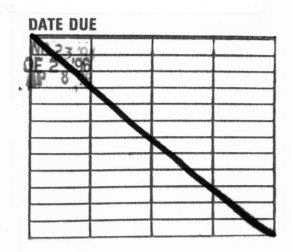

American Constitutional Law

Stephen J. Wayne, GENERAL EDITOR
Georgetown University

American Constitutional Law by Louis Fisher is available in two formats:

single volume
American Constitutional Law
hardcover edition

volume 1
Constitutional Structures:
Separated Powers and Federalism
paperback edition

volume 2
Constitutional Rights:
Civil Rights and Civil Liberties
paperback edition

ALSO BY THE AUTHOR

President and Congress: Power and Policy (*1972*)
Presidential Spending Power (*1975*)
The Constitution between Friends: Congress, the President, and the Law (*1978*)
The Politics of Shared Power: Congress and the Executive (*1981, 1987*)
Constitutional Conflicts between Congress and the President (*1985*)
Constitutional Dialogues: Interpretation as Political Process (*1988*)

American Constitutional Law

Louis Fisher

Congressional Research Service
The Library of Congress

McGRAW-HILL PUBLISHING COMPANY

New York   St. Louis   San Francisco   Auckland   Bogotá   Caracas   Hamburg
Lisbon   London   Madrid   Mexico   Milan   Montreal   New Delhi
Oklahoma City   Paris   San Juan   São Paulo   Singapore   Sydney   Tokyo   Toronto

AMERICAN CONSTITUTIONAL LAW

1 2 3 4 5 6 7 8 9 0   DOC DOC   8 9 4 3 2 1 0 9

ISBN 0-07-557125-0

This book was set in Aster by Black Dot, Inc.
The editors were Bert Lummus and Carolyn Viola-John;
the designer was Joan Greenfield;
the production supervisor was Laura Lamorte.
R. R. Donnelley & Sons Company was printer and binder.

Library of Congress Cataloging-in-Publication Data

Fisher, Louis.
  American constitutional law / Louis Fisher.
    p.   cm.
  Includes bibliographical references.
  ISBN 0-07-557125-0
  1. United States—Constitutional law—Cases.   I. Title.
KF4549.F57   1990b
342.73—dc20
[347.302]   89-13353

Acknowledgments
The author gratefully acknowledges permission from the following sources to use their copyrighted materials:

Reading on pages 18–21 from Abram Chayes, "Public Law Litigation and the Burger Court," 96 Harv. L. Rev. 4 (1982).

Reading on pages 21–23 from Donald L. Horowitz, *The Courts and Social Policy* (Washington, D.C.: The Brookings Institution, 1977).

Reading on pages 26–28 from Samuel Krislov, "The Amicus Curias Brief: From Friendship to Advocacy," 72 Yale L. J. 694 (1963).

Reading on pages 29–31 from Kathryn Mickle Werdeger, "The Solicitor General and Administrative Due Process: A Quarter-Century of Advocacy," 36 G.W. L. Rev. 481 (1968).

Reading on pages 34–35 from Carl McGowan, "Congressmen in Court: The New Plaintiffs," 15 Ga. L. Rev. 241 (1981).

Reading on pages 35–38 from Frank M. Johnson, "The Constitution and the Federal District Judge," 54 Texas L. Rev. 903 (1976).

Reading on pages 38–40 from Tinsley E. Yarbrough, "The Judge as Manager: The Case of Judge Frank Johnson," 1 J. Policy Analyis & Mgt. 386 (1982).

Reading on pages 66–71 from William W. Van Alstyne, "A Critical Guide to *Marbury* v. *Madison*," 1969 Duke L. J. 1.

Reading on pages 83–86 from "Constitutional Interpretation: An Interview with Justice Lewis Powell," Kenyon College Alumni Bulletin (Summer 1979), pp. 14–18.

Reading on pages 86–91 from 27 South Texas Law Review 433–466 (1986).

Reading on pages 124–126 from Gene R. Nichol, Jr., "Rethinking Standing," 72 Cal. L. Rev. 68 (1984).

Reading on pages 135–138 from Alexander M. Bickel, "Foreword: The Passive Virtues," 75 Harv. L. Rev. 40 (1961).

Reading on pages 138–141 from Gerald Gunther, "The Subtle Vices of the 'Passive Virtues'—A Comment on Principle and Expediency in Judicial Review," 64 Colum. L. Rev. 1 (1964).

Reading on pages 165–168 from Jonathan C. Rose, "Shortsightedness Plagues Bankruptcy Courts' History," Legal Times, February 27, 1984.

Reading on pages 168–169, David F. Pike, "The Court-Packing Plans," The National Law Journal, August 29, 1983.

Reading on pages 206–207 from David Lauter, "The Fine Art of Creating a Certiorari Petition," The National Law Journal, December 10, 1984.

Reading on pages 209–210 from Frank M. Coffin, *The Ways of a Judge: Reflections from the Federal Appellate Bench* (Boston: Houghton Mifflin, 1980).

Reading on pages 213–215 from William O. Douglas, "The Dissent: A Safeguard of Democracy," 32 J. Amer. Judicature Soc. 104 (1948).

Reading on pages 215–216 from Robert H. Jackson, *The Supreme Court in the American System of Government* (Cambridge, Mass.: Harvard University Press, 1955).

Reading on pages 280–283 from Louis Fisher, "Judicial Misjudgments About the Lawmaking Process: The Legislative Veto Case," 45 Pub. Adm. Rev. 705 (Special Issue, November 1985).

Reading on pages 352–354 from Erwin N. Griswold, "Secrets Not Worth Keeping," Washington Post, February 15, 1989.

Reading on pages 862–863 from Lewis Powell, Jr., "Death Penalty? Society Has Ruled," Legal Times, August 15, 1988.

Reading on pages 1343–1344 from Association of the Bar of the City of New York, "Jurisdiction-Stripping Proposals in Congress: The Threat to Judicial Constitutional Review" (December 1981).

Reading on pages 1350–1352 from David E. Rosenbaum, "Prayer in Many Schoolrooms Continues Despite '62 Ruling," The New York Times, March 11, 1984.

ABOUT THE AUTHOR

LOUIS FISHER received his B.S. from the College of William and Mary and his Ph.D. from the New School for Social Research. After teaching political science at Queens College, he joined the Congressional Research Service of the Library of Congress in 1970, where he is Senior Specialist in Separation of Powers. He has testified before congressional committees on such issues as executive privilege, impoundment of funds, legislative vetoes, the item veto, the pocket veto, executive reorganization authority, executive spending discretion, and the congressional budget process. During 1987 he served as Research Director for the House Iran-Contra Committee.

The books by Louis Fisher are listed at the front of this volume. His articles have appeared in the following law journals and law periodicals: *Administrative Law Review, American Journal of International Law, Buffalo Law Review, California Law Review, Catholic University Law Review, Cumberland Law Review, George Mason University Law Review, George Washington Law Review, Georgetown Law Journal, Georgia Law Review, Harvard Journal on Legislation, Journal of Public Law, Law and Contemporary Problems, Legal Times, National Law Journal, North Carolina Law Review*, and *University of Pennsylvania Law Review*.

His articles have been published in a number of journals of political science and public administration: *Administrative Science Quarterly, Annals, Canadian Parliamentary Review, Congress & the Presidency, Congressional Studies, Corruption and Reform, Journal of American Studies, Journal of Political Science, Journal of Politics, Political Science Quarterly, Political Science Reviewer, Presidential Studies Quarterly, Public Administration Review, Public Budgeting & Finance, State Legislatures,* and *Western Political Quarterly*. His articles appear frequently in encyclopedias, magazines, newspapers, and edited books.

TO THE
NEW SCHOOL FOR SOCIAL RESEARCH

CONTENTS

INTRODUCTION

To accommodate the leading cases on constitutional law, textbooks concentrate on court decisions and overlook the political, historical, and social framework in which these decisions are handed down. Constitutional law is thus reduced to the judicial exercise of divining the meaning of textual provisions. The larger process, including judicial as well as nonjudicial actors, is ignored. The consequence, as noted recently by a law professor, is the absence of a "comprehensive course on constitutional law in any meaningful sense in American law schools."[1]

The political process must be understood because it establishes the boundaries for judicial activity and influences the substance of specific decisions, if not immediately then within a few years. This book keeps legal issues in a broad political context. Cases should not be torn from their environment. A purely legalistic approach to constitutional law misses the constant, creative interplay between the judiciary and the political branches. The Supreme Court is not the exclusive source of constitutional law. It is not the sole or even dominant agency in deciding constitutional questions. The Constitution is interpreted initially by a private citizen, legislator, or executive official. Someone from the private or public sector decides that an action violates the Constitution; political pressures build in ways to reshape fundamental constitutional doctrines.

These developments affect the entire public. Justice Blackmun, in a 1982 interview, emphasized that the Court "doesn't belong to me, or to the nine of us, or to the Chief Justice. It's an instrument of government. And I try to preach the gospel that lay people, as well as lawyers, should take an interest in the Court and what it's doing."[2] Constitutional law, pared to its essentials, expresses how we want to live as

---

[1]W. Michael Reisman, "International Incidents: Introduction to a New Genre in the Study of International Law," 10 Yale J. Int'l L. 1, 8 n.13 (1984).

[2]"A Justice Speaks Out: A Conversation with Harry A. Blackmun," Cable News Network, Inc., conducted November 25, 1982, at 20.

individuals within a society. What powers shall government exercise? What rights and liberties remain with us? Basic questions of political philosophy and conscience are at stake.

Constitutional questions are considered when Congress debates legislation and when Presidents decide to sign or veto bills presented to them. The Attorney General and the Comptroller General analyze (and resolve) many constitutional questions, as do general counsels in the agencies. Actions by the political branches, over the course of years, help determine the direction and result of a Supreme Court decision. Constitutional issues are often hammered out without the need for litigation.

Charles Evans Hughes, in a widely quoted epigram, said that "We are under the Constitution, but the Constitution is what the judges say it is."[3] The Supreme Court nevertheless recognizes that each branch of government, in the performance of its duties, must initially interpret the Constitution.[4] Those interpretations are given great weight by the Court; sometimes they are the controlling factor.[5] A number of issues never reach the courts because of self-limiting conditions imposed by judges: the doctrines of ripeness, mootness, standing, political questions, and prudential considerations.

When the Supreme Court decides a question, the ruling must be translated into action by lower courts, executive agencies, Congress, and local government. Ambiguities and generalities in a ruling produce broad choices of interpretation and implementation. Decisions usually provide only a broad framework for public officials and citizens. As Justice Frankfurter once noted, the Court "can only hope to set limits and point the way."[6] If Congress, the President, and the public oppose a decision, it is often only a matter of time before the issue is back in the political stream to test and usually alter what the Court has announced.

Books on constitutional law sometimes focus exclusively on Supreme Court decisions and stress its doctrines, as though lower courts and governmental officials are unimportant. Other studies describe constitutional decisionmaking as lacking in legal principle, based on low-level political haggling by various actors. I see an open and vigorous system struggling to produce principled constitutional law. Principles are important. Constitutional interpretations are not idiosyncratic events or the result of a political free-for-all. If they were, our devotion to the rule of law would be either absurd or a matter of whimsy.

It is traditional to focus on constitutional rather than statutory interpretation, and yet the boundaries between these categories are unclear. Issues of constitutional dimension usually form a backdrop to "statutory" questions. Preoccupation with the Supreme Court as the principal or final arbiter of constitutional questions fosters a misleading impression. A dominant business of the Court is statutory construction, and through that function it interacts with other branches of government in a process that refines the meaning of the Constitution. The judicial branch has fashioned guidelines to avoid many of the constitutional issues pressed upon it. If a

---

[3]Charles Evans Hughes, Addresses and Papers 139 (1908).

[4]United States v. *Nixon*, 418 U.S. 683, 703 (1974).

[5]Rostker v. *Goldberg*, 453 U.S. 57 (1981), concerning male-only registration for military service.

[6]Niemotko v. Maryland, 340 U.S. 268, 275 (1951) (concurring opinion).

case can be decided either on constitutional grounds or as a question of statutory construction, the courts prefer to deal only with the latter.[7]

This study treats the Supreme Court and lower courts as one branch of a political system with a difficult but necessary task to perform. They often share with the Legislature and the Executive the responsibility for defining political values, resolving political conflict, and protecting the political process. Through commentary and reading selections, I try to bridge the artificial gap in the literature that presently separates law from politics. Lord Radcliffe advised that "we cannot learn law by learning law." Law must be "a part of history, a part of economics and sociology, a part of ethics and a philosophy of life. It is not strong enough in itself to be a philosophy in itself."[8]

A Note on Citations. The introductory essays to each chapter contain many citations to court cases, public laws, congressional reports, and floor debates. The number of these citations may seem confusing and even overwhelming. In part I want to encourage the reader to consult these documents and develop a richer appreciation for the complex process that shapes constitutional law. Repeated citations to federal statutes help underscore the ongoing role of Congress and the executive branch in constitutional interpretation. To permit deeper exploration of certain issues, either for a term paper or scholarly research, footnotes contain leads to supplementary cases. Bibliographies are provided for each chapter. The appendices include a glossary of legal terms and a primer on researching the law.

If the coverage is too detailed, the instructor may always advise students to skip some of the material. Another option is to ask the student to understand two or three departures from a general doctrine, such as the famous *Miranda* warning developed by the Warren Court but whittled away by the Burger and Rehnquist Courts. Even if a student is dumbfounded by the complexity of constitutional law, it is better to be aware of the delicate shadings that exist than to believe that the Court paints with bold, permanent strokes.

At various points in the chapters I give examples where state courts, refusing to follow the lead of the Supreme Court, conferred greater constitutional rights than available at the federal level. These are examples only. They could have been multiplied many times over. No one should assume that rulings from the Supreme Court represent the last word on constitutional law, even for lower courts.

Compared to other texts written by political scientists, this book offers much more in the way of citations to earlier decisions. I do this for several reasons. The citations allow the reader to research areas in greater depth. They also highlight the process of trial-and-error used by the Court to clarify constitutional principles. Concentration on contemporary cases would obscure the Court's record of veering down side roads, backtracking, and reversing direction. Focusing on landmark cases prevents the reader from understanding the *development* of constitutional law: the dizzying exceptions to "settled" doctrines, the laborious manner in which the Court struggles to fix the meaning of the Constitution, the twists and turns, the detours and dead ends. Describing major cases without these tangled patterns would presume an

[7]Ashwander v. TVA, 297 U.S. 288, 347 (1936) (Brandeis, J., concurring). See also Rescue Army v. Municipal Court, 331 U.S. 549, 568–572 (1947).

[8]Lord Radcliffe, The Law & Its Compass 92–93 (1960).

orderly and static system that mocks the dynamic, fitful, creative, and consensus-building process that exists. No one branch of government prevails. The process is polyarchal, not hierarchical. The latter, perhaps attractive for architectural structures, is inconsistent with our aspiration for self-government.

In all court cases and other documents included as readings, footnotes have been deleted. For footnotes in the introductory essays, standard reference works are abbreviated as follows:

Elliot   Jonathan Elliot, ed., The Debates in the Several State Conventions, on the Adoption of the Federal Constitution (5 vols., Washington, D.C., 1836–1845).

Farrand   Max Farrand, ed., The Records of the Federal Convention of 1787 (4 vols., New Haven: Yale University Press, 1937).

Richardson   James D. Richardson, ed., A Compilation of the Messages and Papers of the Presidents (20 vols., New York: Bureau of National Literature, 1897–1925).

Wkly Comp.   Weekly Compilation of Presidential Documents, published each
Pres. Doc.   week by the Government Printing Office since 1965.

ACKNOWLEDGMENTS

This book, in gestation for years, has many contributors and abettors. Morton Rosenberg of the Congressional Research Service lent a guiding hand, giving encouragement when I needed it and offering importunings I sometimes ignored. I needed both signals. In reviewing the manuscript and selections for readings, he was my major source of counsel and enlightenment. Phillip J. Cooper of the State University of New York at Albany has been a valuable friend, alerting me to new dimensions of constitutional law. His views are incorporated especially in Chapters 2 and 3.

Neal Devins of the William and Mary Law School is a specialist in questions of civil rights and church and state. I am indebted to his comments on these chapters and providing thoughtful insights into the intersections of law and politics. Jacob Landynski of the New School for Social Research and Christopher Pyle of Mount Holyoke College reviewed the chapter on search and seizure. They provided an important check on my effort to discover rhyme or reason to what the Court has done. Robert Meltz of the CRS read the sections on the Just Compensation Clause and property rights. His expertise in these areas added clarity and depth to one of the more baffling sectors of constitutional law. Harold Relyea, another CRS colleague and friend for many years, read the chapters on free press and free speech. His broad understanding of the legal and historical development of the First Amendment enriched both chapters.

I would also like to thank the following professional reviewers for McGraw-Hill: Glen Abernathy, University of South Carolina; John Brigham, University of Massachusetts; Thomas Eimerman, Illinois State University; James Foster, Oregon State University; Mark Gibney, Purdue University; Barbara Graham, University of Missouri; Mary Harada, Northern Essex College; Thomas Hensley, Kent State University; Albert Matheny, University of Florida; Jeremy Rabkin, Cornell University; and Jerry L. Simich, University of Nevada. Their critiques were on the mark and much appreciated.

Bertrand W. Lummus, Senior Editor, suggested that I write this book (more years ago than either of us like to remember). I value his support and patience and look forward to new editions and supplements. Stephen J. Wayne of the George Washington University served as Advisory Editor. I have worked with Steve for several decades on various projects and could not have asked for a better colleague. Carolyn Viola-John, the project editor, very ably transformed a sprawling manuscript into an attractive and coherent book. Tina Barland, the copy editor, made a number of excellent suggestions for tightening and clarifying the text.

Some of the material in this book originally appeared as articles in the following journals: *American Journal of International Law, California Law Review, Cumberland Law Review, Georgia Law Review, Journal of Political Science, Legal Times, North Carolina Law Review, Public Administration Review, State Legislatures,* and the *University of Pennsylvania Law Review.* I also presented papers and addresses at conferences sponsored by the American Enterprise Institute, the American Political Science Association, Claremont Institute, Cumberland Law School, Dickinson College, George Mason University, Kennesaw College, the National War College, Northwestern University, Princeton University, State University of New York, the University of Cincinnati, the University of Dallas, the U.S. District Court for the Northern District of California, Wake Forest University, the Law School at Melbourne University in Australia, the National Autonomous University of Mexico in Mexico City, the Philippine Bar Association in Manila, and the Hebrew University in Jerusalem.

This is my seventh book since graduating from the New School for Social Research in 1967. I had received a bachelor's degree in chemistry, completed some graduate work in physical chemistry, and did technical writing for a few years before taking undergraduate classes in the social sciences at the New School. In 1963, after a conference with Joseph Greenbaum, Dean of the Graduate Faculty of Political and Social Science at the New School, I was accepted into the graduate program. As I walked down the hall, exhilarated by my new venture, he stuck his head out of his office and shouted: "Don't take any more chemistry." I haven't. Grateful for four stimulating years of graduate work at an institution that urges interdisciplinary research, I am happy to dedicate this book to the New School.

LOUIS FISHER

American Constitutional Law

1 Public Law and Politics

For those who teach constitutional law, the relationship between the judiciary and politics remains an awkward subject. Technical details of a decision have a way of driving out the political events that generate a case and influence its disposition. To infuse law with dignity, majesty, and perhaps a touch of mystery, it is tempting to separate the courts from the rest of government and make unrealistic claims of judicial independence.

Legal scholars who explored this relationship early in the twentieth century were discouraged by traditional leaders of the legal profession. To speak the truth, or even search for it, threatened judicial symbols and concepts of long standing. In 1914, when legal philosopher Morris Raphael Cohen began describing how judges make law, he faced opposition from his colleagues. The deans of major law schools advised him that his findings, although unquestionably correct, might invite even greater recourse to "judicial legislation."

Undeterred by these warnings, Cohen had "an abiding conviction that to recognize the truth and adjust oneself to it is in the end the easiest and most advisable course." He denied that the law is a "closed, independent system having nothing to do with economic, political, social, or philosophical science." If courts were in fact constantly making and remaking the law, it became "of the utmost social importance that the law should be made in accordance with the best available information, which it is the object of science to supply." Morris R. Cohen, Law and the Social Order 380–381 n.86 (1933).

For more than a century, the legal profession claimed that judges "found" the law rather than made it. This doctrine of mechanical jurisprudence, joined with the supposed nonpolitical nature of the judiciary, provided convenient reasons for separating courts from the rest of government. A perceptive essay by political scientist C. Herman Pritchett noted that the disciplines of law and political science drifted apart for semantic, philosophical, and practical reasons: "Law is a prestigious symbol, whereas politics tends to be a dirty word. Law is stability; politics is chaos. Law is impersonal; politics is personal. Law is given; politics is free choice. Law is reason; politics is prejudice and self-interest. Law is justice; politics is who gets there first with the most." Joel B. Grossman and Joseph Tanenhaus, eds., *Frontiers of Judicial Research* 31 (1969).

Chief Justice Warren believed that law could be distinguished from politics. Progress in politics "could be made and most often was made by compromising and taking half a loaf where a whole loaf could not be obtained." He insisted that the "opposite is true so far as the judicial process was concerned." Through the judicial process, "and particularly in the Supreme Court, the basic ingredient of decision is principle, and it should not be compromised and parceled out a little in one case, a little more in another, until eventually someone receives the full benefit." *The Memoirs of Earl Warren* 6 (1977).

Yet the piecemeal approach applies quite well to the judicial process. The Supreme Court prefers to avoid general rules that exceed the necessities of a particular case. Especially in the realm of constitutional law it recognizes the "embarrassment" that may result from formulating rules or deciding questions "beyond the necessities of the immediate issue." *Euclid v. Ambler Co.*, 272 U.S. 365, 397 (1926). Compromise, expediency, and ad hoc action are no less a part of the process by which a multimember court gropes incrementally toward a consensus and decision. The desegregation case, *Brown* v. *Board of Education* (1954), was preceded by two decades of halting progress toward the eventual abandonment of the "separate but equal" doctrine enunciated in 1896. After he left the Court, Potter Stewart reflected on the decision to exclude from the courtroom evidence that had been illegally obtained: "Looking back, the exclusionary rule seems a bit jerry-built—like a roller coaster track constructed while the roller coaster sped along. Each new piece of track was attached hastily and imperfectly to the one before it, just in time to prevent the roller coaster from crashing, but without an opportunity to measure the curves and dips preceding it or to contemplate the twists and turns that inevitably lay ahead." 83 Colum. L. Rev. 1365, 1366 (1983).

The desegregation case of 1954 plunged the Court into a political maelstrom that pitted blacks against whites, the North against the South, and states righters against advocates of national power. Justice Jackson, viewing the briefs as sociology rather than law, was reluctant to rule segregation as unconstitutional. When he finally decided to join the majority, he said that the case was basically a question of politics: "I don't know how to justify the abolition of segregation as a judicial act. Our problem is to make a judicial decision out of a political conclusion . . ." Bernard Schwartz, *Super Chief* 89 (1983).

LITIGATION AS A POLITICAL PROCESS

The decision of many political scientists in recent decades to ignore the substance of Supreme Court opinions came at a most peculiar time. The Court had moved from narrow nineteenth-century questions of private law (estates, trusts, admiralty, real property, contracts, and commercial law) to contemporary issues of public law (federal regulation, criminal law, immigration, equal protection, and federal taxation). The period after World War II is generally considered a high-water mark in judicial policymaking. Decisions with nationwide impact were issued, affecting desegregation in 1954, reapportionment and school prayers in 1962, criminal justice in the 1960s, and abortion in 1973.

Although members of Congress criticize "judicial activism," they do their part to encourage judicial policymaking. Congress passes statutes that give standing to litigants, provide fees for attorneys, and establish separate agencies (such as the Legal Services Corporation) to initiate suits on broad public issues. Class-action suits open the doors of the courts even wider. Instead of merely resolving private disputes between private individuals, courts develop and articulate public values on major social, economic, and political questions. Increasingly, their decisions are prospective rather than retrospective. Judges actively participate in negotiating a resolution and maintain their involvement after issuing an initial decree (pp. 18–21). This activist role has been criticized by those who believe that federal judges lack both the legitimacy and the capacity to decide questions of broad social policy (pp. 21–23).

Justices of the Supreme Court have encouraged the belief that a gulf does indeed separate law from politics. Chief Justice John Marshall insisted that "Questions in their nature political . . . can never be made in this court." Marbury v. Madison, 5 U.S. 137, 170 (1803). In that very same decision, however, he established a precedent of far-reaching political importance: the right of the judiciary to review and overturn the actions of Congress and the executive. As noted by one scholar, Marshall "more closely associated the art of judging with the positive qualities of impartiality and disinterestedness, and yet he had made his office a vehicle for the expression of his views about the proper foundations of American government." G. Edward White, The American Judicial Tradition 35 (1976).

During his days as law school professor, Felix Frankfurter referred to constitutional law as "applied politics." Archibald MacLeish and E. F. Prichard, eds., Law and Politics 6 (1962). "The simple truth of the matter," he said, "is that decisions of the Court denying or sanctioning the exercise of federal power, as in the first child labor case, largely involve a judgment about practical matters, and not at all any esoteric knowledge of the Constitution." Id. at 12. He regarded courts as "less than ever technical expounders of technical provisions of the Constitution. They are arbiters of the economic and social life of vast regions and at times of the whole country." Felix Frankfurter and James M. Landis, The Business of the Supreme Court 173 (1928).

Once on the bench, however, Frankfurter did his part to perpetuate the law-politics dichotomy. Refusing to take a reapportionment case in 1946, he said it was "hostile to a democratic system to involve the judiciary in the politics of the people." Colegrove v. Green, 328 U.S. 549, 553–554 (1946). In *Baker* v. *Carr* (1962) the Supreme Court liberated itself from this narrow holding and has demonstrated throughout its history a keen sense of the political system in which it operates daily. Writing in 1921, Justice Cardozo dismissed the idea that judges "stand aloof on these chill and distant heights; and we shall not help the cause of truth by acting and speaking as if they do. The great tides and currents which engulf the rest of men do not turn aside in their course and pass the judges by." The Nature of the Judicial Process 168 (1921).

Although the Supreme Court is an independent branch, it is not isolated. It is buffeted by the same social winds that press upon the executive and legislative branches, even if it does not respond in precisely the same way. It does not, and cannot, operate in a vacuum.

From the late nineteenth century to the 1930s, the courts struck down a number of federal and state efforts to ameliorate industrial conditions. Laws that established maximum hours or minimum wages were declared an unconstitutional interference with the "liberty of contract." Lawyers from the corporate sector helped translate the philosophy of laissez faire into legal terms and constitutional doctrine. These judicial rulings were so spiced with conservative business values that Justice Holmes protested that cases were "decided upon an economic theory which a large part of the country does not entertain." He chided his brethren: "The Fourteenth Amendment does not enact Mr. Herbert Spencer's Social Statics." Lochner v. New York, 198 U.S. 45, 75 (1905). When it was evident that the country would no longer tolerate interference by the courts, the judiciary backed off. After retiring from the Court, Justice Roberts explained the expansion of national power over economic conditions: "Looking back, it is difficult to see how the Court could have resisted the popular urge for uniform standards throughout the country—for what in effect was a unified economy." Owen J. Roberts, The Court and the Constitution 61 (1951).

In 1927, the Supreme Court upheld Virginia's compulsory sterilization law. Buck v. Bell, 274 U.S. 200. The decision was handed down in the midst of the eugenics movement, which sanctioned efforts to prevent reproduction of the "unfit." In the hands of reformers and progressives, eugenics became a respected argument for opposing miscegenation and excluding "lower stock" immigrants coming from the Mediterranean countries, Eastern Europe, and Russia. After odious efforts in Nazi Germany to conduct biological experiments on and exterminate millions of Jews, Poles, gypsies, and other groups to produce a "master race," the eugenics movement had run its course.

Racism in totalitarian countries combined with the emergence of the United States as a world leader after World War II helped set the stage for *Brown* v. *Board of Education* in 1954. America could not fight world communism and appeal to dark-skinned peoples in foreign lands if it maintained racial segregation in its own school system. The executive branch made the Court mindful of these realities (pp. 990–992). On the foundation of court cases that established rights for black Americans, the feminist movement pressed for fundamental changes in women's rights, leading to the Supreme Court's abortion decision in 1973. This case triggered a strong countermovement among "right-to-lifers," who pressed for administrative, legislative, and judicial remedies.

To associate litigation with social forces is not meant to demean the courts or reduce adjudication to just another form of politics. Judges make policy, but not in the same manner as legislators and executives. Unlike the elected branches, the judiciary is not expected to satisfy the needs of the majority or respond to electoral pressures; instead, it has a special responsibility to protect minority interests and constitutional rights. Although judges have an opportunity to engage in their own form of lobbying, they are not supposed to publicly debate a pending issue or participate in ex parte meetings that are open to only one party—privileges routinely exercised by legislators and administrators. Most lobbying by the executive and legislative branches is open and direct; lobbying by the judiciary is filtered through legal briefs, professional meetings, and law review articles.

The executive and legislative branches have elaborate mechanisms for handling public relations, self-promotion, and contacts with the press. For the most part, judges release their opinions and remain silent. If executive officials and legislators are criticized in the press, they can respond in kind. Judges, with rare exceptions, take their lumps without retaliation.

Judges must wait for a case to present itself. They cannot initiate policy with the same ease as members of the political branches. As Judge David Bazelon once remarked, a federal judge "can't wake up one morning and simply decide to give a helpful little push to a school system, a mental hospital, or the local housing agency." 52 Ind. L. J. 101, 103 (1976). Furthermore, judges cannot be as willful as legislators and executives. They are expected to base their decisions on reason and precedent. Courts may overrule themselves, and frequently do, but they must explain (or attempt to explain) why it is necessary to break with a prior holding.

Even so, the operations of the judiciary are sometimes difficult to distinguish from Congress and the executive. In reviewing the work of federal courts in tax matters, Judge Charles E. Wyzanski witnessed the constant interaction between the judiciary and Congress. The disputes generally were "not about a fundamental value but about the choice of insistent interests or pressing policies to be preferred. In short, here again we have an emphasis on those aspects of the law which relate to bargain and compromise, not to 'absolutes' and not even to principles or 'standards'." 26 U. Chi. L. Rev. 237, 242 (1959).

The operations of the political branches can resemble those of the courts. Although responsive to majoritarian pressures, Congress and the President are also sensitive to minority rights. Since the days of President Franklin D. Roosevelt, executive orders and congressional statutes have advanced the cause of civil rights. The political branches are more at liberty to engage in ad hoc actions, but they usually follow general principles and precedents of their own and feel an obligation to present a reasoned explanation for their decisions.

LOBBYING THE COURTS

Private organizations do not hesitate to treat litigation as a political process. They regularly conclude that their interests will be better served through court action than through the legislative and executive branches. Many of the major labor-management struggles were fought out in the courts, with unions and employers hiring counsel to represent their interests. In 1963 Justice Brennan called litigation "a form of political expression." Groups unable to achieve their objectives through the electoral process often turn to the judiciary: "under the conditions of modern government, litigation may well be the sole practicable avenue open to a minority to petition for redress of grievances." NAACP v. BUTTON, 371 U.S. 415 (1963). For groups such as the National Association for the Advancement of Colored People (NAACP) and the American Civil Liberties Union (ACLU), litigation is not merely a technique for resolving private differences. It is a form of political expression and association. In re Primus, 436 U.S. 412, 428 (1978).

The use of litigation in the 1940s and 1950s to shape social policy led to broader public participation and produced fundamental changes in the amicus curiae (friend of the court) brief. Originally, such briefs permitted third parties, without any direct interest in the case, to bring certain facts to the attention of the court to avoid judicial error. Over the years it lost this innocent quality and became an instrument used by private groups to advance their cause. The amicus curiae brief moved "from neutrality to partisanship, from friendship to advocacy" (pp. 26–28). The briefs are now regularly used as part of the interest-group struggle in the courts.

The number of amicus briefs increased so rapidly that the Supreme Court adopted a rule in November 1949 to discourage their filing. With the exception of government units, all parties must consent to the filing of an amicus brief. If a party objects, the applicant must request the Court's permission to file.

The political nature of litigation is underscored by many familiar examples. Through dozens of court actions the Jehovah's Witnesses secured such rights as the refusal to salute or pledge allegiance to the American flag, the right to solicit from house to house, and the right to preach in the streets without a license. Those objectives were not available from legislatures responsive to majoritarian pressures. The NAACP created a Legal Defense and Educational Fund to pursue rights denied blacks by Congress and state legislatures. A series of victories in the courts established basic rights for blacks in voting, housing, education, and jury service. The National Consumers' League channeled its resources into litigation and won important protections for factory workers. The American Liberty League, organized by conservative businessmen, turned to litigation in an effort to prevent the enactment of economic regulation by Congress.

Political motivations dominated each dispute. Encouraged by Congress and the courts, private groups decided that the judiciary was the best arena to further their interests. When the Reagan administration appeared to make an inadequate commitment to environmental protection, private organizations responded with more lawsuits. A senior staff attorney for the Natural Resources Defense Council protested in 1981 that the administration was "massively disobeying these laws because they don't like them. In this context, the only mechanism we have for enforcement is the courts." National Journal, Dec. 19, 1981, at 2233. Labeling this activity "legal" rather than "political" would surprise these attorneys.

Through the publication of articles, books, and commission reports, authors hope to influence a future court decision. Reliance on this body of literature has been of deep concern to many legislators who fear that the judiciary indiscriminately considers "unknown, unrecognized and nonauthoritative text books, law review articles, and other writings of propaganda artists and lobbyists." 103 Cong. Rec. 16160 (1957). The author of this statement, Congressman Wright Patman, complained in 1957 that the Supreme Court had turned increasingly for guidance to private publications and studies promoted by the administration. The research was designed, he said, not to study an issue objectively but to advance the particular views of private interests trying, through the medium of publication, to influence the judiciary's disposition of public policy questions. Experts have pointed out that the members of these study committees and commissions are aware that lawyers will cite the reports in their briefs "and that the real impact of this might very well be in the decisions made by courts and administrative agencies." Id. at 16167 (Prof. Louis B. Schwartz).

The practice of citing professional journals goes back at least to Justice Brandeis in the 1920s. Other Justices, like Cardozo and Stone, adopted this technique as a way of keeping law current with changes in American society. Brandeis' opinions introduced a new meaning to the word "authority." He believed that an opinion "derives its authority, just as law derives its existence, from all the facts of life. The judge is free to draw upon these facts wherever he can find them, if only they are helpful." Chester A. Newland, 48 Geo. L. J. 105, 140 (1959).

The courts are political institutions operating within a political climate. Their decisions determine the ongoing struggle between individual rights and the state, between the national and state governments, and between the three branches of the federal government. The courts are part of this system and respond to it. Sharp protests from Congress, including the threat to withdraw appellate jurisdiction or to take other court-curbing actions, change the climate for future judicial decisions. Professional associations, business and labor groups, consumer and environmental associations, law reviews and scholars all organize their time and talents to influence future court decisions. The following sections describe how the three branches of government intersect in their legal activities: the executive in court, congressional duties, and judge as lawmaker and administrator.

THE EXECUTIVE IN COURT

The Judiciary Act of 1789 established an Attorney General to prosecute and conduct all suits in the Supreme Court concerning the government. He represented Congress as well as the President. Despite some ambiguity in the original statute as to whether the Attorney General was an executive officer in the same sense as the department heads of State, Treasury, and War, the first Attorney General (Edmund Randolph) attended Cabinet meetings and was identified early on as an administrative official.

Unlike the heads of the executive departments, who received full-time salaries, the Attorney General received a nominal sum and was expected to maintain a private practice to supplement his income. Randolph complained that he was "sort of a mongrel between the State and the U.S.; called an officer of some rank here under the latter, and yet thrust out to get a livelihood in the former,—perhaps in a petty mayor's or county court." Leonard D. White, The Federalists 164–165 (1948). The staff of the Attorney General was so small that outside counsel had to be hired to conduct the government's business in court. Partly to do away with this expense, in 1870 Congress established a Department of Justice and created the office of Solicitor General to assist the Attorney General. To the Solicitor General fell the primary responsibility of representing the federal government in court.

Contemporary duties of the Solicitor General are broad-ranging. After consulting agency officials, the Solicitor General conducts (or assigns and supervises) Supreme Court cases, including appeals, petitions regarding certiorari, and the preparation of briefs and arguments; authorizes or declines to authorize appeals by the federal government to appellate courts; authorizes the filing of amicus briefs by the government in all appellate courts; and may, in consultation with each agency, authorize intervention by the government in cases involving the constitutionality of acts of Congress. 28 C.F.R. § 0.20–0.21 (1981). When only private interests are at stake, the Solicitor General may still intervene to advise the Court to accept or deny a case.

The cases that flow through the office of Solicitor General raise complex and specialized issues, but, as a former Solicitor General remarked, the incumbent "must try to discover the social tensions, the reverberations of strife and passion, the political issues, the clashes of interest that are dressed up in technical legal forms." Simon E. Sobeloff, 41 A.B.A.J. 229, 279 (1955). To carry out this responsibility, the Solicitor General juggles several conflicting assignments. As the federal government's lawyer, he is an advocate. However, he is also positioned to play a somewhat detached role, similar to that of an appellate judge. By entering only at the appellate level, he does not begin with the same emotional attachment as the original parties in district court (including agency attorneys). He must also decide, out of a multitude of cases requested by the agencies, which ones deserve the attention of the Supreme Court.

Because the Solicitor General appears before the Supreme Court with such frequency, he has been characterized as the Court's "ninth-and-a-half" member. He serves many functions for the Court:

> The Supreme Court's frequent invitation to the Solicitor General to participate as amicus in constitutional cases is one indication of his useful role. The Solicitor General and his staff have unparalleled experience in constitutional litigation. Their access to and knowledge of the government apparatus not only enable them to inform the Court of factors unknown to private parties, but also to proffer statutory grounds for a decision avoiding the constitutional issues raised. The Solicitor General may indicate the relationship of the case to others pending on the docket, or the particular infirmities or strengths of the case for resolving constitutional or statutory issues. Knowing the Justices' proclivities, the Solicitor General may be able to offer a compromise solution that can gain a majority vote of the Court. The Supreme Court, lacking an extensive staff of its own, often benefits from the Solicitor General's impartial and sophisticated analysis of such constitutional cases. 78 Yale L. J. 1442, 1480 (1969).

The long-term and "impartial" objectives of the Solicitor General compete with, and are sometimes subordinated to, the particular and immediate needs of the President. This relationship is especially common in the field of national security. In arguing cases involving the discharge of federal employees, exclusion and deportation of aliens, and actions against conscientious objectors, Solicitors General in the past have shown little sympathy for fundamental notions of due process (pp. 29–31).

Attorneys General and Solicitors General are legal officers, sometimes operating as members of the bar and therefore officers of the court. But they are also executive officials responsible to the President. As underscored by the actions against Japanese-Americans during World War II, Justice Department attorneys at times swallow their doubts and defend government actions that seem to them not merely unwise but unconstitutional. Under these conditions, constitutional issues are subordinated to the task of behaving as the "President's lawyers." Peter H. Irons, Justice at War 350–361 (1982). Rex Lee, Solicitor General during the Reagan administration, said that one of his duties is "to represent his client, the president of the United States. One of the ways to implement the president's policies is through positions taken in court. When I have that opportunity, I'm going to take it." 69 A.B.A.J. 734, 736 (1983). But if a Solicitor General becomes too partisan, he risks losing the trust and confidence of the Supreme Court.

During the Carter presidency, Attorney General Bell complained about White House interference in litigation that involved questions of church-state separation, affirmative action, and civil rights. Vice President Mondale, his aide Bert Carp, domestic adviser Stuart Eizenstat, and other White House officials treated many of these matters as broad policy questions rather than technical legal issues. In one case, after the Justice Department had taken a position on a church-state question, President Carter responded to political considerations and personally intervened to overrule the decision. Griffin B. Bell, Taking Care of the Law 24–25 (1982).

Part of the lesson supposedly learned from the Watergate affair was the need to keep the Justice Department independent of White House pressures. After Attorney General John Mitchell was convicted and sent to prison, there was broad agreement that never again should a close personal friend of the President be appointed to that office. Nevertheless, President Carter selected Griffin Bell, a personal friend, to head the Justice Department. Bell appeared to make a concerted effort to resist White House pressures, but the line between the White House and the Justice Department narrowed again when President Reagan chose William French Smith, a friend and legal adviser for many years, to be Attorney General. In 1983 Smith announced that he was leaving the Justice Department to help Reagan's reelection effort. To replace Smith, Reagan nominated Edwin Meese III, another close friend. Members of Congress have introduced legislation to depoliticize the Department of Justice (pp. 31–32).

Efforts to subordinate constitutional principles to political tactics can backfire against the President. Faced with a nationwide strike in 1952, President Truman decided to attack the steel companies and work informally with the labor unions rather than invoke the Taft-Hartley Act, which he had vetoed. When that strategy failed, he seized the steel mills and claimed that he could act "for whatever is for the best of the country." Public Papers of the Presidents, 1952, at 273. Realizing that his definition of presidential authority had shocked the country, raising questions about his power to seize even the press and the radio, he hastily explained that his powers were derived from the Constitution and that individual rights were protected. Id. at 301.

In district court, however, the Justice Department told Judge Pine that the courts had no power to constrain the President. Presidential power could be curbed only by the ballot box or impeachment. This audacious and ill-advised presentation may have provoked the judiciary to act boldly to reject a sweeping and dangerous theory of inherent executive authority (pp. 32–33). The political climate invited a rebuff to presidential power. As Chief Justice Rehnquist noted in 1987, the Steel Seizure Case was "one of those celebrated constitutional issues where what might be called the tide of public opinion suddenly began to run against the government, for a number of reasons, and that this tide of public opinion had a considerable influence on the Court." William H. Rehnquist, The Supreme Court 95 (1987).

The Justice Department urged the Supreme Court to adopt an expansive interpretation of presidential power. It supported this thesis by citing statements that Attorney General Jackson had made while serving under Franklin D. Roosevelt. Jackson, by now a member of the Court, found the reference to his earlier pronouncements unconvincing: "While it is not surprising that counsel should grasp support from such unadjudicated claims of power, a judge cannot accept self-serving press statements of the attorney for one of the interested parties as authority in answering a constitutional question, even if the advocate was himself." Youngstown Co. v. Sawyer, 343 U.S. 579, 647 (1952).

The Justice Department has made a concerted effort to retain exclusive control over agency litigation policy. Loss of authority to the agencies can produce an incoherent and ineffective strategy in court. Some of the legal setbacks of the New Deal can be traced to the splintering of litigating authority in the Roosevelt administration. The Justice Department had to compete with autonomous and unsuccessful efforts by the Interior Department and other agencies. Peter H. Irons, The New Deal Lawyers (1982).

The tremendous growth of litigation since the 1930s, coupled with a decision by Congress to restrict the number of attorneys in the Justice Department, has made decentralization inevitable. Congress has given several agencies independent litigating authority. In addition, the Justice Department enters into special agreements called Memoranda of Understanding (MOU's), which allow agencies to litigate certain types of cases at the district and appellate levels.

An unusual situation occurred during the Reagan administration when the Supreme Court appointed a special counsel to argue against the Justice Department. Since 1970, the Internal Revenue Service (IRS) had denied tax exemptions to private schools that practiced racial discrimination. In January 1982, the Reagan administration announced that it was abandoning this decade-old policy (on the ground that it lacked statutory authority) and would move to dismiss two cases brought by the Bob Jones University and Goldsboro Christian School. The Acting Solicitor General, Lawrence G. Wallace, had previously stated the Justice Department's position that the IRS possessed statutory authority to deny the two schools tax-exempt status. Having already announced that position in a September 1981 brief and in a draft brief of early January 1982, which had been circulated to two congressional committees, Wallace felt an obligation to call the Court's attention to this change and to dissociate himself from the administration's new position. 136 P. Kurland and G. Casper, eds., Landmark Briefs and Arguments of the Supreme Court of the United States: Constitutional Law 95 (asterisked material) (1984).

The Supreme Court responded by appointing William T. Coleman, Jr., former law clerk to Justice Frankfurter and Secretary of Transportation during the Ford administration, to defend the IRS policy. In 1983, the Supreme Court decided in favor of the IRS and against the Reagan administration. Tax exemption could not be granted to institutions that discriminate on the basis of race. Bob Jones University v. United States, 461 U.S. 574 (1983).

CONGRESSIONAL DUTIES

During the nineteenth century it was not unusual for members of Congress to maintain a flourishing business in the federal courts. Daniel Webster is the most prominent example of a Congressman with a dual career as lawyer and legislator. While serving in Congress as a Representative and a Senator, he delivered forceful arguments in major cases before the Supreme Court, which at that time was located in a chamber beneath the Senate. Congressmen supplemented their incomes by "duck[ing] into the lower chamber, so to speak, for a lucrative hour or two. After all, should not those who made laws help interpret them?" Maurice G. Baxter, Daniel Webster & the Supreme Court 31 (1966).

Although Congress depends on the Justice Department to protect its interests, members of Congress may intervene on an individual basis. In *Myers* v. *United States* (1926), which involved the President's power to remove executive officials, the Supreme Court invited Senator George Wharton Pepper to serve as amicus curiae. His oral argument and an extract of his brief, together with those of the appellant and the Solicitor General, are printed immediately before the Court's opinion. 272 U.S. 52, 65–88 (1926).

During the impoundment disputes of the Nixon administration, members of Congress submitted an amicus brief on behalf of the plaintiff suing the administration. State Highway Commission of Missouri v. Volpe, 479 F.2d 1099 n.1 (8th Cir. 1973). In the abortion case eventually decided by the Supreme Court in 1980, the district court permitted Senator James L. Buckley, Senator Jesse A. Helms, and

Congressman Henry J. Hyde to intervene as defendants. Harris v. McRae, 448 U.S. 297, 303 (1980). The Ninth Circuit invited both the House and the Senate to submit briefs concerning a legislative veto used by Congress in deportation cases. When the case reached the Supreme Court, both Houses of Congress intervened to protect their interests and fully participated before the Court during oral argument. INS v. Chadha, 462 U.S. 919 (1983). The attorneys for Congress defended the legislative veto, but in a separate brief nine members of the House of Representatives urged the Supreme Court to declare the legislative veto unconstitutional.

Legislative precedents in the House and the Senate do not permit the Speaker or the Chair to rule on questions of constitutionality. Points of order, raising the issue of unconstitutional provisions, are referred to the full chamber for decision. In the Senate, a member may raise a point of order that a bill or an amendment is legislation that changes the Constitution. If there is substantial doubt within Congress concerning the constitutionality of a provision, legislators can place within the bill a procedure authorizing expedited review by the courts. Examples include the Federal Election Campaign Act Amendments of 1974. 86 Stat. 1285, § 315. Two years later the Supreme Court declared the contested provision unconstitutional. Buckley v. Valeo, 424 U.S. 1 (1976). A similar procedure was adopted in the Gramm-Rudman-Hollings Act of 1985. 99 Stat. 1098, § 274 (1985). The provision in question was struck down a year later. Bowsher v. Synar, 478 U.S. 714 (1986).

A striking development over the past decade is the frequency with which members of Congress take issues directly to the courts for resolution. Senator Edward M. Kennedy was successful at both the district court and appellate court levels in challenging Nixon's attempt to use the "pocket veto" during brief recesses of the House and Senate. Kennedy v. Sampson, 364 F.Supp. 1075 (D.D.C. 1973); Kennedy v. Sampson, 511 F.2d 430 (D.C. Cir. 1974). As a result of those lower court decisions, the Ford administration announced that it would use the pocket veto only during the final adjournment at the end of a Congress. 121 Cong. Rec. 41884 (1975); 122 Cong. Rec. 11202 (1976). The Carter administration honored that agreement. President Reagan, however, reopened the issue by using a pocket veto in December 1981 between the first and second sessions of the 97th Congress and again two years later, between the first and second sessions of the 98th Congress. A political agreement, provoked by earlier court decisions, was now pushed back into the judicial arena. In 1985 an appeals court decided in favor of Congress and the matter was taken to the Supreme Court for a "final" determination. Barnes v. Kline, 759 F.2d 21 (D.C. Cir. 1985). Nevertheless, the Court held the case moot because the bill in question had expired, thus tossing the issue back to the two political branches for possible resolution. Burke v. Barnes, 479 U.S. 361 (1987).

Senator Kennedy was successful because his prerogative to vote (to override a presidential veto) had been denied by the pocket veto. Other members of Congress have been unsuccessful when they have tried to achieve political goals from the courts that are available through the regular legislative process. In such cases the members have been told by the courts that (1) they lack standing to sue, (2) the issue is not ripe for adjudication, or (3) the matter is a "political question" to be decided by Congress and the President. Legislators must overcome the standing hurdles (faced by any litigant) by showing that (1) they have suffered injury, (2) the interests are within the zone protected by the statute or constitutional provision, (3) the injury is caused by the challenged action, and (4) the injury can be redressed by a favorable court decision. But legislators face an additional obstacle. If they suffer from an injury that can be redressed by colleagues acting through the regular legislative process, a court may exercise "equitable discretion" to dismiss the action. 90 Harv. L. Rev. 1632 (1977); 11 Harv. J. on Legis. 352 (1974).

Throughout these cases there is a general wariness on the part of judges that the controversy is really not between Congress and the executive. Rather, it is one group of legislators pitted against another. Federal judges may suspect that members of Congress turn to the courts because they have been unable to attract sufficient votes from colleagues to pass a bill. When legislators fail to make use of remedies available within Congress, they have been denied standing to resolve the issue in court (pp. 34–35).

The Legislative Reorganization Act of 1970 explicitly recognized the need within Congress for a more systematic and continuing review of court decisions that affect legislative prerogatives. Congress had been represented in court by the Department of Justice, and sometimes through appearances of Senators, Congressmen, and attorneys acting as amicus curiae, but these ad hoc remedies were unsatisfactory to Congress. A Senate committee concluded in 1966 that the effect on Congress of court decisions "should be a matter of continuous concern for which some agency of the Congress should take responsibility." S. Rept. No. 1414, 89th Cong., 2d Sess. 47 (1966).

The 1970 statute created a Joint Committee on Congressional Operations and made it responsible for identifying "any court proceeding or action which, in the opinion of the Joint Committee, is of vital interest to the Congress, or to either House of the Congress, as a constitutionally established institution of the Federal Government . . ." Congress directed the Joint Committee to make periodic reports and recommendations to the Senate and House. 84 Stat. 1187, § 402 (1970).

In 1971, the Joint Committee on Congressional Operations began publishing a series of reports on legal proceedings of interest to Congress. After the Joint Committee expired in 1977, the task of publishing the report fell to a newly created House Select Committee on Congressional Operations, working in conjunction with the Senate Committee on Rules and Administration. When the House decided to discontinue the Select Committee, the House Judiciary Committee inherited the responsibility for producing the reports on legal proceedings. Moreover, Senate Rule XXV charges the Senate Committee on Rules and Administration with the duty of identifying "any court proceeding or action which, in the opinion of the committee, is of vital interest to the Congress as a constitutionally established institution of the Federal Government and call such proceeding or action to the attention of the Senate."

In recent years members of Congress have become concerned about the refusal of the Justice Department to defend the constitutionality of certain statutory provisions. Sometimes the Department took this position after deciding that a statute infringed on presidential power or was so patently unconstitutional that it could not be defended, as in the bill of attainder case in 1946. United States v. Lovett, 328 U.S. 303 (1946). As a result of language placed in authorization acts for the Justice Department, the Attorney General must now report to Congress whenever the Department does not intend to defend the constitutionality of a law passed by Congress. These reports specify the statutory provision and contain a detailed explanation by the Department for calling the provision unconstitutional.

Congress has always been able to hire private counsel to defend itself, as it did in the civil action brought against it by Congressman Adam Clayton Powell in the 1960s. Yet there was no established procedure for Congress to defend its statutes when the Justice Department chose not to. The institutional interests of Congress, as noted by the Senate Committee on Governmental Affairs in 1977, made it "inappropriate as a matter of principle and of the constitutional separation of powers for the legislative branch to rely upon and entrust the defense of its vital constitutional powers to the advocate for the executive branch, the Attorney General." S. Rept. No. 170, 95th Cong., 1st Sess. 11. The committee recalled that in two cases involving the power of Congress to investigate, the Justice Department withdrew its representation of Congress just as the litigation reached the Supreme Court, after having represented Congress in the district and appellate courts. Id. at 12.

As part of the Ethics in Government Act of 1978, the Senate established an Office of Senate Legal Counsel. The Senate Legal Counsel and the Deputy Legal Counsel are appointed by the President pro tempore of the Senate from among recommendations submitted by the majority and minority leaders of the Senate. Appointments become effective upon approval by resolution of the Senate.

The principal duty of the Counsel is to defend the Senate or a committee, subcommittee, member, officer, or employee of the Senate when directed by two-thirds of the members of the Joint Leadership Group or by the adoption of a Senate resolution. The Joint Leadership Group consists of the Majority and Minority Leaders, the President pro tempore, and the chairmen and ranking minority members of the Committees on the Judiciary and on Rules and Administration. When directed by Senate resolution, the Counsel brings a civil action to enforce a subpoena issued by the Senate, or by a Senate committee or subcommittee, and intervenes or appears as amicus curiae in cases involving the powers and responsibilities of Congress. Individual Senators may initiate suits on their own. In the House of Representatives, the office of the Clerk of the House handles litigation that involves members, House officers, and staff. Decisions to go to court are made by a bipartisan leadership committee.

JUDGE AS LAWMAKER

From the common law of England to the decisions of American courts, judge-made law has been a fact of life. Lawmaking by legislature was a late development in our history, and one that judges opposed because of its blunt and imprecise quality. It is an act of dissembling to pretend that judges "find" the law rather than "make" it. Jeremiah Smith, who taught law at Harvard after a career on the New Hampshire Supreme Court, was refreshingly candid on this point. When asked "Do judges make law?" he responded: "'Course they do. Made some myself." Paul A. Freund, The Supreme Court of the United States 28 (1961). See Lawrence M. Friedman, A History of American Law 316 (1973); Roscoe Pound, The Formative Era of American Law 45, 59–72 (1938).

Throughout its history the federal judiciary has been accused of engaging in "judicial legislation." Few statutes or constitutional provisions are clear in meaning. Judicial interpretation, broadly exercised, becomes a substitute for legislation. Because judges fill in the "interstices" of law, Holmes said he recognized "without hesitation that judges do and must legislate." Southern Pacific Co. v. Jensen, 244 U.S. 205, 221 (1917).

There have been periods when judicial interpretations became so flagrant and arbitrary that they provoked biting criticism. At the end of the nineteenth century, after legislative attempts to regulate the economy were frustrated by Supreme Court decisions, certain members of the Court condemned what they regarded as a judicial assumption of power. When the Court in 1890 decided that the judiciary, not the legislature, was the final arbiter in regulating railroad fares, freight rates, and other charges on the public, Justice Bradley's dissent considered this an arrogation of authority the Court had no right to make. Chicago, Milwaukee & St. Paul R.R. Co. v. Minnesota, 134 U.S. 418, 462–463 (1890). In the Income Tax Case of 1895, Justice White's dissent accused his brethren of amending the Constitution by judicial fiat. For more than a century the federal government and constitutional scholars had confined the definition of direct tax to capitation and land taxes. The Court decided to add a third category: the income tax. White said that the Constitution should have been amended directly rather than by the judiciary. Pollock v. Farmers' Home & Trust Co., 157 U.S. 429, 639 (1895). It took a constitutional amendment—the Sixteenth—to override the Court.

Dissenting in a 1904 case, Justice Harlan charged that the court "entrenches upon the domain of the legislative department. . . . It has made, not declared, law." Schick v. United States, 195 U.S. 65, 99 (1904). In an antitrust decision in 1911 he assailed the Court for converting the formula of the Sherman Act from restraint of trade to "rule of reason." Borrowing language from an earlier decision, he charged that the Court had read into the Act *"by way of judicial legislation an exception that is not placed there by the lawmaking branch of the Government, and this is to be done upon the theory that the impolicy of such legislation is so clear that it cannot be supposed Congress intended the natural import of the language it used. This we cannot and ought not to do . . ."* By mere interpretation, he said, the Court had modified an act of Congress and deprived it of its force in combating monopoly practices. The most ominous part of the decision for Harlan was "the usurpation by the judicial branch of the Government of the functions of the legislative department." Standard Oil v. United States, 221 U.S. 1, 88, 99, 103 (1911).

Judges answer that they must make law because of general language in the Constitution and because of gaps and inadequacies in the statutes enacted by Congress. Jack G. Day, 26 Case West. Res. L. Rev. 563 (1976); Henry J. Friendly, 63 Colum. L. Rev. 787 (1963). Even Justice Rehnquist, who objects to loose notions of a "living Constitution" that allow judges to adapt it constantly for contemporary needs, recognizes that the framers spoke in general language and "left to succeeding generations the task of applying that language to the unceasingly changing environment in which they would live." 54 Tex. L. Rev. 693, 694 (1976). Ironically, judges are more likely to confine their lawmaking if they are conscious of their role and the need to transcend bias and prejudice. Lawmaking may be more pronounced by judges who believe that they adhere to judicial objectivity and follow neutral formulas. Charles E. Clark and David M. Trubek, 71 Yale L. J. 255, 270 (1961).

Although the Supreme Court no longer substitutes its judgment for what Congress considers necessary in economic legislation, or at least not to the degree that the judiciary interfered up to the 1930s, courts still play an active legislative role by interpreting such general concepts as "equal protection" and "due process." Other opportunities are available for judicial legislation. In 1966 the Supreme Court interpreted a congressional statute, passed in 1865, to prohibit not merely obscene materials but those in which the publisher "pandered" (deliberately appealed to the customer's erotic interests). In his dissent, Justice Harlan said he feared that what the Court "has done today is in effect to write a new statute, but without the sharply focused definitions and standards necessary in such a sensitive area. Casting such a dubious gloss over a straightforward 101-year-old statute . . . is for me an astonishing piece of judicial improvisation." Ginzburg v. United States, 383 U.S. 463, 494–495 (1966).

The abortion decisions in 1973 represent for many scholars a spectacular example of judicial legislation. Writing for the majority, Justice Blackmun declared that during the first trimester of pregnancy a physician, after consulting with the woman, is free to perform an abortion without interference by the state. During the second trimester, the state may regulate and even prevent abortion except where it is necessary to preserve the life or health of the mother. The state's interest expands during the third trimester. Roe v. Wade, 410 U.S. 113, 162–163 (1973); Doe v. Bolton, 410 U.S. 179, 195, 199 (1973). In one of the two dissents, Justice Rehnquist said that the Court's "conscious weighing of competing factors . . . is far more appropriate to a legislative judgment than to a judicial one." Roe v. Wade, 410 U.S. at 173.

If the weighing of competing factors constitutes an act of lawmaking, the courts do little else. Questions of federalism and the commerce power turn on the competing interests of the federal government and the states. The courts regularly balance the government's national security interests against the rights of individual freedom. The needs of law enforcement collide with the rights to privacy. A judge's decision to close a trial conflicts with the right of the press and the public to attend. The power of Congress to investigate the executive branch must be weighed against the President's privilege to withhold information.

In addition to this level of involvement, federal judges act on issues that are within the jurisdiction of Congress and could have been addressed through the regular legislative process. Justice Powell noted that much of the expanded role of the Warren Court "was a reaction to the sluggishness of the legislative branch in addressing urgent needs for reform." 62 A.B.A.J. 1454, 1455 (1976). There are other pressures on judges to legislate. If one section or provision of a statute is unconstitutional, courts may decide to "sever" that portion while retaining the balance of the statute. Such decisions require courts to judge whether the altered statute, as redesigned by the judiciary, is consistent with legislative objectives. Judicial rewriting can provoke comments from colleagues that the majority opinion erred by "simply deleting the crucial statutory language and using the words that remain as the raw materials for a new statute of his own making." Regan v. Time, Inc., 468 U.S. 641, 673 (1984). Justice Harlan once complained that the Court, in the name of interpreting the will of Congress, had resorted to "judicial surgery" to remove an offending section, so transforming the statute that the Court performed "a lobotomy." Welsh v. United States, 398 U.S. 333, 351 (1970).

If a statute is unconstitutional because it excludes a legitimate party or group, the courts may prefer to include the party rather than declare the entire statute invalid, even if the effect is to rewrite the law. Still more controversial is judicial rewriting that creates an additional charge on the public purse. If legislators dislike the judiciary's handiwork, they can rewrite the statute along constitutional lines. Until they do, the judicially amended statute continues in force. Ruth Bader Ginsburg, 28 Cleveland State L. Rev. 301 (1979).

JUDGE AS ADMINISTRATOR

Judicial lawmaking is a venerable and long-debated topic. A more contemporary issue, linked to the public-law litigation explosion, concerns judges who actually *administer* a political system to protect legal rights. Attorney General William French Smith offered this criticism in 1981:

> . . . federal courts have attempted to restructure entire school systems in desegregation cases—and to maintain continuing review over basic administrative decisions. They have asserted similar control over entire prison systems and public housing projects. They have restructured the employment criteria to be used by American business and government—even to the extent of mandating numerical results based upon race or gender. No area seems immune from judicial administration. At least one federal judge even attempted to administer a local sewer system. 21 Judges' Journal 4, 7 (Winter 1982).

Involvement in administrative affairs is not a totally new phenomenon for the courts. Nineteenth-century judges reviewed dismissals of federal employees, ordered administrators to carry out "ministerial" (nondiscretionary) duties, and decided questions about the liability of federal officials subjected to lawsuits. With the rise of federal regulatory commissions toward the end of the nineteenth century and the early decades of the twentieth, federal courts became involved in reviewing agency rulemaking and adjudication.

The Administrative Procedure Act (APA) of 1946 provides that any person suffering legal wrong because of agency action is entitled to judicial review. The reviewing court "shall decide all relevant questions of law, interpret constitutional and statutory provisions, and determine the meaning or applicability of the terms of any agency action." Courts shall hold unlawful and set aside agency actions found to be arbitrary, capricious, an abuse of discretion, or contrary to law; contrary to constitutional right, power, privilege, or immunity; or unsupported by substantial evidence in cases subject to formal rulemaking. Although courts often defer to agency expertise and grant a presumption of regularity in favor of the federal government, judges also require agencies to take a "hard look" at the decisions entrusted to their jurisdiction and insist on adequate documentation to support the agency's determinations.

The breadth of judicial administration is reflected in the efforts of District Judge W. Arthur Garrity, Jr., to desegregate the Boston school system. In 1975 he placed South Boston High School in temporary receivership under a supervisor appointed by him. His ruling came after more than a decade of racial discrimination by the local school board. Barry Stuart Roberts, 12 N.E. L. Rev. 55 (1976). Another federal judge, seeking to promote school desegregation in Wilmington, Delaware, "set a tax rate for the school district, ordered state payments to the district, required new training programs for teachers and administrators, mandated specific curricular offerings, ordered the reassignment of staff and called for the development of an 'appropriate human relations program'. . . ." Terry W. Hartle, 41 Pub. Adm. Rev. 595, 599 (1981).

District Judge Frank M. Johnson, Jr., was deeply involved for more than a decade in administering certain institutions in Alabama. "The history of Alabama," he explained, "is replete with instances of state officials who could have chosen one of any number of courses to alleviate unconstitutional conditions but who chose instead to do nothing but punt the problem to the courts." Steven Brill, New York Magazine, April 26, 1976, at 38. Because of the failure of state officials to correct shocking deficiencies in state prisons, mental hospitals, and institutions for the retarded, Johnson repeatedly found violations of the Eighth and Fourteenth Amendments. He graphically described the conditions: "the evidence reflected that one resident was scalded to death when a fellow resident hosed water from one of the bath facilities on him; another died as a result of the insertion of a running water hose into his rectum by a working resident who was cleaning him; one died when soapy water was forced into his mouth; another died of a self-administered overdose of inadequately stored drugs; and authorities restrained another resident in a straightjacket for *nine years* to prevent him from sucking his hands and fingers" (pp. 35–38).

Rather than devise specific steps to improve conditions, Johnson at first directed the state to design its own plan for upgrading the system to meet constitutional standards. After two deadlines passed without acceptable progress, Johnson intervened to define the minimal constitutional standards. The story suggests a solitary judge pitted against the state, but other parties intervened in the suit, including the Department of Justice, the American Psychological Association, the American Orthopsychiatric Association, and the American Civil Liberties Union. Wyatt v. Stickney, 334 F.Supp. 1341 (M.D. Ala. 1971). Johnson was able to forge an effective alliance of state officials and private citizens to bring pressure on the legislature and the governor (pp. 38–40). A case of "judicial activism"? It is difficult to reach that judgment when the attorney for the state of Alabama admitted in open court that every prisoner in the state system was subjected to cruel and inhuman treatment within the meaning of the Eighth Amendment. Pugh v. Locke, 406 F.Supp. 318, 322, 329 & n.13 (M.D. Ala. 1976).

These vignettes from the three branches of government show the extent to which the line between law and politics blurs and becomes indistinct. Subsequent chapters explore the effort of the judiciary to maintain its legitimacy and strength against the other, popularly elected, branches. The posture is not always adversary, for the courts often combine forces with one branch to restrain the other.

Selected Readings

BALL, HOWARD. *Courts and Politics: The Federal Judicial System.* Englewood Cliffs, N.J.: Prentice-Hall, 1980.

BETH, LOREN P. *Politics, the Constitution, and the Supreme Court.* Evanston, Ill.: Row, Peterson, 1962.

CAPLAN, LINCOLN. *The Tenth Justice: The Solicitor General and the Rule of Law.* New York: Knopf, 1987.

CHAYES, ABRAM. "The Role of the Judge in Public Law Litigation." 89 *Harvard Law Review* 1281 (1976).

COOPER, PHILLIP J. *Hard Judicial Choices: Federal District Court Judges and State and Local Officials.* New York: Oxford University Press, 1988.

EPSTEIN, LEE. *Conservatives in Court.* Knoxville: University of Tennessee Press, 1985.

FISHER, LOUIS. "Social Influences on Constitutional Law." 15 *Journal of Political Science* 7 1987.

——. "Constitutional Interpretation by Members of Congress." 63 *North Carolina Law Review* 707 (1985).

GILMOUR, ROBERT J. "Agency Administration by Judiciary." 6 *Southern Review of Public Administration* 26 (1982).

GINGER, ANN FAGAN. "Litigation as a Form of Political Action." 9 *Wayne Law Review* 458 1963.

GINSBURG, RUTH BADER. "Some Thoughts on Judicial Authority to Repair Unconstitutional Legislation." 28 *Cleveland State Law Review* 301 1979.

GLAZER, NATHAN. "Should Judges Administer Social Services?" 50 *The Public Interest* (1978).

GOLDMAN, SHELDON, AND THOMAS JAHNIGE. *The Federal Courts as a Political System.* New York: Harper & Row, 1976.

GRIFFITH, J. A. G. *The Politics of the Judiciary.* Glasgow: Fontana Press, 1985.

HARRIMAN, LINDA, AND JEFFREY D. STRAUSSMAN. "Do Judges Determine Budget Decisions? Federal Court Decisions in Prison Reform and State Spending for Corrections." 43 *Public Administration Review* 343 (1983).

HODDER-WILLIAMS, RICHARD. *The Politics of the U.S. Supreme Court.* London: George Allen & Unwin, 1980.

LASSER, WILLIAM. *The Limits of Judicial Power: The Supreme Court in American Politics.* Chapel Hill: University of North Carolina Press, 1988.

LATHAM, EARL. "The Supreme Court as a Political Institution." 31 *Minnesota Law Review* 205 (1947).

LIEBERMAN, JETHRO K. *The Litigious Society.* New York: Basic Books, 1981.

MURPHY, WALTER, AND C. HERMAN PRITCHETT, eds. *Courts, Judges, and Politics.* New York: Random House, 1986.

NEIER, ARYEH. *Only Judgment: The Limits of Litigation in Social Change.* Middletown, Conn.: Wesleyan University Press, 1982.

O'BRIEN, DAVID M. *Storm Center: The Supreme Court in American Politics.* New York: Norton, 1986.

O'CONNOR, KAREN, AND LEE EPSTEIN. "Amicus Curiae Participation in U.S. Supreme Court Litigation: An Appraisal of Hakman's 'Forklore'." 16 *Law and Society Review* 311 (1981–1982).

PELTASON, JACK. *Federal Courts in the Political Process.* New York: Random House, 1955.

ROSENBLUM, VICTOR G. *Law as a Political Instrument.* New York: Random House, 1955.

VOSE, CLEMENT E. *Caucasians Only: The Supreme Court, the NAACP, and the Restrictive Covenant Cases.* Berkeley: University of California Press, 1959.

WASBY, STEPHEN L. *The Supreme Court in the Federal Judicial System.* New York: Holt, Rinehart and Winston, 1978.

Abram Chayes

Public Law Litigation and the Burger Court

Some years ago in this journal, I called attention to what I saw as a transformation of the role of federal (and to a lesser extent state) judges, a transformation attendant on a far-reaching change in the nature and form of the judicial business that judges are called upon to perform. With some diffidence, I called the new kind of lawsuit "public law litigation." The label was designed to emphasize that in such cases the federal courts are no longer called upon to resolve private disputes between private individuals according to the principles of private law. Instead, they are asked to deal with grievances over the administration of some public or quasi-public

SOURCE: 96 Harv. L. Rev. 4 (1982). Footnotes omitted.

program and to vindicate the public policies embodied in the governing statutes or constitutional provisions. As a result, courts are inevitably cast in an affirmative, political—activist, if you must— role, a role that contrasts with the passive umpireship we are taught to expect.

The main elements of this contrast should be stated in somewhat greater, though still compressed detail. In the classical model, litigation is viewed as a mode of dispute settlement. The dispute is between private parties, and it concerns the consequences of the parties' actions for the legal relationships—rights and obligations— between them. This central focus on the dispute more or less determines the other basic elements of the traditional model. First, litigation is bipolar:

two parties are locked in a confrontational, winner-take-all controversy. Second, the process is retrospective, directed to determining the legal consequences of a closed set of past events. Third, right and remedy are linked in a close, mutually defining logical relationship. Fourth, the lawsuit is a self-contained entity. It is bounded in time: judicial involvement ends with the determination of the disputed issues. It is bounded in effect: the impact is limited to the (two) parties before the court. Finally, the whole process is party initiated and party controlled. The judge is passive, a neutral umpire. Lon Fuller, in his *Forms and Limits of Adjudication*, posits that the typical classical-model litigation is a suit between businessmen for breach of contract. The chief function of adjudication is the settlement of contract disputes.

In the contemporary model, the subject matter of the litigation is not a dispute between private parties, but a grievance about the content or conduct of policy—most often governmental policy, but frequently the policy of nongovernmental aggregates. Again, this characteristic dictates the main features of the litigation. First, the party structure and the matter in controversy are both amorphous, defined ad hoc as the proceedings unfold rather than exogenously determined by legal theories and concepts. Second, the temporal orientation of the lawsuit is prospective rather than historical. Third, because the relief sought looks to the future and is corrective rather than compensatory, it is not derived logically from the right asserted. Instead, it is fashioned ad hoc, usually by a quasi-negotiating process. Fourth, prospective relief implies continuing judicial involvement. And because the relief is directed at government or corporate policies, it will have a direct impact that extends far beyond the immediate parties to the lawsuit. All of these features press the trial judge into an active stance, with large responsibilities for organizing the case and supervising the implementation of relief.

At the time I wrote, the trend toward public law litigation seemed to be on the rise and gathering momentum. Many trace the start of the new era to the great desegregation decisions of the mid-1950's. True, the Court spent most of the next fifteen years in a not-too-successful effort to con-

vince southern school officials to accept what *Brown* had said was their responsibility for school desegregation. It was not until 1971 in *Swann* v. *Charlotte-Mecklenburg Board of Education* that the Court approved a judicially constructed affirmative desegregation plan. Still, there can be little doubt that, whether they fully realized it or not, the Justices in *Brown* had committed the federal courts to an enterprise of profound social reconstruction.

Meanwhile, in 1963, *Baker* v. *Carr* had set off an almost equally far-reaching political upheaval— the remapping of federal and state legislative districts to achieve substantial equality of voter population. In the late 1960's and early 1970's came the passage of the Civil Rights Act prohibitions of discrimination in employment, housing, and education, the Clean Air and Clean Water Acts, the Truth in Lending, Consumer Products Safety, Occupational Safety and Health, and Freedom of Information Acts, and other sweeping acts of Congress, all mandating or inviting affirmative enforcement by the courts. Liberalization of the class action rules in 1966, in the midst of this legislative movement, seemed to reinforce the invitation. In 1971, Judge Frank Johnson in *Wyatt* v. *Stickney* entered the paradigm structural reform decree directing detailed changes in the management of Alabama's Partlow State Hospital for the mentally retarded. A year earlier, one of the first comprehensive decrees against conditions of confinement in a state prison was issued in *Holt* v. *Sarver*.

Observers of this unfolding pattern, whether they applauded or deplored it, seemed to foretell the future (in the usual manner of prophets) as largely a straight-line extrapolation of current events. In fact, however, by the mid-1970's countertendencies were beginning to emerge. The long summer of social reform that occupied the middle third of the century was drawing to a close. This broad change in political mood inevitably was reflected in the reactions of scholars, pundits, and public, and ultimately in the pronouncements of the Supreme Court. *Milliken* v. *Bradley (Milliken I)*, the first case in which the Court rejected a desegregation decree, was handed down in 1974, only three years after *Swann*. Academic criticism began with the publication of Nathan Glazer's *Imperial Judiciary* in 1975 and Donald Horowitz's *The Courts and Social Policy* two years later. Since then the general tone of scholarly, journalistic, and political commentary has been increasingly skeptical of judicial efforts to ride herd on state and federal bureaucracies. Congress has contemplated restrictions on federal court jurisdiction, and the Attorney General has set about by word and deed to bring the judges to heel. Thus, the time seems ripe to consider how the phenomena of public law litigation have fared at the hands of the Burger Court.

My 1977 article was received, not inappropriately, as an endorsement of the enhanced public law role of the federal judiciary. As such, it was greeted with enthusiasm by "liberals" and with scorn or dismay by "conservatives" or "neo-conservatives." On this crude spectrum, there is little doubt where the Burger Court has positioned itself. Hence we would expect—as we shall find— that its decisions have been something less than hospitable to the procedures and elements of public law litigation.

But at a different level, the earlier article made the claim that the public law trend does not simply reflect the political or ideological coloration of a generation of federal judges. The development is rooted in much more pervasive changes in the contemporary "legal consciousness"—our ways of thinking about law and the legal system—that are in turn related to changes in the larger social, political, and cultural environment. If this claim is valid, it implies that the development in question can be affected only marginally even by sustained resistance in the Supreme Court. A fundamental reversal would require a transformation of the underlying political and legal culture as vast as that by which it was initially produced. The Supreme Court can contribute to such a transformation over time but cannot accomplish it . . .

. . . today even a conservative Court is reduced, perforce, to practicing public law litigation. When, for example, the Court pronounces on the constitutionality of an indemnity scheme for nuclear accidents or the existence of a statutory requirement for deinstitutionalization of retarded persons, the essential character of the litigation is

the same whether the Court upholds the claim or rejects it. Whatever the outcome, the Court is not engaged in settling a dispute between private individuals, or even between an individual and a public official. It is resolving a controversy growing out of "the systemic effects" of governmental action. Such decisions will necessarily have far-reaching effects on myriads of persons not individually before the Court and on political, economic, and institutional structures. Whatever the result, the determination rests more-or-less directly on considerations of public policy. The Supreme Court (or the lower courts) must articulate and enforce the public values and policies it finds in the governing constitutional or statutory provisions. It is these characteristics that define public law litigation and that account for the departures from the traditional model at the level of procedure and judicial role . . .

. . . Judicial review in the constitutional sense —the limitation of substantive legislative power— is only a limited element, and a long-familiar one, in the public law function of courts today. What is new, and I believe predominant, is the extensive use of the judiciary to challenge and control the actions of state and federal administrative agencies and large private institutions. The new claims on judicial attention are thus traceable to the central phenomenon of the modern administrative state—bureaucratic decisionmakers exercising broadly delegated powers to run institutions and programs affecting very large numbers of people, and indeed affecting the economic and social structures of society. It is possible to conceive of all challenges to such activity as assertions, in something like the classical sense, of personal rights against the government or the institution from which the challenged decision emanates. But at best this conception would be a severe distortion.

It is more accurate or at least more helpful, I believe, to think of the courts in these cases as institutions exercising an oversight function on behalf of the interests and groups as well as the individuals affected by the challenged bureaucratic actions. In this oversight role, courts need not be seen to be in conflict with the legislature or the politically responsible elements of the executive branch. For in the contemporary administrative state, bureaucratic actions do not necessarily bear a stamp of legitimacy as outcomes of a democratic process. Indeed, the political branches are also struggling to make the bureaucracy behave—not only in the traditional sense of preventing official imposition on the individual, but also in the newer and equally important sense of trying to ensure that the bureaucracy carries out the positive programs assigned to it. The courts have been essential partners in this endeavor. . . .

Donald L. Horowitz
The Courts and Social Policy

LEGITIMACY AND CAPACITY

The appropriate scope of judicial power in the American system of government has periodically been debated, often intensely. For the most part, what has been challenged has been the power to declare legislative and executive action unconstitutional. Accordingly, the debate has been cast in terms of legitimacy. A polity accustomed to question unchecked power views with unease judicial authority to strike down laws enacted by democratically elected legislatures. Where, after all, is the accountability of life-tenured judges? This question of democratic theory has been raised insistently, especially in times of constitutional crisis, notably in the 1930s and again in the 1950s.

The last word has not been heard in these debates, and it will not soon be heard. The structure of American government guarantees the issue a long life. But, for the moment, the debate seems to have waned with the growing recognition that there are elements of overstatement in the case against judicial review. The courts are more democratically accountable, through a variety of formal and informal mechanisms, than they have been accused of being. Equally important, the other branches are in many ways less democratically accountable than they in turn were said to be by those who emphasized the special disabilities under which judges labor. Hence the many aca-

demic discussions of the need for "representative bureaucracy," for a less insular presidency, and for reform of the procedures and devices that make Congress undemocratic internally and unrepresentative externally. (That students of any single institution often tend to see that institution as the flawed one is a useful indication of the limited perspective that comes from singleminded attention to any one institution. It should properly make us chary of drawing inferences about the courts without an institutionally comparative frame of reference.)

As the debate over the democratic character of judicial review wanes, there is another set of issues in the offing. It relates not to legitimacy but to capacity, not to whether the courts *should* perform certain tasks but to whether they *can* perform them competently.

Of course, legitimacy and capacity are related. A court wholly without capacity may forfeit its claim to legitimacy. A court wholly without legitimacy will soon suffer from diminished capacity. The cases for and against judicial review have always rested in part on assessments of judicial capacity: on the one hand, the presumably superior ability of the courts "to build up a body of coherent and intelligible constitutional principle"; on the other, the presumably inferior ability of courts to make the political judgments on which exercises of the power of judicial review so often turn. If the separation of powers reflects a division of labor according to expertise, then relative institutional capacity becomes relevant to

SOURCE: Washington, D.C.: The Brookings Institution, 1977. Footnotes omitted.

defining spheres of power and particular exercises of power.

The recent developments that I have described necessarily raise the previously subsidiary issue of capacity to a more prominent place. Although the assumption of new responsibilities can, as I have observed, be traced to exercises of the traditional power to declare laws unconstitutional, they now transcend that power. Traditional judicial review meant forbidding action, saying "no" to the other branches. Now the judicial function often means requiring action, and there is a difference between foreclosing an alternative and choosing one, between constraining and commanding. Among other things, it is this difference, and the problematic character of judicial resources to manage the task of commanding, that make the question of capacity so important. . . .

THE ADJUDICATIVE PROCESS

Each decision process leaves its distinctive mark on the issues it touches. Each of them snatches a few transactions from the flow of events, brings them to the foreground and blurs others into the background. Each applies its own mode of analysis to these magnified phenomena. Each has its own set of tools that it uses to devise solutions to problems it has analyzed. No one tool kit is exactly the same as any other. Equally important, each decision process decides some things and leaves other things undecided. There are significant and characteristic patterns of non-decision, as there are patterns of decision.

Adjudication, of course, has its own devices for choosing problems, its own habits of analysis, its own criteria of the relevance of phenomena to issues, its own repertoire of solutions. These hallmarks of adjudication have, as I have already suggested, a common origin: judicial preoccupation with the unique case. This admirable preoccupation imparts to the judicial process many of the characteristics that differentiate it in degree or in kind from the legislative and administrative processes, both of which accord greater explicitness and legitimacy to their general policymaking functions.

In what follows, I attempt to elicit some of these distinctive characteristics of adjudication. . . .

1. *Adjudication is focused.* The usual question before the judge is simply: Does one party have a *right?* Does another party have a *duty?* This should be contrasted with the question before a "planner," whether legislative or bureaucratic: What are the *alternatives?* These are quite different ways of casting problems for decision. For the judge, alternatives may be relevant, but they are relevant primarily to the subsequent issue of what "remedies" are appropriate to redress "wrongs" done to those who possess "rights." In other words, the initial focus on rights tends to defer the question of alternatives to a later stage of the inquiry and to consider it a purely technical question.

As this suggests, the initial focus on rights is also a serious impediment to the analysis of costs, for, in principle at least, if rights exist they are not bounded by considerations of cost. If a person possesses a right, he possesses it whatever the cost.

Costing may, to be sure, creep into litigation through the back door, in a variety of disguises. One of the masks it wears is the "balancing of convenience" that occurs in deciding whether an injunction will issue and to what activities it will extend. Judges, confronted with a plaintiff's assertion that he has a right to a hearing before a governmental body acts in a matter affecting his interests, have been known to inquire how many such additional hearings would be required if the plaintiff's right to one were recognized and how much disruption that might inflict on the work of the governmental body. But they tend to regard such questions as tangential and, if pressed on this front, are likely to recoil from a judgment that would make rights stand or fall on considerations of such an order.

Adjudication, then, is narrow in a double sense. The format of decision inhibits the presentation of an array of alternatives and the explicit matching of benefits to costs. . . .

2. *Adjudication is piecemeal.* The lawsuit is the supreme example of incremental decisionmaking. As such, it shares the advantages and the defects of the species. The outcome of litigation may give the illusion of a decisive victory, but the victory is

often on a very limited point. The judge's power to decide extends, in principle, only to those issues that are before him. Related issues, not raised by the instant dispute, must generally await later litigation. So it is at least in traditional conception.

Incrementalism may be entirely appropriate for some kinds of policy. For others, it may be simply too slow or too disjointed.

Incrementalism is, of course, well suited to decisionmaking when information is scarce. Since adequate information is so often scarce when decisions must be confronted, many decisions are of an incremental character, regardless of where they are made. The less the change imposed by the decision, the less the potential error. With courts, this is an especially important consideration. Judges do not choose their cases and so may often have to act in matters in which they lack complete confidence in their information base. . . .

3. *Courts must act when litigants call.* The passivity of the judicial process is one of its most prominent characteristics. Judges sit to hear disputes brought to them by parties; they do not initiate action. This makes the sequencing of judicially ordered change dependent on the capricious timing of litigants rather than the planning of a public body. It also makes it difficult to ascertain the extent to which the situation of the litigants faithfully represents or illustrates the dimensions of the problem they bring to court. . . .

4. *Fact-finding in adjudication is ill-adapted to the ascertainment of social facts.* The fact that judges function at some distance from the social milieu from which their cases spring puts them at an initial disadvantage in understanding the dimensions of social policy problems. The focused, piecemeal quality of adjudication implies that judicial decisions tend to be abstracted from social contexts broader than the immediate setting in which the litigation arises, and, as already indicated, the potentially unrepresentative character of the litigants makes it hazardous to generalize from their situation to the wider context.

The judicial fact-finding process carries forward this abstraction of the case from its more general social context. To make this clear, it is necessary to distinguish between two kinds of facts: historical facts and social facts. *Historical facts* are the events that have transpired between the parties to a lawsuit. *Social facts* are the recurrent patterns of behavior on which policy must be based. . . .

Social facts are nothing new in litigation. Courts have always had to make assumptions or inferences about general conditions that would guide their decisions. The broader the issue, the more such imponderables there are. The breadth of the issues in constitutional law has always made it a fertile field for empirical speculation. Does a civil service law barring alleged subversives from public employment have a "chilling effect" on free speech? Is the use of third-degree methods by the police sufficiently widespread to justify a prophylactic rule that would exclude from evidence even some confessions that are not coerced? Does pornography stimulate the commission of sex crimes, or does it provide cathartic release for those who might otherwise commit such crimes? . . .

The increasing involvement of the courts in social policy questions has increased the number and importance of social fact questions in litigation. As the courts move into new, specialized, unfamiliar policy areas, they are confronted by a plethora of questions about human behavior that are beyond their ability to answer on the basis of common experience or the usual modicum of expert testimony. . . .

5. *Adjudication makes no provision for policy review.* As the judicial process neglects social facts in favor of historical facts, so, too, does it slight what might be called *consequential facts.* Judges base their decisions on *antecedent facts,* on behavior that antedates the litigation. Consequential facts—those that relate to the impact of a decision on behavior—are equally important but much neglected.

This, of course, is a result of the focus on rights and duties rather than alternatives. Litigation is geared to rectifying the injustices of the past and present rather than to planning for some change to occur in the future. The very notion of planning is alien to adjudication. . . .

NAACP v. Button

371 U.S. 415 (1963)

A Virginia statute, designed to restrict the solicitation of legal business, prohibited the acceptance of employment or compensation from any person or organization not a party to a judicial proceeding and having no pecuniary right or liability in it. The National Association for the Advancement of Colored People, organized to assist persons in defending their constitutional rights, sued to enjoin enforcement of the statute and for a declaratory judgment that, as applied to the NAACP, the provision violated the Fourteenth Amendment. The Supreme Court held that the legal activities of the NAACP were modes of expression and association protected by the First and Fourteenth Amendments which Virginia could not prohibit. Footnotes omitted.

MR. JUSTICE BRENNAN delivered the opinion of the Court.

This case originated in companion suits by the National Association for the Advancement of Colored People, Inc. (NAACP), and the NAACP Legal Defense and Educational Fund, Inc. (Defense Fund), brought in 1957 in the United States District Court for the Eastern District of Virginia. . . .

There is no substantial dispute as to the facts; the dispute centers about the constitutionality under the Fourteenth Amendment of Chapter 33, as construed and applied by the Virginia Supreme Court of Appeals to include NAACP's activities within the statute's ban against "the improper solicitation of any legal or professional business."

The NAACP was formed in 1909 and incorporated under New York law as a nonprofit membership corporation in 1911. It maintains its headquarters in New York and presently has some 1,000 active unincorporated branches throughout the Nation. The corporation is licensed to do business in Virginia, and has 89 branches there. The Virginia branches are organized into the Virginia State Conference of NAACP Branches (the Conference), an unincorporated association, which in 1957 had some 13,500 members. The activities of the Conference are financed jointly by the national organization and the local branches from contributions and membership dues. NAACP policy, binding upon local branches and conferences, is set by the annual national convention.

The basic aims and purposes of NAACP are to secure the elimination of all racial barriers which deprive Negro citizens of the privileges and burdens of equal citizenship rights in the United States. To this end the Association engages in extensive educational and lobbying activities. It also devotes much of its funds and energies to an extensive program of assisting certain kinds of litigation on behalf of its declared purposes. For more than 10 years, the Virginia Conference has concentrated upon financing litigation aimed at ending racial segregation in the public schools of the Commonwealth. . . .

Petitioner challenges the decision of the Supreme Court of Appeals on many grounds. But we reach only one: that Chapter 33 as construed and applied abridges the freedoms of the First Amendment, protected against state action by the Fourteenth. More specifically, petitioner claims that the chapter infringes the right of the NAACP and its members and lawyers to associate for the purpose of assisting persons who seek legal redress for infringements of their constitutionally guaranteed and other rights. We think petitioner may assert this right on its own behalf, because, though a corporation, it is directly engaged in those activities, claimed to be constitutionally protected, which the statute would curtail. Cf. *Grosjean* v. *American Press Co.*, 297 U.S. 233. We also think petitioner has standing to assert the corresponding rights of its members. . . .

We reverse the judgment of the Virginia Supreme Court of Appeals. We hold that the activities of the NAACP, its affiliates and legal staff shown on this record are modes of expression and association protected by the First and Fourteenth Amendments which Virginia may not prohibit. . . .

We meet at the outset the contention that "solicitation" is wholly outside the area of freedoms protected by the First Amendment. To this contention there are two answers. The first is that a State cannot foreclose the exercise of constitutional rights by mere labels. The second is that abstract discussion is not the only species of communication which the Constitution protects; the First Amendment also protects vigorous advocacy, certainly of lawful ends, against governmental intrusion. . . . In the context of NAACP objectives, litigation is not a technique of resolving private differences; it is a means for achieving the lawful objectives of equality of treatment by all government, federal, state and local, for the members of the Negro community in this country. It is thus a form of political expression. Groups which find themselves unable to achieve their objectives through the ballot frequently turn to the courts. Just as it was true of the opponents of New Deal legislation during the 1930's, for example, no less is it true of the Negro minority today. And under the conditions of modern government, litigation may well be the sole practicable avenue open to a minority to petition for redress of grievances. . . .

The NAACP is not a conventional political party; but the litigation it assists, while serving to vindicate the legal rights of members of the American Negro community, at the same time and perhaps more importantly, makes possible the distinctive contribution of a minority group to the ideas and beliefs of our society. For such a group, association for litigation may be the most effective form of political association.

MR. JUSTICE DOUGLAS, concurring.

While I join the opinion of the Court, I add a few words. This Virginia Act is not applied across the board to all groups that use this method of obtaining and managing litigation, but instead reflects a legislative purpose to penalize the N. A. A. C. P. because it promotes desegregation of the races. Our decision in *Brown* v. *Board of Education*, 347 U. S. 483, holding that maintenance of public schools segregated by race violated the Equal Protection Clause of the Fourteenth Amendment, was announced May 17, 1954. The amendments to Virginia's code, here in issue, were enacted in 1956. Arkansas, Florida, Georgia, Mississippi, South Carolina, and Tennessee also passed laws following our 1954 decision which brought within their barratry statutes attorneys paid by an organization such as the N. A. A. C. P. and representing litigants without charge.

The bill, here involved, was one of five that Virginia enacted "as parts of the general plan of massive resistance to the integration of schools of the state under the Supreme Court's decrees." Those are the words of Judge Soper, writing for the court in *N. A. A. C. P.* v. *Patty*, 159 F. Supp. 503, 515. He did not indulge in guesswork. He reviewed the various steps taken by Virginia to resist our *Brown* decision, starting with the Report of the Gray Commission on November 11, 1955. *Id.*, at 512. He mentioned the "interposition resolution" passed by the General Assembly on February 1, 1956, the constitutional amendment made to carry out the recommendation of the Report of the Gray Commission, and the address of the Governor before the General Assembly that enacted the five laws, including the present one. *Id.*, at 513–515. These are too lengthy to repeat here. But they make clear the purpose of the present law— as clear a purpose to evade our prior decisions as was the legislation in *Lane* v. *Wilson*, 307 U. S. 268, another instance of a discriminatory state law. The fact that the contrivance used is subtle and indirect is not material to the question. "The Amendment nullifies sophisticated as well as simple-minded modes of discrimination." *Id.*, at 275. There we looked to the origins of the state law and the setting in which it operated to find its discriminatory nature. It is proper to do the same here.

Samuel Krislov

The Amicus Curiae Brief: From Friendship to Advocacy

The pretense by the lawyer that all precedents are, in Holmes' phrase, "born free and equal" all too often produces a curious portrait of a static legal universe where instruments and decisions alike avoid both decay and development. Yet, scholars have demonstrated many times over that imaginative utilization of the historical approach can produce insights which have been concealed by a fallacious assumption of homogeneity.

One device that, when not altogether ignored, has been thought of primarily in this antihistorical vein is the amicus curiae brief. Its delusive innocuousness, its seemingly static function and terminology, taken together with the offhand manner of its usual use in court, have in combination forestalled intensive scholarly study. Inasmuch as the device was apparently known in Roman law and was an early instrument of the common law, the assumption has been that it has remained functionally unchanged as long as the term has remained constant.

Yet, the Supreme Court's first promulgation of a written rule on the subject of such briefs in 1937 followed by two modifications of this newly codified provision within a span of twenty years belies the assumption of permanence. Quietly but unmistakably, such change demonstrates the transition that has occurred and continues to occur in the use of the brief.

THE AMICUS CURIAE AT COMMON LAW

The early use of the device is still preserved in the standard definitions, and may be found today in such sources as *Corpus Juris Secundum*. As Abbott's *Dictionary of Terms and Phrases* describes it, the amicus curiae is:

"A friend of the court. A term applied to a bystander, who without having an interest in the

SOURCE: 72 Yale L. J. 694 (1963). Footnotes omitted.

cause, of his own knowledge makes suggestion on a point of law or of fact for the information of the presiding judge."

Holthouse's *Law Dictionary*, of older vintage, puts it in even more stately fashion:

"When a judge is doubtful or mistaken in matter of law, a bystander may inform the court thereof as *amicus curiae*. Counsel in court frequently act in this capacity when they happen to be in possession of a case which the judge has not seen or does not at the moment remember."

The function of the amicus curiae at common law was one of oral "Shepardizing," the bringing up of cases not known to the judge. The *Yearbooks* cite many instances of such aid by bystanders, who not only acted on behalf of infants, but also called attention to manifest error, to the death of a party to the proceeding, and to existing appropriate statutes. Occasionally, however, other information was adduced. In one extreme instance, Sir George Treby, a member of Parliament, informed the court that he had been present at the passage of the statute whose meaning was contested and, as amicus curiae, wished to inform the court of the intent of Parliament in passing the legislation. The amicus did not even have to be an attorney to intervene, and the general attitude of the courts was to welcome such aid, since "it is for the honor of a court of justice to avoid error." . . .

THE AMICUS CURIAE IN THE UNITED STATES—THE SHIFT FROM NEUTRALITY TO ADVOCACY

The problems of representation of third party interests under the common law system were, if anything, exacerbated by the American system. The creation of a complex federal system meant not only that state and national interests were potentially in conflict, but also that an even greater number of conflicting public interests were potentially unrepresented in the course of private suits. Legal doctrines espoused by the Supreme Court also multiplied these problems. The assertion of judicial review and of the Court's role as "umpire to the federal system" meant that disputes taking the form of litigation between private citizens were in many instances to shape the constitutional contours of the federal system.

. . . until legislative clarification of the situation —most of which occurred in this century—the Court began to expand the right of participation of private litigants. At times as intervenors, at times as amicus curiae, depending on the situation and requests of the litigants or agreements of the counsel, litigants of similar cases pending before the lower courts and parties to lower court proceedings in a case before the Supreme Court who had not joined in the appeal were allowed to state their views by brief or oral presentation. Others claiming to be "real parties" in the case, or persons who could be directly injured by a decision, were sometimes extended similar privileges.

. . . The amicus is no longer a neutral, amorphous embodiment of justice, but an active participant in the interest group struggle.

Where the stakes are highest for the groups, and where the needs on the part of the judges for information and for the sharing of responsibility through consultation are at a peak, access has appropriately, and almost inevitably, been at its greatest. Occasionally a lower court will refuse an amicus brief for being "excessively partisan." Or, a state court will, like the Michigan court, strike its permission to participate in view of the fact that a party "is acting (though under disguise) not as a friend of the court but as a friend of one of the contestant litigants before said court."

The Supreme Court of the United States makes no pretense of such disinterestedness on the part of "its friends." The amicus is treated as a potential litigant in future cases, as an ally of one of the parties, or as the representative of an interest not otherwise represented. At this level the transition is complete; at the other court levels it is in process. Thus the institution of the amicus curiae brief has moved from neutrality to partisanship, from friendship to advocacy. . . .

One major development which has contributed to the use of the amicus brief has been the emergence of administrative agencies. The regulatory agencies enforcing and establishing administrative policies have necessarily been involved with a broad complex of interests. Their policies, in turn, affect a broader skein of interests, both in direct and indirect fashion, than those of the older executive agencies. In short, the activities of these agencies have involved potential interests and actual participants beyond the normal course of individual social and political interaction with governmental agencies. The fact that this has been explicitly recognized has also reinforced the trend. Many administrative agencies, acting by legislative provision or on their own initiative, have broadened the base of official participation in hearings before them. They, thus, have mobilized and alerted groups to issues and stakes involved at a stage prior to judicial litigation. So alerted, groups and individuals have sought means of strengthening favorable policies, both at the administrative level and at the judicial level.

A transitional link between governmental agents acting as interest articulators and private interest group activity in the judicial sphere was the participation of government officials in the guise of organized groups. So, in 1913 the railroad commissions of eight states were conjoined in a single amicus curiae brief. The 1916 term of the Court saw the National Association of Attorneys General participate in cases, as well as groups of attorneys general.

Among the private interest groups which were the first to utilize the opportunities of broader access were racial minority groups, securities and insurance interests, railroad interests, and miscellaneous groups under severe attack, notably the liquor interests in the first quarter of this century. Sheer familiarity with the intricacies of the existing system, strong dissatisfaction with it, and relative desperation seemingly can all function as sufficient motives for the seeking out and the finding of new channels of influence for self-protection or aggrandizement.

. . . the identification of the NAACP with such briefs is not merely a contemporary one, for that organization has, almost from its inception, participated as amicus curiae in litigation. An early case in point is *Guinn* v. *United States,* the famous Grandfather Clause case, where the NAACP justified its participation on the grounds that "the vital importance of these questions to every citizen of the United States, whether white or colored, seems amply to warrant the submission of this brief."

Highly regulated groups also were early participants. Since before the turn of the century, litigation involving the ICC regulatory powers has involved extensive non-party participation of interest groups (though not necessarily as amicus curiae). Following the principle enunciated by Merle Fainsod that interest structure often arises in response to governmental patterns, the transportation industry has continued to be the most highly and intricately organized area of the interest group spectrum. Not only has there been continued representation paralleling the political struggles of the railroad with the trucking interests, of railroad management with laborers, or even individual members with leaders; but also the report of *Noble* v. *United States* records the appearance on opposite sides of the fence of both the Regular Common Carriers Conference of the American Trucking Association and the Contract Carriers Conference of the ATA. . . .

While a series of "discrete and insular minorities" of a fiscal and commercial nature early found the amicus curiae brief a useful and potent instrument, it was the use of the device by civil rights organizations which drew widespread public attention. The American Civil Liberties Union was most active in this, as in other aspects of fostering minority group activity. In accordance with its standard policy of developing groups so as to encourage self-defense, the ACLU has characteristically contracted its activities as each minority group has become capable of handling its own litigation, participating only by invitation. Thus, numerous organizations which developed under ACLU tutelage are now largely independent in orientation and activities. Despite sharp differentiation in attitudes toward, and methods of, litigation, some lessons of legal strategy have remained a common legacy of the various civil rights groups. They also have retained some minimal

cohesion in many of the efforts to affect court rulings, as well as in their political activities, although hardly to the extent sometimes portrayed by opponents.

Vose has shown that by informal and nonsystematic cooperation civil rights groups did tend to coordinate their activities in the conduct of litigation, although the vagaries of chance and the actions of legal participants often thwarted any of the vague efforts at coordination. An increased reliance on litigation as a means of vindicating minority rights otherwise difficult to obtain through the political process, however, resulted in civil rights organizations such as the ACLU, and the American Jewish Congress, being among the most active filers of amicus curiae briefs over the past few years. In addition, labor organizations have been active, and not only in labor cases. Important civil rights cases such as the desegregation decision or the restrictive covenant cases saw a turnout of large numbers of amicus curiae briefs from varying minority group organizations. All of this focused attention and provoked criticism of the amicus curiae brief. . . .

On occasion, the amicus curiae has been an agent of the court acting as champion of the court's point of view, vigorously pursuing and defending a legal position at the request of the bench itself. In the main, however, the amicus curiae has been a means of fostering partisan third party involvement through the encouragement of group representation by a self-conscious bench. The judges have sought to gain information from political groups as well as to give them a feeling of participation in the process of decision. Access to the legal process on the part of such organizations is a logical extension of realistic awareness of law as a process of social choice and policy making. Even criticism of the amicus curiae brief as "political propaganda," court embarrassment at such criticism, and changes in the rules which have hampered such briefs in the short run have not seriously stemmed the growing reliance upon it.

Kathryn Mickle Werdeger

The Solicitor General and Administrative Due Process: A Quarter-Century of Advocacy

The Solicitor General, as chief appellate officer for the United States Government and its foremost advocate before the Supreme Court, holds vast discretionary powers and necessarily has a significant impact on the development of the law. His determination whether the Government should appeal an adverse decision by a lower court or permit it to stand is one aspect of his control over the development of the law. It is in those cases which reach the Supreme Court, however, whether on the initiative of the Government or of another party, that his pervasive influence is most readily discernible. Not only is the United States the most frequent litigant before the Court, it is also a highly successful one, winning an average of forty-eight per cent of its cases over the past eleven years. With a few exceptions, the Solicitor General is ultimately responsible for the Government's arguments in every case to reach the Supreme Court.

As counsel before the Supreme Court the Solicitor General fills a complex role: he is viewed simultaneously as advocate for the Government, representative of the public interest, and officer of the Court. Like all attorneys he has a client whom he is expected to represent, but his client is not only the particular agency or officer who is party to a given case; it is the United States citizenry as a whole. "The United States," reads a plaque outside the Attorney General's door, "wins its point whenever justice is done its citizens in the courts." Adherence to this philosophy should imbue the advocacy of the Solicitor General with a measure of judiciousness foreign to the private practitioner. As described by a former Solicitor General, this sense of loyalty is reflected in the efforts made by

SOURCE: 36 G.W. L. Rev. 481 (1968). Footnotes omitted.

lawyers in the Office to suggest to the Court "how it can decide the case in the way which will be best for the Court, and for the handling of its precedents, instead of seeking the sweeping decision most favorable to the Government's short-run interests." Finally, the Solicitor General's advocacy should be colored by the "permanency" of the Government's relation to the Court—its repeated appearances term after term, a relation which has led some to characterize the Solicitor General as the Court's "ninth-and-a-half" member. Unlike the private attorney, who may feel neither a need to be consistent from one case to the next nor a responsibility for the development of the law, the Solicitor General must temper his arguments with the realization that what he says today will face him tomorrow, and that beyond his duty vigorously and fairly to represent the United States in a particular case is his responsibility to the Court and the public to foster the orderly development of the law and to establish justice.

The unique role of the Solicitor General as counsel and the demonstrable impact his views have on the development of the law warrant analysis of the principles he has espoused and the arguments he has advanced before the Court, particularly in the context of administrative law, with respect to one of the most vital guarantees of our Bill of Rights—the guarantee of procedural due process. "Due process," Mr. Justice Frankfurter has stated, "is perhaps the most majestic concept in our whole constitutional system. While it contains the garnered wisdom of the past in assuring fundamental justice, it is also a living principle not confined to past instances." "The history of liberty has largely been the history of procedural safeguards." Moreover, as Mr. Justice Jackson has observed, "[D]ue process of law is not for the sole benefit of an accused. It is the best insurance for the Government itself against those blunders which leave lasting stains on a system of justice . . ."

The responsibility of the Solicitor General in formulating the Government's position in procedural due process cases is particularly heavy since the answer is rarely clear-cut and necessarily involves a balancing of conflicting interests. While the problem in the administrative law cases considered below is frequently characterized as a conflict between the demands of national security and the rights of an individual petitioner, it would be more precise to describe the process as a balancing of two vital public interests: the interest in the effective preservation of our national security, which may involve protecting confidential sources and techniques of investigation; and the interest in the integrity of our concepts of fair play, concepts which form the basis of our "scheme of ordered liberty" and give us reasonable assurance that truth and thus justice will be achieved. Analysis of the position of the Solicitor General in this regard over the past quarter-century is not merely historical. What the Government argues today will have to be faced tomorrow; what the Government argues today may be tomorrow's law of the land.

. . . the Solicitor General has concluded the procedures of the program *[for discharging federal employees]* represent the informed judgment of the Executive as to the best possible means of reconciling the national security interest of the United States in keeping the identity of informants and methods of investigation confidential, with the interest of the individual in full disclosure of his accusers. "That appraisal of the competing interests, based as it is on extensive information not available to the courts, would seem necessarily to be controlling . . ." Moreover, it was urged, there are no acceptable alternatives. Judicial review of the executive determination that the interests of national security preclude disclosure would require the Executive either to reveal the very information it seeks to protect, or to support its judgment without adequate documentation. A system of ad hoc determinations by the agency head as to the need in each case for nondisclosure would ignore the basic purpose of the regulations,

which is to preserve the entire intelligence systems, and not simply the particular items of information in an individual case. Finally, application in loyalty-security cases of the criminal rule that the Government must either reveal the identity of its informants or drop the prosecution, would require the Government to compromise the national security in one of two ways: either by retaining in federal service an employee of doubtful loyalty, or by exposing to public scrutiny information of a confidential nature.

. . . The Government, as much as the individual, has an immediate and vital interest in abiding by our traditional concepts of fair play, and in preserving the procedural protections embodied in the concept of due process. It might be expected, therefore, that the Solicitor General, charged with representing the public interest as well as the interest of a particular governmental client, would emerge as an important champion of procedural rights—rights which in the long-run benefit both the Government and its citizens. However, an analysis of his position in the administrative law cases discussed above would seem to compel a contrary conclusion. Rather than seeking a strong presumption in favor of procedural safeguards, relinquishing them only in cases where the Executive interest is clearly established, he has seemed to justify even the more spurious government claims once the question of security has been raised.

While the Solicitor General doubtless recognizes the protection of procedural rights to be a positive good for both Government and the individual, and is aware further of the impact his position is likely to have on the development of procedural law, this recognition alone has not been determinative of the position he has adopted in procedural cases. Our adversary system presupposes that both sides will be heard and it is one, though not the sole, duty of the Solicitor General effectively to represent his particular governmental client. Thus, competing with and often submerging the interest in procedural fairness have been the Executive's view of the needs of national security, and the administrator's view of what is required for efficient and effective implementation of his agency's program. Following disposition of a case it has often become apparent, however, that the asserted needs of national security and efficiency were exaggerated. It would seem, therefore, that the Solicitor General might better use the influence of his office to encourage concessions in many of these cases, rather than supporting the Government in its frequently unwarranted restriction of procedural rights so vigorously before the Court.

In addition to the restraints imposed by his role as advocate in our adversary system, however, practical considerations operate to inhibit the Solicitor General's freedom of choice in advancing procedural arguments before the Court. In this respect, Professor Frank C. Newman's observation regarding the role of government lawyers generally applies with particular force to the Solicitor General. "[T]heir counsel is sought," he stated,

"not when other officials wish to design a procedure, so that the lessons of 'the very essence of a scheme of ordered liberty' may be put to good use. Rather they answer calls of alarm. They are shock troops to be rushed in when a lawsuit impends. Their job, with awful consistence, is to demonstrate that a procedure already set is really legitimate, though they and other lawyers . . . might now concede that de novo a more fair procedure should have been designed."

So long as the Solicitor General is cast in the role not of statesman, but of defender of the judgment of administrators who doubtless are concerned primarily with the achievement of their immediate ends, the Court, and ultimately the law, cannot benefit fully from the expertise and breadth of view which is his, and the ideals of his office must remain unfulfilled.

Attorney General Qualifications

Partisanship within the Justice Department has long been a concern of reformers who want to depoliticize the post of Attorney General. This issue was reopened with the Watergate affair and has remained highly visible since then. In 1984, Senator Max Baucus introduced legislation to upgrade the offices of Attorney General and Deputy Attorney General. His statement appears at 130 Cong. Rec. S2020 (daily ed. February 29, 1984), introducing S. 2377.

Mr. BAUCUS. Mr. President, I am today introducing legislation that will prevent any individual who has held a leading partisan position in the election of a President from becoming Attorney General or Deputy Attorney General of the United States. This legislation would institute reforms suggested by the Watergate special prosecution force in their 1975 report and would go a long way to depoliticizing the Department of Justice.

The Members of this body have been asked too many times in the past to give their constitutional advice and consent to the nomination of an individual who served as the President's chief political adviser and campaign manager to become the chief law enforcement officer of the Nation. We

will apparently be asked to do so again. We must stop viewing the job of Attorney General as a political plum to be awarded to the politically faithful. Instead we should view it as a position of responsibility. First this requires an individual who can assure that our laws are strictly and fairly enforced.

The Watergate special prosecution force put it in these words: The President should not nominate and the Senate should not confirm as Attorney General, or as any other appointee in high Department of Justice posts, a person who has served as the President's campaign manager or in a similar high-level campaign role. A campaign manager seeks support for his candidate and necessarily incurs obligations to political leaders and other individuals throughout wide geographical areas. If he then takes a high position in the Justice Department, he may take—or appear to take—official actions on the basis of those commitments rather than on appropriate legal and policy grounds. The Attorney General and other Justice Department appointees should be lawyers with their own reputations in the legal profession, with capacity and willingness to make independent judgments, and with the authority to choose similarly qualified persons for subordinate positions.

Mr. President, we in this body ought to insist that this advice be followed. In fact, the Senate has agreed to legislation similar to mine twice before, once in 1976 and once in 1977, when the Senate by unanimous consent agreed to exclude high Presidential campaign officials from serving as Attorney General. Unfortunately, the House did not agree to the legislation and it was never enacted into law. I believe it is now time to do so.

We need to avoid even the appearance of a conflict of interest when it comes to enforcing the laws of the Nation. The Attorney General, as chief law enforcement official, is in a particularly sensitive position and ought to be completely beyond any taint of conflict of interest or favoritism. Such simply cannot be the case if the Attorney General has incurred political debts as campaign manager of a Presidential campaign.

Unfortunately, too often in recent history Congress has been asked to confirm a political operative as Attorney General. I do not know how Mr. Meese will fare in the confirmation process. But as I review his past record, I have become convinced that the Senate should not be put in this position in the future.

Mr. President, this legislation can only help this Nation. We do not lack for well-qualified individuals who would be excellent Attorneys General. We need not ask high campaign officials to balance their political promises with impartial enforcement of the Nation's laws.

Steel Seizure Case of 1952: Oral Argument Before the District Court

On April 24, 1952, in oral argument before U.S. District Judge David A. Pine, Assistant Attorney General Holmes Baldridge presented the government's case in defense of the seizure of steel companies by Secretary of Commerce Charles Sawyer. Judge Pine's decision, declaring the seizure illegal, was later affirmed by the Supreme Court. The following excerpt of the oral argument comes from House Document No. 534 (Part I), 82d Cong., 2d Sess. (1952), pp. 362–363, 371–373.

Mr. Baldridge: Our position is that there is no power in the Courts to restrain the President and, as I say, Secretary Sawyer is the alter ego of the President and not subject to injunctive order of the Court.

The Court: If the President directs Mr. Sawyer to take you into custody, right now, and have you executed in the morning you say there is no power by which the Court may intervene even by habeas corpus?

Mr. Baldridge: If there are statues protecting me I would have a remedy.

The Court: What statute would protect you?

Mr. Baldridge: I do not recall any at the moment.

The Court: But on the question of the deprivation of your rights you have the Fifth Amendment; that is what protects you.

I would like an answer to that—what about that?

Mr. Baldridge: Well, as I was going to point out in a little while——

The Court (interposing): I will give you a chance to think about that overnight and you may answer me tomorrow. . . .

The Court: Now, Mr. Attorney General, it is

getting near the time when we shall have to stop. I wonder if you would give me such assistance as you can before we stop so that I can think about your viewpoint overnight, as to your power, or as to your client's power.

As I understand it, you do not assert any statutory power.

Mr. Baldridge: That is correct.

The Court: And you do not assert any express constitutional power.

Mr. Baldridge: Well, your Honor, we base the President's power on Sections 1, 2 and 3 of Article II of the Constitution, and whatever inherent, implied or residual powers may flow therefrom.

We do not propose to get into a discussion of semantics with counsel for plaintiffs. We say that when an emergency situation in this country arises that is of such importance to the entire welfare of the country that something has to be done about it and has to be done now, and there is no statutory provision for handling the matter, that it is the duty of the Executive to step in and protect the national security and the national interests. We say that Article II of the Constitution, which provides that the Executive power of the Government shall reside in the President, that he shall faithfully execute the laws of the office and he shall be Commander-in-Chief of the Army and of the Navy and that he shall take care that the laws be faithfully executed, are sufficient to permit him to meet any national emergency that might arise, be it peace time, technical war time, or actual war time.

The Court: So you contend the Executive has unlimited power in time of an emergency?

Mr. Baldridge: He has the power to take such action as is necessary to meet the emergency.

The Court: If the emergency is great, it is unlimited, is it?

Mr. Baldridge: I suppose if you carry it to its logical conclusion, that is true. But I do want to point out that there are two limitations on the Executive power. One is the ballot box and the other is impeachment.

The Court: Then, as I understand it, you claim that in time of emergency the Executive has this great power.

Mr. Baldridge: That is correct.

The Court: And that the Executive determines the emergencies and the Courts cannot even review whether it is an emergency.

Mr. Baldridge: That is correct.

The Court: Do you have any case that sustains such a proposition as that?

Mr. Baldridge: Yes, indeed, your Honor.

The only case in which an attempt was made by the Courts to interfere with the exercise of inherent executive power is the case of Mississippi vs. Johnson, reported in 4 Wall. 475. I think your Honor may be familiar with the facts of that case.

The Court: Yes.

Mr. Baldridge: There the Court held——

The Court: There is no seizure in that.

Mr. Baldridge: Well, there was an attempt to stay executive power, and the Court decided they did not have that power.

The Court: There is no attempt to stay executive power here. It is to stay Mr. Sawyer's act. That is what they claim.

Mr. Baldridge: Well, Mr. Sawyer in this case is the alter ego of the President.

Suppose your Honor could enjoin Mr. Sawyer. The President could immediately appoint somebody else to operate the steel mills, or he could undertake that himself.

The Court: That bridge would be crossed when it is reached. The only case you have, then, is the Mississippi vs. Johnson case?

Mr. Baldridge: The only case in which there has been an attempt——

The Court: Do you have any case of a seizure except a seizure authorized by statute during wartime, which made the statute constitutional?

Mr. Baldridge: Well, we have set out in our brief a number of instances, your Honor, in which seizure occurred in the absence of statutory authorization.

The Court: I mean where the Courts approved it.

Mr. Baldridge: I do not know of any——

The Court: I do not think a seizure without judicial interference is relevant. The fact that a man reaches in your pocket and steals your wallet is not a precedent for making that a valid act.

Carl McGowan

Congressmen in Court: The New Plaintiffs

The last decade has seen the birth and the coming of age of a new kind of lawsuit: one brought by a member of Congress challenging an action of the executive branch as injurious to some interest he or she claims to have as a legislator. Senators and Representatives, either singly or in small groups, have invoked the judicial power for purposes such as forcing the executive to publish as law a bill that had been the subject of an allegedly improper pocket veto, granting the House of Representatives the right to vote on the cession of the Panama Canal, and continuing in effect our mutual-defense treaty with Taiwan despite presidential action purportedly terminating it. In these and other cases, the congressional plaintiffs arguably attempted to circumvent the political process by obtaining in court a remedy that could be obtained from Congress.

Serious separation-of-powers questions inevitably accompany any effort by members of the legislature to enlist the judiciary's aid in a dispute with the executive. The issues involved typically are poorly suited for judicial resolution. Moreover, any intrusion by the judiciary into a dispute between its coequal branches seems fraught with difficulties. The problems are multiplied when the plaintiff could have obtained from Congress the substantial equivalent of the judicial relief sought, because in such cases the court is asked to intrude into the internal functionings of the legislative branch itself.

These problems have troubled congressmen and judges alike. In a lengthy discussion on the Senate floor two days after oral argument on the Taiwan treaty case in the court of appeals, several Senators decried judicial-branch involvement in the dispute. Majority Leader Robert Byrd said that "treaty termination . . . should be resolved be-

SOURCE: 15 Ga. L. Rev. 241 (1981). Footnotes omitted. When he wrote this article, McGowan was Chief Judge of the U.S. Court of Appeals for the District of Columbia.

tween the Senate of the United States and the President. It should not be left to the judicial branch to decide an issue we should confront here." Senator Jacob Javits was "very unhappy . . . to see the procedures of the Senate and the relationships between the Senate and the President under the Constitution determined by a court." Senator Harry F. Byrd, Jr., while maintaining that Senate approval was required, declared it to be "unfortunate . . . that the courts are involved in this."

These comments coincided with those of a very distinguished and uniquely qualified witness who earlier had testified by invitation before the Senate Foreign Relations Committee on a sense of the Senate resolution stating that Senate approval is required to terminate any mutual-defense treaty. That witness was the Honorable Dean Rusk of the University of Georgia School of Law. Professor Rusk said to the Committee:

"I, myself, believe that the question of the continuing validity of a treaty, and especially a mutual defense treaty, is not a matter for the courts. This is a political matter of the highest importance, on which the courts have neither the competence nor the responsibility. It is a question for the political branches of the Government, and if there are differences between a President and a Congress, these differences should be worked out and resolved by political processes.

The late Chief Justice Earl Warren visited our law school shortly before his death and, on that occasion, reminded us that if each branch of the Federal Government were to pursue its own constitutional powers to the end of the trail, our system simply could not function. It would freeze up like an engine without oil. . . ."

Judges have also been acutely aware of the problems inherent in these suits. In a 1977 case holding that a member of the House of Representatives lacked standing to complain of allegedly illegal CIA activities and appropriations when his own legislative reform proposals to this end had failed of enactment, Judge Wilkey noted that expansive concepts of standing in this context "would lead inevitably to the intrusion of the courts into the proper affairs of the co-equal branches of government." In the Taiwan treaty case, Judge Wright, speaking for himself and Judge Tamm as the two members of the court of appeals *en banc* who concluded that the congressional plaintiffs lacked standing, commented that the issue was "rooted in the dynamic relationship between the two political branches" and that hearing the suit would invite "additional unnecessary, and potentially dangerous, judicial incursions into the area."

Frank M. Johnson

The Constitution and the Federal District Judge

Modern American society depends upon our judicial system to play a critical role in maintaining the balance between governmental powers and individual rights. The increasing concern paid by our courts toward the functioning of government and its agencies has received much comment and some criticism recently. As governmental institutions at all levels have assumed a greater role in providing public services, courts increasingly have been confronted with the unavoidable duty of determining whether those services meet basic constitutional requirements. Time and again citizens have brought to the federal courts, and those courts reluctantly have decided, such basic questions as how and when to make available equal quality public education to all our children; how to guarantee all citizens an opportunity to serve on juries, to vote, and to have their votes counted equally; under what minimal living conditions criminal offenders may be incarcerated; and what minimum standards of care and treatment state institutions must provide the mentally ill and mentally retarded who have been involuntarily committed to the custody of the state.

The reluctance with which courts and judges have undertaken the complex task of deciding such questions has at least three important sources. First, one of the founding principles of our

SOURCE: 54 Tex. L. Rev. 903 (1976). Footnotes omitted. When he wrote this article, Johnson was Chief Judge, U.S. District Court for the Middle District of Alabama.

Government, a principle derived from the French philosophers of the eighteenth century, is that the powers of government should be separate and distinct, lest all the awesome power of government unite as one force unchecked in its exercise. The drafters of our Constitution formulated the doctrine of separation of powers to promote the independence of each branch of government in its sphere of operation. To the extent that courts respond to requests to look to the future and to change existing conditions by making new rules, however, they become subject to the charge of usurping authority from the legislative or executive branch.

Second, our Constitution and laws have strictly limited the power of the federal judiciary to participate in what are essentially political affairs. The tenth amendment reserves any power not delegated to the United States to the individual states or to the people. Reflecting the distrust of centralized government expressed by this amendment, courts and citizens alike since the Nation's beginning have regarded certain governmental functions as primarily, if not exclusively, state responsibilities. Among these are public education; maintenance of state and local penal institutions; domestic relations; and provision for the poor, homeless, aged, and infirm. A further limitation on the role of federal courts with respect to other governmental bodies lies in the creation and maintenance of these courts as courts of limited jurisdiction.

Last, federal judges properly hesitate to make decisions either that require the exercise of political judgment or that necessitate expertise they lack. Judges are professionally trained in the law —not in sociology, education, medicine, penology, or public administration. In an ideal society, elected officials would make all decisions relating to the allocation of resources; experts trained in corrections would make all penological decisions; physicians would make all medical decisions; scientists would make all technological decisions; and educators would make all educational decisions. Too often, however, we have failed to achieve this ideal system. Many times, those persons to whom we have entrusted these responsibilities have acted or failed to act in ways that do not fall within the bounds of discretion permitted by the Constitution and the laws. When such transgressions are properly and formally brought before a court—and increasingly before federal courts—it becomes the responsibility of the judiciary to ensure that the Constitution and laws of the United States remain, in fact as well as in theory, the supreme law of the land.

On far too many occasions the intransigent and unremitting opposition of state officials who have neglected or refused to correct unconstitutional or unlawful state policies and practices has necessitated federal intervention to enforce the law. Courts in all sections of the Nation have expended and continue to expend untold resources in repeated litigation brought to compel local school officials to follow a rule of law first announced by the Supreme Court almost twenty-two years ago. In addition to deciding scores of school cases, federal courts in Alabama alone have ordered the desegregation of mental institutions, penal facilities, public parks, city buses, interstate and intrastate buses and bus terminals, airport terminals, and public libraries and museums. Although I refer to Alabama and specific cases litigated in the federal courts of Alabama, I do not intend to suggest that similar problems do not exist in many of our other states.

The history of public school desegregation has been a story of repeated intervention by the courts to overcome not only the threats and violence of extremists attempting to block school desegregation but also the numerous attempts by local and state officials to thwart the orderly, efficient, and lawful resolution of this complicated social problem. Desegregation is not the only area of state responsibility in which Alabama officials have forfeited their decisionmaking powers by such a dereliction of duty as to require judicial intervention. Having found Alabama's legislative apportionment plan unconstitutional, the District Court for the Middle District of Alabama waited ten years for State officials to carry out the duty properly imposed upon them by the Constitution and expressly set out in the court's order. The continued refusal of those officials to comply left the court no choice but to assume that duty itself and to impose its own reapportionment plan. State officers by their inaction have also handed over to the courts property tax assessment plans; standards for the care and treatment of mentally ill and mentally retarded persons committed to the State's custody; and the procedures by which such persons are committed.

Some of these cases are extremely troublesome and time consuming for all concerned. I speak in particular of those lawsuits challenging the operation of state institutions for the custody and control of citizens who cannot or will not function at a safe and self-sustaining capacity in a free society. Ordinarily these cases proceed as class actions seeking to determine the rights of large numbers of people. As a result, the courts' decisions necessarily have wide-ranging effect and momentous importance, whether they grant or deny the relief sought.

A shocking example of a failure of state officials to discharge their duty was forcefully presented in a lawsuit tried before me in 1972, *Newman* v. *Alabama*, which challenged the constitutional sufficiency of medical care available to prisoners in the Alabama penal system. The evidence in that case convincingly demonstrated that correctional officers on occasion intentionally denied inmates the right to examination by a physician or to treatment by trained medical personnel, and that they routinely withheld medicine and other treatments prescribed by physicians. Further evidence showed that untrained inmates served as ward attendants and X-ray, laboratory, and dental technicians; rags were used as bandages; ambulance oxygen tanks remained empty for long periods of time; and unsupervised inmates without formal training pulled teeth, gave injections, sutured, and performed minor surgery. In fact, death resulting from gross neglect and totally inadequate treatment was not unusual.

A nineteen-year-old with an extremely high fever who was diagnosed as having acute pneumonia was left unsupervised and allowed to take cold showers at will for two days before his death. A quadriplegic with bedsores infested with maggots was bathed and had his bandages changed only once in the month before his death. An inmate who could not eat received no nourishment for the three days prior to his death even though intravenous feeding had been ordered by a doctor. A geriatric inmate who had suffered a stroke was made to sit each day on a wooden bench so that he would not soil his bed; he frequently fell onto the floor; his legs became swollen from a lack of circulation, necessitating the amputation of a leg the day before his death. . . .

One of the most comprehensive orders that I have entered concerning the operation and management of state institutions relates to the facilities maintained by the Alabama Department of Mental Health for the mentally ill and mentally retarded. Plaintiffs in *Wyatt* v. *Stickney* brought a class action on behalf of all patients involuntarily confined at Bryce Hospital, the State's largest mental hospital, to establish the minimum standards of care and treatment to which the civilly committed are entitled under the Constitution. Patients at Searcy Hospital in southern Alabama and residents at the Partlow State School and Hospital in Tuscaloosa joined the action as plaintiffs, thereby compelling a comprehensive inquiry into the entire Alabama mental health and retardation treatment and habilitation program.

At trial plaintiffs produced evidence showing that Bryce Hospital, built in the 1850's, was grossly overcrowded, housing more than 5000 patients. Of these 5000 people ostensibly committed to Bryce for treatment of mental illness, about 1600 —almost one-third—were geriatrics neither needing nor receiving any treatment for mental illness. Another 1000 or more of the patients at Bryce were mentally retarded rather than mentally ill. A totally inadequate staff, only a small percentage professionally trained, served these 5000 patients. The hospital employed only six staff members qualified to deal with mental patients— three medical doctors with psychiatric training, one Ph.D psychologist, and two social workers with master's degrees in social work. The evidence indicated that the general living conditions and lack of individualized treatment programs were as intolerable and deplorable as Alabama's rank of fiftieth among the states in per patient expenditures would suggest. For example, the hospital spent less than fifty cents per patient each day for food.

The evidence concerning Partlow State School and Hospital for the retarded proved even more shocking than the evidence relating to the mental hospitals. The extremely dangerous conditions compelled the court to issue an interim emergency order requiring Partlow officials to take immediate steps to protect the lives and safety of the residents. The Associate Commissioner for Mental Retardation for the Alabama Department of Mental Health testified that Partlow was sixty percent overcrowded; that the school, although it had not, could immediately discharge at least 300 residents; *and that seventy percent of the residents should never have been committed at all*. The conclusion that there was no opportunity for habilitation for its residents was inescapable. Indeed, the evidence reflected that one resident was scalded to death when a fellow resident hosed water from one of the bath facilities on him; another died as a result of the insertion of a running water hose into his rectum by a working resident who was cleaning him; one died when soapy water was forced into his mouth; another died of a self-administered overdose of inadequately stored drugs; and authorities restrained another resident in a straitjacket for *nine years* to prevent him from sucking his hands and fingers. Witnesses described the Partlow facilities as barbaric and primitive; some residents had no place to sit to eat meals, and coffee cans served as toilets in some areas of the institution.

With the exception of the interim emergency order designed to eliminate hazardous conditions at Partlow, the court at first declined to devise specific steps to improve existing conditions in Alabama's mental health and retardation facilities. Instead, it directed the Department of Mental

Health to design its own plan for upgrading the system to meet constitutional standards. Only after two deadlines had passed without any signs of acceptable progress did the court itself, relying upon the proposals of counsel for all parties and amici curiae, define the minimal constitutional standards of care, treatment, and habilitation for which the case of *Wyatt* v. *Stickney* has become generally known. . . .

As long as those state officials entrusted with the responsibility for fair and equitable governance completely disregard that responsibility, the judiciary must and will stand ready to intervene on behalf of the deprived. Judge Richard T. Rives of the Court of Appeals for the Fifth Circuit, in joining a three-judge panel that struck down attempts by state officials to frustrate the registration of black voters, eloquently expressed the reluctance with which the vast majority of federal judges approach intervention in state affairs:

"I look forward to the day when the State and its political subdivisions will again take up their mantle of responsibility, treating all of their citizens equally, and thereby relieve the federal Government of the necessity of intervening in their affairs. Until that day arrives, the responsibility for this intervention must rest with those who through their ineptitude and public disservice have forced it."

We in the judiciary await the day when the Alabama Federal Intervention Syndrome, in that State and elsewhere, will become a relic of the past. To reclaim responsibilities passed by default to the judiciary—most often the federal judiciary—and to find solutions for ever-changing challenges, the states must preserve their ability to respond flexibly, creatively, and with due regard for the rights of all. State officials must confront their governmental responsibilities with the diligence and honesty that their constituencies deserve. When lawful rights are being denied, only the exercise of conscientious, responsible leadership, which is usually long on work and short on complimentary news headlines, can avoid judicial intervention. The most fitting Bicentennial observance I can conceive would be for all government officials to take up the constitutional mantle and diligently strive to protect the basic human rights recognized by the founders of our Republic two hundred years ago.

Tinsley E. Yarbrough

The Judge as Manager: The Case of Judge Frank Johnson

Judge Frank M. Johnson, Jr., Chief Judge of the U.S. District Court for the Middle District of Alabama, placed a number of Alabama's mental institutions under federal court order, including Bryce Hospital in Tuscaloosa, Searcy Hospital in Mt. Vernon, and Partlow State School and Hospital for the mentally retarded, also located in Tuscaloosa. *Wyatt* v. *Stickney* was one of a series of cases charging unconstitutional conditions at these institutions. The following excerpt explains how Judge Johnson was able to create a broad base of support for change.

The sheer scope of the mental health and prison orders dictated a more elaborate implementation mechanism than simply the usual filing of periodic compliance reports. The plaintiffs had

SOURCE: 1 J. Policy Analysis and Management 386 (1982). Footnotes omitted.

urged Judge Johnson to turn over operation of Alabama's prisons and mental institutions to court-appointed masters; various organizations and government agencies that had associated themselves with the case by filing briefs as "friends of the court" were offering the same advice. Instead, Judge Johnson opted for creation of committees of laymen to assist him in monitoring compliance. In the 1972 mental health order, he established a human rights committee for each of Alabama's major mental institutions. These committees were authorized to review all treatment programs and proposals for experiments on patients for evidence of human rights violations; they could advise and assist patients who alleged violations of their legal rights; and they could inspect institutional records, interview patients and staff, and consult with independent specialists. The 1976 order provided for a single human rights committee for the state prison system, with a charge similar to that given the mental health committees. The chairman of the prison committee created various subcommittees: four to monitor compliance at each of the four major state prisons; a fifth subcommittee for other facilities; another composed of physicians to monitor compliance with the court's medical care standards; and yet another to review inmate complaints. . . .

. . . the hostility of the mental health and prison personnel to the lay committees was acute, at least at first. Judge Johnson probably viewed the committees as a less drastic alternative to the appointment of masters. Moreover, the committees were assisted by professional consultants and included in their membership a large number of physicians, lawyers, and others with relevant career backgrounds. In addition, the committees were in a position to involve citizens from every part of the state, thereby fostering greater public awareness of the problems confronting Alabama's mental institutions and prisons. Even so, the wisdom of empowering lay committees to monitor compliance with the detailed requirements of the court, particularly those of a technical nature, was debatable; in fact, the Fifth Circuit panel which ultimately reviewed the prison orders rejected the committee approach, suggesting as a "more reasonable, less intrusive, more effective approach" the appointment of a single qualified monitor, with full authority to observe and report, but without power to intervene in daily prison operations.

State personnel resented the lay committee members, and the hostility was especially evident in Alabama's mental institutions. Even before issuance of the *Wyatt* order in 1972, counsel for the plaintiffs in that case, as well as some of the "friends" associated with the case, had frequently and vehemently attacked conditions in the state's mental institutions; and their comments were widely circulated in the state press. Mental health personnel—who believed that they were being unfairly blamed for years of neglect by the state—bristled at such criticism and at the presence of the often outspoken human rights committee members in the state facilities. State officials complained to the court and asked that the roles of the mental health committees be clarified. The superintendent of the Partlow facility went so far as to issue an order forbidding his personnel to meet with the Partlow committee without his approval.

In September 1974, Judge Johnson overturned the superintendent's order and clarified the committees' roles, emphasizing that "free and easy communication should be established between the committees and the patients and staff" at each institution. Relations between state personnel and human rights committee members would remain somewhat strained, however, throughout the committees' existence.

Like the human rights committees, compliance reports and hearings on motions to modify the court's initial orders were important elements in the implementation structure. Judge Johnson also frequently resorted to conferences with counsel for the parties and friends of the court, as well as others connected with the prison and mental health cases. Such sessions often served purposes other than that of monitoring compliance, becoming a pulpit from which the judge could exhort, warn, and reassure. . . .

Critical in the implementation process was Alabama's social and political environment. In his monumental *Southern Politics,* V.O. Key wrote of the factionalism in Alabama politics built on networks of "friends and neighbors." Whatever the accuracy of such a generalization may be, the elaborate web of interpersonal relationships linking principal actors in the mental health and prison cases appears to have been an important element in the implementation process.

A sampling of the relationships pervading the two cases should suffice to suggest their intricate scope. During his tenure, Ira DeMent, the U.S. Attorney for the Middle District, who was chief representative for the United States as a friend of the court in these cases, established close ties with Judge Johnson. DeMent had also been a University of Alabama law school classmate of George Dean, chief counsel for the *Wyatt* plaintiffs. Drawing on those ties, Dean persuaded DeMent, early in the litigation, to make several surprise tours of state mental institutions; and accompanying newsmen and photographers produced graphic reports and photographs for state papers ("We figured judges read the newspapers," Dean later remarked). A University of Alabama psychologist who helped to initiate the *Wyatt* proceedings and who was Judge Johnson's choice to head a team reclassifying Alabama prison inmates had been DeMent's undergraduate roommate at the University. Lecil Gray, a former state probate judge who served as chairman of the Bryce human rights committee and became the court's monitor of mental health compliance under the receivership scheme, was one of Judge Johnson's closest friends, their association reaching back to the judge's earliest years of law practice.

Such personal ties extended, of course, to state officials involved in the litigation. William Baxley, state attorney general through much of the implementation process and a progressive politician by Alabama standards, was Judge Johnson's close friend and an admirer of his judicial record; moreover, Judge Johnson's son served as an aide in Baxley's office. At the other end of the spectrum was Judge Johnson's relationship with Alabama governor George Wallace. Law school classmates and former friends, Johnson and Wallace had become principal antagonists in Alabama's racial wars of the 1960s; Wallace excoriated "lying" federal judges and resisted civil rights reform at every turn, while the judge subjected the state to a seemingly limitless variety of human rights orders.

In the mental health and prison cases, the importance of such relationships occasionally emerged with clarity. In the prison litigation, for example, the state initially was perhaps most concerned about those portions of Judge Johnson's order relating to minimum cell size requirements and the judge's decision that a team of psychologists from the University of Alabama create and implement a program of inmate classification. The provisions regarding cell sizes posed serious financial burdens, and the university faculty had assisted the plaintiffs in the key cases of 1972 and 1976. Attorney General Baxley indicated that he would drop state appeal efforts if a compromise could be reached on these points of contention. Informal negotiations ensued between the judge and the attorney general, with Ira DeMent serving as intermediary. Their efforts were ultimately unsuccessful but do reflect the importance of informal relationships to an understanding of the politics of judicial implementation.

2 The Doctrine of Judicial Review

J udicial review in America survives a number of nagging, unanswered questions. By what right do life-tenured judges invalidate policies adopted by popularly elected officials? If judicial review is of such crucial importance for a written Constitution, why did the framers omit it? Why is it based on implied, rather than explicit, power? If judicial review is essential for a constitutional democracy, how do other nations preserve their constitutions without judicial review?

At some point, judicial review assumes the characteristics of lawmaking. Constitutional interpretation is more than a technical exercise or display of judicial erudition. The power to interpret the law is the power to make the law. Judicial review can be another name for judicial legislation. As Bishop Hoadley announced in 1717: "Whosoever hath an absolute authority to interpret any written or spoken laws, it is he who is truly the lawgiver, to all intents and purposes, and not the person who first wrote or spoke them." James Bradley Thayer, 7 Harv. L. Rev. 129, 152 (1893).

Courts may overturn a government action, find support for it, or refuse to rule at all. Judicial review applies not only to Congress but to the chief executive, administrative agencies, state legislatures, and rulings of state courts. Although the holding of the Supreme Court is of utmost importance, it often serves as but one stage of an ongoing constitutional process shared with lower courts, the executive branch, and the legislature.

SOURCES OF JUDICIAL REVIEW AUTHORITY

When legislators or the chief executive make unpopular decisions, the voters may remove them at the next election. The ballot box represents a periodic test of the legitimacy of elected officers, a reaffirmation of authority they are quite happy to cite. The federal judiciary, however, cannot draw legitimacy from elections. When judges announce an unpopular decision, citizens want to know on what authority courts may overturn the judgments of elected officials who also take an oath to uphold the Constitution. Judges must be able to cite persuasive and authoritative sources: constitutional language, pre-*Marbury* precedents, principles announced by the Marshall Court, and convincing evidence that has accumulated since that time.

Constitutional Language

Article III, Section 1, of the Constitution provides that "The judicial Power of the United States, shall be vested in one Supreme Court, and in such inferior Courts as the Congress may from time to time ordain and establish. . . ." Section 2 extends the judicial power to various cases and controversies, but there is no specific grant of power to declare an act of Congress, the President, or state government unconstitutional. The absence of an explicit grant is not conclusive. An implied power may exist. For example, although the Constitution provides no authority for the President to assert executive privilege, remove appointees from office, issue executive orders with the force of law, or enter into international agreements without the advice and consent of the Senate, the Supreme Court has considered those powers implicit in Article II.[1] Similarly, the Court has found an implied power for Congress to investigate, issue subpoenas, and exercise the power of contempt.[2]

The power of judicial review can be implied from two sources. Under Article III, § 2, the judicial power extends to all cases *"arising under this Constitution,* the Laws of the United States, and Treaties made" (emphasis added). Moreover, the Supremacy Clause in Article VI provides that the Constitution, federal laws "made in Pursuance thereof," and all treaties shall be the supreme law of the land, "and the Judges in every State shall be bound thereby, any Thing in the Constitution or Laws of any State to the Contrary notwithstanding." This language requires federal courts to review the actions of state governments and might invite review of congressional statutes that are not "in pursuance" of the Constitution. However, judicial review over presidential and congressional acts raises a wholly different dimension: the relations between coordinate branches of the national government. Justice Holmes once remarked: "I do not think the United States would come to an end if [the Supreme Court] lost [its] power to declare an act of Congress void. I do think the Union would be imperiled if we could not make that declaration as to the laws of the several States." Collected Legal Papers 295–296 (1920).

The Pre-*Marbury* Precedents

A number of precedents for judicial review before *Marbury* prepared the way for Marshall's famous opinion in 1803. British efforts in the 1760s to reestablish control over America provoked accusations by colonists that the laws of Parliament had violated the "common law" and the "law of reason" and were therefore void. These charges became important ingredients in the case presented to a "candid world" in 1776.

---

[1]United States v. Nixon, 418 U.S. 683 (1974) (executive privilege); Myers v. United States, 272 U.S. 52 (1926) (removal power); Contractors Ass'n of Eastern Pa. v. Secretary of Labor, 442 F.2d 159 (3d Cir. 1971), cert. denied, 404 U.S. 854 (1971) (executive orders); and Dames & Moore v. Regan, 453 U.S. 654 (1981) (executive agreements).

[2]McGrain v. Daugherty, 273 U.S. 135 (1927) (investigations); Eastland v. United States Servicemen's Fund, 421 U.S. 491, 505 (1975) (subpoenas); Anderson v. Dunn, 19 U.S. (6 Wheat.) 204, 228 (1821) (contempt power).

The best-known American challenge to an act of Parliament came in 1761 when James Otis argued the Writs of Assistance Case in Boston. He claimed that British customs officials were not empowered by Parliament to use general search warrants. Even if Parliament had authorized the writs of assistance, Otis said that the statute would be "against the constitution," "against natural equity," and therefore void. Edward S. Corwin, The Doctrine of Judicial Review 30 (1914). In 1766 a Virginia court held the Stamp Act unconstitutional. On the eve of the Declaration of Independence, a Massachusetts judge instructed the jury to treat acts of Parliament as violations of fundamental law and as "void" and "inoperative." Id. at 32.

The proposition that courts could void an act of Parliament appears in Chief Justice Coke's opinion in *Dr. Bonham's Case* (1610). He said that when an act of Parliament "is against common right and reason, or repugnant, or impossible to be performed, the common law will controul it, and adjudge such Act to be void." 77 Eng. Rep. 646, 652. A few British judges in the seventeenth and eighteenth centuries cited Coke's argument, but the principle of judicial review never took root on English soil. Day v. Savadge, 80 Eng. Rep. 235, 237 (1614) and The City of London v. Wood, 88 Eng. Rep. 1592, 1602 (1702). In 1884 the Supreme Court noted: "notwithstanding what was attributed to Lord Coke in *Bonham's Case* . . . the omnipotence of Parliament over the common law was absolute, even against common right and reason." Hurtado v. California, 110 U.S. 516, 531 (1884).

For their understanding of British law the framers relied mainly on Blackstone's *Commentaries,* which states the case for parliamentary supremacy with singular clarity. For those who believed that acts of Parliament contrary to reason were void, he offered this advice:

> But if the parliament will positively enact a thing to be done which is unreasonable, I know of no power that can control it: and the examples usually alleged in support of this sense of the rule do none of them prove, that, where the main object of a statute is unreasonable, the judges are at liberty to reject it; for that were to set the judicial power above that of the legislature, which would be subversive of all government. W. Blackstone, Commentaries, Book One, § 3, at 91 (Oxford 1775).

Although *Dr. Bonham's Case* provides inadequate support for the American concept of judicial review, it was accepted as good law and precedent by those who wanted to break with England. Intellectual justifications were needed to neutralize the appearance of impetuous and impulsive behavior. But "voiding" the acts of Parliament did not automatically deliver the power of judicial review to American courts, especially those at the national level.

From independence to the framing of the Constitution, some of the state judges challenged the acts of their legislatures. Although scholars disagree on the strength of those precedents, decisions providing support for the theory of judicial review were handed down by judges in Virginia, New Jersey, New York, Connecticut, Rhode Island, and North Carolina. The language used by judges in holding state laws invalid was often more bold than the results they achieved. Charles Grove Haines, The American Doctrine of Judicial Supremacy 88–120 (1932).

THE FRAMERS' INTENT

By the time of the convention, some of the framers expected judicial review to be part of the new government. In reading their statements at the convention and during the ratification debates, we need to keep their thoughts in context and recognize conflicting statements. The framers did not have a clear or fully developed theory of judicial review.

The framers wanted to replace the Articles of Confederation to make the central government more effective, resolve disputes among the states over legal and monetary systems, and limit legislative abuses. Each goal depended on the structure and power of the federal judiciary. Instead of the legislative supremacy that prevailed under the Articles of Confederation, the new Congress would be only one of three coordinate and coequal branches. Both the Virginia Plan presented by Edmund Randolph and the New Jersey Plan advocated by William Paterson called for the creation of an independent judiciary headed by a Supreme Court. Although the new judicial article left undecided such questions as whether to create lower federal courts or rely solely on state courts, it did grant broad authority to the Supreme Court.

The framers were worried that thirteen sets of state courts would announce contradictory rulings on matters of national concern. In Federalist No. 80, Alexander Hamilton said that thirteen independent courts of final jurisdiction "over the same causes, arising upon the same laws, is a hydra in government from which nothing but contradiction and confusion can proceed." The convention resolved that problem by adopting the Supremacy Clause. Judicial review over presidential and congressional actions, however, was a subject of much greater delicacy. By 1787 the framers had become alarmed about legislative overreaching. In Federalist No. 48, James Madison wrote that the "legislative department is everywhere extending the sphere of its activity and drawing all power into its impetuous vortex." Several delegates to the Philadelphia Convention expressed the same concern. 1 Farrand 254 (Wilson) and 2 Farrand 35 (Madison), 110 (Madison) and 288 (Mercer). But giving the courts the final say over congressional acts was an extremely radical notion.

A common pastime of constitutional scholars is counting the heads of framers who favored judicial review. Depending on which year he wrote, Edward S. Corwin vacillated on the statistics, ranging from a high of seventeen framers to a low of five or six. Leonard D. Levy, ed., Judicial Review and the Supreme Court 3–4 (1967). Other studies were also flavored by a crusading spirit, either to "prove" the legitimacy of judicial review or to chop away at its foundations.[3] The issue remains unsettled; this very ambiguity adds an inhibiting force on judicial activism.

Judicial review was discussed at the convention as a means of checking Congress and the states. The most important debate was over the veto of legislation passed by Congress. Randolph proposed a Council of Revision consisting of the "Executive and a convenient number of the National Judiciary . . . with authority to examine every act of the National Legislature before it shall operate, & every act of a particular Legislature before a Negative thereon shall be final; and that the dissent of the said Council shall amount to a rejection, unless the Act of the National Legislature be again passed . . ." 1 Farrand 21. Some commentators accept the elimination of the revisionary council as proof that the framers rejected judicial review. However, one of the arguments against the Council was the *availability* of judicial review. As reported by Madison: "Mr. Gerry doubts whether the Judiciary

---

[3]For support of judicial review, see Charles A. Beard, The Supreme Court and the Constitution (1912) and Raoul Berger, Congress v. The Supreme Court (1969). Critics include Louis B. Boudin, Government by Judiciary (1932) and William W. Crosskey, Politics and the Constitution (1953).

ought to form a part of it, as they will have a sufficient check agst. encroachments on their own department by their exposition of the laws, which involved a power of deciding on their Constitutionality. In some States the Judges had ⟨actually⟩ set aside laws as being agst. the Constitution. This was done too with general approbation." Id. at 97. Rufus King supported Gerry's argument after observing that the Justices of the Supreme Court "ought to be able to expound the law as it should come before them, free from the bias of having participated in its formation." This comment provides broad support for judicial review, whereas Gerry appeared to restrict it to legislative encroachments.

After debating a congressional veto over proposed state legislation, that idea was rejected for two reasons. The addition of the Supremacy Clause would presumably handle any conflicts between national law and state legislation. Moreover, the state courts could exercise judicial review to control legislative excesses. They "would not consider as valid any law contravening the Authority of the Union," and if such laws were not set aside by the judiciary they "may be repealed by a Nationl. law." 2 Farrand 27–28 (Sherman and Morris). Madison later said that a law "violating a constitution established by the people themselves, would be considered by the Judges as null & void." Id. at 93. These statements were clearly limited to judicial review at the *state*, not the national, level. A year later, writing to Thomas Jefferson, Madison denied that the Constitution empowered the Court to strike down acts of Congress, for that would have made the judiciary "paramount in fact to the Legislature, which was never intended and can never be proper." 5 Writings of James Madison 294 (Hunt ed. 1904).

James Wilson, soon to be a member of the Supreme Court, defended the concept of judicial review at the Pennsylvania ratification convention. He said the legislature would be "kept within its prescribed bounds" by the judiciary. 2 Elliot 445. At the Connecticut ratifying convention, Oliver Ellsworth (destined to be the third Chief Justice of the Supreme Court) expected federal judges to void any legislative acts that were contrary to the Constitution. Id. at 196; see also Samuel Adams's comments in Massachusetts, id. at 131. At the Virginia ratifying convention, John Marshall anticipated that the federal judiciary would strike down unconstitutional legislative acts. Id. at 553; see also George Nicholas, id. at 443. The context of these remarks suggests that the availability of judicial review was used to reassure the states that national power would be held in check.

The *Federalist Papers* include several essays that speak strongly for judicial review. The principal essay, Hamilton's Federalist No. 78 (pp. 59–60), is designed partly to allay state fears about the power of the central government. The arguments in Federalist No. 78 were later borrowed by John Marshall to buttress his *Marbury* opinion. Hamilton's enthusiasm is somewhat suspect; he appears to have been a late convert to the cause of judicial review. His plan of government presented to the 1787 convention did not grant this power to the judiciary. 1 Farrand 282–293, 302–311; 3 Farrand 617–630. State laws contrary to the Constitution would be "utterly void" but the judiciary is not identified as the voiding agency. 1 Farrand 293.

In the years between ratification and *Marbury* v. *Madison*, the issue of judicial review was debated often in Congress, but not with any consistency. When Madison introduced the Bill of Rights in the House of Representatives, he predicted that once they were incorporated into the Constitution, "independent tribunals of justice will consider themselves in a peculiar manner the guardians of those rights; they will be an impenetrable bulwark against every assumption of power in the Legislative or

Executive." 1 Annals of Congress 439 (June 8, 1789). But nine days later, during debate on the President's removal power, Madison denied that Congress should defer to the courts on this constitutional issue. He begged to know on what principle could it be contended "that any one department draws from the Constitution greater powers than another, in marking out the limits of the powers of the several departments?" If questions arose on the boundaries between the branches, he did not see "that any one of these independent departments has more right than another to declare their sentiments on that point." Id. at 500 (June 17, 1789). In 1791, when proponents of a national bank cited judicial review as a possible check on unconstitutional legislation, Madison was unpersuaded and voted against the bank. 3 Annals of Congress 1978–1979 (February 4, 1791).

THE ROAD TO *MARBURY*

Federal courts reviewed both national and state legislation prior to *Marbury*. In *Hayburn's Case* (1792), three circuit courts held divergent views on an act of Congress that appointed federal judges to serve as commissioners for claims settlement. Their decisions could be set aside by the Secretary of War. One of the courts agreed to serve. The other two believed that the statute was "unwarranted" because it required federal judges to perform nonjudicial duties and to render what was essentially an advisory opinion. The Supreme Court postponed decision until the next term, and by that time Congress had repealed the offending sections and removed the Secretary's authority to veto decisions rendered by judges. 2 Dall. 409 (1792); see 1 Stat. 243 (1792) and 1 Stat. 324 (1793). In 1794, a year after Congress repaired the statute, the Supreme Court decided that the original statute would have been unconstitutional if it sought to place nonjudicial powers on the circuit courts. United States v. Yale Todd (not published until 1851; 13 How. 51). The use of this 1794 case as a precedent for judicial review is rendered suspect by the fact that the statutory provision no longer existed.

Between 1791 and 1799, federal courts began to challenge and strike down a number of state laws. 1 Charles Warren, The Supreme Court in United States History 65–69 (1937). With regard to national legislation, in *Hylton* v. *United States* (1796) the Supreme Court upheld the constitutionality of a congressional statute that imposed a tax on carriages. If the Court had authority to uphold an act of Congress, presumably it had authority to strike one down. Otherwise, it would be engaged in a frivolous and idle enterprise. Justice Chase said it was unnecessary *"at this time,* for me to determine, whether this court, *constitutionally* possesses the power to declare an act of Congress *void* . . . but if the court have such power, I am free to declare, that I will never exercise it, *but in a very clear case."* 3 Dall. 171, 175 (1796). Two years later the Court upheld the constitutionality of another congressional act, this time involving the process of constitutional amendment. Hollingsworth v. Virginia, 3 Dall. 378 (1798).

Three other cases between 1795 and 1800 explored the authority of federal judges to declare state acts unconstitutional. In the first case, a circuit court decided that a Pennsylvania law was unconstitutional and void. Vanhorne's Lessee v. Dorrance, 2 Dall. 304 (1795). In the second, Supreme Court Justices offered differing views on the existence and scope of judicial review. Calder v. Bull, 3 Dall. 386 (1798). In the third, Justice Chase said that even if it were agreed that a statute contrary to the Constitution would be void, "it still remains a question, where the power resides to declare it void?" The "general opinion," he said, is that the Supreme Court could declare an act of Congress unconstitutional, "but there is no adjudication of the Supreme Court itself upon the point." Cooper v. Telfair, 4 Dall. 14, 19 (1800).

From 1789 to 1802, eleven state judiciaries exercised judicial review over state statutes. Charles Grove Haines, The American Doctrine of Judicial Supremacy, at 148–164. The assertion of power by the national judiciary was much more sensitive, and yet even the Jeffersonian Republicans rebuked the federal courts for not striking down the repressive Alien and Sedition Acts of 1798. 1 Warren, The Supreme Court in United States History, at 215. In that same year Jefferson looked to the courts to protect basic rights: "the laws of the land, administered by upright judges, would protect you from any exercise of power unauthorized by the Constitution of the United States." 10 Writings of Thomas Jefferson 61 (Memorial ed. 1903).

Marshall Court Foundations

By 1801 the Supreme Court had yet to solidify its position as a coequal branch of government. It had upheld the constitutionality of a congressional statute. In a series of dicta, it gingerly explored the theory that it could hold one unconstitutional. In four decisions from 1803 to 1821, the Court held that it had the power to determine the constitutionality of statutes passed by Congress and state legislatures, as well as authority to review judgments by state courts in cases raising federal questions.

The election of 1800 marked a pivotal point for the nation. Although formally neutral between Britain and France, America rapidly divided into two warring camps. The Federalist party was pro-British, whereas the Jeffersonian Republicans supported the French. Efforts by the Adams administration to limit Republican criticism led to the Alien and Sedition Acts, further exacerbating partisan strife. When the Jeffersonians swept the elections of 1800, the Federalists looked for ways to salvage their dwindling political power.

Early in 1801, with a few weeks remaining for the Federalist Congress, two bills were passed to create a number of federal judges and justices of the peace in the District of Columbia. 2 Stat. 89, 103 (1801). Within a matter of days President Adams nominated Federalists to the new posts, much to the outrage of Republicans. John Marshall was at that point serving as Secretary of State, although he had already been appointed to the Supreme Court for the next term. The commissions of office were processed, sent to the Senate, and confirmed. Some of the commissions, William Marbury's among them, were never delivered.

Upon assuming the presidency, Thomas Jefferson ordered that the commissions be withheld. The administration also urged Congress to repeal the Circuit Court Act (with its additional judgeships) and to block the anticipated 1802 term of the Supreme Court. Congress complied. 2 Stat. 132, 156 (1802). Partisan bitterness increased in the spring of 1801 when two Federalist judges instructed a district attorney to prosecute a newspaper that had published an attack on the judiciary. The jury refused to indict, but the Republicans saw this as additional evidence that the Federalists were engaged in a national conspiracy.[4] As part of a counterattack, the House of Representatives impeached District Judge John Pickering (a Federalist), contemplated the removal of Justice Chase from the Supreme Court,

---

[4]George Lee Haskins and Herbert A. Johnson, 2 History of the Supreme Court of the United States: Foundations of Power: John Marshall 161–162 (1981).

and planned the removal of other Federalist judges, including John Marshall. Jerry W. Knudson, 14 Am. J. Leg. Hist. 55 (1970).

In this tense political climate, William Marbury and his colleagues appealed to the former Attorney General, Charles Lee, for legal assistance. Lee brought the action directly to the Supreme Court under Section 13 of the Judiciary Act of 1789, which empowered the Court to issue writs of mandamus "in cases warranted by the principles and usages of law, to any courts appointed, or persons holding office, under the authority of the United States." 1 Stat. 81. Lee argued that the Court had jurisdiction under Section 13 because Madison was a person holding office (Secretary of State) under the authority of the United States. He asked the Court to issue a writ of mandamus, ordering Madison to deliver the commissions.

Marshall's options were circumscribed by one overpowering fact: whatever technical ground he used to rule against the administration, any order directing Madison to deliver the commissions was sure to be ignored. If the Court's order could be dismissed with impunity, the judiciary's power and prestige would suffer greatly. As Chief Justice Burger has noted: "The Court could stand hard blows, but not ridicule, and the ale house would rock with hilarious laughter" had Marshall issued a mandamus ignored by Jefferson.[5] Marshall chose a tactic he used in future years. He would appear to absorb a short-term defeat in exchange for a long-term victory. The decision has been called "a masterwork of indirection, a brilliant example of Marshall's capacity to sidestep danger while seeking to court it, to advance in one direction while his opponents are looking in another." Robert G. McCloskey, The American Supreme Court 40 (1960).

The opinion acknowledged the merits of Marbury's case but denied that the Court had power to issue the mandamus. Through a strained reading, Marshall concluded that Section 13 expanded the original jurisdiction of the Court and thereby violated Article III of the Constitution. He maintained that Congress could alter the boundaries only of appellate jurisdiction. Announcing that the statute conflicted with the Constitution and that judges take an oath of office to support the Constitution, Marshall claimed that the power of constitutional interpretation was vested exclusively in the judiciary. MARBURY v. MADISON, 5 U.S. (1 Cr.) 137 (1803).

The decision in *Marbury* has stimulated a number of critiques. Marshall's analysis of original and appellate jurisdiction is less than compelling. He could have read Section 13 to connect mandamus action to appellate jurisdiction. Even if he related it to original jurisdiction, the Constitution did not explicitly prohibit Congress from adding to original jurisdiction. And if the Court did indeed lack jurisdiction, why did Marshall reach further and explore the merits of Marbury's claim and expound on novel questions of judicial authority? Finally, given his previous involvement in the matter, there was strong reason for Marshall to disqualify himself (pp. 66–71).

Encircled by hostile political forces, Marshall decided that it was time to strike boldly for judicial independence. Instead of citing historical and legal precedents, all of which could have been challenged and picked apart by his opponents, Marshall reached to a higher plane and grounded his case on what appeared to be self-evident, universal principles. His decision seems to march logically and inexorably toward the only possible conclusion.

[5]Warren E. Burger, "The Doctrine of Judicial Review: Mr. Marshall, Mr. Jefferson, and Mr. Marbury," in Mark W. Cannon and David M. O'Brien, eds., Views From the Bench 14 (1985).

Developments after *Marbury*

The power to strike down unconstitutional actions by coordinate branches of government was not used again until 1857, in *Dred Scott* v. *Sandford*, 60 U.S. (19 How.) 393. Judicial review of state actions, however, was more frequent. In two sets of decisions, the Court established its authority to review state statutes and state judicial decisions.

United States v. *Peters* (1809) and *Fletcher* v. *Peck* (1810) were decided in a difficult political period. Some states, reacting against the growth of national power, threatened secession and nullification. Richard Peters, a federal judge in Pennsylvania, was unable to compel state officials to obey a decree he had issued. The state legislature passed a law declaring the decree a usurpation of power and ordered the governor to resist any attempt to enforce it. Marshall then issued a mandamus ordering enforcement on the ground that state legislatures cannot interfere with the operation of the federal judicial process. 9 U.S. (5 Cr.) 115 (1809). The governor called out the militia to prevent a federal marshal from executing the court order. He also sought President Madison's assistance, but the state's resistance collapsed when Madison replied that the President "is not only unauthorized to prevent the execution of a decree sanctioned by the Supreme Court of the United States, but is expressly enjoined, by statute, to carry into effect any such decree where opposition may be made to it." Annals of Congress, 11th Cong. 2269.

In *Fletcher* v. *Peck* (1810), the Court struck down an act of a state legislature as unconstitutional. Several land companies had obtained a huge land grant at a bargain price from the Georgia legislature, offering bribes to a number of legislators. After elections, the new legislature revoked the land grant. In the meantime, innocent third parties had bought property from the corrupt land companies. Some of the purchasers challenged the revocation, claiming impairment of the obligations of a contract protected by Article I, Section 10, of the Constitution. Justice Marshall, recognizing the delicate task of reviewing state legislation, concluded that the revocation did constitute a violation of the impairments clause. 10 U.S. (6 Cr.) 87, 136–139 (1810).

A second pair of cases was decided after the War of 1812, following a substantial change in the Supreme Court's membership. The most important addition was Joseph Story. Though appointed by James Madison, he became as ardent a defender of national interests as Marshall. He wrote the decision that established the Court's authority to review state court decisions involving federal questions. MARTIN v. HUNTER'S LESSEE, 1 Wheat. 304 (1816). The dispute in *Martin* was between two private parties. In 1821, with a state as one of the parties, Marshall solidified the relationship of the Court to state courts and breathed new life into the Supremacy Clause. COHENS v. VIRGINIA, 6 Wheat. 264 (1821).

CONSTRAINTS ON JUDICIAL REVIEW

By the time of his visit to America in the 1830s, Alexis de Tocqueville could write of judicial review: "I am aware that a similar right has been sometimes claimed, but claimed in vain, by courts of justice in other countries, but in America it is recognized by all the authorities; and not a party, not so much as an individual, is found to contest it." 1 Alexis de Tocqueville, Democracy in America 100 (Bradley ed. 1951). In fact, judicial review was challenged at every level of government. State courts and state legislatures regularly challenged the jurisdiction of the Supreme Court, not only up to the Civil War but afterward as well. Charles Warren, 47 Am. L. Rev. 1, 161 (1913).

Justice John Gibson's dissent in *Eakin* v. *Raub* (1825) represents a trenchant rebuttal of Marshall's position on judicial review. Gibson, a Pennsylvania judge, conceded that the Supremacy Clause required judges to strike down state laws in conflict with the Federal Constitution, but he rejected judicial review as a means of policing Congress and the President. Although a constitution was superior to a statute, that fact alone did not elevate judges to be the sole interpreters. The oath to support the Constitution was not unique to judges. The political branches had an equal right to put a construction on the Constitution. If a legislature were to abuse its powers and overstep the boundaries established by the Constitution, Gibson preferred that correction come at the hands of the people. Judicial errors were more difficult to correct, for they required constitutional amendment. Eakin v. Raub, 12 S. & R. 330, 343 (Pa. 1825). In subsequent years, Gibson resigned himself to a more generous definition of judicial review. Norris v. Clymer, 2 Pa. 277, 281 (1845).

President Jackson, who inherited some of the Jeffersonian distrust toward the judiciary, disagreed sharply with John Marshall on both personal and policy grounds. Every public officer, he said in 1832, took an oath to support the Constitution "as he understands it, and not as it is understood by others." The opinion of judges "has no more authority over Congress than the opinion of Congress has over the judges, and on that point the President is independent of both" (pp. 78–80). But Jackson appreciated the value of judicial independence. He saw the courts as natural allies in his fight against the Nullifiers, who wanted to release the states from judgments of federal courts. Richard P. Longaker, 71 Pol. Sci. Q. 341, 358-361 (1956). Jackson's theory of the President's independent duty to interpret the Constitution provoked a sharp debate in the Senate (pp. 80–82).

Concern about judicial overreaching prompted some judges to advocate a philosophy of self-restraint. To temper criticism, they offered to presume the validity of government actions and to uphold the legislature in doubtful cases. Fletcher v. Peck, 10 U.S. at 128; Dartmouth College v. Woodward, 17 U.S. 517, 625 (1819). Similar guidelines were issued when reviewing lower court decisions. For judges who felt comfortable with the legitimacy of judicial review, the power was wielded actively and aggressively.

A major challenge to judicial review arose late in the nineteenth century when federal judges began to impose their own philosophies of economic laissez faire. Repeatedly the courts struck down state and federal statutes designed to relieve economic hardship. Legislative efforts to deal with monopoly, prices, minimum wages, maximum work hours, and organized labor were either rejected by the courts or severely restricted. The philosophy of judicial restraint, the presumption of legislative validity, and avoidance of decisions based on the wisdom of government action seemed virtually abandoned.

The judges reached outside the Constitution to discover a "liberty of contract" and read narrowly the scope of interstate commerce and the taxing power. These decisions stood in the path of progressive legislation and threatened effective government. Justice Stone lectured his colleagues in 1936 that courts "are not the only agency of government that must be assumed to have capacity to govern." United States v. Butler, 297 U.S. 1, 87 (1936).

Changes in the composition of the Supreme Court after 1937 removed the judicial impediment to economic regulation. The era of "substantive due process" appeared to be over. But the Warren Court sparked another round of debate over judicial review, this time raising the claim that courts had tilted in a liberal direction. The opinions outlawing desegregation, requiring legislative reapportionment, providing right of counsel, and announcing novel constitutional rights of association and privacy, all supported the weak and politically disfranchised.

Critics who had called for judicial self-restraint during the 1930s now found themselves applauding the substantive results of the activist Warren Court. Others warned that the Court risked losing popular support by issuing broad decisions in social and political areas. Reacting against Judge Learned Hand's plea in 1958 for judicial restraint, Herbert Wechsler maintained that the issue was not whether judges possessed judicial review but rather how they exercised that authority. He objected to what he regarded as idiosyncratic, ad hoc, and poorly reasoned decisions and urged the courts to follow principled rules, deciding on grounds of "adequate neutrality and generality, tested not only by the instant application but by others that the principles imply." 73 Harv. L. Rev. 1, 15 (1959). See Learned Hand, The Bill of Rights (1958).

Many scholars agree that the Warren Court opinions should have been better crafted to clarify statements of principles. If a majority opinion simply announced a result without adequately explaining the underlying argument, the courts would rule by fiat and decree. However, the concept of "neutral principles" has remained elusive and confusing. It appears to run counter to Holmes's dictum that "The life of the law has not been logic: it has been experience." The Common Law 1 (1881). Elsewhere Holmes said: "Behind the logical form lies a judgment as to the relative worth and importance of competing legislative grounds, often an inarticulate and unconscious judgment, it is true, and yet the very root and nerve of the whole proceeding." Collected Legal Papers 181 (1920). In such areas as separation of church and state or in search-and-seizure operations, it is difficult to discover general principles that guide the Court. The process has been characterized by starts and stops, direction and redirection, trial and error. Others point out that an insistence on principled decisions might prevent judges from discovering novel responses for unprecedented conditions. Charles E. Clark, 49 Va. L. Rev. 660, 665 (1963). Rigid adherence to fixed principles would prevent the tactical use of threshold arguments (such as standing, mootness, and ripeness) needed to protect the Court's prestige and effectiveness.

The post-Warren Court years were marked by continued controversy over the scope of judicial decisions. Presidents used rulings on such contentious issues as school desegregation, the death penalty, criminal procedures, and birth control as political rallying points. Courts were accused of deciding too many cases and overtaxing their institutional capacity. They were urged to use their power to control court access to divert issues from the courthouse to the legislative arena.

Despite President Nixon's vow to nominate "strict constructionists" to the bench, the Burger Court continued to play an activist role. It created a constitutional right of "commercial free speech," struck down death-penalty statutes, initiated busing to overcome segregated schools, began the process of reversing sex discrimination, and authored the abortion decision. Many commentators viewed the abortion case as a revival of the era of "substantive due process" that prevailed before 1937. The

Court's decision against the legislative veto in 1983, Justice White noted, struck down in "one fell swoop provisions in more laws enacted by Congress than the Court has cumulatively invalidated in its history." INS v. Chadha, 462 U.S. 919, 1002. The conditions that encourage judges to play an activist role were discussed by Justice Powell in a revealing interview in 1979 (pp. 83–86).

Some critics of contemporary courts argue that the main objection to judicial review is that it runs counter to American democratic values. One study advised judges to limit their work to supporting broad participation in the democratic process and protecting minority rights. John Hart Ely, Democracy and Distrust (1980). Another study endorsed judicial review for protecting individual rights, but proposed that the courts withdraw from almost all areas of federalism and separation of powers. Jesse H. Choper, Judicial Review and the National Political Process (1980).

It is tempting, but misleading, to call judicial review antidemocratic. The Constitution establishes a limited republic, not a direct or pure democracy. Popular sentiment is filtered through a system of representation. Majority vote is limited by various restrictions in the Constitution: candidates must be a certain age, Presidents may not serve a third term—regardless of what the people want. Although states range in population from less than a million to more than twenty million, each state receives the same number of Senators. Filibusters conducted by a minority of Senators can prevent the Senate from acting. Majority rule is further constrained by checks and balances, separation of powers, federalism, a bicameral legislature, and the Bill of Rights.

To the extent that the judiciary protects constitutional principles, including minority rights, it upholds the values of the people who drafted and ratified the Constitution. Throughout much of its history, the judiciary gave little support to civil liberties or civil rights. The record does not support the assertion that judicial review has been a force for protecting individual liberties. Henry W. Edgerton, 22 Corn. L. Q. 299 (1937). But in a number of decisions over the past few decades affecting reapportionment, the right of association, and the "white primary" cases, the Supreme Court opened the door to broader public participation in the political process. In many ways the contemporary judiciary has helped strengthen democracy. Through its decisions, it performs an "informing function" previously associated with legislative bodies.

The judiciary performs other positive, legitimizing functions. Actions by executive and legislative officials are contested and brought before the courts for review. When upheld, citizens can see some standard at work other than the power of majorities and the raw force of politics. Alexander Bickel wrote: "The Court's prestige, the spell it casts as a symbol, enable it to entrench and solidify measures that may have been tentative in the conception or that are on the verge of abandonment in the execution." 75 Harv. L. Rev. 40, 48 (1961). But what happens when the Court faces a repressive executive or legislative action? If judges lend their support, as in the curfew and imprisonment of Japanese-Americans during World War II, the reputation of the judiciary as the guarantor of constitutional liberties is tarnished. Yet if courts refuse to take such a case, they risk communicating the message that might is right and no independent judicial check exists.

If the judiciary behaves in ways intolerable to the public, there are many methods available to legislators and executives to invoke court-curbing pressures. Presidential appointments and Senate confirmations supply a steady stream of influence by popularly elected public officials. Court decisions can be overturned by constitutional amendment, a process that is directly controlled by national and state legislatures. Short of such drastic remedies, judges remain sensitive and responsive to public opinion, notwithstanding traditional claims of judicial isolation from political forces. As witnessed by the "court-packing" effort of 1937 (discussed in Chapter 19), there exists within the public a strong reservoir of support for the independence of the judiciary and the exercise of judicial review.

METHODS OF CONSTITUTIONAL INTERPRETATION

Justice Jackson once remarked that "Nothing has more perplexed generations of conscientious judges than the search in juridical science, philosophy and practice for objective and impersonal criteria for solution of politico-legal questions put to our courts." Vital Speeches, No. 24, Vol. XIX, at 759 (October 1, 1953). No completely satisfactory guide to judicial review has ever been fashioned. Different techniques are available, including the literalist, natural law, historical, and eclectic approaches.

Literalism

Advocates of strict constructionism (or what some scholars call "interpretivism") argue that judges should enforce only those norms that are stated or clearly implicit in the Constitution. Attorney General Edwin Meese III, in a speech in 1985, advocated a "Jurisprudence of Original Intention." He argued that judges should restrict themselves to the original meaning of constitutional provisions. Justice Brennan, in a speech later that year, rejected the search for the framers' intent as "little more than arrogance cloaked as humility" (pp. 86–91).

Judges who offer interpretations that cannot be discovered within the "four corners" of the Constitution are considered activists or noninterpretivists. Most judges try to interpret the Constitution in accordance with the framers' intent, so far as that is possible, but they sift through conflicting evidence and reach different results. They also differ on whether the framers intended the Constitution to be interpreted statically or dynamically. Although some politicians equate strict constructionism with conservative law-and-order views, it can be applied equally well to liberal support for individual rights and religious freedom. Nor does strict constructionism mean judicial restraint. It can be synonymous, and often is, with judicial activism. Arthur J. Goldberg, Equal Justice 35–63 (1971). A recent example is the legislative veto case of 1983, which used strict constructionism with a vengeance to invalidate dozens of statutory provisions.

An example of the literalist approach is Justice Black's position on the First Amendment, which provides that "Congress shall make no law . . . abridging the freedom of speech or of the press." Black insisted that those words mean precisely what they say. Allowing no exceptions, he accused his brethren of rewriting the Constitution to produce a new amendment: "Congress shall pass no law abridging freedom of speech, press, assembly, and petition, unless Congress and the Supreme Court reach the joint conclusion that on balance the interests of the government in stifling these freedoms is greater than the interest of the people in having them exercised." A Constitutional Faith 50 (1968). Black did not want judges deciding on such vague grounds as what is reasonable, fair, fundamental, or decent. He urged us

"to follow what our Constitution says, not what judges think it should have said."
Boddie v. Connecticut, 401 U.S. 371, 393 (1971). But the Constitution "says" nothing
about an indigent's right to counsel, segregated housing, segregated schools, or
many other issues that Black agreed to decide.

Extreme literalists demand that textual ambiguities be resolved solely by constitutional amendment instead of judicial interpretation. Although the literalist approach
may have some superficial appeal, its impracticalities are immense. Madison went to
great lengths in Federalist No. 44 to point out that a constitution, to survive, must be
phrased in general terms. His comments were in support of the Necessary and
Proper Clause of Article I, Section 8, which had been attacked for its vague grant of
power to Congress. He said that the framers might have copied the Articles of
Confederation, which prohibited the exercise of any power not *expressly* delegated
by the states, or they might have attempted to enumerate congressional powers. The
first alternative risked leaving the national government with insufficient power,
whereas the second meant "a complete digest of laws on every subject to which the
Constitution relates; accommodated not only to the existing state of things, but to all
the possible changes which futurity may produce . . ."

Chief Justice Taney, in *Dred Scott* v. *Sandford* (1857), authored what is widely
regarded as one of the major self-inflicted wounds on the Supreme Court. He did so
by insisting that the meaning of "citizens" in Article III was restricted to what it
meant in 1787: "No one, we presume, supposes that any change in public opinion or
feeling, in relation to this unfortunate race [of blacks], in the civilized nations of
Europe or in this country, should induce the court to give to the words of the
Constitution a more liberal construction in their favor than they were intended to
bear when the instrument was framed and adopted. . . . [Constitutional language]
must be construed now as it was understood at the time of its adoption. It is not only
the same in words, but the same in meaning . . ." 60 U.S. at 426.

Justice Holmes rejected this reasoning. To him, a word "is not a crystal,
transparent and unchanged, it is the skin of a living thought and may vary greatly in
color and content according to the circumstances and the time in which it is used."
Towne v. Eisner, 245 U.S. 418, 425 (1918). Literalism would create intolerable
demands on the amending process, subjecting the country to costly delays and
uncertainties in response to issues never anticipated by the framers. Moreover, a
literalist is at sea when two commands of the Constitution, such as free press and fair
trial, collide. How is one constitutional principle to be "balanced" against another?
What guides the Court in deciding between civil rights and state rights? When does
government regulation give way to individual privacy? What "weight" should be
given to protect a free press against searches and seizures by law enforcement
officers? Where in the Constitution do we find answers to conflicts between workers
and employers? Do certain rights, such as those enumerated in the First Amendment, have a "preferred" status?[6] Even if they do, are those rights subordinated to
the needs of the government during time of national emergency?

Natural Law

Judges sometimes reach outside the Constitution to discover fundamental or
universal principles to guide their decisions. This natural law approach, however,

[6]Palko v. Connecticut, 302 U.S. 319, 326–327 (1937); Marsh v. Alabama, 326 U.S. 501, 509 (1946); Kovacs v.
Cooper, 336 U.S. 77, 106 (1949) (Rutledge, J., dissenting).

remains a continuing source of dispute. Writing in *Calder* v. *Bull* (1798), Justice Iredell urged his colleagues to base their decisions on substantial constitutional grounds rather than mere declarations of opinions regarding the laws of nature. Courts should not declare a statute unconstitutional "merely because it is, in their judgment, contrary to the opinions of natural justice. The ideas of natural justice are regulated by no fixed standard: the ablest and the purest men have differed on the subject." 3 U.S. at 399.

Justices react defensively to the charge that they merely read their own predilections into the Constitution, especially when interpreting such vague phrases as "due process," "equal protection," "unreasonable searches and seizures," and "cruel and unusual punishments." Nevertheless, Justices who oppose the death penalty argue that it violates the "human dignity" protected by the Constitution and is "no longer morally tolerable in our civilized society."[7] The law of defamation has been drawn not just from the First Amendment but from "our basic concept of the essential dignity and worth of every human being—a concept at the root of any decent system of ordered liberty." Rosenblatt v. Baer, 383 U.S. 75, 92 (1966).

Justice Frankfurter, remembered as the champion of judicial restraint, objected to those who called the interpretation of "due process" a mere matter of judicial caprice. Notwithstanding his general doctrine, he struck down actions that "shock the conscience" and "offend the community's sense of fair play and decency." Justice Black, a perennial critic of these opinions, charged that Frankfurter derived his standards basically from natural law, not constitutional law, and that such methods allowed judges to propound their own personal philosophies (pp. 91–94). In fact, the Constitution does have a "higher law" heritage.[8] From the very start, federal judges recognized that "there are certain great principles of justice, whose authority is universally acknowledged, that ought not to be entirely disregarded." Fletcher v. Peck, 10 U.S. at 132.

Historical Development

To shed further light on constitutional meaning, judges turn to historical analysis. Justice O'Connor has said that when the intent of the framers is unclear, "we must employ both history and reason in our analysis." Wallace v. Jaffree, 472 U.S. 38, 81 (1985). The legal historian Willard Hurst regarded the general political, economic, and social history of the United States as "legally competent and relevant evidence for the interpretation of the Constitution." Edmond Cahn, ed., Supreme Court and Supreme Law 56 (1954). The meaning of "interstate commerce" could not be restricted to the methods of commerce available at the time the Constitution was adopted. The phrase had to keep pace with the progress of the country, extending from stagecoaches to steamboats, from railroads to the telegraph. Pensacola Telegraph Co. v. Western Union Telegraph Co., 96 U.S. 1, 9 (1877). More than a century of practice became a justification for supporting the exercise of presidential power despite the absence of any express or statutory authority: "long continued practice, known to and acquiesced in by Congress, would raise a presumption . . . of a recognised administrative power of the Executive in the management of the public

[7]Furman v. Georgia, 408 U.S. 238, 270 (1972) (Brennan, J., dissenting); Gregg v. Georgia, 428 U.S. 153, 229 (1976) (Brennan, J., dissenting). Footnote omitted.

[8]Edward S. Corwin, The "Higher Law" Background of American Constitutional Law (1928); J. A. C. Grant, "The Natural Law Background of Due Process," 31 Colum. L. Rev. 56 (1931).

lands."[9] Justice Holmes, writing in 1920, said that a case before the Court has to be considered "in the light of our whole experience and not merely in that of what was said a hundred years ago." Missouri v. Holland, 252 U.S. 416, 433 (1920).

Historical analysis is sometimes confined to discovering the intentions of the framers. Justice Jackson said despairingly at one point: "Just what our forefathers did envision, or would have envisioned had they foreseen modern conditions, must be divined from materials almost as enigmatic as the dreams Joseph was called upon to interpret for Pharaoh." Youngstown Co. v. Sawyer, 343 U.S. 579, 634 (1952). Efforts to discover the intent of the framers are complicated by incomplete and unreliable records. Which framers do we select, and during what periods of their lives? Do we reconstruct intentions partly from private letters, memoranda, and diaries? Do we focus on the debates at the Philadelphia Convention or also at the state ratifying conventions? How much British, American colonial, and early national history is applicable? Efforts by the Supreme Court to introduce historical evidence have been dismissed by some historians as mere law-office efforts: special pleading for a particular point of view. Alfred H. Kelly, 1965 Sup. Ct. Rev. 119.

The judiciary has been profoundly influenced by the prevailing views of social scientists, be they conservative or liberal. It has been customary for the Court to go outside the legal record and take "judicial notice" of writings by experts. The philosophy of Social Darwinism in the late nineteenth and twentieth centuries supplied part of the theoretical justification for a laissez-faire state. This doctrine, reshaped in the hands of judges, helped support their opposition to social and economic regulation. In time, laissez-faire principles were challenged by the "Brandeis brief," which introduced social and economic facts to justify regulation of factory and working conditions. The use of extralegal data helped undermine the Court's reliance on abstract reasoning about "liberty of contract." Paul L. Rosen, The Supreme Court and Social Science 23–101 (1972). Eventually, lawyers on both sides learned how to put together a Brandeis brief to support their case.

Eclecticism

If the Constitution is to guide future generations, there must be some flexibility in applying its language. Speaking of a New Deal dispute over the contract clause, the Supreme Court observed: "It is no answer to say that this public need was not apprehended a century ago, or to insist that what the provision of the Constitution meant to the vision of that day it must mean to the vision of our time. If by the statement that what the Constitution meant at the time of its adoption it means to-day, it is intended to say that the great clauses of the Constitution must be confined to the interpretation which the framers, with the conditions and outlook of their time, would have placed upon them, the statement carries its own refutation." Home Bldg. & Loan Ass'n v. Blaisdell, 290 U.S. 398, 442–443 (1934).

In interpreting the Constitution, we look partly at the "judicial gloss" added by the courts. It is the responsibility of the judiciary to interpret the law, and under the

[9]United States v. Midwest Oil Co., 236 U.S. 459, 472–474 (1915). See also Charles E. Miller, The Supreme Court and the Uses of History (1969); Paul Brest, "The Misconceived Quest for the Original Understanding," 60 B.U.L. Rev. 204 (1980); Frederick Bernays Wiener, Uses and Abuses of Legal History (1962); Sister Marie Carolyn Klinkhamer, "The Use of History in the Supreme Court, 1789–1935," 36 U. Det. L. J. 553 (1959); John Woodford, "The Blinding Light: The Uses of History in Constitutional Interpretation," 31 U. Chi. L. Rev. 502 (1964).

doctrine of *stare decisis* (stand by the precedents) judges try to honor prior rulings. Nevertheless, sufficient variations and discord among existing precedents allow any number of directions for future decisions. Which elements of an opinion were essential for the result and therefore binding on subsequent courts? Which were peripheral *(obiter dicta)?* At what point do we comb concurring and dissenting opinions?

Judges hold different views about the doctrine of stare decisis. Some are more willing than others to break with prior holdings. The Supreme Court's practice is to apply stare decisis less rigidly to constitutional than to nonconstitutional cases. Glidden Co. v. Zdanok, 370 U.S. 530, 543 (1962). If the Court "errs" on nonconstitutional matters, legislatures may respond by passing a new statute. Errors of constitutional dimension, however, need attention by the judiciary. Burnet v. Coronado Oil & Gas Co., 285 U.S. 393, 406-407 (1932). Continuity is important for statutory law, for it permits citizens to arrange their business affairs with confidence. Courts should not disturb this sense of security and stability by needlessly disrupting the law. National Bank v. Whitney, 103 U.S. 99, 102 (1880). But errors of constitutional doctrine require correction. In the words of Justice Douglas, judges swear to support and defend the Constitution, "not the gloss which his predecessors may have put on it." 49 Colum. L. Rev. 735, 736 (1949).

Justice Roberts once complained that the Court's change of views "tends to bring adjudications of this tribunal into the same class as a restricted railroad ticket, good for this day and train only." Smith v. Allwright, 321 U.S. 649, 669 (1944). Justice Stewart argued that even if he believed the Court decided wrongly, and he dissented at the time, subsequent rulings should be governed by what the majority decided. Donovan v. Dewey, 452 U.S. 594, 609 (1981). Most judges, however, would consider it irresponsible if they failed to correct a previous decision containing a mistake in constitutional law. The initial embarrassment of having the Court reverse itself is more than offset by the enhanced reputation of a Court willing to acknowledge its own errors. Justice Jackson declined to bind himself "hand and foot" to prior decisions, even when they were his own. He saw "no reason why I should be consciously wrong today because I was unconsciously wrong yesterday." Massachusetts v. United States, 333 U.S. 611, 639–640 (1948). Two years later, he penned an elegant justification for rejecting prior opinions that have lost their persuasive quality (pp. 94–95).

Outright reversal of a ruling is rare. More frequent is the practice of ignoring a precedent or "distinguishing" it from the pending case. These silent or tacit overrulings prompted Justice Black to remark of such cases: "Their interment is tactfully accomplished, without ceremony, eulogy, or report of their demise." Hood & Sons v. Du Mond, 336 U.S. 525, 555 (1949). Judges may argue that the current facts are different or simply reinterpret the precedent. Such techniques avoid the costs of overruling a precedent, but also produce conflicting case law and uncertainty for those who must obey, interpret, enforce, and practice law.

After reviewing the various approaches to constitutional interpretation, Justice Cardozo described the judge's task as an eclectic exercise that blends in varying proportions the methods of philosophy, history, tradition, logic, and sociology. Rules are replaced by working hypotheses. The Nature of the Judicial Process (1921). The pressure of deadlines eliminates many options. Time, political constraints, and other limitations often make it impossible for judges to examine the entire record, pursue promising leads, review all the precedents, and produce original research. The complexity of the task has been summarized by Walter Murphy:

> To interpret a constitution requires more than ingenious guesses about what its draftsmen were thinking. Constitutional interpretation is an art, an art that must sometimes be both creative and political in the highest sense of that word, for it must apply imperfectly stated general principles to concrete and complex problems of human life and it must produce an authoritative solution. An interpreter who wishes to uphold, defend, maintain, or preserve the American Constitution cannot rationally treat it either as a detailed code or as a compact computer whose machine language is locked in the minds of men long dead. 87 Yale L. J. 1752, 1771 (1978).

Philip Bobbitt identified a broad range of techniques used by judges to interpret the Constitution. They go far beyond the concept of original intent. He suggested that if someone took colored pencils to mark through passages of a Supreme Court opinion, using a different color for each technique, the reader would end up with a multicolored picture. Constitutional Fate 93–94 (1982). This approach to the judicial art of opinion writing describes the work of judges whether they are "activists" or believers in original intent.

Judicial power must be understood in terms of the methods used by courts to preserve their institutional integrity, prestige, and power; the organizational evolution and politics of the courts; and the dynamics of decision making within the judiciary. Those issues are explored in the next three chapters.

Selected Readings

AGRESTO, JOHN. *The Supreme Court and Constitutional Democracy*. Ithaca, N.Y.: Cornell University Press, 1984.

ALFANGE, DEAN, JR. "On Judicial Policymaking and Constitutional Change: Another Look at the 'Original Intent' Theory of Constitutional Interpretation." 5 *Hastings Constitutional Law Quarterly* 603 (1978).

BERGER, RAOUL. *Congress v. The Supreme Court*. Cambridge, Mass.: Harvard University Press, 1969.

BICKEL, ALEXANDER M. *The Least Dangerous Branch*. New York: Bobbs-Merrill, 1962.

BISHIN, WILLIAM R. "Judicial Review in Democratic Theory." 50 *Southern California Law Review* 1099 (1977).

BLACK, CHARLES L., JR. *The People and the Court*. New York: Macmillan, 1960.

CARR, ROBERT K. *The Supreme Court and Judicial Review*. New York: Farrar and Rinehart, 1942.

COMMAGER, HENRY STEELE. *Majority Rule and Minority Rights*. New York: Oxford University Press, 1943.

CORWIN, EDWARD S. *The Doctrine of Judicial Review*. Princeton, N.J.: Princeton University Press, 1914.

———. *Court over Constitution*. Princeton, N.J.: Princeton University Press, 1938.

DAHL, ROBERT A. "Decision-Making in a Democracy: The Role of the Supreme Court as a National Policy-Maker." 6 *Journal of Public Law* 279 (1957).

DUCAT, CRAIG R. *Modes of Constitutional Interpretation*. St. Paul, Minn.: West, 1978.

FISHER, LOUIS. "Methods of Constitutional Interpretation: The Limits of Original Intent." 18 *Cumberland Law Review* 43 (1987-1988).

HAINES, CHARLES GROVES. *The American Doctrine of Judicial Supremacy*. Berkeley: University of California Press, 1932.

HENKIN, LOUIS. "Some Reflections on Current Constitutional Controversy." 109 *University of Pennsylvania Law Review* 637 (1961).

JAFFE, LOUIS L. "The Right to Judicial Review." 71 *Harvard Law Review* 401, 769 (1958).

KURLAND, PHILIP B. *Politics, the Constitution, and the Warren Court*. Chicago: University of Chicago Press, 1970.

LEVY, LEONARD W. *Original Intent and the Framers' Constitution*. New York: Macmillan, 1988.

MILLER, ARTHUR S., AND RONALD F. HOWELL. "The Myth of Neutrality in Constitutional Adjudication." 27 *University of Chicago Law Review* 661 (1960).

NELSON, WILLIAM E. "Changing Conceptions of Judicial Review: The Evolution of Constitutional Theory in the States, 1790–1860." 120 *University of Pennsylvania Law Review* 1166 (1972).

O'BRIEN, DAVID M. "Judicial Review and Constitutional Politics: Theory and Practice." 48 *University of Chicago Law Review* 1052 (1981).

POLLAK, LOUIS H. "Racial Discrimination and Judicial Integrity: A Reply to Professor Wechsler." 108 *University of Pennsylvania Law Review* 1 (1959).

ROSTOW, EUGENE V. *The Sovereign Prerogative.* New Haven, Conn.: Yale University Press, 1962.

WELLINGTON, HARRY H. "The Nature of Judicial Review." 91 *Yale Law Journal* 486 (1982).

WOLFE, CHRISTOPHER. *The Rise of Modern Judicial Review.* New York: Basic Books, 1986.

WRIGHT, J. SKELLY. "The Role of the Supreme Court in a Democratic Society—Judicial Activism or Restraint." 54 *Cornell Law Review* 1 (1968).

——. "Professor Bickel, the Scholarly Tradition, and the Supreme Court." 84 *Harvard Law Review* 769 (1971).

Alexander Hamilton

Federalist No. 78

We proceed now to an examination of the judiciary department of the proposed government.

In unfolding the defects of the existing Confederation, the utility and necessity of a federal judicature have been clearly pointed out. . . .

Whoever attentively considers the different departments of power must perceive, that, in a government in which they are separated from each other, the judiciary, from the nature of its functions, will always be the least dangerous to the political rights of the Constitution; because it will be least in a capacity to annoy or injure them. The Executive not only dispenses the honors, but holds the sword of the community. The legislature not only commands the purse, but prescribes the rules by which the duties and rights of every citizen are to be regulated. The judiciary, on the contrary, has no influence over either the sword or the purse; no direction either of the strength or of the wealth of the society; and can take no active resolution whatever. It may truly be said to have neither FORCE NOR WILL, but merely judgment; and must ultimately depend upon the aid of the executive arm even for the efficacy of its judgments. . . .

The complete independence of the courts of justice is peculiarly essential in a limited Constitution. By a limited Constitution, I understand one which contains certain specified exceptions to the legislative authority; such, for instance, as that it shall pass no bills of attainder, no *ex-post-facto* laws, and the like. Limitations of this kind can be preserved in practice no other way than through the medium of courts of justice, whose duty it must be to declare all acts contrary to the manifest tenor of the Constitution void. Without this, all the reservations of particular rights or privileges would amount to nothing.

Some perplexity respecting the rights of the courts to pronounce legislative acts void, because contrary to the constitution, has arisen from an imagination that the doctrine would imply a superiority of the judiciary to the legislative power. It is urged that the authority which can declare the acts of another void, must necessarily be superior to the one whose acts may be declared void. As this doctrine is of great importance in all the American constitutions, a brief discussion of the ground on which it rests cannot be unacceptable.

There is no position which depends on clearer principles, than that every act of a delegated authority, contrary to the tenor of the commission under which it is exercised, is void. No legislative act, therefore, contrary to the Constitution, can be valid. To deny this, would be to affirm, that the deputy is greater than his principal; that the servant is above his master; that the representatives of the people are superior to the people themselves; that men acting by virtue of powers, may do not only what their powers do not authorize, but what they forbid.

If it be said that the legislative body are themselves the constitutional judges of their own powers, and that the construction they put upon them is conclusive upon the other departments, it may be answered, that this cannot be the natural presumption, where it is not to be collected from any particular provisions in the Constitution. It is not otherwise to be supposed, that the Constitution could intend to enable the representatives of the people to substitute their *will* to that of their constituents. It is far more rational to suppose, that the courts were designed to be an intermediate body between the people and the legislature, in order, among other things, to keep the latter within the limits assigned to their authority. The interpretation of the laws is the proper and peculiar province of the courts. A constitution is, in fact, and must be regarded by the judges, as a fundamental law. It therefore belongs to them to ascertain its meaning, as well as the meaning of any particular act proceeding from the legislative body. If there should happen to be an irreconcilable variance between the two, that which has the

superior obligation and validity ought, of course, to be preferred; or, in other words, the Constitution ought to be preferred to the statute, the intention of the people to the intention of their agents.

Nor does this conclusion by any means suppose a superiority of the judicial to the legislative power. It only supposes that the power of the people is superior to both; and that where the will of the legislature, declared in its statutes, stands in opposition to that of the people, declared in the Constitution, the judges ought to be governed by the latter rather than the former. They ought to regulate their decisions by the fundamental laws, rather than by those which are not fundamental. . . .

This independence of the judges is equally requisite to guard the Constitution and the rights of individuals from the effects of those ill humors, which the arts of designing men, or the influence of particular conjunctures, sometimes disseminate among the people themselves, and which, though they speedily give place to better information, and more deliberate reflection, have a tendency, in the meantime, to occasion dangerous innovations in the government, and serious oppressions of the minor party in the community.

Marbury v. Madison

5 U.S. (1 Cr.) 137 (1803)

William Marbury and several colleagues were nominated by President John Adams to be justices of the peace in the District of Columbia. The Senate confirmed their names, Adams signed their commissions, and the seal of the United States was affixed to the commissions. However, in the confusion of the remaining days of the Adams administration, some of the commissions, including Marbury's, were not delivered. When President Thomas Jefferson entered office, he ordered that the commissions not be delivered. Marbury sued the Secretary of State, James Madison. The opinion in this case is written by Chief Justice John Marshall.

Opinion of the Court.

At the last term on the affidavits then read and filed with the clerk, a rule was granted in this case, requiring the secretary of state to show cause why a *mandamus* should not issue, directing him to deliver to William Marbury his commission as a

justice of the peace for the county of Washington, in the district of Columbia.

No cause has been shown, and the present motion is for a *mandamus*. The peculiar delicacy of this case, the novelty of some of its circumstances, and the real difficulty attending the points which occur in it, require a complete exposition of the principles on which the opinion to be given by the court is founded. . . .

The first object of inquiry is,

1st. Has the applicant a right to the commission he demands?

His right originates in an act of congress passed in February, 1801, concerning the district of Columbia.

After dividing the district into two counties, the 11th section of this law enacts, "that there shall be appointed in and for each of the said counties, such number of discreet persons to be justices of the peace as the president of the United States shall, from time to time, think expedient, to continue in office for five years.

It appears, from the affidavits, that in compliance with this law, a commission for William Marbury, as a justice of peace for the county of Washington, was signed by John Adams, then President of the United States; after which the seal of the United States was affixed to it; but the commission has never reached the person for whom it was made out. . . .

The last act to be done by the president is the signature of the commission. He has then acted on the advice and consent of the senate to his own nomination. The time for deliberation has then passed. He has decided. His judgment, on the advice and consent of the senate concurring with his nomination, has been made, and the officer is appointed. This appointment is evidenced by an open, unequivocal act; and being the last act required from the person making it, necessarily excludes the idea of its being, so far as respects the appointment, an inchoate and incomplete transaction. . . .

The commission being signed, the subsequent duty of the secretary of state is prescribed by law, and not to be guided by the will of the president. He is to affix the seal of the United States to the commission, and is to record it.

This is not a proceeding which may be varied, if the judgment of the executive shall suggest one more eligible; but is a precise course accurately marked out by law, and is to be strictly pursued. It is the duty of the secretary of state to conform to the law, and in this he is an officer of the United States, bound to obey the laws. He acts, in this respect, as has been very properly stated at the bar, under the authority of law, and not by the instructions of the president. It is a ministerial act which the law enjoins on a particular officer for a particular purpose. . . .

Mr. Marbury, then, since his commission was signed by the president, and sealed by the secretary of state, was appointed; and as the law creating the office, gave the officer a right to hold for five years, independent of the executive, the appointment was not revocable, but vested in the officer legal rights, which are protected by the laws of his country.

To withhold his commission, therefore, is an act deemed by the court not warranted by law, but violative of a vested legal right.

This brings us to the second inquiry; which is,

2dly, If he has a right, and that right has been violated, do the laws of his country afford him a remedy?

The very essence of civil liberty certainly consists in the right of every individual to claim the protection of the laws, whenever he receives an injury. One of the first duties of government is to afford that protection. In Great Britain the king himself is sued in the respectful form of a petition, and he never fails to comply with the judgment of his court. . . .

The government of the United States has been emphatically termed a government of laws, and not of men. It will certainly cease to deserve this high appellation, if the laws furnish no remedy for the violation of a vested legal right. . . .

. . . Is the act of delivering or withholding a commission to be considered as a mere political act, belonging to the executive department alone, for the performance of which entire confidence is placed by our constitution in the supreme executive; and for any misconduct respecting which, the injured individual has no remedy?

That there may be such cases is not to be questioned; but that every act of duty, to be performed in any of the great departments of government, constitutes such a case, is not to be admitted. . . .

By the constitution of the United States, the president is invested with certain important political powers, in the exercise of which he is to use his own discretion, and is accountable only to his country in his political character and to his own conscience. To aid him in the performance of these duties, he is authorized to appoint certain officers, who act by his authority, and in conformity with his orders.

In such cases, their acts are his acts; and whatever opinion may be entertained of the manner in which executive discretion may be used, still there exists, and can exist, no power to control that discretion. The subjects are political. They respect the nation, not individual rights, and being intrusted to the executive, the decision of the executive is conclusive. The application of this remark will be perceived by adverting to the act of congress for establishing the department of foreign affairs. This officer, as his duties were prescribed by that act, is to conform precisely to the will of the president. He is the mere organ by whom that will is communicated. The acts of such an officer, as an officer, can never be examinable by the courts.

But when the legislature proceeds to impose on that officer other duties; when he is directed peremptorily to perform certain acts; when the rights of individuals are dependent on the performance of those acts; he is so far the officer of the law; is amenable to the laws for his conduct; and cannot at his discretion sport away the vested rights of others.

The conclusion from this reasoning is, that where the heads of departments are the political or confidential agents of the executive, merely to execute the will of the president, or rather to act in cases in which the executive possesses a constitutional or legal discretion, nothing can be more perfectly clear than that their acts are only politically examinable. But where a specific duty is assigned by law, and individual rights depend upon the performance of that duty, it seems equally clear that the individual who considers himself injured, has a right to resort to the laws of his country for a remedy. . . .

The question whether a right has vested or not, is, in its nature, judicial, and must be tried by the judicial authority. If, for example, Mr. Marbury had taken the oaths of a magistrate, and proceeded to act as one; in consequence of which a suit had been instituted against him, in which his defence had depended on his being a magistrate, the validity of his appointment must have been determined by judicial authority. . . .

It is, then, the opinion of the court,

1st. That by signing the commission of Mr. Marbury, the President of the United States appointed him a justice of peace for the county of Washington, in the district of Columbia; and that the seal of the United States, affixed thereto by the secretary of state, is conclusive testimony of the verity of the signature, and of the completion of the appointment; and that the appointment conferred on him a legal right to the office for the space of five years.

2dly. That, having this legal title to the office, he has a consequent right to the commission; a refusal to deliver which is a plain violation of that right, for which the laws of his country afford him a remedy.

It remains to be inquired whether,

3dly. He is entitled to the remedy for which he applies. This depends on,

1st. The nature of the writ applied for; and,

2dly. The power of this court.

1st. The nature of the writ.

Blackstone, in the 3d volume of his Commentaries, page 110, defines a *mandamus* to be "a command issuing in the king's name from the court of king's bench, and directed to any person, corporation, or inferior court of judicature within the king's dominions, requiring them to do some particular thing therein specified, which appertains to their office and duty, and which the court of king's bench has previously determined, or at least supposes, to be consonant to right and justice." . . .

Still, to render the *mandamus* a proper remedy, the officer to whom it is to be directed, must be one to whom, on legal principles, such writ may be directed; and the person applying for it must be without any other specific and legal remedy.

1st. With respect to the officer to whom it would be directed. The intimate political relation subsisting between the President of the United States and the heads of departments, necessarily renders any legal investigation of the acts of one of those high officers peculiarly irksome, as well as delicate; and excites some hesitation with respect to the propriety of entering into such investigation. Impressions are often received without much reflection or examination, and it is not wonderful that in such a case as this the assertion, by an individual, of his legal claims in a court of justice, to which claims it is the duty of that court to attend, should at first view be considered by some, as an attempt to intrude into the cabinet, and to intermeddle with the prerogatives of the executive.

It is scarcely necessary for the court to disclaim all pretensions to such a jurisdiction. An extravagance, so absurd and excessive, could not have been entertained for a moment. The province of the court is, solely, to decide on the rights of individuals, not to inquire how the executive, or executive officers, perform duties in which they have a discretion. Questions in their nature political, or which are, by the constitution and laws, submitted to the executive, can never be made in this court. . . .

It is not by the office of the person to whom the writ is directed, but the nature of the thing to be done, that the propriety or impropriety of issuing a *mandamus* is to be determined. . . .

This, then, is a plain case for a *mandamus*, either to deliver the commission, or a copy of it from the record; and it only remains to be inquired,

Whether it can issue from this court.

The act to establish the judicial courts of the United States authorizes the supreme court "to issue writs of *mandamus*, in cases warranted by the principles and usages of law, to any courts appointed, or persons holding office, under the authority of the United States."

The secretary of state, being a person holding an office under the authority of the United States, is precisely within the letter of the description; and if this court is not authorized to issue a writ of *mandamus* to such an officer, it must be because the law is unconstitutional, and therefore absolutely incapable of conferring the authority, and assigning the duties which its words purport to confer and assign.

The constitution vests the whole judicial power of the United States in one supreme court, and such inferior courts as congress shall, from time to time, ordain and establish. This power is expressly extended to all cases arising under the laws of the United States; and, consequently, in some form, may be exercised over the present case; because the right claimed is given by a law of the United States.

In the distribution of this power it is declared that "the supreme court shall have original jurisdiction in all cases affecting ambassadors, other public ministers and consuls, and those in which a state shall be a party. In all other cases, the supreme court shall have appellate jurisdiction."

It has been insisted, at the bar, that as the original grant of jurisdiction, to the supreme and inferior courts, is general, and the clause, assigning original jurisdiction to the supreme court, contains no negative or restrictive words, the power remains to the legislature, to assign original jurisdiction to that court in other cases than those specified in the article which has been recited; provided those cases belong to the judicial power of the United States.

If it had been intended to leave it in the discretion of the legislature to apportion the judicial power between the supreme and inferior courts according to the will of that body, it would certainly have been useless to have proceeded further than to have defined the judicial power, and the tribunals in which it should be vested. The subsequent part of the section is mere surplusage, is entirely without meaning, if such is to be the construction. If congress remains at liberty to give this court appellate jurisdiction, where the constitution has declared their jurisdiction shall be original; and original jurisdiction where the constitution has declared it shall be appellate; the distribution of jurisdiction, made in the constitution, is form without substance.

Affirmative words are often, in their operation, negative of other objects than those affirmed; and in this case, a negative or exclusive sense must be given to them, or they have no operation at all.

It cannot be presumed that any clause in the constitution is intended to be without effect; and, therefore, such a construction is inadmissible, unless the words require it.

If the solicitude of the convention, respecting our peace with foreign powers, induced a provision that the supreme court should take original jurisdiction in cases which might be supposed to affect them; yet the clause would have proceeded no further than to provide for such cases, if no further restriction on the powers of congress had been intended. That they should have appellate jurisdiction in all other cases, with such exceptions as congress might make, is no restriction; unless the words be deemed exclusive of original jurisdiction.

When an instrument organizing fundamentally a judicial system, divides it into one supreme, and so many inferior courts as the legislature may ordain and establish; then enumerates its powers, and proceeds so far to distribute them, as to define the jurisdiction of the supreme court by declaring the cases in which it shall take original jurisdiction, and that in others it shall take appellate jurisdiction; the plain import of the words seems to be, that in one class of cases its jurisdiction is original, and not appellate; in the other it is appellate, and not original. If any other construction would render the clause inoperative, that is an additional reason for rejecting such other construction, and for adhering to their obvious meaning.

To enable this court, then, to issue a *mandamus*, it must be shown to be an exercise of appellate jurisdiction, or to be necessary to enable them to exercise appellate jurisdiction.

It has been stated at the bar that the appellate jurisdiction may be exercised in a variety of forms, and that if it be the will of the legislature that a *mandamus* should be used for that purpose, that will must be obeyed. This is true, yet the jurisdiction must be appellate, not original.

It is the essential criterion of appellate jurisdiction, that it revises and corrects the proceedings in a cause already instituted, and does not create that cause. Although, therefore, a *mandamus* may be directed to courts, yet to issue such a writ to an officer for the delivery of a paper, is in effect the same as to sustain an original action for that paper, and, therefore, seems not to belong to appellate, but to original jurisdiction. Neither is it necessary in such a case as this, to enable the court to exercise its appellate jurisdiction.

The authority, therefore, given to the supreme court, by the act establishing the judicial courts of the United States, to issue writs of *mandamus* to public officers, appears not to be warranted by the constitution; and it becomes necessary to inquire whether a jurisdiction so conferred can be exercised.

The question, whether an act, repugnant to the constitution, can become the law of the land, is a question deeply interesting to the United States; but, happily, not of an intricacy proportioned to its interest. It seems only necessary to recognise certain principles, supposed to have been long and well established, to decide it.

That the people have an original right to establish, for their future government, such principles as, in their opinion, shall most conduce to their own happiness is the basis on which the whole American fabric has been erected. The exercise of this original right is a very great exertion; nor can it, nor ought it, to be frequently repeated. The principles, therefore, so established, are deemed fundamental. And as the authority from which they proceed is supreme, and can seldom act, they are designed to be permanent.

This original and supreme will organizes the government, and assigns to different departments their respective powers. It may either stop here, or establish certain limits not to be transcended by those departments.

The government of the United States is of the latter description. The powers of the legislature are defined and limited; and that those limits may not be mistaken, or forgotten, the constitution is written. To what purpose are powers limited, and to what purpose is that limitation committed to writing, if these limits may, at any time, be passed by those intended to be restrained? The distinction between a government with limited and unlimited powers is abolished, if those limits do not confine the persons on whom they are imposed, and if acts prohibited and acts allowed, are of equal obligation. It is a proposition too plain to be contested, that the constitution controls any legislative act repugnant to it; or, that the legislature may alter the constitution by an ordinary act.

Between these alternatives there is no middle ground. The constitution is either a superior paramount law, unchangeable by ordinary means, or it is on a level with ordinary legislative acts, and, like other acts, is alterable when the legislature shall please to alter it.

If the former part of the alternative be true, then a legislative act contrary to the constitution is not law: if the latter part be true, then written constitutions are absurd attempts, on the part of the people, to limit a power in its own nature illimitable.

Certainly all those who have framed written constitutions contemplate them as forming the fundamental and paramount law of the nation, and, consequently, the theory of every such government must be, that an act of the legislature, repugnant to the constitution, is void.

This theory is essentially attached to a written constitution, and, is consequently, to be considered, by this court, as one of the fundamental principles of our society. It is not therefore to be lost sight of in the further consideration of this subject.

If an act of the legislature, repugnant to the constitution, is void, does it, notwithstanding its invalidity, bind the courts, and oblige them to give it effect? Or, in other words, though it be not law, does it constitute a rule as operative as if it was a law? This would be to overthrow in fact what was established in theory; and would seem, at first view, an absurdity too gross to be insisted on. It shall, however, receive a more attentive consideration.

It is emphatically the province and duty of the judicial department to say what the law is. Those who apply the rule to particular cases, must of necessity expound and interpret that rule. If two laws conflict with each other, the courts must decide on the operation of each.

So if a law be in opposition to the constitution; if both the law and the constitution apply to a particular case, so that the court must either decide that case conformably to the law, disregarding the constitution; or conformably to the constitution, disregarding the law; the court must determine which of these conflicting rules governs the case. This is of the very essence of judicial duty.

If, then, the courts are to regard the constitution, and the constitution is superior to any ordinary act of the legislature, the constitution, and not such ordinary act, must govern the case to which they both apply.

Those, then, who controvert the principle that the constitution is to be considered, in court, as a paramount law, are reduced to the necessity of maintaining that courts must close their eyes on the constitution, and see only the law.

This doctrine would subvert the very foundation of all written constitutions. It would declare that an act which, according to the principles and theory of our government, is entirely void, is yet, in practice, completely obligatory. It would declare that if the legislature shall do what is expressly forbidden, such act, notwithstanding the express prohibition, is in reality effectual. It would be giving to the legislature a practical and real omnipotence, with the same breath which professes to restrict their powers within narrow limits. It is prescribing limits, and declaring that those limits may be passed at pleasure.

That it thus reduces to nothing what we have deemed the greatest improvement on political institutions, a written constitution, would of itself be sufficient, in America, where written constitutions have been viewed with so much reverence, for rejecting the construction. But the peculiar expressions of the constitution of the United States furnish additional arguments in favour of its rejection.

The judicial power of the United States is extended to all cases arising under the constitution.

Could it be the intention of those who gave this power, to say that in using it the constitution should not be looked into? That a case arising under the constitution should be decided without examining the instrument under which it arises?

This is too extravagant to be maintained.

In some cases, then, the constitution must be looked into by the judges. And if they can open it at all, what part of it are they forbidden to read or to obey?

There are many other parts of the constitution which serve to illustrate this subject.

It is declared that "no tax or duty shall be laid on articles exported from any state." Suppose a duty on the export of cotton, of tobacco, or of flour; and a suit instituted to recover it. Ought judgment to be rendered in such a case? ought the judges to close their eyes on the constitution, and only see the law.

The constitution declares "that no bill of attainder or *ex post facto* law shall be passed."

If, however, such a bill should be passed, and a person should be prosecuted under it; must the court condemn to death those victims whom the constitution endeavours to preserve?

"No person," says the constitution, "shall be convicted of treason unless on the testimony of two witnesses to the same overt act, or on confession in open court."

Here the language of the constitution is addressed especially to the courts. It prescribes, directly for them, a rule of evidence not to be departed from. If the legislature should change that rule, and declare *one* witness, or a confession *out* of court, sufficient for conviction, must the constitutional principle yield to the legislative act?

From these, and many other selections which might be made, it is apparent, that the framers of the constitution contemplated that instrument as a rule for the government of *courts*, as well as of the legislature.

Why otherwise does it direct the judges to take an oath to support it? This oath certainly applies in an especial manner, to their conduct in their official character. How immoral to impose it on them, if they were to be used as the instruments, and the knowing instruments, for violating what they swear to support!

The oath of office, too, imposed by the legislature, is completely demonstrative of the legislative opinion on this subject. It is in these words: "I do solemnly swear that I will administer justice without respect to persons, and do equal right to the poor and to the rich; and that I will faithfully and impartially discharge all the duties incumbent on me as   , according to the best of my abilities and understanding, agreeably to *the constitution* and laws of the United States."

Why does a judge swear to discharge his duties agreeably to the constitution of the United States, if that constitution forms no rule for his government? if it is closed upon him, and cannot be inspected by him?

If such be the real state of things, this is worse than solemn mockery. To prescribe, or, to take this oath, becomes equally a crime.

It is also not entirely unworthy of observation, that in declaring what shall be the *supreme* law of the land, the *constitution* itself is first mentioned; and not the laws of the United States generally, but those only which shall be made in *pursuance* of the constitution, have that rank.

Thus, the particular phraseology of the constitution of the United States confirms and strengthens the principle, supposed to be essential to all written constitutions, that a law repugnant to the constitution is void; and that *courts*, as well as other departments, are bound by that instrument.

The rule must be discharged.

William W. Van Alstyne

A Critical Guide to Marbury *v.* Madison

THE FIRST ISSUE

Rather than writing about the opinion in general, we may more successfully deal with it in the manner in which one is in fact expected to analyze cases—by taking them on their own terms, raising

SOURCE: 1969 Duke L. J. 1. Footnotes omitted.

and resolving questions each step of the way. Thus, it seems logical to begin with the Court's own beginning.

The Court declares that the "first" issue presented by the case is: "Has the applicant a right to the commission he demands?" At least two criticisms of this beginning have been made. Both arise in answer to the question: Was Marbury's entitlement to the commission he demanded really the issue which the Court should have examined first? Arguably, it was not.

Surely the Court ought first determine whether it has any authority to decide any issues whatever respecting the merits of the case, *i.e.*, it should first resolve the preliminary question of its own jurisdiction. The Court's jurisdiction was ostensibly based on section 13 of the Judiciary Act of 1789 which Marbury alleged to empower the Court to issue a writ of mandamus in this sort of case. But if the Act did not in fact provide for such jurisdiction, or if it were invalid in attempting to provide for such jurisdiction, the Court would be without proper authority to consider the merits of Marbury's claim. Thus, it may be said, the "first" issue was solely the question of the Court's jurisdiction and it should have spoken to that issue at the beginning. The logic of such an approach was subsequently well stated in Ex parte *McCardle:*

"Without jurisdiction the court cannot proceed at all in any cause. Jurisdiction is power to declare the law, and when it ceases to exist, the only function remaining to the court is that of announcing the fact and dismissing the cause."

. . . there is clearly an "issue" of sorts which preceded any of those touched upon in the opinion. Specifically, it would appear that Marshall should have recused himself in view of his substantial involvement in the background of this controversy. Remember, too, that the Court thought it important to establish whether Marbury's commission had already been signed and sealed before it was withdrawn—to determine whether Marbury's interest had "vested" and whether Madison was refusing to carry out a merely ministerial duty, or whether the commission was sufficiently incomplete that matters of executive discretion were involved. Proof of the status of Marbury's commission not only involved circumstances within the Chief Justice's personal knowledge, it was furnished in the Supreme Court by Marshall's own younger brother who had been with him in his office when, as Secretary of State, he had made out the commissions. Arguably the first issue, then, was the appropriateness of Marshall's participation in the decision.

MARBURY'S "RIGHT" TO THE COMMISSION

On the basis of the Act of 1801 providing for the appointment of justices of the peace for a five-year term plus findings of fact that the appointment had "vested," the Court held that Marbury had a "right" to the commission. The Act itself was based on the power of Congress granted by the Constitution in Article I, section 8, clause 17, "to exercise Legislation in all Cases whatsoever, over" the District of Columbia. Marshall concludes that once the commission had been signed and sealed by President Adams, Marbury's claim to the office was complete.

Marshall reasonably could have concluded, however, that no interest actually "vested" in Marbury prior to actual delivery of the commission. Jefferson evidently thought that the better conclusion, subsequently insisting that Marshall's decision on this point was a "perversion of law," and maintaining that "if there is any principle of law never yet contradicted, it is that delivery is one of the essentials to the validity of the deed." Even if Jefferson overstated the law, and even assuming authority could be found urging that certain interests "vest" prior to delivery, it would not necessarily be dispositive of this case. The Court is reviewing an aspect of executive power and passing judgment upon the propriety of conduct by a coordinate branch of government here, a consideration not present in an ordinary civil suit between private litigants. . . .

STATUTORY INTERPRETATION

Certainly the first question is the following one of statutory interpretation which was just barely treated in the opinion: Did section 13 of the Judiciary Act authorize this action to originate in the Supreme Court? The section provides:

"And be it further enacted, That the Supreme Court shall have exclusive jurisdiction of all controversies of a civil nature, where a state is a party, except between a state and its citizens; and except also between a state and citizens of other states, or aliens, in which latter case it shall have original but not exclusive jurisdiction. And shall have exclusively all such jurisdiction of suits or proceedings against ambassadors, or other public minis-

ters, or their domestics, or domestic servants, as a court of law can have or exercise consistently with the law of nations; and original, but not exclusive jurisdiction of all suits brought by ambassadors, or other public ministers, or in which a consul, or vice consul, shall be a party. And the trial of issues in fact in the Supreme Court, in all actions at law against citizens of the United States, shall be by jury. The Supreme Court shall also have appellate jurisdiction from the circuit courts and courts of the several states, in the cases herein after specially provided for; and shall have power to issue writs of prohibition to the district courts, when proceeding as courts of admiralty and maritime jurisdiction, and writs of *mandamus*, in cases warranted by the principles and usages of law, to any courts appointed, or persons holding office, under the authority of the United States."

Marshall quotes only the fragment at the end, perfunctorily notes that Madison holds office under the authority of the United States and therefore "is precisely within the letter of the description," and since he has already established that mandamus would otherwise be an appropriate remedy he quickly concludes that section 13 purports to authorize this case. But there is no discussion of whether this section *confers* original jurisdiction over suits seeking mandamus against persons holding office under the authority of the United States, or whether it merely authorizes mandamus to be so employed by the Court in cases properly *on appeal* or in aid of its original jurisdiction in cases involving foreign ministers or states. If it means only the latter, and if Marbury has no other basis for commencing his case in the Supreme Court, then the Court should simply dismiss the case for want of (statutory) jurisdiction and it need not, and ought not, examine the constitutionality of section 13 under some other construction. An argument can be made, of course, that section 13 did not attempt to grant original jurisdiction in Marbury's case.

The section opens by describing the Court's original jurisdiction and then moves on to describe appellate jurisdiction ("hereinafter specially provided for"). Textually, the provision regarding mandamus says nothing expressly as to whether it is part of original or appellate jurisdic-

tion or both, and the clause itself does not speak at all of "conferring jurisdiction" on the court. The grant of "power" to issue the writ, however, is juxtaposed with the section of appellate jurisdiction and, in fact, follows the general description of appellate jurisdiction in the same sentence, being separated only by a semicolon. No textual mangling is required to confine it to appellate jurisdiction. Moreover, no mangling is required even if it attaches both to original and to appellate jurisdiction, not as an enlargement of either, but simply as a specification of power which the Court is authorized to use in cases which are *otherwise* appropriately under consideration. Since this case is not otherwise within the specified type of original jurisdiction (*e.g.*, it is not a case in which a state is a party or a case against an ambassador), it should be dismissed. . . .

JUDICIAL REVIEW

Assuming that section 13 of the Judiciary Act of 1789 does confer original jurisdiction in this case, is its constitutionality subject to judicial review? Marshall initially responds to this question, which, of course, is the issue which has made the case of historic importance, by posing his own rhetorical question: "whether an Act repugnant to the Constitution can become the law of the land." That it cannot is clear, he says, from the following considerations.

The people in an exercise of their "original right," established the government pursuant to a written constitution which defines and limits the powers of the legislature. A "legislative act contrary to the constitution is not law," therefore, as it is contrary to the original and supreme will which organized the legislature itself.

"To what purpose are powers limited, and to what purpose is that limitation committed to writing, if these limits may, at any time, be passed by those intended to be restrained? . . . It is a proposition too plain to be contested, that the constitution controls any legislative act repugnant to it; or, that the legislature may alter the constitution by an ordinary act.

Between these alternatives there is no middle ground. The constitution is either a superior paramount law, unchangeable by ordinary means, or it is on a level with ordinary legislative acts, and, like other acts, is alterable when the legislature shall please to alter it. . . .

Certainly all those who have framed written constitutions contemplate them as forming the fundamental and paramount law of the nation, and consequently, the theory of every such government must be, that an act of the legislature, repugnant to the constitution, is void.

This theory is essentially attached to a written constitution. . . .

It is also not entirely unworthy of observation, that in declaring what shall be the *supreme* law of the land, the *constitution* itself is first mentioned: and not the laws of the United States generally, but those only which shall be made in *pursuance* of the constitution, have that rank.

Thus, the particular phraseology of the Constitution of the United States confirms and strengthens the principle, supposed to be essential to all written constitutions, that a law repugnant to the constitution is void. . . ."

That the Constitution is a "written" one yields little or nothing as to whether acts of Congress may be given the force of positive law notwithstanding the opinion of judges, the executive, a minority or majority of the population, or even of Congress itself (assuming that Congress might sometimes be pressed by political forces to adopt a law against its belief that it lacked power to do so) that such Acts are repugnant to the Constitution. That this is so is clear enough simply from the fact that even in Marshall's time (and to a great extent today), a number of nations maintained written constitutions and yet gave national legislative acts the full force of positive law without providing any constitutional check to guarantee the compatibility of those acts with their constitutions.

This observation, moreover, leads to the conclusion that Marshall presents a false dilemma in insisting that "[t]he constitution is *either* a superior or paramount law, unchangeable by ordinary means, *or* it is on a level with ordinary legislative acts, and, like other acts, is alterable when the legislature shall please to alter it." Remember, the

question he has posed is "whether an Act repugnant to the Constitution can become the law of the land." The question is not whether Congress can alter the Constitution by means other than those provided by Article V, and the case raises no issue concerning an alteration of any provision in the Constitution. We may assume that Congress cannot, by simple act, alter the Constitution and still we may maintain that an act which the Court or someone else *believes* to be repugnant to the Constitution shall be given the full force of positive law until repealed. Again, this is the situation which prevails in many other countries, and no absurdity is felt to exist where such a condition obtains.

To be sure, situations can be imagined (and may arise in fact) where an act of Congress seems so clearly repugnant to the Constitution that one may wonder what function the Constitution can usefully serve if such a law is nevertheless given the full force of positive law until repealed. Marshall's illustrations of such situations are quite compelling in this regard, *e.g.*, an act of Congress providing that one may be convicted of treason upon testimony of a single witness, or confession out of court, in the "very teeth" of the provision in Article III, section 3, that "no person shall be convicted of treason unless on the testimony of two witnesses to the same overt Act, or on Confession in open Court." . . .

Finally, however, there is the reference to the supremacy clause in Article VI which Marshall uses partly to show, again, "that a law repugnant to the constitution is void" (as well as to show that it does not bind the judiciary). To be sure, the clause does provide that "[t]his Constitution, and the Laws of the United States which shall be made in *Pursuance* thereof . . . shall be the supreme Law of the Land," and thus the text appears to require that acts of Congress be made "pursuant" to the authority (and limitations) of the Constitution to be effective as supreme law. But this does not necessarily support Marshall's conclusion that no act of Congress believed by the Court to be repugnant to the Constitution shall be given full positive-law effect.

The phrase "in pursuance thereof" might as easily mean *in the manner prescribed by this Constitution,*" in which case acts of Congress might be judicially reviewable as to their procedural integrity, but not as to their substance. . . .

The phrase might also mean merely that only those statutes adopted by Congress *after* the reestablishment and reconstitution of Congress pursuant to the Constitution itself shall be the supreme law of the land, whereas acts of the earlier Continental Congress, constituted merely under the Articles of Confederation, would not necessarily be supreme and binding upon the several states. Under this view, acts of Congress, like acts of Parliament, *are* the supreme law and not to be second-guessed by any court, state or federal, so long as they postdate ratification of the Constitution.

. . .

CONSTITUTIONALITY OF SECTION 13

Assuming that section 13 of the Judiciary Act of 1789 does confer original jurisdiction in this case, and assuming also that its substantive constitutionality is subject to independent judicial review, is that section constitutional? In view of the extended discussion above, this issue is almost anticlimactic. Still, it has its own practical and legal importance. If the Court had concluded that the act was constitutional, presumably it would have issued the writ against Madison. If Madison, on Jefferson's instruction, had refused to honor that writ how would it have been enforced? Who would enforce it? The prospect of this problem may well have influenced the decision as to the constitutionality of section 13.

Essentially, Marshall's argument that the act is unconstitutional comes to this: Article III *restricts* the original jurisdiction of the Supreme Court to certain limited types of cases, those "affecting Ambassadors, other public Ministers and Consuls, and those in which a State shall be a Party." Section 13 of the Judiciary Act attempts to expand the Court's original jurisdiction beyond the limitation provided in Article III, and section 13 is therefore repugnant to the Constitution. Since a close reading of Article III itself will not discover any explicit statement clearly providing that the Court's original jurisdiction cannot be expanded to absorb some cases that might otherwise fall

only within its appellate jurisdiction, however, it becomes necessary to study Marshall's opinion to determine on what basis he correctly, or incorrectly, inferred such a limitation. Marshall acknowledges the point just made and attempts to answer in the following fashion:

"If it had been intended to leave it in the discretion of the legislature to apportion the judicial power between the supreme and inferior courts according to the will of that body, it would certainly have been useless to have proceeded further than to have defined the judicial power, and the tribunals in which it should be vested. The subsequent part of the section is mere surplusage, is entirely without meaning, if such is to be the construction. If Congress remains at liberty to give this court appellate jurisdiction, where the constitution has declared their jurisdiction shall be original; and original jurisdiction where the constitution has declared it shall be appellate; the distribution of jurisdiction, made in the constitution, is form without substance.

Affirmative words are often, in their operation, negative of other objects than those affirmed; and in this case, a negative or exclusive sense must be given to them, or they have no operation at all.

It cannot be presumed that any clause in the constitution is intended to be without effect; and, therefore, such a construction is inadmissible, unless the words require it."

Here, as elsewhere, Marshall's essential point is that any interpretation other than the one he finds would leave the text being interpreted without any significance and would have to serve no useful purpose. In this, he has clearly overstated the situation. Indeed his own interpretation may *weaken* the Court's power far more than another interpretation wholly compatible with the text of Article III, section 2, clause two.

The clause readily supports a meaningful interpretation that the Court's original jurisdiction may not be *reduced* by Congress, but that it may be supplemented by adding to it original jurisdiction over some cases which would otherwise fall only within its appellate jurisdiction. Such a reading makes sense and makes no part of the clause surplusage. . . .

III. A Specification of the Holding on Constitutional Review

In litigation before the Supreme Court, the Court may refuse to give effect to an act of Congress where the act pertains to the judicial power itself. In deciding whether to give effect to such an act, the Court may determine its decision according to its own interpretation of constitutional provisions which describe the judicial power.

Thus described, the holding in *Marbury* v. *Madison* is less remarkable than generally supposed. It is also, however, far more defensible because it draws upon one's sympathy to maintain the Court as a co-ordinate branch of government, and not as a superior branch. It represents a defensive use of constitutional review alone, acquiring considerable support from the concept of *separated* powers. It merely minds the Court's *own* business (*i.e.,* what cases shall originate in the Court, what cases shall be treated on appeal or otherwise). Were the Court to lack *this* capacity, it could scarcely be able to maintain even the ordinary function of *non*constitutional judicial review.

. . . It does not mean, for instance, that either Congress or the President need defer to Supreme Court interpretations of the Constitution so far as their own deliberations are concerned and so far as the efficacy of their power does not depend upon judicial co-operation.

When a bill is under consideration, for example, Congress might conscientiously reject the bill believing that bill to be unconstitutional even assuming that the Court has provided no precedent for that belief and even assuming that the Court has itself upheld similar legislation adopted by an earlier Congress. Similarly, the President may veto the bill on the grounds of his own interpretation of the Constitution—whether or not it is the same as the Court's. So, too, might he decline to enforce an act of Congress on such a basis.

The concept of national, substantive judicial *review,* moreover, does not preclude independent prerogatives of Congress and the President to prefer their own constitutional interpretations even when the Court, for its part, has interpreted the Constitution in such a manner as to sustain the bill. A clear instance might involve the use of the executive clemency power, used by Jefferson to pardon those convicted under the Alien and Sedition Acts which had been upheld in the lower federal courts, on the grounds that in the President's own view those acts were repugnant to the Constitution. A harder instance might involve the decision of the President not to enforce an act of Congress because of his own belief that it was unconstitutional, even after the act had been tested and upheld in the Supreme Court.

There is, then, no doctrine of national, substantive judicial *supremacy* which inexorably flows from *Marbury* v. *Madison* itself, *i.e.,* no doctrine that the only interpretation of the Constitution which all branches of the national government must employ is the interpretation which the Court may provide in the course of litigation. . . .

Martin v. Hunter's Lessee

14 U.S. (1 Wheat.) 304 (1816)

A federal district court upheld Martin's land claim, which was based on a treaty between America and Great Britain. The Virginia Court of Appeals, the highest court in that state, regarded the issue as solely one of state law and reversed the district court. The conflict escalated when the U.S. Supreme Court set aside the state ruling and the state court refused to obey. The Virginia Court of Appeals claimed that the Supreme Court had no authority to review its judgment, and to the extent that Section 25 of the Judiciary Act of 1789 attempted to extend the appellate jurisdiction of the Supreme Court to the state courts, the statute was unconstitutional. Chief Justice Marshall did not participate since he had earlier served as attorney for one of the parties.

STORY, J., delivered the opinion of the court.

. . .

The constitution of the United States was ordained and established, not by the states in their sovereign capacities, but emphatically, as the preamble of the constitution declares, by "the People of the United States." There can be no doubt, that it was competent to the people to invest the general government with all the powers which they might deem proper and necessary; to extend or restrain these powers according to their own good pleasure, and to give them a paramount and supreme authority. As little doubt can there be, that the people had a right to prohibit to the states the exercise of any powers which were, in their judgment, incompatible with the objects of the general compact; to make the powers of the state governments, in given cases, subordinate to those of the nation, or to reserve to themselves those sovereign authorities which they might not choose to delegate to either. The constitution was not, therefore, necessarily carved out of existing state sovereignties, nor a surrender of powers already existing in state institutions, for the powers of the states depend upon their own constitutions; and the people of every state had the right to modify and restrain them, according to their own views of policy or principle. On the other hand, it is perfectly clear, that the sovereign powers vested in the state governments, by their respective constitutions, remained unaltered and unimpaired, except so far as they were granted to the government of the United States . . .

. . . The constitution was for a new government, organized with new substantive powers, and not a mere supplementary charter to a government already existing. The confederation was a compact between states; and its structure and powers were wholly unlike those of the national government. The constitution was an act of the people of the United States to supersede the confederation, and not to be engrafted on it, as a stock through which it was to receive life and nourishment. . . .

This leads us to the consideration of the great question, as to the nature and extent of the appellate jurisdiction of the United States. We have already seen, that appellate jurisdiction is given by

the constitution to the supreme court, in all cases where it has not original jurisdiction; subject, however, to such exceptions and regulations as congress may prescribe. It is, therefore, capable of embracing every case enumerated in the constitution, which is not exclusively to be decided by way of original jurisdiction. But the exercise of appellate jurisdiction is far from being limited, by the terms of the constitution, to the supreme court. There can be no doubt, that congress may create a succession of inferior tribunals, in each of which it may vest appellate as well as original jurisdiction. The judicial power is delegated by the constitution, in the most general terms, and may, therefore, be exercised by congress, under every variety of form of appellate or original jurisdiction. And as there is nothing in the constitution which restrains or limits this power, it must, therefore, in all other cases, subsist in the utmost latitude of which, in its own nature, it is susceptible.

As, then, by the terms of the constitution, the appellate jurisdiction is not limited as to the supreme court, and as to this court, it may be exercised in all other cases than those of which it has original cognisance, what is there to restrain its exercise over state tribunals, in the enumerated cases? The appellate power is not limited by the terms of the third article to any particular courts. The words are, "the judicial power (which includes appellate power) shall extend to all cases," &c., and "in all other cases before mentioned the supreme court shall have appellate jurisdiction." It is the case, then, and not the court, that gives the jurisdiction. If the judicial power extends to the case, it will be in vain to search in the letter of the constitution for any qualification as to the tribunal where it depends. It is incumbent, then, upon those who assert such a qualification, to show its existence, by necessary implication. If the text be clear and distinct, no restriction upon its plain and obvious import ought to be admitted, unless the inference be irresistible.

If the constitution meant to limit the appellate jurisdiction to cases pending in the courts of the United States, it would necessarily follow, that the jurisdiction of these courts would, in all the cases enumerated in the constitution, be exclusive of state tribunals. How, otherwise, could the jurisdiction extend to *all* cases arising under the constitution, laws and treaties of the United States, or to *all* cases of admiralty and maritime jurisdiction? If some of these cases might be entertained by state tribunals, and no appellate jurisdiction as to them should exist, then the appellate power would not extend to *all*, but to *some*, cases. If state tribunals might exercise concurrent jurisdiction over all or some of the other classes of cases in the constitution, without control, then the appellate jurisdiction of the United States might, as to such cases, have no real existence, contrary to the manifest intent of the constitution. . . .

But it is plain, that the framers of the constitution did contemplate that cases within the judicial cognisance of the United States, not only might, but would, arise in the state courts, in the exercise of their ordinary jurisdiction. With this view, the sixth article declares, that "this constitution, and the laws of the United States which shall be made in pursuance thereof, and all treaties made, or which shall be made, under the authority of the United States, shall be the supreme law of the land, and the judges in every state shall be bound thereby, anything in the constitution or laws of any state to the contrary notwithstanding." It is obvious, that this obligation is imperative upon the state judges, in their official, and not merely in their private, capacities. From the very nature of their judicial duties, they would be called upon to pronounce the law applicable to the case in judgment. They were not to decide merely according to the laws or constitution of the state, but according to the constitution, laws and treaties of the United States—"the supreme law of the land." . . .

It must, therefore, be conceded, that the constitution not only contemplated, but meant to provide for cases within the scope of the judicial power of the United States, which might yet depend before state tribunals. It was foreseen, that in the exercise of their ordinary jurisdiction, state courts would incidentally take cognisance of cases arising under the constitution, the laws and treaties of the United States. Yet, to all these cases, the judicial power, by the very terms of the constitution, is to extend. It cannot extend, by original jurisdiction, if that was already rightfully and exclusively attached in the state courts, which (as has been already shown) may occur; it must, therefore, extend by appellate jurisdiction, or not

at all. It would seem to follow, that the appellate power of the United States must, in such cases, extend to state tribunals; and if, in such cases, there is no reason why it should not equally attach upon all others, within the purview of the constitution.

It has been argued, that such an appellate jurisdiction over state courts is inconsistent with the genius of our governments, and the spirit of the constitution. That the latter was never designed to act upon state sovereignties, but only upon the people, and that if the power exists, it will materially impair the sovereignty of the states, and the independence of their courts. We cannot yield to the force of this reasoning; it assumes principles which we cannot admit, and draws conclusions to which we do not yield our assent.

. . . The courts of the United States can, without question, revise the proceedings of the executive and legislative authorities of the states, and if they are found to be contrary to the constitution, may declare them to be of no legal validity. Surely, the exercise of the same right over judicial tribunals is not a higher or more dangerous act of sovereign power.

Nor can such a right be deemed to impair the independence of state judges. It is assuming the very ground in controversy, to assert that they possess an absolute independence of the United States. In respect to the powers granted to the United States, they are not independent; they are expressly bound to obedience, by the letter of the constitution; and if they should unintentionally transcend their authority, or misconstrue the constitution, there is no more reason for giving their judgments an absolute and irresistible force, than for giving it to the acts of the other co-ordinate departments of state sovereignty. . . .

It is further argued, that no great public mischief can result from a construction which shall limit the appellate power of the United States to cases in their own courts: first, because state judges are bound by an oath to support the constitution of the United States, and must be presumed to be men of learning and integrity; and secondly, because congress must have an unquestionable right [to] remove all cases within the scope of the judicial power from the state courts to the courts of the United States, at any time before final judgment, though not after final judgment. As to the first reason—admitting that the judges of the state courts are, and always will be, of as much learning, integrity and wisdom, as those of the courts of the United States (which we very cheerfully admit), it does not aid the argument. It is manifest, that the constitution has proceeded upon a theory of its own, and given or withheld powers according to the judgment of the American people, by whom it was adopted. We can only construe its powers, and cannot inquire into the policy or principles which induced the grant of them. The constitution has presumed (whether rightly or wrongly, we do not inquire), that state attachments, state prejudices, state jealousies, and state interests, might sometimes obstruct, or control, or be supposed to obstruct or control, the regular administration of justice. Hence, in controversies between states; between citizens of different states; between citizens claiming grants under different states; between a state and its citizens, or foreigners, and between citizens and foreigners, it enables the parties, under the authority of congress, to have the controversies heard, tried and determined before the national tribunals. No other reason than that which has been stated can be assigned, why some, at least, of those cases should not have been left to the cognisance of the state courts. In respect to the other enumerated cases—the cases arising under the constitution, laws and treaties of the United States, cases affecting ambassadors and other public ministers, and cases of admiralty and maritime jurisdiction—reasons of a higher and more extensive nature, touching the safety, peace and sovereignty of the nation, might well justify a grant of exclusive jurisdiction.

This is not all. A motive of another kind, perfectly compatible with the most sincere respect for state tribunals, might induce the grant of appellate power over their decisions. That motive is the importance, and even necessity of uniformity of decisions throughout the whole United States, upon all subjects within the purview of the constitution. Judges of equal learning and integrity, in different states, might differently interpret the statute, or a treaty of the United States, or even the constitution itself: if there were no revising authority to control these jarring and discordant judgments, and harmonize them into uniformity, the laws, the treaties and the constitution of the United States would be different, in different states, and might, perhaps, never have precisely the same construction, obligation or efficiency, in any two states. The public mischiefs that would attend such a state of things would be truly deplorable; and it cannot be believed, that they could have escaped the enlightened convention which formed the constitution. What, indeed, might then have been only prophecy, has now become fact; and the appellate jurisdiction must continue to be the only adequate remedy for such evils. . . .

On the whole, the court are of opinion, that the appellate power of the United States does extend to cases pending in the state courts; and that the 25th section of the judiciary act, which authorizes the exercise of this jurisdiction in the specified cases, by a writ of error, is supported by the letter and spirit of the constitution. We find no clause in that instrument which limits this power; and we dare not interpose a limitation, where the people have not been disposed to create one.

Strong as this conclusion stands, upon the general language of the constitution, it may still derive support from other sources. It is an historical fact, that this exposition of the constitution, extending its appellate power to state courts, was, previous to its adoption, uniformly and publicly avowed by its friends, and admitted by its enemies, as the basis of their respective reasonings, both in and out of the state conventions. It is an historical fact, that at the time when the judiciary act was submitted to the deliberations of the first congress, composed, as it was, not only of men of great learning and ability, but of men who had acted a principal part in framing, supporting or opposing that constitution, the same exposition was explicitly declared and admitted by the friends and by the opponents of that system. It is an historical fact, that the supreme court of the United States have, from time to time, sustained this appellate jurisdiction, in a great variety of cases, brought from the tribunals of many of the most important states in the Union, and that no state tribunal has ever breathed a judicial doubt on the subject, or declined to obey the mandate of the supreme court, until the present occasion. This weight of contemporaneous exposition by all parties, this acquiescence of enlightened state courts, and these judicial decisions of the supreme court, through so long a period, do, as we think, place the doctrine upon a foundation of authority which cannot be shaken, without delivering over the subject to perpetual and irremediable doubts. . . .

We have thus gone over all the principal questions in the cause, and we deliver our judgment with entire confidence, that it is consistent with the constitution and laws of the land. We have not thought it incumbent on us to give any opinion upon the question, whether this court have authority to issue a writ of *mandamus* to the court of appeals, to enforce the former judgments, as we did not think it necessarily involved in the decision of this cause.

It is the opinion of the whole court, that the judgment of the court of appeals of Virginia, rendered on the mandate in this cause, be reversed, and the judgment of the district court, held at Winchester, be, and the same is hereby affirmed.

Cohens v. Virginia

19 U.S. (6 Wheat.) 264 (1821)

This case involved the question of Supreme Court jurisdiction to review a criminal case in which the state itself was a party. The Cohen brothers were convicted by a Virginia court for selling lottery tickets, contrary to state law. The lottery had been established by an act of Congress to operate in the District of Columbia. The Cohens argued that state courts had no jurisdiction to review a congressional statute. The Virginia Court of Appeals, the state's highest court, rejected that defense and denied that the Supreme Court had power under the Constitution to review its ruling. Section 25 of the Judiciary Act of 1789 was again at issue.

Mr. Chief Justice MARSHALL delivered the opinion of the Court.

. . .

The counsel who opened the cause said, that the want of jurisdiction was shown by the subject matter of the case. The counsel who followed him said, that jurisdiction was not given by the judiciary act. The Court has bestowed all its attention on the arguments of both gentlemen, and supposes that their tendency is to show that this Court has no jurisdiction of the case, or, in other words, has no right to review the judgment of the State Court, because neither the constitution nor any law of the United States has been violated by that judgment.

The questions presented to the Court by the two first points made at the bar are of great magnitude, and may be truly said vitally to affect the Union. They exclude the inquiry whether the constitution and laws of the United States have been violated by the judgment which the plaintiffs in error seek to review; and maintain that, admitting such violation, it is not in the power of the government to apply a corrective. They maintain that the nation does not possess a department capable of restraining peaceably, and by authority of law, any attempts which may be made, by a part, against the legitimate powers of the whole; and that the government is reduced to the alternative of submitting to such attempts, or of resisting them by force. They maintain that the constitution of the United States has provided no tribunal for the final construction of itself, or of the laws or treaties of the nation; but that this power may be exercised in the last resort by the Courts of every State in the Union. That the constitution, laws, and treaties, may receive as many constructions as there are States; and that this is not a mischief, or, if a mischief, is irremediable. . . .

1st. The first question to be considered is, whether the jurisdiction of this Court is excluded by the character of the parties, one of them being a State, and the other a citizen of that State?

The second section of the third article of the constitution defines the extent of the judicial power of the United States. Jurisdiction is given to the Courts of the Union in two classes of cases. In the first, their jurisdiction depends on the character of the cause, whoever may be the parties. This class comprehends "all cases in law and equity arising under this constitution, the laws of the United States, and treaties made, or which shall be made, under their authority." This clause extends the jurisdiction of the Court to all the cases described, without making in its terms any exception whatever, and without any regard to the condition of the party. If there be any exception, it is to be implied against the express words of the article.

In the second class, the jurisdiction depends entirely on the character of the parties. In this are comprehended "controversies between two or more States, between a State and citizens of another State," "and between a State and foreign States, citizens or subjects." If these be the parties, it is entirely unimportant what may be the subject of controversy. Be it what it may, these parties have a constitutional right to come into the Courts of the Union.

. . .

When we consider the situation of the government of the Union and of a State, in relation to each other; the nature of our constitution; the subordination of the State governments to that constitution; the great purpose for which jurisdiction over all cases arising under the constitution and laws of the United States, is confided to the judicial department; are we at liberty to insert in this general grant, an exception of those cases in which a State may be a party? Will the spirit of the constitution justify this attempt to control its words? We think it will not. We think a case arising under the constitution or laws of the United States, is cognizable in the Courts of the Union, whoever may be the parties to that case.

Had any doubt existed with respect to the just construction of this part of the section, that doubt would have been removed by the enumeration of those cases to which the jurisdiction of the federal Courts is extended, in consequence of the character of the parties.

. . . It would be hazarding too much to assert, that the judicatures of the States will be exempt from the prejudices by which the legislatures and people are influenced, and will constitute perfectly impartial tribunals. In many States the judges are dependent for office and for salary on the will of the legislature. The constitution of the United States furnishes no security against the universal adoption of this principle. When we observe the importance which that constitution attaches to the independence of judges, we are the less inclined to suppose that it can have intended to leave these constitutional questions to tribunals where this independence may not exist, in all cases where a State shall prosecute an individual who claims the protection of an act of Congress. These prosecutions may take place even without a legislative act. A person making a seizure under an act of Congress, may be indicted as a trespasser, if force has been employed, and of this a jury may judge. How extensive may be the mischief if the first decisions in such cases should be final! . . .

It is most true that this Court will not take jurisdiction if it should not: but it is equally true, that it must take jurisdiction if it should. The judiciary cannot, as the legislature may, avoid a measure because it approaches the confines of the constitution. We cannot pass it by because it is doubtful. With whatever doubts, with whatever difficulties, a case may be attended, we must decide it, if it be brought before us. We have no more right to decline the exercise of jurisdiction which is given, than to usurp that which is not given. The one or the other would be treason to the constitution. Questions may occur which we would gladly avoid; but we cannot avoid them. All we can do is, to exercise our best judgment, and conscientiously to perform our duty. In doing this, on the present occasion, we find this tribunal invested with appellate jurisdiction in *all* cases arising under the constitution and laws of the United States. We find no exception to this grant, and we cannot insert one. . . .

2d. The second objection to the jurisdiction of the Court is, that its appellate power cannot be exercised, in any case, over the judgment of a State Court.

This objection is sustained chiefly by arguments drawn from the supposed total separation of the judiciary of a State from that of the Union, and their entire independence of each other. The argument considers the federal judiciary as completely foreign to that of a State; and as being no more connected with it in any respect whatever, than the Court of a foreign State. . . .

That the United States form, for many, and for most important purposes, a single nation, has not yet been denied. In war, we are one people. In making peace, we are one people. In all commercial regulations, we are one and the same people. In many other respects, the American people are one, and the government which is alone capable of controlling and managing their interests in all these respects, is the government of the Union. It is their government, and in that character they have no other. America has chosen to be, in many respects, and to many purposes, a nation; and for all these purposes, her government is complete; to all these objects, it is competent. The people have declared, that in the exercise of all powers given for these objects, it is supreme. It can, then, in effecting these objects, legitimately control all individuals or governments within the American territory. The constitution and laws of a State, so far as they are repugnant to the constitution and laws of the United States, are absolutely void. These States are constituent parts of the United States. They are members of one great empire—for some purposes sovereign, for some purposes subordinate.

In a government so constituted, is it unreasonable that the judicial power should be competent to give efficacy to the constitutional laws of the legislature? That department can decide on the validity of the constitution or law of a State, if it be repugnant to the constitution or to a law of the United States. Is it unreasonable that it should also be empowered to decide on the judgment of a State tribunal enforcing such unconstitutional law? Is it so very unreasonable as to furnish a justification for controling the words of the constitution?

We think it is not. We think that in a government acknowledgedly supreme, with respect to objects of vital interest to the nation, there is nothing inconsistent with sound reason, nothing incompatible with the nature of government, in making all its departments supreme, so far as respects those objects, and so far as is necessary to their attainment. The exercise of the appellate power over those judgments of the State tribunals which may contravene the constitution or laws of the United States, is, we believe, essential to the attainment of those objects. . . .

3d. We come now to the third objection, which, though differently stated by the counsel, is substantially the same. One gentleman has said that the judiciary act does not give jurisdiction in the case.

The cause was argued in the State Court, on a case agreed by the parties, which states the prosecution under a law for selling lottery tickets, which is set forth, and further states the act of Congress by which the City of Washington was authorized to establish the lottery. It then states that the lottery was regularly established by virtue of the act, and concludes with referring to the Court the questions, whether the act of Congress be valid? whether, on its just construction, it constitutes a bar to the prosecution? and, whether the act of Assembly, on which the prosecution is founded, be not itself invalid? These questions were decided against the operation of the act of Congress, and in favour of the operation of the act of the State.

If the 25th section of the judiciary act be inspected, it will at once be perceived that it comprehends expressly the case under consideration. . . .

After having bestowed upon this question the most deliberate consideration of which we are capable, the Court is unanimously of opinion, that the objections to its jurisdiction are not sustained, and that the motion ought to be overruled.

Motion denied.

[Having ruled against Virginia's motion to dismiss the case for want of jurisdiction, the Court heard arguments on the merits of the Cohens' claim that the congressional sponsorship of the lottery barred a state prosecution for the sale of tickets. The Court affirmed the Virginia conviction by reasoning that the congressional statute was not a piece of national

legislation but rather an exercise of congressional power over the District of Columbia. As local legisla- *tion, the lottery law did not override state penal laws.]*

Jackson's Veto of the Bank Bill

President Andrew Jackson received a bill in 1832 to renew the Bank of the United States. Although the bill had been passed by Congress, and the constitutionality of the Bank had been upheld by the Supreme Court in *McCulloch* v. *Maryland* (1819), Jackson exercised his veto. His veto message of July 10, 1832, explains the independence of the President in determining constitutional questions notwithstanding the judgments reached by the legislative and judicial branches.

To the Senate:

The bill "to modify and continue" the act entitled "An act to incorporate the subscribers to the Bank of the United States" was presented to me on the 4th July instant. Having considered it with that solemn regard to the principles of the Constitution which the day was calculated to inspire, and come to the conclusion that it ought not to become a law, I herewith return it to the Senate, in which it originated, with my objections.

A bank of the United States is in many respects convenient for the Government and useful to the people. Entertaining this opinion, and deeply impressed with the belief that some of the powers and privileges possessed by the existing bank are unauthorized by the Constitution, subversive of the rights of the States, and dangerous to the liberties of the people, I felt it my duty at an early period of my Administration to call the attention of Congress to the practicability of organizing an institution combining all its advantages and obviating these objections. I sincerely regret that in the act before me I can perceive none of those modifications of the bank charter which are necessary, in my opinion, to make it compatible with justice, with sound policy, or with the Constitution of our country.

[Jackson states his objections that various features of the bill grant monopoly and exclusive privileges to *the rich at the expense of the poor. He also regarded the Bank as injurious to the states.]*

It is maintained by the advocates of the bank that its constitutionality in all its features ought to be considered as settled by precedent and by the decision of the Supreme Court. To this conclusion I can not assent. Mere precedent is a dangerous source of authority, and should not be regarded as deciding questions of constitutional power except where the acquiescence of the people and the States can be considered as well settled. So far from this being the case on this subject, an argument against the bank might be based on precedent. One Congress, in 1791, decided in favor of a bank; another, in 1811, decided against it. One Congress, in 1815, decided against a bank; another, in 1816, decided in its favor. Prior to the present Congress, therefore, the precedents drawn from that source were equal. If we resort to the States, the expressions of legislative, judicial, and executive opinions against the bank have been probably to those in its favor as 4 to 1. There is nothing in precedent, therefore, which, if its authority were admitted, ought to weigh in favor of the act before me.

If the opinion of the Supreme Court covered the whole ground of this act, it ought not to control the coordinate authorities of this Government. The Congress, the Executive, and the Court, must each for itself be guided by its own opinion of the Constitution. Each public officer who takes an oath to support the Constitution swears that he

SOURCE: The full veto message appears in 3 Messages and Papers of the Presidents 1139–1143 (Richardson ed.).

will support it as he understands it, and not as it is understood by others. It is as much the duty of the House of Representatives, of the Senate, and of the President to decide upon the constitutionality of any bill or resolution which may be presented to them for passage or approval as it is of the supreme judges when it may be brought before them for judicial decision. The opinion of the judges has no more authority over Congress than the opinion of Congress has over the judges, and on that point the President is independent of both. The authority of the Supreme Court must not, therefore, be permitted to control the Congress or the Executive when acting in their legislative capacities, but to have only such influence as the force of their reasoning may deserve.

But in the case relied upon the Supreme Court have not decided that all the features of this corporation are compatible with the Constitution. It is true that the court have said that the law incorporating the bank is a constitutional exercise of power by Congress; but taking into view the whole opinion of the court and the reasoning by which they have come to that conclusion, I understand them to have decided that inasmuch as a bank is an appropriate means for carrying into effect the enumerated powers of the General Government, therefore the law incorporating it is in accordance with that provision of the Constitution which declares that Congress shall have power "to make all laws which shall be necessary and proper for carrying those powers into execution." Having satisfied themselves that the word *"necessary"* in the Constitution means *"needful,"* *"requisite,"* *"essential,"* *"conducive to,"* and that *"a bank"* is a convenient, a useful, and essential instrument in the prosecution of the Government's "fiscal operations," they conclude that to "use one must be within the discretion of Congress" and that "the act to incorporate the Bank of the United States is a law made in pursuance of the Constitution;" "but," say they, *"where the law is not prohibited and is really calculated to effect any of the objects intrusted to the Government, to undertake here to inquire into the degree of its necessity would be to pass the line which circumscribes the judicial department and to tread on legislative ground."*

The principle here affirmed is that the "degree of its necessity," involving all the details of a banking institution, is a question exclusively for legislative consideration. A bank is constitutional, but it is the province of the Legislature to determine whether this or that particular power, privilege, or exemption is "necessary and proper" to enable the bank to discharge its duties to the Government, and from their decision there is no appeal to the courts of justice. Under the decision of the Supreme Court, therefore, it is the exclusive province of Congress and the President to decide whether the particular features of this act are *necessary* and *proper* in order to enable the bank to perform conveniently and efficiently the public duties assigned to it as a fiscal agent, and therefore constitutional, or *unnecessary* and *improper,* and therefore unconstitutional.

Without commenting on the general principle affirmed by the Supreme Court, let us examine the details of this act in accordance with the rule of legislative action which they have laid down. It will be found that many of the powers and privileges conferred on it can not be supposed necessary for the purpose for which it is proposed to be created, and are not, therefore, means necessary to attain the end in view, and consequently not justified by the Constitution.

[After citing a number of provisions in the bill that appeared to Jackson unnecessary under the constitutional command, he turns to the following points.]

It is maintained by some that the bank is a means of executing the constitutional power "to coin money and regulate the value thereof." Congress have established a mint to coin money and passed laws to regulate the value thereof. The money so coined, with its value so regulated, and such foreign coins as Congress may adopt are the only currency known to the Constitution. But if they have other power to regulate the currency, it was conferred to be exercised by themselves, and not to be transferred to a corporation. If the bank be established for that purpose, with a charter unalterable without its consent, Congress have parted with their power for a term of years, during which the Constitution is a dead letter. It is neither necessary nor proper to transfer its legislative power to such a bank, and therefore unconstitutional.

By its silence, considered in connection with the decision of the Supreme Court in the case of McCulloch against the State of Maryland, this act takes from the States the power to tax a portion of the banking business carried on within their limits, in subversion of one of the strongest barriers which secured them against Federal encroachments.

. . .

Upon the formation of the Constitution the States guarded their taxing power with peculiar jealousy. They surrendered it only as it regards imports and exports. In relation to every other object within their jurisdiction, whether persons, property, business, or professions, it was secured in as ample a manner as it was before possessed. All persons, though United States officers, are liable to a poll tax by the States within which they reside. The lands of the United States are liable to the usual land tax, except in the new States, from whom agreements that they will not tax unsold lands are exacted when they are admitted into the Union. Horses, wagons, any beasts or vehicles, tools, or property belonging to private citizens, though employed in the service of the United States, are subject to State taxation. Every private business, whether carried on by an officer of the General Government or not, whether it be mixed with public concerns or not, even if it be carried on by the Government of the United States itself, separately or in partnership, falls within the scope of the taxing power of the State. Nothing comes more fully within it than banks and the business of banking, by whomsoever instituted and carried on. Over this whole subject-matter it is just as absolute, unlimited, and uncontrollable as if the Constitution had never been adopted, because in the formation of that instrument it was reserved without qualification.

The principle is conceded that the States can not rightfully tax the operations of the General Government. They can not tax the money of the Government deposited in the State banks, nor the agency of those banks in remitting it; but will any man maintain that their mere selection to perform this public service for the General Government would exempt the State banks and their ordinary business from State taxation? Had the United States, instead of establishing a bank at Philadelphia, employed a private banker to keep and transmit their funds, would it have deprived Pennsylvania of the right to tax his bank and his usual banking operations? It will not be pretended. Upon what principle, then, are the banking establishments of the Bank of the United States and their usual banking operations to be exempted from taxation? It is not their public agency or the deposits of the Government which the States claim a right to tax, but their banks and their banking powers, instituted and exercised within State jurisdiction for their private emolument— those powers and privileges for which they pay a bonus, and which the States tax in their own banks. . . .

The Senate Debates Jackson's Veto Message

President Jackson's veto of the U.S. Bank reached the Senate on July 10, 1832. Before sustaining the veto, the Senate engaged in a major debate on the substantive reasons given by Jackson in opposing the Bank. Several Senators also concentrated on the legitimacy of the veto itself. Did the President have the power to veto a proposal that had been previously passed by Congress, signed by a President (Madison), and upheld by the Supreme Court (in *McCulloch* v. *Maryland*)? Senator Daniel Webster argued that Jackson had no such right. Senator Hugh Lawson White strongly defended Jackson's action.

[Senator Webster:] Does the President, then, reject the authority of all precedent, except what is suitable to his own purposes to use? And does he use, without stint or measure, all precedents which may augment his own power, or gratify his wishes? But if the President thinks lightly of the authority of Congress, in construing the constitution, he thinks still more lightly of the authority of the Supreme Court. He asserts a right of individual judgment on constitutional questions, which is totally inconsistent with any proper administration of the Government, or any regular execution of the laws. Social disorder, entire uncertainty in regard to individual rights and individual duties, the cessation of legal authority, confusion, the dissolution of free Government—all these are the inevitable consequences of the principles adopted by the message, whenever they shall be carried to their full extent. Hitherto it has been thought that the final decision of constitutional questions belonged to the supreme judicial tribunal. The very nature of free Government, it has been supposed, enjoins this: and our constitution, moreover, has been understood so to provide, clearly and expressly. It is true that each branch of the Legislature has an undoubted right, in the exercise of its functions, to consider the constitutionality of a law proposed to be passed. This is naturally a part of its duty, and neither branch can be compelled to pass any law, or do any other act, which it deems to be beyond the reach of its constitutional power. The President has the same right when a bill is presented for his approval; for he is, doubtless, bound to consider, in all cases, whether such bill be compatible with the constitution, and whether he can approve it consistently with his oath of office. But when a law has been passed by Congress, and approved by the President, it is now no longer in the power, either of the same President, or his successors, to say whether the law is constitutional or not. He is not at liberty to disregard it: he is not at liberty to feel or to affect "constitutional scruples," and to sit in judgment himself on the validity of a statute of the Government, and to nullify it if he so chooses. After a law has passed through all the requisite forms: after it

SOURCE: *Congressional Debates*, 22nd Cong., 1st Sess. 1231–1244 (1832).

has received the requisite legislative sanction and the Executive approval, the question of its constitutionality then becomes a judicial question, and a judicial question alone. In the courts, that question may be raised, argued, and adjudged; it can be adjudged nowhere else.

The President is as much bound by the law as any private citizen, and can no more contest its validity than any private citizen. He may refuse to obey the law, and so may a private citizen; but both do it at their own peril, and neither of them can settle the question of its validity. The President may say a law is unconstitutional but he is not the judge. Who is to decide that question? The judiciary, alone, possesses this unquestionable and hitherto unquestioned right. The judiciary is the constitutional tribunal of appeal, for the citizens, against both Congress and the Executive, in regard to the constitutionality of laws. It has this jurisdiction expressly conferred upon it; and when it has decided the question, its judgment must, from the very nature of all judgments that are final, and from which there is no appeal, be conclusive. . . .

According to the doctrines put forth by the President, although Congress may have passed a law, and although the Supreme Court may have pronounced it constitutional, yet it is, nevertheless, no law at all, if he, in his good pleasure, sees fit to deny its effect; in other words, to repeal and annul it. Sir, no President, and no public man, ever before advanced such doctrines in the face of the nation. . . .

If these opinions of the President be maintained, there is an end of all law and all judicial authority. Statutes are but recommendations, judgments no more than opinions. Both are equally destitute of binding force. Such a universal power as is now claimed for him, a power of judging over the laws, and over the decisions of the tribunal, is nothing else than pure despotism. If conceded to him, it makes him, at once, what Louis the Fourteenth proclaimed himself to be, when he said, "I am the State."

. . .

[Senator White:] The honorable Senator argues that the constitution has constituted the Supreme Court a tribunal to decide great constitutional

questions, such as this, and that, when they have done so, the question is put at rest, and every other department of the Government must acquiesce. This doctrine I deny. The constitution vests "the judicial power in a Supreme Court, and in such inferior courts as Congress may from time to time ordain and establish." Whenever a suit is commenced and prosecuted in the courts of the United States, of which they have jurisdiction, and such suit is decided by the Supreme Court, as that is the court of the last resort, its decision is final and conclusive between the parties. But as an authority, it does not bind either the Congress or the President of the United States. If either of these co-ordinate departments is afterwards called upon to perform an official act, and conscientiously believe the performance of that act will be a violation of the constitution, they are not bound to perform it, but, on the contrary, are as much at liberty to decline acting, as if no such decision had been made. In examining the extent of their constitutional power, the opinion of so enlightened a tribunal as our Supreme Court has been, and I hope ever will be, will always be entitled to great weight; and, without doubt, either Congress or the President would always be disposed, in a doubtful case, to think its decisions correct; but I hope neither will ever view them as authority binding upon them. They ought to examine the extent of their constitutional powers for themselves; and when they have had access to all sources of information within their reach, and given to every thing its due weight, if they are satisfied the constitution has not given a power to do the act required, I insist they ought to refrain from doing it.

Suppose the House of Representatives to have passed an act on a given subject for a number of successive sessions, and from want of time the Senate had not acted on it, and the constitutionality of such an act to come before the Senate, would any member think those opinions of the House authorities by which he was bound? Certainly not. They would have due weight, and be respectfully considered, but disregarded in the decision made by the Senate, if shown to be incorrect. In principle there can be no difference between such cases and the judicial decisions. Suppose the President to recommend, never so often, the passage of an act which he may think constitutional, would the Senate, the House of Representatives, or the courts, feel themselves bound by his opinions? I think not. Each co-ordinate department, within its appropriate sphere of action, must judge of its own powers, when called upon to do its official duties; and if either blindly follows the others, without forming an opinion for itself, an essential check against the exercise of unconstitutional power is destroyed. A mistake by Congress in passing an act, inconsistent with the constitution, followed by a like mistake by the Supreme Court, in deciding such act to be constitutional, might be attended with the most fatal consequences. Let each department judge for itself, and we are safe. If different interpretations are put upon the constitution by the different departments, the people is the tribunal to settle the dispute. Each of the departments is the agent of the people, doing their business according to the powers conferred; and where there is a disagreement as to the extent of these powers, the people themselves, through the ballot boxes, must settle it. The Senator, if I heard him correctly, has said that the President has asserted that the Supreme Court has no power to decide upon the constitutionality of an act of Congress. The gentleman has not attended to the message with his usual accuracy. No such opinion is advanced, but the contrary, that each department within its appropriate sphere of action has the right to judge for itself, and is not bound by the opinion of both, or either of the others; and this I incline to think is the correct constitutional view of the subject. The honorable Senator thinks the President entirely mistaken when he supposes Congress cannot deprive itself of some of its legislative powers. Let us for a few minutes attend to the view of this part of the subject presented by the message, and then examine its correctness.

The Boundaries of Judicial Review: Interview with Justice Powell

In an extraordinarily candid interview in 1979, Justice Lewis F. Powell discussed with Professor Harry M. Clor some of the considerations that determine the scope of judicial review and the reasons for judicial activism.

CLOR: I would like to begin with a rather broad and somewhat philosophic question. We can get more specific later on as you choose. This is a question about the role of the federal judiciary and particularly the Supreme Court in the American system of constitutional democracy. Do you see the Court as primarily a political institution, sharing responsibility for governing and making of public policy, or do you see it having a rather narrower function, simply to interpret the Constitution and the law?

POWELL: The judicial branch of government in the United States, of course, is a political branch in the broad sense. In view of the special role it has in our system, the Supreme Court is more than just an ordinary court. It is empowered to decide whether the other two branches of government live within the Constitution. You perhaps would know more accurately than I, but I do not think there is any other country in the world in which the judiciary has the power to invalidate decisions made by the legislative bodies of the country, both federal and state, and by the executive branch also. That's a rather awesome power and it's one that makes our system and our Court distinctive. A good many of the questions that involve constitutionality of statutes, and executive branch conduct, fairly can be viewed as political in the broadest sense. I suppose one could say our function, in that sense and to that degree, is politically oriented, yet basically we think of ourselves as judges guided by the Constitution as the law of the land.

CLOR: It is sometimes said that a certain judge or justice is a judicial statesman, or has acted in a

statesmanlike way, which seems to suggest that something more is involved than just reading or interpreting the text of the Constitution or a law. Do you think there is such a thing as judicial statesmanship?

POWELL: Possibly, though in a limited sense. The Constitution was framed in rather sweeping language, some of which is susceptible to interpretations that not only *may* change but *have* changed over the decades. The clauses that people think about more frequently in this connection are the due process and equal protection clauses, the commerce clause and a number of other quite general phrases. The Court has to give meaning to those provisions of the Constitution, particularly the Bill of Rights, and as history demonstrates the views taken by the Court in one era do not necessarily survive a different era. That has happened with a good deal of frequency. The Constitution has been described, properly I think, as a sort of living political organism. The Court has helped, by its decisions, to keep the Constitution abreast of the vast changes that occur in the life of our nation.

CLOR: Do you think that judicial statesmanship, to the extent that there is such a thing, consists primarily of insight into the needs or demands of the times or into the changing conditions to which Constitutional clauses are to be applied?

POWELL: I'd rather not phrase it quite that way. It's well to bear in mind that the Court is composed of judges who are elected for life. We, therefore, are not directly responsible to the people in any political sense. This is both an asset and perhaps a liability. It could mean that the Court could move too far away from our democratic system. I don't think the Court has done that.

SOURCE: *Kenyon College Alumni Bulletin*, issue of Summer 1979.

Perhaps on very rare occasions. Yet, our independence does give the Court a freedom to make decisions that perhaps are necessary for our society, decisions that the legislative branch may be reluctant to make. The classic case that comes to mind is *Brown* v. *Board of Education*. The Congress had adequate authority under the Constitution to enact the sort of legislation that has been adopted since *Brown*. But it was the Supreme Court that finally decided in 1954 that segregation in our society must come to an end. It also was the Supreme Court that made the difficult decision, one the Congress apparently did not want to make, to lower the voting age to 18. There was nothing in the Constitution that could have suggested that result. In the simplest of terms, the Court decided that when young people were being drafted and asked to go to war and risk their lives at age 18, the time had come to extend to them the right to participate as citizens in the decisions that affected them so seriously.

CLOR: One thing that fascinates me about the desegregation decision of *Brown* v. *Board of Education* is that the Court interpreted the equal protection clause quite differently from the earlier interpretation in 1896 of *Plessy* v. *Ferguson*. The Court virtually reversed its interpretation of the equal protection clause. How do you do that, Mr. Justice Powell?

POWELL: The Court has felt far freer to reverse Constitutional decisions than it has to reverse the interpretation of statutes. The Court's peculiar responsibility is to decide what the Constitution means. This country had moved a long ways by 1954 from the public mores and public perceptions that existed at the time of *Plessy* v. *Ferguson*. If you read the history of the post-Civil War, civil rights legislation, legislation that enacted Section 1983 of the statute which now produces a vast amount of litigation, I think you would have a hard time justifying the decision of our Court in 1954. One would have to strain to find an intention on the part of the Congress in 1866, and again in 1870 and 1871, to provide that there should be integration in education. Of course, there weren't very many public schools, but if the Court had gone strictly by what the Congress had intended, or probably intended, it would have reaffirmed *Plessy* v. *Ferguson*.

CLOR: I believe such schools that they had were segregated in most of the states that ratified the Fourteenth Amendment.

POWELL: I think that is correct. And it's hard now, particularly for young people, to think in terms of the society in which you and I grew up. In my state of Virginia, which is an enlightened part of the South, people took segregation for granted. There was no protest of any consequence either by our Negro citizens, or by the segments of the white society deemed to be liberal. It was a way of life, but had to come to an end; it should have come to an end earlier. The point I am making is that the Supreme Court perceived that vast changes had occurred not only in the United States but worldwide. It was long overdue to bring our Negro citizens into full citizenship.

CLOR: Does that mean the Court was remaking the Constitution, reading into the equal protection clause a meaning that it did not originally have?

POWELL: The Court cannot rely solely on what the founding fathers intended, or even on congressional intent when the Fourteenth Amendment was adopted. Conditions change as our country matures. Take the commerce clause for example. That clause envisioned the need to prevent tariff barriers between the new states. In other words, it was a provision intended primarily to ensure free trade. But over the years the commerce clause has been construed broadly. There are decisions that hold that the people who wash the windows of the great office building in a city are engaged in commerce because the offices are occupied by business executives whose businesses are engaged in interstate commerce. This could not have been envisioned by the founding fathers. These general clauses that were very wisely adopted, are flexible enough to accommodate significant changes in our society. . . .

POWELL: . . . Our duty is to decide whether legislation can be squared with the Constitution, whether we approve of the legislation or not. In this connection, the public often thinks we approve of action that the Constitution—in our judgment—permits. For example, we still receive mail criticizing the Court's 1973 decision sustaining the right of a woman, with the approval of her doctor, to have an abortion during the first trimester. Contrary to public opinion, the Court expressed no view as to the wisdom or morality of abortions. We simply made a constitutional judgment.

CLOR: Well, the Court decided that there is a privacy right to choose an abortion free from the coercive intervention of the state. When the Court makes such decisions do they have in mind some general conception of democratic principle or liberty or human dignity, or do they tend to avoid such broad and theoretical conceptions?

POWELL: We certainly have perceptions of liberty and human dignity very much in mind. It is difficult to think of a decision that's more personal or more important to a pregnant woman than whether or not she will bear a child. The Fifth and Fourteenth Amendments provide that neither the state nor federal government may deprive a person of life, liberty or property without due process of law. There's nothing in the Constitution about privacy, but the concept of liberty was the underlying principle of the abortion case—the liberty to make certain highly personal decisions that are terribly important to people.

CLOR: But there seems to have been a conception in the Court majority that certain things, at least in a liberal democracy such as ours, are private matters, including the choice to bear or not bear a child.

POWELL: Yes. Another example is the decision whether to use contraceptives. This involves a personal and private relationship that should be free from state regulation.

CLOR: How do you respond to charges sometimes made, even frequently made, that federal courts engage in judicial imperialism or excessive judicial activism reaching out beyond anything mandated by the language of the Constitution, results in political decisions or making public policy that really should be left to legislatures?

POWELL: Well such charges do not surprise me because the United States Supreme Court does exercise power considerably beyond that of an ordinary court. Indeed, as I have said, under our Constitution as interpreted in *Marbury* v. *Madison*, the Court has authority to invalidate action deemed to be contrary to the Constitution. Also, as we have discussed earlier, the broad clauses in the Constitution often do not afford specific guid-

ance. Thus, we exercise a judicial judgment that often is criticized as either being judicial activism or as not being bold enough. The Court also undoubtedly has made decisions that should have been considered and acted upon by the legislative branch. Examples include *Brown* v. *Board of Education* and *Baker* v. *Carr* (one man one vote). We do feel, however, a special responsibility to protect the liberties guaranteed by the Bill of Rights. Thus, a fairly high percentage of the cases that we take for review involve claims by citizens —often quite humble citizens—that government has infringed upon their rights under the Constitution. The provisions of the Constitution that come before us most frequently include the First, Fourth, Fifth, Sixth and Eighth Amendments. We do not view our decisions as political except in the broadest sense, and we certainly do not view ourselves as politicians. We have life tenure, and each Justice feels a deep responsibility to preserve the Constitution but also to do this in a manner compatible with the late 20th century rather than the late 18th century.

CLOR: Do you see the Court as performing a somewhat aristocratic function in American democracy when it does that—a non-elected body saying, "no," to majorities in the legislature?

POWELL: One can certainly say that, and other countries in the world might make that judgment. All I would say is that the founding fathers made a different judgment nearly 200 years ago and the people have supported it so far. As a matter of fact—and I don't assert this myself, but you've seen it in print—a good many people think the legislative branch bucks tough decisions to the judicial branch by drawing statutes in quite general and vague terms. Thus, a role sometimes viewed as legislative—I would not say "aristocratic"—is thrust upon us.

CLOR: The Congress hands the tough problem to the Court?

POWELL: It has been said a number of times that Congress does that, and perhaps if I were there I'd think it was a good idea on some issues. In this way members of Congress do not have to go on record on a tough issue.

CLOR: So, we haven't a pure democracy, and don't particularly want one; we seem to want a kind of a mixed system.

POWELL: We do have a pure democracy so far as voting is concerned. I think that's fair to say. And there is an egalitarian spirit, perhaps a general acceptance of democracy in its broadest sweep, but also with an acceptance of the important role of the judiciary . . .

The Doctrine of Original Intent:
Attorney General Meese Versus Justice Brennan

Reliance on the "framers' intent" to interpret the Constitution has been debated almost continuously. A particularly interesting exchange of views occurred in 1985. Attorney General Edwin Meese III, in a speech to the American Bar Association on July 9, 1985, advocated a "Jurisprudence of Original Intention." He insisted that the only legitimate method of constitutional interpretation consists of resurrecting the original meaning of constitutional provisions. In a speech delivered at Georgetown University on October 12, 1985, Justice William J. Brennan, Jr., rejected primary dependence on original intent. The task of judges, he said, was to adapt the Constitution to current problems and current needs.

Attorney General Meese:

. . .

The intended role of the judiciary generally, and the Supreme Court in particular, was to serve as the "bulwark of a limited constitution." The Founders believed that judges would not fail to regard the Constitution as fundamental law and would regulate their decisions by it. As the "faithful guardians of the Constitution," the judges were expected to resist any political effort to depart from the literal provisions of the Constitution. The standard of interpretation applied by the judiciary must focus on the text and the drafter's original intent.

You will recall that Alexander Hamilton, defending the federal courts to be created by the new Constitution, remarked that the want of a judicial power under the Articles of Confederation had been the crowning defect of that first effort at a national constitution. Ever the consummate lawyer, Hamilton pointed out that "laws are a dead letter without courts to expound and define their true meaning and operation."

The anti-Federalist, Brutus, took Hamilton to task in the New York press for what the critics of the Constitution considered his naivete. This prompted Hamilton to write his classic defense of judicial power in *The Federalist*, No. 78.

An independent judiciary under the Constitution, Hamilton said, would prove to be the "citadel of public justice and the public security." Courts were peculiarly essential in a limited Constitution. Without the courts, there would be no security against "the encroachments and oppressions of the representative body," and no protection against unjust and partial laws.

Hamilton, like his colleague James Madison, knew that *all* political power is of an encroaching nature. In order to keep the powers created by the Constitution within the boundaries marked out by the Constitution, an independent—but constitutionally bound—judiciary was essential. The purpose of the Constitution was the creation of limited but energetic government with structures to keep the power in check. As Madison stated, the Constitution enabled the government to control the governed, but also obliged it "to control itself."

But even beyond the institutional role, the Court serves the American republic in yet another, more subtle way. The problem of any popular government, of course, is assuring that the people obey the laws. There are but two ways: either by physical or by moral force. In many ways the

SOURCE: *South Texas Law Review*, Vol. 27, pp. 433–466 (1986). Footnotes omitted.

Court remains the primary moral force in American politics.

The great French observer Tocqueville was correct when he said:

"The great end of justice is to substitute the notion of right for that of violence; and to place a legal barrier between the power of the Government and the use of its physical force. . . . The moral force which courts of justice possess renders the introduction of physical force exceedingly rare . . . if [physical force] proves to be indispensable, its power is doubled by the association of the idea of law."

By fulfilling its proper function, the Supreme Court contributes not only to institutional checks and balances, but also to the moral undergirding of the entire constitutional edifice. The Supreme Court is the only national institution that daily grapples with the most fundamental political questions—and defends them with written expositions. Nothing less than proper functioning of the Court would serve to perpetuate the sanctity of the rule of law so effectively.

But that is not to suggest that the Justices are a body of platonic guardians. Far from it. The Court is what it was understood to be when the Constitution was framed—a political body. The judicial process is, at its most fundamental level, a *political* process. While not a partisan political process, it is political in the truest sense of that word. It is a process wherein public deliberations occur over what constitutes the common good under the terms of a written constitution.

As Benjamin Cardozo pointed out, "[t]he great tides and currents which engulf the rest of men do not turn aside in their course and pass the judges by." Granting that this is true, Tocqueville knew what was required. He wrote:

"The Federal judges must not only be good citizens, and men possessed of that information . . . which [is] indispensable to magistrates, but they must be statesmen—politicians, not unread in the signs of the times, not afraid to brave the obstacles which can be subdued, nor slow to turn aside such encroaching elements as may threaten the supremacy of the Union and the obedience which is due to the laws."

[At this point in his address, Attorney General Meese reviews three areas of constitutional law—federalism, criminal law, and freedom of religion—in which he claimed that recent decisions of the Supreme Court failed to adhere to original intent.]

In considering these areas of adjudication—Federalism, criminal law, and religion—one may conclude that far too many of the Court's opinions were, on the whole, mere policy choices rather than articulations of constitutional principle. The voting blocs and the arguments all reveal a greater allegiance to what the Court thinks constitutes sound public policy rather than a deference to what the Constitution, its text and intention, may demand.

One may also say that until there emerges a coherent jurisprudential stance, the work of the Court will continue in this ad hoc fashion. But that is not to argue for just *any* jurisprudence. In my opinion, a drift back toward the radical egalitarianism and expansive civil libertarianism of the Warren Court would once again be a threat to the notion of a limited but energetic government.

What, then, should a constitutional jurisprudence actually be? It should be a *jurisprudence of original intention.* By seeking to judge policies in light of principles, rather than remold principles in light of policies, the Court could avoid both the charge of incoherence *and* the charge of being either too conservative or too liberal.

A jurisprudence seriously aimed at the explication of original intention would produce defensible principles of government that would not be tainted by ideological predilection.

This belief in a *jurisprudence of original intention* also reflects a deeply rooted commitment to the idea of democracy. The Constitution represents the consent of the governed to the structures and powers of the government. The Constitution is the fundamental will of the people; that is the reason the Constitution is the fundamental law. To allow the courts to govern simply by what it views at the time as fair and decent, is a scheme of government no longer popular; the idea of democracy has suffered. The permanence of the Constitution has been weakened. A constitution that is viewed as only what the judges say it is, is no longer a constitution in the true sense of the term.

Those who framed the Constitution chose their words carefully; they debated at great length the most minute points. The language they chose meant something. It is incumbent upon the Court to determine what that meaning was. This is not a shockingly new theory; nor is it arcane or archaic.

Joseph Story, a lawyer's everyman—lawyer, justice, and teacher of law—had a theory of judging that merits reconsideration. Though speaking specifically of the Constitution, his logic reaches to statutory construction as well.

"In construing the Constitution of the United States, we are, in the first instance, to consider, what are its nature and objects, its scope and design, as apparent from the structure of the instrument, viewed as a whole, and also viewed in its component parts. Where its words are plain, clear, and determinate, they require no interpretation. . . . Where the words admit of two senses, each of which is conformable to common usage, that sense is to be adopted, which, without departing from the literal import of the words, best harmonizes with the nature and objects, the scope and design of the instrument."

A *jurisprudence of original intention* would take seriously the admonition of Justice Story's friend and colleague, John Marshall, in *Marbury* v. *Madison*, that the Constitution is a limitation on judicial power as well as executive and legislative. That is what Chief Justice Marshall meant in *McCulloch* v. *Maryland* when he cautioned judges never to forget that it is a Constitution they are expounding.

It has been and will continue to be the policy of this administration to press for a *jurisprudence of original intention*. In the cases we file and those we join as amicus, we will endeavor to resurrect the original meaning of constitutional provisions and statutes as the only reliable guide for judgment.

Within this context, let me reaffirm our commitment to pursuing the policies most necessary to public justice. We will continue our vigorous enforcement of civil rights laws; we will not rest until unlawful discrimination ceases. We will continue our all-out war on drugs—both supply and demand, both national and international in scope. We intend to bolster public safety by a persistent war on crime. We will endeavor to stem the growing tide of pornography and its attendant costs: sexual and child abuse. We will battle the heretofore largely ignored legal cancer of white collar crime and its cousin, defense procurement fraud. And finally, as we still reel as a people, I pledge to you our commitment to fight terrorism here and abroad. As long as the innocent are fair prey for the barbarians of this world, civilization is not safe.

We will pursue our agenda within the context of our written Constitution of limited yet energetic powers. Our guide in every case will be the sanctity of the rule of law and the proper limits of governmental power.

Our belief is that only the sense in which the Constitution was accepted and ratified by the nation, and only the sense in which laws were drafted and passed provide a solid foundation for adjudication. Any other standard suffers the defect of pouring new meaning into old words, thus creating new powers and new rights totally at odds with the logic of our Constitution and its commitment to the rule of law.

Justice Brennan:

The amended Constitution of the United States entrenches the Bill of Rights and the Civil War amendments and draws sustenance from the bedrock principles of another great text, the Magna Carta. So fashioned, the Constitution embodies the aspiration to social justice, brotherhood, and human dignity that brought this nation into being. The Declaration of Independence, the Constitution, and the Bill of Rights solemnly committed the United States to be a country where the dignity and rights of all persons were equal before all authority. In all candor we must concede that part of this egalitarianism in America has been more pretension than realized fact. But we are an aspiring people, a people with faith in progress. Our amended Constitution is the lodestar for our aspirations. Like every text worth reading, it is not crystalline. The phrasing is broad and the limitations of its provisions are not clearly marked. Its majestic generalities and ennobling pronouncements are both luminous and obscure. This ambiguity, of course, calls forth interpretation, the interaction of reader and text. The encounter with the constitutional text has been, in many senses, my life's work. What is it we do when we interpret the Constitution? I will attempt to elucidate my approach to the text as well as my substantive interpretation.

My encounters with the constitutional text are not purely or even primarily introspective; the Constitution cannot be for me simply a contemplative haven for private moral reflection. My relation to this great text is inescapably public. That is not to say that my reading of the text is not a personal reading, only that the personal reading perforce occurs in a public context and is open to critical scrutiny from all quarters.

The Constitution is fundamentally a public text—the monumental charter of a government and a people—and a Justice of the Supreme Court must apply it to resolve public controversies. From our beginnings, a most important consequence of the constitutionally created separation of powers has been the American habit, extraordinary to other democracies, of casting social, economic, philosophical, and political questions in the form of lawsuits in an attempt to secure ultimate resolution by the Supreme Court. In this way, important aspects of the most fundamental issues confronting our democracy may finally arrive in the Supreme Court for judicial determination. Not infrequently, these are the issues upon which contemporary society is most deeply divided. They arouse our deepest emotions. The main burden of my twenty-nine Terms on the Supreme Court has thus been to wrestle with the Constitution in this heightened public context, to draw meaning from the text in order to resolve public controversies.

Two other aspects of my relation to this text warrant mention. First, constitutional interpretation for a federal judge is, for the most part, obligatory. When litigants approach the bar of court to adjudicate a constitutional dispute, they may justifiably demand an answer. Judges cannot avoid a definitive interpretation because they feel unable to, or would prefer not to, penetrate to the full meaning of the Constitution's provisions. Unlike literary critics, judges cannot merely savor the tensions or revel in the ambiguities inherent in the text—judges must resolve them.

Second, consequences flow from a Justice's interpretation in a direct and immediate way. A judicial decision respecting the incompatibility of Jim Crow with a constitutional guarantee of equality is not simply a contemplative exercise in defining the shape of a just society. It is an order—supported by the full coercive power of the State—that the present society change in a fundamental aspect. Under such circumstances, the process of deciding can be a lonely, troubling experience for fallible human beings conscious that their best may not be adequate to the challenge. We Justices are certainly aware that "[w]e are not final because we are infallible, but we are infallible only because we are final." One does not forget how much may depend on the decision. More than the litigants may be affected. Decisions may direct the course of vital social, economic, and political currents.

These three defining characteristics of my relation to the constitutional text—its public nature, obligatory character, and consequentialist aspect—cannot help but influence the way I read that text. When Justices interpret the Constitution, they speak for their community, not for themselves alone. The act of interpretation must be undertaken with full consciousness that it is, in a very real sense, the community's interpretation that is sought. Justices are not platonic guardians appointed to wield authority according to their personal moral predilections. Precisely because coercive force must attend any judicial decision to countermand the will of a contemporary majority, the Justices must render constitutional interpretations that are received as legitimate. The source of legitimacy is, of course, a wellspring of controversy in legal and political circles. At the core of the debate is what the late Yale Law School professor, Alexander Bickel, labeled "the counter-majoritarian difficulty." Our commitment to self-governance in a representative democracy must be reconciled with vesting in electorally unaccountable Justices the power to invalidate the expressed desires of representative bodies on the ground of inconsistency with higher law. Because judicial power resides in the authority to give meaning to the Constitution, the debate is really a debate about how to read the text, about constraints on what is legitimate interpretation.

There are those who find legitimacy in fidelity to what they call "the intentions of the Framers." In its most doctrinaire incarnation, this view demands that Justices discern exactly what the Framers thought about the question under consideration and simply follow that intention in resolving the case before them. It is a view that feigns self-effacing deference to the specific judgments of those who forged our original social compact. But in truth it is little more than arrogance cloaked as humility. It is arrogant to pretend that from our vantage we can gauge accurately the intent of the Framers on application of principle to specific, contemporary questions. All too often, sources of potential enlightenment such as records of the ratification debates provide sparse or ambiguous evidence of the original intention. Typically, all that can be gleaned is that the Framers themselves did not agree about the application or meaning of particular constitutional provisions and hid their differences in cloaks of generality. Indeed, it is far from clear whose intention is relevant—that of the drafters, the congressional disputants, or the ratifiers in the states—or even whether the idea of an original intention is a coherent way of thinking about a jointly drafted document drawing its authority from a general assent of the states. Apart from the problematic nature of the sources, our distance of two centuries cannot but work as a prism refracting all we perceive. One cannot help but speculate that the chorus of lamentations calling for interpretation faithful to "original intention"—and proposing nullification of interpretations that fail this quick litmus test—must inevitably come from persons who have no familiarity with the historical record.

Perhaps most importantly, while proponents of this facile historicism justify it as a depoliticization of the judiciary, the political underpinnings of such a choice should not escape notice. A position that upholds constitutional claims only if they were within the specific contemplation of the Framers in effect establishes a presumption of resolving textual ambiguities against the claim of constitutional right. It is far from clear what justifies such a presumption against claims of right. Nothing intrinsic in the nature of interpretation—if there is such a thing as the "nature" of interpretation—commands such a passive approach to ambiguity. This is a choice no less political than any other; it expresses antipathy to claims of the minority to rights against the majority. Those who would restrict claims of right to the values of 1789 specifically articulated in the Constitution turn a blind eye to social progress and eschew adaption of overarching principles to changes of social circumstance.

Another, perhaps more sophisticated response to the potential power of judicial interpretation stresses democratic theory: because ours is a government of the people's elected representatives, substantive value choices should by and large be left to them. This view emphasizes not the transcendent historical authority of the Framers but the predominant contemporary authority of the elected branches of government. Yet it has similar consequences for the nature of proper judicial interpretation. Faith in the majoritarian process counsels restraint. Even under more expansive formulations of this approach, judicial review is appropriate only to the extent of ensuring that our democratic process functions smoothly. Thus, for example, we would protect freedom of speech merely to ensure that the people are heard by their representatives, rather than as a separate, substantive value. When, by contrast, society tosses up to the Supreme Court a dispute that would require invalidation of a legislature's substantive policy choice, the Court generally would stay its hand because the Constitution was meant as a plan of government and not as an embodiment of fundamental substantive values.

The view that all matters of substantive policy should be resolved through the majoritarian process has appeal under some circumstances, but I think it ultimately will not do. Unabashed enshrinement of majoritarianism would permit the imposition of a social caste system or wholesale confiscation of property so long as approved by a majority of the fairly elected, authorized legislative body. Our Constitution could not abide such a situation. It is the very purpose of our Constitution —and particularly of the Bill of Rights—to declare certain values transcendent, beyond the reach of temporary political majorities. The majoritarian process cannot be expected to rectify claims of minority right that arise as a response to the outcomes of that very majoritarian process.

. . .

To remain faithful to the content of the Constitution, therefore, an approach to interpreting the text must account for the existence of these substantive value choices and must accept the ambiguity inherent in the effort to apply them to modern circumstances. The Framers discerned fundamental principles through struggles against particular malefactions of the Crown; the struggle shapes the particular contours of the articulated principles. But our acceptance of the fundamental principles has not and should not bind us to those precise, at times anachronistic, contours. Successive generations of Americans have continued to respect these fundamental choices and adopt them as their own guide to evaluating quite different historical practices. Each generation has the choice to overrule or add to the fundamental principles enunciated by the Framers; the Constitution can be amended or it can be ignored. Yet with respect to its fundamental principles, the text has suffered neither fate. Thus, if I may borrow the words of an esteemed predecessor, Justice Robert Jackson, the burden of judicial interpretation

is to translate "the majestic generalities of the Bill of Rights, conceived as part of the pattern of liberal government in the eighteenth century, into concrete restraints on officials dealing with the problems of the twentieth century. . . ."

Current Justices read the Constitution in the only way that we can: as twentieth-century Americans. We look to the history of the time of framing and to the intervening history of interpretation. But the ultimate question must be: What do the words of the text mean in our time? For the genius of the Constitution rests not in any static meaning it might have had in a world that is dead and gone, but in the adaptability of its great principles to cope with current problems and current needs. What the constitutional fundamentals meant to the wisdom of other times cannot be the measure to the vision of our time. Similarly, what those fundamentals mean for us, our descendants will learn, cannot be the measure to the vision of their time. . . .

The Natural Law Debate: Frankfurter Against Black

In *Rochin* v. *California*, **342 U.S. 165 (1952), Justice Frankfurter overturned the actions of law enforcement officers who took a narcotics suspect to the hospital where an emetic was forced into his stomach against his will. He vomited two capsules containing morphine, and they were later admitted in evidence that led to his conviction. Frankfurter relied on the Due Process Clause of the Fourteenth Amendment to reverse the conviction. In a concurrence, Justice Black criticized Frankfurter for invoking natural law. Later, in *Griswold* v. *Connecticut*, 381 U.S. 479 (1965), in a case that struck down a state law banning contraceptives, Black's dissent summed up his views on the natural law approach. Footnotes omitted.**

MR. JUSTICE FRANKFURTER delivered the opinion of the Court.

. . . Regard for the requirements of the Due Process Clause "inescapably imposes upon this Court an exercise of judgment upon the whole course of the proceedings [resulting in a conviction] in order to ascertain whether they offend those canons of decency and fairness which express the notions of justice of English-speaking peoples even toward those charged with the most heinous offenses." *Malinski* v. *New York, supra,* at

416–417. These standards of justice are not authoritatively formulated anywhere as though they were specifics. Due process of law is a summarized constitutional guarantee of respect for those personal immunities which, as Mr. Justice Cardozo twice wrote for the Court, are "so rooted in the traditions and conscience of our people as to be ranked as fundamental" . . . or are "implicit in the concept of ordered liberty." . . .

The Court's function in the observance of this settled conception of the Due Process Clause does not leave us without adequate guides in subjecting State criminal procedures to constitutional judgment. In dealing not with the machinery of government but with human rights, the absence of formal exactitude, or want of fixity of meaning, is not an unusual or even regrettable attribute of constitutional provisions. . . .

The vague contours of the Due Process Clause do not leave judges at large. We may not draw on our merely personal and private notions and disregard the limits that bind judges in their judicial function. Even though the concept of due process of law is not final and fixed, these limits are derived from considerations that are fused in the whole nature of our judicial process. . . . These are considerations deeply rooted in reason and in the compelling traditions of the legal profession. The Due Process Clause places upon this Court the duty of exercising a judgment, within the narrow confines of judicial power in reviewing State convictions, upon interests of society pushing in opposite directions.

Due process of law thus conceived is not to be derided as resort to a revival of "natural law." To believe that this judicial exercise of judgment could be avoided by freezing "due process of law" at some fixed stage of time or thought is to suggest that the most important aspect of constitutional adjudication is a function for inanimate machines and not for judges, for whom the independence safeguarded by Article III of the Constitution was designed and who are presumably guided by established standards of judicial behavior. Even cybernetics has not yet made that haughty claim. To practice the requisite detachment and to achieve sufficient objectivity no doubt demands of judges the habit of self-discipline and self-criticism, incertitude that one's own views are incontestable and alert tolerance toward views not shared. But these are precisely the presuppositions of our judicial process. They are precisely the qualities society has a right to expect from those entrusted with ultimate judicial power.

Restraints on our jurisdiction are self-imposed only in the sense that there is from our decisions no immediate appeal short of impeachment or constitutional amendment. But that does not make due process of law a matter of judicial caprice. The faculties of the Due Process Clause may be indefinite and vague, but the mode of their ascertainment is not self-willed. In each case "due process of law" requires an evaluation based on a disinterested inquiry pursued in the spirit of science, on a balanced order of facts exactly and fairly stated, on the detached consideration of conflicting claims, see *Hudson County Water Co.* v. *McCarter*, 209 U.S. 349, 355, on a judgment not *ad hoc* and episodic but duly mindful of reconciling the needs both of continuity and of change in a progressive society.

Applying these general considerations to the circumstances of the present case, we are compelled to conclude that the proceedings by which this conviction was obtained do more than offend some fastidious squeamishness or private sentimentalism about combatting crime too energetically. This is conduct that shocks the conscience. Illegally breaking into the privacy of the petitioner, the struggle to open his mouth and remove what was there, the forcible extraction of his stomach's contents—this course of proceeding by agents of government to obtain evidence is bound to offend even hardened sensibilities. They are methods too close to the rack and the screw to permit of constitutional differentiation. . . .

To attempt in this case to distinguish what lawyers call "real evidence" from verbal evidence is to ignore the reasons for excluding coerced confessions. Use of involuntary verbal confessions in State criminal trials is constitutionally obnoxious not only because of their unreliability. They are inadmissible under the Due Process Clause even though statements contained in them may be independently established as true. Coerced confessions offend the community's sense of fair play and decency. So here, to sanction the brutal conduct which naturally enough was condemned by the court whose judgment is before us, would be to afford brutality the cloak of law. Nothing would be more calculated to discredit law and thereby to brutalize the temper of a society.

MR. JUSTICE BLACK, concurring.

. . .

What the majority hold is that the Due Process Clause empowers this Court to nullify any state law if its application "shocks the conscience," offends "a sense of justice" or runs counter to the "decencies of civilized conduct." The majority emphasize that these statements do not refer to their own consciences or to their senses of justice and decency. For we are told that "we may not draw on our merely personal and private notions"; our judgment must be grounded on "considerations deeply rooted in reason and in the compelling traditions of the legal profession." We are further admonished to measure the validity of state practices, not by our reason, or by the traditions of the legal profession, but by "the community's sense of fair play and decency"; by the "traditions and conscience of our people"; or by "those canons of decency and fairness which express the notions of justice of English-speaking peoples." These canons are made necessary, it is said, because of "interests of society pushing in opposite directions."

If the Due Process Clause does vest this Court with such unlimited power to invalidate laws, I am still in doubt as to why we should consider only the notions of English-speaking peoples to determine what are immutable and fundamental principles of justice. Moreover, one may well ask what avenues of investigation are open to discover "canons" of conduct so universally favored that this Court should write them into the Constitution? All we are told is that the discovery must be made by an "evaluation based on a disinterested inquiry pursued in the spirit of science, on a balanced order of facts." . . .

MR. JUSTICE BLACK [*dissenting in* Griswold].

. . .

The due process argument which my Brothers HARLAN and WHITE adopt here is based, as their opinions indicate, on the premise that this Court is vested with power to invalidate all state laws that it considers to be arbitrary, capricious, unreasonable, or oppressive, or on this Court's belief that a particular state law under scrutiny has no "rational or justifying" purpose, or is offensive to a "sense of fairness and justice." If these formulas based on "natural justice," or others which mean the same thing, are to prevail, they require judges to determine what is or is not constitutional on the basis of their own appraisal of what laws are unwise or unnecessary. The power to make such decisions is of course that of a legislative body. Surely it has to be admitted that no provision of the Constitution specifically gives such blanket power to courts to exercise such a supervisory veto over the wisdom and value of legislative policies and to hold unconstitutional those laws which they believe unwise or dangerous.

. . . While I completely subscribe to the holding of *Marbury* v. *Madison*, 1 Cranch 137, and subsequent cases, that our Court has constitutional power to strike down statutes, state or federal, that violate commands of the Federal Constitution, I do not believe that we are granted power by the Due Process Clause or any other constitutional provision or provisions to measure constitutionality by our belief that legislation is arbitrary, capricious or unreasonable, or accomplishes no justifiable purpose, or is offensive to our own notions of "civilized standards of conduct." . . .

My Brother GOLDBERG has adopted the recent discovery that the Ninth Amendment as well as the Due Process Clause can be used by this Court as authority to strike down all state legislation which this Court thinks violates "fundamental principles of liberty and justice," or is contrary to the "traditions and [collective] conscience of our people." He also states, without proof satisfactory to me, that in making decisions on this basis judges will not consider "their personal and private notions." One may ask how they can avoid considering them. Our Court certainly has no machinery with which to take a Gallup Poll. And the scientific miracles of this age have not yet produced a gadget which the Court can use to determine what traditions are rooted in the "[collective] conscience of our people."

. . . And so, I cannot rely on the Due Process Clause or the Ninth Amendment or any mysterious and uncertain natural law concept as a reason for striking down this state law. The Due Process Clause with an "arbitrary and capricious" or "shocking to the conscience" formula was liberally used by this Court to strike down economic legislation in the early decades of this century, threatening, many people thought, the tranquility and stability of the Nation. See, *e.g., Lochner* v. *New York*, 198 U. S. 45. That formula, based on subjective considerations of "natural justice," is no less dangerous when used to enforce this Court's views about personal rights than those about economic rights. I had thought that we had laid that formula, as a means for striking down state legislation, to rest once and for all. . . .

Stare Decisis

In the interest of consistency and predictability, judges prefer to decide cases in accordance with past rulings. This doctrine of stare decisis (stand by the precedents) has particular force when applied to statutory interpretation, but decisions are regularly reviewed and revised to take into account recent developments, new information, and better understanding. In a concurring opinion in *McGrath* v. *Kristensen*, 340 U.S. 162 (1950), Justice Jackson offered a candid, personal, and amusing justification for parting company with opinions that seem, upon reflection, unconvincing.

MR. JUSTICE JACKSON, concurring.

I concur in the judgment and opinion of the Court. But since it is contrary to an opinion which, as Attorney General, I rendered in 1940, I owe some word of explanation. 39 Op. Atty. Gen. 504. I am entitled to say of that opinion what any discriminating reader must think of it—that it was as foggy as the statute the Attorney General was asked to interpret. It left the difficult borderline questions posed by the Secretary of War unanswered, covering its lack of precision with generalities which, however, gave off overtones of assurance that the Act applied to nearly every alien from a neutral country caught in the United States under almost any circumstances which required him to stay overnight.

The opinion did not at all consider aspects of our diplomatic history, which I now think, and should think I would then have thought, ought to be considered in applying any conscription Act to aliens.

In times gone by, many United States citizens by naturalization have returned to visit their native lands. There they frequently were held for military duty by governments which refused to recognize a general right of expatriation. The United States consistently has asserted the right of its citizens to be free from seizure for military duty by reason of temporary and lawful presence in foreign lands. Immunities we have asserted for our own citizens we should not deny to those of other friendly nations. Nor should we construe our legislation to penalize or prejudice such aliens for asserting a right we have consistently asserted as a matter of national policy in dealing with other nations. Of course, if an alien is not a mere sojourner but acquires residence here in any permanent sense, he submits himself to our law and assumes the obligations of a resident toward this country.

The language of the Selective Service Act can be interpreted consistently with this history of our international contentions. I think the decision of the Court today does so. Failure of the Attorney General's opinion to consider the matter in this light is difficult to explain in view of the fact that he personally had urged this history upon this Court in arguing *Perkins* v. *Elg*, 307 U. S. 325. Its details may be found in the briefs and their cited sources. It would be charitable to assume that neither the nominal addressee nor the nominal author of the opinion read it. That, I do not doubt, explains Mr. Stimson's acceptance of an answer so inadequate to his questions. But no such confession and avoidance can excuse the then Attorney General.

Precedent, however, is not lacking for ways by which a judge may recede from a prior opinion that has proven untenable and perhaps misled others. See Chief Justice Taney, *License Cases*, 5 How. 504, recanting views he had pressed upon the Court as Attorney General of Maryland in *Brown* v. *Maryland*, 12 Wheat. 419. Baron

Bramwell extricated himself from a somewhat similar embarrassment by saying, "The matter does not appear to me now as it appears to have appeared to me then." *Andrews* v. *Styrap*, 26 L. T. R. (N. S.) 704, 706. And Mr. Justice Story, accounting for his contradiction of his own former opinion, quite properly put the matter: "My own error, however, can furnish no ground for its being adopted by this Court . . . ." *United States* v. *Gooding*, 12 Wheat. 460, 478. Perhaps Dr. Johnson really went to the heart of the matter when he explained a blunder in his dictionary—"Ignorance, sir, ignorance." But an escape less self-depreciating was taken by Lord Westbury, who, it is said, rebuffed a barrister's reliance upon an earlier opinion of his Lordship: "I can only say that I am amazed that a man of my intelligence should have been guilty of giving such an opinion." If there are other ways of gracefully and good-naturedly surrendering former views to a better considered position, I invoke them all.

3 Threshold Requirements: Husbanding Power and Prestige

The scope of judicial review is circumscribed by rules of self-restraint fashioned by judges. Various court doctrines sketch out the minimum conditions needed to adjudicate a case. These thresholds (or "gatekeeping rules") do more than limit access by litigants. They shield judges from cases that threaten their independence and institutional effectiveness. They ration scarce judicial resources and postpone or avoid decisions on politically sensitive issues.

Chief Justice Marshall suggested that the boundaries for judicial action were quite fixed: "It is most true that this Court will not take jurisdiction if it should not: but it is equally true, that it must take jurisdiction if it should." Cohens v. Virginia, 6 Wheat. 264, 404 (1821). The record of the judiciary, however, is quite different. What the Court should or should not accept is largely a matter of judicial discretion. Reflecting on his work at the Supreme Court, Justice Brandeis confided: "The most important thing we do is not doing." Alexander M. Bickel, The Unpublished Opinions of Mr. Justice Brandeis 17 (1957). The deliberate withholding of judicial power often reflects the fact that courts lack ballot-box legitimacy. Although couched in technical jargon, jurisdictional requirements raise fundamental questions of democratic theory.

Judges invoke access rules to promote the adversary system, preserve public support, avoid conflicts with other branches of government, and provide flexibility of action for the judiciary. The doctrines used to pursue those goals include justiciability, standing, mootness, ripeness, political questions, and prudential considerations, all of which help protect an unelected and unrepresentative judiciary. Although efforts are made to distinguish these doctrines, inevitably they overlap. As noted by the Supreme Court: "The standing question thus bears close affinity to questions of ripeness—whether the harm asserted has matured sufficiently to warrant judicial intervention—and of mootness—whether the occasion for judicial intervention persists." Warth v. Seldin, 422 U.S. 490, 499 n.10 (1975).

CASES AND CONTROVERSIES

Article III of the Constitution limits the jurisdiction of federal courts to "cases" and "controversies." Courts must determine that they have jurisdiction to hear the case. Jurisdiction is granted both by the Constitution and by statute. Even after accepting jurisdiction, courts may decide that the subject matter is inappropriate for judicial consideration—what the courts call "nonjusticiable." This latter concept, at times synonymous with "political questions," is used to avoid collisions with Congress and the President. Baker v. Carr, 369 U.S. 186, 198, 208–234 (1962). It is also applied more broadly to cover issues outside the separation of powers. Flast v. Cohen, 392 U.S. 83, 95 (1968).

As a way to minimize error, miscalculation, and political conflict, courts adopt guidelines to avoid judgment on a large number of constitutional questions. These guidelines only provide very broad direction for judicial activity. If judges want to ignore them, they can. However, the rules supply a convenient list of justifications for refusing to decide a case. ASHWANDER v. TVA, 297 U.S. 288 (1936).

To resolve a legal claim, courts need to know that parties have been adversely affected. Abstract or hypothetical questions, removed from a concrete factual setting, prevent courts from reaching an informed judgment. The words "cases" and "controversies" limit the federal courts "to questions presented in an adversary context and in a form historically viewed as capable of resolution through the judicial process." Flast v. Cohen, 392 U.S. at 95.

Adverseness

The adversary system seeks truth by having judges and juries observe a contest between two sets of professional advocates. It assumes that two antagonistic parties, each with a sufficient stake in the outcome, will marshal the best arguments to defend their interests. This clash between rival parties "sharpens the presentation of issues upon which the court so largely depends for illumination of difficult constitutional questions." Baker v. Carr, 369 at 204. A case brought by two parties with the same interest loses its adversary character. South Spring Gold Co. v. Amador Gold Co., 145 U.S. 300 (1892). Nor is there adverseness when two attorneys bring a collusive or "friendly suit" or when both parties agree on a constitutional issue and want the same result.[1]

Courts occasionally consider a case even when both parties agree on the issue. In *United States* v. *Lovett* (1946), the Justice Department agreed with the plaintiff that a provision in a congressional statute was unconstitutional. To protect its interests, Congress passed legislation to create a special counsel. Functioning officially as amicus curiae, the counsel in effect served as counsel for the United States to assure adverseness. 328 U.S. 303, 304 (1946). In other cases the courts have appointed a special counsel to satisfy the requirement for a genuinely adversary proceeding. Granville-Smith v. Granville-Smith, 349 U.S. 1, 4 (1955).

---

[1] United States v. Johnson, 319 U.S. 302 (1943). See also Lord v. Veazie, 49 U.S. 251 (1850), in which the plaintiff and defendant had the same interest, and Moore v. Board of Education, 402 U.S. 47 (1971). In some cases the Court will allow a president to sue his own company because the board of directors, backed by the stockholders, voted against him to create adverseness. Carter v. Carter Coal Co., 298 U.S. 238, 286–287 (1936).

There appeared to be lack of adverseness in the legislative veto case decided by the Supreme Court in 1983. The plaintiff, Jagdish Rai Chadha, sued the Immigration and Naturalization Service (INS), charging that its statutory procedure for deportation was unconstitutional. The government agreed with him. The Ninth Circuit asked both the House of Representatives and the Senate to file briefs as amici curiae. The House argued that Chadha's claim lacked the necessary adverseness because INS agreed that the statute was invalid, and further argued that its appearance as amicus did not supply the adverseness needed for a case or controversy. The court rejected this reasoning because it would "implicitly approve the untenable result that all agencies could insulate unconstitutional orders and procedures from appellate review simply by agreeing that what they did was unconstitutional." Chadha v. INS, 634 F.2d 408, 420 (9th Cir. 1980).

In affirming the judgment of the Ninth Circuit, the Supreme Court also refused to regard the case as a "friendly, non-adversary, proceeding" between Chadha and the INS. As the Court noted, it would be "a curious result if, in the administration of justice, a person could be denied access to the courts because the Attorney General of the United States agreed with the legal arguments asserted by the individual." From the moment of Congress' formal intervention as amicus, adverseness was "beyond doubt." Even prior to intervention there was "adequate Art. III adverseness." INS v. Chadha, 462 U.S. 919, 939 (1983).

Advisory Opinions

The case or controversy requirement was tested in 1790 when Secretary of the Treasury Alexander Hamilton sought the advice of Chief Justice John Jay. Resolutions adopted by the Virginia House of Representatives had challenged the right of the national government to assume state debts. Hamilton regarded this resistance as "the first symptom of a spirit which must either be killed or it will kill the Constitution of the United States," and urged that the "collective weight" of the three branches be employed to repudiate the resolutions. Jay replied that it was inadvisable to take any action. 1 Charles Warren, Supreme Court in United States History 52–53 (1937). Similar efforts by Secretary of State Jefferson in 1793 to obtain advisory opinions were rebuffed by the Court. The Justices considered it improper to make extrajudicial decisions, especially because the Constitution gave the President the express power to obtain opinions from the heads of the executive departments. Manley O. Hudson, 37 Harv. L. Rev. 970, 976 (1924).

This same period, however, yields contrary evidence. Chief Justice Jay and his colleagues on the Court advised President Washington in 1790 that the statutory requirement for them to "ride circuit" (travel around the country hearing appellate cases) was unconstitutional. Robert A. Dahlquist, 14 Sw. U. L. Rev. 46, 50–54 (1983). And in *Hayburn's Case* (1792), two circuit courts explained to President Washington their constitutional objections to a statute passed by Congress.[2] In both of these disputes, however, the interests of the courts were directly involved: having to ride circuit and to perform nonjudicial duties.

---

[2]U.S. (2 Dall.) at 410–414 nn (1792). The statute was constitutionally objectionable because judicial decisions could be set aside by the Secretary of War, in effect converting a judicial decision into a mere advisory opinion. For similar reasons, the Court has opposed procedures that make its decisions dependent on executive and legislative actions before being carried out; Gordon v. United States, 117 U.S. 697 (1864).

The Supreme Court's formal position on advisory opinions appears in *Muskrat* v. *United States* (1911). Congress had authorized certain Indians to bring suit to determine the constitutionality of a statute. They were given expedited treatment by the Court of Claims and a right of appeal to the Supreme Court. Justice Day reviewed earlier instances in which federal judges decided that Congress could not impose nonjudicial duties on the courts. The suit, even though authorized by Congress, did not create a case or controversy between adverse parties. It was an effort to obtain the Court's opinion on the validity of congressional statutes. Day said it was inappropriate for the judiciary "to give opinions in the nature of advice concerning legislative action, a function never conferred upon it by the Constitution and against the exercise of which this court has steadily set its face from the beginning." 219 U.S. 346, 362 (1911). In 1948, the Court voiced its constitutional objections to a statute that allowed the President to override the judgment of a federal court. The procedure amounted to "an advisory opinion in its most obnoxious form." C. & S. Air Lines v. Waterman Corp., 333 U.S. 103, 113–114 (1948).

Nevertheless, judges find ways to offer advice to the political branches. Many of them have met with Presidents, legislators, and agency administrators to discuss matters that were being, or could be, litigated. Walter Murphy, The Elements of Judicial Strategy 132–155 (1964). As a nonjudicial function, the Judicial Conference performs an advisory role by commenting on pending legislation.

In their off-bench activities, federal judges have not hesitated to comment on the constitutionality of legislative proposals. After the Supreme Court in *INS* v. *Chadha* (1983) struck down the legislative veto, D.C. Circuit Judge Abner J. Mikva told a House committee that he did not think "there is any question" that a joint resolution of approval or disapproval, as a substitute for the discredited one-House and two-House vetoes, "would pass constitutional muster."[3]

Even in the course of writing an opinion, judges often resort to dicta to advise executive and legislative officers. For example, in *Duke Power Co.* v. *Carolina Environmental Study Group* (1978), Chief Justice Burger rejected a number of procedural attempts to postpone adjudication of the Price-Anderson Act. He said that any delay in interpreting the statute would frustrate one of its key purposes: "the elimination of doubts concerning the scope of private liability in the event of major nuclear accident." All parties would be adversely affected, he claimed, by deferring a decision. 438 U.S. 59, 82 (1978). Justice Stevens admitted that the decision would serve the national interest by removing doubts concerning the constitutionality of the Price-Anderson Act, but he did not include among judicial functions the duty to provide advisory opinions on important subjects:

> We are not statesmen; we are judges. When it is necessary to resolve a constitutional issue in the adjudication of an actual case or controversy, it is our duty to do so. But whenever we are persuaded by reasons of expediency to engage in the business of giving legal advice, we chip away a part of the foundation of our independence and our strength. Id. at 103 (concurring opinion).

A year later, Justice Stevens and three colleagues accused the Court of rendering an advisory opinion for the state of Massachusetts. In defense, Justice Powell explained that his decision merely provided "some guidance" to the state legislators.

---

[3]"Legislative Veto After Chadha," hearings before the House Committee on Rules, 98th Cong., 2d Sess. 600 (1984).

This exchange took place in two intriguing footnotes. BELLOTTI v. BAIRD, 443 U.S. 622 (1979).

Declaratory Judgments

Parties uncertain of their legal rights want courts to determine those rights before injury is done. Otherwise, they might have to violate a law to bring a test case or forgo possible rights because of a fear of litigation. By issuing "declaratory judgments," courts can offer preventive relief. Representative Ralph Gilbert explained the advantages of declaratory judgments: "Under the present law [in 1928] you take a step in the dark and then turn on the light to see if you stepped into a hole. Under the declaratory law you turn on the light and then take a step." 69 Cong. Rec. 2030 (1928). Unlike other judgments, declaratory relief decides only legal rights; it does not determine damages or the right to coercive relief. To avoid the ban on advisory opinions, such judgments are limited to actual controversies.

Before 1934, declaratory judgments had been issued by Great Britain, India, Scotland, Canada, Australia, and other nations. More than two dozen American states had adopted the practice. H. Rept. No. 1264, 73d Cong., 2d Sess. 1 (1934). Federal courts had also issued what were in effect declaratory judgments, because they determined rights and duties before a law was violated and even before a law had taken effect. Pierce v. Society of Sisters, 268 U.S. 510, 525 (1925); Village of Euclid v. Ambler Realty Co., 272 U.S. 365 (1926). To remove the legal uncertainty, Congress in 1934 passed the Declaratory Judgments Act. In "cases of actual controversy," it gives federal courts the power to declare "rights and other legal relations of any interested party petitioning for such declaration, whether or not further relief is or could be prayed, and such declaration shall have the force and effect of a final judgment or decree and be reviewable as such." 48 Stat. 955 (1934); 28 U.S.C. § 2201 (1982). In a unanimous decision, the Supreme Court upheld the constitutionality of this statute. Aetna Life Insurance Co. v. Haworth, 300 U.S. 227 (1937).

STANDING TO SUE

To satisfy the requirement of a case or controversy, parties bringing an action must have standing to sue. "Generalizations about standing to sue," Justice Douglas said with customary bluntness, "are largely worthless as such." Data Processing Service v. Camp, 397 U.S. 150, 151 (1970). Judges frequently accuse one another of circular reasoning. After the Supreme Court announced that the requirements of standing are met if a taxpayer has the "requisite personal stake in the outcome" of his suit, Justice Harlan chided the Court: "This does not, of course, resolve the standing problem; it merely restates it." Flast v. Cohen, 392 U.S. at 121 (dissenting opinion).

The reader forewarned, here are some generalizations. To demonstrate standing, parties must show injury to a legally protected interest, an injury that is real rather than abstract or hypothetical. O'Shea v. Littleton, 414 U.S. 488, 494 (1974). Injuries may be economic or noneconomic. Data Processing Service v. Camp, 397 U.S. at 154. They may be actual or threatened.[4] Injuries may afflict organizations as well as

[4]Linda R.S. v. Richard D., 410 U.S. 614, 617 (1973); Gladstone, Realtors v. Village of Bellwood, 441 U.S. 91, 99 (1979); Muller Optical Co. v. EEOC, 574 F.Supp. 946, 950 (W.D. Tenn. 1983).

persons. Havens v. Realty Corp. v. Coleman, 455 U.S. 363, 379 n.19 (1982); Warth v. Seldin, 422 U.S. at 511. A "threatened" injury can be close cousin to the hypothetical. Five members of the Supreme Court in 1973 held that *allegations* of injury were sufficient to establish standing. Proof of actual injury was not necessary.[5] On the other hand, actual injury may be inadequate to establish standing if the Court wishes to defer to the states. City of Los Angeles v. Lyons, 461 U.S. 95 (1983).

Individuals, functioning in the role of private attorneys general, may have standing as "representatives of the public interest." Scenic Hudson Preservation Conf. v. FPC, 354 F.2d 608, 615–616 (2d Cir. 1965). This principle sometimes permits one party to assert the rights of third parties *(jus tertii)*. Federal courts are reluctant to resolve a controversy on the basis of the rights of third persons who are not parties to the litigation. There are two reasons:

> First, the courts should not adjudicate such rights unnecessarily, and it may be that in fact the holders of those rights either do not wish them, or will be able to enjoy them regardless of whether the in-court litigant is successful or not. . . . Second, third parties themselves usually will be the best proponents of their own rights. The courts depend on effective advocacy, and therefore should prefer to construe legal rights only when the most effective advocates of those rights are before them. Singleton v. Wulff, 428 U.S. 106, 113–114 (1976).

When genuine obstacles prevent a third party from appearing in court (such as the need to maintain anonymity to avoid the loss of rights), the courts allow exceptions.[6]

Although standing is basically a judge-made rule, courts recognize that Congress can, by statute, confer standing upon an individual or a group, and courts may defer to Congress on such matters.[7] However, such statutory phrases as "any person aggrieved" or "adversely affected" allow the courts broad discretion in interpreting what Congress means by standing. Furthermore, Congress cannot compel the courts to grant standing for a suit that, in the opinion of judges, lacks the necessary ingredients of a case or controversy. Congressional efforts to confer standing are limited by the judiciary's exclusive responsibility to determine Article III requirements.[8]

Courts raise and lower the standing barrier depending on circumstances. In *Frothingham* v. *Mellon* (1923), an individual taxpayer was denied standing to challenge the constitutionality of a federal statute that provided appropriations to the states for maternal and infant care. The taxpayer claimed that Congress had exceeded its Article I powers and had invaded territory reserved to the states by the Tenth Amendment. The Supreme Court decided that a federal taxpayer's interest in

---

[5]United States v. SCRAP, 412 U.S. 669 (1973). Justice Stewart was satisfied with an "attenuated line of causation" linking litigant to an injury; id. at 688. Justices Blackmun and Brennan accepted allegations of harm as sufficient; id. at 699. Justice Douglas agreed with their position; id. at 703. Justice Marshall agreed with the holding on standing; id. at 724.

[6]NAACP v. Alabama, 357 U.S. 449 (1958). See also Singleton v. Wulff, 428 U.S. at 114–116, and Note, "Standing to Assert Constitutional Jus Tertii," 88 Harv. L. Rev. 423 (1974).

[7]Sierra Club v. Morton, 405 U.S. 727, 732 n.3 (1972); Trafficante v. Metropolitan Life Ins., 409 U.S. 205, 209 (1972); Linda R.S. v. Richard D., 410 U.S. at 617 n.3; Warth v. Seldin, 422 U.S. at 501.

[8]Data Processing Service v. Camp, 397 U.S. at 154; Simon v. Eastern Kentucky Welfare Rights Org., 426 U.S. 26, 41 n.22 (1976). For a strict reading of statutory authorization to bring suit, see Bread PAC v. FEC, 455 U.S. 577 (1982).

financing the program was "comparatively minute and indeterminable," and the effect on future taxation "so remote, fluctuating and uncertain" that there was no possibility of a direct injury to confer standing. 262 U.S. 447, 487 (1923).

The Court's decision appeared to be driven largely by policy rather than by constitutional considerations. Lowering the barrier for standing meant increased casework for the judiciary. Other taxpayers could challenge federal statutes involving the outlay of public funds. Id. Lowering the barrier might bring the administrative process to a standstill, as each disappointed party looked automatically to the courts for relief. The Court insisted that a party must not only show that a statute is invalid but that "he has sustained or is immediately in danger of sustaining some direct injury as the result of its enforcement, and not merely that he suffers in some indefinite way in common with people generally." Id. at 488.

The decision was criticized because it was unclear whether the Court had announced a constitutional bar to taxpayer suits (compelled by Article III limitations on federal court jurisdiction) or whether the Court had temporarily imposed a rule of self-restraint to be lifted in the future. In later years the Supreme Court admitted that *Frothingham* could be read either way. Flast v. Cohen, 392 U.S. at 92–93.

The Justice Department interpreted *Frothingham* as an absolute prohibition on taxpayer suits. The Supreme Court discarded that notion in *Flast* v. *Cohen* (1968), which involved a taxpayer's challenge to the use of public funds for religious education. Such a doctrine would put the government in the position of conceding that a taxpayer lacked standing "even if Congress engaged in such palpably unconstitutional conduct as providing funds for the construction of churches for particular sects." 392 U.S. at 98 n.17. The Court decided to liberalize the rule on standing but only at the cost of creating substantial doctrinal confusion. It claimed that standing focuses on the party, not the issue: "when standing is placed in issue in a case, the question is whether the person whose standing is challenged is a proper party to request an adjudication of a particular issue and not whether the issue is justiciable." Id. at 99–100.

The party/issue dichotomy lost its crispness when the Court explained why Mrs. Flast had standing and Mrs. Frothingham did not. The Court looked to the substantive issues to determine whether a logical "nexus" existed between the status asserted and the claim adjudicated. The Court identified two aspects of nexus: (1) the taxpayer must establish a logical link between his status and the legislative statute attacked, and (2) the taxpayer must connect his status with "the precise nature of the constitutional infringement alleged." Id. at 102. The Court concluded that both Frothingham and Flast satisfied the first but only Flast satisfied the second. Justice Harlan dissented, unable to understand how the Court could classify the Article I/Tenth Amendment position in *Frothingham* as too general, while accepting the First Amendment/Establishment Clause in *Flast* as sufficiently "precise."

The Court decided that it was time to retreat from the absolute barrier of *Frothingham* but could not adequately explain why. The party/issue distinction was unpersuasive. Even the questions of party and injury had become muddled. Did Mrs. Flast have to be a taxpayer to bring suit? Could she have had standing if she lived on interest from tax-exempt bonds and was therefore unable to show injury or a monetary stake? Such fundamental questions were left unanswered.

By lowering the barrier for standing, the Supreme Court not only encouraged more lawsuits but invited collisions with other branches of government. In a later case, Justice Powell warned that a relaxed standing policy would expand judicial power: "It seems to be inescapable that allowing unrestricted taxpayer or citizen standing would significantly alter the allocation of power at the national level, with a shift away from a democratic form of government." United States v. Richardson, 418 U.S. 166, 188 (1974) (concurring opinion).

The Burger Court raised the requirements for standing. In 1972 it denied standing to an environmental group that wanted to prevent construction of a ski resort in a national park. The Court was deeply split, four Justices arrayed against three. Sierra Club v. Morton, 405 U.S. 727 (1972). In that same year it refused to decide whether the Army's surveillance of domestic activities constituted a chilling effect on First Amendment liberties. A majority of five Justices, with four dissenting, held that there was insufficient evidence of a direct injury to present a case for resolution in the courts.[9]

The close link between standing and issue is highlighted by a 1974 decision in which the Supreme Court denied standing to a taxpayer who challenged the constitutionality of covert spending by the Central Intelligence Agency. The Court specifically looked at the issues raised before dismissing the case on standing, even though the constitutional provision (the Statement and Account Clause) is quite as "precise" as the Establishment Clause at stake in *Flast*. More to the point, the Court noted that relief was available through the regular political process. What was dismissed on standing appeared to turn basically on questions of separation of power.[10] In concurring in this 5–4 opinion, Justice Powell urged the Court to abandon *Flast's* two-part "nexus" test as hopeless. He also said that a failure by the judiciary to exercise self-restraint might provoke retaliation by the political branches. UNITED STATES v. RICHARDSON, 418 U.S. 166 (1974).

The connection between standing and sensitive political issues was evident again in 1975 when the Court announced that the inquiry into standing "involves both constitutional limitations on federal-court jurisdiction and prudential limitations on its exercise. . . . In both dimensions it is founded in concern about the proper—and properly limited—role of the courts in a democratic society." Warth v. Seldin, 422 U.S. at 498. Prudential rules of standing are not constitutionally required but they "serve to limit the role of the courts in resolving public disputes." Id. at 500. In a dissenting opinion joined by Justices White and Marshall, Justice Brennan picked additional holes in the Court's doctrine that standing was unrelated to the issue being litigated:

> While the Court gives lip service to the principle, often repeated in recent years, that "standing in no way depends on the merits of the plaintiff's contention that particular conduct is illegal," . . . in fact the opinion, which tosses out of court almost every conceivable kind of plaintiff who could be injured by the activity claimed to be unconstitutional, can be explained only by an indefensible hostility to the claim on the merits.

---

[9]Laird v. Tatum, 408 U.S. 1 (1972). Curiously, a year later the Court gave standing to five law students to bring an environmental suit against the Interstate Commerce Commission; United States v. SCRAP, 412 U.S. 669 (1973). Evidently, standing *does* depend on the issue.

[10]United States v. Richardson, 418 U.S. 166 (1974). See also Schlesinger v. Reservists to Stop the War, 418 U.S. 208 (1974), which denied plaintiffs standing to challenge the constitutionality of members of Congress who served in the military reserves, in apparent conflict with the Ineligibility Clause. For reliance on separation of powers to deny standing, see Allen v. Wright, 468 U.S. 737, 752, 759–761 (1984).

The *Flast* doctrine was further shaken by *Valley Forge College* v. *Americans United* (1982), which denied plaintiffs standing to challenge the transfer of federal property to a Christian college. Justice Rehnquist, writing for the Court, first argued that the plaintiffs could not sue as taxpayers because the land was transferred under the Property Clause, not the Taxing and Spending Clause. He then denied that the Establishment Clause gave citizens a personal constitutional right to bring suit. Four Justices dissented, accusing the majority of using a "threshold question" to decide substantive issues and obfuscate legal rights. VALLEY FORGE COLLEGE v. AMERICANS UNITED, 454 U.S. 464 (1982).

Much of the confusion about the standing doctrine has its source in the Court's habit of spinning awkward theories that are, at bottom, techniques of deferring to the states and to the legislative and executive branches (pp. 124–126).

MOOTNESS

Mootness raises some of the same issues as standing and advisory opinions. Litigants able to establish standing at the outset of a case may find their personal stake diluted or eliminated by subsequent events. Because of a change in law or facts, the case or controversy may disappear and leave insufficient adverseness to guide the courts. If the action that triggered the complaint ceases, a court may have no means of granting relief.[11] At that point a decision could become, in effect, an advisory opinion. When the states failed to ratify the Equal Rights Amendment, pending suits regarding the extension of its deadline from March 22, 1979, to June 30, 1982, were mooted. National Organization for Women v. Idaho, 459 U.S. 809 (1982).

A case is not mooted simply because one party discontinues a contested action. Judicial review cannot be circumvented merely through a strategy of starts and stops. If the controversy is likely to reappear, judicial scrutiny "ought not to be, as they might be, defeated, by short term orders, capable of repetition, yet evading review . . . "[12] Complaints about an election process, even after a particular election is over, may remain a continuing controversy that requires decision by the courts. Moore v. Ogilvie, 394 U.S. 814, 816 (1969).

If the judiciary is unprepared or unwilling to decide an issue, mootness is one avenue of escape. In 1952, the Supreme Court held that a public school Bible-reading case was moot because the child had graduated by the time the case had reached the Supreme Court. Although other students would be subjected to the same school policy in the future, the Court declared that "no decision we could render now would protect any rights she may once have had, and this Court does not sit to decide arguments after events have put them to rest." Doremus v. Board of Education, 342 U.S. 429, 433 (1952).

In a 1974 case, a white student denied admission to a law school claimed that the school's affirmative action policy discriminated against him, allowing minorities with lower test scores to enter. He was admitted after winning in trial court. By the

---

[11]California v. San Pablo and Tulare Railroad Co., 149 U.S. 308 (1893); Jones v. Montague, 194 U.S. 147 (1904); Richardson v. McChesney, 218 U.S. 487 (1910). See also Sidney A. Diamond, "Federal Jurisdiction to Decide Moot Cases," 94 U. Pa. L. Rev. 125 (1946); United States v. Hamburg-American Co., 239 U.S. 466 (1916); United States v. Alaska S.S. Co., 253 U.S. 113 (1920); Brockington v. Rhodes, 396 U.S. 41 (1969); Hall v. Beals, 396 U.S. 45 (1969).

[12]Southern Pacific Terminal Co. v. ICC, 219 U.S. 498, 515 (1911). See United States v. Phosphate Export Corp., 393 U.S. 199, 203 (1968) and United States v. W. T. Grant Co., 345 U.S. 629, 632 (1953).

time the case reached the Supreme Court he was in his third and final year. The school assured the Court that he would be allowed to complete his legal studies, regardless of the disposition of the case. The Court refused to reach the merits of the case, considering it moot. Four Justices dissented, predicting that the issue would inevitably return to the Supreme Court. DeFUNIS v. ODEGAARD, 416 U.S. 312 (1974). Within a few years another case challenging a university's affirmative action program found its way to the Supreme Court, in *Regents of the University of California v. Bakke* (1978), and this time the Court confronted the merits. 438 U.S. 265 (1978).

When the judiciary is ready to decide an issue, "mootness" will not stand in its way. For example, in March 1967, the House of Representatives refused to seat Adam Clayton Powell. He was reelected in 1968 and seated in 1969. Was the case moot? The Supreme Court agreed that one of Powell's claims for relief remained a case or controversy: the salary withheld after his exclusion. Powell v. McCormack, 395 U.S. 486, 496 (1969). The Court proceeded to examine the merits of the case and decided that the House had acted unconstitutionally.

In *Roe* v. *Wade* (1973), plaintiffs argued that the Texas criminal abortion laws were unconstitutionally vague and infringed upon their right of privacy. The laws prohibited abortion except on medical advice to save the mother's life. Texas responded that one of the suits, brought by a pregnant single woman, was moot because her pregnancy had terminated. Justice Blackmun, writing for the majority, rejected that position:

> But when, as here, pregnancy is a significant fact in the litigation, the normal 266-day human gestation period is so short that the pregnancy will come to term before the usual appellate process is complete. If that termination makes a case moot, pregnancy litigation seldom will survive much beyond the trial stage, and appellate review will be effectively denied. Our law should not be that rigid. Pregnancy often comes more than once to the same woman, and in the general population, if man is to survive, it will always be with us. Pregnancy provides a classic justification for a conclusion of nonmootness. It truly could be "capable of repetition, yet evading review." 410 U.S. 113, 125 (1973).

In 1984, the Supreme Court had an opportunity to dismiss as moot an affirmative action case involving a court order for the dismissal or demotion of white employees who had more seniority than black employees retained. All white employees laid off as a result of the order were restored to duty a month later. Those demoted were later offered their old positions. Those facts did not prevent the Supreme Court in *Firefighters* v. *Stotts* from deciding the case and reversing the lower court actions. 467 U.S. 561, 568–572 (1984). Although some of the dissenters accused the majority of issuing an advisory opinion, the Court was evidently ready and willing to circumscribe the reach of affirmative action. The twists and turns of the mootness doctrine reflect the Court's effort to maintain a proper relationship with the other political branches.

RIPENESS

Just as a case brought too late can be moot, a case brought too early may not yet be ripe. Sometimes this results from a failure to exhaust administrative and state remedies. Plaintiffs must show that they have explored all avenues of relief before turning to the federal courts. Premature consideration by the courts does more than create unnecessary workload. It deprives judges of information needed for informed adjudication and forces them to deal at an abstract, speculative, and hypothetical level. It also discourages settlement in the administrative arena, which may be the most appropriate forum for resolution.

The issue of ripeness was present in a 1947 case brought by twelve federal employees against the Civil Service Commission. They wanted to prevent the Commission from enforcing a section of the Hatch Act that prohibited them from taking "any active part in political management or in political campaigns." The federal workers complained that the statute deprived them of their First Amendment rights of speech, press, and assembly. The Supreme Court regarded the employees' fears of losing their jobs as too speculative:

> The power of courts, and ultimately of this Court, to pass upon the constitutionality of acts of Congress arises only when the interests of litigants require the use of this judicial authority for their protection against actual interference. A hypothetical threat is not enough. We can only speculate as to the kinds of political activity the appellants desire to engage in or as to the contents of their proposed public statements or the circumstances of their publication. It would not accord with judicial responsibility to adjudge, in a matter involving constitutionality, between the freedom of the individual and the requirements of public order except when definite rights appear upon the one side and definite prejudicial interferences upon the other. United Public Workers v. Mitchell, 330 U.S. 75, 90 (1947).

The situation of one of the federal employees, George P. Poole, was not hypothetical. He faced dismissal unless he could refute the charges of the Commission that his political activities had violated the Hatch Act. Accepting his suit as a justiciable case, the Court held that disciplinary action under the Hatch Act would not violate the Constitution. Justices Black and Douglas dissented, believing that the Court should have heard the cases of all twelve litigants. The threat of discharge, they said, was real rather than fanciful, immediate not remote. Douglas observed:

> . . . to require these employees first to suffer the hardship of a discharge is not only to make them incur a penalty; it makes inadequate, if not wholly illusory, any legal remedy which they might have. Men who must sacrifice their means of livelihood in order to test their jobs must either pursue prolonged and expensive litigation as unemployed persons or pull up their roots, change their life careers, and seek employment in other fields.

The issue of preventive relief often splits the courts. Should judges rule on a statute before its sanctions are invoked? A decision might offer relief to threatened individuals, but it also requires the courts to rule in advance of a concrete case or controversy. It forces judgments on hypothetical situations that raise remote and abstract issues. And yet judicial inaction can lead to irreparable harm to individuals once the statute is enforced. Longshoremen's Union v. Boyd, 347 U.S. 222, 224–226 (1954). Judicial review may be both necessary and appropriate to protect individuals before an agency enforces a regulation.[13]

The extreme point is reached when a suit lingers so long in the courts that it becomes "overripe." Justice Black described a case that bounced around for ten

---

[13]Abbott Laboratories v. Gardner, 387 U.S. 136 (1967). See also Toilet Goods Assn. v. Gardner, 387 U.S. 158 (1967) and Gardner v. Toilet Goods Assn., 387 U.S. 167 (1967).

years before the Supreme Court sent it back to the lower courts "because of the staleness of the record." A Constitutional Faith 17 (1968).

As with mootness, disposing of a case on the ground of ripeness may delay but not necessarily avoid decision. In 1943 and 1961, the Supreme Court refused to rule on the constitutionality of Connecticut laws that prohibited married couples from using contraceptives or physicians from giving advice about their use. Tileson v. Ullman, 318 U.S. 44 (1943); Poe v. Ullman, 367 U.S. 497 (1961). Because the record suggested that the state was unlikely to prosecute offenders, the Court held that it lacked jurisdiction to decide hypothetical cases. In the 1961 case, the Court ignored the fact that the state had closed several birth-control clinics. POE v. ULLMAN, 367 U.S. 497 (1961). After that decision, the state arrested physicians who had operated a birth-control clinic in New Haven. They were found guilty and fined $100 each. In 1965, the Supreme Court held that they had standing and declared the Connecticut statute invalid under the "penumbra" of the Bill of Rights. Griswold v. Connecticut, 381 U.S. 479 (1965).

"Ripeness" may provide the means to sidestep momentarily a socially sensitive issue. Immediately after the Court had decided *Brown* v. *Board of Education* in 1954, it was faced with the constitutionality of a Virginia miscegenation statute. To strike down a law banning interracial marriages would stimulate the fears of critics of the decision who predicted that integrated schools would lead to "mongrelization" of the white race. The Court returned the case to the lower courts by citing the "inadequacy of the record" and the lack of a "properly-presented federal question." Naim v. Naim, 350 U.S. 891 (1955); 350 U.S. 985 (1956). In essence, the Court decided to buy some time. Years later, after the principle of desegregation had been safely established, the Court struck down the Virginia statute. Loving v. Virginia, 388 U.S. 1 (1967).

Judicial doctrine and political practicalities were joined in a 1978 case involving a congressional limitation on liability for accidents by private nuclear plants. A "hypothetical" issue, to be sure, but it was intuitively unappealing to insist that the courts await a nuclear catastrophe before deciding. The Court was satisfied that the test of ripeness had been met by two effects already evident from the operation of nuclear power plants: the emission of small quantities of radiation in the air and water, and an increase in the temperature of two lakes used for recreational purposes.[14]

Ripeness sometimes involves the unwillingness of Congress to challenge presidential actions. President Carter's termination of the Taiwan defense treaty was met initially by a Senate resolution declaring that Senate approval was necessary to terminate a mutual defense treaty. But no final vote was ever taken on the resolution. Justice Powell considered the case insufficiently ripe for judicial review. "Prudential considerations" convinced him that disputes between Congress and the President should not be reviewed by the courts "unless and until each branch has taken action asserting its constitutional authority." He said that only when the political branches reach a "constitutional impasse" should the judiciary decide issues affecting the allocation of power between Congress and the President: "Otherwise, we would encourage small groups or even individual Members of

---

[14]Duke Power Co. v. Carolina Environment Study Group, 438 U.S. 59, 72-74, 81–82 (1978). Also on the need for courts to avoid premature decisions: Adler v. Board of Education, 342 U.S. 485, 497–508 (Frankfurter, J., dissenting); Socialist Labor Party v. Gilligan, 406 U.S. 583 (1972).

Congress to seek judicial resolution of issues before the normal political process has the opportunity to resolve the conflict." Goldwater v. Carter, 444 U.S. 996, 997 (1979).

POLITICAL QUESTIONS

The "political question" doctrine survives to some extent on circular reasoning. In *Marbury* v. *Madison,* Chief Justice Marshall claimed that "Questions in their nature political . . . can never be made in this court." 5 U.S. (1 Cr.) 137, at 170 (1803). Yet every question that reaches a court is, by its very nature, political. Justice Holmes, hearing a litigant claim that a question concerning a party primary was nonjusticiable because of its political character, said that such an objection "is little more than a play upon words." Nixon v. Herndon, 273 U.S. 536, 540 (1927).

Definitional problems are legion. After refusing to decide a war powers case in 1968, a federal judge declared: "Though it is not always a simple matter to define the meaning of the term 'political question,' it is generally used to encompass all questions outside the sphere of judicial power." Velvel v. Johnson, 287 F.Supp. 846, 850 (D. Kans. 1968). That definition recalls this dictionary explanation: "violins are small cellos, and cellos are large violins." Roche, 49 Am. Pol. Sci. Rev. 762, 768 (1955).

Beyond questions of definition, there is some doubt whether a political question doctrine even exists in the sense that courts refuse to adjudicate certain issues. After reviewing political question cases, Louis Henkin concluded: "the court does not refuse judicial review; it exercises it. It is not dismissing the case or the issue as nonjusticiable; it adjudicates it. It is not refusing to pass on the power of the political branches; it passes upon it, only to affirm that they had the power which had been challenged and that nothing in the Constitution prohibited the particular exercise of it." Henkin, 85 Yale L. J. 597, 606 (1976).

In 1962, the Court identified the areas that are generally classified as political questions. BAKER v. CARR, 369 U.S. 186 (1962). Six criteria indicate the kinds of questions not subject to judicial resolution. The first criterion is "a textually demonstrable constitutional commitment of the issue to a coordinate political department." 369 U.S. at 217. However, the very question of whether an issue has been textually committed to a coordinate branch requires judicial interpretation. Powell v. McCormack, 395 U.S. at 519. Moreover, the fact that an area *is* committed to Congress or the President does not automatically produce a political question. As the Supreme Court noted in 1983, "virtually every challenge to the constitutionality of a statute would be a political question" under that reasoning. INS v. Chadha, 462 U.S. 919, 941. The Court further pointed out:

> It is correct that this controversy may, in a sense, be termed "political." But the presence of constitutional issues with significant political overtones does not automatically invoke the political question doctrine. Resolution of litigation challenging the constitutional authority of one of the three branches cannot be evaded by courts because the issues have political implications in the sense urged by Congress. *Marbury* v. *Madison,* 1 Cranch 137 (1803), was also a "political" case, involving as it did claims under a judicial commission alleged to have been duly signed by the President but not delivered. Id. at 942–943.

Consider the language of Article I, Section 5, of the Constitution: "Each House shall be the Judge of the Elections, Returns and Qualifications of its own Members." A study in 1954 concluded: "it is up to Congress to pass upon the qualifications of its own members, the Constitution says as much, leaving nothing for the judges to do." Edmond Cahn, ed., Supreme Court and Supreme Law 39 (1954). Nevertheless, the courts play a significant role. After the House of Representatives excluded Adam Clayton Powell in 1967, it was widely assumed that no court would or could second-guess that decision. Yet, in 1969 the Supreme Court ruled that the House had a duty to seat Powell because he satisfied the standing qualifications provided in the Constitution. Although the power of Congress to judge the qualifications of its members was a "textually demonstrable constitutional commitment," it was a power to judge only the qualifications expressly provided in the Constitution. The Court said that Congress could not add to them.

Attorneys for the House of Representatives argued that the case was not justiciable because it was impossible for a court to offer effective relief. They said that federal courts could not issue mandamus or injunctions compelling officers or employees of the House to perform certain acts. But coercive relief was not at issue. Powell sought a declaratory judgment to determine his rights independent of the question of relief.

Three years later the same section of the Constitution was before the Court in the case of a contested election. Senator Vance Hartke, a narrow winner in an Indiana race, claimed that the appointment of a recount commission by a state court was prohibited by Article I, Section 5, which grants Congress the power to judge the elections, returns, and qualifications of its members. But another section of the Constitution was involved. Article I, Section 4, gives states the power to prescribe the times, places, and manner of holding elections for Senators and Representatives, subject to alterations by Congress.

The issue was thus the power of Indiana under Section 4 to call for a recount. The Senate had not challenged the recount procedure. It was waiting for the final tally before carrying out its powers under Section 5. Unless Congress acted, Section 4 empowered Indiana to regulate the conduct of senatorial elections. Roudebush v. Hartke, 405 U.S. 15, 24 (1972). The Court said that the Senate would not be bound by the recount: "The Senate is free to accept or reject the apparent winner in either count, and, if it chooses, to conduct its own recount." Id. at 25–26.

Another state case during this period concerned the deaths of several students at Kent State University in Ohio after the governor had called out the National Guard. The students sought injunctive relief to prevent the governor from taking such actions in the future and to prevent the Guard from future violations of students' constitutional rights. Basically, the students wanted the courts to supervise the future training and operations of the Guard. The Supreme Court regarded those duties as vested solely in Congress by Article I, Section 8, Clause 16, which empowers Congress to provide "for organizing, arming, and disciplining the Militia, and for governing such Part of them as may be employed in the Service of the United States, reserving to the States respectively, the Appointment of the Officers, and the Authority of training the Militia according to the discipline prescribed by Congress." The Court said that such actions were meant to be exercised by the political branches: "it is difficult to conceive of an area of governmental activity in which the courts have less competence." Gilligan v. Morgan, 413 U.S. 1, 10 (1973).

The Court agreed that the concept of political questions was not of fixed content, and that "nonjusticiable" voting rights cases came to be accepted by the courts. But those cases, it said, "represented the Court's efforts to strengthen the political system by assuring a higher level of fairness and responsiveness to the political processes, not the assumption of a continuing judicial review of substantive political judgments entrusted expressly to the coordinate branches of government." Id. at 11. There has been no uncertainty about the exclusive responsibility of Congress to determine whether a state satisfies the language of Article IV, Section 4, which requires that the United States "shall guarantee to every State in this Union a Republican Form of Government." Luther v. Borden, 7 How. 1 (1849).

The second criterion in *Baker* v. *Carr* is "a lack of judicially discoverable and manageable standards for resolving" a dispute. One example comes from *Coleman* v. *Miller* (1939). Thirteen years had elapsed before Kansas ratified the Child Labor Amendment. Was that too long a time for state action? The Court decided that it lacked statutory and constitutional criteria for judicial determination. The question of a reasonable time involved "an appraisal of a great variety of relevant conditions, political, social and economic, which can hardly be said to be within the appropriate range of evidence receivable in a court of justice . . . " 307 U.S. 433, 453 (1939).

Another example is *C. & S. Airlines* v. *Waterman Corp.* (1948). The courts were asked to review certain orders issued by the Civil Aeronautics Board involving overseas and foreign air transportation. The orders were subject to presidential review, possibly thrusting the courts into an advisory opinion role. But the Supreme Court stated that the President, "both as Commander-in-Chief and as the Nation's organ for foreign affairs, has available intelligence services whose reports are not and ought not to be published to the world. It would be intolerable that courts, without the relevant information, should review and perhaps nullify actions of the Executive taken on information properly held secret." 333 U.S. 103, 111 (1948).

The Court went on to say that "the very nature of executive decisions as to foreign policy is political, not judicial. Such decisions are wholly confided by our Constitution to the political departments of the government, Executive and Legislature." This statement is far too broad. As the Court later noted in *Baker* v. *Carr:* "it is error to suppose that every case or controversy which touches foreign relations lies beyond judicial cognizance." 369 U.S. at 211.

Certain matters of foreign policy are too sensitive for the courts to handle. When President Carter terminated the defense treaty with Taiwan, Senator Goldwater asked the courts to declare the termination invalid. The case reached the Supreme Court a few weeks before the scheduled termination. Justice Rehnquist attracted three other colleagues to his position that the issue represented a nonjusticiable political question. The Court was being asked to settle a dispute between the executive and legislative branches, "each of which has resources available to protect and assert its interests, resources not available to private litigants outside the judicial forum." Goldwater v. Carter, 444 U.S. at 1004.

The third criterion is "the impossibility of deciding without an initial policy determination of a kind clearly for nonjudicial discretion." This criterion is laced with circularity and basically restates the issue. It would cover reapportionment in 1946 but not after 1962. Colegrove v. Green 328 U.S. 549 (1946); Baker v. Carr, 369 U.S. 186 (1962). At the present time, it covers the issue of whether President Reagan violated the War Powers Resolution by sending military advisers to El Salvador. A district court held that the fact-finding necessary to resolve the dispute rendered the case nonjusticiable. The questions were "appropriate for congressional, not judicial, investigation and determination." Crockett v. Reagan, 558 F.Supp. 893, 898 (D.D.C. 1982).

The fourth criterion is "the impossibility of a court's undertaking independent resolution without expressing lack of the respect due coordinate branches of government." This factor exists in every case involving separation of powers, but it offers little guidance in resolving particular controversies. Whether in the Nixon tapes case (*United States* v. *Nixon*) or the exclusion of Powell by the House of Representatives, the Court's judgment often challenges and overrides decisions made by coordinate branches.

Criterion five is "an unusual need for unquestioning adherence to a political decision already made." Professor Henkin said that he did not know "of any case from which Justice Brennan might have derived such a principle." 85 Yale L. J. at 605–606 n.26. Some recent possibilities might include President Carter's termination of the Taiwan defense treaty and his handling of Iranian assets.[15]

Finally, the sixth criterion is "the potentiality of embarrassment from multifarious pronouncements by various departments on one question." Despite this guideline, the Supreme Court told the House of Representatives that Adam Clayton Powell should be seated. However, this criterion retains usefulness in matters regarding the recognition of foreign governments, political boundaries, envoys, the dates for beginning and ending wars, calling out the militia, and an alien's eligibility for federal benefits.[16]

Rules of self-restraint are part of the complex process of drawing limits on judicial power. Some scholars argue that prudence dictates restrictions on judicial activity. Others warn that the contemporary Court has confused the concept of justiciability and abdicated its duty to decide proper cases and controversies. The use of threshold requirements to avoid or delay judicial decision has sparked a number of lively debates. A particularly stimulating exchange was between Alexander M. Bickel and Gerald Gunther (pp. 135–141).

The next two chapters explore judicial activity from other vantage points. Chapter 4 views the power contest in the areas of court structure, legislative courts, appointments, tenure, compensation, and judicial lobbying. Chapter 5 examines the decision-making process of the courts, placing special emphasis on the negotiations required of members of a collegial body.

Selected Readings

ALBERT, LEE A. "Justiciability and Theories of Judicial Review: A Remote Relationship." 50 *Southern California Law Review* 1139 (1977).

BRILMAYER, LEA. "The Jurisprudence of Article III: Perspectives on the 'Case or Controversy' Requirement." 93 *Harvard Law Review* 297 (1979).

[15]Goldwater v. Carter, 444 U.S. 996 (1979); Dames & Moore v. Regan, 453 U.S. 654 (1981). See also Idaho v. Freeman, 529 F.Supp. 1107, 1140–1141 (D. Idaho 1981), regarding Idaho's rescission of its vote to ratify the Equal Rights Amendment.

[16]Recognizing foreign governments: Rose v. Himely, 4 Cr. 241 (1808); Gelston v. Hoyt, 3 Wheat. 246 (1818). Political boundaries: Foster v. Neilson, 2 Pet. 253 (1829); Williams v. Suffolk Insurance Co., 13 Pet. 415 (1839). Envoys: Ex parte Hitz, 111 U.S. 766 (1884). Beginning and ending wars: Martin v. Mott, 12 Wheat. 19 (1827); Commercial Trust Co. v. Miller, 262 U.S. 51 (1923). Calling out the militia: Martin v. Mott, 12 Wheat. 19 (1827). Federal benefits: Mathews v. Diaz, 426 U.S. 67, 81–84 (1976).

CONDON, DANIEL PATRICK. "The Generalized Grievance Restriction: Prudential Restraint or Constitutional Mandate?" 70 *Georgetown Law Journal* 1157
(1982).

HUGHES, GRAHAM. "Civil Disobedience and the Political Question Doctrine." 43 *New York University
Law Review* 1 (1968).

JACKSON, R. BROOKE. "The Political Question Doctrine: Where Does It Stand After *Powell* v. *McCormack*, *O'Brien* v. *Brown*, and *Gilligan* v. *Morgan*?"
44 *University of Colorado Law Review* 477 (1973).

KATES, DON B., JR., AND WILLIAM T. BARKER. "Mootness in Judicial Proceedings: Toward a Coherent
Theory." 62 *California Law Review* 1385 (1974).

LOGAN, DAVID A. "Standing to Sue: A Proposed Separation of Powers Analysis." 1984 *Wisconsin Law
Review* 37.

MONAGHAN, HENRY P. "Constitutional Adjudication:
The Who and When." 82 *Yale Law Journal* 1363
(1973).

MORRISON, ALAN B. "Rights Without Remedies: The
Burger Court Takes the Federal Courts Out of the
Business of Protecting Federal Rights." 30 *Rutgers
Law Review* 841 (1977).

NICHOL, GENE R., JR. "Causation as a Standing Requirement: The Unprincipled Use of Judicial Restraint." 69 *Kentucky Law Journal* 185 (1980).

ORREN, KAREN. "Standing to Sue: Interest Group
Conflict in the Federal Courts." 70 *American Political Science Review* 723 (1976).

POST, CHARLES GORDON, JR. *The Supreme Court and
Political Questions.* Baltimore: The Johns Hopkins
Press, 1936.

RADCLIFFE, JAMES E. *The Case-or-Controversy Provision.* University Park: Pennsylvania State University
Press, 1978.

ROSENBLUM, VICTOR G. "Justiciability and Justice:
Elements of Restraint and Indifference." 15 *Catholic University Law Review* 141 (1966).

SCALIA, ANTONIN. "The Doctrine of Standing as an
Essential Element of the Separation of Powers." 17
Suffolk University Law Review 881 (1983).

SCHARPF, FRITZ W. "Judicial Review and the Political
Question: A Functional Analysis." 75 *Yale Law
Journal* 517 (1966).

SCOTT, KENNETH E. "Standing in the Supreme
Court—A Functional Analysis." 86 *Harvard Law
Review* 645 (1973).

SEDLER, ROBERT ALLEN. "Standing and the Burger Court: An Analysis and Some Proposals for Legislative Reform." 30 *Rutgers Law Review* 863
(1977).

STRUM, PHILIPPA. *The Supreme Court and "Political
Questions."* University: University of Alabama
Press, 1974.

TIGAR, MICHAEL E. "Judicial Power, the 'Political
Question Doctrine,' and Foreign Relations." 17
UCLA Law Review 1135 (1970).

TUCKER, EDWIN W. "The Metamorphosis of the
Standing to Sue Doctrine." 17 *New York Law
Forum* 911 (1972).

TUSHNET, MARK V. "The Sociology of Article III: A
Response to Professor Brilmayer." 93 *Harvard Law
Review* 1698 (1980).

The Brandeis Rules: Ashwander v. TVA

297 U.S. 288 (1936)

**In a concurring opinion, Justice Brandeis reviewed the rules used by the courts to limit
their exercise of judicial review. Footnotes omitted.**

The Court has frequently called attention to the
"great gravity and delicacy" of its function in
passing upon the validity of an act of Congress;
and has restricted exercise of this function by rigid
insistence that the jurisdiction of federal courts is
limited to actual cases and controversies; and that
they have no power to give advisory opinions. On
this ground it has in recent years ordered the

dismissal of several suits challenging the constitutionality of important acts of Congress. . . .

The Court developed, for its own governance in
the cases confessedly within its jurisdiction, a
series of rules under which it has avoided passing
upon a large part of all the constitutional questions pressed upon it for decision. They are:

1. The Court will not pass upon the constitu-

tionality of legislation in a friendly, non-adversary, proceeding, declining because to decide such questions "is legitimate only in the last resort, and as a necessity in the determination of real, earnest and vital controversy between individuals. It never was the thought that, by means of a friendly suit, a party beaten in the legislature could transfer to the courts an inquiry as to the constitutionality of the legislative act." . . .

2. The Court will not "anticipate a question of constitutional law in advance of the necessity of deciding it." . . .

3. The Court will not "formulate a rule of constitutional law broader than is required by the precise facts to which it is to be applied." . . .

4. The Court will not pass upon a constitutional question although properly presented by the record, if there is also present some other ground upon which the case may be disposed of. This rule has found most varied application. Thus, if a case can be decided on either of two grounds, one

involving a constitutional question, the other a question of statutory construction or general law, the Court will decide only the latter. . . . Appeals from the highest court of a state challenging its decision of a question under the Federal Constitution are frequently dismissed because the judgment can be sustained on an independent state ground. . . .

5. The Court will not pass upon the validity of a statute upon complaint of one who fails to show that he is injured by its operation. . . .

6. The Court will not pass upon the constitutionality of a statute at the instance of one who has availed himself of its benefits.

7. "When the validity of an act of the Congress is drawn in question, and even if a serious doubt of constitutionality is raised, it is a cardinal principle that this Court will first ascertain whether a construction of the statute is fairly possible by which the question may be avoided." . . .

Advisory Opinions: Bellotti v. Baird

443 U.S. 622 (1979)

A Massachusetts statute required parental consent before an abortion could be performed on an unmarried woman under the age of 18. If one or both parents refused, a judge could order the abortion "for good cause shown." Justice Stevens, joined by Justices Brennan, Marshall, and Blackmun, wrote a footnote in *Bellotti* v. *Baird*, 443 U.S. 622 (1979) that the Supreme Court's majority opinion was, in effect, an advisory opinion to the Massachusetts legislature. The author of the opinion, Justice Powell, prepared a footnote of his own to justify the direction he had given.

Justice Stevens:

Until and unless Massachusetts or another State enacts a less restrictive statutory scheme, this Court has no occasion to render an advisory opinion on the constitutionality of such a scheme. A real statute—rather than a mere outline of a possible statute—and a real case or controversy may well present questions that appear quite different from the hypothetical questions MR. JUSTICE POWELL has elected to address. Indeed, there is a certain irony in his suggestion that a statute that is

intended to vindicate "the special interest of the State in encouraging an unmarried pregnant minor to seek the advice of her parents in making the important decision whether or not to bear a child," see *ante*, at 639, need not require notice to the parents of the minor's intended decision. That irony makes me wonder whether any legislature concerned with parental consultation would, in the absence of today's advisory opinion, have enacted a statute comparable to the one my Brethren have discussed.

Justice Powell:

The opinion of MR. JUSTICE STEVENS, concurring in the judgment, joined by three Members of the Court, characterizes this opinion as "advisory" and the questions it addresses as "hypothetical." Apparently, this is criticism of our attempt to provide some guidance as to how a State constitutionally may provide for adult involvement—either by parents or a state official such as a judge—in the abortion decisions of minors. In view of the importance of the issue raised, and the protracted litigation to which these parties already have been subjected, we think it would be irresponsible simply to invalidate § 12S without stating our views as to the controlling principles.

The statute before us today is the same one that was here in *Bellotti I*. The issues it presents were not then deemed "hypothetical." In a unanimous opinion, we remanded the case with directions that appropriate questions be certified to the Supreme Judicial Court of Massachusetts "concern-

ing the meaning of [§ 12S] and the procedure it imposes." 428 U.S., at 151. We directed that this be done because, as stated in the opinion, we thought the construction of § 12S urged by appellants would "avoid or substantially modify the federal constitutional challenge to the statute." *Id.*, at 148. The central feature of § 12S was its provision that a state-court judge could make the ultimate decision, when necessary, as to the exercise by a minor of the right to an abortion. See *id.*, at 145. We held that this "would be fundamentally different from a statute that creates a 'parental veto' [of the kind rejected in *Danforth*.]" *Ibid.* (footnote omitted). Thus, all Members of the Court agreed that providing for decisionmaking authority in a judge was not the kind of veto power held invalid in *Danforth*. The basic issues that were before us in *Bellotti I* remain in the case, sharpened by the construction of § 12S by the Supreme Judicial Court.

United States v. Richardson

418 U.S. 166 (1974)

A taxpayer sued to obtain detailed expenditures of the Central Intelligence Agency. In the majority opinion, which denied standing, Chief Justice Burger tried to preserve the doctrines set forth in *Flast* v. *Cohen*. Justice Powell, concurring, urged that *Flast* be abandoned as intellectually incoherent. Footnotes omitted.

MR. CHIEF JUSTICE BURGER delivered the opinion of the Court.

We granted certiorari in this case to determine whether the respondent has standing to bring an action as a federal taxpayer alleging that certain provisions concerning public reporting of expenditures under the Central Intelligence Agency Act of 1949, 63 Stat. 208, 50 U. S. C. § 403a *ct seq.*, violate Art. I, § 9, cl. 7, of the Constitution which provides:

"No Money shall be drawn from the Treasury, but in Consequence of Appropriations made by Law; and a regular Statement and Account of the Receipts and Expenditures of all public Money shall be published from time to time."

. . .

Although the recent holding of the Court in *Flast* v. *Cohen, supra*, is a starting point in an examination of respondent's claim to prosecute this suit as a taxpayer, that case must be read with reference to its principal predecessor, *Frothingham* v. *Mellon*, 262 U. S. 447 (1923). In *Frothingham*, the injury alleged was that the congressional enactment challenged as unconstitutional would, if implemented, increase the complainant's future federal income taxes. Denying standing, the *Frothingham* Court rested on the "comparatively minute[,] remote, fluctuating and uncertain," *id.*, at 487, impact on the taxpayer, and the failure to allege the kind of direct injury required for standing.

"The party who invokes the [judicial] power must be able to show not only that the statute is invalid but that he has sustained or is immediately in danger of sustaining some direct injury as the result of its enforcement, and not merely that he suffers in some indefinite way in common with people generally." *Id.*, at 488.

When the Court addressed the question of standing in *Flast,* Mr. Chief Justice Warren traced what he described as the "confusion" following *Frothingham* as to whether the Court had announced a constitutional doctrine barring suits by taxpayers challenging federal expenditures as unconstitutional or simply a policy rule of judicial self-restraint. In an effort to clarify the confusion and to take into account intervening developments, of which class actions and joinder under the Federal Rules of Civil Procedure were given as examples, the Court embarked on "a fresh examination of the limitations upon standing to sue in a federal court and the application of those limitations to taxpayer suits." 392 U. S., at 94. That re-examination led, however, to the holding that a "taxpayer will have standing *consistent with Article III* to invoke federal judicial power when he alleges that congressional action under the taxing and spending clause is in derogation of those constitutional provisions *which operate to restrict the exercise of the taxing and spending power.*" *Id.*, at 105–106. (Emphasis supplied.) In so holding, the Court emphasized that Art. III requirements are the threshold inquiry:

"The 'gist of the question of standing' is whether the party seeking relief has 'alleged such a personal stake in the outcome of the controversy as to assure that concrete adverseness . . . upon which the court so largely depends for illumination of difficult constitutional questions.'" *Id.*, at 99, citing *Baker* v. *Carr,* 369 U. S., at 204.

The Court then announced a two-pronged standing test which requires allegations: (a) challenging an enactment under the Taxing and Spending Clause of Art. I, § 8, of the Constitution; and (b) claiming that the challenged enactment exceeds specific constitutional limitations imposed on the taxing and spending power. 392 U. S., at 102–103. While the "impenetrable barrier to suits against Acts of Congress brought by individuals who can assert only the interest of federal taxpayers," *id.*, at 85, had been slightly lowered, the Court made clear it was reaffirming the principle of *Frothingham* precluding a taxpayer's use of "a federal court as a forum in which to air his generalized grievances about the conduct of government or the allocation of power in the Federal System." *Id.*, at 106. The narrowness of that holding is emphasized by the concurring opinion of Mr. Justice Stewart in *Flast:*

"In concluding that the appellants therefore have standing to sue, we do not undermine the salutary principle, established by *Frothingham* and reaffirmed today, that a taxpayer may not 'employ a federal court as a forum in which to air his generalized grievances about the conduct of government or the allocation of power in the Federal System.'" *Id.*, at 114.

II

Although the Court made it very explicit in *Flast* that a "fundamental aspect of standing" is that it focuses primarily on the *party* seeking to get his complaint before the federal court rather than "on the issues he wishes to have adjudicated," *id.*, at 99, it made equally clear that

"in ruling on [taxpayer] standing, it is both appropriate and necessary to look to the substantive issues for another purpose, namely, to determine whether there is a logical nexus between the status asserted and the claim sought to be adjudicated." *Id.*, at 102.

We therefore turn to an examination of the issues sought to be raised by respondent's complaint to determine whether he is "a proper and appropriate party to invoke federal judicial power," *ibid.*, with respect to those issues.

We need not and do not reach the merits of the constitutional attack on the statute; our inquiry into the "substantive issues" is for the limited purpose indicated above. The mere recital of the respondent's claims and an examination of the statute under attack demonstrate how far he falls short of the standing criteria of *Flast* and how neatly he falls within the *Frothingham* holding left undisturbed. . . .

MR. JUSTICE POWELL, concurring.

I join the opinion of the Court because I am in accord with most of its analysis, particularly insofar as it relies on traditional barriers against federal taxpayer or citizen standing. And I agree that *Flast* v. *Cohen*, 392 U. S. 83 (1968), which set the boundaries for the arguments of the parties before us, is the most directly relevant precedent and quite correctly absorbs a major portion of the Court's attention. I write solely to indicate that I would go further than the Court and would lay to rest the approach undertaken in *Flast.* I would not overrule *Flast* on its facts, because it is now settled that federal taxpayer standing exists in Establishment Clause cases. I would not, however, perpetuate the doctrinal confusion inherent in the *Flast* two-part "nexus" test. That test is not a reliable indicator of when a federal taxpayer has standing, and it has no sound relationship to the question whether such a plaintiff, with no other interest at stake, should be allowed to bring suit against one of the branches of the Federal Government. In my opinion, it should be abandoned.

I

My difficulties with *Flast* are several. The opinion purports to separate the question of standing from the merits, *id.*, at 99–101, yet it abruptly returns to the substantive issues raised by a plaintiff for the purpose of determining "whether there is a logical nexus between the status asserted and the claim sought to be adjudicated." *Id.*, at 102. Similarly, the opinion distinguishes between constitutional and prudential limits on standing. *Id.*, at 92–94, 97. I find it impossible, however, to determine whether the two-part "nexus" test created in *Flast* amounts to a constitutional or a prudential limitation, because it has no meaningful connection with the Court's statement of the bare-minimum constitutional requirements for standing.

Drawing upon *Baker* v. *Carr*, 369 U. S. 186, 204 (1962), the Court in *Flast* stated the " 'gist of the question of standing' " as "whether the party seeking relief has 'alleged such a personal stake in the

outcome of the controversy as to assure that concrete adverseness which sharpens the presentation of issues upon which the court so largely depends for illumination of difficult constitutional questions.' " 392 U. S., at 99. As the Court today notes, *ante*, at 173, this is now the controlling definition of the irreducible Art. III case-or-controversy requirements for standing. But, as Mr. Justice Harlan pointed out in his dissent in *Flast*, 392 U. S., at 116 *et seq.*, it is impossible to see how an inquiry about the existence of "concrete adverseness" is furthered by an application of the *Flast* test.

Flast announced the following two-part "nexus" test:

"The nexus demanded of federal taxpayers has two aspects to it. First, the taxpayer must establish a logical link between that status and the type of legislative enactment attacked. Thus, a taxpayer will be a proper party to allege the unconstitutionality only of exercises of congressional power under the taxing and spending clause of Art. I, § 8, of the Constitution. It will not be sufficient to allege an incidental expenditure of tax funds in the administration of an essentially regulatory statute. . . . Secondly, the taxpayer must establish a nexus between that status and the precise nature of the constitutional infringement alleged. Under this requirement, the taxpayer must show that the challenged enactment exceeds specific constitutional limitations imposed upon the exercise of the congressional taxing and spending power and not simply that the enactment is generally beyond the powers delegated to Congress by Art. I, § 8. When both nexuses are established, the litigant will have shown a taxpayer's stake in the outcome of the controversy and will be a proper and appropriate party to invoke a federal court's jurisdiction." *Id.*, at 102–103.

Relying on history, the Court identified the Establishment Clause as a specific constitutional limitation upon the exercise by Congress of the taxing and spending power conferred by Art. I, § 8. 392 U. S., at 103–105. On the other hand, the Tenth Amendment, and apparently the Due Process Clause of the Fifth Amendment, were determined not to be such "specific" limitations. The bases for these determinations are not wholly clear, but it appears that the Court found the Tenth Amendment addressed to the interests of the States, rather than of taxpayers, and the Due Process Clause no protection against increases in tax liability. *Id.,* at 105.

In my opinion, Mr. Justice Harlan's critique of the *Flast* "nexus" test is unanswerable. As he pointed out, "the Court's standard for the determination of standing [*i.e.,* sufficiently concrete adverseness] and its criteria for the satisfaction of that standard are entirely unrelated." *Id.,* at 122. Assuming that the relevant constitutional inquiry is the intensity of the plaintiff's concern, as the Court initially posited, *id.,* at 99, the *Flast* criteria "are not in any sense a measurement of any plaintiff's interest in the outcome of any suit." *Id.,* at 121 (Harlan, J., dissenting). A plaintiff's incentive to challenge an expenditure does not turn on the "unconnected fact" that it relates to a regulatory rather than a spending program, *id.,* at 122, or on whether the constitutional provision on which he relies is a "specific limitation" upon Congress' spending powers. *Id.,* at 123.

The ambiguities inherent in the *Flast* "nexus" limitations on federal taxpayer standing are illustrated by this case. There can be little doubt about respondent's fervor in pursuing his case, both within administrative channels and at every level of the federal courts. The intensity of his interest appears to bear no relationship to the fact that, literally speaking, he is not challenging directly a congressional exercise of the taxing and spending power. On the other hand, if the involvement of the taxing and spending power has some relevance, it requires no great leap in reasoning to conclude that the Statement and Account Clause, Art. I, § 9, cl. 7, on which respondent relies, is inextricably linked to that power. And that Clause might well be seen as a "specific" limitation on congressional spending. Indeed, it could be viewed as the most democratic of limitations. Thus, although the Court's application of *Flast* to the instant case is probably literally correct, adherence to the *Flast* test in this instance suggests, as does *Flast* itself, that the test is not a sound or logical limitation on standing.

The lack of real meaning and of principled content in the *Flast* "nexus" test renders it likely that it will in time collapse of its own weight, as MR.

JUSTICE DOUGLAS predicted in his concurring opinion in that case. 392 U. S., at 107. . . .

Relaxation of standing requirements is directly related to the expansion of judicial power. It seems to me inescapable that allowing unrestricted taxpayer or citizen standing would significantly alter the allocation of power at the national level, with a shift away from a democratic form of government. I also believe that repeated and essentially head-on confrontations between the life-tenured branch and the representative branches of government will not, in the long run, be beneficial to either. The public confidence essential to the former and the vitality critical to the latter may well erode if we do not exercise self-restraint in the utilization of our power to negative the actions of the other branches. We should be ever mindful of the contradictions that would arise if a democracy were to permit general oversight of the elected branches of government by a nonrepresentative, and in large measure insulated, judicial branch. Moreover, the argument that the Court should allow unrestricted taxpayer or citizen standing underestimates the ability of the representative branches of the Federal Government to respond to the citizen pressure that has been responsible in large measure for the current drift toward expanded standing. Indeed, taxpayer or citizen advocacy, given its potentially broad base, is precisely the type of leverage that in a democracy ought to be employed against the branches that were intended to be responsive to public attitudes about the appropriate operation of government. . . .

The power recognized in *Marbury* v. *Madison,* 1 Cranch 137 (1803), is a potent one. Its prudent use seems to me incompatible with unlimited notions of taxpayer and citizen standing. Were we to utilize this power as indiscriminately as is now being urged, we may witness efforts by the representative branches drastically to curb its use. Due to what many have regarded as the unresponsiveness of the Federal Government to recognized needs or serious inequities in our society, recourse to the federal courts has attained an unprecedented popularity in recent decades. Those courts have often acted as a major instrument of social reform. But this has not always been the case, as experiences under the New Deal illustrate. The public reaction to the substantive due process holdings of the federal courts during that period requires no elaboration, and it is not unusual for history to repeat itself.

Quite apart from this possibility, we risk a progressive impairment of the effectiveness of the federal courts if their limited resources are diverted increasingly from their historic role to the resolution of public-interest suits brought by litigants who cannot distinguish themselves from all taxpayers or all citizens. The irreplaceable value of the power articulated by Mr. Chief Justice Mar-

shall lies in the protection it has afforded the constitutional rights and liberties of individual citizens and minority groups against oppressive or discriminatory government action. It is this role, not some amorphous general supervision of the operations of government, that has maintained public esteem for the federal courts and has permitted the peaceful coexistence of the countermajoritarian implications of judicial review and the democratic principles upon which our Federal Government in the final analysis rests. . . .

Valley Forge College v. Americans United

454 U.S. 464 (1982)

In 1973, the Secretary of Defense closed the Valley Forge General Hospital and the General Services Administration declared the land and the buildings "surplus property." In 1976, the federal government conveyed seventy-seven acres of the property to the Valley Forge Christian College. The Americans United for Separation of Church and State brought suit in federal court to declare the conveyance a violation of the Establishment Clause of the First Amendment. The case was disposed of partly on grounds of standing.

JUSTICE REHNQUIST delivered the opinion of the Court.

I

Article IV, § 3, cl. 2, of the Constitution vests Congress with the "Power to dispose of and make all needful Rules and Regulations respecting the . . . Property belonging to the United States." Shortly after the termination of hostilities in the Second World War, Congress enacted the Federal Property and Administrative Services Act of 1949, 63 Stat. 377, as amended, 40 U. S. C. § 471 *et seq.* (1976 ed. and Supp. III). The Act was designed, in part, to provide "an economical and efficient system for . . . the disposal of surplus property." 63 Stat. 378, 40 U. S. C. § 471. In furtherance of this policy, federal agencies are directed to maintain adequate inventories of the property under their control and to identify excess property for transfer to other agencies able to use it. See 63 Stat. 384, 40 U. S. C. §§ 483(b), (c). Property that

has outlived its usefulness to the Federal Government is declared "surplus" and may be transferred to private or other public entities. See generally 63 Stat. 385, as amended, 40 U. S. C. § 484.

The Act authorizes the Secretary of Health, Education, and Welfare (now the Secretary of Education) to assume responsibility for disposing of surplus real property "for school, classroom, or other educational use." 63 Stat. 387, as amended, 40 U. S. C. § 484(k)(1). Subject to the disapproval of the Administrator of General Services, the Secretary may sell or lease the property to nonprofit, tax exempt educational institutions for consideration that takes into account "any benefit which has accrued or may accrue to the United States" from the transferee's use of the property. 63 Stat. 387, 40 U. S. C. §§ 484(k)(1)(A), (C). By regulation, the Secretary has provided for the computation of a "public benefit allowance," which discounts the transfer price of the property "on the basis of benefits to the United States from the use of such property for educational purposes." 34 CFR § 12.9(a) (1980).

The property which spawned this litigation was acquired by the Department of the Army in 1942, as part of a larger tract of approximately 181 acres of land northwest of Philadelphia. The Army built on that land the Valley Forge General Hospital, and for 30 years thereafter, that hospital provided medical care for members of the Armed Forces. In April 1973, as part of a plan to reduce the number of military installations in the United States, the Secretary of Defense proposed to close the hospital, and the General Services Administration declared it to be "surplus property."

The Department of Health, Education, and Welfare (HEW) eventually assumed responsibility for disposing of portions of the property, and in August 1976, it conveyed a 77-acre tract to petitioner, the Valley Forge Christian College. The appraised value of the property at the time of conveyance was $577,500. This appraised value was discounted, however, by the Secretary's computation of a 100% public benefit allowance, which permitted petitioner to acquire the property without making any financial payment for it. . . .

In September 1976, respondents Americans United for Separation of Church and State, Inc. (Americans United), and four of its employees, learned of the conveyance through a news release. Two months later, they brought suit in the United States District Court for the District of Columbia, later transferred to the Eastern District of Pennsylvania, to challenge the conveyance on the ground that it violated the Establishment Clause of the First Amendment. See App. 10. In its amended complaint, Americans United described itself as a nonprofit organization composed of 90,000 "taxpayer members." The complaint asserted that each member "would be deprived of the fair and constitutional use of his (her) tax dollar for constitutional purposes in violation of his (her) rights under the First Amendment of the United States Constitution." *Ibid.* Respondents sought a declaration that the conveyance was null and void, and an order compelling petitioner to transfer the property back to the United States. *Id.*, at 12.

On petitioner's motion, the District Court granted summary judgment and dismissed the complaint. App. to Pet. for Cert. A42. The court found that respondents lacked standing to sue as taxpayers under *Flast* v. *Cohen*, 392 U. S. 83 (1968), and had "failed to allege that they have suffered any actual or concrete injury beyond a generalized grievance common to all taxpayers." App. to Pet. for Cert. A43.

Respondents appealed to the Court of Appeals for the Third Circuit, which reversed the judgment of the District Court by a divided vote. *Americans United* v. *U. S. Dept. of HEW*, 619 F. 2d 252 (1980). All members of the court agreed that respondents lacked standing as taxpayers to challenge the conveyance under *Flast* v. *Cohen, supra,* since that case extended standing to taxpayers *qua* taxpayers only to challenge congressional exercises of the power to tax and spend conferred by Art. I, § 8, of the Constitution, and this conveyance was authorized by legislation enacted under the authority of the Property Clause, Art. IV, § 3, cl. 2. Notwithstanding this significant factual difference from *Flast,* the majority of the Court of Appeals found that respondents also had standing merely as "citizens," claiming "'injury in fact' to their shared individuated right to a government that 'shall make no law respecting the establishment of religion.'" 619 F. 2d, at 261. In the majority's view, this "citizen standing" was sufficient to satisfy the "case or controversy" requirement of Art. III. One judge, perhaps sensing the doctrinal difficulties with the majority's extension of standing, wrote separately, expressing his view that standing was necessary to satisfy "the need for an available plaintiff," without whom "the Establishment Clause would be rendered virtually unenforceable" by the Judiciary. *Id.*, at 267, 268. The dissenting judge expressed the view that respondents' allegations constituted a "generalized grievance . . . too abstract to satisfy the injury in fact component of standing." *Id.*, at 269. He therefore concluded that their standing to contest the transfer was barred by this Court's decisions in *Schlesinger* v. *Reservists Committee to Stop the War,* 418 U. S. 208 (1974), and *United States* v. *Richardson,* 418 U. S. 166 (1974). 619 F. 2d, at 270–271.

Because of the unusually broad and novel view of standing to litigate a substantive question in the federal courts adopted by the Court of Appeals, we granted certiorari, 450 U. S. 909 (1981), and we now reverse.

II

Article III of the Constitution limits the "judicial power" of the United States to the resolution of "cases" and "controversies." The constitutional power of federal courts cannot be defined, and indeed has no substance, without reference to the necessity "to adjudge the legal rights of litigants in actual controversies." *Liverpool S.S. Co.* v. *Commissioners of Emigration*, 113 U. S. 33, 39 (1885). The requirements of Art. III are not satisfied merely because a party requests a court of the United States to declare its legal rights, and has couched that request for forms of relief historically associated with courts of law in terms that have a familiar ring to those trained in the legal process. The judicial power of the United States defined by Art. III is not an unconditioned authority to determine the constitutionality of legislative or executive acts. The power to declare the rights of individuals and to measure the authority of governments, this Court said 90 years ago, "is legitimate only in the last resort, and as a necessity in the determination of real, earnest and vital controversy." *Chicago & Grand Trunk R. Co.* v. *Wellman*, 143 U. S. 339, 345 (1892). Otherwise, the power "is not judicial . . . in the sense in which judicial power is granted by the Constitution to the courts of the United States." *United States* v. *Ferreira*, 13 How. 40, 48 (1852).

As an incident to the elaboration of this bedrock requirement, this Court has always required that a litigant have "standing" to challenge the action sought to be adjudicated in the lawsuit. The term "standing" subsumes a blend of constitutional requirements and prudential considerations, see *Warth* v. *Seldin*, 422 U. S. 490, 498 (1975), and it has not always been clear in the opinions of this Court whether particular features of the "standing" requirement have been required by Art. III *ex proprio vigore*, or whether they are requirements that the Court itself has erected and which were not compelled by the language of the Constitution. See *Flast* v. *Cohen*, 392 U. S., at 97.

A recent line of decisions, however, has resolved that ambiguity, at least to the following

extent: at an irreducible minimum, Art. III requires the party who invokes the court's authority to "show that he personally has suffered some actual or threatened injury as a result of the putatively illegal conduct of the defendant," *Gladstone, Realtors* v. *Village of Bellwood*, 441 U. S. 91, 99 (1979), and that the injury "fairly can be traced to the challenged action" and "is likely to be redressed by a favorable decision," *Simon* v. *Eastern Kentucky Welfare Rights Org.*, 426 U. S. 26, 38, 41 (1976). In this manner does Art. III limit the federal judicial power "to those disputes which confine federal courts to a role consistent with a system of separated powers and which are traditionally thought to be capable of resolution through the judicial process." *Flast* v. *Cohen, supra*, at 97. . . .

We need not mince words when we say that the concept of "Art. III standing" has not been defined with complete consistency in all of the various cases decided by this Court which have discussed it, nor when we say that this very fact is probably proof that the concept cannot be reduced to a one-sentence or one-paragraph definition. But of one thing we may be sure: Those who do not possess Art. III standing may not litigate as suitors in the courts of the United States. Article III, which is every bit as important in its circumscription of the judicial power of the United States as in its granting of that power, is not merely a troublesome hurdle to be overcome if possible so as to reach the "merits" of a lawsuit which a party desires to have adjudicated; it is a part of the basic charter promulgated by the Framers of the Constitution at Philadelphia in 1787, a charter which created a general government, provided for the interaction between that government and the governments of the several States, and was later amended so as to either enhance or limit its authority with respect to both States and individuals. . . .

Unlike the plaintiffs in *Flast*, respondents fail the first prong of the test for taxpayer standing. Their claim is deficient in two respects. First, the source of their complaint is not a congressional action, but a decision by HEW to transfer a parcel of federal property. *Flast* limited taxpayer standing to challenges directed "only [at] exercises of congressional power." *Id.*, at 102. See *Schlesinger* v.

Reservists Committee to Stop the War, 418 U. S., at 228 (denying standing because the taxpayer plaintiffs "did not challenge an enactment under Art. I, § 8, but rather the action of the Executive Branch").

Second, and perhaps redundantly, the property transfer about which respondents complain was not an exercise of authority conferred by the Taxing and Spending Clause of Art. I, § 8. The authorizing legislation, the Federal Property and Administrative Services Act of 1949, was an evident exercise of Congress' power under the Property Clause, Art. IV, § 3, cl. 2. Respondents do not dispute this conclusion, see Brief for Respondents Americans United et al. 10, and it is decisive of any claim of taxpayer standing under the *Flast* precedent. . . .

Respondents, therefore, are plainly without standing to sue as taxpayers. The Court of Appeals apparently reached the same conclusion. It remains to be seen whether respondents have alleged any other basis for standing to bring this suit.

IV

Although the Court of Appeals properly doubted respondents' ability to establish standing solely on the basis of their taxpayer status, it considered their allegations of taxpayer injury to be "essentially an assumed role." 619 F. 2d, at 261.

"Plaintiffs have no reason to expect, nor perhaps do they care about, any personal tax saving that might result should they prevail. The crux of the interest at stake, the plaintiffs argue, is found in the Establishment Clause, not in the supposed loss of money as such. As a matter of primary identity, therefore, the plaintiffs are not so much taxpayers as separationists. . . ." *Ibid.*

In the court's view, respondents had established standing by virtue of an " 'injury in fact' to their shared individuated right to a government that 'shall make no law respecting the establishment of religion.' " . . .

In finding that respondents had alleged something more than "the generalized interest of all citizens in constitutional governance," *Schlesinger, supra*, at 217, the Court of Appeals relied on factual differences which we do not think amount to legal distinctions. The court decided that respondents' claim differed from those in *Schlesinger* and *Richardson*, which were predicated, respectively, on the Incompatibility and Accounts Clauses, because "it is at the very least arguable that the Establishment Clause creates in each citizen a 'personal constitutional right' to a government that does not establish religion." . . .

Nor can *Schlesinger* and *Richardson* be distinguished on the ground that the Incompatibility and Accounts Clauses are in some way less "fundamental" than the Establishment Clause. Each establishes a norm of conduct which the Federal Government is bound to honor—to no greater or lesser extent than any other inscribed in the Constitution. To the extent the Court of Appeals relied on a view of standing under which the Art. III burdens diminish as the "importance" of the claim on the merits increases, we reject that notion. The requirement of standing "focuses on the party seeking to get his complaint before a federal court and not on the issues he wishes to have adjudicated." *Flast* v. *Cohen, supra*, at 99. Moreover, we know of no principled basis on which to create a hierarchy of constitutional values or a complementary "sliding scale" of standing which might permit respondents to invoke the judicial power of the United States.

. . . It is evident that respondents are firmly committed to the constitutional principle of separation of church and State, but standing is not measured by the intensity of the litigant's interest or the fervor of his advocacy.

. . . Their claim that the Government has violated the Establishment Clause does not provide a special license to roam the country in search of governmental wrongdoing and to reveal their discoveries in federal court. The federal courts were simply not constituted as ombudsmen of the general welfare. . . .

Were we to accept respondents' claim of standing in this case, there would be no principled basis for confining our exception to litigants relying on the Establishment Clause. Ultimately, that exception derives from the idea that the judicial power requires nothing more for its invocation than important issues and able litigants. The existence of injured parties who might not wish to bring suit becomes irrelevant. Because we are unwilling to countenance such a departure from the limits on judicial power contained in Art. III, the judgment of the Court of Appeals is reversed.

It is so ordered.

JUSTICE BRENNAN, with whom JUSTICE MARSHALL and JUSTICE BLACKMUN join, dissenting.

A plaintiff's standing is a jurisdictional matter for Art. III courts, and thus a "threshold question" to be resolved before turning attention to more "substantive" issues. See *Linda R. S.* v. *Richard D.,* 410 U. S. 614, 616 (1973). But in consequence there is an impulse to decide difficult questions of substantive law obliquely in the course of opinions purporting to do nothing more than determine what the Court labels "standing"; this accounts for the phenomenon of opinions, such as the one today, that tend merely to obfuscate, rather than inform, our understanding of the meaning of rights under the law. The serious by-product of that practice is that the Court disregards its constitutional responsibility when, by failing to acknowledge the protections afforded by the Constitution, it uses "standing to slam the courthouse door against plaintiffs who are entitled to full consideration of their claims on the merits."

The opinion of the Court is a stark example of this unfortunate trend of resolving cases at the "threshold" while obscuring the nature of the underlying rights and interests at stake. The Court waxes eloquent on the blend of prudential and constitutional considerations that combine to create our misguided "standing" jurisprudence. *But not one word is said about the Establishment Clause right that the plaintiff seeks to enforce.* And despite its pat recitation of our standing decisions, the opinion utterly fails, except by the sheerest form of *ipse dixit,* to explain why this case is unlike *Flast* v. *Cohen,* 392 U. S. 83 (1968), and is controlled instead by *Frothingham* v. *Mellon,* 262 U. S. 447 (1923). . . .

It may of course happen that a person believing himself injured in some obscure manner by government action will be held to have no legal right under the constitutional or statutory provision upon which he relies, and will not be permitted to complain of the invasion of another person's "rights." It is quite another matter to employ the rhetoric of "standing" to deprive a person, whose interest is clearly protected by the law, of the opportunity to prove that his own rights have been violated. It is in precisely that dissembling enterprise that the Court indulges today. . . .

In 1947, nine Justices of this Court recognized that the Establishment Clause does impose a very definite restriction on the power to tax. The Court held in *Everson* v. *Board of Education,* 330 U. S., at 15, that the "'establishment of religion' clause of the First Amendment means at least this:"

"No tax in any amount, large or small, can be levied to support any religious activities or institutions, whatever they may be called, or whatever form they may adopt, to teach or practice religion." *Id.,* at 16. . . .

It is at once apparent that the test of standing formulated by the Court in *Flast* sought to reconcile the developing doctrine of taxpayer "standing" with the Court's historical understanding that the Establishment Clause was intended to prohibit the Federal Government from using tax funds for the advancement of religion, and thus the constitutional imperative of taxpayer standing in certain cases brought pursuant to the Establishment Clause. . . .

It may be that Congress can tax for *almost* any reason, or for no reason at all. There is, so far as I have been able to discern, but one constitutionally imposed limit on that authority. Congress cannot use tax money to support a church, or to encourage religion. That is *"the* forbidden exaction." *Everson* v. *Board of Education,* 330 U. S., at 45 (Rutledge, J., dissenting) (emphasis added). See *Flast, supra,* at 115–116 (Fortas, J., concurring). In absolute terms the history of the Establishment Clause of the First Amendment makes this clear. . . .

Blind to history, the Court attempts to distinguish this case from *Flast* by wrenching snippets of language from our opinions, and by perfunctorily applying that language under color of the first prong of *Flast*'s two-part nexus test. The tortuous distinctions thus produced are specious, at best: at worst, they are pernicious to our constitutional heritage.

First, the Court finds this case different from *Flast* because here the "source of [plaintiff's] complaint is not a *congressional* action, but a decision by HEW to transfer a parcel of federal property." *Ante,* at 479 (emphasis added). This attempt at distinction cannot withstand scrutiny. *Flast* involved a challenge to the actions of the Commissioner of Education, and other officials of HEW, in disbursing funds under the Elementary and Secondary Education Act of 1965 to "religious and sectarian" schools. Plaintiffs disclaimed "any intent[ion] to challenge . . . all programs under . . . the Act." *Flast, supra,* at 87. Rather, they claimed that defendant-administrators' approval of such expenditures was not authorized by the Act, or alternatively, to the extent the expenditures were authorized, the Act was "unconstitutional and void." *Ibid.* In the present case, respondents challenge HEW's grant of property pursuant to the Federal Property and Administrative Services Act of 1949, seeking to enjoin HEW "from making a grant of this and other property to the [defendant] so long as such a grant will violate the Establishment Clause." App. 12. It may be that the Court is concerned with the adequacy of respondents' pleading; respondents have not, in so many words, asked for a declaration that the "Federal Property and Administrative Services Act is unconstitutional and void to the extent that it authorizes HEW's actions." I would not construe their complaint so narrowly.

More fundamentally, no clear division can be drawn in this context between actions of the Legislative Branch and those of the Executive Branch. To be sure, the First Amendment is phrased as a restriction on Congress' legislative authority; this is only natural since the Constitution assigns the authority to legislate and appropriate only to the Congress. But it is difficult to conceive of an expenditure for which the last governmental actor, either implementing directly the legislative will, or acting within the scope of legislatively delegated authority, is not an Executive Branch official. The First Amendment binds the Government as a whole, regardless of which branch is at work in a particular instance.

The Court's second purported distinction between this case and *Flast* is equally unavailing. The majority finds it "decisive" that the Federal Property and Administrative Services Act of 1949 "was an evident exercise of Congress' power under the Property Clause, Art. IV, § 3, cl.2," *ante,* at 480, while the Government action in *Flast* was taken under Art. I, § 8. The Court relies on *United States v. Richardson,* 418 U. S. 166 (1974), and *Schlesinger* v. *Reservists Committee to Stop the War,* 418 U. S. 208 (1974), to support the distinction between the two Clauses, noting that those cases involved alleged deviations from the requirements of Art. I, § 9, cl. 7, and Art. I, § 6, cl. 2, respectively. The standing defect in each case was *not,* however, the failure to allege a violation of the Spending Clause; rather, the taxpayers in those cases had not complained of the distribution of Government largesse, and thus failed to meet the essential requirement of taxpayer standing recognized in *Doremus.*

It can make no constitutional difference in the case before us whether the donation to the petitioner here was in the form of a cash grant to build a facility, see *Tilton* v. *Richardson,* 403 U. S. 672 (1971), or in the nature of a gift of property including a facility already built. That this is a meaningless distinction is illustrated by *Tilton.* In that case, taxpayers were afforded standing to object to the fact that the Government had not received adequate assurance that if the property that it financed for use as an educational facility was later converted to religious uses, it would receive full value for the property, as the Constitution requires. The complaint here is precisely that, although the property at issue is actually being used for a sectarian purpose, the Government has not received, nor demanded, full value payment. Whether undertaken pursuant to the Property Clause or the Spending Clause, the breach of the Establishment Clause, and the relationship of the taxpayer to that breach, is precisely the same.

IV

Plainly hostile to the Framers' understanding of the Establishment Clause, and *Flast*'s enforcement of that understanding, the Court vents that hostility under the guise of standing, "to slam the courthouse door against plaintiffs who [as the

Framers intended] are entitled to full consideration of their [Establishment Clause] claims on the merits." *Barlow* v. *Collins*, 397 U. S. 159, 178 (1970) (Brennan, J., concurring in result and dissenting). Therefore, I dissent.

JUSTICE STEVENS, dissenting.

In Parts I, II, and III of his dissenting opinion, JUSTICE BRENNAN demonstrates that respondent taxpayers have standing to mount an Establishment Clause challenge against the Federal Government's transfer of property worth $1,300,000 to the Assemblies of God. For the Court to hold that plaintiffs' standing depends on whether the Government's transfer was an exercise of its power to spend money, on the one hand, or its power to dispose of tangible property, on the other, is to trivialize the standing doctrine. . . .

Today the Court holds, in effect, that the Judiciary has no greater role in enforcing the Establishment Clause than in enforcing other "norm[s] of conduct which the Federal Government is bound to honor," *ante*, at 484, such as the Accounts Clause, *United States* v. *Richardson*, 418 U. S. 166, and the Incompatibility Clause, *Schlesinger* v. *Reservists Committee to Stop the War*, 418 U. S. 208. Ironically, however, its decision rests on the premise that the difference between a disposition of funds pursuant to the Spending Clause and a disposition of realty pursuant to the Property Clause is of fundamental jurisprudential significance. With all due respect, I am persuaded that the essential holding of *Flast* v. *Cohen* attaches special importance to the Establishment Clause and does not permit the drawing of a tenuous distinction between the Spending Clause and the Property Clause. . . .

Gene R. Nichol, Jr.

The Tactical Uses of Standing

The confused nature of the standing doctrine results in part from the habit of treating standing as a series of technical, rather than tactical, exercises. The following article concludes that it is a mistake to read standing cases solely as a question of "injury in fact." Other factors are present, including concerns about separation of powers and federalism.

We need not mince words when we say that the concept of "Art. III standing" has not been defined with complete consistency. . . .
　—Valley Forge Christian College v. Americans United for Separation of Church & State, Inc.

When Justice Rehnquist penned this quotation, he employed no false sense of modesty. To the contrary, describing the law of standing merely as less than consistent reflects a talent for understatement not often associated with the controversial Justice. In perhaps no other area of constitutional law has scholarly commentary been so

uniformly critical. Observers, with just cause, regularly accuse the Supreme Court of applying standing principles in a fashion that is not only erratic, but also eminently frustrating in view of the supposed threshold nature of the standing inquiry. The judicial eye appears to be peering beyond preliminary access issues to take into account a variety of interests traditionally considered irrelevant to the standing determination. As a result, the Court's existing body of law reflects a state of "intellectual crisis."

Nor will the "crisis" soon subside. Current judicial opinions make little effort to recognize—let alone to ameliorate—the vagaries of the law of standing. The Court has been more articulate—or at least more energetic—in describing what it will

SOURCE: "Rethinking Standing," 72 *California Law Review* 68 (1984). Footnotes omitted.

not do than what it will. To an extent, commentators have followed suit. With a few notable exceptions, academics have challenged the results in a particular case or line of cases, without questioning the standing framework as a whole or offering alternative methods with which to measure judicial power.

The standing principle can no longer appropriately be written off as merely a "complicated specialty of federal jurisdiction." It has become, rather, a burgeoning, constitutionally grounded doctrine, with a significant impact upon federal litigation. Standing law provides, in essence, the law of "judicial control of public officers." Given the tremendous growth of public law in the United States over the past three decades, access decisions influence in a major way our constitutional structure. If such decisions are unprincipled, the entire process of constitutional adjudication suffers.

This Article will examine the standing doctrine in its broadest contours. Specifically, in Part I the analytical foundations of the Burger Court's standing jurisprudence will be criticized. My principal claim is that the Court has applied one aspect of standing analysis—namely, the demand for concrete, particularized injury—to areas of article III investigation for which the requirement is ill suited. The results of judicial preoccupation with injury in fact have been numerous. First, the Court has so severely manipulated the injury standard that the foundation of standing law is essentially incomprehensible. Second, by treating the injury standard as if it were an objective measure of interest, the Court has refused to initiate a much-needed dialogue on the appropriate boundaries of constitutional harm. Third, the decisions reflect the influence of issues extraneous to the standing inquiry. The result is a schizophrenic body of law in which the Court announces that one set of interests are dispositive (the plaintiff's stake in the litigation), while in the bulk of the major cases other factors appear to prevail (separation of powers, federalism concerns, the desirability of the claim on the merits, etc.). Finally, by dwelling on concrete injury and ignoring the distinct concerns posed by harms to legally cognizable interests, standing analysis denigrates less tangible values created by law.

It is my position, therefore, that the Supreme Court should reconsider its present use of the particularized injury standard. The demonstration of distinct, concrete harm is one appropriate method of invoking federal jurisdiction. It is not, however, the only manner of showing legally cognizable interest. Statutory and constitutionally created interests often provide independent bases for judicial access. By attempting to fit all of standing analysis within the injury rubric, decisions confuse not only what is required to achieve standing but also what it means to be injured.

A second, and perhaps less controversial claim made here, is that standing law has been made to serve too many masters. Decisions examining the plaintiff's interests in the litigation, the breadth of various protections of substantive law, and the appropriate scope of judicial authority in our system of government have all passed for standing analysis. Even with such divergent goals, however, the Court typically explains its decisions only by conclusory declarations about the presence or absence of injury. If such factors are to be introduced into the standing calculus they should be addressed both openly and individually. To that end, in Part II, I will suggest a method of standing review designed to segregate the various interests that are brought to bear on the modern standing decision. I propose that the Court develop distinctions between (a) access standing—measuring the plaintiff's interest in the litigation to determine whether he is a proper party to invoke federal jurisdiction; (b) issue standing—asking whether the plaintiff is a proper party to assert the particular legal rights he claims; and (c) decision standing—considering whether the issue to be litigated is a political one, entrusted to another branch of state or federal government. So analyzed, it is hoped that scrutiny of the case or controversy requirement can be made both more focused and more finely attuned to the protections afforded by substantive law.

. . .

Standing law, like the proverbial politician, speaks out of both sides of its mouth. On the one hand, in order to segregate the standing inquiry from consideration of the claim on the merits and general justiciability concerns, the entire doctrine has been founded upon an overarching principle —particularized harm. In the years since the adoption of the injury standard, however, the Supreme Court has used the standing doctrine to accomplish far more than the mere determination that the plaintiff is an appropriate party to invoke federal jurisdiction. The Court has also employed standing law to measure the appropriate scope of judicial authority and to mitigate federal judicial interference with local concerns. As a result, in the process of defining actionable injury, the Court has reinserted the very factors into the standing calculus which the particularized harm standard was designed to remove. Further, federalism and separation of powers issues have generally been concealed behind a standing discussion concerning the directness of injury or the generalized nature of the claim. The result has not been beneficial to either standing law or the analysis of the appropriate role of the judiciary in our system of government.

I have argued that standing analysis would be better served if the Court were to separate the various issues reflected in its case or controversy decisions and address them openly and independently. The core of standing is, of course, whether the plaintiff has shown sufficient interest to obtain access to federal judicial power. Yet access standing should require no more than that a litigant assert injury to an interest arguably cognizable by law. Issue standing, on the other hand, should be focused primarily on the breadth of protections offered by various substantive guarantees. As a result, its standards may be tailored appropriately to meet the ends of various substantive principles —extending, for example, overbreadth analysis when free expression rights are at stake but contracting the doctrine in privacy cases. Finally, decision standing, pursuant to which the Court has denied standing based upon the justiciability of the claim, should be abandoned. Measuring the proper expanse of judicial authority vis-a-vis other institutions of government should be accomplished under the political question doctrine. So envisioned, the standing doctrine would likely prove a less formidable obstacle to the acquisition of federal jurisdiction. If it is true, as I have argued, that the standing principle has been made to carry the baggage of other concerns, it should not be surprising that a "cleaning" of the doctrine would result in a lowered access threshold.

Standing law, as presently constructed, is so unfocused that it seems to serve no useful or at least no ascertainable ends. That will likely remain the case so long as standing determinations appear to take into account first one set of interests and then another, but all the while employ conclusory declarations concerning the nature of injury as the basis for decision. As Lincoln argued, "[I]f we could first know *where* we are and *whither* we are tending, we could better judge *what* to do, and *how* to do it." Recognizing the complexity of the injury determination and segregating the numerous interests that have affected past standing decisions are essential first steps in learning where we are, and even perhaps "whither we are tending" in case or controversy analysis. Without such preliminaries, however, we stand little chance of knowing what to do, and how to do it.

DeFunis v. Odegaard

416 U.S. 312 (1974)

Marcos DeFunis, Jr., was denied admission to the University of Washington Law School, although his test scores were higher than those of some of the minorities admitted. He was accepted after a trial court found in his favor, and was in his third and final year when the case reached the Supreme Court. The question was whether the case should be dismissed on grounds of mootness.

PER CURIAM.

In 1971 the petitioner Marco DeFunis, Jr., applied for admission as a first-year student at the University of Washington Law School, a state-operated institution. The size of the incoming first-year class was to be limited to 150 persons, and the Law School received some 1,600 applications for these 150 places. DeFunis was eventually notified that he had been denied admission. He thereupon commenced this suit in a Washington trial court, contending that the procedures and criteria employed by the Law School Admissions Committee invidiously discriminated against him on account of his race in violation of the Equal Protection Clause of the Fourteenth Amendment to the United States Constitution.

DeFunis brought the suit on behalf of himself alone, and not as the representative of any class, against the various respondents, who are officers, faculty members, and members of the Board of Regents of the University of Washington. He asked the trial court to issue a mandatory injunction commanding the respondents to admit him as a member of the first-year class entering in September 1971, on the ground that the Law School admissions policy had resulted in the unconstitutional denial of his application for admission. The trial court agreed with his claim and granted the requested relief. DeFunis was, accordingly, admitted to the Law School and began his legal studies there in the fall of 1971. On appeal, the Washington Supreme Court reversed the judgment of the trial court and held that the Law School admissions policy did not violate the Constitution. By this time DeFunis was in his second year at the Law School.

He then petitioned this Court for a writ of certiorari, and MR. JUSTICE DOUGLAS, as Circuit Justice, stayed the judgment of the Washington Supreme Court pending the "final disposition of the case by this Court." By virtue of this stay, DeFunis has remained in law school, and was in the first term of his third and final year when this Court first considered his certiorari petition in the fall of 1973. Because of our concern that DeFunis' third-year standing in the Law School might have rendered this case moot, we requested the parties to brief the question of mootness before we acted on the petition. In response, both sides contended that the case was not moot. The respondents indicated that, if the decision of the Washington Supreme Court were permitted to stand, the petitioner could complete the term for which he was then enrolled but would have to apply to the faculty for permission to continue in the school before he could register for another term.

We granted the petition for certiorari on November 19, 1973. 414 U.S. 1038. The case was in due course orally argued on February 26, 1974.

In response to questions raised from the bench during the oral argument, counsel for the petitioner has informed the Court that DeFunis has now registered "for his final quarter in law school." Counsel for the respondents have made clear that the Law School will not in any way seek to abrogate this registration. In light of DeFunis' recent registration for the last quarter of his final law school year, and the Law School's assurance that his registration is fully effective, the insistent question again arises whether this case is not moot, and to that question we now turn.

The starting point for analysis is the familiar proposition that "federal courts are without power to decide questions that cannot affect the rights of litigants in the case before them." *North Carolina v. Rice,* 404 U.S. 244, 246 (1971). The inability of the federal judiciary "to review moot cases derives from the requirement of Art. III of the Constitution under which the exercise of judicial power depends upon the existence of a case or controversy." *Liner v. Jafco, Inc.,* 375 U.S. 301, 306 n. 3 (1964); see also *Powell v. McCormack,* 395 U.S. 486, 496 n. 7 (1969); *Sibron v. New York,* 392 U.S. 40, 50 n. 8 (1968). Although as a matter of Washington state law it appears that this case would be saved from mootness by "the great public interest in the continuing issues raised by this appeal," 82 Wash. 2d 11, 23 n. 6, 507 P. 2d 1169, 1177 n. 6 (1973), the fact remains that under Art. III "[e]ven in cases arising in the state courts, the question of mootness is a federal one which a federal court must resolve before it assumes jurisdiction." *North Carolina v. Rice, supra,* at 246.

The respondents have represented that, without regard to the ultimate resolution of the issues in this case, DeFunis will remain a student in the

Law School for the duration of any term in which he has already enrolled. Since he has now registered for his final term, it is evident that he will be given an opportunity to complete all academic and other requirements for graduation, and, if he does so, will receive his diploma regardless of any decision this Court might reach on the merits of this case. In short, all parties agree that DeFunis is now entitled to complete his legal studies at the University of Washington and to receive his degree from that institution. A determination by this Court of the legal issues tendered by the parties is no longer necessary to compel that result, and could not serve to prevent it. DeFunis did not cast his suit as a class action, and the only remedy he requested was an injunction commanding his admission to the Law School. He was not only accorded that remedy, but he now has also been irrevocably admitted to the final term of the final year of the Law School course. The controversy between the parties has thus clearly ceased to be "definite and concrete" and no longer "touch[es] the legal relations of parties having adverse legal interests." *Aetna Life Ins. Co.* v. *Haworth*, 300 U. S. 227, 240–241 (1937).

It matters not that these circumstances partially stem from a policy decision on the part of the respondent Law School authorities. The respondents, through their counsel, the Attorney General of the State, have professionally represented that in no event will the status of DeFunis now be affected by any view this Court might express on the merits of this controversy. And it has been the settled practice of the Court, in contexts no less significant, fully to accept representations such as these as parameters for decision. See *Gerende* v. *Election Board*, 341 U.S. 56 (1951); *Whitehill* v. *Elkins*, 389 U.S. 54, 57–58 (1967); *Ehlert* v. *United States*, 402 U. S. 99, 107 (1971); cf. *Law Students Research Council* v. *Wadmond*, 401 U. S. 154, 162–163 (1971).

There is a line of decisions in this Court standing for the proposition that the "voluntary cessation of allegedly illegal conduct does not deprive the tribunal of power to hear and determine the case, *i.e.*, does not make the case moot." *United States* v. *W. T. Grant Co.*, 345 U.S. 629, 632 (1953); *United States* v. *Trans-Missouri Freight Assn.*, 166 U. S. 290, 308–310 (1897); *Walling* v. *Helmerich &*

Payne, Inc., 323 U.S. 37, 43 (1944); *Gray* v. *Sanders*, 372 U. S. 368, 376 (1963); *United States* v. *Phosphate Export Assn.*, 393 U.S. 199, 202–203 (1968). These decisions and the doctrine they reflect would be quite relevant if the question of mootness here had arisen by reason of a unilateral change in the *admissions procedures* of the Law School. For it was the admissions procedures that were the target of this litigation, and a voluntary cessation of the admissions practices complained of could make this case moot only if it could be said with assurance "that 'there is no reasonable expectation that the wrong will be repeated.'" *United States* v. *W. T. Grant Co., supra*, at 633. Otherwise, "[t]he defendant is free to return to his old ways," *id.*, at 632, and this fact would be enough to prevent mootness because of the "public interest in having the legality of the practices settled." *Ibid.* But mootness in the present case depends not at all upon a "voluntary cessation" of the admissions practices that were the subject of this litigation. It depends, instead, upon the simple fact that DeFunis is now in the final quarter of the final year of his course of study, and the settled and unchallenged policy of the Law School to permit him to complete the term for which he is now enrolled.

It might also be suggested that this case presents a question that is "capable of repetition, yet evading review," *Southern Pacific Terminal Co.* v. *ICC*, 219 U.S. 498, 515 (1911); *Roe* v. *Wade*, 410 U.S. 113, 125 (1973), and is thus amenable to federal adjudication even though it might otherwise be considered moot. But DeFunis will never again be required to run the gantlet of the Law School's admission process, and so the question is certainly not "capable of repetition" so far as he is concerned. Moreover, just because this particular case did not reach the Court until the eve of the petitioner's graduation from law school, it hardly follows that the issue he raises will in the future evade review. If the admissions procedures of the Law School remain unchanged, there is no reason to suppose that a subsequent case attacking those procedures will not come with relative speed to this Court, now that the Supreme Court of Washington has spoken. This case, therefore, in no way presents the exceptional situation in which the *Southern Pacific Terminal* doctrine might permit a departure from "[t]he usual rule in federal cases . . . that an actual controversy must exist at stages of appellate or certiorari review, and not simply at the date the action is initiated." *Roe* v. *Wade, supra,* at 125; *United States* v. *Munsingwear, Inc.,* 340 U.S. 36 (1950).

Because the petitioner will complete his law school studies at the end of the term for which he has now registered regardless of any decision this Court might reach on the merits of this litigation, we conclude that the Court cannot, consistently with the limitations of Art. III of the Constitution, consider the substantive constitutional issues tendered by the parties. Accordingly, the judgment of the Supreme Court of Washington is vacated, and the cause is remanded for such proceedings as by that court may be deemed appropriate.

It is so ordered.

[Justice Douglas dissented; he could not conclude that the admissions procedure violated the Equal Protection Clause.]

MR. JUSTICE BRENNAN, with whom MR. JUSTICE DOUGLAS, MR. JUSTICE WHITE, and MR. JUSTICE MARSHALL concur, dissenting.

I respectfully dissent. Many weeks of the school term remain, and petitioner may not receive his degree despite respondents' assurances that petitioner will be allowed to complete this term's schooling regardless of our decision. Any number of unexpected events—illness, economic necessity, even academic failure—might prevent his graduation at the end of the term. Were that misfortune to befall, and were petitioner required to register for yet another term, the prospect that he would again face the hurdle of the admissions policy is real, not fanciful; for respondents warn that "Mr. DeFunis would have to take some appropriate action to request continued admission for the remainder of his law school education, and *some discretionary action by the University on such request would have to be taken.*" Respondents' Memorandum on the Question of Mootness 3–4 (emphasis supplied). Thus, respondents' assurances have not dissipated the possibility that petitioner might once again have to run the gantlet of the University's allegedly unlawful admissions policy. The Court therefore proceeds on an erro-

neous premise in resting its mootness holding on a supposed inability to render any judgment that may affect one way or the other petitioner's completion of his law studies. For surely if we were to reverse the Washington Supreme Court, we could insure that, if for some reason petitioner did not graduate this spring, he would be entitled to re-enrollment at a later time on the same basis as others who have not faced the hurdle of the University's allegedly unlawful admissions policy.

In these circumstances, and because the University's position implies no concession that its admissions policy is unlawful, this controversy falls squarely within the Court's long line of decisions holding that the "[m]ere voluntary cessation of allegedly illegal conduct does not moot a case." *United States* v. *Phosphate Export Assn.,* 393 U.S. 199, 203 (1968); see *Gray* v. *Sanders,* 372 U.S. 368 (1963); *United States* v. *W. T. Grant Co.,* 345 U.S. 629 (1953); *Walling* v. *Helmerich & Payne, Inc.,* 323 U.S. 37 (1944); *FTC* v. *Goodyear Tire & Rubber Co.,* 304 U.S. 257 (1938); *United States* v. *Trans-Missouri Freight Assn.,* 166 U.S. 290 (1897). Since respondents' voluntary representation to this Court is only that they will permit petitioner to complete this term's studies, respondents have not borne the "heavy burden," *United States* v. *Phosphate Export Assn., supra,* at 203, of demonstrating that there was not even a "mere possibility" that petitioner would once again be subject to the challenged admissions policy. *United States* v. *W. T. Grant Co., supra,* at 633. On the contrary, respondents have positioned themselves so as to be "free to return to [their] old ways." *Id.,* at 632.

I can thus find no justification for the Court's straining to rid itself of this dispute. While we must be vigilant to require that litigants maintain a personal stake in the outcome of a controversy to assure that "the questions will be framed with the necessary specificity, that the issues will be contested with the necessary adverseness and that the litigation will be pursued with the necessary vigor to assure that the constitutional challenge will be made in a form traditionally thought to be capable of judicial resolution," *Flast* v. *Cohen,* 392 U.S. 83, 106 (1968), there is no want of an adversary contest in this case. Indeed, the Court concedes that, if petitioner has lost his stake in this controversy, he did so only when he registered for the

spring term. But petitioner took that action only
after the case had been fully litigated in the state
courts, briefs had been filed in this Court, and oral
argument had been heard. The case is thus ripe
for decision on a fully developed factual record
with sharply defined and fully canvassed legal
issues. Cf. *Sibron* v. *New York,* 392 U. S. 40, 57
(1968).

Moreover, in endeavoring to dispose of this
case as moot, the Court clearly disserves the
public interest. The constitutional issues which
are avoided today concern vast numbers of people, organizations, and colleges and universities,
as evidenced by the filing of twenty-six *amicus
curiae* briefs. Few constitutional questions in recent history have stirred as much debate, and they
will not disappear. They must inevitably return to
the federal courts and ultimately again to this

Court. Cf. *Richardson* v. *Wright,* 405 U. S. 208, 212
(1972) (dissenting opinion). Because avoidance of
repetitious litigation serves the public interest,
that inevitability counsels against mootness determinations, as here, not compelled by the record.
Cf. *United States* v. *W. T. Grant Co., supra,* at 632;
Parker v. *Ellis,* 362 U. S. 574, 594 (1960) (dissenting
opinion). Although the Court should, of course,
avoid unnecessary decisions of constitutional
questions, we should not transform principles of
avoidance of constitutional decisions into devices
for sidestepping resolution of difficult cases. Cf.
Cohens v. *Virginia,* 6 Wheat. 264, 404–405 (1821)
(Marshall, C.J.).

On what appears in this case, I would find that
there is an extant controversy and decide the
merits of the very important constitutional questions presented.

Poe v. Ullman
367 U.S. 497 (1961)

**A married couple, a married woman, and a doctor sued for declaratory relief against the
threatened enforcement of Connecticut's birth-control laws that prohibited married
couples from using contraceptives and physicians from advising married couples about
their use. Footnotes omitted.**

MR. JUSTICE FRANKFURTER announced the
judgment of the Court and an opinion in which
THE CHIEF JUSTICE, MR. JUSTICE CLARK and MR.
JUSTICE WHITTAKER join.

These appeals challenge the constitutionality,
under the Fourteenth Amendment, of Connecticut
statutes which, as authoritatively construed by the
Connecticut Supreme Court of Errors, prohibit
the use of contraceptive devices and the giving of
medical advice in the use of such devices. In
proceedings seeking declarations of law, not on
review of convictions for violation of the statutes,
that court has ruled that these statutes would be
applicable in the case of married couples and even
under claim that conception would constitute a
serious threat to the health or life of the female
spouse. . . .

. . . The State's Attorney intends to prosecute
offenses against the State's laws, and claims that
the giving of contraceptive advice and the use of
contraceptive devices would be offenses forbidden
by Conn. Gen. Stat. Rev., 1958, §§ 53–32 and
54–196. . . .

Appellants' complaints in these declaratory
judgment proceedings do not clearly, and certainly do not in terms, allege that appellee Ullman
threatens to prosecute them for use of, or for
giving advice concerning, contraceptive devices.
The allegations are merely that, in the course of
his public duty, he intends to prosecute any offenses against Connecticut law, and that he claims that
use of and advice concerning contraceptives
would constitute offenses. The lack of immediacy
of the threat described by these allegations might

alone raise serious questions of non-justiciability of appellants' claims. See *United Public Workers* v. *Mitchell*, 330 U.S. 75, 88. But even were we to read the allegations to convey a clear threat of imminent prosecutions, we are not bound to accept as true all that is alleged on the face of the complaint and admitted, technically, by demurrer, any more than the Court is bound by stipulation of the parties. *Swift & Co.* v. *Hocking Valley R. Co.*, 243 U.S. 281, 289. Formal agreement between parties that collides with plausibility is too fragile a foundation for indulging in constitutional adjudication.

The Connecticut law prohibiting the use of contraceptives has been on the State's books since 1879. Conn. Acts 1879, c. 78. During the more than three-quarters of a century since its enactment, a prosecution for its violation seems never to have been initiated, save in *State* v. *Nelson*, 126 Conn. 412, 11 A. 2d 856. . . .

The fact that Connecticut has not chosen to press the enforcement of this statute deprives these controversies of the immediacy which is an indispensable condition of constitutional adjudication. This Court cannot be umpire to debates concerning harmless, empty shadows. To find it necessary to pass on these statutes now, in order to protect appellants from the hazards of prosecution, would be to close our eyes to reality. . . .

Justiciability is of course not a legal concept with a fixed content or susceptible of scientific verification. Its utilization is the resultant of many subtle pressures, including the appropriateness of the issues for decision by this Court and the actual hardship to the litigants of denying them the relief sought. Both these factors justify withholding adjudication of the constitutional issue raised under the circumstances and in the manner in which they are now before the Court.

Dismissed.

MR. JUSTICE BLACK dissents because he believes that the constitutional questions should be reached and decided.

MR. JUSTICE BRENNAN, concurring in the judgment.

I agree that this appeal must be dismissed for failure to present a real and substantial controversy which unequivocally calls for adjudication of the rights claimed in advance of any attempt by the State to curtail them by criminal prosecution. I am not convinced, on this skimpy record, that these appellants as individuals are truly caught in an inescapable dilemma. The true controversy in this case is over the opening of birth-control clinics on a large scale; it is that which the State has prevented in the past, not the use of contraceptives by isolated and individual married couples. It will be time enough to decide the constitutional questions urged upon us when, if ever, that real controversy flares up again. Until it does, or until the State makes a definite and concrete threat to enforce these laws against individual married couples—a threat which it has never made in the past except under the provocation of litigation—this Court may not be compelled to exercise its most delicate power of constitutional adjudication.

MR. JUSTICE DOUGLAS, dissenting. . . .

A public clinic dispensing birth-control information has indeed been closed by the State. Doctors and a nurse working in that clinic were arrested by the police and charged with advising married women on the use of contraceptives. That litigation produced *State* v. *Nelson*, 126 Conn. 412, 11 A. 2d 856, which upheld these statutes. That same police raid on the clinic resulted in the seizure of a quantity of the clinic's contraception literature and medical equipment and supplies. The legality of that seizure was in question in *State* v. *Certain Contraceptive Materials*, 126 Conn. 428, 11 A. 2d 863.

The Court refers to the *Nelson* prosecution as a "test case" and implies that it had little impact. Yet its impact was described differently by a contemporary observer who concluded his comment with this sentence: "This serious setback to the birth control movement [the *Nelson* case] led to the closing of all the clinics in the state, just as they had been previously closed in the state of Massachusetts." At oral argument, counsel for appellants confirmed that the clinics are still closed. In response to a question from the bench, he affirmed that "no public or private clinic" has dared give birth-control advice since the decision in the *Nelson* case. . . .

When the Court goes outside the record to determine that Connecticut has adopted "The undeviating policy of nullification . . . of its anti-contraceptive laws," it selects a particularly poor case in which to exercise such a novel power. This is not a law which is a dead letter. Twice since 1940, Connecticut has re-enacted these laws as part of general statutory revisions. Consistently, bills to remove the statutes from the books have been rejected by the legislature. In short, the statutes—far from being the accidental left-overs of another era—are the center of a continuing controversy in the State. . . .

What are these people—doctor and patients—to do? Flout the law and go to prison? Violate the law surreptitiously and hope they will not get caught? By today's decision we leave them no other alternatives. It is not the choice they need have under the regime of the declaratory judgment and our constitutional system. It is not the choice worthy of a civilized society. A sick wife, a concerned husband, a conscientious doctor seek a dignified, discrete, orderly answer to the critical problem confronting them. We should not turn them away and make them flout the law and get arrested to have their constitutional rights determined. . . .

MR. JUSTICE HARLAN, dissenting.

I am compelled, with all respect, to dissent from the dismissal of these appeals. In my view the course which the Court has taken does violence to established concepts of "justiciability," and unjustifiably leaves these appellants under the threat of unconstitutional prosecution.

. . . I do not think these appeals may be dismissed for want of "ripeness" as that concept has been understood in its "varied applications." There is no lack of "ripeness" in the sense that is exemplified by cases such as *Stearns* v. *Wood*, 236 U.S. 75; *Electric Bond & Share Co.* v. *Securities & Exchange Comm'n*, 303 U. S. 419; *United Public Workers* v. *Mitchell*, 330 U. S. 75; *International Longshoremen's Union* v. *Boyd*, 347 U.S. 222; and perhaps again *Parker* v. *Los Angeles County*, *supra*.

In all of those cases the lack of ripeness inhered in the fact that the need for some further procedure, some further contingency of application or interpretation, whether judicial, administrative or executive, or some further clarification of the intentions of the claimant, served to make remote the issue which was sought to be presented to the Court.

. . . I cannot see what further elaboration is required to enable us to decide the appellants' claims, and indeed neither the plurality opinion nor the concurring opinion—notwithstanding the latter's characterization of this record as "skimpy"—suggests what more grist is needed before the judicial mill could turn.

. . . I find it difficult to believe that doctors generally—and not just those operating specialized clinics—would continue openly to disseminate advice about contraceptives after *Nelson* in reliance on the State's supposed unwillingness to prosecute, or to consider that high-minded members of the profession would in consequence of such inaction deem themselves warranted in disrespecting this law so long as it is on the books. Nor can I regard as "chimerical" the fear of enforcement of these provisions that seems to have caused the disappearance of at least nine birth-control clinics. In short, I fear that the Court has indulged in a bit of sleight of hand to be rid of this case. . . .

The Court's disposition assumes that to decide the case now, in the absence of any consummated prosecutions, is unwise because it forces a difficult decision in advance of any exigent necessity therefor. Of course it is abundantly clear that this requisite necessity can exist prior to any actual prosecution, for that is the theory of anticipatory relief, and is by now familiar law. . . .

In this light it is not surprising that the Court's position is without support in the precedents. Indeed it seems to me that *Pierce* v. *Society of Sisters*, 268 U.S. 510, provides very clear authority contrary to the position of the Court in this case, for there a Court which included Justices Holmes, Brandeis, and Stone rejected a claim of prematureness and then passed upon and held unconstitutional a state statute whose sanctions were not even to become effective for more than seventeen months after the time the case was argued to this Court. The Court found allegations of present loss of business, caused by the threat of the statute's future enforcement against the Society's clientele, sufficient to make the injury to the Society "present and very real." 268 U. S., at 536. I cannot regard as less present, or less real, the tendency to discourage the exercise of the liberties of these appellants, caused by reluctance to submit their freedoms from prosecution and conviction to the discretion of the Connecticut prosecuting authorities. . . .

MR. JUSTICE STEWART, dissenting.

For the reasons so convincingly advanced by both MR. JUSTICE DOUGLAS and MR. JUSTICE HARLAN, I join them in dissenting from the dismissal of these appeals. Since the appeals are nonetheless dismissed, my dissent need go no further. However, in refraining from a discussion of the constitutional issues, I in no way imply that the ultimate result I would reach on the merits of these controversies would differ from the conclusions of my dissenting Brothers.

Baker v. Carr

369 U.S. 186 (1962)

In this case, in which the Supreme Court accepts jurisdiction over the apportionment of legislative seats, the Court sets forth the criteria for determining whether a case falls within the category of a "political question."

MR. JUSTICE BRENNAN delivered the opinion of the Court. . . .

Our discussion, even at the price of extending this opinion, requires review of a number of political question cases, in order to expose the attributes of the doctrine—attributes which, in various settings, diverge, combine, appear, and disappear in seeming disorderliness. Since that review is undertaken solely to demonstrate that neither singly nor collectively do these cases support a conclusion that this apportionment case is nonjusticiable, we of course do not explore their implications in other contexts. That review reveals that in the Guaranty Clause cases and in the other "political question" cases, it is the relationship between the judiciary and the coordinate branches of the Federal Government, and not the federal judiciary's relationship to the States, which gives rise to the "political question."

We have said that "In determining whether a question falls within [the political question] category, the appropriateness under our system of government of attributing finality to the action of the political departments and also the lack of

satisfactory criteria for a judicial determination are dominant considerations." *Coleman* v. *Miller*, 307 U. S. 433, 454–455. The nonjusticiability of a political question is primarily a function of the separation of powers. Much confusion results from the capacity of the "political question" label to obscure the need for case-by-case inquiry. Deciding whether a matter has in any measure been committed by the Constitution to another branch of government, or whether the action of that branch exceeds whatever authority has been committed, is itself a delicate exercise in constitutional interpretation, and is a responsibility of this Court as ultimate interpreter of the Constitution. To demonstrate this requires no less than to analyze representative cases and to infer from them the analytical threads that make up the political question doctrine. We shall then show that none of those threads catches this case.

Foreign relations: There are sweeping statements to the effect that all questions touching foreign relations are political questions. Not only does resolution of such issues frequently turn on standards that defy judicial application, or involve the exercise of a discretion demonstrably committed to the executive or legislature; but many such questions uniquely demand single-voiced statement of the Government's views. Yet it is error to suppose that every case or controversy which touches foreign relations lies beyond judicial cognizance. Our cases in this field seem invariably to show a discriminating analysis of the particular question posed, in terms of the history of its management by the political branches, of its susceptibility to judicial handling in the light of its nature and posture in the specific case, and of the possible consequences of judicial action. . . .

While recognition of foreign governments so strongly defies judicial treatment that without executive recognition a foreign state has been called "a republic of whose existence we know nothing," and the judiciary ordinarily follows the executive as to which nation has sovereignty over disputed territory, once sovereignty over an area is politically determined and declared, courts may examine the resulting status and decide independently whether a statute applies to that area. Similarly, recognition of belligerency abroad is an executive responsibility, but if the executive proclamations fall short of an explicit answer, a court may construe them seeking, for example, to determine whether the situation is such that statutes designed to assure American neutrality have become operative. *The Three Friends*, 166 U.S. 1, 63, 66. Still again, though it is the executive that determines a person's status as representative of a foreign government, *Ex parte Hitz*, 111 U.S. 766, the executive's statements will be construed where necessary to determine the court's jurisdiction, *In re Baiz*, 135 U.S. 403. Similar judicial action in the absence of a recognizedly authoritative executive declaration occurs in cases involving the immunity from seizure of vessels owned by friendly foreign governments. Compare *Ex parte Peru*, 318 U.S. 578, with *Mexico* v. *Hoffman*, 324 U.S. 30, 34–35.

Dates of duration of hostilities: Though it has been stated broadly that "the power which declared the necessity is the power to declare its cessation, and what the cessation requires," *Commercial Trust Co.* v. *Miller*, 262 U.S. 51, 57, here too analysis reveals isolable reasons for the presence of political questions, underlying this Court's refusal to review the political departments' determination of when or whether a war has ended. Dominant is the need for finality in the political determination, for emergency's nature demands "A prompt and unhesitating obedience," *Martin* v. *Mott*, 12 Wheat. 19, 30 (calling up of militia). Moreover, "the cessation of hostilities does not necessarily end the war power. It was stated in *Hamilton* v. *Kentucky Distilleries & W. Co.*, 251 U.S. 146, 161, that the war power includes the power 'to remedy the evils which have arisen from its rise and progress' and continues during that emergency. *Stewart* v. *Kahn*, 11 Wall. 493, 507." *Fleming* v. *Mohawk Wrecking Co.*, 331 U.S. 111, 116. But deference rests on reason, not habit. . . .

Validity of enactments: In *Coleman* v. *Miller, supra,* this Court held that the questions of how long a proposed amendment to the Federal Constitution remained open to ratification, and what effect a prior rejection had on a subsequent ratification, were committed to congressional resolution and involved criteria of decision that necessarily escaped the judicial grasp. Similar considerations apply to the enacting process: "The respect due to coequal and independent departments," and the need for finality and certainty about the status of a statute contribute to judicial reluctance to inquire whether, as passed, it complied with all requisite formalities. *Field* v. *Clark*, 143 U.S. 649, 672, 676–677; see *Leser* v. *Garnett*, 258 U.S. 130, 137. But it is not true that courts will never delve into a legislature's records upon such a quest: If the enrolled statute lacks an effective date, a court will not hesitate to seek it in the legislative journals in order to preserve the enactment. *Gardner* v. *The Collector*, 6 Wall. 499. The political question doctrine, a tool for maintenance of governmental order, will not be so applied as to promote only disorder.

The status of Indian tribes: This Court's deference to the political departments in determining whether Indians are recognized as a tribe, while it reflects familiar attributes of political questions, *United States* v. *Holliday*, 3 Wall. 407, 419, also has a unique element in that "the relation of the Indians to the United States is marked by peculiar and cardinal distinctions which exist no where else. . . . [The Indians are] domestic dependent nations . . . in a state of pupilage. Their relation to the United States resembles that of a ward to his guardian." *The Cherokee Nation* v. *Georgia,* 5 Pet. 1, 16, 17. Yet, here too, there is no blanket rule. While "'It is for [Congress] . . . and not for the courts, to determine when the true interests of the Indian require his release from [the] condition of tutelage' . . . , it is not meant by this that Congress may bring a community or body of people within the range of this power by arbitrarily calling them an Indian tribe. . . . " *United States* v. *Sandoval,* 231 U.S. 28, 46. Able to discern what is "distinctly Indian," *ibid.,* the courts will strike down any heedless extension of that label. They will not stand impotent before an obvious instance of a manifestly unauthorized exercise of power.

It is apparent that several formulations which vary slightly according to the settings in which the questions arise may describe a political question, although each has one or more elements which identify it as essentially a function of the separation of powers. Prominent on the surface of any case held to involve a political question is found a textually demonstrable constitutional commitment of the issue to a coordinate political department; or a lack of judicially discoverable and manageable standards for resolving it; or the impossibility of deciding without an initial policy determination of a kind clearly for nonjudicial discretion; or the impossibility of a court's undertaking independent resolution without expressing lack of the respect due coordinate branches of government; or an unusual need for unquestioning adherence to a political decision already made; or the potentiality of embarrassment from multifarious pronouncements by various departments on one question. . . .

Republican form of government: Luther v. *Borden,* 7 How. 1, though in form simply an action for damages for trespass was, as Daniel Webster said in opening the argument for the defense, "an unusual case." The defendants, admitting an otherwise tortious breaking and entering, sought to justify their action on the ground that they were agents of the established lawful government of Rhode Island, which State was then under martial law to defend itself from active insurrection; that the plaintiff was engaged in that insurrection; and that they entered under orders to arrest the plaintiff. . . .

Clearly, several factors were thought by the Court in *Luther* to make the question there "political": the commitment to the other branches of the decision as to which is the lawful state government; the unambiguous action by the President, in recognizing the charter government as the lawful authority; the need for finality in the executive's decision; and the lack of criteria by which a court could determine which form of government was republican.

* * *

Virtues and Vices: Bickel Versus Gunther

In a foreword entitled "The Passive Virtues," written for the 1960 term of the Supreme Court and published in the *Harvard Law Review* in 1961, Alexander M. Bickel urged the Court to avoid adjudication by making greater use of its doctrines on standing, case and controversy, ripeness, and political questions. A rebuttal, "The Subtle Vices of the 'Passive Virtues'—A Comment on Principle and Expediency in Judicial Review," was prepared by Gerald Gunther and published in the January 1964 issue of the *Columbia Law Review.* Footnotes omitted.

ALEXANDER M. BICKEL:

The volume of the Supreme Court's business is steadily on the rise. It seems to be, quite simply, a direct function of the birth rate. But the number of important and far-reaching issues offered up for decision in any single Term is, in some part at least, a matter of the accidents of litigation. . . .

One is tempted to deal with the resultant

prodigious output by passing a Solomonic judgment on it, something like Dean Griswold's on the subject of Professor Hart's *Foreword* of two years ago. Mr. Hart, Dean Griswold observed, should have cut what he had written in two, and printed the latter half at another time and perhaps in another place. The next best way out from under may be to talk not about what the Court did, but about whether it needed to do it; not so much, that is, about the Bill of Rights and the fourteenth amendment as about the Court's place in the scheme of American government. It happens that a number of this Term's most celebrated cases were as significant for having brought into focus the uses and nonuses of techniques of withholding ultimate constitutional adjudication, as for having wrought changes in substantive law. It may also be that questions of when, whether, and how much to adjudicate come as near as anything else to explaining the frequent divisions within the Court. . . .

I. "STANDING," "CASE AND CONTROVERSY," "RIPENESS," "POLITICAL QUESTION," AND THE RATIONALE OF *MARBURY* v. *MADISON*

In the beginning was the reasoning of *Marbury* v. *Madison*, against the background of *The Correspondence of the Justices* and *Hayburn's Case*. The background was faint, but it assumed sharper outline once *Marbury* v. *Madison* had been decided. If, as Marshall argued, the judiciary's power to construe and enforce the Constitution against the other departments is to be deduced from the obligation of the courts to decide cases conformably to law, which may sometimes be the Constitution, then it must follow that the power may be exercised only in a case. Marshall offered no other coherent justification for lodging it in the courts, and the text of the Constitution, whatever other supports it may or may not offer for Marshall's argument, extends the judicial power only "to all Cases" and "to Controversies." It follows that courts may make no pronouncements in the large and in the abstract, by way of opinions advising the other departments upon request; that they may give no opinions, even in a concrete case, which are advisory because they are not finally

decisive, the power of ultimate disposition of the case having been reserved elsewhere; and that they may not decide noncases, which are not adversary situations and in which nothing of immediate consequence to the parties turns on the results. These are ideas at the heart of the reasoning in *Marbury* v. *Madison*. They constitute not so much limitations of the power of judicial review as necessary supports for the argument which established it. The words of art that are shorthand for these ideas are "case and controversy" and "standing."

It would seem also to follow from *Marbury* v. *Madison* that, except as stated, "all Cases" are justiciable and must be heard. Indeed Marshall, assuming the tone of absolute assertion that he deemed suitable when the Court's basic powers were in issue, said in *Cohens* v. *Virginia*:

"It is most true that this court will not take jurisdiction if it should not; but it is equally true, that it must take jurisdiction if it should. The judiciary cannot, as the legislature may, avoid a measure because it approaches the confines of the constitution. We cannot pass it by because it is doubtful. With whatever doubts, with whatever difficulties, a case may be attended, we must decide it if it be brought before us. We have no more right to decline the exercise of jurisdiction which is given, than to usurp that which is not given. The one or the other would be treason to the constitution."

But the doctrines of standing and case and controversy have in time come to mean also something entirely unrelated to the reasoning of *Marbury* v. *Madison*. They have encompassed numerous instances in which the Court did nothing else but to "decline the exercise of jurisdiction which is given . . ." And to this end they have been abetted by, or used interchangeably (and rather unanalytically) with, other doctrines, such as "ripeness" and "political question." This has caused great difficulties for those who would rest the institution of judicial review on the foundation of the opinion in *Marbury* v. *Madison*, or even on an independent, more scrupulous but quite similar process of deduction from the constitutional text.

Professor Wechsler, who is in this respect a strict constructionist, believes that "the power of the courts [to exercise judicial review] is grounded in the language of the Constitution. . . ." He is, of course, quite aware of the consequences for the legitimacy of any discretionary option to withhold the exercise of jurisdiction. "For me, as for anyone who finds the judicial power anchored in the Constitution, there is no such escape from the judicial obligation; the duty cannot be attenuated in this way." Mr. Wechsler, indeed, goes on to quote with approval the passage from *Cohens* v. *Virginia* given above. But he makes some room for what the courts have done in fact by arguing that the "judicial Power" extends to "all Cases arising under the Constitution" only when a remedy is made available by the general law of remedies, statutory or decisional. Some cases answer to this formulation. The general law may show that the plaintiff had no existing rights in the premises that a statute claimed to be unconstitutional could have infringed. Therefore the statute, even if in fact unconstitutional, could not have injured him. Therefore, in the pure sense, he has no standing, there is no case. This is what Brandeis showed in *Ashwander* v. *TVA*. But in most instances the formulation will not avail. . . .

. . . How can there be a duty to decide "all Cases" conformably to the Constitution, acts of Congress to the contrary notwithstanding, if Congress can defeat this duty by a jurisdictional act? Would not this be "to overthrow in fact what was established in theory"? Would it not seem "an absurdity too gross to be insisted on"? Congress, to be sure, is authorized to regulate the Court's appellate jurisdiction and to make exceptions in it, but that cannot be the whole answer.

Mr. Wechsler's explanation of the political-question doctrine, potentially the widest and most radical avenue of escape from adjudication, runs along different lines. The explanation is that when the Court declines jurisdiction of a case as "political," or when, having taken the case, it declines to adjudicate the merits of a particular issue on the same ground, what it does, in conformity with *Marbury* v. *Madison,* is to render a constitutional adjudication that the matter in question is confided to the uncontrolled discretion of another department. This is sometimes an adequate statement of the result. It also represents, however, for Mr. Wechsler, "all the doctrine can defensibly imply." He puts it quite plainly that

"the only proper judgment that may lead to an abstention from decision is that the Constitution has committed the determination of the issue to another agency of government than the courts. Difficult as it may be to make that judgment wisely, whatever factors may be rightly weighed in situations where the answer is not clear, what is involved is in itself an act of constitutional interpretation, to be made and judged by standards that should govern the interpretive process generally. That, I submit, is *toto caelo* different from a broad discretion to abstain or intervene."

It is different, just so; but only by means of a play on words can the broad discretion that the courts have in fact exercised be turned into an act of constitutional interpretation. The political-question doctrine simply resists being domesticated in this fashion. There is something different about it, in kind, not in degree, from the general "interpretive process"; something greatly more flexible, something of prudence, not construction and not principle. And it is something that cannot exist within the four corners of *Marbury* v. *Madison.*

The strict-constructionist position also has difficulty reconciling itself to the Court's two commonest devices of declining "the exercise of jurisdiction which is given": denials of certiorari and dismissals of appeals "for the want of a substantial federal question." Chief Justice Warren, speaking generally, has allowed that it "is only accurate to a degree to say that our jurisdiction in cases on appeal is obligatory as distinguished from discretionary on certiorari." It can be said, and indeed it is commonly assumed, that dismissals for the want of a substantial federal question are decisions on the merits, albeit without opinion. But what of the alternative of summary reversal or affirmance? There is, and has been for many years, a great deal that is fiction in this explanation. Many are the dismissals for the want of a convenient, or timely, or suitably presented question. The certiorari jurisdiction is of course professedly discretionary and based on few articulated standards. It may be said of it that it does not deny judicial review, but rather denies it in a particular court only. But constitutional adjudication in the lower courts is not the equivalent of what can be had in the Supreme Court. It lacks the general authoritativeness. And judgment, even as it affects the immediate litigant, is constrained. . . .

II. THE POWER TO DECLINE THE EXERCISE OF JURISDICTION WHICH IS GIVEN

I have tried to show that the Supreme Court's well-established if imperfectly understood practice of declining on occasion to exercise the power of judicial review is difficult to reconcile with the strict-constructionist conception of the foundation of that power. If this were all what is called merely academic, it would be none the worse for it. Actually, however, important consequences are in play. Of course, no concept, strict-, loose-, or medium-constructionist, can get around the sheer necessity of limiting each year's business to what nine men can fruitfully deal with. But strict-constructionist compunctions cause the techniques for meeting this necessity to be viewed with misgiving and to be encumbered with fictive explanations. So are other techniques of avoiding adjudication, and I would suggest that herein lies at least part of the reason for the confusion and lack of direction that has characterized their development. Some of the confusion may be in the eye of the beholder, but not all. Beyond this, and more fundamentally, the consequences of the strict-constructionist position are in the alternative. Either literal reliance on *Marbury* v. *Madison* leads to a rampant activism that takes pride in not "ducking" anything and takes comfort, and as Mr. Wechsler says, finds "protection," in the dictum of *Cohens* v. *Virginia*. Or, for those like Mr. Wechsler who are not unaware that judicial review is at least potentially a deviant institution in a democratic society, the consequence is an effort to limit the power of review and render it tolerable through a radical restriction on the category of substantive principles that the Court is allowed to evolve and declare; the consequence is, indeed, a radical constriction of the quality of the Court's function. . . .

Quite obviously, no society, certainly not a large and heterogeneous one, can fail in time to explode if it is deprived of the arts of compromise, if it knows no ways to muddle through. No good society can be unprincipled; and no viable society can be principle-ridden. But it is not true in our society that we are generally governed wholly by principle in some matters and indulge a rule of expediency exclusively in others. There is no such neat dividing line. There are exceptions, some of which are delineated by the political-question doctrine. Most often, however, and as often as not in matters of the widest and deepest concern such as the racial problem, both requirements exist most imperatively side by side: guiding principle and expedient compromise. The role of principle, when it cannot be the inflexible governing rule, is to affect the tendency of policies of expediency. And it is a potent role. . . .

It follows that the techniques and allied devices for staying the Court's hand, as is avowedly true at least of certiorari, cannot themselves be principled in the sense in which we have a right to expect adjudications on the merits to be principled. They mark the point at which the Court gives the electoral institutions their head and itself stays out of politics, and there is nothing paradoxical in finding that here the Court is most a political animal. But this is not to concede unchanneled, undirected, unchartered discretion. It is not to concede judgment proceeding from impulse, hunch, sentiment, predilection, inarticulable and unreasoned. The antithesis of principle in an institution that represents decency and reason is not whim, nor even expediency, but prudence. . . .

GERALD GUNTHER:

. . .

Unfortunately, we have not had an adequate, comprehensive critique of Bickel's thesis. The time and space that can be allotted to a comment cannot fill that gap. Yet, whether his analysis is valid and beneficial or, as I believe, vulnerable and dangerous, it is too important to go undebated. I accordingly propose to suggest some difficulties in its content and application, to the end of encouraging a continuing discussion. . . .

Bickel's delineation of Wechsler's principle of "neutral principles" is one of the best in the books. The volume of criticism elicited by Wechsler's lecture may be "the most genuine kind of tribute to him," but the content of much of the commentary is no tribute to the quality of American legal criticism. Bickel is among the few who have read closely, who have taken time for thought, and who have understood. Wechsler's principle, he concludes, is "neither trivial nor fatuous," nor truly "enigmatic." And he accepts the principle as essential to judicial review—sometimes. The Court "must act rigorously on principle, else it undermines the justification for its power"—at least when the Court "strikes down legislative policy." Principled adjudication is the standard—to a degree; it must be the standard—in some areas of constitutional decisions, to that degree only. There indeed lies the novelty and vulnerability of the Bickel thesis: the emphasis on principle as the highest Court duty, but only in a limited sphere of Court actions; the 100% insistence on principle, 20% of the time. . . .

Bickel's targets are well chosen, his shots well aimed. But the prime interest here is not in his shooting gallery prowess but in his ammunition. Bickel is neither neo-realist nor absolutist. But Bickel's thesis must be examined in light of Bickel's warnings—warnings against polluting the decisional process through excessive preoccupation with the political market place; warnings against fostering menacing illusions, against suppressing candor; warnings against misrepresenting the is, against confusing the is with the ought. His critical premises are admirable: "the integrity of the Court's principled process should remain unimpaired"; "the Court does not involve itself in compromises and expedient actions." Do Bickel's creative contributions meet the standards of Bickel's devastating criticism?

II.

Principle and reason are hard taskmasters. Insistence on these essential ingredients is Bickel's starting point; but, as he contemplates their impact on the judicial process, unpalatable consequences loom ever larger. He cannot bear to abandon the requirement of principle in constitu-

tional adjudication; he cannot bear the inexpedient results of unflinching adherence to principle. He is put to an excruciating choice; his response is to avoid the choice, to seek escape routes.

He derives the philosophic basis for his ingenious solution from his contemplation of American democracy at large: "No good society can be unprincipled; and no viable society can be principle-ridden. . . . Our democratic system of government exists in this Lincolnian tension between principle and expediency, and within it judicial review must play its role." These cosmic observations may be sound; but their relevance and utility as applied to a specific process and institution, to judicial review and the Supreme Court, are questionable. And the inferences Bickel draws ultimately fail to satisfy: they rest on faulty perceptions of the adjudicatory process; and they yield guidelines which invite not accommodation but surrender of principle to expediency. . . .

Bickel's ambitious survey of the avoidance techniques, his "passive virtues," is the most comprehensive we have had, and his examination of this tangled field is of significance quite independent of his purposes. . . .

The result is a strange mixture. He covers an enormous range of techniques; he describes and applies his concepts with skill; he offers some fresh insights and much helpful clarification; yet the total product is essentially unpersuasive, profoundly disturbing, and ultimately subversive of the very values it professes to serve. Two major flaws, I submit, help to explain why so many superior parts add up to such an unsatisfying whole. First, the discrete analyses of the varied avoidance devices are too much influenced by Bickel's underlying premises and overriding purposes: in his anxiety to enlarge Court discretion not to adjudicate, some of the techniques are subjected to greater strains than they can bear. Second, as Bickel criticized some commentators as neo-realists, so it can be said that he suffers from the neo-Brandeisian fallacy: invoking the well-known *Ashwander* statement by Brandeis, regarding avoidance of constitutional questions in adjudication, to assert an amorphous authority to withhold adjudication altogether—a power far broader than any suggested by the examples given by Brandeis, a discretion far wider than any that can be independently justified. . . .

One watches with fascination as Bickel walks his tightrope, as he manipulates his nonprincipled techniques of accommodation to preserve a precarious balance. There is considerable courage and artistry in his attempts to secure a foothold on some minimal intellectual content of these techniques. But he cannot maintain the balance; the support from the tangled net of "prudence," "wisdom," and "principle" proves illusory; and he plunges into "unchanneled, undirected, uncharted discretion." And so, ultimately, the effort is a failure—noble, not total; not without its useful by-products; but nevertheless a failure. . . .

Bickel's manipulative use of jurisdictional doctrines is the ultimate outgrowth of a tendency to blur the fact that jurisdiction under our system is rooted in Article III and congressional enactments, that it is not a domain solely within the Court's keeping. It is a tendency that frequently professes to find support in the Brandeis opinion in the *Ashwander* case; but it is a notion that has about as much relationship to Brandeis as the contentions of the neo-realists—the latter-day "arrested realists" so effectively criticized by Bickel —have to the founders of that school.

Brandeis stated seven rules developed by the Court "for its own governance in the cases confessedly within its jurisdiction"—rules "under which it has avoided passing upon a large part of all the constitutional questions pressed upon it for decision." The statement, in the context of the rules given, is sound and of principled content; it is not an assertion of a vague Court discretion to deny a decision on the merits in a case within the statutory and constitutional bounds of jurisdiction. The Brandeis rules are a far cry from the neo-Brandeisian fallacy that there is a general "Power To Decline the Exercise of Jurisdiction Which Is Given," that there is a general discretion not to adjudicate though statute, Constitution, and remedial law present a "case" for decision and confer no discretion.

Of course the Court often may and should avoid "passing upon a large part of all of the constitutional questions pressed upon it for decision." Four of the seven Brandeis rules involve well-known instances of such avoidance—

avoidance only of some or all of the constitutional questions argued, *not* avoidance of all decision on the merits of the case. Thus, when the Court does not "formulate a rule of constitutional law broader than is required by the precise facts," it merely narrows the constitutional ground of decision, but does not even avoid all constitutional decision. Similarly, when the Court does not decide a constitutional question presented by the case because there is a nonconstitutional ground "upon which the case may be disposed of," it only avoids constitutional decision, not a decision on the merits of the case. Nor, of course, does the Court withhold adjudication of the case when it makes a ruling on the constitutionality of a federal law unnecessary by finding a construction of the statute which is "fairly possible" and which avoids the constitutional doubts. These are all in a sense avoidance devices, and Bickel includes these and similar ones in his catalogue of techniques—but they are devices which go to the choice of the ground of decision of a case, not devices which avoid decision on the merits, not devices which "decline to exercise" the jurisdiction to decide. . . .

Ultimately, it is Bickel's starting point—his rigorous insistence that constitutional adjudication must be truly principled—that gives his thesis such importance and that proves to be its undoing. The predilectional school of Court criticism, the vacuous commentary which is content with reciting agreements and disagreements with particular results, would have no difficulty with the problems posed by Bickel—indeed, would hardly recognize his concerns as problems. Bickel is not of that school, and his writing has depth and substance. My emphasis on weaknesses in his thesis stems from my high estimate of its importance and over-all quality.

Bickel's "passive virtues" are seductively attractive, in purpose and presentation. They are offered as means for achieving simultaneously "a wide-ranging and effective rule of principle" and "the necessary leeway to expedient accommodation." The offer is appealing, and there is great temptation to accept it uncritically. But the temptation must be resisted, for, despite the merit of some of the components, acceptance of the total package would be lethal. Constitutional interpretation tolerates many paradoxes and rejects compulsive doctrinal neatness. Yet, if devotion to principled adjudication is to be taken seriously, tolerance must have its bounds, doctrinal integrity must be more than a sometime goal.

Bickel fears the conclusions drawn from "the premise of an obligation always to decide." There is no such obligation, if that obligation is thought to require decision of the broadest constitutional questions at every opportunity. There is legitimate discretion not to review, as in the certiorari jurisdiction; there is not only discretion but obligation not to decide the broad constitutional question if narrower grounds of decision are available. "Passive virtues" such as these have their proper and important place. But, as I have attempted to illustrate, there is an obligation to decide in some cases; there is a limit beyond which avoidance devices cannot be pressed and constitutional dicta cannot be urged without enervating principle to an impermissible degree. Bickel's "virtues" are "passive" in name and appearance only: a virulent variety of free-wheeling interventionism lies at the core of his devices of restraint. And what Bickel says of some solutions based on the premise of an obligation always to decide is, after all, more aptly applied to his own prescriptions: they "lead either to a manipulative process, whose inherent, if high-minded, lack of candor raises issues of its own, or to the abandonment of principle and the involvement of the Court in judgments of expediency, as a second-guesser of the political institutions; or, more commonly, to both."

4 Judicial Organization

Q uestions of judicial organization are sometimes dismissed as too technical or esoteric. Yet organizational issues present questions of power. Changes in institutional boundaries and processes dramatically affect the flow of power at the federal-state level and among the three branches of the national government. The process of appointing judges is heavily lobbied by all sectors, public and private. Judicial tenure, removal, and compensation are perennial sources of conflict. The appropriate scope of judicial lobbying remains a subject of great sensitivity.

FEDERAL COURT SYSTEM

Long before the American colonies declared their separation from England, the idea of an independent judiciary had secured a firm foothold. The Act of Settlement, passed by England in 1701, contributed to judicial autonomy by guaranteeing tenure for judges during good behavior. The power to constitute courts in the American colonies, however, was vested in the governor and council, creatures of the King. The assemblies were allowed to create courts only for small causes, subject always to the King's veto.[1]

The principle of judicial independence appears in several sections of the Declaration of Independence, which charged that the King had "obstructed the Administration of Justice, by refusing his Assent to Laws for establishing Judiciary Powers." Because of disputes between the British Crown and several of the colonies, laws establishing courts of justice were struck down repeatedly, sometimes eliminating courts for long stretches of time. Edward Dumbauld, The Declaration of Independence and What It Means Today 108–112 (1950). The Declaration of Independence also criticized the King for making judges "dependent on his Will

[1]Julius Goebel, Jr., 1 History of the Supreme Court of the United States: Antecedents and Beginnings 12–13 (1971).

alone, for the Tenure of their Offices, and the Amount and Payment of Their Salaries." Despite the Act of Settlement, the English government insisted that colonial judges serve at the King's pleasure. This policy provoked bitter resistance in New York, New Jersey, Pennsylvania, North Carolina, South Carolina, and Massachusetts, where colonial legislatures wanted judges to have tenure during good behavior. Id. at 112–115. Following the break with England, several American colonies included tenure and salary provisions in their constitutions to secure judicial independence.

After the colonies cut ties with England, state governments authorized vessels to prey on British shipping. A judicial system was needed to dispose of "prizes" taken during those raids. State admiralty courts made the initial determination, but appeals beyond that level required the attention of the Continental Congress. From 1776 to 1780, appeals were handled first by temporary committees and then by a standing committee, until Congress, in May 1780, created a "Court of Appeals in Cases of Capture." This tribunal took direction from the Continental Congress and even from the Secretary for Foreign Affairs.[2] The Court of Appeals continued to function until delegates arrived at Philadelphia in May 1787 to draft a new constitution.

The delegates to the Philadelphia Convention recognized the need for executive and judicial independence. They explored the possibility of setting up a Council of Revision, consisting of the executive and "a convenient number of the National Judiciary," to examine all bills from the legislature before they became law. Rejection by the Council could be overridden by the legislature. 1 Farrand 21. The convention turned down the proposal because the delegates wanted the Supreme Court to interpret the law without any prior participation. Id. at 97–98. The framers decided to vest the veto power exclusively in the President.

Article III of the Constitution created a separate judicial branch. The judges, both of the Supreme and inferior courts, "shall hold their Offices during good Behaviour, and shall, at stated Times, receive for their Services, a Compensation, which shall not be diminished during their Continuance in Office." The Constitution vests the judicial power of the United States "in one supreme Court, and in such inferior Courts as the Congress may from time to time ordain and establish." The word "may" implies that the establishment of lower courts is discretionary, and some members of the First Congress proposed to do only the minimum: create a Supreme Court for national issues and rely on existing state courts for most local needs. The Judiciary Bill of 1789, as first drafted by the Senate, opted for federal district courts. Senator Richard Henry Lee's amendment, which would have restricted those courts to cases of admiralty and maritime matters (like the Court of Appeals in Cases of Capture), was rejected. Warren, 37 Harv. L. Rev. 49, 67 (1923).

During debate on the Bill of Rights, there were similar efforts in the House of Representatives to limit inferior courts to questions of admiralty. 1 Annals of Cong. 762, 777–778. These, too, were unsuccessful. Action on the Judiciary Bill of 1789 produced new resistance against the creation of federal district courts, but again the House rejected the idea of relying on state courts. Id. at 783. Madison warned that the courts in many states "cannot be trusted with the execution of Federal laws." Because of limited tenure and possible salary reductions, some courts were too

[2]Goebel, supra note 1, at 178-179; Henry J. Bourguignon, The First Federal Court: The Federal Appellate Prize Court of the American Revolution (1977).

dependent on state legislatures. Making federal laws dependent on these courts "would throw us back into all the embarrassments which characterized our former situation." Id. at 812–813. By a vote of 31 to 11, the House decisively rejected a motion to establish only State Courts of Admiralty with no federal district courts. Id. at 834.

The Judiciary Act of 1789 provided for a Chief Justice and five Associate Justices for the Supreme Court. It divided the United States into thirteen districts, with a federal judge for each district, and created three circuits to handle appellate cases: the eastern, middle, and southern circuits. The circuit courts met twice a year in each district and consisted of any two Justices of the Supreme Court and one district judge from that circuit. District judges could not vote in any case of appeal or error from their decisions. Section 25 of the Judiciary Act also solidified federal control over the states by conferring upon the Supreme Court a supervisory role over state courts.

The Justices of the Supreme Court complained bitterly about their circuit court duties. In addition to handling cases on the Court's docket, Justices had to "ride circuit" by traveling around the country to hear appellate cases in the circuit courts. Riding circuit was an arduous and hazardous enterprise. Participation in circuit cases had another drawback: a Justice might have to review his own decision if the case reached the Supreme Court. All six Justices appealed to President Washington and Congress to reduce their labors. Congress offered modest relief in 1793 by allowing the attendance of only one Justice for the holding of circuit court. 1 Am. State Papers 24, 52 (1834); 1 Stat. 333 (1793).

With six Justices to cover three circuits, each Justice now had to ride circuit only once a year. Pressure for relief resulted in the ill-fated Judiciary Act of 1801, which divided the country into six circuits and promised to terminate circuit riding by creating sixteen circuit judges. President John Adams elevated six district judges to those positions and also named three Senators and one Representative to the vacant district judgeships. Farrand, 5 Am. Hist. Rev. 682 (1900); 2 Stat. 89, § 7 (1801).

Although the creation of circuit judges had been proposed for several years, the statute creating them was not signed until the closing days of the Adams administration. After President Adams hastily filled the positions and allotted them to loyal Federalists, the Jeffersonians condemned the "midnight judges bill" as unconscionable. They accused the Federalists of trying to accomplish through judicial appointments what had just been denied them in the national election. The Judiciary Act of 1801 also reduced the number of Supreme Court Justices from six to five, effective with the next vacancy. The reduction might have been justified because the work of the Justices had been cut back by eliminating circuit duties. Moreover, five Justices would avoid the possibility of tie votes. The Jeffersonians interpreted the statute less charitably. The reduction decreased Jefferson's opportunity to appoint his own candidate to the High Court. The new Congress promptly repealed the Judiciary Act of 1801.

The size of the Supreme Court fluctuated throughout the nineteenth century, keeping pace with the addition of new circuits. A seventh Justice was added in 1807 to reflect the creation of a new judicial circuit. The size of the Supreme Court rose to nine in 1837, again reflecting the westward expansion, and to ten by 1863 (to accommodate the Pacific circuit). Three years later Congress lowered the permanent size of the Court to seven, although the membership never fell below eight. The reduction is usually interpreted as a slap against President Andrew Johnson, depriving him of an opportunity to fill vacancies. The Radical Republicans feared that his appointees to the Court would oppose Reconstruction policies. S. Rept. No. 711, 75th Cong., 1st Sess. 13 (1937). His nomination of Henry Stanbery as an Associate Justice had to be withdrawn because Congress reduced the Court's size. But Johnson signed the bill and its legislative history does not suggest an attack on the Court. In fact, Chief Justice Salmon P. Chase, in pursuit of higher salaries for the Supreme Court, supported a reduction to seven members.[3]

Legislation in 1869 brought the Court back to its present size of nine members. A major step in judicial reorganization occurred in 1891 when Congress created a separate system of appellate courts, producing three tiers: district (trial) courts, circuit (appellate) courts, and the Supreme Court. A comprehensive "Judges Bill" in 1925 gave the Supreme Court greater discretion to grant or deny petitions of appeal from the lower courts.

By 1891 there were nine circuit courts of appeals. The Tenth Circuit, split from the Eighth, appeared in 1929. When the workload of the Fifth Circuit grew too large, Congress divided it in 1981, forming the Eleventh Circuit. Together with the D.C. Circuit, that made twelve courts of appeals. In 1982 Congress established the Court of Appeals for the Federal Circuit (CAFC), which inherits the work of the Court of Customs and Patent Appeals and hears cases coming from the U.S. Claims Court. Unlike the other twelve circuits, which cover a specific geographical area and possess general jurisdiction, the CAFC is nationwide and limited in subject matter jurisdiction (see chart on page 160).

As a means of expediting action, Congress requires the submission of some disputes to a three-judge court consisting of a mix of district and appellate judges. 28 U.S.C. § 2284 (1982). Initially, these courts were established to limit the interference of federal courts with state statutes. Instead of allowing a single federal district judge to nullify a state law, Congress required three federal judges (including at least one circuit judge) to hear applications to enjoin the enforcement of state statutes on constitutional grounds. Their determinations are appealable directly to the Supreme Court. Note, 85 Yale L. J. 564 (1976). Three-judge courts place an administrative burden on the federal judiciary, requiring three judges to do what might be done by one. In 1976, Congress eliminated three-judge courts for certain situations. 90 Stat. 1119 (1976). Over the years, the jurisdiction of three-judge courts has been cut substantially. Stern & Gressman, Supreme Court Practice 70–74, 90–98 (1978).

Congress has established various organizations to help the judiciary. In 1922 it created the Judicial Conference to coordinate the legislative requests and administrative actions of the federal courts. Two years after Roosevelt's abortive court-packing scheme in 1937, Congress created judicial councils in each circuit to improve the efficiency of court administration. It had been the responsibility of the Justice Department to handle the administrative needs of the courts, creating an obvious separation of powers problem. In 1939, Congress established the Adminis-

---

[3]Charles Fairman, 6 History of the Supreme Court of the United States: Reconstruction and Reunion 163–171 (1971); Cong. Globe, 39th Cong. 3909 (July 18, 1866); Stanley I. Kutler, Judicial Power and Reconstruction Politics 48–63 (1968). As a U.S. Senator, Chase had proposed that no vacancies be filled until the Court's membership fell to six. He justified this smaller number because of reduced duties once Justices were relieved of their responsibilities for riding circuit. Cong. Globe, 33d Cong., 2d Sess. 216–217 (1855).

trative Office of the United States Courts to take care of the managerial, research, statistical, and budgetary needs of the national judiciary. In 1967, Congress created a Federal Judicial Center to study methods of improving judicial administration.

LEGISLATIVE AND SPECIALIZED COURTS

In addition to "constitutional courts" established by Congress pursuant to Article III of the Constitution, Congress creates other courts to carry out legislative duties. Drawing on various sections of the Constitution, Congress has set up territorial courts, legislative courts, military courts, and the courts of the District of Columbia. Judges sitting on those courts are not automatically entitled to the rights of life tenure and irreducible compensation guaranteed to Article III federal judges.

Territorial Courts

Section 3 of Article IV gives Congress the power "to dispose of and make all needful Rules and Regulations respecting the Territory or other Property belonging to the United States." After Spain ceded Florida to the United States in 1819, Congress established a territorial government in Florida and its legislature created a court system that gave judges a term of four years. This system was challenged as a violation of the requirement in Article III that judges serve "during good Behaviour." The Supreme Court ruled that the territorial courts of Florida were not constitutional courts. They were legislative courts, created under Section 3 of Article IV.[4]

Under its authority to govern territories, Congress established district courts in Puerto Rico, Guam, the Virgin Islands, the former Canal Zone, and the Northern Mariana Islands. The district court of Puerto Rico is classified as an Article III federal district court. Its judges hold office during good behavior; territorial judges serve eight-year terms. Similar to territorial courts are the consular courts established by Congress to carry out the constitutional powers regarding treaties and commerce with foreign nations. Ex parte Bakelite Corp., 279 U.S. 438, 451 (1929).

Legislative Courts

Congress has established a number of Article I legislative courts. It created the Court of Claims in 1855 to help Congress handle the large number of claims presented by citizens against the United States. The responsibility for determining these claims "belongs primarily to Congress as an incident of its power to pay the debts of the United States." Ex parte Bakelite, 279 U.S. at 452. At the beginning, the Court of Claims served an advisory role, but subsequent statutes made some of the judgments binding, gradually transforming the Court of Claims from an investigative body to an adjudicatory agency. As long as the Court of Claims rendered advisory opinions on legislative questions referred to it by Congress, the Supreme Court treated it as an Article I court. Its judges lacked the constitutional protections of tenure and salary. Williams v. United States, 289 U.S. 553, 569 (1933). In 1953, Congress made the Court of Claims an Article III court. 67 Stat. 226 (1953).

---

[4]American Ins. Co. v. Canter, 26 U.S. (1 Pet.) 511, 545 (1828). Also on territorial courts see Benner v. Porter, 9 How. 235 (1850); Hornbuckle v. Toombs, 18 Wall. 648 (1874); Reynolds v. United States, 98 U.S. 145 (1878); The "City of Panama," 101 U.S. 453 (1880); and Romeu v. Todd, 206 U.S. 358 (1907).

The United States Customs Court also illustrates the congressional need to delegate some of its constitutional responsibilities to other bodies. In 1890, Congress established within the Department of Treasury a Board of General Appraisers to review the decisions of appraisers and collectors at U.S. ports. In 1926 the Board was replaced by the United States Customs Court and in 1956 Congress made the Customs Court an Article III court. Its name was changed in 1980 to the Court of International Trade. 70 Stat. 532 (1956); 94 Stat. 1727 (1980).

Congress created a Court of Customs Appeal in 1909 to review final decisions of the Board of General Appraisers. The Court was established pursuant to the power of Congress to lay and collect duties on imports. Ex parte Bakelite, 279 U.S. at 458–459. The statute had been silent about judicial tenure. Congress granted the judges life tenure in 1930. 46 Stat. 590, 762 (1930). In 1958 Congress changed the court (by now called the Court of Customs and Patent Appeals) to an Article III court. Legislation in 1982 folded this court into the Court of Appeals for the Federal Circuit. 72 Stat. 848 (1958); 96 Stat. 25 (1982).

The authority of the Supreme Court to exercise appellate jurisdiction over legislative courts depends on the finality of their judgments. If a legislative court merely renders an advisory opinion there is no appeal (and nothing to appeal). Constitutional courts should not perform nonjudicial functions. But if a legislative court exercises judicial duties, the Supreme Court may review its decisions. The Court has also held that legislative courts may handle only disputes between government and private citizens in noncriminal matters (except for military crimes). Issues between individuals are matters of private rights to be adjudicated solely by Article III courts. Northern Pipeline Const. v. Marathon Pipe Line Co., 458 U.S. 50 (1982) (see notes 24 and 25).

From this record it is clear that Congress may choose to resolve questions within its own chambers, delegate them to executive agencies, or vest them in adjudicatory bodies—either Article I or Article III. Functions therefore float from one branch to another as Congress searches for the most effective means of discharging its duties. What is "legislative" at one stage becomes "administrative" at another and "judicial" still later.

The United States Tax Court is one of the few legislative courts to retain its Article I status. Created in 1924 as the Board of Tax Appeals, it was placed within the Treasury Department as "an independent agency in the executive branch of the Government." 43 Stat. 338 (1924). In 1929 the Supreme Court regarded the Board of Tax Appeals not as a court but as an executive or administrative board. Old Colony Trust Co. v. Commissioner of Internal Revenue, 279 U.S. 716, 725 (1929). Studies treated it "for all practical purposes" as a legislative court. Cushman, 24 Corn. L. Q. 13, 44 (1938). Legislation in 1942 and 1969 changed the name of the Board to the "Tax Court of the United States" and gave it Article I status. 56 Stat. 957 (1942); 83 Stat. 30 (1969). All decisions of the Tax Court, other than small tax cases, are subject to review by the United States Court of Appeals and by the Supreme Court.

Military Courts

A third class of specialized courts derives from the power of Congress under Article I, Section 8, to "make Rules for the Government and Regulation of the land and naval Forces." Congress has provided that criminal behavior in the military shall be tried by court-martial proceedings, not by courts established under Article III. The United States Court of Military Appeals, composed of three judges with fifteen-year terms, is an Article I court. Military courts need not satisfy all of the specific procedural protections offered by Article III courts.[5]

In 1969 the Supreme Court attempted to subject certain military questions to the jurisdiction of civilian courts. It held that a crime must be "service connected" to be under military jurisdiction. O'Callahan v. Parker, 395 U.S. 258 (1969). The service-connected doctrine became so confusing that the Court abandoned it in 1987. Jurisdiction of a court-martial now depends solely on the accused's status as a member of the armed forces. Solorio v. United States, 107 S.Ct. 2924 (1987). The rights of servicemen now depend on action by Congress, not the courts.

District of Columbia Courts

Under Article I, Section 8, Congress exercises "exclusive Legislation in all Cases whatsoever, over such District." Initially, the Supreme Court regarded the District of Columbia courts as legislative, not constitutional.[6] In 1933 the Court reasoned that because the District was formed from territory belonging to Maryland and Virginia, District inhabitants should continue to enjoy their former constitutional rights and protections. D.C. courts were therefore considered constitutional courts established under Article III. O'Donoghue v. United States, 289 U.S. 516 (1933). We now distinguish between two types of D.C. courts: federal courts with Article III judges (the U.S. District Court for the District of Columbia and the U.S. Court of Appeals for the D.C. Circuit) and the local courts created pursuant to Article I (the Superior Court and the D.C. Court of Appeals). Defendants charged with a felony under the D.C. Code may be tried by a judge who lacks Article III protections of tenure and salary. The Court compared a District resident to that of a citizen in any other state charged with violating a state criminal law. Citizens in the D.C. courts are "no more disadvantaged and no more entitled to an Art. III judge than any other citizen of any of the 50 States who is tried for a strictly local crime." Palmore v. United States, 411 U.S. 389, 410 (1973).

Bankruptcy Courts

The demarcation between Article I and Article III courts remains a source of disagreement among Justices of the Supreme Court. In 1982 the Court struck down as unconstitutional a court system created by Congress in 1978 to handle thousands of bankruptcy cases. The 1978 legislation established a bankruptcy court in each federal district. The judges of those courts were appointed by the President (subject to Senate advice and consent) for fourteen-year terms and could be removed by the judicial council of the circuit. Their salaries could be decreased by Congress. Technically, the bankruptcy courts were not considered legislative courts but "adjuncts" to the district courts.

---

[5]Palmore v. United States, 411 U.S. 389, 404 (1973). See Toth v. Quarles, 350 U.S. 11, 17–18 (1955). For additional material on military courts, see Chapter 7, pp. 311–312.

[6]Keller v. Potomac Electric Power Co., 261 U.S. 428, 441–443 (1923); Postum Cereal Co. v. Calif. Fig Nut Co., 272 U.S. 693, 700 (1927); Ex parte Bakelite Corp., 279 U.S. 438, 450 (1929); Federal Radio Comm'n v. Gen'l Elec. Co., 281 U.S. 464, 468 (1930).

In its 1982 decision, the Supreme Court denied that Congress could establish specialized courts to carry out every one of its Article I powers. Although Congress has constitutional authority under Article I, Section 8, to establish "uniform Laws on the subject of Bankruptcies throughout the United States," this authority did not permit Congress to rely on a non-Article III court. Such reasoning, said the Court, "threatens to supplant completely our system of adjudication in independent Art. III tribunals and replace it with a system of 'specialized' legislative courts." The Court concluded that the Bankruptcy Act of 1978 had removed essential attributes of judicial power from the Article III district court and vested them in a non-Article III body. NORTHERN PIPELINE CONST. CO. v. MARATHON PIPE LINE CO., 458 U.S. 50 (1982).

If the statute was defective, the judiciary shared the blame. After the House of Representatives had given bankruptcy judges life tenure within an Article III system, federal judges lobbied to defeat that proposal in the Senate. They did not want bankruptcy judges elevated to their status (pp. 165–168). Two years after the Supreme Court's decision, Congress passed legislation to reinstate the bankruptcy courts. The bankruptcy judges were made adjuncts of the district courts and given fourteen-year terms. 98 Stat. 2704 (1984).

The strict ruling of the Supreme Court on bankruptcy judges should not obscure the extent of adjudication that takes place outside Article III courts. In 1985 a unanimous Court upheld the arbitration provision of the Federal Insecticide, Fungicide, and Rodenticide Act. The Court decided that agency adjudication posed only a minimum threat to Article III judicial powers: "practical attention to substance rather than doctrinaire reliance on formal categories should inform application of Article III." Thomas v. Union Carbide Agric. Products Co., 473 U.S. 568, 587 (1985). A year later, the Court upheld another case of agency adjudication, again declining to "adopt formalistic and unbending rules." Commodity Futures Trading Comm'n v. Schor, 478 U.S. 833, 851 (1986). For the routes by lower courts to the Supreme Court, see the chart on page 161.

THE APPOINTMENT PROCESS

The delegates at the Constitutional Convention rejected the British system of executive appointment, associating it with official corruption and debasement of the judiciary. At first, they placed the power to select judges with Congress. Next, they considered vesting that responsibility solely in the Senate. Only late in the convention did they settle on joint action by the President and the Senate. 1 Farrand 21, 63, 119–128, 232–233; 2 Farrand 41–44, 80–83, 121. The President, under Article II of the Constitution, shall nominate "and by and with the Advice and Consent of the Senate, shall appoint . . . Judges of the supreme Court." The Constitution also permits Congress to vest the appointment of "inferior officers" in the President alone, in the courts, or in the heads of the executive departments.

Subjecting federal judges to presidential nomination and Senate confirmation creates an intensely political process. From an early date, Senators wielded considerable power in choosing nominees for federal judgeships. Members of the Supreme Court (especially Chief Justice Taft) have lobbied vigorously for their candidates. Other sectors of government are active. Private organizations participate. The American Bar Association (ABA) plays a key role. Its influence increased during the Truman administration when it established a special committee to judge the professional qualifications of candidates. Acting on names submitted by the Attorney General, the committee informs the chairman of the Senate Judiciary Committee whether a nominee for the Supreme Court fits the categories of "well qualified," "not opposed," or "not qualified." The ABA categories for the lower courts are "exceptionally well qualified," "well qualified," "qualified," and "not qualified."

President Carter altered the selection process for appellate judges by establishing nominating panels. They were directed to recommend five candidates for each vacancy, allowing the President to select the nominee. As part of an accommodation, Senators continued to control nominations for district judges, although some opted for a panel system. Using this procedure, Carter was able to place on the federal courts an unprecedented number of blacks, women, and Hispanics, far exceeding the record of previous Presidents. When President Reagan took office, he abolished the judicial nominating commissions for appellate judges. The effect was to increase the Senate's influence. He also placed far less emphasis on recruiting women and minorities (pages 168–169).

The power to nominate Supreme Court Justices can produce sudden shifts in judicial policy. Slight changes in the composition of the Supreme Court have reversed previous rulings. In 1870, the Court reviewed a congressional statute that treated paper money as legal tender for discharging prior debts. Voting 4–3, the Court declared the statute unconstitutional. The partisanship that raged throughout the post-Civil War period did not bypass the courts. The four Justices in the majority were Democrats; the three dissenters were Republicans. In the lower federal courts, almost every Democratic judge pronounced the statute unconstitutional; nearly every Republican judge sustained it. Hepburn v. Griswold, 8 Wall. (75 U.S.) 603 (1870); Fairman, 54 Harv. L. Rev. 1128, 1131 (1941).

The retirement of Justice Grier and the authorization by Congress the previous year of a new Justice allowed President Grant to appoint two members. His first two appointments were ill-starred. The Senate rejected his Attorney General, Ebenezer Hoar, while his second nominee, Edwin Stanton, died four days after being confirmed. Those nominations were made before the Court's decision. Grant had reason to believe that his next two appointments, submitted after the decision, would support the statute. William Strong, as a member of the Supreme Court of Pennsylvania, had already sustained the Legal Tender Act. Joseph P. Bradley appeared to be no less sympathetic. Fifteen months after the Legal Tender Act had been declared unconstitutional, the reconstituted Court upheld the Act by a 5–4 margin. Strong and Bradley joined the original three dissenters to form the majority; the four Justices who decided the case in 1870 now found themselves in the minority. Legal Tender Cases, 12 Wall. (79 U.S.) 457 (1871).

The transition from the Warren Court to the Burger Court also produced reversals of prior decisions (or efforts by the Court to "distinguish" prior holdings from current judicial policy). In 1971, a 5–4 majority—including two newcomers, Chief Justice Burger and Justice Blackmun—upheld a statutory procedure that stripped an individual of citizenship. The Court thus narrowed earlier holdings that citizenship could not be taken away unless voluntarily renounced. Justice Black protested that protections for American citizenship "should not be blown a-round by every passing political wind that changes the composition of this Court." Rogers v. Bellei, 401 U.S. 815, 837 (1971). No doubt Black was frustrated by policy shifts from the Warren Court to the Burger Court, but he himself had been part of the Roosevelt nominations that helped chart a new course in constitutional interpretation.

Changes in the Court's composition enable it to incorporate contemporary ideas and attitudes. Justice Jackson denied that this fact did any violence to the notion of an independent, nonpolitical judiciary: "let us not deceive ourselves; long-sustained public opinion does influence the process of constitutional interpretation. Each new member of the ever-changing personnel of our courts brings to his task the assumptions and accustomed thought of a later period. The practical play of the forces of politics is such that judicial power has often delayed but never permanently defeated the persistent will of a substantial majority." Vital Speeches, No. 24, Vol. XIX, p. 761 (Oct. 1, 1953).

The Senate has refused to confirm almost one out of every five presidential nominations to the Supreme Court. Twenty-five nominees have either been rejected, had their names submitted without Senate action, or been forced to withdraw. Most of those actions (eighteen) occurred before 1900. After the Senate rejected John J. Parker in 1930, confirmation of Supreme Court nominees seemed an automatic step. That pattern ended in 1968 when the Senate refused to advance Associate Justice Abe Fortas to the position of Chief Justice. Fortas, subjected to embarrassing questions about his acceptance of fees from private parties, eventually asked President Johnson to withdraw his nomination. Homer Thornberry, picked by Johnson to fill Fortas' seat as Associate Justice, then withdrew his name. A year later, with impeachment proceedings gearing up against him because of financial and personal improprieties, Fortas resigned from the Court.

The Supreme Court remained embroiled in political controversy in 1969 when the Senate rejected Nixon's nomination of Clement F. Haynsworth, Jr., to the Supreme Court. The ethical test applied by Republicans against Fortas was now used by Democrats against Haynsworth. A year later, the Senate rejected Nixon's next nominee, G. Harrold Carswell, who lacked the qualifications needed for Associate Justice. Nixon finally nominated Lewis Powell, Jr., and William Rehnquist, both of whom the Senate confirmed.

The emphasis given by Nixon to the sociopolitical views of judicial candidates merely underscores the entanglement of law and politics. Senators, too, in expressing their advice and consent, feel at liberty to evaluate a nominee's political and constitutional philosophy in order to maintain a balance of views on the Court.[7] As shown by the 1981 hearings on the nomination of Sandra Day O'Connor to the Court, her personal and judicial philosophy on the exceedingly sensitive issue of abortion was a matter of recurrent interest to Senators and one on which she was willing to state her views (pages 170–173).

The Senate's rejection of two nominees by Nixon to the Supreme Court was duplicated in 1987. President Reagan nominated Judge Robert H. Bork, a conservative member of the D.C. Circuit, to replace the more moderate Justice Powell. Everyone recognized the nomination as pivotal, especially after Reagan's selection of O'Connor in 1981, Antonin Scalia in 1986, and the elevation of Rehnquist as Chief

[7]Senate Committee on the Judiciary, "Advice and Consent on Supreme Court Nominations," 94th Cong., 2d Sess. (Committee Print 1976). See L. A. Powe, Jr., "The Senate and the Court: Questioning a Nominee," 54 Tex. L. Rev. 891 (1976).

Justice in 1986. Powell, a centrist, had supplied a swing vote on the Burger Court. The addition of Bork threatened to reverse a number of important decisions.

Major groups in the country mounted an intensive campaign against Bork, whose writings and speeches contained provocative views on civil rights, women's rights, the First Amendment, abortion, privacy, reapportionment, and criminal law. Four members of the ABA committee found him "not qualified." One voted "not opposed" (which means minimally qualified and not among the best available). Bork did not fare well during the hearings, and the White House committed a number of tactical blunders, such as trying to paint Bork as a moderate. The Senate voted 58 to 42 to reject Bork.

To replace Bork, a vindictive Reagan turned to Judge Douglas H. Ginsburg of the D.C. Circuit. The nomination unraveled almost hour by hour because of Ginsburg's thin credentials and serious questions of conflict of interest while he served in the Justice Department. Finally, after he admitted smoking marijuana into his thirties, while a professor of law, conservative support for his nomination took flight. The disclosure was particularly damaging because of Reagan's strong campaign against drugs and the administration's heavy emphasis on law and order. Within nine days of the nomination, Reagan received Ginsburg's request to withdraw his name. The next nominee, Judge Anthony Kennedy of the Ninth Circuit, went through the confirmation process without difficulty.

The Senate is denied a role in the confirmation process when the President makes recess appointments to the Supreme Court. Under Article II, Section 2, the President "shall have Power to fill up all Vacancies that may happen during the Recess of the Senate, by granting Commissions which may expire at the End of their next Session." During the 1950s, President Eisenhower placed three men on the Supreme Court while the Senate recessed: Earl Warren, William J. Brennan, Jr., and Potter Stewart. All three joined the Court and participated in decisions before the Senate had an opportunity to review their qualifications and vote on their confirmation. In each case, the Senate gave its advice and consent, but the experience convinced most Senators that the procedure was unhealthy both for the Senate and the Court. How could federal judges serving under a recess appointment maintain total independence of mind? The anticipation of questions by a Senate committee during confirmation hearings might influence the direction and content of a nominee's decision.

In 1960, Senator Philip Hart introduced a resolution to discourage recess appointments to the courts. The Senate passed the resolution, 48 to 37, voting essentially along party lines. The resolution stated that the making of recess appointments to the Supreme Court may be inconsistent with the interests of the Court, the nominee, litigants before the Court, and the people of the United States. Such appointments should "not be made except under unusual circumstances and for the purpose of preventing or ending a demonstrable breakdown in the administration of the Court's business." 106 Cong. Rec. 18130–18145 (1960). Although the resolution is not legally binding, no President after Eisenhower has made recess appointments to the Supreme Court. The President's constitutional authority to make recess appointments to the lower federal courts was upheld in 1985. United States v. Woodley, 751 F.2d 1008 (9th Cir. 1985), cert. denied, 475 U.S. 1048 (1986). However, the dissenters noted that although there have been approximately 300 judicial recess appointments since 1789, there has been only one such appointment since 1964.

TENURE AND REMOVAL

Under Article III of the Constitution, judges "both of the supreme and inferior Courts, shall hold their Offices during good Behaviour." Article I gives the House of Representatives the sole power of impeachment and the Senate has the sole power to try all impeachments. A two-thirds majority of the Senate is required for conviction. Judges may be removed from office "on Impeachment for, and Conviction of, Treason, Bribery, or other high Crimes and Misdemeanors."

The impeachment process is cumbersome and suitable only for grave offenses. The need to remove judges for lesser offenses has long been recognized. In Federalist 79, Alexander Hamilton said that "insanity, without any formal or express provision, may be safely pronounced to be a virtual disqualification" for federal judges. However, he did not explain how judges would be removed for that cause. If insanity is a basis for removal, what of senility, incompetence, disability, alcoholism, laziness, and other deficiencies that may fall short of an impeachable offense?

A rare example of a federal judge impeached and removed from office occurred in 1803 in the case of John Pickering. He was charged with misconduct in a trial and for being on the bench while intoxicated. Supreme Court Justice Samuel Chase was impeached in 1804 but acquitted. Actions were brought against a number of other federal judges, many of whom preferred to resign from office rather than defend themselves against the charges. Shipley, 35 Law & Contemp. Prob. 178, 190–191 (1970). Still other federal judges withdrew quietly from the bench before prosecutors could launch a full-scale investigation. J. Borkin, The Corrupt Judge (1962).

To encourage aged and infirm judges to leave the bench, Congress passed legislation in 1869 to authorize the payment of full salary to any federal judge who resigned at or after age 70 after completing at least ten years' service on the bench. 16 Stat. 44, § 5 (1869). For Justices with less than the required ten years, Congress has passed special statutes to provide full retirement benefits. 22 Stat. 2 (1882); Fairman, 51 Harv. L. Rev. 397 (1938).

Article I judges, such as territorial judges, have been removed by Presidents because they were not entitled to life tenure.[8] Article III judges are immune from removal, other than by impeachment. Nevertheless, they are subject to prosecution by the Justice Department for criminal offenses. The First Congress passed legislation providing that judges convicted of accepting a bribe "shall forever be disqualified to hold any office of honour, trust or profit under the United States." 1 Stat. 117, § 21 (1790). Moreover, any federal judge who engages in the practice of law "is guilty of a high misdemeanor." 28 U.S.C. § 454 (1982).

Criminal prosecutions have been used to drive corrupt judges from the bench. In 1973, Judge Otto Kerner, Jr., of the Seventh Circuit was found guilty of bribery, perjury, tax evasion, and other crimes, most of which occurred during his previous service as governor of Illinois. On appeal, Kerner argued that the Constitution provides only one way to remove a judge: impeachment. The Seventh Circuit decided that judicial immunity did not exempt judges from the operation of criminal laws and affirmed Kerner's conviction. United States v. Isaacs, 493 F.2d 1124 (7th Cir. 1974).

---

[8]United States v. Guthrie, 58 U.S. (17 How.) 284, 288–289 (1854); 5 Op. Att'y Gen. 288, 291 (1851); and McAllister v. United States, 141 U.S. 174 (1891).

Kerner's prosecution primarily concerned his actions before joining the bench. A different issue arose in the early 1980s when the Justice Department charged U.S. District Judge Alcee L. Hastings with criminal activities while sitting as a judge. The Eleventh Circuit decided in 1982 that Hastings could be prosecuted. United States v. Hastings, 681 F.2d 706 (11th Cir. 1982), cert. denied, 459 U.S. 1203 (1983). After a jury acquitted Hastings in 1983, a judicial inquiry panel conducted its own investigation into charges of misconduct. Hastings claimed that this inquiry undermined his independence as a federal judge, but the investigative and disciplinary procedure was upheld by the courts. Hastings v. Judicial Conference of United States, 593 F.Supp. 1371 (D.D.C. 1984); In the Matter of Certain Complaints Under Investigation, 783 F.2d 1488 (11th Cir. 1986). In 1984, U.S. District Judge Harry Claiborne was found guilty of income tax evasion. United States v. Claiborne, 727 F.2d 842 (9th Cir. 1984). Two years later he was impeached and removed by Congress. In 1986 U.S. District Judge Walter L. Nixon, Jr., of Mississippi was convicted of lying to a federal grand jury; in 1989 he was impeached by the House of Representatives.

Once nominated and appointed to the bench, a few judges have been vulnerable to the charge that they violated the "ineligibility clause" of the Constitution. Article I, Section 6, Clause 2, provides that no Senator or Representative "shall, during the Time for which he was elected, be appointed to any Civil Office under the Authority of the United States, which shall have been created, or the Emoluments whereof shall have been encreased during such time." Hugo Black's nomination to the Supreme Court in 1937 was challenged because a retirement system for the judiciary had been enacted that year while Black served as U.S. Senator. The Supreme Court avoided the issue by holding that the plaintiff lacked standing to bring suit. Ex parte Levitt, 302 U.S. 633 (1937).

A more recent challenge concerned Abner Mikva, a member of Congress nominated by President Carter to the D.C. Circuit. Working through Senator James McClure, who served as plaintiff, the National Rifle Association argued that the salaries of federal judges had been increased during Mikva's term in Congress. A three-judge court ruled that McClure lacked standing to challenge the validity of an appointment of a federal judge. The court said that McClure and his colleagues had had their opportunity to vote against Mikva's confirmation. Senators on the losing side could not then ask the judiciary to reverse the Senate's action. McClure v. Carter, 513 F.Supp. 265 (D. Idaho 1981), aff'd sub nom. McClure v. Reagan, 454 U.S. 1025 (1981).

Statutory procedures are available for judges to retire on grounds of disability. If a judge fails to certify to the President his disability, a majority of the members of the judicial council of his circuit may sign a certificate of disability and submit it to the President. Once the President finds that the judge is "unable to discharge efficiently all the duties of his office by reason of permanent mental or physical disability," and that an additional judge is needed, the President may make the appointment with the advice and consent of the Senate. 28 U.S.C. § 372(b) (1982).

Each judicial council is authorized to make all necessary orders for the effective administration of court business. Judges "shall promptly carry into effect all orders of the judicial council." 28 U.S.C. § 332(d) (1982). The judicial council for the Tenth Circuit relied on this provision in the 1960s to order Judge Stephen S. Chandler of the Western District of Oklahoma to "take no action whatsoever in any case or proceeding now or hereafter pending in his court." The order did not remove

Chandler from office; instead, it removed the office from him. In 1966 the Supreme Court denied an application to stay the council's order. Chandler v. Judicial Council, 382 U.S. 1003 (1966). The judicial council later modified its order, allowing Chandler to retain his cases but withholding any new assignments. The Supreme Court denied a motion by Chandler to nullify the new order. Chandler v. Judicial Council, 398 U.S. 74 (1970).

By 1979, all judicial councils had implemented rules for the processing of complaints against federal judges. Building on this system, Congress passed legislation in 1980 that assigns to the councils the responsibility for investigating charges against judges. The statute contemplates charges of inefficiency or ineffectiveness resulting from mental or physical disability (conditions that may not be impeachable). The legislation does not encompass complaints regarding the merits of a decision or the conduct of judges unconnected with their judicial duties.[9] The 1980 statute was upheld by a district court in 1984 and by the Eleventh Circuit in 1986.[10]

The statute also allows a judicial council, after determining that a judge has engaged in conduct constituting one or more grounds for impeachment, to certify this determination for the Judicial Conference, which may then present a report to the House of Representatives for possible impeachment proceedings. This statutory procedure was upheld by the D.C. Circuit in 1987. Hastings v. Judicial Conference of U.S., 829 F.2d 91 (D.C. Cir. 1987). The Judicial Conference invoked the statute in 1987 to vote unanimously for a recommendation to the House of Representatives that it consider impeaching U.S. District Court Judge Alcee L. Hastings. A year later, the House acted to impeach Hastings.

COMPENSATION

Judicial independence would be shortlived if the salaries of judges could be cut by legislators. Federal judges appointed to Article III courts are entitled to a compensation "which shall not be diminished during their Continuance in Office." In Federalist No. 79, Hamilton said that next to permanency in office "nothing can contribute more to the independence of the judges than a fixed provision for their support. . . . In the general course of human nature, a power over a man's subsistence amounts to a power over his will." That principle had been embodied in the Declaration of Independence, which attacked the British King for making colonial judges "dependent on his Will alone, for the Tenure of their Offices, and the Amount and Payment of their Salaries."

The No-Diminution Clause of the Constitution was challenged in 1802 when Congress repealed the Judiciary Act of the previous year. The effect was to abolish sixteen circuit judges and their salaries. Supporters of the repeal argued that it was irrational to expect a judge to hold office during good behavior and to continue

---

[9]94 Stat. 2035 (1980). See S. Rept. No. 362, 96th Cong., 1st Sess. (1979) and H. Rept. No. 1313, 96th Cong., 2d Sess. (1980).

[10]Hastings v. Judicial Conference of the United States, 593 F.Supp. 1371 (D.D.C. 1984). This decision was vacated in part and remanded in Hastings v. Judicial Conference of the United States, 770 F.2d 1093 (D.C. Cir. 1985). The appellate court ruled that the question of constitutionality of the 1980 statute was premature. The Eleventh Circuit not only upheld the statute but regarded it as a means of protecting judicial independence. In the Matter of Certain Complaints Under Investigation, 783 F.2d 1488 (11th Cir. 1986).

receiving payment if the office no longer existed. A salary could not exist without an office. A case challenging the right of Congress to abolish the circuit courts reached the Supreme Court in 1803, but the Court declined to overturn the statute. Stuart v. Laird, 5 U.S. (1 Cr.) 298 (1803).

In 1920, the Supreme Court held unconstitutional a federal income tax that had been levied against Article III judges. Justice Holmes, in a dissent that would later become the majority position, denied that the No-Diminution Clause relieved federal judges "from the ordinary duties of a citizen." To require someone from the judicial branch to pay taxes like other people "cannot possibly be made an instrument to attack his independence as a judge." Evans v. Gore, 253 U.S. 245, 265 (1920). Nineteen years later the Supreme Court held that a federal tax could be applied to Article III judges. O'Malley v. Woodrough, 307 U.S. 277 (1939).

Nothing in this line of cases prevents Congress from giving judges a smaller pay raise than other federal employees or no increase at all. In 1964, members of Congress raised their pay by $7,500 while limiting the increase for Supreme Court Justices to $4,500. The legislative debate suggests that some members of Congress may have wanted to use the power of the purse to penalize the Court for its recent decisions. However, the smaller raise for the judiciary could be justified on other grounds: the more generous retirement system for the courts, the need for Congressmen to maintain two residences, and the extra costs they bear in traveling home to see constituents. 110 Cong. Rec. 17912, 18032–18033 (1964).

As a way to protest their salary levels, 140 federal judges brought an action in the 1970s to argue that their salaries had been diminished unconstitutionally because pay had not kept pace with inflation. The courts dismissed this claim as meritless. Atkins v. United States, 556 F.2d 1028 (Ct. Cl. 1977), cert. denied, 434 U.S. 1009 (1978). The case did call attention to the problem of adjusting federal salaries. In 1967, Congress decided to abandon its periodic efforts to adjust federal salaries and delegated that politically sensitive task to a Quadrennial Commission and to the President. Subsequent delegations allowed annual cost-of-living raises to take effect without congressional action, which critics called the "Look, Ma, no hands" approach. In four consecutive years (1976–1979) Congress passed statutes to stop or reduce authorized cost-of-living increases for all federal employees, including judges. A number of federal judges filed suit, claiming that these actions violated the No-Diminution Clause of the Constitution. In 1980 the Supreme Court held that Congress, under the provisions of the salary statutes, could disapprove scheduled pay increases for the judiciary provided it acted before October 1 of a new fiscal year (when they automatically took effect). The Court allowed two of the statutory actions taken prior to October 1 and struck down two others that came too late. UNITED STATES v. WILL, 449 U.S. 200 (1980).

As a result of this decision, judicial salaries moved well ahead of executive and legislative pay schedules. Congress retaliated in 1981 by passing legislation to require specific congressional authorization before any future pay raise for federal judges could take effect. The language effectively eliminated future automatic increases for the judiciary. 95 Stat. 1200, § 140 (1981). Recent legislation allows judicial salaries to be increased unless Congress, within a thirty-day period, passes a joint resolution of disapproval. 99 Stat. 1322, § 135 (1985). Congress used that procedure in 1989 to defeat a substantial raise for all federal officials, including judges.

JUDICIAL LOBBYING

To preserve their reputation for impartiality, objectivity, and independence, judges traditionally abstain from political activities that are the daily fare of executives and legislators. Judicial activities, both on and off the bench, are expected to be free from impropriety and the *appearance* of impropriety.

Before coming to the bench, most judges have been active in legislatures, government agencies, and other political activities. They are unlikely, upon confirmation, to adopt the manner and habits of a cloistered judge; nor should they. Legislation often has a direct bearing on the courts, justifying the active participation of judges at the bill-drafting and congressional hearing stages. Canon 4 of the American Bar Association's Code of Judicial Conduct permits a judge to "appear at a public hearing before an executive or legislative body or official on matters concerning the law, the legal system, and the administration of justice, and he may otherwise consult with an executive or legislative body or official, but only on matters concerning the administration of justice" and never by casting doubt on his capacity to decide impartially any issue that may come before him. See 2 O.L.C. 30 (1978).

With the 1982 release of *The Brandeis/Frankfurter Connection* by Bruce Allen Murphy, the public learned that Justice Brandeis, over a period of years, had secretly paid more than $50,000 to Felix Frankfurter to advance Brandeis' political agenda. The financial arrangement ended when Brandeis left the Court in 1939. Frankfurter joined the Court that year and remained deeply enmeshed in politics. He drafted legislative proposals for the Roosevelt administration, helped staff the upper echelons of the War Department, and assisted Roosevelt's reelection campaign in 1940.

The details of Frankfurter's activities were particularly noteworthy. As a member of the Court he described himself as a "political eunuch," claiming that the Court "has no excuse for being unless it's a monastery." In 1944 he confided to a friend that "I have an austere and even sacerdotal view of the position of a judge on this Court, and that means I have nothing to say on matters that come within a thousand miles of what may fairly be called politics." Murphy, The Brandeis/Frankfurter Connection 9, 259–269. In a dissenting opinion, Frankfurter insisted that the authority of the Supreme Court depended on its "complete detachment, in fact and in appearance, from political entanglements." Baker v. Carr, 369 U.S. 186, 267 (1962).

Although Frankfurter distinguished himself for hypocrisy, other Justices also participated in off-the-bench activities. The contacts between Brandeis and President Franklin D. Roosevelt had already been noted in the literature.[11] Taft, Frankfurter, Byrnes, and Fortas, while on the Court, met frequently with Presidents and discussed public issues.[12]

Much earlier examples illustrate the difficulty that some members of the Supreme Court have had in drawing a line between law and politics. During the

[11]Philippa Strum, "Justice Brandeis and President Roosevelt," reprinted in Walter F. Murphy and C. Herman Pritchett, eds., Courts, Judges, and Politics 187–190 (1979).

[12]See Max Freedman, ed., Roosevelt and Frankfurter: Their Correspondence (1967); John P. MacKenzie, The Appearance of Justice 1–33 (1974); and "Nonjudicial Activities of Supreme Court Justices and Other Federal Judges," hearings before the Senate Committee on the Judiciary, 91st Cong., 1st Sess. (1969).

Court's first two decades, individual Justices campaigned for political candidates, ran for political office, and accepted political duties that came their way. Chief Justice John Jay was sent as special envoy to negotiate a treaty with England. Chief Justice Oliver Ellsworth followed that precedent by negotiating a treaty with France. Murphy, The Brandeis/Frankfurter Connection 345–363.

After Chief Justice Marshall issued his decision in *McCulloch* v. *Maryland* (1819), arguing in favor of broad implied powers for the federal government, a series of anonymous articles appeared in a Richmond newspaper attacking the decision and championing states' rights. The first few critiques were probably written by William Brockenbrough, a state judge from Virginia. Marshall could not bear to let the charges go unanswered. Working through his colleague Justice Bushrod Washington, Marshall penned a number of anonymous rebuttals (signed "A Friend of the Union") and published them in a Philadelphia newspaper. Four more critiques appeared in the Richmond newspaper, this time by Judge Spencer Roane of the Virginia Court of Appeals (using the pseudonym Hampden). Marshall answered those as well, signing them "A Friend of the Constitution." G. Gunther, ed., John Marshall's Defense of *McCulloch* v. *Maryland* (1969). Justice Story, while serving for over twenty years as president of a Massachusetts branch of the United States Bank, tried to influence Treasury Department officials to secure large deposits in his bank and helped Daniel Webster draft a reply to President Jackson's veto of the Bank's charter in 1832.[13]

Many avenues are available to Justices who want to affect the course of political events. Public addresses, law review articles, and contacts with reporters, scholars, and magazine writers are methods of extending judicial influence beyond official actions. The Chief Justice prepares an annual "year-ender," summing up the problems, needs, and accomplishments of federal courts. He also delivers an annual report on the state of the judiciary, sometimes using these forums to criticize Congress for its actions and inactions. Proposals have been introduced for an annual "State of the Judiciary" address, to be delivered by the Chief Justice to a joint session of Congress. This proposal passed the Senate in 1980, but the House took no action. 126 Cong. Rec. 23397 (1980).

The Judicial Conference is the principal institutional body for preparing a legislative agenda. The organization dates back to 1922, when Congress directed the Chief Justice to call an annual conference of the senior circuit judges. The objective was to make a comprehensive survey of cases pending before the federal courts: their number and character, cases disposed of, and backlog. The potential for judicial lobbying did not go unnoticed. Representative Clarence F. Lea predicted that the Conference "will become the propaganda organization for legislation for the benefit of the Federal judiciary." 62 Cong. Rec. 203 (1921).

As the law now reads, the Chief Justice submits to Congress "an annual report of the proceedings of the Judicial Conference and its recommendations for legislation." 28 U.S.C. § 331 (1982). These reports are submitted twice a year, covering the spring and fall meetings of the Conference. Because the meetings are largely devoted to administrative and legislative matters rather than judicial duties, there has been pressure to open them to the public. Opponents of this reform proposal concede that the Conference is a creature of Congress and subject to further

---

[13]G. Edward White, The American Political Tradition 41 (1976); Gerald T. Dunne, Justice Joseph Story and the Rise of the Supreme Court 301–302, 328–331 (1970).

statutory change, but they argue that the principle of judicial independence should protect the proceedings of the Judicial Conference (pp. 175–179). The Judicial Conference came under fire in 1984 for improper lobbying, as well as a private group called the Federal Judges Association (pp. 179–183).

The lobbying activities of Chief Justice Burger attracted press attention in 1978. On the eve of a Senate vote on the bankruptcy bill, he called Senator Dennis DeConcini and several other members of the Senate Judiciary Committee. DeConcini told reporters that Burger accused him of being "irresponsible" for supporting the legislation and said that the bill "was a political sale and he was going to the President and have him veto it." Calling the charge "a slap in the face of the entire Senate," DeConcini described Burger as being "very, very irate and rude." He "just screamed at me" and "not only lobbied, but pressured and attempted to be intimidating."[14] Representative Don Edwards, head of the House subcommittee responsible for the bankruptcy bill, said that he welcomed the views of judges but only when presented in "a scholarly, judicious way, in writing or in hearings, not in telephone calls once a bill has gone to the floor."[15]

As is customary for most members of the judiciary, Chief Justice Burger did not respond directly to DeConcini's charges. Within a month, however, while accepting an award in New York City, Burger defended his participation in the legislative process (pp. 183–185). He also resisted activities he viewed as inappropriate. In 1981, a number of federal judges wanted to form an association to lobby Congress for higher salaries and fringe benefits. Interested judges would contribute $200 and list the members of Congress they felt comfortable contacting about judicial salaries. Burger advised the judges that the position of the federal judiciary should be expressed through the Judicial Conference.[16]

Selected Readings

ABRAHAM, HENRY J. *Justices and Presidents: A Political History of Appointments to the Supreme Court.* New York: Oxford University Press, 1974.

BALL, HOWARD. *Courts and Politics: The Federal Judicial System.* Englewood Cliffs, N.J.: Prentice-Hall, 1980.

BLACK, CHARLES L., JR. "A Note on Senatorial Consideration of Supreme Court Nominees." 79 *Yale Law Journal* 657 (1970).

CARP, ROBERT A., AND C. K. ROWLAND. *Policymaking and Politics in the Federal District Courts.* Knoxville: University of Tennessee Press, 1983.

CHASE, HAROLD W. *Federal Judges: The Appointing Process.* Minneapolis: University of Minnesota, 1972.

DANELSKI, DAVID J. *A Supreme Court Justice Is Appointed.* New York: Random House, 1964.

EARLY, STEPHEN T., JR. *Constitutional Courts of the U.S.* Totowa, N.J.: Littlefield, Adams, 1977.

FISH, PETER GRAHAM. *The Politics of Federal Judicial Administration.* Princeton, N.J.: Princeton University Press, 1973.

GROSSMAN, JOEL B. *Lawyers and Judges: The ABA and the Politics of Judicial Selection.* New York: Wiley, 1965.

HARRIS, JOSEPH P. *The Advice and Consent of the Senate.* Berkeley: University of California Press, 1953.

HAYNES, EVAN. *The Selection and Tenure of Judges.* Newark, N.J.: National Conference of Judicial Councils, 1944.

HOWARD, J. WOODFORD, JR. *Courts of Appeals in the Federal Judicial System.* Princeton, N.J.: Princeton University Press, 1981.

[14]"Senator Slams Burger on Move to Thwart Bill," National Law Journal, October 16, 1978; "Burger Wants Judges to Speak Up to Congress," Washington Post, October 26, 1978, at A13.

[15]"Lobbying by Burger Provokes Criticism," New York Times, November 19, 1978, at 39.

[16]"U.S. Judges Want Lobby; Burger Against Proposal," National Law Journal, June 29, 1981, at 2, 10.

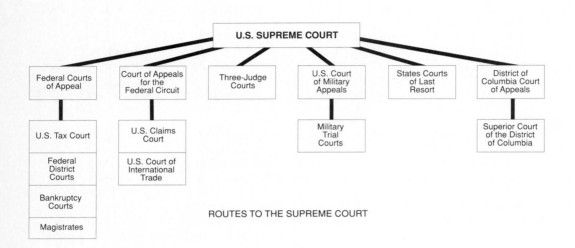

ROUTES TO THE SUPREME COURT

HULBARY, WILLIAM E., AND THOMAS G. WALKER. "The Supreme Court Selection Process: Presidential Motivations and Judicial Performance." 33 *Western Political Quarterly* 185 (1980).

KAHN, MICHAEL A. "The Politics of the Appointment Process: An Analysis of Why Learned Hand Was Never Appointed to the Supreme Court." 25 *Stanford Law Review* 251 (1973).

KURLAND, PHILIP B. "The Constitution and the Tenure of Federal Judges: Some Notes From History." 36 *University of Chicago Law Review* 665 (1969).

MASON, ALPHEUS THOMAS. "Extra-Judicial Work for Judges: The Views of Chief Justice Stone." 67 *Harvard Law Review* 193 (1953).

MURPHY, WALTER. "In His Own Image: Mr. Chief Justice Taft and Supreme Court Appointments." 1961 *Supreme Court Review* 159.

SCHMIDHAUSER, JOHN R. "The Justices of the Supreme Court: A Collective Portrait." 3 *Midwest Journal of Political Science* 1 (1959).

———. *Judges and Justices: The Federal Appellate Judiciary.* Boston: Little, Brown, 1979.

SCIGLIANO, ROBERT. *The Supreme Court and the Presidency.* New York: The Free Press, 1971.

TRIBE, LAURENCE H. *God Save This Honorable Court.* New York: Random House, 1985.

WHEELER, RUSSELL. "Extrajudicial Activities of the Early Supreme Court." 1973 *Supreme Court Review* 123.

WINTERS, GLENN R., ed. *Selected Readings: Judicial Selection and Tenure.* Chicago: American Judicature Society, 1973.

THE FEDERAL JUDICIAL CIRCUIT

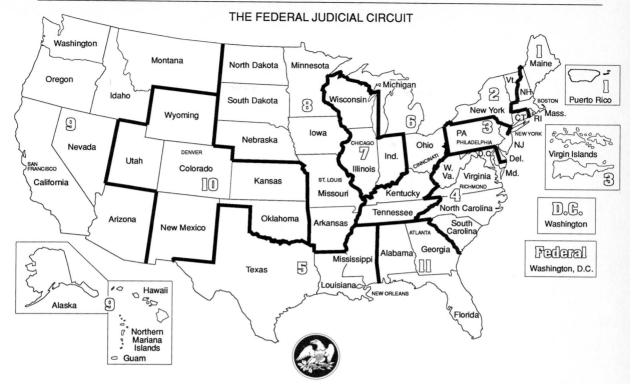

Northern Pipeline Co. v. Marathon Pipe Line Co.

458 U.S. 50 (1982)

The Bankruptcy Reform Act of 1978 established a federal bankruptcy court in each district as an adjunct to district courts. Bankruptcy judges were appointed for fourteen-year terms, subject to removal by the judicial councils for specified causes; their salaries could be reduced by Congress. The Act was challenged as unconstitutional on the ground that it conferred Article III judicial powers on judges who lacked the protections of life tenure and irreducible salaries. The Court's opinion did not attract a majority. Brennan wrote for a four-justice plurality. Rehnquist and O'Connor concurred with Brennan's judgment but on a narrower ground. White, joined by Burger and Powell, dissented. Footnotes omitted.

JUSTICE BRENNAN announced the judgment of the Court and delivered an opinion, in which JUSTICE MARSHALL, JUSTICE BLACKMUN, and JUSTICE STEVENS joined.

. . .

Appellants suggest two grounds for upholding the Act's conferral of broad adjudicative powers upon judges unprotected by Art. III. First, it is urged that "pursuant to its enumerated Article I powers, Congress may establish legislative courts that have jurisdiction to decide cases to which the Article III judicial power of the United States extends." Brief for United States 9. Referring to our precedents upholding the validity of "legislative courts," appellants suggest that "the plenary grants of power in Article I permit Congress to establish non-Article III tribunals in 'specialized areas having particularized needs and warranting distinctive treatment,'" such as the area of bankruptcy law. *Ibid.*, quoting *Palmore* v. *United States, supra,* at 408. Second, appellants contend that even if the Constitution does require that this bankruptcy-related action be adjudicated in an Art. III court, the Act in fact satisfies that requirement. "Bankruptcy jurisdiction was vested in the district court" of the judicial district in which the bankruptcy court is located, "and the exercise of that jurisdiction by the adjunct bankruptcy court was made subject to appeal as of right to an Article III court." Brief for United States 12. Analogizing the role of the bankruptcy court to that of a special master, appellants urge us to conclude that this "adjunct" system established by Congress satisfies the requirements of Art. III. We consider these arguments in turn.

III

Congress did not constitute the bankruptcy courts as legislative courts. Appellants contend, however, that the bankruptcy courts could have been so constituted, and that as a result the "adjunct" system in fact chosen by Congress does not impermissibly encroach upon the judicial power. In advancing this argument, appellants rely upon cases in which we have identified certain matters that "congress may or may not bring within the cognizance of [Art. III courts], as it may deem proper." *Murray's Lessee* v. *Hoboken Land & Improvement Co.*, 18 How. 272, 284 (1856). But when properly understood, these precedents represent no broad departure from the constitutional command that the judicial power of the United States must be vested in Art. III courts. Rather, they reduce to three narrow situations not subject to that command, each recognizing a circumstance in which the grant of power to the Legislative and Executive Branches was historically and constitutionally so exceptional that the congressional assertion of a power to create legislative courts was consistent with, rather than threatening to, the constitutional mandate of separation of powers. These precedents simply acknowledge that the literal command of Art. III, assigning the judicial power of the United States to courts insulated from Legislative or Executive interference, must be interpreted in light of the historical context in which the Constitution was written, and of the structural imperatives of the Constitution as a whole.

Appellants first rely upon a series of cases in which this Court has upheld the creation by Congress of non-Art. III "territorial courts." This exception from the general prescription of Art. III dates from the earliest days of the Republic, when it was perceived that the Framers intended that as to certain geographical areas, in which no State operated as sovereign, Congress was to exercise the general powers of government. For example, in *American Ins. Co.* v. *Canter,* 1 Pet. 511 (1828), the Court observed that Art. IV bestowed upon Congress alone a complete power of government over territories not within the States that comprised the United States. . . .

The Court followed the same reasoning when it reviewed Congress' creation of non-Art. III courts in the District of Columbia. . . .

Appellants next advert to a second class of cases—those in which this Court has sustained the exercise by Congress and the Executive of the power to establish and administer courts-martial. The situation in these cases strongly resembles the situation with respect to territorial courts: It too involves a constitutional grant of power that has been historically understood as giving the political branches of Government extraordinary control over the precise subject matter at issue. Article I, § 8, cls. 13, 14, confer upon Congress the power "[t]o provide and maintain a Navy," and "[t]o make Rules for the Government and Regulation of the land and naval Forces." The Fifth Amendment, which requires a presentment or indictment of a grand jury before a person may be held to answer for a capital or otherwise infamous crime, contains an express exception for "cases arising in the land or naval forces." . . .

Finally, appellants rely on a third group of cases, in which this Court has upheld the constitutionality of legislative courts and administrative agencies created by Congress to adjudicate cases involving "public rights." The "public rights" doctrine was first set forth in *Murray's Lessee* v. *Hoboken Land & Improvement Co.*, 18 How. 272 (1856):

"[W]e do not consider congress can either withdraw from judicial cognizance any matter which, from its nature, is the subject of a suit at the common law, or in equity, or admiralty; nor, on the other hand, can it bring under the judicial power a matter which, from its nature, is not a subject for judicial determination. At the same time there are matters, *involving public rights*, which may be presented in such form that the judicial power is capable of acting on them, and which are susceptible of judicial determination, but which congress may or may not bring within the cognizance of the courts of the United States, as it may deem proper." *Id.*, at 284 (emphasis added).

This doctrine may be explained in part by reference to the traditional principle of sovereign immunity, which recognizes that the Government may attach conditions to its consent to be sued. See *id.*, at 283–285; see also *Ex parte Bakelite Corp.*, 279 U. S. 438, 452 (1929). But the public-rights doctrine also draws upon the principle of separation of powers, and a historical understanding that certain prerogatives were reserved to the political branches of government. . . .

The distinction between public rights and private rights has not been definitively explained in our precedents. Nor is it necessary to do so in the present cases, for it suffices to observe that a matter of public rights must at a minimum arise "between the government and others." *Ex parte Bakelite Corp., supra,* at 451. In contrast, "the liability of one individual to another under the law as defined," *Crowell* v. *Benson, supra,* at 51, is a matter of private rights. Our precedents clearly establish that *only* controversies in the former category may be removed from Art. III courts and delegated to legislative courts or administrative agencies for their determination. See *Atlas Roofing Co.* v. *Occupational Safety and Health Review Comm'n,* 430 U. S. 442, 450, n. 7 (1977); *Crowell* v. *Benson, supra,* at 50–51. See also Katz, Federal Legislative Courts, 43 Harv. L. Rev. 894, 917–918 (1930). Private-rights disputes, on the other hand, lie at the core of the historically recognized judicial power. . . .

The flaw in appellants' analysis is that it provides no limiting principle. It thus threatens to supplant completely our system of adjudication in independent Art. III tribunals and replace it with a system of "specialized" legislative courts. True, appellants argue that under their analysis Con-

gress could create legislative courts pursuant only to some "specific" Art. I power, and "only when there is a particularized need for distinctive treatment." Brief for United States 22–23. They therefore assert that their analysis would not permit Congress to replace the independent Art. III Judiciary through a "wholesale assignment of federal judicial business to legislative courts." *Ibid.* But these "limitations" are wholly illusory. For example, Art. I, § 8, empowers Congress to enact laws, *inter alia,* regulating interstate commerce and punishing certain crimes. Art. I, § 8, cls. 3, 6. On appellants' reasoning Congress could provide for the adjudication of these and "related" matters by judges and courts within Congress' exclusive control. The potential for encroachment upon powers reserved to the Judicial Branch through the device of "specialized" legislative courts is dramatically evidenced in the jurisdiction granted to the courts created by the Act before us. . . .

Appellants advance a second argument for upholding the constitutionality of the Act: that "viewed within the entire judicial framework set up by Congress," the bankruptcy court is merely an "adjunct" to the district court, and that the delegation of certain adjudicative functions to the bankruptcy court is accordingly consistent with the principle that the judicial power of the United States must be vested in Art. III courts. See Brief for United States 11–13, 37–45. As support for their argument, appellants rely principally upon *Crowell* v. *Benson,* 285 U. S. 22 (1932), and *United States* v. *Raddatz,* 447 U. S. 667 (1980), cases in which we approved the use of administrative agencies and magistrates as adjuncts to Art. III courts.

. . . By contrast, the bankruptcy courts exercise all ordinary powers of district courts, including the power to preside over jury trials, 28 U. S. C. § 1480 (1976 ed., Supp. IV), the power to issue declaratory judgments, § 2201, the power to issue writs of habeas corpus, § 2256, and the power to issue any order, process, or judgment appropriate for the enforcement of the provisions of Title 11, 11 U. S. C. § 105(a) (1976 ed., Supp. IV). . . . the bankruptcy courts issue final judgments, which are binding and enforceable even in the absence of an appeal. In short, the "adjunct" bankruptcy courts created by the Act exercise jurisdiction behind the facade of a grant to the district courts, and are exercising powers far greater than those lodged in the adjuncts approved in either *Crowell* or *Raddatz*.

We conclude that 28 U. S. C. § 1471 (1976 ed., Supp. IV), as added by § 241(a) of the Bankruptcy Act of 1978, has impermissibly removed most, if not all, of "the essential attributes of the judicial power" from the Art. III district court, and has vested those attributes in a non-Art. III adjunct. Such a grant of jurisdiction cannot be sustained as an exercise of Congress' power to create adjuncts to Art. III courts. . . .

JUSTICE REHNQUIST, with whom JUSTICE O'CONNOR joins, concurring in the judgment.

Were I to agree with the plurality that the question presented by this case is "whether the assignment by Congress to bankruptcy judges of the jurisdiction granted in 28 U. S. C. § 1471 (1976 ed., Supp IV) by § 241(a) of the Bankruptcy Act of 1978 violates Art. III of the Constitution," *ante*, at 52, I would with considerable reluctance embark on the duty of deciding this broad question. But appellee Marathon Pipe Line Co. has not been subjected to the full range of authority granted Bankruptcy Courts by § 1471. . . .

CHIEF JUSTICE BURGER, dissenting.

I join JUSTICE WHITE's dissenting opinion, but I write separately to emphasize that, notwithstanding the plurality opinion, the Court does *not* hold today that Congress' broad grant of jurisdiction to the new bankruptcy courts is generally inconsistent with Article III of the Constitution. Rather, the Court's holding is limited to the proposition stated by JUSTICE REHNQUIST in his concurrence in the judgment—that a "traditional" state common-law action, not made subject to a federal rule of decision, and related only peripherally to an adjudication of bankruptcy under federal law, must, absent the consent of the litigants, be heard by an "Article III court" if it is to be heard by any court or agency of the United States. This limited holding, of course, does not suggest that there is something inherently unconstitutional about the new bankruptcy courts; nor does it preclude such courts from adjudicating all but a relatively narrow category of claims "arising under" or "arising in or related to cases under" the Bankruptcy Act.

It will not be necessary for Congress, in order to meet the requirements of the Court's holding, to undertake a radical restructuring of the present system of bankruptcy adjudication. The problems arising from today's judgment can be resolved simply by providing that ancillary common-law actions, such as the one involved in these cases, be routed to the United States district court of which the bankruptcy court is an adjunct.

JUSTICE WHITE, with whom THE CHIEF JUSTICE and JUSTICE POWELL join, dissenting.

. . .

Even if there are specific powers now vested in bankruptcy judges that should be performed by Art. III judges, the great bulk of their functions are unexceptionable and should be left intact. Whatever is invalid should be declared to be such; the rest of the 1978 Act should be left alone. I can account for the majority's inexplicably heavy hand in this case only by assuming that the Court has once again lost its conceptual bearings when confronted with the difficult problem of the nature and role of Art. I courts. . . .

Instead of telling us what it is Art. I courts can and cannot do, the plurality presents us with a list of Art. I courts. When we try to distinguish those courts from their Art. III counterparts, we find—apart from the obvious lack of Art. III judges—a series of non-distinctions. By the plurality's own admission, Art. I courts can operate throughout the country, they can adjudicate both private and public rights, and they can adjudicate matters arising from congressional actions in those areas in which congressional control is "extraordinary." I cannot distinguish this last category from the general "arising under" jurisdiction of Art. III courts. . . .

The complicated and contradictory history of the issue before us leads me to conclude that Chief Justice Vinson and Justice Harlan reached the correct conclusion: There is no difference in principle between the work that Congress may assign to an Art. I court and that which the Constitution assigns to Art. III courts. Unless we want to overrule a large number of our precedents upholding a variety of Art. I courts—not to speak of those Art. I courts that go by the contemporary name of "administrative agencies"—this conclusion is inevitable. It is too late to go back that far; too late to return to the simplicity of the principle pronounced in Art. III and defended so vigorously and persuasively by Hamilton in The Federalist Nos. 78–82.

To say that the Court has failed to articulate a principle by which we can test the constitutionality of a putative Art. I court, or that there is no such abstract principle, is not to say that this Court must always defer to the legislative decision to create Art. I, rather than Art. III, courts. Article III is not to be read out of the Constitution; rather, it should be read as expressing one value that must be balanced against competing constitutional values and legislative responsiblities. This Court retains the final word on how that balance is to be struck. . . .

. . . no one seriously argues that the Bankruptcy Act of 1978 represents an attempt by the political branches of government to aggrandize themselves at the expense of the third branch or an attempt to undermine the authority of constitutional courts in general. Indeed, the congressional perception of a lack of judicial interest in bankruptcy matters was one of the factors that led to the establishment of the bankruptcy courts: Congress feared that this lack of interest would lead to a failure by federal district courts to deal with bankruptcy matters in an expeditious manner. . . .

. . . My own view is that the very fact of extreme specialization may be enough, and certainly has been enough in the past, to justify the creation of a legislative court. Congress may legitimately consider the effect on the federal judiciary of the addition of several hundred specialized judges: We are, on the whole, a body of generalists. The addition of several hundred specialists may substantially change, whether for good or bad, the character of the federal bench. Moreover, Congress may have desired to maintain some flexibility in its possible future responses to the general problem of bankruptcy. There is no question that the existence of several hundred bankruptcy judges with life tenure would have severely limited Congress' future options. Furthermore, the number of bankruptcies may fluctuate producing a substantially reduced need for bankruptcy judges. Congress may have thought that, in that event, a bankruptcy specialist should not as a general matter serve as a judge in the countless nonspecialized cases that come before the federal district courts. It would then face the prospect of large numbers of idle federal judges. Finally, Congress may have believed that the change from bankruptcy referees to Art. I judges was far less dramatic, and so less disruptive of the existing bankruptcy and constitutional court systems, than would be a change to Art. III judges.

For all of these reasons, I would defer to the congressional judgment. Accordingly, I dissent.

Jonathan C. Rose

Bankruptcy Courts

In *Northern Pipeline Construction Co.* v. *Marathon Pipe Line Co.* (1982), the Supreme Court declared unconstitutional a bill passed by Congress in 1978 which established bankruptcy courts as "adjuncts" of the federal district courts. The Court argued that Congress had tried to give Article III powers to a legislative court created under Article I. It also expressed concern that if Congress could prevail in this instance, it could gradually undermine the independence of the national judiciary. The following article, entitled "Shortsightedness Plagues Bankruptcy Courts' History," appeared in the *Legal Times*, February 27, 1984. Rose, formerly with the Department of Justice's Office of Legal Policy, was an Assistant Attorney General primarily responsible for the department's

work on the bankruptcy court system. He explains the judiciary's own role in the legislative process and its administration of the bankruptcy courts while Congress searched for a solution. Footnotes omitted.

The ongoing crisis in the nation's bankruptcy courts will reach its decisive stage at the end of March. In order to understand that crisis and the decisions that will have to be made in the very near future, it is necessary to understand the history of the bankruptcy court system, which recently has been one of accident, neglect, short-sightedness, miscalculation, and intransigence. This article traces that history, from the unsatisfactory system that existed for nearly 80 years, through the congressional reform that was held unconstitutional, to the deadlock in Congress today.

Federal judiciary responsibility for bankruptcy actions in something approaching modern form began with the Bankruptcy Act of 1898. That act, periodically amended, created a court system somewhat lacking in coherence. Most issues relating directly to the assets of the debtor—over which the bankruptcy court had summary or in rem jurisdiction—were handled by bankruptcy referees, specialists appointed by the district courts. Other federal questions went to district judges under their plenary jurisdiction, while some matters of state law remained in the hands of state courts. . . .

The attitude of the district judges toward this situation often was strangely inconsistent. District judges usually valued their control over the bankruptcy system, both for its considerable patronage and on the theory that without their supervision, the referees, whom they considered to be lesser judicial lights, frequently would produce injustices. On the other hand, few district judges were willing to become bankruptcy experts. Evidently, their image of bankruptcy was of the small and vaguely embarrassing individual bankruptcy in which a profligate debtor seeks discharge of his debts. As far as most district judges were concerned, bankruptcy was a technical, trivial affair. They wished neither to be effectively responsible for bankruptcy adjudication nor to surrender it to an independent court.

Gradually, the inadequacies of the bankruptcy courts became widely known. Bankruptcy practi-

tioners, academics, and those who had been forced to go through the bankruptcy maze pressed for changes in both the court system and the arcane substance of title 11 itself. This led, in 1970, to the appointment of a Commission on the Bankruptcy Laws of the United States. The commission studied the issue for two years, relying principally on bankruptcy practitioners and commentators to develop a picture of the bankruptcy laws and courts, and the most desirable ways to reform each.

In 1973, the commission issued its report, which proposed systematic overhaul of both the substantive and procedural law of bankruptcy. According to the commission, the administration and adjudication of bankruptcy matters needed to be separated from each other, and both needed to be independent of the district courts. The report proposed creation of a U. S. Bankruptcy Administration, which would have performed the day-to-day functions of liquidating bankrupts or keeping them operational. This administration was to be an executive branch agency.

The suggested changes in the bankruptcy courts were sweeping; the commission favored creation of an essentially independent federal bankruptcy tribunal. This court was not to be an Article III forum. Rather, it would be staffed with presidential appointees serving for terms of years, subject to removal for cause (rather than for lack of "good behavior"). In large measure the commission modeled its proposed bankruptcy court on the Tax Court, an executive agency operating in the form of a court with decisions subject to review in the Article III courts on a deferential standard. . . .

[The House Judiciary Committee decided that bankruptcy judges required the independence of Article III judges, including life tenure.]

Stepped-up lobbying by the advocates of an Article III solution, including numerous personal conversations among members on the constitutional issue, turned the tide in the House three months later. Despite growing involvement by the federal judiciary, which opposed any measure to raise bankruptcy referees' status, the proponents of H.R. 8200 remained firm, especially in their claim that only an Article III court would be constitutional. On Feb. 8, 1978, after some further procedural maneuvers, the House passed the original form of H.R. 8200, which provided life tenure to the new judges.

Defeated in the House, opponents of the Article III solution switched their focus to the Senate. This time they succeeded, in large measure because of the close personal ties between senators and federal district judges and a wariness on the part of conservative senators about the creation of a new, life-tenure court. In the Senate, the House version of H.R. 8200 was wholly changed by an "amendment in the nature of a substitute" that replaced the independent, life-tenure court with a limited-tenure adjunct of the district court. The Senate passed this form of the new bankruptcy courts on September 22, 1978. At this point, of course, the 95th Congress was drawing to a close and midterm elections were approaching. To the other complications—which included numerous controversies over changes to the substance of title 11—was added end-of-session confusion.

Normally, when House and Senate pass different versions of a bill, it goes to a conference committee. But one theme of the history of this legislation is that things were done a little differently. The bills went into conference committee but never came out, and the final form of H.R. 8200 was passed, not as a conference product, but as a pair of identical amendments to amendments to amendments in the nature of a substitute. While this approach was necessary to comply with the rules of the House, the final complexities were not wholly procedural. At one point a compromise, which would have made the new bankruptcy courts adjuncts of the courts of appeals, was nearly reached; it was defeated largely because of the chief justice's personal intervention. On the House floor, uncertainty prevailed until the last minute, but on Oct. 6 the House passed the final version of H.R. 8200. After another delay, President Carter, reportedly relying heavily on the advice of Attorney General Griffin B. Bell, signed into law the Bankruptcy Reform Act of 1978. . . .

This new "adjunct" court was to be staffed with presidentially appointed judges serving 14-year terms, subject to removal for cause by their local judicial councils. It was hoped that this would provide sufficient prestige and independence to attract first-rate jurists to the bankruptcy court. Having managed to come to this compromise, Congress did not decide how many bankruptcy judges there should be and where they should serve. Instead, the Judicial Conference of the United States was to report in January 1983, recommending numbers and duty stations of new bankruptcy judges. A lengthy transition period was to precede the effective date of the new court system, April 1, 1984. Thus, the January 1983 data still would have left ample time for Congress to establish—and the President and Senate to fill—bankruptcy judgeships.

During the transition period the "courts of bankruptcy," which are departments of the district courts composed of bankruptcy referees and district judges sitting in bankruptcy, were to continue. But instead of exercising the old bifurcated jurisdiction from the 1898 act they—or more specifically the bankruptcy referees—were immediately to have the new, expanded jurisdiction provided for by the reform act. . . .

[Before the system could go into operation, the Supreme Court declared the Bankruptcy Act of 1978 unconstitutional on June 28, 1982.]

Having created what some may term chaos in legal theory, the Court sought to avoid chaos in judicial practice. The judgment of *Marathon* was not effective retroactively, so that cases decided previously were not overturned. Indeed, the Court also stayed its judgment from June 1982 to the beginning of the October 1982 term, in order to give Congress time to unravel the situation. When Congress failed to act, the solicitor general sought and obtained an extension of the stay, through Dec. 24, 1982. After the 97th Congress adjourned without action the Department of Justice sought yet another extension, which the justices denied; *Marathon* became effective on Dec. 25, 1982.

However, *Marathon* did not become very effective. In September 1982, Burger moved to obtain through the Judicial Conference of the United

States what he had not been able to obtain in conference of the Supreme Court: a temporary restructuring of the bankruptcy system. Under the chief justice's leadership, the Judicial Conference promulgated a "proposed rule" to the various circuit councils, urging them to direct their district courts to adopt an emergency rule. That rule, in effect, accomplished what the chief justice had urged in his dissent. Jurisdiction was found to vest in the district courts, which referred such matters as could be referred to bankruptcy judges, subject to a nondeferential standard of review. The circuit councils and district courts did indeed implement the Judicial Conference's suggestion. What the judges took away by deciding a case, they gave back by passing rules. Even though *Marathon* and the emergency rule came from different parts of the judiciary, they both originated in the third branch. Needless to say, this created the impression of judicial irresolution and relieved whatever pressure had been building on Congress to solve the bankruptcy puzzle.

The emergency rule is problematic on a number of grounds. For one thing, under the emergency rule, decisions by bankruptcy judges ostensibly are to be reviewed de novo by district judges. The new bankruptcy rules, which are based on the Reform Act's structure but which the Supreme Court promulgated unchanged after *Marathon*, provide for a "clearly erroneous" standard of review. But the emergency rule is issued only by the local courts (albeit with the circuit councils and Judicial Conference behind them), while the bankruptcy rules proper were promulgated by the Supreme Court under a statutory power and thus take precedence. One court of appeals has admitted this problem and held the emergency rule's standard of review invalid as contrary to the bankruptcy rules.

More generally, the emergency rule represents, in some sense, a departure from normal allocations of constitutional power. It can be viewed as an attempt by the courts, acting through their rulemaking power, to control their own jurisdiction. To be sure, the statutory basis underlying the emergency rule is a good one; I certainly do not mean to suggest that the courts are acting improperly or in bad faith. But perhaps, given the emergency, the judges have not fully appreciated what they have done. The emergency rule was written by the judiciary, it was sustained by the judiciary after being challenged on constitutional and statutory grounds, and it is largely administered by the judiciary. Any such fusion of governmental functions must give pause to friends of a constitutional system whose fundamental premise is separation of powers. This example of one branch of government promulgating a rule, implementing that rule in its daily work, and then adjudicating challenges to the rule's validity serves as a reminder of the value of the separation of powers doctrine. . . .

David F. Pike

The Court-Packing Plans

It's rare for President Reagan to follow his predecessor's lead. But in the Carter administration's unprecedented use of lifetime judicial appointments to stamp a lasting mark on the nation, the Reagan administration clearly has found an idea worth emulating.

SOURCE: The National Law Journal, August 29, 1983, pp. 1, 26, 27, 31.

The Carter administration used a record number of judicial vacancies to experiment with new nomination procedures in order to appoint record numbers of women and blacks to the bench—many of whom have been described as lawyers willing to use the courts to overcome social ills.

The Reagan administration, meanwhile, has quickly shifted back to a more conventional political process to put judges on the bench who believe in judicial restraint. Almost all of those appointed so far are white and male.

The Reagan administration has been aided in its drive for a more conservative judiciary by a shift in those who control the advise and consent powers of the Senate. Under the Carter administration, the Senate Judiciary Committee was headed by Sen. Edward M. Kennedy, D-Mass.; now, under the Republicans, Sen. Strom Thurmond, R-S.C., is at the helm and is a powerful ally in the administration's quest for judicial restraint. . . .

As for the Reagan administration's effect on the federal judiciary's demographics, the shift is clear. During the Carter years, 243 federal judges were appointed, with women winning 19.6 percent of the circuit court slots and 14.4 percent of the district court seats, and with blacks netting 16.1 percent of the circuit slots and 13.9 percent of the district court positions.

FEWER "ACTIVISTS"

With 106 Reagan appointees now confirmed, women have captured none of the 21 circuit court seats filled and 7 percent of the district court slots, while blacks have garnered 4.7 percent of the circuit posts (one seat—a district court judge who was elevated) and none of the district court posts.

Although the administration's effect on the judicial philosophy is harder to assess, most observers say the president and Senator Thurmond have gotten what they wanted: judges who are not inclined to be "activists" in asserting the power of the federal courts over legislatures and other government agencies.

"It is fair to observe that the Reagan administration is making maximum use of the prerogatives of office to shape the federal bench (and particularly the appeals courts) in its image," Sheldon Goldman, a professor of political science at the University of Massachusetts at Amherst, concluded recently in an article in Judicature magazine. "It may even surpass the Carter administration's record of ideological and political screening of candidates."

The fact that the current administration's screening has brought a sharp decline in the number of women and minority lawyers nominated to the federal bench has, as might be expected, raised an outcry on behalf of those groups.

The U.S. Commission on Civil Rights, in a June report entitled "Equal Opportunity in Presidential Appointments," said it is "concerned about the low representation of women and minority men among presidential appointees to the federal judiciary and to the U.S. attorney and U.S. marshal positions. These positions are especially sensitive because the appointees play vital roles in interpreting and enforcing the nation's laws."

NO OUTREACH EFFORTS?

D.C. Superior Court Judge Gladys Kessler, the president of the National Association of Women Judges, told members of the ABA's Judicial Administration Division late last month in Atlanta that "our present national leadership has made it clear, by its failure to name blacks to the federal bench and its near-total failure to name women, that it is disinterested in finding qualified women and minorities and that it is disinclined to engage in any outreach efforts to identify appropriate judicial candidates."

Recruiting qualified members of "historically underrepresented" groups for appointment to judicial positions, said Judge Kessler, is not only "right," but also "just."

And Warren Hope Dawson, president of the National Bar Association, called the administration's record on appointing black judges "sad," adding: "They had a great opportunity to continue the move in this area made by the Carter administration."

He noted that there still are no black federal judges in several southern states and in some circuits with large black populations, and, like Judge Kessler, he lamented the fact that his group now has no input in the selection process, as it did in the Carter years.

President Reagan, however, defended his administration's record in his speech before the ABA's annual meeting in Atlanta earlier this month, stating: "We aim for a cross-section of appointments that fully reflects the rich diversity and talent of our people. But we do not, and we never will, select individuals just because they are men or women, whites or blacks, Jews, Catholics or whatever . . . I believe you rob people of their dignity and confidence when you impose quotas."

Nomination Hearings of Sandra Day O'Connor

During the 1981 hearings on the nomination of Sandra Day O'Connor to be Associate Justice of the Supreme Court, Senators were interested in learning about the personal and philosophical views of the first woman nominated to the High Bench. Although the Senators wanted a nominee who would possess certain general qualities—integrity, honesty, technical knowledge, and proper judicial temperament—they also probed her position on the highly controversial issue of abortion, a question that had been decided already by the Court and was likely to be relitigated in the future. The selections below come from "Nomination of Sandra Day O'Connor," hearings before the Senate Committee on the Judiciary, 97th Cong., 1st Sess., September 9, 1981, pp. 60–63, 98, 106.

PERSONAL AND JUDICIAL PHILOSOPHY ON ABORTION

The CHAIRMAN *[Strom Thurmond]*. Judge O'Connor, there has been much discussion regarding your views on the subject of abortion. Would you discuss your philosophy on abortion, both personal and judicial, and explain your actions as a State senator in Arizona on certain specific matters: First, your 1970 committee vote in favor of House bill No. 20, which would have repealed Arizona's felony statutes on abortion. Then I have three other instances I will inquire about.

Judge O'CONNOR. Very well. May I preface my response by saying that the personal views and philosophies, in my view, of a Supreme Court Justice and indeed any judge should be set aside insofar as it is possible to do that in resolving matters that come before the Court.

Issues that come before the Court should be resolved based on the facts of that particular case or matter and on the law applicable to those facts, and any constitutional principles applicable to those facts. They should not be based on the personal views and ideology of the judge with regard to that particular matter or issue.

Now, having explained that, I would like to say that my own view in the area of abortion is that I am opposed to it as a matter of birth control or otherwise. The subject of abortion is a valid one, in my view, for legislative action subject to any constitutional restraints or limitations.

I think a great deal has been written about my vote in a Senate Judiciary Committee in 1970 on a bill called House bill No. 20, which would have repealed Arizona's abortion statutes. Now in reviewing that, I would like to state first of all that that vote occurred some 11 years ago, to be exact, and was one which was not easily recalled by me, Mr. Chairman. In fact, the committee records when I looked them up did not reflect my vote nor that of other members, with one exception.

It was necessary for me, then, to eventually take time to look at news media accounts and determine from a contemporary article a reflection of the vote on that particular occasion. The bill did not go to the floor of the Senate for a vote; it was held in the Senate Caucus and the committee vote was a vote which would have taken it out of that committee with a recommendation to the full Senate.

The bill is one which concerned a repeal of Arizona's then statutes which made it a felony, punishable by from 2 to 5 years in prison, for anyone providing any substance or means to procure a miscarriage unless it was necessary to save the life of the mother. It would have, for example, subjected anyone who assisted a young woman who, for instance, was a rape victim in securing a D. & C. procedure within hours or even days of that rape.

At that time I believed that some change in Arizona statutes was appropriate, and had a bill been presented to me that was less sweeping than

House bill No. 20, I would have supported that. It was not, and the news accounts reflect that I supported the committee action in putting the bill out of committee, where it then died in the caucus.

I would say that my own knowledge and awareness of the issues and concerns that many people have about the question of abortion has increased since those days. It was not the subject of a great deal of public attention or concern at the time it came before the committee in 1970. I would not have voted, I think, Mr. Chairman, for a simple repealer thereafter.

The CHAIRMAN. Now the second instance was your cosponsorship in 1973 of Senate bill No. 1190, which would have provided family planning services, including surgical procedures, even for minors without parental consent.

Judge O'CONNOR. Senate bill No. 1190 in 1973 was a bill in which the prime sponsor was from the city of Tucson, and it had nine other cosigners on the bill. I was one of those cosigners.

I viewed the bill as a bill which did not deal with abortion but which would have established as a State policy in Arizona, a policy of encouraging the availability of contraceptive information to people generally. The bill at the time, I think, was rather loosely drafted, and I can understand why some might read it and say, "What does this mean?"

That did not particularly concern me at the time because I knew that the bill would go through the committee process and be amended substantially before we would see it again. That was a rather typical practice, at least in the Arizona legislature. Indeed, the bill was assigned to a public health and welfare committee where it was amended in a number of respects.

It did not provide for any surgical procedure for an abortion, as has been reported inaccurately by some. The only reference in the bill to a surgical procedure was the following. It was one that said:

"A physician may perform appropriate surgical procedures for the prevention of conception upon any adult who requests such procedure in writing."

That particular provision, I believe, was subsequently amended out in committee but, be that as it may, it was in the bill on introduction.

Mr. Chairman, I supported the availability of contraceptive information to the public generally. Arizona had a statute or statutes on the books at that time, in 1973, which did restrict rather dramatically the availability of information about contraception to the public generally. It seemed to me that perhaps the best way to avoid having people who were seeking abortions was to enable people not to become pregnant unwittingly or without the intention of doing so.

The CHAIRMAN. The third instance, your 1974 vote against House Concurrent Memorial No. 2002, which urged Congress to pass a constitutional amendment against abortion.

Judge O'CONNOR. Mr. Chairman, as you perhaps recall, the *Rowe [sic]* v. *Wade* decision was handed down in 1973. I would like to mention that in that year following that decision, when concerns began to be expressed, I requested the preparation in 1973 of Senate bill No. 1333 which gave hospitals and physicians and employees the right not to participate in or contribute to any abortion proceeding if they chose not to do so and objected, notwithstanding their employment. That bill did pass the State Senate and became law.

The following year, in 1974, less than a year following the *Rowe [sic]* v. *Wade* decision, a House Memorial was introduced in the Arizona House of Representatives. It would have urged Congress to amend the Constitution to provide that the word person in the 5th and 14th amendments applies to the unborn at every stage of development, except in an emergency when there is a reasonable medical certainty that continuation of the pregnancy would cause the death of the mother. The amendment was further amended in the Senate Judiciary Committee.

I did not support the memorial at that time, either in committee or in the caucus.

The CHAIRMAN. Excuse me. My time is up, but you are right in the midst of your question. We will finish abortion, one more instance, and we will give the other members the same additional time, if you will proceed.

Judge O'CONNOR. I voted against it, Mr. Chairman, because I was not sure at that time that we had given the proper amount of reflection or consideration to what action, if any, was appropriate by way of a constitutional amendment in connection with the *Rowe [sic]* v. *Wade* decision.

It seems to me, at least, that amendments to the Constitution are very serious matters and should be undertaken after a great deal of study and thought, and not hastily. I think a tremendous amount of work needs to go into the text and the concept being expressed in any proposed amendment. I did not feel at that time that that kind of consideration had been given to the measure. I understand that the Congress is still wrestling with that issue after some years from that date, which was in 1974.

Thank you, Mr. Chairman.

The CHAIRMAN. Now the last instance is concerning a vote in 1974 against a successful amendment to a stadium construction bill which limited the availability of abortions.

Judge O'CONNOR. Also in 1974, which was an active year in the Arizona Legislature with regard to the issue of abortion, the Senate had originated a bill that allowed the University of Arizona to issue bonds to expand its football stadium. That bill passed the State Senate and went to the House of Representatives.

In the House it was amended to add a nongermane rider which would have prohibited the performance of abortions in any facility under the jurisdiction of the Arizona Board of Regents. When the measure returned to the Senate, at that time I was the Senate majority leader and I was very concerned because the whole subject had become one that was controversial within our own membership.

I was concerned as majority leader that we not encourage a practice of the addition of nongermane riders to Senate bills which we had passed without that kind of a provision. Indeed, Arizona's constitution has a provision which prohibits the putting together of bills or measures or riders dealing with more than one subject. I did oppose the addition by the House of the nongermane rider when it came back.

It might be of interest, though, to know, Mr. Chairman, that also in 1974 there was another Senate bill which would have provided for a medical assistance program for the medically needy. That was Senate bill No. 1165. It contained a provision that no benefits would be provided for abortions except when deemed medically necessary to save the life of the mother, or where the pregnancy had resulted from rape, incest, or criminal action. I supported that bill together with that provision and the measure did pass and become law. . . .

PERSONAL PHILOSOPHY OF ABORTION

Senator DeCONCINI. Returning to the subject— and I am sure it probably will never end—of abortion, you have expressed your views a number of times here today and just now with Senator Dole. I wonder if you could share with us for just a few minutes not the voting record—I know you have had no judicial decisions on the subject matter that we could find—but your personal philosophy or feeling as to abortion so the record would be clear today?

Judge O'CONNOR. OK, Senator. Again let me preface a comment by saying that my personal views and beliefs in this area and in other areas have no place in the resolution of any legal issues that will come before the Court. I think these are matters that of necessity a judge must attempt to set aside in resolving the cases that come before the Court.

I have indicated to you the position that I have held for a long time—my own abhorrence of abortion as a remedy. It is a practice in which I would not have engaged, and I am not trying to criticize others in that process. There are many who have very different feelings on this issue. I recognize that, and I am sensitive to it.

But my view is the product, I suppose, merely of my own upbringing and my religious training, my background, my sense of family values, and my sense of how I should lead my own life.

Senator DeCONCINI. Judge O'Connor, along that line I have one last comment about it. This is not something that has come upon you in the last year or two or the last 6 or 7 weeks; this is a commitment and a feeling that you have had for a long period of time, I assume from the answer to the question.

Judge O'CONNOR. I have had my own personal views on the subject for many years. It is just an outgrowth of what I am, if you will.

Senator DeCONCINI. Thank you. I appreciate that response in depth regarding your own personal background.

I regret to some extent that it is necessary to delve into that, but I believe—as you can appreciate here—it is a sensitive subject among many Members on the many sides of this issue. I think it is very important that it be laid out clearly and precisely, and I think you have done just that. . . .

Senator EAST. Let me cut through this gordian knot and get to the heart of one issue which has been alluded to before—there is no question about it; namely, this very difficult, hotly debated issue of abortion in the United States.

I wish to say again that I do not think it is the sole test for qualification. I do not think it is the only thing that ought to be pursued, nor has it been the only thing that has been pursued, but certainly it is fair game as a part of a whole panoply of items—concept cases—that we might pursue.

As I understand, Mrs. O'Connor, your basic personal position on this issue of abortion—just stating your personal values—is that abortion on demand as a form of birth control—you are personally opposed to that? Is that correct?

Judge O'CONNOR. Yes, Senator.

United States v. Will

449 U.S. 200 (1980)

Congress has enacted a number of statutes designed to bring federal pay into line with salaries of the private sector. The basic thrust of these statutes—the Salary Act of 1967, the Comparability Act of 1970, and the Adjustment Act of 1975—allows pay increases to occur automatically unless Congress intervenes. In this case, the Supreme Court reviews four congressional statutes from 1976 to 1979 that blocked cost-of-living pay raises for federal employees, including judges. The Court decided that late passage of two of the statutes violated Article III's Compensation Clause, which prohibits diminution of pay for federal judges. Chief Justice Burger delivered the Court's opinion in which all members joined except Justice Blackmun, who took no part.

. . .

In October 1975, GS salaries were increased by an average of 5% under the terms of the Comparability Act. Federal judges and the other officials covered by the Adjustment Act received similar increases. In each of the following four years, however, Congress adopted a statute that altered the application of the Adjustment Act for the officials of the three branches subject to it. To avoid the confusion generated by a fiscal year's having a number different from the calendar year in which it begins, we refer to these as Years 1, 2, 3, and 4. We turn now to the specific actions taken for each of the four years in question.

. . .

YEAR 1

The statute applying to Year 1 was signed by the President during the business day of October 1, 1976. By that time, the 4.8% increase under the Adjustment Act already had taken effect, since it was operative with the start of the month—and the new fiscal year—at the beginning of the day. The statute became law only upon the President's signing it on October 1; it therefore purported to repeal a salary increase already in force. Thus it "diminished" the compensation of federal judges.

The Government contends that Congress could reduce compensation as long as it did not "discriminate" against judges, as such, during the process. That the "freeze" applied to various officials in the Legislative and the Executive Branches, as well as judges, does not save the statute, however. This is quite different from the situation in *O'Malley* v. *Woodrough*, 307 U. S. 277 (1939). There the Court held that the Compensation Clause was not offended by an income tax levied on Article III judges as well as on all other taxpayers; there was no discrimination against the plaintiff judge. Federal judges, like all citizens, must share "the material burden of the government . . ." *Id.*, at 282. The inclusion in the freeze of other officials who are not protected by the Compensation Clause does not insulate a direct diminution in judges' salaries from the clear mandate of that Clause; the Constitution makes no exceptions for "nondiscriminatory" reductions. Accordingly, we hold that the statute with respect to Year 1, as applied to compensation of members of the certified class, violates the Compensation Clause of Art. III.

YEAR 2

Unlike the statute for Year 1, the statute for Year 2 was signed by the President before October 1, when the 7.1% raise under the Comparability Act was due to take effect. Year 2 thus confronts us squarely with the question of whether Congress may, before the effective date of a salary increase, rescind such an increase scheduled to take effect at a later date. The District Court held that by including an annual cost-of-living adjustment in the statutory definitions of the salaries of Article III judges . . . Congress made the annual adjustment, from that moment on, a part of judges' compensation for constitutional purposes. Subsequent action reducing those adjustments "diminishes" compensation within the meaning of the Compensation Clause. Relying on *Evans* v. *Gore*, 253 U. S., at 254, the District Court held that such action reduces the amount "a judge . . . has been promised," and all amounts thus promised fall within the protection of the Clause.

We are unable to agree with the District Court's analysis and result. Our discussion of the Framers' debates over the Compensation Clause . . . led to a conclusion that the Compensation Clause does

not erect an absolute ban on all legislation that conceivably could have an adverse effect on compensation of judges. Rather, that provision embodies a clear rule prohibiting decreases but allowing increases, a practical balancing by the Framers of the need to increase compensation to meet economic changes, such as substantial inflation, against the need for judges to be free from undue congressional influence. The Constitution delegated to Congress the discretion to fix salaries and of necessity placed faith in the integrity and sound judgment of the elected representatives to enact increases when changing conditions demand.

Congress enacted the Adjustment Act based on this delegated power to fix and, periodically, increase judicial compensation. It did not thereby alter the *compensation* of judges; it modified only the *formula* for determining that compensation. Later, Congress decided to abandon the formula as to the particular years in question. For Year 2, as opposed to Year 1, the statute was passed before the Adjustment Act increases had taken effect — before they had become a part of the compensation due Article III judges. Thus, the departure from the Adjustment Act policy in no sense diminished the compensation Article III judges were receiving; it refused only to apply a previously enacted formula.

A paramount—indeed, an indispensable— ingredient of the concept of powers delegated to coequal branches is that each branch must recognize and respect the limits on its own authority and the boundaries of the authority delegated to the other branches. To say that the Congress could not alter a method of calculating salaries before it was executed would mean the Judicial Branch could command Congress to carry out an announced future intent as to a decision the Constitution vests exclusively in the Congress. We therefore conclude that a salary increase "vests" for purposes of the Compensation Clause only when it takes effect as part of the compensation due and payable to Article III judges. With regard to Year 2, we hold that the Compensation Clause did not prohibit Congress from repealing the planned but not yet effective cost-of-living adjustment of October 1, 1977, when it did so before October 1, the time it first was scheduled to become part of judges' compensation. The statute in Year 2 thus represents a constitutionally valid exercise of legislative authority.

YEAR 3

For our purposes, the legal issues presented by the statute in Year 3 are indistinguishable from those in Year 2. Each statute eliminated—before October 1—the Adjustment Act salary increases contemplated but not yet implemented. Each statute was passed and signed by the President *before* the Adjustment Act increases took effect, in the case of Year 3, on September 30. For the reasons set forth in our discussion of the issues for Year 2, we hold that the statute in Year 3 did not violate the Compensation Clause.

YEAR 4

Before reaching the constitutional issues implicated in Year 4, we must resolve a problem of statutory construction. On its face, the statute in Year 4 applies in terms to "executive employees, which includes Members of Congress." . . . It does not expressly mention judges. Appellees contend that even if Congress constitutionally could freeze the salaries of Article III judges, it did not do so in this statute.

We are satisfied that Congress' use of the phrase "executive employees," in context, was intended to include Article III judges. The full title of the Adjustment Act is the *Executive* Salary Cost-of-Living Adjustment Act, but it is clear that it was intended to apply to officials in the Legislative and the Judicial Branches as well. The title does not control over the terms of the statute. The statutes in the three preceding years undeniably applied to judges, and we can discern no indication that the Congress chose to single them out for an exemption when it was including Executive and Legislative officials. Most important, both the Conference Report and the Chairman of the House Appropriations Committee, speaking on the floor, made explicit what already was implicit: the limiting statute would apply to judges as well. . . .

Having concluded that the statute in Year 4 was intended to apply to judges as well as other high-level federal officials, we are confronted with a situation similar to that in Year 1. Here again, the statute purported to revoke an increase in judges' compensation *after* those statutes had taken effect. For the reasons governing the statute as to Year 1, we hold that the statute revoking the increase for Year 4 violated the Compensation Clause insofar as it applied to members of the certified class.

Opening the Judicial Conference to the Public

The Senate Committee on the Judiciary held hearings in 1980 on a bill to permit public observation of the Judicial Conference. Senator Dennis DeConcini, author of the bill, chaired the hearing and made an opening statement. Collins J. Seitz, chief judge of the Third Circuit, testified in its favor. Elmo B. Hunter, federal judge from Missouri, presented the views of the Judicial Conference in opposition to the bill. These excerpts are from the committee's published hearing, *Judicial Conference and Councils in the Sunshine Act, S. 2045*, 96th Cong., 2d Sess., March 7, 1980, pp. 1–2, 4–5, 11, 14, 19–21.

Senator DeCONCINI. The Subcommittee on Improvements in Judicial Machinery will come to order.

This morning we will be hearing testimony on S. 2045, the Judicial Conference and Councils in the Sunshine Act.

Democracy does not prosper in darkness. In a free and open society, secrecy should be the exception, not the rule. It has been only within the last decade that Congress has opened the doors of the Federal agencies as well as its own to public scrutiny.

At the time these important steps were taken, there were the forecasters of doom who told us that government could not possibly or effectively function without the closed door. Nonetheless, both Congress and the executive branch have appeared to survive this public scrutiny intact, and the integrity of the decisionmaking process has been unaffected. Rather, I believe that the growing openness in government has contributed to a far better understanding within the public and the media of the processes by which policies are formulated. Knowledge can only strengthen the institutions of our government.

The legislation we are discussing this morning seeks to apply some of the lessons we have thus far learned and apply them to the judicial branch of government. At the outset, let me be absolutely clear and unambiguous about one point. The legislation I introduced in no way contemplates opening the process by which judges reach individual decisions—at the trial or appellate court levels—to public inspection. I do not believe that any responsible individuals or groups would advocate such a radical position.

Rather, what I am proposing is that those aspects of the judicial branch that involve policymaking be open to public observation. The focus of the legislation is on the Judicial Conference and the Judicial Councils. At their respective levels, these two bodies represent the policymaking organizations of the Federal judiciary. Since its establishment in 1922, the Judicial Conference has taken the lead in modernizing and adapting the Federal judiciary to changing conditions. I might add a personal note at this point—that I have the utmost respect for the work they have done and this subcommittee has enjoyed a close working relationship with representatives of the Conference during the last 3 years.

However, the work of the Judicial Conference is not per se judicial; rather, it is more accurately quasi-legislative and quasi-administrative. For example, the Judicial Conference issues position statements on matters of general policy, including legislation pending in Congress; it enacts regulations governing the behavior and conduct of judges; and, most significant, it proposes and makes procedural rules that are binding on the Nation's courts.

The Judicial Councils can, for the sake of convenience, be regarded as miniature versions of the Conference in terms of their overall functions. In other words, they address the general management of the courts within their jurisdiction but do not involve themselves in the substance of specific judicial decisions.

It seems to me that there is no more justification in maintaining a veil of secrecy around the discussions and processes of the Judicial Conference and the Judicial Councils than there is in forbidding the public to witness the give-and-take associated with a House-Senate conference. Indeed, until recently, those conferences were generally held behind closed doors. Today, however, they are conducted in full view of all citizens unless there is some overwhelming need for secrecy, as in the case of classified national security materials.

The point is that when judges are acting in their capacity as members of the Judicial Conference or the Judicial Councils, they are playing a role which is not purely judicial. The decisions they reach in proposing a new rule or changing an old one that affect, for example, class action cases, may have as much ultimate effect on the Nation as an act of Congress. And the issues involved in no way touch the guilt or innocence of specific parties or the outcome of a specific civil case; rather, they are matters of broad policy which affect us all as citizens.

Judge SEITZ. . . . I am happy to be here at the invitation of the Subcommittee on Improvements in Judicial Machinery to speak in support of the substance of S. 2045, known as the Judicial Conference and Councils in the Sunshine Act.

First off, since both the Judicial Conference of the United States and the Judicial Councils are creations of Congress, the Congress certainly has the power within constitutional limitations to tailor their operations to reflect the congressional will.

Next, I stress that this bill deals exclusively with the administrative operations of Federal courts. I cannot overemphasize that it is not designed to encroach in any way on the process of deciding cases. I know this subcommittee would be as vigilant as the judiciary to avoid the slightest impingement on the decisionmaking process itself.

Denial of reasonable public access to the functions of public institutions, without purpose, breeds suspicion that some of its business cannot withstand public scrutiny. In consequence, respect for such institutions is lowered and their credibility lessened.

It is important then, in this period of lessening public respect for our public institutions, that we in responsible positions convey a reasonable sense of openness in the discharge of our responsibilities, that we let the sunshine in.

Indeed, it is in the interest of the judiciary in discharging its administrative and policy roles that the public be made aware of the depth and the scope of the work done and the care given to the administrative process in the Federal courts. Thus, rather than viewing S. 2045 in the negative, I view it as a vehicle to enhance the public image of the Federal court system, both nationally and at the circuit level.

What are the principal objections to sunshine legislation with respect to the Conference and Council proceedings? It seems to me that there may be three: First, a fear that public pressure might chill discussion or impede decisions; second, some delicate, for example, personnel, matters should not be public; and third, that implementing procedures are much too elaborate.

I will speak on the basis of my 9 years experience as a member of the Judicial Conference of the United States and almost 14 years on a circuit council, for almost 9 of which I have served as the chairman. Both at the Conference and Council levels, consideration is given to elaborate committee reports and recommendations.

In my experience the agendas of the Conference and our Council are primarily concerned with the "nuts and bolts" of judicial administration. We consider, for example, as we did in the last 2 days, changes in the rules of court, the need for more judicial and supporting personnel, the operation of the jury system, the impact of proposed legislation and so on.

A public presence during the discussion of nearly all agenda items would in no way, in my view, chill discussion or otherwise impede a determination of the merits of any committee recommendation. On the contrary, as I have indicated, the proceedings would demonstrate the care and consideration given to the business and policy ends of our Federal courts. . . .

Judge HUNTER. . . . Mr. Chairman, I have been directed by the Judicial Conference to make known to you that there is deep concern that regulation of the court's right to administer its own administrative affairs may call for serious consideration of possible violation of the separation of powers doctrine. I note that you have already undertaken to secure legal advice on that question.

Aside and beyond that consideration remains the question of whether S. 2045 and its provisions hinder the ability of the judiciary to carry out its proper function. To answer that question it is necessary to have an understanding of the way the Judicial Conference of the United States and its committees and subcommittees operate.

It is also necessary to have an understanding of the operation of each of the 11 circuit councils and how each of them operates, because each operates somewhat differently from the others.

. . .

With the exception of one chief judge, one whom you have invited and heard this morning, all of the other chief judges have expressed the view that S. 2045 will substantially hinder and cripple the ability of their particular circuit council to carry out its legitimate function.

I might also say that all of the other judges who attended the Judicial Conference are of the same view.

. . .

The Judicial Conference of the United States is the highest administrative body of the third branch of Government. Its ability to handle its sensitive internal matters should not be impaired by requiring compliance with the provisions of S. 2045.

I turn again more specifically to some of those provisions. Some of those provisions simply are not tailored to the judiciary, and they do seriously hinder and greatly impair the function of the Judicial Conference or circuit councils and its committees and subcommittees. First is the requirement that with two narrow exceptions all meetings of the Judicial Conference, circuit councils, committees, and subcommittees are prohibited from the joint conduct or disposition of business of the judiciary entity other than in accordance with S. 2045. It is mandated that every portion of every meeting of each judicial entity shall be open to public observation.

This raises with us many questions, Mr. Chairman. Does public observation include the use of cameras, television, the right to speak out at the meetings and participate in them, that type of thing?

Other provisions make it clear that these judicial entities are prohibited from conducting business through the use of the mails or telephone, although that has been an accepted and time-honored practice, particularly in the larger circuits such as the ninth which runs from Alaska to old Mexico.

. . .

Senator DeConcini. . . . Let me go to one other area. Do you agree that the Judicial Conference is involved in what might be termed to be lobbying, or at least bringing to the Congress certain information in order to persuade them that certain laws should be changed as they relate to the court?

Judge Hunter. Senator, I give a qualified yes to that. We do not ask you or tell you or advise you how to pass on bills unless you invite our comments. We are very careful.

My committee simply will not respond concerning legislation unless the invitation originates with one or the other of the bodies of the Congress.

You have in your statute, in setting up the Judicial Conference of the United States, charged that Conference with the duty in some instances of calling matters to your attention which affect the judiciary or affect the ability of the judiciary to carry out its function. We respond to that statutory duty which you have placed upon us.

If you want to remove that statutory duty, you will hear no more from us on that subject.

Senator DeConcini. You are saying, Judge, you respond only when asked?

Judge Hunter. That is our policy, sir.

Senator DeConcini. You see, when we had the matter of the judicial conduct and disability we didn't ask but every member of the committee received a lengthy letter in the Senate explaining the opposition to it. We did not ask you to do that.

I do not object to your doing it. My point is only that I do not think that it is quite correct when you say that the Judicial Conference responds only to requests. I think they are, and properly so, interested in bringing the proper information before the Congress.

Judge Hunter. Senator, I am glad you raised that problem because between the two of us I hope there is utter frankness.

Senator DeConcini. Indeed there is.

Judge Hunter. I wish to respond fully. If there was any violation of our policy that we respond only at the request of Congress, you can lay that blame on me. The policy is firm and intact. Perhaps I misjudged the application of it.

I attended the seminar which was held in Virginia in which Members of the House and Senate were invited and attended, together with members of the judiciary, together with the Attorney General, and it was a very helpful seminar. Out of that seminar I thought that I heard an invitation to advise the Congress at any time of any pressing need or problem of the judiciary. Perhaps I misunderstood that message.

In other appearances before other subcommittees of the Congress I thought that I heard the message that Congress wanted us to reply more directly, more to the point, and really to express ourselves fully on legislative matters which directly impacted on the judiciary.

If I misread those things, I of course apologize.

Senator DeConcini. I am not asking for an apology.

Judge Hunter. It is the policy of the Judicial Conference——

Senator DeConcini. Apologies are not necessary. My point is only this: It seems to me that the Judicial Conference, and rightfully so, is equivalent to many other interested groups in improving government, or whatever affects their particular interest. I do not think there should be any apologies for that. I think it is the proper course for the Judicial Conference to offer suggestions so as to improve the machinery, whether asked or not. I encourage you to do it.

My point is that I think you do do it, and I see nothing wrong with it except the fact that by doing it you are, for all intents and purposes, attempting to influence the Congress in one manner or another.

That being the case, I think it is healthy and good. That also being the case, I question why should you not be subject at least to having your meetings open?

Judge HUNTER. If you want to consider opening any meeting which results in lobbying, if the gun will be centered on that subject, perhaps there is fertile ground. Frankly, Senator, the judges are poor lobbyists, ill equipped for it.

Senator DECONCINI. They do pretty well.

Judge HUNTER. Their atmosphere is just totally different. I am example "A."

Senator DECONCINI. Judge, you are very convincing. Many of your colleagues are also very good. I won't use the term "lobbyists" but they are good promoters of the Judicial Conference positions. In your conclusion you questioned the need for the statutory provision in any event, not only these specifics.

Judicial Lobbying

In a floor statement on March 2, 1984, Senator Jeremiah Denton expressed concern that federal judges might be violating statutory prohibitions on the use of federal funds to lobby Congress. In his statement, and in the articles he introduced into the Congressional Record, the activities of judges are described through the Judicial Conference of the United States, which was created by statute, and through a private organization called the Federal Judges Association. Denton's statement appears at 130 Cong. Rec. S2267–2270 (daily ed. March 2, 1984).

Mr. DENTON. Mr. President, I have become concerned that members of the Federal judiciary may be violating statutory prohibitions on the use of Federal funds to lobby the Congress. The possible violations were brought to my attention by a November 4, 1983, Los Angeles Times article by Jim Mann, entitled "U.S. Judges Now Court Legislators." I ask that the Times article be printed in full in the RECORD immediately following my remarks.

Mr. President, as my colleagues are aware, section 1913 of title 18, United States Code, prohibits the use of Federal funds to lobby Congress ". . . in the absence of express authorization by the Congress." The only exception that is provided by the law is that Federal officers and employees may communicate with Congress "on the request of any Member or to Congress, through the proper official channels, requests for legislation or appro-

priations which they deem necessary for the efficient conduct of the public business."

Yet the Times article describes two general kinds of judicial lobbying activities: First, lobbying by or on behalf of the Judicial Conference of the United States; and second, lobbying by or on behalf of the Federal Judges Association (FJA). The Judicial Conference of the United States stands as the only group that arguably has "express authorization by the Congress" for lobbying "through the proper official channels." That is because, unlike the FJA, the Judicial Conference is an official governmental body. The FJA is a purely private group, formed in 1981, which asks its approximately 300 dues-paying members "to contact their 'friends' in Congress to seek 'such friends' support' for legislation benefiting the judges." I ask that a June 13, 1981, Washington Post article entitled "Judges Act To Organize for Salaries,

Benefits," which describes the purpose of the FJA, be printed in full in the RECORD following my remarks.

Mr. President, under 28 U.S.C. 331, the Chief Justice of the U.S. Supreme Court, as the statutory head of the Judicial Conference, is authorized and directed to "submit to Congress an annual report of the proceedings of the Judicial Conference and its recommendations for legislation." It can, therefore, be said that the statutory language expressly authorizes only the Chief Justice to recommend legislation. No other Federal judge is expressly authorized to do so, and not even the Chief Justice can be said to be expressly authorized to go beyond recommending legislation to lobbying for its passage.

The Times article, however, discusses lobbying activities by the Chief Justice and by other Federal judges who hold positions within the committee structure of the Judicial Conference. In addition, the Times article discusses how the Judicial Conference has retained two former Senate Judiciary Committee staff members to advise it about influencing the Congress. That kind of activity may violate 18 U.S.C. 1913, and therefore justifies an inquiry by the U.S. General Accounting Office.

Although Federal judges obviously enjoy a constitutional freedom of association that allows them to form a private organization such as the FJA, any "contact" with "friends" in the Congress that involves the use of federally funded support staff, telephones, office equipment, and the like, almost surely would violate section 1913. The Times article raises suspicions in that regard that are sufficient to warrant a GAO inquiry. . . .

[From the Los Angeles Times, Nov. 4, 1983]
U.S. JUDGES NOW COURT LEGISLATORS
(By Jim Mann)

WASHINGTON.—The federal judiciary, long accustomed to deciding questions of public policy on the bench, is becoming more deeply involved than ever before in trying to set or influence public policy off the bench as well.

Over the last few years, the nation's 684 life-tenured federal judges gradually have begun shedding traditional inhibitions about participating in the political process. Now, they are calling congressmen, forming trade associations, conducting grass-roots campaigns, hiring legislative representatives and even filing lawsuits in an effort to alter the course of various disputes, in the legislative and executive branches of government.

ANOTHER SPECIAL-INTEREST GROUP

Through these endeavors, the federal judiciary—which in the past has adopted a posture of Olympian detachment from the day-to-day affairs of the other branches of government—is now beginning to act like the many other special-interest groups in American society. On issues ranging from budget and tax legislation to the requirements for bail or the minimum length of a jail sentence, the judges have become a constituency seeking to be heard.

Indeed, earlier this year, after a group of federal judges hosted a Capitol Hill reception for important legislators, including Senate Judiciary Committee Chairman Strom Thurmond (R-S.C.), U.S. Circuit Judge Abner J. Mikva—himself a former congressman—confessed that the event had seemed "like a traditional lobbying activity, sort of like the realtors and the used-car dealers."

SUCCESSFUL IN KILLING BILL

The judges' efforts are beginning to pay off. During a lame-duck session of Congress late last year, the federal judiciary succeeded in killing a bill that would have given life tenure, the federal judges' most treasured perquisite, to the judges who handle bankruptcy cases, who currently are appointed for fixed terms. One key step in heading off the legislation was a phone call from U.S. District Judge Harold Barefoot Sanders Jr. of Dallas to his old friend and political ally, House Majority Leader Jim Wright (D-Tex.).

"I've found that with Congress, you're most effective with the people you know," explained the judge, who once worked as a legislative aide to President Lyndon B. Johnson.

The judges' unprecedented off-the-bench activism is to some extent a reflection of their concern about getting the salary increases and other benefits they believe are necessary to maintain their standard of living. (Federal district or trial judges are now paid $73,100 a year, while federal appeals court judges receive $77,300.)

In addition, the judges, like many others in America, have discovered that virtually every aspect of their lives—their taxes and pensions, their working conditions and life insurance—may be affected by the laws Congress passes.

"We know which judges are friendly with which congressmen," said U.S. District Judge Spencer M. Williams of San Francisco. "When there's a problem, the judges can contact the congressmen in their home districts and talk to them. . . . The judges are merely exercising their rights. Every other group in this country has an organization to talk to Congress."

ETHICAL QUESTIONS

Yet a number of scholars and lawyers—and a few dissenting judges—say they are disturbed by the judges' new activities. Some believe it is harmful to the judges' dignified image and could jeopardize their special status in American society to be seen as seeking aid and favors from the other branches of government.

"The position of being an authority figure and being a supplicant are inconsistent. I think the judges are compromising their role a little bit," Yale Law School professor Geoffrey C. Hazard Jr. said.

Others go further. They say the judges' behavior raises troublesome questions about the possibilities for ethical conflict between the judges' strong stands off the bench and their need to remain impartial and dispassionate in the courtroom. Critics also point out that, unlike Congress and the executive branch, federal judges have life tenure and are therefore accountable to no one for their actions in the political or legislative domain.

"It's unseemly and inappropriate," Hofstra University law professor Monroe H. Freedman said of the judges' attempts to influence the other branches of government.

OFF-THE-BENCH OPINIONS

In some instances, the judges have taken positions in Congress on issues or legislation whose constitutionality may be tested in the federal courts. In addition, an examination of the judges' activities by The Times turned up several examples of judges' giving off-the-bench opinions about how a decision should be interpreted or whether a particular bill might be constitutional—matters that could later come before them on the bench.

Generally, federal judges are not supposed to give off-the-bench "advisory" opinions concerning constitutional questions that might arise in court. But when it comes to legislation affecting the judiciary, judges frequently have volunteered out-of-court opinions to Congress about what might pass constitutional muster.

Three years ago, for example, when Sen. Dennis DeConcini (D-Ariz.) proposed legislation that would have required the Judicial Conference of the United States, the judiciary's official policymaking board, to open its meetings to the public, U.S. Circuit Judge Irving R. Kaufman of New York bluntly informed DeConcini in writing that his bill would be "an unconstitutional violation of the separation of powers." And last year, when the Supreme Court struck down the legislation setting up the nation's bankruptcy courts, the Judicial Conference sent Congress a written report explaining how it felt the high court's decision should be interpreted. . . .

BURGER SET EXAMPLE

In taking such positions, the federal judiciary is following the example of Chief Justice Warren E. Burger, who has devoted more time to off-the-bench activities than any of his predecessors since Chief Justice William Howard Taft six decades ago. In a 1978 speech, Burger said he believes that "participation in legislative and executive decisions that affect the judicial system is an absolute obligation of judges just as it is of lawyers."

The number of lawyers and staff aides assigned to represent federal judges in Congress and elsewhere in Washington has increased markedly over the past few years.

The Judicial Conference had no full-time staff member assigned to keep track of legislation until 1976. Now, a three-person legislative affairs office keeps track of developments in Congress, regularly contacting important committee members to let them know what the judges want.

LOBBYING LAW CITED

In addition, last spring one committee of the Judicial Conference hired two well-connected Washington lawyer-lobbyists to work on what it

called "congressional strategies designed to im-
prove the personal financial security of federal
judges." One of the attorneys, Kenneth R.
Feinberg, had served as a counsel to the Senate
Judiciary Committee when it was headed by Sen.
Edward M. Kennedy (D-Mass); the other, Emory
M. Sneeden, had served as counsel for the com-
mittee under Thurmond, the current chairman.

The two men will work for the judiciary on a
pro bono basis—that is, without pay. Asked about
his work for the judges, Feinberg said recently:
"Everybody in America is entitled to a lawyer."

The federal lobbying law makes it a crime to
use public money for the purpose of attempting to
influence members of Congress. Like virtually
every other agency of the federal government, the
Judicial Conference maintains that its activities on
Capitol Hill are not lobbying, but merely an effort
to respond to congressional requests. Five years
ago, in a fit of pique after a bankruptcy bill was
passed over his opposition, Burger remarked privately, "If I'm a lobbyist, I'm just about the lousi-
est lobbyist there could ever be."

Many judges, indeed, complain that the efforts
of the Judicial Conference do not go far enough.

Two years ago, some of these judges formed a
separate private group, the Federal Judges Assn.,
with the aim of getting a better deal from Congress on such matters as salaries, pensions and
other benefits. At the time, Burger strenuously
opposed formation of the new organization, saying it would "obstruct, rather than advance, accomplishment of those things needed by the judiciary."

JUDGES' GROUP THRIVES

But the Federal Judges Assn. now is thriving.
Nearly half, or about 300, of the life-tenured
federal judges have joined, with each of them
contributing dues of $200 per year.

In August, these judges hired former Republican Rep. Charles Wiggins of California, who once
served on the House Judiciary Committee, to be
their "federal coordinator." Wiggins says he will
merely "monitor" legislation in Congress for the
association.

"It's not my function to lobby for the judges,"
he said. "They'll make contact on their own with
people in the Senate and the House."

The Federal Judges Assn. is headed by Williams, who sometimes refers to the Judicial
Conference—which is led by the chief justice and
the chief judges of the nation's federal appeals
courts—as "the Establishment." The judges' association, he said, is not only a private organization
but a "grass-roots movement." . . .

"There is some concern in my mind that we
may look like any other group of organized professionals or organized workers that is speaking for
its own personal interests rather than the interests
of the country as a whole," said Circuit Judge
Levin H. Campbell, chief judge of the U.S. 1st
Circuit Court of Appeals in Boston. "Possibly
we're stronger in the long run if we're content just
to do our job."

DISSENTING JUDGES

Campbell acknowledged that his view might be
an "outmoded" one. "Pressure groups have become more common in the past 20 years," he said.

Another federal judge, who spoke only on the
condition that he not be identified, reported that
although others in his courthouse had joined the
judges' association, he had decided not to sign up.
"I sometimes feel like out of a spirit of
camaraderie, I ought to join, too," the judge said.
Asked whether he was being pressured to do so, he
asserted, "of course, if I didn't eat with them (the
other judges), I wouldn't have any pressure at all."

Others are even more critical. "When the judges go around to congressmen asking for something, they give what amounts to an IOU," said
U.S. Bankruptcy Judge Richard L. Merrick, former president of the National Conference of Bankruptcy Judges. "You know how congressmen
work. When they do something for you, they
expect you'll do something for them. Some congressmen might have a constituent who wants to
have a sentence modified. Some might have an
arrangement with a law firm that practices in the
federal courts."

Those in the federal judiciary who have joined
the Federal Judges Assn. say they see nothing
wrong with forming a trade group.

"When it comes to issues that affected the
judiciary directly—their salaries, protection for
their widows and dependents, preservation of the
independence of the judiciary—the judges have

both a right and a duty to speak up and deal with Congress," U.S. District Judge Irving Hill of Los Angeles said, "because if they don't, nobody will."

Wiggins, the former congressman now representing the federal judges, contended that the judiciary needs special help because judges are viewed "with some hostility" in the legislative branch. "The guys on the (Capitol) Hill, who have

to stand for reelection every two years, have a feeling of animosity toward people who are appointed for life," he explained.

Nevertheless, some scholars say they believe judges should speak only from the bench and should avoid attempting to influence the other branches of government. . . .

Participation by Judges in the Legislative Process

On October 25, 1978, while accepting the Fordham-Stein Award in New York City, Chief Justice Burger delivered the following remarks on judicial intervention in the legislative process. Footnotes omitted.

. . .

From time to time the question comes up as to whether the activities of those of our profession who are judges and who try to see that the needs of the courts are met in some way violate the concept of separation of powers.

I hope that you will not mind if I reflect with you tonight on the real meaning of the separation of powers in our tripartite constitutional system— and what it does not mean.

Justice Jackson had some relevant observations on this subject:

"While the Constitution diffuses power the better to secure liberty, it also contemplates that practice will integrate the dispersed powers into a workable government. It enjoins upon its branches separateness but interdependence, autonomy but reciprocity."

The separation of powers concept was never remotely intended to preclude cooperation, coordination, communication and joint efforts by the members of each branch with the members of the others. Examples of this are legion: The executive, represented by the Solicitor General, volunteers, or is invited by the Supreme Court, to file briefs advising the Supreme Court on questions of law. This happens countless times each term. Mem-

bers of the Congress—sometimes singly, sometimes a dozen or more of them together—file briefs *amicus curiae* before the Court, advising us how a matter should be decided. These briefs are always welcomed by the Court.

We all remember that President Washington formally asked the Supreme Court for advice on certain policy questions but wisely the Court decided that it would not advise him on such matters. Justices have come to realize that they should avoid advising Presidents and the Congress on substantive policy questions but on matters relating to the courts there must be joint consultation. The separation of powers does not preclude such consultation.

From the beginning of the republic, members of the Congress have appeared as advocates before the Supreme Court. Indeed, they have been some of our great advocates, from Daniel Webster, Henry Clay and John Quincy Adams, and later William Seward. Webster was a Senator when he argued the famous *Dartmouth College* case. In more recent times other Senators, including Sam Ervin and William Saxbe, have appeared.

To be sure, there is a great and necessary tradition of insulation of judges and Justices from political activities generally. But participation in legislative and executive decisions which affect the judicial system is an absolute obligation of judges, as it is of lawyers. One manifestation of the desirable aloofness of judges from controversy is found in the tradition that they do not answer criticism or respond to attacks, no matter how scurrilous or unwarranted. *But* reasons for refusing to answer attacks must not be used as reasons to abdicate responsibility when Congress is legislating on matters directly affecting the courts. Indeed, the contrary is most emphatically true.

It is entirely appropriate for judges to comment upon issues which affect the courts. The Judicial Conference of the United States and the Administrative Office of the United States courts receive requests from Congress from fifty to one hundred times each year to comment on pending bills.

Historically, the most valuable judicial improvements are made when the judiciary makes proposals and consults with Congress. Indeed, even after Congress acts, the President regularly requests the views of the Judicial Conference before he passes on legislation which relates to the federal courts. This has been going on for nearly two hundred years. It was more than forty years ago that Congress created the Judicial Conference of the United States, which as you know is made up of twenty-five judges from district courts, courts of appeals and special courts. It made the Chief Justice of the United States the chairman of that Conference. It meets approximately five or six days each year. It has committees dealing with special subjects—a committee on court administration, a committee on appellate rules, on criminal rules, on civil rules, on bankruptcy, on magistrates and similar subjects. These committees regularly confer with Congress and its staffs and the executive branch.

In creating the Judicial Conference, it was contemplated that the Conference would comment on legislation directly affecting the operation of the federal judicial system. The Conference has been doing that routinely for more than forty years. Any notion, therefore, that each of these branches should remain in solitary isolation or logic-tight compartments has no basis in reason, law, history or tradition. And, of course, we will continue to do this.

When a congressional committee asks the Judicial Conference of the United States to comment on particular bills, the Judicial Conference invari-

ably responds. Sometimes, however, the Conference decides that the legislation is purely a matter of substantive policy not relating directly to the courts, and accordingly it declines comment on that ground.

We see, therefore, that by statutes, history, and tradition—and simple common sense—the federal judiciary must work constantly with Congress and the President for improved methods of providing justice. On judicial problems, it must also advise the public, as well as the other branches, so that intelligent action can be taken. If the judges, whose lives are devoted to these problems, are not qualified to advise on such matters, one may well ask "who is." Such advice takes nothing away from the prerogatives of Congress or the executive. It simply supplies them with needed information. We cannot assume that the members and committees of Congress desire our views only when we judges agree with them.

The problems of the courts do not have high visibility. They reach the attention of other branches and the public only if they are pressed forward by someone—and often not even then. The good citizen or the busy Congressman can be excused if he is not very familiar with the need to expand United States magistrates' jurisdiction, for example, or to abolish diversity jurisdiction, the need for court administrators or the need for more judges or changes in the court structure or rules of procedure. Someone must make these problems of the courts known to the public if intelligent choices are to be made. Someone must make these problems real to the busy members of the Congress, overwhelmed as they are with a host of other more visible problems.

This is, very clearly, one of the obligations of the office I occupy. The ultimate responsibility for much judicial improvement rests with the Congress—especially if questions of rules of procedure, jurisdiction or appropriations are involved. When Congress enacts laws, the President must sign or veto them. But given all the burdens and distractions of the political process, the judiciary would fail dismally to perform its duty if it stood mute. If a Chief Justice, as spokesman for the Judicial Conference, failed to participate in the process, he would be shirking his obligations.

When we look back at some of my fourteen predecessors, it may well be that I have been too circumspect, too cautious, too restrained in pressing the needs of the courts.

Probably the most striking example of what at the time was thought by some to be a serious breach of the separation of powers was the famous letter of Chief Justice Hughes to Senator Burton Wheeler. This letter was written for public use during the heat of the "court packing" fight. Historians regard that letter as the "deathblow" to President Roosevelt's proposal to enlarge the Supreme Court. This drew Hughes into the vortex of one of the most bitter political controversies in the history of the Supreme Court. This was not an agreeable position for a Chief Justice to be in but he had a duty to provide to Congress and the people relevant facts relating to a proposal which would have distorted the structure of the judicial system as politicized by the Court.

The Chief Justice of the United States must wear two hats: As a judge he must always try to be insulated from political controversy and substantive policy issues. But he must also speak out—to the Congress, to the legal profession, and to the public—so that the courts can be made more effective in serving the people.

I assure you that I have no thought of being deterred from letting the Congress, the President, and the people of this country know what is needed in the judicial system. I will always seek cooperation with the legislative and executive branches and the legal profession to improve the quality of justice and the prompt delivery of justice at the lowest possible cost.

5 Decision Making: Process and Strategy

Publication of *The Brethren* in 1979 promised a rare glimpse into the inner sanctum of the Supreme Court. The authors claimed that for nearly two centuries the Supreme Court had made its decisions "in absolute secrecy." In fact, the deliberative process of the Court has been studied and scrutinized for years. Scholars have had access to internal memoranda, conference notes, diaries, draft opinions, and correspondence by the Justices. Members of the Court and their law clerks publish widely. Drawing on those materials, we have a fairly detailed picture of the process that Justices use to make decisions.[1]

The Supreme Court begins its term on the first Monday in October and ends in late June or early July of the following year. A term is designated by the October date (the 1988 Term began October 3, 1988). During these approximately nine months, the Court selects cases, hears oral argument, writes opinions, and announces decisions. After recessing for the summer, the Justices continue to review petitions in preparation for the new term and decide emergency petitions brought to their attention. Although decisions by the Supreme Court require a quorum of six, in certain cases individual Justices may stay the execution and enforcement of lower court orders and give aggrieved parties time to petition the full Court for review. Each Justice performs other duties when assigned to one of the judicial circuits.

On rare occasions the Court convenes in the summer in special session to deal with urgent matters. For example, the Court met on June 18, 1953, to consider Justice Douglas' stay in the execution of Ethel and Julius Rosenberg, convicted of delivering atomic bomb information to the Soviet Union. On June 19, the Court vacated the stay and the Rosenbergs were executed that day. Another special session

---

[1]Of many commendable studies, special note should be made of J. Woodford Howard, Jr., Mr. Justice Murphy 231–496 (1968); Walter F. Murphy, Elements of Judicial Strategy (1964); and Alpheus Thomas Mason, Harlan Fiske Stone: Pillar of the Law (1956). See Bob Woodward and Scott Armstrong, The Brethren: Inside the Supreme Court 1 (1979).

occurred on August 28, 1958, when the Court convened to consider a lower court order enforcing a desegregation plan for Little Rock High School. The Court unanimously upheld the lower court on September 12, three days before the school's scheduled opening.

JURISDICTION: ORIGINAL AND APPELLATE

The Constitution assigns to the Supreme Court judicial power in "all Cases, in Law and Equity, arising under this Constitution, the Laws of the United States, and Treaties made, or which shall be made under their Authority . . . " The types of cases identified in the Constitution are those affecting (1) ambassadors, other public ministers, and consuls; (2) admiralty and maritime controversies; (3) controversies in which the United States is a party; and (4) controversies between two or more states, between a state and a citizen of another state, between citizens of different states, between citizens of the same state claiming lands under grants of different states, and between a state (or its citizens) and foreign states, citizens, or subjects.

This jurisdiction is divided between original and appellate. In all cases affecting ambassadors, other public ministers, and consuls, and those in which a state shall be a party, the Supreme Court has original jurisdiction. These cases may be taken directly to the Court without action by lower courts. Only rarely does a case of original jurisdiction concern ambassadors, diplomats, and consuls. Most of the cases involve litigation between states, such as disputes over boundaries and water rights.

"Original" appears to imply exclusivity, suggesting that what is granted by the Constitution cannot be abridged or altered by Congress. Nevertheless, Congress has passed legislation that divides original jurisdiction into two categories: (1) original and exclusive jurisdiction, and (2) original but not exclusive jurisdiction. 28 U.S.C. § 1251 (1982). For the latter, lower federal courts share concurrent jurisdiction.

Congress has restricted the jurisdiction of federal courts by establishing criteria for "federal questions." Until 1980, certain federal court cases required at least $10,000 in dispute. The purpose was to reduce case congestion in federal courts. That amount was eliminated in 1980. 94 Stat. 2369. Congress wanted to resolve the anomaly faced by persons whose rights had been violated but were barred from the courts because they had not suffered a sufficient economic injury. Dollar thresholds remain for "diversity" jurisdiction (where federal courts consider cases involving state law if the parties are from different states). 31 U.S.C. § 1332 (1982).

Court jurisdiction may seem like a technical matter of interest only to specialists and practitioners of the law. But jurisdiction means political power. A question of jurisdiction provoked the first constitutional amendment adopted after the Bill of Rights. In 1793, the Court held that states could be sued in federal courts by citizens of another state. Chisholm v. Georgia, 2 Dall. (2 U.S.) 419. The public outcry was so deep and swift that the Eleventh Amendment, overriding *Chisholm*, passed both Houses of Congress in 1794 and was ratified in 1798.

Dockets

Each year the Supreme Court receives about 5,000 petitions for review. A few cases concern original jurisdiction and are placed on the Original Docket. This class is not obligatory on the Court. To fall within the category of original jurisdiction, the case must constitute a proper "controversy." Maryland v. Louisiana, 451 U.S. 725, 735–736 (1981). Original jurisdiction is used sparingly to protect the Court's increased workload with its appellate docket. The Court is especially reluctant to become a court of first instance and assume the fact-finding function of a trial court, a task for which the Court considers itself "ill-equipped." Ohio v. Wyandotte, 401 U.S. 493, 498 (1971). To assist in the handling of its original jurisdiction docket, the Court appoints special masters to study an issue and present recommendations.

Most of the petitions concern appeals. Over the past century, several major court reforms have alleviated the Supreme Court's burden of appellate cases. First, Congress created circuit courts of appeals in 1891. Next, in 1925 it limited appeals to the Supreme Court by substituting the discretionary writ of certiorari.

Cases reach the Supreme Court by one of four routes. First, some parties come to the Court as a matter of statutory right. Congress has passed a number of statutes that provide for direct appeal, preferred treatment, and expedited action. In recent years, however, Congress has begun converting some of these statutes to discretionary review. H. Rept. No. 824 (Part 1), 97th Cong., 2d Sess. 6 (1982). All members of the Court have actively sought to eliminate mandatory jurisdiction (pp. 203–204). In 1988, Congress passed legislation to substantially eliminate the Court's mandatory or obligatory jurisdiction. 102 Stat. 662 (1988).

To handle its workload, the Court often disposes of cases without written opinion. It has been estimated that the Court decided more than 80 percent of the appeals summarily in recent years without oral argument or further briefing. Stern & Gressman, Supreme Court Practice 503 (1978). There is substantial disagreement as to how lower courts should accept the precedential value of summary dismissals and affirmances. In 1975 the Court instructed lower courts that these summary decisions are on the merits and should be treated with the same substantive respect as other holdings. Hicks v. Miranda, 422 U.S. 332, 343–345. But in subsequent decisions, the Court has pointed out that summary actions do not have the same authority as decisions reached after plenary consideration. Metromedia, Inc. v. San Diego, 453 U.S. 490, 500 (1981). The issue remains a source of great confusion (pp. 204–206).

Writs of certiorari are a second route to the Supreme Court. By "granting cert" the Court calls up the records of a lower court, a decision that is wholly discretionary. Third, petitions for review are submitted by indigents, including prison inmates, sometimes in the form of handwritten notes. These requests, called *in forma pauperis* (in the manner of a pauper), numbered a few dozen in 1930 and now are in the range of two thousand a term. Fourth, an appellate court may submit a writ of certification to seek instruction on a question of law. 28 U.S.C. § 1254 (1982). This procedure is seldom used, for it forces the Court to decide questions of law without the guidance of findings and conclusions by the lower courts.

The Writ of Certiorari

The Supreme Court controls its workload largely by exercising discretionary authority over cases coming to it for review. The discretionary writ of certiorari was initiated by the Evarts Act of 1891 and the Judicial Code of 1911, but the primary source of discretion awaited the "Judges Bill" of 1925. That statute eliminated direct review by the Supreme Court of decisions in the district courts and greatly expanded the use of the writ of certiorari. 43 Stat. 936 (1925).

Most of the decisions of the Supreme Court involve "cert" denials. Under Rule 17 of the Supreme Court, a review on writ of certiorari "is not a matter of right, but of judicial discretion, and will be granted only when there are special and important reasons therefor." Among the reasons listed in Rule 17 are conflicts between federal courts of appeals, between a federal court of appeals and a state court of last resort, and over federal questions decided by different state courts of last resort. Justices look for cases that pose questions of general importance: broad issues on the administration of the law, substantive constitutional questions, the construction of important federal statutes, and serious questions of public law. In a 1949 address, Chief Justice Vinson advised lawyers who prepare petitions for certiorari to spend "a little less time discussing the merits of their cases and a little more time demonstrating why it is important that the Court should hear them. . . . If [a petition for certiorari] only succeeds in demonstrating that the decision below may be erroneous, it has not fulfilled its purpose." 69 S.Ct. vi (1949). Lawyers learn how to get the Court's attention (pp. 206–207).

Other factors explain why the Court accepts a writ of certiorari. The literature on "cue theory" points to a key ingredient: the federal government's decision to seek review. The Court relies heavily on the seasoned judgment of the Solicitor General to bring only those cases that merit appeal. When that factor combines with other elements (the presence of a civil liberty issue, conflict between circuits, a lower court decision in which judges are divided), granting a petition is even more likely.

At various times in its history the Court has accepted an issue from a lower court because it appeared that the executive and legislative branches were unwilling to act. An appellate judge said that "waiting for the legislature is not productive. The legislature doesn't legislate. Courts have had to do a good deal of stuff that would be better for the legislature to have done. But it's better for courts to do them than no one." J. Woodford Howard, Jr., Courts of Appeals in the Federal Judicial System 163 n. (1981). Presumably the same attitude prevailed on the Supreme Court, but only recently have its members publicly admitted this function. Justice Powell has said that judicial independence gives the Court "a freedom to make decisions that perhaps are necessary for our society, decisions that the legislative branch may be reluctant to make." Kenyon College Alumni Bulletin, Summer 1979, at 15. Justice Blackmun elaborated on that point in 1982. Asked whether desegregation was an example where the courts had to do more because other branches did less, he replied:

> Well, one can come up with a lot of possible examples. That is one. One man, one vote is another one. And many of the sex discrimination cases perhaps are others. If one goes back twenty-five years, certainly things are different because of judicial intervention. I can remember when I was a law clerk a case came up concerning the possibility of a federal judge intervening in the administration of a prison and it was unheard of in those days. That was a problem for the prison administrative authorities. And now, of course, in recent years—and by that I mean twenty years anyway—there have been many instances where the courts, in effect, have taken constitutional rights inside the prison doors, not all of them. "A Justice Speaks Out: A Conversation with Harry A. Blackmun," Cable News Network, Inc., conducted November 25, 1982, at 10–11.

Of the approximately 5,000 cases received each year, less than 200 are accepted for oral argument and full opinions. In evaluating the petitions, Justices dismiss many as frivolous and "dead-list" them (deny them "cert") without further deliberation. In recent years the Court has replaced the "dead list" with a "discuss list," which includes the cases deemed worthy of discussion. Examples of frivolous petitions include: "Are Negroes in fact Indians and therefore entitled to Indians' exemptions from federal income taxes?"; "Are the federal income tax laws unconstitutional insofar as they do not provide a deduction for depletion of the human body?"; and "Does a ban on drivers turning right on a red light constitute an unreasonable burden on interstate commerce?" Brennan, 40 U. Chi. L. Rev. 473, 478 (1973). When an appeal or petition for writ of certiorari is frivolous, Rule 49 of the Supreme Court authorizes the award of appropriate damages to the party sued. In a rare invocation of this rule in 1983, the Court ordered an individual to pay $500 in legal expenses incurred by University of Nebraska regents in responding to his suit. The action appeared to reflect a growing concern among members of the Court that its caseload was becoming unmanageable. Tatum v. Regents of the University of Nebraska-Lincoln, 462 U.S. 1117 (1983). See Washington Post, June 15, 1983, at A16.

Justices try to avoid cases where the legal issue is overpowered by emotional ingredients. When the Court reviewed cert petitions in 1975 to clarify the rights available to criminal defendants, it deliberately passed over the petition of someone who had been convicted of strangling, raping, and beheading a woman, followed by an attempt to skin her. Liva Baker, Miranda 105 (1983). It would have been impossible for the Court to announce legal principles in the midst of such ghastly circumstances.

In theory, Justices make a personal judgment on each of the thousands of petitions received annually. However, they depend on their law clerks to prepare memoranda that summarize the facts of a case and recommend acceptance or rejection. Some of the Justices, including Rehnquist, White, Blackmun, O'Connor, and Scalia, participate in a "cert pool" to divvy up the work. In 1982, Justice Stevens said that he found it necessary to delegate "a great deal of responsibility in the review of certiorari petitions to my law clerks." He estimated that he looked at the papers in less than 20 percent of the cases filed. Stevens, 66 Judicature 177, 179 (1982).

Justices meet at a Friday conference to discuss and vote on the petitions that survive their initial review. A single Justice may set a case for decision at conference. As a symbol of unity, Justices shake hands upon entering the conference room. These gestures preserve an atmosphere of civility in an institution compelled to deal with some of the most fractious issues in society. Maintaining a measure of collegiality among nine strong personalities is no small feat. Members of the Court work together over long periods and under intense pressures. Someone who alienates colleagues one week may need their votes to control a close question the following week.

To preserve confidentiality in the conference room, only the Justices are present. The junior Justice sits closest to the door, receiving and delivering messages that flow in and out of the room. Some political scientists reported that the rectangular table in the conference room had been chopped into three pieces by Chief Justice Burger and converted into an inverted U, supposedly to prevent the liberal Douglas from sitting opposite him in direct confrontation. Justice Powell reassured his readers in 1975 that the conference table "retains its pristine shape; there has been no hacking or sawing; the justices occupy their seats in the traditional order of seniority."[2] Visitors to the room find the table intact.

The Chief Justice begins the discussion of each case. He summarizes the facts, analyzes the law, and announces his proposed vote. He is followed by the other Justices, in order of seniority, from the senior Associate Justice down to the newest Justice. Before the Warren Court, voting was done in the opposite manner: the junior Justice voted first and the Chief Justice last. Toward the end of his service, Warren persuaded the Justices to vote in the same order as they had spoken.[3] Four votes are needed to grant certiorari. Leiman, 57 Colum. L. Rev. 975 (157). There have been cases where the Court grants cert and later, on the basis of changed circumstances, dismisses the writ of certiorari as "improvidently granted." Conway v. California Adult Authority, 396 U.S. 107 (1969).

Justices must address a wide range of complex cases at each conference. Docket sheets are provided to record each step of the process from deciding to hear a case to postconference voting. Conference notes are a summary record of the arguments of each Justice on the merits of the case. Whoever is selected to draft the opinion can review the conference notes and weave an argument that will attract the maximum number of votes. At any point, however, votes may be changed before the opinion of the Court reaches its final stage.

In denying cert, the Court seldom offers an explanation. When it does, the reason is usually brief if not cryptic. More light is shed when Justices write a dissenting opinion on cert denials. This practice, which has grown significantly in recent decades, complicates the Court's traditional position that cert denial means a refusal to take a case and nothing more. Darr v. Burford, 339 U.S. 200, 226 (1950). If dissenting Justices strongly voice their reasons and argue the merits, it may appear that the majority denying cert considered and rejected those arguments. Justices often differ on the significance to be attached to dissents on cert denials.[4] Speculation as to intent is hazardous. Even when Justices think that a lower court is wrong, they may vote to deny an application simply because they regard the federal question as insubstantial, poorly timed for review, or inappropriate because of the need for judicial restraint (pp. 207–209).

---

[2]Lewis F. Powell, Jr., "Myths and Misconceptions About the Supreme Court," 61 A.B.A.J. 1344 (1975). See Glendon Schubert, Judicial Policy Making 134 (1977) and Howard Ball, Courts and Politics 254 (1980). For a discussion of some of the practices in conference, see William H. Rehnquist, "Sunshine in the Third Branch," 16 Washburn L. J. 559 (1977).

[3]Walter F. Murphy and C. Herman Pritchett, eds., Courts, Judges, and Politics 657 (1979). This account is supported by a 1982 interview with Justice Blackmun; "A Justice Speaks Out: A Conversation with Harry A. Blackmun," Cable News Network, Inc., conducted November 25, 1982, at 21. In a 1963 article, Justice Brennan stated that voting began with the junior Justice; William J. Brennan, Jr., "Inside View of the High Court," New York Times Magazine, October 6, 1963, at 100. Justice Clark, in 1956, also said that the junior Justice voted first, 19 F.R.D. 303, 307, as did Justice Frankfurter in 1953, "Chief Justices I Have Known," 39 Va. L. Rev. 883, 903.

[4]See differing views of Justices Blackmun and Marshall in United States v. Kras, 409 U.S. 434, 443, 460–461 (1973). Justices Stevens, Brennan, and Stewart objected when the Court gave a brief reason for denying cert ("for failure to file petition within time provided"); County of Sonoma v. Isbell, 439 U.S. 996 (1978). See also Peter Linzer, "The Meaning of Certiorari Denials," 79 Colum. L. Rev. 1127 (1979).

FROM ORAL ARGUMENT TO DECISION

After a case receives four votes from Justices meeting in conference, it is transferred to the oral argument list. If Justices conclude that a question is clearly controlled by one of the Court's earlier decisions, they may summarily dispose of a lower court decision without oral argument. Of the cases the Court accepts each year, about ten are decided summarily. In 1980, for example, the Court decided a case involving press and speech restrictions on former government employees without hearing oral argument. Snepp v. United States, 444 U.S. 507. Summary disposition carries the risk of depriving the Court of crucial information. It can also suggest a "rush to judgment."

The Pentagon Papers Case of 1971 marked another occasion when the Court moved with extraordinary speed. Beginning with the *New York Times'* publication of a secret Pentagon study on the origins and conduct of the Vietnam war, only seventeen days were consumed for action by two district courts, two appellate courts, and the Supreme Court. The *New York Times'* petitions and motions were filed with the Supreme Court on June 24 at about 11 a.m. The government filed its motion later that evening. Oral argument took place on June 26. The record in the *Times* case did not arrive until seven or eight o'clock the previous evening. The briefs of the parties were received less than two hours before oral argument. Four days later the Court announced its decision, upholding the right of the press to publish material from the Pentagon study. Despite protests from several Justices, the Court moved quickly to protect the First Amendment right of the press to publish without prior restraint. New York Times v. United States, 403 U.S. 713 (1971).

The number of full opinions each year ranges between 140 and 150. In preparation for oral argument, counsel for each side submits briefs and records which are distributed to each Justice. The Court hears oral argument in public session from Monday through Thursday, listening to cases from 10 a.m. to noon and from 1 to 3 p.m. Usually one hour is set aside for each case. Although briefs are important, members of the judiciary have noted that there are some judges "who listen better than they read and who are more receptive to the spoken than the written word." Harlan, 41 Corn. L. Q. 6 (1955). The impressions they receive during oral argument often carry with them into the conference room at the end of the week. Moreover, oral argument gives an opportunity for judges to explore with counsel key issues left undeveloped in the briefs.

During oral argument, the Chief Justice sits in the center of a raised bench with the senior Associate Justice to his right and the next ranking Justice to his left. Other Justices are arrayed by seniority alternately to his right and left, leaving the most junior Justice positioned farthest to his left. Some Justices rely on a "bench memorandum" prepared by law clerks to digest the facts and arguments of both sides and provide guidance during the questioning of counsel. Judicial styles differ at oral argument. Justice Douglas asked few questions and regarded many of them from colleagues as attempts to lobby Justices for votes rather than to illuminate issues. William O. Douglas, The Court Years 181 (1981).

To divide the time between hearing cases and writing opinions, the Court alternates between several weeks of oral argument and several weeks of recess to write opinions and study appeals and cert petitions. If the Chief Justice has voted with the majority in conference, he assigns the majority opinion either to himself or to another Justice. When the Chief Justice is in the minority, the senior Justice voting with the majority assigns the case. The decision by William Rehnquist to dissent in many cases during his first year as Chief Justice allowed Justice Brennan, a liberal colleague, to control assignment. The dissenters decide who shall write the dissenting opinion. Each Justice may write a separate opinion, concurrence, or dissent.

The assignment of opinions recognizes the need to distribute workload fairly, the different speeds with which Justices complete their research and writing, and the availability of expertise within the Court. Chief Justice Vinson, a former member of the House Ways and Means Committee and Secretary of the Treasury, preferred to handle tax cases. 49 Nw. U. L. Rev. 26, 31–32 (1954).

Although Justices are appointed for life and are immune from periodic campaigning for electoral office, they know that the ability to write acceptable opinions depends on sensitivity to the public. This consideration affects the assignment of opinions. In 1944, Chief Justice Stone initially assigned the Texas "white primary" case to Justice Frankfurter. Justice Jackson shared his misgivings to both Frankfurter and Stone, suggesting that because of "Southern sensibilities" it was unwise to have a Vienna-born Jew, raised in New England (the seat of the abolition movement), write the majority opinion striking down the Texas statute. With Frankfurter's knowledge and consent, Stone transferred the assignment to Stanley Reed, a native-born, Protestant, and old-line Kentuckian. Reed was also a Democrat of long standing, whereas Frankfurter's past ties to the Democratic party were suspect. Alpheus T. Mason, Harlan Fiske Stone: Pillar of the Law 614-615 (1968).

Recusal

Under English common law, judges could be disqualified for direct interest in a case but never for bias. Such an admission would have conceded the capacity for partiality or favoritism in a judge. Frank, 56 Yale L. J. 605, 609–610 (1947); Forer, 73 Harv. L. Rev. 1325, 1327 (1960). Many of the early Justices on the Supreme Court failed to recuse (remove) themselves from cases that, under today's standards, would call for disqualification. Justice Story decided cases involving the United States Bank while serving as president of a Massachusetts branch of the National Bank. Chief Justice Marshall wrote *Marbury* v. *Madison* after serving as the Secretary of State who had neglected to deliver the commission of office. However, Marshall withdrew from *Stuart* v. *Laird* (1803) because he had tried the case earlier in the circuit court.

Based on statutory guidelines, court decisions, judicial codes, and personal standards, judges withdraw from certain cases. 28 U.S.C. §§ 144, 455 (1982). Judges disqualify themselves to maintain the appearance of impartiality and due process. Chief Justice Stone and Justice Jackson did not take part in a 1942 decision because as former Attorneys General they had helped prosecute the case. United States v. Bethlehem Steel Corp., 315 U.S. 289, 309 (1942). Judge Haynsworth's failure to recuse himself in several cases in the Fourth Circuit became a key reason for the Senate's rejecting him to the Supreme Court in 1969.

Justice Jackson shocked the country in June 1946 by issuing a blistering attack on Justice Black. This extraordinary public revelation of a bitter feud between two members of the Supreme Court had its origins in a 1945 decision in which Black was part of a 5–4 majority upholding the right of coal miners. Jewell Ridge Corp. v. Local No. 6167, 325 U.S. 161 (1945). Jackson's dissent in that case quoted from a Senate debate in 1937 to show that Black, as a Senator, provided legislative history contrary to the majority's decision. It was also known that the chief counsel for the miners in the 1945 case was Black's former law partner.

The coal company petitioned for a rehearing, asking whether Black could render impartial justice given his connection with the legislation and the chief counsel. All members of the Court agreed that the motion for a rehearing should be denied, because the decision to disqualify oneself is purely a personal judgment to be made by each Justice. However, Jackson did not want to imply, by silence, that everyone on the Court supported Black's decision. When the Court denied the motion, Jackson wrote a concurring opinion, explaining that disqualification was not a decision for the full Court. Each Justice had to make that determination for himself. Frankfurter joined Jackson's concurrence. Jewell Ridge Coal Corp. v. Local No. 6167, 325 U.S. 897 (1945). Black's supporters were outraged by the concurrence because it drew attention to the issue of disqualification.

A newspaper article in May 1946 reported that Black regarded Jackson's concurrence as a gratuitous insult and a slur on Black's honor. The dispute was exacerbated by the pending selection of a Chief Justice by President Truman. Jackson hoped to be named; Black was dead-set against it. According to the newspaper story, Black threatened to resign if Truman selected Jackson as Chief Justice. Fleeson, "Supreme Court Feud," [Washington] Evening Star, May 16, 1946, at A-15. Black refused to comment on these newspaper stories.

While Jackson was in Nuremberg serving as Special Prosecutor for the Nazi trials, Truman nominated Fred Vinson to be Chief Justice. Jackson concluded that Black played a hand in denying him the promotion. From Nuremberg, Jackson cabled the Judiciary Committees to elaborate on the 1945 dispute. He said that after he announced his decision to write a concurrence on the petition for a rehearing, Black became "very angry" and said that any opinion that discussed the subject at all would mean "a declaration of war." Jackson told Black that he would "not stand for any more of his bullying and that, whatever I would otherwise do, I would now have to write my opinion to keep self-respect in the face of threats." Alluding to rumors that had been published critical of his role, Jackson remarked: "If war is declared on me I propose to wage it with the weapons of the open warrior, not those of the stealthy assassin." Jackson warned that if Black failed to disqualify himself in comparable situations in the future, "I will make my Jewell Ridge opinion look like a letter of recommendation by comparison." New York Times, June 11, 1946, at 2:6.

Justice Rehnquist was asked to recuse himself from Laird v. Tatum because he had earlier testified on the subject while serving as an official in the Justice Department. In a highly unusual memorandum, Rehnquist agreed that disqualification would have been required had he signed a pleading or brief in the case or actively participated in it. In two earlier cases he withdrew for those reasons. 409 U.S. 824, 828–829 (1972). But he disagreed that testimony or the expression of one's views were adequate grounds for recusal. He also pointed out that disqualification of a Supreme Court Justice presents problems that do not exist in a lower court where one judge may substitute for another. Id. at 837–838. This issue resurfaced in 1986 during Rehnquist's nomination hearings to be Chief Justice.

Drafting Opinions

The process of writing opinions begins with the briefs prepared by opposing counsel, research by law clerks and library staff, and the knowledge that Justices acquire from decades of experience in public and private life. These drafts are printed within the Court building and circulated among the Justices. Comments are written on the drafts; memoranda are exchanged. Often, a forceful dissent may persuade members of the majority to change their position, creating a new majority from the old dissenting position. Chief Justice Vinson once remarked that an opinion circulated as a dissent "sometimes has so much in logic, reason, and authority to support it that it becomes the opinion of the Court." 69 S.Ct. x (1949). Draft opinions may be so influential in modifying the Court's final decision that they are never published. Alexander M. Bickel, The Unpublished Opinions of Mr. Justice Brandeis (1967). The threat of a dissent can force changes in the majority opinion.

The role of law clerks is sometimes described in sensational terms, as though they displace the functions of judges. Because of the growing importance of law clerks, Senator John Stennis suggested in 1958 that it might be appropriate to subject them to confirmation by the Senate. 104 Cong. Rec. 8107–8108 (1958). Publication of *The Brethren* in 1979 catapulted clerks to a seemingly pivotal role in making judicial policy. But this study depended heavily on interviews with clerks who no doubt found it tempting to embroider a bit on their contributions to public law.

Judges in the prime of life are unlikely to defer to the opinions of clerks fresh out of law school, however much the clerks may stimulate new ideas and approaches. Clerks come and go, but the persistence in decisions of a unique writing style is compelling evidence that judges do their own work. Yet clerks do more than check footnotes, review cert petitions, and perform minor editing tasks. Depending on the judge they work for, they might be asked to prepare a "prototype or aspirant opinion" to guide the thinking of the court. Frank M. Coffin, The Ways of a Judge 69 (1980). Because of heavy court workload, judges are often inclined to let clerks do the preliminary draft of an opinion (pp. 209–211).

The legal profession no longer suggests that the sole duty of a judge is to place a constitutional provision beside a challenged statute to see if the latter squares with the former. United States v. Butler, 297 U.S. 1, 62 (1936). Still, the belief that judges, in the act of deciding, are able to put aside their personal value systems retains a following. Justice Frankfurter made an eloquent plea for this concept of judicial deliberation:

> It is asked with sophomoric brightness, does a man cease to be himself when he becomes a Justice? Does he change his character by putting on a gown? No, he does not change his character. He brings his whole experience, his training, his outlook, his social, intellectual and moral environment with him when he takes a seat on the Supreme Bench. But a judge worth his salt is in the grip of his function. The intellectual habits of self-discipline which govern his mind are as much a part of him as the influence of the interest he may have represented at the bar, often much more so. 98 Proceedings Am. Phil. Soc. 233, 238 (1954).

It would be superficial to suggest that judges use their office simply to disseminate personal views, but decisions of individual judges flow at least in part from their own values and attitudes. Justice Miller, who served on the Supreme Court from 1862 to 1890, despaired of the fixed views and predispositions of those on the bench: "It is vain to contend with judges who have been at the bar the advocates for forty years of rail road companies, and all the forms of associated capital, when they are called upon to decide cases where such interests are in contest. All their training, all their feelings are from the start in favor of those who need no such influence." Charles Fairman, Mr. Justice Miller and the Supreme Court 374 (1939).

Although the votes of judges cannot be predicted with mathematical accuracy, attorneys are sophisticated enough to engage in "forum shopping" to find the court that augurs best for their client. Judicial independence and objectivity remain important values in the administration of justice, but by now it is routine to recognize definite alignments and alliances among judges. Even members of the judiciary acknowledge the existence of blocs. When Justice Blackmun joined the Supreme Court he calculated that there were two Justices on the right, two on the left, and "five of us in the center." "A Justice Speaks Out: A Conversation with Harry A. Blackmun," Cable News Network, Inc., conducted November 25, 1982, at 22. Justice O'Connor's appearance in 1981 added another conservative voice to that of Chief Justice Burger and Justice Rehnquist. Blackmun, meanwhile, now found himself voting more frequently with the liberal bloc of Justices Brennan and Marshall. Blocs are not necessarily stable. They change over time and vary with the issue. A well-known shift occurred in 1937 when Hughes and Roberts altered their interpretation of the commerce power of Congress. During the Burger Court, Justices Blackmun, Powell, Stevens, and White formed part of a "floating center," casting the votes necessary to build a majority by joining either with the liberal votes of Brennan and Marshall or the conservative wing of Burger, O'Connor, and Rehnquist.

Members of the judiciary sometimes complain that their decisions are distorted by the press. Mistakes and misconceptions by reporters are likely, given the time pressures between the announcement of a decision and the deadlines imposed by newspapers, magazines, and broadcast services. These pressures have been partly relieved by several changes over the past few decades. In 1965, the Supreme Court, instead of handing down all opinions on "Decision Monday," began delivering some of its decisions on other days of the week. The Court also started meeting at 10 a.m. rather than noon; these extra hours eased deadlines for reporters. To assure more accurate and sophisticated coverage, major newspapers and wire services began selecting reporters with law degrees or special training in the law.

Some of the "distortions" in the press come from Justices who use careless language in concurring and dissenting opinions, or from those who fail, in the statement for the Court, to correct misconceptions that appear in separate opinions. When the Supreme Court announced the School Prayer Decision in 1962, Justice Douglas' concurrence suggested that the decision would cover ceremonial observances of a religious nature, such as the Court's traditional invocation when it convenes and the offering of a daily prayer by a chaplain in Congress. Engel v. Vitale, 370 U.S. 421, 439–442 (1962). Such speculations, well beyond the issue before the Court, helped fuel public confusion and outrage. When opinions contain sharp crossfire between Justices, "news reporters and the public at large are likely to lose sight of the law in what appears (to the uninitiated at least) to be a battle of men and not of law." Newland, 17 West. Pol. Q. 15, 24–25 (1964). The Prayer Case was also grossly misrepresented by the president of the American Bar Association, who weighed in with the warning that the decision would require elimination of the motto "In God We Trust" from all coins. Id. at 28. The public impression never recovered from these irresponsible readings.

The judiciary's ability to communicate accurately to the public requires a writing style that is precise and economical. Judges advise opinion writers to use familiar words and short sentences. They prefer simplicity, clarity, brevity, and a direct and vigorous style. Justice Jackson gloried in the "short Saxon word that pierces the mind like a spear and the simple figure that lights the understanding." 37 A.B.A.J. 801, 863–864 (1951). Nevertheless, judges have personal idiosyncrasies that produce affectation, ornate prose, and verbosity. Ambiguity is also likely when several strong-minded individuals must agree on a single statement.

In deciding a particular case, judges often stray from the central issue and add extraneous matter in the form of *obiter dicta*. Because these remarks are not necessary to the basic decision, they are not binding as legal precedent. But they can serve as the functional equivalent of an advisory opinion, supplying guidance to the future direction of legal thinking. In striking down a statute, a court might suggest to legislators how the law could be rewritten. Albertsworth, 23 Geo. L. J. 643, 650–663 (1935). As Griffin Bell noted during his service as a federal appellate judge, "the role of courts under our system of separation of powers and federalism may call such a practice into play in some situations." 15 J. Pub. L. 214, 217 (1966).

Coherence and "principled decision making" are difficult virtues to achieve for a multimembered Court that operates necessarily as a committee, attempting to stitch together a decision that can attract a majority. Compromises are needed. The difficulty is compounded by the practice of moving a step at a time, responding to the concrete case at hand. As noted by one scholar, the Court "is in the unenviable posture of a committee attempting to draft a horse by placing very short lines on a very large drawing-board at irregular intervals during which the membership of the committee constantly changes." Amsterdam, 58 Minn. L. Rev. 349, 350 (1974).

UNANIMITY AND DISSENT

The Supreme Court initially followed the British practice of allowing each Justice to write opinions seriatim (in a series). Rather than announce a single opinion representing the collective position of the majority, the Justices delivered separate statements. Before John Marshall's appointment as Chief Justice, the Court had begun to deliver an opinion for the entire Court rather than a string of seriatim opinions. Marshall reinforced that direction, believing that a single decision strengthened the Court's power and dignity. He selected one Justice (usually himself) to write the majority opinion. Dissents were rare. Jefferson delivered a stinging rebuke to the Chief Justice for departing from seriatim decisions: "An opinion is huddled up in conclave, perhaps by a majority of one, delivered as if unanimous, and with the silent acquiescence of lazy or timid associates, by a crafty chief judge, who sophisticates the law to his own mind, by the turn of his own reasoning." 15 Writings of Thomas Jefferson 298 (Memorial ed. 1904).

Jefferson's critique was written in 1820, about two decades after Marshall had joined the Court, and appeared to be triggered by Marshall's broad nationalist ruling in *McCulloch* v. *Maryland* (1819). Seriatim opinions had offered a definite benefit: each Justice was accountable for articulating the rationale behind a decision. But

Marshall wanted the Court to develop an institutional view, moving away from personal positions to a more generalized principle for the majority.

The harmony within the early Marshall Court depended partly on residential arrangements. The Justices lived together in the same boarding house on Capitol Hill, taking their meals at a common table. Justice Story described the members of the Marshall Court as "united as one. . . . We moot every question as we proceed, and . . . conferences at our lodgings often come to a very quick, and, I trust, a very accurate opinion, in a few hours." James Sterling Young, The Washington Community 77 (1966).

This cohesiveness did not survive. Dissents became more frequent in later years of the Marshall Court and under future Chief Justices. At various times throughout history, however, members of the Court have placed a premium on unanimity. In 1922, Justice McReynolds wrote a majority opinion that provoked dissents from Brandeis, Clarke, and Pitney. Chief Justice Taft scheduled a reargument and by the time he wrote the new majority opinion, Clarke and Pitney had retired. Taft sought Brandeis' views and eventually produced a unanimous opinion, with which McReynolds concurred.[5]

At the urging of colleagues who fear that dissents will damage the corporate reputation of the Supreme Court, Justices have been willing to convert a dissent into a concurring opinion. Labeling it a concurrence, however, is often an inadequate mask to cover the dissenting view.[6] It is not unusual for Justices to concur in the judgment or result while shredding the logic, reasoning, and precedents contained in the opinion of the Court.[7] Justices also withhold dissents when the case is less significant to them. Such accommodations create a reservoir of good will, promote institutional harmony, and allow the acquiescent Justice to call upon a colleague at some future time for reciprocal favors—perhaps a fourth vote to grant certiorari. Walter F. Murphy, Elements of Judicial Strategy 52–53 (1964).

During preparation for *Brown* v. *Board of Education*, members of the Court felt strongly that unanimity was crucial in building public acceptance for desegregation. Discreet pressure was applied to Justices to ward off concurring and dissenting opinions. Chief Justice Warren realized that once a Justice had announced his position, it would be more difficult for him to change his thinking, "so we decided that we could dispense with our usual custom of formally expressing our individual views at the first conference and would confine ourselves for a time to informal discussion of the briefs, the arguments made at the hearing, and our own independent research for each conference day, reserving our final opinions until the discussions were concluded." By following this process, the Court agreed unanimously that the "separate but equal" doctrine had no place in public education. Warren, 239 Atlantic Monthly 35–36 (April 1977).

[5]Alpheus Thomas Mason, "William Howard Taft," in Leon Friedman and Fred L. Israel, eds., The Justices of the United States Supreme Court (New York: Chelsea House, 1969), III, 2114, and Alexander M. Bickel, The Unpublished Opinions of Mr. Justice Brandeis, at 111–113. The case was Sonneborn Bros. v. Cureton, 262 U.S. 506 (1923).

[6]Justice Murphy, under the urgings of colleagues, changed his dissent in *Hirabayashi* v. *United States* to a concurrence. See Murphy, supra note 1, at 46–47, and Howard, supra note 1, at 302–309.

[7]Murphy v. Waterfront Comm'n, 378 U.S. 52, 80–92 (Harlan, J., concurring) (1964); Warden v. Hayden, 387 U.S. 294, 310–312 (Fortas, J., and Warren, C.J., concurring) (1967); Argersinger v. Hamlin, 407 U.S. 25, 41–44 (Burger, C.J., concurring) and 44–46 (Powell, J., concurring, joined by Rehnquist, J.) (1972).

In earlier rulings, the Court relied on per curiam opinions (unsigned opinions "for the court") to reduce friction. This technique permitted the Justices to present a united front and avoid details or legal interpretations that might have fractured the Court and communicated more information to the public than the Court thought prudent. In one of the early racial discrimination cases before *Brown*, Justice Frankfurter explained in a letter to Chief Justice Vinson that the per curiam "should set forth as briefly and as unargumentatively as possible" the Court's position. "In short," Frankfurter wrote, "our *per cur.* should avoid every possibility of serving as a target for contention . . ." Hutchinson, 68 Geo. L. J. 1, 9 (1979).

When Governor Orval Faubus and the Arkansas legislature fought to retain the state's system of segregated schools, the Supreme Court reaffirmed the principle it had enunciated in 1954. To underscore its unanimity, the names of all nine Justices were listed, including the three who had joined the Court since 1954. Frankfurter frustrated this strategy by insisting on a separate concurrence, agreeing to file it a week after the Court released its opinion (pp. 211–213). Warren, Black, and Brennan were furious. Frankfurter's only justification for the extra statement was that he had a special responsibility to lecture Southern lawyers and law professors who had been his students at Harvard Law School. Bernard Schwartz, Super Chief 302–303 (1983).

In 1974, with President Nixon threatening to defy any judicial effort to make him surrender the Watergate tapes, the Supreme Court once again produced a unanimous ruling. United States v. Nixon, 418 U.S. 683 (1974). By forging a united front and rejecting Nixon's broad claim of executive privilege, the Court played a crucial role in bringing about his resignation. But the very process of generating a unanimous opinion invited generalization at so high a plane that the result obfuscated the law of executive privilege.[8] This is an everpresent risk. Attracting a few additional votes may dilute legal principles to such an extent that some Justices in the original majority may decide to write concurring or even dissenting opinions.

Unanimity in these cases helped prepare the public for important rulings. In other situations, however, a multiplicity of opinions may be enlightening. In *Youngstown Co.* v. *Sawyer* (1952), every member of the six-man majority wrote a separate opinion discussing the limits of presidential power, which in this case concerned the seizure of steel mills. The country was therefore privy to nuances and complexities that would have been obscured by a broad ruling satisfactory to the majority. Multiplicity gave room for sophisticated explorations of the source and scope of executive powers. Concurring opinions may anticipate future developments in the direction of law.

With the growth in the number of cases that determine constitutional issues, separate concurring and dissenting opinions have increased dramatically. Justice Rehnquist suggested that it "may well be that the nature of constitutional adjudication invites, at least, if it does not require, more separate opinions than does adjudication of issues of law in other areas." Rehnquist, 59 A.B.A.J. 361, 363 (1973). Of special concern is the Court's inability to prepare a decision that attracts a majority of the Justices. Instead, the Court delivers a plurality opinion that creates

---

[8]Louis Henkin, "Executive Privilege: Mr. Nixon Loses but the Presidency Largely Prevails," 22 UCLA L. Rev. 40 (1974); William Van Alstyne, "A Political and Constitutional Review of *United States* v. *Nixon*," 22 UCLA 116 (1974).

confusion in the lower courts and other branches of government. The number of plurality opinions by the Burger Court exceeded the number of all previous Courts. Note, 94 Harv. L. Rev. 1127 (1981); Davis & Reynolds, 1974 Duke L. J. 59.

Dissents

Shortly before returning to the Supreme Court, this time as Chief Justice, Charles Evans Hughes wrote eloquently on the deliberative process of the judiciary. He recognized that a dissenting opinion can damage the appearance of justice that the public needs in a court of last resort. However, he felt it far more injurious to obtain unanimity by concealing genuine differences, for "what must ultimately sustain the court in public confidence is the character and independence of the judges." While not encouraging dissents born of a captious spirit or an inability to cooperate with others, he believed that a dissenting opinion based on deep thought and feeling could be "an appeal to the brooding spirit of the law, to the intelligence of a future day, when a later decision may possibly correct the error into which the dissenting judge believes the court to have been betrayed." Charles Evans Hughes, The Supreme Court of the United States 68 (1928). Following this tradition, Justice Douglas said that "Certainty and unanimity in the law are possible both under the fascist and communist systems. They are not only possible; they are indispensable . . ." (pp. 213–215).

Dissents may force the majority to clarify and tighten its opinion. They can also serve as a precursor for a future majority holding. Justice Harlan's dissents in the *Civil Rights Cases* (1883), in *Plessy v. Ferguson* (1895), and in other race cases offered a broad interpretation of the Fourteenth Amendment in protecting the rights of blacks. This doctrine gained strength in some of the lower courts more than a half century later and foreshadowed the eventual overruling of *Plessy*. The dissents of Justice Holmes, especially in economic regulation cases, later carried the day for the Court. Justice Stone was a lone dissenter in the first flag-salute case in 1940, involving the religious freedoms of Jehovah's Witnesses. Two years later, three Justices from the majority (Black, Douglas, and Murphy) publicly announced that the decision "was wrongly decided." The following year, the Court reversed its 1940 ruling, vindicating Stone's position.[9] In 1942, the Court split 6–3, deciding that indigent defendants did not have a right to counsel in state court for all felonies. By 1963, the position of the three dissenters had been elevated to the majority viewpoint. Betts v. Brady, 316 U.S. 455, 474 (1942); Gideon v. Wainwright, 372 U.S. 335 (1963).

For a judicial body, dissent carries substantial costs. Justice Edward D. White, himself dissenting in an 1895 opinion, said that the "only purpose which an elaborate dissent can accomplish, if any, is to weaken the effect of the opinion of the majority, and thus engender want of confidence in the conclusions of courts of last resort." Pollock v. Farmers' Loan & Trust Co., 157 U.S. 429, 608 (1895). Dissents detract from institutional unity and may exacerbate tensions within a court, which is by nature a collegial body. Those tensions are heightened by sarcastic dissents that question the integrity or intellectual ability of a fellow judge. Dissents can be

---

[9]Minersville School District v. Gobitis, 310 U.S. 586 (1940); Jones v. Opelika, 316 U.S. 584, 624 (1942); West Virginia Board of Education v. Barnette, 319 U.S. 624 (1943).

especially irresponsible when they confuse or dissort the holding of the Court (pp. 215–216).

Some members of the judiciary feel a special obligation to express their dissent when constitutional questions are at stake. Said Justice Moody in a 1908 dissent:

> Under ordinary circumstances, where the judgment rests exclusively, as it does here, upon a mere interpretation of the words of a law, which may be readily changed by the lawmaking branches of the Government, if they be so minded, a difference of opinion may well be left without expression. But where the judgment is a judicial condemnation of an act of a coordinate branch of our Government it is so grave a step that no member of the court can escape his own responsibility, or be justified in suppressing his own views, if unhappily they have not found expression in those of his associates. The Employers' Liability Cases, 207 U.S. 463, 504–505 (1908).

The choice between writing a dissent and joining the majority remains an individual matter. Although Justice Harlan dissented in *Miranda* v. *Arizona* (1966), the principle of stare decisis and the goal of institutional continuity and cohesiveness prompted him to acquiesce in future applications of *Miranda*. Orozco v. Texas, 394 U.S. 324, 328 (1969). Other Justices will persist with their dissents.

CASELOAD BURDENS

The number of cases before the Supreme Court has increased dramatically over the years, especially in recent decades. In this era of "rights consciousness," a larger number of individuals and organizations go to court either to secure rights or to enforce rights already established by statute. The creation of additional district and appellate judgeships allows more plaintiffs and attorneys to enter the courts. Further aggravating the workload are dozens of statutes passed by Congress creating new causes of action, providing expedited methods of appeal, imposing duties on the judiciary, and awarding fees for attorneys.

In 1971, Chief Justice Burger appointed a group to study the growing caseload of the Supreme Court. Called the Freund Committee, the group recommended that Congress establish a seven-member National Court of Appeals to screen petitions filed with the Supreme Court and to certify 400 or so cases considered the most worthy. The Supreme Court would select from that list, but no appeal would lie from the cases rejected by the National Court of Appeals. The Committee's recommendation paralleled those announced earlier by Burger. U.S. News & World Report, December 14, 1970, at 43. The previous Chief Justice, Earl Warren, criticized the Committee's screening idea as a naive proposal from people who were unfamiliar with the Court's decisional process. He also objected to giving the National Court limited power to resolve conflicting decisions among the circuits. Warren, 28 Record Ass'n Bar of the City of N.Y. 627, 637, 642 (1973).

A second study, prepared by the Hruska Commission, was released in 1975. It, too, proposed a National Court of Appeals, but not to screen cases for the Supreme Court. A new court would be established to handle cases referred to it by the Supreme Court or appellate courts. In 1983, Chief Justice Burger offered his own version of a National Court of Appeals. He suggested a temporary court, drawn from appellate judges in each circuit, to resolve conflicts between appellate courts. A major restructuring of the judicial system, he warned, was necessary to "avoid a breakdown of the system—or of some of the justices." Washington Post, February 7, 1983, at A-l.

Although a majority of the Justices of the present Court share a common concern about heavy caseloads, specific solutions are not so obvious. The Court's docket is largely discretionary in character, so to that extent its workload is self-imposed and self-inflicted. Moreover, the workload increases when the Court reaches out to decide matters that might have been left to state courts or to the process of slow percolation in the federal courts. In 1985, Justice Stevens (joined by Justices Brennan and Marshall) noted in dissent:

> Much of the Court's "burdensome" workload is a product of its own aggressiveness in this area [of Fourth Amendment cases]. By promoting the Supreme Court of the United States as the High Magistrate for every warrantless search and seizure, this practice has burdened the argument docket with cases presenting fact bound errors of minimal significance. It has also encouraged state legal officers to file petitions for certiorari in even the most frivolous search and seizure cases. California v. Carney, 471 U.S. 386, 396 (1985).

Justice Brennan has been a persistent critic of proposals to allow a special court to screen cases for the Supreme Court. He called the screening function "second to none in importance." Brennan, 40 U. Chi. L. Rev. 473, 477 (1973). From his perspective, the dissenting opinions in denying cert represent an important foundation for the development of legal doctrine and the formation of future majority positions. He would not delegate to a separate court the responsibility for screening cases, a process he calls "inherently subjective" in nature and one that helps educate Justices on contemporary issues. Id. at 480–481.

The workload problem could be relieved partly by withdrawing some nonjudicial duties from the Court. At present, the Chief Justice is a member of the Board of Regents of the Smithsonian Institution. He is also a trustee of the National Gallery of Art and of the Joseph H. Hirshhorn Museum and Sculpture Garden. He is responsible for appointing someone from the judicial branch to the National Historical Publications and Records Commission. Carrying out these extraneous duties seems to belie the claim that the Court is pressed to the limit with its caseload.

Selected Readings

BARTH, ALAN. *Prophets with Honor: Great Dissents and Great Dissenters in the Supreme Court.* New York: Knopf, 1974.

CANNON, MARK W., AND DAVID M. O'BRIEN, eds. *Views from the Bench: The Judiciary and Constitutional Politics.* Chatham, N.J.: Chatham House Publishers, 1985.

CASPER, GERHARD, AND RICHARD A. POSNER. *The Workload of the Supreme Court.* Chicago: American Bar Foundation, 1976.

FRANK, JOHN P. *Marble Palace: The Supreme Court in American Life.* New York: Knopf, 1958.

HART, HENRY M., JR. "Foreword: The Time Chart of the Justices." 73 *Harvard Law Review* 84 (1959).

HELLMAN, ARTHUR D. "Caseload, Conflicts, and Decisional Capacity: Does the Supreme Court Need Help?" 67 *Judicature* 29 (1983).

HOWARD, J. WOODFORD, JR. *Mr. Justice Murphy.* Princeton, N.J.: Princeton University Press, 1968.

MASON, ALPHEUS THOMAS. *Harlan Fiske Stone: Pillar of the Law.* New York: Viking, 1956.

MILLER, ARTHUR SELWYN, AND D. S. SASTRI. "Secrecy and the Supreme Court—On the Need for Piercing the Red Velour Curtain." 22 *Buffalo Law Review* 799 (1973). See also accompanying comments by Eugene Gressman, Joel B. Grossman, J. Woodford Howard, Jr., Walter Probert, Glendon Schubert, and Roland Young.

MURPHY, WALTER F. *Elements of Judicial Strategy.* Chicago: University of Chicago Press, 1964.

NEWLAND, CHESTER A. "Personal Assistants to Supreme Court Justices: The Law Clerks." 40 *Oregon Law Review* 299 (1961).

O'BRIEN, DAVID M. *Storm Center: The Supreme Court in American Politics.* New York: Norton, 1986.

PELTASON, JACK W. *Federal Courts in the Political Process.* New York: Random House, 1955.

PROVINE, DORIS MARIE. *Case Selection in the United States Supreme Court.* Chicago: University of Chicago Press, 1980.

RICHARDSON, RICHARD J., AND KENNETH N. VINES. *The Politics of Federal Courts: Lower Courts in the United States.* Boston: Little, Brown, 1970.

ROHDE, DAVID W., AND HAROLD J. SPAETH. *Supreme Court Decision Making.* San Francisco: W. H. Freeman, 1976.

SPAETH, HAROLD J. *Supreme Court Policy Making.* San Francisco: W. H. Freeman, 1979.

STERN, ROBERT L., AND EUGENE GRESSMAN. *Supreme Court Practice,* 5th ed. Washington, D.C.: The Bureau of National Affairs, 1978.

ULMER, S. SIDNEY. "Bricolage and Assorted Thoughts on Working in the Papers of the Supreme Court Justices." 35 *Journal of Politics* 286 (1973).

WESTIN, ALAN F., ed. *The Supreme Court: Views from Inside.* New York: Norton, 1961.

——. *An Autobiography of the Supreme Court.* New York: Macmillan, 1963.

WILKINSON, J. HARVIE, III. *Serving Justice: A Supreme Court Clerk's View.* New York: Charterhouse, 1974.

WOODWARD, BOB, AND SCOTT ARMSTRONG. *The Brethren: Inside the Supreme Court* New York: Simon and Schuster, 1979.

Eliminating Mandatory Jurisdiction

SUPREME COURT OF THE UNITED STATES, *Washington, D.C., June 17, 1982.*

Re H.R. 2406.

DEAR CONGRESSMAN KASTENMEIER: In response to your invitation, we write to express our complete support for the proposals contained in H.R. 2406 substantially to eliminate the Supreme Court's mandatory jurisdiction. A letter to this effect was signed by all the members of the Court on June 22, 1978. Your invitation enables us again to renew our request for elimination of the Court's mandatory jurisdiction.

We endorse H.R. 2406 without reservation and urge the Congress its prompt enactment. Our reasons are similar to those presented to the Senate on June 20, 1978 by Solicitor General Wade McCree, Assistant Attorney General Daniel J. Meador, Professor Eugene Gressman and others. We also agree with the Freund Committee's recommendation urging the elimination of the Supreme Court's mandatory jurisdiction; that report was presented to your subcommittee in the summer of 1977 during the hearings held on the State of the Judiciary. At those hearings Professor

Leo Levin and former Solicitor General Robert Bork also testified in favor of the elimination of the Court's mandatory jurisdiction.

The present mandatory jurisdiction provisions permit litigants to require cases to be decided by the Supreme Court of the United States without regard to the importance of the issue presented or their impact on the general public. Unfortunately, there is no correlation between the difficulty of the legal issues presented in a case and the importance of the issue to the general public. For this reason, the Court must often call for full briefing and oral argument in difficult issues which are of little significance. At present, the Court must devote a great deal of its limited time and resources on cases which do *not,* in Chief Justice Taft's words, "involve principles, the application of which are of wide public importance or governmental interest, and which should be authoritatively declared by the final court."

This is acutely important as we close a Term with the highest number of filings in history. The more time the Court must devote to cases of this type the less time it has to spend on the more important cases facing the nation. Because the volume of complex and difficult cases continues to grow, it is even more important that the Court not be burdened by having to deal with cases that are of significance only to the individual litigants but of no "wide public importance."

Attached in the appendix is a table showing the recent growth of filings at the Supreme Court. Also attached are statistical tables covering the October 1976 and 1980 Terms. These tables reveal that during the 1980 Term, thirty-six percent of the cases decided by the Court were cases arising out of mandatory jurisdiction. The percentage of mandatory jurisdiction cases has decreased since 1976, chiefly because of the action taken by Congress to confine the jurisdiction of three-judge federal district courts. Further decline in the percentage of mandatory jurisdiction cases is not expected however, since the curtailment of three-judge court cases has by now been reflected in the Court's caseload. The remaining burdens posed by the mandatory jurisdiction provisions still on the books are nevertheless substantial and continue to cause the Court to expend its limited resources on cases that are better left to other courts.

It is impossible for the Court to give plenary consideration to all the mandatory appeals it receives; to have done so, for example, during the 1980 Term would have required at least 9 additional weeks of oral argument of a seventy-five percent increase in the argument calendar. To handle the volume of appeals presently being received, the Court must dispose of many cases summarily, often without written opinion. Unfortunately, these summary decisions are decisions on the merits which are binding on state courts and other federal courts. See *Mandel* v. *Bradley*,

432 U.S. 172 (1977); *Hicks* v. *Miranda*, 422 U.S. 332 (1975). Because they are summary in nature these dispositions often also provide uncertain guidelines for the courts that are bound to follow them and, not surprisingly, such decisions sometimes create more confusion than they seek to resolve. The only solution to the problem, and one that is consistent with the intent of the Judiciary Act of 1925 to give the Supreme Court discretion to select those cases it deems most important, is to eliminate or curtail the Court's mandatory jurisdiction.

Because the Court has to devote a great deal of time to deciding mandatory jurisdiction cases, it is imperative that mandatory jurisdiction of the Court be substantially eliminated. For these reasons we endorse H.R. 2406 and urge its immediate adoption.

Cordially and respectfully,

WARREN E. BURGER
WILLIAM J. BRENNAN
BYRON R. WHITE
HARRY A. BLACKMUN
WILLIAM H. REHNQUIST
THURGOOD MARSHALL
LEWIS F. POWELL
JOHN P. STEVENS
SANDRA D. O'CONNOR

Supreme Court Filings

	Cases
October term 1981	[1]4,400
October term 1980	4,174
October term 1979	3,985

[1]Estimated as of June 15, 1982 the actual figure was 4,209, which is 5 percent higher than last Term at the same time.

Summary Dispositions of Appeals

Lower courts have been uncertain as to what weight to give Supreme Court summary dismissals or affirmances of appeals. Some regarded them as binding on the merits; others gave them little precedential value. In 1976, dissenting in *Colorado Springs Amusements, Ltd.* v. *Rizzo*, 428 U.S. 913, Justice Brennan reviewed the extent of the confusion. Footnotes omitted.

MR. JUSTICE BRENNAN, dissenting.

We depreciate the precedential weight of summary dispositions in our decisional process, expressly holding in *Edelman* v. *Jordan*, 415 U.S. 651, 671 (1974), that such dispositions "are not of the same precedential value as would be an opinion of this Court treating the question on the merits." I would not require district courts, courts of appeals, and state courts to ascribe any greater precedential weight to summary dispositions than this Court does. Accordingly, I did not join the holding in *Hicks* v. *Miranda*, 422 U.S. 332, 344–345 (1975), that "the lower courts are bound by summary decisions by this Court," which requires state and lower federal courts to treat our summary dispositions of appeals as conclusive precedents regarding constitutional challenges to like state statutes or ordinances. . . .

. . . We accord summary dispositions less precedential value than dispositions by opinion after full briefing and oral argument, because jurisdictional statements, and motions to affirm or dismiss addressed to them, rarely contain more than brief discussions of the issues presented—certainly not the full argument we expect in briefs where plenary hearing is granted. And, of course, neither the statements nor the motions are argued orally. Actually, the function of the jurisdictional statement and motion to dismiss or affirm is very limited: It is to apprise the Court of issues believed by the appellant to warrant, and by the appellee not to warrant, this Court's plenary review and decision. Thus each paper is addressed to its particular objective in that regard and eschews any extended treatment of the merits. The appellant often concentrates on trying to persuade us that the appealed decision conflicts with the decision of another court and that the conflict requires our resolution. The motions to dismiss or affirm will try to persuade us to the contrary. This treatment is fully in compliance with our Rules, which call for discussion of whether "the questions presented are so substantial as to require plenary consideration, with briefs on the merits and oral argument," and not for treatment of the merits. This Court's Rules 15 (1) (e), (f), 16 (1). Thus, the nature of materials before us when we vote summarily to dispose of a case rarely suffices as a basis for regarding the summary disposition

as a conclusive resolution of an important constitutional question, and we therefore do not treat it as such. . . .

Moreover, summary dispositions are rarely supported even by a brief opinion identifying the federal questions presented or stating the reasons or authority upon which the disposition rests. A mere "affirmed" or "dismissed for want of a substantial federal question" appears on the order list announcing the disposition, even in cases some of us believe present major constitutional issues. See, *e. g., Doe* v. *Commonwealth's Attorney*, 425 U.S. 901 (1976) (BRENNAN, MARSHALL, and STEVENS, JJ., dissenting); *Ringgold* v. *Borough of Collingswood*, 426 U.S. 901 (1976) (BRENNAN, MARSHALL, and BLACKMUN, JJ., dissenting). When presented with the contention that our unexplained dispositions are conclusively binding, puzzled state and lower court judges are left to guess as to the meaning and scope of our unexplained dispositions. We ourselves have acknowledged that summary dispositions are "somewhat opaque," *Gibson* v. *Berryhill*, 411 U.S. 564, 576 (1973), and we cannot deny that they have sown confusion.

It is no answer that a careful examination of the jurisdictional statements in prior cases—a task required by *Hicks* and fully performed by the Court of Appeals in this case—will resolve the ambiguity. As long as we give no explanation of the grounds supporting our summary disposition, such examination cannot disclose, for example, that there is no rationale accepted by a majority of the Court. Plainly, six Members of the Court may vote to dismiss or affirm an appeal without any agreement on a rationale. It is precisely in these areas of the law, however, that there probably is the greatest need for this Court to clarify the law.

In addition, there will always be the puzzling problem of how to deal with cases that are similar, but not identical, to some case that has been summarily disposed of in this Court. Courts should, of course, not feel bound to treat a summary disposition as binding beyond those situations in which the issues are the same. *Hicks* v. *Miranda*, 422 U.S., at 345 n. 14. But there is a significant risk that some courts may try to resolve the ambiguity inherent in summary dispositions by attaching too much weight to dicta or overbroad language contained in opinions from which appeals were taken and resolved summarily in this Court. THE CHIEF JUSTICE has noted that "[w]hen we summarily affirm, without opinion, the judgment of a three-judge district court we affirm the judgment but not necessarily the reasoning by which it was reached." *Fusari* v. *Steinberg*, 419 U.S. 379, 391 (1975) (concurring opinion). The same principle obviously applies to dismissals for want of a substantial federal question. Moreover, it ought to be clear to state and lower federal courts that principles set forth in full opinions cannot be limited merely by a summary disposition; a summary disposition "settles the issues for the parties, and is not to be read as a renunciation by this Court of doctrines previously announced in our opinions after full argument." *Id.*, at 392. See also *Edelman* v. *Jordan*, 415 U.S., at 671.

Further ambiguity is created by the Court's practice of summarily affirming only in federal cases and dismissing for want of a substantial federal question only in state cases—a practice that, I confess, I have accepted uncritically for nearly 20 years. When we summarily affirm in an appeal from a three-judge district court, we necessarily hold that a three-judge court was required; otherwise, we would be without jurisdiction under 28 U. S. C. § 1253. This affirmance, then, encompasses a holding that there was a "substantial federal question" requiring convening of a three-judge court under 28 U. S. C. § 2281. Yet, we would "dismiss for want of a substantial federal question" an appeal from a state appellate court raising the identical issue. The language used to dispose of appeals in state cases is clearly misleading; the Court may be saying either that the federal question is insufficiently substantial to support jurisdiction *or* that a substantial federal question was correctly decided and that this conclusion will not be affected by full briefing and oral argument. Even these alternatives are not mutually exclusive, however, since the six or more Members of the Court voting to dismiss might not agree in a particular case; at least where a majority of the Court votes to dismiss on the latter ground, we ought not create still more confusion by dismissing for want of a substantial federal question. . . .

Certiorari Strategies

In the following article by David Lauter, "The Fine Art of Creating a Certiorari Petition," the considerations of obtaining four votes for a successful cert petition are explained. The article appeared in the *National Law Journal*, December 10, 1984.

Several years ago, Bruce J. Ennis, then legal director of the American Civil Liberties Union, wrote a law review article about how to write a brief for the Supreme Court.

The theme of the piece was that a lawyer should not write for an abstract court, but should concentrate on catching the attention of each of the nine justices who actually will be reviewing the case.

Last week, Mr. Ennis, now in private practice in Washington, D.C.'s Ennis, Friedman, Bersoff & Ewing, provided an object lesson on how the job is done, persuading the Supreme Court to grant certiorari in a libel case involving a candidate for U.S. attorney, a man who didn't like him and a letter to President Reagan. *McDonald* v. *Smith*, 84–476.

The letter, written in 1980 by Robert McDonald, Mr. Ennis' client, told the president that he should not appoint David I. Smith to the U.S. attorney's job in Greensboro, N.C. Mr. Smith did not get the job, found out about the letter and sued for libel.

Mr. Ennis' argument, so far unsuccessful in federal district court and the 4th U.S. Circuit Court of Appeals, is that Mr. McDonald should be absolutely immune from civil liability for the letter under the First Amendment right to "petition the Government for a redress of grievances." The decisions rejecting that argument appear to be the first times the issue has been considered in federal court.

Mr. Ennis started out with the assumption that Justices William J. Brennan Jr. and Thurgood Marshall, who have been sympathetic to defense claims in libel cases, might be interested in hearing the case. Then he set about trying to find two more votes.

First, he noted, "the court has sort of gotten interested in libel issues again. From a law clerk's perspective it's a very juicy question and I thought the law clerks would push it."

The petition for certiorari made a particular point of emphasizing the venerable nature of the petition clause, arguing that the right to petition is far older than the rights of free speech and press. That argument, Mr. Ennis noted, was specially designed to appeal to the interest that several of the justices have in history. Justices John Paul Stevens and Lewis F. Powell Jr. frequently mention historical antecedents in their opinions as does Chief Justice Warren E. Burger.

In addition, the case posed an unusual conflict between state- and federal-court interpretations of constitutional law that Mr. Ennis hoped would appeal to several other justices.

Two state high courts within the 4th Circuit— West Virginia and Maryland—have held that petitions to the government cannot be the basis for a civil suit. With the 4th Circuit holding the other way, Mr. Ennis' petition argued, federal district courts in those two states sitting in diversity actions would be forced to follow the law of the circuit, rejecting the law of the state, implying "a premise that federal courts have greater wisdom, or at least authority, in interpreting the federal Constitution than do state courts."

"Justice [Sandra Day] O'Connor has written law review articles about the need to allow state court judges to make decisions," Mr. Ennis noted, hoping that argument might particularly appeal to her. In addition, Justice William H. Rehnquist might be interested in the federalism aspect of the argument, he said.

Having now gotten the court's attention, Mr. Ennis, of course, faces the more difficult matter of winning the case. "It's a long way to go to convince this court to grant a new absolute right," he said.

* * *

Denying Certiorari

In *Singleton* v. *Commissioner of Internal Revenue*, 439 U.S. 940 (1978), the Supreme Court denied certiorari in a federal income tax case. Blackmun, joined by Marshall and Powell, dissented from the Court's action. Stevens reviewed the significance of denying cert and the value of writing separate opinions of dissent. Footnotes omitted.

Opinion of MR. JUSTICE STEVENS respecting the denial of the petition for writ of certiorari.

What is the significance of this Court's denial of certiorari? That question is asked again and again; it is a question that is likely to arise whenever a dissenting opinion argues that certiorari should have been granted. Almost 30 years ago Mr. Justice Frankfurter provided us with an answer to that question that should be read again and again.

"This Court now declines to review the decision of the Maryland Court of Appeals. The sole significance of such denial of a petition for writ of certiorari need not be elucidated to those versed in the Court's procedures. It simply means that fewer than four members of the Court deemed it desirable to review a decision of the lower court as a matter 'of sound judicial discretion.' Rule 38, paragraph 5. A variety of considerations underlie denials of the writ, and as to the same petition different reasons may lead different Justices to the same result. This is especially true of petitions for review on writ of certiorari to a State court. Narrowly technical reasons may lead to denials. Review may be sought too late; the judgment of the lower court may not be final; it may not be the judgment of a State court of last resort; the decision may be supportable as a matter of State law, not subject to review by this Court, even though the State court also passed on issues of federal law. A decision may satisfy all these technical requirements and yet may commend itself for review to fewer than four members of the Court. Pertinent considerations of judicial policy here come into play. A case may raise an important question but the record may be cloudy. It may be desirable to have different aspects of an issue further illumined by the lower courts. Wise adjudication has its own time for ripening.

"Since there are these conflicting and, to the uninformed, even confusing reasons for denying petitions for certiorari, it has been suggested from time to time that the Court indicate its reasons for denial. Practical considerations preclude. In order that the Court may be enabled to discharge its indispensable duties, Congress has placed the control of the Court's business, in effect, within the Court's discretion. During the last three terms the Court disposed of 260, 217, 224 cases, respectively, on their merits. For the same three terms the Court denied, respectively, 1,260, 1,105, 1,189 petitions calling for discretionary review. If the Court is to do its work it would not be feasible to give reasons, however brief, for refusing to take these cases. The time that would be required is prohibitive, apart from the fact as already indicated that different reasons not infrequently move different members of the Court in concluding that a particular case at a particular time makes review undesirable. It becomes relevant here to note that failure to record a dissent from a denial of a petition for writ of certiorari in nowise implies that only the member of the Court who notes his dissent thought the petition should be granted.

"Inasmuch, therefore, as all that a denial of a petition for a writ of certiorari means is that fewer than four members of the Court thought it should be granted, this Court has rigorously insisted that such a denial carries with it no implication whatever regarding the Court's views on the merits of a case which it has declined to review. The Court has said this again and again; again and again the admonition has to be repeated." Opinion respecting the denial of the petition for writ of certiorari in *Maryland* v. *Baltimore Radio Show*, 338 U. S. 912, 917–919.

When those words were written, Mr. Justice Frankfurter and his colleagues were too busy to spend their scarce time writing dissents from denials of certiorari. Such opinions were almost nonexistent. It was then obvious that if there was no need to explain the Court's action in denying the writ, there was even less reason for individual expressions of opinion about why certiorari should have been granted in particular cases.

Times have changed. Although the workload of the Court has dramatically increased since Mr. Justice Frankfurter's day, most present Members of the Court frequently file written dissents from certiorari denials. It is appropriate to ask whether the new practice serves any important goals or contributes to the strength of the institution.

One characteristic of all opinions dissenting from the denial of certiorari is manifest. They are totally unnecessary. They are examples of the purest form of dicta, since they have even less legal significance than the orders of the entire Court which, as Mr. Justice Frankfurter reiterated again and again, have no precedential significance at all.

Another attribute of these opinions is that they are potentially misleading. Since the Court provides no explanation of the reasons for denying certiorari, the dissenter's arguments in favor of a grant are not answered and therefore typically appear to be more persuasive than most other opinions. Moreover, since they often omit any reference to valid reasons for denying certiorari, they tend to imply that the Court has been unfaithful to its responsibilities or has implicitly reached a decision on the merits when, in fact, there is no basis for such an inference.

In this case, for example, the dissenting opinion suggests that the Court may have refused to grant certiorari because the case is "devoid of glamour and emotion." I am puzzled by this suggestion because I have never witnessed any indication that any of my colleagues has ever considered "glamour and emotion" as a relevant consideration in the exercise of his discretion or in his analysis of the law. With respect to the Court's action in this case, the absence of any conflict among the Circuits is plainly a sufficient reason for denying certiorari. Moreover, in allocating the Court's scarce resources, I consider it entirely appropriate to disfavor complicated cases which turn largely on unique facts. A series of decisions by the courts of appeals may well provide more meaningful guidance to the bar than an isolated or premature opinion of this Court. As Mr. Justice Frankfurter reminded us, "wise adjudication has its own time for ripening."

Admittedly these dissenting opinions may have some beneficial effects. Occasionally a written statement of reasons for granting certiorari is more persuasive than the Justice's oral contribution to the Conference. For that reason the written document sometimes persuades other Justices to change their votes and a petition is granted that would otherwise have been denied. That effect, however, merely justifies the writing and circulating of these memoranda within the Court; it does not explain why a dissent which has not accomplished its primary mission should be published.

It can be argued that publishing these dissents enhances the public's understanding of the work of the Court. But because they are so seldom answered, these opinions may also give rise to misunderstanding or incorrect impressions about how the Court actually works. Moreover, the selected bits of information which they reveal tend to compromise the otherwise secret deliberations in our Conferences. There are those who believe that these Conferences should be conducted entirely in public or, at the very least, that the votes on all Conference matters should be publicly recorded. The traditional view, which I happen to share, is that confidentiality makes a valuable contribution to the full and frank exchange of views during the decisional process; such confidentiality is especially valuable in the exercise of the kind of discretion that must be employed in processing the thousands of certiorari petitions that are reviewed each year. In my judgment, the importance of preserving the tradition of confidentiality outweighs the minimal educational value of these opinions.

In all events, these are the reasons why I have thus far resisted the temptation to publish opinions dissenting from denials of certiorari.

Frank M. Coffin

The Process of Writing a Decision

A remarkably effective device for detecting fissures in accuracy and logic is the reduction to writing of the results of one's thought processes. The custom of American courts of embodying decision in a written opinion setting forth facts, law, logic, and policy is not the least of their strengths. Somehow, a decision mulled over in

SOURCE: From Frank M. Coffin, The Ways of a Judge: Reflections from the Federal Appellate Bench (Boston: Houghton Mifflin, 1980), pp. 57–63. When this book was published, Coffin was Chief Judge of the First Circuit.

one's head or talked about in conference looks different when dressed up in written words and sent out into the sunlight. Sometimes the passage of time or a new way of looking at the issue makes us realize that an opinion will simply not do, and back we go to the drawing board. Or we may be in the very middle of an opinion, struggling to reflect the reasoning all judges have agreed on, only to realize that it simply "won't write." The act of writing tells us what was wrong with the act of thinking.

One can canvass other kinds of deciders who come to mind and find few who accompany their routine decisions with written explanations. If explanations there are, they are likely to be incomplete, informal, oral, and perhaps meant to be forgotten. Or, if in writing, there is little guarantee that they reveal the real reason for decision. A legislature may vote down a tax increase, invoking impressive economic data; one may suspect that the prospect of an impending election had more to do with the result. A chief executive may announce a policy decision and marshal sophisticated reasons in support; in reality he may have been reacting to interest groups or congressional pressures.

What makes the "in writing" tradition a demanding one for appellate courts is that judges do not write on a clean slate. Prior decisions in other cases of different degrees of similarity demand to be reconciled with, or distinguished from, the present one. If results differ, the court must explain why. While conscientious and competent judges may disagree, the rigors of dealing honestly with facts, of recognizing and respectably treating precedent, and of reasoning logically, reduce the occasions for differences and narrow the gulf of such as remain.

A COLLEGIAL DECISION

Every important appellate court decision is made by a group of equals. This fact reflects the shrewd judgment of the architects of our state and federal judicial systems that an appellate judge is no wiser than a trial judge. His only claim to superior judgment lies in numbers; three, five, seven, or nine heads are usually better than one.

This element of collegiality is not unique. As the very word implies, the governance of colleges and universities relies heavily on faculties. Boards of directors, committees, commissions, and legislative bodies act collegially. But there are differences. An appellate court is a small "college." The members may differ in seniority, but each holds rank equal to the others. Most important, almost everything an appellate judge is called on to do he must do with his colleagues. He does not practice a specialty in his own chambers, joining his peers only to make top policy decisions. Virtually all decisions are made by a panel of at least three.

There is intimacy, continuity, and dynamism in the relations among judges, at least on the smaller courts. They do not come together just to vote. They interact with each other, influence each other, and have each other in mind almost from the time they first read briefs for the next session of court. In a sense, the relationship among judges who differ in their values and views is a bargaining one, yet it is a continuing negotiation, where each player lays his cards on the table just as soon as he discovers what cards he has. There is, on a serene court, no suggestion that anyone seeks to manipulate anyone else.

In short, there is a difference between arriving at a yes or no decision through majority vote and working up an opinion on a close case so that three or more judges of different sensitivities, values, and backgrounds can join not only in the result, but in the rationale, tone, nuances, and reservations. Although the task of building toward a unanimous opinion, or even of carpentering a majority, demands a certain amount of sacrifice of ego and substantive concession, collegiality has its solid satisfactions. One quickly realizes that he is not the only source of useful insights. He learns to rejoice when he sees an opinion he has written measurably strengthened by the suggestion of one of his colleagues. Then, too, decisions are sometimes unpleasant, hard, risky, controversial, when the public and the press are hot and quick in their criticism. On such occasions, the comfort of collegiality is a pearl of no little worth.

THE INTENSITY OF INDIVIDUAL INVOLVEMENT

One of the paradoxes about appellate courts is that there can coexist the kind of intimate collegiality I have sketched and a profound, almost antique individualism. Indeed, perhaps the collegiality is the more enduring because it feeds on, cherishes, and respects the individualism nourished by appellate courts. In any case I make so bold as to say that in this supertechnical, industrialized, computerized, organized age, appellate courts are among the last redoubts of individual work.

While reliance on machines and staff proliferates apace in corporations, legislatures, and executive bureaucracies, the appellate judge still lives and works in his chamber with his law clerks.

Although, unlike his predecessor, he can no longer write the first draft of every opinion, he is, as we shall see, in the very heart of creation of every opinion at every stage.

The kind of individualism I refer to is not the individualism of style, flair, or color, though these, happily, are not absent. Rather, every work product of an appellate court, a judicial opinion, bears the individual trademarks of, and is freighted with, the personal scrutiny and reflection of each member to a greater extent than that of any other collegial body. An appellate court's work is the least delegable of that of any major public institution. That this is so is made manifest by the concern of the bar and the Congress that judicial involvement not be diluted by too much reliance on central staff attorneys or parajudicial officers. This is not to say that this preindustrial stronghold is beyond assault. Computer-assisted legal research, elaborate memoried typewriters, word-processing equipment, and machines that can instantaneously reproduce a draft opinion in the chambers of one's colleagues have already made their entry on the scene. . . .

Perhaps there are appellate judges who, on hearing the essential facts of such a case, can confidently announce a sound decision without pause. I have seen professors in the classroom so respond; also panelists, lecturers, and cocktail-party pundits. But I am thankful that nothing said under such circumstances affects the rights of parties. Judges do have their share of excellent talkers. The best of them are called brilliant. Brilliance, however, seems to me more associated with the pyrotechnics of speech and writing; as the word suggests, it has to do with how thoughts can be made to shine and sparkle. Sound decision, on the other hand, is more than result; it is an edifice made up of rationale, tone, and direction. It is faithful to the past, settles the present, and foreshadows the future. Such a decision is rarely made quickly.

I see decision-making as neither a process that results in an early conviction based on instant exposure to competing briefs nor one in which the judge keeps an open mind through briefs, discussion in chambers, argument, and conference, and then summons up the will to decide. I see the process, rather, as a series of shifting biases. It is much like tracing the source of a river, following various minor tributaries, which are found to rise in swamps, returning to the channel, which narrows as one goes upstream.

One reads a good brief from the appellant; the position seems reasonable. But a good brief from appellee, bolstered perhaps by a trial judge's opinion, seems incontrovertible. Discussion with the law clerks in chambers casts doubt on any tentative position. Any such doubt may be demolished by oral argument, only to give rise to a new bias, which in turn may be shaken by the postargument conference among the judges. As research and writing reveal new problems, the tentative disposition of the panel of judges may appear wrong. The opinion is written and circulated, producing reactions from the other judges, which again change the thrust, the rationale, or even the result. Only when the process has ended can one say that the decision has been made, after as many as seven turns in the road. The guarantee of a judge's impartiality lies not in suspending judgment throughout the process but in recognizing that each successive judgment is tentative, fragile, and likely to be modified or set aside as a consequence of deepened insight. The nonlawyer looks on the judge as a model of decisiveness. The truth is more likely that the appellate judge in a difficult case is committed to the unpleasant state of prolonged indecisiveness.

Cooper v. Aaron

358 U.S. 1 (1958)

After the governor and legislature of Arkansas had openly resisted the Supreme Court's school desegregation decision of 1954, the Court unanimously reasserted its supremacy in determining constitutional law. Instead of an unsigned, per curiam decision, the Court

decided to underscore its unity by naming each Justice, including three who had joined the Court since 1954. Justice Frankfurter broke the spirit of unanimity and unity by preparing a concurring opinion, which he released one week after the Court filed its statement.

Opinion of the Court by THE CHIEF JUSTICE, MR. JUSTICE BLACK, MR. JUSTICE FRANKFURTER, MR. JUSTICE DOUGLAS, MR. JUSTICE BURTON, MR. JUSTICE CLARK, MR. JUSTICE HARLAN, MR. JUSTICE BRENNAN, and MR. JUSTICE WHITTAKER.

As this case reaches us it raises questions of the highest importance to the maintenance of our federal system of government. It necessarily involves a claim by the Governor and Legislature of a State that there is no duty on state officials to obey federal court orders resting on this Court's considered interpretation of the United States Constitution. Specifically it involves actions by the Governor and Legislature of Arkansas upon the premise that they are not bound by our holding in *Brown* v. *Board of Education*, 347 U.S. 483. That holding was that the Fourteenth Amendment forbids States to use their governmental powers to bar children on racial grounds from attending schools where there is state participation through any arrangement, management, funds or property. We are urged to uphold a suspension of the Little Rock School Board's plan to do away with segregated public schools in Little Rock until state laws and efforts to upset and nullify our holding in *Brown* v. *Board of Education* have been further challenged and tested in the courts. We reject these contentions. . . .

Article VI of the Constitution makes the Constitution the "supreme Law of the Land." In 1803, Chief Justice Marshall, speaking for a unanimous Court, referring to the Constitution as "the fundamental and paramount law of the nation," declared in the notable case of *Marbury* v. *Madison*, 1 Cranch 137, 177, that "It is emphatically the province and duty of the judicial department to say what the law is." This decision declared the basic principle that the federal judiciary is supreme in the exposition of the law of the Constitution, and that principle has ever since been respected by this Court and the Country as a permanent and indispensable feature of our constitutional system. It follows that the interpretation of the Fourteenth Amendment enunciated by this Court in the *Brown* case is the supreme law of

the land, and Art. VI of the Constitution makes it of binding effect on the States "any Thing in the Constitution or Laws of any State to the Contrary notwithstanding." Every state legislator and executive and judicial officer is solemnly committed by oath taken pursuant to Art. VI, cl. 3, "to support this Constitution." Chief Justice Taney, speaking for a unanimous Court in 1859, said that this requirement reflected the framers' "anxiety to preserve it [the Constitution] in full force, in all its powers, and to guard against resistance to or evasion of its authority, on the part of a State . . ." *Ableman* v. *Booth*, 21 How. 506, 524.

No state legislator or executive or judicial officer can war against the Constitution without violating his undertaking to support it. Chief Justice Marshall spoke for a unanimous Court in saying that: "If the legislatures of the several states may, at will, annul the judgments of the courts of the United States, and destroy the rights acquired under those judgments, the constitution itself becomes a solemn mockery . . . " *United States* v. *Peters*, 5 Cranch 115, 136. A Governor who asserts a power to nullify a federal court order is similarly restrained. If he had such power, said Chief Justice Hughes, in 1932, also for a unanimous Court, "it is manifest that the fiat of a state Governor, and not the Constitution of the United States, would be the supreme law of the land; that the restrictions of the Federal Constitution upon the exercise of state power would be but impotent phrases . . ." *Sterling* v. *Constantin*, 287 U.S. 378, 397–398.

It is, of course, quite true that the responsibility for public education is primarily the concern of the States, but it is equally true that such responsibilities, like all other state activity, must be exercised consistently with federal constitutional requirements as they apply to state action. The Constitution created a government dedicated to equal justice under law. The Fourteenth Amendment embodied and emphasized that ideal. State support of segregated schools through any arrangement, management, funds, or property cannot be squared with the Amendment's command that no State shall deny to any person within its jurisdiction the equal protection of the laws. The right of a student not to be segregated on racial grounds in schools so maintained is indeed so fundamental and pervasive that it is embraced in the concept of due process of law. *Bolling* v. *Sharpe*, 347 U.S. 497. The basic decision in *Brown* was unanimously reached by this Court only after the case had been briefed and twice argued and the issues had been given the most serious consideration. Since the first *Brown* opinion three new Justices have come to the Court. They are at one with the Justices still on the Court who participated in that basic decision as to its correctness, and that decision is now unanimously reaffirmed. The principles announced in that decision and the obedience of the States to them, according to the command of the Constitution, are indispensable for the protection of the freedoms guaranteed by our fundamental charter for all of us. Our constitutional ideal of equal justice under law is thus made a living truth.

Concurring opinion of MR. JUSTICE FRANKFURTER.

While unreservedly participating with my brethren in our joint opinion, I deem it appropriate also to deal individually with the great issue here at stake. . . .

William O. Douglas

The Dissent: A Safeguard of Democracy

All of us in recent years have heard and read many criticisms of the dissenting or concurring opinion. Separate opinions have often been deplored. Courts have been severely criticized for tolerating them. And that is why I rise to their defense.

About ten years ago when I took my seat on the bench, Chief Justice Hughes said this to me: "I think you will find after you have been on the bench for a while that in a great majority of the cases, perhaps in two-thirds of them, the judges will ultimately reach agreement and announce opinions that are unanimous. But in at least a third of the cases, agreement will not be possible. In those cases there will be dissents—no matter how carefully the judges were chosen—whether one President or several Presidents selected them."

Chief Justice Hughes spoke from a long experience both at the bar and in the conference room. In these days of uneasiness and confusion what he said to me is important not only to judges and lawyers but to everyone. It is indeed only when the meaning of his words is clear that the true nature of the judicial process is brought home to the community.

SEARCH FOR CERTAINTY

Holmes, perhaps better than anyone either before or after him, pointed out how illusory was the lawyer's search for certainty. Law is not what has been or is—law in the lawyer's sense is the prediction of things to come, the prediction of what decree will be written by designated judges on specified facts. In layman's language law is the prediction of what will happen to you if you do certain things. This was the lesson Holmes taught; and every lawyer on reflection knows that it is sound.

There are many reasons why this is so. No matter how clear and precise the code or other legal rule may be, the proof may be surrounded with doubt. And even though the proof is clear to the advocate, the credibility of the witnesses may raise serious questions for judge or jury. Uncer-

SOURCE: Journal of the American Judicature Society, Vol. 32, pp. 104–107 (December 1948). Justice Douglas served on the Supreme Court from 1939 to 1975.

tainty is increased when new and difficult problems under ambiguous statutes arise. And when constitutional questions emerge, the case is, as we lawyers say, "at large." For the federal constitution, like most state constitutions, is not a code but a rule of action—a statement of philosophy and point of view, a summation of general principles, a delineation of the broad outlines of a regime which the Fathers designed for us.

These are the things that Holmes summed up when he described the lawyer's continuing and uncertain search for certainty. They indeed suggest why philosophers of the democratic faith will rejoice in the uncertainty of the law and find strength and glory in it.

Certainty and unanimity in the law are possible both under the fascist and communist systems. They are not only possible; they are indispensable; for complete subservience to the political regime is a *sine qua non* to judicial survival under either system. One cannot imagine the courts of Hitler engaged in a public debate over the principles of Der Feuhrer [sic], with a minority of one or four deploring or denouncing the principles themselves. One cannot imagine a judge of a Communist court dissenting against the decrees of the Kremlin.

Disagreement among judges is as true to the character of democracy as freedom of speech itself. The dissenting opinion is as genuinely American as Otis' denunciation of the general warrants, as Thomas Paine's, Thomas Jefferson's, or James Madison's briefs for civil liberties. . . .

LEGISLATIVE PROCESS ONE OF COMPROMISE

Those who have followed the legislative process can produce examples on end. That process is one of compromise—of qualifying absolutes, of creating exceptions to general rules. At times the process of compromise or conciliation involves well-nigh impossible adjustments. The clash of ideas may be so violent that a meeting of the minds seems out of the question. Where such cleavage is great and involves major issues, it may even tear a society apart. By the same token it can stop the legislative process or render it impotent, and thus deprive society of lawful and nonviolent

means and methods of solving its problems. When the breach between the *pros* and *cons* is not too great, the legislative process functions. Even then, the compromise between competing ideas that emerges in the final legislation may be more apparent than real. For the legislative solution is often to write two opposing ideas into a statute. Without that solution enactment of the measure might, indeed, be impossible.

INTERPRETATION HAS LEGISLATIVE CHARACTERISTICS

And so the bill becomes the law and the law arrives before judges for interpretation. The battle that raged before the legislature is now transferred to the court. The passage of the legislation quieted the conflict only temporarily. It breaks out anew in the process of interpretation in the courts. A storm hits the court room, and the advocates take up the fight where the legislators left off. The same cleavage that appeared in legislative halls now shows up among the judges. Each side has eminent authority for its view since two conflicting ideas found their way into the legislation. It is therefore easy for judge or lawyer or editor to accuse the judge, who takes the opposing view, of usurping the role of the legislature. A more honest, a more objective view would concede that interpretation has legislative as well as judicial characteristics. It cannot be otherwise where the legislature has left the choice of competing theories or ideas to the judges.

The legislative process breeds dissension among judges in other ways. An hiatus may be left in a law. The crucial matter may have been too explosive for the legislators to handle. For that or for other reasons they passed it over entirely or left it vague and undefined. The necessity to fill in the gap is then presented to the court. And the judges are left at large in a field that the legislature lacked capacity to define. To a degree the same problem is presented to the judiciary when vague and general language is employed like the words "fair" or "just" or "equitable." The law is not a series of calculating machines where definitions and answers come tumbling out when the right levers are pushed. A judge's reaction to vague statutory language is bound to be like his reaction to the generalities of constitutional clauses. The language that he construes gathers meaning and overtones, significance and relevancy in terms of his own life and experience, his personal set of values, his training and education, and the genes of the blood stream of his ancestors. It would be as futile to argue that judges are not human, as it would to prove that politics and legislatures can be divorced.

STARE DECISIS HAS SMALL PLACE IN CONSTITUTIONAL LAW

When we move to constitutional questions, uncertainty necessarily increases. A judge who is asked to construe or interpret the Constitution often rejects the gloss which his predecessors have put on it. For the gloss may, in his view, offend the spirit of the Constitution or do violence to it. That has been the experience of this generation and of all those that have preceded. It will likewise be the experience of those which follow. And so it should be. For it is the Constitution which we have sworn to defend, not some predecessor's interpretation of it. *Stare decisis* has small place in constitutional law. The Constitution was written for all time and

all ages. It would lose its great character and become feeble, if it were allowed to become encrusted with narrow, legalistic notions that dominated the thinking of one generation.

UNCERTAINTY NECESSARY FOR DEMOCRACY

So it is that the law will always teem with uncertainty. It has always been the case—and it always will remain that way under the democratic scheme of things. The truth is that the law is the highest form of compromise between competing interests; it is a substitute for force and violence— the only path to peace man has yet devised. It is the product of attempted reconciliation between the many diverse groups in a society. The reconciliation is not entirely a legislative function. The judiciary is also inescapably involved. When judges do not agree, it is a sign that they are dealing with problems on which society itself is divided. It is the democratic way to express dissident views. Judges are to be honored rather than criticized for following that tradition, for proclaiming their articles of faith so that all may read. . . .

Robert H. Jackson
The Limitation of Dissent

In argued cases, conferences are followed by the preparation and circulation of opinions by Justices designated by the Chief Justice when he is with the prevailing view and, if not, by the senior Associate who is. But any Justice is free to write as he will, and there may be one or more opinions concurring in the result but reaching it by different reasons, and there may be a dissenting opinion or opinions. This occasions complaint by laymen and the bar that they are required to piece all these contributions together in order to make out

SOURCE: From Justice Jackson's book, The Supreme Court in the American System of Government 16–19 (1955). Footnotes omitted.

where the Supreme Court really stands as an institution.

All of this is at odds with the practice of most courts of continental Europe, which make it a rule to announce the decision in one statement only and to issue no dissents or concurrences. Moreover, their work is institutionalized and depersonalized. The court's opinion bears the name of no author. Like our *per curiam* opinion, it may be the work of any member or of several in collaboration. This anonymity diminishes any temptation to exploit differences within the court, but it may also diminish the incentive for hard work on opinions. In any event, I am sure that not only Anglo-

American tradition but judicial and professional opinion favors the identification of writers and the full disclosure of important differences within the Court. Mr. Jefferson would have required each Justice to write his reasons in every case, as proof that he gave it consideration and did not merely follow a leader.

The dissenting opinion strives to undermine the Court's reasoning and discredit its result. At its best, the dissent, as Mr. Hughes said, is "an appeal to the brooding spirit of the law, to the intelligence of a future day. . . ." But Judge Cardozo has written:

"... Comparatively speaking at least, the dissenter is irresponsible. The spokesman of the court is cautious, timid, fearful of the vivid word, the heightened phrase. He dreams of an unworthy brood of scions, the spawn of careless *dicta*, disowned by the *ratio decidendi*, to which all legitimate offspring must be able to trace their lineage. The result is to cramp and paralyze. One fears to say anything when the peril of misunderstanding puts a warning finger to the lips. Not so, however, the dissenter. . . . For the moment, he is the gladiator making a last stand against the lions. The poor man must be forgiven a freedom of expression, tinged at rare moments with a touch of bitterness, which magnanimity as well as caution would reject for one triumphant."

Dissent has a popular appeal, for it is an underdog judge pleading for an underdog litigant. Of course, one party or the other must always be underdog in a lawsuit, the purpose of which really is to determine which one it shall be. But the tradition of great dissents built around such names as Holmes, Brandeis, Cardozo, and Stone is not due to the frequency or multiplicity of their dissents, but to their quality and the importance of the few cases in which they carried their disagreement beyond the conference table. Also, quite contrary to the popular notion, relatively few of all the dissents recorded in the Supreme Court have later become law, although some of these are of great importance.

There has been much undiscriminating eulogy of dissenting opinions. It is said they clarify the issues. Often they do the exact opposite. The technique of the dissenter often is to exaggerate the holding of the Court beyond the meaning of the majority and then to blast away at the excess. So the poor lawyer with a similar case does not know whether the majority opinion meant what it seemed to say or what the minority said it meant. Then, too, dissenters frequently force the majority to take positions more extreme than was originally intended. The classic example is the *Dred Scott Case*, in which Chief Justice Taney's extreme statements were absent in his original draft and were inserted only after Mr. Justice McLean, then a more than passive candidate for the presidency, raised the issue in dissent.

The *right of dissent* is a valuable one. Wisely used on well-chosen occasions, it has been of great service to the profession and to the law. But there is nothing good, for either the Court or the dissenter, in dissenting per se. Each dissenting opinion is a confession of failure to convince the writer's colleagues, and the true test of a judge is his influence in leading, not in opposing, his court.

6 Separation of Powers: Domestic Conflicts

T he "doctrine" of separation of powers remains an elusive concept. In both theory and practice, it teems with subtleties, ironies, and apparent contradictions. Just what the framers intended remains a subject of continuing dispute, spawning a vast literature with varying interpretations. Even if we could agree on the "framers' intent," the relationships among the three branches of government have changed fundamentally in two centuries to produce novel arrangements and peculiar overlappings. Chapters 6 and 7 cover these general principles as well as specific applications of the separation of powers.

THE SEPARATION DOCTRINE

Critics of separated powers in America claim that this system produces intolerable deadlocks and inefficiency, especially for a twentieth-century government expected to exercise worldwide responsibilities. However, there is no necessary link between separated powers and inefficiency. The framers did not adopt a separation of powers to obstruct government. They wanted to create a system in 1787 that would operate more effectively and efficiently than the discredited Articles of Confederation, written in 1777 and ratified in 1781.

Only one branch of national government existed before 1787: the Continental Congress. There was no executive or judiciary. Members of the Congress had to legislate and then serve on committees to administer and adjudicate what they had passed. Within a few years the system proved to be so exhausting, inept, and embarrassing that it became necessary to delegate administrative and judicial duties to outside bodies. To relieve committees of administrative details, Congress turned to boards staffed by people outside the legislature. When these multiheaded boards failed to supply energy and accountability, Congress appointed single executive officers in 1781 to run the executive departments. These departments supplied a vital link in administrative structures between the Continental Congress and the

217

national government established in 1787. Louis Fisher, President and Congress 1–27, 253–270 (1972).

The Continental Congress also established the beginnings of a national judiciary by setting up Courts of Admiralty to decide all controversies over naval captures and the distribution of war prizes. By 1780 Congress had created the Court of Appeals in Cases of Capture, which functioned until its last session on May 16, 1787, at the State House in Philadelphia across the hall from the room in which delegates were assembling for the Constitutional Convention.

This separation of legislative, executive, and judicial functions reflects the framers' search for more efficient government. The separation was determined principally by events, not theory. In a striking phrase, the historian Francis Wharton said that the Constitution "did not make this distribution of power. It would be more proper to say that this distribution of power made the Constitution of the United States." 1 Francis Wharton, The Revolutionary Correspondence of the United States 663 (1889). Justice Brandeis spoke a half-truth when he claimed that the doctrine of separated powers was "adopted by the Convention of 1787, not to promote efficiency but to preclude the exercise of arbitrary power." Myers v. United States, 272 U.S. 52, 293 (1926). Efficiency was a key objective.

It is often said that powers are separated to preserve liberties. It is equally true that a rigid separation can *destroy* liberties. The historic swings in France between executive and legislative dominance suggest the danger of extreme separation. The constitutions of 1791 and 1848, which established a pure separation of powers, ended in absolutism and reaction. M.J.C. Vile, Constitutionalism and the Separation of Powers 176-211 (1967). The framers wanted to avoid political fragmentation and paralysis of power. They knew that a rigid adherence to separated powers "in all cases would be subversive of the efficiency of the government, and result in the destruction of the public liberties." 1 Joseph Story, Commentaries on the Constitution of the United States 396 (1905 ed.). Justice Jackson described the complex elements that coexist in America's separation doctrine: "While the Constitution diffuses power the better to secure liberty, it also contemplates that the practice will integrate the dispersed powers into a workable government. It enjoins upon its branches separateness but interdependence, autonomy but reciprocity." Youngstown Co. v. Sawyer, 343 U.S. 579, 635 (1952).

Although the separation of powers doctrine is not expressly stated in the Constitution, it is implied in the allocation of legislative powers to the Congress in Article I, executive powers to the President in Article II, and judicial powers to the Supreme Court in Article III. Several provisions help reinforce the separation. Article I, Section 6, prohibits members of either House of Congress from holding any other civil office (the Incompatibility Clause). This provision has been difficult to litigate. In 1974, the Court denied standing to plaintiffs who challenged the right of members of Congress to hold a commission in the armed forces reserves. Schlesinger v. Reservists to Stop the War, 418 U.S. 208 (1974). Article I, Section 6, also prohibits Members of Congress from being appointed to any federal office created during their term of office, or to any federal position whose salary has been increased during their term of office (the Ineligibility Clause). The framers were aware that members of the British Parliament had been corrupted by appointments to office from the Crown. But they were also reluctant to exclude qualified and able people from public office. 1 Farrand 379–382, 386–390; 2 Farrand 283–284, 489–492.

To reconcile these conflicting goals, Congress has at times reduced the salary of an executive position to permit someone from the House or the Senate to be appointed to the post. For example, after Congress had increased the salary of the Secretary of State from $8,000 to $12,000, President Taft wanted to name Senator Philander Knox to that office in 1909. A special bill was drafted to reduce the compensation of the Secretary of State to the original figure. The bill inspired heated debate in the House of Representatives, 43 Cong. Rec. 2390–2404, 2408–2415, but was enacted into law (35 Stat. 626). Knox was then nominated by President Taft and confirmed by the Senate. A similar situation arose in 1973 concerning the nomination of Senator William Saxbe as Attorney General after Congress had increased the salary of that office from $35,000 to $60,000. Legislation was enacted to keep Saxbe's compensation at $35,000. 87 Stat. 697 (1973). The debate offers a good example of the manner in which Congress engages in constitutional interpretation (pp. 237–240).

Other safeguards for the separation doctrine exist. Congress is prohibited from reducing the compensation of the President and members of the judiciary. United States v. Will, 449 U.S. 200 (1980). The Speech or Debate Clause, covered later in this chapter, provides legislative immunity to protect members of Congress from executive or judicial harassment.

Several sections of the Constitution produce combinations, not separations, of the branches. The President may veto legislation, subject to a two-thirds override vote of each House. Some of the Anti-Federalists objected that the veto allowed the President to encroach upon the legislature. Alexander Hamilton, in Federalist 73, defended the qualified veto on two grounds: it protected the President's office against legislative "depredations," and it served as a check on bad laws. In signing legislation into law, Presidents often interpret provisions of a bill to avoid what they consider to be constitutional infirmities (pp. 240–241).

Presidents also exercise a "pocket veto." The Constitution provides that any bill not returned by the President within ten days (Sundays excepted) shall become law unless the adjournment by Congress prevents the bill's return. In such cases, the bill does not become law and is pocket-vetoed. Several decisions have effectively eliminated the use of a pocket veto *during* a congressional session.[1] The remaining legal issue concerns the President's power to pocket-veto a bill *between* the first and second sessions. This issue reached the Supreme Court but was dismissed in 1987 as moot. Barnes v. Kline, 759 F.2d 21 (D.C. Cir. 1985); Burke v. Barnes, 479 U.S. 361 (1987). There is no question about the President's power to invoke the pocket veto at the end of the second session when Congress adjourns.

The Constitution contains other overlappings. The President nominates officers but the Senate confirms. He submits treaties that the Senate must ratify. The House of Representatives may impeach executive and judicial officers, subject to the Senate's conviction in a trial presided over by the Chief Justice (for presidential impeachment). The courts decide criminal cases but the President may pardon offenders. These mixtures led to complaints by several delegates at the state ratifying conventions. They objected that the branches of government had been intermingled instead of being kept separate. By the time of the Philadelphia Convention, however, the doctrine of separated powers had been overtaken by the system of checks and

---

[1]Kennedy v. Sampson, 511 F.2d 430 (D.C. Cir. 1974); Wright v. United States, 302 U.S. 583 (1938). See also The Pocket Veto Case, 279 U.S. 644 (1929).

balances. One contemporary pamphleteer dismissed the separation doctrine, in its pure form, as a "hackneyed principle" and a "trite maxim." M.J.C. Vile, Constitutionalism and the Separation of Powers 153.

Madison devoted several of his *Federalist* essays to the need for overlapping powers, claiming that the concept was superior to the impracticable partitioning of powers demanded by some of the Anti-Federalists (pp. 241–246). Alexander Hamilton, in Federalist 75, defended the combination of the executive with the Senate in the treaty process and bristled at "the trite topic of the intermixture of powers." Opponents were not satisfied. Three states—Virginia, North Carolina, and Pennsylvania—wanted a separation clause added to the national bill of rights. They proposed that neither branch could exercise the powers vested in the others. Congress rejected that proposal as well as a substitute amendment to make the three departments "separate and distinct."[2]

Enumerated and Implied Powers

Strict constructionists regard the American Constitution as one of enumerated powers. They oppose the notion of implied powers, inherent powers, powers derived from custom, or any other extraconstitutional power not explicitly granted to one of the three branches. Although there is legitimate concern about the scope of implied powers, all three branches find it necessary to exercise powers not stated in the Constitution. Congress has the power to investigate as a necessary function of its legislative power; the President has the power to remove certain administrative officials to maintain executive accountability and responsibility; the Supreme Court has acquired the power to review legislative, executive, and state actions on questions of federal constitutionality.

The framers recognized the need for implied powers. Madison noted in Federalist 44: "No axiom is more clearly established in law, or in reason, than that whenever the end is required, the means are authorized; whenever a general power to do a thing is given, every particular power necessary for doing it is included." Congress is granted not merely the enumerated powers found within Article I but is also authorized to "make all Laws which shall be necessary and proper for carrying into Execution the foregoing Powers, and all other Powers vested by this Constitution in the Government of the United States, or in any Department or Officer thereof." The history of the Tenth Amendment underscores the need for implied powers (p. 374).[3]

The boundaries between the three branches of government are also strongly affected by the role of custom and acquiescence. When one branch engages in a certain practice and the other branches acquiesce, the practice gains legitimacy and can fix the meaning of the Constitution. Stuart v. Laird, 5 U.S. (1 Cr.) 299, 309 (1803). The President's power to remove officials was upheld in a 1903 ruling based largely on the "universal practice of the government for over a century." Shurtleff v. United

---

[2]Proposed by three states: 3 Elliot 280; 4 Elliot 116, 121; John Bach McMaster and Frederick D. Stone, eds., Pennsylvania and the Federal Constitution 475–477 (1888). Amendment language: Edward Dumbauld, The Bill of Rights and What It Means Today 174–175, 183, 199 (1957). Rejection: 1 Annals of Congress 435–436 (June 8, 1789) and 789–790 (August 18, 1789); 1 Senate Journals 64, 73–74 (1820).

[3]Implied powers have been upheld in such cases as In re Neagle, 135 U.S. 1 (1890), which recognized the President's inherent authority to assign a U.S. marshal to protect a threatened federal judge, and In re Debs, 158 U.S. 1 (1895), supporting presidential use of military force to break a railroad strike.

States, 189 U.S. 311, 316 (1903). See also United States v. Midwest Oil Co., 236 U.S. 459, 469–471 (1915). Justice Frankfurter explained how executive power can grow when unchallenged: "A systematic, unbroken executive practice, long pursued to the knowledge of the Congress and never before questioned, engaged in by Presidents who have also sworn to uphold the Constitution, making as it were such exercise of power part of the structure of our government, may be treated as a gloss on 'executive Power' vested in the President by § 1 of Art. II." Youngstown Co. v. Sawyer, 343 U.S. 579, 610–611 (1952) (concurring opinion).[4]

CREATING THE EXECUTIVE DEPARTMENTS

The Constitution establishes only a shell for government. It was left to the First Congress, by statute, to create executive departments and federal courts. In so doing, it necessarily debated and decided a number of fundamental constitutional issues. At that time, there was neither a judiciary nor federal judicial precedents. From 1789 to the present, it has been primarily the responsibility of Congress to determine the structure of government, the powers and functions of agencies, limitations on the President's power to remove executive officials, and the qualifications of appointees.

Since each department had to be created by statute, the First Congress could have placed departments under a single individual or a board of commissioners. The experience under the Articles of Confederation convinced most legislators that the board system lacked responsibility, energy, and order. The House of Representatives in 1789 voted for single executives to head the departments. Congress treated the Secretary of Foreign Affairs and the Secretary of War as executive officials, which had been the practice under the Articles. In contrast, Congress regarded the Secretary of the Treasury partly as a *legislative* agent, reflecting the mixed record during the Articles when the duties shifted back and forth between a Superintendent of Finance and a Board of Treasury. The first Secretary of the Treasury, Alexander Hamilton, performed essentially as an arm of the President, not Congress, and so it has been ever since. Under President Andrew Jackson, Congress tried to treat the Secretary of the Treasury as a legislative agent. Jackson eventually prevailed in his argument that the Secretary is "wholly an executive officer," but he had to remove two Secretaries of the Treasury to effectuate his policy and was censured by the Senate for his action. Three years later the Senate ordered its resolution of censure expunged from the record. Louis Fisher, Constitutional Conflicts Between Congress and the President 67–68 (1985).

Some of the officers within the Treasury Department had duties that were not wholly executive in nature. During debate on the Department in 1789, Madison admitted that the comptroller's office "seemed to bear a strong affinity" to the legislative branch, while its settlement and adjustment of legal claims "partake too much of the Judicial capacity to be blended with the Executive." 1 Annals of Congress 613, 614 (June 29, 1789). When Congress created the General Accounting Office (GAO) in 1921, it transferred to it not merely the powers and duties of the

[4]The failure of Congress to repeal or revise a grant of statutory authority in the face of administrative interpretation has been held by the courts as "persuasive evidence" that the interpretation was intended by Congress. Zemel v. Rusk, 381 U.S. 1, 11 (1965). See also Dames & Moore v. Regan; 453 U.S. 654, 678–688 (1981); Norwegian Nitrogen Co. v. United States, 288 U.S. 294, 313 (1933); Costanzo v. Tillinghast, 287 U.S. 341, 345 (1932).

comptroller but even the personnel. GAO functions as a mixed agency. It is "legislative" when it audits accounts and investigates programs and "executive" when it approves payments and settles and adjusts accounts.[5]

This hybrid status was attacked by the Reagan administration in 1985 when it challenged the Comptroller General's authority to determine "bid protests." Disappointed bidders of government contracts could appeal to GAO and have the award of the contract delayed while GAO studied the dispute. The Justice Department regarded GAO as part of the legislative branch and therefore without authority to participate in executive duties. GAO's bid-protest powers were upheld in the lower courts.[6] The confrontation heightened at the end of 1985 when Congress passed the Gramm-Rudman-Hollings Act. The statue, which required federal deficits to decline to zero by fiscal 1991, authorized the Comptroller General under certain circumstances to order program cuts to be carried out by the President through a "sequestration" process. The administration claimed that Congress could not give executive duties to a legislative officer. The Supreme Court in 1986 agreed that the Comptroller General's sequestration duties were unconstitutional because Congress could not vest executive functions in an officer removable by Congress. BOWSHER v. SYNAR, 478 U.S. 714 (1986).

Another dispute concerns the President's authority to supervise the officers within the executive branch. A careless reading of the Constitution gives the President the power to execute the laws. In fact, he is to "take Care that the Laws be faithfully executed" (Article II, Section 3). What happens if a statute places the execution of a program outside his control? Does this violate the principle of responsibility and accountability vested in a single executive? The short answer is that the heads of executive departments function only in part as political agents of the President. They also perform legal duties assigned to them by Congress. In *Marbury* v. *Madison* (1803), Chief Justice Marshall distinguished between two types of duties for a Cabinet head: ministerial and discretionary. The first duty allows Congress to direct a Secretary to carry out certain activities. The second duty is owed to the President alone. When a Secretary performs the first duty he is bound to obey the laws: "He acts . . . under the authority of law, and not by the instructions of the president. It is a ministerial act which the law enjoins on a particular officer for a particular purpose." 5 U.S. (1 Cr.) 137, 157.

The concept of ministerial duties reappears in *Kendall* v. *United States*, 37 U.S. 522 (1838). Congress could mandate that certain payments be made, and neither the head of the executive department nor the President could deny or control these ministerial acts.[7] In 1854, the Attorney General stated that when laws "define what is to be done by a given head of department, and how he is to do it, there the President's discretion stops . . ." 6 Op. Att'y Gen. 326, 341. Opinions by Attorneys

---

[5]United States ex rel. Brookfield Const. Co., Inc. v. Stewart, 234 F.Supp. 94, 99–100 (D.D.C. 1964), aff'd, 339 F.2d 754 (D.C. Cir. 1964).

[6]See the case of Ameron, Inc. v. U.S. Army Corps of Engineers reported at 607 F.Supp. 962 (D. N.J. 1985); 610 F.Supp. 750 (D. N.J. 1985); 787 F.2d 875 (3d Cir. 1986); 809 F.2d 979 (3d Cir. 1986). The statute was also upheld in Lear Siegler, Inc. v. Lehman, 842 F.2d 1102 (9th Cir. 1988). In response to a Justice Department request, the Supreme Court agreed to dismiss its writ of certiorari. 109 S.Ct. 297 (1988).

[7]See also United States v. Schurz, 102 U.S. 378 (1880); United States v. Price, 116 U.S. 43 (1885); United States v. Louisville, 169 U.S. 249 (1898); and Clackamus County, Ore. v. McKay, 219 F.2d 479, 496 (D.C. Cir. 1954), vacated as moot, 349 U.S. 909 (1955).

General advised various Presidents of substantial political and legal constraints on their ability to intervene in certain departmental matters (pp. 251–253). The President is responsible for seeing that administrative officers faithfully perform their duties, "but the statutes regulate and prescribe these duties, and he has no more power to add to, or subtract from, the duties imposed upon subordinate executive and administrative officers by the law, than those officers have to add or subtract from his duties."[8] Departmental heads recognize the limitations that prevent them from interfering with decisions by administrative law judges (ALJ's). Nash v. Califano, 613 F.2d 10 (2d Cir. 1980).

Federal courts invoked the ministerial-discretionary distinction on a regular basis during the Nixon administration to force the release of impounded funds. Cabinet heads were ordered to allocate or obligate funds. Berends v. Butz, 357 F.Supp. 143 (D. Minn. 1973); Train v. City of New York, 420 U.S. 35 (1975). Statutory duties also apply to the President. In 1974, an appellate court held that President Nixon had violated the law by refusing to carry out a statute on federal pay. National Treasury Employees Union v. Nixon, 492 F.2d 587 (D.C. Cir. 1974).

APPOINTMENTS AND REMOVALS

Three steps are required to fill offices created by Congress: (1) nomination by the President, (2) confirmation by the Senate, and (3) commissioning of the appointee by the President. For lesser officers, the Constitution permits Congress to dispense with the confirmation process and place the power of appointment directly in the President, the courts, or department heads.

In legal theory, the power to nominate is the "sole act of the president" and "completely voluntary." Marbury v. Madison, 5 U.S. at 155. Congress cannot designate the person to fill the office it creates. United States v. Ferreira, 54 U.S. (13 How.) 39, 50–51 (1852); Myers v. United States, 272 U.S. at 128. Nevertheless, it can stipulate the qualifications of appointees, and legislators frequently select the names of judges, U.S. attorneys, and marshals for their state. In such cases the roles are reversed: Congress nominates and the President "advises and consents." If the names submitted by Congress are unacceptable, the White House and the Justice Department can object and request substitute proposals. Interest groups and professional organizations are also active in submitting names for consideration and evaluating those who are nominated.

There are limits to congressional intervention. In 1976, the Supreme Court reviewed a statute giving Congress the power to appoint four members to the Federal Election Commission, which monitors the financing and conduct of congressional and presidential elections. All six voting members (including two nominated by the President) required confirmation by the majority of *both* Houses of Congress. The Court ruled that Congress could not select officers responsible for carrying out executive and judicial duties. Such functions could be exercised only by "Officers of the United States" appointed pursuant to Article II, Section 2, Clause

---

[8] 19 Op. Att'y Gen. 685, 686–687 (1890). See also 1 Op. Att'y Gen. 624 (1823); 1 Op. Att'y Gen. 636 (1824); 1 Op. Att'y Gen. 678 (1824); 1 Op. Att'y Gen. 705 (1825); 1 Op. Att'y Gen. 706 (1825); 2 Op. Att'y Gen. 480 (1831); 2 Op. Att'y Gen. 507 (1832); 2 Op. Att'y Gen. 544 (1832); 4 Op. Att'y Gen. 515 (1846); 5 Op. Att'y Gen. 287 (1851); 10 Op. Att'y Gen. 526 (1863); 11 Op. Att'y Gen. 14 (1864); 13 Op. Att'y Gen. 28 (1869); 18 Op. Att'y Gen. 31 (1884).

2. For the Court, this meant either one of two constitutional options: nomination by the President, subject to the advice and consent of the Senate; or vesting the appointment power in the President alone, in the courts of law, or in department heads. Congress took the first option when it rewrote the statute. The decision explains how the appointment process is related to presidential responsibility and the separation doctrine. BUCKLEY v. VALEO, 424 U.S. 1 (1976).

The framers recognized that the Senate would not always be in session to give advice and consent to presidential nominations. To cover these periods, the President is authorized to make recess appointments: "The President shall have Power to fill up all Vacancies that may happen during the Recess of the Senate, by granting Commissions which shall expire at the End of their next Session" (Article II, Section 3, Clause 3). "Happen" is interpreted broadly to mean "happen to exist," even if a vacancy occurs while the Senate is in session. 1 Op. Att'y Gen. 631 (1823). The meaning of "recess" remains uncertain, although the Justice Department agrees that adjournments "for 5 or even 10 days" are too short to justify the use of the recess power. 3 Op. Att'y Gen. 20, 25 (1921); 3 O.L.C. 311, 314 (1979).

In 1863, when it appeared that Presidents were abusing the power to make recess appointments and were deliberately circumventing the Senate's confirmation role, Congress passed legislation to prohibit the use of funds to pay the salary of anyone appointed during a Senate recess to fill a vacancy that existed "while the Senate was in session and is by law required to be filled by and with the advice and consent of the Senate, until such appointee shall have been confirmed by the Senate." 12 Stat. 646 (1863). The law was liberalized in 1940 to permit payment under three conditions. 54 Stat. 751 (1940); 5 U.S.C. § 5503 (1982). Legislation has also been passed to prohibit funds to pay the salary of any recess appointee who is later rejected by the Senate. E.g., 93 Stat. 574, § 604 (1979); Fisher, Constitutional Conflicts 47–59.

Removing Officials

Although the Constitution provides no express authority for the President to remove officials in the executive branch, it was agreed by the First Congress that responsible government requires the President to dismiss incompetent, corrupt, or unreliable administrators. If anything by nature is executive, Madison said, "it must be that power which is employed in superintending and seeing that the laws are faithfully executed." 1 Annals of Congress 500 (June 17, 1789).

These debates of 1789 were interpreted by Chief Justice Taft to leave not the "slightest doubt" that the power to remove officers appointed by the President and confirmed by the Senate is "vested in the President alone." MYERS v. UNITED STATES, 272 U.S. at 114. Taft reached too far; the debates reveal deep divisions among House members and close votes on the Senate side. Fisher, Constitutional Conflicts 61–66. Moreover, the debates in 1789 focused on the President's power to remove the Secretary of Foreign Affairs, which Congress conceded to be an agent of the President and executive in nature. Madison anticipated other types of officers in the executive branch who might have a mix of legislative and judicial duties, requiring greater independence from the President. 1 Annals of Congress 611–614 (June 29, 1789). Congress can place statutory limitations on the removal power, and the Supreme Court had recognized, before Taft made his sweeping claim, that

Congress could identify the grounds for removal. Shurtleff v. United States, 189 U.S. 311 (1903).

A balance must be struck between the President's authority to remove executive officials and Congress' power under the Necessary and Proper Clause to create an office and attach conditions to it. Taft's decision was later modified to permit Congress to limit the President's power to remove commissioners with quasi-legislative and quasi-judicial powers. Humphrey's Executor v. United States, 295 U.S. 602 (1935); Wiener v. United States, 357 U.S. 349 (1958). Depending on statutory language or commitments by the President and his subordinates to maintain an officer's independence, presidential power to remove officers may face other constraints.[9]

Beyond the occasional lawsuit are the more frequent interventions by Congress. Congress may remove an individual by abolishing the office. A term of office created by one statute can be reduced or eliminated by a subsequent statute, requiring the discharge of a federal employee. Crenshaw v. United States, 134 U.S. 99 (1890). Through the passage of nonbinding resolutions, committee investigations, the contempt power, and other pressures, Congress can precipitate a person's resignation or removal. Congress also intervenes to *protect* an officeholder, particularly a "whistleblower" who alerts Congress to agency deficiencies. Members intervene for reasons of simple justice and to keep open the channels of communication between agencies and Congress. Louis Fisher, "Congress and the Removal Power," 10 Congress & the Presidency 63 (1983).

Following the scandals of the Watergate period, Congress passed legislation in 1978 to establish a "special prosecutor" with the authority to investigate wrongdoing by high-level executive branch officials. This official (later called "independent counsel") was made independent of the Attorney General. Congress concluded that the Attorney General, as a key member of the President's cabinet, might face a conflict of interest in prosecuting the suspected official. The statute authorizes a special panel of federal judges to appoint the independent counsel. To assure accountability, Congress provided that the independent counsel could be removed by the Attorney General only for causes specified in the statute. The bill was supported by the Justice Department and the American Bar Association.

During the latter part of the Reagan administration, however, the Justice Department maintained that the statute was unconstitutional because it vested part of law enforcement in an officer who was not appointed by the President. The Constitution authorizes Congress to place part of the appointment power in "the Courts of Law." The Supreme Court had upheld, in a case after the Civil War, the appointment by judges of supervisors of elections. Ex parte Siebold, 100 U.S. 371 (1880). In 1988, a federal appellate court ruled that the independent counsel violated the constitutional principle of separation of powers. The Supreme Court, however, upheld the statute. The extraordinary 7–1 majority opinion overwhelmingly rejects the Justice Department's theory that a "unitary Executive" must be responsible for all administrative matters. MORRISON v. OLSON, 108 S.Ct. 2597 (1988).

[9]Nader v. Bork, 366 F. Supp. 104 (D.D.C. 1973); Borders v. Reagan, 518 F.Supp. 250 (D.D.C. 1981); Stephen Gettinger, "The Power Struggle Over Federal Parole," 8 Corrections Magazine 41 (1982); Berry v. Reagan, Civil Action No. 83–3182 (D.D.C. November 14, 1983).

DELEGATION OF LEGISLATIVE POWER

The boundaries between the legislative and executive branches are further obscured by the large grants of power delegated by Congress. This delegation supposedly violates a fundamental principle, dating back to John Locke. The legislature "cannot transfer the power of making laws to any other hands, for it being but a delegated power from the people, they who have it cannot pass it over to others." John Locke, Second Treatise on Civil Government, § 141. This concept is embodied in the ancient maxim *delegata potestas non potest delegari* ("delegated power cannot be delegated").

This principle is essential to prevent Congress from delegating its legislative power to private groups. In 1936, the Supreme Court struck down a statute partly because it delegated power to representatives of the coal industry to set up a code of mandatory regulations. This was "legislative delegation in its most obnoxious form; for it is not even delegation to an official or an official body, presumptively disinterested, but to private persons whose interests may be and often are adverse to the interests of others in the same business." Carter v. Carter Coal Co., 298 U.S. 238, 311 (1936).

With the exception of two cases handed down in 1935, Panama Refining Co. v. Ryan, 293 U.S. 388 and Schechter Corp. v. United States, 295 U.S. 495, Congress has encountered little opposition from the courts in delegating legislative power to the President, executive agencies, and independent commissions. In sustaining these delegations, the judiciary typically waxes eloquent about the serious breach were Congress ever to transfer its legislative power to other parties, after which it finds a way to uphold the delegation. Field v. Clark, 143 U.S. 649, 692 (1891) and Hampton & Co. v. United States, 276 U.S. 394, 406 (1928).

The courts justify vast delegations of legislative power after satisfying themselves that the powers are confined either by congressional guidelines or procedural safeguards. Statutory guidelines are often absent, however, when Congress orders the Interstate Commerce Commission to protect the "public interest," directs the Federal Trade Commission to police "unfair methods of competition," supplies the standard of "public convenience, interest, or necessity" for the Federal Communications Commission, and requires the Securities and Exchange Commission to ensure that corporations do not "unduly or unnecessarily complicate the structure" or "unfairly or inequitably distribute voting power among security holders."[10]

The structure of these commissions supplies some built-in safeguards. They operate on a multimember (collegial) basis, rather than the system of single administrators selected for the executive departments. The collegial structure supplies a check on possible abuses. Moreover, the terms of commissioners are lengthy and staggered, serving to insulate them somewhat from presidential transitions and the pressure of biennial elections. Congress also limits the number of commissioners who may belong to the same political party and restricts the ability of the President to remove commissioners. Finally, standardless delegations have been

---

[10]The "public interest" guideline was upheld in ICC v. Goodrich Transit Co., 224 U.S. 194, 214–215 (1912), Intermountain Rate Cases, 234 U.S. 476, 486–488 (1914), Avent v. United States, 266 U.S. 127, 130 (1924), and N.Y. Central Securities Co. v. United States, 287 U.S. 12, 24–25 (1932). "Unfair method of competition" passed muster in FTC v. Gratz, 253 U.S. 421, 427–428 (1920), while "public convenience" survived judicial scrutiny in FCC v. Pottsville Broadcasting Co., 309 U.S. 134, 137–188 (1940). The SEC guideline was upheld in American Power Co. v. SEC, 329 U.S. 90, 104–106 (1946).

upheld when the accumulated customs of a regulated industry and the practices developed by states have served to narrow the discretion of a federal agency.[11]

Standardless delegations have also been upheld when the legislative history supplies guidelines for administrative action. A massive delegation of wage-price controls to President Nixon in 1970 was justified by guidelines placed in committee reports and the legislative history. A three-judge court claimed that whether legislative purposes are included in committee reports or the public law "is largely a matter of drafting style." Amalgamated Meat Cutters & Butcher Work. v. Connally, 337 F.Supp. 737, 750 (D.D.C. 1971)(three-judge court). However, agencies are not as tightly bound by legislative history and nonstatutory controls.

The two occasions on which the Supreme Court struck down a delegation of legislative authority to the President involved the National Industrial Recovery Act (NIRA), which authorized industrial and trade associations to draw up codes that minimized competition, raised prices, and restricted production. If the President found the codes unacceptable he could prescribe his own and enforce them as law. The Court held that Congress had failed to establish guidelines or congressional policy to control the President's actions. Although Justice Cardozo argued in the first decision that Congress had supplied adequate standards, in the second he exclaimed: "This is delegation running riot." SCHECHTER CORP. v. UNITED STATES, 295 U.S. at 553. The drafting of the NIRA was dominated by industries and trade associations; executive officials appeared to have little interest in constitutional questions or procedural safeguards. Peter H. Irons, The New Deal Lawyers 22–107 (1982).

During the course of this litigation, the Court discovered that the government had brought an indictment and taken an appeal only to learn, to its embarrassment, that the regulation justifying this action had been repealed by an executive order. Panama Refining Co. v. Ryan, 293 U.S. at 412–413. The House Judiciary Committee in 1935 condemned the "utter chaos" regarding the publication and distribution of administrative rules and pronouncements. H. Rept. No. 280, 74th Cong., 1st Sess. 1–2 (1935). Congress passed legislation that year to provide for publication in a "Federal Register" of all presidential and agency documents having the effect of law. 49 Stat. 500 (1935).

Other reforms are embodied in the Administrative Procedure Act (APA) of 1946, which establishes standards for agency rulemaking to assure fairness and openness. Agencies are required to give notice and a hearing before issuing a rule or regulation. Findings of fact are supplied for the record; procedures exist for appeal. Through such procedural standards Congress tries to eliminate or minimize the opportunity for executive caprice and arbitrariness. The APA relies on the doctrine of separated powers by prohibiting investigative or prosecuting personnel from participating in agency adjudications. 5 U.S.C. §§ 553–554 (1982).

Although the courts have permitted extensive delegations of legislative power, they are active in scrutinizing agency actions. Through the "hard look" doctrine, courts closely supervise the manner in which agencies exercise their delegated authority. Agencies are expected to maintain a rulemaking record that explains their methodology and chain of reasoning. State Farm Mutual Automobile Ins. Co. v. Dept. of Transportation, 680 F.2d 206 (D.C. Cir. 1982), aff'd sub nom. Motor

[11]Fahey v. Mallonee, 332 U.S. 245, 250, 253 (1947), concerning the Home Owners' Loan Act of 1933 and the Federal Home Loan Bank Board. For the various structure and political constraints that operate on the independent regulatory agencies, see Louis Fisher, The Politics of Shared Power 161–189 (1987).

Vehicles Manufacturers Assn. v. State Farm Mutual Automobile Ins. Co., 463 U.S. 29 (1983).

The standards for delegation need not be stricter when the power to tax is involved. Skinner v. Mid-America Pipeline Co., 109 S. Ct. 1726 (1989). Also in 1989, all nine Justices rejected a claim that Congress had delegated excessively in creating the U.S. Sentencing Commission. Mistretta v. United States, 109 S. Ct. 647 (1989).

Presidential Legislation

Agency regulations are not supposed to be a substitute for the general policymaking that Congress supplies in the form of a public law. 6 Op. Att'y Gen. 10 (1853). Agency rulemaking draws its authority from power granted directly or indirectly by Congress.[12] The situation is different when the President "legislates" by issuing executive orders and proclamations. Here the President draws not necessarily on statutory authority but on power he believes is his under the Constitution.

Executive orders and proclamations are subject to legislative and judicial controls. When Congress objected to an executive order used by President Nixon to rejuvenate the Subversive Activities Control Board, Congress used its power of the purse to prohibit the agency from using any funds to carry out the order. As a result, the agency eventually disappeared. Fisher, Constitutional Conflicts 131–133. The federal courts have also been active in declaring proclamations and executive orders illegal.[13]

The scope of presidential lawmaking is clearly evident in two executive orders issued by President Reagan. Executive orders 12291 and 12498 authorized the Office of Management and Budget to use cost-benefit formulas for reviewing agency regulations. The orders cover not only regulations issued by the agencies but also those still in the planning stage. The manner in which these orders have been implemented raises serious questions about their compliance with the Administrative Procedure Act and the risks of ex parte ("off the record") meetings between OMB officials and private industry.[14]

CONGRESSIONAL OVERSIGHT

Congress maintains control over delegated power through a variety of methods: the power to appropriate funds; changes in authorization language; reliance on nonstatutory controls; and different forms of the "legislative veto" (which retains some vitality even after the Supreme Court declared it unconstitutional in 1983). Another form of control, the power to investigate, is covered in the next section.

[12]Chrysler Corp. v. Brown, 441 U.S. 281, 306–308 (1979). See Lincoln Electric Co. v. Commissioner of Int. Rev., 190 F.2d 326, 330 (6th Cir. 1951); American Broadcasting Co. v. United States, 110 F.Supp. 374, 384 (S.D. N.Y. 1953), aff'd, 347 U.S. 284 (1954); and Independent Meat Packers Ass'n v. Butz, 526 F.2d 228, 234–236 (8th Cir. 1975), cert. denied, 424 U.S. 966 (1976).

[13]Independent Gasoline Marketers Council v. Duncan, 492 F.Supp. 614, 620–621 (D.D.C. 1980); Kaplan v. Johnson, 409 F.Supp. 190, 206 (N.D.Ill. 1976); Cole v. Young, 351 U.S. 536, 555 (1956); Youngstown Co. v. Sawyer, 343 U.S. 579 (1952); Schechter Corp. v. United States, 295 U.S. 495, 525–526 (1935); Panama Refining Co. v. Ryan, 295 U.S. 388, 433 (1935); United States v. Symonds, 120 U.S. 46 (1887); Little v. Barreme, 2 Cr. 170 (1804). See Louis Fisher, Constitutional Conflicts Between Congress and the President 125–139.

[14]Morton Rosenberg, "Beyond the Limits of Executive Power: Presidential Control of Agency Rulemaking Under Executive Order 12,291," 80 Mich. L. Rev. 193 (1981).

Power of the Purse

In Federalist 58, James Madison regarded the power of the purse as the "most complete and effectual weapon with which any constitution can arm the immediate representatives of the people, for obtaining a redress of every grievance, and for carrying into effect every just and salutary measure." Article I, Section 9, of the Constitution places this weapon squarely in the hands of Congress: "No Money shall be drawn from the Treasury, but in Consequence of Appropriations made by Law."

There are relatively few restrictions on this power of the purse. Congress cannot lawfully use its funding power to establish a religion.[15] It may not diminish the compensation of federal judges. It may neither increase nor decrease the compensation of the President during his term in office. It may not include language in appropriations bills to deny funds to named "subversives," for such legislative punishment is a bill of attainder prohibited by Article III, Section 3. United States v. Lovett, 328 U.S. 303 (1946); Blitz v. Donovan, 538 F.Supp. 1119 (D.D.C. 1982). A proviso in an appropriations bill may not interfere with the President's power to issue a pardon or prescribe for the judiciary the effect of a pardon. United States v. Klein, 13 Wall. 128 (1872); Hart v. United States, 118 U.S. 62 (1886).

For the most part, Congress may invoke the power of the purse to control almost every facet of executive activity. Appropriations can be lump-sum or itemized. If lump-sum (to give administrators discretion), congressional committees can insist on an informal veto over certain agency actions. Congress can attach "riders" to appropriations bills to prohibit the use of funds for specified purposes. Executive officials may object to "micromanagement" by legislators, but Congress has the constitutional authority to control administrative activity in minute detail.

Presidents share the power of the purse in several ways. The Budget and Accounting Act of 1921 gave the President authority to submit a national budget each year. Through this submission the President has an important means of setting the legislative agenda for Congress. Moreover, Presidents and their assistants are generally given a substantial amount of discretion in withholding funds (impoundment), transferring funds from one appropriation account to another, and "reprogramming" funds within an account. Louis Fisher, Presidential Spending Power (1975).

Changing Authorizations

With the exception of the offices of the President, the Vice President, and the Supreme Court, every other agency of government depends on Congress for its existence. In creating an agency, Congress determines its mission, structure, personnel, and ceilings for appropriations. It is for Congress to decide whether the agency has a permanent authorization or must return to Congress every year or every few years for reauthorization. Through its action on authorization bills, Congress can redirect agency activities, require reports to Congress, redefine missions, or reorganize the agency out of existence.

---

[15]U.S. Constitution, Amend. I; Flast v. Cohen, 392 U.S. 83, 104–105 (1968). However, plaintiffs who challenge federal assistance to religious institutions may be unable to establish standing as a litigant; Valley Forge College v. Americans United, 454 U.S. 464 (1982).

Nonstatutory Controls

Although agencies are subject to authorization and appropriation actions through public law, much of the congressional control is maintained outside the statutory process. Committee reports, committee hearings, correspondence from review committees, and other nonstatutory techniques allow Congress to monitor and direct agency activity without passing another public law. Because these controls are informal and not legally binding, the system functions on a "keep the faith" attitude. Agencies receive lump-sum funds and broad authority from Congress; in return they acquiesce to a multitude of nonstatutory controls. Agencies follow these controls for practical, not legal, reasons. Violation of congressional trust may result in budget cutbacks, restrictive statutory language, and line-item appropriations. Agencies may ignore nonstatutory controls but only "at the peril of strained relations with the Congress." 55 Comp. Gen. 307, 319, 325–326 (1975). See also 55 Comp. Gen. 812 (1976) and 1 O.L.C. 133 (1977).

Legislative Vetoes

During the 1930s, executive officials wanted to "make law" without passage of a statute. President Hoover obtained authority to reorganize the executive branch without having to submit a bill to Congress for hearings, amendments, and enactment by both Houses. Congress agreed only on the condition that either House could reject a reorganization plan by passing a resolution of disapproval. Through this accommodation was born the "legislative veto." Congress experimented with the one-House veto, the two-House veto (passage of a concurrent resolution), and even a committee veto. Fisher, Constitutional Conflicts 162–174.

This procedure obviously departs from the Presentment Clause in Article I, Section 7, which provides that "Every Order, Resolution, or Vote to which the Concurrence of the Senate and House of Representatives may be necessary (except on a question of Adjournment)" shall be presented to the President. Legislative vetoes are not presented to the President. President Hoover accepted the compromise because it simplified executive reorganization. This *quid pro quo* was extended to other areas, including immigration, arms sales, the war power, impoundment, and agency regulations. Eventually, the Justice Department and the White House decided that the bargain no longer favored the executive branch. A test case, involving an immigration statute, was soon on its way to the Supreme Court.

In the 1930s, the executive branch had prevailed upon Congress to delegate discretionary authority over the deportation of aliens. Congress agreed to allow the Attorney General to suspend deportations provided that the suspensions were subject to a one-House legislative veto. Congress exercised this power on numerous occasions. The test case arose in 1975 when the House of Representatives disapproved the suspension of deportation for six aliens. One of the aliens was Jagdish Rai Chadha. After exhausting his administrative remedies in the Immigration and Naturalization Service, he won a court victory in the Ninth Circuit in 1980. The Supreme Court granted certiorari and twice heard the case on oral argument.

In a sweeping decision handed down in 1983, the Supreme Court declared the legislative veto unconstitutional. All legislative vetoes were unconstitutional because they violated the Presentment Clause. In addition, the one-House veto was unconstitutional because it violated the principle of bicameralism (which requires action by both Houses). Chief Justice Burger, writing for the majority, said that whenever congressional action has the "purpose and effect of altering the legal rights, duties and relations of persons" outside the legislative branch, Congress must act through both Houses in a bill presented to the President. INS v. CHADHA, 462 U.S. 919 (1983).

The Court's opinion suffers from a number of deficiencies. It claimed that the convenience of the legislative veto could not overcome the framers' view that efficiency was not a primary objective or hallmark of democratic government, and yet the framers ranked efficiency highly. The Court also argued that the legislative veto threatened the independence of the President by evading his veto power, but Presidents encouraged the legislative veto to obtain greater authority. Under the legislative veto procedure, Congress could not amend a President's proposal. The general veto was therefore not needed for presidential self-defense. More important-ly, the decision did not, and could not, eliminate the conditions that gave rise to the legislative veto: the desire of executive officials for broad delegations of power, and the insistence of Congress that it control those delegations without having to pass another public law. The executive-legislative accommodations that prevailed before *Chadha* continue to exist, sometimes in forms that are indistinguishable from the legislative veto supposedly struck down by the Court (pp. 280–283).

INVESTIGATIONS AND EXECUTIVE PRIVILEGE

The impact of implied powers is nowhere more evident than in the struggle for information. Although the Constitution does not expressly give Congress the power to investigate, the Supreme Court in 1927 announced that a legislative body "cannot legislate wisely or effectively in the absence of information respecting the conditions which the legislation is intended to affect or change." McGrain v. Daugherty, 273 U.S. 135, 175. Similarly, the Constitution does not give the President the privilege of withholding information from Congress, and yet in 1974 the Court decided that the President's interest in withholding information to protect confidentiality with his advisers is implied in the Constitution: "to the extent this interest relates to the effective discharge of a President's powers, it is constitutionally based." United States v. Nixon, 418 U.S. 683, 711 (1974).

There is an inevitable collision when Congress attempts to carry out its investiga-tive function and the President invokes executive privilege. Which branch should surrender to the other? Major confrontations require some type of compromise, prodded by Congress' power to punish for contempt and the judiciary's ability to steer both branches toward an acceptable accommodation.

Congressional Investigations

Congress relies on its investigative power to enact legislation, to oversee the administration of programs, to inform the public, and to protect its integrity, dignity, reputation, and privileges. To enforce each of these responsibilities, Congress possesses an inherent power to punish for contempt. Anderson v. Dunn, 6 Wheat. 204 (1821). Congress may prefer to enforce its will through the courts. Failure of witnesses to appear before congressional committees or the refusal to answer pertinent questions can lead to indictment and conviction as a misdemean-or. 11 Stat. 155 (1857); 2 U.S.C. §§ 192–194 (1982). This law, as amended, was upheld in In re Chapman, 166 U.S. 661 (1897). Congress created a third option in 1978. If an individual from the private sector refuses to comply with a Senate subpoena (an order requiring certain action under threat of punishment), the Senate may request a court order to require compliance with the subpoena. Failure to obey the court order can lead to civil contempt. The sanction is lifted once the individual complies with the Senate's request. 28 U.S.C. § 1364 (1982).

Because of such spectacles as the McCarthy hearings of the 1950s, which deteriorated into a witch hunt for "subversives," congressional investigations are often associated with careless and damaging intrusions into personal lives. Most investigations, however, are conducted in a responsible manner and pose no threat to individual liberties or the separation of powers. In fact, congressional investigations often enhance individual liberties by challenging and exposing executive abuses.

Because of the adverse publicity from the 1950s, Congress adopted a set of procedures for committee investigations to assure fairness. The courts also insisted that committee hearings be properly authorized by Congress and their scope defined. United States v. Rumely, 345 U.S. 41 (1953); Gojack v. United States, 384 U.S. 702 (1966). Witnesses must be given adequate guidance in determining the pertinency of a question. WATKINS v. UNITED STATES, 354 U.S. 178 (1957). At times, the Court adopts a "balancing test" to permit the government's interest in self-preservation to outweigh the individual's right to remain silent. BARENBLATT v. UNITED STATES, 360 U.S. 109 (1959). Witnesses may invoke the Fifth Amendment privilege against self-incrimination. Quinn v. United States, 349 U.S. 155 (1955) and Emspak v. United States, 349 U.S. 190 (1955). An immunity procedure is available to displace the Fifth Amendment right. Witnesses may receive full immunity or partial immunity. Colonel Oliver North received the latter when he testified before the Iran-Contra hearings in 1987.[16]

The judiciary has attempted to place other restrictions on congressional investigations. In 1881, it struck down an investigation and a contempt action because the matter was already pending before a court. Kilbourn v. Thompson, 103 U.S. 168, 182. Such a doctrine would put congressional investigations on the back burner for years while awaiting the outcome of a lawsuit. Executive agencies could sidetrack an embarrassing committee hearing simply by filing suit and pursuing appeals. Congress may decide to defer its investigation until the completion of a criminal trial or refuse to wait for the results of long, drawn-out litigation. The latter course was followed during the Reagan administration when Congress investigated corruption within the Environmental Protection Agency. In such circumstances, Congress has the right to proceed, even at the cost of postponing a trial.[17]

Initially, the courts held that congressional investigations must relate to some legislative purpose. Congress should not conduct "fruitless" inquiries without the prospect of legislation. Kilbourn v. Thompson, 103 U.S. at 194–195. Later, however, the Court admitted that a "potential" for legislation is sufficient. McGrain v. Daugherty, 273 U.S. at 177. Even this is too restrictive a test. Committee efforts to

---

[16]18 U.S.C. §§ 6001–6005 (1982). The immunity procedure, as a substitute for the Fifth Amendment, was upheld in Ullmann v. United States, 350 U.S. 422 (1956); Kastigar v. United States, 406 U.S. 441 (1972); and Application of U.S. Senate Select Com. on Pres. Cam. Act., 361 F.Supp. 1270 (D.D.C. 1973).

[17]Delaney v. United States, 199 F.2d 107, 114–115 (1st Cir. 1952). See also Hutcheson v. United States, 369 U.S. 599, 612–613, 623–624 (1962), Sinclair v. United States, 279 U.S. 263, 295 (1929), and Fisher, Constitutional Conflicts 184–196.

oversee executive agencies may take researchers up "blind alleys" and into nonproductive enterprises: "To be a valid legislative inquiry there need be no predictable end result." Eastland v. United States Servicemen's Fund, 421 U.S. 491, 509 (1975). Attorney General William French Smith was misinformed in 1981 when he claimed that congressional requests for information were on stronger ground if Congress had specific legislation in mind than when it simply probed as part of a general oversight effort.[18]

Impeachment

The ultimate form of the investigative power is impeachment. The President, Vice President, and all civil officers of the United States shall be removed from office upon "Impeachment for, and Conviction of, Treason, Bribery, or other high Crimes and Misdemeanors" (Article II, Section 4). Treason is defined in Article III, Section 3, while bribery has a fairly clear statutory meaning. What constitutes "other high Crimes and Misdemeanors"? The framers rejected vague grounds for impeachment, such as "maladministration," because this would be equivalent to having the President serve at the pleasure of Congress. 3 Farrand 65–66, 550. However, impeachment need not require indictable crimes or specific statutory offenses. In Federalist 65, Alexander Hamilton included "political crimes" (abuses in office or violation of the public trust) as legitimate grounds for impeachment. Madison also supported impeachment for political abuses or neglect of office. 1 Annals of Congress 372–373 (May 19, 1789). The purpose of impeachment is to remove someone from office, not to punish for a crime. Impeachable conduct need not be criminal. That was the conclusion of the House Committee on the Judiciary during the impeachment proceedings of Richard Nixon.

Executive Privilege

President George Washington and his cabinet complied with a request by the House of Representatives in 1792 for papers regarding a military defeat, but also concluded that it would be appropriate in the future to refuse documents "the disclosure of which would injure the public." 1 Writings of Thomas Jefferson 303–305 (Mem. ed. 1903). In general, Presidents agree to make papers and documents available for impeachment inquiries or congressional investigations into administrative corruption. While upholding a very broad theory of executive privilege in 1982, Attorney General Smith said he would not try to "shield documents [from Congress] which contain evidence of criminal or unethical conduct by agency officials from proper review." H. Rept. No. 968, 97th Cong., 2d Sess. 41 (1982).

If executive officials refuse congressional requests for information, a move by Congress to cite the person for contempt is often an effective way to get the official's attention and cooperation. For example, in 1982 the House of Representatives voted 259 to 105 to hold Anne Gorsuch, administrator of the Environmental Protection Agency, in contempt. In an unprecedented action, the U.S. Attorney did not take the contempt citation to the grand jury, as required by statute. Instead, the administra-

---

[18]"Executive Privilege: Legal Opinions Regarding Claim of President Ronald Reagan in Response to a Subpoena Issued to James G. Watt, Secretary of the Interior," prepared for the use of the House Committee on Energy and Commerce, 97th Cong., 1st Sess. 3 (Comm. Print November 1981).

tion asked a district court to declare the House action an unconstitutional intrusion into the President's authority to withhold information from Congress. This tactic failed and the documents were released. United States v. House of Representatives, 556 F. Supp. 150 (D.D.C. 1963).

The major "executive privilege" case—*United States* v. *Nixon*—did not involve a congressional request for executive documents. The request came from the courts as part of the effort to prosecute Watergate crimes. A unanimous Court rejected the argument that the decision to release such documents is up to the President, not the courts. To permit Nixon absolute control over the documents would have prevented the judiciary from carrying out its duties. UNITED STATES v. NIXON, 418 U.S. 683 (1974).

Conflicts between the executive and legislative branches are sometimes resolved with the assistance of federal judges. A deadlock between a House committee and the Justice Department during the 1970s, regarding the release of "national security" information, was eventually broken through the efforts of Circuit Judge Harold Leventhal. He convinced each branch that a compromise worked out between them would be better than a solution dictated by the courts. Practical accommodations are required instead of rigid abstractions about the power of Congress to investigate or the power of the President to withhold information (pp. 297–301).

CONGRESSIONAL MEMBERSHIP AND PREROGATIVES

Under Article I, Section 5, each House of Congress "may determine the rules of its proceedings, punish its members for disorderly behavior, and, with the concurrence of two thirds, expel a member." Each House is also "the judge of the elections, returns and qualifications of its own members." Qualifications for office are set forth in Article I, Sections 2 and 3: age (25 for Representatives and 30 for Senators), citizenship (seven years for Representatives and nine years for Senators), and residency (members must be "inhabitants" of the state in which they are chosen). The custom is for Representatives to also reside in the district for which they are elected.

There have been occasions where the House of Representatives has refused to seat someone elected to office. A prominent example was Victor Berger of Wisconsin, a Socialist denied his seat in 1919 because he had been convicted for opposing World War I. A case that eventually reached the Supreme Court involved Adam Clayton Powell, a flamboyant black Congressman from New York. He was reelected in 1966 but the House refused to seat him, in part because of criminal proceedings against him. A special election was held but he won that also. Many observers thought that the issue was a political question to be decided solely by the House, but in 1969 the Supreme Court held that neither House could deny a seat to a duly elected member who satisfied the qualifications for office specified in the Constitution: age, citizenship, and residency. Congress could not add to that list of qualifications. Powell v. McCormack, 395 U.S. 486 (1969).

If the House wanted to exclude Powell, it had to first seat him and then expel him by the two-thirds majority required by the Constitution. Previously, the Court had held that the Georgia legislature had violated Julian Bond's First Amendment rights by refusing to seat him because he had expressed his opposition to the Vietnam war.

Bond v. Floyd, 385 U.S. 116 (1966). In addition to expulsion, Congress may censure a member for dishonorable or disreputable behavior.

Speech or Debate Clause

Article I, Section 6, provides that "for any Speech or Debate in either House," Senators and Representatives "shall not be questioned in any other Place." The courts have consistently held that the immunities offered by this Clause exist not simply for the personal or private benefit of members "but to protect the integrity of the legislative process by insuring the independence of individual legislators." United States v. Brewster, 408 U.S. 501, 507 (1972). It protects members from executive or judicial harassment. United States v. Johnson, 383 U.S. 177 (1966). The Clause covers not only words spoken in debate but anything required to conduct legislative business: remarks made in the course of committee hearings; speeches printed in the *Congressional Record,* even when not delivered; and information acquired by congressional staff.[19] Other activities, which the courts call "political" rather than "legislative," are not protected: contacts with executive agencies, assistance to constituents seeking federal contracts, the preparation of news releases and newsletters, and speeches or documents delivered outside the Congress.[20]

To protect its prerogatives, Congress has not hesitated to engage in direct confrontations with the judiciary. In 1970, the House Committee on Internal Security prepared a report entitled "Limited Survey of Honoraria Given Guest Speakers for Engagements at Colleges and Universities." By including the names of leftist or anti-war speakers and the amounts they received, the committee hoped that alumni would complain about the use of college funds and threaten to withhold future contributions. The ACLU obtained a copy of the galleys of the committee report and asked a federal judge to issue an injunction prohibiting its publication. U.S. District Judge Gesell did just that, ordering the Public Printer and the Superintendent of Documents not to print the report or even any "fascimile" of it. He suggested that Congress could print the report in the *Congressional Record* if it wanted to. Hentoff v. Ichord, 318 F.Supp. 1175 (D.D.C. 1970).

The House of Representatives responded with a resolution that told everyone, including the courts, to get out of the way. During debate on the resolution, it was pointed out that Congress does not print committee reports in the *Congressional Record.* Supporters of the resolution argued that Judge Gesell's order violated the Speech and Debate Clause and interfered with the authority of each House to determine the rules of its proceedings and to publish them. After the resolution passed by a large bipartisan margin of 302 to 54, the report was printed without any further judicial involvement. 116 Cong. Rec. 41358–374 (1970); H. Rept. No. 1732, 91st Cong., 2d Sess. (1970).

Article I, Section 6, also provides that members of Congress "shall in all cases, except treason, felony and breach of the peace, be privileged from arrest during

---

[19]Kilbourn v. Thompson, 103 U.S. 168, 204 (1881); Doe v. McMillan, 412 U.S. 306, 311–313 (1973) (committee hearings and reports); Hutchinson v. Proxmire, 433 U.S. 111, 116 n.3 (1979) (speeches in the Congressional Record); Tavoulareas v. Piro, 527 F.Supp. 676, 680 (D.D.C. 1981) and Gravel v. United States, 408 U.S. 606, 616–617 (1972) (congressional staff).

[20]United States v. Brewster, 408 U.S. at 513; Hutchinson v. Proxmire, 443 U.S. at 130–133.

their attendance at the session of their respective houses, and in going to and returning from the same." Immunity from arrest during sessions of the legislature can be traced back to struggles between the English Parliament and the King.

CONCLUSIONS

Most of the conflicts between Congress and the President are resolved through informal negotiations and accommodations. Rarely does an issue enter the judicial arena. When it does, the courts are reluctant to set hard-and-fast rules in such complex areas as executive privilege, delegation, and congressional investigations. An emphasis is placed on middle-ground remedies that protect the essential interests of each branch. Beyond the statutory framework agreed to by executive and legislative officials, the two branches have evolved an elaborate system of informal, nonstatutory agreements that satisfy the competing needs of executive flexibility and congressional control.

In recent decades, the Supreme Court has fluctuated between conflicting theories of separated powers. At times, it adopts a flexible, pragmatic model that tolerates an overlapping of powers. On other occasions, it embraces a rigid, formalistic view, announcing that the separation between the branches must be kept pure and immaculate. There is also substantial evidence that the Burger Court used a different methodology depending on the issue, resorting to fixed and original principles to strike down congressional actions but accepting executive actions as within the permissible bounds of an evolving, dynamic Constitution. The Rehnquist Court appears to be moving back to a pragmatic reading of the separation doctrine.[21]

Selected Readings

BARBER, SOTIRIOS A. *The Constitution and the Delegation of Congressional Power*. Chicago: University of Chicago Press, 1975.

BESSETTE, JOSEPH M., AND JEFFREY TULIS, eds. *The Presidency in the Constitutional Order*. Baton Rouge: Louisiana State University Press, 1981.

BRECKENRIDGE, ADAM CARLYLE. *The Executive Privilege*, Lincoln: University of Nebraska Press, 1974.

COOPER, PHILLIP J. "By Order of the President: Administration by Executive Order and Proclamation." 18 *Administration & Society* 233 (1986).

CRAIG, BARBARA HINKSON. *Chadha*. New York: Oxford University Press, 1988.

FISHER, LOUIS. *The Politics of Shared Power: Congress and the Executive*. Washington, D.C.: Congressional Quarterly, 1987.

——. *Constitutional Conflicts Between Congress and the President*. Princeton, N.J.: Princeton University Press, 1985.

GLENNON, MICHAEL J. "The Use of Custom in Resolving Separation of Powers Disputes." 64 *Boston University Law Review* 109 (1984).

GOLDWIN, ROBERT A, AND ART KAUFMAN, eds. *Separation of Powers—Does It Still Work?* Washington, D.C.: American Enterprise Institute, 1986.

GWYN, W. B. "The Meaning of Separation of Powers." *Tulane Series in Political Science*, Vol. IX (1965).

HAMILTON, JAMES. *The Power to Probe: A Study of Congressional Investigations*. New York: Random House, 1976.

HARRIS, JOSEPH P. *The Advice and Consent of the Senate: A Study of the Confirmation of Appointments*

[21]See Erwin Chermerinsky, "A Paradox Without a Principle: A Comment on the Burger Court's Jurisprudence in Separation of Powers Cases," 60 S.Cal. L.Rev. 1083 (1987). For two significant Rehnquist Court opinions, see the independent counsel case of Morrison v. Olson, 108 S.Ct. 2597 (1988) and the U.S. Sentencing Commission case of Mistretta v. United States, 109 S.Ct. 647 (1989). Flexible models were used by the Burger Court in United States v. Nixon, 418 U.S. 683 (1974) and Nixon v. Administrator of General Services, 433 U.S. 425 (1977). Rigid theories were presented in Northern Pipeline Co. v. Marathon Pipe Line Co., 458 U.S. 50 (1982); INS v. Chadha, 462 U.S. 919 (1983); and Bowsher v. Synar, 478 U.S. 714 (1986).

by the United States Senate. Berkeley: University of California Press, 1953.

KADEN, ALAN SCOTT. "Judicial Review of Executive Action in Domestic Affairs." 80 *Columbia Law Review* 1535 (1980).

KAISER, FREDERICK M. "Congressional Control of Executive Actions in the Aftermath of the *Chadha* Decision." 36 *Administrative Law Review* 239 (1984).

MCGOWAN, CARL "Congress, Court and Control of Delegated Powers." 77 *Columbia Law Review* 1119 (1977).

ROSENBERG, MORTON. "Beyond the Limits of Execu-

tive Power: Presidential Control of Agency Rulemaking Under Executive Order 12,291." 80 *Michigan Law Review* 193 (1981).

STATHIS, STEPHEN W. "Executive Cooperation: Presidential Recognition of the Investigative Authority of Congress and the Courts." 3 *Journal of Law & Politics* 183 (1986).

VILE, M.J.C. *Constitutionalism and the Separation of Powers.* London: Oxford University Press, 1967.

WINTERTON, GEORGE. "The Concept of Extra-Constitutional Executive Power in Domestic Affairs." 7 *Hastings Constitutional Law Quarterly* 1 (1979).

Congress Interprets the Ineligibility Clause

During debate in 1973, Congress interpreted the Ineligibility (or Emoluments) Clause, which provides that no Senator or Representative shall, during the time for which he is elected, be appointed to any civil office "the Emoluments whereof shall have been increased during such time." President Nixon intended to nominate Senator William Saxbe to be Attorney General. Because of the constitutional prohibition, legislation was introduced with the support of the administration. The debate is an excellent example of the choice between the literal language of the Constitution and going behind the language to determine the framers' intent. The debate below occurred in the Senate on November 28, 1973, and can be found at 119 Cong. Rec. 38315–38349. Senator Hiram Fong defended the bill; Senator Robert C. Byrd opposed it.

Mr. FONG. Mr. President, S. 2673 is a very simple bill. It merely sets the compensation and emoluments of the Office of Attorney General at that which existed on January 1, 1969. The proposed nomination of our colleague, Senator WILLIAM SAXBE, to the office of Attorney General has raised the question of the eligibility of a Member of Congress for appointment to a high executive office when the emoluments of that office have been increased during the term of the Member.

Senator SAXBE was elected a Senator from the State of Ohio. He took his oath January 4, 1969, and commenced his term of office. Prior thereto, Public Law 90–206, effective December 16, 1967, had been enacted. That bill set up a Commission on Executive, Legislative, and Judicial Salaries. The Commission, at 4-year intervals, recommends rates of pay for such officials. The President then

sets forth his recommendations in the next budget he submits to Congress. These recommendations become effective 30 days after transmittal of the budget, unless other rates are fixed by law or either House disapproves all or part of the President's recommendations.

The President transmitted to Congress on January 15, 1969, recommendations which included the increase of the salary of the Attorney General from $35,000 to $60,000 a year. On February 4, 1969, the Senate defeated Senate Resolution No. 82, which would have disapproved the Presidential recommendation. Senator SAXBE voted with the majority.

The pay raise, including that of the Attorney General, became effective shortly thereafter.

This is the increased emolument now making Senator SAXBE ineligible for appointment to the Office of Attorney General.

S. 2673 is designed to reduce the emolument of the Office of Attorney General to what it was at the time Senator SAXBE took office as Senator in 1969 and thus remove his ineligibility for appointment to that office.

. . .

Insofar as newly created offices are concerned, the consistent practice appears to have been to hold that a person is not eligible to hold such office until after the term for which he has been elected to Congress has expired—whether or not the individual occupied the congressional office at the time of his proposed nomination to any newly created "civil office under the authority of the United States".

2. APPOINTMENT TO OFFICE WHERE EMOLUMENT INCREASED

The relevant portion of the clause where an emolument has been increased states:

"No Senator or Representative shall, during the Time for which he was elected, be appointed to any civil Office under the Authority of the United States . . . the Emoluments whereof shall have been encreased during such time;" . . .

What has been permissible under this portion of this clause?

First, in 1871, Senator Morrill became the Senator from the State of Maine. In 1873, all cabinet officers were given a raise in salary from $8,000 to $10,000 a year. Under the Retrenchment Act, in 1874 the salary of all cabinet officers was returned to $8,000. In 1876 and "during the time for which he was elected," Senator Morrill's nomination to be Secretary of the Treasury was confirmed by the Senate. The proceedings, I understand, took about 6 minutes and there was no challenge to Senator Morrill's eligibility to serve as Secretary of the Treasury.

It should be pointed out that although the emolument of the office to which he was appointed had been increased, then decreased and that thereafter his confirmation took place "during the time for which he was elected," the emolument of the "civil office under the authority of the United States" to which he was appointed was, at the time of his appointment, not "encreased" over what it had been at the time he was elected.

. . . in 1904, Senator Knox was elected Senator from the State of Pennsylvania for a term ending March 1911. In 1907 the compensation of the Secretary of State had been increased from $8,000 to $12,000 a year. In 1909, President Taft announced that he intended to appoint Senator Knox as Secretary of State. As the situation then stood, Senator Knox was ineligible for appointment as the emolument of the office to which he was to be appointed was at a rate in excess of what it had been at the time he was elected, having "been encreased during such time" of his office.

Remedial legislation, similar to S.2673, the bill now under consideration, which Senator MCGEE and I introduced on November 9, 1973, was introduced to reduce the salary in question to what it had been when Senator Knox' term commenced and before the increase in emolument was approved. The constitutionality of the 1909 action was vigorously debated.

. . .

The bill passed the Senate without debate. After heated debate in the House, the bill passed by a vote of 178–123. The law became effective on March 4, 1909, 35 Stat. 626.

Thereafter, Senator Knox was nominated to the office of Secretary of State, at the reduced salary existent at the time he was elected to the Senate; was confirmed by the Senate; and served as Secretary of State.

. . .

Our precedents for the bill before us, S.2673, go back almost 100 years, to 1876 in the case of Senator Morrill and to 1909 in the case of Senator Knox.

In any event, as the Supreme Court stated in *Lake County* v. *Rollins,* 130 U.S. 662, 670 (1889) (a case involving an interpretation of a county debt ceiling limitation in a State constitution):

"The object of construction, applied to a constitution, is to give effect to the intent of its framers, and of the people in adopting it."

True, the opinion continued, at page 670:

"This intent is to be found in the instrument itself; and when the text of a constitutional provision is not ambiguous, the courts, in giving construction thereto, are not at liberty to search for its meaning beyond the instrument."

Nonetheless, we must remember that the Constitution does not have, nor should it have, the specificity of a statute.

As Chief Justice Marshall stated in *McCulloch* v. *Maryland*, 17 U.S. 316, 406 (1819):

"A constitution, to contain an accurate detail of all the subdivisions of which its great powers will admit, and of all the means by which they may be carried into execution, would partake of the prolixity of a legal code, and could scarcely be embraced by the human mind. . . . Its nature, therefore, requires, that only its great outlines should be marked, its important objects designated, and the minor ingredients which compose those objects be deduced from the nature of the objects themselves. . . . [W]e must never forget that it is a *constitution* we are expounding."

And, Chief Justice Marshall continued, at p. 406:

"Can we adopt that construction (unless the words imperiously require it), which would impute to the framers of that instrument, when granting [these] powers for the public good, the intention of impeding their exercise, by withholding a choice of means?"

. . .

The provision in question—that is article I, section 6, clause 2, insofar as the emolument provision is concerned, as I previously indicated, was intended mainly to prevent two evils:

First. To protect legislators from unscrupulous executives using the enticement of public office to influence the actions of the legislators, and

Second. To avoid legislators viewing their election to Congress as a stepping stone to lucrative public office and utilizing their positions in the legislature as a means of creating offices or increasing the compensation of the offices they seek.

This being so, clearly the intent was not to prevent able and qualified Members of Congress from taking civil office.

Surely, the action of this Congress in reducing the emolument of the office of Attorney General from $60,000 to $35,000 cannot be said to be corruptive of the Members of this Congress nor can it be said that Senator SAXBE used his $42,500 Senate office as a stepping stone to a $35,000 office of Attorney General.

. . .

The Senate continued with the consideration of the bill (S. 2673) to insure that the compensation and other emoluments attached to the Office of Attorney General are those which were in effect on January 1, 1969.

Mr. ROBERT C. BYRD. Mr. President, I yield myself such time as I may require.

The President of the United States has indicated his intention to nominate Senator WILLIAM SAXBE, our distinguished colleague from Ohio, to be Attorney General of the United States. The nomination raises a constitutional question as to whether Mr. SAXBE is eligible for appointment against the prohibition contained in article I, section 6, clause 2, of the Constitution.

. . .

On February 4, 1969, the Senate debated Senate Resolution 82, which would have disapproved the Presidential recommendation. The resolution was defeated; the pay raises, including that of the office of Attorney General, became effective shortly thereafter. Meanwhile, Mr. SAXBE'S term of office as a U.S. Senator had begun on January 3, 1969—about 6 weeks before the salary increase for the Attorney General became effective.

Hence, it seems clear beyond doubt that the proposed nomination of Mr. SAXBE, would fly squarely into the face of the prohibition contained in article 1, section 6, clause 2 of the Constitution —which says, I repeat:

"No Senator or Representative shall, during the time for which he was elected, be appointed to any civil office under the authority of the United States, which shall have been created, or the emoluments whereof shall have been increased during such time;" . . .

Clearly, the emoluments of the Office of Attorney General were increased from $35,000 to

$60,000 during the term for which Mr. SAXBE was elected—which term will not expire until January 3, 1975.

. . .

We, as legislators, have a responsibility to consider the constitutional aspects of the actions we take in the performance of our senatorial duties. We cannot be fully responsive to the high calling of our office by simply saying, "We will act to do thus and so; leave it to the courts to determine the constitutional rectitude of what we have done."

Ours is a higher duty. It is a duty that requires us—especially when great constitutional questions confront us in the first instance and on the first impression—to examine and to determine, according to our best lights, the constitutionality of actions we are called upon to take.

The nomination of Mr. SAXBE, under the circumstances peculiar to the nomination, fits almost squarely as a constitutional question heretofore essentially untested and unexplored.

Returning now to the matter before us: Can the constitutional bar be lifted by legislation? I say not.

Mr. President, the Constitution is a legal document. It is the organic law on which rests the foundation of this unique republic. Any law repugnant to the Constitution is void, and both courts and legislatures are bound by that instrument.

The process of constitutional interpretation is a process of determining the meaning of words. And the framers of the Constitution and the people who adopted it must be understood to have employed words in their natural, usual, and commonly understood sense, and to have intended what the words clearly say.

I submit that the words of article 1, section 6, clause 2, are clear, plain, simple, and easily understood by any citizen of this country.

. . .

Mr. FONG. Mr. President, we are not flouting the Constitution of the United States. We are not making one law for one man and another law for another man. We are trying to uphold the intent of the framers of the Constitution by the means provided by the Constitution.

What did the framers intend to accomplish by this article?

First, they sought to protect legislators from an unscrupulous executive using the enticement of office to influence their actions.

Second, they sought to prevent legislators from viewing their election to Congress as a stepping stone to lucrative office. They sought to prevent legislators from using their positions to create unnecessary offices or increase the compensation of offices they hope to attain.

Clearly, the intent was not to prevent able and qualified Members of Congress from taking civil office, but to make the legislature "as uncorrupt as possible."

This Congress in reducing the emolument of the Office of Attorney General from $60,000 to $35,000 cannot be said to be seeking to corrupt the Members of this Congress, nor can it be said that Senator SAXBE used his $42,500 Senate office as a stepping stone to a $35,000 Office of Attorney General.

[The Senate passed the bill, 75 to 16, and the House passed it on December 3. It became law on December 10, 1973 (P.L. 93–178, 87 Stat. 697)].

Constitutional Interpretations by the President in Signing Statements

When signing a bill into law, Presidents in recent years have adopted the practice of offering interpretations of various provisions in the bill that effectively amend the bill to bring about what the President and his advisers consider a constitutional result. Below is the statement by President Reagan on October 28, 1986, signing a federal debt collection bill.

I am pleased to approve S. 209, which authorizes the Attorney General to contract with private counsel in pilot program districts to collect debts owed the United States. I have been advised by the Department of Justice that two provisions of this bill raise constitutional questions. These provisions must, of course, be implemented consistent with the Constitution.

First, I am approving S. 209 knowing that the Attorney General will take all steps necessary to ensure that any contract entered into with private counsel contains provisions requiring ongoing supervision of the private counsel so that all fundamental decisions, including whether to initiate litigation and whether to settle or compromise a claim, are executed by an officer of the United States, as required by the Constitution.

Second, sections 3718 (b)(1)(B) and (b)(3) will require the Attorney General and all executive and legislative agencies to use their best efforts to assure that not less than 10 percent of all claims referred to private counsel will be referred to law firms owned and controlled by socially and economically disadvantaged individuals. I am signing this bill on the understanding that those objectives will be pursued in a race-neutral manner with respect to the actual award of contracts and that the criteria for identifying socially and economically disadvantaged contractors will not contain preferences or presumptions based on race or ethnicity. Implementation of these provisions in any other manner would be of doubtful constitutional validity because the goal is not premised on findings of actual discrimination in the granting of contracts. Moreover, even if such discrimination were established, any racial or ethnic preferences provided by these sections would not be narrowly tailored to remedy such discrimination. Thus, the authority of the Attorney General and the heads of agencies under this law must be read with these constitutional requirements in mind.

The very premise of America is equal opportunity without regard to irrelevant characteristics such as race. Therefore, all Americans, regardless of race, who seek one of these contracts must be allowed an equal chance to demonstrate social and economic disadvantage in order to obtain a contract.

Note: As enacted, S. 209 is Public Law 99–578, approved October 28.

Madison's Analysis of the Separation Doctrine

Some of the Anti-Federalists were astonished to find in the draft Constitution a variety of overlappings among the three branches of government: the President's power to veto legislation, the Senate's involvement in treaties and appointments, and other features of what we now call the system of checks and balances. In Federalist Nos. 37, 47, 48, and 51, James Madison refutes these objections by reviewing the British Constitution, the theory of Montesquieu, and the practices adopted by the American states, all for the purpose of demonstrating that checks and balances are necessary to give the three branches adequate power to resist encroachments.

FEDERALIST NO. 37

. . .

Not less arduous must have been the task of marking the proper line of partition between the authority of the general and that of the State governments. Every man will be sensible of this difficulty, in proportion as he has been accustomed to contemplate and discriminate objects extensive and complicated in their nature. The faculties of the mind itself have never yet been distinguished and defined, with satisfactory precision, by all the efforts of the most acute and metaphysical philosophers. Sense, perception, judgment, desire, volition, memory, imagination, are found to be separated by such delicate shades and minute gradations that their boundaries have eluded the most subtle investigations, and remain a pregnant source of ingenious disquisition and controversy. The boundaries between the great kingdoms of nature, and, still more, between the various provinces, and lesser portions, into which they are subdivided, afford another illustration of the same important truth. The most sagacious and laborious naturalists have never yet succeeded in tracing with certainty the line which separates the district of vegetable life from the neighboring region of unorganized matter, or which marks the termination of the former and the commencement of the animal empire. A still greater obscurity lies in the distinctive characters by which the objects in each of these great departments of nature have been arranged and assorted.

When we pass from the works of nature, in which all the delineations are perfectly accurate, and appear to be otherwise only from the imperfection of the eye which surveys them, to the institutions of man, in which the obscurity arises as well from the object itself as from the organ by which it is contemplated, we must perceive the necessity of moderating still further our expectations and hopes from the efforts of human sagacity. Experience has instructed us that no skill in the science of government has yet been able to discriminate and define, with sufficient certainty, its three great provinces—the legislative, executive, and judiciary; or even the privileges and powers of the different legislative branches. Questions daily occur in the course of practice, which prove the obscurity which reigns in these subjects, and which puzzle the greatest adepts in political science.

. . . Besides the obscurity arising from the complexity of objects, and the imperfection of the human faculties, the medium through which the conceptions of men are conveyed to each other adds a fresh embarrassment. The use of words is to express ideas. Perspicuity, therefore, requires not only that the ideas should be distinctly formed, but that they should be expressed by words distinctly and exclusively appropriate to them. But no language is so copious as to supply words and phrases for every complex idea, or so correct as

not to include many equivocally denoting different ideas. Hence it must happen that however accurately objects may be discriminated in themselves, and however accurately the discrimination may be considered, the definition of them may be rendered inaccurate by the inaccuracy of the terms in which it is delivered. And this unavoidable inaccuracy must be greater or less, according to the complexity and novelty of the objects defined. When the Almighty himself condescends to address mankind in their own language, his meaning, luminous as it must be, is rendered dim and doubtful by the cloudy medium through which it is communicated.

. . .

FEDERALIST NO. 47

Having reviewed the general form of the proposed government and the general mass of power allotted to it, I proceed to examine the particular structure of this government, and the distribution of this mass of power among its constituent parts.

One of the principal objections inculcated by the more respectable adversaries to the Constitution, is its supposed violation of the political maxim, that the legislative, executive, and judiciary departments ought to be separate and distinct. In the structure of the federal government, no regard, it is said, seems to have been paid to this essential precaution in favor of liberty. The several departments of power are distributed and blended in such a manner as at once to destroy all symmetry and beauty of form, and to expose some of the essential parts of the edifice to the danger of being crushed by the disproportionate weight of other parts.

No political truth is certainly of greater intrinsic value, or is stamped with the authority of more enlightened patrons of liberty, than that on which the objection is founded. The accumulation of all powers, legislative, executive, and judiciary, in the same hands, whether of one, a few, or many, and whether hereditary, self-appointed, or elective, may justly be pronounced the very definition of tyranny. Were the federal Constitution, therefore, really chargeable with the accumulation of power, or with a mixture of powers, having a dangerous tendency to such an accumulation, no further arguments would be necessary to inspire a universal reprobation of the system. I persuade myself, however, that it will be made apparent to every one, that the charge cannot be supported, and that the maxim on which it relies has been totally misconceived and misapplied. In order to form correct ideas on this important subject, it will be proper to investigate the sense in which the preservation of liberty requires that the three great departments of power should be separate and distinct.

The oracle who is always consulted and cited on this subject is the celebrated Montesquieu. If he be not the author of this invaluable precept in the science of politics, he has the merit at least of displaying and recommending it most effectually to the attention of mankind. Let us endeavor, in the first place, to ascertain his meaning on this point.

The British Constitution was to Montesquieu what Homer has been to the didactic writers on epic poetry. As the latter have considered the work of the immortal bard as the perfect model from which the principles and rules of the epic art were to be drawn, and by which all similar works were to be judged, so this great political critic appears to have viewed the Constitution of England as the standard, or to use his own expression, as the mirror of political liberty; and to have delivered, in the form of elementary truths, the several characteristic principles of that particular system. That we may be sure, then, not to mistake his meaning in this case, let us recur to the source from which the maxim was drawn.

On the slightest view of the British Constitution, we must perceive that the legislative, executive, and judiciary departments are by no means totally separate and distinct from each other. The executive magistrate forms an integral part of the legislative authority. He alone has the prerogative of making treaties with foreign sovereigns, which, when made, have, under certain limitations, the force of legislative acts. All the members of the judiciary department are appointed by him, can be removed by him on the address of the two Houses of Parliament, and form, when he pleases to consult them, one of his constitutional councils. One branch of the legislative department forms

also a great constitutional council to the executive chief, as, on another hand, it is the sole depositary of judicial power in cases of impeachment, and is invested with the supreme appellate jurisdiction in all other cases. The judges, again, are so far connected with the legislative department as often to attend and participate in its deliberations, though not admitted to a legislative vote.

From these facts, by which Montesquieu was guided, it may clearly be inferred that, in saying "There can be no liberty where the legislative and executive powers are united in the same person, or body of magistrates," or, "if the power of judging be not separated from the legislative and executive powers," he did not mean that these departments ought to have no *partial agency* in, or no *control* over, the acts of each other. His meaning, as his own words import, and still more conclusively as illustrated by the example in his eye, can amount to no more than this, that where the *whole* power of one department is exercised by the same hands which possess the *whole* power of another department, the fundamental principles of a free constitution are subverted. . . .

If we look into the constitutions of the several States, we find that, notwithstanding the emphatical and, in some instances, the unqualified terms in which this axiom has been laid down, there is not a single instance in which the several departments of power have been kept absolutely separate and distinct.

[Here Madison proceeds, state by state, to explain how the state constitutions mix the three powers of government.]

FEDERALIST NO. 48

It was shown in the last paper that the political apothegm there examined does not require that the legislative, executive, and judiciary departments should be wholly unconnected with each other. I shall undertake, in the next place, to show that unless these departments be so far connected and blended as to give to each a constitutional control over the others, the degree of separation which the maxim requires, as essential to a free government, can never in practice be duly maintained.

It is agreed on all sides, that the powers properly belonging to one of the departments ought not to be directly and completely administered by either of the other departments. It is equally evident, that none of them ought to possess, directly or indirectly, an overruling influence over the others, in the administration of their respective powers. It will not be denied, that power is of an encroaching nature, and that it ought to be effectually restrained from passing the limits assigned to it. After discriminating, therefore, in theory, the several classes of power, as they may in their nature be legislative, executive, or judiciary, the next and most difficult task is to provide some practical security for each, against the invasion of the others. What this security ought to be, is the great problem to be solved.

Will it be sufficient to mark, with precision, the boundaries of these departments, in the constitution of the government, and to trust to these parchment barriers against the encroaching spirit of power? This is the security which appears to have been principally relied on by the compilers of most of the American constitutions. But experience assures us, that the efficacy of the provision has been greatly overrated; and that some more adequate defence is indispensably necessary for the more feeble, against the more powerful, members of the government. The legislative department is everywhere extending the sphere of its activity, and drawing all power into its impetuous vortex.

The founders of our republics have so much merit for the wisdom which they have displayed, that no task can be less pleasing than that of pointing out the errors into which they have fallen. A respect for truth, however, obliges us to remark, that they seem never for a moment to have turned their eyes from the danger to liberty from the overgrown and all-grasping prerogative of an hereditary magistrate, supported and fortified by an hereditary branch of the legislative authority. They seem never to have recollected the danger from legislative usurpations, which, by assembling all power in the same hands, must lead to the same tyranny as is threatened by executive usurpations.

In a government where numerous and extensive prerogatives are placed in the hands of an hereditary monarch, the executive department is very justly regarded as the source of danger, and watched with all the jealousy which a zeal for liberty ought to inspire. In a democracy, where a multitude of people exercise in person the legislative functions, and are continually exposed, by their incapacity for regular deliberation and concerted measures, to the ambitious intrigues of their executive magistrates, tyranny may well be apprehended, on some favorable emergency, to start up in the same quarter. But in a representative republic, where the executive magistracy is carefully limited, both in the extent and the duration of its power; and where the legislative power is exercised by an assembly, which is inspired, by a supposed influence over the people, with an intrepid confidence in its own strength; which is sufficiently numerous to feel all the passions which actuate a multitude, yet not so numerous as to be incapable of pursuing the objects of its passions, by means which reason prescribes; it is against the enterprising ambition of this department that the people ought to indulge all their jealousy and exhaust all their precautions.

The legislative department derives a superiority in our governments from other circumstances. Its constitutional powers being at once more extensive, and less susceptible of precise limits, it can, with the greater facility, mask, under complicated and indirect measures, the encroachments which it makes on the coördinate departments. It is not unfrequently a question of real nicety in legislative bodies, whether the operation of a particular measure will, or will not, extend beyond the legislative sphere. On the other side, the executive power being restrained within a narrower compass, and being more simple in its nature, and the judiciary being described by landmarks still less uncertain, projects of usurpation by either of these departments would immediately betray and defeat themselves. Nor is this all: the legislative department alone has access to the pockets of the people, and has in some constitutions full discretion, and in all a prevailing influence, over the pecuniary rewards of those who fill the other departments, a dependence is thus created in the latter, which gives still greater facility to encroachments of the former.

[Starting with Virginia, Madison details various examples of legislative usurpations of executive and judicial power. He also cites instances of executive encroachments.]

The conclusion which I am warranted in drawing from these observations is, that a mere demarcation on parchment of the constitutional limits of the several departments, is not a sufficient guard against those encroachments which lead to a tyrannical concentration of all the powers of government in the same hands.

FEDERALIST NO. 51

To what expedient, then, shall we finally resort, for maintaining in practice the necessary partition of power among the several departments, as laid down in the Constitution? The only answer that can be given is, that as all these exterior provisions are found to be inadequate, the defect must be supplied, by so contriving the interior structure of the government as that its several constituent parts may, by their mutual relations, be the means of keeping each other in their proper places. Without presuming to undertake a full development of this important idea, I will hazard a few general observations, which may perhaps place it in a clearer light, and enable us to form a more correct judgment of the principles and structure of the government planned by the convention.

In order to lay a due foundation for that separate and distinct exercise of the different powers of government, which to a certain extent is admitted on all hands to be essential to the preservation of liberty, it is evident that each department should have a will of its own; and consequently should be so constituted that the members of each should have as little agency as possible in the appointment of the members of the others. Were this principle rigorously adhered to, it would require that all the appointments for the supreme executive, legislative, and judiciary magistracies should be drawn from the same fountain of authority, the people, through channels having no communication whatever with one another. Perhaps such a plan of constructing the several departments would be less difficult in practice than it may in contemplation appear. Some difficulties, however, and some additional expense would attend the execution of it. Some deviations, therefore, from the principle must be admitted. In the constitution of the judiciary department in particular, it might be inexpedient to insist rigorously on the principle: first, because peculiar qualifications being essential in the members, the primary consideration ought to be to select that mode of choice which best secures these qualifications; secondly, because the permanent tenure by which the appointments are held in that department, must soon destroy all sense of dependence on the authority conferring them.

It is equally evident, that the members of each department should be as little dependent as possible on those of the others, for the emoluments annexed to their offices. Were the executive magistrate, or the judges, not independent of the legislature in this particular, their independence in every other would be merely nominal.

But the great security against a gradual concentration of the several powers in the same department, consists in giving to those who administer each department the necessary constitutional means and personal motives to resist encroachments of the others. The provision for defence must in this, as in all other cases, be made commensurate to the danger of attack. Ambition must be made to counteract ambition. The interest of the man must be connected with the constitutional rights of the place. It may be a reflection on human nature, that such devices should be necessary to control the abuses of government. But what is government itself, but the greatest of all reflections on human nature? If men were angels, no government would be necessary. If angels were to govern men, neither external nor internal controls on government would be necessary. In framing a government which is to be administered by men over men, the great difficulty lies in this: you must first enable the government to control the governed; and in the next place oblige it to control itself. A dependence on the people is, no doubt, the primary control on the government; but experience has taught mankind the necessity of auxiliary precautions.

. . .

But it is not possible to give to each department an equal power of self-defence. In republican government, the legislative authority necessarily predominates. The remedy for this inconveniency is to divide the legislature into different branches; and to render them, by different modes of election and different principles of action, as little connected with each other as the nature of their common functions and their common dependence on the society will admit. . . .

Bowsher v. Synar

478 U.S. 714 (1986)

In an effort to gain control over the budget deficits that had mushroomed during the Reagan administration, Congress passed the Gramm-Rudman-Hollings Act in 1985. The statute established a multiyear schedule designed to bring the federal deficit to zero by 1991. If Congress and the President failed to abide by the statutory schedule, automatic cuts (called "sequestration") would occur. Under the sequestration process, the Comptroller General would receive budget estimates from the Office of Management and Budget (OMB) and the Congressional Budget Office (CBO) and proceed to draft the sequestration order, to be signed and issued by the President without change. The principal constitutional question was whether Congress could use the Comptroller General, generally thought to be within the legislative branch, to play a role in the execution of the laws. A three-judge federal court in 1986 held that the statute was unconstitutional as a violation of the separation of powers doctrine because the Comptroller General is removable only by a joint resolution initiated by Congress or by impeachment. Congressman Mike Synar initiated the suit, attacking the constitutionality of Gramm-Rudman. One of the defendants was Charles A. Bowsher, the Comptroller General.

Chief Justice BURGER delivered the opinion of the Court.

The question presented by these appeals is whether the assignment by Congress to the Comptroller General of the United States of certain functions under the Balanced Budget and Emergency Deficit Control Act of 1985 violates the doctrine of separation of powers.

I

A

On December 12, 1985, the President signed into law the Balanced Budget and Emergency Deficit Control Act of 1985, Pub.L. 99–177, 99 Stat. 1038, 2 U.S.C.A. § 901 *et seq.* (Supp.1986), popularly known as the "Gramm-Rudman-Hollings Act." The purpose of the Act is to eliminate the federal budget deficit. To that end, the Act sets a "maximum deficit amount" for federal spending for each of fiscal years 1986 through 1991. The size of that maximum deficit amount progressively reduces to zero in fiscal year 1991. If in any fiscal year the federal budget deficit exceeds the maximum deficit amount by more than a specified sum, the Act requires across-the-board cuts in federal spending to reach the targeted deficit level, with half of the cuts made to defense programs and the other half made to non-defense programs. The Act exempts certain priority programs from these cuts. § 255.

These "automatic" reductions are accomplished through a rather complicated procedure, spelled out in § 251, the so-called "reporting provisions" of the Act. Each year, the Directors of the Office of Management and Budget (OMB) and the Congressional Budget Office (CBO) independently estimate the amount of the federal budget deficit for the upcoming fiscal year. If that deficit exceeds the maximum targeted deficit amount for that fiscal year by more than a specified amount, the Directors of OMB and CBO independently calculate, on a program-by-program basis, the budget reductions necessary to ensure that the deficit does not exceed the maximum deficit amount. The Act then requires the Directors to report jointly their deficit estimates and budget reduction calculations to the Comptroller General.

The Comptroller General, after reviewing the Directors' reports, then reports his conclusions to the President. § 251(b). The President in turn must issue a "sequestration" order mandating the spending reductions specified by the Comptroller General. § 252. There follows a period during which Congress may by legislation reduce spending to obviate, in whole or in part, the need for the sequestration order. If such reductions are not enacted, the sequestration order becomes effective and the spending reductions included in that order are made.

Anticipating constitutional challenge to these procedures, the Act also contains a "fallback" deficit reduction process to take effect "[i]n the event that any of the reporting procedures described in section 251 are invalidated." § 274(f). Under these provisions, the report prepared by the Directors of OMB and the CBO is submitted directly to a specially-created Temporary Joint Committee on Deficit Reduction, which must report in five days to both Houses a joint resolution setting forth the content of the Directors' report. Congress then must vote on the resolution under special rules, which render amendments out of order. If the resolution is passed and signed by the President, it then serves as the basis for a Presidential sequestration order.

B

Within hours of the President's signing of the Act, Congressman Synar, who had voted against the Act, filed a complaint seeking declaratory relief that the Act was unconstitutional. Eleven other Members later joined Congressman Synar's suit. A virtually identical lawsuit was also filed by the National Treasury Employees Union. The Union alleged that its members had been injured as a result of the Act's automatic spending reduction provisions, which have suspended certain cost-of-living benefit increases to the Union's members.

A three-judge District Court, appointed pursuant to 2 U.S.C.A. § 922(a)(5) (Supp. 1986), invalidated the reporting provisions. *Synar* v. *United States*, 626 F.Supp. 1374 (DC 1986) (Scalia, Johnson, Gasch, JJ.).

. . .

II

A threshold issue is whether the Members of Congress, members of the National Treasury Employees Union, or the Union itself have standing to challenge the constitutionality of the Act in question. It is clear that members of the Union, one of whom is an appellee here, will sustain injury by not receiving a scheduled increase in benefits. See § 252(a)(6)(C)(i); 626 F.Supp., at 1381. This is sufficient to confer standing under § 274(a)(2) and Article III. We therefore need not consider the standing issue as to the Union or Members of Congress. . . . Accordingly, we turn to the merits of the case.

III

We noted recently that "[t]he Constitution sought to divide the delegated powers of the new Federal Government into three defined categories, Legislative, Executive, and Judicial." *INS* v. *Chadha*, 462 U.S. 919, 951 (1983). The declared purpose of separating and dividing the powers of government, of course, was to "diffus[e] power the better to secure liberty." *Youngstown Sheet & Tube Co.* v. *Sawyer*, 343 U.S. 579, 635 (1952) (Jackson, J., concurring). Justice Jackson's words echo the famous warning of Montesquieu, quoted by James Madison in The Federalist No. 47, that " 'there can be no liberty where the legislative and executive powers are united in the same person, or body of magistrates'. . . ." The Federalist No. 47, p. 325 (J. Cooke ed. 1961).

. . .

The Constitution does not contemplate an active role for Congress in the supervision of officers charged with the execution of the laws it enacts. The President appoints "Officers of the United States" with the "Advice and Consent of the

Senate. . . . " Article II, § 2. Once the appointment has been made and confirmed, however, the Constitution explicitly provides for removal of Officers of the United States by Congress only upon impeachment by the House of Representatives and conviction by the Senate. An impeachment by the House and trial by the Senate can rest only on "Treason, Bribery or other high Crimes and Misdemeanors." Article II, § 4. A direct congressional role in the removal of officers charged with the execution of the laws beyond this limited one is inconsistent with separation of powers.

This was made clear in debate in the First Congress in 1789. . . .

[The Court summarizes the holdings in Myers v. United States, 272 U.S. 52 (1926), Humphrey's Executor v. United States, 295 U.S. 602 (1935), and Weiner v. United States, 357 U.S. 349 (1958).]

In light of these precedents, we conclude that Congress cannot reserve for itself the power of removal of an officer charged with the execution of the laws except by impeachment. To permit the execution of the laws to be vested in an officer answerable only to Congress would, in practical terms, reserve in Congress control over the execution of the laws. As the District Court observed, "Once an officer is appointed, it is only the authority that can remove him, and not the authority that appointed him, that he must fear and, in the performance of his functions, obey." 626 F.Supp., at 1401. The structure of the Constitution does not permit Congress to execute the laws; it follows that Congress cannot grant to an officer under its control what it does not possess.

Our decision in INS v. Chadha, 462 U.S. 919 (1983), supports this conclusion. In Chadha, we struck down a one house "legislative veto" provision by which each House of Congress retained the power to reverse a decision Congress had expressly authorized the Attorney General to make:

"Disagreement with the Attorney General's decision on Chadha's deportation—that is, Congress' decision to deport Chadha—no less than Congress' original choice to delegate to the Attorney General the authority to make that decision,

involves determinations of policy that Congress can implement in only one way; bicameral passage followed by presentment to the President. Congress must abide by its delegation of authority until that delegation is legislatively altered or revoked." Id., at 954–955.

To permit an officer controlled by Congress to execute the laws would be, in essence, to permit a congressional veto. Congress could simply remove, or threaten to remove, an officer for executing the laws in any fashion found to be unsatisfactory to Congress. This kind of congressional control over the execution of the laws, Chadha makes clear, is constitutionally impermissible.

. . .

IV

Appellants urge that the Comptroller General performs his duties independently and is not subservient to Congress. We agree with the District Court that this contention does not bear close scrutiny.

The critical factor lies in the provisions of the statute defining the Comptroller General's office relating to removability. Although the Comptroller General is nominated by the President from a list of three individuals recommended by the Speaker of the House of Representatives and the President pro tempore of the Senate, see 31 U.S.C. § 703(a)(2), and confirmed by the Senate, he is removable only at the initiative of Congress. He may be removed not only by impeachment but also by Joint Resolution of Congress "at any time" resting on any one of the following bases:

"(i) permanent disability;
"(ii) inefficiency;
"(iii) neglect of duty;
"(iv) malfeasance; or
"(v) a felony or conduct involving moral turpitude." 31 U.S.C. § 703(e)(1).

. . .

. . . The statute permits removal for "inefficiency," "neglect of duty," or "malfeasance." These terms are very broad and, as interpreted by Congress, could sustain removal of a Comptroller General for any number of actual or perceived transgressions of the legislative will. . . .

. . . In constitutional terms, the removal powers over the Comptroller General's office dictate that he will be subservient to Congress.

. . .

Against this background, we see no escape from the conclusion that, because Congress had retained removal authority over the Comptroller General, he may not be entrusted with executive powers. The remaining question is whether the Comptroller General has been assigned such powers in the Balanced Budget and Emergency Deficit Control Act of 1985.

V

The primary responsibility of the Comptroller General under the instant Act is the preparation of a "report." This report must contain detailed estimates of projected federal revenues and expenditures. The report must also specify the reductions, if any, necessary to reduce the deficit to the target for the appropriate fiscal year. The reductions must be set forth on a program-by-program basis.

. . .

. . . we view these functions as plainly entailing execution of the law in constitutional terms. Interpreting a law enacted by Congress to implement the legislative mandate is the very essence of "execution" of the law. Under § 251, the Comptroller General must exercise judgment concerning facts that affect the application of the Act. He must also interpret the provisions of the Act to determine precisely what budgetary calculations are required. Decisions of that kind are typically made by officers charged with executing a statute. . . . as Chadha makes clear, once Congress makes its choice in enacting legislation, its participation ends. Congress can thereafter control the execution of its enactment only indirectly—by passing new legislation. Chadha, 462 U.S., at 958. By placing the responsibility for execution of the Balanced Budget and Emergency Deficit Control

Act in the hands of an officer who is subject to removal only by itself, Congress in effect has retained control over the execution of the Act and has intruded into the executive function. The Constitution does not permit such intrusion.

VI

[Appellants argued that rather than strike down the sequestration powers of the Comptroller General, the Court should nullify the provision of the Budget and Accounting Act of 1921 giving Congress authority to remove the Comptroller General. The Court rejected this option, concluding that this might make the Comptroller General subservient to the President, a result not intended by Congress.]

VII

No one can doubt that Congress and the President are confronted with fiscal and economic problems of unprecedented magnitude, but "the fact that a given law or procedure is efficient, convenient, and useful in facilitating functions of government, standing alone, will not save it if it is contrary to the Constitution. Convenience and efficiency are not the primary objectives—or the hallmarks—of democratic government . . ." Chadha, supra, 462 U.S., at 944.

We conclude the District Court correctly held that the powers vested in the Comptroller General under § 251 violate the command of the Constitution that the Congress play no direct role in the execution of the laws. Accordingly, the judgment and order of the District Court are affirmed.

Our judgment is stayed for a period not to exceed 60 days to permit Congress to implement the fallback provisions.

Justice STEVENS, with whom Justice MARSHALL joins, concurring in the judgment.

[They disagree that the power of Congress to remove the Comptroller General "represents the primary constitutional evil." They disagree also on the attempt to label the functions assigned to the Comptroller General as "executive." They view the statute as unconstitutional because it allows Congress, through the agency of the Comptroller General, to

*make policy that binds the nation without following
the procedures mandated by Article I: passage of a
bill by both Houses and presentment of the bill to the
President. Stevens and Marshall also reject the
premise in the majority opinion that a definite line
distinguishes executive power from legislative power.]*

. . .

Justice WHITE, dissenting.

The Court, acting in the name of separation of
powers, takes upon itself to strike down the
Gramm-Rudman-Hollings Act, one of the most
novel and far-reaching legislative responses to a
national crisis since the New Deal. The basis of the
Court's action is a solitary provision of another
statute that was passed over sixty years ago and has
lain dormant since that time. I cannot concur in
the Court's action. Like the Court, I will not
purport to speak to the wisdom of the policies
incorporated in the legislation the Court invalidates; that is a matter for the Congress and the
Executive, *both* of which expressed their assent to
the statute barely half a year ago. I will, however,
address the wisdom of the Court's willingness to
interpose its distressingly formalistic view of separation of powers as a bar to the attainment of
governmental objectives through the means chosen by the Congress and the President in the
legislative process established by the Constitution.
Twice in the past four years I have expressed my
view that the Court's recent efforts to police the
separation of powers have rested on untenable
constitutional propositions leading to regrettable
results. See *Northern Pipeline Construction Co.* v.
Marathon Pipe Line Co., 458 U.S. 50, 92–118
(1982) (WHITE, J., dissenting); *INS* v. *Chadha,* 462
U.S. 919, 967–1003. (WHITE, J., dissenting).
Today's result is even more misguided. . . .

I

The Court's argument is straightforward: the
Act vests the Comptroller General with "executive" powers, that is, powers to "[i]nterpre[t] a law
enacted by Congress [in order] to implement the
legislative mandate," *ante,* at 3192; such powers
may not be vested by Congress in itself or its
agents, see *Buckley* v. *Valeo,* 424 U.S. 1, 120–141

(1976), for the system of government established
by the Constitution for the most part limits Congress to a legislative rather than an executive or
judicial role, see *INS* v. *Chadha, supra;* the Comptroller General is an agent of Congress by virtue of
a provision in the Budget and Accounting Act of
1921, 43 Stat. 23, 31 U.S.C. § 703(e)(1), granting
Congress the power to remove the Comptroller for
cause through joint resolution; therefore the
Comptroller General may not constitutionally exercise the executive powers granted him in the
Gramm-Rudman Act, and the Act's automatic
budget-reduction mechanism, which is premised
on the Comptroller's exercise of those powers,
must be struck down.

Before examining the merits of the Court's
argument, I wish to emphasize what it is that the
Court quite pointedly and correctly does *not* hold:
namely, that "executive" powers of the sort granted the Comptroller by the Act may only be exercised by officers removable at will by the
President. . . . In an earlier day, in which simpler
notions of the role of government in society prevailed, it was perhaps plausible to insist that all
"executive" officers be subject to an unqualified
presidential removal power, see *Myers* v. *United
States,* 272 U.S. 52 (1926); but with the advent and
triumph of the administrative state and the accompanying multiplication of the tasks undertaken by
the Federal Government, the Court has been virtually compelled to recognize that Congress may
reasonably deem it "necessary and proper" to vest
some among the broad new array of governmental
functions in officers who are free from the partisanship that may be expected of agents wholly
dependent upon the President.

. . .

It is evident (and nothing in the Court's opinion
is to the contrary) that the powers exercised by the
Comptroller General under the Gramm-Rudman
Act are not such that vesting them in an officer not
subject to removal at will by the President would
in itself improperly interfere with Presidential
powers. Determining the level of spending by the
Federal Government is not by nature a function
central either to the exercise of the President's
enumerated powers or to his general duty to
ensure execution of the laws; rather, appropriat-

ing funds is a peculiarly legislative function, and one expressly committed to Congress by Art. I, § 9, which provides that "[n]o Money shall be drawn from the Treasury, but in Consequence of Appropriations made by Law." . . .

Justice BLACKMUN, dissenting.

The Court may be correct when it says that Congress cannot constitutionally exercise removal authority over an official vested with the budget-reduction powers that § 251 of the Balanced Budget and Emergency Deficit Control Act of 1985 gives to the Comptroller General. This, however, is not because "[t]he removal powers over the Comptroller General's office dictate that he will be subservient to Congress," *ante*, at 3190; I agree with JUSTICE WHITE that any such claim is unrealistic. Furthermore, I think it is clear under *Humphrey's Executor* v. *United States*, 295 U.S. 602 (1935), that "executive" powers of the kind delegated to the Comptroller General under the Deficit Control Act need not be exercised by an officer who serves at the President's pleasure; Congress certainly could prescribe the standards and procedures for removing the Comptroller General. . . .

II

Assuming that the Comptroller General's functions under § 251 of the Deficit Control Act cannot be exercised by an official removable by joint resolution of Congress, we must determine whether legislative goals would be frustrated more by striking down § 251 or by invalidating the 1921 removal provision. . . .

In the absence of express statutory direction, I think it is plain that, as both Houses urge, invalidating the Comptroller General's functions under the Deficit Control Act would frustrate congressional objectives far more seriously than would refusing to allow Congress to exercise its removal authority under the 1921 law. . . .

Attorney General Opinion on Ministerial Duties

As early as *Marbury* v. *Madison* (1803), the Supreme Court distinguished between two types of executive duties: ministerial and discretionary. For the latter, the duty of an executive official and adviser is to the President alone. For ministerial actions, however, the duty is to the statute, and the head of a department acts "under the authority of the law, and not by the instructions of the president. It is a ministerial act which the law enjoins on a particular officer for a particular purpose." 5 U.S. 137, 157. Beginning in 1823, Attorneys General regularly informed Presidents that they had no authority to interfere with certain statutory duties assigned by Congress to executive officers. An opinion by Attorney General Cushing in 1854 (6 Op. Att'y Gen. 326), directed to President Pierce, summarizes the law on ministerial duties.

SIR: At the expiration of a year's experience in the discharge of my present official duties, and observation of their relation to other branches of federal administration, it seems to me not unseasonable now to lay before you some suggestions of possible improvement in the manner of conducting the legal business of the Government.

The Constitution of the United States provides, that "the executive power shall be vested in the President of the United States," who shall be Commander-in-chief of the Army and Navy; who shall, by and with the advice and consent of the Senate, make treaties; who shall nominate and, by and with the advice and consent of the Senate, appoint, all officers of the United States, military, judicial, diplomatic, or administrative, whose appointments are not otherwise provided for, and which shall be established by law; who shall have a qualified participation in the enactment of laws, and take care that they be faithfully executed; and who shall, from time to time, give to Congress information of the state of the Union.

The President is thus made the responsible depositary and chief functionary, for the time being, of the ministerial powers and administrative duties of the United States regarded as a political sovereignty.

But the Constitution does not specify the subordinate, ministerial, or administrative functionaries, by whose agency or counsels the details of the public business are to be transacted. It recognises the existence of such official agents and advisers, in saying, that the President "may require the opinion, in writing, of the principal officer in each of the executive departments, upon any subject relating to the duties of their respective offices;" and these officers are again recognised by the Constitution in the clause which vests the appointment of certain inferior officers "in the heads of departments;" and it leaves the number and the organization of those departments to be determined by Congress.

. . .

It is impossible for Congress to foresee, and circumstantially provide for, all the possible future contingencies of executive business, either in respect of the business itself or the manner of conducting it. A necessary discretion must exist in the nature of things somewhere as to all such matters. And that ultimate discretion, when the law does not speak, must reside, as to all executive matters, with the President, who has the power to appoint and remove, and whose duty it is to take care that the laws be faithfully executed. Where the laws define what is to be done by a given head of department, and how he is to do it, there the President's discretion stops; but if the law require an executive act to be performed, without saying how or by whom, it must be for him to supply the direction, in virtue of his powers under the Constitution, he remaining subject always to that, to the analogies of statute, and to the general rules of law and of right. And this view of the question has been followed, uniformly, in the practical administration of the Government.

We shall appreciate the value of this conclusion in the sequel, when we come to perceive that great branches of public business are to be found,

which are not assigned by statute to any particular department, or as to which there is no provision of statute deciding all questions of the manner of transacting such business.

The Supreme Court has recognised the existence of such a discretion, as being reposed for numerous contingencies, not only in the President in regard to the business of the departments, but in the heads of the departments themselves, by implication of law or as the executive agents of the President. The court say, that to attempt to regulate by law the minute movements of every part of the complicated machinery of administration, would evince complete disregard of the limits of the possible and the impossible. While the great lines of its movements may be marked out, and limitations be thus imposed on the exercise of its powers, there are numberless things to be done which cannot be anticipated or defined, but are, nevertheless, indispensable to the action of the Government. These things must of necessity be left to a wise and judicious discretion. (United States *v.* McDaniel, vii Peters, 1; United States *v.* Bailey, ix Peters, 238.)

Question has existed as to the relation of the President and the respective heads of departments to the chiefs of bureaus, and especially the accounting officers of the Treasury.

It is not the duty of the President, and in general it is not convenient for him, to entertain appeals from the departments on the various matters of business, and especially the private claims, on which they have occasion from time to time to pass. Though he is to take care that the laws be faithfully executed, still it is physically impossible that he should do everything in person. Therefore, the Constitution and the laws give to him agents, through whose instrumentality the executive business may be transacted. Among these are the Heads of Departments, and other subordinate officers of the Government.

Now, from the fact that the executive agents, primary and secondary, are assigned by law to particular duties, it has been somewhat hastily inferred, that while it is indubitably true that he may direct the heads of departments, yet he has no authority over the chiefs of bureaus, and especially those in the department of Treasury. It needed only to carry this course of thought one step further, to say that the heads of departments themselves had no authority over those officers. This step was taken, and the doctrine it involves was, for a time, asserted. If maintained, it would have been the singular condition of a great government, in which the executive power was vested by Constitution in the President, and he had authority over the primary executive officers, but neither he nor they had any authority over the secondary executive officers, and, of course, it would be in the power of the latter to arrest, at any time, all the action of the Government.

Such a doctrine was against common sense, which assumes that the superior shall overrule the subordinate, not the latter the former. It was contrary to the settled constitutional theory. That theory, as we shall hereafter see, while it supposes, in all matters not purely ministerial, that executive discretion exists, and that judgment is continually to be exercised, yet requires unity of executive action, and, of course, unity of executive decision; which, by the inexorable necessity of the nature of things, cannot be obtained by means of a plurality of persons wholly independent of one another, without corporate conjunction, and released from subjection to one determining will; and the doctrine is contradicted by a series of

expositions of the rule of administrative law by successive Attorneys General.

. . .

Upon the whole, then, heads ᴕf departments have a threefold relation, namely: 1. To the President, whose political or confidential ministers they are, to execute his will, or rather to act in his name and by his constitutional authority, in cases in which the President possesses a constitutional or legal discretion. 2. To the law; for where the law has directed them to perform certain acts, and where the rights of individuals are dependent on those acts, then, in such cases, a head of department is an officer of the law, and amenable to the laws for his conduct. (Marbury *v.* Madison, i Cranch, 49–61.) And 3. To Congress, in the conditions contemplated by the Constitution.

This latter relation, that of the departments to Congress, is one of the great elements of responsibility and legality in their action. They are created by law; most of their duties are prescribed by law; Congress may at all times call on them for information or explanation in matters of official duty; and it may, if it see fit, interpose by legislation concerning them, when required by the interests of the Government.

. . .

Buckley v. Valeo

424 U.S. 1 (1976)

As part of the Federal Election Campaign Act Amendments of 1974, which responded to the scandals during the election of 1972, Congress enacted a number of reforms, including the creation of the Federal Election Commission (FEC). Because Congress appointed some of the commissioners, the Supreme Court reviewed the framers' intent with respect to the Appointments Clause and the separation of powers theory. Footnotes omitted.

PER CURIAM.

These appeals present constitutional challenges to the key provisions of the Federal Election Campaign Act of 1971 (Act), and related provisions of the Internal Revenue Code of 1954, all as amended in 1974.

. . .

IV. THE FEDERAL ELECTION COMMISSION

The 1974 amendments to the Act create an eight-member Federal Election Commission (Commission) and vest in it primary and substantial responsibility for administering and enforcing the Act. The question that we address in this portion of the opinion is whether, in view of the manner in which a majority of its members are appointed, the Commission may under the Constitution exercise the powers conferred upon it. We find it unnecessary to parse the complex statutory provisions in order to sketch the full sweep of the Commission's authority. It will suffice for present purposes to describe what appear to be representative examples of its various powers.

Chapter 14 of Title 2 makes the Commission the principal repository of the numerous reports and statements which are required by that chapter to be filed by those engaging in the regulated political activities. Its duties under § 438 (a) with respect to these reports and statements include filing and indexing, making them available for public inspection, preservation, and auditing and field investigations. It is directed to "serve as a national clearinghouse for information in respect to the administration of elections." § 438 (b).

Beyond these recordkeeping, disclosure, and investigative functions, however, the Commission is given extensive rulemaking and adjudicative powers. Its duty under § 438 (a)(10) is "to prescribe suitable rules and regulations to carry out the provisions of . . . chapter [14]." Under § 437d (a)(8) the Commission is empowered to make such rules "as are necessary to carry out the provisions of this Act." Section 437d (a)(9) authorizes it to "formulate general policy with respect to the administration of this Act" and enumerated sections of Title 18's Criminal Code, as to all of which provisions the Commission "has primary jurisdiction with respect to [their] civil enforcement." § 437c (b). The Commission is authorized under § 437f (a) to render advisory opinions with respect to activities possibly violating the Act, the Title 18 sections, or the campaign funding provisions of Title 26, the effect of which is that "[n]otwithstanding any other provision of law, any person with respect to whom an advisory opinion is rendered . . . who acts in good faith in accordance with the provisions and findings [thereof] shall be presumed to be in compliance with the [statutory provision] with respect to which such advisory opinion is rendered." § 437f (b). In the course of administering the provisions for Presidential campaign financing, the Commission may

authorize convention expenditures which exceed the statutory limits. 26 U. S. C. § 9008(d)(3) (1970 ed., Supp. IV).

The Commission's enforcement power is both direct and wide ranging. It may institute a civil action for (i) injunctive or other relief against "any acts or practices which constitute or will constitute a violation of this Act," § 437g (a)(5); (ii) declaratory or injunctive relief "as may be appropriate to implement or con[s]true any provisions" of Chapter 95 of Title 26, governing administration of funds for Presidential election campaigns and national party conventions, 26 U. S. C. § 9011 (b) (1) (1970 ed., Supp. IV); and (iii) "such injunctive relief as is appropriate to implement any provision" of Chapter 96 of Title 26, governing the payment of matching funds for Presidential primary campaigns, 26 U. S. C. § 9040 (c) (1970 ed., Supp. IV). If after the Commission's postdisbursement audit of candidates receiving payments under Chapter 95 or 96 it finds an overpayment, it is empowered to seek repayment of all funds due the Secretary of the Treasury. 26 U. S. C. §§ 9010 (b), 9040 (b) (1970 ed., Supp. IV). In no respect do the foregoing civil actions require the concurrence of or participation by the Attorney General; conversely, the decision not to seek judicial relief in the above respects would appear to rest solely with the Commission. With respect to the referenced Title 18 sections, § 437g (a)(7) provides that if, after notice and opportunity for a hearing before it, the Commission finds an actual or threatened criminal violation, the Attorney General "upon request by the Commission. . . shall institute a civil action for relief." Finally, as "[a]dditional enforcement authority," § 456 (a) authorizes the Commission, after notice and opportunity for hearing, to make "a finding that a person . . . while a candidate for Federal office, failed to file" a required report of contributions or expenditures. If that finding is made within the applicable limitations period for prosecutions, the candidate is thereby "disqualified from becoming a candidate in any future election for Federal office for a period of time beginning on the date of such finding and ending one year after the expiration of the term of the Federal office for which such person was a candidate."

The body in which this authority is reposed consists of eight members. The Secretary of the Senate and the Clerk of the House of Representatives are *ex officio* members of the Commission without the right to vote. Two members are appointed by the President *pro tempore* of the Senate "upon the recommendations of the majority leader of the Senate and the minority leader of the Senate." Two more are to be appointed by the Speaker of the House of Representatives, likewise upon the recommendations of its respective majority and minority leaders. The remaining two members are appointed by the President. Each of the six voting members of the Commission must be confirmed by the majority of both Houses of Congress, and each of the three appointing authorities is forbidden to choose both of their appointees from the same political party.

. . .

[After concluding that the Commission's composition was ripe for review, the Court analyzed the substantive issues.]

B. The Merits

Appellants urge that since Congress has given the Commission wide-ranging rulemaking and enforcement powers with respect to the substantive provisions of the Act, Congress is precluded under the principle of separation of powers from vesting in itself the authority to appoint those who will exercise such authority. Their argument is based on the language of Art. II, § 2, cl. 2, of the Constitution, which provides in pertinent part as follows:

"[The President] shall nominate, and by and with the Advice and Consent of the Senate, shall appoint . . . all other Officers of the United States, whose Appointments are not herein otherwise provided for, and which shall be established by Law: but the Congress may by Law vest the Appointment of such inferior Officers, as they think proper, in the President alone, in the Courts of Law, or in the Heads of Departments."

Appellants' argument is that this provision is the exclusive method by which those charged with executing the laws of the United States may be chosen. Congress, they assert, cannot have it both ways. If the Legislature wishes the Commission to exercise all of the conferred powers, then its members are in fact "Officers of the United States" and must be appointed under the Appointments Clause. But if Congress insists upon retaining the power to appoint, then the members of the Commission may not discharge those many functions of the Commission which can be performed only by "Officers of the United States," as that term must be construed within the doctrine of separation of powers.

Appellee Commission and *amici* in support of the Commission urge that the Framers of the Constitution, while mindful of the need for checks and balances among the three branches of the National Government, had no intention of denying to the Legislative Branch authority to appoint its own officers. Congress, either under the Appointments Clause or under its grants of substantive legislative authority and the Necessary and Proper Clause in Art. I, is in their view empowered to provide for the appointment to the Commission in the manner which it did because the Commission is performing "appropriate legislative functions."

. . .

1. Separation of Powers

We do not think appellants' arguments based upon Art. II, § 2, cl. 2, of the Constitution may be so easily dismissed as did the majority of the Court of Appeals. Our inquiry of necessity touches upon the fundamental principles of the Government established by the Framers of the Constitution, and all litigants and all of the courts which have addressed themselves to the matter start on common ground in the recognition of the intent of the Framers that the powers of the three great branches of the National Government be largely separate from one another.

. . . the Constitution by no means contemplates total separation of each of these three essential branches of Government. The President is a participant in the lawmaking process by virtue of his authority to veto bills enacted by Congress. The Senate is a participant in the appointive process by virtue of its authority to refuse to confirm persons nominated to office by the President. The men who met in Philadelphia in the summer of 1787 were practical statesmen, experienced in politics, who viewed the principle of separation of powers as a vital check against tyranny. But they likewise saw that a hermetic sealing off of the three branches of Government from one another would preclude the establishment of a Nation capable of governing itself effectively.

. . .

2. The Appointments Clause

The principle of separation of powers was not simply an abstract generalization in the minds of the Framers: it was woven into the document that they drafted in Philadelphia in the summer of 1787. . . .

It is in the context of these cognate provisions of the document that we must examine the language of Art. II. § 2, cl. 2, which appellants contend provides the only authorization for appointment of those to whom substantial executive or administrative authority is given by statute. Because of the importance of its language, we again set out the provision:

"[The President] shall nominate, and by and with the Advice and Consent of the Senate, shall appoint Ambassadors, other public Ministers and Consuls, Judges of the supreme Court, and all other Officers of the United States, whose Appointments are not herein otherwise provided for, and which shall be established by Law: but the Congress may by Law vest the Appointment of such inferior Officers, as they think proper, in the President alone, in the Courts of Law, or in the Heads of Departments."

The Appointments Clause could, of course, be read as merely dealing with etiquette or protocol in describing "Officers of the United States," but the drafters had a less frivolous purpose in mind. . . .

We think that the term "Officers of the United States" . . . is a term intended to have substantive meaning. We think its fair import is that any appointee exercising significant authority pursuant to the laws of the United States is an "Officer of the United States," and must, therefore, be appointed in the manner prescribed by § 2, cl. 2, of that Article.

. . .

Although two members of the Commission are initially selected by the President, his nominations are subject to confirmation not merely by the Senate, but by the House of Representatives as well. The remaining four voting members of the Commission are appointed by the President *pro tempore* of the Senate and by the Speaker of the House. While the second part of the Clause authorizes Congress to vest the appointment of the officers described in that part in "the Courts of Law, or in the Heads of Departments," neither the Speaker of the House nor the President *pro tempore* of the Senate comes within this language.

The phrase "Heads of Departments," used as it is in conjunction with the phrase "Courts of Law," suggests that the Departments referred to are themselves in the Executive Branch or at least have some connection with that branch. While the Clause expressly authorizes Congress to vest the appointment of certain officers in the "Courts of Law," the absence of similar language to include Congress must mean that neither Congress nor its officers were included within the language "Heads of Departments" in this part of cl. 2.

Thus with respect to four of the six voting members of the Commission, neither the President, the head of any department, nor the Judiciary has any voice in their selection.

. . .

Appellee Commission and *amici* contend somewhat obliquely that because the Framers had no intention of relegating Congress to a position below that of the co-equal Judicial and Executive Branches of the National Government, the Appointments Clause must somehow be read to include Congress or its officers as among those in whom the appointment power may be vested. But the debates of the Constitutional Convention, and the Federalist Papers, are replete with expressions of fear that the Legislative Branch of the National Government will aggrandize itself at the expense of the other two branches. The debates during the Convention, and the evolution of the draft version of the Constitution, seem to us to lend considerable support to our reading of the language of the Appointments Clause itself.

An interim version of the draft Constitution had vested in the Senate the authority to appoint Ambassadors, public Ministers, and Judges of the Supreme Court, and the language of Art. II as finally adopted is a distinct change in this regard. We believe that it was a deliberate change made by the Framers with the intent to deny Congress any authority itself to appoint those who were "Officers of the United States." The debates on the floor of the Convention reflect at least in part the way the change came about.

. . .

3. The Commission's Powers

Thus, on the assumption that all of the powers granted in the statute may be exercised by an agency whose members *have been* appointed in accordance with the Appointments Clause, the ultimate question is which, if any, of those powers may be exercised by the present voting Commissioners, none of whom *was* appointed as provided by that Clause. Our previous description of the statutory provisions, see *supra,* at 109–113, disclosed that the Commission's powers fall generally into three categories: functions relating to the flow of necessary information—receipt, dissemination, and investigation; functions with respect to the Commission's task of fleshing out the statute—rulemaking and advisory opinions; and functions necessary to ensure compliance with the statute and rules—informal procedures, administrative determinations and hearings, and civil suits.

Insofar as the powers confided in the Commission are essentially of an investigative and informative nature, falling in the same general category as those powers which Congress might delegate to one of its own committees, there can be no question that the Commission as presently constituted may exercise them. . . .

But when we go beyond this type of authority to the more substantial powers exercised by the Commission, we reach a different result. The Commission's enforcement power, exemplified by its discretionary power to seek judicial relief, is authority that cannot possibly be regarded as merely in aid of the legislative function of Congress. A lawsuit is the ultimate remedy for a

breach of the law, and it is to the President, and not to the Congress, that the Constitution entrusts the responsibility to "take Care that the Laws be faithfully executed." Art. II, § 3.

. . .

We hold that these provisions of the Act, vesting in the Commission primary responsibility for conducting civil litigation in the courts of the United States for vindicating public rights, violate Art. II, § 2, cl. 2, of the Constitution. Such functions may be discharged only by persons who are "Officers of the United States" within the language of that section.

. . .

MR. JUSTICE STEVENS took no part in the consideration or decision of these cases.

. . .

MR. CHIEF JUSTICE BURGER, concurring in part and dissenting in part.

. . . I agree with the Court that the members of the Federal Election Commission were unconstitutionally appointed. However, I disagree that we should give blanket *de facto* validation to all actions of the Commission undertaken until today. The issue is not before us and we cannot know what acts we are ratifying. I would leave this issue to the District Court to resolve if and when any challenges are brought.

. . .

MR. JUSTICE WHITE, concurring in part and dissenting in part.

. . . it is plain that the FEC is the primary agency for the enforcement and administration of major parts of the election laws. It does not replace or control the executive agencies with respect to criminal prosecutions, but within the wide zone of its authority the FEC is independent of executive as well as congressional control except insofar as certain of its regulations must be laid before and not be disapproved by Congress. § 438 (c); 26 U. S. C. §§ 9009 (c), 9039 (c) (1970 ed., Supp. IV). With duties and functions such as these, members of the FEC are plainly "officers of the United States" as that term is used in Art. II, § 2, cl. 2.

It is thus not surprising that the FEC, in defending the legality of its members' appointments, does not deny that they are "officers of the United States" as that term is used in the Appointments Clause of Art. II. Instead, for reasons the Court outlines, *ante*, at 131–132, 133–134, its position appears to be that even if its members are officers of the United States, Congress may nevertheless appoint a majority of the FEC without participation by the President. This position that Congress may itself appoint the members of a body that is to administer a wide-ranging statute will not withstand examination in light of either the purpose and history of the Appointments Clause or of prior cases in this Court.

. . .

MR. JUSTICE MARSHALL, concurring in part and dissenting in part.

[Justice Marshall concurred in the Court's opinion on FEC appointments.]

MR. JUSTICE BLACKMUN, concurring in part and dissenting in part.

[Justice Blackmun concurred in the Court's opinion on FEC appointments.]

MR. JUSTICE REHNQUIST, concurring in part and dissenting in part.

[Justice Rehnquist concurred in the Court's opinion on FEC appointments.]

Myers v. United States

272 U.S. 52 (1926)

A statute of 1876 provided that postmasters of the first, second, and third classes shall be appointed and may be removed by the President "by and with the advice and consent of the Senate. . . ." President Wilson removed Frank S. Myers, a postmaster of the first class, without seeking or obtaining Senate approval. The constitutional question was whether Congress could interfere with or restrict the President's power of removal, which the Solicitor General and the heirs of Myers argued was essential to preserve the President's responsibility as chief executive officer. They claimed that the President had an implied power to remove subordinates in the executive branch as a means of maintaining accountability. The issue of the removal power was limited to officers subject to Senate confirmation.

MR. CHIEF JUSTICE TAFT delivered the opinion of the Court.

This case presents the question whether under the Constitution the President has the exclusive power of removing executive officers of the United States whom he has appointed by and with the advice and consent of the Senate.

Myers, appellant's intestate, was on July 21, 1917, appointed by the President, by and with the advice and consent of the Senate, to be a postmaster of the first class at Portland, Oregon, for a term of four years. On January 20, 1920, Myers' resigna-

tion was demanded. He refused the demand. On February 2, 1920, he was removed from office by order of the Postmaster General, acting by direction of the President. . . . On April 21, 1921, [Myers] brought this suit in the Court of Claims for his salary from the date of his removal. . . .

The Court of Claims gave judgment against Myers, and this is an appeal from that judgment. . . .

By the 6th section of the Act of Congress of July 12, 1876, 19 Stat. 80, 81, c. 179, under which Myers was appointed with the advice and consent of the Senate as a first-class postmaster, it is provided that

"Postmasters of the first, second and third classes shall be appointed and may be removed by the President by and with the advice and consent of the Senate and shall hold their offices for four years unless sooner removed or suspended according to law."

The Senate did not consent to the President's removal of Myers during his term. . . .

The question where the power of removal of executive officers appointed by the President by and with the advice and consent of the Senate was vested, was presented early in the first session of the First Congress. There is no express provision respecting removals in the Constitution, except as Section 4 of Article II, above quoted, provides for removal from office by impeachment. The subject was not discussed in the Constitutional Convention. Under the Articles of Confederation, Congress was given the power of appointing certain executive officers of the Confederation, and during the Revolution and while the Articles were given effect, Congress exercised the power of removal. . . .

Consideration of the executive power was initiated in the Constitutional Convention by the seventh resolution in the Virginia Plan, introduced by Edmund Randolph. 1 Farrand, Records of the Federal Convention, 21. It gave to the Executive "all the executive powers of the Congress under the Confederation," which would seem therefore to have intended to include the power of removal which had been exercised by that body as incident to the power of appointment.

[Later modifications vested the executive in a single person, elected by an electoral college, with the power to appoint officers and the duty to see that all laws are faithfully observed.]

In the House of Representatives of the First Congress, on Tuesday, May 18, 1789, Mr. Madison moved in the Committee of the Whole that there should be established three executive departments—one of Foreign Affairs, another of the Treasury, and a third of War—at the head of each of which there should be a Secretary, to be appointed by the President by and with the advice

and consent of the Senate, and to be removable by the President. The committee agreed to the establishment of a Department of Foreign Affairs, but a discussion ensued as to making the Secretary removable by the President. 1 Annals of Congress, 370, 371. "The question was now taken and carried, by a considerable majority, in favor of declaring the power of removal to be in the President." 1 Annals of Congress, 383.

On June 16, 1789, the House resolved itself into a Committee of the Whole on a bill proposed by Mr. Madison for establishing an executive department to be denominated the Department of Foreign Affairs, in which the first clause, after stating the title of the officer and describing his duties, had these words: "to be removable from office by the President of the United States." 1 Annals of Congress, 455. After a very full discussion the question was put: shall the words "to be removable by the President" be struck out? It was determined in the negative—yeas 20, nays 34. 1 Annals of Congress, 576.

On June 22, in the renewal of the discussion, "Mr. Benson moved to amend the bill, by altering the second clause, so as to imply the power of removal to be in the President alone. The clause enacted that there should be a chief clerk, to be appointed by the Secretary of Foreign Affairs, and employed as he thought proper, and who, in case of vacancy, should have the charge and custody of all records, books, and papers appertaining to the department. The amendment proposed that the chief clerk, 'whenever the said principal officer shall be removed from office by the President of the United States, or in any other case of vacancy,' should during such vacancy, have the charge and custody of all records, books, and papers appertaining to the department." 1 Annals of Congress, 578.

"Mr. Benson stated that his objection to the clause 'to be removable by the President' arose from an idea that the power of removal by the President hereafter might appear to be exercised by virtue of a legislative grant only, and consequently be subjected to legislative instability, when he was well satisfied in his own mind that it was fixed by a fair legislative construction of the Constitution." 1 Annals of Congress, 579.

"Mr. Benson declared, if he succeeded in this amendment, he would move to strike out the words in the first clause, 'to be removable by the President' which appeared somewhat like a grant. Now, the mode he took would evade that point and establish a legislative construction of the Constitution. He also hoped his amendment would succeed in reconciling both sides of the House to the decision, and quieting the minds of gentlemen." 1 Annals of Congress, 578.

Mr. Madison admitted the objection made by the gentleman near him (Mr. Benson) to the words in the bill. He said: "They certainly may be construed to imply a legislative grant of the power. He wished everything like ambiguity expunged, and the sense of the House explicitly declared, and therefore seconded the motion. Gentlemen have all along proceeded on the idea that the Constitution vests the power in the President; and what arguments were brought forward respecting the convenience or inconvenience of such disposition of the power, were intended only to throw light upon what was meant by the compilers of the Constitution. Now, as the words proposed by the gentleman from New York expressed to his mind the meaning of the Constitution, he should be in favor of them, and would agree to strike out those agreed to in the committee." 1 Annals of Congress, 578, 579.

Mr. Benson's first amendment to alter the second clause by the insertion of the italicized words, made that clause to read as follows:

"That there shall be in the State Department an inferior officer to be appointed by the said principal officer, and to be employed therein as he shall deem proper, to be called the Chief Clerk in the Department of Foreign Affairs, *and who, whenever the principal officer shall be removed from office by the President of the United States,* or in any other case of vacancy, shall, during such vacancy, have charge and custody of all records, books and papers appertaining to said department."

The first amendment was then approved by a vote of thirty to eighteen. 1 Annals of Congress, 580. Mr. Benson then moved to strike out in the first clause the words "to be removable by the President," in pursuance of the purpose he had already declared, and this second motion of his

was carried by a vote of thirty-one to nineteen. 1 Annals of Congress, 585.

The bill as amended was ordered to be engrossed, and read the third time the next day, June 24, 1789, and was then passed by a vote of twenty-nine to twenty-two, and the Clerk was directed to carry the bill to the Senate and desire their concurrence. 1 Annals of Congress, 591.

It is very clear from this history that the exact question which the House voted upon was whether it should recognize and declare the power of the President under the Constitution to remove the Secretary of Foreign Affairs without the advice and consent of the Senate. That was what the vote was taken for. Some effort has been made to question whether the decision carries the result claimed for it, but there is not the slightest doubt, after an examination of the record, that the vote was, and was intended to be, a legislative declaration that the power to remove officers appointed by the President and the Senate vested in the President alone, and until the Johnson Impeachment trial in 1868, its meaning was not doubted even by those who questioned its soundness.

The discussion was a very full one. Fourteen out of the twenty-nine who voted for the passage of the bill, and eleven of the twenty-two who voted against the bill took part in the discussion. Of the members of the House, eight had been in the Constitutional Convention, and of these, six voted with the majority, and two, Roger Sherman and Eldridge Gerry, the latter of whom had refused to sign the Constitution, voted in the minority. After the bill as amended had passed the House, it was sent to the Senate, where it was discussed in secret session, without report. The critical vote there was upon the striking out of the clause recognizing and affirming the unrestricted power of the President to remove. The Senate divided by ten to ten, requiring the deciding vote of the Vice-President, John Adams, who voted against striking out, and in favor of the passage of the bill as it had left the House. Ten of the Senators had been in the Constitutional Convention, and of them six voted that the power of removal was in the President alone. The bill having passed as it came from the House was signed by President Washington and became a law. Act of July 27, 1789, 1 Stat. 28, c.4.

The bill was discussed in the House at length and with great ability. The report of it in the Annals of Congress is extended. James Madison was then a leader in the House, as he had been in the Convention. His arguments in support of the President's constitutional power of removal independently of Congressional provision, and without the consent of the Senate, were masterly, and he carried the House.

[Taft summarizes the reasons advanced by Madison and his associates for vesting the removal power in the President: the need to separate the legislature from the executive functions; the intention to create a strong President; the use of the removal power to permit the President to take responsibility for the conduct of the executive branch and to see that the laws are faithfully executed; the power of removal is incident to the power of appointment; and the need for the President to have full confidence in his subordinates. But Taft acknowledges that Congress can place certain duties in executive officers to make presidential removal inappropriate:]

. . . Of course there may be duties so peculiarly and specifically committed to the discretion of a particular officer as to raise a question whether the President may overrule or revise the officer's interpretation of his statutory duty in a particular instance. Then there may be duties of a quasi-judicial character imposed on executive officers and members of executive tribunals whose decisions after hearing affect interests of individuals, the discharge of which the President can not in a particular case properly influence or control. But even in such a case he may consider the decision after its rendition as a reason for removing the officer, on the ground that the discretion regularly entrusted to that officer by statute has not been on the whole intelligently or wisely exercised. Otherwise he does not discharge his own constitutional duty of seeing that the laws be faithfully executed.

. . .

For the reasons given, we must therefore hold that the provision of the law of 1876, by which the unrestricted power of removal of first class post-masters is denied to the President, is in violation of the Constitution, and invalid. This leads to an affirmance of the judgment of the Court of Claims.

. . .

MR. JUSTICE HOLMES, dissenting.

My brothers MCREYNOLDS and BRANDEIS have discussed the question before us with exhaustive research and I say a few words merely to emphasize my agreement with their conclusion.

The arguments drawn from the executive power of the President, and from his duty to appoint officers of the United States (when Congress does not vest the appointment elsewhere), to take care that the laws be faithfully executed, and to commission all officers of the United States, seem to me spider's webs inadequate to control the dominant facts.

We have to deal with an office that owes its existence to Congress and that Congress may abolish tomorrow. Its duration and the pay attached to it while it lasts depend on Congress alone. Congress alone confers on the President the power to appoint to it and at any time may transfer the power to other hands. With such power over its own creation, I have no more trouble in believing that Congress has power to prescribe a term of life for it free from any interference than I have in accepting the undoubted power of congress to decree its end. I have equally little trouble in accepting its power to prolong the tenure of an incumbent until Congress or the Senate shall have assented to his removal. The duty of the President to see that the laws be executed is a duty that does not go beyond the laws or require him to achieve more than Congress sees fit to leave within his power.

The separate opinion of MR. JUSTICE MCREYNOLDS.

[In this sixty-two-page dissent, McReynolds reviews the succession of statutes that have limited the President's power of removal: civil service reforms; the laws creating commissions, boards, the Comptroller General, and the Board of Tax Appeals; and the general history of congressional control over

postal affairs. He also refutes Taft's claim that a majority of the First Congress believed that the President's removal power was a constitutional grant. McReynolds pulls together his critique in the following section]

X.

Congress has long and vigorously asserted its right to restrict removals and there has been no common executive practice based upon a contrary view. The President has often removed, and it is admitted that he may remove, with either the express or implied assent of Congress; but the present theory is that he may override the declared will of that body. This goes far beyond any practice heretofore approved or followed; it conflicts with the history of the Constitution, with the ordinary rules of interpretation, and with the construction approved by Congress since the beginning and emphatically sanctioned by this court. To adopt it would be revolutionary.

MR. JUSTICE BRANDEIS, dissenting.

[Brandeis followed with a fifty-six-page dissent, spelling out in great detail the power of Congress to fix the tenure of inferior officers and to limit the President's power of removal. Some of the statutes provided that removal shall be made only for specified causes. Others provided for removal only after a hearing. Congress also passed legislation restricting the President's power of nomination.]

The historical data submitted present a legislative practice, established by concurrent affirmative action of Congress and the President, to make consent of the Senate a condition of removal from statutory inferior, civil, executive offices to which the appointment is made for a fixed term by the President with such consent. They show that the practice has existed, without interruption, continuously for the last fifty-eight years; that, throughout this period, it has governed a great majority of all such offices; that the legislation applying the removal clause specifically to the office of postmaster was enacted more than half a century ago; and that recently the practice has, with the President's approval, been extended to several newly created offices. The data show further, that the insertion of the removal clause in acts creating inferior civil offices with fixed tenures is part of the broader legislative practice, which has prevailed since the formation of our Government, to restrict or regulate in many ways both removal from and nomination to such offices. A persistent legislative practice which involves a delimitation of the respective powers of Congress and the President, and which has been so established and maintained, should be deemed tantamount to judicial construction, in the absence of any decision by any court to the contrary. *United States* v. *Midwest Oil Co.*, 236 U. S. 459, 469.

. . .

Nor does the debate show that the majority of those then in Congress thought that the President had the uncontrollable power of removal. The Senators divided equally in their votes. As to their individual views we lack knowledge; for the debate was secret. In the House only 24 of the 54 members voting took part in the debate. Of the 24, only 6 appear to have held the opinion that the President possessed the uncontrollable power of removal. . . .

. . .

The separation of the powers of government did not make each branch completely autonomous. It left each, in some measure, dependent upon the others, as it left to each power to exercise, in some respects, functions in their nature executive, legislative and judicial. Obviously the President cannot secure full execution of the laws, if Congress denies to him adequate means of doing so. Full execution may be defeated because Congress declines to create offices indispensable for that purpose. Or, because Congress, having created the office, declines to make the indispensable appropriation. Or, because Congress, having both created the office and made the appropriation, prevents, by restrictions which it imposes, the appointment of officials who in quality and character are indispensable to the efficient execution of the law.

. . .

Checks and balances were established in order that this should be "a government of laws and not of men." . . . The doctrine of the separation of powers was adopted by the Convention of 1787, not to promote efficiency but to preclude the exercise of arbitrary power. The purpose was, not to avoid friction, but, by means of the inevitable friction incident to the distribution of the governmental powers among three departments, to save the people from autocracy. In order to prevent arbitrary executive action, the Constitution provided in terms that presidential appointments be made with the consent of the Senate, unless Congress should otherwise provide; and this clause was construed by Alexander Hamilton in The Federalist, No. 77, as requiring like consent to removals. Limiting further executive prerogatives

customary in monarchies, the Constitution empowered Congress to vest the appointment of inferior officers, "as they think proper, in the President alone, in the Courts of Law, or in the Heads of Departments." Nothing in support of the claim of uncontrollable power can be inferred from the silence of the Convention of 1787 on the subject of removal. For the outstanding fact remains that every specific proposal to confer such uncontrollable power upon the President was rejected. In America, as in England, the conviction prevailed then that the people must look to representative assemblies for the protection of their liberties. And protection of the individual, even if he be an official, from the arbitrary or capricious exercise of power was then believed to be an essential of free government.

Morrison v. Olson

108 S.Ct. 2597 (1988)

The Ethics in Government Act of 1978, as amended, created an "independent counsel" to investigate high-ranking officials in the executive branch. Under the provisions of the statute, if the Attorney General concludes that the actions of an official exceed a certain threshold, he applies to a panel of three federal judges who are authorized to appoint an independent counsel and to define the counsel's prosecutorial jurisdiction. The Attorney General may remove the independent counsel only "for cause." The statute was challenged in court on a number of constitutional grounds: the appointment power, the removal power, the separation of powers doctrine, and the President's obligation to see that the laws are faithfully executed. In this lawsuit, Independent Counsel Alexia Morrison prosecuted Theodore B. Olson, a former official with the Department of Justice. The statute was declared unconstitutional by a divided (2 to 1) panel of the D.C. Circuit

Chief Justice REHNQUIST delivered the opinion of the Court.

This case presents us with a challenge to the independent counsel provisions of the Ethics in Government Act of 1978, 28 U.S.C.A. §§ 49, 591 *et seq.* (Supp. 1988). We hold today that these provisions of the Act do not violate the Appointments Clause of the Constitution, Art. II, § 2, cl. 2, or the limitations of Article III, nor do they impermissibly interfere with the President's authority under Article II in violation of the constitutional principle of separation of powers.

I

Briefly stated, Title VI of the Ethics of Government Act (Title VI or the Act), 28 U.S.C.A. §§ 591–599 (Supp.1988), allows for the appointment of an "independent counsel" to investigate and, if appropriate, prosecute certain high ranking government officials for violations of federal criminal laws. The Act requires the Attorney General, upon receipt of information that he determines is "sufficient to constitute grounds to investigate whether any person [covered by the Act] may have violated any Federal criminal law," to conduct a preliminary investigation of the matter. When the Attorney General has completed this investigation, or 90 days has elapsed, he is required to report to a special court (the Special Division) created by the Act "for the purpose of appointing independent counsels." 28 U.S.C.A. § 49 (Supp.1988). If the Attorney General determines that "there are no reasonable grounds to believe that further investigation is warranted," then he must notify the Special Division of this result. In such a case, "the division of the court shall have no power to appoint an independent counsel." § 592(b)(1). If, however, the Attorney General has determined that there are "reasonable grounds to believe that further investigation or prosecution is warranted," then he "shall apply to the division of the court for the appointment of an independent counsel." The Attorney General's application to the court "shall contain sufficient information to assist the [court] in selecting an independent counsel and in defining that independent counsel's prosecutorial jurisdiction." § 592(d). Upon receiving this application, the Special Division "shall appoint an appropriate independent counsel and shall define that independent counsel's prosecutorial jurisdiction." § 593(b).

With respect to all matters within the independent counsel's jurisdiction, the Act grants the counsel "full power and independent authority to exercise all investigative and prosecutorial functions and powers of the Department of Justice, the Attorney General, and any other officer or employee of the Department of Justice." § 594(a). The functions of the independent counsel include conducting grand jury proceedings and other investigations, participating in civil and criminal court proceedings and litigation, and appealing any decision in any case in which the counsel participates in an official capacity. §§ 594(a)(1)-(3). . . .

Two statutory provisions govern the length of an independent counsel's tenure in office. The first defines the procedure for removing an independent counsel. Section 596(a)(1) provides:

"An independent counsel appointed under this chapter may be removed from office, other than by impeachment and conviction, only by the personal action of the Attorney General and only for good cause, physical disability, mental inca-

pacity, or any other condition that substantially impairs the performance of such independent counsel's duties."

If an independent counsel is removed pursuant to this section, the Attorney General is required to submit a report to both the Special Division and the Judiciary Committees of the Senate and the House "specifying the facts found and the ultimate grounds for such removal." § 596(a) (2). . . .

The other provision governing the tenure of the independent counsel defines the procedures for "terminating" the counsel's office. Under § 596(b)(1), the office of an independent counsel terminates when he notifies the Attorney General that he has completed or substantially completed any investigations or prosecutions undertaken pursuant to the Act. In addition, the Special Division, acting either on its own or on the suggestion of the Attorney General, may terminate the office of an independent counsel at any time if it finds that "the investigation of all matters within the prosecutorial jurisdiction of such independent counsel . . . have been completed or so substantially completed that it would be appropriate for the Department of Justice to complete such investigations and prosecutions." § 596(b)(2).

[Here the Court reviews the developments that led to the appointment of Alexia Morrison to investigate Theodore B. Olson. In 1982, two subcommittees of the House of Representatives issued subpoenas directing the Environmental Protection Agency (EPA) to produce certain documents related to the "Superfund" program that Congress had enacted to clean up hazardous-waste sites. President Reagan invoked executive privilege to keep the documents from Congress, but they were released after the House voted to hold the EPA Administrator in contempt. A report by the House Judiciary Committee in 1985 suggested that Mr. Olson, in his capacity as Assistant Attorney General for the Office of Legal Counsel, had given false and misleading testimony to Congress. After the House Judiciary Committee requested the Attorney General to seek the appointment of an independent counsel to investigate the allegations against Olson, and after the Attorney General completed a preliminary investigation, the Attorney Gen-

eral sought the appointment of an independent counsel and Ms. Morrison was selected.]

III

The Appointments Clause of Article II reads as follows:

"[The President] shall nominate, and by and with the Advice and Consent of the Senate, shall appoint Ambassadors, other public Ministers and Consuls, Judges of the Supreme Court, and all other Officers of the United States, whose Appointments are not herein otherwise provided for, and which shall be established by Law: but the Congress may by Law vest the Appointment of such inferior Officers, as they think proper, in the President alone, in the Courts of Law, or in the Heads of Departments." U.S. Const., Art. II, § 2, cl. 2.

The parties do not dispute that "[t]he Constitution for purposes of appointment . . . divides all its officers into two classes." *United States* v. *Germaine*, 99 U.S. (9 Otto) 508, 509 (1879). As we stated in *Buckley* v. *Valeo*, 424 U.S. 1, 132 (1976), "[p]rincipal officers are selected by the President with the advice and consent of the Senate. Inferior officers Congress may allow to be appointed by the President alone, by the heads of departments, or by the Judiciary." The initial question is, accordingly, whether appellant is an "inferior" or a "principal" officer. If she is the latter, as the Court of Appeals concluded, then the Act is in violation of the Appointments Clause.

The line between "inferior" and "principal" officers is one that is far from clear, and the Framers provided little guidance into where it should be drawn. . . .We need not attempt here to decide exactly where the line falls between the two types of officers, because in our view appellant clearly falls on the "inferior officer" side of that line. Several factors lead to this conclusion.

First, appellant is subject to removal by a higher Executive Branch official. Although appellant may not be "subordinate" to the Attorney General (and the President) insofar as she possesses a degree of independent discretion to exercise the powers delegated to her under the Act, the fact that she can be removed by the Attorney General indicates that she is to some degree "inferior" in rank and authority. Second, appellant is empowered by the Act to perform only certain, limited duties. An independent counsel's role is restricted primarily to investigation and, if appropriate, prosecution for certain federal crimes. . . . this grant of authority does not include any authority to formulate policy for the Government or the Executive Branch. . . .

Third, appellant's office is limited in jurisdiction. Not only is the Act itself restricted in applicability to certain federal officials suspected of certain serious federal crimes, but an independent counsel can only act within the scope of the jurisdiction that has been granted by the Special Division pursuant to a request by the Attorney General. Finally, appellant's office is limited in tenure. There is concededly no time limit on the appointment of a particular counsel. Nonetheless, the office of independent counsel is "temporary" in the sense that an independent counsel is appointed essentially to accomplish a single task, and when that task is over the office is terminated, either by the counsel herself or by action of the Special Division. . . . In our view, these factors relating to the "ideas of tenure, duration . . . and duties" of the independent counsel, *Germaine, supra,* 9 Otto, at 511, are sufficient to establish that appellant is an "inferior" officer in the constitutional sense.

. . .

This does not, however, end our inquiry under the Appointments Clause. Appellees argue that even if appellant is an "inferior" officer, the Clause does not empower Congress to place the power to appoint such an officer outside the Executive Branch. They contend that the Clause does not contemplate congressional authorization of "interbranch appointments," in which an officer of one branch is appointed by officers of another branch. The relevant langauge of the Appointments Clause is worth repeating. It reads: ". . . but the Congress may by Law vest the Appointment of such inferior Officers, as they think proper, in the President alone, in the courts of Law, or in the Heads of Departments." On its face, the language of this "excepting clause" admits of no limitation on interbranch appointments. Indeed, the inclusion of "as they think proper" seems clearly to give Congress significant discretion to determine whether it is "proper" to vest the appointment of, for example, executive officials in the "courts of Law." . . .

We do not mean to say that Congress' power to provide for interbranch appointments of "inferior officers" is unlimited. In addition to separation of powers concerns, which would arise if such provisions for appointment had the potential to impair the constitutional functions assigned to one of the branches, *Siebold* itself suggested that Congress' decision to vest the appointment power in the courts would be improper if there was some "incongruity" between the functions normally performed by the courts and the performance of their duty to appoint. . . . We have recognized that courts may appoint private attorneys to act as prosecutor for judicial contempt judgments. See *Young* v. *United States ex rel. Vuitton et Fils S.A.*, 481 U.S.——(1987). . . .

IV

Appellees next contend that the powers vested in the Special Division by the Act conflict with Article III of the Constitution. We have long recognized that by the express provision of Article III, the judicial power of the United States is limited to "Cases" and "Controversies." . . . As a general rule, we have broadly stated that "executive or administrative duties of a nonjudicial nature may not be imposed on judges holding office under Art. III of the Constitution." *Buckley*, 424 U.S., at 123. . . . The purpose of this limitation is to help ensure the independence of the Judicial Branch and to prevent the judiciary from encroaching into areas reserved for the other branches. . . .

Most importantly, the Act vests in the Special Division the power to choose who will serve as independent counsel and the power to define his or her jurisdiction. § 593(b). Clearly, once it is accepted that the Appointments Clause gives Congress the power to vest the appointment of officials such as the independent counsel in the "courts of Law," there can be no Article III objection to the Special Division's exercise of that power, as the power itself derives from the Appointments Clause, a source of authority for judicial action

that is independent of Article III. Appellees contend, however, that the Division's Appointments Clause powers do not encompass the power to define the independent counsel's jurisdiction. We disagree. In our view, Congress' power under the Clause to vest the "Appointment" of inferior officers in the courts may, in certain circumstances, allow Congress to give the courts some discretion in defining the nature and scope of the appointed official's authority. . . .

We are more doubtful about the special Division's power to terminate the office of the independent counsel pursuant to § 596(b)(2). As appellees suggest, the power to terminate, especially when exercised by the Division on its own motion, is "administrative" to the extent that it requires the Special Division to monitor the progress of proceedings of the independent counsel and come to a decision as to whether the counsel's job is "completed." § 596(b)(2). It also is not a power that could be considered typically "judicial," as it has few analogues among the court's more traditional powers. Nonetheless, we do not, as did the Court of Appeals, view this provision as a significant judicial encroachment upon executive power or upon the prosecutorial discretion of the independent counsel.

. . . As we see it, "termination" may occur only when the duties of the counsel are truly "completed" or "so substantially completed" that there remains no need for any continuing action by the independent counsel. It is basically a device for removing from the public payroll an independent counsel who has served her purpose, but is unwilling to acknowledge the fact. So construed, the Special Division's power to terminate does not pose a sufficient threat of judicial intrusion into matters that are more properly within the Executive's authority to require that the Act be invalidated as inconsistent with Article III.

. . .

V

We now turn to consider whether the Act is invalid under the constitutional principle of separation of powers. Two related issues must be addressed: The first is whether the provision of the

Act restricting the Attorney General's power to remove the independent counsel to only those instances in which he can show "good cause," taken by itself, impermissibly interferes with the President's exercise of his constitutionally appointed functions. The second is whether, taken as a whole, the Act violates the separation of powers by reducing the President's ability to control the prosecutorial powers wielded by the independent counsel.

A

Two Terms ago we had occasion to consider whether it was consistent with the separation of powers for Congress to pass a statute that authorized a government official who is removable only by Congress to participate in what we found to be "executive powers." *Bowsher* v. *Synar*, 478 U.S. 714, 730 (1986). We held in *Bowsher* that "Congress cannot reserve for itself the power of removal of an officer charged with the execution of the laws except by impeachment." *Id.,* at 726. A primary antecedent for this ruling was our 1925 decision in *Myers* v. *United States*, 272 U.S. 52 (1926). . . . As we observed in *Bowsher*, the essence of the decision in *Myers* was the judgment that the Constitution prevents Congress from "draw[ing] to itself . . . the power to remove or the right to participate in the exercise of that power. To do this would be to go beyond the words and implications of the [Appointments Clause] and to infringe the constitutional principle of the separation of governmental powers." *Myers, supra,* at 161.

Unlike both *Bowsher* and *Myers*, this case does not involve an attempt by Congress itself to gain a role in the removal of executive officials other than its established powers of impeachment and conviction. The Act instead puts the removal power squarely in the hands of the Executive Branch; an independent counsel may be removed from office, "only by the personal action of the Attorney General, and only for good cause." . . . In our view, the removal provisions of the Act make this case more analogous to *Humphrey's Executor* v. *United States*, 295 U.S. 602 (1935), and *Wiener* v. *United States*, 357 U.S. 349 (1958), than to *Myers* or *Bowsher*.

. . .

Considering for the moment the "good cause" removal provision in isolation from the other parts of the Act at issue in this case, we cannot say that the imposition of a "good cause" standard for removal by itself unduly trammels on executive authority. There is no real dispute that the functions performed by the independent counsel are "executive" in the sense that they are law enforcement functions that typically have been undertaken by officials within the Executive Branch. As we noted above, however, the independent counsel is an inferior officer under the Appointments Clause, with limited jurisdiction and tenure and lacking policymaking or significant administrative authority. Although the counsel exercises no small amount of discretion and judgment in deciding how to carry out her duties under the Act, we simply do not see how the President's need to control the exercise of that discretion is so central to the functioning of the Executive Branch as to require as a matter of constitutional law that the counsel be terminable at will by the President.

. . .

B

The final question to be addressed is whether the Act, taken as a whole, violates the principle of separation of powers by unduly interfering with the role of the Executive Branch. . . .

We observe first that this case does not involve an attempt by Congress to increase its own powers at the expense of the Executive Branch. Cf. *Commodity Futures Trading Comm'n* v. *Schor*, 478 U.S., at 856. Unlike some of our previous cases, most recently *Bowsher* v. *Synar*, this case simply does not pose a "dange[r] of congressional usurpation of Executive Branch functions." 478 U.S., at 727; see also *INS* v. *Chadha*, 462 U.S. 919, 958 (1983). Indeed, with the exception of the power of impeachment—which applies to all officers of the United States—Congress retained for itself no powers of control or supervision over an independent counsel. . . .

Similarly, we do not think that the Act works any *judicial* usurpation of properly executive functions. As should be apparent from our discussion of the Appointments Clause above, the power to appoint inferior officers such as independent counsels is not in itself an "executive" function in the constitutional sense, at least when Congress has exercised its power to vest the appointment of an inferior office in the "courts of Law." We note nonetheless that under the Act the Special Division has no power to appoint an independent counsel *sua sponte;* it may only do so upon the specific request of the Attorney General, and the courts are specifically prevented from reviewing the Attorney General's decision not to seek appointment, § 592(f). . . .

Finally, we do not think that the Act "impermissibly undermine[s]" the powers of the Executive Branch, *Schor, supra,* 478 U.S., at 856, or "disrupts the proper balance between the coordinate branches [by].prevent[ing] the Executive Branch from accomplishing its constitutionally assigned functions," *Nixon* v. *Administrator of General Services, supra,* 433 U.S., at 443. It is undeniable that the Act reduces the amount of control or supervision that the Attorney General and, through him, the President exercises over the investigation and prosecution of a certain class of alleged criminal activity. The Attorney General is not allowed to appoint the individual of his choice; he does not determine the counsel's jurisdiction; and his power to remove a counsel is limited. Nonetheless, the Act does give the Attorney General several means of supervising or controlling the prosecutorial powers that may be wielded by an independent counsel. Most importantly, the Attorney General retains the power to remove the counsel for "good cause," a power that we have already concluded provides the Executive with substantial ability to ensure that the laws are "faithfully executed" by an independent counsel. No independent counsel may be appointed without a specific request by the Attorney General, and the Attorney General's decision not to request appointment if he finds "no reasonable grounds to believe that further investigation is warranted" is committed to his unreviewable discretion. The Act thus gives the Executive a degree of control over the power to initiate an investigation by the independent counsel. In addition, the jurisdiction of the independent counsel is defined with reference to the facts submitted by the Attorney General, and once a counsel is appointed, the Act requires that the counsel abide by Justice Department policy unless it is not "possible" to do so. Notwithstanding the fact that the counsel is to some degree "independent" and free from Executive supervision to a greater extent than other federal prosecutors, in our view these features of the Act give the Executive Branch sufficient control over the independent counsel to ensure that the President is able to perform his constitutionally assigned duties.

VI

In sum, we conclude today that it does not violate the Appointments Clause for Congress to vest the appointment of independent counsels in the Special Division; that the powers exercised by the Special Division under the Act do not violate Article III; and that the Act does not violate the separation of powers principle by impermissibly interfering with the functions of the Executive Branch. The decision of the Court of Appeals is therefore

Reversed.

Justice KENNEDY took no part in the consideration or decision of this case.

Justice SCALIA, dissenting.
. . . the founders conspicuously and very consciously declined to sap the executive's strength in the same way they had weakened the legislature: by dividing the executive power. Proposals to have multiple executives, or a council of advisors with separate authority were rejected. See 1 M. Farrand, Records of the Federal Convention of 1787, pp. 66, 71–74, 88, 91–92 (rev. ed. 1966); 2 *id.,* at 335–337, 533, 537, 542. Thus, while "[a]ll legislative Powers herein granted shall be vested in a Congress of the United States, which shall consist of a Senate *and* House of Representatives," U.S. Const., Art I, § 1 (emphasis added), "[t]he executive Power shall be vested in *a President of the United States,*" Art. II, § 1, cl. 1 (emphasis added).

That is what this suit is about. Power. The allocation of power among Congress, the President and the courts in such fashion as to preserve the equilibrium the Constitution sought to establish—so that "a gradual concentration of the several powers in the same department," Federalist No. 51, p. 321 (J. Madison), can effectively be resisted. Frequently an issue of this sort will come before the Court clad, so to speak, in sheep's clothing: the potential of the asserted principle to effect important change in the equilibrium of power is not immediately evident, and must be discerned by a careful and perceptive analysis. But this wolf comes as a wolf.

I

[In this section, Justice Scalia reviews the history of Congress' investigation of the EPA scandal and concludes that the Attorney General, as a "practical matter," had no choice but to seek the appointment of an independent counsel to prosecute Olson.]

II

If to describe this case is not to decide it, the concept of a government of separate and coordinate powers no longer has meaning. The Court devotes most of its attention to such relatively technical details as the Appointments Clause and the removal power, addressing briefly and only at the end of its opinion the separation of powers. As my prologue suggest, I think that has it backwards. . . .

To repeat, Art. II, § 1, cl. 1 of the Constitution provides:

"The executive Power shall be vested in a President of the United States."

As I described at the outset of this opinion, this does not mean *some of* the executive power, but *all of* the executive power. It seems to me, therefore, that the decision of the Court of Appeals invalidating the present statute must be upheld on fundamental separation-of-powers principles if the following two questions are answered affirmatively: (1) Is the conduct of a criminal prosecution (and of an investigation to decide whether to prosecute) the exercise of purely executive power? (2) Does the statute deprive the President of the United States of exclusive control over the exercise of that power? Surprising to say, the Court appears to concede an affirmative answer to both questions, but seeks to avoid the inevitable conclusion that since the statute vests some purely executive power in a person who is not the President of the United States it is void.

The Court concedes that "[t]here is no real dispute that the functions performed by the independent counsel are 'executive'," though it qualifies that concession by adding "in the sense that they are 'law enforcement' functions that typically have been undertaken by officials within the Executive Branch." *Ante*, at 2619. The qualifier adds nothing but atmosphere. In what *other* sense can one identify "the executive Power" that is supposed to be vested in the President (unless it includes everything the Executive Branch is given to do) *except* by reference to what has always and everywhere—if conducted by Government at all —been conducted never by the legislature, never by the courts, and always by the executive. . . .

As for the second question, whether the statute before us deprives the President of exclusive control over that quintessentially executive activity: The Court does not, and could not possibly, assert that it does not. That is indeed the whole object of the statute. Instead, the Court points out that the President, through his Attorney General, has at least *some* control. That concession is alone enough to invalidate the statute, but I cannot refrain from pointing out that the Court greatly exaggerates the extent of that "some" presidential control. "Most importan[t]" among these controls, the Court asserts, is the Attorney General's "power to remove the counsel for 'good cause.'" *Ante*, at 2621. This is somewhat like referring to shackles as an effective means of locomotion. . . .

. . . It effects a revolution in our constitutional jurisprudence for the Court, once it has determined that (1) purely executive functions are at issue here, and (2) those functions have been given to a person whose actions are not fully within the supervision and control of the President, nonetheless to proceed further to sit in judgment of whether "the President's need to control the exercise of [the independent counsel's] discretion is *so central* to the functioning of the Executive Branch" as to require complete control, *ante*, at 2619 (emphasis added), whether the conferral of his powers upon someone else "*sufficiently* deprives the President of control over the independent counsel to interfere impermissibly with [his] constitutional obligation to ensure the faithful execution of the laws," *ante*, at 2619–2620 (emphasis added), and whether "the Act give[s] the Executive Branch *sufficient* control over the independent counsel to ensure that the President is able to perform his constitutionally assigned duties," *ante*, at 2621 (emphasis added). It is not for us to determine, and we have never presumed to determine, how much of the purely executive powers of government must be within the full control of the President. The Constitution prescribes that they *all* are.

The utter incompatibility of the Court's approach with our constitutional traditions can be made more clear, perhaps, by applying it to the powers of the other two Branches. Is it conceivable that if Congress passed a statute depriving itself of less than full and entire control over some insignificant area of legislation, we would inquire whether the matter was "*so central* to the functioning of the Legislative Branch" as really to require complete control, or whether the statute gives Congress "*sufficient* control over the surrogate legislator to ensure that Congress is able to perform its constitutionally assigned duties"? Of course we would have none of that. Once we determined that a purely legislative power was at issue we would require it to be exercised, wholly and entirely, by Congress. Or to bring the point closer to home, consider a statute giving to non-Article III judges just a tiny bit of purely judicial power in a relatively insignificant field, with substantial control, though not total control, in the courts—perhaps "clear error" review, which would be a fair judicial equivalent of the Attorney General's "for cause" removal power here. Is there any doubt that we would not pause to inquire whether the matter was "*so central* to the functioning of the Judicial Branch" as really to require complete control, or whether we retained "*sufficient* control over the matters to be decided that we are able to perform our constitutionally assigned duties"? We would say that our "constitutionally assigned duties" include *complete* control over all exercises of the judicial power—or, as the plurality opinion said in *Northern Pipeline Construction Co.* v. *Marathon Pipe Line Co.,* 458 U.S. 50, 58–59 (1982), that "[t]he inexorable command of

[Article III] is clear and definite: The judicial power of the United States must be exercised by courts having the attributes prescribed in Art. III." . . .

The Court has nonetheless, replaced the clear constitutional prescription that the executive power belongs to the President with a "balancing test." What are the standards to determine how the balance is to be struck, that is, how much removal of presidential power is too much? Many countries of the world get along with an Executive that is much weaker than ours—in fact, entirely dependent upon the continued support of the legislature. Once we depart from the text of the Constitution, just where short of that do we stop? The most amazing feature of the Court's opinion is that it does not even purport to give an answer. It simply *announces*, with no analysis, that the ability to control the decision whether to investigate and prosecute the President's closest advisors, and indeed the President himself, is not "so central to the functioning of the Executive Branch" as to be constitutionally required to be within the President's control. Apparently that is so because we say it is so. . . .

[In Sections III and IV, Scalia concludes that the independent counsel is a principal (not inferior) officer and therefore must be nominated by the President and confirmed by the Senate, and he agrees with the lower court's decision that the restrictions placed on the removal of the independent counsel violate established precedent.]

V

The purpose of the separation and equilibration of powers in general, and of the unitary Executive in particular, was not merely to assure effective government but to preserve individual freedom. Those who hold or have held offices covered by the Ethics in Government Act are entitled to that protection as much as the rest of us, and I conclude my discussion by considering the effect of the Act upon the fairness of the process they receive.

Only someone who has worked in the field of law enforcement can fully appreciate the vast power and the immense discretion that are placed in the hands of a prosecutor with respect to the objects of his investigation. . . .

Under our system of government, the primary check against prosecutorial abuse is a political one. The prosecutors who exercise this awesome discretion are selected and can be removed by a President, whom the people have trusted enough to elect. Moreover, when crimes are not investigated and prosecuted fairly, nonselectively, with a reasonable sense of proportion, the President pays the cost in political damage to his administration. If federal prosecutors "pick people that [they] thin[k] [they] should get, rather than cases that need to be prosecuted, " if they amass many more resources against a particular prominent individual, or against a particular class of political protestors, or against members of a particular political party, than the gravity of the alleged offenses or the record of successful prosecutions seems to warrant, the unfairness will come home to roost in the Oval Office. I leave it to the reader to recall the examples of this in recent years. That result, of course, was precisely what the Founders had in mind when they provided that all executive powers would be exercised by a *single* Chief Executive. . . .

. . . How frightening it must be to have your own independent counsel and staff appointed,

with nothing else to do but to investigate you until investigation is no longer worthwhile—with whether it is worthwhile not depending upon what such judgments usually hinge on, competing responsibilities. And to have that counsel and staff decide, with no basis for comparison, whether what you have done is bad enough, willful enough, and provable enough, to warrant an indictment. How admirable the constitutional system that provides the means to avoid such a distortion. And how unfortunate the judicial decision that has permitted it.

. . .

The ad hoc approach to constitutional adjudication has real attraction, even apart from its work-saving potential. It is guaranteed to produce a result, in every case, that will make a majority of the Court happy with the law. The law is, by definition, precisely what the majority thinks, taking all things into account, it *ought* to be. I prefer to rely upon the judgment of the wise men who constructed our system, and of the people who approved it, and of two centuries of history that have shown it to be sound. Like it or not, that judgment says, quite plainly, that "[t]he executive Power shall be vested in a President of the United States."

Schechter Corp. v. United States

295 U.S. 495 (1935)

In *Panama Refining Co.* v. *Ryan*, 293 U.S. 388 (1935), the Supreme Court struck down part of the National Industrial Recovery Act as an invalid delegation of legislative power from Congress to the President. The statute placed upon industrial and trade associations the responsibility for drawing up codes to minimize competition, raise prices, and restrict production. If the President regarded the codes as unacceptable he could prescribe his own codes and enforce them by law. *Panama Refining* held that a section of the statute governing controls on petroleum production failed to establish criteria to govern the President's course. Only Justice Cardozo dissented. In *Schechter*, the "Sick Chicken Case," the Court examines the constitutionality of the remainder of the statute.

MR. CHIEF JUSTICE HUGHES delivered the opinion of the Court.

Petitioners . . . were convicted in the District Court of the United States for the Eastern District

of New York on eighteen counts of an indictment charging violations of what is known as the "Live Poultry Code," and on an additional count for conspiracy to commit such violations. By demurrer to the indictment and appropriate motions on the trial, the defendants contended (1) that the Code had been adopted pursuant to an unconstitutional delegation by Congress of legislative power; (2) that it attempted to regulate intrastate transactions which lay outside the authority of Congress; and (3) that in certain provisions it was repugnant to the due process clause of the Fifth Amendment.

[The Second Circuit sustained the conviction on the conspiracy count and on sixteen counts of code violations.]

[The Court described New York City as the largest live-poultry market in the United States, 96 percent of the poultry coming from other states. The Schechter Corporation usually purchased their live poultry from a market in New York City, or at the railroad terminals serving the City, but occasionally they bought in Philadelphia. They trucked the poultry to their slaughterhouse markets in Brooklyn for sale to retail dealers and butchers. They did not sell the poultry in interstate commerce.]

The "Live Poultry Code" was promulgated under § 3 of the National Industrial Recovery Act. That section . . . authorizes the President to approve "codes of fair competition." Such a code may be approved for a trade or industry, upon application by one or more trade or industrial associations or groups, if the President finds (1) that such associations or groups "impose no inequitable restrictions on admission to membership therein and are truly representative," and (2) that such codes are not designed "to promote monopolies or to eliminate or oppress small enterprises and will not operate to discriminate against them, and will tend to effectuate the policy" of Title I of the Act. Such codes "shall not permit monopolies or monopolistic practices." As a condition of his approval, the President may "impose such conditions (including requirements for the making of reports and the keeping of accounts) for the protection of consumers, competitors, employees, and others, and in furtherance of the public interest, and may provide such exceptions to and

exemptions from the provisions of such code as the President in his discretion deems necessary to effectuate the policy herein declared." Where such a code has not been approved, the President may prescribe one, either on his own motion or on complaint. Violation of any provision of a code (so approved or prescribed) "in any transaction in or affecting interstate or foreign commerce" is made a misdemeanor punishable by a fine of not more than $500 for each offense, and each day the violation continues is to be deemed a separate offense.

The "Live Poultry Code" was approved by the President on April 13, 1934. . . .

[The code fixed the number of hours for workdays, the minimum pay, the minimum number of employees, and prohibited the employment of any person under sixteen years of age. The Code was administered through an "industry advisory committee" selected by trade associations and members of the industry. A "code supervisor" was appointed with the approval of the committee by agreement between the Secretary of Agriculture and the Administrator for Industrial Recovery.]

First. Two preliminary points are stressed by the Government with respect to the appropriate approach to the important questions presented. We are told that the provision of the statute authorizing the adoption of codes must be viewed in the light of the grave national crisis with which Congress was confronted. Undoubtedly, the conditions to which power is addressed are always to be considered when the exercise of power is challenged. Extraordinary conditions may call for extraordinary remedies. But the argument necessarily stops short of an attempt to justify action which lies outside the sphere of constitutional authority. Extraordinary conditions do not create or enlarge constitutional power. The Constitution established a national government with powers deemed to be adequate, as they have proved to be both in war and peace, but these powers of the national government are limited by the constitutional grants. . . .

The further point is urged that the national crisis demanded a broad and intensive coöperative effort by those engaged in trade and industry, and that this necessary coöperation was sought to be fostered by permitting them to initiate the adoption of codes. But the statutory plan is not simply one for voluntary effort. It does not seek merely to endow voluntary trade or industrial associations or groups with privileges or immunities. It involves the coercive exercise of the law-making power. The codes of fair competition which the statute attempts to authorize are codes of laws. If valid, they place all persons within their reach under the obligation of positive law, binding equally those who assent and those who do not assent. Violations of the provisions of the codes are punishable as crimes.

Second. The question of the delegation of legislative power. We recently had occasion to review the pertinent decisions and the general principles which govern the determination of this question. *Panama Refining Co.* v. *Ryan,* 293 U. S. 388. The Constitution provides that "All legislative powers herein granted shall be vested in a Congress of the United States, which shall consist of a Senate and House of Representatives." Art I, § 1. And the Congress is authorized "To make all laws which shall be necessary and proper for carrying into execution" its general powers. Art. I, § 8, par. 18. The Congress is not permitted to abdicate or to transfer to others the essential legislative functions with which it is thus vested. We have repeatedly recognized the necessity of adapting legislation to complex conditions involving a host of details with which the national legislature cannot deal directly. We pointed out in the *Panama Company* case that the Constitution has never been regarded as denying to Congress the necessary resources of flexibility and practicality, which will enable it to perform its function in laying down policies and establishing standards, while leaving to selected instrumentalities the making of subordinate rules within prescribed limits and the determination of facts to which the policy as declared by the legislature is to apply. But we said that the constant recognition of the necessity and validity of such provisions, and the wide range of administrative authority which has been developed by means of them, cannot be allowed to obscure the limitations of the authority to delegate, if our constitutional system is to be maintained. *Id.,* p. 421.

Accordingly, we look to the statute to see whether Congress has overstepped these limitations,—whether Congress in authorizing "codes of fair competition" has itself established the standards of legal obligation, thus performing its essential legislative function, or, by the failure to enact such standards, has attempted to transfer that function to others.

The aspect in which the question is now presented is distinct from that which was before us in the case of the *Panama Company.* There, the subject of the statutory prohibition was defined. National Industrial Recovery Act, § 9 (c). That subject was the transportation in interstate and foreign commerce of petroleum and petroleum products which are produced or withdrawn from storage in excess of the amount permitted by state authority. The question was with respect to the range of discretion given to the President in prohibiting that transportation. *Id.,* pp. 414, 415, 430. As to the "codes of fair competition," under § 3 of the Act, the question is more fundamental. It is whether there is any adequate definition of the subject to which the codes are to be addressed.

What is meant by "fair competition" as the term is used in the Act? Does it refer to a category established in the law, and is the authority to make codes limited accordingly? Or is it used as a convenient designation for whatever set of laws the formulators of a code for a particular trade or industry may propose and the President may approve (subject to certain restrictions), or the President may himself prescribe, as being wise and beneficent provisions for the government of the trade or industry in order to accomplish the broad purposes of rehabilitation, correction and expansion which are stated in the first section of Title I?

The Act does not define "fair competition." . . .

The Government urges that the codes will "consist of rules of competition deemed fair for each industry by representative members of that industry—by the persons most vitally concerned and most familiar with its problems." Instances are cited in which Congress has availed itself of such assistance; as *e. g.,* in the exercise of its authority over the public domain, with respect to the recognition of local customs or rules of miners as to mining claims, or, in matters of a more or less technical nature, as in designating the standard height of drawbars. But would it be seriously contended that Congress could delegate its legislative authority to trade or industrial associations or groups so as to empower them to enact the laws they deem to be wise and beneficent for the rehabilitation and expansion of their trade or industries? Could trade or industrial associations or groups be constituted legislative bodies for that purpose because such associations or groups are familiar with the problems of their enterprises? And, could an effort of that sort be made valid by such a preface of generalities as to permissible aims as we find in section 1 of title I? The answer is obvious. Such a delegation of legislative power is unknown to our law and is utterly inconsistent with the constitutional prerogatives and duties of Congress.

The question, then, turns upon the authority which § 3 of the Recovery Act vests in the President to approve or prescribe. If the codes have standing as penal statutes, this must be due to the effect of the executive action. But Congress cannot delegate legislative power to the President to exercise an unfettered discretion to make whatever laws he thinks may be needed or advisable for the rehabilitation and expansion of trade or industry. . . .

. . . Section 3 of the Recovery Act is without precedent. It supplies no standards for any trade, industry or activity. It does not undertake to prescribe rules of conduct to be applied to particular states of fact determined by appropriate administrative procedure. Instead of prescribing rules of conduct, it authorizes the making of codes to prescribe them. For that legislative undertaking, § 3 sets up no standards, aside from the statement of the general aims of rehabilitation, correction and expansion described in section

one. In view of the scope of that broad declaration, and of the nature of the few restrictions that are imposed, the discretion of the President in approving or prescribing codes, and thus enacting laws for the government of trade and industry throughout the country, is virtually unfettered. We think that the code-making authority thus conferred is an unconstitutional delegation of legislative power.

. . .

MR. JUSTICE CARDOZO, concurring.

The delegated power of legislation which has found expression in this code is not canalized within banks that keep it from overflowing. It is unconfined and vagrant, if I may borrow my own words in an earlier opinion. *Panama Refining Co.* v. *Ryan*, 293 U. S. 388, 440.

This court has held that delegation may be unlawful though the act to be performed is definite and single, if the necessity, time and occasion of performance have been left in the end to the discretion of the delegate. *Panama Refining Co.* v. *Ryan, supra.* I thought that ruling went too far. I pointed out in an opinion that there had been "no grant to the Executive of any roving commission to inquire into evils and then, upon discovering them, do anything he pleases." 293 U. S. at p. 435. Choice, though within limits, had been given him "as to the occasion, but none whatever as to the means." *Ibid.* Here, in the case before us, is an attempted delegation not confined to any single act nor to any class or group of acts identified or described by reference to a standard. Here in effect is a roving commission to inquire into evils and upon discovery correct them.

. . . This is delegation running riot. No such plenitude of power is susceptible of transfer. . . .

I am authorized to state that MR. JUSTICE STONE joins in this opinion.

INS v. Chadha

462 U.S. 919 (1983)

Congress authorized the Attorney General to suspend the deportation of aliens. Suspensions, however, were subject to the disapproval of either House. Along with a list of 340 names, the Attorney General suspended the deportation of Jagdish Rai Chadha, an East Indian who was born in Kenya and who held a British passport. In 1975, the House of Representatives adopted a resolution disapproving six names, including Chadha. He moved to suspend the deportation proceedings on the ground that the portion of the statute giving Congress a one-House veto was unconstitutional. In 1980, the Ninth Circuit held that the legislative veto violated the doctrine of separation of powers. The Supreme Court twice held oral argument before deciding the case.

CHIEF JUSTICE BURGER delivered the opinion of the Court.

We granted certiorari in Nos. 80–2170 and 80–2171, and postponed consideration of the question of jurisdiction in No. 80–1832. Each presents a challenge to the constitutionality of the provision in § 244(c)(2) of the Immigration and Nationality Act, 66 Stat. 216, as amended, 8 U. S. C. § 1254(c)(2), authorizing one House of Congress, by resolution, to invalidate the decision of the Executive Branch, pursuant to authority delegated by Congress to the Attorney General of the United States, to allow a particular deportable alien to remain in the United States.

I

Chadha is an East Indian who was born in Kenya and holds a British passport. He was lawfully admitted to the United States in 1966 on a nonimmigrant student visa. His visa expired on June 30, 1972. On October 11, 1973, the District Director of the Immigration and Naturalization Service ordered Chadha to show cause why he should not be deported for having "remained in the United States for a longer time than permitted." App. 6. Pursuant to § 242(b) of the Immigration and Nationality Act (Act), 8 U. S. C. § 1252(b), a deportation hearing was held before an Immigration Judge on January 11, 1974. Chadha conceded that he was deportable for overstaying his visa and the hearing was adjourned to enable him

to file an application for suspension of deportation under § 244(a)(1) of the Act. . . .

[The Immigration Judge suspended Chadha's deportation and a report of the suspension was transmitted. Acting under § 244(c)(2) of the Act, and without debate or recorded vote, the House of Representatives disapproved Chadha's suspension. Before addressing the constitutionality of the one-House veto, the Court concluded that (1) it had jurisdiction to entertain the INS appeal, (2) the legislative veto could be severed from the Act without affecting the Attorney General's authority to suspend deportations, (3) Chadha had standing to bring the suit, (4) there was no reason to avoid the constitutional issue because Chadha might have alternative means of relief, (5) the Ninth Circuit had jurisdiction to decide the case, (6) the case represented a genuine case or controversy with the necessary concrete adverseness, and (7) the case did not constitute a nonjusticiable political question.]

III
A

We turn now to the question whether action of one House of Congress under § 244(c)(2) violates strictures of the Constitution. We begin, of course, with the presumption that the challenged statute is valid. Its wisdom is not the concern of the courts; if a challenged action does not violate the Constitution, it must be sustained:

"Once the meaning of an enactment is discerned and its constitutionality determined, the judicial process comes to an end. We do not sit as a committee of review, nor are we vested with the power of veto." *TVA* v. *Hill*, 437 U.S. 153, 194–195 (1978).

By the same token, the fact that a given law or procedure is efficient, convenient, and useful in facilitating functions of government, standing alone, will not save it if it is contrary to the Constitution. Convenience and efficiency are not the primary objectives—or the hallmarks—of democratic government and our inquiry is sharpened rather than blunted by the fact that congressional veto provisions are appearing with increasing frequency in statutes which delegate authority to executive and independent agencies:

"Since 1932, when the first veto provision was enacted into law, 295 congressional veto-type procedures have been inserted in 196 different statutes as follows: from 1932 to 1939, five statutes were affected; from 1940–49, nineteen statutes; between 1950–59, thirty-four statutes; and from 1960–69, forty-nine. From the year 1970 through 1975, at least one hundred sixty-three such provisions were included in eighty-nine laws." Abourezk, The Congressional Veto: A Contemporary Response to Executive Encroachment on Legislative Prerogatives, 52 Ind. L. Rev. 323, 324 (1977).

See also Appendix to JUSTICE WHITE'S dissent, *post*, at 1003.

JUSTICE WHITE undertakes to make a case for the proposition that the one-House veto is a useful "political invention," *post*, at 972, and we need not challenge that assertion. We can even concede this utilitarian argument although the long-range political wisdom of this "invention" is arguable. It has been vigorously debated, and it is instructive to compare the views of the protagonists. . . . But policy arguments supporting even useful "political inventions" are subject to the demands of the Constitution which defines powers and, with respect to this subject, sets out just how those powers are to be exercised.

Explicit and unambiguous provisions of the Constitution prescribe and define the respective functions of the Congress and of the Executive in the legislative process. Since the precise terms of

those familiar provisions are critical to the resolution of these cases, we set them out verbatim. Article I provides:

"All legislative Powers herein granted shall be vested in a Congress of the United States, which shall consist of a Senate *and* House of Representatives." Art. I, § 1. (Emphasis added.)

"Every Bill which shall have passed the House of Representatives *and* the Senate, *shall*, before it becomes a law, be presented to the President of the United States. . . ." Art. I, § 7, cl. 2. (Emphasis added.)

"*Every* Order, Resolution, or Vote to which the Concurrence of the Senate and House of Representatives may be necessary (except on a question of Adjournment) *shall be* presented to the President of the United States; and before the Same shall take Effect, *shall be* approved by him, or being disapproved by him, *shall be* repassed by two thirds of the Senate and House of Representatives, according to the Rules and Limitations prescribed in the Case of a Bill." Art. I, § 7, cl. 3. (Emphasis added.)

. . .

B

The Presentment Clauses

The records of the Constitutional Convention reveal that the requirement that all legislation be presented to the President before becoming law was uniformly accepted by the Framers. Presentment to the President and the Presidential veto were considered so imperative that the draftsmen took special pains to assure that these requirements could not be circumvented. During the final debate on Art. I, § 7, cl. 2, James Madison expressed concern that it might easily be evaded by the simple expedient of calling a proposed law a "resolution" or "vote" rather than a "bill." 2 Farrand 301–302. As a consequence, Art. I, § 7, cl. 3, *supra*, at 945–946, was added. 2 Farrand 304–305.

The decision to provide the President with a limited and qualified power to nullify proposed legislation by veto was based on the profound conviction of the Framers that the powers conferred on Congress were the powers to be most carefully circumscribed. It is beyond doubt that lawmaking was a power to be shared by both Houses and the President. In The Federalist No. 73 (H. Lodge ed. 1888), Hamilton focused on the President's role in making laws:

"If even no propensity had ever discovered itself in the legislative body to invade the rights of the Executive, the rules of just reasoning and theoretic propriety would of themselves teach us that the one ought not to be left to the mercy of the other, but ought to possess a constitutional and effectual power of self-defence." *Id.,* at 458.

. . .

C

Bicameralism

The bicameral requirement of Art. I, §§ 1, 7, was of scarcely less concern to the Framers than was the Presidential veto and indeed the two concepts are interdependent. By providing that no law could take effect without the concurrence of the prescribed majority of the Members of both Houses, the Framers reemphasized their belief, already remarked upon in connection with the Presentment Clauses, that legislation should not be enacted unless it has been carefully and fully considered by the Nation's elected officials. In the Constitutional Convention debates on the need for a bicameral legislature, James Wilson, later to become a Justice of this Court, commented:

"Despotism comes on mankind in different shapes, sometimes in an Executive, sometimes in a military, one. Is there danger of a Legislative despotism? Theory & practice both proclaim it. If the Legislative authority be not restrained, there can be neither liberty nor stability; and it can only be restrained by dividing it within itself, into distinct and independent branches. In a single house there is no check, but the inadequate one, of the virtue & good sense of those who compose it." 1 Farrand 254.

. . .

We see therefore that the Framers were acutely conscious that the bicameral requirement and the Presentment Clauses would serve essential constitutional functions. The President's participation in the legislative process was to protect the Executive Branch from Congress and to protect the whole people from improvident laws. The division of the Congress into two distinctive bodies assures that the legislative power would be exercised only after opportunity for full study and debate in separate settings. The President's unilateral veto power, in turn, was limited by the power of two-thirds of both Houses of Congress to overrule a veto thereby precluding final arbitrary action of one person. See *id.,* at 99–104. It emerges clearly that the prescription for legislative action in Art. I, §§ 1, 7, represents the Framers' decision that the legislative power of the Federal Government be exercised in accord with a single, finely wrought and exhaustively considered, procedure.

IV

The Constitution sought to divide the delegated powers of the new Federal Government into three defined categories, Legislative, Executive, and Judicial, to assure, as nearly as possible, that each branch of government would confine itself to its assigned responsibility. The hydraulic pressure inherent within each of the separate Branches to exceed the outer limits of its power, even to accomplish desirable objectives, must be resisted.

Although not "hermetically" sealed from one another, *Buckley* v. *Valeo*, 424 U. S., at 121, the powers delegated to the three Branches are functionally identifiable. When any Branch acts, it is presumptively exercising the power the Constitution has delegated to it. See *J.W. Hampton & Co.* v. *United States*, 276 U.S. 394, 406 (1928). When the Executive acts, he presumptively acts in an executive or administrative capacity as defined in Art. II. And when, as here, one House of Congress purports to act, it is presumptively acting within its assigned sphere.

. . .

Examination of the action taken here by one House pursuant to § 244(c)(2) reveals that it was essentially legislative in purpose and effect. In purporting to exercise power defined in Art. I, § 8, cl. 4, to "establish an uniform Rule of Naturalization," the House took action that had the purpose and effect of altering the legal rights, duties, and relations of persons, including the Attorney General, Executive Branch officials and Chadha, all outside the Legislative Branch. Section 244(c)(2) purports to authorize one House of Congress to require the Attorney General to deport an individual alien whose deportation otherwise would be canceled under § 244. The one-House veto operated in these cases to overrule the Attorney General and mandate Chadha's deportation; absent the House action, Chadha would remain in the United States. Congress has *acted* and its action has altered Chadha's status.

. . .

[The Court acknowledges that the Constitution authorizes one House of Congress to act alone without the check of the President's veto: the power of the House of Representatives to initiate impeachment, the Senate's power to try impeachments, the Senate's action on appointments, and the Senate's action on treaties.]

The veto authorized by § 244(c)(2) doubtless has been in many respects a convenient shortcut; the "sharing" with the Executive by Congress of its authority over aliens in this manner is, on its face, an appealing compromise. In purely practical terms, it is obviously easier for action to be taken by one House without submission to the President; but it is crystal clear from the records of the Convention, contemporaneous writings and debates, that the Framers ranked other values higher than efficiency. The records of the Convention and debates in the states preceding ratification underscore the common desire to define and limit the exercise of the newly created federal powers affecting the states and the people. There is unmistakable expression of a determination that legislation by the national Congress by a step-by-step, deliberate and deliberative process.

The choices we discern as having been made in the Constitutional Convention impose burdens on governmental processes that often seem clumsy, inefficient, even unworkable, but those hard choices were consciously made by men who had lived under a form of government that permitted arbitrary governmental acts to go unchecked. There is no support in the Constitution or decisions of this Court for the proposition that the cumbersomeness and delays often encountered in complying with explicit constitutional standards may be avoided, either by the Congress or by the President. See *Youngstown Sheet & Tube Co.* v. *Sawyer*, 343 U. S. 579 (1952). With all the obvious flaws of delay, untidiness, and potential for abuse, we have not yet found a better way to preserve freedom than by making the exercise of power subject to the carefully crafted restraints spelled out in the Constitution.

V

We hold that the congressional veto provision in § 244(c)(2) is severable from the Act and that it is unconstitutional. Accordingly, the judgment of the Court of Appeals is

Affirmed.

JUSTICE POWELL, concurring in the judgment.

The Court's decision, based on the Presentment Clauses, Art. I, § 7, cls. 2 and 3, apparently will invalidate every use of the legislative veto. The breadth of this holding gives one pause. Congress has included the veto in literally hundreds of statutes, dating back to the 1930's. Congress clearly views this procedure as essential to controlling the delegation of power to administrative agencies. One reasonably may disagree with Congress' assessment of the veto's utility, but the respect due its judgment as a coordinate branch of Government cautions that our holdings should be no more extensive than necessary to decide these cases. In my view, the cases may be decided on a narrower ground. When Congress finds that a particular person does not satisfy the statutory criteria for permanent residence in this country it has assumed a judicial function in violation of the principle of separation of powers. Accordingly, I concur only in the judgment.

. . .

JUSTICE WHITE, dissenting.

Today the Court not only invalidates § 244(c)(2) of the Immigration and Nationality Act, but also sounds the death knell for nearly 200 other statutory provisions in which Congress has reserved a "legislative veto." For this reason, the Court's decision is of surpassing importance. And it is for this reason that the Court would have been well advised to decide the cases, if possible, on the narrower grounds of separation of powers, leaving for full consideration the constitutionality of other congressional review statutes operating on such varied matters as war powers and agency rulemaking, some of which concern the independent regulatory agencies.

The prominence of the legislative veto mechanism in our contemporary political system and its importance to Congress can hardly be overstated. It has become a central means by which Congress secures the accountability of executive and independent agencies. Without the legislative veto, Congress is faced with a Hobson's choice: either to refrain from delegating the necessary authority, leaving itself with a hopeless task of writing laws with the requisite specificity to cover endless special circumstances across the entire policy landscape, or in the alternative, to abdicate its lawmaking function of the Executive Branch and independent agencies. To choose the former leaves major national problems unresolved; to opt for the latter risks unaccountable policymaking by those not elected to fill that role. Accordingly, over the past five decades, the legislative veto has been placed in nearly 200 statutes. The device is known in every field of governmental concern: reorganization, budgets, foreign affairs, war powers, and regulation of trade, safety, energy, the environment, and the economy.

I

[White explains that the legislative veto arose in 1929 when President Hoover sought authority to reorganize the executive branch and expressed willingness to have Congress check his actions by exercising a one-House veto. In subsequent actions, the two branches applied this quid pro quo to other areas: the President gaining new authority and Congress holding a legislative veto to control the delegated authority.]

The history of the legislative veto also makes clear that it has not been a sword with which Congress has struck out to aggrandize itself at the expense of the other branches—the concerns of Madison and Hamilton. Rather, the veto has been a means of defense, a reservation of ultimate authority necessary if Congress is to fulfill its designated role under Art. I as the Nation's lawmaker. While the President has often objected to particular legislative vetoes, generally those left in the hands of congressional Committees, the Executive has more often agreed to legislative review as the price for a broad delegation of authority. To be sure, the President may have preferred unrestricted power, but that could be precisely why Congress thought it essential to retain a check on the exercise of delegated authority.

. . .

III

. . .

The central concern of the presentment and bicameralism requirements of Art. I is that when a departure from the legal status quo is undertaken, it is done with the approval of the President and both Houses of Congress—or, in the event of a Presidential veto, a two-thirds majority in both Houses. This interest is fully satisfied by the operation of § 244(c)(2). The President's approval is found in the Attorney General's action in recommending to Congress that the deportation order for a given alien be suspended. The House and the Senate indicate their approval of the Executive's action by not passing a resolution of disapproval within the statutory period. Thus, a change in the legal status quo—the deportability of the alien— is consummated only with the approval of each of the three relevant actors. The disagreement of any one of the three maintains the alien's pre-existing status: the Executive may choose not to recommend suspension; the House and Senate may each veto the recommendation. The effect on the rights and obligations of the affected individuals and upon the legislative system is precisely the same as if a private bill were introduced but failed to receive the necessary approval. . . .

V

I regret that I am in disagreement with my colleagues on the fundamental questions that these cases present. But even more I regret the destructive scope of the Court's holding. It reflects a profoundly different conception of the Constitution than that held by the courts which sanctioned the modern administrative state. Today's decision strikes down in one fell swoop provisions in more laws enacted by Congress than the Court has cumulatively invalidated in its history. I fear it will now be more difficult to "insur[e] that the fundamental policy decisions in our society will be made not by an appointed official but by the body immediately responsible to the people," *Arizona* v. *California*, 373 U.S. 546, 626 (1963) (Harlan, J., dissenting in part). I must dissent.

. . .

JUSTICE REHNQUIST, with whom JUSTICE WHITE joins, dissenting.

[Rehnquist states his belief that Congress did not intend the one-House veto to be severable from § 244(c)(2). Because the Court had held the legislative veto unconstitutional, Rehnquist would strike down the delegated authority as well.]

Legislative Vetoes After Chadha

After the Supreme Court in *INS* v. *Chadha* (1983) held the legislative veto unconstitutional, Congress continued to place legislative vetoes in bills and President Reagan continued to sign them into law. Many of these new statutory controls required executive agencies to seek the approval of specific congressional committees before implementing an agency action. The various methods available to Congress for finding substitutes for the legislative veto, and in fact for using legislative vetoes, are explored by Louis Fisher in "Judicial Misjudgments About the Lawmaking Process: The Legislative Veto Case," 45 Pub. Adm. Rev. 705 (Special Issue, November 1985). Footnotes omitted.

In past years the Supreme Court has damaged its reputation by issuing decisions based on misconceptions about the political and economic system. After trying to impose archaic and mechanical concepts about federalism, the taxing power, the commerce power, and other clauses of the Constitution, the court was forced to retreat from pronouncements that were simply unacceptable for a developing nation. To minimize what Charles Evans Hughes once called the court's penchant for "self-inflicted wounds," justices evolved a number of rules to limit their exercise of judicial review. One mainstay is the principle that the court will not "formulate a rule of constitutional law broader than is required by the precise facts to which it is to be applied."

That guideline was not followed in 1983 when the Supreme Court issued *INS* v. *Chadha*, which declared the legislative veto unconstitutional in all its forms. The court announced that future congressional efforts to alter "the legal rights, duties and relations of persons" outside the legislative branch must follow the full lawmaking process:

passage of a bill or joint resolution by both Houses and presentment of that measure to the president for his signature or veto. The court lectured Congress that it could no longer rely on the legislative veto as "a convenient shortcut" to control executive agencies. Instead, "legislation by the national Congress [must] be a step-by-step, deliberate and deliberative process." According to the court, the framers insisted that "the legislative power of the Federal Government be exercised in accord with a single, finely wrought and exhaustively considered, procedure."

A HISTORY OF ACCOMMODATIONS

All three branches reached agreement long ago that the step-by-step, deliberate and deliberative process is not appropriate for each and every exercise of the legislative power. Despite occasional invocations of the non-delegation doctrine, the court itself has accepted the inevitable delegation of legislative power to executive agencies and independent commissions. Administrative bodies routinely "make law" through the rulemaking process. Efforts are made to subject this lawmaking activity to procedural safeguards, but the persistence of the Administrative State is ample proof that the theoretical model of legislative action envisioned by the framers applies only in the most general sense to the 20th century.

Notwithstanding 50 years of delicate accommodations between the executive and legislative branches regarding the legislative veto, the Supreme Court decided to strike it down in one fell swoop. In his dissent, Justice White claimed that the court "sounds the death knell for nearly 200 other statutory provisions in which Congress has reserved a 'legislative veto.'" Although White demonstrated better than his colleagues an appreciation of the realities and subtleties of lawmaking in contemporary times, he too framed the issue too starkly. He argued that without the legislative veto, Congress "is faced with a Hobson's choice: either to refrain from delegating the necessary authority, leaving itself with a hopeless task of writing laws with the requisite specificity to cover endless special circumstances across the entire policy landscape, or in the alternative, to abdicate its lawmaking function to the Executive Branch and independent agencies." In fact, Congress and the agencies have access to a number of middle-range options that serve much the same purpose as the legislative veto. In some cases, current practices are difficult to distinguish from what supposedly vanished with the death knell.

. . .

THE PERSISTENCE OF LEGISLATIVE VETOES

It came as a surprise to some observers that Congress continued to place legislative vetoes in bills after the court's decision and President Reagan continued to sign the bills into law. In the 16 months between *Chadha* and the adjournment of the 98th Congress, an additional 53 legislative vetoes were added to the books.

[By the end of the 99th Congress, which adjourned in October 1986, the list of new legislative vetoes had increased to 102. More than forty new legislative vetoes were enacted during the 100th Congress.]

A flagrant case of non-compliance? A sign of disrespect for the courts? An alarming challenge to the time-honored belief that the Supreme Court has the last word on constitutional questions? Perhaps, but the court painted with too broad a brush and offered a simplistic solution that is unacceptable to the political branches. Its decision will be eroded by open defiance and subtle evasion. Neither consequence is attractive, but much of the responsibility for this condition belongs on the doorstep of the court.

Some of the legislative vetoes enacted since *Chadha* are easy to spot. Most of them vest control in the appropriations committees. For example, construction grants by the Environmental Protection Agency are subject to the approval of the appropriations committees (97 Stat. 226). The approval of the appropriations committees is required before exceeding certain dollar amounts in the National Flood Insurance Fund (97 Stat. 227). With the approval of the appropriations committees, up to 5 percent may be transferred between specified accounts of the National Aeronautics and Space Administration (NASA) (97 Stat. 229). Reimbursement of certain funds for the Ventura Marina project, administered by the Corps of Engineers, requires the prior approval of the appropriations committees (97 Stat. 312). Appropriations may not be available for the acquisition, sale, or transference of Washington's Union Station without the prior approval of the appropriations committees (97 Stat. 462).

Other legislative vetoes are more subtle. A continuing resolution provided that foreign assistance funds allocated to each country "shall not exceed those provided in fiscal year 1983 or those provided in the budget estimates for each country, whichever are lower, unless submitted through the regular reprogramming procedures of the Committees on Appropriations" (97 Stat. 736). Those procedures provide for committee priorapproval. The District of Columbia Appropriation Act for fiscal 1984 prohibited funds from being obligated or spent by reprogramming "except pursuant to advance approval of the reprogramming granted according to the procedure set forth" in two House reports, both of which require prior approval by the appropriations committees (97 Stat. 827).

One year after *Chadha*, President Reagan received the HUD-Independent Agencies Appropriations bill which contained a number of committee vetoes. In his signing statement, he took note of those vetoes and asked Congress to stop adding provisions that the Supreme Court had held to be unconstitutional. He said that "the time has come, with more than a year having passed since the Supreme Court's decision in *Chadha*, to make clear that legislation containing legislative veto devices that comes to me for my approval or disapproval will be implemented in a manner consistent with the *Chadha* decision." The clear import was that the administration did not feel bound by the statutory requirements to seek the approval of congressional committees before implementing certain actions.

The House Appropriations Committee responded to the president's statement by reviewing an agreement it had entered into with NASA four years previously. Caps were set on various NASA programs, usually at the level requested in the president's budget. The agreement allowed NASA to exceed the caps with the approval of the appropriations committees. The House Appropriations Committee thought that the procedure had "worked well during the past four years, and has provided a mechanism by which the Congress and the Committee can be assured that funds are used solely for the purpose for which they were appropriated." Because of Reagan's statement and the threat to ignore committee controls, the committee said it was necessary to repeal the accommodation that had lasted for four years. Repeal language was inserted in the second supplemental bill for fiscal 1984. Both sides stood to lose. The appropriations committees would not be able to veto NASA proposals; NASA would not be able to exceed ceilings without enacting new language in a separate appropriation bill.

Neither NASA nor the appropriations committees wanted to enact a separate public law just to exceed a cap. To avoid this kind of administrative rigidity, NASA Administrator James M. Beggs wrote to both committees on August 9, 1984. His letter reveals the pragmatic sense of give-and-take that is customary between executive agencies and congressional committees. His letter also under-

scores the impracticality and unreality of the doctrines enunciated by the Supreme Court in *Chadha:*

"We have now operated under the present operating plan and reprogramming procedures for several years and have found them to be workable. In light of the constitutional questions raised concerning the legislative veto provisions included in P.L. 98–371 [the HUD-Independent Agencies Appropriations Act], however, the House Committee on Appropriations has proposed in H.R. 6040, the FY 1984 general supplemental, deletion of all Committee approval provisions, leaving inflexible, binding funding limitations on several programs. Without some procedure for adjustment, other than a subsequent separate legislative enactment, these ceilings could seriously impact the ability of NASA to meet unforeseen technical changes or problems that are inherent in challenging R&D programs. We believe that the present legislative procedure could be converted by this letter into an informal agreement by NASA not to exceed amounts for Committee designated programs without the approval of the Committees on Appropriations. This agreement would assume that both the statutory funding ceilings and the Committee approval mechanisms would be deleted from the FY 1985 legislation, and that it would not be the normal practice to include either mechanism in future appropriations bills. Further, the agreement would assume that future program ceiling amounts would be identified by the Committees in the Conference Report accompanying NASA's annual appropriations act and confirmed by NASA in its submission of the annual operating plan. NASA would not expend any funds over the ceilings identified in the Conference Report for these programs without the prior approval of the Committees."

In short, the agency would continue to honor legislative vetoes. But they would be informal rather than statutory. Beggs ended his letter by assuring the appropriations committees that NASA "will comply with any ceilings imposed by the Committees without the need for legislative ceilings which could cause serious damage to NASA's ongoing programs." By converting the legislative veto to an informal and non-statutory status, NASA is not legally bound by the agreement. Violation of the agreement, however, could provoke the appropriations committees to place caps in the appropriation bill and force the agency to lift them only through the enactment of another public law.

. . .

CONCLUSIONS

Through its misreading of history, congressional procedures, and executive-legislative relations, the Supreme Court has commanded the political branches to follow a lawmaking process that is impracticable and unworkable. Neither agencies nor committees want the static model of government offered by the court. The inevitable result is a record of non-compliance, subtle evasion, and a system of lawmaking that is now more convoluted, cumbersome, and covert than before. In many cases the court's decision simply drives underground a set of legislative and committee vetoes that had previously operated in plain sight. No one should be misled if the number of legislative vetoes placed in statutes gradually declines over the years. Fading from view will not mean disappearance. In one form or another legislative vetoes will remain an important method for reconciling legislative and executive interests.

Watkins v. United States

354 U.S. 178 (1957)

Beginning in the early 1950s, congressional committees conducted searching inquiries into left-wing activities of American citizens. The atmosphere of the Cold War permitted little toleration of "disloyal" thoughts and conduct. In this case, the House Committee on Un-American Activities called John Watkins, a labor organizer, to testify. He agreed to describe his past participation in the Communist Party and identify current members. However, he refused to answer questions about those who had left the movement. His refusal led to conviction for contempt of Congress. A panel of the D.C. Circuit reversed the conviction, but the full bench, sitting *en banc*, affirmed the conviction.

MR. CHIEF JUSTICE WARREN delivered the opinion of the Court.

This is a review by certiorari of a conviction under 2 U. S. C. § 192 for "contempt of Congress." The misdemeanor is alleged to have been committed during a hearing before a congressional investigating committee. It is not the case of a truculent or contumacious witness who refuses to answer all questions or who, by boisterous or discourteous conduct, disturbs the decorum of the committee room. Petitioner was prosecuted for refusing to make certain disclosures which he asserted to be beyond the authority of the committee to demand. The controversy thus rests upon fundamental principles of the power of the Congress and the limitations upon that power. We approach the questions presented with conscious awareness of the far-reaching ramifications that can follow from a decision of this nature.

On April 29, 1954, petitioner appeared as a witness in compliance with a subpoena issued by a Subcommittee of the Committee on Un-American Activities of the House of Representatives. The Subcommittee elicited from petitioner a description of his background in labor union activities. . . .

Petitioner's name had been mentioned by two witnesses who testified before the Committee at prior hearings. In September 1952, one Donald O. Spencer admitted having been a Communist from 1943 to 1946. He declared that he had been recruited into the Party with the endorsement and prior approval of petitioner, whom he identified as the then District Vice-President of the Farm Equipment Workers. Spencer also mentioned that petitioner had attended meetings at which only card-carrying Communists were admitted. A month before petitioner testified, one Walter Rumsey stated that he had been recruited into the Party by petitioner. Rumsey added that he had paid Party dues to, and later collected dues from, petitioner, who had assumed the name, Sam Brown. Rumsey told the Committee that he left the Party in 1944.

Petitioner answered these allegations freely and without reservation. His attitude toward the inquiry is clearly revealed from the statement he made when the questioning turned to the subject of his past conduct, associations and predilections:

"I am not now nor have I ever been a card-carrying member of the Communist Party. Rumsey was wrong when he said I had recruited him into the party, that I had received his dues, that I paid dues to him, and that I had used the alias Sam Brown.

"Spencer was wrong when he termed any meetings which I attended as closed Communist Party meetings.

"I would like to make it clear that for a period of time from approximately 1942 to 1947 I cooperated with the Communist Party and participated in Communist activities to such a degree that some persons may honestly believe that I was a member of the party.

"I have made contributions upon occasions to Communist causes. I have signed petitions for Communist causes. I attended caucuses at an FE convention at which Communist Party officials were present."

. . .

The Subcommittee, too, was apparently satisfied with petitioner's disclosures. After some further discussion elaborating on the statement, counsel for the Committee turned to another aspect of Rumsey's testimony. Rumsey had identified a group of persons whom he had known as members of the Communist Party, and counsel began to read this list of names to petitioner.

Petitioner stated that he did not know several of the persons. Of those whom he did know, he refused to tell whether he knew them to have been members of the Communist Party. He explained to the Subcommittee why he took such a position:

"I am not going to plead the fifth amendment, but I refuse to answer certain questions that I believe are outside the proper scope of your committee's activities. I will answer any questions which this committee puts to me about myself. I will also answer questions about those persons whom I knew to be members of the Communist Party and whom I believe still are. I will not, however, answer any questions with respect to others with whom I associated in the past. I do not believe that any law in this country requires me to testify about persons who may in the past have been Communist Party members or otherwise engaged in Communist Party activity but who to my best knowledge and belief have long since removed themselves from the Communist movement.

"I do not believe that such questions are relevant to the work of this committee nor do I believe that this committee has the right to undertake the public exposure of persons because of their past activities. I may be wrong, and the committee may have this power, but until and unless a court of law so holds and directs me to answer, I most firmly refuse to discuss the political activities of my past associates."

The Chairman of the Committee submitted a report of petitioner's refusal to answer questions to the House of Representatives. H. R. Rep. No. 1579, 83d Cong., 2d Sess. The House directed the Speaker to certify the Committee's report to the United States Attorney for initiation of criminal prosecution. H. Res. 534, 83d Cong., 2d Sess. A seven-count indictment was returned. Petitioner waived his right to jury trial and was found guilty on all counts by the court. The sentence, a fine of $100 and one year in prison, was suspended, and petitioner was placed on probation.

An appeal was taken to the Court of Appeals for the District of Columbia. The conviction was reversed by a three-judge panel, one member dissenting. Upon rehearing *en banc*, the full bench affirmed the conviction with the judges of the original majority in dissent. 98 U.S. App. D.C. 190, 233 F. 2d 681. We granted certiorari because of the very important questions of constitutional law presented. 352 U. S. 822.

We start with several basic premises on which there is general agreement. The power of the Congress to conduct investigations is inherent in the legislative process. That power is broad. It encompasses inquiries concerning the administration of existing laws as well as proposed or possibly needed statutes. It includes surveys of defects in our social, economic or political system for the purpose of enabling the Congress to remedy them. It comprehends probes into departments of the Federal Government to expose corruption, inefficiency or waste. But, broad as is this power of inquiry, it is not unlimited. There is no general authority to expose the private affairs of individuals without justification in terms of the functions of the Congress. This was freely conceded by the Solicitor General in his argument of this case. *["Now, we don't claim on behalf of the Government that there is any right to expose for the purposes of exposure. And I don't know that Congress has ever claimed any such right. But we do say, in the same breath, that there is a right to inform the public at the same time you inform the Congress."]* Nor is the Congress a law enforcement or trial agency. These are functions of the executive and judicial departments of government. No inquiry is an end in itself; it must be related to, and in furtherance of, a legitimate task of the Congress. Investigations conducted solely for the personal aggrandizement of the investigators or to "punish" those investigated are indefensible.

It is unquestionably the duty of all citizens to cooperate with the Congress in its efforts to obtain the facts needed for intelligent legislative action. It is their unremitting obligation to respond to subpoenas, to respect the dignity of the Congress and its committees and to testify fully with respect to matters within the province of proper investigation. This, of course, assumes that the constitutional rights of witnesses will be respected by the Congress as they are in a court of justice. The Bill of Rights is applicable to investigations as to all forms of governmental action. Witnesses cannot be compelled to give evidence against themselves.

They cannot be subjected to unreasonable search and seizure. Nor can the First Amendment freedoms of speech, press, religion, or political belief and association be abridged.

[The Court describes the English Parliament's abuse of its contempt power, which was immune even from judicial review. Citizens who made comments critical of Parliament could be punished, fined, and imprisoned. Parliamentary probes were eventually replaced by investigations conducted by Royal Commissions of Inquiry, comprised of experts who rarely had the authority to compel the testimony of witnesses or the production of documents.]

The history of contempt of the legislature in this country is notably different from that of England. In the early days of the United States, there lingered the direct knowledge of the evil effects of absolute power. Most of the instances of use of compulsory process by the first Congresses concerned matters affecting the qualification or integrity of their members or came about in inquiries dealing with suspected corruption or mismanagement of government officials. Unlike the English practice, from the very outset the use of contempt power by the legislature was deemed subject to judicial review.

. . .

It is not surprising, from the fact that the Houses of Congress so sparingly employed the power to conduct investigations, that there have been few cases requiring judicial review of the power. The Nation was almost one hundred years old before the first case reached this Court to challenge the use of compulsory process as a legislative device *[Kilbourn v.* Thompson, *103 U.S. 168 (1881). Relatively few congressional investigations thereafter were contested in the courts.]* . . .

In the decade following World War II, there appeared a new kind of congressional inquiry unknown in prior periods of American history. Principally this was the result of the various investigations into the threat of subversion of the United States Government, but other subjects of congressional interest also contributed to the changed scene. This new phase of legislative inquiry involved a broad-scale intrusion into the lives and affairs of private citizens. It brought before the courts novel questions of the appropriate limits of congressional inquiry. . . .

. . . The critical element is the existence of, and the weight to be ascribed to, the interest of the Congress in demanding disclosures from an unwilling witness. We cannot simply assume, however, that every congressional investigation is justified by a public need that overbalances any private rights affected. To do so would be to abdicate the responsibility placed by the Constitution upon the judiciary to insure that the Congress does not unjustifiably encroach upon an individual's right to privacy nor abridge his liberty of speech, press, religion or assembly.

. . .

We have no doubt that there is no congressional power to expose for the sake of exposure. The public is, of course, entitled to be informed concerning the workings of its government. That cannot be inflated into a general power to expose where the predominant result can only be an invasion of the private rights of individuals. But a solution to our problem is not to be found in testing the motives of committee members for this purpose. Such is not our function. Their motives alone would not vitiate an investigation which had been instituted by a House of Congress if that assembly's legislative purpose is being served.

. . .

The authorizing resolution of the Un-American Activities Committee was adopted in 1938. . . . It defines the Committee's authority as follows:

"The Committee on Un-American Activities, as a whole or by subcommittee, is authorized to make from time to time investigations of (1) the extent, character, and objects of un-American propaganda activities in the United States, (2) the diffusion within the United States of subversive and un-American propaganda that is instigated from foreign countries or of a domestic origin and attacks the principle of the form of government as guaranteed by our Constitution, and (3) all other questions in relation thereto that would aid Congress in any necessary remedial legislation."

It would be difficult to imagine a less explicit authorizing resolution. Who can define the meaning of "un-American"? What is that single, solitary "principle of the form of government as guaranteed by our Constitution"? There is no need to dwell upon the language, however. At one time, perhaps, the resolution might have been read narrowly to confine the Committee to the subject of propaganda. The events that have transpired in the fifteen years before the interrogation of petitioner make such a construction impossible at this date.

The members of the Committee have clearly demonstrated that they did not feel themselves restricted in any way to propaganda in the narrow sense of the word. Unquestionably the Committee conceived of its task in the grand view of its name. Un-American activities were its target, no matter how or where manifested. . . .

Combining the language of the resolution with the construction it has been given, it is evident that the preliminary control of the Committee exercised by the House of Representatives is slight or non-existent. No one could reasonably deduce from the charter the kind of investigation that the Committee was directed to make.

[In order for a reviewing court to determine whether a committee investigation is fulfilling a legislative purpose, the committee's activity must be properly authorized by resolution. In order for a witness to understand the pertinency of a question directed by a committee member or committee staff, and to avoid being held in contempt, the witness must have knowledge of the subject of the inquiry and the pertinency of a question to that inquiry. This knowledge can come from the authorizing resolution, remarks by committee members, and the nature of the proceedings.]

. . . Unless the subject matter has been made to appear with undisputable clarity, it is the duty of the investigative body, upon objection of the witness on grounds of pertinency, to state for the record the subject under inquiry at that time and the manner in which the propounded questions are pertinent thereto. To be meaningful, the explanation must describe what the topic under inquiry is and the connective reasoning whereby the precise questions asked relate to it.

The statement of the Committee Chairman in this case, in response to petitioner's protest, was woefully inadequate to convey sufficient information as to the pertinency of the questions to the subject under inquiry. Petitioner was thus not accorded a fair opportunity to determine whether he was within his rights in refusing to answer, and his conviction is necessarily invalid under the Due Process Clause of the Fifth Amendment.

The judgment of the Court of Appeals is reversed, and the case is remanded to the District Court with instructions to dismiss the indictment.

It is so ordered.

MR. JUSTICE BURTON and MR. JUSTICE WHITTAKER took no part in the consideration or decision of this case.

MR. JUSTICE FRANKFURTER, concurring.

. . .

MR. JUSTICE CLARK, dissenting.

As I see it the chief fault in the majority opinion is its mischievous curbing of the informing function of the Congress. While I am not versed in its procedures, my experience in the Executive Branch of the Government leads me to believe that the requirements laid down in the opinion for the operation of the committee system of inquiry are both unnecessary and unworkable. . . .

III.

Coming to the merits of Watkins' case, the Court reverses the judgment because: (1) The subject matter of the inquiry was not "made to appear with undisputable clarity" either through its "charter" or by the Chairman at the time of the hearing and, therefore, Watkins was deprived of a clear understanding of "the manner in which the propounded questions [were] pertinent thereto"; and (2) the present committee system of inquiry of the House, as practiced by the Un-American Activities Committee, does not provide adequate safeguards for the protection of the constitutional right of free speech. I subscribe to neither conclusion.

. . .

V.

. . . While there may be no restraint by the Government of one's beliefs, the right of free belief has never been extended to include the withholding of knowledge of past events or transactions. There is no general privilege of silence. The First Amendment does not make speech or silence permissible to a person in such measure as he chooses. Watkins has here exercised his own choice as to when he talks, what questions he answers, and when he remains silent. A witness is not given such a choice by the Amendment. . . .

Barenblatt v. United States

360 U.S. 109 (1959)

The Court's "lecture" to Congress in *Watkins* v. *United States* (1957) was one of several cases that convinced many Members of Congress that the judiciary was overstepping its bounds. A number of court-curbing bills were introduced and acted upon. There is reason to believe that the Court recognized a serious collision with Congress and moved in this case, as well as others, to reduce the friction. Lloyd Barenblatt, a college professor, refused to answer certain questions put to him by a subcommittee of the House Committee on Un-American Activities. For his refusal he was convicted, fined, and sentenced to six months in prison.

MR. JUSTICE HARLAN delivered the opinion of the Court.

Once more the Court is required to resolve the conflicting constitutional claims of congressional power and of an individual's right to resist its exercise. The congressional power in question concerns the internal process of Congress in moving within its legislative domain; it involves the utilization of its committees to secure "testimony needed to enable it efficiently to exercise a legislative function belonging to it under the Constitution." *McGrain* v. *Daugherty*, 273 U. S. 135, 160. The power of inquiry has been employed by Congress throughout our history, over the whole range of the national interests concerning which Congress might legislate or decide upon due investigation not to legislate; it has similarly been utilized in determining what to appropriate from the national purse, or whether to appropriate. The scope of the power of inquiry, in short, is as penetrating and far-reaching as the potential power to enact and appropriate under the Constitution.

Broad as it is, the power is not, however, without limitations. Since Congress may only investigate into those areas in which it may potentially legislate or appropriate, it cannot inquire into matters which are within the exclusive province of one of the other branches of the Government. Lacking the judicial power given to the Judiciary, it cannot inquire into matters that are exclusively the concern of the Judiciary. Neither can it supplant the Executive in what exclusively belongs to the Executive. And the Congress, in common with all branches of the Government, must exercise its powers subject to the limitations placed by the Constitution on governmental action, more particularly in the context of this case the relevant limitations of the Bill of Rights.

The congressional power of inquiry, its range and scope, and an individual's duty in relation to it, must be viewed in proper perspective. . . . The power and the right of resistance to it are to be judged in the concrete, not on the basis of abstractions. In the present case congressional efforts to learn the extent of a nation-wide, indeed worldwide, problem have brought one of its investigating committees into the field of education. Of course, broadly viewed, inquiries cannot be made into the teaching that is pursued in any of our educational institutions. When academic teaching-freedom and its corollary learning-freedom, so essential to the well-being of the Nation, are claimed, this Court will always be on the alert against intrusion by Congress into this constitutionally protected domain. But this does not mean that the Congress is precluded from interrogating a witness merely because he is a teacher. An educational institution is not a constitutional sanctuary from inquiry into matters that may otherwise be within the constitutional legislative domain merely for the reason that inquiry is made of someone within its walls.

In the setting of this framework of constitutional history, practice and legal precedents, we turn to the particularities of this case.

We here review petitioner's conviction under 2 U.S.C. § 192 for contempt of Congress, arising from his refusal to answer certain questions put to him by a Subcommittee of the House Committee on Un-American Activities during the course of an inquiry concerning alleged Communist infiltration into the field of education.

[§ 192 provides: "Every person who having been summoned as a witness by the authority of either House of Congress to give testimony or to produce papers upon any matter under inquiry before either House, or any joint committee established by a joint or concurrent resolution of the two Houses of Congress, or any committee of either House of Congress, willfully makes default, or who, having appeared, refuses to answer any question pertinent to the question under inquiry, shall be deemed guilty of a misdemeanor, punishable by a fine of not more than $1,000 nor less than $100 and imprisonment in a common jail for not less than one month nor more than twelve months."]

. . .

Pursuant to a subpoena, and accompanied by counsel, petitioner on June 28, 1954, appeared as a witness before this congressional Subcommittee. After answering a few preliminary questions and testifying that he had been a graduate student and teaching fellow at the University of Michigan from 1947 to 1950 and an instructor in psychology at Vassar College from 1950 to shortly before his appearance before the Subcommittee, petitioner objected generally to the right of the Subcommittee to inquire into his "political" and "religious" beliefs or any "other personal and private affairs" or "associational activities," upon grounds set forth in a previously prepared memorandum which he was allowed to file with the Subcommittee. Thereafter petitioner specifically declined to answer each of the following five questions:

"Are you now a member of the Communist Party? [Count One.]

"Have you ever been a member of the Communist Party? [Count Two.]

"Now, you have stated that you knew Francis Crowley. Did you know Francis Crowley as a member of the Communist Party? [Count Three.]

"Were you ever a member of the Haldane Club of the Communist Party while at the University of Michigan? [Count Four.]

"Were you a member while a student of the University of Michigan Council of Arts, Sciences, and Professions?" [Count Five.]

In each instance the grounds of refusal were those set forth in the prepared statement. Petitioner expressly disclaimed reliance upon "the Fifth Amendment."

. . .

. . . As we conceive the ultimate issue in this case to be whether petitioner could properly be convicted of contempt for refusing to answer questions relating to his participation in or knowledge of alleged Communist Party activities at educational institutions in this country, we find it unnecessary to consider the validity of his conviction under the Third and Fifth Counts, the only ones involving questions which on their face do not directly relate to such participation or knowledge.

Petitioner's various contentions resolve themselves into three propositions: First, the compelling of testimony by the Subcommittee was neither legislatively authorized nor constitutionally permissible because of the vagueness of Rule XI of the House of Representatives, Eighty-third Congress, the charter of authority of the parent Committee. Second, petitioner was not adequately apprised of the pertinency of the Subcommittee's questions to the subject matter of the inquiry. Third, the questions petitioner refused to answer infringed rights protected by the First Amendment.

[After deciding that Rule XI was not constitutionally infirm on the ground of vagueness, and that the questions put to Barenblatt were clearly pertinent and that he had been adequately informed, the Court turns to the First Amendment issue.]

CONSTITUTIONAL CONTENTIONS.

Our function, at this point, is purely one of constitutional adjudication in the particular case and upon the particular record before us, not to pass judgment upon the general wisdom or efficacy of the activities of this Committee in a vexing and complicated field.

The precise constitutional issue confronting us is whether the Subcommittee's inquiry into petitioner's past or present membership in the Communist Party transgressed the provisions of the First Amendment, which of course reach and limit congressional investigations. *Watkins, supra,* at 197.

The Court's past cases establish sure guides to decision. Undeniably, the First Amendment in some circumstances protects an individual from being compelled to disclose his associational relationships. However, the protections of the First Amendment, unlike a proper claim of the privilege against self-incrimination under the Fifth Amendment, do not afford a witness the right to resist inquiry in all circumstances. Where First Amendment rights are asserted to bar governmental interrogation resolution of the issue always involves a balancing by the courts of the competing private and public interests at stake in the particular circumstances shown. These principles were recognized in the *Watkins* case, where, in speaking of the First Amendment in relation to congressional inquiries, we said (at p. 198): "It is manifest that despite the adverse effects which follow upon compelled disclosure of private matters, not all such inquiries are barred. . . . The critical element is the existence of, and the weight to be ascribed to, the interest of the Congress in demanding disclosures from an unwilling witness." . . .

. . . in stating in the *Watkins* case, p. 200, that "there is no congressional power to expose for the sake of exposure," we at the same time declined to inquire into the "motives of committee members," and recognized that their "motives alone would not vitiate an investigation which had been instituted by a House of Congress if that assembly's legislative purpose is being served." Having scrutinized this record we cannot say that the unanimous panel of the Court of Appeals which first considered this case was wrong in concluding that "the primary purposes of the inquiry were in aid of legislative processes." 240 F. 2d, at 881. Certainly this is not a case like *Kilbourn* v. *Thompson*, 103 U.S. 168, 192, where "the House of Representatives not only exceeded the limit of its own authority, but assumed a power which could only be properly exercised by another branch of the government, because it was in its nature clearly judicial." See *McGrain* v. *Daugherty*, 273 U. S. 135, 171. The constitutional legislative power of Congress in this instance is beyond question.

. . .

We conclude that the balance between the individual and the governmental interests here at stake must be struck in favor of the latter, and that therefore the provisions of the First Amendment have not been offended.

We hold that petitioner's conviction for contempt of Congress discloses no infirmity, and that the judgment of the Court of Appeals must be

Affirmed.

MR. JUSTICE BLACK, with whom THE CHIEF JUSTICE and MR. JUSTICE DOUGLAS concur, dissenting.

. . .

. . . I cannot agree with this disposition of the case for I believe that the resolution establishing the House Un-American Activities Committee and the questions that Committee asked Barenblatt violate the Constitution in several respects. (1) Rule XI creating the Committee authorizes such a sweeping, unlimited, all-inclusive and undiscrimi-

nating compulsory examination of witnesses in the field of speech, press, petition and assembly that it violates the procedural requirements of the Due Process Clause of the Fifth Amendment. (2) Compelling an answer to the questions asked Barenblatt abridges freedom of speech and association in contravention of the First Amendment. (3) The Committee proceedings were part of a legislative program to stigmatize and punish by public identification and exposure all witnesses considered by the Committee to be guilty of Communist affiliations, as well as all witnesses who refused to answer Committee questions on constitutional grounds; the Committee was thus improperly seeking to try, convict, and punish suspects, a task which the Constitution expressly denies to Congress and grants exclusively to the courts, to be exercised by them only after indictment and in full compliance with all the safeguards provided by the Bill of Rights.

I.

It goes without saying that a law to be valid must be clear enough to make its commands understandable. For obvious reasons, the standard of certainty required in criminal statutes is more exacting than in noncriminal statutes. This is simply because it would be unthinkable to convict a man for violating a law he could not understand. This Court has recognized that the stricter standard is as much required in criminal contempt cases as in all other criminal cases, and has emphasized that the "vice of vagueness" is especially pernicious where legislative power over an area involving speech, press, petition and assembly is involved. In this area the statement that a statute is void if it "attempts to cover so much that it effectively covers nothing," see *Musser* v. *Utah*, 333 U. S. 95, 97, takes on double significance. For a statute broad enough to support infringement of speech, writings, thoughts and public assemblies, against the unequivocal command of the First Amendment necessarily leaves all persons to guess just what the law really means to cover, and fear of a wrong guess inevitably leads people to forego the very rights the Constitution sought to protect above all others. Vagueness becomes even more intolerable in this area if one accepts, as the Court today does, a balancing test to decide if First Amendment rights shall be protected. It is difficult at best to make a man guess—at the penalty of imprisonment—whether a court will consider the State's need for certain information superior to society's interest in unfettered freedom. It is unconscionable to make him choose between the right to keep silent and the need to speak when the statute supposedly establishing the "state's interest" is too vague to give him guidance. Cf. *Scull* v. *Virginia*, 359 U. S. 344.

Measured by the foregoing standards, Rule XI cannot support any conviction for refusal to testify. In substance it authorizes the Committee to compel witnesses to give evidence about all "un-American propaganda," whether instigated in this country or abroad. The word "propaganda" seems to mean anything that people say, write, think or associate together about. The term "un-American" is equally vague. As was said in *Watkins* v. *United States*, 354 U. S. 178, 202, "Who can define [its] meaning . . . ? What is that single, solitary 'principle of the form of government as guaranteed by our Constitution'?" I think it clear that the boundaries of the Committee are, to say the least, "nebulous." Indeed, "It would be difficult to imagine a less explicit authorizing resolution." *Ibid.*

. . .

II.

The First Amendment says in no equivocal language that Congress shall pass no law abridging freedom of speech, press, assembly or petition. The activities of this Committee, authorized by Congress, do precisely that, through exposure, obloquy and public scorn. See *Watkins* v. *United States*, 354 U. S. 178, 197–198. The Court does not really deny this fact but relies on a combination of three reasons for permitting the infringement: (a) The notion that despite the First Amendment's command Congress can abridge speech and association if this Court decides that the governmental interest in abridging speech is greater than an individual's interest in exercising that freedom, (b) the Government's right to "preserve itself," (c) the fact that the Committee is only after Communists or suspected Communists in this investigation.

(A) I do not agree that laws directly abridging First Amendment freedoms can be justified by a congressional or judicial balancing process. . . .

To apply the Court's balancing test under such circumstances is to read the First Amendment to say "Congress shall pass no law abridging freedom of speech, press, assembly and petition, unless Congress and the Supreme Court reach the joint conclusion that on balance the interest of the Government in stifling these freedoms is greater than the interest of the people in having them exercised." This is closely akin to the notion that neither the First Amendment nor any other provision of the Bill of Rights should be enforced unless the Court believes it is *reasonable* to do so. . . .

But even assuming what I cannot assume, that some balancing is proper in this case, I feel that the Court after stating the test ignores it completely. At most it balances the right of the Government to preserve itself, against Barenblatt's right to refrain from revealing Communist affiliations. Such a balance, however, mistakes the factors to be weighed. In the first place, it completely leaves out the real interest in Barenblatt's silence, the interest of the people as a whole in being able to join organizations, advocate causes and make political "mistakes" without later being subjected to governmental penalties for having dared to think for themselves. It is this right, the right to err politically, which keeps us strong as a Nation. For no number of laws against communism can have as much effect as the personal conviction which comes from having heard its arguments and rejected them, or from having once accepted its tenets and later recognized their worthlessness. Instead, the obloquy which results from investigations such as this not only stifles "mistakes" but prevents all but the most courageous from hazarding any views which might at some later time become disfavored. This result, whose importance cannot be overestimated, is doubly crucial when it affects the universities, on which we must largely rely for the experimentation and development of new ideas essential to our country's welfare. It is these interests of society, rather than Barenblatt's own right to silence, which I think the Court should put on the balance against the demands of the Government, if any balancing process is to be tolerated. Instead they are not mentioned, while on the other side the demands of the Government are vastly overstated and called "self preservation." . . .

(B) Moreover, I cannot agree with the Court's notion that First Amendment freedoms must be abridged in order to "preserve" our country. That notion rests on the unarticulated premise that this Nation's security hangs upon its power to punish people because of what they think, speak or write about, or because of those with whom they associate for political purposes. The Government, in its brief, virtually admits this position when it speaks of the "communication of unlawful ideas." I challenge this premise, and deny that ideas can be proscribed under our Constitution. . . .

(C) The Court implies, however, that the ordinary rules and requirements of the Constitution do not apply because the Committee is merely after Communists and they do not constitute a political party but only a criminal gang. "[T]he long and widely accepted view," the Court says, is "that the tenets of the Communist Party include the ultimate overthrow of the Government of the United States by force and violence." . . .

. . . no matter how often or how quickly we repeat the claim that the Communist Party is not a political party, we cannot outlaw it, as a group, without endangering the liberty of all of us. The reason is not hard to find, for mixed among those aims of communism which are illegal are perfectly normal political and social goals. And muddled with its revolutionary tenets is a drive to achieve power through the ballot, if it can be done. . . .

The fact is that once we allow any group which has some political aims or ideas to be driven from the ballot and from the battle for men's minds because some of its members are bad and some of its tenets are illegal, no group is safe. Today we deal with Communists or suspected Communists. In 1920, instead, the New York Assembly suspended duly elected legislators on the ground that, being Socialists, they were disloyal to the country's principles. In the 1830's the Masons were hunted as outlaws and subversives, and abolition-

ists were considered revolutionaries of the most dangerous kind in both North and South. Earlier still, at the time of the universally unlamented alien and sedition laws, Thomas Jefferson's party was attacked and its members were derisively called "Jacobins." Fisher Ames described the party as a "French faction" guilty of "subversion" and "officered, regimented and formed to subordination." Its members, he claimed, intended to "take arms against the laws as soon as they dare." History should teach us then, that in times of high emotional excitement minority parties and groups which advocate extremely unpopular social or governmental innovations will always be typed as criminal gangs and attempts will always be made to drive them out. . . .

. . .

Ultimately all the questions in this case really boil down to one—whether we as a people will try fearfully and futilely to preserve democracy by adopting totalitarian methods, or whether in accordance with our traditions and our Constitution we will have the confidence and courage to be free.

I would reverse this conviction.

MR. JUSTICE BRENNAN, dissenting.

I would reverse this conviction. It is sufficient that I state my complete agreement with my Brother BLACK that no purpose for the investigation of Barenblatt is revealed by the record except exposure purely for the sake of exposure. This is not a purpose to which Barenblatt's rights under the First Amendment can validly be subordinated. An investigation in which the processes of law-making and law-evaluating are submerged entirely in exposure of individual behavior—in adjudication, of a sort, through the exposure process—is outside the constitutional pale of congressional inquiry. *Watkins* v. *United States*, 354 U. S. 178, 187, 200; see also *Sweezy* v. *New Hampshire*, 354 U. S. 234; *NAACP* v. *Alabama*, 357 U. S. 449; *Uphaus* v. *Wyman*, *ante*, p. 82 (dissenting opinion).

United States v. Nixon

418 U.S. 683 (1974)

The Special Prosecutor investigating the Watergate affair filed a motion for a subpoena to produce certain tapes and documents relating to conversations and meetings between President Nixon and others. President Nixon, claiming executive privilege, filed a motion to quash the subpoena. A district judge rejected that motion and issued an order for an *in camera* **examination of the subpoenaed material. This order was stayed pending appellate review.**

MR. CHIEF JUSTICE BURGER delivered the opinion of the Court.

This litigation presents for review the denial of a motion, filed in the District Court on behalf of the President of the United States, in the case of *United States* v. *Mitchell* (D. C. Crim. No. 74–110), to quash a third-party subpoena *duces tecum* issued by the United States District Court for the District of Columbia, pursuant to Fed. Rule Crim. Proc. 17 (c). The subpoena directed the President to produce certain tape recordings and documents relating to his conversations with aides and advisers. The court rejected the President's claims of absolute executive privilege, of lack of jurisdiction, and of failure to satisfy the requirements of Rule 17 (c). The President appealed to the Court of Appeals. We granted both the United States' petition for certiorari before judgment (No. 73–1766), and also the President's cross-petition for certiorari before judgment (No. 73–1834), because of the public importance of the issues presented and the need for their prompt resolution. 417 U. S. 927 and 960 (1974).

On March 1, 1974, a grand jury of the United States District Court for the District of Columbia returned an indictment charging seven named individuals *[Attorney General John N. Mitchell, White House aides H. R. Haldeman and John D. Ehrlichman, Charles W. Colson, Robert C. Mardian, Kenneth W. Parkinson, and Gordon Strachan. The latter four were either on the White House staff or with the Committee for the Re-election of the President.]* with various offenses, including conspiracy to defraud the United States and to obstruct justice. Although he was not designated as such in the indictment, the grand jury named the President, among others, as an unindicted coconspirator. On April 18, 1974, upon motion of the Special Prosecutor, see n. 8, *infra*, a subpoena *duces tecum* was issued pursuant to Rule 17 (c) to the President by the United States District Court and made returnable on May 2, 1974. This subpoena required the production, in advance of the September 9 trial date, of certain tapes, memoranda, papers, transcripts, or other writings relating to certain precisely identified meetings between the President and others. The Special Prosecutor was able to fix the time, place, and persons present at these discussions because the White House daily logs and appointment records had been delivered to him. On April 30, the President publicly released edited transcripts of 43 conversations; portions of 20 conversations subject to subpoena in the present case were included. On May 1, 1974, the President's counsel filed a "special appearance" and a motion to quash the subpoena under Rule 17 (c). This motion was accompanied by a formal claim of privilege.

. . .

II.
JUSTICIABILITY

In the District Court, the President's counsel argued that the court lacked jurisdiction to issue the subpoena because the matter was an intrabranch dispute between a subordinate and superior officer of the Executive Branch and hence not subject to judicial resolution. That argument has been renewed in this Court with emphasis on the contention that the dispute does not present a "case" or "controversy" which can be adjudicated in the federal courts. The President's counsel argues that the federal courts should not intrude into areas committed to the other branches of Government. He views the present dispute as essentially a "jurisdictional" dispute within the Executive Branch which he analogizes to a dispute between two congressional committees. Since the Executive Branch has exclusive authority and absolute discretion to decide whether to prosecute a case, *Confiscation Cases*, 7 Wall. 454 (1869); *United States* v. *Cox*, 342 F. 2d 167, 171 (CA5), cert. denied *sub nom. Cox* v. *Hauberg*, 381 U. S. 935 (1965), it is contended that a President's decision is final in determining what evidence is to be used in a given criminal case. Although his counsel concedes that the President has delegated certain specific powers to the Special Prosecutor, he has not "waived nor delegated to the Special Prosecutor the President's duty to claim privilege as to all materials . . . which fall within the President's inherent authority to refuse to disclose to any executive officer." Brief for the President 42. The Special Prosecutor's demand for the items therefore presents, in the view of the President's counsel, a political question under *Baker* v. *Carr*, 369 U. S. 186 (1962), since it involves a "textually demonstrable" grant of power under Art. II.

The mere assertion of a claim of an "intrabranch dispute," without more, has never operated to defeat federal jurisdiction; justiciability does not depend on such a surface inquiry. In *United States* v. *ICC*, 337 U. S. 426 (1949), the Court observed, "courts must look behind names that symbolize the parties to determine whether a justiciable case or controversy is presented." *Id.*, at 430.

. . .

[The Court reviews the following facts: under authority of Art. II, § 2, Congress vested in the Attorney General the power to conduct criminal litigation and to appoint subordinate officers; acting pursuant to statutory authority, the Attorney General delegated authority to a Special Prosecutor with unique authority and tenure; the regulation delegating this authority gave the Special Prosecutor explicit power to contest claims of executive privilege; this regulation had the force of law and had not been amended or revoked.]

In light of the uniqueness of the setting in which the conflict arises, the fact that both parties are officers of the Executive Branch cannot be viewed as a barrier to justiciability. It would be inconsistent with the applicable law and regulation, and the unique facts of this case to conclude other than that the Special Prosecutor has standing to bring this action and that a justiciable controversy is presented for decision.

. . .

IV.

THE CLAIM OF PRIVILEGE
A

. . . we turn to the claim that the subpoena should be quashed because it demands "confidential conversations between a President and his close advisors that it would be inconsistent with the public interest to produce." App. 48a. The first contention is a broad claim that the separation of powers doctrine precludes judicial review of a President's claim of privilege. The second contention is that if he does not prevail on the claim of absolute privilege, the court should hold as a matter of constitutional law that the privilege prevails over the subpoena *duces tecum*.

In the performance of assigned constitutional duties each branch of the Government must initially interpret the Constitution, and the interpretation of its powers by any branch is due great respect from the others. The President's counsel, as we have noted, reads the Constitution as providing an absolute privilege of confidentiality for all Presidential communications. Many decisions of this Court, however, have unequivocally reaffirmed the holding of *Marbury* v. *Madison*, 1 Cranch 137 (1803), that "[i]t is emphatically the province and duty of the judicial department to say what the law is." *Id.*, at 177.

No holding of the Court has defined the scope of judicial power specifically relating to the enforcement of a subpoena for confidential Presidential communications for use in a criminal prosecution, but other exercises of power by the Executive Branch and the Legislative Branch have been found invalid as in conflict with the Constitution. *Powell* v. *McCormack*, 395 U. S. 486 (1969);

Youngstown Sheet & Tube Co. v. *Sawyer*, 343 U. S. 579 (1952).

Notwithstanding the deference each branch must accord the others, the "judicial Power of the United States" vested in the federal courts by Art. III, § 1, of the Constitution can no more be shared with the Executive Branch than the Chief Executive, for example, can share with the Judiciary the veto power, or the Congress share with the Judiciary the power to override a Presidential veto. Any other conclusion would be contrary to the basic concept of separation of powers and the checks and balances that flow from the scheme of a tripartite government. The Federalist, No. 47, p. 313 (S. Mittell ed. 1938). We therefore reaffirm that it is the province and duty of this Court "to say what the law is" with respect to the claim of privilege presented in this case. *Marbury* v. *Madison, supra,* at 177.

B

In support of his claim of absolute privilege, the President's counsel urges two grounds, one of which is common to all governments and one of which is peculiar to our system of separation of powers. The first ground is the valid need for protection of communications between high Government officials and those who advise and assist them in the performance of their manifold duties; the importance of this confidentiality is too plain to require further discussion. Human experience teaches that those who expect public dissemination of their remarks may well temper candor with a concern for appearances and for their own interests to the detriment of the decisionmaking process. Whatever the nature of the privilege of confidentiality of Presidential communications in the exercise of Art. II powers, the privilege can be said to derive from the supremacy of each branch within its own assigned area of constitutional duties. Certain powers and privileges flow from the nature of enumerated powers; the protection of the confidentiality of Presidential communications has similar constitutional underpinnings.

The second ground asserted by the President's counsel in support of the claim of absolute privilege rests on the doctrine of separation of powers. Here it is argued that the independence of the Executive Branch within its own sphere,

Humphrey's Executor v. *United States*, 295 U. S. 602, 629–630 (1935); *Kilbourn* v. *Thompson*, 103 U. S. 168, 190–191 (1881), insulates a President from a judicial subpoena in an ongoing criminal prosecution, and thereby protects confidential Presidential communications.

However, neither the doctrine of separation of powers, nor the need for confidentiality of high-level communications, without more, can sustain an absolute, unqualified Presidential privilege of immunity from judicial process under all circumstances. The President's need for complete candor and objectivity from advisers calls for great deference from the courts. However, when the privilege depends solely on the broad, undifferentiated claim of public interest in the confidentiality of such conversations, a confrontation with other values arises. Absent a claim of need to protect military, diplomatic, or sensitive national security secrets, we find it difficult to accept the argument that even the very important interest in confidentiality of Presidential communications is significantly diminished by production of such material for *in camera* inspection with all the protection that a district court will be obliged to provide.

The impediment that an absolute, unqualified privilege would place in the way of the primary constitutional duty of the Judicial Branch to do justice in criminal prosecutions would plainly conflict with the function of the courts under Art. III. In designing the structure of our Government and dividing and allocating the sovereign power among three co-equal branches, the Framers of the Constitution sought to provide a comprehensive system, but the separate powers were not intended to operate with absolute independence.

"While the Constitution diffuses power the better to secure liberty, it also contemplates that practice will integrate the dispersed powers into a workable government. It enjoins upon its branches separateness but interdependence, autonomy but reciprocity." *Youngstown Sheet & Tube Co.* v. *Sawyer*, 343 U. S., at 635 (Jackson, J., concurring).

To read the Art. II powers of the President as providing an absolute privilege as against a subpoena essential to enforcement of criminal statutes on no more than a generalized claim of the public interest in confidentiality of nonmilitary and nondiplomatic discussions would upset the constitutional balance of "a workable government" and gravely impair the role of the courts under Art. III.

C

Since we conclude that the legitimate needs of the judicial process may outweigh Presidential privilege, it is necessary to resolve those competing interests in a manner that preserves the essential functions of each branch. The right and indeed the duty to resolve that question does not free the Judiciary from according high respect to the representations made on behalf of the President. *United States* v. *Burr*, 25 F. Cas. 187, 190, 191–192 (No. 14,694) (CC Va. 1807).

The expectation of a President to the confidentiality of his conversations and correspondence, like the claim of confidentiality of judicial deliberations, for example, has all the values to which we accord deference for the privacy of all citizens and, added to those values, is the necessity for protection of the public interest in candid, objective, and even blunt or harsh opinions in Presidential decisionmaking. A President and those who assist him must be free to explore alternatives in the process of shaping policies and making decisions and to do so in a way many would be unwilling to express except privately. These are the considerations justifying a presumptive privilege for Presidential communications. The privilege is fundamental to the operation of Government and inextricably rooted in the separation of powers under the Constitution. . . .

But this presumptive privilege must be considered in light of our historic commitment to the rule of law. This is nowhere more profoundly manifest than in our view that "the twofold aim [of criminal justice] is that guilt shall not escape or innocence suffer." *Berger* v. *United States*, 295 U. S., at 88. We have elected to employ an adversary system of criminal justice in which the parties contest all issues before a court of law. The need to develop all relevant facts in the adversary system is both fundamental and comprehensive. The ends of criminal justice would be defeated if judgments were to be founded on a partial or speculative presentation of the facts. The very integrity of the judicial system and public confi-

dence in the system depend on full disclosure of all the facts, within the framework of the rules of evidence. To ensure that justice is done, it is imperative to the function of courts that compulsory process be available for the production of evidence needed either by the prosecution or by the defense.

. . .

In this case the President challenges a subpoena served on him as a third party requiring the production of materials for use in a criminal prosecution; he does so on the claim that he has a privilege against disclosure of confidential communications. He does not place his claim of privilege on the ground they are military or diplomatic secrets. As to these areas of Art. II duties the courts have traditionally shown the utmost deference to Presidential responsibilities. . . .

. . .

In this case we must weigh the importance of the general privilege of confidentiality of Presidential communications in performance of the President's responsibilities against the inroads of such a privilege on the fair administration of criminal justice. *[The Court, in a Footnote, adds: "We are not here concerned with the balance between the President's generalized interest in confidentiality and the need for relevant evidence in civil litigation, nor with that between the confidentiality interest and congressional demands for information, nor with the President's interest in preserving state secrets. We address only the conflict between the President's assertion of a generalized privilege of confidentiality and the constitutional need for relevant evidence in criminal trials."]* The interest in preserving confidentiality is weighty indeed and entitled to great respect. However, we cannot conclude that advisers will be moved to temper the candor of their remarks by the infrequent occasions of disclosure because of the possibility that such conversations will be called for in the context of a criminal prosecution.

On the other hand, the allowance of the privilege to withhold evidence that is demonstrably relevant in a criminal trial would cut deeply into the guarantee of due process of law and gravely impair the basic function of the courts. A President's acknowledged need for confidentiality in the communications of his office is general in nature, whereas the constitutional need for production of relevant evidence in a criminal proceeding is specific and central to the fair adjudication of a particular criminal case in the administration of justice. Without access to specific facts a criminal prosecution may be totally frustrated. The President's broad interest in confidentiality of communications will not be vitiated by disclosure of a limited number of conversations preliminarily shown to have some bearing on the pending criminal cases.

We conclude that when the ground for asserting privilege as to subpoenaed materials sought for use in a criminal trial is based only on the generalized interest in confidentiality, it cannot prevail over the fundamental demands of due process of law in the fair administration of criminal justice. The generalized assertion of privilege must yield to the demonstrated, specific need for evidence in a pending criminal trial.

D

We have earlier determined that the District Court did not err in authorizing the issuance of the subpoena. . . . Here the District Court treated the material as presumptively privileged, proceeded to find that the Special Prosecutor had made a sufficient showing to rebut the presumption, and ordered an *in camera* examination of the subpoenaed material. On the basis of our examination of the record we are unable to conclude that the District Court erred in ordering the inspection. Accordingly we affirm the order of the District Court that subpoenaed materials be transmitted to that court. We now turn to the important question of the District Court's responsibilities in conducting the *in camera* examination of Presidential materials or communications delivered under the compulsion of the subpoena *duces tecum*.

E

Enforcement of the subpoena *duces tecum* was stayed pending this Court's resolution of the issues raised by the petitions for certiorari. . . . Statements that meet the test of admissibility and relevance must be isolated; all other material must be excised. At this stage the District Court is not limited to representations of the Special Prosecutor as to the evidence sought by the subpoena; the material will be available to the District Court. It is elementary that *in camera* inspection of evidence is always a procedure calling for scrupulous protection against any release or publication of material not found by the court, at that stage, probably admissible in evidence and relevant to the issues of the trial for which it is sought. . . . The need for confidentiality even as to idle conversations with associates in which casual reference might be made concerning political leaders within the country or foreign statesmen is too obvious to call for further treatment. . . .

Since this matter came before the Court during the pendency of a criminal prosecution, and on representations that time is of the essence, the mandate shall issue forthwith.

Affirmed.

MR. JUSTICE REHNQUIST took no part in the consideration or decision of these cases.

Negotiating the Limits of Executive Privilege: The AT&T Cases

Executive documents are routinely shared with Congress, including documents that are highly classified and confidential. When there is a conflict between the executive and legislative branches, accommodations are usually discovered that avoid litigation. Even when a case is brought to court, the usual resolution is to force the two branches to find an intermediate position that will satisfy executive as well as congressional interests. The

two cases below, involving national-security wiretaps, illustrate the practical efforts to iron out executive-legislative collisions. In a series of steps, Federal Judge Harold Leventhal of the D.C. Circuit helped resolve a dispute between the Justice Department and a congressional committee. The two cases are *United States* v. *AT&T*, 551 F.2d 384 (D.C. Cir. 1976) and *United States* v. *AT&T*, 567 F.2d 121 (D.C. Cir. 1977). The first selection is from the 1976 case.

LEVENTHAL, Circuit Judge.

This unusual case involves a portentous clash between the executive and legislative branches, the executive branch asserting its authority to maintain tight control over information related to our national security, and the legislative branch asserting its authority to gather information necessary for the formulation of new legislation.

In the name of the United States, the Justice Department sued to enjoin the American Telephone and Telegraph Co. (AT&T) from complying with a subpoena of a subcommittee of the House of Representatives issued in the course of an investigation into warrantless "national security" wiretaps. Congressman Moss, chairman of the subcommittee, intervened on behalf of the House, the real defendant in interest since AT&T, while prepared to comply with the subpoena in the absence of a protective court order, has no stake in the controversy beyond knowing whether its legal obligation is to comply with the subpoena or not. The District Court issued the injunction requested by plaintiff and Chairman Moss appeals.

The case presents difficult problems, preliminary questions of jurisdiction and justiciability (application of the political question doctrine) and the ultimate issue on the merits of resolving or balancing the constitutional powers asserted by the legislative and executive branches.

In order to avoid a possibly unnecessary constitutional decision, we suggest the outlines of a possible settlement which may meet the mutual needs of the congressional and executive parties, without requiring a judicial resolution of a head-on confrontation, and we remand without decision at this time in order to permit exploration of this solution by the parties, under District Court guidance if needed.

If the parties reach an impasse this will be reported to us by the District Court. We would then be confronted with the need to enter an order disposing of the appeal pending.

I. BACKGROUND

The controversy arose out of an investigation by the Subcommittee on Oversight and Investigations of the House Committee on Interstate and Foreign Commerce. The Subcommittee was interested in determining the nature and extent of warrantless wiretapping in the United States for asserted national security purposes. It was concerned with the possible abuse of that power and its effect on privacy and other interests of U.S. citizens, and with the possible need for limiting legislation.

The warrantless wiretaps which became the focus of this part of the investigation used facilities provided by AT&T upon its receipt from the FBI of "request" letters. Each request letter specified a target line to be tapped, identified by telephone number, address, or other numerical designation. The letter requested a "leased line" to carry the tapped communications from the target location to a designated monitoring station manned by federal agents.

On June 22, 1976, the Subcommittee authorized and the Committee Chairman issued a subpoena requiring the president of AT&T to turn over to the Subcommittee copies of all national security request letters sent to AT&T and its subsidiaries by the FBI as well as records of such taps prior to the time when the practice of sending such letters was initiated. After the subpoena was issued, AT&T stood ready to comply.

At this point the White House approached Subcommittee Chairman John Moss in search of an alternative arrangement meeting the Subcommittee's information needs. The basic thrust of the ensuing negotiations between the Subcommittee and the Justice Department was to substitute, for the request letters, expurgated copies of the back-up memoranda upon which the Attorney General based his decision to authorize the warrantless taps. These memoranda, providing information on the purpose and nature of the surveillance, might have been more informative to Congress than the request letters, which merely contained numerical identification of the line to be tapped. The Justice Department agreed, at least informally and tentatively, to provide the Subcommittee staff expurgated copies of the backup memo pertaining to foreign intelligence taps, with all information which would identify the target replaced by generic description, such as "Middle Eastern diplomat." The negotiations came close to success, but broke down over the issue of verification by the Subcommittee of the accuracy of the executive's generic descriptions by inspection of a sample of the original memoranda.

. . .

III. QUESTIONS PRESENTED

. . .

D. Clash of Absolutes

In this case we are faced with patently conflicting assertions of absolute authority. Each branch of government claims that as long as it is exercising its authority for a legitimate purpose, its actions are unreviewable by the courts.

1. Congressional Investigatory Power

Congress relies on the Speech or Debate Clause, as interpreted in *Eastland* v. *United States Servicemen's Fund*, 421 U.S. 491, 95 S.Ct. 1813, 44 L.Ed.2d 324 (1975) in support of its contention that its subpoena power cannot be impeded by the Executive. *Eastland* held that, even on an allegation of infringement of First Amendment rights, the courts could not interfere with a subpoena concerning a legitimate area of congressional investigation. . . .

2. Executive National Security Power

The Justice Department claims the President retains ultimate authority to decide what risks to national security are acceptable. Thus, where documents are subpoenaed by Congress, the court's role would be at an end once it determined that there was some risk to national security. At that point, it would have to defer to the President. . . .

E. Strength of the Constitutional Interests

1. Executive

The President asserts the power to maintain the secrecy of information pertaining to national security and finds this power inherent in the responsibility given him in article II of the Constitution for foreign and military affairs, hence intelligence and espionage. Of another executive privilege, the Supreme Court said:

"Nowhere in the Constitution, as we have noted earlier, is there any explicit reference to a privilege of confidentiality, yet to the extent this interest relates to the effective discharge of a President's powers, it is constitutionally based." [United States v. Nixon, *418 U.S. 683, 711 (1974).]

The constitutional basis, indeed the statutory legality, of the foreign intelligence surveillance underlying this controversy, was explicitly left open by the *Keith* case, *United States* v. *United States District Court*, 407 U.S. 297, 309 & n.8, 321–22, 92 S.Ct. 2125, 32 L.Ed.2d 752 (1972).

There is constitutional power, under the Necessary and Proper Clause, in the federal government to keep national security information secret. This is typically a government power, to be exercised by the legislative and executive branches acting together. . . .

2. Congressional

Congressional power to investigate and acquire information by subpoena is on a firm constitutional basis, as indicated by *Eastland* v. *United States Servicemen's Fund*, 421 U.S. 491, 504, 95 S.Ct. 1813, 44 L.Ed.2d 324 (1975); *McGrain* v. *Daugherty*, 273 U.S. 135, 47 S.Ct. 319, 71 L.Ed. 580 (1927). . . .

It is conceded that in the present instance, the Subcommittee is inquiring into a suitable area of federal legislation—interception of interstate telephone communication. *See* Section 605 of the Federal Communications Act of 1934, 47 U.S.C. § 605, and Title III of the Omnibus Crime Control and Safe Streets Act of 1968, 18 U.S.C. §§ 2510–2520. Nor is there any allegation that Congress is seeking to "expose for the sake of exposure."

Watkins v. *United States*, 354 U.S. 178, 200, 77 S.Ct. 1173, 1185, 1 L.Ed.2d 1273 (1957).

Also, we are not confronted here by the possibility of a wayward committee acting contrary to the will of the House.

F. Balancing by the Courts

A court seeking to balance the legislative and executive interests asserted here would face severe problems in formulating and applying standards. Granted that the subpoenas are clearly within the proper legislative investigatory sphere, it is difficult to "weigh" Congress's need for the request letters. Congress's power to monitor executive actions is implicit in the appropriations power. Here, for instance, if the President has the inherent power claimed to block the subpoena, how is Congress to assure that appropriated funds are not being used for illegal warrantless domestic electronic surveillance?

As to the danger to national security, a court would have to consider the Subcommittee's track record for security, the likelihood of a leak if other members of the House sought access to the material. In addition to this delicate and possibly unseemly determination, the court would have to weigh the effect of a leak on intelligence activities and diplomatic relations. Finally, the court would have to consider the reasonableness of the alternatives offered by the parties and decide which would better reconcile the competing constitutional interests.

IV. REASONS FOR EXPLORATION OF SETTLEMENT

Before moving on to a decision of such nerve-center constitutional questions, we pause to allow for further efforts at a settlement. We think that suggestion is particularly appropriate in this case and may well be productive. . . . The legislative and executive branches have a long history of settlement of disputes that seemed irreconcilable. There was almost a settlement in 1976. It may well be attainable in 1977.

Furthermore, our own reflections may be of some assistance. As a prelude to settlement conference, it may be helpful if we review pertinent considerations:

1. This dispute between the legislative and executive branches has at least some elements of the political-question doctrine. A court decision selects a victor, and tends thereafter to tilt the scales. A compromise worked out between the branches is most likely to meet their essential needs and the country's constitutional balance.

. . .

[1977 decision:]

LEVENTHAL, Circuit Judge:

This case brings to us for a second time conflicting assertions by the executive and legislative branches, contentions that require the third branch to decide whether its constitutional mandate to decide controversies extends to such a conflict, and if so what measure of judicial resolution is sound and appropriate.

. . .

When we first came to the case, we developed a novel and somewhat gingerly approach for the delicate problem of accommodating the needs and powers of two coordinate branches in a situation where each claimed absolute authority. *See United States* v. *AT&T*, 179 U.S.App.D.C. 198, 551 F.2d 384 (1976). To the extent possible, we wished to avoid a resolution that might disturb the balance of power between the two branches and inaccurately reflect their true needs. We therefore refrained from deciding the merits of their claims, and indeed did not resolve the preliminary issue of whether the dispute presented a nonjusticiable political question. Instead we remanded the record to the District Court for further proceedings during which the parties and counsel were requested to attempt to negotiate a settlement. We called for a report by the District Court within three months. That time was later extended, to permit the new officials of the incoming administration to grapple with the problem. On April 22, 1977, District Judge Gasch made his report. We heard oral argument on June 3, 1977.

Negotiation has narrowed but not bridged the gap between the parties. Accordingly, we must adopt a somewhat more traditional approach. We begin by deciding that complete judicial abstention on political question grounds is not warranted. In addressing the merits, however, we continue to move cautiously. Taking full account of the negotiating positions, we have chartered the course that we think is most likely to accommodate the substantial needs of the parties. Doubtless, neither will be satisfied. But in our view there is good reason to believe that the procedure set forth in this opinion will prove feasible in practice, with such adjustments and refinements as may be evolved by the parties and the district court. What we decide is only that, so long as this procedure gives promise of satisfying the substantial needs of both parties, this court may appropriately continue to refrain from a decision upholding either of the claims of absolute authority. Should the parties test our approach and encounter difficulties, we may have to determine whether further relief is warranted. In that effort we will be aided by the experience of the parties.

. . .

II. QUESTIONS PRESENTED
A. Political Question

Preliminarily, we must consider whether this case calls for judicial abstention, under the political question doctrine. The issues are the possible unseemliness of a judicial exploration of the needs and motives of the other two branches, and the question whether there are "judicially discoverable and manageable standards" for balancing the conflicting constitutional powers asserted by the parties. We noted these considerations in our earlier opinion.

. . .

In our view, neither the traditional political question doctrine nor any close adaptation thereof is appropriate where neither of the conflicting political branches has a clear and unequivocal constitutional title, and it is or may be possible to establish an effective judicial settlement.

As Judge Friendly recalled in his 1976 Bicentennial lecture, it is one of the major strengths of the Constitution, and far from a weakness, that conflicting viewpoints have been resolved through intermediate positions. Much of this spirit of compromise is reflected in the generality of language found in the Constitution—generality which allows for dispute as to which of the coordinate branches may exercise authority in a particular fact situation.

The framers, rather than attempting to define and allocate all governmental power in minute detail, relied, we believe, on the expectation that where conflicts in scope of authority arose between the coordinate branches, a spirit of dynamic compromise would promote resolution of the dispute in the manner most likely to result in efficient and effective functioning of our governmental system. Under this view, the coordinate branches do not exist in an exclusively adversary relationship to one another when a conflict in authority arises. Rather, each branch should take cognizance of an implicit constitutional mandate to seek optimal accommodation through a realistic evaluation of the needs of the conflicting branches in the particular fact situation. This aspect of our constitutional scheme avoids the mischief of polarization of disputes. . . .

[The case was dismissed on December 21, 1978, after the Justice Department and the subcommittee amicably resolved their differences.]

7 Separation of Powers: Emergencies and Foreign Affairs

T he doctrine of separated powers carries its share of subtleties and puzzles in domestic disputes. Even more enigmatic is the doctrine's application to external affairs and emergency powers. This chapter begins by examining the distinction between external and internal affairs. It analyzes the scope of the "executive prerogative," which allows Presidents to exercise powers not expressly stated in the Constitution, even when their actions are contrary to laws passed by Congress. Other sections in this chapter explore the scope of treaties and executive agreements, the war power, and questions of citizenship.

EXTERNAL AND INTERNAL AFFAIRS

Those who believe that the lion's share of authority in foreign affairs belongs with the President rely heavily on Justice Sutherland's decision in *United States* v. *Curtiss-Wright* (1936). The case could have been confined to a single question: May Congress delegate to the President the authority to prohibit the shipment of arms or munitions to any country in South America whenever he decided that the material would promote domestic violence? The Court agreed that legislation over the international field must often accord to the President greater discretion than would be admissible for domestic affairs. But Sutherland went beyond the issue of delegation to add pages of obiter dicta to describe the far-reaching dimensions of executive power in foreign affairs. He assigned to the President a number of powers not found in the Constitution. *Curtiss-Wright* is cited frequently to justify not only broad grants of legislative power to the President but the exercise of inherent, extraconstitutional powers. UNITED STATES v. CURTISS-WRIGHT, 299 U.S. 304 (1936)

Curtiss-Wright echoed positions Sutherland had taken as a United States Senator and as a member of the Senate Foreign Relations Committee. It closely tracks his article, "The Internal and External Powers of the National Government," printed as

Senate Document No. 417 in 1910, which claimed that national sovereignty "inhered in the United States from the beginning" rather than in the colonies or the states. In his book, *Constitutional Power and World Affairs* (1919), he advanced the same themes.

The contemporary Supreme Court continues to look more sympathetically on delegation that involves external affairs. Even Chief Justice Rehnquist, the strongest advocate of the nondelegation doctrine on the present Court, adopts a different standard for international crises, "the nature of which Congress can hardly have been expected to anticipate in any detail." Dames & Moore v. Regan, 453 U.S. 654, 669 (1981). He agrees that Congress "is permitted to legislate both with greater breadth and with greater flexibility" when a statute governs military affairs. Rostker v. Goldberg, 453 U.S. 57, 66 (1981), quoting Parker v. Levy, 417 U.S. 733, 756 (1974). More importantly, *Curtiss-Wright* is used to support the existence of independent, implied, and inherent powers for the President.[1]

Sutherland believed that foreign and domestic affairs were fundamentally different because the powers of external sovereignty passed from the Crown "not to the colonies severally, but to the colonies in their collective and corporate capacity as the United States of America." But the colonies and states from 1774 to 1788 operated as sovereign entities, not as parts of a collective body. They acted free and independent of one another. The creation of the Continental Congress did not disturb the sovereign capacity of the states to make treaties, borrow money, solicit arms, lay embargoes, collect tariff duties, and conduct separate military campaigns.

Even if the power of external sovereignty had somehow passed intact from the Crown to the "United States," the Constitution divides that power between Congress and the President. The President and the Senate share the treaty power. Congress has the responsibility to raise and support military forces, to lay and collect duties on foreign trade, to regulate commerce with foreign nations, and to fund the armed services. Contemporary conditions make it increasingly difficult to draw a crisp line between external and internal affairs. Oil embargoes imposed by foreign governments have an immediate impact on America's economy, raising the price at home and producing long lines at the neighborhood gas station. The President's decision to ship or withhold wheat from the Soviet Union has a major effect on farming communities. Trade policies are both international and domestic in scope.

Officials of the Reagan administration took a number of actions known collectively as the Iran-Contra affair: sending arms to Iran, diverting funds to the Contras in Nicaragua, and soliciting funds from private donors and foreign countries because Congress refused to appropriate funds for the Contras. Some defenders of these executive actions pointed to *Curtiss-Wright* as legal justification. A report, prepared jointly by the House and the Senate, rejects this reliance on *Curtiss-Wright* (pp. 320-322).

Right to Travel

Claiming both constitutional and statutory authority, Presidents and their administrations use the control over passports and visas to restrict travel by foreigners to this country and by Americans to other countries. Administrations advance a number of

[1]United States v. Pink, 315 U.S. 203, 229 (1942); Knauff v. Shaughnessy, 338 U.S. 537, 542 (1950); United States v. Mazurie, 419 U.S. 544, 566–567 (1975).

foreign policy and national security justifications, while opponents of restraints on foreign travel raise First Amendment issues of access to information and right of association. There is broad agreement among both groups that the government is justified in banning travel to regions affected by pestilence or war.

The interesting fact about these cases is that the Court generally decides them on statutory grounds. This keeps the door fully open for participation by Congress and the President in shaping the law on the right to travel. In 1958, the Supreme Court reviewed the State Department's action in withholding passports from several Americans because of their association with the Communist Party. Although the Court referred to the right to travel as part of a citizen's constitutional "liberty" that could not be denied without due process of law, it avoided the constitutional issue and held that the Secretary of State had exceeded the authority delegated to him by Congress. Kent v. Dulles, 357 U.S. 116 (1958); Dayton v. Dulles, 357 U.S. 144 (1958). Legislation was introduced to strengthen the authority of the Secretary of State, but none of the bills passed Congress.

In 1964, the Court struck down a congressional provision that prevented individuals from applying for a passport if they belonged to a "Communist-action" or "Communist-front" organization. If they already held a passport, it would be revoked. The Court decided that the provision was too broad and indiscriminate in restricting the right to travel. Aptheker v. United States, 378 U.S. 500 (1964). A year later, however, the Court upheld the authority of the State Department to impose *area* restrictions (in this case, involving Cuba). The Court argued that it was permissible to deny all citizens the right to travel to a certain country, in contrast to the 1958 case which involved an individual's belief or association. Zemel v. Rusk, 381 U.S. 1 (1965).

Subsequent cases circumscribed the State Department's authority to impose area restrictions.[2] Moreover, in 1978 Congress passed legislation to limit area restrictions. In the spirit of the Helsinki Accords of 1975, which encouraged the free movement of people and ideas, Congress adopted the following amendment to the Passport Act: "Unless authorized by law, a passport may not be designated as restricted for travel to or for use in any country other than a country with which the United States is at war, where armed hostilities are in progress, or where there is imminent danger to the public health or the physical safety of United States travellers." 92 Stat. 971, § 124 (1978); 22 U.S.C. § 211a (1982). Congress also made it unlawful to travel abroad without a passport. 92 Stat. 993, § 707(b) (1978); 8 U.S.C. § 1185(b) (1982).

Recent cases have given broad support to executive restrictions on foreign travel. In 1981, the Court upheld the authority of the Secretary of State to revoke the passport of Philip Agee, a former CIA employee who had announced his intention to identify undercover CIA agents and intelligences sources in foreign countries. The Court said that the revocation inhibited Agee's action, not his speech. The Secretary's decision was based on a departmental regulation, a broad interpretation of the 1978 amendments, and the "silence" of Congress in acquiescing to the department's action. Specific authorization from Congress, said the Court, was not required. HAIG v. AGEE, 453 U.S. 280 (1981). The broadness of this ruling suggests

---

[2]On area restrictions, see also United States v. Laub, 385 U.S. 475 (1967); Travis v. United States, 385 U.S. 491 (1967); Lynd v. Rusk, 389 F.2d 940 (D.C. Cir. 1967). Congress can limit welfare payments to recipients who travel abroad for thirty days or more; Califano v. Aznavorian, 439 U.S. 170 (1978).

that an administration may prevent the foreign travel of anyone who is apt to question or embarrass the President's foreign policy.

In 1984, the Court upheld (5–4) a Treasury Department regulation in 1982 that prohibited general tourist and business travel to Cuba. The Reagan administration decided to retaliate against Cuba for its political and military interventions in Latin America and in Africa. Congress had passed the International Emergency Economic Powers Act in 1977 to limit the President's power, but the Court read the Act broadly to permit the sanctions against Cuba. Regan v. Wald, 468 U.S. 222 (1984).

EXECUTIVE PREROGATIVE

Theodore Roosevelt and William Howard Taft supposedly championed opposite theories of presidential power. Roosevelt asserted that it was the President's right and duty to do "anything that the needs of the Nation demanded, unless such action was forbidden by the Constitution or by the laws." 20 Works of Theodore Roosevelt 347 (1926). Through this theory the President could enter and occupy any vacuum. In contrast, Taft maintained that the President "can exercise no power which cannot be fairly and reasonably traced to some specific grant of power or justly implied and included within such express grant as proper and necessary to its exercise. Such specific grant must be either in the Federal Constitution or in an act of Congress passed in pursuance thereof." William Howard Taft, Our Chief Magistrate and His Powers 139–140 (1916).

This passage appears to make Taft an advocate of enumerated powers, but he did not believe that every use of presidential power required a specific constitutional or statutory grant. He recognized the need for implied powers: powers that can be "fairly and reasonably traced" or "justly implied." He even adds a "necessary and proper" clause for the President. His book on the presidency promotes a broad view of executive power: incidental powers to remove officers, inferable powers to protect the lives and property of American citizens living abroad, powers created by custom, and emergency powers (such as Lincoln's suspension of the writ of habeas corpus during the Civil War). Taft concluded that executive power was limited "so far as it is possible to limit such a power consistent with that discretion and promptness of action that are essential to preserve the interests of the public in times of emergency, or legislative neglect or inaction."

Taft's formulation follows what is known as the Lockean prerogative: the executive's power to act for the public good in the absence of law and sometimes even against it. Lincoln claimed this authority in April 1861 while Congress was in recess. He issued proclamations calling forth state militias, suspending the writ of habeas corpus, and placing a blockade on the rebellious states. He told Congress that his actions, "whether strictly legal or not," were necessary for the public good. 7 Richardson, Messages and Papers of the Presidents 3225. Congress subsequently passed a statute legalizing his proclamations "as if they had been issued and done under the previous express authority and direction of the Congress of the United States." 12 Stat. 326. Legislative sanction is an essential ingredient of the prerogative. In times of emergency, the executive may act outside the law but must submit his case to the legislature and the people for approval.

Lincoln's use of emergency power to justify the blockade was upheld by a sharply divided Supreme Court. In a 5–4 decision, the Court held that Lincoln could take the actions he did despite the absence of a declaration of war by Congress. The

President was bound to meet the emergency "in the shape it presented itself, without waiting for Congress to baptize it with a name; and no name given to it by him or them could change the fact." THE PRIZE CASES, 2 Black (67 U.S.) 635, 669 (1863). Lincoln's suspension of the writ of habeas corpus was challenged by Chief Justice Taney, sitting in his circuit in Baltimore. Taney held that the President had no power to suspend the writ or imprison someone without trial. Ex parte Merryman, 17 Fed. Case No. 9,487 (1861). Lincoln ignored Taney's opinion and obtained a statement from his Attorney General that justified his action because of the "great and dangerous insurrection." 10 Op. Att'y Gen. 74, 81 (1861). Not until the war was over and Lincoln was dead did the Supreme Court breathe some life into the privilege of the writ of habeas corpus. EX PARTE MILLIGAN, 4 Wall. (71 U.S.) 2 (1866). The Court is reluctant to interfere with the duties of the President, especially when exercising the powers of commander in chief. Mississippi v. Johnson, 4 Wall. 475 (1867).

A notorious use of emergency power was President Roosevelt's decision during World War II to put a curfew on more than 100,000 Americans of Japanese descent (about two-thirds of whom were natural-born U.S. citizens) and then place them in detention camps. A unanimous Supreme Court sustained the curfew, although Justice Murphy remarked that it "bears a melancholy resemblance to the treatment accorded to the members of the Jewish race in Germany and in other parts of Europe." Hirabayashi v. United States, 320 U.S. 81 (1943). Putting Japanese-Americans in detention camps split the Court, the Justices voting 6–3 to uphold this action. The dissents by Murphy and Jackson, objecting that the exclusion order resulted from racism, were particularly vehement. KOREMATSU v. UNITED STATES, 323 U.S. 214, 243 (1944).[3] Congress passed legislation in 1988 to offer the nation's apology for this tragic episode and to provide cash reparations to survivors and their families. 102 Stat. 903 (1988).

President Truman used the emergency power in 1952 to seize steel mills during the Korean war. The Supreme Court overturned his action, but the 6–3 decision revealed almost as many positions as there were Justices. All six Justices in the majority wrote separate opinions, each taking a slightly different view of emergency power. Only Justices Black and Douglas advocated a doctrine of express and enumerated powers. The other seven Justices, in four concurrences and three dissents, recognized that implied and emergency powers might have to be invoked. Jackson developed a theory of extraconstitutional powers that had three scenarios. Presidential authority reaches its highest level when the President acts pursuant to congressional authorization. His power is at its "lowest ebb" when he takes measures incompatible with the will of Congress. In between these two categories lay a "zone of twilight" in which Congress neither grants nor denies authority. In such circumstances, "congressional inertia, indifference or quiescence may sometimes, at least as a practical matter, enable, if not invite, measures of independent presidential responsibility." YOUNGSTOWN CO. v. SAWYER, 343 U.S. 579, 637 (1952). Jackson's opinion underscores the fact that the Constitution is shaped not by textual interpretations from the courts but by a political dialectic among the branches.

[3]See also Yasui v. United States, 320 U.S. 115 (1943); Ex parte Endo, 323 U.S. 283 (1944); Eugene V. Rostow, "The Japanese American Cases—A Disaster," 54 Yale L. J. 489 (1945); Nanette Dembitz, "Racial Discrimination and the Military Judgment: The Supreme Court's Korematsu and Endo Decisions," 45 Colum. L. Rev. 175 (1945); Peter Irons, Justice at War: The Story of the Japanese American Internment Cases (1983).

The concept of "national security" is often employed as an umbrella term to justify a broad range of emergency actions by the President. The Nixon administration was especially active in invoking the term. It asked the courts to enjoin two newspapers from publishing the Pentagon Papers, a confidential report which the administration had prepared to study the origins and conduct of the Vietnam war. The report had been leaked to the newspapers, raising the question of prior restraint on a free press. The Supreme Court decided against the administration. The word "security," warned Justice Black, "is a broad, vague generality whose contours should not be invoked to abrogate the fundamental law embodied in the First Amendment." NEW YORK TIMES CO. v. UNITED STATES, 403 U.S. 713, 719 (1971). Erwin N. Griswold, who served as Solicitor General at the time of the Pentagon Papers Case, and who argued in oral argument that publication of the documents would damage national security, admitted in 1989 that no such damage had occurred (pp. 352–354). Although First Amendment freedoms were protected in the Pentagon Papers Case, the Court upheld the right of the Central Intelligence Agency to require its employees to sign secrecy agreements promising not to publish information about the agency without the Director's prior approval. Snepp v. United States, 444 U.S. 507 (1980).

Beginning in the 1920s, a succession of administrations resorted to wiretapping for the purpose of controlling domestic crime and protecting national security. The Communications Act of 1934 made it a crime to intercept and divulge wire or radio communications, but President Roosevelt in 1940 instructed his Attorney General that wiretapping should continue for "grave matters involving the defense of the nation." Francis Biddle, In Brief Authority 167 (1962). The tension between the statute and Roosevelt's instruction was relieved in part by the practice of intercepting but not divulging communications or using them in court for evidence.

The Omnibus Crime Control Act of 1968 allowed domestic wiretaps if authorized by judicial warrants. The government claimed that warrantless surveillances for "national security" purposes were lawful as a reasonable exercise of presidential power. A section of the 1968 Act stated that nothing in the statute limited the President's constitutional power to protect against the overthrow of the government or against "any other clear and present danger to the structure or existence of the Government." An 8–0 decision by the Supreme Court in 1972 held that the section merely disclaimed congressional intent to define presidential powers in matters affecting national security and did not authorize warrantless national security surveillances. Moreover, the Fourth Amendment required prior judicial approval for surveillances of *domestic* organizations. The Court carefully avoided the question of surveillances over foreign powers, whether within or outside the country. UNITED STATES v. UNITED STATES DISTRICT COURT, 407 U.S. 297 (1972).

Congress passed legislation in 1978 to restrict presidential actions. A court order is now required to engage in electronic surveillance within the United States for purposes of obtaining foreign intelligence information. A special court, appointed by the Chief Justice, reviews applications submitted by government attorneys. 93 Stat. 1783.

Congress enacted legislation in the 1970s to limit the President's use of emergency powers. A number of statutes had contained latent or dormant authority for the President, ready to spring to life whenever he issued a proclamation declaring the nation to be in a state of emergency. Legislation in 1977 and 1978 terminated emergency authorities and subjected future emergencies to procedural safeguards and congressional control. 90 Stat. 1255 (1976); 91 Stat. 1625 (1977). Congressional control depended partly on a concurrent resolution of disapproval, but the Supreme Court declared the legislative veto unconstitutional in *INS* v. *Chadha* (1983). Two years later, Congress complied with the Court ruling by changing the control to a joint resolution of disapproval. 99 Stat. 448, § 801 (1985).

TREATIES AND EXECUTIVE AGREEMENTS

Under Article VI of the Constitution, federal statutes made pursuant to the Constitution, and all treaties "shall be the supreme Law of the Land." State judges are bound by those actions, "any Thing in the Constitution or Laws of any State to the Contrary Notwithstanding." In passing legislation to carry out a treaty, Congress may act in ways that might not have been sustained in the form of a free-standing statute. See Missouri v. Holland (pp. 404–406).

The President makes treaties "by and with the Advice and Consent of the Senate." The process of treaty making need not be divided into two exclusive and sequential stages: negotiation solely by the President, followed by Senate advice and consent. When President Washington first communicated with the Senate regarding the appropriate procedure for treaties, he considered oral communications with Senators "indispensably necessary." Treaties seemed to him "of a legislative nature," inviting deliberation in the Senate's chamber. 30 Writings of Washington 373, 378. On August 22, 1789, he met with Senators to secure their advice and consent to an Indian treaty. The Senators felt uncomfortable in his presence and disliked having to rely solely on information provided by the Secretary of War, who was present. Washington returned two days later and obtained the Senate's consent, but decided against a repeat performance.

This incident has been misinterpreted to suggest that Washington negotiated all future treaties without Senate involvement. In fact, he continued to seek the Senate's advice by written communications rather than personal appearances. Senators were asked to approve the appointment of treaty negotiators and even to advise on their negotiating instructions. Far from being a "presidential monopoly," the negotiation of treaties has often been shared with the Senate in order to obtain legislative understanding and support. Presidential insistence to "go it alone" in negotiating treaties has often had disastrous results. Fisher, Constitutional Conflicts between Congress and the President 255–257 (1985).

Although the Senate is the only House of Congress with a constitutional role in the treaty process, the House of Representatives plays a crucial role. As early as 1796, members of the House of Representatives insisted that the House possessed "a discretionary power of carrying the Treaty into effect, or refusing it their sanction." Annals of Congress, 4th Cong., 1st Sess. 426–428. Certain powers delegated to Congress as a whole, such as the authority to regulate foreign commerce or to set tariffs, could not be set aside by the treaty-making power. The general power of appropriating funds to execute a treaty represents another constraint on the President and the Senate. When two-thirds of the Senate fail to ratify a treaty, Presidents have turned to Congress as a whole to accomplish the same purpose by obtaining a simple majority vote in both Houses for a joint resolution. The annexation of Texas and Hawaii and the adoption of the St. Lawrence Seaway plan were accomplished in this manner. The position of the House of Representatives is enhanced when treaties contain language requiring that funds be made available through the normal procedures of Congress, including prior authorization and annual appropriations. This language requires action not only by the Senate Foreign Relations Committee and the House Foreign Affairs Committee but also by both Appropriations Committees.

The constitutional issue of treaty termination was raised in 1978 when President Jimmy Carter terminated a defense treaty with Taiwan. The Senate considered a resolution which would have required the approval of the Senate or both Houses of Congress before the President could terminate any defense treaty, but final action was never taken on the measure. A federal district judge decided that some form of congressional concurrence was required, either the approval of a majority of both Houses or the consent of two-thirds of the Senate. Goldwater v. Carter, 481 F.Supp. 949, 963–964 (D.D.C. 1979). This decision was rejected by an appellate court and the Supreme Court, in part because of the failure of Congress to confront the President directly. In the words of Justice Jackson, Carter had acted in a "zone of twilight." Goldwater v. Carter, 617 F.2d 697 (D.C. Cir. 1979); GOLDWATER v. CARTER, 444 U.S. 996 (1979). The Justices of the Supreme Court split along so many lines that their opinions shed little light on future treaty terminations. Congress has yet to pass legislation to define executive and legislative roles in this matter.

Treaties differ from executive agreements in several regards. Treaties require the advice and consent of the Senate, while executive agreements do not. Treaties (unlike executive agreements) may supersede prior conflicting statutes. United States v. Schooner Peggy, 5 U.S. (1 Cr.) 103 (1801). Otherwise, officials in the executive branch have considerable latitude in entering into international compacts either by treaty or by executive agreement. Among the more controversial executive agreements are the destroyers-bases deal with Great Britain in 1940, the Yalta and Potsdam agreements of 1945, the Vietnam peace agreement of 1973, the Sinai agreements of 1975, and recent military base agreements with Spain, Diego Garcia, and Bahrain.

The vast majority of executive agreements are based on statutory authority or treaty language. Although these agreements lack what the Supreme Court calls the "dignity" of a treaty, since they do not require Senate approval, they are nevertheless valid international compacts. Altman & Co. v. United States, 224 U.S. 583, 600–601 (1912). In addition to statutory and treaty authority, the executive branch claims four sources of constitutional authority that allow the President to enter into executive agreements: (1) his duty as chief executive to represent the nation in foreign affairs, (2) his authority to receive ambassadors and other public ministers, (3) his authority as commander in chief, and (4) his duty to "take care that the laws be faithfully executed." 11 FAM [Foreign Affairs Manual] 721.2(b)(3) (October 25, 1974). The scope of these unilaterial initiatives has been narrowed by judicial and congressional actions.

Few would deny that the President has constitutional authority to recognize foreign governments. President Roosevelt's recognition of Soviet Russia led to the "Litvinov Assignment" in 1933 and subsequent property claims in the courts. His decision was upheld by the Supreme Court. United States v. Belmont, 301 U.S. 324 (1937); United States v. Pink, 315 U.S. 203 (1942). Left undecided was the President's power to enter into agreements that violate such constitutional provisions as the Due Process and Just Compensation Clauses of the Fifth Amendment.

The State Department concedes that an executive agreement cannot be "inconsistent with legislation enacted by Congress in the exercise of its constitutional authority." 11 FAM 721.2(b)(3) (1974). For example, an agreement cannot survive if it conflicts with a commercial statute concerning another country. Foreign commerce is "subject to regulation, so far as this country is concerned, by Congress alone." United States v. Guy W. Capps, Inc., 204 F.2d 655, 660 (4th Cir. 1953), aff'd on other grounds, 348 U.S. 296 (1955). Other executive agreements have been struck down because they violate the Just Compensation Clause or deprive an accused of trial by jury. Seery v. United States, 127 F.Supp. 601 (Ct. Cl. 1955); Reid v. Covert, 354 U.S. 1 (1957).

The Iranian hostage crisis of 1979 produced a series of extraordinary moves by President Carter, including the freezing of Iran's assets in America and the suspension of claims pending in American courts. Although the Supreme Court found no specific authority for the suspension of claims, legal justifications were discovered somewhere in the combination of past presidential practices to settle claims by executive agreement, the history of "implicit" congressional approval, and the failure of Congress to contest the Iranian Agreement. The Court, straining to uphold an agreement it could not possibly overturn, limited the reach of its opinion by confining it to the specific circumstances in the case. Dames & Moore v. Regan, 453 U.S. 654 (1981).

A number of secret agreements were entered into without the knowledge of Congress. Legislation in 1972 (the Case Act) requires the Secretary of State to transmit to Congress within sixty days the text of "any international agreement, other than a treaty," to which the United States is a party. If the President decides that publication would be prejudicial to national security, he may transmit an agreement to the Senate Committee on Foreign Relations and the House Committee on Foreign Affairs under an injunction of secrecy removable only by the President. 86 Stat. 619 (1972); 1 U.S.C. § 112b (1982). Because the executive branch circumvented the statute by calling some agreements "arrangements," Congress passed legislation to tighten the reporting statute. 91 Stat. 224, § 5 (1977); 92 Stat. 993, § 708 (1978). Legislative control is strengthened even more by requiring that Congress approve certain agreements or appropriate funds to carry them out. Fisher, Constitutional Conflicts between Congress and the President, at 279-283.

THE WAR POWER

Congress is given specific power in the Constitution to declare war and to provide for the armed forces. However, Congress has declared war only five times. On all other occasions the President has entered into combat or hostilities without a declaration. As early as 1800 and 1801, the Supreme Court recognized the constitutionality of undeclared wars, which the Court called limited, partial, imperfect, or "quasi" wars. Bas v. Tingy, 4 U.S. (4 Dall.) 36 (1800); Talbot v. Seeman, 5 U.S. (1 Cr.) 1 (1801). The history of the past two centuries has been one of balancing and reconciling these two powers: war-declaring by Congress and war-making by the President.

Article I, Section 2, makes the President "Commander in Chief of the Army and Navy of the United States, and of the Militia of the several States, when called into the actual Service of the United States." Scholars disagree whether this merely confers a title (commander in chief) or implies additional powers for the President. Where the power begins or ends has mystified the courts. Youngstown Co. v. Sawyer, 343 U.S. 579, 641 (1952). The Justice Department has argued that the President is commander in chief not because he is skilled in the art of war but to preserve civilian supremacy over the military. 10 Op. Att'y Gen. 74, 79 (1861).

The delegates at the Philadelphia Convention recognized an implied power for the President to "repel sudden attacks." When it was proposed that Congress be empowered to "make war," Charles Pinckney objected that legislative proceedings "were too slow" for the safety of the country in an emergency. Madison and Elbridge Gerry successfully inserted "declare" for "make," thereby "leaving to the Executive the power to repel sudden attacks." 2 Farrand 318–319. When Congress delegates to the President its power to call forth the militia to suppress insurrections or to repel invasions, the decision to use force belongs solely to the President. In order to respond effectively to emergencies and avoid divided control, the power to respond is centered in the commander in chief. Martin v. Mott, 25 U.S. (12 Wheat.) 19 (1827).

The Supreme Court stated in 1850 that the President as commander in chief "is authorized to direct the movements of the naval and military forces placed by law at his command, and to employ them in the manner he may deem most effectual to harass and conquer and subdue the enemy." Fleming v. Page, 50 U.S. (9 How.) 602, 614. But what is the power to move forces "placed by *law* at his command"? How much does the President depend on Congress to provide the authorizations and appropriations necessary for military action? Under the Constitution, it is the responsibility of Congress to raise and support the military forces, to make military regulations, to provide for calling up the militia to suppress insurrections and to repel invasions, and to provide for the organization and disciplining of the militia. Art. I, § 8.

Military Courts

The use of military courts during the Civil War in states where federal courts were open and operating had been curbed by *Ex parte Milligan* (pp. 332–335). The issue returned during and after World War II. A unanimous Court in 1942 held that aliens who entered the country with the intention of committing sabotage could be tried by military commission. Alien offenders against the law of war were not entitled to trial by jury before a civilian court. Ex parte Quirin, 317 U.S. 1 (1942). This exception did not allow governors to operate under martial law and substitute military for judicial trials of civilians who were not charged with violations of the law of war. Duncan v. Kahanamoku, 327 U.S. 304 (1946). Nor may the military arrest someone who has been honorably discharged and try that person before a court-martial. Prosecution must be conducted by civilian courts. Toth v. Quarles, 350 U.S. 11 (1955).

In 1969, the Supreme Court attempted to subject certain military questions to the jurisdiction of civilian courts. It held that to be under military jurisdiction, a crime must be "service connected." Otherwise, members of the military were entitled to a civilian trial, including the constitutional right to indictment by grand jury and trial by jury. O'Callahan v. Parker, 395 U.S. 258 (1969). So confusing was the service-connected doctrine that the Court abandoned it in 1987. Jurisdiction of a court-martial now depends solely on the accused's status as a member of the armed forces. The Court announced that Congress "has primary responsibility for the delicate task of balancing the rights of servicemen against the needs of the military." Solorio v.

United States, 483 U.S. 435, 447 (1987). See also United States v. Johnson, 481 U.S. 681 (1987) and United States v. Stanley, 483 U.S. 669 (1987).

War Powers Resolution

Presidential war powers have expanded because of several developments. The idea of "defensive war" was originally limited to protective actions against the borders of the United States or naval wars against the Barbary pirates and France. After World War II, defensive war assumed a much broader meaning. American bases were spread throughout the world; military commitments were added to defense pacts and treaties. Under these agreements, an attack on an ally became an attack on the United States. Presidents also used military force on numerous occasions to protect American lives and property, often stretching those objectives to achieve foreign policy or military objectives, as in the Dominican Republic in 1965, Cambodia in 1970, and Grenada in 1983. The bombing of Libya in 1986 was defended as an antiterrorist response.

The exercise of presidential war power by Lyndon Johnson and Richard Nixon provoked Congress to pass legislation in an effort to curb executive initiatives and promote collective efforts between Congress and the President. The War Powers Resolution of 1973 (pp. 363–366) has three main provisions: presidential consultation with Congress, presidential reports to Congress, and congressional termination of military action. The purpose of the Resolution, as stated in § 2(a), is "to insure that the collective judgment" of both branches will apply to the introduction of U.S. forces into hostilities. Yet, an examination of other sections, together with executive interpretations, judicial decisions, and congressional behavior, supplies ample evidence that collective judgment is by no means assured.

The President is to consult with Congress "in every possible instance." This language obviously leaves considerable discretion to the President on both the form and timing of consultation. The framers of the Resolution did not expect the President to consult with 535 legislators. But whom should he contact? The leadership? The chairmen and ranking members of designated committees? Selected advisers? Congress has yet to select a group that can work with the President on an emergency basis. It is agreed that consultation means more than being briefed. Consultation means an opportunity to influence a pending decision. H. Rept. No. 287, 93d Cong., 1st Sess. 6–7 (1973).

The Resolution requires that the President, after introducing forces into hostilities, report to Congress within forty-eight hours. Precisely what conditions require a report is unclear from the legislation, and if a report is delayed, so are the mechanisms for congressional control. Under the Resolution, military action must terminate within sixty days after the report unless Congress (1) declares war or enacts a specific authorization, (2) extends by law the sixty-day period, or (3) is physically unable to meet as a result of an armed attack on the United States. The President may extend the period by an additional thirty days if he determines that force is needed to protect and remove American troops.

Congress has two means of control: (1) a decision not to support the President during the sixty-to-ninety days or (2) passage of a concurrent resolution at any time to direct the President to remove forces engaged in hostilities. The force of a concurrent resolution has been weakened by two developments. The executive branch takes the position that if the President has power to put men into combat, "that power could not be taken away by concurrent resolution because the power is constitutional in nature." "War Powers: A Test of Compliance," hearings before the House Committee on International Relations, 94th Cong., 1st Sess. 91 (1975). Executive officials argue that the President has a number of constitutional reasons for using military force without congressional approval, such as rescuing Americans living abroad, rescuing foreign nationals under certain circumstances, and protecting U.S. embassies and legations. Id. at 90–91. Moreover, the Supreme Court in 1983 struck down all one-House and two-House (concurrent) resolutions as legislative vetoes that have no binding effect on the executive branch. INS v. Chadha, 462 U.S. 919. Still, passage of a concurrent resolution would mean that a majority of legislators in each House opposed the President's actions. It is difficult to conceive of a President persisting in the face of that opposition.

Members of Congress have gone to court to contest military initiatives by the President, but these efforts have been turned aside by federal judges on the ground that the determination of what constitutes hostilities or imminent hostilities is essentially a fact-finding matter reserved to Congress, not the courts. CROCKETT v. REAGAN, 558 F.Supp. 893 (D.D.C. 1982), aff'd, 720 F.2d 1355 (D.C. Cir. 1983), cert. denied, 467 U.S. 1251 (1984).[4] When President Reagan sent ships into the Persian Gulf in 1987 without reporting to Congress under the War Powers Resolution, 110 members of the House of Representatives took the matter to court. Similar to the other cases, a district court declined to accept jurisdiction and dismissed the case. Lowry v. Reagan, 676 F.Supp. 333 (D.D.C. 1987).

Beginning in 1974 and continuing through the Reagan years, Congress enacted a number of statutes and amendments to restrict covert actions by the Central Intelligence Agency. Part of the accommodation of a 1980 statute required the President to fully inform the House and Senate Intelligence Committees in a "timely fashion" of covert operations in foreign countries. Congress discovered in November 1986 that President Reagan had been sending arms to Iran for ten months, without any notification to Congress. As a result, the Senate passed legislation in 1988 to tighten the requirement so that notification could be delayed for no more than forty-eight hours, but the House of Representatives did not act on the bill.

Although the War Powers Resolution has been criticized as unworkable and an encroachment of presidential responsibilities, there is greater appreciation in contemporary times that presidential military actions must have the support and understanding of Congress. As a postmortem on the Vietnam war, Secretary of State Henry Kissinger offered this perspective in 1975: "Comity between the executive and legislative branches is the only possible basis for national action. The decade-long struggle in this country over executive dominance in foreign affairs is over. The recognition that the Congress is a coequal branch of government is the dominant fact of national politics today. The executive accepts that the Congress must have both the sense and the reality of participation: foreign policy must be a shared enterprise." 72 Dep't State Bull. 562 (1975). The "collective judgment" contem-

---

[4]See also Sanchez-Espinoza v. Reagan, 568 F.Supp. 596 (D.D.C. 1983), aff'd, Sanchez-Espinoza v. Reagan, 770 F.2d 202 (D.C. Cir. 1985) (Nicaragua); Conyers v. Reagan, 578 F.Supp. 324 (D.D.C. 1984), dismissed as moot, Conyers v. Reagan, 765 F.2d 1124 (D.C. Cir. 1985) (Grenada).

plated in § 2(a) of the War Powers Resolution is an essential condition for creating effective policies in military and foreign affairs.

RIGHTS OF CITIZENSHIP

All three branches have been active in determining questions of citizenship and aliens. Article I, Section 8, Clause 4, gives Congress the power to establish a "uniform Rule of Naturalization," but Congress has conferred jurisdiction upon the courts to naturalize aliens as citizens and the executive branch has been active in asserting its notion of prerogatives concerning both citizenship and aliens.

Part of the controversy concerns the ability of aliens to obtain citizenship if they oppose war. In 1929, the Supreme Court held that the government was entitled to deny a woman an application for naturalization because, as a pacifist, she answered that she "would not take up arms personally" to defend the country. The Court said that the duty of citizens to defend the country against enemies was a "fundamental principle" of the Constitution. United States v. Schwimmer, 279 U.S. 644, 650 (1929). In one of his famous dissents, Justice Holmes noted that the woman was over fifty years of age and could not bear arms if she wanted to. He added:

> . . . if there is any principle of the Constitution that more imperatively calls for attachment than any other it is the principle of free thought—not free thought for those who agree with us but freedom for the thought that we hate. . . . I would suggest that the Quakers have done their share to make the country what it is, that many citizens agree with the applicant's belief and that I had not supposed hitherto that we regretted our inability to expel them because they believe more than some of us do in the teachings of the Sermon on the Mount.

Two years later, the Court again upheld the government's action in denying an application for citizenship from someone who would not promise to bear arms in defense of the United States unless he believed the war to be morally justified. He based his belief not on pacifism but on the principles of Christianity. The Court acknowledged that Congress could, as it had, relieve the conscientious objector from the obligation to bear arms, but this policy applied only to citizens, not to aliens seeking citizenship. The dissenters in this 5–4 decision argued that Congress had never expressly required that aliens promise to bear arms as a condition of obtaining citizenship and that courts should not act on the basis of implications. United States v. Macintosh, 283 U.S. 605, 623–624 (1931); United States v. Bland, 283 U.S. 636 (1931).

These decisions were shaken and finally overturned by cases in the 1940s. The first concerned someone who had been granted citizenship in 1927 but the government began proceedings in 1939 to cancel the citizenship, claiming that during the five years preceding naturalization the man had been affiliated with certain Communist organizations. The government charged that he had obtained citizenship by "fraud." The Court held that it was not enough for the government to prevail on a bare preponderance of the evidence. The evidence had to be clear, unequivocal, and convincing. The government could not sustain this higher burden. Schneiderman v. United States, 320 U.S. 118 (1943). See also In re Summers, 325 U.S. 561 (1945) and Klapprott v. United States, 335 U.S. 601 (1949).

In 1946, the Court overruled its earlier decisions in *Schwimmer*, *Macintosh*, and *Bland*. It held that an alien who is willing to take the oath of allegiance and to serve in the army as a noncombatant but who, because of religious beliefs, is unwilling to bear arms in defense of the country, may be admitted nonetheless to citizenship. The Court pointed out that many citizens—nurses, engineers, doctors, chaplains, litter bearers—contribute to the war effort without bearing arms. Girouard v. United States, 328 U.S. 61, 64 (1946).

In 1958, the Court decided whether a native-born American could be stripped of his citizenship because he had been convicted by court-martial for wartime desertion. The Army had sentenced him to three years of hard labor, forfeited his pay and allowances, and gave him a dishonorable discharge. When he later applied for a passport it was denied because a congressional statute required loss of citizenship for wartime desertion or a dishonorable discharge. The Court held that a person must voluntarily renounce or abandon citizenship. Citizenship was not "a license that expires upon misbehavior." Trop v. Dulles, 356 U.S. 86, 92 (1958). Denationalization violated the Eighth Amendment because it resulted in "the total destruction of the individual's status in organized society. It is a form of punishment more primitive than torture, for it destroys for the individual the political existence that was centuries in the development." Id. at 101.

The Court divided 5–4 on this case and split by the same margin in a companion case that upheld the power of Congress to strip someone of citizenship if he votes in a foreign political election. The Court deferred to Congress on this occasion because of foreign policy considerations and the possibility of serious international embarrassment. Perez v. Brownell, 356 U.S. 44 (1958). The dissenters maintained that citizenship "*is* man's basic right for it is nothing less than the right to have rights. Remove this priceless possession and there remains a stateless person, disgraced and degraded in the eyes of his countrymen." Id. at 64.

Another 5–4 decision in 1963 held that Congress could not use expatriation as punishment for draft evaders without providing for the procedural safeguards in the Fifth and Sixth Amendments: indictment, notice, confrontation, jury trial, assistance of counsel, and compulsory process for obtaining witnesses. Kennedy v. Mendoza-Martinez, 372 U.S. 144 (1963). Obviously, this decision was inconsistent with the result five years before in *Perez*, which permitted expatriation without criminal trial, and the Court was parting company from earlier decisions that had ruled expatriation unconstitutional under the Eighth Amendment. Another ruling in 1964 struck down a statutory provision because it favored native-born citizens over naturalized citizens. Schneider v. Rusk, 377 U.S. 163 (1964).

The confusion continued in 1967 with a 5–4 decision overruling *Perez*. This brought the Court back to where it was in 1958: citizenship could be renounced only voluntarily. Even acting under the foreign affairs power, Congress has no power to divest a person of his citizenship. Afroyim v. Rusk, 387 U.S. 253 (1967). However, this decision and *Schneider* were "distinguished" in 1971 when the Court allowed citizenship to be lost under certain conditions. If someone acquires citizenship by being born abroad to parents, one of whom is an American citizen, citizenship can be retained only by satisfying residency requirements established by Congress. Rogers v. Bellei, 401 U.S. 815 (1971).[5]

[5]See also Fedorenko v. United States, 449 U.S. 490 (1981); John P. Roche, "The Expatriation Cases: 'Breathes There the Man, With Soul So Dead . . .'?" 1963 Sup. Ct. Rev. 325; P. Allan Dionisopoulos, "Afroyim v. Rusk: The Evolution, Uncertainty and Implications of a Constitutional Principle," 55 Minn. L. Rev. 235 (1970).

CONCLUSIONS

Much of the debate on the allocation of foreign affairs powers between Congress and the President revolves around two competing models. Under the *Curtiss-Wright* model, the President is blessed with extraconstitutional, inherent powers. The necessities of international affairs and diplomacy make the President the dominant figure. On the other hand, the *Steel Seizure Case* assumes that Congress is the basic lawmaker in both domestic and foreign affairs. Inherent powers are denied, although congressional inertia, silence, or acquiescence may invite independent and conclusive actions by the executive.

The lesson to be drawn from either model is that Congress has ample powers to legislate for emergencies, at home or abroad, but those powers must be exercised. Congressional influence depends on its willingness to act and to take responsibility. Presidential influence, at least for long-term commitments, cannot survive on assertions of inherent power. The President needs the support and understanding of both Congress and the public.

Selected Readings

BOROSAGE, ROBERT L. "Para-Legal Authority and Its Perils." 40 *Law and Contemporary Problems* 166 (1976).

COHEN, RICHARD. "Self-Executing Executive Agreements: A Separation of Powers Problem." 24 *Buffalo Law Review* 137 (1974).

EDGAR, HAROLD, AND BENNO C. SCHMIDT, JR. *"Curtiss-Wright* Comes Home: Executive Power and National Security Secrecy." 21 *Harvard Civil Rights–Civil Liberties Law Review* 349 (1986).

FARBER, DANIEL A. "National Security, the Right to Travel, and the Courts." 1981 *Supreme Court Review* 263.

FISHER, LOUIS. "Foreign Policy Powers of the President and Congress." 499 *The Annals* 148 (1988).

FRANCK, THOMAS M., AND EDWARD WEISBAND. *Foreign Policy by Congress.* New York: Oxford University Press, 1979.

——, AND MICHAEL J. GLENNON. *Foreign Relations and National Security Law.* St. Paul, Minn.: West, 1987.

HENKIN, LOUIS. *Foreign Affairs and the Constitution.* New York: Foundation Press, 1972.

HURTGEN, JAMES R. "The Case for Presidential Prerogative." 7 *University of Toledo Law Review* 59 (1975).

LOFGREN, CHARLES A. "U.S. v. Curtiss-Wright Export Corporation: An Historical Reassessment." 83 *Yale Law Journal* 1 (1973).

——. "War-Making Under the Constitution: The Original Understanding." 81 *Yale Law Journal* 672 (1972).

MARCUS, MAEVA. *Truman and the Steel Seizure Case:*

The Limits of Presidential Power. New York: Columbia University Press, 1977.

MURPHY, JOHN F. "Treaties and International Agreements Other Than Treaties: Constitutional Allocation of Power and Responsibility Among the President, the House of Representatives, and the Senate." 23 *University of Kansas Law Review* 221 (1975).

O'DONNELL, THOMAS A. "Illumination or Elimination of the 'Zone of Twilight'? Congressional Acquiescence and Presidential Authority in Foreign Affairs." 51 *Cincinnati Law Review* 95 (1982).

OHLY, D. CHRISTOPHER. "Advice and Consent: International Executive Claims Settlement Agreements." 5 *Californian Western International Law Journal* 271 (1975).

PAUST, JORDAN J. "Is the President Bound by the Supreme Law of the Land?—Foreign Affairs and National Security Reexamined." 9 *Hastings Constitutional Law Quarterly* 719 (1982).

REVELEY, W. TAYLOR, III. *War Powers of the President and Congress.* Charlottesville: University Press of Virginia, 1981.

ROVINE, ARTHUR W. "Separation of Powers and International Executive Agreements." 52 *Indiana Law Review* 297 (1977).

SOFAER, ABRAHAM D. *War, Foreign Affairs and Constitutional Power: The Origins.* Cambridge, Mass.: Ballinger Publishing, 1976.

STEVENS, CHARLES J. "The Use and Control of Executive Agreements: Recent Congressional Initiatives." 20 *Orbis* 905 (1977).

United States v. Curtiss-Wright Corp.

299 U.S. 304 (1936)

In 1935, in the *Panama Refining* and *Schechter* cases, the Supreme Court struck down the National Industrial Recovery Act and its delegation of legislative power to the President. The *Curtiss-Wright* case involves the delegation of legislative power to the President in foreign rather than domestic affairs. In 1934, Congress authorized the President to place an embargo on the sale of arms and munitions to countries engaged in armed conflict in South America if the President determined that an embargo would contribute to the establishment of peace. Justice Sutherland, writing for the Court, upholds the statute partly on the distinction he drew between external and internal affairs.

MR. JUSTICE SUTHERLAND delivered the opinion of the Court.

On January 27, 1936, an indictment was returned in the court below, the first count of which charges that appellees, beginning with the 29th day of May, 1934, conspired to sell in the United States certain arms of war, namely fifteen machine guns, to Bolivia, a country then engaged in armed conflict in the Chaco, in violation of the Joint Resolution of Congress approved May 28, 1934, and the provisions of a proclamation issued on the same day by the President of the United States pursuant to authority conferred by § 1 of the resolution. In pursuance of the conspiracy, the commission of certain overt acts was alleged, details of which need not be stated. The Joint Resolution (c. 365, 48 Stat. 811) follows:

"Resolved by the Senate and House of Representatives of the United States of America in Congress assembled, That if the President finds that the prohibition of the sale of arms and munitions of war in the United States to those countries now engaged in armed conflict in the Chaco may contribute to the reëstablishment of peace between those countries, and if after consultation with the governments of other American Republics and with their coöperation, as well as that of such other governments as he may deem necessary, he makes proclamation to that effect, it shall be unlawful to sell, except under such limitations and exceptions as the President prescribes, any arms or munitions of war in any place in the United States to the countries now engaged in that armed conflict, or to any person, company, or association acting in the interest of either country, until otherwise ordered by the President or by Congress.

"Sec. 2. Whoever sells any arms or munitions of war in violation of section 1 shall, on conviction, be punished by a fine not exceeding $10,000 or by imprisonment not exceeding two years, or both."

The President's proclamation (48 Stat. 1744), after reciting the terms of the Joint Resolution, declares:

"Now, therefore, I, Franklin D. Roosevelt, President of the United States of America, acting under and by virtue of the authority conferred in me by the said joint resolution of Congress, do hereby declare and proclaim that I have found that the prohibition of the sale of arms and munitions of war in the United States to those countries now engaged in armed conflict in the Chaco may contribute to the reëstablishment of peace between those countries . . . *[This proclamation was revoked by President Roosevelt on November 14, 1935.]*

. . .

First. It is contended that by the Joint Resolution, the going into effect and continued operation of the resolution was conditioned (a) upon the President's judgment as to its beneficial effect upon the reëstablishment of peace between the countries engaged in armed conflict in the Chaco; (b) upon the making of a proclamation, which was left to his unfettered discretion, thus constituting an attempted substitution of the President's will for that of Congress; (c) upon the making of a proclamation putting an end to the operation of the resolution, which again was left to the President's unfettered discretion; and (d) further, that the extent of its operation in particular cases was subject to limitation and exception by the President, controlled by no standard. In each of these particulars, appellees urge that Congress abdicated its essential functions and delegated them to the Executive.

Whether, if the Joint Resolution had related solely to internal affairs it would be open to the challenge that it constituted an unlawful delegation of legislative power to the Executive, we find it unnecessary to determine. The whole aim of the resolution is to affect a situation entirely external to the United States, and falling within the category of foreign affairs. The determination which we are called to make, therefore, is whether the Joint Resolution, as applied to that situation, is vulnerable to attack under the rule that forbids a delegation of the law-making power. In other words, assuming (but not deciding) that the challenged delegation, if it were confined to internal affairs, would be invalid, may it nevertheless be sustained on the ground that its exclusive aim is to afford a remedy for a hurtful condition within foreign territory?

It will contribute to the elucidation of the question if we first consider the differences between the powers of the federal government in respect of foreign or external affairs and those in respect of domestic or internal affairs. That there are differences between them, and that these differences are fundamental, may not be doubted.

The two classes of powers are different, both in respect of their origin and their nature. The broad statement that the federal government can exercise no powers except those specifically enumerated in the Constitution, and such implied powers as are necessary and proper to carry into effect the enumerated powers, is categorically true only in respect of our internal affairs. In that field, the primary purpose of the Constitution was to carve from the general mass of legislative powers *then possessed by the states* such portions as it was thought desirable to vest in the federal government, leaving those not included in the enumera-

tion still in the states. *Carter* v. *Carter Coal Co.,* 298 U.S. 238, 294. That this doctrine applies only to powers which the states had, is self evident. And since the states severally never possessed international powers, such powers could not have been carved from the mass of state powers but obviously were transmitted to the United States from some other source. During the colonial period, those powers were possessed exclusively by and were entirely under the control of the Crown. By the Declaration of Independence, "the Representatives of the United States of America" declared the United [not the several] Colonies to be free and independent states, and as such to have "full Power to levy War, conclude Peace, contract Alliances, establish Commerce and to do all other Acts and Things which Independent States may of right do."

As a result of the separation from Great Britain by the colonies acting as a unit, the powers of external sovereignty passed from the Crown not to the colonies severally, but to the colonies in their collective and corporate capacity as the United States of America. Even before the Declaration, the colonies were a unit in foreign affairs, acting through a common agency—namely the Continental Congress, composed of delegates from the thirteen colonies. That agency exercised the powers of war and peace, raised an army, created a navy, and finally adopted the Declaration of Independence. Rulers come and go; governments end and forms of government change; but sovereignty survives. A political society cannot endure without a supreme will somewhere. Sovereignty is never held in suspense. When, therefore, the external sovereignty of Great Britain in respect of the colonies ceased, it immediately passed to the Union. *See Penhallow* v. *Doane,* 3 Dall. 54, 80–81. That fact was given practical application almost at once. The treaty of peace, made on September 23, 1783, was concluded between his Brittanic Majesty and the "United States of America." 8 Stat.— European Treaties—80.

The Union existed before the Constitution, which was ordained and established among other things to form "a more perfect Union." Prior to that event, it is clear that the Union, declared by the Articles of Confederation to be "perpetual," was the sole possessor of external sovereignty and in the Union it remained without change save in so far as the Constitution in express terms qualified its exercise. . . .

Not only, as we have shown, is the federal power over external affairs in origin and essential character different from that over internal affairs, but participation in the exercise of the power is significantly limited. In this vast external realm, with its important, complicated, delicate and manifold problems, the President alone has the power to speak or listen as a representative of the nation. He *makes* treaties with the advice and consent of the Senate; but he alone negotiates. Into the field of negotiation the Senate cannot intrude; and Congress itself is powerless to invade it. As Marshall said in his great argument of March 7, 1800, in the House of Representatives, "The President is the sole organ of the nation in its external relations, and its sole representative with foreign nations." Annals, 6th Cong., col. 613. The Senate Committee on Foreign Relations at a very early day in our history (February 15, 1816), reported to the Senate, among other things, as follows:

"The President is the constitutional representative of the United States with regard to foreign nations. He manages our concerns with foreign nations and must necessarily be most competent to determine when, how, and upon what subjects negotiation may be urged with the greatest prospect of success. For his conduct he is responsible to the Constitution. The committee consider this responsibility the surest pledge for the faithful discharge of his duty. They think the interference of the Senate in the direction of foreign negotiations calculated to diminish that responsibility and thereby to impair the best security for the national safety. The nature of transactions with foreign nations, moreover, requires caution and unity of design, and their success frequently depends on secrecy and dispatch." U. S. Senate, Reports, Committee on Foreign Relations, vol. 8, p. 24.

It is important to bear in mind that we are here dealing not alone with an authority vested in the President by an exertion of legislative power, but with such an authority plus the very delicate, plenary and exclusive power of the President as the sole organ of the federal government in the field of international relations—a power which does not require as a basis for its exercise an act of Congress, but which, of course, like every other governmental power, must be exercised in subordination to the applicable provisions of the Constitution. It is quite apparent that if, in the maintenance of our international relations, embarrassment—perhaps serious embarrassment—is to be avoided and success for our aims achieved, congressional legislation which is to be made effective through negotiation and inquiry within the international field must often accord to the President a degree of discretion and freedom from statutory restriction which would not be admissible were domestic affairs alone involved. Moreover, he, not Congress, has the better opportunity of knowing the conditions which prevail in foreign countries, and especially is this true in time of war. He has his confidential sources of information. He has his agents in the form of diplomatic, consular and other officials. Secrecy in respect of information gathered by them may be highly necessary, and the premature disclosure of it productive of harmful results. Indeed, so clearly is this true that the first President refused to accede to a request to lay before the House of Representatives the instructions, correspondence and documents relating to the negotiation of the Jay Treaty—a refusal the wisdom of which was recognized by the House itself and has never since been doubted. In his reply to the request, President Washington said:

"The nature of foreign negotiations requires caution, and their success must often depend on secrecy; and even when brought to a conclusion a full disclosure of all the measures, demands, or eventual concessions which may have been proposed or contemplated would be extremely impolitic; for this might have a pernicious influence on future negotiations, or produce immediate inconveniences, perhaps danger and mischief, in relation to other powers. The necessity of such caution and secrecy was one cogent reason for vesting the power of making treaties in the President, with the advice and consent of the Senate, the principle on which that body was formed confining it to a small number of members. To admit, then, a right in the

House of Representatives to demand and to have as a matter of course all the papers respecting a negotiation with a foreign power would be to establish a dangerous precedent." 1 Messages and Papers of the Presidents, p. 194.

[Sutherland neglected to point out that Washington had already submitted the documents to the Senate. It could also have been noted that when treaties require implementing legislation and appropriations, as most do, Presidents have submitted treaty documents to both Houses of Congress.]

. . .

We deem it unnecessary to consider, *seriatim,* the several clauses which are said to evidence the unconstitutionality of the Joint Resolution as involving an unlawful delegation of legislative power. It is enough to summarize by saying that, both upon principle and in accordance with precedent, we conclude there is sufficient warrant for the broad discretion vested in the President to determine whether the enforcement of the statute will have a beneficial effect upon the reëstablishment

of peace in the affected countries; whether he shall make proclamation to bring the resolution into operation; whether and when the resolution shall cease to operate and to make proclamation accordingly; and to prescribe limitations and exceptions to which the enforcement of the resolution shall be subject.

. . .

The judgment of the court below must be reversed and the cause remanded for further proceedings in accordance with the foregoing opinion.

Reversed.

MR. JUSTICE MCREYNOLDS does not agree. He is of opinion that the court below reached the right conclusion and its judgment ought to be affirmed.

MR. JUSTICE STONE took no part in the consideration or decision of this case.

Congress Interprets Curtiss-Wright: *The Iran-Contra Report*

Several witnesses before the Iran-Contra Committees in 1987 testified that the actions by the Reagan administration could be justified in terms of *United States* v. *Curtiss-Wright* (1936), which they claimed recognized broad powers for the President in foreign affairs. The majority report rejected this position. The passage below appeared in *Iran-Contra Affair,* H. Rept. No. 100–433, S. Rept. No. 100–216, 100th Cong., 1st Sess., 388–390 (November 1987). Footnotes omitted.

In urging a broad interpretation of presidential power, various witnesses before these Committees invoked the Supreme Court's 1936 decision in *United States* v. *Curtiss-Wright Export Corporation.* Their reliance on this case is misplaced.

In *Curtiss-Wright,* Congress, by statute, had delegated to the President the power to prohibit the sale of arms to countries in an area of South America if the President believed the prohibition would promote peace. The Curtiss-Wright Corpo-

ration claimed that the power to make this determination was a legislative power that Congress could not delegate to the President.

Witnesses at the hearings misread this case to justify their claim that the President had broad inherent foreign policy powers to the virtual exclusion of Congress. *Curtiss-Wright* did not present any such issue. The case involved the question of the powers of the President in foreign policy where Congress expressly authorizes him to act; it did not involve the question of the President's foreign policy powers when Congress expressly forbids him to act.

In *Curtiss-Wright*, the Court upheld broad delegations by Congress of power to the President in matters of foreign affairs. Writing for the Court, Justice Sutherland said that legislation within "the international field must often accord to the President a degree of discretion and freedom from statutory restriction which would not be admissible were domestic affairs alone involved."

In language frequently seized on by those seeking to claim that the President's role in foreign policy is exclusive, Justice Sutherland noted that the President was acting not only with a delegation of power by the legislature, but also with certain powers the Constitution gave directly to him:

"It is important to bear in mind that we are here dealing not alone with an authority vested in the President by an exertion of legislative power, but with such an authority plus the very delicate, plenary and exclusive power of the President as the sole organ of the federal government in the field of international relations—a power which does not require as a basis for its exercise an act of Congress, but which, of course, like every other governmental power, must be exercised in subordination to applicable provisions of the Constitution."

Some have tried to interpret this passage as stating that the President may act in foreign affairs against the will of Congress. But that is not what it says. As Justice Jackson later observed, the most that can be drawn from Justice Sutherland's language is the intimation "that the President might act in external affairs without congressional authority, but not that he might act contrary to an Act of Congress." More recently, in *Dames & Moore* v. *Regan*, the Supreme Court cautioned that the broad language in *Curtiss-Wright* must be viewed only in context of that case. Writing for the majority, Justice (now Chief Justice) Rehnquist expressed the Court's view of the appropriate relationship between the executive and the legislative branches in the conduct of foreign policy:

"When the President acts pursuant to an express or implied authorization from Congress, he exercises not only his powers but also those delegated by Congress. In such a case the executive action 'would be supported by the strongest presumptions and widest latitude of judicial interpretation, and the burden of persuasion would rest heavily upon any who might attack it.' . . . When the President acts in the absence of congressional authorization he may enter a 'zone of twilight in which he and Congress may have concurrent authority, or in which its distribution is uncertain.' . . . In such a case, the analysis becomes more complicated, and the validity of the President's action, at least so far as separation-of-powers principles are concerned, hinges on a consideration of all the circumstances which might shed light on the views of the Legislative Branch toward such action, including 'congressional inertia, indifference or quiescence.' . . . Finally, when the President acts in contravention of the will of Congress, 'his power is at its lowest ebb' and the Court can sustain his actions 'only by disabling the Congress from action on the subject.'"

Similarly, in 1981, the D.C. Circuit cautioned against undue reliance on the quoted passage from *Curtiss-Wright*: "To the extent that denominating the President as the 'sole organ' of the United States in international affairs constitutes a blanket endorsement of plenary Presidential power over any matter extending beyond the borders of this country, we reject that characterization."

In calling the President the "sole organ" of the Nation in its relations with other countries, Justice Sutherland quoted from a speech by John Marshall in 1800 when Marshall was a Member of the House of Representatives: "As Marshall said in his great argument of March 7, 1800, in the House of Representative, 'The President is the sole organ of the nation in its external relations, and its sole representative with foreign nations.' Annals, 6th Cong., col. 613."

The reader might assume from this passage that Marshall advocated an exclusive, independent power for the President in the area of foreign affairs, free from legislative control. When his statement is placed in the context of the "great argument of March 7, 1800," however, it is clear that Marshall regarded the President as simply carrying out the law as established by statute or treaty. The House had been debating a decision by President John Adams to turn over to England a person charged with murder. Some members thought the President should be impeached for encroaching upon the judiciary, since the case was already pending in court. Marshall replied that President Adams was executing a treaty approved by the Senate that had the force of law. Here is the full context of Marshall's "sole organ" statement:

"The case was in its nature a national demand made upon the nation. The parties were the two nations. They cannot come into court to litigate their claims, nor can a court decide on them. Of consequence, the demand is not a case for judicial cognizance.

"The President is the sole organ of the nation in its external relations, and its sole representative with foreign nations. Of consequence, the demand of a foreign nation can only be made on him.

"He possesses the whole Executive power. He holds and directs the force of the nation. Of consequence, any act to be performed by the force of the nation is to be performed through him.

"He is charged to execute the laws. A treaty is declared to be law. He must then execute a treaty, where he, and he alone, possesses the means of executing it.

"The treaty, which is a law, enjoins the performance of a particular object. The person who is to perform this object is marked out by the Constitution, since the person is named who conducts the foreign intercourse, and is to take care that the laws be faithfully executed. The means by which it is to be performed, the force of the nation, are in the hands of this person. Ought not this person to perform the object, although the particular mode of using the means has not been prescribed? Congress, unquestionably, may prescribe the mode, and Congress may devolve on others the whole execution of the contract; but, till this be done, it seems the duty of the Executive department to execute the contract by any means it possesses."

. . .

Haig v. Agee
453 U.S. 280 (1981)

In this case, the "right to travel" collides with the President's interests over foreign policy and national security. Philip Agee, a former employee of the Central Intelligence Agency, had announced a campaign to expose CIA officers and agents. His activities abroad resulted in the identification of CIA agents and intelligence sources in foreign countries. After Secretary of State Alexander Haig revoked his passport, Agee filed suit claiming that the regulation cited by Haig had not been authorized by Congress and was impermissibly overbroad. Agee also argued that the passport revocation violated his freedom to travel and his First Amendment right to criticize governmental policies. Moreover, he charged that the failure to accord him a hearing before the revocation constituted a violation of procedural due process under the Fifth Amendment. The district court and the D.C. Circuit agreed that the regulation exceeded Haig's authority.

CHIEF JUSTICE BURGER delivered the opinion of the Court.

The question presented is whether the Presi-dent, acting through the Secretary of State, has authority to revoke a passport on the ground that the holder's activities in foreign countries are causing or are likely to cause serious damage to the national security or foreign policy of the United States.

I

A

Philip Agee, an American citizen, currently resides in West Germany. From 1957 to 1968, he was employed by the Central Intelligence Agency. He held key positions in the division of the Agency that is responsible for covert intelligence gathering in foreign countries. In the course of his duties at the Agency, Agee received training in clandestine operations, including the methods used to protect the identities of intelligence employees and sources of the United States overseas. He served in undercover assignments abroad and came to know many Government employees and other persons supplying information to the United States. The relationships of many of these people to our Government are highly confidential; many are still engaged in intelligence gathering.

In 1974, Agee called a press conference in London to announce his "campaign to fight the United States CIA wherever it is operating." He declared his intent "to expose CIA officers and agents and to take the measures necessary to drive them out of the countries where they are operating." Since 1974, Agee has, by his own assertion, devoted consistent effort to that program, and he has traveled extensively in other countries in order to carry it out. To identify CIA personnel in a particular country, Agee goes to the target country and consults sources in local diplomatic circles whom he knows from his prior service in the United States Government. He recruits collaborators and trains them in clandestine techniques designed to expose the "cover" of CIA employees and sources. Agee and his collaborators have repeatedly and publicly identified individuals and organizations located in foreign countries as undercover CIA agents, employees, or sources. The record reveals that the identifications divulge classified information, violate Agee's express contract not to make any public statements about Agency matters without prior clearance by the Agency,

have prejudiced the ability of the United States to obtain intelligence, and have been followed by episodes of violence against the persons and organizations identified.

In December 1979, the Secretary of State revoked Agee's passport and delivered an explanatory notice to Agee in West Germany. The notice states in part:

"The Department's action is predicated upon a determination made by the Secretary under the provisions of [22 CFR] Section 51.70 (b)(4) that your activities abroad are causing or are likely to cause serious damage to the national security or the foreign policy of the United States. . . ."

The notice also advised Agee of his right to an administrative hearing and offered to hold such a hearing in West Germany on 5 days' notice.

Agee at once filed suit against the Secretary. He alleged that the regulation invoked by the Secretary, 22 CFR § 51.70 (b)(4) (1980), has not been authorized by Congress and is invalid; that the regulation is impermissibly overbroad; that the revocation prior to a hearing violated his Fifth Amendment right to procedural due process; and that the revocation violated a Fifth Amendment liberty interest in a right to travel and a First Amendment right to criticize Government policies. He sought declaratory and injunctive relief, and he moved for summary judgment on the question of the authority to promulgate the regulation and on the constitutional claims.

[The district court held that the regulation exceeded the statutory powers of the Secretary under the Passport Act and ordered the Secretary to restore Agee's passport. The D.C. Circuit held that the Secretary was required to show that Congress had authorized the regulation either by an express delegation or by an implied approval. The Court found that the regulation exceeded authority granted by Congress.]

II

The principal question before us is whether the statute authorizes the action of the Secretary pursuant to the policy announced by the challenged regulation.

A

1

Although the historical background that we develop later is important, we begin with the language of the statute. See, *e.g.*, *Universities Research Assn.* v. *Coutu*, 450 U. S. 754, 771 (1981); *Zemel, supra*, at 7–8. The Passport Act of 1926 provides in pertinent part:

"The Secretary of State may grant and issue passports, and cause passports to be granted, issued, and verified in foreign countries by diplomatic representatives of the United States . . . under such rules as the President shall designate and prescribe for and on behalf of the United States, and no other person shall grant, issue, or verify such passports." 22 U. S. C. § 211a (1976 ed., Supp. IV).

This language is unchanged since its original enactment in 1926.

The Passport Act does not in so many words confer upon the Secretary a power to revoke a passport. Nor, for that matter, does it expressly authorize denials of passport applications. Neither, however, does any statute expressly limit those powers. It is beyond dispute that the Secretary has the power to deny a passport for reasons not specified in the statutes. For example, in *Kent* v. *Dulles*, 357 U. S. 116 (1958), the Court recognized congressional acquiescence in Executive policies of refusing passports to applicants "participating in illegal conduct, trying to escape the toils of the law, promoting passport frauds, or otherwise engaging in conduct which would violate the laws of the United States." *Id.*, at 127. In *Zemel*, the Court held that "the weightiest considerations of national security" authorized the Secretary to restrict travel to Cuba at the time of the Cuban missile crisis. 381 U. S., at 16. Agee concedes that if the Secretary may deny a passport application for a certain reason, he may revoke a passport on the same ground.

2

Particularly in light of the "broad rule-making authority granted in the [1926] Act," *Zemel*, 381

U.S., at 12, a consistent administrative construction of that statute must be followed by the courts "'unless there are compelling indications that it is wrong.'" *E. I. du Pont de Nemours & Co.* v. *Collins*, 432 U. S. 46, 55 (1977), quoting *Red Lion Broadcasting Co.* v. *FCC*, 395 U. S. 367, 381 (1969); see *Zemel, supra*, at 11. This is especially so in the areas of foreign policy and national security, where congressional silence is not to be equated with congressional disapproval. In *United States* v. *Curtiss-Wright Export Corp.*, 299 U. S. 304 (1936), the volatile nature of problems confronting the Executive in foreign policy and national defense was underscored:

"In this vast external realm, with its important, complicated, delicate and manifold problems, the President alone has the power to speak or listen as a representative of the nation. . . . As Marshall said in his great argument of March 7, 1800, in the House of Representatives, 'The President is the sole organ of the nation in its external relations, and its sole representative with foreign nations.'" *Id.*, at 319.

Applying these considerations to statutory construction, the *Zemel* Court observed:

"[B]ecause of the changeable and explosive nature of contemporary international relations, and the fact that the Executive is immediately privy to information which cannot be swiftly presented to, evaluated by, and acted upon by the legislature, *Congress—in giving the Executive authority over matters of foreign affairs—must of necessity paint with a brush broader than that it customarily wields in domestic areas.*" 381 U. S., at 17 (emphasis supplied).

Matters intimately related to foreign policy and national security are rarely proper subjects for judicial intervention. In *Harisiades* v. *Shaughnessy*, 342 U. S. 580 (1952), the Court observed that matters relating "to the conduct of foreign relations . . . are so exclusively entrusted to the political branches of government as to be largely immune from judicial inquiry or interference." *Id.*, at 589; accord, *Chicago & Southern Air Lines, Inc.* v. *Waterman S.S. Corp.*, 333 U. S. 103, 111 (1948).

B

1

A passport is, in a sense, a letter of introduction in which the issuing sovereign vouches for the bearer and requests other sovereigns to aid the bearer. . . .

. . . As a travel control document, a passport is both proof of identity and proof of allegiance to the United States. Even under a travel control statute, however, a passport remains in a sense a document by which the Government vouches for the bearer and for his conduct.

The history of passport controls since the earliest days of the Republic shows congressional recognition of Executive authority to withhold passports on the basis of substantial reasons of national security and foreign policy. Prior to 1856, when there was no statute on the subject, the common perception was that the issuance of a passport was committed to the sole discretion of the Executive and that the Executive would exercise this power in the interests of the national security and foreign policy of the United States. This derived from the generally accepted view that foreign policy was the province and responsibility of the Executive [citing United States v. Curtiss-Wright and Federalist No. 64]. From the outset, Congress endorsed not only the underlying premise of Executive authority in the areas of foreign policy and national security, but also its specific application to the subject of passports. Early Congresses enacted statutes expressly recognizing the Executive authority with respect to passports.

The first Passport Act, adopted in 1856, provided that the Secretary of State "shall be authorized to grant and issue passports . . . under such rules as the President shall designate and prescribe for and on behalf of the United States. . . ." § 23, 11 Stat. 60. This broad and permissive language worked no change in the power óf the Executive to issue passports; nor was it intended to do so. The Act was passed to centralize passport authority in the Federal Government and specifically in the Secretary of State. . . .

[Here follows a series of actions by the President and the Secretary of State asserting their authority to deny passports for reasons of national security. The Court concludes that Congress, in the Passport Act of 1926, adopted these administrative constructions. In addition to this "congressional acquiescence," the Court argues that a statute enacted in 1978 is "weighty evidence" that Congress approved of executive interpretations.]

III

Agee also attacks the Secretary's action on three constitutional grounds: first, that the revocation of his passport impermissibly burdens his freedom to travel; second, that the action was intended to penalize his exercise of free speech and deter his criticism of Government policies and practices; and third, that failure to accord him a prerevocation hearing violated his Fifth Amendment right to procedural due process.

In light of the express language of the passport regulations, which permits their application only in cases involving likelihood of "serious damage" to national security or foreign policy, these claims are without merit.

Revocation of a passport undeniably curtails travel, but the freedom to travel abroad with a "letter of introduction" in the form of a passport issued by the sovereign is subordinate to national security and foreign policy considerations; as such, it is subject to reasonable governmental regulation. . . .

. . .

We reverse the judgment of the Court of Appeals and remand for further proceedings consistent with this opinion.

Reversed and remanded.

JUSTICE BLACKMUN, concurring.

There is some force, I feel, in Justice Brennan's observations, *post*, at 312–318, that today's decision cannot be reconciled fully with all the reasoning of *Zemel* v. *Rusk*, 381 U. S. 1 (1965), and, particularly, of *Kent* v. *Dulles*, 357 U. S. 116 (1958), and that the Court is cutting back somewhat upon the opinions in those cases *sub silentio*. I would have preferred to have the Court disavow forthrightly the aspects of *Zemel* and *Kent* that may suggest that evidence of a long-standing Executive policy or construction in this area is not probative of the issue of congressional authorization. Nonetheless, believing this is what the Court in effect has done, I join its opinion.

JUSTICE BRENNAN, with whom JUSTICE MARSHALL joins, dissenting.

Today the Court purports to rely on prior decisions of this Court to support the revocation of a passport by the Secretary of State. Because I believe that such reliance is fundamentally misplaced, and that the Court instead has departed from the express holdings of those decisions, I dissent.

. . .

II

This is not a complicated case. The Court has twice articulated the proper mode of analysis for determining whether Congress has delegated to the Executive Branch the authority to deny a passport under the Passport Act of 1926. *Zemel* v. *Rusk,* 381 U. S. 1 (1965); *Kent* v. *Dulles,* 357 U. S. 116 (1958). The analysis is hardly confusing, and I expect that had the Court faithfully applied it, today's judgment would affirm the decision below.

In *Kent* v. *Dulles, supra,* the Court reviewed a challenge to a regulation of the Secretary denying passports to applicants because of their alleged Communist beliefs and associations and their refusals to file affidavits concerning present or past membership in the Communist Party. Observing that the right to travel into and out of this country is an important personal right included within the "liberty" guaranteed by the Fifth Amendment, *id.,* at 125–127, the Court stated that any infringement of that liberty can only "be pursuant to the lawmaking functions of the Congress," and that delegations to the Executive Branch that curtail that liberty must be construed narrowly, *id.,* at 129. Because the Passport Act of 1926—the same statute at issue here—did not expressly authorize the denial of passports to alleged Communists, the Court examined cases of actual passport refusals by the Secretary to determine whether "it could be fairly argued" that this category of passport refusals was "adopted by Congress in light of prior administrative practice." *Id.,* at 128. The Court was unable to find such prior administrative practice, and therefore held that the regulation was unauthorized.

In *Zemel* v. *Rusk, supra,* the issue was whether the Secretary could restrict travel for all citizens to Cuba. In holding that he could, the Court expressly approved the holding in *Kent:*

"We have held, *Kent* v. *Dulles, supra,* and reaffirm today, that the 1926 Act must take its content from history: it authorizes only those passport refusals and restrictions 'which it could fairly be argued were adopted by Congress in light of prior administrative practice.' *Kent* v. *Dulles, supra,* at 128. So limited, the Act does not constitute an invalid delegation." 381 U. S., at 17–18.

In reaching its decision, the Court in *Zemel* relied upon numerous occasions when the State Department had restricted travel to certain international areas . . .

As in *Kent* and *Zemel,* there is no dispute here that the Passport Act of 1926 does not *expressly* authorize the Secretary to revoke Agee's passport. *Ante,* at 290. Therefore, the sole remaining inquiry is whether there exists "with regard to the sort of passport [revocation] involved [here], an administrative *practice* sufficiently substantial and consistent to warrant the conclusion that Congress had implicitly approved it." *Zemel* v. *Rusk, supra,* at 12 (emphasis added). The Court today, citing to this same page in *Zemel,* applies a test markedly different from that of *Zemel* and *Kent* and in fact expressly disavowed by the latter. The Court states: "We hold that the *policy* announced in the challenged regulations is 'sufficiently substantial and consistent' to compel the conclusion that Congress has approved it. See *Zemel,* 381 U. S., at 12." *Ante,* at 306 (emphasis added). The Court also observes that "a consistent administrative *construction* of [the Passport Act] must be followed by the courts 'unless there are compelling indications that it is wrong.'" *Ante,* at 291 (emphasis added).

But clearly neither *Zemel* nor *Kent* holds that a longstanding Executive *policy* or *construction* is sufficient proof that Congress has implicitly authorized the Secretary's action. The cases hold that an administrative *practice* must be demonstrated; in fact *Kent* unequivocally states that mere *construction* by the Executive—no matter how longstanding and consistent—is *not* sufficient. . . .

. . . Only when Congress had maintained its silence in the face of a consistent and substantial pattern of actual passport denials or revocations —where the parties will presumably object loudly, perhaps through legal action, to the Secretary's exercise of discretion—can this Court be sure that Congress is aware of the Secretary's actions and has implicitly approved that exercise of discretion. Moreover, broad statements by the Executive Branch relating to its discretion in the passport area lack the precision of definition that would follow from concrete applications of that discretion in specific cases. Although Congress might register general approval of the Executive's overall policy, it still might disapprove of the Executive's pattern of applying that broad rule in specific categories of cases.

. . .

The Court's reliance on material expressly abjured in *Kent* becomes understandable only when one appreciates the paucity of recorded administrative practice—the only evidence upon which *Kent* and *Zemel* permit reliance—with respect to passport denials or revocations based on foreign policy or national security considerations relating to an individual. The Court itself identifies only three occasions over the past 33 years when the Secretary has revoked passports for such reasons. *Ante,* at 302. And only one of these cases involved a revocation pursuant to the regulations challenged in this case. Yet, in 1979 alone, there were 7,835,000 Americans traveling abroad. U. S. Dept. of Commerce, Bureau of Census, Statistical Abstract of the United States 253 (101st ed., 1980).

. . .

III

I suspect that this case is a prime example of the adage that "bad facts make bad law." Philip Agee is hardly a model representative of our Nation. And the Executive Branch has attempted to use one of the only means at its disposal, revocation of a passport, to stop respondent's damaging statements. But just as the Constitution protects both popular and unpopular speech, it likewise protects both popular and unpopular travelers. And it is important to remember that this decision applies not only to Philip Agee, whose activities could be perceived as harming the national security, but also to other citizens who may merely disagree with Government foreign policy and express their views.

The Constitution allocates the lawmaking function to Congress, and I fear that today's decision has handed over too much of that function to the Executive. In permitting the Secretary to stop this unpopular traveler and critic of the CIA, the Court professes to rely on, but in fact departs from, the two precedents in the passport regulation area, *Zemel* and *Kent.* Of course it is always easier to fit oneself within the safe haven of *stare decisis* than boldly to overrule precedents of several decades' standing. Because I find myself unable to reconcile those cases with the decision in this case, however, and because I disagree with the Court's *sub silentio* overruling of those cases, I dissent.

The Prize Cases

2 Black (67 U.S.) 635 (1863)

Among other emergency actions in 1861, President Lincoln declared a blockade of ports controlled by persons in armed rebellion against the government. To justify the blockade and seizure of neutral vessels, a state of war had to exist, but Congress had made no such declaration. Under what constitutional authority did Lincoln act? Does a state of war

require a formal declaration? The three Lincoln appointees—Swayne, Miller, and Davis—joined Grier and Wayne to uphold presidential power.

Mr. Justice GRIER. There are certain propositions of law which must necessarily affect the ultimate decision of these cases, and many others, which it will be proper to discuss and decide before we notice the special facts peculiar to each.

They are, 1st. Had the President a right to institute a blockade of ports in possession of persons in armed rebellion against the Government, on the principles of international law, as known and acknowledged among civilized States?

2d. Was the property of persons domiciled or residing within those States a proper subject of capture on the sea as "enemies' property?"

I. Neutrals have a right to challenge the existence of a blockade *de facto*, and also the authority of the party exercising the right to institute it. They have a right to enter the ports of a friendly nation for the purposes of trade and commerce, but are bound to recognize the rights of a belligerent engaged in actual war, to use this mode of coercion, for the purpose of subduing the enemy.

That a blockade *de facto* actually existed, and was formally declared and notified by the President on the 27th and 30th of April, 1861, is an admitted fact in these cases.

That the President, as the Executive Chief of the Government and Commander-in-chief of the Army and Navy, was the proper person to make such notification, has not been, and cannot be disputed.

The right of prize and capture has its origin in the *"jus belli,"* and is governed and adjudged under the law of nations. To legitimate the capture of a neutral vessel or property on the high seas, a war must exist *de facto*, and the neutral must have a knowledge or notice of the intention of one of the parties belligerent to use this mode of coercion against a port, city, or territory, in possession of the other.

Let us enquire whether, at the time this blockade was instituted, a state of war existed which would justify a resort to these means of subduing the hostile force.

War has been well defined to be, "That state in which a nation prosecutes its right by force."

The parties belligerent in a public war are independent nations. But it is not necessary to constitute war, that both parties should be acknowledged as independent nations or sovereign States. A war may exist where one of the belligerents, claims sovereign rights as against the other.

Insurrection against a government may or may not culminate in an organized rebellion, but a civil war always begins by insurrection against the lawful authority of the Government. A civil war is never solemnly declared; it becomes such by its accidents—the number, power, and organization of the persons who originate and carry it on. When the party in rebellion occupy and hold in a hostile manner a certain portion of territory; have declared their independence; have cast off their allegiance; have organized armies; have commenced hostilities against their former sovereign, the world acknowledges them as belligerents, and the contest a *war.* . . .

As a civil war is never publicly proclaimed, *eo nomine*, against insurgents, its actual existence is a fact in our domestic history which the Court is bound to notice and to know.

The true test of its existence, as found in the writings of the sages of the common law, may be thus summarily stated: "When the regular course of justice is interrupted by revolt, rebellion, or insurrection, so that the Courts of Justice cannot be kept open, *civil war exists* and hostilities may be prosecuted on the same footing as if those opposing the Government were foreign enemies invading the land."

By the Constitution, Congress alone has the power to declare a national or foreign war. It cannot declare war against a State, or any number of States, by virtue of any clause in the Constitution. The Constitution confers on the President the whole Executive power. He is bound to take care that the laws be faithfully executed. He is Commander-in-chief of the Army and Navy of the United States, and of the militia of the several States when called into the actual service of the United States. He has no power to initiate or declare a war either against a foreign nation or a domestic State. But by the Acts of Congress of February 28th, 1795, and 3d of March, 1807, he is authorized to call out the militia and use the military and naval forces of the United States in case of invasion by foreign nations, and to suppress insurrection against the government of a State or of the United States.

If a war be made by invasion of a foreign nation, the President is not only authorized but bound to resist force by force. He does not initiate the war, but is bound to accept the challenge without waiting for any special legislative authority. And whether the hostile party be a foreign invader, or States organized in rebellion, it is none the less a war, although the declaration of it be *"unilateral."* Lord Stowell (1 Dodson, 247) observes, "It is not the less a war on *that account,* for war may exist without a declaration on either side. It is so laid down by the best writers on the law of nations. A declaration of war by one country only, is not a mere challenge to be accepted or refused at pleasure by the other."

The battles of Palo Alto and Resaca de la Palma had been fought before the passage of the Act of Congress of May 13th, 1846, which recognized *"a state of war as existing by the act of the Republic of Mexico."* This act not only provided for the future prosecution of the war, but was itself a vindication and ratification of the Act of the President in accepting the challenge without a previous formal declaration of war by Congress.

This greatest of civil wars was not gradually developed by popular commotion, tumultuous assemblies, or local unorganized insurrections. However long may have been its previous conception, it nevertheless sprung forth suddenly from the parent brain, a Minerva in the full panoply of *war.* The President was bound to meet it in the shape it presented itself, without waiting for Congress to baptize it with a name; and no name given to it by him or them could change the fact.

. . .

The law of nations is also called the law of nature; it is founded on the common consent as well as the common sense of the world. It contains no such anomalous doctrine as that which this Court are now for the first time desired to pronounce, to wit: That insurgents who have risen in rebellion against their sovereign, expelled her Courts, established a revolutionary government,

organized armies, and commenced hostilities, are not *enemies* because they are *traitors;* and a war levied on the Government by traitors, in order to dismember and destroy it, is not a *war* because it is an "insurrection."

Whether the President in fulfilling his duties, as Commander-in-chief, in suppressing an insurrection, has met with such armed hostile resistance, and a civil war of such alarming proportions as will compel him to accord to them the character of belligerents, is a question to be decided *by him,* and this Court must be governed by the decisions and acts of the political department of the Government to which this power was entrusted. "He must determine what degree of force the crisis demands." The proclamation of blockade is itself official and conclusive evidence to the Court that a state of war existed which demanded and authorized a recourse to such a measure, under the circumstances peculiar to the case.

The correspondence of Lord Lyons with the Secretary of State admits the fact and concludes the question.

If it were necessary to the technical existence of a war, that it should have a legislative sanction, we find it in almost every act passed at the extraordinary session of the Legislature of 1861, which was wholly employed in enacting laws to enable the Government to prosecute the war with vigor and efficiency. And finally, in 1861, we find Congress *"ex majore cautela"* and in anticipation of such astute objections, passing an act "approving, legalizing, and making valid all the acts, proclamations, and orders of the President, &c., as if they had been *issued and done under the previous express authority* and direction of the Congress of the United States."

. . .

The objection made to this act of ratification, that it is *expost facto,* and therefore unconstitutional and void, might possibly have some weight on the trial of an indictment in a criminal Court. But precedents from that source cannot be received as authoritative in a tribunal administering public and international law.

On this first question therefore we are of the opinion that the President had a right, *jure belli,* to institute a blockade of ports in possession of the

States in rebellion, which neutrals are bound to regard.

. . .

[The Court then decides whether the property of all persons residing within the territory of the states in rebellion, captured on the high seas, is to be treated as "enemies' property" whether the owner be in arms against the government or not.]

Mr. Justice NELSON, dissenting.

. . .

We are of opinion . . . that, according to the very terms of the proclamation, neutral ships were entitled to a warning by one of the blockading squadron and could be lawfully seized only on the second attempt to enter or leave the port.

It is remarkable, also, that both the President and the Secretary, in referring to the blockade, treat the measure, not as a blockade under the law of nations, but as a restraint upon commerce at the interdicted ports under the municipal laws of the Government.

Another objection taken to the seizure of this vessel and cargo is, that there was no existing war between the United States and the States in insurrection within the meaning of the law of nations, which drew after it the consequences of a public or civil war. A contest by force between independent sovereign States is called a public war; and, when duly commenced by proclamation or otherwise, it entitles both of the belligerent parties to all the rights of war against each other, and as respects neutral nations. Chancellor Kent observes, "Though a solemn declaration, or previous notice to the enemy, be now laid aside, it is essential that some formal public act, proceeding directly from the competent source, should announce to the people at home their new relations and duties growing out of a state of war, and which should equally apprize neutral nations of the fact, to enable them to conform their conduct to the rights belonging to the new state of things." . . .

This power in all civilized nations is regulated by the fundamental laws or municipal constitution of the country.

By our Constitution this power is lodged in Congress. Congress shall have power "to declare war, grant letters of marque and reprisal, and make rules concerning captures on land and water."

We have thus far been considering the status of the citizens or subjects of a country at the breaking out of a public war when recognized or declared by the competent power.

In the case of a rebellion or resistance of a portion of the people of a country against the established government, there is no doubt, if in its progress and enlargement the government thus sought to be overthrown sees fit, it may by the competent power recognize or declare the existence of a state of civil war, which will draw after it all the consequences and rights of war between the contending parties as in the case of a public war. Mr. Wheaton observes, speaking of civil war, "But the general usage of nations regards such a war as entitling both the contending parties to all the rights of war as against each other, and even as respects neutral nations." It is not to be denied, therefore, that if a civil war existed between that portion of the people in organized insurrection to overthrow this Government at the time this vessel and cargo were seized, and if she was guilty of a violation of the blockade, she would be lawful prize of war. But before this insurrection against the established Government can be dealt with on the footing of a civil war, within the meaning of the law of nations and the Constitution of the United States, and which will draw after it belligerent rights, it must be recognized or declared by the war-making power of the Government. No power short of this can change the legal status of the Government or the relations of its citizens from that of peace to a state of war, or bring into existence all those duties and obligations of neutral third parties growing out of a state of war. The war power of the Government must be exercised before this changed condition of the Government and people and of neutral third parties can be admitted. There is no difference in this respect between a civil or a public war.

. . .

. . . But we are asked, what would become of the peace and integrity of the Union in case of an insurrection at home or invasion from abroad if this power could not be exercised by the President in the recess of Congress, and until that body could be assembled?

The framers of the Constitution fully comprehended this question, and provided for the contingency. Indeed, it would have been surprising if they had not, as a rebellion had occurred in the State of Massachusetts while the Convention was in session, and which had become so general that it was quelled only by calling upon the military power of the State. The Constitution declares that Congress shall have power "to provide for calling forth the militia to execute the laws of the Union, suppress insurrections, and repel invasions." Another clause, "that the President shall be Commander-in-chief of the Army and Navy of the United States, and of the militia of the several States when called into the actual service of the United States;" and, again, "He shall take care that the laws shall be faithfully executed." Congress passed laws on this subject in 1792 and 1795. 1 United States Laws, pp. 264, 424.

The last Act provided that whenever the United States shall be invaded or be in imminent danger of invasion from a foreign nation, it shall be lawful for the President to call forth such number of the militia most convenient to the place of danger, and in case of insurrection in any State against the Government thereof, it shall be lawful for the President, on the application of the Legislature of such State, if in session, or if not, of the Executive of the State, to call forth such number of militia of any other State or States as he may judge sufficient to suppress such insurrection.

The 2d section provides, that when the laws of the United States shall be opposed, or the execution obstructed in any State by combinations too powerful to be suppressed by the course of judicial proceedings, it shall be lawful for the President to call forth the militia of such State, or of any other State or States as may be necessary to suppress such combinations; and by the Act 3 March, 1807, (2 U. S. Laws, 443,) it is provided that in case of insurrection or obstruction of the laws, either in the United States or of any State or Territory, where it is lawful for the President to call forth the militia for the purpose of suppressing such insurrection, and causing the laws to be executed, it shall be lawful to employ for the same purpose such part of the land and naval

forces of the United States as shall be judged necessary.

. . .

The Acts of 1795 and 1807 did not, and could not under the Constitution, confer on the President the power of declaring war against a State of this Union, or of deciding that war existed, and upon that ground authorize the capture and confiscation of the property of every citizen of the State whenever it was found on the waters. The laws of war, whether the war be civil or *inter gentes*, as we have seen, convert every citizen of the hostile State into a public enemy, and treat him accordingly, whatever may have been his previous conduct. This great power over the business and property of the citizen is reserved to the legislative department by the express words of the Constitution. It cannot be delegated or surrendered to the Executive. Congress alone can determine whether war exists or should be declared; and until they have acted, no citizen of the State can be punished in his person or property, unless he has committed some offence against a law of Congress passed before the act was committed, which made it a crime, and defined the punishment. The penalty of confiscation for the acts of others with which he had no concern cannot lawfully be inflicted.

. . .

Congress on the 6th of August, 1862, passed an Act confirming all acts, proclamations, and orders of the President, after the 4th of March, 1861, respecting the army and navy, and legalizing them, so far as was competent for that body. . . .

. . . Here the captures were without any Constitutional authority, and void; and, on principle, no subsequent ratification could make them valid.

Upon the whole, after the most careful consideration of this case which the pressure of other duties has admitted, I am compelled to the conclusion that no civil war existed between this Government and the States in insurrection till recognized by the Act of Congress 13th of July, 1861; that the President does not possess the power under the Constitution to declare war or recognize its existence within the meaning of the law of nations, which carries with it belligerent rights, and thus change the country and all its citizens from a state of peace to a state of war; that this power belongs exclusively to the Congress of the United States, and, consequently, that the President had no power to set on foot a blockade under the law of nations, and that the capture of the vessel and cargo in this case, and in all cases before us in which the capture occurred before the 13th of July, 1861, for breach of blockade, or as enemies' property, are illegal and void, and that the decrees of condemnation should be reversed and the vessel and cargo restored.

Mr. Chief Justice TANEY, Mr. Justice CATRON and Mr. Justice CLIFFORD, concurred in the dissenting opinion of Mr. Justice NELSON.

Ex Parte Milligan

4 Wall. (71 U.S.) 2 (1866)

Lambdin P. Milligan, a U.S. citizen from Indiana, was arrested by the military in 1864 on charges of conspiracy. He was found guilty before a military commission and sentenced to be hanged. He presented a petition of habeas corpus to the federal courts, asking to be discharged from unlawful imprisonment because the military had no jurisdiction over him. He insisted that he was entitled to trial by jury in a civilian court. The question was whether the President, in times of emergency, could suspend the writ of habeas corpus and declare martial law.

Mr. Justice DAVIS delivered the opinion of the court.

On the 10th day of May, 1865, Lambdin P. Milligan presented a petition to the Circuit Court of the United States for the District of Indiana, to be discharged from an alleged unlawful imprisonment. The case made by the petition is this: Milligan is a citizen of the United States; has lived for twenty years in Indiana; and, at the time of the grievances complained of, was not, and never had been in the military or naval service of the United States. On the 5th day of October, 1864, while at home, he was arrested by order of General Alvin P. Hovey, commanding the military district of Indiana; and has ever since been kept in close confinement.

On the 21st day of October, 1864, he was brought before a military commission, convened at Indianapolis, by order of General Hovey, tried on certain charges and specifications; found guilty, and sentenced to be hanged; and the sentence ordered to be executed on Friday, the 19th day of May, 1865.

On the 2d day of January, 1865, after the proceedings of the military commission were at an end, the Circuit Court of the United States for Indiana met at Indianapolis and empanelled a grand jury, who were charged to inquire whether the laws of the United States had been violated; and, if so, to make presentments. The court adjourned on the 27th day of January, having, prior thereto, discharged from further service the grand jury, who did not find any bill of indictment or make any presentment against Milligan for any offence whatever; and, in fact, since his imprisonment, no bill of indictment has been found or presentment made against him by any grand jury of the United States.

Milligan insists that said military commission had no jurisdiction to try him upon the charges preferred, or upon any charges whatever; because he was a citizen of the United States and the State of Indiana, and had not been, since the commencement of the late Rebellion, a resident of any of the States whose citizens were arrayed against the government, and that the right of trial by jury was guaranteed to him by the Constitution of the United States.

The prayer of the petition was, that under the act of Congress, approved March 3d, 1863, entitled, "An act relating to *habeas corpus* and regulating judicial proceedings in certain cases," he may be brought before the court, and either turned over to the proper civil tribunal to be proceeded against according to the law of the land or discharged from custody altogether.

With the petition were filed the order for the commission, the charges and specifications, the findings of the court, with the order of the War Department reciting that the sentence was approved by the President of the United States, and directing that it be carried into execution without delay. The petition was presented and filed in open court by the counsel for Milligan; at the same time the District Attorney of the United States for Indiana appeared, and, by the agreement of counsel, the application was submitted to the court. The opinions of the judges of the Circuit Court were opposed on three questions, which are certified to the Supreme Court:

1st. "On the facts stated in said petition and exhibits, ought a writ of *habeas corpus* to be issued?"

2d. "On the facts stated in said petition and exhibits, ought the said Lambdin P. Milligan to be discharged from custody as in said petition prayed?"

3d. "Whether, upon the facts stated in said petition and exhibits, the military commission mentioned therein had jurisdiction legally to try and sentence said Milligan in manner and form as in said petition and exhibits is stated?"

The importance of the main question presented by this record cannot be overstated; for it involves the very framework of the government and the fundamental principles of American liberty.

During the late wicked Rebellion, the temper of the times did not allow that calmness in deliberation and discussion so necessary to a correct conclusion of a purely judicial question. *Then*, considerations of safety were mingled with the exercise of power; and feelings and interests prevailed which are happily terminated. *Now* that the public safety is assured, this question, as well as all others, can be discussed and decided without passion or the admixture of any element not required to form a legal judgment. We approach the investigation of this case, fully sensible of the magnitude of the inquiry and the necessity of full and cautious deliberation.

. . .

The controlling question in the case is this: Upon the *facts* stated in Milligan's petition, and the exhibits filed, had the military commission mentioned in it *jurisdiction*, legally, to try and sentence him? Milligan, not a resident of one of the rebellious states, or a prisoner of war, but a citizen of Indiana for twenty years past, and never in the military or naval service, is, while at his home, arrested by the military power of the United States, imprisoned, and, on certain criminal charges preferred against him, tried, convicted, and sentenced to be hanged by a military commission, organized under the direction of the military commander of the military district of Indiana. Had this tribunal the *legal* power and authority to try and punish this man?

No graver question was ever considered by this court, nor one which more nearly concerns the rights of the whole people; for it is the birthright of every American citizen when charged with crime, to be tried and punished according to law.

[The Court reviews such fundamental constitutional rights as grand jury, trial by jury, confrontation of witnesses against the accused, obtaining witnesses in the accused's favor, and assistance of counsel.]

Time has proven the discernment of our ancestors; for even these provisions, expressed in such plain English words, that it would seem the ingenuity of man could not evade them, are *now*, after the lapse of more than seventy years, sought to be avoided. Those great and good men foresaw that troublous times would arise, when rulers and people would become restive under restraint, and seek by sharp and decisive measures to accomplish ends deemed just and proper; and that the principles of constitutional liberty would be in peril, unless established by irrepealable law. The history of the world had taught them that what was done in the past might be attempted in the future. The Constitution of the United States is a law for rulers and people, equally in war and in peace, and covers with the shield of its protection all classes of men, at all times, and under all circumstances. No doctrine, involving more pernicious consequences, was ever invented by the wit of man than that any of its provisions can be suspended during any of the great exigencies of government. Such a doctrine leads directly to anarchy or despotism, but the theory of necessity on which it is based is false; for the government, within the Constitution, has all the powers granted to it, which are necessary to preserve its existence; as has been happily proved by the result of the great effort to throw off its just authority.

. . .

This court has judicial knowledge that in Indiana the Federal authority was always unopposed, and its courts always open to hear criminal accusations and redress grievances; and no usage of war could sanction a military trial there for any offence whatever of a citizen in civil life, in nowise connected with the military service. Congress could grant no such power; and to the honor of our national legislature be it said, it has never been provoked by the state of the country even to attempt its exercise. One of the plainest constitutional provisions was, therefore, infringed when Milligan was tried by a court not ordained and established by Congress, and not composed of judges appointed during good behavior.

. . .

This nation, as experience has proved, cannot always remain at peace, and has no right to expect that it will always have wise and humane rulers, sincerely attached to the principles of the Constitution. Wicked men, ambitious of power, with hatred of liberty and contempt of law, may fill the place once occupied by Washington and Lincoln; and if this right is conceded, and the calamities of war again befall us, the dangers to human liberty are frightful to contemplate.

It is essential to the safety of every government that, in a great crisis, like the one we have just passed through, there should be a power somewhere of suspending the writ of *habeas corpus*. . . . The Constitution . . . does not say after a writ of *habeas corpus* is denied a citizen, that he shall be

tried otherwise than by the course of the common law; if it had intended this result, it was easy by the use of direct words to have accomplished it. . . .

. . . Martial rule can never exist where the courts are open, and in the proper and unobstructed exercise of their jurisdiction. It is also confined to the locality of actual war. Because, during the late Rebellion it could have been enforced in Virginia, where the national authority was overturned and the courts driven out, it does not follow that it should obtain in Indiana, where that authority was never disputed, and justice was always administered. And so in the case of a foreign invasion, martial rule may become a necessity in one state, when, in another, it would be "mere lawless violence." . . .

The **CHIEF JUSTICE** delivered the following opinion.

Four members of the court, concurring with their brethren in the order heretofore made in this cause, but unable to concur in some important particulars with the opinion which has just been read, think it their duty to make a separate statement of their views of the whole case.

We do not doubt that the Circuit Court for the District of Indiana had jurisdiction of the petition of Milligan for the writ of *habeas corpus*.

. . .

It is clear . . . that the Circuit Court was bound to hear Milligan's petition for the writ of *habeas corpus*, called in the act an order to bring the prisoner before the judge or the court, and to issue the writ, or, in the language of the act, to make the order.

The first question, therefore—Ought the writ to issue?—must be answered in the affirmative.

And it is equally clear that he was entitled to the discharge prayed for.

It must be borne in mind that the prayer of the petition was not for an absolute discharge, but to be delivered from military custody and imprisonment, and if found probably guilty of any offence, to be turned over to the proper tribunal for inquiry and punishment; or, if not found thus probably guilty, to be discharged altogether.

. . .

That the third question, namely: Had the military commission in Indiana, under the facts stated, jurisdiction to try and sentence Milligan? must be answered negatively is an unavoidable inference from affirmative answers to the other two.

. . .

But the opinion which has just been read goes further; and as we understand it, asserts not only that the military commission held in Indiana was not authorized by Congress, but that it was not in the power of Congress to authorize it; from which it may be thought to follow, that Congress has no power to indemnify the officers who composed the commission against liability in civil courts for acting as members of it.

We cannot agree to this.

We agree in the proposition that no department of the government of the United States—neither President, nor Congress, nor the Courts—possesses any power not given by the Constitution.

We assent, fully, to all that is said, in the opinion, of the inestimable value of the trial by jury, and of the other constitutional safeguards of civil liberty. And we concur, also, in what is said of the writ of *habeas corpus,* and of its suspension, with two reservations: (1.) That, in our judgment, when the writ is suspended, the Executive is authorized to arrest as well as to detain; and (2.) that there are cases in which, the privilege of the writ being suspended, trial and punishment by military commission, in states where civil courts are open, may be authorized by Congress, as well as arrest and detention.

We think that Congress had power, though not exercised, to authorize the military commission which was held in Indiana.

. . .

Congress has the power not only to raise and support and govern armies but to declare war. It has, therefore, the power to provide by law for carrying on war. This power necessarily extends to all legislation essential to the prosecution of war with vigor and success, except such as interferes with the command of the forces and the conduct of campaigns. . . .

We cannot doubt that, in such a time of public danger, Congress had power, under the Constitution, to provide for the organization of a military commission, and for trial by that commission of persons engaged in this conspiracy. The fact that the Federal courts were open was regarded by Congress as a sufficient reason for not exercising the power; but that fact could not deprive Congress of the right to exercise it. Those courts might be open and undisturbed in the execution of their functions, and yet wholly incompetent to avert threatened danger, or to punish, with adequate promptitude and certainty, the guilty conspirators.

In Indiana, the judges and officers of the courts were loyal to the government. But it might have been otherwise. In times of rebellion and civil war it may often happen, indeed, that judges and marshals will be in active sympathy with the rebels, and courts their most efficient allies.

. . .

We think that the power of Congress, in such times and in such localities, to authorize trials for crimes against the security and safety of the national forces, may be derived from its constitutional authority to raise and support armies and to declare war, if not from its constitutional authority to provide for governing the national forces.

We have no apprehension that this power, under our American system of government, in which all official authority is derived from the people, and exercised under direct responsibility to the people, is more likely to be abused than the power to regulate commerce, or the power to borrow money. And we are unwilling to give our assent by silence to expressions of opinion which seem to us calculated, though not intended, to cripple the constitutional powers of the government, and to augment the public dangers in times of invasion and rebellion.

Mr. Justice WAYNE, Mr. Justice SWAYNE, and MR. JUSTICE MILLER concur with me in these views.

Korematsu v. United States

323 U.S. 214 (1944)

Under authority of President Roosevelt's Executive Order 9066 and a congressional statute enacted in 1942, the Commanding General of the Western Defense Command issued an order directing the exclusion of all Japanese-Americans from a West Coast military area. Exclusion meant imprisonment in barbed wire stockades, called assembly centers, until the individuals could be transported inland to "relocation centers" under military guard. The military order, covering both aliens and U.S. citizens, was based on the belief of Commanding General J. L. DeWitt that all individuals of Japanese descent were "subversive" and belonged to an "enemy race" whose "racial strains are undiluted." Fred Korematsu, an American citizen of Japanese descent, was convicted for violating the exclusion order. His conviction was affirmed by the Ninth Circuit.

MR. JUSTICE BLACK delivered the opinion of the Court.

The petitioner, an American citizen of Japanese descent, was convicted in a federal district court for remaining in San Leandro, California, a "Military Area," contrary to Civilian Exclusion Order No. 34 of the Commanding General of the Western Command, U. S. Army, which directed that after May 9, 1942, all persons of Japanese ancestry should be excluded from that area. No question was raised as to petitioner's loyalty to the United States. The Circuit Court of Appeals affirmed, and the importance of the constitutional question involved caused us to grant certiorari.

It should be noted, to begin with, that all legal restrictions which curtail the civil rights of a single racial group are immediately suspect. That is not to say that all such restrictions are unconstitutional. It is to say that courts must subject them to the most rigid scrutiny. Pressing public necessity may sometimes justify the existence of such restrictions; racial antagonism never can.

. . .

Exclusion Order No. 34, which the petitioner knowingly and admittedly violated, was one of a number of military orders and proclamations, all of which were substantially based upon Executive Order No. 9066, 7 Fed. Reg. 1407. That order, issued after we were at war with Japan, declared that "the successful prosecution of the war requires every possible protection against espionage and against sabotage to national-defense material, national-defense premises, and national-defense utilities. . . ."

One of the series of orders and proclamations, a curfew order, which like the exclusion order here was promulgated pursuant to Executive Order 9066, subjected all persons of Japanese ancestry in prescribed West Coast military areas to remain in their residences from 8 p. m. to 6 a. m. As is the case with the exclusion order here, that prior curfew order was designed as a "protection against espionage and against sabotage." In *Hirabayashi* v. *United States*, 320 U.S. 81, we sustained a conviction obtained for violation of the curfew order. The Hirabayashi conviction and this one thus rest on the same 1942 Congressional Act and the same basic executive and military orders, all of which orders were aimed at the twin dangers of espionage and sabotage.

The 1942 Act was attacked in the *Hirabayashi* case as an unconstitutional delegation of power; it was contended that the curfew order and other orders on which it rested were beyond the war powers of the Congress, the military authorities and of the President, as Commander in Chief of the Army; and finally that to apply the curfew order against none but citizens of Japanese ancestry amounted to a constitutionally prohibited discrimination solely on account of race. To these questions, we gave the serious consideration which their importance justified. We upheld the curfew order as an exercise of the power of the government to take steps necessary to prevent espionage and sabotage in an area threatened by Japanese attack.

In the light of the principles we announced in the *Hirabayashi* case, we are unable to conclude that it was beyond the war power of Congress and the Executive to exclude those of Japanese ancestry from the West Coast war area at the time they did. True, exclusion from the area in which one's home is located is a far greater deprivation than constant confinement to the home from 8 p. m. to 6 a. m. Nothing short of apprehension by the proper military authorities of the gravest imminent danger to the public safety can constitutionally justify either. But exclusion from a threatened area, no less than curfew, has a definite and close relationship to the prevention of espionage and sabotage. The military authorities, charged with the primary responsibility of defending our shores, concluded that curfew provided inadequate protection and ordered exclusion. They did so, as pointed out in our *Hirabayashi* opinion, in accordance with Congressional authority to the military to say who should, and who should not, remain in the threatened areas.

. . .

We uphold the exclusion order as of the time it was made and when the petitioner violated it. Cf. *Chastleton Corporation* v. *Sinclair*, 264 U. S. 543, 547; *Block* v. *Hirsh*, 256 U. S. 135, 154–5. In doing so, we are not unmindful of the hardships imposed by it upon a large group of American citizens. Cf. *Ex parte Kawato*, 317 U.S. 69, 73. But hardships are part of war, and war is an aggregation of hardships. All citizens alike, both in and out of uniform, feel the impact of war in greater or lesser measure. Citizenship has its responsibilities as well as its privileges, and in time of war the burden is always heavier. Compulsory exclusion of large groups of citizens from their homes, except under circumstances of direst emergency and peril, is inconsistent with our basic governmental institutions. But when under conditions of modern warfare our shores are threatened by hostile forces, the power to protect must be commensurate with the threatened danger.

. . .

It is said that we are dealing here with the case of imprisonment of a citizen in a concentration camp solely because of his ancestry, without evidence or inquiry concerning his loyalty and good disposition towards the United States. Our task would be simple, our duty clear, were this a case involving the imprisonment of a loyal citizen in a concentration camp because of racial prejudice. Regardless of the true nature of the assembly and relocation centers—and we deem it unjustifiable to call them concentration camps with all the ugly connotations that term implies—we are dealing specifically with nothing but an exclusion order. To cast this case into outlines of racial prejudice, without reference to the real military dangers which were presented, merely confuses the issue. Korematsu was not excluded from the Military Area because of hostility to him or his race. He *was* excluded because we are at war with the Japanese Empire, because the properly constituted military authorities feared an invasion of our West Coast and felt constrained to take proper security measures, because they decided that the military urgency of the situation demanded that all citizens of Japanese ancestry be segregated from the West Coast temporarily, and finally, because Congress, reposing its confidence in this time of war in our military leaders—as inevitably it must—determined that they should have the power to do just this. There was evidence of disloyalty on the part of some, the military authorities considered that the need for action was great, and time was short. We cannot—by availing ourselves of the calm perspective of hindsight—now say that at that time these actions were unjustified.

Affirmed.

MR. JUSTICE FRANKFURTER, concurring.

. . .

MR. JUSTICE ROBERTS.

I dissent, because I think the indisputable facts exhibit a clear violation of Constitutional rights.

This is not a case of keeping people off the streets at night as was *Hirabayashi* v. *United States*, 320 U.S. 81, nor a case of temporary exclusion of a citizen from an area for his own safety or that of the community, nor a case of offering him an opportunity to go temporarily out of an area where his presence might cause danger to himself or to his fellows. On the contrary, it is the case of convicting a citizen as a punishment for not submitting to imprisonment in a concentration camp, based on his ancestry, and solely because of his ancestry, without evidence or inquiry concerning his loyalty and good disposition towards the United States. If this be a correct statement of the facts disclosed by this record, and facts of which we take judicial notice, I need hardly labor the conclusion that Constitutional rights have been violated.

. . .

MR. JUSTICE MURPHY, dissenting.

This exclusion of "all persons of Japanese ancestry, both alien and non-alien," from the Pacific Coast area on a plea of military necessity in the absence of martial law ought not to be approved. Such exclusion goes over "the very brink of constitutional power" and falls into the ugly abyss of racism.

In dealing with matters relating to the prosecution and progress of a war, we must accord great respect and consideration to the judgments of the military authorities who are on the scene and who have full knowledge of the military facts. The scope of their discretion must, as a matter of necessity and common sense, be wide. And their judgments ought not to be overruled lightly by those whose training and duties ill-equip them to deal intelligently with matters so vital to the physical security of the nation.

At the same time, however, it is essential that there be definite limits to military discretion, especially where martial law has not been declared. Individuals must not be left impoverished of their constitutional rights on a plea of military necessity that has neither substance nor support. Thus, like other claims conflicting with the asserted constitutional rights of the individual, the military claim must subject itself to the judicial process of having its reasonableness determined and its conflicts with other interests reconciled. "What are the allowable limits of military discretion, and whether or not they have been overstepped in a particular case, are judicial questions." Sterling v. Constantin, 287 U. S. 378, 401.

The judicial test of whether the Government, on a plea of military necessity, can validly deprive an individual of any of his constitutional rights is whether the deprivation is reasonably related to a public danger that is so "immediate, imminent, and impending" as not to admit of delay and not to permit the intervention of ordinary constitutional processes to alleviate the danger. United States v. Russell, 13 Wall. 623, 627–8; Mitchell v. Harmony, 13 How. 115, 134–5; Raymond v. Thomas, 91 U. S. 712, 716. Civilian Exclusion Order No. 34, banishing from a prescribed area of the Pacific Coast "all persons of Japanese ancestry, both alien and non-alien," clearly does not meet that test. Being an obvious racial discrimination, the order deprives all those within its scope of the equal protection of the laws as guaranteed by the Fifth Amendment. It further deprives these individuals of their constitutional rights to live and work where they will, to establish a home where they choose and to move about freely. In excommunicating them without benefit of hearings, this order also deprives them of all their constitutional rights to procedural due process. Yet no reasonable relation to an "immediate, imminent, and impending" public danger is evident to support this racial restriction which is one of the most sweeping and complete deprivations of constitutional rights in the history of this nation in the absence of martial law.

. . .

That this forced exclusion was the result in good measure of this erroneous assumption of racial guilt rather than bona fide military necessity is evidenced by the Commanding General's Final Report on the evacuation from the Pacific Coast area. In it he refers to all individuals of Japanese descent as "subversive," as belonging to "an enemy race" whose "racial strains are undiluted," and as constituting "over 112,000 potential enemies . . . at large today" along the Pacific Coast. In support of this blanket condemnation of all persons of Japanese descent, however, no reliable evidence is cited to show that such individuals were generally disloyal, or had generally so conducted themselves in this area as to constitute a special menace to defense installations or war industries, or had otherwise by their behavior furnished reasonable ground for their exclusion as a group.

Justification for the exclusion is sought, instead, mainly upon questionable racial and sociological grounds not ordinarily within the realm of expert military judgment, supplemented by certain semi-military conclusions drawn from an unwarranted use of circumstantial evidence. Individuals of Japanese ancestry are condemned because they are said to be "a large, unassimilated, tightly knit racial group, bound to an enemy nation by strong ties of race, culture, custom and religion." They are claimed to be given to "emperor worshipping ceremonies" and to "dual citizenship." . . .

. . .

The military necessity which is essential to the validity of the evacuation order thus resolves itself into a few intimations that certain individuals actively aided the enemy, from which it is inferred that the entire group of Japanese Americans could not be trusted to be or remain loyal to the United States. No one denies, of course, that there were some disloyal persons of Japanese descent on the Pacific Coast who did all in their power to aid their ancestral land. Similar disloyal activities have been engaged in by many persons of German, Italian and even more pioneer stock in our country. But to infer that examples of individual disloyalty prove group disloyalty and justify discriminatory action against the entire group is to deny that under our system of law individual guilt is the sole basis for deprivation of rights. Moreover, this inference, which is at the very heart of the evacuation orders, has been used in support of the abhorrent and despicable treatment of minority groups by the dictatorial tyrannies which this nation is now pledged to destroy. To give constitutional sanction to that inference in this case, however well-intentioned may have been the military command on the Pacific Coast, is to adopt one of the cruelest of the rationales used by our enemies to destroy the dignity of the individual and to encourage and open the door to discriminatory actions against other minority groups in the passions of tomorrow.

. . .

I dissent, therefore, from this legalization of racism. Racial discrimination in any form and in any degree has no justifiable part whatever in our democratic way of life. It is unattractive in any setting but it is utterly revolting among a free people who have embraced the principles set forth in the Constitution of the United States. All residents of this nation are kin in some way by blood or culture to a foreign land. Yet they are primarily and necessarily a part of the new and distinct civilization of the United States. They must accordingly be treated at all times as the heirs of the American experiment and as entitled to all the rights and freedoms guaranteed by the Constitution.

MR. JUSTICE JACKSON, dissenting.

Korematsu was born on our soil, of parents born in Japan. The Constitution makes him a citizen of the United States by nativity and a citizen of California by residence. No claim is made that he is not loyal to this country. There is no suggestion that apart from the matter involved here he is not law-abiding and well disposed. Korematsu, however, has been convicted of an act not commonly a crime. It consists merely of being present in the state whereof he is a citizen, near the place where he was born, and where all his life he has lived.

Even more unusual is the series of military orders which made this conduct a crime. They forbid such a one to remain, and they also forbid him to leave. They were so drawn that the only way Korematsu could avoid violation was to give himself up to the military authority. This meant submission to custody, examination, and transportation out of the territory, to be followed by indeterminate confinement in detention camps.

A citizen's presence in the locality, however, was made a crime only if his parents were of Japanese birth. Had Korematsu been one of four —the others being, say, a German alien enemy, an Italian alien enemy, and a citizen of American-born ancestors, convicted of treason but out on parole—only Korematsu's presence would have violated the order. The difference between their innocence and his crime would result, not from anything he did, said, or thought, different than they, but only in that he was born of different racial stock.

Now, if any fundamental assumption underlies our system, it is that guilt is personal and not inheritable. Even if all of one's antecedents had been convicted of treason, the Constitution forbids its penalties to be visited upon him, for it provides that "no attainder of treason shall work corruption of blood, or forfeiture except during the life of the person attainted." But here is an attempt to make an otherwise innocent act a crime merely because this prisoner is the son of parents as to whom he had no choice, and belongs to a race from which there is no way to resign. If Congress in peace-time legislation should enact such a criminal law, I should suppose this Court would refuse to enforce it.

But the "law" which this prisoner is convicted of disregarding is not found in an act of Congress, but in a military order. Neither the Act of Congress nor the Executive Order of the President, nor both together, would afford a basis for this conviction. It rests on the orders of General DeWitt. And it is said that if the military commander had reasonable military grounds for

promulgating the orders, they are constitutional and become law, and the Court is required to enforce them. . . .

. . . I cannot say, from any evidence before me, that the orders of General DeWitt were not reasonably expedient military precautions, nor could I say that they were. But even if they were permissible military procedures, I deny that it follows that they are constitutional. If, as the Court holds, it does follow, then we may as well say that any military order will be constitutional and have done with it.

. . .

My duties as a justice as I see them do not require me to make a military judgment as to whether General DeWitt's evacuation and detention program was a reasonable military necessity. I do not suggest that the courts should have attempted to interfere with the Army in carrying out its task. But I do not think they may be asked to execute a military expedient that has no place in law under the Constitution. I would reverse the judgment and discharge the prisoner.

Youngstown Co. v. Sawyer

343 U.S. 579 (1952)

In April 1952, to avert a nationwide strike of steelworkers that threatened U.S. military needs in the Korean war, President Truman issued an executive order directing Secretary of Commerce Sawyer to seize and operate most of the steel mills. The order was not based on specific statutory authority. In fact, Truman decided not to use the statutory remedy available in the Taft-Hartley Act of 1947, which was enacted into law over his veto. In court, the administration justified the executive order on the basis of inherent presidential power. The district court issued a preliminary injunction against the seizure, rejecting the theory of inherent power, and the D.C. Circuit stayed this injunction pending review by the Supreme Court.

MR. JUSTICE BLACK delivered the opinion of the Court.

We are asked to decide whether the President was acting within his constitutional power when he issued an order directing the Secretary of

Commerce to take possession of and operate most of the Nation's steel mills. The mill owners argue that the President's order amounts to lawmaking, a legislative function which the Constitution has expressly confided to the Congress and not to the

President. The Government's position is that the order was made on findings of the President that his action was necessary to avert a national catastrophe which would inevitably result from a stoppage of steel production, and that in meeting this grave emergency the President was acting within the aggregate of his constitutional powers as the Nation's Chief Executive and the Commander in Chief of the Armed Forces of the United States. The issue emerges here from the following series of events:

In the latter part of 1951, a dispute arose between the steel companies and their employees over terms and conditions that should be included in new collective bargaining agreements. Long-continued conferences failed to resolve the dispute. On December 18, 1951, the employees' representative, United Steelworkers of America, C. I. O., gave notice of an intention to strike when the existing bargaining agreements expired on December 31. The Federal Mediation and Conciliation Service then intervened in an effort to get labor and management to agree. This failing, the President on December 22, 1951, referred the dispute to the Federal Wage Stabilization Board to investigate and make recommendations for fair and equitable terms of settlement. This Board's report resulted in no settlement. On April 4, 1952, the Union gave notice of a nation-wide strike called to begin at 12:01 a. m. April 9. The indispensability of steel as a component of substantially all weapons and other war materials led the President to believe that the proposed work stoppage would immediately jeopardize our national defense and that governmental seizure of the steel mills was necessary in order to assure the continued availability of steel. Reciting these considerations for his action, the President, a few hours before the strike was to begin, issued Executive Order 10340, a copy of which is attached as an appendix, *post*, p. 589. The order directed the Secretary of Commerce to take possession of most of the steel mills and keep them running. The Secretary immediately issued his own possessory orders, calling upon the presidents of the various seized companies to serve as operating managers for the United States. They were directed to carry on their activities in accordance with regulations and directions of the Secretary. The next morning

the President sent a message to Congress reporting his action. Cong. Rec., April 9, 1952, p. 3962. Twelve days later he sent a second message. Cong. Rec., April 21, 1952, p. 4192. Congress has taken no action.

Obeying the Secretary's orders under protest, the companies brought proceedings against him in the District Court. Their complaints charged that the seizure was not authorized by an act of Congress or by any constitutional provisions. The District Court was asked to declare the orders of the President and the Secretary invalid and to issue preliminary and permanent injunctions restraining their enforcement. Opposing the motion for preliminary injunction, the United States asserted that a strike disrupting steel production for even a brief period would so endanger the well-being and safety of the Nation that the President had "inherent power" to do what he had done— power "supported by the Constitution, by historical precedent, and by court decisions." The Government also contended that in any event no preliminary injunction should be issued because the companies had made no showing that their available legal remedies were inadequate or that their injuries from seizure would be irreparable. Holding against the Government on all points, the District Court on April 30 issued a preliminary injunction restraining the Secretary from "continuing the seizure and possession of the plants . . . and from acting under the purported authority of Executive Order No. 10340." 103 F. Supp. 569. On the same day the Court of Appeals stayed the District Court's injunction. 90 U. S. App. D. C.—, 197 F. 2d 582. Deeming it best that the issues raised be promptly decided by this Court, we granted certiorari on May 3 and set the cause for argument on May 12. 343 U. S. 937.

Two crucial issues have developed: *First*. Should final determination of the constitutional validity of the President's order be made in this case which has proceeded no further than the preliminary injunction stage? *Second*. If so, is the seizure order within the constitutional power of the President?

I.

[The Court rejects the administration's argument that the case should be resolved on nonconstitu-

tional grounds. The constitutional question is "ripe for determination on the record presented."]

II.

The President's power, if any, to issue the order must stem either from an act of Congress or from the Constitution itself. There is no statute that expressly authorizes the President to take possession of property as he did here. Nor is there any act of Congress to which our attention has been directed from which such a power can fairly be implied. Indeed, we do not understand the Government to rely on statutory authorization for this seizure. . . .

. . .

Moreover, the use of the seizure technique to solve labor disputes in order to prevent work stoppages was not only unauthorized by any congressional enactment; prior to this controversy, Congress had refused to adopt that method of settling labor disputes. When the Taft-Hartley Act was under consideration in 1947, Congress rejected an amendment which would have authorized such governmental seizures in cases of emergency. Apparently it was thought that the technique of seizure, like that of compulsory arbitration, would interfere with the process of collective bargaining. Consequently, the plan Congress adopted in that Act did not provide for seizure under any circumstances. Instead, the plan sought to bring about settlements by use of the customary devices of mediation, conciliation, investigation by boards of inquiry, and public reports. In some instances temporary injunctions were authorized to provide cooling-off periods. All this failing, unions were left free to strike after a secret vote by employees as to whether they wished to accept their employers' final settlement offer.

It is clear that if the President had authority to issue the order he did, it must be found in some provision of the Constitution. And it is not claimed that express constitutional language grants this power to the President. The contention is that presidential power should be implied from the aggregate of his powers under the Constitution. Particular reliance is placed on provisions in Article II which say that "The executive Power

shall be vested in a President . . ."; that "he shall take Care that the Laws be faithfully executed"; and that he "shall be Commander in Chief of the Army and Navy of the United States."

The order cannot properly be sustained as an exercise of the President's military power as Commander in Chief of the Armed Forces. The Government attempts to do so by citing a number of cases upholding broad powers in military commanders engaged in day-to-day fighting in a theater of war. Such cases need not concern us here. Even though "theater of war" be an expanding concept, we cannot with faithfulness to our constitutional system hold that the Commander in Chief of the Armed Forces has the ultimate power as such to take possession of private property in order to keep labor disputes from stopping production. This is a job for the Nation's lawmakers, not for its military authorities.

Nor can the seizure order be sustained because of the several constitutional provisions that grant executive power to the President. In the framework of our Constitution, the President's power to see that the laws are faithfully executed refutes the idea that he is to be a lawmaker. The Constitution limits his functions in the lawmaking process to the recommending of laws he thinks wise and the vetoing of laws he thinks bad. And the Constitution is neither silent nor equivocal about who shall make laws which the President is to execute. The first section of the first article says that "All legislative Powers herein granted shall be vested in a Congress of the United States . . . ." After granting many powers to the Congress, Article I goes on to provide that Congress may "make all Laws which shall be necessary and proper for carrying into Execution the foregoing Powers, and all other Powers vested by this Constitution in the Government of the United States, or in any Department or Officer thereof."

The President's order does not direct that a congressional policy be executed in a manner prescribed by Congress—it directs that a presidential policy be executed in a manner prescribed by the President. The preamble of the order itself, like that of many statutes, sets out reasons why the President believes certain policies should be adopted, proclaims these policies as rules of conduct to be followed, and again, like a statute, authorizes a government official to promulgate additional rules and regulations consistent with the policy proclaimed and needed to carry that policy into execution. The power of Congress to adopt such public policies as those proclaimed by the order is beyond question. It can authorize the taking of private property for public use. It can make laws regulating the relationships between employers and employees, prescribing rules designed to settle labor disputes, and fixing wages and working conditions in certain fields of our economy. The Constitution does not subject this lawmaking power of Congress to presidential or military supervision or control.

It is said that other Presidents without congressional authority have taken possession of private business enterprises in order to settle labor disputes. But even if this be true, Congress has not thereby lost its exclusive constitutional authority to make laws necessary and proper to carry out the powers vested by the Constitution "in the Government of the United States, or any Department or Officer thereof."

The Founders of this Nation entrusted the lawmaking power to the Congress alone in both good and bad times. It would do no good to recall the historical events, the fears of power and the hopes for freedom that lay behind their choice. Such a review would but confirm our holding that this seizure order cannot stand.

The judgment of the District Court is

Affirmed.

MR. JUSTICE FRANKFURTER.

Although the considerations relevant to the legal enforcement of the principle of separation of powers seem to me more complicated and flexible than may appear from what MR. JUSTICE BLACK has written, I join his opinion because I thoroughly agree with the application of the principle to the circumstances of this case. Even though such differences in attitude toward this principle may be merely differences in emphasis and nuance, they can hardly be reflected by a single opinion for the Court. Individual expression of views in reaching a common result is therefore important.

. . .

MR. JUSTICE FRANKFURTER, concurring.

. . . Not so long ago it was fashionable to find our system of checks and balances obstructive to effective government. It was easy to ridicule that system as outmoded—too easy. The experience through which the world has passed in our own day has made vivid the realization that the Framers of our Constitution were not inexperienced doctrinaires. These long-headed statesmen had no illusion that our people enjoyed biological or psychological or sociological immunities from the hazards of concentrated power. It is absurd to see a dictator in a representative product of the sturdy democratic traditions of the Mississippi Valley. The accretion of dangerous power does not come in a day. It does come, however slowly, from the generative force of unchecked disregard of the restrictions that fence in even the most disinterested assertion of authority.

. . .

The issue before us can be met, and therefore should be, without attempting to define the President's powers comprehensively. I shall not attempt to delineate what belongs to him by virtue of his office beyond the power even of Congress to contract; what authority belongs to him until Congress acts; what kind of problems may be dealt with either by the Congress or by the President or by both, cf. *La Abra Silver Mng. Co.* v. *United States*, 175 U.S. 423; what power must be exercised by the Congress and cannot be delegated to the President.

. . .

To be sure, the content of the three authorities of government is not to be derived from an abstract analysis. The areas are partly interacting, not wholly disjointed. The Constitution is a framework for government. Therefore the way the framework has consistently operated fairly establishes that it has operated according to its true nature. Deeply embedded traditional ways of conducting government cannot supplant the Constitution or legislation, but they give meaning to the words of a text or supply them. It is an inadmissibly narrow conception of American constitutional law to confine it to the words of the Constitution and to disregard the gloss which life has written upon them. In short, a systematic, unbroken, executive practice, long pursued to the knowledge of the Congress and never before questioned, engaged in by Presidents who have also sworn to uphold the Constitution, making as it were such exercise of power part of the structure of our government, may be treated as a gloss on "executive Power" vested in the President by § 1 of Art. II.

. . .

MR. JUSTICE DOUGLAS, concurring.

There can be no doubt that the emergency which caused the President to seize these steel plants was one that bore heavily on the country. But the emergency did not create power; it merely marked an occasion when power should be exercised. And the fact that it was necessary that measures be taken to keep steel in production does not mean that the President, rather than the Congress, had the constitutional authority to act. The Congress, as well as the President, is trustee of the national welfare.

. . .

The method by which industrial peace is achieved is of vital importance not only to the parties but to society as well. A determination that sanctions should be applied, that the hand of the law should be placed upon the parties, and that the force of the courts should be directed against them, is an exercise of legislative power. In some nations that power is entrusted to the executive branch as a matter of course or in case of emergencies. We chose another course. We chose to place the legislative power of the Federal Government in the Congress.

. . .

We pay a price for our system of checks and balances, for the distribution of power among the three branches of government. It is a price that today may seem exorbitant to many. Today a kindly President uses the seizure power to effect a wage increase and to keep the steel furnaces in production. Yet tomorrow another President might use the same power to prevent a wage increase, to curb trade-unionists, to regiment la-

bor as oppressively as industry thinks it has been regimented by this seizure.

MR. JUSTICE JACKSON, concurring in the judgment and opinion of the Court.

. . .

A judge, like an executive adviser, may be surprised at the poverty of really useful and unambiguous authority applicable to concrete problems of executive power as they actually present themselves. Just what our forefathers did envision, or would have envisioned had they foreseen modern conditions, must be divined from materials almost as enigmatic as the dreams Joseph was called upon to interpret for Pharaoh. A century and a half of partisan debate and scholarly speculation yields no net result but only supplies more or less apt quotations from respected sources on each side of any question. They largely cancel each other. And court decisions are indecisive because of the judicial practice of dealing with the largest questions in the most narrow way.

The actual art of governing under our Constitution does not and cannot conform to judicial definitions of the power of any of its branches based on isolated clauses or even single Articles torn from context. While the Constitution diffuses power the better to secure liberty, it also contemplates that practice will integrate the dispersed powers into a workable government. It enjoins upon its branches separateness but interdependence, autonomy but reciprocity. Presidential powers are not fixed but fluctuate, depending upon their disjunction or conjunction with those of Congress. We may well begin by a somewhat over-simplified grouping of practical situations in which a President may doubt, or others may challenge, his powers, and by distinguishing roughly the legal consequences of this factor of relativity.

1. When the President acts pursuant to an express or implied authorization of Congress, his authority is at its maximum, for it includes all that he possesses in his own right plus all that Congress can delegate. In these circumstances, and in these only, may he be said (for what it may be worth) to personify the federal sovereignty. If his act is held unconstitutional under these circumstances, it

usually means that the Federal Government as an undivided whole lacks power. A seizure executed by the President pursuant to an Act of Congress would be supported by the strongest of presumptions and the widest latitude of judicial interpretation, and the burden of persuasion would rest heavily upon any who might attack it.

2. When the President acts in absence of either a congressional grant or denial of authority, he can only rely upon his own independent powers, but there is a zone of twilight in which he and Congress may have concurrent authority, or in which its distribution is uncertain. Therefore, congressional inertia, indifference or quiescence may sometimes, at least as a practical matter, enable, if not invite, measures on independent presidential responsibility. In this area, any actual test of power is likely to depend on the imperatives of events and contemporary imponderables rather than on abstract theories of law.

3. When the President takes measures incompatible with the expressed or implied will of Congress, his power is at its lowest ebb, for then he can rely only upon his own constitutional powers minus any constitutional powers of Congress over the matter. Courts can sustain exclusive presidential control in such a case only by disabling the Congress from acting upon the subject. Presidential claim to a power at once so conclusive and preclusive must be scrutinized with caution, for what is at stake is the equilibrium established by our constitutional system.

. . .

We should not use this occasion to circumscribe, much less to contract, the lawful role of the President as Commander in Chief. I should indulge the widest latitude of interpretation to sustain his exclusive function to command the instruments of national force, at least when turned against the outside world for the security of our society. But, when it is turned inward, not because of rebellion but because of a lawful economic struggle between industry and labor, it should have no such indulgence. His command power is not such an absolute as might be implied from that office in a militaristic system but is subject to limitations consistent with a constitu-

tional Republic whose law and policy-making branch is a representative Congress. . . .

. . . I have no illusion that any decision by this Court can keep power in the hands of Congress if it is not wise and timely in meeting its problems. A crisis that challenges the President equally, or perhaps primarily, challenges Congress. If not good law, there was worldly wisdom in the maxim attributed to Napoleon that "The tools belong to the man who can use them." We may say that power to legislate for emergencies belongs in the hands of Congress, but only Congress itself can prevent power from slipping through its fingers.

The essence of our free Government is "leave to live by no man's leave, underneath the law"—to be governed by those impersonal forces which we call law. Our Government is fashioned to fulfill this concept so far as humanly possible. The Executive, except for recommendation and veto, has no legislative power. The executive action we have here originates in the individual will of the President and represents an exercise of authority without law. No one, perhaps not even the President, knows the limits of the power he may seek to exert in this instance and the parties affected cannot learn the limit of their rights. We do not know today what powers over labor or property would be claimed to flow from Government possession if we should legalize it, what rights to compensation would be claimed or recognized, or on what contingency it would end. With all its defects, delays and inconveniences, men have discovered no technique for long preserving free government except that the Executive be under the law, and that the law be made by parliamentary deliberations.

Such institutions may be destined to pass away. But it is the duty of the Court to be last, not first, to give them up.

MR. JUSTICE BURTON, concurring in both the opinion and judgment of the Court.

. . .

. . . The present situation is not comparable to that of an imminent invasion or threatened attack. We do not face the issue of what might be the President's constitutional power to meet such catastrophic situations. Nor is it claimed that the current seizure is in the nature of a military command addressed by the President, as Commander-in-Chief, to a mobilized nation waging, or imminently threatened with, total war.

. . .

MR. JUSTICE CLARK, concurring in the judgment of the Court.

. . .

. . . In my view . . . the Constitution does grant to the President extensive authority in times of grave and imperative national emergency. In fact, to my thinking, such a grant may well be necessary to the very existence of the Constitution itself. As Lincoln aptly said, "[is] it possible to lose the nation and yet preserve the Constitution?" In describing this authority I care not whether one calls it "residual," "inherent," "moral," "implied," "aggregate," "emergency," or otherwise. I am of the conviction that those who have had the gratifying experience of being the President's lawyer have used one or more of these adjectives only with the utmost of sincerity and the highest of purpose.

I conclude that where Congress has laid down specific procedures to deal with the type of crisis confronting the President, he must follow those procedures in meeting the crisis; but that in the absence of such action by Congress, the President's independent power to act depends upon the gravity of the situation confronting the nation. I cannot sustain the seizure in question because here . . . Congress had prescribed methods to be followed by the President in meeting the emergency at hand.

. . .

MR. CHIEF JUSTICE VINSON, with whom MR. JUSTICE REED and MR. JUSTICE MINTON join, dissenting.

. . .

I.

In passing upon the question of Presidential powers in this case, we must first consider the context in which those powers were exercised.

Those who suggest that this is a case involving extraordinary powers should be mindful that these are extraordinary times. A world not yet recovered from the devastation of World War II has been forced to face the threat of another and more terrifying global conflict.

Accepting in full measure its responsibility in the world community, the United States was instrumental in securing adoption of the United Nations Charter, approved by the Senate by a vote of 89 to 2. The first purpose of the United Nations is to "maintain international peace and security, and to that end: to take effective collective measures for the prevention and removal of threats to the peace, and for the suppression of acts of aggression or other breaches of the peace, . . ." In 1950, when the United Nations called upon member nations "to render every assistance" to repel aggression in Korea, the United States furnished its vigorous support. For almost two full years, our armed forces have been fighting in Korea, suffering casualties of over 108,000 men. Hostilities have not abated. The "determination of the United Nations to continue its action in Korea to meet the aggression" has been reaffirmed. Congressional support of the action in Korea has been manifested by provisions for increased military manpower and equipment and for economic stabilization, as hereinafter described.

. . .

Congress recognized the impact of these defense programs upon the economy. Following the attack in Korea, the President asked for authority to requisition property and to allocate and fix priorities for scarce goods. In the Defense Production Act of 1950, Congress granted the powers requested and, *in addition*, granted power to stabilize prices and wages and to provide for settlement of labor disputes arising in the defense program. The Defense Production Act was extended in 1951, a Senate Committee noting that in the dislocation caused by the programs for purchase of military equipment "lies the seed of an economic disaster that might well destroy the military might we are straining to build." Significantly, the Committee examined the problem "in terms of just one commodity, steel," and found "a graphic picture of the over-all inflationary danger growing out of reduced civilian supplies and rising incomes." Even before Korea, steel production at levels above theoretical 100% capacity was not capable of supplying civilian needs alone. Since Korea, the tremendous military demand for steel has far exceeded the increases in productive capacity. This Committee emphasized that the shortage of steel, even with the mills operating at full capacity, coupled with increased civilian purchasing power, presented grave danger of disastrous inflation.

The President has the duty to execute the foregoing legislative programs. Their successful execution depends upon continued production of steel and stabilized prices for steel. . . .

III.

A review of executive action demonstrates that our Presidents have on many occasions exhibited the leadership contemplated by the Framers when they made the President Commander in Chief, and imposed upon him the trust to "take Care that the Laws be faithfully executed." With or without explicit statutory authorization, Presidents have at such times dealt with national emergencies by acting promptly and resolutely to enforce legislative programs, at least to save those programs until Congress could act. Congress and the courts have responded to such executive initiative with consistent approval.

. . .

VI.

The diversity of views expressed in the six opinions of the majority, the lack of reference to authoritative precedent, the repeated reliance upon prior dissenting opinions, the complete disregard of the uncontroverted facts showing the gravity of the emergency and the temporary nature of the taking all serve to demonstrate how far afield one must go to affirm the order of the District Court.

The broad executive power granted by Article II to an officer on duty 365 days a year cannot, it is said, be invoked to avert disaster. Instead, the President must confine himself to sending a message to Congress recommending action. Under this messenger-boy concept of the Office, the President cannot even act to preserve legislative programs from destruction so that Congress will have something left to act upon. There is no judicial finding that the executive action was unwarranted because there was in fact no basis for the President's finding of the existence of an emergency for, under this view, the gravity of the emergency and the immediacy of the threatened disaster are considered irrelevant as a matter of law.

. . .

New York Times Co. v. United States

403 U.S. 713 (1971)

The Nixon administration brought action in federal court to prevent publication in the *New York Times* and the *Washington Post* of certain materials collectively called the "Pentagon Papers." The documents consisted of a classified study prepared by the Defense Department, entitled "History of U.S. Decision-Making Process on Viet Nam Policy." The administration claimed that publication of the materials would be injurious to national security. The newspapers maintained that the First Amendment protected against prior restraint on the right to publish.

PER CURIAM.

We granted certiorari in these cases in which the United States seeks to enjoin the New York Times and the Washington Post from publishing the contents of a classified study entitled "History of U.S. Decision-Making Process on Viet Nam Policy." *Post*, pp. 942, 943.

"Any system of prior restraints of expression comes to this Court bearing a heavy presumption against its constitutional validity." *Bantam Books, Inc.* v. *Sullivan*, 372 U.S. 58, 70 (1963); see also *Near* v. *Minnesota*, 283 U.S. 697 (1931). The Government "thus carries a heavy burden of showing justification for the imposition of such a restraint." *Organization for a Better Austin* v. *Keefe*, 402 U.S. 415, 419 (1971). The District Court for the Southern District of New York in the *New York Times* case and the District Court for the District of Columbia and the Court of Appeals for the District of Columbia Circuit in the *Washington Post* case held that the Government had not met that burden. We agree.

The judgment of the Court of Appeals for the District of Columbia Circuit is therefore affirmed. The order of the Court of Appeals for the Second Circuit is reversed and the case is remanded with directions to enter a judgment affirming the judgment of the District Court for the Southern District of New York. The stays entered June 25, 1971, by the Court are vacated. The judgments shall issue forthwith.

So ordered.

MR. JUSTICE BLACK, with whom MR. JUSTICE DOUGLAS joins, concurring.

I adhere to the view that the Government's case against the Washington Post should have been dismissed and that the injunction against the New York Times should have been vacated without oral argument when the cases were first presented to this Court. I believe that every moment's continuance of the injunctions against these newspapers amounts to a flagrant, indefensible, and continuing violation of the First Amendment. . . .

. . . Madison and the other Framers of the First Amendment, able men that they were, wrote in language they earnestly believed could never be misunderstood: "Congress shall make no law . . . abridging the freedom . . . of the press. . . ." Both the history and language of the First Amendment support the view that the press must be left free to publish news, whatever the source, without censorship, injunctions, or prior restraints.

In the First Amendment the Founding Fathers gave the free press the protection it must have to fulfill its essential role in our democracy. The press was to serve the governed, not the governors. The Government's power to censor the press was abolished so that the press would remain forever free to censure the Government. The press was protected so that it could bare the secrets of government and inform the people. Only a free and unrestrained press can effectively expose deception in government. And paramount among the responsibilities of a free press is the duty to prevent any part of the government from deceiving the people and sending them off to distant lands to die of foreign fevers and foreign shot and shell. In my view, far from deserving condemnation for their courageous reporting, the New York Times, the Washington Post, and other newspapers should be commended for serving the purpose that the Founding Fathers saw so clearly. In revealing the workings of government that led to the Vietnam war, the newspapers nobly did precisely that which the Founders hoped and trusted they would do.

. . .

. . . the Government argues in its brief that in spite of the First Amendment, "[t]he authority of the Executive Department to protect the nation against publication of information whose disclosure would endanger the national security stems from two interrelated sources: the constitutional power of the President over the conduct of foreign affairs and his authority as Commander-in-Chief."

. . .

The word "security" is a broad, vague generality whose contours should not be invoked to abrogate the fundamental law embodied in the First Amendment. The guarding of military and diplomatic secrets at the expense of informed representative government provides no real security for our Republic. . . .

MR. JUSTICE DOUGLAS, with whom MR. JUSTICE BLACK joins, concurring.

While I join the opinion of the Court I believe it necessary to express my views more fully.

It should be noted at the outset that the First Amendment provides that "Congress shall make no law . . . abridging the freedom of speech, or of the press." That leaves, in my view, no room for governmental restraint on the press.

There is, moreover, no statute barring the publication by the press of the material which the Times and the Post seek to use. . . .

The Government says that it has inherent powers to go into court and obtain an injunction to protect the national interest, which in this case is alleged to be national security.

Near v. *Minnesota*, 283 U. S. 697, repudiated that expansive doctrine in no uncertain terms.

The dominant purpose of the First Amendment was to prohibit the widespread practice of governmental suppression of embarrassing information. It is common knowledge that the First Amendment was adopted against the widespread use of the common law of seditious libel to punish the dissemination of material that is embarrassing to the powers-that-be. . . .

MR. JUSTICE BRENNAN, concurring.

I

I write separately in these cases only to emphasize what should be apparent: that our judgments in the present cases may not be taken to indicate the propriety, in the future, of issuing temporary stays and restraining orders to block the publication of material sought to be suppressed by the Government. So far as I can determine, never before has the United States sought to enjoin a newspaper from publishing information in its possession. . . .

II

. . . only governmental allegation and proof that publication must inevitably, directly, and immediately cause the occurrence of an event kindred to imperiling the safety of a transport already at sea can support even the issuance of an interim restraining order. In no event may mere conclu-

sions be sufficient: for if the Executive Branch seeks judicial aid in preventing publication, it must inevitably submit the basis upon which that aid is sought to scrutiny by the judiciary. And therefore, every restraint issued in this case, whatever its form, has violated the First Amendment— and not less so because that restraint was justified as necessary to afford the courts an opportunity to examine the claim more thoroughly. Unless and until the Government has clearly made out its case, the First Amendment commands that no injunction may issue.

MR. JUSTICE STEWART, with whom MR. JUSTICE WHITE joins, concurring.

. . .

. . . If the Constitution gives the Executive a large degree of unshared power in the conduct of foreign affairs and the maintenance of our national defense, then under the Constitution the Executive must have the largely unshared duty to determine and preserve the degree of internal security necessary to exercise that power successfully. It is an awesome responsibility, requiring judgment and wisdom of a high order. I should suppose that moral, political, and practical considerations would dictate that a very first principle of that wisdom would be an insistence upon avoiding secrecy for its own sake. For when everything is classified, then nothing is classified, and the system becomes one to be disregarded by the cynical or the careless, and to be manipulated by those intent on self-protection or self-promotion. . . .

. . . in the cases before us we are asked neither to construe specific regulations nor to apply specific laws. We are asked, instead, to perform a function that the Constitution gave to the Executive, not the Judiciary. We are asked, quite simply, to prevent the publication by two newspapers of material that the Executive Branch insists should not, in the national interest, be published. I am convinced that the Executive is correct with respect to some of the documents involved. But I cannot say that disclosure of any of them will surely result in direct, immediate, and irreparable damage to our Nation or its people. That being so, there can under the First Amendment be but one judicial resolution of the issues before us. I join the judgments of the Court.

MR. JUSTICE WHITE, with whom MR. JUSTICE STEWART joins, concurring.

I concur in today's judgments, but only because of the concededly extraordinary protection against prior restraints enjoyed by the press under our constitutional system. I do not say that in no circumstances would the First Amendment permit an injunction against publishing information about government plans or operations. Nor, after examining the materials the Government characterizes as the most sensitive and destructive, can I deny that revelation of these documents will do substantial damage to public interests. Indeed, I am confident that their disclosure will have that result. But I nevertheless agree that the United States has not satisfied the very heavy burden that it must meet to warrant an injunction against publication in these cases, at least in the absence of express and appropriately limited congressional authorization for prior restraints in circumstances such as these.

. . .

MR. JUSTICE MARSHALL, concurring.

The Government contends that the only issue in these cases is whether in a suit by the United States, "the First Amendment bars a court from prohibiting a newspaper from publishing material whose disclosure would pose a 'grave and immediate danger to the security of the United States.'" Brief for the United States 7. With all due respect, I believe the ultimate issue in these cases is even more basic than the one posed by the Solicitor General. The issue is whether this Court or the Congress has the power to make law.

In these cases there is no problem concerning the President's power to classify information as "secret" or "top secret." Congress has specifically recognized Presidential authority, which has been formally exercised in Exec. Order 10501 (1953), to classify documents and information. See, e. g., 18 U.S.C. § 798; 50 U.S.C. § 783. Nor is there any issue here regarding the President's power as Chief Executive and Commander in Chief to protect national security by disciplining employees who disclose information and by taking precautions to prevent leaks.

The problem here is whether in these particular cases the Executive Branch has authority to invoke the equity jurisdiction of the courts to protect what it believes to be the national interest. See *In re Debs*, 158 U. S. 564, 584 (1895). The Government argues that in addition to the inherent power of any government to protect itself, the President's power to conduct foreign affairs and his position as Commander in Chief give him authority to impose censorship on the press to protect his ability to deal effectively with foreign nations and to conduct the military affairs of the country. Of course, it is beyond cavil that the President has broad powers by virtue of his primary responsibility for the conduct of our foreign affairs and his position as Commander in Chief. *Chicago & Southern Air Lines* v. *Waterman S. S. Corp.*, 333 U. S. 103 (1948); *Hirabayashi* v. *United States*, 320 U. S. 81, 93 (1943); *United States* v. *Curtiss-Wright Corp.*, 299 U. S. 304 (1936). And in some situations it may be that under whatever inherent powers the Government may have, as well as the implicit authority derived from the President's mandate to conduct foreign affairs and to act as Commander in Chief, there is a basis for the invocation of the equity jurisdiction of this Court as an aid to prevent the publication of material damaging to "national security," however that term may be defined.

It would, however, be utterly inconsistent with the concept of separation of powers for this Court to use its power of contempt to prevent behavior that Congress has specifically declined to prohibit. There would be a similar damage to the basic concept of these co-equal branches of Government if when the Executive Branch has adequate authority granted by Congress to protect "national security" it can choose instead to invoke the contempt power of a court to enjoin the threatened conduct. The Constitution provides that Congress shall make laws, the President execute laws, and courts interpret laws. *Youngstown Sheet & Tube Co.* v. *Sawyer*, 343 U. S. 579 (1952). It did not provide for government by injunction in which the courts and the Executive Branch can "make law" without regard to the action of Congress.

. . .

MR. CHIEF JUSTICE BURGER, dissenting.

So clear are the constitutional limitations on prior restraint against expression, that from the time of *Near* v. *Minnesota*, 283 U. S. 697 (1931), until recently in *Organization for a Better Austin* v. *Keefe*, 402 U. S. 415 (1971), we have had little occasion to be concerned with cases involving prior restraints against news reporting on matters of public interest. There is, therefore, little variation among the members of the Court in terms of resistance to prior restraints against publication. Adherence to this basic constitutional principle, however, does not make these cases simple. In these cases, the imperative of a free and unfettered press comes into collision with another imperative, the effective functioning of a complex modern government and specifically the effective exercise of certain constitutional powers of the Executive. Only those who view the First Amendment as an absolute in all circumstances—a view I respect, but reject—can find such cases as these to be simple or easy.

These cases are not simple for another and more immediate reason. We do not know the facts of the cases. No District Judge knew all the facts. No Court of Appeals judge knew all the facts. No member of this Court knows all the facts.

Why are we in this posture, in which only those judges to whom the First Amendment is absolute and permits of no restraint in any circumstances or for any reason, are really in a position to act?

I suggest we are in this posture because these cases have been conducted in unseemly haste. MR. JUSTICE HARLAN covers the chronology of events demonstrating the hectic pressures under which these cases have been processed and I need not restate them. The prompt settling of these cases reflects our universal abhorrence of prior restraint. But prompt judicial action does not mean unjudicial haste.

. . .

The consequence of all this melancholy series of events is that we literally do not know what we are acting on. As I see it, we have been forced to deal with litigation concerning rights of great magnitude without an adequate record, and surely without time for adequate treatment either in the prior proceedings or in this Court. [*Counsel frequently could not answer factual points.*] This Court is in no better posture. I agree generally with MR. JUSTICE HARLAN and MR. JUSTICE BLACKMUN but I am not prepared to reach the merits.

. . .

MR. JUSTICE HARLAN, with whom THE CHIEF JUSTICE and MR. JUSTICE BLACKMUN join, dissenting.

These cases forcefully call to mind the wise admonition of Mr. Justice Holmes, dissenting in *Northern Securities Co.* v. *United States*, 193 U. S. 197, 400–401 (1904):

"Great cases like hard cases make bad law. For great cases are called great, not by reason of their real importance in shaping the law of the future, but because of some accident of immediate overwhelming interest which appeals to the feelings and distorts the judgment. These immediate interests exercise a kind of hydraulic pressure which makes what previously was clear seem doubtful, and before which even well settled principles of law will bend."

With all respect, I consider that the Court has been almost irresponsibly feverish in dealing with these cases.

Both the Court of Appeals for the Second Circuit and the Court of Appeals for the District of Columbia Circuit rendered judgment on June 23. The New York Times' petition for certiorari, its motion for accelerated consideration thereof, and its application for interim relief were filed in this Court on June 24 at about 11 a.m. The application of the United States for interim relief in the *Post* case was also filed here on June 24 at about 7:15 p.m. This Court's order setting a hearing before us on June 26 at 11 a.m., a course which I joined only to avoid the possibility of even more peremptory action by the Court, was issued less than 24 hours before. The record in the *Post* case was filed with the Clerk shortly before 1 p.m. on June 25; the record in the *Times* case did not arrive until 7 or 8 o'clock that same night. The briefs of the parties were received less than two hours before argument on June 26.

This frenzied train of events took place in the name of the presumption against prior restraints created by the First Amendment. Due regard for the extraordinarily important and difficult questions involved in these litigations should have led the Court to shun such a precipitate timetable.

. . .

MR. JUSTICE BLACKMUN, dissenting.

. . .

With such respect as may be due to the contrary view, this, in my opinion, is not the way to try a lawsuit of this magnitude and asserted importance. It is not the way for federal courts to adjudicate, and to be required to adjudicate,

issues that allegedly concern the Nation's vital welfare. The country would be none the worse off were the cases tried quickly, to be sure, but in the customary and properly deliberative manner. The most recent of the material, it is said, dates no later than 1968, already about three years ago, and the Times itself took three months to formulate its plan of procedure and, thus, deprived its public for that period.

The First Amendment, after all, is only one part of an entire Constitution. Article II of the great document vests in the Executive Branch primary power over the conduct of foreign affairs and places in that branch the responsibility for the Nation's safety. Each provision of the Constitution is important, and I cannot subscribe to a doctrine of unlimited absolutism for the First Amendment at the cost of downgrading other provisions. . . .

Erwin N. Griswold

How Sensitive Were the "Pentagon Papers"?

In the administration's brief to the Supreme Court on *New York Times* v. *United States*, Solicitor General Erwin N. Griswold described all of the materials in the forty-seven volumes as classified "Top Secret-Sensitive," "Top Secret," or "Secret." By the time the case reached the Court, the administration wanted to bar only the publication of a smaller number of documents, the disclosure of which would pose a "grave and immediate danger to the security of the United States." During oral argument, Griswold told the Court that the broaching of one of the documents "would be of extraordinary seriousness to the security of the United States." Publication of the documents, according to Griswold, "will affect lives. It will affect the process of the termination of the war. It will affect the process of recovering prisoners of war." Later in the oral argument he warned the Court that publication would interfere with the conduct of "delicate negotiations now in process, or contemplated for the future . . ." Yet in an article for the *Washington Post* on February 15, 1989, entitled "Secrets Not Worth Keeping" (p. A25), he admits that publication produced no trace of a threat to the national security. As he explains, the principal concern of classifiers "is not with national security, but rather with government embarrassment of one sort or another."

It may be relevant at this time to recount some details of events which attracted widespread attention several years ago. The occasion was the presentation of the Pentagon Papers case *(New York Times v. United States* and *United States v.*

Washington Post) before the United States Supreme Court, and the year was 1971.

At that time, I held the office of solicitor general of the United States. The government then in office, under the presidency of Richard Nixon, was determined to do everything in its power to prevent the press from publishing some 47 volumes of mimeographed papers preserved primarily in the office of the Secretary of Defense in the Pentagon, and thus known as the Pentagon Papers. These papers were *in toto* classified as Top Secret. We know now that one of the reasons for President Nixon's concern was that, at that very time, Henry Kissinger was en route to China, and there was fear that these negotiations would be frustrated if the Chinese came to believe that we could not keep secrets involved in the dealings between the two countries.

It was my responsibility to represent the interests of the United States before the Supreme Court. Everything happened very fast. The U.S. Court of Appeals for the District of Columbia decided the case on Thursday, June 24, 1971. On Friday, at noon, I was advised by Chief Justice Warren Burger that the case would be heard by the Supreme Court on Saturday morning, June 26, and that "briefs will be exchanged between the parties in the courtroom immediately before the argument."

At that time, no briefs had been written, and, indeed, I had never seen the *outside* of the Pentagon Papers. I immediately arranged for a set of the papers to be brought to my office. It was obvious that I could not read all of the materials in the time available. In this situation, I arranged to have three high officials, one each from the Defense Department, the State Department and the National Security Agency come to my office. I asked them to tell me what items in the 47 volumes were really bad—what items, if disclosed, would be a real threat to the security of the United States.

This produced a total of about 40 items over which these officers expressed concern. I then read each of these items, but quickly came to the conclusion that most of them presented no serious threat to national security, and that there was simply no prospect that the Supreme Court would ban the publication of all of these items. Eventually, I reduced the list to a total of 11 items. My deputy, Daniel M. Friedman, wrote the main or "open" brief for the United States, while I wrote the "secret" brief, contending that these 11 items presented a threat to the national security.

That task kept me up most of the night. At about 8:30 on Saturday morning, I telephoned Attorney General John M. Mitchell. I advised him that I was waiving objections to the printing of most of the documents in the Pentagon Papers and was relying on only 11 items.

"This is an important matter," I said, "and I think I should have your approval."

I can still hear his voice when he replied, "Well, Dean, I don't see how I can approve that."

My heart sank, for the argument before the court was only about an hour away. There was a pause. Then Mr. Mitchell said, "You know, I have never seen these papers. I don't know what is in them. I don't see how I can approve your plan."

There was a further pause, and then he said: "But you are in charge of the case, and if you think that is the way it should be handled, you have my complete support."

So, I went ahead and presented the case before the court, relying only on the 11 items. As is well known, we lost, by a six-to-three vote, with three members of the majority saying there could never be a prior restraint, while three others said that a prior restraint would be appropriate in a proper case, but that there was no adequate threat to national security in this case.

Accordingly, the newspapers printed many items from the Pentagon Papers. And within a few weeks, under the auspices of Sen. Mike Gravel of Alaska, the entire contents of all the papers were printed. I have never seen any trace of a threat to the national security from the publication. Indeed, I have never seen it even suggested that there was such an actual threat. Sen. Gravel's edition is now almost completely forgotten, and I doubt if there is more than a handful of persons who have ever undertaken to examine the Pentagon Papers in any detail—either with respect to national security or with respect to the policies of the country relating to Vietnam.

It quickly becomes apparent to any person who has considerable experience with classified material that there is massive overclassification and that the principal concern of the classifiers is not with national security, but rather with governmental embarrassment of one sort or another. There may be some basis for short-term classification while plans are being made, or negotiations are going on, but apart from details of weapons systems, there is very rarely any real risk to current national security from the publication of facts relating to transactions in the past, even the fairly recent past. This is the lesson of the Pentagon Papers experience, and it may be relevant now.

United States v. United States District Court

407 U.S. 297 (1972)

Although Title III of the Omnibus Crime Control and Safe Streets Act of 1968 required court-approved electronic surveillance, the government claimed that the President had inherent authority to approve warrantless wiretaps to gather intelligence needed to protect the nation from threats by domestic organizations. The U.S. District Court for the Eastern District of Michigan held that the presidentially authorized surveillance violated the Fourth Amendment. The Sixth Circuit affirmed that judgment.

MR. JUSTICE POWELL delivered the opinion of the Court.

The issue before us is an important one for the people of our country and their Government. It involves the delicate question of the President's power, acting through the Attorney General, to authorize electronic surveillance in internal security matters without prior judicial approval. Successive Presidents for more than one-quarter of a century have authorized such surveillance in varying degrees, without guidance from the Congress or a definitive decision of this Court. This case brings the issue here for the first time. Its resolution is a matter of national concern, requiring sensitivity both to the Government's right to protect itself from unlawful subversion and attack and to the citizen's right to be secure in his privacy against unreasonable Government intrusion.

This case arises from a criminal proceeding in the United States District Court for the Eastern District of Michigan, in which the United States charged three defendants with conspiracy to destroy Government property in violation of 18 U. S. C. § 371. One of the defendants, Plamondon, was charged with the dynamite bombing of an office of the Central Intelligence Agency in Ann Arbor, Michigan.

During pretrial proceedings, the defendants moved to compel the United States to disclose certain electronic surveillance information and to conduct a hearing to determine whether this information "tainted" the evidence on which the indictment was based or which the Government intended to offer at trial. In response, the Government filed an affidavit of the Attorney General, acknowledging that its agents had overheard conversations in which Plamondon had participated. The affidavit also stated that the Attorney General approved the wiretaps "to gather intelligence information deemed necessary to protect the nation from attempts of domestic organizations to attack and subvert the existing structure of the Government." The logs of the surveillance were filed in a sealed exhibit for *in camera* inspection by the District Court.

On the basis of the Attorney General's affidavit and the sealed exhibit, the Government asserted that the surveillance was lawful, though conducted without prior judicial approval, as a reasonable exercise of the President's power (exercised through the Attorney General) to protect the national security.

. . .

I

Title III of the Omnibus Crime Control and Safe Streets Act, 18 U. S. C. §§ 2510–2520, authorizes the use of electronic surveillance for classes of crimes carefully specified in 18 U. S. C. § 2516. Such surveillance is subject to prior court order. Section 2518 sets forth the detailed and particularized application necessary to obtain such an order as well as carefully circumscribed conditions for its use. The Act represents a comprehensive attempt by Congress to promote more effective control of crime while protecting the privacy of individual thought and expression. Much of Title III was drawn to meet the constitutional requirements for electronic surveillance enunciated by this Court in *Berger* v. *New York*, 388 U. S. 41 (1967), and *Katz* v. *United States*, 389 U. S. 347 (1967).

Together with the elaborate surveillance requirements in Title III, there is the following proviso, 18 U. S. C. § 2511 (3):

"Nothing contained in this chapter or in section 605 of the Communications Act of 1934 (48 Stat. 1143; 47 U. S. C. 605) shall limit the constitutional power of the President to take such measures as he deems necessary to protect the Nation against actual or potential attack or other hostile acts of a foreign power, to obtain foreign intelligence information deemed essential to the security of the United States, or to protect national security information against foreign intelligence activities. *Nor shall anything contained in this chapter be deemed to limit the constitutional power of the President to take such measures as he deems necessary to protect the United States against the overthrow of the Government by force or other unlawful means, or against any other clear and present danger to the structure or existence of the Government.* The contents of any wire or oral communication intercepted by authority of the President in the exercise of the foregoing powers may be received in evidence in any trial hearing, or other proceeding only where such interception was reasonable, and shall not be otherwise used or disclosed except as is necessary to implement that power." (Emphasis supplied.)

The Government relies on § 2511 (3). It argues that "in excepting national security surveillances from the Act's warrant requirement Congress recognized the President's authority to conduct such surveillances without prior judicial approval." Brief for United States 7, 28. The section thus is viewed as a recognition or affirmance of a constitutional authority in the President to conduct warrantless domestic security surveillance such as that involved in this case.

We think the language of § 2511 (3), as well as the legislative history of the statute, refutes this interpretation. The relevant language is that:

"Nothing contained in this chapter . . . shall limit the constitutional power of the President to take such measures as he deems necessary to protect . . ."

against the dangers specified. At most, this is an implicit recognition that the President does have certain powers in the specified areas. Few would doubt this, as the section refers—among other things—to protection "against actual or potential attack or other hostile acts of a foreign power." But so far as the use of the President's electronic surveillance power is concerned, the language is essentially neutral.

Section 2511 (3) certainly confers no power, as the language is wholly inappropriate for such a purpose. It merely provides that the Act shall not be interpreted to limit or disturb such power as the President may have under the Constitution. In short, Congress simply left presidential powers where it found them. This view is reinforced by the general context of Title III. Section 2511 (1) broadly prohibits the use of electronic surveillance "[e]xcept as otherwise specifically provided in this chapter." Subsection (2) thereof contains four specific exceptions. In each of the specified exceptions, the statutory language is as follows:

"'It shall not be unlawful . . . to intercept' the particular type of communication described."

The language of subsection (3), here involved, is to be contrasted with the language of the exceptions set forth in the preceding subsection. Rather than stating that warrantless presidential uses of electronic surveillance "shall not be unlawful" and thus employing the standard language of exception, subsection (3) merely disclaims any intention to "limit the constitutional power of the President."

The express grant of authority to conduct surveillances is found in § 2516, which authorizes the Attorney General to make application to a federal judge when surveillance may provide evidence of certain offenses. These offenses are described with meticulous care and specificity.

Where the Act authorizes surveillance, the procedure to be followed is specified in § 2518. Subsection (1) thereof requires application to a judge of competent jurisdiction for a prior order of approval, and states in detail the information required in such application. Subsection (3) prescribes the necessary elements of probable cause which the judge must find before issuing an order authorizing an interception. Subsection (4) sets forth the required contents of such an order. Subsection (5) sets strict time limits on an order. Provision is made in subsection (7) for "an emergency situation" found to exist by the Attorney General (or by the principal prosecuting attorney of a State) "with respect to conspiratorial activities threatening the national security interest." In such a situation, emergency surveillance may be conducted "if an application for an order approving the interception is made . . . within forty-eight hours." If such an order is not obtained, or the application therefor is denied, the interception is deemed to be a violation of the Act.

In view of these and other interrelated provisions delineating permissible interceptions of particular criminal activity upon carefully specified conditions, it would have been incongruous for Congress to have legislated with respect to the important and complex area of national security in a single brief and nebulous paragraph. This would not comport with the sensitivity of the problem involved or with the extraordinary care Congress exercised in drafting other sections of the Act. We therefore think the conclusion inescapable that Congress only intended to make clear that the Act simply did not legislate with respect to national security surveillances.

. . .

II

It is important at the outset to emphasize the limited nature of the question before the Court. This case raises no constitutional challenge to electronic surveillance as specifically authorized by Title III of the Omnibus Crime Control and Safe Streets Act of 1968. Nor is there any question or doubt as to the necessity of obtaining a warrant in the surveillance of crimes unrelated to the national security interest. *Katz* v. *United States*, 389 U. S. 347 (1967); *Berger* v. *New York*, 388 U. S. 41 (1967). Further, the instant case requires no judgment on the scope of the President's surveillance power with respect to the activities of foreign powers, within or without this country. The Attorney General's affidavit in this case states that the surveillances were "deemed necessary to protect the nation from attempts of *domestic organizations* to attack and subvert the existing structure of Government" (emphasis supplied). There is no evidence of any involvement, directly or indirectly, of a foreign power.

Our present inquiry, though important, is therefore a narrow one. It addresses a question left open by *Katz, supra*, at 358 n. 23:

"Whether safeguards other than prior authorization by a magistrate would satisfy the Fourth Amendment in a situation involving the national security . . ."

The determination of this question requires the essential Fourth Amendment inquiry into the "reasonableness" of the search and seizure in question, and the way in which that "reasonableness" derives content and meaning through reference to the warrant clause. *Coolidge* v. *New Hampshire*, 403 U. S. 443, 473–484 (1971).

We begin the inquiry by noting that the President of the United States has the fundamental duty, under Art. II, § 1, of the Constitution, to "preserve, protect and defend the Constitution of the United States." Implicit in that duty is the power to protect our Government against those who would subvert or overthrow it by unlawful means. In the discharge of this duty, the President —through the Attorney General—may find it necessary to employ electronic surveillance to obtain intelligence information on the plans of those who plot unlawful acts against the Government. The use of such surveillance in internal security cases has been sanctioned more or less continuously by various Presidents and Attorneys General since July 1946.

. . .

But a recognition of these elementary truths does not make the employment by Government of electronic surveillance a welcome development— even when employed with restraint and under judicial supervision. There is, understandably, a deep-seated uneasiness and apprehension that this capability will be used to intrude upon cherished privacy of law-abiding citizens. We look to the Bill of Rights to safeguard this privacy. Though physical entry of the home is the chief evil against which the wording of the Fourth Amendment is directed, its broader spirit now shields private speech from unreasonable surveillance. *Katz* v. *United States, supra; Berger* v. *New York, supra; Silverman* v. *United States*, 365 U. S. 505 (1961).

. . .

National security cases, moreover, often reflect a convergence of First and Fourth Amendment values not present in cases of "ordinary" crime. Though the investigative duty of the executive may be stronger in such cases, so also is there greater jeopardy to constitutionally protected speech. "Historically the struggle for freedom of speech and press in England was bound up with the issue of the scope of the search and seizure power." *Marcus* v. *Search Warrant*, 367 U. S. 717, 724 (1961). History abundantly documents the tendency of Government—however benevolent and benign its motives—to view with suspicion those who most fervently dispute its policies. Fourth Amendment protections become the more necessary when the targets of official surveillance may be those suspected of unorthodoxy in their political beliefs. The danger to political dissent is acute where the Government attempts to act under so vague a concept as the power to protect "domestic security."

. . .

III

As the Fourth Amendment is not absolute in its terms, our task is to examine and balance the basic values at stake in this case: the duty of Government to protect the domestic security, and the potential danger posed by unreasonable surveillance to individual privacy and free expression. . . .

The Government argues that the special circumstances applicable to domestic security surveillances necessitate a further exception to the warrant requirement. It is urged that the requirement of prior judicial review would obstruct the President in the discharge of his constitutional duty to protect domestic security. We are told further that these surveillances are directed primarily to the collecting and maintaining of intelligence with respect to subversive forces, and are not an attempt to gather evidence for specific criminal prosecutions. It is said that this type of surveillance should not be subject to traditional warrant requirements which were established to govern investigation of criminal activity, not ongoing intelligence gathering. Brief for United States 15–16, 23–24; Reply Brief for United States 2–3.

The Government further insists that courts "as a practical matter would have neither the knowledge nor the techniques necessary to determine whether there was probable cause to believe that surveillance was necessary to protect national security." These security problems, the Government contends, involve "a large number of complex and subtle factors" beyond the competence of courts to evaluate. Reply Brief for United States 4.

. . .

We cannot accept the Government's argument that internal security matters are too subtle and complex for judicial evaluation. Courts regularly deal with the most difficult issues of our society. There is no reason to believe that federal judges will be insensitive to or uncomprehending of the issues involved in domestic security cases. Certainly courts can recognize that domestic security surveillance involves different considerations from the surveillance of "ordinary crime." If the threat is too subtle or complex for our senior law enforcement officers to convey its significance to a court, one may question whether there is probable cause for surveillance.

Nor do we believe prior judicial approval will fracture the secrecy essential to official intelligence gathering. The investigation of criminal activity has long involved imparting sensitive information to judicial officers who have respected the confidentialities involved. Judges may be counted upon to be especially conscious of security requirements in national security cases. Title III of the Omnibus Crime Control and Safe Streets Act already has imposed this responsibility on the judiciary in connection with such crimes as espionage, sabotage, and treason, §§ 2516 (1)(a) and (c), each of which may involve domestic as well as foreign security threats. Moreover, a warrant application involves no public or adversary proceedings: it is an *ex parte* request before a magistrate or judge. Whatever security dangers clerical and secretarial personnel may pose can be minimized by proper administrative measures, possibly to the point of allowing the Government itself to provide the necessary clerical assistance.

. . .

IV

We emphasize, before concluding this opinion, the scope of our decision. As stated at the outset, this case involves only the domestic aspects of national security. We have not addressed, and express no opinion as to, the issues which may be involved with respect to activities of foreign powers or their agents. Nor does our decision rest on the language of § 2511 (3) or any other section of Title III of the Omnibus Crime Control and Safe Streets Act of 1968. That Act does not attempt to define or delineate the powers of the President to meet domestic threats to the national security.

Moreover, we do not hold that the same type of standards and procedures prescribed by Title III are necessarily applicable to this case. We recognize that domestic security surveillance may involve different policy and practical considerations from the surveillance of "ordinary crime." The gathering of security intelligence is often long range and involves the interrelation of various sources and types of information. The exact targets of such surveillance may be more difficult to identify than in surveillance operations against many types of crime specified in Title III. Often, too, the emphasis of domestic intelligence gathering is on the prevention of unlawful activity or the enhancement of the Government's preparedness for some possible future crisis or emergency. Thus, the focus of domestic surveillance may be less precise than that directed against more conventional types of crime.

Given these potential distinctions between Title III criminal surveillances and those involving the domestic security, Congress may wish to consider protective standards for the latter which differ from those already prescribed for specified crimes in Title III. Different standards may be compatible with the Fourth Amendment if they are reasonable both in relation to the legitimate need of Government for intelligence information and the protected rights of our citizens. . . .

V

As the surveillance of Plamondon's conversations was unlawful, because conducted without prior judicial approval, the courts below correctly held that *Alderman* v. *United States*, 394 U.S. 165 (1969), is controlling and that it requires disclosure to the accused of his own impermissibly intercepted conversations. As stated in *Alderman*, "the trial court can and should, where appropriate, place a defendant and his counsel under enforceable orders against unwarranted disclosure of the materials which they may be entitled to inspect." 394 U. S., at 185.

The judgment of the Court of Appeals is hereby

Affirmed.

THE CHIEF JUSTICE concurs in the result.

MR. JUSTICE REHNQUIST took no part in the consideration or decision of this case.

MR. JUSTICE DOUGLAS, concurring.

. . .

APPENDIX TO OPINION OF DOUGLAS, J., CONCURRING

FEDERAL WIRETAPPING AND BUGGING 1969–1970

	Court Ordered Devices		Executive Ordered Devices		
				Days in Use	
Year	Number	Days in Use	Number	Minimum (Rounded)	Maximum (Rounded)
1969	30	462	94	8,100	20,800
1970	180	2,363	113	8,100	22,600

	Ratio of Days Used Executive Ordered:		Average Days in Use Per Device		
	Court Ordered		Court Ordered Devices	Executive Ordered Devices	
Year	Minimum	Maximum		Minimum	Maximum
1969	17.5*	45.0*	15.4	86.2	221.3
1970	3.4	9.6	13.1	71.7	200.0

*Ratios for 1969 are less meaningful than those for 1970, since court-ordered surveillance program was in its initial stage in 1969.

MR. JUSTICE WHITE, concurring in the judgment.

. . .

Goldwater v. Carter

444 U.S. 996 (1979)

On December 15, 1978, President Carter terminated a defense treaty with Taiwan. Under the terms of the treaty, either party could end the pact after giving the other country a year's notice. By the time the case had traveled through the district court and the appellate court, the treaty was about to be terminated. Acting without oral argument, the Court dismissed the complaint by Senator Barry Goldwater that Carter's action was unconstitutional. Goldwater argued that a treaty, being law, required legislative action for its repeal.

MR. JUSTICE POWELL, concurring in the judgment.

Although I agree with the result reached by the Court, I would dismiss the complaint as not ripe for judicial review.

I

This Court has recognized that an issue should not be decided if it is not ripe for judicial review. *Buckley* v. *Valeo*, 424 U.S. 1, 113-114 (1976) (*per curiam*). Prudential considerations persuade me that a dispute between Congress and the President is not ready for judicial review unless and until each branch has taken action asserting its constitutional authority. Differences between the President and the Congress are commonplace under our system. The differences should, and almost invariably do, turn on political rather than legal considerations. The Judicial Branch should not decide issues affecting the allocation of power between the President and Congress until the political branches reach a constitutional impasse. Otherwise, we would encourage small groups or even individual Members of Congress to seek judicial resolution of issues before the normal political process has the opportunity to resolve the conflict.

In this case, a few Members of Congress claim that the President's action in terminating the treaty with Taiwan has deprived them of their constitutional role with respect to a change in the supreme law of the land. Congress has taken no official action. In the present posture of this case, we do not know whether there ever will be an actual confrontation between the Legislative and Executive Branches. Although the Senate has considered a resolution declaring that Senate approval is necessary for the termination of any mutual defense treaty, see 125 Cong. Rec. 13672, 13695–13697 (1979), no final vote has been taken on the resolution. See *id.*, at 32522-32531. Moreover, it is unclear whether the resolution would have retroactive effect. See *id.*, at 13711–13721; *id.*, at 15210. It cannot be said that either the Senate or the House has rejected the President's claim. If the Congress chooses not to confront the President, it is not our task to do so. I therefore concur in the dismissal of this case.

II

MR. JUSTICE REHNQUIST suggests, however, that the issue presented by this case is a nonjusticiable political question which can never be considered by this Court. I cannot agree. In my view, reliance upon the political-question doctrine is inconsistent with our precedents. As set forth in the seminal case of *Baker* v. *Carr*, 369 U.S. 186, 217 (1962), the doctrine incorporates three inquir-

ies: (i) Does the issue involve resolution of questions committed by the text of the Constitution to a coordinate branch of Government? (ii) Would resolution of the question demand that a court move beyond areas of judicial expertise? (iii) Do prudential considerations counsel against judicial intervention? In my opinion the answer to each of these inquiries would require us to decide this case if it were ready for review.

First, the existence of "a textually demonstrable constitutional commitment of the issue to a coordinate political department," *ibid.*, turns on an examination of the constitutional provisions governing the exercise of the power in question. *Powell* v. *McCormack*, 395 U.S. 486, 519 (1969). No constitutional provision explicitly confers upon the President the power to terminate treaties. Further, Art. II, § 2, of the Constitution authorizes the President to make treaties with the advice and consent of the Senate. Article VI provides that treaties shall be a part of the supreme law of the land. These provisions add support to the view that the text of the Constitution does not unquestionably commit the power to terminate treaties to the President alone. Cf. *Gilligan* v. *Morgan*, 413 U.S. 1, 6 (1973); *Luther* v. *Borden*, 7 How. 1, 42 (1849).

Second, there is no "lack of judicially discoverable and manageable standards for resolving" this case; nor is a decision impossible "without an initial policy determination of a kind clearly for nonjudicial discretion." *Baker* v. *Carr, supra*, at 217. We are asked to decide whether the President may terminate a treaty under the Constitution without congressional approval. Resolution of the question may not be easy, but it only requires us to apply normal principles of interpretation to the constitutional provisions at issue. See *Powell* v. *McCormack, supra*, at 548–549. The present case involves neither review of the President's activities as Commander in Chief nor impermissible interference in the field of foreign affairs. Such a case would arise if we were asked to decide, for example, whether a treaty required the President to order troops into a foreign country. But "it is error to suppose that every case or controversy which touches foreign relations lies beyond judicial cognizance." *Baker* v. *Carr, supra*, at 211. This case "touches" foreign relations, but the question presented to us concerns only the constitutional division of power between Congress and the President.

A simple hypothetical demonstrates the confusion that I find inherent in MR. JUSTICE REHNQUIST's opinion concurring in the judgment. Assume that the President signed a mutual defense treaty with a foreign country and announced that it would go into effect despite its rejection by the Senate. Under MR. JUSTICE REHNQUIST's analysis that situation would present a political question even though Art. II, § 2, clearly would resolve the dispute. . . .

Finally, the political-question doctrine rests in part on prudential concerns calling for mutual respect among the three branches of Government. Thus, the Judicial Branch should avoid "the potentiality of embarrassment [that would result] from multifarious pronouncements by various departments on one question." Similarly, the doctrine restrains judicial action where there is an "unusual need for unquestioning adherence to a political decision already made." *Baker* v. *Carr, supra,* at 217.

If this case were ripe for judicial review, see Part I, *supra,* none of these prudential considerations would be present. Interpretation of the Constitution does not imply lack of respect for a coordinate branch. *Powell* v. *McCormack, supra,* at 548. If the President and the Congress had reached irreconcilable positions, final disposition of the question presented by this case would eliminate, rather than create, multiple constitutional interpretations. The specter of the Federal Government brought to a halt because of the mutual intransigence of the President and the Congress would require this Court to provide a resolution pursuant to our duty " 'to say what the law is.' " *United States* v. *Nixon,* 418 U.S. 683, 703 (1974), quoting *Marbury* v. *Madison,* 1 Cranch 137, 177 (1803).

III

In my view, the suggestion that this case presents a political question is incompatible with this Court's willingness on previous occasions to decide whether one branch of our Government has impinged upon the power of another. See *Buckley* v. *Valeo,* 424 U.S., at 138; *United States* v. *Nixon, supra,* at 707; *The Pocket Veto Case,* 279 U.S. 655, 676–678 (1929); *Myers* v. *United States,* 272 U.S. 52 (1926). Under the criteria enunciated in *Baker* v. *Carr,* we have the responsibility to decide whether both the Executive and Legislative Branches have constitutional roles to play in termination of a treaty. If the Congress, by appropriate formal action, had challenged the President's authority to terminate the treaty with Taiwan, the resulting uncertainty could have serious consequences for our country. In that situation, it would be the duty of this Court to resolve the issue.

MR. JUSTICE REHNQUIST, with whom THE CHIEF JUSTICE, MR. JUSTICE STEWART, and MR. JUSTICE STEVENS join, concurring in the judgment.

I am of the view that the basic question presented by the petitioners in this case is "political" and therefore nonjusticiable because it involves the authority of the President in the conduct of our country's foreign relations and the extent to which the Senate or the Congress is authorized to negate the action of the President. In *Coleman* v. *Miller,* 307 U.S. 433 (1939), a case in which members of the Kansas Legislature brought an action attacking a vote of the State Senate in favor of the ratification of the Child Labor Amendment, Mr. Chief Justice Hughes wrote in what is referred to as the "Opinion of the Court":

"We think that . . . the question of the efficacy of ratifications by state legislatures, in the light of previous rejection or attempted withdrawal, should be regarded as a political question pertaining to the political departments, with the ultimate authority in the Congress in the exercise of its control over the promulgation of the adoption of the Amendment.

"The precise question as now raised is whether, when the legislature of the State, as we have found, has actually ratified the proposed amendment, the Court should restrain the state officers from certifying the ratification to the Secretary of State, because of an earlier rejection, and thus prevent the question from coming before the political departments. We find no basis in either Constitution or statute for such judicial action. Article V, speaking solely of ratification, contains no provision as to rejection. . . ." *Id.*, at 450.

Thus, Mr. Chief Justice Hughes' opinion concluded that "Congress in controlling the promulgation of the adoption of a constitutional amendment has the final determination of the question whether by lapse of time its proposal of the amendment had lost its vitality prior to the required ratifications." *Id.*, at 456.

I believe it follows *a fortiori* from *Coleman* that the controversy in the instant case is a nonjusticiable political dispute that should be left for resolution by the Executive and Legislative Branches of the Government. Here, while the Constitution is express as to the manner in which the Senate shall participate in the ratification of a treaty, it is silent as to that body's participation in the abrogation of a treaty. In this respect the case is directly analogous to *Coleman, supra.* As stated in *Dyer* v. *Blair*, 390 F. Supp. 1291, 1302 (ND Ill. 1975) (three-judge court):

"A question that might be answered in different ways for different amendments must surely be controlled by political standards rather than standards easily characterized as judicially manageable."

In light of the absence of any constitutional provision governing the termination of a treaty, and the fact that different termination procedures may be appropriate for different treaties . . . the instant case in my view also "must surely be controlled by political standards."

I think that the justifications for concluding that the question here is political in nature are even more compelling than in *Coleman* because it involves foreign relations—specifically a treaty commitment to use military force in the defense of a foreign government if attacked. In *United States* v. *Curtiss-Wright Corp.*, 299 U.S. 304 (1936), this Court said:

"Whether, if the Joint Resolution had related solely to internal affairs it would be open to the challenge that it constituted an unlawful delegation of legislative power to the Executive, we find it unnecessary to determine. The whole aim of the resolution is to affect a situation entirely external to the United States, and falling within the category of foreign affairs. . . ." *Id.*, at 315.

The present case differs in several important respects from *Youngstown Sheet & Tube Co.* v. *Sawyer*, 343 U.S. 579 (1952), cited by petitioners as authority both for reaching the merits of this dispute and for reversing the Court of Appeals. In *Youngstown*, private litigants brought a suit contesting the President's authority under his war powers to seize the Nation's steel industry, an action of profound and demonstrable domestic impact. Here, by contrast, we are asked to settle a dispute between coequal branches of our Government, each of which has resources available to protect and assert its interests, resources not available to private litigants outside the judicial forum. Moreover, as in *Curtiss-Wright*, the effect of this action, as far as we can tell, is "entirely external to the United States, and [falls] within the category of foreign affairs." Finally, as already noted, the situation presented here is closely akin to that presented in *Coleman*, where the Constitution spoke only to the procedure for ratification of an amendment, not to its rejection.

Having decided that the question presented in this action is nonjusticiable, I believe that the appropriate disposition is for this Court to vacate the decision of the Court of Appeals and remand with instructions for the District Court to dismiss the complaint. . . .

MR. JUSTICE BLACKMUN, with whom MR. JUSTICE WHITE joins, dissenting in part.

In my view, the time factor and its importance are illusory; if the President does not have the power to terminate the treaty (a substantial issue that we should address only after briefing and oral argument), the notice of intention to terminate surely has no legal effect. It is also indefensible, without further study, to pass on the issue of justiciability or on the issues of standing or ripeness. While I therefore join in the grant of the petition for certiorari, I would set the case for oral argument and give it the plenary consideration it so obviously deserves.

MR. JUSTICE BRENNAN, dissenting.

I respectfully dissent from the order directing the District Court to dismiss this case, and would affirm the judgment of the Court of Appeals in-so-far as it rests upon the President's well-established authority to recognize, and withdraw recognition from, foreign governments. App. to Pet. for Cert. 27A-29A.

In stating that this case presents a non-justiciable "political question," MR. JUSTICE REHNQUIST, in my view, profoundly misapprehends the political-question principle as it applies to matters of foreign relations. Properly understood, the political-question doctrine restrains courts from reviewing an exercise of foreign policy judgment by the coordinate political branch to which authority to make that judgment has been "constitutional[ly] commit[ted]." *Baker* v. *Carr*, 369 U.S. 186, 211–213, 217 (1962). But the doctrine does not pertain when a court is faced with the *antecedent* question whether a particular branch has been constitutionally designated as the repository of political decisionmaking power. Cf.

Powell v. *McCormack*, 395 U.S. 486, 519–521 (1969). The issue of decisionmaking authority must be resolved as a matter of constitutional law, not political discretion; accordingly, it falls within the competence of the courts.

The constitutional question raised here is prudently answered in narrow terms. Abrogation of the defense treaty with Taiwan was a necessary incident to Executive recognition of the Peking Government, because the defense treaty was predicated upon the now-abandoned view that the Taiwan Government was the only legitimate political authority in China. Our cases firmly establish that the Constitution commits to the President alone the power to recognize, and withdraw recognition from, foreign regimes. See *Banco Nacional de Cuba* v. *Sabbatino*, 376 U.S. 398, 410 (1964); *Baker* v. *Carr, supra*, at 212; *United States* v. *Pink*, 315 U.S. 203, 228–230 (1942). That mandate being clear, our judicial inquiry into the treaty rupture can go no further. See *Baker* v. *Carr, supra*, at 212; *United States* v. *Pink, supra*, at 229.

War Powers Resolution of 1973

After several years of hearings and floor action, Congress passed legislation in 1973 to provide a framework for "collective judgment" between Congress and the President in the exercise of the war power. Although President Nixon vetoed the bill, he was overridden by both Houses and the bill became law. It establishes procedures for the introduction of U.S. forces into combat and it sets forth a number of important policies in section 8. The legislation, P.L. 93–148, is found at 87 Stat. 555 (1973), 50 U.S.C. § 1541–1548 (1982).

JOINT RESOLUTION

Concerning the war powers of Congress and the President.

Resolved by the Senate and House of Representatives of the United States of America in Congress assembled,

Short Title

SECTION 1. This joint resolution may be cited as the "War Powers Resolution".

Purpose and Policy

SEC. 2. (a) It is the purpose of this joint resolution to fulfill the intent of the framers of the Constitution of the United States and insure that the collective judgment of both the Congress and the President will apply to the introduction of United States Armed Forces into hostilities, or into situations where imminent involvement in hostilities is clearly indicated by the circumstances, and to the continued use of such forces in hostilities or in such situations.

(b) Under article I, section 8, of the Constitution, it is specifically provided that the Congress shall have the power to make all laws necessary and proper for carrying into execution, not only its own powers but also all other powers vested by the Constitution in the Government of the United States, or in any department or officer thereof.

(c) The constitutional powers of the President as Commander-in-Chief to introduce United States Armed Forces into hostilities, or into situations where imminent involvement in hostilities is clearly indicated by the circumstances, are exercised only pursuant to (1) a declaration of war, (2) specific statutory authorization, or (3) a national emergency created by attack upon the United States, its territories or possessions, or its armed forces.

Consultation

SEC. 3. The President in every possible instance shall consult with Congress before introducing United States Armed Forces into hostilities or into situations where imminent involvement in hostilities is clearly indicated by the circumstances, and after every such introduction shall consult regularly with the Congress until United States Armed Forces are no longer engaged in hostilities or have been removed from such situations.

Reporting

SEC. 4. (a) In the absence of a declaration of war, in any case in which United States Armed Forces are introduced—

(1) into hostilities or into situations where imminent involvement in hostilities is clearly indicated by the circumstances;

(2) into the territory, airspace or waters of a foreign nation, while equipped for combat, except for deployments which relate solely to supply, replacement, repair, or training of such forces; or

(3) in numbers which substantially enlarge United States Armed Forces equipped for combat already located in a foreign nation;

the President shall submit within 48 hours to the Speaker of the House of Representatives and to the President pro tempore of the Senate a report, in writing, setting forth—

(A) the circumstances necessitating the introduction of United States Armed Forces;

(B) the constitutional and legislative authority under which such introduction took place; and

(C) the estimated scope and duration of the hostilities or involvement.

(b) The President shall provide such other information as the Congress may request in the fulfillment of its constitutional responsibilities with respect to committing the Nation to war and to the use of United States Armed Forces abroad.

(c) Whenever United States Armed Forces are introduced into hostilities or into any situation described in subsection (a) of this section, the President shall, so long as such armed forces continue to be engaged in such hostilities or situation, report to the Congress periodically on the status of such hostilities or situation as well as on the scope and duration of such hostilities or situation, but in no event shall he report to the Congress less often than once every six months.

Congressional Action

SEC. 5. (a) Each report submitted pursuant to section 4(a) (1) shall be transmitted to the Speaker of the House of Representatives and to the President pro tempore of the Senate on the same calendar day. Each report so transmitted shall be referred to the Committee on Foreign Affairs of the House of Representatives and to the Committee on Foreign Relations of the Senate for appropriate action. If, when the report is transmitted, the Congress has adjourned sine die or has adjourned for any period in excess of three calendar days, the Speaker of the House of Representatives and the President pro tempore of the Senate, if they deem it advisable (or if petitioned by at least 30 percent of the membership of their respective Houses) shall jointly request the President to convene Congress in order that it may consider the report and take appropriate action pursuant to this section.

(b) Within sixty calendar days after a report is submitted or is required to be submitted pursuant to section 4(a) (1), whichever is earlier, the President shall terminate any use of United States Armed Forces with respect to which such report was submitted (or required to be submitted), unless the Congress (1) has declared war or has enacted a specific authorization for such use of United States Armed Forces, (2) has extended by law such sixty-day period, or (3) is physically unable to meet as a result of an armed attack upon the United States. Such sixty-day period shall be extended for not more than an additional thirty days if the President determines and certifies to the Congress in writing that unavoidable military necessity respecting the safety of United States Armed Forces requires the continued use of such armed forces in the course of bringing about a prompt removal of such forces.

(c) Notwithstanding subsection (b), at any time that United States Armed Forces are engaged in hostilities outside the territory of the United States, its possessions and territories without a declaration of war or specific statutory authorization, such forces shall be removed by the President if the Congress so directs by concurrent resolution.

Congressional Priority Procedures for Joint Resolution or Bill

SEC. 6. (a) Any joint resolution or bill introduced pursuant to section 5(b) at least thirty calendar days before the expiration of the sixty-day period specified in such section shall be referred to the Committee on Foreign Affairs of the House of Representatives or the Committee on Foreign Relations of the Senate, as the case may be, and such committee shall report one such joint resolution or bill, together with its recommendations, not later than twenty-four calendar days before the expiration of the sixty-day period specified in such section, unless such House shall otherwise determine by the yeas and nays.

(b) Any joint resolution or bill so reported shall become the pending business of the House in question (in the case of the Senate the time for debate shall be equally divided between the proponents and the opponents), and shall be voted on within three calendar days thereafter, unless such House shall otherwise determine by yeas and nays.

(c) Such a joint resolution or bill passed by one House shall be referred to the committee of the other House named in subsection (a) and shall be reported out not later than fourteen calendar days before the expiration of the sixty-day period specified in section 5(b). The joint resolution or bill so reported shall become the pending business of the House in question and shall be voted on within three calendar days after it has been reported, unless such House shall otherwise determine by yeas and nays.

(d) In the case of any disagreement between the two Houses of Congress with respect to a joint resolution or bill passed by both Houses, conferees shall be promptly appointed and the committee of conference shall make and file a report with respect to such resolution or bill not later than four calendar days before the expiration of the sixty-day period specified in section 5(b). In the event the conferees are unable to agree within 48 hours, they shall report back to their respective Houses in disagreement. Notwithstanding any rule in either House concerning the printing of conference reports in the Record or concerning any delay in the consideration of such reports, such report shall be acted on by both Houses not later than the expiration of such sixty-day period.

Congressional Priority Procedures for Concurrent Resolution

SEC. 7. (a) Any concurrent resolution introduced pursuant to section 5(c) shall be referred to the Committee on Foreign Affairs of the House of Representatives or the Committee on Foreign Relations of the Senate, as the case may be, and one such concurrent resolution shall be reported out by such committee together with its recommendations within fifteen calendar days, unless such House shall otherwise determine by the yeas and nays.

(b) Any concurrent resolution so reported shall become the pending business of the House in question (in the case of the Senate the time for debate shall be equally divided between the proponents and the opponents) and shall be voted on within three calendar days thereafter, unless such House shall otherwise determine by yeas and nays.

(c) Such a concurrent resolution passed by one

House shall be referred to the committtee of the other House named in subsection (a) and shall be reported out by such committee together with its recommendations within fifteen calendar days and shall thereupon become the pending business of such House and shall be voted upon within three calendar days, unless such House shall otherwise determine by yeas and nays.

(d) In the case of any disagreement between the two Houses of Congress with respect to a concurrent resolution passed by both Houses, conferees shall be promptly appointed and the committee of conference shall make and file a report with respect to such concurrent resolution within six calendar days after the legislation is referred to the committee of conference. Notwithstanding any rule in either House concerning the printing of conference reports in the Record or concerning any delay in the consideration of such reports, such report shall be acted on by both Houses not later than six calendar days after the conference report is filed. In the event the conferees are unable to agree within 48 hours, they shall report back to their respective Houses in disagreement.

Interpretation of Joint Resolution

SEC. 8. (a) Authority to introduce United States Armed Forces into hostilities or into situations wherein involvement in hostilities is clearly indicated by the circumstances shall not be inferred—

(1) from any provision of law (whether or not in effect before the date of the enactment of this joint resolution), including any provision contained in any appropriation Act, unless such provision specifically authorizes the introduction of United States Armed Forces into hostilities or into such situations and states that it is intended to constitute specific statutory authorization within the meaning of this joint resolution; or

(2) from any treaty heretofore or hereafter ratified unless such treaty is implemented by legislation specifically authorizing the introduction of United States Armed Forces into hostilities or into such situations and stating that it is intended to constitute specific statu-

tory authorization within the meaning of this joint resolution.

(b) Nothing in this joint resolution shall be construed to require any further specific statutory authorization to permit members of United States Armed Forces to participate jointly with members of the armed forces of one or more foreign countries in the headquarters operations of high-level military commands which were established prior to the date of enactment of this joint resolution and pursuant to the United Nations Charter or any treaty ratified by the United States prior to such date.

(c) For purposes of this joint resolution, the term "introduction of United States Armed Forces" includes the assignment of members of such armed forces to command, coordinate, participate in the movement of, or accompany the regular or irregular military forces of any foreign country or government when such military forces are engaged, or there exists an imminent threat that such forces will become engaged, in hostilities.

(d) Nothing in this joint resolution—

(1) is intended to alter the constitutional authority of the Congress or of the President, or the provisions of existing treaties; or

(2) shall be construed as granting any authority to the President with respect to the introduction of United States Armed Forces into hostilities or into situations wherein involvement in hostilities is clearly indicated by the circumstances which authority he would not have had in the absence of this joint resolution.

Separability Clause

SEC. 9. If any provision of this joint resolution or the application thereof to any person or circumstance is held invalid, the remainder of the joint resolution and the application of such provision to any other person or circumstance shall not be affected thereby.

Effective Date

SEC. 10. This joint resolution shall take effect on the date of its enactment.

Crockett v. Reagan

558 F.Supp. 893 (D.D.C. 1982)

Members of Congress sought declaratory judgments of the actions of President Reagan and his Secretaries of Defense and State for supplying military assistance to El Salvador. The Members claimed a violation of the War Powers Resolution and the Foreign Assistance Act. The case was before Judge Joyce Hens Green, U.S. District Court, District of Columbia. Footnotes omitted.

JOYCE HENS GREEN, District Judge.

This case was brought by 29 Members of Congress against Ronald Reagan, individually and in his capacity as President of the United States, Caspar W. Weinberger, individually and in his capacity as Secretary of Defense, and Alexander M. Haig, Jr., individually and in his capacity as Secretary of State. Plaintiffs have alleged that defendants have supplied military equipment and aid to the government of El Salvador in violation of the War Powers Clause of the Constitution, the War Powers Resolution, 50 U.S.C. §§ 1541–1548, and Section 502B of the Foreign Assistance Act of 1961, 22 U.S.C. § 2304. More specifically, plaintiffs aver that a civil war is now in progress throughout El Salvador, with the Salvadoran Revolutionary Government Junta and its armed forces on one side, and the Democratic Revolutionary Front and its armed forces known as the Faribundo Marti National Liberation Front (FMLN) on the other. According to the complaint, in addition to the provision of monetary aid and military equipment, the defendants have dispatched at least 56 members of the United States Armed Forces to El Salvador in aid of the Junta. These forces allegedly are in situations where imminent involvement in hostilities is clearly indicated by the circumstances, and are allegedly taking part in the war effort and assisting in planning operations against the FMLN. Plaintiffs claim that this involvement violates Article 1, Section 8, Clause 11 of the Constitution, granting to Congress the exclusive power to declare war, as implemented by the War Powers Resolution (WPR). The WPR requires that absent a declaration of war, a report be made to the Congress within 48 hours of any time when United States Armed Forces have been introduced into hostilities or into situations where imminent involvement in hostilities is clearly indicated by the circumstances, and that 60 days after a report is submitted or is required to be submitted, the President shall terminate any use of United States Armed Forces unless Congress declares war, enacts a specific authorization for such use of United States Armed Forces, or extends the 60-day period for 30 additional days. WPR §§ 4, 5(b), 50 U.S.C. §§ 1543, 1544(b). No report pursuant to the WPR has been made, and American forces have remained more than 60 days since they allegedly were introduced into a situation of hostilities or imminent hostilities without a declaration of war.

A cause of action is also stated under Section 502B of the Foreign Assistance Act of 1961, which prohibits the provision of security assistance to "any country the government of which engages in a consistent pattern of gross violations of internationally recognized human rights," which, plaintiffs contend, is the situation in El Salvador. A separate cause of action was originally stated under various provisions of international law (First Amended Complaint, Third Cause of Action), but plaintiffs have since stated that they recognize that there is no cause of action under international law, except as specifically implemented by Section 502B of the Foreign Assistance Act. Statement of Points and Authorities in Opposition to Defendants' Motion to Dismiss at 15–16.

Plaintiffs seek declaratory judgments that the actions of defendants have violated the above-described provisions of law, and a writ of mandamus and/or an injunction directing that defendants immediately withdraw all United States Armed Forces, weapons, and military equipment and aid from El Salvador and prohibiting any further aid of any nature.

Oral argument was held on defendants' motion to dismiss, and *amicus curiae* briefs were accepted from the group of 16 Senators and 13 Members of Congress which had previously moved to intervene. . . .

THE WAR POWERS RESOLUTION

If the merits were reached, the Court would have to decide whether the Resolution is applicable to the American military presence in El Salvador, and if so, what remedial action is appropriate. The Court decides that the cause of action under the WPR in its present posture is non-justiciable because of the nature of the factfinding that would be required, and that the 60-day automatic termination provision is not operative unless a report has been submitted or required to be submitted by Congress or a court.

Although defendants have not emphasized the factual issues, which need not be reached if their motion to dismiss is granted, their pleadings and exhibits do make clear that the position of the government is that the factual circumstances in El Salvador do not trigger the WPR, that is, U.S. Armed Forces have not been "introduced into hostilities or into situations where imminent involvement in hostilities is clearly indicated by the circumstances." Plaintiffs present a significantly different picture of what is actually occurring in El Salvador, and the relationship of U.S. military personnel to it. Although consideration of the merits might reveal disagreements about the meaning of WPR terms such as "imminent involvement in hostilities," the most striking feature of the pleadings at this stage of the case is the discrepancy as to the facts.

In support of their position, defendants have submitted the declaration of Lieutenant General Ernest Graves, Director of the Defense Security Assistance Agency, whose responsibilities include the administration and oversight of all security assistance programs conducted by the Department of Defense (Ex. 8 to Defendants' Motion to Dismiss), and a statement by the Department of State provided to Congressman William Broomfield in response to questions about the applicability of the WPR to the dispatch of military personnel to El Salvador and reprinted in the Congressional Record. (Ex. 17 to Defendants' Motion to Dismiss.) According to General Graves, the Military Mobile Training Teams which have been dispatched to El Salvador since November, 1979 have the sole function of training Salvadoran military personnel so as to create a self-training capability in particular skills, and have never served as advisors, accompanied military units on combat operations, or given those units advice on or worked with them to plan or coordinate the actual performance of offensive or defensive combat operations. Although not exactly claiming that American military personnel have never been exposed to hostile fire, Graves asserts that at no time has insurgent activity directly or immediately threatened the security of training personnel sufficiently to warrant withdrawal of those individuals. The State Department statement echoes General Graves' assessment of the situation. It states that U.S. forces in El Salvador have not and will not act as combat advisors, accompany Salvadoran forces in combat, on operational patrols, or in any situation where combat is likely, and that they have not been subject to attack.

In contrast, plaintiffs contend that American military personnel in El Salvador are taking part in coordinating the war effort and are assisting in planning specific operations against the FMLN. Also, many of the 56 military personnel are alleged to work in and around areas where there is heavy combat. First Amended Complaint at 5–7. Two armed attacks on locations where U.S. military personnel were stationed are described in the Complaint, and another is described in Plaintiffs' Opposition to Defendants' Motion to Dismiss and Exhibit 4X thereto.

More recently, plaintiffs have supplemented their pleadings to bolster their contention that American forces in El Salvador have been introduced into hostilities or imminent hostilities. They rely upon two news articles. The first is to the effect that U.S. Armed Forces are "fighting side by side" with government troops battling against the

FMLN. The second concerns a General Accounting Office (GAO) report which reportedly disclosed that U.S. military personnel in El Salvador are drawing "hostile fire pay," and that a tentative Pentagon ruling that all of El Salvador qualified as a "hostile fire area" was reversed for "policy reasons," possibly to avoid the necessity of reporting to Congress under the WPR. (The actual GPO report has not been submitted.)

In sum, if plaintiffs' allegations are correct, the executive branch does not merely have a different view of the application of the WPR to the facts, but also is distorting the reality of our involvement in El Salvador. This discrepancy as to factual matters is also evident in the contrast between plaintiffs' allegations regarding the human rights situation in El Salvador, and the President's certifications under the Foreign Assistance Act, discussed *infra*. Plaintiffs' allegations, which are to be accepted as true for the purpose of a motion to dismiss, are, at a minimum, disturbing. This nonetheless does not mean that judicial resolution is appropriate to vindicate, allay or obviate plaintiffs' concerns.

The Court concludes that the factfinding that would be necessary to determine whether U.S. forces have been introduced into hostilities or imminent hostilities in El Salvador renders this case in its current posture non-justiciable. The questions as to the nature and extent of the United States' presence in El Salvador and whether a report under the WPR is mandated because our forces have been subject to hostile fire or are taking part in the war effort are appropriate for congressional, not judicial, investigation and determination. Further, in order to determine the application of the 60-day provision, the Court would be required to decide at exactly what point in time U.S. forces had been introduced into hostilities or imminent hostilities, and whether that situation continues to exist. This inquiry would be even more inappropriate for the judiciary.

. . . Even if the plaintiffs could introduce admissible evidence concerning the state of hostilities in various geographical areas in El Salvador where U.S. forces are stationed and the exact nature of U.S. participation in the conflict (and this information may well be unavailable except through inadmissible newspaper articles), the Court no doubt would be presented conflicting evidence on those issues by defendants. The Court lacks the resources and expertise (which are accessible to the Congress) to resolve disputed questions of fact concerning the military situation in El Salvador. *See Atlee* v. *Laird*, 347 F.Supp. 689 (E.D.Pa.1972) (three judge court), *aff'd without opinion*, 411 U.S. 921, 93 S.Ct. 1545, 36 L.Ed.2d 304 (1973); *Holtzman* v. *Schlesinger*, 484 F.2d 1307 (2d Cir.1973), *cert. denied*, 416 U.S. 936, 94 S.Ct. 1935, 40 L.Ed.2d 286 (1974).

. . . here the Court faces a dispute as to whether a small number of American military personnel who apparently have suffered no casualties have been introduced into hostilities or imminent hostilities. The subtleties of factfinding in this situation should be left to the political branches. If Congress doubts or disagrees with the Executive's determination that U.S. forces in El Salvador have not been introduced into hostilities or imminent hostilities, it has the resources to investigate the matter and assert its wishes. The Court need not decide here what type of congressional statement or action would constitute an official congressional stance that our involvement in El Salvador is subject to the WPR, because Congress has taken absolutely no action that could be interpreted to have that effect. Certainly, were Congress to pass a resolution to the effect that a report was required under the WPR, or to the effect that the forces should be withdrawn, and the President disregarded it, a constitutional impasse appropriate for judicial resolution would be presented. *Goldwater* v. *Carter*, 444 U.S. 996, 100 S.Ct. 533, 62 L.Ed.2d 428 (1976) (Powell, J., concurring). . . .

The doctrine of equitable discretion in congressional plaintiff cases was set forth for this Circuit in *Riegle* v. *Federal Open Market Committee*, 656 F.2d 873 (D.C. Cir.1981). When a member of Congress is a plaintiff in a lawsuit, concern about separation of powers counsels judicial restraint even where a private plaintiff may be entitled to relief. Where the plaintiff's dispute appears to be primarily with his fellow legislators, "[j]udges are presented not with a chance to mediate between two political branches but rather with the possibility of thwarting Congress's will by allowing a plaintiff to circumvent the processes of democratic decisionmaking." . . .

While a court upon scrutiny of detailed discovery might not agree with the President's assessment of the human rights situation in El Salvador, and could possibly conclude that the provision of security assistance under these circumstances violates section 502B of the Foreign Assistance Act, the equitable discretion doctrine prevents consideration of these issues on behalf of congressional plaintiffs. Their dispute is primarily with their fellow legislators. Action by this Court would not serve to mediate between branches of government, but merely aid plaintiffs in circumventing the democratic processes available to them.

8   Federal-State Relations

Federalism divides political power and sovereignty between the national government and the states. This broad principle cuts across almost every constitutional issue in this book, including law enforcement, civil liberties, civil rights, sex discrimination, voting rights, reapportionment, privacy, and welfare payments. This chapter covers the following topics: the principle of federalism; state immunity against suits; the Commerce Clause; the spending and taxing power; the doctrines of preemption and abstention; and the application of the Bill of Rights to the states.

Under Chief Justice Marshall, the Supreme Court gave broad support to congressional efforts to exercise its commerce powers. Later, the Court attempted to restrain Congress, but a variety of judicial doctrines did little more than slow the growth of national power. Congress developed its own independent view of federal-state relations. The law in this area has been shaped more by Congress than by the courts. As the Supreme Court noted in 1946: "the history of judicial limitation of congressional power over commerce, when exercised affirmatively, has been more largely one of retreat than of ultimate victory." Prudential Ins. Co. v. Benjamin, 328 U.S. 408, 415.

THE PRINCIPLE OF FEDERALISM

In Federalist 39, James Madison responded to the criticism that the Constitution had framed a national government instead of a "federal form" (a confederation of sovereign states). Madison identified some features of the Constitution that gave it a national character; other provisions vested power directly in the states. He concluded that the proposed Constitution "is, in strictness, neither a national nor a federal Constitution, but a composition of both."

Independence from England left the thirteen American states without a central government. Under the Articles of Confederation, drafted in 1777 and ratified in 1781, each state retained "its sovereignty, freedom and independence" with the exception of a few powers expressly delegated to the national government. The weakness of the confederation became of increasing concern, forcing the states to seek some form of regional cooperation to deal with commercial problems. Representatives of Virginia and Maryland met in 1785 at the home of George Washington, but it was decided that an interstate compact would be of more value if it included additional states. All states were invited to Annapolis in 1786 to discuss commercial issues. Poor attendance and the need to address other problems led to the convention at Philadelphia the following year "to devise such further provisions as shall appear to them necessary to render the constitution of the Federal Government adequate to the exigencies of the Union."

What emerged from Philadelphia was an entirely new structure of government that divided power functionally (among three separate branches) and spatially (between the national government and the states). The Constitution rejected Montesquieu's theory that republican government could flourish only in small countries. He believed that as the size of the country increased, popular control had to be surrendered, yielding power to aristocracies in moderate-sized countries and to monarchies in large countries. Madison turned this theory on its head in Federalist 10 by arguing that republican government was unlikely to survive in a small territory. A dominant faction would oppress the minority. "Extend the sphere," however, "and you take in a greater variety of parties and interests; you make it less probable that a majority of the whole will have a common motive to invade the rights of other citizens." Dividing this large territory into distinct states added further stability. As Hamilton said in Federalist 28, the national government and the states could check the usurpations of each other: "The people, by throwing themselves into either scale, will infallibly make it preponderate. If their rights are invaded by either, they can make use of the other as the instrument of redress."

The Virginia Plan submitted to the Philadelphia Convention called for a strong central government. The rival New Jersey Plan, espousing a confederation with power left largely to the states, attracted little support. The eventual compromise gave the central government power to collect taxes, regulate commerce, declare war, and other express functions, including the Necessary and Proper Clause to carry into effect the enumerated powers. The power of Congress was divided between two chambers: a House of Representatives elected by the people, with its membership based on population; and a Senate elected by state legislatures, with two Senators for each state. This struck an accommodation between the preference of the big states (representation by population) and the demand of the small states (equal voting power for each state).

The Virginia Plan proposed a congressional veto over all state laws "contravening in the opinion of the National Legislature the articles of Union." Although this provision was initially agreed to without debate or dissent, it was later eliminated. 1 Farrand 21, 54. Instead, the Constitution prohibits a number of actions. Under Article I, Section 9, "No tax or duty shall be laid on articles exported from any State" and no preference shall be given to the ports of one state over another. Article I, Section 10, prohibits any state from entering into any treaty, alliance, or confederation; granting letters of marque and reprisal; coining money; emitting bills of credit; making anything but gold and silver coin a tender in payment of debts; passing any bill of attainder, ex post facto law, or law impairing the obligation of contracts; or granting any title of nobility. Under Article I, Section 10, no state shall, without the consent of Congress, lay any imposts or duties on imports or exports, except what is "absolutely necessary" to execute its inspection laws. Finally, under Article I, Section 10, no state shall, without the consent of Congress, "lay any duty of tonnage, keep troops, or ships of war in time of peace, enter into any agreement or compact with another State, or with a foreign power, or engage in war, unless actually invaded, or in such imminent danger as will not admit of delay."

The Constitution provides for the admission of new states in Article IV, Section 3: "no new State shall be formed or erected within the Jurisdiction of any other State; nor any State be formed by the Junction of two or more States, or Parts of States, without the consent of the legislatures of the States concerned as well as of the Congress." National powers are further reinforced by the Supremacy Clause in Article IV, Section 2: "This Constitution, and the laws of the United States which shall be made in pursuance thereof; and all treaties made, or which shall be made, under the authority of the United States, shall be the supreme law of the land; and the judges in every State shall be bound thereby, anything in the constitution or laws of any State to the contrary notwithstanding." Early in its history, the Supreme Court decided that in cases of conflict between state law and a treaty, the latter prevails. Ware v. Hylton, 3 U.S. (3 Dall.) 198 (1796).

State sovereignty is limited by the power of Congress under the Property Clause "to dispose of and make all needful Rules and Regulations respecting the Territory or other Property belonging to the United States" (Art. IV, § 3, Cl. 2). Under this grant of authority, Congress exercises control over vast stretches of public land located inside the states, particularly those in the West. Kleppe v. New Mexico, 426 U.S. 529 (1976). State sovereignty is also limited by the Privileges and Immunities Clause: "The Citizens of each State shall be entitled to all Privileges and Immunities of Citizens in the several States" (Art. IV, § 2). Along with the Commerce Clause, this was intended to create a "national economic union." Supreme Court of New Hampshire v. Piper, 470 U.S. 274, 280 (1985).[1]

National powers were regularly threatened by state efforts to secede from the Union or to assert the doctrines of interposition and nullification. After the Federalist party passed the Alien and Sedition Acts, the Jeffersonian Republicans protested this exercise of national power. Jefferson drafted the Kentucky Resolutions of 1798, which stated that unauthorized actions by the federal government were "void, and of no force." Here was the doctrine of nullification. The Virginia Resolutions of 1798, which Madison helped write, used somewhat softer language. In cases where the federal government overstepped its powers, the states "have the right and are in duty bound to interpose for arresting the progress of the evil, and for maintaining within their respective limits the authorities, rights, and liberties appertaining to them." Some years later the Federalists complained about Republican policies in the national government. Meeting at the Hartford Convention of 1814, Federalists considered secession and registered the opposition of New England states to the measures taken by Republicans. In 1832, South Carolina's ordinance of nullification maintained that the tariff acts enacted by Congress were "null, void, and no law."

The spirit of nullification led eventually to the South's secession from the Union and the start of the Civil War. In 1869, the Supreme Court determined that the rebel states never left the Union: "The Constitution, in all its provisions, looks to an

[1]See also Hicklin v. Orbeck, 437 U.S. 518 (1978); Baldwin v. Montana Fish and Game Comm'n, 436 U.S. 371 (1978); Austin v. New Hampshire, 420 U.S. 656 (1975); Toomer v. Witsell, 334 U.S. 385 (1948).

indestructible Union, composed of indestructible States." Texas v. White, 7 Wall. (74 U.S.) 700, 725. In admitting new states to the Union, Congress cannot impose conditions that would make a state unequal to others. It cannot, for example, dictate to a state the location of its capital. Coyle v. Oklahoma, 221 U.S. 559 (1911).

The Tenth Amendment

Throughout the nineteenth and twentieth centuries, there have been efforts to reassert the notion of sovereign states by relying on the Tenth Amendment, which provides that the powers "not delegated to the United States by the Constitution, nor prohibited by it to the States, are reserved to the States respectively, or to the people." The Articles of Confederation had given greater protection to the states, which retained all powers except those "expressly delegated" to the national government. When that phrase was proposed for the Tenth Amendment, Madison objected to the word "expressly" because the functions and responsibilities of the federal government could not be delineated with such precision. It was impossible to confine a government to the exercise of express powers, for there "must necessarily be admitted powers by implication, unless the Constitution descended to recount every minutiae." 1 Annals 761 (Aug. 18, 1789). On the strength of his argument, the word "expressly" was eliminated. Chief Justice Marshall relied on this legislative history when he upheld the power of Congress to establish a national bank, even though such power is not expressly included in the Constitution. This endorsement of incidental or implied powers signaled a major advance for both national and congressional powers. McCULLOCH v. MARYLAND, 17 U.S. (4 Wheat.) 315 (1819).

The idea that the Tenth Amendment contains substantive powers for the states is revived on occasion when the Supreme Court tries to rewrite the Constitution by shoehorning the word "expressly" into the Tenth Amendment. Lane County v. Oregon, 74 U.S. (7 Wall.) 71, 76 (1868); Hammer v. Dagenhart, 247 U.S. 251, 275 (1918). Most decisions, however, accept the Amendment as merely declaratory of a general relationship between the federal government and the states. In 1920, the Court denied that the treaty power was restricted in any way "by some invisible radiation from the general terms of the Tenth Amendment." MISSOURI v. HOLLAND, 252 U.S. 416, 434. A decade later, the Court held that the Tenth Amendment added nothing to the Constitution as originally ratified. United States v. Sprague, 282 U.S. 716, 733 (1931). Justice Stone dismissed the Tenth Amendment in 1941 as a "truism," rephrasing it to read "that all is retained which has not been surrendered." United States v. Darby, 312 U.S. 100, 124. As a declaratory statement, however, the Amendment "is not without significance." Fry v. United States, 421 U.S. 542, 547 n.7 (1975).

STATE AND MUNICIPAL IMMUNITY AGAINST SUITS

States were fearful that they would be sued by citizens from other states or citizens from foreign countries. At the Virginia ratifying convention, Madison offered words of reassurance. He explained that the Supreme Court's jurisdiction over controversies between a state and citizens of another state did not give individuals the power to call any state into court. A citizen might initiate an action, but federal courts would have jurisdiction only if a state consented to be a party. 3 Elliot 533. In Federalist 81,

Hamilton claimed that states would be shielded by the general principle of immunity: "It is inherent in the nature of sovereignty not to be amenable to the suit of an individual *without its consent.*"

One of the first cases brought to the Supreme Court involved a suit by Dutch bankers to recover funds from Maryland. In this case, the state's Attorney General voluntarily appeared. Vanstophorst v. Maryland, 2 Dall. 401 (1791). The issue of state immunity reached explosive proportions when two citizens from South Carolina, acting as executors of a British creditor, filed suit against Georgia. In 1793, the Supreme Court decided that the suit was consistent with Article III, Section 2, which gave the federal courts jurisdiction over controversies "between a State and Citizens of another State." Chisholm v. Georgia, 2 U.S. (2 Dall.) 419. To prevent a rash of citizen suits, Congress and the states promptly overturned the Court's ruling by passing the Eleventh Amendment: "The Judicial power of the United States shall not be construed to extend to any suit in law or equity, commenced or prosecuted against one of the United States by Citizens of another State, or by Citizens or Subjects of any foreign state." Although the Amendment does not expressly bar suits against a state by its own citizens, the Court has consistently held that a state is subject to such suits only if it consents.[2]

As interpreted by the Court, the Eleventh Amendment does not give states total immunity from suits filed by citizens from other states. The doctrine that a state may not be sued in its own courts, without its consent, does not provide absolute immunity from suits in the courts of another state. Nevada v. Hall, 440 U.S. 410 (1979). Moreover, the Eleventh Amendment has been substantially limited by the Fourteenth Amendment. The Eleventh Amendment only prohibits suits directed against the *states*. Suits are allowed against state *officers* who are charged with denying due process or equal protection under the Fourteenth Amendment. The theory is that an officer acting illegally is functioning as an individual rather than a state official. Ex parte Young, 209 U.S. 123 (1908); Smyth v. Ames, 169 U.S. 466, 518–519 (1898).[3] This theory does not support a suit against a state official who is used simply as a conduit to recover money from the state. Even if not named in such a case, the state is the real party and is entitled to sovereign immunity. Ford Motor Co. v. Department of Treasury, 323 U.S. 459 (1945); Alabama v. Pugh, 438 U.S. 781 (1978).

State governments regularly invoke sovereign immunity to protect their budgets. In 1974, the Supreme Court held that a suit could not force a state to make retroactive payments for a program it administered for the aged, blind, and disabled. Although the suit was filed against various state officials who administered the program, the funds for retroactive payments would come from the state. The fact that the program was funded equally by state and federal funds was insufficient to establish state consent to be sued in federal courts. Edelman v. Jordan, 415 U.S. 651,

---

[2]Employees v. Missouri Public Health Dept., 411 U.S. 279, 280 (1973); Parden v. Terminal R. Co., 377 U.S. 184, 186 (1964); Great Northern Life Ins. Co. v. Read, 322 U.S. 47, 51 (1944); Duhne v. New Jersey, 251 U.S. 311 (1920); Hans v. Louisiana, 134 U.S. 1 (1890). The theory that the Eleventh Amendment forbids federal courts to hear suits against a state by a citizen of that state has been rejected by four Justices in Atascadero State Hospital v. Scanlon, 473 U.S. 234 (1985) and Welch v. Texas Dept. of Highways, 107 S.Ct. 2941 (1987).

[3]See Truax v. Raich, 239 U.S. 33 (1915); William A. Fletcher, "A Historical Interpretation of the Eleventh Amendment: A Narrow Construction of an Affirmative Grant of Jurisdiction Rather than a Prohibition Against Jurisdiction," 35 Stan. L. Rev. 1033 (1983); Doyle Mathis, "The Eleventh Amendment: Adoption and Interpretation," 2 Ga. L. Rev. 207 (1968).

673 (1974). Some of the dissenters in this 5–4 decision argued that the Eleventh Amendment did not apply when litigants rely on a post–Civil War statute to sue state officials who deprive them "of any rights, privileges, or immunities secured by the [Federal] Constitution and laws." 42 U.S.C. § 1983. Congress enacted the statute in 1871 to enforce the Fourteenth Amendment.

This issue returned two years later. The Court decided that whenever there is a collision between the Eleventh Amendment and Section 5 of the Fourteenth Amendment, which grants Congress authority to enforce "by appropriate legislation" the substantive provisions of the Fourteenth Amendment, the congressional statute prevails. This policy allows suits against states even for retroactive payments from their treasuries. Fitzpatrick v. Bitzer, 427 U.S. 445 (1976). Principles of federalism "that might otherwise be an obstacle to congressional authority are necessarily overridden by the power to enforce the Civil War Amendments 'by appropriate legislation.' Those Amendments were specifically designed as an expansion of federal power and an intrusion on state sovereignty." Rome v. United States, 446 U.S. 156, 179 (1980). Unless Congress expresses in unmistakable terms its intent to abrogate the Eleventh Amendment, states may not be sued in federal court without their consent. Atascadero State Hospital v. Scanlon, 473 U.S. 234 (1985). The same principle was driven home in *Dellmuth* v. *Muth*, 109 S.Ct. 2397 (1989). In that same year the Court ruled that neither states nor state officials acting in their official capacities can be sued under Section 1983, unless Congress specifically applies that law to the states. Will v. Michigan Dept. of Police, 109 S.Ct. 2304 (1989).

Other than its enforcement powers under the Fourteenth Amendment, may Congress use its Article I powers to abrogate the Eleventh Amendment? The Court has held that Congress may use the Commerce Clause to set aside the sovereign immunity of states. Pennsylvania v. Union Gas Co., 109 S.Ct 2273 (1989). It has also ruled that the Bankruptcy Code, based on the Aricle I power of Congress to establish uniform laws for bankruptcies, does not abrogate the states' Eleventh Amendment immunity. Hoffman v. Connecticut Income Maint. Dept, 109 S.Ct. 2818 (1989).

The Eleventh Amendment does not protect states from court awards that compel a state to pay the plaintiff's attorney fees. These awards are treated like a remedial fine imposed for contempt against a court ruling. Hutto v. Finney, 437 U.S. 678 (1978). However, in 1984 the Supreme Court held that the Eleventh Amendment prohibits federal judges from ordering state officials to conform to state law. This case, decided 5–4, reviews the twists and turns of the Eleventh Amendment. Pennhurst State School & Hosp. v. Halderman, 465 U.S. 89 (1984). Confusion over the scope of the Eleventh Amendment continued in a decision in 1987, with the Court split 5–4 over the framers' intent and the literal meaning of the Amendment. Welch v. Texas Dept. of Highways, 483 U.S 468 (1987).

Municipal Liability

Cases involving the immunity of local governments are decided on statutory grounds, giving Congress the ultimate control in determining the extent of immunity, and yet the constitutional principle of federalism is always present. Initially, the Supreme Court held that city or municipal officials were immune from suits charging violations of federally protected civil rights. Monroe v. Pape, 365 U.S. 167

(1961).[4] This result was not consistent with other federal court decisions involving local governments. Furthermore, Congress refused to extend *Monroe* to school boards and even authorized attorney's fees for the prevailing parties in civil rights suits. Under these pressures the Court reversed itself in 1978 and decided that municipal employees can be sued for civil rights injuries resulting from their official actions. Monell v. New York City Dept. of Social Services, 436 U.S. 658, 698–699 (1978). Cities may not reduce their liabilities in these suits by asserting that their officers acted in good faith. Owen v. City of Independence, 445 U.S. 622 (1980). The liability of state and local officials has been expanded by other holdings, covering not only cases involving civil rights and equal protection but *any* federal law. Maine v. Thiboutot, 448 U.S. 1 (1980). Although bills have been introduced in Congress to limit municipal liability under the civil rights statute, no final action has been taken.[5] However, Congress did enact legislation to limit municipal liability under antitrust suits (see p. 380).

THE COMMERCE CLAUSE

Commercial friction among the states during the 1770s and 1780s created the need for stronger national powers. The Continental Congress had no power to raise revenue or to regulate commerce among the states. Its power to conclude treaties with foreign nations meant little unless it could control commerce coming into state ports. With each state guarding its sphere of sovereignty, thirteen conflicting systems of commercial regulation and duty schedules governed trade in the country. These commercial disputes led to the Annapolis Convention in 1786 and the Philadelphia Convention a year later. Among the enumerated duties given to Congress was the power to "regulate commerce with foreign nations, and among the several States, and with the Indian tribes." Art. I, § 8, Cl. 2.

The scope of the Commerce Clause reached the Supreme Court in 1824. The decision by Chief Justice Marshall is significant for two reasons. First, although Marshall was a strong defender of private property and contractual rights, he advanced a broad interpretation of the power of Congress to regulate commerce. Second, the decision represents one of the most articulate rebuttals of "strict constructionism." GIBBONS v. OGDEN, 22 U.S. (9 Wheat.) 1 (1824).

Three years later, Marshall again supported national power by striking down a Maryland statute because it violated two constitutional provisions: the prohibition on states to lay a duty on imports, and the power of Congress to regulate interstate commerce. To distinguish between congressional and state powers, Marshall devel-

---

[4]Affirmed in Moor v. County of Alameda, 411 U.S. 693 (1973); Kenosha v. Bruno, 412 U.S. 507 (1973); Aldinger v. Howard, 427 U.S. 1 (1976). Federally protected civil rights include actions under § 1983, which provides that all persons under color of state law who deprive others of rights secured under the Constitution and laws shall be liable to the injured party.

[5]See 126 Cong. Rec. 25292–25295 (1980); 127 Cong. Rec. 3209–3212 (1981); 133 Cong. Rec. S922–926 (daily ed. Jan. 20, 1987). In Newport v. Fact Concerts, Inc., 453 U.S. 247 (1981), the Court held that municipalities were not subject to punitive damages. Municipal liability was also eased by Middlesex Cty. Sewage Auth. v. Sea Clammers, 453 U.S. 1 (1981); Hallie v. Eau Claire, 471 U.S. 34 (1985); and St. Louis v. Praprotnik, 108 S.Ct. 915 (1988). But see Pembaur v. Cincinnati, 475 U.S. 469 (1986). Municipal liability was further defined in Canton v. Harris, 109 S.Ct. 1197 (1989), and Jett v. Dallas Independent School Dist., 109 S.Ct. 2702 (1989).

oped the "original package" concept. States could not tax an import in its original form or package, but after the imported article became "incorporated and mixed up with the mass of property in the country," it was vulnerable to state taxes. Brown v. Maryland, 25 U.S. (12 Wheat.) 419, 441 (1827). In areas where Congress had not exercised its commerce power, Marshall recognized the authority of states to regulate commerce within their own borders. Willson v. Black-bird Creek Marsh Co., 27 U.S. (2 Pet.) 244 (1829).

Concurrent Powers

Other cases elaborated on the jurisdiction between the national and state governments. The broad nationalistic interpretation of Marshall was supplanted by rulings of the Taney Court. A decision in 1837 permitted states to adopt regulations for passengers arriving from foreign countries. The Court considered packages, not people, as subjects of commerce. States could exercise the "police power" to protect the general welfare of their citizens. New York v. Miln, 36 U.S. (11 Pet.) 102 (1837). Under this doctrine of concurrent powers, states could regulate commerce within their borders unless preempted by Congress. For example, if Congress authorized the importation of liquor from foreign countries, states had to accept the liquor in its "original package." Once the cask became part of retail or domestic traffic, the state police power justified the imposition of taxes, licenses, or total prohibition of liquor. The same reasoning applied to liquor shipped from neighboring states. License Cases, 46 U.S. (5 How.) 504 (1847). The Supreme Court even allowed states to collect "fees" from foreign vessels by distinguishing fees from the imposts and duties forbidden by Article I, Section 10. Cooley v. Board of Wardens, 53 U.S. (12 How.) 299 (1852). During this same period, however, the Court denied states the right to impose taxes on alien passengers arriving at state ports, even when states used "health" as a justification. Passenger Cases, 48 U.S. (7 How.) 282 (1849).

The Supreme Court also created the doctrine of exclusive jurisdictions. Under the theory of "dual federalism," the states and the national government exercised mutually exclusive powers. "The powers which one possesses, the other does not." United States v. Cruikshank, 92 U.S. (2 Otto.) 542, 550 (1876). In 1890, the Court ruled that a state's prohibition of intoxicating liquors could not be applied to original packages or kegs. The power of Congress over commerce, even if not expressly stated in a statute, appeared to override state police powers and local options. The Court qualified its opinion by saying that the states could not exclude incoming articles "without congressional permission." Leisy v. Hardin, 135 U.S. 100, 125 (1890).

Congress promptly overturned the decision by passing legislation that made intoxicating liquors, upon their arrival in a state or territory, subject to the police powers "to the same extent and in the same manner as though such liquids or liquors had been produced in such State or Territory, and shall not be exempt therefrom by reason of being introduced therein in original packages or otherwise." 26 Stat. 313 (1890). The Supreme Court upheld the constitutionality of this statute. In re Rahrer, 140 U.S. 545 (1891). Excerpts from the congressional debate are reprinted on pages 411–415. Three years later, the Court reviewed a state statute that prohibited the sale of oleomargarine that had been colored to look like butter, including oleomargarine manufactured outside the state. The Court supported the statute even though Congress had previously legislated on oleomargarine. Plumley v. Massachusetts, 155 U.S. 461 (1894).

Antitrust Cases

In an effort to curb the concentration of economic power after the Civil War, Congress passed the Sherman Antitrust Act in 1890 to prohibit combinations and conspiracies that restrained trade. Through a series of rulings, the Supreme Court largely nullified the law's effectiveness. In 1895, the Court held that the Act did not apply to monopolies engaged in the *manufacture* of items necessary for life. Through this reasoning the Act exempted (by judicial fiat) the "Sugar Trust": the American Sugar Refining Company, which was incorporated in New Jersey and controlled about 98 percent of the sugar refining business in the country. The Court argued that manufacturing precedes commerce and is not part of it, and that the power to regulate the manufacture of a "necessary of life" belongs to the police power of the states. The Court regarded the sugar monopoly's restraint on trade as "indirect," not direct. United States v. E.C. Knight Co., 156 U.S. 1 (1895).

The Court narrowly upheld the application of the Sherman Antitrust Act to holding companies that rival railroad companies had established to combine their forces and restrain interstate commerce. Northern Securities Co. v. United States, 193 U.S. 197 (1904). The Act was gravely weakened in 1911 when the Court adopted the "rule of reason" doctrine. Previously, the Court had applied the literal and strict language of the Act, which made no exceptions. It prohibited *every* contract, combination, or conspiracy in restraint of interstate or foreign trade. *Every* person engaged in such activity was guilty of a misdemeanor. In this early period, the Court refused to limit the Act to "unreasonable" restraints of trade. United States v. Trans-Missouri Freight Assn., 166 U.S. 290, 327–341 (1897); United States v. Joint Traffic Assn., 171 U.S. 505, 573–578 (1898). If companies entered into contracts that restrained interstate or foreign commerce to any extent, Congress could nullify the contracts. Addyston Pipe & Steel Co. v. United States, 175 U.S. 211 (1899).

Matters changed abruptly in 1911 with the "rule of reason." The Sherman Act was judicially amended to prohibit only *unreasonable* or *undue* restraints. In a dissent, Justice Harlan condemned the use of judicial construction to amend the Constitution and rewrite statutes. Standard Oil Co. v. United States, 221 U.S. 1, 105 (1911); United States v. American Tobacco Co., 221 U.S. 106 (1911). Judgments of "reasonable" rates are now exercised by administrative agencies, not the judiciary. Moreover, the Court has long since abandoned the artificial separation between "manufacturing" and "commerce." Mandeville Farms v. Sugar Co., 334 U.S. 219, 229 (1948).

The give-and-take between Congress and the judiciary is illustrated by the insurance cases. In 1869, the Supreme Court held that states could regulate insurance because it was not a "transaction of commerce." Paul v. Virginia, 8 Wall. 168. That holding, along with 150 years of precedents, was overturned in 1944 when the Court interpreted the transaction of insurance business across state lines as interstate commerce subject to congressional regulation. The Court said that Congress had not intended to exempt the insurance business from the Sherman Antitrust Act. United States v. South-Eastern Underwriters Assn., 322 U.S. 533 (1944). Congress quickly passed the McCarran Act, essentially reversing the Court by authorizing states to regulate insurance. 59 Stat. 33 (1945). Acting under cover of this statute, states were once again allowed to regulate and tax the business of insurance. Prudential Ins. Co. v. Benjamin, 328 U.S. 408 (1946).

The application of the Antitrust Act to professional sports produced some anomalous results. Although baseball players traveled from state to state, the Court held that baseball games were not part of interstate commerce and were therefore exempt from antitrust actions. Federal Baseball Club v. National League, 259 U.S. 200 (1922). See also Toolson v. New York Yankees, 346 U.S. 356 (1953) and Flood v. Kuhn, 407 U.S. 258 (1972). Other professional sports, however, were subject to antitrust laws. United States v. International Boxing Club, 348 U.S. 236 (1955); Radovich v. National Football League, 352 U.S. 445 (1957). Correction of this aberration depended on legislative, not judicial, action, but Congress did not act. With no one at the national level willing to decide, eventually the baseball owners and players worked out an agreement.

The Antitrust Act has been extended in recent years to prohibit the "learned professions" (lawyers, doctors, etc.) from fixing prices and fees. Goldfarb v. Virginia State Bar, 421 U.S. 773 (1975). As recognition of the sovereign status of states, the Antitrust Act does not apply to anticompetitive conduct of a state acting through its legislature. Parker v. Brown, 317 U.S. 341 (1943). However, the Act has been applied to *business* activities of cities, Lafayette v. Louisiana Power & Light Co., 435 U.S. 380 (1978), and to state pricing systems that are not actively supervised by the state, California Retail Liquor Dealers v. Midcal Aluminum, 445 U.S. 97 (1980). The Act does not apply to city activities that are pursuant to state policy. Hallie v. Eau Claire, 471 U.S. 34 (1985). See also Fisher v. Berkeley, 475 U.S. 260 (1986).

A decision in 1982 left some municipalities exposed to treble-damage antitrust suits, especially local governments autonomous from the state because of "home rule" status. Such entities did not enjoy the notion of sovereign immunity available to the states. Community Communications Co. v. Boulder, 455 U.S. 40, 53–54 (1982). In response to more than 100 antitrust suits seeking treble damages against cities, counties, and townships, Congress passed legislation in 1984 to shield municipalities from antitrust actions. Courts in the future can enjoin cities and villages from carrying out anticompetitive practices, but may not award monetary damages. 98 Stat. 2750 (1984).

Nationalization of the Economy

Fundamental changes in economic structures over the past century gradually washed away many traditional boundaries between intrastate and interstate commerce. In 1886, the Supreme Court struck down an Illinois railroad statute because it affected, even for the part of the journey within the state, commerce among the states. Wabash, &c., Railway Co. v. Illinois, 118 U.S. 557 (1886). This decision made national regulation imperative and Congress responded a year later by creating the Interstate Commerce Commission. Another decision allowed Congress to prohibit national and interstate traffic in lottery tickets even if its motivation—such as morality—competed with the state police power. Champion v. Ames (Lottery Case), 188 U.S. 321 (1903). Two years later, a unanimous Court upheld a congressional statute that prevented a company from restraining trade even when the company's cattle came to rest within a stockyard of a particular state. The movement of cattle from state to state created a "current of commerce" subject to congressional control. Swift & Co. v. United States, 196 U.S. 375, 399 (1905). In later years, the Court evoked a similar image, calling the stockyards a temporary resting place for cattle moving interstate, serving as "a throat through which the current of commerce flows." Stafford v. Wallace, 258 U.S. 495, 516 (1922).

These decisions supported congressional regulation only in selected areas: railroads, morals, and health. For example, in 1914 the Supreme Court rejected artificial distinctions between intrastate and interstate by holding that Congress could regulate actions inside a state that were *related* to interstate commerce. Through this reasoning it allowed a congressional commission to set railroad rates within a state. Shreveport Rate Case, 234 U.S. 342. Under the Commerce Clause, Congress could establish an eight-hour day for all railroad workers engaged in interstate commerce, especially when needed to resolve a nationwide strike. Wilson v. New, 243 U.S. 332 (1917). Other decisions upheld the power of Congress to seize and condemn prohibited articles, to forbid the interstate transportation of women engaged in prostitution, and to make it a crime to transport stolen motor vehicles in interstate or foreign commerce.[6] During time of war, commercial operations normally regulated by the states fall within the domain of the national government.[7]

This pattern of sustaining congressional power did not apply to factory conditions, hours, or wages. In 1918, the Court held that a child labor law exceeded the commerce power and invaded responsibilities left to the states. HAMMER v. DAGENHART, 247 U.S. 251 (1918). A congressional effort to accomplish the same objective through the taxing power was struck down four years later. Child Labor Tax Case, 259 U.S. 20 (1922). Not until 1941, after the composition of the Court had been drastically altered and restrictive judicial doctrines abandoned, was child labor legislation upheld. UNITED STATES v. DARBY, 312 U.S. 100 (1941).

THE NEW DEAL WATERSHED

During the New Deal, the Supreme Court at first resisted, but eventually capitulated, to a wholesale expansion of congressional power over commerce. Initially, the Court prohibited Congress from regulating commercial activities that were regarded as production and manufacture, as "local" or intrastate, or that affected commerce only "indirectly." These formulas were variations of dual federalism. By 1936 the Court began to embrace what it had accepted intermittently in the past: intrastate activities having a substantial relation to interstate commerce could be regulated by Congress.

In two cases in 1935, the Court declared unconstitutional the National Industrial Recovery Act of 1933. A provision involving production quotas for petroleum products was struck down as an excessive delegation of legislative power to the President. Panama Refining Co. v. Ryan, 293 U.S. 388 (1935). The remainder of the NIRA was invalidated a few months later when a unanimous Court decided that the statute violated the delegation doctrine and exceeded Congress' power to regulate commerce. The Court refused to apply the "current of commerce" concept to intrastate commerce that involved purchases or transportation of goods outside the state. Once a commodity became "commingled with the mass of property within the State," the flow of interstate commerce ceased. Schechter Corp. v. United States, 295 U.S. 495, 543 (1935).

The Court struck down the Railroad Retirement Act, which transferred funds from railroad carriers to retirees. The Court, refusing to justify the statute under the Commerce Clause, treated it as a taking of property requiring just compensation.

---

[6]Hipolite Egg Co. v. United States, 220 U.S. 45 (1911) (seizing and condemning articles); Hoke v. United States, 227 U.S. 308 (1913) and Caminetti v. United States, 242 U.S. 470 (1917) (White Slave Traffic Act); Brooks v. United States, 267 U.S. 432 (1925) (stolen cars). See also Atlantic Coast Line v. Riverside Mills, 219 U.S. 186 (1911).

[7]Case v. Bowles, 327 U.S. 92, 102 (1946); Dakota Cent. Tel. Co. v. South Dakota, 250 U.S. 163 (1919); Northern Pac. Ry. Co. v. North Dakota, 250 U.S. 135 (1919).

Railroad Retirement Board v. Alton R. Co., 295 U.S. 330 (1935). Also invalidated was the Bituminous Coal Conservation Act of 1935, which relied on the Commerce Clause to regulate mining and the distribution of coal. The Court said that the commerce power did not permit Congress to control the conditions in which coal is produced (such as labor conditions) before coal became an article of commerce. Labor conditions affected commerce only "indirectly." Production and manufacture did not constitute commerce, said the Court, even when done with intent to sell or transport the commodities out of the state. Carter v. Carter Coal Co., 298 U.S. 238 (1936). The processing tax of the Agricultural Adjustment Act was declared unconstitutional in *United States* v. *Butler* (see pp. 384–388 on the spending and taxing powers).

After Roosevelt's election in 1936 and his attempt to pack the judiciary, the Supreme Court began to accommodate New Deal legislation. Without a change in the Court's composition, but with Chief Justice Hughes and Justice Roberts now solidly supporting the three liberals (Brandeis, Cardozo, and Stone), the Court upheld the National Labor Relations Act. The Court accepted Congress' argument that labor disputes directly burdened or obstructed interstate or foreign commerce and could be regulated by the Commerce Clause. The Act gave employees in industry a fundamental right to organize and engage in collective bargaining. Any intrastate activity that had a close and substantial relation to interstate commerce could be brought within the control of Congress. To enforce the Act, Congress established a National Labor Relations Board with the power to prevent any person from engaging in unfair labor practices "affecting commerce." NLRB v. JONES & LAUGHLIN, 301 U.S. 1 (1937).

In 1939, the Court sustained the Agricultural Adjustment Act, which used marketing controls to limit the amount of commodities that could be sold. Through the use of quotas, Congress hoped to stabilize prices and limit production. Farmers who exceeded their allotment had to pay a penalty at the warehouses, the "throat" where commodities entered "the stream of commerce." Mulford v. Smith, 307 U.S. 38, 47 (1939). Wheat marketing quotas were upheld three years later by a unanimous Court, even for wheat not intended for commerce but produced wholly for consumption on the farm. Wickard v. Filburn, 317 U.S. 111 (1942). The Fair Labor Standards Act of 1938 was upheld, allowing Congress to regulate the wages and hours of manufacturing employees. The Court rejected the argument that manufacturing was an intrastate activity and therefore outside the Commerce Clause. Congress could regulate intrastate activities where they have a "substantial effect" on interstate commerce. United States v. Darby, 312 U.S. 100, 119 (1941).

State efforts to limit the length of railroad cars traveling interstate could not be justified for reasons of safety or the police power. Southern Pacific Co. v. Arizona, 325 U.S. 761 (1945). Although states may impose burdensome regulations in the interest of local health and safety, they may not restrain interstate commerce for the purpose of advancing their own commercial interests or promoting local economic advantages. Hood v. Du Mond, 336 U.S. 525 (1949). The Supreme Court has developed a number of criteria to indicate when state actions burden interstate commerce, but the enforcement and implementation of these judicial tests depend largely on congressional action. Commonwealth Edison Co. v. Montana, 453 U.S. 609 (1981).

These decisions did not permit Congress to preempt every area of commerce that might affect interstate activities. States could still control local conditions and affect interstate commerce incidentally while protecting their citizens' welfare. Milk

Board v. Eisenberg Co., 306 U.S. 346 (1939). Even when 90 to 95 percent of a state product was shipped in interstate or foreign commerce, states could adopt marketing and price-stabilization programs in the interest of the "safety, health and well-being of local communities," especially when the activity "may never be adequately dealt with by Congress." Parker v. Brown, 317 U.S. 341, 362–363 (1943).[8] To protect their environmental and natural resources, states may enact regulations even when the incidental effect creates some burden on interstate commerce. Minnesota v. Clover Leaf Creamery Co., 449 U.S. 456 (1981).

The commerce power allows Congress to control such local activity as "loan sharking" (using threats and extortion to collect loans). Although local, these techniques are part of organized crime that affect interstate and foreign commerce. Perez v. United States, 402 U.S. 146 (1971). The breadth of the New Deal revolution is reflected in two decisions in 1981 that upheld congressional regulation of surface coal mining. The statute authorized states to propose a program of environmental protection to meet federal minimum standards. If states failed to prepare a program, they would be forced to adopt a federal plan. A unanimous Court upheld the statute. Hodel v. Virginia Surface Mining & Recl. Assn., 452 U.S. 264 (1981); Hodel v. Indiana, 452 U.S. 314 (1981).

From *National League* to *Garcia*

The most contentious issue of federalism in recent decades involves the extension of federal hours-and-wages standards to state employees. The Court halted this trend toward national control in *National League of Cities* v. *Usery* (1976) but reversed itself in *Garcia* (1985), giving Congress almost total power under the Commerce Clause.

In 1968, the Court had upheld the extension of federal minimum wages and overtime pay to state-operated hospitals and schools. The Court concluded that Congress had a rational basis for the extension, including the effect on interstate competition and the promotion of labor peace. Maryland v. Wirtz, 392 U.S. 183. Building on that decision, in 1975 the Court upheld the short-term power of the President to stabilize wages and salaries of state employees. Fry v. United States, 421 U.S. 542, 549–559. A year later, however, Justice Rehnquist attracted four votes to his position that federal minimum-wage and maximum-hour provisions could not displace state powers in such "traditional governmental functions" as fire prevention, police protection, sanitation, public health, and parks and recreation. Amendments to the Fair Labor Standards Act in 1974 had extended the wage-and-hour provisions to almost all state employees. The 5–4 decision by Rehnquist overruled *Wirtz* by holding that the 1974 amendments threatened the independent existence of states. Justice Blackmun, in a tentative concurrence, supplied the fifth vote. The dissents were sharply worded. NATIONAL LEAGUE OF CITIES v. USERY, 426 U.S. 833 (1976).

Rehnquist's opinion failed to take root as a workable doctrine. In 1981, a unanimous Court rejected a district court's argument that land use regulation was a "traditional governmental function" reserved to the states under *National League*. The Court held that *National League* applied to "states as states" and not to private business operations within a state. Hodel v. Virginia Surface Mining & Recl. Assn.,

---

[8]See also Carter v. Virginia, 321 U.S. 131 (1944) for the power of states to regulate shipments entering into and passing out of their borders, and Milk Board v. Eisenberg Co., 306 U.S. 346, 351 (1939) for the ability of states to regulate local conditions even when they incidentally or indirectly involve interstate commerce.

452 U.S. 264 (1981). A year later, the Court again rejected a district court's reliance on *National League* and the Tenth Amendment. FERC v. Mississippi, 456 U.S. 742 (1982). Operation of a railroad engaged in interstate commerce was not considered a traditional governmental function. United Transportation Union v. Long Island R. Co., 455 U.S. 678 (1982). In a fourth case, a federal district court held that the Age Discrimination in Employment Act violated the Tenth Amendment theory articulated in *National League*. At issue was age discrimination against an employee of Wyoming's Game and Fish Department (*National League* had identified parks and recreation services as a traditional state activity protected by the Tenth Amendment). Nevertheless, the Supreme Court reversed the district court. A concurrence by Justice Stevens stated that the only basis for questioning the age discrimination statute "is the pure judicial fiat" found in *National League*. He suggested that Rehnquist's ruling deserved to be placed in the same category as other decisions repudiated by the Court: "the law would be well served by a prompt rejection of *National League of Cities'* modern embodiment of the spirit of the Articles of Confederation." EEOC v. Wyoming, 460 U.S. 226, 250 (1983).

National League was overturned in 1985 by a 5–4 Court. Justice Blackmun's majority opinion nullified the decision with which he had concurred less than ten years before. He pointed out the difficulty that courts had experienced in distinguishing between "traditional" and "nontraditional" state functions. The effect of the decision is to leave the protection of federalism largely to the political process of Congress. The dissents by Rehnquist and O'Connor imply that, in time, they may form a new majority to overturn Blackmun. GARCIA v. SAN ANTONIO METROPOLITAN TRANSIT AUTHORITY, 469 U.S. 528 (1985).

Garcia threatened the states with massive budgetary obligations. Most state employees were already receiving at least the minimum wage, but the cost of meeting the overtime provisions of the Fair Labor Standards Act could have reached several billion dollars, much of it for firefighters and police in local government. Congress passed legislation to postpone the effective date of *Garcia* (decided February 19, 1985) to April 15, 1986, and permitted the use of compensatory time as a substitute for paying overtime. 99 Stat. 787 (1985).

THE SPENDING AND TAXING POWERS

The pattern of federal spending and taxing powers has been similar to the Commerce Clause. The courts initially placed constraints on congressional power and offered protection to "local" activities in the states. Over time, however, these constraints have been largely removed because the judiciary recognizes the need for national powers and regulation.

The Constitution speaks clearly on only one aspect of the taxing power: "No tax or duty shall be laid on articles exported from any State" (Art. I, § 9). Other tax questions have provoked extensive litigation. Difficulties in distinguishing between direct and indirect taxes created major conflicts between Congress and the judiciary. Indirect taxes must follow the rule of uniformity: "The Congress shall have Power to lay and collect Taxes, Duties, Imposts, and Excises, to pay the Debts and provide for the common Defense and general Welfare of the United States; but all Duties, Imposts and Excises shall be uniform throughout the United States" (Art. I, § 8). The rule of uniformity protects states from discriminatory actions by the national government, although federal taxes do not have to fall equally on each state, nor is

Congress barred from adopting tax exemptions for certain regions. United States v. Psasynski, 462 U.S. 74 (1983).

Direct taxes are covered in Article I, Section 9: "No capitation, or other direct, tax shall be laid, unless in proportion to the census or enumeration herein before directed to be taken." Capitation taxes, or "head taxes," have never been enacted by Congress. Other direct taxes must be levied among the states in accordance with the rule of apportionment. The question of a direct tax was first decided by the Supreme Court in 1796. A carriage tax imposed by Congress was attacked as a direct tax, requiring that it be apportioned among the states on the basis of population. A unanimous Court, however, ruled that the tax was indirect. The decision appeared to limit direct taxes to two kinds: a capitation or poll tax, imposed without regard to property, and a tax on land. Hylton v. United States, 3 Dall. 171, 175 (1796). From 1798 to 1816, the federal government imposed direct taxes on real estate and slaves. In 1861, the federal tax applied to real estate only. Veazie Bank v. Fenno, 75 U.S. (8 Wall.) 533, 543 (1869). Federal taxes on currency and bank circulation were not considered a direct tax. Id. at 546–547.

Income Tax

In 1881, a unanimous Court again limited the meaning of direct taxes to capitation taxes and taxes on real estate. The Court interpreted the federal income tax of 1864, as amended in 1865, as an indirect tax. Springer v. United States, 102 U.S. 586 (1881). In 1895, after a hundred years of agreement on the meaning of direct taxes, the Court reversed direction and struck down a federal income tax, treating it as a direct tax to be apportioned on the basis of population. The statute was invalidated in two steps. The first decision held that the tax on rents or income of real estate was a direct tax and violated the Constitution by not following the apportionment rule. Pollock v. Farmers' Loan & Trust Co., 157 U.S. 429 (1895). A second decision struck down the income tax, in part because the Court concluded that invalidation of the other taxes left a tax scheme that Congress could not have intended. POLLOCK v. FARMERS' LOAN & TRUST CO., 158 U.S. 601, 637 (1895).

The Court acted under the shadow of class warfare and threats of socialism. During oral argument, Joseph H. Choate warned the Justices that the tax was "communistic in its purposes and tendencies." 157 U.S. at 532. After the first hearing, the Court split 4–4 on the question of the income tax. Upon rehearing, a 5–4 decision invalidated the tax. The member missing from the first decision, Justice Jackson, voted to *sustain* the tax in the second case. All things being equal, this should have yielded a 5–4 tally supporting the income tax. One Justice obviously switched his vote. Who he was, and why he switched, has never been revealed. Because of the vote-switching and razor-thin majority, the decision became known as one of three "self-inflicted wounds" on the Court (the other two being *Dred Scott* in 1857 and the Legal Tender Cases of 1870). Charles Evans Hughes, The Supreme of the United States 54 (1928). It was not until 1913 that Congress and the states overrode *Pollock* by passing the Sixteenth Amendment. Brushaber v. Union Pac. R.R. Co., 240 U.S. 1 (1916).

The Income Tax Cases marked an unusual setback for the power of Congress to tax. In 1904, the Court held that the judiciary would not limit the taxing power simply because it had been exercised in an unwise, oppressive, or injurious manner. Nor could the courts inquire into the motive or purpose of Congress in passing a tax, or discover a limitation in the Due Process Clause of the Fifth Amendment.

Congressional abuses in such cases had to be corrected by the voters. McCray v. United States, 195 U.S. 27 (1904). In 1911, a unanimous Court upheld a corporation income tax passed by Congress. The Court called it an excise, not a direct tax, and said it complied with the rule of uniformity. Flint Stone Tracy Co., 220 U.S. 107 (1911). When Congress tried to use the taxing power to regulate matters the Court considered within the police power of the states, the congressional statute was declared invalid. Child Labor Tax Case, 259 U.S. 20 (1922); Hill v. Wallace, 259 U.S. 44 (1922).

New Deal Cases

The question of Congress intruding upon "local" matters within the jurisdiction of the states resulted in the invalidation of several New Deal statutes. In 1936, the Supreme Court struck down a so-called excise tax in the Bituminous Coal Conservation Act of 1935 because it coerced coal producers to submit to the price-fixing and labor provisions of the Act. Carter v. Carter Coal Co., 298 U.S. 238, 288–289 (1936). Also in 1936, the Court declared unconstitutional a "processing tax" enacted by Congress as part of the Agricultural Adjustment Act. In return for limiting their acreage and crops, farmers received payments from this tax. The Court held that the power of taxation exists to support government, not to expropriate money from one group to benefit another as part of a general regulatory scheme. Moreover, the Court held that the tax was coercive on farmers and invaded state powers by trying to regulate the "local" matter of agriculture. The decision suggests that had Congress explicitly invoked its commerce power, the Act might have been sustained. In writing the opinion for the Court, Justice Roberts unveiled his famous mechanical formula for determining the constitutionality of a statute. UNITED STATES v. BUTLER, 297 U.S. 1 (1936).

Spending and Regulatory Power

Roberts abandoned his conservative brethren a year later by joining a 5–4 decision upholding Title IX of the Social Security Act. Congress imposed a tax on employers to support a national unemployment compensation plan. Funds from state unemployment laws were paid over to the Secretary of the Treasury and credited to an unemployment trust fund. Title IX was upheld even though it seemed to conflict with *Butler* by pressuring states to adopt unemployment compensation laws as part of a regulatory, and not merely revenue-raising, effort. Steward Machine Co. v. Davis, 301 U.S. 548 (1937). Congress responded to *Butler* by passing the Soil Conservation and Domestic Allotment Act of 1936 and the Agricultural Adjustment Act of 1938. These statutes avoided the processing tax but pursued the same objective of controlling production by relying on the federal appropriations power and the Commerce Clause.

By attaching conditions to federal funds, Congress can regulate certain state activities. States acquiesce by accepting federal strings with the funds. Oklahoma v. CSC, 330 U.S. 127, 143–144 (1947). Thus, Congress may direct the Secretary of Transportation to withhold a percentage of federal funds from states that allow persons under twenty-one to buy alcoholic beverages. SOUTH DAKOTA v. DOLE, 107 S.Ct. 2793 (1987). The Court has invoked the spending power to justify the use of racial and ethnic criteria by Congress as a condition attached to federal grants (a 10 percent "set-aside" for minority businesses). Fullilove v. Klutznick, 448 U.S. 448 (1980), reprinted on pp. 000–000.

If the conditions are offensive to state interests, there is no obligation to accept the funds. When states violate the conditions, the federal government may assess deficiencies and recover misused funds. Bell v. New Jersey, 461 U.S. 773 (1983). Of greater controversy is the question of Congress using interstate councils and states as administrative bodies to implement federal policy. FERC v. Mississippi, 456 U.S. at 761–763; Seattle Master Builders Assn. v. Northwest Power Planning Council, No. 88–7585 (9th Cir. April 10, 1986).

The states and the federal government are generally free to exercise their taxing power if they proceed on a rational basis and do not resort to classifications that are "palpably arbitrary." Allied Stores of Ohio v. Bowers, 358 U.S. 522, 527 (1959); Lehnhausen v. Lake Shore Auto Parts Co., 410 U.S. 356 (1973). Congress has had mixed results in using the taxing power to regulate narcotics, gambling, liquor, and firearms. The application of the taxing power to narcotics has been repeatedly upheld. United States v. Doremus, 249 U.S. 86 (1919); Nigro v. United States, 276 U.S. 332 (1928); United States v. Sanchez, 340 U.S. 42 (1950). Questions have been raised in some cases as to whether compliance with these laws automatically exposes someone to the risk of self-incrimination. Leary v. United States, 395 U.S. 6 (1969); United States v. Covington, 395 U.S. 57 (1969); Minor v. United States, 396 U.S. 87 (1969). The Court has held that a federal liquor tax operated not as a tax but as a penalty that usurped the police powers of the states. United States v. Constantine, 296 U.S. 287 (1935); United States v. Kesterson, 296 U.S. 299 (1935).

The taxing power has been used to regulate firearms, with the Court pointing out that every tax "is in some measure regulatory." Sonzinsky v. United States, 300 U.S. 506, 513 (1937). Such statutes, however, cannot force gun dealers to incriminate themselves. Haynes v. United States, 390 U.S. 85 (1968). The same issue applies to federal taxes on gambling. At first, the Court determined that federal taxes and requirements to register with the Internal Revenue Service did not violate the Self-Incrimination Clause. United States v. Kahriger, 345 U.S. 22 (1953); Lewis v. United States, 348 U.S. 419 (1955). The Court later held that such statutes unconstitutionally compel gamblers to incriminate themselves. Marchetti v. United States, 390 U.S. 39 (1968); Grosso v. United States, 390 U.S. 62 (1968).

Intergovernmental Tax Immunity

The theory of dual federalism, which created exclusive jurisdictions for the federal government and the states, spawned the sister doctrine of intergovernmental tax immunity. Chief Justice Marshall struck down a state tax on the U.S. Bank by arguing extravagantly that the power to tax is the power to destroy. McCULLOCH v. MARYLAND, 17 U.S. (4 Wheat.) 315 (1819). If states could not tax federal instrumentalities, presumably the federal government could not tax state activities, and indeed the Court reached that conclusion in 1871 by holding that Congress could not tax the salary of a state judge. Justice Bradley, in the solitary dissent, objected to the doctrine that "the general government is to be regarded in any sense foreign or antagonistic to the State governments, their officers, or people." He correctly predicted that the decision would lead to impractical and mischievous results. Collector v. Day, 78 U.S. (11 Wall.) 113, 128–129 (1871).

The doctrine of intergovernmental tax immunity did not exempt state activities from federal taxation when states entered the field of ordinary business operations. Nongovernmental functions are taxed in the same manner as private businesses. South Carolina v. United States, 199 U.S. 437 (1905). The doctrine was shaken in 1928 when four Justices dissented against a rigid application of reciprocal tax immunity. In one of the dissents, Justice Holmes remarked: "The power to tax is not the power to destroy while this Court sits." Panhandle Oil Co. v. Knox, 277 U.S. 218, 223 (1928). By 1939, the Court decided to overrule *Collector* v. *Day* to the extent that it recognized "an implied constitutional immunity from income taxation of the salaries of officers or employees of the national or a state government or their instrumentalities." Graves v. N.Y. ex rel. O'Keefe, 306 U.S. 466, 486 (1939).[9]

Congressional legislation also changed the substance of intergovernmental tax immunity. Beginning in 1864, Congress allowed the states to tax certain activities of national banks. 13 Stat. 111 (1864); see 12 U.S.C. § 548 (1982). Any changes in state taxation of national banks must come from Congress, not from the courts. First Agricultural Nat'l Bank v. State Tax Comm'n, 392 U.S. 339, 346 (1968). Recent decisions have struck down state taxes on military installations operated by the federal government, but the judgment in these cases turned not on abstract constitutional doctrines but on congressional intent (the Buck Act of 1940).[10]

A decision in 1989 struck down state laws that impose discriminatory taxes on state and federal workers. Michigan taxed federal government pensions but exempted state and local government retirees. The 8–1 ruling will require costly refunds by more than a dozen states, especially Virginia. Davis v. Michigan Dept. of Treasury, 109 S.Ct. 1500 (1989).

PREEMPTION AND ABSTENTION

Federal-state relationships are shaped by two cross-cutting doctrines. Under the preemption doctrine, certain matters have such a national character that federal laws must supersede state laws. The abstention doctrine works in the opposite direction. As an exercise of discretionary authority, federal courts relinquish jurisdiction under various circumstances in order to avoid needless friction with the administration of state affairs. Both doctrines are complex and change over time.

The Preemption Doctrine

The preemption doctrine draws its force from the Supremacy Clause of Article VI of the Constitution, which declares that all laws made in pursuance to the Constitution and all treaties made under the authority of the United States shall be the "supreme

---

[9]See also Massachusetts v. United States, 435 U.S. 444 (1978); New York v. United States, 326 U.S. 572 (1946); Helvering v. Gerhardt, 304 U.S. 405 (1938); Brush v. Commissioner, 300 U.S. 352 (1937); United States v. California, 297 U.S. 187 (1936); Helvering v. Powers, 293 U.S. 214 (1934); Ohio v. Helvering, 292 U.S. 360 (1934).

[10]United States v. Tax Comm'n of Mississippi, 421 U.S. 599 (1975); United States v. State Tax Comm'n of Mississippi, 412 U.S. 363 (1973). Massachusetts v. United States, 435 U.S. 444 (1978), held that a registration tax by Congress in the Airport and Airway Revenue Act of 1970 did not violate the tax immunity of states. South Carolina v. Baker, 108 S.Ct. 1355 (1988), upheld a congressional statute that removed the federal tax exemption for interest earned on nonregistered (bearer) state and local bonds. A state sales or use tax on a federal bankruptcy liquidation sale has been upheld. California Equalization Bd. v. Sierra Summit, 109 S.Ct. 2228 (1989).

Law of the Land." Federal actions of this character are superior to any conflicting provision of a state constitution or law. When Congress exercises its express powers, as it does by adopting uniform laws of bankruptcy, national legislation preempts state legislation. Perez v. Campbell, 402 U.S. 637 (1971). If compliance with both federal and state regulations in interstate commerce is a physical impossibility, federal law also preempts state law. Florida Lime & Avocado Growers, Inc. v. Paul, 373 U.S. 132, 142–143 (1963).

The preemption doctrine also covers powers not expressly stated. In the area of foreign affairs, including regulation of aliens, state statutes may not stand "as an obstacle to the accomplishment and execution of the full purposes and objectives of Congress." Hines v. Davidowitz, 312 U.S. 52, 67 (1941). In 1956, the Supreme Court invalidated a state sedition law because the Smith Act, passed by Congress, regulated the same subject. The Court concluded that it had been the intent of Congress to occupy the whole field of sedition. PENNSYLVANIA v. NELSON, 350 U.S. 497, 504. The author of the Smith Act promptly denied that he had ever intended the result reached by the Court. Congressional committees reported legislation to permit federal-state concurrent jurisdiction in the area of sedition and subversion, and to prohibit courts from using intent or implication to decide preemption (see debate on pp. 453–455).[11] Although these bills were never enacted, in the midst of their consideration the Court held that a state could investigate subversive activities against itself. To this extent state and federal sedition laws could coexist. Uphaus v. Wyman, 360 U.S. 72, 76 (1959). A potential legislative-judicial clash was averted. Outside the area of sedition, in matters affecting foreign affairs and international relations, the courts have excluded state involvement. Zschernig v. Miller, 389 U.S. 429, 436 (1968). However, state governments maintain direct contact with both private and government officials in foreign countries in order to promote export trade and foreign investments.

Congress has used its preemption power to regulate major areas of environmental law. The Water Quality Act of 1965, the Air Quality Act of 1967, and the Clean Water Act of 1972 illustrate this trend toward national standards. States can attempt to forestall federal controls by forming interstate compacts to handle problems of a regional nature. These compacts, however, require the approval of Congress if they tend to increase the political power of the states or encroach upon the Supremacy Clause. Cuyler v. Adams, 449 U.S. 433, 440 (1981).

The field of nuclear energy has been largely preempted by Congress, especially over questions of safety and plant construction. States retain authority over economic questions, such as the need for additional plants, the type of facility to be licensed, land use, and setting rates. Pacific Gas & Elec. v. Energy Resources Comm'n, 461 U.S. 190, 212 (1983). The exclusive authority of the federal government over safety questions was compromised a year later when the Court allowed a jury to award punitive damages against a company in a case where Karen Silkwood, a laboratory analyst, was contaminated by plutonium. Silkwood v. Kerr-McGee Corp., 464 U.S. 238 (1984). Recent preemption cases involve pension plans. In response to pension benefits lost by employees because of bankruptcies, mergers, and theft, Congress passed the Employee Retirement Income Security Act of 1974

[11]H. Rept. No. 2576, 84th Cong., 2d Sess. (1956); S. Rept. No. 2117, 84th Cong., 2d Sess. (1956); S. Rept. No. 2230, 84th Cong., 2d Sess. (1956); H. Rept. No. 1878, 85th Cong., 2d Sess. (1958); 104 Cong. Rec. 13844–13865, 13993–14023, 14138–14162 (1958); H. Rept. No. 422, 86th Cong., 1st Sess. (1959); 105 Cong. Rec. 11486–11508, 11625–11667, 11789–11808 (1959).

(ERISA). With certain exceptions, the statute preempts all state laws that "relate to" any employee benefit plan. The Supreme Court has given a broad reading to the statute's preemption clause.[12]

The dominant role of Congress in determining preemption was emphasized by Justice Rehnquist in 1986 during his confirmation hearings to be Chief Justice. He said that Congress "is probably the ultimate decider as to what the proper relationship between State and Federal law is in most situations. . . . How much is going to be Federal law in any area in which the Congress power reaches and how much is going to be State law, really in the last analysis, depends upon Congress." "Nomination of Justice William Hubbs Rehnquist," hearings before the Senate Committee on the Judiciary, 99th Cong., 2d Sess., 131 (1986).

The Abstention Doctrine

The abstention doctrine helps refute the periodic, apocalyptic announcements that "federalism is dead." To cultivate comity and mutual respect between the national and state levels, federal courts abstain in some areas. It would be impossible and self-destructive for federal courts to intervene in every state matter. The policy of abstention can be traced back to a congressional statute in 1793: "nor shall a writ of injunction [by federal courts] be granted to stay proceedings in any court of a state." 1 Stat. 335, § 5.

The Fourteenth Amendment opened the door to a much larger federal role. After the Supreme Court in *Ex parte Young* (1908) suggested that federal courts would intervene extensively in state affairs, Congress acted to limit judicial interference. Instead of allowing a single federal judge to strike down a state statute or enjoin its operation, Congress required a three-judge court to hear and decide such actions.[13] The policy of abstention crystallized as court doctrine in 1941. A unanimous Supreme Court held that it should withhold judgment until state courts reach a definitive construction of a state statute. Federal courts should avoid "needless friction with state policies" and promote "harmonious relation between state and federal authority" by waiting until the highest state court has disposed of a constitutional issue. Railroad Commission v. Pullman, 312 U.S. 496, 500–501. Acting under this authority, the Supreme Court has returned cases to state courts to permit interpretation of questions that were not considered or resolved.[14]

Abstention is a general policy and can be waived. Abstention is inappropriate where state statutes are vulnerable on their face for abridging free expression or discouraging protected activities. Federal courts intervene in these cases to prevent state officials from invoking a statute in bad faith, with no hope for success, simply to harass minorities or their organizations. This exception to the abstention doctrine is aimed at statutes that are so vague or overbroad that they threaten First Amendment

---

[12]Metropolitan Life Ins. Co. v. Massachusetts, 471 U.S. 724 (1985); Shaw v. Delta Air Lines, 463 U.S. 85 (1983); Alessi v. Raybestos-Manhattan, Inc., 451 U.S. 504 (1981). Other preemption cases include California Coastal Comm'n v. Granite Rock Co., 107 S.Ct. 1419 (1987); Exxon Corp. v. Governor of Maryland, 437 U.S. 117 (1978); Ray v. Atlantic Richfield Co., 435 U.S. 151 (1978). For a case in which federal regulations did not preempt state and local regulation because Congress had not expressed that intent, see Hillsborough County v. Automated Medical Labs, 471 U.S. 707 (1985).

[13]36 Stat. 557, § 17 (1910); 36 Stat. 1162, § 266 (1911); 37 Stat. 1013 (1913); 38 Stat. 220 (1913). These statutes are codified at 28 U.S.C. § 2284 (1982).

[14]Reetz v. Bozanich, 397 U.S. 82 (1970); Henry v. Mississippi, 379 U.S. 443 (1965); Meridian v. Southern Bell T. & T. Co., 358 U.S. 639 (1959); Musser v. Utah, 333 U.S. 95 (1948).

freedoms. Dombrowski v. Pfister, 380 U.S. 479 (1965); Zwickler v. Koota, 389 U.S. 241 (1967). In the case of a pending state criminal proceeding, however, federal courts intervene only under extraordinary circumstances: where the danger of irreparable loss is both great and immediate, and where the threat to federally protected rights cannot be eliminated during the course of the trial. Younger v. Harris, 401 U.S. 37 (1971); Samuels v. Mackell, 401 U.S. 66 (1971). The policy of noninterference also applies to certain state civil proceedings. Huffman v. Pursue, Ltd., 420 U.S. 592 (1975).[15]

Noninterference by the Supreme Court often provokes biting dissents that regard federalism as a cloak used to cover constitutional violations by state officials. Justice Brennan, for example, remarked: "Under the banner of vague, undefined notions of equity, comity, and federalism, the Court has embarked upon the dangerous course of condoning both isolated . . . and systematic . . . violations of civil liberties." Juidice v. Vail, 430 U.S. 327, 346 (1977). See also the dissents in Paul v. Davis, 424 U.S. 693 (1976), and Rizzo v. Goode, 423 U.S. 362 (1976).

In addition to congressional statutes that require three-judge federal courts to hear and decide certain state actions, Congress also prohibits a federal court from granting an injunction to stay proceedings in a state court "except as expressly authorized by Act of Congress, or where necessary in aid of its jurisdiction, or to protect or effectuate its judgments." 28 U.S.C. § 2283 (1982). See Mitchum v. Foster, 407 U.S. 225 (1972).

NATIONALIZATION OF THE BILL OF RIGHTS

Two months before the First Congress met, James Madison supported constitutional amendments to provide "for all essential rights, particularly the rights of Conscience in the fullest latitude, the freedom of the press, trials by jury, security against general warrants &c." 5 The Writings of James Madison 320 (letter to George Eve, Jan. 2, 1789). The responsibility for moving these amendments through the House of Representatives fell to Madison, who argued that a Bill of Rights would remove apprehensions that the people felt toward the new national government. 1 Annals of Congress 431–433 (1789). He also wanted to place restrictions on the states and proposed that "No State shall violate the equal rights of conscience, of the freedom of the press, or the trial by jury in criminal cases." Id. at 435. The states "are as liable to attack these invaluable privileges as the General Government . . ." Id. at 441. As finally drafted and ratified, however, the first ten amendments to the Constitution— the Bill of Rights—limited only the federal government.

In 1833, the Supreme Court explicitly held that the Bill of Rights restrained only the federal government, not the states. At issue was the Just Compensation Clause of the Fifth Amendment. Barron v. Baltimore, 32 U.S. (7 Pet.) 243. The Civil War and passage of the Fourteenth Amendment in 1868 worked a fundamental change in federal-state relations. The Amendment prohibited states from making or enforcing any law "which shall abridge the privileges or immunities of citizens of the United States; nor shall any State deprive any person of life, liberty, or property, without

---

[15]For other cases governing federal court supervision of state courts, see Middlesex Ethics Comm. v. Garden State Bar Assn., 457 U.S. 423 (1982); Fair Assessment in Real Estate Assn. v. McNary, 454 U.S. 100 (1981); Moore v. Sims, 422 U.S. 415 (1979); Colorado River Water Cons. Dist. v. United States, 424 U.S. 800 (1976); Doran v. Salem Inn, Inc., 422 U.S. 922 (1975); Hicks v. Miranda, 422 U.S. 332 (1975); MTM, Inc. v. Baxley, 420 U.S. 799 (1975); Gonzales v. Employees Credit Union, 419 U.S. 90 (1974); Steffel v. Thompson, 415 U.S. 452 (1974); North Dakota Pharmacy Bd. v. Snyder's Stores, 414 U.S. 156 (1973).

due process of law; nor deny to any person within its jurisdiction the equal protection of the laws." The Due Process Clause would become the vehicle for applying most of the Bill of Rights to the states.

The idea of imposing a national standard on the states was rejected by the Supreme Court in 1873 when it held that the primary purpose of the Civil War amendments (the Thirteenth, Fourteenth, and Fifteenth Amendments) was to guarantee freedom for blacks. Moreover, privileges and immunities were to be protected by the states, not the national government. Slaughter-House Cases, 16 Wall. 36, 77–79. Other decisions during this period also refused to apply the Bill of Rights to the states.[16] However, the Equal Protection Clause of the Fourteenth Amendment was available to prevent states from acting in a discriminatory or arbitrary manner. Yick Wo v. Hopkins, 118 U.S. 356 (1886).

By the end of the century, the Court had decided that certain portions of the Bill of Rights should be applied to the states. The Court began with the Just Compensation Clause of the Fifth Amendment, reflecting the judiciary's commitment at that time to business and corporate interests. Missouri Pacific Railway Co. v. Nebraska, 164 U.S. 403 (1896); Chicago, B. & Q. Railway Co. v. Chicago, 166 U.S. 226 (1897). Thus began the process of "incorporating" the Bill of Rights in the Due Process Clause of the Fourteenth Amendment and extending these guarantees to the states. Although in 1904 the Court held that the Confrontation Clause of the Sixth Amendment did not apply to the states (West v. Louisiana, 194 U.S. 258), and four years later refused to extend the Self-Incrimination Clause of the Fifth Amendment to the states (Twining v. New Jersey, 211 U.S. 78), within a few decades the Court began the step-by-step process of bringing the states under the Bill of Rights. Almost every provision of the Bill of Rights now covers the states (see Table 1). This process is sometimes called the doctrine of absorption or the selective incorporation of the Bill of Rights.

Selective incorporation reflects a contest between two schools of thought. Justice Harlan II believed that courts have a duty to see that due process follows principles consistent with the people's "traditions and conscience." In re Gault, 387 U.S. 1, 67 (1967). Justice Black opposed this philosophy because it requires judges to impose personal notions of natural law. Duncan v. Louisiana, 391 U.S. 145, 168 (1968). To limit judicial activism, at least in the incremental form supported by Harlan, Black promoted the wholesale incorporation of the Bill of Rights. ADAMSON v. CALIFORNIA, 332 U.S. 46, 75 (1947). Almost all of the Bill of Rights has been incorporated, with little current opposition from members of the Supreme Court (pp. 461–463).

The selective incorporation of the Bill of Rights does not mean that a national standard has been forced upon the states. For example, the First Amendment applies to all states, and yet court rulings on obscenity allow wide discretion to accommodate local community standards. Miller v. California, 413 U.S. 15, 30–34 (1973). The

---

[16]Pervear v. Commonwealth, 5 Wall. (72 U.S.) 475 (1867); Twitchell v. The Commonwealth, 7 Wall. (74 U.S.) 321 (1869); The Justices v. Murray, 9 Wall. (76 U.S.) 274 (1870); Walker v. Saüvinet, 92 U.S. (2 Otto.) 90, 92 (1876); United States v. Cruikshank, 92 U.S. 542, 552 (1876); Hurtado v. California, 110 U.S. 516, 538 (1884); Presser v. Illinois, 116 U.S. 252, 265 (1886); Spies v. Illinois, 123 U.S. 131, 166 (1887); In re Kemmler, 136 U.S. 436, 446 (1890); McElvaine v. Brush, 142 U.S. 155, 158 (1891); O'Neil v. Vermont, 144 U.S. 323, 332 (1892). See also Maxwell v. Dow, 176 U.S. 581 (1900), which declined to apply the guarantees of the Fifth and Sixth Amendments to the states.

TABLE 1   Incorporation of Bill of Rights

Amendment	Clause	Decision
First	Congress shall make no law respecting an establishment of religion, . . .	Everson v. Board of Education, 330 U.S. 1, 15 (1947).
	or prohibiting the free exercise thereof; . . .	Cantwell v. Connecticut, 310 U.S. 296, 303 (1940).
	or abridging the freedom of speech, . . .	Gitlow v. New York, 268 U.S. 652, 666 (1925); Fiske v. Kansas, 274 U.S. 380, 387 (1927).
	or of the press; . . .	Near v. Minnesota, 283 U.S. 697, 707 (1931). See also Gitlow v. New York, 268 U.S. 652, 666 (1925).
	or the right of the people peaceably to assemble, and to petition the Government for a redress of grievances.	DeJonge v. Oregon, 299 U.S. 352, 364 (1937).
Second	A well regulated Militia, being necessary to the security of a free State, the right of the people to keep and bear arms, shall not be infringed.	——
Third	No soldier shall, in time of peace be quartered in any house, without the consent of the Owner, nor in time of war, but in a manner to be prescribed by law.	——
Fourth	The right of the people to be secure in their persons, houses, papers, and effects, against unreasonable searches and seizures, shall not be violated, and no Warrants shall issue, but upon probable cause, supported by Oath or affirmation, and partiularly describing the place to be searched, and the persons or things to be seized.	Wolf v. Colorado, 338 U.S. 25, 27–28 (1949); Mapp v. Ohio, 367 U.S. 643, 655 (1961); Ker v. California, 374 U.S. 23 (1963).
Fifth	No person shall be held to answer for a capital, or otherwise infamous crime, unless on a presentment or indictment of a Grand Jury, except in cases arising in the land or naval forces, or in the Militia, when in actual service in time of War or public danger; . . .	——
	nor shall any person be subject for the same offence to be twice put in jeopardy of life or limb; . . .	Benton v. Maryland, 395 U.S. 784, 787 (1969).
	nor shall be compelled in any Criminal Case to be a witness against himself; . . .	Malloy v. Hogan, 378 U.S. 1, 3 (1964).
	nor be deprived of life, liberty, or property, without due process of law; . . .	[Parallel to Fourteenth Amendment.]
	nor shall private property be taken for public use, without just compensation.	Missouri Pacific Railway Co. v. Nebraska, 164 U.S. 403, 417 (1896); Chicago, B. &

TABLE 1   **Incorporation of Bill of Rights (*Continued*)**

Amendment	Clause	Decision
		Q. R.R. Co. v. Chicago, 166 U.S. 226, 241 (1897).
Sixth	In all criminal prosecutions, the accused shall enjoy the right to a speedy and public trial, . . .	In re Oliver, 333 U.S. 257, 273 (1948) [right to public trial] and Klopfer v. North Carolina, 386 U.S. 213, 222 (1967) [right to speedy trial.]
	by an impartial jury of the State and district wherein the crime shall have been committed, which district shall have been previously ascertained by law, and to be informed of the nature and cause of the accusation; . . .	Duncan v. Louisiana, 391 U.S. 145, 149 (1968); Parker v. Gladden, 385 U.S. 363, 364 (1966). See also Irvin v. Dowd, 366 U.S. 717 (1961) and Turner v. Louisiana, 379 U.S. 466 (1965).
	to be confronted with the witness against him; . . .	Pointer v. Texas, 380 U.S. 400, 403 (1965).
	to have compulsory process for obtaining witnesses in his favor; . . .	Washington v. Texas, 388 U.S. 14, 19 (1967).
	and to have the Assistance of Counsel for his defence.	Powell v. Alabama, 287 U.S. 45, 67–68 (1932) [counsel for young and illiterate in a capital case]; Gideon v. Wainright, 372 U.S. 335, 344 (1963) [counsel for felony trials]; Douglas v. California, 372 U.S. 353, 357–358 (1963) [counsel for first appeals]; Argersinger v. Hamlin, 407 U.S. 25 (1972) [counsel for felony or misdemeanor trials involving jail term].
Seventh	In suits at common law, where the value in Controversy shall exceed twenty dollars, the right of trial by jury shall be preserved, and no fact tried by a jury, shall be otherwise re-examined in any Court of the United States, than according to the rules of the common law.	——
Eighth	Excessive bail shall not be required . . .	Schilb v. Kuebel, 404 U.S. 357, 365 (1971).
	nor excessive fines imposed . . .	——
	nor cruel and unusual punishment inflicted.	Robinson v. California, 370 U.S. 660, 666 (1962).
Ninth	The enumeration in the Constitution, of certain rights, shall not be construed to deny or disparage others retained by the people.	Griswold v. Connecticut, 381 U.S. 479, 484 (1965) [also invoked other parts of the Bill of Rights].
Tenth	The powers not delegated to the United States by the Constitution, nor prohibited by it to the States, are reserved to the States respectively, or to the people.	——

right to a jury trial applies to the states, but states are at liberty to depart from federal standards by establishing juries with less than twelve members and by accepting nonunanimous verdicts (pp. 789–790). Also, state courts can insulate themselves from national standards by basing their rulings not on the U.S. Constitution but on rights guaranteed in their state constitutions. State courts are able to interpret individual liberties more expansively than the federal government. PruneYard Shopping Center v. Robins, 447 U.S. 74, 81 (1980); Collins et al., 13 Hast. Const. L. Q. 599 (1986). Subsequent chapters will offer many specific examples where state courts reject doctrines issued by the U.S. Supreme Court.

CONCLUSIONS

Areas in which state and local governments were once virtually supreme, including agriculture, mining, manufacturing, and labor, eventually gave way to federal controls when transportation systems and economic markets assumed a national character. Over time, much of intrastate commerce became interstate commerce. Other areas long identified with local government, including education, health, welfare, and law enforcement, are now largely a matter of federal-state cooperation. The federal taxing power, magnified by the Sixteenth Amendment and the income tax, ushered in hundreds of federal grant programs.

Questions of federalism, state immunity from suit, the commerce and taxing powers, preemption, and abstention call for the highest legal talents by states to defend their interests. State governments recognized that they were being poorly represented in cases argued before the Supreme Court. The briefs and oral arguments by state attorneys general were generally outmatched by groups challenging state practices. In 1983, a State and Local Legal Center was established in Washington, D.C., to coordinate strategy, sharpen advocacy skills, and prepare amicus briefs. The National Association of Attorneys General (NAAG) is also available to assist with litigation strategy. A National Center for State Courts was established in Williamsburg, Virginia, in 1971. The intervention of various groups and interests have helped hammer out the changing dimensions of federal-state relations.

Although litigation continues to define federal-state relations, it operates mostly at the margins. Basic questions of federalism are left to the determination of Congress. During his confirmation hearings in 1986 to be Associate Justice to the Supreme Court, Antonin Scalia testified that "the primary defender of the constitutional balance, the Federal Government versus the states . . . the primary institution to strike the right balance is the Congress. . . . on the basis of the court's past decisions . . . the main protection for that is in the policymaking area, is in the Congress. The court's struggles to prescribe what is the proper role of the Federal Government vis-à-vis the State have essentially been abandoned for quite a while." "Nomination of Judge Antonin Scalia," hearings before the Senate Committee on the Judiciary, 99th Cong., 2d Sess., 81–82 (1986).

Selected Readings

ABRAMS, KATHRYN. "On Reading and Using the Tenth Amendment." 93 *Yale Law Journal* 723 (1984).
ALFANGE, DEAN, JR. "Congressional Regulation of the 'States Qua States': From National League of Cities to EEOC v. Wyoming." 1983 *Supreme Court Review* 215.

ANDERSON, WILLIAM. *The Nation and the States: Rivals or Partners?* Minneapolis: University of Minnesota Press, 1955.

BENSON, PAUL R., JR. *The Supreme Court and the Commerce Clause, 1937–1970.* New York: Dunellen, 1970.

BRENNAN, WILLIAM J., JR. "The Bill of Rights and the States." 36 *New York University Law Review* 761 (1961).

BRIGHTON, ROBERT CHARLES, JR. "Separating Myth from Reality in Federalism Decisions: A Perspective of American Federalism—Past and Present." 35 *Vanderbilt Law Review* 161 (1982).

CORWIN, EDWARD S. *The Commerce Power Versus States, Rights.* Princeton, N.J.: Princeton University Press, 1936.

——. "The Passing of Dual Federalism." 36 *Virginia Law Review* 1 (1950).

FAIRMAN, CHARLES. "Does the Fourteenth Amendment Incorporate the Bill of Rights?" 2 *Stanford Law Review* 5 (1949).

FISHER, LOUIS. "How the States Shape Constitutional Law." 15 *State Legislatures* 37 (August 1989).

GIBBONS, JOHN J. "The Eleventh Amendment and State Sovereign Immunity: A Reinterpretation." 83 *Columbia Law Review* 1889 (1983).

GREEN, JOHN RAYBURN. "The Bill of Rights, the Fourteenth Amendment, and the Supreme Court." 46 *Michigan Law Review* 869 (1948).

HENKIN, LOUIS. " 'Selective Incorporation' in the Fourteenth Amendment." 73 *Yale Law Journal* 74 (1963).

HOWARD, A. E. DICK. "The States and the Supreme Court." 31 *Catholic University Law Review* 380 (1982).

LOFGREN, CHARLES A. "The Origins of the Tenth Amendment: History, Sovereignty, and the Problem of Constitutional Intention," in Ronald K. L. Collins, ed., *Constitutional Government in America.* Durham, N.C.: Carolina Academic Press, 1980.

MICHELMAN, FRANK I. "States' Rights and States' Roles: Permutations of 'Sovereignty' in *National League of Cities* v. *Usery.*" 86 *Yale Law Journal* 1165 (1977).

MORRISON, STANLEY. "Does the Fourteenth Amendment Incorporate the Bill of Rights?" 2 *Stanford Law Review* 140 (1949).

NAGEL, ROBERT F. "Federalism as a Fundamental Value: National League of Cities in Perspective." 1981 *Supreme Court Review* 81.

NEUBORNE, BURT. "The Myth of Parity." 90 *Harvard Law Review* 1105 (1977).

SCHMIDHAUSER, JOHN R. *The Supreme Court as Final Arbiter in Federal-State Relations, 1789–1957.* Chapel Hill: University of North Carolina Press, 1958.

SHAPIRO, DAVID L. "Wrong Terms: The Eleventh Amendment and the *Pennhurst* Case." 98 *Harvard Law Review* 61 (1984).

VILE, M.J.C. *The Structure of American Federalism.* London: Oxford University Press, 1961.

WELLS, MICHAEL. "The Role of Comity in the Law of Federal Courts." 60 *North Carolina Law Review* 59 (1981).

McCulloch v. Maryland

17 U.S. (4 Wheat.) 315 (1819)

Congress passed legislation in 1816 to create a Bank of the United States. The power to incorporate a national bank is not expressly granted in the Constitution. One issue, therefore, was whether an implied power existed, and here Chief Justice Marshall supplies a classic interpretation of the meaning of the Constitution. In 1818, Maryland passed legislation to impose a tax on all banks, or branches of banks, in the state not chartered by the legislature. James W. McCulloch, the Bank's cashier in Baltimore, refused to pay the tax. The dispute gave Marshall an opportunity to define the relationship between the national government and the states.

March 7th, 1819. MARSHALL, Ch. J., delivered the opinion of the court.—In the case now to be determined, the defendant, a sovereign state, denies the obligation of a law enacted by the legisla-ture of the Union, and the plaintiff, on his part, contests the validity of an act which has been passed by the legislature of that state. The constitution of our country, in its most interesting and vital parts, is to be considered; the conflicting powers of the government of the Union and of its members, as marked in that constitution, are to be discussed; and an opinion given, which may essentially influence the great operations of the government. No tribunal can approach such a question without a deep sense of its importance, and of the awful responsibility involved in its decision. But it must be decided peacefully, or remain a source of hostile legislation, perhaps, of hostility of a still more serious nature; and if it is to be so decided, by this tribunal alone can the decision be made. On the supreme court of the United States has the constitution of our country devolved this important duty.

The first question made in the cause is—has congress power to incorporate a bank? It has been truly said, that this can scarcely be considered as an open question, entirely unprejudiced by the former proceedings of the nation respecting it. The principle now contested was introduced at a very early period of our history, has been recognised by many successive legislatures, and has been acted upon by the judicial department, in cases of peculiar delicacy, as a law of undoubted obligation.

It will not be denied, that a bold and daring usurpation might be resisted, after an acquiescence still longer and more complete than this. But it is conceived, that a doubtful question, one on which human reason may pause, and the human judgment be suspended, in the decision of which the great principles of liberty are not concerned, but the respective powers of those who are equally the representatives of the people, are to be adjusted; if not put at rest by the practice of the government, ought to receive a considerable impression from that practice. An exposition of the constitution, deliberately established by legislative acts, on the faith of which an immense property has been advanced, ought not to be lightly disregarded.

The power now contested was exercised by the first congress elected under the present constitution. The bill for incorporating the Bank of the United States did not steal upon an unsuspecting legislature, and pass unobserved. Its principle was completely understood, and was opposed with equal zeal and ability. After being resisted, first, in the fair and open field of debate, and afterwards, in the executive cabinet, with as much persevering talent as any measure has ever experienced, and being supported by arguments which convinced minds as pure and as intelligent as this country can boast, it became a law. The original act was permitted to expire; but a short experience of the embarrassments to which the refusal to revive it exposed the government, convinced those who were most prejudiced against the measure of its necessity, and induced the passage of the present law. It would require no ordinary share of intrepidity, to assert that a measure adopted under these circumstances, was a bold and plain usurpation, to which the constitution gave no countenance. These observations belong to the cause; but they are not made under the impression, that, were the question entirely new, the law would be found irreconcilable with the constitution.

In discussing this question, the counsel for the state of Maryland have deemed it of some importance, in the construction of the constitution, to consider that instrument, not as emanating from the people, but as the act of sovereign and independent states. The powers of the general government, it has been said, are delegated by the states, who alone are truly sovereign; and must be exercised in subordination to the states, who alone possess supreme dominion. It would be difficult to sustain this proposition. The convention which framed the constitution was indeed elected by the state legislatures. But the instrument, when it came from their hands, was a mere proposal, without obligation, or pretensions to it. It was reported to the then existing congress of the United States, with a request that it might "be submitted to a convention of delegates, chosen in each state by the people thereof, under the recommendation of its legislature, for their assent and ratification." This mode of proceeding was adopted; and by the convention, by congress, and by the state legislatures, the instrument was submitted to the *people*. They acted upon it in the only manner in which they can act safely, effectively and wisely, on such a subject, by assembling in convention. It is true, they assembled in their several states— and where else should they have assembled? No political dreamer was ever wild enough to think of breaking down the lines which separate the states, and of compounding the American people into one common mass. Of consequence, when they act, they act in their states. But the measures they adopt do not, on that account, cease to be the measures of the people themselves, or become the measures of the state governments.

From these conventions, the constitution derives its whole authority. The government proceeds directly from the people; is "ordained and established," in the name of the people; and is declared to be ordained, "in order to form a more perfect union, establish justice, insure domestic tranquility, and secure the blessings of liberty to themselves and to their posterity." The assent of the states, in their sovereign capacity, is implied, in calling a convention, and thus submitting that instrument to the people. But the people were at perfect liberty to accept or reject it; and their act was final. It required not the affirmance, and could not be negatived, by the state governments. The constitution, when thus adopted, was of complete obligation, and bound the state sovereignties.

. . .

This government is acknowledged by all, to be one of enumerated powers. The principle, that it can exercise only the powers granted to it, would seem too apparent, to have required to be enforced by all those arguments, which its enlightened friends, while it was depending before the people, found it necessary to urge; that principle is now universally admitted. But the question respecting the extent of the powers actually granted, is perpetually arising, and will probably continue to arise, so long as our system shall exist. In discussing these questions, the conflicting powers of the general and state governments must be brought into view, and the supremacy of their respective laws, when they are in opposition, must be settled.

If any one proposition could command the universal assent of mankind, we might expect it would be this—that the government of the Union, though limited in its powers, is supreme within its sphere of action. This would seem to result, necessarily, from its nature. It is the government of all; its powers are delegated by all; it represents all, and acts for all. Though any one state may be willing to control its operations, no state is willing to allow others to control them. The nation, on those subjects on which it can act, must necessarily bind its component parts. But this question is not left to mere reason: the people have, in express terms, decided it, by saying, "this constitution, and the laws of the United States, which shall be made in pursuance thereof," "shall be the supreme law of the land," and by requiring that the members of the state legislatures, and the officers of the executive and judicial departments of the states, shall take the oath of fidelity to it. The government of the United States, then, though limited in its powers, is supreme; and its laws, when made in pursuance of the constitution, form the supreme law of the land, "anything in the constitution or laws of any state to the contrary notwithstanding."

Among the enumerated powers, we do not find that of establishing a bank or creating a corporation. But there is no phrase in the instrument which, like the articles of confederation, excludes incidental or implied powers; and which requires that everything granted shall be expressly and minutely described. Even the 10th amendment, which was framed for the purpose of quieting the excessive jealousies which had been excited, omits the word "expressly," and declares only, that the powers "not delegated to the United States, nor prohibited to the states, are reserved to the states or to the people;" thus leaving the question, whether the particular power which may become the subject of contest, has been delegated to the one government, or prohibited to the other, to depend on a fair construction of the whole instrument. The men who drew and adopted this amendment had experienced the embarrassments resulting from the insertion of this word in the articles of confederation, and probably omitted it, to avoid those embarrassments. A constitution, to contain an accurate detail of all the subdivisions of which its great powers will admit, and of all the means by which they may be carried into execution, would partake of the prolixity of a legal code, and could scarcely be embraced by the human mind. It would, probably, never be understood by the public. Its nature, therefore, requires, that only its great outlines should be marked, its important objects designated, and the minor ingredients which compose those objects, be deduced from the nature of the objects themselves. That this idea was entertained by the framers of the American constitution, is not only to be inferred from the nature of the instrument, but from the language. Why else were some of the limitations, found in the 9th section of the 1st article, introduced? It is also, in some degree, warranted, by their having omitted to use any restrictive term which might prevent its receiving a fair and just interpretation. In considering this question, then, we must never forget that it is a *constitution* we are expounding.

Although, among the enumerated powers of government, we do not find the word "bank" or "incorporation," we find the great powers, to lay and collect taxes; to borrow money; to regulate commerce; to declare and conduct a war; and to raise and support armies and navies. The sword and the purse, all the external relations, and no inconsiderable portion of the industry of the nation, are intrusted to its government. It can never be pretended, that these vast powers draw after them others of inferior importance, merely because they are inferior. Such an idea can never be advanced. But it may with great reason be contended, that a government, intrusted with such ample powers, on the due execution of which the happiness and prosperity of the nation so vitally depends, must also be intrusted with ample means for their execution. The power being given, it is the interest of the nation to facilitate its execution. It can never be their interest, and cannot be presumed to have been their intention, to clog and embarrass its execution, by withholding the most appropriate means. Throughout this vast republic, from the St. Croix to the Gulf of Mexico, from the Atlantic to the Pacific, revenue is to be collected and expended, armies are to be marched and supported. The exigencies of the nation may require, that the treasure raised in the north should be transported to the south, that raised in the east, conveyed to the west, or that this order should be reversed. Is that construction of the constitution to be preferred, which would render these operations difficult, hazardous and expensive? Can we adopt that construction (unless the words imperiously require it), which would impute to the framers of that instrument, when

granting these powers for the public good, the intention of impeding their exercise, by withholding a choice of means? If, indeed, such be the mandate of the constitution, we have only to obey; but that instrument does not profess to enumerate the means by which the powers it confers may be executed; nor does it prohibit the creation of a corporation, if the existence of such a being be essential, to the beneficial exercise of those powers. It is, then, the subject of fair inquiry, how far such means may be employed.

. . .

. . . the constitution of the United States has not left the right of congress to employ the necessary means, for the execution of the powers conferred on the government, to general reasoning. To its enumeration of powers is added, that of making "all laws which shall be necessary and proper, for carrying into execution the foregoing powers, and all other powers vested by this constitution, in the government of the United States, or in any department thereof." The counsel for the state of Maryland have urged various arguments, to prove that this clause, though, in terms, a grant of power, is not so, in effect; but is really restrictive of the general right, which might otherwise be implied, of selecting means for executing the enumerated powers. In support of this proposition, they have found it necessary to contend, that this clause was inserted for the purpose of conferring on congress the power of making laws. That, without it, doubts might be entertained, whether congress could exercise its powers in the form of legislation.

But could this be the object for which it was inserted? A government is created by the people, having legislative, executive and judicial powers. Its legislative powers are vested in a congress, which is to consist of a senate and house of representatives. Each house may determine the rule of its proceedings; and it is declared, that every bill which shall have passed both houses, shall, before it becomes a law, be presented to the president of the United States. The 7th section describes the course of proceedings, by which a bill shall become a law; and, then, the 8th section enumerates the powers of congress. Could it be necessary to say, that a legislature should exercise legislative powers, in the shape of legislation?

After allowing each house to prescribe its own course of proceeding, after describing the manner in which a bill should become a law, would it have entered into the mind of a single member of the convention, that an express power to make laws was necessary, to enable the legislature to make them? That a legislature, endowed with legislative powers, can legislate, is a proposition too self-evident to have been questioned.

But the argument on which most reliance is placed, is drawn from that peculiar language of this clause. Congress is not empowered by it to make all laws, which may have relation to the powers conferred on the government, but such only as may be *"necessary and proper"* for carrying them into execution. The word *"necessary"* is considered as controlling the whole sentence, and as limiting the right to pass laws for the execution of the granted powers, to such as are indispensable, and without which the power would be nugatory. That it excludes the choice of means, and leaves to congress, in each case, that only which is most direct and simple.

Is it true, that this is the sense in which the word "necessary" is always used? Does it always import an absolute physical necessity, so strong, that one thing to which another may be termed necessary, cannot exist without that other? We think it does not. If reference be had to its use, in the common affairs of the world, or in approved authors, we find that it frequently imports no more than that one thing is convenient, or useful, or essential to another. To employ the means necessary to an end, is generally understood as employing any means calculated to produce the end, and not as being confined to those single means, without which the end would be entirely unattainable. . . .

Let this be done in the case under consideration. The subject is the execution of those great powers on which the welfare of a nation essentially depends. It must have been the intention of those who gave these powers, to insure, so far as human prudence could insure, their beneficial execution. This could not be done, by confiding the choice of means to such narrow limits as not to leave it in the power of congress to adopt any which might be appropriate, and which were conducive to the end. This provision is made in a

constitution, intended to endure for ages to come, and consequently, to be adapted to the various *crises* of human affairs. To have prescribed the means by which government should, in all future time, execute its powers, would have been to change, entirely, the character of the instrument, and give it the properties of a legal code. It would have been an unwise attempt to provide, by immutable rules, for exigencies which, if foreseen at all, must have been seen dimly, and which can be best provided for as they occur. To have declared, that the best means shall not be used, but those alone, without which the power given would be nugatory, would have been to deprive the legislature of the capacity to avail itself of experience, to exercise its reason, and to accommodate its legislation to circumstances.

. . .

[Marshall rejects Maryland's argument that the Necessary and Proper Clause was intended to abridge the powers of Congress.] 1st. The clause is placed among the powers of congress, not among the limitations on those powers. 2d. Its terms purport to enlarge, not to diminish the powers vested in the government. It purports to be an additional power, not a restriction on those already granted. No reason has been, or can be assigned, for thus concealing an intention to narrow the discretion of the national legislature, under words which purport to enlarge it. The framers of the constitution wished its adoption, and well knew that it would be endangered by its strength, not by its weakness. Had they been capable of using language which would convey to the eye one idea, and, after deep reflection, impress on the mind, another, they would rather have disguised the grant of power, than its limitation. If, then, their intention had been, by this clause, to restrain the free use of means which might otherwise have been implied, that intention would have been inserted in another place, and would have been expressed in terms resembling these. "In carrying into execution the foregoing powers, and all others," &c., "no laws shall be passed but such as are necessary and proper." Had the intention been to make this clause restrictive, it would unquestionably have been so in form as well as in effect.

The result of the most careful and attentive consideration bestowed upon this clause is, that if it does not enlarge, it cannot be construed to restrain the powers of congress, or to impair the right of the legislature to exercise its best judgment in the selection of measures to carry into execution the constitutional powers of the government. If no other motive for its insertion can be suggested, a sufficient one is found in the desire to remove all doubts respecting the right to legislate on that vast mass of incidental powers which must be involved in the constitution, if that instrument be not a splendid bauble.

We admit, as all must admit, that the powers of the government are limited, and that its limits are not to be transcended. But we think the sound construction of the constitution must allow to the national legislature that discretion, with respect to the means by which the powers it confers are to be carried into execution, which will enable that body to perform the high duties assigned to it, in the manner most beneficial to the people. Let the end be legitimate, let it be within the scope of the constitution, and all means which are appropriate, which are plainly adapted to that end, which are not prohibited, but consist with the letter and spirit of the constitution, are constitutional.

That a corporation must be considered as a means not less usual, not of higher dignity, not more requiring a particular specification than other means, has been sufficiently proved. If we look to the origin of corporations, to the manner in which they have been framed in that government from which we have derived most of our legal principles and ideas, or to the uses to which they have been applied, we find no reason to suppose, that a constitution, omitting, and wisely omitting, to enumerate all the means for carrying into execution the great powers vested in government, ought to have specified this. Had it been intended to grant this power, as one which should be distinct and independent, to be exercised in any case whatever, it would have found a place among the enumerated powers of the government. But being considered merely as a means, to be employed only for the purpose of carrying into execution the given powers, there could be no motive for particularly mentioning it.

. . .

After the most deliberate consideration, it is the unanimous and decided opinion of this court, that the act to incorporate the Bank of the United States is a law made in pursuance of the constitution, and is a part of the supreme·law of the land.

The branches, proceeding from the same stock, and being conducive to the complete accomplishment of the object, are equally constitutional. It would have been unwise, to locate them in the charter, and it would be unnecessarily inconvenient, to employ the legislative power in making those subordinate arrangements. The great duties of the bank are prescribed; those duties require branches; and the bank itself may, we think, be safely trusted with the selection of places where those branches shall be fixed; reserving always to the government the right to require that a branch shall be located where it may be deemed necessary.

It being the opinion of the court, that the act incorporating the bank is constitutional; and that the power of establishing a branch in the state of Maryland might be properly exercised by the bank itself, we proceed to inquire—

2. Whether the state of Maryland may, without violating the constitution, tax that branch? That the power of taxation is one of vital importance; that it is retained by the states; that it is not abridged by the grant of a similar power to the government of the Union; that it is to be concurrently exercised by the two governments—are truths which have never been denied. But such is the paramount character of the constitution, that is capacity to withdraw any subject from the action of even this power, is admitted. The states are expressly forbidden to lay any duties on imports or exports, except what may be absolutely necessary for executing their inspection laws. If the obligation of this prohibition must be conceded—if it may restrain a state from the exercise of its taxing power on imports and exports—the same paramount character would seem to restrain, as it certainly may restrain, a state from such other exercise of this power, as is in its nature incompatible with, and repugnant to, the constitutional laws of the Union. A law, absolutely repugnant to another, as entirely repeals that other as if express terms of repeal were used.

On this ground, the counsel for the bank place its claim to be exempted from the power of a state to tax its operations. There is no express provision for the case, but the claim has been sustained on a principle which so entirely pervades the constitution, is so intermixed with the materials which compose it, so interwoven with its web, so blended with its texture, as to be incapable of being separated from it, without rending it into shreds. This great principle is, that the constitution and the laws made in pursuance thereof are supreme; that they control the constitution and laws of the respective states, and cannot be controlled by them. From this, which may be almost termed an axiom, other propositions are deduced as corollaries, on the truth or error of which, and on their application to this case, the cause has been supposed to depend. These are, 1st. That a power to create implies a power to preserve: 2d. That a power to destroy, if wielded by a different hand, is hostile to, and incompatible with these powers to create and to preserve: 3d. That where this repugnancy exists, that authority which is supreme must control, not yield to that over which it is supreme.

These propositions, as abstract truths, would, perhaps, never be controverted. Their application to this case, however, has been denied; and both in maintaining the affirmative and the negative, a splendor of eloquence, and strength of argument, seldom, if ever, surpassed, have been displayed.

The power of congress to create, and of course, to continue, the bank, was the subject of the preceding part of this opinion; and is no longer to be considered as questionable. That the power of taxing it by the states may be exercised so as to destroy it, is too obvious to be denied. But taxation is said to be an absolute power, which acknowledges no other limits than those expressly prescribed in the constitution, and like sovereign power of every other description, is intrusted to the discretion of those who use it. But the very terms of this argument admit, that the sovereignty of the state, in the article of taxation itself, is subordinate to, and may be controlled by the constitution of the United States. How far it has been controlled by that instrument, must be a question of construction. In making this construction, no principle, not declared, can be admissi-

ble, which would defeat the legitimate operations of a supreme government. It is of the very essence of supremacy, to remove all obstacles to its action within its own sphere, and so to modify every power vested in subordinate governments, as to exempt its own operations from their own influence. This effect need not be stated in terms. It is so involved in the declaration of supremacy, so necessarily implied in it, that the expression of it could not make it more certain. We must, therefore, keep it in view, while construing the constitution.

. . .

The sovereignty of a state extends to everything which exists by its own authority, or is introduced by its permission; but does it extend to those means which are employed by congress to carry into execution powers conferred on that body by the people of the United States? We think it demonstrable, that it does not. Those powers are not given by the people of a single state. They are given by the people of the United States, to a government whose laws, made in pursuance of the constitution, are declared to be supreme. Consequently, the people of a single state cannot confer a sovereignty which will extend over them.

If we measure the power of taxation residing in a state, by the extent of sovereignty which the people of a single state possess, and can confer on its government, we have an intelligible standard, applicable to every case to which the power may be applied. We have a principle which leaves the power of taxing the people and property of a state unimpaired; which leaves to a state the command of all its resources, and which places beyond its reach, all those powers which are conferred by the people of the United States on the government of the Union, and all those means which are given for the purpose of carrying those powers into execution. We have a principle which is safe for the states, and safe for the Union. We are relieved, as we ought to be, from clashing sovereignty; from interfering powers; from a repugnancy between a right in one government to pull down, what there is an acknowledged right in another to build up; from the incompatibility of a right in one government to destroy, what there is a right in another to preserve. We are not driven to the perplexing inquiry, so unfit for the judicial department, what degree of taxation is the legitimate use, and what degree may amount to the abuse of the power. The attempt to use it on the means employed by the government of the Union, in pursuance of the constitution, is itself an abuse, because it is the usurpation of a power which the people of a single state cannot give. We find, then, on just theory, a total failure of this original right to tax the means employed by the government of the Union, for the execution of its powers. The right never existed, and the question whether it has been surrendered, cannot arise.

But, waiving this theory for the present, let us resume the inquiry, whether this power can be exercised by the respective states, consistently with a fair construction of the constitution? That the power to tax involves the power to destroy; that the power to destroy may defeat and render useless the power to create; that there is a plain repugnance in conferring on one government a power to control the constitutional measures of another, which other, with respect to those very measures, is declared to be supreme over that which exerts the control, are propositions not to be denied. But all inconsistencies are to be reconciled by the magic of the word *confidence*. Taxation, it is said, does not necessarily and unavoidably destroy. To carry it to the excess of destruction, would be an abuse, to presume which, would banish that confidence which is essential to all government. But is this a case of confidence? Would the people of any one state trust those of another with a power to control the most insignificant operations of their state government? We know they would not. Why, then, should we suppose, that the people of any one state should be willing to trust those of another with a power to control the operations of a government to which they have confided their most important and most valuable interests? In the legislature of the Union alone, are all represented. The legislature of the

Union alone, therefore, can be trusted by the people with the power of controlling measures which concern all, in the confidence that it will not be abused. This, then, is not a case of confidence, and we must consider it is as it really is.

If we apply the principle for which the state of Maryland contends, to the constitution, generally, we shall find it capable of changing totally the character of that instrument. We shall find it capable of arresting all the measures of the government, and of prostrating it at the foot of the states. The American people have declared their constitution and the laws made in pursuance thereof, to be supreme; but this principle would transfer the supremacy, in fact, to the states. If the states may tax one instrument, employed by the government in the execution of its powers, they may tax any and every other instrument. They may tax the mail; they may tax the mint; they may tax patent-rights; they may tax the papers of the custom-house; they may tax judicial process; they may tax all the means employed by the government, to an excess which would defeat all the ends of government. This was not intended by the American people. They did not design to make their government dependent on the states.

. . .

The court has bestowed on this subject its most deliberate consideration. The result is a conviction that the states have no power, by taxation or otherwise, to retard, impede, burden, or in any manner control, the operations of the constitutional laws enacted by congress to carry into execution the powers vested in the general government. This is, we think, the unavoidable consequence of that supremacy which the constitution has declared. We are unanimously of opinion, that the law passed by the legislature of Maryland, imposing a tax on the Bank of the United States, is unconstitutional and void.

. . .

Missouri v. Holland

252 U.S. 416 (1920)

The United States and Great Britain entered into a treaty in 1916 to protect migratory birds in the United States and Canada. Congress passed legislation in 1918 to enforce the treaty, providing for prohibitions on the killing, capturing, or selling any of the migratory birds included within the terms of the treaty, except as permitted by regulations compatible with the treaty. Ray P. Holland, U.S. Game Warden, threatened to arrest and prosecute citizens of Missouri for violating the Migratory Bird Treaty Act. Missouri claimed that the treaty and the statute invaded the rights reserved to the states by the Tenth Amendment.

MR. JUSTICE HOLMES delivered the opinion of the court.

This is a bill in equity brought by the State of Missouri to prevent a game warden of the United States from attempting to enforce the Migratory Bird Treaty Act of July 3, 1918, c. 128, 40 Stat. 755, and the regulations made by the Secretary of Agriculture in pursuance of the same. The ground of the bill is that the statute is an unconstitutional interference with the rights reserved to the States by the Tenth Amendment, and that the acts of the defendant done and threatened under that authority invade the sovereign right of the State and contravene its will manifested in statutes. The State also alleges a pecuniary interest, as owner of the wild birds within its borders and otherwise, admitted by the Government to be sufficient, but it is enough that the bill is a reasonable and proper means to assert the alleged quasi sovereign rights of a State. *Kansas* v. *Colorado*, 185 U. S. 125, 142. *Georgia* v. *Tennessee Copper Co.*, 206 U. S. 230, 237. *Marshall Dental Manufacturing Co.* v. *Iowa*, 226 U. S. 460, 462. A motion to dismiss was sustained by the District Court on the ground that the act of Congress is constitutional. 258 Fed. Rep. 479. Acc. *United States* v. *Thompson*, 258 Fed. Rep. 257; *United States* v. *Rockefeller*, 260 Fed. Rep. 346. The State appeals.

On December 8, 1916, a treaty between the United States and Great Britain was proclaimed by the President. It recited that many species of birds in their annual migrations traversed certain parts of the United States and of Canada, that they were of great value as a source of food and in destroying insects injurious to vegetation, but were in danger of extermination through lack of adequate protection. It therefore provided for specified close seasons and protection in other forms, and agreed that the two powers would take or propose to their law-making bodies the necessary measures for carrying the treaty out. 39 Stat. 1702. The above mentioned Act of July 3, 1918, entitled an act to give effect to the convention, prohibited the killing, capturing or selling any of the migratory birds included in the terms of the treaty except as permitted by regulations compatible with those terms, to be made by the Secretary of Agriculture. Regulations were proclaimed on July 31, and October 25, 1918. 40 Stat. 1812; 1863. It is unnecessary to go into any details, because, as we have said, the question raised is the general one whether the treaty and statute are void as an interference with the rights reserved to the States.

To answer this question it is not enough to refer to the Tenth Amendment, reserving the powers not delegated to the United States, because by Article II, § 2, the power to make treaties is delegated expressly, and by Article VI treaties made under the authority of the United States, along with the Constitution and laws of the United States made in pursuance thereof, are declared the supreme law of the land. If the treaty is valid there can be no dispute about the validity of the statute under Article I, § 8, as a necessary and proper means to execute the powers of the Government. The language of the Constitution as to the supremacy of treaties being general, the question before us is narrowed to an inquiry into the ground upon which the present supposed exception is placed.

It is said that a treaty cannot be valid if it infringes the Constitution, that there are limits, therefore, to the treatymaking power, and that one such limit is that what an act of Congress could not do unaided, in derogation of the powers reserved to the States, a treaty cannot do. An earlier act of Congress that attempted by itself and not in pursuance of a treaty to regulate the killing of migratory birds within the States had been held bad in the District Court. *United States* v. *Shauver,* 214 Fed. Rep. 154. *United States* v. *McCullagh,* 221 Fed. Rep. 288. Those decisions were supported by arguments that migratory birds were owned by the States in their sovereign capacity for the benefit of their people, and that under cases like *Geer* v. *Connecticut,* 161 U. S. 519, this control was one that Congress had no power to displace. The same argument is supposed to apply now with equal force.

Whether the two cases cited were decided rightly or not they cannot be accepted as a test of the treaty power. Acts of Congress are the supreme law of the land only when made in pursuance of the Constitution, while treaties are declared to be so when made under the authority of the United States. It is open to question whether the authority of the United States means more than the formal acts prescribed to make the convention. We do not mean to imply that there are no qualifications to the treaty-making power; but they must be ascertained in a different way. It is obvious that there may be matters of the sharpest exigency for the national well being that an act of Congress could not deal with but that a treaty followed by such an act could, and it is not lightly to be assumed that, in matters requiring national action, "a power which must belong to and somewhere reside in every civilized government" is not to be found. *Andrews* v. *Andrews,* 188 U.S. 14, 33. What was said in that case with regard to the powers of the States applies with equal force to the powers of the nation in cases where the States individually are incompetent to act. We are not yet discussing the particular case before us but only are considering the validity of the test proposed. With regard to that we may add that when we are dealing with words that also are a constituent act, like the

Constitution of the United States, we must realize that they have called into life a being the development of which could not have been foreseen completely by the most gifted of its begetters. It was enough for them to realize or to hope that they had created an organism; it has taken a century and has cost their successors much sweat and blood to prove that they created a nation. The case before us must be considered in the light of our whole experience and not merely in that of what was said a hundred years ago. The treaty in question does not contravene any prohibitory words to be found in the Constitution. The only question is whether it is forbidden by some invisible radiation from the general terms of the Tenth Amendment. We must consider what this country has become in deciding what that Amendment has reserved.

The State as we have intimated founds its claim of exclusive authority upon an assertion of title to migratory birds, an assertion that is embodied in statute. No doubt it is true that as between a State and its inhabitants the State may regulate the killing and sale of such birds, but it does not follow that its authority is exclusive of paramount powers. To put the claim of the State upon title is to lean upon a slender reed. Wild birds are not in the possession of anyone; and possession is the beginning of ownership. The whole foundation of the State's rights is the presence within their jurisdiction of birds that yesterday had not arrived, tomorrow may be in another State and in a week a thousand miles away. If we are to be accurate we cannot put the case of the State upon higher ground than that the treaty deals with creatures that for the moment are within the state borders, that it must be carried out by officers of the United States within the same territory, and that but for the treaty the State would be free to regulate this subject itself.

As most of the laws of the United States are carried out within the States and as many of them deal with matters which in the silence of such laws the State might regulate, such general grounds are not enough to support Missouri's claim. Valid treaties of course "are as binding within the territorial limits of the States as they are elsewhere throughout the dominion of the United States." *Baldwin* v. *Franks,* 120 U. S. 678, 683. No doubt the great body of private relations usually fall within the control of the State, but a treaty may override its power. We do not have to invoke the later developments of constitutional law for this proposition; it was recognized as early as *Hopkirk* v. *Bell*, 3 Cranch, 454, with regard to statutes of limitation, and even earlier, as to confiscation, in *Ware* v. *Hylton*, 3 Dall. 199. It was assumed by Chief Justice Marshall with regard to the escheat of land to the State in *Chirac* v. *Chirac*, 2 Wheat. 259, 275. *Hauenstein* v. *Lynham*, 100 U.S. 483. *Geofroy* v. *Riggs*, 133 U.S. 258. *Blythe* v. *Hinckley*, 180 U.S. 333, 340. So as to a limited jurisdiction of foreign consuls within a State. *Wildenhus's Case*, 120 U.S. 1. See *Ross* v. *McIntyre*, 140 U. S. 453. Further illustration seems unnecessary, and it only remains to consider the application of established rules to the present case.

Here a national interest of very nearly the first magnitude is involved. It can be protected only by national action in concert with that of another power. The subject-matter is only transitorily within the State and has no permanent habitat therein. But for the treaty and the statute there soon might be no birds for any powers to deal with. We see nothing in the Constitution that compels the Government to sit by while a food supply is cut off and the protectors of our forests and our crops are destroyed. It is not sufficient to rely upon the States. The reliance is vain, and were it otherwise, the question is whether the United States is forbidden to act. We are of opinion that the treaty and statute must be upheld. *Carey* v. *South Dakota*, 250 U. S. 118.

Decree affirmed.

MR. JUSTICE VAN DEVANTER and MR. JUSTICE PITNEY dissent.

Gibbons v. Ogden

22 U.S. (9 Wheat.) 1 (1824)

New York granted to Robert R. Livingston and Robert Fulton the exclusive privilege to operate steamboats on all waters within the jurisdiction of the state. Other states enacted similar laws, and soon friction emerged as states required out-of-state boats to pay substantial fees to be admitted. The retaliation that resulted was similar to the commercial warfare among the states prior to the adoption of the Constitution. This case involved the issue of whether New York could require a steamboat operating between New York and New Jersey to secure a New York license. Was this within the power of a state or did it infringe on the commerce power given to Congress? Thomas Gibbons and Aaron Ogden had been partners, operating a steamboat between New Jersey and New York, but they became antagonists in this tangled suit.

March 2d, 1824. MARSHALL, Ch. J., delivered the opinion of the court, and, after stating the case, proceeded as follows:—The appellant contends, that this decree is erroneous, because the laws which purport to give the exclusive privilege it sustains, are repugnant to the constitution and laws of the United States. They are said to be repugnant—1st. To that clause in the constitution which authorizes congress to regulate commerce.

2d. To that which authorizes congress to promote the progress of science and useful arts.

The state of New York maintains the constitutionality of these laws; and their legislature, their council of revision, and their judges, have repeatedly concurred in this opinion. It is supported by great names—by names which have all the titles to consideration that virtue, intelligence and office can bestow. No tribunal can approach the decision of this question, without feeling a just and real respect for that opinion which is sustained by such authority; but it is the province of this court, while it respects, not to bow to it implicitly; and the judges must exercise, in the examination of the subject, that understanding which Providence has bestowed upon them, with that independence which the people of the United States expect from this department of the government.

As preliminary to the very able discussions of the constitution, which we have heard from the bar, and as having some influence on its construction, reference has been made to the political situation of these states, anterior to its formation. It has been said, that they were sovereign, were completely independent, and were connected with each other only by a league. This is true. But when these allied sovereigns converted their league into a government, when they converted their congress of ambassadors, deputed to deliberate on their common concerns, and to recommend measures of general utility, into a legislature, empowered to enact laws on the most interesting subjects, the whole character in which the states appear, underwent a change, the extent of which must be determined by a fair consideration of the instrument by which that change was effected.

This instrument contains an enumeration of powers expressly granted by the people to their government. It has been said, that these powers ought to be construed strictly. But why ought they to be so construed? Is there one sentence in the constitution which gives countenance to this rule? In the last of the enumerated powers, that which grants, expressly, the means for carrying all others into execution, congress is authorized "to make all laws which shall be necessary and proper" for the purpose. But this limitation on the means which may be used, is not extended to the powers which are conferred; nor is there one sentence in the constitution, which has been pointed out by the gentlemen of the bar, or which we have been able to discern, that prescribes this rule. We do not, therefore, think ourselves justified in adopting it. What do gentlemen mean, by a strict construction? If they contend only against that enlarged construction, which would extend words

beyond their natural and obvious import, we might question the application of the term, but should not controvert the principle. If they contend for that narrow construction which, in support of some theory not to be found in the constitution, would deny to the government those powers which the words of the grant, as usually understood, import, and which are consistent with the general views and objects of the instrument—for that narrow construction, which would cripple the government, and render it unequal to the objects for which it is declared to be instituted, and to which the powers given, as fairly understood, render it competent—then we cannot perceive the propriety of this strict construction, nor adopt it as the rule by which the constitution is to be expounded. . . .

The words are, "congress shall have power to regulate commerce with foreign nations, and among the several states, and with the Indian tribes." The subject to be regulated is commerce; and our constitution being, as was aptly said at the bar, one of enumeration, and not of definition, to ascertain the extent of the power, it becomes necessary to settle the meaning of the word. The counsel for the appellee would limit it to traffic, to buying and selling, or the interchange of commodities, and do not admit that it comprehends navigation. This would restrict a general term, applicable to many objects, to one of its significations. Commerce, undoubtedly, is traffic, but it is something more—it is intercourse. It describes the commercial intercourse between nations, and parts of nations, in all its branches, and is regulated by prescribing rules for carrying on that intercourse. The mind can scarcely conceive a system for regulating commerce between nations, which shall exclude all laws concerning navigation, which shall be silent on the admission of the vessels of the one nation into the ports of the other, and be confined to prescribing rules for the conduct of individuals, in the actual employment of buying and selling, or of barter. If commerce does not include navigation, the government of the Union has no direct power over that subject, and can make no law prescribing what shall constitute American vessels, or requiring that they shall be navigated by American seamen. Yet this power has been exercised from the commencement of the government, has been exercised with the consent of all, and has been understood by all to be a commercial regulation. All America understands, and has uniformly understood, the word "commerce," to comprehend navigation. It was so understood, and must have been so understood, when the constitution was framed. The power over commerce, including navigation, was one of the primary objects for which the people of America adopted their government, and must have been contemplated in forming it. The convention must have used the word in that sense, because all have understood it in that sense; and the attempt to restrict it comes too late.

If the opinion that "commerce," as the word is used in the constitution, comprehends navigation also, requires any additional confirmation, that additional confirmation is, we think, furnished by the words of the instrument itself. It is a rule of construction, acknowledged by all, that the exceptions from a power mark its extent; for it would be absurd, as well as useless, to except from a granted power, that which was not granted—that which the words of the grant could not comprehend. If, then, there are in the constitution plain exceptions from the power over navigation, plain inhibitions to the exercise of that power in a particular way, it is a proof that those who made these exceptions, and prescribed these inhibitions, understood the power to which they applied as being granted. The 9th section of the last article declares, that "no preference shall be given, by any regulation of commerce or revenue, to the ports of one state over those of another." This clause cannot be understood as applicable to those laws only which are passed for the purposes of revenue, because it is expressly applied to commercial regulations; and the most obvious preference which can be given to one port over another, in regulating commerce, relates to navigation. But the subsequent part of the sentence is still more explicit. It is, "nor shall vessels bound to or from one state, be obliged to enter, clear or pay duties in another." These words have a direct reference to navigation.

The universally acknowledged power of the government to impose embargoes, must also be considered as showing, that all America is united in that construction which comprehends navigation in the word commerce. Gentlemen have said, in argument, that this is a branch of the war-making power, and that an embargo is an instrument of war, not a regulation of trade. That it may be, and often is, used as an instrument of war, cannot be denied. An embargo may be imposed, for the purpose of facilitating the equipment or manning of a fleet, or for the purpose of concealing the progress of an expedition preparing to sail from a particular port. In these, and in similar cases, it is a military instrument, and partakes of the nature of war. But all embargoes are not of this description. They are sometimes resorted to, without a view to war, and with a single view to commerce. In such case, an embargo is no more a war measure, than a merchantman is a ship of war, because both are vessels which navigate the ocean with sails and seamen. When congress imposed that embargo which, for a time, engaged the attention of every man in the United States, the avowed object of the law was, the protection of commerce, and the avoiding of war. By its friends and its enemies, it was treated as a commercial, not as a war measure. The persevering earnestness and zeal with which it was opposed, in a part of our country which supposed its interests to be vitally affected by the act, cannot be forgotten. . . .

The word used in the constitution, then, comprehends, and has been always understood to comprehend, navigation within its meaning; and a power to regulate navigation, is as expressly granted, as if that term had been added to the word "commerce." To what commerce does this power extend? The constitution informs us, to commerce "with foreign nations, and among the several states, and with the Indian tribes." It has, we believe, been universally admitted, that these words comprehend every species of commercial intercourse between the United States and foreign nations. No sort of trade can be carried on between this country and any other, to which this power does not extend. It has been truly said, that commerce, as the word is used in the constitution, is a unit, every part of which is indicated by the term.

If this be the admitted meaning of the word, in its application to foreign nations, it must carry the same meaning throughout the sentence, and remain a unit, unless there be some plain intelligible cause which alters it. The subject to which the power is next applied, is to commerce, "among the several states." The word "among" means intermingled with. A thing which is among others, is intermingled with them. Commerce among the states, cannot stop at the external boundary line of each state, but may be introduced into the interior. It is not intended to say, that these words comprehend that commerce, which is completely internal, which is carried on between man and man in a state, or between different parts of the same state, and which does not extend to or affect other states. Such a power would be inconvenient, and is certainly unnecessary. Comprehensive as the word "among" is, it may very properly be restricted to that commerce which concerns more states than one. The phrase is not one which would probably have been selected to indicate the completely interior traffic of a state, because it is not an apt phrase for that purpose; and the enumeration of the particular classes of commerce to which the power was to be extended, would not have been made, had the intention been to extend the power to every description. The enumeration presupposes something not enumerated; and that something, if we regard the language or the subject of the sentence, must be the exclusively internal commerce of a state.

. . .

But in regulating commerce with foreign nations, the power of congress does not stop at the jurisdictional lines of the several states. It would be a very useless power, if it could not pass those lines. The commerce of the United States with foreign nations, is that of the whole United States; every district has a right to participate in it. The deep streams which penetrate our country in every direction, pass through the interior of almost every state in the Union, and furnish the means of exercising this right. If congress has the power to regulate it, that power must be exercised whenever the subject exists. If it exists within the states, if a foreign voyage may commence or terminate at a port within a state, then the power of congress may be exercised within a state.

This principle is, if possible, still more clear, when applied to commerce "among the several

states." They either join each other, in which case they are separated by a mathematical line, or they are remote from each other, in which case other states lie between them. What is commerce "among" them; and how is it to be conducted? Can a trading expedition between two adjoining states, commence and terminate outside of each? And if the trading intercourse be between two states remote from each other, must it not commence in one, terminate in the other, and probably pass through a third? Commerce among the states must, of necessity, be commerce with the states. In the regulation of trade with the Indian tribes, the action of the law, especially, when the constitution was made, was chiefly within a state. The power of congress, then, whatever it may be, must be exercised within the territorial jurisdiction of the several states. The sense of the nation on this subject, is unequivocally manifested by the provisions made in the laws for transporting goods, by land, between Baltimore and Providence, between New York and Philadelphia, and between Philadelphia and Baltimore.

We are now arrived at the inquiry—what is this power? It is the power to regulate; that is, to prescribe the rule by which commerce is to be governed. This power, like all others vested in congress, is complete in itself, may be exercised to its utmost extent, and acknowledges no limitations, other than are prescribed in the constitution. These are expressed in plain terms, and do not affect the questions which arise in this case, or which have been discussed at the bar. If, as has always been understood, the sovereignty of congress, though limited to specified objects, is plenary as to those objects, the power over commerce with foreign nations, and among the several states, is vested in congress as absolutely as it would be in a single government, having in its constitution the same restrictions on the exercise of the power as are found in the constitution of the United States. The wisdom and the discretion of congress, their identity with the people, and the influence which their constituents possess at elections, are, in this, as in many other instances, as that, for example, of declaring war, the sole restraints on which they have relied, to secure them from its abuse. They are the restraints on which the people must often rely solely, in all representative governments. The power of congress, then, comprehends navigation, within the limits of every state in the Union; so far as that navigation may be, in any manner, connected with "commerce with foreign nations, or among the several states, or with the Indian tribes." It may, of consequence, pass the jurisdictional line of New York, and act upon the very waters to which the prohibition now under consideration applies.

. . .

. . . When . . . each government exercises the power of taxation, neither is exercising the power of the other. But when a state proceeds to regulate commerce with foreign nations, or among the several states, it is exercising the very power that is granted to congress, and is doing the very thing which congress is authorized to do. There is no analogy, then, between the power of taxation and the power of regulating commerce.

. . .

[Marshall concludes that the licenses for the steamboats operated by Gibbons, which were granted under an act of Congress, gave full authority to those vessels to navigate the waters of the United States, notwithstanding any law of New York to the contrary. Conflicting New York laws were unconstitutional and void.]

Powerful and ingenious minds, taking, as postulates, that the powers expressly granted to the government of the Union, are to be contracted, by construction, into the narrowest possible compass, and that the original powers of the states are retained, if any possible construction will retain them, may, by a course of well-digested, but refined and metaphysical reasoning, founded on these premises, explain away the constitution of our country, and leave it, a magnificent structure, indeed, to look at, but totally unfit for use. They may so entangle and perplex the understanding, as to obscure principles, which were before thought quite plain, and induce doubts where, if the mind were to pursue its own course, none would be perceived. In such a case, it is peculiarly necessary to recur to safe and fundamental principles, to sustain those principles, and, when sustained, to

make them the tests of the arguments to be examined.

JOHNSON, Justice.—The judgment entered by the court in this cause, has my entire approbation; but having adopted my conclusions on views of the subject materially different from those of my brethren, I feel it incumbent on me to exhibit those views. I have also another inducement: in questions of great importance and great delicacy, I feel my duty to the public best discharged, by an effort to maintain my opinions in my own way.

In attempts to construe the constitution, I have never found much benefit resulting from the inquiry, whether the whole, or any part of it, is to be construed strictly or liberally. The simple, classical, precise, yet comprehensive language in which it is couched, leaves, at most, but very little latitude for construction; and when its intent and meaning are discovered, nothing remains but to execute the will of those who made it, in the best manner to effect the purposes intended. The great and paramount purpose was, to unite this mass of wealth and power, for the protection of the humblest individual; his rights, civil and political, his interests and prosperity, are the sole end; the rest are nothing but the means. But the principal of those means, one so essential as to approach nearer the characteristics of an end, was the independence and harmony of the states, that they may the better subserve the purposes of cherishing and protecting the respective families of this great republic.

The strong sympathies, rather than the feeble government, which bound the states together during a common war, dissolved on the return of peace; and the very principles which gave rise to the war of the revolution, began to threaten the confederacy with anarchy and ruin. The states had resisted a tax imposed by the parent state, and now reluctantly submitted to, or altogether rejected, the moderate demands of the confederation. Every one recollects the painful and threatening discussions, which arose on the subject of the five per cent duty. Some states rejected it altogether; others insisted on collecting it themselves; scarcely any acquiesced without reservations which deprived it altogether of the character of a national measure; and at length, some repealed the laws by which they had signified their acquiescence.

For a century, the states had submitted, with murmurs, to the commercial restrictions imposed by the parent state; and now, finding themselves in the unlimited possession of those powers over their own commerce, which they had so long been deprived of, and so earnestly coveted, that selfish principle which, well controlled, is so salutary, and which, unrestricted, is so unjust and tyrannical, guided by inexperience and jealousy, began to show itself in iniquitous laws and impolitic measures, from which grew up a conflict of commercial regulations, destructive to the harmony of the states, and fatal to their commercial interests abroad. This was the immediate cause that led to the forming of a convention.

As early as 1778, the subject had been pressed upon the attention of congress, by a memorial from the state of New Jersey; and in 1781, we find a resolution presented to that body, by one of the most enlightened men of his day (Dr. Witherspoon), affirming, that "it is indispensably necessary, that the United States, in congress assembled, should be vested with a right of superintending the commercial regulations of every state, that none may take place that shall be partial or contrary to the common interests." The resolution of Virginia (January 21st, 1786), appointing her commissioners, to meet commissioners from other states, expresses their purpose to be, "to take into consideration the trade of the United States, to consider how far an uniform system in their commercial regulations may be necessary to their common interests and their permanent har-

mony." And Mr. Madison's resolution, which led to that measure, is introduced by a preamble entirely explicit to this point: "Whereas, the relative situation of the United States has been found, on trial, to require uniformity in their commercial regulations, as the only effectual policy for obtaining, in the ports of foreign nations, a stipulation of privileges reciprocal to those enjoyed by the subjects of such nations in the ports of the United States, for preventing animosities, which cannot fail to arise among the several states, from the interference of partial and separate regulations," &c., "therefore, resolved," &c.

The history of the times will, therefore, sustain the opinion, that the grant of power over commerce, if intended to be commensurate with the evils existing, and the purpose of remedying those evils, could be only commensurate with the power of the states over the subject. And this opinion is supported by a very remarkable evidence of the general understanding of the whole American people, when the grant was made. There was not a state in the Union, in which there did not, at that time, exist a variety of commercial regulations; concerning which it is too much to suppose, that the whole ground covered by those regulations was immediately assumed by actual legislation, under the authority of the Union. But where was the existing statute on this subject, that a state attempted to execute? or by what state was it ever thought necessary to repeal those statutes? By common consent, those laws dropped lifeless from their statute books, for want of the sustaining power that had been relinquished to congress.

. . .

Congress Overturns Leisy *v.* Hardin

In *Leisy* v. *Hardin*, 135 U.S. 100 (1890), the Supreme Court held that an Iowa law violated the Commerce Clause by prohibiting the sale of intoxicating liquors except for pharmaceutical, medicinal, chemical, or sacramental purposes. The law applied to "original packages" or kegs, unbroken and unopened, from the importer. Under the decision, states were forbidden from regulating commerce between the states "without congress-

ional permission." Id. at 125. Within a matters of months, Congress passed legislation to override the Court. Portions of the Senate debate are reproduced here (21 Cong. Rec. 4642, 4954–4955, 4964) as well as the statute (26 Stat. 313). The statute was upheld in *In re Rahrer*, 140 U.S. 545 (1891).

Mr. WILSON, of Iowa. From the Committee on the Judiciary I report favorably, with an amendment, the bill (S. 398) subjecting imported liquors to the provisions of the laws of the several States. I also present a written report to accompany the bill, and with it the concurring view of the Senator from Mississippi [Mr. GEORGE], which I ask may, under the rule, be printed.

I wish also to state in connection with this subject, in view of the conditions surrounding it, that I shall ask the Senate at an early day to take up the bill for consideration. I hope that it may receive favorable action and go to the other House for its concurrence.

The VICE-PRESIDENT. The bill will be placed on the Calendar, and the report and accompanying papers will be printed.

Mr. HOAR. I desire to make a brief statement in regard to the matter. This bill is rendered necessary, in the opinion of the committee, by the late decision of the Supreme Court of the United States, which holds, as I understand it, that intoxicating liquor manufactured in one State, conveyed into another, and there sold by the manufacturer or his agent, is protected by the Constitution of the United States from any regulation or prohibition of that sale by the State law on the ground that such prohibition or regulation is an interference with the regulation of commerce between the States. The court, in their opinion, say that the States can not pass such prohibitory or regulating statutes without the permission of Congress, which is understood to imply an opinion on the part of the court that Congress may give that permission, and that with that permission the States may pass the regulation or prohibitory enactment which they see fit.

I wholly concur in the propriety of this bill, but I suppose the principle of the opinion of the Supreme Court applies as well to gunpowder that a State may deem insecure and may desire to regulate the sale of as dangerous to safety, or to opinum, a deadly drug, and poisons of all kinds. I should have preferred, myself, that the bill should

apply to all articles the prohibition or regulation of the sale of which a State thinks necessary for its health, morals, or safety; but, as so large a number of State laws in regard to the sale of intoxicating liquors are affected by this proposed legislation, it is quite important that it should not be delayed, and therefore I agree with the rest of the committee in this bill.

Mr. EDMUNDS. I wish simply to say on this same subject that I was of the opinion that philosophically the bill ought to be a comprehensive one to cover all the things that the States fairly under their constitutions should have a right to treat as related to their health and domestic safety, but for the reasons stated by the Senator from Massachusetts I assented to this bill limited to intoxicating liquors.

Mr. HALE. From the Committee on Census I report—

Mr. VEST. Before the Senator from Maine proceeds, if he will permit me, as a member of the committee from which the bill was reported, I desire to say that I do not concur with the report of the majority. I have in my hand a report made by the majority of the committee upon a bill having the same object as that now reported to the Senate, that report having been made at the last Congress and before the recent decision by the Supreme Court. I simply want to repeat that my opinions are not changed upon this subject at all, although the shape in which the matter is brought before the Senate is changed. In that majority report (and here is the essence of it) the Judiciary Committee declare:

"It is equally clear that Congress can not part with or delegate to a State any power which has not been reserved to it. Congress can not return to the States a power given by the Constitution to Congress; much more can not Congress delegate or surrender a granted power to any portion of the States, for that would *pro tanto* invest those States with powers not possessed by the others."

This was the opinion of the majority of the

Judiciary Committee at the last Congress. Afterwards the Supreme Court of the United States delivered an opinion in the Iowa case, in which there is a dictum, and nothing else, declaring that certainly until Congress gave permission to a State to exclude liquor in the original packages the State of Iowa had no power to pass the act which was then before the Supreme Court for construction.

I do not believe the Supreme Court of the United States ever intended to assert that Congress could permit a State to invade the exclusive interstate-commerce power of the National Congress. This bill, although it comes in a different shape from the other, does the same thing. . . .

[Mr. WILSON, of Iowa.] The effect of the bill, if it shall become a law, will be to leave every State in the Union free to determine for itself what its policy shall be in respect of the traffic in intoxicating liquors. If a State shall desire prohibition it can adopt it and exercise it and enforce it under the provisions of this bill. If it shall desire license, high or low, the same conditions will attend that policy so far as this bill is concerned. If it shall prefer to adopt the policy denominated local option, it may do that, so that the traffic may be allowed in such counties or cities as desire it and prohibited in others. But that each State shall be left to determine for itself what its policy in this regard shall be is the scope of the bill, its purpose and its effect.

Unless this bill or something which shall be its equivalent shall be enacted by Congress, then the several States are at the mercy of the citizens of other of the several States, and not only that, but the subjects of the Emperor of Germany, of the Queen of England, of the Republic of France, of the King of Spain, of all foreign Governments, will have in the States of this Union greater rights and privileges than the citizens of the States have themselves.

So, too, in respect of the several States, the citizens of Missouri, of Illinois, New York, of whatsoever State in the Union, can have greater rights within the State of Iowa than the citizens of that State will possess; and, Mr. President, that State, which I in part represent in this body, elected as its policy the prohibition of the manufacture and sale of intoxicating liquors. The people of the State are satisfied with it; they desire the

enforcement of their law; but, since the decision from which I have read an extract was announced, agents of distilleries and breweries in other States of the Union are already traversing Iowa and organizing "the original-package saloon" within the State, and there is no limitation as to what "the original package" may be. It may be a pint or a half-pint bottle of whisky; it may be a bottle or a keg of beer; it may be in any quantity and whatsoever form of package agreed upon between the manufacturer of another State and the agent that he may send to transact his business in Iowa.

All the States of this Union do not want prohibition. Some of them want license; some of them want local option; they have various desires in this respect. Some of them may want unrestrained traffic in the sale of intoxicants. The State of Iowa does not want that. She wants her present policy; at least, she should have an opportunity to administer it until her people determine to adopt something else in its place; and so with all the States.

Mr. BUTLER. The Senator from Iowa will allow me to interrupt him for an inquiry.

Mr. WILSON, of Iowa. Certainly.

Mr. BUTLER. Does the Senator hold that under the decision of the Supreme Court the State of Iowa would have the right, after the package gets into that State, to prevent the sale or take control of it in any way after it crosses the line?

Mr. WILSON, of Iowa. Undoubtedly the decision of the Supreme Court protects every package that may be transported into that State from abroad, from foreign countries or from other States, until it shall have passed from the hands of the importer and thereby become mingled with the common property of the State.

Mr. BUTLER. Then the State has the right to interpose by its laws and prevent the sale or any disposition of the article imported?

Mr. WILSON, of Iowa. After it shall have passed from the hands of the importer or his agent. But under this decision, whatever package may be introduced there—for instance, the brewer in Illinois, the distiller in Illinois or any other State may arrange to send his package in there, even in the shape of a vial containing a single drink, and organize his saloon on that basis, the importer holding possession, protected by the decision of the Supreme Court, until that package shall pass from his possession into the hands of his customer and that customer may drink a single drink of whisky in that original-package saloon in the good State of Iowa, and in spite of her laws.

. . .

[Mr. VEST]: All of us are familiar with the history of the clause in the Constitution. All of us know that it originated from the defect in the old Articles of Confederation which permitted one State or colony to tax the product of another. That resulted in "confusion worse confounded." It resulted in anarchy as to taxation. Massachusetts taxed the products of New Hampshire and New Hampshire retaliated upon Massachusetts; Virginia taxed South Carolina and South Carolina retaliated upon Virginia, until, instead of union between the States, there was hostility, antagonism in regard to the great right of taxation.

In order to do away with that condition of things this clause was inserted in the Constitution, and if reference is made to the debates on the Constitution in the Madison Papers it will be found that that was the controlling reason when, after a discussion of days and weeks, it was finally determined to put into the Constitution of 1789 the clause which reads as it does now:

"The Congress shall have power to regulate commerce with foreign nations and among the several States and with the Indian tribes."

The Supreme Court has decided, as I have shown, that this is an exclusive power, and now it is proposed by this bill to delegate that power to one of the States of this Union. If that power can be delegated in regard to an article of merchandise, which alcoholic stimulants are admitted to be, it can be delegated, if sufficient political influence can be brought to bear in these halls, as to wheat, or corn, or oats, or oleomargarine, or any other article which is the subject of interstate commerce.

Are we to make this new departure? Are we upon the dictum of the Supreme Court to tear down the barriers of the Constitution? Are we to uproot the settled doctrine based upon the highest motives of policy to prevent confusion between the States and create uniformity? What is the meaning of the clause in the Constitution that taxation shall be uniform? It means exactly the same thing that this clause in the Constitution means, that the Congress shall have power to regulate commerce among the States.

. . .

Mr. EDMUNDS. Mr. President, it is a very curious circumstance, an interesting one, that we have reached a condition of things where, according to the debate here and the judgments of the Supreme Court of the United States, the States, as the Supreme Court say, have no power to deal with this subject; and now we are told here that Congress has not any power to deal with it. So the result of the performance is that under the Constitution of the United States there must be an inherent, individual, civil, personal right in every man in one State to carry whatever another State considers to be injurious to its safety and life and welfare into it and sell it; that Congress can not stop it; the States can not stop it, say the Supreme Court, unless Congress does something, and we all say Congress can not do that something.

Is not that a perfectly absurd result to come to in the Government and country, unless you say that it is one of the innate human rights that the Declaration of Independence intended to include when it said that every man had a right to pursue the avocations of peace, happiness, and prosperity, or whatever the phrase was (I have not quoted it correctly, but that is the idea), and therefore the right to carry dynamite, and smallpox, and rum, and deleterious drugs, and adulterated teas, and obscene literature from one State to another was one of the few things that the Declaration of Independence and the fundamental Constitution of the United States had put in such a position that, as the Supreme Court says, the State can not do anything about it, and, as gentlemen say here, that Congress can not do anything about it. It is only enough to state such a proposition to show that somewhere there is a fault in the logic of somebody.

Now, let us begin with the Supreme Court. The Supreme Court of the United States is an independent and co-ordinate branch of the Government. Its mission is to decide causes between parties, and its decision of causes between parties all good order and government require shall be carried out and respected as between parties. But, as it regards the Congress of the United States, its opinions are of no more value to us than ours are to it. We are just as independent of the Supreme Court of the United States as it is of us, and every judge will admit it.

Suppose we think that this court has gone wrong and has made a mistake in deciding a given case between A and B that involves the safety and happiness of all the people of the United States in their respective States covering a continent, and that an internal policy may be good for the Pacific coast and bad for a State on the Atlantic coast, are we to stop and say that is the end of the law and the mission of civilization in the United States for that reason? I take it not. It may be that when the next case comes up on a further and wider consideration the very gentlemen who now compose the court, differing as some of them did with the majority, may come to the conclusion that they had been led into an error and that they may still hold that the States of the United States in respect of what shall be done in those States and not among them is a matter that the Constitution leaves to those States to regulate as they will.

So I do not feel absolutely condemned and overpersuaded and feel myself as put in a box by what the Supreme Court of the United States have so recently said. It is their mission to decide causes between parties as they think they ought to be decided; and, as they have often done, it may be their mission next year to change their opinion and say that the rule ought to be the other way. So I do not feel deeply embarrassed by the fact that the Supreme Court of the United States has taken the largest step that in the whole hundred years of the Republic has ever been taken toward the centralization of power somewhere, either in the Supreme Court or in Congress, one or the other.

I do not believe, for one, in the centralization of power. I believe in its segregation and separation in every respect that concerns the internal affairs of the body of the people in every one of the States, leaving out of the question those universal human rights that everybody agrees are intrinsic in man and citizen.

So I am not greatly disturbed in respect of what the Supreme Court of the United States have said and done, except so far as it makes it now the mission of Congress to exert its power upon the subjects according to the light that it thought it had shone upon it, in order to preserve the internal policy and police of every State for itself, whether you call it an independent right or the execution of a national power under agencies that Congress provides, whichever way you choose to state it.

. . .

Be it enacted by the Senate and House of Representatives of the United States of America in Congress assembled, That all fermented, distilled, or other intoxicating liquors or liquids transported into any State or Territory or remaining therein for use, consumption, sale or storage therein, shall upon arrival in such State or Territory be subject to the operation and effect of the laws of such State or Territory enacted in the exercise of its police powers, to the same extent and in the same manner as though such liquids or liquors had been produced in such State or Territory, and shall not be exempt therefrom by reason of being introduced therein in original packages or otherwise.

Approved, August 8, 1890.

Hammer v. Dagenhart

247 U.S. 251 (1918)

In 1916, Congress passed legislation to prohibit the transportation in interstate commerce of goods made at a factory where children under the age of 14 years worked, or children between the ages of 14 and 16 worked more than eight hours a day, or more than six days a week, or after 7 p.m. or before 6 a.m. Roland H. Dagenhart filed this suit on his

own behalf and for his two minor sons who were employed in a cotton mill. After a district court declared the statute unconstitutional, the U.S. Attorney, W.C. Hammer, brought an appeal to the Supreme Court.

MR. JUSTICE DAY delivered the opinion of the court.

A bill was filed in the United States District Court for the Western District of North Carolina by a father in his own behalf and as next friend of his two minor sons, one under the age of fourteen years and the other between the ages of fourteen and sixteen years, employees in a cotton mill at Charlotte, North Carolina, to enjoin the enforcement of the act of Congress intended to prevent interstate commerce in the products of child labor. Act of Sept. 1, 1916, c. 432, 39 Stat. 675.

The District Court held the act unconstitutional and entered a decree enjoining its enforcement. This appeal brings the case here. . . .

Other sections of the act contain provisions for its enforcement and prescribe penalties for its violation.

The attack upon the act rests upon three propositions: First: It is not a regulation of interstate and foreign commerce; Second: It contravenes the Tenth Amendment to the Constitution; Third: It conflicts with the Fifth Amendment to the Constitution.

The controlling question for decision is: Is it within the authority of Congress in regulating commerce among the States to prohibit the transportation in interstate commerce of manufactured goods, the product of a factory in which, within thirty days prior to their removal therefrom, children under the age of fourteen have been employed or permitted to work, or children between the ages of fourteen and sixteen years have been employed or permitted to work more than eight hours in any day, or more than six days in any week, or after the hour of seven o'clock P.M. or before the hour of 6 o'clock A.M.?

The power essential to the passage of this act, the Government contends, is found in the commerce clause of the Constitution which authorizes Congress to regulate commerce with foreign nations and among the States.

In *Gibbons* v. *Ogden*, 9 Wheat. 1, Chief Justice Marshall, speaking for this court, and defining the extent and nature of the commerce power, said, "It is the power to regulate; that is, to prescribe the rule by which commerce is to be governed." In other words, the power is one to control the means by which commerce is carried on, which is directly the contrary of the assumed right to forbid commerce from moving and thus destroy it as to particular commodities. But it is insisted that adjudged cases in this court establish the doctrine that the power to regulate given to Congress incidentally includes the authority to prohibit the movement of ordinary commodities and therefore that the subject is not open for discussion. The cases demonstrate the contrary. They rest upon the character of the particular subjects dealt with and the fact that the scope of governmental authority, state or national, possessed over them is such that the authority to prohibit is as to them but the exertion of the power to regulate.

The first of these cases is *Champion* v. *Ames*, 188 U.S. 321, the so-called *Lottery Case*, in which it was held that Congress might pass a law having the effect to keep the channels of commerce free from use in the transportation of tickets used in the promotion of lottery schemes. In *Hipolite Egg Co.* v. *United States*, 220 U.S. 45, this court sustained the power of Congress to pass the Pure Food and Drug Act which prohibited the introduction into the States by means of interstate commerce of impure foods and drugs. In *Hoke* v. *United States*, 227 U. S. 308, this court sustained the constitutionality of the so-called "White Slave Traffic Act" whereby the transportation of a woman in interstate commerce for the purpose of prostitution was forbidden. . . .

In each of these instances the use of interstate transportation was necessary to the accomplishment of harmful results. In other words, although the power over interstate transportation was to regulate, that could only be accomplished by prohibiting the use of the facilities of interstate commerce to effect the evil intended.

This element is wanting in the present case. The thing intended to be accomplished by this statute is the denial of the facilities of interstate commerce to those manufacturers in the States who employ children within the prohibited ages. The act in its effect does not regulate transportation among the States, but aims to standardize the ages at which children may be employed in mining and manufacturing within the States. The goods shipped are of themselves harmless. The act permits them to be freely shipped after thirty days from the time of their removal from the factory. When offered for shipment, and before transportation begins, the labor of their production is over, and the mere fact that they were intended for interstate commerce transportation does not make their production subject to federal control under the commerce power.

. . .

It is further contended that the authority of Congress may be exerted to control interstate commerce in the shipment of child-made goods because of the effect of the circulation of such goods in other States where the evil of this class of labor has been recognized by local legislation, and the right to thus employ child labor has been more rigorously restrained than in the State of production. In other words, that the unfair competition, thus engendered, may be controlled by closing the channels of interstate commerce to manufacturers in those States where the local laws do not meet what Congress deems to be the more just standard of other States.

There is no power vested in Congress to require the States to exercise their police power so as to prevent possible unfair competition. Many causes may coöperate to give one State, by reason of local laws or conditions, an economic advantage over others. The Commerce Clause was not intended to give to Congress a general authority to equalize such conditions. In some of the States laws have been passed fixing minimum wages for women, in others the local law regulates the hours of labor of women in various employments. Business done in such States may be at an economic disadvantage when compared with States which have no such regulations; surely, this fact does not give Congress the power to deny transportation in interstate commerce to those who carry on business where the hours of labor and the rate of compensation for women have not been fixed by a standard in use in other States and approved by Congress.

The grant of power to Congress over the subject of interstate commerce was to enable it to regulate such commerce, and not to give it authority to control the States in their exercise of the police power over local trade and manufacture.

The grant of authority over a purely federal matter was not intended to destroy the local power always existing and carefully reserved to the States in the Tenth Amendment to the Constitution.

. . .

That there should be limitations upon the right to employ children in mines and factories in the interest of their own and the public welfare, all will admit. That such employment is generally deemed to require regulation is shown by the fact that the brief of counsel states that every State in the Union has a law upon the subject, limiting the right to thus employ children. In North Carolina, the State wherein is located the factory in which the employment was had in the present case, no child under twelve years of age is permitted to work.

It may be desirable that such laws be uniform, but our Federal Government is one of enumerated powers; "this principle," declared Chief Justice Marshall in *McCulloch* v. *Maryland*, 4 Wheat. 316, "is universally admitted."

A statute must be judged by its natural and reasonable effect. *Collins* v. *New Hampshire*, 171 U. S. 30, 33, 34. The control by Congress over interstate commerce cannot authorize the exercise of authority not entrusted to it by the Constitution. *Pipe Line Cases*, 234 U. S. 548, 560. The maintenance of the authority of the States over matters purely local is as essential to the preservation of our institutions as is the conservation of the supremacy of the federal power in all matters entrusted to the Nation by the Federal Constitution.

In interpreting the Constitution it must never be forgotten that the Nation is made up of States to which are entrusted the powers of local government. And to them and to the people the powers not expressly delegated to the National Government are reserved. *Lane County* v. *Oregon*, 7 Wall. 71, 76. The power of the States to regulate their purely internal affairs by such laws as seem wise to the local authority is inherent and has never been surrendered to the general government.

. . .

In our view the necessary effect of this act is, by means of a prohibition against the movement in interstate commerce of ordinary commercial commodities, to regulate the hours of labor of children in factories and mines within the States, a purely state authority. Thus the act in a twofold sense is repugnant to the Constitution. It not only transcends the authority delegated to Congress over commerce but also exerts a power as to a purely local matter to which the federal authority does not extend. The far reaching result of upholding the act cannot be more plainly indicated than by pointing out that if Congress can thus regulate matters entrusted to local authority by prohibition of the movement of commodities in interstate commerce, all freedom of commerce will be at an end, and the power of the States over local matters may be eliminated, and thus our system of government be practically destroyed.

For these reasons we hold that this law exceeds the constitutional authority of Congress. It follows that the decree of the District Court must be

Affirmed.

MR. JUSTICE HOLMES, dissenting.

The single question in this case is whether Congress has power to prohibit the shipment in interstate or foreign commerce of any product of a cotton mill situated in the United States, in which within thirty days before the removal of the product children under fourteen have been employed, or children between fourteen and sixteen have been employed more than eight hours in a day, or more than six days in any week, or between seven in the evening and six in the morning. The objection urged against the power is that the States have exclusive control over their methods of production and that Congress cannot meddle with them, and taking the proposition in the sense of direct

intermeddling I agree to it and suppose that no one denies it. But if an act is within the powers specifically conferred upon Congress, it seems to me that it is not made any less constitutional because of the indirect effects that it may have, however obvious it may be that it will have those effects, and that we are not at liberty upon such grounds to hold it void.

The first step in my argument is to make plain what no one is likely to dispute—that the statute in question is within the power expressly given to Congress if considered only as to its immediate effects and that if invalid it is so only upon some collateral ground. The statute confines itself to prohibiting the carriage of certain goods in interstate or foreign commerce. Congress is given power to regulate such commerce in unqualified terms. It would not be argued today that the power to regulate does not include the power to prohibit. . . .

The question then is narrowed to whether the exercise of its otherwise constitutional power by Congress can be pronounced unconstitutional because of its possible reaction upon the conduct of the States in a matter upon which I have admitted that they are free from direct control. I should have thought that that matter had been disposed of so fully as to leave no room for doubt. I should have thought that the most conspicuous decisions of this Court had made it clear that the power to regulate commerce and other constitutional powers could not be cut down or qualified by the fact that it might interfere with the carrying out of the domestic policy of any State.

The manufacture of oleomargarine is as much a matter of state regulation as the manufacture of cotton cloth. Congress levied a tax upon the compound when colored so as to resemble butter that was so great as obviously to prohibit the manufacture and sale. In a very elaborate discussion the present Chief Justice excluded any inquiry into the purpose of an act which apart from that purpose was within the power of Congress. *McCray* v. *United States*, 195 U. S. 27. . . .

The notion that prohibition is any less prohibition when applied to things now thought evil I do not understand. But if there is any matter upon which civilized countries have agreed—far more unanimously than they have with regard to intoxicants and some other matters over which this country is now emotionally aroused—it is the evil of premature and excessive child labor. I should have thought that if we were to introduce our own moral conceptions where in my opinion they do not belong, this was preëminently a case for upholding the exercise of all its powers by the United States.

But I had thought that the propriety of the exercise of a power admitted to exist in some cases was for the consideration of Congress alone and that this Court always had disavowed the right to intrude its judgment upon questions of policy or morals. It is not for this Court to pronounce when prohibition is necessary to regulation if it ever may be necessary—to say that it is permissible as against strong drink but not as against the product of ruined lives.

The act does not meddle with anything belonging to the States. They may regulate their internal affairs and their domestic commerce as they like. But when they seek to send their products across the state line they are no longer within their rights. If there were no Constitution and no Congress their power to cross the line would depend upon their neighbors. Under the Constitution such commerce belongs not to the States but to Congress to regulate. It may carry out its views of public policy whatever indirect effect they may have upon the activities of the States. . . .

MR. JUSTICE MCKENNA, MR. JUSTICE BRANDEIS and MR. JUSTICE CLARKE concur in this opinion.

United States v. Darby

312 U.S. 100 (1941)

The Fair Labor Standards Act of 1938 provided for minimum wages and maximum hours for employees engaged in the production of goods for interstate commerce. The statute forced the Court to rethink its doctrine on "manufacture." If manufacture is not of itself interstate commerce, would the shipment of manufactured goods interstate bring it within the authority of Congress to regulate? The statute also excluded the products of child labor from interstate commerce, requiring the Court to revisit its holding in _Hammer_ v. _Dagenhart_ (1918), which had struck down the use of the Commerce Clause to regulate child labor. In this case the government prosecutes Fred W. Darby, owner of a lumber company, for violating the 1938 statute.

MR. JUSTICE STONE delivered the opinion of the Court.

The two principal questions raised by the record in this case are, _first_, whether Congress has constitutional power to prohibit the shipment in interstate commerce of lumber manufactured by employees whose wages are less than a prescribed minimum or whose weekly hours of labor at that wage are greater than a prescribed maximum, and, _second_, whether it has power to prohibit the employment of workmen in the production of goods "for interstate commerce" at other than prescribed wages and hours. A subsidiary ques-

tion is whether in connection with such prohibitions Congress can require the employer subject to them to keep records showing the hours worked each day and week by each of his employees including those engaged "in the production and manufacture of goods to-wit, lumber, for 'interstate commerce.' "

. . .

The indictment charges that appellee is engaged, in the State of Georgia, in the business of acquiring raw materials, which he manufactures into finished lumber with the intent, when manufactured, to ship it in interstate commerce to customers outside the state, and that he does in fact so ship a large part of the lumber so produced. There are numerous counts charging appellee with the shipment in interstate commerce from Georgia to points outside the state of lumber in the production of which, for interstate commerce, appellee has employed workmen at less than the prescribed minimum wage or more than the prescribed maximum hours without payment to them of any wage for overtime. Other counts charge the employment by appellee of workmen in the production of lumber for interstate commerce at wages at less than 25 cents an hour or for more than the maximum hours per week without payment to them of the prescribed overtime wage. Still another count charges appellee with failure to keep records showing the hours worked each day a week by each of his employees as required by § 11 (c) and the regulation of the administrator, Title 29, Ch. 5, Code of Federal Regulations, Part 516, and also that appellee unlawfully failed to keep such records of employees engaged "in the production and manufacture of goods, to-wit, lumber, for interstate commerce."

The demurrer, so far as now relevant to the appeal, challenged the validity of the Fair Labor Standards Act under the Commerce Clause and the Fifth and Tenth Amendments. The district court quashed the indictment in its entirety upon the broad grounds that the Act, which it interpreted as a regulation of manufacture within the states, is unconstitutional. It declared that manufacture is not interstate commerce and that the regulation by the Fair Labor Standards Act of wages and hours of employment of those engaged in the manufacture of goods which it is intended at the time of production "may or will be" after production "sold in interstate commerce in part or in whole" is not within the congressional power to regulate interstate commerce.

The effect of the court's decision and judgment is thus to deny the power of Congress to prohibit shipment in interstate commerce of lumber produced for interstate commerce under the proscribed substandard labor conditions of wages and hours, its power to penalize the employer for his failure to conform to the wage and hour provisions in the case of employees engaged in the production of lumber which he intends thereafter to ship in interstate commerce in part or in whole according to the normal course of his business and its power to compel him to keep records of hours of employment as required by the statute and the regulations of the administrator.

. . .

The prohibition of shipment of the proscribed goods in interstate commerce. . . .

While manufacture is not of itself interstate commerce, the shipment of manufactured goods interstate is such commerce and the prohibition of such shipment by Congress is indubitably a regulation of the commerce. The power to regulate commerce is the power "to prescribe the rule by which commerce is governed." *Gibbons* v. *Ogden,* 9 Wheat. 1, 196. It extends not only to those regulations which aid, foster and protect the commerce, but embraces those which prohibit it. . . . It is conceded that the power of Congress to prohibit transportation in interstate commerce includes noxious articles, . . . stolen articles, . . . kidnapped persons, . . . and articles such as intoxicating liquor or convict made goods, traffic in which is forbidden or restricted by the laws of the state of destination. . . .

But it is said that the present prohibition falls within the scope of none of these categories; that while the prohibition is nominally a regulation of the commerce its motive or purpose is regulation of wages and hours of persons engaged in manufacture, the control of which has been reserved to the states and upon which Georgia and some of the states of destination have placed no restriction; . . .

The power of Congress over interstate commerce "is complete in itself, may be exercised to its utmost extent, and acknowledges no limitations other than are prescribed in the Constitution." *Gibbons* v. *Ogden, supra,* 196. That power can neither be enlarged nor diminished by the exercise or non-exercise of state power. . . . Congress, following its own conception of public policy concerning the restrictions which may appropriately be imposed on interstate commerce, is free to exclude from the commerce articles whose use in the states for which they are destined it may conceive to be injurious to the public health, morals or welfare, even though the state has not sought to regulate their use. . . .

Such regulation is not a forbidden invasion of state power merely because either its motive or its consequence is to restrict the use of articles of commerce within the states of destination; and is not prohibited unless by other Constitutional provisions. It is no objection to the assertion of the power to regulate interstate commerce that its exercise is attended by the same incidents which attend the exercise of the police power of the states. . . .

In the more than a century which has elapsed since the decision of *Gibbons* v. *Ogden*, these principles of constitutional interpretation have been so long and repeatedly recognized by this Court as applicable to the Commerce Clause, that there would be little occasion for repeating them now were it not for the decision of this Court twenty-two years ago in *Hammer* v. *Dagenhart*, 247 U.S. 251. In that case it was held by a bare majority of the Court over the powerful and now classic dissent of Mr. Justice Holmes setting forth the fundamental issues involved, that Congress was without power to exclude the products of child labor from interstate commerce. The reasoning and conclusion of the Court's opinion there cannot be reconciled with the conclusion which we have reached, that the power of Congress under the Commerce Clause is plenary to exclude any article from interstate commerce subject only to the specific prohibitions of the Constitution.

Hammer v. *Dagenhart* has not been followed. The distinction on which the decision was rested that Congressional power to prohibit interstate commerce is limited to articles which in themselves have some harmful or deleterious property—a distinction which was novel when made and unsupported by any provision of the Constitution—has long since been abandoned. . . . The thesis of the opinion that the motive of the prohibition or its effect to control in some measure the use or production within the states of the article thus excluded from the commerce can operate to deprive the regulation of its constitutional authority has long since ceased to have force. . . . And finally we have declared "The authority of the federal government over interstate commerce does not differ in extent or character from that retained by the states over intrastate commerce." *United States* v. *Rock Royal Co-operative*, 307 U.S. 533, 569.

The conclusion is inescapable that *Hammer* v. *Dagenhart* was a departure from the principles which have prevailed in the interpretation of the Commerce Clause both before and since the decision and that such vitality, as a precedent, as it then had has long since been exhausted. It should be and now is overruled.

. . .

Our conclusion is unaffected by the Tenth Amendment which provides: "The powers not delegated to the United States by the Constitution, nor prohibited by it to the States, are reserved to the States respectively, or to the people." The amendment states but a truism that all is retained which has not been surrendered. There is nothing in the history of its adoption to suggest that it was more than declaratory of the relationship between the national and state governments as it had been established by the Constitution before the amendment or that its purpose was other than to allay fears that the new national government might seek to exercise powers not granted, and that the states might not be able to exercise fully their reserved powers. See e.g., II Elliot's Debates, 123, 131; III *id*. 450, 464, 600; IV *id*. 140, 149; I Annals of Congress, 432, 761, 767–768; Story, Commentaries on the Constitution, §§ 1907–1908.

From the beginning and for many years the amendment has been construed as not depriving the national government of authority to resort to all means for the exercise of a granted power which are appropriate and plainly adapted to the permitted end. . . .

The Act is sufficiently definite to meet constitutional demands. One who employs persons, without conforming to the prescribed wage and hour conditions, to work on goods which he ships or expects to ship across state lines, is warned that he may be subject to the criminal penalties of the Act. No more is required. *Nash* v. *United States*, 229 U.S. 373, 377.

We have considered, but find it unnecessary to discuss other contentions.

Reversed.

NLRB v. Jones & Laughlin

301 U.S. 1 (1937)

In the National Labor Relations Act of 1935, Congress concluded that labor disputes had a direct burden on interstate or foreign commerce and could be regulated by the Commerce Clause. Even activities taking place within a state, if they had a close and substantial relation to interstate commerce, could be brought within the control of Congress. Under the shadow of Roosevelt's court-packing plan, the Court decided whether this exertion of national power invaded the rights reserved to the states.

MR. CHIEF JUSTICE HUGHES delivered the opinion of the Court.

In a proceeding under the National Labor Relations Act of 1935, the National Labor Relations Board found that the respondent, Jones & Laughlin Steel Corporation, had violated the Act by engaging in unfair labor practices affecting commerce. The proceeding was instituted by the Beaver Valley Lodge No. 200, affiliated with the Amalgamated Association of Iron, Steel and Tin Workers of America, a labor organization. The unfair labor practices charged were that the corporation was discriminating against members of the union with regard to hire and tenure of employment, and was coercing and intimidating its employees in order to interfere with their self-organization. The discriminatory and coercive action alleged was the discharge of certain employees.

The National Labor Relations Board, sustaining the charge, ordered the corporation to cease and desist from such discrimination and coercion, to offer reinstatement to ten of the employees named, to make good their losses in pay, and to post for thirty days notices that the corporation would not discharge or discriminate against members, or those desiring to become members, of the labor union. As the corporation failed to comply, the Board petitioned the Circuit Court of Appeals to enforce the order. The court denied the petition, holding that the order lay beyond the range of federal power. 83 F. (2d) 998. We granted certiorari.

The scheme of the National Labor Relations Act—which is too long to be quoted in full—may be briefly stated. The first section sets forth findings with respect to the injury to commerce resulting from the denial by employers of the right of employees to organize and from the refusal of employers to accept the procedure of collective bargaining. There follows a declaration that it is the policy of the United States to eliminate these causes of obstruction to the free flow of commerce. The Act then defines the terms it uses, including the terms "commerce" and "affecting commerce." § 2. It creates the National Labor Relations Board and prescribes its organization. §§ 3–6. It sets forth the right of employees to self-organization and to bargain collectively through representatives of their own choosing. § 7. It defines "unfair labor practices." § 8. It lays down rules as to the representation of employees for the purpose of collective bargaining. § 9. The Board is empowered to prevent the described unfair labor practices affecting commerce and the Act prescribes the procedure to that end. The Board is authorized to petition designated courts to secure the enforcement of its orders. The findings of the Board as to the facts, if supported by evidence, are to be conclusive. If either party on application to the court shows that additional evidence is material and that there were reasonable grounds for the failure to adduce such evidence in the hearings before the Board, the court may order the additional evidence to be taken. Any person aggrieved by a final order of the Board may obtain a review in the designated courts with the same procedure as in the case of an application by the Board for the enforcement of its order. § 10. The Board has broad powers of investigation. § 11.

Interference with members of the Board or its agents in the performance of their duties is punishable by fine and imprisonment. § 12. Nothing in the Act is to be construed to interfere with the right to strike. § 13. There is a separability clause to the effect that if any provision of the Act or its application to any person or circumstances shall be held invalid, the remainder of the Act or its application to other persons or circumstances shall not be affected. § 15. The particular provisions which are involved in the instant case will be considered more in detail in the course of the discussion.

. . .

Contesting the ruling of the Board, the respondent argues (1) that the Act is in reality a regulation of labor relations and not of interstate commerce; (2) that the Act can have no application to the respondent's relations with its production employees because they are not subject to regulation by the federal government; and (3) that the provisions of the Act violate § 2 of Article III and the Fifth and Seventh Amendments of the Constitution of the United States.

The facts as to the nature and scope of the business of the Jones & Laughlin Steel Corporation have been found by the Labor Board and, so far as they are essential to the determination of this controversy, they are not in dispute. The Labor Board has found: The corporation is organized under the laws of Pennsylvania and has its principal office at Pittsburgh. It is engaged in the business of manufacturing iron and steel in plants situated in Pittsburgh and nearby Aliquippa, Pennsylvania. It manufactures and distributes a widely diversified line of steel and pig iron, being the fourth largest producer of steel in the United States. With its subsidiaries—nineteen in number—it is a completely integrated enterprise, owning and operating ore, coal and limestone properties, lake and river transportation facilities and terminal railroads located at its manufacturing plants. It owns or controls mines in Michigan and Minnesota. It operates four ore steamships on the Great Lakes, used in the transportation of ore to its factories. It owns coal mines in Pennsylvania. It operates towboats and steam barges used in carrying coal to its factories. It owns limestone prop-

erties in various places in Pennsylvania and West Virginia. It owns the Monongahela connecting railroad which connects the plants of the Pittsburgh works and forms an interconnection with the Pennsylvania, New York Central and Baltimore and Ohio Railroad systems. It owns the Aliquippa and Southern Railroad Company which connects the Aliquippa works with the Pittsburgh and Lake Erie, part of the New York Central system. Much of its product is shipped to its warehouses in Chicago, Detroit, Cincinnati and Memphis,—to the last two places by means of its own barges and transportation equipment. In Long Island City, New York, and in New Orleans it operates structural steel fabricating shops in connection with the warehousing of semi-finished materials sent from its works. Through one of its wholly-owned subsidiaries it owns, leases and operates stores, warehouses and yards for the distribution of equipment and supplies for drilling and operating oil and gas wells and for pipe lines, refineries and pumping stations. It has sales offices in twenty cities in the United States and a wholly-owned subsidiary which is devoted exclusively to distributing its product in Canada. Approximately 75 per cent. of its product is shipped out of Pennsylvania.

Summarizing these operations, the Labor Board concluded that the works in Pittsburgh and Aliquippa "might be likened to the heart of a self-contained, highly integrated body. They draw in the raw materials from Michigan, Minnesota, West Virginia, Pennsylvania in part through arteries and by means controlled by the respondent; they transform the materials and then pump them out to all parts of the nation through the vast mechanism which the respondent has elaborated."

. . .

First. The scope of the Act.—The Act is challenged in its entirety as an attempt to regulate all industry, thus invading the reserved powers of the States over their local concerns. . . .

There can be no question that the commerce thus contemplated by the Act (aside from that within a Territory or the District of Columbia) is interstate and foreign commerce in the constitutional sense. The Act also defines the term "affecting commerce" (§ 2 (7)):

"The term 'affecting commerce' means in commerce, or burdening or obstructing commerce or the free flow of commerce, or having led or tending to lead to a labor dispute burdening or obstructing commerce or the free flow of commerce."

This definition is one of exclusion as well as inclusion. The grant of authority to the Board does not purport to extend to the relationship between all industrial employees and employers. Its terms do not impose collective bargaining upon all industry regardless of effects upon interstate or foreign commerce. It purports to reach only what may be deemed to burden or obstruct that commerce and, thus qualified, it must be construed as contemplating the exercise of control within constitutional bounds. It is a familiar principle that acts which directly burden or obstruct interstate or foreign commerce, or its free flow, are within the reach of the congressional power. . . .

Second. The unfair labor practices in question.— The unfair labor practices found by the Board are those defined in § 8, subdivisions (1) and (3). These provide:

Sec. 8. It shall be an unfair labor practice for an employer—

"(1) To interfere with, restrain, or coerce employees in the exercise of the rights guaranteed in section 7."

"(3) By discrimination in regard to hire or tenure of employment or any term or condition of employment to encourage or discourage membership in any labor organization: . . ."

Section 8, subdivision (1), refers to § 7, which is as follows:

"Sec. 7. Employees shall have the right to self-organization, to form, join, or assist labor organizations, to bargain collectively through representatives of their own choosing, and to engage in concerted activities, for the purpose of collective bargaining or other mutual aid or protection."

Thus, in its present application, the statute goes no further than to safeguard the right of employees to self-organization and to select representatives of their own choosing for collective bargaining or other mutual protection without restraint or coercion by their employer.

That is a fundamental right. Employees have as clear a right to organize and select their representatives for lawful purposes as the respondent has to organize its business and select its own officers and agents. Discrimination and coercion to prevent the free exercise of the right of employees to self-organization and representation is a proper subject for condemnation by competent legislative authority. Long ago we stated the reason for labor organizations. We said that they were organized out of the necessities of the situation; that a single employee was helpless in dealing with an employer; that he was dependent ordinarily on his daily wage for the maintenance of himself and family; that if the employer refused to pay him the wages that he thought fair, he was nevertheless unable to leave the employ and resist arbitrary and unfair treatment; that union was essential to give laborers opportunity to deal on an equality with their employer. . . .

Third. The application of the Act to employees engaged in production.—*The principle involved.*— Respondent says that whatever may be said of employees engaged in interstate commerce, the industrial relations and activities in the manufacturing department of respondent's enterprise are not subject to federal regulation. The argument rests upon the proposition that manufacturing in itself is not commerce. . . .

. . . Although activities may be intrastate in character when separately considered, if they have such a close and substantial relation to interstate commerce that their control is essential or appropriate to protect that commerce from burdens and obstructions, Congress cannot be denied the power to exercise that control. . . .

Fourth. Effects of the unfair labor practice in respondent's enterprise.—Giving full weight to respondent's contention with respect to a break in the complete continuity of the "stream of commerce" by reason of respondent's manufacturing operations, the fact remains that the stoppage of those operations by industrial strife would have a most serious effect upon interstate commerce. In view of respondent's far-flung activities, it is idle to say that the effect would be indirect or remote. It is obvious that it would be immediate and might be catastrophic. We are asked to shut our eyes to the plainest facts of our national life and to deal with the question of direct and indirect effects in an intellectual vacuum. . . .

Experience has abundantly demonstrated that the recognition of the right of employees to self-organization and to have representatives of their own choosing for the purpose of collective bargaining is often an essential condition of industrial peace. Refusal to confer and negotiate has been one of the most prolific causes of strife. This is such an outstanding fact in the history of labor disturbances that it is a proper subject of judicial notice and requires no citation of instances. . . .

. . .

Our conclusion is that the order of the Board was within its competency and that the Act is valid as here applied. The judgment of the Circuit Court of Appeals is reversed and the cause is remanded for further proceedings in conformity with this opinion.

Reversed.

[On the same day, the Court handed down other decisions that upheld actions by the National Labor Relations Board.]

MR. JUSTICE MCREYNOLDS delivered the following dissenting opinion in the cases preceding:

MR. JUSTICE VAN DEVANTER, MR. JUSTICE SUTHERLAND, MR. JUSTICE BUTLER and I are unable to agree with the decisions just announced.

We conclude that these causes were rightly decided by the three Circuit Courts of Appeals and that their judgments should be affirmed. The opinions there given without dissent are terse, well-considered and sound. They disclose the meaning ascribed by experienced judges to what this Court has often declared, and are set out below in full.

. . .

V.

In each cause the Labor Board formulated and then sustained a charge of unfair labor practices towards persons employed only in production. It ordered restoration of discharged employees to former positions with payment for losses sus-tained. These orders were declared invalid below upon the ground that respondents while carrying on production operations were not thereby engaging in interstate commerce; that labor practices in the course of such operations did not directly affect interstate commerce; consequently respondents' actions did not come within Congressional power.

Respondent in No. 419 is a large, integrated manufacturer of iron and steel products—the fourth largest in the United States. It has two production plants in Pennsylvania where raw materials brought from points outside the state are converted into finished products, which are thereafter distributed in interstate commerce throughout many states. The Corporation has assets amounting to $180,000,000, gross income $47,000,000, and employs 22,000 people—10,000 in the Aliquippa plant where the complaining employees worked. . . .

Any effect on interstate commerce by the discharge of employees shown here, would be indirect and remote in the highest degree, as consideration of the facts will show. In No. 419 ten men out of ten thousand were discharged; in the other cases only a few. The immediate effect in the factory may be to create discontent among all those employed and a strike may follow, which, in turn, may result in reducing production, which ultimately may reduce the volume of goods moving in interstate commerce. By this chain of indirect and progressively remote events we finally reach the evil with which it is said the legislation under consideration undertakes to deal. A more remote and indirect interference with interstate commerce or a more definite invasion of the powers reserved to the states is difficult, if not impossible, to imagine.

The Constitution still recognizes the existence of states with indestructible powers; the Tenth Amendment was supposed to put them beyond controversy.

We are told that Congress may protect the "stream of commerce" and that one who buys raw material without the state, manufactures it therein, and ships the output to another state is in that stream. Therefore it is said he may be prevented from doing anything which may interfere with its flow.

This, too, goes beyond the constitutional limitations heretofore enforced. If a man raises cattle and regularly delivers them to a carrier for interstate shipment, may Congress prescribe the conditions under which he may employ or discharge helpers on the ranch? The products of a mine pass daily into interstate commerce; many things are brought to it from other states. Are the owners and the miners within the power of Congress in respect of the miners' tenure and discharge? May a mill owner be prohibited from closing his factory or discontinuing his business because so to do would stop the flow of products to and from his plant in interstate commerce? May employees in a factory be restrained from quitting work in a body because this will close the factory and thereby stop the flow of commerce? May arson of a factory be made a Federal offense whenever this would interfere with such flow? If the business cannot continue with the existing wage scale, may Congress command a reduction? If the ruling of the Court just announced is adhered to these questions suggest some of the problems certain to arise.

. . .

It is gravely stated that experience teaches that if an employer discourages membership in "any organization of any kind" "in which employees participate, and which exists for the purpose in whole or in part of dealing with employers concerning grievances, labor disputes, wages, rates of pay, hours of employment or conditions of work," discontent may follow and this in turn may lead to a strike, and as the outcome of the strike there may be a block in the stream of interstate commerce. Therefore Congress may inhibit the discharge! Whatever effect any cause of discontent may ultimately have upon commerce is far too indirect to justify Congressional regulation. Almost anything —marriage, birth, death—may in some fashion affect commerce.

VIII.

That Congress has power by appropriate means, not prohibited by the Constitution, to prevent direct and material interference with the conduct of interstate commerce is settled doctrine. But the interference struck at must be direct and material, not some mere possibility contingent on wholly uncertain events; and there must be no impairment of rights guaranteed. . . .

IX.

. . .

The right to contract is fundamental and includes the privilege of selecting those with whom one is willing to assume contractual relations. This right is unduly abridged by the Act now upheld. A private owner is deprived of power to manage his own property by freely selecting those to whom his manufacturing operations are to be entrusted. We think this cannot lawfully be done in circumstances like those here disclosed.

It seems clear to us that Congress has transcended the powers granted.

National League of Cities v. Usery

426 U.S. 833 (1976)

This case marks an effort by Justice Rehnquist to devise a doctrine to protect states' rights against federal intrusion. In 1974, Congress amended the Fair Labor Standards Act to extend minimum wage and maximum hour provisions to cover almost all employees of states and their political divisions. The National League of Cities, supported by a number of cities and states, brought an action against Secretary of Labor W. J. Usery, Jr., challenging the validity of the 1974 amendments and seeking declaratory and injunctive

relief. A three-judge district court dismissed the complaint for failure to state a claim upon which relief might be granted.

MR. JUSTICE REHNQUIST delivered the opinion of the Court.

Nearly 40 years ago Congress enacted the Fair Labor Standards Act, and required employers covered by the Act to pay their employees a minimum hourly wage and to pay them at one and one-half times their regular rate of pay for hours worked in excess of 40 during a workweek. . . . This Court unanimously upheld the Act as a valid exercise of congressional authority under the commerce power in *United States* v. *Darby*, 312 U. S. 100 (1941). . . .

The original Fair Labor Standards Act passed in 1938 specifically excluded the States and their political subdivisions from its coverage. . . .

I

In a series of amendments beginning in 1961 Congress began to extend the provisions of the Fair Labor Standards Act to some types of public employees. The 1961 amendments to the Act extended its coverage to persons who were employed in "enterprises" engaged in commerce or in the production of goods for commerce. And in 1966, with the amendment of the definition of employers under the Act, the exemption heretofore extended to the States and their political subdivisions was removed with respect to employees of state hospitals, institutions, and schools. We nevertheless sustained the validity of the combined effect of these two amendments in *Maryland* v. *Wirtz*, 392 U.S. 183 (1968).

In 1974, Congress again broadened the coverage of the Act, 88 Stat. 55. . . . By its 1974 amendments, . . . Congress has now entirely removed the exemption previously afforded States and their political subdivisions, substituting only the Act's general exemption for executive, administrative, or professional personnel, 29 U. S. C. § 213 (a)(1), which is supplemented by provisions excluding from the Act's coverage those individuals holding public elective office or serving such an officeholder in one of several specific capacities. 29 U. S. C. § 203 (e)(2)(C) (1970 ed.,

Supp. IV). The Act thus imposes upon almost all public employment the minimum wage and maximum hour requirements previously restricted to employees engaged in interstate commerce. . . .

II

It is established beyond peradventure that the Commerce Clause of Art. I of the Constitution is a grant of plenary authority to Congress. That authority is, in the words of Mr. Chief Justice Marshall in *Gibbons* v. *Ogden*, 9 Wheat. 1 (1824), "the power to regulate; that is, to prescribe the rule by which commerce is to be governed." *Id.*, at 196.

. . .

Appellants in no way challenge these decisions establishing the breadth of authority granted Congress under the commerce power. Their contention, on the contrary, is that when Congress seeks to regulate directly the activities of States as public employers, it transgresses an affirmative limitation on the exercise of its power akin to other commerce power affirmative limitations contained in the Constitution. . . .

This Court has never doubted that there are limits upon the power of Congress to override state sovereignty, even when exercising its otherwise plenary powers to tax or to regulate commerce which are conferred by Art. I of the Constitution. In *Wirtz*, for example, the Court took care to assure the appellants that it had "ample power to prevent . . . 'the utter destruction of the State as a sovereign political entity,'" which they feared. 392 U. S., at 196. Appellee Secretary in this case, both in his brief and upon oral argument, has agreed that our federal system of government imposes definite limits upon the authority of Congress to regulate the activities of the States as States by means of the commerce power. See, *e. g.*, Brief for Appellee 30–41; Tr. of Oral Arg. 39–43. In *Fry, supra*, the Court recognized that an express declaration of this limitation is found in the Tenth Amendment:

"While the Tenth Amendment has been characterized as a 'truism,' stating merely that 'all is retained which has not been surrendered,' *United States* v. *Darby*, 312 U. S. 100, 124 (1941), it is not without significance. The Amendment expressly declares the constitutional policy that Congress may not exercise power in a fashion that impairs the States' integrity or their ability to function effectively in a federal system." 421 U. S., at 547 n. 7.

. . .

One undoubted attribute of state sovereignty is the States' power to determine the wages which shall be paid to those whom they employ in order to carry out their governmental functions, what hours those persons will work, and what compensation will be provided where these employees may be called upon to work overtime. The question we must resolve here, then, is whether these determinations are " 'functions essential to separate and independent existence' " . . . so that Congress may not abrogate the States' otherwise plenary authority to make them.

. . .

Judged solely in terms of increased costs in dollars, [the Act makes] a significant impact on the functioning of the governmental bodies involved. The Metropolitan Government of Nashville and Davidson County, Tenn., for example, asserted that the Act will increase its costs of providing essential police and fire protection, without any increase in service or in current salary levels, by $938,000 per year. . . . The State of California, which must devote significant portions of its budget to fire-suppression endeavors, estimated that application of the Act to its employment practices will necessitate an increase in its budget of between $8 million and $16 million.

Increased costs are not, of course, the only adverse effects which compliance with the Act will visit upon state and local governments, and in turn upon the citizens who depend upon those governments. In its complaint in intervention, for example, California asserted that it could not comply with the overtime costs (approximately $750,000 per year) which the Act required to be paid to California Highway Patrol cadets during their academy training program. California reported that it had thus been forced to reduce its academy training program from 2,080 hours to only 960 hours, a compromise undoubtedly of substantial importance to those whose safety and welfare may depend upon the preparedness of the California Highway Patrol.

. . .

Our examination of the effect of the 1974 amendments, as sought to be extended to the States and their political subdivisions, satisfies us that both the minimum wage and the maximum hour provisions will impermissibly interfere with the integral governmental functions of these bodies. . . . [E]ven if we accept appellee's assessments concerning the impact of the amendments, their application will nonetheless significantly alter or displace the States' abilities to structure employer-employee relationships in such areas as fire prevention, police protection, sanitation, public health, and parks and recreation. These activities are typical of those performed by state and local governments in discharging their dual functions of administering the public law and furnishing public services. Indeed, it is functions such as these which governments are created to provide, services such as these which the States have traditionally afforded their citizens. We hold that insofar as the challenged amendments operate to directly displace the States' freedom to structure integral operations in areas of traditional governmental functions, they are not within the authority granted Congress by Art. I, § 8, cl. 3.

. . .

The judgment of the District Court is accordingly reversed, and the cases are remanded for further proceedings consistent with this opinion.

So ordered.

MR. JUSTICE BLACKMUN, concurring.

The Court's opinion and the dissents indicate the importance and significance of this litigation as it bears upon the relationship between the Federal Government and our States. Although I am not untroubled by certain possible implications of the Court's opinion—some of them suggested by the dissents—I do not read the opinion so despairingly as does my Brother BRENNAN. In my view, the result with respect to the statute under challenge here is necessarily correct. I may misinterpret the Court's opinion, but it seems to me that it adopts a balancing approach, and does not outlaw federal power in areas such as environmental protection, where the federal interest is demonstrably greater and where state facility compliance with imposed federal standards would be essential. See *ante,* at 852–853. With this understanding on my part of the Court's opinion, I join it.

MR. JUSTICE BRENNAN, with whom MR. JUSTICE WHITE and MR. JUSTICE MARSHALL join, dissenting.

The Court concedes, as of course it must, that Congress enacted the 1974 amendments pursuant to its exclusive power under Art. I, § 8, cl. 3, of the Constitution "[t]o regulate Commerce . . . among the several States." It must therefore be surprising that my Brethren should choose this bicentennial year of our independence to repudiate principles governing judicial interpretation of our Constitution settled since the time of Mr. Chief Justice John Marshall, discarding his postulate that the Constitution contemplates that restraints upon exercise by Congress of its plenary commerce power lie in the political process and not in the judicial process. For 152 years ago Mr. Chief Justice Marshall enunciated that principle to which, until today, his successors on this Court have been faithful.

"[T]he power over commerce . . . is vested in Congress as absolutely as it would be in a single government, having in its constitution the same restrictions on the exercise of the power as are found in the constitution of the United States. *The wisdom and the discretion of Congress, their identity with the people, and the influence which their constituents possess at elections, are . . . the sole restraints on which they have relied, to secure them from its abuse. They are the restraints on which the people must often rely solely, in all representative*

governments." Gibbons v. *Ogden,* 9 Wheat. 1, 197 (1824) (emphasis added).

. . .

Today's repudiation of this unbroken line of precedents that firmly reject my Brethren's ill-conceived abstraction can only be regarded as a transparent cover for invalidating a congressional judgment with which they disagree. The only analysis even remotely resembling that adopted today is found in a line of opinions dealing with the Commerce Clause and the Tenth Amendment that ultimately provoked a constitutional crisis for the Court in the 1930's. *E. g., Carter* v. *Carter Coal Co.,* 298 U. S. 238 (1936); *United States* v. *Butler,* 297 U. S. 1 (1936); *Hammer* v. *Dagenhart,* 247 U. S. 251 (1918). See Stern, The Commerce Clause and the National Economy, 1933–1946, 59 Harv. L. Rev. 645 (1946). We tend to forget that the Court invalidated legislation during the Great Depression, not solely under the Due Process Clause, but also and primarily under the Commerce Clause and the Tenth Amendment. It may have been the eventual abandonment of that overly restrictive construction of the commerce power that spelled defeat for the Court-packing plan, and preserved the integrity of this institution. . . .

. . . I cannot recall another instance in the Court's history when the reasoning of so many decisions covering so long a span of time has been discarded in such a roughshod manner. That this is done without any justification not already often advanced and consistently rejected, clearly renders today's decision an *ipse dixit* reflecting nothing but displeasure with a congressional judgment.

. . .

My Brethren do more than turn aside long-standing constitutional jurisprudence that emphatically rejects today's conclusion. More alarming is the startling restructuring of our federal system, and the role they create therein for the federal judiciary. This Court is simply not at liberty to erect a mirror of its own conception of a desirable governmental structure. If the 1974 amendments have any "vice," *ante,* at 849, my Brother STEVENS is surely right that it represents "merely . . . a policy issue which has been firmly resolved by the branches of government having power to decide such questions." *Post*, at 881. It bears repeating "that effective restraints on . . . exercise [of the commerce power] must proceed from political rather than from judicial processes." *Wickard* v. *Filburn*, 317 U. S., at 120.

It is unacceptable that the judicial process should be thought superior to the political process in this area. Under the Constitution the Judiciary has no role to play beyond finding that Congress has not made an unreasonable legislative judgment respecting what is "commerce." My Brother BLACKMUN suggests that controlling judicial supervision of the relationship between the States and our National Government by use of a balancing approach diminishes the ominous implications of today's decision. Such an approach, however, is a thinly veiled rationalization for judicial supervision of a policy judgment that our system of government reserves to Congress.

Judicial restraint in this area merely recognizes that the political branches of our Government are structured to protect the interests of the States, as well as the Nation as a whole, and that the States are fully able to protect their own interests in the premises. Congress is constituted of representatives in both the Senate and House *elected from the States*. The Federalist No. 45, pp. 311–312, No. 46, pp. 317–318 (J. Cooke ed. 1961) (J. Madison). Decisions upon the extent of federal intervention under the Commerce Clause into the affairs of the States are in that sense decisions of the States themselves. Judicial redistribution of powers granted the National Government by the terms of the Constitution violates the fundamental tenet of our federalism that the extent of federal intervention into the States' affairs in the exercise of delegated powers shall be determined by the States' exercise of political power through their representatives in Congress. See Wechsler, The Political Safeguards of Federalism: The Role of the States in the Composition and Selection of the National Government, 54 Col. L. Rev. 543 (1954). . . .

. . .

A sense of the enormous impact of States' political power is gained by brief reference to the federal budget. The largest estimate by any of the appellants of the cost impact of the 1974 amendments—$1 billion—pales in comparison with the financial assistance the States receive from the Federal Government. In fiscal 1977 the President's proposed budget recommends $60.5 billion in federal assistance to the States, exclusive of loans. Office of Management and Budget, Special Analyses: Budget of the United States Government, Fiscal Year 1977, p. 255. Appellants complain of the impact of the amended FLSA on police and fire departments, but the 1977 budget contemplates outlays for law enforcement assistance of $716 million. *Id.*, at 258. Concern is also expressed about the diminished ability to hire students in the summer if States must pay them a minimum wage, but the Federal Government's "summer youth program" provides $400 million for 670,000 jobs. *Ibid.* Given this demonstrated ability to obtain funds from the Federal Government for needed state services, there is little doubt that the States' influence in the political process is adequate to safeguard their sovereignty.

. . .

We are left then with a catastrophic judicial body blow at Congress' power under the Commerce Clause. Even if Congress may nevertheless accomplish its objectives—for example, by conditioning grants of federal funds upon compliance with federal minimum wage and overtime standards, cf. *Oklahoma* v. *CSC*, 330 U. S. 127, 144 (1947)—there is an ominous portent of disruption of our constitutional structure implicit in today's mischievous decision. I dissent.

MR. JUSTICE STEVENS, dissenting.

The Court holds that the Federal Government may not interfere with a sovereign State's inherent right to pay a substandard wage to the janitor at the state capitol. The principle on which the holding rests is difficult to perceive.

The Federal Government may, I believe, require the State to act impartially when it hires or fires the janitor, to withhold taxes from his paycheck, to observe safety regulations when he is performing his job, to forbid him from burning too much soft coal in the capitol furnace, from dumping untreated refuse in an adjacent waterway, from overloading a state-owned garbage truck, or from driving either the truck or the Governor's limousine over 55 miles an hour. Even though these and many other activities of the capitol janitor are activities of the State *qua* State, I have no doubt that they are subject to federal regulation.

I agree that it is unwise for the Federal Government to exercise its power in the ways described in the Court's opinion. For the proposition that regulation of the minimum price of a commodity—even labor—will increase the quantity consumed is not one that I can readily understand. That concern, however, applies with even greater force to the private sector of the economy where the exclusion of the marginally employable does the greatest harm and, in all events, merely reflects my views on a policy issue which has been firmly resolved by the branches of government having power to decide such questions. As far as the

complexities of adjusting police and fire departments to this sort of federal control are concerned, I presume that appropriate tailor-made regulations would soon solve their most pressing problems. After all, the interests adversely affected by this legislation are not without political power.

My disagreement with the wisdom of this legislation may not, of course, affect my judgment with respect to its validity. On this issue there is no dissent from the proposition that the Federal Government's power over the labor market is adequate to embrace these employees. Since I am unable to identify a limitation on that federal power that would not also invalidate federal regulation of state activities that I consider unquestionably permissible, I am persuaded that this statute is valid. Accordingly, with respect and a great deal of sympathy for the views expressed by the Court, I dissent from its constitutional holding.

Garcia v. San Antonio Metro. Transit Auth.

469 U.S. 528 (1985)

The federalism doctrine of *National League of Cities* (1976) rested on a narrow 5–4 decision, with Justice Blackmun's concurrence supplying the fifth vote. The doctrine's attempt to distinguish between "traditional" and "nontraditional" governmental functions produced vast confusion in the lower courts. Blackmun eventually concluded that the doctrine was not only unworkable but also inconsistent with established principles of federalism. By switching sides, he created a new 5–4 majority to overturn *National League of Cities*. The *Garcia* case began in 1979 when the Department of Labor issued an opinion that the operations of the San Antonio Metropolitan Transit Authority (SAMTA) were not immune from the minimum-wage and overtime requirements of the Fair Labor Standards Act, notwithstanding *National League of Cities*. SAMTA filed an action in federal district court, seeking declaratory relief. On the same day, Joe G. Garcia and several other SAMTA employees brought suit against SAMTA for overtime pay under the Fair Labor Standards Act.

JUSTICE BLACKMUN delivered the opinion of the Court.

We revisit in these cases an issue raised in *National League of Cities* v. *Usery*, 426 U. S. 833 (1976). In that litigation, this Court, by a sharply divided vote, ruled that the Commerce Clause does not empower Congress to enforce the mini-

mum-wage and overtime provisions of the Fair Labor Standards Act (FLSA) against the States "in areas of traditional governmental functions." *Id.*, at 852. Although *National League of Cities* supplied some examples of "traditional governmental functions," it did not offer a general explanation of how a "traditional" function is to be distinguished from a "nontraditional" one. Since then, federal and state courts have struggled with the task, thus imposed, of identifying a traditional function for purposes of state immunity under the Commerce Clause.

In the present cases, a Federal District Court concluded that municipal ownership and operation of a mass-transit system is a traditional governmental function and thus, under *National League of Cities,* is exempt from the obligations imposed by the FLSA. Faced with the identical question, three Federal Courts of Appeals and one state appellate court have reached the opposite conclusion.

Our examination of this "function" standard applied in these and other cases over the last eight years now persuades us that the attempt to draw the boundaries of state regulatory immunity in terms of "traditional governmental function" is not only unworkable but is also inconsistent with established principles of federalism and, indeed, with those very federalism principles on which *National League of Cities* purported to rest. That case, accordingly, is overruled.

I

The history of public transportation in San Antonio, Tex., is characteristic of the history of local mass transit in the United States generally. Passenger transportation for hire within San Antonio originally was provided on a private basis by a local transportation company. In 1913, the Texas Legislature authorized the State's municipalities to regulate vehicles providing carriage for hire. 1913 Tex. Gen. Laws, ch. 147, § 4, ¶12, now codified, as amended, as Tex. Rev. Civ. Stat. Ann., Art. 1175, §§ 20 and 21 (Vernon 1963). Two years later, San Antonio enacted an ordinance setting forth franchising, insurance, and safety requirements for passenger vehicles operated for hire. The city continued to rely on such publicly regulated private mass transit until 1959, when it purchased the privately owned San Antonio Transit Company and replaced it with a public authority known as the San Antonio Transit System (SATS). SATS operated until 1978, when the city transferred its facilities and equipment to appellee San Antonio Metropolitan Transit Authority

(SAMTA), a public mass-transit authority organized on a countywide basis. See generally Tex. Rev. Civ. Stat. Ann., Art. 1118x (Vernon Supp. 1984). SAMTA currently is the major provider of transportation in the San Antonio metropolitan area; between 1978 and 1980 alone, its vehicles traveled over 26 million route miles and carried over 63 million passengers.

As did other localities, San Antonio reached the point where it came to look to the Federal Government for financial assistance in maintaining its public mass transit. SATS managed to meet its operating expenses and bond obligations for the first decade of its existence without federal or local financial aid. By 1970, however, its financial position had deteriorated to the point where federal subsidies were vital for its continued operation. SATS' general manager that year testified before Congress that "if we do not receive substantial help from the Federal Government, San Antonio may . . . join the growing ranks of cities that have inferior [public] transportation or may end up with no [public] transportation at all."

The principal federal program to which SATS and other mass-transit systems looked for relief was the Urban Mass Transportation Act of 1964 (UMTA), Pub. L. 88–365, 78 Stat. 302, as amended, 49 U. S. C. App. § 1601 *et seq.,* which provides substantial federal assistance to urban mass-transit programs. . . . SATS received its first UMTA subsidy, a $4.1 million capital grant, in December 1970. From then until February 1980, SATS and SAMTA received over $51 million in UMTA grants —more than $31 million in capital grants, over $20 million in operating assistance, and a minor amount in technical assistance. During SAMTA's first two fiscal years, it received $12.5 million in UMTA operating grants, $26.8 million from sales taxes, and only $10.1 million from fares. Federal subsidies and local sales taxes currently account for about 75 percent of SAMTA's operating expenses.

. . .

II

. . . The District Court voiced a common concern: "Despite the abundance of adjectives, identifying which particular state functions are immune *[from regulation under the Fair Labor Standards Act]* remains difficult." 557 F. Supp., at 447. Just how troublesome the task has been is revealed by the results reached in other federal cases. . . . We find it difficult, if not impossible, to identify an organizing principle that places each of the cases in the first group *[protected under National League of Cities]* on one side of a line and each of the cases in the second group *[not protected]* on the other side. The constitutional distinction between licensing drivers *[protected]* and regulating traffic *[not protected]*, for example, or between operating a highway authority *[protected]* and operating a mental health facility *[not protected]*, is elusive at best.

. . .

We believe, however, that there is a more fundamental problem at work here. . . . The essence of our federal system is that within the realm of authority left open to them under the Constitution, the States must be equally free to engage in any activity that their citizens choose for the common weal, no matter how unorthodox or unnecessary anyone else—including the judiciary —deems state involvement to be. Any rule of state immunity that looks to the "traditional," "integral," or "necessary" nature of governmental functions inevitably invites an unelected federal judiciary to make decisions about which state policies it favors and which ones it dislikes. "The science of government . . . is the science of experiment," *Anderson* v. *Dunn*, 6 Wheat. 204, 226 (1821), and the States cannot serve as laboratories for social and economic experiment, see *New State Ice Co.* v. *Liebmann*, 285 U. S. 262, 311 (1932) (Brandeis, J., dissenting), if they must pay an added price when they meet the changing needs of their citizenry by taking up functions that an earlier day and a different society left in private hands. In the words of Justice Black:

"There is not, and there cannot be, any unchanging line of demarcation between essential and non-essential governmental functions. Many governmental functions of today have at some time in the past been nongovernmental. The genius of our government provides that, within the

sphere of constitutional action, the people— acting not through the courts but through their elected legislative representatives—have the power to determine as conditions demand, what services and functions the public welfare requires." *Helvering* v. *Gerhardt*, 304 U. S., at 427 (concurring opinion).

We therefore now reject, as unsound in principle and unworkable in practice, a rule of state immunity from federal regulation that turns on a judicial appraisal of whether a particular governmental function is "integral" or "traditional." . . .

III

The central theme of *National League of Cities* was that the States occupy a special position in our constitutional system and that the scope of Congress' authority under the Commerce Clause must reflect that position. . . .

We doubt that courts ultimately can identify principled constitutional limitations on the scope of Congress' Commerce Clause powers over the States merely by relying on *a priori* definitions of state sovereignty. In part, this is because of the elusiveness of objective criteria for "fundamental" elements of state sovereignty, a problem we have witnessed in the search for "traditional governmental functions." . . .

IV

This analysis makes clear that Congress' action in affording SAMTA employees the protections of the wage and hour provisions of the FLSA contravened no affirmative limit on Congress' power under the Commerce Clause. The judgment of the District Court therefore must be reversed.

Of course, we continue to recognize that the States occupy a special and specific position in our constitutional system and that the scope of Congress' authority under the Commerce Clause must reflect that position. But the principal and basic limit on the federal commerce power is that inherent in all congressional action—the built-in restraints that our system provides through state participation in federal governmental action. The political process ensures that laws that unduly burden the States will not be promulgated. In the factual setting of these cases the internal safeguards of the political process have performed as intended.

These cases do not require us to identify or define what affirmative limits the constitutional structure might impose on federal action affecting the States under the Commerce Clause. See *Coyle v. Oklahoma*, 221 U. S. 559 (1911). We note and accept Justice Frankfurter's observation in *New York v. United States*, 326 U. S. 572, 583 (1946):

"The process of Constitutional adjudication does not thrive on conjuring up horrible possibilities that never happen in the real world and devising doctrines sufficiently comprehensive in detail to cover the remotest contingency. Nor need we go beyond what is required for a reasoned disposition of the kind of controversy now before the Court."

Though the separate concurrence providing the fifth vote in *National League of Cities* was "not untroubled by certain possible implications" of the decision, 426 U. S., at 856, the Court in that case attempted to articulate affirmative limits on the Commerce Clause power in terms of core governmental functions and fundamental attributes of state sovereignty. But the model of democratic decisionmaking the Court there identified underestimated, in our view, the solicitude of the national political process for the continued vitality of the States. Attempts by other courts since then to draw guidance from this model have proved it both impracticable and doctrinally barren. In sum, in *National League of Cities* the Court tried to repair what did not need repair.

We do not lightly overrule recent precedent. We have not hesitated, however, when it has become apparent that a prior decision has departed from a proper understanding of congressional power under the Commerce Clause. See *United States v. Darby*, 312 U. S. 100, 116–117 (1941). Due respect for the reach of congressional power within the federal system mandates that we do so now.

National League of Cities v. Usery, 426 U. S. 833 (1976), is overruled. The judgment of the District Court is reversed, and these cases are remanded to that court for further proceedings consistent with this opinion.

It is so ordered.

JUSTICE POWELL, with whom THE CHIEF JUSTICE, JUSTICE REHNQUIST, and JUSTICE O'CONNOR join, dissenting.

The Court today, in its 5–4 decision, overrules *National League of Cities v. Usery*, 426 U. S. 833 (1976), a case in which we held that Congress lacked authority to impose the requirements of the Fair Labor Standards Act on state and local governments. Because I believe this decision substantially alters the federal system embodied in the Constitution, I dissent.

I

There are, of course, numerous examples over the history of this Court in which prior decisions have been reconsidered and overruled. There have been few cases, however, in which the principle of *stare decisis* and the rationale of recent decisions were ignored as abruptly as we now witness. . . .

. . .

Although the doctrine is not rigidly applied to constitutional questions, "any departure from the doctrine of *stare decisis* demands special justification." *Arizona v. Rumsey*, 467 U. S. 203, 212 (1984). See also *Oregon v. Kennedy*, 456 U. S. 667, 691–692, n. 34 (1982) (STEVENS, J., concurring in judgment). In the present cases, the five Justices who compose the majority today participated in *National League of Cities* and the cases reaffirming it. The stability of judicial decision, and with it respect for the authority of this Court, are not served by the precipitate overruling of multiple precedents that we witness in these cases.

Whatever effect the Court's decision may have in weakening the application of *stare decisis*, it is likely to be less important than what the Court has done to the Constitution itself. A unique feature of the United States is the *federal* system of government guaranteed by the Constitution and implicit in the very name of our country. Despite some genuflecting in the Court's opinion to the concept of federalism, today's decision effectively reduces the Tenth Amendment to meaningless rhetoric when Congress acts pursuant to the Commerce Clause. The Court holds that the Fair Labor Standards Act (FLSA) "contravened no affirmative limit on Congress' power under the Commerce Clause" to determine the wage rates and hours of employment of all state and local employees. *Ante,* at 556. In rejecting the traditional view of our federal system, the Court states:

"Apart from the limitation on federal authority inherent in the delegated nature of Congress' Article I powers, the principal means chosen by the Framers to ensure the role of the States in the federal system lies in the *structure* of the Federal Government itself." *Ante,* at 550 (emphasis added).

To leave no doubt about its intention, the Court renounces its decision in *National League of Cities* because it "inevitably invites an unelected federal judiciary to make decisions about which state policies its favors and which ones it dislikes." *Ante,* at 546. In other words, the extent to which the States may exercise their authority, when Congress purports to act under the Commerce Clause, henceforth is to be determined from time to time by political decisions made by members of the Federal Government, decisions the Court says will not be subject to judicial review. I note that it does not seem to have occurred to the Court that *it*—an unelected majority of five Justices—today rejects almost 200 years of the understanding of the constitutional status of federalism. In doing so, there is only a single passing reference to the Tenth Amendment. Nor is so much as a dictum of any court cited in support of the view that the role of the States in the federal system may depend upon the grace of elected federal officials, rather than on the Constitution as interpreted by this Court.

. . .

II

The Court finds that the test of state immunity approved in *National League of Cities* and its progeny is unworkable and unsound in principle. In finding the test to be unworkable, the Court begins by mischaracterizing *National League of Cities* and subsequent cases. In concluding that efforts to define state immunity are unsound in principle, the Court radically departs from long-settled constitutional values and ignores the role of judicial review in our system of government.

A

Much of the Court's opinion is devoted to arguing that it is difficult to define *a priori* "traditional governmental functions." *National League of Cities* neither engaged in, nor required, such a task. The Court discusses and condemns as standards "traditional governmental functions," "purely historical" functions, " 'uniquely' governmental functions," and " 'necessary' governmental services." *Ante,* at 539, 543, 545. But nowhere does it mention that *National League of Cities* adopted a familiar type of balancing test for determining whether Commerce Clause enactments transgress constitutional limitations imposed by the federal nature of our system of government. This omission is noteworthy, since the author of today's opinion joined *National League of Cities* and concurred separately to point out that the Court's opinion in that case "adopt[s] a balancing approach [that] does not outlaw federal power in areas . . . where the federal interest is demonstrably greater and where state . . . compliance with imposed federal standards would be essential." 426 U. S., at 856 (BLACKMUN, J., concurring).

. . .

B

Today's opinion does not explain how the States' role in the electoral process guarantees that particular exercises of the Commerce Clause power will not infringe on residual state sovereignty. Members of Congress are elected from the various States, but once in office they are Members of the Federal Government. Although the States participate in the Electoral College, this is hardly a reason to view the President as a representative of the States' interest against federal encroachment. We noted recently "[t]he hydraulic pressure inherent within each of the separate

Branches to exceed the outer limits of its power. . . ." *INS* v. *Chadha*, 462 U. S. 919, 951 (1983). The Court offers no reason to think that this pressure will not operate when Congress seeks to invoke its powers under the Commerce Clause, notwithstanding the electoral role of the States.

The Court apparently thinks that the States' success at obtaining federal funds for various projects and exemptions from the obligations of some federal statutes is indicative of the "effectiveness of the federal political process in preserving the States' interests. . . ." *Ante*, at 552. But such political success is not relevant to the question whether the political *processes* are the proper means of enforcing constitutional limitations. The fact that Congress generally does not transgress constitutional limits on its power to reach state activities does not make judicial review any less necessary to rectify the cases in which it does do so. The States' role in our system of government is a matter of constitutional law, not of legislative grace. "The powers not delegated to the United States by the Constitution, nor prohibited by it to the States, are reserved to the States, respectively, or to the people." U. S. Const., Amdt. 10.

More troubling than the logical infirmities in the Court's reasoning is the result of its holding, *i.e.*, that federal political officials, invoking the Commerce Clause, are the sole judges of the limits of their own power. This result is inconsistent with the fundamental principles of our constitutional system. See, *e. g.*, The Federalist No. 78 (Hamilton). At least since *Marbury* v. *Madison*, 1 Cranch 137, 177 (1803), it has been the settled province of the federal judiciary "to say what the law is" with respect to the constitutionality of Acts of Congress. In rejecting the role of the judiciary in protecting the States from federal overreaching, the Court's opinion offers no explanation for ignoring the teaching of the most famous case in our history.

. . .

JUSTICE REHNQUIST, dissenting.

I join both JUSTICE POWELL's and JUSTICE O'CONNOR's thoughtful dissents. JUSTICE POWELL's reference to the "balancing test" approved in *National League of Cities* is not identical with the language in that case, which recognized that Congress could not act under its commerce power to infringe on certain fundamental aspects of state sovereignty that are essential to "the States' separate and independent existence." Nor is either test, or JUSTICE O'CONNOR's suggested approach, precisely congruent with JUSTICE BLACKMUN's views in 1976, when he spoke of a balancing approach which did not outlaw federal power in areas "where the federal interest is demonstrably greater." But under any one of these approaches the judgment in these cases should be affirmed, and I do not think it incumbent on those of us in dissent to spell out further the fine points of a principle that will, I am confident, in time again command the support of a majority of this Court.

JUSTICE O'CONNOR, with whom JUSTICE POWELL and JUSTICE REHNQUIST join, dissenting.

The Court today surveys the battle scene of federalism and sounds a retreat. Like JUSTICE POWELL, I would prefer to hold the field and, at the very least, render a little aid to the wounded. I join JUSTICE POWELL's opinion. I also write separately to note my fundamental disagreement with the majority's views of federalism and the duty of this Court.

The Court overrules *National League of Cities* v. *Usery*, 426 U. S. 833 (1976), on the grounds that it is not "faithful to the role of federalism in a democratic society." *Ante*, at 546. "The essence of our federal system," the Court concludes, "is that within the realm of authority left open to them under the Constitution, the States must be equally free to engage in any activity that their citizens choose for the common weal. . . ." *Ibid.* *National League of Cities* is held to be inconsistent with this narrow view of federalism because it attempts to protect only those fundamental aspects of state sovereignty that are essential to the States' separate and independent existence, rather than protecting all state activities "equally."

In my view, federalism cannot be reduced to the weak "essence" distilled by the majority today. There is more to federalism than the nature of the constraints that can be imposed on the States in "the realm of authority left open to them by the Constitution." The central issue of federalism, of course, is whether any realm *is* left open to the States by the Constitution—whether any area remains in which a State may act free of federal interference. "The issue . . . is whether the federal system has any *legal* substance, any core of constitutional right that courts will enforce." C. Black, Perspectives in Constitutional Law 30 (1963). The true "essence" of federalism is that the States *as States* have legitimate interests which the National Government is bound to respect even though its laws are supreme. . . .

. . .

. . . With the abandonment of *National League of Cities,* all that stands between the remaining essentials of state sovereignty and Congress is the latter's underdeveloped capacity for self-restraint.

. . .

Pollock v. Farmers' Loan & Trust Co.

158 U.S. 601 (1895)

The Constitution retained for the states the power of direct taxation. The federal government could also invoke that power, but only on the condition that such taxes be apportioned among the states in accordance with their numbers. Congress passed an income tax in 1894. The task for the Court was to distinguish between direct and indirect taxes and specify the conditions for the latter. Earlier in 1895, the Court decided that the statute's tax on rents or income of real estate represented a direct tax and was therefore unconstitutional for failure to follow the apportionment rule. Pollock v. Farmers' Loan & Trust Co., 157 U.S. 429 (1895). That left a remaining issue from the statute: the income tax.

MR. CHIEF JUSTICE FULLER delivered the opinion of the court.

Whenever this court is required to pass upon the validity of an act of Congress as tested by the fundamental law enacted by the people, the duty imposed demands in its discharge the utmost deliberation and care, and invokes the deepest sense of responsibility. And this is especially so when the question involves the exercise of a great governmental power, and brings into consideration, as vitally affected by the decision, that complex system of government, so sagaciously framed to secure and perpetuate "an indestructible Union, composed of indestructible States."

. . . the Constitution divided Federal taxation into two great classes, the class of direct taxes, and the class of duties, imposts, and excises; and prescribed two rules which qualified the grant of power as to each class.

The power to lay direct taxes apportioned among the several States in proportion to their representation in the popular branch of Congress, a representation based on population as ascer-tained by the census, was plenary and absolute; but to lay direct taxes without apportionment was forbidden. The power to lay duties, imposts, and excises was subject to the qualification that the imposition must be uniform throughout the United States.

Our previous decision was confined to the consideration of the validity of the tax on the income from real estate, and on the income from municipal bonds. The question thus limited was whether such taxation was direct or not, in the meaning of the Constitution; and the court went no farther, as to the tax on the income from real estate, than to hold that it fell within the same class as the source whence the income was derived, that is, that a tax upon the realty and a tax upon the receipts therefrom were alike direct; while as to the income from municipal bonds, that could not be taxed because of want of power to tax the source, and no reference was made to the nature of the tax as being direct or indirect.

We are now permitted to broaden the field of inquiry, and to determine to which of the two great classes a tax upon a person's entire income, whether derived from rents, or products, or otherwise, of real estate, or from bonds, stocks, or other forms of personal property, belongs; and we are unable to conclude that the enforced subtraction from the yield of all the owner's real or personal property, in the manner prescribed, is so different from a tax upon the property itself, that it is not a direct, but an indirect tax, in the meaning of the Constitution.

. . .

The founders anticipated that the expenditures of the States, their counties, cities, and towns, would chiefly be met by direct taxation on accumulated property, while they expected that those of the Federal government would be for the most part met by indirect taxes. And in order that the power of direct taxation by the general government should not be exercised, except on necessity; and, when the necessity arose, should be so exercised as to leave the States at liberty to discharge their respective obligations, and should not be so exercised, unfairly and discriminatingly, as to particular States or otherwise, by a mere majority vote, possibly of those whose constituents were intentionally not subjected to any part of the burden, the qualified grant was made. Those who made it knew that the power to tax involved the power to destroy . . .

It is said that a tax on the whole income of property is not a direct tax in the meaning of the Constitution, but a duty, and, as a duty, leviable without apportionment, whether direct or indirect. We do not think so. Direct taxation was not restricted in one breath, and the restriction blown to the winds in another.

. . .

According to the census, the true valuation of real and personal property in the United States in 1890 was $65,037,091,197, of which real estate with improvements thereon made up $39,544,544,333. Of course, from the latter must be deducted, in applying these sections, all unproductive property and all property whose net yield does not exceed four thousand dollars; but, even with such deductions, it is evident that the income from realty formed a vital part of the scheme for taxation embodied therein. If that be stricken out, and also the income from all invested personal property, bonds, stocks, investments of all kinds, it is obvious that by far the largest part of the anticipated revenue would be eliminated, and this would leave the burden of the tax to be borne by professions, trades, employments, or vocations; and in that way what was intended as a tax on capital would remain in substance a tax on occupations and labor. We cannot believe that such was the intention of Congress. We do not mean to say that an act laying by apportionment a direct tax on all real estate and personal property, or the income thereof, might not also lay excise taxes on business, privileges, employments, and vocations. But this is not such an act; and the scheme must be considered as a whole. Being invalid as to the greater part, and falling, as the tax would, if any part were held valid, in a direction which could not have been contemplated except in connection with the taxation considered as an entirety, we are constrained to conclude that sections twenty-seven to thirty-seven, inclusive, of the act, which became a law without the signature of the President on August 28, 1894, are wholly inoperative and void.

Our conclusions may, therefore, be summed up as follows:

First. We adhere to the opinion already announced, that, taxes on real estate being indisputably direct taxes, taxes on the rents or income of real estate are equally direct taxes.

Second. We are of opinion that taxes on personal property, or on the income of personal property, are likewise direct taxes.

Third. The tax imposed by sections twenty-seven to thirty-seven, inclusive, of the act of 1894, so far as it falls on the income of real estate and of personal property, being a direct tax within the meaning of the Constitution, and, therefore, unconstitutional and void because not apportioned according to representation, all those sections, constituting one entire scheme of taxation, are necessarily invalid.

The decrees hereinbefore entered in this court will be vacated; the decrees below will be reversed, and the cases remanded, with instructions to grant the relief prayed.

MR. JUSTICE HARLAN dissenting.

. . .

It is appropriate now to say that however objectionable the law would have been, after the provision for taxing incomes arising from rents was stricken out, I did not then, nor do I now, think it within the province of the court to annul the provisions relating to incomes derived from other specified sources, and take from the government the entire revenue contemplated to be raised by the taxation of incomes, simply because the clause relating to rents was held to be unconstitutional. The reasons for this view will be stated in another connection.

. . .

What are "direct taxes" within the meaning of the Constitution? In the convention of 1787, Rufus King asked what was the precise meaning of *direct* taxation, and no one answered. Madison Papers, 5 Elliott's Debates, 451. The debates of that famous body do not show that any delegate attempted to give a clear, succinct definition of what, in his opinion, was a direct tax. Indeed, the report of those debates, upon the question now before us, is very meagre and unsatisfactory. . . .

A question so difficult to be answered by able statesmen and lawyers directly concerned in the organization of the present government, can now, it seems, be easily answered, after a reexamination of documents, writings, and treatises on political economy, all of which, without any exception worth noting, have been several times directly brought to the attention of this court. And whenever that has been done the result always, until now, has been that a duty on incomes, derived from taxable subjects, of whatever nature, was held not to be a direct tax within the meaning of the Constitution, to be apportioned among the States on the basis of population, but could be laid, according to the rule of uniformity, upon individual citizens, corporations, and associations without reference to numbers in the particular States in which such citizens, corporations, or associations were domiciled. . . .

. . .

. . . The recent civil war, involving the very existence of the nation, was brought to a successful end, and the authority of the Union restored, in part, by the use of vast amounts of money raised under statutes imposing duties on incomes derived from every kind of property, real and personal, not by the unequal rule of apportionment among the States on the basis of numbers, but by the rule of uniformity, operating upon individuals and corporations in all the States. And we are now asked to declare—and the judgment this day rendered in effect declares—that the enormous sums thus taken from the people, and so used, were taken in violation of the supreme law of the land. The supremacy of the nation was reëstablished against armed rebellion seeking to destroy its life, but, it seems, that that consummation, so devoutly wished, and to effect which so many valuable lives were sacrificed, was attended with a disregard of the Constitution by which the Union was ordained.

. . .

In my judgment—to say nothing of the disregard of the former adjudications of this court, and of the settled practice of the government—this decision may well excite the gravest apprehensions. It strikes at the very foundations of national authority, in that it denies to the general government a power which is, or may become, vital to the very existence and preservation of the Union in a national emergency, such as that of war with a great commercial nation, during which the collection of all duties upon imports will cease or be materially diminished. It tends to reëstablish that condition of helplessness in which Congress found itself during the period of the Articles of Confederation, when it was without authority by laws operating directly upon individuals, to lay and collect, through its own agents, taxes sufficient to pay the debts and defray the expenses of government, but was dependent, in all such matters, upon the good will of the States, and their promptness in meeting requisitions made upon them by Congress.

. . .

MR. JUSTICE BROWN dissenting.

. . .

It is difficult to overestimate the importance of these cases. I certainly cannot overstate the regret I feel at the disposition made of them by the court. It is never a light thing to set aside the deliberate will of the legislature, and in my opinion it should never be done, except upon the clearest proof of its conflict with the fundamental law. Respect for the Constitution will not be inspired by a narrow and technical construction which shall limit or impair the necessary powers of Congress. Did the reversal of these cases involve merely the striking down of the inequitable features of this law, or even the whole law, for its want of uniformity, the consequences would be less serious; but as it implies a declaration that every income tax must be laid according to the rule of apportionment, the decision involves nothing less than a surrender of the taxing power to the moneyed class. By resuscitating an argument that was exploded in the *Hylton case*, and has lain practically dormant for a hundred years, it is made to do duty in nullifying, not this law alone, but every similar law that is not based upon an impossible theory of apportionment. Even the spectre of socialism is conjured up to frighten Congress from laying taxes upon the people in proportion to their ability to pay them. It is certainly a strange commentary upon the Constitution of the United States and upon a democratic government that Congress has no power to lay a tax which is one of the main sources of revenue of nearly every civilized State. It is a confession of feebleness in which I find myself wholly unable to join.

. . .

MR. JUSTICE JACKSON dissenting.

. . .

The decision disregards the well-established canon of construction to which I have referred, that an act passed by a coördinate branch of the government has every presumption in its favor, and should never be declared invalid by the courts unless its repugnancy to the Constitution is clear beyond all reasonable doubt. It is not a matter of conjecture; it is the established principle that it must be clear beyond a reasonable doubt. I cannot

see, in view of the past, how this case can be said to be free of doubt.

Again, the decision not only takes from Congress its rightful power of fixing the rate of taxation, but substitutes a rule incapable of application without producing the most monstrous inequality and injustice between citizens residing in different sections of their common country, such as the framers of the Constitution never could have contemplated, such as no free and enlightened people can ever possibly sanction or approve.

The practical operation of the decision is not only to disregard the great principles of equality in taxation, but the further principle that in the imposition of taxes for the benefit of the government the burdens thereof should be imposed upon those having most *ability* to bear them. This decision, in effect, works out a directly opposite result, in relieving the citizens having the greater *ability*, while the burdens of taxation are made to fall most heavily and oppressively upon those having the least ability. It lightens the burden upon the larger number, in some States subject to the tax, and places it most unequally and disproportionately on the smaller number in other States. Considered in all its bearings, this decision is, in my judgment, the most disastrous blow ever struck at the constitutional power of Congress. It strikes down an important portion of the most vital and essential power of the government in practically excluding any recourse to incomes from real and personal estate for the purpose of raising needed revenue to meet the government's wants and necessities under any circumstances.

I am therefore compelled to enter my dissent to the judgment of the court.

MR. JUSTICE WHITE dissenting.

. . .

. . . The suggestion that if the construction now adopted, by the court, brings about hurtful results, it can be cured by an amendment to the Constitution instead of sustaining the conclusion reached, shows its fallacy. The *Hylton case* was decided more than one hundred years ago. The income tax laws of the past were enacted also years ago. At the time they were passed, the debates and reports conclusively show that they were made to conform to the rulings in the *Hylton* case. Since all these things were done, the Constitution has been repeatedly amended. These amendments followed the civil war, and were adopted for the purpose of supplying defects in the national power. Can it be doubted that if an intimation had been conveyed that the decisions of this court would or could be overruled, so as to deprive the government of an essential power of taxation, the amendments would have rendered such a change of ruling impossible? The adoption of the amendments, none of which repudiated the uniform policy of the government, was practically a ratification of that policy and an acquiescence in the settled rule of interpretation theretofore adopted.

. . .

United States v. Butler

297 U.S. 1 (1936)

Processors of farm products challenged the "processing and floor taxes" included in the Agricultural Adjustment Act of 1933. The question was whether a tax could expropriate money from one group to be expended by another, as a necessary means for regulation. The suit was brought by William M. Butler and the Hoosac Mills Corporation. Questions of state power were involved, as well as the distinction between "local" and "national" methods of agriculture.

MR. JUSTICE ROBERTS delivered the opinion of the Court.

In this case we must determine whether certain provisions of the Agricultural Adjustment Act, 1933, conflict with the Federal Constitution.

Title I of the statute is captioned "Agricultural Adjustment." Section 1 recites that an economic emergency has arisen, due to disparity between the prices of agricultural and other commodities, with consequent destruction of farmers' purchasing power and breakdown in orderly exchange, which, in turn, have affected transactions in agricultural commodities with a national public interest and burdened and obstructed the normal currents of commerce, calling for the enactment of legislation.

[Section 8 empowered the Secretary of Agriculture to enter into agreements with agricultural producers for the purpose of reducing acreage and production, thus supporting prices by limiting supply. In connection with this reduction on production, the Secretary was authorized to provide producers with "rental or benefit payments" and to issue licenses for processors engaged in the handling, "in the current of interstate or foreign commerce," of agricultural commodities and products.]

Section 9 (a) enacts:

"To obtain revenue for extraordinary expenses incurred by reason of the national economic emergency, there shall be levied processing taxes as hereinafter provided. When the Secretary of Agriculture determines that rental or benefit payments are to be made with respect to any basic agricultural commodity, he shall proclaim such determination, and a processing tax shall be in effect with respect to such commodity from the beginning of the marketing year therefor next following the date of such proclamation. The processing tax shall be levied, assessed, and collected upon the first domestic processing of the commodity, whether of domestic production or imported, and shall be paid by the processor. . . ."

. . .

By § 16 a floor tax is imposed upon the sale or other disposition of any article processed wholly or in chief value from any commodity with respect to which a processing tax is to be levied in amount equivalent to that of the processing tax which would be payable with respect to the commodity from which the article is processed if the processing had occurred on the date when the processing tax becomes effective.

On July 14, 1933, the Secretary of Agriculture, with the approval of the President, proclaimed that he had determined rental and benefit payments should be made with respect to cotton; that the marketing year for that commodity was to begin August 1, 1933; and calculated and fixed the rates of processing and floor taxes on cotton in accordance with the terms of the act.

The United States presented a claim to the respondents as receivers of the Hoosac Mills Corporation for processing and floor taxes on cotton levied under §§ 9 and 16 of the act. The receivers recommended that the claim be disallowed. The District Court found the taxes valid and ordered them paid. Upon appeal the Circuit Court of Appeals reversed the order. The judgment under review was entered prior to the adoption of the amending act of August 24, 1935, and we are therefore concerned only with the original act.

. . .

The tax can only be sustained by ignoring the avowed purpose and operation of the act, and holding it a measure merely laying an excise upon processors to raise revenue for the support of government. Beyond cavil the sole object of the legislation is to restore the purchasing power of agricultural products to a parity with that prevailing in an earlier day; to take money from the processor and bestow it upon farmers who will reduce their acreage for the accomplishment of the proposed end, and, meanwhile to aid these farmers during the period required to bring the prices of their crops to the desired level.

The tax plays an indispensable part in the plan of regulation. As stated by the Agricultural Adjustment Administrator, it is "the heart of the law"; a means of "accomplishing one or both of two things intended to help farmers attain parity prices and purchasing power." A tax automatically goes into effect for a commodity when the Secretary of Agriculture determines that rental or benefit payments are to be made for reduction of production of that commodity. The tax is to cease when rental or benefit payments cease. The rate is fixed with the purpose of bringing about crop-reduction and price-raising. It is to equal the difference between the "current average farm price" and "fair exchange value." . . .

. . .

It is inaccurate and misleading to speak of the exaction from processors prescribed by the challenged act as a tax, or to say that as a tax it is subject to no infirmity. A tax, in the general understanding of the term, and as used in the Constitution, signifies an exaction for the support of the Government. The word has never been thought to connote the expropriation of money from one group for the benefit of another. We may concede that the latter sort of imposition is constitutional when imposed to effectuate regulation of a matter in which both groups are interested and in respect of which there is a power of legislative regulation. But manifestly no justification for it can be found unless as an integral part of such regulation. The exaction cannot be wrested out of its setting, denominated an excise for raising revenue and legalized by ignoring its purpose as a mere instrumentality for bringing about a desired end. To do this would be to shut our eyes to what all others than we can see and understand. *Child Labor Tax Case*, 259 U.S. 20, 37.

We conclude that the act is one regulating agricultural production; that the tax is a mere incident of such regulation and that the respondents have standing to challenge the legality of the exaction.

. . .

Second. The Government asserts that even if the respondents may question the propriety of the appropriation embodied in the statute their attack must fail because Article I, § 8 of the Constitution authorizes the contemplated expenditure of the funds raised by the tax. This contention presents the great and the controlling question in the case. We approach its decision with a sense of our grave responsibility to render judgment in accordance with the principles established for the governance of all three branches of the Government.

There should be no misunderstanding as to the function of this court in such a case. It is sometimes said that the court assumes a power to overrule or control the action of the people's representatives. This is a misconception. The Constitution is the supreme law of the land ordained and established by the people. All legislation must conform to the principles it lays down. When an act of Congress is appropriately challenged in the courts as not conforming to the constitutional mandate the judicial branch of the Government has only one duty,—to lay the article of the Constitution which is invoked beside the statute which is challenged and to decide whether the latter squares with the former. All the court does, or can do, is to announce its considered judgment upon the question. The only power it has, if such it may be called, is the power of judgment. This court neither approves nor condemns any legislative policy. Its delicate and difficult office is to ascertain and declare whether the legislation is in accordance with, or in contravention of, the provisions of the Constitution; and, having done that, its duty ends.

. . .

Article I, § 8, of the Constitution vests sundry powers in the Congress. But two of its clauses have any bearing upon the validity of the statute under review.

The third clause endows the Congress with power "to regulate Commerce . . . among the several States." Despite a reference in its first section to a burden upon, and an obstruction of the normal currents of commerce, the act under review does not purport to regulate transactions in interstate or foreign commerce. Its stated purpose is the control of agricultural production, a purely local activity, in an effort to raise the prices paid the farmer. Indeed, the Government does not attempt to uphold the validity of the act on the basis of the commerce clause, which, for the purpose of the present case, may be put aside as irrelevant.

The clause thought to authorize the legislation, —the first,—confers upon the Congress power "to lay and collect Taxes, Duties, Imposts and Excises, to pay the Debts and provide for the common Defence and general Welfare of the United States. . . ." It is not contended that this provision grants power to regulate agricultural production upon the theory that such legislation would promote the general welfare. The Government concedes that the phrase "to provide for the general welfare" qualifies the power "to lay and collect taxes." The view that the clause grants power to provide for the general welfare, independently of the taxing power, has never been authoritatively accepted. Mr. Justice Story points out that if it were adopted "it is obvious that under color of the generality of the words, to 'provide for the common defence and general welfare,' the government of the United States is, in reality, a government of general and unlimited powers, notwithstanding the subsequent enumeration of specific powers." The true construction undoubtedly is that the only thing granted is the power to tax for the purpose of providing funds for payment of the nation's debts and making provision for the general welfare.

Nevertheless the Government asserts that warrant is found in this clause for the adoption of the Agricultural Adjustment Act. The argument is that Congress may appropriate and authorize the spending of moneys for the "general welfare"; that the phrase should be liberally construed to cover anything conducive to national welfare; that decision as to what will promote such welfare rests with Congress alone, and the courts may not review its determination; and finally that the appropriation under attack was in fact for the general welfare of the United States.

. . .

We are not now required to ascertain the scope of the phrase "general welfare of the United States" or to determine whether an appropriation in aid of agriculture falls within it. Wholly apart from that question, another principle embedded in our Constitution prohibits the enforcement of the Agricultural Adjustment Act. The act invades the reserved rights of the states. It is a statutory plan to regulate and control agricultural production, a matter beyond the powers delegated to the federal government. The tax, the appropriation of the funds raised, and the direction for their disbursement, are but parts of the plan. They are but means to an unconstitutional end.

From the accepted doctrine that the United States is a government of delegated powers, it follows that those not expressly granted, or reasonably to be implied from such as are conferred, are reserved to the states or to the people. To forestall any suggestion to the contrary, the Tenth Amendment was adopted. The same proposition, otherwise stated, is that powers not granted are prohibited. None to regulate agricultural production is given, and therefore legislation by Congress for that purpose is forbidden.

. . .

Third. If the taxing power may not be used as the instrument to enforce a regulation of matters of state concern with respect to which the Congress has no authority to interfere, may it, as in the present case, be employed to raise the money necessary to purchase a compliance which the Congress is powerless to command? The Government asserts that whatever might be said against the validity of the plan if compulsory, it is constitutionally sound because the end is accomplished by voluntary co-operation. There are two sufficient answers to the contention. The regulation is not in fact voluntary. The farmer, of course, may refuse to comply, but the price of such refusal is the loss of benefits. The amount offered is intended to be sufficient to exert pressure on him to agree to the proposed regulation. The power to confer or withhold unlimited benefits is the power to coerce or destroy. If the cotton grower elects not to accept the benefits, he will receive less for his crops; those who receive payments will be able to undersell him. The result may well be financial ruin. . . . This is coercion by economic pressure. The asserted power of choice is illusory.

. . .

But if the plan were one for purely voluntary co-operation it would stand no better so far as federal power is concerned. At best it is a scheme for purchasing with federal funds submission to federal regulation of a subject reserved to the states.

. . .

MR. JUSTICE STONE, dissenting.

I think the judgment should be reversed.

The present stress of widely held and strongly expressed differences of opinion of the wisdom of the Agricultural Adjustment Act makes it important, in the interest of clear thinking and sound result, to emphasize at the outset certain propositions which should have controlling influence in determining the validity of the Act. They are:

1. The power of courts to declare a statute unconstitutional is subject to two guiding principles of decision which ought never to be absent from judicial consciousness. One is that courts are concerned only with the power to enact statutes, not with their wisdom. The other is that while unconstitutional exercise of power by the executive and legislative branches of the government is subject to judicial restraint, the only check upon our own exercise of power is our own sense of self-restraint. For the removal of unwise laws from the statute books appeal lies not to the courts but to the ballot and to the processes of democratic government.

2. The constitutional power of Congress to levy an excise tax upon the processing of agricultural products is not questioned. The present levy is held invalid, not for any want of power in Congress to lay such a tax to defray public expenditures, including those for the general welfare, but because the use to which its proceeds are put is disapproved.

3. As the present depressed state of agriculture is nation wide in its extent and effects, there is no basis for saying that the expenditure of public money in aid of farmers is not within the specifically granted power of Congress to levy taxes to "provide for the . . . general welfare." The opinion of the Court does not declare otherwise.

4. No question of a variable tax fixed from time to time by fiat of the Secretary of Agriculture, or of unauthorized delegation of legislative power, is now presented. The schedule of rates imposed by the Secretary in accordance with the original command of Congress has since been specifically adopted and confirmed by Act of Congress, which has declared that it shall be the lawful tax. Act of August 24, 1935, 49 Stat. 750. That is the tax which the government now seeks to collect. Any defects there may have been in the manner of laying the

tax by the Secretary have now been removed by the exercise of the power of Congress to pass a curative statute validating an intended, though defective, tax. *United States* v. *Heinszen & Co.*, 206 U. S. 370; *Graham & Foster* v. *Goodcell*, 282 U. S. 409; cf. *Milliken* v. *United States*, 283 U. S. 15. The Agricultural Adjustment Act as thus amended declares that none of its provisions shall fail because others are pronounced invalid.

It is with these preliminary and hardly controverted matters in mind that we should direct our attention to the pivot on which the decision of the Court is made to turn. It is that a levy unquestionably within the taxing power of Congress may be treated as invalid because it is a step in a plan to regulate agricultural production and is thus a forbidden infringement of state power. . . .

. . .

Congress through the Interstate Commerce Commission has set aside intrastate railroad rates. It has made and destroyed intrastate industries by raising or lowering tariffs. These results are said to be permissible because they are incidents of the commerce power and the power to levy duties on imports. See *Minnesota Rate Cases*, 230 U. S. 352; *Shreveport Case*, 234 U. S. 342; *Board of Trustees of the University of Illinois* v. *United States*, 289 U. S. 48. The only conclusion to be drawn is that results become lawful when they are incidents of those powers but unlawful when incident to the similarly granted power to tax and spend.

Such a limitation is contradictory and destructive of the power to appropriate for the public welfare, and is incapable of practical application. The spending power of Congress is in addition to the legislative power and not subordinate to it. This independent grant of the power of the purse, and its very nature, involving in its exercise the duty to insure expenditure within the granted power, presuppose freedom of selection among divers ends and aims, and the capacity to impose such conditions as will render the choice effective. It is a contradiction in terms to say that there is power to spend for the national welfare, while rejecting any power to impose conditions reasonably adapted to the attainment of the end which alone would justify the expenditure.

The limitation now sanctioned must lead to absurd consequences. The government may give seeds to farmers, but may not condition the gift upon their being planted in places where they are most needed or even planted at all. The government may give money to the unemployed, but may not ask that those who get it shall give labor in return, or even use it to support their families. It may give money to sufferers from earthquake, fire, tornado, pestilence or flood, but may not impose conditions—health precautions designed to prevent the spread of disease, or induce the movement of population to safer or more sanitary areas. All that, because it is purchased regulation infringing state powers, must be left for the states, who are unable or unwilling to supply the necessary relief. The government may spend its money for vocational rehabilitation, 48 Stat. 389, but it may not, with the consent of all concerned, supervise the process which it undertakes to aid. It may spend its money for the suppression of the boll weevil, but may not compensate the farmers for suspending the growth of cotton in the infected areas. It may aid state reforestation and forest fire prevention agencies, 43 Stat. 653, but may not be permitted to supervise their conduct. It may support rural schools, 39 Stat. 929, 45 Stat. 1151, 48 Stat. 792, but may not condition its grant by the requirement that certain standards be maintained. It may appropriate moneys to be expended by the Reconstruction Finance Corporation "to aid in financing agriculture, commerce and industry," and to facilitate "the exportation of agricultural and other products." Do all its activities collapse because, in order to effect the permissible purpose, in myriad ways the money is paid out upon terms and conditions which influence action of the recipients within the states, which Congress cannot command? The answer would seem plain. If the expenditure is for a national public purpose, that purpose will not be thwarted because payment is on condition which will advance that purpose. . . .

. . . Courts are not the only agency of government that must be assumed to have capacity to govern. Congress and the courts both unhappily may falter or be mistaken in the performance of their constitutional duty. But interpretation of our great charter of government which proceeds on any assumption that the responsibility for the preservation of our institutions is the exclusive concern of any one of the three branches of government, or that it alone can save them from destruction is far more likely, in the long run, "to obliterate the constituent members" of "an indestructible union of indestructible states" than the frank recognition that language, even of a constitution, may mean what it says: that the power to tax and spend includes the power to relieve a nationwide economic maladjustment by conditional gifts of money.

MR. JUSTICE BRANDEIS and MR. JUSTICE CARDOZO join in this opinion.

South Dakota v. Dole

107 S.Ct. 2793 (1987)

Congress passed legislation in 1984 directing the Secretary of Transportation to withhold a percentage of federal highway funds from states that refuse to adopt age 21 as the minimum drinking age. An issue before the Court was the extent to which Congress can use its spending power, and more particularly conditions attached to federal funds, to achieve national objectives. South Dakota challenged the constitutionality of the statute. A district court dismissed the complaint and the Eighth Circuit affirmed.

Chief Justice REHNQUIST delivered the opinion of the Court.

Petitioner South Dakota permits persons 19 years of age or older to purchase beer containing up to 3.2% alcohol. S.D.Codified Laws § 35–6-27 (1986). In 1984 Congress enacted 23 U.S.C. § 158 (1982 ed., Supp. III) ("§ 158"), which directs the Secretary of Transportation to withhold a percentage of federal highway funds otherwise allocable from States "in which the purchase or public possession of any alcoholic beverage by a person who is less than twenty-one years of age is lawful." The State sued in United States District Court seeking a declaratory judgment that § 158 violates the constitutional limitations on congressional exercise of the spending power and violates the Twenty-first Amendment to the United States Constitution. The District Court rejected the State's claims, and the Court of Appeals for the Eighth Circuit affirmed. 791 F.2d 628 (1986).

In this Court, the parties direct most of their efforts to defining the proper scope of the Twenty-first Amendment. Relying on our statement in *California Retail Liquor Dealers Assn.* v. *Midcal Aluminum, Inc.*, 445 U.S. 97, 110 (1980), that the "Twenty-first Amendment grants the States virtu-ally complete control over whether to permit importation or sale of liquor and how to structure the liquor distribution system," South Dakota asserts that the setting of minimum drinking ages is clearly within the "core powers" reserved to the States under § 2 of the Amendment. Brief for Petitioner 43–44. Section 158, petitioner claims, usurps that core power. The Secretary in response asserts that the Twenty-first Amendment is simply not implicated by § 158; the plain language of § 2 confirms the States' broad power to impose restrictions on the sale and distribution of alcoholic beverages but does not confer on them any power to *permit* sales that Congress seeks to *prohibit*. Brief for Respondent 25-26. That Amendment, under this reasoning, would not prevent Congress from affirmatively enacting a national minimum drinking age more restrictive than that provided by the various state laws; and it would follow *a fortiori* that the indirect inducement involved here is compatible with the Twenty-first Amendment.

These arguments present questions of the meaning of the Twenty-first Amendment, the bounds of which have escaped precise definition. *Bacchus Imports Ltd.* v. *Dias*, 468 U.S. 263, 274–276 (1984); *Craig* v. *Boren*, 429 U.S. 190, 206

(1976). Despite the extended treatment of the question by the parties, however, we need not decide in this case whether that Amendment would prohibit an attempt by Congress to legislate directly a national minimum drinking age. Here, Congress has acted indirectly under its spending power to encourage uniformity in the States' drinking ages. As we explain below, we find this legislative effort within constitutional bounds even if Congress may not regulate drinking ages directly.

The Constitution empowers Congress to "lay and collect Taxes, Duties, Imposts, and Excises, to pay the Debts and provide for the common Defence and general Welfare of the United States." Art. I, § 8, cl. 1. Incident to this power, Congress may attach conditions on the receipt of federal funds, and has repeatedly employed the power "to further broad policy objectives by conditioning receipt of federal moneys upon compliance by the recipient with federal statutory and administrative directives." *Fullilove* v. *Klutznick*, 448 U.S. 448, 474 (1980) (Opinion of Burger, C.J.). See *Lau* v. *Nichols*, 414 U.S. 563, 569 (1974); *Ivanhoe Irrigation Dist.* v. *McCracken*, 357 U.S. 275, 295 (1958); *Oklahoma* v. *Civil Service Comm'n*, 330 U.S. 127, 143–144 (1947); *Steward Machine Co.* v. *Davis*, 301 U.S. 548 (1937). The breadth of this power was made clear in *United States* v. *Butler*, 297 U.S. 1, 66 (1936), where the Court, resolving a longstanding debate over the scope of the Spending Clause, determined that "the power of Congress to authorize expenditure of public moneys for public purposes is not limited by the direct grants of legislative power found in the Constitution." Thus, objectives not thought to be within Article I's "enumerated legislative fields," *id.*, at 65, may nevertheless be attained through the use of the spending power and the conditional grant of federal funds.

The spending power is of course not unlimited, *Pennhurst State School and Hospital* v. *Halderman*, 451 U.S. 1, 17, and n. 13 (1981), but is instead subject to several general restrictions articulated in our cases. The first of these limitations is derived from the language of the Constitution itself: the exercise of the spending power must be in pursuit of "the general welfare." . . . In considering whether a particular expenditure is intend-

ed to serve general public purposes, courts should defer substantially to the judgment of Congress. . . . Second, we have required that if Congress desires to condition the States' receipt of federal funds, it "must do so unambiguously . . . , enabl[ing] the States to exercise their choice knowingly, cognizant of the consequences of their participation." . . . Third, our cases have suggested (without significant elaboration) that conditions on federal grants might be illegitimate if they are unrelated "to the federal interest in particular national projects or programs." . . . Finally, we have noted that other constitutional provisions may provide an independent bar to the conditional grant of federal funds. . . .

South Dakota does not seriously claim that § 158 is inconsistent with any of the first three restrictions mentioned above. We can readily conclude that the provision is designed to serve the general welfare. . . . Congress found that the differing drinking ages in the States created particular incentives for young persons to combine their desire to drink with their ability to drive, and that this interstate problem required a national solution. The means it chose to address this dangerous situation were reasonably calculated to advance the general welfare. The conditions upon which States receive the funds, moreover, could not be more clearly stated by Congress. See 23 U.S.C. § 158 (1982 ed., Supp. III). And the State itself, rather than challenging the germaneness of the condition to federal purposes, admits that it "has never contended that the congressional action was . . . unrelated to a national concern in the absence of the Twenty-first Amendment." Brief for Petitioner 52. Indeed, the condition imposed by Congress is directly related to one of the main purposes for which highway funds are expended —safe interstate travel. See 23 U.S.C. § 101(b). This goal of the interstate highway system had been frustrated by varying drinking ages among the States. A presidential commission appointed to study alcohol-related accidents and fatalities on the Nation's highways concluded that the lack of uniformity in the States' drinking ages created "an incentive to drink and drive" because "young persons commut[e] to border States where the drinking age is lower." Presidential Commission on Drunk Driving, Final Report 11 (1983). By enacting § 158, Congress conditioned the receipt of federal funds in a way reasonably calculated to address this particular impediment to a purpose for which the funds are expended.

The remaining question about the validity of § 158—and the basic point of disagreement between the parties—is whether the Twenty-first Amendment constitutes an "independent constitutional bar" to the conditional grant of federal funds. *Lawrence County* v. *Lead-Deadwood School Dist., supra,* at 269–270. Petitioner, relying on its view that the Twenty-first Amendment prohibits *direct* regulation of drinking ages by Congress, asserts that "Congress may not use the spending power to regulate that which it is prohibited from regulating directly under the Twenty-first Amendment." Brief for Petitioner 52–53. But our cases show that this "independent constitutional bar" limitation on the spending power is not of the kind petitioner suggests. *United States* v. *Butler,* 297 U.S., at 66, for example, established that the constitutional limitations on Congress when exercising its spending power are less exacting than those on its authority to regulate directly.

· · ·

These cases establish that the "independent constitutional bar" limitation on the spending power is not, as petitioner suggests, a prohibition on the indirect achievement of objectives which Congress is not empowered to achieve directly. Instead, we think that the language in our earlier opinions stands for the unexceptionable proposition that the power may not be used to induce the States to engage in activities that would themselves be unconstitutional. Thus, for example, a grant of federal funds conditioned on invidiously discriminatory state action or the infliction of cruel and unusual punishment would be an illegitimate exercise of the Congress' broad spending power. But no such claim can be or is made here. Were South Dakota to succumb to the blandishments offered by Congress and raise its drinking age to 21, the State's action in so doing would not violate the constitutional rights of anyone.

Our decisions have recognized that in some circumstances the financial inducement offered by Congress might be so coercive as to pass the point at which "pressure turns into compulsion."

Steward Machine Co. v. *Davis, supra,* 301 U.S., at 590. Here, however, Congress has directed only that a State desiring to establish a minimum drinking age lower than 21 lose a relatively small percentage of certain federal highway funds. Petitioner contends that the coercive nature of this program is evident from the degree of success it has achieved. We cannot conclude, however, that a conditional grant of federal money of this sort is unconstitutional simply by reason of its success in achieving the congressional objective.

When we consider, for a moment, that all South Dakota would lose if she adheres to her chosen course as to a suitable minimum drinking age is 5% of the funds otherwise obtainable under specified highway grant programs, the argument as to coercion is shown to be more rhetoric than fact. As we said a half century ago in *Steward Machine Co.* v. *Davis:*

"[E]very rebate from a tax when conditioned upon conduct is in some measure a temptation. But to hold that motive or temptation is equivalent to coercion is to plunge the law in endless difficulties. The outcome of such a doctrine is the acceptance of a philosophical determinism by which choice becomes impossible. Till now the law has been guided by a robust common sense which assumes the freedom of the will as a working hypothesis in the solution of its problems." *Id.,* at 589–590.

Here Congress has offered relatively mild encouragement to the States to enact higher minimum drinking ages than they would otherwise choose. But the enactment of such laws remains the prerogative of the States not merely in theory but in fact. Even if Congress might lack the power to impose a national minimum drinking age directly, we conclude that encouragement to state action found in § 158 is a valid use of the spending power. Accordingly, the judgment of the Court of Appeals is

Affirmed.

Justice BRENNAN, dissenting.

I agree with Justice O'CONNOR that regulation of the minimum age of purchasers of liquor falls squarely within the ambit of those powers reserved to the States by the Twenty-first Amendment. . . . Since States possess this constitutional power, Congress cannot condition a federal grant in a manner that abridges this right. The Amendment, itself, strikes the proper balance between federal and state authority. I therefore dissent.

Justice O'CONNOR, dissenting.

The Court today upholds the National Minimum Drinking Age Amendment, 23 U.S.C. § 158 (1982 ed., Supp. III), as a valid exercise of the Spending Power conferred by Article I, § 8. But § 158 is not a condition on spending reasonably related to the expenditure of federal funds and cannot be justified on that ground. Rather, it is an attempt to regulate the sale of liquor, an attempt that lies outside Congress' power to regulate commerce because it falls within the ambit of § 2 of the Twenty-first Amendment.

My disagreement with the Court is relatively narrow on the Spending Power issue: it is a disagreement about the application of a principle rather than a disagreement on the principle itself. . . .

. . .

But the Court's application of the requirement that the condition imposed be reasonably related to the purpose for which the funds are expended, is cursory and unconvincing. We have repeatedly said that Congress may condition grants under the Spending Power only in ways reasonably related to the purpose of the federal program. . . . In my view, establishment of a minimum drinking age of 21 is not sufficiently related to interstate highway construction to justify so conditioning funds appropriated for that purpose.

In support of its contrary conclusion, the Court relies on a supposed concession by counsel for South Dakota that the State "has never contended that the congressional action was . . . unrelated to a national concern in the absence of the Twenty-first Amendment." Brief for Petitioner 52. In the absence of the Twenty-first Amendment, however, there is a strong argument that the Congress might regulate the conditions under which liquor is sold under the Commerce Power, just as it regulates the sale of many other commodities that are in or

affect interstate commerce. The fact that the Twenty-first Amendment is crucial to the State's argument does not, therefore, amount to a concession that the condition imposed by § 158 is reasonably related to highway construction. . . .

. . . if the purpose of § 158 is to deter drunken driving, it is far too over- and under-inclusive. It is over-inclusive because it stops teenagers from drinking even when they are not about to drive on interstate highways. It is under-inclusive because teenagers pose only a small part of the drunken driving problem in this Nation. See, *e.g.*, 130 Cong.Rec. § 8216 (June 26, 1984) (remarks of Sen. Humphrey) ("Eighty-four percent of all highway fatalities involving alcohol occur among those whose ages exceed 21"); *id.*, at § 8219 (remarks of Sen. McClure) ("Certainly, statistically, if you use that one set of statistics, then the mandatory drinking age ought to be raised at least to 30"); *ibid.* (remarks of Sen. Symms) ("most of the studies point out that the drivers of age 21–24 are the worst offenders").

. . .

Of the other possible sources of congressional authority for regulating the sale of liquor only the Commerce Power comes to mind. But in my view, the regulation of the age of the purchasers of liquor, just as the regulation of the price at which liquor may be sold, falls squarely within the scope of those powers reserved to the States by the Twenty-first Amendment. *Capital Cities Cable, Inc.* v. *Crisp*, 467 U.S. 691, 716 (1984). As I emphasized in *324 Liquor Corp.* v. *Duffy*, 479 U.S.——,—— (1987) (dissenting opinion):

"The history of the Amendment strongly supports Justice Black's view that the Twenty-first Amendment was intended to return absolute control of the liquor trade to the States, and that the Federal Government could not use its Commerce Clause powers to interfere in any manner with the States' exercise of the power conferred by the Amendment."

Accordingly, Congress simply lacks power under the Commerce Clause to displace state regulation of this kind. *Ibid.*

The immense size and power of the Government of the United States ought not obscure its fundamental character. It remains a Government of enumerated powers. *McCulloch* v. *Maryland*, 4 Wheat. 316, 405 (1819). Because 23 U.S.C. § 158 (1982 ed., Supp. III) cannot be justified as an exercise of any power delegated to the Congress, it is not authorized by the Constitution. The Court errs in holding it to be the law of the land, and I respectfully dissent.

Pennsylvania v. Nelson

350 U.S. 497 (1956)

Steve Nelson was convicted for violating the Pennsylvania Sedition Act. The question here is whether Congress, by passing the Smith Act of 1940, preempted the enforcement of state sedition acts.

MR. CHIEF JUSTICE WARREN delivered the opinion of the Court.

The respondent Steve Nelson, an acknowledged member of the Communist Party, was convicted in the Court of Quarter Sessions of Allegheny County, Pennsylvania, of a violation of the Pennsylvania Sedition Act and sentenced to imprisonment for twenty years and to a fine of $10,000 and to costs of prosecution in the sum of $13,000. The Superior Court affirmed the conviction. 172 Pa. Super. 125, 92 A. 2d 431. The Supreme Court of Pennsylvania, recognizing but not reaching many alleged serious trial errors and conduct of the trial court infringing upon respondent's right to due process of law, decided the case on the narrow issue of supersession of the state law by the Federal Smith Act. In its opinion, the court stated:

"And, while the Pennsylvania statute proscribes sedition against either the Government of the United States or the Government of Pennsylvania, it is only alleged sedition against the United States with which the instant case is concerned. Out of all the voluminous testimony, we have not found, nor has anyone pointed to, a single word indicating a seditious act or even utterance directed against the Government of Pennsylvania."

The precise holding of the court, and all that is before us for review, is that the Smith Act of 1940, as amended in 1948, which prohibits the knowing advocacy of the overthrow of the Government of the United States by force and violence, super-sedes the enforceability of the Pennsylvania Sedition Act which proscribes the same conduct.

Many State Attorneys General and the Solicitor General of the United States appeared as *amici curiae* for petitioner, and several briefs were filed on behalf of the respondent. Because of the important question of federal-state relationship involved, we granted certiorari. 348 U. S. 814.

It should be said at the outset that the decision in this case does not affect the right of States to enforce their sedition laws at times when the Federal Government has not occupied the field and is not protecting the entire country from seditious conduct. The distinction between the two situations was clearly recognized by the court below. Nor does it limit the jurisdiction of the States where the Constitution and Congress have specifically given them concurrent jurisdiction, as was done under the Eighteenth Amendment and the Volstead Act. *United States* v. *Lanza*, 260 U. S. 377. Neither does it limit the right of the State to protect itself at any time against sabotage or attempted violence of all kinds. Nor does it prevent the State from prosecuting where the same act constitutes both a federal offense and a state offense under the police power, as was done in *Fox* v. *Ohio*, 5 How. 410, and *Gilbert* v. *Minnesota*, 254 U. S. 325. . . .

Where, as in the instant case, Congress has not stated specifically whether a federal statute has occupied a field in which the States are otherwise free to legislate, different criteria have furnished touchstones for decision. Thus, "[t]his Court, in considering the validity of state laws in the light of . . . federal laws touching the same subject, has made use of the following expressions: conflicting; contrary to; occupying the field; repugnance; difference; irreconcilability; inconsistency; violation; curtailment; and interference. But none of these expressions provides an infallible constitutional test or an exclusive constitutional yardstick. In the final analysis, there can be no one crystal clear distinctly marked formula." *Hines* v. *Davidowitz,* 312 U. S. 52, 67.

And see *Rice* v. *Santa Fe Elevator Corp.,* 331 U.S. 218, 230–231. In this case, we think that each of several tests of supersession is met.

First, "[t]he scheme of federal regulation [is] so pervasive as to make reasonable the inference that Congress left no room for the States to supplement it." *Rice* v. *Santa Fe Elevator Corp.,* 331 U. S., at 230. The Congress determined in 1940 that it was necessary for it to re-enter the field of antisubversive legislation, which had been abandoned by it in 1921. In that year, it enacted the Smith Act which proscribes advocacy of the overthrow of any government—federal, state or local —by force and violence and organization of and knowing membership in a group which so advocates. Conspiracy to commit any of these acts is punishable under the general criminal conspiracy provisions in 18 U. S. C. § 371. The Internal Security Act of 1950 is aimed more directly at Communist organizations. It distinguishes between "Communist-action organizations" and "Communist-front organizations," requiring such organizations to register and to file annual reports with the Attorney General giving complete details as to their officers and funds. Members of Communist-action organizations who have not been registered by their organization must register as individuals. Failure to register in accordance with the requirements of Sections 786–787 is punishable by a fine of not more than $10,000 for an offending organization and by a fine of not more than $10,000 or imprisonment for not more than five years or both for an individual offender —each day of failure to register constituting a separate offense. And the Act imposes certain sanctions upon both "action" and "front" organizations and their members. The Communist Con-

trol Act of 1954 declares "that the Communist Party of the United States, although purportedly a political party, is in fact an instrumentality of a conspiracy to overthrow the Government of the United States" and that "its role as the agency of a hostile foreign power renders its existence a clear present and continuing danger to the security of the United States." It also contains a legislative finding that the Communist Party is a "Communist-action organization" within the meaning of the Internal Security Act of 1950 and provides that "knowing" members of the Communist Party are "subject to all the provisions and penalties" of that Act. It furthermore sets up a new classification of "Communist-infiltrated organizations" and provides for the imposition of sanctions against them.

We examine these Acts only to determine the congressional plan. Looking to all of them in the aggregate, the conclusion is inescapable that Congress has intended to occupy the field of sedition. Taken as a whole, they evince a congressional plan which makes it reasonable to determine that no room has been left for the States to supplement it. . . .

Second, the federal statutes "touch a field in which the federal interest is so dominant that the federal system [must] be assumed to preclude enforcement of state laws on the same subject." *Rice* v. *Santa Fe Elevator Corp.,* 331 U. S., at 230, citing *Hines* v. *Davidowitz, supra.* Congress has devised an all-embracing program for resistance to the various forms of totalitarian aggression. Our external defenses have been strengthened, and a plan to protect against internal subversion has been made by it. It has appropriated vast sums, not only for our own protection, but also to strengthen freedom throughout the world. It has charged the Federal Bureau of Investigation and the Central Intelligence Agency with responsibility for intelligence concerning Communist seditious activities against our Government, and has denominated such activities as part of a world conspiracy. . . .

Third, enforcement of state sedition acts presents a serious danger of conflict with the administration of the federal program. Since 1939, in order to avoid a hampering of uniform enforcement of its program by sporadic local prosecutions, the Federal Government has urged local authorities not to intervene in such matters, but to turn over to the federal authorities immediately and unevaluated all information concerning subversive activities.

. . .

The judgment of the Supreme Court of Pennsylvania is

Affirmed.

MR. JUSTICE REED, with whom MR. JUSTICE BURTON and MR. JUSTICE MINTON join, dissenting.

The problems of governmental power may be approached in this case free from the varied viewpoints that focus on the problems of national security. This is a jurisdictional problem of general importance because it involves an asserted limitation on the police power of the States when it is applied to a crime that is punishable also by the Federal Government. As this is a recurring problem, it is appropriate to explain our dissent.

Congress has not, in any of its statutes relating to sedition, specifically barred the exercise of state power to punish the same Acts under state law. And, we read the majority opinion to assume for this case that, absent federal legislation, there is no constitutional bar to punishment of sedition against the United States by both a State and the Nation. The majority limits to the federal courts the power to try charges of sedition against the Federal Government.

First, the Court relies upon the pervasiveness of the antisubversive legislation embodied in the Smith Act of 1940, 18 U.S.C. § 2385, the Internal Security Act of 1950, 64 Stat. 987, and the Communist Control Act of 1954, 68 Stat. 775. It asserts that these Acts in the aggregate mean that Congress has occupied the "field of sedition" to the exclusion of the States. The "occupation of the field" argument has been developed by this Court for the Commerce Clause and legislation thereunder to prevent partitioning of this country by locally erected trade barriers. In those cases this Court has ruled that state legislation is superseded when it conflicts with the comprehensive regulatory scheme and purpose of a federal plan. . . .

But the federal sedition laws are distinct criminal statutes that punish willful advocacy of the use of force against "the government of the United States or the government of any State." These criminal laws proscribe certain local activity without creating any statutory or administrative regulation. There is, consequently, no question as to whether some general congressional regulatory scheme might be upset by a coinciding state plan. In these circumstances the conflict should be clear and direct before this Court reads a congressional intent to void state legislation into the federal sedition acts. . . .

We cannot agree that the federal criminal sanctions against sedition directed at the United States are of such a pervasive character as to indicate an intention to void state action.

Secondly, the Court states that the federal sedition statutes touch a field "in which the federal interest is so dominant" they must preclude state laws on the same subject. This concept is suggested in a comment on *Hines* v. *Davidowitz,* 312 U. S. 52, in the *Rice* case, at 230. The Court in *Davidowitz* ruled that federal statutes compelling alien registration preclude enforcement of state statutes requiring alien registration. We read *Davidowitz* to teach nothing more than that, when the Congress provided a single nation-wide integrated system of regulation so complete as that for aliens' registration (with fingerprinting, a scheduling of activities, and continuous information as to their residence), the Act bore so directly on our foreign relations as to make it evident that Congress intended only one uniform national alien registration system.

. . .

Thirdly, the Court finds ground for abrogating Pennsylvania's antisedition statute because, in the Court's view, the State's administration of the Act may hamper the enforcement of the federal law. Quotations are inserted from statements of President Roosevelt and Mr. Hoover, the Director of the Federal Bureau of Investigation, to support the Court's position. But a reading of the quotations leads us to conclude that their purpose was to gain prompt knowledge of evidence of subversive activities so that the federal agency could be fully advised. We find no suggestion from any official source that state officials should be less alert to ferret out or punish subversion. The Court's attitude as to interference seems to us quite contrary to that of the Legislative and Executive Departments. Congress was advised of the existing state sedition legislation when the Smith Act was enacted and has been kept current with its spread. No declaration of exclusiveness followed. . . .

Finally, and this one point seems in and of itself decisive, there is an independent reason for reversing the Pennsylvania Supreme Court. The Smith Act appears in Title 18 of the United States Code, which Title codifies the federal criminal laws. Section 3231 of that Title provides:

"Nothing in this title shall be held to take away or impair the jurisdiction of the courts of the several States under the laws thereof."

That declaration springs from the federal character of our Nation. It recognizes the fact that maintenance of order and fairness rests primarily with the States. The section was first enacted in 1825 and has appeared successively in the federal criminal laws since that time. This Court has interpreted the section to mean that States may provide concurrent legislation in the absence of explicit congressional intent to the contrary. *Sexton* v. *California*, 189 U. S. 319, 324–325. The majority's position in this case cannot be reconciled with that clear authorization of Congress.

The law stands against any advocacy of violence to change established governments. Freedom of speech allows full play to the processes of reason. The state and national legislative bodies have legislated within constitutional limits so as to allow the widest participation by the law enforcement officers of the respective governments. The individual States were not told that they are powerless to punish local acts of sedition, nominally directed against the United States. Courts should not interfere. We would reverse the judgment of the Supreme Court of Pennsylvania.

Congress Reacts to Nelson

In *Pennsylvania* v. *Nelson*, 350 U.S. 497 (1956), the Supreme Court decided that a congressional statute regarding advocacy for the overthrow of the U.S. government by force or violence supersedes state efforts to regulate sedition. The author of the congressional statute, Howard Smith of Virginia, objected that it was never his intent to preempt state actions. He introduced legislation stating that no act of Congress shall be construed by the courts as indicating an intent by Congress to occupy the field covered by a statute unless the statute contains an express provision to that effect. The House of Representatives passed legislation of this nature in 1958, but no action was taken by the Senate. The House again passed legislation in 1959, but by that time the Supreme Court, in *Uphaus* v. *Wyman*, 360 U.S. 72, had decided that states could proceed with prosecutions for sedition against the state itself. The House debates below appear at 102 Cong. Rec. 6385 (1956) and 104 Cong. Rec. 14139-14140 (1958).

Mr. SMITH of Virginia. . . . I do want to make 1 or 2 comments on . . . a bill of which I am the author, H. R. 3, to correct a decision of the Supreme Court of the United States in the Steve Nelson and other cases. I am glad to announce at this moment that I have been advised the Judiciary Committee will proceed to conclude hearings on the bill this coming Friday. I do hope that the House will have that bill before it in a reasonable time so that we may explore the situation much further.

. . .

I introduced the bill, H. R. 3, in another form in

the last Congress and under another number immediately after the decision in the Steve Nelson case. I did not draft the bill to correct merely the Steve Nelson case. That is just one phase of a very broad situation, a situation where the Supreme Court has assumed out of a clear sky to say what the Congress intended when the Congress has not said it. If anything is to be done upon this subject, I think it is very important that we have a general law which will simply say that when Congress means to do away with State laws the Congress shall say so. If your bill is going to correct one Supreme Court decision at a time, we are just neglecting our constitutional duty and we are placing just a shin plaster on a broken leg.

. . .

[1958 debate]:

Mr. SMITH of Virginia. Mr. Chairman, this is a serious, a far-reaching bill that is deserving of your most careful and deliberate consideration. . . . This bill does exactly two things. It is very brief. It just does two things. It says to the Supreme Court—

First. Do not undertake to read the minds of the Congress; we, in the Congress, think ourselves more capable of knowing our minds than the Supreme Court has proved itself capable of in the past; and we will do our own mind reading; and we are telling you that when we get ready to repeal a State law or preempt a field, we will say so and we will not leave it to the Supreme Court to guess whether we are or not. That is No. 1.

Second. The other thing this bill does is to say that the Supreme Court must not knock down State laws unless they are in irreconcilable conflict with a Federal law. What that means is that the Federal law shall always be supreme when it is in conflict with State law, but if it is not in conflict with the State law that the Supreme Court must not go out of its way to knock down State laws unless the Congress has told them to do so. That part of the law has been the law for 99 years by the word of the Supreme Court of the United States in the case of Sinnot against Davenport decided in 1859. In that case the Supreme Court in its opinion used the identical language that is used in this bill. The language of this bill was copied from the decision of the Supreme Court which said that there must be a conflict between the State and the Federal law, otherwise the States shall be permitted to carry on their local affairs. It is that simple. Here is the language which was used, and if you have the bill before you, you can follow it. It is in the next to last section of the bill, the last two lines. Here is the language that the Supreme Court used and this bill quotes that language: That the conflict between the State and the Federal law must be direct and positive so that the two acts cannot be reconciled or consistently stand together.

What all that means is what this Government started with, and that is the old Jeffersonian principle that the best government is the local government and that we should let our States write our laws as far as they reasonably can when it does not conflict with Federal law. This whole argument has been a mystery to me and it is still a mystery to me. Why the opponents of this bill are afraid to trust the people who sent them here to the Congress from back home. That is the mystery about this bill to me. What are you afraid of? Why are you not willing to let your people back home be governed by the laws of your home State? Are you afraid of the people who trusted you and who were not afraid of you when they sent you here to the Congress to represent them? Let us take some of the things that have been brought up in this bill. I want to tell you what position has been taken by outstanding people. We have had a lot of lawyers talking here—and a lot of good lawyers, but I think I can quote you some better lawyers. I will first, however, quote to you the words of a man who is not a lawyer. What did the President of the United States *[Eisenhower]* say on this general subject? He said this in his campaign pledge:

"I want to see maintained the constitutional relationships between the Federal and State Governments. . . . For, if the States lose their meaning, our entire system of government loses its meaning. And the next step is the rise of the centralized, national state in which the seeds of autocracy can take root and grow. . . . We will see that the legitimate rights of the States and local communities are respected. . . . We will not reach into the States and take from them their powers and responsibilities to serve their citizens."

That is what the President of the United States said and he has never retreated from that position. But what did he do to carry it out? As soon as he was elected President the first time, he appointed a commission. That was the Commission on Intergovernmental Relations to look into this very type of thing. They studied it for over a year and came out with a report, a copy of which I hold in my hand, and they dealt with this subject that H. R. 3 deals with. Here is what they said. Here is the recommendation of the President's own Commission. On this subject they say:

"Second. National laws should be so framed that they will not be construed to preempt any field against State action unless this intent is stated."

That is what H. R. 3 says. I did not know this was in there when I introduced H. R. 3. It was brought to my attention by a member of the Commission long after. Then it says:

"Third. Exercise of national power on any subject should not bar State action on the same subject unless there is positive inconsistency."

There are the two features I have just described to you contained in H. R. 3. They are in exactly the same words as H. R. 3. That is the President's Commission. That is what the President has said. That is what his Commission has said, appointed pursuant to his campaign promises.

. . .

Let us see what the Attorney General said. The Attorney General is opposed to this bill. We will take him next. When the Supreme Court decided the Nelson case in favor of the Communists the Attorney General filed a brief amicus curiae in the Supreme Court and he made some speeches about it. And here is what the Attorney General, who is opposed to this bill, said—

"To warrant a holding that State legislation which is otherwise a valid exercise of the State's police power has been superseded or suspended by an act of Congress dealing with the same subject matter, the Congressional act must be in irreconcilable conflict with the State act, or the Congressional intent to occupy the field exclusively must otherwise appear."

There is the position of the Attorney General. What are they afraid of? Why do they not trust the people back home?

It was said here that the American Bar Association was against the bill. Let us see what the American Bar Association said after due deliberation. Now, Mr. Chairman, the American Bar Association has nothing to gain in this except to approve of good law. Here are the people who have to live with the law. Any good lawyer will tell you if you ask him that this law and other laws have become so confused by recent decisions of the Court that no lawyer can safely advise his client what the law is today or what it will be tomorrow. Here is what the American Bar Association in convention assembled said:

"*Resolved,* That the American Bar Association favors the enactment into law of H. R. 3, entitled "A bill to establish rules of interpretation governing questions of the effect of acts of Congress on State laws," and authorizes and directs the standing committee on Jurisdiction of Law Reform to advocate by all appropriate means its passage by the Congress of the United States."

. . .

Adamson v. California

332 U.S. 46 (1947)

Admiral Dewey Adamson was convicted of a murder charge and sentenced to death. Under California's constitution and its penal laws, Adamson's failure to explain or to deny evidence against him could be commented on by the court and by counsel and

considered by the court and the jury. The immediate question was whether this procedure violated the guaranty in the Fifth Amendment that no person "shall be compelled in any criminal case to be a witness against himself." The Court held that his privilege is not inherent in the right to a fair trial and is not protected by the Due Process Clause of the Fourteenth Amendment. In his dissent, Justice Black lays the groundwork for arguing that the entire Bill of Rights should be incorporated in the Due Process Clause of the Fourteenth Amendment and applied against the states.

MR. JUSTICE REED delivered the opinion of the Court.

The appellant, Adamson, a citizen of the United States, was convicted, without recommendation for mercy, by a jury in a Superior Court of the State of California of murder in the first degree. After considering the same objections to the conviction that are pressed here, the sentence of death was affirmed by the Supreme Court of the state. 27 Cal. 2d 478, 165 P. 2d 3. Review of that judgment by this Court was sought and allowed under Judicial Code § 237; 28 U. S. C. § 344. The provisions of California law which were challenged in the state proceedings as invalid under the Fourteenth Amendment to the Federal Constitution are those of the state constitution and penal code. . . . They permit the failure of a defendant to explain or to deny evidence against him to be commented upon by court and by counsel and to be considered by court and jury. The defendant did not testify. As the trial court gave its instructions and the District Attorney argued the case in accordance with the constitutional and statutory provisions just referred to, we have for decision the question of their constitutionality in these circumstances under the limitations of § 1 of the Fourteenth Amendment.

. . .

In the first place, appellant urges that the provision of the Fifth Amendment that no person "shall be compelled in any criminal case to be a witness against himself" is a fundamental national privilege or immunity protected against state abridgment by the Fourteenth Amendment or a privilege or immunity secured, through the Fourteenth Amendment, against deprivation by state action because it is a personal right, enumerated in the federal Bill of Rights.

Secondly, appellant relies upon the due process of law clause of the Fourteenth Amendment to invalidate the provisions of the California law. . . .

We shall assume, but without any intention thereby of ruling upon the issue, that permission by law to the court, counsel and jury to comment upon and consider the failure of defendant "to explain or to deny by his testimony any evidence or facts in the case against him" would infringe defendant's privilege against self-incrimination under the Fifth Amendment if this were a trial in a court of the United States under a similar law. Such an assumption does not determine appellant's rights under the Fourteenth Amendment. It is settled law that the clause of the Fifth Amendment, protecting a person against being compelled to be a witness against himself, is not made effective by the Fourteenth Amendment as a protection against state action on the ground that freedom from testimonial compulsion is a right of national citizenship, or because it is a personal privilege or immunity secured by the Federal Constitution as one of the rights of man that are listed in the Bill of Rights.

The reasoning that leads to those conclusions starts with the unquestioned premise that the Bill of Rights, when adopted, was for the protection of the individual against the federal government and its provisions were inapplicable to similar actions done by the states. *Barron* v. *Baltimore*, 7 Pet. 243; *Feldman* v. *United States*, 322 U. S. 487, 490. With the adoption of the Fourteenth Amendment, it was suggested that the dual citizenship recognized by its first sentence ["All persons born or naturalized in the United States, and subject to the jurisdiction thereof, are citizens of the United States and of the State wherein they reside"] secured for citizens federal protection for their elemental privileges and immunities of state citizenship. The *Slaughter-House Cases* decided, contrary to the suggestion, that these rights, as privileges and immunities of state citizenship, remained under the sole protection of the state governments. This Court, without the expression of a contrary view upon that phase of the issues before the Court, has approved this determination. *Maxwell* v. *Bugbee*, 250 U. S. 525, 537; *Hamilton* v. *Regents*, 293 U. S. 245, 261. The power to free defendants in state trials from self-incrimination was specifically determined to be beyond the scope of the privileges and immunities clause of the Fourteenth Amendment in *Twining* v. *New Jersey*, 211 U. S. 78, 91–98. "The privilege against self-incrimination may be withdrawn and the accused put upon the stand as a witness for the state." . . .

. . .

Appellant secondly contends that if the privilege against self-incrimination is not a right protected by the privileges and immunities clause of the Fourteenth Amendment against state action, this privilege, to its full scope under the Fifth Amendment, inheres in the right to a fair trial. A right to a fair trial is a right admittedly protected by the due process clause of the Fourteenth Amendment. Therefore, appellant argues, the due process clause of the Fourteenth Amendment protects his privilege against self-incrimination. The due process clause of the Fourteenth Amendment, however, does not draw all the rights of the federal Bill of Rights under its protection. That contention was made and rejected in *Palko* v. *Connecticut*, 302 U. S. 319, 323. It was rejected with citation of the cases excluding several of the rights, protected by the Bill of Rights, against infringement by the National Government. Nothing has been called to our attention that either the framers of the Fourteenth Amendment or the states that adopted intended its due process clause to draw within its scope the earlier amendments to the Constitution. *Palko* held that such provisions of the Bill of Rights as were "implicit in the concept of ordered liberty," p. 325, became secure from state interference by the clause. But it held nothing more.

. . .

MR. JUSTICE FRANKFURTER, concurring.

. . .

Between the incorporation of the Fourteenth Amendment into the Constitution and the beginning of the present membership of the Court—a period of seventy years—the scope of that Amendment was passed upon by forty-three judges. Of all these judges, only one, who may respectfully be called an eccentric exception, ever indicated the belief that the Fourteenth Amendment was a shorthand summary of the first eight Amendments theretofore limiting only the Federal Government, and that due process incorporated those eight Amendments as restrictions upon the powers of the States. . . .

. . .

Indeed, the suggestion that the Fourteenth Amendment incorporates the first eight Amendments as such is not unambiguously urged. Even the boldest innovator would shrink from suggesting to more than half the States that they may no longer initiate prosecutions without indictment by grand jury, or that thereafter all the States of the Union must furnish a jury of twelve for every case involving a claim above twenty dollars. There is suggested merely a selective incorporation of the first eight Amendments into the Fourteenth Amendment. Some are in and some are out, but we are left in the dark as to which are in and which are out. Nor are we given the calculus for determining which go in and which stay out. If the basis of selection is merely that those provisions of the first eight Amendments are incorporated which commend themselves to individual justices as indispensable to the dignity and happiness of a free man, we are thrown back to a merely subjective test. . . .

MR. JUSTICE BLACK, dissenting.

. . .

This decision reasserts a constitutional theory spelled out in *Twining* v. *New Jersey*, 211 U. S. 78, that this Court is endowed by the Constitution with boundless power under "natural law" periodically to expand and contract constitutional standards to conform to the Court's conception of what at a particular time constitutes "civilized decency" and "fundamental liberty and justice." Invoking this *Twining* rule, the Court concludes that although comment upon testimony in a federal court would violate the Fifth Amendment, identical comment in a state court does not violate today's fashion in civilized decency and fundamentals and is therefore not prohibited by the Federal Constitution as amended.

. . .

My study of the historical events that culminated in the Fourteenth Amendment, and the expressions of those who sponsored and favored, as well as those who opposed its submission and passage, persuades me that one of the chief objects that the provisions of the Amendment's first section, separately, and as a whole, were intended to accomplish was to make the Bill of Rights applicable to the states. With full knowledge of the import of the *Barron* decision, the framers and backers of the Fourteenth Amendment proclaimed its purpose to be to overturn the constitutional rule that case had announced. This historical purpose has never received full consideration or exposition in any opinion of this Court interpreting the Amendment.

In construing other constitutional provisions, this Court has almost uniformly followed the precept of *Ex parte Bain*, 121 U. S. 1, 12, that "It is never to be forgotten that, in the construction of the language of the Constitution . . . , as indeed in all other instances where construction becomes necessary, we are to place ourselves as nearly as possible in the condition of the men who framed that instrument." See also *Everson* v. *Board of Education*, 330 U. S. 1, 8, 28, 33; *Thornhill* v. *Alabama*, 310 U. S. 88, 95, 102; *Knowlton* v. *Moore*, 178 U. S. 41, 89, 106; *Reynolds* v. *United States*, 98 U. S. 145, 162; *Barron* v. *Baltimore, supra* at 250–251; *Cohens* v. *Virginia*, 6 Wheat. 264, 416–420.

Investigation of the cases relied upon in *Twining* v. *New Jersey* to support the conclusion there reached that neither the Fifth Amendment's prohibition of compelled testimony, nor any of the Bill of Rights, applies to the States, reveals an unexplained departure from this salutary practice. Neither the briefs nor opinions in any of these

cases, except *Maxwell* v. *Dow*, 176 U. S. 581, make reference to the legislative and contemporary history for the purpose of demonstrating that those who conceived, shaped, and brought about the adoption of the Fourteenth Amendment intended it to nullify this Court's decision in *Barron* v. *Baltimore, supra*, and thereby to make the Bill of Rights applicable to the States. In *Maxwell* v. *Dow, supra*, the issue turned on whether the Bill of Rights guarantee of a jury trial was, by the Fourteenth Amendment, extended to trials in state courts. In that case counsel for appellant did cite from the speech of Senator Howard, Appendix, *infra*, p. 104, which so emphatically stated the understanding of the framers of the Amendment —the Committee on Reconstruction for which he spoke—that the Bill of Rights was to be made applicable to the states by the Amendment's first section. The Court's opinion in *Maxwell* v. *Dow, supra*, 601, acknowledged that counsel had "cited from the speech of one of the Senators," but indicated that it was not advised what other speeches were made in the Senate or in the House. The Court considered, moreover, that "What individual Senators or Representatives may have urged in debate, in regard to the meaning to be given to a proposed constitutional amendment, or bill or resolution, does not furnish a firm ground for its proper construction, nor is it important as explanatory of the grounds upon which the members voted in adopting it." *Id.* at 601–602.

In the *Twining* case itself, the Court was cited to a then recent book, Guthrie, Fourteenth Amendment to the Constitution (1898). A few pages of that work recited some of the legislative background of the Amendment, emphasizing the speech of Senator Howard. But Guthrie did not emphasize the speeches of Congressman Bingham, nor the part he played in the framing and adoption of the first section of the Fourteenth Amendment. Yet Congressman Bingham may, without extravagance, be called the Madison of the first section of the Fourteenth Amendment. In the *Twining* opinion, the Court explicitly declined to give weight to the historical demonstration that the first section of the Amendment was intended to apply to the states the several protections of the Bill of Rights. It held that that question was "no longer open" because of previous decisions of this

Court which, however, had not appraised the historical evidence on that subject. *Id.* at 98. The Court admitted that its action had resulted in giving "much less effect to the Fourteenth Amendment than some of the public men active in framing it" had intended it to have. *Id.* at 96. With particular reference to the guarantee against compelled testimony, the Court stated that "Much might be said in favor of the view that the privilege was guaranteed against state impairment as a privilege and immunity of National citizenship, but, as has been shown, the decisions of this court have foreclosed that view." *Id.* at 113. Thus the Court declined, and again today declines, to appraise the relevant historical evidence of the intended scope of the first section of the Amendment. Instead it relied upon previous cases, none of which had analyzed the evidence showing that one purpose of those who framed, advocated, and adopted the Amendment had been to make the Bill of Rights applicable to the States. None of the cases relied upon by the Court today made such an analysis.

For this reason, I am attaching to this dissent an appendix which contains a résumé, by no means complete, of the Amendment's history. In my judgment that history conclusively demonstrates that the language of the first section of the Fourteenth Amendment, taken as a whole, was thought by those responsible for its submission to the people, and by those who opposed its submission, sufficiently explicit to guarantee that thereafter no state could deprive its citizens of the privileges and protections of the Bill of Rights. Whether this Court ever will, or whether it now should, in the light of past decisions, give full effect to what the Amendment was intended to accomplish is not necessarily essential to a decision here. However that may be, our prior decisions, including *Twining*, do not prevent our carrying out that purpose, at least to the extent of making applicable to the states, not a mere part, as the Court has, but the full protection of the Fifth Amendment's provision against compelling evidence from an accused to convict him of crime. And I further contend that the "natural law" formula which the Court uses to reach its conclusion in this case should be abandoned as an incongruous excrescence on our Constitution. I believe that formula to be itself a violation of our Constitution, in that it subtly conveys to courts, at the expense of legislatures, ultimate power over public policies in fields where no specific provision of the Constitution limits legislative power. . . .

. . .

I cannot consider the Bill of Rights to be an outworn 18th Century "strait jacket" as the *Twining* opinion did. Its provisions may be thought outdated abstractions by some. And it is true that they were designed to meet ancient evils. But they are the same kind of human evils that have emerged from century to century wherever excessive power is sought by the few at the expense of the many. In my judgment the people of no nation can lose their liberty so long as a Bill of Rights like ours survives and its basic purposes are conscientiously interpreted, enforced and respected so as to afford continuous protection against old, as well as new, devices and practices which might thwart those purposes. I fear to see the consequences of the Court's practice of substituting its own concepts of decency and fundamental justice for the language of the Bill of Rights as its point of departure in interpreting and enforcing that Bill of Rights. If the choice must be between the selective process of the *Palko* decision applying some of the Bill of Rights to the States, or the *Twining* rule applying none of them, I would choose the *Palko* selective process. But rather than accept either of these choices, I would follow what I believe was the original purpose of the Fourteenth Amendment—to extend to all the people of the nation the complete protection of the Bill of Rights. To hold that this Court can determine what, if any, provisions of the Bill of Rights will be enforced, and if so to what degree, is to frustrate the great design of a written Constitution.

Conceding the possibility that this Court is now wise enough to improve on the Bill of Rights by substituting natural law concepts for the Bill of Rights, I think the possibility is entirely too speculative to agree to take that course. I would therefore hold in this case that the full protection of the Fifth Amendment's proscription against compelled testimony must be afforded by California. This I would do because of reliance upon the original purpose of the Fourteenth Amendment.

It is an illusory apprehension that literal application of some or all of the provisions of the Bill of Rights to the States would unwisely increase the sum total of the powers of this Court to invalidate state legislation. The Federal Government has not been harmfully burdened by the requirement that enforcement of federal laws affecting civil liberty conform literally to the Bill of Rights. Who would advocate its repeal? It must be conceded, of course, that the natural-law-due-process formula, which the Court today reaffirms, has been interpreted to limit substantially this Court's power to prevent state violations of the individual civil liberties guaranteed by the Bill of Rights. But this formula also has been used in the past, and can be used in the future, to license this Court, in considering regulatory legislation, to roam at large in the broad expanses of policy and morals and to trespass, all too freely, on the legislative domain of the States as well as the Federal Government.

Since *Marbury* v. *Madison*, 1 Cranch 137, was decided, the practice has been firmly established, for better or worse, that courts can strike down legislative enactments which violate the Constitution. This process, of course, involves interpretation, and since words can have many meanings, interpretation obviously may result in contraction or extension of the original purpose of a constitutional provision, thereby affecting policy. But to pass upon the constitutionality of statutes by looking to the particular standards enumerated in the Bill of Rights and other parts of the Constitution is one thing; to invalidate statutes because of application of "natural law" deemed to be above and undefined by the Constitution is another. "In the one instance, courts proceeding within clearly marked constitutional boundaries seek to execute policies written into the Constitution; in the other, they roam at will in the limitless area of their own beliefs as to reasonableness and actually select policies, a responsibility which the Constitution entrusts to the legislative representatives of the people." *Federal Power Commission* v. *Pipeline Co.*, 315 U. S. 575, 599, 601, n. 4.

MR. JUSTICE DOUGLAS joins in this opinion.

[At this point, Black inserts a thirty-one-page appendix describing the origin and legislative history of the *Fourteenth Amendment, concluding that the Bill of Rights applies to the states. He also quotes from Justices who believed that the Privileges and Immunities Clause of the Fourteenth Amendment applies to the states.]*

MR. JUSTICE MURPHY, with whom MR. JUSTICE RUTLEDGE concurs, dissenting.

While in substantial agreement with the views of MR. JUSTICE BLACK, I have one reservation and one addition to make.

I agree that the specific guarantees of the Bill of Rights should be carried over intact into the first section of the Fourteenth Amendment. But I am not prepared to say that the latter is entirely and necessarily limited by the Bill of Rights. Occasions may arise where a proceeding falls so far short of conforming to fundamental standards of procedure as to warrant constitutional condemnation in terms of a lack of due process despite the absence of a specific provision in the Bill of Rights.

That point, however, need not be pursued here inasmuch as the Fifth Amendment is explicit in its provision that no person shall be compelled in any criminal case to be a witness against himself. That provision, as MR. JUSTICE BLACK demonstrates, is a constituent part of the Fourteenth Amendment.

Moreover, it is my belief that this guarantee against self-incrimination has been violated in this case. Under California law, the judge or prosecutor may comment on the failure of the defendant in a criminal trial to explain or deny any evidence or facts introduced against him. As interpreted and applied in this case, such a provision compels a defendant to be a witness against himself in one of two ways:

1. If he does not take the stand, his silence is used as the basis for drawing unfavorable inferences against him as to matters which he might reasonably be expected to explain. Thus he is compelled, through his silence, to testify against himself. And silence can be as effective in this situation as oral statements.

2. If he does take the stand, thereby opening himself to cross-examination, so as to overcome the effects of the provision in question, he is necessarily compelled to testify against himself. In that case, his testimony on cross-examination is

the result of the coercive pressure of the provision rather than his own volition.

Much can be said pro and con as to the desirability of allowing comment on the failure of the accused to testify. But policy arguments are to no avail in the face of a clear constitutional command. This guarantee of freedom from self-incrimination is grounded on a deep respect for those who might prefer to remain silent before their accusers. To borrow language from *Wilson v. United States*, 149 U. S. 60, 66: "It is not every one who can safely venture on the witness stand though entirely innocent of the charge against him. Excessive timidity, nervousness when facing others and attempting to explain transactions of a suspicious character, and offences charged against him, will often confuse and embarrass him to such a degree as to increase rather than remove prejudices against him. It is not every one, however honest, who would, therefore, willingly be placed on the witness stand."

We are obliged to give effect to the principle of freedom from self-incrimination. That principle is as applicable where the compelled testimony is in the form of silence as where it is composed of oral statements. Accordingly, I would reverse the judgment below.

The Incorporation Doctrine: Testimony by Justice Rehnquist

In 1986, during Senate hearings for his nomination for Chief Justice of the Supreme Court, Justice Rehnquist was asked by Senator Arlen Specter about the "incorporation doctrine": the gradual incorporation of the Bill of Rights into the Due Process Clause of the Fourteenth Amendment to be applied against the states. Originally, the Bill of Rights restricted only the federal government. Attorney General Edwin Meese III, as one of the more vocal critics of the incorporation doctrine, had written that "nowhere else has the principle of Federalism been dealt such a politically violent and constitutionally suspect blow as by the theory of incorporation." Meese, "The Supreme Court of the United States: Bulwark of a Limited Constitution," 27 So. Tex. L. Rev. 455, 463–464 (1986). The testimony below comes from "Nomination of Justice William Hubbs Rehnquist," hearings before the Senate Committee on the Judiciary, 99th Cong., 2d Sess., 191–192, 350–351, 356 (1986).

Justice REHNQUIST. . . . if you are looking at the language of the due process clause, as I recall it, Senator, it says: "No State shall deprive any person of life, liberty or property without due process of law."

And the question then becomes, you know, as you know perfectly well, what is included under liberty, or, what provisions from the Bill of Rights are carried over by that language? And I would say that, from the language itself, it is not evident that any particular provisions are carried over, not inexorable; but if you look at the word liberty, and you wonder what kind of liberty are they talking about, surely one liberty was freedom of speech, freedom of the press.

So, it seems to me it is quite natural to carry those over. But I do not know that the language of the due process clause, nor necessarily, what I happen to recall about the debates, and that sort of thing, necessarily indicates that the full rigors of the first amendment as applied to Congress, necessarily were to be applied to the States.

Senator SPECTER. Well, the difficulty with that, it seems to me—and I am just probing to get your line of reasoning on it—is that it is so speculative. If you are picking out a portion of the first amendment, the freedom of speech—if you seek to avoid putting your own personal views, as they arise in a case, which I know you have testified in the 1971 proceedings, that you are very much opposed to—how can you really separate the various aspects of something as fundamental as speech?

Isn't it really all in there? Once you say that the due process clause incorporates freedom of speech under the first amendment, isn't that all there is to it? How can you separate any of it out as not incorporated?

Justice REHNQUIST. Well, if you say that the due process clause incorporates and makes applicable against the States, the first amendment in haec verba, so to speak, the question is answered. If it does that, it does carry it over in precisely the terms that it is applicable to Congress against the State.

But I think the argument on the other side, is that—and I think this is made very well in Justice Jackson's dissent in the *Beauharnais* case—is that there was a good deal of understanding of what freedom of speech meant at the time the Constitution was adopted, that was undoubtedly applicable against the States, but that there were perhaps slightly more latitude allowed to the States than were allowed to the Federal Government.

Justice Harlan took that position in his opinion in the *Roth* case. That the States could proscribe certain kinds of obscenity but that the Federal Government could not.

Senator SPECTER. Mr. Justice Rehnquist, at the risk of asking questions which may come before the Court, I think these are pretty well established principles, but, there is considerable concern on the part of this Senator about the applicability of the due process clause of the 14th amendment to certain fundamental liberties, as embodied in the first 10 amendments.

And I would like to ask your view as to the inclusion of the free exercise of religion in *Cantwell* v. *Connecticut*. It was a unanimous opinion. Does that matter rest, so far as you are concerned?

Justice REHNQUIST. Most certainly, yes.

Senator SPECTER. And the establishment clause in *Everson* v. *Board of Education?*

Justice REHNQUIST. No. I think I criticized the *Everson* case in my dissent in Wallace against Jaffrey, not for the result it reached at all, but for its use of the term "wall of separation between church and state," which I felt was simply not historically justified.

. . .

Senator SPECTER. . . . Mr. Justice Rehnquist, on the subject of the scope of the incorporation doctrine, I had started asking these questions before. You commented that as to the first amendment, the free exercise of religion was incorporated by the due process clause of the 14th amendment. You started to make a distinction with respect to the establishment clause.

Is there any question in your mind that the due process clause of the 14th amendment incorporates freedom of speech?

Justice REHNQUIST. Other than the point I made yesterday. It, obviously, incorporates freedom of speech. I took the position in a couple of opinions I wrote in following Justice Jackson and Justice Harlan that some of the details might be different as applied against the States as opposed to the Federal Government.

Senator SPECTER. Would you repeat the distinction you see as to the scope of the due process clause incorporating the establishment clause of the first amendment?

Justice REHNQUIST. No; I think that is settled by the *Everson* case.

Senator SPECTER. All right.

There is no question that the due process clause of the 14th amendment incorporates freedom of the press under the first amendment?

Justice REHNQUIST. I do not think so.

Senator SPECTER. Are the right of assembly and petition incorporated by the due process clause of the 14th amendment?

Justice REHNQUIST. Yes; I think they are.

Senator SPECTER. Is the search and seizure clause of the fourth amendment incorporated by the due process clause of the fourteenth amendment?

Justice REHNQUIST. That was held in *Mapp* v. *Ohio.*

Senator SPECTER. Do you agree with that? Do you believe it is a decided matter?

Justice REHNQUIST. It is certainly a settled matter, yes.

Senator SPECTER. Is double jeopardy under the fifth amendment incorporated in the due process clause of the 14th amendment?

Justice REHNQUIST. I think that was in the— Senator, I am going to draw back a little. Because in a case like *Benton* v. *Maryland* that came to the Court where—before I got there. I did not participate in that case. I have followed *Benton* v. *Maryland* many times when I have been on the Court. But to say whether I agree with a case that was decided before I came on the Court, I think it is better to phrase it that my record in voting on the case has certainly shown that I have followed that case.

Senator SPECTER. Well, I am not asking whether you agree with it. I am asking whether you consider it a settled issue that the incorporation doctrine covers that issue.

The concern I have is whether the incorporation doctrine is going to be undercut. Although I do not think that you and I have any difference of opinion on this, I just want to be sure.

Justice REHNQUIST. I think in a case—I cannot remember—a case coming up from Montana, I took the—Justice Stewart joined my opinion, I joined Justice Stewart's opinion—saying that some of the nuances of the double jeopardy clause should not apply the same to the States as to the Federal Government.

I think this was a case involving when the trial started, for the purposes of—when jeopardy attached. And the rule in the Federal cases was when a witness is first sworn. But Montana had a wholly different procedure. And it just seemed that a fair translation of the Federal rule to the State rule would not give you an identical situation.

. . .

Senator SPECTER. . . . I had gone through a number of the provisions of the Bill of Rights on the incorporation doctrine, Mr. Justice Rehnquist, because I think it is important to lay to rest the conclusion that the 14th amendment due process clause does incorporate certain provisions of the Bill of Rights.

I have only gone over the ones which have been incorporated. I have not gone into the ones which have not been, because I do not want to move into a lot of areas of the law which are not settled.

There are two remaining areas I want to ask you about. Do you regard it as settled law that the speedy trial provision is incorporated under the due process clause of the 14th amendment?

Justice REHNQUIST. Yes, I think that is settled law, and my opinions reflect it.

Senator SPECTER. What about the cruel and unusual punishment provision of the eighth amendment, is that incorporated into the due process clause of the 14th amendment?

Justice REHNQUIST. Again, my opinions reflect the fact.

9 Property Rights

From the late nineteenth century to the 1930s, the courts struck down efforts by Congress and state legislatures to ease the harshness of industrial conditions. Statutes that established maximum hours or minimum wages were declared unconstitutional interferences with property rights, due process, and "liberty of contract." The courts held that government existed to protect life, liberty, and property, with property accorded the greatest protection. Over those decades the judiciary promoted an exceptionally narrow definition of property and restricted the government's police power to protect the health and safety of citizens.

THE MEANING OF PROPERTY

Few words evoke more powerful emotions than *property*. Pierre Proudhon, the French anarchist of the nineteenth century, equated property with theft. Jesus warned that it would be easier for a camel to pass through the eye of a needle than for a rich man to enter the kingdom of God. Others elevated property to a position of reverence and respect. Machiavelli advised a prince not to take property, for "men forget more easily the death of their father than the loss of their patrimony."

Many of us have been taught from childhood to think of property in narrow terms: land, buildings, personal property, business, and wealth. The word itself, however, suggests a larger meaning. It derives from *proprius:* something private or peculiar to oneself. This general concept embraces intangible possessions, including reputation, ideas, and religious opinions. As a result of court decisions in recent decades, property rights have expanded to cover welfare payments, job rights, garnishment procedures, unemployment compensation, and environmental rights. Property in America acquires specific meaning from custom, statutes, and court decisions.

Property, as a legal creation, fluctuates in meaning over time. Before the War of Independence, a landed aristocracy in America was protected by *entail* (making land inalienable) and *primogeniture* (transferring land to the eldest son). Gradually those laws were abolished. Up until the Civil War, property extended to black slaves, who were auctioned off at the market, bought and sold as human merchandise. Congress enacted fugitive slave laws to return "property" to its owners. In *Dred Scott v. Sandford* (1857), Chief Justice Taney said that the right of property in a slave was "distinctly and expressly affirmed in the Constitution. The right to traffic in it, like an ordinary article of merchandise and property, was guaranteed to the citizens of the United States, in every State that might desire it, for twenty years." 60 U.S. at 451.

Well into the twentieth century the courts continued to treat wives as the property of the husband. The concept of *coverture*, described by Blackstone two centuries ago, maintained its influence. Upon marriage, a woman's legal existence was submerged into that of the man. Marriage made husband and wife "one person in law." Under the husband's "wing, protection, and *cover*, she performs every thing." 2 Commentaries *442. Performance included availability for sex, making it legally impossible in some states for a man to rape his wife. Adultery with a man's wife was considered a violation of the *husband's* property rights. Tinker v. Colwell, 193 U.S. 473 (1904).

To the framers of the Constitution, property represented a broad concept. They knew that when John Locke spoke of property, he meant "lives, liberties and estates"—not simply the latter. To Locke, individuals possessed property in their persons as well as in their goods. Every man had a property in the labor of his body and the work of his hands. The act of labor invested part of one's personality in an object.

James Madison developed a comprehensive view of property. In Federalist 10 he spoke of the "diversity in the faculties of men, from which the rights of property originate." Because mankind consists of different and unequal faculties, different and unequal kinds of property result. But Madison did not say that the most important function of government was to protect property. Rather, the "protection of these faculties is the first object of government." It is no accident that the Constitution authorizes Congress to "promote the progress of science and useful arts, by securing for limited times to authors and inventors the exclusive right to their respective writings and discoveries." Art. I, § 8, Cl. 8. Madison's views are elaborated in an essay written in 1792. People had property in their opinions, in the free communication of ideas, in religious beliefs, and the free use of faculties and "free choice of the objects on which to employ them." Because conscience is the "most sacred of all property," it is a greater violation to invade a man's conscience than to invade his home. MADISON'S ESSAY ON PROPERTY.

This broad view of property rights was obscured by the Supreme Court during America's industrial growth in the nineteenth century. The Court invoked the Due Process Clause of the Fifth and Fourteenth Amendments to control the substantive content of federal and state legislation. In upholding the right of business to operate free of government control, the Court was said to protect property. But it did not protect property in its larger sense, including the community's interest in health and safety. Walton Hamilton and Irene Till explained that it is "incorrect to say that the judiciary protected property; rather they called that property to which they accorded protection." 12 Encycl. Soc. Sci. 536 (1934).

Property has come to represent a "bundle of rights." Kaiser Aetna v. United States, 444 U.S. 164, 176 (1979). These rights have little in common except that they are asserted by persons and enforced by government. Felix S. Cohen, for many years a gifted lecturer at the Yale Law School, underscored the enforcement aspect by proposing that the following label be affixed to all property: "To the world: 'Keep off X unless you have my permission, which I may grant or withhold.' Signed: Private citizen. Endorsed: The state." 9 Rutgers L. Rev. 347, 374 (1954). Although legislative actions and judicial decisions help determine the boundaries of property, the state does not create interests. The active, driving force behind property is the individual who remains conscious of rights and insists on their protection.

THE CONTRACT CLAUSE

The Constitution prohibits any state from passing any law "impairing the Obligation of Contracts." Art. I, § 10. Objections were raised at the Philadelphia Convention that this provision was far too broad and impractical, 2 Farrand 439–440, and so it has proven to be. Madison stated in Federalist 44 that the constitutional prohibitions against bills of attainder, ex post facto laws, and laws impairing the obligation of contracts were added in the interest of "personal security and private rights" and to protect the people from the "fluctuating policy which had directed the public councils." However, under the police power and emergency conditions, state actions that impair the obligation of contracts have been upheld repeatedly by the courts. As the Court noted in 1987, "it is well settled that the prohibition against impairing the obligation of contracts is not to be read literally." Keystone Bituminous Coal Assn. v. DeBenedictis, 480 U.S. 470, 502 (1987).

The prohibition against ex post facto laws might have been used to protect contracts and property rights, but in 1798 the Court restricted this constitutional provision to criminal statutes. The Court said that "Every *ex post facto* law must necessarily be retrospective; but every retrospective law is not an *ex post facto* law: the former only are prohibited." CALDER v. BULL, 3 U.S. (3 Dall.) 385, 390 (1798).

The first major case involving the Contract Clause arose in Georgia. The state legislature, in what became known as the "Yazoo Land Fraud," sold vast tracts of land in 1795 to four companies. With a single exception, every legislator voting for the measure sold his vote either for money or for shares of stock in the companies. In response to this blatant bribery, a mob marched on the state capital and threatened the lives of the lawmakers. Benjamin Wright, The Contract Clause of the Constitution 21 (1938). Public outrage forced the new legislature a year later to rescind the statute. Did this repeal of a corrupt statute violate the contractual rights of speculators and prospective settlers who purchased land from the companies?

Writing for the Supreme Court, Chief Justice Marshall held that the legislature of 1795 possessed constitutional authority to pass the initial statute. The innocent third parties who bought land from the companies, he said, were not responsible for legislative corruption or fraud. On a good-faith basis they had entered into contracts with the companies. Marshall further pointed out that it was inappropriate to expect courts to annul a statute by inquiring into the purity of legislative motives. Fletcher v. Peck, 10 U.S. (6 Cr.) 87 (1810). This decision made it clear that the Contract Clause covered not only "private contracts" but "state contracts" as well. Another reading of the Contract Clause in defense of property rights was announced in New Jersey v.

Wilson, 11 U.S. (7 Cr.) 164 (1812). The overriding theme over history has been a balancing between the right of private property and the right of government to regulate property for the general public.

The Dartmouth College case of 1819 stands as a famous legal landmark, but its unique circumstances apply to relatively few contract disputes. The college had been created in 1754 as a charity school to instruct Indians in the Christian religion. In 1769, it was chartered by the British crown as a private corporation. The college continued to be funded entirely by private donations. In 1816, New Hampshire passed legislation to increase the number of trustees in the college and thereby transfer control to appointees of the governor.

In his decision for the Court, Chief Justice Marshall said that the British parliament could have annulled the charter at any time. New Hampshire could have altered the charter after the break with England and before ratification of the U.S. Constitution. But the Contract Clause prohibited the state from impairing the contract of a "private eleemosynary institution": an institution created by private parties, sustained by private funds, and devoted to charitable goals. Marshall explained that had the college been created by the legislature and supported by public funds, the state could have altered the contract. Under those circumstances the college would have existed as a public corporation to satisfy a public purpose. Dartmouth, however, had a right to continue under its private charter without interference by the state. Otherwise, Marshall warned, all charitable and educational institutions would fall under the control of government. DARTMOUTH COLLEGE v. WOODWARD, 17 U.S. (4 Wheat.) 517 (1819).

This case has few applications today. The line between "public" and "private" is less clear, and even private institutions are subject to state regulation and control. Henry J. Friendly, The Dartmouth College Case and the Public-Private Penumbra (1969). Nevertheless, the case established important limits on the power of government to interfere with academic freedom and certain kinds of contracts. It also reassured Federalist property holders who feared the reach of majority rule and state legislatures.

The Charles River Bridge case of 1837 illustrates that the right of contract is never absolute. In 1785, the legislature of Massachusetts incorporated a company to build a bridge and take tolls. About four decades later it created another company to build a bridge nearby. The second bridge took tolls for a few years and then became free. Travelers, of course, switched to the new bridge and proprietors of the first bridge complained that the legislature had impaired the obligations of a contract. The Supreme Court, balancing the rights of property against the rights reserved to the states, held that a state law may be retrospective in character and alter rights formerly vested by law without violating the Contract Clause. Although corporations are given certain rights by law, the community also has rights in a dynamic economy to improved public accommodations and travel. CHARLES RIVER BRIDGE v. WARREN BRIDGE, 36 U.S. (11 Pet.) 419 (1837).

The principle of *Charles River* has been affirmed in many cases. The Contract Clause does not prevent a state from granting a right and repealing or modifying that right in future years. A legislature may grant a monopoly and decide at a later time that it is in the interest of the state to abolish the monopoly and allow other companies to enter the field. Slaughter-House Cases, 83 U.S. (16 Wall.) 36 (1873); Butchers' Union Co. v. Crescent City Co., 111 U.S. 746 (1884). In matters affecting public health or public morals, one legislature may not bind future legislatures.[1]

Private contracts are subject to government control. The right of an owner of a building to contract with tenants may be limited by rent-control laws. Block v. Hirsh, 256 U.S. 135 (1921). Although contracts may create rights of property, when they concern a subject matter within the control of Congress "they have a congenital infirmity." Norman v. Baltimore & Ohio R. Co., 294 U.S. 240, 307–308 (1935), cited in Connolly v. Pension Benefit Guaranty Corp., 475 U.S. 211, 223–224 (1986).

If a state passes a bankruptcy law to relieve debtors of their liabilities, does this impair the obligation of contracts? The Supreme Court in an early case decided that states are not prevented from passing bankruptcy laws unless Congress preempts the field by passing a uniform law authorized by Article I, Section 8, Clause 4. In this particular case, the Court determined that the state law did impair the obligation of contracts. Sturges v. Crowninshield, 17 U.S. (4 Wheat.) 120 (1819). The following decade the Court again held that congressional inaction on uniform bankruptcy laws permitted the states to legislate on the subject. Moreover, states could pass laws discharging a debtor from liability if the law preceded the contract. If a bankruptcy act operated prospectively, it did not violate the Contract Clause. Ogden v. Saunders, 25 U.S. (12 Wheat.) 212 (1827). Contracts are then entered into in light of the bankruptcy policy established by law.

The question of a retrospective law was decided by the Supreme Court in 1934. A 5–4 decision upheld a Minnesota law, passed during the Great Depression, that gave homeowners a delay of up to two years in meeting their mortgage payments. Although the law clearly impaired contracts entered into prior to the statute, both the state court and the Supreme Court agreed that the police power had sufficient scope in an emergency to set aside, for a limited period, the Contract Clause. HOME BLDG. & LOAN ASSN. v. BLAISDELL, 290 U.S. 398 (1934).

A year later, by a 5–4 vote, the Court upheld the power of Congress to abrogate the "gold clauses" in private contracts. To prevent a run on the banks and the hoarding of gold, President Franklin D. Roosevelt and Congress had taken emergency actions in 1933 to prevent individuals from requiring payment in gold or a particular kind of coin. Norman v. B.&O. R. Co., 294 U.S. 240 (1935). For other "gold clause" cases, see Nortz v. United States, 294 U.S. 317 (1935) and Perry v. United States, 294 U.S. 330 (1935). In several other cases, where state actions were not restricted to an emergency period, statutes were declared invalid under the Contract Clause.[2]

The Contract Clause does not carry the same importance today as it did in the era of *Fletcher* and *Dartmouth College*. As a limitation on state power, it has been largely replaced by the Due Process and Equal Protection Clauses of the Fourteenth Amendment. There are still circumstances, however, where the Contract Clause is

---

[1]Stone v. Mississippi, 101 U.S. 814 (1880); Fertilizing Co. v. Hyde Park, 97 U.S. 659 (1879); Beer Co. v. Massachusetts, 97 U.S. 25 (1878).

[2]Treigle v. Acme Homestead Assn., 297 U.S. 189 (1936); Worthen Co. v. Kavanaugh, 295 U.S. 56 (1935); Worthen Co. v. Thomas, 292 U.S. 426 (1934). But see also El Paso v. Simmons, 379 U.S. 497 (1965); East New York Bank v. Hahn, 326 U.S. 230 (1945); Faitoute Co. v. Asbury Park, 316 U.S. 502 (1942); Veix v. Sixth Ward Assn., 310 U.S. 32 (1940).

successfully invoked to strike down a state statute. A contemporary case involved the Port Authority of New York and New Jersey. In 1962, the two states passed a statutory covenant that limited the ability of the Authority to subsidize rail passenger transportation by using revenues and reserves that had been pledged as security for consolidated bonds issued by the Authority. In 1974, the two states repealed the 1962 statutory covenant. Although the New Jersey courts upheld the repeal as a valid exercise of the police power, the Supreme Court in 1977 ruled that the repeal violated the Contract Clause by eliminating an important security provision for stockholders. United States Trust Co. v. New Jersey, 431 U.S. 1 (1977).

The three dissenters in this 4–3 decision accused the Court of "dusting off" the Contract Clause and giving it a meaning broader than intended by the framers. According to their analysis and some other studies, the Contract Clause was conceived of "primarily as protection for economic transactions entered into by purely private parties, rather than obligations involving the State itself." Id. at 45. This philosophy would allow each new legislature to rescind the policies of the previous legislature. The problem is that state obligations frequently involve investments by private parties, as in the Port Authority case. The dissent concluded with a warning that the Court "can actively intrude into such economic and policy matters only if my Brethren are prepared to bear enormous institutional and social costs. . . . I consider the potential dangers of such judicial interference to be intolerable . . ."

A year later, the Court struck down a Minnesota law for violating the Contract Clause, pointing out that the police power did not give the states unlimited authority to abridge existing contractual relationships. Moreover, the Minnesota law did not deal with grave economic or social emergencies, as in the 1934 *Blaisdell* case. Justices Brennan, White, and Marshall dissented from what they regarded as the Court's extension of the Contract Clause beyond its original intent. Allied Structural Steel Co. v. Spannaus, 438 U.S. 234 (1978).

THE TAKING CLAUSE

The Fifth Amendment states that private property shall not "be taken for public use, without just compensation." This is referred to variously as the Taking Clause, the Public Use Clause, or the Just Compensation Clause. Under the Due Process Clause of the Fourteenth Amendment, as well as under their own constitutions, states are also forbidden from taking private property for public use without just compensation. Chicago, B. & Q. R.R. Co. v. Chicago, 166 U.S. 226, 236–237, 241 (1897). The taking of property constitutes an exercise of the power of eminent domain, which gives the sovereign the right to condemn or expropriate private property for a public purpose upon payment of just compensation.

The decision to invoke the power of eminent domain is purely a legislative function. Whether compensation is "just" or whether property has been taken for "public use" are questions that might be taken to the courts. Berman v. Parker, 348 U.S. 26 (1954); Hawaii Housing Authority v. Midkiff, 467 U.S. 229 (1984). Every deprivation of property does not require compensation. PruneYard Shopping Center v. Robins, 447 U.S. 74, 82 (1980); Chicago, B. & Q. Railway Co. v. Drainage Comm'rs., 200 U.S. 561 (1906). Even when compensation is paid, a number of 5–4 decisions by the Supreme Court reveal fundamental disagreements about the proper method of calculating what is "just."[3]

The dimensions of land property are of broad and changing scope. The ancient *ad coelum* doctrine gave landowners control of their property downward to the core of the earth and upward to the heavens. A landowner's rights to the column of air above his land led to successful actions against overhanging eaves, protruding structures, and the firing of projectiles or the stringing of wires across someone's land. See Portsmouth Co. v. United States, 260 U.S. 327 (1922). Another case in 1922 involved a deed under which a coal company conveyed land surface to homeowners but reserved the right to remove all the coal under the property. Any damages to the surface resulting from mining were waived. The homeowners tried to prevent the company from burrowing under their property and removing supporting structures for their house and land. Despite the existence of a state statute passed after the deed, forbidding mining that would cause land under a home to sink, an 8–1 decision by the Supreme Court held that the police power could not protect shortsighted homeowners who acquired only surface rights and not the right of support. Pennsylvania Coal Co. v. Mahon, 260 U.S. 393 (1922).

Homeowners in the vicinity of transportation systems may be entitled to some compensation for damages. Landowners next to a railroad tunnel had no right to be compensated for normal operations (vibration from trains and the emission of smoke, cinders, and gases). However, they were entitled to the recovery of some damages if fans within the tunnel pumped additional smoke and gases onto their property. Richards v. Washington Terminal Co., 233 U.S. 546 (1914). And if military bombers skim so close to a person's home and chicken farm that chickens are killed by crashing into the walls from fright and homeowners are unable to sleep, the flights constitute a "taking" of property requiring just compensation. United States v. Causby, 328 U.S. 256 (1946). See also Griggs v. Allegheny County, 369 U.S. 84 (1962).[4]

Under conditions of war, private property may be demolished to prevent use by the enemy. Compensation need not be given to the owner. United States v. Caltex, 344 U.S. 149 (1952). Through its power to regulate commerce and other matters, Congress may diminish the value of private property without triggering the Taking Clause. The Supreme Court noted in 1986 that Congress "routinely creates burdens for some that directly benefit others." In setting minimum wages, controlling prices, or regulating other actions, "it cannot be said that the Taking Clause is violated whenever legislation requires one person to use his or her assets for the benefit of another." Connolly v. Pension Benefit Guaranty Corp., 475 U.S. at 223. Statutes may be interpreted as merely regulatory rather than a taking. FCC v. Florida Power Corp., 480 U.S. 245 (1987). When property is diminished without a taking, the decision to

---

[3]United States v. Fuller, 409 U.S. 488 (1973); Almota Farmers Elevator & Whse. Co. v. United States, 409 U.S. 470 (1973); United States v. Cors, 337 U.S. 325 (1949); United States ex rel. TVA v. Powelson, 319 U.S. 266 (1943).

[4]Other "taking" cases include Andrus v. Allard, 444 U.S. 51 (1979); United States v. Reynolds, 397 U.S. 14 (1970); YMCA v. United States, 395 U.S. 85 (1969); Goldblatt v. Hempstead, 369 U.S. 590 (1962); Armstrong v. United States, 364 U.S. 40 (1960); United States v. Central Eureka Mining Co., 357 U.S. 155 (1958); United States v. Petty Motor Co., 327 U.S. 372 (1946); Miller v. Schoene, 276 U.S. 272 (1928); Hadacheck v. Sebastian, 239 U.S. 394 (1915).

provide compensation is a question for the legislative branch, not the courts. Batten v. United States, 306 F.2d 580, 585 (10th Cir. 1962).

Zoning laws may restrict, diminish, or destroy the value of property but they do not necessarily represent a taking. Communities use zoning ordinances as part of the police power to promote public health, safety, and morals. Restrictions are placed on the height of buildings and the materials and methods of construction, and certain industries are excluded from residential areas. These regulations usually do not represent unconstitutional deprivations of property or takings.[5] Zoning ordinances that attempted to segregate neighborhoods on the basis of race have been struck down as unconstitutional. Buchanan v. Warley, 245 U.S. 60 (1917). Moreover, zoning ordinances that arbitrarily or unreasonably interfere with a family's right to remain as a unit within their home have been declared unconstitutional. Moore v. East Cleveland, 431 U.S. 494 (1977).

Zoning ordinances apply equally to all property owners in a designated area. However, laws passed to preserve historic buildings and neighborhoods affect only particular property owners. Any alterations to these structures must be approved by local officials or commissions. In a case decided by the Supreme Court in 1978, a company claimed that the application of New York City's landmarks law to the Grand Central Terminal constituted a taking of property in violation of the Fifth and Fourteenth Amendments. The decision, which denied that property had been taken, reveals the difficulty the Court has experienced in defining the meaning of the Taking Clause. PENN CENTRAL TRANSP. CO. v. NEW YORK CITY, 438 U.S. 104 (1978).

Recent cases highlight the complexity and broad reach of the Taking Clause. If a private developer deepens a pond to form a marina and connects it to a navigable bay used by the public, the marina loses its character as private property. However, if the government wishes to make the marina a public aquatic park, it must pay just compensation. Kaiser Aetna v. United States, 444 U.S. 164 (1979). A state may not force landlords to permit a company to install cable television in return for nominal payments (such as a one-time one-dollar payment). Although the state may determine that cable TV offers important educational and community benefits, the permanent physical occupation of an owner's property constitutes a taking and requires just compensation. Loretto v. Teleprompter Manhattan CATV Corp., 458 U.S. 419 (1972). Company data supplied to the government in the form of trade secrets can be treated as property entitled to protection under the Taking Clause. Ruckelshaus v. Monsanto Co., 467 U.S. 986 (1984). The use of eminent domain to condemn land as a means of redistributing private property and combating oligarchy is a valid "public use." HAWAII HOUSING AUTHORITY v. MIDKIFF, 467 U.S. 229 (1984).

Three decisions in 1987 demonstrate the Court's continuing difficulty in reaching agreement about the meaning of the Taking Clause. The Justices split 5–4 in two cases and 6–3 in the other. The first case concerned a Pennsylvania law that

---

[5]San Diego Gas & Electric Co. v. San Diego, 450 U.S. 621 (1981); Agins v. Tiburon, 447 U.S. 255 (1980); Village of Belle Terre v. Boraas, 416 U.S. 1 (1974); Zahn v. Bd. of Public Works, 274 U.S. 325 (1927); Euclid v. Ambler Co., 272 U.S. 365 (1926); Welch v. Swasey, 214 U.S. 91 (1909). See also MacDonald, Sommer & Frates v. Yolo County, 477 U.S. 340 (1986) and Williamson Planning Comm'n v. Hamilton Bank, 473 U.S. 172 (1985), for the ripeness hurdle that can prevent courts from reaching the taking issue.

prohibits underground coal mining when it causes subsidence damage (sinking) to public buildings, dwellings, and cemeteries. To implement the statute, a state agency required that 50 percent of the coal beneath statutorily protected structures be kept in place to provide surface support. Was this merely state regulation or a taking? A 5–4 Court concluded that the coal companies bringing the case had failed to satisfy their burden of showing that a taking had occurred. To the four dissenters, there had been a taking. Keystone Bituminous Coal Assn. v. DeBenedictis, 480 U.S. 470 (1987).

The second case involved a county's decision to prohibit the construction of buildings on a campground after there had been extensive damage from a flood. A church, which had purchased land in the area, sought to recover damages from loss of use. Was this only a regulatory taking that did not require just compensation? Could the county simply reverse its decision, in the face of a ruling against it, and not pay compensation? A 6–3 Court announced that once a taking has been determined, government must compensate the owner for the period during which the taking was effective. "Temporary" takings, without compensation, are impermissible. First Lutheran Church v. Los Angeles County, 482 U.S. 304 (1987).

In the final case, the California Coastal Commission granted a permit to a couple to replace a small bungalow on their beachfront lot with a larger house. As a condition, however, the Commission insisted that the couple allow the public to pass across their beach, which was located between two public beaches. A 5–4 Court held that the condition did not serve public purposes related to the permit requirement. None of the purposes advanced by the Commission was plausible to the majority. Nollan v. California Coastal Commission, 483 U.S. 825 (1987).

THE POLICE POWER

The courts of the nineteenth century permitted legislatures and municipalities broad discretion under the "police power" to regulate public health and safety. The power of states to "impose restraints and burdens upon persons and property in conservation and promotion of the public health, good order and prosperity, is a power originally and always belonging to the States, not surrendered by them to the general government nor directly restrained by the Constitution of the United States, and essentially exclusive." In re Rahrer, 140 U.S. 545, 554 (1891).

In a major case in 1873, a 5–4 decision by the Supreme Court upheld a monopoly that Louisiana had granted to a slaughterhouse. The Court ruled that the statute represented a valid police regulation for the health and comfort of the people. The decision proved pivotal for two other reasons. First, it concluded that the privileges and immunities under the Fourteenth Amendment were to be protected by the states, not the national government. Second, the powerful dissents influenced future proponents of property rights and liberty of contract. SLAUGHTER-HOUSE CASES, 83 U.S. (16 Wall.) 36 (1873). Just as the police power could justify a monopoly, so could the same state a few years later invoke that power to abolish the monopoly and reintroduce competition. Butchers' Union Co. v. Crescent City Co., 111 U.S. 746 (1884).

There were some hints at the state level that legislative efforts to control business activities could be curbed by the courts. Wynehamer v. People, 13 N.Y. 378 (1856). However, the Supreme Court provided broad support for state regulatory efforts. An Illinois law setting maximum charges for storing grain in warehouses and elevators was upheld in 1877 as a legitimate exercise of state authority to regulate businesses affected with a public interest. MUNN v. ILLINOIS, 94 U.S. 113 (1877). Other cases during this period supported use of the police power for economic regulation. Fertilizing Co. v. Hyde Park, 97 U.S. 659 (1879); Patterson v. Kentucky, 97 U.S. 501 (1879); Beer Co. v. Massachusetts, 97 U.S. 25 (1878).

A unanimous decision in 1885 upheld a law prohibiting public laundries from operating from 10 p.m. to 6 a.m. Barbier v. Connolly, 113 U.S. 27. A year later, the Court upheld the power of a state railroad commission to fix freight and passenger rates. Railroad Commission Cases, 116 U.S. 307, 347, 353 (1886). A unanimous ruling in 1887 allowed states to prohibit the manufacture and sale of intoxicating liquors within the state. It belonged to the legislative branch "to exert what are known as the police powers of the State, and to determine, primarily, what measures are appropriate or needful for the protection of the public morals, the public health, or the public safety." Mugler v. Kansas, 123 U.S. 623, 661. The constitutional provision against impairing contracts did not restrict states from placing restrictions on contracts. Id. at 665, citing New Orleans Gas Co. v. Louisiana Light Co., 115 U.S. 650, 672 (1885).

In 1890, the Supreme Court declared unconstitutional a Minnesota law not because it exceeded the police power but because the judiciary of that state had decided that the reasonableness of rates established by a railroad and warehouse commission was final and conclusive, prohibiting review by the courts. This case did not prevent regulation by the state. It merely required the courts to determine whether the rates satisfied due process of law. Chicago, Milwaukee and St. Paul Railway Co. v. Minnesota, 134 U.S. 418 (1890). Also that year, the Court invalidated a Minnesota "police power" statute because it interfered with commerce among the states and thus invaded the province of Congress. Minnesota v. Barber, 136 U.S. 313.

In 1897, a unanimous Supreme Court used the magic phrase "liberty to contract" and spoke strongly about a citizen's right to be free to earn his livelihood. Allgeyer v. Louisiana, 165 U.S. 578, 589, 591. This general philosophy did not prevent the Court the next year from upholding an eight-hour day for workers in coal mines and smelters. The Court flatly rejected the idea that workers and employers stood on equal footing in reaching a contract. Holden v. Hardy, 169 U.S. 366, 397 (1898). The Court perceptively noted that the police power had been greatly expanded in the nineteenth century "owing to the enormous increase in the number of occupations which are dangerous, or so far detrimental to the health of employees as to demand special precautions for their well-being and protection . . ." Id. at 391–392. In 1903, the Court upheld an eight-hour law in Kansas covering all persons employed by the state or local governments, including work contracted by the state. Atkin v. Kansas, 191 U.S. 207.

SUBSTANTIVE DUE PROCESS

Up to this point the Court had sustained an eight-hour day for the public sector and for certain industries in the private sector (coal mining and smelting). Over the next three decades the courts regularly invalidated legislative efforts to establish maximum hours or minimum wages—efforts the judiciary regarded as an unconstitutional interference with the "liberty of contract." Lawyers from the corporate sector helped translate the philosophy of laissez faire into legal terms and constitutional doctrine. One of the intellectual pillars was Thomas M. Cooley, whose *Constitutional*

Limitations appeared in 1868. Cooley emphasized limits on legislative authority in order to protect personal liberty and private property. Herbert Spencer's *Social Statics* (1851) counseled against government efforts to protect the weak, preferring instead a kind of Darwinian struggle for survival of the "fittest." Christopher G. Tiedeman's *Treatise on the Limitations of the Police Power* (1886) also developed the theory of laissez faire and liberty of contract. See Benjamin R. Twiss, Lawyers and the Constitution (1942).

The climate of the years following the Civil War promoted the pursuit of material goals, especially after the heavy sacrifices demanded by the war. Elitism by corporate leaders could not be justified on tradition (feudalism) or the will of God (Calvinism). Neither belief system fitted an age devoted to materialist thinking, scientific discovery, and industrial capitalism. Justification took the form of Social Darwinism: the belief in ruthless individualism in which only the strongest were allowed to survive. Material success became the overriding value. The American Bar Association, founded in 1878, campaigned to limit legislative interference with property rights. The specter of "socialism" and "communism" gave added force and urgency to these efforts.

Judicial tolerance of the police power came to an abrupt halt in 1905 when the Court invalidated a New York law limiting bakery workers to sixty hours a week or ten hours a day. Justice Peckham, writing for a 5–4 majority, converted the general right to make a contract into laissez-faire rigidity. He found no "reasonable ground" to interfere with the liberty of a person to contract for as many hours of work as desired. LOCHNER v. NEW YORK, 198 U.S. 45, 57 (1905). The statute seemed to him to serve no purpose in safeguarding public health or the health of the worker. Such laws were "mere meddlesome interferences" with the rights of an individual to enter into contracts. Lawyers who opposed the law argued that it was not a health measure but rather "a labor law" to promote paternalism.

In their dissent, Justices Harlan, White, and Day reviewed previous holdings of the Court that had interpreted the police power generously to support economic regulation. They cited statistical studies to show the need for remedial legislation. Peckham's opinion was so flavored with conservative business doctrines that Justice Holmes, in his dissent, accused the majority of deciding "upon an economic theory which a large part of the country does not entertain." The Constitution, he said, is "not intended to embody a particular economic theory, whether of paternalism and the organic relation of the citizen to the state or of *laissez faire*." However, laissez faire did not mean a free market. Corporations were busily involved in forming pools, trusts, "community of interests," and other devices to protect themselves from competition. The marketplace of many competing units was becoming a relic of the past.

The Court equivocated on the principle of laissez faire. In 1908, it struck down a congressional statute that made it unlawful for the railroads to fire workers because of their union membership. A 6–2 decision maintained the fiction of *Lochner* that the employer and employee had "equality of right" to enter into a contract, "and any legislation that disturbs that equality is an arbitrary interference with the liberty of contract over which no government can legally justify in a free land." Adair v. United States, 208 U.S. 161, 175 (1908). See also Coppage v. Kansas, 236 U.S. 1 (1915). In that same year, however, the Court sustained Oregon's ten-hour day for women. The statistical record referred to by the dissenters in *Lochner* supplied a good tactical clue for Louis D. Brandeis, who argued the case for Oregon. His sister-in-law, Josephine Goldmark, was closely associated with the National Consumers' League, which had long advocated improved working conditions. She supervised an intensive search of library holdings and helped produce a brief of 113 pages, almost all of which consisted of copious data extracted from sociological studies supporting the need for limiting working hours for women. The Court called attention to what is now known as the "Brandeis brief": a compilation of state and foreign statutes that imposed restrictions on the hours of labor required of women, followed by extracts from over ninety reports of committees, bureaus of statistics, commissioners of hygiene, and inspectors of factories. These studies, drawn primarily from Europe, concluded that long hours of labor "are dangerous for women, primarily because of their special physical organization." Muller v. Oregon, 208 U.S. 412, 419–420 n.1 (1908). Could the constitutional principle announced in *Lochner* be displaced by sociological data? The Court engaged in a bit of judicial doubletalk:

> The legislation and opinions referred to in the margin may not be, technically speaking, authorities, and in them is little or no discussion of the constitutional question presented to us for determination, yet they are significant of a widespread belief that woman's physical structure, and the functions she performs in consequence thereof, justify special legislation restricting or qualifying the conditions under which she should be permitted to toil. Constitutional questions, it is true, are not settled by even a consensus of present public opinion, for it is the peculiar value of a written constitution that it places in unchanging form limitations upon legislative action, and thus gives a permanence and stability to popular government which otherwise would be lacking. At the same time, when a question of fact is debated and debatable, and the extent to which a special constitutional limitation goes is affected by the truth in respect to that fact, a widespread and long continued belief concerning it is worthy of consideration. We take judicial cognizance of all matters of general knowledge.[6]

"Liberty of contract" did not prevent the Court in 1911 from unanimously upholding an Iowa statute that prohibited certain contracts by railroad companies, or delivering another unanimous opinion three years later to sustain a New York law requiring certain industries to pay employees semimonthly and in cash. Chicago, Burlington & Quincy R.R. Co. v. McGuire, 219 U.S. 543 (1911) and Erie R.R. Co. v. Williams, 233 U.S. 685 (1914). Rent-control laws were also upheld, preventing a landlord from freely contracting with his tenants. Block v. Hirsh, 256 U.S. 135 (1921).

In 1917, the Court upheld the constitutionality of Oregon's ten-hour day for men and women, including a provision for overtime pay. Brandeis was now on the Court as an Associate Justice. Because of his previous involvement in litigating this type of case, he did not participate in the decision. Felix Frankfurter of the Harvard Law School argued the case for Oregon and prepared a "Brandeis brief" that contained an array of facts and statistics to demonstrate the effects of overtime on the physical and moral health of the worker. His brief reviewed industrial conditions and labor

[6]Muller v. Oregon, 208 U.S. 412, 420–421 (1908). For unanimous rulings that upheld other state statutes setting maximum hours for women, see Bosley v. McLaughlin, 236 U.S. 385 (1915); Miller v. Wilson, 236 U.S. 373 (1915); and Riley v. Massachusetts, 232 U.S. 671 (1914). A 5–4 Court upheld a congressional statute setting an eight-hour day for railroad workers engaged in interstate commerce; Wilson v. New, 243 U.S. 332 (1917).

experiences in England and the United States. A 5–3 Court sustained the statute. Bunting v. Oregon, 243 U.S. 426 (1917).

Frankfurter was again lead counsel in defending a congressional statute that provided for minimum wages for women and children in the District of Columbia. Despite his lengthy sociological brief, the Court held the statute invalid. Writing for a 5–3 majority, Justice Sutherland found the mass of data compiled by Frankfurter "interesting but only mildly persuasive." ADKINS v. CHILDREN'S HOSPITAL, 261 U.S. 525, 560 (1923). Because of progress in contractual, political, and civil status of women since the *Muller* decision of 1908, Sutherland said that the continuation of protective legislation could not be justified. Although the Court had sustained statutes setting maximum hours, the minimum wage law seemed dangerous territory to the majority. What was next, Sutherland asked, maximum wages? In one of the dissents, Chief Justice Taft thought that the line drawn between hours and wages was imaginary. Justice Holmes's dissent described how the phrase "due process of law" had evolved into the "dogma, Liberty of Contract."

Between 1923 and 1934, the Court repeatedly struck down statutes on the ground that the activity regulated was not "affected with a public interest."[7] At the same time, new areas of economic life were becoming national in scope and gradually brought within Congress' power over interstate commerce (see Chapter 8). Finally, the onset of the Great Depression of 1929 shattered the dream of a self-correcting free economy.

The philosophy of *Adkins* survived as late as 1936, although a decision that year striking down New York's minimum wage law for women and children could muster only a 5–4 majority. "Freedom of contract," said the Court, "is the general rule and restraint the exception." Morehead v. N.Y. ex rel. Tipaldo, 298 U.S. 587, 610–611. Chief Justice Hughes dissented, joined by Brandeis, Stone, and Cardozo. Stone, in a separate dissent, criticized the basis on which the majority had declared the New York law invalid: "It is difficult to imagine any grounds, other than our own personal economic predilections, for saying that the contract of employment is any the less an appropriate subject of legislation than are scores of others, in dealing with which this Court has held that legislatures may curtail individual freedom in the public interest." Stone emphasized the changes that had occurred in economic conditions: "In the years that have intervened since the *Adkins* case we have had opportunity to learn that a wage is not always the resultant of free bargaining between employers and employees; that it may be one forced upon employees by their economic necessities and upon employers by the most ruthless of their competitors. . . . Because of their nature and extent these are public problems. A generation ago they were for the individual to solve; today they are the burden of the nation."

Adkins was finally overruled in 1937. Sutherland, Van Devanter, McReynolds, and Butler, who had provided four of the majority votes in *Morehead*, dissented. Roberts, the fifth member of that majority, now joined the four dissenters from *Morehead* to uphold a minimum wage law for women and minors in the state of Washington. WEST COAST HOTEL CO. v. PARRISH, 300 U.S. 379 (1937). Since the Washington

---

[7]New State Ice Co. v. Liebmann, 285 U.S. 262 (1932); Williams v. Standard Oil Co., 278 U.S. 235 (1929); Ribnik v. McBride, 277 U.S. 350 (1928); Tyson & Brother v. Banton, 273 U.S. 418 (1927); Wolff Co. v. Industrial Court, 262 U.S. 522 (1923).

case was decided about two months after President Franklin D. Roosevelt had unveiled his court-packing plan, much has been made of Roberts' "switch in time that saved nine." However, Roberts had already broken with his doctrinaire laissez-faire colleagues. He wrote the 5–4 opinion in *Nebbia* v. *New York*, 291 U.S. 502 (1934), which upheld a price-setting statute. With his support, the Court was prepared to sustain minimum wage legislation in the fall of 1936 but had delayed its ruling because Justice Stone was ill.[8]

Justice Sutherland, speaking for the four dissenters in *West Coast Hotel*, assailed the theory that decisions of the Supreme Court should be reconsidered because of economic conditions: "the meaning of the Constitution does not change with the ebb and flow of economic events." His phrase "ebb and flow" suggests a seasonal if not spasmodic quality, which seems offensive to a constitution grounded on fundamental principles. But the record of the Court on economic regulation was decidedly one of ebb and flow. Over a period of about four decades the Court had tried to impose a liberty-of-contract theory at a time when power was shifting dramatically from the employee to the employer. A countervailing force was needed and government intervened to redress the imbalance.

By 1941, the composition of the Court had been radically altered, especially with Reed, Murphy, and Black replacing Sutherland, Butler, and Van Devanter. A unanimous Court that year upheld a congressional statute setting minimum wages and maximum hours for men and women. The statute was within the power of Congress to regulate interstate commerce and to protect public health, morals, and welfare. No conflict was found with the due process of law or with the rights of states under the Tenth Amendment. United States v. Darby, 312 U.S. 100 (1941). Another unanimous decision in 1941 overruled the laissez-faire doctrine of *Ribnik* v. *McBride*. Olsen v. Nebraska, 313 U.S. 236 (1941). A combination of social, economic, and political forces had finally reversed the constitutional doctrines of the Court. In the future, decisions about economic or social philosophy would be left largely to legislatures, not to the courts. FERGUSON v. SKRUPA, 372 U.S. 726 (1963). See also Williamson v. Lee Optical Co., 348 U.S. 483, 488 (1955) and Day-Brite Lighting, Inc. v. Missouri, 342 U.S. 421 (1952). However, there are still occasions when the judiciary will strike down social and economic legislation. Morey v. Doud, 354 U.S. 457 (1957).

An artificial line between property rights and human rights continues to be drawn. With forceful prose, Justice Stewart attempted to join the two concepts: "the dichotomy between personal liberties and property rights is a false one. Property does not have rights. People have rights. The right to enjoy property without unlawful deprivation, no less than the right to speak or the right to travel, is in truth a 'personal' right, whether the 'property' in question be a welfare check, a home, or a savings account. In fact, a fundamental interdependence exists between the personal right to liberty and the personal right in property. Neither could have meaning without the other." Lynch v. Household Finance Corp., 405 U.S. 538, 552 (1972).

---

[8]Felix Frankfurter, "Mr. Justice Roberts," 104 U. Pa. L. Rev. 311 (1955); 2 Merlo J. Pusey, Charles Evans Hughes 757 (1963). For a challenge to Roberts' recollection of key events in 1936, see Clement E. Vose, Constitutional Change 228–234 (1972).

Selected Readings

ACKERMAN, BRUCE. *Private Property and the Constitution*. New Haven, Conn.: Yale University Press, 1977.

BERGER, LAWRENCE. "A Policy Analysis of the Taking Problem." 49 *New York University Law Review* 165 (1974).

BLUME, LAWRENCE, AND DANIEL L. RUBINFELD. "Compensation for Takings: An Economic Analysis." 72 *California Law Review* 569 (1984).

BRIGHAM, JOHN. "Property & the Supreme Court: Do the Justices Make Sense?" 16 *Polity* 242 (1983).

COHEN, FELIX S. "Dialogue on Private Property." 9 *Rutgers Law Review* 357 (1954).

DUNHAM, ALLISON. "Griggs v. Allegheny County in Perspective: Thirty Years of Supreme Court Expropriation Law." 1962 *Supreme Court Review* 63.

EPSTEIN, RICHARD A. *Takings: Private Property and the Power of Eminent Domain*. Cambridge, Mass.: Harvard University Press, 1985.

HALE, ROBERT L. "The Supreme Court and the Contract Clause." 57 *Harvard Law Review* 512, 621, 852 (1944).

HORWITZ, MORTON J. "The Transformation in the Conception of Property in American Law." 40 *University of Chicago Law Review* 248 (1973).

HUMBACH, JOHN A. "A Unifying Theory for the Just-Compensation Cases: Takings, Regulation and Public Use." 34 *Rutgers Law Review* 243 (1982).

JOHNSON, CORWIN W. "Compensation for Invalid Land-Use Regulations." 15 *Georgia Law Review* 559 (1981).

LERNER, MAX. "The Supreme Court and American Capitalism." 42 *Yale Law Journal* 668 (1933).

MANDELKER, DANIEL R. "Land Use Takings: The Compensation Issue." 8 *Hastings Constitutional Law Quarterly* 491 (1981).

McCLOSKEY, ROBERT G. "Economic Due Process and the Supreme Court: An Exhumation and Reburial." 1962 *Supreme Court Review* 34.

MICHELMAN, FRANK I. "Property, Utility, and Fairness: Comments on the Ethical Foundations of 'Just Compensation' Law." 80 *Harvard Law Review* 1165 (1967).

OAKES, JAMES L. " 'Property Rights' in Constitutional Analysis Today." 56 *Washington Law Review* 583 (1981).

REICH, CHARLES A. "The New Property." 73 *Yale Law Journal* 733 (1964).

ROSE, CAROL M. "*Mahon* Reconsidered: Why the Takings Issue Is Still a Muddle." 57 *Southern California Law Review* 561 (1984).

SALLET, JONATHAN B. "Regulatory 'Takings' and Just Compensation: The Supreme Court's Search for a Solution Continues." 18 *Urban Lawyer* 635 (1986).

SAX, JOSEPH L. "Takings and the Police Power." 74 *Yale Law Journal* 36 (1964).

——. "Takings, Private Property, and Public Rights." 81 *Yale Law Journal* 149 (1971).

STOEBUCK, WILLIAM B. "Police Power, Takings, and Due Process." 37 *Washington and Lee Law Review* 1057 (1980).

WRIGHT, BENJAMIN F., JR. *The Contract Clause of the Constitution*. Cambridge, Mass.: Harvard University Press, 1938.

Madison's Essay on Property

This term in its particular application means "that dominion which one man claims and exercises over the external things of the world, in exclusion of every other individual."

In its larger and juster meaning, it embraces every thing to which a man may attach a value and have a right; and *which leaves to every one else the like advantage.*

In the former sense, a man's land, or merchandize, or money is called his property.

In the latter sense, a man has property in his opinions and the free communication of them.

He has a property of peculiar value in his religious opinions, and in the profession and practice dictated by them.

SOURCE: This essay, by James Madison, appeared in *The National Gazette*, March 29, 1792, and was reprinted in *The Writings of James Madison*, edited by Gaillard Hunt, Vol. 6, pp. 101–103.

He has property very dear to him in the safety and liberty of his person.

He has an equal property in the free use of his faculties and free choice of the objects on which to employ them.

In a word, as a man is said to have a right to his property, he may be equally said to have a property in his rights.

Where an excess of power prevails, property of no sort is duly respected. No man is safe in his opinions, his person, his faculties or his possessions.

Where there is an excess of liberty, the effect is the same, tho' from an opposite cause.

Government is instituted to protect property of every sort; as well that which lies in the various rights of individuals, as that which the term particularly expresses. This being the end of government, that alone is a *just* government, which *impartially* secures to every man, whatever is his *own*.

According to this standard of merit, the praise of affording a just security to property, should be sparingly bestowed on a government which, however scrupulously guarding the possessions of individuals, does not protect them in the enjoyment and communication of their opinions, in which they have an equal, and in the estimation of some, a more valuable property.

More sparingly should this praise be allowed to a government, where a man's religious rights are violated by penalties, or fettered by tests, or taxed by a hierarchy. Conscience is the most sacred of all property; other property depending in part on positive law, the exercise of that, being a natural and inalienable right. To guard a man's house as his castle, to pay public and enforce private debts with the most exact faith, can give no title to invade a man's conscience which is more sacred than his castle, or to withold from it that debt of protection, for which the public faith is pledged, by the very nature and original conditions of the social pact.

That is not a just government, nor is property secure under it, where the property which a man has in his personal safety and personal liberty, is violated by arbitrary seizures of one class of citizens for the service of the rest. A magistrate issuing warrants to a press gang, would be in his proper functions in Turkey or Indostan, under appellations proverbial of the most compleat despotism.

That is not a just government, nor is property secure under it, where arbitrary restrictions, exemptions, and monopolies deny to part of its citizens that free use of their faculties, and free choice of their occupations, which not only constitute their property in the general sense of the word; but are the means of acquiring property strictly so called. What must be the spirit of legislation where a manufacturer of linen cloth is forbidden to bury his own child in a linen shroud, in order to favour his neighbour who manufactures woolen cloth; where the manufacturer and wearer of woolen cloth are again forbidden the economical use of buttons of that material, in favor of the manufacturer of buttons of other materials!

A just security to property is not afforded by that government under which unequal taxes oppress one species of property and reward another species: where arbitrary taxes invade the domestic sanctuaries of the rich, and excessive taxes grind the faces of the poor; where the keenness and competitions of want are deemed an insufficient spur to labor, and taxes are again applied by an unfeeling policy, as another spur; in violation of that sacred property, which Heaven, in decreeing man to earn his bread by the sweat of his brow, kindly reserved to him, in the small repose that could be spared from the supply of his necessities.

If there be a government then which prides itself on maintaining the inviolability of property; which provides that none shall be taken *directly* even for public use without indemnification to the owner, and yet *directly* violates the property which individuals have in their opinions, their religion, their persons, and their faculties; nay more, which *indirectly* violates their property, in their actual possessions, in the labor that acquires their daily subsistence, and in the hallowed remnant of time which ought to relieve their fatigues and soothe their cares, the inference will have been anticipated, that such a government is not a pattern for the United States.

If the United States mean to obtain or deserve the full praise due to wise and just governments, they will equally respect the rights of property, and the property in rights: they will rival the government that most sacredly guards the former; and by repelling its example in violating the latter, will make themselves a pattern to that and all other governments.

Calder v. Bull

3 U.S. (3 Dall.) 385 (1798)

The Constitution prohibits any state from passing any law "impairing the Obligation of Contracts." The Constitution also prohibits states from passing ex post facto laws, which might apply to protect contracts and property rights. The issue in this case is whether the prohibition against ex post facto laws applies only to criminal statutes.

CHASE, Justice.—The decision of one question determines (in my opinion) the present dispute. I shall, therefore, state from the record no more of the case, than I think necessary for the consideration of that question only.

The legislature of Connecticut, on the 2d Thursday of May 1795, passed a resolution or law, which, for the reasons assigned, set aside a decree of the Court of Probate for Hartford, on the 21st of March 1793, which decree disapproved of the will of Normand Morrison (the grandson), made the 21st of August 1779, and refused to record the said will; and granted a new hearing by the said court of probate, with liberty of appeal therefrom, in six months. A new hearing was had, in virtue of this resolution or law, before the said court of probate, who, on the 27th of July 1795, approved the said will, and ordered it to be recorded. At August 1795, appeal was then had to the superior court at Hartford, who, at February term 1796, affirmed the decree of the court of probate. Appeal was had to the supreme court of errors of Connecticut, who, in June 1796, adjudged that there were no errors. More than eighteen months elapsed from the decree of the court of probate (on the 1st of March 1793), and thereby Caleb Bull and wife were barred of all right of appeal, by a statute of Connecticut. There was no law of that state whereby a new hearing or trial, before the said court of probate, might be obtained. Calder and wife claimed the premises in question, in right of the wife, as heiress of N. Morrison, physician; Bull and wife claimed under the will of N. Morrison, the grandson.

The counsel for the plaintiffs in error contend, that the said resolution or law of the legislature of Connecticut, granting a new hearing, in the above case, is an *ex post facto* law, prohibited by the constitution of the United States; that any law of the federal government, or of any of the state government, contrary to the constitution of the United States, is void; and that this court possesses the power to declare such law void.

It appears to me a self-evident proposition, that the several state legislatures retain all the powers of legislation, delegated to them by the state constitutions; which are not expressly taken away by the constitution of the United States. The establishing courts of justice, the appointment of judges, and the making regulations for the administration of justice within each state, according to its laws, on all subjects not intrusted to the federal government, appears to me to be the peculiar and exclusive province and duty of the state legislatures. . . .

The effect of the resolution or law of Connecticut, above stated, is to revise a decision of one of its inferior courts, called the court of probate for Hartford, and to direct a new hearing of the case by the same court of probate, that passed the decree against the will of Normand Morrison. By the existing law of Connecticut, a right to recover certain property had vested in Calder and wife (the appellants), in consequence of a decision of a court of justice, but in virtue of a subsequent resolution or law, and the new hearing thereof, and the decision in consequence, this right to recover certain property was divested, and the right to the property declared to be in Bull and wife, the appellees. The sole inquiry is, whether this resolution or law of Connecticut, having such operation, is an *ex post facto* law, within the prohibition of the federal constitution?

. . .

The constitution of the United States, article I., section 9, prohibits the legislature of the United States from passing any *ex post facto* law; and, in § 10, lays several restrictions on the authority of the legislatures of the several states; and, among them, "that no state shall pass any *ex post facto* law."

It may be remembered, that the legislatures of several of the states, to wit, Massachusetts, Pennsylvania, Delaware, Maryland, and North and South Carolina, are expressly prohibited, by their state constitutions, from passing any *ex post facto* law.

I shall endeavor to show what law is to be considered an *ex post facto* law, within the words and meaning of the prohibition in the federal constitution. The prohibition, "that no state shall pass any *ex post facto* law," necessarily requires some explanation; for, naked and without explanation, it is unintelligible, and means nothing. . . . [T]he plain and obvious meaning and intention of the prohibition is this: that the legislatures of the several states, shall not pass laws, after a fact done by a subject or citizen, which shall have relation to such fact, and shall punish him for having done it. The prohibition, considered in this light, is an additional bulwark in favor of the personal security of the subject, to protect his person from punishment by legislative acts, having a retrospective operation. I do not think it was inserted, to secure the citizen in his private rights of either property or contracts. The prohibitions not to make anything but gold and silver coin a tender in payment of debts, and not to pass any law impairing the obligation of contracts, were inserted to secure private rights; but the restriction not to pass any *ex post facto* law, was to secure the person

of the subject from injury or punishment, in consequence of such law. If the prohibition against making *ex post facto* laws was intended to secure personal rights from being affected or injured by such laws, and the prohibition is sufficiently extensive for that object, the other restraints I have enumerated, were unnecessary, and therefore, improper; for both of them are retrospective.

I will state what laws I consider *ex post facto* laws, within the words and the intent of the prohibition. 1st. Every law that makes an action done before the passing of the law, and which was innocent when done, criminal; and punishes such action. 2d. Every law that aggravates a crime, or makes it greater than it was, when committed. 3d. Every law that changes the punishment, and inflicts a greater punishment, than the law annexed to the crime, when committed. 4th. Every law that alters the legal rules of evidence, and receives less, or different testimony, than the law required at the time of the commission of the offence, in order to convict the offender. All these, and similar laws, are manifestly unjust and oppressive. In my opinion, the true distinction is between *ex post facto* laws, and retrospective laws. Every *ex post facto* law must necessarily be retrospective; but every retrospective law is not an *ex post facto* law: the former only are prohibited. Every law that takes away or impairs rights vested, agreeable to existing laws, is retrospective, and is generally unjust, and may be oppressive; and it is a good general rule, that a law should have no retrospect: but there are cases in which laws may justly, and for the benefit of the community, and also of individuals, relate to a time antecedent to their commencement; as statutes of oblivion or of pardon. They are certainly retrospective, and literally both concerning and after the facts committed. But I do not consider any law *ex post facto*, within the prohibition, that mollifies the rigor of the criminal law: but only those that create or aggravate the crime; or increase the punishment, or change the rules of evidence, for the purpose of conviction. . . .

It is not to be presumed, that the federal or state legislatures will pass laws to deprive citizens of rights vested in them by existing laws; unless for the benefit of the whole community; and on making full satisfaction. The restraint against making any *ex post facto* laws was not considered by the framers of the constitution, as extending to prohibit the depriving a citizen even of a vested right to property; or the provision "that private property should not be taken for public use, without just compensation," was unnecessary.

. . .

I am of opinion, that the decree of the supreme court of errors of Connecticut be affirmed, with costs.

PATERSON, Justice.—
. . . the words of the constitution of the United States are, "That no state shall pass any bill of attainder, *ex post facto* law, or law impairing the obligation of contracts." Article I., § 10. Where is the necessity or use of the latter words, if a law impairing the obligation of contracts, be comprehended within the terms *ex post facto* law? It is obvious, from the specification of contracts in the last member of the clause, that the framers of the constitution did not understand or use the words in the sense contended for on the part of the plaintiffs in error. They understood and used the words in their known and appropriate significacation, as referring to crimes, pains and penalties, and no further. The arrangement of the distinct members of this section, necessarily points to this meaning.

. . .

IREDELL, Justice.—Though I concur in the general result of the opinions which have been delivered, I cannot entirely adopt the reasons that are assigned upon the occasion.

. . . it has been the policy of all the American states, which have, individually, framed their state constitutions, since the revolution, and of the people of the United States, when they framed the federal constitution, to define with precision the objects of the legislative power, and to restrain its exercise within marked and settled boundaries. If any act of congress, or of the legislature of a state, violates those constitutional provisions, it is unquestionably void; though, I admit, that as the authority to declare it void is of a delicate and awful nature, the court will never resort to that authority, but in a clear and urgent case. If, on the other hand, the legislature of the Union, or the legislature of any member of the Union, shall pass a law, within the general scope of their constitutional power, the court cannot pronounce it to be void, merely because it is, in their judgment, contrary to the principles of natural justice. The ideas of natural justice are regulated by no fixed standard: the ablest and the purest men have differed upon the subject; and all that the court could properly say, in such an event, would be, that the legislature (possessed of an equal right of opinion) had passed an act which, in the opinion of the judges, was inconsistent with the abstract principles of natural justice. . . .

CUSHING, Justice.—The case appears to me to be clear of all difficulty, taken either way. If the act is a judicial act, it is not touched by the federal constitution: and if it is a legislative act, it is maintained and justified by the ancient and uniform practice of the state of Connecticut.

Judgment affirmed.

Dartmouth College v. Woodward

17 U.S. (4 Wheat.) 517 (1819)

Dartmouth College functioned as a private school, funded entirely by private donations, until New Hampshire passed legislation in 1816 to increase the number of trustees at the college and thereby transfer control to appointees of the governor. The constitutional question was whether the Contract Clause prohibited the state from impairing the contract of a "private eleemosynary institution."

February 2d, 1819. The opinion of the court was delivered by MARSHALL, Ch. J.—This is an action of trover, brought by the Trustees of Dartmouth College against William H. Woodward, in the state court of New Hampshire, for the book of records, corporate seal, and other corporate property, to which the plaintiffs allege themselves to be entitled. A special verdict, after setting out the rights of the parties, finds for the defendant, if certain acts of the legislature of New Hampshire, passed on the 27th of June, and on the 18th of December 1816, be valid, and binding on the trustees, without their assent, and not repugnant to the constitution of the United States; otherwise, it finds for the plaintiffs. The superior court of judicature of New Hampshire rendered a judgment upon this verdict for the defendant, which judgment has been brought before this court by writ of error. The single question now to be considered is, do the acts to which the verdict refers violate the constitution of the United States?

This court can be insensible neither to the magnitude nor delicacy of this question. The validity of a legislative act is to be examined; and the opinion of the highest law tribunal of a state is to be revised—an opinion which carries with it intrinsic evidence of the diligence, of the ability, and the integrity, with which it was formed. On more than one occasion, this court has expressed the cautious circumspection with which it approaches the consideration of such questions; and has declared, that in no doubtful case, would it pronounce a legislative act to be contrary to the constitution. But the American people have said, in the constitution of the United States, that "no state shall pass any bill of attainder, *ex post facto* law, or law impairing the obligation of contracts." In the same instrument, they have also said, "that the judicial power shall extend to all cases in law and equity arising under the constitution." On the judges of this court, then, is imposed the high and solemn duty of protecting, from even legislative violation, those contracts which the constitution of our country has placed beyond legislative control; and, however irksome the task may be, this is a duty from which we dare not shrink.

The title of the plaintiffs originates in a charter dated the 13th day of December, in the year 1769, incorporating twelve persons therein mentioned, by the name of "The Trustees of Dartmouth College," granting to them and their successors the usual corporate privileges and powers, and authorizing the trustees, who are to govern the college, to fill up all vacancies which may be created in their own body.

The defendant claims under three acts of the legislature of New Hampshire, the most material of which was passed on the 27th of June 1816, and is entitled, "an act to amend the charter, and enlarge and improve the corporation of Dartmouth College." Among other alterations in the charter, this act increases the number of trustees to twenty-one, gives the appointment of the additional members to the executive of the state, and creates a board of overseers, with power to inspect and control the most important acts of the trustees. This board consists of twenty-five persons. The president of the senate, the speaker of the house of representatives, of New Hampshire, and the governor and lieutenant-governor of Vermont, for the time being, are to be members *ex officio*. The board is to be completed by the governor and council of New Hampshire, who are also empowered to fill all vacancies which may occur. The acts of the 18th and 26th of December are supplemental to that of the 27th of June, and are principally intended to carry that act into effect. The majority of the trustees of the college have refused to accept this amended charter, and have brought this suit for the corporate property, which is in possession of a person holding by virtue of the acts which have been stated.

It can require no argument to prove, that the circumstances of this case constitute a contract. An application is made to the crown for a charter to incorporate a religious and literary institution. In the application, it is stated, that large contributions have been made for the object, which will be conferred on the corporation, as soon as it shall be created. The charter is granted, and on its faith the property is conveyed. Surely, in this transaction every ingredient of a complete and legitimate contract is to be found. The points for consideration are, 1. Is this contract protected by the constitution of the United States? 2. Is it impaired by the acts under which the defendant holds?

1. On the first point, it has been argued, that the word "contract," in its broadest sense, would

comprehend the political relations between the government and its citizens, would extend to offices held within a state, for state purposes, and to many of those laws concerning civil institutions, which must change with circumstances, and be modified by ordinary legislation; which deeply concern the public, and which, to preserve good government, the public judgment must control. That even marriage is a contract, and its obligations are affected by the laws respecting divorces. That the clause in the constitution, if construed in its greatest latitude, would prohibit these laws. Taken in its broad, unlimited sense, the clause would be an unprofitable and vexatious interference with the internal concerns of a state, would unnecessarily and unwisely embarrass its legislation, and render immutable those civil institutions, which are established for purposes of internal government, and which, to subserve those purposes, ought to vary with varying circumstances. That as the framers of the constitution could never have intended to insert in that instrument, a provision so unnecessary, so mischievous, and so repugnant to its general spirit, the term "contract" must be understood in a more limited sense. That it must be understood as intended to guard against a power, of at least doubtful utility, the abuse of which had been extensively felt; and to restrain the legislature in future from violating the right to property. That, anterior to the formation of the constitution, a course of legislation had prevailed in many, if not in all, of the states, which weakened the confidence of man in man, and embarrassed all transactions between individuals, by dispensing with a faithful performance of engagements. To correct this mischief, by restraining the power which produced it, the state legislatures were forbidden "to pass any law impairing the obligation of contracts," that is, of contracts respecting property, under which some individual could claim a right to something beneficial to himself; and that, since the clause in the constitution must in construction receive some limitation, it may be confined, and ought to be confined, to cases of this description; to cases within the mischief it was intended to remedy.

. . . If the act of incorporation be a grant of political power, if it create a civil institution, to be employed in the administration of the government, or if the funds of the college be public property, or if the state of New Hampshire, as a government, be alone interested in its transactions, the subject is one in which the legislature of the state may act according to its own judgment, unrestrained by any limitation of its power imposed by the constitution of the United States.

But if this be a private eleemosynary institution, endowed with a capacity to take property, for objects unconnected with government, whose funds are bestowed by individuals, on the faith of the charter; if the donors have stipulated for the future disposition and management of those funds, in the manner prescribed by themselves; there may be more difficulty in the case. . . .

[After determining that the funds of Dartmouth College consisted entirely of private donations, Chief Justice Marshall raises broader issues.]

. . . Are the trustees and professors public officers, invested with any portion of political power, partaking in any degree in the administration of civil government, and performing duties which flow from the sovereign authority? That education is an object of national concern, and a proper subject of legislation, all admit. That there may be an institution, founded by government, and placed entirely under its immediate control, the officers of which would be public officers, amenable exclusively to government, none will deny. But is Dartmouth College such an institution? Is education altogether in the hands of government? Does every teacher of youth become a public officer, and do donations for the purpose of education necessarily become public property, so far that the will of the legislature, not the will of the donor, becomes the law of the donation? These questions are of serious moment to society, and deserve to be well considered.

. . .

From this review of the charter, it appears, that Dartmouth College is an eleemosynary institution, incorporated for the purpose of perpetuating the application of the bounty of the donors, to the specified objects of that bounty; that its trustees or governors were originally named by the founder, and invested with the power of perpetuating themselves; that they are not public officers, nor is it a civil institution, participating in the administration of government; but a charity school, or a seminary of education, incorporated for the preservation of its property, and the perpetual application of that property to the objects of its creation.

. . .

The opinion of the court, after mature deliberation, is, that this is a contract, the obligation of which cannot be impaired, without violating the constitution of the United States. This opinion appears to us to be equally supported by reason, and by the former decisions of this court.

2. We next proceed to the inquiry, whether its obligation has been impaired by those acts of the legislature of New Hampshire, to which the special verdict refers?

From the review of this charter, which has been taken, it appears that the whole power of governing the college, of appointing and removing tutors, of fixing their salaries, of directing the course of study to be pursued by the students, and of filling up vacancies created in their own body, was vested in the trustees. On the part of the crown, it was expressly stipulated, that this corporation, thus constituted, should continue for ever; and that the number of trustees should for ever consist of twelve, and no more. By this contract, the crown was bound, and could have made no violent alteration in its essential terms, without impairing its obligation.

By the revolution, the duties, as well as the powers, of government devolved on the people of New Hampshire. It is admitted, that among the latter was comprehended the transcendent power of parliament, as well as that of the executive department. It is too clear, to require the support of argument, that all contracts and rights respecting property, remained unchanged by the revolution. The obligations, then, which were created by the charter to Dartmouth College, were the same in the new, that they had been in the old government. The power of the government was also the same. A repeal of this charter, at any time prior to the adoption of the present constitution of the United States, would have been an extraordinary and unprecedented act of power, but one which could have been contested only by the restrictions upon the legislature, to be found in the constitution of the state. But the constitution of the United States has imposed this additional limitation, that the legislature of a state shall pass no act "impairing the obligation of contracts."

It has been already stated, that the act "to amend the charter, and enlarge and improve the corporation of Dartmouth College," increases the number of trustees to twenty-one, gives the appointment of the additional members to the executive of the state, and creates a board of overseers, to consist of twenty-five persons, of whom twenty-one are also appointed by the executive of New Hampshire, who have power to inspect and control the most important acts of the trustees.

. . .

It results from this opinion, that the acts of the legislature of New Hampshire, which are stated in the special verdict found in this cause, are repugnant to the constitution of the United States; and that the judgment on this special verdict ought to have been for the plaintiffs. The judgment of the state court must, therefore, be reversed.

WASHINGTON, Justice.—*[concurred.]*

JOHNSON, Justice, concurred, for the reasons stated by the Chief Justice.

LIVINGSTON, Justice, concurred, for the reasons stated by the Chief Justice, and Justices WASHINGTON and STORY.

Story, Justice.—*[concurred.]*

DUVALL, Justice, dissented.

Charles River Bridge v. Warren Bridge

36 U.S. (11 Pet.) 419 (1837)

In 1785, the legislature of Massachusetts incorporated a company ("The Proprietors of the Charles River Bridge") to build a bridge and accept tolls. Decades later it established "The Proprietors of the Warren Bridge" to build a bridge nearby; over the course of time this bridge became free to travelers. The first bridge filed a lawsuit, claiming that the legislature had impaired the obligation of a contract. This significant decision by Chief Justice Taney balances the rights of private property against the public's need for economic development.

TANEY, Ch. J., delivered the opinion of the court.—The questions involved in this case are of the gravest character, and the court have given to them the most anxious and deliberate consideration. The value of the right claimed by the plaintiffs is large in amount; and many persons may, no doubt, be seriously affected in their pecuniary interests, by any decision which the court may pronounce; and the questions which have been raised as to the power of the several states, in relation to the corporations they have chartered, are pregnant with important consequences; not only to the individuals who are concerned in the corporate franchises, but to the communities in which they exist. The court are fully sensible, that it is their duty, in exercising the high powers conferred on them by the constitution of the United States, to deal with these great and extensive interests, with the utmost caution; guarding, so far as they have the power to do so, the rights of property, and at the same time, carefully abstaining from any encroachment on the rights reserved to the states.

. . .

The plaintiffs in error insist, mainly, upon two grounds: 1st. That by virtue of the grant of 1650, Harvard College was entitled, in perpetuity, to the right of keeping a ferry between Charlestown and Boston; that this right was exclusive; and that the legislature had not the power to establish another ferry on the same line of travel, because it would infringe the rights of the college; and that these rights, upon the erection of the bridge in the place

of the ferry, under the charter of 1785, were transferred to, and became vested in "The Proprietors of the Charles River Bridge;" and that under, and by virtue of this transfer of the ferry-right, the rights of the bridge company were as exclusive in that line of travel, as the rights of the ferry. 2d. That independently of the ferry-right, the acts of the legislature of Massachusetts, of 1785 and 1792, by their true construction, necessarily implied, that the legislature would not authorize another bridge, and especially, a free one, by the side of this, and placed in the same line of travel, whereby the franchise granted to the "Proprietors of the Charles River Bridge" should be rendered of no value; and the plaintiffs in error contend, that the grant of the ferry to the college, and of the charter to the proprietors of the bridge, are both contracts on the part of the state; and that the law authorizing the erection of the Warren bridge in 1828, impairs the obligation of one or both of these contracts.

. . . it is apparent, that the plaintiffs in error cannot sustain themselves here, either upon the ferry-right, or the charter to the bridge; upon the ground, that vested rights of property have been divested by the legislature. And whether they claim under the ferry-right, or the charter to the bridge, they must show that the title which they claim, was acquired by contract, and that the terms of that contract have been violated by the charter to the Warren bridge. In other words, they must show, that the state had entered into a contract with them, or those under whom they claim, not to establish a free bridge at the place where the Warren bridge is erected. Such, and such only, are the principles upon which the plaintiffs in error can claim relief in this case.

. . .

But upon what ground can the plaintiffs in error contend, that the ferry-rights of the college have been transferred to the proprietors of the bridge? If they have been thus transferred, it must be by some mode of transfer known to the law; and the evidence relied on to prove it, can be pointed out in the record. How was it transferred? It is not suggested, that there ever was, in point of fact, a deed of conveyance executed by the college to the bridge company. Is there any evidence in the record, from which such a conveyance may, upon legal principle, be presumed? The testimony before the court, so far from laying the foundation for such a presumption, repels it, in the most positive terms. . . .

. . .

This brings us to the act of the legislature of Massachusetts, of 1785, by which the plaintiffs were incorporated by the name of "The Proprietors of the Charles River Bridge;" and it is here, and in the law of 1792, prolonging their charter, that we must look for the extent and nature of the franchise conferred upon the plaintiffs. Much has been said in the argument of the principles of construction by which this law is to be expounded, and what undertakings, on the part of the state, may be implied. The court think there can be no serious difficulty on that head. It is the grant of certain franchises, by the public, to a private corporation, and in a matter where the public interest is concerned. . . .

. . . the object and end of all government is to promote the happiness and prosperity of the community by which it is established; and it can never be assumed, that the government intended to diminish its power of accomplishing the end for which it was created. And in a country like ours, free, active and enterprising, continually advancing in numbers and wealth, new channels of communication are daily found necessary, both for travel and trade, and are essential to the comfort, convenience and prosperity of the peo-

ple. A state ought never to be presumed to surrender this power, because, like the taxing power, the whole community have an interest in preserving it undiminished. And when a corporation alleges, that a state has surrendered, for seventy years, its power of improvement and public accommodation, in a great and important line of travel, along which a vast number of its citizens must daily pass, the community have a right to insist, in the language of this court, above quoted, "that its abandonment ought not to be presumed, in a case, in which the deliberate purpose of the state to abandon it does not appear." The continued existence of a government would be of no great value, if, by implications and presumptions, it was disarmed of the powers necessary to accomplish the ends of its creation, and the functions it was designed to perform, transferred to the hands of privileged corporations. . . . While the rights of private property are sacredly guarded, we must not forget, that the community also have rights, and that the happiness and well-being of every citizen depends on their faithful preservation.

Adopting the rule of construction above stated as the settled one, we proceed to apply it to the charter of 1785, to the proprietors of the Charles River bridge. This act of incorporation is in the usual form, and the privileges such as are commonly given to corporations of that kind. It confers on them the ordinary faculties of a corporation, for the purpose of building the bridge; and establishes certain rates of toll, which the company are authorized to take: this is the whole grant. There is no exclusive privilege given to them over the waters of Charles river, above or below their bridge; no right to erect another bridge themselves, nor to prevent other persons from erecting one; no engagement from the state, that another shall not be erected; and no undertaking not to sanction competition, nor to make improvements that may diminish the amount of its income. Upon all these subjects, the charter is silent; and nothing is said in it about a line of travel, so much insisted on in the argument, in which they are to have exclusive privileges. No words are used, from which an intention to grant any of these rights can be inferred; if the plaintiff is entitled to them, it must be implied, simply, from the nature of the grant; and cannot be inferred, from the words by which the grant is made.

The relative position of the Warren bridge has already been described. It does not interrupt the passage over the Charles River bridge, nor make the way to it, or from it, less convenient. None of the faculties or franchises granted to that corporation, have been revoked by the legislature; and its right to take the tolls granted by the charter remains unaltered. In short, all the franchises and rights of property, enumerated in the charter, and there mentioned to have been granted to it, remain unimpaired. But its income is destroyed by the Warren bridge; which, being free, draws off the passengers and property which would have gone over it, and renders their franchise of no value. This is the gist of the complainant; for it is not pretended, that the erection of the Warren bridge would have done them any injury, or in any degree affected their right of property, if it had not diminished the amount of their tolls. In order, then, to entitle themselves to relief, it is necessary to show, that the legislature contracted not to do the act of which they complain; and that they impaired, or in other words, violated, that contract, by the erection of the Warren bridge.

The inquiry, then, is, does the charter contain such a contract on the part of the state? Is there any such stipulation to be found in that instrument? It must be admitted on all hands, that there is none; no words that even relate to another bridge, or to the diminution of their tolls, or to the line of travel. . . .

Indeed, the practice and usage of almost every state in the Union, old enough to have commenced the work of internal improvement, is opposed to the doctrine contended for on the part of the plaintiffs in error. Turnpike roads have been made in succession, on the same line of travel; the later ones interfering materially with the profits of the first. These corporations have, in some instances, been utterly ruined by the introduction of newer and better modes of transportation and traveling. In some cases, railroads have rendered the turnpike roads on the same line of travel so entirely useless, that the franchise of the turnpike corporation is not worth preserving. Yet in none of these cases have the corporation supposed that their

privileges were invaded, or any contract violated on the part of the state. . . .

The judgment of the supreme judicial court of the commonwealth of Massachusetts, dismissing the plaintiffs' bill, must, therefore, be affirmed, with costs.

McLEAN, Justice. *[Favored dismissing the case for lack of jurisdiction.]*

BALDWIN, Justice.— *[Concurred.]*

STORY, Justice. *(Dissenting.)*

. . .

But it has been argued, and the argument has been pressed in every form which ingenuity could suggest, that if grants of this nature are to be construed liberally, as conferring any exclusive rights on the grantees, it will interpose an effectual barrier against all general improvements of the country. For myself, I profess not to feel the cogency of this argument, either in its general application to the grant of franchises, or in its special application to the present grant. This is a subject upon which different minds may well arrive at different conclusions, both as to policy and principle. Men may, and will, complexionally differ upon topics of this sort, according to their natural and acquired habits of speculation and opinion. For my own part, I can conceive of no surer plan to arrest all public improvements, founded on private capital and enterprise, than to make the outlay of that capital uncertain and questionable, both as to security and as to productiveness. No man will hazard his capital in any enterprise, in which, if there be a loss, it must be borne exclusively by himself; and if there be success, he has not the slightest security of enjoying the rewards of that success, for a single moment. If the government means to invite its citizens to enlarge the public comforts and conveniences, to establish bridges, or turnpikes, or canals, or railroads, there must be some pledge, that the property will be safe; that the enjoyment will be co-extensive with the grant; and that success will not be the signal of a general combination to overthrow its rights and to take away its profits. The very agitation of a question of this sort is sufficient to alarm every stockholder in every public enterprise of this sort, throughout the whole country. Already, in my native state, the legislature has found it necessary expressly to concede the exclusive privilege here contended against; in order to insure the accomplishment of a railroad for the benefit of the public. And yet, we are told, that all such exclusive grants are to the detriment of the public.

. . .

Upon the whole, my judgment is, that the act of the legislature of Massachusetts granting the charter of Warren Bridge, is an act impairing the obligation of the prior contract and grant to the proprietors of Charles River bridge; and, by the constitution of the United States, it is, therefore, utterly void. I am for reversing the decree to the state court (dismissing the bill); and for remanding the cause to the state court for further proceedings, as to law and justice shall appertain.

THOMPSON, Justice.—The opinion delivered by my brother, Mr. Justice STORY, I have read over and deliberately considered. On this full consideration, I concur entirely in all the principles and reasonings contained in it; and I am of opinion, the decree of the supreme judicial court of Massachusetts should be reversed.

Home Bldg. & Loan Assn. v. Blaisdell

290 U.S. 398 (1934)

A Minnesota statute, enacted in 1933, declared that the Great Depression created an emergency demanding an exercise of the police power to protect the public and promote the general welfare. It temporarily extended the time allowed by existing law for redeeming real property from foreclosure and sale under existing mortgages. It became known as the Minnesota Mortgage Moratorium Law. At issue was Article I, § 10, of the U.S. Constitution, which provides that no state shall pass any law "impairing the Obligation of Contracts." Could this constitutional prohibition be waived during time of emergency?

MR. CHIEF JUSTICE HUGHES delivered the opinion of the Court.

Appellant contests the validity of Chapter 339 of the Laws of Minnesota of 1933, p. 514, approved April 18, 1933, called the Minnesota Mortgage Moratorium Law, as being repugnant to the contract clause (Art. I, § 10) and the due process and equal protection clauses of the Fourteenth Amendment, of the Federal Constitution. The statute was sustained by the Supreme Court of Minnesota, 189 Minn. 422, 448; 249 N.W. 334, 893, and the case comes here on appeal.

[The Act provided for judicial relief with respect to foreclosures of mortgages and execution sales of real estate. Sales could be postponed and redemption periods extended. The Act remained in effect "only during the continuance of the emergency and in no event beyond May 1, 1935." The Court was concerned with the provisions authorizing the district court of the county to extend the period of redemption from foreclosure sales.]

Invoking the relevant provision of the statute, appellees applied to the District Court of Hennepin County for an order extending the period of redemption from a foreclosure sale. Their petition stated that they owned a lot in Minneapolis which they had mortgaged to appellant; that the mortgage contained a valid power of sale by advertisement and that by reason of their default the mortgage had been foreclosed and sold to appellant on May 2, 1932, for $3700.98; that appellant was the holder of the sheriff's certificate of sale; that because of the economic depression appellees had been unable to obtain a new loan or to redeem, and that unless the period of redemption were extended the property would be irretrievably lost; and that the reasonable value of the property greatly exceeded the amount due on the mortgage including all liens, costs and expenses.

On the hearing, appellant objected to the introduction of evidence upon the ground that the statute was invalid under the federal and state constitutions, and moved that the petition be dismissed. The motion was granted and a motion for a new trial was denied. On appeal, the Supreme Court of the State reversed the decision of the District Court. 189 Minn. 422; 249 N.W. 334. Evidence was then taken in the trial court and appellant renewed its constitutional objections without avail. . . .

[The trial court extended the period of redemption to May 1, 1935, and ordered Blaisdell to pay the loan association a certain amount each month over that period.]

The state court upheld the statute as an emergency measure. Although conceding that the obligations of the mortgage contract were impaired, the court decided that what it thus described as an impairment was, notwithstanding the contract clause of the Federal Constitution, within the police power of the State as that power was called into exercise by the public economic emergency which the legislature had found to exist. . . .

. . .

In determining whether the provision for this temporary and conditional relief exceeds the power of the State by reason of the clause in the Federal Constitution prohibiting impairment of the obligations of contracts, we must consider the relation of emergency to constitutional power, the historical setting of the contract clause, the development of the jurisprudence of this Court in the construction of that clause, and the principles of construction which we may consider to be established.

Emergency does not create power. Emergency does not increase granted power or remove or diminish the restrictions imposed upon power granted or reserved. The Constitution was adopted in a period of grave emergency. Its grants of power to the Federal Government and its limitations of the power of the States were determined in the light of emergency and they are not altered by emergency. What power was thus granted and what limitations were thus imposed are questions which have always been, and always will be, the subject of close examination under our constitutional system.

While emergency does not create power, emergency may furnish the occasion for the exercise of power. "Although an emergency may not call into life a power which has never lived, nevertheless emergency may afford a reason for the exertion of a living power already enjoyed." *Wilson* v. *New,* 243 U.S. 332, 348. . . . emergency would not permit a State to have more than two Senators in the Congress, or permit the election of President by a general popular vote without regard to the number of electors to which the States are respectively entitled, or permit the States to "coin money" or to "make anything but gold and silver coin a tender in payment of debts." But where constitutional grants and limitations of power are set forth in general clauses, which afford a broad outline, the process of construction is essential to fill in the details. That is true of the contract clause. . . .

In the construction of the contract clause, the debates in the Constitutional Convention are of little aid. But the reasons which led to the adoption of that clause, and of the other prohibitions of Section 10 of Article I, are not left in doubt and have frequently been described with eloquent emphasis. The widespread distress following the revolutionary period, and the plight of debtors, had called forth in the States an ignoble array of legislative schemes for the defeat of creditors and the invasion of contractual obligations. Legislative interferences had been so numerous and extreme that the confidence essential to prosperous trade had been undermined and the utter destruction of credit was threatened. "The sober people of America" were convinced that some "thorough reform" was needed which would "inspire a general prudence and industry, and give a regular course to the business of society." *The Federalist,* No. 44. It was necessary to interpose the restraining power of a central authority in order to secure the foundations even of "private faith." . . .

But full recognition of the occasion and general purpose of the clause does not suffice to fix its precise scope. Nor does an examination of the details of prior legislation in the States yield criteria which can be considered controlling. To ascertain the scope of the constitutional prohibition we examine the course of judicial decisions in its application. These put it beyond question that the prohibition is not an absolute one and is not to be read with literal exactness like a mathematical formula. Justice Johnson, in *Ogden* v. *Saunders, supra*, p. 286, adverted to such a misdirected effort in these words:. . . "[T]o assign to contracts, universally, a literal purport, and to exact for them a rigid literal fulfillment, could not have been the intent of the constitution. It is repelled by a hundred examples. Societies exercise a positive control as well over the inception, construction and fulfillment of contracts, as over the form and measure of the remedy to enforce them."

. . .

Not only is the constitutional provision qualified by the measure of control which the State retains over remedial processes, but the State also continues to possess authority to safeguard the vital interests of its people. It does not matter that legislation appropriate to that end "has the result of modifying or abrogating contracts already in effect." *Stephenson* v. *Binford*, 287 U.S. 251, 276. Not only are existing laws read into contracts in order to fix obligations as between the parties, but the reservation of essential attributes of sovereign power is also read into contracts as a postulate of the legal order. The policy of protecting contracts against impairment presupposes the maintenance of a government by virtue of which contractual relations are worth while,—a government which retains adequate authority to secure the peace and good order of society. This principle of harmonizing the constitutional prohibition with the necessary residuum of state power has had progressive recognition in the decisions of this Court.

While the charters of private corporations constitute contracts, a grant of exclusive privilege is not to be implied as against the State. *Charles River Bridge* v. *Warren Bridge*, 11 Pet. 420. And all contracts are subject to the right of eminent domain. *West River Bridge* v. *Dix*, 6 How. 507. The reservation of this necessary authority of the State is deemed to be a part of the contract. . . .

It is no answer to say that this public need was not apprehended a century ago, or to insist that what the provision of the Constitution meant to the vision of that day it must mean to the vision of our time. If by the statement that what the Constitution meant at the time of its adoption it means to-day, it is intended to say that the great clauses of the Constitution must be confined to the interpretation which the framers, with the conditions and outlook of their time, would have placed upon them, the statement carries its own refutation. It was to guard against such a narrow conception that Chief Justice Marshall uttered the memorable warning—"We must never forget that it is a *constitution* we are expounding" (*McCulloch* v. *Maryland*, 4 Wheat. 316, 407)—"a constitution intended to endure for ages to come, and consequently, to be adapted to the various *crises* of human affairs." *Id.*, p. 415. When we are dealing with the words of the Constitution, said this Court in *Missouri* v. *Holland*, 252 U.S. 416, 433, "we must realize that they have called into life a being the development of which could not have been foreseen completely by the most gifted of its begetters. . . . The case before us must be considered in the light of our whole experience and not merely in that of what was said a hundred years ago."

. . .

We are of the opinion that the Minnesota statute as here applied does not violate the contract clause of the Federal Constitution. Whether the legislation is wise or unwise as a matter of policy is a question with which we are not concerned.

What has been said on that point is also applicable to the contention presented under the due process clause. *Block* v. *Hirsh, supra*.

Nor do we think that the statute denies to the appellant the equal protection of the laws. The classification which the statute makes cannot be said to be an arbitrary one. *Magoun* v. *Illinois Trust & Savings Bank*, 170 U.S. 283; *Clark* v. *Titusville*, 184 U.S. 329; *Quong Wing* v. *Kirkendall*, 223 U.S. 59; *Ohio Oil Co.* v. *Conway*, 281 U.S. 146; *Sproles* v. *Binford*, 286 U.S. 374.

The judgment of the Supreme Court of Minnesota is affirmed.

Judgment affirmed.

MR. JUSTICE SUTHERLAND, dissenting.

Few questions of greater moment than that just decided have been submitted for judicial inquiry during this generation. He simply closes his eyes to the necessary implications of the decision who fails to see in it the potentiality of future gradual but ever-advancing encroachments upon the sanctity of private and public contracts. The effect of the Minnesota legislation, though serious enough in itself, is of trivial significance compared with the far more serious and dangerous inroads upon the limitations of the Constitution which are almost certain to ensue as a consequence naturally following any step beyond the boundaries fixed by that instrument. And those of us who are thus apprehensive of the effect of this decision would, in a matter so important, be neglectful of our duty should we fail to spread upon the permanent records of the court the reasons which move us to the opposite view.

A provision of the Constitution, it is hardly necessary to say, does not admit of two distinctly opposite interpretations. It does not mean one thing at one time and an entirely different thing at another time. If the contract impairment clause, when framed and adopted, meant that the terms of a contract for the payment of money could not be altered *in invitum* by a state statute enacted for the relief of hardly pressed debtors to the end and with the effect of postponing payment or enforcement during and because of an economic or financial emergency, it is but to state the obvious to say that it means the same now. . . . The true rule was forcefully declared in *Ex parte Milligan*, 4 Wall. 2, 120–121, in the face of circumstances of national peril and public unrest and disturbance far greater than any that exist today. . . . [I]n words the power and truth of which have become increasingly evident with the lapse of time, there was laid down the rule without which the Constitution would cease to be the "supreme law of the land," binding equally upon governments and governed at all times and under all circumstances, and become a mere collection of political maxims

to be adhered to or disregarded according to the prevailing sentiment or the legislative and judicial opinion in respect of the supposed necessities of the hour:

"The Constitution of the United States is a law for rulers and people, equally in war and in peace, and covers with the shield of its protection all classes of men, at all times, and under all circumstances. No doctrine, involving more pernicious consequences, was ever invented by the wit of man than that any of its provisions can be suspended during any of the great exigencies of government. Such a doctrine leads directly to anarchy or despotism, . . ."

Chief Justice Taney, in *Dred Scott* v. *Sandford*, 19 How. 393, 426, said that while the Constitution remains unaltered it must be construed now as it was understood at the time of its adoption; that it is not only the same in words but the same in meaning, "and as long as it continues to exist in its present form, it speaks not only in the same words, but with the same meaning and intent with which it spoke when it came from the hands of its framers, and was voted on and adopted by the people of the United States. Any other rule of construction would abrogate the judicial character of this court, and make it the mere reflex of the popular opinion or passion of the day." . . .

The provisions of the Federal Constitution, undoubtedly, are pliable in the sense that in appropriate cases they have the capacity of bringing within their grasp every new condition which falls within their meaning. But, their *meaning* is changeless; it is only their *application* which is extensible. . . .

. . .

The present exigency is nothing new. From the beginning of our existence as a nation, periods of depression, of industrial failure, of financial distress, of unpaid and unpayable indebtedness, have alternated with years of plenty. The vital lesson that expenditure beyond income begets poverty, that public or private extravagance, financed by promises to pay, either must end in complete or partial repudiation or the promises be fulfilled by self-denial and painful effort, though constantly taught by bitter experience, seems never to be learned; and the attempt by legislative devices to shift the misfortune of the debtor to the shoulders of the creditor without coming into conflict with the contract impairment clause has been persistent and oft-repeated.

The defense of the Minnesota law is made upon grounds which were discountenanced by the makers of the Constitution and have many times been rejected by this court. That defense should not now succeed, because it constitutes an effort to overthrow the constitutional provision by an appeal to facts and circumstances identical with those which brought it into existence. With due regard for the processes of logical thinking, it legitimately cannot be urged that conditions which produced the rule may now be invoked to destroy it.

The lower court, and counsel for the appellees in their argument here, frankly admitted that the statute does constitute a material impairment of the contract, but contended that such legislation is brought within the state power by the present emergency. If I understand the opinion just delivered, this court is not wholly in accord with that view. The opinion concedes that emergency does not create power, or increase granted power, or remove or diminish restrictions upon power granted or reserved. It then proceeds to say, however, that while emergency does not create power, it may furnish the occasion for the exercise of power. I can only interpret what is said on that subject as meaning that while an emergency does not diminish a restriction upon power it furnishes an occasion for diminishing it; and this, as it seems to me, is merely to say the same thing by the use of another set of words, with the effect of affirming that which has just been denied.

. . .

I quite agree with the opinion of the court that whether the legislation under review is wise or unwise is a matter with which we have nothing to do. Whether it is likely to work well or work ill presents a question entirely irrelevant to the issue. The only legitimate inquiry we can make is whether it is constitutional. If it is not, its virtues, if it have any, cannot save it; if it is, its faults cannot be invoked to accomplish its destruction. If the provisions of the Constitution be not upheld when they pinch as well as when they comfort, they may as well be abandoned. Being unable to reach any other conclusion than that the Minnesota statute infringes the constitutional restriction under review, I have no choice but to say so.

I am authorized to say that MR. JUSTICE VAN DEVANTER, MR. JUSTICE MCREYNOLDS and MR. JUSTICE BUTLER concur in this opinion.

Penn Central Transp. Co. v. New York City

438 U.S. 104 (1978)

New York City passed legislation to protect historic landmarks and neighborhoods from quick decisions that might destroy or fundamentally alter their character. The law authorized a commission to designate a building to be a "landmark" on a particular "landmark site." It could also designate an area to be a "historic district." The designation could be modified or disapproved by the City's Board of Estimate, with the final designation decision subject to judicial review. Owners of a designated landmark were required to keep the building's exterior "in good repair" and secure commission approval before making exterior alterations. The Grand Central Terminal, owned by the Penn Central Transportation Co., was designated a landmark and the block it occupies as a "landmark site." Penn Central opposed the designation but did not seek judicial review. When the commission rejected Penn Central's plans to construct a multistory office building over the terminal, Penn Central brought suit in state court claiming that the application of the landmarks law had "taken" its property without just compensation

in violation of the Fifth and Fourteenth Amendments and arbitrarily deprived it of its property without due process of law in violation of the Fourteenth Amendment. The trial court granted relief but was reversed by the New York Court of Appeals. In this decision the Court attempts to identify the principles that establish when regulatory burdens imposed by the state become a "taking."

MR. JUSTICE BRENNAN delivered the opinion of the Court.

The question presented is whether a city may, as part of a comprehensive program to preserve historic landmarks and historic districts, place restrictions on the development of individual historic landmarks—in addition to those imposed by applicable zoning ordinances—without effecting a "taking" requiring the payment of "just compensation." Specifically, we must decide whether the application of New York City's Landmarks Preservation Law to the parcel of land occupied by Grand Central Terminal has "taken" its owners' property in violation of the Fifth and Fourteenth Amendments.

I

A

Over the past 50 years, all 50 States and over 500 municipalities have enacted laws to encourage or require the preservation of buildings and areas with historic or aesthetic importance. These nationwide legislative efforts have been precipitated by two concerns. The first is recognition that, in recent years, large numbers of historic structures, landmarks, and areas have been destroyed without adequate consideration of either the values represented therein or the possibility of preserving the destroyed properties for use in economically productive ways. The second is a widely shared belief that structures with special historic, cultural, or architectural significance enhance the quality of life for all.

. . .

[The New York City Landmarks Preservation Law of 1965 established an eleven-member Landmarks Preservation Commission, empowered to conduct a hearing for interested parties and then designate a building to be a "landmark" that is situated on a "landmark site" or designate an area as a "historic district."]

B

This case involves the application of New York City's Landmarks Preservation Law to Grand Central Terminal (Terminal). The Terminal, which is owned by the Penn Central Transportation Co. and its affiliates (Penn Central), is one of New York City's most famous buildings. Opened in 1913, it is regarded not only as providing an ingenious engineering solution to the problems presented by urban railroad stations, but also as a magnificent example of the French beaux-arts style.

The Terminal is located in midtown Manhattan. Its south facade faces 42d Street and that street's intersection with Park Avenue. At street level, the Terminal is bounded on the west by Vanderbilt Avenue, on the east by the Commodore Hotel, and on the north by the Pan-American Building. Although a 20-story office tower, to have been located above the Terminal, was part of the original design, the planned tower was never constructed. The Terminal itself is an eight-story structure which Penn Central uses as a railroad station and in which it rents space not needed for railroad purposes to a variety of commercial interests. . . .

On August 2, 1967, following a public hearing, the Commission designated the Terminal a "landmark" and designated the "city tax block" it occupies a "landmark site." The Board of Estimate confirmed this action on September 21, 1967. Although appellant Penn Central had opposed the designation before the Commission, it did not seek judicial review of the final designation decision.

On January 22, 1968, appellant Penn Central, to increase its income, entered into a renewable 50-year lease and sublease agreement with appellant UGP Properties, Inc. (UGP), a wholly owned subsidiary of Union General Properties, Ltd., a United Kingdom corporation. Under the terms of the agreement, UGP was to construct a multistory office building above the Terminal. UGP promised to pay Penn Central $1 million annually during construction and at least $3 million annually thereafter. The rentals would be offset in part by a loss of some $700,000 to $1 million in net rentals presently received from concessionaires displaced by the new building.

Appellants UGP and Penn Central then applied to the Commission for permission to construct an office building atop the Terminal. Two separate plans, both designed by architect Marcel Breuer and both apparently satisfying the terms of the applicable zoning ordinance, were submitted to the Commission for approval. The first, Breuer I, provided for the construction of a 55-story office building, to be cantilevered above the existing facade and to rest on the roof of the Terminal. The second, Breuer II Revised, called for tearing down a portion of the Terminal that included the 42d Street facade, stripping off some of the remaining features of the Terminal's facade, and constructing a 53-story office building. The Commission denied a certificate of no exterior effect on September 20, 1968. Appellants then applied for a certificate of "appropriateness" as to both proposals. After four days of hearings at which over 80 witnesses testified, the Commission denied this application as to both proposals.

. . . appellants filed suit in New York Supreme Court, Trial Term, claiming, *inter alia*, that the application of the Landmarks Preservation Law had "taken" their property without just compensation in violation of the Fifth and Fourteenth Amendments and arbitrarily deprived them of their property without due process of law in violation of the Fourteenth Amendment. Appellants sought a declaratory judgment, injunctive relief barring the city from using the Landmarks Law to impede the construction of any structure that might otherwise lawfully be constructed on the Terminal site, and damages for the "temporary taking" that occurred between August 2, 1967, the designation date, and the date when the restrictions arising from the Landmarks Law would be lifted. The trial court granted the injunctive and declaratory relief, but severed the question of damages for a "temporary taking."

[New York City appealed and the New York Supreme Court, Appellate Division, reversed. The New York Court of Appeals affirmed, rejecting the "taking" argument.]

. . .

II

The issues presented by appellants are (1) whether the restrictions imposed by New York City's law upon appellants' exploitation of the Terminal site effect a "taking" of appellants' property for a public use within the meaning of the Fifth Amendment, which of course is made applicable to the States through the Fourteenth Amendment, see *Chicago, B. & Q. R. Co.* v. *Chicago*, 166 U.S. 226, 239 (1897), and, (2), if so, whether the transferable development rights afforded appellants constitute "just compensation" within the meaning of the Fifth Amendment. We need only address the question whether a "taking" has occurred.

A

Before considering appellants' specific contentions, it will be useful to review the factors that have shaped the jurisprudence of the Fifth Amendment injunction "nor shall private property be taken for public use, without just compensation." The question of what constitutes a "taking" for purposes of the Fifth Amendment has proved to be a problem of considerable difficulty. While this Court has recognized that the "Fifth Amendment's guarantee . . . [is] designed to bar Government from forcing some people alone to bear public burdens which, in all fairness and justice, should be borne by the public as a whole," *Armstrong* v. *United States*, 364 U.S. 40, 49 (1960), this Court, quite simply, has been unable to develop any "set formula" for determining when "justice and fairness" require that economic injuries caused by public action be compensated by the government, rather than remain disproportionately concentrated on a few persons. . . .

In engaging in these essentially ad hoc, factual inquiries, the Court's decisions have identified several factors that have particular significance.

The economic impact of the regulation on the claimant and, particularly, the extent to which the regulation has interfered with distinct investment-backed expectations are, of course, relevant considerations. See *Goldblatt* v. *Hempstead, supra,* at 594. So, too, is the character of the governmental action. A "taking" may more readily be found when the interference with property can be characterized as a physical invasion by government, see, *e. g., United States* v. *Causby,* 328 U.S. 256 (1946), than when interference arises from some public program adjusting the benefits and burdens of economic life to promote the common good.

"Government hardly could go on if to some extent values incident to property could not be diminished without paying for every such change in the general law," *Pennsylvania Coal Co.* v. *Mahon,* 260 U.S. 393, 413 (1922), and this Court has accordingly recognized, in a wide variety of contexts, that government may execute laws or programs that adversely affect recognized economic values. Exercises of the taxing power are one obvious example. A second are the decisions in which this Court has dismissed "taking" challenges on the ground that, while the challenged government action caused economic harm, it did not interfere with interests that were sufficiently bound up with the reasonable expectations of the claimant to constitute "property" for Fifth Amendment purposes. . . .

More importantly for the present case, in instances in which a state tribunal reasonably concluded that "the health, safety, morals, or general welfare" would be promoted by prohibiting particular contemplated uses of land, this Court has upheld land-use regulations that destroyed or adversely affected recognized real property interests. See *Nectow* v. *Cambridge,* 277 U.S. 183, 188 (1928). Zoning laws are, of course, the classic example, see *Euclid* v. *Ambler Realty Co.,* 272 U.S. 365 (1926) (prohibition of industrial use); *Gorieb* v. *Fox,* 274 U.S. 603, 608 (1927) (requirement that portions of parcels be left unbuilt); *Welch* v. *Swasey,* 214 U.S. 91 (1909) (height restriction), which have been viewed as permissible governmental action even when prohibiting the most beneficial use of the property. See *Goldblatt* v. *Hempstead, supra,* at 592–593, and cases cited; see

also *Eastlake* v. *Forest City Enterprises, Inc.,* 426 U.S. 668, 674 n. 8 (1976).

Zoning laws generally do not affect existing uses of real property, but "taking" challenges have also been held to be without merit in a wide variety of situations when the challenged governmental actions prohibited a beneficial use to which individual parcels had previously been devoted and thus caused substantial individualized harm. *Miller* v. *Schoene,* 276 U.S. 272 (1928), is illustrative. In that case, a state entomologist, acting pursuant to a state statute, ordered the claimants to cut down a large number of ornamental red cedar trees because they produced cedar rust fatal to apple trees cultivated nearby. Although the statute provided for recovery of any expense incurred in removing the cedars, and permitted claimants to use the felled trees, it did not provide compensation for the value of the standing trees or for the resulting decrease in market value of the properties as a whole. A unanimous Court held that this latter omission did not render the statute invalid. The Court held that the State might properly make "a choice between the preservation of one class of property and that of the other" and since the apple industry was important in the State involved, concluded that the State had not exceeded "its constitutional powers by deciding upon the destruction of one class of property [without compensation] in order to save another which, in the judgment of the legislature, is of greater value to the public." *Id.,* at 279.

. . .

B

In contending that the New York City law has "taken" their property in violation of the Fifth and Fourteenth Amendments, appellants make a series of arguments, which, while tailored to the facts of this case, essentially urge that any substantial restriction imposed pursuant to a landmark law must be accompanied by just compensation if it is to be constitutional. . . .

. . . Appellants . . . do not dispute that a showing of diminution in property value would not establish a "taking" if the restriction had been imposed as a result of historic-district legislation, see generally *Maher* v. *New Orleans*, 516 F. 2d 1051 (CA5 1975), but appellants argue that New York City's regulation of individual landmarks is fundamentally different from zoning or from historic-district legislation because the controls imposed by New York City's law apply only to individuals who own selected properties.

Stated baldly, appellants' position appears to be that the only means of ensuring that selected owners are not singled out to endure financial hardship for no reason is to hold that any restriction imposed on individual landmarks pursuant to the New York City scheme is a "taking" requiring the payment of "just compensation." Agreement with this argument would, of course, invalidate not just New York City's law, but all comparable landmark legislation in the Nation. We find no merit in it.

. . . It is, of course, true that the Landmarks Law has a more severe impact on some landowners than on others, but that in itself does not mean that the law effects a "taking." Legislation designed to promote the general welfare commonly burdens some more than others. The owners of the brickyard in *Hadacheck*, of the cedar trees in *Miller* v. *Schoene*, and of the gravel and sand mine in *Goldblatt* v. *Hempstead*, were uniquely burdened by the legislation sustained in those cases. Similarly, zoning laws often affect some property owners more severely than others but have not been held to be invalid on that account.

. . .

C

Rejection of appellants' broad arguments is not, however, the end of our inquiry, for all we thus far have established is that the New York City law is not rendered invalid by its failure to provide "just compensation" whenever a landmark owner is restricted in the exploitation of property interests, such as air rights, to a greater extent than provided for under applicable zoning laws. We now must consider whether the interference with appellants' property is of such a magnitude that "there must be an exercise of eminent domain and compensation to sustain [it]." *Pennsylvania Coal Co.* v. *Mahon*, 260 U.S., at 413. . . .

. . . the New York City law does not interfere in any way with the present uses of the Terminal. Its designation as a landmark not only permits but contemplates that appellants may continue to use the property precisely as it has been used for the past 65 years: as a railroad terminal containing office space and concessions. . . .

. . . While the Commission's actions in denying applications to construct an office building in excess of 50 stories above the Terminal may indicate that it will refuse to issue a certificate of appropriateness for any comparably sized structure, nothing the Commission has said or done suggests an intention to prohibit *any* construction above the Terminal. . . .

On this record, we conclude that the application of New York City's Landmarks Law has not effected a "taking" of appellants' property. The restrictions imposed are substantially related to the promotion of the general welfare and not only permit reasonable beneficial use of the landmark site but also afford appellants opportunities further to enhance not only the Terminal site proper but also other properties.

Affirmed.

MR. JUSTICE REHNQUIST, with whom THE CHIEF JUSTICE and MR. JUSTICE STEVENS join, dissenting.

Of the over one million buildings and structures in the city of New York, appellees have singled out 400 for designation as official landmarks. The owner of a building might initially be pleased that his property has been chosen by a distinguished committee of architects, historians, and city planners for such a singular distinction. But he may well discover, as appellant Penn Central Transportation Co. did here, that the landmark designation imposes upon him a substantial cost, with little or no offsetting benefit except for the honor of the designation. The question in this case is whether the cost associated with the city of New York's desire to preserve a limited number of "landmarks" within its borders must be borne by all of its taxpayers or whether it can instead be imposed entirely on the owners of the individual properties.

Only in the most superficial sense of the word can this case be said to involve "zoning." Typical zoning restrictions may, it is true, so limit the prospective uses of a piece of property as to diminish the value of that property in the abstract because it may not be used for the forbidden purposes. But any such abstract decrease in value will more than likely be at least partially offset by an increase in value which flows from similar restrictions as to use on neighboring properties. All property owners in a designated area are placed under the same restrictions, not only for the benefit of the municipality as a whole but also for the common benefit of one another. . . .

I

The Fifth Amendment provides in part: "nor shall private property be taken for public use, without just compensation." In a very literal sense, the actions of appellees violated this constitutional prohibition. Before the city of New York declared Grand Central Terminal to be a landmark, Penn Central could have used its "air rights" over the Terminal to build a multistory office building, at an apparent value of several million dollars per year. Today, the Terminal cannot be modified in *any* form, including the erection of additional stories, without the permission of the Landmark Preservation Commission, a permission which appellants, despite good-faith attempts, have so far been unable to obtain. Because the Taking Clause of the Fifth Amendment has not always been read literally, however, the constitutionality of appellees' actions requires a closer scrutiny of this Court's interpretation of the three key words in the Taking Clause—"property," "taken," and "just compensation."

A

Appellees do not dispute that valuable property rights have been destroyed. And the Court has frequently emphasized that the term "property" as used in the Taking Clause includes the entire "group of rights inhering in the citizen's [ownership]." *United States* v. *General Motors Corp.*, 323 U.S. 373 (1945). . . .

B

Appellees have thus destroyed—in a literal sense, "taken"—substantial property rights of Penn Central. While the term "taken" might have been narrowly interpreted to include only physical seizures of property rights, "the construction of the phrase has not been so narrow. The courts have held that the deprivation of the former owner rather than the accretion of a right or interest to the sovereign constitutes the taking." *Id.*, at 378. . . .

C

Appellees, apparently recognizing that the constraints imposed on a landmark site constitute a taking for Fifth Amendment purposes, do not leave the property owner empty-handed. As the Court notes, *ante*, at 113–114, the property owner may theoretically "transfer" his previous right to develop the landmark property to adjacent properties if they are under his control. Appellees have coined this system "Transfer Development Rights," or TDR's.

Of all the terms used in the Taking Clause, "just compensation" has the strictest meaning. The Fifth Amendment does not allow simply an approximate compensation but requires "a full and perfect equivalent for the property taken." *Monongahela Navigation Co.* v. *United States*, 148 U.S., at 326.

. . .

II

Over 50 years ago, Mr. Justice Holmes, speaking for the Court, warned that the courts were "in danger of forgetting that a strong public desire to improve the public condition is not enough to warrant achieving the desire by a shorter cut than the constitutional way of paying for the change." *Pennsylvania Coal Co.* v. *Mahon*, 260 U.S., at 416. The Court's opinion in this case demonstrates that the danger thus foreseen has not abated. The city of New York is in a precarious financial state, and some may believe that the costs of landmark preservation will be more easily borne by corporations such as Penn Central than the overburdened individual taxpayers of New York. But these concerns do not allow us to ignore past precedents construing the Eminent Domain Clause to the end that the desire to improve the public condition is, indeed, achieved by a shorter cut than the constitutional way of paying for the change.

Hawaii Housing Authority v. Midkiff

467 U.S. 229 (1984)

How much may legislatures exercise their police powers without effecting a "taking" of property in violation of the Fifth and Fourteenth Amendments? Such questions necessarily involve a sharing of judgments and jurisdiction by legislatures and courts. In this case, the Hawaii Legislature enacted a land reform act in 1967 in an effort to reduce the social and economic evils of a land oligopoly that could be traced back to the early high chiefs of the Hawaiian Islands. The statute created a land condemnation scheme and provoked a suit that claimed a violation of constitutional rights.

JUSTICE O'CONNOR delivered the opinion of the Court.

The Fifth Amendment of the United States Constitution provides, in pertinent part, that "private property [shall not] be taken for public use, without just compensation." These cases present the question whether the Public Use Clause of that Amendment, made applicable to the States through the Fourteenth Amendment, prohibits the State of Hawaii from taking, with just compensation, title in real property from lessors and transferring it to lessees in order to reduce the concentration of ownership of fees simple in the State. We conclude that it does not.

I

A

The Hawaiian Islands were originally settled by Polynesian immigrants from the western Pacific. These settlers developed an economy around a feudal land tenure system in which one island high chief, the ali'i nui, controlled the land and assigned it for development to certain subchiefs. The subchiefs would then reassign the land to other lower ranking chiefs, who would administer the land and govern the farmers and other tenants working it. All land was held at the will of the ali'i nui and eventually had to be returned to his trust. There was no private ownership of land. See generally Brief for Office of Hawaiian Affairs as *Amicus Curiae* 3–5.

Beginning in the early 1800's, Hawaiian leaders and American settlers repeatedly attempted to divide the lands of the kingdom among the crown, the chiefs, and the common people. These efforts proved largely unsuccessful, however, and the land remained in the hands of a few. In the mid-1960's, after extensive hearings, the Hawaii Legislature discovered that, while the State and Federal Governments owned almost 49% of the State's land, another 47% was in the hands of only 72 private landowners. See Brief for the Hou Hawaiians and Maui Loa, Chief of the Hou Hawaiians, as *Amici Curiae* 32. The legislature further found that 18 landholders, with tracts of 21,000 acres or more, owned more than 40% of this land and that on Oahu, the most urbanized of the islands, 22 landowners owned 72.5% of the fee simple titles. *Id.*, at 32–33. The legislature concluded that concentrated land ownership was responsible for skewing the State's residential fee simple market, inflating land prices, and injuring the public tranquility and welfare.

To redress these problems, the legislature decided to compel the large landowners to break up their estates. The legislature considered requiring large landowners to sell lands which they were leasing to homeowners. However, the landowners strongly resisted this scheme, pointing out the significant federal tax liabilities they would incur. Indeed, the landowners claimed that the federal tax laws were the primary reason they previously had chosen to lease, and not sell, their lands. Therefore, to accommodate the needs of both lessors and lessees, the Hawaii Legislature enacted the Land Reform Act of 1967 (Act), Haw. Rev. Stat., ch. 516, which created a mechanism for condemning residential tracts and for transferring ownership of the condemned fees simple to existing lessees. By condemning the land in question, the Hawaii Legislature intended to make the land sales involuntary, thereby making the federal tax consequences less severe while still facilitating the redistribution of fees simple. See Brief for Appellants in Nos. 83–141 and 83–283, pp. 3–4, and nn. 6–8.

Under the Act's condemnation scheme, tenants living on single-family residential lots within developmental tracts at least five acres in size are entitled to ask the Hawaii Housing Authority (HHA) to condemn the property on which they live. Haw. Rev. Stat. §§ 516–1(2), (11), 516–22 (1977). When 25 eligible tenants, or tenants on half the lots in the tract, whichever is less, file appropriate applications, the Act authorizes HHA to hold a public hearing to determine whether acquisition by the State of all or part of the tract will "effectuate the public purposes" of the Act. § 516–22. If HHA finds that these public purposes will be served, it is authorized to designate some or all of the lots in the tract for acquisition. It then acquires, at prices set either by condemnation trial or by negotiation between lessors and lessees, the former fee owners' full "right, title, and interest" in the land. § 516–25.

After compensation has been set, HHA may sell the land titles to tenants who have applied for fee simple ownership. HHA is authorized to lend these tenants up to 90% of the purchase price, and it may condition final transfer on a right of first refusal for the first 10 years following sale. §§ 516–30, 516–34, 516–35. If HHA does not sell the lot to the tenant residing there, it may lease the lot or sell it to someone else, provided that public notice has been given. § 516–28. However, HHA may not sell to any one purchaser, or lease to any one tenant, more than one lot, and it may not operate for profit. §§ 516–28, 516–32. In practice, funds to satisfy the condemnation awards have been supplied entirely by lessees. See App. 164. While the Act authorizes HHA to issue bonds and appropriate funds for acquisition, no bonds have issued and HHA has not supplied any funds for condemned lots. See *ibid.*

B

In April 1977, HHA held a public hearing concerning the proposed acquisition of some of appellees' lands. HHA made the statutorily required finding that acquisition of appellees' lands would effectuate the public purposes of the Act. Then, in October 1978, it directed appellees to negotiate with certain lessees concerning the sale of the designated properties. Those negotiations failed, and HHA subsequently ordered appellees to submit to compulsory arbitration.

Rather than comply with the compulsory arbitration order, appellees filed suit, in February 1979, in United States District Court, asking that the Act be declared unconstitutional and that its enforcement be enjoined. The District Court temporarily restrained the State from proceeding against appellees' estates. Three months later, while declaring the compulsory arbitration and compensation formulae provisions of the Act unconstitutional, the District Court refused preliminarily to enjoin appellants from conducting the statutory designation and condemnation proceedings. Finally, in December 1979, it granted partial summary judgment to appellants, holding the remaining portion of the Act constitutional under the Public Use Clause. See 483 F. Supp. 62 (Haw. 1979). The District Court found that the Act's goals were within the bounds of the State's police powers and that the means the legislature had chosen to serve those goals were not arbitrary, capricious, or selected in bad faith.

The Court of Appeals for the Ninth Circuit reversed. 702 F. 2d 788 (1983). First, the Court of Appeals decided that the District Court had permissibly chosen not to abstain from the exercise of its jurisdiction. Then, the Court of Appeals determined that the Act could not pass the requisite judicial scrutiny of the Public Use Clause. It found that the transfers contemplated by the Act were unlike those of takings previously held to constitute "public uses" by this Court. The court further determined that the public purposes offered by the Hawaii Legislature were not deserving of judicial deference. The court concluded that the Act was simply "a naked attempt on the part of the state of Hawaii to take the private property of A and transfer it to B solely for B's private use and benefit." *Id.*, at 798. One judge dissented.

On applications of HHA and certain private appellants who had intervened below, this Court noted probable jurisdiction. 464 U.S. 932 (1983). We now reverse.

II

We begin with the question whether the District Court abused its discretion in not abstaining from the exercise of its jurisdiction. The appellants have suggested as one alternative that perhaps abstention was required under the standards announced in *Railroad Comm'n* v. *Pullman Co.*, 312 U.S. 496 (1941), and *Younger* v. *Harris*, 401 U.S. 37 (1971). We do not believe that abstention was required.

. . .

III

The majority of the Court of Appeals next determined that the Act violates the "public use" requirement of the Fifth and Fourteenth Amendments. On this argument, however, we find ourselves in agreement with the dissenting judge in the Court of Appeals.

A

The starting point for our analysis of the Act's constitutionality is the Court's decision in *Berman* v. *Parker*, 348 U.S. 26 (1954). In *Berman*, the Court held constitutional the District of Columbia Redevelopment Act of 1945. That Act provided both for the comprehensive use of the eminent domain power to redevelop slum areas and for the possible sale or lease of the condemned lands to private

interests. In discussing whether the takings authorized by that Act were for a "public use," *id.*, at 31, the Court stated:

"We deal, in other words, with what traditionally has been known as the police power. An attempt to define its reach or trace its outer limits is fruitless, for each case must turn on its own facts. The definition is essentially the product of legislative determinations addressed to the purposes of government, purposes neither abstractly nor historically capable of complete definition. Subject to specific constitutional limitations, when the legislature has spoken, the public interest has been declared in terms well-nigh conclusive. In such cases the legislature, not the judiciary, is the main guardian of the public needs to be served by social legislation, whether it be Congress legislating concerning the District of Columbia . . . or the States legislating concerning local affairs. . . . This principle admits of no exception merely because the power of eminent domain is involved. . . ." *Id.*, at 32 (citations omitted).

The Court explicitly recognized the breadth of the principle it was announcing, noting:

"Once the object is within the authority of Congress, the right to realize it through the exercise of eminent domain is clear. For the power of eminent domain is merely the means to the end. . . . Once the object is within the authority of Congress, the means by which it will be attained is also for Congress to determine. Here one of the means chosen is the use of private enterprise for redevelopment of the area. Appellants argue that this makes the project a taking from one businessman for the benefit of another businessman. But the means of executing the project are for Congress and Congress alone to determine, once the public purpose has been established." *Id.*, at 33.

The "public use" requirement is thus coterminous with the scope of a sovereign's police powers.

There is, of course, a role for courts to play in reviewing a legislature's judgment of what constitutes a public use, even when the eminent domain power is equated with the police power. But the Court in *Berman* made clear that it is "an extremely narrow" one. *Id.*, at 32. The Court in *Berman* cited with approval the Court's decision in *Old*

Dominion Co. v. *United States,* 269 U.S. 55, 66 (1925), which held that deference to the legislature's "public use" determination is required "until it is shown to involve an impossibility." The *Berman* Court also cited to *United States ex rel. TVA* v. *Welch,* 327 U.S. 546, 552 (1946), which emphasized that "[a]ny departure from this judicial restraint would result in courts deciding on what is and is not a governmental function and in their invalidating legislation on the basis of their view on that question at the moment of decision, a practice which has proved impracticable in other fields." In short, the Court has made clear that it will not substitute its judgment for a legislature's judgment as to what constitutes a public use "unless the use be palpably without reasonable foundation." *United States* v. *Gettysburg Electric R. Co.,* 160 U.S. 668, 680 (1896).

To be sure, the Court's cases have repeatedly stated that "one person's property may not be taken for the benefit of another private person without a justifying public purpose, even though compensation be paid." *Thompson* v. *Consolidated Gas Corp.,* 300 U.S. 55, 80 (1937). . . . Where the exercise of the eminent domain power is rationally related to a conceivable public purpose, the Court has never held a compensated taking to be proscribed by the Public Use Clause. . . .

On this basis, we have no trouble concluding that the Hawaii Act is constitutional. The people of Hawaii have attempted, much as the settlers of the original 13 Colonies did, to reduce the perceived social and economic evils of a land oligopoly traceable to their monarchs. The land oligopoly has, according to the Hawaii Legislature, created artificial deterrents to the normal functioning of the State's residential land market and forced thousands of individual homeowners to lease, rather than buy, the land underneath their homes. Regulating oligopoly and the evils associated with it is a classic exercise of a State's police powers. See *Exxon Corp.* v. *Governor of Maryland,* 437 U.S. 117 (1978); *Block* v. *Hirsh, supra;* see also *People of Puerto Rico* v. *Eastern Sugar Associates,* 156 F. 2d 316 (CA1), cert. denied, 329 U.S. 772 (1946). We cannot disapprove of Hawaii's exercise of this power.

Nor can we condemn as irrational the Act's approach to correcting the land oligopoly prob-

lem. The Act presumes that when a sufficiently large number of persons declare that they are willing but unable to buy lots at fair prices the land market is malfunctioning. When such a malfunction is signalled, the Act authorizes HHA to condemn lots in the relevant tract. The Act limits the number of lots any one tenant can purchase and authorizes HHA to use public funds to ensure that the market dilution goals will be achieved. This is a comprehensive and rational approach to identifying and correcting market failure.

. . .

B

. . . the fact that a state legislature, and not the Congress, made the public use determination does not mean that judicial deference is less appropriate. Judicial deference is required because, in our system of government, legislatures are better able to assess what public purposes should be advanced by an exercise of the taking power. State legislatures are as capable as Congress of making such determinations within their respective spheres of authority. See *Berman* v. *Parker,* 348 U.S., at 32. Thus, if a legislature, state or federal, determines there are substantial reasons for an exercise of the taking power, courts must defer to its determination that the taking will serve a public use.

IV

The State of Hawaii has never denied that the Constitution forbids even a compensated taking of property when executed for no reason other than to confer a private benefit on a particular private party. A purely private taking could not withstand the scrutiny of the public use requirement; it would serve no legitimate purpose of government and would thus be void. But no purely private taking is involved in these cases. The Hawaii Legislature enacted its Land Reform Act not to benefit a particular class of identifiable individuals but to attack certain perceived evils of concentrated property ownership in Hawaii—a legitimate public purpose. Use of the condemnation power to achieve this purpose is not irrational. Since we assume   for   purposes   of   these   appeals that the weighty demand of just compensation has been met, the requirements of the Fifth and Fourteenth Amendments have been satisfied. Accordingly, we reverse the judgment of the Court of Appeals, and remand these cases for further proceedings in conformity with this opinion.

It is so ordered.

JUSTICE MARSHALL took no part in the consideration or decision of these cases.

Slaughter-House Cases

16 Wall. 36 (1873)

The legislature of Louisiana passed an act granting to a corporation, which it created, the exclusive right for twenty-five years to operate slaughterhouses, landings for cattle, and yards for enclosing cattle intended for sale or slaughter. The corporation operated within three parishes, including the city of New Orleans, and prohibited other persons from competing with the corporation. The constitutional issue was whether this exclusive grant of monopoly privilege was a police regulation for the health and comfort of the people or whether it violated the constitutional rights of other citizens to exercise their trade and occupation. The Supreme Court's decision is significant because it is the first interpretation of the Civil War Amendments, especially the reach and purpose of the Fourteenth Amendment and the power of the federal government to direct state activities.

Mr. Justice MILLER, now, April 14th, 1873, delivered the opinion of the court.

These cases are brought here by writs of error to the Supreme Court of the State of Louisiana. They arise out of the efforts of the butchers of New Orleans to resist the Crescent City Live-Stock Landing and Slaughter-House Company in the exercise of certain powers conferred by the charter which created it, and which was granted by the legislature of that State.

The cases . . . have been brought here and dismissed by agreement, were all decided by the Supreme Court of Louisiana in favor of the Slaughter-House Company, as we shall hereafter call it for the sake of brevity, and these writs are brought to reverse those decisions.

. . .

The records show that the plaintiffs in error relied upon, and asserted throughout the entire course of the litigation in the State courts, that the grant of privileges in the charter of defendant,

which they were contesting, was a violation of the most important provisions of the thirteenth and fourteenth articles of amendment of the Constitution of the United States. The jurisdiction and the duty of this court to review the judgment of the State court on those questions is clear and is imperative.

. . .

This statute is denounced not only as creating a monopoly and conferring odious and exclusive privileges upon a small number of persons at the expense of the great body of the community of New Orleans, but it is asserted that it deprives a large and meritorious class of citizens—the whole of the butchers of the city—of the right to exercise their trade, the business to which they have been trained and on which they depend for the support of themselves and their families; and that the unrestricted exercise of the business of butchering is necessary to the daily subsistence of the population of the city.

But a critical examination of the act hardly justifies these assertions.

It is true that it grants, for a period of twenty-five years, exclusive privileges. And whether those privileges are at the expense of the community in the sense of a curtailment of any of their fundamental rights, or even in the sense of doing them an injury, is a question open to considerations to be hereafter stated. But it is not true that it deprives the butchers of the right to exercise their trade, or imposes upon them any restriction incompatible with its successful pursuit, or furnishing the people of the city with the necessary daily supply of animal food.

The act divides itself into two main grants of privilege,—the one in reference to stock-landings and stock-yards, and the other to slaughter-houses. That the landing of livestock in large droves, from steamboats on the bank of the river, and from railroad trains, should, for the safety and comfort of the people and the care of the animals, be limited to proper places, and those not numerous, it needs no argument to prove. Nor can it be injurious to the general community that while the duty of making ample preparation for this is imposed upon a few men, or a corporation, they should, to enable them to do it successfully, have the exclusive right of providing such landing-places, and receiving a fair compensation for the service.

It is, however, the slaughter-house privilege, which is mainly relied on to justify the charges of gross injustice to the public, and invasion of private right.

It is not, and cannot be successfully controverted, that it is both the right and the duty of the legislative body—the supreme power of the State or municipality—to prescribe and determine the localities where the business of slaughtering for a great city may be conducted. To do this effectively it is indispensable that all persons who slaughter animals for food shall do it in those places *and nowhere else.*

The statute under consideration defines these localities and forbids slaughtering in any other. It does not, as has been asserted, prevent the butcher from doing his own slaughtering. On the contrary, the Slaughter-House Company is required, under a heavy penalty, to permit any person who wishes to do so, to slaughter in their houses; and they are bound to make ample provision for the convenience of all the slaughtering for the entire city. The butcher then is still permitted to slaughter, to prepare, and to sell his own meats; but he is required to slaughter at a specified place and to pay a reasonable compensation for the use of the accommodations furnished him at that place.

The wisdom of the monopoly granted by the legislature may be open to question, but it is difficult to see a justification for the assertion that the butchers are deprived of the right to labor in their occupation, or the people of their daily service in preparing food, or how this statute, with the duties and guards imposed upon the company, can be said to destroy the business of the butcher, or seriously interfere with its pursuit.

. . .

It cannot be denied that the statute under consideration is aptly framed to remove from the more densely populated part of the city, the noxious slaughter-houses, and large and offensive collections of animals necessarily incident to the slaughtering business of a large city, and to locate them where the convenience, health, and comfort of the people require they shall be located. And it must be conceded that the means adopted by the act for this purpose are appropriate, are stringent, and effectual. . . .

. . .

The plaintiffs in error accepting this issue, allege that the statute is a violation of the Constitution of the United States in these several particulars:

That it creates an involuntary servitude forbidden by the thirteenth article of amendment;

That it abridges the privileges and immunities of citizens of the United States;

That it denies to the plaintiffs the equal protection of the laws; and,

That it deprives them of their property without due process of law; contrary to the provisions of the first section of the fourteenth article of amendment.

This court is thus called upon for the first time to give construction to these articles.

. . .

The most cursory glance at these articles *[the Thirteenth, Fourteenth, and Fifteenth Amendments]* discloses a unity of purpose, when taken in connection with the history of the times, which cannot fail to have an important bearing on any question of doubt concerning their true meaning. Nor can such doubts, when any reasonably exist, be safely and rationally solved without a reference to that history; for in it is found the occasion and the necessity for recurring again to the great source of power in this country, the people of the States, for additional guarantees of human rights; additional powers to the Federal government; additional restraints upon those of the States. Fortunately that history is fresh within the memory of us all, and its leading features, as they bear upon the matter before us, free from doubt.

The institution of African slavery, as it existed in about half the States of the Union, and the contests pervading the public mind for many years, between those who desired its curtailment and ultimate extinction and those who desired additional safeguards for its security and perpetuation, culminated in the effort, on the part of most of the States in which slavery existed, to separate from the Federal government, and to resist its authority. This constituted the war of the rebellion, and whatever auxiliary causes may have contributed to bring about this war, undoubtedly the overshadowing and efficient cause was African slavery.

. . . the war being over, those who had succeeded in re-establishing the authority of the Federal government were . . . determined to place this main and most valuable result *[emancipation]* in the Constitution of the restored Union as one of its fundamental articles. Hence the thirteenth article of amendment of that instrument. Its two short sections seem hardly to admit of construction, so vigorous is their expression and so appropriate to the purpose we have indicated.

"1. Neither slavery nor involuntary servitude, except as a punishment for crime, whereof the party shall have been duly convicted, shall exist within the United States or any place subject to their jurisdiction.

"2. Congress shall have power to enforce this article by appropriate legislation."

. . .

[The Court summarizes the adoption of the Fourteenth Amendment, as a response to the "black codes" used by southern states to suppress blacks, and the Fifteenth Amendment.]

We repeat, then, in the light of this recapitulation of events, almost too recent to be called history, but which are familiar to us all; and on the most casual examination of the language of these amendments, no one can fail to be impressed with the one pervading purpose found in them all, lying at the foundation of each, and without which none of them would have been even suggested; we mean the freedom of the slave race, the security and firm establishment of that freedom, and the protection of the newly-made freeman and citizen from the oppressions of those who had formerly exercised unlimited dominion over him. It is true that only the fifteenth amendment, in terms, mentions the negro by speaking of his color and his slavery. But it is just as true that each of the other articles was addressed to the grievances of that race, and designed to remedy them as the fifteenth.

We do not say that no one else but the negro can share in this protection. Both the language and spirit of these articles are to have their fair and just weight in any question of construction. Undoubtedly while negro slavery alone was in the mind of the Congress which proposed the thirteenth article, it forbids any other kind of slavery, now or hereafter. If Mexican peonage or the Chinese coolie labor system shall develop slavery of the Mexican or Chinese race within our territory, this amendment may safely be trusted to make it void. And so if other rights are assailed by the States which properly and necessarily fall within the protection of these articles, that protection will apply, though the party interested may not be of African descent. But what we do say, and what we wish to be understood is, that in any fair and just construction of any section or phrase of these amendments, it is necessary to look to the purpose which we have said was the pervading spirit of them all, the evil which they were designed to remedy, and the process of continued addition to the Constitution, until that purpose was supposed to be accomplished, as far as constitutional law can accomplish it.

The first section of the fourteenth article, to which our attention is more specially invited, opens with a definition of citizenship. . . .

"All persons born or naturalized in the United States, and subject to the jurisdiction thereof, are citizens of the United States and of the State wherein they reside."

. . .

It is quite clear, then, that there is a citizenship of the United States, and a citizenship of a State, which are distinct from each other, and which depend upon different characteristics or circumstances in the individual.

We think this distinction and its explicit recognition in this amendment of great weight in this argument, because the next paragraph of this same section, which is the one mainly relied on by the plaintiffs in error, speaks only of privileges and immunities of citizens of the United States, and does not speak of those of citizens of the several States. The argument, however, in favor of the plaintiffs rests wholly on the assumption that the citizenship is the same, and the privileges and immunities guaranteed by the clause are the same.

The language is, "No State shall make or enforce any law which shall abridge the privileges or immunities of citizens of *the United States.*" It is a little remarkable, if this clause was intended as a protection to the citizen of a State against the legislative power of his own State, that the word citizen of the State should be left out when it is so carefully used, and used in contradistinction to citizens of the United States, in the very sentence which precedes it. It is too clear for argument that the change in phraseology was adopted understandingly and with a purpose.

Of the privileges and immunities of the citizen of the United States, and of the privileges and immunities of the citizen of the State, and what they respectively are we will presently consider; but we wish to state here that it is only the former which are placed by this clause under the protection of the Federal Constitution, and that the latter, whatever they may be, are not intended to have any additional protection by this paragraph of the amendment.

. . .

Having shown that the privileges and immunities relied on in the argument are those which belong to citizens of the States as such, and that they are left to the State governments for security and protection, and not by this article placed under the special care of the Federal government, we may hold ourselves excused from defining the privileges and immunities of citizens of the United States which no State can abridge, until some case involving those privileges may make it necessary to do so.

. . .

"All persons born or naturalized in the United States, and subject to the jurisdiction thereof, are citizens of the United States and of the State wherein they reside. No State shall make or enforce any law which shall abridge the privileges or immunities of citizens of the United States; nor shall any State deprive any person of life, liberty, or property without due process of law, nor deny to any person within its jurisdiction the equal protection of its laws."

The argument has not been much pressed in these cases that the defendant's charter deprives the plaintiffs of their property without due process of law, or that it denies to them the equal protection of the law. The first of these paragraphs has been in the Constitution since the adoption of the fifth amendment, as a restraint upon the Federal power. It is also to be found in some form of expression in the constitutions of nearly all the States, as a restraint upon the power of the States. This law, then, has practically been the same as it now is during the existence of the government, except so far as the present amendment may place the restraining power over the States in this matter in the hands of the Federal government.

We are not without judicial interpretation, therefore, both State and National, of the meaning of this clause. And it is sufficient to say that under no construction of that provision that we have ever seen, or any that we deem admissible, can the restraint imposed by the State of Louisiana upon the exercise of their trade by the butchers of New Orleans be held to be a deprivation of property within the meaning of that provision.

"Nor shall any State deny to any person within its jurisdiction the equal protection of the laws."

In the light of the history of these amendments, and the pervading purpose of them, which we have already discussed, it is not difficult to give a meaning to this clause. The existence of laws in the States where the newly emancipated negroes resided, which discriminated with gross injustice and hardship against them as a class, was the evil to be remedied by this clause, and by it such laws are forbidden.

If, however, the States did not conform their laws to its requirements, then by the fifth section of the article of amendment Congress was authorized to enforce it by suitable legislation. We doubt very much whether any action of a State not directed by way of discrimination against the negroes as a class, or on account of their race, will ever be held to come within the purview of this provision. It is so clearly a provision for that race and that emergency, that a strong case would be necessary for its application to any other. . . .

. . . we do not see in *[the Civil War]* amendments any purpose to destroy the main features of the general *[federal]* system. Under the pressure of all the excited feeling growing out of the war, our statesmen have still believed that the existence of the States with powers for domestic and local government, including the regulation of civil rights—the rights of person and of property—was essential to the perfect working of our complex form of government, though they have thought proper to impose additional limitations on the States, and to confer additional power on that of the Nation.

But whatever fluctuations may be seen in the history of public opinion on this subject during the period of our national existence, we think it will be found that this court, so far as its functions required, has always held with a steady and an even hand the balance between State and Federal power, and we trust that such may continue to be the history of its relation to that subject so long as it shall have duties to perform which demand of it a construction of the Constitution, or of any of its parts.

The judgments of the Supreme Court of Louisiana in these cases are

Affirmed.

Mr. Justice FIELD, dissenting:

I am unable to agree with the majority of the court in these cases, and will proceed to state the reasons of my dissent from their judgment.

. . .

It is contended in justification for the act in question that it was adopted in the interest of the city, to promote its cleanliness and protect its health, and was the legitimate exercise of what is termed the police power of the State. That power undoubtedly extends to all regulations affecting the health, good order, morals, peace, and safety of society, and is exercised on a great variety of subjects, and in almost numberless ways.

. . .

The act of Louisiana presents the naked case, unaccompanied by any public considerations, where a right to pursue a lawful and necessary calling, previously enjoyed by every citizen, and in connection with which a thousand persons were daily employed, is taken away and vested exclusively for twenty-five years, for an extensive district and a large population, in a single corporation, or its exercise is for that period restricted to the establishments of the corporation, and there allowed only upon onerous conditions.

. . .

[After reviewing a number of court decisions, Field concludes:] In all these cases there is a recognition of the equality of right among citizens in the pursuit of the ordinary avocations of life, and a declaration that all grants of exclusive privileges, in contravention of this equality, are against common right, and void.

This equality of right, with exemption from all disparaging and partial enactments, in the lawful pursuits of life, throughout the whole country, is the distinguishing privilege of citizens of the United States. To them, everywhere, all pursuits, all professions, all avocations are open without other restrictions than such as are imposed equally upon all others of the same age, sex, and condition. . . . it is to me a matter of profound regret that its validity is not recognized by a majority of this court, for by it the right of free labor, one of the most sacred and imprescriptible rights of man, is violated. As stated by the Supreme Court of Connecticut, in the case cited, grants of exclusive privileges, such as is made by the act in question, are opposed to the whole theory of free government, and it requires no aid from any bill of rights to render them void. That only is a free government, in the American sense of the term, under which the inalienable right of every citizen to pursue his happiness is unrestrained, except by just, equal, and impartial laws.

I am authorized by the CHIEF JUSTICE, Mr. Justice SWAYNE, and Mr. Justice BRADLEY, to state that they concur with me in this dissenting opinion.

Mr. Justice BRADLEY, also dissenting:

I concur in the opinion which has just been read by Mr. Justice Field; but desire to add a few observations for the purpose of more fully illustrating my views on the important question decided in these cases, and the special grounds on which they rest.

· · ·

Every citizen . . . being primarily a citizen of the United States, and, secondarily, a citizen of the State where he resides, what, in general, are the privileges and immunities of a citizen of the United States? Is the right, liberty, or privilege of choosing any lawful employment one of them?

If a State legislature should pass a law prohibiting the inhabitants of a particular township, county, or city, from tanning leather or making shoes, would such a law violate any privileges or immunities of those inhabitants as citizens of the United States, or only their privileges and immunities as citizens of that particular State? Or if a State legislature should pass a law of caste, making all trades and professions, or certain enumerated trades and professions, hereditary, so that no one could follow any such trades or professions except that which was pursued by his father, would such a law violate the privileges and immunities of the people of that State as citizens of the United States, or only as citizens of the State? Would they have no redress but to appeal to the courts of that particular State?

This seems to me to be the essential question before us for consideration. And, in my judgment,

the right of any citizen to follow whatever lawful employment he chooses to adopt (submitting himself to all lawful regulations) is one of his most valuable rights, and one which the legislature of a State cannot invade, whether restrained by its own constitution or not.

· · ·

. . . the Declaration of Independence, which was the first political act of the American people in their independent sovereign capacity, lays the foundation of our National existence upon this broad proposition: "That all men are created equal; that they are endowed by their Creator with certain inalienable rights; that among these are life, liberty, and the pursuit of happiness." Here again we have the great threefold division of the rights of freemen, asserted as the rights of man. Rights to life, liberty, and the pursuit of happiness are equivalent to the rights of life, liberty, and property. These are the fundamental rights which can only be taken away by due process of law, and which can only be interfered with, or the enjoyment of which can only be modified, by lawful regulations necessary or proper for the mutual good of all; and these rights, I contend, belong to the citizens of every free government.

For the preservation, exercise, and enjoyment of these rights the individual citizen, as a necessity, must be left free to adopt such calling, profession, or trade as may seem to him most conducive to that end. Without this right he cannot be a freeman. This right to choose one's calling is an essential part of that liberty which it is the object of government to protect; and a calling, when chosen, is a man's property and right. Liberty and property are not protected where these rights are arbitrarily assailed.

· · ·

Lastly: Can the Federal courts administer relief to citizens of the United States whose privileges and immunities have been abridged by a State? Of this I entertain no doubt. Prior to the fourteenth amendment this could not be done, except in a few instances, for the want of the requisite authority.

· · ·

Admitting, therefore, that formerly the States were not prohibited from infringing any of the fundamental privileges and immunities of citizens of the United States, except in a few specified cases, that cannot be said now, since the adoption of the fourteenth amendment. In my judgment, it was the intention of the people of this country in adopting that amendment to provide National security against violation by the States of the fundamental rights of the citizen.

. . .

It is futile to argue that none but persons of the African race are intended to be benefited by this amendment. They may have been the primary cause of the amendment, but its language is general, embracing all citizens, and I think it was purposely so expressed.

. . .

Mr. Justice SWAYNE, dissenting:

I concur in the dissent in these cases and in the views expressed by my brethren, Mr. Justice Field and Mr. Justice Bradley. I desire, however, to submit a few additional remarks.

. . .

It is admitted that the plaintiffs in error are citizens of the United States, and persons within the jurisdiction of Louisiana. The cases before us, therefore, present but two questions.

(1.) Does the act of the legislature creating the monopoly in question abridge the privileges and immunities of the plaintiffs in error as citizens of the United States?

(2.) Does it deprive them of liberty or property without due process of law, or deny them the equal protection of the laws of the State, they being *persons* "within its jurisdiction?"

Both these inquiries I remit for their answer as to the facts to the opinions of my brethren, Mr. Justice Field and Mr. Justice Bradley. They are full and conclusive upon the subject. A more flagrant and indefensible invasion of the rights of many for the benefit of a few has not occurred in the legislative history of the country. The response to both inquiries should be in the affirmative. In my opinion the cases, as presented in the record, are clearly within the letter and meaning of both the negative categories of the sixth section. The judgments before us should, therefore, be reversed.

. . .

Munn v. Illinois

94 U.S. 113 (1877)

This case illustrates the need to balance two conflicting interests: the property rights of private individuals against the duty of the state to regulate economic conditions for the public good. Although economic regulation is sometimes regarded as a phenomenon of the twentieth century, this case makes clear that it has been customary "from time immemorial." Statutes regulating private property do not necessarily deprive an owner of his property without due process of law. When the owner of property devotes it to a use "in which the public has an interest," the owner must submit to some degree of public control. The issue in this case concerns a law passed by Illinois fixing the maximum rate for storing grain in warehouses in Chicago and other places in the state.

MR. CHIEF JUSTICE WAITE delivered the opinion of the court.

The question to be determined in this case is whether the general assembly of Illinois can, under the limitations upon the legislative power of the States imposed by the Constitution of the United States, fix by law the maximum of charges for the storage of grain in warehouses at Chicago and other places in the State having not less than one hundred thousand inhabitants, "in which grain is stored in bulk, and in which the grain of different owners is mixed together, or in which grain is stored in such a manner that the identity of different lots or parcels cannot be accurately preserved."

It is claimed that such a law is repugnant—

1. To that part of sect. 8, art. 1, of the Constitution of the United States which confers upon Congress the power "to regulate commerce with foreign nations and among the several States;"

2. To that part of sect. 9 of the same article which provides that "no preference shall be given by any regulation of commerce or revenue to the ports of one State over those of another;" and

3. To that part of amendment 14 which ordains that no State shall "deprive any person of life, liberty, or property, without due process of law, nor deny to any person within its jurisdiction the equal protection of the laws."

We will consider the last of these objections first.

Every statute is presumed to be constitutional. The courts ought not to declare one to be unconstitutional, unless it is clearly so. If there is doubt, the expressed will of the legislature should be sustained.

The Constitution contains no definition of the word "deprive," as used in the Fourteenth Amendment. To determine its signification, therefore, it is necessary to ascertain the effect which usage has given it, when employed in the same or a like connection.

While this provision of the amendment is new in the Constitution of the United States, as a limitation upon the powers of the States, it is old as a principle of civilized government. It is found in Magna Charta, and, in substance if not in form, in nearly or quite all the constitutions that have been from time to time adopted by the several States of the Union. By the Fifth Amendment, it was introduced into the Constitution of the United States as a limitation upon the powers of the national government, and by the Fourteenth, as a guaranty against any encroachment upon an acknowledged right of citizenship by the legislatures of the States.

When the people of the United Colonies separated from Great Britain, they changed the form, but not the substance, of their government. They retained for the purposes of government all the powers of the British Parliament, and through their State constitutions, or other forms of social compact, undertook to give practical effect to such as they deemed necessary for the common good and the security of life and property. . . .

When one becomes a member of society, he necessarily parts with some rights or privileges which, as an individual not affected by his relations to others, he might retain. "A body politic," as aptly defined in the preamble of the Constitution of Massachusetts, "is a social compact by which the whole people covenants with each citizen, and each citizen with the whole people, that all shall be governed by certain laws for the common good." This does not confer power upon the whole people to control rights which are purely and exclusively private, *Thorpe* v. *R. & B. Railroad Co.*, 27 Vt. 143; but it does authorize the establishment of laws requiring each citizen to so conduct himself, and so use his own property, as not unnecessarily to injure another. . . . Under these *[police]* powers the government regulates the conduct of its citizens one towards another, and the manner in which each shall use his own property, when such regulation becomes necessary for the public good. In their exercise it has been customary in England from time immemorial, and in this country from its first colonization, to regulate ferries, common carriers, hackmen, bakers, millers, wharfingers, innkeepers, &c., and in so doing to fix a maximum of charge to be made for services rendered, accommodations furnished, and articles sold. To this day, statutes are to be found in many of the States upon some or all these subjects; and we think it has never yet been successfully contended that such legislation came within any of the constitutional prohibitions against interference with private property. . . .

From this it is apparent that, down to the time of the adoption of the Fourteenth Amendment, it was not supposed that statutes regulating the use, or even the price of the use, of private property necessarily deprived an owner of his property without due process of law. Under some circumstances they may, but not under all. The amendment does not change the law in this particular: it simply prevents the States from doing that which will operate as such a deprivation.

This brings us to inquire as to the principles upon which this power of regulation rests, in order that we may determine what is within and what without its operative effect. Looking, then, to the common law, from whence came the right which the Constitution protects, we find that when private property is "affected with a public interest, it ceases to be *juris privati* only." This was said by Lord Chief Justice Hale more than two hundred years ago, in his treatise *De Portibus Maris*, 1 Harg. Law Tracts, 78, and has been accepted without objection as an essential element in the law of property ever since. Property does become clothed with a public interest when used in a manner to make it of public consequence, and affect the community at large. When, therefore, one devotes his property to a use in which the public has an interest, he, in effect, grants to the public an interest in that use, and must submit to be controlled by the public for the common good, to the extent of the interest he has thus created. He may withdraw his grant by discontinuing the use; but, so long as he maintains the use, he must submit to the control.

. . .

. . . the same principle came under consideration in the Supreme Court of Alabama. That court was called upon, in 1841, to decide whether the power granted to the city of Mobile to regulate the weight and price of bread was unconstitutional, and it was contended that "it would interfere with the right of the citizen to pursue his lawful trade or calling in the mode his judgment might dictate;" but the court said, "there is no motive . . . for this interference on the part of the legislature with the lawful actions of individuals, or the mode in which private property shall be enjoyed, unless such calling affects the public interest, or private property is employed in a manner which directly affects the body of the people. Upon this principle, in this State, tavern-keepers are licensed; . . . and the County Court is required, at least once a year, to settle the rates of innkeepers. Upon the same principle is founded the control which the legislature has always exercised in the establishment and regulation of mills, ferries, bridges, turnpike roads, and other kindred subjects." *Mobile* v. *Yuille*, 3 Ala. N.S. 140.

. . .

But we need not go further. Enough has already been said to show that, when private property is devoted to a public use, it is subject to public regulation. It remains only to ascertain whether the warehouses of these plaintiffs in error, and the business which is carried on there, come within the operation of this principle.

For this purpose we accept as true the statements of fact contained in the elaborate brief of one of the counsel of the plaintiffs in error. From these it appears that "the great producing region of the West and North-west sends its grain by water and rail to Chicago, where the greater part of it is shipped by vessel for transportation to the seaboard by the Great Lakes, and some of it is forwarded by railway to the Eastern ports. . . . Vessels, to some extent, are loaded in the Chicago harbor, and sailed through the St. Lawrence directly to Europe. . . . The quantity [of grain] received in Chicago has made it the greatest grain market in the world. This business has created a demand for means by which the immense quantity of grain can be handled or stored, and these have been found in grain warehouses, which are commonly called elevators, because the grain is elevated from the boat or car, by machinery operated by steam, into the bins prepared for its reception, and elevated from the bins, by a like process, into the vessel or car which is to carry it on. . . . In this way the largest traffic between the citizens of the country north and west of Chicago and the citizens of the country lying on the Atlantic coast north of Washington is in grain which passes through the elevators of Chicago. In this way the trade in grain is carried on by the inhabitants of seven or eight of the great States of the West with four or five of the States lying on the sea-shore, and forms the largest part of inter-state commerce in these States. The grain warehouses or elevators in Chicago are immense structures, holding from 300,000 to 1,000,000 bushels at one time, according to size. They are divided into bins of large capacity and great strength. . . . They are located with the river harbor on one side and the railway tracks on the other; and the grain is run through them from car to vessel, or boat to car, as may be demanded in the course of business. It has been found impossible to preserve each owner's grain separate, and this has given rise to a system of inspection and grading, by which the grain of different owners is mixed, and receipts issued for the number of bushels which are negotiable, and redeemable in like kind, upon demand. This mode of conducting the business was inaugurated more than twenty years ago, and has grown to immense proportions. The railways have found it impracticable to own such elevators, and public policy forbids the transaction of such business by the carrier; the ownership has, therefore, been by private individuals, who have embarked their capital and devoted their industry to such business as a private pursuit."

In this connection it must also be borne in mind that, although in 1874 there were in Chicago fourteen warehouses adapted to this particular business, and owned by about thirty persons, nine business firms controlled them, and that the prices charged and received for storage were such "as have been from year to year agreed upon and established by the different elevators or warehouses in the city of Chicago, and which rates have been annually published in one or more newspapers printed in said city, in the month of January in each year, as the established rates for the year then next ensuing such publication." Thus it is apparent that all the elevating facilities through which these vast productions "of seven or eight great States of the West" must pass on the way "to four or five of the States on the sea-shore" may be a "virtual" monopoly.

Under such circumstances it is difficult to see why, if the common carrier, or the miller, or the ferryman, or the innkeeper, or the wharfinger, or the baker, or the cartman, or the hackney-coachman, pursues a public employment and exercises "a sort of public office," these plaintiffs in error do not. They stand, to use again the language of their counsel, in the very "gateway of commerce," and take toll from all who pass. Their business most certainly "tends to a common charge, and is become a thing of public interest and use." Every bushel of grain for its passage "pays a toll, which is a common charge," and, therefore, according to Lord Hale, every such warehouseman "ought to be under public regulation, viz., that he . . . take but reasonable toll."

Certainly, if any business can be clothed "with a public interest, and cease to be *juris privati* only," this has been. It may not be made so by the operation of the Constitution of Illinois or this statute, but it is by the facts.

We also are not permitted to overlook the fact that, for some reason, the people of Illinois, when they revised their Constitution in 1870, saw fit to make it the duty of the general assembly to pass laws "for the protection of producers, shippers, and receivers of grain and produce," art. 13, sect. 7; and by sect. 5 of the same article, to require all railroad companies receiving and transporting grain in bulk or otherwise to deliver the same at any elevator to which it might be consigned, that could be reached by any track that was or could be used by such company, and that all railroad companies should permit connections to be made with their tracks, so that any public warehouse, &c., might be reached by the cars on their railroads. This indicates very clearly that during the twenty years in which this peculiar business had been assuming its present "immense proportions," something had occurred which led the whole body of the people to suppose that remedies such as are usually employed to prevent abuses by virtual monopolies might not be inappropriate here. For our purposes we must assume that, if a state of facts could exist that would justify such legislation, it actually did exist when the statute now under consideration was passed. For us the question is one of power, not of expediency. If no state of circumstances could exist to justify such a statute, then we may declare this one void, because in excess of the legislative power of the State. But if it could we must presume it did. Of the propriety of legislative interference within the scope of legislative power, the legislature is the exclusive judge.

. . .

It is insisted, however, that the owner of property is entitled to a reasonable compensation for its use, even though it be clothed with a public interest, and that what is reasonable is a judicial and not a legislative question.

As has already been shown, the practice has been otherwise. In countries where the common law prevails, it has been customary from time immemorial for the legislature to declare what shall be a reasonable compensation under such circumstances, or, perhaps more properly speaking, to fix a maximum beyond which any charge made would be unreasonable. Undoubtedly, in mere private contracts, relating to matters in which the public has no interest, what is reasonable must be ascertained judicially. But this is because the legislature has no control over such a contract. . . .

We know that *[the police power]* is a power which may be abused; but that is no argument against its existence. For protection against abuses by legislatures the people must resort to the polls, not to the courts.

. . .

We come now to consider the effect upon this statute of the power of Congress to regulate commerce.

It was very properly said in the case of the *State Tax on Railway Gross Receipts*, 15 Wall. 293, that "it is not every thing that affects commerce that amounts to a regulation of it, within the meaning of the Constitution." The warehouses of these plaintiffs in error are situated and their business carried on exclusively within the limits of the State of Illinois. They are used as instruments by those engaged in State as well as those engaged in inter-state commerce, but they are no more necessarily a part of commerce itself than the dray or the cart by which, but for them, grain would be transferred from one railroad station to another. Incidentally they may become connected with inter-state commerce, but not necessarily so. Their regulation is a thing of domestic concern, and, certainly, until Congress acts in reference to their inter-state relations, the State may exercise all the powers of government over them, even though in so doing it may indirectly operate upon commerce outside its immediate jurisdiction. . . .

Judgment affirmed.

MR. JUSTICE FIELD and MR. JUSTICE STRONG dissented.

MR. JUSTICE FIELD. I am compelled to dissent from the decision of the court in this case, and from the reasons upon which that decision is founded. The principle upon which the opinion of the majority proceeds is, in my judgment, subversive of the rights of private property, heretofore believed to be protected by constitutional guaranties against legislative interference, and is in conflict with the authorities cited in its support.

. . .

. . . it would seem from its opinion that the court holds that property loses something of its private character when employed in such a way as to be generally useful. The doctrine declared is that property "becomes clothed with a public interest when used in a manner to make it of public consequence, and affect the community at large;" and from such clothing the right of the legislature is deduced to control the use of the property, and to determine the compensation which the owner may receive for it. . . .

If this be sound law, if there be no protection, either in the principles upon which our republican government is founded, or in the prohibitions of the Constitution against such invasion of private rights, all property and all business in the State are held at the mercy of a majority of its legislature. The public has no greater interest in the use of buildings for the storage of grain than it has in the use of buildings for the residences of families, nor, indeed, any thing like so great an interest; and, according to the doctrine announced, the legislature may fix the rent of all tenements used for residences, without reference to the cost of their erection. If the owner does not like the rates prescribed, he may cease renting his houses. He has granted to the public, says the court, an interest in the use of the buildings, and "he may withdraw his grant by discontinuing the use; but, so long as he maintains the use, he must submit to the control." The public is interested in the manufacture of cotton, woollen, and silken fabrics, in the construction of machinery, in the printing and publication of books and periodicals, and in the making of utensils of every variety, useful and ornamental; indeed, there is hardly an enterprise or business engaging the attention and labor of any considerable portion of the community, in which the public has not an interest in the sense in which that term is used by the court in its opinion; and the doctrine which allows the legislature to interfere with and regulate the charges which the owners of property thus employed shall make for its use, that is, the rates at which all these different kinds of business shall be carried on, has never before been asserted, so far as I am aware, by any judicial tribunal in the United States.

. . .

MR. JUSTICE STRONG. When the judgment in this case was announced by direction of a majority of the court, it was well known by all my brethren that I did not concur in it. It had been my purpose to prepare a dissenting opinion, but I found no time for the preparation, and I was reluctant to dissent in such a case without stating my reasons. Mr. Justice Field has now stated them as fully as I can, and I concur in what he has said.

Lochner v. New York

198 U.S. 45 (1905)

New York passed a law prohibiting employees from working in bakeries more than sixty hours a week or ten hours a day. The statute, sustained by the state courts, was similar to other labor laws passed by states to protect workers from industrial conditions that threatened health and safety. The case represented a conflict between two values: the police power of the state to regulate economic activities versus the "liberty" protected by the Fourteenth Amendment to contract without unreasonable interference by the state.

MR. JUSTICE PECKHAM, after making the foregoing statement of the facts, delivered the opinion of the court.

The indictment, it will be seen, charges that the plaintiff in error violated the one hundred and tenth section of article 8, chapter 415, of the Laws of 1897, known as the labor law of the State of New York, in that he wrongfully and unlawfully required and permitted an employé working for him to work more than sixty hours in one week. There is nothing in any of the opinions delivered in this case, either in the Supreme Court or the Court of Appeals of the State, which construes the section, in using the word "required," as referring to any physical force being used to obtain the labor of an employé. It is assumed that the word means nothing more than the requirement arising from voluntary contract for such labor in excess of the number of hours specified in the statute. There is no pretense in any of the opinions that the statute was intended to meet a case of involuntary labor in any form. All the opinions assume that there is no real distinction, so far as this question is concerned, between the words "required" and "permitted." The mandate of the statute that "no employé shall be required or permitted to work," is the substantial equivalent of an enactment that "no employé shall contract or agree to work," more than ten hours per day, and as there is no provision for special emergencies the statute is mandatory in all cases. It is not an act merely fixing the number of hours which shall constitute a legal day's work, but an absolute prohibition upon the employer, permitting, under any circumstances, more than ten hours work to be done in his establishment. The employé may desire to earn the extra money, which would arise from his working more than the prescribed time, but this statute forbids the employer from permitting the employé to earn it.

The statute necessarily interferes with the right of contract between the employer and employés, concerning the number of hours in which the latter may labor in the bakery of the employer. The general right to make a contract in relation to his business is part of the liberty of the individual protected by the Fourteenth Amendment of the Federal Constitution. *Allgeyer* v. *Louisiana*, 165

U.S. 578. Under that provision no State can deprive any person of life, liberty or property without due process of law. The right to purchase or to sell labor is part of the liberty protected by this amendment, unless there are circumstances which exclude the right. There are, however, certain powers, existing in the sovereignty of each State in the Union, somewhat vaguely termed police powers, the exact description and limitation of which have not been attempted by the courts. Those powers, broadly stated and without, at present, any attempt at a more specific limitation, relate to the safety, health, morals and general welfare of the public. Both property and liberty are held on such reasonable conditions as may be imposed by the governing power of the State in the exercise of those powers, and with such conditions the Fourteenth Amendment was not designed to interfere. *Mugler* v. *Kansas,* 123 U.S. 623; *In re Kemmler,* 136 U.S. 436; *Crowley* v. *Christensen,* 137 U.S. 86; *In re Converse,* 137 U.S. 624.

The State, therefore, has power to prevent the individual from making certain kinds of contracts, and in regard to them the Federal Constitution offers no protection. If the contract be one which the State, in the legitimate exercise of its police power, has the right to prohibit, it is not prevented from prohibiting it by the Fourteenth Amendment. Contracts in violation of a statute, either of the Federal or state government, or a contract to let one's property for immoral purposes, or to do any other unlawful act, could obtain no protection from the Federal Constitution, as coming under the liberty of person or of free contract. Therefore, when the State, by its legislature, in the assumed exercise of its police powers, has passed an act which seriously limits the right to labor or the right of contract in regard to their means of livelihood between persons who are *sui juris* (both employer and employé), it becomes of great importance to determine which shall prevail—the right of the individual to labor for such time as he may choose, or the right of the State to prevent the individual from laboring or from entering into any contract to labor, beyond a certain time prescribed by the State.

This court has recognized the existence and upheld the exercise of the police powers of the States in many cases which might fairly be considered as border ones, and it has, in the course of its determination of questions regarding the asserted invalidity of such statutes, on the ground of their violation of the rights secured by the Federal Constitution, been guided by rules of a very liberal nature, the application of which has resulted, in numerous instances, in upholding the validity of state statutes thus assailed. Among the later cases where the state law has been upheld by this court is that of *Holden* v. *Hardy,* 169 U.S. 366. A provision in the act of the legislature of Utah was there under consideration, the act limiting the employment of workmen in all underground mines or workings, to eight hours per day, "except in cases of emergency, where life or property is in imminent danger." It also limited the hours of labor in smelting and other institutions for the reduction or refining of ores or metals to eight hours per day, except in like cases of emergency. The act was held to be a valid exercise of the police powers of the State. A review of many of the cases on the subject, decided by this and other courts, is given in the opinion. It was held that the kind of employment, mining, smelting, etc., and the character of the employés in such kinds of labor, were such as to make it reasonable and proper for the State to interfere to prevent the employés from being constrained by the rules laid down by the proprietors in regard to labor. The following citation from the observations of the Supreme Court of Utah in that case was made by the judge writing the opinion of this court, and approved: "The law in question is confined to the protection of that class of people engaged in labor in underground mines, and in smelters and other works wherein ores are reduced and refined. This law applies only to the classes subjected by their employment to the peculiar conditions and effects attending underground mining and work in smelters, and other works for the reduction and refining of ores. Therefore it is not necessary to discuss or decide whether the legislature can fix the hours of labor in other employments."

. . .

It must, of course, be conceded that there is a limit to the valid exercise of the police power by the State. There is no dispute concerning this general proposition. Otherwise the Fourteenth

Amendment would have no efficacy and the legislatures of the States would have unbounded power, and it would be enough to say that any piece of legislation was enacted to conserve the morals, the health or the safety of the people; such legislation would be valid, no matter how absolutely without foundation the claim might be. The claim of the police power would be a mere pretext— become another and delusive name for the supreme sovereignty of the State to be exercised free from constitutional restraint. This is not contended for. In every case that comes before this court, therefore, where legislation of this character is concerned and where the protection of the Federal Constitution is sought, the question necessarily arises: Is this a fair, reasonable and appropriate exercise of the police power of the State, or is it an unreasonable, unnecessary and arbitrary interference with the right of the individual to his personal liberty or to enter into those contracts in relation to labor which may seem to him appropriate or necessary for the support of himself and his family? Of course the liberty of contract relating to labor includes both parties to it. The one has as much right to purchase as the other to sell labor.

This is not a question of substituting the judgment of the court for that of the legislature. If the act be within the power of the State it is valid, although the judgment of the court might be totally opposed to the enactment of such a law. But the question would still remain: Is it within the police power of the State? and that question must be answered by the court.

The question whether this act is valid as a labor law, pure and simple, may be dismissed in a few words. There is no reasonable ground for interfering with the liberty of person or the right of free contract, by determining the hours of labor, in the occupation of a baker. There is no contention that bakers as a class are not equal in intelligence and capacity to men in other trades or manual occupations, or that they are not able to assert their rights and care for themselves without the protecting arm of the State, interfering with their independence of judgment and of action. They are in no sense wards of the State. Viewed in the light of a purely labor law, with no reference whatever to the question of health, we think that a law like the one before us involves neither the safety, the

morals nor the welfare of the public, and that the interest of the public is not in the slightest degree affected by such an act. The law must be upheld, if at all, as a law pertaining to the health of the individual engaged in the occupation of a baker. It does not affect any other portion of the public than those who are engaged in that occupation. Clean and wholesome bread does not depend upon whether the baker works but ten hours per day or only sixty hours a week. The limitation of the hours of labor does not come within the police power on that ground.

. . .

We think that there can be no fair doubt that the trade of a baker, in and of itself, is not an unhealthy one to that degree which would authorize the legislature to interfere with the right to labor, and with the right of free contract on the part of the individual, either as employer or employé. In looking through statistics regarding all trades and occupations, it may be true that the trade of a baker does not appear to be as healthy as some other trades, and is also vastly more healthy than still others. To the common understanding the trade of a baker has never been regarded as an unhealthy one. Very likely physicians would not recommend the exercise of that or of any other trade as a remedy for ill health. Some occupations are more healthy than others, but we think there are none which might not come under the power of the legislature to supervise and control the hours of working therein, if the mere fact that the occupation is not absolutely and perfectly healthy is to confer that right upon the legislative department of the Government. It might be safely affirmed that almost all occupations more or less affect the health. There must be more than the mere fact of the possible existence of some small amount of unhealthiness to warrant legislative interference with liberty. It is unfortunately true that labor, even in any department, may possibly carry with it the seeds of unhealthiness. But are we all, on that account, at the mercy of legislative majorities? A printer, a tinsmith, a locksmith, a carpenter, a cabinetmaker, a dry goods clerk, a bank's, a lawyer's or a physician's clerk, or a clerk in almost any kind of business, would all come under the power of the legislature, on this assumption. No trade, no occupation, no mode of earning one's living, could escape this all-pervading power, and the acts of the legislature in limiting the hours of labor in all employments would be valid, although such limitation might seriously cripple the ability of the laborer to support himself and his family. In our large cities there are many buildings into which the sun penetrates for but a short time in each day, and these buildings are occupied by people carrying on the business of bankers, brokers, lawyers, real estate, and many other kinds of business, aided by many clerks, messengers, and other employés. Upon the assumption of the validity of this act under review, it is not possible to say that an act, prohibiting lawyers' or bank clerks, or others, from contracting to labor for their employers more than eight hours a day, would be invalid. . . .

. . . The act is not, within any fair meaning of the term, a health law, but is an illegal interference with the rights of individuals, both employers and employés, to make contracts regarding labor upon such terms as they may think best, or which they may agree upon with the other parties to such contracts. Statutes of the nature of that under review, limiting the hours in which grown and intelligent men may labor to earn their living, are mere meddlesome interferences with the rights of the individual, and they are not saved from condemnation by the claim that they are passed in the exercise of the police power and upon the subject of the health of the individual whose rights are interfered with, unless there be some fair ground, reasonable in and of itself, to say that there is material danger to the public health or to the health of the employés, if the hours of labor are not curtailed. . . .

. . . In our judgment it is not possible in fact to discover the connection between the number of hours a baker may work in the bakery and the healthful quality of the bread made by the workman. The connection, if any exists, is too shadowy and thin to build any argument for the interference of the legislature. If the man works ten hours a day it is all right, but if ten and a half or eleven his health is in danger and his bread may be unhealthful, and, therefore, he shall not be permitted to do it. This, we think, is unreasonable and entirely arbitrary. When assertions such as we have advert-

ed to become necessary in order to give, if possible, a plausible foundation for the contention that the law is a "health law," it gives rise to at least a suspicion that there was some other motive dominating the legislature than the purpose to subserve the public health or welfare.

This interference on the part of the legislatures of the several States with the ordinary trades and occupations of the people seems to be on the increase. In the Supreme Court of New York, in the case of *People* v. *Beattie*, Appellate Division, First Department, decided in 1904, 89 N.Y. Supp. 193, a statute regulating the trade of horseshoeing, and requiring the person practicing such trade to be examined and to obtain a certificate from a board of examiners and file the same with the clerk of the county wherein the person proposes to practice such trade, was held invalid, as an arbitrary interference with personal liberty and private property without due process of law. The attempt was made, unsuccessfully, to justify it as a health law.

. . .

The judgment of the Court of Appeals of New York as well as that of the Supreme Court and of the County Court of Oneida County must be reversed and the case remanded to the County Court for further proceedings not inconsistent with this opinion.

Reversed.

MR. JUSTICE HARLAN, with whom MR. JUSTICE WHITE and MR. JUSTICE DAY concurred, dissenting.

. . .

It is plain that this statute was enacted in order to protect the physical well-being of those who work in bakery and confectionery establishments. It may be that the statute had its origin, in part, in the belief that employers and employés in such establishments were not upon an equal footing, and that the necessities of the latter often compelled them to submit to such exactions as unduly taxed their strength. Be this as it may, the statute must be taken as expressing the belief of the people of New York that, as a general rule, and in the case of the average man, labor in excess of sixty hours during a week in such establishments may endanger the health of those who thus labor. Whether or not this be wise legislation it is not the province of the court to inquire. Under our systems of government the courts are not concerned with the wisdom or policy of legislation. So that in determining the question of power to interfere with liberty of contract, the court may inquire whether the means devised by the State are germane to an end which may be lawfully accomplished and have a real or substantial relation to the protection of health, as involved in the daily work of the persons, male and female, engaged in bakery and confectionery establishments. But when this inquiry is entered upon I find it impossible, in view of common experience, to say that there is here no real or substantial relation between the means employed by the State and the end sought to be accomplished by its legislation. *Mugler* v. *Kansas, supra.* Nor can I say that the statute has no appropriate or direct connection with that protection to health which each State owes to her citizens, *Patterson* v. *Kentucky, supra;* or that it is not promotive of the health of the employés in question, *Holden* v. *Hardy, Lawton* v. *Steele, supra;* or that the regulation prescribed by the State is utterly unreasonable and extravagant or wholly arbitrary, *Gundling* v. *Chicago, supra.* Still less can I say that the statute is, beyond question, a plain, palpable invasion of rights secured by the fundamental law. *Jacobson* v. *Massachusetts, supra.* Therefore I submit that this court will transcend its functions if it assumes to annul the statute of New York. It must be remembered that this statute does not apply to all kinds of business. It applies only to work in bakery and confectionery establishments, in which, as all know, the air constantly breathed by workmen is not as pure and healthful as that to be found in some other establishments or out of doors.

[Justice Harlan summarizes a number of studies that describe the health hazards of working in a bakery, including the inhalation of flour dust that causes inflammation of the lungs and the bronchial tubes.]

MR. JUSTICE HOLMES dissenting.

I regret sincerely that I am unable to agree with the judgment in this case, and that I think it my duty to express my dissent.

This case is decided upon an economic theory which a large part of the country does not entertain. If it were a question whether I agreed with that theory, I should desire to study it further and long before making up my mind. But I do not conceive that to be my duty, because I strongly believe that my agreement or disagreement has nothing to do with the right of a majority to embody their opinions in law. It is settled by various decisions of this court that state constitutions and state laws may regulate life in many ways which we as legislators might think as injudicious or if you like as tyrannical as this, and which equally with this interfere with the liberty to contract. Sunday laws and usury laws are ancient examples. A more modern one is the prohibition of lotteries. The liberty of the citizen to do as he likes so long as he does not interfere with the liberty of others to do the same, which has been a shibboleth for some well-known writers, is interfered with by school laws, by the Post Office, by every state or municipal institution which takes his money for purposes thought desirable, whether he likes it or not. The Fourteenth Amendment does not enact Mr. Herbert Spencer's Social Statics. The other day we sustained the Massachusetts vaccination law. *Jacobson* v. *Massachusetts,* 197 U.S. 11. United States and state statutes and decisions cutting down the liberty to contract by way of combination are familiar to this court. *Northern Securities Co.* v. *United States,* 193 U.S. 197. Two years ago we upheld the prohibition of sales of stock on margins or for future delivery in the constitution of California. *Otis* v. *Parker,* 187 U.S. 606. The decision sustaining an eight hour law for miners is still recent. *Holden* v. *Hardy,* 169 U.S. 366. Some of these laws embody convictions or prejudices which judges are likely to share. Some may not. But a constitution is not intended to embody a particular economic theory, whether of paternalism and the organic relation of the citizen to the State or of *laissez faire.* It is made for people of fundamentally differing views, and the accident of our finding certain opinions natural and familiar or novel and even shocking ought not to conclude our judgment upon the question whether statutes embodying them conflict with the Constitution of the United States.

General propositions do not decide concrete cases. The decision will depend on a judgment or intuition more subtle than any articulate major premise. But I think that the proposition just stated, if it is accepted, will carry us far toward the end. Every opinion tends to become a law. I think that the word liberty in the Fourteenth Amendment is perverted when it is held to prevent the natural outcome of a dominant opinion, unless it can be said that a rational and fair man necessarily would admit that the statute proposed would infringe fundamental principles as they have been understood by the traditions of our people and our law. It does not need research to show that no such sweeping condemnation can be passed upon the statute before us. A reasonable man might think it a proper measure on the score of health. Men whom I certainly could not pronounce unreasonable would uphold it as a first instalment of a general regulation of the hours of work. Whether in the latter aspect it would be open to the charge of inequality I think it unnecessary to discuss.

Adkins v. Children's Hospital

261 U.S. 525 (1923)

In 1918, Congress passed a law setting minimum wages for women and children in the District of Columbia. As in other cases, the question was one of balancing the police power of Congress to regulate health and safety with the right of individuals to conduct their own affairs without legislative interference.

MR. JUSTICE SUTHERLAND delivered the opinion of the Court.

The question presented for determination by these appeals is the constitutionality of the Act of September 19, 1918, providing for the fixing of minimum wages for women and children in the District of Columbia. 40 Stat. 960, c. 174.

The act provides for a board of three members, to be constituted, as far as practicable, so as to be equally representative of employers, employees and the public. The board is authorized to have public hearings, at which persons interested in the matter being investigated may appear and testify, to administer oaths, issue subpoenas requiring the attendance of witnesses and production of books, etc., and to make rules and regulations for carrying the act into effect.

[The act authorized the board to investigate wages for women and minors and to order changes in wages after giving public notice and holding a public hearing. Questions of fact determined by the board could not be appealed.]

The appellee in the first case is a corporation maintaining a hospital for children in the District. It employs a large number of women in various capacities, with whom it had agreed upon rates of wages and compensation satisfactory to such employees, but which in some instances were less than the minimum wage fixed by an order of the board made in pursuance of the act. The women with whom appellee had so contracted were all of full age and under no legal disability. The instant suit was brought by the appellee in the Supreme Court of the District to restrain the board from enforcing or attempting to enforce its order on the ground that the same was in contravention of the Constitution, and particularly the due process clause of the Fifth Amendment.

In the second case the appellee, a woman twenty-one years of age, was employed by the

Congress Hall Hotel Company as an elevator operator, at a salary of $35 per month and two meals a day. She alleges that the work was light and healthful, the hours short, with surroundings clean and moral, and that she was anxious to continue it for the compensation she was receiving and that she did not earn more. Her services were satisfactory to the Hotel Company and it would have been glad to retain her but was obliged to dispense with her services by reason of the order of the board and on account of the penalties prescribed by the act. The wages received by this appellee were the best she was able to obtain for any work she was capable of performing and the enforcement of the order, she alleges, deprived her of such employment and wages. She further averred that she could not secure any other position at which she could make a living, with as good physical and moral surroundings, and earn as good wages, and that she was desirous of continuing and would continue the employment but for the order of the board. An injunction was prayed as in the other case.

[The lower courts held the statute to be unconstitutional.]

. . .

The judicial duty of passing upon the constitutionality of an act of Congress is one of great gravity and delicacy. The statute here in question has successfully borne the scrutiny of the legislative branch of the government, which, by enacting it, has affirmed its validity; and that determination must be given great weight. This Court, by an unbroken line of decisions from Chief Justice Marshall to the present day, has steadily adhered to the rule that every possible presumption is in favor of the validity of an act of Congress until overcome beyond rational doubt. But if by clear and indubitable demonstration a statute be opposed to the Constitution we have no choice but to say so. The Constitution, by its own terms, is the supreme law of the land, emanating from the people, the repository of ultimate sovereignty under our form of government. A congressional statute, on the other hand, is the act of an agency of this sovereign authority and if it conflict with the Constitution must fall; for that which is not

supreme must yield to that which is. To hold it invalid (if it be invalid) is a plain exercise of the judicial power—that power vested in courts to enable them to administer justice according to law. From the authority to ascertain and determine the law in a given case, there necessarily results, in case of conflict, the duty to declare and enforce the rule of the supreme law and reject that of an inferior act of legislation which, transcending the Constitution, is of no effect and binding on no one. This is not the exercise of a substantive power to review and nullify acts of Congress, for no such substantive power exists. It is simply a necessary concomitant of the power to hear and dispose of a case or controversy properly before the court, to the determination of which must be brought the test and measure of the law.

The statute now under consideration is attacked upon the ground that it authorizes an unconstitutional interference with the freedom of contract included within the guaranties of the due process clause of the Fifth Amendment. That the right to contract about one's affairs is a part of the liberty of the individual protected by this clause, is settled by the decisions of this Court and is no longer open to question. *Allgeyer* v. *Louisiana*, 165 U.S. 578, 591; *New York Life Insurance Co.* v. *Dodge*, 246 U.S. 357, 373–374; *Coppage* v. *Kansas*, 236 U.S. 1, 10, 14; *Adair* v. *United States*, 208 U.S. 161; *Lochner* v. *New York*, 198 U.S. 45; *Butchers' Union Co.* v. *Crescent City Co.*, 111 U.S. 746; *Muller* v. *Oregon*, 208 U.S. 412, 421. Within this liberty are contracts of employment of labor: In making such contracts, generally speaking, the parties have an equal right to obtain from each other the best terms they can as the result of private bargaining.

. . .

There is, of course, no such thing as absolute freedom of contract. It is subject to a great variety of restraints. But freedom of contract is, nevertheless, the general rule and restraint the exception; and the exercise of legislative authority to abridge it can be justified only by the existence of exceptional circumstances. Whether these circumstances exist in the present case constitutes the question to be answered. It will be helpful to this end to review some of the decisions where the interference has been upheld and consider the grounds upon which they rest.

[Justice Sutherland reviews cases in which the Court upheld statutes fixing rates and charges to be exacted on businesses impressed with a public interest; statutes relating to contracts for the performance of public work; statutes prescribing the character, methods, and time for payment of wages; and statutes fixing hours of labor.]

Wilson v. *New*, 243 U.S. 332, involved the validity of the so-called Adamson Law, which established an eight-hour day for employees of interstate carriers for which it fixed a scale of minimum wages with proportionate increases for overtime, to be enforced, however, only for a limited period. The act was sustained primarily upon the ground that it was a regulation of a business charged with a public interest. The Court, speaking through the Chief Justice, pointed out that regarding "the private right and private interest as contradistinguished from the public interest the power exists between the parties, the employers and employees, to agree as to a standard of wages free from legislative interference" but that this did not affect the power to deal with the matter with a view to protect the public right, and then said (p. 353):

"And this emphasizes that there is no question here of purely private right since the law is concerned only with those who are engaged in a business charged with a public interest where the subject dealt with as to all the parties is one involved in that business and which we have seen comes under the control of the right to regulate to the extent that the power to do so is appropriate or relevant to the business regulated."

Moreover, in sustaining the wage feature, of the law, emphasis was put upon the fact (p. 345) that it was in this respect temporary "leaving the employers and employees free as to the subject of wages to govern their relations by their own agreements after the specified time." The act was not only temporary in this respect, but it was passed to meet a sudden and great emergency. This feature of the law was sustained principally because the parties, for the time being, could not or would not agree. Here they are forbidden to agree.

. . .

In the *Muller Case* the validity of an Oregon statute, forbidding the employment of any female in certain industries more than ten hours during any one day was upheld. The decision proceeded upon the theory that the difference between the sexes may justify a different rule respecting hours of labor in the case of women than in the case of men. It is pointed out that these consist in differences of physical structure, especially in respect of the maternal functions, and also in the fact that historically woman has always been dependent upon man, who has established his control by superior physical strength. The cases of *Riley, Miller* and *Bosley* follow in this respect the *Muller Case.* But the ancient inequality of the sexes, otherwise than physical, as suggested in the *Muller Case* (p. 421) has continued "with diminishing intensity." In view of the great—not to say revolutionary—changes which have taken place since that utterance, in the contractual, political and civil status of women, culminating in the Nineteenth Amendment, it is not unreasonable to say that these differences have now come almost, if not quite, to the vanishing point. In this aspect of the matter, while the physical differences must be recognized in appropriate cases, and legislation fixing hours or conditions of work may properly take them into account, we cannot accept the doctrine that women of mature age, *sui juris,* require or may be subjected to restrictions upon their liberty of contract which could not lawfully be imposed in the case of men under similar circumstances. To do so would be to ignore all the implications to be drawn from the present day trend of legislation, as well as that of common thought and usage, by which woman is accorded emancipation from the old doctrine that she must be given special protection or be subjected to special restraint in her contractual and civil relationships. . . .

If now, in the light furnished by the foregoing exceptions to the general rule forbidding legislative interference with freedom of contract, we examine and analyze the statute in question, we shall see that it differs from them in every material respect. It is not a law dealing with any business charged with a public interest or with public work, or to meet and tide over a temporary emergency. It has nothing to do with the character, methods or periods of wage payments. It does not prescribe hours of labor or conditions under which labor is to be done. It is not for the protection of persons under legal disability or for the prevention of fraud. It is simply and exclusively a price-fixing law, confined to adult women (for we are not now considering the provisions relating to minors), who are legally as capable of contracting for themselves as men. . . .

The standard furnished by the statute for the guidance of the board is so vague as to be impossible of practical application with any reasonable degree of accuracy. What is sufficient to supply the necessary cost of living for a woman worker and maintain her in good health and protect her morals is obviously not a precise or unvarying sum—not even approximately so. The amount will depend upon a variety of circumstances: the individual temperament, habits of thrift, care, ability to buy necessaries intelligently, and whether the woman live alone or with her family. To those who practice economy, a given sum will afford comfort, while to those of contrary habit the same sum will be wholly inadequate. The coöperative economies of the family group are not taken into account though they constitute an important consideration in estimating the cost of living, for it is obvious that the individual expense will be less in the case of a member of a family than in the case of one living alone. The relation between earnings and morals is not capable of standardization. It cannot be shown that well paid women safeguard their morals more carefully than those who are poorly paid. Morality rests upon other considerations than wages; and there is, certainly, no such prevalent connection between the two as to justify a broad attempt to adjust the latter with reference to the former. . . .

It is said that great benefits have resulted from the operation of such statutes, not alone in the District of Columbia but in the several States, where they have been in force. A mass of reports, opinions of special observers and students of the subject, and the like, has been brought before us in support of this statement, all of which we have found interesting but only mildly persuasive. . . .

Finally, it may be said that if, in the interest of the public welfare, the police power may be invoked to justify the fixing of a minimum wage, it may, when the public welfare is thought to require it, be invoked to justify a maximum wage. The power to fix high wages connotes, by like course of reasoning, the power to fix low wages. If, in the face of the guaranties of the Fifth Amendment, this form of legislation shall be legally justified, the field for the operation of the police power will have been widened to a great and dangerous degree. . . .

It has been said that legislation of the kind now under review is required in the interest of social justice, for whose ends freedom of contract may lawfully be subjected to restraint. The liberty of the individual to do as he pleases, even in innocent matters, is not absolute. It must frequently yield to the common good, and the line beyond which the power of interference may not be pressed is neither definite nor unalterable but may be made to move, within limits not well defined, with changing need and circumstance. Any attempt to fix a rigid boundary would be unwise as well as futile. But, nevertheless, there are limits to the power, and when these have been passed, it becomes the plain duty of the courts in the proper exercise of their authority to so declare. To sustain the individual freedom of action contemplated by the Constitution, is not to strike down the common good but to exalt it; for surely the good of society as a whole cannot be better served than by the preservation against arbitrary restraint of the liberties of its constituent members.

It follows from what has been said that the act in question passes the limit prescribed by the Constitution, and, accordingly, the decrees of the court below are

Affirmed.

MR. JUSTICE BRANDEIS took no part in the consideration or decision of these cases.

MR. CHIEF JUSTICE TAFT, dissenting.

I regret much to differ from the Court in these cases.

The boundary of the police power beyond which its exercise becomes an invasion of the guaranty of liberty under the Fifth and Fourteenth

Amendments to the Constitution is not easy to mark. Our Court has been laboriously engaged in pricking out a line in successive cases. We must be careful, it seems to me, to follow that line as well as we can and not to depart from it by suggesting a distinction that is formal rather than real.

Legislatures in limiting freedom of contract between employee and employer by a minimum wage proceed on the assumption that employees, in the class receiving least pay, are not upon a full level of equality of choice with their employer and in their necessitous circumstances are prone to accept pretty much anything that is offered. They are peculiarly subject to the overreaching of the harsh and greedy employer. The evils of the sweating system and of the long hours and low wages which are characteristic of it are well known. Now, I agree that it is a disputable question in the field of political economy how far a statutory requirement of maximum hours or minimum wages may be a useful remedy for these evils, and whether it may not make the case of the oppressed employee worse than it was before. But it is not the function of this Court to hold congressional acts invalid simply because they are passed to carry out economic views which the Court believes to be unwise or unsound.

. . .

[Chief Justice Taft cites earlier cases in which the Court upheld legislation setting maximum hours.]

. . . I assume that the conclusion in this case rests on the distinction between a minimum of wages and a maximum of hours in the limiting of liberty to contract. I regret to be at variance with the Court as to the substance of this distinction. In absolute freedom of contract the one term is as important as the other, for both enter equally into the consideration given and received, a restriction as to one is not any greater in essence than the other, and is of the same kind. One is the multiplier and the other the multiplicand.

If it be said that long hours of labor have a more direct effect upon the health of the employee than the low wage, there is very respectable authority from close observers, disclosed in the record and in the literature on the subject quoted at length in the briefs, that they are equally harmful in this

regard. Congress took this view and we can not say it was not warranted in so doing.

With deference to the very able opinion of the Court and my brethren who concur in it, it appears to me to exaggerate the importance of the wage term of the contract of employment as more inviolate than its other terms. Its conclusion seems influenced by the fear that the concession of the power to impose a minimum wage must carry with it a concession of the power to fix a maximum wage. This, I submit, is a *non sequitur*. A line of distinction like the one under discussion in this case is, as the opinion elsewhere admits, a matter of degree and practical experience and not of pure logic. Certainly the wide difference between prescribing a minimum wage and a maximum wage could as a matter of degree and experience be easily affirmed.

. . .

I am not sure from a reading of the opinion whether the Court thinks the authority of *Muller* v. *Oregon* is shaken by the adoption of the Nineteenth Amendment. The Nineteenth Amendment did not change the physical strength or limitations of women upon which the decision in *Muller* v. *Oregon* rests. The Amendment did give women political power and makes more certain that legislative provisions for their protection will be in accord with their interests as they see them. But I don't think we are warranted in varying constitutional construction based on physical differences between men and women, because of the Amendment.

But for my inability to agree with some general observations in the forcible opinion of MR. JUSTICE HOLMES who follows me, I should be silent and merely record my concurrence in what he says. It is perhaps wiser for me, however, in a case of this importance, separately to give my reasons for dissenting.

I am authorized to say that MR. JUSTICE SANFORD concurs in this opinion.

MR. JUSTICE HOLMES, dissenting.
The question in this case is the broad one, Whether Congress can establish minimum rates of wages for women in the District of Columbia with

due provision for special circumstances, or whether we must say that Congress has no power to meddle with the matter at all. To me, notwithstanding the deference due to the prevailing judgment of the Court, the power of Congress seems absolutely free from doubt. The end, to remove conditions leading to ill health, immorality and the deterioration of the race, no one would deny to be within the scope of constitutional legislation. The means are means that have the approval of Congress, of many States, and of those governments from which we have learned our greatest lessons. When so many intelligent persons, who have studied the matter more than any of us can, have thought that the means are effective and are worth the price, it seems to me impossible to deny that the belief reasonably may be held by reasonable men. If the law encountered no other objection than that the means bore no relation to the end or that they cost too much I do not suppose that anyone would venture to say that it was bad. I agree, of course, that a law answering the foregoing requirements might be invalidated by specific provisions of the Constitution. For instance it might take private property without just compensation. But in the present instance the only objection that can be urged is found within the vague contours of the Fifth Amendment, prohibiting the depriving any person of liberty or property without due process of law. To that I turn.

The earlier decisions upon the same words in the Fourteenth Amendment began within our memory and went no farther than an unpretentious assertion of the liberty to follow the ordinary callings. Later that innocuous generality was expanded into the dogma, Liberty of Contract. Contract is not specially mentioned in the text that we have to construe. It is merely an example of doing what you want to do, embodied in the word liberty. But pretty much all law consists in forbidding men to do some things that they want to do, and contract is no more exempt from law than other acts. Without enumerating all the restrictive laws that have been upheld I will mention a few that seem to me to have interfered with liberty of contract quite as seriously and directly as the one before us. Usury laws prohibit contracts by which a man receives more than so much interest for the money that he lends. Statutes of frauds restrict many contracts to certain forms. Some Sunday laws prohibit practically all contracts during one-seventh of our whole life. Insurance rates may be regulated. . . .

I confess that I do not understand the principle on which the power to fix a minimum for the wages of women can be denied by those who admit the power to fix a maximum for their hours of work. I fully assent to the proposition that here as elsewhere the distinctions of the law are distinctions of degree, but I perceive no difference in the kind or degree of interference with liberty, the only matter with which we have any concern, between the one case and the other. The bargain is equally affected whichever half you regulate. *Muller* v. *Oregon*, I take it, is as good law today as it was in 1908. It will need more than the Nineteenth Amendment to convince me that there are no differences between men and women, or that legislation cannot take those differences into account. I should not hesitate to take them into account if I thought it necessary to sustain this act. *Quong Wing* v. *Kirkendall*, 223 U.S. 59, 63. But after *Bunting* v. *Oregon*, 243 U.S. 426, I had supposed that it was not necessary, and that *Lochner* v. *New York*, 198 U.S. 45, would be allowed a deserved repose.

. . .

I am of opinion that the statute is valid and that the decree should be reversed.

West Coast Hotel Co. v. Parrish

300 U.S. 379 (1937)

This case overruled *Adkins* v. *Children's Hospital* (1923) and, with it, the doctrine that courts can continually second-guess legislative judgments about the need for statutes governing minimum wages, maximum hours, and other aspects of industrial working conditions. Similarly, this case rejects the exalted notion of "liberty of contract" which presupposed an equality of power between employer and employee to work out a mutually satisfactory contract. The issue before the Court in this case was a statute of the state of Washington providing for the establishment of minimum wages for women.

MR. CHIEF JUSTICE HUGHES delivered the opinion of the Court.

. . .

The appellant conducts a hotel. The appellee Elsie Parrish was employed as a chambermaid and (with her husband) brought this suit to recover the difference between the wages paid her and the minimum wage fixed pursuant to the state law. The minimum wage was $14.50 per week of 48 hours. The appellant challenged the act as repugnant to the due process clause of the Fourteenth Amendment of the Constitution of the United States. The Supreme Court of the State, reversing the trial court, sustained the statute and directed judgment for the plaintiffs. *Parrish* v. *West Coast Hotel Co.*, 185 Wash. 581; 55 P. (2d) 1083. The case is here on appeal.

The appellant relies upon the decision of this Court in *Adkins* v. *Children's Hospital*, 261 U.S. 525, which held invalid the District of Columbia Minimum Wage Act, which was attacked under the due process clause of the Fifth Amendment. On the argument at bar, counsel for the appellees attempted to distinguish the *Adkins* case upon the ground that the appellee was employed in a hotel and that the business of an innkeeper was affected with a public interest. That effort at distinction is obviously futile, as it appears that in one of the cases ruled by the *Adkins* opinion the employee was a woman employed as an elevator operator in a hotel. *Adkins* v. *Lyons*, 261 U.S. 525, at p. 542.

The recent case of *Morehead* v. *New York ex rel. Tipaldo*, 298 U.S. 587, came here on certiorari to the New York court, which had held the New York minimum wage act for women to be invalid. A minority of this Court thought that the New York statute was distinguishable in a material feature from that involved in the *Adkins* case, and that for that and other reasons the New York statute should be sustained. But the Court of Appeals of New York had said that it found no material difference between the two statutes, and this Court held that the "meaning of the statute" as fixed by the decision of the state court "must be accepted here as if the meaning had been specifically expressed in the enactment." *Id.*, p. 609. That view led to the affirmance by this Court of the judgment in the *Morehead* case, as the Court considered that the only question before it was whether the *Adkins* case was distinguishable and that reconsideration of that decision had not been sought. Upon that point the Court said: "The petition for the writ sought review upon the ground that this case [Morehead] is distinguishable from that one [Adkins]. No application has been made for reconsideration of the constitutional question there decided. The validity of the principles upon which that decision rests is not challenged. This court confines itself to the ground upon which the writ was asked or granted . . . Here the review granted was no broader than that sought by the petitioner . . . He is not entitled and does not ask to be heard upon the question whether the *Adkins* case should be overruled. He maintains that it may be distinguished on the ground that the statutes are vitally dissimilar." *Id.*, pp. 604, 605.

We think that the question which was not deemed to be open in the *Morehead* case is open and is necessarily presented here. The Supreme Court of Washington has upheld the minimum wage statute of that State. It has decided that the statute is a reasonable exercise of the police power of the State. In reaching that conclusion the state court has invoked principles long established by this Court in the application of the Fourteenth Amendment. The state court has refused to regard the decision in the *Adkins* case as determinative and has pointed to our decisions both before and since that case as justifying its position. We are of the opinion that this ruling of the state court demands on our part a reëxamination of the *Adkins* case. The importance of the question, in which many States having similar laws are concerned, the close division by which the decision in the *Adkins* case was reached, and the economic conditions which have supervened, and in the light of which the reasonableness of the exercise of the protective power of the State must be considered, make it not only appropriate, but we think imperative, that in deciding the present case the subject should receive fresh consideration.

. . .

The principle which must control our decision is not in doubt. The constitutional provision invoked is the due process clause of the Fourteenth Amendment governing the States, as the due process clause invoked in the *Adkins* case governed Congress. In each case the violation alleged by those attacking minimum wage regulation for women is deprivation of freedom of contract. What is this freedom? The Constitution does not speak of freedom of contract. It speaks of liberty and prohibits the deprivation of liberty without due process of law. In prohibiting that deprivation the Constitution does not recognize an absolute and uncontrollable liberty. Liberty in each of its phases has its history and connotation. But the liberty safeguarded is liberty in a social organization which requires the protection of law against the evils which menace the health, safety, morals and welfare of the people. Liberty under the Constitution is thus necessarily subject to the restraints of due process, and regulation which is reasonable in relation to its subject and is adopted in the interests of the community is due process.

This essential limitation of liberty in general governs freedom of contract in particular. More than twenty-five years ago we set forth the applicable principle in these words, after referring to the cases where the liberty guaranteed by the Fourteenth Amendment had been broadly described:

"But it was recognized in the cases cited, as in many others, that freedom of contract is a qualified and not an absolute right. There is no absolute freedom to do as one wills or to contract as one chooses. The guaranty of liberty does not withdraw from legislative supervision that wide department of activity which consists of the making of contracts, or deny to government the power to provide restrictive safeguards. Liberty implies the absence of arbitrary restraint, not immunity from reasonable regulations and prohibitions imposed in the interests of the community." *Chicago, B. & Q. R. Co.* v. *McGuire,* 219 U.S. 549, 567.

This power under the Constitution to restrict freedom of contract has had many illustrations. That it may be exercised in the public interest with respect to contracts between employer and employee is undeniable. Thus statutes have been sustained limiting employment in underground mines and smelters to eight hours a day (*Holden* v. *Hardy,* 169 U.S. 366); in requiring redemption in cash of store orders or other evidences of indebtedness issued in the payment of wages (*Knoxville Iron Co.* v. *Harbison,* 183 U.S. 13); in forbidding the payment of seamen's wages in advance (*Patterson* v. *Bark Eudora,* 190 U.S. 169); in making it unlawful to contract to pay miners employed at quantity rates upon the basis of screened coal instead of the weight of the coal as originally produced in the mine (*McLean* v. *Arkansas,* 211 U.S. 539); in prohibiting contracts limiting liability for injuries to employees *(Chicago, B. & Q. R. Co.* v. *McGuire, supra);* in limiting hours of work of employees in manufacturing establishments (*Bunting* v. *Oregon,* 243 U.S. 426); and in maintaining workmen's compensation laws (*New York Central R. Co.* v. *White,* 243 U.S. 188; *Mountain Timber Co.* v. *Washington,* 243 U.S. 219). In dealing with the relation of employer and employed, the legislature has necessarily a wide field of discretion in order that there may be suitable protection of health and safety, and that peace and good order may be promoted through regulations designed to insure wholesome conditions of work and freedom from oppression. *Chicago, B. & Q. R. Co.* v. *McGuire, supra,* p. 570.

The point that has been strongly stressed that adult employees should be deemed competent to make their own contracts was decisively met nearly forty years ago in *Holden* v. *Hardy, supra,* where we pointed out the inequality in the footing of the parties. We said (*Id.,* 397):

"The legislature has also recognized the fact, which the experience of legislators in many States has corroborated, that the proprietors of these establishments and their operatives do not stand upon an equality, and that their interests are, to a certain extent, conflicting. The former naturally desire to obtain as much labor as possible from their employes, while the latter are often induced by the fear of discharge to conform to regulations which their judgment, fairly exercised, would pronounce to be detrimental to their health or strength. In other words, the proprietors lay down the rules and the laborers are practically constrained to obey them. In such cases self-interest is often an unsafe guide, and the legislature may properly interpose its authority."

. . .

It is manifest that this established principle is peculiarly applicable in relation to the employment of women in whose protection the State has a special interest. That phase of the subject received elaborate consideration in *Muller* v. *Oregon* (1908), 208 U.S. 412, where the constitutional authority of the State to limit the working hours of women was sustained. . . .

[After reviewing the dissents of Justice Holmes and Chief Justice Taft in Adkins, *and citing cases after* Adkins *that upheld state statutes on economic regulation, the Court concludes:]*

With full recognition of the earnestness and vigor which characterize the prevailing opinion in the *Adkins* case, we find it impossible to reconcile that ruling with these well-considered declara-

tions. What can be closer to the public interest than the health of women and their protection from unscrupulous and overreaching employers? And if the protection of women is a legitimate end of the exercise of state power, how can it be said that the requirement of the payment of a minimum wage fairly fixed in order to meet the very necessities of existence is not an admissible means to that end? The legislature of the State was clearly entitled to consider the situation of women in employment, the fact that they are in the class receiving the least pay, that their bargaining power is relatively weak, and that they are the ready victims of those who would take advantage of their necessitous circumstances. . . .

There is an additional and compelling consideration which recent economic experience has brought into a strong light. The exploitation of a class of workers who are in an unequal position with respect to bargaining power and are thus relatively defenceless against the denial of a living wage is not only detrimental to their health and well being but casts a direct burden for their support upon the community. What these workers lose in wages the taxpayers are called upon to pay. The bare cost of living must be met. We may take judicial notice of the unparalleled demands for relief which arose during the recent period of depression and still continue to an alarming extent despite the degree of economic recovery which has been achieved. It is unnecessary to cite official statistics to establish what is of common knowledge through the length and breadth of the land. While in the instant case no factual brief has been presented, there is no reason to doubt that the State of Washington has encountered the same social problem that is present elsewhere. The community is not bound to provide what is in effect a subsidy for unconscionable employers. . . .

. . .

Our conclusion is that the case of *Adkins* v. *Children's Hospital, supra,* should be, and it is, overruled. The judgment of the Supreme Court of the State of Washington is

Affirmed.

MR. JUSTICE SUTHERLAND, dissenting:

MR. JUSTICE VAN DEVANTER, MR. JUSTICE McREYNOLDS, MR. JUSTICE BUTLER and I think the judgment of the court below should be reversed.

. . .

Under our form of government, where the written Constitution, by its own terms, is the supreme law, some agency, of necessity, must have the power to say the final word as to the validity of a statute assailed as unconstitutional. The Constitution makes it clear that the power has been intrusted to this court when the question arises in a controversy within its jurisdiction; and so long as the power remains there, its exercise cannot be avoided without betrayal of the trust.

It has been pointed out many times, as in the *Adkins* case, that this judicial duty is one of gravity and delicacy; and that rational doubts must be resolved in favor of the constitutionality of the statute. But whose doubts, and by whom resolved? Undoubtedly it is the duty of a member of the court, in the process of reaching a right conclusion, to give due weight to the opposing views of his associates; but in the end, the question which he must answer is not whether such views seem sound to those who entertain them, but whether they convince him that the statute is constitutional or engender in his mind a rational doubt upon that issue. The oath which he takes as a judge is not a composite oath, but an individual one. And in passing upon the validity of a statute, he discharges a duty imposed upon *him*, which cannot be consummated justly by an automatic acceptance of the views of others which have neither convinced, nor created a reasonable doubt in, his mind. If upon a question so important he thus surrender his deliberate judgment, he stands forsworn. He cannot subordinate his convictions to that extent and keep faith with his oath or retain his judicial and moral independence.

The suggestion that the only check upon the exercise of the judicial power, when properly invoked, to declare a constitutional right superior to an unconstitutional statute is the judge's own faculty of self-restraint, is both ill considered and mischievous. Self-restraint belongs in the domain of will and not of judgment. The check upon the judge is that imposed by his oath of office, by the Constitution and by his own conscientious and informed convictions; and since he has the duty to make up his own mind and adjudge accordingly, it is hard to see how there could be any other restraint. This court acts as a unit. It cannot act in any other way; and the majority (whether a bare majority or a majority of all but one of its members), therefore, establishes the controlling rule as the decision of the court, binding, so long as it remains unchanged, equally upon those who disagree and upon those who subscribe to it. Otherwise, orderly administration of justice would cease. But it is the right of those in the minority to disagree, and sometimes, in matters of grave importance, their imperative duty to voice their disagreement at such length as the occasion demands—always, of course, in terms which, however forceful, do not offend the proprieties or impugn the good faith of those who think otherwise.

It is urged that the question involved should now receive fresh consideration, among other reasons, because of "the economic conditions which have supervened"; but the meaning of the Constitution does not change with the ebb and flow of economic events. We frequently are told in more general words that the Constitution must be construed in the light of the present. If by that it is meant that the Constitution is made up of living words that apply to every new condition which they include, the statement is quite true. But to say, if that be intended, that the words of the Constitution mean today what they did not mean when written—that is, that they do not apply to a situation now to which they would have applied then—is to rob that instrument of the essential element which continues it in force as the people have made it until they, and not their official agents, have made it otherwise.

. . .

Coming, then, to a consideration of the Washington statute, it first is to be observed that it is in every substantial respect identical with the statute involved in the *Adkins* case. Such vices as existed in the latter are present in the former. And if the

Adkins case was properly decided, as we who join in this opinion think it was, it necessarily follows that the Washington statute is invalid.

In support of minimum-wage legislation it has been urged, on the one hand, that great benefits will result in favor of underpaid labor, and, on the other hand, that the danger of such legislation is that the minimum will tend to become the maximum and thus bring down the earnings of the more efficient toward the level of the less-efficient employees. But with these speculations we have nothing to do. We are concerned only with the question of constitutionality.

That the clause of the Fourteenth Amendment which forbids a state to deprive any person of life, liberty or property without due process of law includes freedom of contract is so well settled as to be no longer open to question. Nor reasonably can it be disputed that contracts of employment of labor are included in the rule. *Adair* v. *United States*, 208 U.S. 161, 174–175; *Coppage* v. *Kansas*, 236 U.S. 1, 10, 14. In the first of these cases, Mr. Justice Harlan, speaking for the court, said, "The right of a person to sell his labor upon such terms as he deems proper is, in its essence, the same as the right of the purchaser of labor to prescribe the conditions upon which he will accept such labor from the person offering to sell. . . . In all such particulars the employer and employé have equality of right, and any legislation that disturbs that equality is an arbitrary interference with the liberty of contract which no government can legally justify in a free land."

In the *Adkins* case we referred to this language, and said that while there was no such thing as absolute freedom of contract, but that it was subject to a great variety of restraints, nevertheless, freedom of contract was the general rule and restraint the exception; and that the power to abridge that freedom could only be justified by the existence of exceptional circumstances. This statement of the rule has been many times affirmed; and we do not understand that it is questioned by the present decision.

. . .

The Washington statute, like the one for the District of Columbia, fixes minimum wages for adult women. Adult men and their employers are left free to bargain as they please; and it is a significant and an important fact that all state statutes to which our attention has been called are of like character. The common-law rules restricting the power of women to make contracts have, under our system, long since practically disappeared. Women today stand upon a legal and political equality with men. There is no longer any reason why they should be put in different classes in respect of their legal right to make contracts; nor should they be denied, in effect, the right to compete with men for work paying lower wages which men may be willing to accept. And it is an arbitrary exercise of the legislative power to do so.

. . .

Ferguson v. Skrupa

372 U.S. 726 (1963)

For a period of about four or five decades, ending in 1937, the Supreme Court overturned dozens of statutes enacted by Congress and state legislatures to ameliorate the conditions of industrialization. Laws establishing minimum wages and maximum hours, regulating child labor, and governing other aspects of industrial society were struck down. In this decision, the Court explains that such matters are left essentially to legislatures, not courts.

MR. JUSTICE BLACK delivered the opinion of the Court.

In this case, properly here on appeal under 28 U.S.C. § 1253, we are asked to review the judgment of a three-judge District Court enjoining, as being in violation of the Due Process Clause of the Fourteenth Amendment, a Kansas statute making it a misdemeanor for any person to engage "in the business of debt adjusting" except as an incident to "the lawful practice of law in this state." The statute defines "debt adjusting" as "the making of a contract, express or implied, with a particular debtor whereby the debtor agrees to pay a certain amount of money periodically to the person engaged in the debt adjusting business who shall for a consideration distribute the same among certain specified creditors in accordance with a plan agreed upon."

The complaint, filed by appellee Skrupa doing business as "Credit Advisors," alleged that Skrupa was engaged in the business of "debt adjusting" as defined by the statute, that his business was a "useful and desirable" one, that his business activities were not "inherently immoral or dangerous" or in any way contrary to the public welfare, and that therefore the business could not be "absolutely prohibited" by Kansas. The three-judge court heard evidence by Skrupa tending to show the usefulness and desirability of his business and evidence by the state officials tending to show that "debt adjusting" lends itself to grave abuses against distressed debtors, particularly in the lower income brackets, and that these abuses are of such gravity that a number of States have strictly regulated "debt adjusting" or prohibited it altogether. The court found that Skrupa's business did fall within the Act's proscription and concluded, one judge dissenting, that the Act was prohibitory, not regulatory, but that even if construed in part as regulatory it was an unreasonable regulation of a "lawful business," which the court held amounted to a violation of the Due Process Clause of the Fourteenth Amendment. The court accordingly enjoined enforcement of the statute.

The only case discussed by the court below as support for its invalidation of the statute was *Commonwealth* v. *Stone*, 191 Pa. Super. 117, 155 A. 2d 453 (1959), in which the Superior Court of Pennsylvania struck down a statute almost identical to the Kansas act involved here. In *Stone* the Pennsylvania court held that the State could regulate, but could not prohibit, a "legitimate" business. Finding debt adjusting, called "budget planning" in the Pennsylvania statute, not to be "against the public interest" and concluding that it could "see no justification for such interference" with this business, the Pennsylvania court ruled that State's statute to be unconstitutional. In doing so, the Pennsylvania court relied heavily on *Adams* v. *Tanner*, 244 U.S. 590 (1917), which held that the Due Process Clause forbids a State to prohibit a business which is "useful" and not "inherently immoral or dangerous to public welfare."

Both the District Court in the present case and the Pennsylvania court in *Stone* adopted the philosophy of *Adams* v. *Tanner*, and cases like it, that it is the province of courts to draw on their own views as to the morality, legitimacy, and usefulness of a particular business in order to decide whether a statute bears too heavily upon that business and by so doing violates due process. Under the system of government created by our Constitution, it is up to legislatures, not courts, to decide on the wisdom and utility of legislation. There was a time when the Due Process Clause was used by this Court to strike down laws which were thought unreasonable, that is, unwise or incompatible with some particular economic or social philosophy. In this manner the Due Process Clause was used, for example, to nullify laws prescribing maximum hours for work in bakeries, *Lochner* v. *New York*, 198 U.S. 45 (1905), outlawing "yellow dog" contracts, *Coppage* v. *Kansas*, 236 U.S. 1 (1915), setting minimum wages for women, *Adkins* v. *Children's Hospital*, 261 U.S. 525 (1923), and fixing the weight of loaves of bread, *Jay Burns Baking Co.* v. *Bryan*, 264 U.S. 504 (1924). This intrusion by the judiciary into the realm of legislative value judgments was strongly objected to at the time, particularly by Mr. Justice Holmes and Mr. Justice Brandeis. Dissenting from the Court's invalidating a state statute which regulated the resale price of theatre and other tickets, Mr. Justice Holmes said,

"I think the proper course is to recognize that a state legislature can do whatever it sees fit to do unless it is restrained by some express prohibition in the Constitution of the United States or of the State, and that Courts should be careful not to extend such prohibitions beyond their obvious meaning by reading into them conceptions of public policy that the particular Court may happen to entertain."

And in an earlier case he had emphasized that, "The criterion of constitutionality is not whether we believe the law to be for the public good."

The doctrine that prevailed in *Lochner*, *Coppage*, *Adkins*, *Burns*, and like cases—that due process authorizes courts to hold laws unconstitutional when they believe the legislature has acted unwisely—has long since been discarded. We have returned to the original constitutional proposition that courts do not substitute their social and economic beliefs for the judgment of legislative bodies, who are elected to pass laws. As this Court stated in a unanimous opinion in 1941, "We are not concerned . . . with the wisdom, need, or appropriateness of the legislation." Legislative bodies have broad scope to experiment with economic problems, and this Court does not sit to "subject the State to an intolerable supervision hostile to the basic principles of our Government and wholly beyond the protection which the general clause of the Fourteenth Amendment was intended to secure." It is now settled that States "have power to legislate against what are found to be injurious practices in their internal commercial and business affairs, so long as their laws do not run afoul of some specific federal constitutional prohibition, or of some valid federal law."

In the face of our abandonment of the use of the "vague contours" of the Due Process Clause to nullify laws which a majority of the Court believed to be economically unwise, reliance on *Adams* v. *Tanner* is as mistaken as would be adherence to *Adkins* v. *Children's Hospital*, overruled by *West Coast Hotel Co.* v. *Parrish*, 300 U.S. 379 (1937). Not only has the philosophy of *Adams* been abandoned, but also this Court almost 15 years ago expressly pointed to another opinion of this Court

as having "clearly undermined" *Adams*. We conclude that the Kansas Legislature was free to decide for itself that legislation was needed to deal with the business of debt adjusting. Unquestionably, there are arguments showing that the business of debt adjusting has social utility, but such arguments are properly addressed to the legislature, not to us. We refuse to sit as a "superlegislature to weigh the wisdom of legislation," and we emphatically refuse to go back to the time when courts used the Due Process Clause "to strike down state laws, regulatory of business and industrial conditions, because they may be unwise, improvident, or out of harmony with a particular school of thought." Nor are we able or willing to draw lines by calling a law "prohibitory" or "regulatory." Whether the legislature takes for its textbook Adam Smith, Herbert Spencer, Lord Keynes, or some other is no concern of ours. The Kansas debt adjusting statute may be wise or unwise. But relief, if any be needed, lies not with us but with the body constituted to pass laws for the State of Kansas.

Nor is the statute's exception of lawyers a denial of equal protection of the laws to nonlawyers. Statutes create many classifications which do not deny equal protection; it is only "invidious discrimination" which offends the Constitution. The business of debt adjusting gives rise to a relationship of trust in which the debt adjuster will, in a situation of insolvency, be marshalling assets in the manner of a proceeding in bankruptcy. The debt adjuster's client may need advice as to the legality of the various claims against him, remedies existing under state laws governing debtor-creditor relationships, or provisions of the Bankruptcy Act—advice which a nonlawyer cannot lawfully give him. If the State of Kansas wants to limit debt adjusting to lawyers, the Equal Protection Clause does not forbid it. We also find no merit in the contention that the Fourteenth Amendment is violated by the failure of the Kansas statute's title to be as specific as appellee thinks it ought to be under the Kansas Constitution.

Reversed.

MR. JUSTICE HARLAN concurs in the judgment on the ground that this state measure bears a rational relation to a constitutionally permissible objective. See *Williamson* v. *Lee Optical Co.,* 348 U.S. 483, 491.

10 Free Speech in a Democratic Society

T he foundations for a free and open society are contained in the First Amendment: "Congress shall make no law respecting an establishment of religion, or prohibiting the free exercise thereof; or abridging the freedom of speech, or of the press; or the right of the people peaceably to assemble, and to petition the Government for a redress of grievances." Through these words the framers attempted to secure the freedom of conscience and the free communication of ideas. To Justice Cardozo, the freedom of thought and speech forms "the matrix, the indispensable condition, of nearly every other form of freedom." Palko v. Connecticut, 302 U.S. 319, 327 (1937).

Free speech fulfills a number of personal, social, and political functions. The right of free speech, however, is not absolute. It has been constrained for reasons of "national security" and necessary state regulations. A related right, the "freedom of association," is not mentioned in the Constitution, but is considered an implied right and has been protected both by courts and legislatures. After discussing these issues, this chapter analyzes the different forms of speech: symbolic speech, "speech plus," commercial speech, and the rights of broadcasters.

The First Amendment protects a number of values. In part, it strengthens individual growth and self-fulfillment. In the words of Justice Brandeis, it exists to "make men free to develop their faculties." Whitney v. California, 274 U.S. 357, 375 (1927). The First Amendment also protects the "marketplace" of ideas, the promotion of knowledge, and the search for truth. Finally, the First Amendment "serves to ensure that the individual citizen can effectively participate in and contribute to our republican system of self-government." Globe Newspaper Co. v. Superior Court, 457 U.S. 596, 604 (1982). In this sense it reinforces the full political debate needed in a vigorous and healthy democratic society. The House debate on the First Amendment, as proposed by James Madison, is reprinted on pages 551–554.

Only by tolerating different ideas and beliefs can democracy function and survive, especially in a culture as heterogeneous and heterodox as the United States. The history of America is largely the repudiation of orthodoxy by the spirit of individualism and nonconformism. Diversity is a value in itself. In a famous dissent in 1929,

Justice Holmes said that "if there is any principle of the Constitution that more imperatively calls for attachment than any other it is the principle of free thought— not free thought for those who agree with us but freedom for the thought that we hate." United States v. Schwimmer, 279 U.S. 644, 654–655 (1929). The spirit of the First Amendment is captured with extraordinary eloquence by Justice Brandeis in his concurrence in WHITNEY v. CALIFORNIA, 274 U.S. 357 (1927).

Even if the Constitution lacked a First Amendment, representative government requires that citizens be free to discuss government and debate its policies. Some forms of speech make government impossible, such as actions that disrupt legislatures and courts. The following sections identify the major tests used to scrutinize governmental limitations placed on speech.

FREE SPEECH AND NATIONAL SECURITY

In certain periods of our history speech has been suppressed and punished. The heavy hand of the majority fell against sympathizers with France during the 1790s; labor organizers, anarchists, and socialists in the late nineteenth and early twentieth centuries; opponents of World War I; the Communists during and after World War II; and those who spoke out against the Vietnam war. Throughout these periods the Supreme Court attempted to fashion doctrines to protect pure speech but not action, activity, and advocacy. Distinctions between these categories remain opaque.

Sedition

In 1798, the Federalist party passed the notorious Alien and Sedition Acts to silence the opposition within the United States, particularly Republicans and "Francophiles." The Alien Acts increased the years of residence for aliens seeking citizenship, authorized deportation of "dangerous" aliens, and imposed other sanctions. 1 Stat. 566, 570, 577 (1798). The Sedition Act prohibited any person from printing or uttering "any false, scandalous and malicious" statement against the federal government, either House of Congress, or the President. 1 Stat. 596, § 2 (1798). This statute is analyzed more closely in the next chapter (pp. 620, 638–643).

The issue of sedition rarely surfaces in American politics. Not until the United States entered World War I did Congress pass another sedition act. Section 3 of the Espionage Act of 1917 prohibited acts that interfered with or obstructed military recruitment or morale. 40 Stat. 219. When opponents of the war attacked conscription and urged opposition to the draft, the government responded with criminal prosecutions. A unanimous Supreme Court upheld the indictments on the basis of wartime conditions and circumstances. Writing for the Court, Justice Holmes penned his famous admonition against "shouting fire in a theatre" and offered his "clear and present danger" test. SCHENCK v. UNITED STATES, 249 U.S. 47 (1919).

The Court issued similar rulings against war protesters that same month. Frohwerk v. United States, 294 U.S. 204 (1919); Debs v. United States, 249 U.S. 211 (1919). This line of cases developed the "bad tendency" test to curb speech that posed threats or a danger to society. Under this test, there need be no clear and present danger. The mere tendency to create evil justifies suppression.

In a penetrating critique in the *Harvard Law Review* in 1919, Zechariah Chafee, Jr., argued that the First Amendment declared a national policy "in favor of the public discussion of all public questions. Such a declaration should make Congress reluctant and careful in the enactment of all restrictions upon utterance, even though the courts will not refuse to enforce them as unconstitutional." 32 Harv. L. Rev. 932, 934 (1919). Chafee claimed that the framers adopted the First Amendment to give "the right of unrestricted discussion of public affairs," both in time of war and peace. The First Amendment protected not merely an individual's interest in speaking out but society's interest in hearing criticism and vigorous debate. Id. at 946, 955–959.

Following the appearance of this article, Holmes and Brandeis dissented in a free-speech case later that year. Five antiwar activists had been convicted for writing publications that criticized U.S. involvement in World War I, encouraged resistance, and urged workers not to produce war materials. Holmes wrote one of his memorable dissents, appealing for tolerance and the "free trade in ideas." ABRAMS v. UNITED STATES, 250 U.S. 616 (1919). The clear-and-present-danger test supposedly favors free speech more than the bad-tendency test, but these standards are applied unevenly.

The Sedition Act of 1918 made it illegal to utter "any disloyal, profane, scurrilous, or abusive language" about the form of government, the Constitution, soldiers and sailors, the flag, or uniform of the armed forces. 40 Stat. 553. State laws that declared it a misdemeanor to teach or advocate that citizens should not assist the United States in carrying on a war with its enemies were upheld. Gilbert v. Minnesota, 254 U.S. 325 (1920). A New York law punished persons for advocating the overthrow of government. The Court sustained the statute, treating such advocacy as "a call to action" rather than abstract doctrine. GITLOW v. NEW YORK, 268 U.S. 652 (1925). Holmes and Brandeis dissented, objecting that "[e]very idea is an incitement." In *Gitlow*, the Court also ruled that freedoms of speech and press are among the personal rights and liberties protected by the Due Process Clause of the Fourteenth Amendment. Just three years before, the Court had held that the Fourteenth Amendment did *not* impose upon the states an obligation to confer the right of free speech. Prudential Ins. Co. v. Cheek, 259 U.S. 530, 538, 542–543 (1922).

In two decisions in 1927, the Court tackled the issue of syndicalism: the doctrine that workers could use force to seize control of the economy and the government. A unanimous Court upheld California's statute against criminal syndicalism, but Justice Brandeis in his concurrence prepared a masterful essay on the principles of free speech. WHITNEY v. CALIFORNIA, 274 U.S. 357 (1927). Another unanimous opinion that year struck down Kansas' syndicalism statute because it punished class struggles unrelated to crime, violence, or other unlawful acts. Fiske v. Kansas, 274 U.S. 380 (1927). A California statute making it a felony to display a red flag to symbolize opposition to government was declared unconstitutionally vague. Stromberg v. California, 283 U.S. 359 (1931). Also on the ground of vagueness, the Court invalidated a Georgia statute that made it a crime to attempt to incite insurrection or resistance by force. Herndon v. Lowry, 301 U.S. 242 (1937).

National security interests were invoked during the Vietnam war to restrain free speech. A series of cases in 1968 and 1969 involved draft-card burning, the wearing of black arm bands to protest the war, and flag burning, all covered in a later section on symbolic speech (pp. 543–544). In addition, in 1970 a unanimous Court struck down a congressional statute that imposed criminal penalties for the unauthorized wearing of an American military uniform except for a theatrical or motion picture production that does not discredit the armed forces. The statute, applied against a skit that expressed opposition to American involvement in the Vietnam war, imposed an unconstitutional restraint on free speech by singling out for punishment productions that were unfavorable to the military. Schacht v. United States, 398 U.S. 58 (1970). (The Pentagon Papers Case, one of the key decisions on national security and the First Amendment, is discussed in Chapter 7 and in the next chapter.)

The Communist Cases

Following World War II, Congress placed a number of restrictions on members of the Communist party. The Labor Management Relations Act of 1947 required union officers to file a non-Communist affidavit. 61 Stat. 146, 9(h). The purpose was to remove obstructions to commerce from "political strikes" instigated by Communists. The Court, by a 4–2 vote, held that the statute bore a reasonable relation to the "evil" it was designed to reach and did not interfere with speech or thought. The statute, said the Court, was designed to regulate *conduct* and "Congress, not the courts, is primarily charged with determination of the need for regulation of activities affecting interstate commerce." American Communications Assn. v. Douds, 339 U.S. 382, 400 (1950). There was no actual conduct, however. The mere threat or capability of obstructing commerce was considered adequate grounds for the statute.

A year later, the Court decided the constitutionality of the Smith Act of 1940, which made it unlawful for any person to advocate the violent overthrow of "any government in the United States" or to conspire to advocate such violence. 54 Stat. 671, § 2. Divided 6–2, the Court upheld the statute against the charge that it violated the First Amendment because of indefiniteness. Although the Smith Act was aimed at potential conduct rather than actual conduct, the Court responded to the free-speech issue by saying that the statute was "directed at advocacy, not discussion." DENNIS v. UNITED STATES, 341 U.S. 494, 502 (1951). "We hold that the statute may be applied where there is a 'clear and present danger' of the substantive evil which the legislature had the right to prevent." Id. at 512. In his concurrence, Frankfurter conceded the difficulty of distinguishing between protected speech and unprotected advocacy: "It is true that there is no divining rod by which we may locate 'advocacy.' Exposition of ideas readily merges into advocacy." Id. at 545.

Dennis was severely circumscribed in 1957 when the Court reversed the convictions of fourteen Communists charged with advocating and teaching the overthrow of the United States government by force and violence. The Court held that the Smith Act did not prohibit advocacy and teaching of forcible overthrow as an abstract principle. As interpreted by the Court, the statute proscribed only the "advocacy of action to that end." The meaning of that phrase remains vague, but the effect has been to extend greater protection to pure advocacy. YATES v. UNITED STATES, 354 U.S. 298 (1957).

A unanimous Court in 1965 struck down a congressional statute that required the Postmaster General to withhold "communist political propaganda" from an addressee unless the person specifically stated in a return post card, within twenty days, that the materials be delivered. The Court held the statute an unconstitutional limitation on First Amendment rights because it imposed on addressees an affirmative obligation before receiving mail and threatened their livelihood by having to inform the government of their desire to receive blacklisted materials. Lamont v. Postmaster General, 381 U.S. 301 (1965).

Both Congress and the courts were involved in monitoring, and finally abolishing, the Subversive Activities Control Board (SACB), which had been authorized to order groups to register with the Attorney General as a "Communist-action" organization. An effort to adjudicate the statute was turned aside in 1956 because of alleged perjuries committed by three government witnesses. Communist Party v. SACB, 351 U.S. 115 (1956). Five years later the Court, with a 5–4 vote, affirmed the Board's finding that the Communist party was a Communist-action organization and therefore required to register with the Attorney General. Sidestepping such constitutional issues as free speech, bill of attainder, and self-incrimination, the Court concluded that the statute was "regulatory" rather than "prohibitory." Communist Party v. SACB, 367 U.S. 1 (1961). On that same day, in two decisions, the Court held that mere membership in the Communist party did not violate the Smith Act. Punishment could be applied only against members who actively advanced the party's aims. It is therefore no longer a crime to advocate, as an abstract doctrine, the forcible overthrow of government. Scales v. United States, 367 U.S. 203 (1961); Noto v. United States, 367 U.S. 290 (1961).

Other cases during this period also relaxed the pattern of rigid anticommunism. In 1965, the Court held that a congressional statute making it a crime for a Communist party member to serve as union officer constituted a bill of attainder. United States v. Brown, 381 U.S. 437. In the same year, a unanimous Court struck down the registration feature as a violation of the Self-Incrimination Clause because information submitted to the Attorney General could be used as evidence toward a criminal prosecution. Albertson v. SACB, 382 U.S. 70 (1965).

Congress rejuvenated the Subversive Activities Control Board in 1968 by authorizing it to determine, through hearings, whether individuals and organizations were Communist. The following year an appellate court declared that the new procedure violated the First Amendment freedom of association. Boorda v. SACB, 421 F.2d 1142 (D.C. Cir. 1969), cert. denied, 397 U.S. 1042 (1970). With the Board facing extinction, President Nixon issued an executive order expanding its power and field of inquiry. After Congress used its power of the purse to deny funds to carry out the executive order, the Board went out of business. Fisher, Constitutional Conflicts Between Congress and the President 132–133 (1985).

ASSOCIATIONAL RIGHTS

The Constitution does not expressly provide for a right of association. Gradually, however, the First Amendment and the "liberty" interest secured by the Fourteenth Amendment have been interpreted to protect a person's right to associate with others who share similar ideas, interests, and goals. Self-government is more than Self. In many ways, America is a nation of joiners. Americans band together to seek friendship, cooperation, and concerted action.

Associational rights were heavily litigated throughout the 1940s and 1950s, usually involving a person's membership in the Communist party or in organizations considered subversive to the national interest. For a time, these memberships were punished by government. In 1943, Congress passed legislation to deny salaries to three federal officials suspected of "subversive" activities. This statute was struck down by the Supreme Court in 1946 (pp. 577–581). However, the Court upheld Maryland's requirement that state candidates for office, before being placed on the ballot, take an oath or sign an affidavit that they were not engaged in an attempt to overthrow the government by force or violence and were not knowingly members of an organization engaged in such attempts. Gerende v. Election Board, 341 U.S. 56 (1951). Municipalities could require public employees to execute affidavits disclosing whether or not they were, or ever had been, members of Communist organizations. Garner v. Los Angeles Board, 341 U.S. 716 (1951). States were allowed to bar employment in public schools for any member of an organization advocating the overthrow of government by force, violence, or unlawful means. Adler v. Board of Education, 342 U.S. 485 (1952).

These cases provoked dissents from Justices who regarded these state laws as constitutionally offensive. In part, they objected to the use of "guilt by association" to punish people, often without even a hearing. The Court did manage to strike down "loyalty oaths" that required state employees to vow that they had not been a member of "Communist front" or "subversive" organizations. Such laws violated due process because membership might have been innocent and unknowing. Wieman v. Updegraff, 344 U.S. 183 (1952). By a 5–4 margin, the Court invalidated a city charter that stripped city employees of their jobs if they invoked the Self-Incrimination Clause before a legislative committee inquiring into their official conduct. These summary dismissals, said the Court, violated due process and made a mockery of the Fifth Amendment. Slochower v. Board of Education, 350 U.S. 551 (1956). The Court also used the Due Process Clause to protect attorneys who were refused permission to take the bar examination, or who were not allowed to practice after passing the bar, because of their associations with Communist organizations. Schware v. Board of Bar Examiners, 353 U.S. 232 (1957); Konigsberg v. State Bar, 353 U.S. 252 (1957).[1]

The Court's record on associational freedom for Communist and subversive organizations during this period was mixed.[2] The right of association in the NAACP was a different matter. When Alabama tried to obtain the membership list of the NAACP's state chapter, a unanimous Court held that members had a constitutional right to associate freely with others as part of the "liberty" protected by the Fourteenth Amendment. NAACP v. Alabama, 357 U.S. 449 (1958). Another unanimous ruling rejected compulsory disclosure of NAACP memberships as an unconstitutional interference with the freedom of association. Bates v. Little Rock, 361 U.S. 516 (1960). See also NAACP v. Button, 371 U.S. 415 (1963) and Gibson v. Florida Legislative Comm., 372 U.S. 539 (1963).[3] Minor parties, such as the Socialist Workers party, need not report the names of campaign contributors if it results in harassment and reprisals. Brown v. Socialist Workers '74 Campaign Comm., 459 U.S. 87 (1982).

By the 1960s, the Supreme Court was striking down loyalty oaths because they were so vague as to violate due process. Cramp v. Bd. of Public Instruction, 368 U.S. 278 (1961); Baggett v. Bullitt, 377 U.S. 360 (1964); Keyishian v. Board of Regents, 385 U.S. 589 (1967). The objection to "guilt by association" gained a Court majority by 1966. Elfbrandt v. Russell, 384 U.S. 11 (1966). In 1967, a 6–2 majority struck

---

[1] But see the confusing array of cases since that time: Konigsberg v. State Bar, 366 U.S. 36 (1961); In re Anastaplo, 366 U.S. 82 (1961); Baird v. State Bar of Arizona, 401 U.S. 1 (1971); In re Stolar, 401 U.S. 23 (1971); Law Students' Research Council v. Wadmond, 401 U.S. 154 (1971); In re Primus, 436 U.S. 412 (1978).

[2] Sweezy v. New Hampshire, 354 U.S. 234 (1957); Beilan v. Board of Education, 357 U.S. 399 (1958); Lerner v. Casey, 357 U.S. 468 (1958); Nelson v. Los Angeles County, 362 U.S. 1 (1960); Shelton v. Tucker, 364 U.S. 479 (1960).

[3] In 1928, the Court allowed states to obtain the membership lists of the Ku Klux Klan, because its conduct was "inimical to personal rights and public welfare." Bryant v. Zimmerman, 278 U.S. 63, 75 (1928).

down a congressional statute that sought to punish any worker at a defense facility who belonged to a Communist organization. The Court held that the statute abridged the right of association by reaching too broadly to include inactive members or those employed in nonsensitive jobs. United States v. Robel, 389 U.S. 258 (1967).

THE REGULATION OF SPEECH

The Free Speech Clause has never been interpreted to confer an absolute right. Although speech is constitutionally protected, government may adopt regulations to protect other societal interests. Citizens are not at liberty to commit perjury, to libel, or to infringe on copyrights. There is no constitutional right to "insist upon a street meeting in the middle of Times Square at the rush hour as a form of freedom of speech or assembly." Cox v. Louisiana, 379 U.S. 536, 554 (1965). To prevent the clogging of sidewalks and public streets, licenses may be required for parades and public processions. Cox v. New Hampshire, 312 U.S. 569 (1941). Sound trucks equipped with amplifiers and capable of generating "loud and raucous noises" may be prohibited. Kovacs v. Cooper, 336 U.S. 77 (1949); Saia v. New York, 334 U.S. 558 (1948). A mailer's right to communicate must stop at the mailbox of an addressee who objects to what is being sent. Rowan v. Post Office Dept., 397 U.S. 728 (1970).

The scope of free speech depends partly on where it is exercised. The Supreme Court has identified three places: the traditional public forum (public parks), a public forum designated by the government (state universities), and the nonpublic forum (private homes). For the first two, restrictions on free speech are subject to heightened scrutiny by the courts. The right of free speech applies to public forums. I have a right to express my views at a public assembly, not in your livingroom. When the state applies restrictions to speech, the general rule is that they be "content neutral." Government is not supposed to be a censor. When regulations are imposed to limit speech they cannot be "overbroad," pulling within their reach speech that is both protected and unprotected. Even for public parks, however, government may adopt "guidelines" to regulate the noise from rock concerts that disturbs park users and nearby apartment residents. Provided that the regulation is content neutral and narrowly tailored to serve "significant governmental interest," reasonable limits may be imposed on the time, place, and manner of protected speech. Ward v. Rock Against Racism, 109 S.Ct. 2746 (1989).

The Supreme Court has stated that regulation and suppression "are not the same, either in purpose or result, and courts of justice can tell the difference." Poulos v. New Hampshire, 345 U.S. 395, 408 (1953). However, regulation can become a code word to suppress speech that is unpopular with the majority or objectionable to local authorities. To compel labor organizers to obtain a card from a state official before soliciting memberships may simply be a guise to discourage trade unionism. Thomas v. Collins, 323 U.S. 516 (1945). It is legitimate to require speakers to fill out applications before using city parks for group meetings, but not when the applications are denied for arbitrary or discriminatory reasons, such as against a disliked minority sect or an objectionable speech. Under these conditions, the requirement for a license or permit constitutes forbidden censorship and prior restraint.

As a regulatory device, "breach of the peace" statutes can translate easily into suppression of speech. A 1963 case involved high school and college students who had been convicted for gathering peacefully on the grounds of the South Carolina legislature to express their grievances about state laws concerning black citizens. By an 8–1 vote, the Court held that the state had infringed the rights of free speech, free assembly, and freedom to petition for a redress of grievances. EDWARDS v. SOUTH CAROLINA, 372 U.S. 229 (1963).[4] More narrowly, by a 5–4 vote, the Court reversed the convictions of five black males who participated in an orderly, nondisruptive sit-in at a branch library to protest segregation. The Court protected their freedom of speech, assembly, and the right to petition. Brown v. Louisiana, 383 U.S. 131 (1966).

Speech is subject to greater restraint when the question is one not of orderly demonstrations, conducted without obstructing the functions of government, but rather disruptive sit-ins and trespasses. The Supreme Court upheld the convictions of students who demonstrated on the premises of a jail. ADDERLEY v. FLORIDA, 385 U.S. 39 (1966). Similarly, sit-in demonstrations, kneel-in demonstrations, and mass street parades may not continue in defiance of a temporary injunction issued by a judicial authority. Walker v. City of Birmingham, 388 U.S. 307 (1967).

Overly broad breach-of-the-peace statutes, directed against actions that "agitate" or arouse citizens "from a state of repose . . . to disquiet," are by their very nature antagonistic to the First Amendment. One function of the Free Speech Clause "is to invite dispute. It may indeed best serve its high purpose when it induces a condition of unrest, creates dissatisfaction with conditions as they are, or even stirs people to anger. Speech is often provocative and challenging." Cox v. Louisiana, 379 U.S. 536, 551–552 (1965), citing Terminiello v. Chicago, 337 U.S. 1, 4 (1949). A unanimous Court in 1969 struck down a state statute that made it illegal to advocate crime or violence to accomplish reform. In this case, involving a gathering of the Ku Klux Klan, the Court held that government may not forbid advocacy unless it is directed to incite imminent lawless action. BRANDENBURG v. OHIO, 395 U.S. 444 (1969).

The Court carefully monitors laws that restrict the solicitation of funds. One village required that charitable organizations use at least 75 percent of their receipts for "charitable purposes" to be eligible for door-to-door or on-street solicitation of contributions. An 8–1 decision found the ordinance unconstitutionally overbroad. Charitable appeals involve a variety of speech interests: communication of information, dissemination of views and ideas, and advocacy of causes. Schaumburg v. Citizens for Better Environ., 444 U.S. 620 (1980).[5]

Freedom of speech also includes the right not to support an ideology. In 1977, the Supreme Court struck down a requirement in New Hampshire that noncommercial vehicles carry license tags bearing the state motto, "Live Free or Die." Jehovah's Witnesses considered the motto repugnant to their moral, religious, and political beliefs. The Court held that a state may not force an individual to advertise an ideological message, using a car as a "mobile billboard." The First Amendment protects the freedom to speak and not to speak. Wooley v. Maynard, 430 U.S. 705 (1977). In that same year, in upholding a Michigan requirement that nonunion members pay a "service charge" to the union, the Court restricted the use of the funds. The union could use the money for collective bargaining, contract administration, and grievance-adjustment purposes, but could not force nonunion employ-

[4]See also Shuttlesworth v. Birmingham, 394 U.S. 147 (1969); Poulos v. New Hampshire, 345 U.S. 395 (1953); Fowler v. Rhode Island, 345 U.S. 67 (1953); Kunz v. New York, 340 U.S. 290 (1951); Niemotko v. Maryland, 340 U.S. 268 (1951).

[5]See also Cornelius v. NAACP Legal Defense & Ed. Fund, 473 U.S. 788 (1985); Secretary of State of Md. v. J. H. Munson Co., 467 U.S. 947 (1984); Breard v. Alexandria, 341 U.S. 622 (1951); Martin v. Struthers, 319 U.S. 141 (1943).

ees to contribute to ideological causes they oppose. Abood v. Detroit Board of Education, 431 U.S. 209 (1977).

Public Employees

The right of free speech for public employees poses unique problems. After much litigation to the contrary, it is now settled that public employees have a constitutional right to comment upon matters "of public concern." Pickering v. Board of Education, 391 U.S. 563 (1968). They do not forfeit First Amendment freedoms when they engage in private communications with their employers, even when the exchange is considered insulting, hostile, loud, and arrogant. Givhan v. Western Line Consol. School Dist., 439 U.S. 410 (1979). Public employees are prohibited by the Hatch Act from participating in certain political party activities. CSC v. Letter Carriers, 413 U.S. 548 (1973); Broadrick v. Oklahoma, 413 U.S. 601 (1973). When Presidents Theodore Roosevelt and William Howard Taft imposed a "gag order" to prohibit federal employees from lobbying Congress, Congress responded with legislation that gave civil servants the right to petition Congress and to furnish information to either House. 37 Stat. 556, § 6 (1912); 48 Cong. Rec. 4513, 5201, 5223, 5235, 10671 (1912).

Beyond these general guideposts, the scope of free speech for public employees is uncertain. In 1983, a 5–4 Court upheld the removal of public employees who object to internal office conditions and attempt to organize opposition to superiors, even when the reasons for dismissal are alleged to be mistaken or unreasonable. Connick v. Myers, 461 U.S. 138 (1983). Four years later, the Court swung around, again by a 5–4 vote, to overturn the removal of a public employee who remarked to a coworker, after learning of the assassination attempt on President Reagan, "If they go for him again, I hope they get him." Justice Powell, the swing vote, explained that this offhand remark by a clerical employee was insufficiently disruptive of the office to justify dismissal. Rankin v. McPherson, 483 U.S. 378 (1987).[6] (Additional discussion on the First Amendment rights of public employees appears in the earlier section on associational rights.)

With regard to free speech in the armed forces, the Court generally treats the military as a separate enclave of constitutional law, permitting restrictions on speech that would be impermissible in civilian society. Elementary rights of circulating petitions and listening to speeches by political candidates are denied in the interests of military discipline and order.[7]

"Fighting Words"

The Supreme Court created, and subsequently altered, the "fighting words" doctrine. A unanimous decision in 1942 upheld a state law that prohibited speech in public that is offensive or derisive of another person. The statutory purpose was to prevent a breach of the peace. Chaplinsky v. New Hampshire, 315 U.S. 568 (1942).

---

[6]For other free speech cases involving public employees, see Branti v. Finkel, 445 U.S. 507 (1980); Mt. Healthy City Board of Ed. v. Doyle, 429 U.S. 274 (1977); Elrod v. Burns, 427 U.S. 347 (1976); Perry v. Sindermann, 408 U.S. 593 (1972).

[7]United States v. Albertini, 472 U.S. 675 (1985); Secretary of Navy v. Huff, 444 U.S. 453 (1980); Brown v. Glines, 444 U.S. 348 (1980); Greer v. Spock, 424 U.S. 828 (1976); Parker v. Levy, 417 U.S. 733 (1974). But see Flower v. United States, 407 U.S. 197 (1972).

That decision was undercut in 1949 when the Court, divided 5–4, struck down a Chicago ordinance that prohibited any breach of the peace. The trial court had interpreted the ordinance to prohibit any speech that "stirs the public to anger" and "invites disputes." The Court declared that a function of free speech is to invite disputes:

> It may indeed best serve its high purpose when it induces a condition of unrest, creates dissatisfaction with conditions as they are, or even stirs people to anger. Speech is often provocative and challenging. It may strike at prejudices and preconceptions and have profound unsettling effects as it presses for acceptance of an idea. Terminiello v. Chicago, 337 U.S. 1, 4 (1949).

The fighting words doctrine was kept alive two years later when the Court split 6–3 in upholding a New York statute that prohibited incitement of a breach of the peace. The Court supported intervention by the police to prevent a riot. Feiner v. New York, 340 U.S. 315 (1951). The following year, a 5–4 decision upheld an Illinois statute that made it illegal to publish anything that exposed the citizens of any race, color, creed, or religion to contempt, derision, or obloquy. At issue was the distribution of racist leaflets that portrayed blacks as depraved, criminal, and unchaste. Beauharnais v. Illinois, 343 U.S. 250 (1952).

In light of recent cases, little remains of the fighting words doctrine. In 1971, a 5–4 Court overturned the conviction of Paul Robert Cohen, who had been sentenced to thirty days for wearing, in a county courthouse, a jacket bearing the words "Fuck the Draft." Unlike its decisions in cases involving obscenity and pornography, the Court found itself unable to "distinguish this from any other offensive word." COHEN v. CALIFORNIA, 403 U.S. 15, 25 (1971).[8] A year later, the Court agreed to set aside the conviction of someone who had said to a police officer: "White son of a bitch, I'll kill you." The Court found the state law, making it a misdemeanor to use "opprobrious words or abusive language, tending to cause a breach of the peace," unconstitutionally vague and overbroad. Gooding v. Wilson, 405 U.S. 518 (1972). When an eighteen-year-old at a small public gathering remarked that if inducted into the army and made to carry a rifle "the first man I want to get in my sights is L.B.J. [President Lyndon B. Johnson]," the Court held that the context of this remark made it political hyperbole rather than a knowing and willful threat against the President. Watts v. United States, 394 U.S. 705 (1969).

An issue of exceptional emotional intensity involved the request of American Nazis to march in Skokie, Illinois. They wanted to march in their uniform, display the swastika, and distribute literature promoting hatred against Jews. After many court rulings, they eventually held a rally in Chicago's Marquette Park. National Socialist Party v. Skokie, 432 U.S. 43 (1977); Collin v. Smith, 447 F.Supp. 676 (N.D. Ill. 1978), aff'd, 578 F.2d 1197 (7th Cir. 1978), cert. denied, 439 U.S. 916 (1978).

FORMS OF SPEECH

The Supreme Court recognizes categories of speech that would have been novel if not inscrutable to the framers. These forms include symbolic speech, "speech plus,"

---

[8]Yet the Court distinguishes language well enough to use code by referring to articles entitled "M-----f----- Acquitted" and organizations known as "Up Against the Wall, M-----f-----." Papish v. University of Missouri Curators, 410 U.S. 667 (1973). Similar cases include Rosenfeld v. New Jersey, 408 U.S. 901 (1972); Lewis v. City of New Orleans, 408 U.S. 913 (1972); Brown v. Oklahoma, 408 U.S. 914 (1972); Cason v. City of Columbus, 409 U.S. 1053 (1972). For other obscenity/breach-of-the-peace cases, see Hess v. Indiana, 414 U.S. 105 (1973) and Lewis v. City of New Orleans, 415 U.S. 130 (1974).

commercial speech, and broadcasting rights. In the area of campaign financing, the Court has decided that "money is speech" (see Chapter 18).

Symbolic Speech

Ideas are communicated by symbols as well as by words. A California statute made it a felony to display a red flag "as a sign, symbol or emblem of opposition to organized government." By a 7–1 majority, the Supreme Court in 1931 held the statute unconstitutionally vague and repugnant to the guaranty of liberty contained in the Fourteenth Amendment. Stromberg v. California, 283 U.S. 359 (1931). There are obvious limits to symbolic speech and "expressive conduct." As Justice Rehnquist noted in a dissent: "One who burns down the factory of a company whose products he dislikes can expect his First Amendment defense to a consequent arson prosecution to be given short shrift by the courts." Smith v. Goguen, 415 U.S. 566, 594 (1974).

A spectacular form of symbolic speech occurred in a 1968 case involving the burning of a draft card to protest the Vietnam war. The act violated a federal statute that applied to any person "who forges, alters, knowingly destroys, knowingly mutilates, or in any manner changes" a draft card. A 7-1 Court held that the statute did not unconstitutionally abridge free speech; government has a legitimate interest in preserving draft cards; and the act of burning a draft card is not "symbolic speech" protected by the First Amendment. United States v. O'Brien, 391 U.S. 367 (1968). On the other hand, school children were permitted to wear black arm bands to protest the Vietnam war. Their conduct, which the Court called "closely akin to 'pure speech,'" had been quiet and nondisruptive. Tinker v. Des Moines School Dist., 393 U.S. 503, 505 (1969), reprinted in Chapter 16.

States and the federal government have adopted a number of laws to prohibit desecration and abuse of the American flag. A 1907 decision by the Supreme Court involved a Nebraska law that punished the desecration of the flag and the use of the flag to advertise the sale of articles. An exception was made for newspapers, periodicals, or books if disconnected from any advertisement. The Court, voting 8–1, upheld the statute's application against a company that printed the flag on a bottle of beer. Halter v. Nebraska, 205 U.S. 34 (1907). A Massachusetts law, prohibiting anyone from publicly treating the flag "contemptuously," was held void for vagueness when used to convict an individual who wore a small U.S. flag sewn to the seat of his blue jeans. Smith v. Goguen, 415 U.S. 566 (1974).

More difficult to resolve are the cases where the flag is used to communicate opposition to the government and its policies. In 1967, opponents of the Vietnam war burned flags in New York City's Central Park. Congress responded the next year with legislation providing that whoever "knowingly casts contempt upon any flag of the United States by publicly mutilating, defacing, defiling, burning, or trampling upon it shall be fined not more than $1,000 or imprisoned for not more than one year, or both." 18 U.S.C. § 700 (1982). The legislative history reveals that Congress intended to punish the war protesters.

A conviction for flag burning was set aside by the Supreme Court in 1969 because the punishment was directed not only for acts against the flag but for words as well. Street v. New York, 394 U.S. 576 (1969). Another flag case involved a conviction for taping a peace symbol to an American flag and hanging it upside down to protest the Vietnam war. The purpose was to associate the flag with peace, not war. The Court, by a 6–3 majority, held that the state law infringed on protected expression: "there can be little doubt that appellant communicated through the use of symbols." Spence v. Washington, 418 U.S. 405, 410 (1974).

During the 1988 presidential campaign, George Bush and Michael Dukakis clashed on the issue of whether public school teachers could be compelled to order students to pledge allegiance to the flag. Dukakis had vetoed this bill as governor of Massachusetts, relying on an advisory opinion by the Massachusetts Supreme Court. Bush claimed that he would have found a way to sign the bill. Thereafter the two candidates tried to see who could stand in front of more flags and sound more patriotic.

The flag issue returned with full force the next year when the Supreme Court, divided 5–4, held that a conviction for flag desecration (burning the flag during a protest) was contrary to the First Amendment. The majority regarded the action as "expressive conduct" protected by the Constitution. TEXAS v. JOHNSON, 109 S.Ct. 2533 (1989). The decision triggered a flurry of bills and constitutional amendments, with President Bush's support, to overturn the decision.

In 1984, the Court grappled with the issue of homeless persons using "tent cities" in public parks to symbolize their plight. They received permission to erect two in Washington, D.C.: one on the Mall and the other in LaFayette Park, directly across from the White House. To underscore the symbol, they wanted to sleep overnight in the tents. The government said this would violate a regulation permitting camping only in designated areas. An appellate court split 6–5 in upholding the right of the demonstrators but the Supreme Court reversed 7–2. Clark v. Community for Creative Non-Violence, 468 U.S. 288 (1984).

"Speech Plus"

The term "speech plus" refers to speech mixed with conduct. For example, picketing is "free speech *plus*, the plus being physical activity that may implicate traffic and related matters." Amalgamated Food Employees v. Logan Plaza, 391 U.S. 308, 326 (1968). To promote an idea or cause, individuals gather together and carry placards, distribute leaflets, and ask passersby to sign petitions. In 1940, the Court held that picketing is protected by the constitutional freedoms of speech, peaceable assembly, and the right to petition government for redress of grievances. Thornhill v. Alabama, 310 U.S. 88 (1940).[9] The Supreme Court said this about the right to assemble:

> The right of the people peaceably to assemble for lawful purposes existed long before the adoption of the Constitution of the United States. In fact, it is, and always has been, one of the attributes of citizenship under a free government. . . . It was not, therefore, a right granted to the people by the Constitution. The government of the United States when established found it in existence, with the obligation on the part of the States to afford it protection. United States v. Cruikshank, 92 U.S. 542, 551 (1876).

A unanimous Court in 1937 held that peaceable assembly cannot be made a crime. De Jonge v. Oregon, 299 U.S. 353 (1937). This case also applied the right of peaceable assembly, guaranteed under the federal Constitution to the states. Id. at

---

[9]Other picketing cases during this period include: New Negro Alliance v. Grocery Co., 303 U.S. 552 (1938); Milk Wagon Drivers Union v. Meadowmoor Co., 312 U.S. 287 (1941); A.F. of L. v. Swing, 312 U.S. 321 (1941); Hotel Employees' Local v. Board, 315 U.S. 437 (1942); Carpenters Union v. Ritter's Cafe, 315 U.S. 722 (1942); Allen-Bradley Local v. Board, 315 U.S. 742 (1942); Bakery Drivers Local v. Wohl, 315 U.S. 769 (1942).

364. See also Hague v. C.I.O., 307 U.S. 496 (1939). Peaceful demonstrators may not be prosecuted and convicted for "disorderly conduct." Gregory v. Chicago, 394 U.S. 111 (1969). Government cannot make it a crime to assemble on a sidewalk and conduct oneself "in a manner annoying to persons passing by." Such laws are invalid for vagueness and for infringing on the right of free assembly. Coates v. City of Cincinnati, 402 U.S. 611 (1971).

After the *Thornhill* decision in 1940, the Court conducted a gradual retreat from the right to picket. Not only could the state regulate picketing to protect against violence and the destruction of property, but could also prohibit peaceful picketing to further state interests, especially dealing with labor conditions. Picketing could be enjoined to prevent efforts to restrain trade, Giboney v. Empire Storage, 336 U.S. 490 (1949), and to protect state policies against racial discrimination, Hughes v. Superior Court, 339 U.S. 460 (1950).[10] In recent years, decisions have been more supportive of peaceful picketing.[11] When picketers concentrate on a single household, government may prohibit such picketing in order to protect the privacy of a homeowner. Frisby v. Schultz, 108 S.Ct. 2495 (1988).

If picketing is done on private property, which constitutional interest should prevail? An early case involved the right of a company town to require a permit before anyone could distribute literature. The Supreme Court ruled that since the town's shopping district was freely accessible to the general public, the town's public nature overshadowed its private claim. The right to distribute literature was therefore upheld. Marsh v. Alabama, 326 U.S. 501 (1946).

From this simple company-town issue came the conundrum of free speech in shopping centers. The Court might well have asked plaintively: "Oh, Founding Fathers, where are you when we need you?" In 1968, the Court divided 6–3 in ruling that peaceful picketing of a business enterprise within a shopping center did not violate property rights. The Court followed the reasoning of *Marsh,* but cautioned in a footnote that its decision was limited to picketing that was directly related to shopping center activities. Amalgamated Food Employees v. Logan Valley Plaza, 391 U.S. 308, 320 n.9 (1968).

The footnote helped justify a modification in 1972. The distribution of handbills inside a shopping center was held to be a violation of property rights. The handbills (protesting the Vietnam war and the draft) had no relation to the purpose of the shopping center. Lloyd Corp. v. Tanner, 407 U.S. 551 (1972). Confusion became rampant four years later when the Court denied striking members of a union the right to enter a shopping center to picket against their employer. Presumably, this kind of picketing was protected by *Logan Valley,* but the Court said that its new doctrine was based on *statutory* grounds, even though it also reached out to dispose of constitutional issues. The Justices couldn't even agree whether *Lloyd* had overruled *Logan Valley.* Hudgens v. NLRB, 424 U.S. 507 (1976).

In 1980, the Supreme Court reviewed a case in which a privately owned shopping center prohibited visitors or tenants from engaging in any publicly expressive activity (including circulation of petitions) that was not directly related to the commercial purposes of the center. The California courts upheld the rights of

---

[10]Injunctions against peaceful picketing were also upheld in International Brotherhood of Teamsters v. Hanke, 339 U.S. 470 (1950); Building Service Union v. Gazzam, 339 U.S. 532 (1950); and International Brotherhood of Teamsters v. Vogt, Inc., 354 U.S. 284 (1957).

[11]Police Department of Chicago v. Mosley, 408 U.S. 92 (1972); Grayned v. City of Rockford, 408 U.S. 104 (1972); Carey v. Brown, 447 U.S. 455 (1980); NAACP v. Claiborne Hardware Co., 458 U.S. 886 (1982).

students to petition on unrelated matters. The Supreme Court, in a unanimous ruling, affirmed. State courts can make independent and authoritative determinations on the balance between free speech and property rights in shopping centers. PRUNEYARD SHOPPING CENTER v. ROBINS, 447 U.S. 74 (1980). Thus, rights not available through the federal courts can be protected by state courts interpreting state constitutions.[12]

COMMERCIAL SPEECH

Free speech has come to include "speech" related to commercial activities. Initially unprotected under the Constitution, commercial speech is now protected in the courts. In part, this reflects the growing appreciation that commercial speech is part of the free flow of information necessary for informed choice and democratic participation.

The concept of commercial speech appeared in a 1942 case involving a municipal ordinance that prohibited the distribution in the streets of printed handbills bearing commercial advertising matter. The disputed handbill in this case was double-faced: half consisting of a protest against the city's police (protected speech), the other half containing an advertisement. The Court held unanimously that such artifices could not so easily evade the prohibition of the ordinance. Although the Constitution protects the dissemination of opinion by handbills, it "imposes no such restraint on government as respects purely commercial advertising." Valentine v. Chrestensen, 316 U.S. 52, 54 (1942).

Other cases explored the notion of commercial speech,[13] but a major step occurred in 1974 when the Supreme Court narrowly upheld (by a 5–4 vote) a city's policy of allowing commercial, religious, and civic advertising in its transit system but prohibiting ads for political candidates. The four dissenters argued that once the city opened a forum for communication by accepting ads, it could not discriminate "among forum uses solely on the basis of message content." Lehman v. City of Shaker Heights, 418 U.S. 298, 310 (1974).

The value of commercial speech was etched sharply a year later when the Supreme Court, divided 5–4, struck down a state law that made it a misdemeanor for anyone to sell or circulate newspapers that contain ads encouraging abortions. Decided in the shadow of the abortion cases of 1973, the Court held that the statute infringed upon constitutionally protected speech. At issue was not merely the right of newspapers to publish commercial material but also the right of the reader to make informed choices. Bigelow v. Virginia, 421 U.S. 809 (1975).

A similar point was made concerning the right of professionals to advertise their services. In earlier cases, the Court had sustained laws that prohibited certain occupations, such as dentists, from advertising. Semler v. Dental Examiners, 294

[12] For state cases upholding free speech rights in privately owned shopping centers and private universities, see Robins v. PruneYard Shopping Center, 592 P.2d 341 (Cal. 1979); State v. Schmid, 423 A.2d 615 (N.J. 1980); Commonwealth v. Tate, 432 A.2d 1382 (Pa. 1981); Alderwood Assoc. v. Wash. Envir. Council, 635 A.2d 108 (Wash. 1981).

[13] In Capital Broadcasting Co. v. Acting Attorney General, 405 U.S. 1000 (1972), the Supreme Court summarily affirmed a district court decision sustaining the constitutionality of 15 U.S.C. § 1335, which prohibited the electronic media from carrying cigarette advertising. The district court called this form of communication commercial speech. See also Pittsburgh Press Co. v. Human Rel. Comm'n, 413 U.S. 376, 384–385 (1973).

U.S. 608 (1935). In 1976, however, an 8–1 Supreme Court decision rejected a state law that declared it unprofessional conduct for a licensed pharmacist to advertise the prices of prescription drugs. The Court explained that it was not just a matter of trade but of health and the free flow of information. Virginia State Board of Pharmacy v. Virginia Citizens Consumer Council, 425 U.S. 748 (1976). See also Linmark Associates v. Willingboro, 431 U.S. 85 (1977).

Building on this line of cases, in 1977 the Court declared unconstitutional a state rule that prohibited attorneys from advertising in newspapers or other media. The Court protected commercial speech on these grounds: "The listener's interest is substantial; the consumer's concern for the free flow of commercial speech often may be far keener than his concern for urgent political dialogue. Moreover, significant societal interests are served by such speech. Advertising, though entirely commercial, may often carry information of import to significant issues of the day." Bates v. State Bar of Arizona, 433 U.S. 350, 364 (1977). Further guidelines on advertising by lawyers were provided in In re R.M.J., 455 U.S. 191 (1982), Zauderer v. Office of Disciplinary Counsel, 471 U.S. 626 (1985), and Shapero v. Kentucky Bar Assn., 108 S.Ct. 1916 (1988). The right to advertise does not protect lawyers from being disciplined by the bar for soliciting clients in person. Ohralik v. Ohio State Bar Assn., 436 U.S. 447 (1978).

The Court showed its concern for the free flow of information in 1978. Split 5–4, it held that a Massachusetts statute violated the First Amendment because it restricted business corporations from making contributions or expenditures to influence votes on questions submitted to the people. Some of the dissenters objected that the Court should have deferred to legislatures "in the context of the political arena where the expertise of legislators is at its peak and that of judges is at its very lowest." First National Bank of Boston v. Bellotti, 435 U.S. 765, 804 (1978).

Commercial speech involves conflicts between state efforts to regulate the economy and business interests to promote their activities. A New York law prohibited an electric utility from placing ads to encourage the use of electricity. The law reflected concern at that time over insufficient fuel supply because of Middle East oil embargoes. By an 8–1 majority, the Court held that the law violated the First Amendment. Although the utility exercised a monopoly over electricity, it faced competition from oil and gas. Central Hudson Gas & Elec. v. Public Service Comm'n, 447 U.S. 557 (1980). Although this case suggested that government had to use the "least restrictive means" in regulating commercial speech, the Court held in 1989 that only a reasonable "fit" is required between the legislature's ends and the means it chooses. Board of Trustees, State Univ. of N.Y. v. Fox, 109 S.Ct. 3028 1989).

Some of the states have tried to regulate billboards. The city of San Diego, in an effort to eliminate dangerous distractions to pedestrians and motorists and improve the appearance of city streets, placed restrictions on billboards and outdoor advertising displays. However, it made exceptions for on-site advertising (signs on the property of the business) and twelve other categories. Because the city seemed to afford greater protection to commercial (on-site) speech than to noncommercial speech, the ordinance was invalid. Metromedia, Inc. v. San Diego, 453 U.S. 490 (1981). Restrictions that are totally neutral, such as the prohibition against the posting of all signs on public property, have been upheld. Cities may decide that a total ban is necessary to prevent visual clutter and to reduce traffic hazards. Because the ban is total, there is no hint of censorship or suppression. City Council v. Taxpayers for Vincent, 466 U.S. 789 (1984).

In 1983, a unanimous Court struck down a congressional statute that prohibited the mailing of unsolicited advertisements for contraceptives. The Court held that the statute violated commercial speech protected by the First Amendment: "where—as in this case—a speaker desires to convey truthful information relevant to important social issues such as family planning and the prevention of venereal disease, we have previously found the First Amendment interest served by such speech paramount." Bolger v. Youngs Drug Products Corp., 463 U.S. 60, 69 (1983).

A recent decision on commercial speech deals with gambling. A Puerto Rico statute legalized certain forms of casino gambling to promote tourism but prohibited gambling rooms from advertising to the public in Puerto Rico. A sharply divided (5–4) Court sustained the statute, rejecting the argument that once Puerto Rico chose to legalize casino gambling it was prohibited by the First Amendment from restricting advertising. Posadas de Puerto Rico Assoc. v. Tourism Co., 478 U.S. 328 (1986). This decision was interpreted to suggest that legislatures could also ban advertising for such products as cigarettes and alcohol.

BROADCASTING RIGHTS

In theory, there is no limit to the number of newspapers. Radio and television stations, however, compete for a finite number of public airwaves. Acting under the Commerce Clause, Congress has established the Federal Communications Commission (FCC) to allocate this limited space. It grants licenses for a specific number of years, subject to various conditions supplied by statute and agency regulation. The FCC may revoke or suspend a license if a station violates these conditions. No one has a free-speech right to use public airwaves without a license. National Broadcasting Co. v. United States, 319 U.S. 190 (1943).

In 1949, the FCC developed a "fairness doctrine" to require broadcasters to present public issues and give each side of an issue fair coverage. 13 FCC 1246 (1949). Although Congress never explicitly authorized this doctrine, a unanimous Court held that the agency regulation was consistent with congressional policy and did not violate the First Amendment. Red Lion Broadcasting Co. v. FCC, 395 U.S. 367 (1969). Next, there was the question of whether broadcasters are required to accept paid editorial advertisements. The Court again deferred to the judgments of the FCC and Congress that no such requirement exists. Columbia Broadcasting System v. Democratic National Committee, 412 U.S. 94 (1973). Congress and the FCC formulated the policy, accepted by the courts, that political candidates are entitled to "reasonable access" to broadcasting stations to promote their campaigns for federal office. CBS, Inc. v. FCC, 453 U.S. 367 (1981). Some congressional initiatives were struck down. The requirement that stations receiving federal funds could not editorialize was declared invalid. FCC v. League of Women Voters of California, 468 U.S. 364 (1984).

Of all forms of communication, broadcasting has the most limited First Amendment protection. Conditions are imposed on radio and television programs that would be intolerable for newspapers. For example, Congress requires that if one political candidate is given time on the air, opponents must receive "equal time." 47 U.S.C. § 315(a) (1982). In 1970, Congress prohibited the advertisement of cigarettes on radio or television. 84 Stat. 87 (1970). It later applied the same restriction to little cigars. 15 U.S.C. § 1335 (1982). In 1986, the ban was extended to smokeless tobacco (snuff). 100 Stat. 32, § 3(f).

The Court gives two reasons for subjecting broadcasting to more severe restrictions: the pervasive presence of the broadcast media, and its unique access to children. The FCC was therefore allowed to prohibit the playing of "indecent" material in the afternoon (George Carlin's monologue on "seven dirty words"). The same material, in a different place or at another time, might have received First Amendment protection. FCC v. PACIFICA FOUNDATION, 438 U.S. 726, 748–751 (1978).

Broadcasting rights fluctuate with technology. In 1973, the Court explained that the problems of regulating broadcasting "are rendered more difficult because the broadcast industry is dynamic in terms of technological change; solutions adequate a decade ago are not necessarily so now, and those acceptable today may well be outmoded 10 years hence." Columbia Broadcasting System v. Democratic National Committee, 412 U.S. 94, 102 (1973). The Fairness Doctrine depends largely on the limited number of access points available to licensees. If outlets increased because of technology, the Doctrine's rationale would be undermined. In a footnote to a 1984 decision, the Court recognized that the emergence of cable and satellite television created new channels for the public. However, "without some signal from Congress or the FCC" that technological development required revision of broadcasting regulation, the Court was not prepared to challenge the Fairness Doctrine. FCC v. League of Women Voters of California, 468 U.S. 364, 377–378 n.11 (1984). See also n.12 at 378–379.

The FCC chairman in the Reagan administration had criticized the Fairness Doctrine as unconstitutional and threatened to abolish it. In 1985, a Commission report concluded that the Doctrine violates the First Amendment and no longer serves the public interest. However, it declined to initiate a new rule to eliminate or modify the Doctrine. On the basis of that report, a party brought suit and asked the D.C. Circuit to consider the constitutionality of the Doctrine. The D.C. Circuit refused on the ground that the report did not constitute "agency action" subject to its review. Radio-Television News Directors Ass'n v. FCC, 809 F.2d 860 (D.C. Cir. 1987). On the same day, the D.C. Circuit returned a case to the FCC because it had failed to give adequate consideration to a station owner's constitutional arguments regarding the Fairness Doctrine. The Commission regarded Congress and the courts as more appropriate arenas for deciding the constitutional question. The D.C. Circuit, however, thought it might benefit from the FCC's analysis, even if the Commission felt political pressure from Congress to avoid a final conclusion. Meredith Corp. v. FCC, 809 F.2d 863, 872 (D.C. Cir. 1987). It noted that federal officials are not only bound by the Constitution but they take an oath to support and defend it: "To enforce a Commission-generated policy that the Commission itself believes is unconstitutional may well constitute a violation of that oath . . ." Id. at 874.

Congress passed legislation in 1987 to codify the Fairness Doctrine, but President Reagan vetoed the bill. He stated that the Doctrine was antagonistic to the First Amendment and was no longer justified because of new media outlets, such as cable television. 23 Wkly Comp. Pres. Doc. 715 (June 19, 1987). On June 23, the Senate voted to refer the vetoed bill to committee. On August 4, the FCC unanimously abolished the Fairness Doctrine, claiming that it represented an unconstitutional restriction on free speech. "FCC Kills 'Fairness Doctrine,' but Congress Will Renew Fight," Cong. Q. Wkly Rept., August 8, 1987, at 1796. Bills have been introduced in Congress to reinstate the Fairness Doctrine.

The concept of "free speech" emerged from political developments in America in the 1780s, related generally to the needs of self-government and self-development. From the laconic formulation in the First Amendment, the right of free speech has become more specialized and complex, expanding to include such twentieth-century technology as broadcasting rights. Various tests have been fashioned to draw a line between liberty and licentiousness, none with much success. There is general agreement on giving broad scope to pure advocacy of ideas, even if threatening to government, and applying restrictions only when advocacy takes the form of action and conduct. For the most part, pure speech—even "fighting words"—is tolerated as part of the process of peaceful political change.

Other dimensions of the First Amendment are examined in the next chapter: the right of a free press, the natural tensions between a free press and a fair trial, and the bedeviled areas of libel and obscenity.

Selected Readings

ANASTAPLO, GEORGE. *The Constitutionalist: Notes on the First Amendment*. Dallas, Tex.: Southern Methodist University Press, 1971.

BARRON, JEROME A., AND C. THOMAS DIENES. *Handbook of Free Speech and Free Press*. Boston: Little, Brown, 1979.

BERNS, WALTER. *Freedom, Virtue, & the First Amendment*. Baton Rouge: Louisiana State University Press, 1957.

——.*The First Amendment and the Future of American Democracy*. Chicago: Gateway Editions, 1985.

BORK, ROBERT H. "Neutral Principles and Some First Amendment Problems." 47 *Indiana Law Journal* 1 (1971).

BRENNAN, WILLIAM J., JR. "The Supreme Court and the Meiklejohn Interpretation of the First Amendment." 79 *Harvard Law Review* 1 (1965).

CAHN, EDMUND. "Mr. Justice Black and First Amendment Absolutes: A Public Interview." 37 *New York University Law Review* 549 (1962).

CHAFEE, ZECHARIAH, JR. "Freedom of Speech in War Time." 32 *Harvard Law Review* 932 (1919).

——. *Free Speech in the United States*. Cambridge, Mass.: Harvard University Press, 1941.

COOPER, PHILLIP J. "The Supreme Court, the First Amendment, and Freedom of Information." 46 *Public Administration Review* 622 (Nov./Dec. 1986).

DORSEN, NORMAN, AND JOEL GORA. "Free Speech, Property, and the Burger Court: Old Values, New Balances." 1982 *Supreme Court Review* 195.

EMERSON, THOMAS I. *The System of Freedom of Expression*. New York: Random House, 1970.

——. "First Amendment Doctrine and the Burger Court." 68 *California Law Review* 422 (1980).

FELLMAN, DAVID. *The Constitutional Right of Association*. Chicago: University of Chicago Press, 1963.

FRIENDLY, FRED W. *The Good Guys, the Bad Guys, and the First Amendment: Free Speech vs. Fairness in Broadcasting*. New York: Random House, 1975.

HAIMAN, FRANKLYN S. *Speech and Law in a Free Society*. Chicago: University of Chicago Press, 1981.

KALVEN, HARRY, JR. "The Concept of the Public Forum: Cox v. Louisiana." 1965 *Supreme Court Review* 1.

MEIKLEJOHN, ALEXANDER. "The First Amendment Is an Absolute." 1961 *Supreme Court Review* 245.

——. *Political Freedom: The Constitutional Powers of the People*. New York: Oxford University Press, 1965.

MENDELSON, WALLACE. "Clear and Present Danger—From Schenck to Dennis." 52 *Columbia Law Review* 313 (1952).

MURPHY, PAUL L. *The Meaning of Freedom of Speech*. Westport, Conn.: Greenwood Publishing, 1972.

O'BRIEN, DAVID M. *The Public's Right to Know: The Supreme Court and the First Amendment*. New York: Praeger, 1981.

RABBAN, DAVID M. "The First Amendment in Its Forgotten Years." 90 *Yale Law Journal* 514 (1981).

SCHIRO, RICHARD. "Commercial Speech: The Demise of a Chimera." 1976 *Supreme Court Review* 45.

SHAPIRO, MARTIN. *Freedom of Speech: The Supreme Court and Judicial Review*. Englewood Cliffs, N.J.: Prentice-Hall, 1966.

House Debate in 1789 on the First Amendment

On June 8, 1789, James Madison submitted a list of proposed amendments to the Constitution. The passages below discuss the freedoms of speech, press, assembly, and right of petition. Also included is Madison's proposal to prohibit the states from violating certain rights. The source is 1 Annals of Congress 424, 431–436, 731–732, 755, 913.

Mr. MADISON rose, and reminded the House that this was the day that he had heretofore named for bringing forward amendments to the Constitution, as contemplated in the fifth article of the Constitution. . . .

I will state my reasons why I think it proper to propose amendments, and state the amendments themselves, so far as I think they ought to be proposed. If I thought I could fulfil the duty which I owe to myself and my constituents, to let the subject pass over in silence, I most certainly should not trespass upon the indulgence of this House. But I cannot do this, and am therefore compelled to beg a patient hearing to what I have to lay before you. And I do most sincerely believe, that if Congress will devote but one day to this subject, so far as to satisfy the public that we do not disregard their wishes, it will have a salutary influence on the public councils, and prepare the way for a favorable reception of our future measures. It appears to me that this House is bound by every motive of prudence, not to let the first session pass over without proposing to the State Legislatures, some things to be incorporated into the Constitution, that will render it as acceptable to the whole people of the United States, as it has been found acceptable to a majority of them. I wish, among other reasons why something should be done, that those who had been friendly to the adoption of this Constitution may have the opportunity of proving to those who were opposed to it that they were as sincerely devoted to liberty and a Republican Government, as those who charged them with wishing the adoption of this Constitution in order to lay the foundation of an aristocracy or despotism. It will be a desirable thing to extinguish from the bosom of every member of the community, any apprehensions that there are those among his countrymen who wish to deprive them of the liberty for which they valiantly fought and honorably bled. And if there are amendments desired of such a nature as will not injure the Constitution, and they can be ingrafted so as to give satisfaction to the doubting part of our fellow-citizens, the friends of the Federal Government will evince that spirit of deference and concession for which they have hitherto been distinguished.

It cannot be a secret to the gentlemen in this House, that, notwithstanding the ratification of this system of Government by eleven of the thirteen United States, in some cases unanimously, in others by large majorities; yet still there is a great number of our constituents who are dissatisfied with it; among whom are many respectable for their talents and patriotism, and respectable for the jealousy they have for their liberty, which, though mistaken in its object, is laudable in its motive. There is a great body of the people falling under this description, who at present feel much inclined to join their support to the cause of Federalism, if they were satisfied on this one point. We ought not to disregard their inclination, but, on principles of amity and moderation, conform to their wishes, and expressly declare the great rights of mankind secured under this Constitution. . . .

The Amendments which have occurred to me, proper to be recommended by Congress to the State Legislatures, are these:

. . .

The people shall not be deprived or abridged of their right to speak, to write, or to publish their sentiments; and the freedom of the press, as one of the great bulwarks of liberty, shall be invioable.

The people shall not be restrained from peaceably assembling and consulting for their common good; nor from applying to the Legislature by petitions, or remonstrances, for redress of their grievances.

. . .

Fifthly. That in article 1st, section 10, between clauses 1 and 2, be inserted this clause, to wit:

No State shall violate the equal rights of conscience, or the freedom of the press, or the trial by jury in criminal cases.

. . .

The first of these amendments relates to what may be called a bill of rights. I will own that I never considered this provision so essential to the Federal Constitution as to make it improper to ratify it, until such an amendment was added; at the same time, I always conceived, that in a certain form, and to a certain extent, such a provision was neither improper nor altogether useless. I am aware that a great number of the most respectable friends to the Government, and champions for republican liberty, have thought such a provision not only unnecessary, but even improper; nay, I believe some have gone so far as to think it even dangerous. Some policy has been made use of, perhaps, by gentlemen on both sides of the question: I acknowledge the ingenuity of those arguments which were drawn against the Constitution, by a comparison with the policy of Great Britain, in establishing a declaration of rights; but there is too great a difference in the case to warrant the comparison: therefore, the arguments drawn from that source were in a great measure inapplicable. In the declaration of rights which that country has established, the truth is, they have gone no farther than to raise a barrier against the power of the Crown; the power of the Legislature is left altogether indefinite. Although I know whenever the great rights, the trial by jury, freedom of the press, or liberty of conscience, come in question in that body, the invasion of them is resisted by able advocates, yet their Magna Charta does not contain any one provision for the security of those rights, respecting which the people of America are most alarmed. The freedom of the press and rights of conscience, those

choicest privileges of the people, are unguarded in the British Constitution.

But although the case may be widely different, and it may not be thought necessary to provide limits for the legislative power in that country, yet a different opinion prevails in the United States. The people of many States have thought it necessary to raise barriers against power in all forms and departments of Government, and I am inclined to believe, if once bills of rights are established in all the States as well as the Federal Constitution, we shall find, that, although some of them are rather unimportant, yet, upon the whole, they will have a salutary tendency. . . .

. . .

The next clause of the fourth proposition was taken into consideration, and was as follows: "The freedom of speech and of the press, and the right of the people peaceably to assemble and consult for their common good, and to apply to the Government for redress of grievances, shall not be infringed."

Mr. SEDGWICK submitted to those gentlemen who had contemplated the subject, what effect such an amendment as this would have; he feared it would tend to make them appear trifling in the eyes of their constituents; what, said he, shall we secure the freedom of speech, and think it necessary, at the same time, to allow the right of assembling? If people freely converse together, they must assemble for that purpose; it is a self-evident, unalienable right which the people possess; it is certainly a thing that never would be called in question; it is derogatory to the dignity of the House to descend to such minutiæ; he therefore moved to strike out "assemble and."

Mr. BENSON.—The committee who framed this report proceeded on the principle that these rights belonged to the people; they conceived them to be inherent; and all that they meant to provide against was their being infringed by the Government.

Mr. SEDGWICK replied, that if the committee were governed by that general principle, they might have gone into a very lengthy enumeration of rights; they might have declared that a man should have a right to wear his hat if he pleased; that he might get up when he pleased, and go to bed when he thought proper; but he would ask the gentleman whether he thought it necessary to enter these trifles in a declaration of rights, in a Government where none of them were intended to be infringed.

Mr. TUCKER hoped the words would not be struck out, for he considered them of importance; besides, they were recommended by the States of Virginia and North Carolina, though he noticed that the most material part proposed by those States was omitted, which was a declaration that the people should have a right to instruct their representatives. He would move to have those words inserted as soon as the motion for striking out was decided.

Mr. GERRY was also against the words being struck out, because he conceived it to be an essential right; it was inserted in the constitutions of several States; and though it had been abused in the year 1786 in Massachusetts, yet that abuse ought not to operate as an argument against the use of it. The people ought to be secure in the peaceable enjoyment of this privilege, and that can only be done by making a declaration to that effect in the Constitution.

Mr. PAGE.—The gentleman from Massachusetts, (Mr. SEDGWICK,) who made this motion, objects to the clause, because the right is of so trivial a nature. He supposes it no more essential than whether a man has a right to wear his hat or not; but let me observe to him that such rights have been opposed, and a man has been obliged to pull off his hat when he appeared before the face of authority; people have also been prevented from assembling together on their lawful occasions, therefore it is well to guard against such stretches of authority, by inserting the privilege in the declaration of rights. If the people could be deprived of the power of assembling under any pretext whatsoever, they might be deprived of every other privilege contained in the clause.

. . .

The committee then proceeded to the fifth proposition:

Article 1, section 10, between the first and second paragraph, insert "no State shall infringe the equal rights of conscience, nor the freedom of speech, or of the press, nor of the right of trial by jury in criminal cases."

Mr. TUCKER.—This is offered, I presume, as an amendment to the Constitution of the United States, but it goes only to the alteration of the constitutions of particular States. It will be much better, I apprehend, to leave the State Governments to themselves, and not to interfere with them more than we already do; and that is thought by many to be rather too much. I therefore move, sir, to strike out these words.

Mr. MADISON conceived this to be the most valuable amendment in the whole list. If there were any reason to restrain the Government of the United States from infringing upon these essential rights, it was equally necessary that they should be secured against the State Governments. He thought that if they provided against the one, it was as necessary to provide against the other, and was satisfied that it would be equally grateful to the people.

Mr. LIVERMORE had no great objection to the sentiment, but he thought it not well expressed. He wished to make it an affirmative proposition; "the equal rights of conscience, the freedom of speech or of the press, and the right of trial by jury in criminal cases, shall not be infringed by any State."

This transposition being agreed to, and Mr. TUCKER'S motion being rejected, the clause was adopted.

. . .

[September 24, 1789:]

The House proceeded to consider the report of a Committee of Conference, on the subject-matter of the amendments depending between the two Houses to the several articles of amendment to the Constitution of the United States, as proposed by this House: whereupon, it was resolved, that they recede from their disagreement to all the amendments; provided that the two articles, which, by the amendments of the Senate, are now proposed to be inserted as the third and eighth articles, shall be amended to read as follows:

"Art. 3. Congress shall make no law respecting an establishment of religion, or prohibiting a free exercise thereof, or abridging the freedom of speech, or of the press, or the right of the people peaceably to assemble, and to petition the Government for a redress of grievances."

Schenck v. United States

249 U.S. 47 (1919)

Charles T. Schenck, general secretary of the Socialist party, was charged with violating the Espionage Act of 1917. The government claimed that the printing and circulation of 15,000 leaflets, which attacked the draft for World War I, caused insubordination in the military forces and obstructed the recruitment and enlistment of soldiers. Writing for a unanimous Court, Justice Holmes formulated his "clear and present danger" test for deciding First Amendment questions. By the end of the year, in *Abrams* v. *United States*, he showed a greater appreciation for First Amendment interests.

MR. JUSTICE HOLMES delivered the opinion of the court.

This is an indictment in three counts. The first charges a conspiracy to violate the Espionage Act of June 15, 1917, c. 30, § 3, 40 Stat. 217, 219, by causing and attempting to cause insubordination, &c., in the military and naval forces of the United States, and to obstruct the recruiting and enlistment service of the United States, when the United States was at war with the German Empire, to-wit, that the defendants wilfully conspired to have printed and circulated to men who had been called and accepted for military service under the Act of May 18, 1917, a document set forth and alleged to be calculated to cause such insubordination and obstruction. The count alleges overt acts in pursuance of the conspiracy, ending in the distribution of the document set forth. The second count alleges a conspiracy to commit an offence against the United States, to-wit, to use the mails for the transmission of matter declared to be non-mailable by Title XII, § 2 of the Act of June 15, 1917, to-wit, the above mentioned document, with an averment of the same overt acts. The third count charges an unlawful use of the mails for the transmission of the same matter and otherwise as above. The defendants were found guilty on all the counts. They set up the First Amendment to the Constitution forbidding Congress to make any law abridging the freedom of speech, or of the press, and bringing the case here on that ground have argued some other points also of which we must dispose.

It is argued that the evidence, if admissible, was not sufficient to prove that the defendant Schenck was concerned in sending the documents. According to the testimony Schenck said he was general secretary of the Socialist party and had charge of the Socialist headquarters from which the documents were sent. He identified a book found there as the minutes of the Executive Committee of the party. The book showed a resolution of August 13, 1917, that 15,000 leaflets should be printed on the other side of one of them in use, to be mailed to men who had passed exemption boards, and for distribution. Schenck personally attended to the printing. On August 20 the general secretary's report said "Obtained new leaflets from printer and started work addressing envelopes" &c.; and there was a resolve that Comrade Schenck be allowed $125 for sending leaflets through the mail. He said that he had about fifteen or sixteen thousand printed. There were files of the circular in question in the inner office which he said were printed on the other side of the one sided circular and were there for distribution. Other copies were proved to have been sent through the mails to drafted men. Without going into confirmatory details that were proved, no reasonable man could doubt that the defendant Schenck was largely instrumental in sending the circulars about. . . .

The document in question upon its first printed side recited the first section of the Thirteenth Amendment, said that the idea embodied in it was violated by the Conscription Act and that a conscript is little better than a convict. In impassioned language it intimated that conscription was despotism in its worst form and a monstrous wrong against humanity in the interest of Wall Street's chosen few. It said "Do not submit to intimidation," but in form at least confined itself to peaceful measures such as a petition for the repeal of the act. The other and later printed side of the sheet was headed "Assert Your Rights." It stated reasons for alleging that any one violated the Constitution when he refused to recognize "your right to assert your opposition to the draft," and went on "If you do not assert and support your rights, you are helping to deny or disparage rights which it is the solemn duty of all citizens and residents of the United States to retain." It described the arguments on the other side as coming from cunning politicians and a mercenary capitalist press, and even silent consent to the conscription law as helping to support an infamous conspiracy. It denied the power to send our citizens away to foreign shores to shoot up the people of other lands, and added that words could not express the condemnation such cold-blooded ruthlessness deserves, &c., &c., winding up "You must do your share to maintain, support and uphold the rights of the people of this country." Of course the document would not have been sent unless it had been intended to have some effect, and we do not see what effect it could be expected to have upon persons subject to the draft except to influence them to obstruct the carrying of it out. The defendants do not deny that the jury might find against them on this point.

But it is said, suppose that that was the tendency of this circular, it is protected by the First Amendment to the Constitution. Two of the strongest expressions are said to be quoted respectively from well-known public men. It well may be that the prohibition of laws abridging the freedom of speech is not confined to previous restraints, although to prevent them may have been the main

purpose, as intimated in *Patterson* v. *Colorado*, 205 U. S. 454, 462. We admit that in many places and in ordinary times the defendants in saying all that was said in the circular would have been within their constitutional rights. But the character of every act depends upon the circumstances in which it is done. *Aikens* v. *Wisconsin*, 195 U. S. 194, 205, 206. The most stringent protection of free speech would not protect a man in falsely shouting fire in a theatre and causing a panic. It does not even protect a man from an injunction against uttering words that may have all the effect of force. *Gompers* v. *Bucks Stove & Range Co.*, 221 U. S. 418, 439. The question in every case is whether the words used are used in such circumstances and are of such a nature as to create a clear and present danger that they will bring about the substantive evils that Congress has a right to prevent. It is a question of proximity and degree. When a nation is at war many things that might be said in time of peace are such a hindrance to its effort that their utterance will not be endured so long as men fight and that no Court could regard them as protected by any constitutional right. It seems to be admitted that if an actual obstruction of the recruiting service were proved, liability for words that produced that effect might be enforced. The statute of 1917 in § 4 punishes conspiracies to obstruct as well as actual obstruction. If the act, (speaking, or circulating a paper,) its tendency and the intent with which it is done are the same, we perceive no ground for saying that success alone warrants making the act a crime. *Goldman* v. *United States*, 245 U. S. 474, 477. Indeed that case might be said to dispose of the present contention if the precedent covers all *media concludendi*. But as the right to free speech was not referred to specially, we have thought fit to add a few words.

It was not argued that a conspiracy to obstruct the draft was not within the words of the Act of 1917. The words are "obstruct the recruiting or enlistment service," and it might be suggested that they refer only to making it hard to get volunteers. Recruiting heretofore usually having been accomplished by getting volunteers the word is apt to call up that method only in our minds. But recruiting is gaining fresh supplies for the forces, as well by draft as otherwise. It is put as an alternative to enlistment or voluntary enrollment in this act. The fact that the Act of 1917 was enlarged by the amending Act of May 16, 1918, c. 75, 40 Stat. 553, of course, does not affect the present indictment and would not, even if the former act had been repealed. Rev. Stats., § 13.

Judgments affirmed.

Abrams v. United States

250 U.S. 616 (1919)

In another prosecution under the Espionage Act, the government charged five defendants with printing and circulating leaflets that opposed U.S. involvement in World War I. The five defendants, all born in Russia, were Jacob Abrams, Hyman Lachowsky, Samuel Lipman, Hyman Rosansky, and Mollie Steimer. The dissent by Justice Holmes, considering his opinion in *Schenck* earlier in the year, is especially significant.

MR. JUSTICE CLARKE delivered the opinion of the court.

On a single indictment, containing four counts, the five plaintiffs in error, hereinafter designated the defendants, were convicted of conspiring to violate provisions of the Espionage Act of Congress (§ 3, Title I, of Act approved June 15, 1917, as amended May 16, 1918, 40 Stat. 553).

Each of the first three counts charged the defendants with conspiring, when the United States was at war with the Imperial Government of Germany, to unlawfully utter, print, write and publish: In the first count, "disloyal, scurrilous and abusive language about the form of Government of the United States;" in the second count, language "intended to bring the form of Government of the United States into contempt, scorn, contumely and disrepute;" and in the third count, language "intended to incite, provoke and encourage resistance to the United States in said war." The charge in the fourth count was that the defendants conspired "when the United States was at war with the Imperial German Government, . . . unlawfully and wilfully, by utterance, writing, printing and publication, to urge, incite and advocate curtailment of production of things and products, to wit, ordnance and ammunition, necessary and essential to the prosecution of the war." The offenses were charged in the language of the act of Congress.

It was charged in each count of the indictment that it was a part of the conspiracy that the defendants would attempt to accomplish their unlawful purpose by printing, writing and distributing in the City of New York many copies of a leaflet or circular, printed in the English language, and of another printed in the Yiddish language, copies of which, properly identified, were attached to the indictment.

All of the five defendants were born in Russia. They were intelligent, had considerable schooling, and at the time they were arrested they had lived in the United States terms varying from five to ten years, but none of them had applied for naturalization. Four of them testified as witnesses in their own behalf and of these, three frankly avowed that they were "rebels," "revolutionists," "anarchists," that they did not believe in government in any form, and they declared that they had no interest whatever in the Government of the United States. The fourth defendant testified that he was a "socialist" and believed in "a proper kind of government, not capitalistic," but in his classification the Government of the United States was "capitalistic."

It was admitted on the trial that the defendants had united to print and distribute the described circulars and that five thousand of them had been printed and distributed about the 22d day of August, 1918. The group had a meeting place in

New York City, in rooms rented by defendant Abrams, under an assumed name, and there the subject of printing the circulars was discussed about two weeks before the defendants were arrested. The defendant Abrams, although not a printer, on July 27, 1918, purchased the printing outfit with which the circulars were printed and installed it in a basement room where the work was done at night. The circulars were distributed some by throwing them from a window of a building where one of the defendants was employed and others secretly, in New York City.

The defendants pleaded "not guilty," and the case of the Government consisted in showing the facts we have stated, and in introducing in evidence copies of the two printed circulars attached to the indictment, a sheet entitled "Revolutionists United for Action," written by the defendant Lipman, and found on him when he was arrested, and another paper, found at the headquarters of the group, and for which Abrams assumed responsibility.

Thus the conspiracy and the doing of the overt acts charged were largely admitted and were fully established.

On the record thus described it is argued, somewhat faintly, that the acts charged against the defendants were not unlawful because within the protection of that freedom of speech and of the press which is guaranteed by the First Amendment to the Constitution of the United States, and that the entire Espionage Act is unconstitutional because in conflict with that Amendment.

This contention is sufficiently discussed and is definitely negatived in *Schenck* v. *United States* and *Baer* v. *United States*, 249 U.S. 47; and in *Frohwerk* v. *United States*, 249 U.S. 204.

The claim chiefly elaborated upon by the defendants in the oral argument and in their brief is that there is no substantial evidence in the record to support the judgment upon the verdict of guilty and that the motion of the defendants for an instructed verdict in their favor was erroneously denied. A question of law is thus presented, which calls for an examination of the record, not for the purpose of weighing conflicting testimony, but only to determine whether there was some evidence, competent and substantial, before the jury, fairly tending to sustain the verdict. . . .

The first of the two articles attached to the indictment is conspicuously headed, "The Hypocrisy of the United States and her Allies." After denouncing President Wilson as a hypocrite and a coward because troops were sent into Russia, it proceeds to assail our Government in general, saying:

"His [the President's] shameful, cowardly silence about the intervention in Russia reveals the hypocrisy of the plutocratic gang in Washington and vicinity."
It continues:

"He [the President] is too much of a coward to come out openly and say: 'We capitalistic nations cannot afford to have a proletarian republic in Russia.'"

Among the capitalistic nations Abrams testified the United States was included.

Growing more inflammatory as it proceeds, the circular culminates in:

"The Russian Revolution cries: Workers of the World! Awake! Rise! Put down your enemy and mine!

"Yes! friends, there is only one enemy of the workers of the world and that is CAPITALISM."

This is clearly an appeal to the "workers" of this country to arise and put down by force the Government of the United States which they characterize as their "hypocritical," "cowardly" and "capitalistic" enemy.

It concludes:
"Awake! Awake, you Workers of the World!
"REVOLUTIONISTS."

The second of the articles was printed in the Yiddish language and in the translation is headed, "Workers—Wake up." After referring to "his Majesty, Mr. Wilson, and the rest of the gang; dogs of all colors!", it continues:

"Workers, Russian emigrants, you who had the least belief in the honesty of *our* Government," which defendants admitted referred to the United States Government, "must now throw away all confidence, must spit in the face the false, hypocritic, military propaganda which has fooled you so relentlessly, calling forth your sympathy, your help, to the prosecution of the war."

The purpose of this obviously was to persuade the persons to whom it was addressed to turn a deaf ear to patriotic appeals in behalf of the Government of the United States, and to cease to render it assistance in the prosecution of the war.

It goes on:

"With the money which you have loaned, or are going to loan them, they will make bullets not only for the Germans, but also for the Workers Soviets of Russia. *Workers in the ammunition factories, you are producing bullets, bayonets, cannon, to murder not only the Germans, but also your dearest, best, who are in Russia and are fighting for freedom.*"

It will not do to say, as is now argued, that the only intent of these defendants was to prevent injury to the Russian cause. Men must be held to have intended, and to be accountable for, the effects which their acts were likely to produce. Even if their primary purpose and intent was to aid the cause of the Russian Revolution, the plan of action which they adopted necessarily involved, before it could be realized, defeat of the war program of the United States, for the obvious effect of this appeal, if it should become effective, as they hoped it might, would be to persuade persons of character such as those whom they regarded themselves as addressing, not to aid government loans and not to work in ammunition factories, where their work would produce "bullets, bayonets, cannon" and other munitions of war, the use of which would cause the "murder" of Germans and Russians.

Again, the spirit becomes more bitter as it proceeds to declare that—

"America and her Allies have betrayed (the Workers). Their robberish aims are clear to all men. The destruction of the Russian Revolution, that is the politics of the march to Russia.

"*Workers, our reply to the barbaric intervention has to be a general strike! An open challenge* only will let the Government know that not only the Russian Worker fights for freedom, but also *here in America lives the spirit of Revolution.*"

This is not an attempt to bring about a change of administration by candid discussion, for no matter what may have incited the outbreak on the part of the defendant anarchists, the manifest purpose of such a publication was to create an attempt to defeat the war plans of the Government of the United States, by bringing upon the country the paralysis of a general strike, thereby arresting the production of all munitions and other things essential to the conduct of the war.

. . . the plain purpose of their propaganda was to excite, at the supreme crisis of the war, disaffection, sedition, riots, and, as they hoped, revolution, in this country for the purpose of embarrassing and if possible defeating the military plans of the Government in Europe. A technical distinction may perhaps be taken between disloyal and abusive language applied to the *form* of our government or language intended to bring the *form* of our government into contempt and disrepute, and language of like character and intended to produce like results directed against the President and Congress, the agencies through which that form of government must function in time of war. But it is not necessary to a decision of this case to consider whether such distinction is vital or merely formal, for the language of these circulars was obviously intended to provoke and to encourage resistance to the United States in the war, as the third count runs, and, the defendants, in terms, plainly urged and advocated a resort to a general strike of workers in ammunition factories for the purpose of curtailing the production of ordnance and munitions necessary and essential to the prosecution of the war as is charged in the fourth count. Thus it is clear not only that some evidence but that much persuasive evidence was before the jury tending to prove that the defendants were guilty as charged in both the third and fourth counts of the indictment and under the long established rule of law hereinbefore stated the judgment of the District Court must be

Affirmed.

MR. JUSTICE HOLMES dissenting.

This indictment is founded wholly upon the publication of two leaflets which I shall describe in a moment. The first count charges a conspiracy pending the war with Germany to publish abusive language about the form of government of the United States, laying the preparation and publishing of the first leaflet as overt acts. The second count charges a conspiracy pending the war to publish language intended to bring the form of government into contempt, laying the preparation and publishing of the two leaflets as overt acts. The third count alleges a conspiracy to encourage resistance to the United States in the same war and to attempt to effectuate the purpose by publishing the same leaflets. The fourth count lays a conspiracy to incite curtailment of production of things necessary to the prosecution of the war and to attempt to accomplish it by publishing the second leaflet to which I have referred.

. . .

No argument seems to me necessary to show that these pronunciamentos in no way attack the form of government of the United States, or that they do not support either of the first two counts. What little I have to say about the third count may be postponed until I have considered the fourth. With regard to that it seems too plain to be denied that the suggestion to workers in the ammunition factories that they are producing bullets to murder their dearest, and the further advocacy of a general strike, both in the second leaflet, do urge curtailment of production of things necessary to the prosecution of the war within the meaning of the Act of May 16, 1918, c. 75, 40 Stat. 553, amending § 3 of the earlier Act of 1917. But to make the conduct criminal that statute requires that it should be "with intent by such curtailment to cripple or hinder the United States in the prosecution of the war." It seems to me that no such intent is proved.

I am aware of course that the word intent as vaguely used in ordinary legal discussion means no more than knowledge at the time of the act that the consequences said to be intended will ensue. Even less than that will satisfy the general principle of civil and criminal liability. A man may have to pay damages, may be sent to prison, at common law might be hanged, if at the time of his act he knew facts from which common experience showed that the consequences would follow, whether he individually could foresee them or not. But, when words are used exactly, a deed is not done with intent to produce a consequence unless that consequence is the aim of the deed. It may be obvious, and obvious to the actor, that the

consequence will follow, and he may be liable for it even if he regrets it, but he does not do the act with intent to produce it unless the aim to produce it is the proximate motive of the specific act, although there may be some deeper motive behind.

It seems to me that this statute must be taken to use its words in a strict and accurate sense. They would be absurd in any other. A patriot might think that we were wasting money on aeroplanes, or making more cannon of a certain kind than we needed, and might advocate curtailment with success, yet even if it turned out that the curtailment hindered and was thought by other minds to have been obviously likely to hinder the United States in the prosecution of the war, no one would hold such conduct a crime. I admit that my illustration does not answer all that might be said but it is enough to show what I think and to let me pass to a more important aspect of the case. I refer to the First Amendment to the Constitution that Congress shall make no law abridging the freedom of speech.

I never have seen any reason to doubt that the questions of law that alone were before this Court in the cases of *Schenck, Frohwerk* and *Debs*, 249 U.S. 47, 204, 211, were rightly decided. I do not doubt for a moment that by the same reasoning that would justify punishing persuasion to murder, the United States constitutionally may punish speech that produces or is intended to produce a clear and imminent danger that it will bring about forthwith certain substantive evils that the United States constitutionally may seek to prevent. The power undoubtedly is greater in time of war than in time of peace because war opens dangers that do not exist at other times.

But as against dangers peculiar to war, as against others, the principle of the right to free speech is always the same. It is only the present danger of immediate evil or an intent to bring it about that warrants Congress in setting a limit to the expression of opinion where private rights are not concerned. Congress certainly cannot forbid all effort to change the mind of the country. Now nobody can suppose that the surreptitious publishing of a silly leaflet by an unknown man, without more, would present any immediate danger that its opinions would hinder the success of the government arms or have any appreciable tendency to do so. Publishing those opinions for the very purpose of obstructing however, might indicate a greater danger and at any rate would have the quality of an attempt. So I assume that the second leaflet if published for the purposes alleged in the fourth count might be punishable. But it seems pretty clear to me that nothing less than that would bring these papers within the scope of this law. An actual intent in the sense that I have explained is necessary to constitute an attempt, where a further act of the same individual is required to complete the substantive crime. . . .

I return for a moment to the third count. That charges an intent to provoke resistance to the United States in its war with Germany. Taking the clause in the statute that deals with that in connection with the other elaborate provisions of the act, I think that resistance to the United States means some forcible act of opposition to some proceeding of the United States in pursuance of the war. I think the intent must be the specific intent that I have described and for the reasons that I have given I think that no such intent was proved or existed in fact. I also think that there is no hint at resistance to the United States as I construe the phrase.

In this case sentences of twenty years imprisonment have been imposed for the publishing of two leaflets that I believe the defendants had as much right to publish as the Government has to publish the Constitution of the United States now vainly invoked by them. Even if I am technically wrong and enough can be squeezed from these poor and puny anonymities to turn the color of legal litmus paper; I will add, even if what I think the necessary intent were shown; the most nominal punishment seems to me all that possibly could be inflicted, unless the defendants are to be made to suffer not for what the indictment alleges but for the creed that they avow—a creed that I believe to be the creed of ignorance and immaturity when honestly held, as I see no reason to doubt that it was held here, but which, although made the subject of examination at the trial, no one has a right even to consider in dealing with the charges before the Court.

Persecution for the expression of opinions seems to me perfectly logical. If you have no doubt of your premises or your power and want a certain result with all your heart you naturally express your wishes in law and sweep away all opposition. To allow opposition by speech seems to indicate that you think the speech impotent, as when a man says that he has squared the circle, or that you do not care whole-heartedly for the result, or that you doubt either your power or your premises. But when men have realized that time has upset many fighting faiths, they may come to believe even more than they believe the very foundations of their own conduct that the ultimate good desired is better reached by free trade in ideas—that the best test of truth is the power of the thought to get itself accepted in the competition of the market, and that truth is the only ground upon which their wishes safely can be carried out. That at any rate is the theory of our Constitution. It is an experiment, as all life is an experiment. Every year if not every day we have to wager our salvation upon some prophecy based upon imperfect knowledge. While that experiment is part of our system I think that we should be eternally vigilant against attempts to check the expression of opinions that we loathe and believe to be fraught with death, unless they so imminently threaten immediate interference with the lawful and pressing purposes of the law that an immediate check is required to save the country. I wholly disagree with the argument of the Government that the First Amendment left the common law as to seditious libel in force. History seems to me against the notion. I had conceived that the United States through many years had shown its repentance for the Sedition Act of 1798, by repaying fines that it imposed. Only the emergency that makes it immediately dangerous to leave the correction of evil counsels to time warrants making any exception to the sweeping command, "Congress shall make no law . . . abridging the freedom of speech." Of course I am speaking only of expressions of opinion and exhortations, which were all that were uttered here, but I regret that I cannot put into more impressive words my belief that in their conviction upon this indictment the defendants were deprived of their rights under the Constitution of the United States.

MR. JUSTICE BRANDEIS concurs with the foregoing opinion.

Gitlow v. New York

268 U.S. 652 (1925)

Benjamin Gitlow, a member of the Left Wing Section of the Socialist party, was convicted for violating the New York laws of criminal anarchy (which advocates the violent overthrow of the government). This case is significant because it represents a step in the incorporation of part of the First Amendment into the Due Process Clause of the Fourteenth Amendment, thus including these rights and privileges among those protected from impairment by the states.

MR. JUSTICE SANFORD delivered the opinion of the Court.

Benjamin Gitlow was indicted in the Supreme Court of New York, with three others, for the statutory crime of criminal anarchy. New York Penal Laws, §§ 160, 161. He was separately tried, convicted, and sentenced to imprisonment. The judgment was affirmed by the Appellate Division and by the Court of Appeals. 195 App. Div. 773; 234 N. Y. 132 and 539. The case is here on writ of error to the Supreme Court, to which the record was remitted. 260 U. S. 703.

The contention here is that the statute, by its terms and as applied in this case, is repugnant to the due process clause of the Fourteenth Amendment. Its material provisions are:

"§ 160. *Criminal anarchy defined.* Criminal anarchy is the doctrine that organized government should be overthrown by force or violence, or by assassination of the executive head or of any of the executive officials of government, or by any unlawful means. The advocacy of such doctrine either by word of mouth or writing is a felony.

"§ 161. *Advocacy of criminal anarchy.* Any person who:

"1. By word of mouth or writing advocates, advises or teaches the duty, necessity or propriety of overthrowing or overturning organized government by force or violence, or by assassination of the executive head or of any of the executive officials of government, or by any unlawful means; or,

"2. Prints, publishes, edits, issues or knowingly circulates, sells, distributes or publicly displays any book, paper, document, or written or printed matter in any form, containing or advocating, advising or teaching the doctrine that organized government should be overthrown by force, violence or any unlawful means . . . ,

"'Is guilty of a felony and punishable' by imprisonment or fine, or both."

The indictment was in two counts. The first charged that the defendant had advocated, advised and taught the duty, necessity and propriety of overthrowing and overturning organized government by force, violence and unlawful means, by certain writings therein set forth entitled "The Left Wing Manifesto"; the second that he had printed, published and knowingly circulated and distributed a certain paper called "The Revolutionary Age," containing the writings set forth in the first count advocating, advising and teaching the doctrine that organized government should be overthrown by force, violence and unlawful means.

The following facts were established on the trial by undisputed evidence and admissions: The defendant is a member of the Left Wing Section of the Socialist Party, a dissenting branch or faction of that party formed in opposition to its dominant policy of "moderate Socialism." Membership in both is open to aliens as well as citizens. The Left Wing Section was organized nationally at a conference in New York City in June, 1919, attended by ninety delegates from twenty different States. The conference elected a National Council, of which the defendant was a member, and left to it the adoption of a "Manifesto." This was published in The Revolutionary Age, the official organ of the Left Wing. The defendant was on the board of managers of the paper and was its business manager. He arranged for the printing of the paper and took to the printer the manuscript of the first issue which contained the Left Wing Manifesto, and also a Communist Program and a Program of the Left Wing that had been adopted by the conference. Sixteen thousand copies were printed, which were delivered at the premises in New York City used as the office of the Revolutionary Age and the headquarters of the Left Wing, and occupied by the defendant and other officials. These copies were paid for by the defendant, as business manager of the paper. Employees at this office wrapped and mailed out copies of the paper under the defendant's direction; and copies were sold from this office. It was admitted that the defendant signed a card subscribing to the Manifesto and Program of the Left Wing, which all applicants were required to sign before being admitted to membership; that he went to different parts of the State to speak to branches of the Socialist Party about the principles of the Left Wing and advocated their adoption; and that he was responsible for the Manifesto as it appeared, that "he knew of the publication, in a general way and he knew of its publication afterwards, and is responsible for its circulation."

There was no evidence of any effect resulting from the publication and circulation of the Manifesto.

No witnesses were offered in behalf of the defendant.

Extracts from the Manifesto are set forth in the margin. Coupled with a review of the rise of Socialism, it condemned the dominant "moderate Socialism" for its recognition of the necessity of the democratic parliamentary state; repudiated its policy of introducing Socialism by legislative measures; and advocated, in plain and unequivocal language, the necessity of accomplishing the "Communist Revolution" by a militant and "revolutionary Socialism", based on "the class struggle" and mobilizing the "power of the proletariat in action," through mass industrial revolts developing into mass political strikes and "revolutionary mass action", for the purpose of conquering and destroying the parliamentary state and establishing in its place, through a "revolutionary dictatorship of the proletariat", the system of Communist Socialism. . . .

The precise question presented, and the only question which we can consider under this writ of error, then is, whether the statute, as construed and applied in this case by the state courts, deprived the defendant of his liberty of expression in violation of the due process clause of the Fourteenth Amendment.

The statute does not penalize the utterance or publication of abstract "doctrine" or academic discussion having no quality of incitement to any concrete action. It is not aimed against mere historical or philosophical essays. It does not restrain the advocacy of changes in the form of government by constitutional and lawful means. What it prohibits is language advocating, advising or teaching the overthrow of organized government by unlawful means. These words imply urging to action. Advocacy is defined in the Century Dictionary as: "1. The act of pleading for, supporting, or recommending; active espousal." It is not the abstract "doctrine" of overthrowing organized government by unlawful means which is denounced by the statute, but the advocacy of action for the accomplishment of that purpose. It was so construed and applied by the trial judge, who specifically charged the jury that: "A mere grouping of historical events and a prophetic deduction from them would neither constitute advocacy, advice or teaching of a doctrine for the overthrow of government by force, violence or unlawful means. [And] if it were a mere essay on the subject, as suggested by counsel, based upon deductions from alleged historical events, with no teaching, advice or advocacy of action, it would not constitute a violation of the statute. . . ."

The Manifesto, plainly, is neither the statement of abstract doctrine nor, as suggested by counsel, mere prediction that industrial disturbances and revolutionary mass strikes will result spontaneously in an inevitable process of evolution in the economic system. It advocates and urges in fervent language mass action which shall progressively foment industrial disturbances and through political mass strikes and revolutionary mass action overthrow and destroy organized parliamentary government. It concludes with a call to action in these words: "The proletariat revolution and the Communist reconstruction of society—*the struggle for these*—is now indispensable. . . . The Communist International calls the proletariat of the world to the final struggle!" This is not the expression of philosophical abstraction, the mere prediction of future events; it is the language of direct incitement.

. . .

For present purposes we may and do assume that freedom of speech and of the press—which are protected by the First Amendment from abridgment by Congress—are among the fundamental personal rights and "liberties" protected by the due process clause of the Fourteenth Amendment from impairment by the States. . . .

By enacting the present statute the State has determined, through its legislative body, that utterances advocating the overthrow of organized government by force, violence and unlawful means, are so inimical to the general welfare and involve such danger of substantive evil that they may be penalized in the exercise of its police power. That determination must be given great weight. . . . The State cannot reasonably be required to measure the danger from every such utterance in the nice balance of a jeweler's scale. A single revolutionary spark may kindle a fire that, smouldering for a time, may burst into a sweeping and destructive conflagration. It cannot be said that the State is acting arbitrarily or unreasonably when in the exercise of its judgment as to the measures necessary to protect the public peace and safety, it seeks to extinguish the spark without waiting until it has enkindled the flame or blazed into the conflagration. It cannot reasonably be required to defer the adoption of measures for its own peace and safety until the revolutionary utterances lead to actual disturbances of the public peace or imminent and immediate danger of its own destruction; but it may, in the exercise of its judgment, suppress the threatened danger in its incipiency. . . .

And finding, for the reasons stated, that the statute is not in itself unconstitutional, and that it has not been applied in the present case in derogation of any constitutional right, the judgment of the Court of Appeals is

Affirmed.

MR. JUSTICE HOLMES, dissenting.

MR. JUSTICE BRANDEIS and I are of opinion that this judgment should be reversed. The general principle of free speech, it seems to me, must be taken to be included in the Fourteenth Amendment, in view of the scope that has been given to the word 'liberty' as there used, although perhaps it may be accepted with a somewhat larger latitude of interpretation than is allowed to Congress by the sweeping language that governs or ought to govern the laws of the United States. If I am right, then I think that the criterion sanctioned by the full Court in *Schenck* v. *United States*, 249 U.S. 47, 52, applies. "The question in every case is whether the words used are used in such circumstances and are of such a nature as to create a clear and present danger that they will bring about the substantive evils that [the State] has a right to prevent." It is true that in my opinion this criterion was departed from in *Abrams* v. *United States*, 250 U.S. 616, but the convictions that I expressed in that case are too deep for it to be possible for me as yet to believe that it and *Schaefer* v. *United States*, 251 U. S. 466, have settled the law. If what I think the correct test is applied, it is manifest that there was no present danger of an attempt to overthrow the government by force on the part of the admittedly small minority who shared the defendant's views. It is said that this manifesto was more than a theory, that it was an incitement. Every idea is an incitement. It offers itself for belief and if believed it is acted on unless some other belief outweighs it or some failure of energy stifles the movement at its birth. The only difference between the expression of an opinion and an incitement in the narrower sense is the speaker's enthusiasm for the result. Eloquence may set fire to reason. But whatever may be thought of the redundant discourse before us it had no chance of starting a present conflagration. If in the long run the beliefs expressed in proletarian dictatorship are destined to be accepted by the dominant forces of the community, the only meaning of free speech is that they should be given their chance and have their way.

If the publication of this document had been laid as an attempt to induce an uprising against government at once and not at some indefinite time in the future it would have presented a different question. The object would have been one with which the law might deal, subject to the doubt whether there was any danger that the publication could produce any result, or in other words, whether it was not futile and too remote from possible consequences. But the indictment alleges the publication and nothing more.

Whitney v. California

274 U.S. 357 (1927)

Charlotte Anita Whitney was prosecuted for violating California's Criminal Syndicalism Act, which covered efforts of trade unions and industrial workers to gain control of production through general strikes, sabotage, violence, or other criminal means. She was found guilty of having organized and participated in a group assembled to advocate, teach, aid, and abet criminal syndicalism. A unanimous Court upheld the Act, but the case is remembered primarily because of the eloquent exposition of First Amendment values in the concurrence by Brandeis.

MR. JUSTICE SANFORD delivered the opinion of the Court.

By a criminal information filed in the Superior Court of Alameda County, California, the plaintiff in error was charged, in five counts, with violations of the Criminal Syndicalism Act of that State. Statutes, 1919, c. 188, p. 281. She was tried, convicted on the first count, and sentenced to imprisonment. The judgment was affirmed by the District Court of Appeal. 57 Cal. App. 449. Her petition to have the case heard by the Supreme Court was denied. *Ib*. 453. And the case was brought here on a writ of error which was allowed by the Presiding Justice of the Court of Appeal, the highest court of the State in which a decision could be had. Jud. Code, § 237.

On the first hearing in this Court, the writ of error was dismissed for want of jurisdiction. 269 U. S. 530. Thereafter, a petition for rehearing was granted, *Ib*. 538; and the case was again heard and reargued both as to the jurisdiction and the merits.

The pertinent provisions of the Criminal Syndicalism Act are:

"Section 1. The term 'criminal syndicalism' as used in this act is hereby defined as any doctrine or precept advocating, teaching or aiding and abetting the commission of crime, sabotage (which word is hereby defined as meaning wilful and malicious physical damage or injury to physical property), or unlawful acts of force and violence or unlawful methods of terrorism as a means of accomplishing a change in industrial ownership or control, or effecting any political change.

"Sec. 2. Any person who: . . . 4. Organizes or assists in organizing, or is or knowingly becomes a member of, any organization, society, group or assemblage of persons organized or assembled to advocate, teach or aid and abet criminal syndicalism . . .

"Is guilty of a felony and punishable by imprisonment."

The first count of the information, on which the conviction was had, charged that on or about November 28, 1919, in Alameda County, the defendant, in violation of the Criminal Syndicalism Act, "did then and there unlawfully, wilfully, wrongfully, deliberately and feloniously organize and assist in organizing, and was, is, and knowingly became a member of an organization, society, group and assemblage of persons organized and assembled to advocate, teach, aid and abet criminal syndicalism."

. . .

The following facts, among many others, were established on the trial by undisputed evidence:

The defendant, a resident of Oakland, in Alameda County, California, had been a member of the Local Oakland branch of the Socialist Party. This Local sent delegates to the national convention of the Socialist Party held in Chicago in 1919, which resulted in a split between the "radical" group and the old-wing Socialists. The "radicals"—to whom the Oakland delegates adhered—being ejected, went to another hall, and formed the Communist Labor Party of America. Its Constitution provided for the membership of persons subscribing to the principles of the Party and pledging themselves to be guided by its Platform, and for the formation of state organizations conforming to its Platform as the supreme declaration of the Party. In its "Platform and Program" the Party declared that it was in full harmony with "the revolutionary working class parties of all countries" and adhered to the principles of Communism laid down in the Manifesto of the Third International at Moscow, and that its purpose was "to create a unified revolutionary working class movement in America," organizing the workers as a class, in a revolutionary class struggle to conquer the capitalist state, for the overthrow of capitalist rule, the conquest of political power and the establishment of a working class government, the Dictatorship of the Proletariat, in place of the state machinery of the capitalists, which should make and enforce the laws, reorganize society on the basis of Communism and bring about the Communist Commonwealth—advocated, as the most important means of capturing state power, the action of the masses, proceeding from the shops and factories, the use of the political machinery of the capitalist state being only secondary; the organization of the workers into "revolutionary industrial unions"; propaganda pointing out their revolutionary nature and possibilities; and great industrial battles showing the value of the strike as a political weapon—commended the propaganda and example of the Industrial Workers of the World and their struggles and sacrifices in the class war— pledged support and cooperation to "the revolutionary industrial proletariat of America" in their struggles against the capitalist class—cited the Seattle and Winnipeg strikes and the numerous strikes all over the country "proceeding without the authority of the old reactionary Trade Union officials," as manifestations of the new tendency —and recommended that strikes of national importance be supported and given a political character, and that propagandists and organizers be mobilized "who can not only teach, but actually help to put in practice the principles of revolutionary industrial unionism and Communism."

Shortly thereafter the Local Oakland withdrew from the Socialist Party, and sent accredited delegates, including the defendant, to a convention held in Oakland in November, 1919, for the purpose of organizing a California branch of the Communist Labor Party. The defendant, after taking out a temporary membership in the Communist Labor Party, attended this convention as a delegate and took an active part in its proceedings. She was elected a member of the Credentials Committee, and, as its chairman, made a report to the convention upon which the delegates were seated. She was also appointed a member of the Resolutions Committee, and as such signed the following resolution in reference to political action, among others proposed by the Committee: "The C. L. P. of California fully recognizes the value of political action as a means of spreading communist propaganda; it insists that in proportion to the development of the economic strength of the working class, it, the working class, must also develop its political power. The C. L. P. of California proclaims and insists that the capture of political power, locally or nationally by the revolutionary working class can be of tremendous assistance to the workers in their struggle of emancipation. . . ."

. . .

2. It is clear that the Syndicalism Act is not repugnant to the due process clause by reason of vagueness and uncertainty of definition. It has no substantial resemblance to the statutes held void for uncertainty under the Fourteenth and Fifth Amendments in *International Harvester Co.* v. *Kentucky*, 234 U. S. 216, 221; and *United States* v. *Cohen Grocery*, 255 U. S. 81, 89, because not fixing an ascertainable standard of guilt. The language of § 2, subd. 4, of the Act, under which the plaintiff in error was convicted, is clear; the definition of "criminal syndicalism" specific.

The Act, plainly, meets the essential require-

ment of due process that a penal statute be "sufficiently explicit to inform those who are subject to
it, what conduct on their part will render them
liable to its penalties," and be couched in terms
that are not "so vague that men of common
intelligence must necessarily guess at its meaning
and differ as to its application." . . .

. . .

3. Neither is the Syndicalism Act repugnant to
the equal protection clause, on the ground that, as
its penalties are confined to those who advocate a
resort to violent and unlawful methods as a means
of changing industrial and political conditions, it
arbitrarily discriminates between such persons
and those who may advocate a resort to these
methods as a means of maintaining such conditions.

It is settled by repeated decisions of this Court
that the equal protection clause does not take
from a State the power to classify in the adoption
of police laws, but admits of the exercise of a wide
scope of discretion, and avoids what is done only
when it is without any reasonable basis and therefore is purely arbitrary; and that one who assails
the classification must carry the burden of showing that it does not rest upon any reasonable basis,
but is essentially arbitrary. *Lindsley* v. *National Carbonic Gas Co.*, 220 U. S. 61, 78, and cases
cited.

. . .

4. Nor is the Syndicalism Act as applied in this
case repugnant to the due process clause as a
restraint of the rights of free speech, assembly,
and association.

That the freedom of speech which is secured by
the Constitution does not confer an absolute right
to speak, without responsibility, whatever one
may choose, or an unrestricted and unbridled
license giving immunity for every possible use of
language and preventing the punishment of those
who abuse this freedom; and that a State in the
exercise of its police power may punish those who
abuse this freedom by utterances inimical to the
public welfare, tending to incite to crime, disturb
the public peace, or endanger the foundations of
organized government and threaten its overthrow
by unlawful means, is not open to question. *Gitlow*

v. *New York*, 268 U.S. 652, 666–668, and cases
cited.

. . . We cannot hold that, as here applied, the
Act is an unreasonable or arbitrary exercise of the
police power of the State, unwarrantably infringing any right of free speech, assembly or association, or that those persons are protected from
punishment by the due process clause who abuse
such rights by joining and furthering an organization thus menacing the peace and welfare of the
State.

We find no repugnancy in the Syndicalism Act
as applied in this case to either the due process
or equal protection clauses of the Fourteenth
Amendment on any of the grounds upon which its
validity has been here challenged.

The order dismissing the writ of error will be
vacated and set aside, and the judgment of the
Court of Appeal

Affirmed.

MR. JUSTICE BRANDEIS, concurring.

. . .

This Court has not yet fixed the standard by
which to determine when a danger shall be
deemed clear; how remote the danger may be and
yet be deemed present; and what degree of evil
shall be deemed sufficiently substantial to justify
resort to abridgement of free speech and assembly
as the means of protection. To reach sound conclusions on these matters, we must bear in mind
why a State is, ordinarily, denied the power to
prohibit dissemination of social, economic and
political doctrine which a vast majority of its
citizens believes to be false and fraught with evil
consequence.

Those who won our independence believed
that the final end of the State was to make men
free to develop their faculties; and that in its
government the deliberative forces should prevail
over the arbitrary. They valued liberty both as an
end and as a means. They believed liberty to be the
secret of happiness and courage to be the secret of
liberty. They believed that freedom to think as you
will and to speak as you think are means indispensable to the discovery and spread of political truth;
that without free speech and assembly discussion

would be futile; that with them, discussion affords ordinarily adequate protection against the dissemination of noxious doctrine; that the greatest menace to freedom is an inert people; that public discussion is a political duty; and that this should be a fundamental principle of the American government. They recognized the risks to which all human institutions are subject. But they knew that order cannot be secured merely through fear of punishment for its infraction; that it is hazardous to discourage thought, hope and imagination; that fear breeds repression; that repression breeds hate; that hate menaces stable government; that the path of safety lies in the opportunity to discuss freely supposed grievances and proposed remedies; and that the fitting remedy for evil counsels is good ones. Believing in the power of reason as applied through public discussion, they eschewed silence coerced by law—the argument of force in its worst form. Recognizing the occasional tyrannies of governing majorities, they amended the Constitution so that free speech and assembly should be guaranteed.

Fear of serious injury cannot alone justify suppression of free speech and assembly. Men feared witches and burnt women. It is the function of speech to free men from the bondage of irrational fears. To justify suppression of free speech there must be reasonable ground to fear that serious evil will result if free speech is practiced. There must be reasonable ground to believe that the danger apprehended is imminent. There must be reasonable ground to believe that the evil to be prevented is a serious one. Every denunciation of existing law tends in some measure to increase the probability that there will be violation of it. Condonation of a breach enhances the probability. Expressions of approval add to the probability. Propagation of the criminal state of mind by teaching syndicalism increases it. Advocacy of law-breaking heightens it still further. But even advocacy of violation, however reprehensible morally, is not a justification for denying free speech where the advocacy falls short of incitement and there is nothing to indicate that the advocacy would be immediately acted on. The wide difference between advocacy and incitement, between preparation and attempt, between assembling and conspiracy, must be borne in mind. In order to support a finding of clear and present danger it must be shown either that immediate serious violence was to be expected or was advocated, or that the past conduct furnished reason to believe that such advocacy was then contemplated.

Those who won our independence by revolution were not cowards. They did not fear political change. They did not exalt order at the cost of liberty. To courageous, self-reliant men, with confidence in the power of free and fearless reasoning applied through the processes of popular government, no danger flowing from speech can be deemed clear and present, unless the incidence of the evil apprehended is so imminent that it may befall before there is opportunity for full discussion. If there be time to expose through discussion the falsehood and fallacies, to avert the evil by the processes of education, the remedy to be applied is more speech, not enforced silence. Only an emergency can justify repression. Such must be the rule if authority is to be reconciled with freedom. Such, in my opinion, is the command of the Constitution. It is therefore always open to Americans to challenge a law abridging free speech and assembly by showing that there was no emergency justifying it.

. . .

MR. JUSTICE HOLMES joins in this opinion.

Dennis v. United States

341 U.S. 494 (1951)

Leaders of the American Communist party were indicted and found guilty under the Smith Act for willfully and knowingly conspiring to teach and advocate the overthrow of the U.S. government by force or violence. The question before the courts was whether the statute violated First Amendment rights. To do that, the Supreme Court had to give clearer meaning to the *Schenck* test of "clear and present danger."

MR. CHIEF JUSTICE VINSON announced the judgment of the Court and an opinion in which MR. JUSTICE REED, MR. JUSTICE BURTON and MR. JUSTICE MINTON join.

Petitioners were indicted in July, 1948, for violation of the conspiracy provisions of the Smith Act, 54 Stat. 671, 18 U. S. C. (1946 ed.) § 11, during the period of April, 1945, to July, 1948. The pretrial motion to quash the indictment on the grounds, *inter alia*, that the statute was unconstitutional was denied, *United States* v. *Foster*, 80 F. Supp. 479, and the case was set for trial on January 17, 1949. A verdict of guilty as to all the petitioners was returned by the jury on October 14, 1949. The Court of Appeals affirmed the convictions. 183 F. 2d 201. We granted certiorari, 340 U. S. 863, limited to the following two questions: (1) Whether either § 2 or § 3 of the Smith Act, inherently or as construed and applied in the instant case, violates the First Amendment and other provisions of the Bill of Rights; (2) whether either § 2 or § 3 of the Act, inherently or as construed and applied in the instant case, violates the First and Fifth Amendments because of indefiniteness.

Sections 2 and 3 of the Smith Act, 54 Stat. 671, 18 U.S.C. (1946 ed.) §§ 10, 11 (see present 18 U.S.C. § 2385), provide as follows:

"SEC. 2. (a) It shall be unlawful for any person—

"(1) to knowingly or willfully advocate, abet, advise, or teach the duty, necessity, desirability, or propriety of overthrowing or destroying any government in the United States by force or violence, or by the assassination of any officer of any such government;

"(2) with intent to cause the overthrow or destruction of any government in the United States, to print, publish, edit, issue, circulate, sell, distribute, or publicly display any written or printed matter advocating, advising, or teaching the duty, necessity, desirability, or propriety of overthrowing or destroying any government in the United States by force or violence;

"(3) to organize or help to organize any society, group, or assembly of persons who teach, advocate, or encourage the overthrow or destruction of any government in the United States by force or violence; or to be or become a member of, or affiliate with, any such society, group, or assembly of persons, knowing the purposes thereof.

"(b) For the purposes of this section, the term 'government in the United States' means the Government of the United States, the government of any State, Territory, or possession of the United States, the government of the District of Columbia, or the government of any political subdivision of any of them.

"SEC. 3. It shall be unlawful for any person to attempt to commit, or to conspire to commit, any of the acts prohibited by the provisions of this title."

The indictment charged the petitioners with wilfully and knowingly conspiring (1) to organize as the Communist Party of the United States of America a society, group and assembly of persons who teach and advocate the overthrow and destruction of the Government of the United States by force and violence, and (2) knowingly and wilfully to advocate and teach the duty and necessity of overthrowing and destroying the Government of the United States by force and violence.

The indictment further alleged that § 2 of the Smith Act proscribes these acts and that any conspiracy to take such action is a violation of § 3 of the Act.

The trial of the case extended over nine months, six of which were devoted to the taking of evidence, resulting in a record of 16,000 pages. Our limited grant of the writ of certiorari has removed from our consideration any question as to the sufficiency of the evidence to support the jury's determination that petitioners are guilty of the offense charged. Whether on this record petitioners did in fact advocate the overthrow of the Government by force and violence is not before us, and we must base any discussion of this point upon the conclusions stated in the opinion of the Court of Appeals, which treated the issue in great detail. That court held that the record in this case amply supports the necessary finding of the jury that petitioners, the leaders of the Communist Party in this country, were unwilling to work within our framework of democracy, but intended to initiate a violent revolution whenever the propitious occasion appeared. Petitioners dispute the meaning to be drawn from the evidence, contending that the Marxist-Leninist doctrine they advocated taught that force and violence to achieve a Communist form of government in an existing democratic state would be necessary only because the ruling classes of that state would never permit the transformation to be accomplished peacefully, but would use force and violence to defeat any peaceful political and economic gain the Communists could achieve. But the Court of Appeals held that the record supports the following broad conclusions: By virtue of their control over the political apparatus of the Communist Political Association, petitioners were able to transform that organization into the Communist Party; that the policies of the Association were changed from peaceful cooperation with the United States and its economic and political structure to a policy which had existed before the United States and the Soviet Union were fighting a common enemy, namely, a policy which worked for the overthrow of the Government by force and violence; that the Communist Party is a highly disciplined organization, adept at infiltration into strategic positions, use of aliases, and double-meaning language; that

the Party is rigidly controlled; that Communists, unlike other political parties, tolerate no dissension from the policy laid down by the guiding forces, but that the approved program is slavishly followed by the members of the Party; that the literature of the Party and the statements and activities of its leaders, petitioners here, advocate, and the general goal of the Party was, during the period in question, to achieve a successful overthrow of the existing order by force and violence.

I.

[The trial judge charged the jury that the Smith Act required an unlawful intent. The Court agreed with this interpretation.]

II.

The obvious purpose of the statute is to protect existing Government, not from change by peaceable, lawful and constitutional means, but from change by violence, revolution and terrorism. That it is within the *power* of the Congress to protect the Government of the United States from armed rebellion is a proposition which requires little discussion. Whatever theoretical merit there may be to the argument that there is a "right" to rebellion against dictatorial governments is without force where the existing structure of the government provides for peaceful and orderly change. We reject any principle of governmental helplessness in the face of preparation for revolution, which principle, carried to its logical conclusion, must lead to anarchy. No one could conceive that it is not within the power of Congress to prohibit acts intended to overthrow the Government by force and violence. The question with which we are concerned here is not whether Congress has such *power*, but whether the *means* which it has employed conflict with the First and Fifth Amendments to the Constitution.

One of the bases for the contention that the means which Congress has employed are invalid takes the form of an attack on the face of the statute on the grounds that by its terms it prohibits academic discussion of the merits of Marxism-

Leninism, that it stifles ideas and is contrary to all concepts of a free speech and a free press.

. . .

The very language of the Smith Act negates the interpretation which petitioners would have us impose on that Act. It is directed at advocacy, not discussion. Thus, the trial judge properly charged the jury that they could not convict if they found that petitioners did "no more than pursue peaceful studies and discussions or teaching and advocacy in the realm of ideas." . . .

III.

But although the statute is not directed at the hypothetical cases which petitioners have conjured, its application in this case has resulted in convictions for the teaching and advocacy of the overthrow of the Government by force and violence, which, even though coupled with the intent to accomplish that overthrow, contains an element of speech. For this reason, we must pay special heed to the demands of the First Amendment marking out the boundaries of speech.

. . .

No important case involving free speech was decided by this Court prior to *Schenck* v. *United States*, 249 U. S. 47 (1919). Writing for a unanimous Court, Justice Holmes stated that the "question in every case is whether the words used are used in such circumstances and are of such a nature as to create a clear and present danger that they will bring about the substantive evils that Congress has a right to prevent." 249 U. S. at 52. . . .

. . . the literal problem which is presented is what has been meant by the use of the phrase "clear and present danger" of the utterances bringing about the evil within the power of Congress to punish.

Obviously, the words cannot mean that before the Government may act, it must wait until the *putsch* is about to be executed, the plans have been laid and the signal is awaited. If Government is aware that a group aiming at its overthrow is attempting to indoctrinate its members and to commit them to a course whereby they will strike when the leaders feel the circumstances permit, action by the Government is required. . . .

. . .

Chief Judge Learned Hand, writing for the majority below, interpreted the phrase as follows: "In each case [courts] must ask whether the gravity of the 'evil,' discounted by its improbability, justifies such invasion of free speech as is necessary to avoid the danger." 183 F. 2d at 212. We adopt this statement of the rule. As articulated by Chief Judge Hand, it is as succinct and inclusive as any other we might devise at this time. It takes into consideration those factors which we deem relevant, and relates their significances. More we cannot expect from words.

. . . this analysis disposes of the contention that a conspiracy to advocate, as distinguished from the advocacy itself, cannot be constitutionally restrained, because it comprises only the preparation. It is the existence of the conspiracy which creates the danger. Cf. *Pinkerton* v. *United States*, 328 U. S. 640 (1946); *Goldman* v. *United States*, 245 U. S. 474 (1918); *United States* v. *Rabinowich*, 238 U. S. 78 (1915). If the ingredients of the reaction are present, we cannot bind the Government to wait until the catalyst is added.

IV.

[The trial judge instructed the jury that if the defendants were found guilty of violating the Smith Act, he would determine as a matter of law that there was sufficient danger of a substantive evil that Congress has a right to prevent. The Court agreed that this was a question of law for a judge to decide.]

V.

There remains to be discussed the question of vagueness—whether the statute as we have interpreted it is too vague, not sufficiently advising those who would speak of the limitations upon their activity. It is urged that such vagueness contravenes the First and Fifth Amendments. This argument is particularly nonpersuasive when presented by petitioners, who, the jury found, intended to overthrow the Government as speedily as circumstances would permit. . . . A claim of guilelessness ill becomes those with evil intent. . . .

We agree that the standard as defined is not a neat, mathematical formulary. Like all verbalizations it is subject to criticism on the score of indefiniteness. But petitioners themselves contend that the verbalization "clear and present danger" is the proper standard. We see no difference, from the standpoint of vagueness, whether the standard of "clear and present danger" is one contained *in haec verba* within the statute, or whether it is the judicial measure of constitutional applicability. We have shown the indeterminate standard the phrase necessarily connotes. We do not think we have rendered that standard any more indefinite by our attempt to sum up the factors which are included within its scope. We think it well serves to indicate to those who would advocate constitutionally prohibited conduct that there is a line beyond which they may not go—a line which they, in full knowledge of what they intend and the circumstances in which their activity takes place, will well appreciate and understand. . . .

We hold that §§ 2 (a) (1), 2 (a) (3) and 3 of the Smith Act do not inherently, or as construed or applied in the instant case, violate the First Amendment and other provisions of the Bill of Rights, or the First and Fifth Amendments because of indefiniteness. Petitioners intended to overthrow the Government of the United States as speedily as the circumstances would permit. Their conspiracy to organize the Communist Party and to teach and advocate the overthrow of the Government of the United States by force and violence created a "clear and present danger" of an attempt to overthrow the Government by force and violence. They were properly and constitutionally convicted for violation of the Smith Act. The judgments of conviction are

Affirmed.

MR. JUSTICE CLARK took no part in the consideration or decision of this case.

MR. JUSTICE FRANKFURTER, concurring in affirmance of the judgment.

. . .

I.

[Frankfurter discusses the need to weigh the interests of free speech against those of national security.]

But how are competing interests to be assessed? Since they are not subject to quantitative ascertainment, the issue necessarily resolves itself into asking, who is to make the adjustment?— who is to balance the relevant factors and ascertain which interest is in the circumstances to prevail? Full responsibility for the choice cannot be given to the courts. Courts are not representative bodies. They are not designed to be a good reflex of a democratic society. Their judgment is best informed, and therefore most dependable, within narrow limits. Their essential quality is detachment, founded on independence. History teaches that the independence of the judiciary is jeopardized when courts become embroiled in the passions of the day and assume primary responsibility in choosing between competing political, economic and social pressures.

Primary responsibility for adjusting the interests which compete in the situation before us of necessity belongs to the Congress. The nature of the power to be exercised by this Court has been delineated in decisions not charged with the emotional appeal of situations such as that now before us. We are to set aside the judgment of those whose duty it is to legislate only if there is no reasonable basis for it. . . .

MR. JUSTICE JACKSON, concurring.

. . .

IV.

. . .

While I think there was power in Congress to enact this statute and that, as applied in this case, it cannot be held unconstitutional, I add that I have little faith in the long-range effectiveness of this conviction to stop the rise of the Communist movement. Communism will not go to jail with these Communists. No decision by this Court can forestall revolution whenever the existing government fails to command the respect and loyalty of the people and sufficient distress and discontent is allowed to grow up among the masses. Many failures by fallen governments attest that no government can long prevent revolution by outlawry. Corruption, ineptitude, inflation, oppressive taxation, militarization, injustice, and loss of leadership capable of intellectual initiative in domestic or foreign affairs are allies on which the Communists count to bring opportunity knocking to their door. Sometimes I think they may be mistaken. But the Communists are not building just for today—the rest of us might profit by their example.

MR. JUSTICE BLACK, dissenting.

Here again, as in *Breard* v. *Alexandria, post,* p. 622, decided this day, my basic disagreement with the Court is not as to how we should explain or reconcile what was said in prior decisions but springs from a fundamental difference in constitutional approach. Consequently, it would serve no useful purpose to state my position at length.

At the outset I want to emphasize what the crime involved in this case is, and what it is not. These petitioners were not charged with an attempt to overthrow the Government. They were not charged with overt acts of any kind designed to overthrow the Government. They were not even charged with saying anything or writing anything designed to overthrow the Government. The charge was that they agreed to assemble and to talk and publish certain ideas at a later date: The indictment is that they conspired to organize the Communist Party and to use speech or newspapers and other publications in the future to teach and advocate the forcible overthrow of the Government. No matter how it is worded, this is a virulent form of prior censorship of speech and press, which I believe the First Amendment forbids. I would hold § 3 of the Smith Act authorizing this prior restraint unconstitutional on its face and as applied.

But let us assume, contrary to all constitutional ideas of fair criminal procedure, that petitioners although not indicted for the crime of actual advocacy, may be punished for it. Even on this radical assumption, the other opinions in this case show that the only way to affirm these convictions is to repudiate directly or indirectly the estab-

lished "clear and present danger" rule. This the Court does in a way which greatly restricts the protections afforded by the First Amendment. . . .

. . .

So long as this Court exercises the power of judicial review of legislation, I cannot agree that the First Amendment permits us to sustain laws suppressing freedom of speech and press on the basis of Congress' or our own notions of mere "reasonableness." Such a doctrine waters down the First Amendment so that it amounts to little more than an admonition to Congress. The Amendment as so construed is not likely to protect any but those "safe" or orthodox views which rarely need its protection.

. . .

MR. JUSTICE DOUGLAS, dissenting.

If this were a case where those who claimed protection under the First Amendment were teaching the techniques of sabotage, the assassination of the President, the filching of documents from public files, the planting of bombs, the art of street warfare, and the like, I would have no doubts. The freedom to speak is not absolute; the teaching of methods of terror and other seditious conduct should be beyond the pale along with obscenity and immorality. This case was argued as if those were the facts. The argument imported much seditious conduct into the record. That is easy and it has popular appeal, for the activities of Communists in plotting and scheming against the free world are common knowledge. But the fact is that no such evidence was introduced at the trial. There is a statute which makes a seditious conspiracy unlawful. Petitioners, however, were not charged with a "conspiracy to overthrow" the Government. They were charged with a conspiracy to form a party and groups and assemblies of people who teach and advocate the overthrow of our Government by force or violence and with a conspiracy to advocate and teach its overthrow by force and violence. It may well be that indoctrination in the techniques of terror to destroy the Government would be indictable under either statute. But the teaching which is condemned here is of a different character.

. . . The Act, as construed, requires the element of intent—that those who teach the creed believe in it. The crime then depends not on what is taught but on who the teacher is. That is to make freedom of speech turn not on *what is said,* but on the *intent* with which it is said. Once we start down that road we enter territory dangerous to the liberties of every citizen.

There was a time in England when the concept of constructive treason flourished. Men were punished not for raising a hand against the king but for thinking murderous thoughts about him. The Framers of the Constitution were alive to that abuse and took steps to see that the practice would not flourish here. Treason was defined to require overt acts—the evolution of a plot against the country into an actual project. The present case is not one of treason. But the analogy is close when the illegality is made to turn on intent, not on the nature of the act. We then start probing men's minds for motive and purpose; they become entangled in the law not for what they did but *for what they thought;* they get convicted not for what they said but for the purpose with which they said it.

Intent, of course, often makes the difference in the law. An act otherwise excusable or carrying minor penalties may grow to an abhorrent thing if the evil intent is present. We deal here, however, not with ordinary acts but with speech, to which the Constitution has given a special sanction.

. . .

The nature of Communism as a force on the world scene would, of course, be relevant to the issue of clear and present danger of petitioners' advocacy within the United States. But the primary consideration is the strength and tactical position of petitioners and their converts in this country. On that there is no evidence in the record. If we are to take judicial notice of the threat of Communists within the nation, it should not be difficult to conclude that *as a political party* they are of little consequence. Communists in this country have never made a respectable or serious showing in any election. I would doubt that there is a village, let alone a city or county or state, which the Communists could carry. Communism in the world scene is no bogeyman; but Communism as a political faction or party in this country plainly is. Communism has been so thoroughly exposed in this country that it has been crippled as a political force. Free speech has destroyed it as an effective political party. It is inconceivable that those who went up and down this country preaching the doctrine of revolution which petitioners espouse would have any success. In days of trouble and confusion, when bread lines were long, when the unemployed walked the streets, when people were starving, the advocates of a short-cut by revolution might have a chance to gain adherents. But today there are no such conditions. The country is not in despair; the people know Soviet Communism; the doctrine of Soviet revolution is exposed in all of its ugliness and the American people want none of it.

. . .

Yates v. United States

354 U.S. 298 (1957)

Leaders of the Communist party in California were indicted and convicted under the Smith Act. This case allowed the Supreme Court to revisit its holding in *Dennis* v. *United States* (1951) and provide greater protection to First Amendment freedoms.

MR. JUSTIC HARLAN delivered the opinion of the Court.

We brought these cases here to consider certain questions arising under the Smith Act which have not heretofore been passed upon by this Court, and otherwise to review the convictions of these petitioners for conspiracy to violate that Act. Among other things, the convictions are claimed to rest upon an application of the Smith Act which is hostile to the principles upon which its constitutionality was upheld in *Dennis* v. *United States*, 341 U. S. 494.

These 14 petitioners stand convicted, after a jury trial in the United States District Court for the Southern District of California, upon a single count indictment charging them with conspiring (1) to advocate and teach the duty and necessity of overthrowing the Government of the United States by force and violence, and (2) to organize, as the Communist Party of the United States, a society of persons who so advocate and teach, all with the intent of causing the overthrow of the Government by force and violence as speedily as circumstances would permit. . . .

In the view we take of this case, it is necessary for us to consider only the following of petitioners' contentions: (1) that the term "organize" as used in the Smith Act was erroneously construed by the two lower courts; (2) that the trial court's instructions to the jury erroneously excluded from the case the issue of "incitement to action"; (3) that the evidence was so insufficient as to require this Court to direct the acquittal of these petitioners; and (4) that petitioner Schneiderman's conviction was precluded by this Court's judgment in *Schneiderman* v. *United States*, 320 U. S. 118, under the doctrine of collateral estoppel. For reasons given hereafter, we conclude that these convictions must be reversed and the case remanded to the District Court with instructions to enter judgments of acquittal as to certain of the petitioners, and to grant a new trial as to the rest.

I. THE TERM "ORGANIZE."

One object of the conspiracy charged was to violate the third paragraph of 18 U. S. C. § 2385, which provides:

"Whoever organizes or helps or attempts to organize any society, group, or assembly of persons who teach, advocate, or encourage the overthrow or destruction of any [government in the United States] by force or violence . . . [s]hall be fined not more than $10,000 or imprisoned not more than ten years, or both. . . ."

Petitioners claim that "organize" means to "establish," "found," or "bring into existence," and that in this sense the Communist Party was organized by 1945 at the latest. On this basis petitioners contend that this part of the indictment, returned in 1951, was barred by the three-year statute of limitations. The Government, on the other hand, says that "organize" connotes a continuing process which goes on throughout the life of an organization, and that, in the words of the trial court's instructions to the jury, the term includes such things as "the recruiting of new members and the forming of new units, and the regrouping or expansion of existing clubs, classes and other units of any society, party, group or other organization." The two courts below accepted the Government's position. We think, however, that petitioners' position must prevail. . . .

. . . In these circumstances we should follow the familiar rule that criminal statutes are to be strictly construed and give to "organize" its narrow meaning, that is, that the word refers only to acts entering into the creation of a new organization, and not to acts thereafter performed in carrying on its activities, even though such acts may loosely be termed "organizational." . . .

II. INSTRUCTIONS TO THE JURY.

Petitioners contend that the instructions to the jury were fatally defective in that the trial court refused to charge that, in order to convict, the jury must find that the advocacy which the defendants conspired to promote was of a kind calculated to "incite" persons to action for the forcible overthrow of the Government. It is argued that advocacy of forcible overthrow as mere *abstract doctrine* is within the free speech protection of the First Amendment; that the Smith Act, consistently with that constitutional provision, must be taken as proscribing only the sort of advocacy which incites to illegal *action;* and that the trial court's charge, by permitting conviction for mere advocacy, unrelated to its tendency to produce forcible action, resulted in an unconstitutional application of the Smith Act. The Government, which at the trial also requested the court to charge in terms of "incitement," now takes the position, however, that the true constitutional dividing line is not between inciting and abstract advocacy of forcible overthrow, but rather between advocacy as such, irrespective of its inciting qualities, and the mere discussion or exposition of violent overthrow as an abstract theory.

. . .

We are thus faced with the question whether the Smith Act prohibits advocacy and teaching of forcible overthrow as an abstract principle, divorced from any effort to instigate action to that end, so long as such advocacy or teaching is engaged in with evil intent. We hold that it does not.

The distinction between advocacy of abstract doctrine and advocacy directed at promoting unlawful action is one that has been consistently recognized in the opinions of this Court. . . .

. . . The legislative history of the Smith Act and related bills shows beyond all question that Congress was aware of the distinction between the advocacy or teaching of abstract doctrine and the advocacy or teaching of action, and that it did not intend to disregard it. The statute was aimed at the advocacy and teaching of concrete action for the forcible overthrow of the Government, and not of principles divorced from action.

. . .

We recognize that distinctions between advocacy or teaching of abstract doctrines, with evil intent, and that which is directed to stirring people to action, are often subtle and difficult to grasp, for in a broad sense, as Mr. Justice Holmes said in his dissenting opinion in *Gitlow, supra*, 268 U. S., at 673: "Every idea is an incitement." But the very subtlety of these distinctions required the most clear and explicit instructions with reference to them, for they concerned an issue which went to the very heart of the charges against these petitioners. The need for precise and understandable instructions on this issue is further emphasized by the equivocal character of the evidence in this record, with which we deal in Part III of this opinion. Instances of speech that could be considered to amount to "advocacy of action" are so few and far between as to be almost completely overshadowed by the hundreds of instances in the record in which overthrow, if mentioned at all, occurs in the course of doctrinal disputation so remote from action as to be almost wholly lacking in probative value. Vague references to "revolutionary" or "militant" action of an unspecified character, which are found in the evidence, might in addition be given too great weight by the jury in the absence of more precise instructions. Particularly in light of this record, we must regard the trial court's charge in this respect as furnishing wholly inadequate guidance to the jury on this central point in the case. We cannot allow a conviction to stand on such "an equivocal direction to the jury on a basic issue." *Bollenbach* v. *United States*, 326 U.S. 607, 613.

III. THE EVIDENCE.

The determinations already made require a reversal of these convictions. Nevertheless, in the exercise of our power under 28 U. S. C. § 2106 to "direct the entry of such appropriate judgment . . . as may be just under the circumstances," we have conceived it to be our duty to scrutinize this lengthy record with care, in order to determine whether the way should be left open for a new trial of all or some of these petitioners. Such a judgment, we think, should, on the one hand, foreclose further proceedings against those of the petitioners as to whom the evidence in this record would be palpably insufficient upon a new trial, and should, on the other hand, leave the Government free to retry the other petitioners under proper legal standards, especially since it is by no means clear that certain aspects of the evidence against them could not have been clarified to the advantage of the Government had it not been under a misapprehension as to the burden cast upon it by the Smith Act. . . .

[The Court concludes that the evidence against five defendants was so clearly insufficient that their acquittal should be ordered. Nine defendants could be retried.]

IV. COLLATERAL ESTOPPEL.

There remains to be dealt with petitioner Schneiderman's claim based on the doctrine of collateral estoppel by judgment. Petitioner urges that in *Schneiderman* v. *United States*, 320 U. S. 118, a denaturalization proceeding in which he was the prevailing party, this Court made determinations favorable to him which are conclusive in this proceeding under the doctrine of collateral estoppel *[which prevents relitigation of the same issue in a suit upon a different claim or cause of action].*

It is . . . apparent that the determinations made by this Court in *Schneiderman* could not operate as a complete bar to this proceeding. Wholly aside from the fact that the Court was there concerned with the state of affairs existing in 1927, whereas we are concerned here with the period 1948–1951, the issues in the present case are quite different. We are not concerned here with whether petitioner has engaged in "agitation and exhortation calling for present violent action," whether in 1927 or later. Even if it were conclusively established against the Government that neither petitioner nor the Communist Party had ever engaged in such advocacy, that circumstance would constitute no bar to a conviction under 18 U. S. C. § 371 of conspiring to advocate forcible overthrow of government in violation of the Smith Act. It is not necessary for conviction here that advocacy of "present violent action" be proved. Petitioner's demand for judgment of acquittal must therefore be rejected. . . .

. . .

MR. JUSTICE BURTON, concurring in the result.

I agree with the result reached by the Court, and with the opinion of the Court except as to its interpretation of the term "organize" as used in the Smith Act. As to that, I agree with the interpretation given it by the Court of Appeals. 225 F. 2d 146.

MR. JUSTICE BRENNAN and MR. JUSTICE WHITTAKER took no part in the consideration or decision of this case.

MR. JUSTICE BLACK, with whom MR. JUSTICE DOUGLAS joins, concurring in part and dissenting in part.

I.

I would reverse every one of these convictions and direct that all the defendants be acquitted. In my judgment the statutory provisions on which these prosecutions are based abridge freedom of speech, press and assembly in violation of the First Amendment to the United States Constitution. See my dissent and that of MR. JUSTICE DOUGLAS in *Dennis* v. *United States*, 341 U. S. 494, 579, 581. Also see my opinion in *American Communications Assn.* v. *Douds*, 339 U. S. 382, 445.

The kind of trials conducted here are wholly dissimilar to normal criminal trials. Ordinarily these "Smith Act" trials are prolonged affairs lasting for months. In part this is attributable to the routine introduction in evidence of massive collections of books, tracts, pamphlets, newspapers, and manifestoes discussing Communism, Socialism, Capitalism, Feudalism and governmental institutions in general, which, it is not too much to say, are turgid, diffuse, abstruse, and just plain dull. Of course, no juror can or is expected to plow his way through this jungle of verbiage. The testimony of witnesses is comparatively insignificant. Guilt or innocence may turn on what Marx or Engels or someone else wrote or advocated as much as a hundred or more years ago. Elaborate, refined distinctions are drawn between "Communism," "Marxism," "Leninism," "Trotskyism," and "Stalinism." When the propriety of obnoxious or unorthodox views about government is in reality made the crucial issue, as it must be in cases of this kind, prejudice makes conviction inevitable except in the rarest circumstances.

II.

Since the Court proceeds on the assumption that the statutory provisions involved are valid, however, I feel free to express my views about the issues it considers.

First.—I agree with Part I of the Court's opinion that deals with the statutory term, "organize," and holds that the organizing charge in the indictment was barred by the three-year statute of limitations.

Second.— I also agree with the Court insofar as it holds that the trial judge erred in instructing that persons could be punished under the Smith Act for teaching and advocating forceful overthrow as an abstract principle. But on the other hand, I cannot agree that the instruction which the Court indicates it might approve is constitutionally permissible. The Court says that persons can be punished for advocating action to overthrow the Government by force and violence, where those to whom the advocacy is addressed are urged "to *do* something, now or in the future, rather than merely to *believe* in something." Under the Court's approach, defendants could still be convicted simply for agreeing to talk as distinguished from agreeing to act. I believe that the First Amendment forbids Congress to punish people for talking about public affairs, whether or not such discussion incites to action, legal or illegal. . . .

Third.— I also agree with the Court that petitioners, Connelly, Kusnitz, Richmond, Spector, and Steinberg, should be ordered acquitted since there is no evidence that they have ever engaged in anything but "wholly lawful activities." But in contrast to the Court, I think the same action should also be taken as to the remaining nine defendants. . . .

Fourth.— The section under which this conspiracy indictment was brought, 18 U. S. C. § 371, requires proof of an overt act done "to effect the object of the conspiracy." Originally, 11 such

overt acts were charged here. These 11 have now dwindled to 2, and as the Court says:

> "Each was a public meeting held under Party auspices at which speeches were made by one or more of the petitioners extolling leaders of the Soviet Union and criticizing various aspects of the foreign policy of the United States. At one of the meetings an appeal for funds was made. Petitioners contend that these meetings do not satisfy the requirement of the statute that there be shown an act done by one of the conspirators 'to effect the object of the conspiracy.' The Government concedes that nothing unlawful was shown to have been said or done at these meetings, but contends that these occurrences nonetheless sufficed as overt acts under the jury's findings."

The Court holds that attendance at these lawful and orderly meetings constitutes an "overt act" sufficient to meet the statutory requirements. I disagree.

. . .

MR. JUSTICE CLARK, dissenting.

. . .

I would affirm the convictions. However, the Court has freed five of the convicted petitioners and ordered new trials for the remaining nine. As to the five, it says that the evidence is "clearly insufficient." I agree with the Court of Appeals, the District Court, and the jury that the evidence showed guilt beyond a reasonable doubt. . . .

Congress Seeks to Remove "Subversives" from FDR's Administration

In an emergency appropriations bill in 1943, Congress debated an amendment designed to withhold federal salaries from three named individuals: Goodwin B. Watson and William E. Dodd, Jr., of the Federal Communications Commission, and Robert Morse Lovett, governor of the Virgin Islands. They were among a group of federal officials labeled by Congressman Martin Dies as "irresponsible, unrepresentative, crackpot, radical bureaucrats." 89 Cong. Rec. 479 (1943). The debate in the House of Representatives shows most members willing to use the power of the purse to punish individuals for

their opinions and associations. A few members opposed the amendment, regarding it as a violation of the First Amendment, a usurpation of the President's removal power, and a bill of attainder forbidden by the Constitution. The debate below is taken from 89 Cong. Rec. 4482–4487, 4546–4558, 4581–4605.

Mr. CELLER. Mr. Chairman, we are going to vote this afternoon, I presume, on the so-called amendment offered by the Kerr committee. In that connection, I fear that we are embarking upon something rather dangerous. We should think very deeply before we vote approval of the so-called ouster of liberals from various executive departments of the Government.

As I view it, this is an attempt to discharge certain men in the Government service because of their opinions. It is primarily just that.

If we are going to assume the right to fire, we may as well assume the right to hire, and then this august body would become an employment agency.

The Constitution provides for executive removal. Authority to appoint subordinate civil officers whose methods of appointment are not prescribed in the Constitution may be vested by Congress in the President, the department heads, or the courts—article II, section 2, of the Constitution.

Authority to remove subordinate civil officers in the executive branch is recognized to be a part of the power to appoint. The President, acting independently, may even remove civil officers originally appointed with the advice and consent of the Senate, *Myers* v. *The United States*, 1926 (272 U. S. 52). Congress, however, may not remove civil officers except by the specific process of impeachment—article I, sections 2 and 3; article II, section 4; and article III, section 2, of the Constitution.

Therefore, any legislation barring payment of salary to specifically named individuals who were executively appointed will be invalid, and will not be binding upon the executive branch of the Government. In other words, you can do anything you want with reference to barring the right to pay these men out of the appropriation bills, but those men would still have a right to retain those jobs and the executive head would still have the right to maintain them in those positions; so what you intend to do might be purely abortive.

. . .

Mr. OUTLAND. Mr. Chairman, this proposal to remove certain men from the Government service by means of an amendment to an appropriation bill is extremely dangerous. In my judgment, it violates our American concepts of fair play, freedom of speech, and direct action. It sets up no definite standards as to what is subversive and opens wide the path of intolerance. Under the principle here implied, for example, a Cabinet member could be removed from his position by having Congress disapprove his social or economic views, and then follow up such disapproval by an amendment such as we are discussing today.

. . .

And what is the basis for this contemplated action? It is simply that they have belonged to organizations or spoken before groups which do not meet with the approval of certain Members of Congress. Thus it becomes a matter solely of opinion, not of law, and we have prided ourselves that in this democracy of ours we are governed by laws, not by the whims of men. Such action smacks far more of the tactics of the Nazis and the Fascists, against whom we are fighting, than of the spirit of American justice and fair play.

. . .

Mr. COFFEE. . . . What is this crime of which these men are guilty? It is that either they have been the sponsors of some organization, have addressed some organization, donated to some organization which someone, somewhere, somehow said in his opinion was inimical or acting in a manner inimical to the best interests of the United States. There is not a finding anywhere in the report of the Kerr committee that any of the gentlemen so characterized was guilty of advocating the overthrow of the American Government by force and violence. There is no charge anywhere in the committee or in the hearings to the effect that any of these distinguished intellectuals advocated the overthrow of this Government.

. . .

We in Congress are sitting here as judge, as jury, and as prosecutor. . . . We are attempting to do something today which is unconstitutional. We are attempting to impeach men by methods other than impeachment. No articles of impeachment have been drawn up in the House of Representatives nor presented to the Senate against public officials of the United States, and these gentlemen are public officials. No attempt has been made to follow constitutional procedure, but an attempt has been made to circumvent the Constitution by adopting legislation which has the effect of a bill of attainder, one of the fundamental things against which our colonial forefathers sought separation from the mother country 160 years ago.

Mr. Chairman, we are proceeding on a dangerous course. One of the "four freedoms" for which this war is being fought is the freedom of speech and yet we are trying to deny the freedom of speech to distinguished citizens who come from as distinguished ancestors as those from which any Member of Congress in this House of Representatives has descended.

. . .

Mr. DIRKSEN. . . . The real issue is whether or not this body, that is charged under the Constitution as the keeper of the purse, without whose action not one dollar can go out of the Federal Treasury, can, under that authority, spell out that power to determine who shall be on the pay roll and who shall not.

. . .

Their freedom of speech is not involved. Dr. Dodd can go down on Marshall Square tonight and make any kind of a speech he wants to, but I am not going to see him on the pay roll of the Federal Government, the recipient of the taxpayers' money, and do it. That is a different thing.

Dr. Schuman can go down and stand beside the equestrian statue of Andrew Jackson in Lafayette Park this evening, make any kind of a subversive speech he desires, and within reason there will be no arrest and no restraining hand, but he is not going to do it in the terms that he has done it under the interdiction and the record that is before us and remain on the pay roll, if my vote can remove him.

. . .

Mr. KERR. . . . We discovered after organization the fact that there had never been declared judicially or by any legislative body what constituted subversive activities in respect to this Government. Subvert means to turn over, and the committee, in order to have something to go by, undertook to write what it thought constituted subversive activities in respect to the overthrow of this Government.

I may say that the committee fully understood the seriousness of this matter. It understands how serious it is to remove a man from his office and understands that a stigma may be placed upon him when that act is done. I think the committee fully understands the implications involved in one branch of the Government in attempting to remove an employee of another branch. Those things we took into consideration and those things we attempted to handle justly and properly in the light of the evidence in this matter.

You must understand that your subcommittee was not employed to remove anybody from office. We were not delegated to remove anybody from office. This House simply requested this committee to examine the facts and the charges made against various people here who had been charged with activity which was subversive of our form of government and which had for its purpose its overthrow and destruction. The Committee on Appropriations is not undertaking to remove anybody from office. The House Committee on Appropriations is simply bringing here to this Congress and giving you the facts as it has found them, saying to you, "Gentlemen, these are the facts. The duty devolves upon you now to say whether or not these men named in the amendment are fitted to be employees of the United States Government."

. . .

This Congress has the right to say to whom the people's money shall be paid. Congress will not be denied and should never be denied that right. The question involved here is one that simply involves that proposition and that statement.

. . .

Mr. HOLIFIELD. . . . I do not know whether these three men are loyal American citizens or not. I do not believe that such a determination is the prerogative of a Member of Congress or a committee thereof. The transcript of the testimony before the committee was withheld, or unavailable, to the general membership until the time of voting. We were asked to vote on a punitive legislative amendment which was directed against three individuals. In my opinion, any legislation passed by Congress should be general in its impact and not directed either for or against an individual. The civil and Federal courts are the proper places to determine the punishment of an individual. I believe this legislative rider on an appropriation bill is an attempt to punish three individuals. I believe that any punishment of individuals is clearly the prerogative of the civil and Federal courts of our Nation.

. . .

Mr. MARCANTONIO. . . . We have a most fantastic situation. We are to vote on an amendment to an appropriation bill, to expel three people from the Federal Government without a single word of the hearings before us. All we have before us is what we are told by the gentlemen who are on the committee. How can any Member do justice to these men without having before us what they said to the committee in their own defense?

. . .

What method do we employ for this new suppression? We inveigh against them the charge of subversiveness. Hitler used the Reichstag trial, he used the Communist bogey, the same pattern that we employ here for the present restriction and subsequent destruction of democratic rights.

. . .

Mr. BURDICK. Mr. Chairman, many here bemoan the fact that a few Members have seen fit to raise the question of the constitutional right of the Congress to pass a law denying the salary of an officer and thus deprive him of his right to hold office. If ever there was a constitutional question involved in any legislation, it is involved in this amendment. One of the cornerstones of our democracy is attacked—the right of free speech and the freedom of the press. If free speech can be denied in this case, it can, by the same token, be denied in any case.

. . .

In my opinion—and I almost feel like apologizing for expressing this opinion for fear that my salary may be taken away—this Congress does not have the constitutional right to legislate any citizen out of his property, or his salary, which is the same thing, merely because he has expressed an opinion which is not approved by a majority of this Congress.

Heretofore the Supreme Court of the United States has zealously guarded the right of free speech and no opinion can be found to support the intended action of this House. There is little likelihood that the present Supreme Court will fail to protect that right.

Suppose we do pass this amendment and the department paying these men brings action to set this act aside as unconstitutional. Does anyone in this Chamber think the Supreme Court will sustain the action of this House?

. . .

Mr. HOBBS. Mr. Chairman, I am exceedingly loath to oppose the pending amendment. I honor and respect the judgment both of our great Committee on Appropriations and also the special subcommittee on whose reports this amendment stands. I am devoted to the men who compose those committees and in many cases I would bow to their superior wisdom. But in a case such as this, wherein the amendment is clearly unconstitutional, in my opinion, I simply cannot follow their leadership, much as I would like to.

The pending amendment is a bill of pains and penalties within the meaning of the constitutional prohibition:

"No bill of attainder . . . shall be passed (art. I, sec. 9)."

"A bill of attainder is a legislative act which inflicts punishment without a judicial trial. If the punishment be less than death, it is a bill of pains and penalties. As the term 'bill of attainder' is used in the Federal Constitution, it includes both bills of attainder particularly, and bills of pains and penalties. (Cummings v. Missouri (71 U. S. (4 Wall.) 277, 18 L. Ed. 356); Drehman v. Stifle (75 U. S. (8 Wall.), 595, 601, 19 L. Ed. 508); Pierce v. Carskadon (83 U. S. (16 Wall.), 234, 239, 21 L. Ed. 276)."

If, then, the amendment now being considered inflicts punishment, it is a bill of pains and penalties, since there has been no judicial trial. This is not to say that the legislative hearings given by the Kerr committee were not judicial in a sense, but this committee was certainly not a court, and nothing short of a trial by a court constitutes a judicial trial.

[President Roosevelt signed the bill containing this amendment, but later explained that he did so because the bill provided emergency appropriations during the recess of Congress. In noting that the three individuals were being disqualified for federal em-ployment because of "political opinions" attributed to them, he regarded the provision as "not only unwise and discriminary, but unconstitutional as a bill of attainder," which he said the Supreme Court had defined as "a legislative act which inflicts punishment without judicial trial." Public Papers and Addresses of Franklin D. Roosevelt, *1943 Volume, at 386. It was on that ground that the provision was held unconstitutional by the Court of Claims in* Lovett v. United States, *66 F. Supp. 142 (1945), and by the Supreme Court in* United States v. Lovett, *328 U.S. 303 (1946).]*

Edwards v. South Carolina

372 U.S. 229 (1963)

Feeling aggrieved by the laws of South Carolina, 187 black high school and college students assembled peacefully on the grounds of the state legislature. When told by police officers that they must disperse within fifteen minutes or face arrest, they sang patriotic and religious songs. Although there was no violence or threat of violence on their part, they were arrested and convicted of the common-law crime of breach of the peace. James Edwards, a student, is one of the petitioners in this case.

MR. JUSTICE STEWART delivered the opinion of the Court.

The petitioners, 187 in number, were convicted in a magistrate's court in Columbia, South Carolina, of the common-law crime of breach of the peace. Their convictions were ultimately affirmed by the South Carolina Supreme Court, 239 S. C. 339, 123 S. E. 2d 247. We granted certiorari, 369 U. S. 870, to consider the claim that these convictions cannot be squared with the Fourteenth Amendment of the United States Constitution.

There was no substantial conflict in the trial evidence. Late in the morning of March 2, 1961, the petitioners, high school and college students of the Negro race, met at the Zion Baptist Church in Columbia. From there, at about noon, they walked in separate groups of about 15 to the South Carolina State House grounds, an area of two city blocks open to the general public. Their purpose was "to submit a protest to the citizens of South Carolina, along with the Legislative Bodies of South Carolina, our feelings and our dissatisfaction with the present condition of discriminatory actions against Negroes, in general, and to let them know that we were dissatisfied and that we would like for the laws which prohibited Negro privileges in this State to be removed."

Already on the State House grounds when the petitioners arrived were 30 or more law enforcement officers, who had advance knowledge that the petitioners were coming. Each group of petitioners entered the grounds through a driveway and parking area known in the record as the "horseshoe." As they entered, they were told by the law enforcement officials that "they had a right, as a citizen, to go through the State House grounds, as any other citizen has, as long as they were peaceful." During the next half hour or 45 minutes, the petitioners, in the same small groups, walked single file or two abreast in an orderly way through the grounds, each group carrying placards bearing such messages as "I am proud to be a Negro" and "Down with segregation."

During this time a crowd of some 200 to 300 onlookers had collected in the horseshoe area and on the adjacent sidewalks. There was no evidence to suggest that these onlookers were anything but curious, and no evidence at all of any threatening remarks, hostile gestures, or offensive language on the part of any member of the crowd. The City Manager testified that he recognized some of the onlookers, whom he did not identify, as "possible trouble makers," but his subsequent testimony made clear that nobody among the crowd actually caused or threatened any trouble. There was no obstruction of pedestrian or vehicular traffic within the State House grounds. No vehicle was prevented from entering or leaving the horseshoe area. Although vehicular traffic at a nearby street intersection was slowed down somewhat, an officer was dispatched to keep traffic moving. There were a number of bystanders on the public sidewalks adjacent to the State House grounds, but they all moved on when asked to do so, and there was no impediment of pedestrian traffic. Police protection at the scene was at all times sufficient to meet any foreseeable possibility of disorder.

In the situation and under the circumstances thus described, the police authorities advised the petitioners that they would be arrested if they did not disperse within 15 minutes. Instead of dispersing, the petitioners engaged in what the City Manager described as "boisterous," "loud," and "flamboyant" conduct, which, as his later testimony made clear, consisted of listening to a "religious harangue" by one of their leaders, and loudly singing "The Star Spangled Banner" and other patriotic and religious songs, while stamping their feet and clapping their hands. After 15 minutes had passed, the police arrested the petitioners and marched them off to jail.

Upon this evidence the state trial court convicted the petitioners of breach of the peace, and imposed sentences ranging from a $10 fine or five days in jail, to a $100 fine or 30 days in jail. In affirming the judgments, the Supreme Court of South Carolina said that under the law of that State the offense of breach of the peace "is not susceptible of exact definition," but that the "general definition of the offense" is as follows:

"In general terms, a breach of the peace is a violation of public order, a disturbance of the public tranquility, by any act or conduct inciting to violence . . . , it includes any violation of any law enacted to preserve peace and good order. It may consist of an act of violence or an act likely to produce violence. It is not necessary that the peace be actually broken to lay the foundation for a prosecution for this offense. If what is done is unjustifiable and unlawful, tending with sufficient directness to break the peace, no more is required. Nor is actual personal violence an essential element in the offense. . . .

"By 'peace,' as used in the law in this connection, is meant the tranquility enjoyed by citizens of a municipality or community where good order reigns among its members, which is the natural right of all persons in political society." 239 S. C., at 343–344, 123 S. E. 2d, at 249.

The petitioners contend that there was a complete absence of any evidence of the commission of this offense, and that they were thus denied one of the most basic elements of due process of law. *Thompson* v. *Louisville*, 362 U. S. 199; see *Garner* v. *Louisiana*, 368 U. S. 157; *Taylor* v. *Louisiana*, 370 U. S. 154. Whatever the merits of this contention, we need not pass upon it in the present case. The state courts have held that the petitioners' conduct constituted breach of the peace under state law, and we may accept their decision as binding upon us to that extent. But it nevertheless remains our duty in a case such as this to make an independent examination of the whole record. *Blackburn* v. *Alabama*, 361 U. S. 199, 205, n. 5; *Pennekamp* v. *Florida*, 328 U. S. 331, 335; *Fiske* v. *Kansas*, 274 U. S. 380, 385–386. And it is clear to us that in arresting, convicting, and punishing the petitioners under the circumstances disclosed by this record, South Carolina infringed the petitioners' constitutionally protected rights of free speech, free assembly, and freedom to petition for redress of their grievances.

It has long been established that these First Amendment freedoms are protected by the Fourteenth Amendment from invasion by the States. *Gitlow* v. *New York*, 268 U. S. 652; *Whitney* v. *California*, 274 U. S. 357; *Stromberg* v. *California*, 283 U. S. 359; *De Jonge* v. *Oregon*, 299 U. S. 353;

Cantwell v. *Connecticut*, 310 U. S. 296. The circumstances in this case reflect an exercise of these basic constitutional rights in their most pristine and classic form. The petitioners felt aggrieved by laws of South Carolina which allegedly "prohibited Negro privileges in this State." They peaceably assembled at the site of the State Government and there peaceably expressed their grievances "to the citizens of South Carolina, along with the Legislative Bodies of South Carolina." Not until they were told by police officials that they must disperse on pain of arrest did they do more. Even then, they but sang patriotic and religious songs after one of their leaders had delivered a "religious harangue." There was no violence or threat of violence on their part, or on the part of any member of the crowd watching them. Police protection was "ample."

This, therefore, was a far cry from the situation in *Feiner* v. *New York*, 340 U. S. 315, where two policemen were faced with a crowd which was "pushing, shoving and milling around," *id.*, at 317, where at least one member of the crowd "threatened violence if the police did not act," *id.*, at 317, where "the crowd was pressing closer around petitioner and the officer," *id.*, at 318, and where "the speaker passes the bounds of argument or persuasion and undertakes incitement to riot." *Id.*, at 321. And the record is barren of any evidence of "fighting words." See *Chaplinsky* v. *New Hampshire*, 315 U. S. 568.

We do not review in this case criminal convictions resulting from the evenhanded application of a precise and narrowly drawn regulatory statute evincing a legislative judgment that certain specific conduct be limited or proscribed. If, for example, the petitioners had been convicted upon evidence that they had violated a law regulating traffic, or had disobeyed a law reasonably limiting the periods during which the State House grounds were open to the public, this would be a different case. See *Cantwell* v. *Connecticut*, 310 U. S. 296, 307–308; *Garner* v. *Louisiana*, 368 U. S. 157, 202 (concurring opinion). These petitioners were convicted of an offense so generalized as to be, in the words of the South Carolina Supreme Court, "not susceptible of exact definition." And they were convicted upon evidence which showed no more than that the opinions which they were peaceably expressing were sufficiently opposed to the views of the majority of the community to attract a crowd and necessitate police protection.

The Fourteenth Amendment does not permit a State to make criminal the peaceful expression of unpopular views. "[A] function of free speech under our system of government is to invite dispute. It may indeed best serve its high purpose when it induces a condition of unrest, creates dissatisfaction with conditions as they are, or even stirs people to anger. Speech is often provocative and challenging. It may strike at prejudices and preconceptions and have profound unsettling effects as it presses for acceptance of an idea. That is why freedom of speech . . . is . . . protected against censorship or punishment, unless shown likely to produce a clear and present danger of a serious substantive evil that rises far above public inconvenience, annoyance, or unrest. . . . There is no room under our Constitution for a more restrictive view. For the alternative would lead to standardization of ideas either by legislatures, courts, or dominant political or community groups." *Terminiello* v. *Chicago*, 337 U. S. 1, 4–5. As in the *Terminiello* case, the courts of South Carolina have defined a criminal offense so as to permit conviction of the petitioners if their speech "stirred people to anger, invited public dispute, or brought about a condition of unrest. A conviction resting on any of those grounds may not stand." *Id.*, at 5.

As Chief Justice Hughes wrote in *Stromberg* v. *California*, "The maintenance of the opportunity for free political discussion to the end that government may be responsive to the will of the people and that changes may be obtained by lawful means, an opportunity essential to the security of the Republic, is a fundamental principle of our constitutional system. A statute which upon its face, and as authoritatively construed, is so vague and indefinite as to permit the punishment of the fair use of this opportunity is repugnant to the guaranty of liberty contained in the Fourteenth Amendment. . . ." 283 U. S. 359, 369.

For these reasons we conclude that these criminal convictions cannot stand.

Reversed.

MR. JUSTICE CLARK, dissenting.

The convictions of the petitioners, Negro high school and college students, for breach of the peace under South Carolina law are accepted by the Court "as binding upon us to that extent" but are held violative of "petitioners' constitutionally protected rights of free speech, free assembly, and freedom to petition for redress of their grievances." Petitioners, of course, had a right to peaceable assembly, to espouse their cause and to petition, but in my view the manner in which they exercised those rights was by no means the passive demonstration which this Court relates; rather, as the City Manager of Columbia testified, "a dangerous situation was really building up" which South Carolina's courts expressly found had created "an actual interference with traffic and an imminently threatened disturbance of the peace of the community." Since the Court does not attack the state courts' findings and accepts the convictions as "binding" to the extent that the petitioners' conduct constituted a breach of the peace, it is difficult for me to understand its understatement of the facts and reversal of the convictions.

The priceless character of First Amendment freedoms cannot be gainsaid, but it does not follow that they are absolutes immune from necessary state action reasonably designed for the protection of society. See *Cantwell* v. *Connecticut,* 310 U. S. 296, 304 (1940); *Schneider* v. *State,* 308 U. S. 147, 160 (1939). For that reason it is our duty to consider the context in which the arrests here were made. Certainly the city officials would be constitutionally prohibited from refusing petitioners access to the State House grounds merely because they disagreed with their views. See *Niemotko* v. *Maryland,* 340 U. S. 268 (1951). But here South Carolina's courts have found: "There is no indication whatever in this case that the acts of the police officers were taken as a subterfuge or excuse for the suppression of the appellants' views and opinions." It is undisputed that the city officials specifically granted petitioners permission to assemble, imposing only the requirement that they be "peaceful." Petitioners then gathered on the State House grounds, during a General Assembly session, in a large number of almost 200, marching and carrying placards with slogans such as "Down with segregation" and

"You may jail our bodies but not our souls." Some of them were singing.

The activity continued for approximately 45 minutes, during the busy noon-hour period, while a crowd of some 300 persons congregated in front of the State House and around the area directly in front of its entrance, known as the "horseshoe," which was used for vehicular as well as pedestrian ingress and egress. During this time there were no efforts made by the city officials to hinder the petitioners in their rights of free speech and assembly; rather, the police directed their efforts to the traffic problems resulting from petitioners' activities. It was only after the large crowd had gathered, among which the City Manager and Chief of Police recognized potential troublemakers, and which together with the students had become massed on and around the "horseshoe" so closely that vehicular and pedestrian traffic was materially impeded, that any action against the petitioners was taken. Then the City Manager, in what both the state intermediate and Supreme Court found to be the utmost good faith, decided that danger to peace and safety was imminent. Even at this juncture no orders were issued by the City Manager for the police to break up the crowd, now about 500 persons, and no arrests were made. Instead, he approached the recognized leader of the petitioners and requested him to tell the various groups of petitioners to disperse within 15 minutes, failing which they would be arrested. Even though the City Manager might have been honestly mistaken as to the imminence of danger, this was certainly a reasonable request by the city's top executive officer in an effort to avoid a public brawl. But the response of petitioners and their leader was defiance rather than cooperation. The leader immediately moved from group to group among the students, delivering a "harangue" which, according to testimony in the record, "aroused [them] to a fever pitch causing this boisterousness, this singing and stomping."

For the next 15 minutes the petitioners sang "I Shall Not Be Moved" and various religious songs, stamped their feet, clapped their hands, and conducted what the South Carolina Supreme Court found to be a "noisy demonstration in defiance of [the dispersal] orders." 239 S. C. 339, 345, 123 S. E. 2d 247, 250. Ultimately, the petitioners were arrested, as they apparently planned from the beginning, and convicted on evidence the sufficiency of which the Court does not challenge. The question thus seems to me whether a State is constitutionally prohibited from enforcing laws to prevent breach of the peace in a situation where city officials in good faith believe, and the record shows, that disorder and violence are imminent, merely because the activities constituting that breach contain claimed elements of constitutionally protected speech and assembly. To me the answer under our cases is clearly in the negative.

Beginning, as did the South Carolina courts, with the premise that the petitioners were entitled to assemble and voice their dissatisfaction with segregation, the enlargement of constitutional protection for the conduct here is as fallacious as would be the conclusion that free speech necessarily includes the right to broadcast from a sound truck in the public streets. *Kovacs* v. *Cooper*, 336 U. S. 77 (1949). This Court said in *Thornhill* v. *Alabama*, 310 U. S. 88, 105 (1940), that "[t]he power and the duty of the State to take adequate steps to preserve the peace and to protect the privacy, the lives, and the property of its residents cannot be doubted." Significantly, in holding that the petitioner's picketing was constitutionally protected in that case the Court took pains to differentiate it from "picketing *en masse* or otherwise conducted which might occasion . . . imminent and aggravated danger. . . ." *Ibid.* Here the petitioners were permitted without hindrance to exercise their rights of free speech and assembly. Their arrests occurred only after a situation arose in which the law-enforcement officials on the scene considered that a dangerous disturbance was imminent. . . .

In *Cantwell* v. *Connecticut, supra,* at 308, this Court recognized that "[w]hen clear and present danger of riot, disorder, interference with traffic upon the public streets, or other immediate threat to public safety, peace, or order, appears, the power of the State to prevent or punish is obvious." And in *Feiner* v. *New York*, 340 U. S. 315 (1951), we upheld a conviction for breach of the peace in a situation no more dangerous than that found here. There the demonstration was conducted by only one person and the crowd was limited to approximately 80, as compared with the present lineup of some 200 demonstrators and 300 onlookers. There the petitioner was "endeavoring to arouse the Negro people against the whites, urging that they rise up in arms and fight for equal rights." *Id.*, at 317. Only one person—in a city having an entirely different historical background—was exhorting adults. Here 200 youthful Negro demonstrators were being aroused to a "fever pitch" before a crowd of some 300 people who undoubtedly were hostile. Perhaps their speech was not so animated but in this setting their actions, their placards reading "You may jail our bodies but not our souls" and their chanting of "I Shall Not Be Moved," accompanied by stamping feet and clapping hands, created a much greater danger of riot and disorder. It is my belief that anyone conversant with the almost spontaneous combustion in some Southern communities in such a situation will agree that the City Manager's action may well have averted a major catastrophe.

The gravity of the danger here surely needs no further explication. The imminence of that danger has been emphasized at every stage of this proceeding, from the complaints charging that the demonstrations "tended directly to immediate violence" to the State Supreme Court's affirmance on the authority of *Feiner, supra.* This record, then, shows no steps backward from a standard of "clear and present danger." But to say that the police may not intervene until the riot has occurred is like keeping out the doctor until the patient dies. I cannot subscribe to such a doctrine. In the words of my Brother Frankfurter:

"This Court has often emphasized that in the exercise of our authority over state court decisions the Due Process Clause must not be construed in an abstract and doctrinaire way by disregarding local conditions. . . . It is pertinent, therefore, to note that all members of the New York Court accepted the finding that Feiner was stopped not because the listeners or police officers disagreed with his views but because these officers were honestly concerned with preventing a breach of the peace. . . .

"As was said in *Hague* v. *C. I. O., supra,* uncontrolled official suppression of the speaker 'cannot be made a substitute for the duty to maintain order.' 307 U. S. at 516. Where conduct is within the allowable limits of free speech, the police are peace officers for the speaker as well as for his hearers. But the power effectively to preserve order cannot be displaced by giving a speaker complete immunity. Here, there were two police officers present for 20 minutes. They interfered only when they apprehended imminence of vio-lence. It is not a constitutional principle that, in acting to preserve order, the police must proceed against the crowd, whatever its size and temper, and not against the [demonstrators]." 340 U. S., at 288–289 (concurring opinion in *Feiner* v. *New York* and other cases decided that day).

I would affirm the convictions.

Adderley v. Florida

385 U.S. 39 (1966)

Harriett Louise Adderley and thirty-one other college students were members of a group of about 200 who demonstrated against their schoolmates' arrest and perhaps segrega-tion in jail. They assembled on a nonpublic jail driveway, which they blocked. Adjacent to the county jail premises they sang, clapped, and danced. The sheriff, the jail's custodian, advised them that they were trespassing on county property and would have to leave or be arrested. They refused and were convicted under a Florida trespass statute for "trespass with a malicious and mischievous intent."

MR. JUSTICE BLACK delivered the opinion of the Court.

Petitioners, Harriett Louise Adderley and 31 other persons, were convicted by a jury in a joint trial in the County Judge's Court of Leon County, Florida, on a charge of "trespass with a malicious and mischievous intent" upon the premises of the county jail contrary to § 821.18 of the Florida statutes set out below. ["Every trespass upon the property of another, committed with a malicious and mischievous intent, the punishment of which is not specially provided for, shall be punished by imprisonment not exceeding three months, or by fine not exceeding one hundred dollars." Fla. Stat. § 821.18 (1965).] Petitioners, apparently all stu-dents of the Florida A. & M. University in Tallahas-see, had gone from the school to the jail about a mile away, along with many other students, to "demonstrate" at the jail their protests of arrests of other protesting students the day before, and perhaps to protest more generally against state and local policies and practices of racial segrega-tion, including segregation of the jail. The county sheriff, legal custodian of the jail and jail grounds, tried to persuade the students to leave the jail grounds. When this did not work, he notified them that they must leave, that if they did not leave he would arrest them for trespassing, and that if they resisted he would charge them with that as well. Some of the students left but others, including petitioners, remained and they were arrested. On appeal the convictions were affirmed by the Flori-da Circuit Court and then by the Florida District Court of Appeal, 175 So. 2d 249. That being the highest state court to which they could appeal, petitioners applied to us for certiorari contending that, in view of petitioners' purpose to protest against jail and other segregation policies, their conviction denied them "rights of free speech, assembly, petition, due process of law and equal protection of the laws as guaranteed by the Four-teenth Amendment to the Constitution of the United States." On this "Question Presented" we granted certiorari. 382 U. S. 1023. Petitioners present their argument on this question in four separate points, and for convenience we deal with each of their points in the order in which they present them.

I.

Petitioners have insisted from the beginning of this case that it is controlled by and must be reversed because of our prior cases of *Edwards* v. *South Carolina*, 372 U. S. 229, and *Cox* v. *Louisiana*, 379 U. S. 536, 559. We cannot agree.

The *Edwards* case, like this one, did come up when a number of persons demonstrated on public property against their State's segregation policies. They also sang hymns and danced, as did the demonstrators in this case. But here the analogies to this case end. In *Edwards*, the demonstrators went to the South Carolina State Capitol grounds to protest. In this case they went to the jail. Traditionally, state capitol grounds are open to the public. Jails, built for security purposes, are not. The demonstrators at the South Carolina Capitol went in through a public driveway and as they entered they were told by state officials there that they had a right as citizens to go through the State House grounds as long as they were peaceful. Here the demonstrators entered the jail grounds through a driveway used only for jail purposes and without warning to or permission from the sheriff. More importantly, South Carolina sought to prosecute its State Capitol demonstrators by charging them with the common-law crime of breach of the peace. This Court in *Edwards* took pains to point out at length the indefinite, loose, and broad nature of this charge; indeed, this Court pointed out at p. 237, that the South Carolina Supreme Court had itself declared that the "breach of the peace" charge is "not susceptible of exact definition." South Carolina's power to prosecute, it was emphasized at p. 236, would have been different had the State proceeded under a "precise and narrowly drawn regulatory statute evincing a legislative judgment that certain specific conduct be limited or proscribed" such as, for example, "limiting the periods during which the State House grounds were open to the public. . . ." The South Carolina breach-of-the-peace statute was thus struck down as being so broad and all-embracing as to jeopardize speech, press, assembly and petition, under the constitutional doctrine enunciated in *Cantwell* v. *Connecticut*, 310 U. S. 296, 307–308, and followed in many subsequent cases. And it was on this same ground of vagueness that in *Cox* v. *Louisiana, supra*, at 551–552, the Louisiana breach-of-the-peace law used to prosecute Cox was invalidated.

The Florida trespass statute under which these petitioners were charged cannot be challenged on this ground. It is aimed at conduct of one limited kind, that is, for one person or persons to trespass upon the property of another with a malicious and mischievous intent. There is no lack of notice in this law, nothing to entrap or fool the unwary.

Petitioners seem to argue that the Florida trespass law is void for vagueness because it requires a trespass to be "with a malicious and mischievous intent. . . ." But these words do not broaden the scope of trespass so as to make it cover a multitude of types of conduct as does the common-law breach-of-the-peace charge. On the contrary, these words narrow the scope of the offense. The trial court charged the jury as to their meaning and petitioners have not argued that this definition, set out below, [" 'Malicious' means wrongful, you remember back in the original charge, the State has to prove beyond a reasonable doubt there was a malicious and mischievous intent. The word 'malicious' means that the wrongful act shall be done voluntarily, unlawfully and without excuse or justification. The word 'malicious' that is used in these affidavits does not necessarily allege nor require the State to prove that the defendant had actual malice in his mind at the time of the alleged trespass. Another way of stating the definition of 'malicious' is by 'malicious' is meant the act was done knowingly and willfully and without any legal justification.

" 'Mischievous,' which is also required, means that the alleged trespass shall be inclined to cause petty and trivial trouble, annoyance and vexation to others in order for you to find that the alleged trespass was committed with mischievous intent."] is not a reasonable and clear definition of the terms. The use of these terms in the statute, instead of contributing to uncertainty and misunderstanding, actually makes its meaning more understandable and clear.

II.

Petitioners in this Court invoke the doctrine of abatement announced by this Court in *Hamm* v. *City of Rock Hill*, 379 U. S. 306. But that holding was that the Civil Rights Act of 1964, 78 Stat. 241, which made it unlawful for places of public accommodation to deny service to any person because of race, effected an abatement of prosecutions of persons for seeking such services that arose prior to the passage of the Act. But this case in no way involves prosecution of petitioners for seeking service in establishments covered by the Act. It involves only an alleged trespass on jail grounds—a trespass which can be prosecuted regardless of the fact that it is the means of protesting segregation of establishments covered by the Act.

III.

Petitioners next argue that "petty criminal statutes may not be used to violate minorities' constitutional rights." This of course is true but this abstract proposition gets us nowhere in deciding this case.

IV.

Petitioners here contend that "Petitioners' convictions are based on a total lack of relevant evidence." If true, this would be a denial of due process under *Garner* v. *Louisiana*, 368 U. S. 157, and *Thompson* v. *City of Louisville*, 362 U. S. 199. Both in the petition for certiorari and in the brief on the merits petitioners state that their summary of the evidence "does not conflict with the facts contained in the Circuit Court's opinion" which was in effect affirmed by the District Court of Appeal. 175 So. 2d 249. That statement is correct and petitioners' summary of facts, as well as that of the Circuit Court, shows an abundance of facts to support the jury's verdict of guilty in this case.

In summary both these statements show testimony ample to prove this: Disturbed and upset by the arrest of their schoolmates the day before, a large number of Florida A. & M. students assembled on the school grounds and decided to march down to the county jail. Some apparently wanted to be put in jail too, along with the students already there. A group of around 200 marched from the school and arrived at the jail singing and clapping. They went directly to the jail-door entrance where they were met by a deputy sheriff,

evidently surprised by their arrival. He asked them to move back, claiming they were blocking the entrance to the jail and fearing that they might attempt to enter the jail. They moved back part of the way, where they stood or sat, singing, clapping and dancing, on the jail driveway and on an adjacent grassy area upon the jail premises. This particular jail entrance and driveway were not normally used by the public, but by the sheriff's department for transporting prisoners to and from the courts several blocks away and by commercial concerns for servicing the jail. Even after their partial retreat, the demonstrators continued to block vehicular passage over this driveway up to the entrance of the jail. Someone called the sheriff who was at the moment apparently conferring with one of the state court judges about incidents connected with prior arrests for demonstrations. When the sheriff returned to the jail, he immediately inquired if all was safe inside the jail and was told it was. He then engaged in a conversation with two of the leaders. He told them that they were trespassing upon jail property and that he would give them 10 minutes to leave or he would arrest them. Neither of the leaders did anything to disperse the crowd, and one of them told the sheriff that they wanted to get arrested. A local minister talked with some of the demonstrators and told them not to enter the jail, because they could not arrest themselves, but just to remain where they were. After about 10 minutes, the sheriff, in a voice loud enough to be heard by all, told the demonstrators that he was the legal custodian of the jail and its premises, that they were trespassing on county property in violation of the law, that they should all leave forthwith or he would arrest them, and that if they attempted to resist arrest, he would charge them with that as a separate offense. Some of the group then left. Others, including all petitioners, did not leave. Some of them sat down. In a few minutes, realizing that the remaining demonstrators had no intention of leaving, the sheriff ordered his deputies to surround those remaining on jail premises and placed them, 107 demonstrators, under arrest. The sheriff unequivocally testified that he did not arrest any persons other than those who were on the jail premises. Of the three petitioners testifying, two insisted that they were arrested before they had a chance to leave, had they wanted to, and one testified that she did not intend to leave. The sheriff again explicitly testified that he did not arrest any person who was attempting to leave.

Under the foregoing testimony the jury was authorized to find that the State had proven every essential element of the crime, as it was defined by the state court. That interpretation is, of course, binding on us, leaving only the question of whether conviction of the state offense, thus defined, unconstitutionally deprives petitioners of their rights to freedom of speech, press, assembly or petition. We hold it does not. The sheriff, as jail custodian, had power, as the state courts have here held, to direct that this large crowd of people get off the grounds. There is not a shred of evidence in this record that this power was exercised, or that its exercise was sanctioned by the lower courts, because the sheriff objected to what was being sung or said by the demonstrators or because he disagreed with the objectives of their protest. The record reveals that he objected only to their presence on that part of the jail grounds reserved for jail uses. There is no evidence at all that on any other occasion had similarly large groups of the public been permitted to gather on this portion of the jail grounds for any purpose. Nothing in the Constitution of the United States prevents Florida from even-handed enforcement of its general trespass statute against those refusing to obey the sheriff's order to remove themselves from what amounted to the curtilage of the jailhouse. The State, no less than a private owner of property, has power to preserve the property under its control for the use to which it is lawfully dedicated. For this reason there is no merit to the petitioners' argument that they had a constitutional right to stay on the property, over the jail custodian's objections, because this "area chosen for the peaceful civil rights demonstration was not only 'reasonable' but also particularly appropriate. . . ." Such an argument has as its major unarticulated premise the assumption that people who want to propagandize protests or views have a constitutional right to do so whenever and however and wherever they please. That concept of constitutional law was vigorously and forthrightly rejected in two of the cases petitioners rely on, *Cox*

v. *Louisiana, supra,* at 554–555 and 563–564. We reject it again. The United States Constitution does not forbid a State to control the use of its own property for its own lawful nondiscriminatory purpose.

These judgments are

Affirmed.

MR. JUSTICE DOUGLAS, with whom THE CHIEF JUSTICE, MR. JUSTICE BRENNAN, and MR. JUSTICE FORTAS concur, dissenting.

The First Amendment, applicable to the States by reason of the Fourteenth (*Edwards* v. *South Carolina,* 372 U. S. 229, 235), provides that "Congress shall make no law . . . abridging . . . the right of the people peaceably to assemble, and to petition the Government for a redress of grievances." These rights, along with religion, speech, and press, are preferred rights of the Constitution, made so by reason of that explicit guarantee and what Edmond Cahn in Confronting Injustice (1966) referred to as "The Firstness of the First Amendment." With all respect, therefore, the Court errs in treating the case as if it were an ordinary trespass case or an ordinary picketing case.

The jailhouse, like an executive mansion, a legislative chamber, a courthouse, or the statehouse itself (*Edwards* v. *South Carolina, supra*) is one of the seats of government, whether it be the Tower of London, the Bastille, or a small county jail. And when it houses political prisoners or those who many think are unjustly held, it is an obvious center for protest. The right to petition for the redress of grievances has an ancient history and is not limited to writing a letter or sending a telegram to a congressman; it is not confined to appearing before the local city council, or writing letters to the President or Governor or Mayor. See *N. A. A. C. P.* v. *Button,* 371 U. S. 415, 429–431. Conventional methods of petitioning may be, and often have been, shut off to large groups of our citizens. Legislators may turn deaf ears; formal complaints may be routed endlessly through a bureaucratic maze; courts may let the wheels of justice grind very slowly. Those who do not control television and radio, those who cannot afford to advertise in newspapers or circulate elaborate pamphlets may have only a more limited type of access to public officials. Their methods should not be condemned as tactics of obstruction and harassment as long as the assembly and petition are peaceable, as these were.

There is no question that petitioners had as their purpose a protest against the arrest of Florida A. & M. students for trying to integrate public theatres. The sheriff's testimony indicates that he well understood the purpose of the rally. The petitioners who testified unequivocally stated that the group was protesting the arrests, and state and local policies of segregation, including segregation of the jail. This testimony was not contradicted or even questioned. The fact that no one gave a formal speech, that no elaborate handbills were distributed, and that the group was not laden with signs would seem to be immaterial. Such methods are not the *sine qua non* of petitioning for the redress of grievances. The group did sing "freedom" songs. And history shows that a song can be a powerful tool of protest. See *Cox* v. *Louisiana*, 379 U. S. 536, 546–548. There was no violence; no threat of violence; no attempted jail break; no storming of a prison; no plan or plot to do anything but protest. The evidence is uncontradicted that the petitioners' conduct did not upset the jailhouse routine; things went on as they normally would. None of the group entered the jail. Indeed, they moved back from the entrance as they were instructed. There was no shoving, no pushing, no disorder or threat of riot. It is said that some of the group blocked part of the driveway leading to the jail entrance. The chief jailer, to be sure, testified that vehicles would not have been able to use the driveway. Never did the students locate themselves so as to cause interference with persons or vehicles going to or coming from the jail. . . .

We do violence to the First Amendment when we permit this "petition for redress of grievances" to be turned into a trespass action. It does not help to analogize this problem to the problem of picketing. Picketing is a form of protest usually directed against private interests. I do not see how rules governing picketing in general are relevant to this express constitutional right to assemble and to petition for redress of grievances. In the first place the jailhouse grounds were not marked with "NO TRESPASSING!" signs, nor does respondent claim that the public was generally excluded from the grounds. Only the sheriff's fiat transformed lawful conduct into an unlawful trespass. To say that a private owner could have done the same if the rally had taken place on private property is to speak of a different case, as an assembly and a petition for redress of grievances run to government, not to private proprietors.

. . .

There may be some public places which are so clearly committed to other purposes that their use for the airing of grievances is anomalous. There may be some instances in which assemblies and petitions for redress of grievances are not consistent with other necessary purposes of public property. A noisy meeting may be out of keeping with the serenity of the statehouse or the quiet of the courthouse. No one, for example, would suggest that the Senate gallery is the proper place for a vociferous protest rally. And in other cases it may be necessary to adjust the right to petition for redress of grievances to the other interests inhering in the uses to which the public property is normally put. See *Cox* v. *New Hampshire, supra;* *Poulos* v. *New Hampshire*, 345 U. S. 395. But this is quite different from saying that all public places are off limits to people with grievances. See *Hague* v. *C.I.O., supra; Cox* v. *New Hampshire, supra; Jamison* v. *Texas*, 318 U. S. 413, 415–416; *Edwards* v. *South Carolina, supra.* And it is farther yet from saying that the "custodian" of the public property in his discretion can decide when public places shall be used for the communication of ideas, especially the constitutional right to assemble and petition for redress of grievances. . . . For to place such discretion in any public official, be he the "custodian" of the public property or the local police commissioner (cf. *Kunz* v. *New York*, 340 U. S. 290), is to place those who assert their First Amendment rights at his mercy. . . .

Today a trespass law is used to penalize people for exercising a constitutional right. Tomorrow a disorderly conduct statute, a breach-of-the-peace statute, a vagrancy statute will be put to the same end. It is said that the sheriff did not make the arrests because of the views which petitioners espoused. That excuse is usually given, as we know from the many cases involving arrests of minority groups for breaches of the peace, unlawful assemblies, and parading without a permit. The charge against William Penn, who preached a nonconformist doctrine in a street in London, was that he caused "a great concourse and tumult of people" in contempt of the King and "to the great disturbance of his peace." 6 How. St. Tr. 951, 955. That was in 1670. In modern times, also, such arrests are usually sought to be justified by some legitimate function of government. Yet by allowing these orderly and civilized protests against injustice to be suppressed, we only increase the forces of frustration which the conditions of second-class citizenship are generating amongst us.

Brandenburg v. Ohio

395 U.S. 444 (1969)

Charles Brandenburg, a Ku Klux Klan leader, was convicted under an Ohio criminal law for advocating crime or violence as a means of accomplishing industrial or political reform. Neither the indictment nor the trial judge's instructions to the jury refined the statute's definition of the crime in terms of mere advocacy as distinguished from incitement to imminent lawless action. His conviction was affirmed by the intermediate Ohio appellate court without opinion.

PER CURIAM.

The appellant, a leader of a Ku Klux Klan group, was convicted under the Ohio Criminal Syndicalism statute for "advocat[ing] . . . the duty, necessity, or propriety of crime, sabotage, violence, or unlawful methods of terrorism as a means of accomplishing industrial or political reform" and for "voluntarily assembl[ing] with any society, group, or assemblage of persons formed to teach or advocate the doctrines of criminal syndicalism." Ohio Rev. Code Ann. § 2923.13. He was fined $1,000 and sentenced to one to 10 years' imprisonment. The appellant challenged the constitutionality of the criminal syndicalism statute under the First and Fourteenth Amendments to the United States Constitution, but the intermediate appellate court of Ohio affirmed his conviction without opinion. The Supreme Court of Ohio dismissed his appeal, *sua sponte*, "for the reason that no substantial constitutional question exists herein." It did not file an opinion or explain its conclusions. Appeal was taken to this Court, and we noted probable jurisdiction. 393 U. S. 948 (1968). We reverse.

The record shows that a man, identified at trial as the appellant, telephoned an announcer-reporter on the staff of a Cincinnati television station and invited him to come to a Ku Klux Klan "rally" to be held at a farm in Hamilton County. With the cooperation of the organizers, the reporter and a cameraman attended the meeting and filmed the events. Portions of the films were later broadcast on the local station and on a national network.

The prosecution's case rested on the films and on testimony identifying the appellant as the person who communicated with the reporter and who spoke at the rally. The State also introduced into evidence several articles appearing in the film, including a pistol, a rifle, a shotgun, ammunition, a Bible, and a red hood worn by the speaker in the films.

One film showed 12 hooded figures, some of whom carried firearms. They were gathered around a large wooden cross, which they burned. No one was present other than the participants and the newsmen who made the film. Most of the words uttered during the scene were incomprehensible when the film was projected, but scattered phrases could be understood that were derogatory of Negroes and, in one instance, of Jews. Another scene on the same film showed the appellant, in Klan regalia, making a speech. The speech, in full, was as follows:

"This is an organizers' meeting. We have had quite a few members here today which are—we have hundreds, hundreds of members throughout the State of Ohio. I can quote from a newspaper clipping from the Columbus, Ohio Dispatch, five weeks ago Sunday morning. The Klan has more members in the State of Ohio than does any other organization. We're not a revengent organization, but if our President, our Congress, our Supreme Court, continues to suppress the white, Caucasian race, it's possible that there might have to be some revengeance taken.

"We are marching on Congress July the Fourth, four hundred thousand strong. From there we are dividing into two groups, one group to march on St. Augustine, Florida, the other group to march into Mississippi. Thank you."

The second film showed six hooded figures one of whom, later identified as the appellant, repeated a speech very similar to that recorded on the first film. The reference to the possibility of "revengeance" was omitted, and one sentence was added: "Personally, I believe the nigger should be returned to Africa, the Jew returned to Israel." Though some of the figures in the films carried weapons, the speaker did not.

The Ohio Criminal Syndicalism Statute was enacted in 1919. From 1917 to 1920, identical or quite similar laws were adopted by 20 States and two territories. E. Dowell, A History of Criminal Syndicalism Legislation in the United States 21 (1939). In 1927, this Court sustained the constitutionality of California's Criminal Syndicalism Act, Cal. Penal Code §§ 11400–11402, the text of which is quite similar to that of the laws of Ohio. *Whitney* v. *California*, 274 U. S. 357 (1927). The Court upheld the statute on the ground that, without more, "advocating" violent means to effect political and economic change involves such danger to the security of the State that the State may outlaw it. Cf. *Fiske* v. *Kansas*, 274 U. S. 380 (1927). But *Whitney* has been thoroughly discredited by later decisions. See *Dennis* v. *United States*, 341 U. S. 494, at 507 (1951). These later decisions have fashioned the principle that the constitutional guarantees of free speech and free press do not

permit a State to forbid or proscribe advocacy of the use of force or of law violation except where such advocacy is directed to inciting or producing imminent lawless action and is likely to incite or produce such action. As we said in *Noto* v. *United States*, 367 U. S. 290, 297–298 (1961), "the mere abstract teaching . . . of the moral propriety or even moral necessity for a resort to force and violence, is not the same as preparing a group for violent action and steeling it to such action." See also *Herndon* v. *Lowry*, 301 U. S. 242, 259–261 (1937); *Bond* v. *Floyd*, 385 U. S. 116, 134 (1966). A statute which fails to draw this distinction impermissibly intrudes upon the freedoms guaranteed by the First and Fourteenth Amendments. It sweeps within its condemnation speech which our Constitution has immunized from governmental control. Cf. *Yates* v. *United States*, 354 U. S. 298 (1957); *De Jonge* v. *Oregon*, 299 U. S. 353 (1937); *Stromberg* v. *California*, 283 U. S. 359 (1931). See also *United States* v. *Robel*, 389 U. S. 258 (1967); *Keyishian* v. *Board of Regents*, 385 U. S. 589 (1967); *Elfbrandt* v. *Russell*, 384 U. S. 11 (1966); *Aptheker* v. *Secretary of State*, 378 U. S. 500 (1964); *Baggett* v. *Bullitt*, 377 U. S. 360 (1964).

Measured by this test, Ohio's Criminal Syndicalism Act cannot be sustained. The Act punishes persons who "advocate or teach the duty, necessity, or propriety" of violence "as a means of accomplishing industrial or political reform"; or who publish or circulate or display any book or paper containing such advocacy; or who "justify" the commission of violent acts "with intent to exemplify, spread or advocate the propriety of the doctrines of criminal syndicalism"; or who "voluntarily assemble" with a group formed "to teach or advocate the doctrines of criminal syndicalism." Neither the indictment nor the trial judge's instructions to the jury in any way refined the statute's bald definition of the crime in terms of mere advocacy not distinguished from incitement to imminent lawless action.

Accordingly, we are here confronted with a statute which, by its own words and as applied, purports to punish mere advocacy and to forbid, on pain of criminal punishment, assembly with others merely to advocate the described type of action. Such a statute falls within the condemnation of the First and Fourteenth Amendments. The contrary teaching of *Whitney* v. *California, supra,* cannot be supported, and that decision is therefore overruled.

Reversed.

MR. JUSTICE BLACK, concurring.

I agree with the views expressed by MR. JUSTICE DOUGLAS in his concurring opinion in this case that the "clear and present danger" doctrine should have no place in the interpretation of the First Amendment. I join the Court's opinion, which, as I understand it, simply cites *Dennis* v. *United States,* 341 U. S. 494 (1951), but does not indicate any agreement on the Court's part with the "clear and present danger" doctrine on which *Dennis* purported to rely.

MR. JUSTICE DOUGLAS, concurring.

While I join the opinion of the Court, I desire to enter a *caveat.*

The "clear and present danger" test was adumbrated by Mr. Justice Holmes in a case arising during World War I—a war "declared" by the Congress, not by the Chief Executive. The case was *Schenck* v. *United States,* 249 U. S. 47, 52, where the defendant was charged with attempts to cause insubordination in the military and obstruction of enlistment. *[Douglas then summarizes other World War I cases that defined freedom of speech: Frohwerk v. United States, 249 U.S. 204 (1919), Debs v. United States, 249 U.S. 211 (1919), Abrams v. United States, 250 U.S. 616 (1919), Schaefer v. United States, 251 U.S. 466 (1920), and Pierce v. United States, 252 U.S. 239 (1920).]*

Those, then, were the World War I cases that put the gloss of "clear and present danger" on the First Amendment. Whether the war power—the greatest leveler of them all—is adequate to sustain that doctrine is debatable. The dissents in *Abrams, Schaefer,* and *Pierce* show how easily "clear and present danger" is manipulated to crush what Brandeis called "[t]he fundamental right of free men to strive for better conditions through new legislation and new institutions" by argument and discourse *(Pierce* v. *United States, supra,* at 273) even in time of war. Though I doubt if the "clear and present danger" test is congenial to the First Amendment in time of a declared war,

I am certain it is not reconcilable with the First Amendment in days of peace.

The Court quite properly overrules *Whitney* v. *California,* 274 U. S. 357, which involved advocacy of ideas which the majority of the Court deemed unsound and dangerous.

Mr. Justice Holmes, though never formally abandoning the "clear and present danger" test, moved closer to the First Amendment ideal when he said in dissent in *Gitlow* v. *New York,* 268 U. S. 652, 673:

"Every idea is an incitement. It offers itself for belief and if believed it is acted on unless some other belief outweighs it or some failure of energy stifles the movement at its birth. The only difference between the expression of an opinion and an incitement in the narrower sense is the speaker's enthusiasm for the result. Eloquence may set fire to reason. But whatever may be thought of the redundant discourse before us it had no chance of starting a present conflagration. If in the long run the beliefs expressed in proletarian dictatorship are destined to be accepted by the dominant forces of the community, the only meaning of free speech is that they should be given their chance and have their way."

We have never been faithful to the philosophy of that dissent.

The Court in *Herndon* v. *Lowry,* 301 U. S. 242, overturned a conviction for exercising First Amendment rights to incite insurrection because of lack of evidence of incitement. *Id.,* at 259–261. And see *Hartzel* v. *United States,* 322 U. S. 680. In *Bridges* v. *California,* 314 U. S. 252, 261–263, we approved the "clear and present danger" test in an elaborate dictum that tightened it and confined it to a narrow category. But in *Dennis* v. *United States,* 341 U. S. 494, we opened wide the door, distorting the "clear and present danger" test beyond recognition.

In that case the prosecution dubbed an agreement to teach the Marxist creed a "conspiracy." The case was submitted to a jury on a charge that the jury could not convict unless it found that the defendants "intended to overthrow the Government 'as speedily as circumstances would permit.'" *Id.,* at 509–511. The Court sustained convictions under that charge, construing it to mean a determination of "'whether the gravity of the "evil," discounted by its improbability, justifies such invasion of free speech as is necessary to avoid the danger.'" *Id.*, at 510, quoting from *United States* v. *Dennis*, 183 F. 2d 201, 212.

Out of the "clear and present danger" test came other offspring. Advocacy and teaching of forcible overthrow of government as an abstract principle is immune from prosecution. *Yates* v. *United States*, 354 U. S. 298, 318. But an "active" member, who has a guilty knowledge and intent of the aim to overthrow the Government by violence, *Noto* v. *United States*, 367 U. S. 290, may be prosecuted. *Scales* v. *United States*, 367 U. S. 203, 228. And the power to investigate, backed by the powerful sanction of contempt, includes the power to determine which of the two categories fits the particular witness. *Barenblatt* v. *United States*, 360 U. S. 109, 130. And so the investigator roams at will through all of the beliefs of the witness, ransacking his conscience and his innermost thoughts.

Judge Learned Hand, who wrote for the Court of Appeals in affirming the judgment in *Dennis*, coined the "not improbable" test, 183 F. 2d 201, 214, which this Court adopted and which Judge Hand preferred over the "clear and present danger" test. Indeed, in his book, The Bill of Rights 59 (1958), in referring to Holmes' creation of the "clear and present danger" test, he said, "I cannot help thinking that for once Homer nodded."

My own view is quite different. I see no place in the regime of the First Amendment for any "clear and present danger" test, whether strict and tight as some would make it, or free-wheeling as the Court in *Dennis* rephrased it.

When one reads the opinions closely and sees when and how the "clear and present danger" test has been applied, great misgivings are aroused. First, the threats were often loud but always puny and made serious only by judges so wedded to the *status quo* that critical analysis made them nervous. Second, the test was so twisted and perverted in *Dennis* as to make the trial of those teachers of Marxism an all-out political trial which was part and parcel of the cold war that has eroded substantial parts of the First Amendment.

Action is often a method of expression and within the protection of the First Amendment.

Suppose one tears up his own copy of the Constitution in eloquent protest to a decision of this Court. May he be indicted?

Suppose one rips his own Bible to shreds to celebrate his departure from one "faith" and his embrace of atheism. May he be indicted?

Last Term the Court held in *United States* v. *O'Brien*, 391 U. S. 367, 382, that a registrant under Selective Service who burned his draft card in protest of the war in Vietnam could be prosecuted. The First Amendment was tendered as a defense and rejected, the Court saying:

"The issuance of certificates indicating the registration and eligibility classification of individuals is a legitimate and substantial administrative aid in the functioning of this system. And legislation to insure the continuing availability of issued certificates serves a legitimate and substantial purpose in the system's administration." 391 U. S., at 377–378.

But O'Brien was not prosecuted for not having his draft card available when asked for by a federal agent. He was indicted, tried, and convicted for burning the card. And this Court's affirmance of that conviction was not, with all respect, consistent with the First Amendment.

The act of praying often involves body posture and movement as well as utterances. It is nonetheless protected by the Free Exercise Clause. Picketing, as we have said on numerous occasions, is "free speech plus." See *Bakery Drivers Local* v. *Wohl*, 315 U. S. 769, 775 (DOUGLAS, J., concurring); *Giboney* v. *Empire Storage Co.*, 336 U. S. 490, 501; *Hughes* v. *Superior Court*, 339 U. S. 460, 465; *Labor Board* v. *Fruit Packers*, 377 U. S. 58, 77 (BLACK, J., concurring), and *id.*, at 93 (HARLAN, J., dissenting); *Cox* v. *Louisiana*, 379 U. S. 559, 578 (opinion of BLACK, J.); *Food Employees* v. *Logan Plaza*, 391 U. S. 308, 326 (DOUGLAS, J., concurring). That means that it can be regulated when it comes to the "plus" or "action" side of the protest. It can be regulated as to the number of pickets and the place and hours (see *Cox* v. *Louisiana, supra*), because traffic and other community problems would otherwise suffer.

But none of these considerations are implicated in the symbolic protest of the Vietnam war in the burning of a draft card.

One's beliefs have long been thought to be sanctuaries which government could not invade. *Barenblatt* is one example of the ease with which that sanctuary can be violated. The lines drawn by the Court between the criminal act of being an "active" Communist and the innocent act of being a nominal or inactive Communist mark the difference only between deep and abiding belief and casual or uncertain belief. But I think that all matters of belief are beyond the reach of subpoenas or the probings of investigators. That is why the invasions of privacy made by investigating committees were notoriously unconstitutional. That is the deep-seated fault in the infamous loyalty-security hearings which, since 1947 when President Truman launched them, have processed 20,000,000 men and women. Those hearings were primarily concerned with one's thoughts, ideas, beliefs, and convictions. They were the most blatant violations of the First Amendment we have ever known.

The line between what is permissible and not subject to control and what may be made impermissible and subject to regulation is the line between ideas and overt acts.

The example usually given by those who would punish speech is the case of one who falsely shouts fire in a crowded theatre.

This is, however, a classic case where speech is brigaded with action. See *Speiser* v. *Randall*, 357 U. S. 513, 536–537 (DOUGLAS, J., concurring). They are indeed inseparable and a prosecution can be launched for the overt acts actually caused. Apart from rare instances of that kind, speech is, I think, immune from prosecution. Certainly there is no constitutional line between advocacy of abstract ideas as in *Yates* and advocacy of political action as in *Scales*. The quality of advocacy turns on the depth of the conviction; and government has no power to invade that sanctuary of belief and conscience.

Cohen v. California

403 U.S. 15 (1971)

Paul Robert Cohen was convicted of violating a California law that prohibited "maliciously and willfully disturb[ing] the peace or quiet of any neighborhood or person . . . by . . . offensive conduct." In a corridor of the Los Angeles Courthouse, he wore a jacket bearing the words "Fuck the Draft." The issue before the Supreme Court was whether the state had a compelling reason to override First Amendment interests by making the simple display of this single four-letter expletive a criminal offense.

MR. JUSTICE HARLAN delivered the opinion of the Court.

This case may seem at first blush too inconsequential to find its way into our books, but the issue it presents is of no small constitutional significance.

Appellant Paul Robert Cohen was convicted in the Los Angeles Municipal Court of violating that part of California Penal Code § 415 which prohibits "maliciously and willfully disturb[ing] the peace or quiet of any neighborhood or person. . .

by . . . offensive conduct . . . " He was given 30 days' imprisonment. The facts upon which his conviction rests are detailed in the opinion of the Court of Appeal of California, Second Appellate District, as follows:

"On April 26, 1968, the defendant was observed in the Los Angeles County Courthouse in the corridor outside of division 20 of the municipal court wearing a jacket bearing the words 'Fuck the Draft' which were plainly visible. There were women and children present in the corridor. The defendant was arrested. The defendant testified that he wore the jacket knowing that the words were on the jacket as a means of informing the public of the depth of his feelings against the Vietnam War and the draft.

"The defendant did not engage in, nor threaten to engage in, nor did anyone as the result of his conduct in fact commit or threaten to commit any act of violence. The defendant did not make any loud or unusual noise, nor was there any evidence that he uttered any sound prior to his arrest." 1 Cal. App. 3d 94, 97–98, 81 Cal. Rptr. 503, 505 (1969).

In affirming the conviction the Court of Appeal held that "offensive conduct" means "behavior which has a tendency to provoke *others* to acts of violence or to in turn disturb the peace," and that the State had proved this element because, on the facts of this case, "[i]t was certainly reasonably foreseeable that such conduct might cause others to rise up to commit a violent act against the person of the defendant or attempt to forcibly remove his jacket." 1 Cal. App. 3d, at 99–100, 81 Cal. Rptr., at 506. The California Supreme Court declined review by a divided vote. We brought the case here, postponing the consideration of the question of our jurisdiction over this appeal to a hearing of the case on the merits. 399 U.S. 904. We now reverse.

The question of our jurisdiction need not detain us long. Throughout the proceedings below, Cohen consistently claimed that, as construed to apply to the facts of this case, the statute infringed his rights to freedom of expression guaranteed by the First and Fourteenth Amendments of the Federal Constitution. That contention has been rejected by the highest California state court in which review could be had. Accordingly, we are fully satisfied that Cohen has properly invoked our jurisdiction by this appeal. 28 U. S. C. § 1257 (2); *Dahnke-Walker Milling Co.* v. *Bondurant,* 257 U. S. 282 (1921).

I

In order to lay hands on the precise issue which this case involves, it is useful first to canvass various matters which this record does *not* present.

The conviction quite clearly rests upon the asserted offensiveness of the *words* Cohen used to convey his message to the public. The only "conduct" which the State sought to punish is the fact of communication. Thus, we deal here with a conviction resting solely upon "speech," cf. *Stromberg* v. *California,* 283 U. S. 359 (1931), not upon any separately identifiable conduct which allegedly was intended by Cohen to be perceived by others as expressive of particular views but which, on its face, does not necessarily convey any message and hence arguably could be regulated without effectively repressing Cohen's ability to express himself. Cf. *United States* v. *O'Brien,* 391 U. S. 367 (1968). Further, the State certainly lacks power to punish Cohen for the underlying content of the message the inscription conveyed. At least so long as there is no showing of an intent to incite disobedience to or disruption of the draft, Cohen could not, consistently with the First and Fourteenth Amendments, be punished for asserting the evident position on the inutility or immorality of the draft his jacket reflected. *Yates* v. *United States,* 354 U. S. 298 (1957).

Appellant's conviction, then, rests squarely upon his exercise of the "freedom of speech" protected from arbitrary governmental interference by the Constitution and can be justified, if at all, only as a valid regulation of the manner in which he exercised that freedom, not as a permissible prohibition on the substantive message it conveys. This does not end the inquiry, of course, for the First and Fourteenth Amendments have never been thought to give absolute protection to every individual to speak whenever or wherever he pleases, or to use any form of address in any circumstances that he chooses. In this vein, too, however, we think it important to note that several issues typically associated with such problems are not presented here.

In the first place, Cohen was tried under a statute applicable throughout the entire State. Any attempt to support this conviction on the ground that the statute seeks to preserve an appropriately decorous atmosphere in the courthouse where Cohen was arrested must fail in the absence of any language in the statute that would have put appellant on notice that certain kinds of otherwise permissible speech or conduct would nevertheless, under California law, not be tolerated in certain places. See *Edwards* v. *South Carolina*, 372 U. S. 229, 236–237, and n. 11 (1963). Cf. *Adderley* v. *Florida*, 385 U. S. 39 (1966). No fair reading of the phrase "offensive conduct" can be said sufficiently to inform the ordinary person that distinctions between certain locations are thereby created. *[Here the Court adds a footnote: "It is illuminating to note what transpired when Cohen entered a courtroom in the building. He removed his jacket and stood with it folded over his arm. Meanwhile, a policeman sent the presiding judge a note suggesting that Cohen be held in contempt of court. The judge declined to do so and Cohen was arrested by the officer only after he emerged from the courtroom. App. 18–19."]*

In the second place, as it comes to us, this case cannot be said to fall within those relatively few categories of instances where prior decisions have established the power of government to deal more comprehensively with certain forms of individual expression simply upon a showing that such a form was employed. This is not, for example, an obscenity case. Whatever else may be necessary to give rise to the States' broader power to prohibit obscene expression, such expression must be, in some significant way, erotic. *Roth* v. *United States*, 354 U. S. 476 (1957). It cannot plausibly be maintained that this vulgar allusion to the Selective Service System would conjure up such psychic stimulation in anyone likely to be confronted with Cohen's crudely defaced jacket.

This Court has also held that the States are free to ban the simple use, without a demonstration of additional justifying circumstances, of so-called "fighting words," those personally abusive epithets which, when addressed to the ordinary citizen, are, as a matter of common knowledge, inherently likely to provoke violent reaction. *Chaplinsky* v. *New Hampshire*, 315 U. S. 568 (1942). While the four-letter word displayed by Cohen in relation to the draft is not uncommonly employed in a personally provocative fashion, in this instance it was clearly not "directed to the person of the hearer." *Cantwell* v. *Connecticut*, 310 U. S. 296,

309 (1940). No individual actually or likely to be present could reasonably have regarded the words on appellant's jacket as a direct personal insult. Nor do we have here an instance of the exercise of the State's police power to prevent a speaker from intentionally provoking a given group to hostile reaction. Cf. *Feiner* v. *New York*, 340 U. S. 315 (1951); *Terminiello* v. *Chicago*, 337 U. S. 1 (1949). There is, as noted above, no showing that anyone who saw Cohen was in fact violently aroused or that appellant intended such a result.

Finally, in arguments before this Court much has been made of the claim that Cohen's distasteful mode of expression was thrust upon unwilling or unsuspecting viewers, and that the State might therefore legitimately act as it did in order to protect the sensitive from otherwise unavoidable exposure to appellant's crude form of protest. Of course, the mere presumed presence of unwitting listeners or viewers does not serve automatically to justify curtailing all speech capable of giving offense. See, *e. g.*, *Organization for a Better Austin* v. *Keefe*, 402 U. S. 415 (1971). While this Court has recognized that government may properly act in many situations to prohibit intrusion into the privacy of the home of unwelcome views and ideas which cannot be totally banned from the public dialogue, *e. g.*, *Rowan* v. *Post Office Dept.*, 397 U. S. 728 (1970), we have at the same time consistently stressed that "we are often 'captives' outside the sanctuary of the home and subject to objectionable speech." *Id.*, at 738. The ability of government, consonant with the Constitution, to shut off discourse solely to protect others from hearing it is, in other words, dependent upon a showing that substantial privacy interests are being invaded in an essentially intolerable manner. Any broader view of this authority would effectively empower a majority to silence dissidents simply as a matter of personal predilections.

In this regard, persons confronted with Cohen's jacket were in a quite different posture than, say, those subjected to the raucous emissions of sound trucks blaring outside their residences. Those in the Los Angeles courthouse could effectively avoid further bombardment of their sensibilities simply by averting their eyes. . . .

II

. . . The constitutional right of free expression is powerful medicine in a society as diverse and populous as ours. It is designed and intended to remove governmental restraints from the arena of public discussion, putting the decision as to what views shall be voiced largely into the hands of each of us, in the hope that use of such freedom will ultimately produce a more capable citizenry and more perfect polity and in the belief that no other approach would comport with the premise of individual dignity and choice upon which our political system rests. See *Whitney* v. *California*, 274 U. S. 357, 375–377 (1927) (Brandeis, J., concurring).

To many, the immediate consequence of this freedom may often appear to be only verbal tumult, discord, and even offensive utterance. These are, however, within established limits, in truth necessary side effects of the broader enduring values which the process of open debate permits us to achieve. That the air may at times seem filled with verbal cacophony is, in this sense, not a sign of weakness but of strength. We cannot lose sight of the fact that, in what otherwise might seem a trifling and annoying instance of individual distasteful abuse of a privilege, these fundamental societal values are truly implicated. That is why "[w]holly neutral futilities . . . come under the protection of free speech as fully as do Keats' poems or Donne's sermons," *Winters* v. *New York*, 333 U. S. 507, 528 (1948) (Frankfurter, J., dissenting), and why "so long as the means are peaceful, the communication need not meet standards of acceptability," *Organization for a Better Austin* v. *Keefe*, 402 U. S. 415, 419 (1971).

Against this perception of the constitutional policies involved, we discern certain more particularized considerations that peculiarly call for reversal of this conviction. First, the principle contended for by the State seems inherently boundless. How is one to distinguish this from any other offensive word? Surely the State has no right to cleanse public debate to the point where it is grammatically palatable to the most squeamish among us. Yet no readily ascertainable general principle exists for stopping short of that result were we to affirm the judgment below. For, while the particular four-letter word being litigated here is perhaps more distasteful than most others of its genre, it is nevertheless often true that one man's vulgarity is another's lyric. Indeed, we think it is largely because governmental officials cannot make principled distinctions in this area that the Constitution leaves matters of taste and style so largely to the individual.

Additionally, we cannot overlook the fact, because it is well illustrated by the episode involved here, that much linguistic expression serves a dual communicative function: it conveys not only ideas capable of relatively precise, detached explication, but otherwise inexpressible emotions as well. In fact, words are often chosen as much for their emotive as their cognitive force. We cannot sanction the view that the Constitution, while solicitous of the cognitive content of individual speech, has little or no regard for that emotive function which, practically speaking, may often be the more important element of the overall message sought to be communicated. . . .

Finally, and in the same vein, we cannot indulge the facile assumption that one can forbid particular words without also running a substantial risk of suppressing ideas in the process. Indeed, governments might soon seize upon the censorship of particular words as a convenient guise for banning the expression of unpopular views. We have been able, as noted above, to discern little social benefit that might result from running the risk of opening the door to such grave results.

It is, in sum, our judgment that, absent a more particularized and compelling reason for its actions, the State may not, consistently with the First and Fourteenth Amendments, make the simple public display here involved of this single four-letter expletive a criminal offense. Because that is the only arguably sustainable rationale for the conviction here at issue, the judgment below must be

Reversed.

MR. JUSTICE BLACKMUN, with whom THE CHIEF JUSTICE and MR. JUSTICE BLACK join.

I dissent, and I do so for two reasons:

1. Cohen's absurd and immature antic, in my

view, was mainly conduct and little speech. See *Street* v. *New York*, 394 U. S. 576 (1969); *Cox* v. *Louisiana*, 379 U. S. 536, 555 (1965); *Giboney* v. *Empire Storage Co.*, 336 U. S. 490, 502 (1949). The California Court of Appeal appears so to have described it, 1 Cal. App. 3d 94, 100, 81 Cal. Rptr. 503, 507, and I cannot characterize it otherwise. Further, the case appears to me to be well within the sphere of *Chaplinsky* v. *New Hampshire*, 315 U. S. 568 (1942), where Mr. Justice Murphy, a known champion of First Amendment freedoms, wrote for a unanimous bench. As a consequence, this Court's agonizing over First Amendment values seems misplaced and unnecessary.

2. I am not at all certain that the California Court of Appeal's construction of § 415 is now the authoritative California construction. The Court of Appeal filed its opinion on October 22, 1969. The Supreme Court of California declined review by a four-to-three vote on December 17. See 1 Cal. App. 3d, at 104. A month later, on January 27, 1970, the State Supreme Court in another case construed § 415, evidently for the first time. *In re Bushman*, 1 Cal. 3d 767, 463 P. 2d 727. Chief Justice Traynor, who was among the dissenters to his court's refusal to take Cohen's case, wrote the majority opinion. He held that § 415 "is not un-

constitutionally vague and overbroad" and further said:

"[T]hat part of Penal Code section 415 in question here makes punishable only wilful and malicious conduct that is violent and endangers public safety and order or that creates a clear and present danger that others will engage in violence of that nature.

". . . [It] does not make criminal any nonviolent act unless the act incites or threatens to incite others to violence . . ." 1 Cal. 3d, at 773–774, 463 P. 2d, at 731.

Cohen was cited in *Bushman*, 1 Cal. 3d, at 773, 463 P. 2d, at 730, but I am not convinced that its description there and *Cohen* itself are completely consistent with the "clear and present danger" standard enunciated in *Bushman*. Inasmuch as this Court does not dismiss this case, it ought to be remanded to the California Court of Appeal for reconsideration in the light of the subsequently rendered decision by the State's highest tribunal in *Bushman*.

MR. JUSTICE WHITE concurs in Paragraph 2 of MR. JUSTICE BLACKMUN's dissenting opinion.

Texas v. Johnson

109 S.Ct. 2533 (1989)

As a means of protesting against the policies of the Reagan administration and American corporations, Gregory Lee Johnson burned an American flag in front of Dallas City Hall. He was convicted under Texas law for desecrating a flag, but the Texas Court of Criminal Appeals reversed the conviction on the ground that it was inconsistent with the First Amendment. The Supreme Court dealt with the issue of whether Johnson's action was "expressive conduct" protected by the Constitution.

JUSTICE BRENNAN delivered the opinion of the Court.

After publicly burning an American flag as a means of political protest, Gregory Lee Johnson was convicted of desecrating a flag in violation of Texas law. This case presents the question whether his conviction is consistent with the First Amendment. We hold that it is not.

I

While the Republican National Convention was taking place in Dallas in 1984, respondent Johnson participated in a political demonstration dubbed the "Republican War Chest Tour." As explained in literature distributed by the demonstrators and in speeches made by them, the purpose of this event was to protest the policies of the Reagan administration and of certain Dallas-based corporations. The demonstrators marched through the Dallas streets, chanting political slogans and stopping at several corporate locations to stage "die-ins" intended to dramatize the consequences of nuclear war. On several occasions they spray-painted the walls of buildings and overturned potted plants, but Johnson himself took no part in such activities. He did, however, accept an American flag handed to him by a fellow protestor who had taken it from a flag pole outside one of the targeted buildings.

The demonstration ended in front of Dallas City Hall, where Johnson unfurled the American flag, doused it with kerosene, and set it on fire. While the flag burned, the protestors chanted, "America, the red, white, and blue, we spit on you." After the demonstrators dispersed, a witness to the flag-burning collected the flag's remains and buried them in his backyard. No one was physically injured or threatened with injury, though several witnesses testified that they had been seriously offended by the flag-burning.

Of the approximately 100 demonstrators, Johnson alone was charged with a crime. The only criminal offense with which he was charged was the desecration of a venerated object in violation of Tex. Penal Code Ann. § 42.09 (a)(3) (1989). After a trial, he was convicted, sentenced to one year in prison, and fined $2,000. The Court of Appeals for the Fifth District of Texas at Dallas affirmed Johnson's conviction, 706 S. W. 2d 120 (1986), but the Texas Court of Criminal Appeals reversed, 755 S. W. 2d 92 (1988), holding that the State could not, consistent with the First Amendment, punish Johnson for burning the flag in these circumstances.

The Court of Criminal Appeals began by recognizing that Johnson's conduct was symbolic speech protected by the First Amendment: "Given the context of an organized demonstration, speeches, slogans, and the distribution of literature, anyone who observed appellant's act would have understood the message that appellant intended to convey. The act for which appellant was convicted was clearly 'speech' contemplated by the First Amendment." *Id.*, at 95. To justify Johnson's conviction for engaging in symbolic speech,

the State asserted two interests: preserving the flag as a symbol of national unity and preventing breaches of the peace. The Court of Criminal Appeals held that neither interest supported his conviction.

Acknowledging that this Court had not yet decided whether the Government may criminally sanction flag desecration in order to preserve the flag's symbolic value, the Texas court nevertheless concluded that our decision in *West Virginia Board of Education* v. *Barnette*, 319 U. S. 624 (1943), suggested that furthering this interest by curtailing speech was impermissible. "Recognizing that the right to differ is the centerpiece of our First Amendment freedoms," the court explained, "a government cannot mandate by fiat a feeling of unity in its citizens. Therefore, that very same government cannot carve out a symbol of unity and prescribe a set of approved messages to be associated with that symbol when it cannot mandate the status or feeling the symbol purports to represent." 755 S. W. 2d, at 97. Noting that the State had not shown that the flag was in "grave and immediate danger," *Barnette, supra*, at 639, of being stripped of its symbolic value, the Texas court also decided that the flag's special status was not endangered by Johnson's conduct. 755 S. W. 2d, at 97.

As to the State's goal of preventing breaches of the peace, the court concluded that the flag-desecration statute was not drawn narrowly enough to encompass only those flag-burnings that were likely to result in a serious disturbance of the peace. And in fact, the court emphasized, the flag burning in this particular case did not threaten such a reaction. . . .

II

Johnson was convicted of flag desecration for burning the flag rather than for uttering insulting words. This fact somewhat complicates our consideration of his conviction under the First Amendment. We must first determine whether Johnson's burning of the flag constituted expressive conduct, permitting him to invoke the First Amendment in challenging his conviction. See, e. g., *Spence* v. *Washington*, 418 U. S. 405, 409–411 (1974). If his conduct was expressive, we next decide whether the State's regulation is related to the suppression of free expression. See, *e.g.*, *United States* v. *O'Brien*, 391 U. S. 367, 377 (1968); *Spence, supra*, at 414, n. 8. . . .

The First Amendment literally forbids the abridgement only of "speech," but we have long recognized that its protection does not end at the spoken or written word. While we have rejected "the view that an apparently limitless variety of conduct can be labeled 'speech' whenever the person engaging in the conduct intends thereby to express an idea," *United States* v. *O'Brien, supra*, at 376, we have acknowledged that conduct may be "sufficiently imbued with elements of communication to fall within the scope of the First and Fourteenth Amendments." *Spence, supra*, at 409.

In deciding whether particular conduct possesses sufficient communicative elements to bring the First Amendment into play, we have asked whether "[a]n intent to convey a particularized message was present, and [whether] the likelihood was great that the message would be understood by those who viewed it." 418 U.S., at 410–411. Hence, we have recognized the expressive nature of students' wearing of black armbands to protest American military involvement in Vietnam, *Tinker* v. *Des Moines Independent Community School Dist.*, 393 U. S. 503, 505 (1969); of a sit-in by blacks in a "whites only" area to protest segregation, *Brown* v. *Louisiana*, 383 U. S. 131, 141–142 (1966); of the wearing of American military uniforms in a dramatic presentation criticizing American involvement in Vietnam, *Schacht* v. *United States*, 398 U. S. 58 (1970); and of picketing about a wide variety of causes, see, *e. g., Food Employees* v. *Logan Valley Plaza, Inc.*, 391 U. S. 308, 313–314 (1968); *United States* v. *Grace*, 461 U. S. 171, 176 (1983).

Especially pertinent to this case are our decisions recognizing the communicative nature of conduct relating to flags. Attaching a peace sign to the flag, *Spence, supra*, at 409–410; saluting the flag, *Barnette*, 319 U. S., at 632; and displaying a red flag, *Stromberg* v. *California*, 283 U. S. 359, 368–369 (1931), we have held, all may find shelter under the First Amendment. See also *Smith* v. *Goguen*, 415 U. S. 566, 588 (1974) (WHITE, J., concurring in judgment) (treating flag "contemptuously" by wearing pants with small flag sewn

into their seat is expressive conduct). That we have had little difficulty identifying an expressive element in conduct relating to flags should not be surprising. The very purpose of a national flag is to serve as a symbol of our country; it is, one might say, "the one visible manifestation of two hundred years of nationhood." *Id.*, at 603 (REHNQUIST, J., dissenting). Thus, we have observed:

"[T]he flag salute is a form of utterance. Symbolism is a primitive but effective way of communicating ideas. The use of an emblem or flag to symbolize some system, idea, institution, or personality, is a short cut from mind to mind. Causes and nations, political parties, lodges and ecclesiastical groups seek to knit the loyalty of their followings to a flag or banner, a color or design." *Barnette, supra*, at 632.

Pregnant with expressive content, the flag as readily signifies this Nation as does the combination of letters found in "America."

We have not automatically concluded, however, that any action taken with respect to our flag is expressive. Instead, in characterizing such action for First Amendment purposes, we have considered the context in which it occurred. In *Spence*, for example, we emphasized that Spence's taping of a peace sign to his flag was "roughly simultaneous with and concededly triggered by the Cambodian incursion and the Kent State tragedy." 418 U. S., at 410. The State of Washington had conceded, in fact, that Spence's conduct was a form of communication, and we stated that "the State's concession is inevitable on this record." *Id.*, at 409.

The State of Texas conceded for purposes of its oral argument in this case that Johnson's conduct was expressive conduct, Tr. of Oral Arg. 4, and this concession seems to us as prudent as was Washington's in *Spence*. Johnson burned an American flag as part—indeed, as the culmination—of a political demonstration that coincided with the convening of the Republican Party and its renomination of Ronald Reagan for President. The expressive, overtly political nature of this conduct was both intentional and overwhelmingly apparent. At his trial, Johnson explained his reasons for burning the flag as follows: "The American Flag was burned as Ronald Reagan was being renomi-

nated as President. And a more powerful statement of symbolic speech, whether you agree with
it or not, couldn't have been made at that time. It's
quite a just position [juxtaposition]. We had new
patriotism and no patriotism." 5 Record 656. In
these circumstances, Johnson's burning of the flag
was conduct "sufficiently imbued with elements
of communication," *Spence,* 418 U. S., at 409, to
implicate the First Amendment.

III

The Government generally has a freer hand in
restricting expressive conduct than it has in restricting the written or spoken word. See *O'Brien,*
391 U. S. at 376–377; *Clark* v. *Community for
Creative Non-Violence,* 468 U. S. 288, 293 (1984);
Dallas v. *Stanglin,* 490 U. S. ___, ___ (1989) (slip
op., at 5–6). It may not, however, proscribe particular conduct *because* it has expressive elements.
"[W]hat might be termed the more generalized
guarantee of freedom of expression makes the
communicative nature of conduct an inadequate
basis for singling out that conduct for proscription. A law *directed at* the communicative nature
of conduct must, like a law directed at speech
itself, be justified by the substantial showing of
need that the First Amendment requires." *Community for Creative Non-Violence* v. *Watt,* 227 U. S.
App. D. C. 19, 55–56, 703 F. 2d 586, 622–623
(1983) (Scalia, J., dissenting), rev'd *sub nom. Clark*
v. *Community for Creative Non-Violence,* 468 U. S.
288 (1984) (emphasis in original). It is, in short,
not simply the verbal or nonverbal nature of the
expression, but the governmental interest at stake,
that helps to determine whether a restriction on
that expression is valid.

Thus, although we have recognized that where
" 'speech' and 'nonspeech' elements are combined in the same course of conduct, a sufficiently
important governmental interest in regulating the
nonspeech element can justify incidental limitations on First Amendment freedoms," *O'Brien,*
supra, at 376, we have limited the applicability of
O'Brien's relatively lenient standard to those cases
in which "the governmental interest is unrelated
to the suppression of free expression." *Id.,* at 377;
see also *Spence,* 418 U. S., at 414, n. 8. In stating,
moreover, that *O'Brien*'s test "in the last analysis is

little, if any, different from the standard applied to
time, place, or manner restrictions," *Clark, supra,*
at 298, we have highlighted the requirement that
the governmental interest in question be unconnected to expression in order to come under
O'Brien's less demanding rule.

In order to decide whether *O'Brien*'s test applies here, therefore, we must decide whether
Texas has asserted an interest in support of Johnson's conviction that is unrelated to the suppression of expression. If we find that an interest
asserted by the State is simply not implicated on
the facts before us, we need not ask whether
O'Brien's test applies. See *Spence, supra,* at 414,
n. 8. The State offers two separate interests to
justify this conviction: preventing breaches of the
peace, and preserving the flag as a symbol of
nationhood and national unity. We hold that the
first interest is not implicated on this record and
that the second is related to the suppression of
expression.

A

Texas claims that its interest in preventing
breaches of the peace justifies Johnson's conviction for flag desecration. However, no disturbance
of the peace actually occurred or threatened to
occur because of Johnson's burning of the
flag. . . .

The State's position, therefore, amounts to a
claim that an audience that takes serious offense
at particular expression is necessarily likely to
disturb the peace and that the expression may be
prohibited on this basis. Our precedents do not
countenance such a presumption. On the contrary, they recognize that a principal "function of
free speech under our system of government is to
invite dispute. It may indeed best serve its high
purpose when it induces a condition of unrest,
creates dissatisfaction with conditions as they are,
or even stirs people to anger." *Terminiello* v.
Chicago, 337 U. S. 1, 4 (1949). . . .

Nor does Johnson's expressive conduct fall
within that small class of "fighting words" that are
"likely to provoke the average person to retaliation, and thereby cause a breach of the peace."
Chaplinsky v. *New Hampshire,* 315 U. S. 568, 574
(1942). No reasonable onlooker would have regarded Johnson's generalized expression of dissat-

isfaction with the policies of the Federal Government as a direct personal insult or an invitation to exchange fisticuffs. See *id.*, at 572–573; *Cantwell* v. *Connecticut,* 310 U. S. 296, 309 (1940); *FCC* v. *Pacifica Foundation, supra,* at 745 (opinion of STEVENS, J.).

We thus conclude that the State's interest in maintaining order is not implicated on these facts. The State need not worry that our holding will disable it from preserving the peace. We do not suggest that the First Amendment forbids a State to prevent "imminent lawless action." *Brandenburg, supra,* at 447. And, in fact, Texas already has a statute specifically prohibiting breaches of the peace, Tex. Penal Code Ann. § 42.01 (1989), which tends to confirm that Texas need not punish this flag desecration in order to keep the peace. See *Boos* v. *Barry,* 485 U.S., at 327–329.

B

The State also asserts an interest in preserving the flag as a symbol of nationhood and national unity. In *Spence,* we acknowledged that the Government's interest in preserving the flag's special symbolic value "is directly related to expression in the context of activity" such as affixing a peace symbol to a flag. 418 U.S., at 414, n. 8. We are equally persuaded that this interest is related to expression in the case of Johnson's burning of the flag. The State, apparently, is concerned that such conduct will lead people to believe either that the flag does not stand for nationhood and national unity, but instead reflects other, less positive concepts, or that the concepts reflected in the flag do not in fact exist, that is, we do not enjoy unity as a Nation. These concerns blossom only when a person's treatment of the flag communicates some message, and thus are related "to the suppression of free expression" within the meaning of *O'Brien.* We are thus outside of *O'Brien*'s test altogether.

IV

It remains to consider whether the State's interest in preserving the flag as a symbol of nationhood and national unity justifies Johnson's conviction.

As in *Spence,* "[w]e are confronted with a case of prosecution for the expression of an idea through activity," and "[a]ccordingly, we must examine with particular care the interests advanced by [petitioner] to support its prosecution." 418 U. S., at 411. Johnson was not, we add, prosecuted for the expression of just any idea; he was prosecuted for his expression of dissatisfaction with the policies of this country, expression situated at the core of our First Amendment values. See, *e.g., Boos* v. *Barry, supra,* at 318; *Frisby* v. *Schultz,* 487 U. S. ——, —— (1988).

Moreover, Johnson was prosecuted because he knew that his politically charged expression would cause "serious offense." If he had burned the flag as a means of disposing of it because it was dirty or torn, he would not have been convicted of flag desecration under this Texas law: federal law designates burning as the preferred means of disposing of a flag "when it is in such condition that it is no longer a fitting emblem for display," 36 U. S. C. § 176(k), and Texas has no quarrel with this means of disposal. Brief for Petitioner 45. The Texas law is thus not aimed at protecting the physical integrity of the flag in all circumstances, but is designed instead to protect it only against impairments that would cause serious offense to others. Texas concedes as much: "Section 42.09(b) reaches only those severe acts of physical abuse of the flag carried out in a way likely to be offensive. The statute mandates intentional or knowing abuse, that is, the kind of mistreatment that is not innocent, but rather is intentionally designed to seriously offend other individuals." *Id.,* at 44.

Whether Johnson's treatment of the flag violated Texas law thus depended on the likely communicative impact of his expressive conduct. . . .

. . . According to Texas, if one physically treats the flag in a way that would tend to cast doubt on either the idea that nationhood and national unity are the flag's referents or that national unity actually exists, the message conveyed thereby is a harmful one and therefore may be prohibited.

If there is a bedrock principle underlying the First Amendment, it is that the Government may not prohibit the expression of an idea simply because society finds the idea itself offensive or disagreeable. . . .

In holding in *Barnette* . . . Justice Jackson described one of our society's defining principles in words deserving of their frequent repetition: "If there is any fixed star in our constitutional constellation, it is that no official, high or petty, can prescribe what shall be orthodox in politics, nationalism, religion, or other matters of opinion or force citizens to confess by word or act their faith therein." . . .

In short, nothing in our precedents suggests that a State may foster its own view of the flag by prohibiting expressive conduct relating to it. . . .

Texas' focus on the precise nature of Johnson's expression, moreover, misses the point of our prior decisions: their enduring lesson, that the Government may not prohibit expression simply because it disagrees with its message, is not dependent on the particular mode in which one chooses to express an idea. If we were to hold that a State may forbid flag-burning wherever it is likely to endanger the flag's symbolic role, but allow it wherever burning a flag promotes that role—as where, for example, a person ceremoniously burns a dirty flag—we would be saying that when it comes to impairing the flag's physical integrity, the flag itself may be used as a symbol—as a substitute for the written or spoken word or a "short cut from mind to mind"—only in one direction. We would be permitting a State to "prescribe what shall be orthodox" by saying that one may burn the flag to convey one's attitude toward it and its referents only if one does not endanger the flag's representation of nationhood and national unity.

. . .

. . . To conclude that the Government may permit designated symbols to be used to communicate only a limited set of messages would be to enter territory having no discernible or defensible boundaries. Could the Government, on this theory, prohibit the burning of state flags? Of copies of the Presidential seal? Of the Constitution? In evaluating these choices under the First Amendment, how would we decide which symbols were sufficiently special to warrant this unique status? To do so, we would be forced to consult our own political preferences, and impose them on the citizenry, in the very way that the First Amendment forbids us to do. . . .

It is not the State's ends, but its means, to which we object. It cannot be gainsaid that there is a special place reserved for the flag in this Nation, and thus we do not doubt that the Government has a legitimate interest in making efforts to "preserv[e] the national flag as an unalloyed symbol of our country." *Spence*, 418 U. S., at 412. We reject the suggestion, urged at oral argument by counsel for Johnson, that the Government lacks "any state interest whatsoever" in regulating the manner in which the flag may be displayed. Tr. of Oral Arg. 38. Congress has, for example, enacted precatory regulations describing the proper treatment of the flag, see 36 U. S. C. §§ 173–177, and we cast no doubt on the legitimacy of its interest in making such recommendations. To say that the Government has an interest in encouraging proper treatment of the flag, however, is not to say that it may criminally punish a person for burning a flag as a means of political protest. "National unity as an end which officials may foster by persuasion and example is not in question. The problem is whether under our Constitution compulsion as here employed is a permissible means for its achievement." *Barnette*, 319 U. S., at 640.

We are fortified in today's conclusion by our conviction that forbidding criminal punishment for conduct such as Johnson's will not endanger the special role played by our flag or the feelings it inspires. To paraphrase Justice Holmes, we submit that nobody can suppose that this one gesture of an unknown man will change our Nation's attitude towards its flag. See *Abrams* v. *United States*, 250 U. S. 616, 628 (1919) (Holmes, J., dissenting). . . .

We are tempted to say, in fact, that the flag's deservedly cherished place in our community will be strengthened, not weakened, by our holding today. Our decision is a reaffirmation of the principles of freedom and inclusiveness that the flag best reflects, and of the conviction that our toleration of criticism such as Johnson's is a sign and source of our strength. Indeed, one of the proudest images of our flag, the one immortalized in our own national anthem, is of the bombardment it survived at Fort McHenry. It is the Nation's resilience, not its rigidity, that Texas sees reflected in the flag—and it is that resilience that we reassert today.

The way to preserve the flag's special role is not to punish those who feel differently about these matters. It is to persuade them that they are wrong. "To courageous, self-reliant men, with confidence in the power of free and fearless reasoning applied through the processes of popular government, no danger flowing from speech can be deemed clear and present, unless the incidence of the evil apprehended is so imminent that it may befall before there is opportunity for full discussion. If there be time to expose through discussion the falsehood and fallacies, to avert the evil by the processes of education, the remedy to be applied is more speech, not enforced silence." *Whitney* v. *California*, 274 U. S. 357, 377 (1927) (Brandeis, J., concurring). And, precisely because it is our flag that is involved, one's response to the flag-burner may exploit the uniquely persuasive power of the flag itself. We can imagine no more appropriate response to burning a flag than waving one's own, no better way to counter a flag-burner's message than by saluting the flag that burns, no surer means of preserving the dignity even of the flag that burned than by—as one witness here did— according its remains a respectful burial. We do not consecrate the flag by punishing its desecration, for in doing so we dilute the freedom that this cherished emblem represents.

V

Johnson was convicted for engaging in expressive conduct. The State's interest in preventing breaches of the peace does not support his conviction because Johnson's conduct did not threaten to disturb the peace. Nor does the State's interest in preserving the flag as a symbol of nationhood and national unity justify his criminal conviction for engaging in political expression. The judgment of the Texas Court of Criminal Appeals is therefore

Affirmed.

JUSTICE KENNEDY, concurring.

I write not to qualify the words JUSTICE BRENNAN chooses so well, for he says with power all that is necessary to explain our ruling. I join his opinion without reservation, but with a keen sense that this case, like others before us from time to time, exacts its personal toll. This prompts me to add to our pages these few remarks.

The case before us illustrates better than most

that the judicial power is often difficult in its exercise. We cannot here ask another branch to share responsibility, as when the argument is made that a statute is flawed or incomplete. For we are presented with a clear and simple statute to be judged against a pure command of the Constitution. The outcome can be laid at no door but ours.

The hard fact is that sometimes we must make decisions we do not like. We make them because they are right, right in the sense that the law and the Constitution, as we see them, compel the result. And so great is our commitment to the process that, except in the rare case, we do not pause to express distaste for the result, perhaps for fear of undermining a valued principle that dictates the decision. This is one of those rare cases.

. . . I do not believe the Constitution gives us the right to rule as the dissenting members of the Court urge, however painful this judgment is to announce. Though symbols often are what we ourselves make of them, the flag is constant in expressing beliefs Americans share, beliefs in law and peace and that freedom which sustains the human spirit. The case here today forces recognition of the costs to which those beliefs commit us. It is poignant but fundamental that the flag protects those who hold it in contempt.

. . .

CHIEF JUSTICE REHNQUIST, with whom JUSTICE WHITE and JUSTICE O'CONNOR join, dissenting.

In holding this Texas statute unconstitutional, the Court ignores Justice Holmes' familiar aphorism that "a page of history is worth a volume of logic." *New York Trust Co.* v. *Eisner*, 256 U. S. 345, 349 (1921). For more than 200 years, the American flag has occupied a unique position as the symbol of our Nation, a uniqueness that justifies a governmental prohibition against flag burning in the way respondent Johnson did here.

[Here Rehnquist includes various poems, resolutions, and anthems in praise of the flag, written by Ralph Waldo Emerson, Francis Scott Key, and John Greenleaf Whittier. He reviews also the role played by the flag in World War II (with the marines raising the flag on Mount Suribachi at Iwo Jima) and in the Korean War. He further explains that Congress

passed the Flag Desecration Act of 1968 because flag burnings had undermined the morale of American troops in Vietnam.]

The American flag, then, throughout more than 200 years of our history, has come to be the visible symbol embodying our Nation. It does not represent the views of any particular political party, and it does not represent any particular political philosophy. The flag is not simply another "idea" or "point of view" competing for recognition in the marketplace of ideas. Millions and millions of Americans regard it with an almost mystical reverence regardless of what sort of social, political, or philosophical beliefs they may have. I cannot agree that the First Amendment invalidates the Act of Congress, and the laws of 48 of the 50 States, which make criminal the public burning of the flag.

More than 80 years ago in *Halter* v. *Nebraska,* 205 U. S. 34 (1907), this Court upheld the constitutionality of a Nebraska statute that forbade the use of representations of the American flag for advertising purposes upon articles of merchandise. The Court there said:

"For that flag every true American has not simply an appreciation but a deep affection. . . . Hence, it has often occurred that insults to a flag have been the cause of war, and indignities put upon it, in the presence of those who revere it, have often been resented and sometimes punished on the spot." *Id.,* at 41.

. . . Johnson was free to make any verbal denunciation of the flag that he wished; indeed, he was free to burn the flag in private. He could publicly burn other symbols of the Government or effigies of political leaders. He did lead a march through the streets of Dallas, and conducted a rally in front of the Dallas City Hall. He engaged in a "die-in" to protest nuclear weapons. He shouted out various slogans during the march, including: "Reagan, Mondale which will it be? Either one means World War III"; "Ronald Reagan, killer of the hour, Perfect example of U. S. power"; and "red, white and blue, we spit on you, you stand for plunder, you will go under." Brief for Respondent 3. For none of these acts was he arrested or prosecuted; it was only when he proceeded to burn publicly an American flag stolen from its rightful owner that he violated the Texas statute.

. . .

The result of the Texas statute is obviously to deny one in Johnson's frame of mind one of many means of "symbolic speech." Far from being a case of "one picture being worth a thousand words," flag burning is the equivalent of an inarticulate grunt or roar that, it seems fair to say, is most likely to be indulged in not to express any particular idea, but to antagonize others. . . .

Our Constitution wisely places limits on powers of legislative majorities to act, but the declaration of such limits by this Court "is, at all times, a question of much delicacy, which ought seldom, if ever, to be decided in the affirmative, in a doubtful case." *Fletcher* v. *Peck,* 6 Cranch 87, 128 (1810) (Marshall, C. J.). Uncritical extension of constitutional protection to the burning of the flag risks the frustration of the very purpose for which organized governments are instituted. The Court decides that the American flag is just another symbol, about which not only must opinions pro and con be tolerated, but for which the most minimal public respect may not be enjoined. The government may conscript men into the Armed Forces where they must fight and perhaps die for the flag, but the government may not prohibit the public burning of the banner under which they fight. I would uphold the Texas statute as applied in this case.

JUSTICE STEVENS, dissenting.

The value of the flag as a symbol cannot be measured. Even so, I have no doubt that the interest in preserving that value for the future is both significant and legitimate. Conceivably that value will be enhanced by the Court's conclusion that our national commitment to free expression is so strong that even the United States as ultimate guarantor of that freedom is without power to prohibit the desecration of its unique symbol. But I am unpersuaded. The creation of a federal right to post bulletin boards and graffiti on the Washington Monument might enlarge the market for free expression, but at a cost I would not pay. Similarly, in my considered judgment, sanctioning the public desecration of the flag will tarnish its value—

both for those who cherish the ideas for which it waves and for those who desire to don the robes of martyrdom by burning it. That tarnish is not justified by the trivial burden on free expression occasioned by requiring that an available, alternative mode of expression—including uttering words critical of the flag, see *Street* v. *New York*, 394 U. S. 576 (1969)—be employed.

. . . this is not a case in which the fact that "it is the speaker's opinion that gives offense" provides a special "reason for according it constitutional protection," *FCC* v. *Pacifica Foundation*, 438 U. S.

726, 745 (1978) (plurality opinion). The case has nothing to do with "disagreeable ideas," see *ante*, at 11. It involves disagreeable conduct that, in my opinion, diminishes the value of an important national asset.

The Court is therefore quite wrong in blandly asserting that respondent "was prosecuted for his expression of dissatisfaction with the policies of this country, expression situated at the core of our First Amendment values." *Ante*, at 13. Respondent was prosecuted because of the method he chose to express his dissatisfaction with those policies. . . .

PruneYard Shopping Center v. Robins

447 U. S. 74 (1980)

The question of free speech in a shopping center raises two competing interests: the values of the First Amendment and protection to private property. In this case, high school students distributed pamphlets and asked passersby to sign petitions in opposition to a United Nations resolution against Zionism. The activity occurred in PruneYard, a privately owned shopping center in Campbell, California. This case is of special interest because it illustrates that individual rights may receive greater protection under a state constitution than under the federal Constitution.

MR. JUSTICE REHNQUIST delivered the opinion of the Court.

We postponed jurisdiction of this appeal from the Supreme Court of California to decide the important federal constitutional questions it presented. Those are whether state constitutional provisions, which permit individuals to exercise free speech and petition rights on the property of a privately owned shopping center to which the public is invited, violate the shopping center owner's property rights under the Fifth and Fourteenth Amendments or his free speech rights under the First and Fourteenth Amendments.

I

Appellant PruneYard is a privately owned shopping center in the city of Campbell, Cal. It covers approximately 21 acres—5 devoted to parking and 16 occupied by walkways, plazas, sidewalks, and buildings that contain more than

65 specialty shops, 10 restaurants, and a movie theater. The PruneYard is open to the public for the purpose of encouraging the patronizing of its commercial establishments. It has a policy not to permit any visitor or tenant to engage in any publicly expressive activity, including the circulation of petitions, that is not directly related to its commercial purposes. This policy has been strictly enforced in a nondiscriminatory fashion. The PruneYard is owned by appellant Fred Sahadi.

Appellees are high school students who sought to solicit support for their opposition to a United Nations resolution against "Zionism." On a Saturday afternoon they set up a card table in a corner of PruneYard's central courtyard. They distributed pamphlets and asked passersby to sign petitions, which were to be sent to the President and Members of Congress. Their activity was peaceful and orderly and so far as the record indicates was not objected to by PruneYard's patrons.

Soon after appellees had begun soliciting signatures, a security guard informed them that they would have to leave because their activity violated PruneYard regulations. The guard suggested that they move to the public sidewalk at the Prune-Yard's perimeter. Appellees immediately left the premises and later filed this lawsuit in the California Superior Court of Santa Clara County. They sought to enjoin appellants from denying them access to the PruneYard for the purpose of circulating their petitions.

The Superior Court held that appellees were not entitled under either the Federal or California Constitution to exercise their asserted rights on the shopping center property. App. to Juris. Statement A-2. It concluded that there were "adequate, effective channels of communication for [appellees] other than soliciting on the private property of the [PruneYard]." *Id.,* at A-3. The California Court of Appeal affirmed.

The California Supreme Court reversed, holding that the California Constitution protects "speech and petitioning, reasonably exercised, in shopping centers even when the centers are privately owned." 23 Cal. 3d 899, 910, 592 P. 2d 341, 347 (1979). It concluded that appellees were entitled to conduct their activity on PruneYard property. In rejecting appellants' contention that such a result infringed property rights protected by the Federal Constitution, the California Supreme Court observed:

"It bears repeated emphasis that we do not have under consideration the property or privacy rights of an individual homeowner or the proprietor of a modest retail establishment. As a result of advertising and the lure of a congenial environment, 25,000 persons are induced to congregate daily to take advantage of the numerous amenities offered by the [shopping center there]. A handful of additional orderly persons soliciting signatures and distributing handbills in connection therewith, under reasonable regulations adopted by defendant to assure that these activities do not interfere with normal business operations . . ."

. . . Before this Court, appellants contend that their constitutionally established rights under the Fourteenth Amendment to exclude appellees from adverse use of appellants' private property cannot be denied by invocation of a state constitu-

tional provision or by judicial reconstruction of a State's laws of private property. We postponed consideration of the question of jurisdiction until the hearing of the case on the merits. 444 U. S. 949. We now affirm.

II

We initially conclude that this case is properly before us as an appeal under 28 U. S. C. § 1257 (2). It has long been established that a state constitutional provision is a "statute" within the meaning of § 1257 (2). See, *e. g., Torcaso* v. *Watkins,* 367 U. S. 488, 489 (1961); *Adamson* v. *California,* 332 U. S. 46, 48, n. 2 (1947); *Railway Express Agency, Inc.* v. *Virginia,* 282 U. S. 440 (1931). Here the California Supreme Court decided that Art. 1, §§ 2 and 3, of the California Constitution gave appellees the right to solicit signatures on appellants' property in exercising their state rights of free expression and petition. In so doing, the California Supreme Court rejected appellants' claim that recognition of such a right violated appellants' "right to exclude others," which is a fundamental component of their federally protected property rights. Appeal is thus the proper method of review.

III

Appellants first contend that *Lloyd Corp.* v. *Tanner,* 407 U. S. 551 (1972), prevents the State from requiring a private shopping center owner to provide access to persons exercising their state constitutional rights of free speech and petition when adequate alternative avenues of communication are available. *Lloyd* dealt with the question whether under the Federal Constitution a privately owned shopping center may prohibit the distribution of handbills on its property when the handbilling is unrelated to the shopping center's operations. *Id.,* at 552. The shopping center had adopted a strict policy against the distribution of handbills within the building complex and its malls, and it made no exceptions to this rule. *Id.,* at 555. Respondents in *Lloyd* argued that because the shopping center was open to the public, the First Amendment prevents the private owner from enforcing the handbilling restriction on shopping center premises. *Id.*, at 564. In rejecting this claim we substantially repudiated the rationale of *Food Employees* v. *Logan Valley Plaza,* 391 U. S. 308 (1968), which was later overruled in *Hudgens* v. *NLRB,* 424 U. S. 507 (1976). We stated that property does not "lose its private character merely because the public is generally invited to use it for designated purposes," and that "[t]he essentially private character of a store and its privately owned abutting property does not change by virtue of being large or clustered with other stores in a modern shopping center." 407 U. S., at 569.

Our reasoning in *Lloyd,* however, does not *ex proprio vigore* limit the authority of the State to exercise its police power or its sovereign right to adopt in its own Constitution individual liberties more expansive than those conferred by the Federal Constitution. *Cooper* v. *California,* 386 U. S. 58, 62 (1967). See also 407 U. S., at 569–570. In *Lloyd, supra,* there was no state constitutional or statutory provision that had been construed to create rights to the use of private property by strangers, comparable to those found to exist by the California Supreme Court here. It is, of course, well established that a State in the exercise of its police power may adopt reasonable restrictions on private property so long as the restrictions do not amount to a taking without just compensation or contravene any other federal constitutional provision. See, *e. g., Euclid* v. *Ambler Realty Co.,* 272 U. S. 365 (1926); *Young* v. *American Mini Theatres, Inc.,* 427 U. S. 50 (1976). *Lloyd* held that when a shopping center owner opens his private property to the public for the purpose of shopping, the First Amendment to the United States Constitution does not thereby create individual rights in expression beyond those already existing under applicable law. See also *Hudgens* v. *NLRB, supra,* at 517-521.

IV

Appellants next contend that a right to exclude others underlies the Fifth Amendment guarantee against the taking of property without just compensation and the Fourteenth Amendment guarantee against the deprivation of property without due process of law.

It is true that one of the essential sticks in the bundle of property rights is the right to exclude others. *Kaiser Aetna* v. *United States,* 444 U. S. 164, 179–180 (1979). And here there has literally been a "taking" of that right to the extent that the California Supreme Court has interpreted the State Constitution to entitle its citizens to exercise free expression and petition rights on shopping center property. But it is well established that "not every destruction or injury to property by governmental action has been held to be a 'taking' in the constitutional sense." *Armstrong* v. *United States,* 364 U. S. 40, 48 (1960). . . . *[The Court rejects the claim that there had been a "taking" or that property had been denied without due process of law.]*

V

Appellants finally contend that a private property owner has a First Amendment right not to be forced by the State to use his property as a forum for the speech of others. They state that in *Wooley* v. *Maynard,* 430 U. S. 705 (1977), this Court concluded that a State may not constitutionally require an individual to participate in the dissemination of an ideological message by displaying it on his private property in a manner and for the express purpose that it be observed and read by the public. This rationale applies here, they argue, because the message of *Wooley* is that the State may not force an individual to display any message at all.

Wooley, however, was a case in which the government itself prescribed the message, required it to be displayed openly on appellee's personal property that was used "as part of his daily life," and refused to permit him to take any measures to cover up the motto even though the Court found that the display of the motto served no important state interest. Here, by contrast, there are a number of distinguishing factors. Most important, the shopping center by choice of its owner is not limited to the personal use of appellants. It is instead a business establishment that is open to the public to come and go as they please. The views expressed by members of the public in passing out pamphlets or seeking signatures for a petition thus will not likely be identified with those of the owner. Second, no specific message is dictated by the State to be displayed on appellants' property. There consequently is no danger of governmental discrimination for or against a particular message. Finally, as far as appears here appellants can expressly disavow any connection with the message by simply posting signs in the area where the speakers or handbillers stand. Such signs, for example, could disclaim any sponsorship of the message and could explain that the persons are communicating their own messages by virtue of state law.

Appellants also argue that their First Amendment rights have been infringed in light of *West Virginia State Board of Education* v. *Barnette*, 319 U. S. 624 (1943), and *Miami Herald Publishing Co.* v. *Tornillo*, 418 U. S. 241 (1974). *Barnette* is inapposite because it involved the compelled recitation of a message containing an affirmation of belief. This Court held such compulsion unconstitutional because it "require[d] the individual to communicate by word and sign his acceptance" of government-dictated political ideas, whether or not he subscribed to them. 319 U. S., at 633. Appellants are not similarly being compelled to affirm their belief in any governmentally prescribed position or view, and they are free to publicly dissociate themselves from the views of the speakers or handbillers.

Tornillo struck down a Florida statute requiring a newspaper to publish a political candidate's reply to criticism previously published in that newspaper. It rests on the principle that the State cannot tell a newspaper what it must print. The Florida statute contravened this principle in that it "exact[ed] a penalty on the basis of the content of a newspaper." 418 U. S., at 256. There also was a danger in *Tornillo* that the statute would "dampe[n] the vigor and limi[t] the variety of public debate" by deterring editors from publishing controversial political statements that might trigger the application of the statute. *Id.*, at 257. Thus, the statute was found to be an "intrusion into the function of editors." *Id.*, at 258. These concerns obviously are not present here.

We conclude that neither appellants' federally recognized property rights nor their First Amendment rights have been infringed by the California Supreme Court's decision recognizing a right of appellees to exercise state-protected rights of expression and petition on appellants' property. The judgment of the Supreme Court of California is therefore

Affirmed.

MR. JUSTICE BLACKMUN joins the opinion of the Court except that sentence thereof, *ante,* at 84, which reads: "Nor as a general proposition is the United States, as opposed to the several States, possessed of residual authority that enables it to define 'property' in the first instance."

MR. JUSTICE MARSHALL, concurring.

. . .

In the litigation now before the Court, the Supreme Court of California . . . concluded that its State "[C]onstitution broadly proclaims speech and petition rights. Shopping centers to which the public is invited can provide an essential and invaluable forum for exercising those rights." 23 Cal. 3d 899, 910, 592 P. 2d 341, 347 (1979). Like the Court in *Logan Valley*, the California court found that access to shopping centers was crucial to the exercise of rights of free expression. And like the Court in *Logan Valley*, the California court rejected the suggestion that the Fourteenth Amendment barred the intrusion on the property rights of the shopping center owners. I applaud the court's decision, which is a part of a very healthy trend of affording state constitutional provisions a more expansive interpretation than this Court has given to the Federal Constitution. See Brennan, State Constitutions and the Protection of Individual Rights, 90 Harv. L. Rev. 489 (1977).

. . .

MR. JUSTICE WHITE, concurring in part and concurring in the judgment.

I join MR. JUSTICE POWELL's concurring opinion but with these additional remarks.

. . .

I agree that on the record before us there was not an unconstitutional infringement of appellants' property rights. But it bears pointing out that the Federal Constitution does not require that a shopping center permit distributions or solicitations on its property. Indeed, *Hudgens* v. *NLRB*, 424 U. S. 507 (1976), and *Lloyd Corp.* v. *Tanner*, 407 U. S. 551 (1972), hold that the First and Fourteenth Amendments do not prevent the property owner from excluding those who would demonstrate or communicate on his property. Insofar as the Federal Constitution is concerned, therefore, a State may decline to construe its own constitution so as to limit the property rights of the shopping center owner.

. . .

MR. JUSTICE POWELL, with whom MR. JUSTICE WHITE joins, concurring in part and in the judgment.

Although I join the judgment, I do not agree with all of the reasoning in Part V of the Court's opinion. I join Parts I–IV on the understanding that our decision is limited to the type of shopping center involved in this case. Significantly different questions would be presented if a State authorized strangers to picket or distribute leaflets in privately owned, freestanding stores and commercial premises. Nor does our decision today apply to all "shopping centers." This generic term may include retail establishments that vary widely in size, location, and other relevant characteristics. Even large establishments may be able to show that the number or type of persons wishing to speak on their premises would create a substantial annoyance to customers that could be eliminated only by elaborate, expensive, and possibly unenforceable time, place, and manner restrictions. As the Court observes, state power to regulate private property is limited to the adoption of reasonable restrictions that "do not amount to a taking without just compensation or contravene any other federal constitutional provision." . . .

. . .

Appellants have not alleged that they object to the ideas contained in the appellees' petitions. Nor do they assert that some groups who reasonably might be expected to speak at the PruneYard will express views that are so objectionable as to require a response even when listeners will not mistake their source. The record contains no evidence concerning the numbers or types of interest groups that may seek access to this shopping center, and no testimony showing that the appellants strongly disagree with any of them.

Because appellants have not shown that the limited right of access held to be afforded by the California Constitution burdened their First and Fourteenth Amendment rights in the circumstances presented, I join the judgment of the Court. I do not interpret our decision today as a blanket approval for state efforts to transform privately owned commercial property into public forums. Any such state action would raise substantial federal constitutional questions not present in this case.

FCC v. Pacifica Foundation

438 U.S. 726 (1978)

A radio station of Pacifica Foundation made an afternoon broadcast of George Carlin's satiric monologue "Filthy Words," which listed and repeated a variety of colloquial uses of "words you couldn't say on the public airwaves." A father who heard the broadcast while driving with his young son complained to the Federal Communications Commission (FCC), which later issued a declaratory order granting the complaint. Although the FCC did not impose formal sanctions, it stated that the order would be placed in the station's license file and that if subsequent complaints were received it would decide whether to invoke sanctions, including a decision not to renew the license. The FCC also announced that it had the power to regulate indecent broadcasting. A three-judge panel

of the D.C. Circuit reversed the FCC's action, partly on the ground that it was censorship, that the agency rule was overbroad, or that it ran afoul of the First Amendment. The radio station argued that the broadcast was not indecent within the meaning of congressional statutes because there was no "prurient appeal."

MR. JUSTICE STEVENS delivered the opinion of the Court (Parts I, II, III, and IV-C) and an opinion in which THE CHIEF JUSTICE and MR. JUSTICE REHNQUIST joined (Parts IV-A and IV-B).

This case requires that we decide whether the Federal Communications Commission has any power to regulate a radio broadcast that is indecent but not obscene.

A satiric humorist named George Carlin recorded a 12-minute monologue entitled "Filthy Words" before a live audience in a California theater. He began by referring to his thoughts about "the words you couldn't say on the public, ah, airwaves, um, the ones you definitely wouldn't say, ever." He proceeded to list those words and repeat them over and over again in a variety of colloquialisms. The transcript of the recording, which is appended to this opinion, indicates frequent laughter from the audience.

At about 2 o'clock in the afternoon on Tuesday, October 30, 1973, a New York radio station, owned by respondent Pacifica Foundation, broadcast the "Filthy Words" monologue. A few weeks later a man, who stated that he had heard the broadcast while driving with his young son, wrote a letter complaining to the Commission. He stated that, although he could perhaps understand the "record's being sold for private use, I certainly cannot understand the broadcast of same over the air that, supposedly, you control."

The complaint was forwarded to the station for comment. In its response, Pacifica explained that the monologue had been played during a program about contemporary society's attitude toward language and that, immediately before its broadcast, listeners had been advised that it included "sensitive language which might be regarded as offensive to some." Pacifica characterized George Carlin as "a significant social satirist" who "like Twain and Sahl before him, examines the language of ordinary people. . . . Carlin is not mouthing obscenities, he is merely using words to satirize as harmless and essentially silly our attitudes towards those words." Pacifica stated that it was

not aware of any other complaints about the broadcast.

On February 21, 1975, the Commission issued a declaratory order granting the complaint and holding that Pacifica "could have been the subject of administrative sanctions." 56 F.C.C. 2d 94, 99. The Commission did not impose formal sanctions, but it did state that the order would be "associated with the station's license file, and in the event that subsequent complaints are received, the Commission will then decide whether it should utilize any of the available sanctions it has been granted by Congress." *[Congress has empowered the FCC to revoke a station's license, issue a cease and desist order, or impose a monetary forfeiture. The FCC can also deny a license renewal and grant a short-term renewal.]*

In its memorandum opinion the Commission stated that it intended to "clarify the standards which will be utilized in considering" the growing number of complaints about indecent speech on the airwaves. *Id.*, at 94. Advancing several reasons for treating broadcast speech differently from other forms of expression, the Commission found a power to regulate indecent broadcasting in two statutes: 18 U. S. C. § 1464 (1976 ed.), which forbids the use of "any obscene, indecent, or profane language by means of radio communications," and 47 U. S. C. § 303 (g), which requires the Commission to "encourage the larger and more effective use of radio in the public interest."

. . .

. . . the Commission concluded that certain words *[in Carlin's broadcast]* depicted sexual and excretory activities in a patently offensive manner, noted that they "were broadcast at a time when children were undoubtedly in the audience (i. e., in the early afternoon)," and that the prerecorded language, with these offensive words "repeated over and over," was "deliberately broadcast." *Id.*, at 99. In summary, the Commission stated: "We therefore hold that the language as broadcast was indecent and prohibited by 18 U. S. C. § 1464." *Ibid.*

. . .

The United States Court of Appeals for the District of Columbia Circuit reversed, with each of the three judges on the panel writing separately. . . .

. . .

II

The relevant statutory questions are whether the Commission's action is forbidden "censorship" within the meaning of 47 U. S. C. § 326 and whether speech that concededly is not obscene may be restricted as "indecent" under the authority of 18 U. S. C. § 1464 (1976 ed.). The questions are not unrelated, for the two statutory provisions have a common origin. Nevertheless, we analyze them separately.

Section 29 of the Radio Act of 1927 provided:

"Nothing in this Act shall be understood or construed to give the licensing authority the power of censorship over the radio communications or signals transmitted by any radio station, and no regulation or condition shall be promulgated or fixed by the licensing authority which shall interfere with the right of free speech by means of radio communications. No person within the jurisdiction of the United States shall utter any obscene, indecent, or profane language by means of radio communication." 44 Stat. 1172.

The prohibition against censorship unequivocally denies the Commission any power to edit proposed broadcasts in advance and to excise material considered inappropriate for the airwaves. The prohibition, however, has never been construed to deny the Commission the power to review the content of completed broadcasts in the performance of its regulatory duties.

During the period between the original enactment of the provision in 1927 and its re-enactment in the Communications Act of 1934, the courts and the Federal Radio Commission held that the section deprived the Commission of the power to subject "broadcasting matter to scrutiny prior to its release," but they concluded that the Commis-

sion's "undoubted right" to take note of past program content when considering a licensee's renewal application "is not censorship."

. . .

We conclude, therefore, that § 326 does not limit the Commission's authority to impose sanctions on licensees who engage in obscene, indecent, or profane broadcasting.

III

The only other statutory question presented by this case is whether the afternoon broadcast of the "Filthy Words" monologue was indecent within the meaning of § 1464. Even that question is narrowly confined by the arguments of the parties.

The Commission identified several words that referred to excretory or sexual activities or organs, stated that the repetitive, deliberate use of those words in an afternoon broadcast when children are in the audience was patently offensive, and held that the broadcast was indecent. Pacifica takes issue with the Commission's definition of indecency, but does not dispute the Commission's preliminary determination that each of the components of its definition was present. Specifically, Pacifica does not quarrel with the conclusion that this afternoon broadcast was patently offensive. Pacifica's claim that the broadcast was not indecent within the meaning of the statute rests entirely on the absence of prurient appeal.

The plain language of the statute does not support Pacifica's argument. The words "obscene, indecent, or profane" are written in the disjunctive, implying that each has a separate meaning. Prurient appeal is an element of the obscene, but the normal definition of "indecent" merely refers to nonconformance with accepted standards of morality.

. . .

Because neither our prior decisions nor the language or history of § 1464 supports the conclusion that prurient appeal is an essential component of indecent language, we reject Pacifica's construction of the statute. When that construction is put to one side, there is no basis for disagreeing with the Commission's conclusion that indecent language was used in this broadcast.

IV

Pacifica makes two constitutional attacks on the Commission's order. First, it argues that the Commission's construction of the statutory language broadly encompasses so much constitutionally protected speech that reversal is required even if Pacifica's broadcast of the "Filthy Words" monologue is not itself protected by the First Amendment. Second, Pacifica argues that inasmuch as the recording is not obscene, the Constitution forbids any abridgment of the right to broadcast it on the radio.

A

The first argument fails because our review is limited to the question whether the Commission has the authority to proscribe this particular broadcast. As the Commission itself emphasized, its order was "issued in a specific factual context." 59 F. C. C. 2d, at 893. That approach is appropriate for courts as well as the Commission when regulation of indecency is at stake, for indecency is largely a function of context—it cannot be adequately judged in the abstract.

The approach is also consistent with *Red Lion Broadcasting Co.* v. *FCC*, 395 U. S. 367. In that case the Court rejected an argument that the Commission's regulations defining the fairness doctrine were so vague that they would inevitably abridge the broadcasters' freedom of speech. The Court of Appeals had invalidated the regulations because their vagueness might lead to self-censorship of controversial program content. *Radio Television News Directors Assn.* v. *United States*, 400 F. 2d 1002, 1016 (CA7 1968). This Court reversed. After noting that the Commission had indicated, as it has in this case, that it would not impose sanctions without warning in cases in which the applicability of the law was unclear, the Court stated:

"We need not approve every aspect of the fairness doctrine to decide these cases, and we will not now pass upon the constitutionality of these regulations by envisioning the most extreme

applications conceivable, *United States* v. *Sullivan,* 332 U. S. 689, 694 (1948), but will deal with those problems if and when they arise." 395 U. S., at 396.

. . .

B

When the issue is narrowed to the facts of this case, the question is whether the First Amendment denies government any power to restrict the public broadcast of indecent language in any circumstances. For if the government has any such power, this was an appropriate occasion for its exercise.

The words of the Carlin monologue are unquestionably "speech" within the meaning of the First Amendment. It is equally clear that the Commission's objections to the broadcast were based in part on its content. The order must therefore fall if, as Pacifica argues, the First Amendment prohibits all governmental regulation that depends on the content of speech. Our past cases demonstrate, however, that no such absolute rule is mandated by the Constitution.

. . .

. . . the fact that society may find speech offensive is not a sufficient reason for suppressing it. Indeed, if it is the speaker's opinion that gives offense, that consequence is a reason for according it constitutional protection. For it is a central tenet of the First Amendment that the government must remain neutral in the marketplace of ideas. If there were any reason to believe that the Commission's characterization of the Carlin monologue as offensive could be traced to its political content—or even to the fact that it satirized contemporary attitudes about four-letter words—First Amendment protection might be required. But that is simply not this case. These words offend for the same reasons that obscenity offends. Their place in the hierarchy of First Amendment values was aptly sketched by Mr. Justice Murphy when he said: "[S]uch utterances are no essential part of any exposition of ideas, and are of such slight social value as a step to truth that any benefit that may be derived from them is clearly outweighed by the social interest in order and morality." *Chaplinsky* v. *New Hampshire*, 315 U. S., at 572.

. . .

In this case it is undisputed that the content of Pacifica's broadcast was "vulgar," "offensive," and "shocking." Because content of that character is not entitled to absolute constitutional protection under all circumstances, we must consider its context in order to determine whether the Commission's action was constitutionally permissible.

C

We have long recognized that each medium of expression presents special First Amendment problems. *Joseph Burstyn, Inc.* v. *Wilson*, 343 U. S. 495, 502–503. And of all forms of communication, it is broadcasting that has received the most limited First Amendment protection. Thus, although other speakers cannot be licensed except under laws that carefully define and narrow official discretion, a broadcaster may be deprived of his license and his forum if the Commission decides that such an action would serve "the public interest, convenience, and necessity." Similarly, although the First Amendment protects newspaper publishers from being required to print the replies of those whom they criticize, *Miami Herald Publishing Co.* v. *Tornillo*, 418 U. S. 241, it affords no such protection to broadcasters; on the contrary, they must give free time to the victims of their criticism. *Red Lion Broadcasting Co.* v. *FCC*, 395 U. S. 367.

The reasons for these distinctions are complex, but two have relevance to the present case. First, the broadcast media have established a uniquely pervasive presence in the lives of all Americans. Patently offensive, indecent material presented over the airwaves confronts the citizen, not only in public, but also in the privacy of the home, where the individual's right to be left alone plainly outweighs the First Amendment rights of an intruder. *Rowan* v. *Post Office Dept.*, 397 U. S. 728. Because the broadcast audience is constantly tuning in and out, prior warnings cannot completely protect the listener or viewer from unexpected program content. To say that one may avoid further offense by turning off the radio when he hears indecent language is like saying that the remedy for an assault is to run away after the first blow. One may hang up on an indecent phone call, but that option does not give the caller a constitutional immunity or avoid a harm that has already taken place.

Second, broadcasting is uniquely accessible to children, even those too young to read. Although Cohen's written message might have been incomprehensible to a first grader, Pacifica's broadcast could have enlarged a child's vocabulary in an instant. Other forms of offensive expression may be withheld from the young without restricting the expression at its source. Bookstores and motion picture theaters, for example, may be prohibited from making indecent material available to children. We held in *Ginsberg* v. *New York*, 390 U. S. 629, that the government's interest in the "well-being of its youth" and in supporting "parents' claim to authority in their own household" justified the regulation of otherwise protected expression. *Id.*, at 640 and 639. The ease with which children may obtain access to broadcast material, coupled with the concerns recognized in *Ginsberg*, amply justify special treatment of indecent broadcasting.

. . .

The judgment of the Court of Appeals is reversed.

It is so ordered.

Mr. Justice Powell, with whom Mr. Justice Blackmun joins, concurring in part and concurring in the judgment.

I join Parts I, II, III, and IV-C of Mr. Justice Stevens' opinion. The Court today reviews only the Commission's holding that Carlin's monologue was indecent "as broadcast" at two o'clock in the afternoon, and not the broad sweep of the Commission's opinion. . . .

I also agree with much that is said in Part IV of Mr. Justice Stevens' opinion, and with its conclusion that the Commission's holding in this case does not violate the First Amendment. Because I do not subscribe to all that is said in Part IV, however, I state my views separately.

I

It is conceded that the monologue at issue here is not obscene in the constitutional sense. See 56 F. C. C. 2d 94, 98 (1975); Brief for Petitioner 18. Nor, in this context, does its language constitute "fighting words" within the meaning of *Chaplinsky* v. *New Hampshire*, 315 U. S. 568 (1942). Some of the words used have been held protected by the First Amendment in other cases and contexts. *E. g., Lewis* v. *New Orleans*, 415 U. S. 130 (1974); *Hess* v. *Indiana*, 414 U. S. 105 (1973); *Papish* v. *University of Missouri Curators*, 410 U. S. 667 (1973); *Cohen* v. *California*, 403 U. S. 15 (1971); see also *Eaton* v. *Tulsa*, 415 U. S. 697 (1974). I do not think Carlin, consistently with the First Amendment, could be punished for delivering the same monologue to a live audience composed of adults who, knowing what to expect, chose to attend his performance. See *Brown* v. *Oklahoma*, 408 U. S. 914 (1972) (POWELL, J., concurring in result). And I would assume that an adult could not constitutionally be prohibited from purchasing a recording or transcript of the monologue and playing or reading it in the privacy of his own home. Cf. *Stanley* v. *Georgia*, 394 U. S. 557 (1969).

But it also is true that the language employed is, to most people, vulgar and offensive. It was chosen specifically for this quality, and it was repeated over and over as a sort of verbal shock treatment. The Commission did not err in characterizing the narrow category of language used here as "patently offensive" to most people regardless of age.

. . .

II

As the foregoing demonstrates, my views are generally in accord with what is said in Part IV-C of MR. JUSTICE STEVENS' opinion. See *ante*, at 748–750. I therefore join that portion of his opinion. I do not join Part IV-B, however, because I do not subscribe to the theory that the Justices of this Court are free generally to decide on the basis of its content which speech protected by the First Amendment is most "valuable" and hence deserving of the most protection, and which is less "valuable" and hence deserving of less protection. Compare *ante*, at 744–748; *Young* v. *American*

Mini Theatres, Inc., 427 U. S. 50, 63–73 (1976) (opinion of STEVENS, J.), with *id.*, at 73 n. 1 (POWELL, J., concurring). In my view, the result in this case does not turn on whether Carlin's monologue, viewed as a whole, or the words that constitute it, have more or less "value" than a candidate's campaign speech. This is a judgment for each person to make, not one for the judges to impose upon him.

The result turns instead on the unique characteristics of the broadcast media, combined with society's right to protect its children from speech generally agreed to be inappropriate for their years, and with the interest of unwilling adults in not being assaulted by such offensive speech in their homes. Moreover, I doubt whether today's decision will prevent any adult who wishes to receive Carlin's message in Carlin's own words from doing so, and from making for himself a value judgment as to the merit of the message and words. Cf. *id.*, at 77–79 (POWELL, J., concurring). These are the grounds upon which I join the judgment of the Court as to Part IV.

MR. JUSTICE BRENNAN, with whom MR. JUSTICE MARSHALL joins, dissenting.

I agree with MR. JUSTICE STEWART that, under *Hamling* v. *United States*, 418 U. S. 87 (1974), and *United States* v. *12 200-ft. Reels of Film*, 413 U. S. 123 (1973), the word "indecent" in 18 U. S. C. § 1464 (1976 ed.) must be construed to prohibit only obscene speech. I would, therefore, normally refrain from expressing my views on any constitutional issues implicated in this case. However, I find the Court's misapplication of fundamental First Amendment principles so patent, and its attempt to impose *its* notions of propriety on the whole of the American people so misguided, that I am unable to remain silent.

. . .

The Court's balance, of necessity, fails to accord proper weight to the interests of listeners who wish to hear broadcasts the FCC deems offensive. It permits majoritarian tastes completely to preclude a protected message from entering the homes of a receptive, unoffended minority. No decision of this Court supports such a result. . . .

MR. JUSTICE STEWART, with whom MR. JUSTICE BRENNAN, MR. JUSTICE WHITE, and MR. JUSTICE MARSHALL join, dissenting.

The Court today recognizes the wise admonition that we should "avoid the unnecessary decision of [constitutional] issues." *Ante*, at 734. But it disregards one important application of this salutary principle—the need to construe an Act of Congress so as to avoid, if possible, passing upon its constitutionality. It is apparent that the constitutional questions raised by the order of the Commission in this case are substantial. Before deciding them, we should be certain that it is necessary to do so.

The statute pursuant to which the Commission acted, 18 U. S. C. § 1464 (1976 ed.), makes it a federal offense to utter "any obscene, indecent, or profane language by means of radio communication." The Commission held, and the Court today agrees, that "indecent" is a broader concept than "obscene" as the latter term was defined in *Miller* v. *California*, 413 U. S. 15, because language can be "indecent" although it has social, political, or artistic value and lacks prurient appeal. 56 F. C. C. 2d 94, 97–98. But this construction of § 1464, while perhaps plausible, is by no means compelled. To the contrary, I think that "indecent" should properly be read as meaning no more than "obscene." Since the Carlin monologue concededly was not "obscene," I believe that the Commission lacked statutory authority to ban it. Under this construction of the statute, it is unnecessary to address the difficult and important issue of the Commission's constitutional power to prohibit

speech that would be constitutionally protected outside the context of electronic broadcasting.

This Court has recently decided the meaning of the term "indecent" in a closely related statutory context. In *Hamling* v. *United States*, 418 U. S. 87, the petitioner was convicted of violating 18 U. S. C. § 1461, which prohibits the mailing of "[e]very obscene, lewd, lascivious, indecent, filthy or vile article." The Court "construe[d] the generic terms in [§ 1461] to be limited to the sort of 'patently offensive representations or descriptions of that specific "hard core" sexual conduct given as examples in *Miller* v. *California.*'" 418 U. S., at 114, quoting *United States* v. *12 200-ft. Reels of Film*, 413 U. S. 123, 130 n. 7. Thus, the clear holding of *Hamling* is that "indecent" as used in § 1461 has the same meaning as "obscene" as that term was defined in the *Miller* case. See also *Marks* v. *United States*, 430 U. S. 188, 190 (18 U. S. C. § 1465).

Nothing requires the conclusion that the word "indecent" has any meaning in § 1464 other than that ascribed to the same word in § 1461. Indeed, although the legislative history is largely silent, such indications as there are support the view that §§ 1461 and 1464 should be construed similarly. . . .

I would hold, therefore, that Congress intended, by using the word "indecent" in § 1464, to prohibit nothing more than obscene speech. Under that reading of the statute, the Commission's order in this case was not authorized, and on that basis I would affirm the judgment of the Court of Appeals.

11 Freedom of the Press

The Supreme Court generally treats free speech and free press as complementary parts of a larger value designed to promote "freedom of expression." At times, it even demotes freedom of the press, making it a subordinate right derived from freedom of speech. Such formulations distort the historical record. The right to a free press has stronger roots than the right to free speech. Of the eleven original states that adopted revolutionary constitutions, nine protected freedom of press and only one (Pennsylvania) protected speech.

Freedom of the press implies two rights: the right to publish without prior restraint, and the right to publish without prosecution or penalty for the views advanced. The first right is nearly inviolable. A heavy presumption lies against any governmental effort to restrain a publication. The second right is more circumscribed, permitting action against publishers who print materials considered libelous or obscene. A separate issue involves the collision that occurs between the interests of a free press and a fair trial.

THE EVOLUTION OF PRESS FREEDOMS

Many of the battles for individual liberty from the sixteenth to the eighteenth centuries in England centered around the struggle for a free press. Government officials and church authorities took action to suppress writings that threatened their control. Both prosecutions and persecutions were used to silence critics and free thinkers. Authors were punished for views considered to be seditious or heretical. In time, a system of censorship developed to prevent such writings from being published. One of the early protests against censorship and prior restraint came from the pen of the poet John Milton, especially *Areopagitica* (1644), part of which is reproduced on pages 636–637.

English law eventually prohibited prior restraint on publications. As explained by William Blackstone, the liberty of the press "consists in laying no *previous* restraints upon publications, and not in freedom from censure for criminal matter when published." The right to publish was protected, but if an individual published material found to be "improper, mischievous or illegal, he must take the consequence of his own temerity." 4 Blackstone, Commentaries *151–152. These categories encourage the publication only of innocuous material. English law also permitted the government to punish whoever published "seditious libel," another vague realm that invites action against whoever offends or annoys the government.

The trial of John Peter Zenger in 1735 represents a watershed in the fight for a free press in America. William Cosby, New York's royal governor, became embroiled in a local power struggle. The *New-York Weekly Journal* was established to oppose the royal newspaper, the *New-York Gazette*. Zenger, serving as the printer for the opposition newspaper, helped run the first independent journal in America. A series of articles in the *Weekly Journal* promoted the theory of a free press and attacked the Cosby administration.

Cosby placed Zenger in prison for seditious libel. However, a grand jury decided against indicting Zenger and the New York Assembly refused to carry out the request of Cosby's Council that several issues of the *Weekly Journal* be burned. In 1735, Zenger was again imprisoned for seditious libel. Another grand jury rejected indictment. The New York attorney general relied on an information, as an alternative to grand jury action, to charge Zenger for publishing "false, scandalous, malicious, and seditious" libels. Andrew Hamilton, a famous trial attorney in America, argued that Zenger's newspapers had not published "false" material. He said that Zenger had published the truth and had the right to do so. The trial judge advised Hamilton that truth was not a defense under the law; the material was libel even if true. Hamilton appealed to the jury to uphold the cause of liberty and a free press. The verdict they returned was not guilty. Although the law had not changed, the jury action planted a seed to make truth a defense in a libel case. The threat of seditious libel virtually disappeared in America after Zenger's trial.

Except for brief periods in our history, America has placed a high value on the importance of a free press. Leonard Levy, a leading scholar of the First Amendment, wrote an influential work in 1960 in which he challenged the prevailing belief that the framers were deeply committed to press freedoms. In *Legacy of Suppression*, he argued three major theses: the First Amendment was not intended to prevent the state from suppressing seditious libel; American legislatures, especially during the colonial period, were "far more oppressive" than common-law courts; and the Bill of Rights was more the "chance product of political expediency" than of principled commitment to personal liberties. Moreover, Levy concluded that the Jeffersonians, strident critics of the Sedition Act of 1798, were not much more tolerant of political dissent than the Federalists had been.

In a revision of this work in 1985, entitled *Emergence of a Free Press*, Levy admitted that he had overstated his case. After examining new evidence, he now concluded that the American experience with a free press was broad in scope. "Press criticism of government policies and politicians, on both state and national levels, during the war [of Independence] and in the peaceful years of the 1780s and 1790s, raged as contemptuously and scorchingly as it had against Great Britain in the period between the Stamp Act and the battle of Lexington." The presses in the states operated "as if the law of seditious libel did not exist." He explained that if one examines American *practices* rather than American law and theory, there exists not a legacy of suppression but rather a "legacy of liberty" (p. x).

A period of suppression certainly includes the Sedition Act of 1798, which provided penalties for writing, printing, uttering, or publishing "false, scandalous and malicious" statements against the federal government, either House of Congress, or the President. 1 Stat. 596, § 2. Still, the principle from the Zenger trial prevailed. Any person prosecuted under the act had the right to "give in evidence in his defence, the truth of the matter contained in the publication charged as a libel." Moreover, the jury had the right to "determine the law and the fact." Id., § 3. The debate on the Sedition Act demonstrates that the principle of a free press was strongly held at that time (pp. 638–641). The statute was so unpopular that it fatally wounded its sponsor, the Federalist party, and expired under its own terms in 1801.

The constitutionality of the Sedition Act was never determined in the courts. Instead, it was decided by the people in the national elections of 1800, which drove the Federalist party out of office and into oblivion. President Jefferson called the Sedition Act a "nullity" and pardoned every person prosecuted under it. Later, Congress pronounced the statute "unconstitutional, null, and void," and appropriated funds to reimburse those who had been subjected to fines (pp. 641–643). The Supreme Court later acknowledged that the Sedition Act was struck down not by a court of law but by "the court of history." New York Times Co. v. Sullivan, 376 U.S. 254, 276 (1964).

REGULATING THE PRESS

Like other First Amendment freedoms, the press is subject to regulations. A unanimous Court in 1878 upheld the power of Congress to exclude from the mails materials deemed injurious to the public morals, in this case circulars containing lottery prizes. Ex parte Jackson, 96 U.S. 727 (1878). Congress has prohibited the mailing of obscene materials. 13 Stat. 507, § 16 (1865). The Espionage Act of 1917 denied the mails to newspapers and other publications that violated the statute. It was upheld by a 7–2 Court. As administered by the Postmaster General, the statute also required certain publications to pay higher (third-class) rates. Milwaukee Pub. Co. v. Burleson, 255 U.S. 407 (1921).

Initially, state actions that abridged the press were not subject to redress in the federal courts. These matters were left essentially to state and local judgments. Patterson v. Colorado, 205 U.S. 454 (1907); Fox v. Washington, 236 U.S. 273 (1915). In 1931, however, the Court held that a free press is within the liberty safeguarded by the Due Process Clause of the Fourteenth Amendment. Freedom of the press was therefore guaranteed at both a national and a state level. The case involved Minnesota's effort to suppress the "malicious, scandalous and defamatory" articles of Jay Near, an indefatigable critic of corruption in the Minneapolis government. The effect of the state law, said the Court, was to put a publisher under censorship. Except for certain conditions that did not apply in this case, the government could not impose censorship or prior restraint on newspapers and other publications. NEAR v. MINNESOTA, 283 U.S. 697 (1931).

Following this decision, the Court identified a number of unconstitutional regulations on the press. Although publications can be taxed like any other business, taxes may not be applied to discriminate against newspapers, limit their circulation, or subject publications to penalties that amount to previous restraint. Grosjean v. American Press Co., 297 U.S. 233 (1936). The Court has struck down tax systems that pose the risk of discrimination or suppression. Arkansas Writers' Project, Inc. v. Ragland, 481 U.S. 221 (1987); Minneapolis Star v. Minnesota Comm'r of Rev., 460 U.S. 575 (1983).

Government cannot require licenses to distribute literature; this is a form of censorship. Pamphlets and leaflets have been "historic weapons in the defense of liberty." Lovell v. Griffin, 303 U.S. 444, 452 (1938). Government may not require people to print their name and address on a handbill. Anonymity is often necessary for the communication of ideas, as witnessed by the fictitious names of those who wrote the *Federalist Papers*. Talley v. California, 362 U.S. 60, 65 (1960). It is unconstitutional to ban the distribution of handbills by arguing that their prohibition prevents littering of the streets. The purpose of keeping the streets clean "is insufficient to justify an ordinance which prohibits a person rightfully on a public street from handing literature to one willing to receive it. Any burden imposed upon the city authorities in cleaning and caring for the streets as an indirect consequence of such distribution results from the constitutional protection of the freedom of speech and press." Schneider v. State, 308 U.S. 147, 162 (1939). See also Jamison v. Texas, 318 U.S. 413 (1943). The distribution of informational literature is an essential part of a free press and a democratic society. Organization for a Better Austin v. Keefe, 402 U.S. 415 (1971). In 1988, a 4–3 decision by the Supreme Court held that a city ordinance had given the mayor "unbridled discretion" to grant or deny applications from newspapers to place newsracks on public property. City of Lakewood v. Plain Dealer Pub. Co., 108 S.Ct. 2138 (1988).

The Court struck down as overbroad an Ohio ordinance that prohibited people from distributing handbills or circulars to homes. It agreed that a city could punish those who call at a home where the occupant posts an unwillingness to be disturbed. Martin v. Struthers, 319 U.S. 141 (1943). Uninvited door-to-door canvassing can be proscribed as an invasion of privacy. Breard v. Alexandria, 341 U.S. 622 (1951). Although Congress may exclude certain materials from the mails, the Postmaster General cannot act as censor by deciding which items are mailable and which are not. Hannegan v. Esquire, Inc., 327 U.S. 146 (1946). Government must provide adequate safeguards to prevent the inhibition of protected expression. Blount v. Rizzi, 400 U.S. 410 (1971).

Legislatures retain some latitude in regulating the content of newspapers. In 1973, the Court upheld a Pittsburgh ordinance that prohibited newspapers from printing ads that listed job opportunities under headings of "Male Interest" and "Female Interest." Such labels perpetuated sex discrimination and unequal pay. Pittsburgh Press Co. v. Human Rel. Comm'n, 413 U.S. 376 (1973). Advertisements in newspapers can be regulated because they are "classic examples of commercial speech." Id. at 385. The Court said it had "no doubt that a newspaper constitutionally could be forbidden to publish a want ad proposing a sale of narcotics or soliciting prostitutes." Id. at 388.

Regulation of advertisements does not permit regulation of news coverage. A unanimous Court in 1974 held that government may not compel a newspaper to print a response from a political candidate to a critical editorial. Although "access advocates" argued that chain newspapers and nationwide wire services no longer provided a true marketplace of diverse opinions, the Court refused to permit the government to dictate to the press the contents of its news stories and editorials. Miami Herald Publishing Co. v. Tornillo, 418 U.S. 241 (1974). Another unanimous opinion in 1978 struck down a Virginia statute that made it a crime to divulge information regarding proceedings before a state judicial review commission that received complaints about judges' disability or misconduct. The Court held that the First Amendment does not permit the criminal punishment of third persons (in this case the press), who were strangers to the proceedings, from publishing truthful information. Landmark Communications, Inc. v. Virginia, 435 U.S. 829 (1978). See also Smith v. Daily Mail Publishing Co., 443 U.S. 97 (1979). In 1989, the Court reversed a ruling that imposed compensatory and punitive damages against a newspaper that printed the name of a rape victim. Although the publication violated a state law, the woman's full name had appeared in a police report available to the press. The Florida Star v. B.J.F., 109 S.Ct. 2603 (1989). Similarly, a newspaper is free to publish a rape victim's name that was obtained from judicial records open to public inspection. Cox Broadcasting Co. v. Cohn, 420 U.S. 469 (1975).

The interests of a free press suffered a major setback in 1978 when the Court decided that law enforcement officials could obtain a warrant and come onto the premises of a newspaper to conduct a search for evidence regarding another party. Zurcher v. Stanford Daily, 436 U.S. 547 (1978). After the press appealed to Congress for help, legislation was enacted in 1980 to direct police to use subpoenas as a less intrusive method of obtaining documents. The congressional response is described in greater detail in Chapter 14 (pp. 868–869, 890–892).

National Security

In 1931, in striking down Minnesota's law as a prior restraint on the press, the Court noted that censorship would be constitutional under certain conditions. "No one would question but that a government might prevent actual obstruction to its recruiting service or the publication of the sailing dates of transports or the number and location of troops." Near v. Minnesota, 283 U.S. at 716. The Nixon administration thought this type of critical need had arrived when it sought an injunction to prevent the publication of a classified study entitled "History of U.S. Decision-Making Process on Viet Nam Policy." The administration argued that publication of these materials would be injurious to national security. However, the Supreme Court, with a 6–3 majority in *New York Times Co.* v. *United States* (1971), held that the administration had failed to meet the "heavy burden" of justifying prior restraint on a publication. A brief per curiam opinion preceded a collection of concurrences and dissents (pp. 347–352).

Several years later, the Carter administration attempted to prevent the publication in *The Progressive* magazine of an article that claimed to describe the design of an H-bomb. A federal district court judge issued a preliminary injunction against the publication, recognizing that this was the first instance of prior restraint to his knowledge. Balanced against a free press was this consideration by the judge: "A mistake against the United States could pave the way for thermonuclear annihilation for us all. In that event, our right to life is extinguished and the right to publish becomes moot." United States v. Progressive, 467 F.Supp. 990, 996 (W.D. Wis. 1979). As it turned out, essentially the same material appeared in another publication, without a nuclear holocaust, and the case was dismissed. 610 F.2d 819 (7th Cir. 1979); Morland v. Sprecher, 443 U.S. 709 (1979). *The Progressive* published the article in its November 1979 issue.

Questions of press and national security are at issue when the CIA and other federal agencies require employees, as a condition of employment, to sign a statement agreeing not to publish anything relating to the agency without first submitting the manuscript and obtaining approval. This condition applies both during and after employment. Frank Snepp, a former CIA employee, published a critical evaluation of the agency without first seeking approval. Although the book contained no classified information, the Supreme Court affirmed a lower court's injunction on future writings by Snepp, requiring that he submit manuscripts to the CIA. Snepp was also ordered to give the government his earnings from the book *(Decent Interval)* he published without CIA's clearance. Snepp v. United States, 444 U.S. 507 (1980).[1]

Reporter's Privilege

A landmark ruling in 1972 involved the question of whether newspaper reporters can be compelled to respond to a grand jury subpoena and answer questions. Reporters argue that their sources are privileged and cannot be revealed without destroying their access to informers who demand anonymity. They also express concern that the forced disclosure of information to grand juries will make them appear to be agents of government. However, a 5–4 Court decided that the need to investigate and prosecute criminal charges overrides a reporter's rights, including the protection of confidential sources. BRANZBURG v. HAYES, 408 U.S. 665 (1972). Some of the states already had "shield laws" to protect reporters from court orders. Other state laws protecting reporters were added after *Branzburg*. The Supreme Court conceded that Congress has the power to enact similar legislation. Id. at 706.

Free-press conflicts are not always between the government and a publisher. At times, they involve one publisher against another, with the issue decided largely on statutory, not constitutional, grounds. In one case, President Gerald Ford signed a contract with Harper & Row to publish his memoirs. Harper & Row then negotiated a prepublication agreement with *Time* magazine to print parts of the manuscript. Shortly before the scheduled release of *Time*'s article there appeared an unauthorized article in *The Nation* magazine, including at least 300 to 400 words verbatim from the unpublished Ford manuscript. In interpreting the Copyright Act passed by Congress, the Supreme Court held that *The Nation*'s article was not a "fair use" sanctioned by the statute. Harper & Row v. Nation Enterprises, 471 U.S. 539 (1985). For another free-press case that turned on statutory policy (mingled with constitutional considerations), see Lowe v. SEC, 472 U.S. 181 (1985).

States have invoked election laws to curb the press. Statutes on "corrupt practices," prohibiting electioneering or soliciting of votes on election day, cannot be applied against newspapers that publish views on election day. Mills v. Alabama, 384 U.S. 214 (1966). Nor may government prohibit the distribution of magazines on such vague grounds that they consist of bloody and lustful criminal deeds. Winters v. New York, 333 U.S. 507 (1948). However, government may prohibit interviews between prison inmates and reporters who attempt to investigate and publicize prison conditions. Houchins v. KQED, Inc., 438 U.S. 1 (1978); Saxbe v. Washington Post, 417 U.S. 843 (1974); Pell v. Procunier, 417 U.S. 817 (1974).

FREE PRESS VERSUS FAIR TRIAL

The *Branzburg* decision, requiring reporters to testify before a grand jury, is only one of many collisions between the press and the judiciary. A more frequent confronta-

---

[1]See also United States v. Marchetti, 466 F.2d 1309 (4th Cir. 1972), cert. denied, 409 U.S. 1063 (1972); Knopf v. Colby, 509 F.2d 1362 (4th Cir. 1975), cert. denied, 421 U.S. 992 (1975).

tion is when the press wants to cover a trial and a judge wants to close it. For the most part, the Supreme Court has supported the press and the public in such conflicts, but the record is filled with erratic turns and refashioned doctrines.

One of the early cases concerned a newspaper charged with contempt of court because of its unflattering stories about a judge's conduct in a pending case. The contempt was upheld by the Supreme Court. Toledo Newspaper Co. v. United States, 247 U.S. 402 (1918). This decision was later overturned in Nye v. United States, 313 U.S. 33 (1941). Both decisions were efforts to interpret a congressional statute that restricted the power of judges to punish for contempt. 4 Stat. 487 (1831); 18 U.S.C. § 401. The right of the press to publish comments about pending litigation without being held in contempt of court was also upheld in another case in 1941. The Court observed that the "assumption that respect for the judiciary can be won by shielding judges from published criticism wrongly appraises the character of American public opinion." Bridges v. California, 314 U.S. 252, 270 (1941).

There have been many such cases. In 1946, a unanimous Court reversed a state court's action that held a newspaper in contempt for criticizing a trial judge and impugning his integrity. Pennekamp v. Florida, 328 U.S. 331 (1946). Judges claim that newspaper stories can obstruct the fair and impartial administration of justice in pending cases. However, the general record is to protect the freedom of the press, even when state judges are elected for short terms and lack the independence of life-tenured federal judges. Craig v. Harney, 331 U.S. 367 (1947). If misleading and inflammatory newspaper stories create a prejudicial climate and make a fair trial impossible, cases can be postponed, transferred to a different place, and convictions can be reversed. Shepherd v. Florida, 341 U.S. 50 (1951); Estes v. Texas, 381 U.S. 532 (1965); Sheppard v. Maxwell, 384 U.S. 333 (1966). If jurors learn from news accounts that a defendant had prior felony convictions, that information does not automatically invalidate the trial. The Court will examine "the totality of circumstances" to determine whether the defendant was denied a fair trial. Murphy v. Florida, 421 U.S. 794 (1975).

The confrontation between a free press and a fair trial reaches its highest pitch when judges issue "gag orders" to prohibit public comment about a pending trial. In 1976, a unanimous Court reversed the decision of a Nebraska state court judge who, in anticipation of a trial for a multiple murder, restrained newspapers, broadcasters, journalists, news media associations, and national newswire services from publishing or broadcasting statements by the accused to law enforcement officers. The ban extended to statements to third parties, except members of the press. The Supreme Court held that the heavy burden imposed as a condition of prior restraint had not been met. NEBRASKA PRESS ASSN. v. STUART, 427 U.S. 539 (1976). When court proceedings are open to the public, a judge may not enjoin the news media from publishing the name or photograph of someone charged with an offense. Oklahoma Publishing Co. v. District Court, 430 U.S. 308 (1977).

The dialectic between judicial decisions and public opinion is captured vividly in two back-to-back cases in 1979 and 1980. In the first, a 5–4 decision by the Supreme Court supported a trial judge's ruling to close a pretrial hearing to the public and the press. The motion had been made by defendants without objection by the prosecutor. In upholding the need to protect the fair-trial rights of defendants, the Court held that the public has no constitutional right of access to pretrial proceedings. The Court said that the constitutional guarantee of a public trial is for the benefit of the defendant, not the public: "we hold that members of the public have no constitutional right under the Sixth and Fourteenth Amendments to attend criminal trials."

GANNETT CO. v. DE PASQUALE, 443 U.S. 368, 391 (1979). In a concurrence, Chief Justice Burger said that the Sixth Amendment right to public trial applied strictly to the trial, not to pretrial proceedings. Two other concurrences, by Powell and Rehnquist, undercut the strength of the majority opinion.

In response to the Court's fragmented and disjointed opinion, some judges around the country began to close their courtrooms to the public, not only for pretrial proceedings but for the entire trial and even sentencing. In some cases, they allowed the public in but kept the press out. The press mounted a vigorous counterattack. Critics of the decision claimed that it denied citizens the right to keep government accountable and maintain democratic control. Members of the Supreme Court, including Burger, Powell, Blackmun, and Stevens, took the unusual step of telling audiences around the country that *Gannett* had been "misread" to place unacceptable restraints on the press.[2]

Within a year, a 7–1 Supreme Court decided to limit the damage by announcing a more sympathetic understanding of the public's need to attend trials. The Court held that the public's right of access to criminal trials is implicit in the First Amendment. Open trials promote many interests: the yearning to see justice done, the public education that comes from attending a trial, the maintenance of public trust in the judicial system, and the opportunity to check the fairness and accuracy of judicial proceedings. RICHMOND NEWSPAPERS, INC. v. VIRGINIA, 448 U.S. 555 (1980). See also Globe Newspaper Co. v. Superior Court, 457 U.S. 596 (1982). The guarantee of public proceedings in criminal trials has been extended to cover even the *voir dire* screening of potential jurors. Press-Enterprise Co. v. Superior Court of Cal., 464 U.S. 501 (1984). There is also a right of access to preliminary hearings for criminal proceedings. Press-Enterprise Co. v. Superior Court, 478 U.S. 1 (1986).

Public access has reached the point where some judicial proceedings are televised. A unanimous Supreme Court held that the Constitution does not prohibit states from experimenting with televised trials. Chandler v. Florida, 449 U.S. 560 (1981). Chief Justice Burger opposed televising Supreme Court proceedings, but some members of the Rehnquist Court seem more supportive of this prospect. In November 1988, Chief Justice Rehnquist and Justices White and Kennedy attended a brief demonstration of how filming could be done of Supreme Court proceedings.

LIBEL LAW

The press and the media face a battery of costly suits brought by individuals who claim damage to their reputations. Making publishers fully liable for errors that injure others would lead to self-censorship and a diminished free press. In balancing the values between the rights of a free press and safeguards against defamation, the Supreme Court recognizes that the First Amendment "requires that we protect some falsehood in order to protect speech that matters." Gertz v. Robert Welch, Inc., 418 U.S. 323, 341 (1974).

Defamation takes the form of *slander* (oral defamation) and *libel* (written defamation). In addition to defamation of a person, there can also be "product disparagement." Bose Corp. v. Consumers Unions of U.S., Inc., 466 U.S. 485 (1984).

[2]"Burger Suggests Some Judges Err in Closing Trials," New York Times, August 9, 1979, at A-17; "Burger's View on Right to Attend Trial," New York Times, August 11, 1979, at 43; "Powell Says Court Has No Hostility Toward Press," New York Times, August 14, 1979, at A-13; "Appeal Could Clarify Justices' Stand on Closed Courts," New York Times, September 4, 1979, at A-15; "Stevens Says Closed Trials May Justify New Laws," New York Times, September 9, 1979, at 41. See also Anthony Lewis, "A Public's Right to Know About Public Institutions: The First Amendment as Sword," 1980 Supreme Court Review 1.

British libel law permitted punishment of any writing that tended to bring into disrepute the government or established religion, or was likely to provoke a breach of the peace. Truth was not a defense in criminal libel; "the provocation, and not the falsity, is the thing to be punished criminally." 4 Blackstone, Commentaries 150. Contemporary courts recognize truth as a defense, but libel law is engulfed by confusion and tenuous distinctions. "Malice" remains a central and elusive concept; as used by the Supreme Court, it does not carry the conventional meaning of ill-will or hostility.

Although the relationship between malice and defamation was explored in the nineteenth century, White v. Nicholls, 44 U.S. (3 How.) 266 (1845), the benchmark libel case dates from 1964. In response to an advertisement in the *New York Times*, charging Alabama police with acts of terrorism and violence against civil rights demonstrators, a state official responsible for the police brought a libel suit. In a unanimous decision, the Court held that the official could not recover damages unless he could prove that the defamatory information in the advertisement was made with "actual malice," which the Court defined as "knowledge that it was false or with reckless disregard of whether it was false or not." NEW YORK TIMES CO. v. SULLIVAN, 376 U.S. 254, 280 (1964).

Following *Sullivan*, a series of cases have limited the reach of defamation suits. For example, a Louisiana defamation statute permitted critics of public officials to be punished not only for false statements made with ill-will but even true statements made with ill-will. A district attorney in Louisiana, during a news conference, accused state judges of being lazy and inefficient and of hampering his efforts to enforce the laws. He was convicted of violating the state defamation statute. A unanimous Supreme Court held that the Constitution limits state power to impose sanctions for criticism of the official conduct of public officials. Punishment applied only to false statements made with knowledge of their falsity or with reckless disregard of whether they are true or false. "Truth may not be the subject of either civil or criminal sanctions where discussion of public affairs is concerned." Garrison v. Louisiana, 379 U.S. 64, 74 (1964). Concurrences by Justices Black, Douglas, and Goldberg objected to *any* punishment for criticizing public officials. Black and Douglas claimed that fines and jail sentences for "malicious" statements marked a return to the Sedition Act of 1798 and a revival of the law of seditious libel.

In 1966, the Court reversed another libel suit that had awarded damages to an individual employed by three county commissioners. He claimed that a newspaper column accused him of fiscal mismanagement, but the Court ruled that any implication of wrongdoing had not been directed to him personally. Rosenblatt v. Baer, 383 U.S. 75 (1966). Three concurrences by Douglas, Stewart, and Black argued that the Constitution bars any libel actions against government officials. Libel verdicts against newspapers were also reversed in Beckley Newspapers v. Hanks, 389 U.S. 81 (1967) and Greenbelt Pub. Assn. v. Bressler, 398 U.S. 6 (1970).

Apart from libel suits brought by government officials, the Court reviews cases in which private individuals seek damages for defamation or invasion of privacy. An example of the latter involved a suit by James Hill, who had been held hostage in his home, along with his family, by escaped convicts. His ordeal helped inspire a novel and later a play, called "The Desperate Hours." In writing about the play, *Life* magazine related it specifically to the Hill incident and called the play a reenactment. Hill was awarded damages. The Court reversed the judgment with instructions that damages could be given only upon proof that *Life* was knowingly or recklessly false. There had to be calculated falsehoods. Mere negligence, said the Court, would put an intolerable burden on the press. Time, Inc. v. Hill, 385 U.S. 374 (1967).

This case also developed the public-figure doctrine. It distinguished between private citizens (like James Hill) who desired anonymity and those who, because of their prominence in sports, entertainment, and other fields, were "public figures." The latter had a reduced right of privacy. Id. at 384–386. The public-figure doctrine was used in another case in 1967. Libel damages were allowed for an athletic director accused in a magazine article of "fixing" a football game. The falsehood inflicted substantial damage on his reputation and resulted from deficient investigative and reporting techniques. Curtis Publishing Co. v. Butts, 388 U.S. 130 (1967). The Court has issued other guidelines to clarify the public-figure doctrine. Harte-Hanks Communications v. Connaughton, 109 S.Ct. 2678 (1989).

In 1971, a plurality of Supreme Court Justices was ready to float another doctrine. They said that the First Amendment's impact on state libel laws depended not so much on whether the plaintiff was a public official, a public figure, or a private individual, but whether the defamation concerns "an issue of public or general concern." Rosenbloom v. Metromedia, 403 U.S. 29, 44 (1971). Under the latter test, the rights of a free press require special protection and tolerance. In his concurrence, Justice White attempted to summarize the multiple and evolving doctrines of the Court. Public officers and public figures had to prove either knowing or reckless disregard of the truth. Other plaintiffs had to prove at least negligent falsehood, "but if the publication about them was in an area of legitimate public interest, then they too must prove deliberate or reckless error." Id. at 59.

This new formulation did not sit well. Why should a private individual be forced to satisfy the rigorous requirement of knowing-or-reckless falsity simply because the defamatory falsehood became an issue of public or general interest? Within a few years the Court abandoned the *Rosenbloom* doctrine because it gave insufficient protection to private individuals. The Court recognized that public officials and public figures have more opportunities to use the media to rebut defamation. Private individuals are "more vulnerable to injury, and the state interest in protecting them is correspondingly greater." Gertz v. Robert Welch, Inc., 418 U.S. 323, 344 (1974). Although states must follow the knowing-or-reckless-disregard test for public officials and public figures, they "should retain substantial latitude in their efforts to enforce a legal remedy for defamatory falsehood injurious to the reputation of a private individual." Id. at 345–346. In discarding the doctrine of "public or general concern," the Court doubted the wisdom of committing such tasks to the conscience of judges. Id. at 346.

This heightened solicitude for private individuals who seek damages in libel suits was reinforced over the next few years. A series of cases adopted a narrow definition of "public figure," thus allowing private individuals who might be prominent locally a better chance of collecting on a libel suit.[3] However, in 1985 the Court resurrected the public-concern doctrine. In a 5–4 decision, it held that speech on matters of "purely private concern" is entitled to less First Amendment protection than speech involving public concern. Once it is determined that there is a lack of public

---

[3]Wolston v. Reader's Digest Assn., Inc., 443 U.S. 157 (1979); Hutchinson v. Proxmire, 443 U.S. 111 (1979); Time, Inc. v. Firestone, 424 U.S. 448 (1976). In *Hutchinson*, the Court noted: "Clearly, those charged with defamation cannot, by their own conduct, create their own defense by making the claimant a public figure." 443 U.S. at 135.

concern in a libel action, plaintiffs may be awarded damages without having to show actual malice. Dun & Bradstreet, Inc. v. Greenmoss Builders, 472 U.S. 749 (1985). The dissenters objected that the majority had provided "almost no guidance as to what constitutes a protected matter of public concern." The public-concern doctrine was used a year later in another 5–4 decision. The Court held that when a newspaper publishes speech of public concern about a private figure, the individual cannot recover libel damages without showing that the statements are false. Philadelphia Newspapers, Inc. v. Hepps, 475 U.S. 767 (1986).

Although *Sullivan* had made it more difficult for public officials and public figures to win libel verdicts against the press, nothing in that decision prevented the filing of a suit and forcing the press to exhaust funds and resources to defend itself. Celebrities claiming injury sued the press and the media for large sums. For example, General William C. Westmoreland filed a $120 million suit against CBS-TV and its weekly program "60 Minutes" for charging that he and his command had misled the public, the Congress, and the President about enemy troop strength in Vietnam in order to advance the political argument that the war was being won. Ariel Sharon, former Israeli Defense Minister, sued *Time* magazine for $50 million for suggesting that he had encouraged the massacre of hundreds of Lebanese in the Sabra and Shatila refugee camps.

Westmoreland agreed to drop the case in 1985, before verdict, in return for a joint statement in which CBS expressed its respect for his "long and faithful service to his country" and Westmoreland gave his esteem for CBS's "distinguished journalistic tradition." In a separate statement, CBS said it stood by the fairness and accuracy of the program. Also in 1985, a jury in New York issued a split verdict on Sharon, concluding that *Time* had acted negligently and carelessly but not with actual malice or reckless disregard for the truth. In a separate action in Israel, Sharon and *Time* announced an out-of-court settlement in 1986 in which *Time* admitted that its story was "erroneous" and agreed to pay part of Sharon's legal fees. The legal expenses for CBS and *Time* to defend their interests were vast.

A decision by the Supreme Court in 1988 sparked an unusual amount of interest in libel law. A jury had awarded $200,000 to the Reverend Jerry Falwell, founder of the Moral Majority, for damages inflicted by an advertisement in *Hustler* magazine. The ad was a takeoff on a Campari liqueur campaign in which celebrities discussed "their first time." The parody portrays Falwell as a drunkard having sex with his mother in an outhouse. Although the jury said the parody was not libelous because it was patently unbelievable, it assessed damages for the "emotional distress" suffered by Falwell. A unanimous Court ruled that public figures and public officials unable to prove libel cannot recover damages for parodies, no matter how outrageous, that might cause emotional distress. "Outrageousness" was too subjective a test and would interfere with the free flow of ideas protected by the First Amendment. HUSTLER MAGAZINE v. FALWELL, 108 S.Ct. 876 (1988).

The original purpose of the actual-malice test was to safeguard the press by erecting a high shield. How does a plaintiff determine that a falsehood results from malice? What steps must be taken to show that a publisher has "knowledge" or acts with "reckless disregard" in issuing false statements? May plaintiffs interview and depose employees of a newspaper or broadcasting station to discover the state of mind of those who edit, produce, and publish stories? Would this threaten a free press? In 1979, a 6–3 Court held that the First Amendment does not prohibit a plaintiff in a libel case from inquiring into the editorial process. Herbert v. Lando, 441 U.S. 153 (1979).

A 1985 libel case offers another rare example where the Court was able to speak with a unanimous voice. In letters to President Reagan, someone had written false and derogatory statements about a person being considered for U.S. attorney. The author of the letters claimed that the Petition Clause of the First Amendment gave him absolute immunity from liability. The Court held that statements made in a petition are not entitled to greater constitutional protection than other First Amendment expressions. McDonald v. Smith, 472 U.S. 479 (1985).

The law on libel has become so confused and costly for plaintiffs and defendants that alternatives to adjudication are being explored. A 1988 report by the Annenberg Washington Program proposed that lawsuits should be barred if a complainant receives a retraction or an opportunity to reply in a newspaper or broadcast outlet. If the complainant fails to receive that satisfaction, either side could ask a court for a declaratory judgment on the truth or falsity of the statement at issue. Vague standards, including "actual malice" and "public figure," would be eliminated.

OBSCENITY

An author writing on obscenity and pornography approaches the task with heavy heart and wry amusement. Readers are unlikely to comprehend judicial declamations on prurient interest, lascivious matter, lewdness, lust, socially redeeming values, and contemporary community standards. Students are baffled to encounter plaintiffs called "12 200-ft Reels of Super 8 mm. Film." Still, this is a legitimate area of First Amendment law and there is some instruction in the Court's willingness to adjudicate and offer guidance for an overwhelmingly thankless endeavor. The Court is regularly accused of delving into metaphysics and functioning like an ecclesiastical court.

Under English law, the test of obscenity was defined as the tendency of the written matter "to deprave and corrupt those whose minds are open to such immoral influences, and into whose hands a publication of this sort may fall." Regina v. Hicklin, L.R. 3 Q.B. 360, 371 (1868). The effect of this test was to reduce the community to a child's level.

In the United States, the issue of obscenity did not occupy much time for the national government. Congress passed the Comstock Act in 1873 to make it illegal to sell, lend, give away, or exhibit any obscene writings or pictures. The statute also prohibited the mailing of obscene materials. 17 Stat. 598–600. These and other statutes led to several Supreme Court decisions before the century was out.[4] The Supreme Court found it necessary to distinguish between coarse and vulgar writings (not covered by the statute) and lewd, lascivious, and obscene writings which were made illegal. Swearingen v. United States, 161 U.S. 446 (1896). In addition to these prohibited categories, Congress outlawed the mailing of "filthy" books. 35 Stat. 1129, § 211 (1909); United States v. Limehouse, 285 U.S. 424 (1932). A major case in 1931, upholding the rights of a free press, said that "the primary requirements of decency may be enforced against obscene publications." Near v. Minnesota, 283 U.S. 697, 716 (1931).

Significant principles were established in the lower courts. In 1913, Judge Learned Hand rejected the English precedent in *Hicklin*. He did not believe that

---

[4]United States v. Chase, 135 U.S. 255 (1890); Grimm v. United States, 156 U.S. 604 (1895); Rosen v. United States, 161 U.S. 29 (1895); Andrews v. United States, 162 U.S. 420 (1896); Price v. United States, 165 U.S. 311 (1897); Dunlop v. United States, 165 U.S. 486 (1897).

society was content in reducing "our treatment of sex to the standard of a child's library in the supposed interest of a salacious few . . ." United States v. Kennerly, 209 F. 119, 121 (S.D.N.Y. 1913). Further driving home his point: "To put thought in leash to the average conscience of the time is perhaps tolerable, but to fetter it by the necessities of the lowest and least capable seems a fatal policy." Id. With regard to a challenge to James Joyce's *Ulysses*, a district judge held that the courts must determine whether an author *intended* a book to be obscene. The judge concluded that *Ulysses* was a sincere and honest book and that Joyce did not intend to excite sexual impulses or lustful thoughts. United States v. One Book Called "Ulysses," 5 F.Supp. 182 (S.D.N.Y. 1933). Another judge allowed a book to enter the country on the ground that a reading of it "would not stir the sex impulses of any person with a normal mind." United States v. One Book Entitled "Contraception," 51 F.2d 525, 528 (S.D.N.Y. 1931).

The Supreme Court's preoccupation with the issue of obscenity begins in the 1950s. In a censorship case involving a New York law banning "sacrilegious" movies, a unanimous Court held that the statute violated two constitutional principles: the presumption against prior restraint, and the forbidden use of religious objectives to pursue state policy. Joseph Burstyn, Inc. v. Wilson, 343 U.S. 495 (1952). See also Superior Films v. Dept. of Education, 346 U.S. 587 (1954). In 1957, another unanimous ruling struck down a Michigan statute that sought to keep "obscene" books from the general public when the book would have a potentially deleterious effect on youth. As the Court noted, the law would "reduce the adult population of Michigan to reading only what is fit for children." Butler v. Michigan, 352 U.S. 380, 383 (1957).

These two unanimous rulings encouraged the Court's foray into obscenity law, but subsequent cases scattered the Justices in different directions with conflicting theories. Justice Harlan later observed: "The subject of obscenity has produced a variety of views among the members of the Court unmatched in any other course of constitutional interpretation." Interstate Circuit v. Dallas, 390 U.S. 676 (1968). The Court split 5–4 in 1957 in upholding a state law that allowed a court, without a jury trial, to enjoin further distribution of obscene books and to order their destruction. Kingsley Books, Inc. v. Brown, 354 U.S. 436 (1957). In a pivotal case the same year, the Court unveiled a set of new doctrines: obscenity is not within the area of constitutionally protected speech or press; sex and obscenity are not synonymous; the test for obscenity is whether "to the average person, applying contemporary community standards, the dominant theme of the material taken as a whole appeals to prurient interest." The dissenters attacked the vague, ill-defined standards promulgated by the Court. ROTH v. UNITED STATES, 354 U.S. 476 (1957).

To appreciate the complaint of the dissenters, look up *prurient* in the dictionary. Read also the meandering opinions, none of them attracting a majority, in Manual Enterprises v. Day, 370 U.S. 479 (1962). Justice Clark, dissenting, said of this 6–1 decision: "While those in the majority like ancient Gaul are split into three parts . . ." In Jacobellis v. Ohio, 378 U.S. 184 (1964), a 6–3 decision generated five opinions by those in the majority. In one of the concurrences Justice Stewart uttered his famous test for hard-core pornography: "I know it when I see it."

In two 1959 decisions, the Court managed a unanimous ruling on one case and an 8–1 majority on the other. In the first, it held that the denial of a license to show a motion picture *(Lady Chatterly's Lover)* violated the First Amendment freedom to advocate ideas. The movie had been banned because it presented adultery as being right and desirable under certain circumstances. Kingsley Pictures Corp. v. Regents, 360 U.S. 684 (1959). In his concurrence, Justice Black said that if the nation embarked on the road of censorship, "this Court is about the most inappropriate Supreme Court of Censors that could be found." In the other case, the Court ruled that a city ordinance was unconstitutional because its effect would allow a storeowner to sell only the books he had inspected. Under this scheme, restrictions affected the distribution of constitutionally protected as well as obscene literature. Smith v. California, 361 U.S. 147 (1959).

The question of prior restraint returned in 1961, producing a 5–4 decision that upheld the examination of movies before their showing. Licensing could be used to suppress ideas—not only obscene but social and political views as well. The issue was not the standards for censorship but the act of censorship itself. Times Film Corp. v. Chicago, 365 U.S. 43 (1961). The Court supported the screening of movies, a procedure that would be intolerable for newspapers or even broadcasting. The Court later insisted on procedural safeguards whenever films are required to be submitted to a censor.[5]

The tests announced in *Roth* begged for clarification. What are "contemporary community standards"? For Justices Brennan and Goldberg, the phrase referred not to state and local communities but to society at large. Jacobellis v. Ohio, 378 U.S. 184, 193 (1964). This was a liberal standard, for it prohibited censorship by counties and towns. Chief Justice Warren and Justice Clark, in dissent, believed that "contemporary community standards" meant community standards, not a national standard. Id. at 200. Two years later, in a dissent, Justice Black said he was uncertain whether the community standards referred to were worldwide, nationwide, sectionwide, statewide, countrywide, precinctwide, or townshipwide. Ginzburg v. United States, 383 U.S. 463, 479–480 (1966).

What is obscenity? *Roth* said that sex and obscenity are not synonymous. The Court has also held that obscenity means more than vulgarity. To be obscene, an expression must be erotic. Cohen v. California, 403 U.S. 15, 20 (1971). In 1985, the Court found it necessary to distinguish between "lust," which it called a normal sexual response, and the categories of lasciviousness or prurient interest that involve a morbid interest in sex. Brockett v. Spokane Arcades, Inc., 472 U.S. 491 (1985). Also, cities may not outlaw pornography on the ground that it discriminates against women by portraying them as sex objects. The state may not declare one perspective right and silence opponents. Hudnut v. American Booksellers Assn., Inc., 475 U.S. 1001 (1986); 771 F.2d 323.

Nudity, depending on the context, is not necessarily obscene. Kois v. California, 408 U.S. 229 (1972); Jenkins v. Georgia, 418 U.S. 153, 161 (1974); Schad v. Mount Ephraim, 452 U.S. 61 (1981). The Court struck down as overbroad a state law that made it a punishable offense for a drive-in movie to exhibit films showing nudity when the screen is visible from a public street or place. The Court pointed out that the law would bar even "a baby's buttocks, the nude body of a war victim, or scenes from a culture in which nudity is indigenous." Erznoznik v. City of Jacksonville, 422 U.S. 205, 213 (1975). A 6–3 Court deferred to the states on the question of whether nude entertainment could take place simultaneously with the dispensing of liquor.

[5]Freedman v. Maryland, 380 U.S. 51 (1965); Teitel Film Corp. v. Cusack, 390 U.S. 139 (1968); Southeastern Promotions, Ltd. v. Conrad, 420 U.S. 546 (1975); Vance v. Universal Amusement Co., 445 U.S. 308 (1980).

The decision depended partly on the authority of states under the Twenty-First Amendment to control liquor. California v. La Rue, 409 U.S. 109 (1972). See also New York State Liquor Authority v. Bellanca, 452 U.S. 714 (1981) and Newport v. Iacobucci, 479 U.S. 92 (1986).

An interesting twist to *Roth* is that its author, Justice Brennan, took the lead in restricting its scope. Writing an opinion in 1966 joined by Chief Justice Warren and Justice Fortas, he said that even if a book had (1) prurient appeal and (2) was patently offensive to contemporary community standards, it also had to be found (3) *"utterly without redeeming social value"* to be banned. All three elements had to be met. Memoirs v. Massachusetts, 383 U.S. 413, 418–419 (1966). In dissent, Justices White and Clark accused Brennan of rejecting the basic holding of *Roth*. In another dissent, Justice Harlan noted: "The central development that emerges from the aftermath of *Roth* . . . is that no stable approach to the obscenity problem has yet been devised by this Court." He also doubted whether the utterly-without-redeeming test had "any meaning at all."

On the same day, a 5–4 Court affirmed the conviction of someone who had "pandered" to the erotic interests of readers by trying to mail literature at first from Intercourse and Blue Balls, Pennsylvania, and finally settling on Middlesex, New Jersey. Ginzburg v. United States, 383 U.S. 463 (1966). These promotional and advertising techniques appeared to be the decisive factors in justifying the person's conviction. Justice Douglas, dissenting, reminded his brethren of advertisements in national magazines "chock-full of thighs, ankles, calves, bosoms, eyes, and hair, to draw the potential buyer's attention to lotions, tires, food, liquor, clothing, autos, and even insurance policies." See also Mishkin v. New York, 383 U.S. 502 (1966).[6]

By 1973, the legal meaning of obscenity had run in so many directions that the Court needed to formulate new standards. This it did by rejecting the *Memoirs* test that a work must be *"utterly* without redeeming social value." Moreover, the Court said it was not necessary to employ a "national standard." The values of a "forum community" (such as a state) will do. New guidelines for obscenity were announced: (1) whether the "average person, applying contemporary community standards," would find that the work, taken as a whole, appeals to the prurient interest; (2) whether the work depicts or describes, in a patently offensive way, sexual conduct specifically defined by the applicable state law; and (3) whether the work, taken as a whole, lacks "serious literary, artistic, political, or scientific value." MILLER v. CALIFORNIA, 413 U.S. 15 (1973). One of the four dissenters was Justice Brennan, author of *Roth*. He elaborated on his objections while dissenting in another case the same day. PARIS ADULT THEATRE I v. SLATON, 413 U.S. 49 (1973).

The forum-community test does not mean that a jury can operate without limits, allowing it to convict someone for showing a woman with a bare midriff. Jenkins v. Georgia, 418 U.S. 153, 161 (1974). One judge, who was reversed, told the jury that community standards on obscene films meant whatever should not be seen with

[6]For other cases during this period, see Redrup v. New York, 386 U.S. 767 (1967); Interstate Circuit v. Dallas, 390 U.S. 676 (1968); Rabeck v. New York, 391 U.S. 462 (1968). For instructive articles on obscenity, see Harry Kalven, Jr., "The Metaphysics of the Law of Obscenity," 1960 Sup. Ct. Rev. 1; Louis Henkin, "Morals and the Constitution: The Sin of Obscenity," 63 Colum. L. Rev. 391 (1963); Earl Finbar Murphy, "The Value of Pornography," 10 Wayne L. Rev. 655 (1964); C. Peter Magrath, "The Obscenity Cases: Grapes of Roth," 1966 Sup. Ct. Rev. 7.

their mothers sitting next to them. Liles v. Oregon, 425 U.S. 963, 966 (1975). See also Smith v. United States, 431 U.S. 291, 301 (1977). In 1987, the Court held that only the first two prongs of the *Miller* test should be decided by juries on "contemporary community standards." Whether a work has literary, artistic, political, or scientific value need not obtain majority approval to merit protection. The value of a work does not vary from community to community. Pope v. Illinois, 481 U.S. 497 (1987).

Some of the states have refused to adopt the three tests of *Miller* v. *California*. The Oregon Supreme Court said that it could not justify the prosecution of someone who failed to meet such a vague notion as contemporary standards. State citizens would be forced to guess about a future jury's estimate of contemporary state standards of "prurience." The state court also explained that the *Miller* guidelines ran counter to Oregon's political and social culture, which was "dedicated to founding a free society unfettered by the governmental imposition of some people's views of morality on the free expression of others." State v. Henry, 732 P.2d 9, 16 (Ore. 1987).

One of the few areas of agreement in obscenity law is the need to treat children differently from adults. In 1969, a unanimous Court held that the private possession of obscene materials by adults at home cannot be made a crime. Adults may read and watch what they like in the privacy of their own home. Stanley v. Georgia, 394 U.S. 557 (1969) (see reading in Chapter 17). The *Stanley* doctrine does not justify the mailing of obscene materials to adults, the attempt to bring in obscene materials at a port of entry, or the importation of obscene matter intended for an adult's private use. United States v. Reidel, 402 U.S. 351 (1971); United States v. Thirty-Seven Photographs, 402 U.S. 363 (1971); United States v. 12 200-ft Reels of Super 8 mm. Film, 413 U.S. 123 (1973); United States v. Orito, 413 U.S. 139 (1973).

Watching obscene films at home does not create a right to watch them at public theaters. Paris Adult Theatre I v. Slaton, 413 U.S. 49 (1973). Cities may use their zoning authority to disperse adult movie theaters, even if the distinction demands content-based regulation. Young v. American Mini Theatres, 427 U.S. 50 (1976). Cities may also adopt zoning ordinances to keep adult movie theaters away from residential areas, churches, parks, and schools. Renton v. Playtime Theatres, Inc., 475 U.S. 41 (1986). Efforts to regulate "indecent" cable television at home raise unique problems. Wilkinson v. Jones, 480 U.S. 926 (1987), 800 F.2d 989 (10th Cir. 1986).

Congress has been active in legislating against "dial-a-porn": sexually explicit messages available over the telephone. Legislation in 1983 prohibited any party in the District of Columbia or in interstate or foreign communication from providing by telephone, either directly or through use of a recording device, "any obscene or indecent communication for commercial purposes" to any person under eighteen years of age. 97 Stat. 1469, § 8 (1983). The statute had two problems. The provider of these messages had no way of knowing the age of the caller. The FCC, responsible for implementing this statute, found it nearly impossible to enforce it. Second, by permitting persons over eighteen to receive these messages with their consent, the statute in effect legalized dial-a-porn.

Congress passed new legislation in 1988 to completely ban dial-a-porn services, regardless of the age of the caller. 102 Stat. 424, § 6101 (1988). The Court later held that Congress may prohibit the interstate transmission of obscene commercial telephone messages, but that the ban on *indecent* messages violated the First Amendment. There were no legislative findings to justify the conclusion that

Congress was unable to devise constitutionally acceptable and less restrictive means to achieve the government's legitimate interest in protecting minors. The statute, therefore, was not drawn in a sufficiently narrow manner. Sable Communications of Cal. v. FCC, 109 S.Ct. 2829 (1989). In response, Congress began the process of redrafting the statute.

With regard to minors, states may restrict minors under seventeen years of age from reading materials that are not obscene for adults. Ginsberg v. New York, 390 U.S. 629 (1968). Literature can be restricted if there is a "tendency of widely circulated books of this category to reach the impressionable young and have a continuing impact." Kaplan v. California, 413 U.S. 115, 120 (1973). There are continuing disputes as to how booksellers should be required to display sexual publications harmful to juveniles. Virginia v. American Booksellers Assn., 108 S.Ct. 636 (1988).

In one of the rare unanimous decisions on obscenity, the Court upheld a state law directed at child pornography. The statute prohibited persons from knowingly promoting a "sexual performance" by a child under sixteen by distributing material describing such a performance. Sexual performance was defined as actual or simulated sexual intercourse, deviate sexual intercourse, sexual bestiality, mastur- bation, sado-masochistic abuse, or lewd exhibition of the genitals. New York v. Ferber, 458 U.S. 747 (1982). Congress passed legislation in 1978 to make it a federal crime to use children under sixteen for the production of pornographic materials. The law applies to the sale and distribution of obscene materials, mailed or transported in interstate or foreign commerce, that depict children in sexually explicit conduct. 92 Stat. 7 (1978). Those restrictions were strengthened in 1984 by raising the age to eighteen and relying on *New York* v. *Ferber* to remove the requirement in existing law that child pornography be proven "obscene" before convictions could be obtained. 98 Stat. 204 (1984). Amendments in 1986 and 1988 further tightened the statutory prohibitions against child pornography. 100 Stat. 3510 (1986); 102 Stat. 4485–4503 (Subtitle N) (1988).

Some of the efforts to combat obscenity raise Fourth Amendment issues. Police officers may not make ad hoc decisions to search newsstands and seize "obscene" materials. Marcus v. Search Warrant, 367 U.S. 717 (1961). See also A Quantity of Books v. Kansas, 378 U.S. 205 (1964) and Roade v. Kentucky, 413 U.S. 496 (1973). Before issuing a warrant to seize allegedly obscene materials, a magistrate must make some kind of inquiry into the factual basis for the allegation. Lee Art Theatre v. Virginia, 392 U.S. 636 (1968). However, an adversary hearing is not required prior to a seizure. Heller v. New York, 413 U.S. 483 (1973).

The decision by the Warren Court in *New York Times Co.* v. *Sullivan* (1964) appeared to be a ringing endorsement for a free press. Debate on public issues was to be "uninhibited, robust, and wide-open." However, the language and rationale of *Sullivan* paved the way for a series of rulings during the Burger Court that exposed the press to costly settlements and lawsuits in libel cases. There continues to be a presumption against prior restraint, but self-censorship by the press is a possible consequence of expensive litigation. Moreover, the Burger Court held that newsrooms could be searched by law enforcement officials (*Zurcher* in 1978) and reporters could be jailed for refusing to disclose confidential sources (*Branzburg* in 1972). With some starts and stops, the Burger Court generally supported press freedoms with regard to open trials and access to court proceedings. Questions of obscenity and pornography continue to perplex and divide the Court. It is strange that the United States seems preoccupied with the effect of obscenity and pornography on citizens, especially children, while it appears to be unconcerned about the level of violence on television. Studies indicate a causal relationship between televised violence and later aggressive behavior in children.

Freedom of the press depends on the relationship that exists between the government and the citizen. Does government extend the right of a free press to the people or do the people instruct the government on its rights and powers? Remarks by James Madison during House debate in 1794 provide an important context for this question. The House was considering a censure of certain societies involved in an insurrection in western Pennsylvania (the Whiskey Rebellion). Madison warned that opinions could not be the object of legislation. Congressional resolutions of censure might extend improperly to the liberties of speech and of the press, he said, and then concluded: "If we advert to the nature of Republican Government, we shall find that the censorial power is in the people over the Government, and not in the Government over the people." 4 Annals of Congress 934 (1794).

Selected Readings

ANDERSON, DAVID A. "The Origins of the Press Clause." 30 *UCLA Law Review* 455 (1983).

BARRON, JEROME A. *Freedom of the Press for Whom?* Bloomington: Indiana University Press, 1973.

BERNS, WALTER. "Freedom of the Press and the Alien and Sedition Laws: A Reappraisal." 1970 *Supreme Court Review* 109.

BEZANSON, RANDALL P., et al. *Libel Law and the Press: Myth and Reality.* New York: The Free Press, 1987.

BLANCHARD, MARGARET A. "The Institutional Press and its First Amendment Privileges." 1978 *Supreme Court Review* 225.

BLASI, VINCENT. "Toward a Theory of Prior Restraint: The Central Linkage." 66 *Minnesota Law Review* 11 (1981).

BURANELLI, VINCENT. *The Trial of Peter Zenger.* New York: New York University Press, 1957.

EMERSON, THOMAS I. "The Doctrine of Prior Restraint." 20 *Law and Contemporary Problems* 648 (1955).

EMERY, EDWIN. *The Press and America.* Englewood Cliffs, N.J.: Prentice-Hall, 1984.

FRIENDLY, FRED W. *Minnesota Rag.* New York: Random House, 1981.

HUDON, EDWARD G. *Freedom of Speech and Press in America.* Washington, D.C.: Public Affairs Press, 1963.

KALVEN, HARRY, JR. "The Reasonable Man and the First Amendment: Hill, Butts, and Walker." 1967 *Supreme Court Review* 267.

——. "The New York Times Cases: A Note on the 'Central Meaning of the First Amendment'." 1964 *Supreme Court Review* 191.

LAWHORNE, CLIFTON O. *Defamation and Public Officials.* Carbondale: Southern Illinois University Press, 1971.

——. *The Supreme Court and Libel.* Carbondale: Southern Illinois University Press, 1981.

LEVY, LEONARD W. *Emergence of a Free Press.* New York: Oxford University Press, 1985.

——, ed. *Freedom of the Press from Zenger to Jefferson.* Indianapolis, Ind.: Bobbs-Merrill, 1966.

LINDE, HANS. "Courts and Censorship." 66 *Minnesota Law Review* 171 (1981).

LOFTON, JOHN. *The Press as Guardian of the First Amendment.* Columbia: University of South Carolina Press, 1980.

MURPHY, PAUL L. "Near v. Minnesota in the Context of Historical Developments." 66 *Minnesota Law Review* 95 (1981).

NELSON, HAROLD L., ed. *Freedom of the Press: From Hamilton to the Warren Court.* Indianapolis, Ind.: Bobbs-Merrill, 1967.

SHAPIRO, MARTIN, ed. *The Pentagon Papers and the Courts: A Study in Foreign Policy-Making and Freedom of the Press.* San Francisco: Chandler Publishing, 1972.

SMITH, JAMES MORTON. *Freedom's Fetters: The Alien and Sedition Laws and American Civil Liberties.* Ithaca, N.Y.: Cornell University Press, 1956.

UNGAR, SANFORD J. *The Papers & The Papers.* New York: Dutton, 1972.

John Milton

Areopagitica (1644)

In this classic defense of a free press, Milton appeals to the Parliament of England to reject licenses for printing. He had learned of an order that would prohibit the printing of any book, pamphlet, or paper unless first approved and licensed. His essay is one of the most compelling arguments against using prior restraint to suppress written materials.

. . .

If ye be thus resolved, as it were injury to think ye were not, I know not what should withhold me from presenting ye with a fit instance wherein to show both that love of truth which ye eminently profess, and that uprightness of your judgment which is not wont to be partial to yourselves; by judging over again that order which ye have ordained *to regulate printing: that no book, pamphlet, or paper shall be henceforth printed, unless the same be first approved and licensed by such,* or at least one of such, as shall be thereto appointed. For that part which preserves justly every man's copy to himself, or provides for the poor, I touch not; only wish they be not made pretences to abuse and persecute honest and painful men who offend not in either of these particulars. But that other clause of licensing books, which we thought had died with his brother *quadragesimal* and *matrimonial* when the prelates expired, I shall now attend with such a homily as shall lay before ye, first, the inventors of it to be those whom ye will be loth to own; next, what is to be thought in general of reading, whatever sort the books be; and that this order avails nothing to the suppressing of scandalous, seditious, and libelous books, which were mainly intended to be suppressed; last, that it will be primely to the discouragement of all learning, and the stop of truth, not only by disexercising and blunting our abilities in what we know already, but by hindering and cropping the discovery that might be yet further made both in religious and civil wisdom.

I deny not but that it is of greatest concernment in the church and commonwealth to have a vigilant eye how books demean themselves, as well as men, and thereafter to confine, imprison, and do sharpest justice on them as malefactors. For books are not absolutely dead things, but do contain a potency of life in them to be as active as that soul was whose progeny they are; nay, they do preserve as in a vial the purest efficacy and extraction of that living intellect that bred them. I know they are as lively, and as vigorously productive, as those fabulous dragon's teeth; and being sown up and down, may chance to spring up armed men. And yet, on the other hand, unless wariness be used, as good almost kill a man as kill a good book: who kills a man kills a reasonable creature, God's image; but he who destroys a good book, kills reason itself, kills the image of God, as it were, in the eye. Many a man lives a burden to the earth; but a good book is the precious life-blood of a master spirit, embalmed and treasured up on purpose to a life beyond life. 'Tis true, no age can restore a life, whereof, perhaps, there is no great loss; and revolutions of ages do not oft recover the loss of a rejected truth, for the want of which whole nations fare the worse. We should be wary, therefore, what persecution we raise against the living labors of public men, how we spill that seasoned life of man preserved and stored up in books; since we see a kind of homicide may be thus committed, sometimes a martyrdom; and if it extend to the whole impression, a kind of massacre, whereof the execution ends not in the slaying of an elemental life, but strikes at that ethereal and fifth essence, the breath of reason itself, slays an immortality rather than a life.

. . .

. . . If we think to regulate printing, thereby to rectify manners, we must regulate all recreations and pastimes, all that is delightful to man. No music must be heard, no song be set or sung, but what is grave and Doric. There must be licensing dancers, that no gesture, motion, or deportment be taught our youth, but what by their allowance shall be thought honest; for such Plato was provided of. It will ask more than the work of twenty licensers to examine all the lutes, the violins, and the guitars in every house; they must not be suffered to prattle as they do, but must be licensed what they may say. And who shall silence all the airs and madrigals that whisper softness in chambers? The windows also, and the balconies, must be thought on; there are shrewd books, with dangerous frontispieces, set to sale: who shall prohibit them, shall twenty licensers? The villages also must have their visitors to inquire what lectures the bagpipe and the rebeck reads even to the ballatry, and the gamut of every municipal fiddler; for these are the countryman's *Arcadias*, and his Montemayors.

Next, what more national corruption, for which England hears ill abroad, than household gluttony? Who shall be the rectors of our daily rioting? And what shall be done to inhibit the multitudes that frequent those houses where drunkenness is sold and harbored? Our garments also should be referred to the licensing of some more sober work-masters, to see them cut into a less wanton garb. Who shall regulate all the mixed conversation of our youth, male and female together, as is the fashion of this country? Who shall still appoint what shall be discoursed, what presumed, and no further? Lastly, who shall forbid and separate all idle resort, all evil company? These things will be, and must be; but how they shall be least hurtful, how least enticing, herein consists the grave and governing wisdom of a state.

. . .

. . . When a man writes to the world, he summons up all his reason and deliberation to assist him; he searches, meditates, is industrious, and likely consults and confers with his judicious friends; after all which done, he takes himself to be informed in what he writes, as well as any that writ before him. If in this, the most consummate act of his fidelity and ripeness, no years, no industry, no former proof of his abilities can bring him to that state of maturity as not to be still mistrusted and suspected (unless he carry all his considerate diligence, all his midnight watchings and expense of Palladian oil, to the hasty view of an unleisured licenser, perhaps much his younger, perhaps far his inferior in judgment, perhaps one who never knew the labor of book-writing), and if he be not repulsed or slighted, must appear in print like a puny with his guardian, and his censor's hand on the back of his title to be his bail and surety that he is no idiot or seducer; it cannot be but a dishonor and derogation to the author, to the book, to the privilege and dignity of learning.

. . .

What should ye do then, should ye suppress all this flowery crop of knowledge and new light sprung up and yet springing daily in this city? Should ye set an oligarchy of twenty engrossers over it, to bring a famine upon our minds again, when we shall know nothing but what is measured to us by their bushel? Believe it, Lords and Commons, they who counsel ye to such a suppressing do as good as bid ye suppress yourselves; and I will soon show how. If it be desired to know the immediate cause of all this free writing and free speaking, there cannot be assigned a truer than your own mild and free and humane government; it is the liberty, Lords and Commons, which your own valorous and happy counsels have purchased us, liberty which is the nurse of all great wits. This is that which hath rarefied and enlightened our spirits like the influence of heaven; this is that which hath enfranchised, enlarged, and lifted up our apprehensions degrees above themselves. Ye cannot make us now less capable, less knowing, less eagerly pursuing of the truth, unless ye first make yourselves, that made us so, less the lovers, less the founders of our true liberty. We can grow ignorant again, brutish, formal, and slavish, as ye found us; but you then must first become that which ye cannot be, oppressive, arbitrary, and tyrannous, as they were from whom ye have freed us. . . .

House Debate on the Sedition Act of 1798

When John Adams was elected President in 1796, there was concern that the United States might be drawn into war against France. To control foreigners in this country and a press that lashed out against the administration's policy, Congress passed the Alien and Sedition Acts of 1798. The Sedition Act declared that if any person "shall write, print, utter or publish . . . any false, scandalous and malicious writing or writings against the government of the United States, or either house of the Congress of the United States, or the President of the United States, with intent to defame the said government, or either house of the said Congress, or the said President, or to bring them, or either of them, into contempt or disrepute; or to excite against them, or either of them, the hatred of the good people of the United States, or to stir up sedition," the person would be subject to fines and imprisonment. The debate below, from the House of Representatives, is taken from 8 Annals of Congress 2093–2094, 2097, 2105, 2109, 2139–2140, 2147–2148, 2152, 2164, 2167–2168. Jeffersonian Republicans are identified as Democrats. The bill passed the House, 44–41.

[Mr. ALLEN, Federalist of Connecticut]—I hope this bill will not be rejected. If ever there was a nation which required a law of this kind, it is this. Let gentlemen look at certain papers printed in this city and elsewhere, and ask themselves whether an unwarrantable and dangerous combination does not exist to overturn and ruin the Government by publishing the most shameless falsehoods against the Representatives of the people of all denominations, that they are hostile to free Governments and genuine liberty, and of course to the welfare of this country; that they ought, therefore, to be displaced, and that the people ought to raise an *insurrection* against the Government.

In the *Aurora,* of the 28th of June last, we see this paragraph: "It is a curious fact, America is making war with France for *not* treating, at the very moment the Minister for Foreign Affairs fixes upon the very day for opening a negotiation with Mr. Gerry. What think you of this, Americans!"

Such paragraphs need but little comment. The public agents are charged with crimes, for which, if true, they ought to be hung. The intention here is to persuade the people that peace with France is in our power; nay, that she is sincerely desirous of it, on proper terms, but that we reject her offers, and proceed to plunge our country into a destructive war.

. . . Permit me to read a paragraph from "The Time-Piece," a paper printed in New York:

"When such a character attempts by antiquated and exploded sophistry, by Jesuitical arguments, to extinguish the sentiment of liberty, 'tis fit the mask should be torn off from this meaner species of aristocracy than history has condescended to record; where a person without patriotism, without philosophy, without a taste for the fine arts, building his pretensions on a gross and indigested compilation of statutes and precedents, is jostled into the Chief Magistracy by the ominous combination of old Tories with old opinions, and old Whigs with new, 'tis fit this mock Monarch, with his Court, composed of Tories and speculators, should pass in review before the good sense of the world. Monarchies are seen only with indignation and concern; at sight of these terrible establishments, fears accompany the execrations of mankind; but when the champion of the wellborn, with his serene Court, is seen soliciting and answering Addresses, and pronouncing anathemas against France, it shall be my fault if other emotions be not excited; if to tears and execrations be not added derision and contempt."

Gentlemen contend for the liberty of opinions and of the press. Let me ask them whether they seriously think the liberty of the press authorizes such publications? The President of the United States is here called "a person without patriotism, without philosophy, and a mock monarch," and the free election of the people is pronounced "a jostling him into the Chief Magistracy by the ominous combination of old Tories with old opinions, and old Whigs with new."

If this be not a conspiracy against Government and people, I know not what to understand from the "threat of tears, execrations, derision, and contempt." Because the Constitution guaranties the right of expressing our opinions, and the freedom of the press, am I at liberty to falsely call you a thief, a murderer, an atheist? Because I have the liberty of locomotion, of going where I please, have I a right to ride over the footman in the path? The freedom of the press and opinions was never understood to give the right of publishing falsehoods and slanders, nor of exciting sedition, insurrection, and slaughter, with impunity. A man was always answerable for the malicious publication of falsehood; and what more does this bill require?

. . .

[EDWARD LIVINGSTON, Democrat from New York.] . . . The gentleman from South Carolina has said, that provided the law is clear and well defined, and the trial by jury is preserved, he knew of no law which could infringe the liberty of the press. If this be true, Congress might restrict all printing at once. We have, said he, nothing to do but to make the law precise, and then we may forbid a newspaper to be printed, and make it death for any man to attempt it!

If this be the extent to which this bill goes, it is . . . an abridgment of the liberty of the press, which the Constitution has said shall not be abridged . . .

[ALBERT GALLATIN, Democrat from Pennsylvania.] Was the gentleman afraid, or rather was Administration afraid, that in this instance error could not be successfully opposed by truth? The American Government had heretofore subsisted, it had acquired strength, it had grown on the affection of the people, it had been fully supported without the assistance of laws similar to the bill now on the table. It had been able to repel

opposition by the single weapon of argument. And at present, when out of ten presses in the country nine were employed on the side of Administration, such is their want of confidence in the purity of their own views and motives, that they even fear the unequal contest, and require the help of force in order to suppress the limited circulation of the opinions of those who did not approve all their measures.

. . .

[JOHN NICHOLAS, Democrat from Virginia] rose, he said, to ask an explanation of the principles upon which this bill is founded. He confessed it was strongly impressed upon his mind, that it was not within the powers of the House to act upon this subject. He looked in vain amongst the enumerated powers given to Congress in the Constitution, for an authority to pass a law like the present; but he found what he considered as an express prohibition against passing it. He found that, in order to quiet the alarms of the people of the United States with respect to the silence of the Constitution as to the liberty of the press, not being perfectly satisfied that the powers not vested in Congress remained with the people, that one of the first acts of this Government was to propose certain amendments to the Constitution, to put this matter beyond doubt, which amendments are now become a part of the Constitution. It is now expressly declared by that instrument, "that the powers not delegated to the United States by the Constitution, nor prohibited by it to the States, are reserved to the States respectively, or to the people;" and, also, "that Congress shall make no law abridging the freedom of speech, or of the press."

Mr. N. asked whether this bill did not go to the abridgment of the freedom of speech and of the press? If it did not, he would be glad if gentlemen would define wherein the freedom of speech and of the press consists.

Gentlemen have said that this bill is not to restrict the liberty of the press but its licentiousness. He wished gentlemen to inform him where they drew the line between this liberty and licentiousness of which they speak; he wished to know where the one commenced and the other ended?

Will they say the one is truth, and the other falsehood! Gentlemen cannot believe for a moment that such a definition will satisfy the inquiry. The great difficulty which has existed in all free Governments, would, long since, have been done away, if it could have been effected by a simple declaration of this kind. It has been the object of all regulations with respect to the press, to destroy the only means by which the people can examine and become acquainted with the conduct of persons employed in their Government. . . .

. . .

[HARRISON GRAY OTIS, Federalist from Massachusetts.] It was, therefore, most evident to his mind, that the Constitution of the United States, prior to the amendments that have been added to it, secured to the National Government the cognizance of all the crimes enumerated in the bill, and it only remained to be considered whether those amendments divested it of this power. The amendment quoted by the gentleman from Virginia is in these words: "Congress shall make no law abridging the freedom of speech and of the press." The terms "freedom of speech and of the press," he supposed, were a phraseology perfectly familiar in the jurisprudence of every State, and of a certain and technical meaning. It was a mode of expression which we had borrowed from the only country in which it had been tolerated, and he pledged himself to prove that the construction which he should give to those terms, should be consonant not only to the laws of that country, but to the laws and judicial decisions of many of the States composing the Union. This freedom, said Mr. O., is nothing more than the liberty of writing, publishing, and speaking, one's thoughts, under the condition of being answerable to the injured party, whether it be the Government or an individual, for false, malicious, and seditious expressions, whether spoken or written; and the liberty of the press is merely an exemption from all previous restraints. In support of this doctrine, he quoted *Blackstone's Commentaries*, under the head of libels, and read an extract to prove that in England, formerly, the press was subject to a licenser; and that this restraint was afterward removed, by which means the freedom of the press was established. He would not, however, dwell upon the law of En-

gland, the authority of which it might suit the convenience of gentlemen to question; but he would demonstrate that although in several of the State constitutions, the liberty of speech and of the press were guarded by the most express and unequivocal language, the Legislatures and Judicial departments of those States had adopted the definitions of the English law, and provided for the punishment of defamatory and seditious libels. . . .

. . .

[NATHANIEL MACON, Democrat from North Carolina] concluded with observing, that from the best examination which he had been able to give to the subject, he was convinced that Congress does not possess the power to pass a law like the present; but if there be a majority determined to pass it, he could only hope that the Judges would exercise the power placed in them of determining the law an unconstitutional law, if, upon scrutiny, they find it to be so.

. . .

After having given this short sketch of the features of this bill, Mr. *[Gallatin]* said he had intended to make some general remarks on the nature of political libels, or of writings against the measures of the Administration, and on the propriety of interfering at all by law with them. The lateness of the hour prevented him. He would only observe that laws against writings of this kind had uniformly been one of the most powerful engines used by tyrants to prevent the diffusion of knowledge, to throw a veil on their folly or their crimes, to satisfy those mean passions which always denote little minds, and to perpetuate their own tyranny. The principles of the law of political libels were to be found in the rescripts of the worst Emperors of Rome, in the decisions of the Star Chamber. Princes of elevated minds, Governments actuated by pure motives, had ever despised the slanders of malice, and listened to the animadversions made on their conduct. They knew that the proper weapon to combat error was truth, and that to resort to coercion and punishments in order to suppress writings attacking their measures, was to confess that these could not be defended by any other means.

. . .

[ROBERT GOODLOE HARPER, Federalist from South Carolina.] In the other objection, he admitted that there was more plausibility; the objection founded on that part of the Constitution which provides that "Congress shall pass no law to abridge the liberty of speech or of the press." He held this to be one of the most sacred parts of the Constitution, one by which he would stand the longest, and defend with the greatest zeal. But to what, he asked, did this clause amount? Did this liberty of the press include sedition and licentiousness? Did it authorize persons to throw, with impunity, the most violent abuse upon the President and both Houses of Congress? Was this what gentlemen meant by the liberty of the press? As well might it be said that the liberty of action implied the liberty of assault, trespass, or assassination. Every man possessed the liberty of action; but if he used this liberty to the detriment of others, by attacking their persons or destroying their property, he became liable to punishment for this licentious abuse of his liberty. The liberty of the press stood on precisely the same footing. Every man might publish what he pleased; but if he abused this liberty so as to publish slanders against his neighbor, or false, scandalous, and malicious libels against the magistrates, or the Government, he became liable to punishment. What did this law provide? That if "any person should publish any false, scandalous, and malicious libel against the President or Congress, or either House of Congress, with intent to stir up sedition, or to produce any other of the mischievous and wicked effects particularly described in the bill, he should, on conviction before a jury, be liable to fine and imprisonment. A jury is to try the offence, and they must determine, from the evidence and the circumstances of the case, first that the publication is *false*, secondly that it is *scandalous*, thirdly that it is *malicious*, and fourthly that it was made with the *intent* to do some one of the things particularly described in the bill. If in any one of these points the proof should fail, the man must be acquitted; and it is expressly provided that he may give the *truth* of the publication in evidence as a justification. Such is the substance of this law; and yet it is called a law abridging the liberty of the press! That is to say, that the liberty of the press implies the liberty of publishing, with impunity, false, scandalous, and malicious writings, with intent to stir up sedition, &c. As well might it be said that the liberty of *action* implies the liberty to rob and murder with impunity!

Jefferson and Congress Respond to the Sedition Act

The Federalists passed the Alien and Sedition Acts of 1798 to silence domestic opponents of governmental policy. Thomas Jefferson regarded the Sedition Act as unconstitutional, although federal judges did not find it so. After his election as President in 1800, he used his executive authority to discharge whoever had been punished or prosecuted under the Sedition Act. He explains his position in letters to Mrs. John Adams. In 1840, Congress passed a private bill to reimburse the heirs of Matthew Lyon, who had been prosecuted under the Sedition Act. The committee report accompanying the bill stated that the Sedition Act was "unconstitutional, null, and void."

[From Jefferson to Mrs. Adams, July 22, 1804]:

. . . I discharged every person under punishment or prosecution under the sedition law, because I considered, and now consider, that law to be a nullity, as absolute and as palpable as if Congress had ordered us to fall down and worship a golden image; and that it was as much my duty to arrest its execution in every stage, as it would have been to have rescued from the fiery furnace those who should have been cast into it for refusing to worship the image. It was accordingly done in every instance, without asking what the offenders had done, or against whom they had offended, but whether the pains they were suffering were inflicted under the pretended sedition law. . . .

[From Jefferson to Mrs. Adams, September 11, 1804]:

. . .

You seem to think it devolved on the judges to decide on the validity of the sedition law. But nothing in the Constitution has given them a right to decide for the Executive, more than to the Executive to decide for them. Both magistrates are equally independent in the sphere of action assigned to them. The judges, believing the law constitutional, had a right to pass a sentence of fine and imprisonment; because the power was placed in their hands by the Constitution. But the executive, believing the law to be unconstitutional, were bound to remit the execution of it; because that power has been confided to them by the Constitution. That instrument meant that its coordinate branches should be checks on each other. But the opinion which gives to the judges the right to decide what laws are constitutional, and what not, not only for themselves in their own sphere of action, but for the legislature and executive also, in their spheres, would make the judiciary a despotic branch. . . .

[Congress enacted a private bill on July 4, 1840, to refund a fine imposed on Matthew Lyon under the Sedition Act. 6 Stat. 802, c. 45. The committee report accompanying the bill, H. Rept. No. 86, 26th Cong., 1st Sess., March 5, 1840, explains the basis for the bill.]

That in the month of October, 1798, the late Matthew Lyon, the father of the petitioners, at the circuit court held at Rutland, in the State of Vermont, was indicted and found guilty of having printed and published what was alleged to be a libel against Mr. John Adams, the then President of the United States. The alleged libel was in the following words, to wit: "As to the Executive, when I shall see the effects of that power bent on the promotion of the comfort, the happiness, and accommodation of the people, that Executive shall have my zealous and uniform support. But whenever I shall, on the part of our Executive, see

every consideration of public welfare swallowed up in a continual grasp for power, in an unbounded thirst for ridiculous pomp, foolish adulation, and selfish avarice—when I shall behold men of real merit daily turned out of office for no other cause than independency of sentiment—when I shall see men of firmness, merit, years, abilities, and experience, discarded in their applications for office, for fear they possess that independence, and men of meanness preferred for the ease with which they can take up and advocate opinions, the consequence of which they know but little of— when I shall see the sacred name of religion employed as a State engine to make mankind hate and persecute each other, I shall not be their humble advocate!" The second count in the indictment, on which the said Matthew Lyon was convicted, charged him with printing and publishing a seditious writing or libel, entitled "Copy of a letter from an American diplomatic character in France (Mr. Joel Barlow) to a member of Congress in Philadelphia," which was in the following words, to wit: "The misunderstanding between the two Governments has become extremely alarming; confidence is completely destroyed; mistrusts, jealousies, and a disposition to a wrong attribution of motives, are so apparent as to require the utmost caution in every word and action that are to come from your Executive—I mean if your object is to avoid hostilities. Had this truth been understood with you before the recall of Monroe —before the coming and second coming of Pinckney; had it guided the pens that wrote the bullying speech of your President, and stupid answer of your Senate, at the opening of Congress in November last, I should probably have had no occasion to address you this letter. But when we found him borrowing the language of Edmund Burke, and telling the world that, although he should succeed in treating with the French, there was no dependence to be placed in any of their engagements; that their religion and morality were at an end, and they had turned pirates and plunderers, and that it would be necessary to be perpetually armed against them, though you are at peace; we wondered that the answer of both Houses had not been an order to send him to the mad-house. Instead of this, the Senate have echoed the speech with more servility than ever George the Third experienced from either House of Parliament."

The court deemed both the publications above recited libellous, under the 2d section of the act commonly called the sedition law, passed the 4th July, 1798; which section is as follows, viz: "*And be it further enacted*, That if any person shall write, print, utter, or publish, or shall cause or procure to be written, printed, uttered, or published, or shall knowingly and wilfully assist or aid in writing, printing, uttering, or publishing, any false, scandalous, and malicious writing or writings, against the Government of the United States, or either House of the Congress of the United States, or of the President of the United States, with an intent to defame the said Government, or either House of the said Congress, or the President, or to bring them, or either of them, into contempt or disrespect, or to excite against them, or either or any of them, the hatred of the good people of the United States, &c., then such person, being thereof convicted before any court of the United States having jurisdiction thereof, shall be punished by a fine not exceeding two thousand dollars, and by imprisonment not exceeding two years."

Upon this indictment Matthew Lyon was convicted, and sentenced by the court to be imprisoned for four months; to pay a fine of one thousand dollars, and the costs of the prosecution, taxed at sixty dollars and ninety-six cents; and to stand committed until the fine and costs were paid: which were paid, as appears by the exemplification of the record of the said trial and proceedings, now in the archives of this House.

The committee are of opinion that the law above recited was unconstitutional, null, and void, passed under a mistaken exercise of undelegated power, and that the mistake ought to be corrected by returning the fine so obtained, with interest thereon, to the legal representatives of Matthew Lyon.

The committee do not deem it necessary to discuss at length the character of that law, or to assign all the reasons, however demonstrative, that have induced the conviction of its unconstitutionality. No question connected with the liberty of the press ever excited a more universal and intense interest—ever received so acute, able, long-continued, and elaborate investigation—was ever more generally understood, or so conclusively settled by the concurring opinions of all parties, after the heated political contests of the day had passed away. All that now remains to be done by the representatives of a people who condemned this act of their agents as unauthorized, and transcending their grant of power, to place beyond question, doubt, or cavil, that mandate of the constitution prohibiting Congress from abridging the liberty of the press, and to discharge an honest, just, moral, and honorable obligation, is to refund from the Treasury the fine thus illegally and wrongfully obtained from one of their citizens: for which purpose the committee herewith report a bill.

Near v. Minnesota

283 U.S. 697 (1931)

A Minnesota law provided that anyone engaged in the business of publishing "a malicious, scandalous and defamatory newspaper, magazine, or other periodical" was guilty of a nuisance and subject to a suit by the state. The periodicals could be abated and their publishers enjoined from future violations. The punishment of contempt was available for disobeying an injunction. The state prosecuted Jay Near for publishing "The Saturday Press," a hardhitting newspaper that focused largely on corruption and racketeering in Minneapolis. Many of his attacks were directed at the mayor and police chief.

MR. CHIEF JUSTICE HUGHES delivered the opinion of the Court.

Chapter 285 of the Session Laws of Minnesota for the year 1925 provides for the abatement, as a public nuisance, of a "malicious, scandalous and defamatory newspaper, magazine or other periodical." Section one of the Act is as follows:

"Section 1. Any person who, as an individual, or as a member or employee of a firm, or association or organization, or as an officer, director, member or employee of a corporation, shall be engaged in the business of regularly or customarily producing, publishing or circulating, having in possession, selling or giving away.

(a) an obscene, lewd and lascivious newspaper, magazine, or other periodical, or

(b) a malicious, scandalous and defamatory newspaper, magazine or other periodical, is guilty of a nuisance, and all persons guilty of such nuisance may be enjoined, as hereinafter provided.

"Participation in such business shall constitute a commission of such nuisance and render the participant liable and subject to the proceedings, orders and judgments provided for in this Act. Ownership, in whole or in part, directly or indirectly, of any such periodical, or of any stock or interest in any corporation or organization which owns the same in whole or in part, or which publishes the same, shall constitute such participation.

"In actions brought under (b) above, there shall be available the defense that the truth was published with good motives and for justifiable ends and in such actions the plaintiff shall not have the right to report (sic) to issues or editions of periodicals taking place more than three months before the commencement of the action."

. . .

Under this statute, clause (b), the County Attorney of Hennepin County brought this action to enjoin the publication of what was described as a "malicious, scandalous and defamatory newspaper, magazine and periodical," known as "The Saturday Press," published by the defendants in the city of Minneapolis. The complaint alleged that the defendants, on September 24, 1927, and on eight subsequent dates in October and November, 1927, published and circulated editions of that periodical which were "largely devoted to malicious, scandalous and defamatory articles" concerning Charles G. Davis, Frank W. Brunskill, the Minneapolis Tribune, the Minneapolis Journal, Melvin C. Passolt, George E. Leach, the Jewish Race, the members of the Grand Jury of Hennepin County impaneled in November, 1927, and then holding office, and other persons, as more fully appeared in exhibits annexed to the complaint, consisting of copies of the articles described and constituting 327 pages of the record. While the complaint did not so allege, it appears from the briefs of both parties that Charles G. Davis was a special law enforcement officer employed by a civic organization, that George E. Leach was Mayor of Minneapolis, that Frank W. Brunskill was its Chief of Police, and that Floyd B. Olson (the relator in this action) was County Attorney.

Without attempting to summarize the contents of the voluminous exhibits attached to the complaint, we deem it sufficient to say that the articles charged in substance that a Jewish gangster was in control of gambling, bootlegging and racketeering in Minneapolis, and that law enforcing officers and agencies were not energetically performing their duties. Most of the charges were directed against the Chief of Police; he was charged with gross neglect of duty, illicit relations with gangsters, and with participation in graft. The County Attorney was charged with knowing the existing conditions and with failure to take adequate measures to remedy them. The Mayor was accused of inefficiency and dereliction. One member of the grand jury was stated to be in sympathy with the gangsters. A special grand jury and a special prosecutor were demanded to deal with the situation in general, and, in particular, to investigate an attempt to assassinate one Guilford, one of the original defendants, who, it appears from the articles, was shot by gangsters after the first issue of the periodical had been published. There is no question but that the articles made serious accusations against the public officers named and others in connection with the prevalence of crimes and the failure to expose and punish them.

. . .

The District Court made findings of fact, which followed the allegations of the complaint and found in general terms that the editions in question were "chiefly devoted to malicious, scandalous and defamatory articles," concerning the individuals named. The court further found that the defendants through these publications "did engage in the business of regularly and customarily producing, publishing and circulating a malicious, scandalous and defamatory newspaper," and that "the said publication" "under said name of The Saturday Press, or any other name, constitutes a public nuisance under the laws of the State." Judgment was thereupon entered adjudging that "the newspaper, magazine and periodical known as The Saturday Press," as a public nuisance, "be and is hereby abated." The judgment perpetually enjoined the defendants "from producing, editing, publishing, circulating, having in their possession, selling or giving away any publication whatsoever which is a malicious, scandalous or defamatory newspaper, as defined by law," and also "from further conducting said nuisance under the name and title of said The Saturday Press or any other name or title."

. . .

This statute, for the suppression as a public nuisance of a newspaper or periodical, is unusual, if not unique, and raises questions of grave importance transcending the local interests involved in the particular action. It is no longer open to doubt that the liberty of the press, and of speech, is within the liberty safeguarded by the due process clause of the Fourteenth Amendment from invasion by state action. It was found impossible to conclude that this essential personal liberty of the citizen was left unprotected by the general guaranty of fundamental rights of person and property. *Gitlow* v. *New York*, 268 U.S. 652, 666; *Whitney* v. *California*, 274 U.S. 357, 362, 373; *Fiske* v. *Kansas*, 274 U.S. 380, 382; *Stromberg* v. *California*, *ante*, p. 359. In maintaining this guaranty, the authority of the State to enact laws to promote the health, safety, morals and general welfare of its people is necessarily admitted. The limits of this sovereign power must always be determined with appropriate regard to the particular subject of its exercise. . . .

. . .

First. The statute is not aimed at the redress of individual or private wrongs. Remedies for libel remain available and unaffected. The statute, said the state court, "is not directed at threatened libel but at an existing business which, generally speaking, involves more than libel." It is aimed at the distribution of scandalous matter as "detrimental to public morals and to the general welfare," tending "to disturb the peace of the community" and "to provoke assaults and the commission of crime." In order to obtain an injunction to suppress the future publication of the newspaper or periodical, it is not necessary to prove the falsity of the charges that have been made in the publication condemned. In the present action there was no allegation that the matter published was not true. It is alleged, and the statute requires the allegation, that the publication was "malicious." But, as in prosecutions for libel, there is no requirement of proof by the State of malice in fact as distinguished from malice inferred from the mere publication of the defamatory matter. The judgment in this case proceeded upon the mere proof of publication. The statute permits the defense, not of the truth alone, but only that the truth was published with good motives and for justifiable ends. It is apparent that under the statute the publication is to be regarded as defamatory if it injures reputation, and that it is scandalous if it circulates charges of reprehensible conduct, whether criminal or otherwise, and the publication is thus deemed to invite public reprobation and to constitute a public scandal. The court sharply defined the purpose of the statute, bringing out the precise point, in these words: "There is no constitutional right to publish a fact merely because it is true. It is a matter of common knowledge that prosecutions under the criminal libel statutes do not result in efficient repression or suppression of the evils of scandal. Men who are the victims of such assaults seldom resort to the courts. This is especially true if their sins are exposed and the only question relates to whether it was done with good motives and for justifiable ends. This law is not for the protection of the person attacked nor to punish the wrongdoer. It is for the protection of the public welfare."

Second. The statute is directed not simply at the circulation of scandalous and defamatory statements with regard to private citizens, but at the continued publication by newspapers and periodicals of charges against public officers of corruption, malfeasance in office, or serious neglect of duty. Such charges by their very nature create a public scandal. They are scandalous and defamatory within the meaning of the statute, which has its normal operation in relation to publications dealing prominently and chiefly with the alleged derelictions of public officers.

Third. The object of the statute is not punishment, in the ordinary sense, but suppression of the offending newspaper or periodical. The reason for the enactment, as the state court has said, is that prosecutions to enforce penal statutes for libel do not result in "efficient repression or suppression of the evils of scandal." . . .

Fourth. The statute not only operates to suppress the offending newspaper or periodical but to put the publisher under an effective censorship. When a newspaper or periodical is found to be "malicious, scandalous and defamatory," and is suppressed as such, resumption of publication is punishable as a contempt of court by fine or imprisonment. Thus, where a newspaper or periodical has been suppressed because of the circulation of charges against public officers of official misconduct, it would seem to be clear that the renewal of the publication of such charges would constitute a contempt and that the judgment would lay a permanent restraint upon the publisher, to escape which he must satisfy the court as to the character of a new publication. Whether he would be permitted again to publish matter deemed to be derogatory to the same or other public officers would depend upon the court's ruling. . . .

The question is whether a statute authorizing such proceedings in restraint of publication is consistent with the conception of the liberty of the press as historically conceived and guaranteed. In determining the extent of the constitutional protection, it has been generally, if not universally, considered that it is the chief purpose of the guaranty to prevent previous restraints upon publication. The struggle in England, directed against the legislative power of the licenser, resulted in renunciation of the censorship of the press. The liberty deemed to be established was thus described by Blackstone: "The liberty of the press is indeed essential to the nature of a free state; but this consists in laying no *previous* restraints upon publications, and not in freedom from censure for criminal matter when published. Every freeman has an undoubted right to lay what sentiments he pleases before the public; to forbid this, is to destroy the freedom of the press; but if he publishes what is improper, mischievous or illegal, he must take the consequence of his own temerity." 4 Bl. Com. 151, 152; see Story on the Constitution, §§ 1884, 1889. . . .

The criticism upon Blackstone's statement has not been because immunity from previous restraint upon publication has not been regarded as deserving of special emphasis, but chiefly because that immunity cannot be deemed to exhaust the conception of the liberty guaranteed by state and federal constitutions. The point of criticism has been "that the mere exemption from previous restraints cannot be all that is secured by the constitutional provisions"; and that "the liberty of the press might be rendered a mockery and a delusion, and the phrase itself a by-word, if, while every man was at liberty to publish what he pleased, the public authorities might nevertheless punish him for harmless publications." 2 Cooley, Const. Lim., 8th ed., p. 885. But it is recognized that punishment for the abuse of the liberty accorded to the press is essential to the protection of the public, and that the common law rules that subject the libeler to responsibility for the public offense, as well as for the private injury, are not abolished by the protection extended in our constitutions. *id*. pp. 883, 884. . . .

The objection has also been made that the principle as to immunity from previous restraint is stated too broadly, if every such restraint is deemed to be prohibited. That is undoubtedly true; the protection even as to previous restraint is not absolutely unlimited. . . . No one would question but that a government might prevent actual obstruction to its recruiting service or the publication of the sailing dates of transports or the number and location of troops. On similar grounds, the primary requirements of decency may be enforced against obscene publications.

The security of the community life may be protected against incitements to acts of violence and the overthrow by force of orderly government. . . .

The fact that for approximately one hundred and fifty years there has been almost an entire absence of attempts to impose previous restraints upon publications relating to the malfeasance of public officers is significant of the deep-seated conviction that such restraints would violate constitutional right. Public officers, whose character and conduct remain open to debate and free discussion in the press, find their remedies for false accusations in actions under libel laws providing for redress and punishment, and not in proceedings to restrain the publication of newspapers and periodicals. The general principle that the constitutional guaranty of the liberty of the press gives immunity from previous restraints has been approved in many decisions under the provisions of state constitutions.

The importance of this immunity has not lessened. While reckless assaults upon public men, and efforts to bring obloquy upon those who are endeavoring faithfully to discharge official duties, exert a baleful influence and deserve the severest condemnation in public opinion, it cannot be said that this abuse is greater, and it is believed to be less, than that which characterized the period in which our institutions took shape. Meanwhile, the administration of government has become more complex, the opportunities for malfeasance and corruption have multiplied, crime has grown to most serious proportions, and the danger of its protection by unfaithful officials and of the impairment of the fundamental security of life and property by criminal alliances and official neglect, emphasizes the primary need of a vigilant and courageous press, especially in great cities. The fact that the liberty of the press may be abused by miscreant purveyors of scandal does not make any the less necessary the immunity of the press from previous restraint in dealing with official misconduct. Subsequent punishment for such abuses as may exist is the appropriate remedy, consistent with constitutional privilege.

. . .

For these reasons we hold the statute, so far as it authorized the proceedings in this action under clause (b) of section one, to be an infringement of the liberty of the press guaranteed by the Fourteenth Amendment. We should add that this decision rests upon the operation and effect of the statute, without regard to the question of the truth of the charges contained in the particular periodical. The fact that the public officers named in this case, and those associated with the charges of official dereliction, may be deemed to be impeccable, cannot affect the conclusion that the statute imposes an unconstitutional restraint upon publication.

Judgment reversed.

MR. JUSTICE BUTLER, dissenting.

. . .

The record shows, and it is conceded, that defendants' regular business was the publication of malicious, scandalous and defamatory articles concerning the principal public officers, leading newspapers of the city, many private persons and the Jewish race. It also shows that it was their purpose at all hazards to continue to carry on the business. In every edition slanderous and defamatory matter predominates to the practical exclusion of all else. Many of the statements are so highly improbable as to compel a finding that they are false. The articles themselves show malice.

The defendant here has no standing to assert that the statute is invalid because it might be construed so as to violate the Constitution. His right is limited solely to the inquiry whether, having regard to the points properly raised in his case, the effect of applying the statute is to deprive him of his liberty without due process of law. This Court should not reverse the judgment below upon the ground that in some other case the statute may be applied in a way that is repugnant to the freedom of the press protected by the Fourteenth Amendment. *Castillo* v. *McConnico*, 168 U.S. 674, 680. *Williams* v. *Mississippi*, 170 U.S. 213, 225. *Yazoo & Miss. R. Co.* v. *Jackson Vinegar Co.*, 226 U.S. 217, 219–220. *Plymouth Coal Co.* v. *Pennsylvania*, 232 U.S. 531, 544–546.

. . .

Defendant concedes that the editions of the

newspaper complained of are "defamatory *per se*." And he says: "It has been asserted that the constitution was never intended to be a shield for malice, scandal, and defamation when untrue, or published with bad motives, or for unjustifiable ends. . . . The contrary is true; every person *does* have a constitutional right to publish malicious, scandalous, and defamatory matter though untrue, and with bad motives, and for unjustifiable ends, *in the first instance*, though he is subject to responsibility therefor *afterwards*." The record, when the substance of the articles is regarded, requires that concession here. And this Court is required to pass on the validity of the state law on that basis.

. . .

It is of the greatest importance that the States shall be untrammeled and free to employ all just and appropriate measures to prevent abuses of the liberty of the press.

In his work on the Constitution (5th ed.) Justice Story, expounding the First Amendment which declares: "Congress shall make no law abridging the freedom of speech or of the press," said (§ 1880):

"That this amendment was intended to secure to every citizen an absolute right to speak, or write, or print whatever he might please, without any responsibility, public or private, therefor, is a supposition too wild to be indulged by any rational man. This would be to allow to every citizen a right to destroy at his pleasure the reputation, the peace, the property, and even the personal safety of every other citizen. A man might, out of mere malice and revenge, accuse another of the most infamous crimes; might excite against him the indignation of all his fellow-citizens by the most atrocious calumnies; might disturb, nay, overturn, all his domestic peace, and embitter his parental affections; might inflict the most distressing punishments upon the weak, the timid, and the innocent; might prejudice all a man's civil, and political, and private rights; and might stir up sedition, rebellion, and treason even against the government itself, in the wantonness of his passions or the corruption of his heart. Civil society could not go on under

such circumstances. Men would then be obliged to resort to private vengeance to make up for the deficiencies of the law; and assassination and savage cruelties would be perpetrated with all the frequency belonging to barbarous and brutal communities. It is plain, then, that the language of this amendment imports no more than that every man shall have a right to speak, write, and print his opinions upon any subject whatsoever, without any prior restraint, so always that he does not injure any other person in his rights, person, property, or reputation; and so always that he does not thereby disturb the public peace, or attempt to subvert the government. It is neither more nor less than an expansion of the great doctrine recently brought into operation in the law of libel, *that every man shall be at liberty to publish what is true, with good motives and for justifiable ends*. And with this reasonable limitation it is not only right in itself, but it is an inestimable privilege in a free government. Without such a limitation, it might become the scourge of the republic, first denouncing the principles of liberty, and then, by rendering the most virtuous patriots odious through the terrors of the press, introducing despotism in its worst form." (Italicizing added.)

. . .

It is well known, as found by the state supreme court, that existing libel laws are inadequate effectively to suppress evils resulting from the kind of business and publications that are shown in this case. The doctrine that measures such as the one before us are invalid because they operate as previous restraints to infringe freedom of press exposes the peace and good order of every community and the business and private affairs of every individual to the constant and protracted false and malicious assaults of any insolvent publisher who may have purpose and sufficient capacity to contrive and put into effect a scheme or program for oppression, blackmail or extortion.

The judgment should be affirmed.

MR. JUSTICE VAN DEVANTER, MR. JUSTICE MCREYNOLDS, and MR. JUSTICE SUTHERLAND concur in this opinion.

Branzburg v. Hayes

408 U.S. 665 (1972)

In this case, the needs of a free press and criminal prosecution collide. Paul M. Branzburg, a former reporter with the Louisville *Courier-Journal*, was called before a county grand jury after he wrote an article describing how two men made hashish from marijuana. He refused to identify them. Also involved in this case were Paul Pappas, a reporter-cameraman, and Earl Caldwell, a reporter for the *New York Times*, who refused to testify about their coverage of the Black Panthers.

Opinion of the Court by MR. JUSTICE WHITE, announced by THE CHIEF JUSTICE.

The issue in these cases is whether requiring newsmen to appear and testify before state or federal grand juries abridges the freedom of speech and press guaranteed by the First Amendment. We hold that it does not.

I

The writ of certiorari in No. 70–85, *Branzburg v. Hayes* and *Meigs*, brings before us two judgments of the Kentucky Court of Appeals, both involving petitioner Branzburg, a staff reporter for the Courier-Journal, a daily newspaper published in Louisville, Kentucky.

On November 15, 1969, the Courier-Journal carried a story under petitioner's by-line describing in detail his observations of two young residents of Jefferson County synthesizing hashish from marihuana, an activity which, they asserted, earned them about $5,000 in three weeks. The article included a photograph of a pair of hands working above a laboratory table on which was a substance identified by the caption as hashish. The article stated that petitioner had promised not to reveal the identity of the two hashish makers. Petitioner was shortly subpoenaed by the Jefferson County grand jury; he appeared, but refused to identify the individuals he had seen possessing marihuana or the persons he had seen making hashish from marihuana. A state trial court judge ordered petitioner to answer these questions and rejected his contention that the Kentucky reporters' privilege statute, Ky. Rev. Stat. § 421.100 (1962), the First Amendment of the United States

Constitution, or §§ 1, 2, and 8 of the Kentucky Constitution authorized his refusal to answer. Petitioner then sought prohibition and mandamus in the Kentucky Court of Appeals on the same grounds, but the Court of Appeals denied the petition. . . .

The second case involving petitioner Branzburg arose out of his later story published on January 10, 1971, which described in detail the use of drugs in Frankfort, Kentucky. The article reported that in order to provide a comprehensive survey of the "drug scene" in Frankfort, petitioner had "spent two weeks interviewing several dozen drug users in the capital city" and had seen some of them smoking marihuana. A number of conversations with and observations of several unnamed drug users were recounted. Subpoenaed to appear before a Franklin County grand jury "to testify in the matter of violation of statutes concerning use and sale of drugs," petitioner Branzburg moved to quash the summons; the motion was denied, although an order was issued protecting Branzburg from revealing "confidential associations, sources or information" but requiring that he "answer any questions which concern or pertain to any criminal act, the commission of which was actually observed by [him]." Prior to the time he was slated to appear before the grand jury, petitioner sought mandamus and prohibition from the Kentucky Court of Appeals, arguing that if he were forced to go before the grand jury or to answer questions regarding the identity of informants or disclose information given to him in confidence, his effectiveness as a reporter would be greatly damaged. The Court of Appeals once again denied the requested writs. . . .

Petitioner sought a writ of certiorari to review both judgments of the Kentucky Court of Appeals, and we granted the writ. 402 U.S. 942 (1971).

. . .

II

Petitioners Branzburg and Pappas and respondent Caldwell press First Amendment claims that may be simply put: that to gather news it is often necessary to agree either not to identify the source of information published or to publish only part of the facts revealed, or both; that if the reporter is nevertheless forced to reveal these confidences to a grand jury, the source so identified and other confidential sources of other reporters will be measurably deterred from furnishing publishable information, all to the detriment of the free flow of information protected by the First Amendment. Although the newsmen in these cases do not claim an absolute privilege against official interrogation in all circumstances, they assert that the reporter should not be forced either to appear or to testify before a grand jury or at trial until and unless sufficient grounds are shown for believing that the reporter possesses information relevant to a crime the grand jury is investigating, that the information the reporter has is unavailable from other sources, and that the need for the information is sufficiently compelling to override the claimed invasion of First Amendment interests occasioned by the disclosure. Principally relied upon are prior cases emphasizing the importance of the First Amendment guarantees to individual development and to our system of representative government, decisions requiring that official action with adverse impact on First Amendment rights be justified by a public interest that is "compelling" or "paramount," and those precedents establishing the principle that justifiable governmental goals may not be achieved by unduly broad means having an unnecessary impact on protected rights of speech, press, or association. The heart of the claim is that the burden on news gathering resulting from compelling reporters to disclose confidential information outweighs any public interest in obtaining the information.

We do not question the significance of free speech, press, or assembly to the country's welfare. Nor is it suggested that news gathering does not qualify for First Amendment protection; without some protection for seeking out the news, freedom of the press could be eviscerated. But these cases involve no intrusions upon speech or assembly, no prior restraint or restriction on what the press may publish, and no express or implied command that the press publish what it prefers to withhold. No exaction or tax for the privilege of publishing, and no penalty, civil or criminal, related to the content of published material is at issue here. The use of confidential sources by the press is not forbidden or restricted; reporters remain free to seek news from any source by means within the law. No attempt is made to require the press to publish its sources of information or indiscriminately to disclose them on request.

The sole issue before us is the obligation of reporters to respond to grand jury subpoenas as other citizens do and to answer questions relevant to an investigation into the commission of crime. Citizens generally are not constitutionally immune from grand jury subpoenas; and neither the First Amendment nor any other constitutional provision protects the average citizen from disclosing to a grand jury information that he has received in confidence. The claim is, however, that reporters are exempt from these obligations because if forced to respond to subpoenas and identify their sources or disclose other confidences, their informants will refuse or be reluctant to furnish newsworthy information in the future. This asserted burden on news gathering is said to make compelled testimony from newsmen constitutionally suspect and to require a privileged position for them.

. . .

. . . the great weight of authority is that newsmen are not exempt from the normal duty of appearing before a grand jury and answering questions relevant to a criminal investigation. At common law, courts consistently refused to recognize the existence of any privilege authorizing a newsman to refuse to reveal confidential information to a grand jury.

. . .

A number of States have provided newsmen a

statutory privilege of varying breadth, but the majority have not done so, and none has been provided by federal statute. Until now the only testimonial privilege for unofficial witnesses that is rooted in the Federal Constitution is the Fifth Amendment privilege against compelled self-incrimination. We are asked to create another by interpreting the First Amendment to grant newsmen a testimonial privilege that other citizens do not enjoy. This we decline to do. Fair and effective law enforcement aimed at providing security for the person and property of the individual is a fundamental function of government, and the grand jury plays an important, constitutionally mandated role in this process. On the records now before us, we perceive no basis for holding that the public interest in law enforcement and in ensuring effective grand jury proceedings is insufficient to override the consequential, but uncertain, burden on news gathering that is said to result from insisting that reporters, like other citizens, respond to relevant questions put to them in the course of a valid grand jury investigation or criminal trial.

. . .

Thus, we cannot seriously entertain the notion that the First Amendment protects a newsman's agreement to conceal the criminal conduct of his source, or evidence thereof, on the theory that it is better to write about crime than to do something about it. Insofar as any reporter in these cases undertook not to reveal or testify about the crime he witnessed, his claim of privilege under the First Amendment presents no substantial question. The crimes of news sources are no less reprehensible and threatening to the public interest when witnessed by a reporter than when they are not.

There remain those situations where a source is not engaged in criminal conduct but has information suggesting illegal conduct by others. Newsmen frequently receive information from such sources pursuant to a tacit or express agreement to withhold the source's name and suppress any information that the source wishes not published. Such informants presumably desire anonymity in order to avoid being entangled as a witness in a criminal trial or grand jury investigation. They may fear that disclosure will threaten

their job security or personal safety or that it will simply result in dishonor or embarrassment.

The argument that the flow of news will be diminished by compelling reporters to aid the grand jury in a criminal investigation is not irrational, nor are the records before us silent on the matter. But we remain unclear how often and to what extent informers are actually deterred from furnishing information when newsmen are forced to testify before a grand jury. The available data indicate that some newsmen rely a great deal on confidential sources and that some informants are particularly sensitive to the threat of exposure and may be silenced if it is held by this Court that, ordinarily, newsmen must testify pursuant to subpoenas, but the evidence fails to demonstrate that there would be a significant constriction of the flow of news to the public if this Court reaffirms the prior common-law and constitutional rule regarding the testimonial obligations of newsmen. Estimates of the inhibiting effect of such subpoenas on the willingness of informants to make disclosures to newsmen are widely divergent and to a great extent speculative. It would be difficult to canvass the views of the informants themselves; surveys of reporters on this topic are chiefly opinions of predicted informant behavior and must be viewed in the light of the professional self-interest of the interviewees. Reliance by the press on confidential informants does not mean that all such sources will in fact dry up because of the later possible appearance of the newsman before a grand jury. The reporter may never be called and if he objects to testifying, the prosecution may not insist. Also, the relationship of many informants to the press is a symbiotic one which is unlikely to be greatly inhibited by the threat of subpoena: quite often, such informants are members of a minority political or cultural group that relies heavily on the media to propagate its views, publicize its aims, and magnify its exposure to the public. Moreover, grand juries characteristically conduct secret proceedings, and law enforcement officers are themselves experienced in dealing with informers, and have their own methods for protecting them without interference with the effective administration of justice. There is little before us indicating that informants whose interest in avoiding exposure is that it may threaten job security, personal safety, or peace of mind, would in fact be in a worse position, or would think they would be, if they risked placing their trust in public officials as well as reporters. We doubt if the informer who prefers anonymity but is sincerely interested in furnishing evidence of crime will always or very often be deterred by the prospect of dealing with those public authorities characteristically charged with the duty to protect the public interest as well as his.

Accepting the fact, however, that an undetermined number of informants not themselves implicated in crime will nevertheless, for whatever reason, refuse to talk to newsmen if they fear identification by a reporter in an official investigation, we cannot accept the argument that the public interest in possible future news about crime from undisclosed, unverified sources must take precedence over the public interest in pursuing and prosecuting those crimes reported to the press by informants and in thus deterring the commission of such crimes in the future.

. . .

At the federal level, Congress has freedom to determine whether a statutory newsman's privilege is necessary and desirable and to fashion standards and rules as narrow or broad as deemed necessary to deal with the evil discerned and, equally important, to refashion those rules as experience from time to time may dictate. There is also merit in leaving state legislatures free, within First Amendment limits, to fashion their own standards in light of the conditions and problems with respect to the relations between law enforcement officials and press in their own areas. It goes without saying, of course, that we are powerless to bar state courts from responding in their own way and construing their own constitutions so as to recognize a newsman's privilege, either qualified or absolute.

. . .

MR. JUSTICE POWELL, concurring.

I add this brief statement to emphasize what seems to me to be the limited nature of the Court's holding. The Court does not hold that newsmen, subpoenaed to testify before a grand jury, are without constitutional rights with respect to the gathering of news or in safeguarding their sources. Certainly, we do not hold, as suggested in MR. JUSTICE STEWART'S dissenting opinion, that state and federal authorities are free to "annex" the news media as "an investigative arm of government." The solicitude repeatedly shown by this Court for First Amendment freedoms should be sufficient assurance against any such effort, even if one seriously believed that the media—properly free and untrammeled in the fullest sense of these terms—were not able to protect themselves.

As indicated in the concluding portion of the opinion, the Court states that no harassment of newsmen will be tolerated. If a newsman believes that the grand jury investigation is not being conducted in good faith he is not without remedy. Indeed, if the newsman is called upon to give information bearing only a remote and tenuous relationship to the subject of the investigation, or if he has some other reason to believe that his testimony implicates confidential source relationships without a legitimate need of law enforcement, he will have access to the court on a motion to quash and an appropriate protective order may be entered. The asserted claim to privilege should be judged on its facts by the striking of a proper balance between freedom of the press and the obligation of all citizens to give relevant testimony with respect to criminal conduct. The balance of these vital constitutional and societal interests on a case-by-case basis accords with the tried and traditional way of adjudicating such questions.

In short, the courts will be available to newsmen under circumstances where legitimate First Amendment interests require protection.

MR. JUSTICE DOUGLAS, dissenting in No. 70–57, *United States* v. *Caldwell.*

Caldwell, a black, is a reporter for the New York Times and was assigned to San Francisco with the hope that he could report on the activities and attitudes of the Black Panther Party. Caldwell in time gained the complete confidence of its members and wrote in-depth articles about them.

. . .

It is my view that there is no "compelling need" that can be shown which qualifies the reporter's immunity from appearing or testifying before a grand jury, unless the reporter himself is implicated in a crime. His immunity in my view is therefore quite complete, for, absent his involvement in a crime, the First Amendment protects him against an appearance before a grand jury and if he is involved in a crime, the Fifth Amendment stands as a barrier. Since in my view there is no area of inquiry not protected by a privilege, the reporter need not appear for the futile purpose of invoking one to each question. And, since in my view a newsman has an absolute right not to appear before a grand jury, it follows for me that a journalist who voluntarily appears before that body may invoke his First Amendment privilege to specific questions. . . .

The starting point for decision pretty well marks the range within which the end result lies. The New York Times, whose reporting functions are at issue here, takes the amazing position that First Amendment rights are to be balanced against other needs or conveniences of government. My belief is that all of the "balancing" was done by those who wrote the Bill of Rights. By casting the First Amendment in absolute terms, they repudiated the timid, watered-down, emasculated versions of the First Amendment which both the Government and the New York Times advance in the case.

. . .

II

. . .

The intrusion of government into this domain is symptomatic of the disease of this society. As the years pass the power of government becomes more and more pervasive. It is a power to suffocate both people and causes. Those in power, whatever their politics, want only to perpetuate it. Now that the fences of the law and the tradition that has protected the press are broken down, the people are the victims. The First Amendment, as I read it, was designed precisely to prevent that tragedy.

I would also reverse the judgments in No. 70–85, *Branzburg* v. *Hayes,* and No. 70–94, *In re Pappas,* for the reasons stated in the above dissent in No. 70–57, *United States* v. *Caldwell.*

MR. JUSTICE STEWART, with whom MR. JUSTICE BRENNAN and MR. JUSTICE MARSHALL join, dissenting.

The Court's crabbed view of the First Amendment reflects a disturbing insensitivity to the critical role of an independent press in our society. The question whether a reporter has a constitutional right to a confidential relationship with his source is of first impression here, but the principles that should guide our decision are as basic as any to be found in the Constitution. While MR. JUSTICE POWELL'S enigmatic concurring opinion gives some hope of a more flexible view in the future, the Court in these cases holds that a newsman has no First Amendment right to protect his sources when called before a grand jury. . . .

I

The reporter's constitutional right to a confidential relationship with his source stems from the broad societal interest in a full and free flow of information to the public. It is this basic concern that underlies the Constitution's protection of a free press, *Grosjean* v. *American Press Co.,* 297 U.S. 233, 250; *New York Times Co.* v. *Sullivan,* 376 U.S. 254, 269, because the guarantee is "not for the benefit of the press so much as for the benefit of all of us." *Time, Inc.* v. *Hill,* 385 U.S. 374, 389.

Enlightened choice by an informed citizenry is the basic ideal upon which an open society is premised, and a free press is thus indispensable to a free society. Not only does the press enhance personal self-fulfillment by providing the people with the widest possible range of fact and opinion, but it also is an incontestable precondition of self-government. The press "has been a mighty catalyst in awakening public interest in governmental affairs, exposing corruption among public officers and employees and generally informing the citizenry of public events and occurrences . . . ." *Estes* v. *Texas,* 381 U.S. 532, 539; *Mills* v. *Alabama,* 384 U.S. 214, 219; *Grosjean, supra,* at 250. As private and public aggregations of power burgeon in size and the pressures for conformity necessarily mount, there is obviously a continuing need for an independent press to disseminate a robust variety of information and opinion through reportage, investigation, and criticism, if we are to preserve our constitutional tradition of maximizing freedom of choice by encouraging diversity of expression.

. . .

II

Posed against the First Amendment's protection of the newsman's confidential relationships in these cases is society's interest in the use of the grand jury to administer justice fairly and effectively. . . .

Yet the longstanding rule making every person's evidence available to the grand jury is not absolute. The rule has been limited by the Fifth Amendment, the Fourth Amendment, and the evidentiary privileges of the common law. . . .

III

In deciding what protection should be given to information a reporter receives in confidence from a news source, the Court of Appeals for the Ninth Circuit affirmed the holding of the District Court that the grand jury power of testimonial compulsion must not be exercised in a manner

likely to impair First Amendment interests "until there has been a clear showing of a compelling and overriding national interest that cannot be served by any alternative means." *Caldwell* v. *United States*, 434 F. 2d 1081, 1086. It approved the request of respondent Caldwell for specification by the government of the "subject, direction or scope of the Grand Jury inquiry." *Id.*, at 1085. And it held that in the circumstances of this case Caldwell need not divulge confidential information.

I think this decision was correct. On the record before us the United States has not met the burden that I think the appropriate newsman's privilege should require.

. . .

Accordingly, I would affirm the judgment of the Court of Appeals in No. 70-57, *United States* v. *Caldwell*. In the other two cases before us, No. 70–85, *Branzburg* v. *Hayes* and *Meigs*, and No. 70–94, *In re Pappas*, I would vacate the judgments and remand the cases for further proceedings not inconsistent with the views I have expressed in this opinion.

Nebraska Press Assn. v. Stuart

427 U.S. 539 (1976)

A Nebraska state trial judge, anticipating a trial for a multiple murder which had attracted widespread news coverage, entered an order that restrained newspapers, broadcasters, journalists, news media associations, and national newswire services from publishing or broadcasting accounts of confessions or admissions made by the accused to law enforcement officers or third parties. An exception was made for confessions or admissions made to the press. The question was whether the order, intended to prevent pretrial publicity that might jeopardize a fair trial, violated the constitutional guarantee of a free press.

Mr. CHIEF JUSTICE BURGER delivered the opinion of the Court.

The respondent State District Judge entered an order restraining the petitioners from publishing or broadcasting accounts of confessions or admissions made by the accused or facts "strongly

implicative" of the accused in a widely reported murder of six persons. We granted certiorari to decide whether the entry of such an order on the showing made before the state court violated the constitutional guarantee of freedom of the press.

. . .

III

The problems presented by this case are almost as old as the Republic. Neither in the Constitution nor in contemporaneous writings do we find that the conflict between these two important rights was anticipated, yet it is inconceivable that the authors of the Constitution were unaware of the potential conflicts between the right to an unbiased jury and the guarantee of freedom of the press. . . .

The speed of communication and the pervasiveness of the modern news media have exacerbated these problems, however, as numerous appeals demonstrate. The trial of Bruno Hauptmann in a small New Jersey community for the abduction and murder of the Charles Lindberghs' infant child probably was the most widely covered trial up to that time, and the nature of the coverage produced widespread public reaction. Criticism was directed at the "carnival" atmosphere that pervaded the community and the courtroom itself. Responsible leaders of press and the legal profession—including other judges—pointed out that much of this sorry performance could have been controlled by a vigilant trial judge and by other public officers subject to the control of the court. . . .

The excesses of press and radio and lack of responsibility of those in authority in the *Hauptmann* case and others of that era led to efforts to develop voluntary guidelines for courts, lawyers, press, and broadcasters. See generally J. Lofton, Justice and the Press 117–130 (1966). The effort was renewed in 1965 when the American Bar Association embarked on a project to develop standards for all aspects of criminal justice, including guidelines to accommodate the right to a fair trial and the rights of a free press. See Powell, The Right to a Fair Trial, 51 A. B. A. J. 534 (1965). The resulting standards, approved by the Association in 1968, received support from most of the legal profession. . . .

In practice, of course, even the most ideal guidelines are subjected to powerful strains when a case such as Simants' *[arrested for the six murders in Sutherland, Neb.]* arises, with reporters from many parts of the country on the scene. Reporters from distant places are unlikely to consider themselves bound by local standards.

They report to editors outside the area covered by the guidelines, and their editors are likely to be guided only by their own standards. To contemplate how a state court can control acts of a newspaper or broadcaster outside its jurisdiction, even though the newspapers and broadcasts reach the very community from which jurors are to be selected, suggests something of the practical difficulties of managing such guidelines.

The problems presented in this case have a substantial history outside the reported decisions of courts, in the efforts of many responsible people to accommodate the competing interests. We cannot resolve all of them, for it is not the function of this Court to write a code. We look instead to this particular case and the legal context in which it arises.

IV

The Sixth Amendment in terms guarantees "trial, by an impartial jury. . . " in federal criminal prosecutions. Because "trial by jury in criminal cases is fundamental to the American scheme of justice," the Due Process Clause of the Fourteenth Amendment guarantees the same right in state criminal prosecutions. *Duncan* v. *Louisiana,* 391 U. S. 145, 149 (1968).

. . .

In the overwhelming majority of criminal trials, pretrial publicity presents few unmanageable threats to this important right. But when the case is a "sensational" one tensions develop between the right of the accused to trial by an impartial jury and the rights guaranteed others by the First Amendment. The relevant decisions of this Court, even if not dispositive, are instructive by way of background.

In *Irvin* v. *Dowd,* . . . the defendant was convicted of murder following intensive and hostile news coverage. The trial judge had granted a defense motion for a change of venue, but only to an adjacent county, which had been exposed to essentially the same news coverage. At trial, 430 persons were called for jury service; 268 were excused because they had fixed opinions as to guilt. Eight of the 12 who served as jurors thought the defendant guilty, but said they could nevertheless render an impartial verdict. On review the Court vacated the conviction and death sentence and remanded to allow a new trial for, "[w]ith his life at stake, it is not requiring too much that petitioner be tried in an atmosphere undisturbed by so huge a wave of public passion. . . ." 366 U. S., at 728.

Similarly, in *Rideau* v. *Louisiana*, 373 U. S. 723 (1963), the Court reversed the conviction of a defendant whose staged, highly emotional confession had been filmed with the cooperation of local police and later broadcast on television for three days while he was awaiting trial, saying "[a]ny subsequent court proceedings in a community so pervasively exposed to such a spectacle could be but a hollow formality." *Id.*, at 726. And in *Estes* v. *Texas*, 381 U. S. 532 (1965), the Court held that the defendant had not been afforded due process where the volume of trial publicity, the judge's failure to control the proceedings, and the telecast of a hearing and of the trial itself "inherently prevented a sober search for the truth." *Id.*, at 551. See also *Marshall* v. *United States*, 360 U. S. 310 (1959).

. . .

V

The First Amendment provides that "Congress shall make no law . . . abridging the freedom . . . of the press," and it is "no longer open to doubt that the liberty of the press, and of speech, is within the liberty safeguarded by the due process clause of the Fourteenth Amendment from invasion by state action." *Near* v. *Minnesota ex rel. Olson*, 283 U. S. 697, 707 (1931). See also *Grosjean* v. *American Press Co.*, 297 U. S. 233, 244 (1936). The Court has interpreted these guarantees to afford special protection against orders that prohibit the publication or broadcast of particular information or commentary—orders that impose a "previous" or "prior" restraint on speech. None of our decided cases on prior restraint involved restrictive orders entered to protect a defendant's right to a fair and impartial jury, but the opinions on prior restraint have a common thread relevant to this case.

In *Near* v. *Minnesota ex rel. Olson, supra*, the Court held invalid a Minnesota statute providing

for the abatement as a public nuisance of any "malicious, scandalous and defamatory newspaper, magazine or other periodical." . . .

. . .

The Court relied on *Patterson* v. *Colorado ex rel. Attorney General*, 205 U. S. 454, 462 (1907): "[T]he main purpose of [the First Amendment] is 'to prevent all such *previous restraints* upon publications as had been practiced by other governments.'"

[Burger reviews other cases holding that any prior restraint on expression comes to the Court with a "heavy presumption" against its constitutional validity: Organization for a Better Austin *v.* Keefe, *402 U. S. 415 (1971);* New York Times Co. *v.* United States, *403 U. S. 713 (1971).]*

. . . Truthful reports of public judicial proceedings have been afforded special protection against subsequent punishment. See *Cox Broadcasting Corp* v. *Cohn*, 420 U. S. 469, 492–493 (1975); see also, *Craig* v. *Harney*, 331 U. S. 367, 374 (1947). For the same reasons the protection against prior restraint should have particular force as applied to reporting of criminal proceedings, whether the crime in question is a single isolated act or a pattern of criminal conduct.

"A responsible press has always been regarded as the handmaiden of effective judicial administration, especially in the criminal field. Its function in this regard is documented by an impressive record of service over several centuries. The press does not simply publish information about trials but guards against the miscarriage of justice by subjecting the police, prosecutors, and judicial processes to extensive public scrutiny and criticism." *Sheppard* v. *Maxwell*, 384 U. S., at 350.

. . .

VI

We turn now to the record in this case . . . To do so, we must examine the evidence before the trial judge when the order was entered to determine (a) the nature and extent of pretrial news coverage; (b) whether other measures would be likely to mitigate the effects of unrestrained pretrial publicity; and (c) how effectively a restraining order would operate to prevent the threatened danger. The precise terms of the restraining order are also important. We must then consider whether the record supports the entry of a prior restraint on publication, one of the most extraordinary remedies known to our jurisprudence.

A

. . .

Our review of the pretrial record persuades us that the trial judge was justified in concluding that there would be intense and pervasive pretrial publicity concerning this case. He could also reasonably conclude, based on common human experience, that publicity might impair the defendant's right to a fair trial. He did not purport to say more, for he found only "a clear and present danger that pre-trial publicity *could* impinge upon the defendant's right to a fair trial." (Emphasis added.) His conclusion as to the impact of such publicity on prospective jurors was of necessity speculative, dealing as he was with factors unknown and unknowable.

B

We find little in the record that goes to another aspect of our task, determining whether measures short of an order restraining all publication would have insured the defendant a fair trial . . .

We have therefore examined this record to determine the probable efficacy of the measures short of prior restraint on the press and speech. There is no finding that alternative measures would not have protected Simants' rights, and the Nebraska Supreme Court did no more than imply that such measures might not be adequate. Moreover, the record is lacking in evidence to support such a finding.

C

We must also assess the probable efficacy of prior restraint on publication as a workable method of protecting Simants' right to a fair trial, and we cannot ignore the reality of the problems of managing and enforcing pretrial restraining orders. The territorial jurisdiction of the issuing court is limited by concepts of sovereignty . . .

. . . the events disclosed by the record took place in a community of 850 people. It is reasonable to assume that, without any news accounts being printed or broadcast, rumors would travel swiftly by word of mouth. One can only speculate on the accuracy of such reports, given the generative propensities of rumors; they could well be more damaging than reasonably accurate news accounts. But plainly a whole community cannot be restrained from discussing a subject intimately affecting life within it.

Given these practical problems, it is far from clear that prior restraint on publication would have protected Simants' rights.

. . .

E

. . .

Of necessity our holding is confined to the record before us. But our conclusion is not simply a result of assessing the adequacy of the showing made in this case; it results in part from the problems inherent in meeting the heavy burden of demonstrating, in advance of trial, that without prior restraint a fair trial will be denied. The practical problems of managing and enforcing restrictive orders will always be present. In this sense, the record now before us is illustrative rather than exceptional. . . .

. . . We hold that, with respect to the order entered in this case prohibiting reporting or commentary on judicial proceedings held in public, the barriers have not been overcome; to the extent that this order restrained publication of such material, it is clearly invalid. To the extent that it prohibited publication based on information gained from other sources, we conclude that the heavy burden imposed as a condition to securing a prior restraint was not met and the judgment of the Nebraska Supreme Court is therefore

Reversed.

MR. JUSTICE WHITE, concurring.

. . .

MR. JUSTICE POWELL, concurring.

. . .

MR. JUSTICE BRENNAN, with whom MR. JUSTICE STEWART and MR. JUSTICE MARSHALL join, concurring in the judgment.

. . .

MR. JUSTICE STEVENS, concurring in the judgment.

. . .

Gannett Co. v. DePasquale

443 U.S. 368 (1979)

At a pretrial hearing on a motion to suppress allegedly involuntary confessions and certain physical evidence, two defendants in a state prosecution for second-degree murder, robbery, and grand larceny requested that the public be excluded from the hearing. They argued that the unabated buildup of adverse publicity had jeopardized their ability to receive a fair trial. The District Attorney did not oppose the motion and a reporter for the Gannett publishers, whose newspapers had given extensive coverage of the crime through the indictment and arraignment stages, made no objection at the time. Judge DePasquale granted the motion. In response to the reporter's letter the next day asserting a right to cover the hearing and requesting access to the transcript, the judge stated that the suppression hearing had concluded and that any decision on immediate release of the transcript had been reserved. Gannett then moved to have the closure order set aside but Judge DePasquale, after a hearing, refused to vacate the order or grant Gannett immediate access to the transcript, ruling that the interests of the press and the public were outweighed by defendants' right to a fair trial.

MR. JUSTICE STEWART delivered the opinion of the Court.

The question presented in this case is whether members of the public have an independent constitutional right to insist upon access to a pretrial judicial proceeding, even though the accused, the prosecutor, and the trial judge all have agreed to the closure of that proceeding in order to assure a fair trial.

I

Wayne Clapp, aged 42 and residing at Henrietta, a Rochester, N. Y., suburb, disappeared in July 1976. He was last seen on July 16 when, with two male companions, he went out on his boat to fish in Seneca Lake, about 40 miles from Rochester. The two companions returned in the boat the same day and drove away in Clapp's pickup truck. Clapp was not with them. When he failed to return home by July 19, his family reported his absence to the police. An examination of the boat, laced with bulletholes, seemed to indicate

that Clapp had met a violent death aboard it. Police then began an intensive search for the two men. They also began lake-dragging operations in an attempt to locate Clapp's body.

The petitioner, Gannett Co., Inc., publishes two Rochester newspapers, the morning Democrat & Chronicle and the evening Times-Union. On July 20, each paper carried its first story about Clapp's disappearance. Each reported the few details that were then known and stated that the police were theorizing that Clapp had been shot on his boat and his body dumped overboard. Each stated that the body was missing. The Times-Union mentioned the names of respondents Greathouse and Jones and said that Greathouse "was identified as one of the two companions who accompanied Clapp Friday" on the boat; said that the two were aged 16 and 21, respectively; and noted that the police were seeking the two men and Greathouse's wife, also 16. Accompanying the evening story was a 1959 photograph of Clapp. The report also contained an appeal from the state police for assistance.

Michigan police apprehended Greathouse, Jones, and the woman on July 21. This came about when an interstate bulletin describing Clapp's truck led to their discovery in Jackson County, Mich., by police who observed the truck parked at a local motel. The petitioner's two Rochester papers on July 22 reported the details of the capture. The stories recounted how the Michigan police, after having arrested Jones in a park, used a helicopter and dogs and tracked down Greathouse and the woman in some woods. They recited that Clapp's truck was located near the park.

The stories also stated that Seneca County police theorized that Clapp was shot with his own pistol, robbed, and his body thrown into Seneca Lake. The articles provided background on Clapp's life, sketched the events surrounding his disappearance, and said that New York had issued warrants for the arrest of the three persons. *[Newspaper coverage continued on July 23–25. The newspapers reported the indictments of the two men and the woman on August 2 and their arraignments on August 5. Defense attorneys were given ninety days to file pretrial motions. During that period, Greathouse and Jones moved to suppress statements made to the police and to suppress physical evidence seized.]*

The motions to suppress came on before Judge DePasquale on November 4. At this hearing, defense attorneys argued that the unabated buildup of adverse publicity had jeopardized the ability of the defendants to receive a fair trial. They thus requested that the public and the press be excluded from the hearing. The District Attorney did not oppose the motion. Although Carol Ritter, a reporter employed by the petitioner, was present in the courtroom, no objection was made at the time of the closure motion. The trial judge granted the motion.

The next day, however, Ritter wrote a letter to the trial judge asserting a "right to cover this hearing," and requesting that "we . . . be given access to the transcript." The judge responded later the same day. He stated that the suppression hearing had concluded and that any decision on immediate release of the transcript had been reserved. The petitioner then moved the court to set aside its exclusionary order.

[The judge refused to vacate his order. The New York Supreme Court, Appellate Division, vacated the order, but the New York Court of Appeals upheld the exclusion of the press and the public from the pretrial proceeding.]

II

[Shortly before the entry of judgment by the Appellate Division, both defendants pleaded guilty to lesser offenses and a transcript of the suppression hearing was made available to Gannett. In this section the Court holds that, notwithstanding the availability of the transcript, the controversy is not moot.]

III

This Court has long recognized that adverse publicity can endanger the ability of a defendant to receive a fair trial. *E. g., Sheppard* v. *Maxwell*, 384 U. S. 333; *Irvin* v. *Dowd*, 366 U. S. 717; *Marshall* v. *United States*, 360 U. S. 310. Cf. *Estes* v. *Texas*, 381 U. S. 532. To safeguard the due process rights of the accused, a trial judge has an affirmative constitutional duty to minimize the effects of prejudicial pretrial publicity. *Sheppard* v. *Maxwell, supra.* And because of the Constitution's pervasive concern for these due process rights, a trial judge may surely take protective measures even when they are not strictly and inescapably necessary.

Publicity concerning pretrial suppression hearings such as the one involved in the present case poses special risks of unfairness. The whole purpose of such hearings is to screen out unreliable or illegally obtained evidence and insure that this evidence does not become known to the jury. Cf. *Jackson* v. *Denno*, 378 U. S. 368. Publicity concerning the proceedings at a pretrial hearing, however, could influence public opinion against a defendant and inform potential jurors of inculpatory information wholly inadmissible at the actual trial.

The danger of publicity concerning pretrial suppression hearings is particularly acute, because it may be difficult to measure with any degree of certainty the effects of such publicity on the fairness of the trial. After the commencement of the trial itself, inadmissible prejudicial information about a defendant can be kept from a jury by a variety of means. When such information is publicized during a pretrial proceeding, however, it may never be altogether kept from potential jurors. Closure of pretrial proceedings is often one of the most effective methods that a trial judge can employ to attempt to insure that the fairness of a trial will not be jeopardized by the dissemination of such information throughout the community before the trial itself has even begun. Cf. *Rideau* v. *Louisiana*, 373 U. S. 723.

IV

A

The Sixth Amendment, applicable to the States through the Fourteenth, surrounds a criminal trial with guarantees such as the rights to notice, confrontation, and compulsory process that have as their overriding purpose the protection of the accused from prosecutorial and judicial abuses. Among the guarantees that the Amendment provides to a person charged with the commission of a criminal offense, and to him alone, is the "right to a speedy and public trial, by an impartial jury." The Constitution nowhere mentions any right of access to a criminal trial on the part of the public; its guarantee, like the others enumerated, is personal to the accused. See *Faretta* v. *California*, 422 U. S. 806, 848 ("[T]he specific guarantees of the Sixth Amendment are personal to the accused") (BLACKMUN, J., dissenting).

. . .

B

While the Sixth Amendment guarantees to a defendant in a criminal case the right to a public trial, it does not guarantee the right to compel a private trial. "The ability to waive a constitutional right does not ordinarily carry with it the right to insist upon the opposite of that right." *Singer* v. *United States*, 380 U. S. 24, 34–35. But the issue here is not whether the defendant can compel a private trial. Rather, the issue is whether members of the public have an enforceable right to a public trial that can be asserted independently of the parties in the litigation.

There can be no blinking the fact that there is a strong societal interest in public trials. Openness in court proceedings may improve the quality of testimony, induce unknown witnesses to come forward with relevant testimony, cause all trial participants to perform their duties more conscientiously, and generally give the public an opportunity to observe the judicial system. . . .

Recognition of an independent public interest in the enforcement of Sixth Amendment guarantees is a far cry, however, from the creation of a constitutional right on the part of the public. In an adversary system of criminal justice, the public interest in the administration of justice is protected by the participants in the litigation. . . .

V

In arguing that members of the general public have a constitutional right to attend a criminal trial, despite the obvious lack of support for such a right in the structure or text of the Sixth Amendment, the petitioner and *amici* rely on the history of the public-trial guarantee. This history, however, ultimately demonstrates no more than the existence of a common-law rule of open civil and criminal proceedings.

A

Not many common-law rules have been elevated to the status of constitutional rights. The provisions of our Constitution do reflect an incorporation of certain few common-law rules and a rejection of others. . . .

. . . There is no question that the Sixth Amendment permits and even presumes open trials as a norm. But the issue here is whether the Constitution *requires* that a pretrial proceeding such as this one be opened to the public, even though the participants in the litigation agree that it should be closed to protect the defendants' right to a fair trial. The history upon which the petitioner and *amici* rely totally fails to demonstrate that the Framers of the Sixth Amendment intended to create a constitutional right in strangers to attend a pretrial proceeding, when all that they actually did was to confer upon the accused an explicit right to demand a public trial. . . .

B

But even if the Sixth and Fourteenth Amendments could properly be viewed as embodying the common-law right of the public to attend criminal trials, it would not necessarily follow that the petitioner would have a right of access under the circumstances of this case. For there exists no persuasive evidence that at common law members of the public had any right to attend pretrial proceedings; indeed, there is substantial evidence to the contrary. By the time of the adoption of the Constitution, public trials were clearly associated with the protection of the defendant. And pretrial proceedings, precisely because of the same concern for a fair trial, were never characterized by the same degree of openness as were actual trials.

. . .

For these reasons, we hold that members of the public have no constitutional right under the Sixth and Fourteenth Amendments to attend criminal trials.

VI

The petitioner also argues that members of the press and the public have a right of access to the pretrial hearing by reason of the First and Fourteenth Amendments. . . .

Several factors lead to the conclusion that the actions of the trial judge here were consistent with any right of access the petitioner may have had under the First and Fourteenth Amendments. . . . the trial court found that the representatives of the press did have a right of access of constitutional dimension, but held, under the circumstances of this case, that this right was outweighed by the defendants' right to a fair trial. In short, the closure decision was based "on an assessment of the competing societal interests involved . . . rather than on any determination that First Amendment freedoms were not implicated." *Saxbe, supra,* at 860 (POWELL, J., dissenting).

Furthermore, any denial of access in this case was not absolute but only temporary. Once the danger of prejudice had dissipated, a transcript of the suppression hearing was made available. The press and the public then had a full opportunity to scrutinize the suppression hearing. Unlike the case of an absolute ban on access, therefore, the press here had the opportunity to inform the public of the details of the pretrial hearing accurately and completely. Under these circumstan-

ces, any First and Fourteenth Amendment right of the petitioner to attend a criminal trial was not violated.

VII

We certainly do not disparage the general desirability of open judicial proceedings. But we are not asked here to declare whether open proceedings represent beneficial social policy, or whether there would be a constitutional barrier to a state law that imposed a stricter standard of closure than the one here employed by the New York courts. Rather, we are asked to hold that the Constitution itself gave the petitioner an affirmative right of access to this pretrial proceeding, even though all the participants in the litigation agreed that it should be closed to protect the fair-trial rights of the defendants.

For all of the reasons discussed in this opinion, we hold that the Constitution provides no such right. Accordingly, the judgment of the New York Court of Appeals is affirmed.

It is so ordered.

MR. CHIEF JUSTICE BURGER, concurring.

I join the opinion of the Court, but I write separately to emphasize my view of the nature of the proceeding involved in today's decision. By definition, a hearing on a motion before trial to suppress evidence is not a *trial;* it is a *pre*trial hearing.

. . . during the last 40 years in which the pretrial processes have been enormously expanded, it has never occurred to anyone, so far as I am aware, that a pretrial deposition or pretrial interrogatories were other than wholly private to the litigants. A pretrial deposition does not become part of a "trial" until and unless the contents of the deposition are offered in evidence. Pretrial depositions are not uncommon to take the testimony of a witness, either for the defense or for the prosecution. In the entire pretrial period, there is no certainty that a trial will take place. Something in the neighborhood of 85 percent of all criminal charges are resolved by guilty pleas, frequently after pretrial depositions have been taken or motions to suppress evidence have been ruled upon.

For me, the essence of all of this is that by definition "pretrial proceedings" are exactly that.

MR. JUSTICE POWELL, concurring.

. . .

MR. JUSTICE REHNQUIST, concurring.

. . .

The Court today holds, without qualification, that "members of the public have no constitutional right under the Sixth and Fourteenth Amendments to attend criminal trials." *Ante*, at 391. . . .
. . . lower courts should not assume that after today's decision they must adhere to the procedures employed by the trial court in this case or to those advanced by MR. JUSTICE POWELL in his separate opinion in order to avoid running afoul of the First Amendment. To the contrary, in my view and, I think, in the view of a majority of this Court, the lower courts are under no constitutional constraint either to accept or reject those procedures. They remain, in the best tradition of our federal system, free to determine for themselves the question whether to open or close the proceeding. Hopefully, they will decide the question by accommodating competing interests in a judicious manner. But so far as the Constitution is concerned, the question is for them, not us, to resolve.

MR. JUSTICE BLACKMUN, with whom MR. JUSTICE BRENNAN, MR. JUSTICE WHITE, and MR. JUSTICE MARSHALL join, concurring in part and dissenting in part.

. . .

Today's decision, as I view it, is an unfortunate one. . . . That rule is to the effect that if the defense and the prosecution merely agree to have the public excluded from a suppression hearing, and the trial judge does not resist—as trial judges may be prone not to do, since nonresistance is easier than resistance—closure shall take place, and there is nothing in the Sixth Amendment that prevents that happily agreed upon event. The result is that the important interests of the public and the press (as a part of that public) in open judicial proceedings are rejected and cast aside as of little value or significance.

Because I think this easy but wooden approach is without support either in legal history or in the intendment of the Sixth Amendment, I dissent.

I

The Court's review of the facts, *ante*, at 371–377, does not face up to the placid, routine, and innocuous nature of the news articles about the case and, indeed, their comparative infrequency. . . .
. . . there can be no dispute whatsoever that the stories consisted almost entirely of straightforward reporting of the facts surrounding the investigation of Clapp's disappearance, and of the arrests and charges. The stories contained no "editorializing" and nothing that a fairminded person could describe as sensational journalism. Only one picture appeared; it was a photograph of Clapp that accompanied the first story printed by the Times-Union. There is nothing in the record to indicate that the stories were placed on the page or within the paper so as to play up the murder investigation. Headlines were entirely factual. The stories were relatively brief. They appeared only in connection with a development in the investigation, and they gave no indication of being published to sustain popular interest in the case.

. . .

II

This Court confronts in this case another aspect of the recurring conflict that arises whenever a defendant in a criminal case asserts that his right to a fair trial clashes with the right of the public in general, and of the press in particular, to an open proceeding. . . .

Despite MR. JUSTICE POWELL'S concern, *ante*, p. 397, this Court heretofore has not found, and does not today find, any First Amendment right of access to judicial or other governmental proceedings. See, *e. g.*, Nixon v. *Warner Communications, Inc.*, 435 U. S. 589, 608–610 (1978); *Pell* v. *Procunier*, 417 U. S. 817, 834 (1974). One turns then, instead, to that provision of the Constitution that speaks most directly to the question of access to judicial proceedings, namely, the public-trial provision of the Sixth Amendment.

A

The familiar language of the Sixth Amendment reads: "In all criminal prosecutions, the accused shall enjoy the right to a speedy and public trial."

This provision reflects the tradition of our system of criminal justice that a trial is a "public event" and that "[w]hat transpires in the court room is public property." *Craig* v. *Harney*, 331 U. S. 367, 374 (1947). And it reflects, as well, "the notion, deeply rooted in the common law, that 'justice must satisfy the appearance of justice.' " *Levine* v. *United States*, 362 U. S. 610, 616 (1960), quoting *Offutt* v. *United States*, 348 U. S. 11, 14 (1954).

More importantly, the requirement that a trial of a criminal case be public embodies our belief that secret judicial proceedings would be a menace to liberty. The public trial is rooted in the "principle that justice cannot survive behind walls of silence," *Sheppard* v. *Maxwell*, 384 U. S., at 349, and in the "traditional Anglo-American distrust for secret trials," *In re Oliver*, 333 U. S. 257, 268 (1948). This Nation's accepted practice of providing open trials in both federal and state courts "has always been recognized as a safeguard against any attempt to employ our courts as instruments of persecution. The knowledge that every criminal trial is subject to contemporaneous review in the forum of public opinion is an effective restraint on possible abuse of judicial power." *Id.*, at 270.

. . .

B

By its literal terms, the Sixth Amendment secures the right to a public trial only to "the accused." *[By reviewing* Barker *v.* Wingo, *407 U. S. 514 (1972),* Singer *v.* United States, *380 U. S. 24 (1965), and* Faretta *v.* California, *422 U.S. 806 (1975), Blackmun demonstrates that the Sixth Amendment implicates interests beyond those of the accused to include societal interests.]*

C

[The fact that the Sixth Amendment casts the right to a public trial in terms of the right of the accused is not sufficient to Blackmun to permit the inference that the accused may compel a private proceeding simply by waiving that right. Blackmun examines the common-law and colonial antecedents as well as the original understanding of the Sixth Amendment,

and finds no basis for the view that the guarantee of a public trial carries with it a correlative right to compel a private proceeding.]

D

[In this section, Blackmun explains that the Sixth Amendment speaks only of a public "trial," but that the pretrial suppression hearing often is a decisive stage for the defendant and the prosecution. He concludes that the Sixth and Fourteenth Amendments prohibit a state from conducting a pretrial suppression hearing in private, even at the request of the accused, "unless full and fair consideration is first given to the public's interest, protected by the Amendments, in open trials."]

IV

The Sixth Amendment, in establishing the public's right of access to a criminal trial and a pretrial proceeding, also fixes the rights of the press in this regard. Petitioner, as a newspaper publisher, enjoys the same right of access to the *Jackson* v. *Denno* hearing at issue in this case as does the general public. And what petitioner sees and hears in the courtroom it may, like any other citizen, publish or report consistent with the First Amendment. "Of course, there is nothing that proscribes the press from reporting events that transpire in the courtroom." *Sheppard* v. *Maxwell*, 384 U. S., at 362–363. Reporters for newspaper, television, and radio "are entitled to the same rights as the general public" to have access to the courtroom, *Estes* v. *Texas*, 381 U. S., at 540, where they "are always present if they wish to be and are plainly free to report whatever occurs in open court through their respective media." *Id.*, at 541–542. "[O]nce a public hearing ha[s] been held, what transpired there could not be subject to prior restraint." *Nebraska Press Assn.* v. *Stuart*, 427 U. S., at 568.

. . .

Richmond Newspapers, Inc. v. Virginia

448 U.S. 555 (1980)

After three trials on a murder charge had been either reversed on appeal or had resulted in mistrials, a Virginia court granted the motion of the defense counsel to close the trial to the public and to the press. The court's action presented the question to the Supreme Court whether there exists in the Constitution an implied right of the public and press to attend criminal trials.

MR. CHIEF JUSTICE BURGER announced the judgment of the Court and delivered an opinion, in which MR. JUSTICE WHITE and MR. JUSTICE STEVENS joined.

The narrow question presented in this case is whether the right of the public and press to attend criminal trials is guaranteed under the United States Constitution.

I

In March 1976, one Stevenson was indicted for the murder of a hotel manager who had been found stabbed to death on December 2, 1975. Tried promptly in July 1976, Stevenson was convicted of second-degree murder in the Circuit Court of Hanover County, Va. The Virginia Supreme Court reversed the conviction in October 1977, holding that a bloodstained shirt purportedly belonging to Stevenson had been improperly admitted into evidence. *Stevenson* v. *Commonwealth*, 218 Va. 462, 237 S. E. 2d 779.

Stevenson was retried in the same court. This second trial ended in a mistrial on May 30, 1978, when a juror asked to be excused after trial had begun and no alternate was available.

A third trial, which began in the same court on June 6, 1978, also ended in a mistrial. It appears that the mistrial may have been declared because a prospective juror had read about Stevenson's previous trials in a newspaper and had told other prospective jurors about the case before the retrial began. See App. 35a-36a.

Stevenson was tried in the same court for a fourth time beginning on September 11, 1978. Present in the courtroom when the case was called were appellants Wheeler and McCarthy,

reporters for appellant Richmond Newspapers, Inc. Before the trial began, counsel for the defendant moved that it be closed to the public:

"[T]here was this woman that was with the family of the deceased when we were here before. She had sat in the Courtroom. I would like to ask that everybody be excluded from the Courtroom because I don't want any information being shuffled back and forth when we have a recess as to what—who testified to what." Tr. of Sept. 11, 1978 Hearing on Defendant's Motion to Close Trial to the Public 2–3.

The trial judge, who had presided over two of the three previous trials, asked if the prosecution had any objection to clearing the courtroom. The prosecutor stated he had no objection and would leave it to the discretion of the court. *Id.*, at 4. Presumably referring to Va. Code § 19.2–266 (Supp. 1980), the trial judge then announced: "[T]he statute gives me that power specifically and the defendant has made the motion." He then ordered "that the Courtroom be kept clear of all parties except the witnesses when they testify." Tr., *supra*, at 4–5. The record does not show that any objections to the closure order were made by anyone present at the time, including appellants Wheeler and McCarthy.

Later that same day, however, appellants sought a hearing on a motion to vacate the closure order. The trial judge granted the request and scheduled a hearing to follow the close of the day's proceedings. When the hearing began, the court ruled that the hearing was to be treated as part of the trial; accordingly, he again ordered the reporters to leave the courtroom, and they complied.

At the closed hearing, counsel for appellants

observed that no evidentiary findings had been made by the court prior to the entry of its closure order and pointed out that the court had failed to consider any other, less drastic measures within its power to ensure a fair trial. Tr. of Sept. 11, 1978 Hearing on Motion to Vacate 11–12. Counsel for appellants argued that constitutional considerations mandated that before ordering closure, the court should first decide that the rights of the defendant could be protected in no other way.

Counsel for defendant Stevenson pointed out that this was the fourth time he was standing trial. He also referred to "difficulty with information between the jurors," and stated that he "didn't want information to leak out," be published by the media, perhaps inaccurately, and then be seen by the jurors. Defense counsel argued that these things, plus the fact that "this is a small community," made this a proper case for closure. *Id.*, at 16–18.

The trial judge noted that counsel for the defendant had made similar statements at the morning hearing. The court also stated:

"[O]ne of the other points that we take into consideration in this particular Courtroom is lay-out of the Courtroom. I think that having people in the Courtroom is distracting to the jury. Now, we have to have certain people in here and maybe that's not a very good reason. When we get into our new Court Building, people can sit in the audience so the jury can't see them. The rule of the Court may be different under those circumstances. . . ." *Id.*, at 19.

The prosecutor again declined comment, and the court summed up by saying:

"I'm inclined to agree with [defense counsel] that, if I feel that the rights of the defendant are infringed in any way, [when] he makes the motion to do something and it doesn't completely over-ride all rights of everyone else, then I'm inclined to go along with the defendant's motion." *Id.*, at 20.

The court denied the motion to vacate and ordered the trial to continue the following morning "with the press and public excluded." *Id.*, at 27; App. 21a.

. . .

II

We begin consideration of this case by noting that the precise issue presented here has not previously been before this Court for decision. In *Gannett Co.* v. *DePasquale, supra,* the Court was not required to decide whether a right of access to *trials,* as distingushed from hearings on *pre*trial motions, was constitutionally guaranteed. The Court held that the Sixth Amendment's guarantee to the accused of a public trial gave neither the public nor the press an enforceable right of access to a *pre*trial suppression hearing. One concurring opinion specifically emphasized that "a hearing on a motion before trial to suppress evidence is not a *trial.* . . ." 443 U. S., at 394 (BURGER, C. J., concurring). Moreover, the Court did not decide whether the First and Fourteenth Amendments guarantee a right of the public to attend trials, *id.,* at 392, and n. 24; nor did the dissenting opinion reach this issue. *Id.,* at 447 (opinion of BLACKMUN, J.).

In prior cases the Court has treated questions involving conflicts between publicity and a defendant's right to a fair trial; as we observed in *Nebraska Press Assn.* v. *Stuart, supra,* at 547, "[t]he problems presented by this [conflict] are almost as old as the Republic." See also, *e. g., Gannett, supra; Murphy* v. *Florida,* 421 U. S. 794 (1975); *Sheppard* v. *Maxwell,* 384 U. S. 333 (1966); *Estes* v. *Texas,* 381 U. S. 532 (1965). But here for the first time the Court is asked to decide whether a criminal trial itself may be closed to the public upon the unop-posed request of a defendant, without any demonstration that closure is required to protect the defendant's superior right to a fair trial, or that some other overriding consideration requires clo-sure.

. . .

B

. . . the historical evidence demonstrates con-clusively that at the time when our organic laws were adopted, criminal trials both here and in England had long been presumptively open. This is no quirk of history; rather, it has long been recognized as an indispensable attribute of an

Anglo-American trial. Both Hale in the 17th century and Blackstone in the 18th saw the importance of openness to the proper functioning of a trial; it gave assurance that the proceedings were conducted fairly to all concerned, and it discouraged perjury, the misconduct of participants, and decisions based on secret bias or partiality. . . .

. . . The early history of open trials in part reflects the widespread acknowledgment, long before there were behavioral scientists, that public trials had significant community therapeutic value. Even without such experts to frame the concept in words, people sensed from experience and observation that, especially in the administration of criminal justice, the means used to achieve justice must have the support derived from public acceptance of both the process and its results.

When a shocking crime occurs, a community reaction of outrage and public protest often follows. See H. Weihofen, The Urge to Punish 130–131 (1956). Thereafter the open processes of justice serve an important prophylactic purpose, providing an outlet for community concern, hostility, and emotion. Without an awareness that society's responses to criminal conduct are underway, natural human reactions of outrage and protest are frustrated and may manifest themselves in some form of vengeful "self-help," as indeed they did regularly in the activities of vigilante "committees" on our frontiers. . . .

Civilized societies withdraw both from the victim and the vigilante the enforcement of criminal laws, but they cannot erase from people's consciousness the fundamental, natural yearning to see justice done—or even the urge for retribution. The crucial prophylactic aspects of the administration of justice cannot function in the dark; no community catharsis can occur if justice is "done in a corner [or] in any covert manner." *Supra*, at 567. It is not enough to say that results alone will satiate the natural community desire for "satisfaction." A result considered untoward may undermine public confidence, and where the trial has been concealed from public view an unexpected outcome can cause a reaction that the system at best has failed and at worst has been corrupted. To work effectively, it is important that society's criminal process "satisfy the appearance of justice," *Offutt* v. *United States,* 348 U. S. 11, 14

(1954), and the appearance of justice can best be provided by allowing people to observe it.

. . .

C

From this unbroken, uncontradicted history, supported by reasons as valid today as in centuries past, we are bound to conclude that a presumption of openness inheres in the very nature of a criminal trial under our system of justice. This conclusion is hardly novel; without a direct holding on the issue, the Court has voiced its recognition of it in a variety of contexts over the years. . . .

Despite the history of criminal trials being presumptively open since long before the Constitution, the State presses its contention that neither the Constitution nor the Bill of Rights contains any provision which by its terms guarantees to the public the right to attend criminal trials. Standing alone, this is correct, but there remains the question whether, absent an explicit provision, the Constitution affords protection against exclusion of the public from criminal trials.

III

A

The First Amendment, in conjunction with the Fourteenth, prohibits governments from "abridging the freedom of speech, or of the press; or the right of the people peaceably to assemble, and to petition the Government for a redress of grievances." These expressly guaranteed freedoms share a common core purpose of assuring freedom of communication on matters relating to the functioning of government. Plainly it would be difficult to single out any aspect of government of higher concern and importance to the people than the manner in which criminal trials are conducted; as we have shown, recognition of this pervades the centuries-old history of open trials and the opinions of this Court. *Supra*, at 564–575, and n. 9.

The Bill of Rights was enacted against the backdrop of the long history of trials being presumptively open. Public access to trials was then regarded as an important aspect of the process itself; the conduct of trials "before as many of the people as chuse to attend" was regarded as one of "the inestimable advantages of a free English constitution of government." 1 Journals 106, 107. In guaranteeing freedoms such as those of speech and press, the First Amendment can be read as protecting the right of everyone to attend trials so as to give meaning to those explicit guarantees. "[T]he First Amendment goes beyond protection of the press and the self-expression of individuals to prohibit government from limiting the stock of information from which members of the public may draw." *First National Bank of Boston* v. *Bellotti*, 435 U. S. 765, 783 (1978). Free speech carries with it some freedom to listen. "In a variety of contexts this Court has referred to a First Amendment right to 'receive information and ideas.'" *Kleindienst* v. *Mandel*, 408 U. S. 753, 762 (1972). What this means in the context of trials is that the First Amendment guarantees of speech and press, standing alone, prohibit government from summarily closing courtroom doors which had long been open to the public at the time that Amendment was adopted. . . .

B

The right of access to places traditionally open to the public, as criminal trials have long been, may be seen as assured by the amalgam of the First Amendment guarantees of speech and press; and their affinity to the right of assembly is not without relevance. From the outset, the right of assembly was regarded not only as an independent right but also as a catalyst to augment the free exercise of the other First Amendment rights with which it was deliberately linked by the draftsmen. . . . People assemble in public places not only to speak or to take action, but also to listen, observe, and learn . . .

C

The State argues that the Constitution nowhere spells out a guarantee for the right of the public to attend trials, and that accordingly no such right is protected. The possibility that such a contention could be made did not escape the notice of the Constitution's draftsmen; they were concerned that some important rights might be thought disparaged because not specifically guaranteed. It was even argued that because of this danger no Bill of Rights should be adopted. See, *e. g.,* The

Federalist No. 84 (A. Hamilton). In a letter to Thomas Jefferson in October 1788, James Madison explained why he, although "in favor of a bill of rights," had "not viewed it in an important light" up to that time: "I conceive that in a certain degree . . . the rights in question are reserved by the manner in which the federal powers are granted." He went on to state that "there is great reason to fear that a positive declaration of some of the most essential rights could not be obtained in the requisite latitude." 5 Writings of James Madison 271 (G. Hunt ed. 1904).

But arguments such as the State makes have not precluded recognition of important rights not enumerated. Notwithstanding the appropriate caution against reading into the Constitution rights not explicitly defined, the Court has acknowledged that certain unarticulated rights are implicit in enumerated guarantees. For example, the rights of association and of privacy, the right to be presumed innocent, and the right to be judged by a standard of proof beyond a reasonable doubt in a criminal trial, as well as the right to travel, appear nowhere in the Constitution or Bill of Rights. Yet these important but unarticulated rights have nonetheless been found to share constitutional protection in common with explicit guarantees. The concerns expressed by Madison and others have thus been resolved; fundamental rights, even though not expressly guaranteed, have been recognized by the Court as indispensable to the enjoyment of rights explicitly defined.

We hold that the right to attend criminal trials is implicit in the guarantes of the First Amendment; without the freedom to attend such trials, which people have exercised for centuries, important aspects of freedom of speech and "of the press could be eviscerated." *Branzburg*, 408 U. S., at 681.

. . .

MR. JUSTICE POWELL took no part in the consideration or decision of this case.

MR. JUSTICE WHITE, concurring.

. . .

MR. JUSTICE STEVENS, concurring.

This is a watershed case. Until today the Court has accorded virtually absolute protection to the dissemination of information or ideas, but never before has it squarely held that the acquisition of newsworthy matter is entitled to any constitutional protection whatsoever. . . .

MR. JUSTICE BRENNAN, with whom MR. JUSTICE MARSHALL joins, concurring in the judgment.

. . .

MR. JUSTICE STEWART, concurring in the judgment.

. . .

MR. JUSTICE BLACKMUN, concurring in the judgment.

. . .

II

The Court's ultimate ruling in *Gannett*, with such clarification as is provided by the opinions in this case today, apparently is now to the effect that there is no *Sixth* Amendment right on the part of the public—or the press—to an open hearing on a motion to suppress. I, of course, continue to believe that *Gannett* was in error, both in its interpretation of the Sixth Amendment generally, and in its application to the suppression hearing, for I remain convinced that the right to a public trial is to be found where the Constitution explicitly placed it—in the Sixth Amendment.

The Court, however, has eschewed the Sixth Amendment route. The plurality turns to other possible constitutional sources and invokes a veritable potpourri of them—the Speech Clause of the First Amendment, the Press Clause, the Assembly Clause, the Ninth Amendment, and a cluster of penumbral guarantees recognized in past decisions. This course is troublesome, but it is the route that has been selected and, at least for now, we must live with it. . . .

MR. JUSTICE REHNQUIST, dissenting.

In the Gilbert and Sullivan operetta "Iolanthe," the Lord Chancellor recites:

"The Law is the true embodiment
of everything that's excellent,
It has no kind of fault or flaw,
And I, my Lords, embody the Law."

It is difficult not to derive more than a little of this flavor from the various opinions supporting the judgment in this case. The opinion of THE CHIEF JUSTICE states:

"[H]ere for the first time the Court is asked to decide whether a criminal trial itself may be closed to the public upon the unopposed request of a defendant, without any demonstration that closure is required to protect the defendant's superior right to a fair trial, or that some other overriding consideration requires closure." *Ante*, at 564.

The opinion of MR. JUSTICE BRENNAN states:

"Read with care and in context, our decisions must therefore be understood as holding only that any privilege of access to governmental information is subject to a degree of restraint dictated by the nature of the information and countervailing interests in security or confidentiality." *Ante*, at 586.

For the reasons stated in my separate concurrence in *Gannett Co.* v. *DePasquale*, 443 U. S. 368, 403 (1979), I do not believe that either the First or Sixth Amendment, as made applicable to the States by the Fourteenth, requires that a State's reasons for denying public access to a trial, where both the prosecuting attorney and the defendant have consented to an order of closure approved by the judge, are subject to any additional constitutional review at our hands. And I most certainly do not believe that the Ninth Amendment confers upon us any such power to review orders of state trial judges closing trials in such situations. See *ante*, at 579, n. 15.

We have at present 50 state judicial systems and one federal judicial system in the United States, and our authority to reverse a decision by the highest court of the State is limited to only those occasions when the state decision violates some provision of the United States Constitution. And that authority should be exercised with a full sense that the judges whose decisions we review are making the same effort as we to uphold the Constitution.

. . . to gradually rein in, as this Court has done over the past generation, all of the ultimate decisionmaking power over how justice shall be administered, not merely in the federal system but in each of the 50 States, is a task that no Court consisting of nine persons, however gifted, is equal to. Nor is it desirable that such authority be exercised by such a tiny numerical fragment of the 220 million people who compose the population of this country. . . .

The issue here is not whether the "right" to freedom of the press conferred by the First Amendment to the Constitution overrides the defendant's "right" to a fair trial conferred by other Amendments to the Constitution; it is instead whether any provision in the Constitution may fairly be read to prohibit what the trial judge in the Virginia state-court system did in this case. Being unable to find any such prohibition in the First, Sixth, Ninth, or any other Amendment to the United States Constitution, or in the Constitution itself, I dissent.

New York Times Co. v. Sullivan

376 U. S. 254 (1964)

An advertisement in the *New York Times* included statements, some of them false, about actions that Alabama police had taken against civil rights demonstrators. L. B. Sullivan, who supervised the police, brought a libel action against the newspaper and four civil rights leaders. After he won a jury award in the state courts, a unanimous Supreme Court held that the law applied by the Alabama courts gave insufficient protection to free speech and free press. The Court developed the "actual malice" test for recovering damages in a defamation suit.

MR. JUSTICE BRENNAN delivered the opinion of the Court.

We are required in this case to determine for the first time the extent to which the constitutional protections for speech and press limit a State's power to award damages in a libel action brought by a public official against critics of his official conduct.

Respondent L. B. Sullivan is one of the three elected Commissioners of the City of Montgomery, Alabama. He testified that he was "Commissioner of Public Affairs and the duties are supervision of the Police Department, Fire Department, Department of Cemetery and Department of Scales." He brought this civil libel action against the four individual petitioners, who are Negroes and Alabama clergymen, and against petitioner the New York Times Company, a New York corporation which publishes the New York Times, a daily newspaper. A jury in the Circuit Court of Montgomery County awarded him damages of

$500,000, the full amount claimed, against all the petitioners, and the Supreme Court of Alabama affirmed. 273 Ala. 656, 144 So. 2d 25.

Respondent's complaint alleged that he had been libeled by statements in a full-page advertisement that was carried in the New York Times on March 29, 1960. Entitled "Heed Their Rising Voices," the advertisement began by stating that "As the whole world knows by now, thousands of Southern Negro students are engaged in widespread non-violent demonstrations in positive affirmation of the right to live in human dignity as guaranteed by the U. S. Constitution and the Bill of Rights." It went on to charge that "in their efforts to uphold these guarantees, they are being met by an unprecedented wave of terror by those who would deny and negate that document which the whole world looks upon as setting the pattern for modern freedom. . . ." Succeeding paragraphs purported to illustrate the "wave of terror" by describing certain alleged events. The text concluded with an appeal for funds for three purposes: support of the student movement, "the struggle for the right-to-vote," and the legal defense of Dr. Martin Luther King, Jr., leader of the movement, against a perjury indictment then pending in Montgomery.

The text appeared over the names of 64 persons, many widely known for their activities in public affairs, religion, trade unions, and the performing arts. Below these names, and under a line reading "We in the south who are struggling daily for dignity and freedom warmly endorse this appeal," appeared the names of the four individual petitioners and of 16 other persons, all but two of whom were identified as clergymen in various Southern cities. The advertisement was signed at the bottom of the page by the "Committee to Defend Martin Luther King and the Struggle for Freedom in the South," and the officers of the Committee were listed.

Of the 10 paragraphs of text in the advertisement, the third and a portion of the sixth were the basis of respondent's claim of libel. They read as follows:

Third paragraph:

"In Montgomery, Alabama, after students sang 'My Country, 'Tis of Thee' on the State Capitol steps, their leaders were expelled from school, and truckloads of police armed with shotguns and tear-gas ringed the Alabama State College Campus. When the entire student body protested to state authorities by refusing to re-register, their dining hall was padlocked in an attempt to starve them into submission."

Sixth paragraph:

"Again and again the Southern violators have answered Dr. King's peaceful protests with intimidation and violence. They have bombed his home almost killing his wife and child. They have assaulted his person. They have arrested him seven times—for 'speeding,' 'loitering' and similar 'offenses.' And now they have charged him with 'perjury'—a *felony* under which they could imprison him for *ten years. . . ."*

Although neither of these statements mentions respondent by name, he contended that the word "police" in the third paragraph referred to him as

the Montgomery Commissioner who supervised the Police Department, so that he was being accused of "ringing" the campus with police. He further claimed that the paragraph would be read as imputing to the police, and hence to him, the padlocking of the dining hall in order to starve the students into submission. As to the sixth paragraph, he contended that since arrests are ordinarily made by the police, the statement "They have arrested [Dr. King] seven times" would be read as referring to him; he further contended that the "They" who did the arresting would be equated with the "They" who committed the other described acts and with the "Southern violators." Thus, he argued, the paragraph would be read as accusing the Montgomery police, and hence him, of answering Dr. King's protests with "intimidation and violence," bombing his home, assaulting his person, and charging him with perjury. Respondent and six other Montgomery residents testified that they read some or all of the statements as referring to him in his capacity as Commissioner.

It is uncontroverted that some of the statements contained in the two paragraphs were not accurate descriptions of events which occurred in Montgomery. Although Negro students staged a demonstration on the State Capitol steps, they sang the National Anthem and not "My Country, 'Tis of Thee." Although nine students were expelled by the State Board of Education, this was not for leading the demonstration at the Capitol, but for demanding service at a lunch counter in the Montgomery County Courthouse on another day. Not the entire student body, but most of it, had protested the expulsion, not by refusing to register, but by boycotting classes on a single day; virtually all the students did register for the ensuing semester. The campus dining hall was not padlocked on any occasion, and the only students who may have been barred from eating there were the few who had neither signed a preregistration application nor requested temporary meal tickets. Although the police were deployed near the campus in large numbers on three occasions, they did not at any time "ring" the campus, and they were not called to the campus in connection with the demonstration on the State Capitol steps, as the third paragraph implied. Dr. King had not been arrested seven times, but only four; and although he claimed to have been assaulted some years earlier in connection with his arrest for loitering outside a courtroom, one of the officers who made the arrest denied that there was such an assault.

On the premise that the charges in the sixth paragraph could be read as referring to him, respondent was allowed to prove that he had not participated in the events described. Although Dr. King's home had in fact been bombed twice when his wife and child were there, both of these occasions antedated respondent's tenure as Commissioner, and the police were not only not implicated in the bombings, but had made every effort to apprehend those who were. Three of Dr. King's four arrests took place before respondent became Commissioner. Although Dr. King had in fact been indicted (he was subsequently acquitted) on two counts of perjury, each of which carried a possible five-year sentence, respondent had nothing to do with procuring the indictment.

Respondent made no effort to prove that he suffered actual pecuniary loss as a result of the alleged libel. One of his witnesses, a former employer, testified that if he had believed the statements, he doubted whether he "would want to be associated with anybody who would be a party to such things that are stated in that ad," and that he would not re-employ respondent if he believed "that he allowed the Police Department to do the things that the paper say he did." But neither this witness nor any of the others testified that he had actually believed the statements in their supposed reference to respondent.

The cost of the advertisement was approximately $4800, and it was published by the Times upon an order from a New York advertising agency acting for the signatory Committee. The agency submitted the advertisement with a letter from A. Philip Randolph, Chairman of the Committee, certifying that the persons whose names appeared on the advertisement had given their permission. Mr. Randolph was known to the Times' Advertising Acceptability Department as a responsible person, and in accepting the letter as sufficient proof of authorization it followed its established practice. There was testimony that the copy of the advertisement which accompanied the letter listed only the 64 names appearing under the text,

and that the statement, "We in the south . . . warmly endorse this appeal," and the list of names thereunder, which included those of the individual petitioners, were subsequently added when the first proof of the advertisement was received. Each of the individual petitioners testified that he had not authorized the use of his name, and that he had been unaware of its use until receipt of respondent's demand for a retraction. The manager of the Advertising Acceptability Department testified that he had approved the advertisement for publication because he knew nothing to cause him to believe that anything in it was false, and because it bore the endorsement of "a number of people who are well known and whose reputation" he "had no reason to question." Neither he nor anyone else at the Times made an effort to confirm the accuracy of the advertisement, either by checking it against recent Times news stories relating to some of the described events or by any other means.

Alabama law denies a public officer recovery of punitive damages in a libel action brought on account of a publication concerning his official conduct unless he first makes a written demand for a public retraction and the defendant fails or refuses to comply. Alabama Code, Tit. 7, § 914. Respondent served such a demand upon each of the petitioners. None of the individual petitioners responded to the demand, primarily because each took the position that he had not authorized the use of his name on the advertisement and therefore had not published the statements that respondent alleged had libeled him. The Times did not publish a retraction in response to the demand, but wrote respondent a letter stating, among other things, that "we . . . are somewhat puzzled as to how you think the statements in any way reflect on you," and "you might, if you desire, let us know in what respect you claim that the statements in the advertisement reflect on you." Respondent filed this suit a few days later without answering the letter. The Times did, however, subsequently publish a retraction of the advertisement upon the demand of Governor John Patterson of Alabama, who asserted that the publication charged him with "grave misconduct and . . . improper actions and omissions as Governor of Alabama and Ex-Officio Chairman of the State Board of Education of Alabama." When asked to explain why there had been a retraction for the Governor but not for respondent, the Secretary of the Times testified: "We did that because we didn't want anything that was published by The Times to be a reflection on the State of Alabama and the Governor was, as far as we could see, the embodiment of the State of Alabama and the proper representative of the State and, furthermore, we had by that time learned more of the actual facts which the ad purported to recite and, finally, the ad did refer to the action of the State authorities and the Board of Education presumably of which the Governor is the ex-officio chairman. . . ." On the other hand, he testified that he did not think that "any of the language in there referred to Mr. Sullivan."

The trial judge submitted the case to the jury under instructions that the statements in the advertisement were "libelous per se" and were not privileged, so that petitioners might be held liable if the jury found that they had published the advertisement and that the statements were made "of and concerning" respondent. The jury was instructed that, because the statements were libelous *per se*, "the law . . . implies legal injury from the bare fact of publication itself," "falsity and malice are presumed," "general damages need not be alleged or proved but are presumed," and "punitive damages may be awarded by the jury even though the amount of actual damages is neither found nor shown." An award of punitive damages—as distinguished from "general" damages, which are compensatory in nature—apparently requires proof of actual malice under Alabama law, and the judge charged that "mere negligence or carelessness is not evidence of actual malice or malice in fact, and does not justify an award of exemplary or punitive damages." He refused to charge, however, that the jury must be "convinced" of malice, in the sense of "actual intent" to harm or "gross negligence and recklessness," to make such an award, and he also refused to require that a verdict for respondent differentiate between compensatory and punitive damages. The judge rejected petitioners' contention that his rulings abridged the freedoms of speech and of the press that are guaranteed by the First and Fourteenth Amendments.

In affirming the judgment, the Supreme Court of Alabama sustained the trial judge's rulings and instructions in all respects. . . .

Because of the importance of the constitutional issues involved, we granted the separate petitions for certiorari of the individual petitioners and of the Times. 371 U. S. 946. We reverse the judgment. We hold that the rule of law applied by the Alabama courts is constitutionally deficient for failure to provide the safeguards for freedom of speech and of the press that are required by the First and Fourteenth Amendments in a libel action brought by a public official against critics of his official conduct. We further hold that under the proper safeguards the evidence presented in this case is constitutionally insufficient to support the judgment for respondent.

I.

We may dispose at the outset of two grounds asserted to insulate the judgment of the Alabama courts from constitutional scrutiny. The first is the proposition relied on by the State Supreme Court —that "The Fourteenth Amendment is directed against State action and not private action." That proposition has no application to this case. Although this is a civil lawsuit between private parties, the Alabama courts have applied a state rule of law which petitioners claim to impose invalid restrictions on their constitutional freedoms of speech and press. It matters not that the law has been applied in a civil action and that it is common law only, though supplemented by statute. See, *e. g.,* Alabama Code, Tit. 7, §§ 908–917. The test is not the form in which state power has been applied but, whatever the form, whether such power has in fact been exercised. See *Ex parte Virginia,* 100 U. S. 339, 346–347; *American Federation of Labor* v. *Swing,* 312 U. S. 321.

The second contention is that the constitutional guarantees of freedom of speech and of the press are inapplicable here, at least so far as the Times is concerned, because the allegedly libelous statements were published as part of a paid, "commercial" advertisement. The argument relies on *Valentine* v. *Chrestensen,* 316 U. S. 52, where the

Court held that a city ordinance forbidding street distribution of commercial and business advertising matter did not abridge the First Amendment freedoms, even as applied to a handbill having a commercial message on one side but a protest against certain official action on the other. The reliance is wholly misplaced. The Court in *Chrestensen* reaffirmed the constitutional protection for "the freedom of communicating information and disseminating opinion"; its holding was based upon the factual conclusions that the handbill was "purely commercial advertising" and that the protest against official action had been added only to evade the ordinance.

The publication here was not a "commercial" advertisement in the sense in which the word was used in *Chrestensen*. It communicated information, expressed opinion, recited grievances, protested claimed abuses, and sought financial support on behalf of a movement whose existence and objectives are matters of the highest public interest and concern. See *N. A. A. C. P.* v. *Button*, 371 U.S. 415, 435. That the Times was paid for publishing the advertisement is as immaterial in this connection as is the fact that newspapers and books are sold. . . .

II.

Under Alabama law as applied in this case, a publication is "libelous per se" if the words "tend to injure a person . . . in his reputation" or to "bring [him] into public contempt"; the trial court stated that the standard was met if the words are such as to "injure him in his public office, or impute misconduct to him in his office, or want of official integrity, or want of fidelity to a public trust. . . ." The jury must find that the words were published "of and concerning" the plaintiff, but where the plaintiff is a public official his place in the governmental hierarchy is sufficient evidence to support a finding that his reputation has been affected by statements that reflect upon the agency of which he is in charge. Once "libel per se" has been established, the defendant has no defense as to stated facts unless he can persuade the jury that they were true in all their particulars. . . . Unless he can discharge the burden of proving truth,

general damages are presumed, and may be awarded without proof of pecuniary injury. A showing of actual malice is apparently a prerequisite to recovery of punitive damages, and the defendant may in any event forestall a punitive award by a retraction meeting the statutory requirements. Good motives and belief in truth do not negate an inference of malice, but are relevant only in mitigation of punitive damages if the jury chooses to accord them weight. *Johnson Publishing Co.* v. *Davis, supra*, 271 Ala., at 495, 124 So. 2d, at 458.

The question before us is whether this rule of liability, as applied to an action brought by a public official against critics of his official conduct, abridges the freedom of speech and of the press that is guaranteed by the First and Fourteenth Amendments.

. . .

The general proposition that freedom of expression upon public questions is secured by the First Amendment has long been settled by our decisions. The constitutional safeguard, we have said, "was fashioned to assure unfettered interchange of ideas for the bringing about of political and social changes desired by the people." *Roth* v. *United States*, 354 U. S. 476, 484. . . .

. . .

Thus we consider this case against the background of a profound national commitment to the principle that debate on public issues should be uninhibited, robust, and wide-open, and that it may well include vehement, caustic, and sometimes unpleasantly sharp attacks on government and public officials. See *Terminiello* v. *Chicago*, 337 U. S. 1, 4; *De Jonge* v. *Oregon*, 299 U. S. 353, 365. The present advertisement, as an expression of grievance and protest on one of the major public issues of our time, would seem clearly to qualify for the constitutional protection. The question is whether it forfeits that protection by the falsity of some of its factual statements and by its alleged defamation of respondent.

. . .

Injury to official reputation affords no more

warrant for repressing speech that would otherwise be free than does factual error. Where judicial officers are involved, this Court has held that concern for the dignity and reputation of the courts does not justify the punishment as criminal contempt of criticism of the judge or his decision. *Bridges* v. *California*, 314 U. S. 252. This is true even though the utterance contains "half-truths" and "misinformation." *Pennekamp* v. *Florida*, 328 U. S. 331, 342, 343, n. 5, 345. Such repression can be justified, if at all, only by a clear and present danger of the obstruction of justice. See also *Craig* v. *Harney*, 331 U. S. 367; *Wood* v. *Georgia*, 370 U. S. 375. If judges are to be treated as "men of fortitude, able to thrive in a hardy climate," *Craig* v. *Harney, supra*, 331 U. S., at 376, surely the same must be true of other government officials, such as elected city commissioners. Criticism of their official conduct does not lose its constitutional protection merely because it is effective criticism and hence diminishes their official reputations.

If neither factual error nor defamatory content suffices to remove the constitutional shield from criticism of official conduct, the combination of the two elements is no less inadequate. This is the lesson to be drawn from the great controversy over the Sedition Act of 1798, 1 Stat. 596, which first crystallized a national awareness of the central meaning of the First Amendment. . . .

Although the Sedition Act was never tested in this Court, the attack upon its validity has carried the day in the court of history. Fines levied in its prosecution were repaid by Act of Congress on the ground that it was unconstitutional. See, *e. g.,* Act of July 4, 1840, c. 45, 6 Stat. 802, accompanied by H. R. Rep. No. 86, 26th Cong., 1st Sess. (1840). Calhoun, reporting to the Senate on February 4, 1836, assumed that its invalidity was a matter "which no one now doubts." Report with Senate bill No. 122, 24th Cong., 1st Sess., p. 3. Jefferson, as President, pardoned those who had been convicted and sentenced under the Act and remitted their fines, stating: "I discharged every person under punishment or prosecution under the sedition law, because I considered, and now consider, that law to be a nullity, as absolute and as palpable as if Congress had ordered us to fall down and worship a golden image." . . .

. . .

The constitutional guarantees require, we think, a federal rule that prohibits a public official from recovering damages for a defamatory falsehood relating to his official conduct unless he proves that the statement was made with "actual malice"—that is, with knowledge that it was false or with reckless disregard of whether it was false or not. . . .

III.

We hold today that the Constitution delimits a State's power to award damages for libel in actions brought by public officials against critics of their official conduct. Since this is such an action, the rule requiring proof of actual malice is applicable. While Alabama law apparently requires proof of actual malice for an award of punitive damages, where general damages are concerned malice is "presumed." Such a presumption is inconsistent with the federal rule. . . .

Applying these standards, we consider that the proof presented to show actual malice lacks the convincing clarity which the constitutional standard demands, and hence that it would not constitutionally sustain the judgment for respondent under the proper rule of law. The case of the individual petitioners requires little discussion. Even assuming that they could constitutionally be found to have authorized the use of their names on the advertisement, there was no evidence whatever that they were aware of any erroneous statements or were in any way reckless in that regard. The judgment against them is thus without constitutional support.

As to the Times, we similarly conclude that the facts do not support a finding of actual malice. The statement by the Times' Secretary that, apart from the padlocking allegation, he thought the advertisement was "substantially correct," affords no constitutional warrant for the Alabama Supreme Court's conclusion that it was a "cavalier ignoring of the falsity of the advertisement [from which] the jury could not have but been impressed with the bad faith of The Times, and its maliciousness inferable therefrom." The statement does not indicate malice at the time of the publication; even if the advertisement was not "substantially correct" —although respondent's own proofs tend to show that it was—that opinion was at least a reasonable one, and there was no evidence to impeach the witness' good faith in holding it. The Times' failure to retract upon respondent's demand, although it later retracted upon the demand of Governor Patterson, is likewise not adequate evidence of malice for constitutional purposes. Whether or not a failure to retract may ever constitute such evidence, there are two reasons why it does not here. *First,* the letter written by the Times reflected a reasonable doubt on its part as to whether the advertisement could reasonably be taken to refer to respondent at all. *Second,* it was not a final refusal, since it asked for an explanation on this point—a request that respondent chose to ignore. Nor does the retraction upon the demand of the Governor supply the necessary proof. It may be doubted that a failure to retract which is not itself evidence of malice can retroactively become such by virtue of a retraction subsequently made to another party. But in any event that did not happen here, since the explanation given by the Times' Secretary for the distinction drawn between respondent and the Governor was a reasonable one, the good faith of which was not impeached.

Finally, there is evidence that the Times published the advertisement without checking its accuracy against the news stories in the Times' own files. The mere presence of the stories in the files does not, of course, establish that the Times "knew" the advertisement was false, since the state of mind required for actual malice would have to be brought home to the persons in the Times' organization having responsibility for the publication of the advertisement. With respect to the failure of those persons to make the check, the record shows that they relied upon their knowledge of the good reputation of many of those whose names were listed as sponsors of the advertisement, and upon the letter from A. Philip Randolph, known to them as a responsible individual, certifying that the use of the names was authorized. There was testimony that the persons handling the advertisement saw nothing in it that would render it unacceptable under the Times' policy of rejecting advertisements containing "attacks of a personal character"; their failure to reject it on this ground was not unreasonable. We think the evidence against the Times supports at most a finding of negligence in failing to discover the misstatements, and is constitutionally insufficient to show the recklessness that is required for a finding of actual malice. . . .

The judgment of the Supreme Court of Alabama is reversed and the case is remanded to that court for further proceedings not inconsistent with this opinion.

Reversed and remanded.

MR. JUSTICE BLACK, with whom MR. JUSTICE DOUGLAS joins, concurring.

I concur in reversing this half-million-dollar judgment against the New York Times Company and the four individual defendants. In reversing the Court holds that "the Constitution delimits a State's power to award damages for libel in actions brought by public officials against critics of their official conduct." *Ante,* p. 283. I base my vote to reverse on the belief that the First and Fourteenth Amendments not merely "delimit" a State's power to award damages to "public officials against critics of their official conduct" but completely prohibit a State from exercising such a power. The Court goes on to hold that a State can subject such critics to damages if "actual malice" can be proved against them. "Malice," even as defined by the Court, is an elusive, abstract concept, hard to prove and hard to disprove. The requirement that malice be proved provides at best an evanescent protection for the right critically to discuss public affairs and certainly does not measure up to the sturdy safeguard embodied in the First Amendment. Unlike the Court, therefore, I vote to reverse exclusively on the ground that the Times and the individual defendants had an absolute, unconditional constitutional right to publish in the Times advertisement their criticisms of the Montgomery agencies and officials. . . .

MR. JUSTICE GOLDBERG, with whom MR. JUSTICE DOUGLAS joins, concurring in the result.

. . .

In my view, the First and Fourteenth Amendments to the Constitution afford to the citizen and to the press an absolute, unconditional privilege to criticize official conduct despite the harm which may flow from excesses and abuses. The prized American right "to speak one's mind," cf. *Bridges* v. *California,* 314 U. S. 252, 270, about public officials and affairs needs "breathing space to survive," *N. A. A. C. P.* v. *Button,* 371 U. S. 415, 433. The right should not depend upon a probing by the jury of the motivation of the citizen or press. . . .

This is not to say that the Constitution protects defamatory statements directed against the pri-

vate conduct of a public official or private citizen. Freedom of press and of speech insures that government will respond to the will of the people and that changes may be obtained by peaceful means. Purely private defamation has little to do with the political ends of a self-governing society. The imposition of liability for private defamation does not abridge the freedom of public speech or any other freedom protected by the First Amendment.

Hustler Magazine v. Falwell

108 S.Ct. 876 (1988)

Jerry Falwell, a nationally known minister and commentator on politics and public affairs, filed a libel suit against the *Hustler* magazine and its publisher, Larry C. Flynt. The suit sought to recover damages for libel and intentional infliction of emotional distresses arising from the publication of an advertisement parody that displayed Falwell as a drunkard having sex with his mother in an outhouse. The jury rejected the libel claim on the ground that the parody was not believable, but ruled in Falwell's favor on the emotional distress claim. The Fourth Circuit affirmed.

Chief Justice REHNQUIST delivered the opinion of the Court.

Petitioner Hustler Magazine, Inc., is a magazine of nationwide circulation. Respondent Jerry Falwell, a nationally known minister who has been active as a commentator on politics and public affairs, sued petitioner and its publisher, petitioner Larry Flynt, to recover damages for invasion of privacy, libel, and intentional infliction of emotional distress. The District Court directed a verdict against respondent on the privacy claim, and submitted the other two claims to a jury. The jury found for petitioners on the defamation claim, but found for respondent on the claim for intentional infliction of emotional distress and awarded damages. We now consider whether this award is consistent with the First and Fourteenth Amendments of the United States Constitution.

The inside front cover of the November 1983 issue of Hustler Magazine featured a "parody" of an advertisement for Campari Liqueur that contained the name and picture of respondent and

was entitled "Jerry Falwell talks about his first time." This parody was modeled after actual Campari ads that included interviews with various celebrities about their "first times." Although it was apparent by the end of each interview that this meant the first time they sampled Campari, the ads clearly played on the sexual double entendre of the general subject of "first times." Copying the form and layout of these Campari ads, Hustler's editors chose respondent as the featured celebrity and drafted an alleged "interview" with him in which he states that his "first time" was during a drunken incestuous rendezvous with his mother in an outhouse. The Hustler parody portrays respondent and his mother as drunk and immoral, and suggests that respondent is a hypocrite who preaches only when he is drunk. In small print at the bottom of the page, the ad contains the disclaimer, "ad parody—not to be taken seriously." The magazine's table of contents also lists the ad as "Fiction; Ad and Personality Parody."

Soon after the November issue of Hustler became available to the public, respondent brought this diversity action in the United States District Court for the Western District of Virginia against Hustler Magazine, Inc., Larry C. Flynt, and Flynt Distributing Co. Respondent stated in his complaint that publication of the ad parody in Hustler entitled him to recover damages for libel, invasion of privacy, and intentional infliction of emotional distress. The case proceeded to trial. At the close of the evidence, the District Court granted a directed verdict for petitioners on the invasion of privacy claim. The jury then found against respondent on the libel claim, specifically finding that the ad parody could not "reasonably be understood as describing actual facts about [respondent] or actual events in which [he] participated." App. to Pet. for Cert. C1. The jury ruled for respondent on the intentional infliction of emotional distress claim, however, and stated that he should be awarded $100,000 in compensatory damages, as well as $50,000 each in punitive damages from petitioners. Petitioners' motion for judgment notwithstanding the verdict was denied.

On appeal, the United States Court of Appeals for the Fourth Circuit affirmed the judgment against petitioners. *Falwell* v. *Flynt*, 797 F.2d 1270 (CA4 1986). The court rejected petitioners' argument that the "actual malice" standard of *New York Times Co.* v. *Sullivan*, 376 U. S. 254 (1964), must be met before respondent can recover for emotional distress. The court agreed that because respondent is concededly a public figure, petitioners are "entitled to the same level of first amendment protection in the claim for intentional infliction of emotional distress that they received in [respondent's] claim for libel." 797 F.2d, at 1274. But this does not mean that a literal application of the actual malice rule is appropriate in the context of an emotional distress claim. In the court's view, the *New York Times* decision emphasized the constitutional importance not of the falsity of the statement or the defendant's disregard for the truth, but of the heightened level of culpability embodied in the requirement of "knowing . . . or reckless" conduct. Here, the *New York Times* standard is satisfied by the state-law requirement, and the jury's finding, that the defendants have acted intentionally or recklessly. The Court of Appeals then went on to reject the

contention that because the jury found that the ad parody did not describe actual facts about respondent, the ad was an opinion that is protected by the First Amendment. As the court put it, this was "irrelevant," as the issue is "whether [the ad's] publication was sufficiently outrageous to constitute intentional infliction of emotional distress." *Id.*, at 1276. Petitioners then filed a petition for rehearing en banc, but this was denied by a divided court. Given the importance of the constitutional issues involved, we granted certiorari.

This case presents us with a novel question involving First Amendment limitations upon a State's authority to protect its citizens from the intentional infliction of emotional distress. We must decide whether a public figure may recover damages for emotional harm caused by the publication of an ad parody offensive to him, and doubtless gross and repugnant in the eyes of most. Respondent would have us find that a State's interest in protecting public figures from emotional distress is sufficient to deny First Amendment protection to speech that is patently offensive and is intended to inflict emotional injury, even when that speech could not reasonably have been interpreted as stating actual facts about the public figure involved. This we decline to do.

At the heart of the First Amendment is the recognition of the fundamental importance of the free flow of ideas and opinions on matters of public interest and concern. "[T]he freedom to speak one's mind is not only an aspect of individual liberty—and thus a good unto itself—but also is essential to the common quest for truth and the vitality of society as a whole." *Bose Corp.* v. *Consumers Union of United States, Inc.*, 466 U. S. 485, 503–504 (1984). We have therefore been particularly vigilant to ensure that individual expressions of ideas remain free from governmentally imposed sanctions. The First Amendment recognizes no such thing as a "false" idea. *Gertz* v. *Robert Welch, Inc.*, 418 U.S. 323, 339 (1974). As Justice Holmes wrote, "[W]hen men have realized that time has upset many fighting faiths, they may come to believe even more than they believe the very foundations of their own conduct that the ultimate good desired is better reached by free trade in ideas—that the best test of truth is the power of the thought to get itself accepted in the competition of the market . . . ." *Abrams* v. *United States*, 250 U. S. 616, 630 (1919) (dissenting opinion).

The sort of robust political debate encouraged by the First Amendment is bound to produce speech that is critical of those who hold public office or those public figures who are "intimately involved in the resolution of important public questions or, by reason of their fame, shape events in areas of concern to society at large." *Associated Press* v. *Walker*, decided with *Curtis Publishing Co.* v. *Butts*, 388 U.S. 130, 164 (1967) (Warren, C.J., concurring in result). Justice Frankfurter put it succinctly in *Baumgartner* v. *United States*, 322 U.S. 665, 673–674 (1944), when he said that "[o]ne of the prerogatives of American citizenship is the right to criticize public men and measures." Such criticism, inevitably, will not always be reasoned or moderate; public figures as well as public officials will be subject to "vehement, caustic, and sometimes unpleasantly sharp attacks," *New York Times*, *supra*, 376 U.S., at 270. "[T]he candidate who vaunts his spotless record and sterling integrity cannot convincingly cry 'Foul!' when an opponent or an industrious reporter attempts to demonstrate the contrary." *Monitor Patriot Co.* v. *Roy*, 401 U.S. 265, 274 (1971).

Of course, this does not mean that *any* speech about a public figure is immune from sanction in the form of damages. Since *New York Times Co.* v. *Sullivan*, *supra*, we have consistently ruled that a public figure may hold a speaker liable for the damage to reputation caused by publication of a defamatory falsehood, but only if the statement was made "with knowledge that it was false or with reckless disregard of whether it was false or not." *Id.*, 376 U.S., at 279–280. False statements of fact are particularly valueless; they interfere with the truth-seeking function of the marketplace of ideas, and they cause damage to an individual's reputation that cannot easily be repaired by counterspeech, however persuasive or effective. See *Gertz*, 418 U.S., at 340, 344, n. 9. But even though falsehoods have little value in and of themselves, they are "nevertheless inevitable in free debate," *id.*, at 340, and a rule that would impose strict liability on a publisher for false factual assertions would have an undoubted "chilling" effect on

speech relating to public figures that does have constitutional value. "Freedoms of expression require 'breathing space.'" *Philadelphia Newspapers, Inc.* v. *Hepps*, 475 U.S. 767, 772 (1986) (quoting *New York Times*, 376 U.S., at 272). This breathing space is provided by a constitutional rule that allows public figures to recover for libel or defamation only when they can prove *both* that the statement was false and that the statement was made with the requisite level of culpability.

Respondent argues, however, that a different standard should apply in this case because here the State seeks to prevent not reputational damage, but the severe emotional distress suffered by the person who is the subject of an offensive publication. Cf. *Zacchini* v. *Scripps-Howard Broadcasting Co.*, 433 U.S. 562 (1977) (ruling that the "actual malice" standard does not apply to the tort of appropriation of a right of publicity). In respondent's view, and in the view of the Court of Appeals, so long as the utterance was intended to inflict emotional distress, was outrageous, and did in fact inflict serious emotional distress, it is of no constitutional import whether the statement was a fact or an opinion, or whether it was true or false. It is the intent to cause injury that is the gravamen of the tort, and the State's interest in preventing emotional harm simply outweighs whatever interest a speaker may have in speech of this type.

Generally speaking the law does not regard the intent to inflict emotional distress as one which should receive much solicitude, and it is quite understandable that most if not all jurisdictions have chosen to make it civilly culpable where the conduct in question is sufficiently "outrageous." But in the world of debate about public affairs, many things done with motives that are less than admirable are protected by the First Amendment. In *Garrison* v. *Louisiana*, 379 U.S. 64 (1964), we held that even when a speaker or writer is motivated by hatred or ill-will his expression was protected by the First Amendment:

"Debate on public issues will not be uninhibited if the speaker must run the risk that it will be proved in court that he spoke out of hatred; even if he did speak out of hatred, utterances honestly believed contribute to the free interchange of ideas and the ascertainment of truth." *Id.*, at 73.

Thus while such a bad motive may be deemed controlling for purposes of tort liability in other areas of the law, we think the First Amendment prohibits such a result in the area of public debate about public figures.

Were we to hold otherwise, there can be little doubt that political cartoonists and satirists would be subjected to damages awards without any showing that their work falsely defamed its subject. Webster's defines a caricature as "the deliberately distorted picturing or imitating of a person, literary style, etc. by exaggerating features or mannerisms for satirical effect." Webster's New Unabridged Twentieth Century Dictionary of the English Language 275 (2d ed. 1979). The appeal of the political cartoon or caricature is often based on exploration of unfortunate physical traits or politically embarrassing events—an exploration often calculated to injure the feelings of the subject of the portrayal. The art of the cartoonist is often not reasoned or evenhanded, but slashing and onesided. One cartoonist expressed the nature of the art in these words:

"The political cartoon is a weapon of attack, of scorn and ridicule and satire; it is least effective when it tries to pat some politician on the back. It is usually as welcome as a bee sting and is always controversial in some quarters." Long, The Political Cartoon: Journalism's Strongest Weapon, The Quill, 56, 57 (Nov. 1962).

Several famous examples of this type of intentionally injurious speech were drawn by Thomas Nast, probably the greatest American cartoonist to date, who was associated for many years during the post-Civil War era with Harper's Weekly. In the pages of that publication Nast conducted a graphic vendetta against William M. "Boss" Tweed and his corrupt associates in New York City's "Tweed Ring." It has been described by one historian of the subject as "a sustained attack which in its passion and effectiveness stands alone in the history of American graphic art." M. Keller, The Art and Politics of Thomas Nast 177 (1968). Another writer explains that the success of the Nast car-

toon was achieved "because of the emotional impact of its presentation. It continuously goes beyond the bounds of good taste and conventional manners." C. Press, The Political Cartoon 251 (1981).

Despite their sometimes caustic nature, from the early cartoon portraying George Washington as an ass down to the present day, graphic depictions and satirical cartoons have played a prominent role in public and political debate. Nast's castigation of the Tweed Ring, Walt McDougall's characterization of presidential candidate James G. Blaine's banquet with the millionaires at Delmonico's as "The Royal Feast of Belshazzar," and numerous other efforts have undoubtedly had an effect on the course and outcome of contemporaneous debate. Lincoln's tall, gangling posture, Teddy Roosevelt's glasses and teeth, and Franklin D. Roosevelt's jutting jaw and cigarette holder have been memorialized by political cartoons with an effect that could not have been obtained by the photographer or the portrait artist. From the viewpoint of history it is clear that our political discourse would have been considerably poorer without them.

Respondent contends, however, that the caricature in question here was so "outrageous" as to distinguish it from more traditional political cartoons. There is no doubt that the caricature of respondent and his mother published in Hustler is at best a distant cousin of the political cartoons described above, and a rather poor relation at that. If it were possible by laying down a principled standard to separate the one from the other, public discourse would probably suffer little or no harm. But we doubt that there is any such standard, and we are quite sure that the pejorative description "outrageous" does not supply one. "Outrageousness" in the area of political and social discourse has an inherent subjectiveness about it which would allow a jury to impose liability on the basis of the jurors' tastes or views, or perhaps on the basis of their dislike of a particular expression. An "outrageousness" standard thus runs afoul of our longstanding refusal to allow damages to be awarded because the speech in question may have an adverse emotional impact on the audience. See *NAACP* v. *Claiborne Hard-*

ware Co., 458 U.S. 886, 910 (1982) ("Speech does not lose its protected character . . . simply because it may embarrass others or coerce them into action"). And, as we stated in *FCC* v. *Pacifica Foundation*, 438 U.S. 726 (1978):

"[T]he fact that society may find speech offensive is not a sufficient reason for suppressing it. Indeed, if it is the speaker's opinion that gives offense, that consequence is a reason for according it constitutional protection. For it is a central tenet of the First Amendment that the government must remain neutral in the marketplace of ideas." *Id.*, at 745–746.

See also *Street* v. *New York*, 394 U.S. 576, 592 (1969) ("It is firmly settled that . . . the public expression of ideas may not be prohibited merely because the ideas are themselves offensive to some of their hearers").

Admittedly, these oft-repeated First Amendment principles, like other principles, are subject to limitations. We recognized in *Pacifica Foundation*, that speech that is "'vulgar,' 'offensive,' and 'shocking'" is "not entitled to absolute constitutional protection under all circumstances." 438 U.S., at 747. In *Chaplinsky* v. *New Hampshire*, 315 U.S. 568 (1942), we held that a state could lawfully punish an individual for the use of insulting "'fighting' words—those which by their very utterance inflict injury or tend to incite an immediate breach of the peace." *Id.*, at 571–572. These limitations are but recognition of the observation in *Dun & Bradstreet, Inc.* v. *Greenmoss Builders, Inc.*, 472 U.S. 749, 758 (1985), that this Court has "long recognized that not all speech is of equal First Amendment importance." But the sort of expression involved in this case does not seem to us to be governed by any exception to the general First Amendment principles stated above.

We conclude that public figures and public officials may not recover for the tort of intentional infliction of emotional distress by reason of publications such as the one here at issue without showing in addition that the publication contains a false statement of fact which was made with "actual malice," *i.e.*, with knowledge that the statement was false or with reckless disregard as to whether or not it was true. This is not merely a

"blind application" of the *New York Times* standard, see *Time, Inc.* v. *Hill*, 385 U.S. 374, 390 (1967), it reflects our considered judgment that such a standard is necessary to give adequate "breathing space" to the freedoms protected by the First Amendment.

Here it is clear that respondent Falwell is a "public figure" for purposes of First Amendment law. The jury found against respondent on his libel claim when it decided that the Hustler ad parody could not "reasonably be understood as describing actual facts about [respondent] or actual events in which [he] participated." App. to Pet. for Cert. C1. The Court of Appeals interpreted the jury's finding to be that the ad parody "was not reasonably believable," 797 F.2d, at 1278, and in accordance with our custom we accept this finding. Respondent is thus relegated to his claim for damages awarded by the jury for the intentional infliction of emotional distress by "outrageous" conduct. But for reasons heretofore stated this claim cannot, consistently with the First Amendment, form a basis for the award of damages when the conduct in question is the publication of a caricature such as the ad parody involved here. The judgment of the Court of Appeals is accordingly

Reversed.

Justice KENNEDY took no part in the consideration or decision of this case.

Justice WHITE, concurring in the judgment.

As I see it, the decision in *New York Times* v. *Sullivan*, 376 U.S. 254 (1964), has little to do with this case, for here the jury found that the ad contained no assertion of fact. But I agree with the Court that the judgment below, which penalized the publication of the parody, cannot be squared with the First Amendment.

Roth v. United States

354 U.S. 476 (1957)

In this decision, the Supreme Court for the first time sets forth the major doctrines regarding obscenity. Two cases are involved. The *Roth* case (referred to as No. 582) concerns the constitutionality of a federal statute used to convict Roth for mailing an obscene book and obscene circulars and advertising. The companion case, *Alberts* v. *California* (No. 61), deals with a California law that made it a misdemeanor to keep for sale, or to advertise, material that is "obscene or indecent."

MR. JUSTICE BRENNAN delivered the opinion of the Court.

The constitutionality of a criminal obscenity statute is the question in each of these cases. In *Roth*, the primary constitutional question is whether the federal obscenity statute violates the provision of the First Amendment that "Congress shall make no law . . . abridging the freedom of speech, or of the press. . . ." In *Alberts*, the primary constitutional question is whether the obscenity provisions of the California Penal Code invade the freedoms of speech and press as they may be incorporated in the liberty protected from state action by the Due Process Clause of the Fourteenth Amendment.

Other constitutional questions are: whether these statutes violate due process, because too vague to support conviction for crime; whether power to punish speech and press offensive to decency and morality is in the States alone, so that the federal obscenity statute violates the Ninth and Tenth Amendments (raised in *Roth);* and whether Congress, by enacting the federal obscenity statute, under the power delegated by Art. I, § 8, cl. 7, to establish post offices and post roads, pre-empted the regulation of the subject matter (raised in *Alberts).*

Roth conducted a business in New York in the publication and sale of books, photographs and magazines. He used circulars and advertising matter to solicit sales. He was convicted by a jury in the District Court for the Southern District of New York upon 4 counts of a 26-count indictment charging him with mailing obscene circulars and advertising, and an obscene book, in violation of

the federal obscenity statute. His conviction was affirmed by the Court of Appeals for the Second Circuit. We granted certiorari.

Alberts conducted a mail-order business from Los Angeles. He was convicted by the Judge of the Municipal Court of the Beverly Hills Judicial District (having waived a jury trial) under a misdemeanor complaint which charged him with lewdly keeping for sale obscene and indecent books, and with writing, composing and publishing an obscene advertisement of them, in violation of the California Penal Code. The conviction was affirmed by the Appellate Department of the Superior Court of the State of California in and for the County of Los Angeles. We noted probable jurisdiction.

The dispositive question is whether obscenity is utterance within the area of protected speech and press. Although this is the first time the question has been squarely presented to this Court, either under the First Amendment or under the Fourteenth Amendment, expressions found in numerous opinions indicate that this Court has always assumed that obscenity is not protected by the freedoms of speech and press. *Ex parte Jackson*, 96 U. S. 727, 736–737; *United States* v. *Chase*, 135 U. S. 255, 261; *Robertson* v. *Baldwin*, 165 U. S. 275, 281; *Public Clearing House* v. *Coyne*, 194 U. S. 497, 508; *Hoke* v. *United States*, 227 U. S. 308, 322; *Near* v. *Minnesota*, 283 U. S. 697, 716; *Chaplinsky* v. *New Hampshire*, 315 U. S. 568, 571–572; *Hannegan* v. *Esquire, Inc.*, 327 U. S. 146, 158; *Winters* v. *New York*, 333 U. S. 507, 510; *Beauharnais* v. *Illinois*, 343 U. S. 250, 266.

The guaranties of freedom of expression in

effect in 10 of the 14 States which by 1792 had ratified the Constitution, gave no absolute protection for every utterance. Thirteen of the 14 States provided for the prosecution of libel, and all of those States made either blasphemy or profanity, or both, statutory crimes. As early as 1712, Massachusetts made it criminal to publish "any filthy, obscene, or profane song, pamphlet, libel or mock sermon" in imitation or mimicking of religious services. Acts and Laws of the Province of Mass. Bay, c. CV, § 8 (1712), Mass. Bay Colony Charters & Laws 399 (1814). Thus, profanity and obscenity were related offenses.

In light of this history, it is apparent that the unconditional phrasing of the First Amendment was not intended to protect every utterance. This phrasing did not prevent this Court from concluding that libelous utterances are not within the area of constitutionally protected speech. *Beauharnais* v. *Illinois*, 343 U. S. 250, 266. At the time of the adoption of the First Amendment, obscenity law was not as fully developed as libel law, but there is sufficiently contemporaneous evidence to show that obscenity, too, was outside the protection intended for speech and press.

. . . implicit in the history of the First Amendment is the rejection of obscenity as utterly without redeeming social importance. This rejection for that reason is mirrored in the universal judgment that obscenity should be restrained, reflected in the international agreement of over 50 nations, in the obscenity laws of all of the 48 States, and in the 20 obscenity laws enacted by the Congress from 1842 to 1956. . . . We hold that obscenity is not within the area of constitutionally protected speech or press.

. . .

However, sex and obscenity are not synonymous. Obscene material is material which deals with sex in a manner appealing to prurient interest. The portrayal of sex, *e.g.*, in art, literature and scientific works, is not itself sufficient reason to deny material the constitutional protection of freedom of speech and press. Sex, a great and mysterious motive force in human life, has indisputably been a subject of absorbing interest to mankind through the ages; it is one of the vital problems of human interest and public concern. . . .

The early leading standard of obscenity allowed material to be judged merely by the effect of an isolated excerpt upon particularly susceptible persons. *Regina* v. *Hicklin*, [1868] L. R. 3 Q. B. 360. Some American courts adopted this standard but later decisions have rejected it and substituted this test: whether to the average person, applying contemporary community standards, the dominant theme of the material taken as a whole appeals to prurient interest. The *Hicklin* test, judging obscenity by the effect of isolated passages upon the most susceptible persons, might well encompass material legitimately treating with sex, and so it must be rejected as unconstitutionally restrictive of the freedoms of speech and press. On the other hand, the substituted standard provides safeguards adequate to withstand the charge of constitutional infirmity.

Both trial courts below sufficiently followed the proper standard. Both courts used the proper definition of obscenity. In addition, in the *Alberts* case, in ruling on a motion to dismiss, the trial judge indicated that, as the trier of facts, he was judging each item as a whole as it would affect the normal person, and in *Roth*, the trial judge instructed the jury as follows:

". . . The test is not whether it would arouse sexual desires or sexual impure thoughts in those comprising a particular segment of the community, the young, the immature or the highly prudish or would leave another segment, the scientific or highly educated or the so-called worldly-wise and sophisticated indifferent and unmoved. . . .

"The test in each case is the effect of the book, picture or publication considered as a whole, not upon any particular class, but upon all those whom it is likely to reach. In other words, you determine its impact upon the average person in the community. The books, pictures and circulars must be judged as a whole, in their entire context, and you are not to consider detached or separate portions in reaching a conclusion. You judge the circulars, pictures and publications which have been put in evidence by present-day standards of the community. You may ask yourselves does it offend the common conscience of the community by present-day standards.

. . .

"In this case, ladies and gentlemen of the jury,

you and you alone are the exclusive judges of what the common conscience of the community is, and in determining that conscience you are to consider the community as a whole, young and old, educated and uneducated, the religious and the irreligious—men, women and children."

It is argued that the statutes do not provide reasonably ascertainable standards of guilt and therefore violate the constitutional requirements of due process. *Winters* v. *New York*, 333 U. S. 507. The federal obscenity statute makes punishable the mailing of material that is "obscene, lewd, lascivious, or filthy . . . or other publication of an indecent character." The California statute makes punishable, *inter alia*, the keeping for sale or advertising material that is "obscene or indecent." The thrust of the argument is that these words are not sufficiently precise because they do not mean the same thing to all people, all the time, everywhere.

Many decisions have recognized that these terms of obscenity statutes are not precise. This Court, however, has consistently held that lack of precision is not itself offensive to the requirements of due process. ". . . [T]he Constitution does not require impossible standards"; all that is required is that the language "conveys sufficiently definite warning as to the proscribed conduct when measured by common understanding and practices. . . ." *United States* v. *Petrillo*, 332 U. S. 1, 7–8. . . .

In summary, then, we hold that these statutes, applied according to the proper standard for judging obscenity, do not offend constitutional safeguards against convictions based upon protected material, or fail to give men in acting adequate notice of what is prohibited.

. . .

The judgments are

Affirmed.

MR. CHIEF JUSTICE WARREN, concurring in the result.

I agree with the result reached by the Court in these cases, but, because we are operating in a field of expression and because broad language used here may eventually be applied to the arts and sciences and freedom of communication gen-erally, I would limit our decision to the facts before us and to the validity of the statutes in question as applied.

. . .

MR. JUSTICE HARLAN, concurring in the result in No. 61, and dissenting in No. 582.

I regret not to be able to join the Court's opinion. I cannot do so because I find lurking beneath its disarming generalizations a number of problems which not only leave me with serious misgivings as to the future effect of today's decisions, but which also, in my view, call for different results in these two cases.

I.

My basic difficulties with the Court's opinion are threefold. First, the opinion paints with such a broad brush that I fear it may result in a loosening of the tight reins which state and federal courts should hold upon the enforcement of obscenity statutes. Second, the Court fails to discriminate between the different factors which, in my opinion, are involved in the constitutional adjudication of state and federal obscenity cases. Third, relevant distinctions between the two obscenity statutes here involved, and the Court's own definition of "obscenity," are ignored.

. . . Since those standards do not readily lend themselves to generalized definitions, the constitutional problem in the last analysis becomes one of particularized judgments which appellate courts must make for themselves.

I do not think that reviewing courts can escape this responsibility by saying that the trier of the facts, be it a jury or a judge, has labeled the questioned matter as "obscene," for, if "obscenity" is to be suppressed, the question whether a particular work is of that character involves not really an issue of fact but a question of constitutional *judgment* of the most sensitive and delicate kind. Many juries might find that Joyce's "Ulysses" or Bocaccio's "Decameron" was obscene, and yet the conviction of a defendant for selling either book would raise, for me, the gravest constitutional problems, for no such verdict could convince me, without more, that these books are "utterly without redeeming social importance." In short, I do not understand how the Court can resolve the constitutional problems now before it without making its own independent judgment upon the character of the material upon which these convictions were based. I am very much afraid that the broad manner in which the Court has decided these cases will tend to obscure the peculiar responsibilities resting on state and federal courts in this field and encourage them to rely on easy labeling and jury verdicts as a substitute for facing up to the tough individual problems of constitutional judgment involved in every obscenity case.

. . .

II.

I concur in the judgment of the Court in No. 61, *Alberts* v. *California.*

The question in this case is whether the defendant was deprived of liberty without due process of law when he was convicted for selling certain materials found by the judge to be obscene because they would have a "tendency to deprave or corrupt its readers by exciting lascivious thoughts or arousing lustful desire."

In judging the constitutionality of this conviction, we should remember that our function in reviewing state judgments under the Fourteenth Amendment is a narrow one. We do not decide whether the policy of the State is wise, or whether it is based on assumptions scientifically substantiated. We can inquire only whether the state action so subverts the fundamental liberties implicit in the Due Process Clause that it cannot be sustained as a rational exercise of power. . . .

What, then, is the purpose of this California statute? Clearly the state legislature has made the judgment that printed words *can* "deprave or corrupt" the reader—that words can incite to antisocial or immoral action. The assumption seems to be that the distribution of certain types of literature will induce criminal or immoral sexual conduct. It is well known, of course, that the validity of this assumption is a matter of dispute among critics, sociologists, psychiatrists, and penologists. There is a large school of thought, particularly in the scientific community, which denies any causal connection between the reading

of pornography and immorality, crime, or delinquency. Others disagree. Clearly it is not our function to decide this question. That function belongs to the state legislature. Nothing in the Constitution requires California to accept as truth the most advanced and sophisticated psychiatric opinion. It seems to me clear that it is not irrational, in our present state of knowledge, to consider that pornography can induce a type of sexual conduct which a State may deem obnoxious to the moral fabric of society. In fact the very division of opinion on the subject counsels us to respect the choice made by the State.

. . .

III.

I dissent in No. 582, *Roth* v. *United States.*

We are faced here with the question whether the federal obscenity statute, as construed and applied in this case, violates the First Amendment to the Constitution. To me, this question is of quite a different order than one where we are dealing with state legislation under the Fourteenth Amendment. I do not think it follows that state and federal powers in this area are the same, and that just because the State may suppress a particular utterance, it is automatically permissible for the Federal Government to do the same. . . .

The Federal Government has, for example, power to restrict seditious speech directed against it, because that Government certainly has the substantive authority to protect itself against revolution. Cf. *Pennsylvania* v. *Nelson,* 350 U. S. 497. But in dealing with obscenity we are faced with the converse situation, for the interests which obscenity statutes purportedly protect are primarily entrusted to the care, not of the Federal Government, but of the States. Congress has no substantive power over sexual morality. Such powers as the Federal Government has in this field are but incidental to its other powers, here the postal power, and are not of the same nature as those possessed by the States, which bear direct responsibility for the protection of the local moral fabric. . . .

Not only is the federal interest in protecting the Nation against pornography attenuated, but the dangers of federal censorship in this field are far greater than anything the States may do. . . . it seems to me that no overwhelming danger to our freedom to experiment and to gratify our tastes in literature is likely to result from the suppression of a borderline book in one of the States, so long as there is no uniform nation-wide suppression of the book, and so long as other States are free to experiment with the same or bolder books.

Quite a different situation is presented, however, where the Federal Government imposes the ban. The danger is perhaps not great if the people of one State, through their legislature, decide that "Lady Chatterley's Lover" goes so far beyond the acceptable standards of candor that it will be deemed offensive and non-sellable, for the State next door is still free to make its own choice. At least we do not have one uniform standard. But the dangers to free thought and expression are truly great if the Federal Government imposes a blanket ban over the Nation on such a book. The prerogative of the States to differ on their ideas of morality will be destroyed, the ability of States to experiment will be stunted. The fact that the people of one State cannot read some of the works of D. H. Lawrence seems to me, if not wise or desirable, at least acceptable. But that no person in the United States should be allowed to do so seems to me to be intolerable, and violative of both the letter and spirit of the First Amendment.

. . .

MR. JUSTICE DOUGLAS, with whom MR. JUSTICE BLACK concurs, dissenting.

When we sustain these convictions, we make the legality of a publication turn on the purity of thought which a book or tract instills in the mind of the reader. I do not think we can approve that standard and be faithful to the command of the First Amendment, which by its terms is a restraint on Congress and which by the Fourteenth is a restraint on the States.

. . .

By these standards punishment is inflicted for thoughts provoked, not for overt acts nor antisocial conduct. This test cannot be squared with our decisions under the First Amendment. Even the ill-starred *Dennis* case conceded that speech to be punishable must have some relation to action which could be penalized by government. *Dennis v. United States*, 341 U. S. 494, 502–511. Cf. Chafee, The Blessings of Liberty (1956), p. 69. This issue cannot be avoided by saying that obscenity is not protected by the First Amendment. The question remains, what is the constitutional test of obscenity?

The tests by which these convictions were obtained require only the arousing of sexual thoughts. Yet the arousing of sexual thoughts and desires happens every day in normal life in dozens of ways. Nearly 30 years ago a questionnaire sent to college and normal school women graduates asked what things were most stimulating sexually. Of 409 replies, 9 said "music"; 18 said "pictures"; 29 said "dancing"; 40 said "drama"; 95 said "books"; and 218 said "man." Alpert, Judicial Censorship of Obscene Literature, 52 Harv. L. Rev. 40, 73.

The test of obscenity the Court endorses today gives the censor free range over a vast domain. To allow the State to step in and punish mere speech or publication that the judge or the jury thinks has an *undesirable* impact on thoughts but that is not shown to be a part of unlawful action is drastically to curtail the First Amendment. . . .

The standard of what offends "the common conscience of the community" conflicts, in my judgment, with the command of the First Amendment that "Congress shall make no law . . . abridging the freedom of speech, or of the press." Certainly that standard would not be an acceptable one if religion, economics, politics or philosophy were involved. How does it become a constitutional standard when literature treating with sex is concerned?

Any test that turns on what is offensive to the community's standards is too loose, too capricious, too destructive of freedom of expression to be squared with the First Amendment. Under that test, juries can censor, suppress, and punish what they don't like, provided the matter relates to "sexual impurity" or has a tendency "to excite lustful thoughts." This is community censorship in one of its worst forms. It creates a regime where in the battle between the literati and the Philistines, the Philistines are certain to win. If experience in this field teaches anything, it is that "censorship of obscenity has almost always been both irrational and indiscriminate." Lockhart & McClure, *op. cit. supra*, at 371. The test adopted here accentuates that trend.

. . .

Freedom of expression can be suppressed if, and to the extent that, it is so closely brigaded with illegal action as to be an inseparable part of it. *Giboney* v. *Empire Storage Co.*, 336 U. S. 490, 498; *Labor Board* v. *Virginia Power Co.*, 314 U. S. 469, 477–478. As a people, we cannot afford to relax

that standard. For the test that suppresses a cheap tract today can suppress a literary gem tomorrow. All it need do is to incite a lascivious thought or arouse a lustful desire. The list of books that judges or juries can place in that category is endless.

I would give the broad sweep of the First Amendment full support. I have the same confidence in the ability of our people to reject noxious literature as I have in their capacity to sort out the true from the false in theology, economics, politics, or any other field.

Miller v. California

413 U.S. 15 (1973)

After thrashing about in a number of cases on obscenity and pornography, the Court in this case sets forth general principles that have helped to guide subsequent decisions. An interesting feature of this case is that Justice Brennan, author of *Roth* v. *United States* and several other decisions attempting to explain the principles used by courts to restrict obscenity, dissents in both *Miller* and the companion case, *Paris Adult Theatre I.* In those dissents Brennan argues that judicial standards for obscenity have not protected First Amendment rights and that the concept of obscenity cannot be defined with sufficient specificity by the courts to provide fair notice to persons vulnerable to prosecution.

MR. CHIEF JUSTICE BURGER delivered the opinion of the Court.

This is one of a group of "obscenity-pornography" cases being reviewed by the Court in a re-examination of standards enunciated in earlier cases involving what Mr. Justice Harlan called "the intractable obscenity problem." *Interstate Circuit, Inc.* v. *Dallas*, 390 U. S. 676, 704 (1968) (concurring and dissenting).

Appellant conducted a mass mailing campaign to advertise the sale of illustrated books, euphemistically called "adult" material. After a jury trial, he was convicted of violating California Penal Code § 311.2 (a), a misdemeanor, by knowingly distributing obscene matter, and the Appellate Department, Superior Court of California, County of Orange, summarily affirmed the judgment without opinion. Appellant's conviction was

specifically based on his conduct in causing five unsolicited advertising brochures to be sent through the mail in an envelope addressed to a restaurant in Newport Beach, California. The envelope was opened by the manager of the restaurant and his mother. They had not requested the brochures; they complained to the police.

The brochures advertise four books entitled "Intercourse," "Man-Woman," "Sex Orgies Illustrated," and "An Illustrated History of Pornography," and a film entitled "Marital Intercourse." While the brochures contain some descriptive printed material, primarily they consist of pictures and drawings very explicitly depicting men and women in groups of two or more engaging in a variety of sexual activities, with genitals often prominently displayed.

I

This case involves the application of a State's criminal obscenity statute to a situation in which sexually explicit materials have been thrust by aggressive sales action upon unwilling recipients who had in no way indicated any desire to receive such materials. This Court has recognized that the States have a legitimate interest in prohibiting dissemination or exhibition of obscene material when the mode of dissemination carries with it a significant danger of offending the sensibilities of unwilling recipients or of exposure to juveniles. . . . It is in this context that we are called on to define the standards which must be used to identify obscene material that a State may regulate without infringing on the First Amendment as applicable to the States through the Fourteenth Amendment.

The dissent of MR. JUSTICE BRENNAN reviews the background of the obscenity problem, but since the Court now undertakes to formulate standards more concrete than those in the past, it is useful for us to focus on two of the landmark cases in the somewhat tortured history of the Court's obscenity decisions. In *Roth* v. *United States*, 354 U. S. 476 (1957), the Court sustained a conviction under a federal statute punishing the mailing of "obscene, lewd, lascivious or filthy . . ." materials. The key to that holding was the Court's rejection of the claim that obscene materials were protected by the First Amendment. Five Justices joined in the opinion stating:

"All ideas having even the slightest redeeming social importance—unorthodox ideas, controversial ideas, even ideas hateful to the prevailing climate of opinion—have the full protection of the [First Amendment] guaranties, unless excludable because they encroach upon the limited area of more important interests. But implicit in the history of the First Amendment is the rejection of obscenity as utterly without redeeming social importance. . . . This is the same judgment expressed by this Court in *Chaplinsky* v. *New Hampshire*, 315 U. S. 568, 571–572:

"'. . . There are certain well-defined and narrowly limited classes of speech, the prevention and punishment of which have never been thought to raise any Constitutional problem. *These include*

the lewd and obscene. . . . It has been well observed that such utterances are no essential part of any exposition of ideas, and are of such slight social value as a step to truth that any benefit that may be derived from them is clearly outweighed by the social interest in order and morality. . . .' [Emphasis by Court in *Roth* opinion.]

"We hold that obscenity is not within the area of constitutionally protected speech or press." 354 U. S., at 484–485 (footnotes omitted).

Nine years later, in *Memoirs* v. *Massachusetts*, 383 U. S. 413 (1966), the Court veered sharply away from the *Roth* concept and, with only three Justices in the plurality opinion, articulated a new test of obscenity. The plurality held that under the *Roth* definition

"as elaborated in subsequent cases, three elements must coalesce: it must be established that (a) the dominant theme of the material taken as a whole appeals to a prurient interest in sex; (b) the material is patently offensive because it affronts contemporary community standards relating to the description or representation of sexual matters; and (c) the material is utterly without redeeming social value." *Id.*, at 418.

The sharpness of the break with *Roth*, represented by the third element of the *Memoirs* test and emphasized by MR. JUSTICE WHITE'S dissent, *id.*, at 460–462, was further underscored when the *Memoirs* plurality went on to state:

"The Supreme Judicial Court erred in holding that a book need not be 'unqualifiedly worthless before it can be deemed obscene.' A book cannot be proscribed unless it is found to be *utterly* without redeeming social value." *Id.*, at 419 (emphasis in original).

While *Roth* presumed "obscenity" to be "utterly without redeeming social importance," *Memoirs* required that to prove obscenity it must be affirmatively established that the material is *"utterly* without redeeming social value." Thus, even as they repeated the words of *Roth*, the *Memoirs* plurality produced a drastically altered test that called on the prosecution to prove a negative, *i.e.*, that the material was *"utterly* without redeeming social value"—a burden virtually impossible to discharge under our criminal standards of proof. . . .

Apart from the initial formulation in the *Roth* case, no majority of the Court has at any given time been able to agree on a standard to determine what constitutes obscene, pornographic material subject to regulation under the States' police power. . . .

The case we now review was tried on the theory that the California Penal Code § 311 approximately incorporates the three-stage *Memoirs* test, *supra*. But now the *Memoirs* test has been abandoned as unworkable by its author *[Brennan]*, and no Member of the Court today supports the *Memoirs* formulation.

II

. . . we now confine the permissible scope of such regulation to works which depict or describe sexual conduct. That conduct must be specifically defined by the applicable state law, as written or authoritatively construed. A state offense must also be limited to works which, taken as a whole, appeal to the prurient interest in sex, which portray sexual conduct in a patently offensive way, and which, taken as a whole, do not have serious literary, artistic, political, or scientific value.

The basic guidelines for the trier of fact must be: (a) whether "the average person, applying contemporary community standards" would find that the work, taken as a whole, appeals to the prurient interest, *Kois* v. *Wisconsin, supra,* at 230, quoting *Roth* v. *United States, supra,* at 489; (b) whether the work depicts or describes, in a patently offensive way, sexual conduct specifically defined by the applicable state law; and (c) whether the work, taken as a whole, lacks serious literary, artistic, political, or scientific value. We do not adopt as a constitutional standard the *"utterly without redeeming social value"* test of *Memoirs* v. *Massachusetts*, 383 U. S., at 419; that concept has never commanded the adherence of more than three Justices at one time.

. . .

We emphasize that it is not our function to propose regulatory schemes for the States. That must await their concrete legislative efforts. It is possible, however, to give a few plain examples of what a state statute could define for regulation under part (b) of the standard announced in this opinion, *supra:*

(a) Patently offensive representations or descriptions of ultimate sexual acts, normal or perverted, actual or simulated.

(b) Patently offensive representations or descriptions of masturbation, excretory functions, and lewd exhibition of the genitals.

Sex and nudity may not be exploited without limit by films or pictures exhibited or sold in places of public accommodation any more than live sex and nudity can be exhibited or sold without limit in such public places. At a minimum, prurient, patently offensive depiction or description of sexual conduct must have serious literary, artistic, political, or scientific value to merit First Amendment protection. . . .

MR. JUSTICE BRENNAN, author of the opinions of the Court, or the plurality opinions, in *Roth* v. *United States, supra; Jacobellis* v. *Ohio, supra; Ginzburg* v. *United States*, 383 U. S. 463 (1966), *Mishkin* v. *New York*, 383 U. S. 502 (1966); and *Memoirs* v. *Massachusetts, supra*, has abandoned his former position and now maintains that no formulation of this Court, the Congress, or the States can adequately distinguish obscene material unprotected by the First Amendment from protected expression, *Paris Adult Theatre I* v. *Slaton, post,* p. 73 (BRENNAN, J., dissenting). Paradoxically, MR. JUSTICE BRENNAN indicates that suppression of unprotected obscene material is permissible to avoid exposure to unconsenting adults, as in this case, and to juveniles, although he gives no indication of how the division between protected and nonprotected materials may be drawn with greater precision for these purposes than for regulation of commercial exposure to consenting adults only. Nor does he indicate where in the Constitution he finds the authority to distinguish between a willing "adult" one month past the state law age of majority and a willing "juvenile" one month younger.

. . .

It is certainly true that the absence, since *Roth*, of a single majority view of this Court as to proper standards for testing obscenity has placed a strain on both state and federal courts. But today, for the first time since *Roth* was decided in 1957, a majority of this Court has agreed on concrete guidelines to isolate "hard core" pornography from expression protected by the First Amendment. Now we may abandon the casual practice of *Redrup* v. *New York*, 386 U. S. 767 (1967), and attempt to provide positive guidance to federal and state courts alike.

This may not be an easy road, free from difficulty. But no amount of "fatigue" should lead us to adopt a convenient "institutional" rationale—an absolutist, "anything goes" view of the First Amendment—because it will lighten our burdens. . . .

III

Under a National Constitution, fundamental First Amendment limitations on the powers of the States do not vary from community to community, but this does not mean that there are, or should or can be, fixed, uniform national standards of precisely what appeals to the "prurient interest" or is "patently offensive." These are essentially questions of fact, and our Nation is simply too big and too diverse for this Court to reasonably expect that such standards could be articulated for all 50 States in a single formulation, even assuming the prerequisite consensus exists. When triers of fact are asked to decide whether "the average person, applying contemporary community standards" would consider certain materials "prurient," it would be unrealistic to require that the answer be based on some abstract formulation. The adversary system, with lay jurors as the usual ultimate factfinders in criminal prosecutions, has historically permitted triers of fact to draw on the standards of their community, guided always by limiting instructions on the law. To require a State to structure obscenity proceedings around evidence of a *national* "community standard" would be an exercise in futility.

. . .

We conclude that neither the State's alleged failure to offer evidence of "national standards," nor the trial court's charge that the jury consider state community standards, were constitutional

errors. Nothing in the First Amendment requires that a jury must consider hypothetical and unascertainable "national standards" when attempting to determine whether certain materials are obscene as a matter of fact. Mr. Chief Justice Warren pointedly commented in his dissent in *Jacobellis* v. *Ohio, supra,* at 200:

"It is my belief that when the Court said in *Roth* that obscenity is to be defined by reference to 'community standards,' it meant community standards—not a national standard, as is sometimes argued. I believe that there is no provable 'national standard'. . . . At all events, this Court has not been able to enunciate one, and it would be unreasonable to expect local courts to divine one."

It is neither realistic nor constitutionally sound to read the First Amendment as requiring that the people of Maine or Mississippi accept public depiction of conduct found tolerable in Las Vegas, or New York City.

. . .

IV

The dissenting Justices sound the alarm of repression. But, in our view, to equate the free and robust exchange of ideas and political debate with commercial exploitation of obscene material demeans the grand conception of the First Amendment and its high purposes in the historic struggle for freedom. It is a "misuse of the great guarantees of free speech and free press. . . ." *Breard* v. *Alexandria*, 341 U. S., at 645. The First Amendment protects works which, taken as a whole, have serious literary, artistic, political, or scientific value, regardless of whether the government or a majority of the people approve of the ideas these works represent. "The protection given speech and press was fashioned to assure unfettered interchange of *ideas* for the bringing about of political and social changes desired by the people," *Roth* v. *United States, supra,* at 484 (emphasis added). See *Kois* v. *Wisconsin*, 408 U. S., at 230–232; *Thornhill* v. *Alabama*, 310 U. S., at 101–102. But the public portrayal of hard-core sexual conduct for its own sake, and for the ensuing commercial gain, is a different matter.

There is no evidence, empirical or historical, that the stern 19th century American censorship of public distribution and display of material relating to sex, see *Roth* v. *United States, supra,* at 482–485, in any way limited or affected expression of serious literary, artistic, political, or scientific ideas. On the contrary, it is beyond any question that the era following Thomas Jefferson to Theodore Roosevelt was an "extraordinarily vigorous period," not just in economics and politics, but in *belles lettres* and in "the outlying fields of social and political philosophies." We do not see the harsh hand of censorship of ideas—good or bad, sound or unsound—and "repression" of political liberty lurking in every state regulation of commercial exploitation of human interest in sex.

. . .

In sum, we (a) reaffirm the *Roth* holding that obscene material is not protected by the First Amendment; (b) hold that such material can be regulated by the States, subject to the specific safeguards enunciated above, without a showing that the material is *"utterly* without redeeming social value"; and (c) hold that obscenity is to be determined by applying "contemporary community standards," see *Kois* v. *Wisconsin, supra,* at 230, and *Roth* v. *United States, supra,* at 489, not "national standards." The judgment of the Appellate Department of the Superior Court, Orange County, California, is vacated and the case remanded to that court for further proceedings not inconsistent with the First Amendment standards established by this opinion. See *United States* v. *12 200-ft. Reels of Film, post,* at 130 n. 7.

Vacated and remanded.

Mr. Justice Douglas, dissenting.

I

Today we leave open the way for California to send a man to prison for distributing brochures that advertise books and a movie under freshly written standards defining obscenity which until today's decision were never the part of any law.

The Court has worked hard to define obscenity and concededly has failed. In *Roth* v. *United States,* 354 U. S. 476, it ruled that "[o]bscene material is material which deals with sex in a manner appealing to prurient interest." *Id.,* at 487. Obscenity, it was said, was rejected by the First Amendment because it is "utterly without redeeming social importance." *Id.,* at 484. The presence of a "prurient interest" was to be determined by "contemporary community standards." *Id.,* at 489. That test, it has been said, could not be determined by one standard here and another standard there, *Jacobellis* v. *Ohio,* 378 U. S. 184, 194, but "on the basis of a national standard." *Id.,* at 195. My Brother Stewart in *Jacobellis* commented that the difficulty of the Court in giving content to obscenity was that it was "faced with the task of trying to define what may be indefinable." *Id.,* at 197.

. . .

Obscenity cases usually generate tremendous emotional outbursts. They have no business being in the courts. If a constitutional amendment authorized censorship, the censor would probably be an administrative agency. Then criminal prosecutions could follow as, if, and when publishers defied the censor and sold their literature. Under that regime a publisher would know when he was on dangerous ground. Under the present regime—whether the old standards or the new ones are used—the criminal law becomes a trap. A brand new test would put a publisher behind bars under a new law improvised by the courts after the publication. That was done in *Ginzburg* and has all the evils of an *ex post facto* law.

My contention is that until a civil proceeding has placed a tract beyond the pale, no criminal prosecution should be sustained. For no more vivid illustration of vague and uncertain laws could be designed than those we have fashioned. As Mr. Justice Harlan has said:

"The upshot of all this divergence in viewpoint is that anyone who undertakes to examine the Court's decisions since *Roth* which have held particular material obscene or not obscene would find himself in utter bewilderment." *Interstate Circuit, Inc.* v. *Dallas,* 390 U. S. 676, 707.

. . .

III

. . .

We deal with highly emotional, not rational, questions. To many the Song of Solomon is obscene. I do not think we, the judges, were ever given the constitutional power to make definitions of obscenity. If it is to be defined, let the people debate and decide by a constitutional amendment what they want to ban as obscene and what standards they want the legislatures and the courts to apply. Perhaps the people will decide that the path towards a mature, integrated society requires that all ideas competing for acceptance must have no censor. Perhaps they will decide otherwise. Whatever the choice, the courts will have some guidelines. Now we have none except our own predilections.

MR. JUSTICE BRENNAN, with whom MR. JUSTICE STEWART and MR. JUSTICE MARSHALL join, dissenting.

In my dissent in *Paris Adult Theatre I* v. *Slaton, post,* p. 73, decided this date, I noted that I had no occasion to consider the extent of state power to regulate the distribution of sexually oriented material to juveniles or the offensive exposure of such material to unconsenting adults. In the case before us, appellant was convicted of distributing obscene matter in violation of California Penal Code § 311.2, on the basis of evidence that he had caused to be mailed unsolicited brochures advertising various books and a movie. I need not now decide whether a statute might be drawn to impose, within the requirements of the First Amendment, criminal penalties for the precise conduct at issue here. For it is clear that under my dissent in *Paris Adult Theatre I,* the statute under which the prosecution was brought is unconstitutionally overbroad, and therefore invalid on its face. . . .

Paris Adult Theatre I v. Slaton

413 U.S. 49 (1973)

State officials in Georgia sued the owners of two theaters to enjoin the showing of two allegedly obscene films. There was no prior restraint. The trial judge viewed the films and dismissed the complaints on the ground that the showing of the films in commercial theaters to consenting adults, with reasonable precautions taken to exclude minors, was constitutionally permissible. The Georgia Supreme Court reversed, holding that the films constituted "hard core" pornography not within the protection of the First Amendment. This case is significant because of the extensive dissent by Justice Brennan, author of the decision that first excluded obscenity from First Amendment protection, *Roth* v. *United States*.

MR. CHIEF JUSTICE BURGER delivered the opinion of the Court.

Petitioners are two Atlanta, Georgia, movie theaters and their owners and managers, operating in the style of "adult" theaters. On December 28, 1970, respondents, the local state district attorney and the solicitor for the local state trial court, filed civil complaints in that court alleging that petitioners were exhibiting to the public for paid admission two allegedly obscene films, contrary to Georgia Code Ann. § 26–2101. The two films in question, "Magic Mirror" and "It All Comes Out in the End," depict sexual conduct characterized by the Georgia Supreme Court as "hard core pornography" leaving "little to the imagination."

Respondents' complaints, made on behalf of the State of Georgia, demanded that the two films be declared obscene and that petitioners be enjoined from exhibiting the films. The exhibition of the films was not enjoined, but a temporary injunction was granted *ex parte* by the local trial court, restraining petitioners from destroying the films or removing them from the jurisdiction. Petitioners were further ordered to have one print each of the films in court on January 13, 1971, together with the proper viewing equipment.

On January 13, 1971, 15 days after the proceedings began, the films were produced by petitioners at a jury-waived trial. Certain photographs, also produced at trial, were stipulated to portray the single entrance to both Paris Adult Theatre I and Paris Adult Theatre II as it appeared at the time of the complaints. These photographs show a conventional, inoffensive theater entrance, without any pictures, but with signs indicating that the theaters exhibit "Atlanta's Finest Mature Feature Films." On the door itself is a sign saying: "Adult Theatre—You must be 21 and able to prove it. If viewing the nude body offends you, Please Do Not Enter."

The two films were exhibited to the trial court. The only other state evidence was testimony by criminal investigators that they had paid admission to see the films and that nothing on the outside of the theater indicated the full nature of what was shown. In particular, nothing indicated that the films depicted—as they did—scenes of simulated fellatio, cunnilingus, and group sex intercourse. There was no evidence presented that minors had ever entered the theaters. Nor was there evidence presented that petitioners had a systematic policy of barring minors, apart from posting signs at the entrance. On April 12, 1971, the trial judge dismissed respondents' complaints. He assumed "that obscenity is established," but stated:

"It appears to the Court that the display of these films in a commercial theatre, when surrounded by requisite notice to the public of their nature and by reasonable protection against the exposure of these films to minors, is constitutionally permissible."

On appeal, the Georgia Supreme Court unanimously reversed. It assumed that the adult theaters in question barred minors and gave a full warning to the general public of the nature of the films shown, but held that the films were without protection under the First Amendment. . . .

I

It should be clear from the outset that we do not undertake to tell the States what they must do, but rather to define the area in which they may chart their own course in dealing with obscene material. This Court has consistently held that obscene material is not protected by the First Amendment as a limitation on the state police power by virtue of the Fourteenth Amendment. . . .

Georgia case law permits a civil injunction of the exhibition of obscene materials. See *1024 Peachtree Corp.* v. *Slaton,* 228 Ga. 102, 184 S. E. 2d 144 (1971); *Walter* v. *Slaton,* 227 Ga. 676, 182 S. E. 2d 464 (1971); *Evans Theatre Corp.* v. *Slaton,* 227 Ga. 377, 180 S. E. 2d 712 (1971). While this procedure is civil in nature, and does not directly involve the state criminal statute proscribing exhibition of obscene material, the Georgia case law permitting civil injunction does adopt the definition of "obscene materials" used by the criminal statute. Today, in *Miller* v. *California, supra,* we have sought to clarify the constitutional definition of obscene material subject to regulation by the States, and we vacate and remand this case for reconsideration in light of *Miller.*

. . .

II

We categorically disapprove the theory, apparently adopted by the trial judge, that obscene, pornographic films acquire constitutional immunity from state regulation simply because they are exhibited for consenting adults only. This holding was properly rejected by the Georgia Supreme Court. Although we have often pointedly recognized the high importance of the state interest in regulating the exposure of obscene materials to juveniles and unconsenting adults, see *Miller* v. *California, ante,* at 18–20; *Stanley* v. *Georgia,* 394 U. S., at 567; *Redrup* v. *New York,* 386 U. S. 767, 769 (1967), this Court has never declared these to be the only legitimate state interests permitting regulation of obscene material. The States have a long-recognized legitimate interest in regulating the use of obscene material in local commerce and in all places of public accommodation, as long as these regulations do not run afoul of specific constitutional prohibitions.

In particular, we hold that there are legitimate state interests at stake in stemming the tide of commercialized obscenity, even assuming it is feasible to enforce effective safeguards against exposure to juveniles and to passersby. Rights and interests "other than those of the advocates are involved." *Breard* v. *Alexandria*, 341 U. S. 622, 642 (1951). These include the interest of the public in the quality of life and the total community environment, the tone of commerce in the great city centers, and, possibly, the public safety itself. The Hill-Link Minority Report of the Commission on Obscenity and Pornography indicates that there is at least an arguable correlation between obscene material and crime. . . .

. . .

But, it is argued, there are no scientific data which conclusively demonstrate that exposure to obscene material adversely affects men and women or their society. It is urged on behalf of the petitioners that, absent such a demonstration, any kind of state regulation is "impermissible." We reject this argument. It is not for us to resolve empirical uncertainties underlying state legislation, save in the exceptional case where that legislation plainly impinges upon rights protected by the Constitution itself. MR. JUSTICE BRENNAN, speaking for the Court in *Ginsberg* v. *New York*, 390 U. S. 629, 642–643 (1968), said: "We do not demand of legislatures 'scientifically certain criteria of legislation.' *Noble State Bank* v. *Haskell*, 219 U. S. 104, 110." Although there is no conclusive proof of a connection between antisocial behavior and obscene material, the legislature of Georgia could quite reasonably determine that such a connection does or might exist. In deciding *Roth*, this Court implicitly accepted that a legislature could legitimately act on such a conclusion to protect *"the social interest in order and morality."* *Roth* v. *United States*, 354 U. S., at 485, quoting *Chaplinsky* v. *New Hampshire*, 315 U. S. 568, 572 (1942) (emphasis added in *Roth*).

. . .

The States, of course, may follow . . . a "laissez-faire" policy and drop all controls on commercialized obscenity, if that is what they prefer, just as they can ignore consumer protection in the marketplace, but nothing in the Constitution *compels*

the States to do so with regard to matters falling within state jurisdiction. See *United States* v. *Reidel*, 402 U. S., at 357; *Memoirs* v. *Massachusetts*, 383 U. S., at 462 (WHITE, J., dissenting). "We do not sit as a super-legislature to determine the wisdom, need, and propriety of laws that touch economic problems, business affairs, or social conditions." *Griswold* v. *Connecticut*, 381 U. S. 479, 482 (1965). See *Ferguson* v. *Skrupa*, 372 U. S., at 731; *Day-Brite Lighting, Inc.* v. *Missouri*, 342 U. S. 421, 423 (1952).

. . .

Finally, petitioners argue that conduct which directly involves "consenting adults" only has, for that sole reason, a special claim to constitutional protection. Our Constitution establishes a broad range of conditions on the exercise of power by the States, but for us to say that our Constitution incorporates the proposition that conduct involving consenting adults only is always beyond state regulation, is a step we are unable to take. Commercial exploitation of depictions, descriptions, or exhibitions of obscene conduct on commercial premises open to the adult public falls within a State's broad power to regulate commerce and protect the public environment. The issue in this context goes beyond whether someone, or even the majority, considers the conduct depicted as "wrong" or "sinful." The States have the power to make a morally neutral judgment that public exhibition of obscene material, or commerce in such material, has a tendency to injure the community as a whole, to endanger the public safety, or to jeopardize, in Mr. Chief Justice Warren's words, the States' "right . . . to maintain a decent society." *Jacobellis* v. *Ohio*, 378 U. S., at 199 (dissenting opinion).

. . .

Vacated and remanded.

MR. JUSTICE DOUGLAS, dissenting.

. . .

I am sure I would find offensive most of the books and movies charged with being obscene. But in a life that has not been short, I have yet to be trapped into seeing or reading something that would offend me. I never read or see the materials coming to the Court under charges of "obscenity," because I have thought the First Amendment made it unconstitutional for me to act as a censor. I see ads in bookstores and neon lights over theaters that resemble bait for those who seek vicarious exhilaration. As a parent or a priest or as a teacher I would have no compunction in edging my children or wards away from the books and movies that did no more than excite man's base instincts. But I never supposed that government was permitted to sit in judgment on one's tastes or beliefs—save as they involved action within the reach of the police power of government.

I applaud the effort of my Brother BRENNAN to forsake the low road which the Court has followed in this field. The new regime he would inaugurate is much closer than the old to the policy of abstention which the First Amendment proclaims. . . .

MR. JUSTICE BRENNAN, with whom MR. JUSTICE STEWART and MR. JUSTICE MARSHALL join, dissenting.

This case requires the Court to confront once again the vexing problem of reconciling state efforts to suppress sexually oriented expression with the protections of the First Amendment, as applied to the States through the Fourteenth Amendment. No other aspect of the First Amendment has, in recent years, demanded so substantial a commitment of our time, generated such disharmony of views, and remained so resistant to the formulation of stable and manageable standards. I am convinced that the approach initiated 16 years ago in *Roth* v. *United States*, 354 U. S. 476 (1957), and culminating in the Court's decision today, cannot bring stability to this area of the law without jeopardizing fundamental First Amendment values, and I have concluded that the time has come to make a significant departure from that approach.

. . .

II

In *Roth* v. *United States*, 354 U. S. 476 (1957), the Court held that obscenity, although expression, falls outside the area of speech or press constitutionally protected under the First and Fourteenth Amendments against state or federal infringement. But at the same time we emphasized in *Roth* that "sex and obscenity are not synonymous," *id.*, at 487, and that matter which is sexually oriented but not obscene is fully protected by the Constitution. For we recognized that "[s]ex, a great and mysterious motive force in human life, has indisputably been a subject of absorbing interest to mankind through the ages; it is one of the vital problems of human interest and public concern." *Ibid. Roth* rested, in other words, on what has been termed a two-level approach to the question of obscenity. While much criticized, that approach has been endorsed by all but two members of this Court who have addressed the question since *Roth*. Yet our efforts to implement that approach demonstrate that agreement on the existence of something called "obscenity" is still a long and painful step from agreement on a workable definition of the term.

. . .

III

Our experience with the *Roth* approach has certainly taught us that the outright suppression of obscenity cannot be reconciled with the fundamental principles of the First and Fourteenth Amendments. For we have failed to formulate a standard that sharply distinguishes protected from unprotected speech, and out of necessity, we have resorted to the *Redrup* approach, which resolves cases as between the parties, but offers only the most obscure guidance to legislation, adjudication by other courts, and primary conduct. By disposing of cases through summary reversal or denial of certiorari we have deliberately and effectively obscured the rationale underlying the decisions. It comes as no surprise that judicial attempts to follow our lead conscientiously have often ended in hopeless confusion.

Of course, the vagueness problem would be largely of our own creation if it stemmed primarily from our failure to reach a consensus on any one standard. But after 16 years of experimentation and debate I am reluctantly forced to the conclusion that none of the available formulas, including the one announced today, can reduce the vagueness to a tolerable level while at the same time striking an acceptable balance between the protections of the First and Fourteenth Amendments, on the one hand, and on the other the asserted state interest in regulating the dissemination of certain sexually oriented materials. Any effort to draw a constitutionally acceptable boundary on state power must resort to such indefinite concepts as "prurient interest," "patent offensiveness," "serious literary value," and the like. The meaning of these concepts necessarily varies with the experience, outlook, and even idiosyncrasies of the person defining them. Although we have assumed that obscenity does exist and that we "know it when [we] see it," *Jacobellis* v. *Ohio, supra,* at 197 (STEWART, J., concurring), we are manifestly unable to describe it in advance except by reference to concepts so elusive that they fail to distinguish clearly between protected and unprotected speech.

. . .

The vagueness of the standards in the obscenity area produces a number of separate problems, and any improvement must rest on an understanding that the problems are to some extent distinct. First, a vague statute fails to provide adequate notice to persons who are engaged in the type of conduct that the statute could be thought to proscribe. The Due Process Clause of the Fourteenth Amendment requires that all criminal laws provide fair notice of "what the State commands or forbids." *Lanzetta* v. *New Jersey*, 306 U. S. 451, 453 (1939); *Connally* v. *General Construction Co.,* 269 U. S. 385 (1926). . . .

. . .

In addition to problems that arise when any criminal statute fails to afford fair notice of what it forbids, a vague statute in the areas of speech and press creates a second level of difficulty. We have indicated that "stricter standards of permissible statutory vagueness may be applied to a statute having a potentially inhibiting effect on speech; a man may the less be required to act at his peril here, because the free dissemination of ideas may be the loser." *Smith* v. *California*, 361 U. S. 147, 151 (1959). That proposition draws its strength from our recognition that

"[t]he fundamental freedoms of speech and press have contributed greatly to the development and well-being of our free society and are indispensable to its continued growth. Ceaseless vigilance is the watchword to prevent their erosion by Congress or by the States. The door barring federal and state intrusion into this area cannot be left ajar. . . ." *Roth, supra,* at 488.

. . .

The problems of fair notice and chilling protected speech are very grave standing alone. But it does not detract from their importance to recognize that a vague statute in this area creates a third, although admittedly more subtle, set of problems. These problems concern the institutional stress that inevitably results where the line separating protected from unprotected speech is excessively vague. In *Roth* we conceded that "there may be marginal cases in which it is difficult to determine the side of the line on which a particular fact situation falls. . . ." 354 U. S., at 491–492. Our subsequent experience demonstrates that almost every case is "marginal." And since the "margin" marks the point of separation between protected and unprotected speech, we are left with a system in which almost every obscenity case presents a constitutional question of exceptional difficulty. . . .

. . .

But the sheer number of the cases does not define the full extent of the institutional problem. For, quite apart from the number of cases involved and the need to make a fresh constitutional determination in each case, we are tied to the "absurd business of perusing and viewing the miserable stuff that pours into the Court. . . ." *Interstate Circuit, Inc.* v. *Dallas*, 390 U. S., at 707 (separate opinion of Harlan, J.). While the material may have varying degrees of social importance, it is hardly a source of edification to the members of this Court who are compelled to view it before passing on its obscenity. Cf. *Mishkin* v. *New York*, 383 U. S., at 516–517 (Black, J., dissenting).

. . .

IV

1. The approach requiring the smallest deviation from our present course would be to draw a new line between protected and unprotected speech, still permitting the States to suppress all material on the unprotected side of the line. In my view, clarity cannot be obtained pursuant to this approach except by drawing a line that resolves all doubt in favor of state power and against the guarantees of the First Amendment. . . .

2. The alternative adopted by the Court today recognizes that a prohibition against any depiction or description of human sexual organs could not be reconciled with the guarantees of the First Amendment. But the Court does retain the view that certain sexually oriented material can be considered obscene and therefore unprotected by the First and Fourteenth Amendments. To describe that unprotected class of expression, the Court adopts a restatement of the *Roth-Memoirs* definition of obscenity: "The basic guidelines for the trier of fact must be: (a) whether 'the average person, applying contemporary community standards' would find that the work, taken as a whole, appeals to the prurient interest . . . (b) whether the work depicts or describes, in a patently offensive way, sexual conduct specifically defined by the applicable state law, and (c) whether the work, taken as a whole, lacks serious literary, artistic, political, or scientific value." *Miller* v. *California, ante,* at 24. In apparent illustration of "sexual conduct," as that term is used in the test's second element, the Court identifies "(a) Patently offensive representations or descriptions of ultimate sexual acts, normal or perverted, actual or simulated," and "(b) Patently offensive representations or descriptions of masturbation, excretory functions, and lewd exhibition of the genitals." *Id.,* at 25.

The differences between this formulation and the three-pronged *Memoirs* test are, for the most part, academic. The first element of the Court's test is virtually identical to the *Memoirs* requirement that "the dominant theme of the material taken as a whole [must appeal] to a prurient interest in sex." 383 U. S., at 418. Whereas the second prong of the *Memoirs* test demanded that the material be "patently offensive because it

affronts contemporary community standards relating to the description or representation of sexual matters," *ibid.,* the test adopted today requires that the material describe, "in a patently offensive way, sexual conduct specifically defined by the applicable state law." *Miller* v. *California, ante,* at 24. The third component of the *Memoirs* test is that the material must be "utterly without redeeming social value." 383 U. S., at 418. The Court's rephrasing requires that the work, taken as a whole, must be proved to lack "serious literary, artistic, political, or scientific value." *Miller, ante,* at 24.

. . .

. . . Before today, the protections of the First Amendment have never been thought limited to expressions of *serious* literary or political value. See *Gooding* v. *Wilson,* 405 U. S. 518 (1972); *Cohen* v. *California,* 403 U. S. 15, 25–26 (1971); *Terminiello* v. *Chicago,* 337 U. S. 1, 4–5 (1949).

. . .

3. I have also considered the possibility of reducing our own role, and the role of appellate courts generally, in determining whether particular matter is obscene. Thus, we might conclude that juries are best suited to determine obscenity *vel non* and that jury verdicts in this area should not be set aside except in cases of extreme departure from prevailing standards. Or, more generally, we might adopt the position that where a lower federal or state court has conscientiously applied the constitutional standard, its finding of obscenity will be no more vulnerable to reversal by this Court than any finding of fact. . . . while it would mitigate the institutional stress produced by the *Roth* approach, it would neither offer nor produce any cure for the other vices of vagueness. Far from providing a clearer guide to permissible primary conduct, the approach would inevitably lead to even greater uncertainty and the consequent due process problems of fair notice. And the approach would expose much protected, sexually oriented expression to the vagaries of jury determinations. Cf. *Herndon* v. *Lowry,* 301 U. S. 242, 263 (1937). Plainly, the institutional gain would be more than offset by the unprecedented infringement of First Amendment rights.

4. Finally, I have considered the view, urged so forcefully since 1957 by our Brothers Black and Douglas, that the First Amendment bars the suppression of any sexually oriented expression. That position would effect a sharp reduction, although perhaps not a total elimination, of the uncertainty that surrounds our current approach. Nevertheless, I am convinced that it would achieve that desirable goal only by stripping the States of power to an extent that cannot be justified by the commands of the Constitution, at least so long as there is available an alternative approach that strikes a better balance between the guarantee of free expression and the States' legitimate interests.

V

Our experience since *Roth* requires us not only to abandon the effort to pick out obscene materials on a case-by-case basis, but also to reconsider a fundamental postulate of *Roth:* that there exists a definable class of sexually oriented expression that may be totally suppressed by the Federal and State Governments. Assuming that such a class of expression does in fact exist, I am forced to conclude that the concept of "obscenity" cannot be defined with sufficient specificity and clarity to provide fair notice to persons who create and distribute sexually oriented materials, to prevent substantial erosion of protected speech as a byproduct of the attempt to suppress unprotected speech, and to avoid very costly institutional harms. . . .

. . . whatever the strength of the state interests in protecting juveniles and unconsenting adults from exposure to sexually oriented materials, those interests cannot be asserted in defense of the holding of the Georgia Supreme Court in this case. . . .

. . . I would hold, therefore, that at least in the absence of distribution to juveniles or obtrusive exposure to unconsenting adults, the First and Fourteenth Amendments prohibit the State and Federal Governments from attempting wholly to suppress sexually oriented materials on the basis of their allegedly "obscene" contents. Nothing in this approach precludes those governments from taking action to serve what may be strong and legitimate interests through regulation of the manner of distribution of sexually oriented material.

. . .

12 Religious Freedom

The religion clauses in the First Amendment contain two distinct objectives: "Congress shall make no law respecting an establishment of religion or prohibiting the free exercise thereof." These clauses—the Establishment Clause and the Free Exercise Clause—sometimes overlap and compete. Satisfying one clause may violate the other. If Congress grants a tax exemption for church property, is that establishment of religion? Taxing the property, however, might interfere with the free exercise of religion. When Congress provides chaplains for soldiers in the armed forces, is that an act of establishment? Yet denying soldiers access to ministers or rabbis would interfere with free exercise, especially for soldiers assigned to remote outposts. It is well established that the government may accommodate religious practices in various ways without violating the Establishment Clause.

These complexities are not solved by invoking metaphors about the "Wall of Separation" between church and state. In upholding state assistance of transportation to parochial schools, Justice Black claimed that the First Amendment "has erected a wall between church and state. That wall must be kept high and impregnable. We could not approve the slightest breach. New Jersey has not breached it here." EVERSON v. BOARD OF EDUCATION, 330 U.S. 1, 18 (1947). In fact, a breach did occur in this case. A year later, in a concurring opinion, Justice Jackson questioned the Court's reasoning and predicted correctly that the Court would make "the legal 'wall of separation between church and state' as winding as the famous serpentine wall designed by Mr. Jefferson for the University he founded." McCollum v. Board of Education, 333 U.S. 203, 238 (1948). Justice Reed advised: "A rule of law should not be drawn from a figure of speech." Id. at 247.

A complete wall between church and state is neither possible nor desirable. Religious organizations have a right to lobby and petition government for various programs and activities. Ministers may serve in the legislature and hold other public offices. McDaniel v. Paty, 435 U.S. 618 (1978). Sectarian schools are obliged to teach the secular subjects specified by the state and they must adhere to state health and safety standards. "Some relationship between government and religious organizations is inevitable . . . Fire inspections, building and zoning regulations, and state requirements under compulsory school-attendance laws are examples of necessary and permissible contacts." LEMON v. KURTZMAN, 403 U.S. 602, 614 (1971).

How are the religion clauses to be interpreted? On several occasions the Supreme Court has recognized that the clauses "had the same objective and were intended to provide the same protection against governmental intrusion on religious liberty as the Virginia statute." EVERSON v. BOARD OF EDUCATION, 330 U.S. at 13. See also Reynolds v. United States, 98 U.S. 145, 162–164 (1878). The Virginia Statute for Establishing Religious Freedom—the handiwork of Thomas Jefferson and James Madison—provides valuable guidance in understanding the motivations behind the religion clauses. However, it is also true that six states (Connecticut, Georgia, Maryland, Massachusetts, New Hampshire, and South Carolina) continued to provide assistance to established churches after 1786. In 1833, Massachusetts became the last of these states to end their support to established religions.

THE VIRGINIA STATUTE

Religious liberties, which form the basis for political and social rights, had their origin in the long struggle to separate church and state. The three-volume study by Anson Phelps Stokes documents this development: "the study of American history shows that this actual separation, especially in the states, was generally the precursor, and always the surest support of public opinion in guaranteeing freedom of conscience and worship." 1 Stokes, Church and State in the United States 646 (1950). The Virginia statute of 1786 declared "that no man shall be compelled to frequent or support any religious worship, place, or ministry whatsoever, nor shall be enforced, restrained, molested, or burthened in his body or goods, nor shall otherwise suffer on account of his religious opinions or belief . . ." The preamble provided: "to compel a man to furnish contributions of money for the propagation of opinions which he disbelieves, is sinful and tyrannical." The author of the statute was Jefferson; the man who enacted it into Virginia law was Madison. Both men regarded religion and its free exercise as a fundamental human right into which the state could not intrude. Wrote Jefferson: "our rulers can have authority over such natural rights, only as we have submitted to them. The rights of conscience we never submitted, we could not submit." 3 Writings of Thomas Jefferson 263 (Ford ed.).

Neither Madison nor Jefferson had patience for sectarian battles, narrow creeds, or doctrinal wrangling. For them, religion was more of a general moral code to be practiced, not preached. "Of the dogmas of religion," wrote Jefferson, "as distinguished from moral principles, all mankind, from the beginning of the world to this day, have been quarrelling, fighting, burning and torturing one another, for abstractions unintelligible to themselves and to all others, and absolutely beyond the comprehension of the human mind. Were I to enter on that arena, I should only add an unit to the number of Bedlamites." 10 Writings of Thomas Jefferson 67–68 (Ford ed.).

As with other colonies, Virginians suffered from religious cruelty and intolerance among different sects. Madison deplored the "diabolical, hell-conceived principle of persecution" that raged about him in 1774. 1 Writings of James Madison 21 (Hunt ed.). Baptists, Presbyterians, Catholics, Quakers, and other minority groups were whipped, fined, imprisoned, and forced to support the established Anglican Church.

Between 1776 and 1786, Virginia moved a step at a time to establish religious freedom. The state Bill of Rights in 1776 proclaimed that religion "can be directed only by reason and conviction, not by force or violence, and therefore all men are equally entitled to the free exercise of religion, according to the dictates of conscience."

Oppressive laws against dissenters nevertheless remained on the books. In December 1776, Virginia repealed its laws directed against heretics and nonattendance and it exempted dissenters from giving financial support to the Anglican Church. Another step toward disestablishment occurred in 1779 when Virginia repealed all laws requiring even the members of the Anglican Church to support their own ministry. As a substitute for this preferential treatment, the Anglican Church pressed for a general tax to benefit all Christian religions. Bills were introduced to obtain public funds for teachers of Christianity. The final version allowed each taxpayer to designate which church should receive his share of the tax, and even gave the nonreligious taxpayer the option of directing his tax to general educational purposes.

Proponents of the general assessment claimed that Christianity and public morals would be handicapped without state financial aid, but the Baptists and some Presbyterians, who would have benefited financially from the bill, opposed the general assessment. Madison, in his famous "Memorial and Remonstrance Against Religious Assessments," insisted that religion be left to the conviction and conscience of the individual. Religion consisted in voluntary acts "wholly exempt" from the state's jurisdiction. He protested against religious assessments partly because "experience witnesseth that ecclesiastical establishments, instead of maintaining the purity and efficacy of Religion, have had a contrary operation. . . . What have been its fruits? More or less in all places, pride and indolence in the Clergy; ignorance and servility in the laity; in both, superstition, bigotry and persecution." 2 Writings of James Madison 187 (Hunt ed.).

The force and logic of Madison's detailed attack, emphasizing the inherent incompatibility between private religious beliefs and public financial support, led to the defeat of the general assessment bill. Virginia thereby prohibited religious aid even on a nonpreferential basis. Madison seized the opportunity to reintroduce Jefferson's Statute for Establishing Religious Freedom, which passed in January 1786 (pp. 722–723). Years later, in evaluating religious institutions in Virginia after they had been denied public funds, Madison remarked that "it is impossible to deny that Religion prevails with more zeal, and a more exemplary priesthood than it ever did when established and patronised by Public authority." 9 Writings of James Madison 102 (Hunt ed.). A resolution passed by Congress in 1988 contains this Madisonian sentiment: "religion is most free when it is observed voluntarily at private initiative, uncontaminated by Government interference and unconstrained by majority preference." 102 Stat. 1772 (1988).

Madison remained alert to inroads on religious freedom. As President, he vetoed a bill in 1811 that included rules and proceedings for the election and removal of ministers of a Protestant Church. He rejected the bill because it exceeded "the rightful authority to which governments are limited by the essential distinction between civil and religious functions . . ." A week later, he vetoed another bill that reserved a parcel of land in Mississippi for the Baptist Church, pointing out that such legislation would represent "a principle and precedent for the appropriation of funds of the United States for the use and support of religious societies . . ." 1 Richardson 489–490.

Even so small a transgression as the use of public funds for chaplains in Congress was to be resisted. Madison objected to this practice as a harmful and unnecessary precedent. "It would have been a much better proof to their Constituents of their pious feeling if the members had contributed for the purpose, a pittance from their own pockets." 9 Writings of James Madison 100 (Hunt ed.). The comprehensive meaning of "establishment" is evident in Madison's critique: "The establishment of the chaplainship to Congs is a palpable violation of equal rights, as well as of Constitutional principles." Human rights were violated because religious represen- tation in Congress was denied to minority sects such as the Roman Catholics and Quakers. The daily devotions in Congress served to degrade religion by degenerating into "scanty attendance, and a tiresome formality." Elizabeth Fleet, ed., "Madison's 'Detached Memoranda'," 3 Wm. & Mary Q. 534, 558–559 (1946).

Madison's handling of presidential proclamations for fasts and festivals also demonstrates his caution and sensitivity to small erosions. "Every new & successful example therefore of a perfect separation between ecclesiastical and civil matters, is of importance." 9 Writings of James Madison 101–102 (Hunt ed.). Jefferson, as President, refused to proclaim a day of fasting and prayer on the ground that "every one must act according to the dictates of his own reason, & mine tells me that civil powers alone have been given to the President of the U.S. and no authority to direct the religious exercises of his constituents." 9 Writings of Thomas Jefferson 175–176 (Ford ed.). The attitudes of Madison and Jefferson stand in marked contrast to such Presidents as Jimmy Carter and Ronald Reagan who used the Oval Office to promote religion, especially the evangelical wing of Christianity. Richard G. Hutcheson, Jr., God in the White House (1988).

FREE EXERCISE CLAUSE

Before the religion clauses were ratified in 1791 as part of the Bill of Rights, the Constitution had already accorded some protection for religious freedom. It expressly provided that "no religious test shall ever be required as a qualification to any office or public trust under the United States." Art. VI, § 3. Applicants are not to be judged by their creed or belief. Other sections of the Constitution give office- holders the option of being bound "by Oath or Affirmation." Art. II, § 1, Cl. 7; Art. VI, § 3. When Senators sit for trying impeachments, "they shall be on oath or affirmation." Art. I, § 3, Cl. 3. Under the Fourth Amendment, warrants shall not issue but upon probable cause, "supported by Oath or affirmation." An oath is a solemn appeal to God that a promise is true and binding. An affirmation has the same legal value as an oath. Quakers, following the Biblical injunction "Swear not at all," objected to taking an oath, as did Mennonites and nonbelievers.

Many religious fundamentalists believe that government has a positive duty to promote religion. Under their interpretation, the First Amendment seems to extend religious rights only to the believer and the orthodox. Although a treaty with Tripoli in 1796 stated that the United States "is not in any sense founded on the Christian religion" (8 Stat. 155, Art. XI), dicta from a few decisions of the Supreme Court suggest the contrary. The history of the country, said the Court in 1892, confirms that "this is a Christian nation." Church of the Holy Trinity v. United States, 143 U.S. 457,

471. Writing for the Court in 1952, Justice Douglas said "We are a religious people whose institutions presuppose a Supreme Being." Zorach v. Clauson, 343 U.S. 306, 313.

Congressional statutes have endorsed religious belief. Congress has required the inscription "In God We Trust" on coins and paper money.[1] After World War II, Congress engaged in ideological fencing with Soviet Russia by promoting spiritualism over materialism and theism over atheism. It directed the President to "set aside and proclaim a suitable day each year, other than a Sunday, as a National Day of Prayer, on which the people of the United States may turn to God in prayer and meditation at churches, in groups, and as individuals." 66 Stat. 64 (1952); 36 U.S.C. § 169h. Two years later it added the words "under God" to the pledge of allegiance. 68 Stat. 249 (1954); 36 U.S.C. § 172. This flourish of religiosity culminated in a law making "In God We Trust" the national motto. 70 Stat. 732 (1956); 36 U.S.C. § 186. An appellate court concluded that the national motto and the slogan on coinage and currency merely reflected a patriotic or ceremonial quality and had "no theological or ritualistic impact." Aronow v. United States, 432 F.2d 242, 243 (9th Cir. 1970). See also O'Hair v. Blumenthal, 462 F.Supp. 19 (W.D. Tex. 1978).

The executive branch joined in this quest for piety. In 1955, President Eisenhower advised the American Legion: "Without God, there could be no American form of Government, nor an American way of life. Recognition of the Supreme Being is the first—the most basic—expression of Americanism." 1955 Public Papers of the President 274. Recent Presidents, including Richard Nixon, Gerald Ford, Jimmy Carter, and Ronald Reagan, actively used their office to promote religion and prayer.

These congressional and presidential affirmations of religion have been tempered by court decisions calling for neutrality on the part of government—not just between religions but between religion and irreligion. "The law knows no heresy, and is committed to the support of no dogma, the establishment of no sect." Watson v. Jones, 13 Wall. 679, 728 (1872). Neither a state nor the federal government "can force [or] influence a person to go to or to remain away from church against his will or force him to profess a belief or disbelief in any religion. No person can be punished for entertaining or professing religious beliefs or disbeliefs, for church attendance or non-attendance." EVERSON v. BOARD OF EDUCATION, 330 U.S. at 15–16. Justice Jackson, who sent his own children to sectarian schools, warned that the "day that this country ceases to be free for irreligion it will cease to be free for religion—except for the sect that can win political power." Zorach v. Clauson, 343 U.S. at 306 (dissenting opinion).

In 1961, the First Amendment was used explicitly to protect irreligion. Maryland had required public officers to declare their belief in God. A unanimous Supreme Court held that this provision in the state constitution invaded the freedom of belief and religion guaranteed by the First Amendment. Echoing Jackson's warning above, the Court reviewed the history of the early colonists who left Europe to pursue religious freedom. Once in America, however, many who had fled Europe to escape religious persecution "turned out to be perfectly willing, when they had the power to do so, to force dissenters from their faith to take test oaths in conformity with that faith." Torcaso v. Watkins, 367 U.S. 488, 490. In a footnote, the Court listed

[1]E.g., 13 Stat. 518, § 5 (1865); 35 Stat. 164 (1908); 69 Stat. 290 (1955); 31 U.S.C. §§ 5112(d)(1), 5114(b).

Buddhism, Taoism, Ethical Culture, and Secular Humanism as among the religions in America which do not teach "what would generally be considered a belief in the existence of God." Id. at 495.

Conscientious Objectors

The question of religiously based objection to war has occupied the attention of legislatures and courts. Congress passed legislation in 1917 to exempt ministers of religion and theological students from military service. Conscientious objectors were relieved from military action but had to serve in a noncombatant role. The Court held that these laws did not violate the religious clauses. Selective Draft Law Cases, 245 U.S. 366 (1918). State universities were permitted to require male students to take a course in military science and tactics, even if such courses offended the beliefs of conscientious and religious objectors. The Court reasoned that the students were not compelled to attend a state university. If they chose to matriculate they had to comply with the conditions imposed. Hamilton v. Regents, 293 U.S. 245 (1934).

As a result of subsequent decisions, an individual can now be exempt from combat duty without professing a belief in a Supreme Being. Congress exempted from military combat persons whose religious training and belief made them conscientiously opposed to participating in war in any form. As used in the statute, religious training and belief meant "an individual's belief in a relation to a Supreme Being involving duties superior to those arising from any human relation, but [not including] essentially political, sociological or philosophical views or a merely personal code." 62 Stat. 613 (1948). The Court held that the test of "religious belief" is whether it is a sincere and meaningful belief occupying in the individual's life a place parallel to that filled by the God of those explicitly eligible for the exemption. United States v. Seeger, 380 U.S. 163 (1965). Congress rewrote the statute two years later by eliminating the phrase "a relation to a Supreme Being involving duties superior to those arising from any human relation." 81 Stat. 104 (1967); 50 App. U.S.C. § 456(j). Persons may be classified as conscientious objectors even when they do not affirm or deny belief in a Supreme Being.[2]

The congressional requirement that a religious objector be conscientiously opposed to war "in any form" does not apply to a Jehovah's Witness who indicates a willingness to fight in defense of "his ministry, Kingdom Interests and . . . his fellow brethren." The weapons of this warfare are spiritual, not carnal. He is willing to engage in a "theocratic war" if Jehovah so commands. The congressional statute refers to military conflicts in our time, not a fight at Armageddon. Sicurella v. United States, 348 U.S. 385 (1955).

The Free Exercise Clause protects religious belief or opinion, not practice. When government decides that a religious practice is against peace and the public order, such as the Mormon belief in polygamy, it may make such practices a crime. Reynolds v. United States, 98 U.S. 145 (1878); Davis v. Beason, 133 U.S. 333 (1890); Mormon Church v. United States, 136 U.S. 1 (1890). Transporting a woman across

[2]Welsh v. United States, 398 U.S. 333, 337 (1970). See also Gillette v. United States, 401 U.S. 437 (1971) and Clay v. United States, 403 U.S. 698 (1971). Inconsistent statements can cast legitimate doubt on the sincerity of a religious objector. Witmer v. United States, 348 U.S. 375 (1955).

state lines to enter into a plural marriage is prohibited by law even if motivated by a religious belief. Cleveland v. United States, 329 U.S. 14 (1946). To protect the public safety, health, and welfare, states may prevent members of a religious order from handling poisonous reptiles as part of a church service.[3] Religious objections to blood transfusions present difficult questions of constitutional law, especially where the life or health of a child is at stake. Application of the President and Directors of Georgetown College, 331 F.2d 1000 (D.C. Cir. 1964), cert. denied, 377 U.S. 978 (1964).

The Flag-Salute Cases

Periodically, government has prosecuted and harassed minorities whose beliefs did not directly threaten public order. For example, a number of states in the 1930s adopted laws that compelled school children to salute the flag. The Jehovah's Witnesses complained that saluting a secular symbol offended their religious faith. Nonetheless, the compulsory flag-salute survived several test cases.[4]

In 1937, a federal district judge in Pennsylvania found these statutes unconstitutional. If someone on the basis of sincere religious beliefs defied a statute, the individual's rights would prevail unless the state demonstrated that the statute was necessary for the public safety, health, morals, property, or personal rights. The district judge thought that other courts had given insufficient weight to the value of religious liberty. Moreover, he distinguished between the compulsory military courses in state universities sanctioned by Regents v. Hamilton, 293 U.S. 245 (1934), and the compulsory flag-salute imposed on children in grade school and high school. Students attend state universities on their own volition; attendance at the elementary and secondary school level is mandatory. The judge appealed to the heritage of his state: "We may well recall that William Penn, the founder of Pennsylvania, was expelled from Oxford University for his refusal for conscience' sake to comply with regulations not essentially dissimilar [to the compulsory flag-salute], and suffered, more than once, imprisonment in England because of his religious convictions. The commonwealth he founded was intended as a haven for all those persecuted for conscience' sake." Gobitis v. Minersville School Dist., 21 F.Supp. 581, 585 (E.D. Pa. 1937).

Although the religion clauses of the First Amendment had not yet been applied to the states, the federal judge held that the "liberty protected by the due process clause of the Fourteenth Amendment undoubtedly includes the liberty to entertain any religious belief, to practice any religious principle, and to do any act or refrain from doing any act, on conscientious grounds, which does not endanger the public safety, violate the laws of morality or property, or infringe on personal rights." Id. at 587.

[3]Lawson v. Commonwealth, 164 S.W.2d 972 (Ky. 1942); State v. Massey, 51 S.E.2d 179 (N.C. 1949), appeal dismissed for want of a substantial federal question sub nom. Bunn v. North Carolina, 336 U.S. 942 (1949); State ex rel. Swann v. Pack, 527 S.W.2d 99 (Tenn. 1975), cert. denied, 424 U.S. 954 (1976). For recent cases concluding that the government is not required to satisfy every citizen's religious needs and desires, see Lyng v. Northwest Indian Cemetary Prot. Assn., 108 S.Ct. 1323 (1988) and Bowen v. Roy, 476 U.S. 693 (1986).
[4]Leoles v. Landers, 192 S.E. 218; 302 U.S. 656 (1937); Hering v. State Board of Education, 189 A. 629; 303 U.S. 624 (1938); Gabrielli v. Knickerbocker, 82 P.2d 391; 306 U.S. 621 (1939); Johnson v. Deerfield, 25 F.Supp. 918; 306 U.S. 621 (1939).

This judgment was supported by another decision from the same judge, Gobitis v. Minersville School Dist., 24 F.Supp. 271 (1938), and by a federal appellate court, Minersville School Dist. v. Gobitis, 108 F.2d 683 (3d Cir. 1939).

The Supreme Court granted certiorari to review the Pennsylvania flag-salute case. Before issuing its decision, in another case it upheld the right of a Jehovah's Witness who had been prosecuted for violating a state law that prohibited the solicitation of money, services, subscriptions "or any valuable thing" unless approved in advance by a public official. Jesse Cantwell had gone from house to house to solicit money, sell books, and play records on a portable phonograph. Some of the records included attacks on Roman Catholics. A unanimous Court struck down the state law as a violation of the free exercise of religion. The Court also held that the religion clauses in the First Amendment applied to the states. Cantwell v. Connecticut, 310 U.S. 296, 303 (1940).

Two weeks later, the Supreme Court reversed course and upheld Pennsylvania's compulsory flag-salute law. Justice Frankfurter, writing for an 8–1 majority, wrote a decision deeply flawed by contradictions, ipse dixits, and doubletalk. The logic appeared to rest on two assumptions: liberty requires unifying sentiments, and national unity promotes national security. Only Justice Stone dissented. Several Justices in the majority would soon wish they had. MINERSVILLE SCHOOL DISTRICT v. GOBITIS, 310 U.S. 586 (1940).

The decision was excoriated by law journals, the press, and religious organizations. Roman Catholics, although often the prime target of attacks from Jehovah's Witnesses, found Frankfurter's opinion intolerable. By 1942, three members of the *Gobitis* majority publicly apologized for their votes. Justices Black, Douglas, and Murphy now announced that it "was wrongly decided." Jones v. Opelika, 316 U.S. 584, 624. Frankfurter's decision thus commanded at best a slim majority, and two members of the *Gobitis* Court had been replaced by Justices Jackson and Rutledge. The 8–1 majority had evaporated so quickly that a federal district judge in 1942 determined that *Gobitis* was no longer binding even though it had yet to be overruled. He calculated that of the seven Justices on the Supreme Court who had participated in *Gobitis,* "four have given public expression to the view that it is unsound." Barnette v. West Virginia State Board of Ed., 47 F.Supp. 251 (S.D. W.Va. 1942).

The Court overruled *Gobitis* in 1943, almost three years to the date that it was announced. Justice Jackson wrote for a 6–3 majority. Only Justices Roberts and Reed agreed with Frankfurter that *Gobitis* was properly decided. In a lengthy and passionate dissent, Frankfurter sought to vindicate his views. WEST VIRGINIA STATE BOARD OF EDUCATION v. BARNETTE, 319 U.S. 624 (1943).

The flag-salute cases resurfaced during the 1988 presidential campaign when George Bush attacked Michael Dukakis for vetoing a Massachusetts bill requiring a pledge of allegiance in public schools. Bush said he would have found a way to sign the bill. In defense, Dukakis objected that Bush was questioning his patriotism and that his veto was based on an advisory opinion he had received from the Massachusetts Supreme Court, which itself had relied on the 1943 flag-salute case. Dukakis missed an opportunity to articulate the values of diversity, pluralism, and religious freedom that supported the 1943 decision. He also gave the impression of mechanically following Supreme Court opinions, which meant that had he been governor from 1940 to 1943 he would have signed the bill. Like the President, a governor has the duty to reach an independent judgment on constitutional issues.

While the flag-salute cases were being litigated in the 1940s, the Court decided other important issues of religious freedom. A Jehovah's Witness had been convicted for violating a Texas ordinance that required a permit to solicit orders and sell books. The Court held unanimously that the ordinance represented "administrative censorship in an extreme form" and abridged the freedom of religion, press, and speech guaranteed by the Fourteenth Amendment. Largent v. Texas, 318 U.S. 418, 422 (1943). Similarly, it struck down a Pennsylvania ordinance requiring a license tax for those who canvass or solicit orders for books, paintings, pictures, wares, or merchandise. Once again a Jehovah's Witness had been convicted. The Court held that these constraints on missionary evangelism violated the constitutional liberties of speech, press, and religion. Murdock v. Pennsylvania, 319 U.S. 105 (1943). Other state efforts to impose a license tax on the selling of religious merchandise or to require a town's permission before "peddling" religious literature were struck down in Douglas v. Jeannette, 319 U.S. 157 (1943), Follett v. McCormick, 321 U.S. 573 (1944), and Tucker v. Texas, 326 U.S. 517 (1946). A state may not permit one religious organization to conduct services in a public park while denying that same privilege to another religious group. Fowler v. Rhode Island, 345 U.S. 67 (1953).

The state's interest in regulating religious activity is strengthened when a child is involved. In 1944, the Court upheld a Massachusetts statute that prohibited minors (boys under 12, girls under 18) from selling newspapers, magazines, or other articles in public places. A nine-year-old had helped in the distribution of Jehovah's Witness literature. By a 5–4 vote the Court upheld the conviction of the youth's guardian on the ground that the state has a special interest in protecting children. Prince v. Massachusetts, 321 U.S. 158. As the child matures, however, the state's interest declines. In 1972, the Supreme Court decided the case of members of the Amish religious order who had been convicted for violating Wisconsin's requirement that children attend school until age 16. The parents argued that sending their children to public or private schools after the eighth grade endangered the salvation of both parent and child by exposing the children to material, competitive, and modern values. The Court found that the religious interests of the Amish outweighed the interests of the state. Wisconsin v. Yoder, 406 U.S. 205.

Congress exempts self-employed Amish from paying social security taxes because they have a religiously based obligation to provide for their fellow members. 26 U.S.C. § 1402(g). The Supreme Court has held that the exemption applies only to self-employed individuals, not to all employers and employees who are Amish. The state has a compelling interest in avoiding widespread individual voluntary coverage under social security. The accommodation in the *Yoder* case was less disruptive than allowing various exceptions to the social security system. "Because the broad public interest in maintaining a sound tax system is of such a high order, religious belief in conflict with the payment of taxes affords no basis for resisting the tax." United States v. Lee, 455 U.S. 252, 260 (1982).

Other cases illustrate the constant need to reach accommodations between state interests and religious belief. Minnesota required religious organizations at a state fair to sell and distribute religious literature and to solicit funds only at an assigned location within the fairgrounds. Members of those organizations were free to walk around and discuss religious matters in face-to-face contacts. A Krishna group claimed that the rule restricted its religious practices and its ability to proselytize for new members and financial support. The Court agreed that a state, in an effort to control the flow of crowds at a large fair, can restrict the sale of literature and solicitation of funds. Heffron v. Int'l Soc. for Krishna Consciousness, 452 U.S. 640 (1981).

There are limits to the competence of government to delve into religious matters. One case involved the conviction of a cult group for using the mails to defraud the public. The group relied on Guy W. Ballard, deceased, who they said communicated through them certain supernatural powers capable of healing incurable diseases. On the charge of fraudulent practices, the jury was instructed to determine not the truth of this belief but the good-faith intentions of those who claimed to heal. Did members of the cult honestly believe those things? The Supreme Court held that it was a forbidden realm to inquire into the truthfulness of religious beliefs. "Heresy trials are foreign to our Constitution. Men may believe what they cannot prove. They may not be put to the proof of their religious doctrines or beliefs. Religious experiences which are as real as life to some may be incomprehensible to others." United States v. Ballard, 322 U.S. 78, 86 (1944). Property disputes, turning on the question of church doctrine or ecclesiastical law, are beyond the bounds of civil courts.[5]

A 1986 decision illustrates how the First Amendment is shaped not merely by court opinions but by legislative action as well. An Air Force regulation provided that headgear may not be worn indoors except by armed security police in the performance of their duties. An Air Force officer, who was an Orthodox Jew and an ordained rabbi, claimed that the regulation prevented him from wearing his yarmulke (skullcap) and therefore infringed on his freedom to exercise his religious beliefs. The Supreme Court, split 5–4, upheld the regulation as necessary for military discipline, unity, and order. In one of the dissents, Justice Brennan claimed that the Court's response "is to abdicate its role as primary expositor of the Constitution and protector of individual liberties in favor of credulous deference to unsupported assertions of military necessity." GOLDMAN v. WEINBERGER, 475 U.S. 503, 514 (1986). Fortunately, other institutions of government are capable of protecting individual liberties, Congress among them. As Brennan later noted: "Guardianship of this precious liberty [of religious freedom] is not the exclusive domain of federal courts. It is the responsibility as well of the States and of the other branches of the Federal Government." Id. at 523. Congress passed legislation in 1987 to permit military personnel to wear conservative, unobtrusive religious apparel indoors, provided that it does not interfere with their military duties (see floor debate, reprinted on pp. 740–746).

ESTABLISHMENT CLAUSE

The church-state docket since the 1940s has been dominated by two issues: the appropriation of public funds to support sectarian schools, and government encouragement of prayer and religious instruction in public schools. Other cases, however, helped define the boundaries of the Establishment Clause.

In 1899, the Supreme Court upheld the appropriation of funds by Congress to a hospital operated by the Catholic Church. The Court denied that the statute violated the Establishment Clause. Religious ownership did not, by itself, make the hospital

[5]Watson v. Jones, 13 Wall. 679 (1872). See also Jones v. Wolf, 443 U.S. 595 (1979) and Presbyterian Church v. Hull Church, 393 U.S. 440, 449 (1969). State legislatures may not interfere with the selection of clergy to head a church. Kedroff v. St. Nicholas Cathedral, 344 U.S. 94 (1952); Serbian Orthodox Diocese v. Milovojevich, 426 U.S. 696 (1976).

religious or sectarian. The character of an institution is measured by the charter creating it. There was no allegation that the hospital was confined to members of the Catholic Church or that the hospital had violated its charter to serve the poor. Bradfield v. Roberts, 175 U.S. 291. The Court also held that a congressional appropriation to educate Indians in sectarian schools did not violate the Establishment Clause. The tribal and trust funds used for this purpose were not general public moneys. They belonged to the Indians as compensation for lands that they had ceded to the United States. Quick Bear v. Leupp, 210 U.S. 50 (1908).

In a more recent case, a state university allowed student secular groups to meet in university buildings but denied the same privilege to student religious groups. The university reasoned that giving permission to the latter would violate the Establishment Clause. The Supreme Court, voting 8–1, disagreed. State efforts to comply with the Establishment Clause do not permit discrimination against the religious speech of the student group seeking access to buildings for their meetings. Widmar v. Vincent, 454 U.S. 263 (1981). High school students may also form religious groups and meet in school rooms. Bender v. Williamsport Area School Dist., 475 U.S. 534 (1986). Congress passed legislation in 1984 to give student religious groups "equal access" to public high schools (p. 720).

Other state laws have been struck down as violations of the Establishment Clause. A Minnesota law provided that only religious organizations receiving more than half of their total contributions from members or affiliated organizations would be exempt from the registration and reporting requirements of a charitable solicitation statute. A 5–4 Supreme Court held that the statute violated the Establishment Clause because it set up an official denominational preference. The 50 percent rule was not "closely fitted" to the state's asserted interest in preventing fraudulent solicitations. Moreover, the statute presented too great a risk of politicizing religion. Different religious organizations would jockey for support within the legislature to obtain exemptions. Larson v. Valente, 456 U.S. 228 (1982).

In that same year the Court held that a Massachusetts statute violated the Establishment Clause by vesting in the governing bodies of churches the power to prevent issuance of liquor licenses within a 500-foot radius of the churches. The Court regarded the statute as a delegation of legislative zoning power to a nongovernmental entity. Not only was the churches' power under the statute standardless, calling for no reasons or findings for action, but the "mere appearance of a joint exercise of legislative authority by Church and State provides a significant symbolic benefit to religion in the minds of some by reason of the power conferred." Larkin v. Grendel's Den, Inc., 459 U.S. 116, 125–126 (1982).

The Court decided the above case by an 8–1 majority, with only Justice Rehnquist dissenting. Two years later, it split 5–4 in deciding what is called the "crèche case." The city of Pawtucket, R.I., annually erected a Christmas display, including a crèche or Nativity scene. In upholding the city, the Court offended some religious groups by reasoning that the crèche could be displayed because it had a "secular purpose." LYNCH v. DONNELLY, 465 U.S. 668 (1984). The decision opened the door to other governmental practices. The issue returned to the Court in 1989 in two forms: the constitutionality of a crèche on the grand staircase of the Allegheny County Courthouse and an eighteen-foot Chanukah menorah (candelabrum) plus a forty-five-foot decorated Christmas tree placed just outside the City-County Building. In a muddled decision, offering few intelligible principles to guide the lower courts (or state legislatures), the Court struck down the crèche display by the vote of 5-to-4 and upheld the menorah/Christmas tree display 6-to-3. Allegheny County v. Greater Pittsburgh ACLU, 109 S.Ct. 3086 (1989).

To reach this result, the majority concluded that the combination of a Jewish menorah and a Christmas tree somehow recognized "cultural diversity," with little appreciation that the attempt to transform a religious symbol to a cultural event would be offensive to many Jews. By noting that Christmas and Chanukah "are part of the same winter-holiday season, which has attained a secular status in our society," Justice Blackmun's opinion for the majority appeared to secularize, if not Christianize, a Jewish holiday. With regard to the crèche display, Justice Blackmun argued that it offended the Constitution in part because it stood alone, surrounded by a floral decoration, whereas the crèche in *Lynch* v. *Donnelly* was mixed with a Santa Claus house, reindeer pulling Santa's sleigh, candy-striped poles, a Christmas tree, carolers, and cutout figures representing such characters as a clown, an elephant, and a teddy bear. Would the addition of some of those objects save the crèche in Pittsburgh? No one knows. It is not even clear whether the menorah/ Christmas tree combination would be constitutional had the two symbols been transposed, placing the menorah directly in front of the entrance to the City-County Building with the Christmas tree positioned to the side. Finally, if municipalities are free to celebrate Christian and Jewish holidays, what of other sects and of nonbelievers? Does the goal of "cultural diversity" require representation for those groups? Instead of disposing of such questions the Court virtually invited any number of variations to revisit the judiciary.

Laws governing Sunday worship and Sunday closings affect both religion clauses: free exercise and establishment. State interests must be balanced against an individual's preference to worship on a day other than Sunday (so-called Sabbatarians). In one case, a Seventh-Day Adventist had been fired because she would not work on Saturday, the Sabbath Day of her faith. She was later denied unemployment compensation benefits on the ground that she would not accept suitable work when offered. The Court held that the state law violated her religious freedoms. This law was vulnerable on First Amendment grounds because the state expressly saved the Sunday worshipper from having to make the kind of choice faced by the Seventh-Day Adventist. Sherbert v. Verner, 374 U.S. 398, 406 (1963). Government may not put an employee in the predicament of choosing between fidelity to religious beliefs and access to public benefits. Hobbie v. Unemployment Appeals Comm'n of Fla., 480 U.S. 136 (1987); Thomas v. Review Bd., Ind. Empl. Sec. Div., 450 U.S. 707 (1981). It is not necessary to belong to an established religious sect that forbids work on Sundays. A sincere, personal religious belief is sufficient. Frazee v. Employment Security Dept., 109 S.Ct. 1514 (1989).

These cases were decided on constitutional grounds. Other cases revolve around statutory questions, including the intent of Congress when it passed legislation to prohibit religious discrimination. One provision states that employers have an obligation to "reasonably accommodate to an employee's . . . religious observance or practice without undue hardship on the conduct of the employer's business." 42 U.S.C. § 2000e(j) (1982). Congress added this provision after courts had "come down on both sides" of the rights of Sabbatarians. The language was intended to "resolve by legislation . . . that which the courts apparently have not resolved." 118 Cong. Rec. 705–706 (1972). These cases turn on questions of what burden of proof should be placed on the employee to prove discrimination. Ansonia Board of Education v. Philbrook, 479 U.S. 60 (1986). Congress also exempted religious organizations from the prohibition on religious discrimination in employment. 42 U.S.C. § 2000e-1 (1982). The purpose was to shield religious organizations from liability in the case of employment suits. A unanimous Court in 1987 held that this exemption does not offend the Establishment Clause. Corporation of Presiding Bishop v. Amos, 483 U.S. 327 (1987).

Although states may not discriminate against Sabbatarians, they can err by going in the opposite direction to promote their religious practice. In 1985, the Court held that a Connecticut law violated the Establishment Clause because it provided that no person "who states that a particular day of the week is observed as his Sabbath may be required by his employer to work on such day. An employee's refusal to work on his Sabbath shall not constitute grounds for his dismissal." The Court struck down the statute because it lacked neutrality in religious matters. Estate of Thornton v. Caldor, Inc., 472 U.S. 703. What began as an effort to accommodate the free exercise of religion ended up violating the Establishment Clause.

Sunday closing laws (or "blue laws") were challenged in court as a violation of the Establishment Clause. A major case involved a Maryland law that prohibited the sale on Sunday of all merchandise except the retail sale of tobacco products, confectionaries, milk, bread, fruit, gasoline, oils, greases, drugs, medicines, newspapers, and periodicals. After litigation began, the state legislature allowed other exceptions. In reviewing the history of Sunday closing laws, an 8–1 majority for the Supreme Court found that the original motivation had gradually changed from a religious character to a secular purpose in setting aside a day for rest and recreation. The fact that the day was Sunday, "a day of particular significance for the dominant Christian sects, does not bar the State from achieving its secular goals." McGowan v. Maryland, 366 U.S. 420, 445 (1961). The secularization of Sunday was evident in the repeal of earlier laws that had a distinctly religious purpose, such as banning bingo games, pinball machines, slot machines, dancing, and the sale of alcoholic beverages. Id. at 423–424, 448.

Corporations, claiming economic injury, were unsuccessful in challenging the Sunday closing laws. Two Guys v. McGinley, 366 U.S. 582 (1961). The effect of those laws raised more difficult questions when applied to Jewish businesses that closed Friday evening and all day Saturday to observe the Sabbath. The state forced them to close on Sunday as well. Dividing 6–3 on this issue, the Court reasoned that the law did not inconvenience all members of the Orthodox Jewish faith, but only those who chose to work on Sunday. Dodging the question of why Sunday would be selected as the official day of rest, the Court argued that any law was likely to result in an economic disadvantage to some religious sect. Braunfeld v. Brown, 366 U.S. 599 (1961). A Massachusetts law allowing kosher markets to sell kosher meats until 10 a.m. on Sunday was upheld 6–3 even though plaintiffs argued that it was economically impractical for them to stay open from Saturday at sundown until 10 a.m. on Sunday. These laws were saved because they had lost their original religious character. Gallagher v. Crown Kosher Market, 366 U.S. 617 (1961). See also Arlan's Dept. Store v. Kentucky, 371 U.S. 218 (1962). Some of the states changed their laws to permit businesses to operate on Sunday if religious convictions forced them to close on another day. Kroger Co. v. O'Hara Tp., 392 A.2d 266, 273 (Pa. 1978).

Lower courts have also been active in giving content to the Establishment Clause. States may not distribute free maps containing a "motorist's prayer." Although the alleged interest of the state was to promote highway safety, such publications have an undeniable religious purpose. Hall v. Bradshaw, 630 F.2d 1018 (4th Cir. 1980), cert. denied, 450 U.S. 965 (1981). Lower courts have held that the requirement of mandatory chapel attendance for cadets and midshipmen at federal military academies represents a violation of the Establishment Clause. Anderson v. Laird, 466 F.2d 283 (D.C. Cir. 1972), cert. denied, 409 U.S. 1076 (1972). Regarding laws on Sunday closings, a number of state courts concluded that they were so riddled with irrational exceptions that they violated the equal protection of the laws. Kroger Co. v. O'Hara Tp., 392 A.2d at 270; Caldor's, Inc. v. Bedding Barn, Inc., 417 A.2d 343, 346 (Conn. 1979).

In 1988, the Supreme Court decided an important case involving the use of federal funds to discourage adolescent, premarital sex. The statute, known formally as the Adolescent Family Life Act of 1981 and informally as the Teenage Chastity Act, authorized federal grants to public and private groups, including religious organizations. The Court acknowledged that some of the funds had been spent by religious groups impermissibly to promote religious doctrines. Nevertheless, a 5–4 Court held that the statute, *on its face*, did not violate the Establishment Clause. It remanded the case to the district court to determine whether the Act, *as applied*, violates the Clause. Bowen v. Kendrick, 108 S.Ct. 2562 (1988).

FINANCIAL ASSISTANCE TO SECTARIAN SCHOOLS

Before the *Everson* case of 1947, litigation on sectarian schools was limited to such questions as their right to exist. Pierce v. Society of Sisters, 268 U.S. 510 (1925). Other cases dealt with the liberty of private schools to teach certain subjects, such as German. Meyer v. Nebraska, 262 U.S. 390 (1923). Financial aid became an issue when Louisiana used public funds to supply school books to children in private schools, including sectarian schools. A unanimous Supreme Court sustained this legislation on the ground that the books were not religious (they were the same books used by public school students) and that the books benefited children and the state, not the religious schools. The state's interest in education, said the Court, justified the assistance. Cochran v. Board of Education, 281 U.S. 370 (1930). This "child benefit" theory became the basis for upholding other forms of state assistance to sectarian schools. In time, the Court came to recognize that this theory opened the door to almost unlimited public funding of religious schools.

In 1947, a sharply divided Supreme Court upheld a New Jersey statute that reimbursed parents for the cost of sending their children to parochial schools on public buses. The 5–4 decision also declared that the Establishment Clause was applicable to the states just as *Cantwell* in 1940 had applied the Free Exercise Clause to the states. Justice Black's opinion for the Court made a number of unrealistic claims about separating church and state. He said that neither a state nor the federal government "can pass laws which aid one religion, aid all religions, or prefer one religion over another." EVERSON v. BOARD OF EDUCATION, 330 U.S. 1, 15. Yet, New Jersey aided parochial schools by reimbursing transportation costs, and later Court decisions would uphold other forms of assistance. Congress has even passed laws to assist particular religions, such as the social security exemption for the Amish. Black also asserted: "No tax in any amount, large or small, can be levied to support any religious activities or institutions . . ." In fact, taxpayer funds have been used to provide transportation, textbooks, and other types of state and federal aid to religious institutions. Finally, Black claimed that neither a state nor the federal government "can, openly or secretly, participate in the affairs of any religious organizations or groups and *vice versa*." This, too, was superficial. Government may establish health, safety, and curricula standards for sectarian schools, and religious organizations may lobby legislatures, the courts, and the agencies. Four Justices dissented from Black's opinion. Justice Douglas, who joined with Black, later admitted doubts about *Everson*. Engel v. Vitale, 370 U.S. 421, 443 (1962); Walz v. Tax Commission, 397 U.S. 664, 703 (1970).

The next step in supporting financial assistance to sectarian schools came in 1968. A New York law required textbooks to be "lent" free of charge to all students in grades 7 through 12, including children attending private and sectarian schools. A 6–3 decision by the Court held that the statute was constitutional because the benefit was to parents and children, not to schools. Board of Education v. Allen, 392 U.S. 236. The child-benefit theory would look less appealing five years later when the Court struck down a Mississippi law that authorized the lending of books to all-white, nonsectarian private schools. The state argued that the statute benefited children, not schools. The Court dismissed this claim as a way to rationalize state assistance to segregated schools. Norwood v. Harrison, 413 U.S. 455 (1973). The Court was willing to preserve a legal fiction on church-state questions while facing reality on racial segregation.

Interestingly, the opinion for the Court in *Allen* defended the textbook assistance partly on the basis of *Everson*, and yet Black, the author of *Everson*, dissented along with Douglas and Fortas. Black now realized what he had invited with his child-benefit theory in the transportation case: "It requires no prophet to foresee that on the argument used to support this law others could be upheld providing for state or federal government funds to buy property on which to erect religious school buildings or to erect the buildings themselves, to pay the salaries of the religious school teachers, and finally to have the sectarian religious groups cease to rely on voluntary contributions of members of their sects while waiting for the Government to pick up all the bills for the religious schools." Id. at 253. A number of state courts, interpreting highly restrictive language in their constitutions, refused to uphold transportation and textbook assistance to sectarian schools. They specifically rejected the child-benefit theory embraced by the Supreme Court.[6]

In 1970, the Court upheld tax exemptions to religious organizations for properties used solely for religious worship. The Court decided 8–1 that the exemption was not aimed at establishing, sponsoring, or supporting religion; tax exemption created only a minimal and remote involvement between church and state; and government involvement would be far greater with taxation. Apparently decisive for the Court was the persistence of tax exemptions to religious bodies for almost two centuries. Walz v. Tax Commission, 397 U.S. 664, 677. The thrust of *Walz* was limited in 1989 when the Court struck down as a violation of the Establishment Clause a Texas law that exempted religious publications from sales taxes. However, the meaning of this

---

[6]Visser v. Nooksack Valley School Dist. No. 506, 207 P.2d 198 (Wash. 1949); McVey v. Hawkins, 258 S.W.2d 927 (Mo. 1953); Matthews v. Quinton, 362 P.2d 932, 936 (Alas. 1961); Dickman v. School District No. 62C, 366 P.2d 533 (Ore. 1961), cert. denied, 371 U.S. 823 (1962); State v. Nusbaum, 115 N.W.2d 761 (Wis. 1962); Opinion of the Justices, 216 A.2d 668 (Del. 1966); Epeldi v. Engelking, 488 P.2d 860 (Idaho 1971), cert. denied, 406 U.S. 957 (1972); Gaffney v. State Department of Education, 220 N.W.2d 550 (Neb. 1974); Bloom v. School Committee of Springfield, 379 N.E.2d 578 (Mass. 1978); California Teachers Ass'n v. Riles, 632 P.2d 953, 962 (Cal. 1981).

decision was diluted by several concurring opinions. Texas Monthly, Inc. v. Bullock, 109 S.Ct. 890 (1989).

The next year, the Court attempted to restrict the flow of financial assistance to sectarian schools by striking down laws in two states. Pennsylvania had given state funds to nonpublic elementary and secondary schools by reimbursing teachers' salaries, textbooks, and institutional materials in secular subjects. Rhode Island paid teachers in nonpublic elementary schools a supplement of 15 percent of their annual salaries. By a 7–0 vote in the Pennsylvania case and a 7–1 vote in the Rhode Island case, the Court found that these forms of assistance violated the religion clauses. Three tests were developed to determine constitutionality: (1) the statute must have a secular legislative purpose, (2) its principal or primary effect must be one that neither advances nor inhibits religion, and (3) it must not foster excessive entanglement with religion. LEMON v. KURTZMAN, 403 U.S. 602, 612–613 (1971). This three-prong test is frequently waived or ignored by the courts. For example, the government often passes laws that seek to accommodate religious practices (in the form of various exemptions), and these laws are generally sustained even though their primary effect is to advance religion.

On the same day that the Court struck down the Pennsylvania and Rhode Island statutes, it upheld by a 5–4 vote a congressional statute that provided construction grants for church-related colleges and universities. The money was spent for buildings with a nonreligious purpose: libraries, a science building, a language laboratory, and a music, drama, and arts building. It was significant to the Court that there was less religious indoctrination in colleges than in elementary and secondary schools, where student minds are more impressionable. It ruled, however, that the congressional provision allowing the religious use of these buildings after twenty years to be a violation of the religion clauses. Tilton v. Richardson, 403 U.S. 672, 683–684 (1971).

In subsequent decisions the Court confronted new forms of financial assistance to sectarian schools. New York appropriated $28 million to reimburse nonpublic schools for expenses related to examinations, recordkeeping, and reports mandated by the state. The Court held that this aid contravened the Establishment Clause. There was no audit to determine if state payments exceeded costs by the schools, and some of the tests might not be free of religious instruction. The schools had argued that the state should be permitted to pay for any activity mandated by state law or regulation, but the Court rejected this theory because it could require state payments for minimum lighting or sanitary facilities for all school buildings. Levitt v. Committee for Public Education, 413 U.S. 472, 481 (1973). A later effort by New York to reimburse nonpublic schools for expenses incurred before the Court's decision was declared unconstitutional. New York v. Cathedral Academy, 434 U.S. 125 (1977).

Three other cases in 1973 concerned financial assistance to sectarian schools. A South Carolina statute had authorized the issuance of revenue bonds that benefited a Baptist-controlled college. Using *Lemon*'s three-part test, the Court held 6–3 that the statute did not violate the Establishment Clause. The Act had a secular purpose (benefiting higher education), its primary effect was not to advance or inhibit religion, and there was no excessive entanglement with religion. *Tilton* was cited to support state assistance to schools at the university level. The Court found that the Baptist college had no significant religious orientation. The three dissenters viewed the state as deeply involved in the fiscal affairs of the college, even to the extent of fixing tuition rates as part of the state's duty to assure sufficient revenues to meet bond and interest obligations. Hunt v. McNair, 413 U.S. 734, 753 (1973).

Another New York statute provided direct money grants to qualifying nonpublic schools. The money was used to maintain and repair facilities and equipment, to reimburse low-income parents who sent their children to nonpublic elementary and secondary schools, and to provide tax relief for parents failing to qualify for tuition reimbursement. The Supreme Court held that all three forms of assistance violated the Establishment Clause, even if the tuition grants went to the parents rather than directly to the schools. All of the Justices agreed that the maintenance and repair provision was unconstitutional. Chief Justice Burger and Justices White and Rehnquist would have upheld the reimbursement and tax relief provisions. Committee for Public Education v. Nyquist, 413 U.S. 756 (1973).

The Court tried to explain why tax exemptions were permissible in *Walz* (they were "indirect and incidental") while the tax credits at stake in the New York statutes were unconstitutional. The decisive element was that the granting of new tax benefits, in contrast to the extension of tax exemptions, "would tend to increase rather than limit the involvement between Church and State." The Court had to weigh the "potentially divisive political effect of an aid program." Support for maintenance and repair and the grants for tuition would require appropriations each year, opening the door to continuing strife between church and state. Id. at 793-797.

In short, the Court had to do more than interpret constitutional text and case law. It had to make a political judgment about the level of tension and confrontation likely to result from government assistance to sectarian schools. It was for this reason that it also struck down a Pennsylvania statute that reimbursed parents for a portion of tuition expenses incurred in sending their children to nonpublic schools. More than 90 percent of the nonpublic schools were sectarian. The Court rejected the contention that tuition assistance went to parents rather than to schools. Sloan v. Lemon, 413 U.S. 825 (1973).

In other decisions involving financial assistance to sectarian schools the Court split 6–3 or 5–4. Lengthy concurrences made it difficult to chart the positions of individual Justices. A 1975 decision responded to a Pennsylvania statute that authorized "auxiliary services" and textbook loans to all children enrolled in nonpublic elementary and secondary schools. The state could loan instructional materials and equipment. Auxiliary services included counseling, testing, psychological services, and speech and hearing therapy; instructional materials included periodicals, photographs, maps, charts, recordings, and films; instructional equipment embraced such items as projectors, recorders, and laboratory paraphernalia. A 6–3 Court, made more complex by Justices concurring in part and dissenting in part, held that everything but textbook loans violated the Establishment Clause. The Court continued to believe that textbook loans benefited parents and children, not schools. Meek v. Pittenger, 421 U.S. 349, 361.

Would it have made a constitutional difference if instructional materials and equipment had been "lent" to parents and children rather than to schools? Justice Brennan, joined by Justices Douglas and Marshall, said it was "pure fantasy" to treat the textbook program as a loan to students: "The whole business is handled by the school and public authorities and neither parents nor children have a say. The guidelines make crystal clear that the nonpublic school, not its pupils, is the motivating force behind the textbook loan, and that virtually the entire loan transaction is to be, and is in fact, conducted between officials of the nonpublic school, on the one hand, and officers of the State on the other." Id. at 379–380.

A year later the Court, divided 5–4, upheld a Maryland grant of state funds to colleges and universities that refrained from awarding "only seminarian or theological degrees." Funds could not be used for sectarian purposes. The four colleges were affiliated with the Roman Catholic Church. The federal district court had found that the religious colleges were not "pervasively sectarian" or substantially involved in indoctrination. In one of the dissents, Justice Stevens expressed concern about "the pernicious tendency of a state subsidy to tempt religious schools to compromise their religious mission without wholly abandoning it." Roemer v. Maryland Public Works Bd., 426 U.S. 736, 775 (1976).

Ohio authorized various forms of aid to nonpublic schools, most of which were sectarian. Splitting in various directions, the Court upheld the provisions extending assistance for secular textbooks, standardized testing and scoring, diagnostic services, and therapeutic and remedial services. It struck down the portions of the law relating to instructional materials, instructional equipment, and providing transportation and services for field trips. The state statute "loaned" the instructional materials and equipment to the pupils or their parents, but the Court dismissed this mechanism as a patent effort to exploit the *Meek* holding. Parents and students were being used as a conduit to funnel assistance to the schools. Wolman v. Walter, 433 U.S. 229, 250 (1977). Justice Marshall, who had voted with the majority in *Allen* to uphold textbook loans, now announced that it should be overruled and a new line drawn between church and state. Id. at 256–259.

In 1980, the Supreme Court reviewed a New York law similar to the payment system declared unconstitutional in *Levitt* in 1973. The law directed payment to nonpublic schools for their costs in complying with certain state-mandated requirements, including testing, reporting, and recordkeeping. The new law provided for state auditing to assure that public funds would be used only for secular purposes (a safeguard absent from the law struck down in *Levitt*). A 5–4 decision held that the statute did not violate the Establishment Clause. Justice Blackmun's dissent, joined by Brennan and Marshall, pointed out that the "state-mandated" requirements would have been performed by the schools, with or without reimbursement. Justice Stevens, also dissenting, criticized the Court's opinion as "another in a long line of cases making largely ad hoc decisions about what payments may or may not be constitutionally made to nonpublic schools." He said the Court's rationale could be used to justify state subsidies for fire drills or the construction and maintenance of fireproof classrooms. Moreover, he advised that "the entire enterprise of trying to justify various types of subsidies to nonpublic schools should be abandoned." Committee for Public Education v. Regan, 444 U.S. 646, 671 (1980).

Two decisions in 1985 demonstrate the profound disagreement within the Burger Court on public assistance to sectarian schools. One decision, on which the Court divided 5–4, held invalid a New York program that used federal funds to pay the salaries of public school employees who taught in parochial schools. Although the state monitored the content of federally funded classes to avoid the advancement of religion (part of the *Lemon* test), this very involvement produced excessive entanglement of church and state. AGUILAR v. FELTON, 473 U.S. 402. The other decision involved a complicated Michigan program that used public funds to teach nonpublic school students in classrooms located in and leased from nonpublic schools. A "shared time" program offered secular classes during the regular school day. The teachers were full-time employees of the public schools, but a "significant portion" had previously taught in nonpublic schools. A second program, called "community education," was voluntary and offered secular classes after school. These teachers were part-time public school employees generally employed in the nonpublic schools in which the classes were held. Most of the nonpublic schools were sectarian religious schools. A 5–4 decision held that both programs had the primary effect of advancing religion. Grand Rapids School District v. Ball, 473 U.S. 373.

Federal assistance to sectarian schools may also implicate the Property Clause, which empowers Congress "to dispose of and make all needful Rules and Regulations respecting the Territory or other Property belonging to the United States." Art. IV, § 3, Cl. 2. Pursuant to this Clause, Congress passed a law governing the disposition of surplus federal property and the government transferred a military hospital to a church-related college. An organization favoring church-state separation filed suit on the ground that the transfer violated the Establishment Clause. A 5–4 decision by the Supreme Court held that the organization lacked standing to bring the suit. Moreover, the Court reasoned that the transfer was not pursuant to the Taxing and Spending Clause, under which the parties might have had standing, but under the Property Clause. Relying on a legal fiction, the majority claimed that the source of the complaint was not a congressional action but rather an agency action to transfer a parcel of federal property. Through this rationale the parties were unable to challenge the action under the Establishment Clause. The dissenters accused the majority of engaging in a "dissembling exercise." Valley Forge College v. Americans United, 454 U.S. 464, 493 (1982) (reprinted in Chapter 3).

Tax deductions are another source of state assistance to sectarian schools. A Minnesota law allowed taxpayers, in computing their state income tax, to deduct expenses incurred in providing tuition, textbooks, and transportation for their children attending elementary and secondary schools, including schools of a sectarian nature. Another 5–4 decision by the Supreme Court held that the statute did not violate the Establishment Clause. It met the three-part *Lemon* test, even though the law helped fund sectarian textbooks. Mueller v. Allen, 463 U.S. 388 (1983).

In 1986, in a rare unanimous ruling regarding government assistance to sectarian schools, the Court held that state aid under a rehabilitation program to finance an individual's training at a Christian college did not advance religion in a way inconsistent with the Establishment Clause. The assistance was defended on the ground that it went to the student, who then transmitted it to an institution of his or her choice. The majority opinion made no mention of *Mueller*, which four concurring Justices thought should have formed the basis for the decision. Witters v. Wash. Dept. of Services for Blind, 474 U.S. 481 (see Table 2).

RELIGIOUS INSTRUCTION AND PRAYERS IN PUBLIC SCHOOLS

Beginning in 1948, the Supreme Court has had to referee an extraordinarily divisive and emotional issue: efforts to introduce religious instruction and prayers into public schools. Especially with regard to the prayer issue, the Supreme Court has been vilified for "driving God out of the classroom."

A 1948 case dealt with an Illinois law that allowed religious teachers to give religious instruction in public school buildings once a week. Parents could excuse

TABLE 2   Court Decisions Involving Financial Assistance to Sectarian Schools

Assistance Sustained	Assistance Invalidated
Transportation. Everson v. Board of Education, 330 U.S. 1 (1947).	*Teachers' salaries.* Lemon v. Kurtzman, 403 U.S. 602 (1971).
Textbooks. Board of Education v. Allen, 392 U.S. 236 (1968); Meek v. Pittenger, 421 U.S. 349 (1975); Wolman v. Walter, 433 U.S. 229 (1977).	*Examinations, recordkeeping, and reports (without state auditing).* Levitt v. Committee for Public Education, 413 U.S. 472 (1973).
Tax exemptions. Walz v. Tax Commission, 397 U.S. 664 (1970).	*Maintenance and repair of facilities and equipment; reimbursements for low-income parents; tax relief for parents not qualifying for tuition reimbursement.* Committee for Public Education v. Nyquist, 413 U.S. 756 (1973).
Construction grants for colleges. Tilton v. Richardson, 403 U.S. 672 (1971).	
Revenue bonds for colleges. Hunt v. McNair, 413 U.S. 734 (1973).	*Reimbursements for tuition expenses.* Sloan v. Lemon, 413 U.S. 825 (1973).
State grants to colleges. Roemer v. Maryland Public Works Bd., 426 U.S. 736 (1976).	*Counseling, testing, psychological services, and speech and hearing therapy; instructional materials including periodicals, photographs, maps, charts, recordings, and films; instructional equipment including projectors, recorders, and laboratory paraphernalia.* Meek v. Pittenger, 421 U.S. 349 (1975).
Standardized testing and scoring; diagnostic services; therapeutic and remedial services. Wolman v. Walter, 433 U.S. 229 (1977).	
Testing, reporting, and recordkeeping (with state auditing). Committee for Public Education v. Regan, 444 U.S. 646 (1980).	*Instructional materials, instructional equipment, and transportation and services for field trips.* Wolman v. Walter, 433 U.S. 229 (1977).
"Surplus" federal property for colleges. Valley Forge College v. Americans United, 454 U.S. 464 (1982).	*Salaries for public school employees teaching in parochial schools.* Aguilar v. Felton, 473 U.S. 402 (1985).
State aid under a rehabilitation program to finance training at a Christian college. Witters v. Wash. Dept. of Services for Blind, 474 U.S. 481 (1986).	*Public funds to teach nonpublic school students in classrooms located in and leased from nonpublic schools.* Grand Rapids School District v. Ball, 473 U.S. 373 (1985).
Tax deductions for expenses incurred in providing tuition, textbooks, and transportation. Mueller v. Allen, 463 U.S. 388 (1983).	

their children from secular classes to attend religious instruction. The Court held, 8–1, that use of the state's tax-supported public schools for compulsory education to enable sectarian groups to give religious instruction to students in public school buildings violated the religion clauses. In a concurring opinion, joined by Justices Jackson, Rutledge, and Burton, Justice Frankfurter spoke about the dangers of coercing children: "The law of imitation operates, and non-conformity is not an outstanding characteristic of children. The result is an obvious pressure upon children to attend." McCollum v. Board of Education, 333 U.S. 203, 227.

Advocates of religious instruction next proposed that it be done outside the school building. New York City permitted its public schools to release students during school hours, on written requests from their parents, to go to religious centers for religious instruction or devotional exercises. Students not released stayed in the public school classrooms. The churches providing the instruction reported the names of children released for instruction but who failed to appear. The Supreme Court, divided 6–3, held that the "released time" program did not violate the religion clauses. Writing for the majority, Justice Douglas said that when the state "encourages religious instruction or cooperates with religious authorities by adjusting the schedule of public events to sectarian needs, it follows the best of our traditions. For it then respects the religious nature of our people and accommodates the public service to their spiritual needs." Zorach v. Clauson, 343 U.S. 306, 313–314 (1952). This "accommodationist" stance departs from the Court's frequent call for neutrality. Encouragement, urged by Douglas, is not neutrality. Douglas went on to say that no constitutional requirement made it necessary for government "to be hostile to religion and to throw its weight against efforts to widen the effective scope of religious influence." Id. at 314. But why is neutrality (not participating in a released-time program) "hostility"?

Justice Black, who had adopted the accommodationist position when he upheld reimbursement of transportation costs in *Everson*, dissented in the released-time case. He accused the Court of abandoning the neutrality principle by endorsing a law that helped "religious sects get attendants presumably too unenthusiastic to go unless moved to do so by the pressure of this state machinery." Frankfurter, dissenting, agreed with this criticism of the majority's opinion. Jackson, in the third dissent, put the matter forcefully: "Here schooling is more or less suspended during the 'released time' so the nonreligious attendants will not forge ahead of the churchgoing absentees. But it serves as a temporary jail for a pupil who will not go to Church. It takes more subtlety of mind than I possess to deny that this is governmental constraint in support of religion."

If the Court attempted to accommodate religious groups in *Zorach*, in 1962 it set off a storm still raging by holding that a New York "Regents' Prayer" was unconstitutional. State law directed that the following prayer be said aloud by each class of a public school at the beginning of each day: "Almighty God, we acknowledge our dependence upon Thee, and we beg Thy blessings upon us, our parents, our teachers and our Country." The 6–1 decision, written by Black, argued that the Establishment Clause "must at least mean that in this country it is no part of the business of government to compose official prayers for any group of the American people to recite as a part of a religious program carried on by government." ENGEL v. VITALE, 370 U.S. 421, 425. Douglas' concurrence offered unfortunate and unnecessary speculations about the use of prayers in opening the business of the Supreme Court and of Congress. Stewart's dissent also strayed from the issue before the Court. He did not want to deny school children their "wish" to recite the prayer or to interfere with those "who want to begin their day by joining in prayer," but the issue was not the desire of children to pray on their own initiative. It was the constitutionality of a state composing an official prayer for minors in public schools. Congressional hearings revealed broad support by Protestant, Catholic, and Jewish organizations for the Court's ruling (pp. 770–772).

A year later, the Court decided 8–1 that states may not require that passages from the Bible be read or that the Lord's Prayer be recited in the public schools at the beginning of each day, even if individual students may be excused upon written request of their parents. The Court did not bar the study of the Bible or of religion "when presented objectively as part of a secular program of education." Abington School Dist. v. Schempp, 374 U.S. 203, 225 (1963). Stewart was again the lone dissenter.

States have been active in prohibiting the teaching of evolution in the schools. Tennessee's "monkey law," adopted in 1925, led to the famous *Scopes* case in 1927. Scopes v. State, 289 S.W. 363 (Tenn. 1927). When the issue of anti-evolution laws reached the Supreme Court in 1968, a unanimous Court struck down Arkansas' statute making it unlawful for a teacher in any state-supported school or university to teach or use a textbook that claimed that mankind evolved from a lower order of animals. The statute violated the Establishment Clause because a particular religious group considered the evolution theory in conflict with the Book of Genesis. Epperson v. Arkansas, 393 U.S. 97.

In 1987, a 7–2 Court held invalid Louisiana's "Creationism Act," which prohibited the teaching of the theory of evolution in public elementary and secondary schools unless accompanied by instruction in the theory of "creation science." The latter, based on the Book of Genesis, opposes the theory of evolution. The Court rejected the state's assertion that the statute furthered "academic freedom." The legislative record revealed a bias in favor of creationism and religious doctrine. EDWARDS v. AGUILLARD, 482 U.S. 578 (1987). Recent cases in the lower courts concern challenges to textbooks that allegedly promote the "religion" of secular humanism.[7]

The votes on these cases show a remarkable strength for the majority of the Supreme Court: 8–1 in *McCollum*, 6–1 in *Engel*, 8–1 in *Abington*, unanimous in *Epperson*, and 7–2 in *Edwards*. Only in *Zorach* was the Court seriously divided (6–3).

No such agreement marks other decisions on religious instruction and prayer. In 1980, the Court split 5–4 in holding that a Kentucky statute requiring the posting of a copy of the Ten Commandments on the wall of each public school classroom violated the Establishment Clause. Although the copies were purchased with private funds, the mere posting provided official state support for religion. Portions of the Ten Commandments could have been regarded as secular in purpose (the parts concerning honoring one's parents, killing, adultery, stealing, false witness, and covetousness), but other sections were clearly religious in nature (worshiping the Lord God alone, avoiding idolatry, not using the Lord's name in vain, and observing the Sabbath Day). Stone v. Graham, 449 U.S. 39, 41–42. The dissenters were Chief Justice Burger and Justices Blackmun, Stewart, and Rehnquist.

In 1983, the Court divided 6–3 in upholding the practice of the Nebraska legislature to begin each of its sessions with a prayer by a chaplain paid by the state with the legislature's approval. The Court noted that Congress has followed the same practice without interruption for almost 200 years, and that precedents dating back to the First Congress, which drafted the Bill of Rights, shed important light on what the framers intended by the Establishment Clause. Marsh v. Chambers, 463 U.S. 783. As Justice Brennan noted in his dissent, the historical analogy allowed the Court to violate *Lemon*'s three-part test. The Nebraska statute had a religious, not a secular, purpose; its principal or primary effect advanced religion; and it fostered government entanglement with religion.

While the Nebraska chaplain case was wending its way through the courts, a separate challenge concerned the chaplains in the U.S. Senate and the U.S. House of Representatives. A district judge held in 1981 that the taxpayer had no standing to bring the suit. Murray v. Morton, 505 F.Supp. 144 (D.D.C. 1981). However, the

---

[7]A federal judge in Tennessee held that a state requirement for all students in grades 1 through 8 to use a prescribed set of reading textbooks was unconstitutional because the books contained "secular humanist" teachings that offended Christian beliefs. Mozert v. Hawkins County Public Schools, 647 F.Supp. 1194 (E.D. Tenn. 1986). His decision was overturned by a unanimous panel of the Sixth Circuit; 827 F.2d 1058 (6th Cir. 1987), cert. denied, 108 S.Ct. 1029 (1988). A federal judge in Alabama also banned textbooks from public schools in the state because they promoted the "religion" of secular humanism. Smith v. Board of Com'rs of Mobile County, 655 F.Supp. 939 (S.D. Ala. 1987). His decision was reversed by the Eleventh Circuit; 827 F.2d 684 (11th Cir. 1987).

appellate court reinstated the suit and sent the case back to the trial judge for a decision on the merits. Murray v. Buchanan, 674 F.2d 14 (D.C. Cir. 1982). Three weeks later the House of Representatives passed a resolution viewing with "deep concern" the appellate court decision and expressing in strong terms the constitutional power of the House "to determine the rules of its proceedings, to select officers, and otherwise to control its internal affairs." The resolution also stated that the decision of the appellate court "implies a lack of respect due a coordinate branch concerning matters committed to it by the Constitution." The resolution passed by the vote of 388 to zero. 128 Cong. Rec. 5890–5896 (1982). The case was then heard by the D.C. Circuit, sitting en banc. Because of the Supreme Court's decision in *Marsh* v. *Chambers*, the D.C. Circuit held that the complaint against the House and Senate chaplains "retains no vitality" and dismissed the case. Murray v. Buchanan, 720 F.2d 689 (D.C. Cir. 1983) (en banc).

A 1985 decision saw the Court again badly fractured on questions of prayer. The case concerned Alabama's one-minute period of silence in all public schools "for meditation or voluntary prayer." A 6–3 Court, this time using the *Lemon* test, found that the state law violated the religion clauses because the purpose of the statute was to advance religion. WALLACE v. JAFFREE, 472 U.S. 38. A New Jersey "moment of silence" statute reached the Supreme Court in 1987 but the case was dismissed because the parties bringing the case no longer had standing. Karcher v. May, 108 S.Ct. 388 (1987).

Members of Congress have responded to the prayer decisions by introducing legislation to permit voluntary prayer by school children. These bills sometimes propose that federal courts be denied jurisdiction to enter any judgment, decree, or order denying or restricting voluntary prayer in any public school. The Senate has engaged in long filibusters to block action on these bills. Amendments to the Constitution have been introduced to allow voluntary prayer in public schools. President Reagan endorsed this approach and, in 1984, the Senate Judiciary Committee reported the amendment. The measure fell eleven votes short of the necessary two-thirds. Religious groups remain divided on the issue. Some favor governmental sponsorship of prayer as an appropriate means of promoting public morality. Others just as strongly oppose what they consider to be governmental interference with matters of privacy and conscience.

In 1984, Congress passed the "Equal Access" bill. Building on the Court's decision in *Widmar* v. *Vincent* (1981), which upheld the right of student religious groups to have access to university buildings for their meetings, Congress gave students in public high schools the same right. The law prohibits any public secondary school receiving federal funds from denying equal access to students who wish to conduct a meeting devoted to religious objectives. Such meetings are to be voluntary, student-initiated, and without sponsorship by the school. 98 Stat. 1302. See also Bender v. Williamsport Area School Dist., 475 U.S. 534 (1986). The Equal Access Act of 1984 has encountered opposition from some school authorities who find ways to prevent religious clubs from meeting in school. The result is additional litigation to determine the intent of Congress.

NINE JUSTICES IN SEARCH OF A MODEL

The Court has experimented with a number of tests and models in trying to referee church-state disputes. The child-benefit theory, adopted in *Everson*, was largely abandoned after states used it to justify an increasing array of financial assistance to sectarian schools. The three-part *Lemon* test has been more durable, partly because its generality allows the Court to reshape it or ignore it for individual cases. Does a statute have a "secular legislative purpose"? Secular is often redefined to meet the case at hand. Is the "principal or primary effect" of a statute such that it neither "advances nor inhibits" religion? Does the statute foster "excessive entanglement" with religion? These formulations give the Court ample room to maneuver. The tests can even conflict. As Justice Rehnquist noted in one dissent, the entanglement test presents a "Catch-22" paradox. Aid must be supervised by the state to avoid religious content in state-funded secular classes, "but the supervision itself is held to cause an entanglement." Aguilar v. Felton, 473 U.S. at 421.

If the *Lemon* test presents difficulties for the Court, it can switch to a different model and justify a religious practice on the historical record. It used this approach in upholding tax exemptions in *Walz* and state chaplains in *Marsh*. In the latter case, Justice Brennan objected to the Court's sanctioning of a contemporary practice simply because it was done at the time of the First Congress: "Legislators, influenced by the passions and exigencies of the moment, the pressure of constituents and colleagues, and the press of business, do not always pass sober constitutional judgment on every piece of legislation they enact, and this must be assumed to be as true of the members of the First Congress as any other." He also noted that the Court often recognizes that the practices in place "at the time any particular guarantee was enacted into the Constitution do not necessarily fix forever the meaning of that guarantee."

Another test is to distinguish between state aid to primary and secondary schools and state aid to colleges and universities. A more tolerant judicial attitude toward the latter, on the ground that college students are less likely to be indoctrinated to a particular religious creed, was used to sustain financial assistance in *Tilton*, *Hunt*, and *Roemer*.

The Court has not consistently adopted a policy of "neutrality" toward religions. The majority in several cases openly follows a principle of supporting religious belief. Justice Douglas justified the released-time program in *Zorach* because it "encourages religious instruction" and therefore "follows the best of our traditions." When Chief Justice Burger wrote the opinion in 1970 upholding tax exemptions to religious organizations, he claimed that the exemption was "neither the advancement nor the inhibition of religion; it is neither sponsorship nor hostility." Yet, a page later, he explained that the state has an "affirmative policy" to consider religious groups "as beneficial and stabilizing influences in community life . . ." Walz v. Tax Commission, 397 U.S. 664, 672–673. An affirmative and supportive attitude is also reflected in his commitment to a "benevolent neutrality" toward churches and religious exercises. Id. at 676–677. Such remarks appear to make the Court a partisan for one side.

Justice Black warned in *Engel* v. *Vitale* that a union of government and religion injures both parties because it "tends to destroy government and to degrade religion." The cost has been substantial for religion. Its "secularization" has reduced the phrase "In God We Trust" (found on coins, in the national anthem, and in the national motto) to patriotic rather than theological significance. According to the reasoning in *Lynch* v. *Donnelly*, even the crèche has been secularized as part of the Christmas season. Pressure for prayer in public schools risks the formulation of bland language to satisfy all sects. In their quest for state and federal funds, some religious schools are tempted to surrender autonomy and to dilute the sectarian content of their courses.

Selected Readings

BLANCHARD, PAUL. *God and Man in Washington*. Boston: Beacon Press, 1960.

BROWN, ERNEST J. "Quis Custodiet Ipsos Custodes?—The School-Prayer Cases." 1963 *Supreme Court Review* 1.

CAHN, EDMUND. "THE 'ESTABLISHMENT OF RELIGION' PUZZLE." 36 *New York University Law Review* 1274 (1961).

CHOPER, JESSE H. "The Religion Clauses of the First Amendment: Reconciling the Conflict." 41 *University of Pittsburgh Law Review* 673 (1980).

CORD, ROBERT L. *Separation of Church and State: Historical Fact and Current Fiction*. New York: Lambeth Press, 1982.

DOLBEARE, KENNETH M., AND PHILLIP E. HAMMOND. *The School Prayer Decisions*. Chicago: University of Chicago Press, 1971.

GIANNELLA, DONALD A. "Religious Liberty, Nonestablishment, and Doctrinal Development: The Religious Liberty Guarantee." 80 *Harvard Law Review* 1381 (1967).

——. "Religious Liberty, Nonestablishment, and Doctrinal Development: The Nonestablishment Principle." 81 *Harvard Law Review* 513 (1968).

——. "Lemon and Tilton: The Bitter and the Sweet of Church-State Entanglement." 1971 *Supreme Court Review* 147.

GREENAWALT, KENT. "All or Nothing at All: The Defeat of Selective Conscientious Objection." 1971 *Supreme Court Review* 31.

HEUBEL, E. J. "Church and State in England: The Price of Establishment." 18 *Western Political Quarterly* 646 (1965).

KATZ, WILBUR G. "Radiations from Church Tax Exemption." 1970 *Supreme Court Review* 93.

KAUPER, PAUL G. *Religion and the Constitution*. Baton Rouge: Louisiana State University Press, 1964.

——. "Church Autonomy and the First Amendment: The Presbyterian Church Case." 1969 *Supreme Court Review* 347.

KELLY, DEAN M., ed. *Government Intervention in Religious Affairs*. New York: Pilgrim Press, 1982.

KURLAND, PHILIP B. *Religion and the Law: Of Church and State and the Supreme Court*. Chicago: Aldine Publishing, 1962.

——. "The Regents' Prayer Case: 'Full of Sound and Fury, Signifying . . .'" 1962 *Supreme Court Review* 1.

LEVY, LEONARD W. *The Establishment Clause: Religion and the First Amendment*. New York: Macmillan, 1986.

MORGAN, RICHARD E. *The Supreme Court and Religion*. New York: The Free Press, 1972.

——. "The Establishment Clause and Sectarian Schools: A Final Installment?" 1973 *Supreme Court Review* 57.

OAKS, DALLIN H., ed. *The Wall between Church and State*. Chicago: University of Chicago Press, 1963.

PFEFFER, LEO. *Church, State, and Freedom*. Boston: Beacon Press, 1967.

SORAUF, FRANK J. *The Wall of Separation: The Constitutional Politics of Church and State*. Princeton, N.J.: Princeton University Press, 1976.

STOKES, ANSON PHELPS. *Church and State in the United States*. 3 vols. New York: Harper & Row, 1950.

VAN ALSTYNE, WILLIAM W. "Constitutional Separation of Church and State: The Quest for a Coherent Position." 57 *American Political Science Review* 865 (1963).

Virginia Statute for Establishing Religious Freedom (1786)

James Madison, Thomas Jefferson, and George Mason were in the forefront of Virginians who challenged the established Anglican Church and sought to secure religious liberty for all citizens. For them, religious belief was a natural right entrusted to the conscience of the individual and could not be the subject of state interference or coercion. That principle was included in the state Bill of Rights in 1776. Three years later, Virginia repealed its law requiring members of the Anglican Church to support their own ministry. The Church advocated a general tax to benefit all Christian religions, but Madison and others were successful in defeating the bill. Madison was then able to pass,

in 1786, Jefferson's Statute for Establishing Religious Freedom. The bill is reproduced from William Waller Hening, *The Statutes at Large: Being a Collection of All the Laws of Virginia*, Vol. XII, pp. 84–86 (1823).

I. WHEREAS Almighty God hath created the mind free; that all attempts to influence it by temporal punishments or burthens, or by civil incapacitations, tend only to beget habits of hypocrisy and meanness, and are a departure from the plan of the Holy author of our religion, who being Lord both of body and mind, yet chose not to propagate it by coercions on either, as was in his Almighty power to do; that the impious presumption of legislators and rulers, civil as well as ecclesiastical, who being themselves but fallible and uninspired men, have assumed dominion over the faith of others, setting up their own opinions and modes of thinking as the only true and infallible, and as such endeavouring to impose them on others, hath established and maintained false religions over the greatest part of the world, and through all time; that to compel a man to furnish contributions of money for the propagation of opinions which he disbelieves, is sinful and tyrannical; that even the forcing him to support this or that teacher of his own religious persuasion, is depriving him of the comfortable liberty of giving his contributions to the particular pastor, whose morals he would make his pattern, and whose powers he feels most persuasive to righteousness, and is withdrawing from the ministry those temporary rewards, which proceeding from an approbation of their personal conduct, are an additional incitement to earnest and unremitting labours for the instruction of mankind; that our civil rights have no dependence on our religious opinions, any more than our opinions in physics or geometry; that therefore the proscribing any citizen as unworthy the public confidence by laying upon him an incapacity of being called to offices of trust and emolument, unless he profess or renounce this or that religious opinion, is depriving him injuriously of those privileges and advantages to which in common with his fellow-citizens he has a natural right; that it tends only to corrupt the principles of that religion it is meant to encourage, by bribing with a monopoly of wordly honours and emoluments, those who will externally profess and conform to it; that though indeed these are criminal who do not withstand such temptation, yet neither are those innocent who lay the bait in their way; that to suffer the civil magistrate to intrude his powers into the field of opinion, and to restrain the profession or propagation of principles on supposition of their ill tendency, is a dangerous fallacy, which at once destroys all religious liberty, because he being of course judge of that tendency will make his opinions the rule of judgment, and approve or condemn the sentiments of others only as they shall square with or differ from his own; that it is time enough for the rightful purposes of civil government, for its officers to interfere when principles break out into overt acts against peace and good order; and finally, that truth is great and will prevail if left to herself, that she is the proper and sufficient antagonist to error, and has nothing to fear from the conflict, unless by human interposition disarmed of her natural weapons, free argument and debate, errors ceasing to be dangerous when it is permitted freely to contradict them:

II. *Be it enacted by the General Assembly,* That no man shall be compelled to frequent or support any religious worship, place, or ministry whatsoever, nor shall be enforced, restrained, molested, or burthened in his body or goods, nor shall otherwise suffer on account of his religious opinions or belief; but that all men shall be free to profess, and by argument to maintain, their opinion in matters of religion, and that the same shall in no wise diminish, enlarge, or affect their civil capacities.

III. And though we well know that this assembly elected by the people for the ordinary purposes of legislation only, have no power to restrain the acts of succeeding assemblies, constituted with powers equal to our own, and that therefore to declare this act to be irrevocable would be of no effect in law; yet we are free to declare, and do declare, that the rights hereby asserted are of the natural rights of mankind, and that if any act shall be hereafter passed to repeal the present, or to narrow its operation, such act will be an infringement of natural right.

House Debate on the Religion Clauses (1789)

On June 8, 1789, Congressman James Madison proposed the following language as part of a list of amendments to the Constitution: "The civil rights of none shall be abridged on account of religious belief or worship, nor shall any national religion be established, nor shall the full and equal rights of conscience be in any manner, or on any pretext, infringed." He also recommended the following restriction on the states: "No State shall violate the equal rights of conscience, or the freedom of the press, or the trial by jury in criminal cases." 1 Annals of Congress 434, 435. On August 15, the House debated the Religion Clauses. The passages below are taken from 1 Annals of Congress 729–731, 766, 913.

The House again went into a Committee of the Whole on the proposed amendments to the Constitution, Mr. BOUDINOT in the Chair.

The fourth proposition being under consideration, as follows:

Article 1. Section 9. Between paragraphs two and three insert "no religion shall be established by law, nor shall the equal rights of conscience be infringed."

Mr. SYLVESTER had some doubts of the propriety of the mode of expression used in this paragraph. He apprehended that it was liable to a construction different from what had been made by the committee. He feared it might be thought to have a tendency to abolish religion altogether.

Mr. VINING suggested the propriety of transposing the two members of the sentence.

Mr. GERRY said it would read better if it was, that no religious doctrine shall be established by law.

Mr. SHERMAN thought the amendment altogether unnecessary, inasmuch as Congress had no authority whatever delegated to them by the Constitution to make religious establishments; he would, therefore, move to have it struck out.

Mr. CARROLL.—As the rights of conscience are, in their nature, of peculiar delicacy, and will little bear the gentlest touch of governmental hand; and as many sects have concurred in opinion that they are not well secured under the present Constitution, he said he was much in favor of adopting the words. He thought it would tend more towards conciliating the minds of the people to the Government than almost any other amendment he

had heard proposed. He would not contend with gentlemen about the phraseology, his object was to secure the substance in such a manner as to satisfy the wishes of the honest part of the community.

Mr. MADISON said, he apprehended the meaning of the words to be, that Congress should not establish a religion, and enforce the legal observation of it by law, nor compel men to worship God in any manner contrary to their conscience. Whether the words are necessary or not, he did not mean to say, but they had been required by some of the State Conventions, who seemed to entertain an opinion that under the clause of the Constitution, which gave power to Congress to make all laws necessary and proper to carry into execution the Constitution, and the laws made under it, enabled them to make laws of such a nature as might infringe the rights of conscience, and establish a national religion; to prevent these effects he presumed the amendment was intended, and he thought it as well expressed as the nature of the language would admit.

Mr. HUNTINGTON said that he feared, with the gentleman first up on this subject, that the words might be taken in such latitude as to be extremely hurtful to the cause of religion. He understood the amendment to mean what had been expressed by the gentleman from Virginia; but others might find it convenient to put another construction upon it. The ministers of their congregations to the Eastward were maintained by the contributions of those who belonged to their society; the expense of building meeting-houses was contributed in the same manner. These things were regulated by by-laws. If an action was brought before a Federal Court on any of these cases, the person who had neglected to perform his engagements could not be compelled to do it; for a support of ministers or building of places of worship might be construed into a religious establishment.

By the charter of Rhode Island, no religion could be established by law; he could give a history of the effects of such a regulation; indeed the people were now enjoying the blessed fruits of it. He hoped, therefore, the amendment would be made in such a way as to secure the rights of conscience, and a free exercise of the rights of religion, but not to patronise those who professed no religion at all.

Mr. MADISON thought, if the word "national" was inserted before religion, it would satisfy the minds of honorable gentlemen. He believed that the people feared one sect might obtain a preeminence, or two combine together, and establish a religion to which they would compel others to conform. He thought if the word "national" was introduced, it would point the amendment directly to the object it was intended to prevent.

Mr. LIVERMORE was not satisfied with that amendment; but he did not wish them to dwell long on the subject. He thought it would be better if it were altered, and made to read in this manner, that Congress shall make no laws touching religion, or infringing the rights of conscience.

Mr. GERRY did not like the term national, proposed by the gentleman from Virginia, and he hoped it would not be adopted by the House. It brought to his mind some observations that had taken place in the conventions at the time they were considering the present Constitution. It had been insisted upon by those who were called anti-federalists, that this form of Government consolidated the Union; the honorable gentleman's motion shows that he considers it in the same light. Those who were called anti-federalists at that time, complained that they had injustice done them by the title, because they were in favor of a Federal Government, and the others were in favor of a national one; the federalists were for ratifying the Constitution as it stood, and the others not until amendments were made. Their names then

ought not to have been distinguished by federalists and anti-federalists, but rats and anti-rats.

Mr. MADISON withdrew his motion, but observed that the words "no national religion shall be established by law," did not imply that the Government was a national one; the question was then taken on Mr. LIVERMORE'S motion, and passed in the affirmative, thirty-one for, and twenty against it.

. . .

[August 20, 1789:]

On motion of Mr. AMES, the fourth amendment was altered so as to read "Congress shall make no law establishing religion, or to prevent the free exercise thereof, or to infringe the rights of conscience." This being adopted.

[September 24, 1789:]

The House proceeded to consider the report of a Committee of Conference, on the subject-matter of the amendments depending between the two Houses to the several articles of amendment to the Constitution of the United States, as proposed by this House: whereupon, it was resolved, that they recede from their disagreement to all the amendments; provided that the two articles, which, by the amendments of the Senate, are now proposed to be inserted as the third and eighth articles, shall be amended to read as follows:

"Art. 3. Congress shall make no law respecting an establishment of religion, or prohibiting a free exercise thereof, or abridging the freedom of speech, or of the press, or the right of the people peaceably to assemble, and to petition the Government for a redress of grievances."

Minersville School District v. Gobitis

310 U.S. 586 (1940)

Pennsylvania required students in public schools to participate in a daily ceremony of saluting the national flag while reciting in unison a pledge of allegiance to it "and to the Republic for which it stands; one Nation indivisible, with liberty and justice for all." Failure to abide by this requirement resulted in the expulsion of Jehovah's Witnesses, who believed that this gesture of respect for the flag was forbidden by Biblical commands.

MR. JUSTICE FRANKFURTER delivered the opinion of the Court.

A grave responsibility confronts this Court whenever in course of litigation it must reconcile the conflicting claims of liberty and authority. But when the liberty invoked is liberty of conscience, and the authority is authority to safeguard the nation's fellowship, judicial conscience is put to its severest test. Of such a nature is the present controversy.

Lillian Gobitis, aged twelve, and her brother William, aged ten, were expelled from the public schools of Minersville, Pennsylvania, for refusing to salute the national flag as part of a daily school exercise. The local Board of Education required both teachers and pupils to participate in this ceremony. The ceremony is a familiar one. The right hand is placed on the breast and the following pledge recited in unison: "I pledge allegiance to my flag, and to the Republic for which it stands; one nation indivisible, with liberty and justice for all." While the words are spoken, teachers and pupils extend their right hands in salute to the flag. The Gobitis family are affiliated with "Jehovah's Witnesses," for whom the Bible as the Word of God is the supreme authority. The children had been brought up conscientiously to believe that such a gesture of respect for the flag was forbidden by command of Scripture. *[A footnote refers to these verses from Chapter 20 of Exodus: "3. Thou shalt have no other gods before me. 4. Thou shalt not make unto thee any graven image, or any likeness of any thing that is in heaven above, or that is in the earth beneath, or that is in the water under the earth. 5. Thou shalt not bow down thyself to them, nor serve them: . . ."]*

The Gobitis children were of an age for which Pennsylvania makes school attendance compulsory. Thus they were denied a free education, and their parents had to put them into private schools. To be relieved of the financial burden thereby entailed, their father, on behalf of the children and in his own behalf, brought this suit. He sought to enjoin the authorities from continuing to exact participation in the flag-salute ceremony as a condition of his children's attendance at the Minersville school. After trial of the issues, Judge Maris gave relief in the District Court, 24 F. Supp. 271, on the basis of a thoughtful opinion at a preliminary stage of the litigation, 21 F. Supp. 581; his decree was affirmed by the Circuit Court of Appeals, 108 F. 2d 683. . . .

We must decide whether the requirement of participation in such a ceremony, exacted from a child who refuses upon sincere religious grounds, infringes without due process of law the liberty guaranteed by the Fourteenth Amendment.

Centuries of strife over the erection of particular dogmas as exclusive or all-comprehending faiths led to the inclusion of a guarantee for religious freedom in the Bill of Rights. The First Amendment, and the Fourteenth through its absorption of the First, sought to guard against repetition of those bitter religious struggles by prohibiting the establishment of a state religion and by securing to every sect the free exercise of its faith. So pervasive is the acceptance of this precious right that its scope is brought into question, as here, only when the conscience of individuals collides with the felt necessities of society.

Certainly the affirmative pursuit of one's convictions about the ultimate mystery of the universe and man's relation to it is placed beyond the reach of law. Government may not interfere with organized or individual expression of belief or disbelief. Propagation of belief—or even of disbelief—in the supernatural is protected, whether in church or chapel, mosque or synagogue, tabernacle or meeting-house. Likewise the Constitution assures generous immunity to the individual from imposition of penalties for offending, in the course of his own religious activities, the religious views of others, be they a minority or those who are dominant in government. *Cantwell* v. *Connecticut, ante,* p. 296.

But the manifold character of man's relations may bring his conception of religious duty into conflict with the secular interests of his fellowmen. When does the constitutional guarantee compel exemption from doing what society thinks necessary for the promotion of some great common end, or from a penalty for conduct which appears dangerous to the general good? To state the problem is to recall the truth that no single principle can answer all of life's complexities. The right to freedom of religious belief, however dissident and however obnoxious to the cherished beliefs of others—even of a majority—is itself the denial of an absolute. But to affirm that the freedom to follow conscience has itself no limits in the life of a society would deny that very plurality of principles which, as a matter of history, underlies protection of religious toleration. Compare Mr. Justice Holmes in *Hudson Water Co.* v. *McCarter,* 209 U. S. 349, 355. Our present task, then, as so often the case with courts, is to reconcile two rights in order to prevent either from destroying the other. But, because in safeguarding conscience we are dealing with interests so subtle and so dear, every possible leeway should be given to the claims of religious faith.

[Frankfurter refers to earlier cases in which political authority was upheld over conscientious scruples, including laws against bigamy (contrary to Mormonism), drafting conscientious objectors for noncombatant roles, and requiring military training for all male university students.]

. . . Even if it were assumed that freedom of speech goes beyond the historic concept of full opportunity to utter and to disseminate views, however heretical or offensive to dominant opinion, and includes freedom from conveying what may be deemed an implied but rejected affirmation, the question remains whether school children, like the Gobitis children, must be excused from conduct required of all the other children in the promotion of national cohesion. We are dealing with an interest inferior to none in the hierarchy of legal values. National unity is the basis of national security. To deny the legislature the right to select appropriate means for its attainment presents a totally different order of problem from that of the propriety of subordinating the possible ugliness of littered streets to the free expression of opinion through distribution of handbills. Compare *Schneider* v. *State,* 308 U. S. 147.

. . .

Unlike the instances we have cited, the case before us is not concerned with an exertion of legislative power for the promotion of some specific need or interest of secular society—the protection of the family, the promotion of health, the common defense, the raising of public revenues to defray the cost of government. But all these specific activities of government presuppose the existence of an organized political society. The ultimate foundation of a free society is the binding tie of cohesive sentiment. Such a sentiment is fostered by all those agencies of the mind and spirit which may serve to gather up the traditions of a people, transmit them from generation to generation, and thereby create that continuity of a treasured common life which constitutes a civilization. "We live by symbols." The flag is the symbol of our national unity, transcending all internal differences, however large, within the framework of the Constitution. This Court has had occasion to say that ". . . the flag is the symbol of the Nation's power, the emblem of freedom in its truest, best sense. . . . it signifies government resting on the consent of the governed; liberty regulated by law; the protection of the weak against the strong; security against the exercise of arbitrary power; and absolute safety for free institutions against foreign aggression." *Halter* v. *Nebraska,* 205 U. S.

34, 43. And see *United States* v. *Gettysburg Electric Ry. Co.*, 160 U. S. 668.

. . .

The wisdom of training children in patriotic impulses by those compulsions which necessarily pervade so much of the educational process is not for our independent judgment. Even were we convinced of the folly of such a measure, such belief would be no proof of its unconstitutionality. For ourselves, we might be tempted to say that the deepest patriotism is best engendered by giving unfettered scope to the most crotchety beliefs. Perhaps it is best, even from the standpoint of those interests which ordinances like the one under review seek to promote, to give to the least popular sect leave from conformities like those here in issue. But the courtroom is not the arena for debating issues of educational policy. It is not our province to choose among competing considerations in the subtle process of securing effective loyalty to the traditional ideals of democracy, while respecting at the same time individual idiosyncracies among a people so diversified in racial origins and religious allegiances. So to hold would in effect make us the school board for the country. That authority has not been given to this Court, nor should we assume it.

We are dealing here with the formative period in the development of citizenship. Great diversity of psychological and ethical opinion exists among us concerning the best way to train children for their place in society. Because of these differences and because of reluctance to permit a single, iron-cast system of education to be imposed upon a nation compounded of so many strains, we have held that, even though public education is one of our most cherished democratic institutions, the Bill of Rights bars a state from compelling all children to attend the public schools. *Pierce* v. *Society of Sisters*, 268 U. S. 510. But it is a very different thing for this Court to exercise censorship over the conviction of legislatures that a particular program or exercise will best promote in the minds of children who attend the common schools an attachment to the institutions of their country.

What the school authorities are really asserting is the right to awaken in the child's mind consider-

ations as to the significance of the flag contrary to those implanted by the parent. In such an attempt the state is normally at a disadvantage in competing with the parent's authority, so long—and this is the vital aspect of religious toleration—as parents are unmolested in their right to counteract by their own persuasiveness the wisdom and rightness of those loyalties which the state's educational system is seeking to promote. . . .

Judicial review, itself a limitation on popular government, is a fundamental part of our constitutional scheme. But to the legislature no less than to courts is committed the guardianship of deeply-cherished liberties. See *Missouri, K. & T. Ry. Co.* v. *May*, 194 U. S. 267, 270. Where all the effective means of inducing political changes are left free from interference, education in the abandonment of foolish legislation is itself a training in liberty. To fight out the wise use of legislative authority in the forum of public opinion and before legislative assemblies rather than to transfer such a contest to the judicial arena, serves to vindicate the self-confidence of a free people.

Reversed.

MR. JUSTICE MCREYNOLDS concurs in the result.

MR. JUSTICE STONE, dissenting:

I think the judgment below should be affirmed.

Two youths, now fifteen and sixteen years of age, are by the judgment of this Court held liable to expulsion from the public schools and to denial of all publicly supported educational privileges because of their refusal to yield to the compulsion of a law which commands their participation in a school ceremony contrary to their religious convictions. They and their father are citizens and have not exhibited by any action or statement of opinion, any disloyalty to the Government of the United States. They are ready and willing to obey all its laws which do not conflict with what they sincerely believe to be the higher commandments of God. It is not doubted that these convictions are religious, that they are genuine, or that the refusal to yield to the compulsion of the law is in good faith and with all sincerity. It would be a denial of their faith as well as the teachings of most religions to say that children of their age could not have religious convictions.

The law which is thus sustained is unique in the history of Anglo-American legislation. It does more than suppress freedom of speech and more than prohibit the free exercise of religion, which concededly are forbidden by the First Amendment and are violations of the liberty guaranteed by the Fourteenth. For by this law the state seeks to coerce these children to express a sentiment which, as they interpret it, they do not entertain, and which violates their deepest religious convictions. It is not denied that such compulsion is a prohibited infringement of personal liberty, freedom of speech and religion, guaranteed by the Bill of Rights, except in so far as it may be justified and supported as a proper exercise of the state's power over public education. Since the state, in competition with parents, may through teaching in the public schools indoctrinate the minds of the young, it is said that in aid of its undertaking to inspire loyalty and devotion to constituted authority and the flag which symbolizes it, it may coerce the pupil to make affirmation contrary to his belief and in violation of his religious faith. And, finally, it is said that since the Minersville School Board and others are of the opinion that the country will be better served by conformity than by the observance of religious liberty which the Constitution prescribes, the courts are not free to pass judgment on the Board's choice.

Concededly the constitutional guaranties of personal liberty are not always absolutes. Government has a right to survive and powers conferred upon it are not necessarily set at naught by the express prohibitions of the Bill of Rights. . . . But it is a long step, and one which I am unable to take, to the position that government may, as a supposed educational measure and as a means of disciplining the young, compel public affirmations which violate their religious conscience.

. . .

History teaches us that there have been but few infringements of personal liberty by the state which have not been justified, as they are here, in the name of righteousness and the public good, and few which have not been directed, as they are now, at politically helpless minorities. The fram-

ers were not unaware that under the system which they created most governmental curtailments of personal liberty would have the support of a legislative judgment that the public interest would be better served by its curtailment than by its constitutional protection. . . . [While] expressions of loyalty, when voluntarily given, may promote national unity, it is quite another matter to say that their compulsory expression by children in violation of their own and their parents' religious convictions can be regarded as playing so important a part in our national unity as to leave school boards free to exact it despite the constitutional guarantee of freedom of religion. The very terms of the Bill of Rights preclude, it seems to me, any reconciliation of such compulsions with the constitutional guaranties by a legislative declaration that they are more important to the public welfare than the Bill of Rights.

. . .

. . . We have previously pointed to the importance of a searching judicial inquiry into the legislative judgment in situations where prejudice against discrete and insular minorities may tend to curtail the operation of those political processes ordinarily to be relied on to protect minorities. See *United States* v. *Carolene Products Co.*, 304 U. S. 144, 152, note 4. And until now we have not hesitated similarly to scrutinize legislation restricting the civil liberty of racial and religious minorities although no political process was affected. *Meyer* v. *Nebraska*, 262 U. S. 390; *Pierce* v. *Society of Sisters, supra; Farrington* v. *Tokushige*, 273 U. S. 284. Here we have such a small minority entertaining in good faith a religious belief, which is such a departure from the usual course of human conduct, that most persons are disposed to regard it with little toleration or concern. In such circumstances careful scrutiny of legislative efforts to secure conformity of belief and opinion by a compulsory affirmation of the desired belief, is especially needful if civil rights are to receive any protection. Tested by this standard, I am not prepared to say that the right of this small and helpless minority, including children having a strong religious conviction, whether they understand its nature or not, to refrain from an expression obnoxious to their religion, is to be overborne by the interest of the state in maintaining discipline in the schools.

The Constitution expresses more than the conviction of the people that democratic processes must be preserved at all costs. It is also an expression of faith and a command that freedom of mind and spirit must be preserved, which government must obey, if it is to adhere to that justice and moderation without which no free government can exist. For this reason it would seem that legislation which operates to repress the religious freedom of small minorities, which is admittedly within the scope of the protection of the Bill of Rights, must at least be subject to the same judicial scrutiny as legislation which we have recently held to infringe the constitutional liberty of religious and racial minorities.

With such scrutiny I cannot say that the inconveniences which may attend some sensible adjustment of school discipline in order that the religious convictions of these children may be spared, presents a problem so momentous or pressing as to outweigh the freedom from compulsory violation of religious faith which has been thought worthy of constitutional protection.

West Virginia State Board of Education v. Barnette

319 U.S. 624 (1943)

Justice Frankfurter's opinion in *Gobitis*, upholding a compulsory flag-salute for public school children, met with strong criticism from the legal community, the press, civil liberties groups, and religious organizations. In *Jones* v. *Opelika* (1942), three members of Frankfurter's 8–1 majority stated that the decision "was wrongly decided." That reduced the majority to 5–4, and changes in the Court's composition since *Gobitis* pointed to a probable overturning of Frankfurter's decision. One of the new members of the Court, Justice Jackson, wrote for a 6–3 majority striking down the compulsory flag-salute. Frankfurter prepared an emotional dissent; only two other members of the *Gobitis* majority, Roberts and Reed, adhered to the views expressed by that Court.

MR. JUSTICE JACKSON delivered the opinion of the Court.

Following the decision by this Court on June 3, 1940, in *Minersville School District* v. *Gobitis*, 310 U.S. 586, the West Virginia legislature amended its statutes to require all schools therein to conduct courses of instruction in history, civics, and in the Constitution of the United States and of the State "for the purpose of teaching, fostering and perpetuating the ideals, principles and spirit of Americanism, and increasing the knowledge of the organization and machinery of the government." Appellant Board of Education was directed, with advice of the State Superintendent of Schools, to "prescribe the courses of study covering these subjects" for public schools. The Act made it the duty of private, parochial and denominational schools to prescribe courses of study "similar to those required for the public schools."

The Board of Education on January 9, 1942, adopted a resolution containing recitals taken largely from the Court's *Gobitis* opinion and ordering that the salute to the flag become "a regular part of the program of activities in the public schools," that all teachers and pupils "shall be required to participate in the salute honoring the Nation represented by the Flag; provided, however, that refusal to salute the Flag be regarded as an act of insubordination, and shall be dealt with accordingly."

The resolution originally required the "commonly accepted salute to the Flag" which it defined. Objections to the salute as "being too much like Hitler's" were raised by the Parent and Teachers Association, the Boy and Girl Scouts, the Red Cross, and the Federation of Women's Clubs. Some modification appears to have been made in deference to these objections, but no concession was made to Jehovah's Witnesses. What is now required is the "stiff-arm" salute, the saluter to keep the right hand raised with palm turned up while the following is repeated: "I pledge allegiance to the Flag of the United States of America and to the Republic for which it stands; one Nation, indivisible, with liberty and justice for all."

Failure to conform is "insubordination" dealt with by expulsion. Readmission is denied by statute until compliance. Meanwhile the expelled child is "unlawfully absent" and may be proceeded against as a delinquent. His parents or guardians are liable to prosecution, and if convicted are subject to fine not exceeding $50 and jail term not exceeding thirty days.

. . .

The freedom asserted by these appellees does not bring them into collision with rights asserted by any other individual. It is such conflicts which most frequently require intervention of the State to determine where the rights of one end and those of another begin. But the refusal of these persons to participate in the ceremony does not interfere with or deny rights of others to do so. Nor is there any question in this case that their behavior is peaceable and orderly. The sole conflict is between authority and rights of the individual. The State asserts power to condition access to public education on making a prescribed sign and profession and at the same time to coerce attendance by punishing both parent and child. The latter stand on a right of self-determination in matters that touch individual opinion and personal attitude.

. . .

There is no doubt that, in connection with the pledges, the flag salute is a form of utterance. Symbolism is a primitive but effective way of communicating ideas. The use of an emblem or flag to symbolize some system, idea, institution, or personality, is a short cut from mind to mind.

Causes and nations, political parties, lodges and ecclesiastical groups seek to knit the loyalty of their followings to a flag or banner, a color or design. The State announces rank, function, and authority through crowns and maces, uniforms and black robes; the church speaks through the Cross, the Crucifix, the altar and shrine, and clerical raiment. Symbols of State often convey political ideas just as religious symbols come to convey theological ones. Associated with many of these symbols are appropriate gestures of acceptance or respect: a salute, a bowed or bared head, a bended knee. A person gets from a symbol the meaning he puts into it, and what is one man's comfort and inspiration is another's jest and scorn.

. . .

[Jackson analyzes several premises that formed the foundation for Gobitis.*]*

1. It was said that the flag-salute controversy confronted the Court with "the problem which Lincoln cast in memorable dilemma: 'Must a government of necessity be too *strong* for the liberties of its people, or too *weak* to maintain its own existence?'" and that the answer must be in favor of strength. *Minersville School District* v. *Gobitis, supra,* at 596.

We think these issues may be examined free of pressure or restraint growing out of such considerations.

It may be doubted whether Mr. Lincoln would have thought that the strength of government to maintain itself would be impressively vindicated by our confirming power of the State to expel a handful of children from school. Such oversimplification, so handy in political debate, often lacks the precision necessary to postulates of judicial reasoning. If validly applied to this problem, the utterance cited would resolve every issue of power in favor of those in authority and would require us to override every liberty thought to weaken or delay execution of their policies.

Government of limited power need not be anemic government. Assurance that rights are secure tends to diminish fear and jealousy of strong government, and by making us feel safe to live under it makes for its better support. Without promise of a limiting Bill of Rights it is doubtful if our Constitution could have mustered enough strength to enable its ratification. . . .

2. It was also considered in the *Gobitis* case that functions of educational officers in States, counties and school districts were such that to interfere with their authority "would in effect make us the school board for the country." *Id.* at 598.

The Fourteenth Amendment, as now applied to the States, protects the citizen against the State itself and all of its creatures—Boards of Education not excepted. These have, of course, important, delicate, and highly discretionary functions, but none that they may not perform within the limits of the Bill of Rights. That they are educating the young for citizenship is reason for scrupulous protection of Constitutional freedoms of the individual, if we are not to strangle the free mind at its source and teach youth to discount important principles of our government as mere platitudes.

. . .

3. The *Gobitis* opinion reasoned that this is a field "where courts possess no marked and certainly no controlling competence," that it is committed to the legislatures as well as the courts to guard cherished liberties and that it is constitutionally appropriate to "fight out the wise use of legislative authority in the forum of public opinion and before legislative assemblies rather than to transfer such a contest to the judicial arena," since all the "effective means of inducing political changes are left free." *Id.* at 597–598, 600.

The very purpose of a Bill of Rights was to withdraw certain subjects from the vicissitudes of political controversy, to place them beyond the reach of majorities and officials and to establish them as legal principles to be applied by the courts. One's right to life, liberty, and property, to free speech, a free press, freedom of worship and assembly, and other fundamental rights may not be submitted to vote; they depend on the outcome of no elections.

. . .

Nor does our duty to apply the Bill of Rights to assertions of official authority depend upon our possession of marked competence in the field

where the invasion of rights occurs. True, the task of translating the majestic generalities of the Bill of Rights, conceived as part of the pattern of liberal government in the eighteenth century, into concrete restraints on officials dealing with the problems of the twentieth century, is one to disturb self-confidence. These principles grew in soil which also produced a philosophy that the individual was the center of society, that his liberty was attainable through mere absence of governmental restraints, and that government should be entrusted with few controls and only the mildest supervision over men's affairs. We must transplant these rights to a soil in which the *laissez-faire* concept or principle of non-interference has withered at least as to economic affairs, and social advancements are increasingly sought through closer integration of society and through expanded and strengthened governmental controls. These changed conditions often deprive precedents of reliability and cast us more than we would choose upon our own judgment. But we act in these matters not by authority of our competence but by force of our commissions. We cannot, because of modest estimates of our competence in such specialties as public education, withhold the judgment that history authenticates as the function of this Court when liberty is infringed.

4. Lastly, and this is the very heart of the *Gobitis* opinion, it reasons that "National unity is the basis of national security," that the authorities have "the right to select appropriate means for its attainment," and hence reaches the conclusion that such compulsory measures toward "national unity" are constitutional. *Id.* at 595. Upon the verity of this assumption depends our answer in this case.

National unity as an end which officials may foster by persuasion and example is not in question. The problem is whether under our Constitution compulsion as here employed is a permissible means for its achievement.

Struggles to coerce uniformity of sentiment in support of some end thought essential to their time and country have been waged by many good as well as by evil men. Nationalism is a relatively recent phenomenon but at other times and places the ends have been racial or territorial security, support of a dynasty or regime, and particular plans for saving souls. As first and moderate methods to attain unity have failed, those bent on its accomplishment must resort to an ever-increasing severity. As governmental pressure toward unity becomes greater, so strife becomes more bitter as to whose unity it shall be. Probably no deeper division of our people could proceed from any provocation than from finding it necessary to choose what doctrine and whose program public educational officials shall compel youth to unite in embracing. Ultimate futility of such attempts to compel coherence is the lesson of every such effort from the Roman drive to stamp out Christianity as a disturber of its pagan unity, the Inquisition, as a means to religious and dynastic unity, the Siberian exiles as a means to Russian unity, down to the fast failing efforts of our present totalitarian enemies. Those who begin coercive elimination of dissent soon find themselves exterminating dissenters. Compulsory unification of opinion achieves only the unanimity of the graveyard.

It seems trite but necessary to say that the First Amendment to our Constitution was designed to avoid these ends by avoiding these beginnings. There is no mysticism in the American concept of the State or of the nature or origin of its authority. We set up government by consent of the governed, and the Bill of Rights denies those in power any legal opportunity to coerce that consent. Authority here is to be controlled by public opinion, not public opinion by authority.

The case is made difficult not because the principles of its decision are obscure but because the flag involved is our own. Nevertheless, we apply the limitations of the Constitution with no fear that freedom to be intellectually and spiritually diverse or even contrary will disintegrate the social organization. To believe that patriotism will not flourish if patriotic ceremonies are voluntary and spontaneous instead of a compulsory routine is to make an unflattering estimate of the appeal of our institutions to free minds. We can have intellectual individualism and the rich cultural diversities that we owe to exceptional minds only at the price of occasional eccentricity and abnormal attitudes. When they are so harmless to others or to the State as those we deal with here, the price is not too great. But freedom to differ is not limited to things that do not matter much. That would be a mere shadow of freedom. The test of its substance is the right to differ as to things that touch the heart of the existing order.

If there is any fixed star in our constitutional constellation, it is that no official, high or petty, can prescribe what shall be orthodox in politics, nationalism, religion, or other matters of opinion or force citizens to confess by word or act their faith therein. If there are any circumstances which permit an exception, they do not now occur to us.

We think the action of the local authorities in compelling the flag salute and pledge transcends constitutional limitations on their power and invades the sphere of intellect and spirit which it is the purpose of the First Amendment to our Constitution to reserve from all official control.

The decision of this Court in *Minersville School District* v. *Gobitis* and the holdings of those few *per curiam* decisions which preceded and foreshadowed it are overruled, and the judgment enjoining enforcement of the West Virginia Regulation is

Affirmed.

MR. JUSTICE ROBERTS and MR. JUSTICE REED adhere to the views expressed by the Court in *Minersville School District* v. *Gobitis*, 310 U. S. 586, and are of the opinion that the judgment below should be reversed.

MR. JUSTICE BLACK and MR. JUSTICE DOUGLAS, concurring:

. . .

Words uttered under coercion are proof of loyalty to nothing but self-interest. Love of country must spring from willing hearts and free minds, inspired by a fair administration of wise laws enacted by the people's elected representatives within the bounds of express constitutional prohibitions. These laws must, to be consistent with the First Amendment, permit the widest toleration of conflicting viewpoints consistent with a society of free men.

Neither our domestic tranquillity in peace nor our martial effort in war depend on compelling little children to participate in a ceremony which ends in nothing for them but a fear of spiritual condemnation. If, as we think, their fears are groundless, time and reason are the proper antidotes for their errors. The ceremonial, when enforced against conscientious objectors, more likely to defeat than to serve its high purpose, is a handy implement for disguised religious persecution. As such, it is inconsistent with our Constitution's plan and purpose.

MR. JUSTICE MURPHY, concurring:

. . .

I am unable to agree that the benefits that may accrue to society from the compulsory flag salute are sufficiently definite and tangible to justify the invasion of freedom and privacy that is entailed or to compensate for a restraint on the freedom of the individual to be vocal or silent according to his conscience or personal inclination. The trenchant words in the preamble to the Virginia Statute for Religious Freedom remain unanswerable: ". . . all attempts to influence [the mind] by temporal punishments, or burdens, or by civil incapacitations, tend only to beget habits of hypocrisy and meanness, . . ." Any spark of love for country which may be generated in a child or his associates by forcing him to make what is to him an empty gesture and recite words wrung from him contrary to his religious beliefs is overshadowed by the desirability of preserving freedom of conscience to the full. It is in that freedom and the example of persuasion, not in force and compulsion, that the real unity of America lies.

MR. JUSTICE FRANKFURTER, dissenting:
One who belongs to the most vilified and persecuted minority in history is not likely to be insensible to the freedoms guaranteed by our Constitution. Were my purely personal attitude relevant I should wholeheartedly associate myself with the general libertarian views in the Court's opinion, representing as they do the thought and action of a lifetime. But as judges we are neither Jew nor Gentile, neither Catholic nor agnostic. We owe equal attachment to the Constitution and are equally bound by our judicial obligations whether we derive our citizenship from the earliest or the latest immigrants to these shores. As a member of

this Court I am not justified in writing my private notions of policy into the Constitution, no matter how deeply I may cherish them or how mischievous I may deem their disregard. The duty of a judge who must decide which of two claims before the Court shall prevail, that of a State to enact and enforce laws within its general competence or that of an individual to refuse obedience because of the demands of his conscience, is not that of the ordinary person. It can never be emphasized too much that one's own opinion about the wisdom or evil of a law should be excluded altogether when one is doing one's duty on the bench. The only opinion of our own even looking in that direction that is material is our opinion whether legislators could in reason have enacted such a law. In the light of all the circumstances, including the history of this question in this Court, it would require more daring than I possess to deny that reasonable legislators could have taken the action which is before us for review. Most unwillingly, therefore, I must differ from my brethren with regard to legislation like this. I cannot bring my mind to believe that the "liberty" secured by the Due Process Clause gives this Court authority to deny to the State of West Virginia the attainment of that which we all recognize as a legitimate legislative end, namely, the promotion of good citizenship, by employment of the means here chosen.

Not so long ago we were admonished that "the only check upon our own exercise of power is our own sense of self-restraint. For the removal of unwise laws from the statute books appeal lies not to the courts but to the ballot and to the processes of democratic government." *United States* v. *Butler*, 297 U. S. 1, 79 (dissent *[by Stone]*). We have been told that generalities do not decide concrete cases. But the intensity with which a general principle is held may determine a particular issue, and whether we put first things first may decide a specific controversy.

The admonition that judicial self-restraint alone limits arbitrary exercise of our authority is relevant every time we are asked to nullify legislation. The Constitution does not give us greater veto power when dealing with one phase of "liberty" than with another, or when dealing with grade school regulations than with college regulations that offend conscience, as was the case in *Hamil-*

ton v. *Regents,* 293 U. S. 245. In neither situation is our function comparable to that of a legislature or are we free to act as though we were a super-legislature. Judicial self-restraint is equally necessary whenever an exercise of political or legislative power is challenged. There is no warrant in the constitutional basis of this Court's authority for attributing different rôles to it depending upon the nature of the challenge to the legislation. Our power does not vary according to the particular provision of the Bill of Rights which is invoked. . . .

When Mr. Justice Holmes, speaking for this Court, wrote that "it must be remembered that legislatures are ultimate guardians of the liberties and welfare of the people in quite as great a degree as the courts," *Missouri, K. & T. Ry. Co.* v. *May,* 194 U. S. 267, 270, he went to the very essence of our constitutional system and the democratic conception of our society. He did not mean that for only some phases of civil government this Court was not to supplant legislatures and sit in judgment upon the right or wrong of a challenged measure. He was stating the comprehensive judicial duty and rôle of this Court in our constitutional scheme whenever legislation is sought to be nullified on any ground, namely, that responsibility for legislation lies with legislatures, answerable as they are directly to the people, and this Court's only and very narrow function is to determine whether within the broad grant of authority vested in legislatures they have exercised a judgment for which reasonable justification can be offered.

. . .

One's conception of the Constitution cannot be severed from one's conception of a judge's function in applying it. The Court has no reason for existence if it merely reflects the pressures of the day. Our system is built on the faith that men set apart for this special function, freed from the influences of immediacy and from the deflections of worldly ambition, will become able to take a view of longer range than the period of responsibility entrusted to Congress and legislatures. We are dealing with matters as to which legislators and voters have conflicting views. Are we as judges to impose our strong convictions on where wisdom lies? That which three years ago had seemed to five successive Courts to lie within permissible areas of legislation is now outlawed by the deciding shift of opinion of two Justices. What reason is there to believe that they or their successors may not have another view a few years hence? Is that which was deemed to be of so fundamental a nature as to be written into the Constitution to endure for all times to be the sport of shifting winds of doctrine? Of course, judicial opinions, even as to questions of constitutionality, are not immutable. As has been true in the past, the Court will from time to time reverse its position. But I believe that never before these Jehovah's Witnesses cases (except for minor deviations subsequently retraced) has this Court overruled decisions so as to restrict the powers of democratic government. Always heretofore, it has withdrawn narrow views of legislative authority so as to authorize what formerly it had denied.

. . .

Goldman v. Weinberger

475 U.S. 503 (1986)

Captain Goldman, an Orthodox Jew and an ordained rabbi, brought suit against Secretary of Defense Weinberger, claiming that an Air Force regulation prevented him from wearing his yarmulke (skullcap) indoors and infringed on his First Amendment freedom to exercise his religious belief. A federal district court granted an injunction against the Air Force, prohibiting it from denying Goldman the right to wear a yarmulke while in uniform; the D.C. Circuit reversed.

JUSTICE REHNQUIST delivered the opinion of the Court.

Petitioner S. Simcha Goldman contends that the Free Exercise Clause of the First Amendment to the United States Constitution permits him to wear a yarmulke while in uniform, notwithstanding an Air Force regulation mandating uniform dress for Air Force personnel. The District Court for the District of Columbia permanently enjoined the Air Force from enforcing its regulation against petitioner and from penalizing him for wearing his yarmulke. The Court of Appeals for the District of Columbia Circuit reversed on the ground that the Air Force's strong interest in discipline justified the strict enforcement of its uniform dress requirements. We granted certiorari because of the importance of the question, and now affirm.

Petitioner Goldman is an Orthodox Jew and ordained rabbi. In 1973, he was accepted into the Armed Forces Health Professions Scholarship Program and placed on inactive reserve status in the Air Force while he studied clinical psychology at Loyola University of Chicago. During his three years in the scholarship program, he received a monthly stipend and an allowance for tuition, books, and fees. After completing his Ph.D. in psychology, petitioner entered active service in the United States Air Force as a commissioned officer, in accordance with a requirement that participants in the scholarship program serve one year of active duty for each year of subsidized education. Petitioner was stationed at March Air Force Base in Riverside, California, and served as a clinical psychologist at the mental health clinic on the base.

Until 1981, petitioner was not prevented from wearing his yarmulke on the base. He avoided controversy by remaining close to his duty station in the health clinic and by wearing his service cap over the yarmulke when out of doors. But in April 1981, after he testified as a defense witness at a court-martial wearing his yarmulke but not his service cap, opposing counsel lodged a complaint with Colonel Joseph Gregory, the Hospital Commander, arguing that petitioner's practice of wearing his yarmulke was a violation of Air Force Regulation (AFR) 35–10. This regulation states in pertinent part that "[h]eadgear will not be worn . . . [w]hile indoors except by armed security po-

lice in the performance of their duties." AFR 35–10, ¶ 1–6.h(2)(f) (1980).

Colonel Gregory informed petitioner that wearing a yarmulke while on duty does indeed violate AFR 35–10, and ordered him not to violate this regulation outside the hospital. Although virtually all of petitioner's time on the base was spent in the hospital, he refused. Later, after petitioner's attorney protested to the Air Force General Counsel, Colonel Gregory revised his order to prohibit petitioner from wearing the yarmulke even in the hospital. Petitioner's request to report for duty in civilian clothing pending legal resolution of the issue was denied. The next day he received a formal letter of reprimand, and was warned that failure to obey AFR 35–10 could subject him to a court-martial. Colonel Gregory also withdrew a recommendation that petitioner's application to extend the term of his active service be approved, and substituted a negative recommendation.

Petitioner then sued respondent Secretary of Defense and others, claiming that the application of AFR 35–10 to prevent him from wearing his yarmulke infringed upon his First Amendment freedom to exercise his religious beliefs. . . .

Petitioner argues that AFR 35–10, as applied to him, prohibits religiously motivated conduct and should therefore be analyzed under the standard enunciated in *Sherbert* v. *Verner*, 374 U.S. 398, 406 (1963). See also *Thomas* v. *Review Board*, 450 U.S. 707 (1981); *Wisconsin* v. *Yoder*, 406 U.S. 205 (1972). But we have repeatedly held that "the military is, by necessity, a specialized society separate from civilian society." *Parker* v. *Levy*, 417 U.S. 733, 743 (1974). . . .

Our review of military regulations challenged on First Amendment grounds is far more deferential than constitutional review of similar laws or regulations designed for civilian society. The military need not encourage debate or tolerate protest to the extent that such tolerance is required of the civilian state by the First Amendment; to accomplish its mission the military must foster instinctive obedience, unity, commitment, and esprit de corps. . . .

. . .

The considered professional judgment of the Air Force is that the traditional outfitting of personnel in standardized uniforms encourages the subordination of personal preferences and identities in favor of the overall group mission. Uniforms encourage a sense of hierarchical unity by tending to eliminate outward individual distinctions except for those of rank. . . .

To this end, the Air Force promulgated AFR 35–10, a 190-page document, which states that "Air Force members will wear the Air Force uniform while performing their military duties, except when authorized to wear civilian clothes on duty." AFR § 35–10, ¶ 1–6 (1980). The rest of the document describes in minute detail all of the various items of apparel that must be worn as part of the Air Force uniform. It authorizes a few individualized options with respect to certain pieces of jewelry and hair style, but even these are subject to severe limitations. See AFR 35–10, Table 1–1, and ¶ 1–12.b(1)(b) (1980). In general, authorized headgear may be worn only out of doors. See AFR § 35–10, ¶ 1–6.h (1980). Indoors, "[h]eadgear [may] not be worn . . . except by armed security police in the performance of their duties." AFR 35–10, ¶ 1–6.h(2)(f) (1980). A narrow exception to this rule exists for headgear worn during indoor religious ceremonies. See AFR 35–10, ¶ 1–6.h(2)(d) (1980). In addition, military commanders may in their discretion permit visible religious headgear and other such apparel in designated living quarters and nonvisible items generally. See Department of Defense Directive 1300.17 (June 18, 1985).

Petitioner Goldman contends that the Free Exercise Clause of the First Amendment requires the Air Force to make an exception to its uniform dress requirements for religious apparel unless the accoutrements create a "clear danger" of undermining discipline and esprit de corps. He asserts that in general, visible but "unobtrusive" apparel will not create such a danger and must therefore be accommodated. He argues that the Air Force failed to prove that a specific exception for his practice of wearing an unobtrusive yarmulke would threaten discipline. He contends that the Air Force's assertion to the contrary is mere *ipse dixit*, with no support from actual experience or a scientific study in the record, and is contradicted by expert testimony that religious exceptions to AFR 35–10 are in fact desirable and will increase

morale by making the Air Force a more humane place.

But whether or not expert witnesses may feel that religious exceptions to AFR 35–10 are desirable is quite beside the point. The desirability of dress regulations in the military is decided by the appropriate military officials, and they are under no constitutional mandate to abandon their considered professional judgment. Quite obviously, to the extent the regulations do not permit the wearing of religious apparel such as a yarmulke, a practice described by petitioner as silent devotion akin to prayer, military life may be more objectionable for petitioner and probably others. But the First Amendment does not require the military to accommodate such practices in the face of its view that they would detract from the uniformity sought by the dress regulations. The Air Force has drawn the line essentially between religious apparel which is visible and that which is not, and we hold that those portions of the regulations challenged here reasonably and even-handedly regulate dress in the interest of the military's perceived need for uniformity. The First Amendment therefore does not prohibit them from being applied to petitioner even though their effect is to restrict the wearing of the headgear required by his religious beliefs.

The judgment of the Court of Appeals is

Affirmed.

JUSTICE STEVENS, with whom JUSTICE WHITE and JUSTICE POWELL join, concurring.

Captain Goldman presents an especially attractive case for an exception from the uniform regulations that are applicable to all other Air Force personnel. His devotion to his faith is readily apparent. The yarmulke is a familiar and accepted sight. In addition to its religious significance for the wearer, the yarmulke may evoke the deepest respect and admiration—the symbol of a distinguished tradition and an eloquent rebuke to the ugliness of anti-Semitism. Captain Goldman's military duties are performed in a setting in which a modest departure from the uniform regulation creates almost no danger of impairment of the Air Force's military mission. Moreover, on the record before us, there is reason to believe that the policy of strict enforcement against Captain Goldman had a retaliatory motive—he had worn his yarmulke while testifying on behalf of a defendant in a court-martial proceeding. Nevertheless, as the case has been argued, I believe we must test the validity of the Air Force's rule not merely as it applies to Captain Goldman but also as it applies to all service personnel who have sincere religious beliefs that may conflict with one or more military commands.

JUSTICE BRENNAN is unmoved by the Government's concern "that while a yarmulke might not seem obtrusive to a Jew, neither does a turban to a Sikh, a saffron robe to a Satchidananda Ashram-Integral Yogi, nor do dreadlocks to a Rastafarian." *Post*, at 1319. He correctly points out that "turbans, saffron robes, and dreadlocks are not before us in this case," and then suggests that other cases may be fairly decided by reference to a reasonable standard based on "functional utility, health and safety considerations, and the goal of a polished, professional appearance." *Id.*, at 1319. As the Court has explained, this approach attaches no weight to the separate interest in uniformity itself. Because professionals in the military service attach great importance to that plausible interest, it is one that we must recognize as legitimate and rational even though personal experience or admiration for the performance of the "rag-tag band of soldiers" that won us our freedom in the revolutionary war might persuade us that the Government has exaggerated the importance of that interest.

The interest in uniformity, however, has a dimension that is of still greater importance for me. It is the interest in uniform treatment for the members of all religious faiths. The very strength of Captain Goldman's claim creates the danger that a similar claim on behalf of a Sikh or a Rastafarian might readily be dismissed as "so extreme, so unusual, or so faddish an image that public confidence in his ability to perform his duties will be destroyed." *Post*, at 1319. If exceptions from dress code regulations are to be granted on the basis of a multifactored test such as that proposed by JUSTICE BRENNAN, inevitably the decisionmaker's evaluation of the character and the sincerity of the requestor's faith—as well as the probable reaction of the majority to the favored

treatment of a member of that faith—will play a critical part in the decision. For the difference between a turban or a dreadlock on the one hand, and a yarmulke on the other, is not merely a difference in "appearance"—it is also the difference between a Sikh or a Rastafarian, on the one hand, and an Orthodox Jew on the other. The Air Force has no business drawing distinctions between such persons when it is enforcing commands of universal application.

As the Court demonstrates, the rule that is challenged in this case is based on a neutral, completely objective standard—visibility. It was not motivated by hostility against, or any special respect for, any religious faith. An exception for yarmulkes would represent a fundamental departure from the true principle of uniformity that supports that rule. For that reason, I join the Court's opinion and its judgment.

JUSTICE BRENNAN, with whom JUSTICE MARSHALL joins, dissenting.

Simcha Goldman invokes this Court's protection of his First Amendment right to fulfill one of the traditional religious obligations of a male Orthodox Jew—to cover his head before an omnipresent God. The Court's response to Goldman's request is to abdicate its role as principal expositor of the Constitution and protector of individual liberties in favor of credulous deference to unsupported assertions of military necessity. I dissent.

I

In ruling that the paramount interests of the Air Force override Dr. Goldman's free exercise claim, the Court overlooks the sincere and serious nature of his constitutional claim. It suggests that the desirability of certain dress regulations, rather than a First Amendment right, is at issue. . . .

II

A

Dr. Goldman has asserted a substantial First Amendment claim, which is entitled to meaningful review by this Court. The Court, however, evades its responsibility by eliminating, in all but name only, judicial review of military regulations that interfere with the fundamental constitutional rights of service personnel.

Our cases have acknowledged that in order to protect our treasured liberties, the military must be able to command service members to sacrifice a great many of the individual freedoms they enjoyed in the civilian community and to endure certain limitations on the freedoms they retain. See, *e.g., Brown* v. *Glines,* 444 U.S. 348, 354–357 (1980); *Greer* v. *Spock,* 424 U.S. 828 848 (1976) (POWELL, J., concurring); *Parker* v. *Levy,* 417 U.S. 733, 743–744, 751 (1974). Notwithstanding this acknowledgment, we have steadfastly maintained that " 'our citizens in uniform may not be stripped of basic rights simply because they have doffed their civilian clothes.' " *Chappell* v. *Wallace,* 462 U.S. 296, 304 (1983) (quoting Warren, The Bill of Rights and the Military, 37 N.Y.U.L.Rev. 181, 188 (1962). . . .

Today the Court eschews its constitutionally mandated role. It adopts for review of military decisions affecting First Amendment rights a subrational-basis standard—absolute, uncritical "deference to the professional judgment of military authorities." *Ante,* at 1313. If a branch of the military declares one of its rules sufficiently important to outweigh a service person's constitutional rights, it seems that the Court will accept that conclusion, no matter how absurd or unsupported it may be.

. . .

B

1

The Government maintains in its brief that discipline is jeopardized whenever exceptions to military regulations are granted. Service personnel must be trained to obey even the most arbitrary command reflexively. Non-Jewish personnel will perceive the wearing of a yarmulke by an Orthodox Jew as an unauthorized departure from the rules and will begin to question the principle of unswerving obedience. Thus shall our fighting forces slip down the treacherous slope toward unkempt appearance, anarchy, and, ultimately, defeat at the hands of our enemies.

The contention that the discipline of the armed forces will be subverted if Orthodox Jews are allowed to wear yarmulkes with their uniforms surpasses belief. It lacks support in the record of this case and the Air Force offers no basis for it as a general proposition. While the perilous slope permits the services arbitrarily to refuse exceptions requested to satisfy mere personal preferences, before the Air Force may burden free exercise rights it must advance, at the *very least,* a rational reason for doing so.

. . .

2

. . . the purported interests of the Air Force in complete uniformity of dress and in elimination of individuality or visible identification with any group other than itself are belied by the service's own regulations. The dress code expressly abjures the need for total uniformity:

. . .

"(2) Appearance in uniform is an important part of this image. . . . Neither the Air Force nor the public expects absolute uniformity of appearance. Each member has the right, within limits, to express individuality through his or her appearance. However, the image of a disciplined service member who can be relied on to do his or her job excludes the extreme, the unusual, and the fad." AFR 35–10, ¶ 1–12a.(1) & (2) (1978).

It cannot be seriously contended that a serviceman in a yarmulke presents so extreme, so unusual, or so faddish an image that public confidence in his ability to perform his duties will be destroyed. Under the Air Force's own standards, then, Dr. Goldman should have and could have been granted an exception to wear his yarmulke.

The dress code also allows men to wear up to three rings and one identification bracelet of "neat and conservative," but non-uniform design. AFR 35–10, ¶ 1–12b.(1)(b) (1978). This jewelry is apparently permitted even if, as is often the case with rings, it associates the wearer with a denominational school or a religious or secular fraternal organization. If these emblems of religious, social, and ethnic identity are not deemed to be unacceptably divisive, the Air Force cannot rationally justify its bar against yarmulkes on that basis.

Moreover, the services allow, and rightly so, other manifestations of religious diversity. It is clear to all service personnel that some members attend Jewish services, some Christian, some Islamic, and some yet other religious services. Barracks mates see Mormons wearing temple garments, Orthodox Jews wearing tzitzit, and Catholics wearing crosses and scapulars. That they come from different faiths and ethnic backgrounds is not a secret that can or should be kept from them.

. . .

JUSTICE BLACKMUN, dissenting.

I would reverse the judgment of the Court of Appeals, but for reasons somewhat different from those respectively enunciated by JUSTICE BRENNAN and JUSTICE O'CONNOR. I feel that the Air Force is justified in considering not only the costs of allowing Captain Goldman to cover his head indoors, but also the cumulative costs of accommodating constitutionally indistinguishable requests for religious exemptions. Because, however, the Government has failed to make any meaningful showing that either set of costs is significant, I dissent from the Court's rejection of Goldman's claim.

. . .

JUSTICE O'CONNOR, with whom JUSTICE MARSHALL joins, dissenting.

. . .

. . . One can . . . glean at least two consistent themes from this Court's precedents. First, when the government attempts to deny a Free Exercise claim, it must show that an unusually important interest is at stake, whether that interest is denominated "compelling," "of the highest order," or "overriding." Second, the government must show that granting the requested exemption will do substantial harm to that interest, whether by showing that the means adopted is the "least restrictive" or "essential," or that the interest will not "otherwise be served." These two requirements are entirely sensible in the context of the assertion of a free exercise claim. First, because the government is attempting to override an interest specifically protected by the Bill of Rights, the government must show that the opposing interest it asserts is of special importance before there is any chance that its claim can prevail. Second, since the Bill of Rights is expressly designed to protect the individual against the aggregated and sometimes intolerant powers of the state, the government must show that the interest asserted will in fact be substantially harmed by granting the type of exemption requested by the individual.

There is no reason why these general principles should not apply in the military, as well as the civilian, context. . . .

. . .

In the rare instances where the military has not consistently or plausibly justified its asserted need for rigidity of enforcement, and where the individual seeking the exemption establishes that the assertion by the military of a threat to discipline or esprit de corps is in his or her case completely unfounded, I would hold that the Government's policy of uniformity must yield to the individual's assertion of the right of free exercise of religion. On the facts of this case, therefore, I would require the Government to accommodate the sincere religious belief of Captain Goldman. Napoleon may have been correct to assert that, in the military sphere, morale is to all other factors as three is to one, but contradicted assertions of necessity by the military do not on the scales of justice bear a similarly disproportionate weight to sincere religious beliefs of the individual.

I respectfully dissent.

Congress Reverses Goldman

After the Supreme Court in *Goldman* v. *Weinberger* (1986) had upheld an Air Force regulation that prohibited Captain Goldman from wearing his yarmulke (skullcap)

indoors, legislation was immediately introduced to permit members of the armed forces to wear religious apparel indoors if the item is neat and conservative. The legislation permitted the Secretary of Defense to prohibit the wearing of an item of religious apparel if it interfered with the performance of military duties. The House passed the legislation in 1986 but it failed in the Senate. Both Houses acted on the legislation in 1987 and the provision was enacted into law. P.L. 100-180, 101 Stat. 1086–1087, § 508 (1987). Excerpts from the congressional debate in 1987 appear below. The selections are taken from 133 Cong. Rec. H3341–3343 (daily ed. May 8, 1987) and 133 Cong. Rec. S12791–12801 (daily ed. September 25, 1987).

Mrs. SCHROEDER. Mr. Chairman, I offer an amendment.

The CHAIRMAN. The Clerk will designate the amendment.

The text of the amendment is as follows:

Amendment offered by Mrs. SCHROEDER: At the end of title V of division A (page 70, after line 3) add the following new section:
SEC. 509. WEARING OF RELIGIOUS APPAREL BY MEMBERS OF THE ARMED FORCES WHILE IN UNIFORM.

(a) IN GENERAL.—Chapter 45 of title 10, United States Code, is amended—

(1) by redesignating section 774 as section 775; and

(2) by inserting after section 773 the following new section 774:

"§ 774. Religious apparel: wearing while in uniform

"(a) GENERAL RULE.—Except as provided under subsection (b), a member of the armed forces may wear an item of religious apparel while wearing the uniform of the member's armed force.

"(b) EXCEPTIONS.—The Secretary concerned may prohibit the wearing of an item of religious apparel—

"(1) in circumstances with respect to which the Secretary determines that the wearing of the item would interfere with the performance of the member's military duties; or

"(2) if the Secretary determines, under regulations under subsection (c), that the item of apparel is not neat and conservative.

"(c) REGULATIONS.—The Secretary concerned shall prescribe regulations concerning the wearing of religious apparel by members of the armed forces under the Secretary's jurisdiction while the members are wearing the uniform. Such regulations shall be consistent with subsections (a) and (b).

"(d) RELIGIOUS APPAREL DEFINED.—In this section, the term 'religious apparel' means apparel the wearing of which is part of the observance of the religious faith practiced by the member.".

(b) CLERICAL AMENDMENT.—The table of sections at the beginning of such chapter is amended by striking out the item relating to section 774 and inserting in lieu thereof the following:

"774. Religious apparel: wearing while in uniform.

"775. Applicability of chapter.".

(c) REGULATIONS.—The secretary concerned shall prescribe the regulations required by section 774(c) of title 10, United States Code, as added by subsection (a), not later than the end of the 120-day period beginning on the date of the enactment of this Act.

The CHAIRMAN. The gentlewoman from Colorado [Mrs. SCHROEDER] will be recognized for 10 minutes and a Member opposed to the amendment will be recognized for 10 minutes.

The Chair recognizes the gentlewoman from Colorado [Mrs. SCHROEDER].

(Mrs. SCHROEDER asked and was given permission to revise and extend her remarks.)

Mrs. SCHROEDER. Mr. Chairman, I yield myself such time as I may consume.

Mr. Chairman, the amendment permits the wearing of "neat and conservative" religious apparel—that is, Jewish yarmulkes and Sikh turbans—so long as the apparel does not interfere with the performance of military duties.

The "neat and conservative" standard was drawn from existing Air Force regulations, which use that term to define what jewelry members of the military may wear.

The military services have opposed any such legislation.

The Army—but not the other services—accepted Sikhs with turbans from the late 1940's to the early 1960's. When they stopped accepting

Sikhs, they grandfathered those then in service. At least one Sikh remains on active duty. As near as can be learned from the limited records, the Army ceased accepting Sikhs when it was told it must either accept all nonuniform religious apparel— turbans, yarmulkes, saffron robes, dreadlocks, etc.—or none, but could not pick and choose among religious faiths.

Yarmulkes have never been formally permitted —although some have been worn without objection over the years. In the early 1980's, action was taken against an Air Force captain for wearing a yarmulke after he had worn it for 5 years without objection. The complaint was initiated by an Air Force lawyer after the Jewish captain testified for the opposing side in one of the lawyer's cases. The Supreme Court ruled that the military was sufficiently different to permit it to apply rules that might be considered discriminatory in the civilian world.

The amendment arises out of the concerns of Sikhs and Jews resulting from the above two actions.

This year's amendment is identical to language included in the committee-reported bill last year. The same language lost by two votes in the Senate last year and was dropped in conference.

. . .

Mr. DORNAN of California. Mr. Chairman, I rise in support of this amendment.

I cannot think of any religious devotion more unobtrusive than wearing a yarmulke. There are people who have more hair, times 10, than a tiny little skull cap and it can be worn under jet fighter helmets, under garrison hats, under helmets, it can even be worn under a regular flight cap.

I am receiving mail, I have received six letters just within the last 2 weeks, from Americans of Sikh heritage. It is their religious devotion not to ever cut any of their bodily hair. Those beards we see are probably 2 feet long wound up and inside that turban is as much hair as they can grow. They point out how honorably they have served the British Empire, that at one time as 4 percent of the population, they were more than 35 percent of the officer and NCO corps in the British Indian Army and that percentage is still 10 times higher than

their numbers in India now. This is in spite of some religious conflict.

Is there some specificity in this where it leaves—I would like to ask the gentlewoman to respond—where it leaves the military some leeway, Rastafarian hair or something, but where we can be specific in our legislative dialog that this has nothing to do with restricting something as precious, but as tiny and small, as the wearing of a yarmulke by orthodox people?

I yield to the gentlewoman from Colorado.

Mrs. SCHROEDER. Mr. Chairman, I thank the gentleman and I am very honored that the gentleman is backing this amendment.

Yes, indeed, what we are saying here is that the Secretary concerned may prohibit the wearing of any item of religious apparel if the circumstances are that the Secretary determines that the wearing of the item would interfere with the performance of the Member's military duties.

I think if they say it interferes and could make that case, yes; so if some one appeared saying they wanted to say wear a robe and fly an airplane and you could be concerned about getting the robe caught up in the puddles, yes; outside of that, a yarmulke, no.

Mr. DICKINSON. Mr. Chairman, I yield 3 minutes to the gentleman from New York [Mr. GILMAN].

Mr. GILMAN. Mr. Chairman, I thank the gentleman for yielding, and I want to commend the gentlewoman from Colorado for bringing this measure to the floor at this time and the gentleman from New York for being highly supportive of the measure in the past.

I thank the gentleman from California [Mr. DORNAN] for his supportive remarks.

To deny religious individuals the opportunity to serve because of the necessity of wearing an unobstrusive part of their apparel would be a disservice to so many loyal, patriotic Americans.

I merely want to urge my colleagues to be supportive, to give religious orthodox Jews an opportunity to serve by wearing a very small unobstrusive skull cap as part of their military attire.

Mrs. SCHROEDER. Mr. Chairman, I yield 3 minutes to the gentleman from New York [Mr.

SOLARZ], the distinguished author of this amendment and the one who has carried it in prior sessions.

Mr. SOLARZ. Mr. Chairman, I thank the gentlewoman for yielding.

The only really serious concerns that have been expressed about this amendment have to do with the extent to which they might permit members of the armed forces to wear bizarre forms of apparel that could undermine military discipline.

I think it is important for the Members to know that the armed forces of Canada, the armed forces of the United Kingdom, the armed forces of New Zealand, all permit people in their military not only to wear yarmulkes, but also, if they are Sikhs, to wear turbans.

I need hardly remind you that the most effective military force in the Middle East, the Israel Defense Forces, permits its members to wear yarmulkes. I do not think it has handicapped their ability to overcome their enemies in battle.

. . .

We ought to stand up for religious liberty. It is a very simple amendment. The Secretary of Defense can prescribe any item of religious apparel which he believes is neither neat nor conservative, but which interferes in the performance of someones official duties as a member of the armed services.

So I strongly support the gentlewoman's amendment. I would simply say that any amendment which is supported by the gentlewoman from Colorado [Mrs. SCHROEDER] and by the gentleman from California [Mr. DORNAN] must have something going for it.

Mr. DICKINSON. Mr. Chairman, let me say for the benefit of those who are within sound of my voice that the parliamentary situation is such that in order to preserve the time for this side of the aisle on this issue, one must be in opposition to it. I rose in opposition to it and I am representing the position, as I understand it to be that of the Department of Defense, that I do my best to represent here and the administration; but as for my personal preference, I see no objection to an unobstrusive adornment being worn under a hat or without a hat and certainly the Secretary has the right to prescribe what may or may not be worn by the language of the amendment being offered.

. . .

The CHAIRMAN. The question is on the amendment offered by the gentlewoman from Colorado [Mrs. SCHROEDER].

The amendment was agreed to.

[Senate action:]

Mr. LAUTENBERG. Mr. President, today I am offering an amendment to permit the wearing of neat and conservative religious apparel in the military. Under my amendment, such apparel would be permitted only if it does not interfere with the performance of military duty.

. . .

. . . this amendment, and this issue, is broader than any one religion. It concerns the right of people of all faiths to serve their country without having to forsake their religious beliefs and practices, it would affirm the religious and ethnic diversity that have made America strong, not weak.

The primary philosophical objection to this amendment has been that wearing visible items of religious apparel may threaten the military uniformity necessary in building unit cohesion. While I appreciate and agree with the importance of unit cohesion and esprit de corps in the Armed Forces, I do not believe that wearing neat and conservative religious apparel threatens this principle.

To the contrary, it would strengthen morale by affirming that the military is a humane and tolerant institution. And as Justice Brennan made clear in his moving dissent to the majority opinion in Goldman, allowing religious apparel to be worn with a U.S. military uniform is an eloquent reminder that the shared and proud identity of U.S. servicemen embraces and unites religious and ethnic pluralism.

Although uniformity is claimed as an important value, the services easily permit other manifestations of religious diversity. Service members attend Christian, Islamic, Jewish, and other religious services. Barracks mates see Mormons wearing temple garments, and Catholics wearing crosses and scapulars. It is obvious that our services are made up of people from different faiths and ethnic backgrounds, and that diversity is America's greatest asset. It is no secret, nor should it be.

. . .

Our citizens in uniform should not be deprived of their basic constitutional rights, such as the free exercise of religion, the minute they enter the military. There must be a compelling and supportable argument justifying such a prohibition. None has been made.

Some of the services have argued that the neat and conservative standard will be hard to apply, forcing them to make delicate and difficult distinctions between religious garb. But the services have a successful record of using the neat and conservative standard to distinguish acceptable from unacceptable jewelry. If we can make this distinction for neat and conservative jewelry, why can't we make it for religious apparel.

Certainly, the wearing of apparel central to the practice of one's religious beliefs is more important and worthy of review than the wearing of jewelry. The Air Force permits the wearing of up to three rings and one identification bracelet of neat and conservative but nonuniform design. This jewelry is permitted even if, as if is often the case with rings, it associates the wearer with a denominational school or a religious or secular fraternal organization. These items are not deemed to be unacceptably divisive. I cannot see why religious apparel that is neat and conservative would be.

. . .

Mr. MURKOWSKI. I thank the Senator from Ohio.

Mr. President, I rise as the ranking minority member of the Committee on Veterans' Affairs. At the request of numerous organizations representing service members and veterans of all faiths, I feel compelled to express my concern regarding the amendment of the Senator from New Jersey, which would allow service members to wear religious apparel while in uniform. The American Legion, with over 2.5 million members, and the Military Coalition, representing 16 of the largest organizations for military personnel, do not support the amendment of the Senator from New Jersey.

Let me read the list of these organizations. They are as follows: Air Force Sergeants Association, Association of Military Surgeons of the United States, Commissioned Officers Association, Fleet Reserve Association, Marine Corps Reserve Officers Association, National Association for Uniformed Services, National Military Family Association, Naval Enlisted Reserve Association, Naval Reserve Association, Non-Commissioned Officers Association, Reserve Officers Association, the Retired Enlisted Association, the Retired Officers Association, U.S. Army Warrant Officers Association, U.S. Coast Guard CPO Association, and U.S. Coast Guard CWO and WO Association.

. . .

Mr. President, I suggest to my colleagues that this amendment creates many more problems than it solves. The issue is not religious freedoms. The issue is whether we write into law an arbitrary standard and then tell our military leaders to apply it as best as they can. Right now, they apply a very logical, neutral standard. I suggest to my colleagues that they ought to be permitted to continue to apply that visibility standard.

Mr. GLENN. Mr. President, I yield 5 minutes to the Senator from Rhode Island.

Mr. CHAFEE. Mr. President, I consider this an unfortunate amendment and hope that it will not succeed.

First, I should like to emphasize the points that the distinguished Senator from Alaska has made. If this amendment were adopted, it would open the floodgates to all kinds of litigation in the Armed Forces in the interpretation of what the Senator from New Jersey means.

For example, what does his amendment mean in requiring that an allowed item of apparel be "part of the religious observance of the faith practiced by the member?" If the commanding officer attempts to question whether an article that the sailor or soldier is wearing is a piece of religious apparel, there are bound to be disputes as to what qualifies as part of the religious observances. That's point No. 1.

Point No. 2: Who is to judge what is neat and conservative? In my view, it is impossible to judge that. That is a standard that is certainly going to be litigated every time it arises.

Third, the Senator's amendment says that the item must not significantly interfere with the performance of the member's military duties. Note the words "significantly interfere."

Mr. LAUTENBERG. Mr. President, will the Senator yield?

To set the RECORD straight, the word "significantly" is not in the amendment. I just point that out to the Senator.

Mr. CHAFEE. The Senator must have changed the amendment from the one he submitted here, because the word "significantly" was in the printed amendment we have—in the original bill.

Mr. LAUTENBERG. That was last year's.

. . .

Mr. GLENN. Mr. President, I yield myself such time as I may require.

Mr. President, I truly regret having to rise to oppose the amendment by the distinguished Senator from New Jersey. Perhaps this is, of all times of year, the very worst time to be opposing this on the floor of the U.S. Senate, from my standpoint. It is a time of high feelings in the Jewish community. It is the time of Rosh Hashanah, the time of Yom Kippur, of introspection, of family, of very deeply held religious beliefs and thoughts and feelings during this most holy time of the year for people of that faith.

So I truly do regret that I must oppose this amendment to authorize military members to wear religious apparel as part of the official uniform.

I have very great respect and understanding for the motivation of the sponsors of the amendment. Freedom of religious expression was one of the keys upon which this whole Nation of ours was founded and it is one of the freedoms which our military personnel are sworn to defend. I am afraid that this amendment, if passed, could undermine the essential discipline which is so key and so essential to our military services.

. . .

[Senator Glenn placed in the Record a letter from the Secretary of Defense, Caspar Weinberger, opposing the amendment on the ground that it would force commanders to apply subjective criteria ("neat and conservative") in distinguishing among religious apparel. Senator Glenn also placed in the Record a "20-star letter" from the Joint Chiefs of Staff, opposing the amendment. The letter, signed by the chairman of the Joint Chiefs, the general of the Air Force, the general of the Army, the general of the Marine Corps, and the admiral of the Navy, adds up to five four-star officers.]

Mr. ADAMS. Mr. President, I intend to vote for this amendment but I do not do so with enthusiasm. My lack of enthusiasm springs from two sources. First, in my view, this is an issue which should never have gone to the courts and never come before the Congress. In the past, the military services have been able to accommodate individuals on a case by case basis. Those informal agreements seem to have served everyone's interest. I just wish that we were able to return to a time when people spoke with each other instead of sued each other. Second, I have to tell you that I was shocked by the level of lobbying that has gone on about this issue. I have had more calls from constituents on this issue than I had on SDI; I had more requests for visits from DOD on this issue than I did on a comprehensive test ban. There are some really vital issues that need to be addressed in this bill—and while this issue is important, the fate of the nation does not hang on it. I expected that the folks who care about this issue would have taken the opportunity to raise some other concerns when they came to visit—but they never did. And I find that very disturbing.

Having expressed my frustration about the attention this amendment received, let me turn to the substance of the issue. Let me begin, Mr. President, by establishing the basic premise from which I believe both sides are operating: Individuals have the right to be true to their faith while serving their country; and the country has an obligation to do everything it can to make its military a sound functioning organization. I believe that morale and the patriotism of our young people is more important than rigid restrictions which offend their freely and deeply held religious beliefs. I support the amendment.

. . .

Everson v. Board of Education

330 U.S. 1 (1947)

Acting under a New Jersey statute, the township of Ewing reimbursed parents for money spent in transporting their children to school. Part of the money went to children attending Catholic schools. Arch R. Everson, a taxpayer in the local school district, filed suit challenging the right of the Board of Education of the Township of Ewing to reimburse parents of parochial school students. The New Jersey Supreme Court held the statute unconstitutional, but was reversed by the New Jersey Court of Errors and Appeals.

MR. JUSTICE BLACK delivered the opinion of the Court.

A New Jersey statute authorizes its local school districts to make rules and contracts for the transportation of children to and from schools. The appellee, a township board of education, acting pursuant to this statute, authorized reimbursement to parents of money expended by them for the bus transportation of their children on regular busses operated by the public transportation system. Part of this money was for the payment of transportation of some children in the community to Catholic parochial schools. These church schools give their students, in addition to secular education, regular religious instruction conforming to the religious tenets and modes of worship of the Catholic Faith. The superintendent of these schools is a Catholic priest.

The appellant, in his capacity as a district taxpayer, filed suit in a state court challenging the right of the Board to reimburse parents of parochial school students. He contended that the statute and the resolution passed pursuant to it violated both the State and the Federal Constitutions. . . .

[Everson alleged that the statute and township resolution violated the Due Process Clause of the Fourteenth Amendment by authorizing the state to tax the

[After defeating a motion to table the amendment, which lost 42–55, the Senate agreed to the amendment, 55–42.]

private property of some and bestow it upon others, to be used for their own private purposes. Black rejects this argument and turns to the question of the Establishment Clause.]

Second. The New Jersey statute is challenged as a "law respecting an establishment of religion." The First Amendment, as made applicable to the states by the Fourteenth, *Murdock* v. *Pennsylvania,* 319 U. S. 105, commands that a state "shall make no law respecting an establishment of religion, or prohibiting the free exercise thereof. . . ." These words of the First Amendment reflected in the minds of early Americans a vivid mental picture of conditions and practices which they fervently wished to stamp out in order to preserve liberty for themselves and for their posterity. Doubtless their goal has not been entirely reached; but so far has the Nation moved toward it that the expression "law respecting an establishment of religion," probably does not so vividly remind present-day Americans of the evils, fears, and political problems that caused that expression to be written into our Bill of Rights. Whether this New Jersey law is one respecting an "establishment of religion" requires an understanding of the meaning of that language, particularly with respect to the imposition of taxes. Once again, therefore, it is not inappropriate briefly to review the background and environment of the period in which that constitutional language was fashioned and adopted.

A large proportion of the early settlers of this country came here from Europe to escape the bondage of laws which compelled them to support and attend government-favored churches. The centuries immediately before and contemporaneous with the colonization of America had been filled with turmoil, civil strife, and persecutions, generated in large part by established sects determined to maintain their absolute political and religious supremacy. With the power of government supporting them, at various times and places, Catholics had persecuted Protestants, Protestants had persecuted Catholics, Protestant sects had persecuted other Protestant sects, Catholics of one shade of belief had persecuted Catholics of another shade of belief, and all of these had from time to time persecuted Jews. In efforts to force loyalty to whatever religious group happened to be on top and in league with the government of a particular time and place, men and women had been fined, cast in jail, cruelly tortured, and killed. Among the offenses for which these punishments had been inflicted were such things as speaking disrespectfully of the views of ministers of government-established churches, non-attendance at those churches, expressions of nonbelief in their doctrines, and failure to pay taxes and tithes to support them.

These practices of the old world were transplanted to and began to thrive in the soil of the new America. The very charters granted by the English Crown to the individuals and companies designated to make the laws which would control the destinies of the colonials authorized these individuals and companies to erect religious establishments which all, whether believers or nonbelievers, would be required to support and attend. . . .

These practices became so commonplace as to shock the freedom-loving colonials into a feeling of abhorrence. The imposition of taxes to pay ministers' salaries and to build and maintain churches and church property aroused their indignation. It was these feelings which found expression in the First Amendment. No one locality and no one group throughout the Colonies can rightly be given entire credit for having aroused the sentiment that culminated in adoption of the Bill of Rights' provisions embracing religious liberty. But Virginia, where the established church had achieved a dominant influence in political affairs and where many excesses attracted wide public attention, provided a great stimulus and able leadership for the movement. The people there, as elsewhere, reached the conviction that individual religious liberty could be achieved best under a government which was stripped of all power to tax, to support, or otherwise to assist any or all religions, or to interfere with the beliefs of any religious individual or group.

[After summarizing the efforts of Jefferson and Madison in Virginia to enact the Bill for Religious Liberty, and the subsequent adoption of the First Amendment, Black focuses on the meaning of the Establishment Clause.]

The "establishment of religion" clause of the First Amendment means at least this: Neither a state nor the Federal Government can set up a church. Neither can pass laws which aid one religion, aid all religions, or prefer one religion over another. Neither can force nor influence a person to go to or to remain away from church against his will or force him to profess a belief or disbelief in any religion. No person can be punished for entertaining or professing religious beliefs or disbeliefs, for church attendance or nonattendance. No tax in any amount, large or small, can be levied to support any religious activities or institutions, whatever they may be called, or whatever form they may adopt to teach or practice religion. Neither a state nor the Federal Government can, openly or secretly, participate in the affairs of any religious organizations or groups and *vice versa*. In the words of Jefferson, the clause against establishment of religion by law was intended to erect "a wall of separation between church and State." *Reynolds* v. *United States, supra* at 164.

We must consider the New Jersey statute in accordance with the foregoing limitations imposed by the First Amendment. But we must not strike that state statute down if it is within the State's constitutional power even though it approaches the verge of that power. See *Interstate Ry.*

v. *Massachusetts*, Holmes, J., *supra* at 85, 88. New Jersey cannot consistently with the "establishment of religion" clause of the First Amendment contribute tax-raised funds to the support of an institution which teaches the tenets and faith of any church. On the other hand, other language of the amendment commands that New Jersey cannot hamper its citizens in the free exercise of their own religion. Consequently, it cannot exclude individual Catholics, Lutherans, Mohammedans, Baptists, Jews, Methodists, Non-believers, Presbyterians, or the members of any other faith, *because of their faith, or lack of it,* from receiving the benefits of public welfare legislation. While we do not mean to intimate that a state could not provide transportation only to children attending public schools, we must be careful, in protecting the citizens of New Jersey against state-established churches, to be sure that we do not inadvertently prohibit New Jersey from extending its general state law benefits to all its citizens without regard to their religious belief.

Measured by these standards, we cannot say that the First Amendment prohibits New Jersey from spending tax-raised funds to pay the bus fares of parochial school pupils as a part of a general program under which it pays the fares of pupils attending public and other schools. It is undoubtedly true that children are helped to get to church schools. There is even a possibility that some of the children might not be sent to the church schools if the parents were compelled to pay their children's bus fares out of their own pockets when transportation to a public school would have been paid for by the State. The same possibility exists where the state requires a local transit company to provide reduced fares to school children including those attending parochial schools, or where a municipally owned transportation system undertakes to carry all school children free of charge. Moreover, state-paid policemen, detailed to protect children going to and from church schools from the very real hazards of traffic, would serve much the same purpose and accomplish much the same result as state provisions intended to guarantee free transportation of a kind which the state deems to be best for the school children's welfare. And parents might refuse to risk their children to the serious

danger of traffic accidents going to and from parochial schools, the approaches to which were not protected by policemen. Similarly, parents might be reluctant to permit their children to attend schools which the state had cut off from such general government services as ordinary police and fire protection, connections for sewage disposal, public highways and sidewalks. Of course, cutting off church schools from these services, so separate and so indisputably marked off from the religious function, would make it far more difficult for the schools to operate. But such is obviously not the purpose of the First Amendment. That Amendment requires the state to be a neutral in its relations with groups of religious believers and non-believers; it does not require the state to be their adversary. State power is no more to be used so as to handicap religions than it is to favor them.

This Court has said that parents may, in the discharge of their duty under state compulsory education laws, send their children to a religious rather than a public school if the school meets the secular educational requirements which the state has power to impose. See *Pierce* v. *Society of Sisters*, 268 U. S. 510. It appears that these parochial schools meet New Jersey's requirements. The State contributes no money to the schools. It does not support them. Its legislation, as applied, does no more than provide a general program to help parents get their children, regardless of their religion, safely and expeditiously to and from accredited schools.

The First Amendment has erected a wall between church and state. That wall must be kept high and impregnable. We could not approve the slightest breach. New Jersey has not breached it here.

Affirmed.

MR. JUSTICE JACKSON, dissenting.

I find myself, contrary to first impressions, unable to join in this decision. I have a sympathy, though it is not ideological, with Catholic citizens who are compelled by law to pay taxes for public schools, and also feel constrained by conscience and discipline to support other schools for their own children. Such relief to them as this case involves is not in itself a serious burden to taxpayers and I had assumed it to be as little serious in principle. Study of this case convinces me otherwise. The Court's opinion marshals every argument in favor of state aid and puts the case in its most favorable light, but much of its reasoning confirms my conclusions that there are no good grounds upon which to support the present legislation. In fact, the undertones of the opinion, advocating complete and uncompromising separation of Church from State, seem utterly discordant with its conclusion yielding support to their commingling in educational matters. The case which irresistibly comes to mind as the most fitting precedent is that of Julia who, according to Byron's reports, "whispering 'I will ne'er consent,'—consented."

I.

The Court sustains this legislation by assuming two deviations from the facts of this particular case; first, it assumes a state of facts the record does not support, and secondly, it refuses to consider facts which are inescapable on the record.

The Court concludes that this "legislation, as applied, does no more than provide a general program to help parents get their children, regardless of their religion, safely and expeditiously to and from accredited schools," and it draws a comparison between "state provisions intended to guarantee free transportation" for school children with services such as police and fire protection, and implies that we are here dealing with "laws authorizing new types of public services. . . ." This hypothesis permeates the opinion. The facts will not bear that construction.

The Township of Ewing is not furnishing transportation to the children in any form; it is not operating school busses itself or contracting for their operation; and it is not performing any public service of any kind with this taxpayer's money. All school children are left to ride as ordinary paying passengers on the regular busses operated by the public transportation system. What the Township does, and what the taxpayer complains of, is at stated intervals to reimburse parents for the fares paid, provided the children attend either public schools or Catholic Church schools. This expenditure of tax funds has no possible effect on the child's safety or expedition in transit. As passengers on the public busses they travel as fast and no faster, and are as safe and no safer, since their parents are reimbursed as before.

In addition to thus assuming a type of service that does not exist, the Court also insists that we must close our eyes to a discrimination which does exist. The resolution which authorizes disbursement of this taxpayer's money limits reimbursement to those who attend public schools and Catholic schools. That is the way the Act is applied to this taxpayer.

The New Jersey Act in question makes the character of the school, not the needs of the children, determine the eligibility of parents to reimbursement. . . . under the Act and resolution brought to us by this case, children are classified according to the schools they attend and are to be aided if they attend the public schools or private Catholic schools, and they are not allowed to be aided if they attend private secular schools or private religious schools of other faiths.

. . .

II.

Whether the taxpayer constitutionally can be made to contribute aid to parents of students because of their attendance at parochial schools depends upon the nature of those schools and their relation to the Church. . . .

. . .

I should be surprised if any Catholic would deny that the parochial school is a vital, if not the most vital, part of the Roman Catholic Church. If put to the choice, that venerable institution, I should expect, would forego its whole service for mature persons before it would give up education of the young, and it would be a wise choice. Its growth and cohesion, discipline and loyalty, spring from its schools. Catholic education is the rock on which the whole structure rests, and to render tax aid to its Church school is indistinguishable to me from rendering the same aid to the Church itself.

III.

It is of no importance in this situation whether the beneficiary of this expenditure of tax-raised funds is primarily the parochial school and incidentally the pupil, or whether the aid is directly bestowed on the pupil with indirect benefits to the school. The state cannot maintain a Church and it can no more tax its citizens to furnish free carriage to those who attend a Church. The prohibition against establishment of religion cannot be circumvented by a subsidy, bonus or reimbursement of expense to individuals for receiving religious instruction and indoctrination.

. . .

It seems to me that the basic fallacy in the Court's reasoning, which accounts for its failure to apply the principles it avows, is in ignoring the essentially religious test by which beneficiaries of this expenditure are selected. A policeman protects a Catholic, of course—but not because he is a Catholic; it is because he is a man and a member of our society. The fireman protects the Church school—but not because it is a Church school; it is because it is property, part of the assets of our society. Neither the fireman nor the policeman has to ask before he renders aid "Is this man or building identified with the Catholic Church?" But before these school authorities draw a check to reimburse for a student's fare they must ask just that question, and if the school is a Catholic one they may render aid because it is such, while if it is of any other faith or is run for profit, the help must be withheld. To consider the converse of the Court's reasoning will best disclose its fallacy. That there is no parallel between police and fire protection and this plan of reimbursement is apparent from the incongruity of the limitation of this Act if applied to police and fire service. Could we sustain an Act that said the police shall protect pupils on the way to or from public schools and Catholic schools but not while going to and coming from other schools, and firemen shall extinguish a blaze in public or Catholic school buildings but shall not put out a blaze in Protestant Church schools or private schools operated for profit? That is the true analogy to the case we have before us and I should think it pretty plain that such a scheme would not be valid.

. . . This freedom *[of religion]* was first in the Bill of Rights because it was first in the forefathers' minds; it was set forth in absolute terms, and its strength is its rigidity. It was intended not only to keep the states' hands out of religion, but to keep religion's hands off the state, and, above all, to keep bitter religious controversy out of public life by denying to every denomination any advantage from getting control of public policy or the public purse. Those great ends I cannot but think are immeasurably compromised by today's decision.

. . .

MR. JUSTICE FRANKFURTER joins in this opinion.

MR. JUSTICE RUTLEDGE, with whom MR. JUSTICE FRANKFURTER, MR. JUSTICE JACKSON and MR. JUSTICE BURTON agree, dissenting.

. . .

. . . New Jersey's statute sustained is the first, if indeed it is not the second breach to be made by this Court's action. That a third, and a fourth, and still others will be attempted, we may be sure. For just as *Cochran* v. *Board of Education*, 281 U. S. 370, has opened the way by oblique ruling *[supplying secular textbooks to religious schools]* for this decision, so will the two make wider the breach for a third. Thus with time the most solid freedom steadily gives way before continuing corrosive decision.

. . .

Lynch v. Donnelly

465 U.S. 668 (1984)

Each year the city of Pawtucket, R.I., set up a Christmas display in a park owned by a nonprofit organization and located in the city's shopping district. In addition to such objects as a Santa Claus house, a Christmas tree, and a banner that reads "SEASONS GREETINGS," the display includes a crèche (Nativity scene). The crèche has been included in this display for forty years or more. Daniel Donnelly brought an action in federal court, challenging the inclusion of the crèche as a violation of the Establishment Clause. The defendant was Dennis Lynch, Mayor of Pawtucket. The district court upheld the challenge and permanently enjoined the city from including the crèche in the display. The First Circuit affirmed.

CHIEF JUSTICE BURGER delivered the opinion of the Court.

We granted certiorari to decide whether the Establishment Clause of the First Amendment prohibits a municipality from including a crèche, or Nativity scene, in its annual Christmas display.

I

Each year, in cooperation with the downtown retail merchants' association, the city of Pawtucket, R.I., erects a Christmas display as part of its observance of the Christmas holiday season. The display is situated in a park owned by a nonprofit organization and located in the heart of the shopping district. The display is essentially like those to be found in hundreds of towns or cities across the Nation—often on public grounds—during the Christmas season. The Pawtucket display comprises many of the figures and decorations traditionally associated with Christmas, including, among other things, a Santa Claus house, reindeer pulling Santa's sleigh, candy-striped poles, a Christmas tree, carolers, cutout figures representing such characters as a clown, an elephant, and a teddy bear, hundreds of colored lights, a large banner that reads "SEASONS GREETINGS," and the crèche at issue here. All components of this display are owned by the city.

The crèche, which has been included in the display for 40 or more years, consists of the traditional figures, including the Infant Jesus, Mary and Joseph, angels, shepherds, kings, and animals, all ranging in height from 5″ to 5′. In 1973, when the present crèche was acquired, it cost the city $1,365; it now is valued at $200. The erection and dismantling of the crèche costs the city about $20 per year; nominal expenses are incurred in lighting the crèche. No money has been expended on its maintenance for the past 10 years.

. . .

II

A

This Court has explained that the purpose of the Establishment and Free Exercise Clauses of the First Amendment is

"to prevent, as far as possible, the intrusion of either [the church or the state] into the precincts of the other." *Lemon* v. *Kurtzman*, 403 U.S. 602, 614 (1971).

At the same time, however, the Court has recognized that

"total separation is not possible in an absolute sense. Some relationship between government and religious organizations is inevitable." *Ibid.*

. . .

B

The Court's interpretation of the Establishment Clause has comported with what history reveals was the contemporaneous understanding of its guarantees. A significant example of the contemporaneous understanding of that Clause is found in the events of the first week of the First Session of the First Congress in 1789. In the very week that Congress approved the Establishment Clause as part of the Bill of Rights for submission to the states, it enacted legislation providing for paid Chaplains for the House and Senate. In *Marsh* v. *Chambers*, 463 U. S. 783 (1983), we noted that 17 Members of that First Congress had been Delegates to the Constitutional Convention where freedom of speech, press, and religion and antagonism toward an established church were subjects of frequent discussion. We saw no conflict with the Establishment Clause when Nebraska employed members of the clergy as official legislative Chaplains to give opening prayers at sessions of the state legislature. *Id.*, at 791.

. . .

C

[Burger provides other examples of official acknowledgment of religion: making Thanksgiving, with its religious overtones, a national holiday; giving federal employees a holiday for Christmas; putting "In God We Trust" on currency; including "One nation under God" in the Pledge of Allegiance; using public revenue to display religious paintings in art galleries; decorating the Supreme Court with religious motifs; and having Congress direct the President to proclaim a National Day of Prayer.]

III

. . .

The District Court inferred from the religious nature of the crèche that the city has no secular purpose for the display. In so doing, it rejected the city's claim that its reasons for including the crèche are essentially the same as its reasons for sponsoring the display as a whole. The District Court plainly erred by focusing almost exclusively on the crèche. When viewed in the proper context of the Christmas Holiday season, it is apparent that, on this record, there is insufficient evidence to establish that the inclusion of the crèche is a purposeful or surreptitious effort to express some kind of subtle governmental advocacy of a particular religious message. In a pluralistic society a variety of motives and purposes are implicated. The city, like the Congresses and Presidents, however, has principally taken note of a significant historical religious event long celebrated in the Western World. The crèche in the display depicts the historical origins of this traditional event long recognized as a National Holiday. See *Allen* v. *Hickel*, 138 U.S. App. D. C. 31, 424 F. 2d 944 (1970); *Citizens Concerned for Separation of Church and State* v. *City and County of Denver*, 526 F. Supp. 1310 (Colo. 1981).

The narrow question is whether there is a secular purpose for Pawtucket's display of the crèche. The display is sponsored by the city to celebrate the Holiday and to depict the origins of that Holiday. These are legitimate secular purposes. The District Court's inference, drawn from the religious nature of the crèche, that the city has no secular purpose was, on this record, clearly erroneous.

The District Court found that the primary effect of including the crèche is to confer a substantial and impermissible benefit on religion in general and on the Christian faith in particular. Comparisons of the relative benefits to religion of different forms of governmental support are elusive and difficult to make. But to conclude that the primary effect of including the crèche is to advance religion in violation of the Establishment Clause would require that we view it as more beneficial to and more an endorsement of religion, for example, than expenditure of large sums of public money for textbooks supplied throughout the country to students attending church-sponsored schools, *Board of Education* v. *Allen, supra;* expenditure of public funds for transportation of students to church-sponsored schools, *Everson* v. *Board of Education, supra;* federal grants for college buildings of church-sponsored institutions of higher education combining secular and religious education, *Tilton* v. *Richardson*, 403 U.S. 672 (1971); noncategorical grants to church-sponsored colleges and universities, *Roemer* v. *Board of Public Works*, 426 U.S. 736 (1976); and the tax exemptions for church properties sanctioned in *Walz* v. *Tax Comm'n*, 397 U.S. 664 (1970). It would also require that we view it as more of an endorsement of religion than the Sunday Closing Laws upheld in *McGowan* v. *Maryland*, 366 U.S. 420 (1961); the release time program for religious training in *Zorach* v. *Clauson*, 343 U.S. 306 (1952); and the legislative prayers upheld in *Marsh* v. *Chambers*, 463 U.S. 783 (1983).

. . .

IV

. . .

The Court has acknowledged that the "fears and political problems" that gave rise to the Religion Clauses in the 18th century are of far less concern today. *Everson*, 330 U.S., at 8. We are unable to perceive the Archbishop of Canterbury, the Bishop of Rome, or other powerful religious leaders behind every public acknowledgment of the religious heritage long officially recognized by the three constitutional branches of government. Any notion that these symbols pose a real danger of establishment of a state church is farfetched indeed.

V

That this Court has been alert to the constitutionally expressed opposition to the establishment of religion is shown in numerous holdings striking down statutes or programs as violative of the Establishment Clause. See, *e.g., Illinois ex rel. McCollum* v. *Board of Education*, 333 U.S. 203 (1948); *Epperson* v. *Arkansas*, 393 U.S. 97 (1968); *Lemon* v. *Kurtzman, supra; Levitt* v. *Committee for Public Education & Religious Liberty*, 413 U.S. 472 (1973); *Committee for Public Education & Religious Liberty* v. *Nyquist*, 413 U.S. 756 (1973); *Meek* v. *Pittenger*, 421 U.S. 349 (1975); and *Stone* v. *Graham*, 449 U.S. 39 (1980). The most recent example of this careful scrutiny is found in the case invalidating a municipal ordinance granting to a church a virtual veto power over the licensing of liquor establishments near the church. *Larkin* v. *Grendel's Den, Inc.*, 459 U.S. 116 (1982). Taken together these cases abundantly demonstrate the Court's concern to protect the genuine objectives of the Establishment Clause. It is far too late in the day to impose a crabbed reading of the Clause on the country.

VI

We hold that, notwithstanding the religious significance of the crèche, the city of Pawtucket has not violated the Establishment Clause of the First Amendment. Accordingly, the judgment of the Court of Appeals is reversed.

It is so ordered.

JUSTICE O'CONNOR, concurring.

I concur in the opinion of the Court. I write separately to suggest a clarification of our Establishment Clause doctrine. The suggested approach leads to the same result in this case as that taken by the Court, and the Court's opinion, as I read it, is consistent with my analysis.

. . .

II

In this case, as even the District Court found, there is no institutional entanglement. Nevertheless, the respondents contend that the political divisiveness caused by Pawtucket's display of its crèche violates the excessive-entanglement prong of the *Lemon* test. The Court's opinion follows the suggestion in *Mueller* v. *Allen*, 463 U.S. 388, 403–404, n. 11 (1983), and concludes that "no inquiry into potential political divisiveness is even called for" in this case. *Ante*, at 684. In my view, political divisiveness along religious lines should not be an independent test of constitutionality.

. . . Political divisiveness is admittedly an evil addressed by the Establishment Clause. Its existence may be evidence that institutional entanglement is excessive or that a government practice is perceived as an endorsement of religion. But the constitutional inquiry should focus ultimately on the character of the government activity that might cause such divisiveness, not on the divisiveness itself. The entanglement prong of the *Lemon* test is properly limited to institutional entanglement.

. . .

JUSTICE BRENNAN, with whom JUSTICE MARSHALL, JUSTICE BLACKMUN, and JUSTICE STEVENS join, dissenting.

The principles announced in the compact

phrases of the Religion Clauses have, as the Court today reminds us, *ante*, at 678–679, proved difficult to apply. Faced with that uncertainty, the Court properly looks for guidance to the settled test announced in *Lemon* v. *Kurtzman*, 403 U.S. 602 (1971), for assessing whether a challenged governmental practice involves an impermissible step toward the establishment of religion. *Ante*, at 679. Applying that test to this case, the Court reaches an essentially narrow result which turns largely upon the particular holiday context in which the city of Pawtucket's nativity scene appeared. . . .

I

Last Term, I expressed the hope that the Court's decision in *Marsh* v. *Chambers*, 463 U.S. 783 (1983), would prove to be only a single, aberrant departure from our settled method of analyzing Establishment Clause cases. *Id.*, at 796 (BRENNAN, J., dissenting). That the Court today returns to the settled analysis of our prior cases gratifies that hope. At the same time, the Court's less-than-vigorous application of the *Lemon* test suggests that its commitment to those standards may only be superficial. After reviewing the Court's opinion, I am convinced that this case appears hard not because the principles of decision are obscure, but because the Christmas holiday seems so familiar and agreeable. Although the Court's reluctance to disturb a community's chosen method of celebrating such an agreeable holiday is understandable, that cannot justify the Court's departure from controlling precedent. . . .

A

As we have sought to meet new problems arising under the Establishment Clause, our decisions, with few exceptions, have demanded that a challenged governmental practice satisfy the following criteria:

"First, the [practice] must have a secular legislative purpose; second, its principal or primary effect must be one that neither advances nor inhibits religion; finally, [it] must not foster 'an excessive government entanglement with reli-

gion.'" *Lemon* v. *Kurtzman*, 403 U.S., at 612–613 (citations omitted).

. . .

Applying the three-part test to Pawtucket's crèche, I am persuaded that the city's inclusion of the crèche in its Christmas display simply does not reflect a "clearly secular . . . purpose." *Nyquist*, *supra*, at 773. . . .

. . . as was true in *Larkin* v. *Grendel's Den, Inc.*, 459 U.S. 116, 123–124 (1982), all of Pawtucket's "valid secular objectives can be readily accomplished by other means." Plainly, the city's interest in celebrating the holiday and in promoting both retail sales and goodwill are fully served by the elaborate display of Santa Claus, reindeer, and wishing wells that are already a part of Pawtucket's annual Christmas display. More importantly, the nativity scene, unlike every other element of the Hodgson Park display, reflects a sectarian exclusivity that the avowed purposes of celebrating the holiday season and promoting retail commerce simply do not encompass. To be found constitutional, Pawtucket's seasonal celebration must at least be nondenominational and not serve to promote religion. The inclusion of a distinctively religious element like the crèche, however, demonstrates that a narrower sectarian purpose lay behind the decision to include a nativity scene. That the crèche retained this religious character for the people and municipal government of Pawtucket is suggested by the Mayor's testimony at trial in which he stated that for him, as well as others in the city, the effort to eliminate the nativity scene from Pawtucket's Christmas celebration "is a step towards establishing another religion, non-religion that it may be." App. 100. Plainly, the city and its leaders understood that the inclusion of the crèche in its display would serve the wholly religious purpose of "keep[ing] 'Christ in Christmas.'" 525 F. Supp. 1150, 1173 (RI 1981). . . .

Finally, it is evident that Pawtucket's inclusion of a crèche as part of its annual Christmas display does pose a significant threat of fostering "excessive entanglement." As the Court notes, *ante*, at 683, the District Court found no administrative entanglement in this case, primarily because the city had been able to administer the annual display without extensive consultation with religious officials. See 525 F. Supp., at 1179. Of course, there is no reason to disturb that finding, but it is worth noting that after today's decision, administrative entanglements may well develop. Jews and other non-Christian groups, prompted perhaps by the Mayor's remark that he will include a Menorah in future displays, can be expected to press government for inclusion of their symbols, and faced with such requests, government will have to become involved in accommodating the various demands. Cf. *Committee for Public Education & Religious Liberty* v. *Nyquist*, 413 U.S., at 796 ("competing efforts [by religious groups] to gain or maintain the support of government" may "occasio[n] considerable civil strife"). More importantly, although no political divisiveness was apparent in Pawtucket prior to the filing of respondents' lawsuit, that act, as the District Court found, unleashed powerful emotional reactions which divided the city along religious lines. 525 F. Supp., at 1180. The fact that calm had prevailed prior to this suit does not immediately suggest the absence of any division on the point for, as the District Court observed, the quiescence of those opposed to the crèche may have reflected nothing more than their sense of futility in opposing the majority. *Id.*, at 1179. . . .

B

. . . even in the context of Pawtucket's seasonal celebration, the crèche retains a specifically Christian religious meaning. I refuse to accept the notion implicit in today's decision that non-Christians would find that the religious content of the crèche is eliminated by the fact that it appears as part of the city's otherwise secular celebration of the Christmas holiday. The nativity scene is clearly distinct in its purpose and effect from the rest of the Hodgson Park display for the simple reason that it is the only one rooted in a biblical account of Christ's birth. It is the chief symbol of the characteristically Christian belief that a divine Savior was brought into the world and that the purpose of this miraculous birth was to illuminate a path toward salvation and redemption. For Christians, that path is exclusive, precious, and

holy. But for those who do not share these beliefs, the symbolic reenactment of the birth of a divine being who has been miraculously incarnated as a man stands as a dramatic reminder of their differences with Christian faith. When government appears to sponsor such religiously inspired views, we cannot say that the practice is " 'so separate and so indisputably marked off from the religious function,' . . . that [it] may fairly be viewed as reflect[ing] a neutral posture toward religious institutions." *Nyquist*, 413 U.S., at 782 (quoting *Everson*, 330 U.S., at 18). To be so excluded on religious grounds by one's elected government is an insult and an injury that, until today, could not be countenanced by the Establishment Clause.

. . .

JUSTICE BLACKMUN, with whom JUSTICE STEVENS joins, dissenting.

. . .

Not only does the Court's resolution of this controversy make light of our precedents, but also, ironically, the majority does an injustice to the crèche and the message it manifests. While certain persons, including the Mayor of Pawtucket, undertook a crusade to "keep 'Christ' in Christmas," App. 161, the Court today has declared that presence virtually irrelevant. . . . The crèche has been relegated to the role of a neutral harbinger of the holiday season, useful for commercial purposes, but devoid of any inherent meaning and incapable of enhancing the religious tenor of a display of which it is an integral part. The city has its victory—but it is a Pyrrhic one indeed.

The import of the Court's decision is to encourage use of the crèche in a municipally sponsored display, a setting where Christians feel constrained in acknowledging its symbolic meaning and non-Christians feel alienated by its presence. Surely, this is a misuse of a sacred symbol. Because I cannot join the Court in denying either the force of our precedents or the sacred message that is at the core of the crèche, I dissent and join JUSTICE BRENNAN'S opinion.

Lemon v. Kurtzman

403 U.S. 602 (1971)

A number of states passed legislation providing financial assistance to church-related elementary and secondary schools, going far beyond the initial support in the form of transportation and textbooks. These state initiatives required the Court to establish guidelines and principles to distinguish permissible from impermissible aid. This case involves legislation enacted by Rhode Island and Pennsylvania. In the lead case, Alton J. Lemon, a citizen and taxpayer of Pennsylvania as well as a parent of a child attending a public school in Pennsylvania, brings suit against David H. Kurtzman, Superintendent of Public Instruction of Pennsylvania. A three-judge federal court held that the Pennsylvania law violated neither the Establishment nor the Free Exercise Clause of the First Amendment.

MR. CHIEF JUSTICE BURGER delivered the opinion of the Court.

These two appeals raise questions as to Pennsylvania and Rhode Island statutes providing state aid to church-related elementary and secondary schools. Both statutes are challenged as violative of the Establishment and Free Exercise Clauses of the First Amendment and the Due Process Clause of the Fourteenth Amendment.

Pennsylvania has adopted a statutory program that provides financial support to nonpublic elementary and secondary schools by way of reimbursement for the cost of teachers' salaries, textbooks, and instructional materials in specified secular subjects. Rhode Island has adopted a statute under which the State pays directly to teachers in nonpublic elementary schools a supplement of 15% of their annual salary. Under each statute state aid has been given to church-related educational institutions. We hold that both statutes are unconstitutional.

I

The Rhode Island Statute

The Rhode Island Salary Supplement Act was enacted in 1969. It rests on the legislative finding that the quality of education available in nonpublic elementary schools has been jeopardized by the rapidly rising salaries needed to attract competent and dedicated teachers. The Act authorizes state officials to supplement the salaries of teachers of secular subjects in nonpublic elementary schools by paying directly to a teacher an amount not in excess of 15% of his current annual salary. As supplemented, however, a nonpublic school teacher's salary cannot exceed the maximum paid to teachers in the State's public schools, and the recipient must be certified by the state board of education in substantially the same manner as public school teachers.

In order to be eligible for the Rhode Island salary supplement, the recipient must teach in a nonpublic school at which the average per-pupil expenditure on secular education is less than the average in the State's public schools during a specified period. Appellant State Commissioner of Education also requires eligible schools to submit financial data. If this information indicates a per-pupil expenditure in excess of the statutory limitation, the records of the school in question must be examined in order to assess how much of the expenditure is attributable to secular education and how much to religious activity.

The Act also requires that teachers eligible for salary supplements must teach only those subjects that are offered in the State's public schools. They must use "only teaching materials which are used in the public schools." Finally, any teacher applying for a salary supplement must first agree in writing "not to teach a course in religion for so long as or during such time as he or she receives any salary supplements" under the Act.

. . .

A three-judge federal court . . . found that Rhode Island's nonpublic elementary schools accommodated approximately 25% of the State's pupils. About 95% of these pupils attended schools affiliated with the Roman Catholic church. To date some 250 teachers have applied for benefits under the Act. All of them are employed by Roman Catholic schools.

. . .

The Pennsylvania Statute

Pennsylvania has adopted a program that has some but not all of the features of the Rhode Island program. The Pennsylvania Nonpublic Elementary and Secondary Education Act was passed in 1968 in response to a crisis that the Pennsylvania Legislature found existed in the State's nonpublic schools due to rapidly rising costs. The statute affirmatively reflects the legislative conclusion that the State's educational goals could appropriately be fulfilled by government support of "those purely secular educational objectives achieved through nonpublic education. . . ."

The statute authorizes appellee state Superintendent of Public Instruction to "purchase" specified "secular educational services" from nonpublic schools. Under the "contracts" authorized by the statute, the State directly reimburses nonpublic schools solely for their actual expenditures for teachers' salaries, textbooks, and instructional materials. A school seeking reimbursement must maintain prescribed accounting procedures that identify the "separate" cost of the "secular educational service." These accounts are subject to state audit. The funds for this program were originally derived from a new tax on horse and harness racing, but the Act is now financed by a portion of the state tax on cigarettes.

There are several significant statutory restrictions on state aid. Reimbursement is limited to courses "presented in the curricula of the public schools." It is further limited "solely" to courses in the following "secular" subjects: mathematics,

modern foreign languages, physical science, and physical education. Textbooks and instructional materials included in the program must be approved by the state Superintendent of Public Instruction. Finally, the statute prohibits reimbursement for any course that contains "any subject matter expressing religious teaching, or the morals or forms of worship of any sect."

. . . The State has now entered into contracts with some 1,181 nonpublic elementary and secondary schools with a student population of some 535,215 pupils—more than 20% of the total number of students in the State. More than 96% of these pupils attend church-related schools, and most of these schools are affiliated with the Roman Catholic church.

. . .

II

In *Everson* v. *Board of Education*, 330 U.S. 1 (1947), this Court upheld a state statute that reimbursed the parents of parochial school children for bus transportation expenses. There MR. JUSTICE BLACK, writing for the majority, suggested that the decision carried to "the verge" of forbidden territory under the Religion Clauses. *Id.*, at 16. Candor compels acknowledgment, moreover, that we can only dimly perceive the lines of demarcation in this extraordinarily sensitive area of constitutional law.

The language of the Religion Clauses of the First Amendment is at best opaque, particularly when compared with other portions of the Amendment. Its authors did not simply prohibit the establishment of a state church or a state religion, an area history shows they regarded as very important and fraught with great dangers. Instead they commanded that there should be "no law *respecting* an establishment of religion." A law may be one "respecting" the forbidden objective while falling short of its total realization. A law "respecting" the proscribed result, that is, the establishment of religion, is not always easily identifiable as one violative of the Clause. A given law might not *establish* a state religion but nevertheless be one "respecting" that end in the sense of being a step that could lead to such establishment and hence offend the First Amendment.

In the absence of precisely stated constitutional prohibitions, we must draw lines with reference to the three main evils against which the Establishment Clause was intended to afford protection: "sponsorship, financial support, and active involvement of the sovereign in religious activity." *Walz* v. *Tax Commission*, 397 U.S. 664, 668 (1970).

Every analysis in this area must begin with consideration of the cumulative criteria developed by the Court over many years. Three such tests may be gleaned from our cases. First, the statute must have a secular legislative purpose; second, its principal or primary effect must be one that neither advances nor inhibits religion, *Board of Education* v. *Allen*, 392 U.S. 236, 243 (1968); finally, the statute must not foster "an excessive government entanglement with religion." *Walz, supra,* at 674.

Inquiry into the legislative purposes of the Pennsylvania and Rhode Island statutes affords no basis for a conclusion that the legislative intent was to advance religion. On the contrary, the statutes themselves clearly state that they are intended to enhance the quality of the secular education in all schools covered by the compulsory attendance laws. There is no reason to believe the legislatures meant anything else. . . .

The two legislatures, however, have also recognized that church-related elementary and secondary schools have a significant religious mission and that a substantial portion of their activities is religiously oriented. They have therefore sought to create statutory restrictions designed to guarantee the separation between secular and religious educational functions and to ensure that State financial aid supports only the former. All these provisions are precautions taken in candid recognition that these programs approached, even if they did not intrude upon, the forbidden areas under the Religion Clauses. We need not decide whether these legislative precautions restrict the principal or primary effect of the programs to the point where they do not offend the Religion Clauses, for we conclude that the cumulative impact of the entire relationship arising under the statutes in each State involves excessive entanglement between government and religion.

III

. . .

(a) Rhode Island Program

The District Court made extensive findings on the grave potential for excessive entanglement that inheres in the religious character and purpose of the Roman Catholic elementary schools of Rhode Island, to date the sole beneficiaries of the Rhode Island Salary Supplement Act.

. . .

. . . the District Court concluded that the parochial schools constituted "an integral part of the religious mission of the Catholic Church." The various characteristics of the schools make them "a powerful vehicle for transmitting the Catholic faith to the next generation." This process of inculcating religious doctrine is, of course, enhanced by the impressionable age of the pupils, in primary schools particularly. In short, parochial schools involve substantial religious activity and purpose.

. . .

We need not and do not assume that teachers in parochial schools will be guilty of bad faith or any conscious design to evade the limitations imposed by the statute and the First Amendment. We simply recognize that a dedicated religious person, teaching in a school affiliated with his or her faith and operated to inculcate its tenets, will inevitably experience great difficulty in remaining religiously neutral. Doctrines and faith are not inculcated or advanced by neutrals. . . .

. . . The State must be certain, given the Religion Clauses, that subsidized teachers do not inculcate religion—indeed the State here has undertaken to do so. To ensure that no trespass occurs, the State has therefore carefully conditioned its aid with pervasive restrictions. An eligible recipient must teach only those courses that are offered in the public schools and use only those texts and materials that are found in the public schools. In addition the teacher must not engage in teaching any course in religion.

A comprehensive, discriminating, and continuing state surveillance will inevitably be required to ensure that these restrictions are obeyed and the First Amendment otherwise respected. Unlike a book, a teacher cannot be inspected once so as to determine the extent and intent of his or her personal beliefs and subjective acceptance of the limitations imposed by the First Amendment. These prophylactic contacts will involve excessive and enduring entanglement between state and church.

There is another area of entanglement in the Rhode Island program that gives concern. The statute excludes teachers employed by nonpublic schools whose average per-pupil expenditures on secular education equal or exceed the comparable figures for public schools. In the event that the total expenditures of an otherwise eligible school exceed this norm, the program requires the government to examine the school's records in order to determine how much of the total expenditures is attributable to secular education and how much to religious activity. This kind of state inspection and evaluation of the religious content of a religious organization is fraught with the sort of entanglement that the Constitution forbids. . . .

(b) Pennsylvania Program

[The Court found similar problems of excessive entanglement: providing state aid to sectarian schools established to propagate a particular religious faith; state restrictions and surveillance to ensure that teachers play a strictly nonideological role; reimbursement contingent on state approval of courses and teaching materials; and state auditing of a parochial school's financial records.]

IV

A broader base of entanglement of yet a different character is presented by the divisive political potential of these state programs. In a community where such a large number of pupils are served by church-related schools, it can be assumed that state assistance will entail considerable political activity. Partisans of parochial schools, understandably concerned with rising costs and sincerely dedicated to both the religious and secular educational missions of their schools, will inevitably champion this cause and promote political action to achieve their goals. Those who oppose state aid, whether for constitutional, religious, or fiscal reasons, will inevitably respond and employ all of the usual political campaign techniques to prevail. Candidates will be forced to declare and voters to choose. It would be unrealistic to ignore the fact that many people confronted with issues of this kind will find their votes aligned with their faith.

. . .

V

. . . nothing we have said can be construed to disparage the role of church-related elementary and secondary schools in our national life. Their contribution has been and is enormous. Nor do we ignore their economic plight in a period of rising costs and expanding need. Taxpayers generally have been spared vast sums by the maintenance of these educational institutions by religious organizations, largely by the gifts of faithful adherents.

The merit and benefits of these schools, however, are not the issue before us in these cases. The sole question is whether state aid to these schools can be squared with the dictates of the Religion Clauses. Under our system the choice has been made that government is to be entirely excluded from the area of religious instruction and churches excluded from the affairs of government. The Constitution decrees that religion must be a private matter for the individual, the family, and the institutions of private choice, and that while some involvement and entanglement are inevitable, lines must be drawn.

The judgment of the Rhode Island District Court in No. 569 and No. 570 is affirmed. The judgment of the Pennsylvania District Court in No. 89 is reversed, and the case is remanded for further proceedings consistent with this opinion.

Mr. Justice Marshall took no part in the consideration or decision of No. 89 *[the Pennsylvania case]*.

Mr. Justice Douglas, whom Mr. Justice Black joins, concurring.

. . .

MR. JUSTICE MARSHALL, who took no part in the consideration or decision of No. 89, see *ante*, p. 625, while intimating no view as to the continuing vitality of *Everson* v. *Board of Education*, 330 U.S. 1 (1947), concurs in MR. JUSTICE DOUGLAS' opinion covering Nos. 569 and 570 *[the Rhode Island cases]*.

MR. JUSTICE BRENNAN.

. . .

MR. JUSTICE WHITE, concurring in the judgments in No. 153 *[Tilton* v. *Richardson, which sustained federal construction grants to sectarian universities]* and No. 89 and dissenting in Nos. 569 and 570.

. . .

. . . the Court is surely quite wrong in overturning the Pennsylvania and Rhode Island statutes on the ground that they amount to an establishment of religion forbidden by the First Amendment.

. . .

I would sustain both the federal and the Rhode Island programs at issue in these cases, and I therefore concur in the judgment in No. 153 and dissent from the judgments in Nos. 569 and 570. Although I would also reject the facial challenge to the Pennsylvania statute, I concur in the judgment in No. 89 for the reasons given below.

The Court strikes down the Rhode Island statute on its face. . . . The Court . . . finds that impermissible "entanglement" will result from administration of the program. The reasoning is a curious and mystifying blend, but a critical factor appears to be an unwillingness to accept the District Court's express findings that on the evidence before it none of the teachers here involved mixed religious and secular instruction. Rather, the District Court struck down the Rhode Island statute because it concluded that activities outside the secular classroom would probably have a religious content and that support for religious education therefore necessarily resulted from the financial aid to the secular programs, since

that aid generally strengthened the parochial schools and increased the number of their students.

. . .

The Court thus creates an insoluble paradox for the State and the parochial schools. The State cannot finance secular instruction if it permits religion to be taught in the same classroom; but if it exacts a promise that religion not be so taught—a promise the school and its teachers are quite willing and on this record able to give—and enforces it, it is then entangled in the "no entanglement" aspect of the Court's Establishment Clause jurisprudence.

. . .

With respect to Pennsylvania, the Court, accepting as true the factual allegations of the complaint, as it must for purposes of a motion to dismiss, would reverse the dismissal of the complaint and invalidate the legislation. The critical allegations, as paraphrased by the Court, are that "the church-related elementary and secondary schools are controlled by religious organizations, have the purpose of propagating and promoting a particular religious faith, and conduct their operations to fulfill that purpose." *Ante*, at 620. From these allegations the Court concludes that forbidden entanglements would follow from enforcing compliance with the secular purpose for which the state money is being paid.

I disagree. There is no specific allegation in the complaint that sectarian teaching does or would invade secular classes supported by state funds. That the schools are operated to promote a particular religion is quite consistent with the view that secular teaching devoid of religious instruction can successfully be maintained, for good secular instruction is, as Judge Coffin wrote for the District Court in the Rhode Island case, essential to the success of the religious mission of the parochial school. I would no more here than in the Rhode Island case substitute presumption for proof that religion is or would be taught in state-financed secular courses or assume that enforcement measures would be so extensive as to border on a free exercise violation. We should not forget that the

Pennsylvania statute does not compel church schools to accept state funds. I cannot hold that the First Amendment forbids an agreement between the school and the State that the state funds would be used only to teach secular subjects.

. . .

. . . I would reverse the judgment of the District Court and remand the case for trial, thereby holding the Pennsylvania legislation valid on its face but leaving open the question of its validity as applied to the particular facts of this case.

. . .

Aguilar v. Felton

473 U.S. 402 (1985)

New York City received federal funds under the Title I program of the Elementary and Secondary Education Act of 1965. Part of the funds were used to pay the salaries of public school employees who teach in parochial schools in the city. Betty-Louise Felton and five other federal taxpayers filed a complaint in federal court that the use of federal funds for church-affiliated schools violated the Establishment Clause. Yolanda Aguilar and other officials acted as defendants for the Secretary of the U.S. Department of Education and the Chancellor of the Board of Education of New York City. The district court granted the government's motion for summary judgment (sustaining the financial assistance) but the Second Circuit reversed.

JUSTICE BRENNAN delivered the opinion of the Court.

The City of New York uses federal funds to pay the salaries of public employees who teach in parochial schools. In this companion case to *School District of Grand Rapids* v. *Ball, ante,* p. 373, we determine whether this practice violates the Establishment Clause of the First Amendment.

I

A

The program at issue in this case, originally enacted as Title I of the Elementary and Secondary Education Act of 1965, authorizes the Secretary of Education to distribute financial assistance to local educational institutions to meet the needs of educationally deprived children from low-income families. The funds are to be appropriated in accordance with programs proposed by local educational agencies and approved by state educational agencies. . . .

Since 1966, the City of New York has provided instructional services funded by Title I to parochial school students on the premises of parochial schools. Of those students eligible to receive funds in 1981–1982, 13.2% were enrolled in private schools. Of that group, 84% were enrolled in schools affiliated with the Roman Catholic Archdiocese of New York and the Diocese of Brooklyn and 8% were enrolled in Hebrew day schools. With respect to the religious atmosphere of these schools, the Court of Appeals concluded that "the picture that emerges is of a system in which religious considerations play a key role in the selection of students and teachers, and which has as its substantial purpose the inculcation of religious values." 739 F. 2d 48, 68 (CA2 1984).

The programs conducted at these schools include remedial reading, reading skills, remedial mathematics, English as a second language, and guidance services. These programs are carried out by regular employees of the public schools (teachers, guidance counselors, psychologists, psychiatrists, and social workers) who have volunteered to teach in the parochial schools. The amount of time that each professional spends in the parochial school is determined by the number of students in the particular program and the needs of these students.

The City's Bureau of Nonpublic School Reimbursement makes teacher assignments, and the instructors are supervised by field personnel, who attempt to pay at least one unannounced visit per month. The field supervisors, in turn, report to program coordinators, who also pay occasional unannounced supervisory visits to monitor Title I classes in the parochial schools. The professionals involved in the program are directed to avoid involvement with religious activities that are conducted within the private schools and to bar religious materials in their classrooms. All material and equipment used in the programs funded under Title I are supplied by the Government and are used only in those programs. The professional personnel are solely responsible for the selection of the students. Additionally, the professionals are informed that contact with private school personnel should be kept to a minimum. Finally, the administrators of the parochial schools are required to clear the classrooms used by the public school personnel of all religious symbols.

. . .

II

In *School Districts of Grand Rapids* v. *Ball, ante,* p. 373, the Court has today held unconstitutional under the Establishment Clause two remedial and enhancement programs operated by the Grand Rapids Public School District, in which classes were provided to private school children at public expense in classrooms located in and leased from the local private schools. The New York City programs challenged in this case are very similar to the programs we examined in *Ball*. In both cases, publicly funded instructors teach classes composed exclusively of private school students in private school buildings. In both cases, an overwhelming number of the participating private schools are religiously affiliated. In both cases, the publicly funded programs provide not only professional personnel, but also all materials

and supplies necessary for the operation of the programs. Finally, the instructors in both cases are told that they are public school employees under the sole control of the public school system.

The appellants attempt to distinguish this case on the ground that the City of New York, unlike the Grand Rapids Public School District, has adopted a system for monitoring the religious content of publicly funded Title I classes in the religious schools. At best, the supervision in this case would assist in preventing the Title I program from being used, intentionally or unwittingly, to inculcate the religious beliefs of the surrounding parochial school. But appellants' argument fails in any event, because the supervisory system established by the City of New York inevitably results in the excessive entanglement of church and state, an Establishment Clause concern distinct from that addressed by the effects doctrine. Even where state aid to parochial institutions does not have the primary effect of advancing religion, the provision of such aid may nonetheless violate the Establishment Clause owing to the nature of the interaction of church and state in the administration of that aid.

The principle that the state should not become too closely entangled with the church in the administration of assistance is rooted in two concerns. When the state becomes enmeshed with a given denomination in matters of religious significance, the freedom of religious belief of those who are not adherents of that denomination suffers, even when the governmental purpose underlying the involvement is largely secular. In addition, the freedom of even the adherents of the denomination is limited by the governmental intrusion into sacred matters. "[T]he First Amendment rests upon the premise that both religion and government can best work to achieve their lofty aims if each is left free from the other within its respective sphere." *McCollum* v. *Board of Education,* 333 U. S. 203, 212 (1948).

In *Lemon* v. *Kurtzman,* 403 U. S. 602 (1971), the Court held that the supervision necessary to ensure that teachers in parochial schools were not conveying religious messages to their students would constitute the excessive entanglement of church and state:

"A comprehensive, discriminating, and continuing state surveillance will inevitably be required to ensure that these restrictions are obeyed and the First Amendment otherwise respected. Unlike a book, a teacher cannot be inspected once so as to determine the extent and intent of his or her personal beliefs and subjective acceptance of the limitations imposed by the First Amendment. These prophylactic contacts will involve excessive and enduring entanglement between state and church." *Id.*, at 619.

Similarly, in *Meek* v. *Pittenger*, 421 U. S. 349 (1975), we invalidated a state program that offered, *inter alia*, guidance, testing, and remedial and therapeutic services performed by public employees on the premises of the parochial schools. *Id.*, at 352–353. As in *Lemon*, we observed that though a comprehensive system of supervision might conceivably prevent teachers from having the primary effect of advancing religion, such a system would inevitably lead to an unconstitutional administrative entanglement between church and state.

"The prophylactic contacts required to ensure that teachers play a strictly nonideological role, the Court held [in *Lemon*], necessarily give rise to a constitutionally intolerable degree of entanglement between church and state. *Id.*, at 619. The same excessive entanglement would be required for Pennsylvania to be 'certain,' as it must be, that . . . personnel do not advance the religious mission of the church-related schools in which they serve. *Public Funds for Public Schools* v. *Marburger*, 358 F. Supp. 29, 40–41, aff'd, 417 U. S. 961." 421 U. S., at 370.

. . . the elementary and secondary schools here are far different from the colleges at issue in *Roemer, Hunt,* and *Tilton.* 739 F. 2d, at 68–70. Unlike the colleges, which were found not to be "pervasively sectarian," many of the schools involved in this case are the same sectarian schools which had " 'as a substantial purpose the inculcation of religious values' " in *Committee for Public Education & Religious Liberty* v. *Nyquist*, 413 U. S. 756, 768 (1973), quoting *Committee for Public Education & Religious Liberty* v. *Nyquist*, 350 F. Supp. 655, 663 (SDNY 1972). . . . Unlike the schools in *Roemer*, many of the schools here

receive funds and report back to their affiliated church, require attendance at church religious exercises, begin the schoolday or class period with prayer, and grant preference in admission to members of the sponsoring denominations. . . .

. . .

We have long recognized that underlying the Establishment Clause is "the objective . . . to prevent, as far as possible, the intrusion of either [church or state] into the precincts of the other." *Lemon* v. *Kurtzman, supra,* at 614. See also *McCollum* v. *Board of Education,* 333 U. S., at 212. Although "[s]eparation in this context cannot mean absence of all contact," *Walz* v. *Tax Comm'n,* 397 U. S. 664, 676 (1970), the detailed monitoring and close administrative contact required to maintain New York City's Title I program can only produce "a kind of continuing day-to-day relationship which the policy of neutrality seeks to minimize." *Id.*, at 674. The numerous judgments that must be made by agents of the city concern matters that may be subtle and controversial, yet may be of deep religious significance to the controlling denominations. As government agents must make these judgments, the dangers of political divisiveness along religious lines increase. At the same time, "[t]he picture of state inspectors prowling the halls of parochial schools and auditing classroom instruction surely raises more than an imagined specter of governmental 'secularization of a creed.' " *Lemon* v. *Kurtzman, supra,* at 650 (opinion of BRENNAN, , J.).

III

Despite the well-intentioned efforts taken by the City of New York, the program remains constitutionally flawed owing to the nature of the aid, to the institution receiving the aid, and to the constitutional principles that they implicate—that neither the State nor Federal Government shall promote or hinder a particular faith or faith generally through the advancement of benefits or through the excessive entanglement of church and state in the administration of those benefits.

Affirmed.

JUSTICE POWELL, concurring.

. . .

This risk of entanglement is compounded by the additional risk of political divisiveness stemming from the aid to religion at issue here. . . . there remains a considerable risk of continuing political strife over the propriety of direct aid to religious schools and the proper allocation of limited governmental resources. As this Court has repeatedly recognized, there is a likelihood whenever direct governmental aid is extended to some groups that there will be competition and strife among them and others to gain, maintain, or increase the financial support of government. *E. g., Committee for Public Education & Religious Liberty* v. *Nyquist*, 413 U. S. 756, 796–797 (1973); *Lemon* v. *Kurtzman, supra*, at 623. In States such as New York that have large and varied sectarian populations, one can be assured that politics will enter into any state decision to aid parochial schools. Public schools, as well as private schools, are under increasing financial pressure to meet real and perceived needs. Thus, any proposal to extend direct governmental aid to parochial schools alone is likely to spark political disagreement from taxpayers who support the public schools, as well as from nonrecipient sectarian groups, who may fear that needed funds are being diverted from them. . . .

JUSTICE WHITE, dissenting.

As evidenced by my dissenting opinions in *Lemon* v. *Kurtzman*, 403 U. S. 602, 661 (1971) and *Committee for Public Education & Religious Liberty* v. *Nyquist*, 413 U. S. 756, 813 (1973), I have long disagreed with the Court's interpretation and application of the Establishment Clause in the context of state aid to private schools. For the reasons stated in those dissents, I am firmly of the belief that the Court's decisions in these cases, like its decisions in *Lemon* and *Nyquist*, are "not required by the First Amendment and [are] contrary to the long-range interests of the country." 413 U. S., at 820. For those same reasons, I am satisfied that what the States have sought to do in these cases is well within their authority and is not forbidden by the Establishment Clause. Hence, I dissent and would reverse the judgment in each of these cases.

CHIEF JUSTICE BURGER, dissenting.

Under the guise of protecting Americans from the evils of an Established Church such as those of the 18th century and earlier times, today's decision will deny countless schoolchildren desperately needed remedial teaching services funded under Title I. The program at issue covers remedial reading, reading skills, remedial mathematics, English as a second language, and assistance for children needing special help in the learning process. . . .

On the merits of this case, I dissent for the reasons stated in my separate opinion in *Meek* v. *Pittenger*, 421 U. S. 349 (1975). We have frequently recognized that some interaction between church and state is unavoidable, and that an attempt to eliminate all contact between the two would be both futile and undesirable. . . .

I cannot join in striking down a program that, in the words of the Court of Appeals, "has done so much good and little, if any, detectable harm." 739 F. 2d 48, 72 (CA2 1984). The notion that denying these services to students in religious schools is a neutral act to protect us from an Established Church has no support in logic, experience, or history. Rather than showing the neutrality the Court boasts of, it exhibits nothing less than hostility toward religion and the children who attend church-sponsored schools.

JUSTICE REHNQUIST, dissenting.

I dissent for the reasons stated in my dissenting opinion in *Wallace* v. *Jaffree*, 472 U. S. 38, 91 (1985). In this case the Court takes advantage of the "Catch-22" paradox of its own creation, see *Wallace, supra*, at 109–110 (REHNQUIST, J., dissenting), whereby aid must be supervised to ensure no entanglement but the supervision itself is held to cause an entanglement. The Court today strikes down nondiscriminatory nonsectarian aid to educationally deprived children from low-income families. The Establishment Clause does not prohibit such sorely needed assistance; we have indeed traveled far afield from the concerns which prompted the adoption of the First Amendment when we rely on gossamer abstractions to invalidate a law which obviously meets an entirely secular need. I would reverse.

JUSTICE O'CONNOR, with whom JUSTICE REHN-QUIST joins as to Parts II and III, dissenting.

. . .

I

As in *Wallace* v. *Jaffree*, 472 U. S. 38 (1985), and *Thornton* v. *Caldor, Inc.*, 472 U. S. 703 (1985), the Court in this litigation adheres to the three-part Establishment Clause test enunciated in *Lemon* v. *Kurtzman*, 403 U. S. 602, 612–613 (1971). To survive the *Lemon* test, a statute must have both a secular legislative purpose and a principal or primary effect that neither advances nor inhibits religion. Under *Lemon* and its progeny, direct state aid to parochial schools that has the purpose or effect of furthering the religious mission of the schools is unconstitutional. I agree with that principle. According to the Court, however, the New York City Title I program is defective not because of any improper purpose or effect, but rather because it fails the third part of the *Lemon* test: the Title I program allegedly fosters excessive government entanglement with religion. I disagree with the Court's analysis of entanglement, and I question the utility of entanglement as a separate Establishment Clause standard in most cases. . . .

II

Recognizing the weakness of any claim of an improper purpose or effect, the Court today relies entirely on the entanglement prong of *Lemon* to invalidate the New York City Title I program. . . .

This analysis of entanglement, I acknowledge, finds support in some of this Court's precedents. In *Meek* v. *Pittenger*, 421 U. S., at 369, the Court asserted that it could not rely "on the good faith and professionalism of the secular teachers and counselors functioning in church-related schools to ensure that a strictly nonideological posture is maintained." Because "a teacher remains a teacher," the Court stated, there remains a risk that teachers will intertwine religious doctrine with secular instruction. The continuing state surveillance necessary to prevent this from occurring would produce undue entanglement of church and state. *Id.*, at 370–372. The Court's

opinion in *Meek* further asserted that public instruction on parochial school premises creates a serious risk of divisive political conflict over the issue of aid to religion. *Ibid. Meek's* analysis of entanglement was reaffirmed in *Wolman* two Terms later.

I would accord these decisions the appropriate deference commanded by the doctrine of *stare decisis* if I could discern logical support for their analysis. But experience has demonstrated that the analysis in Part V of the *Meek* opinion is flawed. At the time *Meek* was decided, thoughtful dissents pointed out the absence of any record support for the notion that public school teachers would attempt to inculcate religion simply because they temporarily occupied a parochial school classroom, or that such instruction would produce political divisiveness. *Id.*, at 385 (opinion of BURGER, C. J.); *id.*, at 387 (opinion of REHNQUIST, J.). Experience has given greater force to the arguments of the dissenting opinions in *Meek*. It is not intuitively obvious that a dedicated public school teacher will tend to disobey instructions and commence proselytizing students at public expense merely because the classroom is within a parochial school. *Meek* is correct in asserting that a teacher of remedial reading "remains a teacher," but surely it is significant that the teacher involved is a professional, full-time public school employee who is unaccustomed to bringing religion into the classroom. Given that not a single incident of religious indoctrination has been identified as occurring in the thousands of classes offered in Grand Rapids and New York City over the past two decades, it is time to acknowledge that the risk identified in *Meek* was greatly exaggerated.

. . .

The Court's reliance on the potential for political divisiveness as evidence of undue entanglement is also unpersuasive. There is little record support for the proposition that New York City's admirable Title I program has ignited any controversy other than this litigation. . . .

III

Today's ruling does not spell the end of the Title I program of remedial education for disadvantaged children. Children attending public schools may still obtain the benefits of the program. Impoverished children who attend parochial schools may also continue to benefit from Title I programs offered off the premises of their schools—possibly in portable classrooms just over the edge of school property. The only disadvantaged children who lose under the Court's holding are those in cities where it is not economically and logistically feasible to provide public facilities for remedial education adjacent to the parochial school. But this subset is significant, for it includes more than 20,000 New York City schoolchildren and uncounted others elsewhere in the country.

For these children, the Court's decision is tragic. The Court deprives them of a program that offers a meaningful chance at success in life, and it does so on the untenable theory that public school teachers (most of whom are of different faiths than their students) are likely to start teaching religion merely because they have walked across the threshold of a parochial school. I reject this theory and the analysis in *Meek* v. *Pittenger* on which it is based. I cannot close my eyes to the fact that, over almost two decades, New York City's public school teachers have helped thousands of impoverished parochial school children to overcome educational disadvantages without once attempting to inculcate religion. Their praiseworthy efforts have not eroded and do not threaten the religious liberty assured by the Establishment Clause. The contrary judgment of the Court of Appeals should be reversed.

I respectfully dissent.

Engel v. Vitale

370 U.S. 421 (1962)

The New York Board of Regents composed a prayer to be recited in public schools. A group of parents brought action against the state. The parent named first in the suit was Steven I. Engel, who sued William J. Vitale and other members of the Board of Education of Union Free School District. The New York courts upheld the "Regents' prayer," provided that pupils were not compelled to join in the prayer over their objections or the objections of their parents.

MR. JUSTICE BLACK delivered the opinion of the Court.

The respondent Board of Education of Union Free School District No. 9, New Hyde Park, New York, acting in its official capacity under state law, directed the School District's principal to cause the following prayer to be said aloud by each class in the presence of a teacher at the beginning of each school day:

"Almighty God, we acknowledge our dependence upon Thee, and we beg Thy blessings upon us, our parents, our teachers and our Country."

This daily procedure was adopted on the recommendation of the State Board of Regents, a governmental agency created by the State Constitution to which the New York Legislature has granted broad supervisory, executive, and legislative powers over the State's public school system. These state officials composed the prayer which they recommended and published as a part of their "Statement on Moral and Spiritual Training in the Schools," saying: "We believe that this Statement will be subscribed to by all men and women of good will, and we call upon all of them to aid in giving life to our program."

Shortly after the practice of reciting the Regents' prayer was adopted by the School District, the parents of ten pupils brought this action in a New York State Court insisting that use of this official prayer in the public schools was contrary to the beliefs, religions, or religious practices of both themselves and their children. Among other things, these parents challenged the constitutionality of both the state law authorizing the School District to direct the use of prayer in public schools and the School District's regulation ordering the recitation of this particular prayer on the ground that these actions of official governmental agencies violate that part of the First Amendment of the Federal Constitution which commands that "Congress shall make no law respecting an establishment of religion"—a command which was "made applicable to the State of New York by the Fourteenth Amendment of the said Constitution." The New York Court of Appeals, over the dissents of Judges Dye and Fuld, sustained an order of the lower state courts which had upheld the power of New York to use the Regents' prayer as a part of the daily procedures of its public schools so long as the schools did not compel any pupil to join in the prayer over his or his parents' objection. We granted certiorari to review this important decision involving rights protected by the First and Fourteenth Amendments.

We think that by using its public school system to encourage recitation of the Regents' prayer, the State of New York has adopted a practice wholly inconsistent with the Establishment Clause. There can, of course, be no doubt that New York's program of daily classroom invocation of God's blessings as prescribed in the Regents' prayer is a religious activity. It is a solemn avowal of divine faith and supplication for the blessings of the Almighty. . . .

The petitioners contend among other things that the state laws requiring or permitting use of the Regents' prayer must be struck down as a violation of the Establishment Clause because that prayer was composed by governmental officials as a part of a governmental program to further religious beliefs. For this reason, petitioners argue, the State's use of the Regents' prayer in its public school system breaches the constitutional wall of separation between Church and State. We agree with that contention since we think that the constitutional prohibition against laws respecting an establishment of religion must at least mean that in this country it is no part of the business of government to compose official prayers for any group of the American people to recite as a part of a religious program carried on by government.

It is a matter of history that this very practice of establishing governmentally composed prayers for religious services was one of the reasons which caused many of our early colonists to leave England and seek religious freedom in America. The Book of Common Prayer, which was created under governmental direction and which was approved by Acts of Parliament in 1548 and 1549, set out in minute detail the accepted form and content of prayer and other religious ceremonies to be used in the established, tax-supported Church of England. The controversies over the Book and what should be its content repeatedly threatened to disrupt the peace of that country as the accepted forms of prayer in the established church changed with the views of the particular ruler that happened to be in control at the time. Powerful groups representing some of the varying religious views of the people struggled among themselves to impress their particular views upon the Government and obtain amendments of the Book more suitable to their respective notions of how religious services should be conducted in order that the official religious establishment would advance their particular religious beliefs. Other groups, lacking the necessary political power to influence the Government on the matter, decided to leave England and its established church and seek freedom in America from England's governmentally ordained and supported religion.

It is an unfortunate fact of history that when some of the very groups which had most strenuously opposed the established Church of England found themselves sufficiently in control of colonial governments in this country to write their own prayers into law, they passed laws making their own religion the official religion of their respective colonies. Indeed, as late as the time of the Revolutionary War, there were established churches in at least eight of the thirteen former colonies and established religions in at least four of the other five. But the successful Revolution against English political domination was shortly followed by intense opposition to the practice of establishing religion by law. This opposition crystallized rapidly into an effective political force in Virginia where the minority religious groups such as Presbyterians, Lutherans, Quakers and Baptists had gained such strength that the adherents to the established Episcopal Church were actually a minority themselves. In 1785–1786, those opposed to the established Church, led by James Madison and Thomas Jefferson, who, though themselves not members of any of these dissenting religious groups, opposed all religious establishments by law on grounds of principle, obtained the enactment of the famous "Virginia Bill for Religious Liberty" by which all religious groups were placed on an equal footing so far as the State was concerned. Similar though less far-reaching legislation was being considered and passed in other States.

. . . The First Amendment was added to the Constitution to stand as a guarantee that neither the power nor the prestige of the Federal Government would be used to control, support or influence the kinds of prayer the American people can say—that the people's religions must not be subjected to the pressures of government for change each time a new political administration is elected to office. Under that Amendment's prohibition against governmental establishment of religion, as reinforced by the provisions of the Fourteenth Amendment, government in this country, be it state or federal, is without power to prescribe by law any particular form of prayer which is to be used as an official prayer in carrying on any program of governmentally sponsored religious activity.

There can be no doubt that New York's state prayer program officially establishes the religious beliefs embodied in the Regents' prayer. The respondents' argument to the contrary, which is largely based upon the contention that the Regents' prayer is "non-denominational" and the fact that the program, as modified and approved by state courts, does not require all pupils to recite the prayer but permits those who wish to do so to remain silent or be excused from the room, ignores the essential nature of the program's constitutional defects. Neither the fact that the prayer may be denominationally neutral nor the fact that its observance on the part of the students is voluntary can serve to free it from the limitations of the Establishment Clause, as it might from the Free Exercise Clause, of the First Amendment, both of which are operative against the States by virtue of the Fourteenth Amendment. . . . When

the power, prestige and financial support of government is placed behind a particular religious belief, the indirect coercive pressure upon religious minorities to conform to the prevailing officially approved religion is plain. But the purposes underlying the Establishment Clause go much further than that. Its first and most immediate purpose rested on the belief that a union of government and religion tends to destroy government and to degrade religion. The history of governmentally established religion, both in England and in this country, showed that whenever government had allied itself with one particular form of religion, the inevitable result had been that it had incurred the hatred, disrespect and even contempt of those who held contrary beliefs. That same history showed that many people had lost their respect for any religion that had relied upon the support of government to spread its faith. The Establishment Clause thus stands as an expression of principle on the part of the Founders of our Constitution that religion is too personal, too sacred, too holy, to permit its "unhallowed perversion" by a civil magistrate. Another purpose of the Establishment Clause rested upon an awareness of the historical fact that governmentally established religions and religious persecutions go hand in hand. . . .

It has been argued that to apply the Constitution in such a way as to prohibit state laws respecting an establishment of religious services in public schools is to indicate a hostility toward religion or toward prayer. Nothing, of course, could be more wrong. The history of man is inseparable from the history of religion. . . . It is neither sacrilegious nor antireligious to say that each separate government in this country should stay out of the business of writing or sanctioning official prayers and leave that purely religious function to the people themselves and to those the people choose to look to for religious guidance.

It is true that New York's establishment of its Regents' prayer as an officially approved religious doctrine of that State does not amount to a total establishment of one particular religious sect to the exclusion of all others—that, indeed, the governmental endorsement of that prayer seems relatively insignificant when compared to the governmental encroachments upon religion which were commonplace 200 years ago. To those who may subscribe to the view that because the Regents' official prayer is so brief and general there can be no danger to religious freedom in its governmental establishment, however, it may be appropriate to say in the words of James Madison, the author of the First Amendment:

"[I]t is proper to take alarm at the first experiment on our liberties. . . . Who does not see that the same authority which can establish Christianity, in exclusion of all other Religions, may establish with the same ease any particular sect of Christians, in exclusion of all other Sects? That the same authority which can force a citizen to contribute three pence only of his property for the support of any one establishment, may force him to conform to any other establishment in all cases whatsoever?"

The judgment of the Court of Appeals of New York is reversed and the cause remanded for further proceedings not inconsistent with this opinion.

Reversed and remanded.

MR. JUSTICE FRANKFURTER took no part in the decision of this case.

MR. JUSTICE WHITE took no part in the consideration or decision of this case.

MR. JUSTICE DOUGLAS, concurring.

. . .

"We are a religious people whose institutions presuppose a Supreme Being." *Zorach* v. *Clauson,* 343 U. S. 306, 313. Under our Bill of Rights free play is given for making religion an active force in our lives. But "if a religious leaven is to be worked into the affairs of our people, it is to be done by individuals and groups, not by the Government." *McGowan* v. *Maryland,* 366 U. S. 420, 563 (dissenting opinion). By reason of the First Amendment government is commanded "to have no interest in theology or ritual" (*id.,* at 564), for on those matters "government must be neutral." *Ibid.* The First Amendment leaves the Government in a position not of hostility to religion but of neutrality. The philosophy is that the atheist or agnostic—the nonbeliever—is entitled to go his own way. The philosophy is that if government interferes in matters spiritual, it will be a divisive force. The First Amendment teaches that a government neutral in the field of religion better serves all religious interests.

. . .

MR. JUSTICE STEWART, dissenting.

A local school board in New York has provided that those pupils who wish to do so may join in a brief prayer at the beginning of each school day, acknowledging their dependence upon God and asking His blessing upon them and upon their parents, their teachers, and their country. The Court today decides that in permitting this brief nondenominational prayer the school board has violated the Constitution of the United States. I think this decision is wrong.

The Court does not hold, nor could it, that New York has interfered with the free exercise of anybody's religion. For the state courts have made clear that those who object to reciting the prayer must be entirely free of any compulsion to do so, including any "embarrassments and pressures." Cf. *West Virginia State Board of Education* v. *Barnette,* 319 U. S. 624. But the Court says that in permitting school children to say this simple prayer, the New York authorities have established "an official religion."

With all respect, I think the Court has misapplied a great constitutional principle. I cannot see how an "official religion" is established by letting those who want to say a prayer say it. On the contrary, I think that to deny the wish of these school children to join in reciting this prayer is to deny them the opportunity of sharing in the spiritual heritage of our Nation.

The Court's historical review of the quarrels over the Book of Common Prayer in England throws no light for me on the issue before us in this case. England had then and has now an established church. Equally unenlightening, I think, is the history of the early establishment and later rejection of an official church in our own States. For we deal here not with the establishment of a state church, which would, of course, be constitutionally impermissible, but with whether school children who want to begin their day by joining in prayer must be prohibited from doing so. Moreover, I think that the Court's task, in this as in all areas of constitutional adjudication, is not responsibly aided by the uncritical invocation of metaphors like the "wall of separation," a phrase nowhere to be found in the Constitution. What is relevant to the issue here is not the history of an established church in sixteenth century England or in eighteenth century America, but the history of the religious traditions of our people, reflected in countless practices of the institutions and officials of our government.

At the opening of each day's Session of this Court we stand, while one of our officials invokes the protection of God. Since the days of John Marshall our Crier has said, "God save the United States and this Honorable Court." Both the Senate and the House of Representatives open their daily Sessions with prayer. Each of our Presidents, from George Washington to John F. Kennedy, has upon assuming his Office asked the protection and help of God.

The Court today says that the state and federal governments are without constitutional power to prescribe any particular form of words to be recited by any group of the American people on any subject touching religion. One of the stanzas of "The Star-Spangled Banner," made our National Anthem by Act of Congress in 1931, contains these verses:

> "Blest with victory and peace, may the heav'n rescued land

> Praise the Pow'r that hath made and preserved us a nation!
> Then conquer we must, when our cause it is just,
> And this be our motto 'In God is our Trust.'"

In 1954 Congress added a phrase to the Pledge of Allegiance to the Flag so that it now contains the words "one Nation *under God*, indivisible, with liberty and justice for all." In 1952 Congress enacted legislation calling upon the President each year to proclaim a National Day of Prayer. Since 1865 the words "IN GOD WE TRUST" have been impressed on our coins.

Countless similar examples could be listed, but there is no need to belabor the obvious. It was all summed up by this Court just ten years ago in a single sentence: "We are a religious people whose institutions presuppose a Supreme Being." *Zorach* v. *Clauson*, 343 U. S. 306, 313.

I do not believe that this Court, or the Congress, or the President has by the actions and practices I have mentioned established an "official religion" in violation of the Constitution. And I do not believe the State of New York has done so in this case. What each has done has been to recognize and to follow the deeply entrenched and highly cherished spiritual traditions of our Nation —traditions which come down to us from those who almost two hundred years ago avowed their "firm Reliance on the Protection of divine Providence" when they proclaimed the freedom and independence of this brave new world.

I dissent.

Congressional Hearings on School Prayer (1964)

After the Supreme Court in *Engel* v. *Vitale* (1962) struck down state efforts to require students in public schools to recite an official state prayer, many members of Congress introduced constitutional amendments to permit school prayer. Some legislators may have assumed that their initiative would appeal to organized religion, but hearings conducted in 1964 by the House Judiciary Committee revealed broad opposition by Protestant, Catholic, and Jewish organizations. The groups testifying against a constitutional amendment included the American Baptist Convention, the American Jewish

Congress, the American Lutheran Church, the Episcopal Church, the National Council of Churches of Christ, the Synagogue Council of America, and the United Presbyterian Church. The testimony below is by Dr. Edwin H. Tuller, General Secretary, American Baptist Convention, speaking on behalf of the National Council of Churches. These hearings underscore the linkage between constitutional law and the attitudes and values of the private sector.

DR. TULLER: . . . As a result of the Supreme Court decision on the regents' prayer, many constitutional amendments had been proposed by Members of Congress at the time the general board *[of the National Council of Churches]* met, which do not differ appreciably from those now before this committee. In reference to such efforts to rewrite the first amendment, the general board said:

"We express the conviction that the first amendment to our Constitution *in its present wording* has provided the framework within which responsible citizens and our courts have been able to afford maximum protection for the religious liberty of all our citizens."[Emphasis added.]

The general board did not single out a specific proposed amendment for comment, but they were in effect rejecting the current proposals to rewrite the first amendment.

Many people assume that church leaders would of course favor anything designed to "aid religion," and some do not understand why they do not favor prayer and Bible reading in public schools. "What harm can it do"? they ask. It is not possible to know the mind of all members of the general board, but some of them expressed their convictions in debate or discussion on such points as these:

(a) Public institutions belong to all citizens, whatever their religious beliefs or lack of them; it is not right for the majority to impose religious beliefs or practices on the minority in public institutions when adequate provisions are available for those who desire to do so to express such beliefs and follow such practices in nonpublic settings with others of like mind;

(b) Because of American religious variety, our public schools are particularly inappropriate places for corporate religious exercises. Young and impressionable children from a wide variety of religious backgrounds and from no religious back-

ground at all, are present not by choice, but by compulsion of law and are not genuinely free to decide for themselves whether or not they will participate. Many of them are thus compelled to choose between the religious or (nonreligious) intentions of their parents and the expectations of their teachers and fellow pupils;

(c) In such a setting, children are almost always not given a genuinely free choice by glib use of the words "voluntary participation," when the whole atmosphere of the classroom is one of compliance and conformity to group activities.

When the teacher (or a group of pupils) selects a prayer or Bible reading, and all or most of the class members participate in it, at a time and in a procedure instituted by the teacher as the adult bearer of the authority of the public school, it is a rare child indeed who will isolate himself from his fellows by declining to participate. Thus a subtle but no less effective form of duress is present which should never blight the act of worship.

If a completely spontaneous effort should arise among devout children of a fairly uniform religious heritage, we doubt that police action of any community would interfere. We equally doubt that the Bill of Rights has to be amended to permit this possibility, since it already guarantees the "free exercise" of religion.

(d) Who is to compose the prayers, and who is to select the Scriptures? What form of the Lord's Prayer will be used, and which version of the Bible? In those who take their faith seriously, these things are important. They do not consider all prayers or Scriptures interchangeable. Many devout Christians do not want their children to conclude that their transactions with the Most High are something routine, casual, and indiscriminate, in the same category with algebra and spelling;

(e) What a nonsectarian theistic majority can require today in the way of a regents prayer or Bible reading "without comment" a sectarian

majority can require tomorrow in the way of an Augsburg Confession, a "Hail, Mary" or a theistic tract. These things are best not subject to a majority decision, but left to the free choice of each person at the time and place his conscience directs;

(f) Religious practices that are nonsectarian are too vague and generalized to have much meaning or effect for character development or moral motivation; whereas practices which are specific or demanding enough to effect character or motivation are unacceptable to some and therefore sectarian.

As the pronouncement says:

"Major faith groups have not agreed on a formulation of religious beliefs common to all. Even if they had done so, such a body of religious doctrine would tend to become a substitute for the more demanding commitments of historic faiths."

The United Presbyterian General Assembly has said:

"Bible reading and prayers as devotional acts in public schools tend toward indoctrination or meaningless ritual and should be omitted for both reasons." ("Relations Between Church and State," p. 7.)

(g) Protestants believe that prayer can be effectively addressed to God by any believer at any time and in any place. It does not have to be oral or formal, it does not have to be in unison or collective, it does not require a set garb or posture. Any and all children can pray to God in public schools or anywhere else at any time, and no one can stop them.

It is not necessary, however, that the children who happen to be assigned to the same classroom should stop what they are doing to pray with them. God will hear and answer the prayer of one child, though his petition be uttered in the secret places of his inmost self. The effectiveness and the availability of prayer are not enhanced by the intervention of the agencies of the public school or government; in fact, the reverse is as likely to be the case.

(h) Many Christians [*sic*] see in routine formal corporate rituals in public schools at least the danger against which their Lord warned in the Sermon on the Mount—that what begins as a spontaneous and sincere outpouring of devotion can become a public display of hypocrisy, making a show of piety.

For these reasons and others, the leadership of the major Protestant churches, men and women who have given their lives to seek the will of God and attempt to do it, and who have been entrusted by their fellow seekers with position of responsibility and trust, are not convinced, by and large, that God desires an attenuated and conventional worship administered in public school classrooms by the State.

They are not requesting or demanding it on behalf of the churches and churchmen whom they have been called to lead. And most of them are opposed to jeopardizing our long cherished freedom to worship God as conscience dictates by tampering with the first amendment.

. . .

Edwards v. Aguillard

482 U.S. 578 (1987)

Don Aguillard and other parents of children attending public schools in Louisiana, together with teachers and religious leaders, brought this suit against Governor Edwin W. Edwards and Louisiana officials. They challenged a state law that prohibited the teaching of the theory of evolution in public elementary and secondary schools unless accompanied by instruction in the theory of "creation science" (the Biblical belief in the abrupt

appearance of life in complex form). The plaintiffs attacked the statute as a violation of the Establishment Clause because it promoted a particular religious belief. A federal district court held the statute unconstitutional. The Fifth Circuit affirmed.

Justice BRENNAN delivered the opinion of the Court.

The question for decision is whether Louisiana's "Balanced Treatment for Creation-Science and Evolution-Science in Public School Instruction" Act (Creationism Act), La.Rev.Stat. Ann. §§ 17:286.1–17:286.7 (West 1982), is facially invalid as violative of the Establishment Clause of the First Amendment.

I

The Creationism Act forbids the teaching of the theory of evolution in public schools unless accompanied by instruction in "creation science." § 17:286.4A. No school is required to teach evolution or creation science. If either is taught, however, the other must also be taught. *Ibid.* The theories of evolution and creation science are statutorily defined as "the scientific evidences for [creation or evolution] and inferences from those scientific evidences." §§ 17.286.3(2) and (3).

Appellees, who include parents of children attending Louisiana public schools, Louisiana teachers, and religious leaders, challenged the constitutionality of the Act in District Court, seeking an injunction and declaratory relief. Appellants, Louisiana officials charged with implementing the Act, defended on the ground that the purpose of the Act is to protect a legitimate secular interest, namely, academic freedom. Appellees attacked the Act as facially invalid because it violated the Establishment Clause. . . .

. . .

II

The Establishment Clause forbids the enactment of any law "respecting an establishment of religion." The Court has applied a three-pronged test to determine whether legislation comports with the Establishment Clause. First, the legislature must have adopted the law with a secular purpose. Second, the statute's principal or primary effect must be one that neither advances nor

inhibits religion. Third, the statute must not result in an excessive entanglement of government with religion. *Lemon* v. *Kurtzman,* 403 U.S. 602, 612–613 (1971). State action violates the Establishment Clause if it fails to satisfy any of these prongs.

. . .

The Court has been particularly vigilant in monitoring compliance with the Establishment Clause in elementary and secondary schools. Families entrust public schools with the education of their children, but condition their trust on the understanding that the classroom will not purposely be used to advance religious views that may conflict with the private beliefs of the student and his or her family. Students in such institutions are impressionable and their attendance is involuntary. . . .

. . .

III

Lemon's first prong focuses on the purpose that animated adoption of the Act. "The purpose prong of the *Lemon* test asks whether government's actual purpose is to endorse or disapprove of religion." . . . In this case, the petitioners have identified no clear secular purpose for the Louisiana Act.

True, the Act's stated purpose is to protect academic freedom. La.Rev.Stat.Ann. § 17:286.2 (West 1982). This phrase might, in common parlance, be understood as referring to enhancing the freedom of teachers to teach what they will. The Court of Appeals, however, correctly concluded that the Act was not designed to further that goal. We find no merit in the State's argument that the "legislature may not [have] use[d] the terms 'academic freedom' in the correct legal sense. They might have [had] in mind, instead, a basic concept of fairness; teaching all of the evidence." Tr. of Oral Arg. 60. Even if "academic freedom" is read to mean "teaching all of the evidence" with respect to the origin of human beings, the Act does not further this purpose. The goal of providing a more comprehensive science curriculum is not furthered either by outlawing the teaching of evolution or by requiring the teaching of creation science.

A

While the Court is normally deferential to a State's articulation of a secular purpose, it is required that the statement of such purpose be sincere and not a sham. . . .

It is clear from the legislative history that the purpose of the legislative sponsor, Senator Bill Keith, was to narrow the science curriculum. During the legislative hearings, Senator Keith stated: "My preference would be that neither [creationism nor evolution] be taught." 2 App. E621. Such a ban on teaching does not promote— indeed, it undermines—the provision of a comprehensive scientific education.

It is equally clear that requiring schools to teach creation science with evolution does not advance academic freedom. The Act does not grant teachers a flexibility that they did not already possess to supplant the present science curriculum with the presentation of theories, besides evolution, about the origin of life. Indeed, the Court of Appeals found that no law prohibited Louisiana public schoolteachers from teaching any scientific theory. 765 F.2d, at 1257. As the president of the Louisiana Science Teachers Association testified, "[a]ny scientific concept that's based on established fact can be included in our curriculum already, and no legislation allowing this is necessary." 2 App. E616. The Act provides Louisiana schoolteachers with no new authority. Thus the stated purpose is not furthered by it.

. . .

Furthermore, the goal of basic "fairness" is hardly furthered by the Act's discriminatory preference for the teaching of creation science and against the teaching of evolution. While requiring that curriculum guides be developed for creation science, the Act says nothing of comparable guides for evolution. La.Rev.Stat.Ann. § 17:286.7A (West 1982). Similarly, research services are supplied for creation science but not for evolution.

§ 17:286.7B. Only "creation scientists" can serve on the panel that supplies the resource services. *Ibid.* The Act forbids school boards to discriminate against anyone who "chooses to be a creation-scientist" or to teach "creationism," but fails to protect those who choose to teach evolution or any other noncreation science theory, or who refuse to teach creation science. § 17:286.4C.

. . .

B

. . . we need not be blind in this case to the legislature's preeminent religious purpose in enacting this statute. There is a historic and contemporaneous link between the teachings of certain religious denominations and the teaching of evolution. It was this link that concerned the Court in *Epperson* v. *Arkansas,* 393 U.S. 97 (1968), which also involved a facial challenge to a statute regulating the teaching of evolution. In that case, the Court reviewed an Arkansas statute that made it unlawful for an instructor to teach evolution or to use a textbook that referred to this scientific theory. Although the Arkansas anti-evolution law did not explicitly state its predominant religious purpose, the Court could not ignore that "[t]he statute was a product of the upsurge of 'fundamentalist' religious fervor" that has long viewed this particular scientific theory as contradicting the literal interpretation of the Bible. *Id.,* 393 U.S., at 98. After reviewing the history of anti-evolution statutes, the Court determined that "there can be no doubt that the motivation for the [Arkansas] law was the same [as other anti-evolution statutes]: to suppress the teaching of a theory which, it was thought, 'denied' the divine creation of man." *Id.,* at 109. The Court found that there can be no legitimate state interest in protecting particular religions from scientific views "distasteful to them," *id.,* at 107. . . .

These same historic and contemporaneous antagonisms between the teachings of certain religious denominations and the teaching of evolution are present in this case. The preeminent purpose of the Louisiana legislature was clearly to advance the religious viewpoint that a supernatural being created humankind. The term "creation science" was defined as embracing this particular religious doctrine by those responsible for the passage of the Creationism Act. Senator Keith's leading expert on creation science, Edward Boudreaux, testified at the legislative hearings that the theory of creation science included belief in the existence of a supernatural creator. See 1 App. E421–422 (noting that "creation scientists" point to high probability that life was "created by an intelligent mind"). Senator Keith also cited testimony from other experts to support the creation-science view that "a creator [was] responsible for the universe and everything in it." . . .

. . .

We do not imply that a legislature could never require that scientific critiques of prevailing scientific theories be taught. Indeed, the Court acknowledged in *Stone* that its decision forbidding the posting of the Ten Commandments did not mean that no use could ever be made of the Ten Commandments, or that the Ten Commandments played an exclusively religious role in the history of Western Civilization. 449 U.S., at 42, 101 S.Ct., at 194. In a similar way, teaching a variety of scientific theories about the origins of humankind to schoolchildren might be validly done with the clear secular intent of enhancing the effectiveness of science instruction. But because the primary purpose of the Creationism Act is to endorse a particular religious doctrine, the Act furthers religion in violation of the Establishment Clause.

. . .

V

The Louisiana Creationism Act advances a religious doctrine by requiring either the banishment of the theory of evolution from public school classrooms or the presentation of a religious viewpoint that rejects evolution in its entirety. The Act violates the Establishment Clause of the First Amendment because it seeks to employ the symbolic and financial support of government to achieve a religious purpose. The judgment of the Court of Appeals therefore is

Affirmed.

Justice POWELL, with whom Justice O'CONNOR joins, concurring.

I write separately to note certain aspects of the legislative history, and to emphasize that nothing in the Court's opinion diminishes the traditionally broad discretion accorded state and local school officials in the selection of the public school curriculum.

. . .

Justice WHITE, concurring in the judgment.

. . .

Justice SCALIA, with whom THE CHIEF JUSTICE joins, dissenting.

Even if I agreed with the questionable premise that legislation can be invalidated under the Establishment Clause on the basis of its motivation alone, without regard to its effects, I would still find no justification for today's decision. The Louisiana legislators who passed the "Balanced Treatment for Creation-Science and Evolution-Science Act" (Balanced Treatment Act), La.Rev.Stat.Ann. §§ 17:286.1–17:286.7 (West 1982), each of whom had sworn to support the Constitution, were well aware of the potential Establishment Clause problems and considered that aspect of the legislation with great care. After seven hearings and several months of study, resulting in substantial revision of the original proposal, they approved the Act overwhelmingly and specifically articulated the secular purpose they meant it to serve. Although the record contains abundant evidence of the sincerity of that purpose (the only issue pertinent to this case), the Court today holds, essentially on the basis of "its visceral knowledge regarding what *must* have motivated the legislators," 778 F.2d 225, 227 (CA5 1985) (Gee, J., dissenting) (emphasis added), that the members of the Louisiana Legislature knowingly violated their oaths and then lied about it. I dissent. Had requirements of the Balanced Treatment Act that are not apparent on its face been clarified by an interpretation of the Louisiana Supreme Court, or by the manner of its implementation, the Act might well be found unconstitutional; but the question of its constitutionality cannot rightly be disposed of on the gallop, by impugning the motives of its supporters.

I

This case arrives here in the following posture: The Louisiana Supreme Court has never been given an opportunity to interpret the Balanced Treatment Act, State officials have never attempted to implement it, and it has never been the subject of a full evidentiary hearing. We can only guess at its meaning. We know that it forbids instruction in either "creation-science" or "evolution-science" without instruction in the other, § 17:286.4A, but the parties are sharply divided over what creation science consists of. Appellants insist that it is a collection of educationally valuable scientific data that has been censored from classrooms by an embarrassed scientific establishment. Appellees insist it is not science at all but thinly veiled religious doctrine. Both interpretations of the intended meaning of that phrase find considerable support in the legislative history.

At least at this stage in the litigation, it is plain to me that we must accept appellants' view of what the statute means. To begin with, the statute itself *defines* "creation-science" as "the *scientific evidences* for creation and inferences from those *scientific evidences.*" § 17:286.3(2) (emphasis added). If, however, that definition is not thought sufficiently helpful, the means by which the Louisiana Supreme Court will give the term more precise content is quite clear—and again, at this stage in the litigation, favors the appellants' view. "Creation science" is unquestionably a "term of art," see Brief for 72 Nobel Laureates, et al. as *Amici Curiae* 20, and thus, under Louisiana law, is "to be interpreted according to [its] received meaning and acceptation with the learned in the art, trade or profession to which [it] refer[s]." La.Civ. Code Ann., Art. 15 (West 1952). The only evidence in the record of the "received meaning and acceptation" of "creation science" is found in five affidavits filed by appellants. In those affidavits, two scientists, a philosopher, a theologian, and an educator, all of whom claim extensive knowledge of creation science, swear that it is essentially a collection of scientific data support-

ing the theory that the physical universe and life within it appeared suddenly and have not changed substantially since appearing. . . . These experts insist that creation science is a strictly scientific concept that can be presented without religious reference. . . . At this point, then, we must assume that the Balanced Treatment Act does *not* require the presentation of religious doctrine.

. . .

It is important to stress that the purpose forbidden by *Lemon* is the purpose to "advance religion." . . . Our cases in no way imply that the Establishment Clause forbids legislators merely to act upon their religious convictions. We surely would not strike down a law providing money to feed the hungry or shelter the homeless if it could be demonstrated that, but for the religious beliefs of the legislators, the funds would not have been approved. Also, political activism by the religiously motivated is part of our heritage. Notwithstanding the majority's implication to the contrary, . . . we do not presume that the sole purpose of a law is to advance religion merely because it was supported strongly by organized religions or by adherents of particular faiths. . . . To do so would deprive religious men and women of their right to participate in the political process. Today's religious activism may give us the Balanced Treatment Act, but yesterday's resulted in the abolition of slavery, and tomorrow's may bring relief for famine victims.

. . .

. . . few would contend that Title VII of the Civil Rights Act of 1964, which both forbids religious discrimination by private-sector employers, 78 Stat. 255, 42 U.S.C. § 2000e-2(a)(1), and requires them reasonably to accommodate the religious practices of their employees, § 2000e(j), violates the Establishment Clause, even though its "purpose" is, of course, to advance religion, and even though it is almost certainly not required by the Free Exercise Clause. While we have warned that at some point, accommodation may devolve into "an unlawful fostering of religion," *Hobbie* v. *Unemployment Appeals Comm'n of Fla., supra,* 480 U.S., at—, we have not suggested precisely (or even roughly) where that point might be. It is possible, then, that even if the sole motive of those voting for the Balanced Treatment Act was to advance religion, and its passage was not actually required, or even believed to be required, by either the Free Exercise or Establishment Clauses, the Act would nonetheless survive scrutiny under *Lemon's* purpose test.

. . .

II

B

. . .

In sum, even if one concedes, for the sake of argument, that a majority of the Louisiana Legislature voted for the Balanced Treatment Act partly in order to foster (rather than merely eliminate discrimination against) Christian fundamentalist beliefs, our cases establish that that alone would not suffice to invalidate the Act, so long as there was a genuine secular purpose as well. We have, moreover, no adequate basis for disbelieving the secular purpose set forth in the Act itself, or for concluding that it is a sham enacted to conceal the legislators' violation of their oaths of office. I am astonished by the Court's unprecedented readiness to reach such a conclusion, which I can only attribute to an intellectual predisposition created by the facts and the legend of *Scopes* v. *State*, 154 Tenn. 105, 289 S.W. 363 (1927)—an instinctive reaction that any governmentally imposed requirements bearing upon the teaching of evolution must be a manifestation of Christian funda-

mentalist repression. In this case, however, it seems to me the Court's position is the repressive one. The people of Louisiana, including those who are Christian fundamentalists, are quite entitled, as a secular matter, to have whatever scientific evidence there may be against evolution presented in their schools, just as Mr. Scopes was entitled to present whatever scientific evidence there was for it. Perhaps what the Louisiana Legislature has done is unconstitutional because there *is* no such evidence, and the scheme they have established will amount to no more than a presentation of the Book of Genesis. But we cannot say that on the evidence before us in this summary judgment context, which includes ample uncontradicted testimony that "creation science" is a body of scientific knowledge rather than revealed belief. *Infinitely less* can we say (or should we say) that the scientific evidence for evolution is so conclusive that no one could be gullible enough to believe that there is any real scientific evidence to the contrary, so that the legislation's stated purpose must be a lie. Yet that illiberal judgment, that *Scopes*-in-reverse, is ultimately the basis on which the Court's facile rejection of the Louisiana Legislature's purpose must rest.

. . .

Because I believe that the Balanced Treatment Act had a secular purpose, which is all the first component of the *Lemon* test requires, I would reverse the judgment of the Court of Appeals and remand for further consideration.

. . .

Wallace v. Jaffree

472 U.S. 38 (1985)

Alabama passed legislation authorizing a one-minute period of silence in all public schools "for meditation or voluntary prayer." It also authorized teachers to lead "willing students" in a prescribed prayer to "Almighty God . . . the Creator and Supreme Judge of the world." A federal district court upheld the statute, concluding that Alabama could establish a state religion if it wanted to. This ruling was reversed by the Eleventh Circuit. Ishmael Jaffree, a citizen of Alabama and parent of children in public schools, initiated the suit. The appellant is George C. Wallace, Governor of Alabama.

JUSTICE STEVENS delivered the opinion of the Court.

At an early stage of this litigation, the constitutionality of three Alabama statutes was questioned: (1) § 16–1–20, enacted in 1978, which authorized a 1-minute period of silence in all public schools "for meditation"; (2) § 16–1–20.1, enacted in 1981, which authorized a period of silence "for meditation or voluntary prayer"; and (3) § 16–1–20.2, enacted in 1982, which authorized teachers to lead "willing students" in a prescribed prayer to "Almighty God . . . the Creator and Supreme Judge . . . of the world."

. . .

. . . the narrow question for decision is whether § 16–1–20.1, which authorizes a period of silence for "meditation or voluntary prayer," is a law respecting the establishment of religion within the meaning of the First Amendment.

I

Appellee Ishmael Jaffree is a resident of Mobile County, Alabama. On May 28, 1982, he filed a complaint on behalf of three of his minor children; two of them were second-grade students and the third was then in kindergarten. The complaint named members of the Mobile County School Board, various school officials, and the minor plaintiffs' three teachers as defendants. The complaint alleged that the appellees brought the action "seeking principally a declaratory judgment and an injunction restraining the Defendants and each of them from maintaining or allowing the maintenance of regular religious prayer services or other forms of religious observances in the Mobile County Public Schools in violation of the First Amendment as made applicable to states by the Fourteenth Amendment to the United States Constitution." The complaint further alleged that two of the children had been subjected to various acts of religious indoctrination "from the beginning of the school year in September, 1981"; that the defendant teachers had "on a daily basis" led their classes in saying certain prayers in unison; that the minor children were exposed to ostracism from their peer group class members if they did not participate; and that Ishmael Jaffree had repeatedly but unsuccessfully requested that the devotional services be stopped. . . .

On August 2, 1982, the District Court held an evidentiary hearing on appellees' motion for a preliminary injunction. At that hearing, State Senator Donald G. Holmes testified that he was the "prime sponsor" of the bill that was enacted in 1981 as § 16–1–20.1. He explained that the bill was an "effort to return voluntary prayer to our public schools . . . it is a beginning and a step in the right direction." Apart from the purpose to return voluntary prayer to public school, Senator Holmes unequivocally testified that he had "no other purpose in mind." . . .

II

Our unanimous affirmance of the Court of Appeals' judgment concerning § 16–1–20.2 makes it unnecessary to comment at length on the District Court's remarkable conclusion that the Federal Constitution imposes no obstacle to Alabama's establishment of a state religion. Before analyzing the precise issue that is presented to us, it is nevertheless appropriate to recall how firmly embedded in our constitutional jurisprudence is the proposition that the several States have no greater power to restrain the individual freedoms protected by the First Amendment than does the Congress of the United States.

. . .

III

When the Court has been called upon to construe the breadth of the Establishment Clause, it has examined the criteria developed over a period of many years. Thus, in *Lemon* v. *Kurtzman*, 403 U. S. 602, 612–613 (1971), we wrote:

"Every analysis in this area must begin with consideration of the cumulative criteria developed by the Court over many years. Three such tests may be gleaned from our cases. First, the statute must have a secular legislative purpose; second, its principal or primary effect must be one that neither advances nor inhibits religion, *Board of Education* v. *Allen*, 392 U. S. 236, 243 (1968); finally, the statute must not foster 'an excessive government entanglement with religion.' *Walz* v. *Tax Comm'n*, 397 U. S. 664, 674 (1970)]."

It is the first of these three criteria that is most

plainly implicated by this case. As the District Court correctly recognized, no consideration of the second or third criteria is necessary if a statute does not have a clearly secular purpose. For even though a statute that is motivated in part by a religious purpose may satisfy the first criterion, see, *e.g., Abington School District* v. *Schempp,* 374 U. S. 203, 296–303 (1963) (BRENNAN, J., concurring), the First Amendment requires that a statute must be invalidated if it is entirely motivated by a purpose to advance religion.

In applying the purpose test, it is appropriate to ask "whether government's actual purpose is to endorse or disapprove of religion." In this case, the answer to that question is dispositive. For the record not only provides us with an unambiguous affirmative answer, but it also reveals that the enactment of § 16–1–20.1 was not motivated by any clearly secular purpose—indeed, the statute had *no* secular purpose.

IV

The sponsor of the bill that became § 16–1–20.1, Senator Donald Holmes, inserted into the legislative record—apparently without dissent—a statement indicating that the legislation was an "effort to return voluntary prayer" to the public schools. Later Senator Holmes confirmed this purpose before the District Court. In response to the question whether he had any purpose for the legislation other than returning voluntary prayer to public schools, he stated: "No, I did not have no other purpose in mind." The State did not present evidence of *any* secular purpose.

The unrebutted evidence of legislative intent contained in the legislative record and in the testimony of the sponsor of § 16–1–20.1 is confirmed by a consideration of the relationship between this statute and the two other measures that were considered in this case. The District Court found that the 1981 statute and its 1982 sequel had a common, nonsecular purpose. The wholly religious character of the later enactment is plainly evident from its text. When the differences between § 16–1–20.1 and its 1978 predecessor, § 16–1–20, are examined, it is equally clear that the 1981 statute has the same wholly religious character.

There are only three textual differences between § 16–1–20.1 and § 16–1–20: (1) the earlier statute applies only to grades one through six, whereas § 16–1–20.1 applies to all grades; (2) the earlier statute uses the word "shall" whereas § 16–1–20.1 uses the word "may"; (3) the earlier statute refers only to "meditation" whereas § 16–1–20.1 refers to "meditation or voluntary prayer." The first difference is of no relevance in this litigation because the minor appellees were in kindergarten or second grade during the 1981–1982 academic year. The second difference would also have no impact on this litigation because the mandatory language of § 16–1–20 continued to apply to grades one through six. Thus, the only significant textual difference is the addition of the words "or voluntary prayer."

The legislative intent to return prayer to the public schools is, of course, quite different from merely protecting every student's right to engage in voluntary prayer during an appropriate moment of silence during the schoolday. The 1978 statute already protected that right, containing nothing that prevented any student from engaging in voluntary prayer during a silent minute of meditation. Appellants have not identified any secular purpose that was not fully served by § 16–1–20 before the enactment of § 16–1–20.1. Thus, only two conclusions are consistent with the text of § 16–1–20.1: (1) the statute was enacted to convey a message of State endorsement and promotion of prayer; or (2) the statute was enacted for no purpose. No one suggests that the statute was nothing but a meaningless or irrational act.

We must, therefore, conclude that the Alabama Legislature intended to change existing law and that it was motivated by the same purpose that the Governor's answer to the second amended complaint expressly admitted; that the statement inserted in the legislative history revealed; and that Senator Holmes' testimony frankly described. The legislature enacted § 16–1–20.1, despite the existence of § 16–1–20 for the sole purpose of expressing the State's endorsement of prayer activities for one minute at the beginning of each schoolday. The addition of "or voluntary prayer" indicates that the State intended to characterize prayer as a favored practice. Such an endorsement is not consistent with the established principle that the government must pursue a course of complete neutrality toward religion.

The importance of that principle does not permit us to treat this as an inconsequential case involving nothing more than a few words of symbolic speech on behalf of the political majority. For whenever the State itself speaks on a religious subject, one of the questions that we must ask is "whether the government intends to convey a message of endorsement or disapproval of religion." The well-supported concurrent findings of the District Court and the Court of Appeals— that § 16–1–20.1 was intended to convey a message of state approval of prayer activities in the public schools—make it unnecessary, and indeed inappropriate, to evaluate the practical significance of the addition of the words "or voluntary prayer" to the statute. Keeping in mind, as we must, "both the fundamental place held by the Establishment Clause in our constitutional scheme and the myriad, subtle ways in which Establishment Clause values can be eroded," we conclude that § 16–1–20.1 violates the First Amendment.

The judgment of the Court of Appeals is affirmed.

It is so ordered.

JUSTICE POWELL, concurring.

I concur in the Court's opinion and judgment that Ala. Code § 16–1–20.1 (Supp. 1984) violates the Establishment Clause of the First Amendment. My concurrence is prompted by Alabama's persistence in attempting to institute state-sponsored prayer in the public schools by enacting three successive statutes. I agree fully with JUSTICE O'CONNOR's assertion that some moment-of-silence statutes may be constitutional, a suggestion set forth in the Court's opinion as well. *Ante,* at 59.

. . .

JUSTICE O'CONNOR, concurring in the judgment.

Nothing in the United States Constitution as interpreted by this Court or in the laws of the State of Alabama prohibits public school students from voluntarily praying at any time before, during, or after the schoolday. Alabama has facilitated volun-

tary silent prayers of students who are so inclined by enacting Ala. Code § 16–1–20 (Supp. 1984), which provides a moment of silence in appellees' schools each day. The parties to these proceedings concede the validity of this enactment. At issue in these appeals is the constitutional validity of an additional and subsequent Alabama statute, Ala. Code § 16–1–20.1 (Supp. 1984), which both the District Court and the Court of Appeals concluded was enacted solely to officially encourage prayer during the moment of silence. I agree with the judgment of the Court that, in light of the findings of the courts below and the history of its enactment, § 16–1–20.1 of the Alabama Code violates the Establishment Clause of the First Amendment. In my view, there can be little doubt that the purpose and likely effect of this subsequent enactment is to endorse and sponsor voluntary prayer in the public schools. I write separately to identify the peculiar features of the Alabama law that render it invalid, and to explain why moment of silence laws in other States do not necessarily manifest the same infirmity. I also write to explain why neither history nor the Free Exercise Clause of the First Amendment validates the Alabama law struck down by the Court today.

I

. . .

It once appeared that the Court had developed a workable standard by which to identify impermissible government establishments of religion. See *Lemon* v. *Kurtzman,* 403 U. S. 602 (1971). . . . Despite its initial promise, the *Lemon* test has proven problematic. The required inquiry into "entanglement" has been modified and questioned, see *Mueller* v. *Allen,* 463 U. S. 388, 403, n. 11 (1983), and in one case we have upheld state action against an Establishment Clause challenge without applying the *Lemon* test at all. *Marsh* v. *Chambers,* 463 U. S. 783 (1983). The author of *Lemon* himself apparently questions the test's general applicability. See *Lynch* v. *Donnelly,* 465 U. S. 668, 679 (1984). JUSTICE REHNQUIST today suggests that we abandon *Lemon* entirely. . . .

Perhaps because I am new to the struggle, I am not ready to abandon all aspects of the *Lemon* test. I do believe, however, that the standards announced in *Lemon* should be reexamined and refined in order to make them more useful in achieving the underlying purpose of the First Amendment. . . .

. . .

II

In his dissenting opinion, *post*, at 91–106, JUSTICE REHNQUIST reviews the text and history of the First Amendment Religion Clauses. His opinion suggests that a long line of this Court's decisions are inconsistent with the intent of the drafters of the Bill of Rights. He urges the Court to correct the historical inaccuracies in its past decisions by embracing a far more restricted interpretation of the Establishment Clause, an interpretation that presumably would permit vocal group prayer in public schools. See generally R. Cord, *Separation of Church and State* (1982).

. . .

JUSTICE REHNQUIST does not assert, however, that the drafters of the First Amendment expressed a preference for prayer in public schools, or that the practice of prayer in public schools enjoyed uninterrupted government endorsement from the time of enactment of the Bill of Rights to the present era. The simple truth is that free public education was virtually nonexistent in the late 18th century. . . .

This uncertainty as to the intent of the Framers of the Bill of Rights does not mean we should ignore history for guidance on the role of religion in public education. The Court has not done so. See, *e.g.*, *Illinois ex rel. McCollum* v. *Board of Education*, 333 U. S. 203, 212 (1948) (Frankfurter, J., concurring). When the intent of the Framers is unclear, I believe we must employ both history and reason in our analysis. The primary issue raised by JUSTICE REHNQUIST's dissent is whether the historical fact that our Presidents have long called for public prayers of Thanks should be dispositive on the constitutionality of prayer in public schools. I think not. At the very least, Presidential Proclamations are distinguishable from school prayer in that they are received in a noncoercive setting and are primarily directed at adults, who presumably are not readily susceptible to unwilling religious indoctrination. . . .

CHIEF JUSTICE BURGER, dissenting.

Some who trouble to read the opinions in these cases will find it ironic—perhaps even bizarre—that on the very day we heard arguments in the cases, the Court's session opened with an invocation for Divine protection. Across the park a few hundred yards away, the House of Representatives and the Senate regularly open each session with a prayer. These legislative prayers are not just one minute in duration, but are extended, thoughtful invocations and prayers for Divine guidance. They are given, as they have been since 1789, by clergy appointed as official chaplains and paid from the Treasury of the United States. Congress has also provided chapels in the Capitol, at public expense, where Members and others may pause for prayer, meditation—or a moment of silence.

Inevitably some wag is bound to say that the Court's holding today reflects a belief that the historic practice of the Congress and this Court is justified because members of the Judiciary and Congress are more in need of Divine guidance than are schoolchildren. Still others will say that all this controversy is "much ado about nothing," since no power on earth—including this Court and Congress—can stop any teacher from opening the school day with a moment of silence for pupils to meditate, to plan their day—or to pray if they voluntarily elect to do so.

I make several points about today's curious holding.

(a) It makes no sense to say that Alabama has "endorsed prayer" by merely enacting a new statute "to specify expressly that voluntary prayer is *one* of the authorized activities during a moment of silence," *ante*, at 77 (O'CONNOR, J., concurring in judgment) (emphasis added). To suggest that a moment-of-silence statute that includes the word "prayer" unconstitutionally endorses religion, while one that simply provides for a moment of silence does not, manifests not neutrality but hostility toward religion. . . .

(b) The inexplicable aspect of the foregoing opinions, however, is what they advance as support for the holding concerning the purpose of the Alabama Legislature. Rather than determining legislative purpose from the face of the statute as a whole, the opinions rely on three factors in concluding that the Alabama Legislature had a "wholly religious" purpose for enacting the statute under review, Ala. Code § 16–1–20.1 (Supp. 1984): (i) statements of the statute's sponsor, (ii) admissionsin Governor James' answer to the second amended complaint, and (iii) the difference between § 16–1–20.1 and its predecessor statute.

Curiously, the opinions do not mention that *all* of the sponsor's statements relied upon—including the statement "inserted" into the Senate Journal—were made *after* the legislature had passed the statute; indeed, the testimony that the Court finds critical was given well over a year after the statute was enacted. As even the appellees concede, see Brief for Appellees 18, there is not a shred of evidence that the legislature as a whole shared the sponsor's motive or that a majority in either house was even aware of the sponsor's view of the bill when it was passed. . . .

(c) The Court's extended treatment of the "test" of *Lemon* v. *Kurtzman*, 403 U. S. 602 (1971), suggests a naive preoccupation with an easy, bright-line approach for addressing constitutional issues. We have repeatedly cautioned that *Lemon* did not establish a rigid caliper capable of resolving every Establishment Clause issue, but that it sought only to provide "signposts." . . .

(d) The notion that the Alabama statute is a step toward creating an established church borders on, if it does not trespass into, the ridiculous. The statute does not remotely threaten religious liberty; it affirmatively furthers the values of religious freedom and tolerance that the Establishment Clause was designed to protect. Without pressuring those who do not wish to pray, the statute simply creates an opportunity to think, to plan, or to pray if one wishes—as Congress does by providing chaplains and chapels. It accommodates the purely private, voluntary religious choices of the individual pupils who wish to pray while at the same time creating a time for nonreligious reflection for those who do not choose to pray. . . .

JUSTICE WHITE, dissenting.

For the most part agreeing with the opinion of THE CHIEF JUSTICE, I dissent from the Court's judgment invalidating Ala. Code § 16–1–20.1

(Supp. 1984). Because I do, it is apparent that in my view the First Amendment does not proscribe either (1) statutes authorizing or requiring in so many words a moment of silence before classes begin or (2) a statute that provides, when it is initially passed, for a moment of silence for meditation or prayer. . . .

JUSTICE REHNQUIST, dissenting.

[Rehnquist devotes fifteen pages to the history of the adoption of the Bill of Rights, especially the Religion Clauses in the First Amendment. He concludes that the Amendment was designed to prohibit the establishment of a national religion, and perhaps to prevent discrimination among sects, but did not require neutrality on the part of government between religion and irreligion. He also critiques the three-part test of Lemon v. Kurtzman.*]*

These difficulties arise because the *Lemon* test has no more grounding in the history of the First Amendment than does the wall theory upon which it rests. The three-part test represents a determined effort to craft a workable rule from a historically faulty doctrine; but the rule can only be as sound as the doctrine it attempts to service. The three-part test has simply not provided adequate standards for deciding Establishment Clause cases, as this Court has slowly come to realize. Even worse, the *Lemon* test has caused this Court to fracture into unworkable plurality opinions, see n. 6, *supra*, depending upon how each of the three factors applies to a certain state action. The results from our school services cases show the difficulty we have encountered in making the *Lemon* test yield principled results.

. . .

If a constitutional theory has no basis in the history of the amendment it seeks to interpret, is difficult to apply and yields unprincipled results, I see little use in it. The "crucible of litigation," *ante*, at 52, has produced only consistent unpredictability, and today's effort is just a continuation of "the sisyphean task of trying to patch together the 'blurred, indistinct and variable barrier' described in *Lemon* v. *Kurtzman*." *Regan, supra*, at 671 (STEVENS, J., dissenting). We have done much straining since 1947, but still we admit that we can only "dimly perceive" the *Everson* wall. *Tilton, supra.* Our perception has been clouded not by the Constitution but by the mists of an unnecessary metaphor.

. . .

The Court strikes down the Alabama statute because the State wished to "characterize prayer as a favored practice." *Ante,* at 60. It would come as much of a shock to those who drafted the Bill of Rights as it will to a large number of thoughtful Americans today to learn that the Constitution, as construed by the majority, prohibits the Alabama Legislature from "endorsing" prayer. George Washington himself, at the request of the very Congress which passed the Bill of Rights, proclaimed a day of "public thanksgiving and prayer, to be observed by acknowledging with grateful hearts the many and signal favors of Almighty God." History must judge whether it was the Father of his Country in 1789, or a majority of the Court today, which has strayed from the meaning of the Establishment Clause.

The State surely has a secular interest in regulating the manner in which public schools are conducted. Nothing in the Establishment Clause of the First Amendment, properly understood, prohibits any such generalized "endorsement" of prayer. I would therefore reverse the judgment of the Court of Appeals.

13 Rights of the Accused

P robably no area of constitutional law harbors as many public misconceptions and suspicions as the rights available to the accused. The public wonders how many rights flow from the Constitution or from the pen of a judge. The right to a jury trial is generally understood and supported. Juries form an independent check between the government and the defendant. The writ of habeas corpus is another constitutional protection for those unlawfully detained by government. The Bill of Rights contains additional safeguards: use of a grand jury to indict suspects; protections against double jeopardy and self-incrimination; the right to a speedy and public trial by an impartial jury; the right to confront witnesses and obtain witnesses for the defendant; the right to have assistance of counsel; and prohibitions against excessive bail, excessive fines, and cruel and unusual punishment. Still other rights derive from congressional statutes and judicial decisions.

To the popular mind, "legal technicalities" permit known criminals to go free. Public fears and ignorance are easily exploited during political campaigns dominated by law-and-order themes. Candidates routinely attack the courts for handcuffing the police. Strong emotions thus cast a dark shadow across basic values of procedural due process and the right to a fair trial. Although Americans are quick to condemn violations of human rights in other countries, they are often intolerant with the operation of due process at home. Yet Justice Frankfurter reminded us that "the history of liberty has largely been the history of observance of procedural safeguards." McNabb v. United States, 318 U.S. 332, 347 (1943).

Criminal litigation is largely a matter for state courts. The vast bulk of criminal offenses are handled at the state, not the national, level. This chapter reviews developments of criminal law by Congress and the federal courts, identifying the areas in which state courts either took the lead or departed from federal standards.

THE CONCEPT OF DUE PROCESS

Due process is generally traced to the Magna Carta of 1215, in which the English king promised not to proceed against a freeman "unless by the lawful judgment of his peers or by the law of the land." Due process became equivalent to the laws passed by the English Parliament. In America, however, legislative enactments are subjected to the scrutiny of the courts. Murray's Lessee v. Hoboken Land & Improvement Co., 18 How. 272, 276 (1856).

Due process relies partly on the written guarantees in the Constitution. Under the Fifth Amendment, which originally applied only to the federal government, no person shall be "deprived of life, liberty, or property, without due process of law." The Fourteenth Amendment applies the same standard to the states. At a minimum, "due process" means that an accused must be given notice of a charge and adequate opportunity to appear and be heard. Blackmer v. United States, 284 U.S. 421, 440 (1934). Other amendments, from the Fourth through the Eighth, supply additional substance to due process.

Due process also depends on American values of fairness. The Constitution does not specify the standards required to convict, but the requirement that guilt of a criminal charge be proved "beyond a reasonable doubt" is part of custom dating back to the early years of our nation. In re Winship, 397 U.S. 358, 361 (1970). The reasonable-doubt standard "is indispensable to command the respect and confidence of the community in applications of the criminal law. It is critical that the moral force of the criminal law not be diluted by a standard of proof that leaves people in doubt whether innocent men are being condemned." Id. at 364. The requirement of proof beyond a reasonable doubt in a criminal case is "bottomed on a fundamental value determination of our society that it is far worse to convict an innocent man than to let a guilty man go free." Id. at 372 (Harlan, J., concurring). Civil litigation, on the other hand, permits proof by a preponderance of the evidence. Id. at 371.

A presumption of innocence favors the accused. A defendant is innocent until proved guilty. Estelle v. Williams, 425 U.S. 501, 503 (1976); Coffin v. United States, 156 U.S. 432, 453 (1895). The burden of establishing guilt rests on the prosecution "from the beginning to the end of the trial." Agnew v. United States, 165 U.S. 36, 49–50 (1897).

A fair trial cannot be conducted in the presence of a mob-dominated jury. A jury cannot deliberate fairly and reach a just conclusion when threatened by violence from a mob bent on lynching the accused. Such trials violate fundamental notions of due process. A case decided by the Supreme Court in 1915 concerned Leo Frank, who had been charged with the murder of a thirteen-year-old girl. His trial was dominated by angry crowds, chanting "Hang the Jew." After the Supreme Court upheld the conduct of his trial, he was taken from prison by an armed mob and lynched. Frank v. Mangum, 237 U.S. 309 (1915). In 1986, the Georgia Board of Pardons and Paroles gave Frank a posthumous pardon.

Due process is denied when witnesses are whipped and tortured until they testify against the accused. Moore v. Dempsey, 261 U.S. 86, 89 (1923). Even before assistance of counsel was recognized as a constitutional right in state criminal cases, the Supreme Court held in 1932 that due process required counsel for a defendant in a capital case. POWELL v. ALABAMA, 287 U.S. 45 (1932).

Confessions have been extorted by law officers who used violence and brutality. In one case, a black suspect was repeatedly hanged by a rope to the limb of a tree and tied to the tree and whipped until he confessed. Other defendants were stripped and beaten to obtain confessions. These convictions were reversed on the ground that coerced confessions are inherently suspect as evidence. Brown v. Mississippi, 297 U.S. 278 (1936). Even if a confession can be corroborated by independent evidence, the state violates due process if it uses methods that are inquisitorial and threatening. Rogers v. Richmond, 365 U.S. 534 (1961). These forms of persecution are generally inflicted upon "the poor, the ignorant, the numerically weak, the friendless, and the powerless." Chambers v. Florida, 309 U.S. 227, 237–238 (1940). Coercion can involve psychological compulsion, not merely physical beatings. Miller v. Fenton, 474 U.S. 104 (1985). Confessions might result improperly from a "truth serum" administered by a police physician. Townsend v. Sain, 372 U.S. 293 (1963).[1]

In addition to judicial guidance, due process is defined by congressional actions that revise the criminal code. Through this statutory activity, Congress provides standards for culpability, identifies grounds (such as insanity) to defend against prosecution, establishes a structure for sentencing, and sets forth the rules for pretrial and trial procedures, admissibility of evidence, and contempt of court. Congress reviews the Federal Rules of Criminal Procedure submitted by the Supreme Court. These rules, governing such matters as alibis, plea bargaining, and pretrial motions, may be revised or delayed by Congress. Rules of evidence, dealing with privileges, witnesses, and testimony, are also subject to congressional review and action.

Habeas Corpus

Under Article I, Section 9, the privilege of the writ of habeas corpus "shall not be suspended, unless when in Cases of Rebellion or Invasion the public Safety may require it." Through use of this "great writ," judges may determine whether someone is being imprisoned illegally. Authorities who receive the writ (*habeas corpus* means "you have the body") must justify the legality of a detention. Over time, the purpose of the writ has been expanded from protecting rights before conviction to giving relief after conviction. The Warren Court used the writ to enforce Bill of Rights protections in state courts, both broadening federal power over the states and adding substantially to the Court's workload. Fay v. Noia, 372 U.S. 391 (1963). The Burger Court attempted to cut back the scope of the writ. Wainwright v. Sykes, 433 U.S. 72 (1977); Francis v. Henderson, 425 U.S. 536 (1976). Congress has considered legislation to limit the availability of habeas corpus relief for state and federal prisoners. 133 Cong. Rec. E4975 (daily ed. Dec. 22, 1987).

---

[1]For other coerced confessions that were overturned, see Clewis v. Texas, 386 U.S. 707 (1967); Haynes v. Washington, 373 U.S. 503 (1963); Culombe v. Connecticut, 367 U.S. 568 (1961); Reck v. Pate, 367 U.S. 433 (1961); Spano v. New York, 360 U.S. 315 (1959); Payne v. Arkansas, 356 U.S. 560 (1958); Leyra v. Denno, 347 U.S. 556 (1954); Watts v. Indiana, 338 U.S. 49 (1949); Malinski v. New York, 324 U.S. 401 (1945); Ashcraft v. Tennessee, 322 U.S. 143 (1944); White v. Texas, 310 U.S. 530 (1940); and Wan v. United States, 266 U.S. 1 (1924). See also Stein v. New York, 346 U.S. 156 (1953), overruled by Jackson v. Denno, 378 U.S. 368 (1964).

Entrapment

Due process becomes an issue in questions of "entrapment," in which law enforcement officers instigate a crime by trickery and deception. Through such actions they help manufacture or stimulate a crime that might not have occurred without their intervention. Entrapment tactics should not be confused with "sting" operations, in which law officers use deceit to ensnare those who have *already* committed a crime.

As an example of entrapment, government officials lured a citizen into violating the law by making repeated and persistent solicitations, taking advantage of sentiment and friendship to encourage and provoke a crime. The Supreme Court held that the officials implanted in the mind of an innocent person the disposition to commit an offense. Sorrells v. United States, 287 U.S. 435 (1932). In another case, the Court limited law enforcement to the prevention of crime and the apprehension of criminals: "Manifestly, that function does not include the manufacturing of crime." Sherman v. United States, 356 U.S. 369, 372 (1958). The Court attempts to distinguish between two tests: subjective (the defendant's predisposition to commit a crime) and objective (the tactics used by law enforcement officers to instigate a crime). The Supreme Court offers the vague standard that entrapment is no defense unless the government's conduct "is so outrageous" as to violate due process. United States v. Russell, 411 U.S. 423, 431 (1973).[2]

GRAND JURIES AND JURY TRIALS

Procedural safeguards include indictment by a grand jury and trial by (petit) jury. The Fifth Amendment provides that "no person shall be held for a capital, or otherwise infamous crime, unless on a presentment or indictment of a grand jury, except in cases arising in the land or naval forces, or in the militia, when in actual service in time of war or public danger." Definitions of "infamous" vary from one age to another, depending on the severity of the punishment. An offense punishable by death must be prosecuted by indictment; offenses punishable by imprisonment exceeding one year or at hard labor must also be prosecuted by indictment unless the defendant waives indictment and requests prosecution by information. Rule 7 of the Rules of Criminal Procedure; Smith v. United States, 360 U.S. 1 (1959); Ex parte Wilson, 114 U.S. 417 (1885). The grand jury procedure in the Fifth Amendment is one of the few provisions in the Bill of Rights that has not been incorporated into the Due Process Clause of the Fourteenth Amendment and applied against the states.

Grand juries are meant to check government. In England, they acquired an independence "free from control by the Crown or judges." Costello v. United States, 350 U.S. 359, 362 (1956). Before initiating a criminal trial in America, a federal prosecutor must convince a body of laymen (from sixteen to twenty-three members)

---

[2]See also Mathews v. United States, 108 S.Ct. 883 (1988); Hampton v. United States, 425 U.S. 484 (1976); Osborn v. United States, 385 U.S. 323 (1966); Hoffa v. United States, 385 U.S. 293 (1966); Lewis v. United States, 385 U.S. 206 (1966); Massiah v. United States, 377 U.S. 201 (1964); Lopez v. United States, 373 U.S. 427 (1963); Raley v. Ohio, 360 U.S. 423 (1959); United States v. Twigg, 588 F.2d 373 (3d Cir. 1978); United States v. Archer, 486 F.2d 670 (2d Cir. 1973).

that sufficient evidence exists to try a suspect. If satisfied by the evidence, twelve or more jurors may indict, which is a formal charge recommending that the person be brought to trial. When the evidence justifies a criminal trial, grand jurors present an indictment or "true bill" detailing the charges. If the evidence is insufficient, they "ignore" the charges and issue an "ignoramus," which literally means "we are ignorant" of facts adequate to support the prosecutor's accusations. A trial is limited to the charges identified in the indictment. A trial judge may not broaden the charges and allow a jury to decide questions outside the scope of the indictment. Stirone v. United States, 361 U.S. 212 (1960).

Procedures governing federal grand juries are detailed in 18 U.S.C. §§ 3321–3333 and Rules 6 and 7 of the Rules of Criminal Procedure. State grand juries vary in size. The requirement for a grand jury applies only to the federal government. In 1884, the Supreme Court held that the Due Process Clause of the Fourteenth Amendment cannot be used to require states to indict by grand jury. Instead, states may prosecute upon a district attorney's "information," which consists of a prosecutor's accusation under oath. Hurtado v. California, 110 U.S. 516 (1884); Maxwell v. Dow, 176 U.S. 581 (1900); Lem Wood v. Oregon, 229 U.S. 586 (1913).

Grand juries do not follow the same procedural or evidentiary rules as a trial court. The public and the press are excluded. Records, transcripts, and materials are largely secret.[3] No judge is present to monitor grand jury proceedings, which are not adversary hearings to adjudicate guilt or innocence. They merely determine whether criminal proceedings should be instituted. United States v. Calandra, 414 U.S. 338, 343–344 (1974). Unlike a regular trial, grand jurors may decide that "hearsay" evidence is sufficient grounds to indict. Costello v. United States, 350 U.S. at 362.

Grand juries are subject to the test of impartiality required for trial juries. Congress took the initiative in 1875 by prohibiting the use of race to exclude citizens from service as grand or petit jurors. 18 Stat. 336, § 4; 18 U.S.C. § 243 (1982). The Court upheld that statute and has continued to strike down the systematic exclusion of blacks from grand juries.[4] Exclusion of Mexican-Americans from grand juries and regular juries is unconstitutional. Hernandez v. Texas, 347 U.S. 475 (1954). Even inadequate representation of a class, such as Mexican-Americans, is unconstitutional. Castaneda v. Partida, 430 U.S. 482 (1977). When impaneling a grand jury, judges seek to eliminate prejudiced jurors. Beck v. Washington, 369 U.S. 541, 545–549 (1962). In 1984, the Supreme Court decided that discrimination by judges in the selection of grand jury foremen (by excluding blacks and women) does not threaten constitutional rights. Hobby v. United States, 468 U.S. 339.

Witnesses before a grand jury may invoke the Fifth Amendment privilege against self-incrimination. Counselman v. Hitchcock, 142 U.S. 547 (1892). This privilege is

---

[3]Under the general rule of secrecy of Rule 6(e) of the Rules of Criminal Procedure, access to grand jury materials is severely restricted, even for government attorneys. United States v. Baggot, 463 U.S. 476 (1983); United States v. Sells Engineering, Inc., 463 U.S. 418 (1983); Illinois v. Abbott & Associates, Inc., 460 U.S. 557 (1983); Douglas Oil Co. v. Petrol Stops Northwest, 441 U.S. 211 (1979); Pittsburgh Plate Glass Co. v. United States, 360 U.S. 395 (1959); United States v. Procter & Gamble, 356 U.S. 677 (1958).

[4]E.g., Ex parte Virginia, 100 U.S. 339 (1880); Strauder v. West Virginia, 100 U.S. 303, 308 (1880). See also Vasquez v. Hillery, 474 U.S. 254 (1986); Rose v. Mitchell, 443 U.S. 545 (1979); Alexander v. Louisiana, 405 U.S. 625 (1972); Arnold v. North Carolina, 376 U.S. 773 (1964); Eubanks v. Louisiana, 356 U.S. 584 (1958); Pierre v. Louisiana, 306 U.S. 354 (1939).

overridden if the government grants immunity to the witness (p. 232). Witnesses may not refuse to answer because questions are based on illegally obtained evidence. United States v. Calandra, 414 U.S. 338 (1974).

The First Amendment does not protect newspaper reporters from responding to a grand jury subpoena and answering questions. Branzburg v. Hayes, 408 U.S. 665 (1972). This judicial doctrine can be modified by Congress: "At the federal level, Congress has freedom to determine whether a statutory newsman's privilege is necessary and desirable and to fashion standards and rules as narrow or broad as deemed necessary to deal with the evil discerned and, equally important, to refashion those rules as experience from time to time may dictate." Id. at 706. Congress has yet to pass such legislation, but a number of states have enacted "shield laws" to protect reporters from grand jury inquiries.

Grand juries are supposed to be independent checks on a prosecutor's allegations. Instead, they are often criticized as pawns in the hands of zealous and politically-motivated prosecutors. Justice Douglas once said in dissent: "It is, indeed, common knowledge that the grand jury, having been conceived as a bulwark between the citizen and the Government, is now a tool of the Executive." United States v. Mara, 410 U.S. 19, 23 (1973). Indiscriminate use of grand juries can smear the reputation of an individual targeted by an administration. At times, the grand jury becomes an engine of oppression unleashed against radical, nonconformist, and unpopular groups. Grand juries can be exploited to harass and intimidate political opposition.

Jury Trials

Article III, Section 2, provides that the "Trial of all Crimes, except in Cases of Impeachment, shall be by Jury." Under the Sixth Amendment, for all criminal prosecutions the accused is entitled to "an impartial jury." These protections do not apply to aliens who offend the law of war; they may be tried by military commission. Ex parte Quirin, 317 U.S. 1 (1942).

An accused may waive the right to a jury trial and be tried by the court. A defendant waives a jury trial in writing with the approval of the court and the consent of the government. Due process is denied when a suspect is tried before a judge who has a direct, personal, substantial, and pecuniary interest in deciding against the defendant. Tumey v. Ohio, 272 U.S. 510 (1927). Defendants may forgo a trial by entering into a "plea bargain" with the prosecutor. Most criminal cases are disposed of by pleas of guilty. By pleading guilty to a lesser charge, the defendant avoids the risk of a heavier sentence if convicted at trial. Bordenkircher v. Hayes, 434 U.S. 357 (1978). Plea bargaining places great power in the hands of a prosecutor, who can use this tool in a coercive and arbitrary manner.

Federal juries "shall be of 12" but a verdict may be rendered with less than 12 if one or more jurors are excused after the trial begins.[5] A jury verdict in federal courts

---

[5]Rule 23 of 18 U.S.C. Appendix, but see also Patton v. United States, 281 U.S. 276 (1930), which recognized the right of a defendant to waive a full jury after a trial begins, and Schick v. United States, 195 U.S. 65 (1904), which allowed parties to waive the right to a jury trial. In Singer v. United States, 380 U.S. 24 (1965), the Court upheld the procedure in Rule 23 that waiver of a jury trial requires the approval not only of the defendant but of the court and the government.

must be unanimous. Maxwell v. Dow, 176 U.S. 581, 586 (1900), Springfield v. Thomas, 166 U.S. 707 (1897); American Publishing Co. v. Fisher, 166 U.S. 464, 468 (1897). State juries may follow different procedures. The constitutional guarantee of trial by jury does not require a state to provide an accused with a jury of twelve for noncapital cases. The Supreme Court regards twelve as a common-law number and a "historical accident." Williams v. Florida, 399 U.S. 78, 88–89 (1970). However, a jury for a criminal trial in the states must number at least six. BALLEW v. GEORGIA, 435 U.S. 223 (1978).

For noncapital cases, states may allow non-unanimous jury verdicts. APODACA v. OREGON, 406 U.S. 404 (1972); Johnson v. Louisiana, 406 U.S. 346 (1972). If the jury consists of only six persons, a non-unanimous verdict in a state criminal trial for nonpetty offenses violates the Sixth and Fourteenth Amendments. Burch v. Louisiana, 441 U.S. 130 (1979).

The right to a jury trial does not extend to every criminal proceeding. Offenses that are "petty" (as defined by congressional statute) are tried without a jury. Cheff v. Schnackenberg, 384 U.S. 373, 379–380 (1966); District of Columbia v. Clawans, 300 U.S. 617, 624 (1937). Serious offenses require a jury trial. District of Columbia v. Colts, 282 U.S. 63 (1930). The right to a jury trial depends on the potential penalty, not the category of offense. Thus, if someone faces a two-year prison sentence for a "misdemeanor," a jury trial is required. DUNCAN v. LOUISIANA, 391 U.S. 145 (1968). No offense can be regarded as "petty" if imprisonment of more than six months is authorized. Baldwin v. New York, 399 U.S. 66 (1970); Blanton v. North Las Vegas, 109 S.Ct. 1289 (1989).

Those charged with criminal contempt for disobeying a court order are not automatically entitled to a jury trial. The Supreme Court based this exception partly on the constitutional interpretation reached by members of the First Congress, many of whom were delegates to the Philadelphia Convention. United States v. Barnett, 376 U.S. 681, 693 (1964). However, a person convicted of criminal contempt and sentenced to two years' imprisonment is entitled to a jury trial. Bloom v. Illinois, 391 U.S. 194 (1968).

These cases draw attention to an anomaly in constitutional law. Although citizens may be tried for petty offenses without a jury, serving time in jail for up to six months and paying fines of several hundred dollars, the Seventh Amendment contains this language: "In suits at common law, where the value in controversy shall exceed twenty dollars, the right of trial by jury shall be preserved . . ." The purpose was to guarantee a jury not only for criminal trials but for civil trials as well. Nevertheless, the reach of the Seventh Amendment has been limited by several developments. First, it has not been applied to the states. Walker v. Sauvinet, 92 U.S. (12 Otto.) 90, 92 (1876). Second, the trial of civil cases may be conducted before a jury of six persons rather than the twelve required for other federal trials. Colgrove v. Battin, 413 U.S. 149 (1973). Third, the Seventh Amendment does not prevent Congress from assigning to an administrative agency the task of adjudicating violations of federal statutes that create new "public rights" involving the government in its sovereign capacity. The Seventh Amendment "preserved" only the rights to a jury trial in existence at that time. Atlas Roofing Co. v. Occupational Safety Comm'n, 430 U.S. 442 (1977). More than a hundred federal statutes allow civil penalties to be imposed in excess of twenty dollars without a jury trial. 132 Cong. Rec. S13009–13011 (daily ed. Sept. 19, 1986). Fourth, there is no Seventh Amendment right to a jury trial against the federal government. Galloway v. United States, 319 U.S. 372, 388 (1943).[6]

Racial and gender discrimination in jury formation has been a persistent problem in America. Congress passed legislation in 1875 to prohibit the use of race as a factor in selecting jurors. 18 Stat. 336, § 4; 18 U.S.C. § 243 (1982). The Supreme Court has held that due process is denied when blacks are consistently and wholly excluded from jury service. Norris v. Alabama, 294 U.S. 587 (1935). Although these principles existed for almost a century, Congress had to pass legislation in 1968 to supply additional safeguards against discrimination in the selection of jurors (both grand and petit). 82 Stat. 54. Yet the problem of racial exclusion continued.[7] It was not until 1975 that the Supreme Court held that the exclusion of women from petit juries violated the right to a jury trial. Taylor v. Louisiana, 419 U.S. 522 (1975). There were also sharp disputes about the creation of "blue ribbon" jury panels that excluded certain classes of people. Fay v. New York, 332 U.S. 261 (1947).

In *Swain* v. *Alabama* (1965), the Supreme Court reviewed the practice of prosecutors who use "peremptory strikes" (eliminating potential jurors without stating a reason). The Court held that a prosecutor's reliance on peremptory challenges to strike all six blacks, even though it produced an all-white jury, did not constitute racial discrimination unless it could be shown that the prosecutor had engaged in this practice for many years. Swain v. Alabama, 380 U.S. 202 (1965). The Court's ruling was specifically rejected by the Supreme Court of California, which put a much heavier burden on prosecutors to justify peremptory challenges along racial lines. People v. Wheeler, 583 P.2d 748 (Cal. 1978). Other state courts also refused to accept the *Swain* rationale. Commonwealth v. Soares, 387 N.E.2d 499 (Mass. 1979), cert. denied, 444 U.S. 881 (1979); State v. Neil, 457 So.2d 481 (Fla. 1984). The law reviews were uniformly critical of *Swain*. In 1983, in a case denying certiorari to revisit *Swain*, two Justices dissented and three other Justices appeared ready to reconsider the merits of *Swain*, especially in light of its unfriendly reception in the states: "In my judgment it is a sound exercise of discretion for the Court to allow the various States to serve as laboratories in which the issue receives further study before it is addressed by this Court." McCray v. United States, 461 U.S. 961, 963 (1983).

Swain was finally overturned in 1986. The Court held that a prosecutor may not use racial reasons and peremptory challenges to strike all black persons to produce an all-white jury. A prosecutor may not use peremptory challenges on the assumption that black jurors cannot impartially consider a state's case against a black. It is no longer necessary, as under *Swain*, for the defendant to prove discrimination by the prosecutor. If a minority defendant objects to a prosecutor's peremptory challenges, the burden is now on the prosecutor to convince the judge that the exclusions are not racially motivated. Batson v. Kentucky, 476 U.S. 79 (1986).

---

[6]Other important Seventh Amendment cases include Granfinanciera v. Nordberg, 109 S.Ct. 2782 (1989); Tull v. United States, 481 U.S. 412 (1987); Lehman v. Nakshian, 453 U.S. 156 (1981); and Dimick v. Schiedt, 293 U.S. 474 (1935). For a critique of adjudication by executive agencies rather than by Article III courts, see Sun, "Congressional Delegation of Adjudicatory Power to Federal Agencies and the Right to Trial by Jury," 1988 Duke L. J. 539.

[7]See McCray v. New York, 461 U.S. 961 (1983); Peters v. Kiff, 407 U.S. 493 (1972); Carter v. Jury Commission, 396 U.S. 320 (1970).

ELEMENTS OF A FAIR TRIAL

Justice Jackson once remarked that he would rather live under Soviet law enforced by American procedures than under American law enforced by Soviet procedures. Leonard W. Levy, The Origins of the Fifth Amendment ix (1986 ed.). The procedural safeguards treated in this section include a speedy and public trial, protections against double jeopardy, and the right to confront witnesses and call witnesses for the defense.

Speedy and Public Trial

The Sixth Amendment provides that in all criminal prosecutions the accused "shall enjoy the right to a speedy and public trial, by an impartial jury of the State and district wherein the crime shall have been committed, which district shall have been previously ascertained by law, and to be informed of the nature and cause of the accusation . . ." The right to a speedy trial is triggered when a formal criminal charge is instituted and a criminal prosecution begins. United States v. MacDonald, 456 U.S. 1, 6–7 (1982). The needs of public justice may require delays, however. Beavers v. Haubert, 198 U.S. 77, 87 (1905). "While justice should be administered with dispatch, the essential ingredient is orderly expedition and not mere speed." Smith v. United States, 360 U.S. 1, 10 (1959). Procedural safeguards for the accused necessarily slow judicial proceedings to a deliberate pace. United States v. Ewell, 383 U.S. 116, 120 (1966).

When a trial is repeatedly and indefinitely postponed, however, an indicted person is subjected to public scorn without an opportunity to be exonerated in the courts. Under such conditions a defendant is denied a speedy trial, a right now applied against the states. Klopfer v. North Carolina, 386 U.S. 213 (1967). See also Dickey v. Florida, 398 U.S. 30 (1970). In cases in which defendants failed to assert the right to a speedy trial and delays did not seriously prejudice their case, five years could elapse between an arrest and a trial without violating the Speedy Trial Clause. Barker v. Wingo, 407 U.S. 514 (1972).

Congress passed the Speedy Trial Act in 1974 in an effort to prevent these delays in federal court. Charges can be dismissed unless the person is brought to trial within 100 days of arrest. The statute establishes deadlines for indictment and arraignment. Certain delays can be excluded in computing the 100 days. 88 Stat. 2076 (1975); 18 U.S.C. §§ 3161–3174 (1982). Congress has made subsequent amendments to the Speedy Trial Act. See United States v. Rojas-Contreras, 474 U.S. 231 (1985). Moreover, the Court has held that the time during which an accused is not under indictment or under official restraint (subject to bail or in jail) is excluded when determining a speedy trial claim. Under these tests, the government has been permitted to prosecute charges that are ten years old. United States v. Loud Hawk, 474 U.S. 302 (1986). In some jurisdictions, such as the District of Columbia, suspects can still be held a year or more in jail while awaiting trial. Washington Post, April 4, 1987, p. A-1. There have been cases where suspects were held in preventive detention for thirty months. Washington Post, February 11, 1988, p. A-26.

The constitutional right to a "public trial" protects an individual from secret proceedings where there is no opportunity to secure counsel, prepare a defense, cross-examine witnesses, or summon witnesses for the accused. The Anglo-American distrust of secret trials has been traced to the Spanish Inquisition, the

English Star Chamber, and the French *lettre de cachet.* In re Oliver, 333 U.S. 257, 268–269 (1948). Public trials restrain potential abuses of judicial power. Id. at 270. This constitutional protection in the Bill of Rights has been applied to the states. Id. at 273. There have been occasions, however, where a judge has excluded the public while adjudging someone guilty of criminal contempt for refusing to answer questions. Levine v. United States, 362 U.S. 610 (1960). Moreover, there is a constant tension between a judge's interest in closing a trial and the right of the public and the press to attend (see pp. 623–625).

Double Jeopardy

Under the Fifth Amendment, a person shall not be subject "for the same offense to be twice put in jeopardy of life or limb." Litigation exposes a raft of complex issues. What is the "same offense"? What is "jeopardy"? The law of double jeopardy consists of several rules, each rule "marooned in a sea of exceptions." 75 Yale L. J. 262, 263 (1965). The Supreme Court admits that its decisions in this area are "a veritable Sargasso Sea." Albernaz v. United States, 450 U.S. 333, 343 (1981).

As first proposed by Madison in 1789, the Double Jeopardy Clause provided: "No person shall be subject, except in cases of impeachment, to more than one punishment or one trial for the same offence." 1 Annals of Congress 434. Some members of the House of Representatives objected that the limitation of "one trial" would prevent a convicted person from obtaining a second trial if the first was deficient. Id. at 753. The Senate changed the language to its present form. S. Jour., 1st Cong., 1st Sess. 71, 77.

The underlying purpose of the Double Jeopardy Clause is to prohibit the government from making repeated attempts to convict an individual, "subjecting him to embarrassment, expense and ordeal and compelling him to live in a continuing state of anxiety and insecurity." Green v. United States, 355 U.S. 184, 187 (1957). Acquittal acts as an absolute bar on a second trial. United States v. DiFrancesco, 449 U.S. 117, 129 (1980). The meaning of "acquittal," however, often divides the Court. United States v. Scott, 437 U.S. 82 (1978); United States v. Sisson, 399 U.S. 267 (1970).

There is no double jeopardy in trying someone twice for the same offense if the jury is unable to reach a verdict, the jury is discharged, or an appeals court returns the case to the trial court because of defects in the original indictment. United States v. Ball, 163 U.S. 662, 672 (1896); Thompson v. United States, 155 U.S. 271 (1894); Logan v. United States, 144 U.S. 263, 297–298 (1892). Even so, by the time a judge discharges the jury the accused might already have been placed in "jeopardy." When does jeopardy attach? When the jury is empaneled and sworn? the first witness sworn? the first evidence introduced? On such questions the Court splinters to produce 5–4 and 6–3 decisions.[8]

Other difficulties spring from jurisdictional questions. May a state and the federal government (two sovereigns) prosecute someone for the same act? Houston v. Moore, 18 U.S. (5 Wheat.) 1 (1820). In three unanimous rulings, the Supreme Court held that a person may be prosecuted for the same act under federal law and state law. The theory is that there are two distinct offenses rather than the "same offense"

---

[8]Crist v. Bretz, 437 U.S. 28 (1978); Illinois v. Somerville, 410 U.S. 458 (1973); United States v. Jorn, 400 U.S. 470 (1971); Downum v. United States, 372 U.S. 734 (1963); Gori v. United States, 367 U.S. 364 (1961).

under the Fifth Amendment. Jerome v. United States, 318 U.S. 101 (1943); Herbert v. Louisiana, 272 U.S. 312 (1926); United States v. Lanza, 260 U.S. 377 (1922).

When this theory was reaffirmed in 1959, the Court split 5–4. The dissenters regarded double prosecutions as constitutionally repulsive, particularly when the federal government, after losing a case, helps a state try the person for the same offense. Bartkus v. Illinois, 359 U.S. 121 (1959). Because of inherent tribal sovereignty, an Indian can be tried in Tribal Court and in federal court for the same incident. United States v. Wheeler, 435 U.S. 313 (1978). Two states may prosecute a person for the same criminal activity. Heath v. Alabama, 474 U.S. 82 (1985). This theory of "dual sovereignty" does not allow double prosecutions *within* a state: once by the state and again by a municipality. Cities are not sovereign entities. Waller v. Florida, 406 U.S. 916 (1972).

Decisions on double jeopardy initially dealt with the federal government or its territories.[9] In 1937, the Court reviewed a state prosecution of an individual who had been sentenced to life imprisonment but, upon retrial, was sentenced to death. The Court denied that double jeopardy represented a fundamental principle of liberty and justice that must be applied against the states. PALKO v. CONNECTICUT, 302 U.S. 319 (1937). This decision was overturned in 1969 when the Court held that the double jeopardy provision in the Fifth Amendment is fundamental to our constitutional heritage and enforceable against the states through the Fourteenth Amendment. Benton v. Maryland, 395 U.S. 784 (1969).

Other decisions attempted to define the confused contours of the Double Jeopardy Clause. If someone is found guilty and an appeals court orders a new trial, the trial court may not impose a stiffer penalty than the one the defendant received the first time. Arizona v. Rumsey, 467 U.S. 203 (1984); Price v. Georgia, 398 U.S. 323 (1970); Green v. United States, 355 U.S. 184 (1957). If someone is charged with robbing six poker players and is acquitted in a trial involving one of the players, the government may not proceed to prosecute him for robbing one of the other players. Ashe v. Swenson, 397 U.S. 436 (1970). See also Simpson v. Florida, 403 U.S. 384 (1971).

The issue of imposing a more severe sentence when a defendant is convicted in a second trial has occupied both Congress and the courts. In 1969, the Supreme Court decided that there is no constitutional bar to imposing a more severe sentence on reconviction, provided the sentencing judge is not motivated by vindictiveness. The guarantee against double jeopardy, however, requires that punishment already exacted must be fully credited to the new sentence. North Carolina v. Pearce, 395 U.S. 711, 718 (1969); Chaffin v. Stynchcombe, 412 U.S. 17 (1973). If someone is convicted and successfully motions for a new trial because of prosecutorial misconduct, upon reconviction the judge may impose a heavier sentence. Texas v. McCullough, 475 U.S. 134 (1986).

These cases deal with new sentences after a new trial. In 1970, Congress authorized increases in an *existing* sentence; appellate courts may review and increase a trial court's sentence for "dangerous special offenders." 84 Stat. 950, § 3576. The Supreme Court upheld this procedure in United States v. DiFrancesco, 449 U.S. 117 (1980). Legislation in 1984 permits appellate courts to increase existing sentences for offenses in areas other than organized crime. 98 Stat. 2011, § 3742

[9]Diaz v. United States, 223 U.S. 442 (1912); Serra v. Mortiga, 204 U.S. 470 (1907); Kepner v. United States, 195 U.S. 100 (1904); United States v. Ball, 163 U.S. 662 (1896).

(1984). The basis for such statutes is that the scope of punishment is a matter for legislatures, not courts. Missouri v. Hunter, 459 U.S. 359, 368 (1983). Legislatures may authorize multiple punishments and consecutive sentences. Although a person may not be punished more than once for the same offense, a single incident can violate more than one statutory provision and lead to cumulative punishment. These statutes do not violate double jeopardy.[10]

Right of Confrontation

The Sixth Amendment provides that in all criminal prosecutions the accused shall "be confronted with the witnesses against him [and] to have compulsory process for obtaining witnesses in his favor ..." In 1965, the Supreme Court held that the right of confrontation and cross-examination is a fundamental right made obligatory on the states by the Fourteenth Amendment. Pointer v. Texas, 380 U.S. 400 (1965); Douglas v. Alabama, 380 U.S. 415 (1965). Two years later, the Court also applied against the states the right of an accused to have compulsory process for obtaining witnesses. Washington v. Texas, 388 U.S. 14 (1967). The Confrontation and Compulsory Process Clauses give an accused a fair opportunity to present a defense. Pennsylvania v. Ritchie, 480 U.S. 39 (1987); Crane v. Kentucky, 476 U.S. 683 (1986); Lee v. Illinois, 476 U.S. 530 (1986). In 1988, the Court struck down a state law permitting children who claim they are victims of sexual abuse to testify in court behind screens. Coy v. Iowa, 108 S.Ct. 2798 (1988).

Under certain circumstances, a disruptive defendant may be removed from the courtroom without violating his constitutional right to be present and to confront witnesses against him. Illinois v. Allen, 397 U.S. 337 (1970). A trial court's ruling in violation of the Confrontation Clause may even be tolerated if the Supreme Court finds the error "harmless." Delaware v. Van Arsdall, 475 U.S. 673 (1986). Other exceptions to the Confrontation Clause include the use of out-of-court statements in conspiracy trials (permitting hearsay evidence).[11] It is also possible to admit prior-recorded testimony at a trial without the opportunity for confrontation if two conditions are met: the evidence is reliable and the state has made an effort to locate the witness.[12] Under some circumstances, the defendant's attorney (but not the defendant) is allowed to be present at a hearing in the judge's chamber. Kentucky v. Stincer, 482 U.S. 730 (1987).

SELF-INCRIMINATION AND RIGHT TO COUNSEL

Procedural due process includes other protections for the accused: prompt arraignment before a magistrate, the privilege against self-incrimination, and the right to have the assistance of counsel. These issues triggered some of the most bitterly

---

[10]Jones v. Thomas, 109 S.Ct. 2522 (1989); Garrett v. United States, 471 U.S. 773 (1985); Albernaz v. United States, 450 U.S. 333 (1981); Whalen v. United States, 445 U.S. 684 (1980); Gore v. United States, 357 U.S. 386 (1958). See also Brown v. Ohio, 432 U.S. 161 (1977), which held that a person could not be prosecuted for "joyriding" and then later for auto theft if the latter offense includes the former. This holding seems eroded by Ohio v. Johnson, 457 U.S. 493 (1984).

[11]Bourjaily v. United States, 483 U.S. 171 (1987); United States v. Inadi, 475 U.S. 387 (1986); Dutton v. Evans, 400 U.S. 74 (1970).

[12]Ohio v. Roberts, 448 U.S. 56 (1980); Mancusi v. Stubbs, 408 U.S. 204 (1972); Barber v. Page, 390 U.S. 719 (1968).

contested rulings by the Supreme Court: *Mallory* v. *United States* (1957), *Escobedo* v. *Illinois* (1964), and *Miranda* v. *Arizona* (1966).

Prompt Arraignment

Congress and state legislatures have required police officers to take an accused to the nearest judicial officer for arraignment. If officers ignore this procedure and detain the suspect for days in order to extract a confession, the evidence can be excluded by the courts. McNabb v. United States, 318 U.S. 332 (1943). These rulings conform to legislative policy, such as the rule adopted by Congress that requires an arrested person to be taken before a committing magistrate "without unnecessary delay." MALLORY v. UNITED STATES, 354 U.S. 449 (1957). Congress responded to *Mallory* by making confessions admissible if the defendant is arraigned within six hours. 82 Stat. 210 (1968); 18 U.S.C. § 3501(c) (1982).

Self-Incrimination

The Fifth Amendment provides that no person "shall be compelled in any Criminal Case to be a witness against himself." The purpose of this privilege is to prevent repressive and arbitrary methods of prosecution, such as "the horror of Star Chamber proceedings" in England. Quinn v. United States, 349 U.S. 155, 161 (1955). Government officials may not pry incriminating evidence from the lips of the accused. Prosecutors are "forced to search for independent evidence instead of relying upon proof extracted from individuals by force of law." United States v. White, 322 U.S. 694, 698 (1944).

The privilege against self-incrimination is not automatic or self-executing. It can be waived and "must be deemed waived" if a witness does not assert it in a timely manner. Vajtauer v. Comm'n of Immigration, 273 U.S. 103 (1927). Although the privilege against self-incrimination can be waived, even vague and ambiguous references to the "Fifth Amendment" are sufficient to invoke its protection. Quinn v. United States, 349 U.S. at 162–164; Emspak v. United States, 349 U.S. 190 (1955). If a defendant voluntarily takes the stand he may be cross-examined as any other witness, thereby risking the disclosure of incriminating information. Brown v. United States, 356 U.S. 148 (1958); Raffel v. United States, 271 U.S. 494 (1926). Once a defendant offers himself as a witness, "his credibility may be impeached, his testimony may be assailed, and is to be weighed as that of any other witness." Reagan v. United States, 157 U.S. 301, 305 (1895).

In federal proceedings, an accused may request the court to instruct the jury that a defendant's failure to testify does not create a presumption of guilt and must not be used by the jury against him. Bruno v. United States, 308 U.S. 287 (1939). In the states, however, courts and prosecutors were allowed to comment on a defendant's failure to explain or to deny evidence against him. The court or the jury could take that into consideration. Adamson v. California, 332 U.S. 46 (1947) (reprinted in Chapter 8). In this case and in *Twining* v. *New Jersey*, 211 U.S. 78 (1908), the Court applied the Self-Incrimination Clause only to the federal government, not to the states. In 1964, the Court held that the privilege against self-incrimination is incorporated in the Due Process Clause of the Fourteenth Amendment and therefore applicable to the states. Malloy v. Hogan, 378 U.S. 1 (1964). Subsequent cases have attempted to explain when it is appropriate to comment on a defendant's failure to testify.[13]

Problems of federalism provoked the extension of the Self-Incrimination Clause to the states. In 1944, the Court had held that a person could be compelled under a state immunity statute to give testimony and the information could be used later in federal court to convict him. Feldman v. United States, 322 U.S. 487 (1944). This placed the witness in a no-win situation. Agreeing to testify could bring conviction in federal court; refusal to testify risked state imprisonment for contempt of court. Id. at 495 and Knapp v. Schweitzer, 357 U.S. 371 (1958). This dilemma was resolved in 1964 when a unanimous Court held that one jurisdiction within the federal system may not compel a witness (granted immunity) to give testimony that might incriminate him under the laws of another jurisdiction. Murphy v. Waterfront Comm'n, 378 U.S. 52 (1964).

What does the privilege protect? An early case held that seizure of a person's private books and papers, to be used as evidence in court, was the same as compelling the person to be a witness against himself. Boyd v. United States, 116 U.S. 616 (1886). This sweeping interpretation was narrowed by subsequent decisions. Official or business records, including union records, are not protected by the Fourth or Fifth Amendments. The privilege against self-incrimination is a personal one and applies only to natural individuals, not to corporations or organizations.[14] Individuals cannot refuse to file a tax return simply because the government might discover income from criminal activities; if filing part of the return results in self-incrimination, the taxpayer may invoke the Fifth Amendment for that portion. Garner v. United States, 424 U.S. 648 (1976); United States v. Sullivan, 274 U.S. 259 (1927). The IRS can issue a summons for tax and business records, even if the taxpayer transfers them to an accountant or an attorney. Couch v. United States, 409 U.S. 322 (1973); Fisher v. United States, 425 U.S. 391 (1976).

Drivers involved in an accident can be required to stop and provide their name and address, even at the risk of criminal liability. California v. Byers, 402 U.S. 424 (1971). The population regulated here is considered basically noncriminal, but when the target class is suspected of illegal activity, government "regulation" cannot become a means of forcing individuals (such as gun dealers) to incriminate themselves. Haynes v. United States, 390 U.S. 85 (1968). Initially, the Court decided that federal requirements that gamblers register with the IRS did not violate the Self-Incrimination Clause, United States v. Kahriger, 345 U.S. 22 (1953) and Lewis v. United States, 348 U.S. 419 (1955). The Court later reversed itself and held that such

---

[13]If the defendant's attorney is concerned about jury misconceptions regarding the defendant's silence, the judge has an obligation, upon the attorney's request, to instruct the jury that the accused's decision not to testify cannot be used as an inference of guilt. Carter v. Kentucky, 450 U.S. 288 (1981). Instruction can possibly stimulate adverse inferences by calling attention to a defendant's silence. Lakeside v. Oregon, 435 U.S. 333 (1978). Earlier, in Griffin v. California, 380 U.S. 609 (1965), the Court held that state courts were not allowed to comment on a defendant's failure to testify. In cases involving possession of heroin, judges may inform the jury that a defendant's failure to explain possession is sufficient evidence to convict. Turner v. United States, 396 U.S. 398 (1970). See also United States v. Robinson, 108 S.Ct. 864 (1988).

[14]Braswell v. United States, 108 S.Ct. 2284 (1988); United States v. Doe, 465 U.S. 605 (1984); Fisher v. United States, 425 U.S. 391 (1976); Bellis v. United States, 417 U.S. 85 (1974); Campbell Painting Co. v. Reid, 392 U.S. 286 (1968); United States v. White, 322 U.S. 694 (1944); Wilson v. United States, 221 U.S. 361 (1911); Hale v. Henkel, 201 U.S. 43 (1906).

statutes unconstitutionally compel gamblers to incriminate themselves. Marchetti v. United States, 390 U.S. 39 (1968); Grosso v. United States, 390 U.S. 62 (1968).

In an early ruling on the Self-Incrimination Clause, the Supreme Court gave broad protection to a witness compelled to testify against himself, grand jury investigations included. Counselman v. Hitchcock, 142 U.S. 547 (1892). It is a violation to compel a witness to testify before a grand jury and answer questions regarding an activity that is a crime. Hoffman v. United States, 341 U.S. 479 (1951); Blau v. United States, 340 U.S. 159 (1950). Similarly, it is unconstitutional to require a group to register and file a list of its members if that information can be used as evidence toward a criminal prosecution. Albertson v. SACB, 382 U.S. 70 (1965). Witnesses may not be asked to exercise this constitutional privilege at the cost of losing their jobs.[15]

Novel issues suggest the difficulty of relying solely on "framers' intent." The Court has held that the extraction of blood by a physician in a hospital does not offend due process. A blood sample, containing alcohol, can be used to convict someone for involuntary manslaughter. Breithaupt v. Abram, 352 U.S. 432 (1957). A blood test, regarded as "physical or real" evidence rather than testimonial evidence, is unprotected by the Fifth Amendment. Blood may be extracted even if the patient refuses. Schmerber v. California, 384 U.S. 757 (1966). If someone arrested for drunk driving refuses to take a blood-alcohol test, the refusal may be used against him at trial without offending the Self-Incrimination Clause. South Dakota v. Neville, 459 U.S. 553 (1983). Handwriting samples may be taken of a suspect without violating the Self-Incrimination Clause. Gilbert v. California, 388 U.S. 263 (1967). An accused may be compelled to be present at a police lineup and utter the words of the person who committed the crime. United States v. Wade, 388 U.S. 218, 221–223 (1967).

Congress has enacted legislation to compel persons to testify by granting them immunity from prosecution. The Interstate Commerce Act of 1887 compelled persons to testify and produce documents. The claim of a witness that such testimony or evidence "may tend to criminate . . . shall not excuse such witness from testifying," but the evidence or testimony "shall not be used against such person on the trial of any criminal proceeding." 24 Stat. 383, § 12 (1887). The statute was revised two years later. 25 Stat. 858, § 3.

The Supreme Court held that this procedure did not conform to the Self-Incrimination Clause because it did not give a witness absolute immunity against future prosecution. Counselman v. Hitchcock, 142 U.S. 547 (1892). Congress rewrote the statute to provide that no person compelled to testify "shall be prosecuted or subjected to any penalty or forfeiture for or on account of any transaction, matter or thing, concerning which he may testify . . . ." 27 Stat. 443 (1893). This is called "transactional immunity," offering complete immunity for the transaction (offense). In a 5–4 decision, the Supreme Court upheld this statute and rejected a literal interpretation of the Constitution. It concluded that compelled testimony, in the company of absolute immunity, met the essential purpose of the

[15]Lefkowitz v. Turley, 414 U.S. 70 (1973); Sanitation Men v. Sanitation Comm'n, 392 U.S. 280 (1968); Gardner v. Broderick, 392 U.S. 273 (1968); Garrity v. New Jersey, 385 U.S. 493 (1967); Slochower v. Board of Education, 350 U.S. 551 (1956). Lawyers who invoke their privilege against self-incrimination should not face disbarment as a result. Sperack v. Klein, 385 U.S. 511 (1967), overturning Cohen v. Hurley, 366 U.S. 117 (1961).

Self-Incrimination Clause, even if the testimony exposed the witness to public disgrace. Brown v. Walker, 161 U.S. 591, 595 (1896).[16]

In 1954, Congress authorized the granting of immunity by a grand jury, by a majority of one House, or by a two-thirds majority of a congressional committee. Applications are made for a court order to compel testimony. Refusal to testify can result in contempt of court and imprisonment. 68 Stat. 745. The Court upheld this statute in Ullmann v. United States, 350 U.S. 422 (1956). The immunity procedure was codified in 1970 (84 Stat. 926) and appears in 18 U.S.C. §§ 6001–6005 (1982). The immunity offered is called "use immunity." No testimony or other information compelled under a court order, or any information "directly or indirectly" derived from the testimony or other information, "may be used against the witness in any criminal case." 18 U.S.C. § 6002. Use immunity, which Congress invoked in 1987 to force Colonel Oliver North to testify at the Iran-Contra hearings, provides less protection against prosecution than transactional immunity. A witness given use immunity may still be prosecuted for the crime on the basis of evidence obtained from independent sources. The Supreme Court held that the scope of use immunity under Section 6002 is coextensive with the Self-Incrimination Clause. Kastigar v. United States, 406 U.S. 441 (1972). For further exploration on the distinction between transactional and use immunities, see Piccirillo v. New York, 400 U.S. 548 (1971); Application of United States Senate Select Com. on Pres. Camp. Act., 361 F.Supp. 1270 (D.D.C. 1973).

Assistance of Counsel

The Sixth Amendment entitles a person "to have the Assistance of Counsel for his defence." Without counsel, an accused is unable to exercise effectively the rights available in the Constitution: the privilege to remain silent, to cross-examine witnesses, to challenge biased jurors, and a variety of subtle questions of law that tax the resourcefulness even of seasoned lawyers. "A layman is usually no match for the skilled prosecutor whom he confronts in the court room. He needs the aid of counsel lest he be the victim of overzealous prosecutors, of the law's complexity, or his own ignorance or bewilderment." Williams v. Kaiser, 323 U.S. 471, 476 (1945). A defendant may proceed without counsel if the decision is voluntary and the defendant is aware of the dangers and disadvantages of self-representation. Faretta v. California, 422 U.S. 806 (1975); McKaskle v. Wiggins, 465 U.S. 168 (1984). Under certain circumstances, judges may deny the defendant's choice of lawyer. Wheat v. United States, 108 S.Ct. 1692 (1988).

The Court has held that government, in its fight against drug dealers and racketeers, may seize assets from those operations that criminal defendants intended to use to pay their lawyers. The constitutional right to have assistance of counsel is not violated when government seizes ill-gotten gains. United States v. Monsanto, 109 S.Ct. 2657 (1989); Caplin & Drysdale v. United States, 109 S.Ct. 2647 (1989).

The question of providing an attorney for indigent defendants was decided partly

---

[16]Under certain statutes, if a witness appears in response to a subpoena and gives testimony, this action by itself may provide total immunity and prevent prosecution regardless of whether the witness claims the privilege against self-incrimination. United States v. Monia, 317 U.S. 424 (1943). See also Smith v. United States, 337 U.S. 137 (1949); Shapiro v. United States, 335 U.S. 1 (1948); United States v. Hoffman, 335 U.S. 77 (1948).

by the Supreme Court in 1932 when it held that the Due Process Clause of the Fourteenth Amendment requires the appointment of counsel for someone accused of a capital crime. If a defendant is incapable of making his own defense because of "ignorance, feeble mindedness, illiteracy, or the like, it is the duty of the court, whether requested or not, to assign counsel for him as a necessary requisite of due process of law." POWELL v. ALABAMA, 287 U.S. 45, 71 (1932). Six years later, the Court held that indigents charged with a crime in a federal court are entitled by the Sixth Amendment to have the assistance of counsel unless that right is intelligently and competently waived. Johnson v. Zerbst, 304 U.S. 458 (1938).

The question of providing counsel in a *state* court vexed the Court for more than two decades. In 1942, it ruled that a state's refusal to appoint counsel for an indigent in a criminal proceeding did not deny due process. Betts v. Brady, 316 U.S. 455 (1942). The Court divided 6–3 in this case, and dozens and dozens of subsequent decisions whittled away at the majority position. The denial of counsel in a state court brought four dissents in a 1946 case. Carter v. Illinois, 329 U.S. 173. The Court agreed unanimously in 1954 that due process was violated when a state judge denied a defendant the opportunity to obtain counsel on a separate accusation regarding his habitual criminal record. Chandler v. Fretag, 348 U.S. 3. The Court split 5–4 in two cases in 1957 and 1959 in which counsel had been denied in a state proceeding. In re Groban, 352 U.S. 330: Anonymous v. Baker, 360 U.S. 287.

In 1960, the Court held that lack of counsel for an indigent in a state case deprived the accused of due process. As the two dissenters noted, the Court did not even mention *Betts* v. *Brady,* although the decision "cuts serious inroads into that holding." Hudson v. North Carolina, 363 U.S. 697, 704 (1960). A year later, a unanimous Court ruled that due process had been violated by denying counsel to an indigent, ignorant, and mentally ill black. This was a noncapital felony case. Again, the opinion of the Court made no mention of *Betts.* McNeal v. Culver, 365 U.S. 109, 117 (1961). In two other noncapital felony cases, a unanimous Court held that the denial of counsel violated due process. Chewning v. Cunningham, 368 U.S. 443 (1962); Carnley v. Cochran, 369 U.S. 506 (1962).

Betts, left dangling by a thread, was allowed to fall in 1963. A unanimous Court held that the Sixth Amendment right of assistance of counsel is incorporated in the Due Process Clause of the Fourteenth Amendment and applied against the states. GIDEON v. WAINWRIGHT, 372 U.S. 335. An indigent is also entitled to effective assistance of counsel for a first appeal. Douglas v. California, 372 U.S. 353 (1963); Evitts v. Lucey, 469 U.S. 387 (1985). Counsel is not required for additional appeals, such as a petition for certiorari to the U.S. Supreme Court. Ross v. Moffitt, 417 U.S. 600 (1974). For indigent defendants whose main defense is insanity, states are now required to appoint psychiatrists. Ake v. Oklahoma, 470 U.S. 68 (1985). States are not required to provide counsel to death-row inmates seeking postconviction relief. Murray v. Giarratano, 109 S.Ct. 2765 (1989).

The Supreme Court received great credit for issuing *Gideon,* yet it lagged behind many states that had already recognized that the government has a constitutional responsibility to provide counsel for indigents prosecuted by the state. The Supreme Court of Indiana in 1854 held that a "civilized community" could not put a citizen in jeopardy and withhold counsel from the poor. Webb v. Baird, 6 Ind. 13 (1854). In 1859, the Wisconsin Supreme Court called it a "mockery" to promise a pauper a fair trial and then tell him he must employ his own counsel. Carpenter v. Dane, 9 Wis.

249 (1859). Congress passed legislation in 1892 to provide counsel to represent poor persons and extended that provision in 1910. 27 Stat. 252 (1892); 36 Stat. 866 (1910).

No sooner had the Court finally forged a unanimous front to produce *Gideon* than it split on a case that still divides the nation. Danny Escobedo was held in police headquarters for questioning regarding the fatal shooting of his brother-in-law. Although he asked to see his lawyer, who was in the building, the police rejected his request and eventually obtained a damaging statement. The Court, divided 5–4, held that Escobedo had been denied the assistance of counsel in violation of the Sixth and Fourteenth Amendments. ESCOBEDO v. ILLINOIS, 378 U.S. 478 (1964).

Counsel is needed not only at trial but at "critical stages" of the proceedings against the accused. Because of the potential for prejudice and erroneous identifications at police lineups, an accused is entitled to have counsel present. United States v. Wade, 388 U.S. 218 (1967). This decision, announced less as a constitutional principle than as a rule of criminal procedure, allowed Congress to enter the arena and pass legislation stating that eyewitness testimony would be admissible as evidence in any criminal prosecution, regardless of whether the accused had an attorney present at the lineup. 82 Stat. 211 (1968); 18 U.S.C. § 3502 (1982).

The right to counsel exists at the time of a preliminary hearing. Coleman v. Alabama, 399 U.S. 1 (1970). Once adversary proceedings begin, an individual has a right to counsel when the government seeks incriminating testimony. Brewer v. Williams, 430 U.S. 387, 401 (1977). To deprive a person of counsel during the period before trial "may be more damaging than denial of counsel during the trial itself." Maine v. Moulton, 474 U.S. 159, 170 (1985). Under certain circumstances, a suspect may be brought before a witness for the purpose of identification without the assistance of counsel. Stovall v. Denno, 388 U.S. 293 (1967); Kirby v. Illinois, 406 U.S. 682 (1972). This is not allowed, however, if the prosecutor uses a suggestive manner in presenting a suspect to the witness. Moore v. Illinois, 434 U.S. 220 (1977).

Counsel is also required for post-trial proceedings, such as sentencing. Mempa v. Rhay, 389 U.S. 128 (1967). If a sentence involves some imprisonment, indigent persons are entitled to the assistance of counsel whether the offense is classified as felony, misdemeanor, or petty. Argersinger v. Hamlin, 407 U.S. 25 (1972); Scott v. Illinois, 440 U.S. 367 (1979). Recent cases have explored the criteria needed for "effective" assistance of counsel.[17] The Sixth Amendment right to counsel is not violated when an attorney refuses to cooperate with a defendant who wants to present perjured testimony. Nix v. Whiteside, 475 U.S. 157 (1986).

The *Miranda* Warning

Building on cases involving coerced confessions, self-incrimination, and right to counsel, the Supreme Court in 1966 handed down the controversial *Miranda* ruling. The decision announced a cluster of constitutional rights for defendants held in police custody and cut off from the outside world. The atmosphere and environment of incommunicado interrogation was held to be inherently intimidating and hostile to the privilege against self-incrimination. To prevent compulsion by law enforce-

---

[17]Burger v. Kemp, 483 U.S. 776 (1987); Strictland v. Washington, 466 U.S. 688 (1984); United States v. Cronic, 466 U.S. 648 (1984); Jones v. Barnes, 463 U.S. 745 (1983); Wainwright v. Torna, 455 U.S. 586 (1982); Cuyler v. Sullivan, 446 U.S. 335 (1980); Holloway v. Arkansas, 435 U.S. 475 (1978).

ment officials, the person in custody must be clearly informed—before interrogation—of the following: the right to remain silent, anything said may be used in court, the right to consult with an attorney and to have a lawyer present during interrogation, and the right to have a lawyer appointed if the accused is indigent. MIRANDA v. ARIZONA, 384 U.S. 436 (1966).

The decision did not rest solely on constitutional grounds. The Court invited Congress to contribute its handiwork: "Our decision in no way creates a constitutional straitjacket which will handicap sound efforts at reform, nor is it intended to have this effect. We encourage Congress and the States to continue their laudable search for increasingly effective ways of protecting the rights of the individual while promoting efficient enforcement of our criminal laws." Id. at 467. Congress passed legislation in 1968 to allow for the admissibility of confessions if voluntarily given. Trial judges would determine the issue of voluntariness after taking into consideration all the circumstances surrounding the confession, including five elements identified by Congress. 82 Stat. 210 (1968); 18 U.S.C. § 3501(a)(b) (1982). Courts apply these guidelines in determining voluntariness of confession, but may look to other factors that bear on voluntariness. United States v. Crocker, 510 F.2d 1129 (10th Cir. 1975); United States v. Brown, 557 F.2d 541, 548 n.5 (6th Cir. 1977).

Miranda has been bitterly attacked for restricting the efforts of law enforcement officials. During the Reagan administration, Attorney General Edwin Meese III urged that *Miranda* be overturned. However, the Supreme Court correctly noted that its holding was not "an innovation in our jurisprudence." 384 U.S. at 442. Indeed, *Miranda*-type warnings had been given routinely by federal agents in the past. McNabb v. United States, 318 U.S. 332, 336 (1943). They had been given by state officials, as the Court noted in *Michigan* v. *Tucker,* 417 U.S. 433, 447 (1974). Long before *Miranda,* state police recognized that an individual has a constitutional right to remain silent and that suspects must be told that anything said could be used against them in court. Haley v. Ohio, 332 U.S. 596, 598, 604 (1948).

Neither *Miranda* nor *Escobedo* were applied retroactively. Johnson v. New Jersey, 384 U.S. 719 (1966). When applied to future prosecutions, the reversal of a conviction because of a *Miranda* violation does not mean that the suspect goes free. The state can try the case again without the tainted evidence. Orozco v. Texas, 394 U.S. 324 (1969). Nevertheless, law enforcement officers reacted to *Miranda* as the end of justice. In time, they learned to live within its guidelines and discover some exceptions.

Since 1966, *Miranda* has been narrowed by an evergrowing number of exceptions. Although an accused's statement to police may be rendered inadmissible under *Miranda,* it can be used to impeach his credibility if he chooses to take the stand in his own defense. *Miranda* is not a license to commit perjury. Harris v. New York, 401 U.S. 222 (1971); Oregon v. Hass, 420 U.S. 714 (1975). If a defendant takes the stand, it is impermissible during cross-examination to ask why the person failed to supply certain information to the police after receiving *Miranda* warnings.[18] Silence cannot be penalized because the accused was advised in the *Miranda* warning that the right to remain silent will not be used against him. Wainwright v. Greenfield, 474 U.S. 284 (1986). If a defendant takes the stand and tells the jury a story that is inconsistent with what he told the police after being given *Miranda*

[18]Greer v. Miller, 483 U.S. 756 (1987); Doyle v. Ohio, 426 U.S. 610 (1976); United States v. Hale, 422 U.S. 171 (1975).

warnings, cross-examination may probe these conflicting statements. Anderson v. Charles, 447 U.S. 404 (1980).

In cases where *Miranda* rights are not read, silence after an arrest may be used to impeach a defendant's testimony. Fletcher v. Weir, 455 U.S. 603 (1982). Similarly, silence before an arrest may be used to impeach a defendant's testimony. Jenkins v. Anderson, 447 U.S. 231 (1980). If a defendant refuses to cooperate with the government's investigation into related crimes, courts may take that refusal into account when imposing sentence. Roberts v. United States, 445 U.S. 552 (1980).

The reach of the *Miranda* rule is circumscribed by specific conditions. It does not apply to testimony before a grand jury. United States v. Mandujano, 425 U.S. 564 (1976). It applies only after a person is taken into custody. The Court admits that the definition of custody is "a slippery one" and presents "murky and difficult questions" of when it begins. Oregon v. Elstad, 470 U.S. 298, 309, 316 (1985). Although a person in custody is entitled to *Miranda* rights regardless of the nature of the offense (felony or misdemeanor), there is no need to read these rights for routine roadside stops by traffic cops. Berkemer v. McCarty, 468 U.S. 420 (1984). Moreover, if incriminating information can be obtained before a person is taken into custody and given the *Miranda* warning, the information is admissible as evidence. Oregon v. Mathiason, 429 U.S. 492 (1977). Police therefore have an incentive to talk to a suspect without placing him under arrest and reading the *Miranda* rights, in the hopes of uncovering incriminating evidence or eliciting a confession. California v. Beheler, 463 U.S. 1121 (1983). Convicted felons who are required to report to probation officers and be truthful "in all matters" are not considered "in custody." Therefore, any statements they make of an incriminating nature may be used against them in court. Minnesota v. Murphy, 465 U.S. 420 (1984).

Even after a person is in custody and advised of his *Miranda* rights, police officers may engage in a conversation between themselves that leads to an incriminating statement from the suspect. Such conversations are permissible if they are not "interrogations" (questioning intended to elicit an incriminating response). Rhode Island v. Innis, 446 U.S. 291 (1980). How do the courts distinguish between conversations and interrogations and decide whether the police intended to produce an incriminating response?

Police questioning may expand for other reasons. After a suspect is given a *Miranda* warning and declines to comment, police may suspend questioning for a "significant" period, give another warning, and obtain incriminating information that is admissible as evidence. Michigan v. Mosley, 423 U.S. 96 (1975). Once an accused asks for counsel, the police may not return and interrogate him without counsel unless he voluntarily "initiates" the communication. Edwards v. Arizona, 451 U.S. 477 (1981).[19]

In a major weakening of the *Miranda* doctrine in 1985, the Court held that if police officers violate *Miranda* procedures by obtaining a confession before reading a suspect his rights, the mistake may be cured by reading the rights later and

---

[19]See also Michigan v. Jackson, 475 U.S. 625 (1986); Shea v. Louisiana, 470 U.S. 51 (1985); Smith v. Illinois, 469 U.S. 91 (1984); Solem v. Stumes, 465 U.S. 638 (1984); Wyrick v. Fields, 459 U.S. 42 (1982). Further refinements depend on what kind of communication the accused "initiates": a substantive discussion about the crime or merely a routine request for a drink of water or use of the telephone. Oregon v. Bradshaw, 462 U.S. 1039 (1983). A refusal to make a written statement without counsel need not be interpreted to exclude an oral statement that is incriminating. Connecticut v. Barrett, 479 U.S. 523 (1987). See also Colorado v. Spring, 479 U.S. 564 (1987).

obtaining a confession a second time. The suspect, having let the "cat out of the bag" with the first confession, may be more inclined to repeat it. OREGON v. ELSTAD, 470 U.S. 298 (1985). A year later, the Court held that *Miranda* protects the rights of the accused, not the attorney. The police may therefore deceive the latter. Moran v. Burbine, 475 U.S. 412 (1986). Also in 1986, the Court clarified that the involuntariness of a confession after a *Miranda* warning derives only from police coercion, not from a defendant's mental condition (such as being told by the "voice of God" to confess). Colorado v. Connolly, 479 U.S. 157 (1986).

There is also a "public safety" exception to the *Miranda* rule. Its literal language may be waived if there is concern for the public safety. Thus, when an officer frisks a suspect and discovers an empty shoulder holster, it is appropriate to ask where the gun is before making formal arrest and reading the *Miranda* rights. New York v. Quarles, 467 U.S. 649 (1984). Moreover, a 5–4 Court decided that the warning need not be given in the exact form described in *Miranda*, but simply must reasonably convey to a suspect his rights. Thus, informing a suspect that an attorney would be appointed for him "if and when you go to court" does not render the warning inadequate. Duckworth v. Eagan, 109 S.Ct. 2875 (1989).

THE EIGHTH AMENDMENT

The Eighth Amendment, borrowing language from the English Bill of Rights of 1689, provides that "Excessive bail shall not be required, nor excessive fines imposed, nor cruel and unusual punishments inflicted." The first two clauses produce relatively few cases for the Supreme Court. The last six words have generated a massive caseload on the death penalty that is extraordinarily complex and divisive.

Excessive Bail

To gain freedom while awaiting trial, a defendant may have to put up money for a bail bond to guarantee his presence at the trial. Meeting bail allows the accused to prepare a defense and prevents the infliction of punishment prior to conviction. Excessive bail destroys both rights. The level of bail is monitored by criminal rules adopted by Congress (Rule 46) and occasional judicial rulings. Stack v. Boyle, 342 U.S. 1 (1952).

Bail may be denied totally for capital cases. Even for noncapital cases there are instances where bail is refused. Carlson v. Landon, 342 U.S. 524 (1952). In 1966, Congress passed legislation to remove the inequity of holding persons too poor to raise bail. Defendants charged with noncapital offenses shall be released on their own "personal recognizance" unless a court determines that release will not assure the defendant's later appearance in court. 80 Stat. 214 (1966); 18 U.S.C. §§ 3141–3156 (1982). Additional legislation in 1984 requires courts to keep suspects in jail if the government demonstrates by clear and convincing evidence that release will not "reasonably assure" the safety of the community. 98 Stat. 1978–1980. This statute on pretrial detention ("preventive detention") was upheld in *United States* v. *Salerno*, 481 U.S. 739 (1987). The question of excessive bail is sometimes addressed not in terms of the Eighth Amendment but on grounds of equal protection and due process. Schilb v. Kuebel, 404 U.S. 357 (1971).

Excessive Fines

This section of the Constitution is rarely litigated. Ex parte Watkins, 7 Pet. 568 (1833). In contemporary times, the question of excessive fines is more likely attacked under the Equal Protection and Due Process Clauses. In 1970, the Supreme Court unanimously struck down on equal protection grounds a state statute that subjected indigents to additional imprisonment if they failed to pay a fine. Williams v. Illinois, 399 U.S. 235 (1970). See also Tate v. Short, 401 U.S. 395 (1971).

A 7–2 ruling by the Supreme Court in 1989 held that the Excessive Fines Clause does not protect businesses against multi-million dollar awards of punitive damages in civil disputes between private parties. The Clause is restricted to cases in which the government prosecutes a case and has an interest in recovering damages. Every member of the Court (the majority opinion by Blackmun, the concurrence by Brennan and Marshall, and the partial dissent by O'Connor and Stevens) indicated that punitive damage awards may still be limited under the Due Process Clause of the Fourteenth Amendment. Browning-Ferris Industries v. Kelco Disposal, 109 S.Ct. 2909 (1989).

Cruel and Unusual Punishments

The meaning of "cruel and unusual" varies from one American culture to another. A congressional statute in 1790 required the death penalty for forgery. 1 Stat. 115, § 14. Today, that penalty is considered disproportionate to the crime. In 1879, the Supreme Court decided that public shooting was not cruel and unusual, although forms of torture (dragged to the place of execution, embowelled alive, beheaded, quartered, or burned alive) exceeded constitutional limits. Wilkerson v. Utah, 99 U.S. 130 (1879). The framers would have regarded electrocution as "unusual," if not inconceivable, but in 1890 the Court found it constitutionally inoffensive. In re Kemmler, 136 U.S. 436 (1890). Throughout this period the Court held consistently that the states were not bound by the Eighth Amendment.[20]

Even for most of the twentieth century, the Eighth Amendment added little to the Supreme Court's docket. It invoked the amendment in 1910 to strike down the sentence of someone given fifteen years at hard labor and kept in chains day and night for falsifying a public document. The Court said that punishment must be graduated and proportioned to the offense committed. Weems v. United States, 217 U.S. 349 (1910). In 1947, the Court held that the states could try a second time to electrocute someone after it had bungled the first effort. To the 5–4 majority, a second attempt violated neither the Double Jeopardy Clause nor the Cruel and Unusual Punishment Clause. Francis v. Resweber, 329 U.S. 459 (1947).

The extent to which "cruel and unusual" is culturally determined and varies with the times can be seen in two cases decided in 1958 and 1962. In the first, the Court interpreted the Eighth Amendment in light of the "evolving standards of decency that mark the progress of a maturing society." Trop v. Dulles, 356 U.S. 86, 101 (1958). Stripping a native-born American of his citizenship because of wartime desertion constituted cruel and unusual punishment. Four years later the Court, guided by "contemporary human knowledge," decided that it was cruel and

---

[20]O'Neil v. Vermont, 144 U.S. 323 (1892); In re Kemmler, 136 U.S. 436 (1890); Pervear v. The Commonwealth, 5 Wall. (72 U.S.) 475 (1867).

unusual to punish someone for the mere status of being a narcotics addict when the person was not under the influence of narcotics at the time of arrest. Robinson v. California, 370 U.S. 660, 666 (1962). This decision incorporated the Cruel and Unusual Punishment Clause into the Fourteenth Amendment and applied it to the states. In 1968, the Court refused to extend the narcotics decision to strike down a conviction for public drunkenness. It distinguished being drunk in public from the general status of having a narcotics addiction. Powell v. Texas, 392 U.S. 514, 532 (1968).

The overwhelming number of cases on the Eighth Amendment have been decided since 1970. In a series of cases from 1970 to 1973, the Court held that a guilty plea is not invalid or coerced simply because the accused wants to avoid a possible death penalty.[21] In 1971, the Court handed down the first of many long-winded, discursive explorations of the death penalty, deciding in this case that juries could be given absolute discretion to choose between life imprisonment and death, and that juries can decide both guilt and punishment (death) in a single unitary proceeding. Due process did not require a bifurcated trial. McGautha v. California, 402 U.S. 183 (1971).

The number of prisoners executed declined sharply in the 1950s and 1960s. By the late 1960s and early 1970s, there were no persons executed in any of the states. In 1972, the Supreme Court of California declared the death penalty a violation of the state constitutional ban against cruel or unusual punishments. Within nine months, however, the voters of California amended the state constitution to reinstate the death penalty. People v. Anderson, 493 P.2d 880 (Cal. 1972), cert. denied, 406 U.S. 958 (1972); Cal. Const. Art. I, § 27.

In 1972, the Court abruptly struck down death-penalty statutes in Georgia and Texas as cruel and unusual. A brief one-page per curiam—announcing the result— served as a preface for over two hundred pages of concurrences and dissents. Only two Justices (Brennan and Marshall) regarded the death penalty unconstitutional in all cases. The opinions for the 5–4 majority focused on the arbitrariness and inequalities in state practices: the increasing rarity of executions and the application of that punishment to blacks more than whites, to men more than women, and to the poor more than the rich. FURMAN v. GEORGIA, 408 U.S. 238 (1972).

The Court's holding ran counter to explicit language in the Constitution, which acknowledges the death penalty four times. The Fifth Amendment requires a presentment or indictment by grand jury for persons accused of a "capital, or otherwise infamous crime." The Double Jeopardy Clause refers to taking "life or limb." Also in the Fifth Amendment, no person shall be deprived of "life, liberty, or property" without due process of law. Under the Fourteenth Amendment, no state shall deprive any person of "life, liberty, or property" without due process of law. One could argue that *acknowledging* the death penalty in the Constitution does not mandate it or even favor it.

Following the *Furman* decision, the majority of states immediately reinstituted the death penalty for certain kinds of crime. This public endorsement of capital punishment put pressure on the Court to modify *Furman*. In the first of five decisions handed down on July 2, 1976, the Court reviewed the changes in Georgia's statute following *Furman* and upheld, 7–2, the new procedure. GREGG v. GEORGIA, 428

---

[21]Tollett v. Henderson, 411 U.S. 258 (1973); North Carolina v. Alford, 400 U.S. 25 (1970); Parker v. North Carolina, 397 U.S. 790 (1970); Brady v. North Carolina, 397 U.S. 742 (1970).

U.S. 153 (1976). The Court noted that the position of Justices Brennan and Marshall in *Furman* that the Eighth Amendment prohibits the death penalty had been "undercut substantially" by state actions from 1972 to 1976 to enact statutes calling for the death penalty. Id. at 179. Moreover, in 1974 Congress enacted legislation providing the death penalty for aircraft piracy that results in death. Id. at 179–180. The "evolving standards of decency" (Warren's language in *Trop* v. *Dulles*) still tolerated and supported executions. In this and the companion cases, the Court attempted to identify the factors and criteria that are necessary for states to invoke the death penalty. Proffitt v. Florida, 428 U.S. 242 (1976); Jurek v. Texas, 428 U.S. 262 (1976); Woodson v. North Carolina, 428 U.S. 280 (1976); Roberts v. Louisiana, 428 U.S. 325 (1976). However, cases since 1976 demonstrate repeatedly that the Court has been unable to eliminate arbitrariness from death sentences. A recent study identified 350 cases during the twentieth century in which defendants convicted of capital or potentially capital crimes, and in many cases sentenced to death, were later found to be innocent. Bedau & Radelet, 40 Stan. L. Rev. 31 (1987).

Although the death penalty is once again available, executions are often postponed or avoided because the Court finds defects in sentencing procedures or discovers due process problems.[22] In other cases the Court affirms a sentence of death.[23] The Court has gradually broadened the scope of the death penalty to include not only those who intend to kill but those who serve as accomplices to a murder. Compare Tison v. Arizona, 481 U.S. 137 (1987) with Cabana v. Bullock, 474 U.S. 376 (1986) and Enmund v. Florida, 458 U.S. 782 (1982).

At times, the Court decides whether executions are justified for a certain class of crimes. In 1977, it found the death penalty disproportionate punishment for the crime of raping an adult woman. The gradual abandonment of that penalty by most states was accepted by the Court as persuasive evidence of contemporary public judgment. Coker v. Georgia, 433 U.S. 584, 593–596 (1977). Under the principle of proportionality, life imprisonment for certain nonviolent crimes contravenes the Eighth Amendment. Solem v. Helm, 463 U.S. 277 (1983).

In affirming a death sentence, state courts are not required to compare the sentence to others to determine if it is disproportionate. The Court tolerates what it calls "aberrational outcomes" in the application of the death penalty. Pulley v. Harris, 465 U.S. 37, 54 (1984). The Court has held that the execution of prisoners who are insane violates the Eighth Amendment. Ford v. Wainwright, 477 U.S. 399 (1986). The issue of executing the retarded or mentally incapacitated continues to divide the nation. A 5–4 decision by the Supreme Court in 1989 held that the Eighth Amendment does not categorically bar execution of the mentally retarded. The majority cited a lack of "objective indicators" from society to prohibit such

[22]South Carolina v. Gathers, 109 S.Ct. 2207 (1989); Mills v. Maryland, 108 S.Ct. 1860 (1988); Satterwhite v. Texas, 108 S.Ct. 1792 (1988); Booth v. Maryland, 482 U.S. 496 (1987); Skipper v. South Carolina, 476 U.S. 1 (1986); Caldwell v. Mississippi, 472 U.S. 320 (1985); Eddings v. Oklahoma, 455 U.S. 104 (1982); Godfrey v. Georgia, 446 U.S. 420 (1980); Bell v. Ohio, 438 U.S. 637 (1978); Lockett v. Ohio, 438 U.S. 586 (1978); Roberts v. Louisiana, 431 U.S. 633 (1977); Gardner v. Florida, 430 U.S. 349 (1977). A separate issue is the exclusion of jurors who are unwilling or unable to take an oath that a mandatory death penalty or life imprisonment will not affect their deliberations. This practice was struck down in Witherspoon v. Illinois, 391 U.S. 510 (1968) and Adams v. Texas, 448 U.S. 38 (1980).

[23]California v. Brown, 479 U.S. 538 (1987); Baldwin v. Alabama, 472 U.S. 372 (1985); Wainwright v. Witt, 469 U.S. 412 (1985); Spaziano v. Florida, 468 U.S. 447 (1984); Sullivan v. Wainwright, 464 U.S. 109 (1983); California v. Ramos, 463 U.S. 992 (1983); Barclay v. Florida, 463 U.S. 939 (1983); Barefoot v. Estelle, 463 U.S. 880 (1983).

executions. The "clearest and most reliable objective evidence of contemporary values," it said, are the statutes passed by legislative bodies in this country. The Court also looked to data concerning the actions of sentencing jurors. Penry v. Lynaugh, 109 S.Ct. 2934, 2953 (1989).

Statistics demonstrate that the death penalty is applied disproportionately to blacks who kill whites, compared to whites who kill blacks or each race killing one of its own. Nevertheless, the Court refused in 1987 to find a constitutional violation to this pattern. Discretion in sentencing need not mean discrimination. Discretionary judgments by jurors, even when they reveal a strong racial bias at an aggregate level, did not convince the Court that racial discrimination exists for a *particular* case. The Court held that legislatures are better qualified to evaluate and respond to statistical studies regarding racial discrimination in sentencing. McCLESKEY v. KEMP, 481 U.S. 278, 319 (1987). In response to this decision, Congress is considering legislation that would create a federal right to be free from race discrimination in cases of capital punishment. 135 Cong. Rec. E1880–1882 (daily ed. May 24, 1989). See also Turner v. Murray, 476 U.S. 1463 (1986).

Congress has considered a number of bills to establish procedures for imposing the death penalty. At the time of *Furman* v. *Georgia* (1972), federal law authorized capital punishment for such crimes as espionage and treason. Congress tried to pass legislation to remove arbitrary and capricious results. Although the Senate has passed such legislation, the House of Representatives has not supported these measures. S. Rept. No. 98–251, 98th Cong., 1st Sess. (1983); S. Rept. No. 99–282, 99th Cong., 2d Sess. (1986). In 1988, Congress passed legislation to provide constitutional procedures for implementing the death penalty in cases involving certain drug-related murders and the killing of law enforcement officers. 102 Stat. 4387 (1988). The record shows that questions of the death penalty are largely in the hands of legislatures and public opinion (see the views of retired Justice Powell, pp. 862–863).

Questions of cruel and unusual punishment sometimes concern unusually heavy sentences. The Supreme Court held that conviction for three felonies totaling $229.11 could be punished by a mandatory life sentence. Rummel v. Estelle, 445 U.S. 263 (1980). Following the policy of deferring to the legislature for the level of punishment, the Court sustained a forty-year sentence for someone convicted for possessing and selling marijuana. Hutto v. Davis, 454 U.S. 370 (1982).

To correct vast inequities and disparities in sentencing, Congress created a Sentencing Commission in 1984 and received its recommendations in 1987. The recommendations became law when Congress failed to disapprove them within a specified time period. Because of the composition of the Commission (a mixture of judges and nonjudges subject to removal from the Commission by the President), and because the recommendations became law without any congressional action, suits were filed raising a number of constitutional issues. In 1989, the Court upheld the Sentencing Commission and the procedure used to enact its recommendations into law. Justice Scalia was the sole dissenter in this 8–1 decision, which not only upheld the delegation of legislative authority to the Commission and the assignment of extrajudicial duties to judges, but also endorsed the creation of independent agencies that are not directly under the President's control. Mistretta v. United States, 109 S.Ct. 647 (1989).

[For criminal procedures regarding juveniles (including the death penalty) and the rights of prisoners, see Chapter 16.]

Selected Readings

BAKER, LIVA. *Miranda: Crime, Law and Politics*. New York: Atheneum, 1983.

BEDAU, HUGO ADAM, ed. *The Death Penalty in America*. New York: Oxford University Press, 1982.

BLACK, CHARLES L. *Capital Punishment: The Inevitability of Caprice and Mistake*. New York: Norton, 1974.

CLARK, LEROY D. *The Grand Jury: The Use and Abuse of Political Power*. New York: Quadrangle, 1975.

CLARK, RAMSEY. *Crime in America*. New York: Simon and Schuster, 1970.

EDWARDS, GEORGE J., JR. *The Grand Jury*. New York: AMS Press, 1973. Originally published in 1906.

FELLMAN, DAVID. *The Defendant's Rights Today*. Madison: University of Wisconsin Press, 1976.

FRANKEL, MARVIN E., AND GARY P. NAFTALIS. *The Grand Jury*. New York: Hill and Wang, 1975.

GOLDSTEIN, ABRAHAM S. *The Passive Judiciary: Prosecutorial Discretion and the Guilty Plea*. Baton Rouge: Louisiana State University Press, 1981.

GRAHAM, FRED P. *The Self-Inflicted Wound*. New York: Macmillan, 1970.

LEVY, LEONARD W. *Origins of the Fifth Amendment*. New York: Macmillan, 1986.

———. *Against the Law: The Nixon Court and Criminal Justice*. New York: Harper Torchbooks, 1976.

LEWIS, ANTHONY. *Gideon's Trumpet*. New York: Vintage, 1964.

MANSFIELD, JOHN H. "The Albertson Case: Conflict between the Privilege Against Self-Incrimination and the Government's Need for Information." 1966 *Supreme Court Review* 103.

MEDALIE, RICHARD J. *From Escobedo to Miranda: The Anatomy of a Supreme Court Decision*. Washington, D.C.: Lerner Law Book Co., 1966.

MELTSNER, MICHAEL. *Cruel and Unusual: The Supreme Court and Capital Punishment*. New York: William Morrow, 1974.

POLSBY, DANIEL D. "The Death of Capital Punishment? Furman v. Georgia." 1972 *Supreme Court Review* 1.

ROSSUM, RALPH A. *The Politics of the Criminal Justice System: An Organizational Analysis*. New York: Marcel Dekker, 1978.

SEIDMAN, LOUIS MICHAEL. "The Supreme Court, Entrapment, and Our Criminal Justice Dilemma." 1981 *Supreme Court Review* 111.

SELLIN, THORSTEN. *The Penalty of Death*. Beverly Hills, Calif.: Sage Publications, 1980.

SIGLER, JAY A. *Double Jeopardy: The Development of a Legal and Social Policy*. Ithaca, N.Y.: Cornell University Press, 1969.

SPERLICH, PETER W. "Trial by Jury: It May Have a Future." 1978 *Supreme Court Review* 191.

STEPHENS, OTIS H., JR. *The Supreme Court and Confessions of Guilt*. Knoxville: University of Tennessee Press, 1973.

WAY, H. FRANK. *Criminal Justice and the American Constitution*. North Scituate, Mass.: Duxbury Press, 1980.

WESTEN, PETER, AND RICHARD DRUBEL. "Toward a General Theory of Double Jeopardy." 1978 *Supreme Court Review* 81.

YASUDA, TED K. "Entrapment as a Due Process Defense: Developments after *Hampton* v. *United States*." 57 *Indiana Law Journal* 89 (1982).

YOUNGER, RICHARD D. *The People's Panel: The Grand Jury in the United States, 1634–1941*. Providence, R.I.: Brown University Press, 1963.

Powell v. Alabama

287 U.S. 45 (1932)

In this famous trial known as the "Scottsboro Case," black youths in Alabama were charged with raping two white girls. The boys were found guilty and given the death sentence. The case involves basic questions of due process, including the right to a fair trial, assistance of counsel, and the exclusion of blacks from the jury.

MR. JUSTICE SUTHERLAND delivered the opinion of the Court.

These cases were argued together and submitted for decision as one case.

The petitioners, hereinafter referred to as defendants, are negroes charged with the crime of rape, committed upon the persons of two white girls. The crime is said to have been committed on

March 25, 1931. The indictment was returned in a state court of first instance on March 31, and the record recites that on the same day the defendants were arraigned and entered pleas of not guilty. There is a further recital to the effect that upon the arraignment they were represented by counsel. But no counsel had been employed, and aside from a statement made by the trial judge several days later during a colloquy immediately preceding the trial, the record does not disclose when, or under what circumstances, an appointment of counsel was made, or who was appointed. During the colloquy referred to, the trial judge, in response to a question, said that he had appointed all the members of the bar for the purpose of arraigning the defendants and then of course anticipated that the members of the bar would continue to help the defendants if no counsel appeared. Upon the argument here both sides accepted that as a correct statement of the facts concerning the matter.

There was a severance upon the request of the state, and the defendants were tried in three several groups, as indicated above. As each of the three cases was called for trial, each defendant was arraigned, and, having the indictment read to him, entered a plea of not guilty. Whether the original arraignment and pleas were regarded as ineffective is not shown. Each of the three trials was completed within a single day. Under the Alabama statute the punishment for rape is to be fixed by the jury, and in its discretion may be from ten years imprisonment to death. The juries found defendants guilty and imposed the death penalty upon all. The trial court overruled motions for new trials and sentenced the defendants in accordance with the verdicts. The judgments were affirmed by the state supreme court. Chief Justice Anderson thought the defendants had not been accorded a fair trial and strongly dissented. 224 Ala. 524; *id.* 531; *id.* 540; 141 So. 215, 195, 201.

In this court the judgments are assailed upon the grounds that the defendants, and each of them, were denied due process of law and the equal protection of the laws, in contravention of the Fourteenth Amendment, specifically as follows: (1) they were not given a fair, impartial and deliberate trial; (2) they were denied the right of counsel, with the accustomed incidents of consul-

tation and opportunity of preparation for trial; and (3) they were tried before juries from which qualified members of their own race were systematically excluded. These questions were properly raised and saved in the courts below.

The only one of the assignments which we shall consider is the second, in respect of the denial of counsel; and it becomes unnecessary to discuss the facts of the case or the circumstances surrounding the prosecution except in so far as they reflect light upon that question.

The record shows that on the day when the offense is said to have been committed, these defendants, together with a number of other negroes, were upon a freight train on its way through Alabama. On the same train were seven white boys and the two white girls. A fight took place between the negroes and the white boys, in the course of which the white boys, with the exception of one named Gilley, were thrown off the train. A message was sent ahead, reporting the fight and asking that every negro be gotten off the train. The participants in the fight, and the two girls, were in an open gondola car. The two girls testified that each of them was assaulted by six different negroes in turn, and they identified the seven defendants as having been among the number. None of the white boys was called to testify, with the exception of Gilley, who was called in rebuttal.

Before the train reached Scottsboro, Alabama, a sheriff's posse seized the defendants and two other negroes. Both girls and the negroes then were taken to Scottsboro, the county seat. Word of their coming and of the alleged assault had preceded them, and they were met at Scottsboro by a large crowd. It does not sufficiently appear that the defendants were seriously threatened with, or that they were actually in danger of, mob violence; but it does appear that the attitude of the community was one of great hostility. . . . It is perfectly apparent that the proceedings, from beginning to end, took place in an atmosphere of tense, hostile and excited public sentiment. During the entire time, the defendants were closely confined or were under military guard. The record does not disclose their ages, except that one of them was nineteen; but the record clearly indicates that most, if not all, of them were youthful, and they are constantly referred to as "the boys." They were ignorant and illiterate. All of them were residents of other states, where alone members of their families or friends resided.

However guilty defendants, upon due inquiry, might prove to have been, they were, until convicted, presumed to be innocent. It was the duty of the court having their cases in charge to see that they were denied no necessary incident of a fair trial. With any error of the state court involving alleged contravention of the state statutes or constitution we, of course, have nothing to do. The sole inquiry which we are permitted to make is whether the federal Constitution was contravened (*Rogers* v. *Peck*, 199 U.S. 425, 434; *Hebert* v. *Louisiana*, 272 U.S. 312, 316); and as to that, we confine ourselves, as already suggested, to the inquiry whether the defendants were in substance denied the right of counsel, and if so, whether such denial infringes the due process clause of the Fourteenth Amendment.

First. The record shows that immediately upon the return of the indictment defendants were arraigned and pleaded not guilty. Apparently they were not asked whether they had, or were able to employ, counsel, or wished to have counsel appointed; or whether they had friends or relatives who might assist in that regard if communicated with. That it would not have been an idle ceremony to have given the defendants reasonable opportunity to communicate with their families and endeavor to obtain counsel is demonstrated by the fact that, very soon after conviction, able counsel appeared in their behalf. This was pointed out by Chief Justice Anderson in the course of his dissenting opinion. "They were non-residents," he said, "and had little time or opportunity to get in touch with their families and friends who were scattered throughout two other states, and time has demonstrated that they could or would have been represented by able counsel had a better opportunity been given by a reasonable delay in the trial of the cases, judging from the number and activity of counsel that appeared immediately or shortly after their conviction." 224 Ala., at pp. 554–555; 141 So. 201.

It is hardly necessary to say that, the right to counsel being conceded, a defendant should be afforded a fair opportunity to secure counsel of his own choice. Not only was that not done here,

but such designation of counsel as was attempted was either so indefinite or so close upon the trial as to amount to a denial of effective and substantial aid in that regard. . . .

It thus will be seen that until the very morning of the trial no lawyer had been named or definitely designated to represent the defendants. Prior to that time, the trial judge had "appointed all the members of the bar" for the limited "purpose of arraigning the defendants." Whether they would represent the defendants thereafter if no counsel appeared in their behalf, was a matter of speculation only, or, as the judge indicated, of mere anticipation on the part of the court. Such a designation, even if made for all purposes, would, in our opinion, have fallen far short of meeting, in any proper sense, a requirement for the appointment of counsel. How many lawyers were members of the bar does not appear; but, in the very nature of things, whether many or few, they would not, thus collectively named, have been given that clear appreciation of responsibility or impressed with that individual sense of duty which should and naturally would accompany the appointment of a selected member of the bar, specifically named and assigned.

. . . The defendants, young, ignorant, illiterate, surrounded by hostile sentiment, haled back and forth under guard of soldiers, charged with an atrocious crime regarded with especial horror in the community where they were to be tried, were thus put in peril of their lives within a few moments after counsel for the first time charged with any degree of responsibility began to represent them.

. . .

Second. The Constitution of Alabama provides that in all criminal prosecutions the accused shall enjoy the right to have the assistance of counsel; and a state statute requires the court in a capital case, where the defendant is unable to employ counsel, to appoint counsel for him. The state supreme court held that these provisions had not been infringed, and with that holding we are powerless to interfere. The question, however, which it is our duty, and within our power, to decide, is whether the denial of the assistance of counsel contravenes the due process clause of the

Fourteenth Amendment to the federal Constitution.

[Under English common law, a person charged with treason or felony was generally denied the aid of counsel, but parties in civil cases and persons accused of misdemeanors were entitled to the full assistance of counsel. At least twelve of the thirteen colonies rejected the English common law and recognized the right to counsel for most criminal prosecutions. After reviewing this history, the Court turned to the elements of due process and a fair hearing.]

What, then, does a hearing include? Historically and in practice, in our own country at least, it has always included the right to the aid of counsel when desired and provided by the party asserting the right. The right to be heard would be, in many cases, of little avail if it did not comprehend the right to be heard by counsel. Even the intelligent and educated layman has small and sometimes no skill in the science of law. If charged with crime, he is incapable, generally, of determining for himself whether the indictment is good or bad. He is unfamiliar with the rules of evidence. Left without the aid of counsel he may be put on trial without a proper charge, and convicted upon incompetent evidence, or evidence irrelevant to the issue or otherwise inadmissible. He lacks both the skill and knowledge adequately to prepare his defense, even though he have a perfect one. He requires the guiding hand of counsel at every step in the proceedings against him. Without it, though he be not guilty, he faces the danger of conviction because he does not know how to establish his innocence. If that be true of men of intelligence, how much more true is it of the ignorant and illiterate, or those of feeble intellect. If in any case, civil or criminal, a state or federal court were arbitrarily to refuse to hear a party by counsel, employed by and appearing for him, it reasonably may not be doubted that such a refusal would be a denial of a hearing, and, therefore, of due process in the constitutional sense.

. . .

In the light of the facts outlined in the forepart of this opinion—the ignorance and illiteracy of the defendants, their youth, the circumstances of public hostility, the imprisonment and the close surveillance of the defendants by the military forces, the fact that their friends and families were all in other states and communication with them necessarily difficult, and above all that they stood in deadly peril of their lives—we think the failure of the trial court to give them reasonable time and opportunity to secure counsel was a clear denial of due process.

But passing that, and assuming their inability, even if opportunity had been given, to employ counsel, as the trial court evidently did assume, we are of opinion that, under the circumstances just stated, the necessity of counsel was so vital and imperative that the failure of the trial court to make an effective appointment of counsel was likewise a denial of due process within the meaning of the Fourteenth Amendment. Whether this would be so in other criminal prosecutions, or under other circumstances, we need not determine. All that it is necessary now to decide, as we do decide, is that in a capital case, where the defendant is unable to employ counsel, and is incapable adequately of making his own defense because of ignorance, feeble mindedness, illiteracy, or the like, it is the duty of the court, whether requested or not, to assign counsel for him as a necessary requisite of due process of law; and that duty is not discharged by an assignment at such a time or under such circumstances as to preclude the giving of effective aid in the preparation and trial of the case. . . .

The judgments must be reversed and the causes remanded for further proceedings not inconsistent with this opinion.

Judgments reversed.

MR. JUSTICE BUTLER, dissenting.

The Court, putting aside—they are utterly without merit—all other claims that the constitutional rights of petitioners were infringed, grounds its opinion and judgment upon a single assertion of fact. It is that petitioners "were denied the right of counsel, with the accustomed incidents of consultation and opportunity of preparation for trial." . . .

The record wholly fails to reveal that petitioners have been deprived of any right guaranteed by the Federal Constitution, and I am of opinion that the judgment should be affirmed.

MR. JUSTICE MCREYNOLDS concurs in this opinion.

Ballew v. Georgia

435 U.S. 223 (1978)

In 1972, in *Apodaca* v. *Oregon*, the Supreme Court decided that jury verdicts in the states need not be unanimous as in federal courts. The Court also had to resolve questions about the *size* of a jury. *Williams* v. *Florida* (1970) determined that jury trials in the states need not follow the common-law number of twelve. Could it be six? Less than six? What was the magic minimum number for a constitutional trial by jury?

MR. JUSTICE BLACKMUN announced the judgment of the Court and delivered an opinion in which MR. JUSTICE STEVENS joined.

This case presents the issue whether a state criminal trial to a jury of only five persons deprives the accused of the right to trial by jury guaranteed to him by the Sixth and Fourteenth Amendments. Our resolution of the issue requires an application of principles enunciated in *Williams* v. *Florida*, 399 U.S. 78 (1970), where the use of a six-person jury in a state criminal trial was upheld against similar constitutional attack.

I

In November 1973 petitioner Claude Davis Ballew was the manager of the Paris Adult Theatre at 320 Peachtree Street, Atlanta, Ga. On November 9 two investigators from the Fulton County Solicitor General's office viewed at the theater a motion picture film entitled "Behind the Green Door." Record 46–48, 90. After they had seen the film, they obtained a warrant for its seizure, returned to the theater, viewed the film once again, and seized it. *Id.*, at 48–50, 91. Petitioner and a cashier were arrested. Investigators returned to the theater on November 26, viewed the film in its entirety, secured still another warrant, and on November 27 once again viewed the motion picture and seized a second copy of the film. *Id.*, at 53–55.

On September 14, 1974, petitioner was charged in a two-count misdemeanor accusation with

"distributing obscene materials in violation of Georgia Code Section 26–2101 in that the said accused did, knowing the obscene nature thereof, exhibit a motion picture film entitled 'Behind the Green Door' that contained obscene and indecent scenes. . . ." App. 4–6.

Petitioner was brought to trial in the Criminal Court of Fulton County. After a jury of 5 persons had been selected and sworn, petitioner moved that the court impanel a jury of 12 persons. Record 37–38. That court, however, tried its misdemeanor cases before juries of five persons pursuant to Ga. Const., Art. 6 § 16, ¶1, codified as Ga. Code § 2–5101 (1975), and to 1890–1891 Ga. Laws, No. 278, pp. 937–938, and 1935 Ga. Laws, No. 38, p. 498. Petitioner contended that for an obscenity trial, a jury of only five was constitutionally inadequate to assess the contemporary standards of the community. Record 13, 38. He also argued that the Sixth and Fourteenth Amendments required a jury of at least six members in criminal cases. *Id.*, at 38.

The motion for a 12-person jury was overruled, and the trial went on to its conclusion before the 5-person jury that had been impaneled. At the conclusion of the trial, the jury deliberated for 38 minutes and returned a verdict of guilty on both counts of the accusation. *Id.*, at 205–208. The court imposed a sentence of one year and a $1,000 fine on each count, the periods of incarceration to run concurrently and to be suspended upon payment of the fines. *Id.*, at 16–17, 209. After a subsequent hearing, the court denied an amended motion for a new trial.

Petitioner took an appeal to the Court of Appeals of the State of Georgia. There he argued: First, the evidence was insufficient. Second, the trial court committed several First Amendment errors, namely, that the film as a matter of law was not obscene, and that the jury instructions incorrectly explained the standard of scienter, the definition of obscenity, and the scope of community standards. Third, the seizures of the films were illegal. Fourth, the convictions on both counts had placed petitioner in double jeopardy because he had shown only one motion picture. Fifth, the use of the five-member jury deprived him of his Sixth and Fourteenth Amendment right to a trial by jury. *Id.*, at 222–224.

The Court of Appeals rejected petitioner's contentions. 138 Ga. App. 530, 227 S. E. 2d 65 (1976). . . . In its consideration of the five-person-jury issue, the court noted that *Williams* v. *Florida* had not established a constitutional minimum number of jurors. Absent a holding by this Court that a five-person jury was constitutionally inadequate, the Court of Appeals considered itself bound by *Sanders* v. *State*, 234 Ga. 586, 216 S. E. 2d 838 (1975), cert. denied, 424 U. S. 931 (1976), where the constitutionality of the five-person jury had been upheld. The court also cited the earlier case of *McIntyre* v. *State*, 190 Ga. 872, 11 S. E. 2d 5 (1940), a holding to the same general effect but without elaboration.

The Supreme Court of Georgia denied certiorari. App. 26.

In his petition for certiorari here, petitioner raised three issues: the unconstitutionality of the five-person jury; the constitutional sufficiency of the jury instructions on scienter and constructive, rather than actual, knowledge of the contents of the film; and obscenity *vel non*. We granted certiorari. 429 U. S. 1071 (1977). Because we now hold that the five-member jury does not satisfy the jury trial guarantee of the Sixth Amendment, as applied to the States through the Fourteenth, we do not reach the other issues.

II

The Fourteenth Amendment guarantees the right of trial by jury in all state nonpetty criminal cases. *Duncan* v. *Louisiana*, 391 U. S. 145, 159–162 (1968). The Court in *Duncan* applied this Sixth Amendment right to the States because "trial by jury in criminal cases is fundamental to the American scheme of justice." *Id.*, at 149. The right attaches in the present case because the maximum penalty for violating § 26–2101, as it existed at the time of the alleged offenses, exceeded six months' imprisonment. See *Baldwin* v. *New York*, 399 U. S. 66, 68–69 (1970) (opinion of WHITE, J.).

In *Williams* v. *Florida*, 399 U. S., at 100, the Court reaffirmed that the "purpose of the jury trial, as we noted in *Duncan*, is to prevent oppression by the Government. 'Providing an accused with the right to be tried by a jury of his peers gave him an inestimable safeguard against the corrupt or overzealous prosecutor and against the compliant, biased, or eccentric judge.' *Duncan* v. *Louisiana*, [391 U. S.,] at 156." See *Apodaca* v. *Oregon*, 406 U. S. 404, 410 (1972) (opinion of WHITE, J.). This purpose is attained by the participation of the community in determinations of guilt and by the application of the common sense of laymen who, as jurors, consider the case. *Williams* v. *Florida*, 399 U. S., at 100.

Williams held that these functions and this purpose could be fulfilled by a jury of six members. As the Court's opinion in that case explained at some length, *id.*, at 86–90, common-law juries included 12 members by historical accident, "unrelated to the great purposes which gave rise to the jury in the first place." *Id.*, at 89–90. The Court's earlier cases that had *assumed* the number 12 to be constitutionally compelled were set to one side because they had not considered history and the function of the jury. *Id.*, at 90–92. Rather than requiring 12 members, then, the Sixth Amendment mandated a jury only of sufficient size to promote group deliberation, to insulate members from outside intimidation, and to provide a representative cross-section of the community. *Id.*, at 100. Although recognizing that by 1970 little empirical research had evaluated jury performance, the Court found no evidence that the reliability of jury verdicts diminished with six-member panels. Nor did the Court anticipate significant differences in result, including the frequency of "hung" juries. *Id.*, at 101–102, and nn. 47 and 48. Because the reduction in size did not threaten exclusion of any particular class from jury roles, concern that the representative or cross-section character of the jury would suffer with a decrease to six members seemed "an unrealistic one." *Id.*, at 102. As a consequence, the six-person jury was held not to violate the Sixth and Fourteenth Amendments.

III

When the Court in *Williams* permitted the reduction in jury size—or, to put it another way, when it held that a jury of six was not unconstitutional—it expressly reserved ruling on the issue whether a number smaller than six passed constitutional scrutiny. . . .

First, recent empirical data suggest that progressively smaller juries are less likely to foster effective group deliberation. At some point, this decline leads to inaccurate fact-finding and incorrect application of the common sense of the community to the facts. Generally, a positive correlation exists between group size and the quality of both group performance and group productivity. A variety of explanations have been offered for this conclusion. Several are particularly applicable in the jury setting. The smaller the group, the less likely are members to make critical contributions necessary for the solution of a given problem. Because most juries are not permitted to take notes, see Forston, Sense and Non-Sense: Jury Trial Communication, 1975 B. Y. U. L. Rev. 601; 631–633, memory is important for accurate jury deliberations. As juries decrease in size, then, they are less likely to have members who remember each of the important pieces of evidence or argument. Furthermore, the smaller the group, the less likely it is to overcome the biases of its members to obtain an accurate result. When individual and group decisionmaking were compared, it was seen that groups performed better because prejudices of individuals were frequently counterbalanced, and objectivity resulted. Groups also exhibited increased motivation and self-criticism. All these advantages, except, perhaps, self-motivation, tend to diminish as the size of the group diminishes. Because juries frequently face complex problems laden with value choices, the benefits are important and should be retained. In particular, the counterbalancing of various biases

is critical to the accurate application of the common sense of the community to the facts of any given case.

Second, the data now raise doubts about the accuracy of the results achieved by smaller and smaller panels. Statistical studies suggest that the risk of convicting an innocent person (Type I error) rises as the size of the jury diminishes. Because the risk of not convicting a guilty person (Type II error) increases with the size of the panel, an optimal jury size can be selected as a function of the interaction between the two risks. Nagel and Neef concluded that the optimal size, for the purpose of minimizing errors, should vary with the importance attached to the two types of mistakes. After weighting Type I error as 10 times more significant than Type II, perhaps not an unreasonable assumption, they concluded that the optimal jury size was between six and eight. As the size diminished to five and below, the weighted sum of errors increased because of the enlarging risk of the conviction of innocent defendants.

[Here Justice Blackmun draws extensively on statistical studies and results that relate jury size to "correct" decisions, hung juries, and representation on the jury by minority groups in the community.]

IV

While we adhere to, and reaffirm our holding in *Williams* v. *Florida*, these studies, most of which have been made since *Williams* was decided in 1970, lead us to conclude that the purpose and functioning of the jury in a criminal trial is seriously impaired, and to a constitutional degree, by a reduction in size to below six members. We readily admit that we do not pretend to discern a clear line between six members and five. But the assembled data raise substantial doubt about the reliability and appropriate representation of panels smaller than six. Because of the fundamental importance of the jury trial to the American system of criminal justice, any further reduction that promotes inaccurate and possibly biased decisionmaking, that causes untoward differences in verdicts, and that prevents juries from truly representing their communities, attains constitutional significance.

. . .

Petitioner, therefore, has established that his trial on criminal charges before a five-member jury deprived him of the right to trial by jury guaranteed by the Sixth and Fourteenth Amendments.

VI

The judgment of the Court of Appeals is reversed, and the case is remanded for further proceedings not inconsistent with this opinion.

It is so ordered.

MR. JUSTICE STEVENS, concurring.

While I join MR. JUSTICE BLACKMUN'S opinion, I have not altered the views I expressed in *Marks* v. *United States*, 430 U. S. 188.

MR. JUSTICE WHITE, concurring in the judgment.

Agreeing that a jury of fewer than six persons would fail to represent the sense of the community and hence not satisfy the fair cross-section requirement of the Sixth and Fourteenth Amendments, I concur in the judgment of reversal.

MR. JUSTICE POWELL, with whom THE CHIEF JUSTICE and MR. JUSTICE REHNQUIST join, concurring in the judgment.

I concur in the judgment, as I agree that use of a jury as small as five members, with authority to convict for serious offenses, involves grave questions of fairness. As the opinion of MR. JUSTICE BLACKMUN indicates, the line between five- and six-member juries is difficult to justify, but a line has to be drawn somewhere if the substance of jury trial is to be preserved.

I do not agree, however, that every feature of jury trial practice must be the same in both federal and state courts. *Apodaca* v. *Oregon*, 406 U. S. 404, 414 (1972) (POWELL, J., concurring). Because the opinion of MR. JUSTICE BLACKMUN today assumes full incorporation of the Sixth Amendment by the Fourteenth Amendment contrary to my view in *Apodaca*, I do not join it. Also, I have reservations as to the wisdom—as well as the necessity—of MR. JUSTICE BLACKMUN'S heavy reliance on numerology derived from statistical studies. Moreover, neither the validity nor the methodology employed by the studies cited was subjected to the traditional testing mechanisms of the adversary process. The studies relied on merely represent unexamined findings of persons interested in the jury system.

For these reasons I concur only in the judgment.

MR. JUSTICE BRENNAN, with whom MR. JUSTICE STEWART and MR. JUSTICE MARSHALL join.

I join MR. JUSTICE BLACKMUN'S opinion insofar as it holds that the Sixth and Fourteenth Amendments require juries in criminal trials to contain more than five persons. However, I cannot agree that petitioner can be subjected to a new trial, since I continue to adhere to my belief that Ga. Code Ann. § 26–2101 (1972) is overbroad and therefore facially unconstitutional. See *Sanders* v. *Georgia*, 424 U. S. 931 (1976) (dissent from denial of certiorari). See also *Paris Adult Theatre I* v. *Slaton*, 413 U. S. 49, 73 (1973) (BRENNAN, J., dissenting).

Apodaca v. Oregon

406 U.S. 404 (1972)

After the Court had agreed in *Duncan* v. *Louisiana* (1968) that a criminal defendant is entitled to a jury trial in the states, the Court faced a related issue. Could jury verdicts be less than unanimous, even though unanimity is required in the federal courts? Distinctions were necessary between capital and noncapital crimes.

MR. JUSTICE WHITE announced the judgment of the Court and an opinion in which THE CHIEF JUSTICE, MR. JUSTICE BLACKMUN, and MR. JUSTICE REHNQUIST joined.

Robert Apodaca, Henry Morgan Cooper, Jr., and James Arnold Madden were convicted respectively of assault with a deadly weapon, burglary in a dwelling, and grand larceny before separate Oregon juries, all of which returned less-than-unanimous verdicts. The vote in the cases of Apodaca and Madden was 11–1, while the vote in the case of Cooper was 10–2, the minimum requisite vote under Oregon law for sustaining a conviction. After their convictions had been affirmed by the Oregon Court of Appeals, 1 Ore. App. 483, 462 P. 2d 691 (1969), and review had been denied by the Supreme Court of Oregon, all three sought review in this Court upon a claim that conviction of crime by a less-than-unanimous jury violates the right to trial by jury in criminal cases specified by the Sixth Amendment and made applicable to the States by the Fourteenth. See *Duncan* v. *Louisiana*, 391 U. S. 145 (1968). We granted certiorari to consider this claim, 400 U. S. 901 (1970), which we now find to be without merit.

In *Williams* v. *Florida*, 399 U. S. 78 (1970), we had occasion to consider a related issue: whether the Sixth Amendment's right to trial by jury requires that all juries consist of 12 men. After considering the history of the 12-man requirement and the functions it performs in contemporary society, we concluded that it was not of constitutional stature. We reach the same conclusion today with regard to the requirement of unanimity.

I

Like the requirement that juries consist of 12 men, the requirement of unanimity arose during the Middle Ages and had become an accepted feature of the common-law jury by the 18th century. But, as we observed in *Williams*, "the relevant constitutional history casts considerable doubt on the easy assumption . . . that if a given feature existed in a jury at common law in 1789, then it was necessarily preserved in the Constitution." *Id.*, at 92–93. The most salient fact in the scanty history of the Sixth Amendment, which we reviewed in full in *Williams*, is that, as it was introduced by James Madison in the House of Representatives, the proposed Amendment provided for trial

"by an impartial jury of freeholders of the vicinage, with the requisite of unanimity for conviction, of the right of challenge, and other accustomed requisites. . . ." 1 Annals of Cong. 435 (1789).

Although it passed the House with little alteration, this proposal ran into considerable opposition in the Senate, particularly with regard to the vicinage requirement of the House version. The draft of the proposed Amendment was returned to the House in considerably altered form, and a conference committee was appointed. That committee refused to accept not only the original House language but also an alternate suggestion by the House conferees that juries be defined as possessing "the accustomed requisites." Letter from James Madison to Edmund Pendleton, Sept. 23, 1789, in 5 Writings of James Madison 424 (G. Hunt ed. 1904). Instead, the Amendment that ultimately emerged from the committee and then from Congress and the States provided only for trial

"by an impartial jury of the State and district wherein the crime shall have been committed, which district shall have been previously ascertained by law. . . ."

As we observed in *Williams*, one can draw conflicting inferences from this legislative history. One possible inference is that Congress eliminated references to unanimity and to the other "accustomed requisites" of the jury because those requisites were thought already to be implicit in the very concept of jury. A contrary explanation, which we found in *Williams* to be the more plausible, is that the deletion was intended to have some substantive effect. See 399 U. S., at 96–97. Surely one fact that is absolutely clear from this history is that, after a proposal had been made to specify precisely which of the common-law requisites of the jury were to be preserved by the Constitution, the Framers explicitly rejected the proposal and instead left such specification to the future. As in *Williams*, we must accordingly consider what is meant by the concept "jury" and determine whether a feature commonly associated with it is constitutionally required. And, as in *Williams*, our inability to divine "the intent of the Framers" when they eliminated references to the "accustomed requisites" requires that in determining what is meant by a jury we must turn to other than purely historical considerations.

II

Our inquiry must focus upon the function served by the jury in contemporary society. Cf. *Williams* v. *Florida, supra,* at 99–100. As we said in *Duncan,* the purpose of trial by jury is to prevent oppression by the Government by providing a "safeguard against the corrupt or overzealous prosecutor and against the compliant, biased, or eccentric judge." *Duncan* v. *Louisiana,* 391 U. S., at 156. "Given this purpose, the essential feature of a jury obviously lies in the interposition between the accused and his accuser of the commonsense judgment of a group of laymen. . . ." *Williams* v. *Florida, supra,* at 100. A requirement of unanimity, however, does not materially contribute to the exercise of this commonsense judgment. As we said in *Williams,* a jury will come to such a judgment as long as it consists of a group of laymen representative of a cross section of the community who have the duty and the opportunity to deliberate, free from outside attempts at intimidation, on the question of a defendant's guilt. In terms of this function we perceive no difference between juries required to act unanimously and those permitted to convict or acquit by votes of 10 to two or 11 to one. Requiring unanimity would obviously produce hung juries in some situations where nonunanimous juries will convict or acquit. But in either case, the interest of the defendant in having the judgment of his peers interposed between himself and the officers of the State who prosecute and judge him is equally well served.

. . .

IV

Petitioners also cite quite accurately a long line of decisions of this Court upholding the principle that the Fourteenth Amendment requires jury panels to reflect a cross section of the community. See, *e. g., Whitus* v. *Georgia,* 385 U. S. 545 (1967); *Smith* v. *Texas,* 311 U. S. 128 (1940); *Norris* v. *Alabama,* 294 U. S. 587 (1935); *Strauder* v. *West Virginia,* 100 U. S. 303 (1880). They then contend

that unanimity is a necessary precondition for effective application of the cross-section requirement, because a rule permitting less than unanimous verdicts will make it possible for convictions to occur without the acquiescence of minority elements within the community.

There are two flaws in this argument. One is petitioners' assumption that every distinct voice in the community has a right to be represented on every jury and a right to prevent conviction of a defendant in any case. All that the Constitution forbids, however, is systematic exclusion of identifiable segments of the community from jury panels and from the juries ultimately drawn from those panels; a defendant may not, for example, challenge the makeup of a jury merely because no members of his race are on the jury, but must prove that his race has been systematically excluded. See *Swain* v. *Alabama,* 380 U. S. 202, 208–209 (1965); *Cassell* v. *Texas,* 339 U. S. 282, 286–287 (1950); *Akins* v. *Texas,* 325 U. S. 398, 403–404 (1945); *Ruthenberg* v. *United States,* 245 U. S. 480 (1918). No group, in short, has the right to block convictions; it has only the right to participate in the overall legal processes by which criminal guilt and innocence are determined.

We also cannot accept petitioners' second assumption—that minority groups, even when they are represented on a jury, will not adequately represent the viewpoint of those groups simply because they may be outvoted in the final result. They will be present during all deliberations, and their views will be heard. We cannot assume that the majority of the jury will refuse to weigh the evidence and reach a decision upon rational grounds, just as it must now do in order to obtain unanimous verdicts, or that a majority will deprive a man of his liberty on the basis of prejudice when a minority is presenting a reasonable argument in favor of acquittal. We simply find no proof for the notion that a majority will disregard its instructions and cast its votes for guilt or innocence based on prejudice rather than the evidence.

We accordingly affirm the judgment of the Court of Appeals of Oregon.

It is so ordered.

[Justices Blackmun and Powell wrote concurring

opinions. Justices Douglas, Brennan, and Marshall wrote dissenting opinions.]

MR. JUSTICE STEWART, with whom MR. JUSTICE BRENNAN and MR. JUSTICE MARSHALL join, dissenting.

In *Duncan* v. *Louisiana*, 391 U. S. 145, the Court squarely held that the Sixth Amendment right to trial by jury in a federal criminal case is made wholly applicable to state criminal trials by the Fourteenth Amendment. Unless *Duncan* is to be overruled, therefore, the only relevant question here is whether the Sixth Amendment's guarantee of trial by jury embraces a guarantee that the verdict of the jury must be unanimous. The answer to that question is clearly "yes," as my

Brother POWELL has cogently demonstrated in that part of his concurring opinion that reviews almost a century of Sixth Amendment adjudication.

Until today, it has been universally understood that a unanimous verdict is an essential element of a Sixth Amendment jury trial. See *Andres* v. *United States*, 333 U. S. 740, 748; *Patton* v. *United States*, 281 U. S. 276, 288; *Hawaii* v. *Mankichi*, 190 U. S. 197, 211–212; *Maxwell* v. *Dow*, 176 U. S. 581, 586; *Thompson* v. *Utah*, 170 U. S. 343, 351, 353; cf. 2 J. Story, Commentaries on the Constitution § 1779 n. 2 (5th ed. 1891).

I would follow these settled Sixth Amendment precedents and reverse the judgment before us.

Duncan v. Louisiana

391 U.S. 145 (1968)

Gary Duncan was sentenced to sixty days in prison and fined $150 for simple battery. His request for a jury trial was denied. In this case, the Court decides whether trial by jury in criminal cases is so fundamental to the American scheme of justice that it must be available in the states as well as the federal government.

MR. JUSTICE WHITE delivered the opinion of the Court.

Appellant, Gary Duncan, was convicted of simple battery in the Twenty-fifth Judicial District Court of Louisiana. Under Louisiana law simple battery is a misdemeanor, punishable by a maximum of two years' imprisonment and a $300 fine. Appellant sought trial by jury, but because the Louisiana Constitution grants jury trials only in cases in which capital punishment or imprisonment at hard labor may be imposed, the trial judge denied the request. Appellant was convicted and sentenced to serve 60 days in the parish prison and pay a fine of $150. Appellant sought review in the Supreme Court of Louisiana, asserting that the denial of jury trial violated rights guaranteed to him by the United States Constitution. The Supreme Court, finding "[n]o error of law in the ruling complained of," denied appellant a writ of certiorari. Pursuant to 28 U. S. C. § 1257 (2)

appellant sought review in this Court, alleging that the Sixth and Fourteenth Amendments to the United States Constitution secure the right to jury trial in state criminal prosecutions where a sentence as long as two years may be imposed. We noted probable jurisdiction, and set the case for oral argument with No. 52, *Bloom* v. *Illinois, post,* p. 194.

Appellant was 19 years of age when tried. While driving on Highway 23 in Plaquemines Parish on October 18, 1966, he saw two younger cousins engaged in a conversation by the side of the road with four white boys. Knowing his cousins, Negroes who had recently transferred to a formerly all-white high school, had reported the occurrence of racial incidents at the school, Duncan stopped the car, got out, and approached the six boys. At trial the white boys and a white onlooker testified, as did appellant and his cousins. The testimony was in dispute on many points, but the witnesses agreed that appellant and the white boys spoke to each other, that appellant encouraged his cousins to break off the encounter and enter his car, and that appellant was about to enter the car himself for the purpose of driving away with his cousins. The whites testified that just before getting in the car appellant slapped Herman Landry, one of the white boys, on the elbow. The Negroes testified that appellant had not slapped Landry, but had merely touched him. The trial judge concluded that the State had proved beyond a reasonable doubt that Duncan had committed simple battery, and found him guilty.

I

The Fourteenth Amendment denies the States the power to "deprive any person of life, liberty, or property, without due process of law." In resolving conflicting claims concerning the meaning of this spacious language, the Court has looked increasingly to the Bill of Rights for guidance; many of the rights guaranteed by the first eight Amendments to the Constitution have been held to be protected against state action by the Due Process Clause of the Fourteenth Amendment. That clause now protects the right to compensation for property taken by the State; the rights of speech, press, and religion covered by the First Amendment; the Fourth Amendment rights to be free from unreasonable searches and seizures and to have excluded from criminal trials any evidence illegally seized; the right guaranteed by the Fifth Amendment to be free of compelled self-incrimination; and the Sixth Amendment rights to counsel, to a speedy and public trial, to confrontation of opposing witnesses, and to compulsory process for obtaining witnesses.

The test for determining whether a right extended by the Fifth and Sixth Amendments with respect to federal criminal proceedings is also protected against state action by the Fourteenth Amendment has been phrased in a variety of ways in the opinions of this Court. The question has been asked whether a right is among those "'fundamental principles of liberty and justice which lie at the base of all our civil and political institutions,'" *Powell* v. *Alabama*, 287 U. S. 45, 67 (1932); whether it is "basic in our system of

jurisprudence," *In re Oliver*, 333 U. S. 257, 273 (1948); and whether it is "a fundamental right, essential to a fair trial," *Gideon* v. *Wainwright*, 372 U.S. 335, 343–344 (1963); *Malloy* v. *Hogan*, 378 U.S. 1, 6 (1964); *Pointer* v. *Texas*, 380 U. S. 400, 403 (1965). The claim before us is that the right to trial by jury guaranteed by the Sixth Amendment meets these tests. The position of Louisiana, on the other hand, is that the Constitution imposes upon the States no duty to give a jury trial in any criminal case, regardless of the seriousness of the crime or the size of the punishment which may be imposed. Because we believe that trial by jury in criminal cases is fundamental to the American scheme of justice, we hold that the Fourteenth Amendment guarantees a right of jury trial in all criminal cases which—were they to be tried in a federal court— would come within the Sixth Amendment's guarantee. Since we consider the appeal before us to be such a case, we hold that the Constitution was violated when appellant's demand for jury trial was refused.

The history of trial by jury in criminal cases has been frequently told. It is sufficient for present purposes to say that by the time our Constitution was written, jury trial in criminal cases had been in existence in England for several centuries and carried impressive credentials traced by many to Magna Carta. Its preservation and proper operation as a protection against arbitrary rule were among the major objectives of the revolutionary settlement which was expressed in the Declaration and Bill of Rights of 1689. In the 18th century Blackstone could write:

"Our law has therefore wisely placed this strong and two-fold barrier, of a presentment and a trial by jury, between the liberties of the people and the prerogative of the crown. It was necessary, for preserving the admirable balance of our constitution, to vest the executive power of the laws in the prince: and yet this power might be dangerous and destructive to that very constitution, if exerted without check or control, by justices of *oyer* and *terminer* occasionally named by the crown; who might then, as in France or Turkey, imprison, dispatch, or exile any man that was obnoxious to the government, by an instant declaration that such is their will and pleasure. But the founders of the English law have, with excellent forecast, contrived that . . . the truth of every accusation, whether preferred in the shape of indictment, information, or appeal, should afterwards be confirmed by the unanimous suffrage of twelve of his equals and neighbours, indifferently chosen and superior to all suspicion."

Jury trial came to America with English colonists, and received strong support from them. Royal interference with the jury trial was deeply resented. Among the resolutions adopted by the First Congress of the American Colonies (the Stamp Act Congress) on October 19, 1765—resolutions deemed by their authors to state "the most essential rights and liberties of the colonists" —was the declaration:

"That trial by jury is the inherent and invaluable right of every British subject in these colonies."

The First Continental Congress, in the resolve of October 14, 1774, objected to trials before judges dependent upon the Crown alone for their salaries and to trials in England for alleged crimes committed in the colonies; the Congress therefore declared:

"That the respective colonies are entitled to the common law of England, and more especially to the great and inestimable privilege of being tried by their peers of the vicinage, according to the course of that law."

The Declaration of Independence stated solemn objections to the King's making "Judges dependent on his Will alone, for the tenure of their offices, and the amount and payment of their salaries," to his "depriving us in many cases, of the benefits of Trial by Jury," and to his "transporting us beyond Seas to be tried for pretended offenses." The Constitution itself, in Art. III, § 2, commanded:

"The Trial of all Crimes, except in Cases of Impeachment, shall be by Jury; and such Trial shall be held in the State where the said Crimes shall have been committed."

Objections to the Constitution because of the absence of a bill of rights were met by the immedi-

ate submission and adoption of the Bill of Rights. Included was the Sixth Amendment which, among other things, provided:

"In all criminal prosecutions, the accused shall enjoy the right to a speedy and public trial, by an impartial jury of the State and district wherein the crime shall have been committed."

The constitutions adopted by the original States guaranteed jury trial. Also, the constitution of every State entering the Union thereafter in one form or another protected the right to jury trial in criminal cases.

Even such skeletal history is impressive support for considering the right to jury trial in criminal cases to be fundamental to our system of justice. . . .

II.

Louisiana's final contention is that even if it must grant jury trials in serious criminal cases, the conviction before us is valid and constitutional because here the petitioner was tried for simple battery and was sentenced to only 60 days in the parish prison. We are not persuaded. It is doubtless true that there is a category of petty crimes or offenses which is not subject to the Sixth Amendment jury trial provision and should not be subject to the Fourteenth Amendment jury trial requirement here applied to the States. Crimes carrying possible penalties up to six months do not require a jury trial if they otherwise qualify as petty offenses, *Cheff* v. *Schnackenberg*, 384 U. S. 373 (1966). But the penalty authorized for a particular crime is of major relevance in determining whether it is serious or not and may in itself, if severe enough, subject the trial to the mandates of the Sixth Amendment. *District of Columbia* v. *Clawans*, 300 U. S. 617 (1937). . . .

In determining whether the length of the authorized prison term or the seriousness of other punishment is enough in itself to require a jury trial, we are counseled by *District of Columbia* v. *Clawans, supra*, to refer to objective criteria, chiefly the existing laws and practices in the Nation. In the federal system, petty offenses are defined as those punishable by no more than six months in prison and a $500 fine. In 49 of the 50 States crimes subject to trial without a jury, which occasionally include simple battery, are punishable by no more than one year in jail. Moreover, in the late 18th century in America crimes triable without a jury were for the most part punishable by no more than a six-month prison term, although there appear to have been exceptions to this rule. We need not, however, settle in this case the exact location of the line between petty offenses and serious crimes. It is sufficient for our purposes to hold that a crime punishable by two years in prison is, based on past and contemporary standards in this country, a serious crime and not a petty offense. Consequently, appellant was entitled to a jury trial and it was error to deny it.

The judgment below is reversed and the case is remanded for proceedings not inconsistent with this opinion.

[Justice Fortas wrote a concurring opinion. Justice Black, joined by Justice Douglas, wrote a concurrence disputing the position taken in Harlan's dissent, which objects to the selective incorporation of the Bill of Rights into the Fourteenth Amendment and prefers reliance on the Due Process Clause. Black objects to this approach because due process has "no permanent meaning [and shifts] from time to time in accordance with judges' predilections and understandings of what is best for the country."]

MR. JUSTICE HARLAN, whom MR. JUSTICE STEWART joins, dissenting.

Every American jurisdiction provides for trial by jury in criminal cases. The question before us is not whether jury trial is an ancient institution, which it is; nor whether it plays a significant role in the administration of criminal justice, which it does; nor whether it will endure, which it shall. The question in this case is whether the State of Louisiana, which provides trial by jury for all felonies, is prohibited by the Constitution from trying charges of simple battery to the court alone. In my view, the answer to that question, mandated alike by our constitutional history and by the longer history of trial by jury, is clearly "no."

The States have always borne primary responsibility for operating the machinery of criminal justice within their borders, and adapting it to their particular circumstances. In exercising this responsibility, each State is compelled to conform its procedures to the requirements of the Federal Constitution. The Due Process Clause of the Fourteenth Amendment requires that those procedures be fundamentally fair in all respects. It does not, in my view, impose or encourage nationwide uniformity for its own sake; it does not command adherence to forms that happen to be old; and it does not impose on the States the rules that may be in force in the federal courts except where such rules are also found to be essential to basic fairness.

The Court's approach to this case is an uneasy and illogical compromise among the views of various Justices on how the Due Process Clause should be interpreted. The Court does not say that those who framed the Fourteenth Amendment intended to make the Sixth Amendment applicable to the States. And the Court concedes that it finds nothing unfair about the procedure by which the present appellant was tried. Nevertheless, the Court reverses his conviction: it holds, for some reason not apparent to me, that the Due Process Clause incorporates the particular clause of the Sixth Amendment that requires trial by jury in federal criminal cases—including, as I read its opinion, the sometimes trivial accompanying baggage of judicial interpretation in federal contexts.

. . .

Apart from the approach taken by the absolute incorporationists, I can see only one method of analysis that has any internal logic. That is to start with the words "liberty" and "due process of law" and attempt to define them in a way that accords with American traditions and our system of government. This approach, involving a much more discriminating process of adjudication than does "incorporation," is, albeit difficult, the one that was followed throughout the 19th and most of the present century. It entails a "gradual process of judicial inclusion and exclusion," seeking, with due recognition of constitutional tolerance for state experimentation and disparity, to ascertain those "immutable principles . . . of free government which no member of the Union may disregard." Due process was not restricted to rules fixed in the past, for that "would be to deny every quality of the law but its age, and to render it incapable of progress or improvement." Nor did it impose nationwide uniformity in details. . . .

In sum, there is a wide range of views on the desirability of trial by jury, and on the ways to make it most effective when it is used; there is also considerable variation from State to State in local conditions such as the size of the criminal case-load, the ease or difficulty of summoning jurors, and other trial conditions bearing on fairness. We have before us, therefore, an almost perfect example of a situation in which the celebrated dictum of Mr. Justice Brandeis should be invoked. It is, he said,

"one of the happy incidents of the federal system that a single courageous State may, if its citizens choose, serve as a laboratory. . . ." *New State Ice Co.* v. *Liebmann*, 285 U. S. 262, 280, 311 (dissenting opinion).

This Court, other courts, and the political process are available to correct any experiments in criminal procedure that prove fundamentally unfair to defendants. That is not what is being done today: instead, and quite without reason, the Court has chosen to impose upon every State one means of trying criminal cases; it is a good means, but it is not the only fair means, and it is not demonstrably better than the alternatives States might devise.

I would affirm the judgment of the Supreme Court of Louisiana.

Palko v. Connecticut

302 U.S. 319 (1937)

In this opinion, which concerns the Double Jeopardy Clause, Justice Cardozo looks more broadly to determine the respective responsibilities of the federal government and the states and to identify the individual rights "found to be implicit in the concept of ordered liberty."

MR. JUSTICE CARDOZO delivered the opinion of the Court.

A statute of Connecticut permitting appeals in criminal cases to be taken by the state is challenged by appellant as an infringement of the Fourteenth Amendment of the Constitution of the United States. Whether the challenge should be upheld is now to be determined.

Appellant was indicted in Fairfield County, Connecticut, for the crime of murder in the first degree. A jury found him guilty of murder in the second degree, and he was sentenced to confinement in the state prison for life. Thereafter the State of Connecticut, with the permission of the judge presiding at the trial, gave notice of appeal to the Supreme Court of Errors. This it did pursuant to an act adopted in 1886 which is printed in the margin. Public Acts, 1886, p. 560; now § 6494 of the General Statutes. Upon such appeal, the Supreme Court of Errors reversed the judgment and ordered a new trial. *State* v. *Palko*, 121 Conn. 669;

186 Atl. 657. It found that there had been error of law to the prejudice of the state (1) in excluding testimony as to a confession by defendant; (2) in excluding testimony upon cross-examination of defendant to impeach his credibility, and (3) in the instructions to the jury as to the difference between first and second degree murder.

Pursuant to the mandate of the Supreme Court of Errors, defendant was brought to trial again. Before a jury was impaneled and also at later stages of the case he made the objection that the effect of the new trial was to place him twice in jeopardy for the same offense, and in so doing to violate the Fourteenth Amendment of the Constitution of the United States. Upon the overruling of the objection the trial proceeded. The jury returned a verdict of murder in the first degree, and the court sentenced the defendant to the punishment of death. The Supreme Court of Errors affirmed the judgment of conviction, 122 Conn. 529; 191 Atl. 320, adhering to a decision announced in 1894, *State* v. *Lee*, 65 Conn. 265; 30 Atl. 1110, which upheld the challenged statute. Cf. *State* v. *Muolo*, 118 Conn. 373; 172 Atl. 875. The case is here upon appeal. 28 U. S. C., § 344.

1. The execution of the sentence will not deprive appellant of his life without the process of law assured to him by the Fourteenth Amendment of the Federal Constitution.

The argument for appellant is that whatever is forbidden by the Fifth Amendment is forbidden by the Fourteenth also. The Fifth Amendment, which is not directed to the states, but solely to the federal government, creates immunity from double jeopardy. No person shall be "subject for the same offense to be twice put in jeopardy of life or limb." The Fourteenth Amendment ordains, "nor shall any State deprive any person of life, liberty, or property, without due process of law." To retry a defendant, though under one indictment and only one, subjects him, it is said, to double jeopardy in violation of the Fifth Amendment, if the prosecution is one on behalf of the United States. From this the consequence is said to follow that there is a denial of life or liberty without due process of law, if the prosecution is one on behalf of the People of a State. Thirty-five years ago a like argument was made to this court in *Dreyer* v. *Illinois*, 187 U. S. 71, 85, and was passed without consideration of its merits as unnecessary to a decision. The question is now here.

We do not find it profitable to mark the precise limits of the prohibition of double jeopardy in federal prosecutions. The subject was much considered in *Kepner* v. *United States*, 195 U. S. 100, decided in 1904 by a closely divided court. The view was there expressed for a majority of the court that the prohibition was not confined to jeopardy in a new and independent case. It forbade jeopardy in the same case if the new trial was at the instance of the government and not upon defendant's motion. Cf. *Trono* v. *United States*, 199 U. S. 521. All this may be assumed for the purpose of the case at hand, though the dissenting opinions (195 U. S. 100, 134, 137) show how much was to be said in favor of a different ruling. Right-minded men, as we learn from those opinions, could reasonably, even if mistakenly, believe that a second trial was lawful in prosecutions subject to the Fifth Amendment, if it was all in the same case.

Even more plainly, right-minded men could reasonably believe that in espousing that conclusion they were not favoring a practice repugnant to the conscience of mankind. Is double jeopardy in such circumstances, if double jeopardy it must be called, a denial of due process forbidden to the states? The tyranny of labels, *Snyder* v. *Massachusetts*, 291 U. S. 97, 114, must not lead us to leap to a conclusion that a word which in one set of facts may stand for oppression or enormity is of like effect in every other.

We have said that in appellant's view the Fourteenth Amendment is to be taken as embodying the prohibitions of the Fifth. His thesis is even broader. Whatever would be a violation of the original bill of rights (Amendments I to VIII) if done by the federal government is now equally unlawful by force of the Fourteenth Amendment if done by a state. There is no such general rule.

The Fifth Amendment provides, among other things, that no person shall be held to answer for a capital or otherwise infamous crime unless on presentment or indictment of a grand jury. This court has held that, in prosecutions by a state, presentment or indictment by a grand jury may give way to informations at the instance of a public officer. *Hurtado* v. *California*, 110 U. S. 516; *Gaines* v. *Washington*, 277 U. S. 81, 86. The Fifth Amendment provides also that no person shall be compelled in any criminal case to be a witness against himself. This court has said that, in prosecutions by a state, the exemption will fail if the state elects to end it. *Twining* v. *New Jersey*, 211 U. S. 78, 106, 111, 112. Cf. *Snyder* v. *Massachusetts*, *supra*, p. 105; *Brown* v. *Mississippi*, 297 U. S. 278, 285. The Sixth Amendment calls for a jury trial in criminal cases and the Seventh for a jury trial in civil cases at common law where the value in controversy shall exceed twenty dollars. This court has ruled that consistently with those amendments trial by jury may be modified by a state or abolished altogether. *Walker* v. *Sauvinet*, 92 U. S. 90; *Maxwell* v. *Dow*, 176 U. S. 581; *New York Central R. Co.* v. *White*, 243 U. S. 188, 208; *Wagner Electric Mfg. Co.* v. *Lyndon*, 262 U. S. 226, 232. As to the Fourth Amendment, one should refer to *Weeks* v. *United States*, 232 U. S. 383, 398, and as to other provisions of the Sixth, to *West* v. *Louisiana*, 194 U. S. 258.

On the other hand, the due process clause of the Fourteenth Amendment may make it unlawful for a state to abridge by its statutes the freedom of speech which the First Amendment safeguards against encroachment by the Congress, *De Jonge* v. *Oregon*, 299 U. S. 353, 364; *Herndon* v. *Lowry*, 301 U. S. 242, 259; or the like freedom of the press, *Grosjean* v. *American Press Co.*, 297 U. S. 233; *Near* v. *Minnesota ex rel. Olson*, 283 U. S. 697, 707; or the free exercise of religion, *Hamilton* v. *Regents*, 293 U. S. 245, 262; cf. *Grosjean* v. *American Press Co.*, *supra*; *Pierce* v. *Society of Sisters*, 268 U. S. 510; or the right of peaceable assembly, without which speech would be unduly trammeled, *De Jonge* v. *Oregon, supra*; *Herndon* v. *Lowry, supra;* or the right of one accused of crime to the benefit of counsel, *Powell* v. *Alabama*, 287 U. S. 45. In these and other situations immunities that are valid as against the federal government by force of the specific pledges of particular amendments have been found to be implicit in the concept of ordered liberty, and thus, through the Fourteenth Amendment, become valid as against the states.

The line of division may seem to be wavering and broken if there is a hasty catalogue of the cases on the one side and the other. Reflection and analysis will induce a different view. There emerges the perception of a rationalizing principle which gives to discrete instances a proper order and coherence. The right to trial by jury and the immunity from prosecution except as the result of an indictment may have value and importance. Even so, they are not of the very essence of a scheme of ordered liberty. To abolish them is not to violate a "principle of justice so rooted in the traditions and conscience of our people as to be ranked as fundamental." *Snyder* v. *Massachusetts, supra*, p. 105; *Brown* v. *Mississippi, supra*, p. 285; *Hebert* v. *Louisiana*, 272 U. S. 312, 316. Few would be so narrow or provincial as to maintain that a fair and enlightened system of justice would be impossible without them. What is true of jury trials and indictments is true also, as the cases show, of the immunity from compulsory self-incrimination. *Twining* v. *New Jersey, supra*. This too might be lost, and justice still be done. Indeed, today as in the past there are students of our penal system who look upon the immunity as a mischief rather than a benefit, and who would limit its

scope, or destroy it altogether. No doubt there would remain the need to give protection against torture, physical or mental. *Brown* v. *Mississippi, supra*. Justice, however, would not perish if the accused were subject to a duty to respond to orderly inquiry. The exclusion of these immunities and privileges from the privileges and immunities protected against the action of the states has not been arbitrary or casual. It has been dictated by a study and appreciation of the meaning, the essential implications, of liberty itself.

We reach a different plane of social and moral values when we pass to the privileges and immunities that have been taken over from the earlier articles of the federal bill of rights and brought within the Fourteenth Amendment by a process of absorption. These in their origin were effective against the federal government alone. If the Fourteenth Amendment has absorbed them, the process of absorption has had its source in the belief that neither liberty nor justice would exist if they were sacrificed. *Twining* v. *New Jersey, supra*, p. 99. This is true, for illustration, of freedom of thought, and speech. Of that freedom one may say that it is the matrix, the indispensable condition, of nearly every other form of freedom. With rare aberrations a pervasive recognition of that truth can be traced in our history, political and legal. So it has come about that the domain of liberty, withdrawn by the Fourteenth Amendment from encroachment by the states, has been enlarged by latter-day judgments to include liberty of the mind as well as liberty of action. The extension became, indeed, a logical imperative when once it was recognized, as long ago it was, that liberty is something more than exemption from physical restraint, and that even in the field of substantive rights and duties the legislative judgment, if oppressive and arbitrary, may be overridden by the courts. Cf. *Near* v. *Minnesota ex rel. Olson, supra; De Jonge* v. *Oregon, supra*. Fundamental too in the concept of due process, and so in that of liberty, is the thought that condemnation shall be rendered only after trial. *Scott* v. *McNeal*, 154 U. S. 34; *Blackmer* v. *United States*, 284 U. S. 421. The hearing, moreover, must be a real one, not a sham or a pretense. *Moore* v. *Dempsey*, 261 U. S. 86; *Mooney* v. *Holohan*, 294 U. S. 103. For that reason, ignorant defendants in a capital case were held to have been condemned unlawfully when in truth, though not in form, they were refused the aid of counsel. *Powell* v. *Alabama, supra,* pp. 67, 68. The decision did not turn upon the fact that the benefit of counsel would have been guaranteed to the defendants by the provisions of the Sixth Amendment if they had been prosecuted in a federal court. The decision turned upon the fact that in the particular situation laid before us in the evidence the benefit of counsel was essential to the substance of a hearing.

Our survey of the cases serves, we think, to justify the statement that the dividing line between them, if not unfaltering throughout its course, has been true for the most part to a unifying principle. On which side of the line the case made out by the appellant has appropriate location must be the next inquiry and the final one. Is that kind of double jeopardy to which the statute has subjected him a hardship so acute and shocking that our polity will not endure it? Does it violate those "fundamental principles of liberty and justice which lie at the base of all our civil and political institutions"? *Hebert* v. *Louisiana, supra.* The answer surely must be "no." What the answer would have to be if the state were permitted after a trial free from error to try the accused over again or to bring another case against him, we have no occasion to consider. We deal with the statute before us and no other. The state is not attempting to wear the accused out by a multitude of cases with accumulated trials. It asks no more than this, that the case against him shall go on until there shall be a trial free from the corrosion of substantial legal error. *State* v. *Felch*, 92 Vt. 477; 105 Atl. 23; *State* v. *Lee, supra.* This is not cruelty at all, nor even vexation in any immoderate degree. If the trial had been infected with error adverse to the accused, there might have been review at his instance, and as often as necessary to purge the vicious taint. A reciprocal privilege, subject at all times to the discretion of the presiding judge, *State* v. *Carabetta*, 106 Conn. 114; 127 Atl. 394, has now been granted to the state. There is here no seismic innovation. The edifice of justice stands, its symmetry, to many, greater than before.

2. The conviction of appellant is not in derogation of any privileges or immunities that belong to him as a citizen of the United States.

There is argument in his behalf that the privileges and immunities clause of the Fourteenth Amendment as well as the due process clause has been flouted by the judgment.

Maxwell v. *Dow, supra*, p. 584, gives all the answer that is necessary.

The judgment is

Affirmed.

MR. JUSTICE BUTLER dissents.

Mallory v. United States

354 U.S. 449 (1957)

Federal law officers arrested Andrew Mallory on charges of rape and proceeded to question him until he confessed about seven hours later. The issue was whether the police should have taken him before a magistrate "without unnecessary delay" in accordance with the Federal Rules of Criminal Procedure. Some of the issues in this case were later crystallized in *Gideon* v. *Wainwright* (1963), *Escobedo* v. *Illinois* (1964), and *Miranda* v. *Arizona* (1966).

MR. JUSTICE FRANKFURTER delivered the opinion of the Court.

Petitioner was convicted of rape in the United States District Court for the District of Columbia, and, as authorized by the District Code, the jury imposed a death sentence. The Court of Appeals affirmed, one judge dissenting. 98 U. S. App. D. C. 406, 236 F. 2d 701. Since an important question involving the interpretation of the Federal Rules of Criminal Procedure was involved in this capital case, we granted the petition for certiorari. 352 U.S. 877.

The rape occurred at six p. m. on April 7, 1954, in the basement of the apartment house inhabited by the victim. She had descended to the basement a few minutes previous to wash some laundry. Experiencing some difficulty in detaching a hose in the sink, she sought help from the janitor, who lived in a basement apartment with his wife, two grown sons, a younger son and the petitioner, his nineteen-year-old half-brother. Petitioner was alone in the apartment at the time. He detached the hose and returned to his quarters. Very shortly thereafter, a masked man, whose general features were identified to resemble those of petitioner and his two grown nephews, attacked the woman. She had heard no one descend the wooden steps that furnished the only means of entering the basement from above.

Petitioner and one of his grown nephews disappeared from the apartment house shortly after the crime was committed. The former was apprehended the following afternoon between two and two-thirty p. m. and was taken, along with his older nephews, also suspects, to police headquarters. At least four officers questioned him there in the presence of other officers for thirty to forty-five minutes, beginning the examination by telling him, according to his testimony, that his brother had said that he was the assailant. Petitioner strenuously denied his guilt. He spent the rest of the afternoon at headquarters, in the company of the other two suspects and his brother a good part of the time. About four p. m. the three suspects were asked to submit to "lie detector" tests, and they agreed. The officer in charge of the polygraph machine was not located for almost two hours, during which time the suspects received food and drink. The nephews were then examined first. Questioning of petitioner began just after eight p. m. Only he and the polygraph operator were present in a small room, the door to which was closed.

Following almost an hour and one-half of steady interrogation, he "first stated that he could have done this crime, or that he might have done it. He finally stated that he was responsible . . . ."

(Testimony of polygraph operator, R. 70.) Not until ten p. m., after petitioner had repeated his confession to other officers, did the police attempt to reach a United States Commissioner for the purpose of arraignment. Failing in this, they obtained petitioner's consent to examination by the deputy coroner, who noted no indicia of physical or psychological coercion. Petitioner was then confronted by the complaining witness and "[p]ractically every man in the Sex Squad," and in response to questioning by three officers, he repeated the confession. Between eleven-thirty p. m. and twelve-thirty a. m. he dictated the confession to a typist. The next morning he was brought before a Commissioner. At the trial, which was delayed for a year because of doubt about petitioner's capacity to understand the proceedings against him, the signed confession was introduced in evidence.

The case calls for the proper application of Rule 5 (a) of the Federal Rules of Criminal Procedure, promulgated in 1946, 327 U. S. 821. That Rule provides:

"(a) APPEARANCE BEFORE THE COMMISSIONER. An officer making an arrest under a warrant issued upon a complaint or any person making an arrest without a warrant shall take the arrested person without unnecessary delay before the nearest available commissioner or before any other nearby officer empowered to commit persons charged with offenses against the laws of the United States. When a person arrested without a warrant is brought before a commissioner or other officer, a complaint shall be filed forthwith."

This provision has both statutory and judicial antecedents for guidance in applying it. The requirement that arraignment be "without unnecessary delay" is a compendious restatement, without substantive change, of several prior specific federal statutory provisions. (E.g., 20 Stat. 327, 341; 48 Stat. 1008; also 28 Stat. 416.) See Dession, The New Federal Rules of Criminal Procedure: I, 55 Yale L. J. 694, 707. Nearly all the States have similar enactments.

In *McNabb* v. *United States*, 318 U. S. 332, 343–344, we spelled out the important reasons of policy behind this body of legislation:

"The purpose of this impressively pervasive requirement of criminal procedure is plain. . . . The awful instruments of the criminal law cannot be entrusted to a single functionary. The complicated process of criminal justice is therefore divided into different parts, responsibility for which is separately vested in the various participants upon whom the criminal law relies for its vindication. Legislation such as this, requiring that the police must with reasonable promptness show legal cause for detaining arrested persons, constitutes an important safeguard—not only in assuring protection for the innocent but also in securing conviction of the guilty by methods that commend themselves to a progressive and self-confident society. For this procedural requirement checks resort to those reprehensible practices known as the 'third degree' which, though universally rejected as indefensible, still find their way into use. It aims to avoid all the evil implications of secret interrogation of persons accused of crime."

Since such unwarranted detention led to tempting utilization of intensive interrogation, easily gliding into the evils of "the third degree," the Court held that police detention of defendants beyond the time when a committing magistrate was readily accessible constituted "willful disobedience of law." In order adequately to enforce the congressional requirement of prompt arraignment, it was deemed necessary to render inadmissible incriminating statements elicited from defendants during a period of unlawful detention.

. . .

The circumstances of this case preclude a holding that arraignment was "without unnecessary delay." Petitioner was arrested in the early afternoon and was detained at headquarters within the vicinity of numerous committing magistrates. Even though the police had ample evidence from other sources than the petitioner for regarding the petitioner as the chief suspect, they first questioned him for approximately a half hour. When this inquiry of a nineteen-year-old lad of limited intelligence produced no confession, the police asked him to submit to a "lie-detector" test.

He was not told of his rights to counsel or to a preliminary examination before a magistrate, nor was he warned that he might keep silent and "that any statement made by him may be used against him." After four hours of further detention at headquarters, during which arraignment could easily have been made in the same building in which the police headquarters were housed, petitioner was examined by the lie-detector operator for another hour and a half before his story began to waver. Not until he had confessed, when any judicial caution had lost its purpose, did the police arraign him.

We cannot sanction this extended delay, resulting in confession, without subordinating the general rule of prompt arraignment to the discretion of arresting officers in finding exceptional circumstances for its disregard. In every case where the police resort to interrogation of an arrested person and secure a confession, they may well claim, and quite sincerely, that they were merely trying to check on the information given by him. Against such a claim and the evil potentialities of the practice for which it is urged stands Rule 5 (a) as a barrier. Nor is there an escape from the constraint laid upon the police by that Rule in that two other suspects were involved for the same crime. Presumably, whomever the police arrest they must arrest on "probable cause." It is not the function of the police to arrest, as it were, at large and to use an interrogating process at police headquarters in order to determine whom they should charge before a committing magistrate on "probable cause."

Reversed and remanded.

Gideon v. Wainwright

372 U.S. 335 (1963)

In *Betts* v. *Brady* (1942), the Supreme Court held that an indigent defendant was not entitled to be appointed counsel for noncapital cases. That doctrine was undercut repeatedly in cases after *Betts*. In this case, the Supreme Court unanimously overrules the 1942 decision.

MR. JUSTICE BLACK delivered the opinion of the Court.

Petitioner was charged in a Florida state court with having broken and entered a poolroom with intent to commit a misdemeanor. This offense is a felony under Florida law. Appearing in court without funds and without a lawyer, petitioner asked the court to appoint counsel for him, whereupon the following colloquy took place:

"THE COURT: Mr. Gideon, I am sorry, but I cannot appoint Counsel to represent you in this case. Under the laws of the State of Florida, the only time the Court can appoint Counsel to represent a Defendant is when that person is charged with a capital offense. I am sorry, but I will have to deny your request to appoint Counsel to defend you in this case.

"THE DEFENDANT: The United States Supreme Court says I am entitled to be represented by Counsel."

Put to trial before a jury, Gideon conducted his defense about as well as could be expected from a layman. He made an opening statement to the jury, cross-examined the State's witnesses, presented witnesses in his own defense, declined to testify himself, and made a short argument "emphasizing his innocence to the charge contained in the Information filed in this case." The jury returned a verdict of guilty, and petitioner was sentenced to serve five years in the state prison. Later, petitioner filed in the Florida Supreme Court this habeas corpus petition attacking his conviction and sentence on the ground that the trial court's refusal to appoint counsel for him denied him rights "guaranteed by the Constitution and the Bill of Rights by the United States Government." Treating the petition for habeas corpus as

properly before it, the State Supreme Court, "upon consideration thereof" but without an opinion, denied all relief. Since 1942, when *Betts* v. *Brady*, 316 U. S. 455, was decided by a divided Court, the problem of a defendant's federal constitutional right to counsel in a state court has been a continuing source of controversy and litigation in both state and federal courts. To give this problem another review here, we granted certiorari. 370 U.S. 908. Since Gideon was proceeding *in forma pauperis*, we appointed counsel to represent him and requested both sides to discuss in their briefs and oral arguments the following: "Should this Court's holding in *Betts* v. *Brady*, 316 U. S. 455, be reconsidered?"

I.

The facts upon which Betts claimed that he had been unconstitutionally denied the right to have counsel appointed to assist him are strikingly like the facts upon which Gideon here bases his federal constitutional claim. Betts was indicted for robbery in a Maryland state court. On arraignment, he told the trial judge of his lack of funds to hire a lawyer and asked the court to appoint one for him. Betts was advised that it was not the practice in that county to appoint counsel for indigent defendants except in murder and rape cases. He then pleaded not guilty, had witnesses summoned, cross-examined the State's witnesses, examined his own, and chose not to testify himself. He was found guilty by the judge, sitting without a jury, and sentenced to eight years in prison. Like Gideon, Betts sought release by habeas corpus, alleging that he had been denied the right to assistance of counsel in violation of the Fourteenth Amendment. Betts was denied any relief, and on review this Court affirmed. It was held that a refusal to appoint counsel for an indigent defendant charged with a felony did not necessarily violate the Due Process Clause of the Fourteenth Amendment, which for reasons given the Court deemed to be the only applicable federal constitutional provision. The Court said:

"Asserted denial [of due process] is to be tested by an appraisal of the totality of facts in a given case. That which may, in one setting, constitute a denial of fundamental fairness, shocking to the universal sense of justice, may, in other circumstances, and in the light of other considerations, fall short of such denial." 316 U. S., at 462.

Treating due process as "a concept less rigid and more fluid than those envisaged in other specific and particular provisions of the Bill of Rights," the Court held that refusal to appoint counsel under the particular facts and circumstances in the *Betts* case was not so "offensive to the common and fundamental ideas of fairness" as to amount to a denial of due process. Since the facts and circumstances of the two cases are so nearly indistinguishable, we think the *Betts* v. *Brady* holding if left standing would require us to reject Gideon's claim that the Constitution guarantees him the assistance of counsel. Upon full reconsideration we conclude that *Betts* v. *Brady* should be overruled.

II.

The Sixth Amendment provides, "In all criminal prosecutions, the accused shall enjoy the right . . . to have the Assistance of Counsel for his defence." We have construed this to mean that in federal courts counsel must be provided for defendants unable to employ counsel unless the right is competently and intelligently waived. Betts argued that this right is extended to indigent defendants in state courts by the Fourteenth Amendment. In response the Court stated that, while the Sixth Amendment laid down "no rule for the conduct of the States, the question recurs whether the constraint laid by the Amendment upon the national courts expresses a rule so fundamental and essential to a fair trial, and so, to due process of law, that it is made obligatory upon

the States by the Fourteenth Amendment." 316 U.S., at 465. In order to decide whether the Sixth Amendment's guarantee of counsel is of this fundamental nature, the Court in *Betts* set out and considered "relevant data on the subject . . . afforded by constitutional and statutory provisions subsisting in the colonies and the States prior to the inclusion of the Bill of Rights in the national Constitution, and in the constitutional, legislative, and judicial history of the States to the present date." 316 U. S., at 465. On the basis of this historical data the Court concluded that "appointment of counsel is not a fundamental right, essential to a fair trial." 316 U. S., at 471. It was for this reason the *Betts* Court refused to accept the contention that the Sixth Amendment's guarantee of counsel for indigent federal defendants was extended to or, in the words of that Court, "made obligatory upon the States by the Fourteenth Amendment." Plainly, had the Court concluded that appointment of counsel for an indigent criminal defendant was "a fundamental right, essential to a fair trial," it would have held that the Fourteenth Amendment requires appointment of counsel in a state court, just as the Sixth Amendment requires in a federal court.

We think the Court in *Betts* had ample precedent for acknowledging that those guarantees of the Bill of Rights which are fundamental safeguards of liberty immune from federal abridgment are equally protected against state invasion by the Due Process Clause of the Fourteenth Amendment. This same principle was recognized, explained, and applied in *Powell* v. *Alabama*, 287 U. S. 45 (1932), a case upholding the right of counsel, where the Court held that despite sweeping language to the contrary in *Hurtado* v. *California*, 110 U. S. 516 (1884), the Fourteenth Amendment "embraced" those "fundamental principles of liberty and justice which lie at the base of all our civil and political institutions,'" even though they had been "specifically dealt with in another part of the federal Constitution." 287 U. S., at 67. In many cases other than *Powell* and *Betts*, this Court has looked to the fundamental nature of original Bill of Rights guarantees to decide whether the Fourteenth Amendment makes them obligatory on the States. Explicitly recognized to be of this "fundamental nature" and therefore made immune from state invasion by the Fourteenth, or some part of it, are the First Amendment's freedoms of speech, press, religion, assembly, association, and petition for redress of grievances. For the same reason, though not always in precisely the same terminology, the Court has made obligatory on the States the Fifth Amendment's command that private property shall not be taken for public use without just compensation, the Fourth Amendment's prohibition of unreasonable searches and seizures, and the Eighth's ban on cruel and unusual punishment. On the other hand, this Court in *Palko* v. *Connecticut*, 302 U. S. 319 (1937), refused to hold that the Fourteenth Amendment made the double jeopardy provision of the Fifth Amendment obligatory on the States. In so refusing, however, the Court, speaking through Mr. Justice Cardozo, was careful to emphasize that "immunities that are valid as against the federal government by force of the specific pledges of particular amendments have been found to be implicit in the concept of ordered liberty, and thus, through the Fourteenth Amendment, become valid as against the states" and that guarantees "in their origin . . . effective against the federal government alone" had by prior cases "been taken over from the earlier articles of the federal bill of rights and brought within the Fourteenth Amendment by a process of absorption." 302 U.S., at 324–325, 326.

We accept *Betts* v. *Brady's* assumption, based as it was on our prior cases, that a provision of the Bill of Rights which is "fundamental and essential to a fair trial" is made obligatory upon the States by the Fourteenth Amendment. We think the Court in *Betts* was wrong, however, in concluding that the Sixth Amendment's guarantee of counsel is not one of these fundamental rights. Ten years before *Betts* v. *Brady*, this Court, after full consideration of all the historical data examined in *Betts*, had unequivocally declared that "the right to the aid of counsel is of this fundamental character." *Powell* v. *Alabama*, 287 U. S. 45, 68 (1932). While the Court at the close of its *Powell* opinion did by its language, as this Court frequently does, limit its holding to the particular facts and circumstances of that case, its conclusions about the fundamental nature of the right to counsel are unmistakable. Several years later, in 1936, the Court reemphasized what it had said about the fundamental nature of the right to counsel in this language:

"We concluded that certain fundamental rights, safeguarded by the first eight amendments against federal action, were also safeguarded against state action by the due process of law clause of the Fourteenth Amendment, and among them the fundamental right of the accused to the aid of counsel in a criminal prosecution." *Grosjean* v. *American Press Co.*, 297 U. S. 233, 243–244 (1936).

And again in 1938 this Court said:

"[The assistance of counsel] is one of the safeguards of the Sixth Amendment deemed necessary to insure fundamental human rights of life and liberty. . . . The Sixth Amendment stands as a constant admonition that if the constitutional safeguards it provides be lost, justice will not 'still be done.'" *Johnson* v. *Zerbst*, 304 U. S. 458, 462 (1938). To the same effect, see *Avery* v. *Alabama*, 308 U. S. 444 (1940), and *Smith* v. *O'Grady*, 312 U.S. 329 (1941).

In light of these and many other prior decisions of this Court, it is not surprising that the *Betts* Court, when faced with the contention that "one charged with crime, who is unable to obtain counsel, must be furnished counsel by the State," conceded that "[e]xpressions in the opinions of this court lend color to the argument . . . ." 316 U.S., at 462–463. The fact is that in deciding as it did—that "appointment of counsel is not a fundamental right, essential to a fair trial"—the Court in *Betts* v. *Brady* made an abrupt break with its own well-considered precedents. In returning to these old precedents, sounder we believe than the new, we but restore constitutional principles established to achieve a fair system of justice. Not only these precedents but also reason and reflection require us to recognize that in our adversary system of criminal justice, any person haled into court, who is too poor to hire a lawyer, cannot be assured a fair trial unless counsel is provided for him. This seems to us to be an obvious truth. Governments, both state and federal, quite properly spend vast sums of money to establish machinery to try defendants accused of crime. Lawyers to prosecute are everywhere deemed essential to protect the public's interest in an orderly society. Similarly, there are few defendants charged with crime, few indeed, who fail to hire the best lawyers they can get to prepare and present their defenses. That government hires lawyers to prosecute and defendants who have the money hire lawyers to defend are the strongest indications of the widespread belief that lawyers in criminal courts are necessities, not luxuries. The right of one charged with crime to counsel may not be deemed fundamental and essential to fair trials in some countries, but it is in ours. From the very beginning, our state and national constitutions and laws have laid great emphasis on procedural and substantive safeguards designed to assure fair trials before impartial tribunals in which every defendant stands equal before the law. This noble ideal cannot be realized if the poor man charged with crime has to face his accusers without a lawyer to assist him. A defendant's need for a lawyer is nowhere better stated than in the moving words of Mr. Justice Sutherland in *Powell* v. *Alabama:*

"The right to be heard would be, in many cases, of little avail if it did not comprehend the right to be heard by counsel. Even the intelligent and educated layman has small and sometimes no skill in the science of law. If charged with crime, he is incapable, generally, of determining for himself whether the indictment is good or bad. He is unfamiliar with the rules of evidence. Left without the aid of counsel he may be put on trial without a proper charge, and convicted upon incompetent evidence, or evidence irrelevant to the issue or otherwise inadmissible. He lacks both the skill and knowledge adequately to prepare his defense, even though he have a perfect one. He requires the guiding hand of counsel at every step in the proceedings against him. Without it, though he be not guilty, he faces the danger of conviction because he does not know how to establish his innocence." 287 U. S., at 68–69.

The Court in *Betts* v. *Brady* departed from the sound wisdom upon which the Court's holding in *Powell* v. *Alabama* rested. Florida, supported by two other States, has asked that *Betts* v. *Brady* be left intact. Twenty-two States, as friends of the Court, argue that *Betts* was "an anachronism

when handed down" and that it should now be overruled. We agree.

The judgment is reversed and the cause is remanded to the Supreme Court of Florida for further action not inconsistent with this opinion.

Reversed.

Mr. Justice Douglas. [*concurring opinion*] . . .

Mr. Justice Clark, concurring in the result. . . .

Mr. Justice Harlan, concurring.

I agree that *Betts* v. *Brady* should be overruled, but consider it entitled to a more respectful burial than has been accorded, at least on the part of those of us who were not on the Court when that case was decided.

I cannot subscribe to the view that *Betts* v. *Brady* represented "an abrupt break with its own well-considered precedents." *Ante,* p. 344. In 1932, in *Powell* v. *Alabama,* 287 U. S. 45, a capital case, this Court declared that under the particular facts there presented—"the ignorance and illiteracy of the defendants, their youth, the circumstances of public hostility . . . and above all that they stood in deadly peril of their lives" (287 U. S., at 71)—the state court had a duty to assign counsel for the trial as a necessary requisite of due process of law. It is evident that these limiting facts were not added to the opinion as an afterthought; they were repeatedly emphasized, see 287 U. S., at 52, 57–58, 71, and were clearly regarded as important to the result.

Thus when this Court, a decade later, decided *Betts* v. *Brady,* it did no more than to admit of the possible existence of special circumstances in noncapital as well as capital trials, while at the same time insisting that such circumstances be shown in order to establish a denial of due process. . . .

In noncapital cases, the "special circumstances" rule has continued to exist in form while its substance has been substantially and steadily eroded. . . . In truth the *Betts* v. *Brady* rule is no longer a reality.

This evolution, however, appears not to have been fully recognized by many state courts, in this instance charged with the front-line responsibility for the enforcement of constitutional rights. To continue a rule which is honored by this Court only with lip service is not a healthy thing and in the long run will do disservice to the federal system.

. . .

Escobedo v. Illinois

378 U.S. 478 (1964)

Danny Escobedo, a twenty-two-year-old of Mexican extraction, was arrested in connection with the fatal shooting of his brother-in-law. Although his lawyer was in police headquarters, the lawyer was denied access to see his client. The question was whether the refusal by the police to allow Escobedo to consult with his lawyer constituted a denial of the right to counsel.

MR. JUSTICE GOLDBERG delivered the opinion of the Court.

The critical question in this case is whether, under the circumstances, the refusal by the police to honor petitioner's request to consult with his lawyer during the course of an interrogation constitutes a denial of "the Assistance of Counsel" in violation of the Sixth Amendment to the Constitution as "made obligatory upon the States by the Fourteenth Amendment," *Gideon* v. *Wainwright*, 372 U. S. 335, 342, and thereby renders inadmissible in a state criminal trial any incriminating statement elicited by the police during the interrogation.

On the night of January 19, 1960, petitioner's brother-in-law was fatally shot. In the early hours of the next morning, at 2:30 a. m., petitioner was arrested without a warrant and interrogated. Petitioner made no statement to the police and was released at 5 that afternoon pursuant to a state court writ of habeas corpus obtained by Mr. Warren Wolfson, a lawyer who had been retained by petitioner.

On January 30, Benedict DiGerlando, who was then in police custody and who was later indicted for the murder along with petitioner, told the police that petitioner had fired the fatal shots. Between 8 and 9 that evening, petitioner and his sister, the widow of the deceased, were arrested and taken to police headquarters. En route to the police station, the police "had handcuffed the defendant behind his back," and "one of the arresting officers told defendant that DiGerlando had named him as the one who shot" the deceased. Petitioner testified, without contradiction, that the "detectives said they had us pretty well, up pretty tight, and we might as well admit to this crime," and that he replied, "I am sorry but I would like to have advice from my lawyer." A police officer testified that although petitioner was not formally charged "he was in custody" and "couldn't walk out the door."

Shortly after petitioner reached police headquarters, his retained lawyer arrived. The lawyer described the ensuing events in the following terms:

"On that day I received a phone call [from "the mother of another defendant"] and pursuant to that phone call I went to the Detective Bureau at 11th and State. The first person I talked to was the Sergeant on duty at the Bureau Desk, Sergeant Pidgeon. I asked Sergeant Pidgeon for permission to speak to my client, Danny Escobedo. . . . Sergeant Pidgeon made a call to the Bureau lockup and informed me that the boy had been taken from the lockup to the Homicide Bureau. This was between 9:30 and 10:00 in the evening. Before I went anywhere, he called the Homicide Bureau and told them there was an attorney waiting to see Escobedo. He told me I could not see him. Then I went upstairs to the Homicide

Bureau. There were several Homicide Detectives around and I talked to them. I identified myself as Escobedo's attorney and asked permission to see him. They said I could not. . . . The police officer told me to see Chief Flynn who was on duty. I identified myself to Chief Flynn and asked permission to see my client. He said I could not. . . . I think it was approximately 11:00 o'clock. He said I couldn't see him because they hadn't completed questioning. . . . [F]or a second or two I spotted him in an office in the Homicide Bureau. The door was open and I could see through the office. . . . I waved to him and he waved back and then the door was closed, by one of the officers at Homicide. There were four or five officers milling around the Homicide Detail that night. As to whether I talked to Captain Flynn any later that day, I waited around for another hour or two and went back again and renewed by [*sic*] request to see my client. He again told me I could not. . . . I filed an official complaint with Commissioner Phelan of the Chicago Police Department. I had a conversation with every police officer I could find. I was told at Homicide that I couldn't see him and I would have to get a writ of habeas corpus. I left the Homicide Bureau and from the Detective Bureau at 11th and State at approximately 1:00 A. M. [Sunday morning] I had no opportunity to talk to my client that night. I quoted to Captain Flynn the Section of the Criminal Code which allows an attorney the right to see his client."

Petitioner testified that during the course of the interrogation he repeatedly asked to speak to his lawyer and that the police said that his lawyer "didn't want to see" him. The testimony of the police officers confirmed these accounts in substantial detail.

Notwithstanding repeated requests by each, petitioner and his retained lawyer were afforded no opportunity to consult during the course of the entire interrogation.

[During the interrogation, Escobedo made an incriminating statement and was later convicted of murder.]

The interrogation here was conducted before petitioner was formally indicted. But in the context of this case, that fact should make no differ-

ence. When petitioner requested, and was denied, an opportunity to consult with his lawyer, the investigation had ceased to be a general investigation of "an unsolved crime." *Spano* v. *New York*, 360 U. S. 315, 327 (STEWART, J., concurring). Petitioner had become the accused, and the purpose of the interrogation was to "get him" to confess his guilt despite his constitutional right not to do so. At the time of his arrest and throughout the course of the interrogation, the police told petitioner that they had convincing evidence that he had fired the fatal shots. Without informing him of his absolute right to remain silent in the face of this accusation, the police urged him to make a statement. . . .

It is argued that if the right to counsel is afforded prior to indictment, the number of confessions obtained by the police will diminish significantly, because most confessions are obtained during the period between arrest and indictment, and "any lawyer worth his salt will tell the suspect in no uncertain terms to make no statement to police under any circumstances." *Watts* v. *Indiana*, 338 U. S. 49, 59 (Jackson, J., concurring in part and dissenting in part). This argument, of course, cuts two ways. The fact that many confessions are obtained during this period points up its critical nature as a "stage when legal aid and advice" are surely needed. *Massiah* v. *United States, supra,* at 204; *Hamilton* v. *Alabama, supra; White* v. *Maryland, supra.* The right to counsel would indeed be hollow if it began at a period when few confessions were obtained. There is necessarily a direct relationship between the importance of a stage to the police in their quest for a confession and the criticalness of that stage to the accused in his need for legal advice. Our Constitution, unlike some others, strikes the balance in favor of the right of the accused to be advised by his lawyer of his privilege against self-incrimination. See Note, 73 Yale L. J. 1000, 1048–1051 (1964).

We have learned the lesson of history, ancient and modern, that a system of criminal law enforcement which comes to depend on the "confession" will, in the long run, be less reliable and more subject to abuses than a system which depends on extrinsic evidence independently secured through skillful investigation. . . .

. . . This Court also has recognized that "history amply shows that confessions have often been extorted to save law enforcement officials the trouble and effort of obtaining valid and independent evidence . . . ." *Haynes* v. *Washington*, 373 U. S. 503, 519.

We have also learned the companion lesson of history that no system of criminal justice can, or should, survive if it comes to depend for its continued effectiveness on the citizens' abdication through unawareness of their constitutional rights. No system worth preserving should have to *fear* that if an accused is permitted to consult with a lawyer, he will become aware of, and exercise, these rights. If the exercise of constitutional rights will thwart the effectiveness of a system of law enforcement, then there is something very wrong with that system.

We hold, therefore, that where, as here, the investigation is no longer a general inquiry into an unsolved crime but has begun to focus on a particular suspect, the suspect has been taken into police custody, the police carry out a process of interrogations that lends itself to eliciting incriminating statements, the suspect has requested and been denied an opportunity to consult with his lawyer, and the police have not effectively warned him of his absolute constitutional right to remain silent, the accused has been denied "the Assistance of Counsel" in violation of the Sixth Amendment to the Constitution as "made obligatory upon the States by the Fourteenth Amendment," *Gideon* v. *Wainwright*, 372 U. S., at 342, and that no statement elicited by the police during the interrogation may be used against him at a criminal trial.

. . .

Nothing we have said today affects the powers of the police to investigate "an unsolved crime," *Spano* v. *New York*, 360 U. S. 315, 327 (STEWART, J., concurring), by gathering information from witnesses and by other "proper investigative efforts." *Haynes* v. *Washington*, 373 U. S. 503, 519. We hold only that when the process shifts from investigatory to accusatory—when its focus is on the accused and its purpose is to elicit a confession—our adversary system begins to operate, and, under the circumstances here, the accused must be permitted to consult with his lawyer.

The judgment of the Illinois Supreme Court is reversed and the case remanded for proceedings not inconsistent with this opinion.

Reversed and remanded.

MR. JUSTICE HARLAN, dissenting.

I would affirm the judgment of the Supreme Court of Illinois on the basis of *Cicenia* v. *Lagay*, 357 U. S. 504, decided by this Court only six years ago. Like my Brother WHITE, *post*, p. 495, I think the rule announced today is most ill-conceived and that it seriously and unjustifiably fetters perfectly legitimate methods of criminal law enforcement.

MR. JUSTICE STEWART, dissenting.

I think this case is directly controlled by *Cicenia* v. *Lagay*, 357 U. S. 504, and I would therefore affirm the judgment.

. . .

MR. JUSTICE WHITE, with whom MR. JUSTICE CLARK and MR. JUSTICE STEWART join, dissenting.

In *Massiah* v. *United States*, 377 U. S. 201, the Court held that as of the date of the indictment the prosecution is disentitled to secure admissions from the accused. The Court now moves that date back to the time when the prosecution begins to "focus" on the accused. Although the opinion purports to be limited to the facts of this case, it would be naive to think that the new constitutional right announced will depend upon whether the accused has retained his own counsel, cf. *Gideon* v. *Wainright*, 372 U. S. 335; *Griffin* v. *Illinois*, 351 U.S. 12; *Douglas* v. *California*, 372 U. S. 353, or has asked to consult with counsel in the course of interrogation. Cf. *Carnley* v. *Cochran*, 369 U. S. 506. At the very least the Court holds that once the accused becomes a suspect and, presumably, is arrested, any admission made to the police thereafter is inadmissible in evidence unless the accused has waived his right to counsel. The decision is thus another major step in the direction of the goal which the Court seemingly has in mind—to bar from evidence all admissions obtained from an individual suspected of crime, whether involuntarily made or not. It does of course put us one step "ahead" of the English judges who have had the good sense to leave the matter a discretionary one with the trial court. I reject this step and the invitation to go farther which the Court has now issued.

By abandoning the voluntary-involuntary test for admissibility of confessions, the Court seems driven by the notion that it is uncivilized law enforcement to use an accused's own admissions against him at his trial. It attempts to find a home for this new and nebulous rule of due process by attaching it to the right to counsel guaranteed in the federal system by the Sixth Amendment and binding upon the States by virtue of the due process guarantee of the Fourteenth Amendment. *Gideon* v. *Wainwright, supra.* The right to counsel now not only entitles the accused to counsel's advice and aid in preparing for trial but stands as an impenetrable barrier to any interrogation once the accused has become a suspect. From that very moment apparently his right to counsel attaches, a rule wholly unworkable and impossible to administer unless police cars are equipped with public

defenders and undercover agents and police informants have defense counsel at their side.

. . .

. . . The only "inquisitions" the Constitution forbids are those which compel incrimination. Escobedo's statements were not compelled and the Court does not hold that they were.

This new American judges' rule, which is to be applied in both federal and state courts, is perhaps thought to be a necessary safeguard against the possibility of extorted confessions. To this extent it reflects a deep-seated distrust of law enforcement officers everywhere, unsupported by relevant data or current material based upon our own experience. Obviously law enforcement officers can make mistakes and exceed their authority, as today's decision shows that even judges can do, but I have somewhat more faith than the Court evidently has in the ability and desire of prosecutors and of the power of the appellate courts to discern and correct such violations of the law.

Miranda v. Arizona

384 U.S. 436 (1966)

Prior to 1966, Supreme Court decisions had established a number of rights for individuals taken into police custody: defendants had to be arraigned before a neutral magistrate; indigent defendants had a right to court-appointed counsel; confessions could not be coerced. In this landmark decision, the Court announced the rights available to an accused during police interrogation to protect his constitutional privilege against self-incrimination.

MR. CHIEF JUSTICE WARREN delivered the opinion of the Court.

The cases before us raise questions which go to the roots of our concepts of American criminal jurisprudence: the restraints society must observe consistent with the Federal Constitution in prosecuting individuals for crime. More specifically, we deal with the admissibility of statements obtained from an individual who is subjected to custodial police interrogation and the necessity for procedures which assure that the individual is accorded his privilege under the Fifth Amendment

to the Constitution not to be compelled to incriminate himself.

. . .

We start here, as we did in *Escobedo*, with the premise that our holding is not an innovation in our jurisprudence, but is an application of principles long recognized and applied in other settings. We have undertaken a thorough re-examination of the *Escobedo* decision and the principles it announced, and we reaffirm it. That case was but an explication of basic rights that are enshrined in our Constitution—that "No person . . . shall be compelled in any criminal case to be a witness against himself," and that "the accused shall . . . have the Assistance of Counsel"—rights which were put in jeopardy in that case through official overbearing. These precious rights were fixed in our Constitution only after centuries of persecution and struggle. . . .

Our holding will be spelled out with some specificity in the pages which follow but briefly stated it is this: the prosecution may not use statements, whether exculpatory or inculpatory, stemming from custodial interrogation of the defendant unless it demonstrates the use of procedural safeguards effective to secure the privilege against self-incrimination. By custodial interrogation, we mean questioning initiated by law enforcement officers after a person has been taken into custody or otherwise deprived of his freedom of action in any significant way. As for the procedural safeguards to be employed, unless other fully effective means are devised to inform accused persons of their right of silence and to assure a continuous opportunity to exercise it, the following measures are required. Prior to any questioning, the person must be warned that he has a right to remain silent, that any statement he does make may be used as evidence against him, and that he has a right to the presence of an attorney, either retained or appointed. The defendant may waive effectuation of these rights, provided the waiver is made voluntarily, knowingly and intelligently. If, however, he indicates in any manner and at any stage of the process that he wishes to consult with an attorney before speaking there can be no questioning. Likewise, if the individual is alone and indicates in any manner that he does not wish to be interrogated, the police may not question him. The mere fact that he may have answered some questions or volunteered some statements on his own does not deprive him of the right to refrain from answering any further inquiries until he has consulted with an attorney and thereafter consents to be questioned.

I.

The constitutional issue we decide in each of these cases is the admissibility of statements ob-

tained from a defendant questioned while in custody or otherwise deprived of his freedom of action in any significant way. In each, the defendant was questioned by police officers, detectives, or a prosecuting attorney in a room in which he was cut off from the outside world. In none of these cases was the defendant given a full and effective warning of his rights at the outset of the interrogation process. In all the cases, the questioning elicited oral admissions, and in three of them, signed statements as well which were admitted at their trials. They all thus share salient features—incommunicado interrogation of individuals in a police-dominated atmosphere, resulting in self-incriminating statements without full warnings of constitutional rights.

An understanding of the nature and setting of this in-custody interrogation is essential to our decisions today. The difficulty in depicting what transpires at such interrogations stems from the fact that in this country they have largely taken place incommunicado. From extensive factual studies undertaken in the early 1930's, including the famous Wickersham Report to Congress by a Presidential Commission, it is clear that police violence and the "third degree" flourished at that time. In a series of cases decided by this Court long after these studies, the police resorted to physical brutality—beating, hanging, whipping—and to sustained and protracted questioning incommunicado in order to extort confessions. The Commission on Civil Rights in 1961 found much evidence to indicate that "some policemen still resort to physical force to obtain confessions," 1961 Comm'n on Civil Rights Rep., Justice, pt. 5, 17. The use of physical brutality and violence is not, unfortunately, relegated to the past or to any part of the country. Only recently in Kings County, New York, the police brutally beat, kicked and placed lighted cigarette butts on the back of a potential witness under interrogation for the purpose of securing a statement incriminating a third party. *People* v. *Portelli*, 15 N. Y. 2d 235, 205 N. E. 2d 857, 257 N. Y. S. 2d 931 (1965).

The examples given above are undoubtedly the exception now, but they are sufficiently widespread to be the object of concern. Unless a proper limitation upon custodial interrogation is achieved—such as these decisions will advance—there can be no assurance that practices of this nature will be eradicated in the foreseeable future. . . .

Again we stress that the modern practice of in-custody interrogation is psychologically rather than physically oriented. As we have stated before, "Since *Chambers* v. *Florida*, 309 U. S. 227, this Court has recognized that coercion can be mental as well as physical, and that the blood of the accused is not the only hallmark of an unconstitutional inquisition." *Blackburn* v. *Alabama*, 361 U.S. 199, 206 (1960). Interrogation still takes place in privacy. Privacy results in secrecy and this in turn results in a gap in our knowledge as to what in fact goes on in the interrogation rooms. A valuable source of information about present police practices, however, may be found in various police manuals and texts which document procedures employed with success in the past, and which recommend various other effective tactics. These texts are used by law enforcement agencies themselves as guides. It should be noted that these texts professedly present the most enlightened and effective means presently used to obtain statements through custodial interrogation. By considering these texts and other data, it is possible to describe procedures observed and noted around the country.

The officers are told by the manuals that the "principal psychological factor contributing to a successful interrogation is *privacy*—being alone with the person under interrogation." The efficacy of this tactic has been explained as follows:

"If at all practicable, the interrogation should take place in the investigator's office or at least in a room of his own choice. The subject should be deprived of every psychological advantage. In his own home he may be confident, indignant, or recalcitrant. He is more keenly aware of his rights and more reluctant to tell of his indiscretions or criminal behavior within the walls of his home. Moreover his family and other friends are nearby, their presence lending moral support. In his own office, the investigator possesses all the advantages. The atmosphere suggests the invincibility of the forces of the law."

To highlight the isolation and unfamiliar surroundings, the manuals instruct the police to display an air of confidence in the suspect's guilt and from outward appearance to maintain only an interest in confirming certain details. The guilt of the subject is to be posited as a fact. The interrogator should direct his comments toward the reasons why the subject committed the act, rather than court failure by asking the subject whether he did it. Like other men, perhaps the subject has had a bad family life, had an unhappy childhood, had too much to drink, had an unrequited desire for women. The officers are instructed to minimize the moral seriousness of the offense, to cast blame on the victim or on society. These tactics are designed to put the subject in a psychological state where his story is but an elaboration of what the police purport to know already—that he is guilty. Explanations to the contrary are dismissed and discouraged.

. . .

It is obvious that such an interrogation environment is created for no purpose other than to subjugate the individual to the will of his examiner. This atmosphere carries its own badge of intimidation. To be sure, this is not physical intimidation, but it is equally destructive of human dignity. The current practice of incommunicado interrogation is at odds with one of our Nation's most cherished principles—that the individual may not be compelled to incriminate himself. Unless adequate protective devices are employed to dispel the compulsion inherent in custodial surroundings, no statement obtained from the defendant can truly be the product of his free choice.

. . .

III.

Today, then, there can be no doubt that the Fifth Amendment privilege is available outside of criminal court proceedings and serves to protect persons in all settings in which their freedom of action is curtailed in any significant way from being compelled to incriminate themselves. We have concluded that without proper safeguards the process of in-custody interrogation of persons suspected or accused of crime contains inherently compelling pressures which work to undermine the individual's will to resist and to compel him to speak where he would not otherwise do so free-ly. In order to combat these pressures and to per-mit a full opportunity to exercise the privilege against self-incrimination, the accused must be adequately and effectively apprised of his rights and the exercise of those rights must be fully honored.

It is impossible for us to foresee the potential alternatives for protecting the privilege which might be devised by Congress or the States in the exercise of their creative rule-making capacities. Therefore we cannot say that the Constitution necessarily requires adherence to any particular solution for the inherent compulsions of the inter-rogation process as it is presently conducted. Our decision in no way creates a constitutional strait-jacket which will handicap sound efforts at re-form, nor is it intended to have this effect. We encourage Congress and the States to continue their laudable search for increasingly effective ways of protecting the rights of the individual while promoting efficient enforcement of our criminal laws. However, unless we are shown other procedures which are at least as effective in apprising accused persons of their right of silence and in assuring a continuous opportunity to exercise it, the following safeguards must be observed.

At the outset, if a person in custody is to be subjected to interrogation, he must first be in-formed in clear and unequivocal terms that he has the right to remain silent. For those unaware of the privilege, the warning is needed simply to make them aware of it—the threshold require-ment for an intelligent decision as to its exercise. More important, such a warning is an absolute prerequisite in overcoming the inherent pressures of the interrogation atmosphere. . . .

The warning of the right to remain silent must be accompanied by the explanation that anything said can and will be used against the individual in court. This warning is needed in order to make him aware not only of the privilege, but also of the consequences of forgoing it. . . .

The circumstances surrounding in-custody in-terrogation can operate very quickly to overbear the will of one merely made aware of his privilege by his interrogators. Therefore, the right to have counsel present at the interrogation is indispen-sable to the protection of the Fifth Amendment privilege under the system we delineate today. . . .

In order fully to apprise a person interrogated of the extent of his rights under this system then, it is necessary to warn him not only that he has the right to consult with an attorney, but also that if he is indigent a lawyer will be appointed to represent him. Without this additional warning, the admoni-tion of the right to consult with counsel would often be understood as meaning only that he can consult with a lawyer if he has one or has the funds to obtain one. . . .

Over the years the Federal Bureau of Investiga-tion has compiled an exemplary record of effec-tive law enforcement while advising any suspect or arrested person, at the outset of an interview, that he is not required to make a statement, that any statement may be used against him in court, that the individual may obtain the services of an attor-ney of his own choice and, more recently, that he has a right to free counsel if he is unable to pay. . . .

MR. JUSTICE CLARK, dissenting in Nos. 759, 760, and 761, and concurring in the result in No. 584.

It is with regret that I find it necessary to write in these cases. However, I am unable to join the majority because its opinion goes too far on too little, while my dissenting brethren do not go quite far enough. Nor can I join in the Court's criticism of the present practices of police and investigatory agencies as to custodial interrogation. The mat-erials it refers to as "police manuals" are, as I read them, merely writings in this field by professors and some police officers. Not one is shown by the record here to be the official manual of any police department, much less in universal use in crime detection. Moreover, the examples of police bru-tality mentioned by the Court are rare exceptions to the thousands of cases that appear every year in the law reports. . . .

MR. JUSTICE HARLAN, whom MR. JUSTICE STEW-ART and MR. JUSTICE WHITE join, dissenting.

I believe the decision of the Court represents poor constitutional law and entails harmful conse-quences for the country at large. How serious these consequences may prove to be only time can tell. But the basic flaws in the Court's justification seem to me readily apparent now once all sides of the problem are considered. . . .

What the Court largely ignores is that its rules impair, if they will not eventually serve wholly to frustrate, an instrument of law enforcement that has long and quite reasonably been thought worth the price paid for it. There can be little doubt that the Court's new code would markedly decrease the number of confessions. To warn the suspect that he may remain silent and remind him that his confession may be used in court are minor obstructions. To require also an express waiver by the suspect and an end to questioning whenever he demurs must heavily handicap questioning. And to suggest or provide counsel for the suspect simply invites the end of the interrogation. . . .

All four of the cases involved here present express claims that confessions were inadmissible, not because of coercion in the traditional due process sense, but solely because of lack of counsel or lack of warnings concerning counsel and silence. For the reasons stated in this opinion, I would adhere to the due process test and reject the new requirements inaugurated by the Court. . . .

In conclusion: Nothing in the letter or the spirit of the Constitution or in the precedents squares with the heavy-handed and one-sided action that is so precipitously taken by the Court in the name of fulfilling its constitutional responsibilities. The foray which the Court makes today brings to mind the wise and farsighted words of Mr. Justice Jackson in *Douglas* v. *Jeannette*, 319 U. S. 157, 181 (separate opinion): "This Court is forever adding new stories to the temples of constitutional law, and the temples have a way of collapsing when one story too many is added."

MR. JUSTICE WHITE, with whom MR. JUSTICE HARLAN and MR. JUSTICE STEWART join, dissenting.

. . . There is, in my view, every reason to believe that a good many criminal defendants who otherwise would have been convicted on what this Court has previously thought to be the most satisfactory kind of evidence will now, under this new version of the Fifth Amendment, either not be tried at all or will be acquitted if the State's evidence, minus the confession, is put to the test of litigation.

I have no desire whatsoever to share the responsibility for any such impact on the present criminal process.

In some unknown number of cases the Court's rule will return a killer, a rapist or other criminal to the streets and to the environment which produced him, to repeat his crime whenever it pleases him. As a consequence, there will not be a gain, but a loss, in human dignity. The real concern is not the unfortunate consequences of this new decision on the criminal law as an abstract, disembodied series of authoritative proscriptions, but the impact on those who rely on the public authority for protection and who without it can only engage in violent self-help with guns, knives and the help of their neighbors similarly inclined. There is, of course, a saving factor: the next victims are uncertain, unnamed and unrepresented in this case.

Nor can this decision do other than have a corrosive effect on the criminal law as an effective device to prevent crime. A major component in its effectiveness in this regard is its swift and sure enforcement. The easier it is to get away with rape and murder, the less the deterrent effect on those who are inclined to attempt it. This is still good common sense. If it were not, we should posthaste liquidate the whole law enforcement establishment as a useless, misguided effort to control human conduct. . . .

Oregon v. Elstad

470 U.S. 298 (1985)

Police officers picked up Michael James Elstad at his home as a suspect in a burglary. Without being given the warnings required by *Miranda* v. *Arizona* (1966), he made an

incriminating statement. At the station house, after he was advised of and waived his *Miranda* rights, he executed a written confession. Should his confession have been excluded from trial because his first incriminating statement, before the *Miranda* warnings, had let "the cat out of the bag"? Does *Miranda* protect a suspect only after he is officially in custody? When is a person in custody?

JUSTICE O'CONNOR delivered the opinion of the Court.

This case requires us to decide whether an initial failure of law enforcement officers to administer the warnings required by *Miranda* v. *Arizona*, 384 U.S. 436 (1966), without more, "taints" subsequent admissions made after a suspect has been fully advised of and has waived his *Miranda* rights. Respondent, Michael James Elstad, was convicted of burglary by an Oregon trial court. The Oregon Court of Appeals reversed, holding that respondent's signed confession, although voluntary, was rendered inadmissible by a prior remark made in response to questioning without benefit of *Miranda* warnings. We granted certiorari, 465 U.S. 1078 (1984), and we now reverse.

I

In December 1981, the home of Mr. and Mrs. Gilbert Gross, in the town of Salem, Polk County, Ore., was burglarized. Missing were art objects and furnishings valued at $150,000. A witness to the burglary contacted the Polk County Sheriff's Office, implicating respondent Michael Elstad, an 18-year-old neighbor and friend of the Grosses' teenage son. Thereupon, Officers Burke and McAllister went to the home of respondent Elstad, with a warrant for his arrest. Elstad's mother answered the door. She led the officers to her son's room where he lay on his bed, clad in shorts and listening to his stereo. The officers asked him to get dressed and to accompany them into the living room. Officer McAllister asked respondent's mother to step into the kitchen, where he explained that they had a warrant for her son's arrest for the burglary of a neighbor's residence. Officer Burke remained with Elstad in the living room. He later testified:

"I sat down with Mr. Elstad and I asked him if he was aware of why Detective McAllister and myself were there to talk with him. He stated no, he had no idea why we were there. I then asked

him if he knew a person by the name of Gross, and he said yes, he did, and also added that he heard that there was a robbery at the Gross house. And at that point I told Mr. Elstad that I felt he was involved in that, and he looked at me and stated, 'Yes, I was there.' " App. 19–20.

The officers then escorted Elstad to the back of the patrol car. As they were about to leave for the Polk County Sheriff's office, Elstad's father arrived home and came to the rear of the patrol car. The officers advised him that his son was a suspect in the burglary. Officer Burke testified that Mr. Elstad became quite agitated, opened the rear door of the car and admonished his son: "I told you that you were going to get into trouble. You wouldn't listen to me. You never learn." *Id.*, at 21.

Elstad was transported to the Sheriff's headquarters and approximately one hour later, Officers Burke and McAllister joined him in McAllister's office. McAllister then advised respondent for the first time of his *Miranda* rights, reading from a standard card. Respondent indicated he understood his rights, and, having these rights in mind, wished to speak with the officers. Elstad gave a full statement, explaining that he had known that the Gross family was out of town and had been paid to lead several acquaintances to the Gross residence and show them how to gain entry through a defective sliding glass door. The statement was typed, reviewed by respondent, read back to him for correction, initialed and signed by Elstad and both officers. As an afterthought, Elstad added and initialed the sentence, "After leaving the house Robby & I went back to [the] van & Robby handed me a small bag of grass." App. 42. Respondent concedes that the officers made no threats or promises either at his residence or at the Sheriff's office.

Respondent was charged with first-degree burglary. He was represented at trial by retained counsel. Elstad waived his right to a jury, and his case was tried by a Circuit Court Judge. Respondent moved at once to suppress his oral statement and signed confession. He contended that the statement he made in response to questioning at his house "let the cat out of the bag," citing *United States* v. *Bayer*, 331 U.S. 532 (1947), and tainted the subsequent confession as "fruit of the poisonous tree," citing *Wong Sun* v. *United States*, 371 U.S. 471 (1963). The judge ruled that the statement, "I was there," had to be excluded because the defendant had not been advised of his *Miranda* rights. The written confession taken after Elstad's arrival at the Sheriff's office, however, was admitted in evidence. The court found:

"[H]is written statement was given freely, voluntarily and knowingly by the defendant after he had waived his right to remain silent and have counsel present which waiver was evidenced by the card which the defendant had signed. [It] was not tainted in any way by the previous brief statement between the defendant and the Sheriff's Deputies that had arrested him." App. 45.

Elstad was found guilty of burglary in the first degree. He received a 5-year sentence and was ordered to pay $18,000 in restitution.

Following his conviction, respondent appealed to the Oregon Court of Appeals, relying on *Wong Sun* and *Bayer*. The State conceded that Elstad had been in custody when he made his statement, "I was there," and accordingly agreed that this statement was inadmissible as having been given without the prescribed *Miranda* warnings. But the State maintained that any conceivable "taint" had been dissipated prior to the respondent's written confession by McAllister's careful administration of the requisite warnings. The Court of Appeals reversed respondent's conviction, identifying the crucial constitutional inquiry as "whether there was a sufficient break in the stream of events between [the] inadmissible statement and the written confession to insulate the latter statement from the effect of what went before." 61 Ore. App. 673, 676, 658 P. 2d 552, 554 (1983). The Oregon court concluded:

"Regardless of the absence of actual compulsion, the coercive impact of the unconstitutionally obtained statement remains, because in a defendant's mind it has sealed his fate. It is this impact that must be dissipated in order to make a subsequent confession admissible. In determining

whether it has been dissipated, lapse of time, and change of place from the original surroundings are the most important considerations." *Id.*, at 677, 658 P. 2d, at 554.

Because of the brief period separating the two incidents, the "cat was sufficiently out of the bag to exert a coercive impact on [respondent's] later admissions." *Id.*, at 678, 658 P. 2d, at 555.

The State of Oregon petitioned the Oregon Supreme Court for review, and review was declined. This Court granted certiorari to consider the question whether the Self-Incrimination Clause of the Fifth Amendment requires the suppression of a confession, made after proper *Miranda* warnings and a valid waiver of rights, solely because the police had obtained an earlier voluntary but unwarned admission from the defendant.

II

The arguments advanced in favor of suppression of respondent's written confession rely heavily on metaphor. One metaphor, familiar from the Fourth Amendment context, would require that respondent's confession, regardless of its integrity, voluntariness, and probative value, be suppressed as the "tainted fruit of the poisonous tree" of the *Miranda* violation. A second metaphor questions whether a confession can be truly voluntary once the "cat is out of the bag." Taken out of context, each of these metaphors can be misleading. They should not be used to obscure fundamental differences between the role of the Fourth Amendment exclusionary rule and the function of *Miranda* in guarding against the prosecutorial use of compelled statements as prohibited by the Fifth Amendment. The Oregon court assumed and respondent here contends that a failure to administer *Miranda* warnings necessarily breeds the same consequences as police infringement of a constitutional right, so that evidence uncovered following an unwarned statement must be suppressed as "fruit of the poisonous tree." We believe this view misconstrues the nature of the protections afforded by *Miranda* warnings and therefore misreads the consequences of police failure to supply them.

A

. . .

Because *Miranda* warnings may inhibit persons from giving information, this Court has determined that they need be administered only after the person is taken into "custody" or his freedom has otherwise been significantly restrained. *Miranda* v. *Arizona*, 384 U.S., at 478. Unfortunately, the task of defining "custody" is a slippery one, and "policemen investigating serious crimes [cannot realistically be expected to] make no errors whatsoever." *Michigan* v. *Tucker, supra*, at 446. If errors are made by law enforcement officers in administering the prophylactic *Miranda* procedures, they should not breed the same irremediable consequences as police infringement of the Fifth Amendment itself. It is an unwarranted extension of *Miranda* to hold that a simple failure to administer the warnings, unaccompanied by any actual coercion or other circumstances calculated to undermine the suspect's ability to exercise his free will, so taints the investigatory process that a subsequent voluntary and informed waiver is ineffective for some indeterminate period. Though *Miranda* requires that the unwarned admission must be suppressed, the admissibility of any subsequent statement should turn in these circumstances solely on whether it is knowingly and voluntarily made.

B

The Oregon court, however, believed that the unwarned remark compromised the voluntariness of respondent's later confession. It was the court's view that the prior *answer* and not the unwarned questioning impaired respondent's ability to give a valid waiver and that only lapse of time and change of place could dissipate what it termed the "coercive impact" of the inadmissible statement. When a prior statement is actually coerced, the time that passes between confessions, the change in place of interrogations, and the change in identity of the interrogators all bear on whether that coercion has carried over into the second confession. See *Westover* v. *United States*, decided together with *Miranda* v. *Arizona*, 384 U.S., at 494; *Clewis* v. *Texas*, 386 U.S. 707 (1967). The failure of police to administer *Miranda* warn-

ings does not mean that the statements received have actually been coerced, but only that courts will presume the privilege against compulsory self-incrimination has not been intelligently exercised. . . . a careful and thorough administration of *Miranda* warnings serves to cure the condition that rendered the unwarned statement inadmissible.

. . . We must conclude that, absent deliberately coercive or improper tactics in obtaining the initial statement, the mere fact that a suspect has made an unwarned admission does not warrant a presumption of compulsion. A subsequent administration of *Miranda* warnings to a suspect who has given a voluntary but unwarned statement ordinarily should suffice to remove the conditions that precluded admission of the earlier statement. In such circumstances, the finder of fact may reasonably conclude that the suspect made a rational and intelligent choice whether to waive or invoke his rights.

III

Though belated, the reading of respondent's rights was undeniably complete. McAllister testified that he read the *Miranda* warnings aloud from a printed card and recorded Elstad's responses. There is no question that respondent knowingly and voluntarily waived his right to remain silent before he described his participation in the burglary. . . .

. . . The standard *Miranda* warnings explicitly inform the suspect of his right to consult a lawyer before speaking. Police officers are ill-equipped to pinch-hit for counsel, construing the murky and difficult questions of when "custody" begins or whether a given unwarned statement will ultimately be held admissible. . . .

IV

When police ask questions of a suspect in custody without administering the required warnings, *Miranda* dictates that the answers received be presumed compelled and that they be excluded from evidence at trial in the State's case in chief. The Court has carefully adhered to this principle, permitting a narrow exception only where pressing public safety concerns demanded. See *New York* v. *Quarles*, 467 U.S., at 655–656. The Court today in no way retreats from the bright-line rule of *Miranda*. . . .

. . . We hold today that a suspect who has once responded to unwarned yet uncoercive questioning is not thereby disabled from waiving his rights and confessing after he has been given the requisite *Miranda* warnings.

The judgment of the Court of Appeals of Oregon is reversed, and the case is remanded for further proceedings not inconsistent with this opinion.

It is so ordered.

JUSTICE BRENNAN, with whom JUSTICE MARSHALL joins, dissenting.

The Self-Incrimination Clause of the Fifth Amendment guarantees every individual that, if taken into official custody, he shall be informed of important constitutional rights and be given the opportunity knowingly and voluntarily to waive those rights before being interrogated about suspected wrongdoing. . . .

Even while purporting to reaffirm these constitutional guarantees, the Court has engaged of late in a studied campaign to strip the *Miranda* decision piecemeal and to undermine the rights *Miranda* sought to secure. Today's decision not only extends this effort a further step, but delivers a potentially crippling blow to *Miranda* and the ability of courts to safeguard the rights of persons accused of crime. For at least with respect to successive confessions, the Court today appears to strip remedies for *Miranda* violations of the "fruit of the poisonous tree" doctrine prohibiting the use of evidence presumptively derived from official illegality.

Two major premises undergird the Court's decision. The Court rejects as nothing more than "speculative" the long-recognized presumption that an illegally extracted confession causes the accused to confess again out of the mistaken belief that he already has sealed his fate, and it condemns as "'extravagant'" the requirement that the prosecution affirmatively rebut the presumption before the subsequent confession may be admitted. *Ante*, at 307, 313. The Court instead adopts a new rule that, so long as the accused is given the usual *Miranda* warnings before further interrogation, the taint of a previous confession obtained in violation of *Miranda* "ordinarily" must be viewed as *automatically* dissipated. *Ante*, at 311.

. . .

I

. . .

The Court's marble-palace psychoanalysis is tidy, but it flies in the face of our own precedents, demonstrates a startling unawareness of the realities of police interrogation, and is completely out of tune with the experience of state and federal courts over the last 20 years.

[A(2)]

. . .

One police practice that courts have frequently encountered involves the withholding of *Miranda* warnings until the end of an interrogation session. Specifically, the police escort a suspect into a room, sit him down and, without explaining his Fifth Amendment rights or obtaining a knowing and voluntary waiver of those rights, interrogate him about his suspected criminal activity. If the police obtain a confession, it is then typed up, the police hand the suspect a pen for his signature, and—just before he signs—the police advise him of his *Miranda* rights and ask him to proceed. Alternatively, the police may call a stenographer in after they have obtained the confession, advise the suspect for the first time of his *Miranda* rights, and ask him to repeat what he has just told them. In such circumstances, the process of giving *Miranda* warnings and obtaining the final confession is "'merely a formalizing, a setting down almost as a scrivener does, [of] what had already taken [place].'" *People* v. *Raddatz*, 91 Ill. App. 2d 425, 430, 235 N. E. 2d 353, 356 (1968) (quoting trial court). . . .

B

The correct approach, administered for almost 20 years by most courts with no untoward results, is to presume that an admission or confession obtained in violation of *Miranda* taints a subsequent confession unless the prosecution can show that the taint is so attenuated as to justify admission of the subsequent confession. . . .

JUSTICE STEVENS, dissenting.

The Court concludes its opinion with a carefully phrased statement of its holding:

"We hold today that a suspect who has once responded to unwarned yet uncoercive questioning is not thereby disabled from waiving his rights and confessing after he has been given the requisite *Miranda* warnings." *Ante*, at 318.

I find nothing objectionable in such a holding. Moreover, because the Court expressly endorses the "bright-line rule of *Miranda*," which conclusively presumes that incriminating statements obtained from a suspect in custody without administering the required warnings are the product of compulsion, and because the Court places so much emphasis on the special facts of this case, I am persuaded that the Court intends its holding to apply only to a narrow category of cases in which the initial questioning of the suspect was made in a totally uncoercive setting and in which the first confession obviously had no influence on the second. I nevertheless dissent because even such a narrowly confined exception is inconsistent with the Court's prior cases, because the attempt to identify its boundaries in future cases will breed confusion and uncertainty in the administration of criminal justice, and because it denigrates the importance of one of the core constitutional rights that protects every American citizen from the kind of tyranny that has flourished in other societies.

I

The desire to achieve a just result in this particular case has produced an opinion that is somewhat opaque and internally inconsistent. If I read it correctly, its conclusion rests on two untenable premises: (1) that the respondent's first confession was not the product of coercion; and (2) that no constitutional right was violated when respondent was questioned in a tranquil, domestic setting.

Even before the decision in *Miranda* v. *Arizona*, 384 U.S. 436 (1966), it had been recognized that police interrogation of a suspect who has been taken into custody is presumptively coercive. That presumption had its greatest force when the questioning occurred in a police station, when it was prolonged, and when there was evidence that the prisoner had suffered physical injury. To rebut the presumption, the prosecutor had the burden of proving the absence of any actual coercion. Because police officers are generally more credible witnesses than prisoners and because it is always difficult for triers of fact to disregard evidence of guilt when addressing a procedural question, more often than not the presumption of coercion afforded only slight protection to the accused.

The decision in *Miranda* v. *Arizona* clarified the law in three important respects. First, it provided the prosecutor with a simple method of overcoming the presumption of coercion. If the police interrogation is preceded by the warning specified in that opinion, the usual presumption does not attach. Second, it provided an important protection to the accused by making the presumption of coercion irrebuttable if the prescribed warnings are not given. Third, the decision made it clear that a self-incriminatory statement made in response to custodial interrogation was always to be considered "compelled" within the meaning of the Fifth Amendment to the Federal Constitution if the interrogation had not been preceded by appropriate warnings. Thus the irrebuttable presumption of coercion that applies to such a self-incriminatory statement, like a finding of actual coercion, renders the resulting confession inadmissible as a matter of federal constitutional law.

In my opinion, the Court's attempt to fashion a distinction between actual coercion "by physical violence or other deliberate means calculated to break the suspect's will," *ante*, at 312, and irrebuttably presumed coercion cannot succeed. The presumption is only legitimate if it is assumed that there is always a coercive aspect to custodial interrogation that is not preceded by adequate advice of the constitutional right to remain silent. Although I would not support it, I could understand a rule that refused to apply the presumption unless the interrogation took place in an especially coercive setting—perhaps only in the police station itself—but if the presumption arises whenever the accused has been taken into custody or his freedom has been restrained in any significant way, it will surely be futile to try to develop subcategories of custodial interrogation. Indeed, a major purpose of treating the presumption of coercion as irrebuttable is to avoid the kind of fact-bound inquiry that today's decision will surely engender.

. . . surely the fact that an earlier confession was obtained by unlawful methods should add force to the presumption of coercion that attaches to subsequent custodial interrogation and should require the prosecutor to shoulder a heavier burden of rebuttal than in a routine case. Simple logic, as well as the interest in not providing an affirmative incentive to police misconduct, requires that result. I see no reason why the violation of a rule that is as well recognized and easily administered as the duty to give *Miranda* warnings should not also impose an additional burden on the prosecutor. . . .

Furman v. Georgia

408 U.S. 238 (1972)

William Henry Furman was convicted of murder in Georgia and sentenced to death. Another petitioner was sentenced to death after being convicted of rape in Georgia. A third petitioner was sentenced to death in Texas for the crime of rape. The Court was asked whether the death penalty in these cases constituted cruel and unusual punishment and was therefore unconstitutional.

PER CURIAM.

Petitioner in No. 69–5003 was convicted of murder in Georgia and was sentenced to death pursuant to Ga. Code Ann. § 26–1005 (Supp. 1971) (effective prior to July 1, 1969). 225 Ga.253, 167 S. E. 2d 628 (1969). Petitioner in No. 69–5030 was convicted of rape in Georgia and was sentenced to death pursuant to Ga. Code Ann. § 26–1302 (Supp. 1971) (effective prior to July 1, 1969). 225 Ga. 790, 171 S.E. 2d 501 (1969). Petitioner in No. 69–5031 was convicted of rape in Texas and was sentenced to death pursuant to Tex. Penal Code, Art. 1189 (1961). 447 S. W. 2d 932 (Ct. Crim. App. 1969). Certiorari was granted limited to the following question: "Does the imposition and carrying out of the death penalty in [these cases] constitute cruel and unusual punishment in violation of the Eighth and Fourteenth Amendments?" 403 U.S. 952 (1971). The Court holds that the imposition and carrying out of the death penalty in these cases constitute cruel and unusual punishment in violation of the Eighth and Fourteenth Amendments. The judgment in each case is therefore reversed insofar as it leaves undisturbed the death sentence imposed, and the cases are remanded for further proceedings.

So ordered.

MR. JUSTICE DOUGLAS, MR. JUSTICE BRENNAN, MR. JUSTICE STEWART, MR. JUSTICE WHITE, and MR. JUSTICE MARSHALL have filed separate opinions in support of the judgments. THE CHIEF JUSTICE, MR. JUSTICE BLACKMUN, MR. JUSTICE POWELL, and MR. JUSTICE REHNQUIST have filed separate dissenting opinions.

MR. JUSTICE DOUGLAS, concurring.

. . .

The words "cruel and unusual" certainly include penalties that are barbaric. But the words, at least when read in light of the English proscription against selective and irregular use of penalties, suggest that it is "cruel and unusual" to apply the death penalty—or any other penalty—selectively to minorities whose numbers are few, who are outcasts of society, and who are unpopular, but whom society is willing to see suffer though it would not countenance general application of the same penalty across the board. . . .

There is increasing recognition of the fact that the basic theme of equal protection is implicit in "cruel and unusual" punishments. "A penalty . . . should be considered 'unusually' imposed if it is administered arbitrarily or discriminatorily." The same authors add that "[t]he extreme rarity with which applicable death penalty provisions are put to use raises a strong inference of arbitrariness." The President's Commission on Law Enforcement and Administration of Justice recently concluded:

"Finally there is evidence that the imposition of the death sentence and the exercise of dispensing power by the courts and the executive follow discriminatory patterns. The death sentence is disproportionately imposed and carried out on the poor, the Negro, and the members of unpopular groups."

A study of capital cases in Texas from 1924 to 1968 reached the following conclusions:

"Application of the death penalty is unequal: most of those executed were poor, young, and ignorant.

"Seventy-five of the 460 cases involved co-defendants, who, under Texas law, were given separate trials. In several instances where a white and a Negro were co-defendants, the white was sentenced to life imprisonment or a term of years, and the Negro was given the death penalty.

"Another ethnic disparity is found in the type of sentence imposed for rape. The Negro convicted of rape is far more likely to get the death penalty than a term sentence, whereas whites and Latins are far more likely to get a term sentence than the death penalty."

. . .

MR. JUSTICE BRENNAN, concurring.

II

. . .

In determining whether a punishment comports with human dignity, we are aided also by a second principle inherent in the Clause—that the State must not arbitrarily inflict a severe punishment. This principle derives from the notion that the State does not respect human dignity when, without reason, it inflicts upon some people a severe punishment that it does not inflict upon others. Indeed, the very words "cruel and unusual punishments" imply condemnation of the arbitrary infliction of severe punishments. . . .

III

. . .

The question . . . is whether the deliberate infliction of death is today consistent with the command of the Clause that the State may not inflict punishments that do not comport with human dignity. I will analyze the punishment of death in terms of the principles set out above and the cumulative test to which they lead: It is a denial of human dignity for the State arbitrarily to subject a person to an unusually severe punishment that society has indicated it does not regard as acceptable, and that cannot be shown to serve any penal purpose more effectively than a significantly less drastic punishment. Under these principles and this test, death is today a "cruel and unusual" punishment.

. . .

In comparison to all other punishments today, then, the deliberate extinguishment of human life by the State is uniquely degrading to human dignity. I would not hesitate to hold, on that ground alone, that death is today a "cruel and unusual" punishment, were it not that death is a punishment of longstanding usage and acceptance in this country. I therefore turn to the second principle—that the State may not arbitrarily inflict an unusually severe punishment.

The outstanding characteristic of our present practice of punishing criminals by death is the infrequency with which we resort to it. The evidence is conclusive that death is not the ordinary punishment for any crime.

There has been a steady decline in the infliction of this punishment in every decade since the 1930's, the earliest period for which accurate statistics are available. In the 1930's, executions averaged 167 per year; in the 1940's, the average was 128; in the 1950's, it was 72; and in the years 1960–1962, it was 48. There have been a total of 46 executions since then, 36 of them in 1963–1964. Yet our population and the number of capital crimes committed have increased greatly over the past four decades. The contemporary rarity of the infliction of this punishment is thus the end result of a long-continued decline. . . .

When the punishment of death is inflicted in a trivial number of the cases in which it is legally available, the conclusion is virtually inescapable that it is being inflicted arbitrarily. Indeed, it smacks of little more than a lottery system. The States claim, however, that this rarity is evidence not of arbitrariness, but of informed selectivity: Death is inflicted, they say, only in "extreme" cases.

Informed selectivity, of course, is a value not to be denigrated. Yet presumably the States could make precisely the same claim if there were 10 executions per year, or five, or even if there were but one. That there may be as many as 50 per year does not strengthen the claim. When the rate of infliction is at this low level, it is highly implausible that only the worst criminals or the criminals who commit the worst crimes are selected for this punishment. No one has yet suggested a rational basis that could differentiate in those terms the few who die from the many who go to prison. . . .

Although it is difficult to believe that any State today wishes to proclaim adherence to "naked vengeance," *Trop* v. *Dulles,* 356 U. S., at 112 (BRENNAN, J., concurring), the States claim, in reliance upon its statutory authorization, that death is the only fit punishment for capital crimes and that this retributive purpose justifies its infliction. . . . As administered today, however, the punishment of death cannot be justified as a necessary means of exacting retribution from criminals. When the overwhelming number of criminals who commit capital crimes go to prison, it cannot be concluded that death serves the purpose of retribution

more effectively than imprisonment. The asserted public belief that murderers and rapists deserve to die is flatly inconsistent with the execution of a random few. . . .

MR. JUSTICE STEWART, concurring.

The penalty of death differs from all other forms of criminal punishment, not in degree but in kind. It is unique in its total irrevocability. It is unique in its rejection of rehabilitation of the convict as a basic purpose of criminal justice. And it is unique, finally, in its absolute renunciation of all that is embodied in our concept of humanity.

For these and other reasons, at least two of my Brothers have concluded that the infliction of the death penalty is constitutionally impermissible in all circumstances under the Eighth and Fourteenth Amendments. Their case is a strong one. But I find it unnecessary to reach the ultimate question they would decide. See *Ashwander* v. *Tennessee Valley Authority,* 297 U. S. 288, 347 (Brandeis, J., concurring).

. . .

. . . the death sentences now before us are the product of a legal system that brings them, I believe, within the very core of the Eighth Amendment's guarantee against cruel and unusual punishments, a guarantee applicable against the States through the Fourteenth Amendment. *Robinson* v. *California,* 370 U. S. 660. In the first place, it is clear that these sentences are "cruel" in the sense that they excessively go beyond, not in degree but in kind, the punishments that the state legislatures have determined to be necessary. *Weems* v. *United States,* 217 U. S. 349. In the second place, it is equally clear that these sentences are "unusual" in the sense that the penalty of death is infrequently imposed for murder, and that its imposition for rape is extraordinarily rare. But I do not rest my conclusion upon these two propositions alone.

These death sentences are cruel and unusual in the same way that being struck by lightning is cruel and unusual. For, of all the people convicted of rapes and murders in 1967 and 1968, many just as reprehensible as these, the petitioners are among a capriciously selected random handful upon whom the sentence of death has in fact been imposed. My concurring Brothers have demonstrated that, if any basis can be discerned for the selection of these few to be sentenced to die, it is the constitutionally impermissible basis of race. See *McLaughlin* v. *Florida*, 379 U. S. 184. But racial discrimination has not been proved, and I put it to one side. I simply conclude that the Eighth and Fourteenth Amendments cannot tolerate the infliction of a sentence of death under legal systems that permit this unique penalty to be so wantonly and so freakishly imposed.

For these reasons I concur in the judgments of the Court.

MR. JUSTICE WHITE, concurring.

. . .

The imposition and execution of the death penalty are obviously cruel in the dictionary sense. But the penalty has not been considered cruel and unusual punishment in the constitutional sense because it was thought justified by the social ends it was deemed to serve. At the moment that it ceases realistically to further these purposes, however, the emerging question is whether its imposition in such circumstances would violate the Eighth Amendment. It is my view that it would, for its imposition would then be the pointless and needless extinction of life with only marginal contributions to any discernible social or public purposes. A penalty with such negligible returns to the State would be patently excessive and cruel and unusual punishment violative of the Eighth Amendment.

It is also my judgment that this point has been reached with respect to capital punishment as it is presently administered under the statutes involved in these cases. Concededly, it is difficult to prove as a general proposition that capital punishment, however administered, more effectively serves the ends of the criminal law than does imprisonment. But however that may be, I cannot avoid the conclusion that as the statutes before us are now administered, the penalty is so infrequently imposed that the threat of execution is too attenuated to be of substantial service to criminal justice.

. . .

MR. JUSTICE MARSHALL, concurring.

III

Perhaps the most important principle in analyzing "cruel and unusual" punishment questions is one that is reiterated again and again in the prior opinions of the Court: *i. e.*, the cruel and unusual language "must draw its meaning from the evolving standards of decency that mark the progress of a maturing society." Thus, a penalty that was permissible at one time in our Nation's history is not necessarily permissible today.

The fact, therefore, that the Court, or individual Justices, may have in the past expressed an opinion that the death penalty is constitutional is not now binding on us.·. . .

[After rejecting the traditional purposes conceivably served by capital punishment (retribution, deterrence, prevention of repetitive criminal acts, encouragement of guilty pleas and confessions, eugenics, and economy), Marshall turns to other considerations.]

VI

. . . capital punishment is imposed discriminatorily against certain identifiable classes of people; there is evidence that innocent people have been executed before their innocence can be proved; and the death penalty wreaks havoc with our entire criminal justice system. Each of these facts is considered briefly below.

Regarding discrimination, it has been said that "[i]t is usually the poor, the illiterate, the underprivileged, the member of the minority group— the man who, because he is without means, and is defended by a court-appointed attorney—who becomes society's sacrificial lamb . . . ." Indeed, a look at the bare statistics regarding executions is enough to betray much of the discrimination. A total of 3,859 persons have been executed since 1930, of whom 1,751 were white and 2,066 were Negro. Of the executions, 3,334 were for murder; 1,664 of the executed murderers were white and 1,630 were Negro; 455 persons, including 48 whites and 405 Negroes, were executed for rape. It is immediately apparent that Negroes were executed far more often than whites in proportion to their percentage of the population. Studies indicate that while the higher rate of execution among Negroes is partially due to a higher rate of crime, there is evidence of racial discrimination. Racial or other discriminations should not be surprising. In *McGautha* v. *California*, 402 U. S., at 207, this Court held "that committing to the untrammeled discretion of the jury the power to pronounce life or death in capital cases is [not] offensive to anything in the Constitution." This was an open invitation to discrimination.

There is also overwhelming evidence that the death penalty is employed against men and not women. Only 32 women have been executed since 1930, while 3,827 men have met a similar fate. It is difficult to understand why women have received such favored treatment since the purposes allegedly served by capital punishment seemingly are equally applicable to both sexes.

It also is evident that the burden of capital punishment falls upon the poor, the ignorant, and the underprivileged members of society. It is the poor, and the members of minority groups who are least able to voice their complaints against capital punishment. Their impotence leaves them victims of a sanction that the wealthier, better-represented, just-as-guilty person can escape. . . .

Just as Americans know little about who is executed and why, they are unaware of the potential dangers of executing an innocent man. Our "beyond a reasonable doubt" burden of proof in criminal cases is intended to protect the innocent, but we know it is not foolproof. Various studies have shown that people whose innocence is later convincingly established are convicted and sentenced to death.

. . .

While it is difficult to ascertain with certainty the degree to which the death penalty is discriminatorily imposed or the number of innocent persons sentenced to die, there is one conclusion about the penalty that is universally accepted— *i. e.*, it "tends to distort the course of the criminal law." As Mr. Justice Frankfurter said:

"I am strongly against capital punishment . . . When life is at hazard in a trial, it sensationalizes the whole thing almost unwittingly; the effect on juries, the Bar, the public, the Judiciary, I regard as very bad. I think scientifically the claim of deterrence is not worth much. Whatever proof there may be in my judgment does not outweigh the social loss due to the inherent sensationalism of a trial for life."

. . .

MR. CHIEF JUSTICE BURGER, with whom MR. JUSTICE BLACKMUN, MR. JUSTICE POWELL, and MR. JUSTICE REHNQUIST join, dissenting.

At the outset it is important to note that only two members of the Court, MR. JUSTICE BRENNAN and MR. JUSTICE MARSHALL, have concluded that the Eighth Amendment prohibits capital punishment for all crimes and under all circumstances. . . .

I

If we were possessed of legislative power, I would either join with MR. JUSTICE BRENNAN and MR. JUSTICE MARSHALL or, at the very least, restrict the use of capital punishment to a small category of the most heinous crimes. Our constitutional inquiry, however, must be divorced from personal feelings as to the morality and efficacy of the death penalty, and be confined to the meaning and applicability of the uncertain language of the Eighth Amendment. . . .

. . . it disregards the history of the Eighth Amendment and all the judicial comment that has followed to rely on the term "unusual" as affecting the outcome of these cases. Instead, I view these cases as turning on the single question whether capital punishment is "cruel" in the constitutional sense. The term "unusual" cannot be read as limiting the ban on "cruel" punishments or as somehow expanding the meaning of the term "cruel." For this reason I am unpersuaded by the facile argument that since capital punishment has always been cruel in the everyday sense of the word, and has become unusual due to decreased use, it is, therefore, now "cruel and unusual."

. . .

V

Today the Court has not ruled that capital punishment is *per se* violative of the Eighth Amendment; nor has it ruled that the punishment is barred for any particular class or classes of crimes. . . .

While I would not undertake to make a definitive statement as to the parameters of the Court's ruling, it is clear that if state legislatures and the Congress wish to maintain the availability of capital punishment, significant statutory changes will have to be made. Since the two pivotal concurring opinions turn on the assumption that the punishment of death is now meted out in a random and unpredictable manner, legislative bodies may seek to bring their laws into compliance with the Court's ruling by providing standards for juries and judges to follow in determing the sentence in capital cases or by more narrowly defining the crimes for which the penalty is to be imposed.

. . .

MR. JUSTICE BLACKMUN, dissenting.

[Blackman expresses his "abhorrence" for the death penalty and states that if he were a legislator he would vote against the death penalty and that if he were a governor he would be "sorely tempted" to exercise executive clemency. But he concludes that the Court oversteps its constitutional duties by striking down the Georgia and Texas statutes.]

MR. JUSTICE POWELL, with whom THE CHIEF JUSTICE, MR. JUSTICE BLACKMUN, and MR. JUSTICE REHNQUIST join, dissenting.

. . .

In terms of the constitutional role of this Court, the impact of the majority's ruling is all the greater because the decision encroaches upon an area squarely within the historic prerogative of the legislative branch—both state and federal—to protect the citizenry through the designation of penalties for prohibitable conduct. It is the very sort of judgment that the legislative branch is competent to make and for which the judiciary is ill-equipped. . . .

MR. JUSTICE REHNQUIST, with whom THE CHIEF JUSTICE, MR. JUSTICE BLACKMUN, and MR. JUSTICE POWELL join, dissenting.

. . .

. . . The most expansive reading of the leading constitutional cases does not remotely suggest that this Court has been granted a roving commission, either by the Founding Fathers or by the framers of the Fourteenth Amendment, to strike down laws that are based upon notions of policy or morality suddenly found unacceptable by a majority of this Court. . . .

This philosophy of the Framers is best described by one of the ablest and greatest of their number, James Madison, in Federalist No. 51:

"In framing a government which is to be administered by men over men, the great difficulty lies in this: You must first enable the government to controul the governed; and in the next place, oblige it to controul itself."

Madison's observation applies to the Judicial Branch with at least as much force as to the Legislative and Executive Branches. While overreaching by the Legislative and Executive Branches may result in the sacrifice of individual protections that the Constitution was designed to secure against action of the State, judicial overreaching may result in sacrifice of the equally important right of the people to govern themselves. . . .

Gregg v. Georgia
428 U.S. 153 (1976)

After the Supreme Court in *Furman* v. *Georgia* (1972) declared the death penalty unconstitutional as practiced in Georgia and Texas, more than thirty states reinstituted the death penalty. But these states added new procedures in an effort to minimize the arbitrariness of the death sentence. On July 2, 1976, the Court handed down five decisions that reviewed these new state laws. In this case, Troy Leon Gregg was charged with committing armed robbery and murder. He was convicted and the jury returned a sentence of death.

Judgment of the Court, and opinion of MR. JUSTICE STEWART, MR. JUSTICE POWELL, and MR. JUSTICE STEVENS, announced by MR. JUSTICE STEWART.

The issue in this case is whether the imposition of the sentence of death for the crime of murder under the law of Georgia violates the Eighth and Fourteenth Amendments.

I

The petitioner, Troy Gregg, was charged with committing armed robbery and murder. In accordance with Georgia procedure in capital cases, the trial was in two stages, a guilt stage and a sentencing stage. *[The jury found Gregg guilty of two counts of armed robbery and two counts of murder. At the penalty stage, which took place before the same jury, neither the prosecutor nor Gregg's lawyer offered any additional evidence. The trial judge instructed the jury that it could recommend either a death sentence or a life prison sentence on each count. The jury could consider the facts and circumstances, if any, presented by the parties in mitigation or aggravation. To impose the death penalty, the jury had to first find beyond a reasonable doubt one of these aggravating circumstances: (1) that the murder was committed while Gregg was engaged in the armed robbery, (2) that Gregg committed the offense of murder for the purpose of receiving money and the automobile taken during the murder, or (3) the offense of murder was "outrageously and wantonly vile, horrible and inhuman" in that it involved- the "depravity" of Gregg's mind.]*

[The jury found the first and second of these circumstances and returned verdicts of death on each count. The Supreme Court of Georgia affirmed the convictions and the imposition of the death sentences for murder.]

. . .

III

We address initially the basic contention that the punishment of death for the crime of murder is, under all circumstances, "cruel and unusual" in violation of the Eighth and Fourteenth Amendments of the Constitution. In Part IV of this opinion, we will consider the sentence of death imposed under the Georgia statutes at issue in this case.

. . .

B

. . . in assessing a punishment selected by a democratically elected legislature against the constitutional measure, we presume its validity. We may not require the legislature to select the least severe penalty possible so long as the penalty selected is not cruelly inhumane or disproportionate to the crime involved. And a heavy burden rests on those who would attack the judgment of the representatives of the people.

This is true in part because the constitutional test is intertwined with an assessment of contemporary standards and the legislative judgment weighs heavily in ascertaining such standards.

"[I]n a democratic society legislatures, not courts, are constituted to respond to the will and consequently the moral values of the people." *Furman v. Georgia, supra,* at 383 (BURGER, C. J., dissenting). . . .

C

In the discussion to this point we have sought to identify the principles and considerations that guide a court in addressing an Eighth Amendment claim. We now consider specifically whether the sentence of death for the crime of murder is a *per se* violation of the Eighth and Fourteenth Amendments to the Constitution. We note first that history and precedent strongly support a negative answer to this question.

. . .

The most marked indication of society's endorsement of the death penalty for murder is the legislative response to *Furman.* The legislatures of at least 35 States have enacted new statutes that provide for the death penalty for at least some crimes that result in the death of another person. And the Congress of the United States, in 1974, enacted a statute providing the death penalty for aircraft piracy that results in death. These recently adopted statutes have attempted to address the concerns expressed by the Court in *Furman* primarily (i) by specifying the factors to be weighed and the procedures to be followed in deciding when to impose a capital sentence, or (ii) by making the death penalty mandatory for specified crimes. But all of the post-*Furman* statutes make clear that capital punishment itself has not been rejected by the elected representatives of the people.

In the only statewide referendum occurring since *Furman* and brought to our attention, the people of California adopted a constitutional amendment that authorized capital punishment, in effect negating a prior ruling by the Supreme Court of California in *People* v. *Anderson,* 6 Cal. 3d 628, 493 P. 2d 880, cert. denied, 406 U. S. 958 (1972), that the death penalty violated the California Constitution.

The jury also is a significant and reliable objective index of contemporary values because it is so directly involved. . . . the actions of juries in many States since *Furman* are fully compatible with the legislative judgments, reflected in the new statutes, as to the continued utility and necessity of capital punishment in appropriate cases. At the close of 1974 at least 254 persons had been sentenced to death since *Furman,* and by the end of March 1976, more than 460 persons were subject to death sentences.

. . .

. . . we cannot say that the judgment of the Georgia Legislature that capital punishment may be necessary in some cases is clearly wrong. Considerations of federalism, as well as respect for the ability of a legislature to evaluate, in terms of its particular State, the moral consensus concerning the death penalty and its social utility as a sanction, require us to conclude, in the absence of more convincing evidence, that the infliction of death as a punishment for murder is not without justification and thus is not unconstitutionally severe.

. . . we cannot say that the punishment is invariably disproportionate to the crime. It is an extreme sanction, suitable to the most extreme of crimes.

We hold that the death penalty is not a form of punishment that may never be imposed, regardless of the circumstances of the offense, regardless of the character of the offender, and regardless of the procedure followed in reaching the decision to impose it.

IV

We now consider whether Georgia may impose the death penalty on the petitioner in this case.

A

. . . the concerns expressed in *Furman* that the penalty of death not be imposed in an arbitrary or capricious manner can be met by a carefully drafted statute that ensures that the sentencing authority is given adequate information and guidance. As a general proposition these concerns are best met by a system that provides for a bifurcated proceeding at which the sentencing authority is apprised of the information relevant to the imposition of sentence and provided with standards to guide its use of the information.

We do not intend to suggest that only the above-described procedures would be permissible under *Furman* or that any sentencing system constructed along these general lines would inevitably satisfy the concerns of *Furman*, for each distinct system must be examined on an individual basis. Rather, we have embarked upon this general exposition to make clear that it is possible to construct capital-sentencing systems capable of meeting *Furman's* constitutional concerns.

B

We now turn to consideration of the constitutionality of Georgia's capital-sentencing procedures. In the wake of *Furman*, Georgia amended its capital punishment statute, but chose not to narrow the scope of its murder provisions. See Part II, *supra*. Thus, now as before *Furman*, in Georgia "[a] person commits murder when he unlawfully and with malice aforethought, either express or implied, causes the death of another human being." Ga. Code Ann., § 26–1101 (a) (1972). All persons convicted of murder "shall be punished by death or by imprisonment for life." § 26–1101 (c) (1972).

Georgia did act, however, to narrow the class of murderers subject to capital punishment by specifying 10 statutory aggravating circumstances, one of which must be found by the jury to exist beyond a reasonable doubt before a death sentence can ever be imposed. In addition, the jury is authorized to consider any other appropriate aggravating or mitigating circumstances. § 27–2534.1 (b) (Supp. 1975). The jury is not required to find any mitigating circumstance in order to make a recommendation of mercy that is binding on the trial court, see § 27–2302 (Supp. 1975), but it must find a *statutory* aggravating circumstance before recommending a sentence of death.

These procedures require the jury to consider the circumstances of the crime and the criminal before it recommends sentence. No longer can a Georgia jury do as Furman's jury did: reach a finding of the defendant's guilt and then, without guidance or direction, decide whether he should live or die. Instead, the jury's attention is directed to the specific circumstances of the crime: Was it committed in the course of another capital felony? Was it committed for money? Was it committed upon a peace officer or judicial officer? Was it committed in a particularly heinous way or in a manner that endangered the lives of many persons? In addition, the jury's attention is focused on the characteristics of the person who committed the crime: Does he have a record of prior convictions for capital offenses? Are there any special facts about this defendant that mitigate against imposing capital punishment (*e. g.*, his youth, the extent of his cooperation with the police, his emotional state at the time of the crime). As a result, while some jury discretion still exists, "the discretion to be exercised is controlled by clear and objective standards so as to produce non-discriminatory application." *Coley* v. *State*, 231 Ga. 829, 834, 204 S. E. 2d 612, 615 (1974).

As an important additional safeguard against arbitrariness and caprice, the Georgia statutory scheme provides for automatic appeal of all death sentences to the State's Supreme Court. That court is required by statute to review each sentence of death and determine whether it was imposed under the influence of passion or prejudice, whether the evidence supports the jury's finding of a statutory aggravating circumstance, and whether the sentence is disproportionate compared to those sentences imposed in similar cases. § 27–2537 (c) (Supp. 1975).

. . .

V

The basic concern of *Furman* centered on those defendants who were being condemned to death capriciously and arbitrarily. Under the procedures before the Court in that case, sentencing authorities were not directed to give attention to the nature or circumstances of the crime committed or to the character or record of the defendant. . . .

For the reasons expressed in this opinion, we hold that the statutory system under which Gregg was sentenced to death does not violate the Constitution. Accordingly, the judgment of the Georgia Supreme Court is affirmed.

It is so ordered.

MR. JUSTICE WHITE, with whom THE CHIEF JUSTICE and MR. JUSTICE REHNQUIST join, concurring in the judgment.

. . .

Statement of THE CHIEF JUSTICE and MR. JUSTICE REHNQUIST:

We concur in the judgment and join the opinion of MR. JUSTICE WHITE, agreeing with its analysis that Georgia's system of capital punishment comports with the Court's holding in *Furman* v. *Georgia*, 408 U. S. 238 (1972).

MR. JUSTICE BLACKMUN, concurring in the judgment.

I concur in the judgment. See *Furman* v. *Georgia*, 408 U. S. 238, 405–414 (1972) (BLACKMUN, J., dissenting), and *id.*, at 375 (BURGER, C. J., dissenting); *id.*, at 414 POWELL, J., dissenting); *id.*, at 465 (REHNQUIST, J., dissenting).

MR. JUSTICE BRENNAN, dissenting.

. . .

The fatal constitutional infirmity in the punishment of death is that it treats "members of the human race as nonhumans, as objects to be toyed with and discarded. [It is] thus inconsistent with the fundamental premise of the Clause that even the vilest criminal remains a human being possessed of common human dignity." *Id.*, at 273. As such it is a penalty that "subjects the individual to a fate forbidden by the principle of civilized treatment guaranteed by the [Clause]." I therefore would hold, on that ground alone, that death is today a cruel and unusual punishment prohibited by the Clause. . . .

MR. JUSTICE MARSHALL, dissenting.

In *Furman* v. *Georgia*, 408 U. S. 238, 314 (1972) (concurring opinion), I set forth at some length my views on the basic issue presented to the Court in these cases. The death penalty, I concluded, is a cruel and unusual punishment prohibited by the Eighth and Fourteenth Amendments. That continues to be my view.

. . .

Since the decision in *Furman*, the legislatures of 35 States have enacted new statutes authorizing the imposition of the death sentence for certain crimes, and Congress has enacted a law providing the death penalty for air piracy resulting in death. 49 U. S. C. §§ 1472 (i), (n) (1970 ed., Supp. IV). I would be less than candid if I did not acknowledge that these developments have a significant bearing on a realistic assessment of the moral acceptability of the death penalty to the American people. But if the constitutionality of the death penalty turns, as I have urged, on the opinion of an *informed* citizenry, then even the enactment of new death statutes cannot be viewed as conclusive. In *Furman*, I observed that the American people are largely unaware of the information critical to a judgment on the morality of the death penalty, and concluded that if they were better informed they would consider it shocking, unjust, and unacceptable. 408 U. S., at 360–369. A recent study, conducted after the enactment of the post-*Furman* statutes, has confirmed that the American people know little about the death penalty, and that the opinions of an informed public would differ significantly from those of a public unaware of the consequences and effects of the death penalty.

. . .

. . . The mere fact that the community demands the murderer's life in return for the evil he has done cannot sustain the death penalty, for as JUSTICES STEWART, POWELL, and STEVENS remind us, "the Eighth Amendment demands more than that a challenged punishment be acceptable to contemporary society." *Ante*, at 182. To be sustained under the Eighth Amendment, the death penalty must "compor[t] with the basic concept of human dignity at the core of the Amendment," *ibid.;* the objective in imposing it must be "[consistent] with our respect for the dignity of [other] men." *Ante*, at 183. See *Trop* v. *Dulles*, 356 U. S. 86, 100 (1958) (plurality opinion). Under these standards, the taking of life "because the wrongdoer deserves it" surely must fall, for such a punishment has as its very basis the total denial of the wrongdoer's dignity and worth.

The death penalty, unnecessary to promote the goal of deterrence or to further any legitimate notion of retribution, is an excessive penalty forbidden by the Eighth and Fourteenth Amendments. I respectfully dissent from the Court's

judgment upholding the sentences of death imposed upon the petitioners in these cases.

McCleskey v. Kemp
481 U.S. 278 (1987)

Warren McCleskey, a black, was convicted of murder and two counts of armed robbery. After his conviction and death sentence were affirmed by the Georgia Supreme Court, he petitioned for habeas corpus relief. A federal district court concluded that he failed to support his claim that Georgia's death sentencing process was unconstitutional. The Eleventh Circuit reversed. The Supreme Court here reviews the question whether the Eighth Amendment was violated because of evidence that the death penalty in Georgia is imposed more often on black defendants and killers of white victims than on white defendants and killers of black victims.

JUSTICE POWELL delivered the opinion of the Court.

This case presents the question whether a complex statistical study that indicates a risk that racial considerations enter into capital sentencing determinations proves that petitioner McCleskey's capital sentence is unconstitutional under the Eighth or Fourteenth Amendment.

I

McCleskey, a black man, was convicted of two counts of armed robbery and one count of murder in the Superior Court of Fulton County, Georgia, on October 12, 1978. McCleskey's convictions arose out of the robbery of a furniture store and the killing of a white police officer during the course of the robbery. The evidence at trial indicated that McCleskey and three accomplices planned and carried out the robbery. All four were armed. McCleskey entered the front of the store while the other three entered the rear. McCleskey secured the front of the store by rounding up the customers and forcing them to lie face down on the floor. The other three rounded up the employees in the rear and tied them up with tape. The manager was forced at gunpoint to turn over the store receipts, his watch, and $6.00. During the course of the robbery, a police officer, answering a silent alarm, entered the store through the front

door. As he was walking down the center aisle of the store, two shots were fired. Both struck the officer. One hit him in the face and killed him.

Several weeks later, McCleskey was arrested in connection with an unrelated offense. He confessed that he had participated in the furniture store robbery, but denied that he had shot the police officer. At trial, the State introduced evidence that at least one of the bullets that struck the officer was fired from a .38 caliber Rossi revolver. This description matched the description of the gun that McCleskey had carried during the robbery. The State also introduced the testimony of two witnesses who had heard McCleskey admit to the shooting.

The jury convicted McCleskey of murder. At the penalty hearing, the jury heard arguments as to the appropriate sentence. Under Georgia law, the jury could not consider imposing the death penalty unless it found beyond a reasonable doubt that the murder was accompanied by one of the statutory aggravating circumstances. Ga.Code Ann. § 17–10–30(c) (1982). The jury in this case found two aggravating circumstances to exist beyond a reasonable doubt: the murder was committed during the course of an armed robbery, § 17–10–30(b)(2); and the murder was committed upon a peace officer engaged in the performance of his duties, § 17–10–30(b)(8). In making its decision whether to impose the death sentence, the jury considered the mitigating and aggravating circumstances of McCleskey's conduct. § 17–10–2(c). McCleskey offered no mitigating evidence. The jury recommended that he be sentenced to death on the murder charge and to consecutive life sentences on the armed robbery charges. The court followed the jury's recommendation and sentenced McCleskey to death.

On appeal, the Supreme Court of Georgia affirmed the convictions and the sentences. . . .

. . .

McCleskey next filed a petition for a writ of habeas corpus in the federal District Court for the Northern District of Georgia. His petition raised 18 claims, one of which was that the Georgia capital sentencing process is administered in a racially discriminatory manner in violation of the Eighth and Fourteenth Amendments to the United States Constitution. In support of his claim, McCleskey proffered a statistical study performed by Professors David C. Baldus, George Woodworth, and Charles Pulaski (the Baldus study) that purports to show a disparity in the imposition of the death sentence in Georgia based on the race of the murder victim and, to a lesser extent, the race of the defendant. The Baldus study is actually two sophisticated statistical studies that examine over 2,000 murder cases that occurred in Georgia during the 1970s. The raw numbers collected by Professor Baldus indicate that defendants charged with killing white persons received the death penalty in 11% of the cases, but defendants charged with killing blacks received the death penalty in only 1% of the cases. The raw numbers also indicate a reverse racial disparity according to the race of the defendant: 4% of the black defendants received the death penalty, as opposed to 7% of the white defendants.

Baldus also divided the cases according to the combination of the race of the defendant and the race of the victim. He found that the death penalty was assessed in 22% of the cases involving black defendants and white victims; 8% of the cases involving white defendants and white victims; 1% of the cases involving black defendants and black victims; and 3% of the cases involving white defendants and black victims. Similarly, Baldus found that prosecutors sought the death penalty in 70% of the cases involving black defendants and white victims; 32% of the cases involving white defendants and white victims; 15% of the cases involving black defendants and black victims; and 19% of the cases involving white defendants and black victims.

Baldus subjected his data to an extensive analysis, taking account of 230 variables that could have explained the disparities on nonracial grounds. One of his models concludes that, even after taking account of 39 nonracial variables, defendants charged with killing white victims were 4.3 times as likely to receive a death sentence as defendants charged with killing blacks. According to this model, black defendants were 1.1 times as likely to receive a death sentence as other defendants. Thus, the Baldus study indicates that black defendants, such as McCleskey, who kill white victims have the greatest likelihood of receiving the death penalty. *[The District Court held that the Baldus study failed to support McCleskey's claim and dismissed the petition. The Eleventh Circuit affirmed the dismissal, concluding that the statistical evidence confirms rather than condemns the Georgia system.]*

II

McCleskey's first claim is that the Georgia capital punishment statute violates the Equal Protection Clause of the Fourteenth Amendment. He argues that race has infected the administration of Georgia's statute in two ways: persons who murder whites are more likely to be sentenced to death than persons who murder blacks, and black murderers are more likely to be sentenced to death than white murderers. As a black defendant who killed a white victim, McCleskey claims that the Baldus study demonstrates that he was discriminated against because of his race and because of the race of his victim. In its broadest form, McCleskey's claim of discrimination extends to every actor in the Georgia capital sentencing process, from the prosecutor who sought the death penalty and the jury that imposed the sentence, to the State itself that enacted the capital punishment statute and allows it to remain in effect despite its allegedly discriminatory application. We agree with the Court of Appeals, and every other court that has considered such a challenge, that this claim must fail.

A

Our analysis begins with the basic principle that a defendant who alleges an equal protection violation has the burden of proving "the existence of purposeful discrimination." *Whitus* v. *Georgia*, 385 U.S. 545, 550 (1967). A corollary to this principle is that a criminal defendant must prove that the purposeful discrimination "had a discriminatory effect" on him. *Wayte* v. *United States*, 470 U.S. 598, 608 (1985). Thus, to prevail under the Equal Protection Clause, McCleskey must prove that the decision-makers in *his* case acted with discriminatory purpose. He offers no evidence specific to his own case that would support an inference that racial considerations played a part in his sentence. Instead, he relies solely on the Baldus study. McCleskey argues that the Baldus study compels an inference that his sentence rests on purposeful discrimination. McCleskey's claim that these statistics are sufficient proof of discrimination, without regard to the facts of a particular case, would extend to all capital cases in Georgia, at least where the victim was white and the defendant is black.

The Court has accepted statistics as proof of intent to discriminate in certain limited contexts. First, this Court has accepted statistical disparities as proof of an equal protection violation in the selection of the jury venire in a particular district. Although statistical proof normally must present a "stark" pattern to be accepted as the sole proof of discriminatory intent under the Constitution, *Arlington Heights* v. *Metropolitan Housing Dev. Corp.*, 429 U.S. 252, 266 (1977), "[b]ecause of the nature of the jury-selection task, . . . we have permitted a finding of constitutional violation even when the statistical pattern does not approach [such] extremes." *Id.*, at 266, n. 13. Second, this Court has accepted statistics in the form of multiple regression analysis to prove statutory violations under Title VII. *Bazemore* v. *Friday*, 478 U.S. 385, 400–401 (1986) (opinion of BRENNAN, J., concurring in part).

But the nature of the capital sentencing decision, and the relationship of the statistics to that decision, are fundamentally different from the corresponding elements in the venire-selection or Title VII cases. Most importantly, each particular decision to impose the death penalty is made by a petit jury selected from a properly constituted venire. Each jury is unique in its composition, and the Constitution requires that its decision rest on consideration of innumerable factors that vary according to the characteristics of the individual defendant and the facts of the particular capital offense. See *Hitchcock* v. *Dugger, post,* at 398–399; *Lockett* v. *Ohio,* 438 U.S. 586, 602–605 (1978) (plurality opinion of Burger, C.J.). . . .

. . . Because discretion is essential to the criminal justice process, we would demand exceptionally clear proof before we would infer that the discretion has been abused. The unique nature of the decisions at issue in this case also counsel against adopting such an inference from the disparities indicated by the Baldus study. Accordingly, we hold that the Baldus study is clearly insufficient to support an inference that any of the decisionmakers in McCleskey's case acted with discriminatory purpose.

. . .

V

Two additional concerns inform our decision in this case. First, McCleskey's claim, taken to its logical conclusion, throws into serious question the principles that underlie our entire criminal justice system. The Eighth Amendment is not limited in application to capital punishment, but applies to all penalties. *Solem* v. *Helm,* 463 U.S. 277, 289–290 (1983); see *Rummel* v. *Estelle,* 445 U.S. 263, 293 (1980) (POWELL, J., dissenting). Thus, if we accepted McCleskey's claim that racial bias has impermissibly tainted the capital sentencing decision, we could soon be faced with similar claims as to other types of penalty. Moreover, the claim that his sentence rests on the irrelevant factor of race easily could be extended to apply to claims based on unexplained discrepancies that correlate to membership in other minority groups, and even to gender. Similarly, since McCleskey's claim relates to the race of his victim, other claims could apply with equally logical force to statistical disparities that correlate with the race or sex of other actors in the criminal justice system, such as defense attorneys, or judges. Also, there is no logical reason that such a claim need be limited to racial or sexual bias. If arbitrary and capricious punishment is the touchstone under the Eighth Amendment, such a claim could—at least in theory—be based upon any arbitrary variable, such as the defendant's facial characteristics, or the physical attractiveness of the defendant or the victim, that some statistical study indicates may be influential in jury decisionmaking. . . .

Second, McCleskey's arguments are best presented to the legislative bodies. It is not the responsibility—or indeed even the right—of this Court to determine the appropriate punishment for particular crimes. It is the legislatures, the elected representatives of the people, that are "constituted to respond to the will and consequently the moral values of the people." *Furman* v. *Georgia*, 408 U.S., at 383 (Burger, C.J., dissenting). Legislatures also are better qualified to weigh and "evaluate the results of statistical studies in terms of their own local conditions and with a flexibility of approach that is not available to the courts," *Gregg* v. *Georgia*, *supra*, at 186. . . . We agree with the District Court and the Court of Appeals for the Eleventh Circuit that this was carefully and correctly done in this case.

VI

Accordingly, we affirm the judgment of the Court of Appeals for the Eleventh Circuit.

It is so ordered.

JUSTICE BRENNAN, with whom JUSTICE MARSHALL joins, and with whom JUSTICE BLACKMUN and JUSTICE STEVENS join in all but Part I, dissenting.

I

Adhering to my view that the death penalty is in all circumstances cruel and unusual punishment forbidden by the Eighth and Fourteenth Amendments, I would vacate the decision below insofar as it left undisturbed the death sentence imposed in this case. *Gregg* v. *Georgia*, 428 U.S. 153, 227 (1976). . . .

II

At some point in this case, Warren McCleskey doubtless asked his lawyer whether a jury was likely to sentence him to die. A candid reply to this question would have been disturbing. First, counsel would have to tell McCleskey that few of the details of the crime or of McCleskey's past criminal conduct were more important than the fact that his victim was white. Petitioner's Supplemental Exhibits (Supp. Exh.) 50. Furthermore, counsel would feel bound to tell McCleskey that defendants charged with killing white victims in Georgia are 4.3 times as likely to be sentenced to death as defendants charged with killing blacks. Petitioner's Exhibit DB 82. In addition, frankness would compel the disclosure that it was more likely than not that the race of McCleskey's victim would determine whether he received a death sentence: 6 of every 11 defendants convicted of killing a white person would not have received the death penalty if their victims had been black, Supp. Exh. 51, while, among defendants with aggravating and mitigating factors comparable to McCleskey, 20 of every 34 would not have been sentenced to die if their victims had been black. *Id.*, at 54. Finally, the assessment would not be complete without the information that cases involving black defendants and white victims are more likely to result in a death sentence than cases featuring any other racial combination of defendant and victim. *Ibid.* The story could be told in a variety of ways, but McCleskey could not fail to grasp its essential narrative line: there was a significant chance that race would play a prominent role in determining if he lived or died.

. . .

. . . Since, according to Professor Baldus, we cannot say "to a moral certainty" that race influenced a decision, *ante*, at 308, n. 23, we can identify only "a likelihood that a particular factor entered into some decisions", *ante*, at 308, and "a discrepancy that appears to correlate with race." *Ante*, at 312. This "likelihood" and "discrepancy," holds the Court, is insufficient to establish a constitutional violation. The Court reaches this conclusion by placing four factors on the scales opposite McCleskey's evidence: the desire to encourage sentencing discretion, the existence of "statutory safeguards" in the Georgia scheme, the fear of encouraging widespread challenges to other sentencing decisions, and the limits of the judicial role. The Court's evaluation of the significance of petitioner's evidence is fundamentally at odds with our consistent concern for rationality in capital sentencing, and the considerations that the majority invokes to discount that evidence cannot justify ignoring its force.

. . .

V

At the time our Constitution was framed 200 years ago this year, blacks "had for more than a century before been regarded as beings of an inferior order, and altogether unfit to associate with the white race, either in social or political relations; and so far inferior, that they had no rights which the white man was bound to respect." *Dred Scott* v. *Sanford*, 19 How. 393, 407 (1857). Only 130 years ago, this Court relied on these observations to deny American citizenship to blacks. *Ibid.* A mere three generations ago, this Court sanctioned racial segregation, stating that "[i]f one race be inferior to the other socially, the Constitution of the United States cannot put them upon the same plane." *Plessy* v. *Ferguson*, 163 U.S. 537, 552 (1896).

In more recent times, we have sought to free ourselves from the burden of this history. Yet it has been scarcely a generation since this Court's first decision striking down racial segregation, and barely two decades since the legislative prohibition of racial discrimination in major domains of national life. These have been honorable steps, but we cannot pretend that in three decades we have completely escaped the grip of an historical legacy spanning centuries. Warren McCleskey's evidence confronts us with the subtle and persistent influence of the past. His message is a disturbing one to a society that has formally repudiated racism, and a frustrating one to a Nation accustomed to regarding its destiny as the product of its own will. Nonetheless, we ignore him at our peril, for we remain imprisoned by the past as long as we deny its influence in the present.

It is tempting to pretend that minorities on death row share a fate in no way connected to our own, that our treatment of them sounds no echoes beyond the chambers in which they die. Such an illusion is ultimately corrosive, for the reverberations of injustice are not so easily confined. "The destinies of the two races in this country are indissolubly linked together," *id.*, at 560 (Harlan, J., dissenting), and the way in which we choose those who will die reveals the depth of moral commitment among the living.

The Court's decision today will not change what attorneys in Georgia tell other Warren McCleskeys about their chances of execution. Nothing will soften the harsh message they must convey, nor alter the prospect that race undoubtedly will continue to be a topic of discussion. McCleskey's evidence will not have obtained judicial acceptance, but that will not affect what is said on death row. However many criticisms of today's decision may be rendered, these painful conversations will serve as the most eloquent dissents of all.

JUSTICE BLACKMUN, with whom JUSTICE MARSHALL and JUSTICE STEVENS join and with whom JUSTICE BRENNAN joins in all but Part IV-B, dissenting.

The Court today sanctions the execution of a man despite his presentation of evidence that establishes a constitutionally intolerable level of racially based discrimination leading to the imposition of his death sentence. I am disappointed with the Court's action not only because of its denial of constitutional guarantees to petitioner McCleskey individually, but also because of its departure from what seems to me to be well-developed constitutional jurisprudence.

JUSTICE BRENNAN has thoroughly demonstrated, *ante*, that, if one assumes that the statistical evidence presented by petitioner McCleskey is valid, as we must in light of the Court of Appeals' assumption, there exists in the Georgia capital-sentencing scheme a risk of racially based discrimination that is so acute that it violates the Eighth Amendment. . . .

II

A

A criminal defendant alleging an equal protection violation must prove the existence of purposeful discrimination. *Washington* v. *Davis*, 426 U.S. 229, 239–240 (1976); *Whitus* v. *Georgia*, 385 U.S., at 550. He may establish a prima facie case of purposeful discrimination "by showing that the totality of the relevant facts gives rise to an inference of discriminatory purpose." *Batson* v. *Kentucky*, 476 U.S., at 94. Once the defendant establishes a prima facie case, the burden shifts to the prosecution to rebut that case. "The State cannot meet this burden on mere general assertions that its officials did not discriminate or that they properly performed their official duties." *Ibid.* The State must demonstrate that the challenged effect was due to " 'permissible racially neutral selection criteria.' " *Ibid.*, quoting *Alexander* v. *Louisiana*, 405 U.S. 625, 632 (1972).

Under *Batson* v. *Kentucky* and the framework established in *Castaneda* v. *Partida*, McCleskey must meet a three-factor standard. First, he must establish that he is a member of a group "that is a recognizable, distinct class, singled out for different treatment." 430 U.S., at 494. Second, he must make a showing of a substantial degree of differential treatment. Third, he must establish that the allegedly discriminatory procedure is susceptible to abuse or is not racially neutral. *Ibid.*

B

There can be no dispute that McCleskey has made the requisite showing under the first prong of the standard. The Baldus study demonstrates that black persons are a distinct group that are singled out for different treatment in the Georgia capital-sentencing system. The Court acknowledges, as it must, that the raw statistics included in the Baldus study and presented by petitioner indicate that it is much less likely that a death sentence will result from a murder of a black person than from a murder of a white person. . . .

With respect to the second prong, McCleskey must prove that there is a substantial likelihood that his death sentence is due to racial factors. . . .

McCleskey produced evidence concerning the role of racial factors at the various steps in the decisionmaking process, focusing on the prosecutor's decision as to which cases merit the death sentence. McCleskey established that the race of the victim is an especially significant factor at the point where the defendant has been convicted of murder and the prosecutor must choose whether to proceed to the penalty phase of the trial and create the possibility that a death sentence may be imposed or to accept the imposition of a sentence of life imprisonment. McCleskey demonstrated this effect at both the statewide level, see S.E. 56, S.E. 57, Tr. 897–910, and in Fulton County where he was tried and sentenced, see S.E. 59, S.E. 60, Tr. 978–981. The statewide statistics indicated that black defendant/white victim cases advanced to the penalty trial at nearly five times the rate of the black defendant/black victim cases (70% v. 15%), and over three times the rate of white defendant/black victim cases (70% v. 19%). . . .

As to the final element of the prima facie case, McCleskey showed that the process by which the State decided to seek a death penalty in his case and to pursue that sentence throughout the prosecution was susceptible to abuse. Petitioner submitted the deposition of Lewis R. Slaton, who, as of the date of the deposition, had been the District Attorney for 18 years in the county in which McCleskey was tried and sentenced. . . .

When questioned directly as to how the office decided whether to seek the death penalty, Slaton listed several factors he thought relevant to that decision, including the strength of the evidence, the atrociousness of the crime, and the likelihood that a jury would impose the death sentence. *Id.*, at 59. He explained that the attorneys did not seek the death penalty in every case in which statutory aggravating factors existed. *Id.*, at 38. Slaton testified that his office still operated in the same manner as it did when he took office in 1964, except that it has not sought the death penalty in any rape cases since this Court's decision in *Coker* v. *Georgia*, 433 U.S. 584 (1977). Deposition, at 60.

. . .

JUSTICE STEVENS, with whom JUSTICE BLACKMUN joins, dissenting.

. . .

In this case it is claimed—and the claim is supported by elaborate studies which the Court properly assumes to be valid—that the jury's sentencing process was likely distorted by racial prejudice. The studies demonstrate a strong probability that McCleskey's sentencing jury . . . was influenced by the fact that McCleskey is black and his victim was white, and that this same outrage would not have been generated if he had killed a member of his own race. This sort of disparity is constitutionally intolerable. It flagrantly violates the Court's prior "insistence that capital punishment be imposed fairly, and with reasonable consistency, or not at all." *Eddings* v. *Oklahoma*, 455 U.S. 104, 112 (1982).

. . .

Like JUSTICE BRENNAN, I would therefore reverse the judgment of the Court of Appeals. I believe, however, that further proceedings are necessary in order to determine whether McCles-

key's death sentence should be set aside. First, the Court of Appeals must decide whether the Baldus study is valid. I am persuaded that it is, but orderly procedure requires that the Court of Appeals address this issue before we actually decide the question. Second, it is necessary for the District Court to determine whether the particular facts of McCleskey's crime and his background place this case within the range of cases that present an unacceptable risk that race played a decisive role in McCleskey's sentencing.

Accordingly, I respectfully dissent.

The Death Penalty and Public Opinion: The Views of Justice Powell

Following his retirement from the Supreme Court, Justice Lewis Powell, Jr., delivered a speech on capital punishment on August 7, 1988, at the American Bar Association's annual meeting in Toronto. He cited language from the Constitution and statutes from the First Congress to indicate that the Founding Fathers approved capital punishment. After summarizing the Court's holdings in *Furman* v. *Georgia* (1972) and *Gregg* v. *Georgia* (1976), he concluded that the decision on capital punishment was basically in the hands of legislatures and public opinion. The excerpts below are taken from "Death Penalty? Society Has Ruled," *Legal Times*, August 15, 1988, pp. 12, 13.

. . .

Since *Gregg*, the Supreme Court has decided— with full opinions—a number of capital cases. In view of the finality of capital punishment, appellate courts—including the Supreme Court—have reviewed each case with great care. Although protective refinements have been enunciated, *Gregg* remains the law. We have recognized, in accordance with Chief Justice Warren's opinion in *Trop* v. *Dulles*, that the Eighth Amendment "must draw its meaning from evolving standards of decency that mark the progress of a maturing society."

Thus, our constitutional decisions have been informed by contemporary judgments of society as evidenced by decisions of state legislatures and sentencing decisions of juries. Thirty-seven states now have capital punishment statutes enacted since the *Furman* decision. In 33 of these states, death sentences have been imposed. Although no

federal death sentences have been imposed in recent years, several federal criminal statutes authorize a penalty of death, and Congress has recently been considering imposition of the death penalty for certain murders committed in connection with drug violations. And juries continue to impose the sentence of death.

The evidence, therefore, is compelling that a large majority of our people consider that for certain crimes, capital punishment is appropriate. In the face of this evidence, it would be difficult for a court—even the Supreme Court—to conclude that the legislatures of a great majority of the states and the Congress are mistaken as to contemporary standards of decency in our society.

. . .

. . . As a co-author of *Gregg* and recently the author of *McCleskey* [v. *Kemp*], I adhere to the view that the death penalty lawfully may be imposed under our Constitution. My concerns relate to the way the system malfunctions and to the shocking murder rate that prevails in our country. In view of the unambiguous public support for capital punishment, one would think that the time has come for Congress to give thoughtful consideration to making reasonable changes in the federal law governing review of criminal convictions.

It is now evident that our unique system of multiple and dual collateral review is abused, particularly in capital cases. If capital punishment cannot be enforced, even where innocence is not an issue and the fairness of the trial is not seriously questioned, perhaps Congress and the state legislatures should take a serious look at whether retention of a punishment that is not being enforced is in the public interest.

14 Search and Seizure

o area of constitutional law is more unsettled, and unsettling, than Supreme Court decisions on search and seizure. The Court must apply eighteenth-century principles to such twentieth-century practices as automobile and aerial searches, the use of trained dogs to detect drugs, body-cavity searches, wiretaps of phone calls, and increasingly sophisticated methods of electronic eavesdropping. All three branches have been active in defining the contours and content of the Fourth Amendment.

EXPECTATIONS OF PRIVACY

The Fourth Amendment is difficult to interpret because it often implicates other sections of the Constitution. The Fourth and Fifth Amendments "throw great light on each other. For the 'unreasonable searches and seizures' condemned in the Fourth Amendment are almost always made for the purpose of compelling a man to give evidence against himself, which in criminal cases is condemned by the Fifth Amendment . . ." Boyd v. United States, 116 U.S. 616, 633 (1886). The two Amendments sometimes "run almost into each other." Id. at 630. Cases lie at the "crossroads" of the Fourth and Fifth Amendments. Brown v. Illinois, 422 U.S. 590, 591 (1975). Searches and seizures also invoke more general constitutional interests, such as the privacy of the individual. In 1965 the Court asked: "Would we allow the police to search the sacred precincts of marital bedrooms for telltale signs of the use of contraceptives? The very idea is repulsive to the notions of privacy surrounding the marriage relationship." Griswold v. Connecticut, 381 U.S. 479, 485–486.

These complexities are compounded by the general language of the Fourth Amendment: "The right of the people to be secure in their persons, houses, papers, and effects, against unreasonable searches and seizures, shall not be violated and no Warrants shall issue, but upon probable cause, supported by Oath or affirmation, and particularly describing the place to be searched, and the persons or things to be seized." It is more than a problem of defining "unreasonable" and "probable cause." Should the Amendment be taken as a unit, requiring warrants to make a search and seizure reasonable? There are too many exceptions to the warrant requirement to accept that construction. Are some searches and seizures inherently unreasonable, even with a warrant? Justice Stevens thought it unlikely that the framers expected private papers to be among the "things" to be seized with a warrant. He considered all such seizures as unreasonable. Zurcher v. Stanford Daily, 436 U.S. 547, 577–578 (1978). That is a distinctly minority position. See Andresen v. Maryland, 427 U.S. 463 (1976).

Does the Amendment split into two discrete halves, allowing warrantless searches and seizures (provided they are "reasonable") in the first clause, followed by a second clause that describes warrants if used? Some Justices appear to emphasize the first clause to the exclusion of the second, insisting on "reasonableness" but not warrants. Florida v. Royer, 460 U.S. 491, 520 (1983) (Rehnquist dissenting). Justices White and Rehnquist and Chief Justice Burger have argued that it was "not generally considered 'unreasonable' at common law for officers to break doors in making warrantless felony arrests." According to their reading, the second clause "does not purport to alter colonial practice." Payton v. United States, 445 U.S. 573, 610 (1980) (dissenting opinion).

This interpretation overlooks the decisive break by America with British and colonial practices. Justice Bradley summarized the conditions that preceded the rupture with England:

> In order to ascertain the nature of the proceedings intended by the Fourth Amendment to the Constitution under the terms "unreasonable searches and seizures," it is only necessary to recall the contemporary or then recent history of the controversies on the subject, both in this country and in England. The practice had obtained in the colonies of issuing writs of assistance to the revenue officers, empowering them, in their discretion, to search suspected places for smuggled goods, which James Otis pronounced "the worst instrument of arbitrary power, the most destructive of English liberty, and the fundamental principles of law, that ever was found in an English law book;" since they placed "the liberty of every man in the hands of every petty officer." This was in February, 1761, in Boston, and the famous debate in which it occurred was perhaps the most prominent event which inaugurated the resistance of the colonies to the oppressions of the mother country. "Then and there," said John Adams, "then and there was the first scene of the first act of opposition to the arbitrary claims of Great Britain. Then and there the child Independence was born." Boyd v. United States, 116 U.S. at 625.

Although Americans were outraged by writs of assistance and the general search warrant, it has been settled practice throughout our history that warrants are not required for every search and seizure. Various exceptions exist, and the list lengthens with each passing decade. The following sections cover the warrant requirement, the exceptions to it, the technological problems of electronic eavesdropping, and the Court's doctrine of excluding illegally obtained evidence (the exclusionary rule).

ARREST AND SEARCH WARRANTS

It is customary for the Court to reiterate that "searches conducted outside the judicial process, without prior approval by judge or magistrate, are *per se* unreasonable under the Fourth Amendment—subject only to a few specifically established and well-delineated exceptions." KATZ v. UNITED STATES, 389 U.S. 347, 357 (1967).

These "exceptions" have grown so rapidly over the years that they threaten to become the rule.

For most of the Court's history it has been axiomatic that the safeguards built into the Fourth Amendment depend upon warrants issued upon probable cause "by a neutral and detached magistrate." Constitutional liberties are not secure when relying on the judgments of the officer "engaged in the often competitive enterprise of ferreting out crime." To allow warrantless action by a law enforcement officer "would reduce the Amendment to a nullity and leave the people's homes secure only in the discretion of police officers." Johnson v. United States, 333 U.S. 10, 14 (1948). Nor is it considered adequate to have warrants issued by someone prosecuting a case. COOLIDGE v. NEW HAMPSHIRE, 403 U.S. 443 (1971). As the Court noted in 1948: "Power is a heady thing; and history shows that the police acting on their own cannot be trusted." McDonald v. United States, 335 U.S. 451, 456. States may not undermine the neutrality and independence of magistrates by paying them only when they issue a warrant, for this would give them a pecuniary and personal reason to grant approval. Connally v. Georgia, 429 U.S. 245 (1977).

To obtain a search warrant, a law enforcement officer must state in an affidavit the reasons for the search. The reasons must show probable cause; mere suspicion or belief is insufficient ground. If an affidavit merely asserts an officer's belief in the truth of statements made by others, without adequate reason to support the statements, the affidavit does not justify a search warrant. Grau v. United States, 287 U.S. 124 (1932). Before authorizing a warrant, a magistrate is supposed to find probable cause from facts or circumstances presented in the affidavit. Nathanson v. United States, 290 U.S. 41 (1933). These principles were substantially weakened in 1984 when the Court allowed the admission of evidence obtained from a search warrant that was later found to be unsupported by probable cause. UNITED STATES v. LEON, 468 U.S. 897.

Since searches are sometimes conducted incident to an arrest, an arrest warrant must also be based on an officer's personal knowledge and belief that someone has committed a crime. Giordenello v. United States, 357 U.S. 480 (1958). If a suspect is arrested without a warrant, he may not be held in custody pending trial without the right to have a neutral magistrate determine that there is probable cause. Gerstein v. Pugh, 420 U.S. 103 (1975). In determining probable cause and reasonable grounds, warrants may be based on information and hearsay supplied by informers who have a record of providing reliable tips and when officers verify the information through their own observations. Draper v. United States, 358 U.S. 307 (1959); Rugendorf v. United States, 376 U.S. 528 (1964).[1]

If a warrant is deficient in some respect, the resulting search and seizure can be declared invalid. Federal warrants have been held defective when the supporting affidavit has been verified by a state official who lacks authority to administer oaths

[1]The magistrate must understand some of the underlying circumstances relied on by the informer and some of the underlying circumstances that prompt an officer to conclude that an informer is creditable and his information reliable. Aguilar v. Texas, 378 U.S. 108 (1964); United States v. Harris, 403 U.S. 573 (1971). A magistrate cannot authorize a warrant simply by accepting an informer's unsubstantiated tip. Spinelli v. United States, 393 U.S. 410 (1969); Whiteley v. Warden, 401 U.S. 560 (1971). These rules evolved into the "totality of the circumstances" approach, under which a magistrate may use independent police work to corroborate an informer's tip. Illinois v. Gates, 462 U.S. 213 (1983); Massachusetts v. Upton, 466 U.S. 727 (1984). A police officer need not disclose an informer's identity. United States v. Ventresca, 380 U.S. 102 (1965); McCray v. Illinois, 386 U.S. 300 (1967).

in federal criminal proceedings. Albrecht v. United States, 273 U.S. 1 (1927). A magistrate is not required for every warrant, however. Municipal court clerks who operate under the supervision of judges may issue *arrest* warrants for breach of municipal ordinances. However, they are not authorized to issue *search* warrants or even arrest warrants for felonies or misdemeanors. Shadwick v. City of Tampa, 407 U.S. 345 (1972).

The Fourth Amendment requires that a search warrant "particularly describe" the items to be seized. A magistrate may not authorize an open-ended search warrant and leave to the discretion of officials (even when he accompanies them) the decision of what objects to seize when they arrive. The warrant must specify the things to be seized at the time the warrant is issued, not after the search and seizure are complete. Lo-Ji Sales, Inc. v. New York, 442 U.S. 319 (1979).[2]

Under some circumstances a defective warrant can nonetheless produce a valid conviction. In one case, several men transported stolen goods to a retail store, which was searched under a defective warrant. The men were unable to contest the admission of the seized evidence because they had no legitimate expectation of privacy or interest of any kind in the store. Brown v. United States, 411 U.S. 223 (1973). See also UNITED STATES v. LEON, 468 U.S. 897 (1984) and Massachusetts v. Shepperd, 468 U.S. 981 (1984).

Although there are occasions when federal officers may search without a warrant, if they have an "abundant" or "adequate" opportunity to obtain a warrant and fail to do so, the entry is wrongful and the search and seizure unreasonable. Taylor v. United States, 286 U.S. 1 (1932); Trupiano v. United States, 334 U.S. 699, 703 (1948). When someone has been under police observation for months, officers are without authority to force their way into that person's dwelling without an arrest warrant or a search warrant. If they do, the evidence seized is inadmissible. McDonald v. United States, 335 U.S. 451 (1948). Even when a homicide occurs in an apartment, the police are not at liberty to conduct a warrantless search and seizure. A police guard at the apartment will minimize the possibility of evidence being lost, destroyed, or removed during the time required to obtain a search warrant. Thompson v. Louisiana, 469 U.S. 17 (1984); Mincey v. Arizona, 437 U.S. 385 (1978).

These restrictions do not apply to automobile searches. The Court has allowed the government to seize a truck and search it three days later without ever obtaining a search warrant. United States v. Johns, 469 U.S. 478 (1985). Even in a private home, the principle of requiring a search warrant when time permits was seriously compromised by *Segura* v. *United States*, 468 U.S. 796 (1984). The Court allowed an illegal entry to occur before application and approval of a search warrant granted nineteen hours later.

In 1980, the Supreme Court struck down a New York law that authorized police officers to enter a private residence without a warrant and with force, if necessary,

---

[2]Searches have been declared unreasonable when federal agents falsely claim to have a search warrant, Go-Bart Co. v. United States, 282 U.S. 344 (1931), or when a search warrant has expired, Sgro v. United States, 287 U.S. 206 (1932). If an officer deliberately misleads a magistrate by making false statements, and those statements are necessary to find probable cause, a defendant is entitled to challenge the truthfulness of the affidavit. If the defendant prevails, the search warrant is declared void and the fruits of the search excluded. Franks v. Delaware, 438 U.S. 154 (1978). On the other hand, if factual inaccuracies do not destroy the integrity of an affidavit, the resulting search is permitted. Rugendorf v. United States, 376 U.S. 528 (1964).

make a routine felony arrest. The statute allowed them to seize evidence after entry. The Court held that, absent "exigent circumstances," officers may not enter a home without a warrant. It is a basic principle of the Fourth Amendment that searches and seizures inside a home without a warrant are "presumptively unreasonable." Payton v. New York, 445 U.S. 573, 586 (1980). A warrantless nighttime entry into a home to arrest someone for a noncriminal, nonjailable traffic offense is prohibited by the Fourth Amendment. Welsh v. Wisconsin, 466 U.S. 740 (1984). Without consent or exigent circumstances, a law enforcement officer with an arrest warrant may not legally search for that person in the home of a third party without first obtaining a search warrant. The Court explained the broad potential for abuse. In one case the police, armed with an arrest warrant for two fugitives, searched 300 homes. Steagald v. United States, 451 U.S. 204, 215 (1981).[3]

The question of third-party searches arose in a 1978 case involving a police search of a student newspaper which had taken photographs of a clash between demonstrators and police. A search warrant was issued to obtain the photographs and learn the identities of those who had assaulted police officers. The Court held that a state is not prevented from issuing a search warrant simply because the owner of a place is not reasonably suspected of criminal involvement. A warrant could be properly drafted to protect the interests of a free press. Zurcher v. Stanford Daily, 436 U.S. 547. The Court invited the other two branches to participate by noting that the Fourth Amendment "does not prevent or advise against legislative or executive efforts to establish nonconstitutional protections against possible abuses of the search warrant procedure . . ." Id. at 567. Although Congress could not pass legislation to weaken the Fourth Amendment, it could act to strengthen its protections. S. Rept. No. 96–874, at 4.

The Court's decision was denounced by newspapers as "a first step toward a police state," an assault that "stands on its head the history of both the first and the fourth amendments," and a threat to the "privacy rights of the law-abiding." S. Rep. No. 874, 96th Cong., 2d Sess. 5 (1980). In an amicus brief, Solicitor General Wade H. McCree had argued that the use of a warrant to search third parties was constitutional and that there was no need to adopt a "subpoena first" policy to obtain materials, even if the parties were newspapers with a First Amendment interest. After the uproar that greeted the Court's decision, the Carter administration realized that it had miscalculated. McCree had a reputation for composing clever limericks. Robert J. Havel, at that time Deputy Director of Public Information for the Justice Department, applied his own hand to this craft:

> A solicitor known fondly as Wade
> Filed a brief supporting a raid
>   By police on the premises
>   Of a newspaper nemesis
> Said the press, what a big egg Wade laid.

Congress responded by passing a bill that limited newsroom searches. With certain exceptions, it required the use of a subpoena instead of a search warrant to obtain documentary materials from those who disseminate newspapers, books, broadcasts, or other similar forms of public communication. 94 Stat. 1879 (1980).

---

[3]Warrantless searches by probation officers, looking for contraband in the home of someone on probation, were sustained by the Supreme Court in Griffin v. Wisconsin, 107 S.Ct. 3164 (1987). Warrants are not required to search students. New Jersey v. T.L.O., 469 U.S. 325 (1985) (reprinted in Chapter 16).

The "dialogue" between Congress and the Court on constitutional matters is captured nicely in the floor debates (excerpts reprinted on pp. 890–892).

The "subpoena-first" policy offers several advantages to newspapers. A subpoena involves a court hearing where the newspaper can state its case; search warrants are issued without any possibility of influence by a newspaper. Moreover, a subpoena allows the newspaper to produce the specific document requested, rather than having police officers enter the premises of a newsroom and disrupt operations while searching through filing cabinets, desks, and wastepaper baskets.

The *Zurcher* case calls attention to the alternatives to search warrants. Nonjudicial officers in federal agencies may issue subpoenas to require private companies to submit records needed to determine whether the company is violating federal statutes. If the subpoena is not obeyed, federal courts are available to help enforce it. Oklahoma Press Publishing Co. v. Walling, 327 U.S. 186 (1946). Because there is no question of an actual search or seizure, a subpoena does not raise a Fourth Amendment issue. A subpoena does not authorize a law enforcement officer to search an office and seize books and records. Mancusi v. DeForte, 392 U.S. 364 (1968). This limitation is important because subpoenas are often issued by prosecuting attorneys rather than by a neutral and detached magistrate. Id. at 371.

Subpoenas may be used to obtain microfilms of checks, deposit slips, and other records from a bank account. In 1976, the Supreme Court held that a Fourth Amendment interest could not be vindicated in court by challenging such a subpoena. The Court treated the materials as business records of a bank, not private papers of a person. The Court did not consider checks as confidential communications; the checks were regarded as negotiable instruments used in commercial transactions. The depositor took the risk that third parties could convey sensitive information to the government. United States v. Miller, 425 U.S. 435 (1976).

In short, private parties could not look to the courts for the protection of Fourth Amendment interests. Justice Brennan noted in a dissent that a depositor "reveals many aspects of his personal affairs, opinions, habits and associations. Indeed, the totality of bank records provides a virtual current biography." Id. at 451. See also California Bankers Assn. v. Shultz, 416 U.S. 21 (1974). Congress responded by passing the Right to Financial Privacy Act of 1978. The statute allows notice to depositors before access is given to governmental agencies to review their financial records, gives the depositor an opportunity to challenge governmental access, and sets forth requirements for administrative subpoena or summons, search warrants, and judicial subpoena. The government can delay notice to the depositor only by obtaining an order from a judge or magistrate. 92 Stat. 3697. In this manner, certain Fourth Amendment safeguards rendered unavailable by the Supreme Court were secured by congressional action. The congressional debate on the Financial Privacy Act is reprinted in Chapter 17.

EXCEPTIONS TO THE WARRANT REQUIREMENT

Law enforcement officials may make warrantless arrests and searches by relying on eight exceptions: (1) border searches, (2) consent, (3) "hot pursuit," (4) the "plain-view" doctrine, (5) automobiles, (6) emergency situations, (7) search incident to arrest, and (8) inspections. Each exception has its own unique, evolutionary history of complex line-drawing.

Border Searches

Long before the Supreme Court discovered exceptions to the warrant requirement, Congress and the executive branch decided that warrants were not necessary for border searches. As the Supreme Court noted in 1985: "Since the founding of our Republic, Congress has granted the Executive plenary authority to conduct routine searches and seizures at the border, without probable cause or a warrant, in order to regulate the collection of duties and to prevent the introduction of contraband into this country." United States v. Montoya de Hernandez, 473 U.S. 531, 535 (1985). A statute in 1789 authorized federal officials to enter any ship or vessel suspected of having concealed goods or merchandise and to search and seize such goods. 1 Stat. 43, § 24. Under contemporary law, any officer authorized to board or search vessels may examine any person on whom he "shall suspect there is merchandise which is subject to duty, or shall have been introduced into the United States in any manner contrary to law . . . and to search any trunk or envelope, wherever found, in which he may have a reasonable cause to suspect there is merchandise which was imported contrary to law." Such merchandise shall be seized and held for trial. 19 U.S.C. § 482.

These laws reflect the judgment of the legislative and executive branches that the expectation of privacy in the interior of the country does not apply to the borders where smuggling and illegal entry are chronic problems. The authority of the United States to search baggage "of arriving international travelers is based on its inherent sovereign authority to protect its territorial integrity." Torres v. Puerto Rico, 442 U.S. 465, 472–473 (1979). Common carriers (such as airlines) have a right to inspect packages to assure that they do not contain contraband or explosive substances. Illinois v. Andreas, 463 U.S. 765, 769 n.1 (1983). When customs officials have reasonable cause to suspect that incoming international mail contains contraband, they may open envelopes and examine the substance inside. The letter itself may not be read without a search warrant. United States v. Ramsey, 431 U.S. 606 (1977); 19 C.F.R. § 145.3. Officers of the Immigration and Naturalization Service are authorized to conduct a warrantless search of any person seeking admission to the United States if the officer has "reasonable cause" to suspect that grounds exist for excluding the person from the United States. 8 U.S.C. § 1357(c). (Border searches for illegal aliens are discussed in the section on automobile searches.)

Years before the courts began to consider Fourth Amendment questions, the First Congress had established the precedents for warrantless searches and seizures at the border. 1 Stat. 164, § 31; 19 U.S.C. § 1581(a). Upon reviewing the constitutionality of a statute that authorized warrantless border searches, Justice Rehnquist traced the law back to 1790 and agreed that "the enactment of this statute by the same Congress that promulgated the constitutional Amendments that ultimately became the Bill of Rights gives the statute an important historical pedigree." United States v. Villamonte-Marquez, 462 U.S. 579, 585 (1983). Acting under this statutory authority, customs officials may board vessels without any suspicion of wrongdoing. All persons coming into the United States from foreign countries "shall be liable to detention and search" by authorized federal officers or agents. 19 U.S.C. § 1582. Customs officials may make arrests without a warrant when narcotics laws are violated in their presence or where the official has reasonable grounds to believe that a person has committed a violation. 26 U.S.C. § 7607.

Border officials must now contend with smugglers who swallow drug capsules or cocaine-filled balloons and condoms. When officials suspected one woman of being a "balloon swallower," attempting what is called alimentary canal smuggling, they held her for sixteen hours during which time they considered sending her home, performing an x-ray (which she refused), and conducting a test to check her claim of being pregnant (the test proved negative). Nature eventually took its course, discharging eighty-eight cocaine-filled balloons over a four-day period. Considering the circumstances, the Court regarded the officials' actions as permissible under the Fourth Amendment. United States v. Montoya de Hernandez, 473 U.S. 531 (1985).

Enforcement officials who seize vessels not on the border but on the "high seas" are subject to special rules defined by treaties, Ford v. United States, 273 U.S. 593 (1927), and federal statutes, Maul v. United States, 274 U.S. 501 (1927) and United States v. Lee, 274 U.S. 559 (1927). See also Dodge v. United States, 272 U.S. 530 (1926). The exception for border searches does not justify a search without warrant or probable cause for "intermediate borders," such as between the United States and the territory of Puerto Rico. Torres v. Puerto Rico, 442 U.S. 465 (1979).

Consent

The protections of the Fourth Amendment may be waived if a person's consent is voluntary and without coercion. Consent is not granted when one submits to authority. Johnson v. United States, 333 U.S. 10, 13 (1948). In one case, government agents entered a suspect's home without a search warrant or arrest warrant but with his wife's permission. The Court held that his constitutional rights had not been waived when his wife, under implied coercion, allowed the agents to enter. Amos v. United States, 255 U.S. 313 (1921). Under other circumstances the Court has allowed a wife or third party to admit officers to make a full search and find incriminating evidence if the consent has been given voluntarily. United States v. Matlock, 415 U.S. 164 (1974).

The use of undercover agents complicates the notion of "consent." A federal narcotics agent, by misrepresenting his identity and expressing his willingness to buy narcotics, was invited into the home of a drug dealer. There was no question of entrapment; the agent did not encourage or stimulate a crime. The Court decided that the dealer, by opening his home as a place of illegal business, had surrendered any expectation of privacy. Lewis v. United States, 385 U.S. 206 (1966).

A search cannot be justified as lawful on the basis of "consent" if a law officer states that he has a warrant: "When a law enforcement officer claims authority to search a home under a warrant, he announces in effect that the occupant has no right to resist the search. The situation is instinct with coercion—albeit colorably lawful coercion." Bumper v. United States, 391 U.S. 543, 550 (1968). When the subject of a search is not in custody, consent must be given voluntarily without duress or coercion, either express or implied.[4] Even when someone has been arrested and is in custody, consent can be given if the custody is on a public street rather than in the confines of a police station. United States v. Watson, 423 U.S. 411, 424 (1976).

[4]Schneckloth v. Bustamonte, 412 U.S. 218, 248 (1973); United States v. Mendenhall, 446 U.S. 544 (1980); Florida v. Rodriguez, 469 U.S. 1 (1984).

"Hot Pursuit"

A 1967 decision by the Supreme Court dealt with an armed robbery suspect who, police learned, had entered a certain house. Minutes later, the police arrived and were told at the door of the house, by the suspect's wife, that she had no objection to their searching the house. Her consent alone did not justify the resulting search. The police acted reasonably by entering the house and searching for the suspect and for weapons which he had used in the robbery or might use against them. The Fourth Amendment did not require the police to delay the investigation and endanger their lives or the lives of others. "Speed here was essential, and only a thorough search of the house for persons and weapons could have insured that [the suspect] was the only man present and that the police had control of all weapons which could be used against them or to effect an escape." Warden v. Hayden, 387 U.S. 294, 298–299.

The Court expanded the police power by rejecting the "mere evidence" rule. Previous decisions had allowed police to seize the instrumentalities of a crime (weapons, stolen property) but prohibited the seizure of "merely evidentiary materials." The Court now rejected that distinction by allowing the officers to seize certain clothing items which were later used to convict the suspect. The Court held that privacy is not disturbed to any greater degree by a search directed to a purely evidentiary object than by a search directed to an instrumentality, fruit, or contraband. Id. at 301–302.

Another case concerned a woman suspected of selling narcotics. When the police approached her to make an arrest she was standing in the doorway holding a paper bag. As she retreated into the house they followed, finding envelopes containing heroin and marked money. The Court held that standing in the doorway put her in a "public place" with no expectation of privacy. United States v. Santana, 427 U.S. 38 (1976).

"Plain-View" Doctrine

Following a brutal murder of a fourteen-year-old girl, the police went to the suspect's home to question him. On later visits they questioned his wife and eventually arrested him. The police searched his car without a warrant, arguing that it was an instrumentality of the crime and could be seized on his property "because it was in plain view." The Supreme Court reviewed previous holdings on the plain-view doctrine and concluded that the police officer in each of them had a justification for an intrusion "in the course of which he came inadvertently across a piece of evidence incriminating the accused." There has to be some valid reason for the officer's presence, for otherwise the doctrine would invite a general exploratory search without a warrant. When the police know in advance the location of the evidence and intend to seize it, a warrant should be obtained. In this case the police had ample opportunity to obtain a warrant and failed to do so, making the seizure and subsequent search of the car unconstitutional. COOLIDGE v. NEW HAMP-SHIRE, 403 U.S. 443, 464–473, (1973).

The plain-view doctrine allows limited searches and seizures following a fire. In one case, after a fire had been brought under control, firefighters discovered containers of a flammable liquid. A police detective took some pictures, and the fire chief and the detective removed the containers. Subsequent visits produced additional evidence and information. At no time was there a warrant. The Supreme Court upheld the removal of the containers without a warrant, as well as materials taken the following morning, but later visits (some coming a month later) required a warrant. A burning building is "an exigency of sufficient proportions" to permit a warrantless entry, and once inside the building firefighters "may seize evidence of arson that is in plain view." Michigan v. Tyler, 436 U.S. 499, 509 (1978). Nevertheless, people retain significant privacy interests in their fire-damaged home. Arson investigators may not conduct a warrantless search of the entire house simply because of a fire. Michigan v. Clifford, 464 U.S. 287 (1984).

Another case involved a university police officer who stopped a student outside a dormitory because he was carrying a bottle of gin and appeared to be under age. The student asked permission to return to his room to retrieve his identification card and the officer followed. From an open doorway he noticed what appeared to be marijuana seeds and a pipe. He entered the room, confirmed that the seeds were marijuana, and determined that the pipe smelled of marijuana. The Court held that the plain-view doctrine permits a law enforcement officer to seize incriminating evidence and contraband "when it is discovered in a place where the officer has a right to be." Washington v. Chrisman, 455 U.S. 1, 6 (1982). Interestingly, when this case was remanded to the Supreme Court of Washington, the state court rejected the plain-view doctrine and held that the evidence—under the state constitution and state laws—could not be admitted in court. State v. Chrisman, 676 P.2d 419 (Wash. 1984).

The plain-view doctrine requires probable cause, not the lesser standard of reasonable suspicion. Arizona v. Hicks, 480 U.S. 321 (1987). Actions by private parties can be instrumental in putting items in "plain view." While examining a damaged package, employees of a private freight carrier saw a white powder and notified the Drug Enforcement Agency. A DEA agent arrived, tested the powder, and determined that it was cocaine. The Court allowed the warrantless search and seizure because the actions of private individuals had placed the powder essentially in plain view of the agent. United States v. Jacobsen, 466 U.S. 109 (1984). However, when a private carrier mistakenly delivers a package to the wrong person, who opens it, the government may not exceed the scope of the private search. A partial invasion of privacy does not justify a total invasion by the government. Walter v. United States, 447 U.S. 649 (1980). In 1988, the Court ruled that police do not need a warrant to look through trash left on a curb for a pickup, and through that examination discover evidence that supports a search warrant for narcotics use. The owner of the trash has no reasonable expectation of privacy. California v. Greenwood, 108 S.Ct. 1625 (1988).

Related to the plain-view exception is the "open-field" doctrine, which permits police officers to enter and search a field without a warrant. Hester v. United States, 265 U.S. 57 (1924). The term "effects" in the Fourth Amendment is considered less inclusive than property, permitting law enforcement officers to bypass locked gates and "No Trespassing" signs to discover marijuana growing in open fields. The Court reasons that open fields are accessible to the public and to the police in ways that a home, office, or commercial structure are not. Oliver v. United States, 466 U.S. 170 (1984). Similarly, police may cross a series of fences to look in a barn that is not considered to be protected by the Fourth Amendment. United States v. Dunn, 480 U.S. 294 (1987).

Two cases in 1986 expanded the government's authority under the open-field or plain-view doctrines. In one, the Court upheld the authority of the Environmental Protection Agency to use aerial observation and photography to implement the Clean Air Act. Without a warrant, EPA took aerial photographs of an industrial plant complex. Dow Chemical Co. v. United States, 476 U.S. 227 (1986). In the second, law enforcement officers flew over a suspect's house at an altitude of 1,000 feet and identified marijuana plants growing in the yard. On the basis of these observations a search warrant was obtained. The Court, divided 5–4, ruled that the suspect had no expectation of privacy from *all* observations of his backyard. CALIFORNIA v. CIRAOLO, 476 U.S. 207 (1986). This case invited variations on the theme, such as flying over at even lower altitudes or using police helicopters to hover over a suspect's home or outside an apartment window. In 1989, the Court (again divided 5–4) upheld the use of police helicopters to conduct surveillance from a height of 400 feet above a greenhouse in a residential backyard. Florida v. Riley, 109 S.Ct. 693 (1989).

Automobiles

No exception to the warrant requirement has experienced as many permutations and perturbations as the exception for automobiles. The framers were fortunate not to have to spell out their "intent" in this area. The automobile exception illustrates how the constitutionality of an issue can be shaped initially by the executive and legislative branches. From an early date, congressional statutes and Attorney General opinions agreed that government agents could make warrantless searches and seizures of ships, automobiles, and other vehicles which could be easily moved outside the jurisdiction of an officer by the time he obtained a warrant. 1 Stat. 43, § 24 (1789); 26 Op. Att'y Gen. 243 (1907). This justification appears in the first Supreme Court decision on automobile searches. If law enforcement officers had probable cause to stop a car, they could search it without a warrant and seize its contents without violating the Fourth Amendment. The Court regarded its decision as consistent with the intent of Congress in the National Prohibition Act.[5]

Some of the early cases attempted to place restrictions on automobile searches. If probable cause was lacking, automobile searches were illegal. Henry v. United States, 361 U.S. 98 (1959). Merely by being in a suspected car did not strip someone of his usual rights regarding search of his person. United States v. Di Re, 332 U.S. 581 (1948). If a car search was too remote in time from an arrest, evidence was inadmissible in federal court. Preston v. United States, 376 U.S. 364 (1964). The Court adopted a more lenient standard for the states, permitting the search of a glove compartment a week after an arrest. Cooper v. California, 386 U.S. 58 (1967). But see Dyke v. Taylor Implement Co., 391 U.S. 216 (1968).

The Court struggled to find reasonable boundaries for car searches. If evidence is in plain sight of an officer who has a right to be in a position of viewing it, the material can be introduced in evidence without a warrant. Harris v. United States, 390 U.S. 234 (1968); Colorado v. Bannister, 449 U.S. 1 (1980); Texas v. Brown, 460 U.S. 730 (1983). Incriminating evidence can be taken from the exterior of an

---

[5]Carroll v. United States, 267 U.S. 132 (1925). See also Husty v. United States, 282 U.S. 694 (1931) and Brinegar v. United States, 338 U.S. 160 (1949). If a car could have been searched on the streets, officers may follow it into a garage and search it there. Scher v. United States, 305 U.S. 251 (1938).

automobile without a search warrant. Cardwell v. Lewis, 417 U.S. 583 (1974). Even when a car is impounded at a police station or towed to a garage, with no risk of its being moved or its contents taken, a warrantless search of the *interior* is valid. The Court argues that such searches are necessary to inventory the vehicle's contents and to prevent dangerous weapons or materials from falling into the hands of vandals.[6]

These cases suggest that expectations of privacy for the contents of an automobile are severely limited. Other decisions, however, imply that the right to privacy exists for such items as personal luggage, especially when fortified by double locks. United States v. Chadwick, 433 U.S. 1 (1977); Arkansas v. Sanders, 442 U.S. 753 (1979). This line of argument was ill-fated. Justice Blackmun warned that left "hanging in limbo, and probably soon to be litigated, are the briefcase, the wallet, the package, the paper bag, and every other kind of container." 442 U.S. at 768. Within a few years the Court decided that officers needed a search warrant before opening packages wrapped in green opaque plastic. Clearly the Court did not want to make what might appear to be class distinctions, upholding the right of privacy for a leather briefcase but denying it for a cardboard box: "What one person may put into a suitcase, another may put into a paper bag." Robbins v. California, 453 U.S. 420, 426 (1981). Justice Powell criticized the law on automobile searches as "intolerably confusing." Id. at 430.

The latitude for automobile searches continues to widen. As an incident to a lawful arrest, a policeman may reach into the interior of a car, remove a jacket, and unzip one of the pockets to discover cocaine. The search is valid because it is incident to a lawful custodial arrest. New York v. Belton, 453 U.S. 454 (1981). But if a policeman stops a car without probable cause or reasonable suspicion, the seizure of contraband—even if in plain view—is unreasonable under the Fourth Amendment. An individual's right of privacy outweighs a patrolman's decision to make random spot checks. Delaware v. Prouse, 440 U.S. 648 (1979). If passengers in an automobile are unable to show ownership of the car or its contents, they have no standing to raise vicarious Fourth Amendment challenges to the search. Rakas v. Illinois, 439 U.S. 128 (1978).

The major expansion of automobile searches came in 1982. Police with probable cause stopped a car, searched the driver, and searched the interior of the car. After arresting the driver, they opened the car's trunk and discovered a closed brown paper bag. Inside, they found glassine bags containing a white powder, later determined to be heroin. They drove the car to police headquarters and conducted another warrantless search, opening a zippered leather pouch. The Court held that police officers who have legitimately stopped an automobile and have probable cause to believe that it contains contraband may conduct a warrantless search that is as thorough as a magistrate could authorize by warrant. UNITED STATES v. ROSS, 456 U.S. 798. The Court insisted that the decision was "faithful to the interpretation of the Fourth Amendment that the Court has followed with substantial consistency throughout our history," id. at 824, but it effectively repealed the Fourth Amendment warrant requirement for automobile searches and the traditional reliance on a neutral and detached magistrate. The Court did not explain why a search warrant

---

[6]See Colorado v. Bertine, 479 U.S. 367 (1987); Illinois v. Lafayette, 462 U.S. 640 (1983); Michigan v. Thomas, 458 U.S. 259 (1982); South Dakota v. Opperman, 428 U.S. 364, 369 (1976); Texas v. White, 423 U.S. 67 (1975); Cady v. Dombrowski, 413 U.S. 433, 448 (1973); Chambers v. Maroney, 399 U.S. 42 (1970).

could not be obtained after arresting a suspect and immobilizing the car. State courts may reject the *Ross* doctrine by adopting standards that offer owners of automobiles greater protection against searches and seizures. State v. Ringer, 674 P.2d 1240 (Wash. 1983).

The Court now allows the government to seize trucks suspected of containing marijuana and wait three days to search the packages, without ever bothering to obtain a search warrant. United States v. Johns, 469 U.S. 478 (1985). The freedom of police officers to search a car extends to mobile motor homes parked in a lot. The Court has largely replaced the mobility rationale of *Carroll* with the argument that the expectation of privacy in a car or motor home is significantly less than for a home or office. New York v. Class, 475 U.S. 106 (1986); California v. Carney, 471 U.S. 386 (1985).

Several automobile cases concern the use of roving patrols and checkpoints near the Mexican border to discover contraband or illegal aliens. Unless there is probable cause or consent, a roving patrol may not conduct a warrantless search of a car twenty-five air miles north of the Mexican border. Almeida-Sanchez v. United States, 413 U.S. 266 (1973). The Court later held that this decision should not be applied retroactively since border patrols had been acting on the basis of a federal statute, administrative regulations, and previous court decisions. United States v. Peltier, 422 U.S. 531 (1975). A roving patrol may not stop vehicles near the Mexican border and question the occupants about their citizenship and immigration status simply because they appear to be of Mexican ancestry. If an officer's observations lead him to suspect that a vehicle contains illegal aliens, he may stop a car briefly and investigate the circumstances that provoked his suspicion. United States v. Brignoni-Ponce, 422 U.S. 873 (1975); United States v. Cortez, 449 U.S. 411 (1981).

Fixed checkpoints present a different issue. Patrol officers at these sites, which are located away from the border, may stop vehicles and inquire about citizenship. In the absence of consent or probable cause, however, officers may not search the interior of a vehicle. For this purpose there is no difference between a checkpoint and a roving patrol. United States v. Ortiz, 422 U.S. 891 (1975); United States v. Martinez-Fuerte, 428 U.S. 543 (1976).

Emergency Situations

Many of the exceptions to the warrant requirement contain variations of "exigent circumstances." This section describes other emergency situations that permit search and seizure without a warrant. The Court has held that a police officer has a right to "stop and frisk" an individual who is behaving suspiciously and yet there is no probable cause to make an arrest. Whenever a "reasonably prudent officer" believes that his safety or that of others is endangered, he may make a reasonable search for weapons of the person he thinks armed and dangerous, regardless of whether he has probable cause for arrest or an absolute certainty that the individual is armed. The Court recognizes that officers on the beat may have to take swift action based upon on-the-spot decisions. TERRY v. OHIO, 392 U.S. 1 (1968).[7] The Fourth Amendment limits on-the-spot decisions by police officers who use deadly force

---

[7]See also United States v. Sokolow, 109 S.Ct. 1581 (1989); Michigan v. Long, 463 U.S. 1032 (1983); Michigan v. Summers, 452 U.S. 692 (1981); Pennsylvania v. Mimms, 434 U.S. 106 (1977); Adams v. Williams, 407 U.S. 143 (1972).

against unarmed, fleeing suspects. Tennessee v. Garner, 471 U.S. 1 (1985). The degree of force used by law enforcement officials in investigatory stops is analyzed under the "objective reasonableness" standard of the Fourth Amendment, rather than the "substantive due process" (shock-the-conscience) standard. Graham v. Connor, 109 S.Ct. 1865 1989.

Brief stops to question a suspect are permissible if police have a reasonable suspicion that is grounded in specific and articulable facts. Reid v. United States, 448 U.S. 438 (1980); United States v. Hensley, 469 U.S. 221 (1985). Individuals suspected of criminal activity can be detained for periods as long as forty minutes when the delay is attributable mainly to their evasive actions. United States v. Sharpe, 470 U.S. 675 (1985). Detentions of ninety minutes are not justified as a *Terry*-type investigative stop, United States v. Place, 462 U.S. 696 (1983), but detention can last for much longer periods at the border when smuggling is suspected, United States v. Montoya de Hernandez, 473 U.S. 531 (1985). These decisions do not justify detaining a suspect or bringing him to police headquarters on less than probable cause with the hope of discovering incriminating evidence.[8]

Suspicious activities and furtive movements may be sufficient reason for an officer to apprehend someone and frisk him for possible weapons or burglar's tools. Sibron v. New York, 392 U.S. 40, 66 (1968). However, unless there is reasonable suspicion based on objective facts that an individual is engaged or has engaged in criminal conduct, an officer may not require someone to identify himself and make an arrest if he refuses. Brown v. Texas, 443 U.S. 47 (1979); Michigan v. DeFillippo, 443 U.S. 31 (1979); Kolender v. Lawson, 461 U.S. 352 (1983). A warrant to search a bartender does not justify frisking everyone in the tavern. Ybarra v. Illinois, 444 U.S. 85 (1979). Based on circumstances arousing suspicion, law enforcement officers may be justified in seizing packages to allow time for additional inquiry and obtaining a search warrant. United States v. Van Leeuwen, 397 U.S. 249 (1970).

Search Incident to Arrest

Police officers may conduct a search incident to a valid arrest. However, allowing a warrantless search and seizure whenever there is an arrest risks swallowing the general principle of the Fourth Amendment in an exception. Trupiano v. United States, 334 U.S. 699, 708 (1948). The government cannot simultaneously justify an arrest because of a search and a search because of an arrest. Johnson v. United States, 333 U.S. 10, 16–17 (1948).

A lawful arrest may be followed by a search of the persons and premises in order to find and seize things connected with the crime. Agnello v. United States, 269 U.S. 20 (1925). Although a search warrant for intoxicating liquors and articles for their manufacture may not be used to seize a ledger and bills of account, if the latter are in plain view they may be picked up as an incident of an arrest. Marron v. United States, 275 U.S. 192 (1927).

What are the limits of a search for articles that are not in plain view? An arrest should not be used as a pretext to conduct a general and exploratory search for incriminating information. United States v. Lefkowitz, 285 U.S. 452 (1932). Nevertheless, in 1947 the Supreme Court allowed an arrest warrant to justify a five-hour

---

[8]Florida v. Royer, 460 U.S. 491 (1983); Taylor v. Alabama, 457 U.S. 687 (1982); Dunaway v. New York, 442 U.S. 200 (1979); Morales v. New York 396 U.S. 102 (1969).

search of an apartment. Beneath clothes in a bedroom bureau drawer federal agents found a sealed envelope marked "personal papers." They tore it open and found several draft cards used to convict the suspect. The Court claimed that the search was incident to the arrest, although the draft cards were unrelated to the crimes for which the suspect had been arrested. Harris v. United States, 331 U.S. 145. Three years later, the Court allowed government agents with an arrest warrant to search a suspect's desk, safe, and file cabinets to seize 573 forged stamps. The search and seizure were considered incident to a lawful arrest. United States v. Rabinowitz, 339 U.S. 56 (1950).

These decisions were overturned in 1969, but first the Court disposed of other issues. It decided that an arrest warrant could not be used to search and seize items in a room if the suspect was not there. United States v. Jeffers, 324 U.S. 48 (1951). Nor could an arrest warrant justify an indiscriminate search and seizure even after an arrest. Kremen v. United States, 353 U.S. 346 (1957). When law requires police officers to make an arrest only after giving notice of their authority and purpose, or when statutes prohibit an unannounced entering of a home, actions contrary to the law invalidated an arrest and the seizure of incriminating goods. Sabbath v. United States, 391 U.S. 585 (1968); Miller v. United States, 357 U.S. 301 (1958).[9]

A search incident to an arrest must be closely connected in time and place. A warrantless search is not incident to an arrest that occurs two days later, Stoner v. California, 376 U.S. 483 (1964); or when an arrest occurs in one place and the police attempt to use it to search a home blocks away, James v. Louisiana, 382 U.S. 36 (1965); or when the police arrest a person outside his house and take him inside for the purpose of conducting a warrantless search, Shipley v. California, 395 U.S. 818 (1969) and Vale v. Louisiana, 399 U.S. 30 (1970). But when a formal arrest quickly follows a search, it may not be "particularly important that the search preceded the arrest rather than vice versa." Rawlings v. Kentucky, 448 U.S. 98, 111 (1980).

In 1969, the Supreme Court tried to limit the reach of searches that are incident to an arrest. The case involved police officers who arrived at a home with an arrest warrant but not a search warrant. The suspect's wife allowed them to enter. When the suspect arrived, he was arrested but he specifically denied the police the right to "look around." They did so anyway, searching the entire house, attic, garage, and small workshop. The Court reversed the conviction, holding that an arresting officer may search a person to discover and remove weapons and may search the area within the immediate control of the suspect, who might grab a weapon or destroy evidence. A broader search requires a search warrant. CHIMEL v. CALIFORNIA, 395 U.S. 752. The Court's decision was not made retroactive. Williams v. United States, 401 U.S. 646 (1971). The *Chimel* doctrine is applied less strictly to automobile searches, for here the Court allows officers to seize evidence which a suspect could not possibly reach. New York v. Belton, 453 U.S. 454 (1981).

When a suspect is detained with probable cause, even though he is not arrested, it is permissible for the police in the course of station-house questioning to take

---

[9]If there is neither reasonable grounds nor probable cause to make an arrest, incriminating statements or materials may not be introduced as evidence. United States v. Crews, 445 U.S. 463 (1980); Davis v. Mississippi, 394 U.S. 721 (1969); Recznik v. City of Lorain, 393 U.S. 166 (1968); Beck v. Ohio, 379 U.S. 89 (1964); Wong Sun v. United States, 371 U.S. 471 (1963). Without probable cause, consent, or judicial authorization, police may not bring someone to headquarters to obtain incriminating evidence. Hayes v. Florida, 470 U.S. 811 (1985); Taylor v. Alabama, 457 U.S. 687 (1982); Dunaway v. New York, 442 U.S. 200 (1979).

samples from his fingernails. Although there was no search warrant and the suspect objected, the search was considered an appropriate action to preserve highly evanescent evidence. Cupp v. Murphy, 412 U.S. 291 (1973). In the case of a lawful custodial arrest, a full search of the person is reasonable under the Fourth Amendment. Police may search outer clothing to remove weapons, search elsewhere for evidence, and inventory possessions as part of the process of booking someone. United States v. Robinson, 414 U.S. 218 (1973); Gustafson v. Florida, 414 U.S. 260 (1973); United States v. Edwards, 415 U.S. 800 (1974); Illinois v. Lafayette, 462 U.S. 640 (1983).

Administrative Inspections

Congressional statutes authorize many types of warrantless inspections by federal officers, and in almost every case of a challenged statute the Supreme Court has upheld the legislative judgment. Beginning with the First Congress, statutes have required certain businesses to have their records available for federal inspectors. Legislation in 1791 provided that the books of distilleries shall "lie open" for inspection officers to take notes. 1 Stat. 207, § 35. Contemporary law authorizes federal inspectors to enter distilleries during business hours to examine records and documents. 26 U.S.C. § 5146(b). The Narcotics Drug Act of 1914 required persons who dispensed narcotics to prepare orders on IRS (Internal Revenue Service) forms and make them available to official inspectors. United States v. Doremus, 249 U.S. 86 (1919). During business hours, federal inspectors may enter the premises of any firearms or ammunition importer, manufacturer, dealer, or collector to examine records and documents. 18 U.S.C. § 923(g).

With the growth of federal regulatory activities, the courts began to monitor the scope of agency inspections. In 1924, the Supreme Court rejected the argument of the Federal Trade Commission that it had unlimited right of access to company records. The spirit and letter of the Fourth Amendment counseled against the belief that Congress intended to authorize a "fishing expedition" into private papers on the possibility that they may disclose a crime. FTC v. American Tobacco Co., 264 U.S. 298. But when federal agents used heavy-handed tactics to investigate a black market operation in gasoline, the Court sustained the warrantless search because the agents found gasoline ration coupons which the Court regarded as public documents, not private property. Davis v. United States, 328 U.S. 582 (1946). Similarly, the Court held that the terms of a government contract allowed federal agents to audit a contractor's books at any time during business hours. By agreeing to permit inspection of his accounts and records, in order to obtain the government's business, a contractor voluntarily waived privacy rights. Zap v. United States, 328 U.S. 624 (1946). Some statutes required permission of a company's owner before agents could enter and inspect a factory. United States v. Cardiff, 344 U.S. 174 (1952).

Beginning in 1950, the Supreme Court upheld the right of government inspectors to enter private homes to inspect for unsanitary conditions. District of Columbia v. Little, 339 U.S. 1 (1950). Homeowners who refused to allow health inspectors to enter could be convicted. Ironically, this meant that someone suspected of criminal activity had a constitutional right to object to warrantless searches of his home, while no such right existed for those not suspected of crime but who merely objected to health inspectors entering. Frank v. Maryland, 359 U.S. 360, 378 (1959).

See also Ohio ex rel. Eaton v. Price, 360 U.S. 246 (1959) and Eaton v. Price, 364 U.S. 263 (1960).

In 1967, the Supreme Court placed restrictions on warrantless inspections of homes and businesses. The Court pointed out that inspections by city officials were not merely "civil" in nature. A refusal to allow an inspection, combined with the discovery of conditions that violate local ordinances, rendered the person subject to criminal process. Unless an emergency required immediate access, owners of homes and businesses had a constitutional right to insist that inspectors first obtain a search warrant. Nevertheless, the warrant need not conform to the Fourth Amendment standard of probable cause. "Reasonableness" or a "suitable" warrant would suffice. Camera v. Municipal Court, 387 U.S. 523 (1967); See v. City of Seattle, 387 U.S. 541 (1967). Although government employees are entitled to Fourth Amendment protections and have a legitimate expectation of privacy in their office, desk, and file cabinets, employers may, without a warrant, conduct a search of the office if there are reasonable grounds related to work or work-related misconduct. O'Connor v. Ortega, 480 U.S. 709 (1987).

Certain businesses (liquor, narcotics, firearms) are particularly susceptible to warrantless inspections. The Court acknowledges that Congress "has broad authority to fashion standards of reasonableness for searches and seizures" in the liquor industry. Colonnade Catering Corp. v. United States, 397 U.S. 72, 77 (1970). Congress also authorized warrantless searches of firearms stores during business hours, and the Court upheld this provision against the charge that it violated the Fourth Amendment. United States v. Biswell, 406 U.S. 311 (1972). Without a warrant, state health inspectors may enter a corporation's outdoor premises in the daylight, without its knowledge or consent, for the purpose of making tests of smoke emitted from chimneys. Air Pollution Variance Bd. v. Western Alfalfa, 416 U.S. 861 (1974).

This pattern of judicial support for congressional judgments on administrative inspections came to a sudden halt in 1978 when the Court held that warrantless inspections of company work areas, in search of safety and health hazards, intruded on Fourth Amendment rights. The Court struck down these OSHA (Occupational Safety and Health Administration) inspections in part because they affected every industry involved in interstate commerce, in contrast to such specific industries as liquor and firearms. The Court held that OSHA inspectors required a warrant, though probable cause is not necessary. Marshall v. Barlow's, Inc., 436 U.S. 307 (1978). Within three years, the Court returned to the customary practice of sustaining congressional judgment. It upheld (with an 8–1 majority) a statute that permitted warrantless inspections of underground and surface mines as part of the procedures needed to assure compliance with health and safety standards. Under the power to regulate interstate commerce, the Court said that Congress has broad power to authorize warrantless searches to further a regulatory scheme. Donovan v. Dewey, 452 U.S. 594 (1981). The scope of warrantless inspections of "closely regulated" industries was extended in 1987 to permit police officers to enter junkyards to discover stolen automobiles and parts. New York v. Burger, 482 U.S. 691 (1987).

Businesses open to the general public do not have the same expectations of privacy as people who live at home or work in offices. Detectives may enter a bookstore, purchase a magazine, and use that as evidence to arrest the owner for selling obscene materials. Examining the books and magazines offered for sale is not a "search" nor is the purchase a "seizure." The bookstore owner had no "reasonable expectation of privacy in areas of the store where the public was invited to enter and to transact business." Maryland v. Macon, 472 U.S. 463, 469 (1985).

Mandatory drug tests for government employees have been reviewed by the courts for compliance with the Fourth Amendment. Two decisions in 1989 by the Supreme Court began the process of establishing some boundaries. In the first case, decided by a 7–2 majority, the Court upheld federal regulations that require blood and urine tests for railroad employees following major train accidents. Such tests are considered reasonable even though they are warrantless and there is no reasonable suspicion that any particular employee is impaired. Skinner v. Railway Labor Executives' Assn., 109 S.Ct. 1402 (1989). In the second case, the Court divided 5–4 in upholding a Customs Service requirement of urine tests for all employees seeking transfer or promotion to positions having a direct involvement in drug interdiction or that involve the carrying of firearms. National Treasury Employees Union v. Von Raab, 109 S.Ct. 1384 (1989). As a result of these two rulings, other federal agencies are reviewing their programs for mandatory drug tests.[10]

ELECTRONIC EAVESDROPPING

The framers were well aware that eavesdropping could intrude upon personal privacy. The use of *electronic* eavesdropping, however, forced Congress and the Supreme Court to interpret eighteenth-century language in the Fourth Amendment in light of the latest technological advances. The use of wiretapping by law enforcement officials requires the active involvement of all three branches.

The Court first confronted electronic eavesdropping when it considered the use of wiretaps by prohibition agents in the 1920s to monitor and intercept telephone calls. Small wires were inserted in telephone wires leading from residences. Taps could be made in the streets near the houses or in the basement of large office buildings. In a bitterly divided 5–4 decision, the Court reasoned that there was no violation of the Fourth Amendment because the taps did not *enter* the premises. Hence, there was neither "search" nor "seizure." This wooden assessment provoked a scathing dissent from Justice Brandeis, who accurately predicted that technology would overwhelm the Fourth Amendment unless the Court met the challenge with open eyes. OLMSTEAD v. UNITED STATES, 277 U.S. 438 (1928).

Chief Justice Taft, writing for the majority, invited Congress to establish boundaries for wiretapping: "Congress may of course protect the secrecy of telephone messages by making them, when intercepted, inadmissible in evidence in federal criminal trials, by direct legislation, and thus depart from the common law of evidence." Id. at 465–466. Section 605 of the Federal Communications Act of 1934 was intended to fill that gap by making it a crime to intercept or to use any wire or radio communication. Because of that statute, the government could not introduce as trial evidence any information obtained from a wiretap. Nardone v. United States, 302 U.S. 379 (1937); Weiss v. United States, 308 U.S. 321 (1939); Nardone v. United States, 308 U.S. 338 (1939). This restriction did not prevent the government from using wiretaps to "induce" people whose conversations had been overheard to turn

---

[10]In 1989, the Court also upheld Conrail's policy of requiring its employees to undergo physical examinations periodically and upon return from leave. Urinalysis drug screening is part of the exam. Consol. Rail Corp. v. Railway Labor Executives, 109 S.Ct. 2477 (1989).

state's evidence and appear as witnesses for the government. Goldstein v. United States, 316 U.S. 114 (1942).

Until *Olmstead* was overturned in 1967, the Court wrestled with new forms of technological intrusion. Federal agents used a "detectaphone" to overhear telephone conversations. This instrument, when placed against the wall of a room, could pick up sound waves on the other side of the wall. A receiver amplified the sound waves and allowed agents to listen to phone conversations. The Court held that there was neither a "communication" nor an "interception" within the meaning of Section 605. Relying on *Olmstead*, the Court found no violation of the Fourth Amendment. Goldman v. United States, 316 U.S. 129 (1942). Undercover agents, equipped with a radio transmitter, were allowed to stand in a laundry and engage a suspect in conversation. His self-incriminating statements were picked up by a radio receiver and used to convict him. There was no "search" or "seizure" because the Court held that the government did not trespass when it entered the suspect's store. On Lee v. United States, 343 U.S. 747 (1952).

The ingenuity of investigators and police easily outpaced the Court's interpretation of the Fourth Amendment. Using a key made by a locksmith, state police entered the home of a suspect and installed a concealed microphone in the hall. A hole was bored in the roof to allow wires to transmit sounds to a neighboring garage. The police returned later and moved the microphone to a bedroom and came back a third time to move it to a closet. Although a trespass and probably a burglary had been committed, the Court found no violation of Section 605 and upheld the action under the state constitution. Irvine v. California, 347 U.S. 128, 132 (1954). The Court blithely noted: "All that was heard through the microphone was what an eavesdropper, hidden in the hall, the bedroom, or the closet, might have heard." Id. at 131.

Other variations of electronic eavesdropping blossomed. Police officers used an extension phone in an adjoining room to listen to a conversation. They had the consent of the subscriber (who was a party to the conversation) but not the consent of the sender, which Section 605 required. Nevertheless, the Court held that the contents of the communication were admissible in a federal criminal trial because there was no "interception" within the meaning of Section 605. The Court remarked that every party to a telephone conversation takes the risk that the other party may have an extension phone, allowing others to overhear the conversation. Rathbun v. United States, 355 U.S. 107, 111 (1957). The use of a four-party line, with one line connected to a phone that permits the police to hear and record all conversations without lifting the receiver, violated Section 605 because it intercepted and divulged a communication. Lee v. Florida, 392 U.S. 378 (1968). The police deliberately arranged to have the four-party line connected to a suspect's house, whereas in *Rathbun* the extension phone had not been installed just for the police.

In another case, government agents pushed an electronic listening device through the wall of an adjoining house until it touched the heating duct of a suspect's house. Through the use of this "spike mike," officers with earphones listened to conversations taking place on both floors of the house. The Court held that this physical penetration into the suspect's house violated the Fourth Amendment. Silverman v. United States, 365 U.S. 505 (1961). Three years later, the Court reversed a state court decision that had upheld the use of evidence obtained by a small microphone that had been stuck in a wall, penetrating to the depth of a thumb tack. Clinton v. Virginia, 377 U.S. 158; 130 S.E.2d 437.

On some occasions federal judges were asked to authorize an electronic device to record conversations. For example, a lawyer was suspected of wanting to bribe a prospective member of a federal jury. He had hired a Nashville policeman to investigate backgrounds of potential jurors, unaware that the policeman had also agreed to report to federal agents any illegal activities he observed. The district court authorized the placement of a tape recorder on the policeman to record future conversations about bribe efforts. The Court upheld the admissibility of these conversations, which led to the lawyer's conviction. Osborn v. United States, 385 U.S. 323 (1966).

Two decisions in 1967 placed major constraints on electronic eavesdropping. A New York law was struck down because it permitted the installation of recording devices without requiring the police to specify that a particular crime had been or was being committed. Also, the police failed to particularly describe the conversations sought. The broad sweep of the statute violated the Fourth Amendment. Berger v. New York, 388 U.S. 41. Also in 1967, the Court finally overturned the "trespass" doctrine of *Olmstead* and *Goldman*. By a 7–1 vote, the Court declared unconstitutional the placing of electronic listening and recording devices on the outside of public telephone booths to obtain incriminating evidence. Although there was no physical entrance into the area occupied by the suspect, he had a legitimate expectation of privacy within the phone booth. In a broadly principled decision capable of accommodating technological ingenuity, the Court held that the Fourth Amendment "protects people, not places." KATZ v. UNITED STATES, 389 U.S. 347, 351. The effect of the decision was prospective, not retroactive. Desist v. United States, 394 U.S. 244 (1969); Kaiser v. New York, 394 U.S. 280 (1969); United States v. White, 401 U.S. 745 (1971).

In response to *Katz*, Congress passed legislation in 1968 requiring law enforcement officers to obtain a warrant before placing taps on phones or installing bugs (concealed microphones). If an "emergency" exists, communications can be intercepted for up to forty-eight hours without a warrant in cases involving organized crime or national security. Warrants are limited to specific periods of time. After a wire intercept is terminated, the person monitored is informed of the fact and date of the entry. 82 Stat. 212; 18 U.S.C. §§ 2510–2520.

Judicial activity after 1968 concentrated more on statutory construction than on constitutional interpretation. A number of cases examined the government's compliance with the wiretap statute.[11] The Court decided that the Fourth Amendment and congressional legislation protect the *content* of communications, not the numbers dialed from a phone. Smith v. Maryland, 442 U.S. 735 (1979). Although the wiretap law does not explicitly authorize covert entry to install bugging equipment, the Court has held that the language and purpose of the statute implicitly authorizes such action without violating the Fourth Amendment. Dalia v. United States, 441 U.S. 238 (1979). (For judicial and congressional action on electronic surveillance for "national security" purposes, see pp. 307, 354–359.)

Court doctrines and congressional statutes are periodically tested and outstripped by new technology. "Beepers" (battery-operated radio transmitters) allow

---

[11]E.g., Scott v. United States, 436 U.S. 128 (1978); United States v. New York Telephone Co., 434 U.S. 159 (1977); United States v. Donovan, 429 U.S. 413 (1977); United States v. Chavez, 416 U.S. 562 (1974); United States v. Giordano, 416 U.S. 505 (1974); United States v. Kahn, 415 U.S. 143 (1974).

law enforcement officers to follow cars and locate illegal operations. United States v. Knotts, 460 U.S. 276 (1983). The use of a beeper to monitor the movement of articles within a private residence, however, is not permitted under the Fourth Amendment. United States v. Karo, 468 U.S. 705 (1984). Other developments include electronic mail, cellular and cordless phones, night vision cameras, parabolic microphones to pick up conversations in homes or offices, satellite communication systems, and closed-circuit video cameras.

These innovations made it necessary for Congress to rethink and rewrite the law on electronic eavesdropping. See Office of Technology Assessment, "Electronic Surveillance and Civil Liberties" (October 1985). Federal judges appealed to Congress to pass legislation that would clarify Fourth Amendment law. United States v. Torres, 751 F.2d 875, 885–886 (7th Cir. 1984). Congress passed legislation in 1986 to modernize the restrictions on electronic eavesdropping. During the debate in the House of Representatives, the floor manager, Congressman Robert Kastenmeier, noted: "We may provide the forum to balance the privacy rights of citizens with the legitimate law enforcement needs of the Government; or we abdicate that role to ad hoc decisions made by the courts and the executive branch." 132 Cong. Rec. H4046 (daily ed. June 23, 1986).

THE EXCLUSIONARY RULE

The term "exclusionary rule" refers to a general doctrine that excludes illegally obtained evidence from trial. Although usually thought of as a Fourth Amendment question, the exclusionary rule also makes inadmissible a confession or statement that violates due process, the Self-Incrimination Clause, or the Sixth Amendment right to counsel. The rule is shaped by Court doctrine as well as by congressional and executive actions. Sometimes the Court invites action by Congress. Olmstead v. United States, 277 U.S. 438, 465–466 (1928). The wiretap statute of 1968 prohibits the admissibility of any evidence "in any trial, hearing or other proceeding in or before any court, grand jury, department, offices, agency, regulatory body, legislative committee, or other authority of the United States, a state, or a political subdivision thereof" if the disclosure of that information violates the statute. 18 U.S.C. § 2514.

The exclusion of coerced confessions dates back to common-law practice, whereas the exclusion of evidence and documents obtained by illegal searches and seizures is largely a twentieth-century development. The practice at the state level was to admit pertinent evidence even if law enforcement officers had acted illegally. Courts did not take notice of how documents or articles were seized. Judges considered only the competence of the evidence, not the method by which it was obtained. Adams v. New York, 192 U.S. 585 (1904). An exception was the Iowa Supreme Court, which announced in 1903 that the admission of evidence illegally obtained would "emasculate" the constitutional guaranty in the state constitution against unreasonable searches and seizures. State v. Sheridan, 96 N.W. 730, 731 (Iowa 1903).

The exclusionary rule originated at the federal level in 1914, when the Supreme Court ruled unanimously that papers illegally seized by federal officers may not be introduced in court as evidence. The details of the case demonstrate that the Court was reacting to the record of law enforcement officials who were willing and able to convict people by any means: unlawful seizures, forced confessions, and other violations of constitutional rights. WEEKS v. UNITED STATES, 232 U.S. 383.

Because the decision did not address papers illegally seized by private parties or state and local officers, federal agents could still profit from violations committed by others. When private parties stole documents and gave them to the federal government for prosecution, a suit had to be directed against the private party. Because the government was not considered responsible for the wrongful seizure, it could use the stolen papers for grand jury action. Burdeau v. McDowell, 256 U.S. 465 (1921). Similarly, federal agents could use the fruits of an illegal search and seizure committed by state officers as long as the federal government did not participate or cooperate in the illegal actions. Byars v. United States, 273 U.S. 28 (1927); Gambino v. United States, 275 U.S. 310 (1927). The crux of the Court's doctrine was "that a search is a search by a federal official if he had a hand in it; it is not a search by a federal official if evidence secured by state authorities is turned over to the federal authorities on a silver platter." Lustig v. United States, 338 U.S. 74, 79 (1949).

When federal officers violated congressional policy by failing to take suspects to the nearest U.S. commissioner or judicial officer for arraignment, and instead held them for several days to obtain incriminating evidence, the Court set aside the convictions and held that the illegally obtained information was inadmissible. McNabb v. United States, 318 U.S. 332 (1943). These convictions were overturned because federal agents violated the Federal Rules of Criminal Procedure devised by Congress to assure that an arrested person is taken before a committing magistrate "without unnecessary delay." Mallory v. United States, 354 U.S. 449 (1957).

In 1949, the Court held squarely that the doctrine of *Weeks,* which made illegally obtained evidence inadmissible in federal courts, was not imposed on the states by the Fourteenth Amendment. In a strange opinion, Justice Frankfurter spoke eloquently about an individual's constitutional right to be protected from arbitrary intrusions by state police; he offered little, however, in the way of practical relief. He suggested two ways to restrain the states from making illegal searches and seizures: "the remedies of private action" against the offending officer, and "the internal discipline of the police, under the eyes of an alert public opinion." He also thought that Congress could pass a statute under Section 5 of the Fourteenth Amendment to make *Weeks* binding on the states. Wolf v. Colorado, 338 U.S. 25, 33. In his dissenting opinion, Justice Murphy dismissed Frankfurter's remedies as unrealistic. Murphy, who had served previously as Attorney General under President Franklin D. Roosevelt, remarked: "Little need be said concerning the possibilities of criminal prosecution. Self-scrutiny is a lofty ideal, but its exaltation reaches new heights if we expect a District Attorney to prosecute himself or his associates for well-meaning violations of the search and seizure clause during a raid the District Attorney or his associates have ordered." Murphy concluded that only one remedy existed to deter violations of the Fourth Amendment: a rule to exclude illegally obtained evidence. In a separate dissent, Justice Rutledge agreed that without the exclusionary rule the Fourth Amendment was "a dead letter."

Two years later, the Supreme Court advised lower federal courts not to intervene in state criminal proceedings to suppress evidence even when there were claims that the evidence had been obtained by unlawful search and seizure. Stefanelli v. Minard, 342 U.S. 117. But when state officers used methods that seemed to the Court "too close to the rack and the screw," evidence was excluded as a violation of the

Due Process Clause. The actions of county sheriffs in entering a home without a warrant, forcing their way into a suspect's bedroom, struggling with him to extract capsules he had placed in his mouth, and then taking him to a hospital where "stomach pumping" caused him to vomit two capsules later identified as morphine, seemed to the Court "conduct that shocks the conscience." Rochin v. California, 342 U.S. 165, 172 (1952). Nevertheless, local police continued to obtain evidence that would have been inadmissible in federal court. Schwartz v. Texas, 344 U.S. 199 (1952); Irvine v. California, 347 U.S. 128 (1954). The practical result was that the Court applied the exclusionary rule in ad hoc fashion to the states whenever a majority of the Court felt sufficiently revolted by local police actions.

A 1960 decision laid the groundwork for overturning *Wolf* and applying *Weeks* to the states. State law enforcement officers had conducted an illegal search and seizure. Because federal agents were not involved, evidence admitted in federal court was used to convict the defendant. The Supreme Court decided that the silver-platter doctrine had become intolerable, and that it did not matter to the victim of police abuse "whether his constitutional right has been invaded by a federal agent or by a state officer." Elkins v. United States, 364 U.S. 206, 215. The decision responded to practical problems of federalism. If the fruit of an unlawful search by state agents could not be admitted in a federal trial, there would be no inducement "to subterfuge and evasion with respect to federal-state cooperation in criminal investigation." Id. at 222. See also Rios v. United States, 364 U.S. 253 (1960).

A year later the Court applied the exclusionary rule to the states. The decision was not so much a federal imposition on the states as a recognition that they were already heading in that direction. Prior to the *Wolf* case in 1949, about one-third of the states supported the exclusionary rule. By 1961, additional states had conceded that the only effective remedy to official lawlessness was the exclusion of evidence illegally obtained. The remedies presented by Frankfurter in *Wolf* now seemed to the Court an exercise in "obvious futility." MAPP v. OHIO, 367 U.S. 643, 652. The Court applied the exclusionary rule to the states for several reasons: to deter unlawful conduct by the government; to provide effective protection to a person's constitutional right to privacy under the Fourth Amendment; to eliminate the double standard practiced by the federal government and the states; and to preserve judicial integrity by forcing the government to obey its own laws.

Mapp was criticized for placing a federal straitjacket on the diverse needs of state police and prosecutors. In fact, *Mapp* has accommodated a variety of circumstances and conditions at both the state and federal level. In 1971, the Court held that a defendant's statement, although ruled inadmissible as evidence, could nevertheless be used by the state to impeach a suspect's credibility if he chooses to testify. The exclusionary rule does not give a defendant the right to commit perjury. Harris v. New York, 401 U.S. 222. In 1974, the Court denied that a grand jury witness could invoke the exclusionary rule as grounds for not testifying. When a grand jury subpoenas an individual for questioning, the person cannot refuse because the evidence at issue was seized illegally. The Court considered the deterrent effect on police misconduct too speculative and minimal to impede the grand jury's role. United States v. Calandra, 414 U.S. 338 (1974).

The largest loophole in the exclusionary rule is the "good faith" defense, which has been actively explored by all three branches. In 1976, the Court held that evidence seized by a state officer acting in good faith (who nonetheless violated the

Fourth and Fourteenth Amendments) is admissible in a *civil* proceeding by the federal government. The Court, pointing out that the exclusionary rule was intended to deter state officers from overzealous criminal investigations, questioned the deterrent effect of excluding evidence at a federal civil proceeding. The societal cost of excluding the evidence seemed too high to the Court. The supervision of law enforcement "is properly the duty of the Executive and Legislative Branches." United States v. Janis, 428 U.S. 433, 459. Justice Stewart, dissenting, expressed concern that the Court was reviving the silver-platter doctrine. On the same day, the Court reviewed a number of state court criminal convictions based on evidence that allegedly was illegally obtained. The defendants had sought relief in a federal district court by filing a petition for a writ of habeas corpus. Notwithstanding the fact that the Fourth Amendment claims might have been meritorious had they been asserted originally, the Court held that federal courts should not consider such petitions when a defendant has already been afforded an opportunity to litigate that claim in a state court. STONE v. POWELL, 428 U.S. 465.

The exclusionary rule suffered further erosion in 1978. The Court decided that while an unconstitutional search could not produce inanimate objects admissible in court, such a search could yield a live witness willing to testify for the government. United States v. Ceccolini, 434 U.S. 268. Two years later, the Court held that the government could use illegally obtained evidence to impeach a witness' credibility with regard to what was said not only on direct examination but on cross-examination as well. United States v. Havens, 446 U.S. 620.

The extent to which the exclusionary rule can be circumvented is evident in a 1980 case. Federal agents had participated in a break-in and theft of papers belonging to a third party. The government used this evidence to convict someone else of falsifying his federal income tax. The Court held that the convicted person had no standing to contest the illegal and unconstitutional search of another party. United States v. Payner, 447 U.S. 727. Similarly, the Court discarded an earlier ruling that persons charged with crimes of possession had "automatic standing" to challenge illegal searches, without regard to whether they had an expectation of privacy in the place searched. The Court now held that defendants charged with crimes of possession may only claim the benefits of the exclusionary rule if their own Fourth Amendment rights had been violated. United States v. Salvucci, 448 U.S. 83 (1980).

The Court continues to carve out other exceptions to the exclusionary rule. If information is obtained from a suspect in violation of the constitutional right to have counsel, and that information would have been discovered anyway without a constitutional violation, the evidence is admissible. Under this "inevitable discovery" exception to the exclusionary rule, prosecutors need not prove good faith of police or the absence of bad faith. Nix v. Williams, 467 U.S. 431, 445 (1984). When a search results from a defective warrant, the incriminating evidence obtained from that search is admissible on the ground that the mistake was made by the judge issuing the warrant, not the police officer. The Court reasoned that suppression of the evidence would have no deterrent effect on the police who thought they were acting in "good faith" that the warrant was valid. Massachusetts v. Shepperd, 468 U.S. 981 (1984); UNITED STATES v. LEON, 468 U.S. 897 (1984). The same reasoning applies to a search conducted by police pursuant to a statute later found to be unconstitutional. Illinois v. Krull, 480 U.S. 340 (1987). Illegal police conduct in the form of a warrantless entry is effectively excused unless it can be shown that the officers acted in bad faith by purposely delaying the obtaining of a warrant. Segura v. United States, 468 U.S. 796 (1984).

The exclusionary rule has been narrowed by the Supreme Court to the point where it exists solely to deter police misconduct. United States v. Leon, 468 U.S. at 916. Largely ignored are other important objectives of the rule identified so carefully in *Weeks* and *Mapp:* protecting an individual's right to privacy; eliminating the double standard between the federal government and the states; shielding the judiciary from the taint of official lawlessness; and forcing the government to obey its own laws. As the Court gradually dilutes the meaning of the exclusionary rule, constitutional rights are now more likely to be protected at the state level. A number of state courts have refused to adopt the *Leon* good-faith doctrine for the state constitution.[12]

By grounding the exclusionary rule almost exclusively on the rationale that it deters unlawful police conduct, the doctrine is simply a judicial choice of remedies cast in the form of a rule of evidence rather than a doctrine that is constitutionally anchored. Congress may therefore pass legislation to modify the rule. S. Rept. No. 350, 98th Cong., 2d Sess. 3–8 (1984). In 1984, the Senate passed a bill that permitted the good-faith exception. 130 Cong. Rec. S104–166 (daily ed. February 7, 1984). Enactment of this exception would place an extraordinary and unrealistic demand on the sensitivity of law enforcement officers to respect constitutional rights and limits. Law enforcers would have to police themselves instead of having their actions monitored by a neutral and detached magistrate. Unless Congress can pass an effective tort remedy to punish officers who violate constitutional rights, the exclusionary rule will remain a necessary constraint on official lawlessness.

In 1971, the Supreme Court held that violations of the Fourth Amendment by federal agents give rise to a cause of action for damages resulting from unconstitutional conduct. Bivens v. Six Unknown Fed. Narcotics Agents, 403 U.S. 388 (1971). Even the Attorney General acting in the realm of national security is not absolutely immune for violating the Fourth Amendment. Mitchell v. Forsyth, 472 U.S. 511 (1985). Similarly, state troopers are entitled only to qualified immunity for Fourth Amendment violations. To be held liable for damages, they must know that their affidavits failed to establish probable cause and that they should not have applied for a warrant. Malley v. Briggs, 475 U.S. 335 (1986). In 1987, the Court eased the liability of law enforcement officers when it held that they may avoid damages by establishing that a "reasonable officer" could have believed that a search met the requirements of the Fourth Amendment even if in fact it did not. Anderson v. Creighton, 483 U.S. 635 (1987).

CONCLUSIONS

While it is important to understand the purpose of the Fourth Amendment in restricting governmental searches, reliance on the "framers' intent" offers only limited assistance. The framers did not anticipate or discuss the types of cases that now bedevil the courts. Is it a permissible search and seizure to extract blood from someone to prove intoxication? Breithaupt v. Abram, 352 U.S. 432 (1957);

---

[12]State v. Novembrino, 519 A.2d 820 (N.J. 1987); People v. Sundling, 395 N.W.2d 308 (Mich. 1986); People v. Bigelow, 488 N.E.2d 451 (N.Y. 1985); State v. Grawien, 367 N.W.2d 816 (Wis. 1985). See also Stringer v. State, 491 So.2d 837, 841–851 (Miss. 1986).

Schmerber v. California, 384 U.S. 757 (1966). May a state force a suspect to undergo surgery to remove a bullet lodged in his chest and then introduce the bullet into evidence? Winston v. Lee, 470 U.S. 753 (1985). Answers to these questions ("yes" for the first, "no" for the second) require the Court each time to balance individual and government rights within the particular fact patterns of a case.

The scope of the Fourth Amendment has broadened considerably since the framers first drafted the language. Although the Amendment refers to the "right of the people" to be secure, it also protects corporations from unlawful search and seizure.[13] Through a series of decisions the Amendment now applies to the states. Wolf v. Colorado, 338 U.S. 25, 27–28 (1949); Mapp v. Ohio, 367 U.S. 643, 655 (1961); Ker v. California, 374 U.S. 23 (1963).

Over the years, the Court has adopted a balancing test that weighs a suspect's right against the needs of government and society. As the Court noted in 1983: "We must balance the nature and quality of the intrusion on the individual's Fourth Amendment interests against the importance of the governmental interests alleged to justify the intrusion." United States v. Place, 462 U.S. 696, 703. This attitude severely weakens the Fourth Amendment. Instead of its serving as a restriction on government, which was the original purpose, the contemporary test is whether the government's interest or society's interest will prevail over a particular suspect. An individual can expect little protection from the Constitution when the odds are so heavily stacked against him.

A more appropriate balance is not one suspect against the government or against society but rather the interest of society against governmental misconduct and overreaching. The former test can produce a crude cost/benefit analysis with "a narcotic effect," creating "an illusion of technical precision and ineluctability." United States v. Leon, 468 U.S. at 929 (Brennan, J., dissenting). To the extent that the court balances an individual's interest in privacy and security against society's interest in law enforcement, it performs essentially a legislative judgment, inviting a sharing of power with Congress and the executive.

As with other branches, Congress can make major mistakes when it interprets the Fourth Amendment. However, the impulsiveness with which Congress sometimes moves in wrong directions allows it just as easily to reverse course and repeal the offending statute. For example, in 1970 Congress passed two ill-considered measures that authorized law enforcement officers to break and enter private dwellings and businesses. 84 Stat. 630–631; 84 Stat. 1274, § 509. Serious doubts about the constitutionality of these bills, combined with shocking reports of federal agents breaking into the wrong homes, prompted Congress four years later to repeal both provisions. 88 Stat. 1455, §§ 3, 4. Compare that performance with the twelve years it took the Court in *Mapp* to overturn *Wolf*, or the thirty-nine years needed for *Katz* to reverse *Olmstead*.

Selected Readings

ALLEN, FRANCIS A. "Federalism and the Fourth Amendment: A Requiem for Wolf." 1961 *Supreme Court Review* 1.

AMSTERDAM, ANTHONY G. "Perspectives on the Fourth Amendment." 58 *Minnesota Law Review* 349 (1974).

[13]G.M. Leasing Corp. v. United States, 429 U.S. 338, 353 (1977); Essgee Co. v. United States, 262 U.S. 151 (1923); Silverthorne Lumber Co. v. United States, 251 U.S. 385 (1920).

BARRETT, EDWARD L., JR. "Personal Rights, Property Rights, and the Fourth Amendment." 1960 *Supreme Court Review* 46.

ERVIN, SAM J., JR. "The Exclusionary Rule: An Essential Ingredient of the Fourth Amendment." 1983 *Supreme Court Review* 283.

FISHER, EDWARD C. *Search and Seizure*. Evanston, Ill.: Northwestern University Press, 1970.

FISHER, LOUIS. "Congress and the Fourth Amendment." 21 *Georgia Law Review* 107 (Special Issue 1986).

KAMISAR, YALE. "Is the Exclusionary Rule an 'Illogical' or 'Unnatural' Interpretation of the Fourth Amendment?" 62 *Judicature* 66 (1978).

——. "The Exclusionary Rule in Historical Perspective: The Struggle to Make the Fourth Amendment More Than 'An Empty Blessing'." 62 *Judicature* 337 (1979).

KAPLAN, JOHN. "The Limits of the Exclusionary Rule." 26 *Stanford Law Review* 1027 (1974).

KITCH, EDMUND W. "Katz v. United States: The Limits of the Fourth Amendment." 1968 *Supreme Court Review* 133.

LAFAVE, WAYNE C. "'Case-by-Case Adjudication' Versus 'Standardized Procedures': The Robinson Dilemma." 1974 *Supreme Court Review* 127.

——. *Search and Seizure: A Treatise on the Fourth Amendment*. 3 vols. St. Paul, Minn.: West, 1978.

LANDYNSKI, JACOB W. *Search and Seizure and the Supreme Court*. Baltimore: Johns Hopkins University Press, 1966.

NOTE. "Border Searches and the Fourth Amendment." 77 *Yale Law Journal* 1007 (1968).

OAKS, DALLIN H. "Studying the Exclusionary Rule in Search and Seizure." 37 *University of Chicago Law Review* 665 (1970).

POSNER, RICHARD A. "Rethinking the Fourth Amendment." 1981 *Supreme Court Review* 49.

SCHLESINGER, STEVEN R. *Exclusionary Injustice*. New York: Marcel Dekker, 1977.

STEWART, POTTER. "The Road to *Mapp* v. *Ohio* and Beyond: The Origins, Development and Future of the Exclusionary Rule in Search-and-Seizure Cases." 83 *Columbia Law Review* 1365 (1983).

TRAYNOR, ROGER J. "Mapp v. Ohio at Large in the Fifty States." 1962 *Duke Law Journal* 319.

U.S. CONGRESS. "The Exclusionary Rule Bills." Hearings before the Senate Committee on the Judiciary, 97th Cong., 1st and 2d Sess. (1981, 1982).

WHITE, JAMES B. "The Fourth Amendment as a Way of Talking about People: A Study of Robinson and Matlock." 1974 *Supreme Court Review* 165.

WILKEY, MALCOLM RICHARD. "The Exclusionary Rule: Why Suppress Valid Evidence?," 62 *Judicature* 214 (1978).

——. "A Call for Alternatives to the Exclusionary Rule: Let Congress and the Courts Speak." 62 *Judicature* 351 (1979).

Congress Responds to Zurcher *v.* Stanford Daily

In *Zurcher* v. *Stanford Daily*, 436 U.S. 547 (1978), the Supreme Court upheld the right of law enforcement officers to use a search warrant on the premises of a newspaper. The newspaper was not a suspected party to a crime. It was a "third party," and in previous cases third-party searches were subject to substantial restraints. This use of a search warrant against a newspaper created a collision between two values: First Amendment rights versus law enforcement needs. In response to *Zurcher*, Congress passed legislation in 1980 to offer greater protection to First Amendment interests. The debate below, from the House of Representatives, is taken from 126 Cong. Rec. 26561–26564, 26567 (1980).

Mr. KASTENMEIER. Mr. Speaker, I move to suspend the rules and pass the bill (H.R. 3486) to limit governmental search and seizure of materials possessed by persons involved in first amendment activities, to provide a remedy for persons aggrieved by violations of the provisions of this act, and for other purposes, as amended.

. . .

Mr. Speaker, sometimes a longstanding principle of constitutional jurisprudence is thrown into doubt by a decision of the Supreme Court which —while it may answer a narrow question based on specific facts—leaves Government officials and members of the public in doubt as to how to interpret the law. When this occurs it is often best for Congress to step in to fill the void, rather than to await the results of many years of potential litigation which will again redefine the principle. This is the case with respect to the matter before us today—legislation to redefine a portion of the law of search and seizure in response to the Supreme Court's decision in Zurcher against Stanford Daily in 1978.

Prior to Stanford Daily, the long established interpretation of the fourth amendment had held that a search warrant was considered to meet the constitutional ban on general searches only if the evidence sought constituted contraband, or fruits or instrumentalities of a crime. This rule was modified in 1967 in Warden against Hayden to permit searches for mere evidence, but the facts of that case involved evidence obtained incidental to an arrest.

In the Stanford Daily case the Supreme Court swept away 200 years of jurisprudence greatly limiting searches directed against innocent third parties. The opinion of the Court, delivered by Mr. Justice White, set forth a new theory governing third party searches—identifying the standard to be applied in issuing such warrants as one of "reasonableness." Further, while recognizing that any reasonableness requirement must be established with "scrupulous exactitude," where a newspaper was involved, the Court's opinion did not conclude that the first amendment placed any additional restraints on such searches.

The public and congressional response to the Supreme Court's decision was immediate. Newspaper editorials appeared all over the country condemning the Court's decision. And in Congress numerous members, of every ideological and political stripe, introduced remedial legislation. Meanwhile, the President ordered the Attorney General to study the issue and make a legislative recommendation to him. After consultation with constitutional scholars, civil libertarians, law enforcement authorities, and Cabinet officers, the President recommended H.R. 3486, the bill before us today.

As introduced the bill before you protected third parties from arbitrary searches only where first amendment interests were involved. Howev-er, with the exception of the Department of Justice, not a single witness in favor of the legislation testified that the protections of the bill should be limited to the press alone. In fact, the representatives of media organizations were among the strongest proponents of expanding the legislation to protect all innocent third parties from arbitrary search and seizure. A great deal of apprehension was expressed about singling out the press for special treatment.

As a result, when the committee met for markup it was agreed that the legislation should be extended to provide guidance to Federal law enforcement officials as to the circumstances under which search warrants should be used to obtain information from innocent third parties other than those engaged in first amendment activities. However, because of the constitutional and policy implications of regulating the police powers of State and local authorities, the committee decided to limit the applicability of any broader third party provisions of the bill to searches by Federal officials only. Of course, we would hope that State legislatures would follow suit, and indeed eight States have already enacted similar legislation. With respect to searches directed against persons preparing materials for broadcast or publication, we retained the features of the original bill—which apply to State and local as well as Federal officials. The justification involved is the historic obligation of the Federal Government to protect the free speech values of the first amendment.

. . .

Mr. DANIELSON. Mr. Speaker, I have come to the well reluctantly but necessarily because I oppose this bill. I think it is a bad bill, and I hope that tomorrow when the time comes to vote, it will be defeated.

I have not seen the amendment which the gentleman from Wisconsin refers to. Apparently it is not in print. I did inquire for it earlier this afternoon. So I do not know for sure what it contains.

However, I must therefore address myself to the bill as it is in print.

In the first place, I respectfuly submit that we are not here dealing with a question of constitutionality. The Supreme Court of the United States in the case of *Zurcher* v. *Stanford Daily*, 1978, reported at 436 U.S. at 547, found that this search, that this issuance of a warrant, was constitutional. We are not confronted with the issue of constitutionality.

I respectfully submit that if these activities are not unconstitutional, we are here, by this law, diminishing the availability of the search warrant to be used in connection with the enforcement of our criminal laws.

If these activities were unconstitutional, this bill would not be necessary because we can neither add to, nor subtract from, the Constitution by legislation.

I oppose the purposes of this bill, H.R. 3486, in their entirety. I believe that there should be no special exceptions from the coverage of the fourth amendment for those persons known as the press, nor for anyone else.

. . .

Mr. HYDE. Mr. Speaker, I rise in reluctant support of this legislation. Since the moment it emerged from the Subcommittee on Courts, Civil Liberties, and the Administration of Justice, I opposed a provision then contained in section 3 of

the bill and which was designed to extend the "subpena-first" rule to "all innocent third parties." At that time, I offered an amendment to strike that section and fully intended to join with my colleague from the other side, Mr. DANIELSON from California, in offering an amendment on the floor to remove that portion of the bill. The Justice Department has since withdrawn its support for this amendment and so I will not offer it.

As has been stated, this legislation is principally designed to protect the public's right to know. It is not designed to make a sweeping change in constitutional law regarding the probable cause standard contained in the fourth amendment. In Zurcher against Stanford Daily, 436 U.S. 597 (1978), the Court held that the fourth amendment's minimal requirement for the issuance of a search warrant is probable cause to believe the evidence exists where you wish to search. Congress, of course, has the power to broaden and build upon that standard. This is what we have done with the creation of the "subpena first" rule now contained in the bill. By this procedure, law enforcement authorities must seek a subpena first before resorting to the issuance of a search warrant. . . .

Coolidge v. New Hampshire
403 U.S. 443 (1971)

This case involves what the Court called a "particularly brutal murder" of a fourteen-year-old girl. It illustrates the need to have warrants issued by a "neutral and detached magistrate" and to have searches and seizures conducted pursuant to judicial process. Also discussed in this case is the "plain view" doctrine and the scope of searches and seizures that are incident to an arrest. The Court divided 5–4 on most of the issues, but a precise count is impossible because several of the Justices never discussed or joined in sections of the majority opinion.

MR. JUSTICE STEWART delivered the opinion of the Court.*

We are called upon in this case to decide issues under the Fourth and Fourteenth Amendments

*Parts II-A, II-B, and II-C of this opinion are joined only by MR. JUSTICE DOUGLAS, MR. JUSTICE BRENNAN, and MR. JUSTICE MARSHALL.

arising in the context of a state criminal trial for the commission of a particularly brutal murder. As in every case, our single duty is to determine the issues presented in accord with the Constitution and the law.

Pamela Mason, a 14-year-old girl, left her home in Manchester, New Hampshire, on the evening of January 13, 1964, during a heavy snowstorm, apparently in response to a man's telephone call for a babysitter. Eight days later, after a thaw, her body was found by the side of a major north-south highway several miles away. She had been murdered. The event created great alarm in the area, and the police immediately began a massive investigation.

On January 28, having learned from a neighbor that the petitioner, Edward Coolidge, had been away from home on the evening of the girl's disappearance, the police went to his house to question him. They asked him, among other things, if he owned any guns, and he produced three, two shotguns and a rifle. They also asked whether he would take a lie-detector test concerning his account of his activities on the night of the disappearance. He agreed to do so on the following Sunday, his day off. The police later described his attitude on the occasion of this visit as fully "cooperative." His wife was in the house throughout the interview.

On the following Sunday, a policeman called Coolidge early in the morning and asked him to come down to the police station for the trip to Concord, New Hampshire, where the lie-detector test was to be administered. That evening, two plainclothes policemen arrived at the Coolidge house, where Mrs. Coolidge was waiting with her mother-in-law for her husband's return. These two policemen were not the two who had visited the house earlier in the week, and they apparently did not know that Coolidge had displayed three guns for inspection during the earlier visit. The plainclothesmen told Mrs. Coolidge that her husband was in "serious trouble" and probably would not be home that night. They asked Coolidge's mother to leave, and proceeded to question Mrs. Coolidge. During the course of the interview they obtained from her four guns belonging to Coolidge, and some clothes that Mrs. Coolidge thought her husband might have been wearing on the evening of Pamela Mason's disappearance.

Coolidge was held in jail on an unrelated charge that night, but he was released the next day. During the ensuing two and a half weeks, the State accumulated a quantity of evidence to support the theory that it was he who had killed Pamela Mason. On February 19, the results of the investigation were presented at a meeting between the police officers working on the case and the State Attorney General, who had personally taken charge of all police activities relating to the murder, and was later to serve as chief prosecutor at the trial. At this meeting, it was decided that there was enough evidence to justify the arrest of Coolidge on the murder charge and a search of his house and two cars. At the conclusion of the meeting, the Manchester police chief made formal application, under oath, for the arrest and search warrants. The complaint supporting the warrant for a search of Coolidge's Pontiac automobile, the only warrant that concerns us here, stated that the affiant "has probable cause to suspect and believe, and does suspect and believe, and herewith offers satisfactory evidence, that there are certain objects and things used in the Commission of said offense, now kept, and concealed in or upon a certain vehicle, to wit: 1951 Pontiac two-door sedan. . . ." The warrants were then signed and issued by the Attorney General himself, acting as a justice of the peace. Under New Hampshire law in force at that time, all justices of the peace were authorized to issue search warrants. N. H. Rev. Stat. Ann. § 595:1 (repealed 1969).

The police arrested Coolidge in his house on the day the warrant issued. Mrs. Coolidge asked whether she might remain in the house with her small child, but was told that she must stay elsewhere, apparently in part because the police believed that she would be harassed by reporters if she were accessible to them. When she asked whether she might take her car, she was told that both cars had been "impounded," and that the police would provide transportation for her. Some time later, the police called a towing company, and about two and a half hours after Coolidge had been taken into custody the cars were towed to the police station. It appears that at the time of the arrest the cars were parked in the Coolidge driveway, and that although dark had fallen they were plainly visible both from the street and from inside the house where Coolidge was actually arrested. The 1951 Pontiac was searched and vacuumed on February 21, two days after it was seized, again a year later, in January 1965, and a third time in April 1965.

At Coolidge's subsequent jury trial on the charge of murder, vacuum sweepings, including particles of gun powder, taken from the Pontiac were introduced in evidence against him, as part of an attempt by the State to show by microscopic analysis that it was highly probable that Pamela Mason had been in Coolidge's car. Also introduced in evidence was one of the guns taken by the police on their Sunday evening visit to the Coolidge house—a .22-caliber Mossberg rifle, which the prosecution claimed was the murder weapon. Conflicting ballistics testimony was offered on the question whether the bullets found in Pamela Mason's body had been fired from this rifle. Finally, the prosecution introduced vacuum sweepings of the clothes taken from the Coolidge house that same Sunday evening, and attempted to show through microscopic analysis that there was a high probability that the clothes had been in contact with Pamela Mason's body. Pretrial motions to suppress all this evidence were referred by the trial judge to the New Hampshire Supreme Court, which ruled the evidence admissible. 106 N. H. 186, 208 A.2d 322. The jury found Coolidge guilty and he was sentenced to life imprisonment. The New Hampshire Supreme Court affirmed the judgment of conviction, 109 N. H. 403, 260 A. 2d 547, and we granted certiorari to consider the constitutional questions raised by the admission of this evidence against Coolidge at his trial. 399 U. S. 926.

I

The petitioner's first claim is that the warrant authorizing the seizure and subsequent search of his 1951 Pontiac automobile was invalid because not issued by a "neutral and detached magistrate." Since we agree with the petitioner that the warrant was invalid for this reason, we need not consider his further argument that the allegations under oath supporting the issuance of the warrant were so conclusory as to violate relevant constitutional standards. Cf. *Giordenello* v. *United States,* 357 U. S. 480; *Aguilar* v. *Texas,* 378 U. S. 108.

The classic statement of the policy underlying the warrant requirement of the Fourth Amendment is that of Mr. Justice Jackson, writing for the Court in *Johnson* v. *United States,* 333 U. S. 10, 13–14:

"The point of the Fourth Amendment, which often is not grasped by zealous officers, is not that it denies law enforcement the support of the usual inferences which reasonable men draw from evidence. Its protection consists in requiring that those inferences be drawn by a neutral and detached magistrate instead of being judged by the officer engaged in the often competitive enterprise of ferreting out crime. Any assumption that evidence sufficient to support a magistrate's disinterested determination to issue a search warrant will justify the officers in making a search without a warrant would reduce the Amendment to a nullity and leave the people's homes secure only in the discretion of police officers. . . . When the right of privacy must reasonably yield to the right of search is, as a rule, to be decided by a judicial officer, not by a policeman or government enforcement agent."

Cf. *United States* v. *Lefkowitz,* 285 U. S. 452, 464; *Giordenello* v. *United States, supra,* at 486. *Wong Sun* v. *United States,* 371 U. S. 471, 481-482; *Katz* v. *United States,* 389 U. S. 347, 356–357.

In this case, the determination of probable cause was made by the chief "government enforcement agent" of the State—the Attorney General—who was actively in charge of the investigation and later was to be chief prosecutor at the trial. To be sure, the determination was formalized here by a writing bearing the title "Search Warrant," whereas in *Johnson* there was no piece of paper involved, but the State has not attempted to uphold the warrant on any such artificial basis. Rather, the State argues that the Attorney General, who was unquestionably authorized as a justice of the peace to issue warrants under then-existing state law, did in fact act as a "neutral and detached magistrate." Further, the State claims that *any* magistrate, confronted with the showing of probable cause made by the Manchester chief of police, would have issued the warrant in question. To the first proposition it is enough to answer that there could hardly be a more appropriate setting than this for a *per se* rule of disqualification rather than a case-by-case evaluation of all the circumstances. Without disrespect to the state law enforcement agent here involved, the whole point of the basic rule so well expressed by Mr. Justice Jackson is that prosecutors and policemen simply cannot be asked to maintain the requisite neutrality with regard to their own investigations—the "competitive enterprise" that must rightly engage their single-minded attention. Cf. *Mancusi* v. *DeForte,* 392 U. S. 364, 371. As for the proposition that the existence of probable cause renders noncompliance with the warrant procedure an irrelevance, it is enough to cite *Agnello* v. *United States,* 269 U. S. 20, 33, decided in 1925:

"Belief, however well founded, that an article sought is concealed in a dwelling house furnishes no justification for a search of that place without a warrant. And such searches are held unlawful notwithstanding facts unquestionably showing probable cause."

See also *Jones* v. *United States,* 357 U. S. 493, 497–498; *Silverthorne Lumber Co.* v. *United States,* 251 U. S. 385, 392. ("[T]he rights . . . against unlawful search and seizure are to be protected even if the same result might have been achieved in a lawful way.")

. . .

II

The State proposes three distinct theories to bring the facts of this case within one or another of the exceptions to the warrant requirement. In considering them, we must not lose sight of the Fourth Amendment's fundamental guarantee. Mr. Justice Bradley's admonition in his opinion for the Court almost a century ago in *Boyd* v. *United States,* 116 U. S. 616, 635, is worth repeating here:

"It may be that it is the obnoxious thing in its mildest and least repulsive form; but illegitimate and unconstitutional practices get their first footing in that way, namely, by silent approaches and slight deviations from legal modes of procedure. This can only be obviated by adhering to the rule that constitutional provisions for the security of person and property should be liberally construed. A close and literal construction deprives them of half their efficacy, and leads to gradual depreciation of the right, as if it consisted more in sound than in substance. It is the duty of courts to be watchful for the constitutional rights of the

citizen, and against any stealthy encroachments thereon."

Thus the most basic constitutional rule in this area is that "searches conducted outside the judicial process, without prior approval by judge or magistrate, are *per se* unreasonable under the Fourth Amendment—subject only to a few specifically established and well-delineated exceptions."

. . .

A

The State's first theory is that the seizure on February 19 and subsequent search of Coolidge's Pontiac were "incident" to a valid arrest. We assume that the arrest of Coolidge inside his house was valid, so that the first condition of a warrantless "search incident" is met. *Whiteley* v. *Warden,* 401 U. S. 560, 567 n. 11. And since the events in issue took place in 1964, we assess the State's argument in terms of the law as it existed before *Chimel* v. *California,* 395 U. S. 752, which substantially restricted the "search incident" exception to the warrant requirement, but did so only prospectively. *Williams* v. *United States,* 401 U. S. 646. But even under pre-*Chimel* law, the State's position is untenable.

The leading case in the area before *Chimel* was *United States* v. *Rabinowitz,* 339 U. S. 56, which was taken to stand "for the proposition, *inter alia,* that a warrantless search 'incident to a lawful arrest' may generally extend to the area that is considered to be in the 'possession' or under the 'control' of the person arrested." *Chimel, supra,* at 760. In this case, Coolidge was arrested inside his house; his car was outside in the driveway. The car was not touched until Coolidge had been removed from the scene. It was then seized and taken to the station, but it was not actually searched until two days later.

First, it is doubtful whether the police could have carried out a contemporaneous search of the car under *Rabinowitz* standards. For this Court has repeatedly held that, even under *Rabinowitz,* "[a] search may be incident to an arrest '"only if it is substantially contemporaneous with the arrest and is confined to the *immediate* vicinity of the arrest. . . ."'" *Vale* v. *Louisiana,* 399 U. S. 30, 33, quoting from *Shipley* v. *California*, 395 U. S. 818, 819, quoting from *Stoner* v. *California*, 376 U. S. 483, 486. (Emphasis in *Shipley*.) Cf. *Agnello* v. *United States*, 269 U. S., at 30–31; *James* v. *Louisiana*, 382 U. S. 36. These cases make it clear beyond any question that a lawful pre-*Chimel* arrest of a suspect outside his house could never by itself justify a warrantless search inside the house. There is nothing in search-incident doctrine (as opposed to the special rules for automobiles and evidence in "plain view," to be considered below) that suggests a different result where the arrest is made inside the house and the search outside and at some distance away.

. . .

B

The second theory put forward by the State to justify a warrantless seizure and search of the Pontiac car is that under *Carroll* v. *United States*, 267 U. S. 132, the police may make a warrantless search of an automobile whenever they have probable cause to do so, and, under our decision last Term in *Chambers* v. *Maroney*, 399 U. S. 42, whenever the police may make a legal contemporaneous search under *Carroll*, they may also seize the car, take it to the police station, and search it there. But even granting that the police had probable cause to search the car, the application of the *Carroll* case to these facts would extend it far beyond its original rationale.

. . .

The word "automobile" is not a talisman in whose presence the Fourth Amendment fades away and disappears. And surely there is nothing in this case to invoke the meaning and purpose of the rule of *Carroll* v. *United States*—no alerted criminal bent on flight, no fleeting opportunity on an open highway after a hazardous chase, no contraband or stolen goods or weapons, no confederates waiting to move the evidence, not even the inconvenience of a special police detail to guard the immobilized automobile. In short, by no possible stretch of the legal imagination can this be made into a case where "it is not practicable to secure a warrant," *Carroll, supra*, at 153, and the "automobile exception," despite its label, is simply irrelevant.

. . .

C

The State's third theory in support of the warrantless seizure and search of the Pontiac car is that the car itself was an "instrumentality of the crime," and as such might be seized by the police on Coolidge's property because it was in plain view. Supposing the seizure to be thus lawful, the case of *Cooper* v. *California*, 386 U. S. 58, is said to support a subsequent warrantless search at the station house, with or without probable cause. Of course, the distinction between an "instrumentality of crime" and "mere evidence" was done away with by *Warden* v. *Hayden*, 387 U. S. 294, and we may assume that the police had probable cause to seize the automobile. But, for the reasons that follow, we hold that the "plain view" exception to the warrant requirement is inapplicable to this case.

. . .

What the "plain view" cases have in common is that the police officer in each of them had a prior justification for an intrusion in the course of which he came inadvertently across a piece of evidence incriminating the accused. The doctrine serves to supplement the prior justification— whether it be a warrant for another object, hot pursuit, search incident to lawful arrest, or some other legitimate reason for being present unconnected with a search directed against the accused —and permits the warrantless seizure. Of course, the extension of the original justification is legitimate only where it is immediately apparent to the police that they have evidence before them; the "plain view" doctrine may not be used to extend a general exploratory search from one object to another until something incriminating at last emerges.

. . .

In the light of what has been said, it is apparent that the "plain view" exception cannot justify the police seizure of the Pontiac car in this case. The police had ample opportunity to obtain a valid warrant; they knew the automobile's exact description and location well in advance; they intended to seize it when they came upon Coolidge's property. And this is not a case involving contraband or stolen goods or objects dangerous in themselves.

The seizure was therefore unconstitutional, and so was the subsequent search at the station house. Since evidence obtained in the course of the search was admitted at Coolidge's trial, the judgment must be reversed and the case remanded to the New Hampshire Supreme Court. *Mapp* v. *Ohio*, 367 U. S. 643.

. . .

MR. JUSTICE HARLAN, concurring.

From the several opinions that have been filed in this case it is apparent that the law of search and seizure is due for an overhauling. State and federal law enforcement officers and prosecutorial authorities must find quite intolerable the present state of uncertainty, which extends even to such an everyday question as the circumstances under which police may enter a man's property to arrest him and seize a vehicle believed to have been used during the commission of a crime.

. . .

MR. CHIEF JUSTICE BURGER, dissenting in part and concurring in part.

I join the dissenting opinion of MR. JUSTICE WHITE and in Parts II and III of MR. JUSTICE BLACK'S concurring and dissenting opinion. I also agree with most of what is said in Part I of MR. JUSTICE BLACK'S opinion, but I am not prepared to accept the proposition that the Fifth Amendment requires the exclusion of evidence seized in violation of the Fourth Amendment. I join in Part III of MR. JUSTICE STEWART'S opinion.

This case illustrates graphically the monstrous price we pay for the exclusionary rule in which we seem to have imprisoned ourselves. See my dissent in *Bivens* v. *Six Unknown Named Agents of Federal Bureau of Narcotics, ante,* p. 411.

On the merits of the case I find not the slightest basis in the record to reverse this conviction. Here again the Court reaches out, strains, and distorts rules that were showing some signs of stabilizing, and directs a new trial which will be held more than seven years after the criminal acts charged.

Mr. Justice Stone, of the Minnesota Supreme Court, called the kind of judicial functioning in which the Court indulges today "bifurcating elements too infinitesimal to be split."

MR. JUSTICE BLACK, concurring and dissenting.

After a jury trial in a New Hampshire state court, petitioner was convicted of murder and sentenced to life imprisonment. Holding that certain evidence introduced by the State was seized during an "unreasonable" search and that the evidence was inadmissible under the judicially created exclusionary rule of the Fourth Amendment, the majority reverses that conviction. Believing that the search and seizure here was reasonable and that the Fourth Amendment properly construed contains no such exclusionary rule, I dissent.

. . .

MR. JUSTICE BLACKMUN joins MR. JUSTICE BLACK in Parts II and III of this opinion and in that portion of Part I thereof which is to the effect that the Fourth Amendment supports no exclusionary rule.

MR. JUSTICE WHITE, with whom THE CHIEF JUSTICE joins, concurring and dissenting.

I would affirm the judgment. In my view, Coolidge's Pontiac was lawfully seized as evidence of the crime in plain sight and thereafter was lawfully searched under *Cooper* v. *California*, 386 U. S. 58 (1967). I am therefore in substantial disagreement with Parts II–C and II–D of the Court's opinion. Neither do I agree with Part II–B, and I can concur only in the result as to Part III.

. . .

California v. Ciraolo
476 U.S. 207 (1986)

California police received an anonymous telephone tip that Dante Ciraolo was growing marijuana in his backyard, which was enclosed by two fences and shielded from view at ground level. Using a private airplane, the police flew over his house at an altitude of 1,000 feet and readily identified marijuana plants growing in the yard. After obtaining a search warrant the marijuana plants were seized. The California trial court denied Ciraolo's motion to suppress the evidence of the search, but the California Court of Appeals reversed on the ground that the warrantless aerial observation violated the Fourth Amendment.

CHIEF JUSTICE BURGER delivered the opinion of the Court.

We granted certiorari to determine whether the Fourth Amendment is violated by aerial observation without a warrant from an altitude of 1,000 feet of a fenced-in backyard within the curtilage of a home.

I

On September 2, 1982, Santa Clara Police received an anonymous telephone tip that marijuana was growing in respondent's backyard. Police were unable to observe the contents of respondent's yard from ground level because of a 6-foot outer fence and a 10-foot inner fence completely enclosing the yard. Later that day, Officer Shutz, who was assigned to investigate, secured a private plane and flew over respondent's house at an altitude of 1,000 feet, within navigable airspace; he was accompanied by Officer Rodriguez. Both officers were trained in marijuana identification. From the overflight, the officers readily identified marijuana plants 8 feet to 10 feet in height growing in a 15- by 25-foot plot in respondent's yard; they photographed the area with a standard 35mm camera.

On September 8, 1982, Officer Shutz obtained a search warrant on the basis of an affidavit describing the anonymous tip and their observations; a photograph depicting respondent's house, the backyard, and neighboring homes was attached to the affidavit as an exhibit. The warrant was execut-

ed the next day and 73 plants were seized; it is not disputed that these were marijuana.

After the trial court denied respondent's motion to suppress the evidence of the search, respondent pleaded guilty to a charge of cultivation of marijuana. The California Court of Appeal reversed, however, on the ground that the warrantless aerial *observation* of respondent's yard which led to the issuance of the warrant violated the Fourth Amendment. 161 Cal. App. 3d 1081, 208 Cal. Rptr. 93 (1984). That court held first that respondent's backyard marijuana garden was within the "curtilage" of his home, under *Oliver* v. *United States*, 466 U. S. 170 (1984). The court emphasized that the height and existence of the two fences constituted "objective criteria from which we may conclude he manifested a reasonable expectation of privacy by any standard." 161 Cal. App. 3d, at 1089, 208 Cal. Rptr., at 97.

Examining the particular method of surveillance undertaken, the court then found it "significant" that the flyover "was not the result of a routine patrol conducted for any other legitimate law enforcement or public safety objective, but was undertaken for the specific purpose of observing this particular enclosure within [respondent's] curtilage." *Ibid.* It held this focused observation was "a direct and unauthorized intrusion into the sanctity of the home" which violated respondent's reasonable expectation of privacy. *Id.*, at 1089–1090, 208 Cal. Rptr., at 98 (footnote omitted). The California Supreme Court denied the State's petition for review.

We granted the State's petition for certiorari, 471 U. S. 1134 (1985). We reverse.

The State argues that respondent has "knowingly exposed" his backyard to aerial observation, because all that was seen was visible to the naked eye from any aircraft flying overhead. The State analogizes its mode of observation to a knothole or opening in a fence: if there is an opening, the police may look.

The California Court of Appeal, as we noted earlier, accepted the analysis that unlike the casual observation of a private person flying overhead, this flight was focused specifically on a small suburban yard, and was not the result of any routine patrol overflight. Respondent contends he has done all that can reasonably be expected to tell the world he wishes to maintain the privacy of his garden within the curtilage without covering his yard. Such covering, he argues, would defeat its purpose as an outside living area; he asserts he has not "knowingly" exposed himself to aerial views.

II

The touchstone of Fourth Amendment analysis is whether a person has a "constitutionally protected reasonable expectation of privacy." *Katz* v. *United States*, 389 U. S. 347, 360 (1967) (Harlan, J., concurring). *Katz* posits a two-part inquiry: first, has the individual manifested a subjective expectation of privacy in the object of the challenged search? Second, is society willing to recognize that expectation as reasonable? See *Smith* v. *Maryland*, 442 U. S. 735, 740 (1979).

Clearly—and understandably—respondent has met the test of manifesting his own subjective intent and desire to maintain privacy as to his unlawful agricultural pursuits. However, we need not address that issue, for the State has not challenged the finding of the California Court of Appeal that respondent had such an expectation. It can reasonably be assumed that the 10-foot fence was placed to conceal the marijuana crop from at least street-level views. So far as the normal sidewalk traffic was concerned, this fence served that purpose, because respondent "took normal precautions to maintain his pri-

vacy." *Rawlings* v. *Kentucky*, 448 U. S. 98, 105 (1980).

Yet a 10-foot fence might not shield these plants from the eyes of a citizen or a policeman perched on the top of a truck or a 2-level bus. Whether respondent therefore manifested a subjective expectation of privacy from *all* observations of his backyard, or whether instead he manifested merely a hope that no one would observe his unlawful gardening pursuits, is not entirely clear in these circumstances. Respondent appears to challenge the authority of government to observe his activity from any vantage point or place if the viewing is motivated by a law enforcement purpose, and not the result of a casual, accidental observation.

We turn, therefore, to the second inquiry under *Katz, i. e.,* whether that expectation is reasonable. In pursuing this inquiry, we must keep in mind that "[t]he test of legitimacy is not whether the individual chooses to conceal assertedly 'private' activity," but instead "whether the government's intrusion infringes upon the personal and societal values protected by the Fourth Amendment." *Oliver, supra,* at 181–183.

Respondent argues that because his yard was in the curtilage of his home, no governmental aerial observation is permissible under the Fourth Amendment without a warrant. The history and genesis of the curtilage doctrine is instructive. "At common law, the curtilage is the area to which extends the intimate activity associated with the 'sanctity of a man's home and the privacies of life.'" *Oliver, supra,* at 180 (quoting *Boyd* v. *United States*, 116 U. S. 616, 630 (1886)). See 4 Blackstone, Commentaries *225. The protection afforded the curtilage is essentially a protection of families and personal privacy in an area intimately linked to the home, both physically and psychologically, where privacy expectations are most heightened. The claimed area here was immediately adjacent to a suburban home, surrounded by high double fences. This close nexus to the home would appear to encompass this small area within the curtilage. Accepting, as the State does, that this yard and its crop fall within the curtilage, the question remains whether naked-eye observation of the curtilage by police from an aircraft lawfully operating at an altitude of 1,000 feet violates an expectation of privacy that is reasonable.

That the area is within the curtilage does not itself bar all police observation. The Fourth Amendment protection of the home has never been extended to require law enforcement officers to shield their eyes when passing by a home on public thoroughfares. Nor does the mere fact that an individual has taken measures to restrict some views of his activities preclude an officer's observations from a public vantage point where he has a right to be and which renders the activities clearly visible. *E. g., United States* v. *Knotts,* 460 U. S. 276, 282 (1983). "What a person knowingly exposes to the public, even in his own home or office, is not a subject of Fourth Amendment protection." *Katz, supra,* at 351.

The observations by Officers Shutz and Rodriguez in this case took place within public navigable airspace, see 49 U. S. C. App. § 1304, in a physically nonintrusive manner; from this point they were able to observe plants readily discernible to the naked eye as marijuana. That the observation from aircraft was directed at identifying the plants and the officers were trained to recognize marijuana is irrelevant. Such observation is precisely what a judicial officer needs to provide a basis for a warrant. Any member of the public flying in this airspace who glanced down could have seen everything that these officers observed. On this record, we readily conclude that respondent's expectation that his garden was protected from such observation is unreasonable and is not an expectation that society is prepared to honor.

The dissent contends that the Court ignores Justice Harlan's warning in his concurrence in *Katz* v. *United States,* 389 U. S., at 361–362, that the Fourth Amendment should not be limited to proscribing only physical intrusions onto private property. *Post,* at 215–216. But Justice Harlan's observations about future electronic developments and the potential for electronic interference with private communications, see *Katz, supra,* at 362, were plainly not aimed at simple visual observations from a public place. Indeed, since *Katz* the Court has required warrants for electronic surveillance aimed at intercepting private conversations. See *United States* v. *United States District Court,* 407 U. S. 297 (1972).

Justice Harlan made it crystal clear that he was resting on the reality that one who enters a telephone booth is entitled to assume that his conversation is not being intercepted. This does not translate readily into a rule of constitutional dimensions that one who grows illicit drugs in his backyard is "entitled to assume" his unlawful conduct will not be observed by a passing aircraft —or by a power company repair mechanic on a pole overlooking the yard. As Justice Harlan emphasized,

"a man's home is, for most purposes, a place where he expects privacy, but objects, activities, or statements that he exposes to the 'plain view' of outsiders are not 'protected' because no intention to keep them to himself has been exhibited. On the other hand, conversations in the open would not be protected against being overheard, for the expectation of privacy under the circumstances would be unreasonable." *Katz, supra,* at 361.

One can reasonably doubt that in 1967 Justice Harlan considered an aircraft within the category of future "electronic" developments that could stealthily intrude upon an individual's privacy. In an age where private and commercial flight in the public airways is routine, it is unreasonable for respondent to expect that his marijuana plants were constitutionally protected from being observed with the naked eye from an altitude of 1,000 feet. The Fourth Amendment simply does not require the police traveling in the public airways at this altitude to obtain a warrant in order to observe what is visible to the naked eye.

Reversed.

JUSTICE POWELL, with whom JUSTICE BRENNAN, JUSTICE MARSHALL, and JUSTICE BLACKMUN join, dissenting.

Concurring in *Katz* v. *United States,* 389 U. S. 347 (1967), Justice Harlan warned that any decision to construe the Fourth Amendment as proscribing only physical intrusions by police onto private property "is, in the present day, bad physics as well as bad law, for reasonable expectations of privacy may be defeated by electronic as well as physical invasion." *Id.,* at 362. Because the Court today ignores that warning in an opinion that departs significantly from the standard developed in *Katz* for deciding when a Fourth Amendment violation has occurred, I dissent.

I

. . . In my view, the Court's holding rests on only one obvious fact, namely, that the airspace generally is open to all persons for travel in airplanes. The Court does not explain why this single fact deprives citizens of their privacy interest in outdoor activities in an enclosed curtilage.

II

A

The Fourth Amendment protects "[t]he right of the people to be secure in their persons, houses, papers, and effects, against unreasonable searches and seizures." While the familiar history of the Amendment need not be recounted here, we should remember that it reflects a choice that our society should be one in which citizens "dwell in reasonable security and freedom from surveillance." *Johnson* v. *United States,* 333 U. S. 10, 14 (1948). Since that choice was made by the Framers of the Constitution, our cases construing the Fourth Amendment have relied in part on the common law for instruction on "what sorts of searches the Framers . . . regarded as reasonable." *Steagald* v. *United States,* 451 U. S. 204, 217 (1981). But we have repeatedly refused to freeze "'into constitutional law those enforcement practices that existed at the time of the Fourth Amendment's passage.'" *Id.,* at 217, n. 10, quoting *Payton* v. *New York,* 445 U. S. 573, 591, n. 33 (1980). See *United States* v. *United States District Court,* 407 U.S. 297, 313 (1972). Rather, we have construed the Amendment "'in light of contemporary norms and conditions,'" *Steagald* v. *United States,* 451 U.S., at 217, n. 10, quoting *Payton* v. *New York, supra,* at 591, n. 33, in order to prevent "any stealthy encroachments" on our citizens' right to be free of arbitrary official intrusion, *Boyd* v. *United States,* 116 U. S. 616, 635 (1886). Since the landmark decision in *Katz* v. *United States,* the

Court has fulfilled its duty to protect Fourth Amendment rights by asking if police surveillance has intruded on an individual's reasonable expectation of privacy.

As the decision in *Katz* held, and dissenting opinions written by Justices of this Court prior to *Katz* recognized, *e. g., Goldman* v. *United States,* 316 U. S. 129, 139–141 (1942) (Murphy, J., dissenting); *Olmstead* v. *United States,* 277 U. S. 438, 474 (1928) (Brandeis, J., dissenting), a standard that defines a Fourth Amendment "search" by reference to whether police have physically invaded a "constitutionally protected area" provides no real protection against surveillance techniques made possible through technology. Technological advances have enabled police to see people's activities and associations, and to hear their conversations, without being in physical proximity. Moreover, the capability now exists for police to conduct intrusive surveillance without any physical penetration of the walls of homes or other structures that citizens may believe shelters their privacy. Looking to the Fourth Amendment for protection against such "broad and unsuspected governmental incursions" into the "cherished privacy of law-abiding citizens," *United States* v. *United States District Court, supra,* at 312–313 (footnote omitted), the Court in *Katz* abandoned its inquiry into whether police had committed a physical trespass. *Katz* announced a standard under which the occurrence of a search turned not on the physical position of the police conducting the surveillance, but on whether the surveillance in question had invaded a constitutionally protected reasonable expectation of privacy.

Our decisions following the teaching of *Katz* illustrate that this inquiry "normally embraces two discrete questions." *Smith* v. *Maryland,* 442 U.S. 735, 740 (1979). "The first is whether the individual, by his conduct, has 'exhibited an actual (subjective) expectation of privacy.'" *Ibid.,* quoting *Katz* v. *United States,* 389 U. S., at 361 (Harlan, J., concurring). The second is whether that subjective expectation "is 'one that society is prepared to recognize as "reasonable."'" *Ibid.,* quoting *Katz* v. *United States,* 389 U. S., at 361 (Harlan, J., concurring). While the Court today purports to reaffirm this analytical framework, its conclusory rejection of respondent's expectation of privacy in the yard of his residence as one that "is unreasonable," *ante,* at 213, represents a turning away from the principles that have guided our Fourth Amendment inquiry. The Court's rejection of respondent's Fourth Amendment claim is curiously at odds with its purported reaffirmation of the curtilage doctrine, both in this decision and its companion case, *Dow Chemical Co.* v. *United States, post,* p. 227, and particularly with its conclusion in *Dow* that society is prepared to recognize as reasonable expectations of privacy in the curtilage, *post,* at 235.

The second question under *Katz* has been described as asking whether an expectation of privacy is "legitimate in the sense required by the Fourth Amendment." *Oliver* v. *United States,* 466 U. S. 170, 182 (1984). The answer turns on "whether the government's intrusion infringes upon the personal and societal values protected by the Fourth Amendment." *Id.,* at 182–183. While no single consideration has been regarded as dispositive, "the Court has given weight to such factors as the intention of the Framers of the Fourth Amendment, . . . the uses to which the individual has put a location, . . . and our societal understanding that certain areas deserve the most scrupulous protection from government invasion." *Id.,* at 178. . . .

B

This case involves surveillance of a home, for as we stated in *Oliver* v. *United States,* the curtilage "has been considered part of the home itself for Fourth Amendment purposes." 466 U. S., at 180. In *Dow Chemical Co.* v. *United States,* decided today, the Court reaffirms that the "curtilage doctrine evolved to protect much the same kind of privacy as that covering the interior of a structure." *Post,* at 235. The Court in *Dow* emphasizes, moreover, that society accepts as reasonable citizens' expectations of privacy in the area immediately surrounding their homes. *Ibid.*

In deciding whether an area is within the curtilage, courts "have defined the curtilage, as did the common law, by reference to the factors that determine whether an individual reasonably may expect that an area immediately adjacent to the home will remain private. . . .

III

A

The Court begins its analysis of the Fourth Amendment issue posed here by deciding that respondent had an expectation of privacy in his backyard. I agree with that conclusion because of the close proximity of the yard to the house, the nature of some of the activities respondent conducted there, and because he had taken steps to shield those activities from the view of passersby. The Court then implicitly acknowledges that society is prepared to recognize his expectation as reasonable with respect to ground-level surveillance, holding that the yard was within the curtilage, an area in which privacy interests have been afforded the "most heightened" protection. *Ante,* at 213. As the foregoing discussion of the curtilage doctrine demonstrates, respondent's yard unquestionably was within the curtilage. Since Officer Shutz could not see into this private family area from the street, the Court certainly would agree that he would have conducted an unreasonable search had he climbed over the fence, or used a ladder to peer into the yard without first securing a warrant. See *United States* v. *Van Dyke, supra;* see also *United States* v. *Williams,* 581 F.2d 451 (CA5 1978).

The Court concludes, nevertheless, that Shutz could use an airplane—a product of modern technology—to intrude visually into respondent's yard. The Court argues that respondent had no reasonable expectation of privacy from aerial observation. It notes that Shutz was "within public navigable airspace," *ante,* at 213, when he looked into and photographed respondent's yard. It then relies on the fact that the surveillance was not accompanied by a physical invasion of the curtilage, *ibid.* Reliance on the *manner* of surveillance is directly contrary to the standard of *Katz,* which identifies a constitutionally protected privacy right by focusing on the interests of the individual and of a free society. Since *Katz,* we have consistently held that the presence or absence of physical trespass by police is constitutionally irrelevant to the question whether society is prepared to recognize an asserted privacy interest as reasonable. *E.g., United States* v. *United States District Court,* 407 U. S., at 313.

The Court's holding, therefore, must rest solely on the fact that members of the public fly in planes and may look down at homes as they fly over them. *Ante*, at 213–214. The Court does not explain why it finds this fact to be significant. One may assume that the Court believes that citizens bear the risk that air travelers will observe activities occurring within backyards that are open to the sun and air. This risk, the Court appears to hold, nullifies expectations of privacy in those yards even as to purposeful police surveillance from the air. The Court finds support for this conclusion in *United States* v. *Knotts*, 460 U. S. 276 (1983). *Ante*, at 213.

This line of reasoning is flawed. First, the actual risk to privacy from commercial or pleasure aircraft is virtually nonexistent. Travelers on commercial flights, as well as private planes used for business or personal reasons, normally obtain at most a fleeting, anonymous, and nondiscriminating glimpse of the landscape and buildings over which they pass. The risk that a passenger on such a plane might observe private activities, and might connect those activities with particular people, is simply too trivial to protect against. It is no accident that, as a matter of common experience, many people build fences around their residential areas, but few build roofs over their backyards. . . .

The Court's reliance on *Knotts* reveals the second problem with its analysis. The activities under surveillance in *Knotts* took place on public streets, not in private homes. 460 U. S., at 281–282. Comings and goings on public streets are public matters, and the Constitution does not disable police from observing what every member of the public can see. The activity in this case, by contrast, took place within the private area immediately adjacent to a home. . . .

B

Since respondent had a reasonable expectation of privacy in his yard, aerial surveillance undertaken by the police for the purpose of discovering evidence of crime constituted a "search" within the meaning of the Fourth Amendment. "Warrantless searches are presumptively unreasonable, though the Court has recognized a few limited exceptions to this general rule." *United States* v. *Karo*, 468 U. S., at 717. This case presents no such exception. The indiscriminate nature of aerial surveillance, illustrated by Officer Shutz' photograph of respondent's home and enclosed yard as well as those of his neighbors, poses "far too serious a threat to privacy interests in the home to escape entirely some sort of Fourth Amendment oversight." *Id.*, at 716 (footnote omitted). Therefore, I would affirm the judgment of the California Court of Appeal ordering suppression of the marijuana plants.

IV

Some may believe that this case, involving no physical intrusion on private property, presents "the obnoxious thing in its mildest and least repulsive form." *Boyd* v. *United States*, 116 U. S., at 635. But this Court recognized long ago that the essence of a Fourth Amendment violation is "not the breaking of [a person's] doors, and the rummaging of his drawers," but rather is "the invasion of his indefeasible right of personal security, personal liberty and private property." *Id.*, at 630. Rapidly advancing technology now permits police to conduct surveillance in the home itself, an area where privacy interests are most cherished in our society, without any physical trespass. While the rule in *Katz* was designed to prevent silent and unseen invasions of Fourth Amendment privacy rights in a variety of settings, we have consistently afforded heightened protection to a person's right to be left alone in the privacy of his house. The Court fails to enforce that right or to give any weight to the longstanding presumption that warrantless intrusions into the home are unreasonable. I dissent.

United States v. Ross

456 U.S. 798 (1982)

Police officers conducted a warrantless search of the interior of a car belonging to Albert Ross, even after the car had been taken to police headquarters and impounded. After a federal district court denied Ross' motion to suppress the evidence found in the car, he was convicted for possessing heroin with intent to distribute it. The Court of Appeals reversed by holding that the officers had probable cause to stop and search the car, including its trunk, without a warrant, but they should not have opened a paper bag or leather pouch discovered in the trunk.

JUSTICE STEVENS delivered the opinion of the Court.

In *Carroll* v. *United States*, 267 U. S. 132, the Court held that a warrantless search of an automobile stopped by police officers who had probable cause to believe the vehicle contained contraband was not unreasonable within the meaning of the Fourth Amendment. The Court in *Carroll* did not explicitly address the scope of the search that is permissible. In this case, we consider the extent to which police officers—who have legitimately stopped an automobile and who have probable cause to believe that contraband is concealed somewhere within it—may conduct a probing search of compartments and containers within the vehicle whose contents are not in plain view. We hold that they may conduct a search of the vehicle that is as thorough as a magistrate could authorize in a warrant "particularly describing the place to be searched."

I

In the evening of November 27, 1978, an informant who had previously proved to be reliable telephoned Detective Marcum of the District of Columbia Police Department and told him that an individual known as "Bandit" was selling narcotics kept in the trunk of a car parked at 439 Ridge Street. The informant stated that he had just observed "Bandit" complete a sale and that "Bandit" had told him that additional narcotics were in the trunk. The informant gave Marcum a detailed description of "Bandit" and stated that the car was

a "purplish maroon" Chevrolet Malibu with District of Columbia license plates.

Accompanied by Detective Cassidy and Sergeant Gonzales, Marcum immediately drove to the area and found a maroon Malibu parked in front of 439 Ridge Street. A license check disclosed that the car was registered to Albert Ross; a computer check on Ross revealed that he fit the informant's description and used the alias "Bandit." In two passes through the neighborhood the officers did not observe anyone matching the informant's description. To avoid alerting persons on the street, they left the area.

The officers returned five minutes later and observed the maroon Malibu turning off Ridge Street onto Fourth Street. They pulled alongside the Malibu, noticed that the driver matched the informant's description, and stopped the car. Marcum and Cassidy told the driver—later identified as Albert Ross, the respondent in this action—to get out of the vehicle. While they searched Ross, Sergeant Gonzales discovered a bullet on the car's front seat. He searched the interior of the car and found a pistol in the glove compartment. Ross then was arrested and handcuffed. Detective Cassidy took Ross' keys and opened the trunk, where he found a closed brown paper bag. He opened the bag and discovered a number of glassine bags containing a white powder. Cassidy replaced the bag, closed the trunk, and drove the car to headquarters.

At the police station Cassidy thoroughly searched the car. In addition to the "lunch-type" brown paper bag, Cassidy found in the trunk a zippered red leather pouch. He unzipped the pouch and discovered $3,200 in cash. The police laboratory later determined that the powder in the paper bag was heroin. No warrant was obtained.

Ross was charged with possession of heroin with intent to distribute, in violation of 21 U. S. C. § 841(a). Prior to trial, he moved to suppress the heroin found in the paper bag and the currency found in the leather pouch. After an evidentiary hearing, the District Court denied the motion to suppress. The heroin and currency were introduced in evidence at trial and Ross was convicted.

A three-judge panel of the Court of Appeals reversed the conviction. It held that the police had probable cause to stop and search Ross' car and that, under *Carroll* v. *United States, supra,* and *Chambers* v. *Maroney,* 399 U. S. 42, the officers lawfully could search the automobile—including its trunk—without a warrant. The court considered separately, however, the warrantless search of the two containers found in the trunk. On the basis of *Arkansas* v. *Sanders,* 442 U. S. 753, the court concluded that the constitutionality of a warrantless search of a container found in an automobile depends on whether the owner possesses a reasonable expectation of privacy in its contents. Applying that test, the court held that the warrantless search of the paper bag was valid but the search of the leather pouch was not. The court remanded for a new trial at which the items taken from the paper bag, but not those from the leather pouch, could be admitted.

The entire Court of Appeals then voted to rehear the case en banc. A majority of the court rejected the panel's conclusion that a distinction of constitutional significance existed between the two containers found in respondent's trunk; it held that the police should not have opened either container without first obtaining a warrant. The court reasoned:

"No specific, well-delineated exception called to our attention permits the police to dispense with a warrant to open and search 'unworthy' containers. Moreover, we believe that a rule under which the validity of a warrantless search would turn on judgments about the durability of a container would impose an unreasonable and unmanageable burden on police and courts. For these

reasons, and because the Fourth Amendment protects all persons, not just those with the resources or fastidiousness to place their effects in containers that decisionmakers would rank in the luggage line, we hold that the Fourth Amendment warrant requirement forbids the warrantless opening of a closed, opaque paper bag to the same extent that it forbids the warrantless opening of a small unlocked suitcase or a zippered leather pouch." 210 U. S. App. D. C. 342, 344, 655 F. 2d 1159, 1161 (1981) (footnote omitted).

The en banc Court of Appeals considered, and rejected, the argument that it was reasonable for the police to open both the paper bag and the leather pouch because they were entitled to conduct a warrantless search of the entire vehicle in which the two containers were found. The majority concluded that this argument was foreclosed by *Sanders.*

Three dissenting judges interpreted *Sanders* differently. Other courts also have read the *Sanders* opinion in different ways. Moreover, disagreement concerning the proper interpretation of *Sanders* was at least partially responsible for the fact that *Robbins* v. *California,* 453 U. S. 420, was decided last Term without a Court opinion.

. . .

II

We begin with a review of the decision in *Carroll* itself. In the fall of 1921, federal prohibition agents obtained evidence that George Carroll and John Kiro were "bootleggers" who frequently traveled between Grand Rapids and Detroit in an Oldsmobile Roadster. On December 15, 1921, the agents unexpectedly encountered Carroll and Kiro driving west on that route in that car. The officers gave pursuit, stopped the roadster on the highway, and directed Carroll and Kiro to get out of the car.

No contraband was visible in the front seat of the Oldsmobile and the rear portion of the roadster was closed. One of the agents raised the rumble seat but found no liquor. He raised the seat cushion and again found nothing. The officer then struck at the "lazyback" of the seat and noticed that it was "harder than upholstery ordinarily is in those backs." 267 U. S., at 174. He tore open the seat cushion and discovered 68 bottles of gin and whiskey concealed inside. No warrant had been obtained for the search.

Carroll and Kiro were convicted of transporting intoxicating liquor in violation of the National Prohibition Act. On review of those convictions, this Court ruled that the warrantless search of the roadster was reasonable within the meaning of the Fourth Amendment. In an extensive opinion written by Chief Justice Taft, the Court held:

"On reason and authority the true rule is that if the search and seizure without a warrant are made upon probable cause, that is, upon a belief, reasonably arising out of circumstances known to the seizing officer, that an automobile or other vehicle contains that which by law is subject to seizure and destruction, the search and seizure are valid. The Fourth Amendment is to be construed in the light of what was deemed an unreasonable search and seizure when it was adopted, and in a manner which will conserve public interests as well as the interests and rights of individual citizens." *Id.*, at 149.

The Court explained at length the basis for this rule. The Court noted that historically warrantless searches of vessels, wagons, and carriages—as opposed to fixed premises such as a home or other building—had been considered reasonable by Congress. After reviewing legislation enacted by Congress between 1789 and 1799, the Court stated:

"Thus contemporaneously with the adoption of the Fourth Amendment we find in the first Congress, and in the following Second and Fourth Congresses, a difference made as to the necessity for a search warrant between goods subject to forfeiture, when concealed in a dwelling house or similar place, and like goods in course of transportation and concealed in a movable vessel where they readily could be put out of reach of a search warrant." *Id.*, at 151.

The Court reviewed additional legislation passed by Congress and again noted that

"the guaranty of freedom from unreasonable searches and seizures by the Fourth Amendment has been construed, practically since the beginning of the Government, as recognizing a necessary difference between a search of a store, dwelling house or other structure in respect of which a proper official warrant readily may be obtained, and a search of a ship, motor boat, wagon or automobile, for contraband goods, where it is not practicable to secure a warrant because the vehicle can be quickly moved out of the locality or jurisdiction in which the warrant must be sought." *Id.*, at 153.

Thus, since its earliest days Congress had recognized the impracticability of securing a warrant in cases involving the transportation of contraband goods. It is this impracticability, viewed in historical perspective, that provided the basis for the *Carroll* decision. Given the nature of an automobile in transit, the Court recognized that an immediate intrusion is necessary if police officers are to secure the illicit substance. In this class of cases, the Court held that a warrantless search of an automobile is not unreasonable.

In defining the nature of this "exception" to the general rule that "[i]n cases where the securing of a warrant is reasonably practicable, it must be used," *id.*, at 156, the Court in *Carroll* emphasized the importance of the requirement that officers have probable cause to believe that the vehicle contains contraband.

"Having thus established that contraband goods concealed and illegally transported in an automobile or other vehicle may be searched for without a warrant, we come now to consider under what circumstances such search may be made. It would be intolerable and unreasonable if a prohibition agent were authorized to stop every automobile on the chance of finding liquor and thus subject all persons lawfully using the highways to the inconvenience and indignity of such a search. Travellers may be so stopped in crossing an international boundary because of national self protection reasonably requiring one entering the country to identify himself as entitled to come in, and his belongings as effects which may be lawfully brought in. But those lawfully within the country, entitled to use the public highways, have a right to free passage without interruption or search unless there is known to a competent official authorized to search, probable cause for believing that their vehicles are carrying contraband or illegal merchandise." *Id.*, at 153–154.

Moreover, the probable-cause determination must be based on objective facts that could justify the issuance of a warrant by a magistrate and not merely on the subjective good faith of the police officers. "'[A]s we have seen, good faith is not enough to constitute probable cause. That faith must be grounded on facts within knowledge of the [officer], which in the judgment of the court would make his faith reasonable.'" *Id.*, at 161–162 (quoting *Director General of Railroads* v. *Kastenbaum*, 263 U. S. 25, 28).

In short, the exception to the warrant requirement established in *Carroll*—the scope of which we consider in this case—applies only to searches of vehicles that are supported by probable cause. In this class of cases, a search is not unreasonable if based on facts that would justify the issuance of a warrant, even though a warrant has not actually been obtained.

III

The rationale justifying a warrantless search of an automobile that is believed to be transporting contraband arguably applies with equal force to any movable container that is believed to be carrying an illicit substance. That argument, however, was squarely rejected in *United States* v. *Chadwick*, 433 U. S. 1.

. . .

IV

In *Carroll* itself, the whiskey that the prohibition agents seized was not in plain view. It was discovered only after an officer opened the rumble seat and tore open the upholstery of the lazyback. The Court did not find the scope of the search unreasonable. Having stopped Carroll and Kiro on a public road and subjected them to the indignity of a vehicle search—which the Court found to be a reasonable intrusion on their privacy because it was based on probable cause that their vehicle was transporting contraband—

prohibition agents were entitled to tear open a portion of the roadster itself. The scope of the search was no greater than a magistrate could have authorized by issuing a warrant based on the probable cause that justified the search. Since such a warrant could have authorized the agents to open the rear portion of the roadster and to rip the upholstery in their search for concealed whiskey, the search was constitutionally permissible.

. . .

A lawful search of fixed premises generally extends to the entire area in which the object of the search may be found and is not limited by the possibility that separate acts of entry or opening may be required to complete the search. Thus, a warrant that authorizes an officer to search a home for illegal weapons also provides authority to open closets, chests, drawers, and containers in which the weapon might be found. A warrant to open a footlocker to search for marihuana would also authorize the opening of packages found inside. A warrant to search a vehicle would support a search of every part of the vehicle that might contain the object of the search. When a legitimate search is under way, and when its purpose and its limits have been precisely defined, nice distinctions between closets, drawers, and containers, in the case of a home, or between glove compartments, upholstered seats, trunks, and wrapped packages, in the case of a vehicle, must give way to the interest in the prompt and efficient completion of the task at hand.

This rule applies equally to all containers, as indeed we believe it must. One point on which the Court was in virtually unanimous agreement in *Robbins* was that a constitutional distinction between "worthy" and "unworthy" containers would be improper. Even though such a distinction perhaps could evolve in a series of cases in which paper bags, locked trunks, lunch buckets, and orange crates were placed on one side of the line or the other, the central purpose of the Fourth Amendment forecloses such a distinction. For just as the most frail cottage in the kingdom is absolutely entitled to the same guarantees of privacy as the most majestic mansion, so also may a traveler who carries a toothbrush and a few articles of clothing in a paper bag or knotted scarf claim an equal right to conceal his possessions from official inspection as the sophisticated executive with the locked attaché case.

. . . an individual's expectation of privacy in a vehicle and its contents may not survive if probable cause is given to believe that the vehicle is transporting contraband. Certainly the privacy interests in a car's trunk or glove compartment may be no less than those in a movable container. An individual undoubtedly has a significant interest that the upholstery of his automobile will not be ripped or a hidden compartment within it opened. These interests must yield to the authority of a search, however, which—in light of *Carroll*—does not itself require the prior approval of a magistrate. The scope of a warrantless search based on probable cause is no narrower—and no broader—than the scope of a search authorized by a warrant supported by probable cause. Only the prior approval of the magistrate is waived; the search otherwise is as the magistrate could authorize.

The scope of a warrantless search of an automobile thus is not defined by the nature of the container in which the contraband is secreted. Rather, it is defined by the object of the search and the places in which there is probable cause to believe that it may be found. Just as probable cause to believe that a stolen lawnmower may be found in a garage will not support a warrant to search an upstairs bedroom, probable cause to believe that undocumented aliens are being transported in a van will not justify a warrantless search of a suitcase. Probable cause to believe that a container placed in the trunk of a taxi contains contraband or evidence does not justify a search of the entire cab.

V

. . . We hold that the scope of the warrantless search authorized by that exception is no broader and no narrower than a magistrate could legitimately authorize by warrant. If probable cause justifies the search of a lawfully stopped vehicle, it justifies the search of every part of the vehicle and its contents that may conceal the object of the search.

The judgment of the Court of Appeals is re-versed. The case is remanded for further proceedings consistent with this opinion.

It is so ordered.

JUSTICE BLACKMUN, concurring.

My dissents in prior cases have indicated my continuing dissatisfaction and discomfort with the Court's vacillation in what is rightly described as "this troubled area." *Ante*, at 817. See *United States* v. *Chadwick*, 433 U. S. 1, 17 (1977); *Arkansas* v. *Sanders*, 442 U. S. 753, 768 (1979); *Robbins* v. *California*, 453 U. S. 420, 436 (1981).

I adhere to the views expressed in those dissents. It is important, however, not only for the Court as an institution, but also for law enforcement officials and defendants, that the applicable legal rules be clearly established. JUSTICE STEVENS' opinion for the Court now accomplishes much in this respect, and it should clarify a good bit of the confusion that has existed. In order to have an authoritative ruling, I join the Court's opinion and judgment.

JUSTICE POWELL, concurring.

. . .

JUSTICE WHITE, dissenting.

I would not overrule *Robbins* v. *California*, 453 U. S. 420 (1981). For the reasons stated by Justice Stewart in that case, I would affirm the judgment of the Court of Appeals. I also agree with much of JUSTICE MARSHALL's dissent in this case.

JUSTICE MARSHALL, with whom JUSTICE BRENNAN joins, dissenting.

The majority today not only repeals all realistic limits on warrantless automobile searches, it repeals the Fourth Amendment warrant requirement itself. By equating a police officer's estimation of probable cause with a magistrate's, the Court utterly disregards the value of a neutral and detached magistrate. For as we recently, and unanimously, reaffirmed:

"The warrant traditionally has represented an independent assurance that a search and arrest will not proceed without probable cause to believe that a crime has been committed and that the person or place named in the warrant is involved in the crime. Thus, an issuing magistrate must meet two tests. He must be neutral and detached, and he must be capable of determining whether probable cause exists for the requested arrest or search. This Court long has insisted that inferences of probable cause be drawn by 'a neutral and detached magistrate instead of being judged by the officer engaged in the often competitive enterprise of ferreting out crime.'" *Shadwick* v. *City of Tampa*, 407 U. S. 345, 350 (1972), quoting *Johnson* v. *United States*, 333 U. S. 10, 14 (1948).

A police officer on the beat hardly satisfies these standards. In adopting today's new rule, the majority opinion shows contempt for these Fourth Amendment values, ignores this Court's precedents, is internally inconsistent, and produces anomalous and unjust consequences. I therefore dissent.

I

According to the majority, whenever police have probable cause to believe that contraband may be found within an automobile that they have stopped on the highway, they may search not only the automobile but also any container found inside it, without obtaining a warrant. The scope of the search, we are told, is as broad as a magistrate could authorize in a warrant to search the automobile. The majority makes little attempt to justify this rule in terms of recognized Fourth Amendment values. The Court simply ignores the critical function that a magistrate serves. And although the Court purports to rely on the mobility of an automobile and the impracticability of obtaining a warrant, it never explains why these concerns permit the warrantless search of a *container*, which can easily be seized and immobilized while police are obtaining a warrant.

The new rule adopted by the Court today is completely incompatible with established Fourth Amendment principles, and takes a first step toward an unprecedented "probable cause" exception to the warrant requirement. In my view, under accepted standards, the warrantless search of the containers in this case clearly violates the Fourth Amendment.

. . .

The only convincing explanation I discern for the majority's broad rule is expediency: it assists police in conducting automobile searches, ensuring that the private containers into which criminal suspects often place goods will no longer be a Fourth Amendment shield. See *ante*, at 820. "When a legitimate search is under way," the Court instructs us, "nice distinctions between . . . glove compartments, upholstered seats, trunks, and wrapped packages . . . must give way to the interest in the prompt and efficient completion of the task at hand." *Ante*, at 821. No "nice distinctions" are necessary, however, to comprehend the well-recognized differences between movable containers (which, even after today's decision, would be subject to the warrant requirement if located outside an automobile), and the automobile itself, together with its integral parts. Nor can I pass by the majority's glib assertion that the "prompt and efficient completion of the task at hand" is paramount to the Fourth Amendment interests of our citizens. I had thought it well established that "the mere fact that law enforcement may be made more efficient can never by itself justify disregard of the Fourth Amendment." *Mincey* v. *Arizona*, 437 U. S., at 393.

This case will have profound implications for the privacy of citizens traveling in automobiles, as the Court well understands. "For countless vehicles are stopped on highways and public streets every day and our cases demonstrate that it is not uncommon for police officers to have probable cause to believe that contraband may be found in a stopped vehicle." *Ante*, at 803–804. A closed paper bag, a toolbox, a knapsack, a suitcase, and an attaché case can alike be searched without the protection of the judgment of a neutral magistrate, based only on the rarely disturbed decision of a police officer that he has probable cause to search for contraband in the vehicle. The Court derives satisfaction from the fact that its rule does not exalt the rights of the wealthy over the rights of the poor. *Ante*, at 822. A rule so broad that all citizens lose vital Fourth Amendment protection is no cause for celebration.

I dissent.

Terry v. Ohio

392 U.S. 1 (1968)

The Fourth Amendment standard of probable cause for searches and seizures was relaxed in this case to permit a "stop and frisk" of three individuals who had been behaving suspiciously. The pat-down by the police officer produced concealed weapons used to convict Terry and his companion. The Ohio Supreme Court dismissed their appeal. As a result of this case, the *Terry*-stop has become a legitimate technique available for law enforcement officers.

MR. CHIEF JUSTICE WARREN delivered the opinion of the Court.

This case presents serious questions concerning the role of the Fourth Amendment in the confrontation on the street between the citizen and the policeman investigating suspicious circumstances.

Petitioner Terry was convicted of carrying a concealed weapon and sentenced to the statutorily prescribed term of one to three years in the penitentiary. Following the denial of a pretrial motion to suppress, the prosecution introduced in evidence two revolvers and a number of bullets seized from Terry and a codefendant, Richard Chilton, by Cleveland Police Detective Martin McFadden. At the hearing on the motion to suppress this evidence, Officer McFadden testified that while he was patrolling in plain clothes in downtown Cleveland at approximately 2:30 in the afternoon of October 31, 1963, his attention was attracted by two men, Chilton and Terry, standing on the corner of Huron Road and Euclid Avenue. He had never seen the two men before, and he was unable to say precisely what first drew his eye to them. However, he testified that he had been a policeman for 39 years and a detective for 35 and that he had been assigned to patrol this vicinity of downtown Cleveland for shoplifters and pickpockets for 30 years. He explained that he had developed routine habits of observation over the years and that he would "stand and watch people or walk and watch people at many intervals of the day." He added: "Now, in this case when I looked over they didn't look right to me at the time."

His interest aroused, Officer McFadden took up a post of observation in the entrance to a store 300

to 400 feet away from the two men. "I get more purpose to watch them when I seen their movements," he testified. He saw one of the men leave the other one and walk southwest on Huron Road, past some stores. The man paused for a moment and looked in a store window, then walked on a short distance, turned around and walked back toward the corner, pausing once again to look in the same store window. He rejoined his companion at the corner, and the two conferred briefly. Then the second man went through the same series of motions, strolling down Huron Road, looking in the same window, walking on a short distance, turning back, peering in the store window again, and returning to confer with the first man at the corner. The two men repeated this ritual alternately between five and six times apiece —in all, roughly a dozen trips. At one point, while the two were standing together on the corner, a third man approached them and engaged them briefly in conversation. This man then left the two others and walked west on Euclid Avenue. Chilton and Terry resumed their measured pacing, peering, and conferring. After this had gone on for 10 to 12 minutes, the two men walked off together, heading west on Euclid Avenue, following the path taken earlier by the third man.

By this time Officer McFadden had become thoroughly suspicious. He testified that after observing their elaborately casual and oft-repeated reconnaissance of the store window on Huron Road, he suspected the two men of "casing a job, a stick-up," and that he considered it his duty as a police officer to investigate further. He added that he feared "they may have a gun." Thus, Officer McFadden followed Chilton and Terry and saw them stop in front of Zucker's store to talk to the same man who had conferred with them earlier on the street corner. Deciding that the situation was ripe for direct action, Officer McFadden approached the three men, identified himself as a police officer and asked for their names. At this point his knowledge was confined to what he had observed. He was not acquainted with any of the three men by name or by sight, and he had received no information concerning them from any other source. When the men "mumbled something" in response to his inquiries, Officer McFadden grabbed petitioner Terry, spun him around so that they were facing the other two, with Terry between McFadden and the others, and patted down the outside of his clothing. In the left breast pocket of Terry's overcoat Officer McFadden felt a pistol. He reached inside the overcoat pocket, but was unable to remove the gun. At this point, keeping Terry between himself and the others, the officer ordered all three men to enter Zucker's store. As they went in, he removed Terry's overcoat completely, removed a .38-caliber revolver from the pocket and ordered all three men to face the wall with their hands raised. Officer McFadden proceeded to pat down the outer clothing of Chilton and the third man, Katz. He discovered another revolver in the outer pocket of Chilton's overcoat, but no weapons were found on Katz. The officer testified that he only patted the men down to see whether they had weapons, and that he did not put his hands beneath the outer garments of either Terry or Chilton until he felt their guns. So far as appears from the record, he never placed his hands beneath Katz' outer garments. Officer McFadden seized Chilton's gun, asked the proprietor of the store to call a police wagon, and took all three men to the station, where Chilton and Terry were formally charged with carrying concealed weapons.

On the motion to suppress the guns the prosecution took the position that they had been seized following a search incident to a lawful arrest. The trial court rejected this theory, stating that it "would be stretching the facts beyond reasonable comprehension" to find that Officer McFadden had had probable cause to arrest the men before he patted them down for weapons. However, the court denied the defendants' motion on the ground that Officer McFadden, on the basis of his experience, "had reasonable cause to believe . . . that the defendants were conducting themselves suspiciously, and some interrogation should be made of their action." Purely for his own protection, the court held, the officer had the right to pat down the outer clothing of these men, who he had reasonable cause to believe might be armed. The court distinguished between an investigatory "stop" and an arrest, and between a "frisk" of the outer clothing for weapons and a full-blown search for evidence of crime. The frisk, it held, was essential to the proper performance of the officer's investigatory duties, for without it "the answer to the police officer may be a bullet, and a loaded pistol discovered during the frisk is admissible."

After the court denied their motion to suppress, Chilton and Terry waived jury trial and pleaded not guilty. The court adjudged them guilty, and the Court of Appeals for the Eighth Judicial District, Cuyahoga County, affirmed. *State* v. *Terry*, 5 Ohio App. 2d 122, 214 N. E. 2d 114 (1966). The Supreme Court of Ohio dismissed their appeal on the ground that no "substantial constitutional question" was involved. We granted certiorari, 387 U. S. 929 (1967), to determine whether the admission of the revolvers in evidence violated petitioner's rights under the Fourth Amendment, made applicable to the States by the Fourteenth. *Mapp* v. *Ohio*, 367 U.S. 643 (1961). We affirm the conviction.

I.

The Fourth Amendment provides that "the right of the people to be secure in their persons, houses, papers, and effects, against unreasonable searches and seizures, shall not be violated. . . ." This inestimable right of personal security belongs as much to the citizen on the streets of our cities as to the homeowner closeted in his study to dispose of his secret affairs.

. . . we approach the issues in this case mindful of the limitations of the judicial function in controlling the myriad daily situations in which policemen and citizens confront each other on the street. The State has characterized the issue here as "the right of a police officer . . . to make an on-the-street stop, interrogate and pat down for weapons (known in street vernacular as 'stop and frisk')." But this is only partly accurate. For the issue is not the abstract propriety of the police conduct, but the admissibility against petitioner of the evidence uncovered by the search and seizure. Ever since its inception, the rule excluding evidence seized in violation of the Fourth Amendment has been recognized as a principal mode of discouraging lawless police conduct. See *Weeks* v. *United States*, 232 U. S. 383, 391–393 (1914). Thus its major thrust is a deterrent one, see *Linkletter* v. *Walker*, 381 U. S. 618, 629–635 (1965), and experience has taught that it is the only effective deterrent to police misconduct in the criminal context, and that without it the constitutional guarantee against unreasonable searches and seizures would be a mere "form of words." *Mapp* v. *Ohio*, 367 U.S. 643, 655 (1961). The rule also serves another vital function—"the imperative of judicial integrity." *Elkins* v. *United States*, 364 U. S. 206, 222 (1960). Courts which sit under our Constitution cannot and will not be made party to lawless invasions of the constitutional rights of citizens by permitting unhindered governmental use of the fruits of such invasions.

. . . No judicial opinion can comprehend the protean variety of the street encounter, and we can only judge the facts of the case before us. Nothing we say today is to be taken as indicating approval of police conduct outside the legitimate investigative sphere. Under our decision, courts still retain their traditional responsibility to guard against police conduct which is overbearing or harassing, or which trenches upon personal security without the objective evidentiary justification which the Constitution requires. When such conduct is identified, it must be condemned by the judiciary and its fruits must be excluded from evidence in criminal trials. And, of course, our approval of legitimate and restrained investigative conduct undertaken on the basis of ample factual justification should in no way discourage the employment of other remedies than the exclusionary rule to curtail abuses for which that sanction may prove inappropriate.

Having thus roughly sketched the perimeters of the constitutional debate over the limits on police

investigative conduct in general and the background against which this case presents itself, we turn our attention to the quite narrow question posed by the facts before us: whether it is always unreasonable for a policeman to seize a person and subject him to a limited search for weapons unless there is probable cause for an arrest. Given the narrowness of this question, we have no occasion to canvass in detail the constitutional limitations upon the scope of a policeman's power when he confronts a citizen without probable cause to arrest him.

II.

Our first task is to establish at what point in this encounter the Fourth Amendment becomes relevant. That is, we must decide whether and when Officer McFadden "seized" Terry and whether and when he conducted a "search." There is some suggestion in the use of such terms as "stop" and "frisk" that such police conduct is outside the purview of the Fourth Amendment because neither action rises to the level of a "search" or "seizure" within the meaning of the Constitution. We emphatically reject this notion. It is quite plain that the Fourth Amendment governs "seizures" of the person which do not eventuate in a trip to the station house and prosecution for crime— "arrests" in traditional terminology. It must be recognized that whenever a police officer accosts an individual and restrains his freedom to walk away, he has "seized" that person. And it is nothing less than sheer torture of the English language to suggest that a careful exploration of the outer surfaces of a person's clothing all over his or her body in an attempt to find weapons is not a "search." Moreover, it is simply fantastic to urge that such a procedure performed in public by a policeman while the citizen stands helpless, perhaps facing a wall with his hands raised, is a "petty indignity." It is a serious intrusion upon the sanctity of the person, which may inflict great indignity and arouse strong resentment, and it is not to be undertaken lightly.

. . .

In this case there can be no question, then, that Officer McFadden "seized" petitioner and subjected him to a "search" when he took hold of him and patted down the outer surfaces of his clothing. We must decide whether at that point it was reasonable for Officer McFadden to have interfered with petitioner's personal security as he did. And in determining whether the seizure and search were "unreasonable" our inquiry is a dual one—whether the officer's action was justified at its inception, and whether it was reasonably related in scope to the circumstances which justified the interference in the first place.

III.

If this case involved police conduct subject to the Warrant Clause of the Fourth Amendment, we would have to ascertain whether "probable cause" existed to justify the search and seizure which took place. However, that is not the case. . . . we deal here with an entire rubric of police conduct —necessarily swift action predicated upon the on-the-spot observations of the officer on the beat—which historically has not been, and as a practical matter could not be, subjected to the warrant procedure. Instead, the conduct involved in this case must be tested by the Fourth Amendment's general proscription against unreasonable searches and seizures.

Nonetheless, the notions which underlie both the warrant procedure and the requirement of probable cause remain fully relevant in this context. In order to assess the reasonableness of Officer McFadden's conduct as a general proposition, it is necessary "first to focus upon the governmental interest which allegedly justifies official intrusion upon the constitutionally protected interests of the private citizen," for there is "no ready test for determining reasonableness other than by balancing the need to search [or seize] against the invasion which the search [or seizure] entails." *Camara* v. *Municipal Court*, 387 U. S. 523, 534–535, 536–537 (1967). And in justifying the particular intrusion the police officer must be able to point to specific and articulable facts which, taken together with rational inferences from those facts, reasonably warrant that intrusion. The scheme of the Fourth Amendment becomes meaningful only when it is assured that at some point the conduct of those charged with enforcing

the laws can be subjected to the more detached, neutral scrutiny of a judge who must evaluate the reasonableness of a particular search or seizure in light of the particular circumstances. And in making that assessment it is imperative that the facts be judged against an objective standard: would the facts available to the officer at the moment of the seizure or the search "warrant a man of reasonable caution in the belief" that the action taken was appropriate? Cf. *Carroll* v. *United States,* 267 U. S. 132 (1925); *Beck* v. *Ohio,* 379 U. S. 89, 96–97 (1964). Anything less would invite intrusions upon constitutionally guaranteed rights based on nothing more substantial than inarticulate hunches, a result this Court has consistently refused to sanction.

. . .

Our evaluation of the proper balance that has to be struck in this type of case leads us to conclude that there must be a narrowly drawn authority to permit a reasonable search for weapons for the protection of the police officer, where he has reason to believe that he is dealing with an armed and dangerous individual, regardless of whether he has probable cause to arrest the individual for a crime. The officer need not be absolutely certain that the individual is armed; the issue is whether a reasonably prudent man in the circumstances would be warranted in the belief that his safety or that of others was in danger. Cf. *Beck* v. *Ohio,* 379 U. S. 89, 91 (1964); *Brinegar* v. *United States,* 338 U. S. 160, 174–176 (1949); *Stacey* v. *Emery,* 97 U. S. 642, 645 (1878). And in determining whether the officer acted reasonably in such circumstances, due weight must be given, not to his inchoate and unparticularized suspicion or "hunch," but to the specific reasonable inferences which he is entitled to draw from the facts in light of his experience. Cf. *Brinegar* v. *United States supra.*

IV.

We must now examine the conduct of Officer McFadden in this case to determine whether his search and seizure of petitioner were reasonable, both at their inception and as conducted. He had observed Terry, together with Chilton and another man, acting in a manner he took to be preface to a "stick-up." We think on the facts and circumstances Officer McFadden detailed before the trial judge a reasonably prudent man would have been warranted in believing petitioner was armed and thus presented a threat to the officer's safety while he was investigating his suspicious behavior. The actions of Terry and Chilton were consistent with McFadden's hypothesis that these men were contemplating a daylight robbery—which, it is reasonable to assume, would be likely to involve the use of weapons—and nothing in their conduct from the time he first noticed them until the time he confronted them and identified himself as a police officer gave him sufficient reason to negate that hypothesis. Although the trio had departed the original scene, there was nothing to indicate abandonment of an intent to commit a robbery at some point. Thus, when Officer McFadden approached the three men gathered before the display window at Zucker's store he had observed enough to make it quite reasonable to fear that they were armed; and nothing in their response to his hailing them, identifying himself as a police officer, and asking their names served to dispel that reasonable belief. We cannot say his decision at that point to seize Terry and pat his clothing for weapons was the product of a volatile or inventive imagination, or was undertaken simply as an act of harassment; the record evidences the tempered act of a policeman who in the course of an investigation had to make a quick decision as to how to protect himself and others from possible danger, and took limited steps to do so.

. . .

The scope of the search in this case presents no serious problem in light of these standards. Officer McFadden patted down the outer clothing of petitioner and his two companions. He did not place his hands in their pockets or under the outer surface of their garments until he had felt weapons, and then he merely reached for and removed the guns. He never did invade Katz' person beyond the outer surfaces of his clothes, since he discovered nothing in his pat-down which might have been a weapon. Officer McFadden confined his search strictly to what was minimally necessary to learn whether the men were armed and to disarm

them once he discovered the weapons. He did not conduct a general exploratory search for whatever evidence of criminal activity he might find.

V.

We conclude that the revolver seized from Terry was properly admitted in evidence against him. At the time he seized petitioner and searched him for weapons, Officer McFadden had reasonable grounds to believe that petitioner was armed and dangerous, and it was necessary for the protection of himself and others to take swift measures to discover the true facts and neutralize the threat of harm if it materialized. The policeman carefully restricted his search to what was appropriate to the discovery of the particular items which he sought. Each case of this sort will, of course, have to be decided on its own facts. We merely hold today that where a police officer observes unusual conduct which leads him reasonably to conclude in light of his experience that criminal activity may be afoot and that the persons with whom he is dealing may be armed and presently dangerous, where in the course of investigating this behavior he identifies himself as a policeman and makes reasonable inquiries, and where nothing in the initial stages of the encounter serves to dispel his reasonable fear for his own or others' safety, he is entitled for the protection of himself and others in the area to conduct a carefully limited search of the outer clothing of such persons in an attempt to discover weapons which might be used to assault him. Such a search is a reasonable search under the Fourth Amendment, and any weapons seized may properly be introduced in evidence against the person from whom they were taken.

Affirmed.

MR. JUSTICE BLACK concurs in the judgment and the opinion except where the opinion quotes from and relies upon this Court's opinion in *Katz* v. *United States* and the concurring opinion in *Warden* v. *Hayden.*

MR. JUSTICE HARLAN, concurring.

. . .

MR. JUSTICE WHITE, concurring.

. . .

MR. JUSTICE DOUGLAS, dissenting.

. . .

To give the police greater power than a magistrate is to take a long step down the totalitarian path. Perhaps such a step is desirable to cope with modern forms of lawlessness. But if it is taken, it should be the deliberate choice of the people through a constitutional amendment. Until the Fourth Amendment, which is closely allied with the Fifth, is rewritten, the person and the effects of the individual are beyond the reach of all government agencies until there are reasonable grounds to believe (probable cause) that a criminal venture has been launched or is about to be launched.

There have been powerful hydraulic pressures throughout our history that bear heavily on the Court to water down constitutional guarantees and give the police the upper hand. That hydraulic pressure has probably never been greater than it is today.

Yet if the individual is no longer to be sovereign, if the police can pick him up whenever they do not like the cut of his jib, if they can "seize" and "search" him in their discretion, we enter a new regime. The decision to enter it should be made only after a full debate by the people of this country.

Chimel v. California

395 U.S. 752 (1969)

In this decision, the Supreme Court attempted to limit the scope of a search that is made incident to an arrest. Police officers, armed with an arrest warrant but not a search warrant, were admitted to a suspect's home by his wife. They served him with the arrest warrant when he arrived and proceeded to search the entire house, finding evidence that led to his conviction for burglary. The conviction was upheld by the state courts.

MR. JUSTICE STEWART delivered the opinion of the Court.

This case raises basic questions concerning the permissible scope under the Fourth Amendment of a search incident to a lawful arrest.

The relevant facts are essentially undisputed. Late in the afternoon of September 13, 1965, three police officers arrived at the Santa Ana, California, home of the petitioner with a warrant authorizing his arrest for the burglary of a coin shop. The officers knocked on the door, identified themselves to the petitioner's wife, and asked if they might come inside. She ushered them into the house, where they waited 10 or 15 minutes until the petitioner returned home from work. When the petitioner entered the house, one of the officers handed him the arrest warrant and asked for permission to "look around." The petitioner objected, but was advised that "on the basis of the lawful arrest," the officers would nonetheless conduct a search. No search warrant had been issued.

Accompanied by the petitioner's wife, the officers then looked through the entire three-bedroom house, including the attic, the garage, and a small workshop. In some rooms the search was relatively cursory. In the master bedroom and sewing room, however, the officers directed the petitioner's wife to open drawers and "to physically move contents of the drawers from side to side so that [they] might view any items that would have come from [the] burglary." After completing the search, they seized numerous items— primarily coins, but also several medals, tokens, and a few other objects. The entire search took between 45 minutes and an hour.

At the petitioner's subsequent state trial on two charges of burglary, the items taken from his house were admitted into evidence against him, over his objection that they had been unconstitutionally seized. He was convicted, and the judgments of conviction were affirmed by both the California Court of Appeal, 61 Cal. Rptr. 714, and the California Supreme Court, 68 Cal. 2d 436, 439 P. 2d 333. Both courts accepted the petitioner's contention that the arrest warrant was invalid because the supporting affidavit was set out in conclusory terms, but held that since the arresting officers had procured the warrant "in good faith," and since in any event they had had sufficient information to constitute probable cause for the petitioner's arrest, that arrest had been lawful. From this conclusion the appellate courts went on to hold that the search of the petitioner's home had been justified, despite the absence of a search warrant, on the ground that it had been incident to a valid arrest. We granted certiorari in order to consider the petitioner's substantial constitutional claims. 393 U. S. 958.

Without deciding the question, we proceed on the hypothesis that the California courts were correct in holding that the arrest of the petitioner was valid under the Constitution. This brings us directly to the question whether the warrantless search of the petitioner's entire house can be constitutionally justified as incident to that arrest. The decisions of this Court bearing upon that question have been far from consistent, as even the most cursory review makes evident.

. . .

In 1950 . . . came *United States* v. *Rabinowitz*, 339 U. S. 56, the decision upon which California primarily relies in the case now before us. In *Rabinowitz*, federal authorities had been informed that the defendant was dealing in stamps bearing forged overprints. On the basis of that information they secured a warrant for his arrest, which they executed at his one-room business office. At the time of the arrest, the officers "searched the desk, safe, and file cabinets in the office for about an hour and a half," *id.*, at 59, and seized 573 stamps with forged overprints. The stamps were admitted into evidence at the defendant's trial, and this Court affirmed his conviction, rejecting the contention that the warrantless search had been unlawful. The Court held that the search in its entirety fell within the principle giving law en-

forcement authorities "[t]he right 'to search the place where the arrest is made in order to find and seize things connected with the crime. . . .'" *Id.*, at 61. . . .

Rabinowitz has come to stand for the proposition, *inter alia*, that a warrantless search "incident to a lawful arrest" may generally extend to the area that is considered to be in the "possession" or under the "control" of the person arrested. And it was on the basis of that proposition that the California courts upheld the search of the petitioner's entire house in this case. That doctrine, however, at least in the broad sense in which it was applied by the California courts in this case, can withstand neither historical nor rational analysis.

Even limited to its own facts, the *Rabinowitz* decision was, as we have seen, hardly founded on an unimpeachable line of authority. As Mr. Justice Frankfurter commented in dissent in that case, the "hint" contained in *Weeks* was, without persuasive justification, "loosely turned into dictum and finally elevated to a decision." 339 U.S., at 75. And the approach taken in cases such as *Go-Bart, Lefkowitz,* and *Trupiano* was essentially disregarded by the *Rabinowitz* Court.

Nor is the rationale by which the State seeks here to sustain the search of the petitioner's house supported by a reasoned view of the background and purpose of the Fourth Amendment. Mr. Justice Frankfurter wisely pointed out in his *Rabinowitz* dissent that the Amendment's proscription of "unreasonable searches and seizures" must be read in light of "the history that gave rise to the words"—a history of "abuses so deeply felt by the Colonies as to be one of the potent causes of the Revolution. . . ." 339 U. S., at 69. The Amendment was in large part a reaction to the general warrants and warrantless searches that had so alienated the colonists and had helped speed the movement for independence. In the scheme of the Amendment, therefore, the requirement that "no Warrants shall issue, but upon probable cause," plays a crucial part. As the Court put it in *McDonald* v. *United States*, 335 U. S. 451:

"We are not dealing with formalities. The presence of a search warrant serves a high function. Absent some grave emergency, the Fourth Amendment has interposed a magistrate between the citizen and the police. This was done not to shield criminals nor to make the home a safe haven for illegal activities. It was done so that an objective mind might weigh the need to invade that privacy in order to enforce the law. The right of privacy was deemed too precious to entrust to the discretion of those whose job is the detection of crime and the arrest of criminals. . . . And so the Constitution requires a magistrate to pass on the desires of the police before they violate the privacy of the home. We cannot be true to that constitutional requirement and excuse the absence of a search warrant without a showing by those who seek exemption from the constitutional mandate that the exigencies of the situation made that course imperative." *Id.*, at 455–456.

. . .

Only last Term in *Terry* v. *Ohio*, 392 U. S. 1, we emphasized that "the police must, whenever practicable, obtain advance judicial approval of searches and seizures through the warrant procedure," *id.*, at 20, and that "[t]he scope of [a] search must be 'strictly tied to and justified by' the circumstances which rendered its initiation permissible." *Id.*, at 19. The search undertaken by the officer in that "stop and frisk" case was sustained under that test, because it was no more than a "protective . . . search for weapons." *Id.*, at 29. . . .

A similar analysis underlies the "search incident to arrest" principle, and marks its proper extent. When an arrest is made, it is reasonable for the arresting officer to search the person arrested in order to remove any weapons that the latter might seek to use in order to resist arrest or effect his escape. Otherwise, the officer's safety might well be endangered, and the arrest itself frustrated. In addition, it is entirely reasonable for the arresting officer to search for and seize any evidence on the arrestee's person in order to prevent its concealment or destruction. And the area into which an arrestee might reach in order to grab a weapon or evidentiary items must, of course, be governed by a like rule. A gun on a table or in a drawer in front of one who is arrested can be as dangerous to the arresting officer as one concealed in the clothing of the person arrested.

There is ample justification, therefore, for a search of the arrestee's person and the area "within his immediate control"—construing that phrase to mean the area from within which he might gain possession of a weapon or destructible evidence.

There is no comparable justification, however, for routinely searching any room other than that in which an arrest occurs—or, for that matter, for searching through all the desk drawers or other closed or concealed areas in that room itself. Such searches, in the absence of well-recognized exceptions, may be made only under the authority of a search warrant. The "adherence to judicial processes" mandated by the Fourth Amendment requires no less.

. . .

Application of sound Fourth Amendment principles to the facts of this case produces a clear result. The search here went far beyond the petitioner's person and the area from within which he might have obtained either a weapon or something that could have been used as evidence against him. There was no constitutional justification, in the absence of a search warrant, for extending the search beyond that area. The scope of the search was, therefore, "unreasonable" under the Fourth and Fourteenth Amendments, and the petitioner's conviction cannot stand.

Reversed.

MR. JUSTICE HARLAN, concurring.

. . .

MR. JUSTICE WHITE, with whom MR. JUSTICE BLACK joins, dissenting.

Few areas of the law have been as subject to shifting constitutional standards over the last 50 years as that of the search "incident to an arrest." There has been a remarkable instability in this whole area, which has seen at least four major shifts in emphasis. Today's opinion makes an untimely fifth. In my view, the Court should not now abandon the old rule.

. . .

If circumstances so often require the warrantless arrest that the law generally permits it, the typical situation will find the arresting officers lawfully on the premises without arrest or search warrant. Like the majority, I would permit the police to search the person of a suspect and the area under his immediate control either to assure the safety of the officers or to prevent the destruction of evidence. And like the majority, I see nothing in the arrest alone furnishing probable cause for a search of any broader scope. However, where as here the existence of probable cause is independently established and would justify a warrant for a broader search for evidence, I would follow past cases and permit such a search to be carried out without a warrant, since the fact of arrest supplies an exigent circumstance justifying police action before the evidence can be removed, and also alerts the suspect to the fact of the search so that he can immediately seek judicial determination of probable cause in an adversary proceeding, and appropriate redress.

This view, consistent with past cases, would not authorize the general search against which the Fourth Amendment was meant to guard, nor would it broaden or render uncertain in any way whatsoever the scope of searches permitted under the Fourth Amendment. The issue in this case is not the breadth of the search, since there was clearly probable cause for the search which was carried out. No broader search than if the officers had a warrant would be permitted. The only issue is whether a search warrant was required as a precondition to that search. It is agreed that such a warrant would be required absent exigent circumstances. I would hold that the fact of arrest supplies such an exigent circumstance, since the police had lawfully gained entry to the premises to effect the arrest and since delaying the search to secure a warrant would have involved the risk of not recovering the fruits of the crime.

. . .

Olmstead v. United States

277 U.S. 438 (1928)

Roy Olmstead and several accomplices were convicted of violating the National Prohibition Act by importing and selling liquor. On the basis of evidence obtained by wiretapping telephone conversations, indictments were handed down against more than seventy individuals involved in an extensive operation that reached across the Canadian border. The Circuit Court of Appeals for the Ninth Circuit upheld the convictions.

MR. CHIEF JUSTICE TAFT delivered the opinion of the Court.

. . .

The information which led to the discovery of the conspiracy and its nature and extent was largely obtained by intercepting messages on the telephones of the conspirators by four federal prohibition officers. Small wires were inserted along the ordinary telephone wires from the residences of four of the petitioners and those leading from the chief office. The insertions were made without trespass upon any property of the defendants. They were made in the basement of the large office building. The taps from house lines were made in the streets near the houses.

The gathering of evidence continued for many months. Conversations of the conspirators of which refreshing stenographic notes were currently made, were testified to by the government witnesses. They revealed the large business transactions of the partners and their subordinates. Men at the wires heard the orders given for liquor by customers and the acceptances; they became auditors of the conversations between the partners. All this disclosed the conspiracy charged in the indictment. Many of the intercepted conversations were not merely reports but parts of the criminal acts. The evidence also disclosed the difficulties to which the conspirators were subjected, the reported news of the capture of vessels, the arrest of their men and the seizure of cases of liquor in garages and other places. It showed the dealing by Olmstead, the chief conspirator, with members of the Seattle police, the messages to them which secured the release of arrested members of the conspiracy, and also direct promises to officers of payments as soon as opportunity offered.

. . .

The [Fourth] Amendment itself shows that the search is to be of material things—the person, the house, his papers or his effects. The description of the warrant necessary to make the proceeding lawful, is that it must specify the place to be searched and the person or *things* to be seized.

It is urged that the language of Mr. Justice Field in *Ex parte Jackson*, already quoted, offers an analogy to the interpretation of the Fourth Amendment in respect of wire tapping. But the analogy fails. The Fourth Amendment may have proper application to a sealed letter in the mail because of the constitutional provision for the Postoffice Department and the relations between the Government and those who pay to secure protection of their sealed letters. See Revised Statutes, §§ 3978 to 3988, whereby Congress monopolizes the carriage of letters and excludes from that business everyone else, and § 3929 which forbids any postmaster or other person to open any letter not addressed to himself. It is plainly within the words of the Amendment to say that the unlawful rifling by a government agent of a sealed letter is a search and seizure of the sender's papers or effects. The letter is a paper, an effect, and in the custody of a Government that forbids carriage except under its protection.

The United States takes no such care of telegraph or telephone messages as of mailed sealed letters. The Amendment does not forbid what was done here. There was no searching. There was no seizure. The evidence was secured by the use of the sense of hearing and that only. There was no entry of the houses or offices of the defendants.

By the invention of the telephone, fifty years ago, and its application for the purpose of extend-

ing communications, one can talk with another at a far distant place. The language of the Amendment can not be extended and expanded to include telephone wires reaching to the whole world from the defendant's house or office. The intervening wires are not part of his house or office any more than are the highways along which they are stretched.

This Court in *Carroll* v. *United States*, 267 U.S. 132, 149, declared:

"The Fourth Amendment is to be construed in the light of what was deemed an unreasonable search and seizure when it was adopted and in a manner which will conserve public interests as well as the interests and rights of individual citizens."

Justice Bradley in the *Boyd* case, and Justice Clark in the *Gouled* case, said that the Fifth Amendment and the Fourth Amendment were to be liberally construed to effect the purpose of the framers of the Constitution in the interest of liberty. But that can not justify enlargement of the language employed beyond the possible practical meaning of houses, persons, papers, and effects, or so to apply the words search and seizure as to forbid hearing or sight.

Hester v. *United States*, 265 U.S. 57, held that the testimony of two officers of the law who trespassed on the defendant's land, concealed themselves one hundred yards away from his house and saw him come out and hand a bottle of whiskey to another, was not inadmissible. While there was a trespass, there was no search of person, house, papers or effects. *United States* v. *Lee*, 274 U.S. 559, 563; *Eversole* v. *State*, 106 Tex. Cr. 567.

Congress may of course protect the secrecy of telephone messages by making them, when intercepted, inadmissible in evidence in federal criminal trials, by direct legislation, and thus depart from the common law of evidence. But the courts may not adopt such a policy by attributing an enlarged and unusual meaning to the Fourth Amendment. The reasonable view is that one who installs in his house a telephone instrument with connecting wires intends to project his voice to those quite outside, and that the wires beyond his house and messages while passing over them are not within the protection of the Fourth Amendment. Here those who intercepted the projected voices were not in the house of either party to the conversation.

. . .

A standard which would forbid the reception of evidence if obtained by other than nice ethical conduct by government officials would make society suffer and give criminals greater immunity than has been known heretofore. In the absence of controlling legislation by Congress, those who realize the difficulties in bringing offenders to justice may well deem it wise that the exclusion of evidence should be confined to cases where rights under the Constitution would be violated by admitting it.

The statute of Washington, adopted in 1909, provides (Remington Compiled Statutes, 1922, § 2656–18) that:

"Every person . . . who shall intercept, read or in any manner interrupt or delay the sending of a message over any telegraph or telephone line . . . shall be guilty of a misdemeanor."

This statute does not declare that evidence obtained by such interception shall be inadmissible, and by the common law, already referred to, it would not be. *People* v. *McDonald*, 177 App. Div. (N.Y.) 806. Whether the State of Washington may prosecute and punish federal officers violating this law and those whose messages were intercepted may sue them civilly is not before us. But clearly a statute, passed twenty years after the admission of the State into the Union can not affect the rules of evidence applicable in courts of the United States in criminal cases. Chief Justice Taney, in *United States* v. *Reid*, 12 How. 361, 363, construing the 34th section of the Judiciary Act, said:

"But it could not be supposed, without very plain words to show it, that Congress intended to give the states the power of prescribing the rules of evidence in trials for offenses against the United States. For this construction would place the criminal jurisprudence of one sovereignty under the control of another." See also *Withaup* v. *United States*, 127 Fed. 530, 534.

The judgments of the Circuit Court of Appeals are affirmed. The mandates will go down forthwith under Rule 31.

Affirmed.

MR. JUSTICE HOLMES:

My brother BRANDEIS has given this case so exhaustive an examination that I desire to add but a few words. While I do not deny it, I am not prepared to say that the penumbra of the Fourth and Fifth Amendments covers the defendant, although I fully agree that Courts are apt to err by sticking too closely to the words of a law where those words import a policy that goes beyond them. *Gooch* v. *Oregon Short Line R.R. Co.*, 258 U.S. 22, 24. But I think, as MR. JUSTICE BRANDEIS says, that apart from the Constitution the Government ought not to use evidence obtained and only obtainable by a criminal act. There is no body of precedents by which we are bound, and which confines us to logical deduction from established rules. Therefore we must consider the two objects of desire, both of which we cannot have, and make up our minds which to choose. It is desirable that criminals should be detected, and to that end that all available evidence should be used. It also is desirable that the Government should not itself foster and pay for other crimes, when they are the means by which the evidence is to be obtained. If it pays its officers for having got evidence by crime I do not see why it may not as well pay them for getting it in the same way, and I can attach no importance to protestations of disapproval if it knowingly accepts and pays and announces that in future it will pay for the fruits. We have to choose, and for my part I think it a less evil that some criminals should escape than that the Government should play an ignoble part.

For those who agree with me, no distinction can be taken between the Government as prosecutor and the Government as judge. If the existing code does not permit district attorneys to have a hand in such dirty business it does not permit the judge to allow such iniquities to succeed. See *Silverthorne Lumber Co.* v. *United States*, 251 U.S. 385. And if all that I have said so far be accepted it makes no difference that in this case wire tapping is made a crime by the law of the State, not by the law of the United States. It is true that a State cannot make rules of evidence for Courts of the United States, but the State has authority over the conduct in question, and I hardly think that the United States would appear to greater advantage when paying for an odious crime against State law than when inciting to the disregard of its own. I am aware of the often repeated statement that in a criminal proceeding the Court will not take notice of the manner in which papers offered in evidence have been obtained. But that somewhat rudimentary mode of disposing of the question has been overthrown by *Weeks* v. *United States,* 232 U.S. 383 and the cases that have followed it. I have said that we are free to choose between two principles of policy. But if we are to confine ourselves to precedent and logic the reason for excluding evidence obtained by violating the Constitution seems to me logically to lead to excluding evidence obtained by a crime of the officers of the law.

MR. JUSTICE BRANDEIS, dissenting.

. . .

. . . Clauses guaranteeing to the individual protection against specific abuses of power, must have a similar capacity of adaptation to a changing world. It was with reference to such a clause that this Court said in *Weems* v. *United States,* 217 U.S. 349, 373: "Legislation, both statutory and constitutional, is enacted, it is true, from an experience of evils, but its general language should not, therefore, be necessarily confined to the form that evil had theretofore taken. Time works changes, brings into existence new conditions and purposes. Therefore a principle to be vital must be capable of wider application than the mischief which gave it birth. This is peculiarly true of constitutions. They are not ephemeral enactments, designed to meet passing occasions. They are, to use the words of Chief Justice Marshall 'designed to approach immortality as nearly as human institutions can approach it.' The future is their care and provision for events of good and bad tendencies of which no prophecy can be made. In the application of a constitution, therefore, our contemplation cannot be only of what has been but of what may be. Under any other rule a constitution would indeed be as easy of applica-

tion as it would be deficient in efficacy and power. Its general principles would have little value and be converted by precedent into impotent and lifeless formulas. Rights declared in words might be lost in reality."

When the Fourth and Fifth Amendments were adopted, "the form that evil had theretofore taken," had been necessarily simple. Force and violence were then the only means known to man by which a Government could directly effect self-incrimination. It could compel the individual to testify—a compulsion effected, if need be, by torture. It could secure possession of his papers and other articles incident to his private life—a seizure effected, if need be, by breaking and entry. Protection against such invasion of "the sanctities of a man's home and the privacies of life" was provided in the Fourth and Fifth Amendments by specific language. *Boyd* v. *United States,* 116 U.S. 616, 630. But "time works changes, brings into existence new conditions and purposes." Subtler and more far-reaching means of invading privacy have become available to the Government. Discovery and invention have made it possible for the Government, by means far more effective than stretching upon the rack, to obtain disclosure in court of what is whispered in the closet.

Moreover, "in the application of a constitution, our contemplation cannot be only of what has been but of what may be." The progress of science in furnishing the Government with means of espionage is not likely to stop with wire-tapping. Ways may some day be developed by which the Government, without removing papers from secret drawers, can reproduce them in court, and by which it will be enabled to expose to a jury the most intimate occurrences of the home. Advances in the psychic and related sciences may bring means of exploring unexpressed beliefs, thoughts and emotions.

. . .

The protection guaranteed by the *[Fourth and Fifth]* Amendments is much broader in scope. The makers of our Constitution undertook to secure conditions favorable to the pursuit of happiness. They recognized the significance of man's spiritual nature, of his feelings and of his intellect. They knew that only a part of the pain, pleasure and satisfactions of life are to be found in material things. They sought to protect Americans in their beliefs, their thoughts, their emotions and their sensations. They conferred, as against the Government, the right to be let alone—the most comprehensive of rights and the right most valued by civilized men. To protect that right, every unjustifiable intrusion by the Government upon the privacy of the individual, whatever the means employed, must be deemed a violation of the Fourth Amendment. And the use, as evidence in a criminal proceeding, of facts ascertained by such intrusion must be deemed a violation of the Fifth.

Applying to the Fourth and Fifth Amendments the established rule of construction, the defendants' objections to the evidence obtained by wire-tapping must, in my opinion, be sustained. It is, of course, immaterial where the physical connection with the telephone wires leading into the defendants' premises was made. And it is also immaterial that the intrusion was in aid of law enforcement. Experience should teach us to be most on our guard to protect liberty when the Government's purposes are beneficent. Men born to freedom are naturally alert to repel invasion of their liberty by evil-minded rulers. The greatest dangers to liberty lurk in insidious encroachment by men of zeal, well-meaning but without understanding.

. . .

Decency, security and liberty alike demand that government officials shall be subjected to the same rules of conduct that are commands to the citizen. In a government of laws, existence of the government will be imperilled if it fails to observe the law scrupulously. Our Government is the potent, the omnipresent teacher. For good or for ill, it teaches the whole people by its example. Crime is contagious. If the Government becomes a lawbreaker, it breeds contempt for law; it invites every man to become a law unto himself; it invites anarchy. To declare that in the administration of the criminal law the end justifies the means—to declare that the Government may commit crimes in order to secure the conviction of a private criminal—would bring terrible retribution. Against that pernicious doctrine this Court should resolutely set its face.

MR. JUSTICE BUTLER, dissenting.

. . .

MR. JUSTICE STONE, dissenting.

. . .

Katz v. United States

389 U.S. 347 (1967)

Charles Katz was convicted for transmitting information on bets and wagers by telephone across state lines. FBI agents overheard his phone conversations by attaching an electronic listening and recording device to the top of a public telephone booth he used. The Court of Appeals affirmed his conviction, finding that there was no Fourth Amendment violation since there was "no physical entrance into the area occupied by" Katz.

MR. JUSTICE STEWART delivered the opinion of the Court.
. . . the parties have attached great significance to the characterization of the telephone booth from which the petitioner placed his calls.

The petitioner has strenuously argued that the booth was a "constitutionally protected area." The Government has maintained with equal vigor that it was not. But this effort to decide whether or not a given "area," viewed in the abstract, is "constitutionally protected" deflects attention from the problem presented by this case. For the Fourth Amendment protects people, not places. What a person knowingly exposes to the public, even in his own home or office, is not a subject of Fourth Amendment protection. See *Lewis* v. *United States*, 385 U.S. 206, 210; *United States* v. *Lee*, 274 U.S. 559, 563. But what he seeks to preserve as private, even in an area accessible to the public, may be constitutionally protected. See *Rios* v. *United States*, 364 U.S. 253; *Ex parte Jackson*, 96 U.S. 727, 733.

The Government stresses the fact that the telephone booth from which the petitioner made his calls was constructed partly of glass, so that he was as visible after he entered it as he would have been if he had remained outside. But what he sought to exclude when he entered the booth was not the intruding eye—it was the uninvited ear. He did not shed his right to do so simply because he made his calls from a place where he might be seen. No less than an individual in a business office, in a friend's apartment, or in a taxicab, a person in a telephone booth may rely upon the protection of the Fourth Amendment. One who occupies it, shuts the door behind him, and pays the toll that permits him to place a call is surely entitled to assume that the words he utters into the mouthpiece will not be broadcast to the world. To read the Constitution more narrowly is to ignore the vital role that the public telephone has come to play in private communication.

The Government contends, however, that the activities of its agents in this case should not be tested by Fourth Amendment requirements, for the surveillance technique they employed involved no physical penetration of the telephone booth from which the petitioner placed his calls. It is true that the absence of such penetration was at one time thought to foreclose further Fourth Amendment inquiry, *Olmstead* v. *United States*, 277 U.S. 438, 457, 464, 466; *Goldman* v. *United States*, 316 U.S. 129, 134–136, for that Amendment was thought to limit only searches and seizures of tangible property. But "[t]he premise that property interests control the right of the Government to search and seize has been discredited." *Warden* v. *Hayden*, 387 U.S. 294, 304. Thus, although a closely divided Court supposed in

Olmstead that surveillance without any trespass and without the seizure of any material object fell outside the ambit of the Constitution, we have since departed from the narrow view on which that decision rested. Indeed, we have expressly held that the Fourth Amendment governs not only the seizure of tangible items, but extends as well to the recording of oral statements, overheard without any "technical trespass under . . . local property law." *Silverman* v. *United States*, 365 U.S. 505, 511. Once this much is acknowledged, and once it is recognized that the Fourth Amendment protects people—and not simply "areas"—against unreasonable searches and seizures, it becomes clear that the reach of that Amendment cannot turn upon the presence or absence of a physical intrusion into any given enclosure.

We conclude that the underpinnings of *Olmstead* and *Goldman* have been so eroded by our subsequent decisions that the "trespass" doctrine there enunciated can no longer be regarded as controlling. The Government's activities in electronically listening to and recording the petitioner's words violated the privacy upon which he justifiably relied while using the telephone booth and thus constituted a "search and seizure" within the meaning of the Fourth Amendment. The fact that the electronic device employed to achieve that end did not happen to penetrate the wall of the booth can have no constitutional significance.

The question remaining for decision, then, is whether the search and seizure conducted in this case complied with constitutional standards. In that regard, the Government's position is that its agents acted in an entirely defensible manner: They did not begin their electronic surveillance until investigation of the petitioner's activities had established a strong probability that he was using the telephone in question to transmit gambling information to persons in other States, in violation of federal law. Moreover, the surveillance was limited, both in scope and in duration, to the specific purpose of establishing the contents of the petitioner's unlawful telephonic communications. The agents confined their surveillance to the brief periods during which he used the telephone booth, and they took great care to overhear only the conversations of the petitioner himself.

Accepting this account of the Government's actions as accurate, it is clear that this surveillance was so narrowly circumscribed that a duly authorized magistrate, properly notified of the need for such investigation, specifically informed of the basis on which it was to proceed, and clearly apprised of the precise intrusion it would entail, could constitutionally have authorized, with appropriate safeguards, the very limited search and seizure that the Government asserts in fact took place. Only last Term we sustained the validity of such an authorization, holding that, under sufficiently "precise and discriminate circumstances," a federal court may empower government agents to employ a concealed electronic device "for the narrow and particularized purpose of ascertaining the truth of the . . . allegations" of a "detailed factual affidavit alleging the commission of a specific criminal offense." *Osborn* v. *United States*, 385 U.S. 323, 329–330. Discussing that holding, the Court in *Berger* v. *New York*, 388 U.S. 41, said that "the order authorizing the use of the electronic device" in *Osborn* "afforded similar protections to those . . . of conventional warrants authorizing the seizure of tangible evidence." Through those protections, "no greater invasion of privacy was permitted than was necessary under the circumstances." *Id.*, at 57. Here, too, a similar judicial order could have accommodated "the legitimate needs of law enforcement" by authorizing the carefully limited use of electronic surveillance.

The Government urges that, because its agents relied upon the decisions in *Olmstead* and *Goldman*, and because they did no more here than they might properly have done with prior judicial sanction, we should retroactively validate their conduct. That we cannot do. It is apparent that the agents in this case acted with restraint. Yet the inescapable fact is that this restraint was imposed by the agents themselves, not by a judicial officer. They were not required, before commencing the search, to present their estimate of probable cause for detached scrutiny by a neutral magistrate. They were not compelled, during the conduct of the search itself, to observe precise limits established in advance by a specific court order. Nor were they directed, after the search had been completed, to notify the authorizing magistrate in detail of all that had been seized. In the absence of such safeguards, this Court has never sustained a search upon the sole ground that officers reasonably expected to find evidence of a particular crime and voluntarily confined their activities to the least intrusive means consistent with that end. Searches conducted without warrants have been held unlawful "notwithstanding facts unquestionably showing probable cause," *Agnello* v. *United States*, 269 U.S. 20, 33, for the Constitution requires "that the deliberate, impartial judgment of a judicial officer . . . be interposed between the citizen and the police. . . ." *Wong Sun* v. *United States*, 371 U.S. 471, 481–482. "Over and again this Court has emphasized that the mandate of the [Fourth] Amendment requires adherence to judicial processes," *United States* v. *Jeffers*, 342 U.S. 48, 51, and that searches conducted outside the judicial process, without prior approval by judge or magistrate, are *per se* unreasonable under the Fourth Amendment—subject only to a few specifically established and well-delineated exceptions.

It is difficult to imagine how any of those exceptions could ever apply to the sort of search and seizure involved in this case. Even electronic surveillance substantially contemporaneous with an individual's arrest could hardly be deemed an "incident" of that arrest. Nor could the use of electronic surveillance without prior authorization be justified on grounds of "hot pursuit." And, of course, the very nature of electronic surveillance precludes its use pursuant to the suspect's consent.

The Government does not question these basic principles. Rather, it urges the creation of a new exception to cover this case. It argues that surveillance of a telephone booth should be exempted from the usual requirement of advance authorization by a magistrate upon a showing of probable cause. We cannot agree. Omission of such authorization

"bypasses the safeguards provided by an objective predetermination of probable cause, and substitutes instead the far less reliable procedure of an after-the-event justification for the . . . search, too likely to be subtly influenced by the familiar shortcomings of hindsight judgment." *Beck* v. *Ohio*, 379 U.S. 89, 96.

And bypassing a neutral predetermination of the

scope of a search leaves individuals secure from Fourth Amendment violations "only in the discretion of the police." *Id.*, at 97.

These considerations do not vanish when the search in question is transferred from the setting of a home, an office, or a hotel room to that of a telephone booth. Wherever a man may be, he is entitled to know that he will remain free from unreasonable searches and seizures. The government agents here ignored "the procedure of antecedent justification . . . that is central to the Fourth Amendment," a procedure that we hold to be a constitutional precondition of the kind of electronic surveillance involved in this case. Because the surveillance here failed to meet that condition, and because it led to the petitioner's conviction, the judgment must be reversed.

It is so ordered.

MR. JUSTICE MARSHALL took no part in the consideration or decision of this case.

MR. JUSTICE DOUGLAS, with whom MR. JUSTICE BRENNAN joins, concurring.

While I join the opinion of the Court, I feel compelled to reply to the separate concurring opinion of my Brother WHITE, which I view as a wholly unwarranted green light for the Executive Branch to resort to electronic eavesdropping without a warrant in cases which the Executive Branch itself labels "national security" matters.

Neither the President nor the Attorney General is a magistrate. In matters where they believe national security may be involved they are not detached, disinterested, and neutral as a court or magistrate must be. Under the separation of powers created by the Constitution, the Executive Branch is not supposed to be neutral and disinterested. Rather it should vigorously investigate and prevent breaches of national security and prosecute those who violate the pertinent federal laws. The President and Attorney General are properly interested parties, cast in the role of adversary, in national security cases. They may even be the intended victims of subversive action. Since spies and saboteurs are as entitled to the protection of the Fourth Amendment as suspected gamblers

like petitioner, I cannot agree that where spies and saboteurs are involved adequate protection of Fourth Amendment rights is assured when the President and Attorney General assume both the position of adversary-and-prosecutor and disinterested, neutral magistrate.

. . .

MR. JUSTICE HARLAN, concurring.

. . .

MR. JUSTICE WHITE, concurring.

I agree that the official surveillance of petitioner's telephone conversations in a public booth must be subjected to the test of reasonableness under the Fourth Amendment and that on the record now before us the particular surveillance undertaken was unreasonable absent a warrant properly authorizing it. This application of the Fourth Amendment need not interfere with legitimate needs of law enforcement.

In joining the Court's opinion, I note the Court's acknowledgment that there are circumstances in which it is reasonable to search without a warrant. In this connection, in footnote 23 the Court points out that today's decision does not reach national security cases. Wiretapping to protect the security of the Nation has been authorized by successive Presidents. The present Administration would apparently save national security cases from restrictions against wiretapping. See *Berger* v. *New York*, 388 U.S. 41, 112–118 (1967) (WHITE, J., dissenting). We should not require the warrant procedure and the magistrate's judgment if the President of the United States or his chief legal officer, the Attorney General, has considered the requirements of national security and authorized electronic surveillance as reasonable.

MR. JUSTICE BLACK, dissenting.

If I could agree with the Court that eavesdropping carried on by electronic means (equivalent to wiretapping) constitutes a "search" or "seizure," I would be happy to join the Court's opinion. . . .

My basic objection is twofold: (1) I do not believe that the words of the Amendment will bear the meaning given them by today's decision, and

(2) I do not believe that it is the proper role of this Court to rewrite the Amendment in order "to bring it into harmony with the times" and thus reach a result that many people believe to be desirable.

. . .

Tapping telephone wires, of course, was an unknown possibility at the time the Fourth Amendment was adopted. But eavesdropping (and wiretapping is nothing more than eavesdropping by telephone) was, as even the majority opinion in *Berger, supra,* recognized, "an ancient practice which at common law was condemned as a nuisance. 4 Blackstone, Commentaries 168. In those days the eavesdropper listened by naked ear under the eaves of houses or their windows, or beyond their walls seeking out private discourse." 388 U.S., at 45. There can be no doubt that the Framers were aware of this practice, and if they had desired to outlaw or restrict the use of evidence obtained by eavesdropping, I believe that they would have used the appropriate language to do so in the Fourth Amendment. They certainly would not have left such a task to the ingenuity of language-stretching judges. No one, it seems to me, can read the debates on the Bill of Rights without reaching the conclusion that its Framers and critics well knew the meaning of the words they used, what they would be understood to mean by others, their scope and their limitations. Under these circumstances it strikes me as a charge against their scholarship, their common sense and their candor to give to the Fourth Amendment's language the eavesdropping meaning the Court imputes to it today.

. . .

Weeks v. United States

232 U.S. 383 (1914)

Without a search warrant, police entered the home of Fremont Weeks and took certain papers used to convict him of transporting lottery tickets through the mails. Weeks filed a petition for the return of his private papers and possessions. The Supreme Court confronted the question of whether illegal and unauthorized actions by the government could produce evidence admissible in a criminal prosecution. A federal district court required the return to Weeks of property that was not pertinent to the charge against him, but permitted the District Attorney to retain papers to be used in evidence in the trial.

MR. JUSTICE DAY delivered the opinion of the court.

. . .

The defendant was arrested by a police officer, so far as the record shows, without warrant, at the Union Station in Kansas City, Missouri, where he was employed by an express company. Other police officers had gone to the house of the defendant and being told by a neighbor where the key was kept, found it and entered the house. They searched the defendant's room and took possession of various papers and articles found there, which were afterwards turned over to the United States Marshal. Later in the same day police officers returned with the Marshal, who thought he might find additional evidence, and, being admitted by someone in the house, probably a boarder, in response to a rap, the Marshal searched the defendant's room and carried away certain letters and envelopes found in the drawer of a chiffonier. Neither the marshal nor the police officers had a search warrant.

. . .

Upon the introduction of such papers during the trial, the defendant objected on the ground that the papers had been obtained without a search warrant and by breaking open his home, in violation of the Fourth and Fifth Amendments to the Constitution of the United States, which objection was overruled by the court. Among the papers retained and put in evidence were a number of lottery tickets and statements with reference to the lottery, taken at the first visit of the police to the defendant's room, and a number of letters written to the defendant in respect to the lottery, taken by the Marshal upon his search of defendant's room.

The defendant assigns error, among other things, in the court's refusal to grant his petition for the return of his property and in permitting the papers to be used at the trial.

. . .

The history of *[the Fourth]* Amendment is given with particularity in the opinion of Mr. Justice Bradley, speaking for the court in *Boyd* v. *United States* 116 U. S. 616. As was there shown, it took its origin in the determination of the framers of the Amendments to the Federal Constitution to provide for that instrument a Bill of Rights, securing to the American people, among other things, those safeguards which had grown up in England to protect the people from unreasonable searches and seizures, such as were permitted under the general warrants issued under authority of the Government by which there had been invasions of the home and privacy of the citizens and the seizure of their private papers in support of charges, real or imaginary, made against them. Such practices had also received sanction under warrants and seizures under the so-called writs of assistance, issued in the American colonies. See 2 Watson on the Constitution, 1414 *et seq.* Resistance to these practices had established the principle which was enacted into the fundamental law in the Fourth Amendment, that a man's house was his castle and not to be invaded by any general authority to search and seize his goods and papers. Judge Cooley, in his Constitutional Limitations, pp. 425, 426, in treating of this feature of our Constitution, said: "The maxim that 'every man's house is his castle,' is made a part of our constitutional law in the clauses prohibiting unreasonable searches and seizures, and has always been looked upon as of high value to the citizen." "According-

ly," says Lieber in his work on Civil Liberty and Self-Government, 62, in speaking of the English law in this respect, "no man's house can be forcibly opened, or he or his goods be carried away after it has thus been forced, except in cases of felony, and then the sheriff must be furnished with a warrant, and take great care lest he commit a trespass. This principle is jealously insisted upon." In *Ex parte Jackson*, 96 U. S. 727, 733, this court recognized the principle of protection as applicable to letters and sealed packages in the mail, and held that consistently with this guaranty of the right of the people to be secure in their papers against unreasonable searches and seizures such matter could only be opened and examined upon warrants issued on oath or affirmation particularly describing the thing to be seized, "as is required when papers are subjected to search in one's own household."

In the *Boyd Case, supra,* after citing Lord Camden's judgment in *Entick* v. *Carrington*, 19 Howell's State Trials, 1029, Mr. Justice Bradley said (630):

"The principles laid down in this opinion affect the very essence of constitutional liberty and security. They reach farther than the concrete form of the case then before the court, with its adventitious circumstances; they apply to all invasions on the part of the government and its employés of the sanctity of a man's home and the privacies of life. It is not the breaking of his doors, and the rummaging of his drawers, that constitutes the essence of the offence; but it is the invasion of his indefeasible right of personal security, personal liberty and private property, where that right has never been forfeited by his conviction of some public offence, — it is the invasion of this sacred right which underlies and constitutes the essence of Lord Camden's judgment."

. . .

The effect of the Fourth Amendment is to put the courts of the United States and Federal officials, in the exercise of their power and authority, under limitations and restraints as to the exercise of such power and authority, and to forever secure the people, their persons, houses, papers and effects against all unreasonable searches and seizures under the guise of law. This protection reaches all alike, whether accused of crime or not, and the duty of giving to it force and effect is obligatory upon all entrusted under our Federal system with the enforcement of the laws. The tendency of those who execute the criminal laws of the country to obtain conviction by means of unlawful seizures and enforced confessions, the latter often obtained after subjecting accused persons to unwarranted practices destructive of rights secured by the Federal Constitution, should find no sanction in the judgments of the courts which are charged at all times with the support of the Constitution and to which people of all conditions have a right to appeal for the maintenance of such fundamental rights.

What then is the present case? Before answering that inquiry specifically, it may be well by a process of exclusion to state what it is not. It is not an assertion of the right on the part of the Government, always recognized under English and American law, to search the person of the accused when legally arrested to discover and seize the fruits or evidences of crime. This right has been uniformly maintained in many cases. 1 Bishop on Criminal Procedure, § 211; Wharton, Crim. Plead. and Practice, 8th ed., § 60; *Dillon* v. *O'Brien and Davis,* 16 Cox C. C. 245. Nor is it the case of testimony offered at a trial where the court is asked to stop and consider the illegal means by which proofs, otherwise competent, were obtained—of which we shall have occasion to treat later in this opinion. Nor is it the case of burglar's tools or other proofs of guilt found upon his arrest within the control of the accused.

The case in the aspect in which we are dealing with it involves the right of the court in a criminal prosecution to retain for the purposes of evidence the letters and correspondence of the accused, seized in his house in his absence and without his authority, by a United States Marshal holding no warrant for his arrest and none for the search of his premises. The accused, without awaiting his trial, made timely application to the court for an order for the return of these letters, as well as other property. This application was denied, the letters retained and put in evidence, after a further application at the beginning of the trial, both applications asserting the rights of the accused under the Fourth and Fifth Amendments to the Constitution. If letters and private documents can thus be seized and held and used in evidence against a citizen accused of an offense, the protection of the Fourth Amendment declaring his right to be secure against such searches and seizures is of no value, and, so far as those thus placed are concerned, might as well be stricken from the Constitution. The efforts of the courts and their officials to bring the guilty to punishment, praiseworthy as they are, are not to be aided by the sacrifice of those great principles established by years of endeavor and suffering which have resulted in their embodiment in the fundamental law of the land. The United States Marshal could only have invaded the house of the accused when armed with a warrant issued as required by the Constitution, upon sworn information and describing with reasonable particularity the thing for which the search was to be made. Instead, he acted without sanction of law, doubtless prompted by the desire to bring further proof to the aid of the Government, and under color of his office undertook to make a seizure of private papers in direct violation of the constitutional prohibition against such action. Under such circumstances, without sworn information and particular description, not even an order of court would have justified such procedure, much less was it within the authority of the United States Marshal to thus invade the house and privacy of the accused.

. . .

We therefore reach the conclusion that the letters in question were taken from the house of the accused by an official of the United States acting under color of his office in direct violation of the constitutional rights of the defendant; that having made a seasonable application for their return, which was heard and passed upon by the court, there was involved in the order refusing the application a denial of the constitutional rights of the accused, and that the court should have restored these letters to the accused. In holding them and permitting their use upon the trial, we think prejudicial error was committed. As to the papers and property seized by the policemen, it does not appear that they acted under any claim of Federal authority such as would make the Amendment applicable to such unauthorized seizures. The record shows that what they did by way of arrest and search and seizure was done before the finding of the indictment in the Federal court, under what supposed right or authority does not appear. What remedies the defendant may have against them we need not inquire, as the Fourth Amendment is not directed to individual misconduct of such officials. Its limitations reach the Federal Government and its agencies. *Boyd Case*, 116 U. S., *supra*, and see *Twining* v. *New Jersey*, 211 U. S. 78.

It results that the judgment of the court below must be reversed, and the case remanded for further proceedings in accordance with this opinion.

Reversed.

Mapp v. Ohio
367 U.S. 643 (1961)

Dollree Mapp was convicted for possessing obscene materials. Cleveland police had arrived at her home looking for a bombing suspect. Without a search warrant, they forced their way in and proceeded to search the entire house, including dresser drawers, suitcases, photo albums, personal papers, and a trunk in the basement. Although the Supreme Court of Ohio admitted that the materials had been "unlawfully seized during an unlawful search," it upheld her conviction.

MR. JUSTICE CLARK delivered the opinion of the Court.

. . .

On May 23, 1957, three Cleveland police officers arrived at appellant's residence in that city pursuant to information that "a person [was] hiding out in the home, who was wanted for questioning in connection with a recent bombing, and that there was a large amount of policy paraphernalia being hidden in the home." Miss Mapp and her daughter by a former marriage lived on the top floor of the two-family dwelling. Upon their arrival at that house, the officers knocked on the door and demanded entrance but appellant, after telephoning her attorney, refused to admit them without a search warrant. They advised their headquarters of the situation and undertook a surveillance of the house.

The officers again sought entrance some three hours later when four or more additional officers arrived on the scene. When Miss Mapp did not come to the door immediately, at least one of the several doors to the house was forcibly opened and the policemen gained admittance. Meanwhile Miss Mapp's attorney arrived, but the officers, having secured their own entry, and continuing in their defiance of the law, would permit him neither to see Miss Mapp nor to enter the house. It appears that Miss Mapp was halfway down the stairs from the upper floor to the front door when the officers, in this highhanded manner, broke into the hall. She demanded to see the search warrant. A paper, claimed to be a warrant, was held up by one of the officers. She grabbed the "warrant" and placed it in her bosom. A struggle ensued in which the officers recovered the piece of paper and as a result of which they handcuffed appellant because she had been "belligerent" in resisting their official rescue of the "warrant" from her person. Running roughshod over appellant, a policeman "grabbed" her, "twisted [her] hand," and she "yelled [and] pleaded with him" because "it was hurting." Appellant, in handcuffs, was then forcibly taken upstairs to her bedroom where the officers searched a dresser, a chest of drawers, a closet and some suitcases. They also looked into a photo album and through personal papers belonging to the appellant. The search spread to the rest of the second floor including the child's bedroom, the living room, the kitchen and a dinette. The basement of the building and a trunk found therein were also searched. The obscene materials for possession of which she was ultimately convicted were discovered in the course of that widespread search.

At the trial no search warrant was produced by the prosecution, nor was the failure to produce one explained or accounted for. At best, "There is, in the record, considerable doubt as to whether there ever was any warrant for the search of defendant's home." 170 Ohio St., at 430, 166 N. E. 2d, at 389. The Ohio Supreme Court believed a "reasonable argument" could be made that the conviction should be reversed "because the 'methods' employed to obtain the [evidence] . . . were such as to 'offend "a sense of justice," ' " but the court found determinative the fact that the evidence had not been taken "from defendant's person by the use of brutal or offensive physical force against defendant." 170 Ohio St., at 431, 166 N. E. 2d, at 389–390.

The State says that even if the search were made without authority, or otherwise unreasonably, it is not prevented from using the unconstitutionally seized evidence at trial, citing *Wolf* v. *Colorado,* 338 U. S. 25 (1949), in which this Court did indeed hold "that in a prosecution in a State court for a State crime the Fourteenth Amendment does not forbid the admission of evidence obtained by an unreasonable search and seizure." At p. 33. On this appeal, of which we have noted probable jurisdiction, 364 U. S. 868, it is urged once again that we review that holding.

I.

Seventy-five years ago, in *Boyd* v. *United States,* 116 U. S. 616, 630 (1886), considering the Fourth and Fifth Amendments as running "almost into each other" on the facts before it, this Court held that the doctrines of those Amendments

"apply to all invasions on the part of the government and its employés of the sanctity of a man's home and the privacies of life. It is not the breaking of his doors, and the rummaging of his drawers, that constitutes the essence of the offence; but it is the invasion of his indefeasible right of personal security, personal liberty and private

property . . . . Breaking into a house and opening boxes and drawers are circumstances of aggravation; but any forcible and compulsory extortion of a man's own testimony or of his private papers to be used as evidence to convict him of crime or to forfeit his goods, is within the condemnation . . . [of those Amendments]."

The Court noted that

"constitutional provisions for the security of person and property should be liberally construed. . . . It is the duty of courts to be watchful for the constitutional rights of the citizen, and against any stealthy encroachments thereon." At p. 635.

. . .

II.

In 1949, 35 years after *Weeks* was announced, this Court, in *Wolf* v. *Colorado, supra,* again for the first time, discussed the effect of the Fourth Amendment upon the States through the operation of the Due Process Clause of the Fourteenth Amendment. It said:

"[W]e have no hesitation in saying that were a State affirmatively to sanction such police incursion into privacy it would run counter to the guaranty of the Fourteenth Amendment." At p. 28.

Nevertheless, after declaring that the "security of one's privacy against arbitrary intrusion by the police" is "implicit in 'the concept of ordered liberty' and as such enforceable against the States through the Due Process Clause," cf. *Palko* v. *Connecticut,* 302 U. S. 319 (1937), and announcing that it "stoutly adhere[d]" to the *Weeks* decision, the Court decided that the *Weeks* exclusionary rule would not then be imposed upon the States as "an essential ingredient of the right." 338 U. S., at 27–29. The Court's reasons for not considering essential to the right to privacy, as a curb imposed upon the States by the Due Process Clause, that which decades before had been posited as part and parcel of the Fourth Amendment's limitation upon federal encroachment of individual privacy, were bottomed on factual considerations.

While they are not basically relevant to a decision that the exclusionary rule is an essential ingredient of the Fourth Amendment as the right it embodies is vouchsafed against the States by the Due Process Clause, we will consider the current validity of the factual grounds upon which *Wolf* was based.

The Court in *Wolf* first stated that "[t]he contrariety of views of the States" on the adoption of the exclusionary rule of *Weeks* was "particularly impressive" (at p. 29); and, in this connection, that it could not "brush aside the experience of States which deem the incidence of such conduct by the police too slight to call for a deterrent remedy . . . by overriding the [States'] relevant rules of evidence." At pp. 31–32. While in 1949, prior to the *Wolf* case, almost two-thirds of the States were opposed to the use of the exclusionary rule, now, despite the *Wolf* case, more than half of those since passing upon it, by their own legislative or judicial decision, have wholly or partly adopted or adhered to the *Weeks* rule. See *Elkins* v. *United States*, 364 U. S. 206, Appendix, pp. 224–232 (1960). Significantly, among those now following the rule is California, which, according to its highest court, was "compelled to reach that conclusion because other remedies have completely failed to secure compliance with the constitutional provisions. . . ." *People* v. *Cahan*, 44 Cal. 2d 434, 445, 282 P. 2d 905, 911 (1955). In connection with this California case, we note that the second basis elaborated in *Wolf* in support of its failure to enforce the exclusionary doctrine against the States was that "other means of protection" have been afforded "the right to privacy." 338 U.S., at 30. The experience of California that such other remedies have been worthless and futile is buttressed by the experience of other States. The obvious futility of relegating the Fourth Amendment to the protection of other remedies has, moreover, been recognized by this Court since *Wolf.* See *Irvine* v. *California*, 347 U. S. 128, 137 (1954).

Likewise, time has set its face against what *Wolf* called the "weighty testimony" of *People* v. *Defore*, 242 N. Y. 13, 150 N. E. 585 (1926). There Justice (then Judge) Cardozo, rejecting adoption of the *Weeks* exclusionary rule in New York, had said that "[t]he Federal rule as it stands is either too strict or too lax." 242 N. Y., at 22, 150 N. E., at 588. However, the force of that reasoning has been largely vitiated by later decisions of this Court. These include the recent discarding of the "silver platter" doctrine which allowed federal judicial use of evidence seized in violation of the Constitution by state agents, *Elkins* v. *United States, supra;* the relaxation of the formerly strict requirements as to standing to challenge the use of evidence thus seized, so that now the procedure of exclusion, "ultimately referable to constitutional safeguards," is available to anyone even "legitimately on [the] premises" unlawfully searched, *Jones* v. *United States,* 362 U.S. 257, 266–267 (1960); and, finally, the formulation of a method to prevent state use of evidence unconstitutionally seized by federal agents, *Rea* v. *United States,* 350 U. S. 214 (1956). Because there can be no fixed formula, we are admittedly met with "recurring questions of the reasonableness of searches," but less is not to be expected when dealing with a Constitution, and, at any rate, "reasonableness is in the first instance for the [trial court] . . . to determine." *United States* v. *Rabinowitz,* 339 U.S. 56, 63 (1950).

It, therefore, plainly appears that the factual considerations supporting the failure of the *Wolf* Court to include the *Weeks* exclusionary rule when it recognized the enforceability of the right to privacy against the States in 1949, while not basically relevant to the constitutional consideration, could not, in any analysis, now be deemed controlling.

. . .

IV.

Since the Fourth Amendment's right of privacy has been declared enforceable against the States through the Due Process Clause of the Fourteenth, it is enforceable against them by the same sanction of exclusion as is used against the Federal Government. Were it otherwise, then just as without the *Weeks* rule the assurance against unreasonable federal searches and seizures would be "a form of words," valueless and undeserving of mention in a perpetual charter of inestimable human liberties, so too, without that rule the freedom from state invasions of privacy would be so ephemeral and so neatly severed from its conceptual nexus with the freedom from all brutish means of coercing evidence as not to merit this Court's high regard as a freedom "implicit in the concept of ordered liberty."

. . .

V.

Moreover, our holding that the exclusionary rule is an essential part of both the Fourth and Fourteenth Amendments is not only the logical dictate of prior cases, but it also makes very good sense. There is no war between the Constitution and common sense. Presently, a federal prosecutor may make no use of evidence illegally seized, but a State's attorney across the street may, although he supposedly is operating under the enforceable prohibitions of the same Amendment. Thus the State, by admitting evidence unlawfully seized, serves to encourage disobedience to the Federal Constitution which it is bound to uphold. Moreover, as was said in *Elkins*, "[t]he very essence of a healthy federalism depends upon the avoidance of needless conflict between state and federal courts." 364 U.S., at 221. Such a conflict, hereafter needless, arose this very Term, in *Wilson* v. *Schnettler*, 365 U. S. 381 (1961), in which, and in spite of the promise made by *Rea*, we gave full recognition to our practice in this regard by refusing to restrain a federal officer from testifying in a state court as to evidence unconstitutionally seized by him in the performance of his duties. Yet the double standard recognized until today hardly put such a thesis into practice. In nonexclusionary States, federal officers, being human, were by it invited to and did, as our cases indicate, step across the street to the State's attorney with their unconstitutionally seized evidence. Prosecution on the basis of that evidence was then had in a state court in utter disregard of the enforceable Fourth Amendment. If the fruits of an unconstitutional search had been inadmissible in both state and federal courts, this inducement to evasion would have been sooner eliminated. There would be no need to reconcile such cases as *Rea* and *Schnettler*, each pointing up the hazardous uncertainties of our heretofore ambivalent approach.

Federal-state cooperation in the solution of crime under constitutional standards will be promoted, if only by recognition of their now mutual obligation to respect the same fundamental criteria in their approaches. "However much in a particular case insistence upon such rules may appear as a technicality that inures to the benefit of a guilty person, the history of the criminal law proves that tolerance of shortcut methods in law enforcement impairs its enduring effectiveness." *Miller* v. *United States*, 357 U. S. 301, 313 (1958). Denying shortcuts to only one of two cooperating law enforcement agencies tends naturally to breed legitimate suspicion of "working arrangements" whose results are equally tainted. *Byars* v. *United States*, 273 U. S. 28 (1927); *Lustig* v. *United States*, 338 U. S. 74 (1949).

There are those who say, as did Justice (then Judge) Cardozo, that under our constitutional exclusionary doctrine "[t]he criminal is to go free because the constable has blundered." *People* v. *Defore*, 242 N. Y., at 21, 150 N. E., at 587. In some cases this will undoubtedly be the result. But, as was said in *Elkins*, "there is another consideration —the imperative of judicial integrity." 364 U. S., at 222. The criminal goes free, if he must, but it is the law that sets him free. Nothing can destroy a government more quickly than its failure to observe its own laws, or worse, its disregard of the charter of its own existence. As Mr. Justice Brandeis, dissenting, said in *Olmstead* v. *United States*, 277 U. S. 438, 485 (1928): "Our Government is the potent, the omnipresent teacher. For good or for ill, it teaches the whole people by its example. . . . If the Government becomes a lawbreaker, it breeds contempt for law; it invites every man to become a law unto himself; it invites anarchy." Nor can it lightly be assumed that, as a practical matter, adoption of the exclusionary rule fetters law enforcement. Only last year this Court expressly considered that contention and found that "pragmatic evidence of a sort" to the contrary was not wanting. *Elkins* v. *United States*, *supra*, at 218. The Court noted that

"The federal courts themselves have operated under the exclusionary rule of *Weeks* for almost half a century; yet it has not been suggested either that the Federal Bureau of Investigation has thereby been rendered ineffective, or that the administration of criminal justice in the federal courts has thereby been disrupted. Moreover, the experience of the states is impressive. . . . The movement towards the rule of exclusion has been halting but seemingly inexorable." *Id.*, at 218–219.

The ignoble shortcut to conviction left open to the State tends to destroy the entire system of constitutional restraints on which the liberties of the people rest. Having once recognized that the right to privacy embodied in the Fourth Amendment is enforceable against the States, and that the right to be secure against rude invasions of privacy by state officers is, therefore, constitutional in origin, we can no longer permit that right to remain an empty promise. Because it is enforceable in the same manner and to like effect as other basic rights secured by the Due Process Clause, we can no longer permit it to be revocable at the whim of any police officer who, in the name of law enforcement itself, chooses to suspend its enjoyment. Our decision, founded on reason and truth, gives to the individual no more than that which the Constitution guarantees him, to the police officer no less than that to which honest law enforcement is entitled, and, to the courts, that judicial integrity so necessary in the true administration of justice.

The judgment of the Supreme Court of Ohio is reversed and the cause remanded for further proceedings not inconsistent with this opinion.

Reversed and remanded.

MR. JUSTICE BLACK, concurring.

. . .

MR. JUSTICE DOUGLAS, concurring.

. . .

Memorandum of MR. JUSTICE STEWART.

Agreeing fully with Part I of MR. JUSTICE HARLAN'S dissenting opinion, I express no view as to the merits of the constitutional issue which the Court today decides. I would, however, reverse the judgment in this case, because I am persuaded that the provision of § 2905.34 of the Ohio Revised Code, upon which the petitioner's conviction was based, is, in the words of MR. JUSTICE HARLAN, not "consistent with the rights of free thought and expression assured against state action by the Fourteenth Amendment."

MR. JUSTICE HARLAN, whom MR. JUSTICE FRANKFURTER and MR. JUSTICE WHITTAKER join, dissenting.

In overruling the *Wolf* case the Court, in my opinion, has forgotten the sense of judicial restraint which, with due regard for *stare decisis*, is one element that should enter into deciding

whether a past decision of this Court should be overruled. Apart from that I also believe that the *Wolf* rule represents sounder Constitutional doctrine than the new rule which now replaces it.

. . .

The preservation of a proper balance between state and federal responsibility in the administration of criminal justice demands patience on the part of those who might like to see things move faster among the States in this respect. Problems of criminal law enforcement vary widely from State to State. One State, in considering the totality of its legal picture, may conclude that the need for embracing the *Weeks* rule is pressing because other remedies are unavailable or inadequate to secure compliance with the substantive Constitutional principle involved. Another, though equally solicitous of Constitutional rights, may choose to pursue one purpose at a time, allowing all evidence relevant to guilt to be brought into a criminal trial, and dealing with Constitutional infractions by other means. Still another may consider the exclusionary rule too rough-and-ready a remedy, in that it reaches only unconstitutional intrusions which eventuate in criminal prosecution of the victims. Further, a State after experimenting with the *Weeks* rule for a time may, because of unsatisfactory experience with it, decide to revert to a non-exclusionary rule. And so on. From the standpoint of Constitutional permissibility in pointing a State in one direction or another, I do not see at all why "time has set its face against" the considerations which led Mr. Justice Cardozo, then chief judge of the New York Court of Appeals, to reject for New York in *People v. Defore*, 242 N. Y. 13, 150 N. E. 585, the *Weeks* exclusionary rule. For us the question remains, as it has always been, one of state power, not one of passing judgment on the wisdom of one state course or another. In my view this Court should continue to forbear from fettering the States with an adamant rule which may embarrass them in coping with their own peculiar problems in criminal law enforcement.

. . .

In conclusion, it should be noted that the majority opinion in this case is in fact an opinion only for the *judgment* overruling *Wolf*, and not for the basic rationale by which four members of the majority have reached that result. For my Brother BLACK is unwilling to subscribe to their view that the *Weeks* exclusionary rule derives from the Fourth Amendment itself (see *ante*, p. 661), but joins the majority opinion on the premise that its end result can be achieved by bringing the Fifth Amendment to the aid of the Fourth (see *ante*, pp. 662–665). *[In a footnote, Justice Harlan stated: "My Brother Stewart concurs in the Court's judgment on grounds which have nothing to do with Wolf."]*

. . .

Stone v. Powell

428 U.S. 465 (1976)

Lloyd Powell was convicted of criminal offenses in a state court. He claimed that evidence used to convict him had been obtained by an illegal search and seizure. He sought relief in a federal district court by filing a petition for a writ of federal habeas corpus. This case examines the following question: Should a federal court consider a claim that evidence has been illegally obtained and introduced when the convicted person already litigated that claim in the state courts? Also at issue is the scope of the exclusionary rule.

MR. JUSTICE POWELL delivered the opinion of the Court.

Respondents in these cases were convicted of criminal offenses in state courts, and their convictions were affirmed on appeal. The prosecution in each case relied upon evidence obtained by searches.and seizures alleged by respondents to have been unlawful. Each respondent subsequently sought relief in a Federal District Court by filing a petition for a writ of federal habeas corpus under 28 U. S. C. § 2254. The question presented is whether a federal court should consider, in ruling on a petition for habeas corpus relief filed by a state prisoner, a claim that evidence obtained by an unconstitutional search or seizure was introduced at his trial, when he has previously been afforded an opportunity for full and fair litigation of his claim in the state courts. The issue is of considerable importance to the administration of criminal justice.

I

We summarize first the relevant facts and procedural history of these cases.

A

Respondent Lloyd Powell was convicted of murder in June 1968 after trial in a California state court. At about midnight on February 17, 1968, he and three companions entered the Bonanza Liquor Store in San Bernardino, Cal., where Powell became involved in an altercation with Gerald Parsons, the store manager, over the theft of a bottle of wine. In the scuffling that followed Powell shot and killed Parsons' wife. Ten hours later an officer of the Henderson, Nev., Police Department arrested Powell for violation of the Henderson vagrancy ordinance, and in the search incident to the arrest discovered a .38-caliber revolver with six expended cartridges in the cylinder.

Powell was extradited to California and convicted of second-degree murder in the Superior Court of San Bernardino County. Parsons and Powell's accomplices at the liquor store testified against him. A criminologist testified that the revolver found on Powell was the gun that killed Parsons' wife. The trial court rejected Powell's contention that testimony by the Henderson police officer as to the search and the discovery of the revolver should have been excluded because the vagrancy ordinance was unconstitutional. In October 1969, the conviction was affirmed by a California District Court of Appeal. Although the issue was duly presented, that court found it unnecessary to pass upon the legality of the arrest and search because it concluded that the error, if any, in admitting the testimony of the Henderson officer was harmless beyond a reasonable doubt under *Chapman* v. *California,* 386 U. S. 18 (1967). The Supreme Court of California denied Powell's petition for habeas corpus relief.

In August 1971 Powell filed an amended petition for a writ of federal habeas corpus under 28 U. S. C. § 2254 in the United States District Court for the Northern District of California, contending that the testimony concerning the .38-caliber revolver should have been excluded as the fruit of an illegal search. He argued that his arrest had been unlawful because the Henderson vagrancy ordinance was unconstitutionally vague, and that the arresting officer lacked probable cause to believe that he was violating it. The District Court concluded that the arresting officer had probable cause and held that even if the vagrancy ordinance was unconstitutional, the deterrent purpose of the exclusionary rule does not require that it be applied to bar admission of the fruits of a search incident to an otherwise valid arrest. In the alternative, that court agreed with the California District Court of Appeal that the admission of the evidence concerning Powell's arrest, if error, was harmless beyond a reasonable doubt.

In December 1974, the Court of Appeals for the Ninth Circuit reversed. 507 F. 2d 93. The court concluded that the vagrancy ordinance was unconstitutionally vague, that Powell's arrest was therefore illegal, and that although exclusion of the evidence would serve no deterrent purpose with regard to police officers who were enforcing statutes in good faith, exclusion would serve the public interest by deterring legislators from enacting unconstitutional statutes. *Id.,* at 98. After an independent review of the evidence the court concluded that the admission of the evidence was not harmless error since it supported the testimony of Parsons and Powell's accomplices. *Id.,* at 99.

. . .

II

The authority of federal courts to issue the writ of habeas corpus *ad subjiciendum* was included in the first grant of federal-court jurisdiction, made by the Judiciary Act of 1789, c. 20, § 14, 1 Stat. 81, with the limitation that the writ extend only to prisoners held in custody by the United States. The original statutory authorization did not define the substantive reach of the writ. It merely stated that the courts of the United States "shall have power to issue writs of . . . *habeas corpus.* . . ." *Ibid.* The courts defined the scope of the writ in accordance with the common law and limited it to an inquiry as to the jurisdiction of the sentencing tribunal. See, *e. g., Ex parte Watkins,* 3 Pet. 193 (1830) (Marshall, C. J.).

In 1867 the writ was extended to state prisoners. Act of Feb. 5, 1867, c. 28, § 1, 14 Stat. 385. Under the 1867 Act federal courts were authorized to give relief in "all cases where any person may be restrained of his or her liberty in violation of the constitution, or of any treaty or law of the United States. . . ." But the limitation of federal habeas corpus jurisdiction to consideration of the jurisdiction of the sentencing court persisted.

. . .

The discussion in *Kaufman [v.* United States, *394 U. S. 217 (1969)]* of the scope of federal habeas corpus rests on the view that the effectuation of the Fourth Amendment, as applied to the States through the Fourteenth Amendment, requires the granting of habeas corpus relief when a prisoner has been convicted in state court on the basis of evidence obtained in an illegal search or seizure since those Amendments were held in *Mapp* v. *Ohio,* 367 U. S. 643 (1961), to require exclusion of such evidence at trial and reversal of conviction upon direct review. Until these cases we have not had occasion fully to consider the validity of this view. See, *e. g., Schneckloth* v. *Bustamonte, supra,* at 249 n. 38; *Cardwell* v. *Lewis, supra,* at 596, and n. 12. Upon examination, we conclude, in light of the nature and purpose of the Fourth Amendment exclusionary rule, that this view is unjustified. We hold, therefore, that where the State has provided an opportunity for full and fair litigation of a Fourth Amendment claim, the Constitution does not require that a state prisoner be granted federal habeas corpus relief on the ground that evidence obtained in an unconstitutional search or seizure was introduced at his trial.

III

. . .

Decisions prior to *Mapp* advanced two principal reasons for application of the rule in federal trials. The Court in *Elkins*, for example, in the context of its special supervisory role over the lower federal courts, referred to the "imperative of judicial integrity," suggesting that exclusion of illegally seized evidence prevents contamination of the judicial process. 364 U. S., at 222.

. . . While courts, of course, must ever be concerned with preserving the integrity of the judicial process, this concern has limited force as a justification for the exclusion of highly probative evidence. The force of this justification becomes minimal where federal habeas corpus relief is sought by a prisoner who previously has been afforded the opportunity for full and fair consideration of his search-and-seizure claim at trial and on direct review.

The primary justification for the exclusionary rule then is the deterrence of police conduct that violates Fourth Amendment rights. . . .

IV

We turn now to the specific question presented by these cases. Respondents allege violations of Fourth Amendment rights guaranteed them through the Fourteenth Amendment. The question is whether state prisoners—who have been afforded the opportunity for full and fair consideration of their reliance upon the exclusionary rule with respect to seized evidence by the state courts at trial and on direct review—may invoke their claim again on federal habeas corpus review. The answer is to be found by weighing the utility of the exclusionary rule against the costs of extending it to collateral review of Fourth Amendment claims.

The costs of applying the exclusionary rule even at trial and on direct review are well known: the focus of the trial, and the attention of the participants therein, are diverted from the ultimate question of guilt or innocence that should be the central concern in a criminal proceeding. Moreover, the physical evidence sought to be excluded is typically reliable and often the most probative information bearing on the guilt or innocence of the defendant. As Mr. Justice Black emphasized in his dissent in *Kaufman:*

"A claim of illegal search and seizure under the Fourth Amendment is crucially different from many other constitutional rights; ordinarily the evidence seized can in no way have been rendered untrustworthy by the means of its seizure and indeed often this evidence alone establishes beyond virtually any shadow of a doubt that the defendant is guilty." 394 U. S., at 237.

Application of the rule thus deflects the truthfinding process and often frees the guilty. The disparity in particular cases between the error committed by the police officer and the windfall afforded a guilty defendant by application of the rule is contrary to the idea of proportionality that is essential to the concept of justice. Thus, although the rule is thought to deter unlawful police activity in part through the nurturing of respect for Fourth Amendment values, if applied indiscriminately it may well have the opposite effect of generating disrespect for the law and administration of justice. These long-recognized costs of the rule persist when a criminal conviction is sought to be overturned on collateral review on the ground that a search-and-seizure claim was erroneously rejected by two or more tiers of state courts.

Evidence obtained by police officers in violation of the Fourth Amendment is excluded at trial in the hope that the frequency of future violations will decrease. Despite the absence of supportive empirical evidence, we have assumed that the immediate effect of exclusion will be to discourage law enforcement officials from violating the Fourth Amendment by removing the incentive to disregard it. More importantly, over the long term, this demonstration that our society attaches serious consequences to violation of constitutional rights is thought to encourage those who formulate law enforcement policies, and the officers who implement them, to incorporate Fourth Amendment ideals into their value system.

We adhere to the view that these considerations support the implementation of the exclusionary rule at trial and its enforcement on direct appeal of state-court convictions. But the additional contribution, if any, of the consideration of search-and-seizure claims of state prisoners on collateral review is small in relation to the costs. To be sure, each case in which such claim is considered may add marginally to an awareness of the values protected by the Fourth Amendment. There is no reason to believe, however, that the overall educative effect of the exclusionary rule would be appreciably diminished if search-and-seizure claims could not be raised in federal habeas corpus review of state convictions. Nor is there reason to assume that any specific disincentive already created by the risk of exclusion of evidence at trial or the reversal of convictions on direct review would be enhanced if there were the further risk that a conviction obtained in state court and affirmed on direct review might be overturned in collateral proceedings often occurring years after the incarceration of the defendant. The view that the deterrence of Fourth Amendment violations would be furthered rests on the dubious assumption that law enforcement authorities would fear that federal habeas review might reveal flaws in a search or seizure that went undetected at trial and on appeal. Even if one rationally could assume that some additional incremental deterrent effect would be present in isolated cases, the resulting advance of the legitimate goal of furthering Fourth Amendment rights would be outweighed by the acknowledged costs to other values vital to a rational system of criminal justice.

In sum, we conclude that where the State has provided an opportunity for full and fair litigation of a Fourth Amendment claim, a state prisoner may not be granted federal habeas corpus relief on the ground that evidence obtained in an unconstitutional search or seizure was introduced at his trial. In this context the contribution of the exclusionary rule, if any, to the effectuation of the Fourth Amendment is minimal and the substantial societal costs of application of the rule persist with special force.

Accordingly, the judgments of the Courts of Appeals are

Reversed.

MR. CHIEF JUSTICE BURGER, concurring.

I concur in the Court's opinion. By way of dictum, and somewhat hesitantly, the Court notes that the holding in this case leaves undisturbed the exclusionary rule as applied to criminal trials. For reasons stated in my dissent in *Bivens* v. *Six Unknown Fed. Narcotics Agents*, 403 U. S. 388, 411 (1971), it seems clear to me that the exclusionary rule has been operative long enough to demonstrate its flaws. The time has come to modify its reach, even if it is retained for a small and limited category of cases.

Over the years, the strains imposed by reality, in terms of the costs to society and the bizarre miscarriages of justice that have been experienced because of the exclusion of reliable evidence when the "constable blunders," have led the Court to vacillate as to the rationale for deliberate exclusion of truth from the factfinding process. The rhetoric has varied with the rationale to the point where the rule has become a doctrinaire result in search of validating reasons.

. . .

MR. JUSTICE BRENNAN, with whom MR. JUSTICE MARSHALL concurs, dissenting.

The Court today holds "that where the State has provided an opportunity for full and fair litigation of a Fourth Amendment claim, a state prisoner may not be granted federal habeas corpus relief on the ground that evidence obtained in an unconstitutional search or seizure was introduced at his trial." *Ante*, at 494. To be sure, my Brethren are hostile to the continued vitality of the exclusionary rule as part and parcel of the Fourth Amendment's prohibition of unreasonable searches and seizures, as today's decision in *United States* v. *Janis, ante*, p. 433, confirms. But these cases, despite the veil of Fourth Amendment terminology employed by the Court, plainly do not involve any question of the right of a defendant to have evidence excluded from use against him in his criminal trial when that evidence was seized in contravention of rights ostensibly secured by the Fourth and Fourteenth Amendments. Rather, they involve the question of the availability of a *federal forum* for vindicating those federally guaranteed rights. Today's holding portends substantial evisceration of federal habeas corpus jurisdiction, and I dissent.

. . .

IV

In summary, while unlike the Court I consider that the exclusionary rule is a constitutional ingredient of the Fourth Amendment, any modification of that rule should at least be accomplished with some modicum of logic and justification not provided today. See, *e. g.,* Dershowitz & Ely, *Harris v. New York:* Some Anxious Observations on the Candor and Logic of the Emerging Nixon Majority, 80 Yale L. J. 1198 (1971). The Court does not disturb the holding of *Mapp* v. *Ohio* that, as a matter of federal constitutional law, illegally obtained evidence must be excluded from the trial of a criminal defendant whose rights were transgressed during the search that resulted in acquisition of the evidence. In light of that constitutional rule it is a matter for Congress, not this Court, to prescribe what federal courts are to review state prisoners' claims of constitutional error committed by state courts. Until this decision, our cases have never departed from the construction of the habeas statutes as embodying a congressional intent that, however substantive constitutional rights are delineated or expanded, those rights may be asserted as a procedural matter under federal habeas jurisdiction. Employing the transparent tactic that today's is a decision construing the Constitution, the Court usurps the authority—vested by the Constitution in the Congress—to reassign federal judicial responsibility for reviewing state prisoners' claims of failure of state courts to redress violations of their Fourth Amendment rights. Our jurisdiction is eminently unsuited for that task, and as a practical matter the only result of today's holding will be that denials by the state courts of claims by state prisoners of violations of their Fourth Amendment rights will go unreviewed by a federal tribunal. I fear that the same treatment ultimately will be accorded state prisoners' claims of violations of other constitutional rights; thus the potential ramifications of this case for federal habeas jurisdiction generally are ominous. The Court, no longer content just to restrict forthrightly the constitutional rights of the citizenry, has embarked on a campaign to water down even such constitutional rights as it purports to acknowledge by the device of foreclosing resort to the federal habeas remedy for their redress.

I would affirm the judgments of the Courts of Appeals.

MR. JUSTICE WHITE, dissenting.

For many of the reasons stated by MR. JUSTICE BRENNAN, I cannot agree that the writ of habeas corpus should be any less available to those convicted of state crimes where they allege Fourth Amendment violations than where other constitutional issues are presented to the federal court. Under the amendments to the habeas corpus statute, which were adopted after *Fay* v. *Noia,* 372 U. S. 391 (1963), and represented an effort by Congress to lend a modicum of finality to state criminal judgments, I cannot distinguish between Fourth Amendment and other constitutional issues.

. . .

United States v. Leon

468 U.S. 897 (1984)

The exclusionary rule prohibits the government from introducing in court evidence that has been illegally obtained. The question in this case is whether the rule covers the actions of law enforcement officers who believe they are acting in "good faith" by

obtaining a search warrant but later discover that the warrant is invalid. The search involved drug trafficking by Alberto Leon and his associates. The District Court rejected the government's good-faith defense and suppressed the evidence against Leon. The Ninth Circuit affirmed.

JUSTICE WHITE delivered the opinion of the Court.

This case presents the question whether the Fourth Amendment exclusionary rule should be modified so as not to bar the use in the prosecution's case in chief of evidence obtained by officers acting in reasonable reliance on a search warrant issued by a detached and neutral magistrate but ultimately found to be unsupported by probable cause. To resolve this question, we must consider once again the tension between the sometimes competing goals of, on the one hand, deterring official misconduct and removing inducements to unreasonable invasions of privacy and, on the other, establishing procedures under which criminal defendants are "acquitted or convicted on the basis of all the evidence which exposes the truth." *Alderman* v. *United States*, 394 U. S. 165, 175 (1969).

I

In August 1981, a confidential informant of unproven reliability informed an officer of the Burbank Police Department that two persons known to him as "Armando" and "Patsy" were selling large quantities of cocaine and methaqualone from their residence at 620 Price Drive in Burbank, Cal. The informant also indicated that he had witnessed a sale of methaqualone by "Patsy" at the residence approximately five months earlier and had observed at that time a shoebox containing a large amount of cash that belonged to "Patsy." He further declared that "Armando" and "Patsy" generally kept only small quantities of drugs at their residence and stored the remainder at another location in Burbank.

On the basis of this information, the Burbank police initiated an extensive investigation focusing first on the Price Drive residence and later on two other residences as well. Cars parked at the Price Drive residence were determined to belong to respondents Armando Sanchez, who had previously been arrested for possession of marihuana,

and Patsy Stewart, who had no criminal record. During the course of the investigation, officers observed an automobile belonging to respondent Ricardo Del Castillo, who had previously been arrested for possession of 50 pounds of marihuana, arrive at the Price Drive residence. The driver of that car entered the house, exited shortly thereafter carrying a small paper sack, and drove away. A check of Del Castillo's probation records led the officers to respondent Alberto Leon, whose telephone number Del Castillo had listed as his employer's. Leon had been arrested in 1980 on drug charges, and a companion had informed the police at that time that Leon was heavily involved in the importation of drugs into this country. Before the current investigation began, the Burbank officers had learned that an informant had told a Glendale police officer that Leon stored a large quantity of methaqualone at his residence in Glendale. During the course of this investigation, the Burbank officers learned that Leon was living at 716 South Sunset Canyon in Burbank.

Subsequently, the officers observed several persons, at least one of whom had prior drug involvement, arriving at the Price Drive residence and leaving with small packages; observed a variety of other material activity at the two residences as well as at a condominium at 7902 Via Magdalena; and witnessed a variety of relevant activity involving respondents' automobiles. The officers also observed respondents Sanchez and Stewart board separate flights for Miami. The pair later returned to Los Angeles together, consented to a search of their luggage that revealed only a small amount of marihuana, and left the airport. Based on these and other observations summarized in the affidavit, App. 34, Officer Cyril Rombach of the Burbank Police Department, an experienced and well-trained narcotics investigator, prepared an application for a warrant to search 620 Price Drive, 716 South Sunset Canyon, 7902 Via Magdalena, and automobiles registered to each of the respondents for an extensive list of items believed to be related to respondents' drug-trafficking activities. Officer

Rombach's extensive application was reviewed by several Deputy District Attorneys.

A facially valid search warrant was issued in September 1981 by a State Superior Court Judge. The ensuing searches produced large quantities of drugs at the Via Magdalena and Sunset Canyon addresses and a small quantity at the Price Drive residence. Other evidence was discovered at each of the residences and in Stewart's and Del Castillo's automobiles. Respondents were indicted by a grand jury in the District Court for the Central District of California and charged with conspiracy to possess and distribute cocaine and a variety of substantive counts.

The respondents then filed motions to suppress the evidence seized pursuant to the warrant. The District Court held an evidentiary hearing and, while recognizing that the case was a close one, see *id.*, at 131, granted the motions to suppress in part. It concluded that the affidavit was insufficient to establish probable cause, but did not suppress all of the evidence as to all of the respondents because none of the respondents had standing to challenge all of the searches. In response to a request from the Government, the court made clear that Officer Rombach had acted in good faith, but it rejected the Government's suggestion that the Fourth Amendment exclusionary rule should not apply where evidence is seized in reasonable, good-faith reliance on a search warrant.

The District Court denied the Government's motion for reconsideration, *id.*, at 147, and a divided panel of the Court of Appeals for the Ninth Circuit affirmed, judgt. order reported at 701 F. 2d 187 (1983). . . .

We have concluded that, in the Fourth Amendment context, the exclusionary rule can be modified somewhat without jeopardizing its ability to perform its intended functions. Accordingly, we reverse the judgment of the Court of Appeals.

II

Language in opinions of this Court and of individual Justices has sometimes implied that the exclusionary rule is a necessary corollary of the Fourth Amendment, *Mapp* v. *Ohio*, 367 U. S. 643, 651, 655–657 (1961); *Olmstead* v. *United States*,

277 U. S. 438, 462–463 (1928), or that the rule is required by the conjunction of the Fourth and Fifth Amendments. *Mapp* v. *Ohio, supra*, at 661–662 (Black, J., concurring); *Agnello* v. *United States*, 269 U. S. 20, 33–34 (1925). These implications need not detain us long. The Fifth Amendment theory has not withstood critical analysis or the test of time, see *Andresen* v. *Maryland*, 427 U. S. 463 (1976), and the Fourth Amendment "has never been interpreted to proscribe the introduction of illegally seized evidence in all proceedings or against all persons." *Stone* v. *Powell*, 428 U. S. 465, 486 (1976).

A

. . .

The substantial social costs exacted by the exclusionary rule for the vindication of Fourth Amendment rights have long been a source of concern. "Our cases have consistently recognized that unbending application of the exclusionary sanction to enforce ideals of governmental rectitude would impede unacceptably the truth-finding functions of judge and jury." *United States* v. *Payner*, 447 U. S. 727, 734 (1980). An objectionable collateral consequence of this interference with the criminal justice system's truth-finding function is that some guilty defendants may go free or receive reduced sentences as a result of favorable plea bargains. Particularly when law enforcement officers have acted in objective good faith or their transgressions have been minor, the magnitude of the benefit conferred on such guilty defendants offends basic concepts of the criminal justice system. . . .

III

A

Because a search warrant "provides the detached scrutiny of a neutral magistrate, which is a more reliable safeguard against improper searches than the hurried judgment of a law enforcement officer 'engaged in the often competitive enterprise of ferreting out crime,'" *United States* v. *Chadwick*, 433 U. S. 1, 9 (1977) (quoting *Johnson* v. *United States*, 333 U. S. 10, 14 (1948)), we have expressed a strong preference for warrants . . .

. . . To the extent that proponents of exclusion rely on its behavioral effects on judges and magistrates in these areas, their reliance is misplaced. First, the exclusionary rule is designed to deter police misconduct rather than to punish the errors of judges and magistrates. Second, there exists no evidence suggesting that judges and magistrates are inclined to ignore or subvert the Fourth Amendment or that lawlessness among these actors requires application of the extreme sanction of exclusion.

. . . most important, we discern no basis, and are offered none, for believing that exclusion of evidence seized pursuant to a warrant will have a significant deterrent effect on the issuing judge or magistrate. Many of the factors that indicate that the exclusionary rule cannot provide an effective "special" or "general" deterrent for individual offending law enforcement officers apply as well to judges or magistrates. And, to the extent that the rule is thought to operate as a "systemic" deterrent on a wider audience, it clearly can have no such effect on individuals empowered to issue search warrants. Judges and magistrates are not adjuncts to the law enforcement team; as neutral judicial officers, they have no stake in the outcome of particular criminal prosecutions. The threat of exclusion thus cannot be expected significantly to deter them. Imposition of the exclusionary sanction is not necessary meaningfully to inform judicial officers of their errors, and we cannot conclude that admitting evidence obtained pursuant to a warrant while at the same time declaring that the warrant was somehow defective will in any way reduce judicial officers' professional incentives to comply with the Fourth Amendment, encourage them to repeat their mistakes, or lead to the granting of all colorable warrant requests.

B

If exclusion of evidence obtained pursuant to a subsequently invalidated warrant is to have any deterrent effect, therefore, it must alter the behavior of individual law enforcement officers or the policies of their departments. One could argue that applying the exclusionary rule in cases where the police failed to demonstrate probable cause in the warrant application deters future inadequate presentations or "magistrate shopping" and thus

promotes the ends of the Fourth Amendment. Suppressing evidence obtained pursuant to a technically defective warrant supported by probable cause also might encourage officers to scrutinize more closely the form of the warrant and to point out suspected judicial errors. We find such arguments speculative and conclude that suppression of evidence obtained pursuant to a warrant should be ordered only on a case-by-case basis and only in those unusual cases in which exclusion will further the purposes of the exclusionary rule.

. . .

[White reviews previous cases that concluded that the exclusionary rule is most justified when a law enforcement officer knows the search was unconstitutional. Where the officer's conduct is objectively reasonable, White said that the exclusion of evidence will not further the ends of the exclusionary rule in any appreciable way. Excluding evidence under these circumstances would not affect future conduct except to make the officer less willing to do his duty.]

This is particularly true, we believe, when an officer acting with objective good faith has obtained a search warrant from a judge or magistrate and acted within its scope. In most such cases, there is no police illegality and thus nothing to deter. It is the magistrate's responsibility to determine whether the officer's allegations establish probable cause and, if so, to issue a warrant comporting in form with the requirements of the Fourth Amendment. . . . Penalizing the officer for the magistrate's error, rather than his own, cannot logically contribute to the deterrence of Fourth Amendment violations.

C

. . .

Suppression . . . remains an appropriate remedy if the magistrate or judge in issuing a warrant was misled by information in an affidavit that the affiant knew was false or would have known was false except for his reckless disregard of the truth. *Franks* v. *Delaware*, 438 U. S. 154 (1978). The exception we recognize today will also not apply in cases where the issuing magistrate wholly abandoned his judicial role in the manner condemned in *Lo-Ji Sales, Inc.* v. *New York*, 442 U. S. 319 (1979); in such circumstances, no reasonably well trained officer should rely on the warrant. Nor would an officer manifest objective good faith in relying on a warrant based on an affidavit "so lacking in indicia of probable cause as to render official belief in its existence entirely unreasonable." *Brown* v. *Illinois*, 422 U. S., at 610–611 (POWELL, J., concurring in part); see *Illinois* v. *Gates, supra*, at 263–264 (WHITE, J., concurring in judgment). Finally, depending on the circumstances of the particular case, a warrant may be so facially deficient—*i. e.*, in failing to particularize the place to be searched or the things to be seized—that the executing officers cannot reasonably presume it to be valid. Cf. *Massachusetts* v. *Sheppard, post*, at 988–991.

. . .

In the absence of an allegation that the magistrate abandoned his detached and neutral role, suppression is appropriate only if the officers were dishonest or reckless in preparing their affidavit or could not have harbored an objectively reasonable belief in the existence of probable cause. Only respondent Leon has contended that no reasonably well trained police officer could have believed that there existed probable cause to search his house; significantly, the other respondents advance no comparable argument. Officer Rombach's application for a warrant clearly was supported by much more than a "bare bones" affidavit. The affidavit related the results of an extensive investigation and, as the opinions of the divided panel of the Court of Appeals make clear, provided evidence sufficient to create disagreement among thoughtful and competent judges as to the existence of probable cause. Under these circumstances, the officers' reliance on the magistrate's determination of probable cause was objectively reasonable, and application of the extreme sanction of exclusion is inappropriate.

Accordingly, the judgment of the Court of Appeals is

Reversed.

JUSTICE BLACKMUN, concurring.

. . .

JUSTICE BRENNAN, with whom JUSTICE MARSHALL joins, dissenting.

Ten years ago in *United States* v. *Calandra*, 414 U. S. 338 (1974), I expressed the fear that the Court's decision "may signal that a majority of my colleagues have positioned themselves to reopen the door [to evidence secured by official lawlessness] still further and abandon altogether the exclusionary rule in search-and-seizure cases." *Id.*, at 365 (dissenting opinion). Since then, in case after case, I have witnessed the Court's gradual but determined strangulation of the rule. It now appears that the Court's victory over the Fourth Amendment is complete. That today's decisions represent the *pièce de résistance* of the Court's past efforts cannot be doubted, for today the Court sanctions the use in the prosecution's case in chief of illegally obtained evidence against the individual whose rights have been violated—a result that had previously been thought to be foreclosed.

The Court seeks to justify this result on the ground that the "costs" of adhering to the exclusionary rule in cases like those before us exceed the "benefits." But the language of deterrence and of cost/benefit analysis, if used indiscriminately, can have a narcotic effect. It creates an illusion of technical precision and ineluctability. It suggests that not only constitutional principle but also empirical data support the majority's result. When the Court's analysis is examined carefully, however, it is clear that we have not been treated to an honest assessment of the merits of the exclusionary rule, but have instead been drawn into a curious world where the "costs" of excluding illegally obtained evidence loom to exaggerated heights and where the "benefits" of such exclusion are made to disappear with a mere wave of the hand.

The majority ignores the fundamental constitutional importance of what is at stake here. While the machinery of law enforcement and indeed the nature of crime itself have changed dramatically since the Fourth Amendment became part of the Nation's fundamental law in 1791, what the Framers understood then remains true today—that the task of combating crime and convicting the guilty will in every era seem of such critical and pressing concern that we may be lured by the temptations of expediency into forsaking our commitment to protecting individual liberty and privacy. It was for that very reason that the Framers of the Bill of Rights insisted that law enforcement efforts be permanently and unambiguously restricted in order to preserve personal freedoms. . . .

I

The Court holds that physical evidence seized by police officers reasonably relying upon a warrant issued by a detached and neutral magistrate is admissible in the prosecution's case in chief, even though a reviewing court has subsequently determined either that the warrant was defective [Massachusetts v. Sheppard, 468 U. S. 981 (1984)], or that those officers failed to demonstrate when applying for the warrant that there was probable cause to conduct the search [United States v. Leon]. . . .

A

At bottom, the Court's decision turns on the proposition that the exclusionary rule is merely a " 'judicially created remedy designed to safeguard Fourth Amendment rights generally through its deterrent effect, rather than a personal constitutional right.' " *Ante*, at 906, quoting *United States* v. *Calandra*, 414 U. S., at 348. . . .

. . . Because seizures are executed principally to secure evidence, and because such evidence generally has utility in our legal system only in the context of a trial supervised by a judge, it is apparent that the admission of illegally obtained evidence implicates the same constitutional concerns as the initial seizure of that evidence. Indeed, by admitting unlawfully seized evidence, the judiciary becomes a part of what is in fact a single governmental action prohibited by the terms of the Amendment. Once that connection between the evidence-gathering role of the police and the evidence-admitting function of the courts is acknowledged, the plausibility of the Court's interpretation becomes more suspect. . . .

B

From the foregoing, it is clear why the question whether the exclusion of evidence would deter future police misconduct was never considered a relevant concern in the early cases from *Weeks* to

Olmstead. In those formative decisions, the Court plainly understood that the exclusion of illegally obtained evidence was compelled not by judicially fashioned remedial purposes, but rather by a direct constitutional command. *[That principle was weakened by* Wolf v. Colorado, 338 U. S. 25 (1949), *bolstered again by* Mapp v. Ohio, 367 U. S. 643 (1961), *but the deterrence theory has been pressed in* United States v. Calandra, 414 U. S. 338 (1974), United States v. Peltier, 422 U. S. 531 (1975), Stone v. Powell, 428 U. S. 465 (1976), and United States v. Janis, 428 U. S. 433 (1976).]

. . .

II

. . . In . . . *United States* v. *Leon* . . . it is conceded by the Government and accepted by the Court that the affidavit filed by the police officers in support of their application for a search warrant failed to provide a sufficient basis on which a neutral and detached magistrate could conclude that there was probable cause to issue the warrant. Specifically, it is conceded that the officers' application for a warrant was based in part on information supplied by a confidential informant of unproven reliability that was over five months old by the time it was relayed to the police. Although the police conducted an independent investigation on the basis of this tip, both the District Court and the Court of Appeals concluded that the additional information gathered by the officers failed to corroborate the details of the informant's tip and was "as consistent with innocence as . . . with guilt." App. to Pet. for Cert. 10a. The warrant, therefore, should never have issued. Stripped of the authority of the warrant, the conduct of these officers was plainly unconstitutional—it amounted to nothing less than a naked invasion of the privacy of respondents' homes without the requisite justification demanded by the Fourth Amendment. . . .

JUSTICE STEVENS, . . . dissenting . . .

It is appropriate to begin with the plain language of the Fourth Amendment:

"The right of the people to be secure in their persons, houses, papers, and effects, against unreasonable searches and seizures, shall not be violated; and no Warrants shall issue but upon probable cause, supported by Oath or affirmation, and particularly describing the place to be searched, and the persons or things to be seized."

The Court assumes that the searches in these cases violated the Fourth Amendment, yet refuses to apply the exclusionary rule because the Court concludes that it was "reasonable" for the police to conduct them. In my opinion an official search and seizure cannot be both "unreasonable" and "reasonable" at the same time. The doctrinal vice in the Court's holding is its failure to consider the separate purposes of the two prohibitory Clauses in the Fourth Amendment.

. . .

III

. . .

In *[Leon,]* the Government now admits—at least for the tactical purpose of achieving what it regards as a greater benefit—that the substance, as well as the letter, of the Fourth Amendment was violated. The Court therefore assumes that the warrant in that case was not supported by probable cause, but refuses to suppress the evidence obtained thereby because it considers the police conduct to satisfy a "newfangled" nonconstitutional standard of reasonableness. Yet if the Court's assumption is correct—if there was no probable cause—it must follow that it was "unreasonable" for the authorities to make unheralded entries into and searches of private dwellings and automobiles. The Court's conclusion that such searches undertaken without probable cause can nevertheless be "reasonable" is totally without support in our Fourth Amendment jurisprudence.

. . .

The majority's contrary conclusion rests on the notion that it must be reasonable for a police officer to rely on a magistrate's finding. Until today that has plainly not been the law; it has been well settled that even when a magistrate issues a warrant there is no guarantee that the ensuing search and seizure is constitutionally reasonable. Law enforcement officers have long been on notice that despite the magistrate's decision a warrant will be invalidated if the officers did not provide sufficient facts to enable the magistrate to evaluate the existence of probable cause responsibly and independently. Reviewing courts have always inquired into whether the magistrate acted properly in issuing the warrant—not merely whether the officers acted properly in executing it. . . .

The notion that a police officer's reliance on a magistrate's warrant is automatically appropriate is one the Framers of the Fourth Amendment would have vehemently rejected. The precise problem that the Amendment was intended to address was *the unreasonable issuance of warrants.* As we have often observed, the Amendment was actually motivated by the practice of issuing general warrants—warrants which did not satisfy the particularity and probable-cause requirements. The resentments which led to the Amendment were directed at the issuance of *warrants* unjustified by particularized evidence of wrongdoing. Those who sought to amend the Constitution to include a Bill of Rights repeatedly voiced the view that the evil which had to be addressed was the issuance of warrants on insufficient evidence. . . .

IV

. . .

The exclusionary rule is designed to prevent violations of the Fourth Amendment. "Its purpose is to deter—to compel respect for the constitutional guaranty in the only effectively available way, by removing the incentive to disregard it." *Elkins* v. *United States*, 364 U. S. 206, 217 (1960). If the police cannot use evidence obtained through warrants issued on less than probable cause, they have less incentive to seek those warrants, and magistrates have less incentive to issue them.

Today's decisions do grave damage to that deterrent function. Under the majority's new rule, even when the police know their warrant application is probably insufficient, they retain an incentive to submit it to a magistrate, on the chance that he may take the bait. No longer must they hesitate and seek additional evidence in doubtful cases. . . .

15 Racial Discrimination

N o issue has dominated American constitutional law as much as the question of race, beginning with slavery and discrimination against blacks, followed by recent efforts to heal the wounds of racism. Two chapters have already addressed the issue of race: First Amendment questions in Chapter 10 (sit-in and demonstration cases) and rights of the accused in Chapter 13 (jury composition and death penalty). The sections on voting rights and reapportionment in Chapter 18 deal heavily with racial questions. This chapter concentrates on slavery, the Civil War amendments, school desegregation, desegregation of public facilities, racial discrimination in housing, and issues of employment and affirmative action.

SLAVERY

At the time the framers met at the Philadelphia Convention, slavery was an established institution in the southern states. How to recognize that reality in the Constitution while laying the groundwork for abolishing slavery represented a matter of tactics and compromise. A more fundamental problem was how to reconcile slavery with the principles in the Declaration of Independence. For this there could be no compromise. A nation could not proclaim that "all men are created equal" and at the same time condone slavery. Thomas Jefferson's original draft of the Declaration of Independence contained a sharp condemnation of slavery:

> [King George III] has waged cruel war against human nature itself, violating its most sacred rights of life & liberty in the persons of a distant people who never offended him, captivating & carrying them into slavery in another hemisphere, or to incur miserable death in their transportation thither, this piratical warfare, the opprobrium of *infidel* powers, is the warfare of the CHRISTIAN king of Great Britain, determined to keep open a market where MEN should be bought & sold, he has prostituted his negative [veto] for suppressing every legislative attempt to prohibit or to restrain this execrable commerce: and that this assemblage of horrors might want no fact of distinguished die, he is now

exciting those very people to rise in arms among us, and to purchase that liberty of which *he* has deprived them, by murdering the people upon whom *he* also obtruded them; thus paying off former crimes committed against the *liberties* of one people, with crimes which he urges them to commit against the *lives* of another.

Because of opposition from southern delegates in the Continental Congress, that passage was struck from Jefferson's draft. However, the Northwest Ordinance of 1787, which governed the territory northwest of the Ohio River, contained this forthright declaration in Article 6: "There shall be neither slavery nor involuntary servitude in the said territory, otherwise than in the punishment of crimes whereof the party shall have been duly convicted . . ."

Although the word "slavery" does not appear in the Constitution drafted at Philadelphia in 1787, it is implied in five places. First, Article V provides that no amendment to the Constitution prior to 1808 "shall in any Manner affect the first and fourth Clauses in the Ninth Section of the first Article . . ." The first clause in Section 9 states that the "Migration or Importation of such Persons as any of the States now Existing shall think proper to admit" shall not be prohibited by Congress before 1808. This grace period for the slave trade prompted Madison to remark: "Twenty years will produce all the mischief that can be apprehended from the liberty to import slaves. So long a term will be more dishonorable to the National Character than to say nothing about it in the Constitution." 2 Farrand 415.

The first clause in Section 9 also permitted a tax or duty on imported slaves "not exceeding ten dollars for each Person." The delegates divided on the merits of this language. Some regarded it as offensive to tax slaves as though they were incoming goods or articles of merchandise. Others thought that a tax might discourage the importation of slaves, but the modest level of the tax suggests that the objective was revenue more than prohibition. 2 Farrand 416. Madison "thought it wrong to admit in the Constitution the idea that there could be property in men." 2 Farrand 417.

Slavery also became mixed with the question of apportioning taxes and Representatives among the states. The fourth clause in Section 9 prohibits capitation or other direct taxes unless in proportion to population. How was population to be measured? Should slaves be counted like whites, giving the southern states additional representation because of their "peculiar institution"? Or should representation be based solely on free inhabitants? William Paterson of New Jersey, objecting to any credit to the south for slaves, did not want to give "an indirect encouragemt. of the slave trade." 1 Farrand 561.

As with other matters, the framers reached a compromise. Under Article I, Representatives and direct taxes were apportioned among the states "according to their respective Numbers, which shall be determined by adding to the whole Number of free Persons, including those bound to Service for a Term of Years, and excluding Indians not taxed, three fifths of all other Persons." The three-fifths formula had been devised by the Continental Congress to deal with taxes. As picked up by the framers, the formula implies that they regarded blacks as three-fifths of a person, or subhuman, but the fraction had a different effect. It penalized the states for practicing slavery. Their number of Representatives was reduced from what it would have been by freeing blacks.

Finally, Article IV, Section 2, provided that persons "held to Service or Labour" in one state shall be delivered back to that state in case they escaped to another. At the Virginia ratifying convention, Madison explained that this clause was inserted to "enable owners of slaves to reclaim them." 3 Farrand 325. This part of the Constitution became the basis for the fugitive slave laws passed by Congress.

The 1790 census showed 757,363 blacks in the United States, or 19.3 percent of the population. Of these, 59,466 were free. States in excess of 20 percent slaves included South Carolina, Virginia, Georgia, Maryland, North Carolina, and Delaware. Slave-holding plantations were not profitable, but the situation changed dramatically in 1793 with Eli Whitney's invention of the cotton gin. The machine made it easier to separate the fiber from the seed, allowing plantation owners to export much greater quantities. Beginning in 1794, Congress passed various bills to regulate and restrict the slave trade. It enacted legislation in 1807 to stop the slave trade altogether, effective January 1, 1808. Slaves continued to enter the country illegally, requiring additional legislation.[1]

Congress passed legislation to implement the constitutional provision on runaway slaves. The Fugitive Slave Act of 1793 authorized the return of slaves to their owners; it was amended in 1850. 1 Stat. 302; 9 Stat. 462. The Supreme Court decided that congressional action preempted fugitive slave laws passed by the states. Prigg v. Pennsylvania, 16 Pet. 539 (1842). A unanimous Court also upheld the constitutionality of the Fugitive Slave Act. Ableman v. Booth, 21 How. 506 (1859). During this period, Congress attempted to maintain a balance between free states and slave states. The Ordinance of 1787 prohibited slavery in the Northwest Territory (the Ohio country). Land acquired by the Louisiana Purchase threatened to upset the balance of slave and nonslave states. As a remedy, the Missouri Compromise Act of 1820 admitted Missouri as a slave state but prohibited slavery in future states north of the 36° 30' line.

The Compromise of 1850, governing the new territory acquired from Mexico, basically dodged the issue of slavery, while the Kansas-Nebraska Act of 1854 specifically repealed the Missouri Compromise. The effect was to leave the question of slavery to the territories (the doctrine of congressional noninterference, or "popular sovereignty"). The Kansas-Nebraska Act also tossed the smoldering issue of slavery to the judiciary, inviting a final disposition by the courts.

The forces clamoring for war gained momentum when the Supreme Court decided *Dred Scott* v. *Sandford*. Dred Scott, a slave from Missouri, argued that he had become free by following his master to a free state (Illinois) and to a free territory (Upper Louisiana). The principal issue was whether Scott, after returning to Missouri, was a citizen capable of suing in the federal courts. Did his stay on free soil give him this right? The Court held that Scott (and all other black slaves and their descendants) was not a citizen of the United States or of Missouri. Chief Justice Taney refused to allow contemporary social beliefs to change the meaning of the Constitution by making blacks citizens. No one, he said, "supposes that any change in public opinion or feeling, in relation to this unfortunate race, in the civilized nations of Europe or in this country, should induce the court to give to the words of the Constitution a more liberal construction in their favor than they were intended to bear when the instrument was framed and adopted." DRED SCOTT v. SANDFORD, 16 How. 393, 426 (1857). Taney also ruled that Congress was without power to prevent the spread of slavery to the territories in the West. Among the opponents

[1] 1 Stat. 347 (1794); 2 Stat. 70 (1800); 2 Stat. 205 (1803); 2 Stat. 426 (1807). Additional legislation was needed after 1808: 3 Stat. 450 (1818); 3 Stat. 532 (1819); 3 Stat. 600, §§ 4, 5 (1820).

of Taney's decision was a Republican candidate for the U.S. Senate, Abraham Lincoln (pp. 976-978).

The Court miscalculated wildly. Concurring in Taney's opinion, Justice Wayne referred to the constitutional issues as so divisive "that the peace and harmony of the country required the settlement of them by judicial decision." Id. at 455. In his Inaugural Address in 1857, President Buchanan spoke confidently that the Dred Scott Case was at the Supreme Court, where the issue of slavery would be "speedily and finally settled." Instead, the country lurched into a bloody civil war that left, out of a population of about 30 million, over 600,000 dead and another 400,000 wounded.

CIVIL WAR AMENDMENTS

Following the war, Congress took steps to eradicate slavery and its evils. The Thirteenth Amendment, adopted in 1865, abolished the institution of slavery. The Fourteenth Amendment, ratified in 1868, provided for the equality of whites and blacks before the law. The Fifteenth Amendment, ratified in 1870, gave blacks the right to vote. Under the express language of these amendments, Congress was empowered to enforce them "by appropriate legislation."

The Fourteenth Amendment was foreshadowed by the Civil Rights Act of 1866. After passage of the Thirteenth Amendment, a number of southern states enacted "Black Codes" to keep the newly freed slaves in a subordinate status economically, politically, and culturally. The 1866 statute made all persons born in the United States, excluding Indians not taxed, citizens of the United States. Such citizens, "of every race and color," had the same right in every state and territory "to make and enforce contracts, to sue, be parties, and give evidence, to inherit, purchase, lease, sell, hold, and convey real and personal property, and to full and equal benefit of all laws and proceedings for the security of person and property, as is enjoyed by white citizens . . ." 14 Stat. 27, § 1 (1866). President Andrew Johnson vetoed the bill, claiming that the power to confer the right of state citizenship "is just as exclusively with the several States as the power to confer the right of Federal citizenship is with Congress." He objected to forcing this policy on the southern states and questioned whether blacks, newly emerged from slavery, had the "requisite qualifications to entitle them to all the privileges and immunities of citizens of the United States." 8 Richardson 3604. Congress overrode the veto, making the Civil Rights Act law on April 9, 1866. Similar objectives were incorporated in the Fourteenth Amendment, passed by Congress on June 13, 1866, and ratified by the states on July 20, 1868.

Legislation in 1875 attempted to close the gap between the Declaration of Independence and the Constitution. The preamble of the statute read: "Whereas, it is essential to just government we recognize the equality of all men before the law . . ." 18 Stat. 335. The statute provided for equality of all races in using public accommodations: inns, "conveyances" (transportation), theaters, and other places of public amusement. This landmark legislation would be struck down by the Supreme Court in 1883 as a federal encroachment on the states.

Before issuing that decision, the Court handled other questions of race. When states attempted to require shared accommodations for public transportation, a unanimous Court held that these statutes, to the extent that they regulated interstate commerce, were unconstitutional and void. Hall v. DeCuir, 95 U.S. 485 (1878). State efforts to deny blacks the right to participate as jurors were struck down as a violation of the Equal Protection Clause of the Fourteenth Amendment. In doing so, however, the Court betrayed a prevailing attitude: "the colored race, as a race, was abject and ignorant, and in that condition was unfitted to command the respect of those who had superior intelligence. Their training had left them mere children, and as such they needed the protection which a wise government extends to those who are unable to protect themselves." Strauder v. West Virginia, 100 U.S. 303, 306 (1880). The Equal Protection Clause was available to offer that protection. As the Court later admitted, however, that Clause was "[v]irtually strangled in infancy by post-civil-war judicial reactionism." Regents of the University of California v. Bakke, 438 U.S. 265, 291 (1978), quoting with approval a law review article.

The Court recognized the authority of Congress, under Section 5 of the Fourteenth Amendment, to enact appropriate legislation to enforce the amendment. State judges who excluded blacks from grand and petit juries could be indicted for violating federal law. The purpose of the Civil War amendments was to "raise the colored race from that condition of inferiority and servitude in which most of them had previously stood, into perfect equality of civil rights with all other persons within the jurisdiction of the States." Ex parte Virginia, 100 U.S. 339, 344–345 (1880). When states excluded blacks from grand juries on the ground that they were "utterly unqualified by want of intelligence, experience, or moral integrity," the Court dismissed the indictments issued by the grand jury. Neal v. Delaware, 103 U.S. 370, 394 (1880). However, when Alabama prohibited interracial cohabitation or marriage, and imposed heavier penalties for interracial cohabitation than for cohabitation by those of the same race, a unanimous Court discovered no violation of the Equal Protection Clause of the Fourteenth Amendment. Pace v. Alabama, 106 U.S. 583 (1883).

The major case of this period was the decision of the Court to strike down the Civil Rights Act of 1875, which had made all public accommodations available regardless of race. The Court held that Section 5 of the Fourteenth Amendment empowered Congress only to enforce the prohibitions placed upon the states. Congress could regulate only "state action," not discrimination by private parties. The Court suggested that Congress might invoke the Commerce Power to regulate rights in public conveyances passing from one state to another, but that question was not before the Court. Justice Harlan issued the sole dissent, pointing out that for centuries the common law had prohibited private parties from acting in a discriminatory fashion toward travelers who needed access to inns and restaurants. What could have been accomplished in 1875 had to await, because of the Court's action, the Civil Rights Act of 1964. CIVIL RIGHTS CASES, 109 U.S. 3 (1883).

The Court initially believed that the "one pervading purpose" of the Civil War amendments was to free enslaved blacks and protect their freedoms. Slaughter-House Cases, 16 Wall. 36, 71 (1873). Although the Fourteenth Amendment appeared to give limited protection to blacks, a unanimous Court in 1886 declared a San Francisco ordinance discriminatory against Chinese operators of laundries. Announced as a fire-prevention measure, the ordinance required all laundries in wooden buildings to obtain a permit. Local authorities denied permission to a majority of Chinese, but all of the non-Chinese laundries, except for one, were allowed to continue. The Court found the ordinance "purely arbitrary" and a violation of the Equal Protection Clause of the Fourteenth Amendment. Yick Wo v. Hopkins, 118 U.S. 356 (1886).

Yick Wo illustrates that the Fourteenth Amendment, intended to grant rights to newly freed blacks, applies literally to "all persons." Yick Wo was not a U.S. citizen; he was still a subject of the Emperor of China. But the Fourteenth Amendment protects all persons, not all citizens. As the nation filled with immigrants, the Equal Protection Clause of the Fourteenth Amendment was extended "to all ethnic groups seeking protection from official discrimination": Celtic Irishmen, Chinese, Austrian resident aliens, Japanese, and Mexican-Americans. Regents of the University of California v. Bakke, 438 U.S. at 292. Similarly, although Congress passed civil rights legislation in 1866 and 1870 to protect blacks (currently §§ 1981 and 1982), those statutory provisions apply to all groups subjected to discrimination solely because of their ancestry or ethnic characteristics, including Jews and Arabs. Shaare Tefila Congregation v. Cobb, 481 U.S. 615 (1987); Saint Francis College v. Al-Khazraji, 481 U.S. 604 (1987).

Separate but Equal

The Fourteenth Amendment extended civil rights to blacks, but a number of states (not only in the South) invoked the police power to require separate facilities. Segregation of races was adopted for transportation, education, housing, parks, hospitals, restaurants, hotels, theaters, waiting rooms, and bathrooms. Statutes and ordinances even required separate phone booths for blacks and whites and separate textbooks. Black and white prostitutes had to be kept in separate districts. Regents of the University of California v. Bakke, 438 U.S. at 393 (Marshall, J.).

Mississippi passed a law in 1888 that required all railroads carrying passengers within the state (other than streetcars) to provide equal, but separate, accommodations for whites and blacks. A 7–2 Court ruled that the statute did not violate the Commerce Clause because the law applied solely to commerce within the state. Louisville &c. Railway Co. v. Mississippi, 133 U.S. 587 (1890).

In *Plessy* v. *Ferguson* (1896), the Supreme Court upheld a Louisiana statute that required railroads to provide equal, but separate, accommodations for white and black passengers. At that time, the tide of public opinion ran strongly against the policy of shared accommodations. The Court said that "in the nature of things" it could not have been intended to force the commingling of the two races. Laws requiring their separation "do not necessarily imply the inferiority of either race to the other" and were within the police power of the states. Justice Harlan was the sole dissenter. PLESSY v. FERGUSON, 163 U.S. 537, 544 (1896).

The separate-but-equal doctrine saddled state governments with heavy financial costs, requiring duplicate facilities for whites and blacks. In 1914, a unanimous Court upheld an Oklahoma statute that required separate-but-equal train accommodations for whites and blacks. As it was restricted to intrastate commerce, the Court found no constitutional infirmity. However, it rejected the railroads' contention that they could provide dining and Pullman (sleeper) cars for whites only, because there were insufficient blacks to justify separate cars. States had to bear the expense of separate facilities. McCabe v. A., T. & S.F. Ry. Co., 235 U.S. 151 (1914).

Bus and train systems changed from an intrastate to an interstate structure, making it difficult for states to defend a separate-but-equal policy. In 1941, a unanimous Court held that the treatment of a black on an interstate journey—denying him the right to use an available seat in a Pullman car after he had payed a first-class fare, and requiring him to leave that car and ride in a second-class car—was unjust and violated the Interstate Commerce Act. Moreover, the Court found that the accommodations for black passengers were substantially inferior to those for white passengers. Mitchell v. United States, 313 U.S. 80 (1941). Another unanimous decision struck down state restrictions on interstate movement as a violation of the Commerce Clause. Some of the concurring opinions would have relied on the Privileges and Immunities Clause of the Fourteenth Amendment Edwards v. California, 314 U.S. 160 (1941).

A Virginia statute required all passenger motor vehicle carriers, both interstate and intrastate, to separate the races. A black was convicted for refusing to move to the back of an interstate bus that traveled from Virginia through the District of Columbia to Baltimore, Maryland. A 7–1 Court held the statute invalid because it interfered with interstate commerce and disrupted the uniformity and convenience required for national travel. To comply with the Virginia law, black passengers traveling from the north would have to change their seats once they entered Virginia. Morgan v. Virginia, 328 U.S. 373 (1946). Finally, a unanimous Court in 1950 decided that an interstate railroad's separation of races in the dining car violated the Interstate Commerce Act, which made it unlawful for a railroad in interstate commerce "to subject any particular person . . . to any undue or unreasonable prejudice or disadvantage in any respect whatsoever." The Court thus disposed of this issue on statutory, not constitutional, grounds. Henderson v. United States, 339 U.S. 816 (1950). Therefore, before the Court handed down its Desegregation Decision in 1954, a combination of factors had chipped away at the policy of separate-but-equal facilities for transportation.

SCHOOL DESEGREGATION

Like transportation, the policy of separate-but-equal in education became increasingly impractical. Various forces helped erode this practice long before the Court struck it down in 1954. Part of the shift toward desegregation reflected a mobile society, with each state receiving new visitors and new challenges to its customs. Another factor was foreign policy. Competition with international communism after World War II put pressure on the United States to abolish segregation and bring practices in line with American ideals.

Plessy reinforced the separate-but-equal doctrine in many fields, including education. A unanimous Court in 1899 ruled that schools, even if segregated, were a matter belonging to the states. The opinion was written by Justice Harlan, the lone dissenter in *Plessy*. Cumming v. Board of Education, 175 U.S. 528 (1899). States were even permitted to outlaw integrated education in private colleges. Berea College v. Kentucky, 211 U.S. 45 (1908). A unanimous ruling held that states had discretion to assign Chinese children to attend public schools with blacks. Gong Lum v. Rice, 275 U.S. 78 (1927).

Opponents of *Plessy* decided to file lawsuits to attack the most vulnerable area: segregated graduate schools. The timing was propitious. During the late 1930s, the courts began to abandon use of the Due Process Clause to protect property interests ("substantive due process") and relied more on the Equal Protection Clause to defend individual rights. Regents of the University of California v. Bakke, 438 U.S. at 291–292. This attitude was expressed most forcefully in a famous footnote by Justice Stone. In reviewing the standards for judicial review and the choice between activism and restraint, he suggested that the courts might have a special responsibility for protecting "discrete and insular minorities," particularly when political processes relied upon to protect minorities have been curtailed. United States v. Carolene Products Co., 304 U.S. 144, 153 n.4 (1938). Although this footnote has never been adopted as the holding of the Court, it expressed a solicitude that captures much of the Court's work in racial discrimination since 1938.

Beginning in 1936, Court decisions on the separate-but-equal policy in higher education gradually painted *Plessy* into an ever-narrowing corner. In one case, black applicants were denied admission to the law school at the University of Maryland. As compensation, the state offered to pay their tuition to a law school outside the state. A unanimous appellate court in Maryland ruled that this policy violated the Equal Protection Clause. Blacks would encounter greater costs traveling to another state and having to pay additional living expenses. Moreover, an education outside the state would not adequately prepare blacks who intended to practice in Maryland. Pearson v. Murray, 182 A. 593 (Md. 1936).

Missouri also wanted to pay black students their tuition costs for a law school education in an adjacent state. The Supreme Court, divided 7–2, held that this policy violated the Equal Protection Clause by creating a privilege for white law students (able to attend the Missouri law school) that was denied to blacks. Missouri ex rel. Gaines v. Canada, 305 U.S. 337 (1938). See also Sipuel v. Board of Regents, 332 U.S. 631 (1948) and Fisher v. Hurst, 333 U.S. 147 (1948).

The next effort to preserve *Plessy* was to create a separate law school for blacks within the state. A unanimous Court in 1950 concluded that the school for blacks did not satisfy the separate-but-equal standard. The University of Texas Law School, attended by whites, was superior in terms of its professional staff, library, law review, moot court facilities, scholarship funds, distinguished alumni, tradition, and prestige. Sweatt v. Painter, 339 U.S. 629 (1950).

Backed into a corner, Oklahoma agreed to admit blacks to the state university but separated them from white students. Blacks had to sit in a special seat in the classroom, a special table in the library, and a special table in the cafeteria. Once again, a unanimous Court found this in violation of the Equal Protection Clause. The restrictions on the black student impaired and inhibited "his ability to study, to engage in discussions and exchange views with other students, and, in general, to learn his profession." McLaurin v. Oklahoma State Regents, 339 U.S. 637 (1950).

These cases laid the groundwork for the Desegregation Case of 1954. Other influences were important. The horrors of racism in Nazi Germany, sending millions of Jews to their death in gas chambers and concentration camps, showed the results of preaching a "master race." After the war, President Truman took steps to eliminate discrimination in federal government and to abolish segregation in the armed forces. The United States, which emerged as a world leader after World War II, could not fight world communism while maintaining racial segregation at home.

By the time of the Desegregation Case of 1954, seventeen states and the District of Columbia required segregated schools. Four other states permitted segregation as a local option. The Supreme Court admitted that in approaching the problem of school segregation "we cannot turn the clock back to 1868 when the [Fourteenth] Amendment was adopted, or even to 1896 when *Plessy* v. *Ferguson* was written." BROWN v. BOARD OF EDUCATION, 347 U.S. 483, 492 (1954). Segregation, said a unanimous Court, generated a feeling of inferiority among black children: "Whatever may have been the extent of psychological knowledge at the time of *Plessy* v. *Ferguson*, this finding [of inequality] is amply supported by modern authority."

Following this sentence was a famous footnote, the wisdom of which has been extensively debated, citing seven psychological and sociological studies on the effects of discrimination and segregation on children.[2]

Foreign policy entered the equation. The NAACP's brief observed: "Survival of our country in the present international situation is inevitably tied to resolution of this domestic issue." The federal government's amicus brief in 1952 explained in great detail the harmful effects of American segregation on the foreign policy of the executive branch. Racial discrimination affected American blacks and dark-skinned visitors from other countries, furnishing "grist for the Communist propaganda mills" (pp. 990–992).

In striking down segregated schools in the states, the Court relied on the Equal Protection Clause of the Fourteenth Amendment. What could be used to overturn segregation in the nation's capital? The Fifth Amendment, applicable to the District of Columbia, does not contain an equal protection clause. It would have been intolerable for the Court to invalidate segregated schools in the states and allow them to operate in the District of Columbia. The Court reached the desired result by holding that racial segregation in the D.C. public schools denied black children the due process of law guaranteed by the Fifth Amendment. The concepts of equal protection and due process, "both stemming from our American ideal of fairness, are not mutually exclusive." Bolling v. Sharpe, 347 U.S. 497, 499 (1954).

In 1955, the Court announced guidelines for implementing its desegregation decision. How quickly were states to make the transition? The Court largely deferred to local school authorities in determining the appropriate course, leaving to federal courts the duty of considering whether school authorities were acting in good faith to comply with desegregation. Several phrases from the Court—including "practical flexibility," "as soon as practicable," "a prompt and reasonable start," and "all deliberate speed"—gave a green light to delay and procrastination. BROWN v. BOARD OF EDUCATION, 349 U.S. 294 (1955).

Civil Rights Acts

In issuing its desegregation decision, the Supreme Court obviously did not have the "last word." The Justice Department had given strong encouragement to the Court to strike down segregated schools, but that was during the Truman administration. The amicus brief filed by the Justice Department, after Dwight D. Eisenhower had become President, was not as strong. Eisenhower failed to give full support to the *Brown* decision, perhaps reflecting his belief in states' rights and limited government. In any event, the record after 1954 was marred by massive state resistance and acts of violence against blacks. A major confrontation occurred in Arkansas, when Governor Orval Faubus defied three court orders to integrate the Little Rock Central High School. On September 24, 1957, President Eisenhower sent in armed troops to prevent the obstruction of justice. In a radio and television address to the nation, Eisenhower spoke of the harm done to America's prestige and influence in the

---

[2]See Abraham L. Davis, The United States Supreme Court and the Uses of Social Science Data 48–61, 65–74, 95–118 (1973); William B. Ball, "Lawyers and Social Sciences—Guiding the Guides," 5 Vill. L. Rev. 215 (1959–60); Kenneth B. Clark, "The Desegregation Cases: Criticism of the Social Scientist's Role," 5 Vill. L. Rev. 224 (1959–60); Herbert Garfinkel, "Social Science Evidence and the School Desegregation Cases," 21 J. Pol. 37 (1959); Jack Greenberg, "Social Scientists Take the Stand," 54 Mich. L. Rev. 953 (1956); Edmond Cahn, "Jurisprudence," 30 N.Y.U. L. Rev. 150 (1955).

world, noting that "enemies are gloating over this incident." 1957 Public Papers of the Presidents 694. In 1958, after calling a special term in August, the Court affirmed the lower court orders in the Little Rock crisis. Cooper v. Aaron, 358 U.S. 1 (1958). (Excerpts from this decision appear in Chapter 5.)

Even the 1958 ruling did not provide the last word on race relations. Some act of finality was needed beyond Court opinions. The resolution required the concerted action of the elected branches: Congress and the President. Three statutes, passed in 1957, 1960, and 1964, put the nation on course in eliminating segregation in public facilities.

The Civil Rights Act of 1957 was the first civil rights measure passed since 1875. It established a Commission on Civil Rights to investigate allegations of discrimination, authorized the President to appoint an additional Assistant Attorney General to head a new Civil Rights Division in the Justice Department, and set fines for those convicted in cases arising from the statute. 71 Stat. 634. The broad investigative powers of the Commission were upheld by the Supreme Court. Hannah v. Larche, 363 U.S. 420 (1960). The Civil Rights Act of 1960 strengthened existing laws on obstruction of court orders, provided criminal penalties for acts of violence and destruction, and authorized court-appointed "referees" to monitor voting rights. 74 Stat. 86.

The major step was the Civil Rights Act of 1964, the most far-reaching civil rights statute since the Reconstruction era. Public pressure for legislative action included sit-ins, demonstrations, picketing, and boycotts. For the first time on a civil rights bill, Senators were able to vote cloture and stop a filibuster. The legislation passed by top-heavy majorities of 289–126 in the House and 73–27 in the Senate. Bipartisan support was solid. The House voted 153–91 Democrat and 136–35 Republican. The party split in the Senate was 46–21 for Democrats and 27–6 for Republicans. Major factions throughout the country had united to give the final word. 78 Stat. 241. In signing the bill, President Johnson reviewed the history of racial discrimination in America and announced: "it cannot continue. Our Constitution, the foundation of our Republic, forbids it. The principles of our freedom forbid it. Morality forbids it. And the law I sign tonight forbids it." 1964(II) Public Papers of the Presidents 842–843.

The statute provided new guarantees for black voters and created a Community Relations Service to help resolve civil rights problems. The most significant sections concerned public accommodations, termination of federal funds, and discrimination in employment. Title IV dealt with desegregation of public education, including elementary, secondary, and higher education. Title VI provided for nondiscrimination in federally assisted programs. If parties receiving federal funds refused to voluntarily comply with the statute, agencies could terminate funds. Termination of assistance was subject to judicial review. Title VII, on equal employment opportunity, outlawed employment practices based on race, color, religion, sex, or national origin. The Act created the Equal Employment Opportunity Commission (EEOC) to enforce the law.

Title VI, threatening a cutoff of federal funds from states that practiced racial discrimination in schools, became more significant as the level of federal assistance increased. The Elementary and Education School Act of 1965 provided large federal grants to school districts. It was the first general school aid in the nation's history. School districts now had to decide what was more important to retain: segregated schools or federal funds.

De Facto Segregation and Busing

For much of the 1950s and 1960s, smug northerners pretended that segregation was a problem only for the South. Little notice was taken of northern school systems that were segregated in fact (de facto) rather than by law (de jure). Increasingly, inner-city blacks were encircled by white suburbs. What was to be done when segregated schools resulted not from state laws but from residential patterns?

Busing was one possibility. Although busing today is associated with efforts to integrate schools, it can be used just as easily to *promote* segregation. In eastern Virginia, where there was no residential segregation, school buses were used heavily to criss-cross students from one corner of the county to another to maintain all-white and all-black schools. Green v. County School Board, 391 U.S. 430, 432 (1969). The Court said that where it was possible to identify a "white school" or a "black school," a prima facie case existed to show deprivation of constitutional rights. Id. at 435.

In 1971, a unanimous Court held that district courts have broad power to fashion remedies for desegregated schools. To achieve greater racial balance, judges could alter school district zones, reassign teachers, and bus students. SWANN v. CHARLOTTE-MECKLENBURG BD. OF ED., 402 U.S. 1 (1971). A unanimous Court also struck down state anti-busing laws. North Carolina State Board of Education v. Swann, 402 U.S. 43 (1971).

These rulings appeared to clash with language in the Civil Rights Act of 1964, which defined "desegregation" as the assignment of students to public schools without regard to their race, color, religion, or national origin, and stated that desegregation "shall not mean the assignment of students to public schools in order to overcome racial imbalance." 78 Stat. 246, § 401(b). In fact, race was regularly taken into account by courts to devise desegregation plans. McDaniel v. Barresi, 402 U.S. 39, 41 (1971). The Civil Rights Act of 1964 did not empower any federal official or court "to issue any order seeking to achieve a racial balance in any school by requiring the transportation of pupils . . ." 78 Stat. 248, § 407(a). The Court finessed this potential conflict by arguing that the busing provision in the statute was directed at de facto, not de jure, segregation. Swann v. Charlotte-Mecklenburg, 402 U.S. at 17–18.

Within a few years busing was used to integrate schools in the North. A Supreme Court decision in 1973 involved the school system in Denver, Colorado. Parents of black children charged that the school board maintained a segregated system through the use of student attendance zones, school-site selection, and a neighborhood school policy. A 7–1 Court found that the school board intended school segregation in one area, thereby practicing de jure segregation, and that the burden appropriately shifted to the board to prove that other segregated schools were not also the result of intentional actions. Several Justices dismissed the difference between de jure and de facto segregation, preferring that whenever segregated public schools exist there is prima facie evidence of a constitutional violation by the school board. This test would avoid the question of whether segregation resulted from "intent" (de jure) or "effect" (de facto). Keyes v. School District No. 1, Denver, Colo., 413 U.S. 189 (1973).

The next northern school system scrutinized by the Court was in Detroit. Black families claimed that schools had been racially segregated because of official policies. The lower courts concluded that a Detroit-only solution was inadequate;

widespread busing, reaching to outlying districts, would be necessary. The string of unanimous or near-unanimous decisions by the Supreme Court on school segregation was now shattered. Divided 5 to 4, the Court dismissed the remedies adopted by the lower courts. It decided that a cross-district busing plan would disrupt school district lines, violate the tradition of local school control, and thrust judges into the role of "school superintendent" for which they are unqualified. The district court had ordered the school board to obtain at least 295 school buses, with the cost borne by the state. The Supreme Court concluded that a metropolitan area remedy punished outlying districts with no showing that they had committed constitutional violations. MILLIKEN v. BRADLEY, 418 U.S. 717 (1974). In a follow-up case for Detroit, a unanimous Court agreed that lower courts can order compensatory or remedial educational programs for schoolchildren subjected to past acts of de jure segregation. Assistance included reading instruction, in-service teacher training, testing, and counseling. Milliken v. Bradley, 433 U.S. 267 (1977).

The Supreme Court scrutinized two other northern school systems, in Columbus and Dayton, Ohio. The Court decided that there had been de jure segregation, requiring officials to take affirmative action in desegregating the school system. Justice Powell had already expressed opposition to widespread busing as a remedy. Chief Justice Burger agreed that it "is becoming increasingly doubtful that massive public transportation really accomplishes the desirable objectives sought." Columbus Board of Education v. Penick, 443 U.S. 449, 469 (1979). In a dissent, Justice Powell warned that parents resentful of court-ordered integration might withdraw their children from public schools by relocating their families ("white flight") or turning to private schools. Either choice would produce resegregation of public schools. Id. at 484. See also Dayton Board of Education v. Brinkman, 433 U.S. 406 (1977) and Dayton Board of Education v. Brinkman, 443 U.S. 526 (1979). Dissenters in these cases objected to having school boards prove that segregated schools did not result from discriminatory intent.

In addition to placing anti-busing language in the Civil Rights Act of 1964, Congress prohibited the use of appropriated funds to bus students for racial balance. However, these restrictions controlled federal agencies, not the courts. States were affected by some limitations that prohibited agencies from forcing states to bus students as a condition for receiving federal funds.[3] In prohibiting the forced busing of students, Congress sometimes softened the language by adding: "Except as required by the Constitution." 84 Stat. 48, §§ 408, 409 (1970). Congress, issuing findings that busing was sometimes harmful, specified appropriate remedies. And yet it also stated that its actions were "not intended to modify or diminish the authority" of U.S. courts to enforce the Fifth and Fourteenth Amendments. 88 Stat. 515, § 203(b) (1974), codified at 20 U.S.C. § 1702(b) (1982). Other limitations applied directly to the courts. 88 Stat. 517, § 215 (1974), codified at 20 U.S.C. § 1714 (1982). The riders on appropriations bills expired at the end of each fiscal year; other restrictions on busing became part of permanent law.[4]

---

[3]81 Stat. 441, § 16 (1967); 82 Stat. 995, § 409 (1968); 84 Stat. 805, §§ 209, 210 (1970); 85 Stat. 107, §§ 309, 310 (1971); 90 Stat. 21–22, §§ 207–209 (1976); 90 Stat. 1433–1434, §§ 206–208 (1976); 92 Stat. 1585–1586, §§ 207–209 (1978);

[4]80 Stat. 1264, § 205(f) (1966), codified at 42 U.S.C. § 3335(f) (1982); 84 Stat. 169, § 422 (1970), codified at 20 U.S.C. § 1232a (1982); 86 Stat. 371–373, Title VIII (1972), codified at 20 U.S.C. §§ 1651–1656 (1982); 88 Stat. 514–521, Title II (1974), codified at 20 U.S.C. §§ 1701-1758 (1982).

A combination of dissenting Justices, public opposition, and restrictions by Congress eventually forced the courts to abandon widespread busing as a remedy for desegregation. Black parents as well as white parents objected to having their children transported on buses for long distances. They preferred other solutions, including "compensatory schools" or "magnet schools" that offered extra teachers, computers, better laboratories, and other resources. With the support of the Supreme Court, cities abandoned busing as a means of racially integrating their schools. Riddick v. School Bd. of City of Norfolk, 784 F.2d 521 (4th Cir. 1986) (en banc), cert. denied, 479 U.S. 938 (1986).

Desegregation was frustrated by other tactics. "Freedom of choice" plans permitted whites to attend all-black schools and blacks to attend all-white schools. Predictably, whites did not attend black schools and few blacks attended white schools. The Court struck down these plans as inadequate remedies for desegregation.[5] "Transfer plans" allowed students to transfer from a school where they would be in a racial minority back to a former segregated school. A unanimous Court declared this procedure invalid. Goss v. Board of Education, 373 U.S. 683 (1963). Also, states were not permitted to create new school districts that had the effect of producing a refuge for white students. United States v. Scotland Neck Bd. of Educ., 407 U.S. 484 (1972).

Private Schools

Southern states attempted to avoid integrated education by closing public schools with white and black enrollment and setting up "private schools" operated for white students only. County funds provided tuition funds for the private schools, euphemistically called a "freedom of choice" program. Federal courts enjoined the counties from paying tuition grants or giving tax credits as long as public schools remained closed. The Supreme Court supported those rulings and announced, in 1964, that its slogan "all deliberate speed" had produced too much deliberation and not enough speed. Griffin v. School Board, 377 U.S. 218, 229 (1964). The time for deliberate speed "has run out." Id. at 234.[6] The IRS denied tax-exempt status to private schools with racially discriminatory admissions policies. See Prince Edward School Foundation v. Commissioner of Internal Revenue, 478 F.Supp. (D.D.C. 1979), cert. denied, 450 U.S. 944 (1981). Some of these schools, such as the Prince Edward Academy in Virginia, regained tax-exempt status after announcing that they were open to all races.

In Mississippi, the number of virtually all-white private secular schools increased substantially after the desegregation ruling in 1954. In 1973, a unanimous Court held that Mississippi could not give free textbooks to private schools that practiced racial or other invidious discrimination. Norwood v. Harrison, 413 U.S. 455 (1973). Another ruling involved private schools that had been set up in Virginia shortly after the 1954 desegregation decision. These schools excluded qualified children solely

[5]Wright v. Council of City of Emporia, 407 U.S. 451 (1972); Monroe v. Board of Commissioners, 391 U.S. 450 (1968); Raney v. Board of Education, 391 U.S. 443 (1968); Green v. County School Board, 391 U.S. 430 (1968).

[6]Other rejections of the "all deliberate speed" formula: Alexander v. Board of Education, 396 U.S. 1218 (1969); Keyes v. Denver School District, 396 U.S. 1215 (1969); Alexander v. Board of Education, 396 U.S. 19 (1969).

because they were black. A 7–2 Court held that federal law prohibited racial discrimination in the making and enforcement of private contracts practiced by these schools. Runyon v. McCrary, 427 U.S. 160 (1976). *Runyon* was reaffirmed in 1989 in a case involving employment, but the reach of the federal statute was restricted by the Court. Patterson v. McLean Credit Union, 109 S.Ct. 2363 (1989). This case is discussed in greater detail later in this chapter under the section covering employment and affirmative action.

In 1970, the IRS announced that it would not give tax-exempt status to private schools that practiced racial discrimination. That policy persisted until 1982 when the Reagan administration said that the IRS had exceeded its statutory powers. A year later, an 8–1 Court sustained the IRS. The national policy of nondiscrimination could not support the granting of tax-exemption to institutions that adopt racial policies. Tax-exemption is a benefit given to organizations that provide a public benefit. Bob Jones University v. United States, 461 U.S. 574 (1983). In other cases, suits brought against the IRS for failing to deny tax-exempt status to racially discriminatory private schools have been set aside for lack of standing by plaintiffs. Allen v. Wright, 468 U.S. 737 (1984).

DESEGREGATING OTHER ACTIVITIES

Aside from schools and transportation, other facilities and activities available to the public have been the subject of segregation laws: housing, parks and playgrounds, golf courses, swimming pools, beaches, courtrooms, restaurants, and marriage. All three branches have searched for remedies.

Race and Housing

Public schools remain segregated because of housing patterns, both within the city and between the city and the suburbs. Some of these patterns result from discriminatory actions by public officials and private homeowners. The process of breaking down racial barriers depends on a combination of judicial rulings, presidential leadership, congressional enactments, state initiatives, and tolerance practiced by private homeowners.

Compared to the tenacious hold of the separate-but-equal doctrine in the fields of education, transportation, and public accommodations, it is surprising to find a number of early judicial rulings against segregated housing. In 1917, a unanimous Court struck down a city ordinance that prohibited blacks from occupying houses in blocks controlled by whites. Such restrictions, said the Court, exceeded the police power and invaded the right to acquire, enjoy, and use property protected by the Fourteenth Amendment. The case was not so much a vindication of racial equality; rather, it supported the freedom of whites to sell their property without interference. The Court based its decision not only on the Fourteenth Amendment but the civil rights acts passed by Congress in 1866 and 1870. Buchanan v. Warley, 245 U.S. 60, 78–79 (1917). See also Corrigan v. Buckley, 271 U.S. 323 (1926); Benjamin v. Tyler, 273 U.S. 668 (1927); City of Richmond v. Deans, 281 U.S. 704 (1930).

Of major importance is a unanimous opinion by the Court in 1948. Private parties in St. Louis, Missouri, agreed to exclude blacks from buying or occupying residences. The Court held that the agreements (restrictive covenants) did not themselves violate the Fourteenth Amendment. However, it would be a constitutional violation for the state courts to enforce them. SHELLEY v. KRAEMER, 334 U.S. 1 (1948). See also Hurd v. Hodge, 334 U.S. 25 (1948) and Barrows v. Jackson, 346 U.S. 249 (1953).

The principle of *Shelley* also prohibited discrimination against blacks in state-owned buildings. A restaurant in a building owned by Delaware refused to serve blacks. The building, constructed with public funds for public purposes, was owned and operated by the state, which leased part of it to a private operator for a restaurant. The Court held that this made the state a joint participant in operating the restaurant. The proscriptions of the Fourteenth Amendment applied to the restaurant just as though they were "binding covenants" written into the lease itself. Burton v. Wilmington Pkg. Auth., 365 U.S. 715 (1961). States may not distance themselves from racial discrimination in housing, and in effect encourage it, by prohibiting state interference with the selling, leasing, or rental of property. Reitman v. Mulkey, 387 U.S. 369 (1967).

In 1962, President Kennedy issued Executive Order 11063 to prohibit racial, ethnic, and religious discrimination in federally owned and assisted housing. The Civil Rights Act of 1964 prohibited racial discrimination in federally assisted programs, including public housing. In 1968, Congress passed the Fair Housing Act to prohibit the use of race, color, religion, or national origin in the sale or rental of most housing. Passage came in the turmoil of urban riots and widespread violence. One week before the House took its final vote to support open housing, Martin Luther King, Jr., was assassinated. 82 Stat. 81 (1968).

While Congress debated this legislation, an open housing case reached the Supreme Court. An interracial couple had been denied the right to buy a house in suburban St. Louis. Two months after enactment of the fair housing bill, a 7–2 Court held that federal law (dating back to the Civil Rights Act of 1866) prohibited every racially motivated refusal to rent or sell property. The Court ruled that Congress had authority under the Thirteenth Amendment to pass the 1866 legislation. The Amendment forbade not only slavery but the "badges and the incidents of slavery." Congress may prohibit both state action and private action that restrict the right of blacks to purchase, lease, and use property. JONES v. MAYER, 392 U.S. 409 (1968).

A year later, the Court held that questions of fair housing may not be put to voters for approval. The rights of minorities cannot be delegated to referenda results. Hunter v. Erickson, 393 U.S. 385 (1969). When the issue is not fair housing but simply low-rent public housing, states may put such matters to the people in the form of a referendum. The question here is not racial but rather income class (poor versus rich). James v. Valtierra, 402 U.S. 137 (1971). The Court also held that "private social clubs" may not use racial discrimination to prevent white owners from leasing their homes to blacks. These practices violate congressional policy dating back to 1866. Sullivan v. Little Hunting Park, 396 U.S. 229 (1969).

Subsequent cases reviewed segregation in public housing projects. Black tenants in Chicago claimed that the housing authority, supported by the Department of Housing and Urban Development (HUD), had deliberately selected public housing sites to avoid placing blacks in white neighborhoods. A unanimous Court agreed that metropolitan area remedies, covering both city and suburbs, might be necessary to alleviate the effects of segregated housing. Areawide action was justified in this case because HUD itself had violated the Constitution and statutes. Hills v. Gautreaux, 425 U.S. 284 (1976).

Segregated housing partly reflects unequal income. Many blacks cannot afford single-family homes in white neighborhoods. Developers may seek a rezoning permit to build racially integrated housing (multiple-family townhouses and apartments). However, if their application is denied and they litigate, they must prove that the denial results from intentional racial discrimination. It is not enough that the "ultimate effect" of a rezoning denial is discrimination on the basis of race. Arlington Heights v. Metropolitan Housing Corp., 429 U.S. 252 (1977). In other cases, challenges to racial discrimination in housing have been denied on grounds of standing. Warth v. Seldin, 422 U.S. 490 (1975).

Segregated housing persists throughout the country. Studies conducted by sending white, black, and Hispanic "testers" to real estate offices reveal that discrimination continues to be practiced against blacks and dark-skinned Hispanics. Havens Realty Corp. v. Coleman, 455 U.S. 363 (1982). The Fair Housing Act of 1968 was never effectively enforced. To maintain integrated housing in public projects, some authorities select tenants according to a racial quota. The result: qualified applicants are often denied housing because of their race, and the use of racial quotas can be challenged in court as a violation of the Civil Rights Act of 1964 and the Fair Housing Act of 1968. Washington Post, November 30, 1985, at El. To strengthen the enforcement of the Fair Housing Act, Congress passed legislation in 1988 to give the executive branch new authority to bring lawsuits when mediation efforts fail. The law permits government to seek large monetary damages for victims of housing discrimination. 102 Stat. 1619 (1988).

Other Public Facilities

Following *Brown* v. *Board of Education*, federal courts struck down a number of laws that discriminated on the basis of race. In 1955, the Court held that cities and states could not use the police power to enforce racial segregation in public beaches and bathhouses. Dawson v. Mayor, 220 F.2d 386 (4th Cir. 1955), aff'd, 350 U.S. 877 (1955). Blacks could not be prohibited from using public golf courses and parks reserved for whites. Holmes v. City of Atlanta, 223 F.2d 93 (5th Cir. 1955), aff'd, 350 U.S. 879 (1955). In 1956, a three-judge court held that an Alabama statute and a city ordinance of Montgomery, Alabama, requiring segregation on buses, violated the Due Process and Equal Protection Clauses of the Fourteenth Amendment. The court's decision, explicitly overruling *Plessy* v. *Ferguson*, was affirmed by the Supreme Court. Browder v. Gayle, 142 F.Supp. 707 (M.D. Ala. 1956), aff'd, 352 U.S. 903 (1956). A unanimous Court held that states may not require segregation in a courtroom. Johnson v. Virginia, 373 U.S. 61 (1963).

Another unanimous decision ruled that the exclusion of blacks from public parks, playgrounds, community centers, and golf courses violated the Fourteenth Amendment. Watson v. Memphis, 373 U.S. 526 (1963). State efforts to designate in primary, general, and special elections the race of the candidates were struck down by a unanimous Court because such designations encouraged voters to discriminate on the basis of race. The fact that the labeling provision applied equally to blacks and whites did not save state actions that arouse racial prejudice. Anderson v. Martin, 375 U.S. 399 (1964). The Court also held that when blacks travel on an interstate bus, and the bus stops at a terminal and restaurant that function as an integral part of the bus system, the restaurant may not be segregated by race. Boynton v. Virginia, 364 U.S. 454 (1960).

Blacks sat at lunch counters to challenge the policy of owners to deny them service. A cluster of cases pushed restaurants in the direction of abandoning that policy, but these cases also implied that the "final word" on this issue would have to come from legislatures, not courts.[7] Mounting pressure for action finally culminated in passage of the Civil Rights Act of 1964. One of its sections on public accommodations barred discrimination on grounds of race, color, religion, or national origin if the operations affected interstate commerce or discrimination was supported by state action. Activities covered within this section included restaurants, cafeterias, lunchrooms, lunch counters, soda fountains, gas stations, movies, theaters, concert halls, sports arenas, stadiums, or any inn, hotel, motel, or lodging house for transient guests other than units with five or less rooms. This section did not apply to private clubs. Congressional action on public accommodations appeared to contradict the Civil Rights Cases of 1883, which had never been overruled by the Supreme Court. Congress avoided this potential conflict by basing the statute not only on the Civil War amendments but also on the Commerce Clause (pp. 1016-1017).

The public accommodation section was sustained in two unanimous rulings by the Court. The first involved a large motel in Atlanta, Georgia, used by interstate travelers. The Court supported the public accommodation provision as a valid exercise of congressional power under the Commerce Clause. HEART OF ATLANTA MOTEL v. UNITED STATES, 379 U.S. 241 (1964). The second case concerned a restaurant in Birmingham, Alabama. Although it catered to local white customers and provided a take-out service for blacks, it served food obtained from interstate commerce and was therefore within the reach of the Commerce Power as exercised by Congress. The Act specifically covers restaurants where "a substantial portion" of the food served "has moved in commerce." Katzenbach v. McClung, 379 U.S. 294 (1964). See also Daniel v. Paul, 395 U.S. 298 (1969).

In a case decided months after the Civil Rights Act of 1964, the Court reviewed the convictions of blacks who had participated in a sit-in. Relying on the Act, a 5–4 Court vacated the convictions and dismissed the prosecutions, even though the conduct in the case had occurred before the Act. Furthermore, the prosecutions were under state law. Hamm v. Rock Hill, 379 U.S. 306 (1964). Similarly, the Court returned to the state of Maryland a case in which blacks had been arrested and convicted for refusing to leave a restaurant. The fact that the state later changed the law and replaced it with a public accommodations law prompted the Court to return the case with the strong suggestion that the convictions be dismissed. Bell v. Maryland, 378 U.S. 226 (1964).

Private Facilities

The public accommodations title of the Civil Rights Act of 1964 did not apply to "a private club or other establishment not in fact open to the public," other than the facilities covered by the title (Section 201(e)). Several decisions fleshed out the scope of this section. Even when a facility is privately owned, action by the state to enforce a private policy of racial segregation violates the Equal Protection Clause of the

---

[7]Bouie v. City of Columbia, 378 U.S. 347 (1964); Bell v. Maryland, 378 U.S. 226 (1964); Avent v. North Carolina, 373 U.S. 375 (1963); Gober v. City of Birmingham, 373 U.S. 374 (1963); Lombard v. Louisiana, 373 U.S. 267 (1963); Shuttlesworth v. City of Birmingham, 373 U.S. 262 (1963); Peterson v. City of Greenville, 373 U.S. 244 (1963); Turner v. City of Memphis, 369 U.S. 350 (1962); Garner v. Louisiana, 368 U.S. 157 (1961).

Fourteenth Amendment. Griffin v. Maryland, 378 U.S. 130 (1964). When private individuals or groups exercise powers or perform functions governmental in nature, such as establishing a park for whites only, they become agencies or instrumentalities of the state and are subject to the restrictions of the Fourteenth Amendment. Evans v. Newton, 382 U.S. 296 (1966).

As with school segregation, opponents of racial equality tried a number of tactics. Residents of Virginia opened playground facilities and a community park for whites only. A 6–3 Court held that this nonstock corporation, acting as a "private social club," practiced racial discrimination in violation of federal law. Sullivan v. Little Hunting Park, 396 U.S. 229 (1969). A unanimous Court in 1973 ruled that a recreation association violated congressional policy by limiting the use of its swimming pool to white members and their white guests. The Court considered this case indistinguishable from *Sullivan*. Tillman v. Wheaton-Haven Recreation Assn., 410 U.S. 431 (1973).

A different result was reached in a 1972 case. A black guest at a private club had been denied service in the dining room and bar solely because of his race. Did the issuance of a state liquor license make the discriminatory practices "state action"? The Court, divided 6–3, relied on the Civil Rights Cases of 1883 to distinguish between discriminatory action by the state, which is prohibited by the Equal Protection Clause, and discriminatory action by private parties, against which the Clause erects no shield. The Court was reluctant to conclude that the provision of state benefits or services, including such necessities as electricity, water, and police and fire protection, was sufficient to implicate the state and automatically convert a private entity into state action. MOOSE LODGE NO. 107 v. IRVIS, 407 U.S. 163 (1972). Private companies and schools that receive almost all of their funds from public sources do not necessarily perform a "state action." Randell-Baker v. Kohn, 457 U.S. 830 (1982).

Marriage and Cohabitation

In 1955, the Court received a miscegenation case from Virginia. Reluctant to strike down a law against mixed marriages, the Court decided to dodge this socially explosive issue. The Court's ruling on desegregation in 1954 had been criticized by opponents who predicted that integrated schools would produce "mongrelization" of the white race. A state court, in upholding the Virginia statute, said that natural law forbade interracial marriage: "the social amalgamation which leads to a corruption of races is as clearly divine as that which imparted to them different natures." Naim v. Naim, 87 S.E.2d 749, 752 (Va. 1955). State regulation of marriages was necessary to prevent "a mongrel breed of citizens." Id. at 756.

The Supreme Court quickly returned the case to Virginia, giving time for its ruling on desegregation to establish itself as the law of the land. Naim v. Naim, 350 U.S. 891 (1955). A unanimous ruling in 1964 held that Florida's statute prohibiting the cohabitation of unmarried interracial couples, singling them out for punishment, was a denial of equal protection. McLaughlin v. Florida, 379 U.S. 184 (1964). By 1967, the Court was prepared to strike down miscegenation laws and did so unanimously. It pointed out that fourteen states in the previous fifteen years had repealed laws prohibiting interracial marriages. Contemporary public opinion thus played a part. The Court rejected the argument that the state law should be upheld because the framers of the Fourteenth Amendment did not intend to prohibit miscegenation laws. "Under our Constitution, the freedom to marry, or not marry, a person of another race resides with the individual and cannot be infringed by the State." Loving v. Virginia, 388 U.S. 1, 12 (1967).

EMPLOYMENT AND AFFIRMATIVE ACTION

Racial segregation persists because of a number of interlocking cycles. Segregated housing contributes to segregated education; segregated education is a factor in segregated employment. One way to combat racial segregation is through job opportunities. Blacks and Hispanics with stable jobs and higher incomes have greater choices in deciding where to live and where to send their children to school. To support these choices, the government has relied on the controversial tools of quotas and affirmative action (or "reverse discrimination").

From 1941 to 1958, Presidents Roosevelt, Truman, and Eisenhower issued a number of Executive Orders to improve employment opportunities for blacks. Under pressure from civil rights activists who protested discrimination in hiring, Roosevelt issued an Executive Order in 1941 to establish the Committee on Fair Employment Practices. The purpose was to increase black employment in the defense industry. Executive Order 8802 declared that "there shall be no discrimination in the employment of workers in defense industries or government because of race, creed, color, or national origin . . ." Outbreaks of racial violence after World War II prompted Truman, in 1946, to issue Executive Order 9808 to establish the President's Committee on Civil Rights. The Committee's report, *To Secure These Rights,* was released in 1947. The Committee attacked segregation and the separate-but-equal doctrine as morally wrong and economically wasteful. In a major address to Congress on February 2, 1948, Truman set forth an agenda for civil rights. The goals he established, including a commission to prevent unfair discrimination in employment, had to await passage of the civil rights bills from 1957 to 1965.

In the meantime, President Kennedy issued Executive Order 10925 in 1961 to establish the President's Committee on Equal Employment Opportunity. There were two goals: equal access to employment within the government, and equal opportunity for those who receive government contracts. As a condition for receiving federal contracts, private companies had to agree to nondiscriminatory policies. Executive Order 11114, issued in 1963, extended the Committee's authority to include federally assisted construction. President Johnson issued Executive Order 11246 in 1965, vesting in the Secretary of Labor the responsibility for ensuring nondiscrimination by government contractors.

The Office of Federal Contract Compliance (OFCC), created to administer Johnson's order, was authorized to withhold or cancel contracts with companies that violated equal employment practices. This agency was later called the Office of Federal Contract Compliance Programs (OFCCP). In 1987, a House report concluded that enforcement at the OFCCP had come to a "virtual standstill" during the Reagan administration. The declining effectiveness of OFCCP reflected Attorney General Meese's attempt to revise Executive Order 11246 to prohibit the use of goals and timetables for affirmative action. In 1987, the head of the OFCCP resigned because he thought the Reagan administration had failed to give its full support.[8]

---

[8]House Committee on Education and Labor, A Report on the Investigation of the Civil Rights Enforcement Activities of the Office of Federal Contract Compliance Programs, U.S. Department of Labor, 100th Cong., 1st Sess. 3, 9–10, 55–57 (October 1987); "Affirmative Action Official Quits Over Staff Cuts, Lack of Support," Washington Post, January 22, 1987, at A19.

Title VII of the Civil Rights Act of 1964 prohibits employment practices based on race, color, religion, sex, or national origin. Congress created the Equal Employment Opportunity Commission (EEOC) to oversee this title, but gave the commission authority only to conciliate complaints of job bias. It had no power to issue cease-and-desist orders to employers or to file suit in court. Enforcement powers were strengthened in 1972 by authorizing the EEOC to take discrimination cases to federal court if conciliation efforts fail. 86 Stat. 103 (1972). The 1972 amendments also extended Title VII coverage to state and local government employees. For example, see Hazelwood School District v. United States, 433 U.S. 299 (1977).

In 1971, a unanimous Court interpreted Title VII to prohibit the use of hiring practices that are not job-related and that operate to exclude blacks. In this case, a company required a high school diploma and the taking of an intelligence test. The Court said it was immaterial whether the employer had a discriminatory intent. Griggs v. Duke Power Co., 401 U.S. 424 (1971). Other decisions clarified the intent of Title VII.[9] The *Griggs* test appeared to require an employee to prove only disparate *results*, not the employer's *intent*. However, that doctrine was undermined in *Wards Cove Packing Co.* v. *Atonio* (1989), discussed in the next section on affirmative action.

Another case on employment tests was decided in 1976. Two blacks, after being rejected as police officers, claimed that the written personnel tests bore no relation to job performance and were racially discriminatory. Although the police department had made affirmative efforts to recruit black officers, the tests excluded a disproportionately high number of black applicants. The tests measured verbal ability, vocabulary, reading, and comprehension. The Court, by a 7–2 vote, held that the tests were not unconstitutional solely because they had a racially disproportionate impact. In an apparent conflict with *Griggs*, the Court said that there must be a purpose to discriminate. The Court justified a different conclusion because this was not a Title VII case. The plaintiffs asserted that the tests violated their rights under the Due Process Clause of the Fifth Amendment, under 42 U.S.C. § 1981, and under the D.C. Code. WASHINGTON v. DAVIS, 426 U.S. 229 (1976).

Affirmative Action

Civil rights legislation appeared to prohibit racial discrimination in any form. For example, Section 703 of Title VII makes it unlawful to "discriminate . . . because of . . . race" in hiring and in the selection of apprentices for training programs. Moreover, Section 703(j) states that nothing in Title VII shall be interpreted to require "preferential treatment" to any individual for reasons of race or color. On the other hand, Section 706(g) authorized a court to order "such affirmative action as may be appropriate, which may include reinstatement or hiring of employees, with or without backpay . . ." This authority was strengthened in 1972 to read: "such

[9]Watson v. Fort Worth Bank & Trust, 108 S.Ct. 2777 (1988); Goodman v. Lukens Steel Co., 482 U.S. 656 (1987); Ford Motor Co. v. EEOC, 458 U.S. 219 (1982); Connecticut v. Teal, 457 U.S. 440 (1982); Pullman-Standard v. Swint, 456 U.S. 273 (1982); Furnco Construction Corp. v. Waters, 438 U.S. 567 (1978); International Brotherhood of Teamsters, 431 U.S. 324 (1977); McDonald v. Sante Fe Trail Transp. Co., 427 U.S. 273 (1976); Franks v. Bowman Transportation Co., 424 U.S. 747 (1976); Albemarle Paper Co. v. Moody, 422 U.S. 405 (1975); Johnson v. Railway Express Agency, 421 U.S. 454 (1975); Alexander v. Gardner-Denver Co., 415 U.S. 36 (1974); Espinoza v. Farah Mfg. Co., 414 U.S. 86 (1973); McDonnel Douglas Corp. v. Green, 411 U.S. 792 (1973). Title VII cases involving sex discrimination are discussed on pp. 1053–1056, 1058.

affirmative action as may be appropriate, which may include, but is not limited to, reinstatement or hiring of employees, with or without back pay . . . or any other equitable relief as the court deems appropriate." 86 Stat. 107. Senator Ervin offered an amendment in 1972 to prohibit any federal agency or office from requiring employers to practice "discrimination in reverse." His amendment was rejected by the lopsided majority of 44–22, in part because it would deprive courts of their power to remedy cases of discrimination. 118 Cong. Rec. 1661–1676 (1972).

A number of government and private programs give preferential treatment to certain races. Little opposition exists to programs that make special efforts to recruit minorities, assuring that a sufficient number will be in the pool of candidates. But should race be a factor in making the selections? Can employers prefer, for reasons of race, a minority over an equally qualified white? Does affirmative action allow the acceptance of a minority who is less qualified? Is racial discrimination an appropriate means to compensate for past injuries and injustices? Should quotas or "goals" be established to guarantee the acceptance of a specific number of blacks, Hispanics, and other minorities?

Initially, the judiciary interpreted congressional policy to require a standard of racial neutrality in hiring. Race was not to be a factor. In 1971, a unanimous Court stated that Congress did not, in Title VII of the Civil Rights Act of 1964, command "that the less qualified be preferred over the better qualified simply because of minority origins. Far from disparaging job qualifications as such, Congress has made such qualifications the controlling factor, so that race, religion, nationality, and sex become irrelevant." Griggs v. Duke Power Co., 401 U.S. at 436. Congress prohibited discriminatory preference "for any group, minority or majority." Id. at 431. A unanimous Court in 1976 held that Title VII prohibits racial discrimination whether the victim is black or white. Employers could not dismiss whites for an offense and retain a black who committed the same offense. McDonald v. Sante Fe Trail Transp. Co., 427 U.S. 273 (1976).

Yet various administrations have used race as a criterion in overseeing the award of federal contracts. Under the "Philadelphia Plan," developed by the Nixon administration, contractors had to set specific goals for hiring members of minority groups as a condition for working on federally assisted projects. Federal courts upheld the legality of the plan in 1970 and 1971, as well as the Executive Order that placed it in operation.[10]

The question of affirmative action first confronted the Court in 1974. Marco DeFunis, Jr., a white applicant to the University of Washington Law School, was denied admission. He claimed that the school's policy discriminated against him. Out of 150 openings for first-year students, the school set aside a specific number of places for minority applicants (blacks, Chicanos, American Indians, and Filipinos). DeFunis scored higher than most of the minorities accepted. Had the minority applicants been considered under the same procedure applied to him, none of those eventually enrolled would have been admitted.

After DeFunis' claim of discrimination was upheld by a state trial court, he was

---

[10]Contractors Ass'n of Eastern Pa. v. Secretary of Labor, 442 F.2d 159 (3d Cir. 1971), cert. denied, 404 U.S. 854 (1971). See also Contractors Ass'n of Eastern Pa. v. Secretary of Labor, 311 F.Supp. 1002 (E.D. Pa. 1970); Robert P. Schuwerk, "The Philadelphia Plan: A Study in the Dynamics of Executive Power," 39 U. Chi. L. Rev. 723 (1972); and "Committee Analysis of Executive Order 11246 (The Affirmative Action Program)," prepared by the Senate Committee on Labor and Human Resources, 97th Cong., 2d Sess. (Comm. Print April 1982).

admitted to the law school. The trial court was reversed by the Washington Supreme Court, but by that time DeFunis was in his second year. The U.S. Supreme Court, reviewing his appeal when he was in his final year, held the case moot. DeFunis v. Odegaard, 416 U.S. 312 (1974). Among the questions the Court was able to avoid: If positions are reserved for blacks, Chicanos, American Indians, and Filipinos, why not Orientals and other "minorities"? How are courts to draw and justify such lines? Excerpts of this decision are reprinted in Chapter 3.

Within a few years the issue of affirmative action returned to the Court, this time involving Allan Bakke's application to the medical school at the University of California at Davis. The school had two admissions programs: a regular admissions program (for Bakke and other nonminority candidates) and a special admissions program for "disadvantaged" minorities (blacks, Chicanos, Asians, and American Indians). Disadvantaged whites were not admitted to the special program, although many applied. Out of 100 openings for entering students, 16 were reserved for special admissions. Bakke was rejected twice; minorities with significantly lower scores were admitted under the special program. The Supreme Court decided that Bakke should be admitted to the medical school and that the special admissions program was invalid. However, it reversed the judgment of lower courts that race could not be taken into account in an admissions program. The judgment of the Court, concurrences, and separate opinions spread across 156 rambling pages. Eight Justices found fault with parts of the opinion of the Court written by Powell. REGENTS OF THE UNIVERSITY OF CALIFORNIA v. BAKKE, 438 U.S. 265 (1978).

The following year, a 5–2 Court supported the use of affirmative action for private employment. It had been the practice in some industries to hire as craftworkers only persons with prior craft experience; blacks were usually excluded from craft unions. To open up opportunities for the well-paying craft jobs, Kaiser Aluminum and the United Steelworkers union agreed upon an affirmative action plan. Fifty percent of craft-training openings were reserved for black employees until the percentage of black craftworkers equaled the percentage of blacks in the local labor force. The most senior black trainee had less seniority than several whites who were rejected. One of the whites, Brian Weber, filed a class action claiming that the plan violated Title VII by discriminating on the basis of race. The Court held that Title VII does not prohibit all private, voluntary, race-conscious affirmative action programs to overcome past discrimination. Chief Justice Burger and Justice Rehnquist dissented, accusing the majority of rewriting Title VII. Justice Blackmun, in a concurrence, pointed out that if the Court "has misperceived the political will, it has the assurance that because the question is statutory Congress may set a different course if it so chooses." United Steelworkers v. Weber, 443 U.S. 193, 216 (1979).

Although language in some of the civil rights acts appeared to announce a race-neutral policy, other statutes endorsed preferential treatment. Two years before *Weber*, Congress passed legislation to set aside 10 percent of public works funds for "minority business enterprises." The statute defined minority group members as U.S. citizens "who are Negroes, Spanish-speaking, Orientals, Indians, Eskimos, and Aleuts." 91 Stat. 117. Congressional action had been preceded by several Executive Orders during the Nixon administration directing federal agencies to increase the proportion of procurement contracts to minority business enteprises.[11]

---

[11]Executive Order 11458, 34 Fed. Reg. 4937 (1969); Executive Order 11518, 35 Fed. Reg. 4939 (1970); Executive Order 11625, 36 Fed. Reg. 19967 (1971); 1969 Public Papers of the Presidents 197–198, 994–995; 1970 Public Papers of the Presidents 284–288.

A 6–3 Court found the set-aside an acceptable exercise of congressional authority under the Spending Power. The Court said the statute could also be justified on the basis of congressional power under the Commerce Clause or Section 5 of the Fourteenth Amendment. The use of racial and ethnic criteria as a condition attached to a federal grant did not violate the equal protection component of the Due Process Clause of the Fifth Amendment. FULLILOVE v. KLUTZNICK, 448 U.S. 448 (1980).

The decision in *Fullilove* did not necessarily support the use of set-asides by states and cities. In 1989 the Court, by a 6–3 vote, struck down a city of Richmond plan that required contractors receiving city construction contracts to subcontract at least 30 percent of the funds to "minority business enterprises" (Blacks, Hispanics, Orientals, Indians, Eskimos, and Aleuts). The Court rejected *Fullilove* as an acceptable precedent, pointing out that the Fourteenth Amendment authorizes Congress, not cities or states, to act against racial discrimination. Also, the plan was not narrowly tailored to accomplish a remedial purpose. With regard to the set-aside for such groups as the Aleuts, the Court remarked: "The gross overinclusiveness of Richmond's racial preference strongly impugns the city's claim of remedial motivation." Richmond v. Croson Co., 109 S.Ct. 706, 728 (1989). The twenty-two states that currently set aside a specific percentage of funds for minority business enterprises must now reexamine them in light of *Croson*'s demand for a detailed, documentary record of past discrimination and the selection of narrowly tailored remedies. They can also shift the emphasis from minority businesses to "disadvantaged businesses" in distressed communities, accomplishing much the same purpose. Waren, "Minority Set-Aside Programs: What Future After *Richmond vs. Croson?*," 15 State Legislatures 32 (July 1989).

After resolving the question of congressional power in *Fullilove*, the Court next turned to another Title VII case. Two black members of a Memphis, Tennessee, fire department filed a complaint of racial discrimination. A consent decree (incorporating the agreement of the two parties) was issued by a district court to remedy the department's hiring and promotion practices. When budget deficits required the release of some city employees, the court enjoined the department from following its seniority system to decide layoffs. A modified layoff plan resulted in white employees, with more seniority than black employees, being laid off. A 6–3 Court held that the injunction exceeded the consent decree, which had made no mention of layoffs, demotions, or departures from the seniority system. Firefighters v. Stotts, 467 U.S. 561 (1984).

Two years later, in another Title VII case, the Court affirmed a lower court's judgment that established a 29 percent nonwhite membership goal in a union, based on the percentage of nonwhites in the local labor force. The decision is significant because the Court agreed that race-conscious relief can be granted to benefit individuals who are not identified victims of unlawful discrimination. The Justice Department, and the Justices who dissented, argued that the legislative history of Title VII indicates that Congress intended that affirmative relief could benefit only those who had been identified as victims of past discrimination. LOCAL 28 OF SHEET METAL WORKERS v. EEOC, 478 U.S. 421 (1986). In a second case issued that day, the Court decided that Title VII does not preclude consent decrees that benefit individuals who were not the actual victims of discriminatory practices. The Court held that a consent decree was not among the "orders" referred to in Section 706(g), which limits the type of affirmative relief that courts can grant. Firefighters v. Cleveland, 478 U.S. 501 (1986). These two decisions represented a direct rebuff to the Reagan administration's argument that remedial relief was available only for identifiable victims of discrimination. Following the decisions, the EEOC dropped its opposition to affirmative action.

Although the Court has deferred to congressional actions that benefit minorities, and has supported private efforts to hire minorities or admit them to universities, a more stringent review is applied to the use of racial classification for layoffs. Nonminority school teachers in Michigan challenged a provision in a collective bargaining agreement that allowed the school board to give preferential protection to minorities in case of layoffs. A 5–4 decision held that the agreement violated the Fourteenth Amendment. The Court reasoned that when affirmative action is used for hiring goals, the burden on innocent individuals is diffused among society generally, whereas layoffs represent a greater and more intrusive loss to specific employees. Wygant v. Jackson Bd. of Educ., 476 U.S. 267 (1986).

The general support for some form of affirmative action is underscored by a 1987 decision. For almost four decades, Alabama had excluded blacks as state troopers. In 1972, a district court ordered a hiring quota and directed the state to refrain from discrimination in hiring practices, including promotions. Other court actions were ineffective in producing promotions for blacks. Finally, under court order, the state promoted eight blacks and eight whites. A 5–4 Court affirmed this remedy, citing the long and systematic exclusion of blacks, the continuous practice of discrimination, and the state's record of delay and resistance. Even the four dissenters did not totally oppose affirmative action or quotas. They merely objected that the district court's particular remedy was not narrowly tailored to achieve the appropriate results. United States v. Paradise, 480 U.S. 149 (1987). Also in 1987, the Court approved affirmative action to increase promotional opportunities for women. Johnson v. Transportation Agency, 480 U.S. 616 (1987), discussed at pp. 1058, 1105–1111.

After Anthony Kennedy replaced Lewis Powell in 1988, the Court began to backtrack from its previous positions on civil rights. This pattern became most pronounced during the spring of 1989, when the Court issued a series of stunning rulings. One decision shifted the burden to employees to prove that racial disparities in the workforce result from employment practices and are not justified by business needs. This new test conflicted with the *Griggs* ruling in 1971, which appeared to require an employee to demonstrate disparate results, not intent. Wards Cove Packing Co. v. Atonio, 109 S.Ct. 2115 (1989). Since this decision is a statutory interpretation of Title VII, Congress can rewrite the statute and overturn the Court. Legislation has already been introduced to do precisely that.

Also disturbing was a decision that limited the reach of a civil rights statute passed in 1866, now codified at 42 U.S.C. § 1981. The law gives blacks the same right to "make and enforce contracts" as whites. Brenda Patterson, a black woman, claimed that her employer had harassed her, withheld promotion, and discharged her for reasons of race. The Court decided that § 1981 is limited to prohibiting discriminatory actions *before* someone is hired, not after, and advised Patterson that she should have acted under Title VII. Patterson v. McLean Credit Union, 109 S.Ct. 2363 (1989). Although Title VII is not a full substitute for § 1981, nothing prevents Congress from changing this statute to prohibit racial harassment on the job.

A third decision gives white men new authority to challenge consent decrees that embody court-approved affirmative action plans. To avoid future challenges, consent decrees must now reach out to all groups that might be affected. Martin v. Wilks, 109 S.Ct. 2180 (1989). How much this will complicate affirmative action settlements is unclear. Since the Court decided the case by interpreting the Federal Rules of Civil Procedure, Congress could enter the fray and reverse the Court. As a practical matter, however, the lack of public consensus on affirmative action makes the prospect for legislative action dim.[12]

The preoccupation with race in American constitutional law continues with little interruption. The first effort to reconcile the Declaration of Independence and the Constitution came from Congress, which passed the three Civil War amendments (the Thirteenth, Fourteenth, and Fifteenth) and the Civil Rights Acts of 1866 and 1875. The nation then turned its back on this commitment for decades. During the 1930s and 1940s, the courts and the President began to take some initiatives to eliminate discrimination against blacks. America's contribution in World War II to combat racism in Europe made it imperative, after the war, for America to honor its democratic ideals. That was especially important to prevent communist leaders from taunting the United States for its betrayal of democratic principles. All of those forces gathered to produce the political momentum for *Brown* v. *Board of Education*.

Since 1954 the effort to eradicate racism has collided with stubborn counterforces: state resistance, housing patterns, and job discrimination. Despite a series of court orders, beginning in 1954 and stretching over the next decade, little was accomplished toward desegregation until Congress and the President in the Civil Rights Act of 1964 confronted the injustices of racism. Judicial remedies in the form of school busing proved counterproductive and were abandoned. Although substantial progress has been achieved in recent decades, the policy of affirmative action has created major strains in a society that wants to eliminate racial discrimination without abandoning the merit principle. Precisely how to implement affirmative action, and for how long, is a task that demands the attention and skills of all sectors of society, public and private, federal and state, and all three branches of government.

Selected Readings

BICKEL, ALEXANDER M. "The Original Understanding and the Segregation Decision." 69 *Harvard Law Review* 1 (1955).

BLAUSTEIN, ALBERT, P., AND CLARENCE CLYDE FERGUSON, JR. *Desegregation and the Law.* New York: Vintage, 1962.

BLAUSTEIN, ALBERT P., AND ROBERT L. ZANGRANDO, eds. *Civil Rights and the American Negro.* New York: Washington Square Press, 1968.

CASPER, GERHARD. "Jones v. Mayer: Clio, Bemused and Confused Muse." 1968 *Supreme Court Review* 89.

DORSEN, NORMAN. *Discrimination and Civil Rights.* Boston: Little, Brown, 1969.

ELY, JOHN HART. "The Constitutionality of Reverse Racial Discrimination." 41 *University of Chicago Law Review* 723 (1974).

FALLON, RICHARD H., JR., AND PAUL C. WEILER. "Firefighters v. Stotts: Conflicting Models of Racial Justice." 1984 *Supreme Court Review* 1.

FINCH, MINNIE. *The NAACP: Its Fight for Justice.* Metuchen, N.J.: Scarecrow Press, 1981.

FRANKLIN, JOHN HOPE. *From Slavery to Freedom: A History of Negro Americans.* New York: Knopf, 1980.

FREED, MAYER G., AND DANIEL D. POLSBY. "Race, Religion, and Public Policy: Bob Jones University v. United States." 1983 *Supreme Court Review* 1.

GLAZER, NATHAN. *Affirmative Discrimination.* New York: Basic Books, 1975.

[12]Also during the spring of 1989 the Court handed down two other rulings restrictive of Title VII rights. Independent Fed. of Flight Attendants v. Zipes, 109 S.Ct. 2732 (1989); Lorance v. AT&T Technologies, Inc., 109 S.Ct. 2261 (1989).

GRAGLIA, LINO A. *Disaster by Decree: The Supreme Court's Decisions on Race and the Schools*. Ithaca, N.Y.: Cornell University Press, 1976.

GREENAWALT, KENT. *Discrimination and Reverse Discrimination*. New York: Knopf, 1983.

HAMILTON, CHARLES V. *The Bench and the Ballot: Southern Federal Judges and Black Voters*. New York: Oxford University Press, 1973.

HYMAN, HAROLD M., AND WILLIAM M. WEICEK. *Equal Justice Under Law*. New York: Harper & Row, 1982.

KITCH, EDMUND W. "The Return of Color-Consciousness to the Constitution: Weber, Dayton and Columbus." 1979 *Supreme Court Review* 1.

KLUGER, RICHARD. *Simple Justice*. New York: Knopf, 1976.

LIVINGSTON, JOHN C. *Fair Game? Inequality and Affirmative Action*. San Francisco: W. H. Freeman, 1979.

MORGAN, RUTH. *The President and Civil Rights: Policy-Making by Executive Order*. New York: St. Martin's Press, 1970.

PELTASON, JACK. *Fifty-Eight Lonely Men: Southern Federal Judges and School Desegregation*. New York: Harcourt, Brace & World, 1961.

POSNER, RICHARD A. "The DeFunis Case and the Constitutionality of Preferential Treatment of Racial Minorities." 1974 *Supreme Court Review* 1.

SINDLER, ALLAN P. *Bakke, DeFunis, and Minority Admissions*. New York: Longman, 1978.

STRAUSS, DAVID A. "The Myth of Colorblindness." 1986 *Supreme Court Review* 99.

VOSE, CLEMENT E. *Causasians Only: The Supreme Court, the NAACP, and the Restrictive Covenant Cases*. Berkeley: University of California Press, 1959.

WILKINSON, J. HARVIE, III. *From Brown to Bakke: The Supreme Court and School Integration*. New York: Oxford University Press, 1979.

WOLK, ALLAN. *The Presidency and Black Civil Rights: Eisenhower to Nixon*. Cranbury, N.J.: Fairleigh Dickinson University Press, 1971.

Dred Scott v. Sandford

16 How. 393 (1857)

Dred Scott, a Negro slave, belonged to Dr. Emerson, who took him in 1834 from Missouri to the free state of Illinois. In 1836, Dr. Emerson took Dred Scott to a military post in the territory known as Upper Louisiana, situated north of 36 degrees, 30 minutes, also free territory. In 1838, they returned to Missouri. Dred Scott and his wife and two daughters were later sold to John F. A. Sanford (incorrectly spelled in the case as Sandford). Dred Scott brought an action in the Circuit Court of the United States, claiming that as a result of his stay in free territory he was a citizen of Missouri capable of suing for his freedom. The case might have been confined to the question whether the Circuit Court had jurisdiction to hear the case, or whether Dred Scott was a citizen. Instead, the issues were broadened to include the power of Congress to exclude slavery in the territories.

Mr. Chief Justice TANEY delivered the opinion of the court.

. . .

The question is simply this: Can a negro, whose ancestors were imported into this country, and sold as slaves, become a member of the political community formed and brought into existence by the Constitution of the United States, and as such become entitled to all the rights, and privileges, and immunities, guaranteed by that instrument to the citizen? One of which rights is the privilege of suing in a court of the United States in the cases specified in the Constitution.

It will be observed, that the plea applies to that class of persons only whose ancestors were negroes of the African race, and imported into this country, and sold and held as slaves. The only matter in issue before the court, therefore, is, whether the descendants of such slaves, when they shall be emancipated, or who are born of parents who had become free before their birth, are citizens of a State, in the sense in which the word citizen is used in the Constitution of the United States. And this being the only matter in dispute on the pleadings, the court must be understood as speaking in this opinion of that class only, that is, of those persons who are the descendants of Africans who were imported into this country, and sold as slaves.

. . .

In discussing this question, we must not confound the rights of citizenship which a State may confer within its own limits, and the rights of citizenship as a member of the Union. It does not by any means follow, because he has all the rights and privileges of a citizen of a State, that he must be a citizen of the United States. He may have all of the rights and privileges of the citizen of a State, and yet not be entitled to the rights and privileges of a citizen in any other State. For previous to the adoption of the Constitution of the United States, every State had the undoubted right to confer on whomsoever it pleased the character of citizen, and to endow him with all its rights. . . .

The question then arises, whether the provisions of the Constitution, in relation to the personal rights and privileges to which the citizen of a State should be entitled, embraced the negro African race, at that time in this country, or who might afterwards be imported, who had then or should afterwards be made free in any State; and to put it in the power of a single State to make him a citizen of the United States, and endue him with the full rights of citizenship in every other State without their consent? Does the Constitution of the United States act upon him whenever he shall be made free under the laws of a State, and raised there to the rank of a citizen, and immediately clothe him with all the privileges of a citizen in every other State, and in its own courts?

The court think the affirmative of these propositions cannot be maintained. And if it cannot, the plaintiff in error could not be a citizen of the State of Missouri, within the meaning of the Constitution of the United States, and, consequently, was not entitled to sue in its courts.

. . .

It becomes necessary, therefore, to determine who were citizens of the several States when the Constitution was adopted. And in order to do this, we must recur to the Governments and institutions of the thirteen colonies, when they separated from Great Britain and formed new sovereignties, and took their places in the family of independent nations. We must inquire who, at that time, were recognised as the people or citizens of a State, whose rights and liberties had been outraged by the English Government; and who declared their independence, and assumed the powers of Government to defend their rights by force of arms.

In the opinion of the court, the legislation and histories of the times, and the language used in the Declaration of Independence, show, that neither the class of persons who had been imported as slaves, nor their descendants, whether they had become free or not, were then acknowledged as a part of the people, nor intended to be included in the general words used in that memorable instrument.

It is difficult at this day to realize the state of public opinion in relation to that unfortunate race, which prevailed in the civilized and enlightened portions of the world at the time of the Declaration of Independence, and when the Constitution of the United States was framed and adopted. But the public history of every European nation displays it in a manner too plain to be mistaken.

They had for more than a century before been regarded as beings of an inferior order, and altogether unfit to associate with the white race, either in social or political relations; and so far inferior, that they had no rights which the white man was bound to respect; and that the negro might justly and lawfully be reduced to slavery for his benefit. He was bought and sold, and treated as an ordinary article of merchandise and traffic, whenever a profit could be made by it. This opinion was at that time fixed and universal in the civilized portion of the white race. It was regarded as an axiom in morals as well as in politics, which no one thought of disputing, or supposed to be open to dispute; and men in every grade and position in society daily and habitually acted upon it in their private pursuits, as well as in matters of public concern, without doubting for a moment the correctness of this opinion.

And in no nation was this opinion more firmly fixed or more uniformly acted upon than by the English Government and English people. They not only seized them on the coast of Africa, and sold them or held them in slavery for their own use; but they took them as ordinary articles of merchandise to every country where they could make a profit on them, and were far more extensively engaged in this commerce than any other nation in the world.

. . .

[Colonial laws and the state of feeling toward blacks] show that a perpetual and impassable barrier was intended to be erected between the white race and the one which they had reduced to slavery, and governed as subjects with absolute and despotic power, and which they then looked upon as so far below them in the scale of created beings, that intermarriages between white persons and negroes or mulattoes were regarded as unnatural and immoral, and punished as crimes, not only in the parties, but in the person who joined them in marriage. And no distinction in this respect was made between the free negro or mulatto and the slave, but this stigma, of the deepest degradation, was fixed upon the whole race.

. . .

[The Declaration of Independence] proceeds to say: "We hold these truths to be self-evident: that all men are created equal; that they are endowed by their Creator with certain unalienable rights; that among them is life, liberty, and the pursuit of happiness; that to secure these rights, Governments are instituted, deriving their just powers from the consent of the governed."

The general words above quoted would seem to embrace the whole human family, and if they were used in a similar instrument at this day would be so understood. But it is too clear for dispute that the enslaved African race were not intended to be included, and formed no part of the people who framed and adopted this declaration; for if the language, as understood in that day, would embrace them, the conduct of the distinguished men who framed the Declaration of Independence would have been utterly and flagrantly inconsistent with the principles they asserted; and instead of the sympathy of mankind, to which they so confidently appealed, they would have deserved and received universal rebuke and reprobation.

Yet the men who framed this declaration were great men—high in literary acquirements—high in their sense of honor, and incapable of asserting principles inconsistent with those on which they were acting. They perfectly understood the meaning of the language they used, and how it would be understood by others; and they knew that it would not in any part of the civilized world be supposed to embrace the negro race, which, by common consent, had been excluded from civilized Governments and the family of nations and doomed to slavery. They spoke and acted according to the then established doctrines and principles, and in the ordinary language of the day, and no one misunderstood them. The unhappy black race were separated from the white by indelible marks, and laws long before established, and were never thought of or spoken of except as property, and when the claims of the owner or the profit of the trader were supposed to need protection.

[Taney states that the words "persons" and "citizens" excluded the negro race and refer to the provisions permitting the slave trade until 1808 and requiring states to return escaped persons held in labor or service. He also discusses the movement in some states, after 1787, to abolish slavery, and the persistence of laws in slaveholding states treating blacks as an inferior class. He cites a law passed by Congress in 1790 limiting the right of becoming citizens "to aliens being free white persons."]

No one, we presume, supposes that any change in public opinion or feeling, in relation to this unfortunate race, in the civilized nations of Europe or in this country, should induce the court to give to the words of the Constitution a more liberal construction in their favor than they were intended to bear when the instrument was framed and adopted. Such an argument would be altogether inadmissible in any tribunal called on to interpret it. If any of its provisions are deemed unjust, there is a mode prescribed in the instrument itself by which it may be amended; but while it remains unaltered, it must be construed now as it was understood at the time of its adoption. It is not only the same in words, but the same in meaning, and delegates the same powers to the Government, and reserves and secures the same rights and privileges to the citizen; and as long as it continues to exist in its present form, it speaks not only in the same words, but with the same meaning and intent with which it spoke when it came from the hands of its framers, and was voted on and adopted by the people of the United States. Any other rule of construction would abrogate the judicial character of this court, and make it the mere reflex of the popular opinion or passion of the day. This court was not created by the Constitution for such purposes. Higher and graver trusts have been confided to it, and it must not falter in the path of duty.

. . .

. . . upon a full and careful consideration of the subject, the court is of opinion, that, upon the facts stated in the plea in abatement, Dred Scott was not a citizen of Missouri within the meaning of the Constitution of the United States, and not entitled as such to sue in its courts; and, consequently, that the Circuit Court had no jurisdiction of the case, and that the judgment on the plea in abatement is erroneous.

. . .

[Taney next turns to the question whether Dred Scott became free by living in a free state or territory. This raised the issue whether Congress was empowered to pass legislation to exclude slavery from certain lands.]

In considering this part of the controversy, two questions arise: 1. Was he, together with his family, free in Missouri by reason of the stay in the territory of the United States herein-before mentioned? And 2. If they were not, is Scott himself free by reason of his removal to Rock Island, in the State of Illinois, as stated in the above admission?

We proceed to examine the first question.

The act of Congress, upon which the plaintiff relies, declares that slavery and involuntary servitude, except as a punishment for crime, shall be forever prohibited in all that part of the territory ceded by France, under the name of Louisiana,

which lies north of thirty-six degrees thirty minutes north latitude, and not included within the limits of Missouri. And the difficulty which meets us at the threshold of this part of the inquiry is, whether Congress was authorized to pass this law under any of the powers granted to it by the Constitution; for if the authority is not given by that instrument, it is the duty of this court to declare it void and inoperative, and incapable of conferring freedom upon any one who is held as a slave under the laws of any one of the States.

The counsel for the plaintiff has laid much stress upon that article in the Constitution which confers on Congress the power "to dispose of and make all needful rules and regulations respecting the territory or other property belonging to the United States;" but, in the judgment of the court, that provision has no bearing on the present controversy, and the power there given, whatever it may be, is confined, and was intended to be confined, to the territory which at that time belonged to, or was claimed by, the United States, and was within their boundaries as settled by the treaty with Great Britain, and can have no influence upon a territory afterwards acquired from a foreign Government. It was a special provision for a known and particular territory, and to meet a present emergency, and nothing more.

. . .

The language used in the clause, the arrangement and combination of the powers, and the somewhat unusual phraseology it uses, when it speaks of the political power to be exercised in the government of the territory, all indicate the design and meaning of the clause to be such as we have mentioned. It does not speak of *any* territory, nor of *Territories*, but uses language which, according to its legitimate meaning, points to a particular thing. The power is given in relation only to *the* territory of the United States—that is, to a territory then in existence, and then known or claimed as the territory of the United States. . . .

Now, as we have already said in an earlier part of this opinion, upon a different point, the right of property in a slave is distinctly and expressly affirmed in the Constitution. The right to traffic in it, like an ordinary article of merchandise and property, was guarantied to the citizens of the

United States, in every State that might desire it, for twenty years. And the Government in express terms is pledged to protect it in all future time, if the slave escapes from his owner. This is done in plain words—too plain to be misunderstood. And no word can be found in the Constitution which gives Congress a greater power over slave property, or which entitles property of that kind to less protection than property of any other description. The only power conferred is the power coupled with the duty of guarding and protecting the owner in his rights.

Upon these considerations, it is the opinion of the court that the act of Congress which prohibited a citizen from holding and owning property of this kind in the territory of the United States north of the line therein mentioned, is not warranted by the Constitution, and is therefore void; and that neither Dred Scott himself, nor any of his family, were made free by being carried into this territory; even if they had been carried there by the owner, with the intention of becoming a permanent resident.

. . .

Mr. Justice WAYNE. *[concurs]*

. . .

Mr. Justice NELSON. *[concurs]*

. . .

Mr. Justice GRIER. *[concurs]*

. . .

Mr. Justice DANIEL. *[concurs]*

. . .

Mr. Justice CAMPBELL. *[concurs]*

. . .

Mr. Justice CATRON. *[concurs]*

. . .

Mr. Justice McLEAN and Mr. Justice CURTIS dissented.

Mr. Justice McLEAN dissenting.

. . .

In the argument, it was said that a colored citizen would not be an agreeable member of society. This is more a matter of taste than of law. Several of the States have admitted persons of color to the right of suffrage, and in this view have recognised them as citizens; and this has been done in the slave as well as the free States. On the question of citizenship, it must be admitted that we have not been very fastidious. Under the late treaty with Mexico, we have made citizens of all grades, combinations, and colors. The same was done in the admission of Louisiana and Florida. No one ever doubted, and no court ever held, that the people of these Territories did not become citizens under the treaty. They have exercised all the rights of citizens, without being naturalized under the acts of Congress.

. . .

In the formation of the Federal Constitution, care was taken to confer no power on the Federal Government to interfere with this institution *[of slavery]* in the States. In the provision respecting the slave trade, in fixing the ratio of representation, and providing for the reclamation of fugitives from labor, slaves were referred to as persons, and in no other respect are they considered in the Constitution.

We need not refer to the mercenary spirit which introduced the infamous traffic in slaves, to show the degradation of negro slavery in our country. This system was imposed upon our colonial settlements by the mother country, and it is due to truth to say that the commercial colonies and States were chiefly engaged in the traffic. But we know as a historical fact, that James Madison, that great and good man, a leading member in the Federal Convention, was solicitous to guard the language of that instrument so as not to convey the idea that there could be property in man.

I prefer the lights of Madison, Hamilton, and Jay, as a means of construing the Constitution in all its bearings, rather than to look behind that period, into a traffic which is now declared to be piracy, and punished with death by Christian nations. I do not like to draw the sources of our domestic relations from so dark a ground. Our independence was a great epoch in the history of freedom; and while I admit the Government was not made especially for the colored race, yet many of them were citizens of the New England States, and exercised the rights of suffrage when the Constitution was adopted, and it was not doubted by any intelligent person that its tendencies would greatly ameliorate their condition.

Many of the States, on the adoption of the Constitution, or shortly afterward, took measures to abolish slavery within their respective jurisdictions; and it is a well-known fact that a belief was cherished by the leading men, South as well as North, that the institution of slavery would gradually decline, until it would become extinct. The increased value of slave labor, in the culture of cotton and sugar, prevented the realization of this expectation. Like all other communities and States, the South were influenced by what they considered to be their own interests.

But if we are to turn our attention to the dark ages of the world, why confine our view to colored slavery? On the same principles, white men were made slaves. All slavery has its origin in power, and is against right.

The power of Congress to establish Territorial Governments, and to prohibit the introduction of slavery therein, is the next point to be considered.

. . .

The prohibition of slavery north of thirty-six degrees thirty minutes, and of the State of Missouri, contained in the act admitting that State into the Union, was passed by a vote of 134, in the House of Representatives, to 42. Before Mr. Monroe signed the act, it was submitted by him to his Cabinet, and they held the restriction of slavery in a Territory to be within the constitutional powers of Congress. It would be singular, if in 1804 Congress had power to prohibit the introduction of slaves in Orleans Territory from any other part of the Union, under the penalty of freedom to the slave, if the same power, embodied in the Missouri compromise, could not be exercised in 1820.

But this law of Congress, which prohibits slavery north of Missouri and of thirty-six degrees

thirty minutes, is declared to have been null and void by my brethren. And this opinion is founded mainly, as I understand, on the distinction drawn between the *[Northwest]* ordinance of 1787 and the Missouri compromise line. In what does the distinction consist? The ordinance, it is said, was a compact entered into by the confederated States before the adoption of the Constitution; and that in the cession of territory authority was given to establish a Territorial Government.

It is clear that the ordinance did not go into operation by virtue of the authority of the Confederation, but by reason of its modification and adoption by Congress under the Constitution. It seems to be supposed, in the opinion of the court, that the articles of cession placed it on a different footing from territories subsequently acquired. I am unable to perceive the force of this distinction. That the ordinance was intended for the government of the Northwestern Territory, and was limited to such Territory, is admitted. It was extended to Southern Territories, with modifications, by acts of Congress, and to some Northern Territories. But the ordinance was made valid by the act of Congress, and without such act could have been of no force. It rested for its validity on the act of Congress, the same, in my opinion, as the Missouri compromise line.

If Congress may establish a Territorial Government in the exercise of its discretion, it is a clear principle that a court cannot control that discretion. This being the case, I do not see on what ground the act is held to be void. It did not purport to forfeit property, or take it for public purposes. It only prohibited slavery; in doing which, it followed the ordinance of 1787.

. . .

Mr. Justice CURTIS dissenting.

. . .

It has been often asserted that the Constitution was made exclusively by and for the white race. It has already been shown that in five of the thirteen original States, colored persons then possessed the elective franchise, and were among those by whom the Constitution was ordained and established. If so, it is not true, in point of fact, that the

Constitution was made exclusively by the white race. And that it was made exclusively for the white race is, in my opinion, not only an assumption not warranted by anything in the Constitution, but contradicted by its opening declaration, that it was ordained and established by the people of the United States, for themselves and their posterity. And as free colored persons were then citizens of at least five States, and so in every sense part of the people of the United States, they were among those for whom and whose posterity the Constitution was ordained and established.

. . .

I dissent, therefore, from that part of the opinion of the majority of the court, in which it is held that a person of African descent cannot be a citizen of the United States; and I regret I must go further, and dissent both from what I deem their assumption of authority to examine the constitutionality of the act of Congress commonly called the Missouri compromise act, and the grounds and conclusions announced in their opinion.

Having first decided that they were bound to consider the sufficiency of the plea to the jurisdiction of the Circuit Court, and having decided that this plea showed that the Circuit Court had not jurisdiction, and consequently that this is a case to which the judicial power of the United States does not extend, they have gone on to examine the merits of the case as they appeared on the trial before the court and jury, on the issues joined on the pleas in bar, and so have reached the question of the power of Congress to pass the act of 1820. On so grave a subject as this, I feel obliged to say that, in my opinion, such an exertion of judicial power transcends the limits of the authority of the court, as described by its repeated decisions, and, as I understand, acknowledged in this opinion of the majority of the court.

. . . I am of opinion that so much of the several acts of Congress as prohibited slavery and involuntary servitude within that part of the Territory of Wisconsin lying north of thirty-six degrees thirty minutes north latitude, and west of the river Mississippi, were constitutional and valid laws.

. . .

Lincoln's Critique of Dred Scott

On July 17, 1858, at Springfield, Illinois, Abraham Lincoln responded to the Supreme Court's decision in *Dred Scott* v. *Sandford* (1857). At the same time, he rejected the defense of that decision by his opponent for the U.S. Senate, Stephen A. Douglas. Lincoln carefully identified the portion of the decision he regarded as legally binding. He considered major parts of the decision a nullity, to be left to political resolution outside the courts.

. . .

Does Judge Douglas, when he says that several of the past years of his life have been devoted to the question of "popular sovereignty," and that all the remainder of his life shall be devoted to it, does he mean to say that he has been devoting his life to securing to the people of the territories the right to exclude slavery from the territories? If he

means so to say, he means to deceive; because he and every one knows that the decision of the Supreme Court, which he approves and makes especial ground of attack upon me for disapproving, forbids the people of a territory to exclude slavery. This covers the whole ground, from the settlement of a territory till it reaches the degree of maturity entitling it to form a State Constitution. So far as all that ground is concerned, the

Judge is not sustaining popular sovereignty, but absolutely opposing it. He sustains the decision which declares that the popular will of the territories has no constitutional power to exclude slavery during their territorial existence. [Cheers] This being so, the period of time from the first settlement of a territory till it reaches the point of forming a State Constitution, is not the thing that the Judge has fought for or is fighting for, but on the contrary, he has fought for, and is fighting for, the thing that annihilates and crushes out that same popular sovereignty.

. . .

Now, as to the Dred Scott decision; for upon that he makes his last point at me. He boldly takes ground in favor of that decision.

This is one-half the onslaught, and one-third of the entire plan of the campaign. I am opposed to that decision in a certain sense, but not in the sense which he puts on it. I say that in so far as it decided in favor of Dred Scott's master and against Dred Scott and his family, I do not propose to disturb or resist the decision.

I never have proposed to do any such thing. I think, that in respect for judicial authority, my humble history would not suffer in a comparison with that of Judge Douglas. He would have the citizen conform his vote to that decision; the Member of Congress, his; the President, his use of the veto power. He would make it a rule of political action for the people and all the departments of the government. I would not. By resisting it as a political rule, I disturb no right of property, create no disorder, excite no mobs.

. . .

. . . I shall read from a letter written by Mr. Jefferson in 1820 . . . . It seems he had been presented by a gentleman of the name of Jarvis with a book, or essay, or periodical, called the "Republican," and he was writing in acknowledgement of the present, and noting some of its contents. After expressing the hope that the work will produce a favorable effect upon the minds of the young, he proceeds to say:

"That it will have this tendency may be expect-ed, and for that reason I feel an urgency to note what I deem an error in it, the more requiring notice as your opinion is strengthened by that of many others. You seem in pages 84 and 148, to consider the judges as the ultimate arbiters of all constitutional questions—a very dangerous doctrine indeed and one which would place us under the despotism of an oligarchy. Our judges are as honest as other men, and not more so. They have, with others, the same passions for party, for power, and the privilege of their corps. Their maxim is, 'boni judicis est ampliare jurisdictionem'; and their power is the more dangerous as they are in office for life, and not responsible, as the other functionaries are, to the elective control. The Constitution has erected no such single tribunal, knowing that to whatever hands confided, with the corruptions of time and party, its members would become despots. It has more wisely made all the departments co-equal and co-sovereign within themselves."

Thus we see the power claimed for the Supreme Court by Judge Douglas, Mr. Jefferson holds, would reduce us to the despotism of an oligarchy.

Now, I have said no more than this—in fact, never quite so much as this—at least I am sustained by Mr. Jefferson.

Let us go a little further. You remember we once had a national bank. Some one owed the bank a debt; he was sued and sought to avoid payment, on the ground that the bank was unconstitutional. The case went to the Supreme Court, and therein it was decided that the bank was constitutional. The whole Democratic party revolted against that decision. General Jackson himself asserted that he, as President, would not be bound to hold a national bank to be constitutional, even though the Court had decided it to be so. He fell in precisely with the view of Mr. Jefferson, and acted upon it under his official oath, in vetoing a charter for a national bank. The declaration that Congress does not possess this constitutional power to charter a bank, has gone into the Democratic platform, at their national conventions, and was brought forward and reaffirmed in their last convention at Cincinnati. They have contended for that declaration, in the very teeth of the Supreme Court, for more than a quarter of a century. In fact, they have reduced the decision to an absolute nullity. That decision, I repeat, is repudiated in the Cincinnati platform; and still, as if to show that effrontery can go no farther, Judge Douglas vaunts in the very speeches in which he denounces me for opposing the Dred Scott decision, that he stands on the Cincinnati platform.

Now, I wish to know what the Judge can charge upon me, with respect to decision of the Supreme Court which does not lie in all its length, breadth, and proportions at his own door. The plain truth is simply this: Judge Douglas is *for* Supreme Court decisions when he likes and against them when he does not like them. He is for the Dred Scott decision because it tends to nationalize slavery— because it is part of the original combination for that object. It so happens, singularly enough, that I never stood opposed to a decision of the Supreme Court till this. On the contrary, I have no recollection that he was ever particularly in favor of one till this. He never was in favor of any, nor opposed to any, till the present one, which helps to nationalize slavery.

Free men of Sangamon—free men of Illinois —free men everywhere—judge ye between him and me, upon this issue.

He says this Dred Scott case is a very small matter at most—that it has no practical effect; that at best, or rather, I suppose, at worst, it is but an abstraction. I submit that the proposition that the thing which determines whether a man is free or a slave, is rather *concrete* than *abstract*. I think you would conclude that it was, if your liberty depended upon it, and so would Judge Douglas if his liberty depended upon it. . . .

. . .

One more thing. Last night Judge Douglas tormented himself with horrors about my disposition to make negroes perfectly equal with white men in social and political relations. He did not stop to show that I have said any such thing, or that it legitimately follows from any thing I have said, but he rushes on with his assertions. I adhere to the Declaration of Independence. If Judge Douglas and his friends are not willing to stand by it, let them come up and amend it. Let them make it read that all men are created equal except negroes. Let us have it decided, whether the Declaration of Independence, in this blessed year of 1858, shall be thus amended.

. . .

My declarations upon this subject of negro slavery may be misrepresented, but can not be misunderstood. I have said that I do not understand the Declaration to mean that all men were created equal in all respects. They are not our equal in color; but I suppose that it does mean to declare that all men are equal in some respects; they are equal in their right to "life, liberty, and the pursuit of happiness." Certainly the negro is not our equal in color—perhaps not in many other respects; still, in the right to put into his mouth the bread that his own hands have earned, he is the equal of every other man, white or black. In pointing out that more has been given you, you can not be justified in taking away the little which has been given him. All I ask for the negro is that if you do not like him, let him alone. If God gave him but little, that little let him enjoy.

. . .

Civil Rights Cases

109 U.S. 3 (1883)

Congress passed the Civil Rights Act of 1875 to extend to blacks the full and equal enjoyment of public accommodations, including inns, transportation on land and water, theaters, and other places of amusement. The statute also provided penalties for anyone

who denied these privileges to black people. The question for the Court was whether the Thirteenth and Fourteenth Amendments prohibited only state action or private action as well.

MR. JUSTICE BRADLEY delivered the opinion of the court. After stating the facts in the above language he continued:

It is obvious that the primary and important question in all the cases is the constitutionality of the law: for if the law is unconstitutional none of the prosecutions can stand.

The sections of the law referred to provide as follows:

"SEC. 1. That all persons within the jurisdiction of the United States shall be entitled to the full and equal enjoyment of the accommodations, advantages, facilities, and privileges of inns, public conveyances on land or water, theatres, and other places of public amusement; subject only to the conditions and limitations established by law, and applicable alike to citizens of every race and color, regardless of any previous condition of servitude.

"SEC. 2. That any person who shall violate the foregoing section by denying to any citizen, except for reasons by law applicable to citizens of every race and color, and regardless of any previous condition of servitude, the full enjoyment of any of the accommodations, advantages, facilities, or privileges in said section enumerated, or by aiding or inciting such denial, shall for every such offence forfeit and pay the sum of five hundred dollars to the person aggrieved thereby, to be recovered in an action of debt, with full costs; and shall also, for every such offence, be deemed guilty of a misdemeanor, and, upon conviction thereof, shall be fined not less than five hundred nor more than one thousand dollars, or shall be imprisoned not less than thirty days nor more than one year: *Provided,* That all persons may elect to sue for the penalty aforesaid, or to proceed under their rights at common law and by State statutes; and having so elected to proceed in the one mode or the other, their right to proceed in the other jurisdiction shall be barred. But this provision shall not apply to criminal proceedings, either under this act or the criminal law of any State: *And provided further,* That a judgment for the penalty in favor of the party aggrieved, or a

judgment upon an indictment, shall be a bar to either prosecution respectively."

. . .

Has Congress constitutional power to make such a law? Of course, no one will contend that the power to pass it was contained in the Constitution before the adoption of the last three amendments. The power is sought, first, in the Fourteenth Amendment, and the views and arguments of distinguished Senators, advanced whilst the law was under consideration, claiming authority to pass it by virtue of that amendment, are the principal arguments adduced in favor of the power. We have carefully considered those arguments, as was due to the eminent ability of those who put them forward, and have felt, in all its force, the weight of authority which always invests a law that Congress deems itself competent to pass. But the responsibility of an independent judgment is now thrown upon this court; and we are bound to exercise it according to the best lights we have.

The first section of the Fourteenth Amendment (which is the one relied on), after declaring who shall be citizens of the United States, and of the several States, is prohibitory in its character, and prohibitory upon the States. It declares that:

"No State shall make or enforce any law which shall abridge the privileges or immunities of citizens of the United States; nor shall any State deprive any person of life, liberty, or property without due process of law; nor deny to any person within its jurisdiction the equal protection of the laws."

It is State action of a particular character that is prohibited. Individual invasion of individual rights is not the subject-matter of the amendment. It has a deeper and broader scope. It nullifies and makes void all State legislation, and State action of every kind, which impairs the privileges and immunities of citizens of the United States, or which injures them in life, liberty or property without due process of law, or which denies to any of them the equal protection of the laws. It not only does this, but, in order that the national will, thus declared, may not be a mere *brutum fulmen*, the last section of the amendment invests Congress with power to enforce it by appropriate legislation. To enforce what? To enforce the prohibition. To adopt appropriate legislation for correcting the effects of such prohibited State laws and State acts, and thus to render them effectually null, void, and innocuous. This is the legislative power conferred upon Congress, and this is the whole of it. It does not invest Congress with power to legislate upon subjects which are within the domain of State legislation; but to provide modes of relief against State legislation, or State action, of the kind referred to. It does not authorize Congress to create a code of municipal law for the regulation of private rights; but to provide modes of redress against the operation of State laws, and the action of State officers executive or judicial, when these are subversive of the fundamental rights specified in the amendment. . . .

. . .

We have discussed the question presented by the law on the assumption that a right to enjoy equal accommodation and privileges in all inns, public conveyances, and places of public amusement, is one of the essential rights of the citizen which no State can abridge or interfere with. Whether it is such a right, or not, is a different question which, in the view we have taken of the validity of the law on the ground already stated, it is not necessary to examine.

We have also discussed the validity of the law in reference to cases arising in the States only; and not in reference to cases arising in the Territories or the District of Columbia, which are subject to the plenary legislation of Congress in every branch of municipal regulation. Whether the law would be a valid one as applied to the Territories and the District is not a question for consideration in the cases before us: they all being cases arising within the limits of States. And whether Congress, in the exercise of its power to regulate commerce amongst the several States, might or might not pass a law regulating rights in public conveyances passing from one State to another, is also a question which is not now before us, as the sections in question are not conceived in any such view.

But the power of Congress to adopt direct and primary, as distinguished from corrective legislation, on the subject in hand, is sought, in the second place, from the Thirteenth Amendment, which abolishes slavery. This amendment declares "that neither slavery, nor involuntary servitude, except as a punishment for crime, whereof the party shall have been duly convicted, shall exist within the United States, or any place subject to their jurisdiction;" and it gives Congress power to enforce the amendment by appropriate legislation.

This amendment, as well as the Fourteenth, is undoubtedly self-executing without any ancillary legislation, so far as its terms are applicable to any existing state of circumstances. By its own unaided force and effect it abolished slavery, and established universal freedom. Still, legislation may be necessary and proper to meet all the various cases and circumstances to be affected by it, and to prescribe proper modes of redress for its violation in letter or spirit. And such legislation may be primary and direct in its character; for the amendment is not a mere prohibition of State laws establishing or upholding slavery, but an absolute declaration that slavery or involuntary servitude shall not exist in any part of the United States.

. . .

. . . it is assumed, that the power vested in Congress to enforce the article by appropriate legislation, clothes Congress with power to pass all laws necessary and proper for abolishing all badges and incidents of slavery in the United States: and upon this assumption it is claimed, that this is sufficient authority for declaring by law that all persons shall have equal accommodations and privileges in all inns, public conveyances, and places of amusement; the argument being, that the denial of such equal accommodations and privileges is, in itself, a subjection to a species of servitude within the meaning of the amendment. . . .

. . .

Now, conceding, for the sake of the argument, that the admission to an inn, a public conveyance, or a place of public amusement, on equal terms with all other citizens, is the right of every man and all classes of men, is it any more than one of those rights which the states by the Fourteenth Amendment are forbidden to deny to any person? And is the Constitution violated until the denial of the right has some State sanction or authority? Can the act of a mere individual, the owner of the inn, the public conveyance or place of amusement, refusing the accommodation, be justly regarded as imposing any badge of slavery or servitude upon the applicant, or only as inflicting an ordinary civil injury, properly cognizable by the laws of the State, and presumably subject to redress by those laws until the contrary appears?

After giving to these questions all the consideration which their importance demands, we are forced to the conclusion that such an act of refusal has nothing to do with slavery or involuntary servitude, and that if it is violative of any right of the party, his redress is to be sought under the laws of the State; or if those laws are adverse to his rights and do not protect him, his remedy will be found in the corrective legislation which Congress has adopted, or may adopt, for counteracting the effect of State laws, or State action, prohibited by the Fourteenth Amendment. It would be running the slavery argument into the ground to make it apply to every act of discrimination which a person may see fit to make as to the guests he will entertain, or as to the people he will take into his coach or cab or car, or admit to his concert or theatre, or deal with in other matters of intercourse or business. Innkeepers and public carriers, by the laws of all the States, so far as we are aware, are bound, to the extent of their facilities, to furnish proper accommodation to all unobjectionable persons who in good faith apply for them. If the laws themselves make any unjust discrimination, amenable to the prohibitions of the Fourteenth Amendment, Congress has full power to afford a remedy under that amendment and in accordance with it.

When a man has emerged from slavery, and by the aid of beneficent legislation has shaken off the inseparable concomitants of that state, there must be some stage in the progress of his elevation when he takes the rank of a mere citizen, and ceases to be the special favorite of the laws, and when his rights as a citizen, or a man, are to be protected in the ordinary modes by which other

men's rights are protected. There were thousands of free colored people in this country before the abolition of slavery, enjoying all the essential rights of life, liberty and property the same as white citizens; yet no one, at that time, thought that it was any invasion of his personal status as a freeman because he was not admitted to all the privileges enjoyed by white citizens, or because he was subjected to discriminations in the enjoyment of accommodations in inns, public conveyances and places of amusement. Mere discriminations on account of race or color were not regarded as badges of slavery. If, since that time, the enjoyment of equal rights in all these respects has become established by constitutional enactment, it is not by force of the Thirteenth Amendment (which merely abolishes slavery), but by force of the Thirteenth and Fifteenth Amendments.

. . .

. . . the answer to be given will be that the first and second sections of the act of Congress of March 1st, 1875, entitled "An Act to protect all citizens in their civil and legal rights," are unconstitutional and void, and that judgment should be rendered upon the several indictments in those cases accordingly.

And it is so ordered.

MR. JUSTICE HARLAN dissenting.

The opinion in these cases proceeds, it seems to me, upon grounds entirely too narrow and artificial. I cannot resist the conclusion that the substance and spirit of the recent amendments of the Constitution have been sacrificed by a subtle and ingenious verbal criticism. "It is not the words of the law but the internal sense of it that makes the law: the letter of the law is the body; the sense and reason of the law is the soul." Constitutional provisions, adopted in the interest of liberty, and for the purpose of securing, through national legislation, if need be, rights inhering in a state of freedom, and belonging to American citizenship, have been so construed as to defeat the ends the people desired to accomplish, which they attempted to accomplish, and which they supposed they had accomplished by changes in their fundamental law. By this I do not mean that the determination of these cases should have been materially controlled by considerations of mere expediency or policy. I mean only, in this form, to express an earnest conviction that the court has departed from the familiar rule requiring, in the interpretation of constitutional provisions, that full effect be given to the intent with which they were adopted.

. . .

That there are burdens and disabilities which constitute badges of slavery and servitude, and that the power to enforce by appropriate legislation the Thirteenth Amendment may be exerted by legislation of a direct and primary character, for the eradication, not simply of the institution, but of its badges and incidents, are propositions which ought to be deemed indisputable. They lie at the foundation of the Civil Rights Act of 1866. Whether that act was authorized by the Thirteenth Amendment alone, without the support which it subsequently received from the Fourteenth Amendment, after the adoption of which it was re-enacted with some additions, my brethren do not consider it necessary to inquire. But I submit, with all respect to them, that its constitutionality is conclusively shown by their opinion. They admit, as I have said, that the Thirteenth Amendment established freedom; that there are burdens and disabilities, the necessary incidents of slavery, which constitute its substance and visible form; that Congress, by the act of 1866, passed in view of the Thirteenth Amendment, before the Fourteenth was adopted, undertook to remove certain burdens and disabilities, the necessary incidents of slavery, and to secure to all citizens of every race and color, and without regard to previous servitude, those fundamental rights which are the essence of civil freedom . . . It remains now to inquire what are the legal rights of colored persons in respect of the accommodations, privileges and facilities of public conveyances, inns and places of public amusement?

First, as to public conveyances on land and water. [*Earlier cases ruled that*] railroads are public highways, established by authority of the State for the public use; that they are none the less public highways, because controlled and owned by private corporations; that it is a part of the function of government to make and maintain highways for the convenience of the public; that

no matter who is the agent, or what is the agency, the function performed is *that of the State;* . . .

Second, as to inns. The same general observations which have been made as to railroads are applicable to inns. The word 'inn' has a technical legal signification. It means, in the act of 1875, just what it meant at common law. A mere private boarding-house is not an inn, nor is its keeper subject to the responsibilities, or entitled to the privileges of a common innkeeper. "To constitute one an innkeeper, within the legal force of that term, he must keep a house of entertainment or lodging for all travellers or wayfarers who might choose to accept the same, being of good character or conduct." Redfield on Carriers, etc., § 575. Says Judge Story:

"An innkeeper may be defined to be the keeper of a common inn for the lodging and entertainment of travellers and passengers, their horses and attendants. An innkeeper is bound to take in all travellers and wayfaring persons, and to entertain them, if he can accommodate them, for a reasonable compensation; and he must guard their goods with proper diligence. . . . If an innkeeper improperly refuses to receive or provide for a guest, he is liable to be indicted therefor. . . . They (carriers of passengers) are no more at liberty to refuse a passenger, if they have sufficient room and accommodations, than an innkeeper is to refuse suitable room and accommodations to a guest." Story on Bailments, §§ 475–6.

. . .

. . . a keeper of an inn is in the exercise of a quasi public employment. The law gives him special privileges and he is charged with certain duties and responsibilities to the public. The public nature of his employment forbids him from discriminating against any person asking admission as a guest on account of the race or color of that person.

Third. As to places of public amusement. It may be argued that the managers of such places have no duties to perform with which the public are, in any legal sense, concerned, or with which the public have any right to interfere; and, that the exclusion of a black man from a place of public amusement, on account of his race, or the denial to him, on that ground, of equal accommodations at such places, violates no legal right for the vindication of which he may invoke the aid of the courts. My answer is, that places of public amusement, within the meaning of the act of 1875, are such as are established and maintained under direct license of the law. The authority to establish and maintain them comes from the public. The colored race is a part of that public. The local government granting the license represents them as well as all other races within its jurisdiction. A license from the public to establish a place of public amusement, imports, in law, equality of right, at such places, among all the members of that public. . . .

It remains now to consider these cases with reference to the power Congress has possessed since the adoption of the Fourteenth Amendment. Much that has been said as to the power of Congress under the Thirteenth Amendment is applicable to this branch of the discussion, and will not be repeated.

. . .

. . . what was secured to colored citizens of the United States—as between them and their respective States—by the national grant to them of State citizenship? With what rights, privileges, or immunities did this grant invest them? There is one, if there be no other—exemption from race discrimination in respect of any civil right belonging to citizens of the white race in the same State. That, surely, is their constitutional privilege when within the jurisdiction of other States. And such must be their constitutional right, in their own State, unless the recent amendments be splendid baubles, thrown out to delude those who deserved fair and generous treatment at the hands of the nation. Citizenship in this country necessarily imports at least equality of civil rights among citizens of every race in the same State. . . .

. . . With all respect for the opinion of others, I insist that the national legislature may, without transcending the limits of the Constitution, do for human liberty and the fundamental rights of American citizenship, what it did, with the sanction of this court, for the protection of slavery and the rights of the masters of fugitive slaves. If fugitive slave laws, providing modes and prescrib-

ing penalties, whereby the master could seize and recover his fugitive slave, were legitimate exertions of an implied power to protect and enforce a right recognized by the Constitution, why shall the hands of Congress be tied, so that—under an express power, by appropriate legislation, to enforce a constitutional provision granting citizenship—it may not, by means of direct legislation, bring the whole power of this nation to bear upon States and their officers, and upon such individuals and corporations exercising public functions as assume to abridge, impair, or deny rights confessedly secured by the supreme law of the land?

. . .

But the court says that Congress did not, in the act of 1866, assume, under the authority given by the Thirteenth Amendment, to adjust what may be called the social rights of men and races in the community. I agree that government has nothing to do with social, as distinguished from technically legal, rights of individuals. No government ever has brought, or ever can bring, its people into social intercourse against their wishes. Whether one person will permit or maintain social relations with another is a matter with which government has no concern. I agree that if one citizen chooses not to hold social intercourse with another, he is not and cannot be made amenable to the law for his conduct in that regard; for no legal right of a citizen is violated by the refusal of others to maintain merely social relations with him, even upon grounds of race. What I affirm is that no State, nor the officers of any State, nor any corporation or individual wielding power under State authority for the public benefit or the public convenience, can, consistently either with the freedom established by the fundamental law, or with that equality of civil rights which now belongs to every citizen, discriminate against freemen or citizens, in those rights, because of their race, or because they once labored under the disabilities of slavery imposed upon them as a race. The rights which Congress, by the act of 1875, endeavored to secure and protect are legal, not social rights. The right, for instance, of a colored citizen to use the accommodations of a public highway, upon the same terms as are permitted to white citizens, is no more a social right than his right, under the law, to use the public streets of a city or a town, or a turnpike road, or a public market, or a post office, or his right to sit in a public building with others, of whatever race, for the purpose of hearing the political questions of the day discussed. Scarcely a day passes without our seeing in this court-room citizens of the white and black races sitting side by side, watching the progress of our business. It would never occur to any one that the presence of a colored citizen in a court-house, or court-room, was an invasion of the social rights of white persons who may frequent such places. And yet, such a suggestion would be quite as sound in law—I say it with all respect—as is the suggestion that the claim of a colored citizen to use, upon the same terms as is permitted to white citizens, the accommodations of public highways, or public inns, or places of public amusement, established under the license of the law, is an invasion of the social rights of the white race.

. . .

My brethren say, that when a man has emerged from slavery, and by the aid of beneficent legislation has shaken off the inseparable concomitants of that state, there must be some stage in the progress of his elevation when he takes the rank of a mere citizen, and ceases to be the special favorite of the laws, and when his rights as a citizen, or a man, are to be protected in the ordinary modes by which other men's rights are protected. It is, I submit, scarcely just to say that the colored race has been the special favorite of the laws. The statute of 1875, now adjudged to be unconstitutional, is for the benefit of citizens of every race and color. What the nation, through Congress, has sought to accomplish in reference to that race, is—what had already been done in every State of the Union for the white race—to secure and protect rights belonging to them as freemen and citizens; nothing more. It was not deemed enough "to help the feeble up, but to support him after." The one underlying purpose of congressional legislation has been to enable the black race to take the rank of mere citizens. The difficulty has been to compel a recognition of the legal right of the black race to take the rank of citizens, and to secure the enjoyment of privileges belonging, under the law, to them as a component part of the people for whose welfare and happiness government is ordained. At every step, in this direction, the nation has been confronted with class tyranny, which a contemporary English historian says is, of all tyrannies, the most intolerable, "for it is ubiquitous in its operation, and weighs, perhaps, most heavily on those whose obscurity or distance would withdraw them from the notice of a single despot." To-day, it is the colored race which is denied, by corporations and individuals wielding public authority, rights fundamental in their freedom and citizenship. At some future time, it may be that some other race will fall under the ban of race discrimination. If the constitutional amendments be enforced, according to the intent with which, as I conceive, they were adopted, there cannot be, in this republic, any class of human beings in practical subjection to another class, with power in the latter to dole out to the former just such privileges as they may choose to grant. The supreme law of the land has decreed that no authority shall be exercised in this country upon the basis of discrimination, in respect of civil rights, against freemen and citizens because of their race, color, or previous condition of servitude. To that decree—for the due enforcement of which, by appropriate legislation, Congress has been invested with express power—every one must bow, whatever may have been, or whatever now are, his individual views as to the wisdom or policy, either of the recent changes in the fundamental law, or of the legislation which has been enacted to give them effect.

For the reasons stated I feel constrained to withhold my assent to the opinion of the court.

Plessy v. Ferguson

163 U.S. 537 (1896)

After the Civil War, and despite the Thirteenth and Fourteenth Amendments, some of the states began to adopt segregationist policies by creating "separate-but-equal" facilities for blacks and whites. Eventually, the policy extended to schools, transportation, parks, and other public accommodations. This case involved a Louisiana law that required separate railway cars for whites and blacks.

MR. JUSTICE BROWN, after stating the case, delivered the opinion of the court.

This case turns upon the constitutionality of an act of the General Assembly of the State of Louisiana, passed in 1890, providing for separate railway carriages for the white and colored races. Acts 1890, No. 111, p. 152.

The first section of the statute enacts "that all railway companies carrying passengers in their coaches in this State, shall provide equal but separate accommodations for the white, and colored races, by providing two or more passenger coaches for each passenger train, or by dividing the passenger coaches by a partition so as to secure separate accommodations: *Provided,* That this section shall not be construed to apply to street railroads. No person or persons, shall be admitted to occupy seats in coaches, other than, the ones, assigned, to them on account of the race they belong to."

[Sections two and three provided for fines and imprisonment for those who failed to comply with the statute, with a proviso that "nothing in this act shall be construed as applying to nurses attending children of the other race."]

The information filed in the criminal District Court charged in substance that Plessy, being a passenger between two stations within the State of Louisiana, was assigned by officers of the company to the coach used for the race to which he belonged, but he insisted upon going into a coach used by the race to which he did not belong. Neither in the information nor plea was his particular race or color averred.

The petition for the writ of prohibition averred that petitioner was seven eighths Caucasian and one eighth African blood; that the mixture of colored blood was not discernible in him, and that he was entitled to every right, privilege and immunity secured to citizens of the United States of the white race; and that, upon such theory, he took possession of a vacant seat in a coach where passengers of the white race were accommodated, and was ordered by the conductor to vacate said coach and take a seat in another assigned to persons of the colored race, and having refused to comply with such demand he was forcibly ejected with the aid of a police officer, and imprisoned in the parish jail to answer a charge of having violated the above act.

The constitutionality of this act is attacked upon the ground that it conflicts both with the Thirteenth Amendment of the Constitution, abolishing slavery, and the Fourteenth Amendment, which prohibits certain restrictive legislation on the part of the States.

1. That it does not conflict with the Thirteenth Amendment, which abolished slavery and involuntary servitude, except as a punishment for crime, is too clear for argument. Slavery implies involuntary servitude—a state of bondage; the ownership of mankind as a chattel, or at least the control of the labor and services of one man for the benefit of another, and the absence of a legal right to the disposal of his own person, property and services. This amendment was said in the *Slaughter-house cases,* 16 Wall. 36, to have been intended primarily to abolish slavery, as it had been previously known in this country, and that it

equally forbade Mexican peonage or the Chinese coolie trade, when they amounted to slavery or involuntary servitude, and that the use of the word "servitude" was intended to prohibit the use of all forms of involuntary slavery, of whatever class or name. It was intimated, however, in that case that this amendment was regarded by the statesmen of that day as insufficient to protect the colored race from certain laws which had been enacted in the Southern States, imposing upon the colored race onerous disabilities and burdens, and curtailing their rights in the pursuit of life, liberty and property to such an extent that their freedom was of little value; and that the Fourteenth Amendment was devised to meet this exigency.

So, too, in the *Civil Rights cases*, 109 U.S. 3, 24, it was said that the act of a mere individual, the owner of an inn, a public conveyance or place of amusement, refusing accommodations to colored people, cannot be justly regarded as imposing any badge of slavery or servitude upon the applicant, but only as involving an ordinary civil injury, properly cognizable by the laws of the State, and presumably subject to redress by those laws until the contrary appears. "It would be running the slavery argument into the ground," said Mr. Justice Bradley, "to make it apply to every act of discrimination which a person may see fit to make as to the guests he will entertain, or as to the people he will take into his coach or cab or car, or admit to his concert or theatre, or deal with in other matters of intercourse or business."

A statute which implies merely a legal distinction between the white and colored races—a distinction which is founded in the color of the two races, and which must always exist so long as white men are distinguished from the other race by color—has no tendency to destroy the legal equality of the two races, or reëstablish a state of involuntary servitude. Indeed, we do not understand that the Thirteenth Amendment is strenuously relied upon by the plaintiff in error in this connection.

2. By the Fourteenth Amendment, all persons born or naturalized in the United States, and subject to the jurisdiction thereof, are made citizens of the United States and of the State wherein they reside; and the States are forbidden from making or enforcing any law which shall abridge the privileges or immunities of citizens of the United States, or shall deprive any person of life, liberty or property without due process of law, or deny to any person within their jurisdiction the equal protection of the laws.

The proper construction of this amendment was first called to the attention of this court in the *Slaughter-house cases*, 16 Wall. 36, which involved, however, not a question of race, but one of exclusive privileges. The case did not call for any expression of opinion as to the exact rights it was intended to secure to the colored race, but it was said generally that its main purpose was to establish the citizenship of the negro; to give definitions of citizenship of the United States and of the States, and to protect from the hostile legislation of the States the privileges and immunities of citizens of the United States, as distinguished from those of citizens of the States.

The object of the amendment was undoubtedly to enforce the absolute equality of the two races before the law, but in the nature of things it could not have been intended to abolish distinctions based upon color, or to enforce social, as distinguished from political equality, or a commingling of the two races upon terms unsatisfactory to either. Laws permitting, and even requiring, their separation in places where they are liable to be brought into contact do not necessarily imply the inferiority of either race to the other, and have been generally, if not universally, recognized as within the competency of the state legislatures in the exercise of their police power. The most common instance of this is connected with the establishment of separate schools for white and colored children, which has been held to be a valid exercise of the legislative power even by courts of States where the political rights of the colored race have been longest and most earnestly enforced.

. . .

So far, then, as a conflict with the Fourteenth Amendment is concerned, the case reduces itself to the question whether the statute of Louisiana is a reasonable regulation, and with respect to this there must necessarily be a large discretion on the part of the legislature. In determining the question of reasonableness it is at liberty to act with reference to the established usages, customs and traditions of the people, and with a view to the promotion of their comfort, and the preservation of the public peace and good order. Gauged by this standard, we cannot say that a law which authorizes or even requires the separation of the two races in public conveyances is unreasonable, or more obnoxious to the Fourteenth Amendment than the acts of Congress requiring separate schools for colored children in the District of Columbia, the constitutionality of which does not seem to have been questioned, or the corresponding acts of state legislatures.

We consider the underlying fallacy of the plaintiff's argument to consist in the assumption that the enforced separation of the two races stamps the colored race with a badge of inferiority. If this be so, it is not by reason of anything found in the act, but solely because the colored race chooses to put that construction upon it. The argument necessarily assumes that if, as has been more than once the case, and is not unlikely to be so again, the colored race should become the dominant power in the state legislature, and should enact a law in precisely similar terms, it would thereby relegate the white race to an inferior position. We imagine that the white race, at least, would not acquiesce in this assumption. The argument also assumes that social prejudices may be overcome by legislation, and that equal rights cannot be secured to the negro except by an enforced commingling of the two races. We cannot accept this proposition. If the two races are to meet upon terms of social equality, it must be the result of natural affinities, a mutual appreciation of each other's merits and a voluntary consent of individuals. . . . If the civil and political rights of both races be equal one cannot be inferior to the other civilly or politically. If one race be inferior to the other socially, the Constitution of the United States cannot put them upon the same plane.

It is true that the question of the proportion of colored blood necessary to constitute a colored person, as distinguished from a white person, is one upon which there is a difference of opinion in the different States, some holding that any visible admixture of black blood stamps the person as belonging to the colored race, (*State* v. *Chavers*, 5 Jones, [N.C.] 1, p. 11); others that it depends upon the preponderance of blood, (*Gray* v. *State*, 4 Ohio, 354; *Monroe* v. *Collins*, 17 Ohio St. 665); and still others that the predominance of white blood must only be in the proportion of three fourths. (*People* v. *Dean*, 14 Michigan, 406; *Jones* v. *Commonwealth*, 80 Virginia, 538.) But these are questions to be determined under the laws of each State and are not properly put in issue in this case. Under the allegations of his petition it may undoubtedly become a question of importance whether, under the laws of Louisiana, the petitioner belongs to the white or colored race.

The judgment of the court below is, therefore,

Affirmed.

MR. JUSTICE HARLAN dissenting.

. . .

However apparent the injustice of such legislation may be, we have only to consider whether it is consistent with the Constitution of the United States.

That a railroad is a public highway, and that the corporation which owns or operates it is in the exercise of public functions, is not, at this day, to be disputed. . . .

In respect of civil rights, common to all citizens, the Constitution of the United States does not, I think, permit any public authority to know the race of those entitled to be protected in the enjoyment of such rights. Every true man has pride of race, and under appropriate circumstances when the rights of others, his equals before the law, are not to be affected, it is his privilege to express such pride and to take such action based upon it as to him seems proper. But I deny that any legislative body or judicial tribunal may have regard to the race of citizens when the civil rights of those citizens are involved. Indeed, such legislation, as that here in question, is inconsistent not only with that equality of rights which pertains to citizenship, National and State, but with the personal liberty enjoyed by every one within the United States.

The Thirteenth Amendment does not permit the withholding or the deprivation of any right necessarily inhering in freedom. It not only struck down the institution of slavery as previously existing in the United States, but it prevents the imposition of any burdens or disabilities that constitute badges of slavery or servitude. It decreed universal civil freedom in this country. This court has so adjudged. But that amendment having been found inadequate to the protection of the rights of those who had been in slavery, it was followed by the Fourteenth Amendment, which added greatly to the dignity and glory of American citizenship, and to the security of personal liberty, by declaring that "all persons born or naturalized in the United States, and subject to the jurisdiction thereof, are citizens of the United States and of the State wherein they reside," and that "no State shall make or enforce any law which shall abridge the privileges or immunities of citizens of the United States; nor shall any State deprive any person of life, liberty or property without due process of law, nor deny to any person within its jurisdiction the equal protection of the laws." These two amendments, if enforced according to their true intent and meaning, will protect all the civil rights that pertain to freedom and citizenship. Finally, and to the end that no citizen should be denied, on account of his race, the privilege of participating in the political control of his country, it was declared by the Fifteenth Amendment that "the right of citizens of the United States to vote shall not be denied or abridged by the United States or by any State on account of race, color or previous condition of servitude."

These notable additions to the fundamental law were welcomed by the friends of liberty throughout the world. They removed the race line from our governmental systems. They had, as this court has said, a common purpose, namely, to secure "to a race recently emancipated, a race that through many generations have been held in slavery, all the civil rights that the superior race enjoy." They declared, in legal effect, this court has further said, "that the law in the States shall be the same for the black as for the white; that all persons, whether colored or white, shall stand equal before the laws of the States, and, in regard to the colored race, for whose protection the amendment was primarily designed, that no discrimination shall be made against them by law because of their color." We also said: "The words

of the amendment, it is true, are prohibitory, but they contain a necessary implication of a positive immunity, or right, most valuable to the colored race—the right to exemption from unfriendly legislation against them distinctively as colored—exemption from legal discriminations, implying inferiority in civil society, lessening the security of their enjoyment of the rights which others enjoy, and discriminations which are steps towards reducing them to the condition of a subject race." It was, consequently, adjudged that a state law that excluded citizens of the colored race from juries, because of their race and however well qualified in other respects to discharge the duties of jurymen, was repugnant to the Fourteenth Amendment. *Strauder* v. *West Virginia*, 100 U.S. 303, 306, 307; *Virginia* v. *Rives*, 100 U.S. 313; *Ex parte Virginia*, 100 U.S. 339; *Neal* v. *Delaware*, 103 U.S. 370, 386; *Bush* v. *Kentucky*, 107 U.S. 110, 116. . . .

It was said in argument that the statute of Louisiana does not discriminate against either race, but prescribes a rule applicable alike to white and colored citizens. But this argument does not meet the difficulty. Every one knows that the statute in question had its origin in the purpose, not so much to exclude white persons from railroad cars occupied by blacks, as to exclude colored people from coaches occupied by or assigned to white persons. . . .

The white race deems itself to be the dominant race in this country. And so it is, in prestige, in achievements, in education, in wealth and in power. So, I doubt not, it will continue to be for all time, if it remains true to its great heritage and holds fast to the principles of constitutional liberty. But in view of the Constitution, in the eye of the law, there is in this country no superior, dominant, ruling class of citizens. There is no caste here. Our Constitution is color-blind, and neither knows nor tolerates classes among citizens. In respect of civil rights, all citizens are equal before the law. The humblest is the peer of the most powerful. The law regards man as man, and takes no account of his surroundings or of his color when his civil rights as guaranteed by the supreme law of the land are involved. It is, therefore, to be regretted that this high tribunal, the final expositor of the fundamental law of the land, has reached the conclusion that it is competent for a State to regulate the enjoyment by citizens of their civil rights solely upon the basis of race.

In my opinion, the judgment this day rendered will, in time, prove to be quite as pernicious as the decision made by this tribunal in the *Dred Scott case*. . . . The recent amendments of the Constitution, it was supposed, had eradicated these principles from our institutions. But it seems that we have yet, in some of the States, a dominant race—a superior class of citizens, which assumes to regulate the enjoyment of civil rights, common to all citizens, upon the basis of race. The present decision, it may well be apprehended, will not only stimulate aggressions, more or less brutal and irritating, upon the admitted rights of colored citizens, but will encourage the belief that it is possible, by means of state enactments, to defeat the beneficent purposes which the people of the United States had in view when they adopted the recent amendments of the Constitution, by one of which the blacks of this country were made citizens of the United States and of the States in which they respectively reside, and whose privileges and immunities, as citizens, the States are forbidden to abridge. Sixty millions of whites are in no danger from the presence here of eight millions of blacks. The destinies of the two races, in this country, are indissolubly linked together, and the interests of both require that the common government of all shall not permit the seeds of race hate to be planted under the sanction of law. What can more certainly arouse race hate, what more certainly create and perpetuate a feeling of distrust between these races, than state enactments, which, in fact, proceed on the ground that colored citizens are so inferior and degraded that they cannot be allowed to sit in public coaches occupied by white citizens? That, as all will admit, is the real meaning of such legislation as was enacted in Louisiana.

. . .

There is a race so different from our own that we do not permit those belonging to it to become citizens of the United States. Persons belonging to it are, with few exceptions, absolutely excluded from our country. I allude to the Chinese race.

But by the statute in question, a Chinaman can ride in the same passenger coach with white citizens of the United States, while citizens of the black race in Louisiana, many of whom, perhaps, risked their lives for the preservation of the Union, who are entitled, by law, to participate in the political control of the State and nation, who are not excluded, by law or by reason of their race, from public stations of any kind, and who have all the legal rights that belong to white citizens, are yet declared to be criminals, liable to imprisonment, if they ride in a public coach occupied by citizens of the white race. . . .

The arbitrary separation of citizens, on the basis of race, while they are on a public highway, is a badge of servitude wholly inconsistent with the civil freedom and the equality before the law established by the Constitution. It cannot be justified upon any legal grounds.

If evils will result from the commingling of the two races upon public highways established for the benefit of all, they will be infinitely less than those that will surely come from state legislation regulating the enjoyment of civil rights upon the basis of race. We boast of the freedom enjoyed by our people above all other peoples. But it is difficult to reconcile that boast with a state of the law which, practically, puts the brand of servitude and degradation upon a large class of our fellow-citizens, our equals before the law. The thin disguise of "equal" accommodations for passengers in railroad coaches will not mislead any one, nor atone for the wrong this day done.

. . .

MR. JUSTICE BREWER did not hear the argument or participate in the decision of this case.

Government's Brief in Brown

In an amicus brief filed December 1952 in the case of *Brown* v. *Board of Education*, the Justice Department explained the interest of the President and the executive branch in abolishing racial discrimination. The importance of civil rights transcended domestic politics. The persistence of segregation in America undermined its claim to democratic values and provided an easy target for exploitation by communist nations. The selection below is from 49 Landmark Briefs and Arguments of the Supreme Court of the United States: Constitutional Law 116–123 (P. Kurland and G. Caspar eds. 1975). Footnotes omitted.

I

The Interest of the United States

In recent years the Federal Government has increasingly recognized its special responsibility for assuring vindication of the fundamental civil rights guaranteed by the Constitution. The President has stated: "We shall not . . . finally achieve the ideals for which this Nation was founded so long as any American suffers discrimination as a result of his race, or religion, or color, or the land of origin of his forefathers. . . . The Federal Government has a clear duty to see that constitutional guaranties of individual liberties and of equal protection under the laws are not denied or abridged anywhere in our Union."

Recognition of the responsibility of the Federal Government with regard to civil rights is not a matter of partisan controversy, even though differences of opinion may exist as to the need for particular legislative or executive action. Few Americans believe that government should pursue a *laissez-faire* policy in the field of civil rights, or that it adequately discharges its duty to the people so long as it does not itself intrude on their civil liberties. Instead, there is general acceptance of an affirmative government obligation to insure respect for fundamental human rights.

The constitutional right invoked in these cases is the basic right, secured to all Americans, to equal treatment before the law. The cases at bar do not involve isolated acts of racial discrimination by private individuals or groups. On the contrary, it is contended in these cases that public school systems established in the states of Kansas, South Carolina, Virginia, and Delaware, and in the District of Columbia, unconstitutionally discriminate against Negroes solely because of their color.

This contention raises questions of the first importance in our society. For racial discriminations imposed by law, or having the sanction or support of government, inevitably tend to undermine the foundations of a society dedicated to freedom, justice, and equality. The proposition that all men are created equal is not mere rhetoric. It implies a rule of law—an indispensable condition to a civilized society—under which all men stand equal and alike in the rights and opportunities secured to them by their government. Under the Constitution every agency of government, national and local, legislative, executive, and judicial, must treat each of our people as an *American*, and not as a member of a particular group classified on the basis of race or some other constitutional irrelevancy. The color of a man's skin—like his religious beliefs, or his political attachments, or the country from which he or his ancestors came to the United States—does not diminish or alter his legal status or constitutional rights. "Our Constitution is color-blind, and neither knows nor tolerates classes among citizens."

The problem of racial discrimination is particularly acute in the District of Columbia, the nation's capital. This city is the window through which the world looks into our house. The embassies, legations, and representatives of all nations are here, at the seat of the Federal Government. Foreign officials and visitors naturally judge this country and our people by their experiences and observations in the nation's capital; and the treatment of colored persons here is taken as the measure of our attitude toward minorities generally. The President has stated that "The District of Columbia should be a true symbol of American freedom and democracy for our own people, and for the people of the world." Instead, as the President's Committee on Civil Rights found, the District of Columbia "is a graphic illustration of a failure of democracy." The Committee summarized its findings as follows:

"For Negro Americans, Washington is not just the nation's capital. It is the point at which all public transportation into the South becomes 'Jim Crow.' If he stops in Washington, a Negro may dine like other men in the Union Station, but as soon as he steps out into the capital, he leaves such democratic practices behind. With very few exceptions, he is refused service at downtown restaurants, he may not attend a downtown movie or play, and he has to go into the poorer section of the city to find a night's lodging. The Negro who decides to settle in the District must often find a home in an overcrowded, substandard area. He must often take a job below the level of his ability. He must send his children to the inferior public schools set aside for Negroes and entrust his family's health to medical agencies which give inferior service. In addition, he must endure the countless daily humiliations that the system of segregation imposes upon the one-third of Washington that is Negro.

. . .

"The shamefulness and absurdity of Washington's treatment of Negro Americans is highlighted by the presence of many dark-skinned foreign visitors. Capital custom not only humiliates colored citizens, but is a source of considerable embarrassment to these visitors. . . . Foreign officials are often mistaken for American Negroes and refused food, lodging and entertainment. However, once it is established that they are not Americans, they are accommodated."

It is in the context of the present world struggle between freedom and tyranny that the problem of racial discrimination must be viewed. The United States is trying to prove to the people of the world, of every nationality, race, and color, that a free democracy is the most civilized and most secure form of government yet devised by man. We must set an example for others by showing firm determination to remove existing flaws in our democracy.

The existence of discrimination against minority groups in the United States has an adverse effect upon our relations with other countries. Racial discrimination furnishes grist for the Communist propaganda mills, and it raises doubts even among friendly nations as to the intensity of our devotion to the democratic faith. In response to the request of the Attorney General for an authoritative statement of the effects of racial discrimination in the United States upon the conduct of foreign relations, the Secretary of State has written as follows:

". . . I wrote the Chairman of the Fair Employment Practices Committee on May 8, 1946, that the existence of discrimination against minority groups was having an adverse effect upon our relations with other countries. At that time I pointed out that discrimination against such groups in the United States created suspicion and resentment in other countries, and that we would have better international relations were these reasons for suspicion and resentment to be removed.

"During the past six years, the damage to our foreign relations attributable to this source has become progressively greater. The United States is under constant attack in the foreign press, over the foreign radio, and in such international bodies as the United Nations because of various practices of discrimination against minority groups in this country. As might be expected, Soviet spokesmen regularly exploit this situation in propaganda against the United States, both within the United Nations and through radio broadcasts and the press, which reaches all corners of the world. Some of these attacks against us are based on falsehood or distortion; but the undeniable existence of racial discrimination gives unfriendly governments the most effective kind of ammunition for their propaganda warfare. The hostile reaction among normally friendly peoples, many of whom are particularly sensitive in regard to the status of non-European races, is growing in alarming proportions. In such countries the view is expressed more and more vocally that the United States is hypocritical in claiming to be the champion of democracy while permitting practices of racial discrimination here in this country.

"The segregation of school children on a racial basis is one of the practices in the United States that has been singled out for hostile foreign comment in the United Nations and elsewhere. Other peoples cannot understand how such a practice can exist in a country which professes to be a staunch supporter of freedom, justice, and de-

mocracy. The sincerity of the United States in this respect will be judged by its deeds as well as by its words.

"Although progress is being made, the continuance of racial discrimination in the United States remains a source of constant embarrassment to this Government in the day-to-day conduct of its foreign relations; and it jeopardizes the effective maintenance of our moral leadership of the free and democratic nations of the world."

. . .

Brown v. Board of Education

347 U.S. 483 (1954)

After chipping away at the foundations of *Plessy* v. *Ferguson*, a unanimous Court in this case resolved that the "separate but equal" doctrine has no place in the field of education. In deciding that the history of the Fourteenth Amendment is inconclusive as to its intended effect on public education, the Court held that the use of race to segregate white and black children in the public schools is a denial to black children of the equal protection of the laws guaranteed by the Fourteenth Amendment.

MR. CHIEF JUSTICE WARREN delivered the opinion of the Court.

These cases come to us from the States of Kansas, South Carolina, Virginia, and Delaware. They are premised on different facts and different local conditions, but a common legal question justifies their consideration together in this consolidated opinion.

In each of the cases, minors of the Negro race, through their legal representatives, seek the aid of the courts in obtaining admission to the public schools of their community on a nonsegregated basis. In each instance, they had been denied admission to schools attended by white children under laws requiring or permitting segregation according to race. This segregation was alleged to deprive the plaintiffs of the equal protection of the laws under the Fourteenth Amendment. In each of the cases other than the Delaware case, a three-judge federal district court denied relief to the plaintiffs on the so-called "separate but equal" doctrine announced by this Court in *Plessy* v.

Ferguson, 163 U.S. 537. Under that doctrine, equality of treatment is accorded when the races are provided substantially equal facilities, even though these facilities be separate. In the Delaware case, the Supreme Court of Delaware adhered to that doctrine, but ordered that the plaintiffs be admitted to the white schools because of their superiority to the Negro schools.

(The plaintiffs contend that segregated public schools are not "equal" and cannot be made "equal," and that hence they are deprived of the equal protection of the laws.) Because of the obvious importance of the question presented, the Court took jurisdiction. Argument was heard in the 1952 Term, and reargument was heard this Term on certain questions propounded by the Court.

Reargument was largely devoted to the circumstances surrounding the adoption of the Fourteenth Amendment in 1868. It covered exhaustively consideration of the Amendment in Congress, ratification by the states, then existing practices in racial segregation, and the views of proponents and opponents of the Amendment. This discussion and our own investigation convince us that, although these sources cast some light, it is not enough to resolve the problem with which we are faced. At best, they are inconclusive. The most avid proponents of the post-War Amendments undoubtedly intended them to remove all legal distinctions among "all persons born or naturalized in the United States." Their opponents, just as certainly, were antagonistic to both the letter and the spirit of the Amendments and wished them to have the most limited effect. What others in Congress and the state legislatures had in mind cannot be determined with any degree of certainty.

An additional reason for the inconclusive nature of the Amendment's history, with respect to segregated schools, is the status of public education at that time. In the South, the movement toward free common schools, supported by general taxation, had not yet taken hold. Education of white children was largely in the hands of private groups. Education of Negroes was almost nonexistent, and practically all of the race were illiterate. In fact, any education of Negroes was forbidden by law in some states. Today, in contrast, many Negroes have achieved outstanding success in the arts and sciences as well as in the business and professional world. It is true that public school education at the time of the Amendment had advanced further in the North, but the effect of the Amendment on Northern States was generally ignored in the congressional debates. Even in the North, the conditions of public education did not approximate those existing today. The curriculum was usually rudimentary; ungraded schools were common in rural areas; the school term was but three months a year in many states; and compulsory school attendance was virtually unknown. As a consequence, it is not surprising that there should be so little in the history of the Fourteenth Amendment relating to its intended effect on public education.

In the first cases in this Court construing the Fourteenth Amendment, decided shortly after its adoption, the Court interpreted it as proscribing all state-imposed discriminations against the Negro race. The doctrine of "separate but equal" did not make its appearance in this Court until 1896 in the case of *Plessy* v. *Ferguson, supra,* involving not education but transportation. American courts have since labored with the doctrine for over half a century. In this Court, there have been six cases involving the "separate but equal" doctrine in the field of public education. In *Cumming* v. *County Board of Education,* 175 U.S. 528, and *Gong Lum* v. *Rice,* 275 U.S. 78, the validity of the doctrine itself was not challenged. In more recent cases, all on the graduate school level, inequality was found in that specific benefits enjoyed by white students were denied to Negro students of the same educational qualifications. *Missouri ex rel. Gaines* v. *Canada,* 305 U.S. 337; *Sipuel* v. *Oklahoma,* 332 U.S. 631; *Sweatt* v. *Painter,* 339 U.S. 629; *McLaurin* v. *Oklahoma State Regents,* 339 U.S. 637. In none of these cases was it necessary to re-examine the doctrine to grant relief to the Negro plaintiff. And in *Sweatt* v. *Painter, supra,* the Court expressly reserved decision on the question whether *Plessy* v. *Ferguson* should be held inapplicable to public education.

In the instant cases, that question is directly presented. Here, unlike *Sweatt* v. *Painter,* there are findings below that the Negro and white schools involved have been equalized, or are being equalized, with respect to buildings, curricula, qualifications and salaries of teachers, and other "tangible" factors. Our decision, therefore, cannot turn on merely a comparison of these tangible factors in the Negro and white schools involved in each of the cases. We must look instead to the effect of segregation itself on public education.

In approaching this problem, we cannot turn the clock back to 1868 when the Amendment was adopted, or even to 1896 when *Plessy* v. *Ferguson* was written. We must consider public education in the light of its full development and its present place in American life throughout the Nation. Only in this way can it be determined if segregation in public schools deprives these plaintiffs of the equal protection of the laws.

Today, education is perhaps the most important function of state and local governments. Compulsory school attendance laws and the great expenditures for education both demonstrate our recognition of the importance of education to our democratic society. It is required in the performance of our most basic public responsibilities, even service in the armed forces. It is the very foundation of good citizenship. Today it is a principal instrument in awakening the child to cultural values, in preparing him for later professional training, and in helping him to adjust normally to his environment. In these days, it is doubtful that any child may reasonably be expected to succeed in life if he is denied the opportunity of an education. Such an opportunity, where the state has undertaken to provide it, is a right which must be made available to all on equal terms.

We come then to the question presented: Does segregation of children in public schools solely on the basis of race, even though the physical facilities and other "tangible" factors may be equal, deprive the children of the minority group of equal educational opportunities? We believe that it does.

In *Sweatt* v. *Painter, supra,* in finding that a segregated law school for Negroes could not provide them equal educational opportunities, this Court relied in large part on "those qualities which are incapable of objective measurement but which make for greatness in a law school." In *McLaurin* v. *Oklahoma State Regents, supra,* the Court, in requiring that a Negro admitted to a white graduate school be treated like all other students, again resorted to intangible considerations: ". . . his ability to study, to engage in discussions and exchange views with other students, and, in general, to learn his profession." Such considerations apply with added force to children in grade and high schools. To separate them from others of similar age and qualifications solely because of their race generates a feeling of inferiority as to their status in the community that may affect their hearts and minds in a way unlikely ever to be undone. The effect of this separation on their educational opportunities was well stated by a finding in the Kansas case by a court which nevertheless felt compelled to rule against the Negro plaintiffs:

"Segregation of white and colored children in public schools has a detrimental effect upon the colored children. The impact is greater when it has the sanction of the law; for the policy of separating the races is usually interpreted as denoting the inferiority of the negro group. A sense of inferiority affects the motivation of a child to learn. Segregation with the sanction of law, therefore, has a tendency to [retard] the educational and mental development of negro children and to deprive them of some of the benefits they would receive in a racial[ly] integrated school system."

Whatever may have been the extent of psychological knowledge at the time of *Plessy* v. *Ferguson,* this finding is amply supported by modern authority. *[Here the Court adds its famous footnote 11: K. B. Clark, Effect of Prejudice and Discrimination on Personality Development (Midcentury White House Conference on Children and Youth, 1950); Witmer and Kotinsky, Personality in the Making (1952), c. VI; Deutscher and Chein, The Psychological Effects of Enforced Segregation: A Survey of Social Science Opinion, 26 J. Psychol. 259 (1948); Chein, What are the Psychological Effects of Segregation Under Conditions of Equal Facilities?, 3 Int. J. Opinion and Attitude Res. 229 (1949); Brameld, Educational Costs, in Discrimination and National Welfare (MacIver, ed., 1949), 44–48; Frazier, The Negro in the United States (1949), 674–681. And see generally Myrdal, An American Dilemma (1944).]* Any language in *Plessy* v. *Ferguson* contrary to this finding is rejected.

We conclude that in the field of public education the doctrine of "separate but equal" has no place. Separate educational facilities are inherently unequal. Therefore, we hold that the plaintiffs and others similarly situated for whom the actions have been brought are, by reason of the segregation complained of, deprived of the equal protection of the laws guaranteed by the Fourteenth Amendment. This disposition makes unnecessary any discussion whether such segregation also violates the Due Process Clause of the Fourteenth Amendment.

Because these are class actions, because of the wide applicability of this decision, and because of the great variety of local conditions, the formulation of decrees in these cases presents problems of considerable complexity. On reargument, the consideration of appropriate relief was necessarily subordinated to the primary question—the constitutionality of segregation in public education. We have now announced that such segregation is a denial of the equal protection of the laws. In order that we may have the full assistance of the parties in formulating decrees, the cases will be restored to the docket, and the parties are requested to present further argument on Questions 4 and 5 previously propounded by the Court for the reargument this Term. The Attorney General of the United States is again invited to participate. The Attorneys General of the states requiring or permitting segregation in public education will also be permitted to appear as *amici curiae* upon request to do so by September 15, 1954, and submission of briefs by October 1, 1954.

It is so ordered.

Brown v. Board of Education

349 U.S. 294 (1955)

In the first *Brown* case, called *Brown I*, the Court held that racial discrimination in public schools is unconstitutional. Having announced the constitutional principle, the Court had to issue instructions on the means used to implement the principle. This case, called *Brown II*, has been heavily criticized for deferring too much to local school districts and thus delaying the implementation of *Brown I*.

MR. CHIEF JUSTICE WARREN delivered the opinion of the Court.

These cases were decided on May 17, 1954. The opinions of that date, declaring the fundamental principle that racial discrimination in public education is unconstitutional, are incorporated herein by reference. All provisions of federal, state, or local law requiring or permitting such discrimination must yield to this principle. There remains for consideration the manner in which relief is to be accorded.

Because these cases arose under different local conditions and their disposition will involve a variety of local problems, we requested further argument on the question of relief. In view of the nationwide importance of the decision, we invited the Attorney General of the United States and the Attorneys General of all states requiring or permitting racial discrimination in public education to present their views on that question. The parties, the United States, and the States of Florida, North Carolina, Arkansas, Oklahoma, Maryland, and Texas filed briefs and participated in the oral argument.

These presentations were informative and helpful to the Court in its consideration of the complexities arising from the transition to a system of public education freed of racial discrimination.

The presentations also demonstrated that substantial steps to eliminate racial discrimination in public schools have already been taken, not only in some of the communities in which these cases arose, but in some of the states appearing as *amici curiae*, and in other states as well. Substantial progress has been made in the District of Columbia and in the communities in Kansas and Delaware involved in this litigation. The defendants in the cases coming to us from South Carolina and Virginia are awaiting the decision of this Court concerning relief.

Full implementation of these constitutional principles may require solution of varied local school problems. School authorities have the primary responsibility for elucidating, assessing, and solving these problems; courts will have to consider whether the action of school authorities constitutes good faith implementation of the governing constitutional principles. Because of their proximity to local conditions and the possible need for further hearings, the courts which originally heard these cases can best perform this judicial appraisal. Accordingly, we believe it appropriate to remand the cases to those courts.

In fashioning and effectuating the decrees, the courts will be guided by equitable principles. Traditionally, equity has been characterized by a practical flexibility in shaping its remedies and by a facility for adjusting and reconciling public and private needs. These cases call for the exercise of these traditional attributes of equity power. At stake is the personal interest of the plaintiffs in admission to public schools as soon as practicable on a nondiscriminatory basis. To effectuate this interest may call for elimination of a variety of obstacles in making the transition to school systems operated in accordance with the constitutional principles set forth in our May 17, 1954, decision. Courts of equity may properly take into account the public interest in the elimination of such obstacles in a systematic and effective manner. But it should go without saying that the vitality of these constitutional principles cannot be allowed to yield simply because of disagreement with them.

While giving weight to these public and private considerations, the courts will require that the defendants make a prompt and reasonable start toward full compliance with our May 17, 1954, ruling. Once such a start has been made, the courts may find that additional time is necessary to carry out the ruling in an effective manner. The burden rests upon the defendants to establish that such time is necessary in the public interest and is consistent with good faith compliance at the earliest practicable date. To that end, the courts may consider problems related to administration, arising from the physical condition of the school plant, the school transportation system, personnel, revision of school districts and attendance areas into compact units to achieve a system of determining admission to the public schools on a nonracial basis, and revision of local laws and regulations which may be necessary in solving the foregoing problems. They will also consider the adequacy of any plans the defendants may propose to meet these problems and to effectuate a transition to a racially nondiscriminatory school system. During this period of transition, the courts will retain jurisdiction of these cases.

The judgments below, except that in the Delaware case, are accordingly reversed and the cases are remanded to the District Courts to take such proceedings and enter such orders and decrees consistent with this opinion as are necessary and proper to admit to public schools on a racially nondiscriminatory basis with all deliberate speed the parties to these cases. The judgment in the Delaware case—ordering the immediate admission of the plaintiffs to schools previously attended only by white children—is affirmed on the basis of the principles stated in our May 17, 1954, opinion, but the case is remanded to the Supreme Court of Delaware for such further proceedings as that Court may deem necessary in light of this opinion.

It is so ordered.

Swann v. Charlotte-Mecklenburg Bd. of Ed.

402 U.S. 1 (1971)

By 1971, there had been little progress in desegregating public schools, despite the Supreme Court's historic decision in 1954. School boards were under pressure from the courts to come forward with desegregation plans *now*. In this case, the Court focuses on remedies available to federal courts to produce a unitary school system free of state-imposed segregation.

MR. CHIEF JUSTICE BURGER delivered the opinion of the Court.

We granted certiorari in this case to review important issues as to the duties of school authorities and the scope of powers of federal courts under this Court's mandates to eliminate racially separate public schools established and maintained by state action. *Brown* v. *Board of Education*, 347 U.S. 483 (1954) *(Brown I)*.

This case and those argued with it arose in

States having a long history of maintaining two sets of schools in a single school system deliberately operated to carry out a governmental policy to separate pupils in schools solely on the basis of race. That was what *Brown* v. *Board of Education* was all about. These cases present us with the problem of defining in more precise terms than heretofore the scope of the duty of school authorities and district courts in implementing *Brown I* and the mandate to eliminate dual systems and establish unitary systems at once. Meanwhile district courts and courts of appeals have struggled in hundreds of cases with a multitude and variety of problems under this Court's general directive. Understandably, in an area of evolving remedies, those courts had to improvise and experiment without detailed or specific guidelines. This Court, in *Brown I,* appropriately dealt with the large constitutional principles; other federal courts had to grapple with the flinty, intractable realities of day-to-day implementation of those constitutional commands. Their efforts, of necessity, embraced a process of "trial and error," and our effort to formulate guidelines must take into account their experience.

I

The Charlotte-Mecklenburg school system, the 43d largest in the Nation, encompasses the city of Charlotte and surrounding Mecklenburg County, North Carolina. The area is large—550 square miles—spanning roughly 22 miles east-west and 36 miles north-south. During the 1968–1969 school year the system served more than 84,000 pupils in 107 schools. Approximately 71% of the pupils were found to be white and 29% Negro. As of June 1969 there were approximately 24,000 Negro students in the system, of whom 21,000 attended schools within the city of Charlotte. Two-thirds of those 21,000—approximately 14,000 Negro students—attended 21 schools which were either totally Negro or more than 99% Negro.

This situation came about under a desegregation plan approved by the District Court at the commencement of the present litigation in 1965, 243 F. Supp. 667 (WDNC), aff'd, 369 F. 2d 29 (CA4 1966), based upon geographic zoning with a free-transfer provision. The present proceedings were initiated in September 1968 by petitioner Swann's motion for further relief based on *Green* v. *County School Board,* 391 U.S. 430 (1968), and its companion cases. All parties now agree that in 1969 the system fell short of achieving the unitary school system that those cases require.

The District Court held numerous hearings and received voluminous evidence. In addition to finding certain actions of the school board to be discriminatory, the court also found that residential patterns in the city and county resulted in part from federal, state, and local government action other than school board decisions. School board action based on these patterns, for example, by locating schools in Negro residential areas and fixing the size of the schools to accommodate the needs of immediate neighborhoods, resulted in segregated education. These findings were subsequently accepted by the Court of Appeals.

In April 1969 the District Court ordered the school board to come forward with a plan for both faculty and student desegregation. Proposed plans were accepted by the court in June and August 1969 on an interim basis only, and the board was ordered to file a third plan by November 1969. In November the board moved for an extension of time until February 1970, but when that was denied the board submitted a partially completed plan. In December 1969 the District Court held that the board's submission was unacceptable and appointed an expert in education administration, Dr. John Finger, to prepare a desegregation plan. Thereafter in February 1970, the District Court was presented with two alternative pupil assignment plans—the finalized "board plan" and the "Finger plan."

The Board Plan. As finally submitted, the school board plan closed seven schools and reassigned their pupils. It restructured school attendance zones to achieve greater racial balance but maintained existing grade structures and rejected techniques such as pairing and clustering as part of a desegregation effort. The plan created a single athletic league, eliminated the previously racial basis of the school bus system, provided racially mixed faculties and administrative staffs, and modified its free-transfer plan into an optional majority-to-minority transfer system.

The board plan proposed substantial assignment of Negroes to nine of the system's 10 high schools, producing 17% to 36% Negro population in each. The projected Negro attendance at the 10th school, Independence, was 2%. The proposed attendance zones for the high schools were typically shaped like wedges of a pie, extending outward from the center of the city to the suburban and rural areas of the county in order to afford residents of the center city area access to outlying schools.

As for junior high schools, the board plan rezoned the 21 school areas so that in 20 the Negro attendance would range from 0% to 38%. The other school, located in the heart of the Negro residential area, was left with an enrollment of 90% Negro.

The board plan with respect to elementary schools relied entirely upon gerrymandering of geographic zones. More than half of the Negro elementary pupils were left in nine schools that were 86% to 100% Negro; approximately half of the white elementary pupils were assigned to schools 86% to 100% white.

The Finger Plan. The plan submitted by the court-appointed expert, Dr. Finger, adopted the school board zoning plan for senior high schools with one modification: it required that an additional 300 Negro students be transported from the Negro residential area of the city to the nearly all-white Independence High School.

The Finger plan for the junior high schools employed much of the rezoning plan of the board, combined with the creation of nine "satellite" zones. [A "satellite zone" is an area which is not contiguous with the main attendance zone surrounding the school.] Under the satellite plan, inner-city Negro students were assigned by attendance zones to nine outlying predominately white junior high schools, thereby substantially desegregating every junior high school in the system.

The Finger plan departed from the board plan chiefly in its handling of the system's 76 elementary schools. Rather than relying solely upon geographic zoning, Dr. Finger proposed use of zoning, pairing, and grouping techniques, with the result that student bodies throughout the system would range from 9% to 38% Negro.

The District Court described the plan thus:

"Like the board plan, the Finger plan does as much by rezoning school attendance lines as can reasonably be accomplished. However, unlike the board plan, it does not stop there. It goes further and desegregates all the rest of the elementary schools by the technique of grouping two or three outlying schools with one black inner city school; by transporting black students from grades one through four to the outlying white schools; and by transporting white students from the fifth and sixth grades from the outlying white schools to the inner city black school."

Under the Finger plan, nine inner-city Negro schools were grouped in this manner with 24 suburban white schools.

On February 5, 1970, the District Court adopted the board plan, as modified by Dr. Finger, for the junior and senior high schools. The court rejected the board elementary school plan and adopted the Finger plan as presented. Implementation was partially stayed by the Court of Appeals for the Fourth Circuit on March 5, and this Court declined to disturb the Fourth Circuit's order, 397 U.S. 978 (1970).

On appeal the Court of Appeals affirmed the District Court's order as to faculty desegregation and the secondary school plans, but vacated the order respecting elementary schools. While agreeing that the District Court properly disapproved the board plan concerning these schools, the Court of Appeals feared that the pairing and grouping of elementary schools would place an unreasonable burden on the board and the system's pupils. The case was remanded to the District Court for reconsideration and submission of further plans. 431 F. 2d 138. This Court granted certiorari, 399 U.S. 926, and directed reinstatement of the District Court's order pending further proceedings in that court.

On remand the District Court received two new plans for the elementary schools: a plan prepared by the United States Department of Health, Education, and Welfare (the HEW plan) based on contiguous grouping and zoning of schools, and a plan prepared by four members of the nine-member school board (the minority plan) achieving substantially the same results as the Finger plan but apparently with slightly less transportation. A majority of the school board declined to amend its proposal. After a lengthy evidentiary hearing the District Court concluded that its own plan (the Finger plan), the minority plan, and an earlier draft of the Finger plan were all reasonable and acceptable. It directed the board to adopt one of the three or in the alternative to come forward with a new, equally effective plan of its own; the court ordered that the Finger plan would remain in effect in the event the school board declined to adopt a new plan. On August 7, the board indicated it would "acquiesce" in the Finger plan, reiterating its view that the plan was unreasonable. The District Court, by order dated August 7, 1970, directed that the Finger plan remain in effect.

II

[The Court summarizes the holdings in the desegregation decisions of 1954 and 1955 and the difficulties encountered in implementing those decisions. This experience convinced the Court of the need to issue new guidelines for school authorities and courts.]

III

The objective today remains to eliminate from the public schools all vestiges of state-imposed segregation. Segregation was the evil struck down by *Brown I* as contrary to the equal protection guarantees of the Constitution. That was the violation sought to be corrected by the remedial measures of *Brown II*. That was the basis for the holding in *Green* that school authorities are "clearly charged with the affirmative duty to take whatever steps might be necessary to convert to a unitary system in which racial discrimination would be eliminated root and branch." 391 U.S., at 437–438.

If school authorities fail in their affirmative obligations under these holdings, judicial authority may be invoked. Once a right and a violation have been shown, the scope of a district court's equitable powers to remedy past wrongs is broad, for breadth and flexibility are inherent in equitable remedies.

. . .

The school authorities argue that the equity powers of federal district courts have been limited by Title IV of the Civil Rights Act of 1964, 42 U.S.C. § 2000c. The language and the history of Title IV show that it was enacted not to limit but to define the role of the Federal Government in the implementation of the *Brown I* decision. It authorizes the Commissioner of Education to provide technical assistance to local boards in the preparation of desegregation plans, to arrange "training institutes" for school personnel involved in desegregation efforts, and to make grants directly to schools to ease the transition to unitary systems. It also authorizes the Attorney General, in specified circumstances, to initiate federal desegregation suits. Section 2000c (b) defines "desegregation" as it is used in Title IV:

" 'Desegregation' means the assignment of students to public schools and within such schools without regard to their race, color, religion, or national origin, but 'desegregation' shall not mean the assignment of students to public schools in order to overcome racial imbalance."

Section 2000c–6, authorizing the Attorney General to institute federal suits, contains the following proviso:

"nothing herein shall empower any official or court of the United States to issue any order seeking to achieve a racial balance in any school by requiring the transportation of pupils or students from one school to another or one school district to another in order to achieve such racial balance, or otherwise enlarge the existing power of the court to insure compliance with constitutional standards."

On their face, the sections quoted purport only to insure that the provisions of Title IV of the Civil Rights Act of 1964 will not be read as granting new powers. The proviso in § 2000c-6 is in terms designed to foreclose any interpretation of the Act as expanding the *existing* powers of federal courts to enforce the Equal Protection Clause. There is no suggestion of an intention to restrict those powers or withdraw from courts their historic equitable remedial powers. The legislative history of Title IV indicates that Congress was concerned that the Act might be read as creating a right of action under the Fourteenth Amendment in the situation of so-called "de facto segregation," where racial imbalance exists in the schools but with no showing that this was brought about by discriminatory action of state authorities. In short, there is nothing in the Act that provides us material assistance in answering the question of remedy for state-imposed segregation in violation of *Brown I*. The basis of our decision must be the prohibition of the Fourteenth Amendment that no State shall "deny to any person within its jurisdiction the equal protection of the laws."

IV

[The Court reviews the major principles identified in previous cases regarding remedies for segregated school systems.]

V

The central issue in this case is that of student assignment, and there are essentially four problem areas:

(1) to what extent racial balance or racial quotas may be used as an implement in a remedial order to correct a previously segregated system;

(2) whether every all-Negro and all-white school must be eliminated as an indispensable part of a remedial process of desegregation;

(3) what the limits are, if any, on the rearrangement of school districts and attendance zones, as a remedial measure; and

(4) what the limits are, if any, on the use of transportation facilities to correct state-enforced racial school segregation.

(1) *Racial Balances or Racial Quotas.*

The constant theme and thrust of every holding from *Brown I* to date is that state-enforced separation of races in public schools is discrimination that violates the Equal Protection Clause. The remedy commanded was to dismantle dual school systems.

. . .

In this case it is urged that the District Court has imposed a racial balance requirement of 71%–29% on individual schools. The fact that no such objective was actually achieved—and would appear to be impossible—tends to blunt that claim . . .

. . .

We see therefore that the use made of mathematical ratios was no more than a starting point in the process of shaping a remedy, rather than an inflexible requirement. From that starting point the District Court proceeded to frame a decree that was within its discretionary powers, as an equitable remedy for the particular circumstances. As we said in *Green*, a school authority's remedial plan or a district court's remedial decree is to be judged by its effectiveness. Awareness of the racial composition of the whole school system is likely to be a useful starting point in shaping a remedy to correct past constitutional violations. In sum, the very limited use made of mathematical ratios was within the equitable remedial discretion of the District Court.

(2) *One-race Schools.*

The record in this case reveals the familiar phenomenon that in metropolitan areas minority groups are often found concentrated in one part of the city. In some circumstances certain schools may remain all or largely of one race until new schools can be provided or neighborhood patterns change. Schools all or predominately of one race in a district of mixed population will require close scrutiny to determine that school assignments are not part of state-enforced segregation.

. . .

(3) *Remedial Altering of Attendance Zones.*

The maps submitted in these cases graphically demonstrate that one of the principal tools employed by school planners and by courts to break up the dual school system has been a frank—and sometimes drastic—gerrymandering of school districts and attendance zones. An additional step was pairing, "clustering," or "grouping" of schools with attendance assignments made deliberately to accomplish the transfer of Negro students out of formerly segregated Negro schools and transfer of white students to formerly all-Negro schools. More often than not, these zones are neither compact nor contiguous; indeed they may be on opposite ends of the city. As an interim corrective measure, this cannot be said to be beyond the broad remedial powers of a court.

. . .

(4) *Transportation of Students.*

The scope of permissible transportation of students as an implement of a remedial decree has never been defined by this Court and by the very nature of the problem it cannot be defined with precision. No rigid guidelines as to student transportation can be given for application to the infinite variety of problems presented in thousands of situations. Bus transportation has been an integral part of the public education system for years, and was perhaps the single most important factor in the transition from the one-room schoolhouse to the consolidated school. Eighteen million of the Nation's public school children, approximately 39%, were transported to their schools by bus in 1969–1970 in all parts of the country.

The importance of bus transportation as a normal and accepted tool of educational policy is readily discernible in this and the companion case, *[Davis v. School Comm'rs of Mobile County, 402 U.S. 33 (1971).]* The Charlotte school authorities did not purport to assign students on the basis of geographically drawn zones until 1965 and then they allowed almost unlimited transfer privileges. The District Court's conclusion that assignment of children to the school nearest their home serving their grade would not produce an effective dismantling of the dual system is supported by the record.

Thus the remedial techniques used in the District Court's order were within that court's power to provide equitable relief; implementation of the decree is well within the capacity of the school authority.

The decree provided that the buses used to implement the plan would operate on direct routes. Students would be picked up at schools near their homes and transported to the schools they were to attend. The trips for elementary school pupils average about seven miles and the District Court found that they would take "not over 35 minutes at the most." This system compares favorably with the transportation plan previously operated in Charlotte under which each day 23,600 students on all grade levels were transported an average of 15 miles one way for an average trip requiring over an hour. . . .

VI

The Court of Appeals, searching for a term to define the equitable remedial power of the district courts, used the term "reasonableness." In *Green, supra,* this Court used the term "feasible" and by implication, "workable," "effective," and "realistic" in the mandate to develop "a plan that promises realistically to work, and . . . to work *now.*" On the facts of this case, we are unable to conclude that the order of the District Court is not reasonable, feasible and workable. However, in seeking to define the scope of remedial power or the limits on remedial power of courts in an area as sensitive as we deal with here, words are poor instruments to convey the sense of basic fairness inherent in equity. Substance, not semantics, must govern, and we have sought to suggest the nature of limitations without frustrating the appropriate scope of equity.

. . .

For the reasons herein set forth, the judgment of the Court of Appeals is affirmed as to those parts in which it affirmed the judgment of the District Court. The order of the District Court, dated August 7, 1970, is also affirmed.

It is so ordered.

Milliken v. Bradley

418 U.S. 717 (1974)

Parents and students in Detroit, Michigan, brought this action against Governor Milliken. They alleged that the Detroit public school system was racially segregated as a result of the official policies and actions of state and city officials. A district court, concluding that official acts had created and perpetuated school segregation, ordered the Detroit Board of Education to submit Detroit-only desegregation plans. The court also ordered the state officials to submit desegregation plans encompassing the three-county metropolitan area, despite the fact that the eighty-five outlying school districts in these three counties were not parties to the action and there was no claim that they had committed constitutional violations. The district court ruled that Detroit-only plans were inadequate to accomplish desegregation and that it was proper to consider metropolitan plans. The Sixth Circuit affirmed that a metropolitan plan was the only feasible solution and was within the district court's equity powers.

MR. CHIEF JUSTICE BURGER delivered the opinion of the Court.

We granted certiorari in these consolidated cases to determine whether a federal court may impose a multidistrict, areawide remedy to a single-district *de jure* segregation problem absent any finding that the other included school districts have failed to operate unitary school systems within their districts, absent any claim or finding that the boundary lines of any affected school district were established with the purpose of fostering racial segregation in public schools, absent any finding that the included districts committed acts which effected segregation within the other districts, and absent a meaningful opportunity for the included neighboring school districts to present evidence or be heard on the propriety of a multidistrict remedy or on the question of constitutional violations by those neighboring districts.

I

The action was commenced in August 1970 by the respondents, the Detroit Branch of the National Association for the Advancement of Colored People and individual parents and students, on behalf of a class later defined by order of the United States District Court for the Eastern District of Michigan, dated February 16, 1971, to include "all school children in the City of Detroit, Michigan, and all Detroit resident parents who have children of school age." The named defendants in the District Court included the Governor of Michigan, the Attorney General, the State Board of Education, the State Superintendent of Public Instruction, the Board of Education of the city of Detroit, its members, and the city's former superintendent of schools. . . . In their complaint respondents attacked the constitutionality of a statute of the State of Michigan known as Act 48 of the 1970 Legislature on the ground that it put the State of Michigan in the position of unconstitutionally interfering with the execution and operation of a voluntary plan of partial high school desegregation, known as the April 7, 1970, Plan, which had been adopted by the Detroit Board of Education to be effective beginning with the fall 1970 semester. The complaint also alleged that the Detroit Public School System was and is segregated on the basis of race as a result of the official policies and actions of the defendants and their predecessors in office, and called for the implementation of a plan that would eliminate "the racial identity of every school in the [Detroit] system and . . . maintain now and hereafter a unitary, nonracial school system."

[After the case bounced back and forth between the district court and the Sixth Circuit, the district court concluded that governmental actions had contribut-

ed to residential segregation and therefore school segregation. Moreover, school segregation had been perpetuated by optional attendance zones created by the Detroit Board of Education, allowing white students to escape black schools. Busing was used to transport black students to distant black schools rather than have them attend closer white schools. With one exception, created by the burning of a white school, white children were not bused to predominantly black schools. As a remedy, the district court designated fifty-three of the eighty-five suburban school districts plus Detroit as the "desegregation area" and ordered the Detroit Board of Education to purchase or lease "at least" 295 school buses to produce a desegregation plan for the metropolitan area. The Sixth Circuit agreed that any solution less comprehensive than a metropolitan area plan would be ineffective.]

II

Ever since *Brown* v. *Board of Education*, 347 U.S. 483 (1954), judicial consideration of school desegregation cases has begun with the standard:

"[I]n the field of public education the doctrine of 'separate but equal' has no place. Separate educational facilities are inherently unequal." *Id.*, at 495.

This has been reaffirmed time and again as the meaning of the Constitution, and the controlling rule of law.

The target of the *Brown* holding was clear and forthright: the elimination of state-mandated or deliberately maintained dual school systems with certain schools for Negro pupils and others for white pupils. This duality and racial segregation were held to violate the Constitution in the cases subsequent to 1954, including particularly *Green* v. *County School Board of New Kent County*, 391 U.S. 430 (1968); *Raney* v. *Board of Education*, 391 U.S. 443 (1968); *Monroe* v. *Board of Comm'rs*, 391 U.S. 450 (1968); *Swann* v. *Charlotte-Mecklenburg Board of Education*, 402 U.S. 1 (1971); *Wright* v. *Council of the City of Emporia*, 407 U.S. 451 (1972); *United States* v. *Scotland Neck Board of Education*, 407 U.S. 484 (1972).

The *Swann* case, of course, dealt

"with the problem of defining in more precise

terms than heretofore the scope of the duty of school authorities and district courts in implementing *Brown I* and the mandate to eliminate dual systems and establish unitary systems at once." 402 U.S., at 6.

In *Brown* v. *Board of Education*, 349 U.S. 294 (1955) *(Brown II)*, the Court's first encounter with the problem of remedies in school desegregation cases, the Court noted:

"In fashioning and effectuating the decrees, the courts will be guided by equitable principles. Traditionally, equity has been characterized by a practical flexibility in shaping its remedies and by a facility for adjusting and reconciling public and private needs." *Id.*, at 300 (footnotes omitted).

In further refining the remedial process, *Swann* held, the task is to correct, by a balancing of the individual and collective interests, "the condition that offends the Constitution." A federal remedial power may be exercised "only on the basis of a constitutional violation" and, "[a]s with any equity case, the nature of the violation determines the scope of the remedy." 402 U.S., at 16.

Proceeding from these basic principles, we first note that in the District Court the complainants sought a remedy aimed at the *condition* alleged to offend the Constitution—the segregation within the Detroit City School District. The court acted on this theory of the case and in its initial ruling on the "Desegregation Area" stated:

"The task before this court, therefore, is now, and . . . has always been, how to desegregate the Detroit public schools." 345 F. Supp., at 921.

Thereafter, however, the District Court abruptly rejected the proposed Detroit-only plans on the ground that "while [they] would provide a racial mix more in keeping with the Black-White proportions of the student population [they] would accentuate the racial identifiability of the [Detroit] district as a Black school system, and would not accomplish desegregation." . . .

Viewing the record as a whole, it seems clear that the District Court and the Court of Appeals shifted the primary focus from a Detroit remedy to the metropolitan area only because of their conclusion that total desegregation of Detroit would not produce the racial balance which they perceived as desirable. . . .

In *Swann*, which arose in the context of a single independent school district, the Court held:

"If we were to read the holding of the District Court to require, as a matter of substantive constitutional right, any particular degree of racial balance or mixing, that approach would be disapproved and we would be obliged to reverse." 402 U.S., at 24.

The clear import of this language from *Swann* is that desegregation, in the sense of dismantling a dual school system, does not require any particular racial balance in each "school, grade or classroom." See *Spencer* v. *Kugler*, 404 U.S. 1027 (1972).

. . . No single tradition in public education is more deeply rooted than local control over the operation of schools; local autonomy has long been thought essential both to the maintenance of community concern and support for public schools and to quality of the educational process. See *Wright* v. *Council of the City of Emporia*, 407 U.S., at 469. Thus, in *San Antonio School District* v. *Rodriguez*, 411 U.S. 1, 50 (1973), we observed that local control over the educational process affords citizens an opportunity to participate in decisionmaking, permits the structuring of school programs to fit local needs, and encourages "experimentation, innovation, and a healthy competition for educational excellence."

. . .

. . . an interdistrict remedy might be in order where the racially discriminatory acts of one or more school districts caused racial segregation in an adjacent district, or where district lines have been deliberately drawn on the basis of race. In such circumstances an interdistrict remedy would be appropriate to eliminate the interdistrict segregation directly caused by the constitutional violation. Conversely, without an interdistrict violation and interdistrict effect, there is no constitutional wrong calling for an interdistrict remedy.

The record before us, voluminous as it is, contains evidence of *de jure* segregated conditions only in the Detroit schools; indeed, that was the theory on which the litigation was initially based and on which the District Court took evidence. See *supra*, at 725–726. With no showing of significant violation by the 53 outlying school districts and no evidence of any interdistrict violation or effect, the court went beyond the original theory of the case as framed by the pleadings and mandated a metropolitan area remedy. To approve the remedy ordered by the court would impose on the outlying districts, not shown to have committed any constitutional violation, a wholly impermissible remedy based on a standard not hinted at in *Brown I* and *II* or any holding of this Court.

. . .

IV

. . .

We conclude that the relief ordered by the District Court and affirmed by the Court of Appeals was based upon an erroneous standard and was unsupported by record evidence that acts of the outlying districts effected the discrimination found to exist in the schools of Detroit. Accordingly, the judgment of the Court of Appeals is reversed and the case is remanded for further proceedings consistent with this opinion leading to prompt formulation of a decree directed to eliminating the segregation found to exist in Detroit city schools, a remedy which has been delayed since 1970.

Reversed and remanded.

MR. JUSTICE STEWART, concurring.

. . .

MR. JUSTICE DOUGLAS, dissenting.

. . .

When we rule against the metropolitan area remedy we take a step that will likely put the problems of the blacks and our society back to the period that antedated the "separate but equal" regime of *Plessy* v. *Ferguson*, 163 U.S. 537. The reason is simple.

The inner core of Detroit is now rather solidly black; and the blacks, we know, in many instances are likely to be poorer, just as were the Chicanos in *San Antonio School District* v. *Rodriguez*, 411 U.S. 1. By that decision the poorer school districts must pay their own way. It is therefore a foregone conclusion that we have now given the States a formula whereby the poor must pay their own way.

Today's decision, given *Rodriguez*, means that there is no violation of the Equal Protection Clause though the schools are segregated by race and though the black schools are not only "separate" but "inferior."

. . .

MR. JUSTICE WHITE, with whom MR. JUSTICE DOUGLAS, MR. JUSTICE BRENNAN, and MR. JUSTICE MARSHALL join, dissenting.

The District Court and the Court of Appeals found that over a long period of years those in charge of the Michigan public schools engaged in various practices calculated to effect the segregation of the Detroit school system. The Court does not question these findings, nor could it reasonably do so. Neither does it question the obligation of the federal courts to devise a feasible and effective remedy. But it promptly cripples the ability of the judiciary to perform this task, which is of fundamental importance to our constitutional system, by fashioning a strict rule that remedies in school cases must stop at the school district line unless certain other conditions are met. As applied here, the remedy for unquestioned violations of the equal protection rights of Detroit's Negroes by the Detroit School Board and the State of Michigan must be totally confined to the limits of the school district and may not reach into adjoining or surrounding districts unless and until it is proved there has been some sort of "interdistrict violation"—unless unconstitutional actions of the Detroit School Board have had a segregative impact on other districts, or unless the segregated condition of the Detroit schools has itself been influenced by segregative practices in those surrounding districts into which it is proposed to extend the remedy.

. . .

MR. JUSTICE MARSHALL, with whom MR. JUSTICE DOUGLAS, MR. JUSTICE BRENNAN, and MR. JUSTICE WHITE join, dissenting.

In *Brown* v. *Board of Education*, 347 U.S. 483 (1954), this Court held that segregation of children in public schools on the basis of race deprives minority group children of equal educational opportunities and therefore denies them the equal protection of the laws under the Fourteenth Amendment. This Court recognized then that remedying decades of segregation in public education would not be an easy task. Subsequent events, unfortunately, have seen that prediction bear bitter fruit. But however imbedded old ways, however ingrained old prejudices, this Court has not been diverted from its appointed task of making "a living truth" of our constitutional ideal of equal justice under law. *Cooper* v. *Aaron*, 358 U.S. 1, 20 (1958).

After 20 years of small, often difficult steps toward that great end, the Court today takes a giant step backwards. Notwithstanding a record showing widespread and pervasive racial segregation in the educational system provided by the State of Michigan for children in Detroit, this Court holds that the District Court was powerless to require the State to remedy its constitutional violation in any meaningful fashion. Ironically purporting to base its result on the principle that the scope of the remedy in a desegregation case should be determined by the nature and the extent of the constitutional violation, the Court's answer is to provide no remedy at all for the violation proved in this case, thereby guaranteeing that Negro children in Detroit will receive the same separate and inherently unequal education in the future as they have been unconstitutionally afforded in the past.

I cannot subscribe to this emasculation of our constitutional guarantee of equal protection of the laws and must respectfully dissent. Our precedents, in my view, firmly establish that where, as here, state-imposed segregation has been demonstrated, it becomes the duty of the State to eliminate root and branch all vestiges of racial discrimination and to achieve the greatest possible degree of actual desegregation. I agree with both the District Court and the Court of Appeals that, under the facts of this case, this duty cannot be fulfilled unless the State of Michigan involves outlying metropolitan area school districts in its desegregation remedy. . . .

I

The great irony of the Court's opinion and, in my view, its most serious analytical flaw may be gleaned from its concluding sentence, in which the Court remands for "prompt formulation of a decree directed to eliminating the segregation found to exist in Detroit city schools, a remedy which has been delayed since 1970." *Ante*, at 753. The majority, however, seems to have forgotten the District Court's explicit finding that a Detroit-only decree, the only remedy permitted under today's decision, "would not accomplish desegregation."

. . .

Contrary to the suggestions in the Court's opinion, the basis for affording a desegregation remedy in this case was not some perceived racial imbalance either between schools within a single school district or between independent school districts. What we confront here is "a systematic program of segregation affecting a substantial portion of the students, schools . . . and facilities within the school system . . . ." *Id.*, at 201. The constitutional violation found here was not some *de facto* racial imbalance, but rather the purposeful, intentional, massive, *de jure* segregation of the Detroit city schools, which under our decision in *Keyes*, forms "a predicate for a finding of the existence of a dual school system," *ibid.*, and justifies "all-out desegregation." *Id.*, at 214.

Having found a *de jure* segregated public school system in operation in the city of Detroit, the District Court turned next to consider which officials and agencies should be assigned the affirmative obligation to cure the constitutional violation. The court concluded that responsibility for the segregation in the Detroit city schools rested not only with the Detroit Board of Education, but belonged to the State of Michigan itself

and the state defendants in this case—that is, the Governor of Michigan, the Attorney General, the State Board of Education, and the State Superintendent of Public Instruction. While the validity of this conclusion will merit more extensive analysis below, suffice it for now to say that it was based on three considerations. First, the evidence at trial showed that the State itself had taken actions contributing to the segregation within the Detroit schools. Second, since the Detroit Board of Education was an agency of the State of Michigan, its acts of racial discrimination were acts of the State for purposes of the Fourteenth Amendment. Finally, the District Court found that under Michigan law and practice, the system of education was in fact a *state* school system, characterized by relatively little local control and a large degree of centralized state regulation, with respect to both educational policy and the structure and operation of school districts.

. . .

III

. . .

Desegregation is not and was never expected to be an easy task. Racial attitudes ingrained in our Nation's childhood and adolescence are not quickly thrown aside in its middle years. But just as the inconvenience of some cannot be allowed to stand in the way of the rights of others, so public opposition, no matter how strident, cannot be permitted to divert this Court from the enforcement of the constitutional principles at issue in this case. Today's holding, I fear, is more a reflection of a perceived public mood that we have gone far enough in enforcing the Constitution's guarantee of equal justice than it is the product of neutral principles of law. In the short run, it may seem to be the easier course to allow our great metropolitan areas to be divided up each into two cities— one white, the other black—but it is a course, I predict, our people will ultimately regret. I dissent.

Shelley v. Kraemer
334 U.S. 1 (1948)

Private agreements, known as restrictive covenants, were used in Missouri to prevent blacks from owning property. Private agreements, standing alone, usually do not violate the Fourteenth Amendment, which is directed against actions by state governments. The question in this case was whether a connection existed between private agreements and the state of Missouri. The Kraemers, a couple in the neighborhood subject to the terms of the restrictive covenant, brought suit to prevent the Shelleys, a black couple, from taking possession of property. The trial court denied the relief but was reversed by the Supreme Court of Missouri.

MR. CHIEF JUSTICE VINSON delivered the opinion of the Court.

These cases present for our consideration questions relating to the validity of court enforcement of private agreements, generally described as restrictive covenants, which have as their purpose the exclusion of persons of designated race or color from the ownership or occupancy of real property. Basic constitutional issues of obvious importance have been raised.

The first of these cases comes to this Court on certiorari to the Supreme Court of Missouri. On February 16, 1911, thirty out of a total of thirty-nine owners of property fronting both sides of Labadie Avenue between Taylor Avenue and Cora Avenue in the city of St. Louis, signed an agreement, which was subsequently recorded, providing in part:

". . . the said property is hereby restricted to the use and occupancy for the term of Fifty (50) years from this date, so that it shall be a condition all the time and whether recited and referred to as [*sic*] not in subsequent conveyances and shall attach to the land as a condition precedent to the sale of the same, that hereafter no part of said property or any portion thereof shall be, for said term of Fifty-years, occupied by any person not of the Caucasian race, it being intended hereby to restirct the use of said property for said period of time against the occupancy as owners or tenants of any portion of said property for resident or other purpose by people of the Negro or Mongolian Race."

The entire district described in the agreement included fifty-seven parcels of land. The thirty owners who signed the agreement held title to forty-seven parcels, including the particular parcel involved in this case. At the time the agreement was signed, five of the parcels in the district were owned by Negroes. One of those had been occupied by Negro families since 1882, nearly thirty years before the restrictive agreement was executed. The trial court found that owners of seven out of nine homes on the south side of Labadie Avenue, within the restricted district and "in the immediate vicinity" of the premises in question, had failed to sign the restrictive agreement in 1911. At the time this action was brought, four of the premises were occupied by Negroes, and had been so occupied for periods ranging from twenty-three to sixty-three years. A fifth parcel had been occupied by Negroes until a year before this suit was instituted.

On August 11, 1945, pursuant to a contract of sale, petitioners Shelley, who are Negroes, for valuable consideration received from one Fitzgerald a warranty deed to the parcel in question. The trial court found that petitioners had no actual knowledge of the restrictive agreement at the time of the purchase.

On October 9, 1945, respondents, as owners of other property subject to the terms of the restrictive covenant, brought suit in the Circuit Court of the city of St. Louis praying that petitioners Shelley be restrained from taking possession of the property and that judgment be entered divesting title out of petitioners Shelley and revesting title in the immediate grantor or in such other person as the court should direct. The trial court denied the requested relief on the ground that the restrictive agreement, upon which respondents based their action, had never become final and complete because it was the intention of the parties to that agreement that it was not to become effective until signed by all property owners in the district, and signatures of all the owners had never been obtained.

The Supreme Court of Missouri sitting *en banc* reversed and directed the trial court to grant the relief for which respondents had prayed. That court held the agreement effective and concluded that enforcement of its provisions violated no rights guaranteed to petitioners by the Federal Constitution. At the time the court rendered its decision, petitioners were occupying the property in question.

[The Court summarizes a second case, coming to it from Michigan, which raises similar issues.]

I.

Whether the equal protection clause of the Fourteenth Amendment inhibits judicial enforcement by state courts of restrictive covenants based on race or color is a question which this Court has not heretofore been called upon to consider. Only two cases have been decided by this Court which in any way have involved the enforcement of such agreements. The first of these was the case of *Corrigan* v. *Buckley*, 271 U.S. 323 (1926). There, suit was brought in the courts of the District of Columbia to enjoin a threatened violation of certain restrictive covenants relating to lands situated in the city of Washington. Relief was granted, and the case was brought here on appeal. It is apparent that that case, which had originated in the federal courts and involved the enforcement of covenants on land located in the District of Columbia, could present no issues under the Fourteenth Amendment; for that Amendment by its terms applies only to the States. Nor was the question of the validity of court enforcement of the restrictive covenants under the Fifth Amendment properly before the Court, as the opinion of this Court specifically recognizes. . . .

The second of the cases involving racial restrictive covenants was *Hansberry* v. *Lee*, 311 U.S. 32 (1940). In that case, petitioners, white property owners, were enjoined by the state courts from violating the terms of a restrictive agreement. The state Supreme Court had held petitioners bound by an earlier judicial determination, in litigation in which petitioners were not parties, upholding the validity of the restrictive agreement, although, in fact, the agreement had not been signed by the number of owners necessary to make it effective under state law. This Court reversed the judgment of the state Supreme Court upon the ground that petitioners had been denied due process of law in being held estopped to challenge the validity of the agreement on the theory, accepted by the state court, that the earlier litigation, in which petitioners did not participate, was in the nature of a class suit. In arriving at its result, this Court did not reach the issues presented by the cases now under consideration.

It is well, at the outset, to scrutinize the terms of the restrictive agreements involved in these cases. In the Missouri case, the covenant declares that no part of the affected property shall be "occupied by any person not of the Caucasian race, it being intended hereby to restrict the use of said property . . . against the occupancy as owners or tenants of any portion of said property for resident or other purpose by people of the Negro or Mongolian Race." Not only does the restriction seek to proscribe use and occupancy of the affected properties by members of the excluded class, but as construed by the Missouri courts, the agreement requires that title of any person who uses his property in violation of the restriction shall be divested. . . .

It cannot be doubted that among the civil rights intended to be protected from discriminatory state action by the Fourteenth Amendment are the rights to acquire, enjoy, own and dispose of property. Equality in the enjoyment of property rights was regarded by the framers of that Amendment as an essential pre-condition to the realization of other basic civil rights and liberties which the Amendment was intended to guarantee. Thus, § 1978 of the Revised Statutes, derived from § 1 of the Civil Rights Act of 1866 which was enacted by Congress while the Fourteenth Amendment was also under consideration, provides:

"All citizens of the United States shall have the same right, in every State and Territory, as is enjoyed by white citizens thereof to inherit, purchase, lease, sell, hold, and convey real and personal property."

This Court has given specific recognition to the same principle. *Buchanan* v. *Warley*, 245 U.S. 60 (1917).

It is likewise clear that restrictions on the right of occupancy of the sort sought to be created by the private agreements in these cases could not be squared with the requirements of the Fourteenth Amendment if imposed by state statute or local ordinance. We do not understand respondents to urge the contrary. . . .

. . .

. . . the present cases . . . do not involve action by state legislatures or city councils. Here the particular patterns of discrimination and the areas in which the restrictions are to operate, are determined, in the first instance, by the terms of agreements among private individuals. Participation of the State consists in the enforcement of the restrictions so defined. The crucial issue with which we are here confronted is whether this distinction removes these cases from the operation of the prohibitory provisions of the Fourteenth Amendment.

Since the decision of this Court in the *Civil Rights Cases*, 109 U.S. 3 (1883), the principle has become firmly embedded in our constitutional law that the action inhibited by the first section of the Fourteenth Amendment is only such action as may fairly be said to be that of the States. That Amendment erects no shield against merely private conduct, however discriminatory or wrongful.

We conclude, therefore, that the restrictive agreements standing alone cannot be regarded as violative of any rights guaranteed to petitioners by the Fourteenth Amendment. So long as the purposes of those agreements are effectuated by voluntary adherence to their terms, it would appear clear that there has been no action by the State

and the provisions of the Amendment have not been violated. Cf. *Corrigan* v. *Buckley, supra.*

But here there was more. These are cases in which the purposes of the agreements were secured only by judicial enforcement by state courts of the restrictive terms of the agreements. The respondents urge that judicial enforcement of private agreements does not amount to state action; or, in any event, the participation of the State is so attenuated in character as not to amount to state action within the meaning of the Fourteenth Amendment. Finally, it is suggested, even if the States in these cases may be deemed to have acted in the constitutional sense, their action did not deprive petitioners of rights guaranteed by the Fourteenth Amendment. We move to a consideration of these matters.

II.

That the action of state courts and judicial officers in their official capacities is to be regarded as action of the State within the meaning of the Fourteenth Amendment, is a proposition which has long been established by decisions of this Court. . . .

. . . the examples of state judicial action which have been held by this Court to violate the Amendment's commands are not restricted to situations in which the judicial proceedings were found in some manner to be procedurally unfair. It has been recognized that the action of state courts in enforcing a substantive common-law rule formulated by those courts, may result in the denial of rights guaranteed by the Fourteenth Amendment, even though the judicial proceedings in such cases may have been in complete accord with the most rigorous conceptions of procedural due process. . . .

The short of the matter is that from the time of the adoption of the Fourteenth Amendment until the present, it has been the consistent ruling of this Court that the action of the States to which the Amendment has reference includes action of state courts and state judicial officials. Although, in construing the terms of the Fourteenth Amendment, differences have from time to time been expressed as to whether particular types of state action may be said to offend the Amendment's prohibitory provisions, it has never been suggested that state court action is immunized from the operation of those provisions simply because the act is that of the judicial branch of the state government.

III.

Against this background of judicial construction, extending over a period of some three-quarters of a century, we are called upon to consider whether enforcement by state courts of the restrictive agreements in these cases may be deemed to be the acts of those States; and, if so, whether that action has denied these petitioners the equal protection of the laws which the Amendment was intended to insure.

We have no doubt that there has been state action in these cases in the full and complete sense of the phrase. The undisputed facts disclose that petitioners were willing purchasers of properties upon which they desired to establish homes. The owners of the properties were willing sellers; and contracts of sale were accordingly consummated. It is clear that but for the active intervention of the state courts, supported by the full panoply of state power, petitioners would have been free to occupy the properties in question without restraint.

. . .

We hold that in granting judicial enforcement of the restrictive agreements in these cases, the States have denied petitioners the equal protection of the laws and that, therefore, the action of the state courts cannot stand. We have noted that freedom from discrimination by the States in the enjoyment of property rights was among the basic objectives sought to be effectuated by the framers of the Fourteenth Amendment. That such discrimination has occurred in these cases is clear. Because of the race or color of these petitioners they have been denied rights of ownership or occupancy enjoyed as a matter of course by other citizens of different race or color. . . .

The historical context in which the Fourteenth Amendment became a part of the Constitution should not be forgotten. Whatever else the framers sought to achieve, it is clear that the matter of primary concern was the establishment of equality in the enjoyment of basic civil and political rights and the preservation of those rights from discriminatory action on the part of the States based on considerations of race or color. Seventy-five years ago this Court announced that the provisions of the Amendment are to be construed with this fundamental purpose in mind. Upon full consideration, we have concluded that in these cases the States have acted to deny petitioners the equal protection of the laws guaranteed by the Fourteenth Amendment. Having so decided, we find it unnecessary to consider whether petitioners have also been deprived of property without due process of law or denied privileges and immunities of citizens of the United States.

For the reasons stated, the judgment of the Supreme Court of Missouri and the judgment of the Supreme Court of Michigan must be reversed.

Reversed.

MR. JUSTICE REED, MR. JUSTICE JACKSON, and MR. JUSTICE RUTLEDGE took no part in the consideration or decision of these cases.

Jones v. Mayer Co.

392 U.S. 409 (1968)

Joseph Lee Jones, a black, claimed in court that the Alfred H. Mayer Company had refused to sell him a home solely because of his race. He relied in part on 42 U.S.C. § 1982, which provides that all citizens "shall have the same right, in every State and Territory, as

is enjoyed by white citizens thereof to inherit, purchase, lease, sell, hold, and convey real and personal property." The district court dismissed the complaint and the Eighth Circuit affirmed, concluding that § 1982 applies only to state action and does not reach private refusals to sell.

MR. JUSTICE STEWART delivered the opinion of the Court.

In this case we are called upon to determine the scope and the constitutionality of an Act of Congress, 42 U.S.C. § 1982, which provides that:

"All citizens of the United States shall have the same right, in every State and Territory, as is enjoyed by white citizens thereof to inherit, purchase, lease, sell, hold, and convey real and personal property."

On September 2, 1965, the petitioners filed a complaint in the District Court for the Eastern District of Missouri, alleging that the respondents had refused to sell them a home in the Paddock Woods community of St. Louis County for the sole reason that petitioner Joseph Lee Jones is a Negro. Relying in part upon § 1982, the petitioners sought injunctive and other relief. The District Court sustained the respondents' motion to dismiss the complaint, and the Court of Appeals for the Eighth Circuit affirmed, concluding that § 1982 applies only to state action and does not reach private refusals to sell. We granted certiorari to consider the questions thus presented. For the reasons that follow, we reverse the judgment of the Court of Appeals. We hold that § 1982 bars *all* racial discrimination, private as well as public, in the sale or rental of property, and that the statute, thus construed, is a valid exercise of the power of Congress to enforce the Thirteenth Amendment.

I.

At the outset, it is important to make clear precisely what this case does *not* involve. Whatever else it may be, 42 U.S.C. § 1982 is not a comprehensive open housing law. In sharp contrast to the Fair Housing Title (Title VIII) of the Civil Rights Act of 1968, Pub. L. 90–284, 82 Stat. 81, the statute in this case deals only with racial discrimination and does not address itself to discrimination on grounds of religion or national

origin. It does not deal specifically with discrimination in the provision of services or facilities in connection with the sale or rental of a dwelling. It does not prohibit advertising or other representations that indicate discriminatory preferences. It does not refer explicitly to discrimination in financing arrangements or in the provision of brokerage services. It does not empower a federal administrative agency to assist aggrieved parties. It makes no provision for intervention by the Attorney General. And, although it can be enforced by injunction, it contains no provision expressly authorizing a federal court to order the payment of damages.

. . .

[There are] vast differences between, on the one hand, a general statute applicable only to racial discrimination in the rental and sale of property and enforceable only by private parties acting on their own initiative, and, on the other hand, a detailed housing law, applicable to a broad range of discriminatory practices and enforceable by a complete arsenal of federal authority. Having noted these differences, we turn to a consideration of § 1982 itself.

II.

This Court last had occasion to consider the scope of 42 U.S.C. § 1982 in 1948, in *Hurd* v. *Hodge*, 334 U.S. 24. That case arose when property owners in the District of Columbia sought to enforce racially restrictive covenants against the Negro purchasers of several homes on their block. *[The Court held that § 1982 was designed to prevent this kind of discrimination, but a federal court had assisted in the enforcement of the racially restrictive agreement. Thus,* Hurd *did not present the question whether "purely private discrimination, unaided by any action on the part of the government, would violate § 1982 if its effect were to deny a citizen the right to rent or buy property solely because of his race or color."]*

III.

We begin with the language of the statute itself. In plain and unambiguous terms, § 1982 grants to all citizens, without regard to race or color, "the same right" to purchase and lease property "as is enjoyed by white citizens." . . .

On its face, therefore, § 1982 appears to prohibit *all* discrimination against Negroes in the sale or rental of property—discrimination by private owners as well as discrimination by public authorities. Indeed, even the respondents seem to concede that, if § 1982 "means what it says"—to use the words of the respondents' brief—then it must encompass every racially motivated refusal to sell or rent and cannot be confined to officially sanctioned segregation in housing. Stressing what they consider to be the revolutionary implications of so literal a reading of § 1982, the respondents argue that Congress cannot possibly have intended any such result. Our examination of the relevant history, however, persuades us that Congress meant exactly what it said.

IV.

In its original form, 42 U.S.C. § 1982 was part of § 1 of the Civil Rights Act of 1866. That section was cast in sweeping terms:

"Be it enacted by the Senate and House of Representatives of the United States of America in Congress assembled, That all persons born in the United States and not subject to any foreign power, . . . are hereby declared to be citizens of the United States; and such citizens, of every race and color, without regard to any previous condition of slavery or involuntary servitude, . . . shall have the same right, in every State and Territory in the United States, to make and enforce contracts, to sue, be parties, and give evidence, to inherit, purchase, lease, sell, hold, and convey real and personal property, and to full and equal benefit of all laws and proceedings for the security of person and property, as is enjoyed by white citizens, and shall be subject to like punishment, pains, and penalties, and to none other, any law, statute, ordinance, regulation, or custom, to the contrary notwithstanding."

The crucial language for our purposes was that which guaranteed all citizens "the same right, in every State and Territory in the United States, . . . to inherit, purchase, lease, sell, hold, and convey real and personal property . . . as is enjoyed by white citizens . . . ." To the Congress that passed the Civil Rights Act of 1866, it was clear that the right to do these things might be infringed not only by "State or local law" but also by "custom, or prejudice." Thus, when Congress provided in § 1 of the Civil Rights Act that the right to purchase and lease property was to be enjoyed equally throughout the United States by Negro and white citizens alike, it plainly meant to secure that right against interference from any source whatever, whether governmental or private.

Indeed, if § 1 had been intended to grant nothing more than an immunity from *governmental* interference, then much of § 2 would have made no sense at all. For that section, which provided fines and prison terms for certain individuals who deprived others of rights "secured or protected" by § 1, was carefully drafted to exempt private violations of § 1 from the criminal sanctions it imposed. There would, of course, have been no private violations to exempt if the only "right" granted by § 1 had been a right to be free of discrimination by public officials. Hence the structure of the 1866 Act, as well as its language, points to the conclusion urged by the petitioners in this case—that § 1 was meant to prohibit *all* racially motivated deprivations of the rights enumerated in the statute, although only those deprivations perpetrated "under color of law" were to be criminally punishable under § 2.

. . .

Nor was the scope of the 1866 Act altered when it was re-enacted in 1870, some two years after the ratification of the Fourteenth Amendment. It is quite true that some members of Congress supported the Fourteenth Amendment "in order to eliminate doubt as to the constitutional validity of the Civil Rights Act as applied to the States." *Hurd* v. *Hodge,* 334 U.S. 24, 32–33. But it certainly does not follow that the adoption of the Fourteenth Amendment or the subsequent readoption of the Civil Rights Act were meant somehow to *limit* its application to state action. The legislative history furnishes not the slightest factual basis for any such speculation, and the conditions prevailing in 1870 make it highly implausible. For by that time most, if not all, of the former Confederate States, then under the control of "reconstructed" legislatures, had formally repudiated racial discrimination, and the focus of congressional concern had clearly shifted from hostile statutes to the activities of groups like the Ku Klux Klan, operating wholly outside the law.

Against this background, it would obviously make no sense to assume, without any historical support whatever, that Congress made a silent decision in 1870 to exempt private discrimination from the operation of the Civil Rights Act of 1866. "The cardinal rule is that repeals by implication are not favored." *Posadas* v. *National City Bank*, 296 U.S. 497, 503. All Congress said in 1870 was that the 1866 law "is hereby re-enacted." That is all Congress meant.

As we said in a somewhat different setting two Terms ago, "We think that history leaves no doubt that, if we are to give [the law] the scope that its origins dictate, we must accord it a sweep as broad as its language." *United States* v. *Price*, 383 U.S. 787, 801. "We are not at liberty to seek ingenious analytical instruments," *ibid.*, to carve from § 1982 an exception for private conduct—even though its application to such conduct in the present context is without established precedent. And, as the Attorney General of the United States said at the oral argument of this case, "The fact that the statute lay partially dormant for many years cannot be held to diminish its force today."

V.

The remaining question is whether Congress has power under the Constitution to do what § 1982 purports to do: to prohibit all racial discrimination, private and public, in the sale and rental of property. Our starting point is the Thirteenth Amendment, for it was pursuant to that constitutional provision that Congress originally enacted what is now § 1982. The Amendment consists of two parts. Section 1 states:

"Neither slavery nor involuntary servitude, except as a punishment for crime whereof the party shall have been duly convicted, shall exist within the United States, or any place subject to their jurisdiction."

Section 2 provides:

"Congress shall have power to enforce this article by appropriate legislation."

As its text reveals, the Thirteenth Amendment "is not a mere prohibition of State laws establishing or upholding slavery, but an absolute declaration that slavery or involuntary servitude shall not exist in any part of the United States." *Civil Rights Cases*, 109 U.S. 3, 20. It has never been doubted, therefore, "that the power vested in Congress to enforce the article by appropriate legislation," *ibid.*, includes the power to enact laws "direct and primary, operating upon the acts of individuals, whether sanctioned by State legislation or not." *Id.*, at 23.

Thus, the fact that § 1982 operates upon the unofficial acts of private individuals, whether or not sanctioned by state law, presents no constitutional problem. If Congress has power under the Thirteenth Amendment to eradicate conditions that prevent Negroes from buying and renting property because of their race or color, then no federal statute calculated to achieve that objective can be thought to exceed the constitutional power of Congress simply because it reaches beyond state action to regulate the conduct of private individuals. The constitutional question in this case, therefore, comes to this: Does the authority of Congress to enforce the Thirteenth Amendment "by appropriate legislation" include the power to eliminate all racial barriers to the acquisition of real and personal property? We think the answer to that question is plainly yes.

. . .

. . . Surely Congress has the power under the Thirteenth Amendment rationally to determine what are the badges and the incidents of slavery, and the authority to translate that determination into effective legislation. Nor can we say that the determination Congress has made is an irrational one . . . .when racial discrimination herds men into ghettos and makes their ability to buy property turn on the color of their skin, then it too is a relic of slavery.

. . .

. . . The judgment is

Reversed.

MR. JUSTICE DOUGLAS, concurring.

. . .

MR. JUSTICE HARLAN, whom MR. JUSTICE WHITE joins, dissenting.

The decision in this case appears to me to be most ill-considered and ill-advised.

The petitioners argue that the respondents' racially motivated refusal to sell them a house entitles them to judicial relief on two separate grounds. First, they claim that the respondents acted in violation of 42 U.S.C. § 1982; second, they assert that the respondents' conduct amounted in the circumstances to "state action" and was therefore forbidden by the Fourteenth Amendment even in the absence of any statute. The Court, without reaching the second ground alleged, holds that the petitioners are entitled to relief under 42 U.S.C. § 1982, and that § 1982 is constitutional as legislation appropriate to enforce the Thirteenth Amendment.

For reasons which follow, I believe that the Court's construction of § 1982 as applying to purely private action is almost surely wrong, and at the least is open to serious doubt. The issues of the constitutionality of § 1982, as construed by the Court, and of liability under the Fourteenth Amendment alone, also present formidable difficulties. Moreover, the political processes of our own era have, since the date of oral argument in this case, given birth to a civil rights statute embodying "fair housing" provisions which would at the end of this year make available to others, though apparently not to the petitioners themselves, the type of relief which the petitioners now seek. It seems to me that this latter factor so diminishes the public importance of this case that by far the wisest course would be for this Court to refrain from decision and to dismiss the writ as improvidently granted.

I.

I shall deal first with the Court's construction of § 1982, which lies at the heart of its opinion. That construction is that the statute applies to purely private as well as to state-authorized discrimination.

A.

The Court's opinion focuses upon the statute's legislative history, but it is worthy of note that the precedents in this Court are distinctly opposed to the Court's view of the statute.

. . .

B.

Like the Court, I begin analysis of § 1982 by examining its language. In its present form, the section provides:

"All citizens of the United States shall have the same right, in every State and Territory, as is enjoyed by white citizens thereof to inherit, purchase, lease, sell, hold, and convey real and personal property."

The Court finds it "plain and unambiguous," *ante,* at 420, that this language forbids purely private as well as state-authorized discrimination. With all respect, I do not find it so. For me, there is an inherent ambiguity in the term "right," as used in § 1982. The "right" referred to may either be a right to equal status under the law, in which case the statute operates only against state-sanctioned discrimination, or it may be an "absolute" right enforceable against private individuals. To me, the words of the statute, taken alone, suggest the former interpretation, not the latter.

Further, since intervening revisions have not been meant to alter substance, the intended meaning of § 1982 must be drawn from the words in which it was originally enacted. Section 1982 originally was a part of § 1 of the Civil Rights Act of 1866, 14 Stat. 27. Sections 1 and 2 of that Act provided in relevant part:

"That all persons born in the United States and not subject to any foreign power . . . are hereby declared to be citizens of the United States; and such citizens, of every race and color . . . , shall have the same right, in every State and Territory in the United States, . . . to inherit, purchase, lease, sell, hold, and convey real and personal property . . . as is enjoyed by white citizens, and shall be subject to like punishment, pains, and penalties, and to none other, any law, statute, ordinance, regulation, or custom, to the contrary notwithstanding.

"Sec. 2. That any person who, under color of any law, statute, ordinance, regulation, or custom, shall subject, or cause to be subjected, any inhabitant of any State or Territory to the deprivation of any right secured or protected by this act . . . shall be deemed guilty of a misdemeanor . . . ."

It seems to me that this original wording indicates even more strongly than the present language that § 1 of the Act (as well as § 2, which is explicitly so limited) was intended to apply only to action taken pursuant to state or community authority, in the form of a "law, statute, ordinance, regulation, or custom." And with deference I suggest that the language of § 2, taken alone, no more implies that § 2 "was carefully drafted to exempt private violations of § 1 from the criminal sanctions it imposed," see *ante*, at 425, than it does that § 2 was carefully drafted to enforce all of the rights secured by § 1.

C.

The Court rests its opinion chiefly upon the legislative history of the Civil Rights Act of 1866. I shall endeavor to show that those debates do not, as the Court would have it, overwhelmingly support the result reached by the Court, and in fact that a contrary conclusion may equally well be drawn. . . .

. . . In the course of the debates, Senator Trumbull, who was by far the leading spokesman for the bill, made a number of statements which can only be taken to mean that the bill was aimed at "state action" alone. For example, on January 29, 1866, Senator Trumbull began by citing a number of recently enacted Southern laws depriving men of rights named in the bill. He stated that "[t]he purpose of the bill under consideration is to destroy *all these discriminations*, and carry into effect the constitutional amendment." . . .

. . .

. . . Residential segregation was the prevailing pattern almost everywhere in the North. There were no state "fair housing" laws in 1866, and it appears that none had ever been proposed. In this historical context, I cannot conceive that a bill thought to prohibit purely private discrimination not only in the sale or rental of housing but in *all* property transactions would not have received a great deal of criticism explicitly directed to this feature. The fact that the 1866 Act received *no* criticism of this kind is for me strong additional evidence that it was not regarded as extending so far.

. . .

II.

. . .

. . . Since, the Court did vote to hear this case, I normally would consider myself obligated to decide whether the petitioners are entitled to relief on either of the grounds on which they rely. After mature reflection, however, I have concluded that this is one of those rare instances in which an event which occurs after the hearing of argument so diminishes a case's public significance, when viewed in light of the difficulty of the questions presented, as to justify this Court in dismissing the writ as improvidently granted.

The occurrence to which I refer is the recent enactment of the Civil Rights Act of 1968, Pub. L. 90–284, 82 Stat. 73. Title VIII of that Act contains comprehensive "fair housing" provisions, which by the terms of § 803 will become applicable on January 1, 1969, to persons who, like the petitioners, attempt to buy houses from developers. Under those provisions, such persons will be entitled to injunctive relief and damages from developers who refuse to sell to them on account of race or color, unless the parties are able to resolve their dispute by other means. Thus, the type of relief which the petitioners seek will be available within seven months' time under the terms of a presumptively constitutional Act of Congress. In these circumstances, it seems obvious that the case has lost most of its public

importance, and I believe that it would be much the wiser course for this Court to refrain from deciding it. . . .

For these reasons, I would dismiss the writ of certiorari as improvidently granted.

Congress Interprets the Commerce Clause

Congressional action on the public accommodations section of the Civil Rights Act of 1964 was jeopardized by the Supreme Court's decision in the *Civil Rights Cases* of 1883. In that case, the Court struck down an earlier congressional effort, based on the Fourteenth Amendment, to pass legislation on public accommodations. Rather than risk a head-on collision with the Court, Congress selected another instrument to achieve its ends: the Commerce Clause. The language below is from Senate Report No. 872, 88th Cong., 2d Sess. 12–14 (1964).

At the outset a formidable obstacle to a favorable determination on S. 1732 appeared to be an 1883 decision by the U.S. Supreme Court holding unconstitutional an 1875 statute providing criminal penalties for denials of service by public facilities or accommodations on account of race, color, or religion. This 1875 law was expressly based on the 14th amendment, but the Supreme Court could not find the requisite "State action" in denials of service by privately owned establishments. There is a large body of legal thought that believes the Court would either reverse the earlier decision if the question were again presented or that changed circumstances in the intervening 80 years would make it possible for the earlier decision to be distinguished. That question, however, was not before the committee, for the instant measure is based on the commerce clause (art. 1, sec. 8, clause 3) of the Constitution. The majority opinion of the Court in the 1883 decision carefully stated that they were not foreclosing a statute based on the broad powers of Congress such as are found in the commerce clause. Mr. Justice Bradley wrote:

"Of course, these remarks do not apply to those cases in which Congress is clothed with direct and plenary powers of legislation over the whole subject, accompanied with an express or implied

denial of such power to the States, as in the regulation of commerce with foreign nations, and among the several States and with the Indian tribes, the coining of money, the establishment of post offices and post roads, the declaring of war, etc. In these cases Congress has power to pass laws for regulating the subjects specified in every detail, and the conduct and transactions of individuals in respect thereof." (109 U.S. 3, 18 (1883))

Attached as an appendix to this report is a brief prepared at the request of the committee by Prof. Paul Freund of the Harvard Law School, a noted authority on the Constitution. In this document Professor Freund concludes that the law proposed by S. 1732 is consistent with the Constitution and the decisions thereunder by the Supreme Court. In the judgment of the committee it would be upheld on review. Similar conclusions were reached by almost all legal scholars or practitioners consulted by the committee or inquired of by witnesses appearing before the committee. Professor Freund wrote: "The commerce power is clearly adequate and appropriate. No impropriety need be felt in using the commerce clause as a response to a deep moral concern." Where social injustices occur in commercial activities the commerce clause has been used to prevent discrimination; it has been used to prohibit racial discrimination; and it has been used to reach intrastate activities if they have a substantial effect (individually or cumulatively) upon commerce. The committee concludes that there is sufficient authority in the Constitution to uphold S. 1732.

Congress, in the exercise of its plenary power over interstate commerce, may regulate commerce or that which affects it for other than purely economic goals.

"The motive and purpose of a regulation of interstate commerce are matters for the legislative judgment upon the exercise of which the Constitution places no restriction and over which the courts are given no control." (Mr. Justice Stone in *United States* v. *Darby*, 312 U.S. 100, 115 (1941))

The fact that S. 1732 would accomplish socially oriented objectives by aid of the commerce clause powers would not detract from its validity. There are many instances in which Congress has discouraged practices which it deems evil, dangerous, or unwise by a regulation of interstate commerce. Examples of this are found in Federal legislation keeping the channels of commerce free from the transportation of tickets used in lottery schemes, sustained in *Champion* v. *Ames*, 188 U.S. 321 (1903); the Pure Food and Drug Act, sustained in *Hipolite Egg Co.* v. *United States*, 220 U.S. 45 (1911). the "White Slave Traffic Act," upheld in *Hoke* v. *United States*, 227 U.S. 308 (1913); strict regulation of the transportation of intoxicating liquors, sustained in *Clark Distilling Co.* v. *Western Maryland Railway Co.*, 242 U.S. 311 (1917); and the Fair Labor Standards Act, imposing wages and hours requirements, sustained in *United States* v. *Darby*, 312 U.S. 100 (1941).

As broad and as deep as are the powers of Congress, there is presented the more difficult problem of how those powers should be utilized. Gov. Farris Bryant of Florida, speaking in opposition to the bill said: "My position is purely and simply that while I believe that the Federal Government has the power to do, I do not believe it has the right to do what it is suggesting be done here." The chairman of the committee, Senator Magnuson, in the initial stages of the public hearings, stated the issue in another way. He observed:

"This is a question of public policy and how far Congress wants to go under the authority of the commerce provision of the Constitution."

The commerce power has served as the basis for Federal action on such national policies as the regulation of agricultural production; requirement of collective bargaining; prohibition of industrial monopolies and unfair trade practices; regulation of the sale of stocks, bonds, and other securities; establishment of hydroelectric, flood control and navigation projects; and an attack upon such crimes as white slavery, kidnaping, trade in narcotics, theft of automobiles, and shipments of gambling devices and lottery tickets. Should it now be used to prohibit denials of service in public facilities when the exclusive reason for the denial is the race, religion, or national origin of the would-be patron?

Heart of Atlanta Motel v. United States

379 U.S. 241 (1964)

Title II of the Civil Rights Act of 1964 prohibits racial discrimination in places of public accommodation affecting interstate commerce. Establishments covered by the Act include inns, hotels, restaurants, cafeterias, and movie theaters. The appellant in this case, the Heart of Atlanta Motel located in Atlanta, Georgia, restricted its clientele to white persons. The motel claimed that the statute exceeded Congress' power under the Commerce Clause and violated other parts of the Constitution. A three-judge court upheld the constitutionality of Title II.

MR. JUSTICE CLARK delivered the opinion of the Court.

This is a declaratory judgment action, 28 U. S. C. § 2201 and § 2202 (1958 ed.), attacking the constitutionality of Title II of the Civil Rights Act of 1964, 78 Stat. 241, 243. In addition to declaratory relief the complaint sought an injunction restraining the enforcement of the Act and damages against appellees based on allegedly resulting injury in the event compliance was required. Appellees counterclaimed for enforcement under § 206 (a) of the Act and asked for a three-judge district court under § 206 (b). A three-judge court, empaneled under § 206 (b) as well as 28 U. S. C. § 2282 (1958 ed.), sustained the validity of the Act and issued a permanent injunction on appellees' counterclaim restraining appellant from continuing to violate the Act which remains in effect on order of MR. JUSTICE BLACK, 85 S. Ct. 1. We affirm the judgment.

1. THE FACTUAL BACKGROUND AND CONTENTIONS OF THE PARTIES.

The case comes here on admissions and stipulated facts. Appellant owns and operates the Heart of Atlanta Motel which has 216 rooms available to transient guests. The motel is located on Courtland Street, two blocks from downtown Peachtree Street. It is readily accessible to interstate highways 75 and 85 and state highways 23 and 41. Appellant solicits patronage from outside the State of Georgia through various national advertising media, including magazines of national circulation; it maintains over 50 billboards and highway signs within the State, soliciting patronage for the motel; it accepts convention trade from outside Georgia and approximately 75% of its registered guests are from out of State. Prior to passage of the Act the motel had followed a practice of refusing to rent rooms to Negroes, and it alleged that it intended to continue to do so. In an effort to perpetuate that policy this suit was filed.

The appellant contends that Congress in passing this Act exceeded its power to regulate commerce under Art. I, § 8, cl. 3, of the Constitution of the United States; that the Act violates the Fifth Amendment because appellant is deprived of the right to choose its customers and operate its business as it wishes, resulting in a taking of its liberty and property without due process of law and a taking of its property without just compensation; and, finally, that by requiring appellant to rent available rooms to Negroes against its will, Congress is subjecting it to involuntary servitude in contravention of the Thirteenth Amendment.

The appellees counter that the unavailability to Negroes of adequate accommodations interferes significantly with interstate travel, and that Congress, under the Commerce Clause, has power to remove such obstructions and restraints; that the Fifth Amendment does not forbid reasonable regulation and that consequential damage does not constitute a "taking" within the meaning of that amendment; that the Thirteenth Amendment claim fails because it is entirely frivolous to say that an amendment directed to the abolition of human bondage and the removal of widespread disabilities associated with slavery places discrimination in public accommodations beyond the reach of both federal and state law.

At the trial the appellant offered no evidence, submitting the case on the pleadings, admissions and stipulation of facts; however, appellees proved the refusal of the motel to accept Negro transients after the passage of the Act. . . .

2. THE HISTORY OF THE ACT.

Congress first evidenced its interest in civil rights legislation in the Civil Rights or Enforcement Act of April 9, 1866. There followed four Acts, with a fifth, the Civil Rights Act of March 1, 1875, culminating the series. In 1883 this Court struck down the public accommodations sections of the 1875 Act in the *Civil Rights Cases*, 109 U. S. 3. No major legislation in this field had been enacted by Congress for 82 years when the Civil Rights Act of 1957 became law. . . .

3. TITLE II OF THE ACT *[of 1964]*.

This Title is divided into seven sections beginning with § 201 (a) which provides that:

"All persons shall be entitled to the full and equal enjoyment of the goods, services, facilities, privileges, advantages, and accommodations of any place of public accommodation, as defined in this section, without discrimination or segregation on the ground of race, color, religion, or national origin."

There are listed in § 201 (b) four classes of business establishments, each of which "serves the public" and "is a place of public accommodation" within the meaning of § 201 (a) "if its operations affect commerce, or if discrimination or segregation by it is supported by State action." The covered establishments are:

"(1) any inn, hotel, motel, or other establishment which provides lodging to transient guests, other than an establishment located within a building which contains not more than five rooms for rent or hire and which is actually occupied by the proprietor of such establishment as his residence;

"(2) any restaurant, cafeteria . . . [not here involved];

"(3) any motion picture house . . . [not here involved];

"(4) any establishment . . . which is physically located within the premises of any establishment otherwise covered by this subsection, or . . . within the premises of which is physically located any such covered establishment . . . [not here involved]."

Section 201 (c) defines the phrase "affect commerce" as applied to the above establishments. It first declares that "any inn, hotel, motel, or other establishment which provides lodging to transient guests" affects commerce *per se*. Restaurants, cafeterias, etc., in class two affect commerce only if they serve or offer to serve interstate travelers or if a substantial portion of the food which they serve or products which they sell have "moved in commerce." . . .

4. APPLICATION OF TITLE II TO HEART OF ALTANTA MOTEL.

It is admitted that the operation of the motel brings it within the provisions of § 201 (a) of the Act and that appellant refused to provide lodging for transient Negroes because of their race or color and that it intends to continue that policy unless restrained.

The sole question posed is, therefore, the constitutionality of the Civil Rights Act of 1964 as applied to these facts. The legislative history of the Act indicates that Congress based the Act on § 5 and the Equal Protection Clause of the Fourteenth Amendment as well as its power to regulate interstate commerce under Art. I, § 8, cl. 3, of the Constitution.

The Senate Commerce Committee made it quite clear that the fundamental object of Title II was to vindicate "the deprivation of personal dignity that surely accompanies denials of equal access to public establishments." At the same time, however, it noted that such an objective has been and could be readily achieved "by congressional action based on the commerce power of the Constitution." S. Rep. No. 872, *supra*, at 16–17. Our study of the legislative record, made in the light of prior cases, has brought us to the conclusion that Congress possessed ample power in this regard, and we have therefore not considered the other grounds relied upon. This is not to say that the remaining authority upon which it acted was not adequate, a question upon which we do not pass, but merely that since the commerce power is sufficient for our decision here we have considered it alone. Nor is § 201 (d) or § 202, having to do with state action, involved here and we do not pass upon either of those sections.

5. THE CIVIL RIGHTS CASES, 109 U. S. 3 (1883), AND THEIR APPLICATION.

In light of our ground for decision, it might be well at the outset to discuss the *Civil Rights Cases, supra*, which declared provisions of the Civil Rights Act of 1875 unconstitutional. 18 Stat. 335, 336. We think that decision inapposite, and without precedential value in determining the constitutionality of the present Act. Unlike Title II of the present legislation, the 1875 Act broadly proscribed discrimination in "inns, public conveyances on land or water, theaters, and other places of public amusement," without limiting the categories of affected businesses to those impinging upon interstate commerce. In contrast, the applicability of Title II is carefully limited to enterprises having a direct and substantial relation to the interstate flow of goods and people, except where state action is involved. Further, the fact that certain kinds of businesses may not in 1875 have been sufficiently involved in interstate commerce to warrant bringing them within the ambit of the commerce power is not necessarily dispositive of the same question today. Our populace had not reached its present mobility, nor were facilities, goods and services circulating as readily in interstate commerce as they are today. . . .

6. THE BASIS OF CONGRESSIONAL ACTION.

While the Act as adopted carried no congressional findings the record of its passage through each house is replete with evidence of the burdens that discrimination by race or color places upon interstate commerce. . . . This testimony included the fact that our people have become increasingly mobile with millions of people of all races traveling from State to State; that Negroes in particular have been the subject of discrimination in transient accommodations, having to travel great distances to secure the same; that often they have been unable to obtain accommodations and have had to call upon friends to put them up overnight . . . ; and that these conditions had become so acute as to require the listing of available lodging for Negroes in a special guidebook which was itself "dramatic testimony to the difficulties" Negroes encounter in travel. . . .

7. THE POWER OF CONGRESS OVER INTERSTATE TRAVEL.

The power of Congress to deal with these obstructions depends on the meaning of the Commerce Clause. . . .

It is said that the operation of the motel here is of a purely local character. But, assuming this to be true, "[i]f it is interstate commerce that feels the pinch, it does not matter how local the operation which applies the squeeze." *United States* v. *Women's Sportswear Mfrs. Assn.*, 336 U.S. 460, 464 (1949). See *Labor Board* v. *Jones & Laughlin Steel Corp.*, *supra*. As Chief Justice Stone put it in *United States* v. *Darby*, *supra*:

"The power of Congress over interstate commerce is not confined to the regulation of commerce among the states. It extends to those activities intrastate which so affect interstate commerce or the exercise of the power of Congress over it as to make regulation of them appropriate means to the attainment of a legitimate end, the exercise of the granted power of Congress to regulate interstate commerce. See *McCulloch* v. *Maryland*, 4 Wheat. 316, 421." At 118.

Thus the power of Congress to promote interstate commerce also includes the power to regulate the local incidents thereof, including local activities in both the States or origin and destination, which might have a substantial and harmful effect upon that commerce. One need only examine the evidence which we have discussed above to see that Congress may—as it has—prohibit racial discrimination by motels serving travelers, however "local" their operations may appear.

Nor does the Act deprive appellant of liberty or property under the Fifth Amendment. The commerce power invoked here by the Congress is a specific and plenary one authorized by the Constitution itself. The only questions are: (1) whether Congress had a rational basis for finding that racial discrimination by motels affected commerce, and (2) if it had such a basis, whether the means it selected to eliminate that evil are reasonable and appropriate. If they are, appellant has no "right" to select its guests as it sees fit, free from governmental regulation.

. . .

We find no merit in the remainder of appellant's contentions, including that of "involuntary servitude." As we have seen, 32 States prohibit racial discrimination in public accommodations. These laws but codify the common-law innkeeper rule which long predated the Thirteenth Amendment. It is difficult to believe that the Amendment was intended to abrogate this principle. Indeed, the opinion of the Court in the *Civil Rights Cases* is to the contrary as we have seen, it having noted with approval the laws of "all the States" prohibiting discrimination. We could not say that the requirements of the Act in this regard are in any way "akin to African slavery." *Butler* v. *Perry,* 240 U. S. 328, 332 (1916).

We, therefore, conclude that the action of the Congress in the adoption of the Act as applied here to a motel which concededly serves interstate travelers is within the power granted it by the Commerce Clause of the Constitution, as interpreted by this Court for 140 years. It may be argued that Congress could have pursued other methods to eliminate the obstructions it found in interstate commerce caused by racial discrimination. But this is a matter of policy that rests entirely with the Congress not with the courts. How obstructions in commerce may be removed —what means are to be employed—is within the sound and exclusive discretion of the Congress. It is subject only to one caveat—that the means chosen by it must be reasonably adapted to the end permitted by the Constitution. We cannot say that its choice here was not so adapted. The Constitution requires no more.

Affirmed.

. . .

MR. JUSTICE BLACK, concurring.

. . .

MR. JUSTICE DOUGLAS, concurring.

I.

Though I join the Court's opinions, I am somewhat reluctant here, as I was in *Edwards* v. *California,* 314 U. S. 160, 177, to rest solely on the Commerce Clause. My reluctance is not due to any conviction that Congress lacks power to regulate commerce in the interests of human rights. It is rather my belief that the right of people to be free of state action that discriminates against them because of race, like the "right of persons to move freely from State to State" (*Edwards* v. *California,* *supra,* at 177), "occupies a more protected position in our constitutional system than does the movement of cattle, fruit, steel and coal across state lines." *Ibid.* Moreover, when we come to the problem of abatement in *Hamm* v. *City of Rock Hill, post,* p. 306, decided this day, the result

reached by the Court is for me much more obvious as a protective measure under the Fourteenth Amendment than under the Commerce Clause. For the former deals with the constitutional status of the individual not with the impact on commerce of local activities or vice versa.

Hence I would prefer to rest on the assertion of legislative power contained in § 5 of the Fourteenth Amendment which states: "The Congress shall have power to enforce, by appropriate legislation, the provisions of this article"—a power which the Court concedes was exercised at least in part in this Act.

A decision based on the Fourteenth Amendment would have a more settling effect, making unnecessary litigation over whether a particular restaurant or inn is within the commerce definitions of the Act or whether a particular customer is an interstate traveler. Under my construction, the Act would apply to all customers in all the enumerated places of public accommodation. And that construction would put an end to all obstructionist strategies and finally close one door on a bitter chapter in American history.

. . .

MR. JUSTICE GOLDBERG, concurring.

I join in the opinions and judgments of the Court, since I agree "that the action of the Congress in the adoption of the Act as applied here . . . is within the power granted it by the Commerce Clause of the Constitution, as interpreted by this Court for 140 years," *ante,* at 261.

The primary purpose of the Civil Rights Act of 1964, however, as the Court recognizes, and as I would underscore, is the vindication of human dignity and not mere economics. The Senate Commerce Committee made this quite clear:

"The primary purpose of . . . [the Civil Rights Act], then, is to solve this problem, the deprivation of personal dignity that surely accompanies denials of equal access to public establishments. Discrimination is not simply dollars and cents, hamburgers and movies; it is the humiliation, frustration, and embarrassment that a person must surely feel when he is told that he is unacceptable as a member of the public because of his race or color. It is equally the inability to explain to a child that regardless of education, civility, courtesy, and morality he will be denied the right to enjoy equal treatment, even though he be a citizen of the United States and may well be called upon to lay down his life to assure this Nation continues." S. Rep. No. 872, 88th Cong., 2d Sess., 16.

Moreover, that this is the primary purpose of the Act is emphasized by the fact that while § 201 (c) speaks only in terms of establishments which "affect commerce," it is clear that Congress based this section not only on its power under the Commerce Clause but also on § 5 of the Fourteenth Amendment. The cases cited in the Court's opinions are conclusive that Congress could exercise its powers under the Commerce Clause to accomplish this purpose. As §§ 201 (b) and (c) are undoubtedly a valid exercise of the Commerce Clause power for the reasons stated in the opinions of the Court, the Court considers that it is unnecessary to consider whether it is additionally supportable by Congress' exertion of its power under § 5 of the Fourteenth Amendment.

In my concurring opinion in *Bell* v. *Maryland*, 378 U. S. 226, 317, however, I expressed my conviction that § 1 of the Fourteenth Amendment guarantees to all Americans the constitutional right "to be treated as equal members of the community with respect to public accommodations," and that "Congress [has] authority under § 5 of the Fourteenth Amendment, or under the Commerce Clause, Art. I, § 8, to implement the rights protected by § 1 of the Fourteenth Amendment. In the give-and-take of the legislative process, Congress can fashion a law drawing the guidelines necessary and appropriate to facilitate practical administration and to distinguish between genuinely public and private accommodations." The challenged Act is just such a law and, in my view, Congress clearly had authority under both § 5 of the Fourteenth Amendment and the Commerce Clause to enact the Civil Rights Act of 1964.

Moose Lodge No. 107 v. Irvis

407 U.S. 163 (1972)

K. Leroy Irvis, a black guest of a member of Moose Lodge No. 107, was refused service at the club's dining room and bar solely because of his race. In suing for injunctive relief, he contended that the discrimination was "state action" and thus a violation of the Equal Protection Clause of the Fourteenth Amendment. He argued that a connection existed between the private club and the state because the Pennsylvania liquor board had issued the lodge a private club liquor license. The district court found the lodge's membership and guest practices discriminatory and agreed that there was state action.

MR. JUSTICE REHNQUIST delivered the opinion of the Court.

Appellee Irvis, a Negro (hereafter appellee), was refused service by appellant Moose Lodge, a local branch of the national fraternal organization located in Harrisburg, Pennsylvania. Appellee then brought this action under 42 U. S. C. § 1983 for injunctive relief in the United States District Court for the Middle District of Pennsylvania. He claimed that because the Pennsylvania liquor board had issued appellant Moose Lodge a private club license that authorized the sale of alcoholic beverages on its premises, the refusal of service to him was "state action" for the purposes of the Equal Protection Clause of the Fourteenth Amendment. He named both Moose Lodge and the Pennsylvania Liquor Authority as defendants, seeking injunctive relief that would have required the defendant liquor board to revoke Moose Lodge's license so long as it continued its discriminatory practices. Appellee sought no damages.

A three-judge district court, convened at appellee's request, upheld his contention on the merits, and entered a decree declaring invalid the liquor license issued to Moose Lodge "as long as it follows a policy of racial discrimination in its membership or operating policies or practices." Moose Lodge alone appealed from the decree, and we postponed decision as to jurisdiction until the hearing on the merits, 401 U. S. 992. Appellant urges, in the alternative, that we either vacate the judgment below because there is not presently a case or controversy between the parties, or that we reverse on the merits.

I

The District Court in its opinion found that "a Caucasian member in good standing brought plaintiff, a Negro, to the Lodge's dining room and bar as his guest and requested service of food and beverages. The Lodge through its employees refused service to plaintiff solely because he is a Negro." 318 F. Supp. 1246, 1247. It is undisputed that each local Moose Lodge is bound by the constitution and general bylaws of the Supreme Lodge, the latter of which contain a provision limiting membership in the lodges to white male Caucasians. The District Court in this connection found that "[t]he lodges accordingly maintain a policy and practice of restricting membership to the Caucasian race and permitting members to bring only Caucasian guests on lodge premises, particularly to the dining room and bar." *Ibid.*

[The Court holds that Irvis, who had not applied for or been denied membership in the lodge, had no standing to contest the lodge's membership practices. He did, however, have standing to litigate the constitutional validity of the lodge's discriminatory policies toward members' guests.]

II

Moose Lodge is a private club in the ordinary meaning of that term. It is a local chapter of a national fraternal organization having well-defined requirements for membership. It conducts all of its activities in a building that is owned by it. It is not publicly funded. Only members and guests are permitted in any lodge of the order; one may become a guest only by invitation of a member or upon invitation of the house committee.

Appellee, while conceding the right of private clubs to choose members upon a discriminatory basis, asserts that the licensing of Moose Lodge to serve liquor by the Pennsylvania Liquor Control Board amounts to such state involvement with the club's activities as to make its discriminatory practices forbidden by the Equal Protection Clause of the Fourteenth Amendment. The relief sought and obtained by appellee in the District Court was an injunction forbidding the licensing by the liquor authority of Moose Lodge until it ceased its discriminatory practices. We conclude that Moose Lodge's refusal to serve food and beverages to a guest by reason of the fact that he was a Negro does not, under the circumstances here presented, violate the Fourteenth Amendment.

In 1883, this Court in *The Civil Rights Cases*, 109 U. S. 3, set forth the essential dichotomy between discriminatory action by the State, which is prohibited by the Equal Protection Clause, and private conduct, "however discriminatory or wrongful," against which that clause "erects no shield," *Shelley* v. *Kraemer*, 334 U. S. 1, 13 (1948). That dichotomy has been subsequently reaffirmed in *Shelley* v. *Kraemer*, *supra*, and in *Burton* v. *Wilmington Parking Authority*, 365 U. S. 715 (1961).

While the principle is easily stated, the question of whether particular discriminatory conduct is private, on the one hand, or amounts to "state action," on the other hand, frequently admits of no easy answer. "Only by sifting facts and weighing circumstances can the nonobvious involvement of the State in private conduct be attributed its true significance." *Burton* v. *Wilmington Parking Authority*, *supra*, at 722.

Our cases make clear that the impetus for the forbidden discrimination need not originate with the State if it is state action that enforces privately originated discrimination. *Shelley* v. *Kraemer*, *supra*. The Court held in *Burton* v. *Wilmington Park-*

ing Authority, supra, that a private restaurant owner who refused service because of a customer's race violated the Fourteenth Amendment, where the restaurant was located in a building owned by a state-created parking authority and leased from the authority. The Court, after a comprehensive review of the relationship between the lessee and the parking authority concluded that the latter had "so far insinuated itself into a position of interdependence with Eagle [the restaurant owner] that it must be recognized as a joint participant in the challenged activity, which, on that account, cannot be considered to have been so 'purely private' as to fall without the scope of the Fourteenth Amendment." 365 U. S., at 725.

The Court has never held, of course, that discrimination by an otherwise private entity would be violative of the Equal Protection Clause if the private entity receives any sort of benefit or service at all from the State, or if it is subject to state regulation in any degree whatever. Since state-furnished services include such necessities of life as electricity, water, and police and fire protection, such a holding would utterly emasculate the distinction between private as distinguished from state conduct set forth in *The Civil Rights Cases, supra,* and adhered to in subsequent decisions. Our holdings indicate that where the impetus for the discrimination is private, the State must have "significantly involved itself with invidious discriminations," *Reitman* v. *Mulkey,* 387 U. S. 369, 380 (1967), in order for the discriminatory action to fall within the ambit of the constitutional prohibition.

. . .

Here there is nothing approaching the symbiotic relationship between lessor and lessee that was present in *Burton,* where the private lessee obtained the benefit of locating in a building owned by the state-created parking authority, and the parking authority was enabled to carry out its primary public purpose of furnishing parking space by advantageously leasing portions of the building constructed for that purpose to commercial lessees such as the owner of the Eagle Restaurant. Unlike *Burton,* the Moose Lodge building is located on land owned by it, not by any public authority. Far from apparently holding itself out as

a place of public accommodation, Moose Lodge quite ostentatiously proclaims the fact that it is not open to the public at large. Nor is it located and operated in such surroundings that although private in name, it discharges a function or performs a service that would otherwise in all likelihood be performed by the State. In short, while Eagle was a public restaurant in a public building, Moose Lodge is a private social club in a private building.

. . .

Even though the Liquor Control Board regulation in question is neutral in its terms, the result of its application in a case where the constitution and bylaws of a club required racial discrimination would be to invoke the sanctions of the State to enforce a concededly discriminatory private rule. State action, for purposes of the Equal Protection Clause, may emanate from rulings of administrative and regulatory agencies as well as from legislative or judicial action. *Robinson* v. *Florida,* 378 U. S. 153, 156 (1964). *Shelley* v. *Kraemer,* 334 U. S. 1 (1948), makes it clear that the application of state sanctions to enforce such a rule would violate the Fourteenth Amendment. Although the record before us is not as clear as one would like, appellant has not persuaded us that the District Court should have denied any and all relief.

Appellee was entitled to a decree enjoining the enforcement of § 113.09 of the regulations promulgated by the Pennsylvania Liquor Control Board insofar as that regulation requires compliance by Moose Lodge with provisions of its constitution and bylaws containing racially discriminatory provisions. He was entitled to no more. The judgment of the District Court is reversed, and the cause remanded with instructions to enter a decree in conformity with this opinion.

Reversed and remanded.

MR. JUSTICE DOUGLAS, with whom MR. JUSTICE MARSHALL joins, dissenting.

My view of the First Amendment and the related guarantees of the Bill of Rights is that they create a zone of privacy which precludes government from interfering with private clubs or groups. The associational rights which our system honors permit all white, all black, all brown, and all yellow clubs to be formed. They also permit all Catholic, all Jewish, or all agnostic clubs to be established. Government may not tell a man or woman who his or her associates must be. The individual can be as selective as he desires. So the fact that the Moose Lodge allows only Caucasians to join or come as guests is constitutionally irrelevant, as is the decision of the Black Muslims to admit to their services only members of their race.

. . .

. . . the fact that a private club gets some kind of permit from the State or municipality does not make it *ipso facto* a public enterprise or undertaking, any more than the grant to a householder of a permit to operate an incinerator puts the householder in the public domain. We must, therefore, examine whether there are special circumstances involved in the Pennsylvania scheme which differentiate the liquor license possessed by Moose Lodge from the incinerator permit.

Pennsylvania has a state store system of alcohol distribution. Resale is permitted by hotels, restaurants, and private clubs which all must obtain licenses from the Liquor Control Board. . . . Once a license is issued the licensee must comply with many detailed requirements or risk suspension or revocation of the license. Among these requirements is Regulation § 113.09 which says: "Every club licensee shall adhere to all of the provisions of its Constitution and By-laws." This regulation means, as applied to Moose Lodge, that it must adhere to the racially discriminatory provision of the Constitution of its Supreme Lodge . . .

. . . we have held that "a State is responsible for the discriminatory act of a private party when the State, by its law, has compelled the act." *Adickes* v. *Kress & Co.,* 398 U. S. 144, 170. . . . The result, as I see it, is the same as though Pennsylvania had put into its liquor licenses a provision that the license may not be used to dispense liquor to blacks, browns, yellows—or atheists or agnostics. Regulation § 113.09 is thus an invidious form of state action.

Were this regulation the only infirmity in Pennsylvania's licensing scheme, I would perhaps agree with the majority that the appropriate relief would be a decree enjoining its enforcement. But there is another flaw in the scheme not so easily cured. Liquor licenses in Pennsylvania, unlike driver's licenses, or marriage licenses, are not freely available to those who meet racially neutral qualifications. There is a complex quota system, which the majority accurately describes. *Ante,* at 176. What the majority neglects to say is that the quota for Harrisburg, where Moose Lodge No. 107 is located, has been full for many years. No more club licenses may be issued in that city.

This state-enforced scarcity of licenses restricts the ability of blacks to obtain liquor, for liquor is commercially available *only* at private clubs for a significant portion of each week. Access by blacks to places that serve liquor is further limited by the fact that the state quota is filled. A group desiring to form a nondiscriminatory club which would serve blacks must purchase a license held by an existing club, which can exact a monopoly price for the transfer. The availability of such a license is speculative at best, however, for, as Moose Lodge itself concedes, without a liquor license a fraternal organization would be hard pressed to survive.

Thus, the State of Pennsylvania is putting the weight of its liquor license, concededly a valued and important adjunct to a private club, behind racial discrimination.

As the first Justice Harlan, dissenting in the *Civil Rights Cases,* 109 U. S. 3, 59, said:

"I agree that government has nothing to do with social, as distinguished from technically legal, rights of individuals. No government ever has brought, or ever can bring, its people into social intercourse against their wishes. Whether one person will permit or maintain social relations with another is a matter with which government has no concern. . . . What I affirm is that no State, nor the officers of any State, nor any corporation or individual wielding power under State authority for the public benefit or the public convenience, can consistently . . . with the freedom established by the fundamental law . . . discriminate against freemen or citizens, in those rights, because of their race . . . ."

The regulation governing this liquor license has in it that precise infirmity.

I would affirm the judgment below.

MR. JUSTICE BRENNAN, with whom MR. JUSTICE MARSHALL joins, dissenting.

When Moose Lodge obtained its liquor license, the State of Pennsylvania became an active participant in the operation of the Lodge bar. Liquor licensing laws are only incidentally revenue measures; they are primarily pervasive regulatory schemes under which the State dictates and continually supervises virtually every detail of the operation of the licensee's business. Very few, if any, other licensed businesses experience such complete state involvement. Yet the Court holds that such involvement does not constitute "state action" making the Lodge's refusal to serve a guest liquor solely because of his race a violation of the Fourteenth Amendment. The vital flaw in the Court's reasoning is its complete disregard of the fundamental value underlying the "state action" concept. That value is discussed in my separate opinion in *Adickes* v. *Kress & Co.*, 398 U. S. 144, 190–191 (1970):

"The state-action doctrine reflects the profound judgment that denials of equal treatment, and particularly denials on account of race or color, are singularly grave when government has or shares responsibility for them. Government is the social organ to which all in our society look for the promotion of liberty, justice, fair and equal treatment, and the setting of worthy norms and goals for social conduct. Therefore something is uniquely amiss in a society where the government, the authoritative oracle of community values, involves itself in racial discrimination. Accordingly, . . . the cases that have come before us [in which] this Court has condemned significant state involvement in racial discrimination, however subtle and indirect it may have been and whatever form it may have taken[,] . . . represent vigilant fidelity to the constitutional principle that no State shall in any significant way lend its authority to the sordid business of racial discrimination."

Plainly, the State of Pennsylvania's liquor regulations intertwine the State with the operation of the Lodge bar in a "significant way [and] lend [the State's] authority to the sordid business of racial discrimination." The opinion of the late Circuit Judge Freedman, for the three-judge District Court, most persuasively demonstrates the "state action" present in this case . . .

I therefore dissent and would affirm the final decree entered by the District Court.

Washington v. Davis

426 U.S. 229 (1976)

Two blacks, after their applications to become police officers in the District of Columbia had been rejected, filed an action against the D.C. Mayor, Walter E. Washington. They claimed that the Police Department's recruiting procedures, including a written personnel test, were racially discriminatory and violated the Due Process Clause of the Fifth Amendment. It was their position that the test bore no relationship to job performance and excluded a disproportionately high number of black applicants. The district court concluded that they were not entitled to relief. The D.C. Circuit reversed, finding that the disproportionate impact sufficed to establish a constitutional violation.

MR. JUSTICE WHITE delivered the opinion of the Court.

This case involves the validity of a qualifying test administered to applicants for positions as police officers in the District of Columbia Metro-politan Police Department. The test was sustained by the District Court but invalidated by the Court of Appeals. We are in agreement with the District Court and hence reverse the judgment of the Court of Appeals.

I

This action began on April 10, 1970, when two Negro police officers filed suit against the then Commissioner of the District of Columbia, the Chief of the District's Metropolitan Police Department, and the Commissioners of the United States Civil Service Commission. An amended complaint, filed December 10, alleged that the promotion policies of the Department were racially discriminatory and sought a declaratory judgment and an injunction. The respondents Harley and Sellers were permitted to intervene, their amended complaint asserting that their applications to become officers in the Department had been rejected, and that the Department's recruiting procedures discriminated on the basis of race against black applicants by a series of practices including, but not limited to, a written personnel test which excluded a disproportionately high number of Negro applicants. These practices were asserted to violate respondents' rights "under the due process clause of the Fifth Amendment to the United States Constitution, under 42 U. S. C. § 1981 and under D. C. Code § 1–320." Defendants answered, and discovery and various other proceedings followed. Respondents then filed a motion for partial summary judgment with respect to the recruiting phase of the case, seeking a declaration that the test administered to those applying to become police officers is "unlawfully discriminatory and thereby in violation of the due process clause of the Fifth Amendment . . . ." No issue under any statute or regulation was raised by the motion. The District of Columbia defendants, petitioners here, and the federal parties also filed motions for summary judgment with respect to the recruiting aspects of the case, asserting that respondents were entitled to relief on neither constitutional nor statutory grounds. The District Court granted petitioners' and denied respondents' motions. 348 F. Supp. 15 (DC 1972).

According to the findings and conclusions of the District Court, to be accepted by the Department and to enter an intensive 17-week training program, the police recruit was required to satisfy certain physical and character standards, to be a high school graduate or its equivalent, and to receive a grade of at least 40 out of 80 on "Test 21," which is "an examination that is used gener-ally throughout the federal service," which "was developed by the Civil Service Commission, not the Police Department," and which was "designed to test verbal ability, vocabulary, reading and comprehension." *Id.*, at 16.

The validity of Test 21 was the sole issue before the court on the motions for summary judgment. The District Court noted that there was no claim of "an intentional discrimination or purposeful discriminatory acts" but only a claim that Test 21 bore no relationship to job performance and "has a highly discriminatory impact in screening out black candidates." *Ibid.* Respondents' evidence, the District Court said, warranted three conclusions: "(a) The number of black police officers, while substantial, is not proportionate to the population mix of the city. (b) A higher percentage of blacks fail the Test than whites. (c) The Test has not been validated to establish its reliability for measuring subsequent job performance." *Ibid.* This showing was deemed sufficient to shift the burden of proof to the defendants in the action, petitioners here; but the court nevertheless concluded that on the undisputed facts respondents were not entitled to relief. The District Court relied on several factors. Since August 1969, 44% of new police force recruits had been black; that figure also represented the proportion of blacks on the total force and was roughly equivalent to 20- to 29-year-old blacks in the 50-mile radius in which the recruiting efforts of the Police Department had been concentrated. It was undisputed that the Department had systematically and affirmatively sought to enroll black officers many of whom passed the test but failed to report for duty. The District Court rejected the assertion that Test 21 was culturally slanted to favor whites and was "satisfied that the undisputable facts prove the test to be reasonably and directly related to the requirements of the police recruit training program and that it is neither so designed nor operates [*sic*] to discriminate against otherwise qualified blacks." *Id.*, at 17. . . .

[*The D. C. Circuit declared*] that lack of discriminatory intent in designing and administering Test 21 was irrelevant; the critical fact was rather that a far greater proportion of blacks—four times as many—failed the test than did whites. This disproportionate impact, standing alone and without regard to whether it indicated a discriminatory purpose, was held sufficient to establish a constitutional violation, absent proof by petitioners that the test was an adequate measure of job performance in addition to being an indicator of probable success in the training program, a burden which the court ruled petitioners had failed to discharge. That the Department had made substantial efforts to recruit blacks was held beside the point and the fact that the racial distribution of recent hirings and of the Department itself might be roughly equivalent to the racial makeup of the surrounding community, broadly conceived, was put aside as a "comparison [not] material to this appeal." *Id.*, at 46 n. 24, 512 F. 2d, at 960 n. 24. The Court of Appeals, over a dissent, accordingly reversed the judgment of the District Court and directed that respondents' motion for partial summary judgment be granted. We granted the petition for certiorari, 423 U. S. 820 (1975), filed by the District of Columbia officials.

II

Because the Court of Appeals erroneously applied the legal standards applicable to Title VII cases in resolving the constitutional issue before it, we reverse its judgment in respondents' favor. . . .

As the Court of Appeals understood Title VII, employees or applicants proceeding under it need not concern themselves with the employer's possibly discriminatory purpose but instead may focus solely on the racially differential impact of the challenged hiring or promotion practices. This is not the constitutional rule. We have never held that the constitutional standard for adjudicating claims of invidious racial discrimination is identical to the standards applicable under Title VII, and we decline to do so today.

The central purpose of the Equal Protection Clause of the Fourteenth Amendment is the prevention of official conduct discriminating on the basis of race. It is also true that the Due Process Clause of the Fifth Amendment contains an equal protection component prohibiting the United States from invidiously discriminating between individuals or groups. *Bolling* v. *Sharpe*, 347 U. S. 497 (1954). But our cases have not embraced the proposition that a law or other official act, without regard to whether it reflects a racially discriminatory purpose, is unconstitutional *solely* because it has a racially disproportionate impact.

. . .

The school desegregation cases have also adhered to the basic equal protection principle that the invidious quality of a law claimed to be racially discriminatory must ultimately be traced to a racially discriminatory purpose. That there are both predominantly black and predominantly white schools in a community is not alone violative of the Equal Protection Clause. The essential element of *de jure* segregation is "a current condition of segregation resulting from intentional state action." *Keyes* v. *School Dist. No. 1*, 413 U. S. 189, 205 (1973). "The differentiating factor between *de jure* segregation and so-called *de facto* segregation . . . is *purpose* or *intent* to segregate." *Id.*, at 208. See also *id.*, at 199, 211, 213.

. . .

As an initial matter, we have difficulty understanding how a law establishing a racially neutral qualification for employment is nevertheless racially discriminatory and denies "any person . . . equal protection of the laws" simply because a greater proportion of Negroes fail to qualify than members of other racial or ethnic groups. Had respondents, along with all others who had failed Test 21, whether white or black, brought an action claiming that the test denied each of them equal protection of the laws as compared with those who had passed with high enough scores to qualify them as police recruits, it is most unlikely that their challenge would have been sustained. Test 21, which is administered generally to prospective Government employees, concededly seeks to ascertain whether those who take it have acquired a particular level of verbal skill; and it is untenable that the Constitution prevents the Government from seeking modestly to upgrade the communicative abilities of its employees rather than to be satisfied with some lower level of competence, particularly where the job requires special ability to communicate orally and in writing.

. . .

III

We also hold that the Court of Appeals should have affirmed the judgment of the District Court granting the motions for summary judgment filed by petitioners and the federal parties. Respondents were entitled to relief on neither constitutional nor statutory grounds.

. . .

MR. JUSTICE STEWART joins Parts I and II of the Court's opinion.

MR. JUSTICE STEVENS, concurring.

. . .

MR. JUSTICE BRENNAN, with whom MR. JUSTICE MARSHALL joins, dissenting.

. . .

III

The Court also says that its conclusion is not foreclosed by *Griggs* and *Albemarle*, but today's result plainly conflicts with those cases. *Griggs* held that "[i]f an employment practice which operates to exclude Negroes cannot be shown to be *related to job performance*, the practice is prohibited." 401 U. S., at 431 (emphasis added). Once a discriminatory impact is shown, the employer carries the burden of proving that the challenged practice "bear[s] a *demonstrable relationship to successful performance of the jobs* for which it was used." *Ibid.* (emphasis added). We observed further:

"Nothing in the Act precludes the use of testing or measuring procedures; obviously they are useful. What Congress has forbidden is giving these devices and mechanisms controlling force unless they are demonstrably a reasonable measure of job performance. . . . What Congress has commanded is that any tests used must measure the person for the job and not the person in the abstract." *Id.,* at 436.

Albemarle read *Griggs* to require that a discriminatory test be validated through proof "by professionally acceptable methods" that it is " 'predictive of or significantly correlated with *important* elements of work behavior *which comprise or are relevant to the job or jobs* for which candidates are being evaluated.' " 422 U. S., at 431 (emphasis added), quoting 29 CFR § 1607.4(c) (1975). Further, we rejected the employer's attempt to validate a written test by proving that it was related to supervisors' job performance ratings, because there was no demonstration that the ratings accurately reflected job performance. We were unable "to determine whether the criteria *actually* considered were sufficiently related to the [employer's] legitimate interest in job-specific ability to justify a testing system with a racially discriminatory impact." 422 U. S., at 433 (emphasis in original). To me, therefore, these cases read Title VII as requiring proof of a significant relationship to job performance to establish the validity of a discriminatory test. See also *McDonnell Douglas Corp.* v. *Green*, 411 U. S. 792, 802, and n. 14 (1973). Petitioners do not maintain that there is a demonstrated correlation between Test 21 scores and job performance. Moreover, their validity study was unable to discern a significant positive relationship between training averages and job performance. Thus, there is no proof of a correlation—either direct or indirect—between Test 21 and performance of the job of being a police officer.

It may well be that in some circumstances, proof of a relationship between a discriminatory qualification test and training performance is an acceptable substitute for establishing a relationship to job performance. But this question is not settled, and it should not be resolved by the minimal analysis in the Court's opinion.

. . .

Today's reduced emphasis on a relationship to job performance is also inconsistent with clearly expressed congressional intent. A section-by-section analysis of the 1972 amendments to Title VII states as follows:

"In any area where the new law does not address itself, or in any areas where a specific contrary intention is not indicated, it was assumed that the present case law as developed by the courts would continue to govern the applicability and construction of Title VII." 118 Cong. Rec. 7166 (1972).

The pre-1972 judicial decisions dealing with

standardized tests used as job qualification requirements uniformly follow the EEOC regulations discussed above and insist upon proof of a relationship to job performance to prove that a test is job related. Furthermore, the Court ignores Congress's explicit hostility toward the use of written tests as job-qualification requirements; Congress disapproved the CSC's "use of general ability tests which are not aimed at any direct relationship to specific jobs." H. R. Rep. No. 92–238, p. 24 (1971). See S. Rep. No. 92–415, pp. 14-15 (1971). Petitioners concede that Test 21 was devised by the CSC for general use and was not designed to be used by police departments.

Finally, it should be observed that every federal court, except the District Court in this case, presented with proof identical to that offered to validate Test 21 has reached a conclusion directly opposite to that of the Court today. Sound policy considerations support the view that, at a minimum, petitioners should have been required to prove that the police training examinations either measure job-related skills or predict job perfor-

mance. Where employers try to validate written qualification tests by proving a correlation with written examinations in a training course, there is a substantial danger that people who have good verbal skills will achieve high scores on both tests due to verbal ability, rather than "job-specific ability." As a result, employers could validate any entrance examination that measures only verbal ability by giving another written test that measures verbal ability at the end of a training course. Any contention that the resulting correlation between examination scores would be evidence that the initial test is "job related" is plainly erroneous. It seems to me, however, that the Court's holding in this case can be read as endorsing this dubious proposition. Today's result will prove particularly unfortunate if it is extended to govern Title VII cases.

Accordingly, accepting the Court's assertion that it is necessary to reach the statutory issue, I would hold that petitioners have not met their burden of proof and affirm the judgment of the Court of Appeals.

Regents of the University of California v. Bakke

438 U. S. 265 (1978)

Allan Bakke, a white applicant to the medical school at the University of California at Davis, was twice rejected by the regular admissions program. "Disadvantaged" applicants from minority groups (blacks, Chicanos, Asians, and American Indians) were screened by a special admissions program. Although these minorities had lower grade point averages from undergraduate school and scored lower on the medical admissions test, they were accepted to fill 16 out of 100 openings for first-year students. The California Supreme Court, agreeing that increasing the number of minorities in the medical profession was a compelling state interest, concluded that the special admissions program was not the least intrusive means of achieving that goal. It held that the Equal Protection Clause of the Fourteenth Amendment required that "no applicant may be rejected because of his race, in favor of another who is less qualified, as measured by standards applied without regard to race." When the University conceded its inability to prove that Bakke would not have been admitted even in the absence of a special admissions program, the California court directed that Bakke be admitted. That order was stayed pending review by the Supreme Court. "Petitioner" in this case is the University of California; the "respondent" is Bakke.

MR. JUSTICE POWELL announced the judgment of the Court.

This case presents a challenge to the special admissions program of the petitioner, the Medical

School of the University of California at Davis, which is designed to assure the admission of a specified number of students from certain minority groups. The Superior Court of California sustained respondent's challenge, holding that petitioner's program violated the California Constitution, Title VI of the Civil Rights Act of 1964, 42 U. S. C. § 2000d *et seq.*, and the Equal Protection Clause of the Fourteenth Amendment. The court enjoined petitioner from considering respondent's race or the race of any other applicant in making admissions decisions. It refused, however, to order respondent's admission to the Medical School, holding that he had not carried his burden of proving that he would have been admitted but for the constitutional and statutory violations. The Supreme Court of California affirmed those portions of the trial court's judgment declaring the special admissions program unlawful and enjoining petitioner from considering the race of any applicant. It modified that portion of the judgment denying respondent's requested injunction and directed the trial court to order his admission.

For the reasons stated in the following opinion, I believe that so much of the judgment of the California court as holds petitioner's special admissions program unlawful and directs that respondent be admitted to the Medical School must be affirmed. For the reasons expressed in a separate opinion, my Brothers THE CHIEF JUSTICE, MR. JUSTICE STEWART, MR. JUSTICE REHNQUIST, and MR. JUSTICE STEVENS concur in this judgment.

I also conclude for the reasons stated in the following opinion that the portion of the court's judgment enjoining petitioner from according any consideration to race in its admissions process must be reversed. For reasons expressed in separate opinions, my Brothers MR. JUSTICE BRENNAN, MR. JUSTICE WHITE, MR. JUSTICE MARSHALL, and MR. JUSTICE BLACKMUN concur in this judgment.

Affirmed in part and reversed in part.

I

The Medical School of the University of California at Davis opened in 1968 with an entering class of 50 students. In 1971, the size of the entering class was increased to 100 students, a level at which it remains. No admissions program for disadvantaged or minority students existed when the school opened, and the first class contained three Asians but no blacks, no Mexican-Americans, and no American Indians. Over the next two years, the faculty devised a special admissions program to increase the representation of "disadvantaged" students in each Medical School class. The special program consisted of a separate admissions system operating in coordination with the regular admissions process.

Under the regular admissions procedure, a candidate could submit his application to the Medical School beginning in July of the year preceding the academic year for which admission was sought. Record 149. Because of the large number of applications, the admissions committee screened each one to select candidates for further consideration. Candidates whose overall undergraduate grade point averages fell below 2.5 on a scale of 4.0 were summarily rejected. *Id.*, at 63. About one out of six applicants was invited for a personal interview. *Ibid.* Following the interviews, each candidate was rated on a scale of 1 to 100 by his interviewers and four other members of the admissions committee. The rating embraced the interviewers' summaries, the candidate's overall grade point average, grade point average in science courses, scores on the Medical College Admissions Test (MCAT), letters of recommendation, extracurricular activities, and other biographical data. *Id.*, at 62. The ratings were added together to arrive at each candidate's "benchmark" score. Since five committee members rated each candidate in 1973, a perfect score was 500; in 1974, six members rated each candidate, so that a perfect score was 600. The full committee then reviewed the file and scores of each applicant and made offers of admission on a "rolling" basis. The chairman was responsible for placing names on the waiting list. They were not placed in strict numerical order; instead, the chairman had discretion to include persons with "special skills." *Id.*, at 63–64.

The special admissions program operated with a separate committee, a majority of whom were members of minority groups. *Id.*, at 163. On the 1973 application form, candidates were asked to indicate whether they wished to be considered as "economically and/or educationally disadvantaged" applicants; on the 1974 form the question was whether they wished to be considered as members of a "minority group," which the Medical School apparently viewed as "Blacks," "Chicanos," "Asians," and "American Indians." *Id.*, at 65–66, 146, 197, 203–205, 216–218. If these questions were answered affirmatively, the application was forwarded to the special admissions committee. No formal definition of "disadvantaged" was ever produced, *id.*, at 163–164, but the chairman of the special committee screened each application to see whether it reflected economic or educational deprivation. Having passed this initial hurdle, the applications then were rated by the special committee in a fashion similar to that used by the general admissions committee, except that special candidates did not have to meet the 2.5 grade point average cutoff applied to regular applicants. About one-fifth of the total number of special applicants were invited for interviews in 1973 and 1974. Following each interview, the special committee assigned each special applicant a benchmark score. The special committee then presented its top choices to the general admissions committee. The latter did not rate or compare the special candidates against the general applicants, *id.*, at 388, but could reject recommended special candidates for failure to meet course requirements or other specific deficiencies. *Id.*, at 171–172. The special committee continued to recommend special applicants until a number prescribed by faculty vote were admitted. While the overall class size was still 50, the prescribed number was 8; in 1973 and 1974, when the class size had doubled to 100, the prescribed number of special admissions also doubled, to 16. *Id.*, at 164, 166.

From the year of the increase in class size—1971—through 1974, the special program resulted in the admission of 21 black students, 30 Mexican-Americans, and 12 Asians, for a total of 63 minority students. Over the same period, the regular admissions program produced 1 black, 6 Mexican-Americans, and 37 Asians, for a total of 44 minority students. Although disadvantaged whites applied to the special program in large numbers, see n. 5, *supra*, none received an offer of admission through that process. Indeed, in 1974,

at least, the special committee explicitly considered only "disadvantaged" special applicants who were members of one of the designated minority groups. Record 171.

Allan Bakke is a white male who applied to the Davis Medical School in both 1973 and 1974. In both years Bakke's application was considered under the general admissions program, and he received an interview. His 1973 interview was with Dr. Theodore C. West, who considered Bakke "a very desirable applicant to [the] medical school." *Id.*, at 225. Despite a strong benchmark score of 468 out of 500, Bakke was rejected. His application had come late in the year, and no applicants in the general admissions process with scores below 470 were accepted after Bakke's application was completed.

[Bakke was also rejected in 1974, after scoring 549 out of 600. In both years, applicants were admitted under the special program with grade point averages, MCAT scores, and benchmark scores significantly lower than Bakke's.]

[After assuming that Bakke could sue under the Civil Rights Act of 1964, Powell explored the meaning of Title VI, especially § 601: "No person in the United States shall, on the ground of race, color, or national origin, be excluded from participation in, be denied the benefits of, or be subjected to discrimination under any program or activity receiving Federal financial assistance." Powell concluded, from the legislative history, that Title VI proscribes only racial classifications that would violate the Equal Protection Clause of the Fourteenth Amendment.]

[III.B]

Petitioner urges us to adopt for the first time a more restrictive view of the Equal Protection Clause and hold that discrimination against members of the white "majority" cannot be suspect if its purpose can be characterized as "benign." The clock of our liberties, however, cannot be turned back to 1868. *Brown* v. *Board of Education, supra,* at 492; accord, *Loving* v. *Virginia, supra,* at 9. It is far too late to argue that the guarantee of equal protection to *all* persons permits the recognition of special wards entitled to a degree of protection greater than that accorded others. "The Fourteenth Amendment is not directed solely against discrimination due to a 'two-class theory'—that is, based upon differences between 'white' and Negro." *Hernandez*, 347 U. S., at 478.

Once the artificial line of a "two-class theory" of the Fourteenth Amendment is put aside, the difficulties entailed in varying the level of judicial review according to a perceived "preferred" status of a particular racial or ethnic minority are intractable. The concepts of "majority" and "minority" necessarily reflect temporary arrangements and political judgments. As observed above, the white "majority" itself is composed of various minority groups, most of which can lay claim to a history of prior discrimination at the hands of the State and private individuals. Not all of these groups can receive preferential treatment and corresponding judicial tolerance of distinctions drawn in terms of race and nationality, for then the only "majority" left would be a new minority of white Anglo-Saxon Protestants. There is no principled basis for deciding which groups would merit "heightened judicial solicitude" and which would not. Courts would be asked to evaluate the extent of the prejudice and consequent harm suffered by various minority groups. Those whose societal injury is thought to exceed some arbitrary level of tolerability then would be entitled to preferential classifications at the expense of individuals belonging to other groups. Those classifications would be free from exacting judicial scrutiny. As these preferences began to have their desired effect, and the consequences of past discrimination were undone, new judicial rankings would be necessary. The kind of variable sociological and political analysis necessary to produce such rankings simply does not lie within the judicial competence—even if they otherwise were politically feasible and socially desirable.

. . .

[V.A]

. . .

It has been suggested that an admissions program which considers race only as one factor is simply a subtle and more sophisticated—but no less effective—means of according racial prefer-

ence than the Davis program. A facial intent to discriminate, however, is evident in petitioner's preference program and not denied in this case. No such facial infirmity exists in an admissions program where race or ethnic background is simply one element—to be weighed fairly against other elements—in the selection process. "A boundary line," as Mr. Justice Frankfurter remarked in another connection, "is none the worse for being narrow." *McLeod* v. *Dilworth*, 322 U. S. 327, 329 (1944). And a court would not assume that a university, professing to employ a facially nondiscriminatory admissions policy, would operate it as a cover for the functional equivalent of a quota system. In short, good faith would be presumed in the absence of a showing to the contrary in the manner permitted by our cases. See, *e. g.*, *Arlington Heights* v. *Metropolitan Housing Dev. Corp.*, 429 U. S. 252 (1977); *Washington* v. *Davis*, 426 U. S. 229 (1976); *Swain* v. *Alabama*, 380 U. S. 202 (1965).

B

In summary, it is evident that the Davis special admissions program involves the use of an explicit racial classification never before countenanced by this Court. It tells applicants who are not Negro, Asian, or Chicano that they are totally excluded from a specific percentage of the seats in an entering class. No matter how strong their qualifications, quantitative and extracurricular, including their own potential for contribution to educational diversity, they are never afforded the chance to compete with applicants from the preferred groups for the special admissions seats. At the same time, the preferred applicants have the opportunity to compete for every seat in the class.

The fatal flaw in petitioner's preferential program is its disregard of individual rights as guaranteed by the Fourteenth Amendment. *Shelley* v. *Kraemer*, 334 U. S., at 22. Such rights are not absolute. But when a State's distribution of benefits or imposition of burdens hinges on ancestry or the color of a person's skin, that individual is entitled to a demonstration that the challenged classification is necessary to promote a substantial state interest. Petitioner has failed to carry this burden. For this reason, that portion of the California court's judgment holding petitioner's special admissions program invalid under the Fourteenth Amendment must be affirmed.

C

In enjoining petitioner from ever considering the race of any applicant, however, the courts below failed to recognize that the State has a substantial interest that legitimately may be served by a properly devised admissions program involving the competitive consideration of race and ethnic origin. For this reason, so much of the California court's judgment as enjoins petitioner from any consideration of the race of any applicant must be reversed.

VI

With respect to respondent's entitlement to an injunction directing his admission to the Medical School, petitioner has conceded that it could not carry its burden of proving that, but for the existence of its unlawful special admissions program, respondent still would not have been admitted. Hence, respondent is entitled to the injunction, and that portion of the judgment must be affirmed.

. . .

Opinion of MR. JUSTICE BRENNAN, MR. JUSTICE WHITE, MR. JUSTICE MARSHALL, and MR. JUSTICE BLACKMUN, concurring in the judgment in part and dissenting in part.

The Court today, in reversing in part the judgment of the Supreme Court of California, affirms the constitutional power of Federal and State Governments to act affirmatively to achieve equal opportunity for all. The difficulty of the issue presented—whether government may use race-conscious programs to redress the continuing effects of past discrimination—and the mature consideration which each of our Brethren has brought to it have resulted in many opinions, no single one speaking for the Court. But this should not and must not mask the central meaning of today's opinions: Government may take race into account when it acts not to demean or insult any racial group, but to remedy disadvantages cast on minorities by past racial prejudice, at least when appropriate findings have been made by judicial,

legislative, or administrative bodies with competence to act in this area.

THE CHIEF JUSTICE and our Brothers STEWART, REHNQUIST, and STEVENS, have concluded that Title VI of the Civil Rights Act of 1964, 78 Stat. 252, as amended, 42 U. S. C. § 2000d *et. seq.*, prohibits programs such as that at the Davis Medical School. On this statutory theory alone, they would hold that respondent Allan Bakke's rights have been violated and that he must, therefore, be admitted to the Medical School. Our Brother POWELL, reaching the Constitution, concludes that, although race may be taken into account in university admissions, the particular special admissions program used by petitioner, which resulted in the exclusion of respondent Bakke, was not shown to be necessary to achieve petitioner's stated goals. Accordingly, these Members of the Court form a majority of five affirming the judgment of the Supreme Court of California insofar as it holds that respondent Bakke "is entitled to an order that he be admitted to the University." 18 Cal. 3d 34, 64, 553 P. 2d 1152, 1172 (1976).

We agree with MR. JUSTICE POWELL that, as applied to the case before us, Title VI goes no further in prohibiting the use of race than the Equal Protection Clause of the Fourteenth Amendment itself. We also agree that the effect of the California Supreme Court's affirmance of the judgment of the Superior Court of California would be to prohibit the University from establishing in the future affirmative-action programs that take race into account. See *ante,* at 271 n. Since we conclude that the affirmative admissions program at the Davis Medical School is constitutional, we would reverse the judgment below in all respects. MR. JUSTICE POWELL agrees that some uses of race in university admissions are permissible and, therefore, he joins with us to make five votes reversing the judgment below insofar as it prohibits the University from establishing race-conscious programs in the future.

[This opinion points out that Congress, in 1977, passed legislation providing for a "set-aside" of 10 percent of public works funds for minority business enterprises. Minority group members were defined as "Negroes, Spanish-speaking, Orientals, Indians, Eskimos, and Aleuts." The Supreme Court upheld

this statute in Fullilove *v. Klutznick, 448 U. S. 448 (1980).]*

MR. JUSTICE WHITE . . . .

MR. JUSTICE MARSHALL.

I agree with the judgment of the Court only insofar as it permits a university to consider the race of an applicant in making admissions decisions. I do not agree that petitioner's admissions program violates the Constitution. For it must be remembered that, during most of the past 200 years, the Constitution as interpreted by this Court did not prohibit the most ingenious and pervasive forms of discrimination against the Negro. Now, when a State acts to remedy the effects of that legacy of discrimination, I cannot believe that this same Constitution stands as a barrier.

. . .

III

I do not believe that the Fourteenth Amendment requires us to accept that fate. Neither its history nor our past cases lend any support to the conclusion that a university may not remedy the cumulative effects of society's discrimination by giving consideration to race in an effort to increase the number and percentage of Negro doctors.

A

This Court long ago remarked that

"in any fair and just construction of any section or phrase of these [Civil War] amendments, it is necessary to look to the purpose which we have said was the pervading spirit of them all, the evil which they were designed to remedy . . . ." *Slaughter-House Cases,* 16 Wall., at 72.

It is plain that the Fourteenth Amendment was not intended to prohibit measures designed to remedy the effects of the Nation's past treatment of Negroes. The Congress that passed the Fourteenth Amendment is the same Congress that passed the 1866 Freedmen's Bureau Act, an Act that provided many of its benefits only to Negroes. Act of July 16, 1866, ch. 200, 14 Stat. 173; see *supra,* at 391. Although the Freedmen's Bureau legislation pro-

vided aid for refugees, thereby including white persons within some of the relief measures, 14 Stat. 174; see also Act of Mar. 3, 1865, ch. 90, 13 Stat. 507, the bill was regarded, to the dismay of many Congressmen, as "solely and entirely for the freedmen, and to the exclusion of all other persons. . . ." Cong. Globe, 39th Cong., 1st Sess. 544 (1866) (remarks of Rep. Taylor). See also *id.,* at 634–635 (remarks of Rep. Ritter); *id.,* at App. 78, 80–81 (remarks of Rep. Chanler). Indeed, the bill was bitterly opposed on the ground that it "undertakes to make the negro in some respects . . . superior . . . and gives them favors that the poor white boy in the North cannot get." *Id.,* at 401 (remarks of Sen. McDougall). See also *id.,* at 319 (remarks of Sen. Hendricks); *id.,* at 362 (remarks of Sen. Saulsbury); *id.,* at 397 (remarks of Sen. Willey); *id.,* at 544 (remarks of Rep. Taylor). The bill's supporters defended it—not by rebutting the claim of special treatment—but by pointing to the need for such treatment:

"The very discrimination it makes between 'destitute and suffering' negroes, and destitute and suffering white paupers, proceeds upon the distinction that, in the omitted case, civil rights and immunities are already sufficiently protected by the possession of political power, the absence of which in the case provided for necessitates governmental protection." *Id.,* at App. 75 (remarks of Rep. Phelps).

Despite the objection to the special treatment the bill would provide for Negroes, it was passed by Congress. *Id.,* at 421, 688. President Johnson vetoed this bill and also a subsequent bill that contained some modifications; one of his principal objections to both bills was that they gave special benefits to Negroes. 8 Messages and Papers of the Presidents 3596, 3599, 3620, 3623 (1897). Rejecting the concerns of the President and the bill's opponents, Congress overrode the President's second veto. Cong. Globe, 39th Cong., 1st Sess., 3842, 3850 (1866).

. . .

MR. JUSTICE BLACKMUN.

I participate fully, of course, in the opinion, *ante,* p. 324, that bears the names of my Brothers BRENNAN, WHITE, MARSHALL, and myself. I add only some general observations that hold particular significance for me, and then a few comments on equal protection.

I

At least until the early 1970's, apparently only a very small number, less than 2%, of the physicians, attorneys, and medical and law students in the United States were members of what we now refer to as minority groups. In addition, approximately three-fourths of our Negro physicians were trained at only two medical schools. If ways are not found to remedy that situation, the country can never achieve its professed goal of a society that is not race conscious.

I yield to no one in my earnest hope that the time will come when an "affirmative action" program is unnecessary and is, in truth, only a relic of the past. I would hope that we could reach this stage within a decade at the most. But the story of *Brown* v. *Board of Education*, 347 U.S. 483 (1954), decided almost a quarter of a century ago, suggests that that hope is a slim one. At some time, however, beyond any period of what some would claim is only transitional inequality, the United States must and will reach a stage of maturity where action along this line is no longer necessary. Then persons will be regarded as persons, and discrimination of the type we address today will be an ugly feature of history that is instructive but that is behind us.

. . .

II

. . .

It is worth noting, perhaps, that governmental preference has not been a stranger to our legal life. We see it in veterans' preferences. We see it in the aid-to-the-handicapped programs. We see it in the progressive income tax. We see it in the Indian programs. We may excuse some of these on the ground that they have specific constitutional protection or, as with Indians, that those benefited are wards of the Government. Nevertheless, these preferences exist and may not be ignored. And in the admissions field, as I have indicated, educational institutions have always used geography, athletic ability, anticipated financial largess, alumni pressure, and other factors of that kind.

I add these only as additional components on the edges of the central question as to which I join my Brothers BRENNAN, WHITE, and MARSHALL in our more general approach. It is gratifying to know that the Court at least finds it constitutional for an academic institution to take race and ethnic background into consideration as one factor, among many, in the administration of its admissions program. I presume that that factor always has been there, though perhaps not conceded or even admitted. It is a fact of life, however, and a part of the real world of which we are all a part. The sooner we get down the road toward accepting and being a part of the real world, and not shutting it out and away from us, the sooner will these difficulties vanish from the scene.

I suspect that it would be impossible to arrange an affirmative-action program in a racially neutral way and have it successful. To ask that this be so is to demand the impossible. In order to get beyond racism, we must first take account of race. There is no other way. And in order to treat some persons equally, we must treat them differently. We cannot —we dare not—let the Equal Protection Clause perpetuate racial supremacy.

. . .

MR. JUSTICE STEVENS, with whom THE CHIEF JUSTICE, MR. JUSTICE STEWART, and MR. JUSTICE REHNQUIST join, concurring in the judgment in part and dissenting in part.

It is always important at the outset to focus precisely on the controversy before the Court. It is particularly important to do so in this case because correct identification of the issues will determine whether it is necessary or appropriate to express any opinion about the legal status of any admissions program other than petitioner's.

I

This is not a class action. The controversy is between two specific litigants. Allan Bakke challenged petitioner's special admissions program, claiming that it denied him a place in medical school because of his race in violation of the Federal and California Constitutions and of Title VI of the Civil Rights Act of 1964, 42 U.S.C. § 2000d *et seq.* . . .

It is . . . perfectly clear that the question whether race can ever be used as a factor in an admissions decision is not an issue in this case, and that discussion of that issue is inappropriate.

II

Both petitioner and respondent have asked us to determine the legality of the University's special admissions program by reference to the Constitution. Our settled practice, however, is to avoid the decision of a constitutional issue if a case can be fairly decided on a statutory ground. . . .

III

Section 601 of the Civil Rights Act of 1964, 78 Stat. 252, 42 U.S.C. § 2000d, provides:

"No person in the United States shall, on the ground of race, color, or national origin, be excluded from participation in, be denied the benefits of, or be subjected to discrimination under any program or activity receiving Federal financial assistance."

The University, through its special admissions policy, excluded Bakke from participation in its program of medical education because of his race. The University also acknowledges that it was, and still is, receiving federal financial assistance. The plain language of the statute therefore requires affirmance of the judgment below. . . .

. . . In the words of the House Report, Title VI stands for "the general principle that *no person* . . . be excluded from participation . . . on the ground of race, color, or national origin under any program or activity receiving Federal financial assistance." H. R. Rep. No. 914, 88th Cong., 1st Sess., pt. 1, p. 25 (1963) (emphasis added). This same broad view of Title VI and § 601 was echoed throughout the congressional debate and was stressed by every one of the major spokesmen for the Act.

. . .

The University's special admissions program violated Title VI of the Civil Rights Act of 1964 by excluding Bakke from the Medical School because of his race. It is therefore our duty to affirm the judgment ordering Bakke admitted to the University.

Accordingly, I concur in the Court's judgment insofar as it affirms the judgment of the Supreme Court of California. To the extent that it purports to do anything else, I respectfully dissent.

Fullilove v. Klutznick

448 U.S. 448 (1980)

Congress passed legislation in 1977 providing that at least 10 percent of federal funds granted for local public works projects must be used to obtain services or supplies from businesses owned by minority groups, defined as United States citizens "who are Negroes, Spanish-speaking, Orientals, Indians, Eskimos, and Aleuts." H. Earl Fullilove and several associations of construction contractors and subcontractors filed suit for declaratory and injunctive relief in federal district court, alleging that they had sustained economic injury due to enforcement of the statute. They claimed that the provision for minority businesses violated, on its face, the Equal Protection Clause of the Fourteenth Amendment and the equal protection component of the Due Process Clause of the Fifth Amendment. The district court upheld the statute; the Second Circuit affirmed. Defending the statute was Philip M. Klutznick, Secretary of Commerce.

MR. CHIEF JUSTICE BURGER announced the judgment of the Court and delivered an opinion, in which MR. JUSTICE WHITE and MR. JUSTICE POWELL joined.

We granted certiorari to consider a facial constitutional challenge to a requirement in a congressional spending program that, absent an administrative waiver, 10% of the federal funds granted for local public works projects must be used by the state or local grantee to procure services or supplies from businesses owned and controlled by members of statutorily identified minority groups. 441 U. S. 960 (1979).

I

In May 1977, Congress enacted the Public Works Employment Act of 1977, Pub. L. 95–28, 91 Stat. 116, which amended the Local Public Works Capital Development and Investment Act of 1976, Pub. L. 94–369, 90 Stat. 999, 42 U.S.C. § 6701 *et seq.* The 1977 amendments authorized an additional $4 billion appropriation for federal grants to be made by the Secretary of Commerce, acting through the Economic Development Administration (EDA), to state and local governmental entities for use in local public works projects. Among the changes made was the addition of the provision that has become the focus of this litigation. Section 103 (f)(2) of the 1977 Act, referred to as the "minority business enterprise" or "MBE" provision, requires that:

"Except to the extent that the Secretary determines otherwise, no grant shall be made under this Act for any local public works project unless the applicant gives satisfactory assurance to the Secretary that at least 10 per centum of the amount of each grant shall be expended for minority business enterprises. For purposes of this paragraph, the term 'minority business enterprise' means a business at least 50 per centum of which is owned by minority group members or, in case of a publicly owned business, at least 51 per centum of the stock of which is owned by minority group members. For the purposes of the preceding sentence, minority group members are citizens of the United States who are Negroes,

Spanish-speaking, Orientals, Indians, Eskimos, and Aleuts."

[The Secretary promulgated regulations to implement the grant program and the EDA issued supplementary guidelines. A district court and the Second Circuit upheld the statute against constitutional challenge on equal protection grounds.]

II

A

The MBE provision was enacted as part of the Public Works Employment Act of 1977, which made various amendments to Title I of the Local Public Works Capital Development and Investment Act of 1976. The 1976 Act was intended as a short-term measure to alleviate the problem of national unemployment and to stimulate the national economy by assisting state and local governments to build needed public facilities. *[The 10 percent provision for minorities originated as an amendment in the House of Representatives, where it was argued that in fiscal year 1976 less than one percent of all federal procurement was concluded with minority business enterprises, although minorities comprised 15 to 18 percent of the population. It was also stated that the concept of a "set-aside" for minorities had been used for ten years in the Small Business Administration. The Senate adopted the amendment, slightly modified, without debate.]*

B

The legislative objectives of the MBE provision must be considered against the background of ongoing efforts directed toward deliverance of the century-old promise of equality of economic opportunity. The sponsors of the MBE provision in the House and the Senate expressly linked the provision to the existing administrative programs promoting minority opportunity in government procurement, particularly those related to § 8 (a) of the Small Business Act of 1953. *[As Congress began consideration of the Public Works Employment Act of 1977, the House Committee on Small Business issued a lengthy report which included an evaluation of the § 8 (a) program, pointing out discriminatory practices against minorities in the economy. Minorities had difficulties gaining access to government contracting opportunities at the federal, state, and local levels.]*

Against this backdrop of legislative and administrative programs, it is inconceivable that Members of both Houses were not fully aware of the objectives of the MBE provision and of the reasons prompting its enactment.

C

Although the statutory MBE provision itself outlines only the bare bones of the federal program, it makes a number of critical determinations: the decision to initiate a limited racial and ethnic preference; the specification of a minimum level for minority business participation; the identification of the minority groups that are to be encompassed by the program; and the provision for an administrative waiver where application of the program is not feasible. Congress relied on the administrative agency to flesh out this skeleton, pursuant to delegated rulemaking authority, and to develop an administrative operation consistent with legislative intentions and objectives.

. . .

III

When we are required to pass on the constitutionality of an Act of Congress, we assume "the gravest and most delicate duty that this Court is called on to perform." *Blodgett* v. *Holden*, 275 U. S. 142, 148 (1927) (opinion of Holmes, J.). A program that employs racial or ethnic criteria, even in a remedial context, calls for close examination; yet we are bound to approach our task with appropriate deference to the Congress, a co-equal branch charged by the Constitution with the power to "provide for the . . . general Welfare of the United States" and "to enforce, by appropriate legislation," the equal protection guarantees of the Fourteenth Amendment. . . .

A

(1)

In enacting the MBE provision, it is clear that Congress employed an amalgam of its specifically delegated powers. The Public Works Employment Act of 1977, by its very nature, is primarily an exercise of the Spending Power. U. S. Const., Art. I, § 8, cl. 1. This Court has recognized that the power to "provide for the . . . general Welfare" is an independent grant of legislative authority, distinct from other broad congressional powers. *Buckley* v. *Valeo*, 424 U. S. 1, 90–91 (1976); *United States* v. *Butler*, 297 U. S. 1, 65–66 (1936). Congress has frequently employed the Spending Power to further broad policy objectives by conditioning receipt of federal moneys upon compliance by the recipient with federal statutory and administrative directives. This Court has repeatedly upheld against constitutional challenge the use of this technique to induce governments and private parties to cooperate voluntarily with federal policy. . . .

Here we need not explore the outermost limitations on the objectives attainable through such an application of the Spending Power. The reach of the Spending Power, within its sphere, is at least as broad as the regulatory powers of Congress. If, pursuant to its regulatory powers, Congress could have achieved the objectives of the MBE program, then it may do so under the Spending Power. And we have no difficulty perceiving a basis for accomplishing the objectives of the MBE program through the Commerce Power insofar as the program objectives pertain to the action of private contracting parties, and through the power to enforce the equal protection guarantees of the Fourteenth Amendment insofar as the program objectives pertain to the action of state and local grantees.

(2)

We turn first to the Commerce Power. U. S. Const., Art. I, § 8, cl. 3. Had Congress chosen to do so, it could have drawn on the Commerce Clause to regulate the practices of prime contractors on federally funded public works projects. *Katzenbach* v. *McClung*, 379 U. S. 294 (1964); *Heart of Atlanta Motel, Inc.* v. *United States*, 379 U. S. 241 (1964). The legislative history of the MBE provision shows that there was a rational basis for Congress to conclude that the subcontracting practices of prime contractors could perpetuate the prevailing impaired access by minority businesses to public contracting opportunities, and that this inequity has an effect on interstate commerce. Thus Congress could take necessary and proper action to remedy the situation. *Ibid.*

It is not necessary that these prime contractors be shown responsible for any violation of antidiscrimination laws. Our cases dealing with application of Title VII of the Civil Rights Act of 1964, 78 Stat. 253, as amended, express no doubt of the congressional authority to prohibit practices "challenged as perpetuating the effects of [not unlawful] discrimination occurring prior to the effective date of the Act." . . . Insofar as the MBE program pertains to the actions of private prime contractors, the Congress could have achieved its objectives under the Commerce Clause. We conclude that in this respect the objectives of the MBE provision are within the scope of the Spending Power.

(3)

In certain contexts, there are limitations on the reach of the Commerce Power to regulate the actions of state and local governments. *National League of Cities* v. *Usery*, 426 U. S. 833 (1976). To avoid such complications, we look to § 5 of the Fourteenth Amendment for the power to regulate the procurement practices of state and local grantees of federal funds. *Fitzpatrick* v. *Bitzer*, 427 U. S. 445 (1976). A review of our cases persuades us that the objectives of the MBE program are within the power of Congress under § 5 "to enforce, by appropriate legislation," the equal protection guarantees of the Fourteenth Amendment.

[After reviewing the holdings in Katzenbach *v.* Morgan, *384 U. S. 641 (1966),* Oregon *v.* Mitchell, *400 U. S. 112 (1970),* City of Rome *v.* United States, *446 U. S. 156 (1980), and* South Carolina *v.* Katzenbach, *383 U. S. 301 (1966), the Court concludes about the MBE provision:]* . . . Congress had abundant evidence from which it could conclude that minority businesses have been denied effective participation in public contracting opportunities by procurement practices that perpetuated the effects of prior discrimination. . . .

B

We now turn to the question whether, as a *means* to accomplish these plainly constitutional objectives, Congress may use racial and ethnic criteria, in this limited way, as a condition attached to a federal grant. . . .

(1)

As a threshold matter, we reject the contention that in the remedial context the Congress must act in a wholly "color-blind" fashion. In *Swann* v. *Charlotte-Mecklenburg Board of Education*, 402 U. S. 1, 18–21 (1971), we rejected this argument in considering a court-formulated school desegregation remedy on the basis that examination of the racial composition of student bodies was an unavoidable starting point and that racially based attendance assignments were permissible so long as no absolute racial balance of each school was required. . . .

Here we deal . . . not with the limited remedial powers of a federal court, for example, but with the broad remedial powers of Congress. It is fundamental that in no organ of government, state or federal, does there repose a more comprehensive remedial power than in the Congress, expressly charged by the Constitution with competence and authority to enforce equal protection guarantees. Congress not only may induce voluntary action to assure compliance with existing federal statutory or constitutional antidiscrimination provisions, but also, where Congress has authority to declare certain conduct unlawful, it may, as here, authorize and induce state action to avoid such conduct. *Supra*, at 473–480.

(2)

. . .

It is not a constitutional defect in this program that it may disappoint the expectations of nonminority firms. When effectuating a limited and properly tailored remedy to cure the effects of prior discrimination, such "a sharing of the burden" by innocent parties is not impermissible. . . .

(3)

Another challenge to the validity of the MBE program is the assertion that it is underinclusive —that it limits its benefit to specified minority groups rather than extending its remedial objectives to all businesses whose access to government contracting is impaired by the effects of disadvantage or discrimination. Such an extension would, of course, be appropriate for Congress to provide; it is not a function for the courts.

. . .

The Congress has not sought to give select minority groups a preferred standing in the construction industry, but has embarked on a remedial program to place them on a more equitable footing with respect to public contracting opportunities. There has been no showing in this case that Congress has inadvertently effected an invidious discrimination by excluding from coverage an identifiable minority group that has been the victim of a degree of disadvantage and discrimination equal to or greater than that suffered by the groups encompassed by the MBE program. . . .

(4)

It is also contended that the MBE program is overinclusive—that it bestows a benefit on businesses identified by racial or ethnic criteria which cannot be justified on the basis of competitive criteria or as a remedy for the present effects of identified prior discrimination. It is conceivable that a particular application of the program may have this effect; however, the peculiarities of specific applications are not before us in this case. We are not presented here with a challenge involving a specific award of a construction contract or the denial of a waiver request; such questions of specific application must await future cases.

. . .

IV

Congress, after due consideration, perceived a pressing need to move forward with new approaches in the continuing effort to achieve the goal of equality of economic opportunity. In this effort, Congress has necessary latitude to try new techniques such as the limited use of racial and ethnic criteria to accomplish remedial objectives; this is especially so in programs where voluntary cooperation with remedial measures is induced by placing conditions on federal expenditures. That the program may press the outer limits of congressional authority affords no basis for striking it down.

Petitioners have mounted a facial challenge to a program developed by the politically responsive branches of Government. For its part, the Congress must proceed only with programs narrowly tailored to achieve its objectives, subject to continuing evaluation and reassessment; administration of the programs must be vigilant and flexible; and, when such a program comes under judicial review, courts must be satisfied that the legislative objectives and projected administration give reasonable assurance that the program will function within constitutional limitations. . . .

. . . The MBE provision of the Public Works Employment Act of 1977 does not violate the Constitution.

Affirmed.

MR. JUSTICE POWELL, concurring.

. . .

V

In the history of this Court and this country, few questions have been more divisive than those arising from governmental action taken on the basis of race. Indeed, our own decisions played no small part in the tragic legacy of government-sanctioned discrimination. See *Plessy* v. *Ferguson,* 163 U. S. 537 (1896); *Dred Scott* v. *Sandford,* 19 How. 393 (1857). At least since the decision in *Brown* v. *Board of Education,* 347 U. S. 483 (1954), the Court has been resolute in its dedication to the principle that the Constitution envisions a Nation where race is irrelevant. The time cannot come too soon when no governmental decision will be based upon immutable characteristics of pigmentation or origin. But in our quest to achieve a society free from racial classification, we cannot ignore the claims of those who still suffer from the effects of identifiable discrimination.

. . . I believe that the use of racial classifications, which are fundamentally at odds with the ideals of a democratic society implicit in the Due Process and Equal Protection Clauses, cannot be imposed simply to serve transient social or political goals, however worthy they may be. But the issue here turns on the scope of congressional power, and Congress has been given a unique constitutional role in the enforcement of the post-Civil War Amendments. In this case, where Congress determined that minority contractors were victims of purposeful discrimination and where Congress chose a reasonably necessary means to effectuate its purpose, I find no constitutional reason to invalidate § 103 (f)(2).

MR. JUSTICE MARSHALL, with whom MR. JUSTICE BRENNAN and MR. JUSTICE BLACKMUN join, concurring in the judgment.

. . .

MR. JUSTICE STEWART, with whom MR. JUSTICE REHNQUIST joins, dissenting.

"Our Constitution is color-blind, and neither knows nor tolerates classes among citizens. . . . The law regards man as man, and takes no account of his surroundings or of his color. . . ." Those words were written by a Member of this Court 84 years ago. *Plessy* v. *Ferguson*, 163 U. S. 537, 559 (Harlan, J., dissenting). His colleagues disagreed with him, and held that a statute that required the separation of people on the basis of their race was constitutionally valid because it was a "reasonable" exercise of legislative power and had been "enacted in good faith for the promotion [of] the public good. . . ." *Id.*, at 550. Today, the Court upholds a statute that accords a preference to citizens who are "Negroes, Spanish-speaking, Orientals, Indians, Eskimos, and Aleuts," for much the same reasons. I think today's decision is wrong for the same reason that *Plessy* v. *Ferguson* was wrong, and I respectfully dissent.

A

The equal protection standard of the Constitution has one clear and central meaning—it abso-

lutely prohibits invidious discrimination by government. . . . Under our Constitution, any official action that treats a person differently on account of his race or ethnic origin is inherently suspect and presumptively invalid. . . .

. . . Under our Constitution, the government may never act to the detriment of a person solely because of that person's race. The color of a person's skin and the country of his origin are immutable facts that bear no relation to ability, disadvantage, moral culpability, or any other characteristics of constitutionally permissible interest to government. "Distinctions between citizens solely because of their ancestry are by their very nature odious to a free people whose institutions are founded upon the doctrine of equality." *Hirabayashi* v. *United States*, 320 U. S. 81, 100, quoted in *Loving* v. *Virginia, supra,* at 11. In short, racial discrimination is by definition individious discrimination.

. . .

No one disputes the self-evident proposition that Congress has broad discretion under its spending power to disburse the revenues of the United States as it deems best and to set conditions on the receipt of the funds disbursed. No one disputes that Congress has the authority under the Commerce Clause to regulate contracting practices on federally funded public works projects, or that it enjoys broad powers under § 5 of the Fourteenth Amendment "to enforce by appropriate legislation" the provisions of that Amendment. But these self-evident truisms do not begin to answer the question before us in this case. For in the exercise of its powers, Congress must obey the Constitution just as the legislatures of all the States must obey the Constitution in the exercise of their powers. If a law is unconstitutional, it is no less unconstitutional just because it is a product of the Congress of the United States.

B

On its face, the minority business enterprise (MBE) provision at issue in this case denies the equal protection of the law. . . . One class of contracting firms—defined solely according to the racial and ethnic attributes of their owners—is, however, excepted from the full rigor of these requirements with respect to a percentage of each federal grant. The statute, on its face and in effect, thus bars a class to which the petitioners belong from having the opportunity to receive a government benefit, and bars the members of that class solely on the basis of their race or ethnic background. This is precisely the kind of law that the guarantee of equal protection forbids.

. . .

C

. . .

The Court, moreover, takes this drastic step without, in my opinion, seriously considering the ramifications of its decision. Laws that operate on the basis of race require definitions of race. Because of the Court's decision today, our statute books will once again have to contain laws that reflect the odious practice of delineating the qualities that make one person a Negro and make another white. . . . Most importantly, by making race a relevant criterion once again in its own affairs the Government implicitly teaches the public that the apportionment of rewards and penalties can legitimately be made according to race— rather than according to merit or ability—and that people can, and perhaps should, view themselves and others in terms of their racial characteristics. Notions of "racial entitlement" will be fostered, and private discrimination will necessarily be encouraged. . . .

There are those who think that we need a new Constitution, and their views may someday prevail. But under the Constitution we have, one practice in which government may never engage is the practice of racism—not even "temporarily" and not even as an "experiment."

For these reasons, I would reverse the judgment of the Court of Appeals.

Mr. Justice Stevens, dissenting.

The 10% set-aside contained in the Public Works Employment Act of 1977 (Act), 91 Stat. 116, creates monopoly privileges in a $400 million market for a class of investors defined solely by racial characteristics. The direct beneficiaries of these monopoly privileges are the relatively small number of persons within the racial classification who represent the entrepreneurial subclass—those who have, or can borrow, working capital.

. . .

I

. . .

Even if we assume that each of the six racial subclasses has suffered its own special injury at some time in our history, surely it does not necessarily follow that each of those subclasses suffered harm of identical magnitude. Although "the Negro was dragged to this country in chains to be sold in slavery," *Bakke, supra,* at 387 (opinion of Marshall, J.), the "Spanish-speaking" subclass came voluntarily, frequently without invitation, and the Indians, the Eskimos and the Aleuts had an opportunity to exploit America's resources before the ancestors of most American citizens arrived. There is no reason to assume, and nothing in the legislative history suggests, much less demonstrates, that each of the subclasses is equally entitled to reparations from the United States Government.

. . .

IV

. . .

. . . a statute of this kind inevitably is perceived by many as resting on an assumption that those who are granted this special preference are less qualified in some respect that is identified purely by their race. Because that perception— especially when fostered by the Congress of the United States—can only exacerbate rather than reduce racial prejudice, it will delay the time when race will become a truly irrelevant, or at least insignificant, factor. Unless Congress clearly articulates the need and basis for a racial classification, and also tailors the classification to its justification, the Court should not uphold this kind of statute.

V

. . . rather than take the substantive position expressed in MR. JUSTICE STEWART'S dissenting opinion, I would hold this statute unconstitutional on a narrower ground. It cannot fairly be characterized as a "narrowly tailored" racial classification because it simply raises too many serious questions that Congress failed to answer or even to address in a responsible way. The risk that habitual attitudes toward classes of persons, rather than analysis of the relevant characteristics of the class, will serve as a basis for a legislative classification is present when benefits are distributed as well as when burdens are imposed. In the past, traditional attitudes too often provided the only explanation for discrimination against women, aliens, illegitimates, and black citizens. Today there is a danger that awareness of past injustice will lead to automatic acceptance of new classifications that are not in fact justified by attributes characteristic of the class as a whole.

When Congress creates a special preference, or a special disability, for a class of persons, it should identify the characteristic that justifies the special treatment. When the classification is defined in racial terms, I believe that such particular identification is imperative.

In this case, only two conceivable bases for differentiating the preferred classes from society as a whole have occurred to me: (1) that they were the victims of unfair treatment in the past and (2) that they are less able to compete in the future. Although the first of these factors would justify an appropriate remedy for past wrongs, for reasons that I have already stated, this statute is not such a remedial measure. The second factor is simply not true. Nothing in the record of this case, the legislative history of the Act, or experience that we may notice judicially provides any support for such a proposition. It is up to Congress to demonstrate that its unique statutory preference is justified by a relevant characteristic that is shared by the members of the preferred class. In my opinion, because it has failed to make that demonstration, it has also failed to discharge its duty to govern impartially embodied in the Fifth Amendment to the United States Constitution.

I respectfully dissent.

Local 28 of Sheet Metal Workers v. EEOC

478 U.S. 421 (1986)

In 1975, a federal district court found a sheet metal union guilty of violating Title VII by discriminating against nonwhite workers in recruitment, selection, training, and admission to the union. The court ordered the union to cease its discriminatory practices, established a 29 percent nonwhite membership goal (based on the percentage of nonwhites in the labor pool in New York City), and ordered the union to implement procedures designed to achieve this goal under the supervision of a court-appointed administrator. These orders were affirmed by the Second Circuit. In 1982 and again in 1983, the district court found the union guilty of civil contempt for failing to obey the court's orders. The district court entered an amended affirmative-action program establishing a 29.23 percent nonwhite membership goal to be met by August 1987. The Second Circuit affirmed the district court's contempt findings (with one exception), the contempt remedies, and the affirmative-action program with modifications, holding that the 29.23 percent goal was proper and did not violate Title VII or the Constitution.

JUSTICE BRENNAN announced the judgment of the Court and delivered the opinion of the Court with respect to Parts I, II, III, and VI, and an opinion with respect to Parts IV, V, and VII in which JUSTICE MARSHALL, JUSTICE BLACKMUN, and JUSTICE STEVENS join.

In 1975, petitioners were found guilty of engaging in a pattern and practice of discrimination against black and Hispanic individuals (nonwhites) in violation of Title VII of the Civil Rights Act of 1964, 42 U.S.C. § 2000e *et seq.*, and ordered to end their discriminatory practices, and to admit a certain percentage of nonwhites to union membership by July 1982. In 1982 and again in 1983, petitioners were found guilty of civil contempt for disobeying the District Court's earlier orders. They now challenge the District Court's contempt finding, and also the remedies the court ordered both for the Title VII violation and for contempt. Principally, the issue presented is whether the remedial provision of Title VII, see 42 U.S.C. 2000e–5(g), empowers a district court to order race-conscious relief that may benefit individuals who are not identified victims of unlawful discrimination.

I

Petitioner Local 28 of the Sheet Metal Workers' International Association (Local 28) represents sheet metal workers employed by contractors in the New York City metropolitan area. Petitioner Local 28 Joint Apprenticeship Committee (JAC) is a management-labor committee which operates a 4-year apprenticeship training program designed to teach sheet metal skills. Apprentices enrolled in the program receive training both from classes and from on the job work experience. Upon completing the program, apprentices become journeyman members of Local 28. Successful completion of the program is the principal means of attaining union membership.

In 1964, the New York State Commission for Human Rights determined that petitioners had excluded blacks from the union and the apprenticeship program in violation of state law. The State Commission found, among other things, that Local 28 had never had any black members or apprentices, and that "admission to apprenticeship is conducted largely on a nepot[is]tic basis involving sponsorship by incumbent union members," App. JA–407, creating an impenetrable barrier for nonwhite applicants. Petitioners were ordered to "cease and desist" their racially discriminatory practices. The New York State Su-

preme Court affirmed the State Commission's findings, and directed petitioners to implement objective standards for selecting apprentices. *State Comm'n for Human Rights* v. *Farrell*, 43 Misc.2d 958, 252 N.Y.S.2d 649 (1964).

When the court's orders proved ineffective, the State Commission commenced other state-court proceedings in an effort to end petitioners' discriminatory practices. Petitioners had originally agreed to indenture two successive classes of apprentices using nondiscriminatory selection procedures, but stopped processing applications for the second apprentice class, thus requiring that the State Commission seek a court order requiring petitioners to indenture the apprentices. *State Comm'n for Human Rights* v. *Farrell*, 47 Misc.2d 244, 262 N.Y.S.2d 526, *aff'd*, 24 App.Div.2d 128, 264 N.Y.S.2d 489 (1st Dept. 1965). The court subsequently denied the union's request to reduce the size of the second apprentice class, and chastized the union for refusing "except for token gestures, to further the integration process." *State Comm'n for Human Rights* v. *Farrell*, 47 Misc.2d 799, 800, 263 N.Y.S.2d 250, 252 (1965). Petitioners proceeded to disregard the results of the selection test for a third apprentice class on the ground that nonwhites had received "unfair tutoring" and had passed in unreasonably high numbers. The state court ordered petitioners to indenture the apprentices based on the examination results. *State Comm'n for Human Rights* v. *Farrell*, 52 Misc.2d 936, 277 N.Y.S.2d 287, *aff'd*, 27 App.Div.2d 327, 278 N.Y.S.2d 982 (1st Dept.), *aff'd* 19 N.Y.2d 974, 281 N.Y.S.2d 521, 228 N.E.2d 691 (1967).

In 1971, the United States initiated this action under Title VII and Executive Order 11246, 3 CFR 339 (1964–1965 Comp.) to enjoin petitioners from engaging in a pattern and practice of discrimination against black and Hispanic individuals (nonwhites). The New York City Commission on Human Rights (City) intervened as plaintiff to press claims that petitioners had violated municipal fair employment laws, and had frustrated the City's efforts to increase job opportunities for minorities in the construction industry. 347 F.Supp. 164 (1972). In 1970, the City had adopted a plan requiring contractors on its projects to employ one minority trainee for every four journeyman union members. Local 28 was the only construction local which refused to comply voluntarily with the plan. In early 1974, the City attempted to assign six minority trainees to sheet metal contractors working on municipal construction projects. After Local 28 members stopped work on the projects, the District Court directed the JAC to admit the six trainees into the apprenticeship program, and enjoined Local 28 from causing any work stoppage at the affected job sites. The parties subsequently agreed to a consent order that required the JAC to admit up to 40 minorities into the apprenticeship program by September 1974. The JAC stalled compliance with the consent order, and only completed the indenture process under threat of contempt.

Following a trial in 1975, the District Court concluded that petitioners had violated both Title VII and New York law by discriminating against nonwhite workers in recruitment, selection, training, and admission to the union. 401 F.Supp. 467 (1975). Noting that as of July 1, 1974, only 3.19% of the union's total membership, including apprentices and journeymen, was nonwhite, the court found that petitioners had denied qualified nonwhites access to union membership through a variety of discriminatory practices. First, the court found that petitioners had adopted discriminatory procedures and standards for admission into the apprenticeship program. The court examined some of the factors used to select apprentices, including the entrance examination and high-school diploma requirement, and determined that these criteria had an adverse discriminatory impact on nonwhites, and were not related to job performance. The court also observed that petitioners had used union funds to subsidize special training sessions for friends and relatives of union members taking the apprenticeship examination.

Second, the court determined that Local 28 had restricted the size of its membership in order to deny access to nonwhites. The court found that Local 28 had refused to administer yearly journeymen's examinations despite a growing demand for members' services. Rather, to meet this increase in demand, Local 28 recalled pensioners who obtained doctors' certificates that they were able to work, and issued hundreds of temporary

work permits to nonmembers; only one of these permits was issued to a nonwhite. . . .

[The District Court also determined that Local 28 had drawn only white employees from nonunion shops and had discriminated in favor of white applicants seeking to transfer from sister locals. After the District Court established a 29 percent nonwhite membership goal, it held the union in contempt for failing to comply with the affirmative action program. The Court also entered an amended affirmative action program, setting a 29.23 percent minority membership goal to be met by August 31, 1987. The Second Circuit found this goal to be proper in light of Local 28's "long continued and egregious racial discrimination."]

. . .

IV

Petitioners, joined by the EEOC, argue that the membership goal, the Fund order, and other orders which require petitioners to grant membership preferences to nonwhites are expressly prohibited by § 706(g), 42 U.S.C. § 2000e-5(g), which defines the remedies available under Title VII. Petitioners and the EEOC maintain that § 706(g) authorizes a district court to award preferential relief only to the actual victims of unlawful discrimination. They maintain that the membership goal and the Fund violate this provision, since they require petitioners to admit to membership, and otherwise to extend benefits to black and Hispanic individuals who are not the identified victims of unlawful discrimination. We reject this argument, and hold that § 706(g) does not prohibit a court from ordering, in appropriate circumstances, affirmative race-conscious relief as a remedy for past discrimination. Specifically, we hold that such relief may be appropriate where an employer or a labor union has engaged in persistent or egregious discrimination, or where necessary to dissipate the lingering effects of pervasive discrimination.

A

Section 706(g) states:

"If the court finds that the respondent has intentionally engaged in or is intentionally engaging in an unlawful employment practice . . . , the court may enjoin the respondent from engaging in such unlawful employment practice, and order such affirmative action as may be appropriate, which may include, but is not limited to, reinstatement or hiring of employees, with or without back pay . . . , or any other equitable relief as the court deems appropriate. . . . No order of the court shall require the admission or reinstatement of an individual as a member of a union, or the hiring, reinstatement, or promotion of an individual as an employee, or the payment to him of any back pay, if such individual was refused admission, suspended, or expelled, or was refused employment or advancement or was suspended or discharged for any reason other than discrimination on account of race, color, religion, sex, or national origin in violation of . . . this title." 42 U.S.C. § 2000e-5(g).

The language of § 706(g) plainly expresses Congress's intent to vest district courts with broad discretion to award "appropriate" equitable relief to remedy unlawful discrimination. . . . Nevertheless, petitioners and the EEOC argue that the last sentence of § 706(g) prohibits a court from ordering an employer or labor union to take affirmative steps to eliminate discrimination which might incidentally benefit individuals who are not the actual victims of discrimination. This reading twists the plain language of the statute.

The last sentence of § 706(g) prohibits a court from ordering a union to admit an individual who was "refused admission . . . for any reason other than discrimination." It does not, as petitioners and the EEOC suggest, say that a court may order relief only for the actual victims of past discrimination. The sentence on its face addresses only the situation where a plaintiff demonstrates that a union (or an employer) has engaged in unlawful discrimination, but the union can show that a particular individual would have been refused admission even in the absence of discrimination, for example because that individual was unqualified. In these circumstances, § 706(g) confirms that a court could not order the union to admit the unqualified individual. . . . In this case, neither the membership goal nor the Fund order required petitioners to admit to membership individuals who had been refused admission for reasons

unrelated to discrimination. Thus, we do not read § 706(g) to prohibit a court from ordering the kind of affirmative relief the District Court awarded in this case.

B

The availability of race-conscious affirmative relief under § 706(g) as a remedy for a violation of Title VII also furthers the broad purposes underlying the statute. Congress enacted Title VII based on its determination that racial minorities were subject to pervasive and systematic discrimination in employment. . . . In order to foster equal employment opportunities, Congress gave the lower courts broad power under § 706(g) to fashion "the most complete relief possible" to remedy past discrimination. . . .

In most cases, the court need only order the employer or union to cease engaging in discriminatory practices, and award make-whole relief to the individuals victimized by those practices. In some instances, however, it may be necessary to require the employer or union to take affirmative steps to end discrimination effectively to enforce Title VII. Where an employer or union has engaged in particularly longstanding or egregious discrimination, an injunction simply reiterating Title VII's prohibition against discrimination will often prove useless and will only result in endless enforcement litigation. In such cases, requiring recalcitrant employers or unions to hire and to admit qualified minorities roughly in proportion to the number of qualified minorities in the work force may be the only effective way to ensure the full enjoyment of the rights protected by Title VII. . . .

[Justice Brennan examined the claim by petitioners and the EEOC that the legislative history indicates Congress intended that affirmative relief under § 706(g) benefit only the identified victims of past discrimination. After reviewing the legislative history, Brennan concluded that Congress did not intend to prohibit a court from exercising its remedial authority to adopt affirmative race-conscious relief, including preferential remedies that might benefit nonvictims. Brennan also referred to the legislative history of the Equal Employment Opportunity Act of 1972, when Senator Ervin offered an amendment to

prohibit an employer from being required "to practice discrimination in reverse by employing persons of a particular race . . . in either fixed or variable numbers, proportions, percentages, quotas, goals, or ranges." The Ervin amendment was defeated by a margin of 2 to 1.]

VII

To summarize our holding today, six members of the Court agree that a district court may, in appropriate circumstances, order preferential relief benefitting individuals who are not the actual victims of discrimination as a remedy for violations of Title VII, see *supra*, Parts IV-A-IV-D (opinion of BRENNAN, J., joined by MARSHALL, J., BLACKMUN, J., and STEVENS, J.); *post*, at 483 (POWELL, J., concurring in part and concurring in the judgment); *post*, at 499 (WHITE, J., dissenting), that the District Court did not use incorrect statistical evidence in establishing petitioners' nonwhite membership goal, see *supra*, Part II-A, that the contempt fines and Fund order were proper remedies for civil contempt, see *supra*, Part III, and that the District Court properly appointed an administrator to supervise petitioners' compliance with the court's orders, see *supra* Part VI. Five members of the Court agree that in this case, the District Court did not err in evaluating petitioners' utilization of the apprenticeship program, see *supra*, Part II-B, and that the membership goal and the Fund order are not violative of either Title VII or the Constitution, see *supra*, Parts IV–E, V (opinion of BRENNAN, J., joined by MARSHALL, J., BLACKMUN, J., and STEVENS, J.); *post*, at 486–487 (POWELL, J., concurring in part and concurring in the judgment). The judgment of the Court of Appeals is hereby

Affirmed.

JUSTICE POWELL, concurring in part and concurring in the judgment.

I join Parts I, II, III, and VI of JUSTICE BRENNAN'S opinion. I further agree that § 706(g) does not limit a court in all cases to granting relief only to actual victims of discrimination. I write separately with respect to the issues raised in parts IV and V to explain why I think the remedy ordered under the circumstances of this case violated neither Title VII nor the Constitution.

. . .

JUSTICE O'CONNOR, concurring in part and dissenting in part.

I join Parts II-A, III, and VI of the Court's opinion. I would reverse the judgment of the Court of Appeals on statutory grounds insofar as the membership "goal" and the Fund order are concerned, and I would not reach petitioners' constitutional claims. I agree with JUSTICE WHITE, however, that the membership "goal" in this case operates as a rigid racial quota that cannot feasibly be met through good-faith efforts by Local 28. In my view, § 703(j), 42 U.S.C. § 2000e–2(j), and § 706(g), 42 U.S.C. § 2000e–5(g), read together, preclude courts from ordering racial quotas such as this. I therefore dissent from the Court's judgment insofar as it affirms the use of these mandatory quotas.

. . .

JUSTICE WHITE, dissenting.

As the Court observes, the general policy under Title VII is to limit relief for racial discrimination in employment practices to actual victims of the discrimination. But I agree that § 706(g) does not bar relief for nonvictims in all circumstances. Hence, I generally agree with Parts I through IV–D of the Court's opinion. It may also be that this is one of those unusual cases where nonvictims of discrimination were entitled to a measure of the relief ordered by the District Court and affirmed by the Court of Appeals. But Judge Winter, in dissent below, was correct in concluding that critical parts of the remedy ordered in this case were excessive under § 706(g), absent findings that those benefiting from the relief had been victims of discriminatory practices by the union. As Judge Winter explained and contrary to the Court's views, the cumulative effect of the revised affirmative action plan and the contempt judgments against the union established not just a minority membership goal but also a strict racial quota that the union was required to attain. We have not heretofore approved this kind of racially discriminatory hiring practice, and I would not do so now. Beyond this, I am convinced, as Judge Winter was, that holding the union in contempt for failing to attain the membership quota during a time of economic doldrums in the construction industry and a declining demand for the union skills involved in this case was for all practical purposes equivalent to a judicial insistence that the union comply even if it required the displacement of nonminority workers by members of the plaintiff class. The remedy is inequitable in my view, and for this reason I dissent from the judgment affirming the Court of Appeals.

JUSTICE REHNQUIST, with whom THE CHIEF JUSTICE joins, dissenting.

Today, in *Firefighters* v. *Cleveland, post,* p. 501 (REHNQUIST, J., dissenting), I express my belief that § 706(g) forbids a court from ordering racial preferences that effectively displace non-minorities except to minority individuals who have been the actual victims of a particular employer's racial discrimination. Although the pervasiveness of the racial discrimination practiced by a particular union or employer is likely to increase the number of victims who are entitled to a remedy under the Act, § 706(g) does not allow us to go further than that and sanction the granting of relief to those who were not victims at the expense of innocent non-minority workers injured by racial preferences. I explain that both the language and the legislative history of § 706(g) clearly support this reading of § 706(g), and that this Court stated as much just two Terms ago in *Firefighters* v. *Stotts,* 467 U. S. 561 (1984). Because of this, I would not reach the equal protection question, see *ante,* at 479–481 (opinion of JUSTICE BRENNAN), *id.,* at 484–489 (opinion of JUSTICE POWELL), but would rely solely on § 706(g) to reverse the Court of Appeals' judgment approving the order of class-based relief for petitioners' past discrimination.

16 The Emergence of Group Rights

uilding on the rights established for black Americans, the feminist movement pressed for fundamental changes in women's rights. Also from this period of "rights consciousness" emerged efforts to secure rights for other groups: Mexican-Americans, Indians, aliens, the indigent, the aged, the handicapped, juveniles, illegitimate children, and institutionalized persons.[1] This extension of individual rights placed heavy demands on Congress and the judiciary.

Several group rights are studied in this chapter. The trio of women, juveniles, and prisoners may seem an odd, even offensive, combination, but all three share certain common characteristics. In each case they were initially denied constitutional rights available to the rest of the population. In each case they had to overcome entrenched ideas and customs. The chapter concludes by examining the constitutional rights of the poor.

GENDER DISCRIMINATION

When the framers proclaimed in the Declaration of Independence that "all men are created equal," they meant men literally, and not even all men. Blacks were excluded from equal treatment, as were nonpropertied white males. On March 31, 1776, Abigail Adams appealed to her husband, John Adams, who was busily engaged with the Continental Congress in Philadelphia. She urged that "in the new code of laws which I suppose it will be necessary for you to make, I desire you would remember the ladies and be more generous and favorable to them than your ancestors. Do not put such unlimited power into the hands of the husbands.

---

[1]In a major alien case in 1982, the Supreme Court struck down a Texas statute that withheld from local school districts any state funds for the education of children who were not "legally admitted" into the United States. The state authorized schools to deny enrollment to such children. The Court held that the statute violated the Equal Protection Clause of the Fourteenth Amendment, which protects *persons*, including illegal aliens. Plyler v. Doe, 457 U.S. 202 (1982).

Remember, all men would be tyrants if they could." His curt reply mirrored the attitude of the times: "As to your extraordinary code of laws, I cannot but laugh." C. F. Adams, ed., Familiar Letters of John Adams and His Wife Abigail Adams During the Revolution 149–150, 155 (1876).

The customs of 1776 included the ancient doctrine of *coverture*, which placed women in a subordinate position to men. Blackstone, the great English jurist, stated that marriage made husband and wife "one person in law: that is, the very being or legal existence of the woman is suspended during the marriage, or at least is incorporated and consolidated into that of the husband: under whose wing, protection, and *cover,* she performs every thing." 2 Commentaries *442.

This philosophy animates the early Supreme Court rulings on women's rights. A prominent example is *Bradwell* v. *State* (1873). Myra Bradwell had a law degree but needed the approval of a panel of judges to practice law in Illinois. They turned her down solely because she was a woman. The Supreme Court denied that her rejection violated the privileges and immunities of the Fourteenth Amendment. The Slaughter-House Cases, announced earlier that year, left those questions to the states, not the federal government. Eight Justices voted against Mrs. Bradwell; only Chief Justice Chase (without a written opinion) dissented.

The concurrence by Justice Bradley in *Bradwell* claimed that the "natural and proper timidity and delicacy which belongs to the female sex evidently unfits it for many of the occupations of civil life." A woman's responsibility to domestic life and to the family institution made it "repugnant" for her to adopt an independent career from that of her husband. Bradley recognized that his argument was irrelevant for unmarried women, but they were exceptions to the general rule: "The paramount destiny and mission of woman are to fulfill the noble and benign offices of wife and mother. This is the law of the Creator. And the rules of civil society must be adapted to the general constitution of things, and cannot be based on exceptional cases." BRADWELL v. STATE, 83 U.S. (16 Wall.) 130 (1873).

Within two years the judiciary delivered another major blow against women's rights. A lawsuit by Mrs. Virginia Minor argued that she was a "citizen" within the meaning of the Constitution and therefore entitled to vote as one of the privileges and immunities protected by the Fourteenth Amendment. A unanimous Court agreed that women are citizens but denied that the Fourteenth Amendment added substantive rights to previous privileges and immunities. According to the Court, Section 2 of the Fourteenth Amendment limited suffrage to male inhabitants. Indeed, it took the Fifteenth Amendment to give blacks the right to vote. Women, like children, were "citizens" and "persons" in the constitutional sense but that status did not automatically entitle either to vote. Minor v. Happersett, 88 U.S. (21 Wall.) 162 (1875). Women did not gain the right to vote until the Nineteenth Amendment was ratified in 1920.

Protective Legislation

Although women later won important victories in the courts, the verdicts were often premised on their inferiority, not their equality. A decision in 1908, in which the Supreme Court unanimously upheld Oregon's ten-hour-day for women, helped perpetuate the stereotype of women advanced in *Bradwell*. Speaking for the Court, Justice Brewer remarked: "Still again, history discloses the fact that woman has always been dependent upon man. He established his control at the outset by superior physical strength, and this control in various forms, with diminishing intensity, has continued to the present." Muller v. Oregon, 208 U.S. 412, 421 (1908). Despite new opportunities for women to acquire knowledge, "it is still true that in the struggle for subsistence she is not an equal competitor with her brother. Though limitations upon personal and contractual rights may be removed by legislation, there is that in her disposition and habits of life which will operate against a full assertion of those rights." Id. at 422. Acknowledging that individual exceptions existed, Brewer felt confident that even with the elimination of political and contractual restrictions "it would still be true that she is so constituted that she will rest upon and look to him for protection." Id. Blackstone still reigned.

By 1923, the Court concluded that protective legislation for women was no longer necessary because of the Nineteenth Amendment and changes in statutory and contractual law. Adkins v. Children's Hospital, 261 U.S. 525, 553 (1923). Chief Justice Taft, in one of the dissents, wondered if the majority believed that previous Court doctrines had been invalidated by the Nineteenth Amendment, which "did not change the physical strength or limitations of women upon which the decision in *Muller* v. *Oregon* rests." Id. at 567. Another dissent by Justice Holmes wryly observed: "It will need more than the Nineteenth Amendment to convince me that there are no differences between men and women, or that legislation cannot take those differences into account." Id. at 569–570.

The Court continued to support certain types of protective legislation for women. In 1924 it upheld a New York law that prohibited women in large cities from working between 10 p.m. and 6 a.m. Radice v. New York, 264 U.S. 292 (1924). But the spirit of *Adkins* survived through 1936 when the Court (divided 5–4) struck down New York's minimum wage law for women and minors. The Court saw no justification for protective legislation for women when men "in need of work are as likely as women to accept the low wages offered by unscrupulous employers." Morehead v. N.Y. ex rel. Tipaldo, 298 U.S. 587, 616 (1936). *Adkins* was overturned the next year. A 5–4 majority accepted minimum wage legislation for women. States were entitled to consider "the fact that they are in the class receiving the least pay, that their bargaining power is relatively weak, and that they are the ready victims of those who would take advantage of their necessitous circumstances." West Coast Hotel Co. v. Parrish, 300 U.S. 379, 398 (1937). The Court also took "judicial notice" of the public relief needed during the Great Depression. Inadequate wages for women had placed demands on state agencies for public assistance: "The community is not bound to provide what is in effect a subsidy for unconscionable employers." Id. at 399.

Court doctrines had not advanced very far by 1948, when the Supreme Court upheld a Michigan law that prohibited female bartenders unless they were the wife or daughter of the male owner. Attitudes in state legislatures and the judiciary had not changed much since *Bradwell*. By a 6–3 vote, the Court decided that Michigan had not violated the Equal Protection Clause of the Fourteenth Amendment. Frankfurter's opinion for the majority has a smug quality: "Beguiling as the subject is, it need not detain us for long. To ask whether or not the Equal Protection of the Laws Clause of the Fourteenth Amendment barred Michigan from making the classification the State has made between wives and daughters of owners of liquor places and wives and daughters of non-owners, is one of those rare instances where to state the question is in effect to answer it." Goeseart v. Cleary, 335 U.S. 464, 465 (1948). Frankfurter concluded that Michigan could, "beyond question," forbid all women from working behind a bar. To the three dissenters, Michigan's statute arbitrarily discriminated between men and women.

In 1960, Frankfurter wrote an opinion rejecting the "medieval view" that husband and wife are one person, with but a single will, and therefore legally incapable of entering into a criminal conspiracy. To the extent that this outmoded doctrine of coverture rested on a legal fiction, three dissenters preferred that it be corrected by Congress, not the judiciary. United States v. Dege, 364 U.S. 51 (1960). Medieval thinking triumphed in 1961 when the Court agreed unanimously that women could be largely exempted from jury service because they are "still regarded as the center of home and family life." Hoyt v. Florida, 368 U.S. 57, 62 (1961). Remnants of the law of coverture persisted until 1966. United States v. Yazell, 382 U.S. 341 (1966).

Abolishing Sexual Stereotypes

Judicial attitudes on sex discrimination did not change until long after the Desegregation Case of 1954. Remedies came first from Congress, not the courts. Using its constitutional power to regulate commerce, Congress passed the Equal Pay Act in 1963 to prohibit employers in the private sector from discriminating on the basis of sex. 77 Stat. 56. The debate (pp. 1072–1075) demonstrates how Congress can respond to constitutional inequities before they are addressed, or redressed, by the courts.

Title VII of the Civil Rights Act of 1964 made it illegal for any employer to discriminate against anyone with respect to "compensation, terms, conditions, or privileges of employment" because of the person's sex. 42 U.S.C. § 2000e-2(a)(1) (1982). It is sometimes claimed that the word "sex" was added to the bill to ridicule and perhaps sabotage the enactment of a civil rights bill. However, the debate suggests a different motivation. By prohibiting discrimination on the basis of race, Members of Congress were concerned that a white woman applying for a job would be at a disadvantage, legally, to a black woman (pp. 1075–1080).

Congress established the Equal Employment Opportunity Commission (EEOC) to investigate claims of discrimination. Much of the agency's workload deals with cases of sex discrimination. Upholding congressional policy and EEOC regulations, the Court held that a company could not deny employment to a woman because she had preschool-age children if the company agreed to hire men with preschool-age children. Phillips v. Martin Marietta Corp., 400 U.S. 542 (1971). In another initiative, Congress passed Title IX of the Education Amendments of 1972 to withdraw federal financial assistance from any educational institution that practices sex discrimination. 86 Stat. 373 (1972).

Supreme Court doctrines began to shift after Warren Burger replaced Earl Warren as Chief Justice in 1969. A unanimous Court in 1971 struck down an Idaho law that preferred men over women in administering estates. The statute, the Court held, arbitrarily discriminated on the basis of sex and violated the Equal Protection Clause of the Fourteenth Amendment. Reed v. Reed, 404 U.S. 71 (1971). Since that time, a flood of cases has gradually challenged and eliminated sexual stereotypes of an earlier age. In 1973, the Court said that sex discrimination had survived in America as "romantic paternalism," whereas the practical effect was to put women "not on a pedestal, but in a cage." Statutes were "laden with gross, stereotyped distinctions between the sexes." FRONTIERO v. RICHARDSON, 411 U.S. 677, 684–685 (1973). Customs of earlier times were "no longer tenable" to exclude women from juries. Taylor v. Louisiana, 419 U.S. 522, 537 (1975). The Court rejected "old notions" about a man's primary responsibility to provide a home. Stanton v. Stanton, 421 U.S. 7, 10 (1975).

The Supreme Court had an opportunity in 1973 to declare sex a "suspect classification" as it had done with race and alienage. Under this classification, the strict-scrutiny test is applied to governmental actions that discriminate and the government must show a compelling interest to support its policy. The more lenient equal-protection standard permits a legislature to make classifications if the statute is rational and furthers an important governmental interest.

The case before the Court in 1973 involved a congressional statute that permitted a serviceman to claim his wife as a "dependent" even if she was not dependent on him. In contrast, a female member of the armed forces could not claim her husband as a dependent (and therefore obtain increased housing allowances and medical and dental benefits) unless he relied on her for over one-half of his support. An 8–1 majority found the statute unconstitutional. Justice Brennan was one of four members of the Court who urged that sex be made a suspect classification. Other Justices thought that the Court should defer to the workings of the constitutional amendment process under way with the ERA. FRONTIERO v. RICHARDSON, 411 U.S. 677 (1973).[2]

In the midst of this revolutionary litigation appeared the Equal Rights Amendment (ERA), passed by the House of Representatives in 1971 and by the Senate in 1972 by overwhelming margins. The Amendment read: "Equality of rights under the law shall not be denied or abridged by the United States or by any state on account of sex." When the amendment failed to be ratified by the end of the seven-year period specified in the amendment, Congress extended the deadline to June 30, 1982. Even with this extra time the amendment fell short of the necessary states.

The ERA failed for a number of reasons. Some women were concerned that they might lose traditional benefits from divorce settlements or be subject to the military draft. The major setback, however, was the Supreme Court's decision in *Roe* v. *Wade* (1973), upholding a woman's right to have an abortion in the first two trimesters of pregnancy (reprinted in Chapter 17). ERA proponents had tried to keep abortion as a separate issue. *Roe* seemed to link ERA with the pro-choice philosophy. Moreover, it appeared throughout the 1970s that many of the goals of the feminist movement could be accomplished by legislative action and judicial decisions.

For example, in 1973 the Court agreed that a city could prohibit a newspaper from printing advertisements that listed job opportunities under headings "Male

---

[2]Two years later, the Court accepted a congressional decision to establish different periods of tenure for servicemen and servicewomen before forcing them out. Male officers were subject to mandatory discharge after nine years unless they were promoted; female officers faced that test after thirteen years. The Court decided that the legislative classification was rational because Congress had taken into account the restrictions placed upon women with regard to combat duty and sea service. Schlesinger v. Ballard, 419 U.S. 498 (1975). Another congressional decision was accepted in *Mathews* v. *De Castro*, 429 U.S. 181 (1976), which concluded that it was not irrational for Congress in the Social Security Act to grant monthly benefits to a married woman under 62 whose husband retires or becomes disabled and she has a minor or dependent child in her care, whereas a divorced woman under 62 whose ex-husband retires or becomes disabled receives no such benefits. Congress recognized that divorced couples typically live separate lives, giving the divorced woman greater financial independence.

Interest" and "Female Interest." The positions available for men offered substantially higher salaries. Pittsburgh Press Co. v. Human Rel. Comm'n, 413 U.S. 376, 392 (1973). Two years later, the Court held that the systematic exclusion of women from jury panels violates the right to a jury trial in the Sixth Amendment. Taylor v. Louisiana, 419 U.S. 522 (1975), overruling Hoyt v. Florida, 368 U.S. 57 (1961). See also Duren v. Missouri, 439 U.S. 357 (1979).

Discrepancies in the age of majority (21 for men and 18 for women) were declared unconstitutional. Old notions of viewing men as the breadwinners, requiring additional years to obtain an education and training before assuming the position as head of the house, were rejected by the Court as justification for the difference between 21 and 18. The Court noted that women are increasingly involved in education, business, the professions, and government. Stanton v. Stanton, 421 U.S. 7, 15 (1975). State laws describing the husband as "head and master" and giving him unilateral power to sell jointly owned property were struck down as a violation of the Equal Protection Clause. Kirchberg v. Feenstra, 450 U.S. 455 (1981).

Increased professional activity by women produced other changes. Women lawyers denied partnership in their firm may take a sex discrimination claim to court. Hishon v. King & Spalding, 467 U.S. 69 (1984). It is still uncertain how much evidence is required to prove discrimination under Title VII. It is clear that employers may not rely on sex-based considerations in denying a woman a promotion. However, a 6–3 decision by the Supreme Court has held that when a woman shows that gender played a motivating part in an unfavorable employment decision, the employer may avoid a finding of liability by proving that it would have made the same decision even if it had not allowed gender to play a role. The plurality of four, plus a concurrence by Justice O'Connor, agreed that employers have to prove their case by a preponderance of the evidence. Price Waterhouse v. Hopkins, 109 S.Ct. 1775 (1989). See also Mt. Healthy City Board of Education v. Doyle, 429 U.S. 274 (1977).

Although some private clubs and organizations have the constitutional freedom of association to exclude women, organizations can be required to accept women when the organizational purpose concerns economic advancement of its members through the use of commercial programs and benefits. Roberts v. United States Jaycees, 468 U.S. 609, 626 (1984). Rotary Clubs, because of their assistance to businesses and professions, have been forced to admit women as members. Bd. of Dirs. of Rotary Int'l v. Rotary Club, 481 U.S. 537 (1987). Other organizations, including the Kiwanis International and the Lions Club International, now accept female members. In 1988, a unanimous Court upheld a New York City law that prohibited discrimination based on sex in any private club with more than 400 members involved directly or indirectly in furthering trade or business. New York State Club Assn. v. City of New York, 108 S. Ct. 2225 (1988).

Discriminatory pension funds have been abolished. Employers may not require female workers to make larger contributions to a pension fund than male workers simply because females on average live longer. Los Angeles Dept. of Water & Power v. Manhart, 435 U.S. 702 (1978). Nor may compensation plans pay lower monthly retirement benefits to a woman than to a man on the ground that women on average have a greater life expectancy. Arizona Governing Committee v. Norris, 463 U.S. 1073 (1983). The retroactivity of these judicial decisions was determined by Florida v. Long, 108 S.Ct. 2354 (1988).

Title VII of the Civil Rights Act of 1964 is not limited to economic or "tangible" discrimination. A claim of "hostile environment" because of sexual harassment by a supervisor is a valid basis for a lawsuit. Meritor Savings Bank v. Vinson, 477 U.S. 57 (1986). Title VII does not require absolute equality between the sexes. In their employment actions, government agencies and private employers may discriminate on the basis of sex if there are "bona fide occupational qualifications" (bfoq's). Obvious examples include male and female actors, male and female models, and wet nurses. See Dothard v. Rawlinson, 433 U.S. 321 (1977).

Discriminations Against Men

Sex discrimination may injure men as well as women. In 1972, the Court struck down an Illinois law that took children from the custody of an unwed father without a hearing, although a hearing was required for an unwed mother. Under state law, his fitness as a father was irrelevant. This procedure violated the Equal Protection Clause of the Fourteenth Amendment. Stanley v. Illinois, 405 U.S. 645 (1972). In cases where an unwed father fails to legitimate a child or take responsibility for the child's care, states can use a "best interests of the child" standard in permitting only the mother's consent for the adoption of an illegitimate child. Quilloin v. Walcott, 434 U.S. 246 (1978); Lehr v. Robertson, 463 U.S. 248 (1983). Variations on this issue can send the Court scattering in various directions. Compare Caban v. Mohammed, 441 U.S. 380 (1979) with Parham v. Hughes, 441 U.S. 347 (1979).[3]

Under a social security law struck down by a unanimous Court in 1975, a man's benefits went to both the widow and the children. If the wife died, the benefits went only to the children, not to the widower. This law violated the Equal Protection Clause by giving a female wage earner and the male survivor less protection. Weinberger v. Wiesenfeld, 420 U.S. 636 (1975). In another social security case, Congress provided benefits to the widow regardless of dependency. However, if the wife died, the widower received benefits only if he was receiving at least half of his support from her. The Court held this an invidious and unconstitutional discrimination. Califano v. Goldfarb, 430 U.S. 199 (1977). In that same year, however, the Court upheld a social security law in which Congress deliberately used classification by gender to compensate for previous economic discrimination against women. Califano v. Webster, 430 U.S. 313 (1977).

An Oklahoma law was invalidated in 1976 on equal protection grounds. It prohibited the sale of 3.2 percent beer to males under 21 while allowing females at age 18 to purchase the beer. The Court dismissed as inconsequential the slight percentage difference between females and males arrested for drunk driving. CRAIG v. BOREN, 429 U.S. 190 (1976). A Missouri law was struck down because it denied a widower the benefits from his wife's work-related death unless he was mentally or physically incapacitated or could prove dependence on the wife's

---

[3]In 1968, the Supreme Court ruled that an illegitimate child is a "person" under the Fourteenth Amendment and capable of challenging practices and laws as a denial of equal protection. Levy v. Louisiana, 391 U.S. 68 (1968). The rights of illegitimate children have been further explored and defined in Glona v. American Guarantee Co., 391 U.S. 73 (1968); Labine v. Vincent, 401 U.S. 532 (1971); Weber v. Aetna Casualty & Surety Co., 406 U.S. 164 (1972); Gomez v. Perez, 409 U.S. 535 (1973); New Jersey Welfare Rights Org. v. Cahill, 411 U.S. 619 (1973); Jimenez v. Weinberger, 417 U.S. 628 (1974); Mathews v. Lucas, 427 U.S. 495 (1976); Norton v. Mathews, 427 U.S. 524 (1976); Trimble v. Gordon, 430 U.S. 762 (1977); Mills v. Habluetzel, 456 U.S. 91 (1982); Pickett v. Brown, 462 U.S. 1 (1983).

earnings. No such test was required for widows. Wengler v. Druggists Mutual Ins. Co., 446 U.S. 142 (1980).

Alimony laws were successfully challenged. In 1979, the Court held that an Alabama statute violated the Equal Protection Clause by requiring husbands, but not wives, to pay alimony. Although assisting needy spouses is "a legitimate and important governmental objective," needy males along with needy females can be helped "with little if any additional burden on the State." Orr v. Orr, 440 U.S. 268, 280–281 (1979).

In 1982, the Court held that a state-supported university could not limit its nursing school to women. The school attempted to justify its admission policy as compensation for past discrimination against women, but the Court concluded that the policy merely perpetuated the stereotype that nursing is exclusively a woman's job. The decision applied only to professional nursing schools; other single-sex colleges are not affected by the ruling. Mississippi University for Women v. Hogan, 458 U.S. 718 (1982).

Some sexual stereotypes persist. In 1974, the Court upheld a Florida statute that granted widows an annual $500 property tax exemption but denied widowers the same benefit. According to the Court, the law was reasonably designed to further the state's policy of cushioning the financial impact when a spouse dies. The Court accepted the generalization that widows are more needy than widowers, even if some heiresses and rich widows have no need for largess from the state. Kahn v. Shevin, 416 U.S. 351 (1974).

State laws on "statutory rape"—sexual intercourse with a female under 18 who is not the wife of the perpetrator—have been upheld even though they discriminate on the basis of gender. Men alone are criminally liable. These laws are based on the premise that young women (but not young men) are legally incapable of consenting to sex. MICHAEL M. v. SONOMA COUNTY SUPERIOR COURT, 450 U.S. 464 (1981).

In another decision in 1981, the Court again placed its imprimatur on discrimination between men and women. By a 6–3 majority it upheld the decision of Congress to require registration of males, but not females, for possible military service. The Court deferred to congressional judgment on this constitutional question, claiming unconvincingly that the exemption for women was not the "accidental byproduct of a traditional way of thinking about females." ROSTKER v. GOLDBERG, 453 U.S. 57, 74 (1981).[4]

Preferential Hiring

Despite efforts to eliminate gender-based employment, a person's sex may still be a factor in hiring decisions. In 1979, the Court upheld a Massachusetts law that gave a lifetime preference to veterans for state jobs. Although a woman received higher test scores than her male competitors, they were entitled under state laws to be considered first if they were veterans. The Court rationalized that the law distinguished between veterans and nonveterans, not men and women. While necessarily admitting that the statute "today benefits an overwhelmingly male class," the Court

---

[4]On the question of granting wives a portion of their husbands' military retired pay (required by certain state laws), the Court has held that federal law preempts state action. McCarty v. McCarty, 453 U.S. 210 (1981).

announced that the law was "neutral on its face." PERSONNEL ADMINISTRATOR OF MASS. v. FEENEY, 442 U.S. 256, 269, 274 (1979).

In 1987, the Court issued a major decision that supported affirmative action programs to hire women. An agency in California had employed 238 workers in a skilled craft position; all had been men. The company took gender into account in selecting the first woman, even though a man had scored slightly higher during an interview. The Court allowed employers to consider as one factor the sex of a qualified applicant. JOHNSON v. TRANSPORTATION AGENCY, 480 U.S. 616 (1987).

Pregnancy

The rights of pregnant women have proved particularly troublesome for Congress and the courts. Total elimination of gender-based discrimination would make it impossible to address the special needs of pregnant workers. In 1974, by a 7–2 majority, the Court struck down the policy of requiring pregnant teachers to quit their jobs without pay several months before expecting a child. Some states forced teachers to quit as much as five months before the delivery date, all done on the quaint ground that schoolchildren should be spared the sight of a pregnant woman. Cleveland Board of Education v. LaFleur, 414 U.S. 632 (1974).

The question of paying benefits to pregnant women was more difficult to resolve. A California law paid benefits to persons temporarily disabled from working and not covered by workmen's compensation. Payment was not made for certain disabilities attributable to pregnancy. The Court upheld the statute in *Geduldig* v. *Aiello*, 417 U.S. 484 (1974). Building on this precedent, two years later the Court supported a company's disability plan that gave benefits for nonoccupational sickness and accidents but not for disabilities arising from pregnancy. The Court decided that the plan did not violate Title VII of the Civil Rights Act of 1964. General Electric Co. v. Gilbert, 429 U.S. 125 (1976). This decision was "distinguished" a year later when the Court held that a company policy on leave of absence for pregnant workers violated Title VII. Nashville Gas Co. v. Satty, 434 U.S. 136 (1977).

Congress passed legislation in 1978 to reverse *Gilbert*. The statute amended Title VII to prohibit employment discrimination on the basis of pregnancy and to require fringe benefit and insurance plans to cover pregnant workers. 92 Stat. 2076 (1978). When a company responded to this statute by amending its health insurance plan to provide female workers with hospitalization benefits for pregnancy-related conditions, it provided less extensive pregnancy benefits for the wives of male employees. The Court held that this plan discriminated against male employees in violation of Title VII of the Civil Rights Act of 1964. Newport News Shipbuilding & Dry Dock v. EEOC, 462 U.S. 669 (1983).

In 1987, the Court upheld state laws that require employers to give female workers an unpaid pregnancy disability leave and guarantee them their jobs when they return. The Court ruled that these laws, granting greater benefits to pregnant women than under the 1978 congressional statute, are not preempted by federal action. Moreover, the state laws necessarily discriminate on the basis of sex because pregnant women are given preferential treatment not available to other workers. California Federal S. & L. v. Guerra, 479 U.S. 272 (1987). See also Wimberly v. Labor & Industrial Rel. Comm'n, 479 U.S. 511 (1987).

Title IX Actions

By enacting Title IX of the Education Amendments of 1972, Congress announced that it would withdraw federal financial assistance from any educational institution that practiced sex discrimination. The Court interprets Title IX broadly to apply not only to students but to employees as well. *North Haven Board of Education v. Bell*, 456 U.S. 512 (1982). Enforcement of Title IX depends largely on the executive branch, but private parties have a right of action to bring disputes to the courts. *Cannon v. University of Chicago*, 441 U.S. 677 (1979).

In 1984 the Court construed Title IX narrowly. The educational institution, Grove City College, did not accept direct federal assistance but some of its students received federal grants. The Court held that the student aid triggered Title IX. However, it declined to make the coverage institutionwide. Title IX therefore applied only to the financial aid program, not to other activities at the college. *Grove City College v. Bell*, 465 U.S. 555 (1984). This meant that Title IX could be used to withhold funds only from the particular program or activity that practiced sex discrimination; federal funds would continue to flow to other programs and activities at the school. Congress tried repeatedly to pass legislation to reverse the decision, but action was stalled by numerous complications, especially language dealing with abortion. In 1988, Congress managed to pass legislation overturning *Grove City*, thereby enacting broad coverage for civil rights. President Reagan vetoed the bill but was overridden.

JUSTICE FOR JUVENILES

Rights for juveniles date largely from the 1960s, although cases decided before that time recognized certain elementary rights. In 1943 the Supreme Court, after first upholding a compulsory flag salute in public schools, declared that it unconstitutionally infringed on a child's free exercise of religion. *West Virginia Board of Education v. Barnette*, 319 U.S. 624 (1943), overturning *Minersville v. Gobitis*, 310 U.S. 586 (1940). Youths charged with serious offenses were protected by basic rules against coerced confessions. *Haley v. Ohio*, 332 U.S. 596 (1948). Children in public schools had a right to be free of segregation. *Brown v. Board of Education*, 347 U.S. 483 (1954).

For most of our history, juvenile rights depended on a paternalistic system. Under the doctrine *parens patriae*, with the government taking the role as parent, juvenile courts served as guardians for youthful offenders. Procedural rights and protections were considered unnecessary because the judge would act in the best interest of the child. In many cases, however, judges acted arbitrarily and harshly toward juveniles, meting out periods of incarceration that exceeded the penalties imposed on adults for the same crime.

Congress passed several statutes during the 1960s to deal with the mounting problem of juvenile delinquency. 75 Stat. 572 (1961); 82 Stat. 462 (1968). Beginning in 1971, the Senate Judiciary Committee held a series of hearings on juvenile delinquency and the methods used for treatment and rehabilitation. With Senator Birch Bayh serving as chairman, the hearings revealed widespread inadequacies in correctional facilities. Eight-year-old youths were placed in these institutions for several years at a time. Initial efforts to protect the constitutional rights of juveniles centered on procedural safeguards, but later spread to free speech, privacy, and other elements of due process.

Criminal Procedures

Many of the procedural safeguards available to adults now protect the rights of juveniles. A 1948 case involved a fifteen-year-old boy who was arrested about midnight on a charge of murder. He was questioned by relays of police from that point until about 5 a.m., without benefit of counsel or friends to advise him. After the police told him that his friends had confessed to the crime, he signed a confession and was later convicted. He was not taken before a magistrate and formally charged with a crime until three days after his confession. A lawyer tried to see him twice but the police refused. The Court held his confession inadmissible. Haley v. Ohio, 332 U.S. 596 (1948). Similar circumstances led the Court to declare inadmissible the confession of a fourteen-year-old boy held for five days without seeing a lawyer, parent, or other friendly adult, although his mother tried twice to see him. Gallegos v. Colorado, 370 U.S. 49 (1962).

After these cases, the Court began to challenge some conventional notions about the protections accorded by juvenile courts. In theory, juvenile courts acted toward a child in a "parental" relationship and not as adversary. Since the proceedings were civil in nature and not criminal, the youth had no opportunity to complain that basic rights of criminal law had been denied.

A major breakthrough occurred in 1966. A sixteen-year-old was accused of housebreaking, robbery, and rape. He was committed to the juvenile court unless it waived jurisdiction after "full investigation" and assigned his case to a federal court. Jurisdiction was waived; he was indicted and convicted. The Court held that such waivers were invalid unless the juvenile received a hearing and his counsel had access to social records and probation reports. Moreover, the juvenile court had to give reasons for a waiver. Under the system existing at that time, a child received "the worst of both worlds: that he gets neither the protections accorded to adults nor the solicitous care and regenerative treatment postulated for children." Kent v. United States, 383 U.S. 541, 556 (1966).

After these ad hoc efforts to protect the rights of juveniles, the Court took a more comprehensive approach in 1967. Gerald Gault, a fifteen-year-old, was taken into custody for allegedly making obscene phone calls. No notice was left at his home for his parents. After hearings, a juvenile court committed him to the State Industrial School until he reached majority (a commitment of almost six years). No appeal was permitted by state law for juvenile cases. The Supreme Court held that minors are entitled to certain procedural rights: adequate notice, right to counsel, privilege against self-incrimination, and the rights of confrontation and sworn testimony. IN RE GAULT, 387 U.S. 1 (1967).

Closely resembling this case was the decision of a state family court to place a twelve-year-old boy in a "training school" for up to six years for stealing $112 from a woman's pocketbook. The Supreme Court held that when a juvenile is charged with an act that would constitute a crime if committed by an adult, due process requires proof beyond a reasonable doubt during the adjudicatory phase. The family court had relied on a preponderance of the evidence. In re Winship, 397 U.S. 358 (1970).

Other rights have been recognized for juveniles. A case in 1975 involved a youth who had been prosecuted as an adult following a finding in juvenile court that he violated a criminal law and was unfit for treatment as a juvenile. The Supreme Court held that the procedure violated the Double Jeopardy Clause. Breed v. Jones, 421 U.S. 519 (1975). See also Swisher v. Brady, 438 U.S. 204 (1978). Questions also concern the *Miranda* warning, Fare v. Michael C., 442 U.S. 707 (1979), and pretrial detention for juvenile delinquents, Schall v. Martin, 467 U.S. 253 (1984).

In extending these rights to juveniles, the Court decided that a jury trial is not constitutionally required for a state juvenile court delinquency proceeding. At least in this area, the Court was "reluctant to disallow the States to experiment further and to seek in new and different ways the elusive answers to the problems of the young . . ." McKeiver v. Pennsylvania, 403 U.S. 528, 547 (1971). See also DeBacker v. Brainard, 396 U.S. 28 (1969). In 1988, the Supreme Court vacated the death sentence of someone who had participated in a murder at age 15. However, a majority of the Court did not agree that the Constitution prohibits the execution of persons who were under 16 at the time of the offense. Although there appears to be a national consensus against executing such minors, the Court allowed state legislatures leeway in determining standards and punishment. Thompson v. Oklahoma, 108 S.Ct. 2687 (1988).

A year later, five Justices of the Supreme Court affirmed the death sentence for Kevin Stanford (17 at the time he committed murder) and Heath Wilkins (16 when he committed murder). In its search for objective criteria to decide the constitutional issue, the Court looked to statutes passed by state legislatures. As Justice Scalia noted with his usual crisp style: "The audience for these arguments, in other words, is not this Court but the citizenry of the United States. It is they, not we, who must be persuaded. . . . our job is to *identify* the 'evolving standards of decency'; to determine, not what they *should* be, but what they *are*." Justice O'Connor joined the majority but wrote a concurrence which rejected Scalia's deference to majority opinion. The Court, she said, has a constitutional obligation to determine that a punishment is proportional to the crime. Stanford v. Kentucky, 109 S.Ct. 2969 (1989).

Student Rights

School authorities and judges have wrestled with novel questions about a student's rights to free speech, due process, and protection against cruel and unusual punishment (corporal punishment), and the scope of search and seizure on school premises.

In a leading First Amendment case, public school children were suspended from a junior high school for wearing black arm bands to protest the Vietnam war. The Court held that their conduct, which was quiet and not disruptive, was protected by the Free Speech Clause of the First Amendment and the Due Process Clause of the Fourteenth Amendment. TINKER v. DES MOINES SCHOOL DIST., 393 U.S. 503 (1969). In deciding which books to remove from school libraries, a board of education may not suppress ideas and impose an orthodoxy. Board of Education v. Pico, 457 U.S. 853 (1982). High school students have successfully resorted to lawsuits to gain the right to hold religious club meetings in school rooms. Bender v. Williamsport Area School Dist., 475 U.S. 534 (1986).

Juveniles do not automatically gain access to First Amendment rights available to adults. States may restrict minors under 17 from reading materials that are not obscene for adults. Ginsberg v. New York, 390 U.S. 629 (1968). Schools may discipline students for lewd and indecent speech that would be permissible for adults. Bethel School Dist. No. 403 v. Fraser, 478 U.S. 675 (1986). School officials may delete from student newspapers articles or stories that might identify and embarrass certain students (such as pregnant students) or that are one-sided accounts critical of parents. Schools can exercise editorial control over the style and content of student speech in school-sponsored newspapers so long as the control is reasonably related to legitimate educational concerns. Hazelwood School District v. Kulhmeier, 108 S.Ct. 562 (1988). In response to this restrictive ruling on students' rights, some states have begun to pass legislation that permits greater freedom of speech by students.

Before students can be suspended from public school, they must be given an informal opportunity to be heard. On the basis of state law, students have legitimate claims of entitlement to a public education, and this entitlement is a property interest protected by the Due Process Clause. "Neither the property interest in educational benefits temporarily denied nor the liberty interest in reputation, which is also implicated, is so insubstantial that suspensions may constitutionally be imposed by any procedure the school chooses, no matter how arbitrary." Goss v. Lopez, 419 U.S. 565, 576 (1975).

The Court split 5–4 on this decision, and divided by the same margin in holding that the Cruel and Unusual Punishment Clause does not apply to disciplinary corporal punishments in public schools. The state law authorized a wooden paddle applied against the buttocks. The evidence in this case showed that the paddling was exceptionally harsh, keeping the child out of school for several days. Nevertheless, the Court held that the Eighth Amendment deals only with criminal punishments. Ingraham v. Wright, 430 U.S. 651 (1977).

Another issue is search and seizure. In 1985, the Court decided that the Fourth Amendment applies to minors on public school property. Although teachers need not obtain a warrant or adhere to the probable cause requirement, their actions must be reasonable under the circumstances in order to search students. NEW JERSEY v. T.L.O, 469 U.S. 325 (1985). For the use of German shepherds to perform "sniff tests" while searching students for drugs in junior and senior high schools, see Doe v. Renfrow, 451 U.S. 1022 (1981).

Other decisions on the rights of juveniles, involving questions of abortion and privacy, are reserved for the next chapter.

PRISONER RIGHTS

Prisoners along with inmates of mental institutions have been kept in a constitutional backwater. Legislators have little incentive to provide adequate funds for shelter, food, clothing, and medical care. Constituents are content, perhaps out of ignorance, to have public funds spent elsewhere.[5] Congressman Robert Kastenmeier reflected on his service as chairman of the Subcommittee on Corrections of the House Judiciary Committee: "few organizations have lobbied for prison reform. This apparent lack of interest creates little external pressure for action, while there is

[5]For basic cases on the rights of inmates in mental institutions, see Youngberg v. Romeo, 457 U.S. 307 (1982); Mills v. Rogers, 457 U.S. 291 (1982); Vitek v. Jones, 445 U.S. 480 (1980); Secretary of Public Welfare v. Institutionalized Juveniles, 442 U.S. 640 (1979); Parham v. J.R., 442 U.S. 584 (1979); O'Connor v. Donaldson, 422 U.S. 563 (1975).

growing and vocal opposition to penal reform based on the widespread sentiment that high crime rates can only be reduced by long and harsh incarceration."[6] Because of the crimes they committed, prisoners are considered undeserving of even minimal care. At one time in our history, an inmate in a penitentiary was considered "the slave of the State." Ruffin v. Commonwealth, 62 Va. 790, 796 (1871).

Litigation has been the chief instrument for initiating prison reform. In the 1960s, professional journals began to focus on the primitive and unconscionable conditions in mental hospitals and prisons. Out of these studies came the concept of a right to treatment for institutionalized persons. U.S. Judge David Bazelon pioneered some of the reforms in mental hospitals, ruling in 1966 that a failure to provide suitable treatment would justify a patient's release. Rouse v. Cameron, 373 F.2d 451 (D.C. Cir. 1966). A few years later, U.S. Judge Frank Johnson held that inadequate treatment for institutionalized persons represented a violation of the basic fundamentals of due process. Wyatt v. Stickney, 325 F.Supp. 781 (M.D. Ala. 1971). It is difficult to criticize Johnson's efforts as an exercise in "judicial activism." The counsel for the state admitted in open court that the evidence conclusively established violations of the Eighth Amendment rights of prisoners. Pugh v. Locke, 406 F.Supp. 318, 322, 329 n.13 (M.D. Ala. 1976). (For additional material on Johnson's efforts, see pp. 16–17, 35–40.)

Even before the attention devoted to prisoner rights in recent years, certain rights were conceded. States cannot impair a prisoner's right to apply to the federal courts for a writ of habeas corpus.[7] Prisoners must be given a reasonable opportunity to pursue their religious faith, but prison officials are not expected to sacrifice their legitimate objectives in accommodating every religious need. O'Lone v. Estate of Shabazz, 482 U.S. 342 (1987); Cruz v. Beto, 405 U.S. 319 (1972); Cooper v. Pate, 378 U.S. 546 (1964). Prisoners may not be segregated by race. Lee v. Washington, 390 U.S. 333 (1968). A prisoner's desire to marry may not be prevented by prison regulations that rely on an exaggerated and unreasonable concern for security. Turner v. Safley, 482 U.S. 78 (1987); Butler v. Wilson, 415 U.S. 953 (1974), aff'd, Johnson v. Rockefeller, 365 F.Supp. 377 (S.D. N.Y. 1973).

Due Process Protections

Beginning in the early 1970s, the Supreme Court announced a series of new rights for prisoners and parolees. Authorities may no longer revoke paroles and return a person to prison without an informal hearing. The parolee must be given written notice of claimed violations, the evidence against him, an opportunity to be heard, to present witnesses and evidence, and to confront and cross-examine adverse witnesses. Morrissey v. Brewer, 408 U.S. 471 (1972). Parole *revocation* is a serious deprivation of liberty, requiring procedural protections, but the possible *granting* of parole does not create the same entitlement of due process. Greenholtz v. Nebraska Penal Inmates, 442 U.S. 1 (1979).

[6]Robert W. Kasternmeier, "The Legislator and the Legislature: Their Roles in Prison Reform," in Michele G. Hermann and Marilyn G. Haft, eds., Prisoners' Rights Sourcebook 456 (1973).

[7]Ex parte Hull, 312 U.S. 546 (1941); Johnson v. Avery, 393 U.S. 483 (1969). See also Procunier v. Martinez, 416 U.S. 421 (1974), in which the Court held that a ban on attorney-client interviews conducted by law students or paralegals constituted an unjustifiable restriction on the inmates' right of access to the courts. States must even assist inmates in preparing and filing legal papers by providing adequate law libraries and assistance from persons trained in the law. Bounds v. Smith, 430 U.S. 817 (1977).

Congress and the executive branch were embroiled in parole issues during President Reagan's first year in office. The U.S. Parole Commission, an independent agency within the executive branch, is responsible for granting, denying, or revoking parole for federal prisoners. Reagan tried to remove one of the Democratic commissioners but backed off after one member went to court and legislators from both Houses criticized Reagan's effort to interfere with the Commission's independence.

Due process does not require a state prisoner to be given a hearing simply because he is being transferred to a prison with less favorable conditions. Meachum v. Fano, 427 U.S. 215 (1976); Montanye v. Haymes, 427 U.S. 236 (1976). These transfers, whether intrastate or interstate, do not invoke a liberty interest protected by the Due Process Clause. Olim v. Wakinekona, 461 U.S. 238 (1983). Only informal, nonadversary review is required before placing a prisoner in confinement, provided he receives notice of the charges and has an opportunity to present his views. Hewitt v. Helms, 459 U.S. 460 (1983).

If a state creates the right to "good time" credits (to reduce a sentence), a prisoner is entitled to minimal procedures to insure that this right is not arbitrarily abrogated. The prisoner must be given advance written notice of the claimed violation, a statement of the evidence, and the reasons for the disciplinary action. The inmate has a right to call witnesses and to present evidence; there is no right of confrontation and cross-examination. Wolff v. McDonnell, 418 U.S. 539 (1974).[8]

Prison Conditions

Prisoners do not have the same rights as other citizens regarding privacy and First Amendment freedoms. Their letters may be turned over and given to government officials. Stroud v. United States, 251 U.S. 15 (1919). Prison officials may censor or restrict personal correspondence if necessary for security, order, and the rehabilitation of inmates. Turner v. Safley, 482 U.S. 78 (1987); Procunier v. Martinez, 416 U.S. 396 (1974). The Supreme Court defers considerably to prison officials who monitor and exclude incoming publications that they find detrimental to the "security, good order, or discipline" of the institution. Prisoners have greater First Amendment rights with regard to *outgoing* correspondence because it presents less of a risk to institutional security. Thornburgh v. Abbott, 109 S.Ct. 1874 (1989). Prisoners have no right to "contact visits" (physical touching) with their spouses, relatives, children, or friends. This privilege may be denied by prison officials concerned about the introduction of drugs, weapons, and other contraband. Block v. Rutherford, 468 U.S. 576 (1984). In deciding which visitors to exclude, prison officials are not bound by the Due Process Clause (such as providing a hearing before the exclusion). Kentucky Dept. of Corrections v. Thompson, 109 S.Ct. 1904 (1989).

Conversations may be monitored and intercepted through electronic listening

---

[8]In 1973, the Court held that prisoners who lose "good time" credits because of disciplinary reasons must use the remedy of a writ of habeas corpus. They were not allowed to rely on 42 U.S.C. § 1983 suits in an effort to circumvent the state courts. Preiser v. Rodriguez, 411 U.S. 475 (1973). Prisoners have brought § 1983 suits since that time, but not with successful results. O'Lone v. Estate of Shabazz, 482 U.S. 342 (1987); Whitley v. Albers, 475 U.S. 312 (1986); Davidson v. Cannon, 474 U.S. 344 (1986); Daniels v. Williams, 474 U.S. 327 (1986); Hudson v. Palmer, 468 U.S. 517 (1984); Rhodes v. Chapman, 452 U.S. 337 (1981); Parratt v. Taylor, 451 U.S. 527 (1981).

devices. Lanza v. New York, 370 U.S. 139 (1962). Because the Court holds that prisoners have no reasonable expectation of privacy in their prison cells, they are not entitled to Fourth Amendment protections against unreasonable searches. HUDSON v. PALMER, 468 U.S. 517 (1984); Brock v. Rutherford, 468 U.S. 576 (1984).

Although the press has an interest in reporting on prison conditions, the government may prohibit interviews between newsmen and inmates in medium-security and maximum-security prisons. Houchins v. KQED, Inc., 438 U.S. 1 (1978); Saxbe v. Washington Post, 417 U.S. 843 (1974); Pell v. Procunier, 417 U.S. 817 (1974). States may prohibit prisoners from soliciting other inmates to join the prisoners' labor union, from holding union meetings, and from making and receiving bulk mailings concerning the union. Jones v. North Carolina Prisoners' Union, 433 U.S. 119 (1977).

In some cases, the judiciary intervenes to put pressure on states to upgrade their prison facilities. The Supreme Court upheld a court order placing a maximum limit of thirty days for Arkansas' isolation cells. Confinement beyond that period constituted cruel and unusual punishment. Conditions in the Arkansas prisons, with a history of overcrowding, physical violence, and malnutrition, were described as "a dark and evil world completely alien to the free world." Hutto v. Finney, 437 U.S. 678, 681 (1978).

For the most part, the judiciary defers to prison officials on questions of "double-bunking," body-cavity searches, and restrictions on incoming packages. BELL v. WOLFISH, 441 U.S. 520 (1979). See also Rhodes v. Chapman, 452 U.S. 337 (1981). Prison rules and regulations are not subject to strict-scrutiny analysis. The Court applies a lesser and more lenient standard of scrutiny. Turner v. Safley, 482 U.S. 78 (1987). The Court recognizes that running a prison "is an inordinately difficult undertaking that requires expertise, planning, and the commitment of resources, all of which are peculiarly within the province of the legislative and executive branches of government." Id. at 84–85.

RIGHTS OF THE POOR

The Constitution extends rights to all persons. The full realization of those rights, however, often depends on one's income. The Sixth Amendment guarantees that the accused may have the assistance of counsel. It did not require the government to provide counsel to a defendant unable to afford an attorney. Not until 1963, in *Gideon* v. *Wainwright,* did the Supreme Court rule that the government must provide a lawyer if an indigent person is accused of a felony. As explained in Chapter 13, this right has been expanded by subsequent decisions. Similarly, in *Harper* v. *Virginia Board of Elections* (1966), the Court struck down the poll tax, concluding that lines drawn on the basis of wealth or property, like those of race, "are traditionally disfavored."

The fact that these decisions did not come until the 1960s suggests a quite different conclusion: tradition has very much favored the distribution of justice on the basis of wealth. Anatole France made his famous remark about the law, "in all its majestic equality," prohibiting both rich and poor from sleeping under bridges, begging in the streets, and stealing bread. Even with a court-appointed attorney, an indigent defendant is unlikely to fare as well as the wealthy defendant capable of hiring three or four attorneys from a major law firm. By creating the Legal Services Corporation in 1974, Congress attempted to provide financial support for legal assistance for low-income people, but this program is designed only for noncriminal proceedings and is funded at minimal levels.

Welfare Rights

There is no constitutional right to receive welfare payments or other forms of public assistance for the indigent. The extent of public funding for these purposes is determined by legislative action. Once granted, however, assistance may be terminated only by observing procedural safeguards. In 1970, the Supreme Court held that individuals receiving financial aid under the federally assisted Aid to Families with Dependent Children (AFDC) program or under New York's general home-relief program could not have their assistance terminated without prior notice and hearing. Although welfare benefits are a matter of statutory entitlement, to be decided by the legislative and executive branches, procedural due process is applicable to the termination of benefits. Goldberg v. Kelly, 397 U.S. 254 (1970). In the case of disability benefits, the Court has ruled that an evidentiary hearing is not required before the initial termination of benefits. The Court distinguished *Goldberg* on the ground that welfare recipients have greater financial need than the disabled. Mathews v. Eldridge, 424 U.S. 319 (1976).

The Court has reviewed state restrictions that make people ineligible for welfare benefits. One-year residency requirements were struck down as an unconstitutional interference with the right of interstate movement. Shapiro v. Thompson, 394 U.S. 618 (1969). Applying the same principle, states may not require a year's residence in a county as a condition for an indigent to receive nonemergency hospitalization or medical care at the county's expense. Memorial Hospital v. Maricopa County, 415 U.S. 250 (1974).

For the most part, judges confine their review of welfare rights to questions of statutory interpretation and congressional intent, not constitutional law. The Supreme Court decided that an Alabama regulation, denying AFDC payments to the children of a mother who kept "a man in the house," was inconsistent with federal law. King v. Smith, 392 U.S. 309 (1968). On the other hand, state efforts to impose a ceiling on AFDC payments, regardless of family size or need, have been sustained as not prohibited by federal law. Dandridge v. Williams, 397 U.S. 471 (1970). The "intractable economic, social, and even philosophical problems presented by public welfare assistance programs are not the business of this Court." Id. at 487.[9]

In 1971, the Court confronted the sensitive issue of caseworkers entering the home of a welfare recipient. New York required caseworkers to visit beneficiaries during working hours and prohibited forcible entry and snooping. A beneficiary under the AFDC program refused to admit caseworkers, contending that home visitation amounted to a search and required either consent or a warrant supported by probable cause. The Court, divided 6–3, decided that constitutional rights had not been violated. Home visitation is not a search within the traditional criminal law context of the Fourth Amendment. Wyman v. James, 400 U.S. 309 (1971).

---

[9]For other statutory interpretations of the AFDC program, see Bowen v. Gilliard, 483 U.S. 587 (1987); Quern v. Mandley, 436 U.S. 725 (1978); Philbrook v. Glodgett, 421 U.S. 707 (1975); Burns v. Alcala, 420 U.S. 575 (1975); Jefferson v. Hackney, 406 U.S. 535 (1972); Townsend v. Swank, 404 U.S. 282 (1971); Rosado v. Wyman, 397 U.S. 397 (1970).

In that same year the Court, with only Justice Black dissenting, ruled that due process is denied by refusing indigents (including welfare recipients) access to the courts to dissolve a marriage simply because of their inability to pay court fees and costs. Such a policy amounts to denying them an opportunity to be heard. Boddie v. Connecticut, 401 U.S. 371 (1971). On other matters the Court has upheld filing fees for indigents when the fee "does not rise to the same constitutional level" as in *Boddie*, especially where alternative procedures are available without payment of a fee. Ortwein v. Schwab, 410 U.S. 656 (1973); United States v. Kras, 409 U.S. 434 (1973).

School Financing

The Supreme Court split 5–4 on a major case in 1973 involving the financing of public schools. In Texas, half of the revenues for public elementary and secondary schools came from a state-funded program. Each district then supplemented that amount through an ad valorem tax on property within its jurisdiction. The higher the value of the properties, the higher the supplement. Rich communities could therefore support better schools than poor neighborhoods. A class action brought by Mexican-American parents argued that the system violated the Equal Protection Clause by favoring students in more affluent districts. The Court held that the system does not disadvantage any suspect class. The fundamental right of education is not interfered with, said the Court, if state-supported revenues assure at least a minimum education. With respect to wealth, the Court announced that the Equal Protection Clause does not require absolute equality of precisely equal advantages. San Antonio School District v. Rodriguez, 411 U.S. 1 (1973).

Justice Marshall, penning one of the dissents, pointed to the inconsistency between this decision and the cases on desegregation: "even before this Court recognized its duty to tear down the barriers of state-enforced racial segregation in public education, it acknowledged that inequality in the educational facilities provided to students may be discriminatory state action as contemplated by the Equal Protection Clause." Id. at 84. However, the Court may have concluded that it lacked the legitimacy or power to dictate funding levels in public schools throughout the states.

State courts have reached different results. The Supreme Court of New Jersey reviewed the state's system of financing public education, which relied heavily on local taxation to cover public school costs and created substantial variations in spending per pupil. The court held that the system violated the provision in the state constitution that requires the state to furnish "thorough and efficient" public schooling. The New Jersey court explained why it could be more demanding on the question of equal protection than the U.S. Supreme Court: "For one thing, there is absent the principle of federalism which cautions against too expansive a view of a federal constitutional limitation upon the power and opportunity of the several States to cope with their own problems in the light of their own circumstances." Robinson v. Cahill, 303 A.2d 273, 282 (N.J. 1973), cert. denied sub nom. Dickey v. Robinson, 414 U.S. 976 (1973).

Four years later, the Supreme Court of California invalidated the state's system of financing public schools because it denied equal protection. By conditioning the availability of school revenues upon the wealth of a district, the system produced unconstitutional disparities in expenditures and quality of education. The state judiciary, by restricting the legal issue to the state constitution, could reach a different result than the U.S. Supreme Court. Serrano v. Priest, 557 P.2d 929 (Cal. 1977). In that same year, the Supreme Court of Connecticut struck down the state's system for financing elementary and secondary education. The reliance on property taxes could not pass the test of "strict judicial scrutiny" or satisfy the state's obligation to provide a substantially equal educational opportunity to its youth. Horton v. Meskill, 376 A.2d 359, 374–375 (Conn. 1977). The Wyoming judiciary issued a similar ruling. Washakie Co. Sch. Dist. No. One v. Herschler, 606 P.2d 310 (Wyo. 1980), cert. denied, 449 U.S. 824 (1980).

Over the next decade, state legislatures restructured their financing systems to provide more equitable funding for schools in poorer communities. Litigation continues, however, to test the constitutionality of school financing. In 1987, a state judge in Texas ruled that the state system of funding public schools discriminates against students in property-poor districts. Average spending in the poorest districts was $2,978 per student; for the 100 wealthiest districts the average spending was $7,233. Washington Post, April 30, 1987, at A22. In 1989, the Kentucky Supreme Court declared the state's public school system unconstitutional because of spending disparities between rich and poor districts. Although suits of this nature are often brought by blacks and Mexican-Americans, the plaintiffs in the Kentucky case were overwhelmingly white and rural. Washington Post, June 9, 1989, at A-16. A 1988 ruling by the U.S Supreme Court emphasized once again that the commitment to education in *Brown* v. *Board of Education* has limited reach. Split 5–4, the Court ruled that education is not a "fundamental right" and that states can require even poor families to pay a fee for bus service to public schools. Kadrmas v. Dickinson Public Schools, 108 S.Ct. 2481 (1988).

Abortion

In 1980, the Supreme Court upheld the "Hyde Amendment," passed by Congress to deny public funds for abortions except to save the mother's life or in cases of rape or incest. Harris v. McRae, 448 U.S. 297 (1980). As with the school financing cases, state courts reached different conclusions. In California, Massachusetts, and New Jersey, state courts struck down state versions of the Hyde Amendment. They held that states have no obligation to provide medical care to the poor, but that it is a violation of the state constitution to give money to indigent women wanting to bear a child and deny funds to those who seek an abortion. This issue is explored more fully in the next chapter.

The group rights studied in this chapter illustrate the strong social forces and customs that help shape constitutional law. They also highlight the pressures applied to legislative and judicial bodies, with one branch or the other initiating action in response to changing conditions. Although the courts take the lead in some instances, the sections on prisoner rights and school financing demonstrate that judges are cautious in ordering remedies that involve vast appropriations. Such allocations of state or federal funds are left generally to legislative action and the priorities established by the two political branches. Furthermore, this chapter offers insights into the complex give-and-take between federal and state governments.

Selected Readings

ALPERT, GEOFFREY P., ed. *Legal Rights of Prisoners*. Beverly Hills, Calif.: Sage Publications, 1980.

BABCOCK, BARBARA A., et al. *Sex Discrimination and the Law*. Boston: Little, Brown, 1975.

BAER, JUDITH. "Sexual Equality and the Burger Court." 31 *Western Political Quarterly* 470 (1978).

BELAIR, ROBERT R., ed. *Legal Rights of Children*. Fair Lawn, N.J.: R. E. Burdick, 1973.

BENNETT, ROBERT W. "The Burger Court and the Poor," in Vincent Blasi, ed. *The Burger Court: The Counter-Revolution That Wasn't*. New Haven, Conn.: Yale University Press, 1983.

CLUTE, PENELOPE D. *The Legal Aspects of Prisons and Jails*. Springfield, Ill.: Charles C. Thomas, 1980.

FAIR, DARYL R. "Prison Reform by the Courts," in Richard A.L. Gambitta et al. *Governing Through Courts*. Beverly Hills, Calif.: Sage Publications, 1981.

FOX, SANFORD J. *The Law of Juvenile Courts*. St. Paul, Minn.: West, 1984.

GETMAN, JULIUS. "The Emerging Constitutional Principle of Sexual Equality." 1972 *Supreme Court Review* 157.

GINSBURG, RUTH BADER. "Gender in the Supreme Court: The 1973 and 1974 Terms." 1975 *Supreme Court Review* 1.

————. "The Burger Court's Grapplings with Sex Discrimination," in Vincent Blasi, ed. *The Burger Court: The Counter-Revolution That Wasn't*. New Haven, Conn.: Yale University Press, 1983.

GUGGENHEIM, MARTIN, AND ALAN SUSSMAN. *The Rights of Young People*. New York: Bantam Books, 1985.

HAPPERLE, WINIFRED, AND LAURA CRITES. *Women in the Courts*. Williamsburg, Va.: National Center for State Court, 1978.

KANOWITZ, LEO. *Women and the Law*. Albuquerque: University of New Mexico Press, 1969.

MANSBRIDGE, JANE J. *Why We Lost the ERA*. Chicago: University of Chicago Press, 1986.

NEIER, ARYEH. "Reforming Asylums: No Other Way," in *Only Judgment*. Middletown, Conn.: Wesleyan University Press, 1982.

O'CONNOR, KAREN. *Women's Organizations' Use of the Courts*. Lexington, Mass.: Lexington Books, 1980.

PAULSEN, MONRAD G. "Kent v. United States: The Constitutional Context of Juvenile Cases." 1966 *Supreme Court Review* 167.

————. "The Constitutional Domestication of the Juvenile Court." 1967 *Supreme Court Review* 233.

ROSS, SUSAN DELLER, AND ANN BARCHER. *The Rights of Women*. New York: Bantam Books, 1983.

RUDOVSKY, DAVID, et al. *The Rights of Prisoners*. New York: Bantam Books, 1983.

SCHEINGOLD, STUART. *The Politics of Rights*. New Haven, Conn.: Yale University Press, 1974.

STEINER, GILBERT Y. *Constitutional Inequality: The Political Fortunes of the Equal Rights Amendment*. Washington, D.C.: The Brookings Institution, 1985.

WILKINSON, J. HARVIE, III. "Goss v. Lopez: The Supreme Court as School Administrator." 1975 *Supreme Court Review* 25.

Bradwell v. State

83 U.S. 130 (1873)

Myra Bradwell, a resident of Illinois, applied to the judges of the Illinois Supreme Court for a license to practice law. In addition to listing her qualifications, she asserted that she was entitled to the license by virtue of the privileges and immunities guaranteed to U.S. citizens under Section 2 of Article IV and under Section 1 of the Fourteenth Amendment. Her application was denied, with only one Justice dissenting. The concurrence by Justice Bradley is of special interest because of his instruction regarding the "mission of woman."

Mr. Justice MILLER delivered the opinion of the court.

The record in this case is not very perfect, but it may be fairly taken that the plaintiff asserted her right to a license on the grounds, among others, that she was a citizen of the United States, and that having been a citizen of Vermont at one time, she was, in the State of Illinois, entitled to any right granted to citizens of the latter State.

The court having overruled these claims of right founded on the clauses of the Federal Constitution before referred to, those propositions may be considered as properly before this court.

As regards the provision of the Constitution that citizens of each State shall be entitled to all the privileges and immunities of citizens in the several States, the plaintiff in her affidavit has stated very clearly a case to which it is inapplicable.

The protection designed by that clause, as has been repeatedly held, has no application to a citizen of the State whose laws are complained of. If the plaintiff was a citizen of the State of Illinois, that provision of the Constitution gave her no protection against its courts or its legislation.

The plaintiff seems to have seen this difficulty, and attempts to avoid it by stating that she was born in Vermont.

While she remained in Vermont that circumstance made her a citizen of that State. But she states, at the same time, that she is a citizen of the United States, and that she is now, and has been for many years past, a resident of Chicago, in the State of Illinois.

The fourteenth amendment declares that citizens of the United States are citizens of the State within which they reside; therefore the plaintiff was, at the time of making her application, a citizen of the United States and a citizen of the State of Illinois.

We do not here mean to say that there may not be a temporary residence in one State, with intent to return to another, which will not create citizenship in the former. But the plaintiff states nothing to take her case out of the definition of citizenship of a State as defined by the first section of the fourteenth amendment.

In regard to that amendment counsel for the plaintiff in this court truly says that there are certain privileges and immunities which belong to a citizen of the United States as such; otherwise it would be nonsense for the fourteenth amendment to prohibit a State from abridging them, and he proceeds to argue that admission to the bar of a State of a person who possesses the requisite learning and character is one of those which a State may not deny.

In this latter proposition we are not able to concur with counsel. We agree with him that there are privileges and immunities belonging to citizens of the United States, in that relation and character, and that it is these and these alone which a State is forbidden to abridge. But the right to admission to practice in the courts of a State is not one of them. This right in no sense depends on citizenship of the United States. It has not, as far as we know, ever been made in any State, or in any case, to depend on citizenship at all. Certainly many prominent and distinguished lawyers have been admitted to practice, both in the State and Federal courts, who were not citizens of the United States or of any State. But, on whatever basis this right may be placed, so far as it can have any relation to citizenship at all, it would seem that, as to the courts of a State, it would relate to citizenship of the State, and as to Federal courts, it would relate to citizenship of the United States.

The opinion just delivered in the *Slaughter-House Cases* renders elaborate argument in the present case unnecessary; for, unless we are wholly and radically mistaken in the principles on which those cases are decided, the right to control and regulate the granting of license to practice law in the courts of a State is one of those powers which are not transferred for its protection to the Federal government, and its exercise is in no manner governed or controlled by citizenship of the United States in the party seeking such license.

It is unnecessary to repeat the argument on which the judgment in those cases is founded. It is sufficient to say they are conclusive of the present case.

JUDGMENT AFFIRMED.

Mr. Justice BRADLEY:

I concur in the judgment of the court in this case, by which the judgment of the Supreme Court of Illinois is affirmed, but not for the reasons specified in the opinion just read.

The claim of the plaintiff, who is a married woman, to be admitted to practice as an attorney and counsellor-at-law, is based upon the supposed right of every person, man or woman, to engage in any lawful employment for a livelihood. The Supreme Court of Illinois denied the application on the ground that, by the common law, which is the basis of the laws of Illinois, only men were admitted to the bar, and the legislature had not made any change in this respect, but had simply provided that no person should be admitted to practice as attorney or counsellor without having previously obtained a license for that purpose from two justices of the Supreme Court, and that no person should receive a license without first obtaining a certificate from the court of some county of his good moral character. In other respects it was left to the discretion of the court to establish the rules by which admission to the profession should be determined. The court, however, regarded itself as bound by at least two limitations. One was that it should establish such terms of admission as would promote the proper administration of justice, and the other that it should not admit any persons, or class of persons, not intended by the legislature to be admitted, even though not expressly excluded by statute. In view of this latter limitation the court felt compelled to deny the application of females to be admitted as members of the bar. Being contrary to the rules of the common law and the usages of Westminster Hall from time immemorial, it could not be supposed that the legislature had intended to adopt any different rule.

The claim that, under the fourteenth amendment of the Constitution, which declares that no State shall make or enforce any law which shall abridge the privileges and immunities of citizens of the United States, the statute law of Illinois, or the common law prevailing in that State, can no longer be set up as a barrier against the right of females to pursue any lawful employment for a livelihood (the practice of law included), assumes that it is one of the privileges and immunities of women as citizens to engage in any and every profession, occupation, or employment in civil life.

It certainly cannot be affirmed, as an historical fact, that this has ever been established as one of the fundamental privileges and immunities of the sex. On the contrary, the civil law, as well as

nature herself, has always recognized a wide difference in the respective spheres and destinies of man and woman. Man is, or should be, woman's protector and defender. The natural and proper timidity and delicacy which belongs to the female sex evidently unfits it for many of the occupations of civil life. The constitution of the family organization, which is founded in the divine ordinance, as well as in the nature of things, indicates the domestic sphere as that which properly belongs to the domain and functions of womanhood. The harmony, not to say identity, of interests and views which belong, or should belong, to the family institution is repugnant to the idea of a woman adopting a distinct and independent career from that of her husband. So firmly fixed was this sentiment in the founders of the common law that it became a maxim of that system of jurisprudence that a woman had no legal existence separate from her husband, who was regarded as her head and representative in the social state; and, notwithstanding some recent modifications of this civil status, many of the special rules of law flowing from and dependent upon this cardinal principle still exist in full force in most States. One of these is, that a married woman is incapable, without her husband's consent, of making contracts which shall be binding on her or him. This very incapacity was one circumstance which the Supreme Court of Illinois deemed important in rendering a married woman incompetent fully to perform the duties and trusts that belong to the office of an attorney and counsellor.

It is true that many women are unmarried and not affected by any of the duties, complications, and incapacities arising out of the married state, but these are exceptions to the general rule. The paramount destiny and mission of woman are to fulfil the noble and benign offices of wife and mother. This is the law of the Creator. And the rules of civil society must be adapted to the general constitution of things, and cannot be based upon exceptional cases.

The humane movements of modern society, which have for their object the multiplication of avenues for woman's advancement, and of occupations adapted to her condition and sex, have my heartiest concurrence. But I am not prepared to say that it is one of her fundamental rights and privileges to be admitted into every office and position, including those which require highly special qualifications and demanding special responsibilities. In the nature of things it is not every citizen of every age, sex, and condition that is qualified for every calling and position. It is the prerogative of the legislator to prescribe regulations founded on nature, reason, and experience for the due admission of qualified persons to professions and callings demanding special skill and confidence. This fairly belongs to the police power of the State; and, in my opinion, in view of the peculiar characteristics, destiny, and mission of woman, it is within the province of the legislature to ordain what offices, positions, and callings

shall be filled and discharged by men, and shall receive the benefit of those energies and responsibilities, and that decision and firmness which are presumed to predominate in the sterner sex.

For these reasons I think that the laws of Illinois now complained of are not obnoxious to the charge of abridging any of the privileges and immunities of citizens of the United States.

Mr. Justice SWAYNE and Mr. Justice FIELD concurred in the foregoing opinion of Mr. Justice BRADLEY.

The CHIEF JUSTICE dissented from the judgment of the court, and from all the opinions.

Equal Pay Act of 1963: Congressional Debate

The federal government had prohibited discrimination on the basis of sex for federal salaries, but the private sector was at liberty to pay women less than men for the same job. Congress passed legislation in 1963 to place restrictions on private employers. Although the bill permitted some exceptions, Congress used its power over commerce to bring a measure of fairness and justice to private wages. The debate below occurred in the House of Representatives on May 23, 1963.

Mr. BOLLING. Mr. Speaker, I yield 30 minutes to the gentlewoman from New York [Mrs. ST. GEORGE] and, pending that, myself such time as I may consume.

Mr. Speaker, House Resolution 362 makes in order the consideration of H.R. 6060, a bill to prohibit discrimination on account of sex in the payment of wages by employers engaged in commerce or in the production of goods for commerce. It is an open rule and provides for 2 hours of debate.

Mr. Speaker, I know of no controversy over the rule, although there is some controversy over the bill, and I therefore reserve the balance of my time.

Mrs. ST. GEORGE. Mr. Speaker, I yield myself such time as I may require.

Mr. Speaker, this resolution, House Resolution 362, makes in order the consideration of H.R.

6060 to prohibit discrimination on account of sex in the payment of wages by employers engaged in commerce or in the production of goods for commerce. Similar bills have been before this House before, but this one, I think, is by all odds the best one, although it is by no means perfect, that we have had so far.

For those who fear this legislation—and there are some—I would like to point out that all women are by no means covered in this act. As a matter of fact, we see, according to the supplemental views in the report, that the prohibition against discrimination because of sex is placed under the Fair Labor Standards Act, with the act's established coverage of employers and employees. All of the Fair Labor Standards exemptions apply; and, this is very noteworthy, agriculture, hotels, motels, restaurants, and laundries are excluded. Also all professional, managerial, and administrative personnel and outside salesmen are excluded. So, a very great quantity of women will not be covered in this act, especially because it considers hotels, motels, restaurants, and laundries, where women are by far the majority of the workers. They will not be included.

Mr. Speaker, I have always felt that these bills would come to us from now on, and I hope that they will, but in every instance it is only one bite of the cherry. In other words, we are just nibbling away at a thing that could have been completely covered by an amendment to the Constitution simply giving women equal rights and letting it go at that. That apparently has not been the will of the House so far. I hope someday that it will be. However, in the meantime, we are going to have to have these bills which will help, which will do a little, which will get a foot in the door, and they will have to continue to come to us.

Mr. Speaker, this bill in my estimation is good. It is a little bit too little and, of course, it is too late. But on the other hand it is the best thing we can get at this time.

Mr. Speaker, I know of no serious objection to it. I feel sure that the House will be glad; in fact, we feel that it is high time for it to pass favorably on this legislation and certainly pass favorably on the rule.

Mr. Speaker, I reserve the balance of my time.

Mr. BOLLING. Mr. Speaker, I yield 5 minutes to the gentleman from Mississippi [Mr. COLMER].

Mr. COLMER. Mr. Speaker, I do not know that I will use the 5 minutes that the gentleman from Missouri [Mr. BOLLING] has so graciously granted me. But I cannot sit idly by without expressing my opinion about this legislation. I recognize that this bill is going to pass. It is going to pass overwhelmingly, I suspect, because it has an appeal to a minority or special group. It deals with women. I recognize the seeming popular appeal and then, too, Mr. Speaker, I recognize in addition to the futility of my stating my position the politically unwise situation in which I find myself. I certainly do not want to be put in the position of opposing the women of this country, and I could dwell at some length on that subject. I am not so sure that the women want this bill. However, I am opposed to this proposal because I think it is basically unsound, just as I have opposed proposals here that were aimed at other minority or special groups.

I doubt seriously, Mr. Speaker, if this bill is constitutional. I do not like the idea of pointing out women here as if they are an inferior group and that the Federal Government with its strong arm must step in and try to protect them. I think they can stand on their own. They have been doing that for many, many generations.

Mr. Speaker, there are many instances where women are entitled to more pay than the opposite sex and why should we just put them on an equal basis? This strikes at the merit system.

Mr. Speaker, I am principally opposed to this legislation because it represents further regimentation of our people.

This sets up another army of Federal agents to go about snooping into every little, as well as every big business in the country to see whether the Federal law is being enforced.

I think women should be paid. I think they should be paid upon an equal basis with men for similar work, and I think generally it is true that they are, where they have the qualifications for that particular position, but this thing of regimentation is something that just does not appeal to me. In fact, our people are already overregimented.

Mr. Speaker, there has grown up a custom in this country that we have to have the Federal Government stick its strong arms out to get into every phase and facet of our local government and of our industry. There is a provision in this bill, Mr. Speaker, that I think throws some light on what I am talking about. There is a provision that an employer who is paying a wage rate differential in violation of this subsection shall not, in order to comply with the provisions of this subsection, reduce the wage rate of an employee. That recognizes the fact that there are many, many women in this country who are receiving better pay than men for equal service, as spelled out in this bill. I recognize, I repeat, the political appeal of this bill. I am not going to ask anyone to oppose this bill, or to cast their ballot against it, but I am going to emphasize, as one who is opposed to the everspreading tentacles of the Federal Government into the management and the conduct of the affairs of the people of this Nation, that the Members had better give some consideration to it and its far-reaching implications.

Moreover, Mr. Speaker, I am not so sure that this proposed legislation in the long run is going to benefit the women employees of this country. It is highly probable that the employers may find it advantageous to employ men in positions now filled by women. Certainly, they would feel inclined so to do in marginal instances where the labor market is plentiful. In other words, it is highly probable that the passage of this bill would result in less employment for women.

Mr. Speaker, finally I am opposed to this bill because I do not think that this subject is any of the Federal Government's business.

Mrs. ST. GEORGE. Mr. Speaker, I yield 2 minutes to the gentlewoman from Ohio [Mrs. BOLTON].

Mrs. FRANCES P. BOLTON. Mr. Speaker, as a long-time advocate of the principle of equal pay for equal work, I am very glad to speak in favor of H.R. 6060. I am very much interested in the remarks of the previous speaker because it is some time since the women of this country have been in the minority. We are rather far ahead of you in that regard, my distinguished colleague. Of course, if you care to be the spokesman for the actual minority. Equal pay legislation has been introduced in every Congress since 1945 by Members of both parties, a truly bipartisan effort.

The bill which is now before us is essentially the same as the one introduced in March of this year by the distinguished gentleman from New York [Mr. GOODELL]. It is a very logical approach to the problem in that it places administration of equal pay under the Fair Labor Standards Act. This alleviates the fear voiced by many that passage of such a bill would lead to the establishment of a new bureaucracy with a new set of rules and a new set of investigators. The procedures under the Fair Labor Standards Act are already well established. However, let me remind you of what the gentlewoman from New York [Mrs. ST. GEORGE] has already told us, that this bill in no way covers all the women workers of this country. Indeed, it leaves out a very great many of them. So I would like to consider this bill and have you consider it as one of the first steps toward an adjustment of balance in pay for women.

As a matter of fact, you know it is going to affect some of you men because there are places where the men do not get paid as much as women for doing the same job.

. . .

It is a matter of simple justice to pay a woman the same rate as a man when she is performing the same duties. We have had equal pay in the Government for some years through the Federal classified civil service. Some 22 States have enacted equal-pay laws, but let me say right there that in many of these they do not work too well. However, a Federal law is needed to give complete and adequate coverage.

. . .

Mr. POWELL. Mr. Chairman, I yield myself such time as I may desire.

Mr. Chairman, I rise in support of H.R. 6060, a bill to prohibit discrimination on account of sex in the payment of wages by employers engaged in commerce or in the production of goods for commerce.

I would like to inform this body that the bill comes out of the Committee on Education and Labor with bipartisan support. Only three committee members opposed the passage of this legislation.

Legislation of this kind has been recommended over a period of years and during the 87th Congress the House acted favorably on an equal-pay bill. However, the Senate appended this legislation to another bill and the 87th Congress closed without final action on the measure.

There is little doubt as to the need for this legislation. The objective sought is wage justice for working men and women. Discriminatory wage practices based upon sex, like other forms of discrimination in employment, are contrary to our basic employment, are contrary to our basic traditions of freedom and fairplay.

The payment of wages on a basis other than that of the job performed is not only harmful to the individual worker and our economy, but also to our Nation's image abroad. The fact that employers still pay lower wage rates to women workers for the same or comparable work as that performed by men workers in the same place is contrary to every concept of equality and justice in which we so strongly believe.

This principle of equality has been endorsed by labor, by leaders in both political parties, and by numerous business organizations and spokesmen. The International Labor Organization—of which we are a member and which I shall attend next week—provides in its constitution that "men and women should receive equal remuneration for work of equal value." Thirty-eight countries have ratified an ILO Convention which sets up standards and procedures for establishing equal pay in fact as well as in principle. The European Common Market agreement, the Rome Treaty, also carries a specific provision for equal pay.

Thus we come to this legislation buttressed by support at home and abroad, from labor and management, from men and women, and from Democrats and Republicans.

. . .

Mr. FRELINGHUYSEN. Mr. Chairman, I yield myself 6 minutes.

Mr. Chairman, I rise in support of H.R. 6060. Perhaps, as the gentlewoman from New York has stated, this proposal is too little and too late. Perhaps, as the gentlewoman from Ohio says, this is only the first step in the right direction.

Mr. Chairman, passage of this bill will mark an important milestone in the campaign for equal rights for women. Its aim is simple, few will argue about the desirability of what it seeks to achieve. Under its provisions, the women of America will be assured of equal pay when they perform equal work. This undeniable right is now to be bolstered and secured by appropriate legislative action.

. . .

Civil Rights Act of 1964: Congressional Debate

During debate on the Civil Rights Act of 1964, Congressman Howard Smith of Virginia offered an amendment to prohibit discrimination not only on the basis of race but on "sex" as well. This amendment has been widely interpreted as an effort by a Southern opponent of civil rights to jeopardize the entire bill by weighing it down with a ludicrous amendment. But the concerns of Congressman Smith and his colleagues from the South were real. If Congress only prohibited discrimination on the basis of race, white women would consistently lose out to black women in the competition for jobs. Employers would tend to favor black women as a way of avoiding discrimination suits. An alternative motivation for the amendment—defending the interests of white women—comes out strongly in the debate, taken from 110 Cong. Rec. 2577–2584 (1964).

AMENDMENT OFFERED BY MR. SMITH OF VIRGINIA

Mr. SMITH of Virginia. Mr. Chairman, I offer an amendment.

The Clerk read as follows:

"Amendment offered by Mr. SMITH of Virginia: On page 68, line 23, after the word 'religion,' insert the word 'sex.'

"On page 69, line 10, after the word 'religion,' insert the word 'sex.'

"On page 69, line 17, after the word 'religion,' insert the word 'sex.'

"On page 70, line 1, after the word 'religion,' insert the word 'sex.'

"On page 71, line 5, after the word 'religion,' insert the word 'sex.'"

Mr. SMITH of Virginia. Mr. Chairman, this amendment is offered to the fair employment practices title of this bill to include within our desire to prevent discrimination against another minority group, the women, but a very essential minority group, in the absence of which the majority group would not be here today.

Now, I am very serious about this amendment. It has been offered several times before, but it was offered at inappropriate places in the bill. Now, this is the appropriate place for this amendment to come in. I do not think it can do any harm to this legislation; maybe it can do some good. I think it will do some good for the minority sex.

I think we all recognize and it is indisputable fact that all throughout industry women are discriminated against in that just generally speaking they do not get as high compensation for their work as do the majority sex. Now, if that is true, I hope that the committee chairman will accept this amendment.

That is about all I have to say about it except, to get off of this subject for just a moment but to show you how some of the ladies feel about discrimination against them, I want to read you an extract from a letter that I received the other day. This lady has a real grievance on behalf of the minority sex. She said that she had seen that I was going to present an amendment to protect the most important sex, and she says:

"I suggest that you might also favor an amendment or a bill to correct the present 'imbalance' which exists between males and females in the United States."

Then she goes on to say—and she has her statistics, which is the reason why I am reading it to you, because this is serious—

"The census of 1960 shows that we had 88,331,000 males living in this country, and 90,992,000 females, which leaves the country with an 'imbalance' of 2,661,000 females."

Now another paragraph:

"Just why the Creator would set up such an imbalance of spinsters, shutting off the 'right' of every female to have a husband of her own, is, of course, known only to nature.

"But I am sure you will agree that this is a grave injustice—"

And I do agree, and I am reading you the letter because I want all the rest of you to agree, you of the majority—

"But I am sure you will agree that this is a grave injustice to womankind and something the Congress and President Johnson should take immediate steps to correct—"

And you interrupted me just now before I could finish reading the sentence, which continues on:

"immediate steps to correct, especially in this election year."

Now, I just want to remind you here that in this election year it is pretty nearly half of the voters in this country that are affected, so you had better sit up and take notice.

She also says this, and this is a very cogent argument, too:

"Up until now, instead of assisting these poor unfortunate females in obtaining their 'right' to happiness, the Government has on several occasions engaged in wars which killed off a large number of eligible males, creating an 'imbalance' in our male and female population that was even worse than before.

"Would you have any suggestions as to what course our Government might pursue to protect our spinster friends in their 'right' to a nice husband and family?"

I read that letter just to illustrate that women have some real grievances and some real rights to be protected. I am serious about this thing. I just hope that the committee will accept it. Now, what harm can you do this bill that was so perfect yesterday and is so imperfect today— what harm will this do to the condition of the bill?

The CHAIRMAN. The time of the gentleman from Virginia has expired.

Mr. CELLER. Mr. Chairman, I rise in opposition to the amendment.

Mr. SMITH of Virginia. Oh, no.

Mr. CELLER. Mr. Chairman, I heard with a great deal of interest the statement of the gentleman from Virginia that women are in the minority. Not in my house. I can say as a result of 49 years of experience—and I celebrate my 50th wedding anniversary next year—that women, indeed, are not in the minority in my house. As a matter of fact, the reason I would suggest that we have been living in such harmony, such delightful accord for almost half a century is that I usually have the last two words, and those words are, "Yes, dear." Of course, we all remember the famous play by George Bernard Shaw, "Man and Superman"; and man was not the superman, the other sex was.

I received a letter this morning from the U.S. Department of Labor which reads as follows:

U.S. DEPARTMENT OF LABOR,
OFFICE OF THE SECRETARY,
Washington, February 7, 1964.

This is in response to your inquiry about the reaction of the Women's Bureau to suggestions that the civil rights bill be amended to prohibit job discrimination on the basis of sex as well as race, creed, color, or national origin.

Assistant Secretary of Labor Esther Peterson who is in charge of the Women's Bureau has replied to requests for support of such an amendment in the following way:

"This question of broadening civil rights legislation to prohibit discriminations based on sex has arisen previously. The President's Commission on the Status of Women gave this matter careful consideration in its discussion of Executive Order 10925 which now prohibits discrimination based on race, creed, color, or national origin in employment under Federal contracts. Its conclusion is stated on page 30 of its report, 'American Women,' as follows:

"'We are aware that this order could be expanded to forbid discrimination based on sex. But discrimination based on sex, the Commission believes, involves problems sufficiently different from discrimination based on the other factors listed to make separate treatment preferable.'

"In view of this policy conclusion reached by representatives from a variety of women's organizations and private and public agencies to attack discriminations based on sex separately, we are of the opinion that to attempt to so amend H.R. 7152 would not be to the best advantage of women at this time."

So we have an expression of opinion from

the Department of Labor to the effect that it will be ill advised to append to this bill the word "sex" and provide for discrimination on the basis of race, color, creed, national origin, and sex as well. Of course, there has been before us for a considerable length of time, before the Judiciary Committee, an equal rights amendment. At first blush it seems fair, just, and equitable to grant these equal rights. But when you examine carefully what the import and repercussions are concerning equal rights throughout American life, and all facets of American life you run into a considerable amount of difficulty.

You will find that there are in the equality of sex that some people glibly assert, and without reason serious problems. I have been reluctant as chairman of the Committee on the Judiciary to give favorable consideration to that constitutional amendment.

The CHAIRMAN. The time of the gentleman from New York has expired.

Mr. CELLER. Mr. Chairman, I ask unanimous consent to proceed for 5 additional minutes.

The CHAIRMAN. Is there objection to the request of the gentleman from New York?

There was no objection.

Mr. CELLER. You know, the French have a phrase for it when they speak of women and men. When they speak of the difference, they say "vive la différence."

I think the French are right.

Imagine the upheaval that would result from adoption of blanket language requiring total equality. Would male citizens be justified in insisting that women share with them the burdens of compulsory military service? What would become of traditional family relationships? What about alimony? Who would have the obligation of supporting whom? Would fathers rank equally with mothers in the right of custody to children? What would become of the crimes of rape and statutory rape? Would the Mann Act be invalidated? Would the many State and local provisions regulating working conditions and hours of employment for women be struck down?

You know the biological differences between the sexes. In many States we have laws favorable to women. Are you going to strike those laws down? This is the entering wedge, an amendment of this sort. The list of foreseeable consequences, I will say to the committee, is unlimited.

What is more, even conceding that some degree of discrimination against women obtains in the area of employment, it is contrary to the situation with respect to civil rights for Negroes. Real and genuine progress is being made in discrimination against women. The Equal Pay Act of 1963, for example, which became law last June, amends the Fair Labor Standards Act of 1938 by prohibiting discrimination between employees on the basis of sex, with respect to wages for equal work on jobs requiring equal skill, effort, and responsibility.

. . .

Mrs. FRANCES P. BOLTON. Mr. Chairman, I rise in support of the amendment.

Mr. Chairman, it is always perfectly delightful when some enchanting gentleman, from the South particularly, calls us the minority group. We used to be but we are not any more. I have just had the figures sent me. You males, as you seem to like to call yourselves, are 88,331,494. We females, as you like to call us, are 90,991,681. So I regret to state that we can no longer be the minority; indeed, we have not been for some time.

. . .

Mrs. GRIFFITHS. Mr. Chairman, I move to strike out the last word and rise in support of the amendment.

Mr. Chairman, I presume that if there had been any necessity to have pointed out that women were a second-class sex, the laughter would have proved it.

Mr. Chairman, I rise in support of the amendment primarily because I feel as a white woman when this bill has passed this House and the Senate and has been signed by the President that white women will be last at the hiring gate.

In his great work "The American Dilemma," the Swedish sociologist pointed out 20 years ago that white women and Negroes occupied relatively the same position in American society.

Before I begin my argument, however, I would like to ask the chairman of the Committee on the Judiciary, the gentleman from New York, a question.

Mr. Chairman, is it your judgment that this bill will protect colored men and colored women at the hiring gate equally?

Mr. CELLER. This bill is all-embracing and will cover everybody in the United States.

Mrs. GRIFFITHS. It will cover every colored man and every colored woman?

Mr. CELLER. Yes, it will cover white men and white women and all Americans.

. . .

Mrs. GRIFFITHS. . . . I come from a city in which there is a university. It is my understanding that there has never been a woman political scientist employed at that university to teach political science. Suppose a colored woman political scientist applied for a job. Could she or could she not invoke the act?

Mr. CELLER. Of course, we are addressing ourselves to business activity. It is conceivable that colleges might be covered. There again, if there were discrimination then there would be a violation.

Mrs. GRIFFITHS. Could a white woman turned away from the college or from the restaurant where all the employees were white invoke the act? Would a white woman have any recourse under the act?

Mr. CELLER. I think we covered that in colloquies we had in the earlier part of the afternoon. There could be discrimination against white people and there could be against colored people.

Mrs. GRIFFITHS. Mr. Chairman, you know well and good if every employee of that restaurant were white, that that woman cannot go to the FEPC or to a district attorney and say, "I was turned away from there because I was white," because every employee is white there.

. . .

Now, Mr. Chairman, I would like to proceed to some of the arguments I have heard on this floor against adding the word "sex." In some of the arguments, I have heard the comment that the chairman is making, which is, that this makes it an equal rights bill. Of course it does not even approach making it an equal rights bill. This is equal employment rights. In one field only—employment. And if you do not add sex to this bill,

I really do not believe there is a reasonable person sitting here who does not by now understand perfectly that you are going to have white men in one bracket, you are going to try to take colored men and colored women and give them equal employment rights, and down at the bottom of the list is going to be a white woman with no rights at all.

. . .

Mrs. ST. GEORGE. Mr. Chairman, I move to strike out the requisite number of words.

Mr. Chairman, I was somewhat amazed when I came on the floor this afternoon to hear the very distinguished chairman of the Committee on the Judiciary make the remark that he considered the amendment at this point illogical. I can think of nothing more logical than this amendment at this point.

. . .

The addition of that little, terrifying word "s-e-x" will not hurt this legislation in any way. In fact, it will improve it. It will make it comprehensive. It will make it logical. It will make it right.

Mrs. GREEN of Oregon. . . . I honestly cannot support the amendment. For every discrimination that has been made against a woman in this country there has been 10 times as much discrimination against the Negro of this country. There has been 10 times maybe 100 times as much humiliation for the Negro woman, for the Negro man and for the Negro child. Yes; and for the Negro baby who is born into a world of discrimination.

From the first day of life that baby is the object of discrimination—sometimes subtle, sometimes cruel, and he or she will feel it far more keenly all of his life than I possibly could. Yes—the Negro will suffer far more from discrimination than any discrimination that has been placed against me as a woman or against any other woman just because of her sex. Whether we want to admit it or not, the main purpose of this legislation today is to try to help end the discrimination that has been practiced against Negroes. . . . I hope that no other amendment will be added to this bill on sex or age or anything else, that would jeopardize our primary purpose in any way.

. . .

Mr. TUTEN. Mr. Chairman, I move to strike out the last word.

Mr. Chairman, I rise to compliment the performance of the brilliant female Members of this great body.

It has been brought out in the debate here today that I am definitely a member of a minority group. In view of the reference to Innsbruck and the brilliant performance here on the floor today, I accept my place, ladies, as a second-class citizen. Although I am second class and a member of a minority group, I rise to inform the House that I always take my stand for the majority.

I have been vigorously opposed to this bill—not as a racist—but in the interest of the rights of all of the citizens of this country. Since I am a man, which places me in the minority and makes me a second-class citizen—and the fact that I am white and from the South—I look forward to claiming my rights under the terms of this legislation.

But, Mr. Chairman, the main purpose of my rising is this: Some men in some areas of the country might support legislation which would discriminate against women, but never let it be said that a southern gentleman would vote for such legislation.

Therefore, Mr. Chairman, I rise in support of this amendment.

Mr. POOL. Mr. Chairman, I move to strike out the last word and rise in support of the amendment.

Mr. Chairman, I arise in support of the amendment and point out that the interests and welfare of all American citizens, without distinction as to sex, shall prevail. This principle of equality of rights under the law for all citizens without distinction as to sex would thereby safeguard American women from such inequities with regard to their civil rights as are now threatened in the pending civil rights bill.

Mr. ANDREWS of Alabama. Mr. Chairman, I move to strike out the last word and rise in support of the amendment.

Mr. Chairman, I rise in support of this amendment offered by the gentleman from Virginia [Mr. SMITH]. Unless this amendment is adopted, the white women of this country would be drastically discriminated against in favor of a Negro woman.

If a white woman and a Negro woman applied for the same job, and each woman had the identical qualifications, the chances are about 99 to 1 that the Negro woman would be given the job because if the employer did not give the job to the Negro woman he could be prosecuted under this bill. Failure to employ the white woman would not subject the employer to such action.

Commonsense tells us that the employer would hire the Negro woman to avoid prosecution. The white woman will be at a great disadvantage in the business world unless this amendment is adopted.

Mr. RIVERS of South Carolina. I rise in support of the amendment offered by the gentleman from Virginia [Mr. SMITH] making it possible for the white Christian woman to receive the same consideration for employment as the colored woman. It is incredible to me that the authors of this monstrosity—whomever they are—would deprive the white woman of mostly Anglo-Saxon or Christian heritage equal opportunity before the employer. I know this Congress will not be a party to such an evil.

Mr. SMITH of Virginia. . . . I put a question to you in behalf of the white women of the United States. Let us assume that two women apply for the same job and both of them are equally eligible, one a white woman and one a Negro woman. The first thing that employer will look at will be the provision with regard to the records he must keep. If he does not employ that colored woman and has to make that record, that employer will say, "Well, now, if I hire the colored woman I will not be in any trouble, but if I do not hire the colored woman and hire the white woman, then the Commission is going to be looking down my throat and will want to know why I did not. I may be in a lawsuit."

That will happen as surely as we are here this afternoon. You all know it.

I have not heard anybody give any valid reason why the amendment should not be adopted.

. . .

The CHAIRMAN. The question is on the amendment offered by the gentleman from Virginia [Mr. SMITH].

Mrs. GRIFFITHS. Mr. Chairman, on that I demand tellers.

Tellers were ordered, and the Chairman appointed as tellers Mr. CELLER and Mrs. GRIFFITHS.

The Committee divided, and the tellers reported that there were—ayes 168, noes 133.

So the amendment was agreed to.

Frontiero v. Richardson
411 U.S. 677 (1973)

Sharron Frontiero, a lieutenant in the U.S. Air Force, sought increased quarters allowances and housing and medical benefits for her husband on the ground that he was her "dependent." The law provided that wives of servicemen automatically were treated as dependents, but husbands of servicewomen were not dependents unless they depended on their wives for over one-half their support. Lt. Frontiero and her husband brought suit on the ground that the congressional statute deprived servicewomen of due process.

MR. JUSTICE BRENNAN announced the judgment of the Court and an opinion in which MR. JUSTICE DOUGLAS, MR. JUSTICE WHITE, and MR. JUSTICE MARSHALL join.

The question before us concerns the right of a female member of the uniformed services to claim her spouse as a "dependent" for the purposes of obtaining increased quarters allowances and medical and dental benefits under 37 U. S. C. §§ 401, 403, and 10 U. S. C. §§ 1072, 1076, on an equal footing with male members. Under these statutes, a serviceman may claim his wife as a "dependent" without regard to whether she is in fact dependent upon him for any part of her support. 37 U. S. C. § 401 (1); 10 U. S. C. § 1072 (2)(A). A servicewoman, on the other hand, may not claim her husband as a "dependent" under these programs unless he is in fact dependent upon her for over one-half of his support. 37 U. S. C. § 401; 10 U. S. C. § 1072 (2)(C). Thus, the question for decision is whether this difference in treatment constitutes an unconstitutional discrimination against servicewomen in violation of the Due Process Clause of the Fifth Amendment. A three-judge District Court for the Middle District of Alabama, one judge dissenting, rejected this contention and sustained the constitutionality of the provisions of the statutes making this distinction. 341 F. Supp. 201 (1972). We noted probable jurisdiction. 409 U. S. 840 (1972). We reverse.

I

In an effort to attract career personnel through reenlistment, Congress established, in 37 U. S. C. § 401 et seq., and 10 U. S. C. § 1071 et seq., a scheme for the provision of fringe benefits to members of the uniformed services on a competitive basis with business and industry. Thus, under 37 U. S. C. § 403, a member of the uniformed services with dependents is entitled to an increased "basic allowance for quarters" and, under 10 U. S. C. § 1076, a member's dependents are provided comprehensive medical and dental care.

Appellant Sharron Frontiero, a lieutenant in the United States Air Force, sought increased quarters allowances, and housing and medical benefits for her husband, appellant Joseph Frontiero, on the ground that he was her "dependent." Although such benefits would automatically have been granted with respect to the wife of a male member of the uniformed services, appellant's application was denied because she failed to demonstrate that her husband was dependent on her for more than one-half of his support. Appellants then commenced this suit, contending that, by making this distinction, the statutes unreasonably discriminate on the basis of sex in violation of the Due Process Clause of the Fifth Amendment. In essence, appellants asserted that the discriminatory impact of the statutes is twofold: first, as a

procedural matter, a female member is required to demonstrate her spouse's dependency, while no such burden is imposed upon male members; and, second, as a substantive matter, a male member who does not provide more than one-half of his wife's support receives benefits, while a similarly situated female member is denied such benefits. Appellants therefore sought a permanent injunction against the continued enforcement of these statutes and an order directing the appellees to provide Lieutenant Frontiero with the same housing and medical benefits that a similarly situated male member would receive.

Although the legislative history of these statutes sheds virtually no light on the purposes underlying the differential treatment accorded male and female members, a majority of the three-judge District Court surmised that Congress might reasonably have concluded that, since the husband in our society is generally the "breadwinner" in the family—and the wife typically the "dependent" partner—"it would be more economical to require married female members claiming husbands to prove actual dependency than to extend the presumption of dependency to such members." 341 F. Supp., at 207. Indeed, given the fact that approximately 99% of all members of the uniformed services are male, the District Court speculated that such differential treatment might conceivably lead to a "considerable saving of administrative expense and manpower." Ibid.

II

At the outset, appellants contend that classifications based upon sex, like classifications based upon race, alienage, and national origin, are inherently suspect and must therefore be subjected to close judicial scrutiny. We agree and, indeed, find at least implicit support for such an approach in our unanimous decision only last Term in Reed v. Reed, 404 U. S. 71 (1971).

In Reed, the Court considered the constitutionality of an Idaho statute providing that, when two individuals are otherwise equally entitled to appointment as administrator of an estate, the male applicant must be preferred to the female. Appellant, the mother of the deceased, and appellee, the father, filed competing petitions for appointment as administrator of their son's estate. Since the parties, as parents of the deceased, were members of the same entitlement class, the statutory preference was invoked and the father's petition was therefore granted. Appellant claimed that this statute, by giving a mandatory preference to males over females without regard to their individual qualifications, violated the Equal Protection Clause of the Fourteenth Amendment.

The Court noted that the Idaho statute "provides that different treatment be accorded to the applicants on the basis of their sex; it thus establishes a classification subject to scrutiny under the Equal Protection Clause." 404 U. S., at 75. Under "traditional" equal protection analysis, a legislative classification must be sustained unless it is "patently arbitrary" and bears no rational relationship to a legitimate governmental interest. See *Jefferson* v. *Hackney*, 406 U. S. 535, 546 (1972); *Richardson* v. *Belcher*, 404 U. S. 78, 81 (1971); *Flemming* v. *Nestor*, 363 U. S. 603, 611 (1960); *McGowan* v. *Maryland*, 366 U. S. 420, 426 (1961); *Dandridge* v. *Williams*, 397 U. S. 471, 485 (1970).

In an effort to meet this standard, appellee contended that the statutory scheme was a reasonable measure designed to reduce the workload on probate courts by eliminating one class of contests. Moreover, appellee argued that the mandatory preference for male applicants was in itself reasonable since "men [are] as a rule more conversant with business affairs than . . . women." Indeed, appellee maintained that "it is a matter of common knowledge, that women still are not engaged in politics, the professions, business or industry to the extent that men are." And the Idaho Supreme Court, in upholding the constitutionality of this statute, suggested that the Idaho Legislature might reasonably have "concluded that in general men are better qualified to act as an administrator than are women."

Despite these contentions, however, the Court held the statutory preference for male applicants unconstitutional. In reaching this result, the Court implicitly rejected appellee's apparently rational explanation of the statutory scheme, and concluded that, by ignoring the individual qualifications of particular applicants, the challenged statute provided "dissimilar treatment for men and wom-

en who are . . . similarly situated." 404 U. S., at 77. The Court therefore held that, even though the State's interest in achieving administrative efficiency "is not without some legitimacy," "[t]o give a mandatory preference to members of either sex over members of the other, merely to accomplish the elimination of hearings on the merits, is to make the very kind of arbitrary legislative choice forbidden by the [Constitution]. . . ." *Id.*, at 76. This departure from "traditional" rational-basis analysis with respect to sex-based classifications is clearly justified.

There can be no doubt that our Nation has had a long and unfortunate history of sex discrimination. Traditionally, such discrimination was rationalized by an attitude of "romantic paternalism" which, in practical effect, put women, not on a pedestal, but in a cage. Indeed, this paternalistic attitude became so firmly rooted in our national consciousness that, 100 years ago, a distinguished Member of this Court was able to proclaim:

"Man is, or should be, woman's protector and defender. The natural and proper timidity and delicacy which belongs to the female sex evidently unfits it for many of the occupations of civil life. The constitution of the family organization, which is founded in the divine ordinance, as well as in the nature of things, indicates the domestic sphere as that which properly belongs to the domain and functions of womanhood. The harmony, not to say identity, of interests and views which belong, or should belong, to the family institution is repugnant to the idea of a woman adopting a distinct and independent career from that of her husband. . . .

". . . The paramount destiny and mission of woman are to fulfil the noble and benign offices of wife and mother. This is the law of the Creator." *Bradwell* v. *State*, 16 Wall. 130, 141 (1873) (Bradley, J., concurring).

As a result of notions such as these, our statute books gradually became laden with gross, stereotyped distinctions between the sexes and, indeed, throughout much of the 19th century the position of women in our society was, in many respects, comparable to that of blacks under the pre-Civil War slave codes. Neither slaves nor women could hold office, serve on juries, or bring suit in their own names, and married women traditionally were denied the legal capacity to hold or convey property or to serve as legal guardians of their own children. See generally L. Kanowitz, Women and the Law: The Unfinished Revolution 5–6 (1969); G. Myrdal, An American Dilemma 1073 (20th anniversary ed. 1962). And although blacks were guaranteed the right to vote in 1870, women were denied even that right—which is itself "preservative of other basic civil and political rights" —until adoption of the Nineteenth Amendment half a century later.

It is true, of course, that the position of women in America has improved markedly in recent decades. Nevertheless, it can hardly be doubted that, in part because of the high visibility of the sex characteristic, women still face pervasive, although at times more subtle, discrimination in our educational institutions, in the job market and, perhaps most conspicuously, in the political arena. See generally K. Amundsen, The Silenced Majority: Women and American Democracy (1971); The President's Task Force on Women's Rights and Responsibilities, A Matter of Simple Justice (1970).

Moreover, since sex, like race and national origin, is an immutable characteristic determined solely by the accident of birth, the imposition of special disabilities upon the members of a particular sex because of their sex would seem to violate "the basic concept of our system that legal burdens should bear some relationship to individual responsibility. . . ." *Weber* v. *Aetna Casualty & Surety Co.*, 406 U. S. 164, 175 (1972). And what differentiates sex from such nonsuspect statuses as intelligence or physical disability, and aligns it with the recognized suspect criteria, is that the sex characteristic frequently bears no relation to ability to perform or contribute to society. As a result, statutory distinctions between the sexes often have the effect of invidiously relegating the entire class of females to inferior legal status without regard to the actual capabilities of its individual members.

We might also note that, over the past decade, Congress has itself manifested an increasing sensitivity to sex-based classifications. In Tit. VII of the Civil Rights Act of 1964, for example, Congress expressly declared that no employer, labor union, or other organization subject to the provisions of the Act shall discriminate against any individual on the basis of "race, color, religion, *sex*, or national origin." Similarly, the Equal Pay Act of 1963 provides that no employer covered by the Act "shall discriminate . . . between employees on the basis of *sex*." And § 1 of the Equal Rights Amendment, passed by Congress on March 22, 1972, and submitted to the legislatures of the States for ratification, declares that "[e]quality of rights under the law shall not be denied or abridged by the United States or by any State on account of sex." Thus, Congress itself has concluded that classifications based upon sex are inherently invidious, and this conclusion of a coequal branch of Government is not without significance to the question presently under consideration. Cf. *Oregon* v. *Mitchell*, 400 U. S. 112, 240, 248–249 (1970) (opinion of BRENNAN, WHITE, and MARSHALL, JJ.); *Katzenbach* v. *Morgan*, 384 U. S. 641, 648–649 (1966).

With these considerations in mind, we can only conclude that classifications based upon sex, like classifications based upon race, alienage, or national origin, are inherently suspect, and must therefore be subjected to strict judicial scrutiny. Applying the analysis mandated by that stricter standard of review, it is clear that the statutory scheme now before us is constitutionally invalid.

. . .

III

. . . We therefore conclude that, by according differential treatment to male and female members of the uniformed services for the sole purpose of achieving administrative convenience, the challenged statutes violate the Due Process Clause of the Fifth Amendment insofar as they require a female member to prove the dependency of her husband.

Reversed.

MR. JUSTICE STEWART concurs in the judgment, agreeing that the statutes before us work an invidious discrimination in violation of the Constitution. *Reed* v. *Reed,* 404 U. S. 71.

MR. JUSTICE REHNQUIST dissents for the reasons stated by Judge Rives in his opinion for the District Court, *Frontiero* v. *Laird,* 341 F. Supp. 201 (1972).

MR. JUSTICE POWELL, with whom THE CHIEF JUSTICE and MR. JUSTICE BLACKMUN join, concurring in the judgment.

I agree that the challenged statutes constitute an unconstitutional discrimination against servicewomen in violation of the Due Process Clause of the Fifth Amendment, but I cannot join the opinion of MR. JUSTICE BRENNAN, which would hold that all classifications based upon sex, "like classifications based upon race, alienage, and national origin," are "inherently suspect and must therefore be subjected to close judicial scrutiny." . . . It is unnecessary for the Court in this case to characterize sex as a suspect classification, with all of the far-reaching implications of such a holding. *Reed* v. *Reed,* 404 U. S. 71 (1971), which abundantly supports our decision today, did not add sex to the narrowly limited group of classifications which are inherently suspect. In my view, we can and should decide this case on the authority of *Reed* and reserve for the future any expansion of its rationale.

There is another, and I find compelling, reason for deferring a general categorizing of sex classifications as invoking the strictest test of judicial scrutiny. The Equal Rights Amendment, which if adopted will resolve the substance of this precise question, has been approved by the Congress and submitted for ratification by the States. If this Amendment is duly adopted, it will represent the will of the people accomplished in the manner prescribed by the Constitution. By acting prematurely and unnecessarily, as I view it, the Court has assumed a decisional responsibility at the very time when state legislatures, functioning within the traditional democratic process, are debating the proposed Amendment. It seems to me that this reaching out to pre-empt by judicial action a major political decision which is currently in process of resolution does not reflect appropriate respect for duly prescribed legislative processes.

There are times when this Court, under our system, cannot avoid a constitutional decision on issues which normally should be resolved by the elected representatives of the people. But democratic institutions are weakened, and confidence in the restraint of the Court is impaired, when we appear unnecessarily to decide sensitive issues of broad social and political importance at the very time they are under consideration within the prescribed constitutional processes.

Craig v. Boren

429 U.S. 190 (1976)

Curtis Craig, a male then between eighteen and twenty-one years old, together with a licensed vendor of 3.2 percent beer, brought an action in federal court for declaratory and injunctive relief, claiming that an Oklahoma law constituted a gender-based discrimination in violation of the Equal Protection Clause. The law prohibited the sale of "nonintoxicating" 3.2 percent beer to males under the age of 21 and to females under the age of 18. A three-judge court held that the state's statistical evidence regarding young males' drunk-driving arrests and traffic injuries demonstrated that the gender-based discrimination was substantially related to the achievement of traffic safety on Oklahoma roads. David Boren was governor of Oklahoma.

MR. JUSTICE BRENNAN delivered the opinion of the Court.

The interaction of two sections of an Oklahoma statute, Okla. Stat., Tit. 37, §§ 241 and 245 (1958 and Supp. 1976), prohibits the sale of "nonintoxicating" 3.2% beer to males under the age of 21 and to females under the age of 18. The question to be decided is whether such a gender-based differential constitutes a denial to males 18–20 years of age of the equal protection of the laws in violation of the Fourteenth Amendment.

. . .

[In Section I, the Court addressed the preliminary question of standing. Craig had turned 21 by the time the Court noted probable jurisdiction. Since only declaratory and injunctive relief against enforcement of the gender-based differential had been sought, the controversy was moot as to Craig. However, the Court held that the licensed vendor (Whitener) who had joined the case with Craig had standing to raise an equal protection challenge to the Oklahoma law.]

II

A

. . .

Analysis may appropriately begin with the reminder that *Reed* emphasized that statutory classifications that distinguish between males and females are "subject to scrutiny under the Equal Protection Clause." 404 U. S., at 75. To withstand constitutional challenge, previous cases establish that classifications by gender must serve important governmental objectives and must be substantially related to achievement of those objectives. . . .

. . . We turn then to the question whether, under *Reed*, the difference between males and females with respect to the purchase of 3.2% beer warrants the differential in age drawn by the Oklahoma statute. We conclude that it does not.

B

The District Court recognized that *Reed* v. *Reed* was controlling. In applying the teachings of that case, the court found the requisite important governmental objective in the traffic-safety goal proffered by the Oklahoma Attorney General. It then concluded that the statistics introduced by the appellees established that the gender-based

distinction was substantially related to achievement of that goal.

C

We accept for purposes of discussion the District Court's identification of the objective underlying §§ 241 and 245 as the enhancement of traffic safety. Clearly, the protection of public health and safety represents an important function of state and local governments. However, appellees' statistics in our view cannot support the conclusion that the gender-based distinction closely serves to achieve that objective and therefore the distinction cannot under *Reed* withstand equal protection challenge.

The appellees introduced a variety of statistical surveys. First, an analysis of arrest statistics for 1973 demonstrated that 18–20-year-old male arrests for "driving under the influence" and "drunkenness" substantially exceeded female arrests for that same age period. Similarly, youths aged 17–21 were found to be overrepresented among those killed or injured in traffic accidents, with males again numerically exceeding females in this regard. *[A footnote by the Court explains that this survey did not draw a correlation between the accident figures for any age group and levels of intoxication found in those killed or injured.]* Third, a random roadside survey in Oklahoma City revealed that young males were more inclined to drive and drink beer than were their female counterparts. Fourth, Federal Bureau of Investigation nationwide statistics exhibited a notable increase in arrests for "driving under the influence." *[The Court notes that the FBI did not attempt to relate the arrest figures either to beer drinking or to an 18–21 age differential.]* Finally, statistical evidence gathered in other jurisdictions, particularly Minnesota and Michigan, was offered to corroborate Oklahoma's experience by indicating the pervasiveness of youthful participation in motor vehicle accidents following the imbibing of alcohol. Conceding that "the case is not free from doubt," 399 F. Supp., at 1314, the District Court nonetheless concluded that this statistical showing substantiated "a rational basis for the legislative judgment underlying the challenged classification." *Id.*, at 1307.

Even were this statistical evidence accepted as

accurate, it nevertheless offers only a weak answer to the equal protection question presented here. The most focused and relevant of the statistical surveys, arrests of 18–20-year-olds for alcohol-related driving offenses, exemplifies the ultimate unpersuasiveness of this evidentiary record. Viewed in terms of the correlation between sex and the actual activity that Oklahoma seeks to regulate—driving while under the influence of alcohol—the statistics broadly establish that .18% of females and 2% of males in that age group were arrested for that offense. While such a disparity is not trivial in a statistical sense, it hardly can form the basis for employment of a gender line as a classifying device. Certainly if maleness is to serve as a proxy for drinking and driving, a correlation of 2% must be considered an unduly tenuous "fit." Indeed, prior cases have consistently rejected the use of sex as a decisionmaking factor even though the statutes in question certainly rested on far more predictive empirical relationships than this.

Moreover, the statistics exhibit a variety of other shortcomings that seriously impugn their value to equal protection analysis. Setting aside the obvious methodological problems, the surveys do not adequately justify the salient features of Oklahoma's gender-based traffic-safety law. None purports to measure the use and dangerousness of 3.2% beer as opposed to alcohol generally, a detail that is of particular importance since, in light of its low alcohol level, Oklahoma apparently considers the 3.2% beverage to be "nonintoxicating." Okla. Stat., Tit. 37, § 163.1 (1958); see *State ex rel. Springer* v. *Bliss*, 199 Okla. 198, 185 P. 2d 220 (1947). Moreover, many of the studies, while graphically documenting the unfortunate increase in driving while under the influence of alcohol, make no effort to relate their findings to age-sex differentials as involved here. Indeed, the only survey that explicitly centered its attention upon young drivers and their use of beer—albeit apparently not of the diluted 3.2% variety—reached results that hardly can be viewed as impressive in justifying either a gender or age classification.

There is no reason to belabor this line of analysis. It is unrealistic to expect either members of the judiciary or state officials to be well versed in the rigors of experimental or statistical technique. But this merely illustrates that proving broad sociological propositions by statistics is a dubious business, and one that inevitably is in tension with the normative philosophy that underlies the Equal Protection Clause. Suffice to say that the showing offered by the appellees does not satisfy us that sex represents a legitimate, accurate proxy for the regulation of drinking and driving. In fact, when it is further recognized that Oklahoma's statute prohibits only the selling of 3.2% beer to young males and not their drinking the beverage once acquired (even after purchase by their 18–20-year-old female companions), the relationship between gender and traffic safety becomes far too tenuous to satisfy *Reed's* requirement that the gender-based difference be substantially related to achievement of the statutory objective.

We hold, therefore, that under *Reed*, Oklahoma's 3.2% beer statute invidiously discriminates against males 18–20 years of age.

D

[In this section, the Court considers Oklahoma's contention that §§ 241 and 245 enforce state policies concerning the sale and distribution of alcohol and by force of the Twenty-first Amendment should therefore be held to withstand the equal protection challenge. The Court holds that the Amendment does not save the invidious gender-based discrimination from invalidation.]

We conclude that the gender-based differential contained in Okla. Stat., Tit. 37, § 245 (1976 Supp.) constitutes a denial of the equal protection of the laws to males aged 18–20 and reverse the judgment of the District Court.

It is so ordered.

MR. JUSTICE POWELL, concurring.

. . .

[In a footnote, Powell refers to the dissatisfaction with the Court's "two-tier" analysis of the Equal Protection Clause, adopting a strict-scrutiny test for discrimination in cases of race and alienage, and a more lenient test that permits a legislature to make

classifications if the statute is rational and furthers an important governmental interest. He even suggests that the holding in the Oklahoma case implies a "middle-tier" approach.]

MR. JUSTICE STEVENS, concurring.

There is only one Equal Protection Clause. It requires every State to govern impartially. It does not direct the courts to apply one standard of review in some cases and a different standard in other cases. Whatever criticism may be leveled at a judicial opinion implying that there are at least three such standards applies with the same force to a double standard.

I am inclined to believe that what has become known as the two-tiered analysis of equal protection claims does not describe a completely logical method of deciding cases, but rather is a method the Court has employed to explain decisions that actually apply a single standard in a reasonably consistent fashion. I also suspect that a careful explanation of the reasons motivating particular decisions may contribute more to an identification of that standard than an attempt to articulate it in all-encompassing terms. It may therefore be appropriate for me to state the principal reasons which persuaded me to join the Court's opinion.

In this case, the classification is not as obnoxious as some the Court has condemned, nor as inoffensive as some the Court has accepted. It is objectionable because it is based on an accident of birth, because it is a mere remnant of the now almost universally rejected tradition of discriminating against males in this age bracket, and because, to the extent it reflects any physical difference between males and females, it is actually perverse. *[Stevens points out in a footnote that because males are generally heavier than females, they have a greater capacity to consume alcohol without impairing their driving ability.]* The question then is whether the traffic safety justification put forward by the State is sufficient to make an otherwise offensive classification acceptable.

The classification is not totally irrational. For the evidence does indicate that there are more males than females in this age bracket who drive and also more who drink. Nevertheless, there are several reasons why I regard the justification as unacceptable. It is difficult to believe that the statute was actually intended to cope with the problem of traffic safety, since it has only a minimal effect on access to a not very intoxicating beverage and does not prohibit its consumption. Moreover, the empirical data submitted by the State accentuate the unfairness of treating all 18–20-year-old males as inferior to their female counterparts. The legislation imposes a restraint on 100% of the males in the class allegedly because about 2% of them have probably violated one or more laws relating to the consumption of alcoholic beverages. It is unlikely that this law will have a significant deterrent effect either on that 2% or on the law-abiding 98%. But even assuming some such slight benefit, it does not seem to me that an insult to all of the young men of the State can be justified by visiting the sins of the 2% on the 98%.

MR. JUSTICE BLACKMUN, concurring in part.

I join the Court's opinion except Part II–D thereof. I agree, however, that the Twenty-first Amendment does not save the challenged Oklahoma statute.

MR. JUSTICE STEWART, concurring in the judgment.

. . .

MR. CHIEF JUSTICE BURGER, dissenting.

I am in general agreement with MR. JUSTICE REHNQUIST's dissent, but even at the risk of compounding the obvious confusion created by those voting to reverse the District Court, I will add a few words.

At the outset I cannot agree that appellant Whitener has standing arising from her status as a saloonkeeper to assert the constitutional rights of her customers. In this Court "a litigant may only assert his own constitutional rights or immunities." *United States* v. *Raines*, 362 U. S. 17, 22 (1960). There are a few, but strictly limited exceptions to that rule; despite the most creative efforts, this case fits within none of them.

. . .

The means employed by the Oklahoma Legislature to achieve the objectives sought may not be agreeable to some judges, but since eight Members of the Court think the means not irrational, I see no basis for striking down the statute as violative of the Constitution simply because we find it unwise, unneeded, or possibly even a bit foolish.

With MR. JUSTICE REHNQUIST, I would affirm the judgment of the District Court.

MR. JUSTICE REHNQUIST, dissenting.

The Court's disposition of this case is objectionable on two grounds. First is its conclusion that *men* challenging a gender-based statute which treats them less favorably than women may invoke a more stringent standard of judicial review than pertains to most other types of classifications. Second is the Court's enunciation of this standard, without citation to any source, as being that "classifications by gender must serve *important* governmental objectives and must be *substantially* related to achievement of those objectives." *Ante*, at 197 (emphasis added). The only redeeming feature of the Court's opinion, to my mind, is that it apparently signals a retreat by those who joined the plurality opinion in *Frontiero* v. *Richardson*, 411 U. S. 677 (1973), from their view that sex is a "suspect" classification for purposes of equal protection analysis. I think the Oklahoma statute challenged here need pass only the "rational basis" equal protection analysis expounded in cases such as *McGowan* v. *Maryland*, 366 U. S. 420 (1961), and *Williamson* v. *Lee Optical Co.*, 348 U. S. 483 (1955), and I believe that it is constitutional under that analysis.

I

In *Frontiero* v. *Richardson*, *supra*, the opinion for the plurality sets forth the reasons of four Justices for concluding that sex should be regarded as a suspect classification for purposes of equal protection analysis. These reasons center on our Nation's "long and unfortunate history of sex discrimination," 411 U.S., at 684, which has been reflected in a whole range of restrictions on the legal rights of women, not the least of which have concerned the ownership of property and partici-

pation in the electoral process. Noting that the pervasive and persistent nature of the discrimination experienced by women is in part the result of their ready identifiability, the plurality rested its invocation of strict scrutiny largely upon the fact that "statutory distinctions between the sexes often have the effect of invidiously relegating the entire class of females to inferior legal status without regard to the actual capabilities of its individual members." *Id.*, at 686–687. See *Stanton* v. *Stanton*, 421 U. S. 7, 14–15 (1975).

Subsequent to *Frontiero*, the Court has declined to hold that sex is a suspect class, *Stanton* v. *Stanton*, *supra*, at 13, and no such holding is imported by the Court's resolution of this case. However, the Court's application here of an elevated or "intermediate" level scrutiny, like that invoked in cases dealing with discrimination against females, raises the question of why the statute here should be treated any differently from countless legislative classifications unrelated to sex which have been upheld under a minimum rationality standard. . . .

Most obviously unavailable to support any kind of special scrutiny in this case, is a history or pattern of past discrimination, such as was relied on by the plurality in *Frontiero* to support its invocation of strict scrutiny. There is no suggestion in the Court's opinion that males in this age group are in any way peculiarly disadvantaged, subject to systematic discriminatory treatment, or otherwise in need of special solicitude from the courts.

The Court does not discuss the nature of the right involved, and there is no reason to believe that it sees the purchase of 3.2% beer as implicating any important interest, let alone one that is "fundamental" in the constitutional sense of invoking strict scrutiny. Indeed, the Court's accurate observation that the statute affects the selling but not the drinking of 3.2% beer, *ante*, at 204, further emphasizes the limited effect that it has on even those persons in the age group involved. There is, in sum, nothing about the statutory classification involved here to suggest that it affects an interest, or works against a group, which can claim under the Equal Protection Clause that it is entitled to special judicial protection.

It is true that a number of our opinions contain broadly phrased dicta implying that the same test should be applied to all classifications based on sex, whether affecting females or males. *E. g., Frontiero* v. *Richardson, supra,* at 688; *Reed* v. *Reed,* 404 U. S. 71, 76 (1971). However, before today, no decision of this Court has applied an elevated level of scrutiny to invalidate a statutory discrimination harmful to males, except where the statute impaired an important personal interest protected by the Constitution. *[In a footnote, Rehnquist refers to* Stanley v. Illinois, *405 U.S. 645 (1972), which struck down a statute allowing separation of illegitimate children from a surviving father but not a surviving mother, without showing parental unfitness.]* There being no such interest here, and there being no plausible argument that this is a discrimination against females, the Court's reliance on our previous sex-discrimination cases is ill-founded. It treats gender classification as a talisman which—without regard to the rights involved or the persons affected—calls into effect a heavier burden of judicial review.

The Court's conclusion that a law which treats males less favorably than females "must serve important governmental objectives and must be substantially related to achievement of those objectives" apparently comes out of thin air. The Equal Protection Clause contains no such language, and none of our previous cases adopt that standard. I would think we have had enough difficulty with the two standards of review which our cases have recognized—the norm of "rational basis," and the "compelling state interest" required where a "suspect classification" is involved—so as to counsel weightily against the insertion of still another "standard" between those two. How is this Court to divine what objectives are important? How is it to determine whether a particular law is "substantially" related to the achievement of such objective, rather than related in some other way to its achievement? Both of the phrases used are so diaphanous and elastic as to invite subjective judicial preferences or prejudices relating to particular types of legislation, masquerading as judgments whether such legislation is directed at "important" objectives or, whether the relationship to those objectives is "substantial" enough.

. . .

Michael M. v. Sonoma County Superior Court

450 U.S. 464 (1981)

Michael M., a 17½-year-old male, was charged with violating California's "statutory rape" law, which defines unlawful sexual intercourse as "an act of sexual intercourse accomplished with a female not the wife of the perpetrator, where the female is under the age of 18 years." He sued on the ground that the statute unlawfully discriminated on the basis of gender since men alone were criminally liable.

JUSTICE REHNQUIST announced the judgment of the Court and delivered an opinion, in which THE CHIEF JUSTICE, JUSTICE STEWART, and JUSTICE POWELL joined.

The question presented in this case is whether California's "statutory rape" law, § 261.5 of the Cal. Penal Code Ann. (West Supp. 1981), violates the Equal Protection Clause of the Fourteenth Amendment. Section 261.5 defines unlawful sexual intercourse as "an act of sexual intercourse accomplished with a female not the wife of the perpetrator, where the female is under the age of 18 years." The statute thus makes men alone criminally liable for the act of sexual intercourse.

In July 1978, a complaint was filed in the Municipal Court of Sonoma County, Cal., alleging that petitioner, then a 17½-year-old male, had had unlawful sexual intercourse with a female under the age of 18, in violation of § 261.5. The evidence adduced at a preliminary hearing showed that at approximately midnight on June 3, 1978, petitioner and two friends approached Sharon, a 16½-year-old female, and her sister as they waited at a bus stop. Petitioner and Sharon, who had already been drinking, moved away from the others and began to kiss. After being struck in the face for rebuffing petitioner's initial advances, Sharon submitted to sexual intercourse with petitioner. Prior to trial, petitioner sought to set aside the information on both state and federal constitutional grounds, asserting that § 261.5 unlawfully discriminated on the basis of gender. The trial court and the California Court of Appeal denied petitioner's request for relief and petitioner sought review in the Supreme Court of California.

The Supreme Court held that "section 261.5 discriminates on the basis of sex because only females may be victims, and only males may violate the section." 25 Cal. 3d 608, 611, 601 P. 2d 572, 574. The court then subjected the classification to "strict scrutiny," stating that it must be justified by a compelling state interest. It found that the classification was "supported not by mere social convention but by the immutable physiological fact that it is the female exclusively who can become pregnant." *Ibid.* Canvassing "the tragic human costs of illegitimate teenage pregnancies," including the large number of teenage abortions, the increased medical risk associated with teenage pregnancies, and the social consequences of teenage childbearing, the court concluded that the State has a compelling interest in preventing such pregnancies. Because males alone can "physiologically cause the result which the law properly seeks to avoid," the court further held that the gender classification was readily justified as a means of identifying offender and victim. For the reasons stated below, we affirm the judgment of the California Supreme Court.

As is evident from our opinions, the Court has had some difficulty in agreeing upon the proper approach and analysis in cases involving challenges to gender-based classifications. The issues posed by such challenges range from issues of standing, see *Orr* v. *Orr*, 440 U.S. 268 (1979), to the appropriate standard of judicial review for the

substantive classification. Unlike the California Supreme Court, we have not held that gender-based classifications are "inherently suspect" and thus we do not apply so-called "strict scrutiny" to those classifications. See *Stanton* v. *Stanton*, 421 U. S. 7 (1975). Our cases have held, however, that the traditional minimum rationality test takes on a somewhat "sharper focus" when gender-based classifications are challenged. See *Craig* v. *Boren*, 429 U. S. 190, 210 n.* (1976) (POWELL, J., concurring). In *Reed* v. *Reed*, 404 U. S. 71 (1971), for example, the Court stated that a gender-based classification will be upheld if it bears a "fair and substantial relationship" to legitimate state ends, while in *Craig* v. *Boren, supra,* at 197, the Court restated the test to require the classification to bear a "substantial relationship" to "important governmental objectives."

. . .

We are satisfied not only that the prevention of illegitimate pregnancy is at least one of the "purposes" of the statute, but also that the State has a strong interest in preventing such pregnancy. At the risk of stating the obvious, teenage pregnancies, which have increased dramatically over the last two decades, have significant social, medical, and economic consequences for both the mother and her child, and the State. Of particular concern to the State is that approximately half of all teenage pregnancies end in abortion. And of those children who are born, their illegitimacy makes them likely candidates to become wards of the State.

We need not be medical doctors to discern that young men and young women are not similarly situated with respect to the problems and the risks of sexual intercourse. Only women may become pregnant, and they suffer disproportionately the profound physical, emotional, and psychological consequences of sexual activity. The statute at issue here protects women from sexual intercourse at an age when those consequences are particularly severe.

The question thus boils down to whether a State may attack the problem of sexual intercourse and teenage pregnancy directly by prohibiting a male from having sexual intercourse with a minor female. We hold that such a statute is sufficiently related to the State's objectives to pass constitutional muster.

Because virtually all of the significant harmful and inescapably identifiable consequences of teenage pregnancy fall on the young female, a legislature acts well within its authority when it elects to punish only the participant who, by nature, suffers few of the consequences of his conduct. It is hardly unreasonable for a legislature acting to protect minor females to exclude them from punishment. Moreover, the risk of pregnancy itself constitutes a substantial deterrence to young females. No similar natural sanctions deter males. A criminal sanction imposed solely on males thus serves to roughly "equalize" the deterrents on the sexes.

. . .

There remains only petitioner's contention that the statute is unconstitutional as it is applied to him because he, like Sharon, was under 18 at the time of sexual intercourse. Petitioner argues that the statute is flawed because it presumes that as between two persons under 18, the male is the culpable aggressor. We find petitioner's contentions unpersuasive. Contrary to his assertions, the statute does not rest on the assumption that males are generally the aggressors. It is instead an attempt by a legislature to prevent illegitimate teenage pregnancy by providing an additional deterrent for men. The age of the man is irrelevant since young men are as capable as older men of inflicting the harm sought to be prevented.

In upholding the California statute we also recognize that this is not a case where a statute is being challenged on the grounds that it "invidiously discriminates" against females. To the contrary, the statute places a burden on males which is not shared by females. But we find nothing to suggest that men, because of past discrimination or peculiar disadvantages, are in need of the special solicitude of the courts. Nor is this a case where the gender classification is made "solely for . . . administrative convenience," as in *Frontiero* v. *Richardson*, 411 U. S. 677, 690 (1973) (emphasis omitted), or rests on "the baggage of sexual stereotypes" as in *Orr* v. *Orr*, 440 U. S., at

283. As we have held, the statute instead reasonably reflects the fact that the consequences of sexual intercourse and pregnancy fall more heavily on the female than on the male.

Accordingly the judgment of the California Supreme Court is

Affirmed.

JUSTICE STEWART, concurring.

Section 261.5, on its face, classifies on the basis of sex. A male who engages in sexual intercourse with an underage female who is not his wife violates the statute; a female who engages in sexual intercourse with an underage male who is not her husband does not. The petitioner contends that this state law, which punishes only males for the conduct in question, violates his Fourteenth Amendment right to the equal protection of the law. The Court today correctly rejects that contention. . . .

JUSTICE BLACKMUN, concurring in the judgment. . . .

JUSTICE BRENNAN, with whom JUSTICES WHITE and MARSHALL join, dissenting.

I

It is disturbing to find the Court so splintered on a case that presents such a straightforward issue: Whether the admittedly gender-based classification in Cal. Penal Code Ann. § 261.5 (West Supp. 1981) bears a sufficient relationship to the State's asserted goal of preventing teenage pregnancies to survive the "mid-level" constitutional scrutiny mandated by *Craig* v. *Boren*, 429 U. S. 190 (1976). Applying the analytical framework provided by our precedents, I am convinced that there is only one proper resolution of this issue: the classification must be declared unconstitutional. I fear that the plurality opinion and JUSTICES STEWART and BLACKMUN reach the opposite result by placing too much emphasis on the desirability of achieving the State's asserted statutory goal—prevention of teenage pregnancy—and not enough emphasis on the fundamental question of whether the sex-based discrimination in the California statute is *substantially* related to the achievement of that goal.

. . .

The State of California vigorously asserts that the "important governmental objective" to be served by § 261.5 is the prevention of teenage pregnancy. It claims that its statute furthers this goal by deterring sexual activity by males—the class of persons it considers more responsible for causing those pregnancies. But even assuming that prevention of teenage pregnancy is an important governmental objective and that it is in fact an objective of § 261.5, see *infra*, at 494–496, California still has the burden of proving that there are fewer teenage pregnancies under its gender-based statutory rape law than there would be if the law were gender neutral. To meet this burden, the State must show that because its statutory rape law punishes only males, and not females, it more effectively deters minor females from having sexual intercourse.

The plurality assumes that a gender-neutral statute would be less effective than § 261.5 in deterring sexual activity because a gender-neutral statute would create significant enforcement problems. The plurality thus accepts the State's assertion that

"a female is surely less likely to report violations of the statute if she herself would be subject to criminal prosecution. In an area already fraught with prosecutorial difficulties, we decline to hold that the Equal Protection Clause requires a legislature to enact a statute so broad that it may well be incapable of enforcement." *Ante*, at 473–474 (footnotes omitted).

However, a State's bare assertion that its gender-based statutory classification substantially furthers an important governmental interest is not enough to meet its burden of proof under *Craig* v. *Boren*. Rather, the State must produce evidence that will persuade the court that its assertion is true. See *Craig* v. *Boren*, 429 U. S., at 200-204.

The State has not produced such evidence in this case. Moreover, there are at least two serious flaws in the State's assertion that law enforcement problems created by a gender-neutral statutory rape law would make such a statute less effective than a gender-based statute in deterring sexual activity.

First, the experience of other jurisdictions, and California itself, belies the plurality's conclusion that a gender-neutral statutory rape law "may well be incapable of enforcement." There are now at least 37 States that have enacted gender-neutral statutory rape laws. Although most of these laws protect young persons (of either sex) from the sexual exploitation of older individuals, the laws of Arizona, Florida, and Illinois permit prosecution of both minor females and minor males for engaging in mutual sexual conduct. California has introduced no evidence that those States have been handicapped by the enforcement problems the plurality finds so persuasive. Surely, if those States could provide such evidence, we might expect that California would have introduced it.

In addition, the California Legislature in recent years has revised other sections of the Penal Code to make them gender-neutral. For example, Cal. Penal Code Ann. §§ 286 (b)(1) and 288a (b)(1) (West Supp. 1981), prohibiting sodomy and oral copulation with a "person who is under 18 years of age," could cause two minor homosexuals to be subjected to criminal sanctions for engaging in mutually consensual conduct. Again, the State has introduced no evidence to explain why a gender-neutral statutory rape law would be any more difficult to enforce than those statutes.

The second flaw in the State's assertion is that even assuming that a gender-neutral statute would be more difficult to enforce, the State has still not shown that those enforcement problems would make such a statute less effective than a gender-based statute in deterring minor females from engaging in sexual intercourse. Common sense, however, suggests that a gender-neutral statutory rape law is potentially a *greater* deterrent of sexual activity than a gender-based law, for the simple reason that a gender-neutral law subjects both men and women to criminal sanctions and thus arguably has a deterrent effect on twice as many potential violators. Even if fewer persons were prosecuted under the gender-neutral law, as the State suggests, it would still be true that twice as many persons would be *subject* to arrest. The State's failure to prove that a gender-neutral law would be a less effective deterrent than a gender-based law, like the State's failure to prove that a gender-neutral law would be difficult to enforce, should have led this Court to invalidate § 261.5.

III

Until very recently, no California court or commentator had suggested that the purpose of California's statutory rape law was to protect young women from the risk of pregnancy. Indeed, the historical development of § 261.5 demonstrates that the law was initially enacted on the premise that young women, in contrast to young men, were to be deemed legally incapable of consenting to an act of sexual intercourse. Because their chastity was considered particularly precious, those young women were felt to be uniquely in need of the State's protection. In contrast, young men were assumed to be capable of making such decisions for themselves; the law therefore did not offer them any special protection.

It is perhaps because the gender classification in California's statutory rape law was initially designed to further these outmoded sexual stereotypes, rather than to reduce the incidence of teenage pregnancies, that the State has been unable to demonstrate a substantial relationship between the classification and its newly asserted goal. Cf. *Califano* v. *Goldfarb*, 430 U. S., at 223 (STEVENS, J., concurring in judgment). But whatever the reason, the State has not shown that Cal. Penal Code § 261.5 is any more effective than a gender-neutral law would be in deterring minor females from engaging in sexual intercourse. It has therefore not met its burden of proving that the statutory classification is substantially related to the achievement of its asserted goal.

I would hold that § 261.5 violates the Equal Protection Clause of the Fourteenth Amendment, and I would reverse the judgment of the California Supreme Court.

JUSTICE STEVENS, dissenting.

Local custom and belief—rather than statutory laws of venerable but doubtful ancestry—will determine the volume of sexual activity among unmarried teenagers. The empirical evidence cited by the plurality demonstrates the futility of the notion that a statutory prohibition will significantly affect the volume of that activity or provide a meaningful solution to the problems created by it. Nevertheless, as a matter of constitutional power, unlike my Brother BRENNAN, see *ante*, at 491, n. 5, I would have no doubt about the validity of a state law prohibiting all unmarried teenagers from engaging in sexual intercourse. The societal interests in reducing the incidence of venereal disease and teenage pregnancy are sufficient, in my judgment, to justify a prohibition of conduct that increases the risk of those harms.

My conclusion that a nondiscriminatory prohibition would be constitutional does not help me answer the question whether a prohibition applicable to only half of the joint participants in the risk-creating conduct is also valid. It cannot be true that the validity of a total ban is an adequate justification for a selective prohibition; otherwise, the constitutional objection to discriminatory rules would be meaningless. The question in this case is whether the difference between males and females justifies this statutory discrimination based entirely on sex.

. . .

In this case, the fact that a female confronts a greater risk of harm than a male is a reason for applying the prohibition to her—not a reason for granting her a license to use her own judgment on whether or not to assume the risk. Surely, if we examine the problem from the point of view of society's interest in preventing the risk-creating conduct from occurring at all, it is irrational to exempt 50% of the potential violators. See dissent of JUSTICE BRENNAN, *ante*, at 493–494. And, if we view the government's interest as that of a *parens patriae* seeking to protect its subjects from harming themselves, the discrimination is actually perverse. Would a rational parent making rules for the conduct of twin children of opposite sex simultaneously forbid the son and authorize the daughter to engage in conduct that is especially harmful to the daughter? That is the effect of this statutory classification.

If pregnancy or some other special harm is suffered by one of the two participants in the prohibited act, that special harm no doubt would constitute a legitimate mitigating factor in deciding what, if any, punishment might be appropriate in a given case. But from the standpoint of fashioning a general preventive rule—or, indeed, in determining appropriate punishment when neither party in fact has suffered any special harm—I regard a total exemption for the members of the more endangered class as utterly irrational.

. . . even if my logic is faulty and there actually is some speculative basis for treating equally guilty males and females differently, I still believe that any such speculative justification would be outweighed by the paramount interest in evenhanded enforcement of the law. A rule that authorizes punishment of only one of two equally guilty wrongdoers violates the essence of the constitutional requirement that the sovereign must govern impartially.

I respectfully dissent.

Rostker v. Goldberg
453 U.S. 57 (1981)

In 1980, Congress reactivated the registration process for military service but denied President Carter the authority he requested to permit the registration and conscription of women as well as men. After President Carter ordered the registration of specified groups of young men, several men, including Robert L. Goldberg, brought a lawsuit challenging the statute's constitutionality. A three-judge district court held that the statute's gender-based discrimination violated the Due Process Clause of the Fifth Amendment and enjoined registration under the statute. Bernard Rostker, Director of Selective Service, brought this appeal to the Supreme Court.

JUSTICE REHNQUIST delivered the opinion of the Court.

The question presented is whether the Military Selective Service Act, 50 U. S. C. App. § 451 *et seq.* (1976 ed. and Supp. III), violates the Fifth Amendment to the United States Constitution in authorizing the President to require the registration of males and not females.

I

Congress is given the power under the Constitution "To raise and support Armies," "To provide and maintain a Navy," and "To make Rules for the Government and Regulation of the land and naval Forces." Art. I, § 8, cls. 12–14. Pursuant to this grant of authority Congress has enacted the Military Selective Service Act, 50 U. S. C. App. § 451 *et seq.* (1976 ed. and Supp. III) (the MSSA or the Act). Section 3 of the Act, 62 Stat. 605, as amended, 50 U. S. C. App. § 453, empowers the President, by proclamation, to require the registration of "every male citizen" and male resident aliens between the ages of 18 and 26. The purpose of this registration is to facilitate any eventual conscription: pursuant to § 4 (a) of the Act, 62 Stat. 605, as amended, 50 U. S. C. App. § 454 (a), those persons required to register under § 3 are liable for training and service in the Armed Forces. The MSSA registration provision serves no other purpose beyond providing a pool for subsequent induction.

Registration for the draft under § 3 was discontinued in 1975. Presidential Proclamation No. 4360, 3 CFR 462 (1971–1975 Comp.), note following 50 U. S. C. App. § 453. In early 1980, President Carter determined that it was necessary to reactivate the draft registration process. The immediate impetus for this decision was the Soviet armed invasion of Afghanistan. . . . He also recommended that Congress take action to amend the MSSA to permit the registration and conscription of women as well as men. . . .

Congress agreed that it was necessary to reactivate the registration process, and allocated funds for that purpose in a Joint Resolution . . . The Resolution did not allocate all the funds originally requested by the President, but only those necessary to register males. See S. Rep. No. 96–789, p. 1, n. 1, and p. 2 (1980); 126 Cong. Rec. 13895 (1980) (Sen. Nunn). Although Congress considered the question at great length, see *infra*, at 72–74, it declined to amend the MSSA to permit the registration of women.

On July 2, 1980, the President, by Proclamation, ordered the registration of specified groups of young men pursuant to the authority conferred by § 3 of the Act. Registration was to commence on July 21, 1980. Proclamation No. 4771, 3 CFR 82 (1980).

[A lawsuit, beginning in 1971, attacked the draft system on several grounds, including an impermissible discrimination between males and females. The case had never been dismissed. On July 1, 1980, the District Court for the Eastern District of Pennsylvania certified a plaintiff class of all male persons subject to registration. On July 18, 1980, the district court found the Act in violation of the Due Process Clause of the Fifth Amendment. It decided only that women should be subject to registration. The question of women serving in combat was not addressed.]

II

Whenever called upon to judge the constitutionality of an Act of Congress—"the gravest and most delicate duty that this Court is called upon to perform," *Blodgett* v. *Holden*, 275 U. S. 142, 148 (1927) (Holmes, J.)—the Court accords "great weight to the decisions of Congress." *Columbia Broadcasting System, Inc.* v. *Democratic National Committee*, 412 U. S. 94, 102 (1973). The Congress is a coequal branch of government whose Members take the same oath we do to uphold the Constitution of the United States. As Justice Frankfurter noted in *Joint Anti-Fascist Refugee Committee* v. *McGrath*, 341 U. S. 123, 164 (1951) (concurring opinion), we must have "due regard to the fact that this Court is not exercising a primary judgment but is sitting in judgment upon those who also have taken the oath to observe the Constitution and who have the responsibility for carrying on

government." The customary deference accorded the judgments of Congress is certainly appropriate when, as here, Congress specifically considered the question of the Act's constitutionality. See, *e. g.*, S. Rep. No. 96–826, pp. 159–161 (1980); 126 Cong. Rec. 13880–13882 (1980) (Sen. Warner); *id.*, at 13896 (Sen. Hatfield).

This is not, however, merely a case involving the customary deference accorded congressional decisions. The case arises in the context of Congress' authority over national defense and military affairs, and perhaps in no other area has the Court accorded Congress greater deference. In rejecting the registration of women, Congress explicitly relied upon its constitutional powers under Art. I, § 8, cls. 12–14. The "specific findings" section of the Report of the Senate Armed Services Committee, later adopted by both Houses of Congress, began by stating:

"Article I, section 8 of the Constitution commits exclusively to the Congress the powers to raise and support armies, provide and maintain a Navy, and make rules for Government and regulation of the land and naval forces, and pursuant to these powers it lies within the discretion of the Congress to determine the occasions for expansion of our Armed Forces, and the means best suited to such expansion should it prove necessary." S. Rep. No. 96–826, *supra*, at 160.

See also S. Rep. No. 96–226, p. 8 (1979). This Court has consistently recognized Congress' "broad constitutional power" to raise and regulate armies and navies, *Schlesinger* v. *Ballard*, 419 U. S. 498, 510 (1975). As the Court noted in considering a challenge to the selective service laws: "The constitutional power of Congress to raise and support armies and to make all laws necessary and proper to that end is broad and sweeping." *United States* v. *O'Brien*, 391 U. S. 367, 377 (1968). See *Lichter* v. *United States*, 334 U. S. 742, 755 (1948).

Not only is the scope of Congress' constitutional power in this area broad, but the lack of competence on the part of the courts is marked. In *Gilligan* v. *Morgan*, 413 U. S. 1, 10 (1973), the Court noted:

"[I]t is difficult to conceive of an area of governmental activity in which the courts have less competence. The complex, subtle, and professional decisions as to the composition, training, equipping, and control of a military force are essentially professional military judgments, subject *always* to civilian control of the Legislative and Executive Branches."

. . .

None of this is to say that Congress is free to disregard the Constitution when it acts in the area of military affairs. In that area, as any other, Congress remains subject to the limitations of the Due Process Clause, see *Ex parte Milligan*, 4 Wall. 2 (1866); *Hamilton* v. *Kentucky Distilleries & Warehouse Co.*, 251 U. S. 146, 156 (1919), but the tests and limitations to be applied may differ because of the military context. We of course do not abdicate our ultimate responsibility to decide the constitutional question, but simply recognize that the Constitution itself requires such deference to congressional choice. . . .

III

This case is quite different from several of the gender-based discrimination cases we have considered in that, despite appellees' assertions, Congress did not act "unthinkingly" or "reflexively and not for any considered reason." Brief for Appellees 35. The question of registering women for the draft not only received considerable national attention and was the subject of wide-ranging public debate, but also was extensively considered by Congress in hearings, floor debate, and in committee. Hearings held by both Houses of Congress in response to the President's request for authorization to register women adduced extensive testimony and evidence concerning the issue. . . .

The MSSA established a plan for maintaining "adequate armed strength . . . to insure the security of [the] Nation." 50 U. S. C. App. § 451 (b). Registration is the first step "in a united and continuous process designed to raise an army speedily and efficiently," *Falbo* v. *United States*, 320 U. S. 549, 553 (1944), see *United States* v. *Nugent*, 346 U. S. 1, 9 (1953), and Congress provided for the reactivation of registration in order to "provid[e] the means for the early delivery of

inductees in an emergency." S. Rep. No. 96–826, *supra*, at 156. Although the three-judge District Court often tried to sever its consideration of registration from the particulars of induction, see, e. g., 509 F. Supp., at 604–605, Congress rather clearly linked the need for renewed registration with its views on the character of a subsequent draft. The Senate Report specifically found that "[a]n ability to mobilize rapidly is essential to the preservation of our national security. . . . A functioning registration system is a vital part of any mobilization plan." S. Rep. No. 96–826, *supra*, at 160. As Senator Warner put it, "I equate registration with the draft." Hearings on S. 2294, at 1197. See also *id.*, at 1195 (Sen. Jepsen), 1671 (Sen. Exon). Such an approach is certainly logical, since under the MSSA induction is interlocked with registration: only those registered may be drafted, and registration serves no purpose beyond providing a pool for the draft. . . .

Women as a group, however, unlike men as a group, are not eligible for combat. The restrictions on the participation of women in combat in the Navy and Air Force are statutory. Under 10 U. S. C. § 6015 (1976 ed., Supp. III), "women may not be assigned to duty on vessels or in aircraft that are engaged in combat missions," and under 10 U. S. C. § 8549 female members of the Air Force "may not be assigned to duty in aircraft engaged in combat missions." The Army and Marine Corps preclude the use of women in combat as a matter of established policy. . . .

The existence of the combat restrictions clearly indicates the basis for Congress' decision to exempt women from registration. The purpose of registration was to prepare for a draft of combat troops. Since women are excluded from combat, Congress concluded that they would not be needed in the event of a draft, and therefore decided not to register them. . . .

. . . assuming that a small number of women could be drafted for noncombat roles, Congress simply did not consider it worth the added burdens of including women in draft and registration plans. "It has been suggested that all women be registered, but only a handful actually be inducted in an emergency. The Committee finds this a confused and ultimately unsatisfactory solution." S. Rep. No. 96–826, *supra*, at 158. As the Senate

Committee recognized a year before, "training would be needlessly burdened by women recruits who could not be used in combat." S. Rep. No. 96–226, p. 9 (1979). See also S. Rep. No. 96–826, *supra*, at 159 ("Other administrative problems such as housing and different treatment with regard to dependency, hardship and physical standards would also exist"). It is not for this Court to dismiss such problems as insignificant in the context of military preparedness and the exigencies of a future mobilization.

Congress also concluded that whatever the need for women for noncombat roles during mobilization, whether 80,000 or less, it could be met by volunteers. See *id.*, at 160; *id.*, at 158 ("Because of the combat restrictions, the need would be primarily for men, and women volunteers would fill the requirements for women"); House Hearings 19 (Rep. Holt). See also Hearings on S. 2294, at 1195 (Gen. Rogers).

Most significantly, Congress determined that staffing noncombat positions with women during a mobilization would be positively detrimental to the important goal of military flexibility.

". . . [T]here are other military reasons that preclude very large numbers of women from serving. Military flexibility requires that a commander be able to move units or ships quickly. Units or ships not located at the front or not previously scheduled for the front nevertheless must be able to move into action if necessary. In peace and war, significant rotation of personnel is necessary. We should not divide the military into two groups—one in permanent combat and one in permanent support. Large numbers of noncombat positions must be available to which combat troops can return for duty before being redeployed." S. Rep. No. 96–826, *supra*, at 158.

The point was repeated in specific findings, *id.*, at 160; see also S. Rep. No. 96–226, *supra.* at 9. In sum, Congress carefully evaluated the testimony that 80,000 women conscripts could be usefully employed in the event of a draft and rejected it in the permissible exercise of its constitutional responsibility. See also Hearing on S. 109 and S. 226, at 16 (Gen. Rogers); Hearings on S. 2294, at 1682. The District Court was quite wrong in undertaking an independent evaluation of this evidence, rather than adopting an appropriately deferential examination of *Congress'* evaluation of that evidence.

In light of the foregoing, we conclude that Congress acted well within its constitutional authority when it authorized the registration of men, and not women, under the Military Selective Service Act. The decision of the District Court holding otherwise is accordingly

Reversed.

JUSTICE WHITE, with whom JUSTICE BRENNAN joins, dissenting.

I assume what has not been challenged in this case—that excluding women from combat positions does not offend the Constitution. Granting that, it is self-evident that if during mobilization for war, all noncombat military positions must be filled by combat-qualified personnel available to be moved into combat positions, there would be no occasion whatsoever to have any women in the Army, whether as volunteers or inductees. The Court appears to say, *ante*, at 76–77, that Congress concluded as much and that we should accept that judgment even though the serious view of the Executive Branch, including the responsible military services, is to the contrary. The Court's position in this regard is most unpersuasive. I perceive little, if any, indication that Congress itself concluded that every position in the military, no matter how far removed from combat, must be filled with combat-ready men. Common sense and experience in recent wars, where women volunteers were employed in substantial numbers, belie this view of reality. It should not be ascribed to Congress, particularly in the face of the testimony of military authorities, hereafter referred to, that there would be a substantial number of positions in the services that could be filled by women, both in peacetime and during mobilization, even though they are ineligible for combat.

. . .

The Court also submits that because the primary purpose of registration and conscription is to supply combat troops and because the great majority of noncombat positions must be filled by combat-trained men ready to be rotated into combat, the absolute number of positions for which women would be eligible is so small as to be *de minimis* and of no moment for equal protection purposes, especially in light of the administrative burdens involved in registering all women of suitable age. There is some sense to this; but at least on the record before us, the number of women who could be used in the military without sacrificing combat readiness is not at all small or insubstantial, and administrative convenience has not been sufficient justification for the kind of outright gender-based discrimination involved in registering and conscripting men but no women at all.

. . .

JUSTICE MARSHALL, with whom JUSTICE BRENNAN joins, dissenting.

The Court today places its imprimatur on one of the most potent remaining public expressions of "ancient canards about the proper role of women," *Phillips* v. *Martin Marietta Corp.*, 400 U. S. 542, 545 (1971) (MARSHALL, J., concurring). It upholds a statute that requires males but not females to register for the draft, and which thereby categorically excludes women from a fundamental civic obligation. Because I believe the Court's decision is inconsistent with the Constitution's guarantee of equal protection of the laws, I dissent.

I

. . .

C

. . . When, as here, a federal law that classifies on the basis of gender is challenged as violating this constitutional guarantee, it is ultimately for this Court, not Congress, to decide whether there exists the constitutionally required "close and substantial relationship" between the discriminatory means employed and the asserted governmental objective. See *Powell* v. *McCormack*, 395 U. S. 486, 549 (1969); *Baker* v. *Carr*, 369 U. S. 186, 211 (1962). In my judgment, there simply is no basis for concluding in this case that excluding women from registration is substantially related to the achievement of a concededly important governmental interest in maintaining an effec-

tive defense. The Court reaches a contrary conclusion only by using an "[a]nnounced degre[e] of 'deference' to legislative judgmen[t]" as a "facile abstractio[n] . . . to justify a result." *Ante*, at 69, 70.

II

A

The Government does not defend the exclusion of women from registration on the ground that preventing women from serving in the military is substantially related to the effectiveness of the Armed Forces. Indeed, the successful experience of women serving in all branches of the Armed Services would belie any such claim. Some 150,000 women volunteers are presently on active service in the military, and their number is expected to increase to over 250,000 by 1985. . . .

III

The Government argues, however, that the "consistent testimony before Congress was to the effect that there is *no military need* to draft women." Brief for Appellant 31 (emphasis in original). And the Government points to a statement in the Senate Report that "[b]oth the civilian and military leadership agreed that there was no military need to draft women. . . . The argument for registration and induction of women . . . is not based on military necessity, but on considerations of equity." S. Rep. No. 96–826, p. 158 (1980). In accepting the Government's contention, the Court asserts that the President's decision to seek authority to register women was based on "equity," and concludes that "Congress was certainly entitled, in the exercise of its constitutional powers to raise and regulate armies and navies, to focus on the question of military need rather than 'equity.'" *Ante*, at 80. In my view, a more careful examination of the concepts of "equity" and "military need" is required.

As previously noted, the Defense Department's recommendation that women be included in registration plans was based on its conclusion that drafting a limited number of women is consistent with, and could contribute to, military effectiveness. See *supra*, at 97–102. It was against this background that the military experts concluded that "equity" favored registration of women. Assistant Secretary Pirie explained:

"Since women have proven that they can serve successfully as volunteers in the Armed Forces, equity suggests that they be liable to serve as draftees if conscription is reinstated." 1980 House Hearings, at 7.

By "considerations of equity," the military experts acknowledged that female conscripts can perform as well as male conscripts in certain positions, and that there is therefore no reason why one group should be totally excluded from registration and a draft. Thus, what the majority so blithely dismisses as "equity" is nothing less than the Fifth Amendment's guarantee of equal protection of the laws which "requires that Congress treat similarly situated persons similarly," *ante*, at 79. Moreover, whether Congress could subsume this constitutional requirement to "military need," in part depends on precisely what the Senate Report meant by "military need."

The Report stated that "[b]oth the civilian and military leadership agreed that there was no military need to draft women." S. Rep. No. 96–826, *supra*, at 158. An examination of what the "civilian and military leadership" meant by "military need" should therefore provide an insight into the Report's use of the term. Several witnesses testified that because personnel requirements in the event of a mobilization could be met by drafting men, including women in draft plans is not a military necessity. . . .

To be sure, there is no "military need" to draft women in the sense that a war could be waged without their participation. This fact is, however, irrelevant to resolving the constitutional issue. As previously noted, see *supra*, at 94–95, it is not appellees' burden to prove that registration of women substantially furthers the objectives of the MSSA. Rather, because eligibility for combat is not a requirement for some of the positions to be filled in the event of a draft, it is incumbent on the Government to show that excluding women from a draft to fill those positions substantially furthers an important governmental objective.

It may be, however, that the Senate Report's allusion to "military need" is meant to convey Congress' expectation that women volunteers will make it unnecessary to draft any women. The majority apparently accepts this meaning when it states: "Congress also concluded that whatever the need for women for noncombat roles during mobilization, whether 80,000 or less, it could be met by volunteers." *Ante.* at 81. But since the purpose of registration is to protect against unanticipated shortages of volunteers, it is difficult to see how excluding women from registration can be justified by conjectures about the expected number of female volunteers. I fail to see why the exclusion of a pool of persons who would be conscripted only *if needed* can be justified by reference to the current supply of volunteers. In any event, the Defense Department's best estimate is that in the event of a mobilization requiring reinstitution of the draft, there will not be enough women volunteers to fill the positions for which women would be eligible. The Department told Congress:

"If we had a mobilization, our present best projection is that we could use women in some 80,000 of the jobs we would be *inducting* 650,000 people for." 1980 Senate Hearings, at 1688 (Principal Deputy Assistant Secretary of Defense Danzig) (emphasis added).

Thus, however the "military need" statement in the Senate Report is understood, it does not provide the constitutionally required justification for the total exclusion of women from registration and draft plans.

· · ·

VI

· · ·

In concluding that the Government has carried its burden in this case, the Court adopts "an appropriately deferential examination of *Congress'* evaluation of [the] evidence," *ante,* at 83 (emphasis in original). The majority then proceeds to supplement Congress' actual findings with those the Court apparently believes Congress could (and should) have made. Beyond that, the Court substitutes hollow shibboleths about "deference to legislative decisions" for constitutional analysis. It is as if the majority has lost sight of the fact that "it is the responsibility of this Court to act as the ultimate interpreter of the Constitution." *Powell* v. *McCormack*, 395 U. S., at 549. See *Baker* v. *Carr*, 369 U. S., at 211. Congressional enactments in the area of military affairs must, like all other laws, be *judged* by the standards of the Constitution. For the Constitution is the supreme law of the land, and *all* legislation must conform to the principles it lays down. As the Court has pointed out, "the phrase 'war power' cannot be invoked as a talismanic incantation to support any exercise of congressional power which can be brought within its ambit." *United States* v. *Robel*, 389 U. S., at 263–264.

Furthermore, "[w]hen it appears that an Act of Congress conflicts with [a constitutional] provisio[n], we have no choice but to enforce the paramount commands of the Constitution. We are sworn to do no less. We cannot push back the limits of the Constitution merely to accommodate challenged legislation." *Trop* v. *Dulles*, 356 U. S. 86, 104 (1958) (plurality opinion). In some 106 instances since this Court was established it has determined that congressional action exceeded the bounds of the Constitution. I believe the same is true of this statute. In an attempt to avoid its constitutional obligation, the Court today "pushes back the limits of the Constitution" to accommodate an Act of Congress.

I would affirm the judgment of the District Court.

Personnel Administrator of Mass. v. Feeney

442 U.S. 256 (1979)

Under a Massachusetts statute, all veterans who qualify for state civil service positions must be considered for appointment ahead of any qualifying nonveteran. The statute made the preference available to "any person, male or female, including a nurse," who was honorably discharged from the United States armed forces after at least ninety days of active service, at least one day of which was during "wartime." Helen B. Feeney, who was not a veteran, passed a number of open competitive civil service examinations but, because of the veterans' preference law, was ranked below male veterans who had lower test scores. She claimed in court that the statute operated overwhelmingly to the advantage of males.

MR. JUSTICE STEWART delivered the opinion of the Court.

This case presents a challenge to the constitutionality of the Massachusetts veterans' preference statute, Mass. Gen. Laws Ann., ch. 31, § 23, on the ground that it discriminates against women in violation of the Equal Protection Clause of the Fourteenth Amendment. Under ch. 31, § 23, all veterans who qualify for state civil service positions must be considered for appointment ahead of any qualifying nonveterans. The preference operates overwhelmingly to the advantage of males.

The appellee Helen B. Feeney is not a veteran. She brought this action pursuant to 42 U. S. C. § 1983, alleging that the absolute-preference for-

mula established in ch. 31, § 23, inevitably operates to exclude women from consideration for the best Massachusetts civil service jobs and thus unconstitutionally denies them the equal protection of the laws. The three-judge District Court agreed, one judge dissenting. *Anthony* v. *Massachusetts*, 415 F. Supp. 485 (Mass. 1976).

The District Court found that the absolute preference afforded by Massachusetts to veterans has a devastating impact upon the employment opportunities of women. Although it found that the goals of the preference were worthy and legitimate and that the legislation had not been enacted for the purpose of discriminating against women, the court reasoned that its exclusionary impact upon women was nonetheless so severe as to require the State to further its goals through a more limited form of preference. Finding that a more modest preference formula would readily accommodate the State's interest in aiding veterans, the court declared ch. 31, § 23, unconstitutional and enjoined its operation.

Upon an appeal taken by the Attorney General of Massachusetts, this Court vacated the judgment and remanded the case for further consideration in light of our intervening decision in *Washington* v. *Davis*, 426 U. S. 229. *Massachusetts* v. *Feeney*, 434 U. S. 884. The *Davis* case held that a neutral law does not violate the Equal Protection Clause solely because it results in a racially disproportionate impact; instead the disproportionate impact must be traced to a purpose to discriminate on the basis of race. 426 U. S., at 238–244.

Upon remand, the District Court, one judge concurring and one judge again dissenting, concluded that a veterans' hiring preference is inherently nonneutral because it favors a class from which women have traditionally been excluded, and that the consequences of the Massachusetts absolute-preference formula for the employment opportunities of women were too inevitable to have been "unintended." Accordingly, the court reaffirmed its original judgment. *Feeney* v. *Massachusetts*, 451 F. Supp. 143. The Attorney General again appealed to this Court pursuant to 28 U. S. C. § 1253, and probable jurisdiction of the appeal was noted. 439 U. S. 891.

I

A

The Federal Government and virtually all of the States grant some sort of hiring preference to veterans. The Massachusetts preference, which is loosely termed an "absolute lifetime" preference, is among the most generous. It applies to all positions in the State's classified civil service, which constitute approximately 60% of the public jobs in the State. It is available to "any person, male or female, including a nurse," who was honorably discharged from the United States Armed Forces after at least 90 days of active service, at least one day of which was during "wartime." Persons who are deemed veterans and who are otherwise qualified for a particular civil

service job may exercise the preference at any time and as many times as they wish.

Civil service positions in Massachusetts fall into two general categories, labor and official. For jobs in the official service, with which the proofs in this action were concerned, the preference mechanics are uncomplicated. All applicants for employment must take competitive examinations. Grades are based on a formula that gives weight both to objective test results and to training and experience. Candidates who pass are then ranked in the order of their respective scores on an "eligible list." Chapter 31, § 23, requires, however, that disabled veterans, veterans, and surviving spouses and surviving parents of veterans be ranked—in the order of their respective scores—above all other candidates.

Rank on the eligible list and availability for employment are the sole factors that determine which candidates are considered for appointment to an official civil service position. When a public agency has a vacancy, it requisitions a list of "certified eligibles" from the state personnel division. Under formulas prescribed by civil service rules, a small number of candidates from the top of an appropriate list, three if there is only one vacancy, are certified. The appointing agency is then required to choose from among these candidates. Although the veterans' preference thus does not guarantee that a veteran will be appointed, it is obvious that the preference gives to veterans who achieve passing scores a well-nigh absolute advantage.

B

The appellee has lived in Dracut, Mass., most of her life. She entered the work force in 1948, and for the next 14 years worked at a variety of jobs in the private sector. She first entered the state civil service system in 1963, having competed successfully for a position as Senior Clerk Stenographer in the Massachusetts Civil Defense Agency. There she worked for four years. In 1967, she was promoted to the position of Federal Funds and Personnel Coordinator in the same agency. The agency, and with it her job, was eliminated in 1975.

During her 12-year tenure as a public employee, Ms. Feeney took and passed a number of open competitive civil service examinations. On several she did quite well, receiving in 1971 the second highest score on an examination for a job with the Board of Dental Examiners, and in 1973 the third highest on a test for an Administrative Assistant position with a mental health center. Her high scores, however, did not win her a place on the certified eligible list. Because of the veterans' preference, she was ranked sixth behind five male veterans on the Dental Examiner list. She was not certified, and a lower scoring veteran was eventually appointed. On the 1973 examination, she was placed in a position on the list behind 12 male veterans, 11 of whom had lower scores. Following the other examinations that she took, her name was similarly ranked below those of veterans who had achieved passing grades.

. . .

C

The veterans' hiring preference in Massachusetts, as in other jurisdictions, has traditionally been justified as a measure designed to reward veterans for the sacrifice of military service, to ease the transition from military to civilian life, to encourage patriotic service, and to attract loyal and well-disciplined people to civil service occupations. . . .

D

The first Massachusetts veterans' preference statute defined the term "veterans" in gender-neutral language. See 1896 Mass. Acts, ch. 517 § 1 ("a person" who served in the United States Army or Navy), and subsequent amendments have followed this pattern, see, e. g., 1919 Mass. Acts, ch. 150, § 1 ("any person who has served . . ."); 1954 Mass. Acts, ch. 627, § 1 ("any person, male or female, including a nurse"). Women who have served in official United States military units during wartime, then, have always been entitled to the benefit of the preference. In addition, Massachusetts, through a 1943 amendment to the definition of "wartime service," extended the preference to women who served in unofficial auxiliary women's units. 1943 Mass. Acts, ch. 194.

When the first general veterans' preference statute was adopted in 1896, there were no women veterans. The statute, however, covered only Civil War veterans. Most of them were beyond middle age, and relatively few were actively competing for public employment. Thus, the impact of the preference upon the employment opportunities of nonveterans as a group and women in particular was slight.

Notwithstanding the apparent attempts by Massachusetts to include as many military women as possible within the scope of the preference, the statute today benefits an overwhelmingly male class. This is attributable in some measure to the variety of federal statutes, regulations, and policies that have restricted the number of women who could enlist in the United States Armed Forces, and largely to the simple fact that women have never been subjected to a military draft. . . .

II

The sole question for decision on this appeal is whether Massachusetts, in granting an absolute lifetime preference to veterans, has discriminated against women in violation of the Equal Protection Clause of the Fourteenth Amendment.

A

The equal protection guarantee of the Fourteenth Amendment does not take from the States all power of classification. *Massachusetts Bd. of Retirement* v. *Murgia*, 427 U. S. 307, 314. Most laws classify, and many affect certain groups unevenly, even though the law itself treats them no differently from all other members of the class described by the law. When the basic classification is rationally based, uneven effects upon particular groups within a class are ordinarily of no constitutional concern. . . .

Certain classifications, however, in themselves supply a reason to infer antipathy. Race is the paradigm. A racial classification, regardless of purported motivation, is presumptively invalid and can be upheld only upon an extraordinary justification. *Brown* v. *Board of Education*, 347 U. S. 483; *McLaughlin* v. *Florida*, 379 U. S. 184. This rule applies as well to a classification that is ostensibly neutral but is an obvious pretext for racial discrimination. *Yick Wo* v. *Hopkins*, 118 U. S. 356; *Guinn* v. *United States*, 238 U. S. 347; cf. *Lane* v. *Wilson*, 307 U. S. 268; *Gomillion* v. *Lightfoot*, 364 U. S. 339. But, as was made clear in

Washington v. *Davis,* 426 U. S. 229, and *Arlington Heights* v. *Metropolitan Housing Dev. Corp.,* 429 U. S. 252, even if a neutral law has a disproportionately adverse effect upon a racial minority, it is unconstitutional under the Equal Protection Clause only if that impact can be traced to a discriminatory purpose.

. . .

III

A

The question whether ch. 31, § 23, establishes a classification that is overtly or covertly based upon gender must first be considered. The appellee has conceded that ch. 31, § 23, is neutral on its face. She has also acknowledged that state hiring preferences for veterans are not *per se* invalid, for she has limited her challenge to the absolute lifetime preference that Massachusetts provides to veterans. The District Court made two central findings that are relevant here: first, that ch. 31, § 23, serves legitimate and worthy purposes; second, that the absolute preference was not established for the purpose of discriminating against women. The appellee has thus acknowledged and the District Court has thus found that the distinction between veterans and nonveterans drawn by ch. 31, § 23, is not a pretext for gender discrimination. The appellee's concession and the District Court's finding are clearly correct.

. . . Veteran status is not uniquely male. Although few women benefit from the preference, the nonveteran class is not substantially all female. To the contrary, significant numbers of nonveterans are men, and all nonveterans—male as well as female—are placed at a disadvantage. Too many men are affected by ch. 31, § 23, to permit the inference that the statute is but a pretext for preferring men over women.

Moreover, as the District Court implicitly found, the purposes of the statute provide the surest explanation for its impact. Just as there are cases in which impact alone can unmask an invidious classification, cf. *Yick Wo* v. *Hopkins,* 118 U. S. 356, there are others, in which—notwithstanding impact—the legitimate noninvidious purposes of a law cannot be missed. This

is one. The distinction made by ch. 31, § 23, is, as it seems to be, quite simply between veterans and nonveterans, not between men and women.

B

The dispositive question, then, is whether the appellee has shown that a gender-based discriminatory purpose has, at least in some measure, shaped the Massachusetts veterans' preference legislation. As did the District Court, she points to two basic factors which in her view distinguish ch. 31, § 23, from the neutral rules at issue in the *Washington* v. *Davis* and *Arlington Heights* cases. The first is the nature of the preference, which is said to be demonstrably gender-biased in the sense that it favors a status reserved under federal military policy primarily to men. The second concerns the impact of the absolute lifetime preference upon the employment opportunities of women, an impact claimed to be too inevitable to have been unintended. The appellee contends that these factors, coupled with the fact that the preference itself has little if any relevance to actual job performance, more than suffice to prove the discriminatory intent required to establish a constitutional violation.

1

The contention that this veterans' preference is "inherently nonneutral" or "gender-biased" presumes that the State, by favoring veterans, intentionally incorporated into its public employment policies the panoply of sex-based and assertedly discriminatory federal laws that have prevented all but a handful of women from becoming veterans. There are two serious difficulties with this argument. First, it is wholly at odds with the District Court's central finding that Massachusetts has not offered a preference to veterans for the purpose of discriminating against women. Second, it cannot be reconciled with the assumption made by both the appellee and the District Court that a more limited hiring preference for veterans could be sustained. Taken together, these difficulties are fatal.

. . .

2

The appellee's ultimate argument rests upon the presumption, common to the criminal and civil law, that a person intends the natural and foreseeable consequences of his voluntary actions. . . .

. . . The decision to grant a preference to veterans was of course "intentional." So, necessarily, did an adverse impact upon nonveterans follow from that decision. And it cannot seriously be argued that the Legislature of Massachusetts could have been unaware that most veterans are men. It would thus be disingenuous to say that the adverse consequences of this legislation for women were unintended, in the sense that they were not volitional or in the sense that they were not foreseeable.

"Discriminatory purpose," however, implies more than intent as volition or intent as awareness of consequences. See *United Jewish Organizations* v. *Carey*, 430 U. S. 144, 179 (concurring opinion). It implies that the decisionmaker, in this case a state legislature, selected or reaffirmed a particular course of action at least in part "because of," not merely "in spite of," its adverse effects upon an identifiable group. Yet nothing in the record demonstrates that this preference for veterans was originally devised or subsequently re-enacted because it would accomplish the collateral goal of keeping women in a stereotypic and predefined place in the Massachusetts Civil Service.

. . .

IV

Veterans' hiring preferences represent an awkward—and, many argue, unfair—exception to the widely shared view that merit and merit alone should prevail in the employment policies of government. After a war, such laws have been enacted virtually without opposition. During peacetime, they inevitably have come to be viewed in many quarters as undemocratic and unwise. Absolute and permanent preferences, as the troubled history of this law demonstrates, have always been subject to the objection that they give the veteran more than a square deal. But the Four-

teenth Amendment "cannot be made a refuge from ill-advised . . . laws." *District of Columbia* v. *Brooke*, 214 U. S. 138, 150. The substantial edge granted to veterans by ch. 31, § 23, may reflect unwise policy. The appellee, however, has simply failed to demonstrate that the law in any way reflects a purpose to discriminate on the basis of sex.

The judgment is reversed, and the case is remanded for further proceedings consistent with this opinion.

It is so ordered.

MR. JUSTICE STEVENS, with whom MR. JUSTICE WHITE joins, concurring. . . .

MR. JUSTICE MARSHALL, with whom MR. JUSTICE BRENNAN joins, dissenting.

Although acknowledging that in some circumstances, discriminatory intent may be inferred from the inevitable or foreseeable impact of a statute . . . the Court concludes that no such intent has been established here. I cannot agree. In my judgment, Massachusetts' choice of an absolute veterans' preference system evinces purposeful gender-based discrimination. And because the statutory scheme bears no substantial relationship to a legitimate governmental objective, it cannot withstand scrutiny under the Equal Protection Clause.

I

The District Court found that the "prime objective" of the Massachusetts veterans' preference statute, Mass. Gen. Laws Ann., ch. 31, § 23, was to benefit individuals with prior military service. . . .

That a legislature seeks to advantage one group does not, as a matter of logic or of common sense, exclude the possibility that it also intends to disadvantage another. Individuals in general and lawmakers in particular frequently act for a variety of reasons. . . . Thus, the critical constitutional inquiry is not whether an illicit consideration was the primary or but-for cause of a decision, but rather whether it had an appreciable role in shaping a given legislative enactment. . . .

II

To survive challenge under the Equal Protection Clause, statutes reflecting gender-based discrimination must be substantially related to the achievement of important governmental objectives. See *Califano* v. *Webster,* 430 U. S. 313, 316–317 (1977); *Craig* v. *Boren,* 429 U. S. 190, 197 (1976); *Reed* v. *Reed,* 404 U. S. 71, 76 (1971). Appellants here advance three interests in support of the absolute-preference system: (1) assisting veterans in their readjustment to civilian life; (2) encouraging military enlistment; and (3) rewarding those who have served their country. Brief for Appellants 24. Although each of those goals is unquestionably legitimate, the "mere recitation of a benign, compensatory purpose" cannot of itself insulate legislative classifications from constitutional scrutiny. *Weinberger* v. *Wiesenfeld, supra,* at 648. And in this case, the Commonwealth has failed to establish a sufficient relationship between its objectives and the means chosen to effectuate them.

With respect to the first interest, facilitating veterans' transition to civilian status, the statute is plainly overinclusive. Cf. *Trimble* v. *Gordon,* 430 U. S. 762, 770–772 (1977); *Jimenez* v. *Weinberger,* 417 U. S. 628, 637 (1974). By conferring a permanent preference, the legislation allows veterans to invoke their advantage repeatedly, without regard to their date of discharge. As the record demonstrates, a substantial majority of those currently enjoying the benefits of the system are not recently discharged veterans in need of readjustment assistance.

Nor is the Commonwealth's second asserted interest, encouraging military service, a plausible justification for this legislative scheme. . . . I am unwilling to assume what appellants made no effort to prove, that the possibility of obtaining an *ex post facto* civil service preference significantly influenced the enlistment decisions of Massachusetts residents. Moreover, even if such influence could be presumed, the statute is still grossly overinclusive in that it bestows benefits on men drafted as well as those who volunteered.

Finally, the Commonwealth's third interest, rewarding veterans, does not "adequately justify the salient features" of this preference system. *Craig* v. *Boren, supra,* at 202-203. See *Orr* v. *Orr, supra,* at 281. Where a particular statutory scheme visits substantial hardship on a class long subject to discrimination, the legislation cannot be sustained unless " 'carefully tuned to alternative considerations.' " *Trimble* v. *Gordon, supra,* at 772. See *Caban* v. *Mohammed,* 441 U. S. 380, 392-393, n. 13 (1979); *Mathews* v. *Lucas,* 427 U. S. 495 (1976). Here, there are a wide variety of less discriminatory means by which Massachusetts could effect its compensatory purposes. For example, a point preference system, such as that maintained by many States and the Federal Government, . . . or an absolute preference for a limited duration would reward veterans without excluding all qualified women from upper level civil service positions. Apart from public employment, the Commonwealth, can, and does, afford assistance to veterans in various ways, including tax abatements, educational subsidies, and special programs for needy veterans. . . .

Johnson v. Transportation Agency

480 U.S. 616 (1987)

Paul E. Johnson, a male employee, was passed over for promotion to the position of road dispatcher. Instead, the Transportation Agency selected a female employee, Diane Joyce. Both were rated as well qualified for the job, but Joyce was picked in part because the Agency took into account her gender as a factor. Johnson filed suit, claiming that the Agency had violated Title VII of the Civil Rights Act of 1964. The district court agreed; the Ninth Circuit reversed.

JUSTICE BRENNAN delivered the opinion of the Court.

Respondent, Transportation Agency of Santa Clara County, California, unilaterally promulgated an Affirmative Action Plan applicable, *inter alia*, to promotions of employees. In selecting applicants for the promotional position of road dispatcher, the Agency, pursuant to the Plan, passed over petitioner Paul Johnson, a male employee, and promoted a female employee applicant, Diane Joyce. The question for decision is whether in making the promotion the Agency impermissibly took into account the sex of the applicants in violation of Title VII of the Civil Rights Act of 1964, 42 U.S.C. § 2000e *et seq.* The District Court for the Northern District of California, in an action filed by petitioner following receipt of a right-to-sue letter from the Equal Employment Opportunity Commission (EEOC), held that respondent had violated Title VII. App. to Pet. for Cert. 1a. The Court of Appeals for the Ninth Circuit reversed. 770 F.2d 752 (1985). We granted certiorari, 478 U.S. 1019 (1986). We affirm.

I

A

In December 1978, the Santa Clara County Transit District Board of Supervisors adopted an Affirmative Action Plan (Plan) for the County Transportation Agency. The Plan implemented a County Affirmative Action Plan, which had been adopted, declared the County, because "mere prohibition of discriminatory practices is not enough to remedy the effects of past practices and to permit attainment of an equitable representation of minorities, women and handicapped persons." App. 31. Relevant to this case, the Agency Plan provides that, in making promotions to positions within a traditionally segregated job classification in which women have been significantly underrepresented, the Agency is authorized to consider as one factor the sex of a qualified applicant.

In reviewing the composition of its work force, the Agency noted in its Plan that women were represented in numbers far less than their proportion of the county labor force in both the Agency

as a whole and in five of seven job categories. Specifically, while women constituted 36.4% of the area labor market, they composed only 22.4% of Agency employees. Furthermore, women working at the Agency were concentrated largely in EEOC job categories traditionally held by women: women made up 76% of Office and Clerical Workers, but only 7.1% of Agency Officials and Administrators, 8.6% of Professionals, 9.7% of Technicians, and 22% of Service and Maintenance workers. As for the job classification relevant to this case, none of the 238 Skilled Craft Worker positions was held by a woman. *Id.*, at 49. The Plan noted that this underrepresentation of women in part reflected the fact that women had not traditionally been employed in these positions, and that they had not been strongly motivated to seek training or employment in them "because of the limited opportunities that have existed in the past for them to work in such classifications." . . .

B

On December 12, 1979, the Agency announced a vacancy for the promotional position of road dispatcher in the Agency's Roads Division. Dispatchers assign road crews, equipment, and materials, and maintain records pertaining to road maintenance jobs. *Id.*, at 23–24. The position requires at minimum four years of dispatch or road maintenance work experience for Santa Clara County. The EEOC job classification scheme designates a road dispatcher as a Skilled Craft worker.

Twelve County employees applied for the promotion, including Joyce and Johnson. Joyce had worked for the County since 1970, serving as an account clerk until 1975. She had applied for a road dispatcher position in 1974, but was deemed ineligible because she had not served as a road maintenance worker. In 1975, Joyce transferred from a senior account clerk position to a road maintenance worker position, becoming the first woman to fill such a job. Tr. 83–84. During her four years in that position, she occasionally worked out of class as a road dispatcher.

Petitioner Johnson began with the county in 1967 as a road yard clerk, after private employment that included working as a supervisor and dispatcher. He had also unsuccessfully applied for the road dispatcher opening in 1974. In 1977, his clerical position was downgraded, and he sought and received a transfer to the position of road maintenance worker. *Id.*, at 127. He also occasionally worked out of class as a dispatcher while performing that job.

Nine of the applicants, including Joyce and Johnson, were deemed qualified for the job, and were interviewed by a two-person board. Seven of the applicants scored above 70 on this interview, which meant that they were certified as eligible for selection by the appointing authority. The scores awarded ranged from 70 to 80. Johnson was tied for second with score of 75, while Joyce ranked next with a score of 73. A second interview was conducted by three Agency supervisors, who ultimately recommended that Johnson be promoted. Prior to the second interview, Joyce had contacted the County's Affirmative Action Office because she feared that her application might not receive disinterested review. The Office in turn contacted the Agency's Affirmative Action Coordinator, whom the Agency's Plan makes responsible for, *inter alia*, keeping the Director informed of opportunities for the Agency to accomplish its objectives under the Plan. At the time, the Agency employed no women in any Skilled Craft position, and had never employed a woman as a road dispatcher. The Coordinator recommended to the Director of the Agency, James Graebner, that Joyce be promoted.

Graebner, authorized to choose any of the seven persons deemed eligible, thus had the benefit of suggestions by the second interview panel and by the Agency Coordinator in arriving at his decision. After deliberation, Graebner concluded that the promotion should be given to Joyce. As he testified: "I tried to look at the whole picture, the combination of her qualifications and Mr. Johnson's qualifications, their test scores, their expertise, their background, affirmative action matters, things like that . . . I believe it was a combination of all those." *Id.*, at 68.

The certification form naming Joyce as the person promoted to the dispatcher position stated that both she and Johnson were rated as well-qualified for the job. The evaluation of Joyce read: "Well qualified by virtue of 18 years of past clerical experience including 3½ years at West Yard plus almost 5 years as a [road maintenance worker]." App. 27. The evaluation of Johnson was as

follows: "Well qualified applicant; two years of [road maintenance worker] experience plus 11 years of Road Yard Clerk. Has had previous outside Dispatch experience but was 13 years ago." *Ibid.* Graebner testified that he did not regard as significant the fact that Johnson scored 75 and Joyce 73 when interviewed by the two-person board. Tr. 57–58.

. . .

II

As a preliminary matter, we note that petitioner bears the burden of establishing the invalidity of the Agency's Plan. Only last term in *Wygant* v. *Jackson Board of Education*, 476 U.S. 267, 277–278 (1986), we held that "[t]he ultimate burden remains with the employees to demonstrate the unconstitutionality of an affirmative-action program," and we see no basis for a different rule regarding a plan's alleged violation of Title VII. . . .

[Justice Brennan states that the legality of the Agency Plan must be guided by Steelworkers *v.* Weber, *443 U.S. 193 (1979), which upheld an employer's decision to select less senior black applicants over a white applicant into a craft training program. The Court found significant the fact that the plan did not require the discharge of white workers.]*

As an initial matter, the Agency adopted as a benchmark for measuring progress in eliminating underrepresentation the long-term goal of a work force that mirrored in its major job classifications the percentage of women in the area labor market. . . .

As the Agency Plan recognized, women were most egregiously underrepresented in the Skilled Craft job category, since *none* of the 238 positions was occupied by a woman. In mid-1980, when Joyce was selected for the road dispatcher position, the Agency was still in the process of refining its short-term goals for Skilled Craft Workers in accordance with the directive of the Plan. This process did not reach fruition until 1982, when the Agency established a short-term goal for that year of three women for the 55 expected openings in that job category—a modest goal of about 6% for that category.

We reject petitioner's argument that, since only the long-term goal was in place for Skilled Craft positions at the time of Joyce's promotion, it was inappropriate for the Director to take into account affirmative action considerations in filling the road dispatcher position. The Agency's Plan emphasized that the long-term goals were not to be taken as guides for actual hiring decisions, but that supervisors were to consider a host of practical factors in seeking to meet affirmative action objectives, including the fact that in some job categories women were not qualified in numbers comparable to their representation in the labor force.

. . . it was plainly not unreasonable for the Agency to determine that it was appropriate to consider as one factor the sex of Ms. Joyce in making its decision. The promotion of Joyce thus satisfies the first requirement enunciated in *Weber*, since it was undertaken to further an affirmative action plan designed to eliminate Agency work force imbalances in traditionally segregated job categories.

We next consider whether the Agency Plan unnecessarily trammeled the rights of male employees or created an absolute bar to their advancement. In contrast to the plan in *Weber*, which provided that 50% of the positions in the craft training program were exclusively for blacks, and to the consent decree upheld last term in *Firefighters* v. *Cleveland*, 478 U.S. 501 (1986), which required the promotion of specific numbers of minorities, the Plan sets aside no positions for women. . . . As the Agency Director testified, the sex of Joyce was but one of numerous factors he took into account in arriving at his decision. . . .

In addition, petitioner had no absolute entitlement to the road dispatcher position. Seven of the applicants were classified as qualified and eligible, and the Agency Director was authorized to promote any of the seven. Thus, denial of the promotion unsettled no legitimate firmly rooted expectation on the part of the petitioner. Furthermore, while the petitioner in this case was denied a promotion, he retained his employment with the Agency, at the same salary and with the same seniority, and remained eligible for other promotions.

. . .

III

. . .

We therefore hold that the Agency appropriately took into account as one factor the sex of Diane Joyce in determining that she should be promoted to the road dispatcher position. The decision to do so was made pursuant to an affirmative action plan that represents a moderate, flexible, case-by-case approach to effecting a gradual improvement in the representation of minorities and women in the Agency's work force. Such a plan is fully consistent with Title VII, for it embodies the contribution that voluntary employer action can make in eliminating the vestiges of discrimination in the workplace. Accordingly, the judgment of the Court of Appeals is

Affirmed.

JUSTICE STEVENS, concurring.

. . .

JUSTICE O'CONNOR, concurring in the judgment.

. . .

JUSTICE WHITE, dissenting.

I agree with Parts I and II of JUSTICE SCALIA'S dissenting opinion. Although I do not join Part III, I also would overrule *Weber*. My understanding of *Weber* was, and is, that the employer's plan did not violate Title VII because it was designed to remedy intentional and systematic exclusion of blacks by the employer and the unions from certain job categories. That is how I understood the phrase "traditionally segregated jobs" we used in that case. The Court now interprets it to mean nothing more than a manifest imbalance between one identifiable group and another in an employer's labor force. As so interpreted, that case, as well as today's decision, as JUSTICE SCALIA so well demonstrates, is a perversion of Title VII. I would overrule *Weber* and reverse the judgment below.

JUSTICE SCALIA, with whom THE CHIEF JUSTICE joins, and with whom JUSTICE WHITE joins in Parts I and II, dissenting.

With a clarity which, had it not proven so

unavailing, one might well recommend as a model of statutory draftsmanship, Title VII of the Civil Rights Act of 1964 declares:

"It shall be an unlawful employment practice for an employer—

"(1) to fail or refuse to hire or to discharge any individual, or otherwise to discriminate against any individual with respect to his compensation, terms, conditions, or privileges of employment, because of such individual's race, color, religion, sex, or national origin; or

"(2) to limit, segregate, or classify his employees or applicants for employment in any way which would deprive or tend to deprive any individual of employment opportunities or otherwise adversely affect his status as an employee, because of such individual's race, color, religion, sex, or national origin." 42 U.S.C. § 2000e–2(a).

The Court today completes the process of converting this from a guarantee that race or sex will *not* be the basis for employment determinations, to a guarantee that it often *will*. Ever so subtly, without even alluding to the last obstacles preserved by earlier opinions that we now push out of our path, we effectively replace the goal of a discrimination-free society with the quite incompatible goal of proportionate representation by race and by sex in the workplace. Part I of this dissent will describe the nature of the plan that the Court approves, and its effect upon this petitioner. Part II will discuss prior holdings that are tacitly overruled, and prior distinctions that are disregarded. Part III will describe the engine of discrimination we have finally completed.

I

. . .

Several salient features of the plan should be noted. Most importantly, the plan's purpose was assuredly not to remedy prior sex discrimination by the Agency. It could not have been, because there was no prior sex discrimination to remedy. The majority, in cataloguing the Agency's alleged misdeeds, *ante*, at 1448, n. 5, neglects to mention the District Court's finding that the Agency "has not discriminated in the past, and does not discriminate in the present against women in regard

to employment opportunities in general and promotions in particular." App. to Pet. for Cert. 13a. This finding was not disturbed by the Ninth Circuit.

. . . the oft-stated goal was to mirror the racial and sexual composition of the entire county labor force, not merely in the Agency work force as a whole, but in each and every individual job category at the Agency. In a discrimination-free world, it would obviously be a statistical oddity for every job category to match the racial and sexual composition of even that portion of the county work force *qualified* for that job; it would be utterly miraculous for each of them to match, as the plan expected, the composition of the *entire* work force. Quite obviously, the plan did not seek to replicate what a lack of discrimination would produce, but rather imposed racial and sexual tailoring that would, in defiance of normal expectations and laws of probability, give each protected racial and sexual group a governmentally determined "proper" proportion of each job category.

. . .

II

The most significant proposition of law established by today's decision is that racial or sexual discrimination is permitted under Title VII when it is intended to overcome the effect, not of the employer's own discrimination, but of societal attitudes that have limited the entry of certain races, or of a particular sex, into certain jobs. Even if the societal attitudes in question consisted exclusively of conscious discrimination by other employers, this holding would contradict a decision of this Court rendered only last Term. *Wygant* v. *Jackson Board of Education*, 476 U.S. 267 (1986), held that the objective of remedying societal discrimination cannot prevent remedial affirmative action from violating the Equal Protection Clause. . . .

III

I have omitted from the foregoing discussion the most obvious respect in which today's decision o'erleaps, without analysis, a barrier that was thought still to be overcome. In *Weber*, this Court held that a private-sector affirmative-action training program that overtly discriminated against white applicants did not violate Title VII. However, although the majority does not advert to the fact, until today the applicability of *Weber* to public employers remained an open question. In *Weber* itself, see 443 U.S., at 200, 204, and in later decisions, see *Firefighters* v. *Cleveland*, 478 U.S., at 517; *Wygant*, 476 U.S., at 282, n.9 (opinion of POWELL, J.), this Court has repeatedly emphasized that *Weber* involved only a private employer. . . .

. . .

. . . It is well to keep in mind just how thoroughly *Weber* rewrote the statute it purported to construe. The language of that statute, as quoted at the outset of this dissent, is unambiguous: it is an unlawful employment practice "to fail or refuse to hire or to discharge any individual, or otherwise to discriminate against any individual with respect to his compensation, terms, conditions, or privileges of employment, because of such individual's race, color, religion, sex, or national origin." 42 U.S.C. § 2000e–2(a). *Weber* disregarded the text of the statute, invoking instead its " 'spirit,' " 443 U.S., at 201 (quoting *Holy Trinity Church* v. *United States*, 143 U.S. 457, 459 (1892)), and "practical and equitable [considerations] only partially perceived, if perceived at all, by the 88th Congress," 443 U.S., at 209 (BLACKMUN, J., concurring). It concluded, on the basis of these intangible guides, that Title VII's prohibition of intentional discrimination on the basis of race and sex does not prohibit intentional discrimination on the basis of race and sex, so long as it is "designed to break down old patterns of racial [or sexual] segregation and hierarchy," "does not unnecessarily trammel the interests of the white [or male] employees," "does not require the discharge of white [or male] workers and their replacement with new black [or female] hirees," "does [not] create an absolute bar to the advancement of white [or male] employees," and "is a temporary measure . . . not intended to maintain racial [or sexual] balance, but simply to eliminate a manifest racial [or sexual] imbalance." *Id.*, at 208. In effect, *Weber* held that the legality of intentional discrimination by private employers against certain disfavored groups or individuals is to be judged not by Title VII but by a judicially crafted code of conduct, the contours of which are determined by no discernible standard, aside from (as the dissent convincingly demonstrated) the divination of congressional "purposes" belied by the face of the statute and by its legislative history. We have been recasting that self-promulgated code of conduct ever since—and what it has led us to today adds to the reasons for abandoning it.

The majority's response to this criticism of *Weber*, *ante*, at 1450, n. 7, asserts that, since "Congress has not amended the statute to reject our construction, . . . we . . . may assume that our interpretation was correct." This assumption, which frequently haunts our opinions, should be put to rest. It is based, to begin with, on the patently false premise that the correctness of statutory construction is to be measured by what the current Congress desires, rather than by what the law as enacted meant. . . . even accepting the flawed premise that the intent of the current Congress, with respect to the provision in isolation, is determinative, one must ignore rudimentary principles of political science to draw any conclusions regarding that intent from the *failure* to enact legislation. The "complicated check on legislation," The Federalist No. 62, p. 378 (C. Rossiter ed. 1961), erected by our Constitution creates an inertia that makes it impossible to assert with any degree of assurance that congressional failure to act represents (1) approval of the status quo, as opposed to (2) inability to agree upon how to alter the status quo, (3) unawareness of the status quo, (4) indifference to the status quo, or even (5) political cowardice. . . .

. . . A statute designed to establish a color-blind and gender-blind workplace has thus been converted into a powerful engine of racism and sexism, not merely *permitting* intentional race- and sex-based discrimination, but often making it, through operation of the legal system, practically compelled.

It is unlikely that today's result will be displeasing to politically elected officials, to whom it provides the means of quickly accommodating the demands of organized groups to achieve concrete, numerical improvement in the economic status of particular constituencies. Nor will it displease the world of corporate and governmental employers (many of whom have filed briefs as *amici* in the present case, all on the side of Santa Clara) for whom the cost of hiring less qualified workers is often substantially less—and infinitely more predictable—than the cost of litigating Title VII cases and of seeking to convince federal agencies by nonnumerical means that no discrimination exists. In fact, the only losers in the process are the Johnsons of the country, for whom Title VII has been not merely repealed but actually inverted. The irony is that these individuals—predominantly unknown, unaffluent, unorganized—suffer this injustice at the hands of a Court fond of thinking itself the champion of the politically impotent. I dissent.

In re Gault

387 U.S. 1 (1967)

Gerald Gault, fifteen years old, was taken into custody for allegedly making obscene phone calls to a woman. The police did not leave notice with his parents. After hearings before a juvenile court judge, he was ordered committed to the State Industrial School as a juvenile delinquent until he reached the age of majority (age 21). His parents challenged the constitutionality of the Arizona Juvenile Code and the procedures used in Gerald's case.

MR. JUSTICE FORTAS delivered the opinion of the Court.

This is an appeal under 28 U. S. C. § 1257 (2) from a judgment of the Supreme Court of Arizona affirming the dismissal of a petition for a writ of habeas corpus. 99 Ariz. 181, 407 P. 2d 760 (1965). The petition sought the release of Gerald Francis Gault, appellants' 15-year-old son, who had been committed as a juvenile delinquent to the State Industrial School by the Juvenile Court of Gila County, Arizona. The Supreme Court of Arizona affirmed dismissal of the writ against various arguments which included an attack upon the constitutionality of the Arizona Juvenile Code because of its alleged denial of procedural due process rights to juveniles charged with being "delinquents." The court agreed that the constitutional guarantee of due process of law is applicable in such proceedings. It held that Arizona's Juvenile Code is to be read as "impliedly" implementing the "due process concept." It then proceeded to identify and describe "the particular elements which constitute due process in a juvenile hearing." It concluded that the proceedings ending in commitment of Gerald Gault did not offend those requirements. We do not agree, and we reverse. We begin with a statement of the facts.

I.

On Monday, June 8, 1964, at about 10 a.m., Gerald Francis Gault and a friend, Ronald Lewis, were taken into custody by the Sheriff of Gila County. Gerald was then still subject to a six months' probation order which had been entered on February 25, 1964, as a result of his having been in the company of another boy who had stolen a wallet from a lady's purse. The police action on June 8 was taken as the result of a verbal complaint by a neighbor of the boys, Mrs. Cook, about a telephone call made to her in which the caller or callers made lewd or indecent remarks. It will suffice for purposes of this opinion to say that the remarks or questions put to her were of the irritatingly offensive, adolescent, sex variety.

At the time Gerald was picked up, his mother and father were both at work. No notice that Gerald was being taken into custody was left at the home. No other steps were taken to advise them that their son had, in effect, been arrested. Gerald was taken to the Children's Detention Home. When his mother arrived home at about 6 o'clock, Gerald was not there. Gerald's older brother was sent to look for him at the trailer home of the Lewis family. He apparently learned then that

Gerald was in custody. He so informed his mother. The two of them went to the Detention Home. The deputy probation officer, Flagg, who was also superintendent of the Detention Home, told Mrs. Gault "why Jerry was there" and said that a hearing would be held in Juvenile Court at 3 o'clock the following day, June 9.

Officer Flagg filed a petition with the court on the hearing day, June 9, 1964. It was not served on the Gaults. Indeed, none of them saw this petition until the habeas corpus hearing on August 17, 1964. The petition was entirely formal. It made no reference to any factual basis for the judicial action which it initiated. It recited only that "said minor is under the age of eighteen years, and is in need of the protection of this Honorable Court; [and that] said minor is a delinquent minor." It prayed for a hearing and an order regarding "the care and custody of said minor." Officer Flagg executed a formal affidavit in support of the petition.

On June 9, Gerald, his mother, his older brother, and Probation Officers Flagg and Henderson appeared before the Juvenile Judge in chambers. Gerald's father was not there. He was at work out of the city. Mrs. Cook, the complainant, was not there. No one was sworn at this hearing. No transcript or recording was made. No memorandum or record of the substance of the proceedings was prepared. Our information about the proceedings and the subsequent hearing on June 15, derives entirely from the testimony of the Juvenile Court Judge, Mr. and Mrs. Gault and Officer Flagg at the habeas corpus proceeding conducted two months later. From this, it appears that at the June 9 hearing Gerald was questioned by the judge about the telephone call. There was conflict as to what he said. His mother recalled that Gerald said he only dialed Mrs. Cook's number and handed the telephone to his friend, Ronald. Officer Flagg recalled that Gerald had admitted making the lewd remarks. Judge McGhee testified that Gerald "admitted making one of these [lewd] statements." At the conclusion of the hearing, the judge said he would "think about it." Gerald was taken back to the Detention Home. He was not sent to his own home with his parents. On June 11 or 12, after having been detained since June 8, Gerald was released and driven home. There is no explanation in the record as to why he was kept in the Detention Home or why he was released. At 5 p. m. on the day of Gerald's release, Mrs. Gault received a note signed by Officer Flagg. It was on plain paper, not letterhead. Its entire text was as follows:

"Mrs. Gault:
"Judge McGHEE has set Monday June 15, 1964 at 11:00 A. M. as the date and time for further Hearings on Gerald's delinquency

"/s/Flagg"

At the appointed time on Monday, June 15, Gerald, his father and mother, Ronald Lewis and his father, and Officers Flagg and Henderson were present before Judge McGhee. Witnesses at the habeas corpus proceeding differed in their recollections of Gerald's testimony at the June 15 hearing. Mr. and Mrs. Gault recalled that Gerald again testified that he had only dialed the number and that the other boy had made the remarks. Officer Flagg agreed that at this hearing Gerald did not admit making the lewd remarks. But Judge McGhee recalled that "there was some admission again of some of the lewd statements. He—he didn't admit any of the more serious lewd statements." Again, the complainant, Mrs. Cook, was not present. Mrs. Gault asked that Mrs. Cook be present "so she could see which boy that done the talking, the dirty talking over the phone." The Juvenile Judge said "she didn't have to be present at that hearing." The judge did not speak to Mrs. Cook or communicate with her at any time. Probation Officer Flagg had talked to her once—over the telephone on June 9.

At this June 15 hearing a "referral report" made by the probation officers was filed with the court, although not disclosed to Gerald or his parents. This listed the charge as "Lewd Phone Calls." At the conclusion of the hearing, the judge committed Gerald as a juvenile delinquent to the State Industrial School "for the period of his minority [that is, until 21], unless sooner discharged by due process of law." An order to that effect was entered. It recites that "after a full hearing and due deliberation the Court finds that said minor is a delinquent child, and that said minor is of the age of 15 years."

No appeal is permitted by Arizona law in juvenile cases. . . .

II.

The Supreme Court of Arizona held that due process of law is requisite to the constitutional validity of proceedings in which a court reaches the conclusion that a juvenile has been at fault, has engaged in conduct prohibited by law, or has otherwise misbehaved with the consequence that he is committed to an institution in which his freedom is curtailed. This conclusion is in accord with the decisions of a number of courts under both federal and state constitutions.

. . .

From the inception of the juvenile court system, wide differences have been tolerated—indeed insisted upon—between the procedural rights accorded to adults and those of juveniles. In practically all jurisdictions, there are rights granted to adults which are withheld from juveniles. In addition to the specific problems involved in the present case, for example, it has been held that the juvenile is not entitled to bail, to indictment by grand jury, to a public trial or to trial by jury. It is frequent practice that rules governing the arrest and interrogation of adults by the police are not observed in the case of juveniles.

The history and theory underlying this development are well-known, but a recapitulation is necessary for purposes of this opinion. The Juvenile Court movement began in this country at the end of the last century. From the juvenile court statute adopted in Illinois in 1899, the system has spread to every State in the Union, the District of Columbia, and Puerto Rico. The constitutionality of Juvenile Court laws has been sustained in over 40 jurisdictions against a variety of attacks.

The early reformers were appalled by adult procedures and penalties, and by the fact that children could be given long prison sentences and mixed in jails with hardened criminals. They were profoundly convinced that society's duty to the child could not be confined by the concept of justice alone. They believed that society's role was not to ascertain whether the child was "guilty" or "innocent," but "What is he, how has he become what he is, and what had best be done in his interest and in the interest of the state to save him from a downward career." The child—essentially good, as they saw it—was to be made "to feel that he is the object of [the state's] care and solicitude," not that he was under arrest or on trial. The rules of criminal procedure were therefore altogether inapplicable. The apparent rigidities, technicalities, and harshness which they observed in both substantive and procedural criminal law were therefore to be discarded. The idea of crime and punishment was to be abandoned. The child was to be "treated" and "rehabilitated" and the procedures, from apprehension through institutionalization, were to be "clinical" rather than punitive.

These results were to be achieved, without coming to conceptual and constitutional grief, by insisting that the proceedings were not adversary, but that the state was proceeding as *parens patriae*. The Latin phrase proved to be a great help to those who sought to rationalize the exclusion of juveniles from the constitutional scheme; but its meaning is murky and its historic credentials are of dubious relevance. The phrase was taken from chancery practice, where, however, it was used to describe the power of the state to act *in loco parentis* for the purpose of protecting the property interests and the person of the child. But there is no trace of the doctrine in the history of criminal jurisprudence. At common law, children under seven were considered incapable of possessing criminal intent. Beyond that age, they were subjected to arrest, trial, and in theory to punishment like adult offenders. In these old days, the state was not deemed to have authority to accord them fewer procedural rights than adults.

. . .

If Gerald had been over 18, he would not have been subject to Juvenile Court proceedings. For the particular offense immediately involved, the maximum punishment would have been a fine of $5 to $50, or imprisonment in jail for not more than two months. Instead, he was committed to custody for a maximum of six years. If he had been over 18 and had committed an offense to which such a sentence might apply, he would have been entitled to substantial rights under the Constitution of the United States as well as under Arizona's laws and constitution. The United States Constitution would guarantee him rights and protections with respect to arrest, search and seizure, and pretrial interrogation. It would assure him of specific notice of the charges and adequate time to decide his course of action and to prepare his defense. He would be entitled to clear advice that he could be represented by counsel, and, at least if a felony were involved, the State would be required to provide counsel if his parents were unable to afford it. If the court acted on the basis of his confession, careful procedures would be required to assure its voluntariness. If the case went to trial, confrontation and opportunity for cross-examination would be guaranteed. So wide a gulf between the State's treatment of the adult and of the child requires a bridge sturdier than mere verbiage, and reasons more persuasive than cliché can provide. As Wheeler and Cottrell have put it, "The rhetoric of the juvenile court movement has developed without any necessarily close correspondence to the realities of court and institutional routines."

. . .

III.

Notice of Charges.

Appellants allege that the Arizona Juvenile Code is unconstitutional or alternatively that the proceedings before the Juvenile Court were constitutionally defective because of failure to provide adequate notice of the hearings. No notice was given to Gerald's parents when he was taken into custody on Monday, June 8. On that night, when Mrs. Gault went to the Detention Home, she was orally informed that there would be a hearing the next afternoon and was told the reason why Gerald was in custody. The only written notice Gerald's parents received at any time was a note on plain paper from Officer Flagg delivered on Thursday or Friday, June 11 or 12, to the effect that the judge had set Monday, June 15, "for further Hearings on Gerald's delinquency."

. . .

We cannot agree with the . . . conclusion that adequate notice was given in this case. Notice, to comply with due process requirements, must be given sufficiently in advance of scheduled court proceedings so that reasonable opportunity to prepare will be afforded, and it must "set forth the alleged misconduct with particularity." It is obvi-

ous, as we have discussed above, that no purpose of shielding the child from the public stigma of knowledge of his having been taken into custody and scheduled for hearing is served by the procedure approved by the court below. The "initial hearing" in the present case was a hearing on the merits. Notice at that time is not timely; and even if there were a conceivable purpose served by the deferral proposed by the court below, it would have to yield to the requirements that the child and his parents or guardian be notified, in writing, of the specific charge or factual allegations to be considered at the hearing, and that such written notice be given at the earliest practicable time, and in any event sufficiently in advance of the hearing to permit preparation. . . .

IV.

Right to Counsel.

Appellants charge that the Juvenile Court proceedings were fatally defective because the court did not advise Gerald or his parents of their right to counsel, and proceeded with the hearing, the adjudication of delinquency and the order of commitment in the absence of counsel for the child and his parents or an express waiver of the right thereto. . . .

We conclude that the Due Process Clause of the Fourteenth Amendment requires that in respect of proceedings to determine delinquency which may result in commitment to an institution in which the juvenile's freedom is curtailed, the child and his parents must be notified of the child's right to be represented by counsel retained by them, or if they are unable to afford counsel, that counsel will be appointed to represent the child.

. . .

V.

Confrontation, Self-Incrimination, Cross-Examination.

Appellants urge that the writ of habeas corpus should have been granted because of the denial of the rights of confrontation and cross-examination in the Juvenile Court hearings, and because the privilege against self-incrimination was not observed. The Juvenile Court Judge testified at the habeas corpus hearing that he had proceeded on the basis of Gerald's admissions at the two hearings. Appellants attack this on the ground that the admissions were obtained in disregard of the privilege against self-incrimination. If the confession is disregarded, appellants argue that the delinquency conclusion, since it was fundamentally based on a finding that Gerald had made lewd remarks during the phone call to Mrs. Cook, is fatally defective for failure to accord the rights of confrontation and cross-examination which the Due Process Clause of the Fourteenth Amendment of the Federal Constitution guarantees in state proceedings generally.

. . .

It would be entirely unrealistic to carve out of the Fifth Amendment all statements by juveniles on the ground that these cannot lead to "criminal" involvement. In the first place, juvenile proceedings to determine "delinquency," which may lead to commitment to a state institution, must be regarded as "criminal" for purposes of the privilege against self-incrimination. To hold otherwise would be to disregard substance because of the feeble enticement of the "civil" label-of-convenience which has been attached to juvenile proceedings. Indeed, in over half of the States, there is not even assurance that the juvenile will be kept in separate institutions, apart from adult "criminals." . . .

We conclude that the constitutional privilege against self-incrimination is applicable in the case of juveniles as it is with respect to adults. We appreciate that special problems may arise with respect to waiver of the privilege by or on behalf of children, and that there may well be some differences in technique—but not in principle—depending upon the age of the child and the presence and competence of parents. The participation of counsel will, of course, assist the police, Juvenile Courts and appellate tribunals in administering the privilege. If counsel was not present for some permissible reason when an admission was obtained, the greatest care must be taken to assure that the admission was voluntary, in the sense not only that it was not coerced or suggested, but also that it was not the product of ignorance of rights or of adolescent fantasy, fright or despair.

. . . Mrs. Cook, the complainant, was not present. The Arizona Supreme Court held that "sworn testimony must be required of all witnesses including police officers, probation officers and others who are part of or officially related to the juvenile court structure." We hold that this is not enough. No reason is suggested or appears for a different rule in respect of sworn testimony in juvenile courts than in adult tribunals. Absent a valid confession adequate to support the determination of the Juvenile Court, confrontation and sworn testimony by witnesses available for cross-examination were essential for a finding of "delinquency" and an order committing Gerald to a state institution for a maximum of six years.

. . .

VI.
Appellate Review and Transcript of Proceedings.

Appellants urge that the Arizona statute is unconstitutional under the Due Process Clause because, as construed by its Supreme Court, "there is no right of appeal from a juvenile court order. . . ." The court held that there is no right to a transcript because there is no right to appeal and because the proceedings are confidential and any record must be destroyed after a prescribed period of time. Whether a transcript or other recording is made, it held, is a matter for the discretion of the juvenile court.

This Court has not held that a State is required by the Federal Constitution "to provide appellate courts or a right to appellate review at all." In view of the fact that we must reverse the Supreme Court of Arizona's affirmance of the dismissal of the writ of habeas corpus for other reasons, we need not rule on this question in the present case or upon the failure to provide a transcript or recording of the hearings—or, indeed, the failure of the Juvenile Judge to state the grounds for his conclusion. . . .

For the reasons stated, the judgment of the Supreme Court of Arizona is reversed and the cause remanded for further proceedings not inconsistent with this opinion.

It is so ordered.

MR. JUSTICE BLACK, concurring.

. . .

MR. JUSTICE WHITE, concurring.

I join the Court's opinion except for Part V. I also agree that the privilege against compelled self-incrimination applies at the adjudicatory stage of juvenile court proceedings. I do not, however, find an adequate basis in the record for determining whether that privilege was violated in this case. . . .

For somewhat similar reasons, I would not reach the questions of confrontation and cross-examination which are also dealt with in Part V of the opinion.

MR. JUSTICE HARLAN, concurring in part and dissenting in part.

[Justice Harlan agreed that juvenile courts must give timely notice, counsel must be present (appointed by the court, if necessary), and a written record must be maintained of the proceedings. He disagreed with the Court's analysis of self-incrimination, confrontation, and cross-examination.]

MR. JUSTICE STEWART, dissenting.

The Court today uses an obscure Arizona case as a vehicle to impose upon thousands of juvenile courts throughout the Nation restrictions that the Constitution made applicable to adversary criminal trials. I believe the Court's decision is wholly unsound as a matter of constitutional law, and sadly unwise as a matter of judicial policy.

Juvenile proceedings are not criminal trials. They are not civil trials. They are simply not adversary proceedings. Whether treating with a delinquent child, a neglected child, a defective child, or a dependent child, a juvenile proceeding's whole purpose and mission is the very opposite of the mission and purpose of a prosecution in a criminal court. The object of the one is correction of a condition. The object of the other is conviction and punishment for a criminal act.

In the last 70 years many dedicated men and women have devoted their professional lives to the enlightened task of bringing us out of the dark world of Charles Dickens in meeting our responsibilities to the child in our society. The result has been the creation in this century of a system of juvenile and family courts in each of the 50 States. There can be no denying that in many areas the performance of these agencies has fallen disappointingly short of the hopes and dreams of the courageous pioneers who first conceived them. For a variety of reasons, the reality has sometimes not even approached the ideal, and much remains to be accomplished in the administration of public juvenile and family agencies—in personnel, in planning, in financing, perhaps in the formulation of wholly new approaches.

I possess neither the specialized experience nor the expert knowledge to predict with any certainty where may lie the brightest hope for progress in dealing with the serious problems of juvenile delinquency. But I am certain that the answer does not lie in the Court's opinion in this case, which serves to convert a juvenile proceeding into a criminal prosecution.

The inflexible restrictions that the Constitution so wisely made applicable to adversary criminal trials have no inevitable place in the proceedings of those public social agencies known as juvenile or family courts. And to impose the Court's long catalog of requirements upon juvenile proceedings in every area of the country is to invite a long step backwards into the nineteenth century. In that era there were no juvenile proceedings, and a child was tried in a conventional criminal court with all the trappings of a conventional criminal trial. So it was that a 12-year-old boy named James Guild was tried in New Jersey for killing Catharine Beakes. A jury found him guilty of murder, and he was sentenced to death by hanging. The sentence was executed. It was all very constitutional.

A State in all its dealings must, of course, accord every person due process of law. And due process may require that some of the same restrictions which the Constitution has placed upon criminal trials must be imposed upon juvenile proceedings. For example, I suppose that all would agree that a brutally coerced confession could not constitutionally be considered in a juvenile court hearing. But it surely does not follow that the testimonial privilege against self-incrimination is applicable in all juvenile proceedings. Similarly, due process clearly requires timely notice of the purpose and scope of any proceedings affecting the relationship of parent and child. *Armstrong* v. *Manzo*, 380 U. S. 545. But it certainly does not follow that notice of a juvenile hearing must be framed with all the technical niceties of a criminal indictment. See *Russell* v. *United States*, 369 U. S. 749.

In any event, there is no reason to deal with issues such as these in the present case. The Supreme Court of Arizona found that the parents of Gerald Gault "knew of their right to counsel, to subpoena and cross examine witnesses, of the

right to confront the witnesses against Gerald and the possible consequences of a finding of delinquency." 99 Ariz. 181, 185, 407 P. 2d 760, 763. It further found that "Mrs. Gault knew the exact nature of the charge against Gerald from the day he was taken to the detention home." 99 Ariz., at 193, 407 P. 2d, at 768. And, as MR. JUSTICE WHITE correctly points out, pp. 64–65, *ante*, no issue of compulsory self-incrimination is presented by this case.

I would dismiss the appeal.

Tinker v. Des Moines School Dist.

393 U.S. 503 (1969)

In the midst of the Vietnam war, three public school students were suspended from school for wearing black arm bands to protest U.S. involvement. They claimed that their protest, which was quiet and nondisruptive, was protected by the Free Speech Clause of the First Amendment. The school argued that school discipline and questions of suspension were within the power and jurisdiction of school authorities.

MR. JUSTICE FORTAS delivered the opinion of the Court.

Petitioner John F. Tinker, 15 years old, and petitioner Christopher Eckhardt, 16 years old, attended high schools in Des Moines, Iowa. Petitioner Mary Beth Tinker, John's sister, was a 13-year-old student in junior high school.

In December 1965, a group of adults and students in Des Moines held a meeting at the Eckhardt home. The group determined to publicize their objections to the hostilities in Vietnam and their support for a truce by wearing black armbands during the holiday season and by fasting on December 16 and New Year's Eve. Petitioners and their parents had previously engaged in similar activities, and they decided to participate in the program.

The principals of the Des Moines schools became aware of the plan to wear armbands. On December 14, 1965, they met and adopted a policy that any student wearing an armband to school would be asked to remove it, and if he refused he would be suspended until he returned without the

armband. Petitioners were aware of the regulation that the school authorities adopted.

On December 16, Mary Beth and Christopher wore black armbands to their schools. John Tinker wore his armband the next day. They were all sent home and suspended from school until they would come back without their armbands. They did not return to school until after the planned period for wearing armbands had expired—that is, until after New Year's Day.

This complaint was filed in the United States District Court by petitioners, through their fathers, under § 1983 of Title 42 of the United States Code. It prayed for an injunction restraining the respondent school officials and the respondent members of the board of directors of the school district from disciplining the petitioners, and it sought nominal damages. After an evidentiary hearing the District Court dismissed the complaint. It upheld the constitutionality of the school authorities' action on the ground that it was reasonable in order to prevent disturbance of school discipline. 258 F. Supp. 971 (1966). The court referred to but expressly declined to follow the Fifth Circuit's holding in a similar case that the wearing of symbols like the armbands cannot be prohibited unless it "materially and substantially interfere[s] with the requirements of appropriate discipline in the operation of the school." *Burnside* v. *Byars*, 363 F. 2d 744, 749 (1966).

On appeal, the Court of Appeals for the Eighth Circuit considered the case *en banc*. The court was equally divided, and the District Court's decision was accordingly affirmed, without opinion. 383 F. 2d 988 (1967). We granted certiorari. 390 U. S. 942 (1968).

I.

The District Court recognized that the wearing of an armband for the purpose of expressing certain views is the type of symbolic act that is within the Free Speech Clause of the First Amendment. See *West Virginia* v. *Barnette*, 319 U. S. 624 (1943); *Stromberg* v. *California*, 283 U. S. 359 (1931). Cf. *Thornhill* v. *Alabama*, 310 U. S. 88 (1940); *Edwards* v. *South Carolina*, 372 U. S. 229 (1963); *Brown* v. *Louisiana*, 383 U. S. 131 (1966). As we shall discuss, the wearing of armbands in the circumstances of this case was entirely divorced from actually or potentially disruptive conduct by those participating in it. It was closely akin to "pure speech" which, we have repeatedly held, is entitled to comprehensive protection under the First Amendment. Cf. *Cox* v. *Louisiana*, 379 U. S. 536, 555 (1965); *Adderley* v. *Florida*, 385 U. S. 39 (1966).

First Amendment rights, applied in light of the special characteristics of the school environment, are available to teachers and students. It can hardly be argued that either students or teachers shed their constitutional rights to freedom of speech or expression at the schoolhouse gate. This has been the unmistakable holding of this Court for almost 50 years. In *Meyer* v. *Nebraska*, 262 U. S. 390 (1923), and *Bartels* v. *Iowa*, 262 U. S. 404 (1923), this Court, in opinions by Mr. Justice McReynolds, held that the Due Process Clause of the Fourteenth Amendment prevents States from forbidding the teaching of a foreign language to young students. Statutes to this effect, the Court held, unconstitutionally interfere with the liberty of teacher, student, and parent. See also *Pierce* v. *Society of Sisters*, 268 U. S. 510 (1925); *West Virginia* v. *Barnette*, 319 U. S. 624 (1943); *McCollum* v. *Board of Education*, 333 U. S. 203 (1948); *Wieman* v. *Updegraff*, 344 U. S. 183, 195 (1952) (concurring opinion); *Sweezy* v. *New Hampshire*, 354 U. S. 234 (1957); *Shelton* v. *Tucker*, 364 U. S. 479, 487 (1960); *Engel* v. *Vitale*, 370 U. S. 421 (1962); *Keyishian* v. *Board of Regents*, 385 U. S. 589, 603 (1967); *Epperson* v. *Arkansas*, ante, p. 97 (1968).

In *West Virginia* v. *Barnette*, supra, this Court held that under the First Amendment, the student in public school may not be compelled to salute the flag. Speaking through Mr. Justice Jackson, the Court said:

"The Fourteenth Amendment, as now applied to the States, protects the citizen against the State itself and all of its creatures—Boards of Education not excepted. These have, of course, important, delicate, and highly discretionary functions, but none that they may not perform within the limits of the Bill of Rights. That they are educating the young for citizenship is reason for scrupulous protection of Constitutional freedoms of the individual, if we are not to strangle the free mind at its source and teach youth to discount important principles of our government as mere platitudes." 319 U. S., at 637.

On the other hand, the Court has repeatedly emphasized the need for affirming the comprehensive authority of the States and of school officials, consistent with fundamental constitutional safeguards, to prescribe and control conduct in the schools. See *Epperson* v. *Arkansas*, supra, at 104; *Meyer* v. *Nebraska*, supra, at 402. Our problem lies in the area where students in the exercise of First Amendment rights collide with the rules of the school authorities.

II.

The problem posed by the present case does not relate to regulation of the length of skirts or the type of clothing, to hair style, or deportment. Cf. *Ferrell* v. *Dallas Independent School District*, 392 F. 2d 697 (1968); *Pugsley* v. *Sellmeyer*, 158 Ark. 247, 250 S. W. 538 (1923). It does not concern aggressive, disruptive action or even group demonstrations. Our problem involves direct, primary First Amendment rights akin to "pure speech."

. . . the school authorities did not purport to prohibit the wearing of all symbols of political or controversial significance. The record shows that students in some of the schools wore buttons relating to national political campaigns, and some even wore the Iron Cross, traditionally a symbol of Nazism. The order prohibiting the wearing of armbands did not extend to these. Instead, a particular symbol—black armbands worn to exhibit opposition to this Nation's involvement in Vietnam—was singled out for prohibition. Clearly, the prohibition of expression of one particular opinion, at least without evidence that it is necessary to avoid material and substantial interference with schoolwork or discipline, is not constitutionally permissible.

In our system, state-operated schools may not be enclaves of totalitarianism. School officials do not possess absolute authority over their students. Students in school as well as out of school are "persons" under our Constitution. They are possessed of fundamental rights which the State must respect, just as they themselves must respect their obligations to the State. In our system, students may not be regarded as closed-circuit recipients of only that which the State chooses to communicate. They may not be confined to the expression of those sentiments that are officially approved. . . .

As we have discussed, the record does not demonstrate any facts which might reasonably have led school authorities to forecast substantial disruption of or material interference with school activities, and no disturbances or disorders on the school premises in fact occurred. These petitioners merely went about their ordained rounds in school. Their deviation consisted only in wearing on their sleeve a band of black cloth, not more than two inches wide. They wore it to exhibit their disapproval of the Vietnam hostilities and their advocacy of a truce, to make their views known, and, by their example, to influence others to adopt them. They neither interrupted school activities nor sought to intrude in the school affairs or the lives of others. They caused discussion outside of the classrooms, but no interference with work and no disorder. In the circumstances, our Constitution does not permit officials of the State to deny their form of expression.

We express no opinion as to the form of relief which should be granted, this being a matter for the lower courts to determine. We reverse and remand for further proceedings consistent with this opinion.

Reversed and remanded.

MR. JUSTICE STEWART, concurring.

Although I agree with much of what is said in the Court's opinion, and with its judgment in this case, I cannot share the Court's uncritical assumption that, school discipline aside, the First Amendment rights of children are co-extensive with those of adults. Indeed, I had thought the Court decided otherwise just last Term in *Ginsberg* v. *New York*, 390 U. S. 629. I continue to hold the view I expressed in that case: "[A] State may permissibly determine that, at least in some precisely delineated areas, a child—like someone in a captive audience—is not possessed of that full capacity for individual choice which is the presupposition of First Amendment guarantees." *Id.*, at 649–650 (concurring in result). Cf. *Prince* v. *Massachusetts*, 321 U. S. 158.

MR. JUSTICE WHITE, concurring.

While I join the Court's opinion, I deem it appropriate to note, first, that the Court continues to recognize a distinction between communicating by words and communicating by acts or conduct which sufficiently impinges on some valid state interest; and, second, that I do not subscribe to everything the Court of Appeals said about free speech in its opinion in *Burnside* v. *Byars*, 363 F. 2d 744, 748 (C. A. 5th Cir. 1966), a case relied upon by the Court in the matter now before us.

MR. JUSTICE BLACK, dissenting.

The Court's holding in this case ushers in what I deem to be an entirely new era in which the power to control pupils by the elected "officials of state supported public schools . . ." in the United States is in ultimate effect transferred to the Supreme Court. . . .

While the record does not show that any of these armband students shouted, used profane language, or were violent in any manner, detailed testimony by some of them shows their armbands caused comments, warnings by other students, the poking of fun at them, and a warning by an older football player that other, nonprotesting students had better let them alone. There is also evidence that a teacher of mathematics had his lesson period practically "wrecked" chiefly by disputes with Mary Beth Tinker, who wore her armband for her "demonstration." Even a casual reading of the record shows that this armband did divert students' minds from their regular lessons, and that talk, comments, etc., made John Tinker "self-conscious" in attending school with his armband. While the absence of obscene remarks or boisterous and loud disorder perhaps justifies the Court's statement that the few armband students did not actually "disrupt" the classwork, I think the record overwhelmingly shows that the armbands did exactly what the elected school officials and principals foresaw they would, that is, took the students' minds off their classwork and diverted them to thoughts about the highly emotional subject of the Vietnam war. And I repeat that if the time has come when pupils of state-supported schools, kindergartens, grammar schools, or high schools, can defy and flout orders of school officials to keep their minds on their own schoolwork, it is the beginning of a new revolutionary era of permissiveness in this country fostered by the judiciary. The next logical step, it appears to me, would be to hold unconstitutional laws that bar pupils under 21 or 18 from voting, or from being elected members of the boards of education. . . .

In my view, teachers in state-controlled public schools are hired to teach there. Although Mr. Justice McReynolds may have intimated to the contrary in *Meyer* v. *Nebraska, supra,* certainly a teacher is not paid to go into school and teach subjects the State does not hire him to teach as a part of its selected curriculum. Nor are public school students sent to the schools at public expense to broadcast political or any other views to educate and inform the public. The original idea of schools, which I do not believe is yet abandoned as worthless or out of date, was that children had not yet reached the point of experience and wisdom which enabled them to teach all of their elders. It may be that the Nation has outworn the old-fashioned slogan that "children are to be seen not heard," but one may, I hope, be permitted to harbor the thought that taxpayers send children to school on the premise that at their age they need to learn, not teach.

. . . groups of students all over the land are already running loose, conducting break-ins, sit-ins, lie-ins, and smash-ins. Many of these student groups, as is all too familiar to all who read the newspapers and watch the television news programs, have already engaged in rioting, property seizures, and destruction. They have picketed schools to force students not to cross their picket lines and have too often violently attacked earnest but frightened students who wanted an education that the pickets did not want them to get. Students engaged in such activities are apparently confident that they know far more about how to operate public school systems than do their parents, teachers, and elected school officials. It is no answer to say that the particular students here have not yet reached such high points in their demands to attend classes in order to exercise their political pressures. Turned loose with lawsuits for damages and injunctions against their teachers as they are here, it is nothing but wishful thinking to imagine that young, immature students will not soon believe it is their right to control the schools rather than the right of the States that collect the taxes to hire the teachers for the benefit of the pupils. This case, therefore, wholly without constitutional reasons in my judgment, subjects all the public schools in the country to the whims and caprices of their loudest-mouthed, but maybe not their brightest, students. I, for one, am not fully persuaded that school pupils are wise enough, even with this Court's expert help from Washington, to run the 23,390 public school systems in our 50 States. I wish, therefore, wholly to disclaim any purpose on my part to hold that the Federal Constitution compels the teachers, parents, and elected school officials to surrender control of the American public school system to public school students. I dissent.

MR. JUSTICE HARLAN, dissenting.

I certainly agree that state public school authorities in the discharge of their responsibilities are not wholly exempt from the requirements of the Fourteenth Amendment respecting the freedoms of expression and association. At the same time I am reluctant to believe that there is any disagreement between the majority and myself on the proposition that school officials should be accorded the widest authority in maintaining discipline and good order in their institutions. To translate that proposition into a workable constitutional rule, I would, in cases like this, cast upon those complaining the burden of showing that a particular school measure was motivated by other than legitimate school concerns—for example, a desire to prohibit the expression of an unpopular point of view, while permitting expression of the dominant opinion.

Finding nothing in this record which impugns the good faith of respondents in promulgating the armband regulation, I would affirm the judgment below.

New Jersey v. T.L.O.

469 U.S. 325 (1985)

T.L.O., a fourteen-year-old high school freshman, was caught smoking in the school bathroom. After being taken to the Principal's office, she denied that she had been smoking and claimed that she did not smoke at all. The Assistant Vice Principal opened her purse, found a pack of cigarettes, and also noticed a package of cigarette rolling papers that are commonly associated with the use of marijuana. A thorough search of the purse uncovered some marijuana, a pipe, plastic bags, a fairly substantial amount of money, an index card containing a list of students who owed her money, and two letters that implicated her in marijuana dealing. The state of New Jersey brought delinquency charges against her in Juvenile Court. After denying her motion to suppress the evidence found in her purse, the court held that the Fourth Amendment applied to searches by school officials but that the search in question was a reasonable one. The Appellate Division of the New Jersey Superior Court affirmed that there had been no Fourth Amendment violation. The New Jersey Supreme Court reversed and ordered the suppression of the evidence on the ground that the search of the purse was unreasonable.

JUSTICE WHITE delivered the opinion of the Court.

We granted certiorari in this case to examine the appropriateness of the exclusionary rule as a remedy for searches carried out in violation of the Fourth Amendment by public school authorities. Our consideration of the proper application of the Fourth Amendment to the public schools, however, has led us to conclude that the search that gave rise to the case now before us did not violate the Fourth Amendment. Accordingly, we here address only the questions of the proper standard for assessing the legality of searches conducted by public school officials and the application of that standard to the facts of this case.

I

On March 7, 1980, a teacher at Piscataway High School in Middlesex County, N. J., discovered two girls smoking in a lavatory. One of the two girls was the respondent T. L. O., who at that time was a 14-year-old high school freshman. Because smoking in the lavatory was a violation of a school rule, the teacher took the two girls to the Principal's office, where they met with Assistant Vice Principal Theodore Choplick. In response to questioning by Mr. Choplick, T. L. O.'s companion admitted that she had violated the rule. T. L. O., however, denied that she had been smoking in the lavatory and claimed that she did not smoke at all.

Mr. Choplick asked T. L. O. to come into his private office and demanded to see her purse. Opening the purse, he found a pack of cigarettes, which he removed from the purse and held before T. L. O. as he accused her of having lied to him. As he reached into the purse for the cigarettes, Mr. Choplick also noticed a package of cigarette rolling papers. In his experience, possession of rolling papers by high school students was closely associated with the use of marihuana. Suspecting that a closer examination of the purse might yield further evidence of drug use, Mr. Choplick proceeded to search the purse thoroughly. The search revealed a small amount of marihuana, a pipe, a number of empty plastic bags, a substantial quantity of money in one-dollar bills, an index card that appeared to be a list of students who owed T. L. O. money, and two letters that implicated T. L. O. in marihuana dealing.

Mr. Choplick notified T. L. O.'s mother and the police, and turned the evidence of drug dealing over to the police. At the request of the police, T. L. O.'s mother took her daughter to police headquarters, where T. L. O. confessed that she had been selling marihuana at the high school. On the basis of the confession and the evidence seized by Mr. Choplick, the State brought delinquency charges against T. L. O. in the Juvenile and Domestic Relations Court of Middlesex County. Contending that Mr. Choplick's search of her purse violated the Fourth Amendment, T. L. O. moved to suppress the evidence found in her purse as well as her confession, which, she argued, was tainted by the allegedly unlawful search.

. . .

Although we originally granted certiorari to decide the issue of the appropriate remedy in juvenile court proceedings for unlawful school searches, our doubts regarding the wisdom of deciding that question in isolation from the broader question of what limits, if any, the Fourth Amendment places on the activities of school authorities prompted us to order reargument on

that question. Having heard argument on the legality of the search of T. L. O.'s purse, we are satisfied that the search did not violate the Fourth Amendment.

II

In determining whether the search at issue in this case violated the Fourth Amendment, we are faced initially with the question whether that Amendment's prohibition on unreasonable searches and seizures applies to searches conducted by public school officials. We hold that it does.

It is now beyond dispute that "the Federal Constitution, by virtue of the Fourteenth Amendment, prohibits unreasonable searches and seizures by state officers." *Elkins* v. *United States*, 364 U. S. 206, 213 (1960); accord, *Mapp* v. *Ohio*, 367 U. S. 643 (1961); *Wolf* v. *Colorado*, 338 U. S. 25 (1949). Equally indisputable is the proposition that the Fourteenth Amendment protects the rights of students against encroachment by public school officials:

"The Fourteenth Amendment, as now applied to the States, protects the citizen against the State itself and all of its creatures—Boards of Education not excepted. These have, of course, important, delicate, and highly discretionary functions, but none that they may not perform within the limits of the Bill of Rights. That they are educating the young for citizenship is reason for scrupulous protection of Constitutional freedoms of the individual, if we are not to strangle the free mind at its source and teach youth to discount important principles of our government as mere platitudes." *West Virginia State Bd. of Ed.* v. *Barnette*, 319 U. S. 624, 637 (1943).

These two propositions—that the Fourth Amendment applies to the States through the Fourteenth Amendment, and that the actions of public school officials are subject to the limits placed on state action by the Fourteenth Amendment—might appear sufficient to answer the suggestion that the Fourth Amendment does not proscribe unreasonable searches by school officials. On reargument, however, the State of New Jersey has argued that the history of the Fourth Amendment indicates that the Amendment was intended to regulate only searches and seizures carried out by law enforcement officers; accordingly, although public school officials are concededly state agents for purposes of the Fourteenth Amendment, the Fourth Amendment creates no rights enforceable against them.

It may well be true that the evil toward which the Fourth Amendment was primarily directed was the resurrection of the pre-Revolutionary practice of using general warrants or "writs of assistance" to authorize searches for contraband by officers of the Crown. See *United States* v. *Chadwick*, 433 U. S. 1, 7–8 (1977); *Boyd* v. *United States*, 116 U. S. 616, 624–629 (1886). But this Court has never limited the Amendment's prohibition on unreasonable searches and seizures to operations conducted by the police. Rather, the Court has long spoken of the Fourth Amendment's strictures as restraints imposed upon "governmental action"—that is, "upon the activities of sovereign authority." . . .

III

To hold that the Fourth Amendment applies to searches conducted by school authorities is only to begin the inquiry into the standards governing such searches. Although the underlying command of the Fourth Amendment is always that searches and seizures be reasonable, what is reasonable depends on the context within which a search takes place. The determination of the standard of reasonableness governing any specific class of searches requires "balancing the need to search against the invasion which the search entails." *Camara* v. *Municipal Court, supra,* at 536–537. On one side of the balance are arrayed the individual's legitimate expectations of privacy and personal security; on the other, the government's need for effective methods to deal with breaches of public order.

. . .

Although this Court may take notice of the difficulty of maintaining discipline in the public schools today, the situation is not so dire that students in the schools may claim no legitimate expectations of privacy. . . .

. . . Students at a minimum must bring to school not only the supplies needed for their studies, but also keys, money, and the necessaries of personal hygiene and grooming. In addition, students may carry on their persons or in purses or wallets such nondisruptive yet highly personal items as photographs, letters, and diaries. Finally, students may have perfectly legitimate reasons to carry with them articles of property needed in connection with extracurricular or recreational activities. In short, schoolchildren may find it necessary to carry with them a variety of legitimate, noncontraband items, and there is no reason to conclude that they have necessarily waived all rights to privacy in such items merely by bringing them onto school grounds.

Against the child's interest in privacy must be set the substantial interest of teachers and administrators in maintaining discipline in the classroom and on school grounds. Maintaining order in the classroom has never been easy, but in recent years, school disorder has often taken particularly ugly forms: drug use and violent crime in the schools have become major social problems. . . .

How, then, should we strike the balance between the schoolchild's legitimate expectations of privacy and the school's equally legitimate need to maintain an environment in which learning can take place? It is evident that the school setting requires some easing of the restrictions to which searches by public authorities are ordinarily subject. The warrant requirement, in particular, is unsuited ⹁o the school environment: requiring a teacher to obtain a warrant before searching a child suspected of an infraction of school rules (or of the criminal law) would unduly interfere with the maintenance of the swift and informal disciplinary procedures needed in the schools. Just as we have in other cases dispensed with the warrant requirement when "the burden of obtaining a warrant is likely to frustrate the governmental purpose behind the search," *Camara* v. *Municipal Court*, 387 U. S., at 532–533, we hold today that school officials need not obtain a warrant before searching a student who is under their authority.

The school setting also requires some modification of the level of suspicion of illicit activity needed to justify a search. Ordinarily, a search—

even one that may permissibly be carried out without a warrant—must be based upon "probable cause" to believe that a violation of the law has occurred. See, *e. g., Almeida-Sanchez* v. *United States*, 413 U. S. 266, 273 (1973); *Sibron* v. *New York*, 392 U. S. 40, 62–66 (1968). However, "probable cause" is not an irreducible requirement of a valid search. The fundamental command of the Fourth Amendment is that searches and seizures be reasonable . . .

We join the majority of courts that have examined this issue in concluding that the accommodation of the privacy interests of schoolchildren with the substantial need of teachers and administrators for freedom to maintain order in the schools does not require strict adherence to the requirement that searches be based on probable cause to believe that the subject of the search has violated or is violating the law. Rather, the legality of a search of a student should depend simply on the reasonableness, under all the circumstances, of the search. Determining the reasonableness of any search involves a twofold inquiry: first, one must consider "whether the . . . action was justified at its inception," *Terry* v. *Ohio*, 392 U. S., at 20; second, one must determine whether the search as actually conducted "was reasonably related in scope to the circumstances which justified the interference in the first place," *ibid.* Under ordinary circumstances, a search of a student by a teacher or other school official will be "justified at its inception" when there are reasonable grounds for suspecting that the search will turn up evidence that the student has violated or is violating either the law or the rules of the school. Such a search will be permissible in its scope when the measures adopted are reasonably related to the objectives of the search and not excessively intrusive in light of the age and sex of the student and the nature of the infraction.

. . .

IV

There remains the question of the legality of the search in this case. We recognize that the "reasonable grounds" standard applied by the New Jersey Supreme Court in its consideration of

this question is not substantially different from the standard that we have adopted today. Nonetheless, we believe that the New Jersey court's application of that standard to strike down the search of T. L. O.'s purse reflects a somewhat crabbed notion of reasonableness. Our review of the facts surrounding the search leads us to conclude that the search was in no sense unreasonable for Fourth Amendment purposes.

. . . T. L. O. had been accused of smoking, and had denied the accusation in the strongest possible terms when she stated that she did not smoke at all. Surely it cannot be said that under these circumstances, T. L. O.'s possession of cigarettes would be irrelevant to the charges against her or to her response to those charges. T. L. O.'s possession of cigarettes, once it was discovered, would both corroborate the report that she had been smoking and undermine the credibility of her defense to the charge of smoking. . . .

Our conclusion that Mr. Choplick's decision to open T. L. O.'s purse was reasonable brings us to the question of the further search for marihuana once the pack of cigarettes was located. The suspicion upon which the search for marihuana was founded was provided when Mr. Choplick observed a package of rolling papers in the purse as he removed the pack of cigarettes. Although T. L. O. does not dispute the reasonableness of Mr. Choplick's belief that the rolling papers indicated the presence of marihuana, she does contend that the scope of the search Mr. Choplick conducted exceeded permissible bounds when he seized and read certain letters that implicated T. L. O. in drug dealing. This argument, too, is unpersuasive. The discovery of the rolling papers concededly gave rise to a reasonable suspicion that T. L. O. was carrying marihuana as well as cigarettes in her purse. This suspicion justified further exploration of T. L. O.'s purse, which turned up more evidence of drug-related activities: a pipe, a number of plastic bags of the type commonly used to store marihuana, a small quantity of marihuana, and a fairly substantial amount of money. Under these circumstances, it was not unreasonable to extend the search to a separate zippered compartment of the purse; and when a search of that compartment revealed an index card containing a list of "people who owe me money" as well as two letters, the inference that T. L. O. was involved in marihuana trafficking was substantial enough to justify Mr. Choplick in examining the letters to determine whether they contained any further evidence. In short, we cannot conclude that the search for marihuana was unreasonable in any respect.

Because the search resulting in the discovery of the evidence of marijuana dealing by T. L. O. was reasonable, the New Jersey Supreme Court's decision to exclude that evidence from T. L. O.'s juvenile delinquency proceedings on Fourth Amendment grounds was erroneous. Accordingly, the judgment of the Supreme Court of New Jersey is

Reversed.

JUSTICE POWELL, with whom JUSTICE O'CONNOR joins, concurring.

. . .

JUSTICE BLACKMUN, concurring in the judgment.

. . .

JUSTICE BRENNAN, with whom JUSTICE MARSHALL joins, concurring in part and dissenting in part.

I fully agree with Part II of the Court's opinion. Teachers, like all other government officials, must conform their conduct to the Fourth Amendment's protections of personal privacy and personal security. As JUSTICE STEVENS points out, *post*, at 373–374, 385–386, this principle is of particular importance when applied to schoolteachers, for children learn as much by example as by exposition. It would be incongruous and futile to charge teachers with the task of embuing their students with an understanding of our system of constitutional democracy, while at the same time immunizing those same teachers from the need to respect constitutional protections. See *Board of Education* v. *Pico*, 457 U. S. 853, 864–865 (1982) (plurality opinion); *West Virginia State Board of Education* v. *Barnette*, 319 U. S. 624, 637 (1943).

I do not, however, otherwise join the Court's opinion. Today's decision sanctions school officials to conduct full-scale searches on a "reason-

ableness" standard whose only definite content is that it is *not* the same test as the "probable cause" standard found in the text of the Fourth Amendment. In adopting this unclear, unprecedented, and unnecessary departure from generally applicable Fourth Amendment standards, the Court carves out a broad exception to standards that this Court has developed over years of considering Fourth Amendment problems. Its decision is supported neither by precedent nor even by a fair application of the "balancing test" it proclaims in this very opinion.

. . .

JUSTICE STEVENS, with whom JUSTICE MARSHALL joins, and with whom JUSTICE BRENNAN joins as to Part I, concurring in part and dissenting in part.

. . .

. . . The Court has . . . seized upon this "no smoking" case to announce "the proper standard" that should govern searches by school officials who are confronted with disciplinary problems far more severe than smoking in the restroom. Although I join Part II of the Court's opinion, I continue to believe that the Court has unnecessarily and inappropriately reached out to decide a constitutional question. See 468 U. S. 1214 (1984) (STEVENS, J., dissenting from reargument order). More importantly, I fear that the concerns that motivated the Court's activism have produced a holding that will permit school administrators to search students suspected of violating only the most trivial school regulations and guidelines for behavior.

I

The question the Court decides today— whether Mr. Choplick's search of T. L. O.'s purse violated the Fourth Amendment—was not raised by the State's petition for writ of certiorari. That petition only raised one question: "Whether the Fourth Amendment's exclusionary rule applies to searches made by public school officials and teachers in school." The State quite properly declined to submit the former question because "[it] did not wish to present what might appear to be solely a factual dispute to this Court." Since this Court has twice had the threshold question argued, I believe that it should expressly consider the merits of the New Jersey Supreme Court's ruling that the exclusionary rule applies.

. . .

Schools are places where we inculcate the values essential to the meaningful exercise of rights and responsibilities by a self-governing citizenry. If the Nation's students can be convicted through the use of arbitrary methods destructive of personal liberty, they cannot help but feel that they have been dealt with unfairly. The application of the exclusionary rule in criminal proceedings arising from illegal school searches makes an important statement to young people that "our society attaches serious consequences to a violation of constitutional rights," and that this is a principle of "liberty and justice for all."

Thus, the simple and correct answer to the question presented by the State's petition for certiorari would have required affirmance of a state court's judgment suppressing evidence. That result would have been dramatically out of character for a Court that not only grants prosecutors relief from suppression orders with distressing regularity, but also is prone to rely on grounds not advanced by the parties in order to protect evidence from exclusion. In characteristic disregard of the doctrine of judicial restraint, the Court avoided that result in this case by ordering reargument and directing the parties to address a constitutional question that the parties, with good reason, had not asked the Court to decide. Because judicial activism undermines the Court's power to perform its central mission in a legitimate way, I dissented from the reargument order. See 468 U. S. 1214 (1984). I have not modified the views expressed in that dissent, but since the majority has brought the question before us, I shall explain why I believe the Court has misapplied the standard of reasonableness embodied in the Fourth Amendment.

. . .

III

. . . The rule the Court adopts today is so open-ended that it may make the Fourth Amendment virtually meaningless in the school context. Although I agree that school administrators must have broad latitude to maintain order and discipline in our classrooms, that authority is not unlimited.

IV

The schoolroom is the first opportunity most citizens have to experience the power of government. Through it passes every citizen and public official, from schoolteachers to policemen and prison guards. The values they learn there, they take with them in life. One of our most cherished ideals is the one contained in the Fourth Amendment: that the government may not intrude on the personal privacy of its citizens without a warrant or compelling circumstance. The Court's decision today is a curious moral for the Nation's youth. Although the search of T. L. O.'s purse does not trouble today's majority, I submit that we are not dealing with "matters relatively trivial to the welfare of the Nation. There are village tyrants as well as village Hampdens, but none who acts under color of law is beyond reach of the Constitution." *West Virginia State Board of Education* v. *Barnette*, 319 U. S. 624, 638 (1943).

I respectfully dissent.

Hudson v. Palmer

468 U. S. 517 (1984)

Russell Palmer, a prisoner in a Virginia penal institution, filed an action in federal district court under 42 U. S. C. § 1983 against Ted Hudson, an officer at the institution. Palmer alleged that Hudson had conducted an unreasonable "shakedown" search of his prison locker and cell and had brought a false charge, under prison disciplinary procedures, of destroying state property solely to harass him. The district court granted summary judgment for Hudson. The Fourth Circuit held that a prisoner has a "limited privacy right" in his cell entitling him to protection against searches conducted solely to harass or to humiliate, and that a remand was necessary to determine the purpose of the search by Hudson.

CHIEF JUSTICE BURGER delivered the opinion of the Court.

We granted certiorari in No. 82–1630 to decide whether a prison inmate has a reasonable expectation of privacy in his prison cell entitling him to the protection of the Fourth Amendment against unreasonable searches and seizures. We also granted certiorari in No. 82–6695, the cross-petition, to determine whether our decision in *Parratt* v. *Taylor,* 451 U. S. 527 (1981), which held that a negligent deprivation of property by state officials does not violate the Fourteenth Amendment if an adequate postdeprivation state remedy exists, should extend to intentional deprivations of property.

I

The facts underlying this dispute are relatively simple. Respondent Palmer is an inmate at the Bland Correctional Center in Bland, Va., serving sentences for forgery, uttering, grand larceny, and bank robbery convictions. On September 16, 1981, petitioner Hudson, an officer at the Correctional Center, with a fellow officer, conducted a "shakedown" search of respondent's prison locker and cell for contraband. During the "shakedown," the officers discovered a ripped pillowcase in a trash can near respondent's cell bunk. Charges against Palmer were instituted under the prison disciplinary procedures for destroying state property. After a hearing, Palmer was found guilty on the charge and was ordered to reimburse the State for the cost of the material destroyed; in addition, a reprimand was entered on his prison record.

Palmer subsequently brought this *pro se* action in United States District Court under 42 U. S. C. § 1983. Respondent claimed that Hudson had conducted the shakedown search of his cell and had brought a false charge against him solely to harass him, and that, in violation of his Fourteenth Amendment right not to be deprived of property without due process of law, Hudson had intentionally destroyed certain of his noncontraband personal property during the September 16 search. Hudson denied each allegation; he moved for and was granted summary judgment. The District Court accepted respondent's allegations as true but held nonetheless, relying on *Parratt* v. *Taylor, supra,* that the alleged destruction of respondent's property, even if intentional, did not violate the Fourteenth Amendment because there were state tort remedies available to redress the deprivation, App. 31 and that the alleged harassment did not "rise to the level of a constitutional deprivation," *id.,* at 32.

The Court of Appeals affirmed in part, reversed in part, and remanded for further proceedings. . . .

II

A

The first question we address is whether respondent has a right of privacy in his prison cell entitling him to the protection of the Fourth Amendment against unreasonable searches. As we have noted, the Court of Appeals held that the District Court's summary judgment in petitioner's favor was premature because respondent had a "limited privacy right" in his cell that might have been breached. The court concluded that, to protect this privacy right, shakedown searches of an individual's cell should be performed only "pursuant to an established program of conducting random searches . . . reasonably designed to deter or discover the possession of contraband" or upon reasonable belief that the prisoner possesses contraband. Petitioner contends that the Court of Appeals erred in holding that respondent had even a limited privacy right in his cell, and urges that we adopt the "bright line" rule that prisoners have no legitimate expectation of privacy in their individual cells that would entitle them to Fourth Amendment protection.

We have repeatedly held that prisons are not beyond the reach of the Constitution. No "iron curtain" separates one from the other. *Wolff* v. *McDonnell*, 418 U. S. 539, 555 (1974). Indeed, we have insisted that prisoners be accorded those rights not fundamentally inconsistent with imprisonment itself or incompatible with the objectives of incarceration. For example, we have held that invidious racial discrimination is as intolerable within a prison as outside, except as may be essential to "prison security and discipline." *Lee* v. *Washington*, 390 U. S. 333 (1968) *(per curiam)*. Like others, prisoners have the constitutional right to petition the Government for redress of their grievances, which includes a reasonable right of access to the courts. *Johnson* v. *Avery*, 393 U. S. 483 (1969).

Prisoners must be provided "reasonable opportunities" to exercise their religious freedom guaranteed under the First Amendment. *Cruz* v. *Beto*, 405 U. S. 319 (1972) *(per curiam)*. Similarly, they retain those First Amendment rights of speech "not inconsistent with [their] status as . . . prisoner[s] or with the legitimate penological objectives of the corrections system." *Pell* v. *Procunier*, 417 U. S. 817, 822 (1974). They enjoy the protection of due process. *Wolff* v. *McDonnell*, *supra*; *Haines* v. *Kerner*, 404 U. S. 519 (1972). And the Eighth Amendment ensures that they will not be subject to "cruel and unusual punishments." *Estelle* v. *Gamble*, 429 U. S. 97 (1976). The continuing guarantee of these substantial rights to prison inmates is testimony to a belief that the way a society treats those who have transgressed against it is evidence of the essential character of that society.

However, while persons imprisoned for crime enjoy many protections of the Constitution, it is also clear that imprisonment carries with it the circumscription or loss of many significant rights. See *Bell* v. *Wolfish*, 441 U. S., at 545. These constraints on inmates, and in some cases the complete withdrawal of certain rights, are "justified by the considerations underlying our penal system." *Price* v. *Johnston*, 334 U. S. 266, 285 (1948); see also *Bell* v. *Wolfish*, *supra*, at 545–546 and cases cited; *Wolff* v. *McDonnell*, *supra*, at 555. The curtailment of certain rights is necessary, as a practical matter, to accommodate a myriad of "institutional needs and objectives" of prison facilities, *Wolff* v. *McDonnell*, *supra*, at 555, chief among which is internal security, see *Pell* v. *Procunier*, *supra*, at 823. Of course, these restrictions or retractions also serve, incidentally, as reminders that, under our system of justice, deterrence and retribution are factors in addition to correction.

We have not before been called upon to decide the specific question whether the Fourth Amendment applies within a prison cell, but the nature of our inquiry is well defined. We must determine here, as in other Fourth Amendment contexts, if a "justifiable" expectation of privacy is at stake. *Katz* v. *United States*, 389 U. S. 347 (1967). The applicability of the Fourth Amendment turns on whether "the person invoking its protection can claim a 'justifiable,' a 'reasonable,' or a 'legitimate expectation of privacy' that has been invaded by government action." *Smith* v. *Maryland*, 442 U. S. 735, 740 (1979), and cases cited. We must decide, in Justice Harlan's words, whether a prisoner's expectation of privacy in his prison cell is the kind of expectation that "society is prepared to recognize as 'reasonable.'" *Katz, supra*, at 360, 361 (concurring opinion).

Notwithstanding our caution in approaching claims that the Fourth Amendment is inapplicable in a given context, we hold that society is not prepared to recognize as legitimate any subjective expectation of privacy that a prisoner might have in his prison cell and that, accordingly, the Fourth Amendment proscription against unreasonable searches does not apply within the confines of the prison cell. The recognition of privacy rights for prisoners in their individual cells simply cannot be reconciled with the concept of incarceration and the needs and objectives of penal institutions.

Prisons, by definition, are places of involuntary confinement of persons who have a demonstrated proclivity for anti-social criminal, and often violent, conduct. Inmates have necessarily shown a lapse in ability to control and conform their behavior to the legitimate standards of society by the normal impulses of self-restraint; they have shown an inability to regulate their conduct in a way that reflects either a respect for law or an appreciation of the rights of others. Even a partial survey of the statistics on violent crime in our Nation's prisons illustrates the magnitude of the problem. During 1981 and the first half of 1982, there were over 120 prisoners murdered by fellow inmates in state and federal prisons. A number of prison personnel were murdered by prisoners during this period. Over 29 riots or similar disturbances were reported in these facilities for the same time frame. And there were over 125 suicides in these institutions. See Prison Violence, 7 Corrections Compendium (Mar. 1983). Additionally, informal statistics from the United States Bureau of Prisons show that in the federal system during 1983, there were 11 inmate homicides, 359 inmate assaults on other inmates, 227 inmate assaults on prison staff, and 10 suicides. There were in the same system in 1981 and 1982 over 750 inmate assaults on other inmates and over 570 inmate assaults on prison personnel.

Within this volatile "community," prison administrators are to take all necessary steps to ensure the safety of not only the prison staffs and administrative personnel, but also visitors. They are under an obligation to take reasonable measures to guarantee the safety of the inmates themselves. They must be ever alert to attempts to introduce drugs and other contraband into the premises which, we can judicially notice, is one of the most perplexing problems of prisons today; they must prevent, so far as possible, the flow of illicit weapons into the prison; they must be vigilant to detect escape plots, in which drugs or weapons may be involved, before the schemes materialize. In addition to these monumental tasks, it is incumbent upon these officials at the same time to maintain as sanitary an environment for the inmates as feasible, given the difficulties of the circumstances.

The administration of a prison, we have said, is "at best an extraordinarily difficult undertaking." *Wolff* v. *McDonnell*, 418 U. S., at 566; *Hewitt* v. *Helms*, 459 U. S. 460, 467 (1983). But it would be literally impossible to accomplish the prison objectives identified above if inmates retained a right of privacy in their cells. Virtually the only place inmates can conceal weapons, drugs, and other contraband is in their cells. Unfettered access to these cells by prison officials, thus, is imperative if drugs and contraband are to be ferreted out and sanitary surroundings are to be maintained.

Determining whether an expectation of privacy is "legitimate" or "reasonable" necessarily entails a balancing of interests. The two interests here are the interest of society in the security of its penal institutions and the interest of the prisoner in privacy within his cell. The latter interest, of course, is already limited by the exigencies of the circumstances: A prison "shares none of the attributes of privacy of a home, an automobile, an office, or a hotel room." *Lanza* v. *New York*, 370 U. S. 139, 143–144 (1962). We strike the balance in favor of institutional security, which we have noted is "central to all other corrections goals," *Pell* v. *Procunier*, 417 U. S., at 823. A right of privacy in traditional Fourth Amendment terms is fundamentally incompatible with the close and continual surveillance of inmates and their cells required to ensure institutional security and internal order. We are satisfied that society would insist that the prisoner's expectation of privacy always yield to what must be considered the paramount interest in institutional security.

. . .

Our holding that respondent does not have a reasonable expectation of privacy enabling him to invoke the protections of the Fourth Amendment does not mean that he is without a remedy for calculated harassment unrelated to prison needs.

Nor does it mean that prison attendants can ride roughshod over inmates' property rights with impunity. The Eighth Amendment always stands as a protection against "cruel and unusual punishments." By the same token, there are adequate state tort and common-law remedies available to respondent to redress the alleged destruction of his personal property. See discussion *infra*, at 534–536.

B

In his complaint in the District Court, in addition to his claim that the shakedown search of his cell violated his Fourth and Fourteenth Amendment privacy rights, respondent alleged under 42 U. S. C. § 1983 that petitioner intentionally destroyed certain of his personal property during the search. This destruction, respondent contended, deprived him of property without due process, in violation of the Due Process Clause of the Fourteenth Amendment. The District Court dismissed this portion of respondent's complaint for failure to state a claim. Reasoning under *Parratt* v. *Taylor*,

"meaningful means by which to assess the propriety of the State's action at some time after the initial taking . . . satisf[ies] the requirements of procedural due process." 451 U. S., at 539 (footnote omitted).

We reasoned that where a loss of property is occasioned by a random, unauthorized act by a state employee, rather than by an established state procedure, the state cannot predict when the loss will occur. *Id.*, at 541. Under these circumstances, we observed:

"It is difficult to conceive of how the State could provide a meaningful hearing before the deprivation takes place. The loss of property, although attributable to the State as action under 'color of law,' is in almost all cases beyond the control of the State. Indeed, in most cases it is not only impracticable, but impossible, to provide a meaningful hearing before the deprivation." *Ibid.*

Two Terms ago, we reaffirmed our holding in *Parratt* in *Logan* v. *Zimmerman Brush Co.*, 455 U. S. 422 (1982), in the course of holding that postdeprivation remedies do not satisfy due process where a deprivation of property is caused by

conduct pursuant to established state procedure, rather than random and unauthorized action.

While *Parratt* is necessarily limited by its facts to negligent deprivations of property, it is evident, as the Court of Appeals recognized, that its reasoning applies as well to intentional deprivations of property. The underlying rationale of *Parratt* is that when deprivations of property are effected through random and unauthorized conduct of a state employee, predeprivation procedures are simply "impracticable" since the state cannot know when such deprivations will occur. We can discern no logical distinction between negligent and intentional deprivations of property insofar as the "practicability" of affording predeprivation process is concerned. The state can no more anticipate and control in advance the random and unauthorized intentional conduct of its employees than it can anticipate similar negligent conduct. Arguably, intentional acts are even more difficult to anticipate because one bent on intentionally depriving a person of his property might well take affirmative steps to avoid signalling his intent.

If negligent deprivations of property do not violate the Due Process Clause because predeprivation process is impracticable, it follows that intentional deprivations do not violate that Clause provided, of course, that adequate state postdeprivation remedies are available. Accordingly, we hold that an unauthorized intentional deprivation of property by a state employee does not constitute a violation of the procedural requirements of the Due Process Clause of the Fourteenth Amendment if a meaningful postdeprivation remedy for the loss is available. For intentional, as for negligent deprivations of property by state employees, the state's action is not complete until and unless it provides or refuses to provide a suitable postdeprivation remedy.

. . .

III

We hold that the Fourth Amendment has no applicability to a prison cell. We hold also that, even if petitioner intentionally destroyed respondent's personal property during the challenged shakedown search, the destruction did not violate the Fourteenth Amendment since the Commonwealth of Virginia has provided respondent an adequate postdeprivation remedy.

Accordingly, the judgment of the Court of Appeals reversing and remanding the District Court's judgment on respondent's claim under the Fourth and Fourteenth Amendments is reversed. The judgment affirming the District Court's decision that respondent has not been denied due process under the Fourteenth Amendment is affirmed.

It is so ordered.

JUSTICE O'CONNOR, concurring.

The courts of this country quite properly share the responsibility for protecting the constitutional rights of those imprisoned for the commission of crimes against society. Thus, when a prisoner's property is wrongfully destroyed, the courts must ensure that the prisoner, no less than any other person, receives just compensation. The Constitution, as well as human decency, requires no less. The issue in these cases, however, does not concern *whether* a prisoner may recover damages for a malicious deprivation of property. Rather, these cases decide only *what* is the appropriate source of the constitutional right and the remedy that corresponds with it. I agree with the Court's treatment of these issues and therefore join its opinion and judgment today. I write separately to elaborate my understanding of why the complaint in this litigation does not state a ripe constitutional claim.

. . . In these cases, the Commonwealth of Virginia has demonstrated that it provides aggrieved inmates with a grievance procedure and various state tort and common-law remedies. The plaintiff inmate has not availed himself of these remedies or successfully proved that they are inadequate. Thus, his complaint cannot be said to have stated a ripe constitutional claim and summary judgment for the defendant was proper.

JUSTICE STEVENS, with whom JUSTICE BRENNAN, JUSTICE MARSHALL, and JUSTICE BLACKMUN join, concurring in part and dissenting in part.

This case comes to us on the pleadings. We must take the allegations in Palmer's complaint as true. Liberally construing this *pro se* complaint as

we must, it alleges that after examining it, prison guard Hudson maliciously took and destroyed a quantity of Palmer's property, including legal materials and letters, for no reason other than harassment.

For the reasons stated in Part II–B of the opinion of the Court, I agree that Palmer's complaint does not allege a violation of his constitutional right to procedural due process. The reasoning in Part II–A of the Court's opinion, however, is seriously flawed—indeed, internally inconsistent. The Court correctly concludes that the imperatives of prison administration require random searches of prison cells, and also correctly states that in the prison context "[o]f course, there is a risk of maliciously motivated searches, and of course, intentional harassment of even the most hardened criminals cannot be tolerated by a civilized society." *Ante*, at 528. But the Court then holds that no matter how malicious, destructive, or arbitrary a cell search and seizure may be, it cannot constitute an unreasonable invasion of any privacy or possessory interest that society is prepared to recognize as reasonable. *Ante*, at 525–526.

Measured by the conditions that prevail in a free society, neither the possessions nor the slight residuum of privacy that a prison inmate can retain in his cell, can have more than the most minimal value. From the standpoint of the prisoner, however, that trivial residuum may mark the difference between slavery and humanity. On another occasion, THE CHIEF JUSTICE wrote:

"It is true that inmates lose many rights when they are lawfully confined, but they do not lose all civil rights. Inmates in jails, prisons, or mental institutions retain certain fundamental rights of privacy; they are not like animals in a zoo to be filmed and photographed at will by the public or by media reporters, however 'educational' the process may be for others." *Houchins* v. *KQED, Inc.*, 438 U. S. 1, 5, n. 2 (1978) (plurality opinion) (citation omitted).

Personal letters, snapshots of family members, a souvenir, a deck of cards, a hobby kit, perhaps a diary or a training manual for an apprentice in a new trade, or even a Bible—a variety of inexpensive items may enable a prisoner to maintain contact with some part of his past and an eye to the possibility of a better future. Are all of these items subject to unrestrained perusal, confiscation, or mutilation at the hands of a possibly hostile guard? Is the Court correct in its perception that "society" is not prepared to recognize *any* privacy or possessory interest of the prison inmate—no matter how remote the threat to prison security may be?

I

Even if it is assumed that Palmer had no reasonable expectation of privacy in most of the property at issue in this case because it could be inspected at any time, that does not mean he was without Fourth Amendment protection. For the Fourth Amendment protects Palmer's possessory interests in this property entirely apart from whatever privacy interest he may have in it.

. . .

The Court suggests that "the interest of society in the security of its penal institutions" precludes prisoners from having any legitimate possessory interests. *Ante*, at 527–528, and n. 8. See also *ante*, at 538 (O'CONNOR, J., concurring). That contention is fundamentally wrong for at least two reasons.

First, Palmer's possession of the material was entirely legitimate as a matter of state law. There is no contention that the material seized was contraband or that Palmer's possession of it was in any way inconsistent with applicable prison regulations. Hence, he had a legal right to possess it. In fact, the Court's analysis of Palmer's possessory interests is at odds with its treatment of his due process claim.

. . . It is well settled that once a State creates such a constitutionally protected interest, the Constitution forbids it to deprive even a prisoner of such an interest arbitrarily. Thus, Palmer had a legitimate right under both state law and the Due Process Clause to possess the material at issue. That being the case, the Court's own analysis indicates that Palmer had a legitimate possessory interest in the material within the Fourth Amendment's proscription on unreasonable seizures.

Second, the most significant of Palmer's possessory interests are protected as a matter of substantive constitutional law, entirely apart from the legitimacy of those interests under state law or the Due Process Clause. The Eighth Amendment forbids "cruel and unusual punishments." Its proscriptions are measured by society's "evolving standards of decency," *Rhodes* v. *Chapman*, 452 U. S. 337, 346–347 (1981); *Estelle* v. *Gamble*, 429 U. S. 97, 102–103 (1976). The Court's implication that prisoners have no possessory interests that by virtue of the Fourth Amendment are free from state interference cannot, in my view, be squared with the Eighth Amendment. To hold that a prisoner's possession of a letter from his wife, or a picture of his baby, has no protection against arbitrary or malicious perusal, seizure, or destruction would not, in my judgment, comport with any civilized standard of decency.

II

Once it is concluded that Palmer has adequately alleged a "seizure," the question becomes whether the seizure was "unreasonable." Questions of Fourth Amendment reasonableness can be resolved only by balancing the intrusion on constitutionally protected interests against the law enforcement interests justifying the challenged conduct.

It is well settled that the discretion accorded prison officials is not absolute. A prisoner retains those constitutional rights not inconsistent with legitimate penological objectives. There can be no penological justification for the seizure alleged here. There is no contention that Palmer's property posed any threat to institutional security. Hudson had already examined the material before he took and destroyed it. The allegation is that Hudson did this for no reason save spite; there is no contention that under prison regulations the material was contraband, and in any event as I have indicated above the Constitution prohibits a State from treating letters and legal materials as contraband. The Court agrees that intentional harassment of prisoners by guards is intolerable, *ante*, at 528. That being the case, there is no room for any conclusion but that the alleged seizure was unreasonable. . . .

Depriving inmates of any residuum of privacy or possessory rights is in fact plainly *contrary* to institutional goals. Sociologists recognize that prisoners deprived of any sense of individuality devalue themselves and others and therefore are more prone to violence toward themselves or others. At the same time, such an approach undermines the rehabilitative function of the institution: "Without the privacy and dignity provided by fourth amendment coverage, an inmate's opportunity to reform, as small as it may be, will further be diminished. It is anomalous to provide a prisoner with rehabilitative programs and services in an effort to build self-respect while simultaneously subjecting him to unjustified and degrading searches and seizures." Gianelli & Gilligan, Prison Searches and Seizures: "Locking" the Fourth Amendment Out of Correctional Facilities, 62 Va. L. Rev. 1045, 1069 (1976).

To justify its conclusion, the Court recites statistics concerning the number of crimes that occur within prisons. For example, it notes that over an 18-month period approximately 120 prisoners were murdered in state and federal facilities. *Ante*, at 526. At the end of 1983 there were 438,830 inmates in state and federal prisons. The Court's homicide rate of 80 per year yields an annual prison homicide rate of 18.26 persons per 100,000 inmates. In 1982, the homicide rate in Miami was 51.98 per 100,000; in New York it was 23.50 per 100,000; in Dallas 31.53 per 100,000; and in the District of Columbia 30.70 per 100,000. Thus, the prison homicide rate, it turns out, is significantly lower than that in many of our major cities. I do not suggest this type of analysis provides a standard for measuring the reasonableness of a search or seizure within prisons, but I do suggest that the Court's use of statistics is less than persuasive.

. . .

III

By adopting its "bright line" rule, the Court takes the "hands off" approach to prison administration that I thought it had abandoned forever when it wrote in *Wolff* v. *McDonnell*, 418 U. S. 539 (1974):

"[T]hough his rights may be diminished by the needs and exigencies of the institutional environment, a prisoner is not wholly stripped of constitutional protections when he is imprisoned for crime. There is no iron curtain drawn between the Constitution and the prisons of this country." *Id.*, at 555–556.

. . . in its eagerness to adopt a rule consistent with what it believes to be wise penal administration, the Court overlooks the purpose of a written Constitution and its Bill of Rights. That purpose, of course, is to ensure that certain principles will not be sacrificed to expediency; these are enshrined as principles of fundamental law beyond the reach of governmental officials or legislative majorities. The Fourth Amendment is part of that fundamental law; it represents a value judgment that unjustified search and seizure so greatly threatens individual liberty that it must be forever condemned as a matter of constitutional principle. The courts, of course, have a special obligation to protect the rights of prisoners. Prisoners are truly the outcasts of society. Disenfranchised, scorned and feared, often deservedly so, shut away from public view, prisoners are surely a "discrete and insular minority." In this case, the destruction of Palmer's property was a seizure; the Judiciary has a constitutional duty to determine whether it was justified. The Court's conclusive presumption that all conduct by prison guards is reasonable is supported by nothing more than its idiosyncratic view of the imperatives of prison administration—a view not shared by prison administrators themselves. Such a justification is nothing less than a decision to sacrifice constitutional principle to the Court's own assessment of administrative expediency.

More than a decade ago I wrote:

"[T]he view once held that an inmate is a mere slave is now totally rejected. The restraints and the punishment which a criminal conviction entails do not place the citizen beyond the ethical tradition that accords respect to the dignity and intrinsic worth of every individual. 'Liberty' and 'custody' are not mutually exclusive concepts." *United States ex rel. Miller* v. *Twomey*, 479 F. 2d 701, 712 (CA7 1973) (footnotes omitted), cert. denied *sub nom. Gutierrez* v. *Department of Public Safety of Illinois*, 414 U. S. 1146 (1974).

By telling prisoners that no aspect of their individuality, from a photo of a child to a letter from a wife, is entitled to constitutional protection, the Court breaks with the ethical tradition that I had thought was enshrined forever in our jurisprudence.

Accordingly, I respectfully dissent from the Court's judgment in No. 82–1630 and from Part II–A of its opinion.

Bell v. Wolfish

441 U.S. 520 (1979)

Louis Wolfish and other inmates brought a class action to challenge the conditions in the Metropolitan Correctional Center (MCC), a federal facility in New York City designed to hold pretrial detainees. The defendant in the suit was Griffin B. Bell, Attorney General of the United States. A federal district court enjoined certain practices as unconstitutional; the Second Circuit affirmed.

MR. JUSTICE REHNQUIST delivered the opinion of the Court.

Over the past five Terms, this Court has in several decisions considered constitutional challenges to prison conditions or practices by convicted prisoners. This case requires us to examine the constitutional rights of pretrial detainees— those persons who have been charged with a crime but who have not yet been tried on the charge. The parties concede that to ensure their presence at trial, these persons legitimately may be incarcerated by the Government prior to a determination of their guilt or innocence, *infra*, at 533–535, and n. 15; see 18 U. S. C. §§ 3146, 3148, and it is the scope of their rights during this period of confinement prior to trial that is the primary focus of this case.

This lawsuit was brought as a class action in the United States District Court for the Southern District of New York to challenge numerous conditions of confinement and practices at the Metropolitan Correctional Center (MCC), a federally operated short-term custodial facility in New York City designed primarily to house pretrial detainees. The District Court, in the words of the Court of Appeals for the Second Circuit, "intervened broadly into almost every facet of the institution" and enjoined no fewer than 20 MCC practices on constitutional and statutory grounds. The

Court of Appeals largely affirmed the District Court's constitutional rulings and in the process held that under the Due Process Clause of the Fifth Amendment, pretrial detainees may "be subjected to only those 'restrictions and privations' which 'inhere in their confinement itself or which are justified by compelling necessities of jail administration.'" *Wolfish* v. *Levi*, 573 F. 2d 118, 124 (1978), quoting *Rhem* v. *Malcolm*, 507 F. 2d 333, 336 (CA2 1974). We granted certiorari to consider the important constitutional questions raised by these decisions and to resolve an apparent conflict among the Circuits. 439 U. S. 816 (1978). We now reverse.

I

The MCC was constructed in 1975 to replace the converted waterfront garage on West Street that had served as New York City's federal jail since 1928. It is located adjacent to the Foley Square federal courthouse and has as its primary objective the housing of persons who are being detained in custody prior to trial for federal criminal offenses in the United States District Courts for the Southern and Eastern Districts of New York and for the District of New Jersey. Under the Bail Reform Act, 18 U. S. C. § 3146, a person in the federal system is committed to a detention facility only because no other less drastic means can reasonably ensure his presence at trial. In addition to pretrial detainees, the MCC also houses some convicted inmates who are awaiting sentencing or transportation to federal prison or who are serving generally relatively short sentences in a service capacity at the MCC, convicted prisoners who have been lodged at the facility under writs of habeas corpus *ad prosequendum* or *ad testificandum* issued to ensure their presence at upcoming trials, witnesses in protective custody, and persons incarcerated for contempt.

The MCC differs markedly from the familiar image of a jail; there are no barred cells, dank, colorless corridors, or clanging steel gates. It was intended to include the most advanced and innovative features of modern design of detention facilities. As the Court of Appeals stated: "[I]t represented the architectural embodiment of the best and most progressive penological planning." 573 F. 2d, at 121. The key design element of the 12-story structure is the "modular" or "unit" concept, whereby each floor designed to house inmates has one or two largely self-contained residential units that replace the traditional cell-block jail construction. Each unit in turn has several clusters or corridors of private rooms or dormitories radiating from a central 2-story "multipurpose" or common room, to which each inmate has free access approximately 16 hours a day. Because our analysis does not turn on the particulars of the MCC concept or design, we need not discuss them further.

When the MCC opened in August 1975, the planned capacity was 449 inmates, an increase of 50% over the former West Street facility. *Id.*, at 122. Despite some dormitory accommodations, the MCC was designed primarily to house these inmates in 389 rooms, which originally were intended for single occupancy. While the MCC was under construction, however, the number of persons committed to pretrial detention began to rise at an "unprecedented" rate. *Ibid.* The Bureau of Prisons took several steps to accommodate this unexpected flow of persons assigned to the facility, but despite these efforts, the inmate population at the MCC rose above its planned capacity within a short time after its opening. To provide sleeping space for this increased population, the MCC replaced the single bunks in many of the individual rooms and dormitories with double bunks. Also, each week some newly arrived inmates had to sleep on cots in the common areas until they could be transferred to residential rooms as space became available. See *id.*, at 127–128.

. . .

II

As a first step in our decision, we shall address "double-bunking" as it is referred to by the parties, since it is a condition of confinement that is alleged only to deprive pretrial detainees of their liberty without due process of law in contravention of the Fifth Amendment. . . .

B

In evaluating the constitutionality of conditions or restrictions of pretrial detention that implicate only the protection against deprivation of liberty without due process of law, we think that the proper inquiry is whether those conditions amount to punishment of the detainee. For under the Due Process Clause, a detainee may not be punished prior to an adjudication of guilt in accordance with due process of law. . . .

Not every disability imposed during pretrial detention amounts to "punishment" in the constitutional sense, however. Once the Government has exercised its conceded authority to detain a person pending trial, it obviously is entitled to employ devices that are calculated to effectuate this detention. Traditionally, this has meant confinement in a facility which, no matter how modern or how antiquated, results in restricting the movement of a detainee in a manner in which he would not be restricted if he simply were free to walk the streets pending trial. . . .

. . . We need not here attempt to detail the precise extent of the legitimate governmental interests that may justify conditions or restrictions of pretrial detention. It is enough simply to recognize that in addition to ensuring the detainees' presence at trial, the effective management of the detention facility once the individual is confined is a valid objective that may justify imposition of conditions and restrictions of pretrial detention and dispel any inference that such restrictions are intended as punishment.

C

Judged by this analysis, respondents' claim that "double-bunking" violated their due process rights fails. Neither the District Court nor the Court of Appeals intimated that it considered "double-bunking" to constitute punishment; instead, they found that it contravened the compelling-necessity test, which today we reject. On this record, we are convinced as a matter of law that "double-bunking" as practiced at the MCC did not amount to punishment and did not, therefore, violate respondents' rights under the Due Process Clause of the Fifth Amendment.

. . .

We disagree with both the District Court and the Court of Appeals that there is some sort of "one man, one cell" principle lurking in the Due Process Clause of the Fifth Amendment. While confining a given number of people in a given amount of space in such a manner as to cause them to endure genuine privations and hardship over an extended period of time might raise serious questions under the Due Process Clause as to whether those conditions amounted to punishment, nothing even approaching such hardship is shown by this record.

Detainees are required to spend only seven or eight hours each day in their rooms, during most or all of which they presumably are sleeping. The rooms provide more than adequate space for sleeping. During the remainder of the time, the detainees are free to move between their rooms and the common area. . . . Nearly all of the detainees are released within 60 days. See n. 3, *supra*. We simply do not believe that requiring a detainee to share toilet facilities and this admittedly rather small sleeping place with another person for generally a maximum period of 60 days violates the Constitution.

III

Respondents also challenged certain MCC restrictions and practices that were designed to promote security and order at the facility on the ground that these restrictions violated the Due Process Clause of the Fifth Amendment, and certain other constitutional guarantees, such as the First and Fourth Amendments. . . .

. . . maintaining institutional security and preserving internal order and discipline are essential goals that may require limitation or retraction of the retained constitutional rights of both convicted prisoners and pretrial detainees. . . . we have held that even when an institutional restriction infringes a specific constitutional guarantee, such as the First Amendment, the practice must be evaluated in the light of the central objective of prison administration, safeguarding institutional security. . . .

. . . the problems that arise in the day-to-day operation of a corrections facility are not susceptible of easy solutions. Prison administrators therefore should be accorded wide-ranging deference in the adoption and execution of policies and practices that in their judgment are needed to preserve internal order and discipline and to maintain institutional security. . . . judicial deference is accorded not merely because the administrator ordinarily will, as a matter of fact in a particular case, have a better grasp of his domain than the reviewing judge, but also because the operation of our correctional facilities is peculiarly the province of the Legislative and Executive Branches of our Government, not the Judicial. . . .

A

[The MCC permitted inmates to receive books and magazines from outside the institution only if the materials were mailed directly from the publisher or a book club. Other items might contain contraband. The policy was later amended to permit the receipt of books and magazines from bookstores as well as publishers and book clubs, and to allow receipt of paperback books, magazines, and other soft-covered materials from any source. The Court concludes that the prohibition against receipt of hardback books unless mailed directly from publishers, book clubs, or bookstores does not violate the First Amendment rights of MCC inmates.]

B

Inmates at the MCC were not permitted to receive packages from outside the facility containing items of food or personal property, except for one package of food at Christmas. This rule was justified by MCC officials on three grounds. First, officials testified to "serious" security problems that arise from the introduction of such packages into the institution, the "traditional file in the cake kind of situation" as well as the concealment of drugs "in heels of shoes [and] seams of clothing." App. 80; see *id.*, at 24, 84–85. As in the case of the "publisher-only" rule, the warden testified that if such packages were allowed, the inspection process necessary to ensure the security of the institution would require a "substantial and inordinate amount of available staff time." *Id.*, at 24. Second, officials were concerned that the introduction of personal property into the facility would increase the risk of thefts, gambling, and inmate conflicts, the "age-old problem of you have it and I don't." *Id.*, at 80; see *id.*, at 85. Finally, they noted storage and sanitary problems that would result from inmates' receipt of food packages. *Id.*, at 67, 80. Inmates are permitted, however, to purchase certain items of food and personal property from the MCC commissary.

[The district court and the Second Circuit rejected MCC's justifications as "dire predictions," but the Supreme Court concluded that the policy was based on legitimate security concerns.] There simply is no basis in this record for concluding that MCC officials have exaggerated their response to these serious problems or that this restriction is irrational. It does not therefore deprive the convicted inmates or pretrial detainees of the MCC of their property without due process of law in contravention of the Fifth Amendment.

C

The MCC staff conducts unannounced searches of inmate living areas at irregular intervals. These searches generally are formal unit "shakedowns" during which all inmates are cleared of the residential units, and a team of guards searches each room. Prior to the District Court's order, inmates were not permitted to watch the searches. Officials testified that permitting inmates to observe room inspections would lead to friction between the inmates and security guards and would allow the inmates to attempt to frustrate the search by distracting personnel and moving contraband from one room to another ahead of the search team.

[The district court and the Second Circuit invalidated the room-search rule, the former stating that the rule infringed the detainee's interest in privacy founded on the Fourth Amendment.]

It is difficult to see how the detainee's interest in privacy is infringed by the room-search rule. No one can rationally doubt that room searches represent an appropriate security measure and neither the District Court nor the Court of Appeals prohibited such searches. And even the most zealous advocate of prisoners' rights would not suggest that a warrant is required to conduct such a search. Detainees' drawers, beds, and personal items may be searched, even after the lower courts' rulings. Permitting detainees to observe the searches does not lessen the invasion of their privacy; its only conceivable beneficial effect would be to prevent theft or misuse by those conducting the search. The room-search rule simply facilitates the safe and effective performance of the search which all concede may be conducted. The rule itself, then, does not render the searches "unreasonable" within the meaning of the Fourth Amendment.

D

Inmates at all Bureau of Prisons facilities, including the MCC, are required to expose their body cavities for visual inspection as a part of a strip search conducted after every contact visit with a person from outside the institution. *[If the inmate is a male, he must lift his genitals and bend over to spread his buttocks for visual inspection. The vaginal and anal cavities of female inmates also are visually inspected. The inmate is not touched by security personnel at any time during the* visual *search procedure.]*

Corrections officials testified that visual cavity searches were necessary not only to discover but also to deter the smuggling of weapons, drugs, and other contraband into the institution. App. 70–72, 83–84. The District Court upheld the strip-search procedure but prohibited the body-cavity searches, absent probable cause to believe that the inmate is concealing contraband. 439 F. Supp., at 147–148. Because petitioners proved only one instance in the MCC's short history where contraband was found during a body-cavity search, the Court of Appeals affirmed. In its view, the "gross violation of personal privacy inherent in such a search cannot be outweighed by the government's security interest in maintaining a practice of so little actual utility." 573 F. 2d, at 131.

Admittedly, this practice instinctively gives us the most pause. However, assuming for present purposes that inmates, both convicted prisoners and pretrial detainees, retain some Fourth Amendment rights upon commitment to a corrections facility, see *Lanza* v. *New York, supra; Stroud* v. *United States*, 251 U. S. 15, 21 (1919), we nonetheless conclude that these searches do not violate that Amendment. The Fourth Amendment prohibits only unreasonable searches, *Carroll* v. *United States*, 267 U. S. 132, 147 (1925), and under the circumstances, we do not believe that these searches are unreasonable.

. . . That there has been only one instance where an MCC inmate was discovered attempting to smuggle contraband into the institution on his person may be more a testament to the effectiveness of this search technique as a deterrent than to any lack of interest on the part of the inmates to secrete and import such items when the opportunity arises.

. . .

V

There was a time not too long ago when the federal judiciary took a completely "hands-off" approach to the problem of prison administration. In recent years, however, these courts largely have discarded this "hands-off" attitude and have waded into this complex arena. The deplorable conditions and Draconian restrictions of some of our Nation's prisons are too well known to require recounting here, and the federal courts rightly have condemned these sordid aspects of our prison systems. But many of these same courts have, in the name of the Constitution, become increasingly enmeshed in the minutiae of prison operations. Judges, after all, are human. They, no less

than others in our society, have a natural tendency to believe that their individual solutions to often intractable problems are better and more workable than those of the persons who are actually charged with and trained in the running of the particular institution under examination. But under the Constitution, the first question to be answered is not whose plan is best, but in what branch of the Government is lodged the authority to initially devise the plan. This does not mean that constitutional rights are not to be scrupulously observed. It does mean, however, that the inquiry of federal courts into prison management must be limited to the issue of whether a particular system violates any prohibition of the Constitution or, in the case of a federal prison, a statute. The wide range of "judgment calls" that meet constitutional and statutory requirements are confided to officials outside of the Judicial Branch of Government.

The judgment of the Court of Appeals is, accordingly, reversed, and the case is remanded for proceedings consistent with this opinion.

It is so ordered.

MR. JUSTICE POWELL, concurring in part and dissenting in part.

I join the opinion of the Court except the discussion and holding with respect to body-cavity searches. In view of the serious intrusion on one's privacy occasioned by such a search, I think at least some level of cause, such as a reasonable suspicion, should be required to justify the anal and genital searches described in this case. I therefore dissent on this issue.

MR. JUSTICE MARSHALL, dissenting.

The Court holds that the Government may burden pretrial detainees with almost any restriction, provided detention officials do not proclaim a punitive intent or impose conditions that are "arbitrary or purposeless." *Ante,* at 539. As if this standard were not sufficiently ineffectual, the Court dilutes it further by according virtually unlimited deference to detention officials' justifications for particular impositions. Conspicuously lacking from this analysis is any meaningful consideration of the most relevant factor, the impact that restrictions may have on inmates. Such an approach is unsupportable, given that all of these detainees are presumptively innocent and many are confined solely because they cannot afford bail.

[Marshall believed that a remand was necessary on the issue of double-bunking to produce further evidence. He took the same position on the rule limiting the sources of hardback books, and concluded that the record did not establish that unobserved searches were substantially necessary to jail administration. Finally, Marshall said that body-cavity searches should be conducted only when there is probable cause to believe that an inmate is concealing contraband.]

MR. JUSTICE STEVENS, with whom MR. JUSTICE BRENNAN joins, dissenting.

This is not an equal protection case. An empirical judgment that most persons formally accused of criminal conduct are probably guilty would provide a rational basis for a set of rules that treat them like convicts until they establish their innocence. No matter how rational such an approach might be—no matter how acceptable in a community where equality of status is the dominant goal—it is obnoxious to the concept of individual freedom protected by the Due Process Clause. If ever accepted in this country, it would work a fundamental change in the character of our free society.

Nor is this an Eighth Amendment case. That provision of the Constitution protects individuals convicted of crimes from punishment that is cruel and unusual. The pretrial detainees whose rights are at stake in this case, however, are innocent men and women who have been convicted of no crimes. Their claim is not that they have been subjected to cruel and unusual punishment in violation of the Eighth Amendment, but that to subject them to any form of punishment at all is an unconstitutional deprivation of their liberty.

This is a due process case. The most significant —and I venture to suggest the most enduring— part of the Court's opinion today is its recognition of this initial constitutional premise. The Court squarely holds that "under the Due Process Clause, a detainee may not be punished prior to an adjudication of guilt in accordance with due process of law." *Ante*, at 535.

This right to be free of punishment is not expressly embodied in any provision in the Bill of Rights. Nor is the source of this right found in any statute. The source of this fundamental freedom is the word "liberty" itself as used in the Due Process Clause, and as informed by "history, reason, the past course of decisions," and the judgment and experience of "those whom the Constitution entrusted" with interpreting that word. *Anti-Fascist Committee* v. *McGrath*, 341 U. S. 123, 162–163 (Frankfurter, J., concurring). See *Leis* v. *Flynt*, 439 U. S. 438, 457 (STEVENS, J., dissenting).

. . .

I

Some of the individuals housed in the Metropolitan Correction Center (MCC) are convicted criminals. As to them, detention may legitimately serve a punitive goal, and there is strong reason, even apart from the rules challenged here, to suggest that it does. But the same is not true of the detainees who are also housed there and whose rights we are called upon to address. Notwithstanding the impression created by the Court's opinion, see, *e. g., ante*, at 562, these people are not "prisoners": they have not been convicted of any crimes, and their detention may serve only a more limited, regulatory purpose. See *Houchins* v. *KQED, Inc.*, 438 U. S. 1, 37–38 (STEVENS, J., dissenting).

. . .

It may well be, as the Court finds, that the rules at issue here were not adopted by administrators eager to punish those detained at MCC. The rules can all be explained as the easiest way for administrators to ensure security in the jail. But the easiest course for jail officials is not always one that our Constitution allows them to take. If fundamental rights are withdrawn and severe harms are indiscriminately inflicted on detainees merely to secure minimal savings in time and effort for administrators, the guarantee of due process is violated.

In my judgment, each of the rules at issue here is unconstitutional. The four rules do indiscriminately inflict harm on all pretrial detainees in MCC. They are all either unnecessary or excessively harmful, particularly when judged against our historic respect for the dignity of the free citizen. I think it is unquestionably a form of punishment to deny an innocent person the right to read a book loaned to him by a friend or relative while he is temporarily confined, to deny him the right to receive gifts or packages, to search his private possessions out of his presence, or to compel him to exhibit his private body cavities to the visual inspection of a guard. Absent probable cause to believe that a specific individual detainee poses a special security risk, none of these practices would be considered necessary, or even arguably reasonable, if the pretrial detainees were confined in a facility separate and apart from convicted prisoners. . . .

17   Rights of Privacy

The right to privacy is invoked repeatedly by Congress and the Supreme Court to uphold basic rights of individual conduct and choice. If privacy includes the right of a person to prevent intrusion into certain thoughts and activities, privacy is protected by the First Amendment (freedom of speech, religion, and association), the Third Amendment (quartering of troops in private homes), the Fourth Amendment (freedom from unreasonable searches and seizures), and the Fifth Amendment (freedom from self-incrimination). At times there is reliance on the Ninth Amendment, which states that the "enumeration in the Constitution, of certain rights, shall not be construed to deny or disparage others retained by the people." The Due Process and Equal Protection Clauses provide other shields for privacy interests.

DIMENSIONS OF PRIVACY

In contemporary times, privacy has a special urgency because of industrialization, urbanization, electronic surveillance methods, and computer data banks. Although litigation highlights such current issues as contraception, abortion, and homosexuality, privacy was no less important to the framers. The Constitution does not mention privacy, and yet a zone of autonomy is implicit in the framers' support for individual rights and limited government. The notion of privacy is part of our presocietal "natural rights." Areas of private conduct and thought have always been protected from state intrusion. James Madison felt strongly that people had a property interest in their opinions, the free communication of ideas, religious beliefs, and conscience (pp. 478–480).

The Declaration of Independence attacked England's practice of "quartering large bodies of armed troops among us." In response, the Third Amendment provides that no soldier shall, "in time of peace be quartered in any house, without the consent of the owner, nor in time of war, but in a manner to be prescribed by law." The Fourth Amendment was adopted to prevent the hated general warrants and writs of assistance used by England to invade the homes and businesses of American colonists.

In a famous dissent in 1928, Justice Brandeis interpreted the trilogy in the Declaration of Independence—life, liberty, and the pursuit of happiness—in these terms:

> The makers of our Constitution undertook to secure conditions favorable to the pursuit of happiness. They recognized the significance of man's spiritual nature, of his feelings and of his intellect. They knew that only a part of his pain, pleasure and satisfactions of life are to be found in material things. They sought to protect Americans in their beliefs, their thoughts, their emotions and their sensations. They conferred, as against the Government, the right to be let alone—the most comprehensive of rights and the right most valued by civilized men. Olmstead v. United States, 277 U.S. 438, 478 (1928).

The phrase "the right to be let alone" appeared earlier in an article published by Brandeis and Samuel D. Warren in 1890. Building on Judge Thomas Cooley's treatise on torts, they concluded that the right to privacy evolved from transformations that had occurred in property rights: from tangible to intangible interests; from actual bodily injury (battery) to the mere threat of injury (assault). Protections were extended to reputation (slander and libel) and to intellectual property (copyright, trademarks, and trade secrets). Brandeis and Warren were especially offended by newsmen and photographers who invaded "the sacred precincts of private and domestic life." 4 Harv. L. Rev. 193, 195 (1890).

The right of citizens to conduct their own lives was recognized by the Supreme Court in 1923 when it struck down a Nebraska law prohibiting the teaching in any school of any modern language other than English to any child who had not passed the eighth grade. The statute, reflecting an anti-German mentality following World War I, interfered with the liberty of individuals to pursue their interests: "the right of the individual to contract, to engage in any of the common occupations of life, to acquire useful knowledge, to marry, to establish a home and bring up children, to worship God according to the dictates of his own conscience, and generally to enjoy those privileges long recognized at common law as essential to the orderly pursuit of happiness by free men." Meyer v. Nebraska, 262 U.S. 390, 399 (1923).

Two years later, the Court invalidated an Oregon law that required all children between the ages of 8 and 16 to attend public school. A Roman Catholic orphanage and a military academy brought suit to defend the rights of parents to send their children to private schools. Following the doctrine of Meyer v. Nebraska, the Court held that the Oregon statute unreasonably interfered with the liberty of parents and guardians to direct the upbringing and education of their children: "The child is not the mere creature of the State; those who nurture him and direct his destiny have the right, coupled with the high duty, to recognize and prepare him for additional obligations." Pierce v. Society of Sisters, 268 U.S. 510, 535 (1925).

Sterilization

At the same time that the Supreme Court defended the right to teach foreign languages and operate private schools, it endorsed a major governmental intrusion into individual privacy: sterilization of the "unfit." Some of the early decisions by federal courts rejected state efforts to sterilize prisoners for eugenic reasons. In 1914, a federal district court struck down a law in Iowa that required a vasectomy for criminals convicted twice of a felony (even if "felonies" consisted of breaking an electric globe and unfastening a strap on a harness). The court regarded vasectomy as a cruel and unusual punishment that "belongs to the Dark Ages." Davis v. Berry, 216 Fed. 413, 416 (S.D. Iowa 1914). A Nevada law on sterilization was struck down in 1918 because it gave judges too much discretion. Mickle v. Henrichs, 262 Fed. 687 (D. Nev. 1918).

A Virginia court in 1925 upheld a sterilization law as a proper use of the police power to prevent the transmission of insanity, idiocy, imbecility, epilepsy, and crime. Buck v. Bell, 143 Va. 310 (1925). The case involved Carrie Buck, committed to a state institution at the age of eighteen. Her mother had been committed to the same institution, and Carrie had just given birth to an illegitimate child which the state claimed was of "defective mentality."

By an 8–1 majority, a three-page opinion by Justice Holmes affirmed the state law. The decision is marred by illogic, hasty assumptions of unproved assertions, and a judgment that is harsh if not cruel. Holmes dashed off one of his famous aphorisms: "Three generations of imbeciles are enough." BUCK v. BELL, 274 U.S. 200, 207 (1927). In fact, Carrie's child was not mentally impaired.[1]

The Court handed down its decision in an environment that believed that crime and other social problems could be controlled by sterilization. Eugenics became a respectable argument for opposing mixed marriages and for excluding "lower stock" immigrants arriving from the Mediterranean countries, Eastern Europe, and Russia. Experts proposed that sterilization be directed against such vague categories as the feeble-minded, the criminalistic (including the delinquent and the "way-ward"), those with "seriously impaired" vision or hearing, the deformed (including the crippled), and dependents "including orphans, neer–do–wells, the homeless, tramps, and paupers." Harry Hamilton Laughlin, Eugenical Sterilization in the United States 446–447 (1922).

The Supreme Court's decision preceded by a few years Nazi Germany's biological experiments and its extermination of millions of Jews, Poles, gypsies, and other groups to produce a "master race." Today, instead of sterilization being forced on the "unfit," the operation is submitted to voluntarily each year by thousands of fit adults for purpose of population control.

Buck v. *Bell* has never been explicitly overruled. However, its tenets were challenged by the Supreme Court in 1942 when it struck down an Oklahoma law that provided for the sterilization of "habitual criminals." A unanimous opinion held that the state statute violated the Equal Protection Clause of the Fourteenth Amendment by making an invidious distinction. Under the statute, someone who stole more than $20 three times would be sterilized, whereas someone who embezzled that amount three times was exempt even though both crimes were a felony under state law.

The opinion for the Court did not comment on the scope of the police power to mandate sterilization. It did note that the case involved "one of the basic civil rights of man. Marriage and procreation are fundamental to the very existence and survival of the race." Skinner v. Oklahoma, 316 U.S. 535, 541 (1942). Chief Justice

[1]For good critiques of *Buck* v. *Bell,* see Paul A. Lombardo, "Three Generations, No Imbeciles: New Light on *Buck* v. *Bell,*" 60 N.Y.U. L. Rev. 30 (1985); Clement E. Vose, Constitutional Change 5–20 (1972); James B. O'Hara and T. Howland Sanks, "Eugenic Sterilization," 45 Geo. L. J. 20 (1956); Walter Berns, "*Buck* v. *Bell:* Due Process of Law?," 6 West. Pol. Q. 762 (1953).

Stone, concurring, thought that a state could, after appropriate inquiry, sterilize someone "to prevent the transmission by inheritance of his socially injurious tendencies." Justice Jackson, also concurring, insisted that there are limits to the extent that legislatures "may conduct biological experiments at the expense of the dignity and personality and natural powers of a minority—even those who have been guilty of what the majority defines as crimes." Jackson's reservations have been underscored by more recent cases involving the rights of marriage, family, and privacy.

Privacy and Family

In 1967, the Supreme Court issued an important decision that recognized the essential value of privacy in the Fourth Amendment. After decades of tortured reasoning on what constitutes a "search," the Court finally came to terms with an individual's constitutional right to preserve certain activities as private, even in an area accessible to the public. Katz v. United States, 389 U.S. 347 (1967), reprinted in Chapter 14.

Two years later, a unanimous Supreme Court held that the private possession of obscene materials by an adult cannot constitutionally be made a crime. State claims that the materials are obscene cannot override an individual's liberty: "If the First Amendment means anything, it means that a State has no business telling a man, sitting alone in his own house, what books he may read or what films he may watch. Our whole constitutional heritage rebels at the thought of giving government the power to control men's minds." STANLEY v. GEORGIA, 394 U.S. 557, 565 (1969).

The relationship between privacy and the choice of family and marriage has been explored in subsequent decisions. A zoning case in 1977 involved a local ordinance that denied a woman the right to remain in her house because she lived with her son and two grandsons (who were first cousins). Because of the latter, she did not qualify under the definition of "family" included in the ordinance. The Court held that the ordinance arbitrarily interfered with the family unit. The Constitution "protects the sanctity of the family precisely because the institution of the family is deeply rooted in this Nation's history and tradition." Moore v. East Cleveland, 431 U.S. 494 (1977). In that same year, a unanimous Court upheld a New York law that provided for expedited procedures for removing a child from foster parents and placing the child with the natural parents. The liberty interest in family privacy "has its source, and its contours are ordinarily to be sought, not in state law, but in intrinsic human rights . . ." Smith v. Organization of Foster Families, 431 U.S. 816, 845 (1977).

The right to marry is a decision that an individual is free to make without unjustified governmental interference. Loving v. Virginia, 388 U.S. 1, 12 (1967). A Wisconsin statute prohibited a certain class of state residents from marrying without first obtaining a court order granting permission. The class was anyone with a child not in his custody and which he is obligated to support by court order or judgment. An 8–1 Court held that the statute violated the Due Process Clause by interfering with the fundamental right to marry. The decision to marry is "among the personal decisions protected by the right of privacy." Zablocki v. Redhail, 434 U.S. 374, 384 (1978).

Reputation

Part of our intangible property is reputation. The precious quality of this commodity is captured in Shakespeare's *Othello:* "Good name in man and woman, dear my lord, is the immediate jewel of their souls: who steals my purse steals trash; 'tis something, nothing; 'twas mine, 'tis his, and has been slave to thousands; but he that filches from me my good name robs me of that which not enriches him, but makes me poor indeed."

A case in 1971 involved the action of a Wisconsin police chief who posted a notice in all retail stores forbidding for one year the sale of liquor to a woman. State law required these postings—without notice or hearing—whenever a designated official decided that the sale of liquor to a particular person would endanger the community or place the individual or the individual's family in a state of want. The Supreme Court, by a 6–3 majority, held that notice and an opportunity to be heard are essential safeguards whenever a person's name, reputation, honor, or integrity is at stake. Wisconsin v. Constantineau, 400 U.S. 433, 437 (1971).

The Court decided a similar case in 1976, but this time left the individual's reputation unprotected. The police in Kentucky authorized the preparation and distribution of a flyer containing the names and mug shots of persons described as "subjects known to be active in this criminal field" of shoplifting. About 800 flyers were distributed to merchants and businessmen in downtown Louisville. A newspaper photographer was arrested, but not convicted, of shoplifting. Although the charges against him were eventually dropped, his name and photograph appeared in the flyer. He filed suit, claiming injury to reputation and impairment of earning ability. The Sixth Circuit rejected the idea that police chiefs can determine the guilt or innocence of an accused. Distinguishing this case from *Constantineau*, a 5–3 Court reversed the Sixth Circuit by holding that distribution of the flyer did not deprive the plaintiff of any "liberty" or "property" rights secured against state deprivation by the Fourteenth Amendment. PAUL v. DAVIS, 424 U.S. 693 (1976).

USE OF CONTRACEPTIVES

Family and marriage cases rely heavily on a landmark case in 1965 regarding the right to privacy. A Connecticut law made it a crime for any person to use any drug or article to prevent conception. This type of statute can be traced to the Comstock Act of 1873, which Congress passed to suppress the circulation of obscene literature and "immoral" articles. Part of this puritanical statute prohibited selling, giving away, exhibiting, possessing, or promoting "any drug or medicine, or any article whatever, for the prevention of contraception . . ." The statute also prohibited the mailing of any article designed to prevent contraception. 17 Stat. 598, §§ 1, 2 (1873).

The constitutional issue of using contraceptives did not reach the Supreme Court until 1943, when it dismissed a case on the ground that the physician bringing it lacked standing to challenge a Connecticut statute. Tileson v. Ullman, 318 U.S. 44 (1943). The Court avoided the issue again in 1961, arguing that the case lacked ripeness because the plaintiff had not been prosecuted. However, two of the four dissents argued that the statute invaded the right to privacy. To Justice Douglas, the Connecticut law "touches the relationship between man and wife [and] reaches into the intimacies of the marriage relationship." Poe v. Ullman, 367 U.S. 497, 519

(1961). Efforts to enforce the law would mark "an invasion of the privacy that is implicit in a free society." Id. at 521. Only in totalitarian regimes, he said, could the government seek to bring the married couple completely within the control of the state: "Can there be any doubt that a Bill of Rights that in time of peace bars soldiers from being quartered in a home 'without the consent of the Owner' should also bar the police from investigating the intimacies of the marriage relation?" Id. at 522.

Justice Harlan's dissent also invoked the right of privacy to condemn the Connecticut law: "I believe that a statute making it a criminal offense for *married couples* to use contraceptives is an intolerable and unjustifiable invasion of privacy in the conduct of the most intimate concerns of an individual's life." Id. at 539. The law was "grossly offensive to this privacy" and forced the machinery of criminal law "into the very heart of marital privacy." Id. at 549, 553. This decision is reprinted in Chapter 3.

By 1965, the Supreme Court was prepared to decide the constitutionality of the Connecticut statute. An administrator and physician had been convicted for giving married persons information and medical advice on how to prevent conception and prescribing a contraceptive device for the wife's use. Writing for the Court, Justice Douglas held that the law violated the Due Process Clause of the Fourteenth Amendment, "emanations" and "penumbras" from the First Amendment (including association and privacy), and other privacy values derived from the Third, Fourth, Fifth, and Ninth Amendments. Justice Goldberg, joined by Chief Justice Warren and Justice Brennan, relied primarily on the Ninth Amendment. GRISWOLD v. CONNECTICUT, 381 U.S. 479 (1965).

The next question was whether contraceptives could be denied to single people. In 1972, the Court struck down a Massachusetts law that made it a felony to give away a drug, medicine, instrument, or article for the prevention of contraception except when registered physicians or registered pharmacists gave them to married persons. A 6–1 Court held that the statute violated the rights of single persons. "If the right of privacy means anything, it is the right of the *individual*, married or single, to be free from unwarranted governmental intrusion into matters so fundamentally affecting a person as the decision whether to bear or beget a child." Eisenstadt v. Baird, 405 U.S. 438, 453 (1972).

Having sustained the use of contraceptives by adults, whether married or single, the next awaiting issue concerned the use of contraceptives by minors. New York argued that the cases striking down state prohibitions on the *use* of contraceptives did not prevent states from prohibiting the *sale* and *manufacture* of contraceptives. This fine distinction did not convince the Court, which held that the New York law prohibiting the selling or distribution of any contraceptive to a minor under 16 was unconstitutional as it applied to nonprescription contraceptives. Restrictions on the distribution of contraceptives necessarily interfered with their use. The Court also struck down New York's prohibition of any advertisement or display of contraceptive devices. The law was considered unreasonable in part because New York allowed girls to marry at age 14 with parental consent. Carey v. Population Services International, 431 U.S. 678 (1977).

In 1983, the Supreme Court reviewed a law passed by Congress that prohibited the mailing of unsolicited advertisements for contraceptives. A unanimous decision held that the statute violated the First Amendment: "where—as in this case—a speaker desires to convey truthful information relevant to important social issues such as family planning and the prevention of venereal disease, we have previously found the First Amendment interest served by such speech paramount." Bolger v. Youngs Drug Products Corp., 463 U.S. 60, 69 (1983). The law was also defective because it denied parents information bearing on their ability to discuss birth control and make informed decisions. Id. at 74.

ABORTION RIGHTS

No contemporary issue has inflamed the country, Congress, and the courts more than the right of a woman to abort her pregnancy. What balance should be struck between a woman's interest in deciding to have an abortion and the state's interest in protecting the health and life of the mother and child? If a wife decides to abort, must the husband first consent? Does government have an obligation to fund abortions? Do abortion rights extend to minors? Is a fetus a "person" entitled to constitutional protection under the Fourteenth Amendment? Other emotional issues bombard the courts, executive agencies, and legislatures.

The question that reached the Supreme Court in 1973 was not the abstract issue of whether abortions should be performed. The record was abundantly clear that they would take place, with or without the law. In states that had prohibited or severely restricted abortion, some women attempted self-abortion by using coat hangers and other life-threatening instruments. Others placed their life and health in the hands of whoever was willing, with or without medical training, to do the job. Women with higher incomes were more fortunate. They could travel to another state or country for the operation. The issue before the Court in 1973 was exceedingly complex: How could abortions be performed within a legal structure that satisfied the conflicting values of those who wanted abortion on demand and those who believed equally strongly in the right to life?

In *Roe* v. *Wade* (1973), the Supreme Court attempted to steer a middle course by rejecting both abortion on demand and the absolute right to life. The Court held that state laws permitting abortions only to save the mother's life violated due process, which the Court said protects the right to privacy and a woman's *qualified* right to terminate her pregnancy. The state has legitimate interests in protecting both the pregnant woman's health and the potential life of the fetus. Each of those interests grows and reaches a "compelling" point at later stages of the woman's pregnancy. Over the first three months (the first trimester) the decision to abort is left to the woman and her physician. After the first trimester, states may regulate the abortion procedure in ways that are reasonably related to the health of the mother. After the fetus becomes viable (about seven months), the state may prohibit abortion except where necessary to preserve the life or health of the mother. ROE v. WADE, 410 U.S. 113 (1973).

This decision has been condemned as the work of an activist Court behaving like a legislature, even to the extent of identifying the stages of pregnancy where the state's interest prevails over the woman's. The decision was also vulnerable to criticism because of the difficulty the Court had in identifying its source of authority. In discussing the right of privacy, the Court pointed to the First Amendment, the Fourth and Fifth Amendments, "the penumbras of the Bill of Rights," the Ninth Amendment, and the "concept of liberty guaranteed by the first section of the Fourteenth Amendment." Precisely where to anchor the decision did not seem to matter: "This right of privacy, whether it be founded in the Fourteenth Amendment's concept of personal liberty and restrictions upon state action, as we feel it is, or, as the District Court determined, in the Ninth Amendment's reservation of rights to the people, is broad enough to encompass a woman's decision whether or not to terminate her pregnancy." Id. at 153.

The Court specifically rejected the argument that a fetus is a "person" within the language and meaning of the Fourteenth Amendment. After examining the various instances in the Constitution where the word "person" is used, the Court concluded that they apply only postnatally. The constitutional meaning of person "does not include the unborn." Id. at 157–158.

The constitutional issue was mixed with factual questions. The ruling depended on "the light of present medical knowledge." Id. at 163. The "compelling" point for state intervention, said the Court, is viability, a condition that is not fixed but varies with medical competence and techniques. As the Court noted in a subsequent case, viability is "a matter of medical judgment, skill, and technical ability, and we preserved the flexibility of the term." Planned Parenthood of Missouri v. Danforth, 428 U.S. 52, 64 (1976). As medical knowledge advances, the Court's identification of trimester stages provides less guidance. In fact, the Court later struck down a Pennsylvania statute that required doctors to first determine the viability of a fetus. If the fetus was viable, the statute mandated that the doctor exercise the same care to preserve the fetus' life and health as would be necessary for a regular birth. The Court held the statute void for vagueness. Colautti v. Franklin, 439 U.S. 379 (1979).

The companion case to Roe v. Wade reviewed the requirement in Georgia's law that abortion be performed in a hospital accredited by a joint commission. The Court determined that the statute was unconstitutional because it unduly restricted a woman's rights, particularly the indigent married woman who brought the case. The state law also required that the abortion procedure be approved by a hospital committee, a condition the Court again found too restrictive on a woman's rights. Finally, by requiring that her doctor's judgment be confirmed by two other licensed physicians, the state law infringed impermissibly on a doctor's right to practice. Doe v. Bolton, 410 U.S. 179 (1973).

Although the Court had apparently settled the constitutional question, full compliance with the ruling was not forthcoming. Dr. Kenneth Edelin, a physician in Boston, was indicted in 1974 for performing an abortion and subsequently found guilty of manslaughter. His conviction was later overturned, but the opposition to Roe v. Wade intensified. Over the following years, "right–to–lifers" would bomb abortion clinics, send letter bombs through the mails, and use other tactics to intimidate and harass women and physicians.

The Court addressed new legal issues in 1976. It upheld Missouri's requirement that a woman consent to an abortion in writing and certify that her consent is freely given. However, the state's requirement for a written consent from the woman's spouse (unless the physician certified that an abortion was necessary to save her life) was struck down. Also, a blanket requirement for parental consent for minors was declared unconstitutional. Planned Parenthood of Missouri v. Danforth, 428 U.S. 52 (1976). See also Bellotti v. Baird, 443 U.S. 622 (1979).

Public Funding

A series of cases involved the issue of providing public funds for abortion. Acting under its interpretation of federal law, Pennsylvania denied women medical assistance for nontherapeutic abortions. State regulations limited assistance to abortion certified by physicians as medically necessary. The Court, split 6–3, held that federal law did not require the funding of nontherapeutic abortions as a condition for states to participate in the federal Medicaid program. This decision turned on statutory construction, not constitutional interpretation. In a bitter dissent, Justice Marshall protested that the challenged statutes "brutally coerce poor women to bear children whom society will scorn for every day of their lives. Many thousands of unwanted minority and mixed–race children now spend blighted lives in foster homes, orphanages, and 'reform' schools." Beal v. Doe, 432 U.S. 438, 456 (1977).

Evidently the Court regarded these issues as moral questions to be resolved by legislatures, not the judiciary. It recognized the risk of trying to direct legislatures how to spend public funds, at least in this area. On the same day, the Court held that the Constitution does not obligate states to pay the pregnancy–related medical expenses of indigent women. Maher v. Roe, 432 U.S. 464 (1977). See also Poelker v. Doe, 432 U.S. 519 (1977).

The major challenge came from the "Hyde Amendment," first passed by Congress in 1976 (pp. 1181–1185). In the version that eventually came to the Supreme Court, the language provided:

> [N]one of the funds provided by this joint resolution shall be used to perform abortions except where the life of the mother would be endangered if the fetus were carried to term; or except for such medical procedures necessary for the victims of rape or incest when such rape or incest has been reported promptly to a law enforcement agency or public health service. 93 Stat. 926, § 109 (1979).

A federal district court, without deciding the constitutional issue, enjoined the Secretary of Health, Education, and Welfare from enforcing the Hyde Amendment. The court order required the Secretary to continue providing federal reimbursement for abortions. McRae v. Mathews, 421 F.Supp. 533 (E.D. N.Y. 1976). The Supreme Court vacated the injunction and remanded the case for reconsideration in light of its holdings. In 1980, the district court held that the Hyde Amendment impermissibly used appropriation language to change substantive (legislative) language in federal law, violated an individual's liberty to terminate pregnancy for medical reasons, and unreasonably denied funds for medically necessary abortions. McRae v. Califano, 491 F.Supp. 630 (E.D. N.Y. 1980).

Clearly a major collision loomed between Congress and the judiciary. In 1980, by a 5–4 vote, the Supreme Court upheld the Hyde Amendment. According to the Court, government may not place obstacles in the path of a woman's decision to choose abortion, but neither has it an obligation to remove obstacles it did not create (including a woman's indigency). Poverty, standing alone, was not considered a suspect classification. The Court concluded that the Hyde Amendment, by encouraging childbirth except in the most urgent circumstances, was rationally related to legitimate governmental objectives of protecting potential life. HARRIS v. McRAE, 448 U.S. 297 (1980). In a companion decision, the Court (again split 5–4) upheld the right of state legislatures to limit public funds for abortions. Williams v. Zbaraz, 448 U.S. 358 (1980).

When the issue of public funding is framed entirely as a state matter to be decided under the state constitution, the results can differ from *Harris* v. *McRae*. California restricted the circumstances under which public funds would be authorized to pay for abortions for Medi-Cal recipients. The California courts struck down these statutes as unconstitutional, holding that the state has no constitutional obligation to provide medical care to the poor, but once it does it bears the heavy burden of justifying a provision that withholds benefits from otherwise qualified individuals solely because they chose to exercise their constitutional right to have an abortion. COMMITTEE TO DEFEND REPROD. RIGHTS v. MYERS, 625 P.2d 779 (Cal. 1981). Similar decisions were issued by the New Jersey and Massachusetts courts, overturning state laws that restricted public funding for abortions. Right to Choose v. Byrne, 450 A.2d 925 (N.J. 1982); Moe v. Secretary of Administration, 417 N.E. 2d 387 (Mass. 1981).

Chronic Challenges

Roe v. *Wade* has not been accepted as the "last word" on the rights of abortion. Legislative efforts by state and local bodies put constant pressure on the Court to clarify and modify the boundaries of its 1973 ruling. A 1981 case involved Utah's statute requiring a physician to notify, if possible, the parents or guardian of a minor facing an abortion. Concluding that the statute did not amount to a parental veto, the Court upheld the law as a legitimate opportunity for parents to supply essential medical and other information to the physician. Three members of the *Roe* majority (Marshall, Brennan, and Blackmun) dissented. H.L. v. Matheson, 450 U.S. 398 (1981).

A cluster of three cases in 1983 raised a multitude of new issues. An Akron, Ohio, ordinance set forth five requirements: (1) all abortions performed after the first trimester had to be performed in a hospital, (2) abortions were prohibited for unmarried minors under age 15 without parental consent or court order, (3) the physician had to inform the woman of various facts concerning the operation, (4) abortions were delayed for at least twenty–four hours after the woman's consent, and (5) the physician had to insure that fetal remains were disposed of in a "humane and sanitary manner." The Court found each provision unconstitutional. Justices White and Rehnquist continued to dissent from the *Roe* doctrine, but Justice O'Connor, added to the Court in 1981, now joined them by penning a major critique of the premises supporting *Roe*. AKRON v. AKRON CENTER FOR REPRODUCTIVE HEALTH, 462 U.S. 416 (1983).

Two other decisions handed down on the same day as *Akron* explored additional restrictions on abortion rights. A Missouri statute required that abortions, after twelve weeks of pregnancy, be performed in a hospital. Consistent with previous rulings, the Court struck down the hospital requirement, but it sustained three other requirements in the Missouri law: a pathology report for each abortion, the presence of a second physician for abortions performed after viability, and either parental or court consent for minors. The latter marked a major departure from past rulings. Planned Parenthood Ass'n v. Ashcroft, 462 U.S. 476 (1983). The 7–2 majority from *Roe* had clearly evaporated. Four Justices (Blackmun, Brennan, Marshall, and Stevens) dissented from the Court's support for pathology reports, second physicians, and parental/court consent.

In the other case, the Court upheld Virginia's law that second trimester abortions be performed either in hospitals or licensed outpatient clinics. The requirement furthered the state's interest in protecting the health of a woman after the end of the first trimester. Justice Stevens was the sole dissenter. Simopoulos v. Virginia, 462 U.S. 506 (1983).

In 1986, the Supreme Court faced another major case on the right to abort. A Pennsylvania statute required that the woman be informed of the following: the physician who would perform the abortion; the "particular medical risks" of the abortion procedure, including physical and psychological effects; the medical assistance benefits available for prenatal care, childbirth, and care immediately after birth; the father's liability to provide financial support for the child; and printed materials that describe fetal characteristics at two–week intervals and that list agencies offering alternatives to abortion. The state also required other procedures, such as the presence of a second physician during an abortion performed when viability is possible. The responsibility of the second physician was to take all reasonable steps to preserve the child's life and health.

With a 5–4 majority, the Court invalidated the statute. It held that states are not free, under the guise of protecting maternal health or potential life, to intimidate women into continuing their pregnancies. The statute impermissibly intruded upon a decision to be made by the woman and her physician. The dissent by Chief Justice Burger was significant, since he formed part of the 7–2 majority in *Roe* v. *Wade*. He agreed with the dissenters that "we should reexamine *Roe*." The three other dissenters (White, Rehnquist, O'Connor) were much more emphatic in rejecting the premises of *Roe*. THORNBURGH v. AMERICAN COLL. OF OBST. & GYN., 476 U.S. 747 (1986).

Support for *Roe* v. *Wade* has been slowly eroding in recent years. With Antonin Scalia replacing Burger in 1986, and Anthony Kennedy taking Powell's seat in 1988, the Court was positioned to overhaul and possibly overrule *Roe*. The opportunity came in 1989, when the Court reviewed a Missouri statute that imposed a number of severe restrictions on a woman's decision to have an abortion. Without overruling *Roe*, four Justices rejected the trimester framework (Justice O'Connor, who declined to join that part of the Court's decision, had criticized the trimester concept in previous opinions). The 5–4 decision upheld key portions of the Missouri statute and allowed governmental regulation that would have been prohibited under earlier decisions. WEBSTER v. REPRODUCTIVE HEALTH SERVICES, 109 S. Ct. 3040 (1989).

This decision was promptly denounced by pro-choice advocates who believe that it is the duty of the Court to resolve the abortion issue. They rebuked the Court for sending this volatile question back to the state level, inviting further political strife and repressive legislation. However, the pro-choice community would not like a definitive resolution from the Rehnquist Court, especially after Harry Blackmun, William Brennan, and Thurgood Marshall retire. By relying on the benign intervention of the national judiciary, supporters of abortion rights have discouraged grass-roots organizational efforts at the state and local level. Those who support a woman's choice must now compete on an equal basis with pro-lifers, who have lobbied state legislatures effectively ever since *Roe* v. *Wade*.

The Court will most likely conduct further retreats from *Roe*, offering little resistance until the ultimate question is posed: may states criminalize abortion? At some point in the next few years the Court may have to decide whether states have it within their power to punish women and physicians who decide to abort. Meanwhile, states will scatter in different directions by offering women assistance or erecting additional hurdles. In states that deny the use of public funds and public facilities, a greater burder will fall on private clinics. Citizens who support a pro-choice policy will have to contribute their own money. Politicizing the issue need not deprive women of the fundamental right to abort early in their pregnancy.

Closely related to the abortion issue is the decision of parents to withhold consent for operations on infants born with severe handicaps. This emotional question became national news in 1982 when a couple in Bloomington, Indiana, opposed surgery on their child "Baby Doe," born with Down's syndrome and a blocked esophagus. The hospital was unsuccessful in challenging the parents' decision in court and the child died six days after its birth.

The Reagan administration warned hospitals receiving federal funds that newborn infants with handicaps such as Down's syndrome were protected by Section 504 of the Rehabilitation Act of 1973. Regulations were drafted and promulgated to allow the administration to intervene in the decision previously left to parents, physicians, and state governments. A federal district court and the Second Circuit rejected the regulation, as did the Supreme Court. Bowen v. American Hospital Assn., 476 U.S. 610 (1986).[2]

The Reagan administration also took steps to limit federal funds for family-planning activities. Congress had passed legislation in 1970 to provide funds for family planning, specifying that none of the funds "shall be used in programs where abortion is a method of family planning." 84 Stat. 1508, § 1008. Family–planning clinics could perform abortions and abortion–related services with state funds or private funds. On September 1, 1987, the Department of Health and Human Services issued a proposed rule to place restrictions on Title X funds for abortion–related activities carried out by family–planning clinics. Under the proposed rule, clinics would have to maintain separate accounts to demonstrate that Title X funds had not been used for such activities as counseling women on abortions or referring them to a doctor for an abortion. Congress adopted language in a conference report stating that changes in existing law must be achieved through the constitutional process and not through the executive's bypassing that process by issuing regulations. H. Rept. No. 100–498, at 943. When the administration persisted by publishing final regulations, the federal courts declared the regulations in violation of congressional intent and constitutional rights.

Members of Congress continue to fashion proposals designed to overrule *Roe* v. *Wade*. One approach is to amend the Constitution to protect the life of the unborn. Sometimes this takes the form of defining "person" in the Fourteenth Amendment to include the human fetus from the moment of conception. None of these proposals has attracted the necessary support to clear Congress, much less gain ratification by the states.

HOMOSEXUALITY

States have attempted to criminalize homosexuality by passing laws that prohibit "crimes against nature," "buggery," "deviancy," and sodomy. States sometimes borrowed English common law to define the offense as "the abominable and detestable crime against nature, either with mankind or with beast." Frequently

[2]Questions of privacy include the "right to die" for the elderly and for patients who survive solely because of life-support systems with no hope of recovery. An especially tragic case concerned Karen Ann Quinlan, who at 22 years of age lay in a New Jersey hospital in what the state court called a "vegetative existence." Her parents wanted to withdraw the life-sustaining mechanism and allow her to die naturally. After lengthy and anguished litigation they gained that right. Matter of Quinlan, 355 A.2d 647 (N.J. 1976).

these laws are challenged for being vague, unenforceable, and an invasion of privacy. It is often unclear whether the laws apply only to homosexuals or to married couples as well.

Opponents of these laws generally limit their attack to governmental efforts to control private consensual sex acts between adults. Where the activity concerns married couples, and there is no issue of force or coercion, legal action has been successful in striking down the statute or reversing a conviction. Buchanan v. Batchelor, 308 F.Supp. 729 (N.D. Tex. 1970); Cotner v. Henry, 394 F.2d 873 (7th Cir. 1968). If force is used, the Court is likely to consider general statutory phrases of "crime against nature" as not unconstitutionally vague when applied to such acts as cunnilingus. Rose v. Locke, 423 U.S. 48 (1975). A state sodomy statute proscribing "the abominable and detestable crime against nature, either mankind or beast," was held to be not unconstitutionally vague when applied against two adult males. Wainwright v. Stone, 414 U.S. 21 (1973).

Opponents of sodomy statutes do not deny that the public has certain legitimate interests if the activity involves minors, unwilling participants, or actions that occur in public.[3] If the activity involves two males, one of them a minor, a conviction is likely to stand. State v. Crawford, 478 S.W.2d 314 (Mo. 1972), appeal dismissed for want of substantial federal question, 409 U.S. 811 (1972). Similarly, if consenting adults commit sodomy in private and allow their activity to become known to a minor, the state can convict them on that ground. Lovisi v. Slayton, 363 F.Supp. 620 (E.D. Va. 1973).

A major homosexual case was decided by a federal court in 1975. An action was brought claiming that a Virginia statute deprived adult males, engaging in homosexual relations consensually and in private, of their constitutional rights to due process, freedom of expression, and privacy. The court upheld the statute by distinguishing between the right of privacy in *Griswold* (the use of contraceptives by married couples in private) and the practices of adultery, homosexuality, and other sexual intimacies which the state may forbid. Interestingly, the court relied on the *dissenting* opinion of Justice Harlan in *Poe* v. *Ullman* in making this distinction. Doe v. Commonwealth, 403 F.Supp. 1199, 1201 (E.D. Va. 1975), aff'd, 425 U.S. 901 (1976). In a dissent, Judge Merhige read *Griswold* and the abortion cases to stand for the principle that "every individual has a right to be free from unwarranted governmental intrusion into one's decisions on private matters of individual concern." More particularly, he said: "A mature individual's choice of an adult sexual partner, in the privacy of his or her own home, would appear to me to be a decision of the utmost private and intimate concern. Private consensual sex acts between adults are matters, absent evidence that they are harmful, in which the state has no legitimate interest." Id. at 1203.

Another significant case reached a federal appeals court in 1984. A Navy officer, discharged for homosexual conduct, brought an action seeking to be reinstated in the service. He acknowledged engaging in homosexual acts in a Navy barracks. The appeals court held that the Navy's policy of mandatory discharge for homosexual conduct does not violate constitutional rights to privacy or equal protection. If government may proscribe homosexual conduct in a civilian context, as in *Doe* v. *Commonwealth*, "then such a regulation is certainly sustainable in a military context" where discipline and good order justify restrictions "that go beyond the

---

[3]"Statement as to Jurisdiction," Buchanan v. Wade, U.S. Supreme Court, October Term, 1969, at 8.

needs of civilian society." Dronenberg v. Zech, 741 F.2d 1388, 1392 (D.C. Cir. 1984). The appeals court read previous privacy cases to protect such values as marriage, procreation, contraception, family relationships, and child rearing and education, none of which is present in homosexual conduct. Id. at 1395–1396. The decision is especially noteworthy because two members of the three–judge panel were Antonin Scalia, appointed to the Supreme Court in 1986, and Robert Bork, rejected for the Court in 1987. Bork wrote the decision.[4]

In 1986, the Supreme Court narrowly sustained—by a 5–4 vote—the constitutionality of a Georgia statute that criminalized sodomy. Michael Hardwick, a homosexual, was arrested for committing sodomy with another adult in the bedroom of his home. After the district attorney decided not to present the matter to the grand jury, Hardwick brought suit to challenge the statute as it applied to private, consensual sodomy. The majority held that the Constitution does not confer a fundamental right upon homosexuals to engage in sodomy. BOWERS v. HARDWICK, 478 U.S. 186 (1986). Justice Powell, concurring in the opinion, suggested that had Hardwick been "tried, much less convicted and sentenced," and had he raised the Eighth Amendment, he might have decided differently. Powell later admitted that he switched his vote to create the majority upholding Georgia's statute. Washington Post, August 13, 1986, at A4; see also Washington Post, July 13, 1986, at A1.

The Court did not pretend to have the "last word" on consensual sodomy. It emphasized that its decision "raises no question about the right or propriety of state legislative decisions to repeal their laws that criminalize homosexual sodomy, or of state–court decisions invalidating those laws on state constitutional grounds." 478 U.S. at 190. In 1988, a 6–2 decision by the Supreme Court held that CIA employees fired for homosexuality may sue the government for violations of their constitutional rights. Webster v. Doe, 108 S.Ct. 2047 (1988).

DEFINING THE LIMITS OF PRIVACY

Privacy has a multitude of meanings. In part, it preserves an individual's interest in seclusion or solitude. At other times it protects against the public disclosure of embarrassing private facts, or avoids placing someone in a "false light" in the public eye. On other occasions it prevents the appropriation of one's name or likeness. Prosser, 48 Cal. L. Rev. 383, 389 (1960).

Alan Westin, in *Privacy and Freedom* (1967), recommended that personal information (the right of decision over one's private personality) be defined as a property right. A citizen would be entitled to have due process of law before his "property" could be taken and misused, including access to information in the person's file and a right to challenge its accuracy. By passing the Fair Credit Reporting Act of 1970, Congress supplied that type of protection. Credit agencies are required to disclose to a consumer information about that person in their files, including the sources of the information. If a consumer successfully challenges the completeness or accuracy of any item in the file, the information must be promptly deleted. 84 Stat. 1127 (1970).

The question of computer files was addressed by the Supreme Court in 1977. As part of its broad police power, New York required the recording in a centralized computer file of the names and addresses of all persons who have obtained, pursuant

---

[4]Bork's decision was later criticized by four members of the D.C. Circuit on a motion for rehearing en banc, which was denied. Dronenberg v. Zech, 746 F.2d 1579 (D.C. Cir. 1984).

to a doctor's prescription, certain drugs for which there is both a lawful and unlawful market. The statute prohibited public disclosure of the patient's identity. In a unanimous opinion, the Court held that the statute did not violate the privacy of the doctor–patient relationship. Whalen v. Roe, 429 U.S. 589 (1977).

Congress intervened to protect the privacy interests of bank depositors. In 1976, the Supreme Court held that a Fourth Amendment interest could not be vindicated in court by challenging a government subpoena for microfilms of checks, deposit slips, and other records in a bank. The Court treated the materials as business records of a bank, not private papers of a person. Justice Brennan noted in a dissent that a depositor "reveals many aspects of his personal affairs, opinions, habits and associations. Indeed, the totality of bank records provides a virtual current biography." United States v. Miller, 425 U.S. 435, 451 (1976). Two years later Congress passed the Right to Financial Privacy Act, giving depositors certain procedural rights and protections that were unavailable from the Court. 92 Stat. 3697 (1978). The legislative debate illustrates that privacy interests left unprotected by the judiciary can be secured by congressional action (1223-1226).

In 1978, the Supreme Court upheld the right of law enforcement officers to use warrants to come onto the premises of a newspaper. Zurcher v. Stanford Daily, 436 U.S. 547 (1978). In quick response, Congress passed the Privacy Protection Act of 1980. With certain exceptions, the statute requires the use of a subpoena instead of a search warrant to obtain documentary materials from those who disseminate newspapers, books, broadcasts, or other similar forms of public communication. 94 Stat. 1879 (1980). The effect is to protect the privacy rights of those engaged in First Amendment activities. Here, too, the congressional debate is instructive (pp. 890-892).

In 1983, the Reagan administration issued a national security decision directive (NSDD 84) that required executive branch employees to submit to polygraph examinations "when appropriate." Polygraph testing, used to determine whether someone is telling the truth, has been criticized both as unreliable and as a serious intrusion on personal privacy. Congressional committees held hearings and urged that the directive be delayed to permit time for further study. Congress passed legislation to place a moratorium on polygraph testing. 97 Stat. 690, § 1218 (1983). When Congress considered legislation for a permanent restriction, the administration agreed to suspend its policy for governmentwide polygraph testing. In 1988, Congress enacted legislation to prohibit most polygraph tests by private employers. 102 Stat. 646 (1988).

During the hearings in 1987 on the nomination of Judge Robert H. Bork to be Associate Justice of the Supreme Court, a reporter obtained from a local video store a list of the movies that Bork and his family had rented. After the list was published in a newspaper, this invasion of Bork's privacy was roundly condemned. Congress responded by enacting the Video Privacy Protection Act of 1988, which makes video stores liable for actions forbidden by the statute. With certain exceptions, stores may be sued for disclosing the video tapes rented by customers. 102 Stat. 3195 (1988).

The right to privacy does not carry with it a comprehensive right to be "let alone." Legitimate actions by private agencies and government may intrude upon the individual. Carried to its extreme, the right to privacy would practically extinguish the freedom of the press. No one would dare publish or broadcast anything for fear of a lawsuit from an aggrieved citizen or public official. Even when state law prohibits the broadcasting of a rape victim's name, this right to privacy yields to the freedom of the press to accurately publish names obtained from judicial records that are open to public inspection. Cox Broadcasting v. Cohn, 420 U.S. 469 (1975). Newspapers may not be punished for publishing the name of a rape victim if the woman's full name appeared in a police report available to the press. The Florida Star v. B.J.F., 109 S.Ct. 2603 (1989).

There are many anomalies to the right of privacy. Entertainers demand both the right to privacy and the right to publicity. In the same year that Congress substantially strengthened the Freedom of Information Act of 1974, which gave the public access to federal agency records, it also passed the Privacy Act. This statute prohibits access by the public to certain materials in agency records, but also provides U.S. citizens the right to examine their own federal agency files and correct erroneous entries.

Although one may object to vaccination and regard it as a deprivation of personal liberty, states may invoke their police power to make it compulsory in order to prevent the spread of contagious diseases, such as smallpox. Jacobson v. Massachusetts, 197 U.S. 11 (1905). Playing radio programs on bus and streetcar systems may seem an invasion of privacy to some passengers, but the practice does not offend the Constitution. Public Utilities Comm'n v. Pollak, 343 U.S. 451 (1952). However, the state does have a right to protect citizens from assault from raucous loudspeakers. Kovacs v. Cooper, 336 U.S. 77 (1949).

In criminal law, a defendant can expect no success when invoking the right of privacy for certain activities, such as incest. Criminal procedures often affect sensitive areas of privacy, particularly those involving the body. Suspects accused of drunk driving can be subjected to compulsory blood tests and breath tests. Breithaupt v. Abram, 352 U.S. 432 (1957); Schmerber v. California, 384 U.S. 757 (1966). The Court has held that no one has an expectation of privacy if law enforcement officers decide to fly over their backyard and take photographs of marijuana plants. California v. Ciraolo, 476 U.S. 207 (1986); Florida v. Riley, 109 S.Ct. 693 (1989).

There are, of course, limits on the search for evidence. The police cannot use stomach pumps on a narcotics suspect to recover forbidden substances. Rochin v. California, 342 U.S. 165 (1952). States have been prohibited from compelling an armed robbery suspect to undergo surgery to remove a bullet lodged in his chest. Winston v. Lee, 470 U.S. 753 (1985). Individuals arrested and booked for misdemeanors may not be subjected to the indignity of strip searches and body-cavity searches, regardless of whether they are reasonably suspected of concealing contraband. Weber v. Dell, 804 F.2d 796 (2nd Cir. 1986), cert. denied, 483 U.S. 1020.

Justice Douglas' decision in *Griswold* v. *Connecticut*, discovering a right of privacy in various "emanations" and "penumbras" in the Constitution, has been the target of harsh critiques and ridicule. However, the nation's commitment to privacy is not grounded in ephemeral judicial doctrine. Citizens harbor a natural resistance to government intrusions. The Senate 1987 hearings on the ill–fated nomination of Robert Bork to the Supreme Court underscore the deep roots of privacy in America (pp. 1226–1232).[5]

---

[5]Another aspect of privacy is associational rights. The compelled disclosure of membership lists can seriously infringe on privacy of association and belief. Brown v. Socialist Workers '74 Campaign Comm., 459 U.S. 87 (1982); Buckley v. Valeo, 424 U.S. 1, 64 (1976); Gibson v. Florida Legislative Comm., 372 U.S. 539 (1963); NAACP v. Button, 371 U.S. 415 (1963).

Selected Readings

ALLEN, KATHERINE M. "*Dronenburg* v. *Zech:* The Wrong Case for Asserting a Right of Privacy for Homosexuals." 63 *North Carolina Law Review* 749 (1985).

BERGER, RAOUL. "The Ninth Amendment." 66 *Cornell Law Review* 1 (1980).

BLOUSTEIN, EDWARD J. "Privacy as an Aspect of Human Dignity: An Answer to Dean Prosser." 39 *New York University Law Review* 962 (1964).

BRECKINRIDGE, ADAM CARLYLE. *The Right to Privacy.* Lincoln: University of Nebraska Press, 1970.

CAPLAN, RUSSELL L. "The History and Meaning of the Ninth Amendment." 69 *Virginia Law Review* 223 (1983).

CRAVEN, J. BRAXTON, JR. "Personhood: The Right to be Let Alone," 1976 *Duke Law Journal* 699.

ELY, JOHN HART. "The Wages of Crying Wolf: A Comment on *Roe* v. *Wade.*" 82 *Yale Law Journal* 920 (1973).

EPSTEIN, RICHARD A. "Substantive Due Process by Any Other Name: The Abortion Cases." 1973 *Supreme Court Review* 159.

FRIED, CHARLES. "Privacy." 77 *Yale Law Journal* 475 (1968).

HAYDEN, TRUDY, AND JACK NOVIK. *Your Rights to Privacy.* New York: Avon Books, 1980.

HENKIN, LOUIS. "Privacy and Autonomy." 74 *Columbia Law Review* 1410 (1974).

LUKER, KRISTIN. *Abortion and the Politics of Motherhood.* Berkeley: University of California Press, 1984.

MAYER, MICHAEL. *Rights of Privacy.* New York: Law-Arts Publishers, 1972.

MCCLELLAN, GRANT S., ed. *The Right to Privacy.* New York: H. W. Wilson, 1976.

MILLER, ARTHUR R. *The Assault on Privacy.* Ann Arbor: University of Michigan Press, 1971.

NOTE. "The Constitutional Status of Sexual Orientation: Homosexuality as a Suspect Classification." 98 *Harvard Law Review* 1285 (1985).

O'BRIEN, DAVID M. *Privacy, Law, and Public Policy.* New York: Praeger, 1979.

PEMBER, DON R. *Privacy and the Press.* Seattle: University of Washington Press, 1972.

PENNOCK, J. ROLAND, AND JOHN W. CHAPMAN, eds. *Privacy.* New York: Atherton, 1971.

Privacy. Criminal Law and Practice. Course Handbook Series, Number 70. New York: Practising Law Institute, 1974.

PROSSER, WILLIAM L. "Privacy." 48 *California Law Review* 383 (1960).

REHNQUIST, WILLIAM H. "Is an Expanded Right of Privacy Consistent with Fair and Effective Law Enforcement? Or, Privacy, You've Come a Long Way, Baby." 23 *University of Kansas Law Review* 1 (1974).

RUBIN, EVA R. *Abortion, Politics, and the Courts:* Roe v. Wade *and Its Aftermath.* New York: Greenwood Press, 1987.

SHATTUCK, JOHN H. F. *Rights of Privacy.* Skokie, Ill.: National Textbook Co., 1977.

STEINER, GILBERT Y., ed. *The Abortion Dispute and the American System.* Washington, D.C.: The Brookings Institution, 1983.

WARREN, SAMUEL D., AND LOUIS D. BRANDEIS. "The Right to Privacy." 4 *Harvard Law Review* 193 (1890).

WESTIN, ALAN F. *Privacy and Freedom.* New York: Atheneum, 1967.

Buck v. Bell

274 U.S. 200 (1927)

A Virginia statute provided for the sexual sterilization of inmates in state institutions who are found to be afflicted with a hereditary form of insanity or imbecility. The state intended to perform on Carrie Buck the operation of salpingectomy, which consists of opening the abdominal cavity and cutting the Fallopian tubes. The statute provided for a hearing before the operation could be performed.

MR. JUSTICE HOLMES delivered the opinion of the Court.

This is a writ of error to review a judgment of the Supreme Court of Appeals of the State of

Virginia, affirming a judgment of the Circuit Court of Amherst County, by which the defendant in error, the superintendent of the State Colony for Epileptics and Feeble Minded, was ordered to perform the operation of salpingectomy upon Carrie Buck, the plaintiff in error, for the purpose of making her sterile. 143 Va. 310. The case comes here upon the contention that the statute authorizing the judgment is void under the Fourteenth Amendment as denying to the plaintiff in error due process of law and the equal protection of the laws.

Carrie Buck is a feeble minded white woman who was committed to the State Colony above mentioned in due form. She is the daughter of a feeble minded mother in the same institution, and the mother of an illegitimate feeble minded child. She was eighteen years old at the time of the trial of her case in the Circuit Court, in the latter part of 1924. An Act of Virginia, approved March 20, 1924, recites that the health of the patient and the welfare of society may be promoted in certain cases by the sterilization of mental defectives, under careful safeguard, &c.; that the sterilization may be effected in males by vasectomy and in females by salpingectomy, without serious pain or substantial danger to life; that the Commonwealth is supporting in various institutions many defective persons who if now discharged would become a menace but if incapable of procreating might be discharged with safety and become self-supporting with benefit to themselves and to society; and that experience has shown that heredity plays an important part in the transmission of insanity, imbecility, &c. The statute then enacts that whenever the superintendent of certain institutions including the above named State Colony shall be of opinion that it is for the best interests of the patients and of society that an inmate under his care should be sexually sterilized, he may have the operation performed upon any patient afflicted with hereditary forms of insanity, imbecility, &c., on complying with the very careful provisions by which the act protects the patients from possible abuse.

The superintendent first presents a petition to the special board of directors of his hospital or colony, stating the facts and the grounds for his opinion, verified by affidavit. Notice of the petition and of the time and place of the hearing in the institution is to be served upon the inmate, and also upon his guardian, and if there is no guardian the superintendent is to apply to the Circuit Court of the County to appoint one. If the inmate is a minor notice also is to be given to his parents if any with a copy of the petition. The board is to see to it that the inmate may attend the hearings if desired by him or his guardian. The evidence is all to be reduced to writing, and after the board has made its order for or against the operation, the superintendent, or the inmate, or his guardian, may appeal to the Circuit Court of the County. The Circuit Court may consider the record of the board and the evidence before it and such other admissible evidence as may be offered, and may affirm, revise, or reverse the order of the board and enter such order as it deems just. Finally any party may apply to the Supreme Court of Appeals, which, if it grants the appeal, is to hear the case upon the record of the trial in the Circuit Court and may enter such order as it thinks the Circuit Court should have entered. There can be no doubt that so far as procedure is concerned the rights of the patient are most carefully considered, and as every step in this case was taken in scrupulous compliance with the statute and after months of observation, there is no doubt that in that respect the plaintiff in error has had due process of law.

The attack is not upon the procedure but upon the substantive law. It seems to be contended that in no circumstances could such an order be justified. It certainly is contended that the order cannot be justified upon the existing grounds. The judgment finds the facts that have been recited and that Carrie Buck "is the probable potential parent of socially inadequate offspring, likewise afflicted, that she may be sexually sterilized without detriment to her general health and that her welfare and that of society will be promoted by her sterilization," and thereupon makes the order. In view of the general declarations of the legislature and the specific findings of the Court, obviously we cannot say as matter of law that the grounds do not exist, and if they exist they justify the result. We have seen more than once that the public welfare may call upon the best citizens for their lives. It would be strange if it could not call upon those who already sap the strength of the State for these lesser sacrifices, often not felt to be such by those concerned, in order to prevent our being swamped with incompetence. It is better for all the world, if instead of waiting to execute degenerate offspring for crime, or to let them starve for their imbecility, society can prevent those who are manifestly unfit from continuing their kind. The principle that sustains compulsory vaccination is broad enough to cover cutting the Fallopian tubes. *Jacobson* v. *Massachusetts*, 197 U. S. 11. Three generations of imbeciles are enough.

But, it is said, however it might be if this reasoning were applied generally, it fails when it is confined to the small number who are in the institutions named and is not applied to the multi-tudes outside. It is the usual last resort of constitutional arguments to point out shortcomings of this sort. But the answer is that the law does all that is needed when it does all that it can, indicates a policy, applies it to all within the lines, and seeks to bring within the lines all similarly situated so far and so fast as its means allow. Of course so far as the operations enable those who otherwise must be kept confined to be returned to the world, and thus open the asylum to others, the equality aimed at will be more nearly reached.

Judgment affirmed.

MR. JUSTICE BUTLER dissents.

Stanley v. Georgia

394 U.S. 557 (1969)

Law enforcement officers obtained a warrant to search Stanley's home for evidence of alleged bookmaking activities. While conducting this search, they found some films in his bedroom, used a projector to view the films, and judged them to be obscene. He was later convicted for violating a Georgia law that prohibits the possession of obscene matter. The conviction was confirmed by the Georgia Supreme Court.

MR. JUSTICE MARSHALL delivered the opinion of the Court.

An investigation of appellant's alleged bookmaking activities led to the issuance of a search warrant for appellant's home. Under authority of this warrant, federal and state agents secured entrance. They found very little evidence of bookmaking activity, but while looking through a desk drawer in an upstairs bedroom, one of the federal agents, accompanied by a state officer, found three reels of eight-millimeter film. Using a projector and screen found in an upstairs living room, they viewed the films. The state officer concluded that they were obscene and seized them. Since a further examination of the bedroom indicated that appellant occupied it, he was charged with possession of obscene matter and placed under arrest. He was later indicted for "knowingly hav-[ing] possession of . . . obscene matter" in violation of Georgia law. Appellant was tried before ajury and convicted. The Supreme Court of Geor-gia affirmed. *Stanley* v. *State*, 224 Ga. 259, 161 S. E. 2d 309 (1968). We noted probable jurisdiction of an appeal brought under 28 U.S.C. § 1257 (2). 393 U.S. 819 (1968).

Appellant raises several challenges to the validity of his conviction. We find it necessary to consider only one. Appellant argues here, and argued below, that the Georgia obscenity statute, insofar as it punishes mere private possession of obscene matter, violates the First Amendment, as made applicable to the States by the Fourteenth Amendment. For reasons set forth below, we agree that the mere private possession of obscene matter cannot constitutionally be made a crime.

The court below saw no valid constitutional objection to the Georgia statute, even though it extends further than the typical statute forbidding commercial sales of obscene material. It held that "[i]t is not essential to an indictment charging one with possession of obscene matter that it be alleged that such possession was 'with intent to sell, expose or circulate the same.'" *Stanley* v. *State, supra,* at 261, 161 S. E. 2d, at 311. The State and appellant both agree that the question here before us is whether "a statute imposing criminal sanctions upon the mere [knowing] possession of obscene matter" is constitutional. In this context, Georgia concedes that the present case appears to be one of "first impression . . . on this exact point," but contends that since "obscenity is not within the area of constitutionally protected speech or press," *Roth* v. *United States,* 354 U. S. 476, 485 (1957), the States are free, subject to the limits of other provisions of the Constitution, see, *e.g., Ginsberg* v. *New York,* 390 U. S. 629, 637–645 (1968), to deal with it any way deemed necessary, just as they may deal with possession of other things thought to be detrimental to the welfare of their citizens. If the State can protect the body of a citizen, may it not, argues Georgia, protect his mind?

It is true that *Roth* does declare, seemingly without qualification, that obscenity is not protected by the First Amendment. That statement has been repeated in various forms in subsequent cases. See, *e.g., Smith* v. *California,* 361 U. S. 147, 152 (1959); *Jacobellis* v. *Ohio,* 378 U. S. 184, 186–187 (1964) (opinion of BRENNAN, J.); *Ginsberg* v. *New York, supra,* at 635. However, neither *Roth* nor any subsequent decision of this Court dealt with the precise problem involved in the present case. Roth was convicted of mailing obscene circulars and advertising, and an obscene book, in violation of a federal obscenity statute. The defendant in a companion case, *Alberts* v. *California,* 354 U. S. 476 (1957), was convicted of "lewdly keeping for sale obscene and indecent books, and [of] writing, composing and publishing an obscene advertisement of them. . . ." *Id.,* at 481. None of the statements cited by the Court in *Roth* for the proposition that "this Court has always assumed that obscenity is not protected by the freedoms of speech and press" were made in the context of a statute punishing mere private possession of obscene material; the cases cited deal for the most part with use of the mails to distribute objectionable material or with some form of public distribution or dissemination. Moreover, none of this Court's decisions subse-

quent to *Roth* involved prosecution for private possession of obscene materials. Those cases dealt with the power of the State and Federal Governments to prohibit or regulate certain public actions taken or intended to be taken with respect to obscene matter. Indeed, with one exception, we have been unable to discover any case in which the issue in the present case has been fully considered.

. . .

It is now well established that the Constitution protects the right to receive information and ideas. "This freedom [of speech and press] . . . necessarily protects the right to receive. . . ." *Martin* v. *City of Struthers,* 319 U. S. 141, 143 (1943); see *Griswold* v. *Connecticut,* 381 U. S. 479, 482 (1965); *Lamont* v. *Postmaster General,* 381 U. S. 301, 307–308 (1965) (BRENNAN, J., concurring); cf. *Pierce* v. *Society of Sisters,* 268 U. S. 510 (1925). This right to receive information and ideas, regardless of their social worth, see *Winters* v. *New York,* 333 U. S. 507, 510 (1948), is fundamental to our free society. Moreover, in the context of this case—a prosecution for mere possession of printed or filmed matter in the privacy of a person's own home—that right takes on an added dimension. For also fundamental is the right to be free, except in very limited circumstances, from unwanted governmental intrusions into one's privacy.

"The makers of our Constitution undertook to secure conditions favorable to the pursuit of happiness. They recognized the significance of man's spiritual nature, of his feelings and of his intellect. They knew that only a part of the pain, pleasure and satisfactions of life are to be found in material things. They sought to protect Americans in their beliefs, their thoughts, their emotions and their sensations. They conferred, as against the Government, the right to be let alone—the most comprehensive of rights and the right most valued by civilized man." *Olmstead* v. *United States,* 277 U. S. 438, 478 (1928) (Brandeis, J., dissenting).

See *Griswold* v. *Connecticut, supra;* cf. *NAACP* v. *Alabama,* 357 U. S. 449, 462 (1958).

These are the rights that appellant is asserting in the case before us. He is asserting the right to read or observe what he pleases—the right to satisfy his intellectual and emotional needs in the privacy of his own home. He is asserting the right to be free from state inquiry into the contents of his library. Georgia contends that appellant does not have these rights, that there are certain types of materials that the individual may not read or even possess. Georgia justifies this assertion by arguing that the films in the present case are obscene. But we think that mere categorization of these films as "obscene" is insufficient justification for such a drastic invasion of personal liberties guaranteed by the First and Fourteenth Amendments. Whatever may be the justifications for other statutes regulating obscenity, we do not think they reach into the privacy of one's own home. If the First Amendment means anything, it means that a State has no business telling a man, sitting alone in his own house, what books he may read or what films he may watch. Our whole constitutional heritage rebels at the thought of giving government the power to control men's minds.

And yet, in the face of these traditional notions of individual liberty, Georgia asserts the right to protect the individual's mind from the effects of obscenity. We are not certain that this argument amounts to anything more than the assertion that the State has the right to control the moral content of a person's thoughts. To some, this may be a noble purpose, but it is wholly inconsistent with the philosophy of the First Amendment. As the Court said in *Kingsley International Pictures Corp.* v. *Regents*, 360 U. S. 684, 688–689 (1959), "[t]his argument misconceives what it is that the Constitution protects. Its guarantee is not confined to the expression of ideas that are conventional or shared by a majority. . . . And in the realm of ideas it protects expression which is eloquent no less than that which is unconvincing." Cf. *Joseph Burstyn, Inc.* v. *Wilson*, 343 U. S. 495 (1952). Nor is it relevant that obscene materials in general, or the particular films before the Court, are arguably devoid of any ideological content. The line between the transmission of ideas and mere entertainment is much too elusive for this Court to draw, if indeed such a line can be drawn at all. See *Winters* v. *New York*, *supra*, at 510. Whatever the power of the state to control public dissemination

of ideas inimical to the public morality, it cannot constitutionally premise legislation on the desirability of controlling a person's private thoughts.

Perhaps recognizing this, Georgia asserts that exposure to obscene materials may lead to deviant sexual behavior or crimes of sexual violence. There appears to be little empirical basis for that assertion. But more important, if the State is only concerned about printed or filmed materials inducing antisocial conduct, we believe that in the context of private consumption of ideas and information we should adhere to the view that "[a]mong free men, the deterrents ordinarily to be applied to prevent crime are education and punishment for violations of the law. . . ." *Whitney* v. *California*, 274 U. S. 357, 378 (1927) (Brandeis, J., concurring). See Emerson, Toward a General Theory of the First Amendment, 72 Yale L. J. 877, 938 (1963). Given the present state of knowledge, the State may no more prohibit mere possession of obscene matter on the ground that it may lead to antisocial conduct than it may prohibit possession of chemistry books on the ground that they may lead to the manufacture of homemade spirits.

It is true that in *Roth* this Court rejected the necessity of proving that exposure to obscene material would create a clear and present danger of antisocial conduct or would probably induce its recipients to such conduct. 354 U. S., at 486–487. But that case dealt with public distribution of obscene materials and such distribution is subject to different objections. For example, there is always the danger that obscene material might fall into the hands of children, see *Ginsberg* v. *New York*, *supra*, or that it might intrude upon the sensibilities or privacy of the general public. See *Redrup* v. *New York*, 386 U. S. 767, 769 (1967). No such dangers are present in this case.

Finally, we are faced with the argument that prohibition of possession of obscene materials is a necessary incident to statutory schemes prohibiting distribution. That argument is based on alleged difficulties of proving an intent to distribute or in producing evidence of actual distribution. We are not convinced that such difficulties exist, but even if they did we do not think that they would justify infringement of the individual's right to read or observe what he pleases. Because that right is so fundamental to our scheme of individual liberty, its restriction may not be justified by the need to ease the administration of otherwise valid criminal laws. See *Smith* v. *California*, 361 U. S. 147 (1959).

We hold that the First and Fourteenth Amendments prohibit making mere private possession of obscene material a crime. *Roth* and the cases following that decision are not impaired by today's holding. As we have said, the States retain broad power to regulate obscenity; that power simply does not extend to mere possession by the individual in the privacy of his own home. Accordingly, the judgment of the court below is reversed and the case is remanded for proceedings not inconsistent with this opinion.

It is so ordered.

MR. JUSTICE BLACK, concurring.

I agree with the Court that the mere possession of reading matter or movie films, whether labeled obscene or not, cannot be made a crime by a State without violating the First Amendment, made applicable to the States by the Fourteenth. My reasons for this belief have been set out in many of my prior opinions, as for example, *Smith* v. *California*, 361 U. S. 147, 155 (concurring opinion), and *Ginzburg* v. *United States*, 383 U. S. 463, 476 (dissenting opinion).

MR. JUSTICE STEWART, with whom MR. JUSTICE BRENNAN and MR. JUSTICE WHITE join, concurring in the result.

Before the commencement of the trial in this case, the appellant filed a motion to suppress the films as evidence upon the ground that they had been seized in violation of the Fourth and Fourteenth Amendments. The motion was denied, and the films were admitted in evidence at the trial. In affirming the appellant's conviction, the Georgia Supreme Court specifically determined that the films had been lawfully seized. The appellant correctly contends that this determination was clearly wrong under established principles of constitutional law. But the Court today disregards this preliminary issue in its hurry to move on to newer constitutional frontiers. I cannot so readily overlook the serious inroads upon Fourth Amendment

guarantees countenanced in this case by the Georgia courts.

The Fourth Amendment provides that "no Warrants shall issue, but upon probable cause, supported by Oath or affirmation, and particularly describing the place to be searched, and the persons or things to be seized." The purpose of these clear and precise words was to guarantee to the people of this Nation that they should forever be secure from the general searches and unrestrained seizures that had been a hated hallmark of colonial rule under the notorious writs of assistance of the British Crown. See *Stanford* v. *Texas*, 379 U. S. 476, 481. This most basic of Fourth Amendment guarantees was frustrated in the present case, I think, in a manner made the more pernicious by its very subtlety. For what happened here was that a search that began as perfectly lawful became the occasion for an unwarranted and unconstitutional seizure of the films.

. . .

The controlling constitutional principle was stated in two sentences by this Court more than 40 years ago:

"The requirement that warrants shall particularly describe the things to be seized makes general searches under them impossible and prevents the seizure of one thing under a warrant describing another. As to what is to be taken, nothing is left to the discretion of the officer executing the warrant." *Marron* v. *United States*, 275 U. S. 192, 196.

This is not a case where agents in the course of a lawful search came upon contraband, criminal activity, or criminal evidence in plain view. For the record makes clear that the contents of the films could not be determined by mere inspection. And this is not a case that presents any questions as to the permissible scope of a search made incident to a lawful arrest. For the appellant had not been arrested when the agents found the films. After finding them, the agents spent some 50 minutes exhibiting them by means of the appellant's projector in another upstairs room. Only then did the agents return downstairs and arrest the appellant.

Even in the much-criticized case of *United*

States v. *Rabinowitz,* 339 U. S. 56, the Court emphasized that "exploratory searches . . . cannot be undertaken by officers with or without a warrant." *Id.,* at 62. This record presents a bald violation of that basic constitutional rule. To condone what happened here is to invite a government official to use a seemingly precise and legal warrant only as a ticket to get into a man's home, and, once inside, to launch forth upon unconfined searches and indiscriminate seizures as if armed with all the unbridled and illegal power of a general warrant.

Because the films were seized in violation of the Fourth and Fourteenth Amendments, they were inadmissible in evidence at the appellant's trial. *Mapp* v. *Ohio,* 367 U. S. 643. Accordingly, the judgment of conviction must be reversed.

Paul v. Davis

24 U.S. 693 (1976)

A photocopy of Edward Charles Davis III, bearing his name, was included in a "flyer" of "active shoplifters" and distributed to area merchants by the police department. Davis had been arrested on a shoplifting charge but the charge was dismissed. He brought an action against Edgar Paul, Chief of Police of the Louisville, Ky., Division of Police, and Russell McDaniel, Chief of Police of the Jefferson County, Ky., Division of Police. Davis claimed that their defamation of him violated 42 U.S.C. § 1983 (official deprivation of rights, privileges, or immunities secured by the Constitution and laws) and the Fourteenth Amendment. His suit was dismissed by the district court but the Sixth Circuit supported his § 1983 complaint.

MR. JUSTICE REHNQUIST delivered the opinion of the Court.

We granted certiorari, 421 U. S. 909 (1975), in this case to consider whether respondent's charge that petitioners' defamation of him, standing alone and apart from any other governmental action with respect to him, stated a claim for relief under 42 U.S.C. § 1983 and the Fourteenth Amendment. For the reasons hereinafter stated, we conclude that it does not.

Petitioner Paul is the Chief of Police of the Louisville, Ky., Division of Police, while petitioner McDaniel occupies the same position in the Jefferson County, Ky., Division of Police. In late 1972 they agreed to combine their efforts for the purpose of alerting local area merchants to possible shoplifters who might be operating during the Christmas season. In early December petitioners distributed to approximately 800 merchants in the Louisville metropolitan area a "flyer," which began as follows:

"TO: BUSINESS MEN IN THE METROPOLITAN AREA

"The Chiefs of The Jefferson County and City of Louisville Police Departments, in an effort to keep their officers advised on shoplifting activity, have approved the attached alphabetically arranged flyer of subjects known to be active in this criminal field.

"This flyer is being distributed to you, the business man, so that you may inform your security personnel to watch for these subjects. These persons have been arrested during 1971 and 1972 or have been active in various criminal fields in high density shopping areas.

"Only the photograph and name of the subject is shown on this flyer, if additional information is desired, please forward a request in writing. . . ."

The flyer consisted of five pages of "mug shot" photos, arranged alphabetically. Each page was headed:

"NOVEMBER 1972
CITY OF LOUISVILLE
JEFFERSON COUNTY
POLICE DEPARTMENTS
ACTIVE SHOPLIFTERS"

In approximately the center of page 2 there appeared photos and the name of the respondent, Edward Charles Davis III.

Respondent appeared on the flyer because on June 14, 1971, he had been arrested in Louisville on a charge of shoplifting. He had been arraigned on this charge in September 1971, and, upon his plea of not guilty, the charge had been "filed away with leave [to reinstate]," a disposition which left the charge outstanding. Thus, at the time petitioners caused the flyer to be prepared and circulated respondent had been charged with shoplifting but his guilt or innocence of that offense had never been resolved. Shortly after circulation of the flyer the charge against respondent was finally dismissed by a judge of the Louisville Police Court.

At the time the flyer was circulated respondent was employed as a photographer by the Louisville Courier-Journal and Times. The flyer, and respondent's inclusion therein, soon came to the attention of respondent's supervisor, the executive director of photography for the two newspapers. This individual called respondent in to hear his version of the events leading to his appearing in the flyer. Following this discussion, the supervisor informed respondent that although he would not be fired, he "had best not find himself in a similar situation" in the future.

Respondent thereupon brought this § 1983 action in the District Court for the Western District of Kentucky, seeking redress for the alleged violation of rights guaranteed to him by the Constitution of the United States. Claiming jurisdiction under 28 U.S.C. § 1343 (3), respondent sought damages as well as declaratory and injunctive relief. Petitioners moved to dismiss this complaint. The District Court granted this motion, ruling that "[t]he facts alleged in this case do not establish that plaintiff has been deprived of any right secured to him by the Constitution of the United States."

Respondent appealed to the Court of Appeals for the Sixth Circuit which recognized that, under our decisions, for respondent to establish a claim cognizable under § 1983 he had to show that petitioners had deprived him of a right secured by the Constitution of the United States, and that any such deprivation was achieved under color of law. *Adickes* v. *Kress & Co.*, 398 U. S. 144, 150 (1970). The Court of Appeals concluded that respondent had set forth a § 1983 claim "in that he has alleged facts that constitute a denial of due process of law." 505 F. 2d 1180, 1182 (1974). In its view our decision in *Wisconsin* v. *Constantineau*, 400 U. S. 433 (1971), mandated reversal of the District Court.

I

Respondent's due process claim is grounded upon his assertion that the flyer, and in particular the phrase "Active Shoplifters" appearing at the head of the page upon which his name and photograph appear, impermissibly deprived him of some "liberty" protected by the Fourteenth Amendment. His complaint asserted that the "active shoplifter" designation would inhibit him from entering business establishments for fear of being suspected of shoplifting and possibly apprehended, and would seriously impair his future employment opportunities. Accepting that such consequences may flow from the flyer in question, respondent's complaint would appear to state a classical claim for defamation actionable in the courts of virtually every State. Imputing criminal behavior to an individual is generally considered defamatory *per se*, and actionable without proof of special damages.

Respondent brought his action, however, not in the state courts of Kentucky, but in a United States District Court for that State. He asserted not a claim for defamation under the laws of Kentucky, but a claim that he had been deprived of rights secured to him by the Fourteenth Amendment of the United States Constitution. Concededly if the same allegations had been made about respondent by a private individual, he would have nothing more than a claim for defamation under state law. But, he contends, since petitioners are respectively an offical of city and of county government, his action is thereby transmuted into one for deprivation by the State of rights secured under the Fourteenth Amendment.

In *Greenwood* v. *Peacock,* 384 U. S. 808 (1966), in the course of considering an important and not wholly dissimilar question of the relationship between the National and the State Governments, the Court said that "[i]t is worth contemplating what the result would be if the strained interpretation of § 1443 (1) urged by the individual petitioners were to prevail." *Id.,* at 832. We, too, pause to consider the result should respondent's interpretation of § 1983 and of the Fourteenth Amendment be accepted.

If respondent's view is to prevail, a person arrested by law enforcement officers who announce that they believe such person to be responsible for a particular crime in order to calm the fears of an aroused populace, presumably obtains a claim against such officers under § 1983. And since it is surely far more clear from the language of the Fourteenth Amendment that "life" is protected against state deprivation than it is that reputation is protected against state injury, it would be difficult to see why the survivors of an innocent bystander mistakenly shot by a policeman or negligently killed by a sheriff driving a government vehicle, would not have claims equally cognizable under § 1983.

It is hard to perceive any logical stopping place to such a line of reasoning. Respondent's construction would seem almost necessarily to result in every legally cognizable injury which may have been inflicted by a state official acting under "color of law" establishing a violation of the Fourteenth Amendment. We think it would come as a great surprise to those who drafted and shepherded the adoption of that Amendment to learn that it worked such a result, and a study of our decisions convinces us they do not support the construction urged by respondent.

II

The result reached by the Court of Appeals, which respondent seeks to sustain here, must be bottomed on one of two premises. The first is that the Due Process Clause of the Fourteenth Amendment and § 1983 make actionable many wrongs inflicted by government employees which had heretofore been thought to give rise only to state-law tort claims. The second premise is that the infliction by state officials of a "stigma" to one's reputation is somehow different in kind from the infliction by the same official of harm or injury to other interests protected by state law, so that an injury to reputation is actionable under § 1983 and the Fourteenth Amendment even if other such harms are not. We examine each of these premises in turn.

A

The first premise would be contrary to pronouncements in our cases on more than one occasion with respect to the scope of § 1983 and of the Fourteenth Amendment. In the leading case of *Screws* v. *United States,* 325 U. S. 91 (1945), the Court considered the proper application of the criminal counterpart of § 1983, likewise intended by Congress to enforce the guarantees of the Fourteenth Amendment. In his opinion for the Court plurality in that case, Mr. Justice Douglas observed:

"Violation of local law does not necessarily mean that federal rights have been invaded. The fact that a prisoner is assaulted, injured, or even murdered by state officials does not necessarily mean that he is deprived of any right protected or secured by the Constitution or laws of the United States." 325 U.S., at 108–109.

. . .

B

The second premise upon which the result reached by the Court of Appeals could be rested— that the infliction by state officials of a "stigma" to one's reputation is somehow different in kind from infliction by a state official of harm to other interests protected by state law—is equally untenable. The words "liberty" and "property" as used in the Fourteenth Amendment do not in terms single out reputation as a candidate for special protection over and above other interests that may be protected by state law. While we have in a number of our prior cases pointed out the frequently drastic effect of the "stigma" which may result from defamation by the government in a variety of contexts, this line of cases does not establish the proposition that reputation alone, apart from some more tangible interests such as employment, is either "liberty" or "property" by itself sufficient to invoke the procedural protection of the Due Process Clause. As we have said, the Court of Appeals, in reaching a contrary conclusion, relied primarily upon *Wisconsin* v. *Constantineau*, 400 U. S. 433 (1971). We think the correct import of that decision, however, must be derived from an examination of the precedents upon which it relied, as well as consideration of the other decisions by this Court, before and after *Constantineau*, which bear upon the relationship between governmental defamation and the guarantees of the Constitution. While not uniform in their treatment of the subject, we think that the weight of our decisions establishes no constitutional doctrine converting every defamation by a public official into a deprivation of liberty within the meaning of the Due Process Clause of the Fifth or Fourteenth Amendment.

. . .

Two things appear from the line of cases beginning *[in 1946]*. The Court has recognized the serious damage that could be inflicted by branding a government employee as "disloyal," and thereby stigmatizing his good name. But the Court has never held that the mere defamation of an individual, whether by branding him disloyal or otherwise, was sufficient to invoke the guarantees of procedural due process absent an accompanying loss of government employment.

. . .

It was against this backdrop that the Court in 1971 decided *Constantineau*. There the Court held that a Wisconsin statute authorizing the practice of "posting" was unconstitutional because it failed to provide procedural safeguards of notice and an opportunity to be heard, prior to an individual's being "posted." Under the statute "posting" consisted of forbidding in writing the sale or delivery of alcoholic beverages to certain persons who were determined to have become hazards to themselves, to their family, or to the community by reason of their "excessive drinking." The statute

also made it a misdemeanor to sell or give liquor to any person so posted. See 400 U. S., at 434 n. 2.

There is undoubtedly language in *Constantineau*, which is sufficiently ambiguous to justify the reliance upon it by the Court of Appeals:

"Yet certainly where the state attaches 'a badge of infamy' to the citizen, due process comes into play. *Wieman* v. *Updegraff*, 344 U. S. 183, 191. '[T]he right to be heard before being condemned to suffer grievous loss of any kind, even though it may not involve the stigma and hardships of a criminal conviction, is a principle basic to our society.' *Anti-Fascist Committee* v. *McGrath*, 341 U. S. 123, 168 (Frankfurter, J., concurring). "Where a person's good name, reputation, honor, or integrity is at stake *because of what the government is doing to him*, notice and an opportunity to be heard are essential." *Id.*, at 437 (emphasis supplied).

. . .

We think that the italicized language in the last sentence quoted, "because of what the government is doing to him," referred to the fact that the governmental action taken in that case deprived the individual of a right previously held under state law—the right to purchase or obtain liquor in common with the rest of the citizenry. "Posting," therefore, significantly altered her status as a matter of state law, and it was that alteration of legal status which, combined with the injury resulting from the defamation, justified the invocation of procedural safeguards. The "stigma" resulting from the defamatory character of the posting was doubtless an important factor in evaluating the extent of harm worked by that act, but we do not think that such defamation, standing alone, deprived Constantineau of any "liberty" protected by the procedural guarantees of the Fourteenth Amendment.

. . .

. . . the interest in reputation alone which respondent seeks to vindicate in this action in federal court is quite different from the "liberty" or "property" recognized in those decisions. Kentucky law does not extend to respondent any legal guarantee of present enjoyment of reputation which has been altered as a result of petitioners' actions. Rather his interest in reputation is simply one of a number which the State may protect against injury by virtue of its tort law, providing a forum for vindication of those interests by means of damages actions. And any harm or injury to that interest, even where as here inflicted by an officer of the State, does not result in a deprivation of any "liberty" or "property" recognized by state or federal law, nor has it worked any change of respondent's status as theretofore recognized under the State's laws. For these reasons we hold that the interest in reputation asserted in this case is neither "liberty" nor "property" guaranteed against state deprivation without due process of law.

. . .

IV

Respondent's complaint also alleged a violation of a "right to privacy guaranteed by the First, Fourth, Fifth, Ninth, and Fourteenth Amendments." The Court of Appeals did not pass upon this claim since it found the allegations of a due process violation sufficient to require reversal of the District Court's order. As we have agreed with the District Court on the due process issue, we find it necessary to pass upon respondent's other theory in order to determine whether there is any support for the litigation he seeks to pursue.

While there is no "right of privacy" found in any specific guarantee of the Constitution, the Court has recognized that "zones of privacy" may be created by more specific constitutional guarantees and thereby impose limits upon government power. See *Roe* v. *Wade*, 410 U. S. 113, 152–153 (1973). Respondent's case, however, comes within none of these areas. He does not seek to suppress evidence seized in the course of an unreasonable search. See *Katz* v. *United States*, 389 U. S. 347, 351 (1967); *Terry* v. *Ohio*, 392 U. S. 1, 8–9 (1968). And our other "right of privacy" cases, while defying categorical description, deal generally with substantive aspects of the Fourteenth Amendment. In *Roe* the Court pointed out that the personal rights found in this guarantee of personal privacy must be limited to those which

are "fundamental" or "implicit in the concept of ordered liberty" as described in *Palko* v. *Connecticut*, 302 U. S. 319, 325 (1937). The activities detailed as being within this definition were ones very different from that for which respondent claims constitutional protection—matters relating to marriage, procreation, contraception, family relationships, and child rearing and education. In these areas it has been held that there are limitations on the States' powers to substantively regulate conduct.

. . .

MR. JUSTICE STEVENS took no part in the consideration or decision of this case.

MR. JUSTICE BRENNAN, with whom MR. JUSTICE MARSHALL concurs and MR. JUSTICE WHITE concurs in part, dissenting.

I dissent. The Court today holds that police officials, acting in their official capacities as law enforcers, may on their own initiative and without trial constitutionally condemn innocent individuals as criminals and thereby brand them with one of the most stigmatizing and debilitating labels in our society. If there are no constitutional restraints on such oppressive behavior, the safeguards constitutionally accorded an accused in a criminal trial are rendered a sham, and no individual can feel secure that he will not be arbitrarily singled out for similar *ex parte* punishment by those primarily charged with fair enforcement of the law. The Court accomplishes this result by excluding a person's interest in his good name and reputation from all constitutional protection, regardless of the character of or necessity for the government's actions. The result, which is demonstrably inconsistent with our prior case law and unduly restrictive in its construction of our precious Bill of Rights, is one in which I cannot concur.

To clarify what is at issue in this case, it is first necessary to dispel some misconceptions apparent in the Court's opinion. Title 42 U. S. C. § 1983 provides:

"Every person who, under color of any statute, ordinance, regulation, custom, or usage, of any State or Territory, subjects, or causes to be subjected, any citizen of the United States or other person within the jurisdiction thereof to the deprivation of any rights, privileges, or immunities secured by the Constitution and laws, shall be liable to the party injured in an action at law, suit in equity, or other proper proceeding for redress."

. . .

The stark fact is that the police here have officially imposed on respondent the stigmatizing label "criminal" without the salutary and constitutionally mandated safeguards of a criminal trial. The Court concedes that this action will have deleterious consequences for respondent. For 15 years, the police had prepared and circulated similiar lists, not with respect to shoplifting alone, but also for other offenses. App. 19, 27–28. Included in the five-page list in which respondent's name and "mug shot" appeared were numerous individuals who, like respondent, were never convicted of any criminal activity and whose only "offense" was having once been arrested. Indeed, respondent was arrested over 17 months before the flyer was distributed, not by state law enforcement authorities, but by a store's private security police, and nothing in the record appears to suggest the existence at that time of even constitutionally sufficient probable cause for that single arrest on a shoplifting charge. Nevertheless, petitioners had 1,000 flyers printed (800 were distributed widely throughout the Louisville business community) proclaiming that the individuals

identified by name and picture were "subjects *known* to be *active* in this criminal field [shoplifting]," and trumpeting the "fact" that each page depicted *"Active Shoplifters"* (emphasis supplied).

. . . The logical and disturbing corollary of this holding is that no due process infirmities would inhere in a statute constituting a commission to conduct *ex parte* trials of individuals, so long as the only official judgment pronounced was limited to the public condemnation and branding of a person as a Communist, a traitor, an "active murderer," a homosexual, or any other mark that "merely" carries social opprobrium. The potential of today's decision is frightening for a free people. That decision surely finds no support in our relevant constitutional jurisprudence.

. . .

I have always thought that one of this Court's most important roles is to provide a formidable bulwark against governmental violation of the constitutional safeguards securing in our free society the legitimate expectations of every person to innate human dignity and sense of worth. It is a regrettable abdication of that role and a saddening denigration of our majestic Bill of Rights when the Court tolerates arbitrary and capricious official conduct branding an individual as a criminal without compliance with constitutional procedures designed to ensure the fair and impartial ascertainment of criminal culpability. Today's decision must surely be a short-lived aberration.

Griswold v. Connecticut

381 U.S. 479 (1965)

The executive director and medical director of the Planned Parenthood League of Connecticut were convicted for giving married persons information and medical advice on how to prevent conception and for prescribing a contraceptive device for the wife's use. A Connecticut statute made it a crime for any person to use any drug or article to prevent conception.

MR. JUSTICE DOUGLAS delivered the opinion of the Court.

Appellant Griswold is Executive Director of the Planned Parenthood League of Connecticut. Appellant Buxton is a licensed physician and a professor at the Yale Medical School who served as Medical Director for the League at its Center in New Haven—a center open and operating from November 1 to November 10, 1961, when appellants were arrested.

They gave information, instruction, and medical advice to *married persons* as to the means of preventing conception. They examined the wife and prescribed the best contraceptive device or material for her use. Fees were usually charged, although some couples were serviced free.

The statutes whose constitutionality is involved in this appeal are §§ 53–32 and 54–196 of the General Statutes of Connecticut (1958 rev.). The former provides:

"Any person who uses any drug, medicinal article or instrument for the purpose of preventing conception shall be fined not less than fifty dollars or imprisoned not less than sixty days nor more than one year or be both fined and imprisoned."

Section 54–196 provides:

"Any person who assists, abets, counsels, causes, hires or commands another to commit any offense may be prosecuted and punished as if he were the principal offender."

The appellants were found guilty as accessories and fined $100 each, against the claim that the accessory statute as so applied violated the Fourteenth Amendment. The Appellate Division of the Circuit Court affirmed. The Supreme Court of Errors affirmed that judgment. 151 Conn. 544, 200 A. 2d 479. We noted probable jurisdiction. 379 U. S. 926.

We think that appellants have standing to raise the constitutional rights of the married people with whom they had a professional relationship. *Tileston* v. *Ullman*, 318 U. S. 44, is different, for there the plaintiff seeking to represent others asked for a declaratory judgment. In that situation we thought that the requirements of standing should be strict, lest the standards of "case or controversy" in Article III of the Constitution become blurred. Here those doubts are removed by reason of a criminal conviction for serving married couples in violation of an aiding-and-abetting statute. Certainly the accessory should have standing to assert that the offense which he is charged with assisting is not, or cannot constitutionally be, a crime.

This case is more akin to *Truax* v. *Raich*, 239 U. S. 33, where an employee was permitted to assert the rights of his employer; to *Pierce* v. *Society of Sisters*, 268 U. S. 510, where the owners of private schools were entitled to assert the rights of potential pupils and their parents; and to *Barrows* v. *Jackson*, 346 U. S. 249, where a white defendant, party to a racially restrictive covenant, who was being sued for damages by the covenantors because she had conveyed her property to Negroes, was allowed to raise the issue that enforcement of the covenant violated the rights of prospective Negro purchasers to equal protection, although no Negro was a party to the suit. And see *Meyer* v. *Nebraska*, 262 U. S. 390; *Adler* v. *Board of Education*, 342 U. S. 485; *NAACP* v. *Alabama*, 357 U. S. 449; *NAACP* v. *Button*, 371 U. S. 415. The rights of husband and wife, pressed here, are likely to be diluted or adversely affected unless those rights are considered in a suit involving those who have this kind of confidential relation to them.

Coming to the merits, we are met with a wide range of questions that implicate the Due Process Clause of the Fourteenth Amendment. Overtones of some arguments suggest that *Lochner* v. *New York*, 198 U. S. 45, should be our guide. But we decline that invitation as we did in *West Coast Hotel Co.* v. *Parrish*, 300 U. S. 379; *Olsen* v. *Nebraska*, 313 U. S. 236; *Lincoln Union* v. *Northwestern Co.*, 335 U. S. 525; *Williamson* v. *Lee Optical Co.*, 348 U. S. 483; *Giboney* v. *Empire Storage Co.*, 336 U. S. 490. We do not sit as a super-legislature to determine the wisdom, need, and propriety of laws that touch economic problems, business affairs, or social conditions. This law, however, operates directly on an intimate relation of husband and wife and their physician's role in one aspect of that relation.

The association of people is not mentioned in the Constitution nor in the Bill of Rights. The right to educate a child in a school of the parents' choice—whether public or private or parochial—is also not mentioned. Nor is the right to study any particular subject or any foreign language. Yet the

First Amendment has been construed to include certain of those rights.

By *Pierce* v. *Society of Sisters, supra,* the right to educate one's children as one chooses is made applicable to the States by the force of the First and Fourteenth Amendments. By *Meyer* v. *Nebraska, supra,* the same dignity is given the right to study the German language in a private school. In other words, the State may not, consistently with the spirit of the First Amendment, contract the spectrum of available knowledge. . . .

In *NAACP* v. *Alabama,* 357 U. S. 449, 462, we protected the "freedom to associate and privacy in one's associations," noting that freedom of association was a peripheral First Amendment right. Disclosure of membership lists of a constitutionally valid association, we held, was invalid "as entailing the likelihood of a substantial restraint upon the exercise by petitioner's members of their right to freedom of association." *Ibid.* In other words, the First Amendment has a penumbra where privacy is protected from governmental intrusion. In like context, we have protected forms of "association" that are not political in the customary sense but pertain to the social, legal, and economic benefit of the members. *NAACP* v. *Button,* 371 U. S. 415, 430–431. . . .

Those cases involved more than the "right of assembly"—a right that extends to all irrespective of their race or ideology. *DeJonge* v. *Oregon,* 299 U. S. 353. The right of "association," like the right of belief (*Board of Education* v. *Barnette,* 319 U. S. 624), is more than the right to attend a meeting; it includes the right to express one's attitudes or philosophies by membership in a group or by affiliation with it or by other lawful means. Association in that context is a form of expression of opinion; and while it is not expressly included in the First Amendment its existence is necessary in making the express guarantees fully meaningful.

The foregoing cases suggest that specific guarantees in the Bill of Rights have penumbras, formed by emanations from those guarantees that help give them life and substance. See *Poe* v. *Ullman,* 367 U. S. 497, 516–522 (dissenting opinion). Various guarantees create zones of privacy. The right of association contained in the penumbra of the First Amendment is one, as we have seen. The Third Amendment in its prohibition

against the quartering of soldiers "in any house" in time of peace without the consent of the owner is another facet of that privacy. The Fourth Amendment explicitly affirms the "right of the people to be secure in their persons, houses, papers, and effects, against unreasonable searches and seizures." The Fifth Amendment in its Self-Incrimination Clause enables the citizen to create a zone of privacy which government may not force him to surrender to his detriment. The Ninth Amendment provides: "The enumeration in the Constitution, of certain rights, shall not be construed to deny or disparage others retained by the people."

The Fourth and Fifth Amendments were described in *Boyd* v. *United States,* 116 U. S. 616, 630, as protection against all governmental invasions "of the sanctity of a man's home and the privacies of life." We recently referred in *Mapp* v. *Ohio,* 367 U. S. 643, 656, to the Fourth Amendment as creating a "right to privacy, no less important than any other right carefully and particularly reserved to the people." . . .

The present case, then, concerns a relationship lying within the zone of privacy created by several fundamental constitutional guarantees. And it concerns a law which, in forbidding the *use* of contraceptives rather than regulating their manufacture or sale, seeks to achieve its goals by means having a maximum destructive impact upon that relationship. Such a law cannot stand in light of the familiar principle, so often applied by this Court, that a "governmental purpose to control or prevent activities constitutionally subject to state regulation may not be achieved by means which sweep unnecessarily broadly and thereby invade the area of protected freedoms." *NAACP* v. *Alabama,* 377 U. S. 288, 307. Would we allow the police to search the sacred precincts of marital bedrooms for telltale signs of the use of contraceptives? The very idea is repulsive to the notions of privacy surrounding the marriage relationship.

We deal with a right of privacy older than the Bill of Rights—older than our political parties, older than our school system. Marriage is a coming together for better or for worse, hopefully enduring, and intimate to the degree of being sacred. It is an association that promotes a way of life, not causes; a harmony in living, not political faiths; a bilateral loyalty, not commercial or social projects. Yet it is an association for as noble a purpose as any involved in our prior decisions.

Reversed.

MR. JUSTICE GOLDBERG, whom THE CHIEF JUSTICE and MR. JUSTICE BRENNAN join, concurring.

I agree with the Court that Connecticut's birth-control law unconstitutionally intrudes upon the right of marital privacy, and I join in its opinion and judgment. Although I have not accepted the view that "due process" as used in the Fourteenth Amendment incorporates all of the first eight Amendments (see my concurring opinion in *Pointer* v. *Texas*, 380 U. S. 400, 410, and the dissenting opinion of MR. JUSTICE BRENNAN in *Cohen* v. *Hurley*, 366 U. S. 117, 154), I do agree that the concept of liberty protects those personal rights that are fundamental, and is not confined to the specific terms of the Bill of Rights. My conclusion that the concept of liberty is not so restricted and that it embraces the right of marital privacy though that right is not mentioned explicitly in the Constitution is supported both by numerous decisions of this Court, referred to in the Court's opinion, and by the language and history of the Ninth Amendment. In reaching the conclusion that the right of marital privacy is protected, as being within the protected penumbra of specific guarantees of the Bill of Rights, the Court refers to the Ninth Amendment, *ante*, at 484. I add these words to emphasize the relevance of that Amendment to the Court's holding.

. . .

The Ninth Amendment reads, "The enumeration in the Constitution, of certain rights, shall not be construed to deny or disparage others retained by the people." The Amendment is almost entirely the work of James Madison. It was introduced in Congress by him and passed the House and Senate with little or no debate and virtually no change in language. It was proffered to quiet expressed fears that a bill of specifically enumerated rights could not be sufficiently broad to cover all essential rights and that the specific mention of certain rights would be interpreted as a denial that others were protected.

In presenting the proposed Amendment, Madison said:

"It has been objected also against a bill of rights, that, by enumerating particular exceptions to the grant of power, it would disparage those rights which were not placed in that enumeration; and it might follow by implication, that those rights which were not singled out, were intended to be assigned into the hands of the General Government, and were consequently insecure. This is one of the most plausible arguments I have ever heard urged against the admission of a bill of rights into this system; but, I conceive, that it may be guarded against. I have attempted it, as gentlemen may see by turning to the last clause of the fourth resolution [the Ninth Amendment]." I Annals of Congress 439 (Gales and Seaton ed. 1834).

Mr. Justice Story wrote of this argument against a bill of rights and the meaning of the Ninth Amendment:

"In regard to . . . [a] suggestion, that the affirmance of certain rights might disparage others, or might lead to argumentative implications in favor of other powers, it might be sufficient to say that such a course of reasoning could never be sustained upon any solid basis . . . . But a conclusive answer is, that such an attempt may be interdicted (as it has been) by a positive declaration in such a bill of rights that the enumeration of certain rights shall not be construed to deny or disparage others retained by the people." II Story, Commentaries on the Constitution of the United States 626–627 (5th ed. 1891).

He further stated, referring to the Ninth Amendment:

"This clause was manifestly introduced to prevent any perverse or ingenious misapplication of the well-known maxim, that an affirmation in particular cases implies a negation in all others; and, *e converso*, that a negation in particular cases implies an affirmation in all others." *Id.*, at 651.

These statements of Madison and Story make clear that the Framers did not intend that the first eight amendments be construed to exhaust the basic and fundamental rights which the Constitution guaranteed to the people.

. . .

. . . To hold that a right so basic and fundamental and so deep-rooted in our society as the right of privacy in marriage may be infringed because that right is not guaranteed in so many words by the first eight amendments to the Constitution is to ignore the Ninth Amendment and to give it no effect whatsoever. Moreover, a judicial construction that this fundamental right is not protected by the Constitution because it is not mentioned in explicit terms by one of the first eight amendments or elsewhere in the Constitution would violate the Ninth Amendment, which specifically states that "[t]he enumeration in the Constitution, of certain rights, shall not be *construed* to deny or disparage others retained by the people." (Emphasis added.)

. . .

MR. JUSTICE HARLAN, concurring in the judgment.

I fully agree with the judgment of reversal, but find myself unable to join the Court's opinion. The reason is that it seems to me to evince an approach to this case very much like that taken by my Brothers BLACK and STEWART in dissent, namely: the Due Process Clause of the Fourteenth Amendment does not touch this Connecticut statute unless the enactment is found to violate some right assured by the letter or penumbra of the Bill of Rights.

In other words, what I find implicit in the Court's opinion is that the "incorporation" doctrine may be used to *restrict* the reach of Fourteenth Amendment Due Process. For me this is just as unacceptable constitutional doctrine as is the use of the "incorporation" approach to *impose* upon the States all the requirements of the Bill of Rights as found in the provisions of the first eight amendments and in the decisions of this Court interpreting them. See, *e. g.*, my concurring opinions in *Pointer* v. *Texas*, 380 U. S. 400, 408, and *Griffin* v. *California*, 380 U. S. 609, 615, and my dissenting opinion in *Poe* v. *Ullman*, 367 U. S. 497, 522, at pp. 539–545.

In my view, the proper constitutional inquiry in this case is whether this Connecticut statute infringes the Due Process Clause of the Fourteenth Amendment because the enactment violates basic values "implicit in the concept of ordered liberty," *Palko* v. *Connecticut*, 302 U. S. 319, 325. For reasons stated at length in my dissenting opinion in *Poe* v. *Ullman, supra,* I believe that it does. While the relevant inquiry may be aided by resort to one or more of the provisions of the Bill of Rights, it is not dependent on them or any of their radiations. The Due Process Clause of the Fourteenth Amendment stands, in my opinion, on its own bottom.

. . .

MR. JUSTICE WHITE, concurring in the judgment.

In my view this Connecticut law as applied to married couples deprives them of "liberty" without due process of law, as that concept is used in the Fourteenth Amendment. I therefore concur in the judgment of the Court reversing these convictions under Connecticut's aiding and abetting statute.

. . .

MR. JUSTICE BLACK, with whom MR. JUSTICE STEWART joins, dissenting.

I agree with my Brother STEWART'S dissenting opinion. And like him I do not to any extent whatever base my view that this Connecticut law is constitutional on a belief that the law is wise or that its policy is a good one. In order that there may be no room at all to doubt why I vote as I do, I feel constrained to add that the law is every bit as offensive to me as it is to my Brethren of the majority and my Brothers HARLAN, WHITE and GOLDBERG who, reciting reasons why it is offensive to them, hold it unconstitutional. There is no single one of the graphic and eloquent strictures and criticisms fired at the policy of this Connecticut law either by the Court's opinion or by those of my concurring Brethren to which I cannot subscribe—except their conclusion that the evil qualities they see in the law make it unconstitutional.

Had the doctor defendant here, or even the nondoctor defendant, been convicted for doing nothing more than expressing opinions to persons coming to the clinic that certain contraceptive devices, medicines or practices would do them good and would be desirable, or for telling people how devices could be used, I can think of no reasons at this time why their expressions of views would not be protected by the First and Fourteenth Amendments, which guarantee freedom of speech. Cf. *Brotherhood of Railroad Trainmen* v. *Virginia ex rel. Virginia State Bar*, 377 U. S. 1; *NAACP* v. *Button*, 371 U. S. 415. But speech is one thing; conduct and physical activities are quite another. See, *e.g., Cox* v. *Louisiana*, 379 U. S. 536, 554–555; *Cox* v. *Louisiana*, 379 U. S. 559, 563–564; *id.*, 575–584 (concurring opinion); *Giboney* v. *Empire Storage & Ice Co.*, 336 U. S. 490; cf. *Reynolds* v. *United States*, 98 U. S. 145, 163–164. The two defendants here were active participants in an organization which gave physical examinations to women, advised them what kind of contraceptive devices or medicines would most likely be satisfactory for them, and then supplied the devices themselves, all for a graduated scale of fees, based on the family income. Thus these defendants admittedly engaged with others in a planned course of conduct to help people violate the Connecticut law. Merely because some speech was used in carrying on that conduct—just as in ordinary life some speech accompanies most kinds of conduct—we are not in my view justified in holding that the First Amendment forbids the State to punish their conduct.

. . . I get nowhere in this case by talk about a constitutional "right of privacy" as an emanation from one or more constitutional provisions. I like my privacy as well as the next one, but I am nevertheless compelled to admit that government has a right to invade it unless prohibited by some specific constitutional provision. For these reasons I cannot agree with the Court's judgment and the reasons it gives for holding this Connecticut law unconstitutional.

. . .

I realize that many good and able men have eloquently spoken and written, sometimes in rhapsodical strains, about the duty of this Court to keep the Constitution in tune with the times. The idea is that the Constitution must be changed from time to time and that this Court is charged with a duty to make those changes. For myself, I must with all deference reject that philosophy. The Constitution makers knew the need for change and provided for it. Amendments suggested by the people's elected representatives can be submitted to the people or their selected agents for ratification. That method of change was good for our Fathers, and being somewhat old-fashioned I must add it is good enough for me. And so, I cannot rely on the Due Process Clause or the Ninth Amendment or any mysterious and uncertain natural law concept as a reason for striking down this state law . . .

MR. JUSTICE STEWART, whom MR. JUSTICE BLACK joins, dissenting.

Since 1879 Connecticut has had on its books a law which forbids the use of contraceptives by anyone. I think this is an uncommonly silly law. As a practical matter, the law is obviously unenforceable, except in the oblique context of the present case. As a philosophical matter, I believe the use of contraceptives in the relationship of marriage should be left to personal and private choice, based upon each individual's moral, ethical, and religious beliefs. As a matter of social policy, I think professional counsel about methods of birth control should be available to all, so that each individual's choice can be meaningfully made. But we are not asked in this case to say whether we think this law is unwise, or even asinine. We are asked to hold that it violates the United States Constitution. And that I cannot do.

In the course of its opinion the Court refers to no less than six Amendments to the Constitution: the First, the Third, the Fourth, the Fifth, the Ninth, and the Fourteenth. But the Court does not say which of these Amendments, if any, it thinks is infringed by this Connecticut law.

. . .

The Court also quotes the Ninth Amendment, and my Brother GOLDBERG'S concurring opinion relies heavily upon it. But to say that the Ninth Amendment has anything to do with this case is to turn somersaults with history. The Ninth Amendment, like its companion the Tenth, which this Court held "states but a truism that all is retained which has not been surrendered," *United States* v. *Darby*, 312 U. S. 100, 124, was framed by James Madison and adopted by the States simply to make clear that the adoption of the Bill of Rights did not alter the plan that the *Federal* Government was to be a government of express and limited powers, and that all rights and powers not delegated to it were retained by the people and the individual States. Until today no member of this Court has ever suggested that the Ninth Amendment meant anything else, and the idea that a federal court could ever use the Ninth Amendment to annul a law passed by the elected representatives of the people of the State of Connecticut would have caused James Madison no little wonder.

What provision of the Constitution, then, does make this state law invalid? The Court says it is the right of privacy "created by several fundamental constitutional guarantees." With all deference, I can find no such general right of privacy in the Bill of Rights, in any other part of the Constitution, or in any case ever before decided by this Court.

At the oral argument in this case we were told that the Connecticut law does not "conform to current community standards." But it is not the function of this Court to decide cases on the basis of community standards. We are here to decide cases "agreeably to the Constitution and laws of the United States." It is the essence of judicial duty to subordinate our own personal views, our own ideas of what legislation is wise and what is not. If, as I should surely hope, the law before us does not reflect the standards of the people of Connecticut, the people of Connecticut can freely exercise their true Ninth and Tenth Amendment rights to persuade their elected representatives to repeal it. That is the constitutional way to take this law off the books.

Roe v. Wade

410 U. S. 113 (1973)

Using the pseudonym "Jane Roe," a pregnant single woman brought a class action challenging the constitutionality of a Texas law that made it a criminal offense to attempt an abortion except for the purpose of saving the mother's life. Other parties were allowed to intervene. A three-judge district court declared the Texas law void as vague and overbroadly infringing the rights under the Ninth and Fourteenth Amendments. Wade, the District Attorney of Dallas County, cross-appealed on the district court's grant of declaratory relief to Roe and to a physician who intervened, while Roe appealed on the district court's ruling to bar injunctive relief.

MR. JUSTICE BLACKMUN delivered the opinion of the Court.

This Texas federal appeal and its Georgia companion, *Doe* v. *Bolton, post,* p. 179, present constitutional challenges to state criminal abortion legislation. The Texas statutes under attack here are typical of those that have been in effect in many States for approximately a century. The Georgia statutes, in contrast, have a modern cast and are a legislative product that, to an extent at least, obviously reflects the influences of recent attitudinal change, of advancing medical knowledge and techniques, and of new thinking about an old issue.

We forthwith acknowledge our awareness of the sensitive and emotional nature of the abortion controversy, of the vigorous opposing views, even among physicians, and of the deep and seemingly absolute convictions that the subject inspires. One's philosophy, one's experiences, one's exposure to the raw edges of human existence, one's religious training, one's attitudes toward life and family and their values, and the moral standards one establishes and seeks to observe, are all likely to influence and to color one's thinking and conclusions about abortion.

In addition, population growth, pollution, poverty, and racial overtones tend to complicate and not to simplify the problem.

Our task, of course, is to resolve the issue by constitutional measurement, free of emotion and of predilection. We seek earnestly to do this, and, because we do, we have inquired into, and in this opinion place some emphasis upon, medical and medical-legal history and what that history reveals about man's attitudes toward the abortion procedure over the centuries. We bear in mind, too, Mr. Justice Holmes' admonition in his now-vindicated dissent in *Lochner* v. *New York*, 198 U. S. 45, 76 (1905):

"[The Constitution] is made for people of fundamentally differing views, and the accident of our finding certain opinions natural and familiar or novel and even shocking ought not to conclude our judgment upon the question whether statutes embodying them conflict with the Constitution of the United States."

I

The Texas statutes that concern us here are Arts. 1191–1194 and 1196 of the State's Penal Code. These make it a crime to "procure an abortion," as therein defined, or to attempt one, except with respect to "an abortion procured or attempted by medical advice for the purpose of saving the life of the mother." Similar statutes are in existence in a majority of the States.

. . .

II

Jane Roe, a single woman who was residing in Dallas County, Texas, instituted this federal action in March 1970 against the District Attorney of the county. She sought a declaratory judgment that the Texas criminal abortion statutes were unconstitutional on their face, and an injunction restraining the defendant from enforcing the statutes.

Roe alleged that she was unmarried and pregnant; that she wished to terminate her pregnancy by an abortion "performed by a competent, licensed physician, under safe, clinical conditions"; that she was unable to get a "legal" abortion in Texas because her life did not appear to be threatened by the continuation of her pregnancy; and that she could not afford to travel to another jurisdiction in order to secure a legal abortion under safe conditions. She claimed that the Texas statutes were unconstitutionally vague and that they abridged her right of personal privacy, protected by the First, Fourth, Fifth, Ninth, and Fourteenth Amendments. By an amendment to her complaint Roe purported to sue "on behalf of herself and all other women" similarly situated.

James Hubert Hallford, a licensed physician, sought and was granted leave to intervene in Roe's action. In his complaint he alleged that he had been arrested previously for violations of the Texas abortion statutes and that two such prosecutions were pending against him.

. . .

John and Mary Doe *[pseudonyms]*, a married couple, filed a companion complaint to that of Roe. . . . The Does alleged that they were a childless couple; that Mrs. Doe was suffering from a "neural-chemical" disorder; that her physician had "advised her to avoid pregnancy until such time as her condition has materially improved" (although a pregnancy at the present time would not present "a serious risk" to her life); that, pursuant to medical advice, she had discontinued use of birth control pills; and that if she should become pregnant, she would want to terminate the pregnancy by an abortion performed by a competent, licensed physician under safe, clinical conditions. . . .

[After deciding that Jane Roe had standing to sue, that she presented a justiciable controversy, that the termination of her 1970 pregnancy did not render the case moot, and that neither Hallford nor the Does had standing, the Court moves to the merits and substance of the case.]

V

The principal thrust of appellant's attack on the Texas statutes is that they improperly invade a right, said to be possessed by the pregnant woman, to choose to terminate her pregnancy. Appellant would discover this right in the concept of personal "liberty" embodied in the Fourteenth Amendment's Due Process Clause; or in personal, marital, familial, and sexual privacy said to be protected by the Bill of Rights or its penumbras, see *Griswold* v. *Connecticut*, 381 U. S. 479 (1965); *Eisenstadt* v. *Baird*, 405 U. S. 438 (1972); *id.*, at 460 (WHITE, J., concurring in result); or among those rights reserved to the people by the Ninth Amendment, *Griswold* v. *Connecticut*, 381 U. S., at 486 (Goldberg, J., concurring). Before addressing this claim, we feel it desirable briefly to survey, in several aspects, the history of abortion, for such insight as that history may afford us, and then to examine the state purposes and interests behind the criminal abortion laws.

VI

It perhaps is not generally appreciated that the restrictive criminal abortion laws in effect in a majority of States today are of relatively recent vintage. Those laws, generally proscribing abortion or its attempt at any time during pregnancy except when necessary to preserve the pregnant woman's life, are not of ancient or even of common-law origin. Instead, they derive from statutory changes effected, for the most part, in the latter half of the 19th century.

[The Court devotes seventeen pages to ancient attitudes toward abortion, the Hippocratic Oath, the common law, the English statutory law, the American law, and the positions of the American Medical Association, the American Public Health Association, and the American Bar Association.]

VII

Three reasons have been advanced to explain historically the enactment of criminal abortion laws in the 19th century and to justify their continued existence.

It has been argued occasionally that these laws were the product of a Victorian social concern to discourage illicit sexual conduct. Texas, however, does not advance this justification in the present case, and it appears that no court or commentator has taken the argument seriously. . . .

A second reason is concerned with abortion as a medical procedure. When most criminal abortion laws were first enacted, the procedure was a hazardous one for the woman. This was particularly true prior to the development of antisepsis. Antiseptic techniques, of course, were based on discoveries by Lister, Pasteur, and others first announced in 1867, but were not generally accepted and employed until about the turn of the century. Abortion mortality was high. Even after 1900, and perhaps until as late as the development of antibiotics in the 1940's, standard modern techniques such as dilation and curettage were not nearly so safe as they are today. Thus, it has been argued that a State's real concern in enacting a criminal abortion law was to protect the pregnant woman, that is, to restrain her from submitting to a procedure that placed her life in serious jeopardy.

Modern medical techniques have altered this situation. Appellants and various *amici* refer to medical data indicating that abortion in early pregnancy, that is, prior to the end of the first trimester, although not without its risk, is now relatively safe. Mortality rates for women undergoing early abortions, where the procedure is legal, appear to be as low as or lower than the rates for normal childbirth. . . .

The third reason is the State's interest—some phrase it in terms of duty—in protecting prenatal life. Some of the argument for this justification rests on the theory that a new human life is present from the moment of conception. The State's interest and general obligation to protect life then extends, it is argued, to prenatal life. Only when the life of the pregnant mother herself is at stake, balanced against the life she carries within her, should the interest of the embryo or fetus not prevail. Logically, of course, a legitimate state interest in this area need not stand or fall on acceptance of the belief that life begins at conception or at some other point prior to live birth. In assessing the State's interest, recognition may be given to the less rigid claim that as long as at least *potential* life is involved, the State may assert interests beyond the protection of the pregnant woman alone.

. . .

VIII

The Constitution does not explicitly mention any right of privacy. In a line of decisions, however, going back perhaps as far as *Union Pacific R. Co.* v. *Botsford,* 141 U. S. 250, 251 (1891), the Court has recognized that a right of personal privacy, or a guarantee of certain areas or zones of privacy, does exist under the Constitution. In varying contexts, the Court or individual Justices have, indeed, found at least the roots of that right in the First Amendment, *Stanley* v. *Georgia,* 394 U. S. 557, 564 (1969); in the Fourth and Fifth Amendments, *Terry* v. *Ohio,* 392 U. S. 1, 8–9 (1968), *Katz* v. *United States,* 389 U. S. 347, 350 (1967), *Boyd* v. *United States,* 116 U. S. 616 (1886), see *Olmstead* v. *United States,* 277 U. S. 438, 478 (1928) (Brandeis, J., dissenting); in the penumbras of the Bill of Rights, *Griswold* v. *Connecticut,* 381 U. S., at 484–485; in the Ninth Amendment, *id.,* at 486 (Goldberg, J., concurring); or in the concept of liberty guaranteed by the first section of the Fourteenth Amendment, see *Meyer* v. *Nebraska,* 262 U. S. 390, 399 (1923). These decisions make it clear that only personal rights that can be deemed "fundamental" or "implicit in the concept of ordered liberty," *Palko* v. *Connecticut,* 302 U. S. 319, 325 (1937), are included in this guarantee of personal privacy. They also make it clear that the right has some extension to activities relating to marriage, *Loving* v. *Virginia,* 388 U. S. 1, 12 (1967); procreation, *Skinner* v. *Oklahoma,* 316 U. S. 535, 541–542 (1942); contraception, *Eisenstadt* v. *Baird,* 405 U. S., at 453–454; *id.,* at 460, 463–465 (WHITE, J., concurring in result); family relationships, *Prince* v. *Massachusetts,* 321 U. S. 158, 166 (1944); and child rearing and education, *Pierce* v. *Society of Sisters,* 268 U. S. 510, 535 (1925), *Meyer* v. *Nebraska, supra.*

This right of privacy, whether it be founded in the Fourteenth Amendment's concept of personal liberty and restrictions upon state action, as we feel it is, or, as the District Court determined, in the Ninth Amendment's reservation of rights to the people, is broad enough to encompass a woman's decision whether or not to terminate her pregnancy. The detriment that the State would impose upon the pregnant woman by denying this choice altogether is apparent. Specific and direct harm medically diagnosable even in early pregnancy may be involved. Maternity, or additional offspring, may force upon the woman a distressful life and future. Psychological harm may be imminent. Mental and physical health may be taxed by child care. There is also the distress, for all concerned, associated with the unwanted child, and there is the problem of bringing a child into a family already unable, psychologically and otherwise, to care for it. In other cases, as in this one, the additional difficulties and continuing stigma of unwed motherhood may be involved. All these are factors the woman and her responsible physician necessarily will consider in consultation.

On the basis of elements such as these, appellant and some *amici* argue that the woman's right is absolute and that she is entitled to terminate her pregnancy at whatever time, in whatever way, and for whatever reason she alone chooses. With this we do not agree. Appellant's arguments that Texas either has no valid interest at all in regulating the abortion decision, or no interest strong enough to support any limitation upon the woman's sole determination, are unpersuasive. The Court's decisions recognizing a right of privacy also acknowledge that some state regulation in areas protected by that right is appropriate. As noted above, a State may properly assert important interests in safeguarding health, in maintaining medical standards, and in protecting potential life. At some point in pregnancy, these respective interests become sufficiently compelling to sustain regulation of the factors that govern the abortion decision. The privacy right involved, therefore, cannot be said to be absolute. In fact, it is not clear to us that the claim asserted by some *amici* that one has an unlimited right to do with one's body as one pleases bears a close relationship to the right of privacy previously articulated in the Court's decisions. The Court has refused to recognize an unlimited right of this kind in the past. *Jacobson* v. *Massachusetts,* 197 U. S. 11 (1905) (vaccination); *Buck* v. *Bell,* 274 U. S. 200 (1927) (sterilization).

We, therefore, conclude that the right of personal privacy includes the abortion decision, but that this right is not unqualified and must be considered against important state interests in regulation.

. . .

IX

. . .

A. The appellee and certain *amici* argue that the fetus is a "person" within the language and meaning of the Fourteenth Amendment. In support of this, they outline at length and in detail the well-known facts of fetal development. If this suggestion of personhood is established, the appellant's case, of course, collapses, for the fetus' right to life would then be guaranteed specifically by the Amendment. . . .

The Constitution does not define "person" in so many words. Section 1 of the Fourteenth Amendment contains three references to "person." The first, in defining "citizens," speaks of "persons born or naturalized in the United States." The word also appears both in the Due Process Clause and in the Equal Protection Clause. "Person" is used in other places in the Constitution: in the listing of qualifications for Representatives and Senators, Art. I, § 2, cl. 2, and § 3, cl. 3; in the Apportionment Clause, Art. I, § 2, cl. 3; in the Migration and Importation provision, Art. I, § 9, cl. 1; in the Emolument Clause, Art. I § 9, cl. 8; in the Electors provisions, Art. II, § 1, cl 2, and the superseded cl. 3; in the provision outlining qualifications for the office of President, Art. II, § 1, cl. 5; in the Extradition provisions, Art. IV, § 2, cl. 2, and the superseded Fugitive Slave Clause 3; and in the Fifth, Twelfth, and Twenty-second Amendments, as well as in §§ 2 and 3 of the Fourteenth Amendment. But in nearly all these instances, the use of the word is such that it has application only postnatally. None indicates, with any assurance, that it has any possible pre-natal application.

. . .

B. . . . Texas urges that, apart from the Fourteenth Amendment, life begins at conception and is present throughout pregnancy, and that, therefore, the State has a compelling interest in protecting that life from and after conception. We need not resolve the difficult question of when life begins. When those trained in the respective disciplines of medicine, philosophy, and theology are unable to arrive at any consensus, the judiciary, at this point in the development of man's knowledge, is not in a position to speculate as to the answer.

. . .

X

In view of all this, we do not agree that, by adopting one theory of life, Texas may override the rights of the pregnant woman that are at stake. We repeat, however, that the State does have an important and legitimate interest in preserving and protecting the health of the pregnant woman, whether she be a resident of the State or a nonresident who seeks medical consultation and treatment there, and that it has still *another* important and legitimate interest in protecting the potentiality of human life. These interests are separate and distinct. Each grows in substantiality as the woman approaches term and, at a point during pregnancy, each becomes "compelling."

With respect to the State's important and legitimate interest in the health of the mother, the "compelling" point, in the light of present medical knowledge, is at approximately the end of the first trimester. This is so because of the now-established medical fact, referred to above at 149, that until the end of the first trimester mortality in abortion may be less than mortality in normal childbirth. It follows that, from and after this point, a State may regulate the abortion procedure to the extent that the regulation reasonably relates to the preservation and protection of maternal health. Examples of permissible state regulation in this area are requirements as to the qualifications of the person who is to perform the abortion; as to the licensure of that person; as to the facility in which the procedure is to be performed, that is, whether it must be a hospital or may be a clinic or some other place of less-than-hospital status; as to the licensing of the facility; and the like.

This means, on the other hand, that, for the period of pregnancy prior to this "compelling" point, the attending physician, in consultation with his patient, is free to determine, without regulation by the State, that, in his medical judgment, the patient's pregnancy should be terminated. If that decision is reached, the judgment may be effectuated by an abortion free of interference by the State.

With respect to the State's important and legitimate interest in potential life, the "compelling" point is at viability. This is so because the fetus then presumably has the capability of meaningful life outside the mother's womb. State regulation protective of fetal life after viability thus has both logical and biological justifications. If the State is interested in protecting fetal life after viability, it may go so far as to proscribe abortion during that period, except when it is necessary to preserve the life or health of the mother.

Measured against these standards, Art. 1196 of the Texas Penal Code, in restricting legal abortions to those "procured or attempted by medical advice for the purpose of saving the life of the mother," sweeps too broadly. The statute makes no distinction between abortions performed early in pregnancy and those performed later, and it limits to a single reason, "saving" the mother's life, the legal justification for the procedure. The statute, therefore, cannot survive the constitutional attack made upon it here.

. . .

XI

To summarize and to repeat:

. . .

(a) For the stage prior to approximately the end of the first trimester, the abortion decision and its effectuation must be left to the medical judgment of the pregnant woman's attending physician.

(b) For the stage subsequent to approximately the end of the first trimester, the State, in promoting its interest in the health of the mother, may, if it chooses, regulate the abortion procedure in ways that are reasonably related to maternal health.

(c) For the stage subsequent to viability, the State in promoting its interest in the potentiality of human life may, if it chooses, regulate, and even proscribe, abortion except where it is necessary,

in appropriate medical judgment, for the preservation of the life or health of the mother.

. . .

MR. CHIEF JUSTICE BURGER, concurring

I agree that, under the Fourteenth Amendment to the Constitution, the abortion statutes of Georgia and Texas impermissibly limit the performance of abortions necessary to protect the health of pregnant women, using the term health in its broadest medical context. . . .

I do not read the Court's holdings today as having the sweeping consequences attributed to them by the dissenting Justices; the dissenting views discount the reality that the vast majority of physicians observe the standards of their profession, and act only on the basis of carefully deliberated medical judgments relating to life and health. Plainly, the Court today rejects any claim that the Constitution requires abortions on demand.

MR. JUSTICE DOUGLAS, concurring

. . .

MR. JUSTICE STEWART, concurring.

. . .

MR. JUSTICE REHNQUIST, dissenting.

. . .

II

. . . I have difficulty in concluding, as the Court does, that the right of "privacy" is involved in this case. Texas, by the statute here challenged, bars the performance of a medical abortion by a licensed physician on a plaintiff such as Roe. A transaction resulting in an operation such as this is not "private" in the ordinary usage of that word. Nor is the "privacy" that the Court finds here even a distant relative of the freedom from searches and seizures protected by the Fourth Amendment to the Constitution, which the Court has referred to as embodying a right to privacy. *Katz* v. *United States*, 389 U. S. 347 (1967).

If the Court means by the term "privacy" no more than that the claim of a person to be free from unwanted state regulation of consensual transactions may be a form of "liberty" protected by the Fourteenth Amendment, there is no doubt that similar claims have been upheld in our earlier decisions on the basis of that liberty. I agree with the statement of MR. JUSTICE STEWART in his concurring opinion that the "liberty," against deprivation of which without due process the Fourteenth Amendment protects, embraces more than the rights found in the Bill of Rights. But that liberty is not guaranteed absolutely against deprivation, only against deprivation without due process of law. The test traditionally applied in the area of social and economic legislation is whether or not a law such as that challenged has a rational relation to a valid state objective. *Williamson* v. *Lee Optical Co.*, 348 U. S. 483, 491 (1955). The Due Process Clause of the Fourteenth Amendment undoubtedly does place a limit, albeit a broad one, on legislative power to enact laws such as this. If the Texas statute were to prohibit an abortion even where the mother's life is in jeopardy, I have little doubt that such a statute would lack a rational relation to a valid state objective under the test stated in *Williamson, supra*. But the Court's sweeping invalidation of any restrictions on abortion during the first trimester is impossible to justify under that standard, and the conscious weighing of competing factors that the Court's opinion apparently substitutes for the established test is far more appropriate to a legislative judgment than to a judicial one.

. . .

While the Court's opinion quotes from the dissent of Mr. Justice Holmes in *Lochner* v. *New York*, 198 U. S. 45, 74 (1905), the result it reaches is more closely attuned to the majority opinion of Mr. Justice Peckham in that case. As in *Lochner* and similar cases applying substantive due process standards to economic and social welfare legislation, the adoption of the compelling state interest standard will inevitably require this Court to examine the legislative policies and pass on the wisdom of these policies in the very process of deciding whether a particular state interest put forward may or may not be "compelling." The decision here to break pregnancy into three distinct terms and to outline the permissible restrictions the State may impose in each one, for example, partakes more of judicial legislation than it does of a determination of the intent of the drafters of the Fourteenth Amendment.

. . .

MR. JUSTICE WHITE, with whom MR. JUSTICE REHNQUIST joins, dissenting.

At the heart of the controversy in these cases are those recurring pregnancies that pose no danger whatsoever to the life or health of the mother but are, nevertheless, unwanted for any one or more of a variety of reasons—convenience, family planning, economics, dislike of children, the embarrassment of illegitimacy, etc. The common claim before us is that for any one of such reasons, or for no reason at all, and without asserting or claiming any threat to life or health, any woman is entitled to an abortion at her request if she is able to find a medical advisor willing to undertake the procedure.

The Court for the most part sustains this position: During the period prior to the time the fetus becomes viable, the Constitution of the United States values the convenience, whim, or caprice of the putative mother more than the life or potential life of the fetus; the Constitution, therefore, guarantees the right to an abortion as against any state law or policy seeking to protect the fetus from an abortion not prompted by more compelling reasons of the mother.

With all due respect, I dissent. I find nothing in the language or history of the Constitution to support the Court's judgment. The Court simply fashions and announces a new constitutional right for pregnant mothers and, with scarcely any reason or authority for its action, invests that right with sufficient substance to override most existing state abortion statutes. The upshot is that the people and the legislatures of the 50 States are constitutionally disentitled to weigh the relative importance of the continued existence and development of the fetus, on the one hand, against a spectrum of possible impacts on the mother, on the other hand. As an exercise of raw judicial power, the Court perhaps has authority to do what it does today; but in my view its judgment is an improvident and extravagant exercise of the power of judicial review that the Constitution extends to this Court.

The Court apparently values the convenience of the pregnant mother more than the continued existence and development of the life or potential life that she carries. Whether or not I might agree with that marshaling of values, I can in no event join the Court's judgment because I find no constitutional warrant for imposing such an order of priorities on the people and legislatures of the States. In a sensitive area such as this, involving as it does issues over which reasonable men may easily and heatedly differ, I cannot accept the Court's exercise of its clear power of choice by interposing a constitutional barrier to state efforts to protect human life and by investing mothers and doctors with the constitutionally protected right to exterminate it. This issue, for the most part, should be left with the people and to the political processes the people have devised to govern their affairs.

. . .

Hyde Amendment of 1976: Congressional Debate

As an amendment to the Labor-HEW appropriations bill for fiscal 1977, Cong. Henry J. Hyde of Illinois offered language to prohibit any of the funds appropriated in the bill "to pay for abortions or to promote or encourage abortions." His amendment passed in the Committee of the Whole, 207–167, and again by the full House, 199–165. After action by the Senate and conference committee, the enacted language read: "None of the funds contained in this Act shall be used to perform abortions except where the life of the mother would be endangered if the fetus were carried to term." 90 Stat. 1434, § 209 (1976).

Mr. HYDE. Mr. Chairman, I offer an amendment.

The Clerk read as follows:

"Amendment offered by Mr. HYDE: On page 36, after line 9, add the following new section:

'SEC. 209. None of the funds appropriated under this Act shall be used to pay for abortions or to promote or encourage abortions.'"

Mr. HYDE. Mr. Chairman, this amendment may stimulate a lot of debate—but it need not—because I believe most Members know how they will vote on this issue.

Nevertheless, there are those of us who believe it is to the everlasting shame of this country that in 1973 approximately 800,000 legal abortions were performed in this country—and so it is fair to assume that this year over a million human lives will be destroyed because they are inconvenient to someone.

The unborn child facing an abortion can best be classified as a member of the innocently inconvenient and since the pernicious doctrine that some lives are more important than others seems to be persuasive with the pro-abortion forces, we who seek to protect that most defenseless and innocent of human lives, the unborn—seek to inhibit the use of Federal funds to pay for and thus encourage abortion as an answer to the human and compelling problem of an unwanted child.

We are all exercised at the wanton killing of the porpoise, the baby seal. We urge big game hunters to save the tiger, but we somehow turn away at the specter of a million human beings being violently destroyed because this great, society does not want them.

And make no mistake, an abortion is violent.

I think in the final analysis, you must determine whether or not the unborn person is human. If you think it is animal or vegetable then, of course, it is disposable like an empty beer can to be crushed and thrown out with the rest of the trash.

But medicine, biology, embryology, say that growing living organism is not animal or vegetable or mineral—but it is a human life.

And if you believe that human life is deserving

of due process of law—of equal protection of the laws, then you cannot in logic and conscience help fund the execution of these innocent defenseless human lives.

If we are to order our lives by the precepts of animal husbandry, then I guess abortion is an acceptable answer. If we human beings are not of a higher order than animals then let us save our pretentious aspirations for a better and more just world and recognize this is an anthill we inhabit and there are no such things as ideals or justice or morality.

Once conception has occurred a new and unique genetic package has been created, not a potential human being, but a human being with potential. For 9 months the mother provides nourishment and shelter, and birth is no substantial change, it is merely a change of address.

We are told that bringing an unwanted child into the world is an obscene act. Unwanted by whom? Is it too subtle a notion to understand it is more important to be a loving person than to be one who is loved. We need more people who are capable of projecting love.

We hear the claim that the poor are denied a right available to other women if we do not use tax money to fund abortions.

Well, make a list of all the things society denies poor women and let them make the choice of what we will give them.

Don't say "poor women, go destroy your young, and we will pay for it."

An innocent, defenseless human life, in a caring and humane society deserves better than to be flushed down a toilet or burned in an incinerator.

The promise of America is that life is not just for the privileged, the planned, or the perfect.

Mr. MYERS of Pennsylvania. Mr. Chairman, will the gentleman yield?

Mr. HYDE. I yield to the gentleman from Pennsylvania.

Mr. MYERS of Pennsylvania. Mr. Chairman, I support the gentleman's amendment. I think the basic question is, as the gentleman has put it, if we believe that human lives, in fact, are the objects which are being disposed of in plastic bags in the abortion clinics, then we certainly have a responsibility to protect them from the use of Federal funds to destroy them.

Mr. Chairman, I respect the gentleman for coming to the floor with this issue.

Mr. SNYDER. Mr. Chairman, will the gentleman yield?

Mr. HYDE. I yield to the gentleman from Kentucky.

Mr. SNYDER. Mr. Chairman, I want to associate myself with the gentleman in the well and commend the gentleman for his initiative in offering this amendment. I support it.

Mr. FLOOD. Mr. Chairman, I rise in opposition to the amendment.

Mr. Chairman, I would like the attention of the Members on this. I will tell them why. Nobody, but nobody in this room, has a better right to be standing here this minute on this subject, and everybody knows this, than the gentleman from Pennsylvania that is talking to the House now.

Mr. Chairman, everybody knows my position for many years with respect to abortion. I believe it is wrong, with a capital "W". It violates the most basic rights, the right of the unborn child, the right to life.

It is for that reason that I have supported for many, many years constitutional amendments which would address this very serious matter, and the Members know it. So, what am I doing down here now? Well, I will tell you. I oppose this amendment, and I will tell you why. Listen. This is blatantly discriminatory; that is why.

The Members do not like that? Of course they do not. It does not prohibit abortion. No, it does not prohibit abortion. It prohibits abortion for poor people. That is what it does. That is a horse of a different rolling stone. That is what it does. It does not require any change in the practice of the middle-income and the upper-income people. Oh, no. They are able to go to their private practitioners and get the service done for a fee. But, it does take away the option from those of our citizens who must rely on medicaid—and other public programs for medical care.

Now abortion, Mr. Chairman, abortion is not an economic issue; not at all. The morality—all right, the morality of abortion is no different for a poor family—the morality of abortion is no different for a poor family than it is for a rich family. Is that right? Of course: a standard of morality is a standard.

To accept—now, this is coming from me—to accept this amendment, the right of this country to impose on its poor citizens, impose on them a morality which it is not willing to impose on the rich as well, we would not dare do that. That is what this amendment does. To me, the choice is clear. Listen: A vote for this amendment is not a vote against abortion. It is a vote against poor people. That is what it is, as plain as the nose on your face.

This is not the place, on an appropriation bill, to address that kind of issue. This is not. Mr. Chairman, this is an appropriation bill. This is not a constitutional amendment.

I urge my colleagues to reject this amendment.

Mr. GUYER. Mr. Chairman, I move to strike the last word.

Mr. Chairman, this issue has all but become threadbare, largely due to the fact that we cannot get action from the proper committee to really correct the wrong by a constitutional amendment that would solve the problem totally and properly. In the meantime, I think that children should have a bill of rights, which the law has indicated. They have legal rights, they have human rights, they have civil rights, they have property rights and they have divine rights. What a woman does with her body is her own business.

What she does with the body of someone else is not her business.

I think that we here should go on record as safeguarding that most precious commodity, the gift of little children from God, who have a right to live.

Mr. BAUMAN. Mr. Chairman, I move to strike the requisite number of words, and I rise in support of the amendment.

Mr. Chairman, I want to compliment the gentleman from Illinois (Mr. HYDE) for taking the leadership in offering this amendment and I am pleased to have worked with him in its drafting. The gentleman from Illinois serves on the Committee on the Judiciary with great distinction. He, as well as the rest of the Members of this body, know that for the 3 years since the Supreme Court held that constitutional limitations against abortion on demand were wiped out, many of us in the Congress have sought a forum on the floor of both bodies so that the people could express their will on this issue through their representatives; and we have been denied that forum. We have had perfunctory hearings in this body this year, in which not even all Members were permitted to testify. In the other body hearings were held which, finally, again resulted in a refusal to permit a bill to come to the floor.

The gentleman from Pennsylvania objects to using an appropriation bill for the purpose of making public policy, but no question was raised against the form of this amendment, and none could be, because it is a legitimate limit on the expenditure of Federal funds.

The gentleman raises an interesting, but I think answerable, point on the grounds that this would discriminate against poor people. The answer is that we have not been able to pass a constitutional amendment that would permit the right to life, regardless of poverty or wealth. But I do not understand that the child of a poor parent has any less right to live than the child of a rich parent. If we could protect the right to life for all children, we would do it. But the fact of the matter is, under medicaid and other programs that are financed in this bill, the Federal Government has been paying for more than 300,000 abortions annually at a cost of $40 to $50 million.

I think the unborn children whose lives are being snuffed out, even though they may not be adults have a right to live, too, regardless of the mistaken and immoral Supreme Court decision. I do not think the taxpayers of the United States have any obligation to permit their money to be used in this manner for federally financed abortions. That is the only issue here today.

The gentleman from Pennsylvania is mistaken. This is indeed a vote on whether or not we are for the right to life for millions of people who are not being permitted to be born. And they are people. The vote we cast on this will show whether or not we are for the right to live. Let us permit, those who are children of the poor to live, and then let us go on and hold up our action as an example. Let the House act on this fundamental issue, so that perhaps one day soon all unborn people in the United States can be permitted to live.

This is the most fundamental issue that this House will ever address; it involves a precious right once accorded to every Member at some time in the past, the right to live. Let us not deny it to others.

I hope the House will support the amendment offered by the distinguished gentleman from Illinois.

. . .

Ms. ABZUG. Mr. Chairman, I move to strike the requisite number of words.

Mr. Chairman, the issue confronting this body is whether it will conduct itself with respect for the normal processes in which we engage and for which we were sent here. The issue being discussed here today is irrelevant, nongermane, and inappropriate as it relates to this measure, because the relief that is being sought by those who have a very particular point of view cannot be accomplished by this amendment.

This amendment is a cruel amendment, as was very ably pointed out by the chairman of the subcommittee presenting this appropriations bill. The passage of this amendment will not overcome the fact that every survey and every poll in this country show that a majority of people support the Supreme Court decision.

This is not to say that I and others who support the Supreme Court decision and the right to privacy that is protected therein do not respect the right of others to differ with us. We do respect the right of those who take an opposite point of view to differ with us on this subject. As a matter of fact, people like myself probably have more contact with those who differ on this subject than those who claim to represent them in the House. They understand our differences, and they and we understand that there is a right to differ with a decision. Still, there must be an understanding that those who differ as a matter of conscience or religious belief have no right to impose their views on others who also wish to exercise their rights in their own way.

The implementation of this amendment or an amendment like this, if agreed to in this House, will mean only one thing, and that will be, as was pointed out by the subcommittee chairman, to deny to some people the rights the majority have in this country.

The fact is that most of the women who would be denied medicaid for the purpose of obtaining an abortion would be forced to carry unwanted pregnancies to term.

I have sat here all day and listened to the enormous concern that the Members of this House have expressed about increasing the budget. Well, the cost to the Government for the fiscal year, after implementation of this particular section in the public assistance area, would be between $450 million and $565 million. That is what those who seek to impose this irrelevant legislation upon an appropriation bill will cost this country—$450 million to $565 million. But it will not achieve the objective that they seek, namely, to create a law that says abortions are not permitted, because those same abortions will continue.

These abortions will continue, but under much more difficult conditions. Up to 25,000 cases involving serious medical complications from self-induced abortions would result, and the hospital costs involved would be anywhere from $375 to $2,000 per patient. And some will die—and you can calculate the social cost of that.

Language in the HEW bill restraining abortion will a neutral position. By refusing medicaid reimbursement for abortions performed on poor women, the Government is de facto putting itself in the position of countenancing abortion for those who can pay for it but denying it to others who cannot. That would be clearly a discriminatory action, one which may result in legal action against the Government, if not indeed against this Congress itself.

Mr. Chairman, it seems to me that we have a form of relief. If this Congress wants to change the law of the Supreme Court, then what it should do so by appropriate procedures. There are hearings taking place in the Judiciary Committee. There have been extensive hearings on amendments which seek to reverse the decision of the Supreme Court. That is the proper and the orderly method in which we should proceed, and that is the path that should be taken by those who wish indeed to put an end to the Supreme Court decision. We should not act in this improper, disorderly way of attempting to put legislation in an appropriation bill. This will not solve the problem.

Hearings have taken place in the Judiciary Committee. That is what was wanted. Petitions were circulated in this House demanding that there be hearings.

I see the chairman of the Committee on the Judiciary here. He has indeed held these hearings.

Some say that is not enough and there are individuals who seek only to reflect their own point of view in this lawless and inappropriate way; and not the point of view of the majority who seek to distort the legislative process; and who seek to deprive the poor person, who always carries the burden of discrimination now once again.

Mr. Chairman, I hope the Members of this House will not take this improper action. The committee has to act. It will act. We can then proceed lawfully.

The CHAIRMAN. The time of the gentlewoman from New York (Ms. ABZUG) has expired.

(On request of Mr. BUTLER and by unanimous consent, Ms. ABZUG was allowed to proceed for 1 additional minute.)

Mr. BUTLER. Mr. Chairman, will the gentlewoman yield?

Ms. ABZUG. I yield to the gentleman from Virginia.

Mr. BUTLER. As a member of the subcommittee which has considered these hearings, I would like to deny the suggestions that they are merely perfunctory.

It seems to me that we have to do this in some detail. The reason there has not been an amendment reported out up to this moment is that I do not find a consensus among our witnesses or among the subcommittee which would indicate that any amendment would pass this House or, indeed, pass the Judiciary Subcommittee.

I would like to support those who oppose this amendment. I would like to join with them. I do not think this is an option which should be denied by us while it remains available to the wealthy under the present state of the law.

For that reason, it is my intention to vote against the amendment offered by the gentleman from Illinois.

Mr. Chairman, I thank the gentlewoman from New York (Ms. ABZUG) for yielding.

Mr. KOCH. Mr. Chairman, I am opposed to the Hyde amendment. And I believe even those who are opposed to the Supreme Court decision allowing abortion as a constitutional right are not for this all encompassing amendment. This amendment would deny an abortion even to a woman whose very life would be lost without the abortion. I cannot believe that the Members here would be so heartless. I urge a no vote.

. . .

Harris v. McRae

448 U.S. 297 (1980)

Title XIX of the Social Security Act established the Medicaid program in 1965 to provide federal financial assistance to states that choose to reimburse certain costs of medical treatment for needy persons. Since 1976, versions of the "Hyde Amendment" passed by Congress severely limited the use of any federal funds to reimburse the cost of abortions under the Medicaid program. Cora McRae brought an action in federal court, seeking to enjoin enforcement of the Hyde Amendment on the ground that it violated the Due Process Clause of the Fifth Amendment and the Religion Clauses of the First Amendment. The defendant was Patricia R. Harris, Secretary of Health and Human Services. The federal court held that the Amendment violated the equal protection component of the Fifth Amendment's Due Process Clause and the Free Exercise Clause of the First Amendment.

MR. JUSTICE STEWART delivered the opinion of the Court.

This case presents statutory and constitutional questions concerning the public funding of abortions under Title XIX of the Social Security Act, commonly known as the "Medicaid" Act, and recent annual Appropriations Acts containing the so-called "Hyde Amendment." The statutory question is whether Title XIX requires a State that participates in the Medicaid program to fund the cost of medically necessary abortions for which federal reimbursement is unavailable under the Hyde Amendment. The constitutional question, which arises only if Title XIX imposes no such requirement, is whether the Hyde Amendment, by denying public funding for certain medically necessary abortions, contravenes the liberty or equal protection guarantees of the Due Process Clause of the Fifth Amendment, or either of the Religion Clauses of the First Amendment.

I

The Medicaid program was created in 1965, when Congress added Title XIX to the Social Security Act, 79 Stat. 343, as amended, 42 U.S.C. § 1396 *et seq.* (1976 ed. and Supp. II), for the purpose of providing federal financial assistance to States that choose to reimburse certain costs of medical treatment for needy persons. Although participation in the Medicaid program is entirely optional, once a State elects to participate, it must comply with the requirements of Title XIX.

One such requirement is that a participating State agree to provide financial assistance to the "categorically needy" with respect to five general areas of medical treatment: (1) inpatient hospital services, (2) outpatient hospital services, (3) other laboratory and X-ray services, (4) skilled nursing facilities services, periodic screening and diagnosis of children, and family planning services, and (5) services of physicians. 42 U.S.C. §§ 1396a (a)(13)(B), 1396d (a)(1)–(5). Although a participating State need not "provide funding for all medical treatment falling within the five general categories, [Title XIX] does require that [a] state Medicaid pla[n] establish 'reasonable standards . . . for determining . . . the extent of medical assistance under the plan which . . . are consistent with the objectives of [Title XIX].' 42 U.S.C. § 1396a (a)(17)." *Beal* v. *Doe*, 432 U.S. 438, 441.

Since September 1976, Congress has prohibited—either by an amendment to the annual appropriations bill for the Department of Health, Education, and Welfare or by a joint resolution—the use of any federal funds to reimburse the cost of abortions under the Medicaid program except under certain specified circumstances. This funding restriction is commonly known as the "Hyde Amendment," after its original congressional sponsor, Representative Hyde. The current version of the Hyde Amendment, applicable for fiscal year 1980, provides:

"[N]one of the funds provided by this joint resolution shall be used to perform abortions except where the life of the mother would be endangered if the fetus were carried to term; or except for such medical procedures necessary for the victims of rape or incest when such rape or incest has been reported promptly to a law enforcement agency or public health service." Pub. L. 96–123, § 109, 93 Stat. 926.

See also Pub. L. 96–86, § 118, 93 Stat. 662. This version of the Hyde Amendment is broader than that applicable for fiscal year 1977, which did not include the "rape or incest" exception, Pub. L. 94–439, § 209, 90 Stat. 1434, but narrower than that applicable for most of fiscal year 1978, and all of fiscal year 1979, which had an additional exception for "instances where severe and long-lasting physical health damage to the mother would result if the pregnancy were carried to term when so determined by two physicians," Pub. L. 95–205, § 101, 91 Stat. 1460; Pub. L. 95–480, § 210, 92 Stat. 1586.

On September 30, 1976, the day on which Congress enacted the initial version of the Hyde Amendment, these consolidated cases were filed in the District Court for the Eastern District of New York. . . .

[The District Court entered a preliminary injunction to prohibit the Secretary from enforcing the Hyde Amendment; the Supreme Court vacated the injunction and remanded the case in light of Beal v. Doe, *432 U.S. 438, and* Maher v. Roe, *432 U.S. 464; the District Court then filed an opinion invalidating all versions of the Hyde Amendment on constitutional grounds, including the equal protection component of the Fifth Amendment's Due Process*

Clause and the Free Exercise Clause of the Fifth Amendment.]

II

It is well settled that if a case may be decided on either statutory or constitutional grounds, this Court, for sound jurisprudential reasons, will inquire first into the statutory question. This practice reflects the deeply rooted doctrine "that we ought not to pass on questions of constitutionality . . . unless such adjudication is unavoidable." *Spector Motor Service, Inc.* v. *McLaughlin*, 323 U.S. 101, 105. Accordingly, we turn first to the question whether Title XIX requires a State that participates in the Medicaid program to continue to fund those medically necessary abortions for which federal reimbursement is unavailable under the Hyde Amendment. If a participating State is under such an obligation, the constitutionality of the Hyde Amendment need not be drawn into question in the present case, for the availability of medically necessary abortions under Medicaid would continue, with the participating State shouldering the total cost of funding such abortions.

[The Court interprets Title XIX as part of "cooperative federalism" in which the federal government contributes to participating states. It concludes that Title XIX does not require a participating state to include in its plan any service for which Congress has withheld federal funding.]

III

Having determined that Title XIX does not obligate a participating State to pay for those medically necessary abortions for which Congress has withheld federal funding, we must consider the constitutional validity of the Hyde Amendment. The appellees assert that the funding restrictions of the Hyde Amendment violate several rights secured by the Constitution—(1) the right of a woman, implicit in the Due Process Clause of the Fifth Amendment, to decide whether to terminate a pregnancy, (2) the prohibition under the Establishment Clause of the First Amendment against any "law respecting an establishment of religion," and (3) the right to freedom of religion protected by the Free Exercise Clause of the First Amendment. The appellees also contend that, quite apart from substantive constitutional rights, the Hyde Amendment violates the equal protection component of the Fifth Amendment.

. . .

A

We address first the appellees' argument that the Hyde Amendment, by restricting the availability of certain medically necessary abortions under Medicaid, impinges on the "liberty" protected by the Due Process Clause as recognized in *Roe* v. *Wade*, 410 U.S. 113, and its progeny.

[Wade recognized a woman's freedom to decide whether to terminate a pregnancy in the early stages, but the interests of a state grew substantially as the woman approached term. In Maher v. Roe, 432 U.S. 464, the Court held that the constitutional freedom recognized in Wade did not prevent a state from making a value judgment by providing funds to favor childbirth over abortion. A state has no constitutional obligation to subsidize abortions.]

The Hyde Amendment, like the Connecticut welfare regulation at issue in *Maher*, places no governmental obstacle in the path of a woman who chooses to terminate her pregnancy, but rather, by means of unequal subsidization of abortion and other medical services, encourages alternative activity deemed in the public interest. The present case does differ factually from *Maher* insofar as that case involved a failure to fund nontherapeutic abortions, whereas the Hyde Amendment withholds funding of certain medically necessary abortions. Accordingly, the appellees argue that because the Hyde Amendment affects a significant interest not present or asserted in *Maher*—the interest of a woman in protecting her health during pregnancy—and because that interest lies at the core of the personal constitutional freedom recognized in *Wade*, the present case is constitutionally different from *Maher*. It is the appellees' view that to the extent that the Hyde Amendment withholds funding for certain medically necessary abortions, it clearly impinges on the constitutional principle recognized in *Wade*.

. . . regardless of whether the freedom of a woman to choose to terminate her pregnancy for health reasons lies at the core or the periphery of the due process liberty recognized in *Wade*, it simply does not follow that a woman's freedom of choice carries with it a constitutional entitlement to the financial resources to avail herself of the full range of protected choices. The reason why was explained in *Maher:* although government may not place obstacles in the path of a woman's exercise of her freedom of choice, it need not remove those not of its own creation. Indigency falls in the latter category. The financial constraints that restrict an indigent woman's ability to enjoy the full range of constitutionally protected freedom of choice are the product not of governmental restrictions on access to abortions, but rather of her indigency. . . .

. . . It cannot be that because government may not prohibit the use of contraceptives, *Griswold* v. *Connecticut*, 381 U.S. 479, or prevent parents from sending their child to a private school, *Pierce* v. *Society of Sisters*, 268 U.S. 510, government, therefore, has an affirmative constitutional obligation to ensure that all persons have the financial resources to obtain contraceptives or send their children to private schools. To translate the limitation on governmental power implicit in the Due Process Clause into an affirmative funding obligation would require Congress to subsidize the medically necessary abortion of an indigent woman even if Congress had not enacted a Medicaid program to subsidize other medically necessary services. Nothing in the Due Process Clause supports such an extraordinary result. Whether freedom of choice that is constitutionally protected warrants federal subsidization is a question for Congress to answer, not a matter of constitutional entitlement. Accordingly, we conclude that the Hyde Amendment does not impinge on the due process liberty recognized in *Wade*.

B

The appellees also argue that the Hyde Amendment contravenes rights secured by the Religion Clauses of the First Amendment. It is the appellees' view that the Hyde Amendment violates the Establishment Clause because it incorporates into law the doctrines of the Roman Catholic Church concerning the sinfulness of abortion and the time at which life commences. Moreover, insofar as a woman's decision to seek a medically necessary abortion may be a product of her religious beliefs under certain Protestant and Jewish tenets, the appellees assert that the funding limitations of the Hyde Amendment impinge on the freedom of religion guaranteed by the Free Exercise Clause.

1

It is well settled that "a legislative enactment does not contravene the Establishment Clause if it has a secular legislative purpose, if its principal or primary effect neither advances nor inhibits religion, and if it does not foster an excessive governmental entanglement with religion." *Committee for Public Education* v. *Regan*, 444 U.S. 646, 653. Applying this standard, the District Court properly concluded that the Hyde Amendment does not run afoul of the Establishment Clause. Although neither a State nor the Federal Government can constitutionally "pass laws which aid one religion, aid all religions, or prefer one religion over another," *Everson* v. *Board of Education*, 330 U.S. 1, 15, it does not follow that a statute violates the Establishment Clause because it "happens to coincide or harmonize with the tenets of some or all religions." *McGowan* v. *Maryland*, 366 U.S. 420, 442. That the Judaeo-Christian religions oppose stealing does not mean that a State or the Federal Government may not, consistent with the Establishment Clause, enact laws prohibiting larceny. *Ibid*. The Hyde Amendment, as the District Court noted, is as much a reflection of "traditionalist" values towards abortion, as it is an embodiment of the views of any particular religion. 491 F. Supp., at 741. See also *Roe* v. *Wade*, 410 U.S., at 138–141. In sum, we are convinced that the fact that the funding restrictions in the Hyde Amendment may coincide with the religious tenets of the Roman Catholic Church does not, without more, contravene the Establishment Clause.

2

We need not address the merits of the appellees' arguments concerning the Free Exercise Clause, because the appellees lack standing to raise a free exercise challenge to the Hyde Amendment. The named appellees fall into three categories: (1) the indigent pregnant women who sued on behalf of other women similarly situated, (2) the two officers of the Women's Division, and (3) the Women's Division itself. The named appellees in the first category lack standing to challenge the Hyde Amendment on free exercise grounds because none alleged, much less proved, that she sought an abortion under compulsion of religious belief. See *McGowan* v. *Maryland, supra*, at 429. Although the named appellees in the second category did provide a detailed description of their religious beliefs, they failed to allege either that they are or expect to be pregnant or that they are eligible to receive Medicaid. These named appellees, therefore, lack the personal stake in the controversy needed to confer standing to raise such a challenge to the Hyde Amendment. See *Warth* v. *Seldin*, 422 U.S. 490, 498–499.

Finally, although the Women's Division alleged that its membership includes "pregnant Medicaid eligible women who, as a matter of religious practice and in accordance with their conscientious beliefs, would choose but are precluded or discouraged from obtaining abortions reimbursed by Medicaid because of the Hyde Amendment," the Women's Division does not satisfy the standing requirements for an organization to assert the rights of its membership. . . . the claim asserted here is one that ordinarily requires individual participation. . . .

C

It remains to be determined whether the Hyde Amendment violates the equal protection component of the Fifth Amendment. This challenge is premised on the fact that, although federal reimbursement is available under Medicaid for medically necessary services generally, the Hyde Amendment does not permit federal reimbursement of all medically necessary abortions. The District Court held, and the appellees argue here, that this selective subsidization violates the constitutional guarantee of equal protection.

The guarantee of equal protection under the Fifth Amendment is not a source of substantive rights or liberties . . .

1

For the reasons stated above, we have already concluded that the Hyde Amendment violates no constitutionally protected substantive rights. We now conclude as well that it is not predicated on a constitutionally suspect classification. In reaching this conclusion, we again draw guidance from the Court's decision in *Maher* v. *Roe*. . . .

It is our view that the present case is indistinguishable from *Maher* in this respect. Here, as in *Maher*, the principal impact of the Hyde Amendment falls on the indigent. But that fact does not itself render the funding restriction constitutionally invalid, for this Court has held repeatedly that poverty, standing alone, is not a suspect classification. See, *e.g., James* v. *Valtierra*, 402 U.S. 137. That *Maher* involved the refusal to fund nontherapeutic abortions, whereas the present case involves the refusal to fund medically necessary abortions, has no bearing on the factors that render a classification "suspect" within the meaning of the constitutional guarantee of equal protection.

2

The remaining question then is whether the Hyde Amendment is rationally related to a legitimate governmental objective. It is the Government's position that the Hyde Amendment bears a rational relationship to its legitimate interest in protecting the potential life of the fetus. We agree.

In *Wade*, the Court recognized that the State has an "important and legitimate interest in protecting the potentiality of human life." 410 U.S., at 162. That interest was found to exist throughout a pregnancy, "grow[ing] in substantiality as the woman approaches term." *Id.*, at 162–163. See also *Beal* v. *Doe*, 432 U.S., at 445–446. Moreover, in *Maher*, the Court held that Connecticut's decision to fund the costs associated with childbirth but not those associated with nontherapeutic abortions was a rational means of advancing the legitimate state interest in protecting potential life by encouraging childbirth. 432 U.S., at 478–479. See also *Poelker* v. *Doe*, 432 U.S. 519, 520–521.

It follows that the Hyde Amendment, by encouraging childbirth except in the most urgent circumstances, is rationally related to the legitimate governmental objective of protecting potential life. By subsidizing the medical expenses of indigent women who carry their pregnancies to term while not subsidizing the comparable expenses of women who undergo abortions (except those whose lives are threatened), Congress has established incentives that make childbirth a more attractive alternative than abortion for persons eligible for Medicaid. These incentives bear a direct relationship to the legitimate congressional interest in protecting potential life. . . .

After conducting an extensive evidentiary hearing into issues surrounding the public funding of abortions, the District Court concluded that "[t]he interests of . . . the federal government . . . in the fetus and in preserving it are not sufficient, weighed in the balance with the woman's threatened health, to justify withdrawing medical assistance unless the woman consents . . . to carry the fetus to term." 491 F. Supp., at 737. In making an independent appraisal of the competing interests involved here, the District Court went beyond the judicial function. Such decisions are entrusted under the Constitution to Congress, not the courts. It is the role of the courts only to ensure that congressional decisions comport with the Constitution.

. . .

IV

For the reasons stated in this opinion, we hold that a State that participates in the Medicaid program is not obligated under Title XIX to continue to fund those medically necessary abortions for which federal reimbursement is unavailable under the Hyde Amendment. We further hold that the funding restrictions of the Hyde Amendment violate neither the Fifth Amendment nor the Establishment Clause of the First Amendment. It is also our view that the appellees lack standing to raise a challenge to the Hyde Amendment under the Free Exercise Clause of the First Amendment. Accordingly, the judgment of the District Court is reversed, and the case is remanded to that court for further proceedings consistent with this opinion.

It is so ordered.

MR. JUSTICE WHITE, concurring.

. . .

MR. JUSTICE BRENNAN, with whom MR. JUSTICE MARSHALL and MR. JUSTICE BLACKMUN join, dissenting.

I agree entirely with my Brother STEVENS that the State's interest in protecting the potential life of the fetus cannot justify the exclusion of financially and medically needy women from the benefits to which they would otherwise be entitled solely because the treatment that a doctor has concluded is medically necessary involves an abortion. See *post*, at 351–352. I write separately to express my continuing disagreement with the Court's mischaracterization of the nature of the fundamental right recognized in *Roe* v. *Wade*, 410 U.S. 113 (1973), and its misconception of the manner in which that right is infringed by federal and state legislation withdrawing all funding for medically necessary abortions.

Roe v. *Wade* held that the constitutional right to personal privacy encompasses a woman's decision whether or not to terminate her pregnancy. *Roe* and its progeny established that the pregnant woman has a right to be free from state interference with her choice to have an abortion—a right which, at least prior to the end of the first trimester, absolutely prohibits any governmental regulation of that highly personal decision. The proposition for which these cases stand thus is not that the State is under an affirmative obligation to ensure access to abortions for all who may desire them; it is that the State must refrain from wielding its enormous power and influence in a manner that might burden the pregnant woman's freedom to choose whether to have an abortion. The Hyde Amendment's denial of public funds for medically necessary abortions plainly intrudes upon this constitutionally protected decision, for both by design and in effect it serves to coerce indigent pregnant women to bear children that they would otherwise elect not to have.

. . .

MR. JUSTICE MARSHALL, dissenting.

. . .

III

The consequences of today's opinion—consequences to which the Court seems oblivious—

are not difficult to predict. Pregnant women denied the funding necessary to procure abortions will be restricted to two alternatives. First, they can carry the fetus to term—even though that route may result in severe injury or death to the mother, the fetus, or both. If that course appears intolerable, they can resort to self-induced abortions or attempt to obtain illegal abortions—not because bearing a child would be inconvenient, but because it is necessary in order to protect their health. The result will not be to protect what the Court describes as "the legitimate governmental objective of protecting potential life," *ante*, at 325, but to ensure the destruction of both fetal and maternal life. "There is another world 'out there,' the existence of which the Court . . . either chooses to ignore or fears to recognize." *Beal* v. *Doe*, 432 U.S., at 463 (BLACKMUN, J., dissenting). In my view, it is only by blinding itself to that other world that the Court can reach the result it announces today.

. . .

MR. JUSTICE BLACKMUN, dissenting.

I join the dissent of MR. JUSTICE BRENNAN and agree wholeheartedly with his and MR. JUSTICE STEVENS' respective observations and descriptions of what the Court is doing in this latest round of "abortion cases." I need add only that I find what I said in dissent in *Beal* v. *Doe*, 432 U.S. 438, 462 (1977), and its two companion cases, *Maher* v. *Roe*, 432 U.S. 464 (1977), and *Poelker* v. *Doe*, 432 U.S. 519 (1977), continues for me to be equally pertinent and equally applicable in these Hyde Amendment cases. There is "condescension" in the Court's holding that "she may go elsewhere for her abortion"; this is "disingenuous and alarming"; the Government "punitively impresses upon a needy minority its own concepts of the socially desirable, the publicly acceptable, and the morally sound"; the "financial argument, of course, is specious"; there truly is "another world 'out there,' the existence of which the Court, I suspect, either chooses to ignore or fears to recognize"; the "cancer of poverty will continue to grow"; and "the lot of the poorest among us," once again, and still, is not to be bettered.

MR. JUSTICE STEVENS, dissenting.

"The federal sovereign, like the States, must govern impartially. The concept of equal justice under law is served by the Fifth Amendment's guarantee of due process, as well as by the Equal Protection Clause of the Fourteenth Amendment." *Hampton* v. *Mow Sun Wong*, 426 U.S. 88, 100. When the sovereign provides a special benefit or a special protection for a class of persons, it must define the membership in the class by neutral criteria; it may not make special exceptions for reasons that are constitutionally insufficient.

. . .

Having decided to alleviate some of the hardships of poverty by providing necessary medical care, the government must use neutral criteria in distributing benefits. It may not deny benefits to a financially and medically needy person simply because he is a Republican, a Catholic, or an Oriental—or because he has spoken against a program the government has a legitimate interest in furthering. In sum, it may not create exceptions for the sole purpose of furthering a governmental interest that is constitutionally subordinate to the individual interest that the entire program was designed to protect. The Hyde Amendments not only exclude financially and medically needy persons from the pool of benefits for a constitutionally insufficient reason; they also require the expenditure of millions and millions of dollars in order to thwart the exercise of a constitutional right, thereby effectively inflicting serious and long-lasting harm on impoverished women who want and need abortions for valid medical reasons. In my judgment, these Amendments constitute an unjustifiable, and indeed blatant, violation of the sovereign's duty to govern impartially.

I respectfully dissent.

Committee to Defend Reprod. Rights v. Myers

625 P.2d 779 (Cal. 1981)

California passed legislation to restrict the circumstances under which public funds would be authorized to pay for abortions for indigent women. Although the Supreme Court in *Harris* v. *McRae* (1980) had upheld restrictions on federal Medicaid funding of abortions similar to those in the California statutes, the Supreme Court of California was at liberty to reach a different conclusion when interpreting the safeguards guaranteed not by the Federal Constitution but by the California Constitution.

TOBRINER, Justice.

Plaintiffs, representing indigent women throughout the state, challenge the constitutionality under the California Constitution of provisions in the 1978, 1979, and 1980 California Budget Acts that limit Medi-Cal funding for abortions. Although the acts differ in minor respects, all afford full funding of medical expenses incurred by indigent women who decide to bear a child, but, except in a few limited circumstances, deny funding to those indigent women who choose to have an abortion. Plaintiffs contend that this selective or discriminatory public funding scheme violates a number of distinct constitutional guarantees, in particular the women's rights of privacy, due process, and equal protection of the laws.

At the outset, to dispel certain misconceptions that have appeared in this case, we must clarify the precise, narrow legal issue before this court. First, this case does not turn on the morality or immorality of abortion, and most decidedly does not concern the personal views of the individual justices as to the wisdom of the legislation itself or the ethical considerations involved in a woman's individual decision whether or not to bear a child. Indeed, although in this instance the Legislature has adopted restrictions which discriminate against women who choose to have an abortion, similar constitutional issues would arise if the Legislature—as a population control measure, for example—funded Medi-Cal abortions but refused to provide comparable medical care for poor women who choose childbirth. Thus, the constitutional question before us does not involve a weighing of the value of abortion as against childbirth, but instead concerns the protection of either procreative choice from discriminatory governmental treatment.

Second, contrary to the suggestion of the defendants and the dissent, the question presented is not whether the state is generally obligated to subsidize the exercise of constitutional rights for those who cannot otherwise afford to do so; plaintiffs do not contend that the state would be required to fund abortions for poor women if the state had not chosen to fund medical services for poor women who choose to bear a child. Rather, we face the much narrower question of whether the state, having enacted a general program to provide medical services to the poor, may selectively withhold such benefits from otherwise qualified persons solely because such persons seek to exercise their constitutional right of procreative choice in a manner which the state does not favor and does not wish to support.

In defending the constitutionality of the provision in question, the Attorney General relies most prominently upon the recent decision of the United States Supreme Court in *Harris* v. *McRae* (1980),——U.S.——, 100 S.Ct. 2671, 65 L.Ed.2d 784 (hereafter *McRae).* In *McRae,* the Supreme Court, by a closely divided vote (five to four), upheld restrictions on federal Medicaid funding of abortions similar to those in the state acts before us. As the Attorney General acknowledges, however, the *McRae* case did not present any question under the California Constitution and consequently the justices of the high court neither addressed nor resolved the question of the compatibility of such a statutory scheme with our state constitutional guarantees. It is this question of state constitutional law, not resolved by *McRae*, which we must decide in the present case.

In addressing this issue, we shall explain initially that the analysis utilized by the majority of the United States Supreme Court in *McRae* differs substantially from the analysis mandated by the controlling California authorities and thus cannot be followed here. In *McRae*, the five-justice majority acknowledged that the governmental program provided unequal treatment in the distribution of public benefits solely on the basis of how an individual woman exercised her basic constitutional right of procreative choice. The court concluded, however, that the federal Constitution required no special justification for such discriminatory treatment so long as the program placed no new obstacles in the path of the woman seeking to exercise her constitutional right. (100 S.Ct. at p. 2688.)

By contrast, the governing California cases, discussed at length below, have long held that a discriminatory or restricted government benefit program demands special scrutiny whether or not it erects some new or additional obstacle that impedes the exercise of constitutional rights. In a series of cases reaching back more than three decades, this court has developed and applied a three-part test for evaluating the constitutionality of statutory schemes, like the program at issue here, that condition the receipt of benefits upon a recipient's waiver of a constitutional right or upon his exercise of such right in a manner which the government approves.

In order to sustain the constitutionality of such a scheme under the California Constitution, the state must demonstrate (1) "that the imposed conditions relate to the purposes of the legislation which confers the benefit or privilege"; (2) that "the utility of imposing the conditions . . . manifestly outweigh[s] any resulting impairment of constitutional rights"; and (3) that there are no "less offensive alternatives" available for achieving the state's objective. *(Bagley* v. *Washington Township Hospital Dist.* (1966) 65 Cal.2d 499, 505–507, 55 Cal. Rptr. 401, 421 P.2d 409.)

As we shall see, when measured against this established standard, the statutory scheme at issue is plainly unconstitutional. First, the Budget Act

restrictions are antithetical to the purpose of the Medi-Cal program—to provide indigents with access to medical services comparable to that enjoyed by more affluent persons. Second, the benefits of the funding restrictions do not manifestly outweigh the impairment of the constitutional rights; the fiscal advantages of the restrictions are illusory, and the asserted state interest in protecting fetal life cannot constitutionally claim priority over the woman's fundamental right of procreative choice. Third, the Medi-Cal program as qualified by the Budget Act restrictions clearly does not aid poor women who choose to bear children in a manner least offensive to the rights of those who choose abortion. Accordingly, we conclude that the challenged restrictions cannot stand.

. . .

2. *Our court bears an independent obligation to resolve plaintiffs' claims under the California Constitution on the basis of the governing state constitutional principles.*

. . . we think it important to reiterate the basic principles of federalism which illuminate our responsibilities in construing our state Constitution. In emphasizing, in *People* v. *Brisendine* (1975) 13 Cal.3d 528, 549–550, 119 Cal.Rptr. 315, 531 P.2d 1099, "the incontrovertible conclusion that the California Constitution is, and always has been, a document of independent force," our court explained that "[i]t is a fiction too long accepted that provisions in state constitutions textually identical to the Bill of Rights were intended to mirror their federal counterpart. The lesson of history is otherwise: the Bill of Rights was based upon the corresponding provisions of the first state constitutions, rather than the reverse. . . . The federal Constitution was designed to guard the states as sovereignties against potential abuses of centralized government; state charters, however, were conceived as the first and at one time the only line of protection of the individual against the excesses of local officials." Accordingly, we affirmed in *Brisendine* that state courts, in interpreting constitutional guarantees contained in state constitutions, are *"independently responsible* for safeguarding the rights of their citizens." (Italics added.) (*Id.* at p. 551, 119 Cal.Rptr. 315, 531 P.2d 1099.)

Contrary to the Attorney General's rhetoric, such independent construction does not represent an unprincipled exercise of power, but a means of fulfilling our solemn and independent constitutional *obligation* to interpret the safeguards guaranteed by the California Constitution in a manner consistent with the governing principles of California law. As we explained very recently in *People* v. *Chavez* (1980) 26 Cal.3d 334, 352, 161 Cal.Rptr. 762, 605 P.2d 401: "[J]ust as the United States Supreme Court bears the ultimate judicial responsibility for determining matters of federal law, this court bears the ultimate judicial responsibility for resolving questions of state law, including the proper interpretation of provisions of the state Constitution. [Citations.] In fulfilling this difficult and grave responsibility, we cannot properly relegate our task to the judicial guardians of the federal Constitution, but instead must recognize our personal obligation to exercise independent legal judgment in ascertaining the meaning and application of state constitutional provisions."

It is from this perspective that we must analyze plaintiffs' claims that the statutes in question are invalid under the California Constitution.

3. *Although the state has no constitutional obligation to provide medical care to the poor, a long line of California decisions establishes that once the state has decided to make such benefits available, it bears a heavy burden of justification in defending any provision which withholds such benefits from otherwise qualified individuals solely because they choose to exercise a constitutional right.*

In analyzing the constitutionality of the challenged statutory scheme, we start from the premise, not challenged by the Attorney General, that under article 1, section 1 of the California Constitution all women in this state—rich and poor alike—possess a fundamental constitutional right to choose whether or not to bear a child. Our court first recognized the existence of this constitutional right of procreative choice in *People* v. *Belous* (1969) 71 Cal.2d 954, 80 Cal.Rptr. 354, 458 P.2d 194, four years before the United States Supreme Court in *Roe* v. *Wade* (1973) 410 U.S. 113, 93 S.Ct. 705, 35 L.Ed.2d, 147 acknowledged

the existence of a comparable constitutional right under the federal Constitution.

In 1972, moreover, the people of this state specifically added the right of "privacy" to the other inalienable rights of individuals enumerated in article I, section 1 of the state Constitution. The federal constitutional right of privacy, by contrast, enjoys no such *explicit* constitutional status. . . .

5. *Conclusion.*

. . .

By virtue of the explicit protection afforded an individual's inalienable right of privacy by article I, section 1 of the California Constitution, . . . the decision whether to bear a child or to have an abortion is so private and so intimate that each woman in this state—rich or poor—is guaranteed the constitutional right to make that decision as an *individual*, uncoerced by governmental intrusion. Because a woman's right to choose whether or not to bear a child is explicitly afforded this constitutional protection, in California the question of whether an individual woman should or should not terminate her pregnancy is not a matter that may be put to a vote of the Legislature.

If the state cannot directly prohibit a woman's right to obtain an abortion, may the state by discriminatory financing indirectly nullify that constitutional right? Can the state tell an indigent person that the state will provide him with welfare benefits only upon the condition that he join a designated political party or subscribe to a particular newspaper that is favored by the government? Can the state tell a poor woman that it will pay for her needed medical care but only if she gives up her constitutional right to choose whether or not to have a child?

There is no greater power than the power of the purse. If the government can use it to nullify constitutional rights, by conditioning benefits only upon the sacrifice of such rights, the Bill of Rights could eventually become a yellowing scrap of paper. Once the state furnishes medical care to poor women in general, it cannot withdraw part of that care solely because a woman exercises her constitutional right to choose to have an abortion.

Indeed, the statutory scheme before us is all the more invidious because its practical effect is to deny to poor women the right of choice guaranteed to the rich. An affluent woman who desires to terminate her pregnancy enjoys the full right to obtain a medical abortion, regardless of the opposition of any legislative majority. By contrast, when the state finances the cost of childbirth, but will not finance the termination of pregnancy, it realistically forces an indigent pregnant woman to choose childbirth even though she has the constitutional right to refuse to do so.

Thus, we conclude that the restrictions in question are invalid under the California Constitution. . . .

Akron v. Akron Center for Reproductive Health
462 U.S. 416 (1983)

An Akron, Ohio, ordinance required all abortions after the first trimester of pregnancy to be performed in a hospital. The ordinance also established other requirements, including regulations for abortion on an unmarried minor, counseling of the patient by the physician, a twenty-four-hour delay in performing an abortion after a pregnant woman signed a consent form, and procedures for disposing of the fetal remains. A federal district court invalidated some of the requirements and upheld others. The Sixth Circuit sustained some of the lower court's rulings but reversed others.

JUSTICE POWELL delivered the opinion of the Court.

In this litigation we must decide the constitutionality of several provisions of an ordinance enacted by the city of Akron, Ohio, to regulate the performance of abortions. Today we also review abortion regulations enacted by the State of Missouri, see *Planned Parenthood Assn. of Kansas City, Mo., Inc.* v. *Ashcroft, post*, p. 476, and by the State of Virginia, see *Simopoulos* v. *Virginia, post*, p. 506.

These cases come to us a decade after we held in *Roe* v. *Wade*, 410 U.S. 113 (1973), that the right of privacy, grounded in the concept of personal liberty guaranteed by the Constitution, encompasses a woman's right to decide whether to terminate her pregnancy. Legislative responses to the Court's decision have required us on several occasions, and again today, to define the limits of a State's authority to regulate the performance of abortions. And arguments continue to be made, in these cases as well, that we erred in interpreting the Constitution. Nonetheless, the doctrine of *stare decisis*, while perhaps never entirely persuasive on a constitutional question, is a doctrine that demands respect in a society governed by the rule of law. We respect it today, and reaffirm *Roe* v. *Wade*.

I

In February 1978 the City Council of Akron enacted Ordinance No. 160–1978, entitled "Regulation of Abortions." The ordinance sets forth 17 provisions that regulate the performance of abortions, see Akron Codified Ordinances, ch. 1870, 5 of which are at issue in this case:

(i) Section 1870.03 requires that all abortions performed after the first trimester of pregnancy be performed in a hospital.

(ii) Section 1870.05 sets forth requirements for notification of and consent by parents before abortions may be performed on unmarried minors.

(iii) Section 1870.06 requires that the attending physician make certain specified statements to the patient "to insure that the consent for an abortion is truly informed consent."

(iv) Section 1870.07 requires a 24-hour waiting period between the time the woman signs a consent form and the time the abortion is performed.

(v) Section 1870.16 requires that fetal remains be "disposed of in a humane and sanitary manner."

A violation of any section of the ordinance is punishable as a criminal misdemeanor. § 1870.18.

If any provision is invalidated, it is to be severed from the remainder of the ordinance. The ordinance became effective on May 1, 1978.

[The district court invalidated four provisions, including §§ 1870.05, 1870.06(B), and 1870.16. The court upheld §§ 1870.03, 1870.06(C), and 1870.07. The Sixth Circuit affirmed that § 1870.03 is constitutional and affirmed that §§ 1870.05, 1870.06(B), and 1870.16 are unconstitutional. It reversed the district court on §§ 1870.06(C) and 1870.07, finding those sections unconstitutional.]

II

In *Roe* v. *Wade*, the Court held that the "right of privacy, . . . founded in the Fourteenth Amendment's concept of personal liberty and restrictions upon state action, . . . is broad enough to encompass a woman's decision whether or not to terminate her pregnancy." 410 U.S., at 153. Although the Constitution does not specifically identify this right, the history of this Court's constitutional adjudication leaves no doubt that "the full scope of the liberty guaranteed by the Due Process Clause cannot be found in or limited by the precise terms of the specific guarantees elsewhere provided in the Constitution." *Poe* v. *Ullman*, 367 U.S. 497, 543 (1961) (Harlan, J., dissenting from dismissal of appeal). Central among these protected liberties is an individual's "freedom of personal choice in matters of marriage and family life." *Roe*, 410 U.S., at 169 (Stewart, J., concurring). See, *e.g.*, *Eisenstadt* v. *Baird*, 405 U.S. 438 (1972); *Loving* v. *Virginia*, 388 U.S. 1 (1967); *Griswold* v. *Connecticut*, 381 U.S. 479 (1965); *Pierce* v. *Society of Sisters*, 268 U.S. 510 (1925); *Meyer* v. *Nebraska*, 262 U.S. 390 (1923). The decision in *Roe* was based firmly on this long-recognized and essential element of personal liberty.

[Justice Powell summarizes the holding in Roe *that a woman's right is strongest in the first trimester and becomes progressively weaker as the state's interest increases in the second and third trimesters.]*

III

Section 1870.03 of the Akron ordinance requires that any abortion performed "upon a pregnant woman subsequent to the end of the first trimester of her pregnancy" must be "performed in a hospital." A "hospital" is "a general hospital or special hospital devoted to gynecology or obstetrics which is accredited by the Joint Commission on Accreditation of Hospitals or by the American Osteopathic Association." § 1870.01(B). Accreditation by these organizations requires compliance with comprehensive standards governing a wide variety of health and surgical services. The ordinance thus prevents the performance of abortions in outpatient facilities that are not part of an acute-care, full-service hospital.

[The district court and Sixth Circuit upheld this section.] We believe that the courts below misinterpreted this Court's prior decisions, and we now hold that § 1870.03 is unconstitutional.

. . .

B

There can be no doubt that § 1870.03's second-trimester hospitalization requirement places a significant obstacle in the path of women seeking an abortion. A primary burden created by the requirement is additional cost to the woman. The Court of Appeals noted that there was testimony that a second-trimester abortion costs more than twice as much in a hospital as in a clinic. See 651 F. 2d, at 1209 (in-hospital abortion costs $850–$900, whereas a dilatation-and-evacuation (D&E) abortion performed in a clinic costs $350–$400). Moreover, the court indicated that second-trimester abortions were rarely performed in Akron hospitals. *Ibid.* (only nine second-trimester abortions performed in Akron hospitals in the year before trial). Thus, a second-trimester hospitalization requirement may force women to travel to find available facilities, resulting in both financial expense and additional health risk. It therefore is apparent that a second-trimester hospitalization requirement may significantly limit a woman's ability to obtain an abortion.

Akron does not contend that § 1870.03 imposes only an insignificant burden on women's access to abortion, but rather defends it as a reasonable health regulation. This position had strong support at the time of *Roe* v. *Wade*, as hospitalization for second-trimester abortions was recommended by the American Public Health Association (APHA), see *Roe*, 410 U.S., at 143–146, and the American College of Obstetricians and Gynecologists (ACOG), see Standards for Obstetric-Gynecologic Services 65 (4th ed. 1974). Since then, however, the safety of second-trimester abortions has increased dramatically.

. . . The evidence is strong enough to have convinced the APHA to abandon its prior recommendation of hospitalization for all second-trimester abortions . . .

. . .

Similarly, the ACOG no longer suggests that all second-trimester abortions be performed in a hospital. . . .

IV

We turn next to § 1870.05(B), the provision prohibiting a physician from performing an abortion on a minor pregnant woman under the age of 15 unless he obtains "the informed written consent of one of her parents or her legal guardian" or unless the minor obtains "an order from a court having jurisdiction over her that the abortion be performed or induced." The District Court invalidated this provision because "[i]t does not establish a procedure by which a minor can avoid a parental veto of her abortion decision by demonstrating that her decision is, in fact, informed. Rather, it requires, in all cases, both the minor's informed consent and either parental consent or a court order." 479 F. Supp., at 1201. The Court of Appeals affirmed on the same basis.

The relevant legal standards are not in dispute. The Court has held that "the State may not impose a blanket provision . . . requiring the consent of a parent or person *in loco parentis* as a condition for abortion of an unmarried minor." *Danforth, supra*, at 74. In *Bellotti* v. *Baird*, 443 U.S. 622 (1979) *(Bellotti II)*, a majority of the Court indicated that a State's interest in protecting immature minors will sustain a requirement of a consent substitute, either parental or judicial. See *id.*, at 640–642 (plurality opinion for four Justices); *id.*, at 656–657 (WHITE, J., dissenting) (expressing approval of absolute parental or judicial consent requirement). See also *Danforth, supra*, at 102–105 (STE-

VENS, J., concurring in part and dissenting in part). The *Bellotti II* plurality cautioned, however, that the State must provide an alternative procedure whereby a pregnant minor may demonstrate that she is sufficiently mature to make the abortion decision herself or that, despite her immaturity, an abortion would be in her best interests. 443 U.S., at 643–644. Under these decisions, it is clear that Akron may not make a blanket determination that *all* minors under the age of 15 are too immature to make this decision or that an abortion never may be in the minor's best interests without parental approval.

. . . we do not think that the Akron ordinance, as applied in Ohio juvenile proceedings, is reasonably susceptible of being construed to create an "opportunity for case-by-case evaluations of the maturity of pregnant minors." *Bellotti II, supra*, at 643, n. 23 (plurality opinion). We therefore affirm the Court of Appeals' judgment that § 1870.05(B) is unconstitutional.

V

The Akron ordinance provides that no abortion shall be performed except "with the informed written consent of the pregnant woman, . . . given freely and without coercion." § 1870.06(A). Furthermore, "in order to insure that the consent for an abortion is truly informed consent," the woman must be "orally informed by her attending physician" of the status of her pregnancy, the development of her fetus, the date of possible viability, the physical and emotional complications that may result from an abortion, and the availability of agencies to provide her with assistance and information with respect to birth control, adoption, and childbirth. § 1870.06(B). In addition, the attending physician must inform her "of the particular risks associated with her own pregnancy and the abortion technique to be employed . . . [and] other information which in his own medical judgment is relevant to her decision as to whether to have an abortion or carry her pregnancy to term." § 1870.06(C).

The District Court found that § 1870.06(B) was unconstitutional, but that § 1870.06(C) was related to a valid state interest in maternal health. See 479 F. Supp., at 1203–1204. The Court of Appeals concluded that both provisions were unconstitutional. See 651 F. 2d, at 1207. We affirm.

. . .

B

Viewing the city's regulations in this light, we believe that § 1870.06(B) attempts to extend the State's interest in ensuring "informed consent" beyond permissible limits. First, it is fair to say that much of the information required is designed not to inform the woman's consent but rather to persuade her to withhold it altogether. Subsection (3) requires the physician to inform his patient that "the unborn child is a human life from the moment of conception," a requirement inconsistent with the Court's holding in *Roe* v. *Wade* that a State may not adopt one theory of when life begins to justify its regulation of abortions. . . . subsection (5), that begins with the dubious statement that "abortion is a major surgical procedure" and proceeds to describe numerous possible physical and psychological complications of abortion, is a "parade of horribles" intended to suggest that abortion is a particularly dangerous procedure.

. . .

C

Section 1870.06(C) presents a different question. Under this provision, the "attending physician" must inform the woman

"of the particular risks associated with her own pregnancy and the abortion technique to be employed including providing her with at least a general description of the medical instructions to be followed subsequent to the abortion in order to insure her safe recovery, and shall in addition provide her with such other information which in his own medical judgment is relevant to her decision as to whether to have an abortion or carry her pregnancy to term."

The information required clearly is related to maternal health and to the State's legitimate purpose in requiring informed consent. Nonetheless, the Court of Appeals determined that it interfered with the physician's medical judgment "in exactly the same way as section 1870.06(B). It requires

the doctor to make certain disclosures in all cases, regardless of his own professional judgment as to the desirability of doing so." 651 F. 2d, at 1207. . . .

. . . we believe that it is unreasonable for a State to insist that only a physician is competent to provide the information and counseling relevant to informed consent. We affirm the judgment of the Court of Appeals that § 1870.06(C) is invalid.

VI

The Akron ordinance prohibits a physician from performing an abortion until 24 hours after the pregnant woman signs a consent form. § 1870.07. The District Court upheld this provision on the ground that it furthered Akron's interest in ensuring "that a woman's abortion decision is made after careful consideration of all the facts applicable to her particular situation." 479 F. Supp., at 1204. The Court of Appeals reversed, finding that the inflexible waiting period had "no medical basis," and that careful consideration of the abortion decision by the woman "is beyond the state's power to require." 651 F. 2d, at 1208. We affirm the Court of Appeals' judgment.

The District Court found that the mandatory 24-hour waiting period increases the cost of obtaining an abortion by requiring the woman to make two separate trips to the abortion facility. See 479 F. Supp., at 1204. Plaintiffs also contend that because of scheduling difficulties the effective delay may be longer than 24 hours, and that such a delay in some cases could increase the risk of an abortion. . . .

VII

Section § 1870.16 of the Akron ordinance requires physicians performing abortions to "insure that the remains of the unborn child are disposed of in a humane and sanitary manner." The Court of Appeals found that the word "humane" was impermissibly vague as a definition of conduct subject to criminal prosecution. The court invalidated the entire provision, declining to sever the word "humane" in order to uphold the requirement that disposal be "sanitary." See 651 F. 2d, at 1211. We affirm this judgment.

Akron contends that the purpose of § 1870.16 is simply " 'to preclude the mindless dumping of aborted fetuses onto garbage piles.' " *Planned Parenthood Assn.* v. *Fitzpatrick,* 401 F. Supp. 554, 573 (ED Pa. 1975) (three-judge court) (quoting State's characterization of legislative purpose), summarily aff'd *sub nom. Franklin* v. *Fitzpatrick,* 428 U.S. 901 (1976). It is far from clear, however, that this provision has such a limited intent. The phrase "humane and sanitary" does, as the Court of Appeals noted, suggest a possible intent to "mandate some sort of 'decent burial' of an embryo at the earliest stages of formation." 651 F. 2d, at 1211. This level of uncertainty is fatal where criminal liability is imposed. See *Colautti* v. *Franklin, supra,* at 396. Because § 1870.16 fails to give a physician "fair notice that his contemplated conduct is forbidden," *United States* v. *Harriss,* 347 U.S. 612, 617 (1954), we agree that it violates the Due Process Clause.

VIII

We affirm the judgment of the Court of Appeals invalidating those sections of Akron's "Regulations of Abortions" ordinance that deal with parental consent, informed consent, a 24-hour waiting period, and the disposal of fetal remains. The remaining portion of the judgment, sustaining Akron's requirement that all second-trimester abortions be performed in a hospital, is reversed.

It is so ordered.

JUSTICE O'CONNOR, with whom JUSTICE WHITE and JUSTICE REHNQUIST join, dissenting.

. . .

I

The trimester or "three-stage" approach adopted by the Court in *Roe,* and, in a modified form, employed by the Court to analyze the regulations in these cases, cannot be supported as a legitimate or useful framework for accommodating the woman's right and the State's interests. The decision of the Court today graphically illustrates why the trimester approach is a completely unworkable method of accommodating the conflicting personal rights and compelling state interests that are involved in the abortion context.

As the Court indicates today, the State's compelling interest in maternal health changes as medical technology changes, and any health regulation must not "depart from accepted medical practice." *Ante,* at 431. In applying this standard, the Court holds that "the safety of second-trimester abortions has increased dramatically" since 1973, when *Roe* was decided. *Ante,* at 435–436 (footnote omitted). Although a regulation such as one requiring that all second-trimester abortions be performed in hospitals "had strong support" in 1973 "as a reasonable health regulation," *ante,* at 435, this regulation can no longer stand because, according to the Court's diligent research into medical and scientific literature, the dilation and evacuation (D&E) procedure, used in 1973 only for first-trimester abortions, "is now widely and successfully used for second-trimester abortions." *Ante,* at 436 (footnote omitted). Further, the medical literature relied on by the Court indicates that the D&E procedure may be performed in an appropriate nonhospital setting for "at least . . . the early weeks of the second trimester. . . ." *Ante,* at 437. The Court then chooses the period of 16 weeks of gestation as that point at which D&E procedures may be performed safely in a nonhospital setting, and thereby invalidates the Akron hospitalization regulation.

It is not difficult to see that despite the Court's purported adherence to the trimester approach adopted in *Roe,* the lines drawn in that decision have now been "blurred" because of what the Court accepts as technological advancement in the safety of abortion procedure. The State may no longer rely on a "bright line" that separates permissible from impermissible regulation, and it is no longer free to consider the second trimester as a unit and weigh the risks posed by all abortion procedures throughout that trimester. Rather, the State must continuously and conscientiously study contemporary medical and scientific literature in order to determine whether the effect of a particular regulation is to "depart from accepted medical practice" insofar as particular procedures and particular periods within the trimester are concerned. Assuming that legislative bodies are able to engage in this exacting task, it is difficult to believe that our Constitution *requires* that they do it as a prelude to protecting the health of their citizens. It is even more difficult to believe that this Court, without the resources available to those bodies entrusted with making legislative choices, believes itself competent to make these inquiries and to revise these standards every time the American College of Obstetricians and Gynecologists (ACOG) or similar group revises its views about what is and what is not appropriate medical procedure in this area. . . .

Just as improvements in medical technology inevitably will move *forward* the point at which the State may regulate for reasons of maternal health, different technological improvements will move *backward* the point of viability at which the State may proscribe abortions except when necessary to preserve the life and health of the mother.

In 1973, viability before 28 weeks was considered unusual. The 14th edition of L. Hellman & J. Pritchard, Williams Obstetrics (1971), on which the Court relied in *Roe* for its understanding of viability, stated, at 493, that "[a]ttainment of a [fetal] weight of 1,000 g [or a fetal age of approximately 28 weeks' gestation] is . . . widely used as the criterion of viability." However, recent studies have demonstrated increasingly earlier fetal via-

bility. It is certainly reasonable to believe that fetal viability in the first trimester of pregnancy may be possible in the not too distant future. . . .

The *Roe* framework, then, is clearly on a collision course with itself. As the medical risks of various abortion procedures decrease, the point at which the State may regulate for reasons of maternal health is moved further forward to actual childbirth. As medical science becomes better able to provide for the separate existence of the fetus, the point of viability is moved further back toward conception. . . .

[O'Connor concludes that (a) the requirement that second-trimester abortions be performed in hospitals is constitutional; (b) the Court should have abstained in declaring the parental-consent provision unconstitutional; (c) with regard to the informed-consent provisions, other than subsections (3), (4), and (5), which Akron conceded were unconstitutional, the provisions do not impose an undue burden or drastic limitation on the abortion decision; (d) the twenty-four-hour waiting period is unconstitutional; and (e) the requirement that fetal remains be disposed of in "a humane and sanitary manner" is not void because of vagueness.]

Thornburgh v. American College of Obst. & Gyn.

476 U.S. 747 (1986)

Pennsylvania passed legislation in 1982 to impose restraints on abortion. The bill, signed into law by Governor Richard Thornburgh, required certain procedures for "informed consent" by the woman; the use of medical techniques after viability to preserve the health and life of both mother and child; and the presence of a second physician during an abortion performed when viability is possible. The lower courts held several portions of the statute unconstitutional, building in part on *Akron* v. *Akron Center for Reproductive Health* (1983).

JUSTICE BLACKMUN delivered the opinion of the Court.

This is an appeal from a judgment of the United States Court of Appeals for the Third Circuit reviewing the District Court's rulings upon a

motion for a preliminary injunction. The Court of Appeals held unconstitutional several provisions of Pennsylvania's current Abortion Control Act, 1982 Pa.Laws, Act No. 138, now codified as 18 Pa.Cons.Stat. § 3201 *et seq.* (1983) (Act). Among the provisions ruled invalid by the Court of Appeals were portions of § 3205, relating to "informed consent"; § 3208, concerning "printed information"; §§ 3210(b) and (c), having to do with postviability abortions; and § 3211(a) and § 3214(a) and (h), regarding reporting requirements.

I

The Abortion Control Act was approved by the Governor of the Commonwealth on June 11, 1982. By its own terms, however, see § 7 of the Act, it was to become effective only 180 days thereafter, that is, on the following December 8. . . .

After the passage of the Act, but before its effective date, the present litigation was instituted in the United States District Court for the Eastern District of Pennsylvania. The plaintiffs, who are the appellees here, were the American College of Obstetricians and Gynecologists, Pennsylvania Section; certain physicians licensed in Pennsylvania; clergymen; an individual who purchases from a Pennsylvania insurer health-care and disability insurance extending to abortions; and Pennsylvania abortion counselors and providers. Alleging that the Act violated the United States Constitution, the plaintiffs, pursuant to 42 U.S.C. § 1983, sought declaratory and injunctive relief. The defendants named in the complaint were the Governor of the Commonwealth, other Commonwealth officials, and the District Attorney for Montgomery County, Pa.

. . .

IV

This case, as it comes to us, concerns the constitutionality of six provisions of the Pennsylvania Act that the Court of Appeals struck down as facially invalid: § 3205 ("informed consent"); § 3208 ("printed information"); § 3214(a) and (h) (reporting requirements); § 3211(a) (determination of viability); § 3210(b) (degree of care required in postviability abortions); and § 3210(c) (second-physician requirement). We have no reason to address the validity of the other sections of the Act challenged in the District Court.

A

. . . The States are not free, under the guise of protecting maternal health or potential life, to intimidate women into continuing pregnancies. Appellants claim that the statutory provisions before us today further legitimate compelling interests of the Commonwealth. Close analysis of those provisions, however, shows that they wholly subordinate constitutional privacy interests and concerns with maternal health in an effort to deter a woman from making a decision that, with her physician, is hers to make.

B

We turn to the challenged statutes:

1. Section 3205 ("informed consent") and § 3208 (printed information). Section 3205(a) requires that the woman give her "voluntary and informed consent" to an abortion. Failure to observe the provisions of § 3205 subjects the physician to suspension or revocation of his license, and subjects any other person obligated to provide information relating to informed consent to criminal penalties. . . .

. . . We conclude that, like Akron's ordinance, §§ 3205 and 3208 fail the *Akron* measurement. The two sections prescribe in detail the method for securing "informed consent." Seven explicit kinds of information must be delivered to the woman at least 24 hours before her consent is given, and five of these must be presented by the woman's physician. The five are: (a) the name of the physician who will perform the abortion, (b) the "fact that there may be detrimental physical and psychological effects which are not accurately foreseeable," (c) the "particular medical risks associated with the particular abortion procedure to be employed," (d) the probable gestational age, and (e) the "medical risks associated with carrying her child to term." The remaining two categories are (f) the "fact that medical assistance benefits may be available for prenatal care, childbirth and neonatal care," and (g) the "fact that the father is liable to assist" in the child's support, "even in instances where the father has offered to pay for the abortion." §§ 3205(a)(1) and (2). The woman also must be informed that materials printed and supplied by the Commonwealth that describe the fetus and that list agencies offering alternatives to abortion are available for her review. If she chooses to review the materials but is unable to read, the materials "shall be read to her," and any answer she seeks must be "provided her in her own language." § 3205(a)(2)(iii). She must certify in writing, prior to the abortion, that all this has been done. § 3205(a)(3). The printed materials "shall include the following statement":

"There are many public and private agencies willing and able to help you to carry your child to term, and to assist you and your child after your child is born, whether you choose to keep your child or place her or him for adoption. The Commonwealth of Pennsylvania strongly urges you to contact them before making a final decision about abortion. The law requires that your physician or his agent give you the opportunity to call agencies like these before you undergo an abortion." § 3208(a)(1).

The materials must describe the "probable anatomical and physiological characteristics of the unborn child at two-week gestational increments from fertilization to full term, including any relevant information on the possibility of the unborn child's survival." § 3208(a)(2).

. . . The printed materials required by §§ 3205 and 3208 seem to us to be nothing less than an outright attempt to wedge the Commonwealth's message discouraging abortion into the privacy of the informed-consent dialogue between the woman and her physician. . . .

2. Sections 3214(a) and (h) (reporting) and § 3211(a) (determination of viability). Section 3214(a)(8), part of the general reporting section, incorporates § 3211(a). Section 3211(a) requires the physician to report the basis for his determination "that a child is not viable." It applies only after the first trimester. The report required by § 3214(a) and (h) is detailed and must include, among other things, identification of the performing and referring physicians and of the facility or agency; information as to the woman's political subdivision and State of residence, age, race, marital status, and number of prior pregnancies; the date of her last menstrual period and the probable gestational age; the basis for any judg-

ment that a medical emergency existed; the basis for any determination of nonviability; and the method of payment for the abortion. The report is to be signed by the attending physician. § 3214(b).

Despite the fact that § 3214(e)(2) provides that such reports "shall not be deemed public records," within the meaning of the Commonwealth's "Right-to-Know Law," Pa.Stat.Ann., Tit. 65, § 66.1 *et seq.* (Purdon 1959 and Supp.1985), each report "shall be made available for public inspection and copying within 15 days of receipt in a form which will not lead to the disclosure of the identity of any person filing a report." Similarly, the report of complications, required by § 3214(h), "shall be open to public inspection and copying." A willful failure to file a report required under § 3214 is "unprofessional conduct" and the noncomplying physician's license "shall be subject to suspension or revocation." § 3214(i)(1).

. . .

A woman and her physician will necessarily be more reluctant to choose an abortion if there exists a possibility that her decision and her identity will become known publicly. Although the statute does not specifically require the reporting of the woman's name, the amount of information about her and the circumstances under which she had an abortion are so detailed that identification is likely. Identification is the obvious purpose of these extreme reporting requirements. . . .

. . . Pennsylvania's reporting requirements raise the spectre of public exposure and harassment of women who choose to exercise their personal, intensely private, right, with their physician, to end a pregnancy. Thus, they pose an unacceptable danger of deterring the exercise of that right, and must be invalidated.

3. Section 3210(b) (degree of care for postviability abortions) and § 3210(c) (second-physician requirement when the fetus is possibly viable). Section 3210(b) sets forth two independent requirements for a postviability abortion. First, it demands the exercise of that degree of care "which such person would be required to exercise in order to preserve the life and health of any unborn child intended to be born and not aborted." Second, "the abortion technique employed shall be that which would provide the best

opportunity for the unborn child to be aborted alive unless," in the physician's good-faith judgment, that technique "would present a significantly greater medical risk to the life or health of the pregnant woman." An intentional, knowing, or reckless violation of this standard is a felony of the third degree, and subjects the violator to the possibility of imprisonment for not more than seven years and to a fine of not more than $15,000. See 18 Pa.Cons.Stat. §§ 1101(2) and 1103(3) (1983).

[The Court finds Section 3210(b) facially invalid because it requires the mother to bear an increased medical risk in order to save her viable fetus.]

Section 3210(c) requires that a second physician be present during an abortion performed when viability is possible. The second physician is to "take control of the child and . . . provide immediate medical care for the child, taking all reasonable steps necessary, in his judgment, to preserve the child's life and health." Violation of this requirement is a felony of the third degree.

In *Planned Parenthood Assn.* v. *Ashcroft*, 462 U.S. 476 (1983), the Court, by a 5–4 vote, but not by a controlling single opinion, ruled that a Missouri statute requiring the presence of a second physician during an abortion performed after viability was constitutional. JUSTICE POWELL, joined by THE CHIEF JUSTICE, concluded that the State had a compelling interest in protecting the life of a viable fetus and that the second physician's presence provided assurance that the State's interest was protected more fully than with only one physician in attendance. *Id.*, at 482–486. JUSTICE POWELL recognized that, to pass constitutional muster, the statute must contain an exception for the situation where the health of the mother was endangered by delay in the arrival of the second physician. Recognizing that there was "no clearly expressed exception" on the face of the Missouri statute for the emergency situation, JUSTICE POWELL found the exception implicit in the statutory requirement that action be taken to preserve the fetus "provided it does not pose an increased risk to the life or health of the woman." *Id.*, at 485, n. 8.

Like the Missouri statute, § 3210(c) of the Pennsylvania statute contains no express exception for

an emergency situation. While the Missouri statute, in the view of JUSTICE POWELL, was worded sufficiently to imply an emergency exception, Pennsylvania's statute contains no such comforting or helpful language and evinces no intent to protect a woman whose life may be at risk. Section 3210(a) provides only a defense to criminal liability for a physician who concluded, in good faith, that a fetus was nonviable "or that the abortion was necessary to preserve maternal life or health." It does not relate to the second-physician requirement and its words are not words of emergency.

It is clear that the Pennsylvania Legislature knows how to provide a medical-emergency exception when it chooses to do so. It defined "[m]edical emergency" in general terms in § 3203, and it specifically provided a medical-emergency exception with respect to informational requirements, § 3205(b); for parental consent, § 3206; for post-first trimester hospitalization, § 3209; and for a public official's issuance of an order for an abortion without the express voluntary consent of the woman, § 3215(f). We necessarily conclude that the legislature's failure to provide a medical-emergency exception in § 3210(c) was intentional. All the factors are here for chilling the performance of a late abortion, which, more than one performed at an earlier date, perhaps tends to be under emergency conditions.

V

Constitutional rights do not always have easily ascertainable boundaries, and controversy over the meaning of our Nation's most majestic guarantees frequently has been turbulent. As judges, however, we are sworn to uphold the law even when its content gives rise to bitter dispute. See *Cooper* v. *Aaron*, 358 U.S. 1 (1958). We recognized at the very beginning of our opinion in *Roe*, 410 U.S., at 116, that abortion raises moral and spiritual questions over which honorable persons can disagree sincerely and profoundly. But those disagreements did not then and do not now relieve us of our duty to apply the Constitution faithfully.

Our cases long have recognized that the Constitution embodies a promise that a certain private sphere of individual liberty will be kept largely beyond the reach of government. . . . That promise extends to women as well as to men. Few decisions are more personal and intimate, more properly private, or more basic to individual dignity and autonomy, than a woman's decision—with the guidance of her physician and within the limits specified in *Roe*—whether to end her pregnancy. A woman's right to make that choice freely is fundamental. Any other result, in our view, would protect inadequately a central part of the sphere of liberty that our law guarantees equally to all.

The Court of Appeals correctly invalidated the specified provisions of Pennsylvania's 1982 Abortion Control Act. Its judgment is affirmed.

It is so ordered.

JUSTICE STEVENS, concurring.

. . .

CHIEF JUSTICE BURGER, dissenting.

. . .

The Court in *Roe* further recognized that the State "has still *another* important and legitimate interest" which is "separate and distinct" from the interest in protecting maternal health, *i.e.*, an interest in "protecting the potentiality of human life." *Ibid*. The point at which these interests become "compelling" under *Roe* is at viability of the fetus. *Id.*, at 163. Today, however, the Court abandons that standard and renders the solemnly stated concerns of the 1973 *Roe* opinion for the interests of the States mere shallow rhetoric. The statute at issue in this case requires that a second physician be present during an abortion performed after viability, so that the second physician can "take control of the child and . . . provide immediate medical care . . . taking all reasonable steps necessary, in his judgment, to preserve the child's life and health." 18 Pa. Cons.Stat. § 3210(c) (1982).

Essentially this provision simply states that a viable fetus is to be cared for, not destroyed. No governmental power exists to say that a viable fetus should not have every protection required to preserve its life. Undoubtedly the Pennsylvania

Legislature added the second physician requirement on the mistaken assumption that this Court meant what it said in *Roe* concerning the "compelling interest" of the states in potential life after viability.

. . .

JUSTICE WHITE, with whom JUSTICE REHNQUIST joins, dissenting.

. . .

[I.A]

If the woman's liberty to choose an abortion is fundamental, then, it is not because any of our precedents (aside from *Roe* itself) commands or justifies that result; it can only be because protection for this unique choice is itself "implicit in the concept of ordered liberty" or, perhaps, "deeply rooted in this Nation's history and tradition." It seems clear to me that it is neither. The Court's opinion in *Roe* itself convincingly refutes the notion that the abortion liberty is deeply rooted in the history or tradition of our people, as does the continuing and deep division of the people themselves over the question of abortion. As for the notion that choice in the matter of abortion is implicit in the concept of ordered liberty, it seems apparent to me that a free, egalitarian, and democratic society does not presuppose any particular rule or set of rules with respect to abortion. And again, the fact that many men and women of good will and high commitment to constitutional government place themselves on both sides of the abortion controversy strengthens my own conviction that the values animating the Constitution do not compel recognition of the abortion liberty as fundamental. In so denominating that liberty, the Court engages not in constitutional interpretation, but in the unrestrained imposition of its own, extra-constitutional value preferences.

. . .

C

. . . Abortion is a hotly contested moral and political issue. Such issues, in our society, are to be resolved by the will of the people, either as expressed through legislation or through the general principles they have already incorporated into the Constitution they have adopted. *Roe* v. *Wade* implies that the people have already resolved the debate by weaving into the Constitution the values and principles that answer the issue. As I have argued, I believe it is clear that the people have never—not in 1787, 1791, 1868, or at any time since—done any such thing. I would return the issue to the people by overruling *Roe* v. *Wade*.

. . .

III

The decision today appears symptomatic of the Court's own insecurity over its handiwork in *Roe* v. *Wade* and the cases following that decision. Aware that in *Roe* it essentially created something out of nothing and that there are many in this country who hold that decision to be basically illegitimate, the Court responds defensively. Perceiving, in a statute implementing the State's legitimate policy of preferring childbirth to abortion, a threat to or criticism of the decision in *Roe* v. *Wade*, the majority indiscriminately strikes down statutory provisions that in no way contravene the right recognized in *Roe*. I do not share the warped point of view of the majority, nor can I follow the tortuous path the majority treads in proceeding to strike down the statute before us. I dissent.

JUSTICE O'CONNOR, with whom JUSTICE REHN-QUIST joins, dissenting.

This Court's abortion decisions have already worked a major distortion in the Court's constitutional jurisprudence. See *Akron* v. *Akron Center for Reproductive Health, Inc.*, 462 U.S. 416, 452 (1983) (O'CONNOR, J., dissenting). Today's decision goes further, and makes it painfully clear that no legal rule or doctrine is safe from ad hoc nullification by this Court when an occasion for its application arises in a case involving state regulation of abortion. The permissible scope of abortion regulation is not the only constitutional issue on which this Court is divided, but—except when it comes to abortion—the Court has generally refused to let such disagreements, however longstanding or deeply felt, prevent it from evenhandedly applying uncontroversial legal doctrines to cases that come before it.

. . .

The Court today holds that "[t]he Court of Appeals correctly invalidated the specified provisions of Pennsylvania's 1982 Abortion Control Act." *Ante*, at 772. In so doing, the Court prematurely decides serious constitutional questions on an inadequate record, in contravention of settled principles of constitutional adjudication and procedural fairness. The constitutionality of the challenged provisions was not properly before the Court of Appeals, and is not properly before this Court. There has been no trial on the merits, and appellants have had no opportunity to develop facts that might have a bearing on the constitutionality of the statute. The only question properly before the Court is whether or not a preliminary injunction should have been issued to restrain enforcement of the challenged provisions pending trial on the merits. . . .

II

. . . By holding that each of the challenged provisions is facially unconstitutional as a matter of law, and that no conceivable facts appellants might offer could alter this result, the Court appears to adopt as its new test a *per se* rule under which any regulation touching on abortion must be invalidated if it poses "an unacceptable danger of deterring the exercise of that right." *Ante*, at 767. Under this prophylactic test, it seems that the mere possibility that some women will be less likely to choose to have an abortion by virtue of the presence of a particular state regulation suffices to invalidate it. Simultaneously, the Court strains to discover "the anti-abortion character of the statute," *ante*, at 764, and, as JUSTICE WHITE points out, invents an unprecedented canon of construction under which "in cases involving abortion, a permissible reading of a statute is to be avoided at all costs." *Ante*, at 812 (dissenting). I shall not belabor the dangerous extravagance of this dual approach, because I hope it represents merely a temporary aberration rather than a portent of lasting change in settled principles of constitutional law. Suffice it to say that I dispute not only the wisdom but the legitimacy of the Court's attempt to discredit and preempt state abortion regulation regardless of the interests it serves and the impact it has.

. . .

Webster v. Reproductive Health Services
109 S. Ct. 3040 (1989)

A Missouri statute, based on the premise that the "life of each human being begins at conception," placed a number of restrictions on abortions: prohibiting public employees and facilities from performing or assisting abortions not necessary to save the mother's life; prohibiting any encouragement or counseling to have an abortion; and requiring physicians to perform a viability test at twenty weeks or more. A federal district court struck down each restriction and enjoined their enforcement. The Eighth Circuit affirmed, ruling that the Missouri law violated the decisions in *Roe* v. *Wade* and subsequent cases.

CHIEF JUSTICE REHNQUIST announced the judgment of the Court and delivered the opinion of the Court with respect to Parts I, II–A, II–B, and II–C, and an opinion with respect to Parts II–D and III, in which JUSTICE WHITE and JUSTICE KENNEDY join.

This appeal concerns the constitutionality of a Missouri statute regulating the performance of abortions. The United States Court of Appeals for the Eighth Circuit struck down several provisions of the statute on the ground that they violated this Court's decision in *Roe* v. *Wade*, 410 U. S. 113 (1973), and cases following it. We noted probable jurisdiction, 488 U. S.—(1989), and now reverse.

I

In June 1986, the Governor of Missouri signed into law Missouri Senate Committee Substitute for House Bill No. 1596 (hereinafter Act or statute), which amended existing state law concerning unborn children and abortions. The Act consisted of 20 provisions, 5 of which are now before the Court. The first provision, or preamble, contains "findings" by the state legislature that "[t]he life of each human being begins at conception," and that "unborn children have protectable interests in life, health, and well-being." Mo. Rev. Stat. §§ 1.205.1(1), (2) (1986). The Act further requires

that all Missouri laws be interpreted to provide unborn children with the same rights enjoyed by other persons, subject to the Federal Constitution and this Court's precedents. § 1.205.2. Among its other provisions, the Act requires that, prior to performing an abortion on any woman whom a physician has reason to believe is 20 or more weeks pregnant, the physician ascertain whether the fetus is viable by performing "such medical examinations and tests as are necessary to make a finding of the gestational age, weight, and lung maturity of the unborn child." § 188.029. The Act also prohibits the use of public employees and facilities to perform or assist abortions not necessary to save the mother's life, and it prohibits the use of public funds, employees, or facilities for the purpose of "encouraging or counseling" a woman to have an abortion not necessary to save her life. §§ 188.205, 188.210, 188.215.

[The district court declared seven provisions in the Act unconstitutional and enjoined their enforcement. The Eighth Circuit affirmed, with one exception not relevant to the appeal to the Supreme Court.]

II

Decision of this case requires us to address four sections of the Missouri Act: (a) the preamble; (b) the prohibition on the use of public facilities or employees to perform abortions; (c) the prohibition on public funding of abortion counseling; and (d) the requirement that physicians conduct viability tests prior to performing abortions. We address these *seriatim*.

A

The Act's preamble, as noted, sets forth "findings" by the Missouri legislature that "[t]he life of each human being begins at conception," and that "[u]nborn children have protectable interests in life, health, and well-being." Mo. Rev. Stat. §§ 1.205.1(1), (2) (1986). The Act then mandates that state laws be interpreted to provide unborn children with "all the rights, privileges, and immunities available to other persons, citizens, and residents of this state," subject to the Constitution and this Court's precedents. § 1.205.2. In invalidating the preamble, the Court of Appeals relied on this Court's dictum that "'a State may not adopt one theory of when life begins to justify its regulation of abortions.'" 851 F. 2d, at 1075–1076, quoting *Akron* v. *Akron Center for Reproductive Health, Inc.,* 462 U. S. 416, 444 (1983), in turn citing *Roe* v. *Wade,* 410 U. S., at 159–162. . . .

The State contends that the preamble itself is precatory and imposes no substantive restrictions on abortions, and that appellees therefore do not have standing to challenge it. . . .

In our view, the Court of Appeals misconceived the meaning of the *Akron* dictum, . . . The Court has emphasized that *Roe* v. *Wade* "implies no limitation on the authority of a State to make a value judgment favoring childbirth over abortion." *Maher* v. *Roe,* 432 U. S., at 474. The preamble can be read simply to express that sort of value judgment.

We think the extent to which the preamble's language might be used to interpret other state statutes or regulations is something that only the courts of Missouri can definitively decide. . . .

It will be time enough for federal courts to address the meaning of the preamble should it be applied to restrict the activities of appellees in some concrete way. . . . We therefore need not pass on the constitutionality of the Act's preamble.

B

Section 188.210 provides that "[i]t shall be unlawful for any public employee within the scope of his employment to perform or assist an abortion, not necessary to save the life of the mother," while § 188.215 makes it "unlawful for any public facility to be used for the purpose of performing or assisting an abortion not necessary to save the life of the mother." The Court of Appeals held that these provisions contravened this Court's abortion decisions. 851 F. 2d, at 1082–1083. We take the contrary view.

As we said earlier this Term in *DeShaney* v. *Winnebago County Dept. of Social Services,* 489 U. S. —, — (1989) (slip op., at 6), "our cases have recognized that the Due Process Clauses generally confer no affirmative right to governmental aid, even where such aid may be necessary to secure life, liberty, or property interests of which the government itself may not deprive the individual." In *Maher* v. *Roe, supra,* the Court upheld a Connecticut welfare regulation under which Medicaid recipients received payments for medical services related to childbirth, but not for nontherapeutic abortions. The Court rejected the claim that this unequal subsidization of childbirth and abortion was impermissible under *Roe* v. *Wade.* . . .

[The Court reinforces that point by referring to Poelker v. Doe, 432 U.S. 519 (1977) and Harris v. McRae, 448 U.S. 297 (1980).]

. . . Nothing in the Constitution requires States to enter or remain in the business of performing abortions. Nor, as appellees suggest, do private physicians and their patients have some kind of constitutional right of access to public facilities for the performance of abortions. Brief for Appellees 46–47. Indeed, if the State does recoup all of its costs in performing abortions, and no state subsidy, direct or indirect, is available, it is difficult to see how any procreational choice is burdened by the State's ban on the use of its facilities or employees for performing abortions.

Maher, Poelker, and *McRae* all support the view that the State need not commit any resources to facilitating abortions, even if it can turn a profit by doing so. . . . Thus we uphold the Act's restrictions on the use of public employees and facilities

for the performance or assistance of nontherapeutic abortions.

C

The Missouri Act contains three provisions
relating to "encouraging or counseling a woman
to have an abortion not necessary to save her life."
Section 188.205 states that no public funds can be
used for this purpose; § 188.210 states that public
employees cannot, within the scope of their employment, engage in such speech; and § 188.215
forbids such speech in public facilities. The Court
of Appeals did not consider § 188.205 separately
from §§ 188.210 and 188.215. It held that all three
of these provisions were unconstitutionally vague,
and that "the ban on using public funds, employees, and facilities to encourage or counsel a woman to have an abortion is an unacceptable infringement of the woman's fourteenth amendment right
to choose an abortion after receiving the medical
information necessary to exercise the right knowingly and intelligently." 851 F. 2d, at 1079.

Missouri has chosen only to appeal the Court of
Appeals' invalidation of the public funding provision, § 188.205. See Juris. Statement I-II. A threshold question is whether this provision reaches
primary conduct, or whether it is simply an instruction to the State's fiscal officers not to allocate funds for abortion counseling. We accept, for
purposes of decision, the State's claim that
§ 188.205 "is not directed at the conduct of any
physician or health care provider, private or public," but "is directed solely at those persons responsible for expending public funds." Brief for
Appellants 43.

Appellees contend that they are not "adversely"
affected under the State's interpretation of
§ 188.205, and therefore that there is no longer a
case or controversy before us on this question.
Brief for Appellees 31–32. Plaintiffs are masters of
their complaints and remain so at the appellate
stage of a litigation. See *Caterpillar Inc.* v. *Williams*,
482 U. S. 386, 398–399 (1987). A majority of the
Court agrees with appellees that the controversy
over § 188.205 is now moot, because appellees'
argument amounts to a decision to no longer seek
a declaratory judgment that § 188.205 is unconstitutional and accompanying declarative relief. . . .

D

Section 188.029 of the Missouri Act provides:

"Before a physician performs an abortion on a
woman he has reason to believe is carrying an
unborn child of twenty or more weeks gestational
age, the physician shall first determine if the
unborn child is viable by using and exercising that
degree of care, skill, and proficiency commonly
exercised by the ordinarily skillful, careful, and
prudent physician engaged in similar practice
under the same or similar conditions. In making
this determination of viability, the physician shall
perform or cause to be performed such medical
examinations and tests as are necessary to make a
finding of the gestational age, weight, and lung
maturity of the unborn child and shall enter such
findings and determination of viability in the
medical record of the mother."

As with the preamble, the parties disagree over the
meaning of this statutory provision. The State
emphasizes the language of the first sentence,
which speaks in terms of the physician's determination of viability being made by the standards of
ordinary skill in the medical profession. Brief for
Appellants 32–35. Appellees stress the language of
the second sentence, which prescribes such "tests
as are necessary" to make a finding of gestational
age, fetal weight, and lung maturity. Brief for
Appellees 26–30.

The Court of Appeals read § 188.029 as requiring that after 20 weeks "doctors *must* perform
tests to find gestational age, fetal weight and lung
maturity." 851 F. 2d, at 1075, n. 5. The court
indicated that the tests needed to determine fetal
weight at 20 weeks are "unreliable and inaccurate" and would add $125 to $250 to the cost of an
abortion. *Ibid.* It also stated that "amniocentesis,
the only method available to determine lung maturity, is contrary to accepted medical practice
until 28–30 weeks of gestation, expensive, and
imposes significant health risks for both the pregnant woman and the fetus." *Ibid.*

. . .

We think the viability-testing provision makes
sense only if the second sentence is read to require

only those tests that are useful to making subsidiary findings as to viability. If we construe this provision to require a physician to perform those tests needed to make the three specified findings *in all circumstances*, including when the physician's reasonable professional judgment indicates that the tests would be irrelevant to determining viability or even dangerous to the mother and the fetus, the second sentence of § 188.029 would conflict with the first sentence's *requirement* that a physician apply his reasonable professional skill and judgment. It would also be incongruous to read this provision, especially the word "necessary," to require the performance of tests irrelevant to the expressed statutory purpose of determining viability. It thus seems clear to us that the Court of Appeals' construction of § 188.029 violates well-accepted canons of statutory interpretation . . .

We think that the doubt cast upon the Missouri statute by these cases is not so much a flaw in the statute as it is a reflection of the fact that the rigid trimester analysis of the course of a pregnancy enunciated in *Roe* has resulted in subsequent cases like *Colautti* and *Akron* making constitutional law in this area a virtual Procrustean bed. . . .

Stare decisis is a cornerstone of our legal system, but it has less power in constitutional cases, where, save for constitutional amendments, this Court is the only body able to make needed changes. See *United States* v. *Scott*, 437 U. S. 82, 101 (1978). We have not refrained from reconsideration of a prior construction of the Constitution that has proved "unsound in principle and unworkable in practice." *Garcia* v. *San Antonio Metropolitan Transit Authority*, 469 U. S. 528, 546 (1985); see *Solorio* v. *United States*, 483 U. S. 435, 448–450 (1987); *Erie R. Co.* v. *Tompkins*, 304 U. S. 64, 74–78 (1938). We think the *Roe* trimester framework falls into that category.

In the first place, the rigid *Roe* framework is hardly consistent with the notion of a Constitution cast in general terms, as ours is, and usually speaking in general principles, as ours does. The key elements of the *Roe* framework—trimesters and viability—are not found in the text of the Constitution or in any place else one would expect to find a constitutional principle. Since the bounds of the inquiry are essentially indeterminate, the result has been a web of legal rules that have become increasingly intricate, resembling a code of regulations rather than a body of constitutional doctrine. . . .

In the second place, we do not see why the State's interest in protecting potential human life should come into existence only at the point of viability, and that there should therefore be a rigid line allowing state regulation after viability but prohibiting it before viability. . . .

The dissent takes us to task for our failure to join in a "great issues" debate as to whether the Constitution includes an "unenumerated" general right to privacy as recognized in cases such as *Griswold* v. *Connecticut*, 381 U. S. 479 (1965), and *Roe*. But *Griswold* v. *Connecticut*, unlike *Roe*, did not purport to adopt a whole framework, complete with detailed rules and distinctions, to govern the cases in which the asserted liberty interest would apply. As such, it was far different from the opinion, if not the holding, of *Roe* v. *Wade*, which sought to establish a constitutional framework for judging state regulation of abortion during the entire term of pregnancy. That framework sought to deal with areas of medical practice traditionally subject to state regulation, and it sought to balance once and for all by reference only to the calendar the claims of the State to protect the fetus as a form of human life against the claims of a woman to decide for herself whether or not to abort a fetus she was carrying. The experience of the Court in applying *Roe* v. *Wade* in later cases, see *supra*, at 20, n. 15, suggests to us that there is wisdom in not unnecessarily attempting to elaborate the abstract differences between a "fundamental right" to abortion, as the Court described it in *Akron*, 462 U. S. at 420, n. 1, a "limited fundamental constitutional right," which JUSTICE BLACKMUN's dissent today treats *Roe* as having established, *post*, at 18, or a liberty interest protected by the Due Process Clause, which we believe it to be. The Missouri testing requirement here is reasonably designed to ensure that abortions are not performed where the fetus is viable—an end which all concede is legitimate—and that is sufficient to sustain its constitutionality.

The dissent also accuses us, *inter alia*, of cowardice and illegitimacy in dealing with "the most politically divisive domestic legal issue of our time." *Post*, at 23. There is no doubt that our holding today will allow some governmental regulation of abortion that would have been prohibited under the language of cases such as *Colautti* v. *Franklin*, 439 U. S. 379 (1979), and *Akron* v. *Akron Center for Reproductive Health, Inc., supra.* But the goal of constitutional adjudication is surely not to remove inexorably "politically divisive" issues from the ambit of the legislative process, whereby the people through their elected representatives deal with matters of concern to them. The goal of constitutional adjudication is to hold true the balance between that which the Constitution puts beyond the reach of the democratic process and that which it does not. We think we have done that today. The dissent's suggestion, *post*, at 1–2, 21–22, that legislative bodies, in a Nation where more than half of our population is women, will treat our decision today as an invitation to enact abortion regulation reminiscent of the dark ages not only misreads our views but does scant justice to those who serve in such bodies and the people who elect them.

III

Both appellants and the United States as *Amicus Curiae* have urged that we overrule our decision in *Roe* v. *Wade.* Brief for Appellants 12–18; Brief for United States as *Amicus Curiae* 8–24. The facts of the present case, however, differ from those at issue in *Roe.* Here, Missouri has determined that viability is the point at which its interest in potential human life must be safeguarded. In *Roe*, on the other hand, the Texas statute criminalized the performance of *all* abortions, except when the mother's life was at stake. 410 U. S., at 117–118. This case therefore affords us no occasion to revisit the holding of *Roe*, which was that the Texas statute unconstitutionally infringed the right to an abortion derived from the Due Process Clause, *id.*, at 164, and we leave it undisturbed. To the extent indicated in our opinion, we would modify and narrow *Roe* and succeeding cases.

Because none of the challenged provisions of the Missouri Act properly before us conflict with the Constitution, the judgment of the Court of Appeals is

Reversed.

————

JUSTICE O'CONNOR, concurring in part and concurring in the judgment.

I concur in Parts I, II–A, II–B, and II–C of the Court's opinion.

I

Nothing in the record before us or the opinions below indicates that subsections 1(1) and 1(2) of the preamble to Missouri's abortion regulation statute will affect a woman's decision to have an abortion. . . . It may be correct that the use of postfertilization contraceptive devices is constitutionally protected by *Griswold* and its progeny but, as with a woman's abortion decision, nothing in the record or the opinions below indicates that the preamble will affect a woman's decision to practice contraception. For that matter, nothing in appellees' original complaint, App. 8–21, or their motion *in limine* to limit testimony and evidence on their challenge to the preamble, App. 57–59, indicates that appellees sought to enjoin potential violations of *Griswold.* Neither is there any indication of the possibility that the preamble might be applied to prohibit the performance of *in vitro* fertilization. I agree with the Court, therefore, that all of these intimations of unconstitutionality are simply too hypothetical to support the use of declaratory judgment procedures and injunctive remedies in this case.

. . .

[Justice O'Connor agrees with the Court's analysis of the provisions of the Missouri statute dealing with the use of public facilities and the lack of a case or controversy regarding § 188.205.]

II

In its interpretation of Missouri's "determination of viability" provision, Mo. Rev. Stat.

§ 188.029 (1986), see *ante,* at 15–23, the plurality has proceeded in a manner unneccessary [*sic*] to deciding the question at hand. I agree with the plurality that it was plain error for the Court of Appeals to interpret the second sentence of Mo. Rev. Stat. § 188.029 as meaning that "doctors *must* perform tests to find gestational age, fetal weight and lung maturity." 851 F. 2d, at 1075, n. 5 (emphasis in original). When read together with the first sentence of § 188.029—which requires a physician to "determine if the unborn child is viable by using and exercising that degree of care, skill, and proficiency commonly exercised by the ordinary skillful, careful, and prudent physician engaged in similar practice under the same or similar conditions"—it would be contradictory nonsense to read the second sentence as requiring a physician to perform viability examinations and tests in situations where it would be careless and imprudent to do so. The plurality is quite correct: "the viability-testing provision makes sense only if the second sentence is read to require only those tests that are useful to making subsidiary findings as to viability," *ante,* at 16, and, I would add, only those examinations and tests that it would not be imprudent or careless to perform in the particular medical situation before the physician.

Unlike the plurality, I do not understand these viability testing requirements to conflict with any of the Court's past decisions concerning state regulation of abortion. Therefore, there is no necessity to accept the State's invitation to reexamine the constitutional validity of *Roe* v. *Wade,* 410 U. S. 113 (1973). . . .

It is clear to me that requiring the performance of examinations and tests useful to determining whether a fetus is viable, when viability is possible, and when it would not be medically imprudent to do so, does not impose an undue burden on a woman's abortion decision. On this ground alone I would reject the suggestion that § 188.029 as interpreted is unconstitutional. More to the point, however, just as I see no conflict between § 188.029 and *Colautti* or any decision of this Court concerning a State's ability to give effect to its interest in potential life, I see no conflict between § 188.029 and the Court's opinion in *Akron.* The second-trimester hospitalization re-

quirement struck down in *Akron* imposed, in the majority's view, "a heavy, and unnecessary, burden," 462 U. S., at 438, more than doubling the cost of "women's access to a relatively inexpensive, otherwise accessible, and safe abortion procedure." *Ibid.;* see also *id.,* at 434. By contrast, the cost of examinations and tests that could usefully and prudently be performed when a woman is 20–24 weeks pregnant to determine whether the fetus is viable would only marginally, if at all, increase the cost of an abortion. See Brief for American Association of Prolife Obstetricians and Gynecologists et al. as *Amici Curiae* 3 ("At twenty weeks gestation, an ultrasound examination to determine gestational age is standard medical practice. It is routinely provided by the plaintiff clinics. An ultrasound examination can effectively provide all three designated findings of sec. 188.029"); . . .

JUSTICE SCALIA, concurring in part and concurring in the judgment.

I join Parts I, II–A, II–B, and II–C of the opinion of THE CHIEF JUSTICE. As to Part II–D, I share JUSTICE BLACKMUN's view, *post,* at 20, that it effectively would overrule *Roe* v. *Wade,* 410 U. S. 113 (1973). I think that should be done, but would do it more explicitly. Since today we contrive to avoid doing it, and indeed to avoid almost any decision of national import, I need not set forth my reasons, some of which have been well recited in dissents of my colleagues in other cases. See, *e.g., Thornburgh* v. *American College of Obstetricians and Gynecologists,* 476 U. S. 747, 786–797 (1986) (WHITE, J., dissenting); *Akron* v. *Akron Center for Reproductive Health, Inc.,* 462 U. S. 416, 453–459 (1983) (O'CONNOR, J., dissenting); *Roe* v. *Wade, supra,* at 172–178 (REHNQUIST, J., dissenting); *Doe* v. *Bolton,* 410 U. S. 179, 221–223 (1973) (WHITE, J., dissenting).

The outcome of today's case will doubtless be heralded as a triumph of judicial statesmanship. It is not that, unless it is statesmanlike needlessly to prolong this Court's self-awarded sovereignty over a field where it has little proper business since the answers to most of the cruel questions posed are political and not juridical—a sovereignty which therefore quite properly, but to the great damage of the Court, makes it the object of the sort of organized public pressure that political institutions in a democracy ought to receive.

JUSTICE O'CONNOR's assertion, *ante*, at 5, that a "'fundamental rule of judicial restraint'" requires us to avoid reconsidering *Roe*, cannot be taken seriously. By finessing *Roe* we do not, as she suggests, *ante*, at 5, adhere to the strict and venerable rule that we should avoid "'decid[ing] questions of a constitutional nature.'" We have not disposed of this case on some statutory or procedural ground, but have decided, and could not avoid deciding, whether the Missouri statute meets the requirements of the United States Constitution. The only choice available is whether, in deciding that constitutional question, we should use *Roe* v. *Wade* as the benchmark, or something else. . . .

The real question, then, is whether there are valid reasons to go beyond the most stingy possible holding today. It seems to me there are not only valid but compelling ones. Ordinarily, speaking no more broadly than is absolutely required avoids throwing settled law into confusion; doing so today preserves a chaos that is evident to anyone who can read and count. Alone sufficient to justify a broad holding is the fact that our retaining control, through *Roe*, of what I believe to be, and many of our citizens recognize to be, a political issue, continuously distorts the public perception of the role of this Court. We can now look forward to at least another Term with carts full of mail from the public, and streets full of demonstrators, urging us—their unelected and life-tenured judges who have been awarded those extraordinary, undemocratic characteristics precisely in order that we might follow the law despite the popular will—to follow the popular will. Indeed, I expect we can look forward to even more of that than before, given our indecisive decision today. . . . It thus appears that the mansion of constitutionalized abortion-law, constructed overnight in *Roe* v. *Wade*, must be disassembled doorjamb by door-jamb, and never entirely brought down, no matter how wrong it may be.

Of the four courses we might have chosen today—to reaffirm *Roe*, to overrule it explicitly, to overrule it *sub silentio*, or to avoid the question— the last is the least responsible. On the question of

the constitutionality of § 188.029, I concur in the judgment of the Court and strongly dissent from the manner in which it has been reached.

———

JUSTICE BLACKMUN, with whom JUSTICE BRENNAN and JUSTICE MARSHALL join, concurring in part and dissenting in part.

Today, *Roe* v. *Wade*, 410 U. S. 113 (1973), and the fundamental constitutional right of women to decide whether to terminate a pregnancy, survive but are not secure. Although the Court extricates itself from this case without making a single, even incremental, change in the law of abortion, the plurality and JUSTICE SCALIA would overrule *Roe* (the first silently, the other explicitly) and would return to the States virtually unfettered authority to control the quintessentially intimate, personal, and life-directing decision whether to carry a fetus to term. Although today, no less than yesterday, the Constitution and the decisions of this Court prohibit a State from enacting laws that inhibit women from the meaningful exercise of that right, a plurality of this Court implicitly invites every state legislature to enact more and more restrictive abortion regulations in order to provoke more and more test cases, in the hope that sometime down the line the Court will return the law of procreative freedom to the severe limitations that generally prevailed in this country before January 22, 1973. Never in my memory has a plurality announced a judgment of this Court that so foments disregard for the law and for our standing decisions.

Nor in my memory has a plurality gone about its business in such a deceptive fashion. At every level of its review, from its effort to read the real meaning out of the Missouri statute, to its intended evisceration of precedents and its deafening silence about the constitutional protections that it would jettison, the plurality obscures the portent of its analysis. With feigned restraint, the plurality announces that its analysis leaves *Roe* "undisturbed," albeit "modif[ied] and narrow[ed]." *Ante*, at 23. But this disclaimer is totally meaningless. The plurality opinion is filled with winks, and nods, and knowing glances to those who would do away with *Roe* explicitly, but turns a stone face to anyone in search of what the plurality conceives as the scope of a woman's right under the Due Process Clause to terminate a pregnancy free from the coercive and brooding influence of the State. The simple truth is that *Roe* would not survive the plurality's analysis, and that the plurality provides no substitute for *Roe's* protective umbrella.

I fear for the future. I fear for the liberty and equality of the millions of women who have lived and come of age in the 16 years since *Roe* was decided. I fear for the integrity of, and public esteem for, this Court.

. . .

[I.A]

At the outset, I note that in its haste to limit abortion rights, the plurality compounds the errors of its analysis by needlessly reaching out to address constitutional questions that are not actually presented. The conflict between § 188.029 and *Roe's* trimester framework, which purportedly drives the plurality to reconsider our past decisions, is a contrived conflict: the product of an aggressive misreading of the viability-testing requirement and a needlessly wooden application of the *Roe* framework.

. . .

Had the plurality read the statute as written, it would have had no cause to reconsider the *Roe* framework. As properly construed, the viability-testing provision does not pass constitutional muster under even a rational-basis standard, the least restrictive level of review applied by this Court. See *Williamson* v. *Lee Optical Co.*, 348 U. S. 483 (1955). By mandating tests to determine fetal weight and lung maturity for every fetus thought to be more than 20 weeks gestational age, the statute requires physicians to undertake procedures, such as amniocentesis, that, in the situation presented, have no medical justification, impose significant additional health risks on both the pregnant woman and the fetus, and bear no rational relation to the State's interest in protecting fetal life. As written, § 188.029 is an arbitrary imposition of discomfort, risk, and expense,

furthering no discernible interest except to make the procurement of an abortion as arduous and difficult as possible. Thus, were it not for the plurality's tortured effort to avoid the plain import of § 188.029, it could have struck down the testing provision as patently irrational irrespective of the *Roe* framework.

The plurality eschews this straightforward resolution, in the hope of precipitating a constitutional crisis. Far from avoiding constitutional difficulty, the plurality attempts to engineer a dramatic retrenchment in our jurisprudence by exaggerating the conflict between its untenable construction of § 188.029 and the *Roe* trimester framework.

No one contests that under the *Roe* framework the State, in order to promote its interest in potential human life, may regulate and even proscribe non-therapeutic abortions once the fetus becomes viable. *Roe*, 410 U. S., at 164–165. If, as the plurality appears to hold, the testing provision simply requires a physician to use appropriate and medically sound tests to determine whether the fetus is actually viable when the estimated gestational age is greater than 20 weeks (and therefore within what the District Court found to be the margin of error for viability, *ante*, at 19), then I see little or no conflict with *Roe*. Nothing in *Roe*, or any of its progeny, holds that a State may not effectuate its compelling interest in the potential life of a viable fetus by seeking to ensure that no viable fetus is mistakenly aborted because of the inherent lack of precision in estimates of gestational age. A requirement that a physician make a finding of viability, one way or the other, for every fetus that falls within the range of possible viability does no more than preserve the State's recognized authority. Although, as the plurality correctly points out, such a testing requirement would have the effect of imposing additional costs on second-trimester abortions where the tests indicated that the fetus was not viable, these costs would be merely incidental to, and a necessary accommodation of, the State's unquestioned right to prohibit non-therapeutic abortions after the point of viability. In short, the testing provision, as construed by the plurality is consistent with the *Roe* framework and could be upheld effortlessly under current doctrine.

. . .

B

Having set up the conflict between § 188.029 and the *Roe* trimester framework, the plurality summarily discards *Roe*'s analytic core as " 'unsound in principle and unworkable in practice.' " *Ante*, at 20, quoting *Garcia* v. *San Antonio Metropolitan Transit Authority*, 469 U. S. 528, 546 (1985). This is so, the plurality claims, because the key elements of the framework do not appear in the text of the Constitution, because the framework more closely resembles a regulatory code than a body of constitutional doctrine, and because under the framework the State's interest in potential human life is considered compelling only after viability, when, in fact, that interest is equally compelling throughout pregnancy. *Ante*, at 21–22. The plurality does not bother to explain these alleged flaws in *Roe*. Bald assertion masquerades as reasoning. The object, quite clearly, is not to persuade, but to prevail.

1

The plurality opinion is far more remarkable for the arguments that it does not advance than for those that it does. The plurality does not even mention, much less join, the true jurisprudential debate underlying this case: whether the Constitution includes an "unenumerated" general right to privacy as recognized in many of our decisions, most notably *Griswold* v. *Connecticut*, 381 U. S. 479 (1965), and *Roe*, and, more specifically, whether and to what extent such a right to privacy extends to matters of childbearing and family life, including abortion. . . .

But rather than arguing that the text of the Constitution makes no mention of the right to privacy, the plurality complains that the critical elements of the *Roe* framework—trimesters and viability—do not appear in the Constitution and are, therefore, somehow inconsistent with a Constitution cast in general terms. *Ante*, at 20. Were this a true concern, we would have to abandon most of our constitutional jurisprudence. As the plurality well knows, or should know, the "critical elements" of countless constitutional doctrines nowhere appear in the Constitution's text. The Constitution makes no mention, for example, of the First Amendment's "actual malice" standard for proving certain libels, see *New York Times* v. *Sullivan*, 376 U. S. 254 (1964), or of the standard for determining when speech is obscene. See *Miller* v. *California*, 413 U. S. 15 (1973). Similarly, the Constitution makes no mention of the rational-basis test, or the specific verbal formulations of intermediate and strict scrutiny by which this Court evaluates claims under the Equal Protection Clause. The reason is simple. Like the *Roe* framework, these tests or standards are not, and do not purport to be, rights protected by the Constitution. Rather, they are judge-made methods for evaluating and measuring the strength and scope of constitutional rights or for balancing the constitutional rights of individuals against the competing interests of government.

. . .

D

Thus, "not with a bang, but a whimper," the plurality discards a landmark case of the last generation, and casts into darkness the hopes and visions of every woman in this country who had come to believe that the Constitution guaranteed her the right to exercise some control over her unique ability to bear children. The plurality does so either oblivious or insensitive to the fact that millions of women, and their families, have ordered their lives around the right to reproductive choice, and that this right has become vital to the full participation of women in the economic and political walks of American life. The plurality would clear the way once again for government to force upon women the physical labor and specific and direct medical and psychological harms that may accompany carrying a fetus to term. The plurality would clear the way again for the State to conscript a woman's body and to force upon her a "distressful life and future." *Roe*, 410 U. S., at 153.

The result, as we know from experience, see Cates & Rocket, Illegal Abortions in the United States: 1972–1974, 8 Family Planning Perspectives 86, 92 (1976), would be that every year hundreds of thousands of women, in desperation, would defy the law, and place their health and safety in the unclean and unsympathetic hands of back-alley abortionists, or they would attempt to perform abortions upon themselves, with disastrous results. Every year, many women, especially poor and minority women, would die or suffer debilitating physical trauma, all in the name of enforced morality or religious dictates or lack of compassion, as it may be.

Of the aspirations and settled understandings of American women, of the inevitable and brutal consequences of what it is doing, the tough-approach plurality utters not a word. This silence is callous. It is also profoundly destructive of this Court as an institution. . . .

. . . Today's decision involves the most politically divisive domestic legal issue of our time. By refusing to explain or to justify its proposed revolutionary revision in the law of abortion, and by refusing to abide not only by our precedents, but also by our canons for reconsidering those precedents, the plurality invites charges of cowardice and illegitimacy to our door. I cannot say that these would be undeserved.

II

For today, at least, the law of abortion stands undisturbed. For today, the women of this Nation still retain the liberty to control their destinies. But the signs are evident and very ominous, and a chill wind blows.

I dissent.

JUSTICE STEVENS, concurring in part and dissenting in part.

Having joined Part II–C of the Court's opinion, I shall not comment on § 188.205 of the Missouri statute. With respect to the challenged portions of §§ 188.210 and 188.215, I agree with JUSTICE BLACKMUN, *ante*, at 2–5, n. 1 (concurring in part and dissenting in part), that the record identifies a sufficient number of unconstitutional applications to support the Court of Appeals' judgment invalidating those provisions. The reasons why I would also affirm that court's invalidation of § 188.029, the viability testing provision, and §§ 1.205.1(1)(2) of the preamble, require separate explanation.

I

It seems to me that in Part II–D of its opinion, the plurality strains to place a construction on § 188.029 that enables it to conclude, "[W]e would modify and narrow *Roe* and succeeding cases," *ante*, at 23. That statement is ill-advised because there is no need to modify even slightly the holdings of prior cases in order to uphold § 188.029. For the most plausible nonliteral construction, as both JUSTICE BLACKMUN, *ante*, at 8–9 (concurring in part and dissenting in part), and JUSTICE O'CONNOR, *ante*, at 4–11 (concurring in part and concurring in judgment), have demonstrated, is constitutional and entirely consistent with our precedents.

I am unable to accept JUSTICE O'CONNOR's construction of the second sentence in § 188.029, however, because I believe it is foreclosed by two controlling principles of statutory interpretation. . . .

. . . the meaning of the second sentence of § 188.029 is too plain to be ignored. The sentence twice uses the mandatory term "shall," and contains no qualifying language. If it is implicitly limited to tests that are useful in determining viability, it adds nothing to the requirement imposed by the preceding sentence.

My interpretation of the plain language is supported by the structure of the statute as a whole, particularly the preamble, which "finds" that life "begins at conception" and further commands that state laws shall be construed to provide the maximum protection to "the unborn child at every stage of development." Mo. Rev. Stat. §§ 1.205.1(1), 1.205.2 (1986). I agree with the District Court that "[o]bviously, the purpose of this law is to protect the potential life of the fetus, rather than to safeguard maternal health." 662 F. Supp., at 420. A literal reading of the statute tends to accomplish that goal. Thus it is not "incongruous," *ante*, at 16, to assume that the Missouri Legislature was trying to protect the potential human life of nonviable fetuses by making the abortion decision more costly. On the contrary, I am satisfied that the Court of Appeals, as well as the District Court, correctly concluded that the Missouri Legislature meant exactly what it said in the second sentence of § 188.029. I am also satisfied, for the reasons stated by JUSTICE BLACKMUN, that the testing provision is manifestly unconstitutional under *Williamson* v. *Lee Optical Co.,* 348 U. S. 483 (1955), "irrespective of the *Roe*[v. *Wade,* 410 U. S. 113 (1973),] framework." *Ante,* at 7 (concurring in part and dissenting in part).

II

The Missouri statute defines "conception" as "the fertilization of the ovum of a female by a sperm of a male," Mo. Rev. Stat. § 188.015(3) (1986), even though standard medical texts equate "conception" with implantation in the uterus, occurring about six days after fertilization. Missouri's declaration therefore implies regulation not only of previability abortions, but also of common forms of contraception such as the IUD and the morning-after pill. Because the preamble, read in context, threatens serious encroachments upon the liberty of the pregnant woman and the health professional, I am persuaded that these plaintiffs, appellees before us, have standing to challenge its constitutionality. Accord, 851 F. 2d, at 1075–1076.

To the extent that the Missouri statute interferes with contraceptive choices, I have no doubt that it is unconstitutional under the Court's holdings in *Griswold* v. *Connecticut,* 381 U. S. 479 (1965), *Eisenstadt* v. *Baird,* 405 U. S. 438 (1972), and *Carey* v. *Population Services International,* 431 U. S. 678 (1977). . . .

. . .

In my opinion the preamble to the Missouri statute is unconstitutional for two reasons. To the extent that it has substantive impact on the freedom to use contraceptive procedures, it is inconsistent with the central holding in *Griswold.* To the extent that it merely makes "legislative findings without operative effect," as the State argues, Brief for Appellants 22, it violates the Establishment Clause of the First Amendment. Contrary to the theological "finding" of the Missouri Legislature, a woman's constitutionally protected liberty encompasses the right to act on her own belief that—to paraphrase St. Thomas Aquinas—until a seed has acquired the powers of sensation and movement, the life of a human being has not yet begun.

Bowers v. Hardwick

478 U.S. 186 (1986)

Michael Hardwick was charged with violating Georgia law by committing sodomy with another adult male in the bedroom of his home. After the district attorney decided not to present the matter to the grand jury, Hardwick brought suit in federal court to have the statute declared unconstitutional because it criminalized consensual sodomy. A district court granted the state's motion to dismiss; the Eleventh Circuit reversed, holding that the statute violated Hardwick's fundamental rights. The defendant in this case is Michael J. Bowers, Attorney General of Georgia. John and Mary Doe joined Hardwick as plaintiffs in the action, claiming that they wished to engage in sexual activity proscribed by the statute. The Court examined only Hardwick's challenge and expressed no opinion on the constitutionality of the Georgia statute as applied to other acts of sodomy.

JUSTICE WHITE delivered the opinion of the Court.

In August 1982, respondent was charged with violating the Georgia statute criminalizing sodomy by committing that act with another adult

male in the bedroom of respondent's home. After a preliminary hearing, the District Attorney decided not to present the matter to the grand jury unless further evidence developed.

Respondent then brought suit in the Federal

District Court, challenging the constitutionality of the statute insofar as it criminalized consensual sodomy. He asserted that he was a practicing homosexual, that the Georgia sodomy statute, as administered by the defendants, placed him in imminent danger of arrest, and that the statute for several reasons violates the Federal Constitution. The District Court granted the defendants' motion to dismiss for failure to state a claim, relying on *Doe* v. *Commonwealth's Attorney for the City of Richmond*, 403 F.Supp. 1199 (ED Va.1975), which this Court summarily affirmed, 425 U.S. 901 (1976).

A divided panel of the Court of Appeals for the Eleventh Circuit reversed. 760 F.2d 1202 (1985). The court first held that, because *Doe* was distinguishable and in any event had been undermined by later decisions, our summary affirmance in that case did not require affirmance of the District Court. Relying on our decisions in *Griswold* v. *Connecticut*, 381 U.S. 479 (1965), *Eisenstadt* v. *Baird*, 405 U.S. 438 (1972), *Stanley* v. *Georgia*, 394 U.S. 557 (1969), and *Roe* v. *Wade*, 410 U.S. 113 (1973), the court went on to hold that the Georgia statute violated respondent's fundamental rights because his homosexual activity is a private and intimate association that is beyond the reach of state regulation by reason of the Ninth Amendment and the Due Process Clause of the Fourteenth Amendment. The case was remanded for trial, at which, to prevail, the State would have to prove that the statute is supported by a compelling interest and is the most narrowly drawn means of achieving that end.

Because other Courts of Appeals have arrived at judgments contrary to that of the Eleventh Circuit in this case, we granted the State's petition for certiorari questioning the holding that its sodomy statute violates the fundamental rights of homosexuals. We agree with the State that the Court of Appeals erred, and hence reverse its judgment.

This case does not require a judgment on whether laws against sodomy between consenting adults in general, or between homosexuals in particular, are wise or desirable. It raises no question about the right or propriety of state legislative decisions to repeal their laws that criminalize homosexual sodomy, or of state court decisions invalidating those laws on state constitutional grounds. The issue presented is whether the Federal Constitution confers a fundamental right upon homosexuals to engage in sodomy and hence invalidates the laws of the many States that still make such conduct illegal and have done so for a very long time. The case also calls for some judgment about the limits of the Court's role in carrying out its constitutional mandate.

We first register our disagreement with the Court of Appeals and with respondent that the Court's prior cases have construed the Constitution to confer a right of privacy that extends to homosexual sodomy and for all intents and purposes have decided this case. The reach of this line of cases was sketched in *Carey* v. *Population Services International*, 431 U.S. 678, 685 (1977). *Pierce* v. *Society of Sisters*, 268 U.S. 510 (1925), and *Meyer* v. *Nebraska*, 262 U.S. 390 (1923), were described as dealing with child rearing and education; *Prince* v. *Massachusetts*, 321 U.S. 158 (1944), with family relationships; *Skinner* v. *Oklahoma ex rel. Williamson*, 316 U.S. 535 (1942), with procreation; *Loving* v. *Virginia*, 388 U.S. 1 (1967), with marriage; *Griswold* v. *Connecticut, supra*, and *Eisenstadt* v. *Baird, supra*, with contraception; and *Roe* v. *Wade*, 410 U.S. 113 (1973), with abortion. The latter three cases were interpreted as construing the Due Process Clause of the Fourteenth Amendment to confer a fundamental individual right to decide whether or not to beget or bear a child. *Carey* v. *Population Services International, supra*, 431 U.S., at 688–689.

Accepting the decisions in these cases and the above description of them, we think it evident that none of the rights announced in those cases bears any resemblance to the claimed constitutional right of homosexuals to engage in acts of sodomy that is asserted in this case. No connection between family, marriage, or procreation on the one hand and homosexual activity on the other has been demonstrated, either by the Court of Appeals or by respondent. Moreover, any claim that these cases nevertheless stand for the proposition that any kind of private sexual conduct between consenting adults is constitutionally insulated from state proscription is unsupportable. Indeed, the Court's opinion in *Carey* twice asserted that the privacy right, which the *Griswold* line of cases found to be one of the protections provided by the Due Process Clause, did not reach so far. 431 U.S., at 688, n. 5, 694, n. 17.

Precedent aside, however, respondent would have us announce, as the Court of Appeals did, a fundamental right to engage in homosexual sodomy. This we are quite unwilling to do. It is true that despite the language of the Due Process Clauses of the Fifth and Fourteenth Amendments, which appears to focus only on the processes by which life, liberty, or property is taken, the cases are legion in which those Clauses have been interpreted to have substantive content, subsuming rights that to a great extent are immune from federal or state regulation or proscription. Among such cases are those recognizing rights that have little or no textual support in the constitutional language. *Meyer, Prince,* and *Pierce* fall in this category, as do the privacy cases from *Griswold* to *Carey.*

Striving to assure itself and the public that announcing rights not readily identifiable in the Constitution's text involves much more than the imposition of the Justices' own choice of values on the States and the Federal Government, the Court has sought to identify the nature of the rights qualifying for heightened judicial protection. In *Palko* v. *Connecticut,* 302 U.S. 319, 325, 326, (1937), it was said that this category includes those fundamental liberties that are "implicit in the concept of ordered liberty," such that "neither liberty nor justice would exist if [they] were sacrificed." A different description of fundamental liberties appeared in *Moore* v. *East Cleveland,* 431 U.S. 494, 503, (1977) (opinion of POWELL, J.), where they are characterized as those liberties that are "deeply rooted in this Nation's history and tradition." *Id.,* at 503, (POWELL, J.). See also *Griswold* v. *Connecticut,* 381 U.S., at 506.

It is obvious to us that neither of these formulations would extend a fundamental right to homosexuals to engage in acts of consensual sodomy. Proscriptions against that conduct have ancient roots. See generally, Survey on the Constitutional Right to Privacy in the Context of Homosexual Activity, 40 U.Miami L. Rev. 521, 525 (1986). Sodomy was a criminal offense at common law and was forbidden by the laws of the original thirteen States when they ratified the Bill of Rights. In 1868, when the Fourteenth Amendment was ratified, all but 5 of the 37 States in the Union had criminal sodomy laws. In fact, until 1961, all 50 States outlawed sodomy, and today, 24 States and the District of Columbia continue to provide criminal penalties for sodomy performed in private and between consenting adults. Survey, U.Miami L.Rev., *supra,* at 524, n. 9. Against this background, to claim that a right to engage in such conduct is "deeply rooted in this Nation's history and tradition" or "implicit in the concept of ordered liberty" is, at best, facetious.

Nor are we inclined to take a more expansive view of our authority to discover new fundamental rights imbedded in the Due Process Clause. The Court is most vulnerable and comes nearest to illegitimacy when it deals with judge-made constitutional law having little or no cognizable roots in the language or design of the Constitution. That this is so was painfully demonstrated by the face-off between the Executive and the Court in the 1930's, which resulted in the repudiation of much of the substantive gloss that the Court had placed on the Due Process Clause of the Fifth and Fourteenth Amendments. There should be, therefore, great resistance to expand the substantive reach of those Clauses, particularly if it requires redefining the category of rights deemed to be fundamental. Otherwise, the Judiciary necessarily takes to itself further authority to govern the country without express constitutional authority. The claimed right pressed on us today falls far short of overcoming this resistance.

. . .

Even if the conduct at issue here is not a fundamental right, respondent asserts that there must be a rational basis for the law and that there is none in this case other than the presumed belief of a majority of the electorate in Georgia that homosexual sodomy is immoral and unacceptable. This is said to be an inadequate rationale to support the law. The law, however, is constantly based on notions of morality, and if all laws representing essentially moral choices are to be invalidated under the Due Process Clause, the courts will be very busy indeed. Even respondent makes no such claim, but insists that majority sentiments about the morality of homosexuality should be declared inadequate. We do not agree, and are unpersuaded that the sodomy laws of some 25 States should be invalidated on this basis.

Accordingly, the judgment of the Court of Appeals is

Reversed.

CHIEF JUSTICE BURGER, concurring.

I join the Court's opinion, but I write separately to underscore my view that in constitutional terms there is no such thing as a fundamental right to commit homosexual sodomy.

As the Court notes, *ante* at 192, the proscriptions against sodomy have very "ancient roots." Decisions of individuals relating to homosexual conduct have been subject to state intervention throughout the history of Western Civilization. Condemnation of those practices is firmly rooted in Judaeo-Christian moral and ethical standards. . . . To hold that the act of homosexual sodomy is somehow protected as a fundamental right would be to cast aside millennia of moral teaching.

This is essentially not a question of personal "preferences" but rather of the legislative authority of the State. I find nothing in the Constitution depriving a State of the power to enact the statute challenged here.

JUSTICE POWELL, concurring.

I join the opinion of the Court. I agree with the Court that there is no fundamental right—*i.e.*, no substantive right under the Due Process Clause—such as that claimed by respondent, and found to exist by the Court of Appeals. This is not to suggest, however, that respondent may not be protected by the Eighth Amendment of the Constitution. The Georgia statute at issue in this case, Ga.Code Ann. § 16–6–2, authorizes a court to imprison a person for up to 20 years for a single private, consensual act of sodomy. In my view, a prison sentence for such conduct—certainly a sentence of long duration—would create a serious Eighth Amendment issue. Under the Georgia statute a single act of sodomy, even in the private setting of a home, is a felony comparable in terms of the possible sentence imposed to serious felonies such as aggravated battery, § 16–5–24, first degree arson, § 16–7–60 and robbery, § 16–8–40.

In this case, however, respondent has not been tried, much less convicted and sentenced. Moreover, respondent has not raised the Eighth Amendment issue below. For these reasons this constitutional argument is not before us.

JUSTICE BLACKMUN, with whom JUSTICE BRENNAN, JUSTICE MARSHALL, and JUSTICE STEVENS join, dissenting.

This case is no more about "a fundamental right to engage in homosexual sodomy," as the Court purports to declare, *ante*, at 191, than *Stanley* v. *Georgia*, 394 U.S. 557 (1969), was about a fundamental right to watch obscene movies, or *Katz* v. *United States*, 389 U.S. 347 (1967), was about a fundamental right to place interstate bets from a telephone booth. Rather, this case is about "the most comprehensive of rights and the right most valued by civilized men," namely, "the right to be let alone." *Olmstead* v. *United States*, 277 U.S. 438, 478 (1928) (Brandeis, J., dissenting).

The statute at issue, Ga.Code Ann. § 16–6–2, denies individuals the right to decide for themselves whether to engage in particular forms of private, consensual sexual activity. The Court concludes that § 16–6–2 is valid essentially because "the laws of . . . many States . . . still make such conduct illegal and have done so for a very long time." *Ante*, at 190. But the fact that the moral judgments expressed by statutes like § 16–6–2 may be "natural and familiar . . . ought not to conclude our judgment upon the question whether statutes embodying them conflict with the Constitution of the United States." *Roe* v. *Wade*, 410 U.S. 113, 117 (1973), quoting *Lochner* v. *New York*, 198 U.S. 45, 76 (1905) (Holmes J., dissenting). Like Justice Holmes, I believe that "[i]t is revolting to have no better reason for a rule of law than that so it was laid down in the time of Henry IV. It is still more revolting if the grounds upon which it was laid down have vanished long since, and the rule simply persists from blind imitation of the past." Holmes, The Path of the Law, 10

Harv.L.Rev. 457, 469 (1897). I believe we must analyze respondent's claim in the light of the values that underlie the constitutional right to privacy. If that right means anything, it means that, before Georgia can prosecute its citizens for making choices about the most intimate apsects of their lives, it must do more than assert that the choice they have made is an "'abominable crime not fit to be named among Christians.'" *Herring* v. *State*, 119 Ga. 709, 721, 46 S.E. 876, 882 (1904).

I

. . . the Court's almost obsessive focus on homosexual activity is particularly hard to justify in light of the broad language Georgia has used. Unlike the Court, the Georgia Legislature has not proceeded on the assumption that homosexuals are so different from other citizens that their lives may be controlled in a way that would not be tolerated if it limited the choices of those other citizens. Cf. *ante*, at 188, n. 2. Rather, Georgia has provided that "[a] person commits the offense of sodomy when he performs or submits to any sexual act involving the sex organs of one person and the mouth or anus of another." Ga.Code Ann. § 16–6–2(a). The sex or status of the persons who engage in the act is irrelevant as a matter of state law. In fact, to the extent I can discern a legislative purpose for Georgia's 1968 enactment of § 16–6–2, that purpose seems to have been to broaden the coverage of the law to reach heterosexual as well as homosexual activity. I therefore see no basis for the Court's decision to treat this case as an "as applied" challenge to § 16–6–2, see *ante*, at 188, n. 2, or for Georgia's attempt, both in its brief and at oral argument, to defend § 16–6–2 solely on the grounds that it prohibits homosexual activity. Michael Hardwick's standing may rest in significant part on Georgia's apparent willingness to enforce against homosexuals a law it seems not to have any desire to enforce against heterosexuals. See Tr. of Oral Arg. 4–5; cf. 760 F.2d 1202, 1205–1206 (CA11 1985). But his claim that § 16–6–2 involves an unconstitutional intrusion into his privacy and his right of intimate association does not depend in any way on his sexual orientation.

Second, I disagree with the Court's refusal to consider whether § 16–6–2 runs afoul of the Eighth or Ninth Amendments or the Equal Protection Clause of the Fourteenth Amendment. *Ante*, at 196, n. 8. Respondent's complaint expressly invoked the Ninth Amendment, see App. 6., and he relied heavily before this Court on *Griswold* v. *Connecticut*, 381 U.S. 479, 484, (1965), which identifies that Amendment as one of the specific constitutional provisions giving "life and substance" to our understanding of privacy. . . . even if respondent did not advance claims based on the Eighth or Ninth Amendments, or on the Equal Protection Clause, his complaint should not be dismissed if any of those provisions could entitle him to relief. I need not reach either the Eighth Amendment or the Equal Protection Clause issues because I believe that Hardwick has stated a cognizable claim that § 16–6–2 interferes with constitutionally protected interests in privacy and freedom of intimate association. But neither the Eighth Amendment nor the Equal Protection Clause is so clearly irrelevant that a claim resting on either provision should be peremptorily dismissed. The Court's cramped reading of the issue before it makes for a short opinion, but it does little to make for a persuasive one.

II

"Our cases long have recognized that the Constitution embodies a promise that a certain private sphere of individual liberty will be kept largely beyond the reach of government." *Thornburgh* v. *American Coll. of Obst. & Gyn.*, 476 U.S. 747, 772 (1986). In construing the right to privacy, the Court has proceeded along two somewhat distinct, albeit complementary, lines. First, it has recognized a privacy interest with reference to certain *decisions* that are properly for the individual to make. *E.g.*, *Roe* v. *Wade*, 410 U.S. 113 (1973); *Pierce* v. *Society of Sisters*, 268 U.S. 510 (1925). Second, it has recognized a privacy interest with reference to certain *places* without regard for the particular activities in which the individuals who occupy them are engaged. *E.g.*, *United States* v. *Karo*, 468 U.S. 705 (1984); *Payton* v. *New York*, 445 U.S. 573 (1980); *Rios* v. *United States*,

364 U.S. 253 (1960). The case before us implicates both the decisional and the spatial aspects of the right to privacy.

A

The Court concludes today that none of our prior cases dealing with various decisions that individuals are entitled to make free of governmental interference "bears any resemblance to the claimed constitutional right of homosexuals to engage in acts of sodomy that is asserted in this case." *Ante*, at 190–191.

Only the most willful blindness could obscure the fact that sexual intimacy is "a sensitive, key relationship of human existence, central to family life, community welfare, and the development of human personality," *Paris Adult Theatre I* v. *Slaton*, 413 U.S. 49, 63 (1973); see also *Carey* v. *Population Services International*, 431 U.S. 678, 685 (1977). The fact that individuals define themselves in a significant way through their intimate sexual relationships with others suggests, in a Nation as diverse as ours, that there may be many "right" ways of conducting those relationships, and that much of the richness of a relationship will come from the freedom an individual has to *choose* the form and nature of these intensely personal bonds. . . .

B

The behavior for which Hardwick faces prosecution occurred in his own home, a place to which the Fourth Amendment attaches special significance. The Court's treatment of this aspect of the case is symptomatic of its overall refusal to consider the broad principles that have informed our treatment of privacy in specific cases. Just as the right to privacy is more than the mere aggregation of a number of entitlements to engage in specific behavior, so too, protecting the physical integrity of the home is more than merely a means of protecting specific activities that often take place there. Even when our understanding of the contours of the right to privacy depends on "reference to a 'place,' " *Katz* v. *United States*, 389 U.S., at 361 (Harlan, J., concurring), "the essence of a Fourth Amendment violation is 'not the breaking of [a person's] doors, and the rummaging of his

drawers,' but rather is 'the invasion of his indefeasible right of personal security, personal liberty and private property.' " *California* v. *Ciraolo*, 476 U.S. 207, 226 (1986) (POWELL, J., dissenting), quoting *Boyd* v. *United States*, 116 U.S. 616, 630 (1886).

. . .

III

. . .

I cannot agree that either the length of time a majority has held its convictions or the passions with which it defends them can withdraw legislation from this Court's scrutiny. See, *e.g.*, *Roe* v. *Wade*, 410 U.S. 113 (1973); *Loving* v. *Virginia*, 388 U.S. 1 (1967); *Brown* v. *Board of Education*, 347 U.S. 483 (1954). As Justice Jackson wrote so eloquently for the Court in *West Virginia Board of Education* v. *Barnette*, 319 U.S. 624, 641–642 (1943), "we apply the limitations of the Constitution with no fear that freedom to be intellectually and spiritually diverse or even contrary will disintegrate the social organization. . . . [F]reedom to differ is not limited to things that do not matter much. That would be a mere shadow of freedom. The test of its substance is the right to differ as to things that touch the heart of the existing order." . . .

The assertion that "traditional Judeo-Christian values proscribe" the conduct involved, Brief for Petitioner 20, cannot provide an adequate justification for § 16–6–2. That certain, but by no means all, religious groups condemn the behavior at issue gives the State no license to impose their judgments on the entire citizenry. . . . A State can no more punish private behavior because of religious intolerance than it can punish such behavior because of racial animus. . . .

IV

It took but three years for the Court to see the error in its analysis in *Minersville School District* v. *Gobitis*, 310 U.S. 586 (1940), and to recognize that the threat to national cohesion posed by a refusal to salute the flag was vastly outweighed by the threat to those same values posed by compelling such a salute. See *West Virginia Board of Education* v. *Barnette,* 319 U.S. 624 (1943). I can only hope that here, too, the Court soon will reconsider its analysis and conclude that depriving individuals of the right to choose for themselves how to conduct their intimate relationships poses a far greater threat to the values most deeply rooted in our Nation's history than tolerance of nonconformity could ever do. Because I think the Court today betrays those values, I dissent.

JUSTICE STEVENS, with whom JUSTICE BRENNAN and JUSTICE MARSHALL join, dissenting.

Like the statute that is challenged in this case, the rationale of the Court's opinion applies equally to the prohibited conduct regardless of whether the parties who engage in it are married or unmarried, or are of the same or different sexes. Sodomy was condemned as an odious and sinful type of behavior during the formative period of the common law. That condemnation was equally damning for heterosexual and homosexual sodomy. Moreover, it provided no special exemption for married couples. The license to cohabit and to produce legitimate offspring simply did not include any permission to engage in sexual conduct that was considered a "crime against nature."

The history of the Georgia statute before us clearly reveals this traditional prohibition of heterosexual, as well as homosexual, sodomy. Indeed, at one point in the 20th century, Georgia's law was construed to permit certain sexual conduct between homosexual women even though such conduct was prohibited between heterosexuals. The history of the statutes cited by the majority as proof for the proposition that sodomy is not constitutionally protected, *ante,* at 192–194, and nn. 5 and 6, similarly reveals a prohibition on heterosexual, as well as homosexual, sodomy.

Because the Georgia statute expresses the traditional view that sodomy is an immoral kind of conduct regardless of the identity of the persons who engage in it, I believe that a proper analysis of its constitutionality requires consideration of two questions: First, may a State totally prohibit the described conduct by means of a neutral law applying without exception to all persons subject to its jurisdiction? If not, may the State save the statute by announcing that it will only enforce the law against homosexuals? The two questions merit separate discussion.

I

Our prior cases make two propositions abundantly clear. First, the fact that the governing majority in a State has traditionally viewed a particular practice as immoral is not a sufficient reason for upholding a law prohibiting the practice; neither history nor tradition could save a law prohibiting miscegenation from constitutional attack. Second, individual decisions by married persons, concerning the intimacies of their physical relationship, even when not intended to produce offspring, are a form of "liberty" protected by the Due Process Clause of the Fourteenth Amendment. *Griswold* v. *Connecticut,* 381 U.S. 479 (1965). Moreover, this protection extends to intimate choices by unmarried as well as married persons. *Carey* v. *Population Services International,* 431 U.S. 678 (1977); *Eisenstadt* v. *Baird,* 405 U.S. 438 (1972).

. . .

Society has every right to encourage its individual members to follow particular traditions in expressing affection for one another and in gratifying their personal desires. It, of course, may prohibit an individual from imposing his will on another to satisfy his own selfish interests. It also may prevent an individual from interfering with, or violating, a legally sanctioned and protected relationship, such as marriage. And it may explain the relative advantages and disadvantages of different forms of intimate expression. But when individual married couples are isolated from observation by others, the way in which they voluntarily choose to conduct their intimate relations is a matter for them—not the State—to decide. . . .

II

If the Georgia statute cannot be enforced as it is written—if the conduct it seeks to prohibit is a protected form of liberty for the vast majority of Georgia's citizens—the State must assume the burden of justifying a selective application of its law. Either the persons to whom Georgia seeks to apply its statute do not have the same interest in "liberty" that others have, or there must be a reason why the State may be permitted to apply a generally applicable law to certain persons that it does not apply to others.

The first possibility is plainly unacceptable. Although the meaning of the principle that "all men are created equal" is not always clear, it surely must mean that every free citizen has the same interest in "liberty" that the members of the majority share. From the standpoint of the individual, the homosexual and the heterosexual have the same interest in deciding how he will live his own life, and, more narrowly, how he will conduct himself in his personal and voluntary associations with his companions. State intrusion into the private conduct of either is equally burdensome.

The second possibility is similarly unacceptable. A policy of selective application must be supported by a neutral and legitimate interest—something more substantial than a habitual dislike for, or ignorance about, the disfavored group. Neither the State nor the Court has identified any such interest in this case. The Court has posited as a justification for the Georgia statute "the presumed belief of a majority of the electorate in Georgia that homosexual sodomy is immoral and unacceptable." *Ante,* at 196. But the Georgia electorate has expressed no such belief—instead, its representatives enacted a law that presumably reflects the belief that *all sodomy* is immoral and unacceptable. Unless the Court is prepared to conclude that such a law is constitutional, it may not rely on the work product of the Georgia Legislature to support its holding. For the Georgia statute does not single out homosexuals as a separate class meriting special disfavored treatment.

Nor, indeed, does the Georgia prosecutor even believe that all homosexuals who violate this statute should be punished. This conclusion is evident from the fact that the respondent in this very case has formally acknowledged in his complaint and in court that he has engaged, and intends to continue to engage, in the prohibited conduct, yet the State has elected not to process criminal charges against him. As JUSTICE POWELL points out, moreover, Georgia's prohibition on private, consensual sodomy has not been enforced for decades. The record of nonenforcement, in this case and in the last several decades, belies the Attorney General's representations about the importance of the State's selective application of its generally applicable law.

Both the Georgia statute and the Georgia prosecutor thus completely fail to provide the Court with any support for the conclusion that homosexual sodomy, *simpliciter,* is considered unacceptable conduct in that State, and that the burden of justifying a selective application of the generally applicable law has been met.

III

The Court orders the dismissal of respondent's complaint even though the State's statute prohibits all sodomy; even though that prohibition is concededly unconstitutional with respect to heterosexuals; and even though the State's *post hoc* explanations for selective application are belied by the State's own actions. At the very least, I think it clear at this early stage of the litigation that respondent has alleged a constitutional claim sufficient to withstand a motion to dismiss.

I respectfully dissent.

Financial Privacy Act of 1978: Congressional Debate

In *United States* v. *Miller,* 425 U.S. 435 (1976), the Supreme Court held that bank depositors were not protected by the Fourth Amendment when the government wanted to gain access to microfilms of checks, deposit slips, or other bank records. These materials were regarded as business records of a bank, not the private papers of a person. Congress responded by passing legislation—the Right to Financial Privacy Act—that gave depositors certain procedural rights and protections. The debate in the House of Representatives illustrates how members of Congress are involved in deciding questions of Fourth Amendment rights and privacy interests. The excerpts below come from 124 Cong. Rec. 33310–33311, 33818–33819, 33835-33836 (1978).

Mr. WHALEN. Mr. Chairman, the legislation now before us, the Financial Institution's Regulatory Act, is a complex bill, for the most part dealing with relatively esoteric questions of banking regulation. One title, however, is of direct and immediate concern to every American and is one with which I have been involved personally.

I am referring, of course, to title XI, the Right to Financial Privacy Act of 1968.

Title XI represents an enormous step forward in the protection of the rights to privacy of American citizens. I am delighted to see this legislation come to the floor of the House.

During the 93rd Congress, Senator CHARLES MATHIAS of Maryland first proposed the Bill of Rights Procedures Act. Its primary purpose was to prevent warrantless Government searches of bank, credit, medical, telephone toll billing, and other records that reveal the nature of one's private affairs. This was the first legislative proposal ever to address the problem of access to third party records.

At the start of the 94th Congress, Senator MATHIAS reintroduced the Bill of Rights Procedures Act with our former colleague, the Honorable Charles A. Mosher, serving as the chief House sponsor. I was pleased to join as a cosponsor of that measure (H.R. 214). The bill underwent more than 40 days of hearings and markup in the House Judiciary Subcommittee on Courts, Civil Liberties and the Administration of Justice, but was reported out of subcommittee too late to reach the floor in 1976.

At the start of the 95th Congress I accepted Senator MATHIAS' invitation to replace former Congressman Mosher as the chief House sponsor of the Bill of Rights Procedure Act. Upon its introduction in January, the new bill, H.R. 215, was referred jointly to the Judiciary and the Banking Committees.

Mr. Chairman, the first drafts of the Right to Financial Privacy Act were derived directly from title I of H.R. 2151 Bill of Rights Procedures Act. As Senator MATHIAS and I have testified, we are pleased to have our bill serve as the model for this legislation.

While H.R. 13471 differs in many details from H.R. 215, the essential elements remain the same. Most important, the new legislation preserves our basic principle that third party records of a personal nature, in this case bank and credit records, should not be accessed by Government agents except with the knowledge of the subject individual or else with the supervision of the courts.

This is a crucial concept. It returns to the individual some measure of control over dissemination of records that contain very detailed information about one's daily life. And it puts the courts into a proper role of resolving conflicts between a citizen's rights to privacy and society's needs for information.

Moreover, it also restores the record holders, the banks, and credit card companies to their proper role as impartial custodians of records. I know that the financial community welcomes this opportunity to get out of the middle of disputes between customers and Government. And they surely will welcome being able once again to assure their clients that they can have a reasonable expectation that the confidentiality of their records will be maintained. Surely, everyone will benefit from the establishment of a clear set of rules and procedures.

. . .

Mr. LAFALCE. Mr. Chairman, I move to strike the last word.

Mr. Chairman, I rise in support of this bill.

The bill which we consider today is the product of many months of investigation, debate, and compromise. The result, in my judgment, is a bill which will go far to improving the image and the actual condition of financial institutions in this country.

. . .

The Right to Financial Privacy Act of 1978, title XI, is one on which I have spent many hours trying to maximize the privacy protections afforded to the individual bank customer without tying the hands of Government law enforcement activities. There is a right, equally as important as the right of an individual to financial privacy, of a society to be relatively free from crime and fear then protection of which is also the responsibility of the Government. The challenge is to find a way to protect both of these interests through the same Government. Hopefully we have done this in the Right to Financial Privacy Act of 1978.

The overriding purpose of this title is to let an individual know when the Federal Government is seeking access to his financial records and what use is made of those records after the Government acquires them. The individual is given an opportunity to challenge the access to his records if he thinks that there is no legitimate reason for the Government to be seeking them. The first step is that the Government informs the individual that it wishes to review his records for a given purpose. The individual is also given a form to fill out which will enable him to challenge the Government's access to the records.

It is then up to the Government to show that the records are relevant to the investigation and that the investigation itself is a legitimate one, and not being conducted to harass an individual for political reasons, to intimidate a witness, or for other bad faith motives. The important point to remember is that we are dealing here with the preliminary stages of an investigation and, especially in cases of white collar crime, financial records are the best, if not the only evidence of the crime. At the beginning of investigations into alleged embezzlement, bribery, public corruption, extortion, drug trafficking and the like, financial records provide the information needed to begin or continue the investigation, and it is not the intent of the framers of this title to inhibit these legitimate activities of Government law enforcement authorities. To require excessively detailed demonstrations of the basis for the investigation at this point in the process would lead to the courts making preliminary decisions on investigations rather than prosecutors, and would be a violation of the separation of powers doctrine.

Some very limited exceptions are included in the title to allow for situations in which prior notice to the individual would cause serious harm to that individual, another person, or to the investigation. In these cases, the Government is required to demonstrate the potential harm to a court, and the individual is notified after the fact that the records have been obtained, and may challenge the access if it was improper. Notice is also given to the individual of transfers of his records between Government agencies, so that at all times, unless there is a compelling reason not to disclose the transfer, he or she will know which agencies in the Federal Government have reviewed the bank records.

. . .

Mr. PATTISON of New York. I thank the gentleman for yielding.

Mr. Chairman, title XI of the Financial Institutions Regulatory Act is truly landmark legislation. This title, known as the Right to Financial Privacy Act, addresses a fundamental constitutional issue: The extent to which an individual's records held in a bank should be protected from government intrusion.

Many of us on both sides of the aisle strongly believe that individual bank records must be afforded basic privacy rights. Furthermore, it is our belief that the framers of the Constitution intended to provide protection for all individual records. At the time the fourth amendment to the Constitution was drafted, however, almost all personal records were kept at home. Protecting those records actually in the possession of the individual citizen was an adequate safeguard. In this century, however, increasingly financial records have been held by banks and other financial institutions. Furthermore, advances in communications and recordkeeping technology now allow financial institutions to store and quickly retrieve vast amounts of information.

These records can tell a complete story about the customer's life and lifestyle: His religious and political affiliations, what medical services he requires, how much he drinks, and a vast array of his personal habits.

Despite their personal nature, these records are not afforded privacy protections. In its 1976 Miller decision, the Supreme Court ruled that, under current law, records held by a financial institution are the property of the institution, rather than the customer's. These records are therefore not entitled to safeguards from unwarranted government access. Therefore, under Miller, a citizen does not have "standing" to sue to prevent unreasonable access to those records.

Clearly, it is an empty gesture to protect individual records held in the home when a much richer store of information is readily available at the individual's bank. This inconsistency led the Privacy Protection Study Commission, in its 1977 report entitled "Personal Privacy in an Information Society," to call for the creation of "a legitimate, enforceable expectation of confidentiality."

The legislation before us today is based on the premise that bank customers have a right to reasonable expectation of privacy. . . .

Mr. CAVANAUGH. Mr. Chairman, the Right to Financial Privacy, title XI of H.R. 13471, the Financial Institutions Regulatory Act of 1978, merits your special consideration and support.

As the Presidential Privacy Protection Study Commission pointed out in its final report:

"Financial records, particularly the information retained in demand deposit accounts, provide another instance where the changing patterns of life took the possession of information about himself out of the control of the individual. Of great importance, checking account records present a situation where alterations in recordkeeping patterns have been exacerbated by government action."

Now, more than ever before, it is important to assure that the substantial majority of our people who do utilize services of depository institutions are not surrendering their rights to privacy by virtue of such a relationship.

The Privacy Protection Study Commission recommended legislation for financial institution depositors in its final report, published in June 1977. This will be the first time that such legislation has reached the House floor for a vote.

To answer the fear of unwarranted Government fishing expeditions, title XI would, for the first time in law, give bank customers three key privacy rights: First, the right to notice before the records are made available to Government investigators; second, the opportunity to challenge the Government's access to those records; and (3) creation of a paper trail tracing all Government acquisitions and transfers of records.

This legislation has been drafted to create a delicate balance between essential individual privacy protections and the legitimate needs of law enforcement. For over a year the Department of Justice and the Department of the Treasury have worked closely with myself and other members of the House Banking Committee and Judiciary Committee. Leaders in the financial community have also given assistance and support to this bill. . . .

The Right to Privacy: The Bork Hearings

During the hearings in 1987 on the nomination of Robert H. Bork to be Associate Justice of the U.S. Supreme Court, questions zeroed in on Bork's position on privacy. The questioning below is directed by the Chairman of the Senate Judiciary Committee, Joseph R. Biden, Jr., followed by questions from Senators Edward M. Kennedy and Alan K. Simpson. These passages come from "Nomination of Robert H. Bork to be Associate Justice of the Supreme Court of the United States," hearings before the Senate Committee on the Judiciary, 100th Cong., 1st Sess. 114–121, 149–151, 240–242 (Part 1 of 5 Parts) (1987).

The CHAIRMAN. Well, let's talk about another case. Let's talk about the *Griswold* case. Now, while you were living in Connecticut, that State had a law—I know you know this, but for the record—that it made it a crime for anyone, even a married couple, to use birth control. You indicated that you thought that law was "nutty," to use your words and I quite agree. Nevertheless, Connecticut, under that "nutty" law, prosecuted and convicted a doctor and the case finally reached the Supreme Court.

The Court said that the law violated a married couple's constitutional right to privacy. You criticized this opinion in numerous articles and speeches, beginning in 1971 and as recently as July 26th of this year. In your 1971 article, "Neutral Principles and Some First Amendment Problems," you said that the right of married couples to have sexual relations without fear of unwanted children is no more worthy of constitutional protection by the courts than the right of public utilities to be free of pollution control laws.

You argued that the utility company's right or gratification, I think you referred to it, to make money and the married couple's right or gratification to have sexual relations without fear of unwanted children, as "the cases are identical." Now, I am trying to understand this. It appears to me that you are saying that the government has as much right to control a married couple's decision about choosing to have a child or not, as that government has a right to control the public utility's right to pollute the air. Am I misstating your rationale here?

Judge BORK. With due respect, Mr. Chairman, I think you are. I was making the point that where the Constitution does not speak—there is no provision in the Constitution that applies to the case—then a judge may not say, I place a higher value upon a marital relationship than I do upon an economic freedom. Only if the Constitution gives him some reasoning. Once the judge begins to say economic rights are more important than marital rights or vice versa, and if there is nothing in the Constitution, the judge is enforcing his own moral values, which I have objected to. Now, on the *Griswold* case itself—

The CHAIRMAN. Can we stick with that point a minute to make sure I understand it?

Judge BORK. Sure.

The CHAIRMAN. So that you suggest that unless the Constitution, I believe in the past you used the phrase, textually identifies, a value that is worthy of being protected, then competing values in society, the competing value of a public utility, in the example you used, to go out and make money —that economic right has no more or less constitutional protection than the right of a married couple to use or not use birth control in their bedroom. Is that what you are saying?

Judge BORK. No, I am not entirely, but I will straighten it out. I was objecting to the way Justice Douglas, in that opinion, *Griswold* v. *Connecticut*, derived this right. It may be possible to derive an objection to an anti-contraceptive statute in some other way. I do not know.

But starting from the assumption, which is an assumption for purposes of my argument, not a proven fact, starting from the assumption that there is nothing in the Constitution, in any legitimate method of constitutional reasoning about either subject, all I am saying is that the judge has no way to prefer one to the other and the matter should be left to the legislatures who will then decide which competing gratification, or freedom, should be placed higher.

The CHAIRMAN. Then I think I do understand it, that is, that the economic gratification of a utility company is as worthy of as much protection as the sexual gratification of a married couple, because neither is mentioned in the Constitution.

Judge BORK. All that means is that the judge may not choose.

The CHAIRMAN. Who does?

Judge BORK. The legislature.

The CHAIRMAN. Well, that is my point, so it is not a constitutional right. I am not trying to be picky here. Clearly, I do not want to get into a debate with a professor, but it seems to me that what you are saying is what I said and that is, that the Constitution—if it were a constitutional right, if the Constitution said anywhere in it, in your view, that a married couple's right to engage in the decision of having a child or not having a child was a constitutionally-protected right of privacy, then you would rule that that right exists. You would not leave it to a legislative body no matter what they did.

Judge BORK. That is right.

The CHAIRMAN. But you argue, as I understand it, that no such right exists.

Judge BORK. No, Senator, that is what I tried to clarify. I argued that the way in which this unstructured, undefined right of privacy that Justice Douglas elaborated, that the way he did it did not prove its existence.

The CHAIRMAN. You have been a professor now for years and years, everybody has pointed out and I have observed, you are one of the most well-read and scholarly people to come before this committee. In all your short life, have you come up with any other way to protect a married couple, under the Constitution, against an action by a government telling them what they can or cannot do about birth control in their bedroom? Is there any constitutional right, anywhere in the Constitution?

Judge BORK. I have never engaged in that exercise. What I was doing was criticizing a doctrine the Supreme Court was creating which was capable of being applied in unknown ways in the future, in unprincipled ways. Let me say something about *Griswold* v. *Connecticut*. Connecticut never tied to prosecute any married couple for the use of contraceptives. That statute was used entirely through an aiding and abetting clause in the general criminal code to prosecute birth control clinics that advertised. That is what it was about.

The CHAIRMAN. But in fact, they did prosecute a doctor, didn't they, for giving advice?

. . . Does a State legislative body, or any legislative body, have a right to pass a law telling a married couple, or anyone else, that behind—let's stick with the married couple for a minute—behind their bedroom door, telling them they can or cannot use birth control? Does the majority have the right to tell a couple that they cannot use birth control?

Judge BORK. There is always a rationality standard in the law, Senator. I do not know what rationale the State would offer or what challenge the married couple would make. I have never decided that case. If it ever comes before me, I will have to decide it. All I have done was point out that the right of privacy, as defined or undefined by

Justice Douglas, was a free-floating right that was not derived in a principled fashion from constitutional materials. That is all I have done.

The CHAIRMAN. Judge, I agree with the rationale offered in the case. Let me just read it to you and it went like this. I happen to agree with it. It said, in part, "would we allow the police to search the sacred precincts of marital bedrooms for telltale signs of contraceptives? The very idea is repulsive to the notions of privacy surrounding the marriage relationship. We deal with the right of privacy older than the Bill of Rights. Marriage is a coming together for better or worse, hopefully enduring, and intimate to the degree of being sacred. The association promotes a way of life, not causes. A harmony of living, not political face. A bilateral loyalty, not a commercial or social projects."

Obviously, that Justice believes that the Constitution protects married couples, anyone.

Judge BORK. I could agree with almost every—I think I could agree with every word you read but that is not, with respect, Mr. Chairman, the rationale of the case. That is the rhetoric at the end of the case. What I objected to was the way in which this right of privacy was created and that was simply this. Justice Douglas observed, quite correctly, that a number of provisions of the Bill of Rights protect aspects of privacy and indeed they do and indeed they should.

But he went on from there to say that since a number of the provisions did that and since they had emanations, by which I think he meant buffer zones to protect the basic right, he would find a penumbra which created a new right of privacy that existed where no provision of the Constitution applied, so that he—

The CHAIRMAN. What about the ninth amendment?

Judge BORK. Wait, let me finish with Justice Douglas.

The CHAIRMAN. All right.

Judge BORK. He did not rest on the ninth amendment. That was Justice Goldberg.

The CHAIRMAN. Right. That is what I was talking about.

Judge BORK. Yes. And I want to discuss first Justice Douglas and then I would be glad to discuss Justice Goldberg.

The CHAIRMAN. OK.

Judge BORK. Now you see, in that way, he could have observed, equally well, the various provisions of the Constitution protect individual freedom and therefore, generalized a general right of freedom that would apply where no provision of the Constitution did. That is exactly what Justice Hugo Black criticized in dissent in that case, in some heated terms—and Justice Potter Stewart also dissented in that case.

So, in observing that *Griswold* v. *Connecticut* does not sustain its burden, the judge's burden of showing that the right comes from constitutional materials, I am by no means alone. A lot of people, including Justices, have criticized that decision.

The CHAIRMAN. I am not suggesting whether you are alone or in the majority. I am just trying to find out where you are. As I hear you, you do not believe that there is a general right of privacy that is in the Constitution.

Judge BORK. Not one derived in *that* fashion. There may be other arguments and I do not want to pass upon those.

The CHAIRMAN. Have you ever thought of any? Have you ever written about any?

Judge BORK. Yes, as a matter of fact, Senator, I taught a seminar with Professor Bickel starting in about 1963 or 1964. We taught a seminar called Constitutional Theory. I was then all in favor of *Griswold* v. *Connecticut*. I thought that was a great way to reason. I tried to build a course around that, only I said: we can call it a general right of freedom, and let's then take the various provisions of the Constitution, treat them the way a lawyer treats common law cases, extract a more general principle and apply that.

I did that for about 6 or 7 years, and Bickel fought me every step of the way; said it was not possible. At the end of 6 or 7 years, I decided he was right.

The CHAIRMAN. Judge, let's go on. There have been a number of cases that flow from the progeny of the *Griswold* case, all relying on *Griswold*, the majority view, with different rationales offered, that there is a right of privacy in the Constitution, a general right of privacy, a right of privacy derived from the due process, from the 14th amendment, a right of privacy, to use the Douglas word—the

penumbra, which you criticize, and a right Goldberg suggested in the *Griswold* case, from the ninth amendment. It seems to me, if you cannot find a rationale for the decision of the *Griswold* case, then all the succeeding cases are up for grabs.

Judge BORK. I have never tried to find a rationale and I have not been offered one. Maybe somebody would offer me one. I do not know if the other cases are up for grabs or not.

The CHAIRMAN. Wouldn't they have to be if they are based on the same rationale?

Judge BORK. Well, it may be that—I have written that some of these cases were wrongly decided, in my opinion. For some of them I can think of rationales that would make them correctly decided but wrongly reasoned. There may be other ways, that a generalized and undefined right of privacy—one of the problems with the right of privacy, as Justice Douglas defined it, or did not define it, is not simply that it comes out of nowhere, that it does not have any rootings in the Constitution, it is also that he does not give it any contours, so you do not know what it is going to mean from case to case.

. . .

The CHAIRMAN. My time is up. Judge, I want to make it clear, I am not suggesting there is anything extreme about your reasoning. I am not suggesting it is conservative or liberal. I just want to make sure I understand it. And as I understand what you have said in the last 30 minutes, a State legislative body, a government, can, if it so chose, pass a law saying married couples cannot use birth control devices.

Judge BORK. Senator, Mr. Chairman, I have not said that; I do not want to say that. What I am saying to you is that if that law is to be struck down, it will have to be done under better constitutional argumentation than was present in the *Griswold* opinion.

The CHAIRMAN. Again I will end, to quote you, sir, you said, "The truth is that the Court could not reach the result in *Griswold* through principle." I assume you are talking about constitutional principle.

Judge BORK. I do not know—what is that from?

The CHAIRMAN. I am referring to your 1971

article. That is the quote in the 1971 article. And then you said—

Judge BORK. Do you have a page number for that, Senator?

The CHAIRMAN. I will get the page. Sorry—a 1982 speech while you were Judge, speaking at Catholic University. You said, "The result in *Griswold* could not have been reached by proper interpretation of the Constitution." End of quote. We will dig it out for you here to show you—I believe you all sent it to us, so that is how we got it.

Judge BORK. OK. Yes.

. . .

Senator KENNEDY. Thank you very much, Mr. Chairman. Judge Bork, I wanted to pick up, for a moment, one aspect of the line of questioning of the Chairman. As I understand your discussion of the *Griswold* case, your view is that there is no right to privacy in the Constitution. It is up to the legislature. Doesn't that lead you to the view that you would uphold a statute requiring say, compulsory abortion, if a legislature enacted it by majority?

. . .

I believe, Mr. Bork, that in your world, the individuals have precious few rights to protect them against the majority and I think this is where the Bill of Rights comes in and what the Bill of Rights is all about, that there are some things in America which no majority can do to the minority or to the individuals. The provisions of the 14th Amendment under section 1, include "nor shall any State deprive any person of life, liberty or property without the due process of law."

Isn't included in the concept of liberty, the right to privacy? In reading that term with the ninth amendment, which provides that "the enumeration in the Constitution of certain rights shall not be construed to deny or disparage others retained by the people," I would be interested in your reaction or response because it seems to me that the issues of privacy have been carefully enshrined within the Constitution by court decisions over the period of the last 60 years.

They are rights which are enshrined in such a way and respected and valued so importantly that

I would think Americans would have serious questions, I certainly do, about placing someone on the Supreme Court that is willing to find some kind of a rationale, or appears to find some rationale, not to respect it.

Judge BORK. Senator Kennedy, at the outset let me say this. I have the greatest respect for the Bill of Rights and I will enforce the Bill of Rights. I have enforced the Bill of Rights. What we were talking about here was a generalized, undefined right of privacy which is not in the Bill of Rights. Now, as I said in my opening statement, a judge has to apply the law and the law comes from the text, the history and the structure of the Constitution.

There are important aspects of privacy in the Bill of Rights. This Congress has increased privacy in many ways by statute. As a society, we value it, but as a judge, I do not think I can tell the American people they may not have a law that in no way conflicts with the written and historical Constitution. Now, you raise the question of—

Senator KENNEDY. I want you to complete your answer. What I was really springing from is your response to the chairman's questions with regard to the *Griswold*. We remember that the majority in that case found that the provisions in a State statute that restricted married couples from using contraception would be violative of their right to privacy. You've indicated that you took issue with the rationale.

I think you continued and said, well, perhaps someone can come up with a different rationale so that you might be able to reach a different decision. But in response, I think, to the chairman's question, you talked about the importance of the majority in the State legislatures. You did not find, at least at this time, that you were prepared to state a philosophy or legal justification for the overruling of that Connecticut statute. I believe, quite frankly, following that rationale, that you could lead yourself into the kinds of situations which I've posed here. If I am wrong, I would like to hear from you on that.

Judge BORK. Well, let me repeat about this created, generalized and undefined right of privacy in *Griswold*. Aside from the fact that the right was not derived by Justice Douglas, in any traditional mode of constitutional analysis, there is this. The right was not—we do not know what it is. We do not know what it covers. It can strike at random. For example the Supreme Court has not applied the right of privacy consistently and I think it is safe to predict that the Supreme Court will not.

For example, if it really is a right of sexual freedom in private, as some people have suggested, then *Bowers* v. *Hardwick*, which upheld a statute against sodomy as applied to homosexuals, is wrongly decided. Privacy to do what, Senator? You know, privacy to use cocaine in private? Privacy for businessmen to fix prices in a hotel room? We just do not know what it is.

Senator KENNEDY. Well, there are some things that people would understand—they would feel that government intrusion, in terms of the married couple in the *Griswold* case, in terms of their use of contraceptives, did go across that line; and in the kind of examples that I have given you, it would seem to me that that would be equally clear, that a State statute that required compulsory abortion would certainly violate what I think most Americans would feel would be the right to privacy. And I believe as well that, once you have the State dictating the size of families, it would do so as well.

What I am interested in is how you reach that conclusion, if that would be the conclusion, under your rationale, that if a State has got a majority and it has got a basis for passing that statute, then it is not up to Judge Bork to look behind that.

Judge BORK. It is not up to Judge Bork to look behind that unless he has got law to apply. I was going to say, furthermore, that I do not think—I have never found it terribly useful, in testing constitutional theories, to use examples that we know the American people will never enact. The founders of this nation banked a good deal upon the good sense of the people, as well as upon the courts.

Senator KENNEDY. I would just say here, Judge Bork, that one State did enact such a law with regard to sterilization. One State did with regards to sterilization and I think that that reaches the same kind of abhorrence, in terms of what I would imagine most Americans, and certainly the Court did, would find abhorrent. I do not think that our Founding Fathers might have imagined that as

well. But I think you have made the point. I would be glad to give you further time on it.

Judge BORK. Well, if you want to talk about *Skinner* v. *Oklahoma*—

Senator KENNEDY. I was basically interested, rather than getting into the cases, just to get at the rationale, the reasoning, the way that you do move to reach a decision. . . .

Senator SIMPSON . . .

Let us get back to privacy. That is a recurring theme here about privacy and judicial restraint and *Griswold* v. *Connecticut,* and we have now talked about contraception, homosexuality, sterility or else sexual preference, sexual gratification. There is no telling where we will get if we keep struggling along in this area. Those are important things. I do not even belittle that. But it has all been taken out of context, every bit of it.

I do not think you had an appropriate time to respond on the issue of privacy, and especially with regard to the *Griswold* case and the *Skinner* case. I guess I want to be sure because there was a line of questioning which I gathered—and I think it was our Chairman, and it was a good line of questioning—it was, well if you do not embrace these things through some method, how are we going to get to that point? How do you protect?

I want to ask you if it is fair to say that you believe that privacy is protected under the Constitution, but that you just do not believe that there is a general and unspecified right that protects everything including homosexual conduct, incest, whatever—and you mentioned that yesterday. Is that correct?

Judge BORK. That is correct, Senator. I think the fact that I did not get everything I wanted to say out was my fault because I was trying to discuss with Senator Biden and others the constitutional problem. But I think it requires a fuller answer than that and that is this: No civilized person wants to live in a society without a lot of privacy in it. And the framers, in fact, of the Constitution protected privacy in a variety of ways.

The first amendment protects free exercise of religion. The free speech provision of the first amendment has been held to protect the privacy of membership lists and a person's associations in order to make the free speech right effective. The fourth amendment protects the individual's home and office from unreasonable searches and seizures, and usually requires a warrant. The Fifth amendment has a right against self-incrimination.

There is much more. There is a lot of privacy in the Constitution. *Griswold*, in which we were talking about a Connecticut statute which was unenforced against any individual except the birth control clinic, *Griswold* involved a Connecticut statute which banned the use of contraceptives. And Justice Douglas entered that opinion with a rather eloquent statement of how awful it would be to have the police pounding into the marital bedroom. And it would be awful, and it would never happen because there is the fourth amendment.

Nobody ever tried to enforce that statute, but the police simply could not get into the bedroom without a warrant, and what magistrate is going to give the police a warrant to go in to search for signs of the use of contraceptives? I mean it is a wholly bizarre and imaginary case.

. . . the only reason that Connecticut statute stayed on the statute book—it was an old, old statute, dating back from the days when Connecticut was entirely a Yankee State—the only reason it stayed on the statute book was that it was not enforced. If anybody had tried to enforce that against a married couple, he would have been out of office instantly and the law would have been repealed. . . .

18 Political Participation

C onstitutional interpretations by all three branches have helped shape the rights and privileges of the political process. Previous chapters discussed political participation in terms of free speech, free press, the right of petition, and freedom of assembly. This chapter focuses on voting rights, the conduct of primaries and general elections, reapportionment, campaign financing, and lobbying. An important subtheme running throughout this history is the effort to disfranchise black citizens, either by depriving them of the right to vote or by diluting their vote through districting schemes.

VOTING RIGHTS

The right to vote would seem inherent in the republican form of government envisaged in the Constitution. "The United States shall guarantee to every State in this Union a Republican Form of Government." Art. IV, § 4. Nevertheless, it took the Fifteenth Amendment, ratified in 1870, to establish the right of blacks to vote. A unanimous Supreme Court in 1875, announcing that the Constitution "does not confer the right of suffrage upon any one," denied that women were entitled to vote as a privilege and immunity protected by the Constitution. Minor v. Happersett, 88 U.S. 162, 178 (1875). Yet in 1886, a unanimous opinion of the Court could refer to voting as "a fundamental political right, because preservative of all rights." Yick Wo v. Hopkins, 118 U.S. 356, 370 (1886). Not until 1920, with the Nineteenth Amendment, did women gain the right to vote.

Voting rights in America have been hammered out by state action, judicial decisions, congressional action, and constitutional amendment. Members of the House of Representatives are chosen directly by the people. Senators were originally selected by state legislatures, but have been elected directly by the people after the Seventeenth Amendment was ratified in 1913. The time, place, and manner of elections of Representatives and Senators are left to the states; Congress may alter state regulations except as to the place of choosing Senators. Art. I, § 4, Cl. 1; Amend. XVII.

Congress passed the Enforcement Act of 1870 to guarantee blacks the right to vote in state elections. 16 Stat. 140. Using a strict dual-federalism model, the Supreme Court eviscerated the statute by holding that it was not "appropriate legislation" under Section 2 of the Fifteenth Amendment. It said that the Amendment "does not confer the right of suffrage upon any one." United States v. Reese, 92 U.S. 214, 217 (1876). Another decision further undermined the Enforcement Act by holding that jurisdiction and sovereignty to bring indictments under the statute rested solely with the states. United States v. Cruikshank, 92 U.S. 542 (1876). The Court did sustain the power of Congress, in elections for U.S. Representatives, to enact penalties for those who stuff the ballot box. Ex parte Siebold, 100 U.S. 371 (1880).

A few years later, a unanimous Court upheld a congressional statute that prohibited two or more persons from conspiring to threaten or intimidate any citizen (in this case a black) from exercising the right to vote for national office. The Court stated that the Fifteenth Amendment conferred upon blacks the right to vote "and Congress has the power to protect and enforce that right." Ex parte Yarbrough, 110 U.S. 651, 665 (1884). See also United States v. Mosley, 238 U.S. 383 (1915); Swafford v. Templeton, 185 U.S. 487 (1902); Wiley v. Sinkler, 179 U.S. 58 (1900).

States tried to nullify the Fifteenth Amendment by adopting a "Grandfather Clause," extending voting rights only to those who were entitled to vote before the Amendment. These tactics were overturned by the Court in 1915. Guinn v. United States, 238 U.S. 347; Myers v. Anderson, 238 U.S. 368. Oklahoma then changed its law to provide that those who had voted in 1914 automatically remained qualified voters. This requirement affected only blacks, forcing them to apply between April 30 and May 11, 1916, or risk permanent disfranchisement. The Court held the statute unconstitutional, remarking that the Fifteenth Amendment "nullifies sophisticated as well as simple-minded modes of discrimination." Lane v. Wilson, 307 U.S. 268, 275 (1939).

Primaries

In one-party states, the result of a primary election victory is tantamount to winning the general election. Although the Fifteenth Amendment protected the right of blacks to vote, some states restricted that right to the general election and used different strategems to bar blacks from participating in primary elections. In the "White Primary" cases, the Supreme Court reviewed a Texas statute that barred blacks from voting in the Democratic party primary for U.S. Senator and Congressmen. A unanimous Court held that this violated the Fourteenth Amendment. Texas claimed that the suit was political and hence inappropriate for the courts, an objection Justice Holmes called "little more than a play upon words." Nixon v. Herndon, 273 U.S. 536, 540 (1927).

Texas tried to achieve the same result through a different method. It gave state political parties the power to prescribe qualifications for party membership, including the right to vote. The Democratic party then adopted a resolution that only white Democrats could participate in primaries. By a 5–4 vote, the Court held the statute in violation of the Fourteenth Amendment. It rejected the argument that the Amendment operates against the states, not private parties (in this case, officials of the Democratic party). The Court pointed out that the statute lodged the power to determine voter qualification in the executive committee of each party; to that extent the parties were organs of the state. Nixon v. Condon, 286 U.S. 73 (1932).

Three years later, however, a unanimous Court agreed that a county clerk in Texas could refuse to give a ballot to a black who wanted to vote in the Democratic party primary. The party convention, acting on its own without state legislation, had voted to restrict party membership to whites. The Court decided that the clerk was not a state officer, there was no "state action," and the conduct did not violate the Federal Constitution. Grovey v. Townsend, 295 U.S. 45 (1935). In 1941, the Court backed away from *Grovey* by holding that election officials in a Louisiana primary (conducted at public expense) acted "under color of" state law in altering and falsely counting ballots. Voters had a right under the Federal Constitution to cast their ballots and have them counted. United States v. Classic, 313 U.S. 299 (1941). *Grovey* was finally overruled by the Court in 1944, when it declared (8 to 1) that Texas could not exclude blacks by limiting participation in state conventions to white citizens. This was held to be state action in violation of the Fifteenth Amendment. SMITH v. ALLWRIGHT, 321 U.S. 649 (1944).

This ruling did not exhaust the bag of tricks. Texas excluded blacks from participating in elections conducted by the "Jaybird Democratic Association," which selected candidates for county offices. These candidates were invariably the ones nominated to run in the Democratic primary and elected to office. The Jaybirds claimed that their association was not a political party but a self-governing voluntary club. Although the elections for candidates were not governed by state laws and did not use state machinery or state funds, an 8–1 Court held that the process violated the Fifteenth Amendment. The Democratic primary and the general election became "no more than the perfunctory ratifiers of the choice that has already been made in Jaybird elections from which Negroes have been excluded." Terry v. Adams, 345 U.S. 461, 469 (1953).

Poll Taxes

Another method of restricting or discouraging the black vote was to require payment of a poll tax before a person could register to vote. This type of tax was upheld by the Court in Breedlove v. Suttles, 302 U.S. 277 (1937). A later case involved the Virginia constitution, which required a poll tax to vote. Although some members of the constitutional convention expressed a desire to eliminate the black vote in Virginia, a three-judge federal court in 1951 found insufficient evidence that the state requirement discriminated against blacks. Butler v. Thompson, 97 F.Supp. 17, 21 (E.D. Va. 1951). A per curiam ruling by the Supreme Court affirmed this judgment. Only Justice Douglas dissented. Butler v. Thompson, 341 U.S. 937 (1951).

Congress took steps to eliminate the poll tax in federal elections. By 1962, when both the House and the Senate passed the Twenty-fourth Amendment, only five states used the tax: Alabama, Arkansas, Mississippi, Texas, and Virginia. The Amendment, ratified in 1964, provides that the right of the U.S. citizens to vote in any primary or other election for federal office "shall not be denied or abridged by the United States or any State by reason of failure to pay any poll tax or other tax."

States were still permitted to use poll taxes for state and local elections. In the Voting Rights Act of 1965, Congress declared that the poll tax placed an unreasonable hardship on voter rights and did not bear a reasonable relationship to any legitimate state interest. It also authorized the Attorney General to institute actions against state poll taxes and gave federal courts jurisdiction to decide these cases. Attorney General Katzenbach supported a challenge to the poll tax brought by Annie E. Harper. With this case as the vehicle, the Supreme Court declared Virginia's poll tax for its elections a violation of the Equal Protection Clause of the Fourteenth Amendment. Writing for the Court, Justice Douglas said that voter qualifications "have no relation to wealth nor to paying or not paying this or any other tax." HARPER v. VIRGINIA BD. OF ELECTIONS, 383 U.S. 663, 666 (1966).

Literacy Tests

Still another contrivance to limit the black vote was the literacy test. A unanimous Court in 1959 held that states may apply a literacy test to all voters irrespective of race or color. The particular statute at issue, a North Carolina law, required that the prospective voter "be able to read and write any section of the Constitution of North Carolina in the English language." The Court concluded that the law did not, on its face, violate the Fifteenth Amendment. Lassiter v. Northampton Election Bd., 360 U.S. 45 (1959).

The Voting Rights Act of 1965 placed temporary suspensions on the use of literacy tests. This provision was upheld in South Carolina v. Katzenbach, 383 U.S. 301 (1966). See also Gaston County v. United States, 395 U.S. 285 (1969). In 1965, a unanimous Court held that election commissioners and voting registrars in Mississippi could be sued for using literacy tests and other devices to disfranchise blacks. State techniques had reduced the percentage of black "qualified" voters from over 50 percent to about 5 percent. To register for voting, a citizen of Mississippi had to read and copy any section of the state constitution, *and* give a reasonable interpretation of that section to the county registrar, *and* demonstrate to the registrar "a reasonable understanding of the duties and obligations of citizenship under a constitutional form of government." The opportunities for racial discrimination and abuse were immense. United States v. Mississippi, 380 U.S. 128 (1965). The use of "interpretation tests" gave the state unbridled discretion to keep blacks from voting. Blacks, even those "with the most advanced education and scholarship, were declared by voting registrars with less education to have an unsatisfactory understanding of the Constitution of Louisiana or of the United States. This is not a test but a trap, sufficient to stop even the most brilliant man on his way to the voting booth." Louisiana v. United States, 380 U.S. 145, 153 (1965).

In the Voting Rights Act Amendments of 1970, Congress enacted a five-year ban on literacy tests for the entire nation. These tests had been used to restrict the registration of blacks, Spanish-Americans, and Indians. The ban was upheld by every member of the Supreme Court. Oregon v. Mitchell, 400 U.S. 112, 131–134, 144–147, 216–217, 231–236, 282–284 (1970).

Residency Requirements

In other cases, the Court ruled that states may not discriminate against servicemen by denying them the right to vote if they moved their home to another state. Carrington v. Rush, 380 U.S. 89 (1965). Residency requirements were also subject to congressional restrictions. In 1970, Congress abolished residency requirements as a precondition to vote for President and Vice President. Such restrictions, it said, bore no "reasonable relationship to any compelling State interest." 84 Stat. 316. This provision was upheld by eight Justices in Oregon v. Mitchell, 400 U.S. 112, 134, 147–150, 236–239, 285–287 (1970). In 1972, the Court struck down residency requirements in excess of thirty days as a prerequisite to register for voting. Such provisions violated the Equal Protection Clause and were not necessary to further a compelling state interest. Dunn v. Blumstein, 405 U.S. 330 (1972). A year later, the Court upheld a fifty-day residency requirement. Marston v. Lewis, 410 U.S. 679 (1973); Burns v. Fortson, 410 U.S. 686 (1973).

Civil Rights Statutes

Congress passed the Civil Rights Act of 1957 to protect the voting rights of blacks. If someone was about to engage in any practice to deprive a person of the right to vote, the U.S. Attorney General could seek an injunction. 71 Stat. 637, § 131. This provision was upheld by a unanimous Court. United States v. Raines, 362 U.S. 17 (1960). The Civil Rights Act of 1960 adopted additional measures, including the appointment of "voting referees" by federal judges, to protect the right of blacks to register and vote. 74 Stat. 86. The voting-rights provision was strengthened again in Title I of the Civil Rights Act of 1964. 78 Stat. 241.

The Voting Rights Act of 1965 represents the most comprehensive measure since 1870 to protect the voting rights of blacks. The statute suspended literacy tests, authorized the appointment of federal voting examiners, and created federal machinery to supervise voter registration. To increase the number of Puerto Rican voters in New York, Congress prohibited a state from conditioning the right to vote on the ability to read, write, understand, or interpret any matter in the English language. The statute waived English language literacy requirements for persons who had completed the sixth grade in a school under the American flag (including the Commonwealth of Puerto Rico) where the language of instruction was other than English.

South Carolina filed an original suit to test the validity of the Voting Rights Act. The state claimed that Congress exceeded its constitutional powers and invaded states' rights. Twenty-one states filed amici briefs supporting the statute; five Southern states joined with South Carolina in opposition. With Justice Black dissenting in part, an 8–1 Court upheld all challenged provisions of the Act. The decision gives broad recognition to the power of Congress to enforce the Fifteenth Amendment. SOUTH CAROLINA v. KATZENBACH, 383 U.S. 301 (1966). See also Allen v. State Board of Education, 393 U.S. 544 (1969).

Another case challenged a provision that waived the English language requirement for Puerto Ricans. A three-judge court found the provision unconstitutional. Judge McGowan, dissenting, said that Congress had power under Article IV, Section 3, of the Constitution, which gives Congress authority to "make all needful rules and regulations" for American territories. Because Congress had sanctioned schools teaching only Spanish in Puerto Rico, McGowan concluded that Congress could protect the voting rights of Puerto Ricans once they moved to the mainland. Morgan v. Katzenbach, 247 F.Supp. 196 (D.D.C. 1965).

A 7–2 Supreme Court held that the waiver was "a proper exercise of the powers granted to Congress by § 5 of the Fourteenth Amendment." Factfinding was a legislative, not a judicial, responsibility. "It was for Congress, as the branch that made this judgment, to assess and weigh the various conflicting considerations . . .

It is not for us to review the congressional resolution of these factors. It is enough that we be able to perceive a basis upon which the Congress might resolve the conflict as it did." Morgan v. Katzenbach, 384 U.S. 641, 653 (1966).

In 1970, Congress extended the Voting Rights Act and lowered the voting age to 18 for federal, state, and local elections. In signing the bill, President Nixon said that this provision for an eighteen-year-old vote was unconstitutional because Congress lacked authority to extend the suffrage by statute. The issue was taken directly to the Supreme Court, as a case of original jurisdiction, where a 5–4 decision held that the voting age provision was constitutional as applied to national elections but invalid for state and local contests. Oregon v. Mitchell, 400 U.S. 112 (1970). The cost and confusion of dual voting rolls (one established for the federal government and another for state and local elections) created sufficient incentive to override the Court. The Twenty-sixth Amendment quickly passed the House and the Senate and was ratified on July 1, 1971, imposing the eighteen-year-old vote for all national, state, and local elections.

Although Section 2 of the Voting Rights Act provides that voting qualifications or practices may not deny or abridge the voting rights of any U.S. citizen on account of race or color, discriminatory impact alone may be insufficient to find a violation of the statute. In 1980, a plurality of the Court held that states are prohibited only from *purposefully* discriminating against the voting rights of blacks. Abridgement of voting rights had to be intentional, not incidental. To be held invalid, the voting plan must be conceived for the purpose of furthering racial discrimination. MOBILE v. BOLDEN, 446 U.S. 55 (1980).

Nevertheless, on the same day, the Court upheld the power of Congress to go beyond discriminatory purpose to include discriminatory effect. At issue was Section 5 of the Voting Rights Act, which requires that changes in state voting practices be submitted for preclearance to the U.S. Attorney General or a federal judge. Section 5 provides that the Attorney General may clear a voting practice only if it "does not have the purpose and will not have the effect of denying or abridging the right to vote on account of race or color." A 6–3 Court held that Congress had deliberately used the conjunctive (purpose *and* effect) and that this objective was within its power to enact "appropriate legislation" to enforce the Fifteenth Amendment. City of Rome v. United States, 446 U.S. 156 (1980).

Congress responded to *Mobile* v. *Bolden* by amending the Voting Rights Act to allow plaintiffs to show discrimination solely on the *effects* of a voting plan. The statute borrowed language from an earlier opinion by the Court in *White* v. *Regester*, 412 U.S. 755 (1973). 96 Stat. 134, § 3 (1982). For the congressional debate, see pp. 1271–1275. The Court accepted the statute's "results test" to invalidate districting plans that have the effect of diluting the black vote, whether intended by the state or not. Thornburg v. Gingles, 478 U.S. 30 (1986).[1]

REAPPORTIONMENT

The "activism" of the Warren Court revolutionized many areas of constitutional law: criminal rights, desegregation, reapportionment, church and state, and other

---

[1]For other cases on preclearance under Section 5, see McCain v. Lybrand, 465 U.S. 236 (1984); Lockhart v. United States, 460 U.S. 125 (1983); Port Arthur v. United States, 459 U.S. 159 (1982); McDaniel v. Sanchez, 452 U.S. 130 (1981).

sensitive issues. Of all these initiatives and innovations, it is widely assumed that the Desegregation Case of 1954 was the most important decision. Chief Justice Warren, author of the 1954 ruling, disagreed. The "accolade," he said, should go to *Baker* v. *Carr* (1962), which opened the door to the "one person, one vote" rule for reapportionment. This decision helped return power to the people, giving them a direct means of protecting their rights and responsibilities through representative government. The Memoirs of Earl Warren 306–308 (1977).

The first major reapportionment case appeared in 1946, involving congressional districts in Illinois. Because of changes in population and the state's failure to reapportion districts for forty years, the districts ranged from a low of 112,116 to a high of 914,053. Voters in the most populous district had one-ninth the voting power of those in the smallest district. A 4–3 decision by the Supreme Court dismissed the complaint. Justice Frankfurter said it was "hostile to a democratic system to involve the judiciary in the politics of the people." COLEGROVE v. GREEN, 328 U.S. 549, 554 (1946). Although nothing in previous decisions suggested that reapportionment was outside the jurisdiction of the courts,[2] Frankfurter warned that courts "ought not to enter this political thicket" and counseled that the ultimate remedy lay with the people to insist on fair apportionment. How the people could protect their interests when disfranchised by malapportioned districts he never explained.

In a concurrence that supplied the fourth vote, Rutledge rejected Frankfurter's position that reapportionment was nonjusticiable. Rutledge believed that the Court had jurisdiction to decide the case, but that the shortness of time remaining before the election (a few months off) prevented judicial action. Thus, a majority of Justices (4–3) agreed that the Court could take jurisdiction in reapportionment cases. Because of Rutledge's position, Frankfurter had actually written a *minority* opinion on the question of jurisdiction. However, the circumstances of the Illinois case did not allow sufficient time to draw new district lines. Declaring them invalid would have forced candidates to run at-large on a statewide ticket. The pressure of an impending election also dictated the Court's decision two years later to refuse jurisdiction. MacDougall v. Green, 335 U.S. 281 (1948).

In a 1950 case, Georgia's apportionment law was considered a political matter unfit for judicial review. South v. Peters, 339 U.S. 276 (1950). Georgia allotted each county a number of unit votes, giving residents of the less populous rural counties an advantage over the more populous counties in the cities. The vote in the least populous county was worth over 120 times the vote of residents in the most populous county (Fulton County). The system did more than disfranchise urban voters. The large cities had a heavy black population. In their dissent, Justices Douglas and Black pointed out that the County Unit System "has indeed been called the 'last loophole' around our decisions holding that there must be no discrimination because of race in primary as well as in general elections." Id. at 278. With regard to the issue of nonjusticiability, Douglas and Black assumed that the Court would strike down state efforts to reduce the votes of blacks, Catholics, or Jews "so that each got only one-tenth of a vote." Id. at 277.

In 1960, a unanimous Court agreed to strike down the political boundaries drawn by the Alabama legislature for the city of Tuskegee. Black citizens challenged the legislature's decision to change the boundaries from a square to an irregular

---

[2]See Wood v. Broom, 287 U.S. 1 (1932); Smiley v. Holm, 285 U.S. 355 (1932); Koenig v. Flynn, 285 U.S. 375 (1932); Carroll v. Becker, 285 U.S. 380 (1932).

twenty-eight-sided figure. Through this process of gerrymandering, the state eliminated all but four or five of the city's 400 black voters without eliminating a single white voter. The Court invalidated the redistricting, but not on the general ground of the Equal Protection Clause. It disposed of the case on the specific commands of the Fifteenth Amendment, which forbids a state to deprive any citizen of the right to vote because of race. Justice Whittaker, concurring, would have decided the case on equal protection grounds. Gomillion v. Lightfoot, 364 U.S. 339 (1960).

With this case the Court stepped into the "political thicket" of redistricting. Two years later it completed the journey. Tennessee had failed to reapportion its state legislature since 1900, despite massive population shifts over the course of six census takings. A single vote in Moore County was worth nineteen votes in Hamilton County. Frankfurter's appeal in *Colegrove* for voters to demand change was simplistic. The ability of disfranchised voters had been systematically diluted by malapportionment. Basing its decision on the Equal Protection Clause, a 6–2 Court held that (1) it possessed jurisdiction over reapportionment; (2) plaintiffs could obtain appropriate relief in the courts; and (3) plaintiffs had standing to challenge the Tennessee apportionment statutes. The particular remedy was left to the district court. BAKER v. CARR, 369 U.S. 186 (1962).

In an impassioned dissent, Frankfurter claimed that the remedy for malapportionment should come from "an aroused popular conscience that sears the conscience of the people's representatives." Id. at 270. But Justice Clark, in a concurrence, pointed out that there were no practical opportunities for voters to correct malapportionment. Tennessee had no initiative or referendum. Constitutional conventions could be called only by the legislature. Appeal to the state courts had been futile. As Clark noted, the majority of voters "have been caught up in a legislative strait jacket." Id. at 259.

The Court explained that the question in the Tennessee case was "the consistency of state action with the Federal Constitution. We have no question decided, or to be decided, by a political branch of government coequal with this Court." Id. at 226. That calculus changed in 1964 when the Court accepted a case involving *congressional* districts and held that it had jurisdiction, plaintiffs had standing, and relief could be granted by the courts. Drawing upon constitutional history and the framers' intent, the Court concluded that the U.S. House of Representatives was bound by the principle of equal representation for equal numbers of people. Although it might not be possible to draw congressional districts with "mathematical precision," the principle of "one person, one vote" applied to the House. WESBERRY v. SANDERS, 376 U.S. 1 (1964). In a dissent, Justice Harlan calculated that the decision impugned the validity of 398 Representatives, leaving a "constitutional" House of thirty-seven members.

In 1968, the Court extended the one-person, one-vote principle to any legislative or administrative body in the state subject to popular election, including units of local government with general governmental powers over the entire geographical area served by the body. Avery v. Midland County, 390 U.S. 474. The Court rejected the idea of limiting equal apportionment to "important" elections. "In some instances the election of a local sheriff may be far more important than the election of a United States Senator." Hadley v. Junior College District, 397 U.S. 50, 55 (1970). On the other hand, nonlegislative state or local officials need not be chosen by election. Their selection is not governed by the one-person, one-vote requirement.

Sailors v. Board of Education, 387 U.S. 105 (1967). The Court also refused to extend the one-person, one-vote principle to specialized state agencies that govern limited jurisdictions.[3]

New York City's Board of Estimate was struck down by a unanimous Court in 1989. The Board consists of the Mayor, the comptroller, and the president of the City Council (all elected citywide and each with two votes on the Board), plus the elected presidents of the city's five boroughs (each casting one vote). This arrangement gave Brooklyn's 2.2 million people, about half of them minorities, the same voting strength on the Board as the 400,000 residents of Staten Island, which is mostly white. The Board exercises major powers with respect to zoning, franchises, sewer and water rates, and city contracts. Although the city offered various arguments to justify the composition of the Board, including efforts to accommodate natural and political boundaries, the Court found that the Board violated the Equal Protection Clause. Board of Estimate of City of New York v. Morris, 109 S.Ct. 1433 (1989).

Singlemember Districts

In requiring a population-based formula for redistricting, the Supreme Court allows state legislatures to experiment with other variations. For example, the Court does not insist that state legislators be selected from singlemember districts. Some districts can be multimember.[4] However, when courts are forced to fashion an apportionment plan, singlemember districts are generally preferable. East Carroll Parish School Bd. v. Marshall, 424 U.S. 636 (1976); Chapman v. Meier, 420 U.S. 1 1975); Connor v. Johnson, 402 U.S. 690 (1971). Under certain conditions, multimember districts are declared unconstitutional if they discriminate against minorities and ethnic groups. The capacity of these groups to elect one of their own is diluted when their votes are cast in a large, multimember district controlled by whites. White v. Regester, 412 U.S. 755 (1973).

The problem is similar with an at-large electoral system, where voters of an entire county elect a multimember governing board. If at-large voting discriminates against blacks or other groups, the county may have to be divided into districts to avoid vote dilution. Rogers v. Lodge, 458 U.S. 613 (1982). These cases generally required plaintiffs to prove that an at-large system was designed with the *intent* to further racial discrimination. There had to be not only a discriminatory effect but also a discriminatory purpose. Mobile v. Bolden, 446 U.S. 55 (1980). The distinction between effect and purpose was also explored in City of Rome v. United States, 446 U.S. 156 (1980).

In response to *Bolden*, Congress amended the Voting Rights Act in 1982 to provide that a violation could be proved by showing discriminatory effect alone. The new language adopted the "results test." 96 Stat. 134, § 3. This amendment has been used to challenge and overturn multimember districting that impairs black voting, but blacks are not automatically guaranteed seats in the legislature because of their

---

[3]Ball v. James, 451 U.S. 355 (1982); Salyer Land Co. v. Tulare Lake Basin Water Storage Dist., 410 U.S. 719 (1973); Associated Enterprises, Inc. v. Toltec District, 410 U. S. 743 (1973).

[4]Reynolds v. Sims, 377 U.S. 533, 577 (1964). See also Fortson v. Dorsey, 379 U.S. 433 (1965) and Burns v. Richardson, 384 U.S. 73, 88–89 (1966). The merits and demerits of multimember voting were explored more fully in Whitcomb v. Chavis, 403 U.S. 124 (1971).

percentage of the population. Thornburg v. Gingles, 478 U.S. 30 (1986). Congress specifically provided that there is no right "to have members of a protected class elected in numbers equal to their proportion of the population." 96 Stat. 134, § 3.

Equality in Population

Over the years, Congress has adopted different policies on the question of making election districts equal in population. The text of the Constitution contradicted the principle of equality of representation. In counting the "whole Number of free Persons," certain Indians were excluded and only "three-fifths of all other Persons" (blacks) were added to the total. Art. I, § 2. The Civil War Amendments eliminated these constitutional supports for racism. In 1872, Congress required Representatives to be elected from districts "containing as nearly as practicable an equal number of inhabitants." 17 Stat. 28, § 2. That standard was continued in 1882, 1891, 1901, and 1911, dropped in 1929, and not revived by subsequent statutes.[5]

In 1963, the Supreme Court held that the concept of political equality could mean only one thing with regard to apportionment systems: "one person, one vote." Gray v. Sanders, 372 U.S. 368, 381. A year later it announced a softer standard. The constitutional command of Article I, Section 2, that members of the U.S. House of Representatives be chosen "by the People of the several States," means that "as nearly as is practicable one man's vote in a congressional election is to be worth as much as another's." Wesberry v. Sanders, 376 U.S. at 8. In 1964, the Court said that "mathematical nicety is not a constitutional requisite." Reynolds v. Sims, 377 U.S. 533, 568 (1964).

Although states are not compelled to achieve mathematical exactness in population among districts, a failure to articulate acceptable reasons for variations can result in the invalidation of a reapportionment plan. In cases involving *congressional* districts, population variations, no matter how small, have to be justified by the state.[6] Even variations of less than one percent from the ideal must be justified by good-faith efforts to achieve population equality. Karcher v. Daggett, 462 U.S. 725 (1983). Efforts to preserve intact whole regions or less populous counties are unacceptable justifications for population variations. Wells v. Rockefeller, 394 U.S. 542 (1969). Computer technology has simplified the task of drawing new district lines.

With regard to apportioning seats in a *state* legislature, the Court permits more flexibility and greater population variations to preserve the integrity of political subdivision lines. Mahan v. Howell, 410 U.S. 315 (1973); Gaffney v. Cummings, 412 U.S. 735 (1973). When state constitutions ensure that each county (no matter how small its population) will have one representative in the state legislature, the Court has upheld population deviations as large as 16 percent as necessary to maintain the integrity of political subdivisions. Brown v. Thomson, 462 U.S. 835 (1983). The Court tolerates "slightly greater percentage deviations" for local government

---

[5]22 Stat. 6, § 3 (1882); 26 Stat. 735, § 3 (1891); 31 Stat. 734, § 3 (1901); 37 Stat. 14, § 3 (1911); 46 Stat. 26, § 22 (1929).

[6]Kirkpatrick v. Preisler, 394 U.S. 526 (1969); White v. Weiser, 412 U.S. 783 (1973). Population variations in state legislatures also had to be explained: Swann v. Adams, 385 U.S. 440 (1967); Kilgarin v. Hill, 386 U.S. 120 (1967).

apportionment schemes than for state and national counterparts. Abate v. Mundt, 403 U.S. 182, 185 (1971). When courts devise a reapportionment plan, they are held to a higher standard than legislatures in making districts as nearly of equal population as is practicable. Connor v. Finch, 431 U.S. 407 (1977).

Bicameralism

The Federal Constitution provides for a House of Representatives based on population, and a Senate that gives two Senators to each state regardless of population. In the states, this "federal analogy" was invoked to argue for a population-based lower house, while allowing for factors other than population to determine seats in the upper house.

In 1964, the Supreme Court extended the principle of equal representation to both houses of a state legislature. Relying on the Equal Protection Clause, the Court held that the seats in both houses of a bicameral state legislature must be apportioned substantially on a population basis. The Court found the federal analogy irrelevant. Whereas the original states surrendered some of their sovereignty to form the Union, and insisted on equal representation in the Senate as part of the Grand Compromise, counties did not form the states. They are creatures of the state and were never sovereign entities. REYNOLDS v. SIMS, 377 U.S. 533 (1964).[7] It mattered not to the Court whether the voters of a state specifically supported a constitutional amendment to allow one house of a state legislature to be apportioned on a basis other than population. The constitutional meaning of the Equal Protection Clause does not depend on majority vote. Lucas v. Colorado Gen. Assembly, 377 U.S. 713, 736–737 (1964).

Senator Everett Dirksen, Republican from Illinois, took the lead in trying to reverse the Court's ruling that both houses of a state legislature had to be based on population. The Republican National Convention adopted a platform plank in 1964 in support of a constitutional amendment to allow one house to be based on other than population. Congressman William Tuck, Democrat of Virginia, introduced a bill to strip the federal courts of jurisdiction to hear apportionment cases. After a pitched battle, these and other court-curbing efforts were defeated.[8]

Compactness and Gerrymandering

The term "gerrymander" originates from an election district so tortured in shape that it resembled a salamander. The district lines were formed in Massachusetts by Governor Elbridge Gerry, a member of the Jeffersonian party. The Federalist party complained that the district was drawn intentionally to disadvantage them. Congress passed legislation to limit gerrymandering. In 1842, it provided that members of the

---

[7] The Court also struck down New York's apportionment law, which gave greater representation to the less populous counties for both houses of the state legislature. WMCA, Inc. v. Lomenzo, 377 U.S. 633 (1964). The Court held that both houses of Maryland's legislature must be apportioned substantially on a population basis. Maryland Committee v. Tawes, 377 U.S. 656 (1964). The same standard was applied to the two houses of the legislatures in Virginia and in Delaware. Davis v. Mann, 377 U.S. 678 (1964); Roman v. Sincock, 377 U.S. 695 (1964).

[8] Richard C. Cortner, The Apportionment Cases 236–246 (1970); Robert G. Dixon, Jr., Democratic Representation 385–435 (1968); Royce Hanson, The Political Thicket 82–101 (1966).

House of Representatives be elected from districts of "contiguous territory." 5 Stat. 491. Over the years, this requirement was periodically dropped and reinstated.[9]

In *Gomillion* (1960), the Supreme Court struck down a gerrymandered district because it deprived blacks of their voting rights. In 1964, however, the Court decided a case in which gerrymandering was used in New York City to *promote* the interests of black voters. The evidence strongly suggests that district lines had been drawn to segregate white voters from black and Puerto Rican voters. The result was a white congressional district and a nonwhite congressional district, giving black voters control of the Representative from the latter. A 7–2 Court decided that the district court's ruling, that plaintiffs had failed to show that the apportionment was motivated by racial considerations, "was not clearly erroneous." The dissent by Douglas and Goldberg claimed that New York supported segregation not on the "separate but equal" theory of *Plessy* v. *Ferguson* but on the theory of "separate but better off." Wright v. Rockefeller, 376 U.S. 52, 62 (1964).

With the Court applying constant pressure on state legislatures to attain mathematical equivalence in the population among districts, states were tempted to create strange configurations through gerrymandering. As Justice Harlan noted in one dissent: "The fact of the matter is that the rule of absolute equality is perfectly compatible with 'gerrymandering' of the worst sort." Wells v. Rockefeller, 394 U.S. at 542, 551 (1969). Justice Stevens remarked in 1983 that advances in computer technology since the time Harlan wrote "have made the task of the gerrymander even easier." Karcher v. Daggett, 462 U.S. 725, 752 (1983).

In the Voting Rights Act of 1965, Congress directed that states were not to adopt practices or procedures that have the purpose or effect "of denying or abridging the right to vote on account of race or color." 79 Stat. 439, § 5 (1965); 42 U.S.C. § 1973c (1982). These practices and procedures include redistricting that discriminates against blacks. Allen v. State Board of Elections, 393 U.S. 544, 569–570 (1969).

Although race may not be used to deny or abridge voting rights, it may be used to enhance the right to vote. That practice was evident in the case of *Wright* v. *Rockefeller* (1964). Race was also used in Brooklyn to divide the Hasidic Jewish community in order to maintain certain percentages in the white and nonwhite districts. In upholding this reapportionment, the Second Circuit reasoned that the Act contemplated that the Attorney General and the state legislature would have "to think in racial terms" to satisfy the Act, which "necessarily deals with race or color." The Supreme Court affirmed this judgment. United Jewish Organizations v. Carey, 430 U.S. 144, 154–155 (1977). Compliance with the Act in apportionment cases "would often necessitate the use of racial considerations in drawing district lines." Id. at 159. The Court recognized that New York "deliberately increased the nonwhite majorities in certain districts in order to enhance the opportunity for election of nonwhite representatives from those districts." Id. at 165.

Race is also a factor when cities annex nearby counties to reduce the percentage of the black population. Part of the compromise may be the creation of wards with

---

[9]The requirement of "contiguous territory" was dropped in 1850, 9 Stat. 432, § 25, and reinstated in 1862, 1872, 1882, and 1891. 12 Stat. 572 (1862); 17 Stat. 28, § 2 (1872); 22 Stat. 6, § 3 (1882); 26 Stat. 735, § 3 (1891). The language in 1901 and 1911 became "contiguous and compact territory." 31 Stat. 734, § 3 (1901); 37 Stat. 14, § 3 (1911). This requirement was dropped in 1929. 46 Stat. 26, § 22 (1929).

substantial black populations.[10] When cities try to annex only white areas, they may be unable to obtain either the approval of the Attorney General or a federal judge. City of Pleasant Grove v. United States, 479 U.S. 462 (1987).

In addition to gerrymanders along racial lines, the Court has reviewed gerrymanders that favor one political party over another. In 1983, it sidestepped a New Jersey political gerrymandering case by deciding it on grounds of equal population. Karcher v. Daggett, 462 U.S. 725 (1983). The political gerrymandering case decided by the Court in 1986 involved the Indiana legislature, which consists of a 100-member House of Representatives and a 50-member Senate. Following the 1980 census, the legislature (controlled by Republicans) reapportioned the districts. The Democrats claimed that the reapportionment plan constituted a political gerrymander that violated their right to equal protection. In a decision marked by confusion of gigantic proportions, a badly fractured Court agreed that it had jurisdiction over political gerrymandering. The standards it established, however, were quite vague. DAVIS v. BANDEMER, 478 U.S. 109 (1986).

CAMPAIGN FINANCING

As a result of court rulings, elections now operate under the broad slogan of "one person, one vote." This superficial equality, giving equal weight to each voter, is seriously skewed by large campaign contributions from individuals, corporations, and political action committees (PACs). Congress has attempted to regulate campaign spending to remove the most serious abuses, but these efforts have been circumscribed by court rulings. The one-person, one-vote principle collides with the reality of wealthy and powerful financial contributors.

Congress has to juggle two conflicting interests: (1) the right of private citizens to make financial contributions to elections, and (2) the need to protect campaigns from corrupting influences. One of the first efforts to reconcile this conflict came in 1907, when Congress responded to the practice of corporations making large contributions to political candidates. Legislation in 1907 prohibited any national bank or any corporation created by Congress from contributing money for political elections. 34 Stat. 864. The Federal Corrupt Practices Act of 1910 limited the amount of money that congressional candidates could contribute to their own nomination or election. Political committees had to record their contributions and make regular reports to Congress. 36 Stat. 822 (1910); 37 Stat. 25 (1911).

The Supreme Court held that this statute, to the extent that it covered primaries, was unconstitutional. Although Article I, Section 4, empowers Congress to alter state regulations concerning the "Manner of holding Elections" for U.S. Senators and Representatives, four members of the Court ruled that elections in the constitutional sense meant "the final choice of an officer." Pushing original intent and strict construction to the limit, the Court said that primaries "were then unknown" at the time of the Constitution. Primaries were "in no sense elections for an office." Newberry v. United States, 256 U.S. 232, 250 (1921). As applied to primaries and nominating conventions, therefore, the statute usurped state power.

---

[10]City of Richmond v. United States, 422 U.S. 358 (1975); Georgia v. United States, 411 U.S. 526 (1973); Perkins v. Matthews, 400 U.S. 379 (1971). See also Beer v. United States, 425 U.S. 130 (1976).

Justice McKenna joined the four Justices in setting aside the conviction but offered no opinion on the constitutional issue.

In one of the dissents, Chief Justice White denounced the appeal to original intent as "suicidal." Id. at 262. To underscore his point, he reviewed the expectation of the framers that members of the electoral college would be free agents, capable of exercising discretion when choosing the President. In 1876, however, when James Russell Lowell was urged to exercise independence and vote for Tilden, he refused on the ground that "whatever the first intent of the Constitution was, usage had made the presidential electors strictly the instruments of the party which chose them." Id. at 266. White concluded that whatever case could have been made for state autonomy in matters of national elections had evaporated in 1913 with the Seventeenth Amendment, which provided for the election of U.S. Senators by the people rather than by state legislatures. Justice Pitney, joined by Justices Brandeis and Clarke, also repudiated the Court's foray into strict construction. Pitney wrote: "It is said primaries were unknown when the Constitution was adopted. So were the steam railway and the electric telegraph. But the authority of Congress to regulate commerce among the several States extended over these instrumentalities . . ." Id. at 282.

Congress rewrote the Federal Corrupt Practices Act to conform to the Court's ruling but also strengthened several provisions in the statute. 43 Stat. 1070 (1925). The Court upheld the power of Congress to require political committees to keep detailed accounts of all financial contributions and to file with Congress a statement containing the name and address of each contributor to a federal election. The Court denied that the statute invaded state power. The operation of the statute was confined to situations which, "if not beyond the power of the state to deal with at all, are beyond its power to deal with adequately." The authority of Congress to safeguard federal elections comes from "the power of self protection." Burroughs v. United States, 290 U.S. 534, 544–545 (1934). Congress enacted additional legislation in 1939 and 1940 to protect campaigns from corruption and "pernicious political activities." 53 Stat. 1147; 54 Stat. 767.

Although the Court in *Newberry* had denied Congress the power to regulate primary elections, the Justice Department challenged the Court's decision by returning to first principles. In a subsequent case, the government argued that the right of voters in congressional primaries is secured by Article I, Section 2, calling for the choice of Representatives "by the People," as well as the Times, Places, and Manner Clause of Section 4. Richard Claude, The Supreme Court and the Electoral Process 33 (1970). The Court reversed *Newberry* and held that congressional power embraced not merely the final election but primaries as well. Even the three dissenters, Justices Douglas, Black, and Murphy, rejected *Newberry*'s conclusion that Congress had no power to control primary elections. United States v. Classic, 313 U.S. 299, 329–330 (1941).

The prohibition that Congress had placed on corporate and national bank campaign contributions was later extended to cover labor organizations. 57 Stat. 167, § 9 (1943); 61 Stat. 159, § 304 (1947). Labor unions responded by setting up PACs (political action committees) to pursue campaign goals. Initially, union members were required to contribute to these political funds, which were used to support the campaigns of candidates friendly to the labor cause. These political funds were later replaced by a "voluntary" organization, with funds segregated from union dues. Congress authorized this type of fund in 1972 by stating that the prohibition on labor contributions did not include "the establishment, administration, and solicitation of contributions to a separate segregated fund to be utilized for political purposes by a corporation or labor organization." 86 Stat. 10, § 205 (1972). Partly on the basis of this law, the Supreme Court upheld political funds operated by labor unions. Pipefitters v. United States, 407 U.S. 385 (1972). See also United States v. Auto. Workers, 352 U.S. 567 (1957).

The high cost of federal campaigns, especially for TV ads, led to the Federal Election Campaign Act of 1971. New limits were placed on campaign contributions and expenditures. 86 Stat. 3. On the heels of the Watergate scandal, which exposed widespread corruption during the presidential campaign of 1972, Congress enacted new legislation. The Federal Election Campaign Act Amendments of 1974 placed limits on contributions and expenditures, created the Federal Election Commission (FEC) to enforce the law, and provided optional public funding for presidential elections. 88 Stat. 1263.

The *Buckley* Case

A strange alliance challenged the constitutionality of the bill. Opponents of the legislation included conservative Senator James L. Buckley, liberal Senator Eugene J. McCarthy, the Conservative party of New York State, the Libertarian party, the New York Civil Liberties Union, and *Human Events*, a conservative publication. They argued that the limits on campaign contributions and expenditures represented a violation of the First Amendment right of expression, both by contributors and candidates.

In *Buckley* v. *Valeo* (1976), the Court upheld limits on how much individuals and political action committees (PACs) may contribute to candidates. These limits serve the important governmental interest of preventing corruption of the political process. The contribution limits on a candidate's personal funds (or family funds) were declared invalid constraints on the ability of persons to become engaged in protected First Amendment expression. The Court upheld the Act's disclosure-recordkeeping provisions and the public financing of presidential campaigns. If presidential candidates accept public funds, expenditure limits are imposed on campaign costs. The Court upheld those limits. Other limits on campaign expenditures were struck down as a violation of the freedoms of speech and association protected by the First Amendment. The Court made a key distinction between contributions and expenditures, concluding that the risk of corruption is greater in *giving*, rather than *spending*, money. Quid pro quos, said the Court, pose a more serious threat with contributions than with expenditures. Finally, the Court found the composition of the FEC to be unconstitutional. BUCKLEY v. VALEO, 424 U.S. 1 (1976).

Congress corrected the defect in the FEC (pp. 223–224) and adopted other reforms, but years of effort have been unsuccessful in providing public funding for congressional campaigns or limiting the amount spent by PACs. Members of Congress and committees are directly influenced by PAC spending. Dairy PACs give money to members of the agriculture committees, corporate PACs contribute to members of the tax committees, and other PACs donate funds to committee members that have jurisdiction over their activities. These issues of *influence* are not covered by the Court's preoccupation with *corruption*. In other cases the Court has expressed concern not only about electoral corruption but the *integrity* of the electoral process.[11]

The cost of running for Congress continues to spiral upwards. The average expenditure by the winning House candidate rose from an estimated $87,000 in 1976 to $393,000 in 1988. Comparable figures for the winning Senate candidate were $609,000 and $3,747,114. As the cost of campaigns goes up, qualified candidates are less able to enter the race. Instead of the "robust debate" promised by the Supreme Court in *Buckley,* including enhanced protection to First Amendment values, the high cost of campaigning may reduce the field of candidates to an ever-narrowing band.

The basic thrust of *Buckley* has been sustained in subsequent decisions. Congress may set limits on how much presidential candidates spend as a condition on their receiving public funds. Republican National Committee v. FEC, 445 U.S. 955 (1980), aff'g summarily, 487 F.Supp. 280 (S.D. N.Y. 1980) (three-judge court) and 616 F.2d 1 (2d Cir. 1980) *(en banc).* Congress can place limits on some contributions. California Medical Assn. v. FEC, 453 U.S. 182 (1982). However, a total ban on contributions runs afoul of First Amendment freedoms. In 1978, a 5–4 Court held that Massachusetts violated the First Amendment by prohibiting business corporations from contributing funds to influence a referendum. The "speech" protected, of course, was not by natural persons but by artificial entities created in the form of corporations. In a dissent, Justice White warned that in the area of campaign financing "the expertise of legislators is at its peak and that of judges is at its very lowest." First National Bank of Boston v. Bellotti, 435 U.S. 765, 804 (1978). Members of the Court have increasing difficulty in understanding the contribution/expenditure distinction in *Buckley.* See the dissents in FEC v. National Conservative PAC, 470 U.S. 480 (1985).

A critical issue of campaign financing is the control of "independent expenditures": the expenses of a person or political committee free of any coordination with a candidate's official campaign committee. The Federal Election Campaign Act Amendments of 1974 imposed a $1,000 limit on independent expenditures, but the Court struck down that limit in *Buckley.* As a result, while federal law limits contributions made directly to political candidates, no such restraints operate on independent expenditures. A three-judge court ruled that the $1,000 limit on independent expenditures of political committees was facially unconstitutional under the First Amendment; Common Cause v. Schmitt, 512 F.Supp. 489 (D.D.C. 1980). This ruling was affirmed by an equally divided (4–4) Supreme Court in a per curiam decision; 455 U.S. 129 (1982). See also FEC v. National Conservative PAC, 470 U.S. 480 (1985). In 1986, a 5–4 Court struck down as unconstitutional FEC's regulation that prohibited political expenditures by nonprofit advocacy groups that take positions on abortion, busing, gun control, and other issues. Under the Court's reading of the First Amendment, those groups may take out advertisements urging voters to support or oppose specific candidates. These independent expenditures are

---

[11]E.g., Storer v. Brown, 415 U.S. 724 (1974); Kusper v. Pontikes, 414 U.S. 51 (1973); Rosario v. Rockefeller, 410 U.S. 752 (1973); Bullock v. Carter, 405 U.S. 134 (1972); Williams v. Rhodes, 393 U.S. 23 (1968).

not subject to federal limits. FEC v. Massachusetts Citizens for Life, Inc., 479 U.S. 238 (1986).[12]

LOBBYING

A variety of interest groups maintain regular contacts with members of Congress, congressional committees, and executive agencies, supplying advice and information they hope will influence government policy. The pejorative term "lobbying" is often applied to these activities, but it is healthy and appropriate in a democracy for private groups to intervene in the process of government. They are expected to make efforts to persuade the executive and legislative branches to take particular actions. As the Supreme Court remarked in 1961, "the whole concept of representation depends upon the ability of the people to make their wishes known to their representatives." Eastern Railroad Presidents Conference v. Noerr Motors, Inc., 365 U.S. 127, 137 (1961). The First Amendment recognizes the right of citizens to petition their government for a redress of grievances. How can this activity be regulated through constitutional means?

It is difficult to conceive of a democratic government operating in a sterile environment never contaminated by private lobbyists. However, the activity of interest groups has been cast in negative terms from the start. In Federalist 10, Madison defined "faction" as a number of citizens "united and actuated by some common impulse of passion, or of interest, adverse to the rights of other citizens, or to the permanent and aggregate interests of the community." Under his definition, almost every interest group in America is rendered suspect. Although Madison disapproved of factions, he did not urge that they be abolished. The answer was not in removing the cause of faction but in "controlling its effects" (pp. 1310–1314).

Regulatory Efforts

In 1919, Congress passed legislation to prevent executive officials from using appropriated funds to stimulate grassroots lobbying against Congress. Officials had used telephones, telegrams, letters, and other forms of communication to drum up pressure against Congress from the private sector. Legislation prohibited this practice and remains part of current law. 41 Stat. 68, § 6 (1919); 18 U.S.C. § 1913 (1982). In 1934, Congress amended the tax code to restrict expenditures by charitable organizations for lobbying. The amendment applied to organizations covered by Section 501(c)(3) of the Internal Revenue Code, which gives tax-exempt status to various groups. As a condition attached to this tax benefit, Congress required that "no substantial part" of the activities of tax-exempt groups should consist of "carrying on propaganda, or otherwise attempting, to influence legislation." 48 Stat. 690 (1934).

A year later, Congress required representatives of public utility holding compa-

---

[12]Government cannot compel minor political parties, such as the Socialist Workers party, to report the names and addresses of campaign contributors and recipients of campaign disbursements if disclosure is likely to result in harassment and reprisals. Brown v. Socialists Workers '74 Campaign Comm., 459 U.S. 87 (1982); Buckley v. Valeo, 424 U.S. at 64–74. Other questions of campaign financing are explored in FEC v. National Right to Work Committee, 459 U.S. 197 (1982) and Citizens Against Rent Control v. Berkeley, 454 U.S. 290 (1981).

nies to file a report with the Securities and Exchange Commission before attempting to influence Congress, the SEC, or the Federal Power Commission. 49 Stat. 825 (1935). Similar requirements were applied in 1936 to lobbyists for the merchant marine and in 1938 to agents of foreign governments. 49 Stat. 2014, § 807 (1936); 52 Stat. 631 (1938).

The most extensive effort to control lobbying is the Federal Regulation of Lobbying Act of 1946, which requires lobbyists to register with Congress and file quarterly reports of their activities. 60 Stat. 839 (1946); 2 U.S.C. §§ 261–270 (1982). The statute was criticized for using vague language to cover activities that carried criminal penalties for violations. The statute has limited reach. It applies only to lobbyists whose "principal purpose" is to influence Congress. A more general critique is that the Act interferes with the First Amendment freedom to petition government. National Ass'n of Mfrs. v. McGrath, 103 F.Supp. 510 (D.D.C. 1952), vacated as moot, 344 U.S. 804 (1952).

Section 307 of the Lobbying Act covers persons who, "directly or indirectly," solicit, collect, or receive money to influence Congress. The House set up a Select Committee on Lobbying Activities to investigate how well the Act was working. The term "lobbying activities" was not used in the Act, but in 1953 the Supreme Court restricted it to "direct" appeals to members of Congress, rather than the more general definition of influencing the thinking of the community. United States v. Rumely, 345 U.S. 41, 47 (1953). That restricted interpretation was followed a year later in a case that dealt more specifically with the Act. The Court dismissed the charge of vagueness leveled against the statute, but agreed with *Rumely* that the statute covered only direct communications with members of Congress. As to the First Amendment challenge, the Court held that Congress is not forbidden to require the disclosure of lobbying activities. United States v. Harriss, 347 U.S. 612 (1954).

The Internal Revenue Code, as interpreted by Treasury Department regulations, forbids the deduction of sums expended for "the promotion or defeat of legislation." In upholding these regulations, a unanimous Court held that they apply to expenditures made in connection with efforts to promote or defeat legislation by persuasion of the general public (as in initiative measures and referenda), as well as efforts to influence legislative bodies directly through "lobbying." Cammarano v. United States, 358 U.S. 498 (1959). In granting tax exemptions to certain nonprofit organizations on the condition that "no substantial part" of their activities involve propaganda or attempts to influence legislation, Congress does not violate the First Amendment. Members of Congress may legitimately choose not to subsidize lobbying activities. Regan v. Taxation With Representation of Wash., 461 U.S. 540 (1983).

In recent decisions, the Supreme Court has recognized a broad right of citizens to demonstrate against governmental policies, including those of the Court itself and also foreign governments. Congress had passed legislation to prohibit the display of any flag, banner, or device in the Supreme Court or on its grounds "to bring into public notice any party, organization, or movement." The statute was meant to insulate the Court from direct lobbying, but in 1983 the Court held that the acts of distributing leaflets and carrying picket signs on the public sidewalk around the building were protected by the First Amendment. United States v. Grace, 461 U.S. 171 (1983).

Five years later, in a case involving demonstrations against foreign governments, the Court issued a decision that illustrates the dialogue between Congress and the judiciary on constitutional questions. The D.C. government made it unlawful for individuals, within 500 feet of a foreign embassy, to display any sign that tended to bring the foreign government into "public odium" or "public disrepute." Congress had also passed an antipicketing provision to protect foreign officials, but repealed it in 1976 because of First Amendment concerns. In 1986, Congress passed legislation to suggest that the D.C. law on demonstrations near foreign missions may be inconsistent with First Amendment rights. The D.C. government repealed the law, contingent on Congress extending to the District the federal law on foreign embassies. Against this background, the Court held that the D.C. law violated the First Amendment because it represented a content-based restriction on political speech in a public forum. Boos v. Barry, 108 S.Ct. 1157 (1988).

The sections in this chapter provide further evidence of the essentially shared nature of constitutional interpretation, involving the combined efforts of legislators, executive officials, and judges. The responsibility for keeping the political process free and open is not entrusted to a single branch. Members of the judiciary must exercise careful judgment in deciding which cases to accept and resolve. Harold Leventhal, for many years a distinguished federal judge on the D.C. Circuit, recognized that the "political thicket" did not constitute a flat ban on judicial involvement: "For me the 'thicket' sign does not mean out of bounds, but a caution to walk carefully in the work of interpreting and determining the validity of the legislature's efforts to structure the political process." 77 Colum. L. Rev. 345, 346 (1977). Other constraints on judicial activism are addressed in the next chapter.

Selected Readings

ALEXANDER, HERBERT E. *Financing Politics: Money, Elections, and Political Reform.* Washington, D.C.: Congressional Quarterly, 1984.

ALFANGE, DEAN, JR. "Gerrymandering and the Constitution: Into the Thorns of the Thicket at Last." 1986 *Supreme Court Review* 175.

AUERBACH, CARL A. "The Reapportionment Cases: One Person, One Vote—One Vote, One Value." 1964 *Supreme Court Review* 1.

BAKER, GORDON E. *The Reapportionment Revolution.* New York: Random House, 1966.

BALL, HOWARD. *The Warren Court's Conceptions of Democracy: An Evaluation of the Supreme Court's Apportionment Cases.* Rutherford, N.J.: Fairleigh Dickinson University Press, 1971.

BICKEL, ALEXANDER. "The Voting Rights Cases." 1966 *Supreme Court Review* 79.

CAIN, BRUCE E. *The Reapportionment Puzzle.* Berkeley: University of California Press, 1984.

CLAUDE, RICHARD. *The Supreme Court and the Electoral Process.* Baltimore, Md.: Johns Hopkins University Press, 1970.

CORTNER, RICHARD C. *The Apportionment Cases.* Knoxville: University of Tennessee Press, 1970.

DIXON, ROBERT G., JR. *Democratic Representation:*

Reapportionment in Law and Politics. New York: Oxford University Press, 1968.

———. "The Warren Court Crusade for the Holy Grail of 'One Man–One Vote.'" 1969 *Supreme Court Review* 219.

ELLIOTT, WARD. "Prometheus, Proteus, Pandora, and Procrustes Unbound: The Political Consequences of Reapportionment." 37 *University of Chicago Law Review* 474 (1970).

HAMILTON, HOWARD D., ed. *Legislative Reapportionment: Key to Power.* New York: Harper & Row, 1964.

HANSON, ROYCE. *The Political Thicket: Reapportionment and Constitutional Democracy.* Englewood Cliffs, N.J.: Prentice-Hall, 1966.

LEVENTHAL, HAROLD. "Courts and Political Thickets." 77 *Columbia Law Review* 345 (1977).

LEWIS, ANTHONY. "Legislative Apportionment and the Federal Courts." 71 *Harvard Law Review* 1057 (1958).

NEAL, PHIL C. "Baker v. Carr: Politics in Search of Law." 1962 *Supreme Court Review* 252.

PENNOCK, J. ROLAND, AND JOHN W. CHAPMAN, eds. *Representation.* New York: Atherton Press, 1968.

POLSBY, DANIEL D. "Buckley v. Valeo: The Special

Nature of Political Speech." 1976 *Supreme Court Review* 1.

POLSBY, NELSON W., ed. *Reapportionment in the 1970s.* Berkeley: University of California Press, 1971.

SORAUF, FRANK J. "Caught in a Political Thicket: The Supreme Court and Campaign Finance." 3 *Constitutional Commentary* 97 (1986).

TAPER, BERNARD. *Gomillion versus Lightfoot: Apartheid in Alabama.* New York: McGraw-Hill, 1967.

WRIGHT, J. SKELLY. "Money and the Pollution of Politics: Is the First Amendment an Obstacle to Political Equality?" 82 *Columbia Law Review* 609 (1982).

Smith v. Allwright

321 U.S. 649 (1944)

The statutes of Texas provided for primary elections for U.S. Senators, Congressmen, and state officers. The Democratic party of Texas, which the Texas Supreme Court called a "voluntary association," adopted in a state convention a resolution permitting only white citizens of the state to participate in the Democratic primary. The issue in this case was whether the resolution constituted "state action" in violation of the Fifteenth Amendment. Lonnie Smith, a black, sued an election judge, S. E. Allwright.

MR. JUSTICE REED delivered the opinion of the Court.

This writ of certiorari brings here for review a claim for damages in the sum of $5,000 on the part of petitioner, a Negro citizen of the 48th precinct of Harris County, Texas, for the refusal of respondents, election and associate election judges respectively of that precinct, to give petitioner a ballot or to permit him to cast a ballot in the primary election of July 27, 1940, for the nomination of Democratic candidates for the United States Senate and House of Representatives, and Governor and other state officers. The refusal is alleged to have been solely because of the race and color of the proposed voter.

The actions of respondents are said to violate §§ 31 and 43 of Title 8 of the United States Code in that petitioner was deprived of rights secured by §§ 2 and 4 of Article I and the Fourteenth, Fifteenth and Seventeenth Amendments to the United States Constitution. The suit was filed in the District Court of the United States for the Southern District of Texas, which had jurisdiction under Judicial Code § 24, subsection 14.

The District Court denied the relief sought and

the Circuit Court of Appeals quite properly affirmed its action on the authority of *Grovey* v. *Townsend*, 295 U. S. 45. We granted the petition for certiorari to resolve a claimed inconsistency between the decision in the *Grovey* case and that of *United States* v. *Classic*, 313 U. S. 299. 319 U. S. 738.

The State of Texas by its Constitution and statutes provides that every person, if certain other requirements are met which are not here in issue, qualified by residence in the district or county "shall be deemed a qualified elector." Constitution of Texas, Article VI, § 2; Vernon's Civil Statutes (1939 ed.), Article 2955. Primary elections for United States Senators, Congressmen and state officers are provided for by Chapters Twelve and Thirteen of the statutes. Under these chapters, the Democratic party was required to hold the primary which was the occasion of the alleged wrong to petitioner. . . .

The Democratic party of Texas is held by the Supreme Court of that State to be a "voluntary association," *Bell* v. *Hill*, 123 Tex. 531, 534, protected by § 27 of the Bill of Rights, Art. 1, Constitution of Texas, from interference by the State except that:

"In the interest of fair methods and a fair expression by their members of their preferences in the selection of their nominees, the State may regulate such elections by proper laws." p. 545.

That court stated further:

"Since the right to organize and maintain a political party is one guaranteed by the Bill of Rights of this State, it necessarily follows that every privilege essential or reasonably appropriate to the exercise of that right is likewise guaranteed,—including, of course, the privilege of determining the policies of the party and its membership. Without the privilege of determining the policy of a political association and its membership, the right to organize such an association would be a mere mockery. We think these rights,—that is, the right to determine the membership of a political party and to determine its policies, of necessity are to be exercised by the state convention of such party, and cannot, under any circumstances, be conferred upon a state or governmental agency." p. 546. Cf. *Waples* v. *Marrast,* 108 Tex. 5, 184 S. W. 180.

The Democratic party on May 24, 1932, in a state convention adopted the following resolution, which has not since been "amended, abrogated, annulled or avoided":

"Be it resolved that all white citizens of the State of Texas who are qualified to vote under the Constitution and laws of the State shall be eligible to membership in the Democratic party and, as such, entitled to participate in its deliberations."

It was by virtue of this resolution that the respondents refused to permit the petitioner to vote.

Texas is free to conduct her elections and limit her electorate as she may deem wise, save only as her action may be affected by the prohibitions of the United States Constitution or in conflict with powers delegated to and exercised by the National Government. The Fourteenth Amendment forbids a State from making or enforcing any law which abridges the privileges or immunities of citizens of the United States and the Fifteenth Amendment specifically interdicts any denial or abridgement by a State of the right of citizens to vote on account of color. Respondents appeared in the District Court and the Circuit Court of Appeals and defended on the ground that the Democratic party of Texas is a voluntary organization with members banded together for the purpose of selecting individuals of the group representing the common political beliefs as candidates in the general election. As such a voluntary organization, it was claimed, the Democratic party is free to select its own membership and limit to whites participation in the party primary. Such action, the answer asserted, does not violate the Fourteenth, Fifteenth or Seventeenth Amendment as officers of government cannot be chosen at primaries and the Amendments are applicable only to general elections where governmental officers are actually elected. Primaries, it is said, are political party affairs, handled by party, not governmental, officers. No appearance for respondents is made in this Court. Arguments presented here by the Attorney General of Texas and the Chairman of the State Democratic Executive Committee of Texas, as amici curiae, urged substantially the same grounds as those advanced by the respondents.

The right of a Negro to vote in the Texas primary has been considered heretofore by this Court. The first case was *Nixon* v. *Herndon,* 273 U.S. 536. At that time, 1924, the Texas statute, Art. 3093a, afterwards numbered Art. 3107 (Rev. Stat. 1925) declared "in no event shall a Negro be eligible to participate in a Democratic Party primary election in the State of Texas." *[The Court held that the statute violated the Equal Protection Clause of the Fourteenth Amendment, after which the legislature of Texas gave the State Executive Committee of a party the power to prescribe the voting qualifications of its members. In* Nixon v. Condon, *286 U.S. 73 (1932), the Court held that the Committee action was state action and invalid as discriminatory under the Fourteenth Amendment. In* Grovey v. *Townsend, 295 U.S. 45 (1935), the Court decided that the refusal of a county clerk in Texas to give a black an absentee ballot, for reasons only of race, was permissible because the clerk was not a state officer and there was no "state action." After* Grovey, *the Court held in* United States v. *Classic, 313 U.S. 299 (1941), that § 4 of Article I of the Constitution authorized Congress to regulate primary as well as general elections.]*

... The fusing by the *Classic* case of the primary and general elections into a single instrumentality for choice of officers has a definite bearing on the permissibility under the Constitution of excluding Negroes from primaries. This is not to say that the *Classic* case cuts directly into the rationale of *Grovey* v. *Townsend*. This latter case was not mentioned in the opinion. *Classic* bears upon *Grovey* v. *Townsend* not because exclusion of Negroes from primaries is any more or less state action by reason of the unitary character of the electoral process but because the recognition of the place of the primary in the electoral scheme makes clear that state delegation to a party of the power to fix the qualifications of primary elections is delegation of a state function that may make the party's action the action of the State. When *Grovey* v. *Townsend* was written, the Court looked upon the denial of a vote in a primary as a mere refusal by a party of party membership. 295 U.S. at 55. As the Louisiana statutes for holding primaries are similar to those of Texas, our ruling in *Classic* as to the unitary character of the electoral process calls for a reexamination as to whether or not the exclusion of Negroes from a Texas party primary was state action.

The statutes of Texas relating to primaries and the resolution of the Democratic party of Texas extending the privileges of membership to white citizens only are the same in substance and effect today as they were when *Grovey* v. *Townsend* was decided by a unanimous Court. The question as to whether the exclusionary action of the party was the action of the State persists as the determinative factor. In again entering upon consideration of the inference to be drawn as to state action from a substantially similar factual situation, it should be noted that *Grovey* v. *Townsend* upheld exclusion of Negroes from primaries through the denial of party membership by a party convention. A few years before, this Court refused approval of exclusion by the State Executive Committee of the party. A different result was reached on the theory that the Committee action was state authorized and the Convention action was unfettered by statutory control. Such a variation in the result from so slight a change in form influences us to consider anew the legal validity of the distinction

which has resulted in barring Negroes from participating in the nominations of candidates of the Democratic party in Texas. Other precedents of this Court forbid the abridgement of the right to vote. *United States* v. *Reese*, 92 U.S. 214, 217; *Neal* v. *Delaware*, 103 U.S. 370, 388; *Guinn* v. *United States*, 238 U.S. 347, 361; *Myers* v. *Anderson*, 238 U.S. 368, 379; *Lane* v. *Wilson*, 307 U.S. 268.

It may now be taken as a postulate that the right to vote in such a primary for the nomination of candidates without discrimination by the State, like the right to vote in a general election, is a right secured by the Constitution. *United States* v. *Classic*, 313 U.S. at 314; *Myers* v. *Anderson*, 238 U.S. 368; *Ex parte Yarbrough*, 110 U.S. 651, 663 *et seq.* By the terms of the Fifteenth Amendment that right may not be abridged by any State on account of race. Under our Constitution the great privilege of the ballot may not be denied a man by the State because of his color.

We are thus brought to an examination of the qualifications for Democratic primary electors in Texas, to determine whether state action or private action has excluded Negroes from participation. ... Texas requires electors in a primary to pay a poll tax. Every person who does so pay and who has the qualifications of age and residence is an acceptable voter for the primary. Art. 2955. As appears above in the summary of the statutory provisions set out in note 6, Texas requires by the law the election of the county officers of a party. These compose the county executive committee. The county chairmen so selected are members of the district executive committee and choose the chairman for the district. Precinct primary election officers are named by the county executive committee. Statutes provide for the election by the voters of precinct delegates to the county convention of a party and the selection of delegates to the district and state conventions by the county convention. The state convention selects the state executive committee. No convention may place in platform or resolution any demand for specific legislation without endorsement of such legislation by the voters in a primary. Texas thus directs the selection of all party officers.

Primary elections are conducted by the party under state statutory authority. The county executive committee selects precinct election officials and the county, district or state executive committees, respectively, canvass the returns. These party committees or the state convention certify the party's candidates to the appropriate officers for inclusion on the official ballot for the general election. No name which has not been so certified may appear upon the ballot for the general election as a candidate of a political party. No other name may be printed on the ballot which has not been placed in nomination by qualified voters who must take oath that they did not participate in a primary for the selection of a candidate for the office for which the nomination is made.

The state courts are given exclusive original jurisdiction of contested elections and of mandamus proceedings to compel party officers to perform their statutory duties.

We think that this statutory system for the selection of party nominees for inclusion on the general election ballot makes the party which is required to follow these legislative directions an agency of the State in so far as it determines the participants in a primary election. The party takes its character as a state agency from the duties imposed upon it by state statutes; the duties do not become matters of private law because they are performed by a political party. . . . This is state action within the meaning of the Fifteenth Amendment. *Guinn* v. *United States*, 238 U.S. 347, 362.

The United States is a constitutional democracy. Its organic law grants to all citizens a right to participate in the choice of elected officials without restriction by any State because of race. This grant to the people of the opportunity for choice is not to be nullified by a State through casting its electoral process in a form which permits a private organization to practice racial discrimination in the election. Constitutional rights would be of little value if they could be thus indirectly denied. *Lane* v. *Wilson*, 307 U.S. 268, 275.

. . .

. . . In reaching this conclusion we are not unmindful of the desirability of continuity of decision in constitutional questions. However, when convinced of former error, this Court has never felt constrained to follow precedent. In constitutional questions, where correction depends upon amendment and not upon legislative action this Court throughout its history has freely exercised its power to reexamine the basis of its constitutional decisions. This has long been accepted practice, and this practice has continued to this day. This is particularly true when the decision believed erroneous is the application of a constitutional principle rather than an interpretation of the Constitution to extract the principle itself. Here we are applying, contrary to the recent decision in *Grovey* v. *Townsend*, the well-established principle of the Fifteenth Amendment, forbidding the abridgement by a State of a citizen's right to vote. *Grovey* v. *Townsend* is overruled.

Judgment reversed.

MR. JUSTICE FRANKFURTER concurs in the result.

MR. JUSTICE ROBERTS:

In *Mahnich* v. *Southern Steamship Co.*, 321 U.S. 96, 105, I have expressed my views with respect to the present policy of the court freely to disregard and to overrule considered decisions and the rules of law announced in them. This tendency, it seems to me, indicates an intolerance for what those who have composed this court in the past have conscientiously and deliberately concluded, and involves an assumption that knowledge and wisdom reside in us which was denied to our predecessors. I shall not repeat what I there said for I consider it fully applicable to the instant decision, which but points the moral anew.

. . .

The reason for my concern is that the instant decision, overruling that announced about nine years ago, tends to bring adjudications of this tribunal into the same class as a restricted railroad ticket, good for this day and train only. I have no assurance, in view of current decisions, that the opinion announced today may not shortly be repudiated and overruled by justices who deem they have new light on the subject. In the present term the court has overruled three cases.

. . .

I do not stop to call attention to the material differences between the primary election laws of Louisiana under consideration in the *Classic* case and those of Texas which are here drawn in question. These differences were spelled out in detail in the Government's brief in the *Classic* case and emphasized in its oral argument. It is enough to say that the Louisiana statutes required the primary to be conducted by state officials and made it a state election, whereas, under the Texas statute, the primary is a party election conducted at the expense of members of the party and by officials chosen by the party. If this court's opinion in the *Classic* case discloses its method of overruling earlier decisions, I can only protest that, in fairness, it should rather have adopted the open and frank way of saying what it was doing than, after the event, characterize its past action as overruling *Grovey* v. *Townsend* though those less sapient never realized the fact.

It is regrettable that in an era marked by doubt and confusion, an era whose greatest need is steadfastness of thought and purpose, this court, which has been looked to as exhibiting consistency in adjudication, and a steadiness which would hold the balance even in the face of temporary ebbs and flows of opinion, should now itself become the breeder of fresh doubt and confusion in the public mind as to the stability of our institutions.

Harper v. Virginia Board of Elections
383 U.S. 663 (1966)

Annie E. Harper and other residents of Virginia brought this action to have Virginia's poll tax declared unconstitutional. A three-judge district court dismissed the complaint. The Supreme Court had to decide whether the poll tax violated the Equal Protection Clause of the Fourteenth Amendment.

MR. JUSTICE DOUGLAS delivered the opinion of the Court.

These are suits by Virginia residents to have declared unconstitutional Virginia's poll tax. The three-judge District Court, feeling bound by our decision in *Breedlove* v. *Suttles*, 302 U.S. 277, dismissed the complaint. See 240 F. Supp. 270. The cases came here on appeal and we noted probable jurisdiction. 380 U.S. 930, 382 U.S. 806.

While the right to vote in federal elections is conferred by Art. I, § 2, of the Constitution (*United States* v. *Classic*, 313 U.S. 299, 314–315), the right to vote in state elections is nowhere expressly mentioned. It is argued that the right to vote in state elections is implicit, particularly by reason of the First Amendment and that it may not constitutionally be conditioned upon the payment of a tax or fee. Cf. *Murdock* v. *Pennsylvania*, 319 U.S. 105, 113. We do not stop to canvass the relation between voting and political expression. For it is enough to say that once the franchise is granted to the electorate, lines may not be drawn which are inconsistent with the Equal Protection Clause of the Fourteenth Amendment. That is to say, the right of suffrage "is subject to the imposition of state standards which are not discriminatory and which do not contravene any restriction that Congress, acting pursuant to its constitutional powers, has imposed." *Lassiter* v. *Northampton Election Board*, 360 U.S. 45, 51. We were speaking there of a state literacy test which we sustained, warning that the result would be different if a literacy test, fair on its face, were used to discriminate against a class. *Id.*, at 53. But the *Lassiter* case does not govern the result here, because, unlike a poll tax, the "ability to read and write . . . has some relation to standards designed to promote intelligent use of the ballot." *Id.*, at 51.

We conclude that a State violates the Equal Protection Clause of the Fourteenth Amendment whenever it makes the affluence of the voter or payment of any fee an electoral standard. Voter qualifications have no relation to wealth nor to paying or not paying this or any other tax. Our cases demonstrate that the Equal Protection Clause of the Fourteenth Amendment restrains the States from fixing voter qualifications which invidiously discriminate. Thus without questioning the power of a State to impose reasonable residence restrictions on the availability of the ballot (see *Pope* v. *Williams*, 193 U.S. 621), we held in *Carrington* v. *Rash*, 380 U.S. 89, that a State may not deny the opportunity to vote to a bona fide resident merely because he is a member of the armed services. "By forbidding a soldier ever to controvert the presumption of non-residence, the Texas Constitution imposes an invidious discrimination in violation of the Fourteenth Amendment." *Id.*, at 96. And see *Louisiana* v. *United States*, 380 U.S. 145. Previously we had said that neither homesite nor occupation "affords a permissible basis for distinguishing between qualified voters within the State." *Gray* v. *Sanders*, 372 U.S. 368, 380. . . .

We say the same whether the citizen, otherwise qualified to vote, has $1.50 in his pocket or nothing at all, pays the fee or fails to pay it. The principle that denies the State the right to dilute a citizen's vote on account of his economic status or other such factors by analogy bars a system which excludes those unable to pay a fee to vote or who fail to pay.

It is argued that a State may exact fees from citizens for many different kinds of licenses; that if it can demand from all an equal fee for a driver's license, it can demand from all an equal poll tax for voting. But we must remember that the interest of the State, when it comes to voting, is limited to the power to fix qualifications. Wealth, like race, creed, or color, is not germane to one's ability to participate intelligently in the electoral process. Lines drawn on the basis of wealth or property, like those of race (*Korematsu* v. *United States*, 323 U.S. 214, 216), are traditionally disfavored. See *Edwards* v. *California*, 314 U.S. 160, 184–185 (Jackson, J., concurring); *Griffin* v. *Illinois*, 351 U.S. 12; *Douglas* v. *California*, 372 U.S. 353. To introduce wealth or payment of a fee as a measure of a voter's qualifications is to introduce a capricious or irrelevant factor. . . .

. . . the Equal Protection Clause is not shackled to the political theory of a particular era. In determining what lines are unconstitutionally discriminatory, we have never been confined to historic notions of equality, any more than we have restricted due process to a fixed catalogue of what was at a given time deemed to be the limits of fundamental rights. See *Malloy* v. *Hogan*, 378 U.S. 1, 5–6. Notions of what constitutes equal treatment for purposes of the Equal Protection Clause *do* change. This Court in 1896 held that laws providing for separate public facilities for white and Negro citizens did not deprive the latter of the equal protection and treatment that the Fourteenth Amendment commands. *Plessy* v. *Ferguson*, 163 U.S. 537. Seven of the eight Justices then sitting subscribed to the Court's opinion, thus joining in expressions of what constituted unequal and discriminatory treatment that sound strange to a contemporary ear. When, in 1954—more than a half-century later—we repudiated the "separate-but-equal" doctrine of *Plessy* as respects public education we stated: "In approaching this problem, we cannot turn the clock back to 1868 when the Amendment was adopted, or even to 1896 when *Plessy* v. *Ferguson* was written." *Brown* v. *Board of Education*, 347 U.S. 483, 492.

In a recent searching re-examination of the Equal Protection Clause, we held, as already noted, that "the opportunity for equal participation by all voters in the election of state legislators" is required. *Reynolds* v. *Sims, supra,* at 566. We decline to qualify that principle by sustaining this poll tax. Our conclusion, like that in *Reynolds* v. *Sims,* is founded not on what we think governmental policy should be, but on what the Equal Protection Clause requires.

We have long been mindful that where fundamental rights and liberties are asserted under the Equal Protection Clause, classifications which might invade or restrain them must be closely scrutinized and carefully confined. See, *e.g., Skinner* v. *Oklahoma*, 316 U.S. 535, 541; *Reynolds* v. *Sims*, 377 U.S. 533, 561–562; *Carrington* v. *Rash, supra; Baxstrom* v. *Herold, ante,* p. 107; *Cox* v.

Louisiana, 379 U.S. 536, 580–581 (BLACK, J., concurring).

Those principles apply here. For to repeat, wealth or fee paying has, in our view, no relation to voting qualifications; the right to vote is too precious, too fundamental to be so burdened or conditioned.

Reversed.

MR. JUSTICE BLACK, dissenting.

[Justice Black points out that the Court in Breedlove *v.* Suttles, *302 U.S. 277 (1937) and* Butler *v.* Thompson, *341 U.S. 937 (1951) upheld poll taxes.]* Since the *Breedlove* and *Butler* cases were decided the Federal Constitution has not been amended in the only way it could constitutionally have been, that is, as provided in Article V of the Constitution. I would adhere to the holding of those cases. The Court, however, overrules *Breedlove* in part, but its opinion reveals that it does so not by using its limited power to interpret the original meaning of the Equal Protection Clause, but by giving that clause a new meaning which it believes represents a better governmental policy. From this action I dissent.

. . . All voting laws treat some persons differently from others in some respects. Some bar a person from voting who is under 21 years of age; others bar those under 18. Some bar convicted felons or the insane, and some have attached a freehold or other property qualification for voting. The *Breedlove* case upheld a poll tax which was imposed on men but was not equally imposed on women and minors, and the Court today does not overrule that part of *Breedlove* which approved those discriminatory provisions. And in *Lassiter* v. *Northampton Election Board*, 360 U.S. 45, this Court held that state laws which disqualified the illiterate from voting did not violate the Equal Protection Clause. From these cases and all the others decided by this Court interpreting the Equal Protection Clause it is clear that some discriminatory voting qualifications can be imposed without violating the Equal Protection Clause.

A study of our cases shows that this Court has refused to use the general language of the Equal Protection Clause as though it provided a handy instrument to strike down state laws which the Court feels are based on bad governmental policy. The equal protection cases carefully analyzed boil down to the principle that distinctions drawn and even discriminations imposed by state laws do not violate the Equal Protection Clause so long as these distinctions and discriminations are not "irrational," "irrelevant," "unreasonable," "arbitrary," or "invidious." These vague and indefinite terms do not, of course, provide a precise formula or an automatic mechanism for deciding cases arising under the Equal Protection Clause. The restrictive connotations of these terms, however (which in other contexts have been used to expand the Court's power inordinately, see, *e. g.,* cases cited at pp. 728–732 in *Ferguson* v. *Skrupa*, 372 U.S. 726), are a plain recognition of the fact that under a proper interpretation of the Equal Protection Clause States are to have the broadest kind of leeway in areas where they have a general constitutional competence to act. In view of the purpose of the terms to restrain the courts from a wholesale invalidation of state laws under the Equal Protection Clause it would be difficult to say that the poll tax requirement is "irrational" or "arbitrary" or works "invidious discriminations." State poll tax legislation can "reasonably," "rationally" and without an "invidious" or evil purpose to injure anyone be found to rest on a number of state policies including (1) the State's desire to collect its revenue, and (2) its belief that voters who pay a poll tax will be interested in furthering the State's welfare when they vote. Certainly it is rational to believe that people may be more likely to pay taxes if payment is a prerequisite to voting.

. . .

The Court's justification for consulting its own notions rather than following the original meaning of the Constitution, as I would, apparently is based on the belief of the majority of the Court that for this Court to be bound by the original meaning of the Constitution is an intolerable and debilitating evil; that our Constitution should not be "shackled to the political theory of a particular era," and that to save the country from the original Constitution the Court must have constant power to renew it and keep it abreast of this Court's more enlightened theories of what is best for our society.

. . .

The people have not found it impossible to amend their Constitution to meet new conditions. The Equal Protection Clause itself is the product of the people's desire to use their constitutional power to amend the Constitution to meet new problems. Moreover, the people, in § 5 of the Fourteenth Amendment, designated the governmental tribunal they wanted to provide additional rules to enforce the guarantees of that Amendment. The branch of Government they chose was not the Judicial Branch but the Legislative. I have no doubt at all that Congress has the power under § 5 to pass legislation to abolish the poll tax in order to protect the citizens of this country if it believes that the poll tax is being used as a device to deny voters equal protection of the laws. . . .

. . .

MR. JUSTICE HARLAN, whom MR. JUSTICE STEWART joins, dissenting.

The final demise of state poll taxes, already totally proscribed by the Twenty-Fourth Amendment with respect to federal elections and abolished by the States themselves in all but four States with respect to state elections, is perhaps in itself not of great moment. But the fact that the *coup de grace* has been administered by this Court instead of being left to the affected States or to the federal political process should be a matter of continuing concern to all interested in maintaining the proper role of this tribunal under our scheme of government.

. . .

. . . in holding unconstitutional state poll taxes and property qualifications for voting and *pro tanto* overruling *Breedlove* v. *Suttles*, 302 U.S. 277, and *Butler* v. *Thompson*, 341 U.S. 937, the Court reverts to the highly subjective judicial approach manifested by *Reynolds*. In substance the Court's analysis of the equal protection issue goes no further than to say that the electoral franchise is "precious" and "fundamental," *ante*, p. 670, and to conclude that "[t]o introduce wealth or payment of a fee as a measure of a voter's qualifications is to introduce a capricious or irrelevant factor," *ante*, p. 668. These are of course captivating phrases, but they are wholly inadequate to satisfy the standard governing adjudication of the equal protection issue: Is there a rational basis for Virginia's poll tax as a voting qualification? I think the answer to that question is undoubtedly "yes."

Property qualifications and poll taxes have been a traditional part of our political structure. In the Colonies the franchise was generally a restricted one. . . .

. . .

Property and poll-tax qualifications . . . are not in accord with current egalitarian notions of how a modern democracy should be organized. It is of course entirely fitting that legislatures should modify the law to reflect such changes in popular attitudes. However, it is all wrong, in my view, for the Court to adopt the political doctrines popularly accepted at a particular moment of our history and to declare all others to be irrational and invidious, barring them from the range of choice by reasonably minded people acting through the political process. It was not too long ago that Mr. Justice Holmes felt impelled to remind the Court that the Due Process Clause of the Fourteenth Amendment does not enact the *laissez-faire* theory of society, *Lochner* v. *New York*, 198 U.S. 45, 75–76. The times have changed, and perhaps it is appropriate to observe that neither does the Equal Protection Clause of that Amendment rigidly impose upon America an ideology of unrestrained egalitarianism.

I would affirm the decision of the District Court.

South Carolina v. Katzenbach

383 U.S. 301 (1966)

By passing the Voting Rights Act of 1965, Congress acted against states that used various tests and devices to prevent blacks from registering and voting. The statute authorized federal examiners to qualify applicants for registration, entitling them to vote in elections. South Carolina filed suit to have the Act declared unconstitutional as an encroachment on states' rights and a violation of due process protections. The case was one of original jurisdiction, with South Carolina supported by Alabama, Georgia, Louisiana, Mississippi, and Virginia, while the states supporting Attorney General Katzenbach included California, Illinois, and Massachusetts, joined by Hawaii, Indiana, Iowa, Kansas, Maine, Maryland, Michigan, Montana, New Hampshire, New Jersey, New York, Oklahoma, Oregon, Pennsylvania, Rhode Island, Vermont, West Virginia, and Wisconsin.

MR. CHIEF JUSTICE WARREN delivered the opinion of the Court.

By leave of the Court, 382 U.S. 898, South Carolina has filed a bill of complaint, seeking a declaration that selected provisions of the Voting Rights Act of 1965 violate the Federal Constitution, and asking for an injunction against enforcement of these provisions by the Attorney General. Original jurisdiction is founded on the presence of a controversy between a State and a citizen of another State under Art. III, § 2, of the Constitution. See *Georgia* v. *Pennsylvania R. Co.*, 324 U.S. 439. Because no issues of fact were raised in the complaint, and because of South Carolina's desire to obtain a ruling prior to its primary elections in June 1966, we dispensed with appointment of a special master and expedited our hearing of the case.

Recognizing that the questions presented were of urgent concern to the entire country, we invited all of the States to participate in this proceeding as friends of the Court. A majority responded by submitting or joining in briefs on the merits, some supporting South Carolina and others the Attorney General. . . .

The Voting Rights Act was designed by Congress to banish the blight of racial discrimination in voting, which has infected the electoral process in parts of our country for nearly a century. The Act creates stringent new remedies for voting discrimination where it persists on a pervasive scale, and in addition the statute strengthens existing remedies for pockets of voting discrimination elsewhere in the country. Congress assumed the power to prescribe these remedies from § 2 of the Fifteenth Amendment, which authorizes the National Legislature to effectuate by "appropriate" measures the constitutional prohibition against racial discrimination in voting. We hold that the sections of the Act which are properly before us are an appropriate means for carrying out Congress' constitutional responsibilities and are consonant with all other provisions of the Constitution. We therefore deny South Carolina's request that enforcement of these sections of the Act be enjoined.

I.

The constitutional propriety of the Voting Rights Act of 1965 must be judged with reference to the historical experience which it reflects. Before enacting the measure, Congress explored with great care the problem of racial discrimination in voting. The House and Senate Committees on the Judiciary each held hearings for nine days and received testimony from a total of 67 witnesses. More than three full days were consumed discussing the bill on the floor of the House, while the debate in the Senate covered 26 days in all. At the close of these deliberations, the verdict of both chambers was overwhelming. The House approved the bill by a vote of 328–74, and the measure passed the Senate by a margin of 79–18.

Two points emerge vividly from the voluminous legislative history of the Act contained in the committee hearings and floor debates. First: Congress felt itself confronted by an insidious and pervasive evil which had been perpetuated in certain parts of our country through unremitting and ingenious defiance of the Constitution. Second: Congress concluded that the unsuccessful remedies which it had prescribed in the past would have to be replaced by sterner and more elaborate measures in order to satisfy the clear commands of the Fifteenth Amendment. . . .

The Fifteenth Amendment to the Constitution was ratified in 1870. Promptly thereafter Congress passed the Enforcement Act of 1870, which made it a crime for public officers and private persons to obstruct exercise of the right to vote. The statute was amended in the following year to provide for detailed federal supervision of the electoral process, from registration to the certification of returns. As the years passed and fervor for racial equality waned, enforcement of the laws became spotty and ineffective, and most of their provisions were repealed in 1894. The remnants have had little significance in the recently renewed battle against voting discrimination.

Meanwhile, beginning in 1890, the States of Alabama, Georgia, Louisiana, Mississippi, North Carolina, South Carolina, and Virginia enacted tests still in use which were specifically designed to prevent Negroes from voting. Typically, they made the ability to read and write a registration qualification and also required completion of a registration form. These laws were based on the fact that as of 1890 in each of the named States, more than two-thirds of the adult Negroes were illiterate while less than one-quarter of the adult whites were unable to read or write. At the same time, alternate tests were prescribed in all of the named States to assure that white illiterates would not be deprived of the franchise. These included grandfather clauses, property qualifications, "good character" tests, and the requirement that registrants "understand" or "interpret" certain matter.

The course of subsequent Fifteenth Amendment litigation in this Court demonstrates the variety and persistence of these and similar institutions designed to deprive Negroes of the right to vote. Grandfather clauses were invalidated in *Guinn* v. *United States*, 238 U.S. 347, and *Myers* v. *Anderson*, 238 U.S. 368. Procedural hurdles were struck down in *Lane* v. *Wilson*, 307 U.S. 268. The white primary was outlawed in *Smith* v. *Allwright*, 321 U.S. 649, and *Terry* v. *Adams*, 345 U.S. 461. Improper challenges were nullified in *United States* v. *Thomas*, 362 U.S. 58. Racial gerrymandering was forbidden by *Gomillion* v. *Lightfoot*, 364 U.S. 339. Finally, discriminatory application of voting tests was condemned in *Schnell* v. *Davis*, 336 U.S. 933: *Alabama* v. *United States*, 371 U.S. 37; and *Louisiana* v. *United States*, 380 U.S. 145.

According to the evidence in recent Justice Department voting suits, the latter stratagem is now the principal method used to bar Negroes from the polls. Discriminatory administration of voting qualifications has been found in all eight Alabama cases, in all nine Louisiana cases, and in all nine Mississippi cases which have gone to final judgment. Moreover, in almost all of these cases, the courts have held that the discrimination was pursuant to a widespread "pattern or practice." White applicants for registration have often been excused altogether from the literacy and understanding tests or have been given easy versions, have received extensive help from voting officials, and have been registered despite serious errors in their answers. *[A footnote observes:* "A white applicant in Louisiana satisfied the registrar of his ability to interpret the state constitution by writing, 'FRDUM FOOF SPETGH.' *United States* v. *Louisiana*, 225 F. Supp. 353, 384. A white applicant in Alabama who had never completed the first grade of school was enrolled after the registrar filled out the entire form for him. *United States* v. *Penton*, 212 F. Supp. 193, 210–211."] Negroes, on the other hand, have typically been required to pass difficult versions of all the tests, without any outside assistance and without the slightest error. The good-morals requirement is so vague and subjective that it has constituted an open invitation to abuse at the hands of voting officials. Negroes obliged to obtain vouchers from registered voters have found it virtually impossible to comply in areas where almost no Negroes are on the rolls.

In recent years, Congress has repeatedly tried to cope with the problem by facilitating case-by-case litigation against voting discrimination. The Civil Rights Act of 1957 authorized the Attorney General to seek injunctions against public and private interference with the right to vote on racial grounds. Perfecting amendments in the Civil Rights Act of 1960 permitted the joinder of States as parties defendant, gave the Attorney General access to local voting records, and authorized courts to register voters in areas of systematic discrimination. Title I of the Civil Rights Act of 1964 expedited the hearing of voting cases before three-judge courts and outlawed some of the tactics used to disqualify Negroes from voting in federal elections.

Despite the earnest efforts of the Justice Department and of many federal judges, these new laws have done little to cure the problem of voting discrimination. According to estimates by the Attorney General during hearings on the Act, registration of voting-age Negroes in Alabama rose only from 14.2% to 19.4% between 1958 and 1964; in Louisiana it barely inched ahead from 31.7% to 31.8% between 1956 and 1965; and in Mississippi it increased only from 4.4% to 6.4% between 1954 and 1964. In each instance, registration of voting-age whites ran roughly 50 percentage points or more ahead of Negro registration.

. . .

II.

The Voting Rights Act of 1965 reflects Congress' firm intention to rid the country of racial discrimination in voting. The heart of the Act is a complex scheme of stringent remedies aimed at areas where voting discrimination has been most flagrant. Section 4(a)–(d) lays down a formula defining the States and political subdivisions to which these new remedies apply. The first of the remedies, contained in § 4(a), is the suspension of literacy tests and similar voting qualifications for a period of five years from the last occurrence of substantial voting discrimination. Section 5 prescribes a second remedy, the suspension of all

new voting regulations pending review by federal authorities to determine whether their use would perpetuate voting discrimination. The third remedy, covered in §§ 6(b), 7, 9, and 13(a), is the assignment of federal examiners on certification by the Attorney General to list qualified applicants who are thereafter entitled to vote in all elections.

Other provisions of the Act prescribe subsidiary cures for persistent voting discrimination. Section 8 authorizes the appointment of federal poll-watchers in places to which federal examiners have already been assigned. Section 10(d) excuses those made eligible to vote in sections of the country covered by § 4(b) of the Act from paying accumulated past poll taxes for state and local elections. Section 12(e) provides for balloting by persons denied access to the polls in areas where federal examiners have been appointed.

The remaining remedial portions of the Act are aimed at voting discrimination in any area of the country where it may occur. Section 2 broadly prohibits the use of voting rules to abridge exercise of the franchise on racial grounds. Sections 3, 6(a), and 13(b) strengthen existing procedures for attacking voting discrimination by means of litigation. Section 4(c) excuses citizens educated in American schools conducted in a foreign language from passing English-language literacy tests. Section 10(a)–(c) facilitates constitutional litigation challenging the imposition of all poll taxes for state and local elections. Sections 11 and 12(a)–(d) authorize civil and criminal sanctions against interference with the exercise of rights guaranteed by the Act.

At the outset, we emphasize that only some of the many portions of the Act are properly before us. . . . the only sections of the Act to be reviewed at this time are §§ 4(a)–(d), 5, 6(b), 7, 9, 13(a), and certain procedural portions of § 14, all of which are presently in actual operation in South Carolina. We turn now to a detailed description of these provisions and their present status.

Coverage Formula.

The remedial sections of the Act assailed by South Carolina automatically apply to any State, or to any separate political subdivision such as a county or parish, for which two findings have been made: (1) the Attorney General has determined that on November 1, 1964, it maintained a "test or device," and (2) the Director of the Census has determined that less than 50% of its voting-age residents were registered on November 1, 1964, or voted in the presidential election of November 1964. *[Under this § 4(b) procedure, coverage was extended to Alabama, Alaska, Georgia, Louisiana, Mississippi, South Carolina, Virginia, twenty-six counties in North Carolina, three counties in Arizona, one county in Hawaii, and one county in Idaho.]*

. . .

Suspension of Tests.

In a State or political subdivision covered by § 4(b) of the Act, no person may be denied the right to vote in any election because of his failure to comply with a "test or device." § 4(a).

. . .

Review of New Rules.

In a State or political subdivision covered by § 4(b) of the Act, no person may be denied the right to vote in any election because of his failure to comply with a voting qualification or procedure different from those in force on November 1, 1964. This suspension of new rules is terminated, however, under either of the following circumstances: (1) if the area has submitted the rules to the Attorney General, and he has not interposed an objection within 60 days, or (2) if the area has obtained a declaratory judgment from the District Court for the District of Columbia, determining that the rules will not abridge the franchise on racial grounds. These declaratory judgment actions are to be heard by a three-judge panel, with direct appeal to this Court. § 5.

. . .

Federal Examiners.

In any political subdivision covered by § 4(b) of the Act, the Civil Service Commission shall appoint voting examiners whenever the Attorney General certifies either of the following facts: (1) that he has received meritorious written complaints from at least 20 residents alleging that they have been disenfranchised under color of law because of their race, or (2) that the appointment of examiners is otherwise necessary to effectuate the guarantees of the Fifteenth Amendment. § 6(b)

. . .

III.

These provisions of the Voting Rights Act of 1965 are challenged on the fundamental ground that they exceed the powers of Congress and encroach on an area reserved to the States by the Constitution. South Carolina and certain of the *amici curiae* also attack specific sections of the Act for more particular reasons. They argue that the coverage formula prescribed in § 4(a)–(d) violates the principle of the equality of States, denies due process by employing an invalid presumption and by barring judicial review of administrative findings, constitutes a forbidden bill of attainder, and impairs the separation of powers by adjudicating guilt through legislation. They claim that the review of new voting rules required in § 5 infringes Article III by directing the District Court to issue advisory opinions. They contend that the assignment of federal examiners authorized in § 6(b) abridges due process by precluding judicial review of administrative findings and impairs the separation of powers by giving the Attorney General judicial functions; also that the challenge procedure prescribed in § 9 denies due process on account of its speed. Finally, South Carolina and certain of the *amici curiae* maintain that §§ 4(a) and 5, buttressed by § 14(b) of the Act, abridge due process by limiting litigation to a distant forum.

Some of these contentions may be dismissed at the outset. The word "person" in the context of the Due Process Clause of the Fifth Amendment cannot, by any reasonable mode of interpretation, be expanded to encompass the States of the Union, and to our knowledge this has never been done by any court. . . . Likewise, courts have consistently regarded the Bill of Attainder Clause of Article I and the principle of the separation of powers only as protections for individual persons and private groups, those who are peculiarly vulnerable to nonjudicial determinations of guilt. . . . Nor does a State have standing as the parent of its citizens to invoke these constitutional provisions against the Federal Government, the ultimate *parens patriae* of every American citizen. . . . The objections to the Act which are raised under these provisions may therefore be considered only as additional aspects of the basic question presented by the case: Has Congress exercised its powers under the Fifteenth Amendment in an appropriate manner with relation to the States?

. . .

. . . § 2 of the Fifteenth Amendment expressly declares that "Congress shall have power to enforce this article by appropriate legislation." By adding this authorization, the Framers indicated that Congress was to be chiefly responsible for implementing the rights created in § 1. "It is the power of Congress which has been enlarged. Congress is authorized to *enforce* the prohibitions by appropriate legislation. Some legislation is contemplated to make the [Civil War] amendments fully effective." *Ex parte Virginia*, 100 U.S. 339, 345. Accordingly, in addition to the courts, Congress has full remedial powers to effectuate the constitutional prohibition against racial discrimination in voting.

. . .

We . . . reject South Carolina's argument that Congress may appropriately do no more than to forbid violations of the Fifteenth Amendment in general terms—that the task of fashioning specific remedies or of applying them to particular localities must necessarily be left entirely to the courts. Congress is not circumscribed by any such artificial rules under § 2 of the Fifteenth Amendment. In the oft-repeated words of Chief Justice Marshall, referring to another specific legislative authorization in the Constitution, "This power, like all others vested in Congress, is complete in itself, may be exercised to its utmost extent, and acknowledges no limitations, other than are prescribed in the constitution." *Gibbons* v. *Ogden*, 9 Wheat. 1, 196.

IV.

Congress exercised its authority under the Fifteenth Amendment in an inventive manner when it enacted the Voting Rights Act of 1965. First: The measure prescribes remedies for voting discrimi-

nation which go into effect without any need for prior adjudication. This was clearly a legitimate response to the problem, for which there is ample precedent under other constitutional provisions. See *Katzenbach* v. *McClung*, 379 U. S. 294, 302–304; *United States* v. *Darby*, 312 U. S. 100, 120–121. Congress had found that case-by-case litigation was inadequate to combat widespread and persistent discrimination in voting, because of the inordinate amount of time and energy required to overcome the obstructionist tactics invariably encountered in these lawsuits. After enduring nearly a century of systematic resistance to the Fifteenth Amendment, Congress might well decide to shift the advantage of time and inertia from the perpetrators of the evil to its victims. . . .

[The Court upholds the sections on coverage formula, suspension of tests, review of new rules, and federal examiners.]

After enduring nearly a century of widespread resistance to the Fifteenth Amendment, Congress has marshalled an array of potent weapons against the evil, with authority in the Attorney General to employ them effectively. Many of the areas directly affected by this development have indicated their willingness to abide by any restraints legitimately imposed upon them. We here hold that the portions of the Voting Rights Act properly before us are a valid means for carrying out the commands of the Fifteenth Amendment. Hopefully, millions of non-white Americans will now be able to participate for the first time on an equal basis in the government under which they live. We may finally look forward to the day when truly "[t]he right of citizens of the United States to vote shall not be denied or abridged by the United States or by any State on account of race, color, or previous condition of servitude."

The bill of complaint is

Dismissed.

MR. JUSTICE BLACK, concurring and dissenting.

I agree with substantially all of the Court's opinion sustaining the power of Congress under § 2 of the Fifteenth Amendment to suspend state literacy tests and similar voting qualifications and to authorize the Attorney General to secure the appointment of federal examiners to register qualified voters in various sections of the country. . . . I also agree with the judgment of the Court upholding § 4 (b) of the Act which sets out a formula for determining when and where the major remedial sections of the Act take effect. I reach this conclusion, however, for a somewhat different reason . . .

Though, as I have said, I agree with most of the Court's conclusions, I dissent from its holding that every part of § 5 of the Act is constitutional. Section 4(a), to which § 5 is linked, suspends for five years all literacy tests and similar devices in those States coming within the formula of § 4(b). Section 5 goes on to provide that a State covered by § 4(b) can in no way amend its constitution or laws relating to voting without first trying to persuade the Attorney General of the United States or the Federal District Court for the District of Columbia that the new proposed laws do not have the purpose and will not have the effect of denying the right to vote to citizens on account of their race or color. I think this section is unconstitutional on at least two grounds.

(a) The Constitution gives federal courts jurisdiction over cases and controversies only. If it can be said that any case or controversy arises under this section which gives the District Court for the District of Columbia jurisdiction to approve or reject state laws or constitutional amendments, then the case or controversy must be between a State and the United States Government. But it is hard for me to believe that a justiciable controversy can arise in the constitutional sense from a desire by the United States Government or some of its officials to determine in advance what legislative provisions a State may enact or what constitutional amendments it may adopt. . . .

The form of words and the manipulation of presumptions used in § 5 to create the illusion of a case or controversy should not be allowed to cloud the effect of that section. By requiring a State to ask a federal court to approve the validity of a proposed law which has in no way become operative, Congress has asked the State to secure precisely the type of advisory opinion our Constitution forbids. . . .

(b) My second and more basic objection to § 5 is that Congress has here exercised its power under § 2 of the Fifteenth Amendment through the adoption of means that conflict with the most basic principles of the Constitution. . . . Section 5, by providing that some of the States cannot pass state laws or adopt state constitutional amendments without first being compelled to beg federal authorities to approve their policies, so distorts our constitutional structure of government as to render any distinction drawn in the Constitution between state and federal power almost meaningless. One of the most basic premises upon which our structure of government was founded was that the Federal Government was to have certain specific and limited powers and no others, and all other power was to be reserved either "to the States respectively, or to the people." Certainly if all the provisions of our Constitution which limit the power of the Federal Government and reserve other power to the States are to mean anything, they mean at least that the States have power to pass laws and amend their constitutions without first sending their officials hundreds of miles away to beg federal authorities to approve them. Moreover, it seems to me that § 5 which gives federal officials power to veto state laws they do not like is in direct conflict with the clear command of our Constitution that "The United States shall guarantee to every State in this Union a Republican Form of Government." I cannot help but believe that the inevitable effect of any such law which forces any one of the States to entreat federal authorities in far-away places for approval of local laws before they can become effective is to create the impression that the State or States treated in this way are little more than conquered provinces. And if one law concerning voting can make the States plead for this approval by a distant federal court or the United States Attorney General, other laws on different subjects can force the States to seek the advance approval not only of the Attorney General but of the President himself or any other chosen members of his staff. . . .

Mobile v. Bolden
446 U.S. 55 (1980)

Wiley L. Bolden and other residents of Mobile, Alabama, brought a class action in federal court against the city on behalf of all black citizens in the city. They alleged that the practice of electing city commissioners at-large unfairly diluted the voting strength of blacks in violation of the Fourteenth and Fifteenth Amendments. Although finding that blacks registered and voted "without hindrance," the district court held that the at-large electoral system violated the Fifteenth Amendment and invidiously discriminated against blacks in violation of the Equal Protection Clause of the Fourteenth Amendment. The Fifth Circuit affirmed.

MR. JUSTICE STEWART announced the judgment of the Court and delivered an opinion, in which THE CHIEF JUSTICE, MR. JUSTICE POWELL, and MR. JUSTICE REHNQUIST joined.

The city of Mobile, Ala., has since 1911 been governed by a City Commission consisting of three members elected by the voters of the city at large. The question in this case is whether this at-large system of municipal elections violates the rights of Mobile's Negro voters in contravention of federal statutory or constitutional law.

The appellees brought this suit in the Federal District Court for the Southern District of Alabama as a class action on behalf of all Negro citizens of Mobile. Named as defendants were the city and its three incumbent Commissioners, who are the appellants before this Court. The complaint alleged that the practice of electing the City Commissioners at large unfairly diluted the voting strength of Negroes in violation of § 2 of the Voting Rights Act of 1965, of the Fourteenth Amendment, and of the Fifteenth Amendment. Following a bench trial, the District Court found that the constitutional rights of the appellees had been violated, entered a judgment in their favor, and ordered that the City Commission be disestablished and replaced by a municipal government consisting of a Mayor and a City Council with members elected from single-member districts. 423 F. Supp. 384. The Court of Appeals affirmed the judgment in its entirety, 571 F. 2d 238, . . .

I

In Alabama, the form of municipal government a city may adopt is governed by state law. Until 1911, cities not covered by specific legislation were limited to governing themselves through a mayor and city council. In that year, the Alabama Legislature authorized every large municipality to adopt a commission form of government. Mobile established its City Commission in the same year, and has maintained that basic system of municipal government ever since.

The three Commissioners jointly exercise all legislative, executive, and administrative power in the municipality. They are required after election to designate one of their number as Mayor, a largely ceremonial office, but no formal provision is made for allocating specific executive or administrative duties among the three. As required by the state law enacted in 1911, each candidate for the Mobile City Commission runs for election in the city at large for a term of four years in one of three numbered posts, and may be elected only by a majority of the total vote. This is the same basic electoral system that is followed by literally thousands of municipalities and other local governmental units throughout the Nation.

II

Although required by general principles of judicial administration to do so, *Spector Motor Service, Inc.* v. *McLaughlin*, 323 U. S. 101, 105;

Ashwander v. *TVA*, 297 U. S. 288, 347 (Brandeis, J., concurring), neither the District Court nor the Court of Appeals addressed the complaint's statutory claim—that the Mobile electoral system violates § 2 of the Voting Rights Act of 1965. Even a cursory examination of that claim, however, clearly discloses that it adds nothing to the appellees' complaint.

Section 2 of the Voting Rights Act provides:

"No voting qualification or prerequisite to voting, or standard, practice, or procedure shall be imposed or applied by any State or political subdivision to deny or abridge the right of any citizen of the United States to vote on account of race or color." 79 Stat. 437, as amended, 42 U. S. C. § 1973.

Assuming, for present purposes, that there exists a private right of action to enforce this statutory provision, it is apparent that the language of § 2 no more than elaborates upon that of the Fifteenth Amendment, and the sparse legislative history of § 2 makes clear that it was intended to have an effect no different from that of the Fifteenth Amendment itself.

Section 2 was an uncontroversial provision in proposed legislation whose other provisions engendered protracted dispute. The House Report on the bill simply recited that § 2 "grants . . . a right to be free from enactment or enforcement of voting qualifications . . . or practices which deny or abridge the right to vote on account of race or color." H. R. Rep. No. 439, 89th Cong., 1st Sess., 23 (1965). See also S. Rep. No. 162, 89th Cong., 1st Sess., pt. 3, pp. 19–20 (1965). The view that this section simply restated the prohibitions already contained in the Fifteenth Amendment was expressed without contradiction during the Senate hearings. Senator Dirksen indicated at one point that all States, whether or not covered by the preclearance provisions of § 5 of the proposed legislation, were prohibited from discriminating against Negro voters by § 2, which he termed "almost a rephrasing of the 15th [A]mendment." Attorney General Katzenbach agreed. See Voting Rights: Hearings on S. 1564 before the Senate Committee on the Judiciary, 89th Cong., 1st Sess., pt. 1, p. 208 (1965).

In view of the section's language and its sparse but clear legislative history, it is evident that this statutory provision adds nothing to the appellees' Fifteenth Amendment claim. We turn, therefore, to a consideration of the validity of the judgment of the Court of Appeals with respect to the Fifteenth Amendment.

III

The Court's early decisions under the Fifteenth Amendment established that it imposes but one limitation on the powers of the States. It forbids them to discriminate against Negroes in matters having to do with voting. See *Ex parte Yarbrough*, 110 U. S. 651, 665; *Neal* v. *Delaware*, 103 U. S. 370, 389–390; *United States* v. *Cruikshank*, 92 U. S. 542, 555–556; *United States* v. *Reese*, 92 U. S. 214. The Amendment's command and effect are wholly negative. "The Fifteenth Amendment does not confer the right of suffrage upon any one," but has "invested the citizens of the United States with a new constitutional right which is within the protecting power of Congress. That right is exemption from discrimination in the exercise of the elective franchise on account of race, color, or previous condition of servitude." *Id.*, at 217–218.

Our decisions, moreover, have made clear that action by a State that is racially neutral on its face violates the Fifteenth Amendment only if motivated by a discriminatory purpose. [*Guinn* v. United States, *238 U. S. 347 (1915)*] . . .

The Court's more recent decisions confirm the principle that racially discriminatory motivation is a necessary ingredient of a Fifteenth Amendment violation. [*Gomillion* v. Lightfoot, *364 U. S. 339 (1960)*] . . .

While other of the Court's Fifteenth Amendment decisions have dealt with different issues, none has questioned the necessity of showing purposeful discrimination in order to show a Fifteenth Amendment violation. The cases of *Smith* v. *Allwright*, 321 U. S. 649, and *Terry* v. *Adams*, 345 U. S. 461, for example, dealt with the question whether a State was so involved with racially discriminatory voting practices as to invoke the Amendment's protection. . . .

[Bolden argued that the at-large system was unconstitutional because the effect of racially polarized voting in Mobile was the same as that of a racially exclusionary primary.]

The answer to the appellees' argument is that, as the District Court expressly found, their freedom to vote has not been denied or abridged by anyone. The Fifteenth Amendment does not entail the right to have Negro candidates elected, and neither *Smith* v. *Allwright* nor *Terry* v. *Adams* contains any implication to the contrary. That Amendment prohibits only purposefully discriminatory denial or abridgment by government of the freedom to vote "on account of race, color, or previous condition of servitude." Having found that Negroes in Mobile "register and vote without hindrance," the District Court and Court of Appeals were in error in believing that the appellants invaded the protection of that Amendment in the present case.

IV

The Court of Appeals also agreed with the District Court that Mobile's at-large electoral system violates the Equal Protection Clause of the Fourteenth Amendment. There remains for consideration, therefore, the validity of its judgment on that score.

A

The claim that at-large electoral schemes unconstitutionally deny to some persons the equal protection of the laws has been advanced in numerous cases before this Court. That contention has been raised most often with regard to multimember constituencies within a state legislative apportionment system. The constitutional objection to multimember districts is not and cannot be that, as such, they depart from apportionment on a population basis in violation of *Reynolds* v. *Sims*, 377 U. S. 533, and its progeny. Rather the focus in such cases has been on the lack of representation multimember districts afford various elements of the voting population in a system of representative legislative democracy. "Criticism [of multimember districts] is rooted in their winner-take-

all aspects, their tendency to submerge minorities . . . , a general preference for legislatures reflecting community interests as closely as possible and disenchantment with political parties and elections as devices to settle policy differences between contending interests." *Whitcomb* v. *Chavis*, 403 U. S. 124, 158–159.

Despite repeated constitutional attacks upon multimember legislative districts, the Court has consistently held that they are not unconstitutional *per se*, *e.g.*, *White* v. *Regester*, 412 U. S. 755; *Whitcomb* v. *Chavis*, *supra*; *Kilgarlin* v. *Hill*, 386 U. S. 120; *Burns* v. *Richardson*, 384 U. S. 73; *Fortson* v. *Dorsey*, 379 U. S. 433. We have recognized, however, that such legislative apportionments could violate the Fourteenth Amendment if their purpose were invidiously to minimize or cancel out the voting potential of racial or ethnic minorities. See *White* v. *Regester*, *supra*; *Whitcomb* v. *Chavis*, *supra*; *Burns* v. *Richardson*, *supra*; *Fortson* v. *Dorsey*, *supra*. To prove such a purpose it is not enough to show that the group allegedly discriminated against has not elected representatives in proportion to its numbers. *White* v. *Regester*, *supra*, at 765–766; *Whitcomb* v. *Chavis*, 403 U. S., at 149–150. A plaintiff must prove that the disputed plan was "conceived or operated as [a] purposeful devic[e] to further racial . . . discrimination," *id.*, at 149.

. . .

[The Court noted that no black had been elected to the Mobile City Commission. However, blacks had the only active "slating" organization in the city. "It may be that Negro candidates have been defeated, but that fact alone does not work a constitutional deprivation."]

V

The judgment is reversed, and the case is remanded to the Court of Appeals for further proceedings.

It is so ordered.

MR. JUSTICE BLACKMUN, concurring in the result.

Assuming that proof of intent is a prerequisite to appellees' prevailing on their constitutional claim of vote dilution, I am inclined to agree with MR. JUSTICE WHITE that, in this case, "the findings of the District Court amply support an inference of purposeful discrimination," *post*, at 103. I concur in the Court's judgment of reversal, however, because I believe that the relief afforded appellees by the District Court was not commensurate with the sound exercise of judicial discretion.

It seems to me that the city of Mobile, and its citizenry, have a substantial interest in maintaining the commission form of government that has been in effect there for nearly 70 years. The District Court recognized that its remedial order, changing the form of the city's government to a mayor-council system, "raised serious constitutional issues." 423 F. Supp. 384, 404 (SD Ala. 1976). Nonetheless, the court was "unable to see how the impermissibly unconstitutional dilution can be effectively corrected by any other approach." *Id.*, at 403.

. . .

MR. JUSTICE STEVENS, concurring in the judgment.

. . .

As MR. JUSTICE STEWART points out, Mobile's basic election system is the same as that followed by literally thousands of municipalities and other governmental units throughout the Nation. *Ante*, at 60. The fact that these at-large systems characteristically place one or more minority groups at a significant disadvantage in the struggle for political power cannot invalidate all such systems. . . .

MR. JUSTICE BRENNAN, dissenting.

I dissent because I agree with MR. JUSTICE MARSHALL that proof of discriminatory impact is sufficient in these cases. I also dissent because, even accepting the plurality's premise that discriminatory purpose must be shown, I agree with MR. JUSTICE MARSHALL and MR. JUSTICE WHITE that the appellees have clearly met that burden.

MR. JUSTICE WHITE, dissenting.

In *White* v. *Regester*, 412 U. S. 755 (1973), this Court unanimously held the use of multimember districts for the election of state legislators in two counties in Texas violated the Equal Protection Clause of the Fourteenth Amendment because, based on a careful assessment of the totality of the circumstances, they were found to exclude Negroes and Mexican-Americans from effective participation in the political processes in the counties. Without questioning the vitality of *White* v. *Regester* and our other decisions dealing with challenges to multimember districts by racial or ethnic groups, the Court today inexplicably rejects a similar holding based on meticulous factual findings and scrupulous application of the principles of these cases by both the District Court and the Court of Appeals. The Court's decision is flatly inconsistent with *White* v. *Regester* and it cannot be understood to flow from our recognition in *Washington* v. *Davis*, 426 U. S. 229 (1976), that the Equal Protection Clause forbids only purposeful discrimination. Both the District Court and the Court of Appeals properly found that an invidious discriminatory purpose could be inferred from the totality of facts in this case. The Court's cryptic rejection of their conclusions ignores the principles that an invidious discriminatory purpose can be inferred from objective factors of the kind relied on in *White* v. *Regester* and that the trial courts are in a special position to make such intensely local appraisals.

I

Prior to our decision in *White* v. *Regester*, we upheld a number of multimember districting schemes against constitutional challenges, but we consistently recognized that such apportionment schemes could constitute invidious discrimination "where the circumstances of a particular case may 'operate to minimize or cancel out the voting strength of racial or political elements of the voting population.'" *Whitcomb* v. *Chavis*, 403 U. S. 124, 143 (1971), quoting from *Fortson* v. *Dorsey*, 379 U. S. 433, 439 (1965); *Burns* v. *Richardson*, 384 U. S. 73, 88 (1966). In *Whitcomb* v. *Chavis*, *supra*, we noted that the fact that the number of members of a particular group who were legislators was not in proportion to the population of the group did not prove invidious discrimination absent evidence and findings that the members of the group had less opportunity than did other persons "to participate in the political processes and to elect legislators of their choice." 403 U. S., at 149.

Relying on this principle, in *White* v. *Regester* we unanimously upheld a District Court's conclusion that the use of multimember districts in Dallas and Bexar Counties in Texas violated the Equal Protection Clause in the face of findings that they excluded Negroes and Mexican-Americans from effective participation in the political processes. With respect to the exclusion of Negroes in Dallas County, "the District Court first referred to the history of official racial discrimination in Texas, which at times touched the right of Negroes to register and vote and to participate in the democratic processes." 412 U. S., at 766. The District Court also referred to Texas' majority vote requirement and "place" rule, "neither in themselves improper nor invidious," but which "enhanced the opportunity for racial discrimination" by reducing legislative elections from the multimember district to "a head-to-head contest for each position." *Ibid.* We deemed more fundamental the District Court's findings that only two Negro state representatives had been elected from Dallas County since Reconstruction and that these were the only two Negroes ever slated by an organization that effectively controlled Democratic Party candidate slating. . . .

With respect to the exclusion of Mexican-Americans from the political process in Bexar County, the District Court referred to the continuing effects of a long history of invidious discrimination against Mexican-Americans in education, employment, economics, health, politics, and other fields. *Id.*, at 768. The impact of this discrimination, coupled with a cultural and language barrier, made Mexican-American participation in the political life of Bexar County extremely difficult. Only five Mexican-Americans had represented Bexar County in the Texas Legislature since 1880, and the county's legislative delegation "was insufficiently responsive to Mexican-American interests." . . .

Because I believe that the findings of the District Court amply support an inference of purposeful discrimination in violation of the Fourteenth and Fifteenth Amendments, I respectfully dissent.

MR. JUSTICE MARSHALL, dissenting.

. . .

[II.B]

The plurality concludes that our prior decisions establish the principle that proof of discriminatory intent is a necessary element of a Fifteenth Amendment claim. In contrast. I continue to adhere to my conclusion in *Beer* v. *United States*, 425 U. S., at 148, n. 4 (dissenting opinion), that "[t]he Court's decisions relating to the relevance of purpose-and/or-effect analysis in testing the constitutionality of legislative enactments are somewhat less than a seamless web." As I there explained, at various times the Court's decisions have seemed to adopt three inconsistent approaches: (1) that purpose alone is the test for unconstitutionality; (2) that effect alone is the test; and (3) that purpose or effect, either alone or in combination, is sufficient to show unconstitutionality. *Ibid.* In my view, our Fifteenth Amendment jurisprudence on the necessity of proof of discriminatory purpose is no less unsettled than was our approach to the importance of such proof in Fourteenth Amendment racial discrimination cases prior to *Washington* v. *Davis*, 426 U. S. 229 (1976). What is called for in the present cases is a fresh consideration—similar to our inquiry in *Washington* v. *Davis*, *supra*, with regard to Fourteenth Amendment discrimination claims—of whether proof of discriminatory purpose is necessary to establish a claim under the Fifteenth Amendment. . . .

. . . it is beyond dispute that a standard based solely upon the motives of official decisionmakers creates significant problems of proof for plaintiffs and forces the inquiring court to undertake an unguided, tortuous look into the minds of officials in the hope of guessing why certain policies were adopted and others rejected. . . . An approach based on motivation creates the risk that officials will be able to adopt policies that are the products of discriminatory intent so long as they sufficiently mask their motives through the use of subtlety and illusion. . . .

I continue to believe, then, that under the Fifteenth Amendment an "[e]valuation of the purpose of a legislative enactment is just too ambiguous a task to be the sole tool of constitutional analysis. . . . [A] demonstration of effect ordinarily should suffice. If, of course, purpose may conclusively be shown, it too should be sufficient to demonstrate a statute's unconstitutionality." *Beer* v. *United States*, 425 U. S., at 149–150, n. 5 (MARSHALL, J., dissenting). The plurality's refusal in this case even to consider this approach bespeaks an indifference to the plight of minorities who, through no fault of their own, have suffered diminution of the right preservative of all other rights.

. . .

IV

The American approach to government is premised on the theory that, when citizens have the unfettered right to vote, public officials will make decisions by the democratic accommodation of competing beliefs, not by deference to the mandates of the powerful. The American approach to civil rights is premised on the complementary theory that the unfettered right to vote is preservative of all other rights. The theoretical foundations for these approaches are shattered where, as in the present cases, the right to vote is granted in form, but denied in substance.

It is time to realize that manipulating doctrines and drawing improper distinctions under the Fourteenth and Fifteenth Amendments, as well as under Congress' remedial legislation enforcing those Amendments, make this Court an accessory to the perpetuation of racial discrimination. The plurality's requirement of proof of *intentional discrimination*, so inappropriate in today's cases, may represent an attempt to bury the legitimate concerns of the minority beneath the soil of a doctrine almost as impermeable as it is specious. If so, the superficial tranquility created by such measures can be but short-lived. If this Court refuses to honor our long-recognized principle that the Constitution "nullifies sophisticated as well as simpleminded modes of discrimination," *Lane* v. *Wilson*, 307 U. S., at 275, it cannot expect the victims of discrimination to respect political channels of seeking redress. I dissent.

Congress Reverses Mobile *v.* Bolden

In *Mobile* v. *Bolden*, **446 U. S. 55 (1980), the Supreme Court held that the Voting Rights Act of 1965, as amended, only prohibits states from purposefully discriminating against the voting rights of blacks. There had to be an *intent* on the part of states to abridge voting rights. In 1982, Congress amended the Act to allow plaintiffs to show discrimination solely on the *effects* of a voting plan. As explained in the congressional debate, members of Congress borrowed language that had appeared in an earlier decision by the Supreme Court, in *White* v. *Regester*, 412 U. S. 755 (1973). The selections below come from 128 Cong. Rec. 14100, 14111, 14113–14115, 14936 (1982).**

Mr. DeCONCINI. Mr. President, for the past several months the attention of the Nation's civil rights community, this Congress, and of the Nation itself has been focused upon the extension of the Voting Rights Act of 1965. I join in this concern, for as the Supreme Court noted almost a century ago,

"the political franchise of voting is . . . a fundamental political right, because preservative of all rights."

My belief in the central nature of voting rights has led me to support and cosponsor S. 1992, the Voting Rights Act Amendments of 1982.

The Voting Rights Act has been hailed as "one of the most important and effective pieces of civil rights legislation ever passed by Congress." Under this act, enormous strides have been made. Prior to the act's enactment, the percentage of black registered voters in the "covered jurisdictions" averaged 29 percent; it is now well in excess of 50 percent. In my own home State of Arizona, Hispanic voter participation has increased markedly, an increase due in large part to the enactment of the bilingual provisions of the act in 1975.

. . .

In the years since the passage of the Voting Rights Act, many subtle and complex means have been developed to avoid inclusion of minority persons in the political process. With the recent Supreme Court decision of *Mobile* v. *Bolden*, 446 U.S. 55 (1980), which requires a finding of discriminatory intent to establish a violation of the 15th amendment, a new statutory tool became necessary to avoid the consequences of such subtle discriminatory mechanisms. S. 1992 would establish a "results" test in section 2 of the act, and thus provide the necessary tool.

. . .

In the course of the debate over a "results" versus an "intent" test for section 2 of the act, opponents of "results" have asserted that intent to discriminate is, and always has been, the standard of proof in civil rights law. This assertion involves a number of misunderstandings of the history of civil rights law.

First, while intentional discrimination has always been clearly prohibited by the 14th and 15th amendments to the Constitution, it has not always been understood to be the sole standard by which discrimination could be attacked under those provisions. Indeed, it was entirely consistent for Attorney General Katzenbach to state in 1965 that section 2 would reach any practice or procedure "if its purpose or effect was to deny or abridge the right to vote on account of race or color," and to agree with Senator Dirksen's assertion that section 2 was "a restatement, in effect, of the 15th amendment." That same year, the Supreme Court had held that multimember district sys-

tems would be unconstitutional if it were shown that—

"*designedly or otherwise*, a multi-member constituency scheme . . . would operate to minimize or cancel out the voting strength of racial . . . elements of the voting population." *Fortson* v. *Dorsey*, 379 U. S. 433 at 439 (1965). (Emphasis added.)

Intent has been expressly required by the Supreme Court as a necessary element of a 14th amendment equal protection case only since 1976. It has been expressly required in 15th amendment cases only since the Mobile against Bolden decision in 1980.

Second, "effect" standards have been used, and are being used today, in civil rights law. Both title VII of the Civil Rights Act of 1964 and section 5 of the Voting Rights Act employ effects-based standards. It is true that the proposed "results" standards of S. 1992 would not be identical to these standards, however. S. 1992 employs language designed to assure that the mere numbers or minorities elected to office would not, by themselves, provide a basis for alleging a violation of section 2 nor provide a standard for remedies of adjudicated violations of section 2. In other words, the section 2 "results" test would be a more difficult test under which to establish a violation than either the section 5 or title VII "effects" tests.

A "results" test would be superior to the present "intent" test for a variety of reasons. First and most fundamentally, "results" language in section 2 of the act would reimpose the standard which most Federal courts used in vote dilution cases prior to the Bolden decision in 1980. This standard was arrived at through interpretation of a number of landmark Supreme Court decisions over the past two decades. Most important among these decisions are Fortson against Dorsey, Burns against Richardson, Whitcomb against Chavis, and White against Regester. These Supreme Court decisions did not create a standard of proof which required discriminatory intent; rather, they outlined objective factors which could be analyzed to determine whether or not minority voting strength had been unconstitutionally diluted by the existing electoral system.

As a result of these decisions, some 23 cases were litigated in the lower Federal courts between 1972 and 1979. Perhaps the clearest expression of the standard of proof in these vote dilution cases may be found in the fifth circuit case of Zimmer against McKeithen. Factors taken into account include lack of minority access to the candidate slating process, a tenuous policy underlying multi-member or at-large districting systems, and the existence of past discrimination. After an inference of minority exclusion had been raised by such factors as these, support could be provided through proof of such electoral mechanisms as majority vote requirements and anti-single-shot voting provisions.

These 23 cases are extremely important in the evaluation of a "results" test which would incorporate their standards into statutory law. It is important to note, for instance, that in these 23 cases, the defendants prevailed 13 times. Thus, a "results" test would not mean automatic victory for plaintiffs in vote dilution cases. Also, violations were not proven under these cases merely by evidence of a lack of racial proportional representation plus some additional scintilla of evidence, as some critics of S. 1992 suggest would be possible under the "results" test. Rather, consideration of the "totality of the circumstances" was required, together with a finding "of an aggregate of these factors."

. . .

Mr. MATHIAS. *[This bill would amend the Voting Rights Act]* to prohibit any voting practice or procedure which results in voting discrimination. This amendment is designed to make clear that proof of discriminatory intent is not required to establish a violation of section 2. It is intended to restore the legislative standard which governed voting discrimination claims prior to the litigation involved in *Mobile* v. *Bolden* (446 U. S. 55 (1980)). Specifically, this amendment adds a subsection to section 2 codifying the standard set forth in the leading pre-Bolden voting case, White against Regester (412 U. S. 755 (1973)).

. . .

The importance of Congress amending section 2 of the act in response to the City of Mobile against Bolden also emerges clearly from the legislative history.

In pre-Bolden voting cases plaintiffs could prevail by showing that a challenged election law or procedure—in the context of the total circumstances of the local electoral process—had the result of denying racial or language minority voters an equal chance to participate effectively in the electoral process. Under this results test, it was not necessary to demonstrate that the challenged election law or procedure was designed or maintained for a discriminatory purpose. In Bolden, a plurality of the Supreme Court broke with precedent and substantially increased the burden on plaintiffs by requiring proof of discriminatory intent. As noted in the committee report, the Bolden intent test is unacceptable for a number of reasons.

First, the intent test asks the wrong question. Rather than focusing on the crucial question of whether or not minority voters now have a fair chance to participate in the electoral process, the intent test diverts the inquiry to an analysis of the subjective motives of public officials. Thus the intent test requires Federal judges to engage in protracted, burdensome inquiries into the motives of lawmakers, which often have little or no bearing on the ability of minority voters to participate in their electoral process. For example, on remand, following the Supreme Court's decision in Bolden, the district court was required to make an inquiry into the motives of legislators to determine if the system was devised or maintained for a discriminatory purpose. In order to comply with Bolden, the district court was forced to recreate events shedding light on the motivation of politicians who held office during the several crucial periods under investigation between 1814 and the present.

Second, as Arthur Flemming, former Chairman of the U.S. Commission on Civil Rights, told the Subcommittee on the Constitution that inquiries under the intent test "can only be divisive, threatening to destroy any existing racial progress in a community."

Third, the intent test places an unacceptable burden on plaintiffs in voting discrimination cases. It creates the risk that electoral systems will be free from challenge even where there is overwhelming evidence of unequal access to the political process. This point is dramatically illustrated by the Edgefield County, S.C., case, McCain against Lybrand. On April 17, 1980, the district court ruled the county's at-large system of electing county council members was unconstitutional. In an exhaustive opinion, the district court faithfully applied the White against Regester results test and concluded that blacks simply did not have a fair chance to participate in the system: "Black participation in Edgefield County has been merely tokenism and even this has been on a very small scale."

Despite the overwhelming evidence of unequal access to the electoral system, the district court's determination could not withstand the impact of Bolden. Shortly after rendering its initial decision the district court vacated the judgment and stated:

"A careful reading of Mobile and a reconsideration of the evidence in the present Edgefield County case convinced the Court that the plaintiffs have not proved that the voting plan for election of members of the County Council in Edgefield County was either conceived or is operated as a purposeful device to further racial discrimination nor was it intended to individually discriminate against blacks in violation of the Equal Protection Clause."

. . .

The constitutionality of the committee bill is beyond question. As the committee report clearly demonstrates, both the revised bailout procedures and the proposed amendment of section 2 are constitutional exercises of congressional power.

With respect to bailout it is essential to note that the Supreme Court has long recognized the constitutionality of the preclearance and bailout procedures contained in the Voting Rights Act. Twice in the last 16 years, in South Carolina against Katzenbach and United States against City of Rome, the Court has sustained these provisions. The Senate Judiciary Committee reached the inescapable conclusion that the proposed revisions of the existing bailout procedures are well within the constitutional limits established by the Court in these cases.

Equally clear is the congressional power to enact the proposed amendment to section 2. In a series of cases over the past 16 years, the Supreme Court has acknowledged that section 5 of the 14th amendment and section 2 of the 15th amendment provide Congress with broad power to enact appropriate legislation to protect the rights secured by those amendments. The proposed amendment to section 2 is a proper exercise of this congressional power, and is not, as some have claimed, a legislative effort to overrule a substantive Supreme Court interpretation of the Constitution.

. . .

[Debate in the House of Representatives produced this colloquy:]

Mr. HYDE . . . I would like to ask the gentleman from California about the test which the Senate incorporated in the proposed section 2 of the act. I have read the language, and I believe it comes virtually word for word from page 766 of the Supreme Court's 1973 decision in White against Regester, and I would like to ask the gentleman whether I am correct.

Mr. EDWARDS of California. If the gentleman will yield, the gentleman from Illinois is correct. It comes right out of the Supreme Court's decision in White against Regester.

Mr. HYDE. I thank the gentleman. . . . Under the Senate amendments, the "results" test remains in the statute but, since it has no precursor in the law, it is explained by the adoption of clarifying language. Specifically, the amendments provide that a violation of the results test can be shown by an examination of the totality of the circumstances surrounding the alleged discrimination, and the determination that "the political processes leading to nomination or election in the State or political subdivision are not equally open to participation by members of the class of citizens protected" by the Voting Rights Act. While this language may give the appearance to some of being an "effects" test, and indeed has been marketed as such in some quarters, it has been taken, virtually word for word, from the Supreme Court's 1973 holding in *White v. Regester*, 412 U. S. 755, 766, a case which, according to its author, Justice Byron White, underscored the requirement that an "invidious discriminatory purpose [must] be inferred from the totality of facts" to constitute a violation. *Mobile* v. *Bolden,* 466 U. S. 55, 95 (1980).

It is also worth noting that the language adopted in the Senate was suggested during the House debate by the minority (see House hearings, page 2053) but was rejected and, during negotiations for a compromise in which I was intimately in-volved, no one would consider it. Therefore, it is clear, and I suspect will be clear by a reviewing court, that the language adopted through the Senate compromise is language which was reject-ed in the House and which, therefore, represents the intent standard articulated by White, not an effects standard as some would suggest.

Colegrove v. Green

328 U.S. 549 (1946)

Congressional districts in Illinois varied widely in population, ranging from 112,116 to 914,000. Kenneth W. Colegrove and two other citizens of Illinois qualified to vote in the upcoming congressional elections brought suit in federal court under the Declaratory Judgment Act to restrain state officers from arranging for an election. They alleged that the congressional districts lacked compactness of territory and approximate equality of population, violating various provisions of the Federal Constitution and the Reapportion-ment Act of 1911. The district court dismissed the complaint. The defendant was Dwight H. Green, an Illinois election official.

MR. JUSTICE FRANKFURTER announced the judgment of the Court and an opinion in which MR. JUSTICE REED and MR. JUSTICE BURTON concur.

This case is appropriately here, under § 266 of the Judicial Code, 28 U. S. C. § 380, on direct review of a judgment of the District Court of the Northern District of Illinois, composed of three judges, dismissing the complaint of the appellants. These are three qualified voters in Illinois districts which have much larger populations than other Illinois Congressional districts. They brought this suit against the Governor, the Secretary of State, and the Auditor of the State of Illinois, as members *ex officio* of the Illinois Primary Certifying Board, to restrain them, in effect, from taking proceed-ings for an election in November 1946, under the provisions of Illinois law governing Congressional districts. Illinois Laws of 1901, p. 3. Formally, the appellants asked for a decree, with its incidental relief. § 274 (d) Judicial Code, 28 U. S. C. § 400, declaring these provisions to be invalid because they violated various provisions of the United States Constitution and § 3 of the Reapportion-ment Act of August 8, 1911, 37 Stat. 13, as amend-ed, 2 U. S. C. § 2a, in that by reason of subsequent changes in population the Congressional districts for the election of Representatives in the Congress created by the Illinois Laws of 1901 (Ill. Rev. Stat. Ch. 46 (1945) §§ 154–56) lacked compactness of territory and approximate equality of population. The District Court, feeling bound by this Court's opinion in *Wood* v. *Broom,* 287 U. S. 1, dismissed the complaint. 64 F. Supp. 632.

The District Court was clearly right in deeming itself bound by *Wood* v. *Broom, supra,* and we could also dispose of this case on the authority of *Wood* v. *Broom.* The legal merits of this controver-sy were settled in that case, inasmuch as it held that the Reapportionment Act of June 18, 1929, 46 Stat. 21, as amended, 2 U. S. C. § 2 (a), has no requirements "as to the compactness, contiguity and equality in population of districts." 287 U. S. at 8. The Act of 1929 still governs the districting for the election of Representatives. It must be remembered that not only was the legislative history of the matter fully considered in *Wood* v. *Broom,* but the question had been elaborately before the Court in *Smiley* v. *Holm,* 285 U. S. 355, *Koenig* v. *Flynn,* 285 U. S. 375, and *Carroll* v. *Becker,* 285 U. S. 380, argued a few months before

Wood v. *Broom* was decided. Nothing has now been adduced to lead us to overrule what this Court found to be the requirements under the Act of 1929, the more so since seven Congressional elections have been held under the Act of 1929 as construed by this Court. No manifestation has been shown by Congress even to question the correctness of that which seemed compelling to this Court in enforcing the will of Congress in *Wood* v. *Broom.*

But we also agree with the four Justices (Brandeis, Stone, Roberts, and Cardozo, JJ.) who were of opinion that the bill in *Wood* v. *Broom, supra,* should be "dismissed for want of equity." To be sure, the present complaint, unlike the bill in *Wood* v. *Broom,* was brought under the Federal Declaratory Judgment Act which, not having been enacted until 1934, was not available at the time of *Wood* v. *Broom.* But that Act merely gave the federal courts competence to make a declaration of rights even though no decree of enforcement be immediately asked. It merely permitted a freer movement of the federal courts within the recognized confines of the scope of equity. The Declaratory Judgment Act "only provided a new form of procedure for the adjudication of rights in conformity" with "established equitable principles." *Great Lakes Co.* v. *Huffman,* 319 U. S. 293, 300. And so, the test for determining whether a federal court has authority to make a declaration such as is here asked, is whether the controversy "would be justiciable in this Court if presented in a suit for injunction . . ." *Nashville, C. & St. L. R. Co.* v. *Wallace,* 288 U. S. 249, 262.

We are of opinion that the appellants ask of this Court what is beyond its competence to grant. This is one of those demands on judicial power which cannot be met by verbal fencing about "jurisdiction." It must be resolved by considerations on the basis of which this Court, from time to time, has refused to intervene in controversies. It has refused to do so because due regard for the effective working of our Government revealed this issue to be of a peculiarly political nature and therefore not meet for judicial determination.

This is not an action to recover for damage because of the discriminatory exclusion of a plaintiff from rights enjoyed by other citizens. The basis for the suit is not a private wrong, but a wrong suffered by Illinois as a polity. Compare *Nixon* v. *Herndon,* 273 U. S. 536 and *Lane* v. *Wilson,* 307 U. S. 268, with *Giles* v. *Harris,* 189 U.S. 475. In effect this is an appeal to the federal courts to reconstruct the electoral process of Illinois in order that it may be adequately represented in the councils of the Nation. Because the Illinois legislature has failed to revise its Congressional Representative districts in order to reflect great changes, during more than a generation, in the distribution of its population, we are asked to do this, as it were, for Illinois.

Of course no court can affirmatively re-map the Illinois districts so as to bring them more in conformity with the standards of fairness for a representative system. At best we could only declare the existing electoral system invalid. The result would be to leave Illinois undistricted and to bring into operation, if the Illinois legislature chose not to act, the choice of members for the House of Representatives on a state-wide ticket. The last stage may be worse than the first. The upshot of judicial action may defeat the vital political principle which led Congress, more than a hundred years ago, to require districting. This requirement, in the language of Chancellor Kent, "was recommended by the wisdom and justice of giving, as far as possible, to the local subdivisions of the people of each state, a due influence in the choice of representatives, so as not to leave the aggregate minority of the people in a state, though approaching perhaps to a majority, to be wholly overpowered by the combined action of the numerical majority, without any voice whatever in the national councils." 1 Kent, *Commentaries* (12th ed., 1873) *230–31, n. (c). Assuming acquiescence on the part of the authorities of Illinois in the selection of its Representatives by a mode that defies the direction of Congress for selection by districts, the House of Representatives may not acquiesce. In the exercise of its power to judge the qualifications of its own members, the House may reject a delegation of Representatives-at-large. Article I, § 5, Cl. 1. For the detailed system by which Congress supervises the election of its members, see *e.g.,* 2 U. S. C. §§ 201–226; Bartlett, *Contested Elections in the House of Representatives* (2 vols.); Alexander, *History and Procedure of the House of Representatives* (1916) c. XVI. Nothing is clearer than that this controversy concerns matters that bring courts into immediate and active relations with party contests. From the determination of such issues this Court has traditionally held aloof. It is hostile to a democratic system to involve the judiciary in the politics of the people. And it is not less pernicious if such judicial intervention in an essentially political contest be dressed up in the abstract phrases of the law.

The appellants urge with great zeal that the conditions of which they complain are grave evils and offend public morality. The Constitution of the United States gives ample power to provide against these evils. But due regard for the Constitution as a viable system precludes judicial correction. Authority for dealing with such problems resides elsewhere. Article I, § 4 of the Constitution provides that "The Times, Places and Manner of holding Elections for . . . Representatives, shall be prescribed in each State by the Legislature thereof; but the Congress may at any time by Law make or alter such Regulations, . . ." The short of it is that the Constitution has conferred upon Congress exclusive authority to secure fair representation by the States in the popular House and left to that House determination whether States have fulfilled their responsibility. If Congress failed in exercising its powers, whereby standards of fairness are offended, the remedy ultimately lies with the people. Whether Congress faithfully discharges its duty or not, the subject has been committed to the exclusive control of Congress. An aspect of government from which the judiciary, in view of what is involved, has been excluded by the clear intention of the Constitution cannot be entered by the federal courts because Congress may have been in default in exacting from States obedience to its mandate.

. . .

To sustain this action would cut very deep into the very being of Congress. Courts ought not to enter this political thicket. The remedy for unfairness in districting is to secure State legislatures that will apportion properly, or to invoke the ample powers of Congress. The Constitution has many commands that are not enforceable by courts because they clearly fall outside the conditions and purposes that circumscribe judicial action. Thus, "on Demand of the executive Authority," Art. IV, § 2, of a State it is the duty of a sister State to deliver up a fugitive from justice. But the fulfilment of this duty cannot be judicially enforced. *Kentucky* v. *Dennison,* 24 How. 66. The duty to see to it that the laws are faithfully executed cannot be brought under legal compulsion, *Mississippi* v. *Johnson,* 4 Wall. 475. Violation of the great guaranty of a republican form of government in States cannot be challenged in the courts. *Pacific Telephone Co.* v. *Oregon,* 223 U. S. 118. The Constitution has left the performance of many duties in our governmental scheme to depend on the fidelity of the executive and legislative action and, ultimately, on the vigilance of the people in exercising their political rights.

Dismissal of the complaint is affirmed.

MR. JUSTICE JACKSON took no part in the consideration or decision of this case.

MR. JUSTICE RUTLEDGE.

I concur in the result. But for the ruling in *Smiley* v. *Holm,* 285 U. S. 355, I should have supposed that the provisions of the Constitution, Art. I, § 4, that "The Times, Places and Manner of holding Elections for . . . Representatives, shall be prescribed in each State by the Legislature thereof; but the Congress may at any time by Law make or alter such Regulations . . ."; Art. I, § 2, vesting in Congress the duty of apportionment of representatives among the several states "according to their respective Numbers"; and Art. I, § 5, making each House the sole judge of the qualifications of its own members, would remove the issues in this case from justiciable cognizance. But, in my judgment, the *Smiley* case rules squarely to the contrary, save only in the matter of degree.

Moreover, we have but recently been admonished again that it is the very essence of our duty to avoid decision upon grave constitutional questions, especially when this may bring our function into clash with the political departments of the Government, if any tenable alternative ground for disposition of the controversy is presented.

I was unable to find such an alternative in that instance. There is one, however, in this case. And I think the gravity of the constitutional questions raised so great, together with the possibilities for collision above mentioned, that the admonition is appropriate to be followed here. Other reasons support this view, including the fact that, in my opinion, the basic ruling and less important ones in *Smiley* v. *Holm, supra,* would otherwise be brought into question.

Assuming that that decision is to stand, I think, with Mr. Justice Black, that its effect is to rule that this Court has power to afford relief in a case of this type as against the objection that the issues are not justiciable.

. . .

The shortness of the time remaining makes it doubtful whether action could, or would, be taken in time to secure for petitioners the effective relief they seek. To force them to share in an election at large might bring greater equality of voting right. It would also deprive them and all other Illinois citizens of representation by districts which the prevailing policy of Congress commands. 46 Stat. 26, as amended; 2 U. S. C. § 2a.

If the constitutional provisions on which appellants rely give them the substantive rights they urge, other provisions qualify those rights in important ways by vesting large measures of control in the political subdivisions of the Government and the state. There is not, and could not be except abstractly, a right of absolute equality in voting. At best there could be only a rough approximation. And there is obviously considerable latitude for the bodies vested with those powers to exercise their judgment concerning how best to attain this, in full consistency with the Constitution.

The right here is not absolute. And the cure sought may be worse than the disease.

I think, therefore, the case is one in which the Court may properly, and should, decline to exercise its jurisdiction. Accordingly, the judgment should be affirmed and I join in that disposition of the cause.

MR. JUSTICE BLACK, dissenting.

The complaint alleges the following facts essential to the position I take: Appellants, citizens and voters of Illinois, live in congressional election districts, the respective populations of which

range from 612,000 to 914,000. Twenty other congressional election districts have populations that range from 112,116 to 385,207. In seven of these districts the population is below 200,000. The Illinois Legislature established these districts in 1901 on the basis of the Census of 1900. The Federal Census of 1910, of 1920, of 1930, and of 1940, each showed a growth of population in Illinois and a substantial shift in the distribution of population among the districts established in 1901. But up to date, attempts to have the State Legislature reapportion congressional election districts so as more nearly to equalize their population have been unsuccessful. A contributing cause of this situation, according to appellants, is the fact that the State Legislature is chosen on the basis of state election districts inequitably apportioned in a way similar to that of the 1901 congressional election districts. The implication is that the issues of state and congressional apportionment are thus so interdependent that it is to the interest of state legislators to perpetuate the inequitable apportionment of both state and congressional election districts. Prior to this proceeding a series of suits had been brought in the state courts challenging the State's local and federal apportionment system. In all these cases the Supreme Court of the State had denied effective relief.

In the present suit the complaint attacked the 1901 State Apportionment Act on the ground that it among other things violates Article I and the Fourteenth Amendment of the Constitution. Appellants claim that since they live in the heavily populated districts their vote is much less effective than the vote of those living in a district which under the 1901 Act is also allowed to choose one Congressman, though its population is sometimes only one-ninth that of the heavily populated districts. Appellants contend that this reduction of the effectiveness of their vote is the result of a wilful legislative discrimination against them and thus amounts to a denial of the equal protection of the laws guaranteed by the Fourteenth Amendment. They further assert that this reduction of the effectiveness of their vote also violates the privileges and immunities clause of the Fourteenth Amendment in abridging their privilege as citizens of the United States to vote for Congressmen, a privilege guaranteed by Article I of the

Constitution. They further contend that the State Apportionment Act directly violates Article I which guarantees that each citizen eligible to vote has a right to vote for Congressmen and to have his vote counted. The assertion here is that the right to have their vote counted is abridged unless that vote is given approximately equal weight to that of other citizens. It is my judgment that the District Court had jurisdiction; that the complaint presented a justiciable case and controversy; and that appellants had standing to sue, since the facts alleged show that they have been injured as individuals. . . .

. . . It is true that declaration of invalidity of the State Act and the enjoining of state officials would result in prohibiting the State from electing Con-

gressmen under the system of the old congressional districts. But it would leave the State free to elect them from the State at large, which, as we held in the *Smiley* case, is a manner authorized by the Constitution. It is said that it would be inconvenient for the State to conduct the election in this manner. But it has an element of virtue that the more convenient method does not have—namely, it does not discriminate against some groups to favor others, it gives all the people an equally effective voice in electing their representatives as is essential under a free government, and it is constitutional.

MR. JUSTICE DOUGLAS and MR. JUSTICE MURPHY join in this dissent.

Baker v. Carr

369 U.S. 186 (1962)

Charles W. Baker and other residents of Tennessee brought this suit against Joe C. Carr, the Secretary of State of Tennessee. They alleged that a state statute passed in 1901 arbitrarily and capriciously apportioned the seats in the General Assembly among the state's ninety-five counties and the state failed to reapportion the seats notwithstanding substantial growth and redistribution of the state's population. Through this "debasement of their votes" they claimed they were denied the equal protection of the laws guaranteed by the Fourteenth Amendment. After dismissing the argument that the matter constituted a "political question" (see the portion of the decision reprinted on pages 133–135), the Court turned to the broader question of whether the issue was justiciable.

MR. JUSTICE BRENNAN delivered the opinion of the Court.

This civil action was brought under 42 U. S. C. §§ 1983 and 1988 to redress the alleged deprivation of federal constitutional rights. The complaint, alleging that by means of a 1901 statute of Tennessee apportioning the members of the General Assembly among the State's 95 counties, "these plaintiffs and others similarly situated, are denied the equal protection of the laws accorded them by the Fourteenth Amendment to the Constitution of the United States by virtue of the debasement of their votes," was dismissed by a three-judge court convened under 28 U. S. C. § 2281 in the Middle District of Tennessee. The

court held that it lacked jurisdiction of the subject matter and also that no claim was stated upon which relief could be granted. 179 F. Supp. 824. We noted probable jurisdiction of the appeal. 364 U. S. 898. We hold that the dismissal was error, and remand the cause to the District Court for trial and further proceedings consistent with this opinion.

The General Assembly of Tennessee consists of the Senate with 33 members and the House of Representatives with 99 members. The Tennessee Constitution provides in Art. II as follows:

"Sec. 3. Legislative authority—Term of office. —The Legislative authority of this State shall be vested in a General Assembly, which shall consist of a Senate and House of Representatives, both dependent on the people; who shall hold their offices for two years from the day of the general election.

"Sec. 4.   Census.—An enumeration of the qualified voters, and an apportionment of the Representatives in the General Assembly, shall be made in the year one thousand eight hundred and seventy-one, and within every subsequent term of ten years.

"Sec. 5. Apportionment of representatives.— The number of Representatives shall, at the several periods of making the enumeration, be apportioned among the several counties or districts, according to the number of qualified voters in each; and shall not exceed seventy-five, until the population of the State shall be one million and a half, and shall never exceed ninety-nine; Provided, that any county having two-thirds of the ratio shall be entitled to one member.

"Sec. 6.   Apportionment of senators.—The number of Senators shall, at the several periods of making the enumeration, be apportioned among the several counties or districts according to the number of qualified electors in each, and shall not exceed one-third the number of representatives. In apportioning the Senators among the different counties, the fraction that may be lost by any county or counties, in the apportionment of members to the House of Representatives, shall be made up to such county or counties in the Senate, as near as may be practicable. When a district is composed of two or more counties, they shall be adjoining; and no county shall be divided in forming a district."

Thus, Tennessee's standard for allocating legislative representation among her counties is the total number of qualified voters resident in the respective counties, subject only to minor qualifications. Decennial reapportionment in compliance with the constitutional scheme was effected by the General Assembly each decade from 1871 to 1901. The 1871 apportionment was preceded by an 1870 statute requiring an enumeration. The 1881 apportionment involved three statutes, the first authorizing an enumeration, the second enlarging the Senate from 25 to 33 members and the House from 75 to 99 members, and the third

apportioning the membership of both Houses. In 1891 there were both an enumeration and an apportionment. In 1901 the General Assembly abandoned separate enumeration in favor of reliance upon the Federal Census and passed the Apportionment Act here in controversy. In the more than 60 years since that action, all proposals in both Houses of the General Assembly for reapportionment have failed to pass.

. . .

We come, finally, to the ultimate inquiry whether our precedents as to what constitutes a nonjusticiable "political question" bring the case before us under the umbrella of that doctrine. A natural beginning is to note whether any of the common characteristics which we have been able to identify and label descriptively are present. We find none: The question here is the consistency of state action with the Federal Constitution. We have no question decided, or to be decided, by a political branch of government coequal with this Court. Nor do we risk embarrassment of our government abroad, or grave disturbance at home if we take issue with Tennessee as to the constitutionality of her action here challenged. Nor need the appellants, in order to succeed in this action, ask the Court to enter upon policy determinations for which judicially manageable standards are lacking. Judicial standards under the Equal Protection Clause are well developed and familiar, and it has been open to courts since the enactment of the Fourteenth Amendment to determine, if on the particular facts they must, that a discrimination reflects *no* policy, but simply arbitrary and capricious action.

This case does, in one sense, involve the allocation of political power within a State, and the appellants might conceivably have added a claim under the Guaranty Clause. Of course, as we have seen, any reliance on that clause would be futile. But because any reliance on the Guaranty Clause could not have succeeded it does not follow that appellants may not be heard on the equal protection claim which in fact they tender. True, it must be clear that the Fourteenth Amendment claim is not so enmeshed with those political question elements which render Guaranty Clause claims nonjusticiable as actually to present a political question itself. But we have found that not to be the case here.

. . .

When challenges to state action respecting matters of "the administration of the affairs of the State and the officers through whom they are conducted" have rested on claims of constitutional deprivation which are amenable to judicial correction, this Court has acted upon its view of the merits of the claim. For example, in *Boyd* v. *Nebraska ex rel. Thayer,* 143 U. S. 135, we reversed the Nebraska Supreme Court's decision that Nebraska's Governor was not a citizen of the United States or of the State and therefore could not continue in office. In *Kennard* v. *Louisiana ex rel. Morgan,* 92 U. S. 480, and *Foster* v. *Kansas ex rel. Johnston,* 112 U. S. 201, we considered whether persons had been removed from public office by procedures consistent with the Fourteenth Amendment's due process guaranty, and held on the merits that they had. And only last Term, in *Gomillion* v. *Lightfoot,* 364 U. S. 339, we applied the Fifteenth Amendment to strike down a redrafting of municipal boundaries which effected a discriminatory impairment of voting rights, in the face of what a majority of the Court of Appeals thought to be a sweeping commitment to state legislatures of the power to draw and redraw such boundaries.

. . .

We conclude that the complaint's allegations of a denial of equal protection present a justiciable constitutional cause of action upon which appellants are entitled to a trial and a decision. The right asserted is within the reach of judicial protection under the Fourteenth Amendment.

The judgment of the District Court is reversed and the cause is remanded for further proceedings consistent with this opinion.

Reversed and remanded.

MR. JUSTICE WHITTAKER did not participate in the decision of this case.

. . .

MR. JUSTICE DOUGLAS, concurring.

While I join the opinion of the Court and, like the Court, do not reach the merits, a word of explanation is necessary. I put to one side the problems of "political" questions involving the distribution of power between this Court, the Congress, and the Chief Executive. We have here a phase of the recurring problem of the relation of the federal courts to state agencies. More particularly, the question is the extent to which a State may weight one person's vote more heavily than it does another's.

. . .

I agree with my Brother CLARK that if the allegations in the complaint can be sustained a case for relief is established. We are told that a single vote in Moore County, Tennessee, is worth 19 votes in Hamilton County, that one vote in Stewart or in Chester County is worth nearly eight times a single vote in Shelby or Knox County. The opportunity to prove that an "invidious discrimination" exists should therefore be given the appellants.

. . .

MR. JUSTICE CLARK, concurring.

One emerging from the rash of opinions with their accompanying clashing of views may well find himself suffering a mental blindness. The Court holds that the appellants have alleged a cause of action. However, it refuses to award relief here—although the facts are undisputed—and fails to give the District Court any guidance whatever. One dissenting opinion, bursting with words that go through so much and conclude with so little, contemns the majority action as "a massive repudiation of the experience of our whole past." Another describes the complaint as merely asserting conclusory allegations that Tennessee's apportionment is "incorrect," "arbitrary," "obsolete," and "unconstitutional." I believe it can be shown that this case is distinguishable from earlier cases dealing with the distribution of political power by a State, that a patent violation of the Equal Protection Clause of the United States Constitution has been shown, and that an appropriate remedy may be formulated.

. . .

III.

Although I find the Tennessee apportionment statute offends the Equal Protection Clause, I would not consider intervention by this Court into so delicate a field if there were any other relief available to the people of Tennessee. But the majority of the people of Tennessee have no "practical opportunities for exerting their political weight at the polls" to correct the existing "invidious discrimination." Tennessee has no initiative and referendum. I have searched diligently for other "practical opportunities" present under the law. I find none other than through the federal courts. The majority of the voters have been caught up in a legislative strait jacket. Tennessee has an "informed, civically militant electorate" and "an aroused popular conscience," but it does not sear "the conscience of the people's representatives." This is because the legislative policy has riveted the present seats in the Assembly to their respective constituencies, and by the votes of their incumbents a reapportionment of any kind is prevented. The people have been rebuffed at the hands of the Assembly; they have tried the constitutional convention route, but since the call must originate in the Assembly it, too, has been fruitless. They have tried Tennessee courts with the same result, and Governors have fought the tide only to flounder. It is said that there is recourse in Congress and perhaps that may be, but from a practical standpoint this is without substance. To date Congress has never undertaken such a task in any State. We therefore must conclude that the people of Tennessee are stymied and without judicial intervention will be saddled with the present discrimination in the affairs of their state government.

. . .

MR. JUSTICE STEWART, concurring.

The separate writings of my dissenting and concurring Brothers stray so far from the subject of today's decision as to convey, I think, a distressingly inaccurate impression of what the Court decides. For that reason, I think it appropriate, in joining the opinion of the Court, to emphasize in a few words what the opinion does and does not say.

The Court today decides three things and no more: "(a) that the court possessed jurisdiction of the subject matter; (b) that a justiciable cause of action is stated upon which appellants would be entitled to appropriate relief; and (c) . . . that the appellants have standing to challenge the Tennessee apportionment statutes." *Ante,* pp. 197–198.

The complaint in this case asserts that Tennessee's system of apportionment is utterly arbitrary—without any possible justification in rationality. The District Court did not reach the merits of that claim, and this Court quite properly expresses no view on the subject. Contrary to the suggestion of my Brother HARLAN, the Court does not say or imply that "state legislatures must be so structured as to reflect with approximate equality the voice of every voter." *Post,* p. 332. The Court does not say or imply that there is anything in the Federal Constitution "to prevent a State, acting not irrationally, from choosing any electoral legislative structure it thinks best suited to the interests, temper, and customs of its people." *Post,* p. 334. And contrary to the suggestion of my Brother DOUGLAS, the Court most assuredly does not decide the question, "may a State weight the vote of one county or one district more heavily than it weights the vote in another?" *Ante,* p. 244.

. . .

MR. JUSTICE FRANKFURTER, whom MR. JUSTICE HARLAN joins, dissenting.

The Court today reverses a uniform course of decision established by a dozen cases, including one by which the very claim now sustained was unanimously rejected only five years ago. The impressive body of rulings thus cast aside reflected the equally uniform course of our political history regarding the relationship between population and legislative representation—a wholly different matter from denial of the franchise to individuals because of race, color, religion or sex. Such a massive repudiation of the experience of our whole past in asserting destructively novel judicial power demands a detailed analysis of the role of this Court in our constitutional scheme. Disregard of inherent limits in the effective exercise of the Court's "judicial Power" not only presages the futility of judicial intervention in the essentially political conflict of forces by which the relation between population and representation has time out of mind been and now is determined. It may well impair the Court's position as the ultimate organ of "the supreme Law of the Land" in that vast range of legal problems, often strongly entangled in popular feeling, on which this Court must pronounce. The Court's authority—possessed of neither the purse nor the sword—ultimately rests on sustained public confidence in its moral sanction. Such feeling must be nourished by the Court's complete detachment, in fact and in appearance, from political entanglements and by abstention from injecting itself into the clash of political forces in political settlements.

. . .

. . . The Framers carefully and with deliberate forethought refused so to enthrone the judiciary. In this situation, as in others of like nature, appeal for relief does not belong here. Appeal must be to an informed, civically militant electorate. In a democratic society like ours, relief must come through an aroused popular conscience that sears the conscience of the people's representatives. In any event there is nothing judicially more unseemly nor more self-defeating than for this Court to make *in terrorem* pronouncements, to indulge in merely empty rhetoric, sounding a word of promise to the ear, sure to be disappointing to the hope.

. . .

IV.

. . .

A federal court enforcing the Federal Constitution is not, to be sure, bound by the remedial doctrines of the state courts. But it must consider as pertinent to the propriety or impropriety of exercising its jurisdiction those state-law effects of its decree which it cannot itself control. A federal court cannot provide the authority requisite to make a legislature the proper governing body of the State of Tennessee. And it cannot be doubted that the striking down of the statute here challenged on equal protection grounds, no less than on grounds of failure to reapportion decennially, would deprive the State of all valid apportionment legislation and . . . deprive the State of an

effective law-based legislative branch. Just such considerations, among others here present, were determinative in *Luther* v. *Borden* and the Oregon initiative cases.

Although the District Court had jurisdiction in the very restricted sense of power to determine whether it could adjudicate the claim, the case is of that class of political controversy which, by the nature of its subject, is unfit for federal judicial action. The judgment of the District Court, in dismissing the complaint for failure to state a claim on which relief can be granted, should therefore be affirmed.

Dissenting opinion of MR. JUSTICE HARLAN, whom MR. JUSTICE FRANKFURTER joins.

The dissenting opinion of MR. JUSTICE FRANKFURTER, in which I join, demonstrates the abrupt departure the majority makes from judicial history by putting the federal courts into this area of state concerns—an area which, in this instance, the Tennessee state courts themselves have refused to enter.

It does not detract from his opinion to say that the panorama of judicial history it unfolds, though evincing a steadfast underlying principle of keeping the federal courts out of these domains, has a tendency, because of variants in expression, to becloud analysis in a given case. With due respect to the majority, I think that has happened here.

Once one cuts through the thicket of discussion devoted to "jurisdiction," "standing," "justiciability," and "political question," there emerges a straightforward issue which, in my view, is determinative of this case. Does the complaint disclose a violation of a federal constitutional right, in other words, a claim over which a United States District Court would have jurisdiction under 28 U. S. C. § 1343 (3) and 42 U. S. C. § 1983? The majority opinion does not actually discuss this basic question, but, as one concurring Justice observes, seems to decide it *"sub silentio." Ante,* p. 261. However, in my opinion, appellants' allegations, accepting all of them as true, do not, parsed down or as a whole, show an infringement by Tennessee of any rights assured by the Fourteenth Amendment. Accordingly, I believe the complaint should have been dismissed for "failure to state a

claim upon which relief can be granted." Fed.
Rules Civ. Proc., Rule 12(b)(6).

It is at once essential to recognize this case for
what it is. The issue here relates not to a method of
state electoral apportionment by which seats in
the *federal* House of Representatives are allocated,
but solely to the right of a State to fix the basis of
representation in its *own* legislature. Until it is
first decided to what extent that right is limited by
the Federal Constitution, and whether what Tennessee has done or failed to do in this instance
runs afoul of any such limitation, we need not
reach the issues of "justiciability" or "political
question" or any of the other considerations
which in such cases as *Colegrove* v. *Green*, 328
U. S. 549, led the Court to decline to adjudicate a
challenge to a state apportionment affecting seats
in the federal House of Representatives, in the
absence of a controlling Act of Congress. See also
Wood v. *Broom*, 287 U. S. 1.

The appellants' claim in this case ultimately
rests entirely on the Equal Protection Clause of
the Fourteenth Amendment. It is asserted that
Tennessee has violated the Equal Protection
Clause by maintaining in effect a system of apportionment that grossly favors in legislative representation the rural sections of the State as against
its urban communities. . . .

I.

I can find nothing in the Equal Protection
Clause or elsewhere in the Federal Constitution
which expressly or impliedly supports the view
that state legislatures must be so structured as to
reflect with approximate equality the voice of
every voter. Not only is that proposition refuted by
history, as shown by my Brother FRANKFURTER,
but it strikes deep into the heart of our federal
system. Its acceptance would require us to turn
our backs on the regard which this Court has
always shown for the judgment of state legislatures and courts on matters of basically local
concern.

In the last analysis, what lies at the core of this
controversy is a difference of opinion as to the
function of representative government. It is surely
beyond argument that those who have the responsibility for devising a system of representation may
permissibly consider that factors other than bare
numbers should be taken into account. The existence of the United States Senate is proof enough
of that. . . .

II.

. . .

Indeed, I would hardly think it unconstitutional if a state legislature's expressed reason for
establishing or maintaining an electoral imbalance between its rural and urban population were
to protect the State's agricultural interests from
the sheer weight of numbers of those residing in
its cities. A State may, after all, take account of the
interests of its rural population in the distribution
of tax burdens, *e. g.*, *American Sugar Rfg. Co.* v.
Louisiana, 179 U. S. 89, and recognition of the
special problems of agricultural interests has repeatedly been reflected in federal legislation, *e. g.*,
Capper-Volstead Act, 42 Stat. 388; Agricultural
Adjustment Act of 1938, 52 Stat. 31. Even the
exemption of agricultural activities from state
criminal statutes of otherwise general application
has not been deemed offensive to the Equal Protection Clause. *Tigner* v. *Texas*, 310 U. S. 141. Does
the Fourteenth Amendment impose a stricter limitation upon a State's apportionment of political
representatives to its central government? I think
not. These are matters of local policy, on the
wisdom of which the federal judiciary is neither
permitted nor qualified to sit in judgment.

. . .

*[In a lengthy appendix, Harlan analyzes the opin-
ions of Stewart and Clark and finds the mathematical formula, used to reject Tennessee's apportionment as arbitrary, to be defective.]*

Wesberry v. Sanders

376 U.S. 1 (1964)

After the Court decided in *Baker* v. *Carr* (1962) to accept jurisdiction in reapportionment cases, it had to determine whether judicial scrutiny would cover only malapportionment in state legislatures or in Congress as well. This case involved Georgia's Fifth Congressional District, which had a population two to three times greater than some other congressional districts in the state. A three-judge district court dismissed the complaint filed by James P. Wesberry, Jr., a citizen of Fulton County, for "want of equity." The defendant was Carl E. Sanders, Governor of Georgia.

MR. JUSTICE BLACK delivered the opinion of the Court.

Appellants are citizens and qualified voters of Fulton County, Georgia, and as such are entitled to vote in congressional elections in Georgia's Fifth Congressional District. That district, one of ten created by a 1931 Georgia statute, includes Fulton, DeKalb, and Rockdale Counties and has a population according to the 1960 census of 823,680. The average population of the ten districts is 394,312, less than half that of the Fifth. One district, the Ninth, has only 272,154 people, less than one-third as many as the Fifth. Since there is only one Congressman for each district, this inequality of population means that the Fifth District's Congressman has to represent from two to three times as many people as do Congressmen from some of the other Georgia districts.

Claiming that these population disparities deprived them and voters similarly situated of a right under the Federal Constitution to have their votes for Congressmen given the same weight as the votes of other Georgians, the appellants brought this action under 42 U. S. C. §§ 1983 and 1988 and 28 U. S. C. § 1343 (3) asking that the Georgia statute be declared invalid and that the appellees, the Governor and Secretary of State of Georgia, be enjoined from conducting elections under it. The complaint alleged that appellants were deprived of the full benefit of their right to vote, in violation of (1) Art. I, § 2, of the Constitution of the United States, which provides that "The House of Representatives shall be composed of Members chosen every second Year by the People of the several States . . ."; (2) the Due Process, Equal Protection, and Privileges and Immunities Clauses of the Fourteenth Amendment; and (3) that part of Section 2 of the Fourteenth Amendment which provides that "Representatives shall be apportioned among the several States according to their respective numbers. . . ."

. . .

I.

[The Court summarizes its holding in Baker *v.* Carr *(1962), concluding that the district court erred in dismissing the complaint.]*

II.

This brings us to the merits. We agree with the District Court that the 1931 Georgia apportionment grossly discriminates against voters in the Fifth Congressional District. A single Congressman represents from two to three times as many Fifth District voters as are represented by each of the Congressmen from the other Georgia congressional districts. The apportionment statute thus contracts the value of some votes and expands that of others. If the Federal Constitution intends that when qualified voters elect members of Congress each vote be given as much weight as any other vote, then this statute cannot stand.

We hold that, construed in its historical context, the command of Art. I, § 2, that Representatives be chosen "by the People of the several States" means that as nearly as is practicable one man's vote in a congressional election is to be worth as much as another's. This rule is followed automatically, of course, when Representatives are chosen as a group on a statewide basis, as was a widespread practice in the first 50 years of our Nation's history. It would be extraordinary to suggest that in such statewide elections the votes of inhabitants of some parts of a State, for example, Georgia's thinly populated Ninth District, could be weighted at two or three times the value of the votes of people living in more populous parts of the State, for example, the Fifth District around Atlanta. Cf. *Gray* v. *Sanders*, 372 U. S. 368. We do not believe that the Framers of the Constitution intended to permit the same vote-diluting discrimination to be accomplished through the device of districts containing widely varied numbers of inhabitants. To say that a vote is worth more in one district than in another would not only run counter to our fundamental ideas of democratic government, it would cast aside the principle of a House of Representatives elected "by the People," a principle tenaciously fought for and established at the Constitutional Convention. The history of the Constitution, particularly that part of it relating to the adoption of Art. I, § 2, reveals that those who framed the Constitution meant that, no matter what the mechanics of an election, whether statewide or by districts, it was population which was to be the basis of the House of Representatives.

. . .

The question of how the legislature should be constituted precipitated the most bitter controversy of the Convention. One principle was uppermost in the minds of many delegates: that, no matter where he lived, each voter should have a voice equal to that of every other in electing members of Congress. In support of this principle, George Mason of Virginia

"argued strongly for an election of the larger branch by the people. It was to be the grand depository of the democratic principle of the Govt."

James Madison agreed, saying "If the power is not immediately derived from the people, in proportion to their numbers, we may make a paper

confederacy, but that will be all." Repeatedly, delegates rose to make the same point: that it would be unfair, unjust, and contrary to common sense to give a small number of people as many Senators or Representatives as were allowed to much larger groups—in short, as James Wilson of Pennsylvania put it, "equal numbers of people ought to have an equal no. of representatives . . ." and representatives "of different districts ought clearly to hold the same proportion to each other, as their respective constituents hold to each other."

[The Court describes the fear of small states that they would be overwhelmed in a legislature based only on population. As part of the Grand Compromise, each state would have two Senators, elected by the state legislatures, while members of the House of Representatives would be chosen directly by the people and "apportioned among the several States . . . according to their respective Numbers."]

It would defeat the principle solemnly embodied in the Great Compromise—equal representation in the House for equal numbers of people—for us to hold that, within the States, legislatures may draw the lines of congressional districts in such a way as to give some voters a greater voice in choosing a Congressman than others. The House of Representatives, the Convention agreed, was to represent the people as individuals, and on a basis of complete equality for each voter. The delegates were quite aware of what Madison called the "vicious representation" in Great Britain whereby "rotten boroughs" with few inhabitants were represented in Parliament on or almost on a par with cities of greater population. Wilson urged that people must be represented as individuals, so that America would escape the evils of the English system under which one man could send two members to Parliament to represent the borough of Old Sarum while London's million people sent but four. The delegates referred to rotten borough apportionments in some of the state legislatures as the kind of objectionable governmental action that the Constitution should not tolerate in the election of congressional representatives.

. . .

Soon after the Constitution was adopted, James Wilson of Pennsylvania, by then an Associate Justice of this Court, gave a series of lectures at Philadelphia in which, drawing on his experience as one of the most active members of the Constitutional Convention, he said:

"[A]ll elections ought to be equal. Elections are equal, when a given number of citizens, in one part of the state, choose as many representatives, as are chosen by the same number of citizens, in any other part of the state. In this manner, the proportion of the representatives and of the constituents will remain invariably the same."

It is in the light of such history that we must construe Art. I, § 2, of the Constitution, which, carrying out the ideas of Madison and those of like views, provides that Representatives shall be chosen "by the People of the several States" and shall be "apportioned among the several States . . . according to their respective Numbers." It is not surprising that our Court has held that this Article gives persons qualified to vote a constitutional right to vote and to have their votes counted. *United States* v. *Mosley*, 238 U. S. 383; *Ex Parte Yarbrough*, 110 U. S. 651. Not only can this right to vote not be denied outright, it cannot, consistently with Article I, be destroyed by alteration of ballots, see *United States* v. *Classic*, 313 U. S. 299, or diluted by stuffing of the ballot box, see *United States* v. *Saylor*, 322 U. S. 385. No right is more precious in a free country than that of having a voice in the election of those who make the laws under which, as good citizens, we must live. Other rights, even the most basic, are illusory if the right to vote is undermined. Our Constitution leaves no room for classification of people in a way that unnecessarily abridges this right. In urging the people to adopt the Constitution, Madison said in No. 57 of *The Federalist*:

"Who are to be the electors of the Fœderal Representatives? Not the rich more than the poor; not the learned more than the ignorant; not the haughty heirs of distinguished names, more than the humble sons of obscure and unpropitious fortune. The electors are to be the great body of the people of the United States. . . ."

Readers surely could have fairly taken this to mean, "one person, one vote." Cf. *Gray* v. *Sanders*, 372 U. S. 368, 381.

While it may not be possible to draw congressional districts with mathematical precision, that is no excuse for ignoring our Constitution's plain objective of making equal representation for equal numbers of people the fundamental goal for the House of Representatives. That is the high standard of justice and common sense which the Founders set for us.

Reversed and remanded.

MR. JUSTICE CLARK, concurring in part and dissenting in part.

Unfortunately I can join neither the opinion of the Court nor the dissent of my Brother HARLAN. It is true that the opening sentence of Art. I, § 2, of the Constitution provides that Representatives are to be chosen "by the People of the several States. . . ." However, in my view, Brother HARLAN has clearly demonstrated that both the historical background and language preclude a finding that Art. I, § 2, lays down the *ipse dixit* "one person, one vote" in congressional elections.

On the other hand, I agree with the majority that congressional districting is subject to judicial scrutiny. . . . I therefore cannot agree with Brother HARLAN that the supervisory power granted to Congress under Art. I, § 4, is the exclusive remedy.

. . .

MR. JUSTICE HARLAN, dissenting.

I had not expected to witness the day when the Supreme Court of the United States would render a decision which casts grave doubt on the constitutionality of the composition of the House of Representatives. It is not an exaggeration to say that such is the effect of today's decision. The Court's holding that the Constitution requires States to select Representatives either by elections at large or by elections in districts composed "as nearly as is practicable" of equal population places in jeopardy the seats of almost all the members of the present House of Representatives.

In the last congressional election, in 1962, Representatives from 42 States were elected from congressional districts. *[Representatives were elect-*

ed at large in Alabama, Alaska, Delaware, Hawaii, Nevada, New Mexico, Vermont, and Wyoming, accounting for seventeen Representatives. In addition, Connecticut, Maryland, Michigan, Ohio, and Texas each elected one of their Representatives at large.] In all but five of those States, the difference between the populations of the largest and smallest districts exceeded 100,000 persons. A difference of this magnitude in the size of districts the average population of which in each State is less than 500,000 is presumably not equality among districts "as nearly as is practicable," although the Court does not reveal its definition of that phrase. Thus, today's decision impugns the validity of the election of 398 Representatives from 37 States, leaving a "constitutional" House of 37 members now sitting.

Only a demonstration which could not be avoided would justify this Court in rendering a decision the effect of which, inescapably as I see it, is to declare constitutionally defective the very composition of a coordinate branch of the Federal Government. The Court's opinion not only fails to make such a demonstration, it is unsound logically on its face and demonstrably unsound historically.

I.

Before coming to grips with the reasoning that carries such extraordinary consequences, it is important to have firmly in mind the provisions of Article I of the Constitution which control this case:

"Section 2. The House of Representatives shall be composed of Members chosen every second Year by the People of the several States, and the Electors in each State shall have the Qualifications requisite for Electors of the most numerous Branch of the State Legislature.

.   .   .   .   .

"Representatives and direct Taxes shall be apportioned among the several States which may be included within this Union, according to their respective Numbers, which shall be determined by adding to the whole Number of free Persons, including those bound to Service for a Term of

Years, and excluding Indians not taxed, three fifths of all other Persons. The actual Enumeration shall be made within three Years after the first Meeting of the Congress of the United States, and within every subsequent Term of ten Years, in such Manner as they shall by Law direct. The Number of Representatives shall not exceed one for every thirty Thousand, but each State shall have at Least one Representative. . . .

"Section 4. The Times, Places and Manner of holding Elections for Senators and Representatives, shall be prescribed in each State by the Legislature thereof; but the Congress may at any time by Law make or alter such Regulations, except as to the Places of chusing Senators.

.   .   .   .   .

"Section 5. Each House shall be the Judge of the Elections, Returns and Qualifications of its own Members. . . ."

As will be shown, these constitutional provisions and their "historical context," *ante*, p. 7, establish:

1. that congressional Representatives are to be apportioned among the several States largely, but not entirely, according to population;

2. that the States have plenary power to select their allotted Representatives in accordance with any method of popular election they please, subject only to the supervisory power of Congress; and

3. that the supervisory power of Congress is exclusive.

.   .   .

II.

Disclaiming all reliance on other provisions of the Constitution, in particular those of the Fourteenth Amendment on which the appellants relied below and in this Court, the Court holds that the provision in Art. I, § 2, for election of Representatives "by the People" *means* that congressional districts are to be "as nearly as is practicable" equal in population, *ante*, pp. 7–8. Stripped of rhetoric and a "historical context," *ante*, p. 7, which bears little resemblance to the evidence found in the pages of history, see *infra*, pp. 30–41, the Court's opinion supports its holding only with the bland assertion that "the principle of a House of Representatives elected 'by the People'" would be "cast aside" if "a vote is worth more in one district than in another," *ante*, p. 8, *i. e.*, if congressional districts within a State, each electing a single Representative, are not equal in population. The fact is, however, that Georgia's 10 Representatives *are* elected "by the People" of Georgia, just as Representatives from other States are elected "by the People of the several States." This is all that the Constitution requires.

Although the Court finds necessity for its artificial construction of Article I in the undoubted importance of the right to vote, that right is not involved in this case. All of the appellants do vote. The Court's talk about "debasement" and "dilution" of the vote is a model of circular reasoning, in which the premises of the argument feed on the conclusion. Moreover, by focusing exclusively on numbers in disregard of the area and shape of a congressional district as well as party affiliations within the district, the Court deals in abstractions which will be recognized even by the politically unsophisticated to have little relevance to the realities of political life.

. . .

Far from supporting the Court, the apportionment of Representatives among the States shows how blindly the Court has marched to its decision. Representatives were to be apportioned among the States on the basis of free population plus three-fifths of the slave population. Since no slave voted, the inclusion of three-fifths of their number in the basis of apportionment gave the favored States representation far in excess of their voting population. If, then, slaves were intended to be without representation, Article I did exactly what the Court now says it prohibited: it "weighted" the vote of voters in the slave States. Alternatively, it might have been thought that Representatives elected by free men of a State would speak also for the slaves. But since the slaves added to the representation only of their own State, Representatives from the slave States could have been thought to speak only for the slaves of their own

States, indicating both that the Convention believed it possible for a Representative elected by one group to speak for another nonvoting group and that Representatives were in large degree still thought of as speaking for the whole population *of a State.*

There is a further basis for demonstrating the hollowness of the Court's assertion that Article I requires "one man's vote in a congressional election . . . to be worth as much as another's," *ante*, p. 8. Nothing that the Court does today will disturb the fact that although in 1960 the population of an average congressional district was 410,481, the States of Alaska, Nevada, and Wyoming each have a Representative in Congress, although their respective populations are 226,167, 285,278, and 330,066. In entire disregard of population, Art. I, § 2, guarantees each of these States and every other State "at Least one Representative." It is whimsical to assert in the face of this guarantee that an absolute principle of "equal representation in the House for equal numbers of people" is "solemnly embodied" in Article I. . . .

. . .

[In the remainder of this lengthy dissent, Harlan states that it is unlikely that "most or many" delegates to the Constitutional Convention would have subscribed to the one-person, one-vote principle; that state legislatures had plenary power to district, subject only to the supervisory power of Congress; and that the Court is not simply undertaking to exercise a power which the Constitution reserves to Congress, but it is also overruling congressional judgment expressed in previous statutes and legislative history.]

This Court, no less than all other branches of the Government, is bound by the Constitution. The Constitution does not confer on the Court blanket authority to step into every situation where the political branch may be thought to have fallen short. The stability of this institution ultimately depends not only upon its being alert to keep the other branches of government within constitutional bounds but equally upon recognition of the limitations on the Court's own functions in the constitutional system.

What is done today saps the political process. The promise of judicial intervention in matters of this sort cannot but encourage popular inertia in efforts for political reform through the political process, with the inevitable result that the process is itself weakened. By yielding to the demand for a judicial remedy in this instance, the Court in my view does a disservice both to itself and to the broader values of our system of government.

Believing that the complaint fails to disclose a constitutional claim, I would affirm the judgment below dismissing the complaint.

. . .

MR. JUSTICE STEWART.

I think it is established that "this Court has power to afford relief in a case of this type as against the objection that the issues are not justiciable," and I cannot subscribe to any possible implication to the contrary which may lurk in MR. JUSTICE HARLAN'S dissenting opinion. With this single qualification I join the dissent because I think MR. JUSTICE HARLAN has unanswerably demonstrated that Art. I, § 2, of the Constitution gives no mandate to this Court or to any court to ordain that congressional districts within each State must be equal in population.

Reynolds v. Sims

377 U.S. 533 (1964)

M.O. Sims and other voters from Alabama brought suit to challenge the apportionment of the state legislature as a violation of the Equal Protection Clause of the Fourteenth Amendment and the Alabama constitution. Under the state constitution, each county was entitled to at least one state representative, no matter how small the population. A three-judge federal court refused to order the May 1962 primary election to be held at large, stating that it should not act until the legislature had an opportunity to take corrective action before the general election. After the legislature acted, the district court held that neither of the two apportionment plans fashioned by the legislature would cure the violation of the Equal Protection Clause, and proceeded to combine features of the two plans to produce a more equitable apportionment. The state appealed, claiming that a federal court lacks power to apportion a legislature. In this case the Court faces the question whether the principle of equal representation applies to both houses of a state legislature, or whether one house, following the federal model (the U.S. Senate), may be apportioned on a basis other than population.

MR. CHIEF JUSTICE WARREN delivered the opinion of the Court.

Involved in these cases are an appeal and two cross-appeals from a decision of the Federal District Court for the Middle District of Alabama holding invalid, under the Equal Protection Clause of the Federal Constitution, the existing and two legislatively proposed plans for the apportionment of seats in the two houses of the Alabama Legislature, and ordering into effect a temporary reapportionment plan comprised of parts of the proposed but judicially disapproved measures.

I.

On August 26, 1961, the original plaintiffs (appellees in No. 23), residents, taxpayers and voters of Jefferson County, Alabama, filed a complaint in the United States District Court for the Middle District of Alabama, in their own behalf and on behalf of all similarly situated Alabama voters, challenging the apportionment of the Alabama Legislature. Defendants below (appellants in No. 23), sued in their representative capacities, were various state and political party officials charged with the performance of certain duties in connection with state elections. The complaint alleged a deprivation of rights under the Alabama Constitution and under the Equal Protection Clause of the Fourteenth Amendment, and asserted that the District Court had jurisdiction under provisions of the Civil Rights Act, 42 U. S. C. §§ 1983, 1988, as well as under 28 U. S. C. § 1343(3).

The complaint stated that the Alabama Legislature was composed of a Senate of 35 members and a House of Representatives of 106 members. It set out relevant portions of the 1901 Alabama Constitution, which prescribe the number of members of the two bodies of the State Legislature and the method of apportioning the seats among the State's 67 counties, and provide as follows:

[Each county was entitled to at least one representative. The state was to be divided into as many senatorial districts as there were senators, with each district as "nearly equal" to each other in population. Representation in the legislature "shall be based upon population." Although the state constitution required that the legislature be apportioned every ten years, the last apportionment was based on the 1900 census. Population-variance ratios of up to about 41-to-1 existed in the Senate, and up to about 16-to-1 in the House.]

II.

Undeniably the Constitution of the United States protects the right of all qualified citizens to vote, in state as well as in federal elections. A consistent line of decisions by this Court in cases involving attempts to deny or restrict the right of suffrage has made this indelibly clear. . . . The right to vote freely for the candidate of one's choice is of the essence of a democratic society, and any restrictions on that right strike at the heart of representative government. And the right of suffrage can be denied by a debasement or dilution of the weight of a citizen's vote just as effectively as by wholly prohibiting the free exercise of the franchise.

[The Court reviews the holdings in Baker v. Carr *(1962),* Gray v. Sanders *(1963), and* Wesberry v. Sanders *(1964).]*

III.

A predominant consideration in determining whether a State's legislative apportionment scheme constitutes an invidious discrimination violative of rights asserted under the Equal Protection Clause is that the rights allegedly impaired are individual and personal in nature. . . . Especially since the right to exercise the franchise in a free and unimpaired manner is preservative of other basic civil and political rights, any alleged infringement of the right of citizens to vote must be carefully and meticulously scrutinized. Almost a century ago, in *Yick Wo* v. *Hopkins,* 118 U. S. 356, the Court referred to "the political franchise of voting" as "a fundamental political right, because preservative of all rights." 118 U. S., at 370.

Legislators represent people, not trees or acres. Legislators are elected by voters, not farms or cities or economic interests. As long as ours is a representative form of government, and our legislatures are those instruments of government elected directly by and directly representative of the people, the right to elect legislators in a free and unimpaired fashion is a bedrock of our political system. It could hardly be gainsaid that a constitutional claim had been asserted by an allegation that certain otherwise qualified voters had been entirely prohibited from voting for members of their state legislature. And, if a State should provide that the votes of citizens in one part of the State should be given two times, or five times, or 10 times the weight of votes of citizens in another part of the State, it could hardly be contended that the right to vote of those residing in the disfavored areas had not been effectively diluted. It would appear extraordinary to suggest that a State could be constitutionally permitted to enact a law providing that certain of the State's voters could vote two, five, or 10 times for their legislative representatives, while voters living elsewhere could vote only once. And it is inconceivable that a state law to the effect that, in counting votes for legislators, the votes of citizens in one part of the State would be multiplied by two, five, or 10, while the votes of persons in another area would be counted only at face value, could be constitutionally sustainable. Of course, the effect of state legislative districting schemes which give the same number of representatives to unequal numbers of constituents is identical. . . .

. . . the concept of equal protection has been traditionally viewed as requiring the uniform treatment of persons standing in the same relation to the governmental action questioned or challenged. . . . Since the achieving of fair and effective representation for all citizens is concededly the basic aim of legislative apportionment, we conclude that the Equal Protection Clause guarantees the opportunity for equal participation by all voters in the election of state legislators. . . .

. . .

. . . A citizen, a qualified voter, is no more nor no less so because he lives in the city or on the farm. This is the clear and strong command of our Constitution's Equal Protection Clause. This is an essential part of the concept of a government of laws and not men. This is at the heart of Lincoln's vision of "government of the people, by the people, [and] for the people." The Equal Protection Clause demands no less than substantially equal state legislative representation for all citizens, of all places as well as of all races.

IV.

We hold that, as a basic constitutional standard, the Equal Protection Clause requires that the seats in both houses of a bicameral state legislature must be apportioned on a population basis. Simply stated, an individual's right to vote for state legislators is unconstitutionally impaired when its weight is in a substantial fashion diluted when compared with votes of citizens living in other parts of the State. Since, under neither the existing apportionment provisions nor either of the proposed plans was either of the houses of the Alabama Legislature apportioned on a population basis, the District Court correctly held that all three of these schemes were constitutionally invalid. . . .

V.

Since neither of the houses of the Alabama Legislature, under any of the three plans consid-

ered by the District Court, was apportioned on a population basis, we would be justified in proceeding no further. However, one of the proposed plans, that contained in the so-called 67-Senator Amendment, at least superficially resembles the scheme of legislative representation followed in the Federal Congress. Under this plan, each of Alabama's 67 counties is allotted one senator, and no counties are given more than one Senate seat. Arguably, this is analogous to the allocation of two Senate seats, in the Federal Congress, to each of the 50 States, regardless of population. Seats in the Alabama House, under the proposed constitutional amendment, are distributed by giving each of the 67 counties at least one, with the remaining 39 seats being allotted among the more populous counties on a population basis. This scheme, at least at first glance, appears to resemble that prescribed for the Federal House of Representatives, where the 435 seats are distributed among the States on a population basis, although each State, regardless of its population, is given at least one Congressman. Thus, although there are substantial differences in underlying rationale and result, the 67-Senator Amendment, as proposed by the Alabama Legislature, at least arguably presents for consideration a scheme analogous to that used for apportioning seats in Congress.

Much has been written since our decision in *Baker* v. *Carr* about the applicability of the so-called federal analogy to state legislative apportionment arrangements. After considering the matter, the court below concluded that no conceivable analogy could be drawn between the federal scheme and the apportionment of seats in the Alabama Legislature under the proposed constitutional amendment. We agree with the District Court, and find the federal analogy inapposite and irrelevant to state legislative districting schemes. . . .

. . .

The system of representation in the two Houses of the Federal Congress is one ingrained in our Constitution, as part of the law of the land. It is one conceived out of compromise and concession indispensable to the establishment of our federal republic. Arising from unique historical circumstances, it is based on the consideration that in establishing our type of federalism a group of formerly independent States bound themselves together under one national government. Admittedly, the original 13 States surrendered some of their sovereignty in agreeing to join together "to form a more perfect Union." But at the heart of our constitutional system remains the concept of separate and distinct governmental entities which have delegated some, but not all, of their formerly held powers to the single national government. . . .

Political subdivisions of States—counties, cities, or whatever—never were and never have been considered as sovereign entities. Rather, they have been traditionally regarded as subordinate governmental instrumentalities created by the State to assist in the carrying out of state governmental functions. . . . The relationship of the States to the Federal Government could hardly be less analogous.

. . .

VI.

By holding that as a federal constitutional requisite both houses of a state legislature must be apportioned on a population basis, we mean that the Equal Protection Clause requires that a State make an honest and good faith effort to construct districts, in both houses of its legislature, as nearly of equal population as is practicable. We realize that it is a practical impossibility to arrange legislative districts so that each one has an identical number of residents, or citizens, or voters. Mathematical exactness or precision is hardly a workable constitutional requirement.

. . .

. . . we affirm the judgment below and remand the cases for further proceedings consistent with the views stated in this opinion.

It is so ordered.

MR. JUSTICE CLARK, concurring in the affirmance.

The Court goes much beyond the necessities of this case in laying down a new "equal population"

principle for state legislative apportionment. This principle seems to be an offshoot of *Gray* v. *Sanders*, 372 U. S. 368, 381 (1963), *i. e.*, "one person, one vote," modified by the "nearly as is practicable" admonition of *Wesberry* v. *Sanders*, 376 U. S. 1, 8 (1964). Whether "nearly as is practicable" means "one person, one vote" qualified by "approximately equal" or "some deviations" or by the impossibility of "mathematical nicety" is not clear from the majority's use of these vague and meaningless phrases. But whatever the standard, the Court applies it to each house of the State Legislature.

It seems to me that all that the Court need say in this case is that each plan considered by the trial court is "a crazy quilt," clearly revealing invidious discrimination in each house of the Legislature and therefore violative of the Equal Protection Clause. See my concurring opinion in *Baker* v. *Carr*, 369 U. S. 186, 253–258 (1962).

I, therefore, do not reach the question of the so-called "federal analogy." But in my view, if one house of the State Legislature meets the population standard, representation in the other house might include some departure from it so as to take into account, on a rational basis, other factors in order to afford some representation to the various elements of the State. See my dissenting opinion in *Lucas* v. *Forty-Fourth General Assembly of Colorado, post*, p. 741, decided this date.

MR. JUSTICE STEWART.

All of the parties have agreed with the District Court's finding that legislative inaction for some 60 years in the face of growth and shifts in population has converted Alabama's legislative apportionment plan enacted in 1901 into one completely lacking in rationality. Accordingly, for the reasons stated in my dissenting opinion in *Lucas* v. *Forty-Fourth General Assembly of Colorado, post*, p. 744, I would affirm the judgment of the District Court holding that this apportionment violated the Equal Protection Clause.

I also agree with the Court that it was proper for the District Court, in framing a remedy, to adhere as closely as practicable to the apportionments approved by the representatives of the people of Alabama, and to afford the State of Alabama full opportunity, consistent with the requirements of the Federal Constitution, to devise its own system of legislative apportionment.

MR. JUSTICE HARLAN, dissenting.

In these cases the Court holds that seats in the legislatures of six States are apportioned in ways that violate the Federal Constitution. Under the Court's ruling it is bound to follow that the legislatures in all but a few of the other 44 States will meet the same fate. These decisions, with *Wesberry* v. *Sanders*, 376 U. S. 1, involving congressional districting by the States, and *Gray* v. *Sanders*, 372 U. S. 368, relating to elections for statewide office, have the effect of placing basic aspects of state political systems under the pervasive overlordship of the federal judiciary. Once again, I must register my protest.

. . .

Had the Court paused to probe more deeply into the matter, it would have found that the Equal Protection Clause was never intended to inhibit the States in choosing any democratic method they pleased for the apportionment of their legislatures. This is shown by the language of the Fourteenth Amendment taken as a whole, by the understanding of those who proposed and ratified it; and by the political practices of the States at the time the Amendment was adopted. It is confirmed by numerous state and congressional actions since the adoption of the Fourteenth Amendment, and by the common understanding of the Amendment as evidenced by subsequent constitutional amendments and decisions of this Court before *Baker* v. *Carr, supra,* made an abrupt break with the past in 1962.

The failure of the Court to consider any of these matters cannot be excused or explained by any concept of "developing" constitutionalism. It is meaningless to speak of constitutional "development" when both the language and history of the controlling provisions of the Constitution are wholly ignored. Since it can, I think, be shown beyond doubt that state legislative apportionments, as such, are wholly free of constitutional limitations, save such as may be imposed by the Republican Form of Government Clause (Const., Art. IV, § 4), the Court's action now bringing them within the purview of the Fourteenth Amendment

amounts to nothing less than an exercise of the amending power by this Court.

. . .

I.

A. *The Language of the Fourteenth Amendment.*

The Court relies exclusively on that portion of § 1 of the Fourteenth Amendment which provides that no State shall "deny to any person within its jurisdiction the equal protection of the laws," and disregards entirely the significance of § 2, which reads:

"Representatives shall be apportioned among the several States according to their respective numbers, counting the whole number of persons in each State, excluding Indians not taxed. *But when the right to vote at any election for* the choice of electors for President and Vice President of the United States, Representatives in Congress, *the Executive and Judicial officers of a State, or the members of the Legislature thereof, is denied* to any of the male inhabitants of such State, being twenty-one years of age, and citizens of the United States, *or in any way abridged,* except for participation in rebellion, or other crime, the basis of representation therein shall be reduced in the proportion which the number of such male citizens shall bear to the whole number of male citizens twenty-one years of age in such State." (Emphasis added.)

The Amendment is a single text. It was introduced and discussed as such in the Reconstruction Committee, which reported it to the Congress. It was discussed as a unit in Congress and proposed as a unit to the States, which ratified it as a unit. A proposal to split up the Amendment and submit each section to the States as a separate amendment was rejected by the Senate. Whatever one might take to be the application to these cases of the Equal Protection Clause if it stood alone, I am unable to understand the Court's utter disregard of the second section which expressly recognizes the States' power to deny "or in any way" abridge the right of their inhabitants to vote for "the members of the [State] Legislature," and its express provision of a remedy for such denial or abridgment. The comprehensive scope of the second section and its particular reference to the state legislatures preclude the suggestion that the first section was intended to have the result reached by the Court today. If indeed the words of the Fourteenth Amendment speak for themselves, as the majority's disregard of history seems to imply, they speak as clearly as may be against the construction which the majority puts on them. But we are not limited to the language of the Amendment itself.

[Justice Harlan proceeds to set forth a detailed account of the proposal and ratification of the Fourteenth Amendment, concluding that Congress deliberately excluded from the Amendment any restriction on the states' power "to control voting rights because it believed that if such restrictions were included," the Amendment would not have been adopted.]

. . .

. . . these decisions give support to a current mistaken view of the Constitution and the constitutional function of this Court. This view, in a nutshell, is that every major social ill in this country can find its cure in some constitutional "principle," and that this Court should "take the lead" in promoting reform when other branches of government fail to act. The Constitution is not a panacea for every blot upon the public welfare, nor should this Court, ordained as a judicial body, be thought of as a general haven for reform movements. The Constitution is an instrument of government, fundamental to which is the premise that in a diffusion of governmental authority lies the greatest promise that this Nation will realize liberty for all its citizens. This Court, limited in function in accordance with that premise, does not serve its high purpose when it exceeds its authority, even to satisfy justified impatience with the slow workings of the political process. For when, in the name of constitutional interpretation, the Court *adds* something to the Constitution that was deliberately excluded from it, the Court in reality substitutes its view of what should be so for the amending process.

. . .

Davis v. Bandemer

478 U.S. 109 (1986)

A suit was brought by Indiana Democrats challenging the constitutionality of Indiana's 1981 state apportionment. They claimed that the apportionment, drawn up by Republicans, unconstitutionally diluted the votes of Democrats. A three-judge court sustained the equal protection challenge. The Supreme Court faced the question whether political gerrymandering cases are properly justiciable under the Equal Protection Clause. State officials, defending the apportionment, are represented here by Susan J. Davis. The position of Indiana Democrats is represented by Irwin C. Bandemer. In an interesting twist, the state Democrats were joined by the Republican National Committee, which hoped to use the case to challenge the reapportionment of other state legislatures, most of which are controlled by Democrats.

JUSTICE WHITE announced the judgment of the Court and delivered the opinion of the Court as to Part II and an opinion as to Parts I, III, and IV, in which JUSTICE BRENNAN, JUSTICE MARSHALL, and JUSTICE BLACKMUN join.

In this case, we review a judgment from a three-judge District Court, which sustained an equal protection challenge to Indiana's 1981 state apportionment on the basis that the law unconstitutionally diluted the votes of Indiana Democrats.

603 F.Supp. 1479 (1984). Although we find such political gerrymandering to be justiciable, we conclude that the District Court applied an insufficiently demanding standard in finding unconstitutional vote dilution. Consequently, we reverse.

I

The Indiana Legislature, also known as the "General Assembly," consists of a House of Representatives and a Senate. There are 100 members of the House of Representatives, and 50 members of the Senate. The members of the House serve two-year terms, with elections held for all seats every 2 years. The members of the Senate serve 4-year terms, and Senate elections are staggered so that half of the seats are up for election every two years. The members of both Houses are elected from legislative districts; but, while all Senate members are elected from single-member districts, House members are elected from a mixture of single-member and multi-member districts. The division of the State into districts is accomplished by legislative enactment, which is signed by the Governor into law. Reapportionment is required every 10 years and is based on the federal decennial census. There is no prohibition against more frequent reapportionments.

In early 1981, the General Assembly initiated the process of reapportioning the State's legislative districts pursuant to the 1980 census. At this time, there were Republican majorities in both the House and the Senate, and the Governor was Republican. Bills were introduced in both Houses, and a reapportionment plan was duly passed and approved by the Governor. This plan provided 50 single-member districts for the Senate; for the House, it provided 7 triple-member, 9 double-member, and 61 single-member districts. In the Senate plan, the population deviation between districts was 1.15%; in the House plan, the deviation was 1.05%. The multi-member districts generally included the more metropolitan areas of the State, although not every metropolitan area was in a multi-member district. Marion County, which includes Indianapolis, was combined with portions of its neighboring counties to form five triple-member districts. Fort Wayne was divided into two parts, and each part was combined with

portions of the surrounding county or counties to make two double-member districts. On the other hand, South Bend was divided and put partly into a double-member district and partly into a single-member district (each part combined with part of the surrounding county or counties). Although county and city lines were not consistently followed, township lines generally were. The two plans, the Senate and the House, were not nested; that is, each Senate district was not divided exactly into two House districts. There appears to have been little relation between the lines drawn in the two plans.

In early 1982, this suit was filed by several Indiana Democrats (here the appellees) against various state officials (here the appellants), alleging that the 1981 reapportionment plans constituted a political gerrymander intended to disadvantage Democrats. Specifically, they contended that the particular district lines that were drawn and the mix of single- and multi-member districts were intended to and did violate their right, as Democrats, to equal protection under the Fourteenth Amendment. A three-judge District Court was convened to hear these claims.

In November 1982, before the case went to trial, elections were held under the new districting plan. All of the House seats and half of the Senate seats were up for election. Over all the House races statewide, Democratic candidates received 51.9% of the vote. Only 43 Democrats, however, were elected to the House. Over all the Senate races statewide, Democratic candidates received 53.1% of the vote. Thirteen (of 25) Democrats were elected. In Marion and Allen Counties, both divided into multi-member House districts, Democratic candidates drew 46.6% of the vote, but only 3 of the 21 House seats were filled by Democrats.

On December 13, 1984, a divided District Court issued a decision declaring the reapportionment to be unconstitutional, enjoining the appellants from holding elections pursuant to the 1981 redistricting, ordering the General Assembly to prepare a new plan, and retaining jurisdiction over the case. See 603 F.Supp. 1479 (1984).

To the District Court majority, the results of the 1982 elections seemed "to support an argument that there is a built-in bias favoring the majority party, the Republicans, which instituted the reapportionment plan." *Id.*, at 1486. Although the court thought that these figures were unreliable predictors of future elections, it concluded that they warranted further examination of the circumstances surrounding the passage of the reapportionment statute. See *ibid.* In the course of this further examination, the court noted the irregular shape of some district lines, the peculiar mix of single- and multi-member districts, and the failure of the district lines to adhere consistently to political subdivision boundaries to define communities of interest. The court also found inadequate the other explanations given for the configuration of the districts, such as adherence to the one-person, one-vote imperative and the Voting Right Act's no retrogression requirement. These factors, concluded the court, evidenced an intentional effort to favor Republican incumbents and candidates and to disadvantage Democratic voters. This was achieved by "stacking" Democrats into districts with large Democratic majorities and "splitting" them in other districts so as to give Republicans safe but not excessive majorities in those districts. Because the 1982 elections indicated that the plan also had a discriminatory effect in that the proportionate voting influence of Democratic voters had been adversely affected and because any scheme "which purposely inhibit[s] or prevent[s] proportional representation cannot be tolerated," *id.*, at 1492, the District Court invalidated the statute.

The defendants appealed, seeking review of the District Court's rulings that the case was justiciable and that, if justiciable, an equal protection violation had occurred. We noted probable jurisdiction. 470 U.S. 1083 (1985).

II

We address first the question whether this case presents a justiciable controversy or a non-justiciable political question. Although the District Court never explicitly stated that the case was justiciable, its holding clearly rests on such a finding. The appellees urge that this Court has in the past acknowledged and acted upon the justiciability of purely political gerrymandering claims. The appellants contend that we have af-

firmed on the merits decisions of lower courts finding such claims to be nonjusticiable.

A

Since *Baker* v. *Carr*, 369 U.S. 186 (1962), we have consistently adjudicated equal protection claims in the legislative districting context regarding inequalities in population between districts. *[The Court reviews its principal holdings, including the principle "one person, one vote"; actions against racial gerrymandering; and decisions that struck down multimember districts that operated to minimize the voting strength of racial or political elements. Although the Court had summarily affirmed some lower-court decisions that rejected the justiciability of purely political gerrymandering, it stated that it was not bound by those affirmances. In addressing the issue of justiciability, the Court restates the political question doctrine announced in* Baker *v.* Carr. *In that case the Court held the state legislative apportionment scheme was justiciable in part because it did not involve a question decided, or to be decided, by a political branch of government coequal with the Supreme Court. Nor was there any risk of embarrassment of the U.S. government abroad or any risk of grave disturbance at home. The Court was also satisfied, in* Baker, *that judicially manageable standards were available.]*

This analysis applies equally to the question now before us. Disposition of this question does not involve us in a matter more properly decided by a coequal branch of our Government. There is no risk of foreign or domestic disturbance, and in light of our cases since *Baker* we are not persuaded that there are no judicially discernible and manageable standards by which political gerrymander cases are to be decided. *[The Court later adds that the fact that the claim "is submitted by a political group, rather than a racial group, does not distinguish it in terms of justiciability."]*

III

Having determined that the political gerrymandering claim in this case is justiciable, we turn to the question whether the District Court erred in holding that appellees had alleged and proved a violation of the Equal Protection Clause.

A

Preliminarily, we agree with the District Court that the claim made by the appellees in this case is a claim that the 1981 apportionment discriminates against Democrats on a statewide basis. Both the appellees and the District Court have cited instances of individual districting within the State which they believe exemplify this discrimination, but the appellees' claim as we understand it is that Democratic voters over the State as a whole, not Democratic voters in particular districts, have been subjected to unconstitutional discrimination. . . .

We also agree with the District Court that in order to succeed the Bandemer plaintiffs were required to prove both intentional discrimination against an identifiable political group and an actual discriminatory effect on that group. See, *e.g.*, *Mobile* v. *Bolden*, 446 U.S., at 67–68. Further, we are confident that if the law challenged here had discriminatory effects on Democrats, this record would support a finding that the discrimination was intentional. Thus, we decline to overturn the District Court's finding of discriminatory intent as clearly erroneous.

Indeed, quite aside from the anecdotal evidence, the shape of the House and Senate Districts, and the alleged disregard for political boundaries, we think it most likely that whenever a legislature redistricts, those responsible for the legislation will know the likely political composition of the new districts and will have a prediction as to whether a particular district is a safe one for a Democratic or Republican candidate or is a competitive district that either candidate might win. . . .

[From Gaffney *v.* Cummings, *412 U.S., at 752-753 (1973), the Court states that the consideration of political factors in a reapportionment plan is not sufficient to invalidate it. "Politics and political considerations are inseparable from districting and apportionment."]*

B

We do not accept, however, the District Court's legal and factual bases for concluding that the 1981 Act visited a sufficiently adverse effect on the appellees' constitutionally protected rights to make out a violation of the Equal Protection Clause. The District Court held that because any apportionment scheme that purposely prevents proportional representation is unconstitutional, Democratic voters need only show that their proportionate voting influence has been adversely affected. 603 F.Supp., at 1492. Our cases, however, clearly foreclose any claim that the Constitution requires proportional representation or that legislatures in reapportioning must draw district lines to come as near as possible to allocating seats to the contending parties in proportion to what their anticipated statewide vote will be. . . .

In cases involving individual multi-member districts, we have required a substantially greater showing of adverse effects than a mere lack of proportional representation to support a finding of unconstitutional vote dilution. Only where there is evidence that excluded groups have "less opportunity to participate in the political processes and to elect candidates of their choice" have we refused to approve the use of multimember districts. *Rogers* v. *Lodge*, 458 U.S., at 624 . . .

[Our] holdings rest on a conviction that the mere fact that a particular apportionment scheme makes it more difficult for a particular group in a particular district to elect the representatives of its choice does not render that scheme constitutionally infirm. This conviction, in turn, stems from a perception that the power to influence the political process is not limited to winning elections. An individual or a group of individuals who votes for a losing candidate is usually deemed to be adequately represented by the winning candidate and to have as much opportunity to influence that candidate as other voters in the district. We cannot presume in such a situation, without actual proof to the contrary, that the candidate elected will entirely ignore the interests of those voters. This is true even in a safe district where the losing group loses election after election. Thus, a group's electoral power is not unconstitutionally diminished by the simple fact of an apportionment scheme that makes winning elections more difficult, and a failure of proportional representation alone does not constitute impermissible discrimination under the Equal Protection Clause. See *Mobile* v.

Bolden, 446 U.S., at 111, n. 7 (MARSHALL, J., dissenting).

As with individual districts, where unconstitutional vote dilution is alleged in the form of statewide political gerrymandering, the mere lack of proportional representation will not be sufficient to prove unconstitutional discrimination. Again, without specific supporting evidence, a court cannot presume in such a case that those who are elected will disregard the disproportionately underrepresented group. Rather, unconstitutional discrimination occurs only when the electoral system is arranged in a manner that will consistently degrade a voter's or a group of voters' influence on the political process as a whole.

. . .

Based on these views, we would reject the District Court's apparent holding that *any* interference with an opportunity to elect a representative of one's choice would be sufficient to allege or make out an equal protection violation, unless justified by some acceptable state interest that the State would be required to demonstrate. In addition to being contrary to the above-described conception of an unconstitutional political gerrymander, such a low threshold for legal action would invite attack on all or almost all reapportionment statutes. District-based elections hardly ever produce a perfect fit between votes and representation. The one-person, one-vote imperative often mandates departure from this result as does the no-retrogression rule required by § 5 of the Voting Rights Act. Inviting attack on minor departures from some supposed norm would too much embroil the judiciary in second-guessing what has consistently been referred to as a political task for the legislature, a task that should not be monitored too closely unless the express or tacit goal is to effect its removal from legislative halls. We decline to take a major step toward that end, which would be so much at odds with our history and experience.

. . .

D

[In his concluding section, Justice White rejects an alternative method proposed by Justice Powell, who suggested a number of factors to consider in judging equal protection claims of political gerrymandering. White disagreed that the intentional drawing of district boundaries for partisan ends and for no other reason violates the Equal Protection Clause in and of itself.]

In sum, we decline to adopt the approach enunciated by JUSTICE POWELL. In our view, that approach departs from our past cases and invites judicial interference in legislative districting whenever a political party suffers at the polls. We recognize that our own view may be difficult of application. Determining when an electoral system has been "arranged in a manner that will consistently degrade a voter's or a group of voters' influence on the political process as a whole," *supra,* at 132, is of necessity a difficult inquiry. Nevertheless, we believe that it recognizes the delicacy of intruding on this most political of legislative functions and is at the same time consistent with our prior cases regarding individual multi-member districts, which have formulated a parallel standard.

IV

In sum, we hold that political gerrymandering cases are properly justiciable under the Equal Protection Clause. We also conclude, however, that a threshold showing of discriminatory vote dilution is required for a prima facie case of an equal protection violation. In this case, the findings made by the District Court of an adverse effect on the appellees do not surmount the threshold requirement. Consequently, the judgment of the District Court is

Reversed.

CHIEF JUSTICE BURGER, concurring in the judgment.

I join JUSTICE O'CONNOR's opinion.

. . .

JUSTICE O'CONNOR, with whom THE CHIEF JUSTICE and JUSTICE REHNQUIST join, concurring in the judgment.

Today the Court holds that claims of political gerrymandering lodged by members of one of the political parties that make up our two-party system are justiciable under the Equal Protection Clause of the Fourteenth Amendment. Nothing in our precedents compels us to take this step, and there is every reason not to do so. I would hold that the partisan gerrymandering claims of major political parties raise a nonjusticiable political question that the judiciary should leave to the legislative branch as the Framers of the Constitution unquestionably intended. Accordingly, I would reverse the District Court's judgment on the grounds that appellees' claim is nonjusticiable.

. . .

To turn these matters over to the federal judiciary is to inject the courts into the most heated partisan issues. It is predictable that the courts will respond by moving away from the nebulous standard a plurality of the Court fashions today and toward some form of rough proportional representation for all political groups. The consequences of this shift will be as immense as they are unfortunate. I do not believe, and the Court offers not a shred of evidence to suggest, that the Framers of the Constitution intended the judicial power to encompass the making of such fundamental choices about how this Nation is to be governed. Nor do I believe that the proportional representation towards which the Court's expansion of equal protection doctrine will lead is consistent with our history, our traditions, or our political institutions.

I

. . .

The step taken today is a momentous one, which if followed in the future can only lead to political instability and judicial malaise. If members of the major political parties are protected by the Equal Protection Clause from dilution of their voting strength, then members of every identifiable group that possesses distinctive interests and tends to vote on the basis of those interests should be able to bring similar claims. Federal courts will have no alternative but to attempt to recreate the complex process of legislative apportionment in the context of adversary litigation in order to reconcile the competing claims of political, religious, ethnic, racial, occupational, and socioeconomic groups. Even if there were some way of limiting such claims to organized political parties, the fact remains that the losing party or the losing group of legislators in every reapportionment will now be invited to fight the battle anew in federal court. . . .

. . . There is no proof before us that political gerrymandering is an evil that cannot be checked or cured by the people or by the parties themselves. Absent such proof, I see no basis for concluding that there is a need, let alone a constitutional basis, for judicial intervention.

. . .

JUSTICE POWELL, with whom JUSTICE STEVENS joins, concurring in Part II, and dissenting.

This case presents the question whether a state legislature violates the Equal Protection Clause by adopting a redistricting plan designed solely to preserve the power of the dominant political party, when the plan follows the doctrine of "one person, one vote" but ignores all other neutral factors relevant to the fairness of redistricting.

In answering this question, the plurality expresses the view, with which I agree, that a partisan political gerrymander violates the Equal Protection Clause only on proof of "both intentional discrimination against an identifiable political group and an actual discriminatory effect on that group." *Ante*, at 127. The plurality acknowledges that the record in this case supports a finding that the challenged redistricting plan was adopted for the purpose of discriminating against Democratic voters. *Ibid.* The plurality argues, however, that appellees failed to establish that their voting strength was diluted statewide despite uncontradicted proof that certain key districts were grotesquely gerrymandered to enhance the election prospects of Republican candidates. This argument appears to rest solely on the ground that the legislature accomplished its gerrymander consistent with "one person, one vote," in the sense that the legislature designed voting districts of approximately equal population and erected no direct barriers to Democratic voters' exercise of the franchise. Since the essence of a gerrymandering claim is that the members of a political party as a group have been denied their right to "fair and effective representation," *Reynolds* v. *Sims*, 377 U.S. 533, 565 (1964), I believe that the claim cannot be tested solely by reference to "one person, one vote." Rather, a number of other relevant neutral factors must be considered. Because the plurality ignores such factors and fails to enunciate standards by which to determine whether a legislature has enacted an unconstitutional gerrymander, I dissent.

. . .

II
A

Gerrymandering is "the deliberate and arbitrary distortion of district boundaries and populations for partisan or personal political purposes." *Kirkpatrick* v. *Preisler*, 394 U.S. 526, 538 (1969) (Fortas, J., concurring). As JUSTICE STEVENS correctly observed, gerrymandering violates the Equal Protection Clause only when the redistricting plan serves "no purpose other than to favor one segment—whether racial, ethnic, religious, economic, or political—that may occupy a position of strength at a particular time, or to disadvantage a politically weak segment of the community." *Karcher* v. *Daggett*, 462 U.S. 725, 748 (1983) concurring opinion).

The term "gerrymandering," however, is also used loosely to describe the common practice of the party in power to choose the redistricting plan that gives it an advantage at the polls. An intent to discriminate in this sense may be present whenever redistricting occurs. . . . Because it is difficult to develop and apply standards that will identify the unconstitutional gerrymander, courts may seek to avoid their responsibility to enforce the Equal Protection Clause by finding that a claim of gerrymandering is nonjusticiable. I agree with the plurality that such a course is mistaken, and that the allegations in this case raise a justiciable issue.

Moreover, I am convinced that appropriate judicial standards can and should be developed. Justice Fortas' definition of unconstitutional gerrymandering properly focuses on whether the boundaries of the voting districts have been distorted deliberately and arbitrarily to achieve illegitimate ends. *Kirkpatrick* v. *Preisler, supra,* at 538. Under this definition, the merits of a gerrymandering claim must be determined by reference to the configurations of the districts, the observance of political subdivision lines, and other criteria that have independent relevance to the fairness of redistricting. See *Karcher* v. *Daggett, supra,* at 755–759. (STEVENS, J., concurring). In this case, the District Court examined the redistricting in light of such factors and found, among other facts, that the boundaries of a number of districts were deliberately distorted to deprive Democratic voters of an equal opportunity to participate in the State's legislative processes. The plurality makes no reference to any of these findings of fact. It rejects the District Court's ultimate conclusion with no explanation of the respects in which appellees' proof fell short of establishing discriminatory effect. A brief review of the Court's jurisprudence in the context of another kind of challenge to redistricting, a claim of malapportionment, demonstrates the pressing need for the Court to enunciate standards to guide legislators who redistrict and judges who determine the constitutionality of the legislative effort.

B

The Equal Protection Clause guarantees citizens that their state will govern them impartially. See *Karcher* v. *Daggett, supra,* at 748 (STEVENS, J., concurring). In the context of redistricting, that guarantee is of critical importance because the franchise provides most citizens their only voice in the legislative process. *Reynolds* v. *Sims*, 377 U.S., at 561–562, 565–566. Since the contours of a voting district powerfully may affect citizens' ability to exercise influence through their vote, district lines should be determined in accordance with neutral and legitimate criteria. When deciding where those lines will fall, the state should treat its voters as standing in the same position, regardless of their political beliefs or party affiliation. *Chapman* v. *Meier*, 420 U.S. 1, 17 (1975); *Gaffney* v. *Cummings, supra,* at 751.

The first cases in which this Court entertained equal protection challenges to redistricting involved allegations that state legislatures had refused to redesign States' voting districts to eliminate gross population disparities among those districts. *E.g., Baker* v. *Carr,* 369 U.S. 186 (1962); *Reynolds* v. *Sims, supra.* The Court's decision in *Reynolds* v. *Sims* illustrates two concepts that are vitally important in evaluating an equal protection challenge to redistricting. First, the Court recognized that equal protection encompasses a guarantee of equal *representation,* requiring a State to seek to achieve through redistricting "fair and effective representation for all citizens." *Reynolds* v. *Sims, supra,* at 565–566; see *Gaffney* v. *Cummings,* 412 U.S., at 748. The concept of "representation" necessarily applies to groups: groups of voters elect representatives, individual voters do not. Gross population disparities violate the mandate of equal representation by denying voters residing in heavily populated districts, *as a group,* the opportunity to elect the number of representatives to which their voting strength otherwise would entitle them. . . .

C

. . .

The final and most basic flaw in the plurality's opinion is its failure to enunciate any standard that affords guidance to legislatures and courts. Legislators and judges are left to wonder whether compliance with "one person, one vote" completely insulates a partisan gerrymander from constitutional scrutiny, or whether a fairer but as yet undefined standard applies. The failure to articulate clear doctrine in this area places the plurality in the curious position of inviting further litigation even as it appears to signal the "constitutional green light" to would-be gerrymanderers.

. . .

Buckley v. Valeo

424 U.S. 1 (1976)

As a response to the scandals uncovered by the Watergate affair, Congress rewrote campaign finance laws to impose stricter limits on contributions and expenditures. The Federal Election Campaign Act Amendments of 1974 also created a Federal Election Commission (FEC) to enforce the statute. In *Buckley* v. *Valeo*, the Supreme Court considered the objectives of Congress in light of First Amendment freedoms of speech and association. It concluded that the restrictions on contributions were legitimate means to accomplish the purpose of combating campaign corruption, but held that the limits on expenditures violated the First Amendment. James L. Buckley, U.S. Senator, was the lead plaintiff in filing this case against Francis R. Valeo, Secretary of the Senate.

PER CURIAM.

These appeals present constitutional challenges to the key provisions of the Federal Election Campaign Act of 1971 (Act), and related provisions of the Internal Revenue Code of 1954, all as amended in 1974.

The Court of Appeals, in sustaining the legislation in large part against various constitutional challenges, viewed it as "by far the most comprehensive reform legislation [ever] passed by Congress concerning the election of the President, Vice-President, and members of Congress." 171

U. S. App. D. C. 172, 182, 519 F. 2d 821, 831 (1975). The statutes at issue summarized in broad terms, contain the following provisions: (a) individual political contributions are limited to $1,000 to any single candidate per election, with an overall annual limitation of $25,000 by any contributor; independent expenditures by individuals and groups "relative to a clearly identified candidate" are limited to $1,000 a year; campaign spending by candidates for various federal offices and spending for national conventions by political parties are subject to prescribed limits; (b) contributions and expenditures above certain threshold levels must be reported and publicly disclosed; (c) a system for public funding of Presidential campaign activities is established by Subtitle H of the Internal Revenue Code; and (d) a Federal Election Commission is established to administer and enforce the legislation.

This suit was originally filed by appellants in the United States District Court for the District of Columbia. Plaintiffs included a candidate for the Presidency of the United States, a United States Senator who is a candidate for re-election, a potential contributor, the Committee for a Constitutional Presidency—McCarthy '76, the Conservative Party of the State of New York, the Mississippi Republican Party, the Libertarian Party, the New York Civil Liberties Union, Inc., the American Conservative Union, the Conservative Victory Fund, and Human Events, Inc. The defendants included the Secretary of the United States Senate and the Clerk of the United States House of Representatives, both in their official capacities and as *ex officio* members of the Federal Election Commission. The Commission itself was named as a defendant. Also named were the Attorney General of the United States and the Comptroller General of the United States.

. . .

[After determining that the lawsuit constituted a "case or controversy" within the meaning of Article III of the Constitution, the Court turned to the merits.]

I. CONTRIBUTION AND EXPENDITURE LIMITATIONS

The intricate statutory scheme adopted by Congress to regulate federal election campaigns includes restrictions on political contributions and expenditures that apply broadly to all phases of and all participants in the election process. The major contribution and expenditure limitations in the Act prohibit individuals from contributing more than $25,000 in a single year or more than $1,000 to any single candidate for an election campaign and from spending more than $1,000 a year "relative to a clearly identified candidate." Other provisions restrict a candidate's use of personal and family resources in his campaign and limit the overall amount that can be spent by a candidate in campaigning for federal office.

The constitutional power of Congress to regulate federal elections is well established and is not questioned by any of the parties in this case. Thus, the critical constitutional questions presented here go not to the basic power of Congress to legislate in this area, but to whether the specific legislation that Congress has enacted interferes with First Amendment freedoms or invidiously discriminates against nonincumbent candidates and minor parties in contravention of the Fifth Amendment.

A. General Principles

The Act's contribution and expenditure limitations operate in an area of the most fundamental First Amendment activities. Discussion of public issues and debate on the qualifications of candidates are integral to the operation of the system of government established by our Constitution. The First Amendment affords the broadest protection to such political expression in order "to assure [the] unfettered interchange of ideas for the bringing about of political and social changes desired by the people." *Roth* v. *United States*, 354 U. S. 476, 484 (1957). . . .

The First Amendment protects political association as well as political expression. The constitutional right of association explicated in *NAACP* v. *Alabama*, 357 U. S. 449, 460 (1958), stemmed from the Court's recognition that "[e]ffective advocacy of both public and private points of view, particularly controversial ones, is undeniably enhanced by group association." . . .

It is with these principles in mind that we consider the primary contentions of the parties with respect to the Act's limitations upon the giving and spending of money in political campaigns. Those conflicting contentions could not more sharply define the basic issues before us. Appellees contend that what the Act regulates is conduct, and that its effect on speech and association is incidental at most. Appellants respond that contributions and expenditures are at the very core of political speech, and that the Act's limitations thus constitute restraints on First Amendment liberty that are both gross and direct.

. . .

A restriction on the amount of money a person or group can spend on political communication during a campaign necessarily reduces the quantity of expression by restricting the number of issues discussed, the depth of their exploration, and the size of the audience reached. This is because virtually every means of communicating ideas in today's mass society requires the expenditure of money. The distribution of the humblest handbill or leaflet entails printing, paper, and circulation costs. Speeches and rallies generally necessitate hiring a hall and publicizing the event. The electorate's increasing dependence on television, radio, and other mass media for news and information has made these expensive modes of communication indispensable instruments of effective political speech.

The expenditure limitations contained in the Act represent substantial rather than merely theoretical restraints on the quantity and diversity of political speech.

. . .

By contrast with a limitation upon expenditures for political expression, a limitation upon the amount that any one person or group may contribute to a candidate or political committee entails only a marginal restriction upon the contributor's ability to engage in free communication. A contribution serves as a general expression of support for the candidate and his views, but does not communicate the underlying basis for the support.

. . .

In sum, although the Act's contribution and expenditure limitations both implicate fundamental First Amendment interests, its expenditure ceilings impose significantly more severe restrictions on protected freedoms of political expression and association than do its limitations on financial contributions.

B. Contribution Limitations

1. The $1,000 Limitation on Contributions by Individuals and Groups to Candidates and Authorized Campaign Committees

Section 608(b) provides, with certain limited exceptions, that "no person shall make contributions to any candidate with respect to any election for Federal office which, in the aggregate, exceed $1,000." . . .

It is unnecessary to look beyond the Act's primary purpose—to limit the actuality and appearance of corruption resulting from large individual financial contributions—in order to find a constitutionally sufficient justification for the $1,000 contribution limitation. Under a system of private financing of elections, a candidate lacking immense personal or family wealth must depend on financial contributions from others to provide the resources necessary to conduct a successful campaign. The increasing importance of the communications media and sophisticated mass-mailing and polling operations to effective campaigning make the raising of large sums of money an ever more essential ingredient of an effective candidacy. To the extent that large contributions are given to secure a political *quid pro quo* from current and potential office holders, the integrity of our system of representative democracy is undermined. Although the scope of such pernicious practices can never be reliably ascertained, the deeply disturbing examples surfacing after the 1972 election demonstrate that the problem is not an illusory one.

. . .

We find that, under the rigorous standard of review established by our prior decisions, the weighty interests served by restricting the size of financial contributions to political candidates are sufficient to justify the limited effect upon First Amendment freedoms caused by the $1,000 contribution ceiling.

. . .

2. The $5,000 Limitation on Contributions by Political Committees

Section 608 (b)(2) permits certain committees, designated as "political committees," to contribute up to $5,000 to any candidate with respect to any election for federal office. In order to qualify for the higher contribution ceiling, a group must have been registered with the Commission as a political committee under 2 U. S. C. § 433 (1970 ed., Supp. IV) for not less than six months, have received contributions from more than 50 persons, and, except for state political party organizations, have contributed to five or more candidates for federal office. Appellants argue that these qualifications unconstitutionally discriminate against *ad hoc* organizations in favor of established interest groups and impermissibly burden free association. The argument is without merit. Rather than undermining freedom of association, the basic provision enhances the opportunity of bona fide groups to participate in the election process, and the registration, contribution, and candidate conditions serve the permissible purpose of preventing individuals from evading the applicable contribution limitations by labeling themselves committees.

3. Limitations on Volunteers' Incidental Expenses

The Act excludes from the definition of contribution "the value of services provided without compensation by individuals who volunteer a portion or all of their time on behalf of a candidate or political committee." § 591(e)(5)(A). Certain expenses incurred by persons in providing volunteer services to a candidate are exempt from the $1,000 ceiling only to the extent that they do not exceed $500. . . .

If, as we have held, the basic contribution limitations are constitutionally valid, then surely these provisions are a constitutionally acceptable accommodation of Congress' valid interest in encouraging citizen participation in political campaigns while continuing to guard against the corrupting potential of large financial contributions to candidates.

. . .

4. The $25,000 Limitation on Total Contributions During any Calendar Year

In addition to the $1,000 limitation on the nonexempt contributions that an individual may make to a particular candidate for any single election, the Act contains an overall $25,000 limitation on total contributions by an individual during any calendar year. § 608(b)(3). A contribution made in connection with an election is considered, for purposes of this subsection, to be made in the year the election is held. Although the constitutionality of this provision was drawn into question by appellants, it has not been separately addressed at length by the parties. The overall $25,000 ceiling does impose an ultimate restriction upon the number of candidates and committees with which an individual may associate himself by means of financial support. But this quite modest restraint upon protected political activity serves to prevent evasion of the $1,000 contribution limitation by a person who might otherwise contribute massive amounts of money to a particular candidate through the use of unearmarked contributions to political committees likely to contribute to that candidate, or huge contributions to the candidate's political party. The limited, additional restriction on associational freedom imposed by the overall ceiling is thus no more than a corollary of the basic individual contribution limitation that we have found to be constitutionally valid.

C. Expenditure Limitations

The Act's expenditure ceilings impose direct and substantial restraints on the quantity of political speech. The most drastic of the limitations restricts individuals and groups, including political parties that fail to place a candidate on the ballot, to an expenditure of $1,000 "relative to a clearly identified candidate during a calendar year." § 608(e)(1). Other expenditure ceilings limit spending by candidates, § 608(a), their campaigns, § 608(c), and political parties in connection with election campaigns, § 608(f). It is clear that a primary effect of these expenditure limitations is to restrict the quantity of campaign speech by individuals, groups, and candidates. . . .

We find that the governmental interest in preventing corruption and the appearance of corruption is inadequate to justify § 608(e)(1)'s ceiling on independent expenditures. First, assuming, *arguendo*, that large independent expenditures pose the same dangers of actual or apparent *quid pro quo* arrangements as do large contributions, § 608(e)(1) does not provide an answer that sufficiently relates to the elimination of those dangers. Unlike the contribution limitations' total ban on the giving of large amounts of money to candidates, § 608(e)(1) prevents only some large expenditures. So long as persons and groups eschew expenditures that in express terms advocate the election or defeat of a clearly identified candidate, they are free to spend as much as they want to promote the candidate and his views. . . .

For the reasons stated, we conclude that § 608(e)(1)'s independent expenditure limitation is unconstitutional under the First Amendment.

2. Limitation on Expenditures by Candidates from Personal or Family Resources

The Act also sets limits on expenditures by a candidate "from his personal funds, or the personal funds of his immediate family, in connection with his campaigns during any calendar year." § 608(a)(1). These ceilings vary from $50,000 for Presidential or Vice Presidential candidates to $35,000 for senatorial candidates, and $25,000 for most candidates for the House of Representatives.

The ceiling on personal expenditures by candidates on their own behalf, like the limitations on independent expenditures contained in § 608(e)(1), imposes a substantial restraint on the ability of persons to engage in protected First Amendment expression. The candidate, no less than any other person, has a First Amendment right to engage in the discussion of public issues and vigorously and tirelessly to advocate his own election and the election of other candidates. . . .

The primary governmental interest served by the Act—the prevention of actual and apparent corruption of the political process—does not support the limitation on the candidate's expenditure of his own personal funds. As the Court of Appeals concluded: "Manifestly, the core problem of avoiding undisclosed and undue influence on candidates from outside interests has lesser application when the monies involved come from the candidate himself or from his immediate family." 171 U. S. App. D. C., at 206, 519 F. 2d, at 855. Indeed, the use of personal funds reduces the candidate's dependence on outside contributions and thereby counteracts the coercive pressures and attendant risks of abuse to which the Act's contribution limitations are directed.

. . .

3. Limitations on Campaign Expenditures
Section 608(c) places limitations on overall campaign expenditures by candidates seeking nomination for election and election to federal office. . . .

No governmental interest that has been suggested is sufficient to justify the restriction on the quantity of political expression imposed by § 608(c)'s campaign expenditure limitations. The major evil associated with rapidly increasing campaign expenditures is the danger of candidate dependence on large contributions. The interest in alleviating the corrupting influence of large contributions is served by the Act's contribution limitations and disclosure provisions rather than by § 608(c)'s campaign expenditure ceilings. The Court of Appeals' assertion that the expenditure restrictions are necessary to reduce the incentive to circumvent direct contribution limits is not persuasive. . . .

II. REPORTING AND DISCLOSURE REQUIREMENTS

Unlike the limitations on contributions and expenditures imposed by 18 U. S. C. § 608 (1970 ed., Supp. IV), the disclosure requirements of the Act, 2 U. S. C. § 431 et seq. (1970 ed., Supp. IV), are not challenged by appellants as per se unconstitutional restrictions on the exercise of First Amendment freedoms of speech and association. Indeed, appellants argue that "narrowly drawn disclosure requirements are the proper solution to virtually all of the evils Congress sought to remedy."

. . .

Each political committee is required to register with the Commission, § 433, and to keep detailed records of both contributions and expenditures, §§ 432(c), (d). These records must include the name and address of everyone making a contribution in excess of $10, along with the date and amount of the contribution. If a person's contributions aggregate more than $100, his occupation and principal place of business are also to be included. § 432(c)(2). These files are subject to periodic audits and field investigations by the Commission. § 438(a)(8).

. . .

In summary, we find no constitutional infirmities in the recordkeeping, reporting, and disclosure provisions of the Act.

III. PUBLIC FINANCING OF PRESIDENTIAL ELECTION CAMPAIGNS

A series of statutes for the public financing of Presidential election campaigns produced the scheme now found in § 6096 and Subtitle H of the Internal Revenue Code of 1954, 26 U. S. C. §§ 6096, 9001–9012, 9031–9042 (1970 ed., Supp. IV). Both the District Court, 401 F. Supp. 1235, and the Court of Appeals, 171 U. S. App. D. C., at 229–238, 519 F. 2d, at 878–887, sustained Subtitle H against a constitutional attack. Appellants renew their challenge here, contending that the legislation violates the First and Fifth Amendments. We find no merit in their claims and affirm.

A. Summary of Subtitle H

Section 9006 establishes a Presidential Election Campaign Fund (Fund), financed from general revenues in the aggregate amount designated by individual taxpayers, under § 6096, who on their income tax returns may authorize payment to the Fund of one dollar of their tax liability in the case of an individual return or two dollars in the case of a joint return. The Fund consists of three separate accounts to finance (1) party nominating conventions, § 9008(a), (2) general election campaigns, § 9006(a), and (3) primary campaigns, § 9037(a).

. . .

For expenses in the general election campaign, § 9004(a)(1) entitles each major-party candidate to $20,000,000. This amount is also adjusted for inflation. See § 9004(a)(1). To be eligible for funds the candidate must pledge not to incur expenses in excess of the entitlement under § 9004(a)(1) and not to accept private contributions except to the extent that the fund is insufficient to provide the full entitlement. § 9003(b). . . .

B. Constitutionality of Subtitle H

Appellants argue that Subtitle H is invalid (1) as "contrary to the 'general welfare,'" Art. I, § 8, (2) because any scheme of public financing of election campaigns is inconsistent with the First Amendment, and (3) because Subtitle H invidiously discriminates against certain interests in violation of the Due Process Clause of the Fifth Amendment. We find no merit in these contentions.

Appellants' "general welfare" contention erroneously treats the General Welfare Clause as a limitation upon congressional power. It is rather a grant of power, the scope of which is quite expansive, particularly in view of the enlargement of power by the Necessary and Proper Clause. *M'Culloch* v. *Maryland,* 4 Wheat. 316, 420 (1819). Congress has power to regulate Presidential elections and primaries, *United States* v. *Classic,* 313 U. S. 299 (1941); *Burroughs* v. *United States,* 290 U. S. 534 (1934); and public financing of Presidential elections as a means to reform the electoral process was clearly a choice within the granted power. It is for Congress to decide which expenditures will promote the general welfare: "[T]he power of Congress to authorize expenditure of public moneys for public purposes is not limited by the direct grants of legislative power found in the Constitution." *United States* v. *Butler,* 297 U. S. 1, 66 (1936). See *Helvering* v. *Davis,* 301 U. S. 619, 640–641 (1937). Any limitations upon the exercise of that granted power must be found elsewhere in the Constitution. In this case, Congress was legislating for the "general welfare"—to reduce the deleterious influence of large contributions on our political process, to facilitate communication by candidates with the electorate, and to free candidates from the rigors of fundraising. See S. Rep. No. 93-689, pp. 1–10 (1974). Whether the chosen means appear "bad," "unwise," or "unworkable" to us is irrelevant; Congress has concluded that the means are "necessary and proper" to promote the general welfare, and we thus decline to find this legislation without the grant of power in Art. I, § 8.

. . .

MR. JUSTICE STEVENS took no part in the consideration or decision of these cases.

. . .

MR. CHIEF JUSTICE BURGER, concurring in part and dissenting in part.

For reasons set forth more fully later, I dissent from those parts of the Court's holding sustaining the statutory provisions (a) for disclosure of small contributions, (b) for limitations on contributions, and (c) for public financing of Presidential campaigns. In my view, the Act's disclosure scheme is impermissibly broad and violative of the First Amendment as it relates to reporting contributions in excess of $10 and $100. The contribution limitations infringe on First Amendment liberties and suffer from the same infirmities that the Court correctly sees in the expenditure ceilings. The system for public financing of Presidential campaigns is, in my judgment, an impermissible intrusion by the Government into the traditionally private political process.

. . . it seems to me that the threshold limits fixed at $10 and $100 for anonymous contributions are constitutionally impermissible on their face. As the Court's opinion notes, *ante*, at 83, Congress gave little or no thought, one way or the other, to these limits, but rather lifted figures out of a 65-year-old statute. As we are all painfully aware, the 1976 dollar is not what it used to be and is surely not the dollar of 1910. Ten dollars in 1976 will, for example, purchase only what $1.68 would buy in 1910. United States Dept. of Labor, Handbook of Labor Statistics 1975, p. 313 (Dec. 1975). To argue that a 1976 contribution of $10 or $100 entails a risk of corruption or its appearance is simply too extravagant to be maintained. No public right to know justifies the compelled disclosure of such contributions, at the risk of discouraging them. There is, in short, no relation whatever between the means used and the legitimate goal of ventilating possible undue influence. Congress has used a shotgun to kill wrens as well as hawks.

. . .

I agree fully with that part of the Court's opinion that holds unconstitutional the limitations the Act puts on campaign expenditures which "place substantial and direct restrictions on the ability of candidates, citizens, and associations to engage in protected political expression, restrictions that the First Amendment cannot tolerate." *Ante*, at 58–59. Yet when it approves similarly stringent limitations on contributions, the Court ignores the reasons it finds so persuasive in the context of expenditures. For me contributions and expenditures are two sides of the same First Amendment coin.

. . . the inappropriateness of subsidizing, from general revenues, the actual political dialogue of the people—the process which begets the Government itself—is as basic to our national tradition as the separation of church and state also deriving from the First Amendment, see *Lemon* v. *Kurtzman*, 403 U. S. 602, 612 (1971); *Walz* v. *Tax Comm'n*, 397 U. S. 664, 668–669 (1970), or the separation of civilian and military authority, see *Orloff* v. *Willoughby*, 345 U. S. 83, 93–94 (1953), neither of which is explicit in the Constitution but both of which have developed through case-by-case adjudication of express provisions of the Constitution.

. . .

MR. JUSTICE WHITE, concurring in part and dissenting in part.

[He dissents from the Court's view that the expenditure limits violate the First Amendment.]

It would make little sense to me, and apparently made none to Congress, to limit the amounts an individual may give to a candidate or spend with his approval but fail to limit the amounts that could be spent on his behalf. Yet the Court permits the former while striking down the latter limitation. No more than $1,000 may be given to a candidate or spent at his request or with his approval or cooperation; but otherwise, apparently, a contributor is to be constitutionally protected in spending unlimited amounts of money in support of his chosen candidate or candidates.

Let us suppose that each of two brothers spends $1 million on TV spot announcements that he has individually prepared and in which he appears, urging the election of the same named candidate in identical words. One brother has sought and obtained the approval of the candidate; the other has not. The former may validly be prosecuted under § 608(e); under the Court's view, the latter may not, even though the candidate could scarcely help knowing about and appreciating the expensive favor. For constitutional purposes it is difficult to see the difference between the two situations. I would take the word of those who know—that limiting independent expenditures is essential to prevent transparent and widespread evasion of the contribution limits.

. . .

I also disagree with the Court's judgment that § 608(a), which limits the amount of money that a candidate or his family may spend on his campaign, violates the Constitution. Although it is true that this provision does not promote any interest in preventing the corruption of candidates, the provision does, nevertheless, serve salutary purposes related to the integrity of federal campaigns. By limiting the importance of personal wealth, § 608(a) helps to assure that only individuals with a modicum of support from others will be viable candidates. This in turn would tend to discourage any notion that the outcome of elections is primarily a function of money. Similarly, § 608(a) tends to equalize access to the political arena, encouraging the less wealthy, unable to bankroll their own campaigns, to run for political office.

As with the campaign expenditure limits, Congress was entitled to determine that personal wealth ought to play a less important role in political campaigns than it has in the past. Nothing in the First Amendment stands in the way of that determination.

. . .

MR. JUSTICE MARSHALL, concurring in part and dissenting in part.

I join in all of the Court's opinion except Part I–C–2, which deals with 18 U. S. C. § 608(a) (1970 ed., Supp. IV). That section limits the amount a candidate may spend from his personal funds, or family funds under his control, in connection with his campaigns during any calendar year. See *ante,* at 51–52, n. 57. The Court invalidates § 608(a) as violative of the candidate's First Amendment rights. "[T]he First Amendment," the Court explains, "simply cannot tolerate § 608(a)'s restriction upon the freedom of a candidate to speak without legislative limit on behalf of his own candidacy." *Ante,* at 54. I disagree.

. . .

MR. JUSTICE BLACKMUN, concurring in part and dissenting in part.

I am not persuaded that the Court makes, or indeed is able to make, a principled constitutional distinction between the contribution limitations, on the one hand, and the expenditure limitations, on the other, that are involved here. I therefore do not join Part I–B of the Court's opinion or those portions of Part I–A that are consistent with Part I–B. As to those, I dissent.

[Justice Blackmun also dissented from the Court's responses to limits on contributions, limits on incidental expenditures by volunteers, and the definition of "political committee."]

MR. JUSTICE REHNQUIST, concurring in part and dissenting in part.

[Justice Rehnquist dissented from the Court's opinion that certain aspects of the statutory treatment of minor parties and independent candidates are constitutionally valid.]

. . . Congress in this legislation has . . . enshrined the Republican and Democratic Parties in a permanently preferred position, and has established requirements for funding minor-party and independent candidates to which the two major parties are not subject. Congress would undoubtedly be justified in treating the Presidential candidates of the two major parties differently from minor-party or independent Presidential candidates, in view of the long demonstrated public support of the former. But because of the First Amendment overtones of the appellants' Fifth Amendment equal protection claim, something more than a merely rational basis for the difference in treatment must be shown, as the Court apparently recognizes. I find it impossible to subscribe to the Court's reasoning that because no third party has posed a credible threat to the two major parties in Presidential elections since 1860, Congress may by law attempt to assure that this pattern will endure forever.

I would hold that, as to general election financing, Congress has not merely treated the two major parties differently from minor parties and independents, but has discriminated in favor of the former in such a way as to run afoul of the Fifth and First Amendments to the United States Constitution.

Madison's Views on Factions

In Federalist No. 10, James Madison defines *faction* as citizens "united and actuated by some common impulse of passion, or of interest, adverse to the rights of other citizens, or to the permanent and aggregate interests of the community." As a very rough and often unfair characterization, the definition could apply to interest groups or the even more pejorative "lobbyists." In a careful and insightful analysis, Madison reconciles the activity of factions to democratic government.

Among the numerous advantages promised by a well-constructed Union, none deserves to be more accurately developed than its tendency to break and control the violence of faction. The friend of popular governments never finds himself so much alarmed for their character and fate, as when he contemplates their propensity to this dangerous vice. He will not fail, therefore, to set a due value on any plan which, without violating the principles to which he is attached, provides a proper cure for it. The instability, injustice, and confusion introduced into the public councils, have, in truth, been the mortal diseases under which popular governments have everywhere perished; as they continue to be the favorite and fruitful topics from which the adversaries to liberty derive their most specious declamations. The valuable improvements made by the American constitutions on the popular models, both ancient and modern, cannot certainly be too much admired; but it would be an unwarrantable partiality, to contend that they have as effectually obviated the danger on this side, as was wished and expected. Complaints are everywhere heard from our most considerate and virtuous citizens, equally the friends of public and private faith, and of public and personal liberty, that our governments are too unstable, that the public good is disregarded in the conflicts of rival parties, and that measures are too often decided, not according to the rules of justice and the rights of the minor party, but by the superior force of an interested and overbearing majority. However anxiously we may wish that these complaints had no foundation, the evidence of known facts will not permit us to deny that they are in some degree true. It will be found, indeed, on a candid review of our situation, that some of the distresses under which we labor have been erroneously charged on the operation of our governments; but it will be found, at the same time, that other causes will not alone account for many of our heaviest misfortunes; and, particularly, for that prevailing and increasing distrust of public engagements, and alarm for private rights, which are echoed from one end of the continent to the other. These must be chiefly, if not wholly, effects of the unsteadiness and injustice with which a factious spirit has tainted our public administrations.

By a faction, I understand a number of citizens, whether amounting to a majority or minority of the whole, who are united and actuated by some common impulse of passion, or of interest, adverse to the rights of other citizens, or to the permanent and aggregate interests of the community.

There are two methods of curing the mischiefs of faction: the one, by removing its causes; the other, by controlling its effects.

There are again two methods of removing the causes of faction: the one, by destroying the liberty which is essential to its existence; the other, by giving to every citizen the same opinions, the same passions, and the same interests.

It could never be more truly said than of the first remedy, that it was worse than the disease. Liberty is to faction what air is to fire, an aliment without which it instantly expires. But it could not be less folly to abolish liberty, which is essential to political life, because it nourishes faction, than it would be to wish the annihilation of air, which is essential to animal life, because it imparts to fire its destructive agency.

The second expedient is as impracticable as the first would be unwise. As long as the reason of man continues fallible, and he is at liberty to exercise it, different opinions will be formed. As long as the connection subsists between his reason and his self-love, his opinions and his passions will have a reciprocal influence on each other: and the former will be objects to which the latter will attach themselves. The diversity in the faculties of men, from which the rights of property originate, is not less an insuperable obstacle to a uniformity of interests. The protection of these faculties is the first object of government. From the protection of different and unequal faculties of acquiring property, the possession of different degrees and kinds of property immediately results; and from the influence of these on the sentiments and views of the respective proprietors, ensues a division of the society into different interests and parties.

The latent causes of faction are thus sown in the nature of man; and we see them everywhere brought into different degrees of activity, according to the different circumstances of civil society. A zeal for different opinions concerning religion, concerning government, and many other points, as well of speculation as of practice; an attachment to different leaders ambitiously contending for pre-eminence and power; or to persons of other descriptions whose fortunes have been interesting to the human passions, have, in turn, divided mankind into parties, inflamed them with mutual animosity, and rendered them much more disposed to vex and oppress each other than to co-operate for their common good. So strong is this propensity of mankind to fall into mutual animosities, that where no substantial occasion presents itself, the most frivolous and fanciful

distinctions have been sufficient to kindle their unfriendly passions and excite their most violent conflicts. But the most common and durable source of factions has been the various and unequal distribution of property. Those who hold and those who are without property have ever formed distinct interests in society. Those who are creditors, and those who are debtors, fall under a like discrimination. A landed interest, a manufacturing interest, a mercantile interest, a moneyed interest, with many lesser interests, grow up of necessity in civilized nations, and divide them into different classes, actuated by different sentiments and views. The regulation of these various and interfering interests forms the principal task of modern legislation, and involves the spirit of party and faction in the necessary and ordinary operations of the government.

No man is allowed to be a judge in his own cause, because his interest would certainly bias his judgment, and, not improbably, corrupt his integrity. With equal, nay with greater reason, a body of men are unfit to be both judges and parties at the same time; yet what are many of the most important acts of legislation, but so many judicial determinations, not indeed concerning the rights of single persons, but concerning the rights of large bodies of citizens? And what are the different classes of legislators but advocates and parties to the causes which they determine? Is a law proposed concerning private debts? It is a question to which the creditors are parties on one side and the debtors on the other. Justice ought to hold the balance between them. Yet the parties are, and must be, themselves the judges; and the most numerous party, or, in other words, the most powerful faction must be expected to prevail. Shall domestic manufactures be encouraged, and in what degree, by restrictions on foreign manufactures? are questions which would be differently decided by the landed and the manufacturing classes, and probably by neither with a sole regard to justice and the public good. The apportionment of taxes on the various descriptions of property is an act which seems to require the most exact impartiality; yet there is, perhaps, no legislative act in which greater opportunity and temptation are given to a predominant party to trample on the rules of justice. Every shilling with which they overburden the inferior number, is a shilling saved to their own pockets.

It is in vain to say that enlightened statesmen will be able to adjust these clashing interests, and render them all subservient to the public good. Enlightened statesmen will not always be at the helm. Nor, in many cases, can such an adjustment be made at all without taking into view indirect and remote considerations, which will rarely prevail over the immediate interest which one party may find in disregarding the rights of another or the good of the whole.

The inference to which we are brought is, that the *causes* of faction cannot be removed, and that relief is only to be sought in the means of controlling its *effects*.

If a faction consists of less than a majority, relief is supplied by the republican principle, which enables the majority to defeat its sinister views by regular vote. It may clog the administration, it may convulse the society; but it will be unable to execute and mask its violence under the forms of the Constitution. When a majority is included in a faction, the form of popular government, on the other hand, enables it to sacrifice to its ruling passion or interest both the public good and the rights of other citizens. To secure the public good and private rights against the danger of such a faction, and at the same time to preserve the spirit and the form of popular government, is then the great object to which our inquiries are directed. Let me add that it is the great desideratum by which this form of government can be rescued from the opprobrium under which it has so long labored, and be recommended to the esteem and adoption of mankind.

By what means is this object attainable? Evidently by one of two only. Either the existence of the same passion or interest in a majority at the same time must be prevented, or the majority, having such coexistent passion or interest, must be rendered, by their number and local situation, unable to concert and carry into effect schemes of oppression. If the impulse and the opportunity be suffered to coincide, we well know that neither moral nor religious motives can be relied on as an adequate control. They are not found to be such

on the injustice and violence of individuals, and lose their efficacy in proportion to the number combined together, that is, in proportion as their efficacy becomes needful.

From this view of the subject it may be concluded that a pure democracy, by which I mean a society consisting of a small number of citizens, who assemble and administer the government in person, can admit of no cure for the mischiefs of faction. A common passion or interest will, in almost every case, be felt by a majority of the whole; a communication and concert result from the form of government itself; and there is nothing to check the inducements to sacrifice the weaker party or an obnoxious individual. Hence it is that such democracies have ever been spectacles of turbulence and contention; have ever been found incompatible with personal security or the rights of property; and have in general been as short in their lives as they have been violent in their deaths. Theoretic politicians, who have patronized this species of government, have erroneously supposed that by reducing mankind to a perfect equality in their political rights, they would, at the same time, be perfectly equalized and assimilated in their possessions, their opinions, and their passions.

A republic, by which I mean a government in which the scheme of representation takes place, opens a different prospect, and promises the cure for which we are seeking. Let us examine the points in which it varies from pure democracy, and we shall comprehend both the nature of the cure and the efficacy which it must derive from the Union.

The two great points of difference between a democracy and a republic are: first, the delegation of the government, in the latter, to a small number of citizens elected by the rest; secondly, the greater number of citizens, and greater sphere of country, over which the latter may be extended.

The effect of the first difference is, on the one hand, to refine and enlarge the public views, by passing them through the medium of a chosen body of citizens, whose wisdom may best discern the true interest of their country, and whose patriotism and love of justice will be least likely to sacrifice it to temporary or partial considerations.

Under such a regulation, it may well happen that the public voice, pronounced by the representatives of the people, will be more consonant to the public good than if pronounced by the people themselves, convened for the purpose. On the other hand, the effect may be inverted. Men of factious tempers, of local prejudices, or of sinister designs, may, by intrigue, by corruption, or by other means, first obtain the suffrages, and then betray the interests, of the people. The question resulting is, whether small or extensive republics are more favorable to the election of proper guardians of the public weal; and it is clearly decided in favor of the latter by two obvious considerations:

In the first place, it is to be remarked that, however small the republic may be, the representatives must be raised to a certain number, in order to guard against the cabals of a few; and that, however large it may be, they must be limited to a certain number, in order to guard against the confusion of a multitude. Hence, the number of representatives in the two cases not being in proportion to that of the two constituents, and being proportionally greater in the small republic, it follows that, if the proportion of fit characters be not less in the large than in the small republic, the former will present a greater option, and consequently a greater probability of a fit choice.

In the next place, as each representative will be chosen by a greater number of citizens in the large than in the small republic, it will be more difficult for unworthy candidates to practise with success the vicious arts by which elections are too often carried; and the suffrages of the people being more free, will be more likely to centre in men who possess the most attractive merit and the most diffusive and established characters.

It must be confessed that in this, as in most other cases, there is a mean, on both sides of which inconveniences will be found to lie. By enlarging too much the number of electors, you render the representative too little acquainted with all their local circumstances and lesser interests; as by reducing it too much, you render him unduly attached to these, and too little fit to comprehend and pursue great and national objects. The federal Constitution forms a happy combination in this respect; the great and aggregate interests being referred to the national, the local and particular to the State legislatures.

The other point of difference is, the greater number of citizens and extent of territory which may be brought within the compass of republican than of democratic government; and it is this circumstance principally which renders factious combinations less to be dreaded in the former than in the latter. The smaller the society, the fewer probably will be the distinct parties and interests composing it; the fewer the distinct parties and interests, the more frequently will a majority be found of the same party; and the smaller the number of individuals composing a majority, and the smaller the compass within which they are placed, the most easily will they concert and execute their plans of oppression. Extend the sphere, and you take in a greater variety of parties and interests; you make it less probable that a majority of the whole will have a common motive to invade the rights of other citizens; or if such a common motive exists, it will be more difficult for all who feel it to discover their own strength, and to act in unison with each other. Besides other impediments, it may be remarked that, where there is a consciousness of unjust or dishonorable purposes, communication is always checked by distrust in proportion to the number whose concurrence is necessary.

Hence, it clearly appears, that the same advantage which a republic has over a democracy, in controlling the effects of faction, is enjoyed by a large over a small republic,—is enjoyed by the Union over the States composing it. Does the advantage consist in the substitution of representatives whose enlightened views and virtuous sentiments render them superior to local prejudices and to schemes of injustice? It will not be denied that the representation of the Union will be most likely to possess these requisite endowments. Does it consist in the greater security afforded by a greater variety of parties, against the event of any one party being able to outnumber and oppress the rest? In an equal degree does the increased variety of parties comprised within the Union, increase this security. Does it, in fine, consist in the greater obstacles opposed to the concert and accomplishment of the secret wishes of an unjust and interested majority? Here, again, the extent of the Union gives it the most palpable advantage.

The influence of factious leaders may kindle a flame within their particular States, but will be unable to spread a general conflagration through the other States. A religious sect may degenerate into a political faction in a part of the Confederacy; but the variety of sects dispersed over the entire face of it must secure the national councils against any danger from that source. A rage for paper money, for an abolition of debts, for an equal division of property, or for any other im-

proper or wicked project, will be less apt to pervade the whole body of the Union than a particular member of it; in the same proportion as such a malady is more likely to taint a particular county or district, than an entire State.

In the extent and proper structure of the Union, therefore, we behold a republican remedy for the diseases most incident to republican government. And according to the degree of pleasure and pride we feel in being republicans, ought to be our zeal in cherishing the spirit and supporting the character of Federalists.

PUBLIUS

19 Efforts to Curb the Court

ustice Stone once lectured his brethren: "the only check upon our own exercise of power is our own sense of self-restraint." United States v. Butler, 297 U.S. 1, 79 (1936). While that is an important check, it is by no means the only one. Judges act within an environment that constantly tests the reasonableness and acceptability of their rulings. Courts issue the "last word" only for an instant, for after the release of an opinion the process of interaction begins: with Congress, the President, executive agencies, states, professional associations, law journals, and the public at large.

Earlier chapters identified some of the constraints that operate on the judiciary: the President's power to appoint; the Senate's power to confirm; congressional powers over the purse, impeachment, and court jurisdiction; and the force of public opinion, the press, and scholarly studies. Other restraints, covered in this chapter, include constitutional amendments, statutory reversals, changing the number of Justices (court packing), withdrawing jurisdiction, and noncompliance with court rulings.

Court-curbing periods often emerge when the judiciary acts by nullifying statutes, particularly those passed by Congress. But the judiciary can also create enemies by *upholding* legislation, such as the broad nationalist rulings issued by Chief Justice John Marshall. To restrain the courts, members of Congress introduce a variety of legislative bills and constitutional amendments. Hearings are held to explore ways to curb the judiciary. State legislatures prepare petitions of protest; state judges pass resolutions of "concern," if not condemnation. To reduce the tension, the federal judiciary may decide to conduct a partial and possibly graceful retreat.

Judicial-congressional confrontations were especially sharp between 1858 and 1869 (reflecting the *Dred Scott* case and congressional efforts to protect Reconstruction legislation), 1935 and 1937 (reacting to the Court's nullification of New Deal legislation), and 1955 and 1959 (triggered by decisions involving desegregation, congressional investigations, and national security).[1] A new round of court-curbing efforts began in the late 1970s to challenge judicial rulings on school prayer, school busing, and abortion.

The judiciary is most likely to be out of step with Congress or the President during periods of electoral and partisan realignment, when the country is undergoing sharp shifts in political directions while the courts retain the orientation of an age gone by.[2] During earlier periods, attacks on the judiciary generally came from liberal groups: Jeffersonians, Jacksonians, Radical Republicans, LaFollette Republicans, and New Deal Democrats. However, conservatives dominated the 1955–1959 confrontation and have inspired most of the court-curbing efforts since then.

CONSTITUTIONAL AMENDMENTS

Whenever two-thirds of both Houses of Congress deem it necessary, they may propose amendments to the Constitution. Ratification requires three-fourths of the states. Alternatively, two-thirds of the states may call a convention for constitutional amendment, but thus far all successful amendments have been initiated by Congress. The process of amending the Constitution is extraordinarily difficult and time-consuming. On only four occasions has Congress successfully used constitutional amendments to reverse Supreme Court decisions.

The Eleventh Amendment responded to *Chisholm* v. *Georgia*, 2 U.S. (2 Dall.) 419 (1793), which decided that a state could be sued in federal court by a plaintiff from another state. The lower house of the Georgia legislature adopted the modest proposal that any federal marshal attempting to enforce that ruling would be guilty of a felony and hanged until death "without the benefit of the clergy." To protect states from a flood of costly citizen suits, Congress quickly passed a constitutional amendment. Although a sufficient number of states ratified it by 1795, not until 1798 did President John Adams notify Congress that the amendment was effective. The Eleventh Amendment reads: "The Judicial power of the United States shall not be construed to extend to any suit in law or equity, commenced or prosecuted against one of the United States by Citizens of another State, or by Citizens or Subjects of any Foreign States."

The Fourteenth Amendment nullified the Supreme Court's decision in *Dred Scott* v. *Sandford*, 60 U.S. (19 How.) 393 (1857), which held that blacks as a class were not citizens protected under the Constitution. After the nation had fought a bloody civil war, North against South, the Fourteenth Amendment was ratified in 1868. Section 1 provides: "All persons born or naturalized in the United States and subject to the jurisdiction thereof, are citizens of the United States and of the State wherein they reside." *Dred Scott* had been partially reversed by statute in 1862 when Congress passed legislation to prohibit slavery in the territories. 12 Stat. 432.

The Sixteenth Amendment overruled *Pollock* v. *Farmers' Loan and Trust Co.*, 157 U.S. 429 (1895), which struck down a federal income tax. The need to finance

---

[1]See Stuart S. Nagel, "Court-Curbing Periods in American History," 18 Vand. L. Rev. 925 (1965). For a review of proposals to remedy judicial activism, see Charles Grove Haines, The American Doctrine of Judicial Supremacy 467–499 (1932).

[2]Richard Funston, "The Supreme Court and Critical Elections," 69 Am. Pol. Sci. Rev. 795 (1975); David Adamany, "Legitimacy, Realigning Elections, and the Supreme Court," 1973 Wisc. L. Rev. 790.

national expansion and new international responsibilities, combined with a desire to reduce the dependence on high tariffs as the main source of revenue, triggered the drive for a constitutional amendment. Ratified in 1913, the Sixteenth Amendment gave Congress the power "to lay and collect taxes on incomes, from whatever source derived, without apportionment among the several States, and without regard to any census or enumeration."

The Twenty-sixth Amendment was ratified in 1971 to overturn *Oregon* v. *Mitchell*, 400 U.S. 112 (1970), a Supreme Court decision of the previous year that had voided a congressional effort to lower the minimum voting age in state elections to eighteen. As a way to encourage youths to participate constructively in the political process and to avoid the cost of a dual registration system of eighteen years for national elections and twenty-one years for state and local elections, Congress sent a constitutional amendment to the states. In record time, three months later, a sufficient number of states ratified this language: "The right of citizens of the United States, who are eighteen years of age or older, to vote shall not be denied or abridged by the United States or any State on account of age."

Other constitutional amendments, driven by seemingly irresistible political forces, have fallen by the wayside. A successful amendment process requires an extraordinary combination of social, economic, and political forces. If any one of these factors is absent, an amendment may fail. For example, Congress made a concerted effort in 1964 to amend the Constitution to overturn the Supreme Court's decisions in the reapportionment and school prayer cases. Because of delays by House committees and filibusters on the Senate side, these efforts proved fruitless.

Even when Congress reacts against a Court decision by clearing an amendment for ratification by the states, the hurdles are immense. After the Supreme Court in 1918 and 1922 denied Congress the right to regulate child labor conditions, opponents of the Court rulings tried unsuccessfully to reverse them by constitutional amendment. Hammer v. Dagenhart, 247 U.S. 251 (1918); Bailey v. Drexel Furniture Co., 259 U.S. 20 (1922). In 1924, both Houses of Congress passed a constitutional amendment to give Congress the power to "limit, regulate and prohibit the labor of persons under 18 years of age." By 1937, only twenty-eight of the necessary thirty-six states had ratified the amendment. The issue became moot after Congress passed the Fair Labor Standards Act of 1938 and the Supreme Court upheld it three years later. United States v. Darby, 312 U.S. 100 (1941).

Once the Constitution is successfully amended to overturn a Court decision, there is no guarantee that the judiciary will interpret the amendment consistent with the intent of the framers and ratifiers. Although the Thirteenth, Fourteenth, and Fifteenth Amendments were meant to overturn *Dred Scott* and protect the rights of blacks, such decisions as *The Civil Rights Cases*, 109 U.S. 3 (1883) and *Plessy* v. *Ferguson*, 163 U.S. 537 (1896), were more in line with racial attitudes that flourished before the Civil War.

In addition to constitutional amendments aimed at particular decisions, there have been other proposals aimed at curbing the Court's strength by imposing certain procedural requirements. These amendments have in every instance been unsuccessful. Of recurring interest are the following: requiring more than a majority of Justices to strike down a statute; subjecting the Court's decisions to another tribunal, such as the Senate or a judicial body consisting of a judge from each state; submitting the Court's decisions to popular referenda; allowing Congress by two-thirds vote to override a Court decision just as it does a presidential veto; and making laws held unconstitutional by the Court valid if reenacted by Congress.

Other amendments are directed at the Court's tenure and qualifications: allowing the removal of Supreme Court Justices and other federal judges by majority vote of each House of Congress; restricting the term of a Justice to a set number of years; having Justices retire at the age of 75 years; requiring direct election from the judicial districts; itemizing the qualifications for Justices, such as requiring prior judicial service in the highest court of a state or excluding anyone who has, within the preceding five years, served in the executive or legislative branch; and vesting the appointment of Justices in judges from the highest state courts.[3] Although unsuccessful in every case, these amendments serve the purpose of venting popular and professional resentment toward Court decisions and may even temper future rulings.

STATUTORY REVERSALS

When decisions turn on the interpretation of federal statutes, Congress may overturn a ruling simply by passing a new statute to clarify legislative intent. The private sector often uses Congress as an "appellate court" to reverse judicial interpretations of a statute. At a congressional hearing in 1959, Congressman Wilbur Mills leaned across the witness table and told a company president: "It seems that it is becoming more and more almost a full-time job of the Congress to correct the Supreme Court's desire to legislate." The company president, seeking to have a major Supreme Court decision modified to his advantage, nodded his approval.[4]

In 1969, the Supreme Court struck down a joint operating agreement by two newspapers on the ground that it violated the Antitrust Act. Citizen Publishing Co. v. United States, 394 U.S. 131 (1969). Congress responded within a year with the Newspaper Preservation Act, specifically exempting from the Act any authorizing agreement needed to prevent newspapers from going out of business. 84 Stat. 466 (1970).

Judicial-legislative conversations helped shape the meaning of the Freedom of Information Act (FOIA). In one case, thirty-three members of the House of Representatives went to court to obtain documents prepared for President Nixon concerning an underground nuclear test. In 1973, the Supreme Court decided that it had no authority to examine the documents *in camera* to sift out "non-secret components" for their release. EPA v. Mink, 410 U.S. 73 (1973). Congress passed legislation a year later to override the decision, clearly authorizing federal courts to examine sensitive records in judges' chambers. 88 Stat. 1562, § 4(B) (1974).

A more recent example of statutory reversal involved *Smith* v. *Robinson*, 468 U.S. 992 (1984), in which the Supreme Court held that parents who brought legal action to obtain schooling for their handicapped child were not entitled to attorney's fees if they prevailed in the litigation. Congress had passed legislation to provide special education to handicapped children, but the Court decided from the statutory

---

[3]Maurice S. Culp, "A Survey of the Proposals to Limit or Deny the Power of Judicial Review by the Supreme Court of the United States," 4 Ind. L. J. 386 (1929); Shelden D. Elliott, "Court-Curbing Proposals in Congress," 33 Notre Dame Lawyer 597, 606 (1958).

[4]Emmette S. Redford, et al., Politics and Government in the United States 518 (1965).

arrangement that Congress had not intended that attorney's fees be awarded. Justice Brennan, writing a dissent joined by Justices Marshall and Stevens, said that "with today's decision . . . Congress will now have to take the time to revisit the matter" of attorney's fees. Id. at 1030–1031. Legislation amended the Education of the Handicapped Act to authorize the award of attorney's fees to prevailing parties. 100 Stat. 796 (1986).

Another successful congressional effort concerned the case of *Grove City College* v. *Bell*, 465 U.S. 555 (1984). Title IX of the Education Amendments of 1972 prohibited sex discrimination in any education program or activity that received federal financial assistance. After the Reagan administration had issued statements indicating that its interpretation of Title IX was not as broad as previous administrations', the House of Representatives on November 16, 1983, passed a resolution by a vote of 414–8 opposing the administration's position. The resolution stated the sense of the House that Title IX and regulations issued pursuant to the title "should not be amended or altered in any manner which will lessen the comprehensive coverage of such statute in eliminating gender discrimination throughout the American educational system." The resolution, of course, was not legally binding, but it was passed because the Supreme Court was about to hear oral argument on the *Grove City* case. As Congressman Paul Simon noted: "Passing this resolution the House can send the Court a signal that we believe that no institution should be allowed to discriminate on the basis of sex if it receives Federal funds." 129 Cong. Rec. H10087 (daily ed. November 16, 1983).

The issue before the Court was whether Title IX required federal funds to be terminated only for specific programs in which discrimination occurs or for the entire educational institution. The Supreme Court adopted the narrower interpretation. Justices Brennan and Marshall dissented in part, stating that the Court was ignoring congressional intent for institution-wide coverage. Within four months the House of Representatives, by a vote of 375–32, passed legislation to amend not only Title IX but also three other statutes to adopt broad coverage of the antidiscrimination provisions. 130 Cong. Rec. 18880 (1984). See reading on pp. 1333–1335. The Senate resisted action that year, and subsequent efforts were complicated by questions of church-state and abortion. Finally, in 1988, Congress was able to forge a compromise. President Reagan vetoed the measure, but both Houses overrode the veto to enact the broader coverage for civil rights that had been rejected in *Grove City*.

Also in 1988, Congress passed two other statutes to reverse the Supreme Court. In one decision, the Court ruled that federal employees could be sued for common law torts committed on the job. They were not entitled to absolute immunity from lawsuit. However, the Court remarked: "Congress is in the best position to provide guidance for the complex and often highly empirical inquiry into whether absolute immunity is warranted in a particular context." Westfall v. Erwin, 108 S.Ct. 580, 585 (1988). Congress passed legislation to overturn this decision by protecting federal employees from personal liability for common law torts committed within the scope of their employment. The statute provides the injured person with a remedy against the United States government. Thus, compensation would come from the U.S. Treasury, not the employee's pocketbook. 102 Stat. 4563 (1988).

The other statutory reversal in 1988 concerned a Supreme Court decision that accepted the definition of the Veterans Administration that alcoholism results from "willful misconduct" rather than from a disease. For those who regarded the

Court's position as erroneous, they were advised that their arguments would be "better presented to Congress than to the courts." Traynor v. Turnage, 108 S.Ct. 1372, 1383–1384 (1988). Legislation enacted by Congress recognized that veterans seeking education or rehabilitation would not be denied those benefits under the willful-misconduct standard. 102 Stat. 4170, § 109 (1988).

These cases involve matters of statutory interpretation, an area in which Congress can ultimately prevail. But even in cases where constitutional rights are present, Congress may pass legislation to modify a Court ruling. A 1957 case involved access by defendants to government files bearing on their trial. On the basis of statements by two informers for the FBI, the government prosecuted Clinton Jencks for failing to state that he was a member of the Communist party. He asked that the FBI reports be turned over to the trial judge for examination to determine whether they had value in impeaching the statements of the two informers. The Supreme Court went beyond Jencks' request by ordering the government to produce for *his* inspection all FBI reports "touching the events and activities" at issue in the trial. Jencks v. United States, 353 U.S. 657, 668 (1957). The Court specifically rejected the option of producing government documents to the trial judge for his determination of relevancy and materiality. Id. at 669.

In their concurrence, Justices Burton and Harlan believed that Jencks was only entitled to have the records submitted to the trial judge. A dissent by Justice Clark agreed that the documents should be delivered only to the trial judge. In a remarkable statement he incited Congress to act: "Unless the Congress changes the rule announced by the Court today, those intelligence agencies of our Government engaged in law enforcement may as well close up shop, for the Court has opened their files to the criminal and thus afforded him a Roman holiday for rummaging through confidential information as well as vital national secrets."

The Court announced its decision on June 3, 1957. Both Houses of Congress quickly held hearings and reported remedial legislation. The "Jencks Bill" (after much redrafting) passed the Senate by voice vote on August 26 and passed the House on August 27 by a vote of 351 to 17. The conference report was adopted with huge majorities: 74–2 in the Senate and 315–0 in the House. The bill became law on September 2. The statute provides that in any federal criminal prosecution, no statement or report in the possession of the government "which was made by a Government witness or prospective Government witness (other than the defendant) to an agent of the Government shall be the subject of subpena, discovery, or inspection unless said witness has testified on direct examination in the trial of the case." If a witness testifies, statements may be delivered to the defendant for examination and use unless the United States claims that the statement contains irrelevant matter, in which case the statement shall be inspected by the court *in camera*. The judge may excise irrelevant portions of the statement before submitting it to the defendant. 71 Stat. 595 (1957); 18 U.S.C. § 3500 (1982).

Members of Congress wanted to overturn other decisions from the 1950s and 1960s affecting criminal rights, but it took a combination of urban riots, high crime rates, and the assassinations of Martin Luther King, Jr., and Robert F. Kennedy to create momentum for the Omnibus Crime Control and Safe Streets Act of 1968. Title II responded to three controversial decisions on criminal procedure: *Mallory* v. *United States*, 354 U.S. 449 (1957), *Miranda* v. *Arizona*, 384 U.S. 436 (1966), and *United States* v. *Wade*, 388 U.S. 218 (1967).

Mallory held that suspects must be taken before a magistrate for arraignment as quickly as possible. Admissions obtained from the suspect during illegal detainment could not be used against him. The Court invited congressional participation by basing its decision not on constitutional interpretation but rather on the Federal Rules of Criminal Procedure. Law enforcement officers had held Mallory for about twenty hours before bringing him before a magistrate. His confession during that period, the Court said, violated the congressional requirement for a prompt arraignment "without unnecessary delay." The decision therefore allowed Congress to enter the arena and modify the rules of criminal procedure. Title II established six hours as a reasonable period before arraignment. 18 U.S.C. § 3501(c) (1982).

Miranda provided that confessions by criminal suspects could not be used unless they had first been informed of their rights by law enforcement officers. It is unclear whether the majority opinion is grounded on constitutional principles or statutory rules of evidence. The Court reviewed the history of the Fifth Amendment privilege against self-incrimination, spoke of the "constitutional issue we decide in each of these cases," and said that "the issues presented are of constitutional dimensions and must be determined by the courts." But it also referred to the Federal Rules of Criminal Procedure and welcomed Congress to contribute its handiwork:

> It is impossible for us to foresee the potential alternatives for protecting the privilege which might be devised by Congress or the States in the exercise of their creative rule-making capacities. Therefore we cannot say that the Constitution necessarily requires adherence to any particular solution for the inherent compulsions of the interrogation process as it is presently conducted. Our decision in no way creates a constitutional straitjacket which will handicap sound efforts at reform, nor is it intended to have this effect. We encourage Congress and the States to continue their laudable search for increasingly effective ways of protecting the rights of the individual while promoting efficient enforcement of our criminal laws. 384 U.S. at 467.

In his dissent, Justice Harlan objected that the Court's decision represented "poor constitutional law" and threatened to harm the country (pp. 1336–1337). The majority's opinion, combined with the force of the dissenting opinions, set the stage for legislative action. Title II allowed for the admissibility of confessions if voluntarily given. Trial judges would determine the issue of voluntariness after taking into consideration all the circumstances surrounding the giving of the confession, including five elements specified by Congress. 18 U.S.C. § 3501(a) and (c) (1982).

In *Wade*, the Court decided that if an accused was denied the right to counsel during a police lineup, identification would be inadmissible. The Court seemed to suggest that legislative or other regulations, such as those developed by local police departments, might eliminate "the risks of abuse and unintentional suggestion at lineup proceedings," but that "neither Congress nor the Federal authorities have seen fit to provide a solution." 388 U.S. at 239. Title II provided that *eyewitness* testimony would be admissible as evidence in any criminal prosecution, regardless of whether the accused had an attorney present at the lineup. 18 U.S.C. § 3502(c) (1982).

COURT PACKING

Congress has altered the number of Justices on the Supreme Court throughout its history. Congress authorized six Justices in 1789, lowered that to five in the ill-fated

Judiciary Act of 1801, returned it to six a year later, and increased the number in subsequent years to keep pace with the creation of new circuits. Since 1869, the number of Justices has remained fixed at nine. Appointments to the Court have often produced marked changes in judicial policy, as witnessed by the abrupt shift in the Legal Tender Cases (p. 150). In none of these earlier examples was the alteration of court size linked so blatantly to changing judicial policy as in FDR's court-packing plan.

In his Inaugural Address in 1933, Franklin D. Roosevelt struck a confident note for presidential-judicial relations. He said that the Constitution "is so simple and practical that it is possible always to meet extraordinary needs by changes in emphasis and arrangement without loss of essential form." Privately, he tempered his hope with the knowledge that members on the Supreme Court were essentially conservative and business-oriented.

Presidential optimism was routed on "Black Monday," May 27, 1935, when the Supreme Court unanimously struck down the National Industrial Recovery Act (NIRA). Schechter Corp. v. United States, 295 U.S. 495 (1935). On that same day it ruled that Presidents could remove members of independent regulatory commissions only by following the statutory reasons for removal, and it held unconstitutional a statute for the relief of farm mortgagors. Humphrey's Executor v. United States, 295 U.S. 602 (1935); Louisville Bank v. Radford, 295 U.S. 555 (1935). The fact that all nine Justices had declared the NIRA unconstitutional suggested the futility of trying to "pack" the Court. Feeling betrayed by the liberal members on the Court, Roosevelt asked plaintively: "Well, where was Ben Cardozo? And what about old Isaiah [Brandeis]?"[5] Direct attacks on the Court were shelved after the public reacted unfavorably to Roosevelt's sneering accusation at a press conference that the Justices had adopted a "horse-and-buggy definition of interstate commerce." At a cabinet meeting in December 1935, Roosevelt reviewed several methods of restraining the Court. Packing the Court, Interior Secretary Harold Ickes recorded in his diary, "was a distasteful idea." 1 The Secret Diary of Harold L. Ickes 495 (1953).

Roosevelt's indignation at the judiciary was further aroused on January 6, 1936, when the Court struck down the processing tax in the Agricultural Adjustment Act. The ruling divided the Court, 6 to 3, with Justice Stone penning a stinging dissent. He reminded his colleagues on the Court that they were not the only branch of government assumed to have the capacity to govern. United States v. Butler, 297 U.S. at 87. This time there appeared to be a ground swell of public support for adding younger Justices more attuned to the temper of the times. Yet Roosevelt bided his time, not wanting to give his opponents in an election year the opportunity to rally behind the Constitution and the Court. Other decisions in 1936, striking down federal and state laws, provided extra incentives to curb the Court. Some of those decisions attracted three or four dissents.[6] The climate for curbing the Court was further encouraged by the national popularity of The Nine Old Men (1936), a caustic portrait of the Justices written by Drew Pearson and Robert Allen. Peppered by such

[5]William E. Leuchtenburg, "The Origins of Franklin D. Roosevelt's 'Court-Packing' Plan," 1966 Sup. Ct. Rev. 347, 357.

[6]Jones v. SEC, 298 U.S. 1 (1936) (Cardozo, Brandeis, and Stone dissenting); St. Joseph Stock Yards Co. v. United States, 298 U.S. 38 (1936) (Cardozo, Brandeis, and Stone dissenting in part); Carter v. Carter Coal Co., 298 U.S. 238 (1936); Morehead v. New York ex rel. Tipaldo, 298 U.S. 587 (1936) (Hughes, Brandeis, Stone, and Cardozo dissenting).

chapters as "The Lord High Executioners," the book charged that "justice has no relation whatsoever to popular will. Administrations may come and go, the temper of the people may reverse itself, economic conditions may be revolutionalized, the Nine Old Men sit on."

Roosevelt's landslide victory in 1936, capturing all but two states, paved the way for a direct assault on the Court. Constitutional amendments seemed to him wholly impracticable. They were difficult to frame and nearly impossible to pass. Statutory remedies, such as requiring a unanimous or 8-to-1 decision in the Supreme Court to invalidate a law, were of doubtful constitutionality and could be easily overturned by the Court. After rejecting a number of alternatives, he considered court packing the only feasible solution.

Working closely with his Attorney General and Solicitor General, but without the advice of congressional leaders, Roosevelt ordered the preparation of a draft bill. The President would be authorized to nominate Justices to the Supreme Court whenever an incumbent over the age of 70 declined to resign or retire. He proposed the same procedure for the lower courts, limiting the number of additional appointments to fifty and setting the maximum size of the Supreme Court at fifteen. Under this scenario, Roosevelt could name as many as six new Justices to the Supreme Court. When he submitted his proposal to Congress on February 5, 1937, he attempted to disguise it primarily as an economy and efficiency measure. Additional Justices would help relieve the delay and congestion he claimed resulted from aged or infirm judges. FDR's "indirection" (a euphemism for his deception and deviousness) offended some potential supporters. Robert H. Jackson, who served as Solicitor General and Attorney General under Roosevelt before being appointed to the Supreme Court in 1941, admitted that the plan "lacked the simplicity and clarity which was the President's genius and, to men not learned in the procedures of the Court, much of it seemed technical and confusing." Robert H. Jackson, The Struggle for Judicial Supremacy 189 (1941).

Roosevelt soon revealed his real purpose: to pack the Supreme Court with liberal Justices. In a "fireside chat" on March 9, 1937, he told the country that he wanted a Supreme Court that "will enforce the Constitution as written." But a mechanical application of that document by six additional Justices would not alleviate the problem Roosevelt faced. Later in that address he called for judges "who will bring to the Courts a present-day sense of the Constitution." He wanted "younger men who have had personal experience and contact with modern facts and circumstances." More concretely, he promised to appoint Justices "who will not undertake to override the judgment of the Congress on legislative policy." The result of this reform, he said, would be a "reinvigorated, liberal-minded Judiciary."

The Senate Judiciary Committee denounced Roosevelt's bill. Its report methodically and mercilessly shreds the bill's premises, structure, content, and motivation. This searing indictment constituted an extraordinary determination on the part of the committee to pulverize Roosevelt's creation and bury it forever. The first of six reasons for rejecting the plan bluntly noted: "the bill does not accomplish any one of the objectives for which it was originally offered." S. Rept. No. 711, 75th Cong., 1st Sess., 3 (1937). Among other points in this scathing attack, the committee said that the courts "with the oldest judges have the best records in the disposition of business." The bill called for retirement only for judges who had served for ten years (penalizing not age itself but age combined with experience). Nothing in the bill prevented Roosevelt from nominating someone 69 years and 11 months of age without prior judicial service. The result could be a Court of fifteen members, all of them over 70, and with no means of altering its composition. To the committee, the bill had one purpose and one purpose only: to apply force to the judiciary.

The committee condemned the bill as a "needless, futile, and utterly dangerous abandonment of constitutional principle." The report's harsh language (pp. 1337–1341) was designed to repudiate the bill so emphatically "that its parallel will never again be presented to the free representatives of the free people of America." The committee's position was reinforced by a letter from Chief Justice Hughes stating that the Court was "fully abreast of its work" and there was "no congestion of cases upon our calendar."

A number of unexpected developments sealed the fate of the court-packing bill. Senate Majority Leader Joe Robinson, who Roosevelt hoped would steer the bill through the Senate, died on July 14 after a week of debate in the sweltering capital. By that time the Court had already begun to modify some of its earlier rulings. On March 29, 1937, it upheld a state law establishing a minimum wage law for women, basically reversing a decision handed down ten months earlier.[7] This reversal occurred because of a change in position by Justice Roberts, or what has been called the "switch in time that saved nine." However, before FDR submitted his court-packing plan, Roberts had already broken with his doctrinaire laissez-faire colleagues. He wrote the opinion for a 5–4 Court in *Nebbia* v. *New York*, 291 U.S. 502 (1934), upholding a New York price-setting statute. With his support, the Court was prepared to sustain minimum-wage legislation in the fall of 1936 but had delayed its ruling because of Justice Stone's illness. Late in 1936, Roberts had voted with the liberals to affirm a state unemployment insurance law.[8]

Other decisions in 1937 confirmed that the Court had become more accepting of New Deal programs. Roosevelt remarked with obvious relish: "The old minority of 1935 and 1936 had become the majority of 1937—without a single new appointment of a justice!"[9] Because Congress finally passed legislation early in 1937 to provide full judicial pay during retirement, Justice Van Devanter stepped down on June 2, 1937, giving Roosevelt his first chance in more than four years to nominate a Justice to the Supreme Court. Other retirements were imminent. Within a matter of months, the need for the court-packing plan had evaporated. President Roosevelt would be able to "reorganize" the Court through the regular constitutional process.

---

[7] West Coast Hotel Co. v. Parrish, 300 U.S. 379 (1937), overturning Adkins v. Children's Hospital, 261 U.S. 525 (1923) and "distinguishing" (in fact reversing) Morehead v. New York ex rel. Tipaldo, 298 U.S. 587 (1936).

[8] W. H. H. Chamberlin, Inc. v. Andrews, 299 U.S. 515, decided November 23, 1936. The Court was equally divided. For Roberts' vote, see John W. Chambers, "The Big Switch: Justice Roberts and the Minimum-Wage Cases," 10 Labor Hist. 44, 57 (1969). See also Felix Frankfurter, "Mr. Justice Roberts," 104 U. Pa. L. Rev. 311 (1955); 2 Merlo J. Pusey, Charles Evans Hughes 757 (1963). For a challenge to Roberts' recollection of key events in 1936, see Clement E. Vose, Constitutional Change: Amendment Politics and Supreme Court Litigation Since 1900 228–234 (1972).

[9] 6 Public Papers and Addresses of Franklin D. Roosevelt 1xviii (1941). See also Virginian Ry. v. Federation, 300 U.S. 515 (1937); Wright v. Vinton Branch, 300 U.S. 440 (1937); NLRB v. Jones & Laughlin, 301 U.S. 1 (1937); NLRB v. Fruehauf Co., 301 U.S. 49 (1937); NLRB v. Clothing Co., 301 U.S. 58 (1937); Steward Machine Co. v. Davis, 301 U.S. 548 (1937); Helvering v. Davis, 301 U.S. 619 (1937).

WITHDRAWING JURISDICTION

During the past decade Congress has been under strong pressure to withdraw the Supreme Court's jurisdiction to hear appeals in cases of abortion, school busing, school prayer, and other issues on the conservatives' "social agenda." This strategy is based on language in Article III of the Constitution: "The Supreme Court shall have appellate jurisdiction, both as to law and fact, with such exceptions, and under such regulations, as the Congress shall make." The Exceptions Clause, it is argued, gives Congress plenary power to determine the Court's appellate jurisdiction.

Although this approach appears to be grounded on constitutional language, the Exceptions Clause must be read in concert with other provisions in the Constitution. An aggressive use of the Exceptions Clause by Congress would make an exception the rule and deny citizens access to the Supreme Court to vindicate constitutional rights. Stripping the Supreme Court of jurisdiction to hear certain issues would vest ultimate judicial authority in the lower federal and state courts, producing contradictory and conflicting legal doctrines.

A more radical proposal would prevent even the lower federal courts from ruling on specific social issues. Under Article III, the judicial power is vested in a Supreme Court "and in such inferior Courts as the Congress may from time to time ordain and establish." Because Congress creates the lower courts, it may by statute confer, define, and withdraw jurisdiction. Sheldon v. Sill, 49 U.S. (8 How.) 441, 449 (1950). Although Congress has withdrawn jurisdiction to adjudicate certain issues, the exercise of that power "is subject to compliance with at least the requirements of the Fifth Amendment. That is to say, while Congress has the undoubted power to give, withhold, and restrict the jurisdiction of courts other than the Supreme Court, it must not so exercise that power as to deprive any person of life, liberty, or property without due process of law or to take private property without just compensation." Battaglia v. General Motors Corp., 169 F.2d 254, 257 (2d Cir. 1948), cert. denied, 335 U.S. 887 (1948). To deny the lower federal courts jurisdiction to hear claims arising under the Constitution would upset the system of checks and balances, alter the balance of power between the national government and the states, and strengthen the force of majority rule over individual rights (pp. 1343–1344).

Withdrawing appellate jurisdiction from the Supreme Court and withdrawing jurisdiction from the lower federal courts would also undercut the Supremacy Clause in Article VI, which states that the Constitution and federal laws "made in Pursuance thereof . . . shall be the supreme Law of the Land; and the Judges in every State shall be bound thereby, any Thing in the Constitution or Laws of any State to the contrary notwithstanding." In 1982, the chief justices of the highest state courts issued a unanimous resolution expressing "serious concerns" about bills introduced in Congress to give the states sole authority to decide certain social issues. Among other objections, the chief justices pointed out that the result of such legislation would be contrary to what conservatives professed to be their goal. Instead of overturning Supreme Court decisions, they would be "cast in stone" when state judges continued to honor their oaths to obey the federal Constitution and to give full force (pursuant to the Supremacy Clause) to Supreme Court precedents. The practical effect, therefore, would be to place a body of legal doctrine outside the reach of federal courts or state courts either to alter or overrule. 128 Cong. Rec. 689–690 (1982).

Members of Congress have also attempted to use their power to enforce the Fourteenth Amendment as a lever to alter the jurisdiction of the federal courts. Section 5 of the Fourteenth Amendment gives Congress the power "to enforce, by appropriate legislation," the provisions of that Amendment. In 1981, the Senate Judiciary Committee held hearings on a bill that looked to Section 5 as the vehicle for overturning the Supreme Court's 1973 abortion decision. The hearings covered the scope of Section 5, the issue of whether Congress would be exercising judgments over "facts" or "law," and a possible shift of balance of power between the national government and the states (pp. 1344–1348).

The McCardle Case

In a number of early decisions, the Supreme Court recognized the power of Congress to make exceptions and to regulate the Court's appellate jurisdiction.[10] For example, in 1847 the Court stated that it possessed "no appellate power in any case, unless conferred upon it by act of Congress; nor can it, when conferred be exercised in any other form, or by any other mode of proceeding than that which the law prescribes." Barry v. Mercein, 5 How. 103, 119 (1847). These early decisions stated the congressional power too broadly, as will be shown.

The leading case for empowering Congress to withdraw appellate jurisdiction from the Supreme Court is *Ex parte McCardle* (1869). In 1868, Congress withdrew the Court's jurisdiction to review circuit court judgments on habeas corpus actions. The clear purpose was to prevent the Court from deciding a case on the constitutionality of the Reconstruction military government in the South, even though the Court had already heard oral argument in the case of William McCardle. He had been held in custody awaiting trial by military commission, charged with publishing articles that incited "insurrection, disorder, and violence." Under an act of February 5, 1867, he petitioned a federal circuit court for the writ of habeas corpus. The writ was issued, directing the military commander to deliver McCardle to a federal marshal. After the commander complied with the writ (denying that the restraint was unlawful), the circuit court rejected McCardle's petition.

At that point McCardle appealed to the Supreme Court. On February 17, 1868, the Court dismissed the government's argument that the Court lacked jurisdiction to hear the case. 73 U.S. (6 Wall.) 318 (1868). The case was argued March 2, 3, 4, and 9. Before the Court could meet in conference to decide the case, Congress passed legislation to nullify McCardle's relief under the act of February 5, 1867. The new legislation provided that the portion of the 1867 statute that authorized an appeal from the judgment of the circuit court to the Supreme Court, "or the exercise of any such jurisdiction by said Supreme Court on appeals which have been or may hereafter be taken, be, and the same is, hereby repealed." 15 Stat. 44 (1868). Congress wanted to sweep McCardle's case from the docket, fearing that the Court might use it to invalidate the Reconstruction laws.

In a unanimous opinion upholding the repeal statute, Chief Justice Chase stated that the Court was "not at liberty to inquire into the motives of the legislature. We can only examine into its power under the Constitution; and the power to make

---

[10]Wiscart v. Dauchy, 3 Dall. 321 (1796); Durousseau v. United States, 10 U.S. (6 Cr.) 306 (1810); Daniels v. Railroad Co., 70 U.S. (3 Wall.) 250, 254 (1866).

exceptions to the appellate jurisdiction of this court is given by express words." EX PARTE MCCARDLE, 74 U.S. (7 Wall.) 506, 514 (1869). The Court dismissed the case for want of jurisdiction. The Court might have used Section 14 of the Judiciary Act of 1789 to review habeas corpus actions. 1 Stat. 81–82, § 14. But to do that in the face of the repeal statute, with the prospect of overturning Reconstruction legislation, invited a high-risk collision with Congress. The House of Representatives had already passed legislation to require a two-thirds majority of the Court to invalidate a federal statute, and some of the more rambunctious Radicals wanted to abolish the Supreme Court.

There is some question whether Congress acted under the Exceptions Clause, even though it forms the basis for the Court's decision. Congress may have merely repealed a special statutory right of access that it had previously granted. As the Court noted a year later, Congress did not repeal alternative rights of access, such as under the Judiciary Act of 1789 and later statutes that expanded the writ of habeas corpus. Ex parte Yerger, 75 U.S. (8 Wall.) 85, 101–102 (1869).

McCardle remains in a shadowy realm, surrounded on both sides by conflicting cases that both limit and legitimate congressional power under the Exceptions Clause. Shortly after *McCardle*, the Supreme Court decided *United States* v. *Klein* (1872), which involved a congressional attempt to use the appropriations power to nullify the President's power to pardon. The Court said that Congress had exceeded its authority, first by trying to limit a presidential power granted by the Constitution, and second by preventing a presidential pardon or amnesty from being admitted as evidence in court. The statute was meant to strip the Supreme Court of its jurisdiction over such cases. The Court agreed that the Exceptions Clause gave Congress the power to deny the right of appeal in a particular class of cases, but it could not withhold appellate jurisdiction "as a means to an end" if the end was forbidden under the Constitution. In this case, the effect of withholding appellate jurisdiction was to prescribe rules of decision for the judiciary in a pending case. 80 U.S. (13 Wall.) 128, 146 (1872).

Other restrictions limit the power of Congress under the Exceptions Clause. For example, Congress could not extend certain rights and then attempt, through the Exceptions Clause, to exclude a particular race or religious group. Such actions would violate the Due Process Clause and the First Amendment. As noted by Laurence H. Tribe of the Harvard Law School, Congress could not deny access to federal courts "to all but white Anglo-Saxon Protestants, or to all who voted in the latest election for a losing candidate." 127 Cong. Rec. 13360 (1981).

The Supreme Court has announced since *McCardle* and *Klein* that its appellate jurisdiction "is confined within such limits as Congress sees fit to prescribe." The "Francis Wright," 105 U.S. 381, 385 (1881). However, the establishment of exceptions and regulations must give "due regard to all the provisions of the Constitution." United States v. Bitty, 208 U.S. 393, 399–400 (1908). For district and appellate courts, Congress "may give, withhold or restrict such jurisdiction at its discretion, provided it be not extended beyond the boundaries fixed by the Constitution." Kline v. Burke Const. Co., 260 U.S. 226, 234 (1922). The Court has allowed Congress to limit the availability of certain judicial remedies, such as prohibiting district courts from issuing injunctions to control labor disputes or the enforcement of price regulations. Lauf v. E.G. Shinner & Co., 303 U.S. 323 (1938); Lockerty v. Phillips, 319 U.S. 182 (1942).

These precedents cannot be read to justify the exclusion of whole areas of constitutional law from the Supreme Court.[11] The mere existence of a power does not mean that it may be used without limit. Such a construction runs counter to the basic principles of constitutionalism, separation of powers, and checks and balances. Congress has the "power" to determine the size of the Supreme Court, but the availability of that power did not support Roosevelt's effort to pack the Court. Indeed, the Senate Judiciary Committee rejected the proposal with such force that it hoped no President would ever dare repeat the suggestion. The President has the "power" to withhold documents and appropriations, but we live under a system that recognizes limits on executive privilege and impoundment. The Court has the "power" to declare presidential and congressional acts unconstitutional, but it can exercise that power effectively only by acknowledging the limits of the political system. The use of the Exceptions Clause must take due regard of an independent judiciary, the Supremacy Clause, and the constitutional rights available to citizens.

NONCOMPLIANCE

In a masterful phrase, rendered almost hypnotic by its elegance, Justice Jackson said: "We are not final because we are infallible, but we are infallible only because we are final." Brown v. Allen, 344 U.S. 443, 540 (1953). The historical record demonstrates convincingly that the Supreme Court is neither infallible nor final. The lack of finality is evident in the fluid quality of its decisions, reshaped over the years by all three branches. Furthermore, the Court often experiences substantial difficulty in obtaining full compliance with decisions when they are handed down. Noncompliance is a direct threat to the Court's dignity, authority, legitimacy, and reputation (pp. 1349–1350).

In theory, judicial opinions are binding on the public and the other branches of government. In practice, judicial opinions are implemented with varying degrees of fidelity by local and federal officials. Noncompliance sometimes results from deliberate evasion, as in the South's "massive resistance" to the desegregation cases. Unintentional violations may also occur but they can be relieved by adequate education and clear judicial rulings. In between these two positions are various shades of avoidance and evasion.

In 1983, the Supreme Court held that the "legislative veto," used by Congress for fifty years to control executive actions, was unconstitutional. INS v. Chadha, 462 U.S. 919 (1983). Over the next five years, however, Congress passed more than one hundred and forty additional legislative vetoes, all signed into law by President Reagan. Moreover, Congress continued to exercise other instruments of control that are the functional equivalent of the legislative veto. Although the Court had announced one of the most important separation of powers cases of all time, the practical effect was not nearly as sweeping as the Court's decision (pp. 280–283).

---

[11]For studies cautioning unbounded use of the Exceptions Clause, see Lawrence Gene Sager, "The Supreme Court, 1980 Term—Foreword: Constitutional Limitations on Congress' Authority to Regulate the Jurisdiction of the Federal Courts," 95 Harv. L. Rev. 17 (1981); Leonard G. Ratner, "Congressional Power over the Appellate Jurisdiction of the Supreme Court," 109 U. Pa. L. Rev. 157 (1960); and Henry M. Hart, Jr., "The Power of Congress to Limit the Jurisdiction of Federal Courts: An Exercise in Dialectic," 66 Harv. L. Rev. 1362 (1953).

One source of noncompliance is poor communication of judicial opinions. Scholars have found that most people do not know or understand decisions rendered by the courts. Instead, the public receives abbreviated interpretations, often erroneous, from the media and local officials. For a variety of reasons, the media have difficulty providing adequate coverage of the courts.

The sheer force of inertia limits compliance. Court decisions must pass through the perceptual screens of citizens who believe that current practices can persist with only slight modifications. Almost thirty years after *Engel* v. *Vitale* (1962), which struck down state-sponsored prayers in public schools, school authorities continue to set aside time during the day for students to say prayers (pp. 1350–1352). Local officials may prefer to reinterpret judicial decisions on church-state separation to minimize the level of conflict and dissension within their communities.[12]

Finally, decisions by the Supreme Court and federal appellate courts are filtered through U.S. district courts and state courts. Lower courts, legislatures, and administrators have a number of ways to avoid full compliance. Lower courts can reinterpret rulings. Parties can relitigate to delay implementation or appeal to legislators to reverse a ruling that turns on statutory interpretation. When the Supreme Court reverses a lower court decision, it may remand the case for disposition "not inconsistent with this opinion." In this new round, the litigant who found success at the Supreme Court level may lose out in the lower courts. 67 Harv. L. Rev. 1251 (1954).

If the Court's opinion is a patchwork quilt, stitched together from disparate strands of conflicting views in the majority, the leeway for lower courts will be substantial. Ambiguities can result from "inadvertence, or because of a deliberate fudging or vagueness built into the opinion to secure the support of a wavering colleague." Davis & Reynolds, 1974 Duke L. J. 59, 71. When the Supreme Court is unable to muster a majority of Justices behind a decision, and instead merely releases a plurality opinion, a confused message is sent to lower courts (state and federal) and to the legislative and executive branches. 94 Harv. L. Rev. 1127 (1981). Even when the opinion is more coherent and principled, judges in the lower courts have considerable latitude in applying Supreme Court doctrine.

After the Supreme Court handed down its Desegregation Decision in 1954, lower court judges followed different paths in implementing the ruling. Some were faithful; others were defiant or evasive. Many federal judges were torn between the edict of the High Court and the sentiments and customs of their local communities. It has been said that the Constitution is what the Supreme Court says it is, but Supreme Court decisions often mean what district courts say they mean. Jack W. Peltason, Federal Courts in the Political Process 14 (1955).

CONSTITUTIONAL DIALOGUES

"Judicial sacrosanctity" can be a useful rallying cry to protect the independence of the courts from external attacks. The concept is a powerful talisman for warding off

---

[12]Kenneth M. Dolbeare and Phillip E. Hammond, The School Prayer Decisions: From Court Policy to Local Practice (1971); Frank J. Sorauf, *"Zorach* v. *Clauson:* The Impact of a Supreme Court Decision," 53 Am. Pol. Sci. Rev. 777 (1959); Gordon Patric, "The Impact of a Court Decision: Aftermath of the McCollum Case," 6 J. Pub. L. 455 (1957).

major court-curbing efforts, such as court packing or the withdrawal of appellate jurisdiction. However, it is ineffective in preventing Congress from passing laws to reverse statutory interpretations by the courts. Because these reversals are well within the realm of political legitimacy, they are buttressed by the intervention of interest groups.

No one doubts the right of Congress to pass legislation that overturns what it considers to be judicial misinterpretations of statutes. But even when the courts render a constitutional interpretation, it is usually only a matter of time before Congress prevails. Through changes in the composition of courts or adjustments in the attitudes of judges who continue to sit, a determined majority in Congress is likely to have its way. At some point a similar statute, struck down in the past as unconstitutional, will find acceptance in the courts. That pattern has been evident in such areas as child labor, regulation of commerce, and federalism.

Do these congressional challenges to the Court threaten to usurp judicial responsibilities? If the Constitution could be interpreted in mechanical fashion, left unchanged over the years and with few dissenting or even concurring opinions, and if the record were barren of instances in which the judiciary had reversed itself, this argument might have merit. But if the function of the Supreme Court is to apply the general language of the Constitution to changing needs, and if the Constitution is developmental rather than static in meaning, there can be no doubt about the propriety of legislation that prompts the Court to reconsider its decisions.

When the Supreme Court struck down the first effort by Congress to regulate child labor, Congress shifted the basis for this federal regulation from the commerce power to the taxing power. That effort was also invalidated by the Supreme Court. By 1938 Congress had returned to the commerce power and this time the legislation was upheld. United States v. Darby, 312 U.S. 100 (1941). Similar examples can be cited. Congress decided to pass the Civil Rights Act of 1964, despite its apparent collision with the *Civil Rights Cases* of 1883. This conflict between judicial doctrine and legislative aspirations did not prevent Congress from acting. It avoided a direct confrontation with the judiciary by basing the statute not only on the Fourteenth Amendment but also on the Commerce Clause. The Supreme Court promptly upheld the Act as a valid exercise of congressional power under the Commerce Clause. Heart of Atlanta Motel, Inc. v. United States, 379 U.S. 241 (1964); Katzenbach v. McClung, 379 U.S. 294 (1964).

Through what Alexander Bickel once called the Court's "continuing colloquy" with the political branches and society at large, the judiciary's search for constitutional principles can be reconciled with democratic values. Bickel, The Least Dangerous Branch 240 (1962). An open dialogue between Congress and the courts is a more fruitful avenue for constitutional interpretation than simply believing that the judiciary possesses certain superior skills.

No one doubts that Congress, like the Court, can reach unconstitutional results. As Justice Brennan said in a 1983 dissent: "Legislators, influenced by the passions and exigencies of the moment, the pressure of constituents and colleagues, and the press of business, do not always pass sober constitutional judgment on every piece of legislation they enact . . ." Marsh v. Chambers, 463 U.S. 783, 814 (1983) (dissenting opinion). Yet, if we count the times that Congress has been "wrong" about the Constitution and compare those lapses with the occasions when the Court has been "wrong" by its own later admissions, the results make a compelling case for legislative confidence and judicial modesty. In a recent evaluation, George Anastaplo said that "in the great crises over the past two hundred years, when Congress and the Supreme Court have differed on major issues, Congress has been correct." Center Magazine, November/December 1986, at 15.

There is no justification for deferring automatically to the judiciary because of its technical skills and political independence. Each decision by a court is subject to scrutiny and rejection by private citizens and public officials. What is "final" at one stage of our political development may be reopened at some later date, leading to revisions, fresh interpretations, and reversals of Court doctrines. Through this process of interaction among the branches, all three institutions are able to expose weaknesses, hold excesses in check, and gradually forge a consensus on constitutional issues. Also through that process, the public has an opportunity to add a legitimacy and a meaning to what might otherwise be an alien and short-lived document.

At certain moments in our constitutional history, there is a compelling need for an authoritative and binding decision by the Supreme Court. The unanimous ruling in 1958, signed by each Justice, was essential in dealing with the Little Rock crisis. Cooper v. Aaron, 358 U.S. 1 (1958). Another unanimous decision in 1974 disposed of the confrontation between President Nixon and the judiciary regarding the Watergate tapes. United States v. Nixon, 418 U.S. 683 (1974). These moments are rare. Usually the Court makes a series of exploratory movements followed by backing and filling—a necessary and sensible tactic for resolving constitutional issues that have profound political, social, and economic ramifications.

For the most part, Court decisions are tentative and reversible like other political events. The Court is not the Constitution. To accept the two as equivalent is to relinquish individual responsibility and the capacity for self-government. Constitutional determinations are not matters that can be left exclusively to the judiciary. Individuals outside the courts have their own judgments to make. Even with our own consent we cannot abdicate the duty to think for ourselves. What is constitutional or unconstitutional must be left for us to explore, ponder, and come to terms with. Attorney General Edwin Meese III presented a controversial speech in 1986, in which he challenged the belief that the Constitution is equivalent to Supreme Court decisions (pp. 1352–1354). The "finality" of Supreme Court decisions was examined during Senate hearings in 1986 on William Rehnquist's nomination as Chief Justice and again in 1987 on Anthony Kennedy's nomination as Associate Justice (pp. 1354–1357).

An "activist" member of the judiciary, Earl Warren, explained the limits of the courts. In times of political stress, the courts may acquiesce to actions that we later deplore. Commenting on the Court's role in upholding the treatment of Japanese-Americans during World War II, he said: "the fact that the Court rules in a case like *Hirabayashi* that a given program is constitutional, does not necessarily answer the question whether, in a broader sense, it actually is." Earl Warren, "The Bill of Rights and the Military," 37 N.Y.U. L. Rev. 181, 193 (1962). That the courts fail to strike down a governmental action does not mean that constitutional standards have been followed. The habit of looking automatically to the courts to protect constitutional liberties is ill-advised. Warren concluded that under our political system the judiciary must play a limited role: "In our democracy it is still the Legislature and the elected Executive who have the primary responsibility for fashioning and executing policy consistent with the Constitution." Id. at 202. Even here he warned against excessive dependence on the political branches: "the day-to-day job of upholding the Constitution really lies elsewhere. It rests, realistically, on the shoulders of every citizen." Id.

The belief in judicial supremacy imposes a burden that the Court cannot carry. It sets up expectations that invite disappointment if not disaster. A President once reassured his country in an inaugural address that an issue over which the nation was seriously divided "legitimately belongs to the Supreme Court of the United States, before whom it is now pending, and will, it is understood, be speedily and finally settled." The President was James Buchanan. The case about to be decided: *Dred Scott* v. *Sandford.*

What qualifications should be placed on the "last word" doctrine? First, the fact that the Supreme Court upholds the constitutionality of a measure, as when it sustained the U.S. Bank in *McCulloch,* places no obligation on executive and legislative branches to adopt that measure in the future. Congress was free to discontinue the Bank. If it passed legislation to renew it, President Jackson was within his rights to veto the bill. A decision by the Supreme Court did not relieve the other branches of their duty or freedom to reach independent interpretations.

Second, a decision by the Supreme Court that a certain practice is not prohibited by the Constitution, such as the use of search warrants in *Stanford Daily* or access to bank records in *Miller,* does not prevent the other branches from passing legislation to prohibit or restrict these practices. Rights unprotected by the courts may be secured by Congress and the President.

Third, when the Supreme Court concludes that an action has no constitutional protection in the federal courts—for example, distributing petitions in a shopping center, as in *PruneYard*—the states are not inhibited in any way from protecting these actions through their own constitutional interpretations. Decisions by the Supreme Court set a floor, or minimum, for constitutional rights. States may exceed those rights through independent interpretations of their own constitutions and unique cultures.

Fourth, many constitutional issues are resolved through rules of evidence, statutes, customs, and accommodations—a common-law method of settling disputes. Through these techniques, institutions outside the courts play a decisive role in shaping not only constitutional values but constitutional doctrines.

Fifth, there are occasions when Supreme Court rulings strike such a discordant note in the body politic that they will be tested again and again with new variations on the same theme. Court decisions are entitled to respect, not adoration. When the Court issues its judgment we should not suspend ours. The Commerce Clause, raising such issues as child labor and economic regulation by the government, is one area in which Congress eventually prevailed over judicial roadblocks. Many other examples could be cited. These challenges and collisions help keep the constitutional dialogue open and vigorous. In the search for a reconciliation between constitutional law and self-government, we must all participate.

Judicial review fits our constitutional system because we like to fragment power. We feel safer with checks and balances, even when an unelected Court tells an elected legislature or elected President that they have overstepped. This very preference for fragmented power denies the Supreme Court an authoritative and final voice for deciding constitutional questions. We do not accept the concentration of legislative power in Congress or executive power in the President. For the same reason, we cannot permit judicial power and constitutional interpretation to reside only in the courts. We reject supremacy in all three branches because of the value placed upon freedom, discourse, democracy, and limited government.

Selected Readings

BECKER, THEODORE L., AND MALCOLM M. FEELEY, eds. *The Impact of Supreme Court Decisions.* New York: Oxford University Press, 1973.

BRECKENRIDGE, ADAM CARLYLE. *Congress Against the Court.* Lincoln: University of Nebraska Press, 1970.

CULP, MAURICE S. "A Survey of the Proposals to Limit or Deny the Power of Judicial Review by the Supreme Court of the United States." 4 *Indiana Law Journal* 386, 474 (1929).

"Efforts in the Congress to Curtail the Federal Courts: Pro & Con." *Congressional Digest,* May 1982.

ELLIOTT, SHELDEN D. "Court-Curbing Proposals in Congress." 33 *Notre Dame Lawyer* 597 (1958).

HALPER, THOMAS. "Supreme Court Responses to Congressional Threats: Strategy and Tactics." 19 *Drake Law Review* 292 (1970).

HANDBERG, ROGER, AND HAROLD F. HILL, JR. "Court Curbing, Court Reversals, and Judicial Review: The Supreme Court Versus Congress." 14 *Law & Society Review* 309 (1980).

HENSCHEN, BETH. "Statutory Interpretations of the Supreme Court: Congressional Responses." 11 *American Politics Quarterly* 441 (1983).

JACKSON, ROBERT H. *The Struggle for Judicial Supremacy.* New York: Knopf, 1941.

LEUCHTENBURG, WILLIAM E. "The Origins of Franklin D. Roosevelt's 'Court-Packing' Plan." 1966 *Supreme Court Review* 347.

LYTLE, CLIFFORD M. "Congressional Response to Supreme Court Decisions in the Aftermath of the School Desegregation Cases." 12 *Journal of Public Law* 290 (1963).

MCDOWELL, GARY L. *Curbing the Courts: The Constitution and the Limits of Judicial Power.* Baton Rouge: Louisiana State University Press.

MURPHY, WALTER F. *Congress and the Court.* Chicago: University of Chicago Press, 1962.

———. "Lower Court Checks on Supreme Court Power." 53 *American Political Science Review* 1017 (1959).

NAGEL, STUART S. "Court-Curbing Periods in American History." 18 *Vanderbilt Law Review* 925 (1965).

NICHOLS, EGBERT RAY, ed. *Congress or the Supreme Court: Which Shall Rule America?* New York: Noble and Noble, 1935.

NOTE. "Congressional Reversal of Supreme Court Decisions: 1945–1957." 71 *Harvard Law Review* 1324 (1958).

———. "Tension Between Judicial and Legislative Powers as Reflected in Confrontations Between Congress and the Courts." 13 *Georgia Law Review* 1513 (1979).

PRITCHETT, C. HERMAN. *Congress Versus the Supreme Court: 1957–1960.* Minneapolis: University of Minnesota Press, 1961.

SCHMIDHAUSER, JOHN R., AND LARRY L. BERG. *The Supreme Court and Congress: Conflict and Interaction, 1945–1968.* New York: The Free Press, 1972.

STEAMER, ROBERT J. *The Supreme Court in Crisis.* Amherst: University of Massachusetts Press, 1971.

STUMPF, HARRY P. "Congressional Response to Supreme Court Rulings: The Interaction of Law and Politics." 14 *Journal of Public Law* 377 (1965).

VOSE, CLEMENT E. *Constitutional Change: Amendment Politics and Supreme Court Litigation Since 1900.* Lexington, Mass.: D.C. Heath, 1972.

WARREN, CHARLES. "Legislative and Judicial Attacks on the Supreme Court of the United States—A History of the Twenty-Fifth Section of the Judiciary Act." 47 *American Law Review* 1, 161 (1913).

Statutory Reversal: Grove City

After the Supreme Court announced *Grove City College* v. *Bell* on February 28, 1984, which restricted the reach of congressional prohibitions on sex discrimination, the House Judiciary Committee reported a bill to overturn the Court's statutory interpretation. The following selection is from the Committee's report, H. Rept. 829 (Part 1), pp. 1,

4, 37. This reading also includes the supplemental views of Congressmen John Erlenborn, Ron Packard, and Howard Nielson from Part 2, pp. 48-49, of that report.

The Committee on the Judiciary, to whom was referred the bill (H.R. 5490) to clarify the application of Title IX of the Education Amendments of 1972, section 504 of the Rehabilitation Act of 1973, the Age Discrimination Act of 1975, and Title VI of the Civil Rights Act of 1964, having considered the same, report favorably thereon without amendment and recommend that the bill do pass.

PURPOSE

H.R. 5490 was introduced on April 12, 1984 in response to the Supreme Court's recent decision in *Grove City College* v. *Bell*, 465 U.S., 104 S. Ct. 1211, 52 U.S.L.W. 4283 (1984). The *Grove City* ruling severely narrows the application of coverage of Title IX of the Education Amendments of 1972. It is anticipated that the other provisions addressed by this bill—Title VI of the 1964 Civil Rights Act, Sec. 504 of the 1973 Rehabilitation Act and the Age Discrimination Act of 1975 will be similarly narrowed in their application as a result of changed agency enforcement practices and subsequent judicial interpretations.

The purpose of this legislation is simple and straight-forward: to reaffirm pre-*Grove City College* judicial and executive branch interpretations and enforcement practices which provided for broad coverage of these antidiscrimination provisions.

By enacting H.R. 5490, Congress will reaffirm its intent with respect to these provisions that they be applied broadly and that fund termination, continue to be more tailored in scope.

. . .

Title IX is modeled after Title VI of the 1964 Civil Rights Act (prohibiting discrimination on the basis of race, color, or national origin). Title VI was also the legislative model for Sec. 504 of the Rehabilitation Act of 1973 (prohibiting discrimination on the basis disability) and the Age Discrimination Act of 1975. Together, all four statutes prohibit discrimination in "programs or activities which receive federal financial assistance." The Committee believes that the Supreme Court's nar-

row construction of the operative phrase "program or activity" conflicts with Executive Branch enforcement of the provisions for the past twenty years.

Although the *Grove City College* decision only addresses Title IX, the Committee believes it is appropriate and necessary to clarify each of the Civil Rights provisions *now* because their legislative and judicial histories are closely related. Also, it is anticipated that the application of these provisions will be similarly narrowed as a result of potential changes in the enforcement practices of federal agencies and subsequent judicial interpretations.

. . .

This legislation is a crucial step in our national effort to end discrimination, particularly that discrimination which is committed by those who receive and enjoy the benefits of federal assistance. It reflects a renewed Congressional commitment to that concept. The discrimination prohibited by these statutes is repugnant to our national consensus about equality of treatment and opportunity, a national consensus reflected in our Constitution and numerous federal statutes. No federal money should be used to support practices repugnant to our national antidiscrimination policy. The clarification in this legislation will assure that federal agencies charged with administering and distributing federal assistance will do so in conformance with our national purpose that such funds should not aid and abet discrimination. The statutes this bill amends have been critical in meeting that purpose.

The supreme Court exercised its proper constitutional role in interpreting one of those statutes, but the result was an incorrect reading of what Congress intended the law to be. Now, mindful of the implications for other statutes, Congress must enact new legislation to preserve the old.

The Committee wishes to emphasize that it cannot anticipate and answer every likely fact situation to be raised by these statutes. This statement of explanation will provide some guidance; and, in addition, we refer those seeking to define the scope of the Civil Rights Act of 1984 to the long and rich history of agency and judicial interpretations of these statutes and their regulations. We are confident that any unusual issue regarding the scope of coverage or enforcement will be referred to the Federal courts for interpretation. It is our intent that these statutes should be construed broadly so that agencies may conduct investigations unimpeded, without tracing funds to determine the jurisdiction over discrimination complaints. We believe the full panoply of remedies must remain available to the government and private parties so that the purpose of these statutes can be realized.

We believe, above all, that the record to date has been guided by a common sense approach. These amendments reaffirm that approach.

[Supplemental views of Congressmen Erlenborn, Packard and Nielson:]

In our view, the Civil Rights Act of 1984 is not ready for House consideration.

Much of our concern stems from discrepancies between the sponsors' explanations of what the bill is designed to do and the actual language of the bill. If, indeed, the sole purpose of this bill is to overturn *Grove City College* v. *Bell*, that goal could be accomplished by a more carefully crafted, narrowly drafted bill. Without claiming any extraordinary prophetic powers, we predict that the questions resolved by passage of this legislation will be few indeed compared to the avalanche of new questions of interpretation that will inevitably fall upon the courts.

Many of these questions could have been answered by a more thorough consideration of the ramifications of the bill by the Committee and a genuine willingness to consider and adopt amendments. Instead, in a mark-up lacking a spirit of receptivity to amendments which could clear up ambiguities in the bill, the Committee surrendered the opportunity—and the obligation—to add needed clarifying language to the bill. What we are left with, then, is a bill drafted in breathtakingly broad terms, subject to conflicting interpretations, and relying only on language in the Committee Report to clear up a few of the ambiguities that have been identified. This is hardly sufficient.

Vagueness still abounds as to the intended scope and application of these amendments to the very heart of our civil rights laws. The bill is amenable to interpretations that would reach far beyond the sponsors' declared purpose. We think it absolutely essential that we agree, first, on exactly what it is we want to accomplish and, second, that we ought to do it in an open, straightforward way, without machinations of "newspeak."

While the bill has been characterized as restoring the original legislative intent underlying this legislation, the Supreme Court found that Congress *had* intended program-specific application. Was not, then, the law always what the Court said it was? The bill's proponents would have us believe that the Supreme Court changed the law, and now it is incumbent upon the Congress to "restore" the law to what it had been before the Court's ruling. More accurately, the bill, to the extent it does overturn *Grove City*, would widen materially the application of Title IX and the other statutes it would amend. In fact, the bill's sponsors have repeatedly stated that the result they seek is "broad and comprehensive coverage."

. . .

We are elected to devise policy and legislate; the courts are not. This bill should not have been treated as sacrosanct, consequently not subject to amendment. We have the duty to perfect the draftsmanship, to legislate precisely. We have not properly discharged our responsibility with the care and attention it demands. In abdicating to the courts the task of making fine distinctions from the vague language in this bill, we are in effect saying: "This new bill is too complicated to understand. We'll just have to pass it to find out what it means."

[Because of differences between the House and the Senate and opposition from the Reagan administration, this legislation was not enacted until 1988.]

Statutory Reversal: Miranda

In *Miranda* v. *Arizona*, 384 U.S. 436 (1966), the Supreme Court ruled that admissibility of a confession depends on a fourfold warning given to a person in custody before he is questioned: that he has a right to remain silent, that anything he says may be used against him, that he has a right to have present an attorney during the questioning, and that if indigent he has a right to a lawyer without charge. Although the Court based its decision on Fifth and Sixth Amendment grounds, Justice Harlan's dissent argued that the Court's "new code" would be harmful to law enforcement and should not be read into the Constitution. This dissent encouraged Congress, in the Omnibus Crime Control and Safe Streets Act of 1968, to modify *Miranda* by making the admissibility of confessions dependent upon their voluntary nature. Footnotes to Harlan's dissent are omitted.

MR. JUSTICE HARLAN, whom MR. JUSTICE STEWART and MR. JUSTICE WHITE join, dissenting.

I believe the decision of the Court represents poor constitutional law and entails harmful consequences for the country at large. How serious these consequences may prove to be only time can tell. But the basic flaws in the Court's justification seem to me readily apparent now once all sides of the problem are considered. . . .

Examined as an expression of public policy, the Court's new regime proves so dubious that there can be no due compensation for its weakness in constitutional law. The foregoing discussion has shown, I think, how mistaken is the Court in implying that the Constitution has struck the balance in favor of the approach the Court takes. . . . Rather, precedent reveals that the Fourteenth Amendment in practice has been construed to strike a different balance, that the Fifth Amendment gives the Court little solid support in this context, and that the Sixth Amendment should have no bearing at all. Legal history has been stretched before to satisfy deep needs of society. In this instance, however, the Court has not and cannot make the powerful showing that its new rules are plainly desirable in the context of our society, something which is surely demanded before those rules are engrafted onto the Constitution and imposed on every State and county in the land. . . .

What the Court largely ignores is that its rules impair, if they will not eventually serve wholly to

frustrate, an instrument of law enforcement that has long and quite reasonably been thought worth the price paid for it. There can be little doubt that the Court's new code would markedly decrease the number of confessions. To warn the suspect that he may remain silent and remind him that his confession may be used in court are minor obstructions. To require also an express waiver by the suspect and an end to questioning whenever he demurs must heavily handicap questioning. And to suggest or provide counsel for the suspect simply invites the end of the interrogation. . . .

How much harm this decision will inflict on law enforcement cannot fairly be predicted with accuracy. Evidence on the role of confessions is notoriously incomplete . . . and little is added by the Court's reference to the FBI experience and the resources believed wasted in interrogation. . . . We do know that some crimes cannot be solved without confessions, that ample expert testimony attests to their importance in crime control, and that the Court is taking a real risk with society's welfare in imposing its new regime on the country. The social costs of crime are too great to call the new rules anything but a hazardous experimentation.

While passing over the costs and risks of its experiment, the Court portrays the evils of normal police questioning in terms which I think are exaggerated. Albeit stringently confined by the due process standards interrogation is no doubt often inconvenient and unpleasant for the suspect. However, it is no less so for a man to be arrested and jailed, to have his house searched, or to stand trial in court, yet all this may properly happen to the most innocent given probable cause, a warrant, or an indictment. Society has always paid a stiff price for law and order, and peaceful interrogation is not one of the dark moments of the law.

This brief statement of the competing considerations seems to me ample proof that the Court's preference is highly debatable at best and therefore not to be read into the Constitution. . . .

In conclusion: Nothing in the letter or the spirit of the Constitution or in the precedents squares with the heavy-handed and one-sided action that is so precipitously taken by the Court in the name of fulfilling its constitutional responsibilities. The foray which the Court makes today brings to mind the wise and farsighted words of Mr. Justice Jackson in *Douglas* v. *Jeannette,* 319 U.S. 157, 181 (separate opinion): "This Court is forever adding new stories to the temples of constitutional law, and the temples have a way of collapsing when one story too many is added."

FDR's Court-Packing Plan: Senate Report

President Franklin D. Roosevelt submitted to Congress on February 5, 1937, a proposal for "judicial reorganization." In actual fact, it was a plan that would have allowed him to pack the Supreme Court and lower federal courts with liberal judges. With top-heavy majorities in both Houses, he hoped for quick passage. His hopes were permanently dashed on June 7, when the Senate Judiciary Committee reported the bill adversely and so excoriated the President's idea that any parallels to it would "never again be presented to the free representatives of the free people of America." S. Rept. No. 711, 75th Cong., 1st Sess.

The Committee on the Judiciary, to whom was referred the bill (S. 1392) to reorganize the judicial branch of the Government, after full consideration, having unanimously amended the measure, hereby report the bill adversely with the recommendation that it do not pass. . . .

THE ARGUMENT

The committee recommends that the measure be rejected for the following primary reasons:

I. The bill does not accomplish any one of the objectives for which it was originally offered.

II. It applies force to the judiciary and in its initial and ultimate effect would undermine the independence of the courts.

III. It violates all precedents in the history of our Government and would in itself be a dangerous precedent for the future.

IV. The theory of the bill is in direct violation of

the spirit of the American Constitution and its employment would permit alteration of the Constitution without the people's consent or approval; it undermines the protection our constitutional system gives to minorities and is subversive of the rights of individuals.

V. It tends to centralize the Federal district judiciary by the power of assigning judges from one district to another at will.

VI. It tends to expand political control over the judicial department by adding to the powers of the legislative and executive departments respecting the judiciary.

BILL DOES NOT DEAL WITH INJUNCTIONS

This measure was sent to the Congress by the President on February 5, 1937, with a message (appendix A) setting forth the objectives sought to be attained.

It should be pointed out here that a substantial portion of the message was devoted to a discussion of the evils of conflicting decisions by inferior courts on constitutional questions and to the alleged abuse of the power of injunction by some of the Federal courts. These matters, however, have no bearing on the bill before us, for it contains neither a line nor a sentence dealing with either of those problems.

Nothing in this measure attempts to control, regulate, or prohibit the power of any Federal court to pass upon the constitutionality of any law—State or National.

Nothing in this measure attempts to control, regulate, or prohibit the issuance of injunctions by any court, in any case, whether or not the Government is a party to it.

If it were to be conceded that there is need of reform in these respects, it must be understood that this bill does not deal with these problems.

OBJECTIVES AS ORIGINALLY STATED

As offered to the Congress, this bill was designed to effectuate only three objectives, described as follows in the President's message:

1. To increase the personnel of the Federal courts "so that cases may be promptly decided in the first instance, and may be given adequate and prompt hearing on all appeals";

2. To "invigorate all the courts by the permanent infusion of new blood";

3. To "grant to the Supreme Court further power and responsibility in maintaining the efficiency of the entire Federal judiciary."

The third of these purposes was to be accomplished by the provisions creating the office of the Proctor and dealing with the assignment of judges to courts other than those to which commissioned.

The first two objectives were to be attained by the provisions authorizing the appointment of not to exceed 50 additional judges when sitting judges of retirement age, as defined in the bill, failed to retire or resign. How totally inadequate the measure is to achieve either of the named objectives, the most cursory examination of the facts reveals.

BILL FAILS OF ITS PURPOSE

In the first place, as already pointed out, the bill does not provide for any increase of personnel unless judges of retirement age fail to resign or retire. Whether or not there is to be an increase of the number of judges, and the extent of the increase if there is to be one, is dependent wholly upon the judges themselves and not at all upon the accumulation of litigation in any court. To state it another way the increase of the number of judges is to be provided, not in relation to the increase of work in any district or circuit, but in relation to the age of the judges and their unwillingness to retire.

In the second place, as pointed out in the President's message, only 25 of the 237 judges serving in the Federal courts on February 5, 1937, were over 70 years of age. Six of these were members of the Supreme Court at the time the bill was introduced. At the present time there are 24 judges 70 years of age or over distributed among the 10 circuit courts, the 84 district courts, and the 4 courts in the District of Columbia and that dealing with customs cases in New York. Of the 24, only 10 are serving in the 84 district courts, so that the remaining 14 are to be found in 5 special courts and in the 10 circuit courts. (Appendix B.) Moreover, the facts indicate that the courts with the oldest judges have the best records in the disposition of business. It follows, therefore, that since there are comparatively few aged justices in service and these are among the most efficient on the bench, the age of sitting judges does not make necessary an increase of personnel to handle the business of the courts.

There was submitted with the President's message a report from the Attorney General to the effect that in recent years the number of cases has greatly increased and that delay in the administration of justice is interminable. It is manifest, however, that this condition cannot be remedied by the contingent appointment of new judges to sit beside the judges over 70 years of age, most of whom are either altogether equal to their duties or are commissioned in courts in which congestion of business does not exist. It must be obvious that the way to attack congestion and delay in the courts is directly by legislation which will increase the number of judges in those districts where the accumulation exists, not indirectly by the contingent appointment of new judges to courts where the need does not exist, but where it may happen that the sitting judge is over 70 years of age. . . .

QUESTION OF AGE NOT SOLVED

The next question is to determine to what extent "the persistent infusion of new blood" may be expected from this bill.

It will be observed that the bill before us does not and cannot compel the retirement of any judge, whether on the Supreme Court or any other court, when he becomes 70 years of age. It will be remembered that the mere attainment of three score and ten by a particular judge does not, under this bill, require the appointment of another. The man on the bench may be 80 years of age, but this bill will not authorize the President to appoint a new judge to sit beside him unless he has served as a judge for 10 years. In other words, age itself is not penalized; the penalty falls only when age is attended with experience.

No one should overlook the fact that under this bill the President, whoever he may be and whether or not he believes in the constant infusion of young blood in the courts, may nominate a man 69 years and 11 months of age to the Supreme Court, or to any court, and, if confirmed, such nominee, if he never had served as a judge, would continue to sit upon the bench unmolested by this law until he had attained the ripe age of 79 years and 11 months.

We are told that "modern complexities call also for a constant infusion of new blood in the courts, just as it is needed in executive functions of the Government and in private business." Does this bill provide for such? The answer is obviously no. As has been just demonstrated, the introduction of old and inexperienced blood into the courts is not prevented by this bill.

More than that, the measure, by its own terms, makes impossible the "constant" or "persistent" infusion of new blood. It is to be observed that the word is "new", not "young." . . .

It thus appears that the bill before us does not

with certainty provide for increasing the personnel of the Federal judiciary, does not remedy the law's delay, does not serve the interest of the "poorer litigant" and does not provide for the "constant" or "persistent infusion of new blood" into the judiciary. What, then, does it do?

THE BILL APPLIES FORCE TO THE JUDICIARY

The answer is clear. It applies force to the judiciary. It is an attempt to impose upon the courts a course of action, a line of decision which, without that force, without that imposition, the judiciary might not adopt.

Can there be any doubt that this is the purpose of the bill? Increasing the personnel is not the object of this measure; infusing young blood is not the object; for if either one of these purposes had been in the minds of the proponents, the drafters would not have written the following clause to be found on page 2, lines 1 to 4, inclusive:

"*Provided*, That no additional judge shall be appointed hereunder if the judge who is of retirement age dies, resigns, or retires prior to the nomination of such additional judge."

Let it also be borne in mind that the President's message submitting this measure contains the following sentence:

"If, on the other hand, any judge eligible for retirement should feel that his Court would suffer because of an increase of its membership, he may retire or resign under already existing provisions of law if he wishes to do so."

Moreover, the Attorney General in testifying before the committee (hearings, pt. 1, p. 33) said:

"If the Supreme Court feels that the addition of six judges would be harmful to that Court, it can avoid that result by resigning."

Three invitations to the members of the Supreme Court over 70 years of age to get out despite all the talk about increasing personnel to expedite the disposition of cases and remedy the law's delay. One by the bill. One by the President's message. One by the Attorney General.

Can reasonable men by any possibility differ

about the constitutional impropriety of such a course?

Those of us who hold office in this Government, however humble or exalted it may be, are creatures of the Constitution. To it we owe all the power and authority we possess. Outside of it we have none. We are bound by it in every official act.

We know that this instrument, without which we would not be able to call ourselves presidents, judges, or legislators, was carefully planned and deliberately framed to establish three coordinate branches of government, every one of them to be independent of the others. For the protection of the people, for the preservation of the rights of the individual, for the maintenance of the liberties of minorities, for maintaining the checks and balances of our dual system, the three branches of the Government were so constituted that the independent expression of honest difference of opinion could never be restrained in the people's servants and no one branch could overawe or subjugate the others. That is the American system. It is immeasurably more important, immeasurably more sacred to the people of America, indeed, to the people of all the world than the immediate adoption of any legislation however beneficial. . . .

A PRECEDENT OF LOYALTY TO THE CONSTITUTION

Shall we now, after 150 years of loyalty to the constitutional ideal of an untrammeled judiciary, duty bound to protect the constitutional rights of the humblest citizen even against the Government itself, create the vicious precedent which must necessarily undermine our system? The only argument for the increase which survives analysis is that Congress should enlarge the Court so as to make the policies of this administration effective.

We are told that a reactionary oligarchy defies the will of the majority, that this is a bill to "unpack" the Court and give effect to the desires of the majority; that is to say, a bill to increase the number of Justices for the express purpose of neutralizing the views of some of the present members. In justification we are told, but without authority, by those who would rationalize this program, that Congress was given the power to determine the size of the Court so that the legisla-

tive branch would be able to impose its will upon the judiciary. This amounts to nothing more than the declaration that when the Court stands in the way of a legislative enactment, the Congress may reverse the ruling by enlarging the Court. When such a principle is adopted, our constitutional system is overthrown!

This, then, is the dangerous precedent we are asked to establish. When proponents of the bill assert, as they have done, that Congress in the past has altered the number of Justices upon the Supreme Court and that this is reason enough for our doing it now, they show how important precedents are and prove that we should now refrain from any action that would seem to establish one which could be followed hereafter whenever a Congress and an executive should become dissatisfied with the decisions of the Supreme Court.

This is the first time in the history of our country that a proposal to alter the decisions of the court by enlarging its personnel has been so boldly made. Let us meet it. Let us now set a salutary precedent that will never be violated. Let us, of the Seventy-fifth Congress, in words that will never be disregarded by any succeeding Congress, declare that we would rather have an independent Court, a fearless Court, a Court that will dare to announce its honest opinions in what it believes to be the defense of the liberties of the people, than a Court that, out of fear or sense of obligation to the appointing power, or factional passion, approves any measure we may enact. We are not the judges of the judges. We are not above the Constitution.

Even if every charge brought against the so-called "reactionary" members of this Court be true, it is far better that we await orderly but inevitable change of personnel than that we impatiently overwhelm them with new members. Exhibiting this restraint, thus demonstrating our faith in the American system, we shall set an example that will protect the independent American judiciary from attack as long as this Government stands. . . .

SUMMARY

We recommend the rejection of this bill as a needless, futile, and utterly dangerous abandonment of constitutional principle.

It was presented to the Congress in a most intricate form and for reasons that obscured its real purpose.

It would not banish age from the bench nor abolish divided decisions.

It would not affect the power of any court to hold laws unconstitutional nor withdraw from any judge the authority to issue injunctions.

It would not reduce the expense of litigation nor speed the decision of cases.

It is a proposal without precedent and without justification.

It would subjugate the courts to the will of Congress and the President and thereby destroy the independence of the judiciary, the only certain shield of individual rights.

It contains the germ of a system of centralized administration of law that would enable an executive so minded to send his judges into every judicial district in the land to sit in judgment on controversies between the Government and the citizen.

It points the way to the evasion of the Constitution and establishes the method whereby the people may be deprived of their right to pass upon all amendments of the fundamental law.

It stands now before the country, acknowledged by its proponents as a plan to force judicial interpretation of the Constitution, a proposal that violates every sacred tradition of American democracy.

Under the form of the Constitution it seeks to do that which is unconstitutional.

Its ultimate operation would be to make this Government one of men rather than one of law, and its practical operation would be to make the Constitution what the executive or legislative branches of the Government choose to say it is—an interpretation to be changed with each change of administration.

It is a measure which should be so emphatically rejected that its parallel will never again be presented to the free representatives of the free people of America.

Ex Parte McCardle

74 U.S. (7 Wall.) 506 (1869)

William H. McCardle, a Southern editor, had been arrested under the Reconstruction Acts and tried before a military commission for publishing articles considered incendiary and libelous. After his petition for a writ of habeas corpus was denied by a federal circuit court in Mississippi, the Supreme Court accepted jurisdiction and held oral argument. It was widely speculated that the Court might hold the Reconstruction Acts unconstitutional. Congress had begun the impeachment of President Andrew Johnson, partly for his opposition to the Reconstruction Acts. To prevent a decision on the constitutionality of the Reconstruction Acts, Congress passed legislation to withdraw the appellate jurisdiction of the Supreme Court in McCardle's case.

The CHIEF JUSTICE delivered the opinion of the court.

The first question necessarily is that of jurisdiction; for, if the act of March, 1868, takes away the jurisdiction defined by the act of February, 1867, it is useless, if not improper, to enter into any discussion of other questions.

It is quite true, as was argued by the counsel for the petitioner, that the appellate jurisdiction of this court is not derived from acts of Congress. It is, strictly speaking, conferred by the Constitution. But it is conferred "with such exceptions and under such regulations as Congress shall make."

It is unnecessary to consider whether, if Congress had made no exceptions and no regulations, this court might not have exercised general appellate jurisdiction under rules prescribed by itself. For among the earliest acts of the first Congress, at its first session, was the act of September 24th, 1789, to establish the judicial courts of the United States. That act provided for the organization of this court; and prescribed regulations for the exercise of its jurisdiction.

The source of that jurisdiction, and the limitations of it by the Constitution and by statute, have been on several occasions subjects of consideration here. In the case of *Durousseau* v. *The United States*, particularly, the whole matter was carefully examined, and the court held, that while "the appellate powers of this court are not given by the judicial act, but are given by the Constitution," they are, nevertheless, "limited and regulated by that act, and by such other acts as have been passed on the subject." The court said, further, that the judicial act was an exercise of the power given by the Constitution to Congress "of making exceptions to the appellate jurisdiction of the Supreme Court." "They have described affirmatively," said the court, "its jurisdiction, and this affirmative description has been understood to imply a negation of the exercise of such appellate power as is not comprehended within it."

The principle that the affirmation of appellate jurisdiction implies the negation of all such jurisdiction not affirmed having been thus established, it was an almost necessary consequence that acts of Congress, providing for the exercise of jurisdiction, should come to be spoken of as acts granting jurisdiction, and not as acts making exceptions to the constitutional grant of it.

The exception to appellate jurisdiction in the case before us, however, is not an inference from the affirmation of other appellate jurisdiction. It is made in terms. The provision of the act of 1867, affirming the appellate jurisdiction of this court in cases of *habeas corpus* is expressly repealed. It is hardly possible to imagine a plainer instance of positive exception.

We are not at liberty to inquire into the motives of the legislature. We can only examine into its power under the Constitution; and the power to make exceptions to the appellate jurisdiction of this court is given by express words.

What, then, is the effect of the repealing act upon the case before us? We cannot doubt as to this. Without jurisdiction the court cannot proceed at all in any cause. Jurisdiction is power to declare the law, and when it ceases to exist, the only function remaining to the court is that of announcing the fact and dismissing the cause. And this is not less clear upon authority than upon principle.

Several cases were cited by the counsel for the petitioner in support of the position that jurisdiction of this case is not affected by the repealing act. But none of them, in our judgment, afford any support to it. They are all cases of the exercise of judicial power by the legislature, or of legislative interference with courts in the exercising of continuing jurisdiction.

On the other hand, the general rule, supported by the best elementary writers, is, that "when an act of the legislature is repealed, it must be considered, except as to transactions past and closed, as if it never existed." And the effect of repealing acts upon suits under acts repealed, has been determined by the adjudications of this court. The subject was fully considered in *Norris* v. *Crocker*, and more recently in *Insurance Company* v. *Ritchie*. In both of these cases it was held that no judgment could be rendered in a suit after the repeal of the act under which it was brought and prosecuted.

It is quite clear, therefore, that this court cannot proceed to pronounce judgment in this case, for it has no longer jurisdiction of the appeal; and judicial duty is not less fitly performed by declining ungranted jurisdiction than in exercising firmly that which the Constitution and the laws confer.

Counsel seem to have supposed, if effect be given to the repealing act in question, that the whole appellate power of the court, in cases of *habeas corpus*, is denied. But this is an error. The act of 1868 does not except from that jurisdiction any cases but appeals from Circuit Courts under the act of 1867. It does not affect the jurisdiction which was previously exercised.

The appeal of the petitioner in this case must be

Dismissed for want of jurisdiction.

Jurisdiction-Stripping Proposals: ABA Report

Congress has authority under Article III of the Constitution to regulate the jurisdiction of federal district and appellate courts and to make "exceptions" to the appellate jurisdiction of the Supreme Court. That authority, however, must be placed in the context of other constitutional principles and restrictions, an issue discussed below by the Association of the Bar of the City of New York, "Jurisdiction-Stripping Proposals in Congress: The Threat to Judicial Constitutional Review," December 1981. Footnotes omitted.

. . . There are pending in both houses of Congress at least 25 bills that, if enacted and upheld as constitutional, would have the effect of scrapping the federal courts' historical role in the system of checks and balances. These bills, listed in the Appendix to this Report, would divest the federal courts of all original and appellate jurisdiction to hear cases relating to (1) the constitutionality of programs of "voluntary" prayer in the public schools or other public places, (2) the constitutionality of laws or regulations affecting abortions, (3) busing as a remedy for school segregation, and (4) the constitutionality of treating men and women differently in connection with the armed forces or the draft. One bill, H.R. 114, may be read to go even further—to eliminate all federal judicial review of state court decisions.

In this Report, we do not address the merits of the various federal court decisions on these subjects that have prompted the proposed legislation, nor do we analyze the individual bills in detail. Rather, we address a question that is raised by all such proposals: Is the elimination of federal court jurisdiction to hear constitutional claims a lawful and appropriate response to judicial decisions of which a current majority in Congress disapproves? That question is fundamental to the structure of our government because, if Congress can legitimately curtail the federal courts' jurisdiction to hear constitutional claims concerning such specific issues as school prayer, abortion, and desegregation, then there is no principled limitation on Congress' power effectively to eliminate the judicial branch as a check on the other branches of the federal government or the states. By enacting any of the present bills, Congress

would necessarily be claiming the power, should it so choose, to forbid the federal courts to hear *any* claim asserted under the Bill of Rights or under any other provision of the Constitution.

Although most of the proponents of these bills generally style themselves as "conservatives," our review of the historical record reveals that their proposals are *radical* in the most extreme sense of that word. They would not only cast doubt upon the abortion, school prayer, and busing decisions of the past few years, but two centuries of historical development and constitutional doctrine. For the reasons set forth below, we conclude that this radical departure from the system of checks and balances that has served our nation well for the past two centuries is unwise and probably unconstitutional. There is no precedent of enacted legislation eliminating all federal court jurisdiction to hear claims of deprivation of constitutional rights. To find any precedent for the present bills, one must look to many bills that have been proposed over the years but *not* enacted. Congress wisely declined these previous invitations to tamper with our constitutional structure of government, and should decline the same invitation presented by the current bills.

Article III of the Constitution does grant Congress power to regulate the jurisdiction of the federal courts. . . . But, as the following analysis shows, this power cannot fairly be construed to permit Congress to deprive the courts of jurisdiction to hear claims arising under the Constitution itself, particularly on an issue-by-issue basis. If Congress' power were so extensive, it would undo the elaborate system of checks and balances that the Framers of the Constitution so carefully crafted. First, it would upset the checks and balances among the three coordinate branches of the federal government, eliminating the judiciary as a check upon unconstitutional actions of the political branches by the simple expedient of removing their jurisdiction to consider challenges to such actions. Second, it would disrupt the allocation of power between the federal government and the states, by eliminating the power of the federal judiciary to restrain acts of the states that violate the Constitution. Third, and perhaps most significant, it would alter the constitutional balance between individual rights and majority will, since the judiciary is the only organ of government that is institutionally suited to protect the rights that our Constitution guarantees to individuals against the wishes of a strong-willed majority.

Another serious objection to legislation of the sort currently proposed is that it is undesirable to deal with complex and controversial social issues, particularly those of constitutional dimension, by eliminating the opportunity for full airing and debate in the federal judiciary. Indeed, one of the ironies of the present bills is that the constitutional interpretations with which the bills' sponsors differ would remain frozen as the supreme law of the land forever, binding upon the state courts under the Supremacy Clause and the doctrine of *stare decisis,* without any possibility of change through the evolution of legal thought or a change in judicial (particularly Supreme Court) personnel. . . .

Human Life Bill: Senate Hearings

In response to the Supreme Court's decision in *Roe* v. *Wade,* 410 U.S. 113 (1973), which upheld a woman's right to an abortion at least in the first trimester of pregnancy, members of Congress looked for ways to overturn the Court's ruling. One approach was to define "person" in the Fourteenth Amendment to include life beginning at conception, allow states to enact anti-abortion laws, and prevent lower federal courts from striking down those state laws. Members argued that a statutory route was available pursuant to the power of Congress under Section 5 of the Fourteenth Amendment "to enforce, by appropriate legislation, the provisions of this article." In the selections below, this approach is defended by Stephen H. Galebach, attorney for Covington & Burling, and is opposed by Professor Laurence H. Tribe of Harvard Law School. The selections are taken from "The Human Life Bill," hearings before the Senate Committee on the Judiciary, 97th Cong., 1st Sess. (1981).

Stephen H. Galebach:

. . .

In its 1973 abortion decision, the Supreme Court declared that it was unable to determine whether unborn children were human beings. The Court also held that unborn children were not persons within the meaning of the 14th amendment and that a woman's right to privacy took precedence over the State's right to protect potential life until a fetus had become viable.

The Supreme Court thus left unresolved the fundamental question of whether unborn children are human beings. The answer to this question necessarily influences the proper resolution of the abortion issue. However, if the Supreme Court is unable to decide when human life begins, who can make that decision? I submit that under the Constitution, Congress can make that decision.

The 5th and 14th amendments to the Constitution provide that no person may be deprived of life without due process of law. The 14th amendment expressly authorizes Congress to enforce its protections by appropriate legislation.

If Congress examines the question the Supreme Court was unable to answer and concludes that unborn children are human beings, then the Court's conclusion that they are not persons would be subject to change, and Congress would have the power to enforce the 14th amendment by declaring that unborn children are persons within the meaning of that amendment.

In my law review, I explained the constitutional justification of the human life bill in terms of two leading theories advanced by Supreme Court Justices concerning the power of Congress to enforce 14th amendment rights.

The first theory is found in Justice Brennan's majority opinion in the landmark case of *Katzenbach* v. *Morgan*. Under this theory, Congress has broad power to define the scope and meaning of the 14th amendment rights so long as it acts to expand those rights.

The second theory is found in Justice Harlan's dissenting opinion in *Katzenbach* v. *Morgan*. Justice Harlan took a narrower view of Congress power, allowing Congress to make legislative findings that influence constitutional determinations, but reserving to the Court the authority to make the ultimate constitutional decision.

The majority opinion in *Katzenbach* v. *Morgan* is controversial because it confers on Congress such broad power to redefine the 14th amendment rights and to force its view on the Supreme Court. There is serious question whether the Court would or should reaffirm such a broad precedent today.

However, the constitutionality of the human life bill does not depend on the validity of such a broad theory of Congress power. The narrow enforcement power described by Justice Harlan is sufficient to justify the human life bill.

For that reason, I would like to focus today on the applicability of Justice Harlan's theory to the human life bill. The key sentence in Justice Harlan's opinion in *Katzenbach* v. *Morgan* is as follows:

"To the extent 'legislative facts' are relevant to a judicial determination, Congress is well equipped to investigate them, and such determinations are of course entitled to due respect."

According to this theory, congressional findings influence the Supreme Court, but do not necessarily control the Court's decisions. For example, in the 1965 and 1970 Voting Rights Acts, Congress influenced the Supreme Court to conclude that literacy tests for voting were racially discriminatory, even though in 1959 the Court held them not to be discriminatory. The Supreme Court was not persuaded, on the other hand, by Congress finding that equal protection requires the extension of voting rights to 18-year-olds in State elections.

Former Solicitor General Robert H. Bork has recognized the power of Congress, within narrow limits, to influence constitutional decisionmaking. In reference to the President's 1972 legislative proposals for busing, Professor Bork wrote that:

"The justices may be persuaded to a different view of a subject by the informed opinion of the legislature. At the very least, a deliberate judgment by Congress on constitutional matters is a powerful brief laid before the Court. A constitutional role of even such limited dimensions is not to be despised."

It is only rarely that Congress can contribute findings that will have such persuasive value as to change a constitutional determination. However, the issue of abortion presents what may well be the most appropriate issue for Congress to influence a constitutional interpretation by means of legislative findings.

The unique aspect of the abortion issue is that the Supreme Court has declared itself unable to decide the basic question of whether unborn children are human beings. Congress is well equipped, in Justice Harlan's words, to investigate and decide the issue.

If Congress finds that a live human being exists from conception, that finding will be entitled to due respect from the Supreme Court. The persuasive value of such a finding will depend on what value should be given to human life under the 14th amendment.

If all human lives are of equal value under the 14th amendment, then Congress finding that unborn children are human beings will necessarily mean that their lives are equally protected with other human lives.

The congressional finding will lack persuasive value only if the 14th amendment does not protect all human lives equally; that is, only if some human beings can by nonpersons under the amendment.

The Supreme Court has never decided whether all human beings are equally entitled to the protection of the 14th amendment's right to life. However, the legislative history of the 14th amendment speaks to this issue.

The proponents of slavery who framed that amendment repeatedly expressed their view that all human beings should be protected under the Constitution. The author of the 14th amendment, Congressman Jonathan Bingham of Ohio, spoke of the rights guaranteed by the amendment as applying to every human being. Senator Jacob M. Howard of Michigan, who sponsored the amendment on the floor of the Senate, spoke of its provisions as protecting the rights of common humanity.

In expressing these views, the framers were echoing the words of the Declaration of Independence that all men are created equal, and that all are endowed by their Creator with certain inalienable rights, among which is the right to life. In other words, any human life which has been created shares equally in the inalienable right to life.

Respect for the sanctity of all human life is thus a basic principle affirmed both at the founding of our Nation and at the framing of the 14th amendment. This basic principle underlying the 14th amendment leaves no room for an argument that some human beings are nonpersons under that amendment.

If fact, the framers of the amendment were reacting specifically against the Supreme Court's decision in the *Dred Scott* case, which held that black people were nonpersons under the law. The 14th amendment was framed after the Civil War for the purpose of insuring that never again in the United States would a class of human beings be treated as nonpersons under the Constitution.

In light of the overall purpose and specific statements of the framers of the 14th amendment, a congressional finding that unborn children are human beings will have strong persuasive value to show that they must be persons entitled to the 14th amendment's protection of life. At the very least, the Supreme Court will have to reexamine the question of personhood in light of Congress' findings on the beginnings of human life.

Of course, the Supreme Court has also said that the Constitution protects a woman's right to privacy. The human life bill does not address this right or deny its existence.

However, the Supreme Court will have to reevaluate the proper balance between the privacy right and the right to life of unborn children. The Supreme Court will still have the final say. The human life bill does not dictate what the result must be. All the bill does is ask the Court to look at the issue again in light of Congress' answer to the question that the Court said it could not resolve, namely, when does human life begin.

The Court's role as the final interpreter of the Constitution is not threatened by this approach. Congress is merely exercising its prerogative to inform the Court of its views in accordance with Justice Harlan's understanding of the appropriate role of Congress and the Court. . . .

If these decisions are left to the private consciences of individuals, if individuals are free to choose whether someone else shall live or die, then life ultimately has no protection.

However, our Constitution does not take such an irresponsible path. The Constitution protects life, and gives Congress power to enforce that protection. That is why the human life bill is in no sense a circumvention of the Constitution, but rather a fulfillment of it.

Laurence H. Tribe:

. . .

The Court, it is true, expressed its inability to give a definitive answer to what it took to be an unanswerable question: When does human life begin?

Mr. Galebach says that some branch of Government must be able to decide this intimate moral question; but I have thought if we have learned anything in the modern era, it is that sometimes Government does not have an answer and cannot have an answer.

The fact that a question is profound and important does not mean that Government must tell us how to answer it. The whole point of the Supreme Court's decision in 1973 was not simply one of judicial incapacity, for right after the Court said that it was unable to answer the question of when human life begins, the Court explained that what it really meant was that no State, by adopting its own answer to that question—choosing one theory of life rather than another—could be permitted to override the fundamental right of the pregnant woman to give an answer for herself.

One may disagree with that view. One may disagree with the view that this fundamental question must be left to the woman. However, if one disagrees with that view, one is not disagreeing on a question of fact—What is the fetus? What is a human being?—but on a basic proposition of constitutional law.

The only way to undo a proposition of constitutional law announced by the Court is by constitutional amendment, not by legislative redefinition of constitutional language and not by waving the magic wand of section 5 of the 14th amendment and saying, "We will now inform the Court as to what the fertilized ovum is."

The Court was not in a deep, dark mystery on that question. It is not as though the Court labored under the misapprehensions of an Aristotle, believing that until some late point in pregnancy the fetus was inert, not alive. There was confusion about that.

I think it is instructive, in this connection, that the National Academy of Sciences at its 118th annual meeting adopted an extraordinary resolution, a resolution which stated that the bill now before this subcommittee purports to derive its conclusions from science, but it deals with a question to which science can provide no answer.

The question of when human life begins is a shorthand for a profound, tragic moral puzzle, one which the Supreme Court said was not for Government to decide. . . .

Let me say a word or two about section 2 of S. 158 because that provision, I think, is also a concern to this subcommittee.

Section two would attempt to prevent lower Federal courts from issuing declaratory or injunctive relief to protect the rights that women were declared to have under *Roe* v. *Wade* under section 2 of the bill. Women seeking abortions could not obtain declaratory or injunctive relief to prevent the enforcement of a restrictive abortion law.

That provision, it seems to me, is as unconstitutional as section 1, redefining "person" under the 14th amendment. The purpose of section 2 is transparent. It is not simply to channel cases dealing with abortion to the State courts. In the words of Chairman East in a question and answer memorandum that I understand was released on April 23, the purpose, quite transparently and, I think, candidly stated, is to assure continued enforcement of a State law outlawing abortion until the Supreme Court itself has ruled on the constitutionality of S. 158. That is its purpose.

Its structure is completely asymmetrical. It does not take abortion questions out of the Federal courts. Rather, it enlists the Federal courts in an antiabortion crusade.

However well-meaning, however ultimately right, perhaps, morally, that is what it does. It does so because, for example, as Senator Baucus pointed out in his questions to Congressman Dougherty, S. 158 would define all fetuses as human beings, as persons from the moment of conception, and if it were to be upheld, it would obviously mean that the State cannot pay for terminating their lives, cannot subsidize abortion of any kind.

A guardian of a fetus or a father could go into Federal court and obtain an injunction to prevent the expenditure of public moneys on abortion. If, for example, a State were to pass various restrictions on abortion but provide a public abortion subsidy, the guardian or the father could go to Federal court to prevent the expenditure of public money on abortion, while the woman could not get similar relief from that Federal court. The deck would thus be completely stacked against her.

It seems to me quite clear that section 2 of the bill is not a housekeeping jurisdictional provision as such. It is essentially a provision designed to assure that until and unless the U.S. Supreme Court strikes this law down, the rights that women were deemed to have had under *Roe* v. *Wade* could not be protected injunctively or through declaratory relief.

CONGRESS SHOULD NOT PASS S. 158 IF IT EXPECTS SUPREME COURT TO INVALIDATE THE LEGISLATION

It is no answer to say that, of course, if it is unconstitutional, as all those experts seem to say and as the six ex-Attorneys General seem to say, then quickly, by an expedited means, the Supreme Court will tell us so.

That kind of buckpassing, if I may say so, is not really worthy of this Congress. If it is the best judgment of Congress that this measure is not constitutional, as the Court has thus far construed the Constitution, then the only responsible path is constitutional amendment, not sending up a constitutional trial balloon that pro- and anti-*Roe* v. *Wade* scholars alike agree is certain be be shot down.

S. 158 WOULD NOT RESTORE STATE AUTONOMY IN ABORTION CONTEXT

Let me close with a concern that I have that would persist even if this law were to be upheld, even if it were deemed to be constitutional.

I believe that S. 158 is inherently and unavoidably defective as measured by its own aims. I think the chairman stated the reasonable aims in a way that I found almost compelling when he said that we are simply trying to return to the States a matter that perhaps ought never to have been taken over by the Federal Government in the first place. If these matters are divisive, if they are unclear, why try to resolve them nationally? Why not decentralize?

However, observe that that is not, despite its intentions, what this law does. To begin with, on the matter of State and local funding for abortions, the law leaves States no choice. In Massachusetts and in California, the State constitutions require public funds to be expended without discrimination against abortion. Under this law, spending on abortion would be forbidden because that would, if this law were upheld, amount to State action which destroys the lives of persons.

To that degree at least, the matter is suddenly nationalized and not restored to its condition as it was in 1973.

Even more fundamentally, if I may just read from the bill for a moment, it says:

"For the purpose of enforcing the obligation of the States under the 14th amendment not to deprive persons of life without due process, human life shall be deemed to exist from conception."

This talks about the obligation of the States. I have heard it said repeatedly in support of S. 158 that it would be up to the State legislatures. If the State legislatures chose not to do anything about the destruction of fetuses—which this statute declares to be human persons from the moment of conception—that would be just fine, proponents of S. 158 assert.

I submit that this is not a responsible reading of the bill's language. If the Constitution says, as Mr. Galebach reminds us, that "persons," once we have agreed that beings are "persons," may not simply be abandoned by the State to wanton slaughter, it would surely follow once we declared that the fetus was a "person" from the moment of conception without regard to "condition of dependency," that for the State to declare open season on fetuses, and to say we are not going to prosecute those who kill them, would be a deprivation of life without due process of law. . . .

It seems to me this measure is clearly unconstitutional. That it would be so held by the Supreme Court is not a matter of guesswork. It is not a responsible thing, however well-intentioned, for this Congress to do. I would regard it as a very sad day were this very serious, difficult issue to become the occasion for futile confrontation between the Congress and the Supreme Court, with a predictable outcome—one that would not enhance respect for either body, and one that would not advance the cause either of women or of unborn life.

Sustaining Public Confidence

In *Baker* v. *Carr*, 369 U.S. 186 (1962), the Supreme Court accepted jurisdiction to decide the politically volatile issue of legislative reapportionment. Justice Frankfurter, who had written the Court's opinion in *Colegrove* v. *Green*, 328 U.S. 549 (1946), describing reapportionment as "of a peculiarly political nature and therefore not meet for judicial determination," dissented in *Baker*. Although he proved to be a false prophet by overstating the difficulties of judicial remedies to malapportionment, his dissent explains that the Court's ultimate authority is not its status as the "court of last resort" but rather its ability to sustain public confidence in the moral force of its opinions. There was "nothing judicially more unseemly nor more self-defeating than for this Court to make *in terrorem* pronouncements, to indulge in merely empty rhetoric, sounding a word of promise to the ear, sure to be disappointing to the hope."

MR. JUSTICE FRANKFURTER, whom MR. JUSTICE HARLAN joins, dissenting.

The Court today reverses a uniform course of decision established by a dozen cases, including one by which the very claim now sustained was unanimously rejected only five years ago. The impressive body of rulings thus cast aside reflected the equally uniform course of our political history regarding the relationship between population and legislative representation—a wholly different matter from denial of the franchise to individuals because of race, color, religion or sex. Such a massive repudiation of the experience of our whole past in asserting destructively novel judicial power demands a detailed analysis of the role of this Court in our constitutional scheme. Disregard of inherent limits in the effective exercise of the Court's "judicial Power" not only presages the futility of judicial intervention in the essentially political conflict of forces by which the relation between population and representation has time out of mind been and now is determined. It may well impair the Court's position as the ultimate organ of "the supreme Law of the Land" in that vast range of legal problems, often strongly entangled in popular feeling, on which this Court must pronounce. The Court's authority—possessed of neither the purse nor the sword—ultimately rests on sustained public confidence in its moral sanction. Such feeling must be nourished by the Court's complete detachment, in fact and in appearance, from political entanglements and by abstention from injecting itself into the clash of political forces in political settlements.

A hypothetical claim resting on abstract assumptions is now for the first time made the basis for affording illusory relief for a particular evil even though it foreshadows deeper and more pervasive difficulties in consequence. The claim is hypothetical and the assumptions are abstract because the Court does not vouchsafe the lower courts—state and federal—guidelines for formulating specific, definite, wholly unprecedented remedies for the inevitable litigations that today's umbrageous disposition is bound to stimulate in connection with politically motivated reapportionments in so many States. In such a setting, to promulgate jurisdiction in the abstract is meaningless. It is as devoid of reality as "a brooding omnipresence in the sky," for it conveys no intimation what relief, if any, a District Court is capable of affording that would not invite legislatures to play ducks and drakes with the judiciary. For this Court to direct the District Court to enforce a claim to which the Court has over the years consistently found itself required to deny legal enforcement and at the same time to find it necessary to withhold any guidance to the lower court how to enforce this turnabout, new legal claim, manifests an odd—indeed an esoteric—conception of judicial propriety. One of the Court's supporting opinions, as elucidated by commentary, unwittingly affords a disheartening preview of the mathematical quagmire (apart from divers judicially inappropriate and elusive determinants) into which this Court today catapults the lower courts of the country without so much as adumbrating the basis for a legal calculus as a means of extrication. Even assuming the indispensable intellectual disinterestedness on the part of judges in such matters, they do not have accepted legal standards or criteria or even reliable analogies to draw upon for making judicial judgments. To charge courts with the task of accommodating the incommensurable factors of policy that underlie these mathematical puzzles is to attribute, however flatteringly, omnicompetence to judges. The Framers of the Constitution persistently rejected a proposal that embodied this assumption and Thomas Jefferson never entertained it.

Recent legislation, creating a district appropriately described as "an atrocity of ingenuity," is not unique. Considering the gross inequality among legislative electoral units within almost every State, the Court naturally shrinks from asserting that in districting at least substantial equality is a constitutional requirement enforceable by courts. Room continues to be allowed for weighting. This of course implies that geography, economics, urban-rural conflict, and all the other non-legal factors which have throughout our history entered into political districting are to some extent not to be ruled out in the undefined vista now opened up by review in the federal courts of state reapportionments. To some extent—aye, there's the rub. In effect, today's decision empowers the courts of the country to devise what should constitute the proper composition of the legislatures of the fifty States. If state courts should for one reason or another find themselves unable to discharge this task, the duty of doing so is put on the federal courts or on this Court, if State views do not satisfy this Court's notion of what is proper districting.

We were soothingly told at the bar of this Court that we need not worry about the kind of remedy a court could effectively fashion once the abstract constitutional right to have courts pass on a state-wide system of electoral districting is recognized as a matter of judicial rhetoric, because legislatures would heed the Court's admonition. This is not only a euphoric hope. It implies a sorry confession of judicial impotence in place of a frank acknowledgment that there is not under our Constitution a judicial remedy for every political mischief, for every undesirable exercise of legislative power. The Framers carefully and with deliberate forethought refused so to enthrone the judiciary. In this situation, as in others of like nature, appeal for relief does not belong here. Appeal must be to an informed, civically militant electorate. In a democratic society like ours, relief must come through an aroused popular conscience that sears the conscience of the people's representatives. In any event there is nothing judicially more unseemly nor more self-defeating than for this Court to make *in terrorem* pronouncements, to indulge in merely empty rhetoric, sounding a word of promise to the ear, sure to be disappointing to the hope.

Prayers in Public Schools

In *Engel* v. *Vitale*, 370 U.S. 421 (1962), the Supreme Court struck down state-sponsored prayers in public schools. Nevertheless, school authorities across the nation permitted prayers to continue, sometimes by acquiescing to the initiatives of individual teachers, sometimes by directly intervening to assure a daily prayer. The following extracts are from an article by David E. Rosenbaum, "Prayer in Many Schoolrooms Continues Despite '62 Ruling," *The New York Times*, March 11, 1984, Section 1, pp. 1, 32.

The 31 children in Alvenia P. Hunter's second-grade class at the Pratt Elementary School in Birmingham, Ala., began the school day Thursday as they do every day, by bowing their heads for prayer.

In unison, they recited: "O, help me please each day to find new ways of just being kind. At home, at work, at school and play, please help me now and every day. Amen."

Mrs. Hunter's class is one of many across the nation where, despite the Supreme Court's prohibition of organized prayer in the schools more than 20 years ago, students continue to recite prayers, sing hymns or read the Bible aloud.

Many more students observe a period of silence in which they can pray if they want, a practice the Supreme Court has neither upheld nor rejected.

There is no organized worship in most of the country's public schools. In the main, educators have accepted the Supreme Court's doctrine that prayer prescribed by government or led by a teacher, a government employee, violates the First Amendment sanction against "establishment of religion." . . .

A spot check of schools in communities from coast to coast last week revealed practices ranging from that in Iowa, where few schools had organized prayers even before the Supreme Court outlawed them in 1962, a practice that continues, to that in North Carolina, where a survey found regular prayer recitation and Bible readings in 39 of the state's 100 counties.

Mrs. Hunter, who has been a teacher for 18 years, said she had never heard an objection to her classroom prayer from a parent or a principal. "I believe in doing things right," she said. "I have been given the strength to come here and the ability to teach. This way I am thanking my God for enabling me to come here to work."

Louis Dale, president of the Birmingham School Board, said that the board had an official policy against organized prayer in the schools but that the policy was not enforced. He said he was personally of two minds about the matter.

SILENT PERIODS IN DISPUTE

Jean Lancaster, who teaches the second grade at Fulwiler Elementary School in Greenville,
Miss., also chooses to lead her pupils in prayer. Every day before lunch, they bow heads and recite: "God is great. God is good. Let us thank him for our food. Amen."

"If I forget to lead it, they remind me," Mrs. Lancaster said. She also said no one had ever objected to her prayer.

Much more common than organized worship in the schools are periods of silence set aside to allow children time to pray or meditate.

Nearly half the states, including New York and Connecticut, have laws that require or permit periods of silent prayer or meditation in the school day. The Federal courts have struck down such statutes as an unconstitutional subterfuge for mandating prayer in some states, including New Jersey, and have upheld them in others, where the courts said there was a difference between periods of silence and organized prayer. The issue is now before the Supreme Court.

Few if any schools in New York City observe periods of silence, but they are part of the regular curriculum in many places. Two weeks ago the school board in Hicksville, L.I., decided to end a 30-second silent period after several residents threatened to sue.

PARENTS OFFER VIEWS

Cheryl Sweet, who has a daughter in the first grade in Shelton, Conn., said of the silent period in that community, "The teacher explains to them they are to think good thoughts. It puts no pressure on them. I don't think parents can find a way to object to it."

Vicky Rohr, a Buddhist who lives in Evanston, Ill., where her daughter is in a public school, said, "Silent prayer wouldn't bother me, but a God-oriented prayer would offend me."

Other parents and teachers, however, do find regular periods of silence objectionable.

"I have no problem with the kids praying individually at any time or place," said Joan Marie Shelley, a French teacher at Lowell High School in San Francisco, "but to create a time for a group activity is absolutely inappropriate."

Proponents of prayer in the schools say that students who do not wish to participate are always free to leave the room.

But Melanie Wolf, a New Haven schoolteacher and mother of two small children, said, "It's not fair to ostracize people like that."

STUDENTS' VIEWS DIFFER

Students also have varied views about silent periods. Jody Kunkel, a ninth grader at Hillcrest Junior High School in Trumbull, Conn., said: "You just stand there. There's a little fooling around, but they're basically quiet."

Isabel Copa, a Roman Catholic eighth-grader at the Pompano Beach Middle School in Florida, said that even a period of silence would be "unfair to some students who don't believe in God."

"I go to church school and we pray over there," she said. "I have friends that are all different kinds of religions. If they want to pray, they can do it at home or at church." . . .

SOME ARE OSTRACIZED

In some places, parents who complained about prayers in the schools have been ostracized, or worse.

Three years ago, two mothers sued to stop organized prayers in the schools in Little Axe,

Okla., a rural community southeast of Oklahoma City. One of the women, JoAnn Bell, a member of the Church of the Nazarene, argued that other people should not tell her children how to pray. She said last week that after she won her suit in Federal court, she was beaten by a school worker and her home was set afire, so she moved.

In some places, the public schools have made accommodations to specific religious groups that dominate the communities.

In Utah, Mormon seminary buildings are situated near every high school in the state, and the schools make time available for students to attend the seminaries for religious education.

At the Swan Meadow School in Gortner, a small community in western Maryland, nearly all the students are Amish or Mennonites, and the morning routine includes the recital of prayers and the singing of such hymns as "His Yoke Is Easy" and "God Put the Rainbow in His Clouds."

County officials allow the prayers and the hymns because they feel it is the only way to keep the Amish and Mennonite children in the public schools. In other communities, the officials said, the religious groups had started their own schools with inferior curriculums. . . .

Is the Supreme Court the Constitution?

On October 21, 1986, Attorney General Edwin Meese III presented an address at Tulane University called "The Law of the Constitution." He referred to the Constitution as fundamental law, capable of change only by constitutional amendment, and compared that "higher law" to the body of law developed by the Supreme Court. He quoted from constitutional historian Charles Warren that "however the Court may interpret the provisions of the Constitution, it is still the Constitution which is the law, not the decisions of the Court." Meese's address sent shock waves across the country. Some columnists called the speech a "stink bomb" that showed disrespect for the Court. One newspaper column claimed that the speech invited anarchy. Other commentators predicted "enormous chaos" if Meese's view ever prevailed. His speech provides an essential backdrop for the next reading, which is a colloquy between Senator Arlen Specter and Judge Anthony Kennedy on the Court's authority and power to issue the "final word" in constitutional law.

. . .

Since becoming Attorney General, I have had the pleasure to speak about the Constitution on several occasions. I have tried to examine it from many angles. I have discussed its moral foundations. I have also addressed on separate occasions its great structural principles—federalism and separation of powers. Tonight I would like to look at it from yet another perspective and try to develop further some of the views that I have already expressed. Specifically, I would like to consider a distinction that is essential to maintaining our limited form of government. That is the necessary distinction between the Constitution and constitutional law. The two are not synonymous.

What, then, is this distinction?

The Constitution is—to put it simply but, one hopes, not simplistically—the Constitution. It is a document of our most fundamental law. It begins "We the People of the United States, in Order to form a more perfect Union . . ." and ends up, some 6,000 words later, with the 26th Amendment. It creates the institutions of our government, it enumerates the powers those institutions may wield, and it cordons off certain areas into which government may not enter. It prohibits the national authority, for example, from passing *ex post facto* laws while it prohibits the states from violating the obligations of contracts.

The Constitution is, in brief, the instrument by which the consent of the governed—the fundamental requirement of any legitimate government —is transformed into a government complete with "the powers to act and a structure designed to make it act wisely or responsibly." Among its various "internal contrivances" (as James Madison called them) we find federalism, separation of powers, bicameralism, representation, an extended commercial republic, an energetic executive, and an independent judiciary. Together, these devices form the machinery of our popular form of government and secure the rights of the people. The Constitution, then, is the Constitution, and as such it is, in its own words, "the supreme Law of the Land."

Constitutional law, on the other hand, is that body of law which has resulted from the Supreme Court's adjudications involving disputes over constitutional provisions or doctrines. To put it a bit more simply, constitutional law is what the Supreme Court says about the Constitution in its decisions resolving the cases and controversies that come before it.

And in its limited role of offering judgment, the Court has had a great deal to say. In almost two hundred years, it has produced nearly 500 volumes of *Reports* of cases. While not all these opinions deal with constitutional questions, of course, a good many do. This stands in marked contrast to the few, slim paragraphs that have been added to the original Constitution as amendments. So, in terms of sheer bulk, constitutional law greatly overwhelms the Constitution. But in substance, it is meant to support and not overwhelm the Constitution whence it is derived.

And this body of law, this judicial handiwork, is, in a fundamental way, unique in our scheme. For the Court is the only branch of our government that routinely, day in and day out, is charged with the awesome task of addressing the most basic, the most enduring political questions: What *is* due process of law? How *does* the idea of separation of powers affect the Congress in certain circumstances? And so forth. The answers the Court gives are very important to the stability of the law so necessary for good government. But as constitutional historian Charles Warren once noted, what's most important to remember is that "however the Court may interpret the provisions of the Constitution, it is still the Constitution which is the law, not the decisions of the Court."

By this, of course, Charles Warren did not mean that a constitutional decision by the Supreme Court lacks the character of law. Obviously it does have binding quality: It binds the parties in a case and also the executive branch for whatever enforcement is necessary. But such a decision does not establish a "supreme Law of the Land" that is binding on all persons and parts of government, henceforth and forevermore.

This point should seem so obvious as not to need elaboration. Consider its necessity in particular reference to the Court's own work. The Supreme Court would face quite a dilemma if its own constitutional decisions really were "the supreme Law of the Land" binding on all persons and governmental entities, including the Court itself, for then the Court would not be able to change its mind. It could not overrule itself in a constitutional case. Yet we know that the Court has done so on numerous occasions. I do not have to remind a New Orleans audience of the fate of *Plessy* v. *Ferguson,* the infamous case involving a Louisiana railcar law, which in 1896 established the legal doctrine of "separate but equal." It finally and fortunately was struck down in 1954, in *Brown* v. *Board of Education.* Just this past term, the Court overruled itself in *Batson* v. *Kentucky* by reversing a 1965 decision that had made preemptory challenges to persons on the basis of race virtually unreviewable under the Constitution.

. . . If a constitutional decision is not the same as the Constitution itself, if it is not binding in the same way that the Constitution is, we as citizens may respond to a decision we disagree with. As Lincoln in effect pointed out, we can make our responses through the presidents, the senators, and the representatives we elect at the national level. We can also make them through those we elect at the state and local levels.

Thus, not only can the Supreme Court respond to its previous constitutional decisions and change them, as it did in *Brown* and has done on many other occasions. So can the other branches of government, and, through them, the American people.

As we know, Lincoln himself worked to overturn *Dred Scott* through the executive branch. The Congress joined him in this effort. Fortunately, *Dred Scott*—the case—lived a very short life.

Once we understand the distinction between constitutional law and the Constitution, once we see that constitutional decisions need not be seen as the last words in constitutional construction, once we comprehend that these decisions do not necessarily determine future public policy—once we see all of this, we can grasp a correlative point: that constitutional interpretation is not the business of the Court only, but also, and properly, the business of all branches of government.

The Supreme Court, then, is not the only interpreter of the Constitution. Each of the three coordinate branches of government created and empowered by the Constitution—the executive and legislative no less than the judicial—has a duty to interpret the Constitution in the performance of its official functions. In fact, every official takes an oath precisely to that effect.

For the same reason that the Constitution cannot be reduced to constitutional law, the Constitution cannot simply be reduced to what Congress or the President say it is either. Quite the contrary. The Constitution, the original document of 1787 plus its amendments, is and must be understood to be the standard against which all laws, policies and interpretations must be measured. It is the consent of the governed with which the actions of the governors must be squared.

And this also applies to the power of judicial review. For as Justice Felix Frankfurter once said, "The ultimate touchstone of constitutionality is the Constitution itself and not what we have said about it."

. . .

The "Finality" of Supreme Court Decisions: Senate Hearings

During the hearings in 1986 on the nomination of William Hubbs Rehnquist as Chief Justice of the U.S. Supreme Court, Senator Arlen Specter referred to the "binding precedent" of *Marbury* v. *Madison* (1803). Specter claimed that the Supreme Court "is the final arbiter, the final decisionmaker of what the Constitution means." Asked whether he agreed with that assessment, Rehnquist responded: "Unquestionably" (p. 187 of Rehnquist's 1986 hearings). A year later, when Senator Specter put that same question to Anthony M. Kennedy during his confirmation hearings for appointment as Associate Justice of the U.S. Supreme Court, Kennedy did not agree that the Court is the final

arbiter of all constitutional issues. Instead, Kennedy develops an interesting picture of the constant interaction between the Court and the political branches (pp. 221–225 of Kennedy's 1987 hearings).

Senator SPECTER. There was a comment in a speech you made before the Los Angeles Patent Lawyers Association back in February of 1982, which I would like to call to your attention and ask you about.

Quote: As I have pointed out, the Constitution, in some of its most critical aspects, is what the political branches of the government have made it, whether the judiciary approves or not.

By making that statement, you didn't intend to undercut, to any extent at all, your conviction that the Supreme Court of the United States has the final word on the interpretation of the Constitution?

Judge KENNEDY. That is my conviction. And I think that the Court has an important role to play in umpiring disputes between the political branches.

Senator SPECTER. What did you mean by that, that in most critical aspects, it is what the political branches of the government have made it, whether the judiciary approves or not?

Judge KENNEDY. I was thinking in two different areas. One in this area of separation of powers and the growth of the office of the presidency. The courts just have had nothing to do with that.

Second, and even more importantly, is the shape of federalism. It seems to me that the independence of the States, or their non-independence, as the case may be, is really largely now committed to the Congress of the United States, in the enactment of its grants-in-aid programs, and in the determination whether or not to impose conditions that the States must comply with in order to receive federal monies; that kind of thing.

Senator SPECTER. Well, this is a very important subject. And I want to refer you to a comment which was made by Attorney General Meese in a speech last year at Tulane, and ask for your reaction to it.

He said this: But as constitutional historian Charles Warren once noted, what is most important to remember is that, quote, however the Court may interpret the provisions of the Constitu-

tion, it is still the Constitution which is the law, not the decisions of the Court.

By this, of course, Charles Warren did not mean that a constitutional decision by the Supreme Court lacks the character of law. Obviously it does have binding quality. It binds the parties in a case, and also the executive branch for whatever enforcement is necessary.

But such a decision does not establish a supreme law of the land that is binding on all persons and parts of government henceforth and evermore.

Do you agree with that?

Judge KENNEDY. Well, I am not sure—I am not sure I read that entire speech. But if we can just take it as a question, whether or not I agree that the decisions of the Supreme Court are or are not the law of the land. They are the law of the land, and they must be obeyed.

I am somewhat reluctant to say that in all circumstances each legislator is immediately bound by the full consequences of a Supreme Court decree.

Senator SPECTER. Why not?

Judge KENNEDY. Well, as I have indicated before, the Constitution doesn't work very well if there is not a high degree of voluntary compliance, and, in the school desegregation cases, I think, it was not permissible for any school board to refuse to implement *Brown* v. *Board of Education* immediately.

On the other hand, without specifying what the situations are, I can think of instances, or I can accept the proposition that a chief executive or a Congress might not accept as doctrine the law of the Supreme Court.

Senator SPECTER. Well, how can that be if the Supreme Court is to have the final word?

Judge KENNEDY. Well, suppose that the Supreme Court of the United States tomorrow morning in a sudden, unexpected development were to overrule in *New York Times* v. *Sullivan*. Newspapers no longer have protection under the libel laws. Could you, as a legislator, say I think that decision is constitutionally wrong and I want to have legislation to change it? I think you could. And I think you should.

Senator SPECTER. Well, there could be legislation——

Judge KENNEDY. And I think you could make that judgment as a constitutional matter.

Senator SPECTER. Well, there could be legislation in the hypothetical you suggest which would give the newspapers immunity for certain categories of writings.

Judge KENNEDY. But I think you could stand up on the floor of the U.S. Senate and say I am introducing this legislation because in my view the Supreme Court of the United States is 180 degrees wrong under the Constitution. And I think you would be fulfilling your duty if you said that.

Senator SPECTER. Well, you can always say it, but the issue is whether or not I would comply with it.

Judge KENNEDY. Well, I am just indicating that it doesn't seem to me that just because the Supreme Court has said it legislators cannot attempt to affect its decision in legitimate ways.

Senator SPECTER. Well, but the critical aspect about the final word that the Supreme Court has is that there is a significant school of thought in this country that the Supreme Court does not have the final word. That the President has the authority to interpret the Constitution as the President chooses and the Congress has the authority to interpret the Constitution as the Congress chooses, and there is separate but equal and the Supreme Court does not have the final word.

And, if *Marbury* v. *Madison* is to have any substance, then it seems to me that we do have to recognize the Supreme Court as the final arbiter of the Constitution, just as rockbed.

Judge KENNEDY. Well, as I have indicated earlier in my testimony, I think it was a landmark in constitutional responsibility for the Presidents in the *Youngstown* case and the *Nixon* case to instantly comply with the Court's decisions. I think that was an exercise of the constitutional obligation on their part. I have no problem with that at all.

Senator SPECTER. Well, there has been compliance because it has been accepted that the Supreme Court is the final arbiter. I just want to be sure that you agree with that proposition.

Judge KENNEDY. Yes, but there just may be instances in which I think it is consistent with constitutional morality to challenge those views. And I am not saying to avoid those views or to refuse to obey a mandate.

Senator SPECTER. Well, I think it is fine to challenge them. You can challenge them by constitutional amendment, you can challenge by taking another case to the Supreme Court. But, as long as the Court has said what the Court concludes the Constitution means, then I think it is critical that there be an acceptance that that is the final word.

Judge KENNEDY. I would agree with that as a general proposition. I am not sure there are not exceptions.

Senator SPECTER. But you can't think of any at the moment?

Judge KENNEDY. Not at the moment.

Senator SPECTER. Okay. If you do think of any between now and the time we vote, would you let me know?

Judge KENNEDY. I will let you know, Senator.

Senator SPECTER. Let me pick up some specific issues on executive power and refer to a speech that you presented in Salzburg, Austria, back in November of 1980, where you talk about the extensive discretion saying, "The blunt fact is that American Presidents have in the past had a significant degree of discretion in defining their constitutional powers."

Then you refer to, "The President in the international sphere can commit us to a course of conduct that is all but irrevocable despite the authority of Congress to issue corrective instructions in appropriate cases." Then you refer to President Truman, saying he committed thousands of troops to Korea without a congressional declaration. And then you say, "My position has always been that as to some fundamental constitutional questions it is best not to insist on definitive answers."

And you say further, "I am not one who believes that all of the important constitutional declarations of most important constitutional evolutions come from pronouncements of the courts."

And, without asking you for a specific statement on the War Powers Act, that is a matter of enormous concern that engulfs us with frequency. Major questions arise under the authority of the Congress to require notice from the President on covert operations coming out of the Iran-contra hearings. What is the appropriate range of redress for the Congress? Do we cut off funding for military action in the Persian Gulf? Do we cut off funding for covert operations? Are these justiciable issues which we can expect the Supreme Court of the United States to decide?

Judge KENNEDY. Well, whether or not they are justiciable issues, of course, depends on the peculiar facts of the case, and I would not like to commit myself on that. But the very examples you gave indicate to me that there are within the political powers of the Congress, within its great arsenal of powers under article I of the Constitution, very strong remedies that it can take to bring a chief executive into compliance with its will, and this is the way the political system was designed to work.

The framers knew about fighting for turf. I don't think they knew that term, but they deliberately set up a system wherein each branch would compete somewhat with the other in an orderly constitutional fashion for control over key policy areas. And these are the kinds of things where the political branches of the government may have a judgment that is much better than that of the courts.

Senator SPECTER. But isn't it unrealistic, Judge Kennedy, to expect the Congress to respond by cutting off funds for U.S. forces in the Persian Gulf? If you accept the proposition that the President can act to involve us in war without a formal declaration, and the President and the Congress ought to decide those questions for themselves, isn't that pretty much an abdication of the Supreme Court's responsibility to be the arbiter and the interpreter of the Constitution?

Judge KENNEDY. Well, I don't know if it is an abdication of responsibility for a nominee not to say that under all circumstances he thinks the Court can decide that broad of an issue. If the issue is presented in a manageable judicial form, in a manageable form, I have no objection to the Court being the umpire between the branches.

On the other hand, I point out that having to rely on the courts may infer, or may imply an institutional weakness on the part of the Congress that is ultimately debilitating. It seems to me that in some instances Congress is better off standing on its own feet and making its position known and then its strength in the federal system will be greater than if it had relied on the assistance of the courts.

. . .

APPENDIX 1

The Constitution of the United States

We the People of the United States, in Order to form a more perfect Union, establish Justice, insure domestic Tranquility, provide for the common defence, promote the general Welfare, and secure the Blessings of Liberty to ourselves and our Posterity, do ordain and establish this Constitution for the United States of America.

ARTICLE 1

Section 1.   All legislative Powers herein granted shall be vested in a Congress of the United States, which shall consist of a Senate and House of Representatives.

Section 2.   The House of Representatives shall be composed of Members chosen every second Year by the People of the several States, and the Electors in each State shall have the Qualifications requisite for Electors of the most numerous Branch of the State Legislature.

No Person shall be a Representative who shall not have attained to the Age of twenty five Years, and been seven Years a Citizen of the United States, and who shall not, when elected, be an Inhabitant of that State in which he shall be chosen.

Representatives and direct Taxes shall be apportioned among the several States which may be included within this Union, according to their respective Numbers, which shall be determined by adding to the whole Number of free Persons, including those bound to Service for a Term of Years, and excluding Indians not taxed, three fifths of all other Persons. The actual Enumeration shall be made within three Years after the first Meeting of the Congress of the United States, and within every subsequent Term of ten Years, in such Manner as they shall by Law direct. The Number of Representatives shall not exceed one for every thirty Thousand, but each State shall have at Least one Representative; and until such enumerations shall be made, the State of New Hampshire shall be entitled to chuse three, Massachusetts eight, Rhode-Island and Providence Plantations one, Connecticut five, New-York six, New Jersey four, Pennsylvania eight, Delaware one, Maryland six, Virginia ten, North Carolina five, South Carolina five, and Georgia three.

When vacancies happen in the Representation from any State, the Executive Authority thereof shall issue Writs of Election to fill such Vacancies.

The House of Representatives shall chuse their speaker and other Officers; and shall have the sole Power of Impeachment.

Section 3. The Senate of the United States shall be composed of two Senators from each State, chosen by the Legislature thereof, for six Years; and each Senator shall have one Vote.

Immediately after they shall be assembled in Consequence of the first Election, they shall be divided as equally as may be into three Classes. The Seats of the Senators of the first Class shall be vacated at the Expiration of the second Year, of the second Class at the Expiration of the fourth Year, and of the third Class at the Expiration of the sixth Year, so that one third may be chosen every second Year; and if Vacancies happen by Resignation, or otherwise, during the Recess of the Legislature of any State, the Executive thereof may make temporary Appointments until the next Meeting of the Legislature, which shall then fill such Vacancies.

No Person shall be a Senator who shall not have attained to the Age of thirty Years, and been nine Years a Citizen of the United States, and who shall not, when elected, be an Inhabitant of that State for which he shall be chosen.

The Vice President of the United States shall be President of the Senate, but shall have no Vote, unless they be equally divided.

The Senate shall chuse their other Officers, and also a President pro tempore, in the Absence of the Vice President, or when he shall exercise the Office of President of the United States.

The Senate shall have the sole Power to try all Impeachments. When sitting for that Purpose, they shall be on Oath or Affirmation. When the President of the United States is tried, the Chief Justice shall preside: And no Person shall be convicted without the concurrence of two thirds of the Members present. Judgment in Cases of Impeachment shall not extend further than to removal from Office, and disqualification to hold and enjoy any Office of honor, Trust or Profit under the United States: but the Party convicted shall nevertheless be liable and subject to Indictment, Trial, Judgment and Punishment, according to law.

Section 4. The Times, Places and Manner of holding Elections for Senators and Representatives, shall be prescribed in each State by the Legislature thereof; but the Congress may at any time by Law make or alter such Regulations, except as to the Places of chusing Senators.

The Congress shall assemble at least once in every Year, and such Meeting shall be on the first Monday in December, unless they shall by Law appoint a different Day.

Section 5. Each House shall be the Judge of the Elections, Returns and Qualifications of its own Members, and a Majority of each shall constitute a Quorum to do business; but a smaller Number may adjourn from day to day, and may be authorized to compel the Attendance of absent Members, in such Manner, and under such Penalties as each House may provide.

Each House may determine the Rules of its Proceedings, punish its Members for disorderly Behaviour, and, with the Concurrence of two thirds, expel a Member.

Each House shall keep a Journal of its Proceedings, and from time to time publish the same, excepting such Parts as may in their Judgment require Secrecy; and the yeas and Nays of the Members of either House on any question shall, at the Desire of one fifth of those Present, be entered on the Journal.

Neither House, during the Session of Congress, shall, without the Consent of the other, adjourn for more than three days, nor to any other place than that in which the two Houses shall be sitting.

Section 6.   The Senators and Representatives shall receive a Compensation for their Services, to be ascertained by Law, and paid out of the Treasury of the United States. They shall in all Cases, except Treason, Felony and Breach of the Peace, be privileged from Arrest during their Attendance at the Session of their respective Houses, and in going to and returning from the same; and for any Speech or Debate in either House, they shall not be questioned in any other Place.

No Senator or Representative shall, during the Time for which he was elected, be appointed to any civil Office under the Authority of the United States, which shall have been created, or the Emoluments whereof shall have been encreased during such time; and no Person holding any Office under the United States, shall be a Member of either House during his Continuance in Office.

Section 7.   All Bills for raising Revenue shall originate in the House of Representatives; but the Senate may propose or concur with Amendments as on other Bills.

Every Bill which shall have passed the House of Representatives and the Senate, shall, before it become a Law, be presented to the President of the United States; If he approve he shall sign it, but if not he shall return it, with his Objections to that House in which it shall have originated, who shall enter the Objections at large on their Journal, and proceed to reconsider it. If after such Reconsideration two thirds of that House shall agree to pass the Bill, it shall be sent, together with the Objections, to the other House, by which it shall likewise be reconsidered, and if approved by two thirds of that House, it shall become a Law. But in all such Cases the Votes of both Houses shall be determined by yeas and Nays, and the Names of the Persons voting for and against the Bill shall be entered on the Journal of each House respectively. If any Bill shall not be returned by the President within ten Days (Sundays excepted) after it shall have been presented to him, the Same shall be a Law, in like Manner as if he had signed it, unless the Congress by their Adjournment prevent its Return, in which Case it shall not be a Law.

Every Order, Resolution, or Vote to which the Concurrence of the Senate and House of Representatives may be necessary (except on a question of Adjournment) shall be presented to the President of the United States; and before the Same shall take Effect, shall be approved by him, or being disapproved by him, shall be repassed by two thirds of the Senate and House of Representatives, according to the Rules and Limitations prescribed in the Case of a Bill.

Section 8.   The Congress shall have Power To lay and collect Taxes, Duties, Imposts and Excises, to pay the Debts and provide for the common Defence and general Welfare of the United States; but all duties, Imposts and Excises shall be uniform throughout the United States;

To borrow Money on the Credit of the United States;

To regulate Commerce with foreign Nations, and among the several States, and with the Indian Tribes;

To establish an uniform Rule of Naturalization, and uniform Laws on the subject of Bankruptcies throughout the United States;

To coin Money, regulate the Value thereof, and of foreign Coin, and fix the Standard of Weights and Measures;

To provide for the Punishment of counterfeiting the Securities and current Coin of the United States;

To establish Post Offices and post Roads;

To promote the Progress of Science and useful Arts, by securing for limited Times to Authors and Inventors exclusive Right to their respective Writings and Discoveries;

To constitute Tribunals inferior to the supreme Court;

To define and punish Piracies and Felonies committed on the high Seas, and Offences against the Law of Nations;

To declare War, grant Letters of Marque and Reprisal, and make rules concerning Captures on Land and Water;

To raise and support Armies, but no Appropriation of Money to that Use shall be for a longer Term than two Years;

To provide and maintain a Navy;

To make rules for the Government and Regulation of the land and naval Forces;

To provide for calling forth the Militia to execute the Laws of the Union, suppress Insurrections and repel Invasions;

To provide for organizing, arming, and disciplining, the Militia, and for governing such Part of them as may be employed in the Service of the United States, reserving to the States respectively, the Appointment of the Officers, and the Authority of training the Militia according to the discipline prescribed by Congress;

To exercise exclusive Legislation in all Cases whatsoever, over such District (not exceeding ten Miles square), as may, by Cession of particular States, and the Acceptance of Congress, become the Seat of the Government of the United States, and to exercise like Authority over all Places purchased by the Consent of the Legislature of the State in which the Same shall be for the Erection of Forts, Magazines, Arsenals, dock-Yards, and other needful Buildings;—And

To make all Laws which shall be necessary and proper for carrying into Execution the foregoing Powers, and all other Powers vested by this Constitution in the Government of the United States, or in any Department or Officer thereof.

Section 9.   The Migration or Importation of such Persons as any of the States now existing shall think proper to admit, shall not be prohibited by the Congress prior to the Year one thousand eight hundred and eight, but a Tax or duty may be imposed on such Importation, not exceeding ten dollars for each Person.

The Privilege of the Writ of Habeas Corpus shall not be suspended, unless when in Cases of Rebellion or Invasion the public Safety may require it.

No Bill of Attainder or ex post facto Law shall be passed.

No Capitation, or other direct, Tax shall be laid, unless in Proportion to the Census or Enumeration herein before directed to be taken.

No Tax or Duty shall be laid on Articles exported from any State.

No Preference shall be given by any Regulation of Commerce or Revenue to the Ports of one State over those of another: nor shall Vessels bound to, or from, one State, be obliged to enter, clear, or pay Duties in another.

No money shall be drawn from the Treasury, but in Consequence of Appropriations made by Law; and a regular Statement and Account of the Receipts and Expenditures of all public Money shall be published from time to time.

No Title of Nobility shall be granted by the United States: And no Person holding any

Office of Profit or Trust under them, shall, without the Consent of the Congress, accept of any present, Emolument, Office, or Title, of any kind whatever, from any King, Prince, or foreign State.

Section 10.   No State shall enter into any Treaty, Alliance, or Confederation; grant Letters of Marque and Reprisal; coin Money; emit Bills of Credit; make any Thing but gold and silver Coin a Tender in Payment of Debts; pass any Bill of Attainder, ex post facto Law, or Law impairing the Obligation of Contracts, or grant any Title of Nobility.

No State shall, without the Consent of the Congress, lay any Imposts or Duties on Imports or Exports, except what may be absolutely necessary for executing it's inspection Laws: and the net Produce of all Duties and Imposts, laid by any State on Imports or Exports, shall be for the Use of the Treasury of the United States; and all such Laws shall be subject to the Revision and Controul of the Congress.

No State shall, without the Consent of Congress, lay any Duty of Tonnage, keep Troops, or Ships of War in time of Peace, enter into any Agreement or Compact with another State, or with a foreign Power, or engage in War, unless actually invaded, or in such imminent Danger as will not admit of delay.

ARTICLE II

Section 1.   The executive Power shall be vested in a President of the United States of America. He shall hold his Office during the Term of four Years, and, together with the Vice President, chosen for the same term, be elected, as follows

Each State shall appoint, in such Manner as the Legislature thereof may direct, a Number of Electors, equal to the whole Number of Senators and Representatives to which the State may be entitled in the Congress: but no Senator or Representative, or Person holding an Office of Trust or Profit under the United States, shall be appointed an Elector.

The Electors shall meet in their respective States, and vote by Ballot for two Persons, of whom one at least shall not be an Inhabitant of the same State with themselves. And they shall make a List of all the Persons voted for, and of the Number of Votes for each; which List they shall sign and certify, and transmit sealed to the Seat of the Government of the United States, directed to the President of the Senate. The President of the Senate shall, in the Presence of the Senate and House of Representatives, open all the Certificates, and the Votes shall then be counted. The Person having the greatest Number of Votes shall be the President, if such Number be a Majority of the whole Number of Electors appointed; and if there be more than one who have such Majority, and have an equal Number of Votes, then the House of Representatives shall immediately chuse by Ballot one of them for President: and if no Person have a Majority, then from the five highest on the List the said House shall in like Manner chuse the President. But in chusing the President, the Votes shall be taken by States, the Representation from each State having one Vote; A quorum for this Purpose shall consist of a Member or Members from two thirds of the States, and a Majority of all the States shall be necessary to a Choice. In every Case, after the Choice of the President, the Person having the greatest Number of Votes of the Electors shall be the Vice President. But if there should remain two or more who have equal Votes, the Senate shall chuse from them by Ballot the Vice President.

The Congress may determine the Time of chusing the Electors, and the Day on which they shall give their Votes; which Day shall be the same throughout the United States.

No Person except a natural born Citizen, or a Citizen of the United States, at the time of the Adoption of this Constitution, shall be eligible to the Office of President; neither shall any Person be eligible to that Office who shall not have attained to the Age of thirty five Years, and been fourteen Years a Resident within the United States.

In Case of the Removal of the President from Office, or of his Death, Resignation, or Inability to discharge the Powers and Duties of the said Office, the Same shall devolve on the Vice President, and the Congress may by Law provide for the Case of Removal, Death, Resignation or Inability, both of the President and Vice President, declaring what Officer shall then act as President, and such Officer shall act accordingly, until the Disability be removed, or a President shall be elected.

The President shall, at stated Times, receive for his Services, a Compensation, which shall neither be encreased nor diminished during the Period for which he shall have been elected, and he shall not receive within that Period any other Emolument from the United States, or any of them.

Before he enter on the Execution of his Office, he shall take the following Oath or Affirmation:—"I do solemnly swear (or affirm) that I will faithfully execute the Office of President of the United States, and will to the best of my Ability, preserve, protect and defend the Constitution of the United States."

Section 2.   The President shall be Commander in Chief of the Army and Navy of the United States, and of the Militia of the several States, when called into the actual Service of the United States; he may require the Opinion, in writing, of the principal Officer in each of the executive Departments, upon any Subject relating to the Duties of their respective Offices, and he shall have Power to grant Reprieves and Pardons for Offences against the United States, except in Cases of Impeachment.

He shall have Power, by and with the Advice and Consent of the Senate, to make Treaties, provided two thirds of the Senators present concur; and he shall nominate, and by and with the Advice and Consent of the Senate, shall appoint Ambassadors, other public Ministers and Consuls, Judges of the supreme Court, and all other Officers of the United States, whose Appointments are not herein otherwise provided for, and which shall be established by Law: but the Congress may by Law vest the Appointment of such inferior Officers, as they think proper, in the President alone, in the Courts of Law, or in the Heads of Departments.

The President shall have Power to fill up all Vacancies that may happen during the Recess of the Senate, by granting Commissions which shall expire at the End of their next Session.

Section 3.   He shall from time to time give to the Congress Information of the State of the Union, and recommend to their Consideration such Measures as he shall judge necessary and expedient; he may, on extraordinary Occasions, convene both Houses, or either of them, and in Case of Disagreement between them, with Respect to the Time of Adjournment, he may adjourn them to such Time as he shall think proper; he shall receive Ambassadors and other public Ministers; he shall take Care that the Laws be faithfully executed, and shall Commission all the Officers of the United States.

Section 4.   The President, Vice President and all civil Officers of the United States, shall be removed from Office on Impeachment for, and Conviction of, Treason, Bribery, or other High Crimes and Misdemeanors.

ARTICLE III

Section 1. The judicial Power of the United States, shall be vested in one supreme Court, and in such inferior Courts as the Congress may from time to time ordain and establish. The Judges, both of the supreme and inferior Courts, shall hold their Offices during good Behaviour, and shall, at stated Times, receive for their Services, a Compensation, which shall not be diminished during their Continuance in Office.

Section 2. The judicial Power shall extend to all Cases, in Law and Equity, arising under this Constitution, the Laws of the United States, and Treaties made, or which shall be made, under their Authority;—to all Cases affecting Ambassadors, other public Ministers and Consuls;—to all Cases of admiralty and maritime Jurisdiction;—to Controversies to which the United States shall be a Party;—to Controversies between two or more States;— between a State and Citizens of another State;—between Citizens of different States;— between Citizens of the same State claiming Lands under Grants of different States, and between a State, or the Citizens thereof, and foreign States, Citizens or Subjects.

In all Cases affecting Ambassadors, other public Ministers and Consuls, and those in which a State shall be Party, the supreme Court shall have original Jurisdiction. In all the other Cases before mentioned, the supreme Court shall have appellate Jurisdiction, both as to Law and Fact, with such Exceptions, and under such Regulations as the Congress shall make.

The Trial of all Crimes, except in Cases of Impeachment, shall be by Jury; and such Trial shall be held in the State where the said Crimes shall have been committed; but when not committed within any State, the Trial shall be at such Place or Places as the Congress may by Law have directed.

Section 3. Treason against the United States, shall consist only in levying War against them, or in adhering to their Enemies, giving them Aid and Comfort. No Person shall be convicted of Treason unless on the Testimony of two Witnesses to the same overt Act, or on Confession in open Court.

The Congress shall have Power to declare the Punishment of Treason, but no Attainder of Treason shall work Corruption of Blood, or Forfeiture except during the Life of the Person attainted.

ARTICLE IV

Section 1. Full Faith and Credit shall be given in each State to the public Acts, Records, and judicial Proceedings of every other State. And the Congress may by general Laws prescribe the Manner in which such Acts, Records and Proceedings shall be proved, and the Effect thereof.

Section 2. The Citizens of each State shall be entitled to all Privileges and Immunities of Citizens in the several States.

A Person charged in any State with Treason, Felony, or other Crime, who shall flee from Justice, and be found in another State, shall on Demand of the executive Authority of the State from which he fled, be delivered up, to be removed to the State having Jurisdiction of the Crime.

No person held to Service or Labour in one State, under the Laws thereof, escaping into another, shall, in Consequence of any Law or Regulation therein, be discharged from such Service or Labour, but shall be delivered up on Claim of the Party to whom such Service or Labour may be due.

Section 3.   New States may be admitted by the Congress into this Union; but no new State shall be formed or erected within the Jurisdiction of any other State; nor any State be formed by the Junction of two or more States, or Parts of States, without the Consent of the Legislatures of the States concerned as well as of the Congress.

The Congress shall have Power to dispose of and make all needful Rules and Regulations respecting the Territory or other Property belonging to the United States; and nothing in this Constitution shall be so construed as to Prejudice any Claims of the United States, or of any particular State.

Section 4.   The United States shall guarantee to every State in this Union a Republican Form of Government, and shall protect each of them against Invasion; and on Application of the Legislature, or of the Executive (when the Legislature cannot be convened) against domestic Violence.

ARTICLE V

The Congress, whenever two thirds of both Houses shall deem it necessary, shall propose Amendments to this Constitution, or, on the Application of the Legislatures of two thirds of the several States, shall call a Convention for proposing Amendments, which, in either Case, shall be valid to all Intents and Purposes, as Part of this Constitution, when ratified by the Legislatures of three fourths of the several States, or by Conventions in three fourths thereof, as the one or the other Mode of Ratification may be proposed by the Congress; Provided that no Amendment which may be made prior to the Year One thousand eight hundred and eight shall in any Manner affect the first and fourth Clauses in the Ninth Section of the first Article; and that no State, without its Consent, shall be deprived of its equal Suffrage in the Senate.

ARTICLE VI

All Debts contracted and Engagements entered into, before the Adoption of this Constitution, shall be as valid against the United States under this Constitution, as under the Confederation.

This Constitution, and the Laws of the United States which shall be made in Pursuance thereof; and all Treaties made, or which shall be made, under the Authority of the United States, shall be the supreme Law of the Land; and the Judges in every State shall be bound thereby, any Thing in the Constitution or Laws of any State to the Contrary notwithstanding.

The Senators and Representatives before mentioned, and the Members of the several State Legislatures, and all executive and judicial Officers, both of the United States and of the several States, shall be bound by Oath or Affirmation, to support this Constitution; but no religious Test shall ever be required as a Qualification to any Office or public Trust under the United States.

ARTICLE VII

The Ratification of the Conventions of nine States, shall be sufficient for the Establishment of this Constitution between the States so ratifying the Same.

AMENDMENTS

(The first 10 Amendments were ratified December 15, 1791, and form what is known as the "Bill of Rights")

AMENDMENT 1

Congress shall make no law respecting an establishment of religion, or prohibiting the free exercise thereof; or abridging the freedom of speech, or of the press; or the right of the people peaceably to assemble, and to petition the Government for a redress of grievances.

AMENDMENT 2

A well regulated Militia, being necessary to the security of a free State, the right of the people to keep and bear Arms, shall not be infringed.

AMENDMENT 3

No Soldier shall, in time of peace be quartered in any house, without the consent of the Owner, nor in time of war, but in a manner to be prescribed by law.

AMENDMENT 4

The right of the people to be secure in their persons, houses, papers, and effects, against unreasonable searches and seizures, shall not be violated, and no Warrants shall issue, but upon probable cause, supported by Oath or affirmation, and particularly describing the place to be searched, and the persons or things to be seized.

AMENDMENT 5

No person shall be held to answer for a capital, or otherwise infamous crime, unless on a presentment or indictment of a Grand Jury, except in cases arising in the land or naval forces, or in the Militia, when in actual service in time of War or public danger; nor shall any person be subject for the same offence to be twice put in jeopardy of life or limb; nor shall be compelled in any criminal case to be a witness against himself, nor be deprived of life, liberty, or property, without due process of law; nor shall private property be taken for public use, without just compensation.

AMENDMENT 6

In all criminal prosecutions, the accused shall enjoy the right to a speedy and public trial, by an impartial jury of the State and district wherein the crime shall have been committed, which district shall have been previously ascertained by law, and to be informed of the nature and cause of the accusation; to be confronted with the witnesses against him; to have compulsory process for obtaining witnesses in his favor, and to have the Assistance of Counsel for his defence.

AMENDMENT 7

In Suits at common law, where the value in controversy shall exceed twenty dollars, the right of trial by jury shall be preserved, and no fact tried by a jury, shall be otherwise re-examined in any Court of the United States, than according to the rules of the common law.

AMENDMENT 8

Excessive bail shall not be required, nor excessive fines imposed, nor cruel and unusual punishments inflicted.

AMENDMENT 9

The enumeration in the Constitution, of certain rights, shall not be construed to deny or disparage others retained by the people.

AMENDMENT 10

The powers not delegated to the United States by the Constitution, nor prohibited by it to the States, are reserved to the States respectively, or to the people.

AMENDMENT 11

(Ratified February 7, 1795)

The Judicial power of the United States shall not be construed to extend to any suit in law or equity, commenced or prosecuted against one of the United States by Citizens of another State, or by Citizens or Subjects of any Foreign State.

AMENDMENT 12

(Ratified July 27, 1804)

The Electors shall meet in their respective states and vote by ballot for President and Vice-President, one of whom, at least, shall not be an inhabitant of the same state with themselves; they shall name in their ballots the person voted for as President, and in distinct ballots the person voted for as Vice-President, and they shall make distinct lists of all persons voted for as President, and of all persons voted for as Vice-President, and of the number of votes for each, which lists they shall sign and certify, and transmit sealed to the seat of the government of the United States, directed to the President of the Senate;—The President of the Senate shall, in the presence of the Senate and House of Representatives, open all the certificates and the votes shall then be counted;—The person having the greatest number of votes for President, shall be the President, if such number be a majority of the whole number of Electors appointed; and if no person have such majority, then from the persons having the highest numbers not exceeding three on the list of those voted for as President, the House of Representatives shall choose immediately, by ballot, the President. But in choosing the President, the votes shall be taken by states, the representation from each state having one vote; a quorum for this purpose shall consist of a member or members from two-thirds of the states, and a majority of all the states shall be necessary to a choice. And if the House of Representatives shall not choose a President whenever the right of choice shall devolve upon them, before the fourth day of March next following, then the Vice-President shall act as President, as in the case of the death or other constitutional disability of the President.— The person having the greatest number of votes as Vice-President, shall be the Vice-President, if such number be a majority of the whole number of Electors appointed, and if no person have a majority, then from the two highest numbers on the list, the Senate shall choose the Vice-President; a quorum for the purpose shall consist of two-thirds of the whole number of Senators, and a majority of the whole number shall be nease of the death or other constitutional disability of the President.—The person having the greatest number of votes as Vice-President, shall be the Vice-President, if such number be a majority of the whole number of Electors appointed, and if no person have a majority, then from the two highest numbers on the list, the Senate shall choose the Vice-President; a quorum for the purpose shall consist of two-thirds of the whole number of Senators, and a majority of the whole number shall be necessary to a choice. But no person constitutionally ineligible to the office of President shall be eligible to that of Vice-President of the United States.

AMENDMENT 13

(Ratified December 6, 1865)

Section 1.   Neither slavery nor involuntary servitude, except as a punishment for crime whereof the party shall have been duly convicted, shall exist within the United States, or any place subject to their jurisdiction.

Section 2.   Congress shall have power to enforce this article by appropriate legislation.

AMENDMENT 14

(Ratified July 9, 1868)

Section 1.   All persons born or naturalized in the United States, and subject to the jurisdiction thereof, are citizens of the United States and of the State wherein they reside. No State shall make or enforce any law which shall abridge the privileges or immunities of citizens of the United States; nor shall any State deprive any person of life, liberty, or property, without due process of law; nor deny to any person within its jurisdiction the equal protection of the laws.

Section 2.   Representatives shall be apportioned among the several States according to their respective numbers, counting the whole number of persons in each State, excluding Indians not taxed. But when the right to vote at any election for the choice of electors for President and Vice President of the United States, Representatives in Congress, the Executive and Judicial officers of a State, or the members of the Legislature thereof, is denied to any of the male inhabitants of such State, being twenty-one years of age, and citizens of the United States, or in any way abridged, except for participation in rebellion, or other crime, the basis of representation therein shall be reduced in the proportion which the number of such male citizens shall bear to the whole number of male citizens twenty-one years of age in such State.

Section 3.   No person shall be a Senator or Representative in Congress, or elector of President and Vice President, or hold any office, civil or military, under the United States, or under any State, who, having previously taken an oath, as a member of Congress, or as an officer of the United States, or as a member of any State legislature, or as an executive or judicial officer of any State, to support the Constitution of the United States, shall have engaged in insurrection or rebellion against the same, or given aid or comfort to the enemies thereof. But Congress may by a vote of two-thirds of each House, remove such disability.

Section 4. The validity of the public debt of the United States, authorized by law, including debts incurred for payment of pensions and bounties for services in suppressing insurrection or rebellion, shall not be questioned. But neither the United States nor any State shall assume or pay any debt or obligation incurred in aid of insurrection or rebellion against the United States, or any claim for the loss or emancipation of any slave; but all such debts, obligations and claims shall be held illegal and void.

Section 5. The Congress shall have power to enforce, by appropriate legislation, the provisions of this article.

AMENDMENT 15

(Ratified February 3, 1870)

Section 1. The right of citizens of the United States to vote shall not be denied or abridged by the United States or by any State on account of race, color, or previous condition of servitude.

Section 2. The Congress shall have power to enforce this article by appropriate legislation.

AMENDMENT 16

(Ratified February 3, 1913)

The Congress shall have power to lay and collect taxes on incomes, from whatever source derived, without apportionment among the several States, and without regard to any census or enumeration.

AMENDMENT 17

(Ratified April 8, 1913)

The Senate of the United States shall be composed of two Senators from each State, elected by the people thereof for six years; and each Senator shall have one vote. The electors in each State shall have the qualifications requisite for electors of the most numerous branch of the State legislatures.

When vacancies happen in the representation of any State in the Senate, the executive authority of such State shall issue writs of election to fill such vacancies: *Provided,* That the legislature of any State may empower the executive thereof to make temporary appointments until the people fill the vacancies by election as the legislature may direct.

This amendment shall not be so construed as to affect the election or term of any Senator chosen before it becomes valid as part of the Constitution.

AMENDMENT 18

(Ratified January 16, 1919. Repealed December 5, 1933 by Amendment 21)

Section 1. After one year from the ratification of this article the manufacture, sale, or transportation of intoxicating liquors within, the importation thereof into, or the exportation thereof from the United States and all territory subject to the jurisdiction thereof for beverage purposes is hereby prohibited.

Section 2. The Congress and the several States shall have concurrent power to enforce this article by appropriate legislation.

Section 3. This article shall be inoperative unless it shall have been ratified as an amendment to the Constitution by the legislatures of the several States as provided in the Constitution, within seven years from the date of the submission hereof to the States by the Congress.

AMENDMENT 19

(Ratified August 18, 1920)

The right of citizens of the United States to vote shall not be denied or abridged by the United States or by any State on account of sex.

Congress shall have power to enforce this article by appropriate legislation.

AMENDMENT 20

(Ratified January 23, 1933)

Section 1. The terms of the President and Vice President shall end at noon on the 20th day of January, and the terms of Senators and Representatives at noon on the 3d day of January, of the years in which such terms would have ended if this article had not been ratified; and the terms of their successors shall then begin.

Section 2. The Congress shall assemble at least once in every year, and such meeting shall begin at noon on the 3d day of January, unless they shall by law appoint a different day.

Section 3. If, at the time fixed for the beginning of the term of the President, the President elect shall have died, the Vice President elect shall become President. If a President shall not have been chosen before the time fixed for the beginning of his term, or if the President elect shall have failed to qualify, then the Vice President elect shall act as President until a President shall have qualified; and the Congress may by law provide for the case wherein neither a President elect nor a Vice President elect shall have qualified, declaring who shall then act as President, or the manner in which one who is to act shall be selected, and such person shall act accordingly until a President or Vice President shall have qualified.

Section 4. The Congress may by law provide for the case of the death of any of the persons from whom the House of Representatives may choose a President whenever the right of choice shall have devolved upon them, and for the case of the death of any of the persons from whom the Senate may choose a Vice President whenever the right of choice shall have devolved upon them.

Section 5. Sections 1 and 2 shall take effect on the 15th day of October following the ratification of this article.

Section 6. This article shall be inoperative unless it shall have been ratified as an amendment to the Constitution by the legislatures of three-fourths of the several States within seven years from the date of its submission.

AMENDMENT 21

(Ratified December 5, 1933)

Section 1. The eighteenth article of amendment to the Constitution of the United States is hereby repealed.

Section 2. The transportation or importation into any State, Territory, or possession of the United States for delivery or use therein of intoxicating liquors, in violation of the laws thereof, is hereby prohibited.

Section 3. This article shall be inoperative unless it shall have been ratified as an amendment to the Constitution by conventions in the several States, as provided in the Constitution, within seven years from the date of the submission hereof to the States by the Congress.

AMENDMENT 22

(Ratified February 27, 1951)

Section 1. No person shall be elected to the office of the President more than twice, and no person who has held the office of President, or acted as President, for more than two years of a term to which some other person was elected President shall be elected to the office of the President more than once. But this Article shall not apply to any person holding the office of President when this Article was proposed by the Congress, and shall not prevent any person who may be holding the office of President, or acting as President, during the term within which this Article becomes operative from holding the office of President or acting as President during the remainder of such term.

Section 2. This article shall be inoperative unless it shall have been ratified as an amendment to the Constitution by the legislatures of three-fourths of the several States within seven years from the date of its submission to the States by the Congress.

AMENDMENT 23

(Ratified March 29, 1961)

Section 1. The District constituting the seat of Government of the United States shall appoint in such manner as the Congress may direct:

A number of electors of President and Vice President equal to the whole number of Senators and Representatives in Congress to which the District would be entitled if it were a State, but in no event more than the least populous State; they shall be in addition to those appointed by the States, but they shall be considered, for the purposes of the election of President and Vice President, to be electors appointed by a State; and they shall meet in the District and perform such duties as provided by the twelfth article of amendment.

Section 2. The Congress shall have power to enforce this article by appropriate legislation.

AMENDMENT 24

(Ratified January 23, 1964)

Section 1. The right of citizens of the United States to vote in any primary or other election for President or Vice President, for electors for President or Vice President, or for Senator or Representative in Congress, shall not be denied or abridged by the United States or any State by reason of failure to pay any poll tax or other tax.

Section 2. The Congress shall have power to enforce this article by appropriate legislation.

AMENDMENT 25

(Ratified February 10, 1967)

Section 1. In case of the removal of the President from office or of his death or resignation, the Vice President shall become President.

Section 2. Whenever there is a vacancy in the office of the Vice President, the President shall nominate a Vice President who shall take office upon confirmation by a majority vote of both Houses of Congress.

Section 3. Whenever the President transmits to the President pro tempore of the Senate and the Speaker of the House of Representatives his written declaration that he is unable to discharge the powers and duties of his office, and until he transmits to them a written declaration to the contrary, such powers and duties shall be discharged by the Vice President as Acting President.

Section 4. Whenever the Vice President and a majority of either the principal officers of the executive departments or of such other body as Congress may by law provide, transmit to the President pro tempore of the Senate and the Speaker of the House of Representatives their written declaration that the President is unable to discharge the powers and duties of his office, the Vice President shall immediately assume the powers and duties of the office as Acting President.

Thereafter, when the President transmits to the President pro tempore of the Senate and the Speaker of the House of Representatives his written declaration that no inability exists, he shall resume the powers and duties of his office unless the Vice President and a majority of either the principal officers of the executive department or of such other body as Congress may by law provide, transmit within four days to the President pro tempore of the Senate and the Speaker of the House of Representatives their written declaration that the President is unable to discharge the powers and duties of his office. Thereupon Congress shall decide the issue, assembling within forty-eight hours for that purpose if not in session. If the Congress, within twenty-one days after receipt of the latter written declaration, or, if Congress is not in session, within twenty-one days after Congress is required to assemble, determines by two-thirds vote of both Houses that the President is unable to discharge the powers and duties of his office, the Vice President shall continue to discharge the same as Acting President; otherwise, the President shall resume the powers and duties of his office.

AMENDMENT 26

(Ratified July 1, 1971)

Section 1.   The right of citizens of the United States, who are eighteen years of age or older, to vote shall not be denied or abridged by the United States or by any State on account of age.

Section 2.   The Congress shall have the power to enforce this article by appropriate legislation.

APPENDIX 2
Justices of the Supreme Court (1789–1989)

YEAR	CHIEF JUSTICE	ASSOCIATE JUSTICES							
1789	Jay	Rutledge	Cushing	Wilson	Blair				
1790	Jay	Rutledge	Cushing	Wilson	Blair	Iredell			
1791	Jay	Johnson	Cushing	Wilson	Blair	Iredell			
1793	Jay	Paterson	Cushing	Wilson	Blair	Iredell			
1795	Rutledge	Paterson	Cushing	Wilson	Blair	Iredell			
1796	Ellsworth	Paterson	Cushing	Wilson	Chase	Iredell			
1798	Ellsworth	Paterson	Cushing	Washington	Chase	Iredell			
1799	Ellsworth	Paterson	Cushing	Washington	Chase	Moore			
1801	Marshall	Paterson	Cushing	Washington	Chase	Moore			
1804	Marshall	Paterson	Cushing	Washington	Chase	Johnson			
1806	Marshall	Livingston	Cushing	Washington	Chase	Johnson			
1807	Marshall	Livingston	Cushing	Washington	Chase	Johnson	Todd		
1811	Marshall	Livingston	Story	Washington	Duvall	Johnson	Todd		
1823	Marshall	Thompson	Story	Washington	Duvall	Johnson	Todd		
1826	Marshall	Thompson	Story	Washington	Duvall	Johnson	Trimble		
1829	Marshall	Thompson	Story	Washington	Duvall	Johnson	McLean		
1830	Marshall	Thompson	Story	Baldwin	Duvall	Johnson	McLean		
1835	Marshall	Thompson	Story	Baldwin	Duvall	Wayne	McLean		
1836	Taney	Thompson	Story	Baldwin	Barbour	Wayne	McLean		
1837	Taney	Thompson	Story	Baldwin	Barbour	Wayne	McLean	Catron	McKinley
1841	Taney	Thompson	Story	Baldwin	Daniel	Wayne	McLean	Catron	McKinley
1845	Taney	Nelson	Woodbury	Baldwin	Daniel	Wayne	McLean	Catron	McKinley
1846	Taney	Nelson	Woodbury	Grier	Daniel	Wayne	McLean	Catron	McKinley
1851	Taney	Nelson	Curtis	Grier	Daniel	Wayne	McLean	Catron	McKinley
1853	Taney	Nelson	Curtis	Grier	Daniel	Wayne	McLean	Catron	Campbell
1858	Taney	Nelson	Clifford	Grier	Daniel	Wayne	McLean	Catron	Campbell
1862	Taney	Nelson	Clifford	Grier	Miller	Wayne	Swayne	Catron	Davis
1863	Taney	Nelson	Clifford	Grier	Miller	Wayne	Swayne	Catron	Davis	Field
1864	Chase	Nelson	Clifford	Grier	Miller	Wayne	Swayne	Catron	Davis	Field
1865	Chase	Nelson	Clifford	Grier	Miller	—	Swayne	Catron	Davis	Field
1867	Chase	Nelson	Clifford	Grier	Miller	—	Swayne	—	Davis	Field

YEAR	CHIEF JUSTICE	ASSOCIATE JUSTICES							
1870	Chase	Nelson	Clifford	Strong	Miller	Bradley	Swayne	Davis	Field
1872	Chase	Hunt	Clifford	Strong	Miller	Bradley	Swayne	Davis	Field
1874	Waite	Hunt	Clifford	Strong	Miller	Bradley	Swayne	Davis	Field
1877	Waite	Hunt	Clifford	Strong	Miller	Bradley	Swayne	Harlan	Field
1880	Waite	Hunt	Clifford	Woods	Miller	Bradley	Swayne	Harlan	Field
1881	Waite	Hunt	Gray	Woods	Miller	Bradley	Matthews	Harlan	Field
1882	Waite	Blatchford	Gray	Woods	Miller	Bradley	Matthews	Harlan	Field
1888	Fuller	Blatchford	Gray	Lamar	Miller	Bradley	Matthews	Harlan	Field
1889	Fuller	Blatchford	Gray	Lamar	Miller	Bradley	Brewer	Harlan	Field
1890	Fuller	Blatchford	Gray	Lamar	Brown	Bradley	Brewer	Harlan	Field
1892	Fuller	Blatchford	Gray	Lamar	Brown	Shiras	Brewer	Harlan	Field
1893	Fuller	Blatchford	Gray	Jackson	Brown	Shiras	Brewer	Harlan	Field
1894	Fuller	White	Gray	Jackson	Brown	Shiras	Brewer	Harlan	Field
1895	Fuller	White	Gray	Peckham	Brown	Shiras	Brewer	Harlan	Field
1898	Fuller	White	Gray	Peckham	Brown	Shiras	Brewer	Harlan	McKenna
1902	Fuller	White	Holmes	Peckham	Brown	Shiras	Brewer	Harlan	McKenna
1903	Fuller	White	Holmes	Peckham	Brown	Day	Brewer	Harlan	McKenna
1906	Fuller	White	Holmes	Peckham	Moody	Day	Brewer	Harlan	McKenna
1909	Fuller	White	Holmes	Lurton	Moody	Day	Brewer	Harlan	McKenna
1910	White	Van Devanter	Holmes	Lurton	Lamar	Day	Hughes	Harlan	McKenna
1912	White	Van Devanter	Holmes	Lurton	Lamar	Day	Hughes	Pitney	McKenna
1914	White	Van Devanter	Holmes	McReynolds	Lamar	Day	Hughes	Pitney	McKenna
1916	White	Van Devanter	Holmes	McReynolds	Brandeis	Day	Clarke	Pitney	McKenna
1921	Taft	Van Devanter	Holmes	McReynolds	Brandeis	Day	Clarke	Pitney	McKenna
1922	Taft	Van Devanter	Holmes	McReynolds	Brandeis	Butler	Sutherland	Pitney	McKenna
1923	Taft	Van Devanter	Holmes	McReynolds	Brandeis	Butler	Sutherland	Sanford	McKenna
1925	Taft	Van Devanter	Holmes	McReynolds	Brandeis	Butler	Sutherland	Sanford	Stone
1930	Hughes	Van Devanter	Holmes	McReynolds	Brandeis	Butler	Sutherland	Roberts	Stone
1932	Hughes	Van Devanter	Cardozo	McReynolds	Brandeis	Butler	Sutherland	Roberts	Stone
1937	Hughes	Black	Cardozo	McReynolds	Brandeis	Butler	Sutherland	Roberts	Stone
1938	Hughes	Black	Cardozo	McReynolds	Brandeis	Butler	Reed	Roberts	Stone
1939	Hughes	Black	Frankfurter	McReynolds	Douglas	Butler	Reed	Roberts	Stone
1940	Hughes	Black	Frankfurter	McReynolds	Douglas	Murphy	Reed	Roberts	Stone
1941	Stone	Black	Frankfurter	Byrnes	Douglas	Murphy	Reed	Roberts	Jackson
1943	Stone	Black	Frankfurter	Rutledge	Douglas	Murphy	Reed	Roberts	Jackson
1945	Stone	Black	Frankfurter	Rutledge	Douglas	Murphy	Reed	Burton	Jackson
1946	Vinson	Black	Frankfurter	Rutledge	Douglas	Murphy	Reed	Burton	Jackson
1949	Vinson	Black	Frankfurter	Minton	Douglas	Clark	Reed	Burton	Jackson
1953	Warren	Black	Frankfurter	Minton	Douglas	Clark	Reed	Burton	Jackson
1955	Warren	Black	Frankfurter	Minton	Douglas	Clark	Reed	Burton	Harlan
1956	Warren	Black	Frankfurter	Brennan	Douglas	Clark	Reed	Burton	Harlan
1957	Warren	Black	Frankfurter	Brennan	Douglas	Clark	Whittaker	Burton	Harlan
1958	Warren	Black	Frankfurter	Brennan	Douglas	Clark	Whittaker	Stewart	Harlan
1962	Warren	Black	Goldberg	Brennan	Douglas	Clark	White	Stewart	Harlan
1965	Warren	Black	Fortas	Brennan	Douglas	Clark	White	Stewart	Harlan
1967	Warren	Black	Fortas	Brennan	Douglas	Marshall	White	Stewart	Harlan
1969	Burger	Black	Fortas	Brennan	Douglas	Marshall	White	Stewart	Harlan
1970	Burger	Black	Blackmun	Brennan	Douglas	Marshall	White	Stewart	Harlan
1972	Burger	Powell	Blackmun	Brennan	Douglas	Marshall	White	Stewart	Rehnquist
1975	Burger	Powell	Blackmun	Brennan	Stevens	Marshall	White	Stewart	Rehnquist
1981	Burger	Powell	Blackmun	Brennan	Stevens	Marshall	White	O'Connor	Rehnquist
1986	Rehnquist	Powell	Blackmun	Brennan	Stevens	Marshall	White	O'Connor	Scalia
1988	Rehnquist	Kennedy	Blackmun	Brennan	Stevens	Marshall	White	O'Connor	Scalia

APPENDIX 3
Glossary of Legal Terms

Abstention doctrine Permits a federal court to relinquish jurisdiction where necessary to avoid needless friction with the state's administration of its own affairs.

Acquittal Certifying the innocence of a person charged with a crime.

Advisory opinion An opinion rendered by a court indicating how the court would rule on a matter; an interpretation of a law without binding effect. Federal courts do not issue advisory opinions.

Affidavit Written statement of facts, made voluntarily, and confirmed by oath or affirmation before a judge or magistrate.

Affirm Appellate court declares that lower court's judgment is valid and right.

Amicus curiae "Friend of the court." A person or group, not a party to a case, that submits a brief detailing its views on a case.

Ante Before.

Appeal Review by a superior court of an inferior court's decision. May also be levels of appeal within an administrative agency.

Appellant The party appealing a case.

Appellate jurisdiction Power of an appellate court to review and revise the judicial action of an inferior court.

Appellee The party responding to a case brought by appellant; sometimes called "respondent."

Arraignment Bringing an accused before a court, stating the criminal charge against him, and calling on him to enter a plea.

Article I court *See* legislative court.

Article III court *See* constitutional court.

Balancing test A constitutional doctrine in which a court weighs an individual's rights with the rights or powers of the state.

Bill of attainder Legislative act that inflicts punishment without judicial proceeding.

Brandeis brief A brief that includes, along with legal citations and principles, references to economic and social surveys. Takes its name from Louis D. Brandeis, who used such practices before joining the Supreme Court.

Brief A written statement prepared by the counsel arguing a case in court.

Case A general term for an action, cause, suit, or controversy, at law or in equity.

Case law The aggregate of reported cases that form a body of jurisdiction, as contrasted with statutory law.

Case or controversy A constitutional prerequisite, from Article III, that determines the justiciability of a question before federal courts.

Cause of action The facts that give a person a right of judicial relief.

Certification, writ of Method of taking a case from a federal appellate court to the Supreme Court; the appellate court may certify any question of law on which it requests instruction from the Court.

Certiorari, writ of Order by Supreme Court when it exercises discretion to hear an appeal. It may grant or deny "cert."

Circuit courts Federal appellate courts with jurisdiction over several states.

Civil law Concerned with private rights and remedies, as contrasted with criminal law.

Class action A suit brought by a person or group of persons to represent the interests of a class.

Collateral estoppel The doctrine that prevents relitigation of the same issue in a suit upon a different claim or cause of action.

Common law Derives its authority from usages and customs or from court decrees regarding these usages and customs. As distinguished from law created by legislative enactments (statutory law).

Compelling state interest Term used to uphold state action in the area of Equal Protection or First Amendment rights because of an overriding need for state action.

Concurrent powers Powers that may be exercised independently by Congress and state legislatures on the same subject matter.

Concurring opinion An opinion that agrees with the decision of the majority but offers separate reasons for reaching that decision.

Consent decree A decree entered by a judge expressing the consent of both parties in resolving their dispute; a contract by the parties made under the sanction of the court.

Constitutional court A court protected by Article III rights (life tenure and no diminution of salary). *See* legislative court.

Criminal law Law created to prevent harm to society, as contrasted with civil law.

Curtilage The land and buildings immediately adjacent to a home.

Declaratory judgment A binding adjudication of the legal rights of litigants but without awarding relief.

De facto In fact; in reality. *See* de jure.

Defendant The party against whom relief is sought in an action or suit; the accused in a criminal case.

De jure By law; result of official action. Contrary to "de facto." Example: de jure segregation is mandated by law; de facto segregation exists but is not officially sanctioned.

Demurrer A defendant admits the facts of a complaint but states that they are insufficient to proceed upon or to oblige the defendant to answer.

Dicta Expressions in a court opinion that go beyond the necessities of the case and are not binding. Singular is dictum. *See* obiter dictum.

Dissenting opinion Disagreement with the majority opinion. A dissent may or may not be accompanied by an opinion.

Distinguish A court's explanation why a previous decision does not apply.

District courts U.S. district courts are the trial courts; each state has one or more federal judicial districts.

Diversity jurisdiction Jurisdiction of federal courts over cases between citizens of different states.

Docket List of cases set to be tried at a specified term.

Eleemosynary Devoted to charity.

En banc The full bench of an appellate court, as distinguished from a panel of three judges.

Enjoin To require; command. To require a person to perform, or desist from, some act. *See* injunction.

Equity Justice administered according to fairness rather than the stricter rules of common law.

Estop To stop, bar, prevent.

Exclusionary rule Prohibits the introduction in a criminal trial of evidence obtained by illegal means, such as from a search or seizure that violates the Fourth Amendment.

Ex parte On one side only; by or for one party.

Ex post facto After the fact.

Ex post facto law A law that inflicts punishment on a person for an act done which, at the time committed, was innocent. Forbidden by U.S. Constitution.

Express Clear; definite; explicit; set forth in words. Contrasted with "implied."

Ex proprio vigore By their own force.

Federal question Case arising under the U.S. Constitution, federal statutes, or treaties; generally involves significant or major issue.

Grand jury A jury of inquiry to hear accusations in criminal cases and find bills of indictment when they are satisfied that the accused should be tried. *See* petit jury.

Habeas corpus "You have the body." A writ commanding a law officer to bring a party before a court or judge. The purpose is to release someone from unlawful imprisonment.

Harmless error An error which was not prejudicial to the substantial rights of a person convicted; not a ground for granting a new trial.

Implied The intention is not manifested by explicit and direct words. The meaning is gathered by necessary deduction. Used in contrast to "express."

Inalienable rights Rights which are not capable of being surrendered without the consent of the person possessing such rights.

In camera In chambers; in private. In camera hearings occur in the judge's private chambers or when all spectators are excluded from the courtroom.

Indictment An accusation in writing presented by a grand jury; charges person named with an act which is a public offense.

In forma pauperis (I.F.P.) In the character or manner of a pauper. Gives permission to a poor person to proceed without liability for court fees or costs.

Information An accusation against a person for some criminal offense; differs from indictment in that it is presented by public officer instead of by grand jury.

Infra Below.

Injunction A prohibitive remedy issued by a court that forbids the defendant to do some act.

In re In the matter of.

Ipse dixit A bare assertion resting on an individual's authority.

Judicial Conference Policymaking organization of the federal judiciary. Annual meetings consisting of the Chief Justice of the United States, the chief judge of each judicial circuit, and a district judge from each judicial circuit.

Judicial council Judges of each circuit meet to assure expeditious and effective administration of the business of the courts.

Judicial review A court's authority to review the constitutionality of legislative and executive acts.

Jurisdiction A term that embraces every kind of judicial action. The authority by which courts take cognizance of and decide cases.

Jurisprudence The philosophy of law. The science that treats the principles of law.

Jury A body of persons sworn to inquire into matters of fact and to declare the truth upon evidence laid before them.

Justiciable Matter appropriate for court review.

Legislative court Courts created by Congress (Article I courts) in contrast to those created by the Constitution (Article III courts).

Litigant A party to a lawsuit.

Magistrate A person clothed with power as a public civil officer; invested with executive or judicial power.

Mandamus "We command." The name of a writ issued from a court, commanding the performance of a particular act.

Mandatory jurisdiction Jurisdiction that a court must accept.

Mootness Question is moot when it presents no actual controversy or where the issues have ceased to exist or have become academic or dead.

Motion Application made to a court or judge for purpose of obtaining a rule or order.

Natural law Natural law, or *jus naturale*, represents a universal system of rules and principles to guide human conduct. Applies to all nations and people. Contrasts with positive law.

Natural rights Rights that grow out of the nature of man. Distinguished from rights created by positive law.

Obiter dictum "A remark by the way." Statement in an opinion that is not essential to the case at hand. Plural is *dicta*.

Order Direction of a court or judge made in writing but not included in the judgment.

Original jurisdiction Jurisdiction in the first instance. Distinguished from appellate jurisdiction.

Overbreadth doctrine Requirement that a statute be aimed specifically at evils within the allowable area of government control. Statute cannot reach conduct that is constitutionally protected.

Per curiam "By the court." An unsigned opinion reflecting a majority of the court.

Petitioner The party filing a petition seeking action or relief from a court.

Petit jury Trial jury; the ordinary jury to try civil or criminal action.

Plaintiff The party bringing an action to obtain relief for a claimed injury.

Plurality opinion   An opinion of an appellate court that has the support of less than a majority of judges.

Police power   The power of government to protect the health, safety, welfare, and morals of citizens.

Political question   An issue that must be resolved by the nonjudicial branches.

Positive law   A law enacted by a governmental body. Contrasted with natural law.

Post   After; same as "infra."

Preemption   Doctrine adopted by the U.S. Supreme Court holding that certain matters are of such a national character that federal laws take precedence over state laws.

Prima facie   "At first sight." A fact presumed to be true unless disproved by contrary evidence.

Pro se   "For himself." One who appears in court without representation by a lawyer.

Quash   To overthrow, vacate, annul; to make void.

Recuse   For a judge to disqualify himself or herself from hearing a case because of interest or prejudice.

Remand   Appellate court sends case back to a lower court with instructions to correct specified irregularities.

Respondent   When the Supreme Court grants a writ of certiorari, the party seeking review is the petitioner and the party responding is the respondent.

Reverse   Appellate court sends case back to a lower court with instructions to change the result reached below.

Ripeness   The doctrine that requires a court to consider whether a case has matured or developed into a controversy worthy of adjudication.

Scienter   "Knowingly." Used to signify the defendant's guilty knowledge.

Seriatim   "One after another." Initially, each Justice of the Supreme Court prepared a separate opinion rather than have one Justice write for the majority.

Standing   To have standing to sue, a person must have a sufficient stake in a controversy to merit judicial resolution.

Stare decisis   "Stand by things decided." To abide by, or adhere to, decided cases.

State action   Term used to determine whether an action complained of has its source in state authority or policy.

Stay   To stop, arrest, or hold in abeyance.

Strict constructionism   A close or rigid reading and interpretation of a law or constitutional provision.

Sub nomine   "Under the name of."

Subpoena   "Under pain." A command to appear at a certain time and place. A *subpoena duces tecum* requires production of books, papers, or objects. A *subpoena ad testificandum* is to testify.

Sub silentio   "Under silence"; without notice taken.

Summary judgment   The Court writes a short opinion without receiving briefs or oral argument.

Supra   Above.

Temporary restraining order (TRO)   An emergency remedy issued by a court until it can hear arguments or evidence on the controversy.

Three-judge court   Panel that combines federal district and appellate judges to expedite review of a challenged action.

Trial court   The first court to consider litigation.

Trover   Remedy for any wrongful interference with or detention of the goods of another.

Ultra vires   "Beyond powers." Acts in excess of powers granted.

Underinclusiveness   The challenge that a statute is invalid because it limits benefits to a specified group rather than making them available to all groups.

Vacate   To annul; to set aside.

Vel non   "Or not." Example: "We now judge the merits vel non of this claim."

Venire   "To come." Summoning a jury.

Vested rights   Rights so settled in a person that they cannot be taken or diminished without the person's consent.

Vicinage   Neighborhood; vicinity.

Voir dire   "To speak the truth." Preliminary examination by a court to determine competency and impartiality of a witness or juror.

Warrant   An *arrest warrant*, made on behalf of the state, commands a law enforcement officer to arrest a person and bring him before a magistrate. A *search warrant*, issued in writing by a judge or magistrate, directs a law enforcement officer to search for and seize specified property.

Writ   An order issued from a court requiring the performance of a specified act.

APPENDIX 4
How to Research the Law

When a bill passes Congress and is signed by the President, or is vetoed by the President and Congress overrides the veto, the bill is printed either as a public law or a private law. The latter series is reserved for legislation intended for the relief of private parties, especially bills dealing with claims against the United States, the waiver of claims by the government against individuals, and exceptions for individuals subject to certain immigration and naturalization requirements.

The enacted bill first appears as a "slip law." The heading indicates the public law number, date of approval, and bill number. For example, the Civil Rights Restoration Act of 1987, which originated as S. 557, was enacted on March 22, 1988, and designated Public Law 100–259 (the 259th public law of the One Hundredth Congress). The heading also indicates the volume and page in the *U.S. Statutes at Large*, where the public law will appear. For the Civil Rights Restoration Act of 1987, the citation is 102 Stat. 28 (Volume 102, page 28). At the end of the slip law is a convenient legislative history that refers to the House and Senate reports and floor debates that preceded the bill's enactment. Private laws are numbered by a separate series, also prefixed by the Congress. Thus, a bill for the relief of Miriama Jones, enacted October 28, 1978, was called Private Law 95–110.

Bound volumes, called the *U.S. Statutes at Large*, contain public laws, private laws, reorganization plans, joint resolutions, concurrent resolutions, and proclamations issued by the President. There is little practical difference between a bill and a joint resolution. Both forms of legislation must be presented to the President for his signature; both are legally binding. Concurrent resolutions, adopted by the House and the Senate, are not presented to the President and do not have the force of law.

Beginning with volume 52 (1938), each volume of the *Statutes at Large* contains the laws enacted during a calendar year. After volume 64, treaties and other international agreements were no longer printed in the *Statutes*. They are printed in a new series of volumes, published by the State Department, called *United States Treaties and Other*

International Agreements. The documents first appear in pamphlet form numbered in the "Treaties and Other International Acts Series" (TIAS). Citations are usually given to both the TIAS number and the volume of *United States Treaties and Other International Agreements,* as in 30 UST 617, TIAS 9207 (1978).

Treaties may supersede prior conflicting statutes.[1] By virtue of Article VI, Section 2, the Constitution, statutes, and treaties are collectively called "the supreme Law of the Land." On the other hand, executive agreements cannot be "inconsistent with legislation enacted by Congress in the exercise of its constitutional authority."[2] In cases where executive agreements violate rights secured by the Constitution, they have been struck down by the courts.[3]

As laws are modified or repealed by subsequent enactments of Congress, the need arises for a publication that consolidates the permanent body of law. The first codification of U.S. laws, enacted June 22, 1874, appeared in the *Revised Statutes.* A second edition was published in 1878, followed by supplements. In 1926, Congress passed a law to provide for a code intended to embrace the laws of the United States that are general and permanent in their character. The first volume, reflecting the laws in force as of December 7, 1925, was printed as volume 44, part I, of the *Statutes at Large.* This series is now known as the *United States Code.* New editions of the code appeared in 1934, 1940, 1946, 1952, 1958, 1964, 1970, 1976, and 1982. Supplements to the code are issued after each session of Congress. The code consists of fifty titles organized by subject matter (Agriculture, Highways, Money and Finance, etc.). Index references are to title, section, and year, as in 7 U.S.C. 443 (1982) and 10 U.S.C. 1437 (Supp. IV, 1986).

Unless superseded by federal statute or invalidated by the courts, presidential proclamations, executive orders, and regulations are other sources of law. Not until 1935 did Congress pass legislation to provide for the custody and publication of these administrative rules and pronouncements. This publication, the *Federal Register,* includes all presidential proclamations and executive orders that have general applicability and legal effect, as well as agency regulations and orders that prescribe a penalty. Based partly on the statutory authority vested in him by the Federal Register Act, President Franklin D. Roosevelt issued an executive order in 1936 that vested in the Bureau of the Budget (now Office of Management and Budget) the responsibility for reviewing all proposed executive orders and proclamations.[4]

The *Federal Register* is published daily, Monday through Friday, except for official holidays. A typical citation would be 46 Fed. Reg. 36707 (1981). The rules, regulations, and orders that constitute the current body of administrative regulations are arranged under fifty titles (generally parallel to those of the *United States Code)* and printed as the *Code of Federal Regulations.* Citations are by title and section, as in 50 C.F.R. 17.13 (1980).

There is continuing controversy over the range and legal effect of executive orders and proclamations. Executive orders cannot supersede a statute or override contradictory

---

[1] United States v. Schooner Peggy, 5 U.S. (1 Cr.) 103 (1801).

[2] 11 Foreign Affairs Manual [FAM] 721.2(b)(3) (1974); United States v. Guy W. Capps, Inc., 204 F.2d 655, 660 (4th Cir. 1953), aff'd on other grounds, 348 U.S. 296 (1955).

[3] Seery v. United States, 127 F.Supp. 601, 606 (Ct. Cl. 1955); Reid v. Covert, 354 U.S. 1, 16 (1956).

[4] 49 Stat. 500, § 5 (1935). Roosevelt's Executive Order 7298, February 18, 1936, appeared too early for the first volume of the Federal Register. It is reprinted in James Hart, "The Exercise of Rule-Making Power," the President's Committee on Administrative Management 355 (1937).

congressional expressions,[5] but the latitude for presidential lawmaking is still substantial and a source of concern.[6] Proclamations also operate in a twilight zone of legality. When a statute prescribes a specific procedure and the President elects to follow a different course, a proclamation by him is illegal and void.[7] Proclamations have been upheld, however, with only tenuous ties to statutory authority.[8]

FOLLOWING INTERPRETATIONS OF THE LAW

As a general guide to the constitutional powers of the president, the student should consult what has become known as the "Annotated Constitution." The actual title is *The Constitution of the United States of America: Analysis and Interpretation*, prepared periodically by the Congressional Research Service of the Library of Congress and printed as a Senate document. Edward S. Corwin wrote the 1952 edition, which has since been substantially revised. Constitutional scholars still turn with profit to Corwin's *The President: Office and Powers, 1787–1957* (New York: New York University Press, 1957). Other basic sources include *The Records of the Federal Convention of 1787*, a four-volume work edited by Max Farrand and published by Yale University Press in 1937, and the *Federalist* papers of Hamilton, Jay, and Madison, the most prominent edition of which was published by Harvard University Press in 1966 under the guidance of Benjamin Fletcher Wright.

Other than brief accounts that appear in daily newspapers announcing major decisions by the Supreme Court, a researcher must rely on more specialized sources to keep track of legal interpretations—especially lower-court decisions. Decisions by federal district and appellate courts are fascinating for two reasons: (1) they are the first step in shaping constitutional and statutory law and (2) often they are the last step, for few of their rulings are reviewed by the Supreme Court.

This huge body of material is conveniently organized by the *United States Law Week*, which appears each Tuesday except the first Tuesday in September and the last Tuesday in December. The *Law Week* consists of four major sections: (1) a summary and analysis of major decisions, with page references to more extended treatment in the *Law Week;* (2) new court decisions and agency rulings (decisions, executive orders, regulations, and administrative interpretations) and a "News in Brief" section that contains book reviews, comments on specialized areas of the law, and lists of executive nominations and confirmations; (3) Supreme Court proceedings, including oral arguments before the Court, reviews granted, summary actions, reviews denied, cases recently filed, and special articles summarizing and analyzing the most significant Supreme Court opinions rendered for each term; and (4) Supreme Court opinions. The *Law Week* is published by

[5]Marks v. CIA, 590 F.2d 997, 1003 (D.C. Cir. 1978); Weber v. Kaiser Aluminum & Chemical Corp., 563 F.2d 216, 227 (5th Cir. 1977), rev'd on other grounds, Steelworkers v. Weber, 443 U.S. 193 (1979). The judiciary has struck down executive orders that exceed presidential authority; e.g., Youngstown Co. v. Sawyer, 343 U.S. 579 (1952) and Panama Refining Co. v. Ryan, 293 U.S. 388, 433 (1935).

[6]Note, "Judicial Review of Executive Action in Domestic Affairs," 80 Colum. L. Rev. 1535 (1980); "Presidential Control of Agency Rulemaking: An Analysis of Constitutional Issues That May be Raised by Executive Order 12291," a Report Prepared for the Use of the House Committee on Energy and Commerce, 97th Cong., 1st Sess. (Comm. Print, June 15, 1981).

[7]Schmidt Pritchard & Co. v. United States, 167 F.Supp. 272 (Cust. Ct. 1958); Carl Zeiss, Inc. v. United States, 76 F.2d 412 (Ct. Cust. & Pa. App. 1935).

[8]United States v. Yoshida Intern., Inc., 526 F.2d 560 (Ct. Cust. & Pat. App. 1975); Louis Fisher, Constitutional Conflicts between Congress and the President 123–134 (1985).

the Bureau of National Affairs. Citations are by volume, page, and year, as in *Maher* v. *Roe,* 45 U.S.L.W. [or L.W.] 4787 (1977).

Two weekly newspapers, catering to the legal profession, are especially valuable. Both newspapers contain stories on appointments to the federal agencies, personnel actions, departmental politics, budget cutbacks, executive-legislative clashes, regulatory policy, and administrative law. They also regularly review the literature. *The National Law Journal* is published weekly by the New York Law Publishing Company. The *Legal Times of Washington* is published weekly by Legal Times of Washington. These periodicals contain incisive, sophisticated, and well-written accounts on current developments. Additional political background on litigation is available from the *Federal Times,* published every Monday by Army Times Publishing Company.

The Supreme Court decisions are printed first in the form of "slip opinions." They may be purchased from the Government Printing Office and are usually available from libraries that serve as depositories for government documents. The full decisions are republished in paperbacks called "preliminary prints" and finally in bound volumes of the *United States Reports.* Citations take this form: *Ohio* v. *Roberts,* 448 U.S. 56 (1980), which indicates that the decision may be found in volume 448, beginning on page 56.

The first ninety volumes of the *Reports* were named after court reporters. Volumes 1 through 4 (1790–1800) were named after Dallas. Later volumes, 5 through 90, carry the names of Cranch, Wheaton, Peters, Howard, Black, and Wallace. Volumes 91–107 (1875–1882) are designated "1 to 17 Otto" as well as "United States Reports 91–107." Reprints of volumes 1 through 90 generally have a dual numbering system to the *Reports* and to court reporters, requiring such citations as *Marbury* v. *Madison,* 5 U.S. (1 Cr.) 137 (1803).

The full text of each Supreme Court decision also appears in the *Supreme Court Reporter,* issued semimonthly during the session of the Court by West Publishing Company. The citations for these decisions are in the form *Maryland* v. *Louisiana,* 101 S.Ct. 2114 (1981).

Another source of Supreme Court decisions is *United States Supreme Court Reports, Lawyers' Edition,* published twice monthly by the Lawyers Co-Operative Publishing Company. A unique feature of the *Lawyers' Edition* is a summary of the arguments in each case for the majority of the Court and for justices who concur and dissent. The first series of the *Lawyers' Edition,* consisting of 100 volumes, covers the period from 1790 to 1956. The second series is now past volume 90. A typical citation is *Steagald* v. *United States,* 68 L.Ed. 2d 38 (1981).

Briefs and oral arguments to the Supreme Court, for major cases, are published in *Landmark Briefs and Arguments of the Supreme Court of the United States: Constitutional Law,* edited by Philip B. Kurland and Gerhard Casper and published by University Publications of America.

Significant decisions by federal district courts are printed in the *Federal Supplement,* issued first in paper edition and later in bound volumes. The citation shows the volume, page, state, and year, as in *United States* v. *Mandel,* 505 F.Supp. 189 (D. Md. 1981). The "D" in parentheses indicates that the decision occurred at the district court level. For decisions that are not reported in the *Federal Supplement,* or in situations where immediate access to a decision is needed, a researcher may call the judge's chamber and receive a copy of the memorandum decision from a law clerk or filing clerk.

To follow appeals of district court decisions, the source is the *Federal Reporter,* consisting of two series. The first series (F. or Fed.) stopped with volume 300; the second series (F.2d) is now in the 800s. Typical citations are *Rowe* v. *Drohen,* 262 F. 15 (2d Cir.

1919) and *Romeo* v. *Youngberg*, 644 F.2d 147 (3d Cir. 1980). These decisions are initially available as slip opinions and in memorandum form either from the court or libraries.

The "citator" or citation book tells the student whether a decision is still valid and authoritative. A decision by a lower court may be affirmed, reversed, or modified. *Shepard's Citations*, a widely used sourcebook, has spawned such words as "Shepardize" and "Shepardizing" to describe the process of determining the current state of the law. *Shepard's United States Citations* includes citations to Supreme Court decisions, U.S. statutes, treaties, and court rules for federal courts. *Shepard's Federal Citations*, covering decisions by federal courts below the Supreme Court, is issued in two series. One series covers the *Federal Supplement*, and the other the *Federal Reporter*. For more specific guidance on legal sources, the student can turn to *Fundamentals of Legal Research*, by J. Myron Jacobstein and Roy M. Mersky (Mineola, N.Y.: Foundation Press, 1987).

Many of the issues that come before the courts have been first explored by the Justice Department and the General Accounting Office. These analyses are published in *Official Opinions of the Attorneys General* and *Decisions of the Comptroller General*. Among his other duties, the Attorney General renders important opinions on legal issues presented to him by Presidents and departmental heads. Citations to these opinions are by volume, page, and year, as in 40 Ops. Att'y Gen. [or Op. A.G.] 469 (1946). A new series, called *Opinions of the Office of Legal Counsel*, is now available to record the memorandum opinions from the Office of Legal Counsel, which advises the President, the Attorney General, and other executive officers. The first volume, published in 1980, covers the period from January 27, 1977, to December 31, 1977.

The Comptroller General determines the legality of payments of appropriated funds by federal officials. This function was vested in the Treasury Department from 1817 to 1921 but passed thereafter to the Comptroller General as the head of the newly created General Accounting Office. The decisions are cited as 49 Comp. Gen. 59 (1969). Although the Comptroller General maintains that his decisions regarding the legality of government expenditures "are binding on the executive departments and agencies,"[9] ever since 1921 the Comptroller General and the Attorney General have been locked in vigorous disagreements as to statutory interpretations and jurisdiction.[10] In 1969 the Comptroller General and the Attorney General disagreed completely about the legality of the Nixon administration's "Philadelphia Plan," designed to increase the number of minority workers in federally assisted contracts.[11] In this dispute the courts sided with the Attorney General's interpretation.[12]

An indispensable guide to the literature is the *Index to Legal Periodicals*, published monthly except September by the H. W. Wilson Company. Currently covering more than 400 legal periodicals, it indexes the articles under subject and author. Entries of special interest to political scientists include administrative agencies, administrative law, administrative procedure, delegation of powers, discrimination, executive agreements, executive power, federalism, freedom of information, freedom of religion, freedom of speech, freedom of the press, government, judicial review, legislation, political science, politics, public finance, separation of powers, United States: Congress, United States: President, and United States: Supreme Court.

[9]Elmer B. Staats, "The GAO: Present and Future," 28 Pub. Adm. Rev. 461 (1968).

[10]E.g., 33 Ops. Att'y Gen. 383, 385–386 (1922); 34 Ops. Att'y Gen. 311 (1924).

[11]49 Comp. Gen. (1969); 42 Ops. Att'y Gen. 405 (1969).

[12]Contractors Ass'n of Eastern Pa. v. Secretary of Labor, 442 F.2d 159 (3d Cir. 1971), cert. denied, 404 U.S. 854 (1971).

The American Bar Association now publishes *Preview*, issued monthly from September through May. It consists of 2–5 page articles that summarize the cases to be argued during the current term of the U.S. Supreme Court. The articles review the principal issue, the facts of the case, the background and significance of the litigation, and the main arguments presented in the briefs (including amicus arguments).

Decisions by state courts are reported in volumes published by each state. They are also published in seven regional reporters. For example, decisions by Connecticut, Delaware, the District of Columbia, Maine, Maryland, New Hampshire, New Jersey, Pennsylvania, Rhode Island, and Vermont appear in the *Atlantic Reporter*. The citation for the second series is A2d. Other state court decisions appear in the following reporters, with citations given to the second series: *North Eastern Reporter* (N.E.2d; Illinois, Indiana, Massachusetts, New York, Ohio); *North Western Reporter* (N.W.2d; Iowa, Michigan, Minnesota, Nebraska, North Dakota, South Dakota, Wisconsin); *Pacific Reporter* (P.2d; Alaska, Arizona, California, Colorado, Hawaii, Idaho, Kansas, Montana, Nevada, New Mexico, Oklahoma, Oregon, Utah, Washington, Wyoming); *South Eastern Reporter* (S.E.2d; Georgia, North Carolina, South Carolina, Virginia, West Virginia); *Southern Reporter* (So.2d; Alabama, Florida, Louisiana, Mississippi); and *South Western Reporter* (S.W.2d; Arkansas, Kentucky, Missouri, Tennessee, Texas).

TABLE OF CASES

This table includes cases discussed in chapter essays and cases excerpted for readings (shown in **bold** for case names and page references). Cases cited in readings are not included in this table.

INDEX